How to Use the
Thesaurus of ERIC Descriptors
for an Effective ERIC Search

FIRST...

1. Identify your specific topic, in your own terms.

2. "Translate" your topic into ERIC Descriptors (subject index terms). The Rotated Descriptor Display in the back of the *Thesaurus* may help you.

3. List the best Descriptors and locate them in the Alphabetical Descriptor Display (the main part of the *Thesaurus).*

    a. Read the Scope Notes (SNs) for information on how ERIC uses the terms.

    b. Check the Broader Terms (BTs), Narrower Terms (NTs), and Related Terms (RTs) under your Descriptors and identify other possible Descriptors relevant to your topic.

    c. Make a list of other Descriptors that you might also use.

    d. Look up those Descriptors and repeat steps 3a-c.

4. Make a final list of the Descriptors most likely to have been used to represent your topic.

THEN...

FOR A MANUAL SEARCH:

Look under your Descriptors in the Subject Index of *Resources in Education (RIE)* and *Current Index to Journals in Education (CIJE)* monthly and cumulative issues to find titles relevant to your search.

FOR A COMPUTER SEARCH:

Follow the directions of your particular library or information retrieval system for a search of the ERIC database (all or any group of years).

NOTE: The Introduction to the *Thesaurus* contains information helpful to searchers on ERIC indexing rules, deleted and invalid Descriptors, and useful parts of the Descriptor entry, such as the date the term was added to the *Thesaurus* and the number of times it has been used.

Thesaurus of

ERICˢᴹ
Educational Resources Information Center

Descriptors

14th Edition

James E. Houston
Editor/Lexicographer
ERIC Processing and Reference Facility
Civil Group
Computer Sciences Corporation

ORYX PRESS

The rare Arabian Oryx is believed to have inspired the myth of the unicorn. This desert antelope became virtually extinct in the early 1960s. At that time, several groups of international conservationists arranged to have 9 animals sent to the Phoenix Zoo to be the nucleus of a captive-breeding herd. Today the Oryx population is over 1,000, and 500 have been returned to reserves in the Middle East.

Copyright © 2001 by The Oryx Press
An imprint of Greenwood Publishing Group, Inc.
88 Post Road West
Westport, CT 06881
(203) 226-3571
(800) 225-5800
http://www.oryxpress.com

The material contained herein was generated under contracts with the National Library of Education, Office of Educational Research and Improvement, U.S. Department of Education. However, the contents do not necessarily reflect the position or policy of that agency, and no U.S. Government endorsement is to be inferred.

Published simultaneously in Canada

Printed and bound in the United States of America

♾ The paper used in this publication meets the minimum requirements of American National Standard for Information Science — Permanence of Paper for Printed Library Materials, ANSI Z39.48-1984.

ISBN 1-57356-330-7
ISSN 1051-2993

Contents

Introduction

Preface

The *Thesaurus of ERIC Descriptors, 14th Edition* 2001, has been developed under the auspices of the Educational Resources Information Center (ERIC) of the National Library of Education, Office of Educational Research and Improvement (OERI), U.S. Department of Education. Its content reflects ERIC's 34 years of monitoring the educational literature. This 14th edition is the result of ERIC's continued efforts to maintain quality in its controlled vocabulary and to respond to the changing nature of education. As in previous editions, the *Thesaurus* reflects ERIC's response to the needs of the educational user community. ERIC remains committed to maintaining a *Thesaurus* that represents the definitive vocabulary for education.

The 2001 edition contains 10,773 vocabulary terms, of which 5,963 are main-entry Descriptors and 4,810 are non-indexable USE references or "Dead" terms. New terms not appearing in previous editions include 206 Descriptors and 210 USE references. This edition also reflects several hundred Scope Notes and cross-reference modifications to earlier Descriptor displays.

Again as in the past, the *Thesaurus* revision has been made possible by the joint efforts and sound judgments of personnel throughout the entire ERIC system responding to both the literature and the users in the field. ERIC vocabulary coordinators, who, as members of the systemwide "Vocabulary Review Group," oversee this effort, are listed below.

ERIC VOCABULARY REVIEW GROUP

ERIC Clearinghouse Vocabulary Coordinators

Jane Atwell, ERIC Document Reproduction Service at DynEDRS, Inc.

Lynne Crane, ERIC Clearinghouse on Disabilities and Gifted Education at the Council for Exceptional Children

Mary Lou Finne, ERIC Clearinghouse on Educational Management at the University of Oregon

Cheryl Gilbert, Oryx Press

Jane Henson, ERIC Clearinghouse for Social Studies/Social Science Education at Indiana University

Hilary Holbrook, ERIC Clearinghouse on Elementary and Early Childhood Education at the University of Illinois

Elaine Howell, ERIC Clearinghouse for Community Colleges at the University of California, Los Angeles

Jim Houston, ERIC Processing and Reference Facility at Computer Sciences Corporation

Jillian Barr Joncas, ERIC Clearinghouse on Counseling and Student Services at the University of North Carolina at Greensboro

Joan Kad, ERIC Clearinghouse on Information and Technology at Syracuse University

Wayne Kemp, National Clearinghouse for Educational Facilities at the National Institute of Building Sciences

Sandra Kerka, ERIC Clearinghouse on Adult, Career, and Vocational Education at Ohio State University

James Lonergan, ERIC Clearinghouse on Urban Education at Teachers College, Columbia University

Mark Lorson, ERIC Clearinghouse for Science, Mathematics, and Environmental Education at Ohio State University

Mark Pioli, ERIC Clearinghouse on Teaching and Teacher Education at the American Association of Colleges for Teacher Education

Jeanne Rennie, ERIC Clearinghouse on Languages and Linguistics at the Center for Applied Linguistics

Lawrence Rudner, ERIC Clearinghouse on Assessment and Evaluation at the University of Maryland

Roger Sensenbaugh, ERIC Clearinghouse on Reading, English, and Communication at Indiana University

Belinda Taheri, ACCESS ERIC at Aspen Systems Corporation

Susan Voelkel, ERIC Clearinghouse on Rural Education and Small Schools at Appalachia Educational Laboratory

Patricia Wood, ERIC Clearinghouse on Higher Education at The George Washington University

ERIC Vocabulary Coordinators in the User Community

Rebecca Augustyniak, Florida Tech Prep/School-to-Work Clearinghouse, Florida State University, Tallahassee, Florida

Susan Cnudde, Outsourcers, Tallahassee, Florida

Jo Ann Davison, Gilman School, Baltimore, Maryland

June Hennig, The SMERC Library, San Mateo County Office of Education, Redwood City, California

Claudine Langlois, International Association of Universities, Paris, France

Suzanne Wise, Belk Library, Appalachian State University, Boone, North Carolina

*International ERIC Coordinators

Margaret Findlay, *Australian Education Index*, Australian Council for Educational Research, The Cunningham Library, Camberwell, Victoria, Australia

Lucy Lemieux, *Canadian Education Index*, Micromedia Ltd., Toronto, Ontario, Canada

Phillip Sheffield, *British Education Index*, Brotherton Library, The University of Leeds, Leeds, Great Britain

---

Users are invited to direct comments on the *Thesaurus* or the ERIC System as a whole to Luna Levinson, Division Director of ERIC, Department of Education, 400 Maryland Avenue, FOB 6, 4th Floor, Washington, DC 20202.

Jeanne Rennie
Chair, Vocabulary Review Group
ERIC Clearinghouse on Languages and Linguistics
Center for Applied Linguistics

Jim Houston
Lexicographer
ERIC Processing and Reference Facility
Computer Sciences Corporation

Kevin Arundel
Project Monitor
ERIC Program/Office of Educational Research and Improvement
U.S. Department of Education

---

*"International ERIC" is a long-term initiative for international cooperation among the major English-language education-related databases (AEI, BEI, CEI, and ERIC).

New Descriptors

These Descriptors have been added to the *Thesaurus* since December 1994 and do not appear in previous editions.

Academic Accommodations
  (Disabilities)
Academic Discourse
Acids
Adolescent Attitudes
Adolescent Behavior
Afrocentrism
Alternative Assessment
American Dream
Asian American Students
Attitudes toward Disabilities

Beginning Principals
Beginning Writing
Benchmarking
Bereavement
Biodiversity
Births to Single Women
Bisexuality
Block Scheduling
Bookstores
Brain
Brain Drain
Brass Instruments
Bullying

Capital Punishment
Career Academies
Case Method (Teaching Technique)
Central Office Administrators
Chaos Theory
Charter Schools
Child Safety
Childrens Writing
Classics (Literature)
Cochlear Implants
Community Needs
Comprehensive School Health
  Education
Concept Mapping
Conjunctions
Corporate Libraries
Crisis Management
Cultural Relevance
Culturally Relevant Education

Cystic Fibrosis

Debt (Financial)
Denial (Psychology)
Density (Matter)
Developmentally Appropriate
  Practices
Dewey Decimal Classification
Discourse Communities
Dissection
Diversity (Faculty)
Diversity (Student)
Document Delivery
Drought

Early Identification
Electronic Journals
Electronic Libraries
Emergent Literacy
Empowerment
English Only Movement
English Teachers
Environmental Interpretation
Ethnomathematics
Euthanasia

Family English Literacy
Family Literacy
Family Needs
Femininity
Feminist Criticism
Floods
Focus Groups
Fraud

Gardening
Gardens
Gender Issues
Genocide
Graphing Calculators
Gun Control
Guns

Hands on Science
Hazing

Health Behavior
Health Maintenance Organizations
High Stakes Tests
Hispanic American Students
Historians
Historic Sites
Historical Interpretation
Honesty
Housework
Hurricanes

Informal Education
Internet
Islam

Japanese Culture
Job Security
Journal Articles
Journalism Research

Keywords
Kyrgyz

Language Minorities
Library Administrators
Library Directors
Library of Congress Classification
Limits (Mathematics)
Listservs

Mandatory Continuing Education
Mandatory Retirement
Manuscripts
Maori
Maori (People)
Masculinity
Mathematics Activities
Mathematics History
Maya (People)
Mental Computation
Middle School Students
Middle School Teachers
Multiple Intelligences
Multiracial Persons
Muslims

National Parks
National Standards
National Teacher Certification
Navigation (Information Systems)
Nongovernmental Organizations
Nuclear Weapons
Nursery Rhymes

Objectivity
Occupational Segregation
Older Workers
Otitis Media
Outcome Based Education
Outdoor Leadership

Pacific Islanders
Parent Empowerment
Parents with Disabilities
Patterns in Mathematics
Pedagogical Content Knowledge
Peer Mediation
Performance Based Assessment
Pets
Phonathons
Political Correctness
Popular Education
Popular Music
Postmodernism
Posttraumatic Stress Disorder
Prenatal Drug Exposure
Preservice Teachers

Problem Based Learning
Process Approach (Writing)
Puberty
Public History

Rainforests
Reading Motivation
Recipes (Food)
Reggio Emilia Approach
Rehearsals (Theater Arts)
Resilience (Personality)
Reunions
Rhyme
Rivers

Scholarly Communication
Scholarly Writing
Scholastic Journalism
School Culture
School Psychology
School Uniforms
Science Achievement
Scoring Rubrics
Self Advocacy
Service Learning
Sexual Orientation
Social Promotion
Sociologists
Spirituality
String Instruments
Student Empowerment

Sudden Infant Death Syndrome

Teacher Collaboration
Teacher Empowerment
Teacher Researchers
Teacher Surveys
Teachers with Disabilities
Tech Prep
Temporary Employment
Time to Degree
Tohono O Odham People
Toilet Training
Tornadoes
Transfer Rates (College)
Transformative Learning

Universal Decimal Classification
University Presses

Velocity
Virtual Reality

Walking
Weapons
Wellness
Wind Instruments
Woodwind Instruments
Word Order
Workplace Literacy
World Views
World Wide Web

Transferred Descriptors

These former Descriptors have been downgraded to USE references. Postings for such terms are transferred to other "preferred" terms. Their entries in the Alphabetical Descriptor Display identify the receiving Descriptors. Postings transfers of approximately 840 Descriptors before December 1980 (when the last reload of the ERIC file occurred) are reflected in the ERIC database, and these Descriptors no longer need to be considered in online or other computer searching. Transfers after December 1980, however, have *not* been fully implemented in the ERIC file, and both old and new versions of a term must be used in retrospective searching. *All* "transferred" ERIC Descriptors that are still searchable are listed below.

Acceleration
After School Day Care
Agricultural Research Projects
Appliance Repairers
Appliance Repairing
Architectural Programing
Audiodisc Recordings
Authoring Aids (Programing)

Bricklayers

Carpenters
Cerebral Dominance
Clinic Personnel (School)
Computer Programs
Cosmetologists
Craftsmen

Data Bases
Delinquent Behavior
Diffusion
Drafters

Food Service Industry
Food Service Occupations
Food Service Workers
Foster Homes

Geographic Mobility

Handicap Discrimination
Handicap Identification

Handwriting Instruction
Handwriting Materials
Handwriting Readiness
Handwriting Skills
High Risk Persons

Ibo
Illegal Immigrants
Illegitimate Births
Inhalation Therapists
Interest

Kirghiz

Language Handicaps
Latent Trait Theory
Linear Programing

Marihuana

Normalization (Handicapped)

Panjabi
Perceptual Handicaps
Practical Nurses
Programed Instruction
Programed Instructional Materials
Programed Tutoring
Programers
Programing
Programing (Broadcast)
Programing Languages

Quantitative Tests

Research Apprenticeships
Retention Studies
Roofers
Rumanian
Rural Dropouts

Self Mutilation
Shared Services
Sheet Metal Workers
Solar Radiation
Spatial Perception
Speech Handicaps
Speech Pathology
Stenographers
Student Teacher Ratio
Student Teacher Relationship
Supervised Farm Practice

Trainable Mentally Handicapped
Transitional Classes
Typists

Urban Dropouts

Videodisc Recordings
Visually Handicapped Mobility

Welders
Wheel Chairs
Women Teachers

Invalid ("Dead") Descriptors

These Descriptors are no longer used in indexing (see p. xxx). They may be used for searching database entries prior to September 1980. (See Invalid Descriptors below marked with [i], [ii], [iii], [iv] for the exceptions.) More recent literature on topics represented by these terms is searchable using related Descriptors. For further reference, see entries for the terms in the Alphabetical Descriptor Display.

Academically Handicapped
Administrative Agencies
Advanced Programs
American Culture
American History
Analytical Criticism
Ancillary Services
Architectural Barriers
Aristotelian Criticism
Assistant Superintendent Role

Basic Reading
Black Housing

Career Opportunities
Caricatures
Child Care
Class Attitudes
Class Average
Classroom Guidance Programs
College Language Programs
Conceptual Schemes
Conference Reports
Congruence
Continuation Education
Controlled Environment
Counseling Instructional Programs
Creative Reading

Developmental Reading
Direction Writing

Educational Problems
Educational Programs
Educational Retardation
Educational Specifications
Elective Reading

English Education
English Neoclassic Literary Period
Episode Teaching
Ethnic Grouping
Exceptional Child Education
Exceptional Child Services
[i]Exceptional Persons
Exercise (Physiology)

Factual Reading
Flexible Schedules
Formal Criticism
Former Teachers

Grade Charts
Group Norms
Group Reading
Growth Patterns

Handicapped Children
Handicapped Students
Health Occupations Centers
Historical Criticism
Human Development
Human Living

Impressionistic Criticism
Individual Reading
Inequalities
Instructional Programs
Interpretive Reading

Laboratory Techniques
Language Ability
Language Aids
Language and Area Centers
Language Guides

Language Instruction
Language Learning Levels
Language Programs
[ii]Legal Education
Literary Discrimination
Literary Influences
Literary Mood
Literary Perspective
Literature Guides
Literature Programs
Low Ability Students

Mathematical Experience
Maturation
Measurement Instruments
Moral Criticism
Mythic Criticism

[iii]Negro Housing
Northern Schools

Performance Criteria
Performance Specifications
Plant Science
Platonic Criticism
Preschool Learning
Pressure
Programing Problems
Project Applications
Projects
Publicize

Racial Characteristics
Racism
Reading Development
Reading Difficulty
Reading Level

---

[i]Invalid since September 1994.
[ii]Invalid since April 1986
[iii]Not used after 1977—see also "Black Housing."
[iv]All postings are earlier than May 1978.

Recognition
Research Criteria
Research Reviews (Publications)

School Planning
ivSecurity
Self Directed Classrooms
Self Evaluation
Sex (Characteristics)
Social Relations
Social Welfare
Sound Tracks
Southern Citizens
Southern Community
Southern Schools

Space Orientation
Spatial Relationship
Speech Education
Stimulus Devices
Structural Analysis
Student Distribution
Studio Floor Plans
Supreme Court Litigation
Supreme Courts
Systems Concepts

Talent Utilization
Task Performance
Teaching
Teaching Assignment

Teaching Programs
TENL
Textbook Publications
Textual Criticism
Theoretical Criticism
Tracking
Training Laboratories
Transfers

Unit Plan
Unwritten Language

Weight
Welfare

Deleted Descriptors

This designation refers to former Descriptors that no longer appear in the *Thesaurus*, even as USE references. No terms were included in this category for the present edition of the *Thesaurus*.

ERIC's Indexing and Retrieval: 2001 Update[1]

THE ERIC SYSTEM

The Educational Resources Information Center (ERIC) is a national information system designed to provide users with ready access to an extensive body of education-related literature.[2] Established in 1966, it is today part of the National Library of Education, and is funded by the Office of Educational Research and Improvement (OERI) of the U.S. Department of Education. The ERIC database, the world's largest source of education information, contains abstracts of more than 1 million documents and journal articles. ERIC collects and disseminates virtually all types of print materials, published and unpublished, that deal with education—for example, descriptions and evaluations of programs, research reports and surveys, curriculum and teaching guides, instructional materials, position papers, machine-readable data files, and resource materials. The AskERIC service handles 40,000+ education-related questions a year, recently reaching a milestone of 200,000 answered questions.[3]

The ERIC Program Office within OERI establishes policy and oversees the operation of the ERIC system. Centers of educational expertise, located primarily at universities or professional associations, operate the 16 decentralized ERIC Clearinghouses and 10 ERIC Adjunct or Affiliate Clearinghouses.[4] These Clearinghouses identify, acquire, and process educational information in such specific subject areas as reading and communication skills, science and mathematics, and social studies, and in such other areas as elementary, secondary, higher, rural, and urban education. Support organizations perform other services for the ERIC system. These services include centralized database management (the ERIC Processing and Reference Facility), document delivery (the ERIC Document Reproduction Service), commercial publishing (Oryx Press), and outreach (ACCESS ERIC).

ERIC acquires and announces the availability of education-related literature, including journal articles. Each item is cataloged, abstracted, and indexed using the key words from the controlled vocabulary—the *Thesaurus of ERIC Descriptors*. Citations for nonjournal literature appear in the monthly bibliographic abstract journal, *Resources in Education (RIE)*; journal article annotations are found in the companion monthly publication, *Current Index to Journals in Education (CIJE)*. With the help of the *Thesaurus*, users can identify information in the ERIC database by manual searches of the printed indexes in *RIE* and *CIJE* or by computer searches of the online, CD-ROM, and Internet ERIC files. ERIC provides convenient access to the actual text of more than 390,000 documents at more than 1,000 libraries and resource centers around the world that subscribe to the ERIC microfiche collection (see footnote 10, on p. xv). Full-text electronic access to 80 percent of the ERIC documents from 1993 to the present is now provided to subscribing institutions[5] via the ERIC E*Subscribe service from EDRS.[6]

The Clearinghouses are important components of the ERIC system. Responsible for locating, acquiring, and selecting literature in their respective areas of education, each Clearinghouse indexes its materials with the terms from the *Thesaurus*. Because Clearinghouses have a stake in the content of the *Thesaurus*, each contributes regularly to updating the ERIC vocabulary.

VOCABULARY MAINTENANCE

In 1977, a unique systemwide project, the Vocabulary Improvement Project, was undertaken to update the

---

[1]The arrangement of this introduction is based on materials in earlier editions of the *Thesaurus of ERIC Descriptors*, written by:
— Lynn Barnett, Director of Academic, Student, and Community Development, American Association of Community Colleges (formerly Associate Director, ERIC Clearinghouse on Higher Education, The George Washington University).
— Anita Colby, Head, Collection Development Division, Science & Engineering Library, University of California at Los Angeles (formerly Associate Director, ERIC Clearinghouse for Community Colleges, UCLA).
[2]See Delmer J. Trester's *ERIC—The First 15 Years. A History of the Educational Resources Information Center* (ED 195 289 from the ERIC Document Reproduction Service [EDRS]). See also Laura J. Colker's *Reminiscences from the Field: The Continuing Story of ERIC* (ED 437 937 from EDRS).
[3]AskERIC is a free, Internet-based service for educators and others interested in the theory and practice of education. Questions can be e-mailed to askeric@askeric.org or submitted via an online form located at http://www.askeric.org.
[4]Note the "scope of interest" statements for the 16 ERIC Clearinghouses in the concluding "ERIC Network Components" section of this Introduction, pp. xxxii-xxxv. These statements show the diversity of the ERIC system and indicate the areas of expertise of the individual Clearinghouses. See also the inside back cover of this publication for a graphic display of the ERIC system components.
[5]Contributors restrict remaining documents for the 1993 to present period to microfiche release.
[6]EDRS is the ERIC Document Reproduction Service, the document-delivery arm of the ERIC database. Address: ERIC Document Reproduction Service (EDRS), DynEDRS, Inc., 7420 Fullerton Road, Suite 110, Springfield, VA 22153-2852. The EDRS Web site is http://edrs.com.

Thesaurus of ERIC Descriptors.[7] The three-year project added and clarified scope notes, rearranged hierarchies, updated terminology, merged synonymous terms, revised cross-references, and modified sexist language. The objective was to improve retrieval by improving indexing consistency. This unprecedented project culminated in a completely revised eighth edition of the *Thesaurus* in 1980. More important, however, it also established new procedures for vocabulary maintenance that have become standard practices in the ERIC system.

At the heart of the new procedures is the commitment to a participative approach to vocabulary development. Three features characterize this approach: a designated vocabulary coordinator at each Clearinghouse to monitor the language of its own scope area (see p. vii); user participation in vocabulary review; and a regular interactive process for thesaurus development. Simply put, ERIC has built a mechanism for considering multiple viewpoints in questions about indexing language.

Those viewpoints are heard through the ERIC Vocabulary Review Group (VRG), whose members are the 16 Clearinghouse vocabulary coordinators, the ERIC lexicographic staff, an ERIC Program Office representative, and members of the user community, including international representatives. User groups that are represented include school and university librarians, practitioners, and online searchers. The VRG is chaired by a Clearinghouse coordinator, who is appointed by the ERIC Program Office. The VRG both initiates and evaluates new terminology or modifications to existing vocabulary. The interactive nature of the evaluation process allows for thorough discussion before final decisions are made in periodic *Thesaurus* updates and revisions. Since mid-1993, all VRG evaluations have occurred via an Internet listserv, resulting in a simplified input and a shortened disposition cycle.[8]

ERIC solicits the viewpoints of the educational community. Users are encouraged to submit comments on this edition and any suggestions for future editions of the *Thesaurus* to: Director, ERIC, Department of Education, 400 Maryland Avenue, SW, Washington, DC 20202-5721, or http://www.accesseric.org. Comments and suggestions may also be submitted to Lexicographer, ERIC Facility,

Computer Sciences Corporation, 4483-A Forbes Boulevard, Lanham, MD 20706. Telephone: 301-552-4200. Fax: 301-552-4700. Email: ericfac@inet.ed.gov or http://ericfacility.org

INFORMATION RETRIEVAL

Information can be retrieved from the ERIC database manually or by computer. For manual searching, ERIC provides several printed reference tools; for computer searching (online, CD-ROM, or via the Internet), immediate access is provided to the same information.

Manual Searching

Manual searching makes use primarily of the monthly printed versions of *Resources in Education* (*RIE*) and *Current Index to Journals in Education* (*CIJE*). Users locate citations in these publications through various indexes. *RIE* provides a Subject Index (consisting of Major Descriptors and Major Identifiers—see pp. xvii and xx); an Author Index[9]; an Institution Index (showing organizations responsible for a document and/or the agency sponsoring it); and a Publication Type Index (see p. xxi). *CIJE* contains a Subject Index, Author Index (see footnote 9), and a Journal Contents Index (which lists by journal name the titles of articles indexed in that issue). Cumulations of *RIE* (annual) and *CIJE* (semiannual), including their indexes are available.[10]

Computer Searching

Computer searching allows a user to quickly review part or all of the ERIC database (*RIE* and *CIJE*) with a single set of commands, eliminating the time-consuming task of scanning separate monthly or annual print indexes. Computers make retrieval possible not only by Major and Minor Descriptors and Identifiers, authors, institutions, specific journals, and Publication Types, but also by unique words or phrases found in titles and abstracts/annotations.

---

[7]See Barbara Booth's "A New ERIC Thesaurus. Fine-Tuned for Searching." *Online* v3 n3 July 1979, pp. 20-29.

[8]See the inside back cover of this publication for a flowchart of the present ERIC vocabulary development procedure. The hub of the procedure is the Internet Vocabulary Listserv, which links every communication and transaction made on every *Thesaurus* recommendation through final disposition and archiving.

[9]Multiple authors may be indexed in ERIC after Sep97 (before that date, for documents/articles listing three or more authors, only the first author was indexed in ERIC). For collected works or proceedings containing works by multiple authors and not listing an editor or compiler of the whole, *no* authors are indexed; however, individual author names appearing in such collections are usually included within the text of the ERIC abstract/annotation and can be retrieved by full-text computer searching.

[10]*RIE*, covering education documents, is issued monthly by the Superintendent of Documents, U.S. Government Printing Office (GPO), Washington, DC 20402-9371.

——*CIJE*, covering education journal articles, is published monthly by The Oryx Press: An imprint of Greenwood Publishing Group, Inc., 88 Post Road West, Westport, CT 06881-5007, 800-225-5800. Oryx Press also publishes the following titles:

——*CIJE Semiannual Cumulations* are one-volume cumulations of all main entries (descriptions of journal articles) and indexes for a six-month period. Prior to 1979, these were published by Macmillan Information, 866 Third Avenue, New York, NY 10022.

——*RIE Annual Cumulations* are published in three volumes—two of cumulated main entries (abstracts) and one of cumulated indexes. Similar cumulations prior to 1979 were published under the title *Educational Documents Abstracts/Index* by Macmillan Information.

Most *RIE* documents, identified by "ED" numbers in the ERIC database, can be ordered in microfiche or paper from the ERIC Document Reproduction Service. EDRS delivers monthly *RIE* microfiche sets to approximately 970 standing-order subscribers. Cumulated *RIE* indexes on microfiche (1966-present) by subject, author, title, and institution are also available from EDRS.

In short, computer searching allows users to access not only indexed data but also almost every word in a database record.

ERIC Web Sites. Through the Internet, ERIC provides a global audience easy access to a variety of education resources, including the ERIC database, full-text ERIC Digests (see "Full-Text," below), virtual libraries, lesson plans, parent publications, and reference directories. Internet users can access these and other resources through a system of ERIC-sponsored Web sites. The gateway to these Web sites is the ERIC systemwide Web site, which is sponsored by ACCESS ERIC and is located at http://www.accesseric.org. Currently, ERIC-sponsored Web sites include:

- AskERIC
  http://ericir.syr.edu
- ERIC Document Reproduction Service
  http://www.edrs.com/
- ERIC Clearinghouse on Assessment and Evaluation
  —Quick Search
  http://ericae.net/aesearch.htm
  —Search Wizard
  http://ericae.net/scripts/ewiz/

ERIC searching on ERIC-sponsored Web sites is free.

NOTE: The Search Wizard program allows users direct access to the ERIC *Thesaurus* displays; Descriptors and their cross-references may be examined and selected for searching and used to build search strategies. An ERIC *Thesaurus* search/browse Web site is offered at http://www.ericfacility.net/extra/pub/ thessearch.cfm by the ERIC Processing and Reference Facility.

The ERIC Clearinghouse on Information and Technology sponsors the AskERIC project, an Internet-based question-answering service for teachers, library media specialists, administrators, and others involved in education. The hallmark of AskERIC is the human intermediary, who interacts with the information seeker and personally selects and delivers information resources within 48 working hours. The benefits of the human-mediated service is that it allows AskERIC staff to determine the precise information needs of the client and to present an array of relevant resources, both from the ERIC system and the vast resources of the Internet. Anyone involved in education can send an Internet inquiry to AskERIC at the following e-mail address: askeric@askeric.org or http://ericir.syr.edu/.

Online Access through Commercial Services. Originally, the only way to access the ERIC database by computer was through a telecommunications link from a modem to a commercial online database vendor. Today only one such vendor, the Dialog Corporation, regularly accesses ERIC in this

manner. ("Classic Dialog" is available via modem or the Web—see Web site below.) Instead, vendors, including Dialog, now commonly use Web-based services to access ERIC. There are currently seven Web-based database vendors offering access to ERIC (and other databases):

- CSA (Cambridge Scientific Abstracts)
  http://www.csa.com/
- Dialog Corporation
  http://www.dialog.com
- EBSCO Host
  http://www-us.ebsco.com/
- NISC BiblioLine
  http://www.nisc.com/
- OCLC FirstSearch
  http://www.oclc.com/home
- Ovid Technologies
  http://www.ovid.com/
- SilverPlatter WebSPIRS
  http://www.silverplatter.com/

Procedures and costs for searching the ERIC database vary with each online vendor. Web-based services offer the most powerful and sophisticated search capabilities, the ability to access the entire database at once, and the ability to conduct complicated searches. Training in the vendors' search language is sometimes required. Costs may include a membership fee and charges based on the number of minutes connected and the number of citations printed or downloaded.

CD-ROM. There are currently five CD-ROM vendors who supply ERIC:

- Dialog OnDisc
  http://www.dialog.com/
- EBSCO Publishing
  http://www.epnet.com
- ERIC Processing and Reference Facility
  http://ericfacility.org/nisc.html
- NISC DISCover
  http://www.nisc.com/
- SilverPlatter SPIRS
  http://www.silverplatter.com

Dialog OnDisc offers the option of using its traditional "Classic Dialog" online commands to retrieve information. CD-ROM searching cannot replace direct online searching for currency and thoroughness, but it has cost advantages. For example, the ERIC Processing and Reference Facility has arranged with NISC to sell the NISC DISCover discs at $100 for a year's subscription to a "current" disc, with an "archival" disc added for an additional $25 completing the set.

Full-Text. ERIC is a bibliographic, rather than a full-text database; therefore, "full-text searching" in ERIC refers to searching individual words of document *resumes* (citation summaries) and not the content of the documents themselves.
ERIC Documents (ED accessions). The texts of

approximately 95 percent of ERIC documents (ED accessions) are available in paper copy or microfiche from the ERIC Document Reproduction Service (EDRS)—see footnotes 6 and 10. Many libraries have ERIC microfiche collections that are available to the public. To find a nearby ERIC collection, consult the *Directory of ERIC Resource Collections*.[11] The complete text of 80 percent of ERIC documents from 1993 to the present may be electronically accessed by subscribing institutions through the E*Subscribe service provided by EDRS.

ERIC Journal Articles (EJ accessions). The texts of ERIC journal articles (EJ accessions) must be obtained from the journals themselves, the journal publishers, or via periodical reprint services like UnCover or ISI.[12]

ERIC Digests. Beginning in October 1989, selected ERIC documents, called "ERIC Digests," have appeared in ERIC in full-text form. ERIC Digests are short reports (1,000 to 1,500 words) prepared by the 16 ERIC Clearinghouses on topics of prime interest in education. Examples are "Equal Mathematics Education for Female Students" (Clearinghouse on Urban Education); "Accreditation of College and University Counseling Services" (Clearinghouse on Counseling and Student Services); and "Beyond Transition: Ensuring Continuity in Early Childhood Services" (Clearinghouse on Early Childhood and Elementary Education). At this writing, nearly 2,300 ERIC Digests are available in full-text format and the Clearinghouses produce approximately 200 new digests each year. A full-text file of the ERIC digests (updated quarterly) is available to Internet users through the U.S. Department of Education's Web site, http://www.ed.gov/databases/ERIC_Digests/index/. Users can also search the full text of the entire current Digest file on any online or CD-ROM version of the ERIC database.

NOTE: Procedures for searching the ERIC database vary with each online/CD-ROM vendor. You may contact ACCESS ERIC (1-800-LET-ERIC) or the most appropriate ERIC Clearinghouse for guidance on searching (see "ERIC Network Components" section of the Introduction).

A review of the procedures outlined in the "ERIC's Indexing" section that follows may help in developing strategies for searching the ERIC database, regardless of the form of database used.

ERIC'S INDEXING

General Guidelines

Knowing how something is stored makes finding it easier. Understanding the methods by which literature is prepared for input into a computerized database facilitates retrieval of that literature. Just as an indexer must consider the user's needs for retrieval, so should a user/searcher be aware of the rules and guidelines of the indexing process.

ERIC's indexing aims to provide subject access to the documents and articles contained in the database and announced in *RIE* and *CIJE*. ERIC has two fundamental indexing rules:

- Index only what is in the document.
- Index at the level of specificity of the document.

These rules mean that implied statements or assumptions are not indexed, and that very general Descriptors are not used unless the document covers a topic very broadly. For example, SCHOOLS would not be indexed on documents about HIGH SCHOOLS, PRIVATE SCHOOLS, or MEDICAL SCHOOLS. In other words, ERIC avoids "indexing up" to a broader Descriptor when an appropriate, more specific one exists. Keeping these basic rules in mind will help ensure effective retrieval.

Indexing rules[13] are detailed in the *ERIC Processing Manual*, the system's official guide. Additional instructions, suggestions, and specific examples are detailed in the 400-page training-oriented *ERIC Abstractor/Indexer Workbook* and the more recent *ERIC Indexing Handbook: Clearinghouse Indexing Practices*.[14]

Major points relevant to retrieval are:

1. "Indexable" concepts, or key words, of a document are translated into Descriptors from the *Thesaurus*. Using the *Thesaurus* helps maintain consistency and prevents proliferation or scattering of concepts in the subject indexes.

2. Precoordinated Descriptors (i.e., multiple-word) are used whenever possible, rather than two or more Descriptors representing their component concepts. Thus, SCIENCE CURRICULUM would be used rather than SCIENCE plus CURRICULUM.

3. Descriptors are assigned to identify subject content, edu-

---

[11] *Directory of ERIC Resource Collections*, available at http://oerid.ed.gov/BASISDB/EROD/eric/SF or in paper copy from ACCESS ERIC (1-800-LET-ERIC).

[12] The UnCover Company, 3801 East Florida Avenue, Suite 300, Denver, CO 80210 / 800-787-7979 / http://uncweb.carl.org; Institute for Scientific Information, ISI Document Solution, 3501 Market Street, Philadelphia, PA 19104 / 800-336-4474 / http://www.isinet.com.

[13] The *ERIC Processing Manual* (1992 edition) is available for $75.00 from the ERIC Processing and Reference Facility, 4483-A Forbes Boulevard, Lanham, MD 20706 / http://ericfacility.org. Sections relevant to retrieval, *Section 6: Abstracting/Annotating and Section 7: Indexing*, may be purchased for $7.50 each from the ERIC Facility. The manual also appears in the ERIC Microfiche Collection (entire manual, ED 348 055; Abstracting Section, ED 348 061; Indexing Section, ED 348 062) and is available from the ERIC Document Reproduction Service (EDRS).

[14] The *ERIC Abstractor/Indexer Workbook* (Revised Edition, 1981) is in the ERIC Microfiche Collection (ED 207 614) and is available from EDRS. *The ERIC Indexing Handbook: Clearinghouse Indexing Practices* (1992 edition) has been incorporated as Appendix C of the *ERIC Processing Manual* and is available as ED 348 069 from EDRS.

cational level, age level, validation status of a program, research methodology employed, tests utilized, form or type of document, etc. (See pp. xviii, xix and xxi for lists of Mandatory Educational Level Descriptors, Optional Age Level Descriptors, and Publication Types.)

4. Up to six "Major" Descriptors are assigned to a single document. They cover the main focus of the document. Major Descriptors appear in the *RIE* and *CIJE* printed Subject Indexes. In the document resume section of *RIE* and the main entry section of *CIJE*, Major Descriptors are identified with an asterisk (*).

5. Additional Descriptors, called "Minor" Descriptors, are also assigned to a document or journal article. They appear in the printed resumes (without an asterisk) but *do not* appear in the printed Subject Indexes of *RIE* or *CIJE*. (See examples that follow.)

6. Major Descriptors cover the main focus or *subject* of a document. Minor Descriptors indicate less important aspects within the document, as well as such nonsubject features as methodology, form, or educational level.

NOTE: Major Descriptors appear in the Subject Indexes of *RIE* and *CIJE* and therefore can be searched manually. Minor Descriptors do not appear in the Subject Indexes but are searchable by computer.

SAMPLE *RIE* ENTRY

ED 312 182　　　　　　　　　　　　SO 020 269
Cramer, Elizabeth, Ed. Hill, Margaret, Ed.
Who Said Learning about the Constitution Isn't Fun? Active Lessons on the U.S. Constitution for Junior and Senior High School Students. Lessons created by participants at "Congress and the Constitution: A Summer Institute for Teachers" (Ontario, California, 1988).
Chaffey Joint Union High School District, Ontario, CA; Commission on the Bicentennial of the United States Constitution, Washington, DC.
Pub Date—1988
Note—136p.
Pub Type—Guides—Classroom—Teacher (052)
EDRS Price—MF01/PC06 Plus Postage.
Descriptors *Citizenship Education, Government (Administrative Body), *History Instruction, Lesson Plans, Secondary Education, Teacher Developed Materials, *United States Government (Course), Units of Study
Identifiers California, *United States Constitution
Twenty-eight lesson plans developed by California teachers who attended a summer institute on Congress and the Constitution are presented in this document. Sample lesson plan titles are: (1) "Geopolitics and the Constitution," (2) "Judicial Review," (3) "Electoral College and the...

SAMPLE *CIJE* ENTRY

EJ 596 813　　　　　　　　　　　　CS 758 144
The Making of a Teacher. Allender, Dale *English Journal*; v89 n1 p20-22 Sep 1999
Descriptors: Beginning Teachers; Collegiality; *English Teachers; *Faculty Development; *Professional Associations; Secondary Education; *Teacher Student Relationship; Teaching Experience
Identifiers: *National Council of Teachers of English
Note: Theme: Research Revisited

Describes teachers who made a difference in the author's literacy development and who fostered his love of learning and teaching. Discusses the importance of teachers growing as professionals. Describes various opportunities through the National Council of Teachers of English (NCTE) for teachers to share the good work that they do. Notes NCTE's "TEACH 2000" initiative for first-year English language arts teachers. (SR)

"Leveling" Descriptors

Since the ERIC database covers literature from all levels—preschool through postdoctoral, infant through adult—it is important, where appropriate, to "tag" documents with "leveling" terms. Leveling terms are classified as Descriptors and will be found in the Descriptor field of the *RIE* and *CIJE* resumes. They refer to either the educational level or age level of the population discussed in the document. Sometimes both educational and age level Descriptors may be assigned. Since a variety of *Thesaurus* terms conceivably could be used to tag these levels, ERIC has developed lists of preferred leveling Descriptors.

Mandatory Educational Level Descriptors. Assignment of at least one of the "Educational Level" Descriptors is mandatory for every document and journal article, unless it is entirely inappropriate (such as an essay on "the role of education in society"). The Mandatory Educational Level Descriptors procedure was implemented in February 1975.

This required assignment of Educational Level Descriptors has a practical implication for the searcher. For example, a computer search of the Descriptor READING SKILLS would pull out all the references in ERIC to reading skills, regardless of educational level. Adding the Descriptor SECONDARY EDUCATION would limit the output to those references dealing with grades 7 through 12; adding HIGH SCHOOLS instead would limit the output to reading skills in the upper secondary grades. Similarly, the Descriptor TWO YEAR COLLEGES would focus a search more discretely than would the term POSTSECONDARY EDUCATION. Thus, the same guideline holds here in searching as in subject indexing: use the most specific Descriptor available for a specific search.

On the other hand, a document indexed at a narrow educational level would, in most instances, not be "indexed up" to a broader level, and exhaustive searches of broader levelers require that each of their respective narrower levelers also be used. For example, one would need to search SECONDARY EDUCATION, JUNIOR HIGH SCHOOLS, HIGH SCHOOLS, and HIGH SCHOOL EQUIVALENCY PROGRAMS to achieve an exhaustive search at the SECONDARY EDUCATION level.

MIDDLE SCHOOLS was added as an educational level Descriptor only in July 1999. Prior to that, indexers were instructed to index the levelers INTERMEDIATE GRADES and/or JUNIOR HIGH SCHOOLS for the middle school grades; the Descriptor MIDDLE SCHOOLS was used only when the document or article itself used it, and only with an appropriate Educational Level Descriptor.

DESCRIPTORS

The Mandatory Educational Level Descriptors are flagged within the body of the *Thesaurus* with a special instruction in the Scope Note:

Secondary Education
SN   Education provided in grade 7, 8, or 9 through grade 12 (Note: Also appears in the list of mandatory educational level Descriptors)

NOTE:
1. Use the most specific Educational Level Descriptor possible. In searching, use broader *and* narrower Educational Level Descriptors to retrieve at broader levels.
2. Educational Level Descriptors are *never* Major Descriptors unless they are the *subject* of the document.
3. As mandatory terms, Educational Level Descriptors always have precedence over the Age Level Descriptors.

The Mandatory Educational Level Descriptors appear with their Scope Notes in the following chart:

MANDATORY "EDUCATIONAL LEVEL" DESCRIPTORS
(Procedure Implemented February 1975)

• EARLY CHILDHOOD EDUCATION
  Scope Note: Activities and/or experiences that are intended to effect developmental changes in children, from birth through the primary units of elementary school (grades K-3).
• • PRESCHOOL EDUCATION
  Scope Note: Activities and/or experiences that are intended to effect developmental changes in children, from birth to entrance in kindergarten (or grade 1 when kindergarten is not attended).
• • PRIMARY EDUCATION
  Scope Note: Education provided in kindergarten through grade 3.
• ELEMENTARY SECONDARY EDUCATION
  Scope Note: Formal education provided in kindergarten or grade 1 through grade 12.
• • ELEMENTARY EDUCATION
  Scope Note: Education provided in kindergarten or grade 1 through grade 6, 7, or 8.
• • • ADULT BASIC EDUCATION
  Scope Note: Education provided for adults at the elementary level (through grade 8), usually with emphasis on communicative, computational, and social skills.
• • • PRIMARY EDUCATION
  Scope Note: (See above.)
• • • INTERMEDIATE GRADES
  Scope Note: Includes the middle and/or upper elementary grades, but usually, 4, 5, and 6.
• • MIDDLE SCHOOLS (Added July 1999 as "educational level" Descriptor—formerly indexed "Intermediate Grades" and/or "Junior High Schools," along with "Middle Schools.")
  Scope Note: Various combinations of grades 5 through 9—mainly 6-8, but also 5-7, 5-8, 7-8, or 7-9.
• • SECONDARY EDUCATION
  Scope Note: Education provided in grade 7, 8, or 9 through grade 12.
• • • JUNIOR HIGH SCHOOLS
  Scope Note: Providing formal education in grades 7, 8, and 9—less commonly 7 and 8, or 8 and 9.
• • • HIGH SCHOOLS (Changed from "Senior High Schools" in March 1980.)

  Scope Note: Providing formal education in grades 9 or 10 through 12.
• • • HIGH SCHOOL EQUIVALENCY PROGRAMS
  Scope Note: Adult educational activities concerned with the preparation for and the taking of tests that lead to a high school equivalency certificate, e.g., General Educational Development programs.
• POSTSECONDARY EDUCATION
  Scope Note: All education beyond the secondary level—includes learning activities and experiences beyond the compulsory school attendance age, with the exception of adult basic education and high school equivalency programs. (Before Apr75, restricted to "education beyond grade 12 and less than the baccalaureate level.")
• • HIGHER EDUCATION
  Scope Note: All education beyond the secondary level leading to a formal degree.
• • TWO YEAR COLLEGES (Changed from "Junior Colleges" in March 1980.)
  Scope Note: Public or private postsecondary institutions providing at least 2, but less than 4, years of academic and/or occupational education.

Optional Age Level Descriptors. Age Level Descriptors were mandatory in ERIC from 1980 until mid-1982, when the requirement was abolished. They are still used as optional indexing points, and have been added to over the years in response to user requests. Each Age Level Descriptor covers an approximate age range, and one or more are used when a document or journal article *is concerned strictly with age-level groups or populations*.

NOTE: The use of specific age-related Descriptors such as ADOPTED CHILDREN and ADULT DROPOUTS usually eliminates the need to also index or search such generic terms as CHILDREN and ADULTS.

The broad age-level Descriptor CHILDREN is defined as "aged birth through approximately 12 years," and its narrower terms (NTs) generally may be regarded as reflective of this range. However, some "children" terms are occasionally indexed more broadly than the 0-12 restriction would appear to allow. For example:

ADOPTED CHILDREN used for "adopted adolescents";
LATCHKEY CHILDREN used for "latchkey youth";
PROBLEM CHILDREN used for "problem teens."

This, of course, occurs because specific alternative Descriptors in these cases, such as "Adopted Adolescents," do not exist in the *Thesaurus*. While this practice violates in a sense normal broader/narrower term (BT/NT) or "class membership" relationships, it is preferable to having multiple pairs of quasi-synonymous terms. In the examples above, each could be coordinated with the age leveler ADOLESCENTS to reflect the proper context. Retrieval is not particularly hampered by this unusual situation. For example, one can search:

ADOPTED CHILDREN for the entire broad 0-17 age range;
ADOPTED CHILDREN *and* ADOLESCENTS for ages

13-17 only;
ADOPTED CHILDREN *not* ADOLESCENTS for ages
0-12 only.

The Age Level Descriptors appear with their Scope
Notes in the following chart:

OPTIONAL "AGE LEVEL" DESCRIPTORS

NEONATES
Scope Note: Aged birth to approximately 1 month.
INFANTS
Scope Note: Aged birth to approximately 24 months.
YOUNG CHILDREN
Scope Note: Aged birth through approximately 8 years.
CHILDREN
Scope Note: Aged birth through approximately 12 years.
TODDLERS
Scope Note: Approximately 1-3 years of age.
PRESCHOOL CHILDREN
Scope Note: Approximately 2-5 years of age.
PREADOLESCENTS
Scope Note: Approximately 9-12 years of age.
EARLY ADOLESCENTS
Scope Note: Approximately 11-15 years of age.
ADOLESCENTS
Scope Note: Approximately 13-17 years of age.
LATE ADOLESCENTS
Scope Note: Approximately 16-23 years of age.
YOUNG ADULTS
Scope Note: Approximately 18-30 years of age.
ADULTS
Scope Note: Approximately 18+ years of age.
ADULTS (30 TO 45)
Scope Note: Age group between "young adults"
and "middle aged adults"—approximately 30-45.
MIDDLE AGED ADULTS
Scope Note: Approximately 45-64 years of age.
YOUNG OLD ADULTS
Scope Note: Approximately 65-75 years of age.
OLDER ADULTS
Scope Note: Approximately 65+ years of age.
OLD OLD ADULTS
Scope Note: Approximately 75+ years of age.

Identifiers

"Identifiers" are key words or "indexable" concepts
intended to add a depth to subject indexing that is not
always possible with Descriptors alone. Identifiers are not
found in the *Thesaurus*, since they are generally: (1) proper
names, or (2) concepts not yet represented by approved
Descriptors. They appear in a separate field below the
Descriptors in the resume sections of *RIE* and *CIJE*. They
may be "majored" with an asterisk just as Descriptors are.
Major Identifiers, like Major Descriptors, appear in the
printed Subject Indexes of *RIE* and *CIJE*.

IDENTIFIERS

EJ 397 738   EA 523 711
Enlisting Parents' Help with Mathematics.
Kahn. Ann P. *Educational Leadership*; v47 n2
p37 Oct 1989
Descriptors: *Mathematics; *Parent Student
Relationship; *Home Programs; Elementary
Secondary Education
→ Identifiers: *Parent Teacher Association
A new national PTA kit, "Math Matters; Kids Are
Counting on You," can help all parents make
a difference in their children's education.
Suggested home activities include doubling
cookie recipes, surveying and graphing fami-
ly ice cream flavor preferences, filling in foot-
ball "stat" charts, and other tasks easily per-
formed on a calculator. (MLH)

Identifiers are used to index geographic locations,
personal names, test or program names, specific legislation,
etc., as well as concepts not found in the *Thesaurus*. The
Identifier field can provide a "tryout" for candidate
Descriptors. Identifiers are examined regularly by the
Vocabulary Review Group for their suitability as
Descriptors. ERIC is a literature-based information system,
and every Descriptor must be supported by a document or
article in the database; Identifiers often provide that evidence and serve as the justification for Clearinghouse
proposals for new *Thesaurus* terms.

Recent examples of former Identifiers that now
appear in the *Thesaurus* as Descriptors are:

ALTERNATIVE ASSESSMENT
BOOKSTORES
BULLYING
CLASSICS (LITERATURE)
DISCOURSE COMMUNITIES
ELECTRONIC LIBRARIES
HAZING
HISTORICAL INTERPRETATION
JOB SECURITY
LISTSERVS
OBJECTIVITY
POSTMODERNISM
REGGIO EMILIA APPROACH
RIVERS
SOCIAL PROMOTION
SPIRITUALITY
TRANSFORMATIVE LEARNING
WORLD VIEWS

New Descriptors are announced in the monthly issues
of *RIE* and *CIJE*. It is rare for Identifiers that are proper
names (person, place, program, organization, etc.) to
become Descriptors.

All terms in the Identifier field must conform in format to terms in the *ERIC Identifier Authority List (IAL)*[15] or
to the rules and guidelines for creating new Identifiers.[16]
Items are purged from the *IAL* when they are upgraded to
Descriptor status and shifted to the *Thesaurus*.

---

[15] The *IAL*, most recent annual edition, is available in paper copy from the ERIC Processing and Reference Facility, 4483-A Forbes Boulevard, Lanham, MD 20706, 800-799-ERIC, http://ericfacility.org. It includes two displays: main *Alphabetical Display*, listing the approximately 56,000 preferred Identifier forms with their postings—some cross-references and scope notes are included; Category Display, listing Identifiers alphabetically within broad categories (e.g., equipment, geographic locations, legislation, persons). The displays are available separately: *Alphabetical Display* ($40)—includes free supplement, when available; *Category Display* ($35).
[16] Guidelines are detailed in the *ERIC Processing Manual, Section 8, Vocabulary Development and Maintenance (Part 2)—Identifiers*, available for $7.50 from the ERIC Facility or as ED 348 064 from the ERIC Document Reproduction Service.

As Identifiers are moved to the *Thesaurus*, their index postings are transferred to the Descriptor field. All such Identifier-to-Descriptor conversions occurring before December 1980 are fully reflected in the ERIC file. December 1980 was the last time a general reload of the ERIC backfile was performed. Conversions since that time, therefore, are *not* fully reflected in the database, and posting counts for Descriptors added after December 1980 may represent combined Descriptor/Identifier usages. (See related discussion under "Transferred Descriptors," p. xi.)

NOTE:

1. Like Major Descriptors, Major Identifiers appear in the Subject Indexes of *RIE* and *CIJE*.
2. Both Major and Minor Identifiers can be searched by computer similarly to the way that Descriptors can be searched.
3. To be safe, searches of Descriptors with add dates after December 1980 (when the last general ERIC reload occurred) should consider usages (postings) not only in the Descriptor field, but in the Identifier field as well.

Publication Types

PUBTYPE Codes. All documents may be categorized by their "form" of publication (i.e., Publication Type or PUB-TYPE) as well as by their subject. A special section of the document resume identifies the PUBTYPE by means of a three-digit code. PUBTYPEs are assigned to every document and journal article (beginning September 1974 for *RIE*, August 1979 for *CIJE*). They appear in the monthly printed issues of *RIE* along with the bibliographic information.

ED 360 238   SO 023 270
Gallagher, Arlene F., Ed.
Acting Together. Readers Theatre: Excerpts from Children's Literature on Themes from the Constitution.
Social Science Education Consortium, Inc., Boulder, Colo.
Spons Agency—Commission on the Bicentennial of the United States Constitution, Washington, DC
Report No.—ISBN-0-89994-363-2
Pub Date—91
Note—123p.
Available from—Social Science Education Consortium, 3300 Mitchell Lane, Suite 240, Boulder, CO 80301-2272.
→ Pub Type—Creative Works—(030)
Guides - Classroom - Learner—(051)
Guides - Classroom - Teacher—(052)
EDRS Price - MF01/PC05 Plus Postage.
Descriptors—*Childrens Literature; Citizenship Education; *Constitutional History; *Constitutional Law; Elementary Education; Law Related Education; Learning Activities; *Readers Theater; *Social Studies
Identifiers—*United States Constitution
This book summarizes itself as "A collection of excerpts from children's literature on themes related to the United States Constitution scripted in Readers Theatre format for elementary school students." It is based on the belief that an integrated curriculum...

Printed issues of *CIJE* do not include PUBTYPE designations. However, all assigned PUBTYPEs for both *RIE* and *CIJE* are searchable by computer.

In *RIE*, they are also searchable manually in the Publication Type Index (first published in July 1979). This index is organized numerically by PUBTYPE code and provides reference to title and accession (ED) number for each document having that code. (The // symbol following an accession number refers to a document that is not available from the ERIC Document Reproduction Service.)

(030) Creative Works
Acting Together. Readers Theatre. Excerpts from Children's Literature on Themes from the Constitution.
ED 360 238
From Puggy to Larry: Poetry from "Gathering Light."
ED 360 226
Pages from Life: Families Write Together = Paginas de la Vida: Familias Escriben Juntas.
ED 360 433//
Storytelling Project. Southeast Asian Women's Alliance.
ED 359 838

Codes and category names for the ERIC PUBTYPEs are as follows:

CODE	PUBLICATION/DOCUMENT TYPES
010	BOOKS
	COLLECTED WORKS
020	—General
021	—Conference Proceedings
022	—Serials
030	CREATIVE WORKS (Literature, Drama, Fine Arts)
	DISSERTATIONS/THESES
040	—Undetermined
041	—Doctoral Dissertations
042	—Masters Theses
043	—Practicum Papers
	GUIDES
050	—General (use more specific code, if possible)
	Classroom Use
051	—Instructional Materials (for Learner)
052	—Teaching Guides (for Teacher)
055	—Non-Classroom Use (for Administrative and Support Staff, and for Teachers, Parents,Clergy, Researchers, Counselors, etc., in Non-Classroom Situations)
060	HISTORICAL MATERIALS
070	INFORMATION ANALYSES (State-of-the-Art Papers, Research Summaries, Reviews of the Literature on a Topic)
071	ERIC Information Analysis Products (IAPs)
072	Book/Product Reviews
073	ERIC Digests (Selected) in Full Text
074	Non-ERIC Digests (Selected) in Full Text
080	JOURNAL ARTICLES
090	LEGAL/LEGISLATIVE/REGULATORY MATERIALS
100	AUDIOVISUAL/NON-PRINT MATERIALS
101	—Computer Programs
102	—Machine-Readable Data Files (MRDFs)
110	STATISTICAL DATA (Numerical, Quantitative, etc.)
120	VIEWPOINTS (Opinion Papers, Position Papers, Essays, etc.)
	REFERENCE MATERIALS
130	—General (use more specific code, if possible)
131	—Bibliographies/Annotated Bibliographies
132	—Directories/Catalogs

(continued)

	(continued)	
133	—Geographic Materials/Maps	
134	—Vocabularies/Classifications/Dictionaries	
	REPORTS	
140	—General (use more specific code, if possible)	
141	—Descriptive (i.e., Project Descriptions)	
142	—Evaluative/Feasibility	
143	—Research/Technical	
150	SPEECHES, CONFERENCE PAPERS	
160	TESTS, EVALUATION INSTRUMENTS	
170	TRANSLATIONS	
171	—Multilingual/Bilingual Materials	

DIRECTORIES	132
DOCTORAL DISSERTATIONS	041
GUIDES	050
JOURNAL ARTICLES	080
MASTERS THESES	042
MULTILINGUAL MATERIALS	171
PRACTICUM PAPERS	043
REFERENCE MATERIALS	130
REPORTS	140
RESEARCH REPORTS	143
SERIALS	022
SPEECHES	150
STATISTICAL DATA	110
TESTS	160
THESES	040
VOCABULARY	134

To determine the proper PUBTYPE code for a document, an ERIC indexer examines the item and then checks the "Guide for Assigning Pubtype Codes" (see pp. xxiv-xxvi). For example, if the document in hand is a feasibility study, the table readily identifies it as a "code 142" item.

Similarly, this cross-reference chart is useful in the retrieval process. For example, if a user wanted samples of facility guidelines, the PUBTYPE code 055 could be searched; or an examination of the PUBTYPE code 060 could be used to help find biographies of historical figures.

NOTE: One PUBTYPE code is required on every ERIC document or article. To allow flexibility in classification, up to three PUBTYPE codes can be assigned (two for *CIJE* journal articles since PUBTYPE code 080 is assigned automatically by computer). All may be searched by computer. PUBTYPE categories assigned to *RIE* documents appear in the *RIE* Publication Type Index. Although PUBTYPES are assigned to *CIJE* articles, there is no comparable *CIJE* publication type index.

Publication Type Descriptors. Labeling of publication type or document characteristics is also done by the use of Descriptors. For example, a document that includes the complete survey instrument (e.g., a questionnaire) used in a research study would be PUBTYPE-coded 143 (Research/Technical Reports) and 160 (Tests, Evaluation Instruments). But it would also carry the Minor Descriptor QUESTIONNAIRES (minor, because "questionnaire" is not the *subject* of the document). The use of specific form terms is not unusual in the Descriptor field. However, as of March 1980, certain very broad form terms that coincide exactly with names of PUBTYPE categories are not used for indexing document form in the Descriptor Field. These 23 form terms and their corresponding PUBTYPE codes are listed below:

DESCRIPTORS CORRESPONDING TO PUBLICATION TYPE CATEGORIES	
DESCRIPTOR	PUBTYPE CODE
AUDIOVISUAL AIDS	100
BIBLIOGRAPHIES	131
BOOKS	010
COMPUTER SOFTWARE	101
CONFERENCE PAPERS	150
CONFERENCE PROCEEDINGS	021
DICTIONARIES	134

These very broad terms may be used as Descriptors (Major or Minor) *if* they apply to the *subject* of the document, as noted in the *Thesaurus*:

PUBTYPE INSTRUCTION

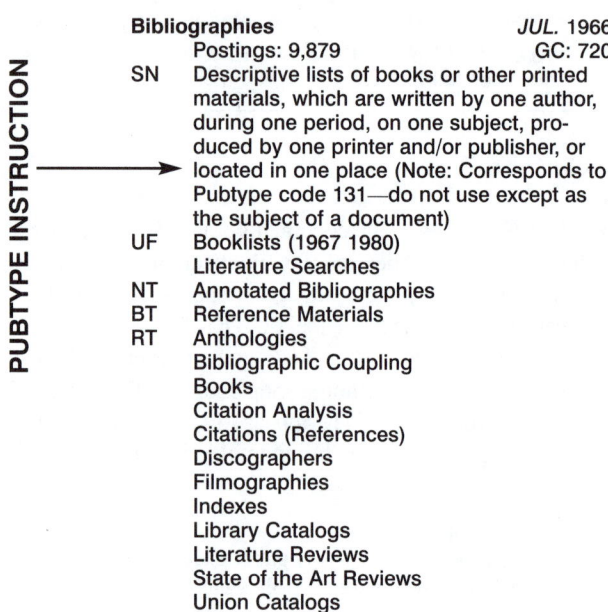

Bibliographies		JUL. 1966
	Postings: 9,879	GC: 720
SN	Descriptive lists of books or other printed materials, which are written by one author, during one period, on one subject, produced by one printer and/or publisher, or located in one place (Note: Corresponds to Pubtype code 131—do not use except as the subject of a document)	
UF	Booklists (1967 1980)	
	Literature Searches	
NT	Annotated Bibliographies	
BT	Reference Materials	
RT	Anthologies	
	Bibliographic Coupling	
	Books	
	Citation Analysis	
	Citations (References)	
	Discographers	
	Filmographies	
	Indexes	
	Library Catalogs	
	Literature Reviews	
	State of the Art Reviews	
	Union Catalogs	

Thus, if a document were a bibliography about how to compile bibliographies, it would have the PUBTYPE 131 (Bibliographies) and also the Major Descriptor BIBLIOGRAPHIES (major, because it is the subject of the document).

NOTE: "Document type" Descriptors (see table on pp. xxiv-xxvi) should *not* be *Major* Descriptors unless they are the *subject* of the document.

FURTHER HINTS FOR RELEVANT RETRIEVAL

Nonsubject Access

The usual approach to finding information in ERIC is by subject area, using Descriptors, Identifiers, and/or free-text phrases. Using ERIC's PUBTYPE codes to locate types of materials further refines the search process. Additional non-subject access points are available through ERIC's cataloging, which can help target computer searches even more precisely. These include document language, geographic origin (country, or country and state/province), and target audience.[17] All three of these data elements are searchable only by computer. Language appears on both *RIE* and *CIJE* citations as of January 1979. Geographic origin, also effective January 1979, is used only for *RIE*.

Target Audience

Documents and journal articles in ERIC are sometimes written for particular audiences. ERIC catalogs these audiences in a special "Target Audience" field. *This field is used when an author clearly specifies an intended audience; otherwise, it is left blank.*

Eleven distinct audiences have been defined by ERIC, as follows:

- Policymakers
- Researchers
- Practitioners
  - Administrators
  - Teachers
  - Counselors
  - Media Staff
  - Support Staff
- Students
- Parents
- Community

NOTE: The ERIC computer system automatically adds the generic audience "Practitioners" to records cataloged by any of the five "Practitioner" subcategories.

The Target Audience field may be used to limit a computer search more narrowly. For example, adding the Target Audience "Teachers" to a computer search of the Descriptor ACQUIRED IMMUNE DEFICIENCY SYNDROME would focus the search on literature on AIDS written specifically for teachers.

Target Audience is an optional cataloging element. Not all documents identify an audience; some identify more than one. There are no limitations on the number of audiences that may be cataloged other than adherence to the prescribed list above. However, if more than two practitioner groups are identified, only the generic "Practitioners" is cataloged.

The Target Audience field has been a fully defined cataloging element for *RIE* since January 1984 and for *CIJE* since September 1984. The terms "Practitioners" and/or "Students" have been added retrospectively to selected May 1975 through December 1983 *RIE* citations. No citations prior to May 1975 contain a Target Audience field.

NOTE:
1. Target Audience was added as a new data element to *RIE* in January 1984 and to *CIJE* in September 1984. There are some retrospective *RIE* postings of "Practitioners" and "Students."
2. Target Audience is not cataloged on all documents and journal articles, but only for those approximately 25 percent that explicitly claim a specific target group.
3. Target Audience does not appear in the printed *RIE* and *CIJE* abstract journals.
4. In searching, Target Audience should be used as a precise "limiter." Its assignment on a document assumes restrictiveness.

CONCLUSION

This brief review of the ERIC system is intended to make users more aware of the system as a whole, of how the literature on education and educational issues is indexed for the database, and how the *Thesaurus* fits into the overall information dissemination process.

ERIC is committed to serving a widely divergent educational community while maintaining high database standards. To do so, ERIC staff encourage direct contact and interaction with users in the field. The ERIC network appreciates feedback and assistance from the clientele it serves.

For further information about ERIC, call ACCESS ERIC 1-800-LET-ERIC
ACCESS ERIC was established in May 1989 to increase awareness of and access to educational information by the educational community and the pubic. ACCESS ERIC staff answer questions, refer callers to education sources, and provide information about the ERIC network.

---

[17] Further details on the Language, Geographic Origin, and Target Audience fields are given in the *ERIC Processing Manual Section 5: Cataloging*, available for $7.50 from the ERIC Facility or as ED 348 060 from the ERIC Document Reproduction Service.

Publication Type	Pubtype Code Most Applicable
Abstracts	131
Administrator Guides	055
Annotated Bibliographies	131
Annual Reports	141
Answer Keys	160
Answer Sheets	160
Anthologies	020
[Archival Documents]	060
Atlases	133
Audiodisks	100
Audiotape Recordings	100
*Audiovisual Aids	100
Autobiographies	060
*Bibliographies	131
[Bilingual Materials]	171
Biographical Inventories	060 (132)
Biographies	060
Book Reviews	072
[Booklists]	131
*Books	010
Bulletins	022
[Bylaws]	090
Cartoons	100 (030)
Case Records [or] Case Studies	141 or 143 or 140
Catalogs	132
Charts	100
Check Lists	130 or 160
[Childrens Books]	010 and 030
Childrens Literature	030 (010)
Chronicles	060 (020)
Citation Indexes	131
[Class Newspapers]	022
[Classroom Games]	051 (100)
[Classroom Materials]	051 or 052
Codes of Ethics	090
Comics (Publications)	030
Computer Output Microfilm	100
*Computer Software	101
Computer Software Reviews	072 (142)
[Concordances]	134
*Conference Papers	150
*Conference Proceedings	021

Publication Type	Pubtype Code Most Applicable
[Conference Summaries]	021
Contracts	090
Course Descriptions	052 or 050 or 051
[Courtroom Transcripts]	090
[Creative Works]	030
Curriculum Guides	052 or 050 or 051
[Data Sheets]	110 or 130
Databases	102
Diagrams	100
Diaries	120 (060 or 030)
*Dictionaries	134
[Dictionary Catalogs]	131
*Directories	132
[Discipline Codes]	090
Discographies	131
*Doctoral Dissertations	041
Documentaries	100 (141)
Drama	030
Editorials	120
Encyclopedias	130
[ERIC Digests in Full Text]	073
[ERIC IAPs]	071
Essays	120 or 030
[Evaluation Studies]	142
Facility Guidelines	055
Facility Handbooks	055
Feasibility Studies	142
Filmographies	131
Films	100
Filmstrips	100
Flow Charts	100
Foreign Language Books	010 (170)
Foreign Language Films	100 (170)
Foreign Language Periodicals	022 (170)
Games	030 or 100
Glossaries	134
Graphs	100
Guidelines	050 or 052 or 055
*Guides	050 or 051 or 052 or 055

FOOTNOTES:

1. All terms not in brackets have been selected from the ERIC *Thesaurus*.
2. Conventions   A or B   =   One or the other category is appropriate, depending on item.
    A and B   =   Two categories are appropriate.
    A (B)   =   A second category might be appropriate, depending on item.
    *   =   Category and term are synonymous. Term should be used in Descriptor field only when it denotes subject matter.
3. These terms, like all other Descriptors identifying the form or type of a document, should be used as major Descriptors only when they represent the subject of the document in hand.

**GUIDE FOR ASSIGNING PUBTYPE CODES
(A CROSS-REFERENCE FROM SPECIFIC KINDS OF DOCUMENTS
TO MOST APPLICABLE PUBLICATION TYPE CODE)**

[Bracketed terms are not Descriptors]

Publication Type	Pubtype Code Most Applicable
Hearings	090
[Historical Reviews]	060
Illustrations	100
Indexes	130 or 131
[Information Analyses]	070 or 071
Instructional Materials	051
Interviews	120 or 160
Item Banks	160
Journal Articles	080
[Journals]	022
[Judicial Materials]	090
Kinescope Recordings	100
Laboratory Manuals	051
[Language Guides]	051 or 030 (170)
Large Type Materials	051
Leaders Guides	052
[Lecture]	150 (051)
[Legal Analysis]	090
Legislation	090
Lesson Plans	052
Letters (Correspondence)	030
[Literature Guides]	131
Literature Reviews	131 (070)
[Lobbying Papers]	090 and 120
Magnetic Tape Cassettes	100
Magnetic Tapes	100
[Manuals]	050 or 051 or 052 or 055
Maps	133
Master Plans	090
[Master Tapes (Audio)]	100
*Masters Theses	042
Matrices	100
Microforms	100
Models	100 or 143
*Multilingual Materials	171
[Musical Materials]	030
Negotiation Agreements	090
Newsletters	022
Newspapers	022
Nonprint Media	100
Opinions	120
[Oral History Transcripts]	060
Pamphlets	Document Dependent

Publication Type	Pubtype Code Most Applicable
[Parent Guides]	055
Patents	090
Periodicals	022
Permuted Indexes	130 or 131
Personal Narratives	060 or 120
[Phonograph Records]	100
Photographs	100
Poetry	030
Position Papers	120
*Practicum Papers	043
Program Descriptions	141
Program Evaluation	142
Program Guides	141
Program Proposals	141
[Programmed Texts]	010 and 051
Puzzles	030 or 100
Questionnaires	160
Rating Scales	160
[Recommendations]	120
Records (Forms)	Document Dependent
*Reference Materials	130 (010)
[Regulations]	090
*Reports	140
[Research Methodology Guides]	055
Research Proposals	143
*Research Reports	143
[Research Reviews (Publications)]	070
Resource Materials	050 or 051 or 052 or 055
Scholarly Journals	022
School Newspapers	022
School Publications	Document Dependent
Scripts	030
*Serials	022
Short Stories	030
Slides	100
Specifications	090
*Speeches	150
Standards	090
State of the Art Reviews	070
*Statistical Data	110
Student Journals	120 (030)
Student Publications	Document Dependent
Study Guides	051
Surveys	160 or 143

GUIDE FOR ASSIGNING PUBTYPE CODES
(A CROSS-REFERENCE FROM SPECIFIC KINDS OF DOCUMENTS
TO MOST APPLICABLE PUBLICATION TYPE CODE)

(see explanatory <u>footnotes</u> on first page

[Bracketed terms are not Descriptors]

Publication Type	Pubtype Code Most Applicable
Tables (Data)	110
Talking Books	100
Tape Recordings	100
[Taxonomy]	134
Teaching Guides	052
[Technical Reports]	143
Test Reviews	072 (142)
*Tests	160
Textbooks	010 and 051
Thesauri	134
*Theses	040
[Transcripts (Interview)]	120

Publication Type	Pubtype Code Most Applicable
[Transcripts (Legal)]	090
[Transcripts (Oral History)]	060
Videodisks	100
Videotape Recordings	100
*Vocabulary	134
Word Lists	134
Workbooks	051
Worksheets	051
Yearbooks	141 (022)

GUIDE FOR ASSIGNING PUBTYPE CODES
(A CROSS-REFERENCE FROM SPECIFIC KINDS OF DOCUMENTS
TO MOST APPLICABLE PUBLICATION TYPE CODE)

(see explanatory <u>footnotes</u> on first page

[Bracketed terms are not Descriptors]

Thesaurus Construction and Format

The *Thesaurus of ERIC Descriptors, 14th Edition*, contains an alphabetical listing of terms used for indexing and searching in the ERIC system. It actually consists of four parts—the main Alphabetical Display, the Rotated Display, the Two-way Hierarchical Term Display, and the Descriptor Group Display.

ALPHABETICAL DESCRIPTOR DISPLAY

The main, word-by-word Alphabetical Display is probably the most familiar since it provides a variety of information (a "display") for each Descriptor. This includes a Scope Note (SN), Add Date, Descriptor Group Code, Posting Notes, Used For (UF) and Use (USE) references, Narrower Terms (NT), Broader Terms (BT), and Related Terms (RT). Each of these segments of the *Thesaurus* display is explained in detail below.

SN (Scope Note)

A Scope Note is a brief statement of the intended usage of a Descriptor. It may be used to clarify an ambiguous term or to restrict the usage of a term. Special indexing notes are often included.

Tests
SN Devices, procedures, or sets of items that are used to measure ability, skill, understanding, knowledge, or achievement (Note: Use a more specific term if possible—this broad term corresponds to Pubtype code 160 and should not be used except as the subject of a document)

Recommends use of a Narrower Term and directs indexers and searchers to PUBTYPE category.

Oral Interpretation
SN The oral interpretation and presentation of a work of literature to an audience (Note: Prior to Mar80, the instruction "Oral Interpretation, USE Interpretive Reading" was carried in the *Thesaurus*)

Alerts indexers and searchers to an earlier Thesaurus instruction.

Reference Groups
SN Real or theoretical groups (social, ethnic, family, etc.) that serve as sources for identification, motivation, aspiration, attitudes, behavior, or modes of living (Note: Do not confuse with "Role Models" or the Identifier "Reference Individuals," both referring to individuals rather than groups, the former emulated in one or a few roles and the latter emulated in many roles)

Suggests another Descriptor or an Identifier that may be more appropriate.

UF (Used For)

The UF reference is employed generally to solve problems of synonymy occurring in natural language. Terms following the UF notation are *not to be used in indexing*. They most often represent either (1) synonymous or variant forms of the main term, or (2) specific terms that, for purposes of storage and retrieval, are indexed under a more general term. The examples below illustrate both types of UFs:

Mainstreaming
UF Desegregation (Disabled Students)
   Integration (Disabled Students)
   Least Restrictive Environment (Disabled)
   Regular Class Placement (1968 1978)

Lifelong Learning
UF Continuous Learning (1967 1980)
   Education Permanente
   Life Span Education
   Lifelong Education
   Permanent Education
   Recurrent Education

Labor Force Development
UF Human Resources Development (Labor)
   Manpower Development (1966 1980)

Physical Disabilities
UF Crippled Children (1968 1980)
   Orthopedically Handicapped (1968 1980)
   Physical Handicaps (1966 1980)
   Physically Handicapped (1966 1980)

A former Descriptor that has been downgraded to the status of a UF term is accompanied by a "life span" notation in parentheses: e.g., (1966 1980). This indicates the time period during which the term was used in indexing. It provides useful information for searching older printed indexes, or computer files that have not been updated.

NOTE: The present status of "downgraded" Descriptors in the ERIC database is discussed under "Transferred Descriptors," p. xi, accompanied by a list of all such terms still searchable on the file.

Sometimes a UF needs more than one Descriptor to represent it adequately. In such cases, a pound sign (#) following the UF term signifies that two or more main terms are to be used in coordination. The term's main entry in the Alphabetical Display shows the appropriate coordination. A footnote to this effect appears at the bottom of each page of the display. Sample "multiple UFs" follow:

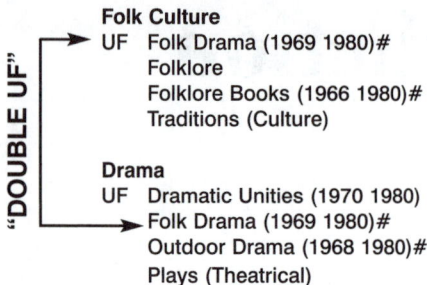

"DOUBLE UF"

Folk Culture
UF   Folk Drama (1969 1980)#
       Folklore
       Folklore Books (1966 1980)#
       Traditions (Culture)

Drama
UF   Dramatic Unities (1970 1980)
       Folk Drama (1969 1980)#
       Outdoor Drama (1968 1980)#
       Plays (Theatrical)

USE

The USE reference, the mandatory reciprocal of the UF, refers an indexer or searcher from a nonusable (nonindexable) term to the preferred indexable term or terms.

In the examples below, there is only one USE term for each entry. This means that there is a direct, one-to-one correlation in the ERIC system from the UF to the USE term.

Regular Class Placement (1968 1978)
USE   Mainstreaming

Continuous Learning (1967 1980)
USE   Lifelong Learning

Orthopedically Handicapped (1968 1980)
USE   Physical Disabilities

Manpower
USE   Labor Force

A coordinate or multiple USE reference (the reciprocal of the "double UF" above) looks a little different. The following example illustrates the use of two main terms together to represent a single concept, both for indexing and searching:

Folk Drama (1969 1980)
USE   Drama
AND   Folk Culture

BT (Broader Term) and NT (Narrower Term)

The BT/NT notations are used to indicate the existence of a hierarchical relationship between a class and its subclasses. Narrower terms (terms following the NT notation) are included in the broader class represented by the main entry.

Libraries
NT   Academic Libraries
       Branch Libraries
       Childrens Libraries
       Depository Libraries
       Electronic Libraries
       Public Libraries
       Research Libraries
       School Libraries
       Special Libraries

Models
NT   Causal Models
       Mathematical Models
       Role Models
       Student Writing Models
       Teaching Models

The Broader Term (BT) is the mandatory reciprocal of the NT. Broader Terms (terms following the BT symbol) include as a subclass the concept represented by the main (narrower) term.

School Libraries
BT   Libraries

Mathematical Models
BT   Models

Sometimes a term may have more than one Broader Term:

Remedial Reading
BT   Reading
       Reading Instruction
       Remedial Instruction

RT (Related Term)

Terms following the RT notation have a close conceptual relationship to the main term, but not the direct class/subclass relationship described by BTs/NTs. Part-whole relationships, near-synonyms, and other conceptually related terms, which might be helpful to the user, appear as RTs.

High School Seniors
RT   College Bound Students
       Grade 12
       High School Freshmen
       High School Graduates
       Noncollege Bound Students

Minimum Competency Testing
RT   Academic Achievement
       Academic Standards
       Basic Skills
       Competence
       Competency Based Education
       Mastery Tests
       Minimum Competencies
       National Competency Tests
       Student Certification
       Teacher Competency Testing
       Test Score Decline

Second Language Programs
RT   Bilingual Education Programs
       Conversational Language Courses
       English (Second Language)
       FLES
       Intensive Language Courses
       Language Enrollment
       Language Laboratories
       Modern Language Curriculum
       Multilevel Classes (Second Language
          Instruction)
       Native Speakers
       Notional Functional Syllabi
       Second Language Instruction
       Second Language Learning
       Second Languages

Two Year Colleges
RT   Associate Degrees
       Multicampus Colleges
       Multicampus Districts
       Postsecondary Education
       State Colleges
       Technical Education
       Trade and Industrial Education

Transfer Rates (College)
Two Year College Students
Undergraduate Study
Upper Division Colleges

Parenthetical Qualifiers

A Parenthetical Qualifier is used to identify a particular indexable meaning of a homograph. In other words, it discriminates between terms (either Descriptors or USE references) that might otherwise be confused with each other. Examples include LETTERS (ALPHABET) and LETTERS (CORRESPONDENCE); SELF EVALUATION (INDIVIDUALS) and SELF EVALUATION (GROUPS).

> NOTE: The Qualifier is considered an integral part of the Descriptor and must be used with the Descriptor in indexing *and* searching.

Add Dates

An Add Date (i.e., date term was entered into the *Thesaurus*) is printed to the right of each Descriptor or main term. The earliest "real" Add Date is Aug. 1968. Month and year of entry into the *Thesaurus* are given for each Descriptor added from Aug. 1968 to the present. All earlier Descriptors have been given the arbitrary Add Date of Jul. 1966, the approximate point in time at which ERIC indexing (only for *RIE* at that point) began. Add Dates are intended to help users in the preparation of search strategies. They represent calendar dates, not *RIE* or *CIJE* issue dates. Rigid interpretation of Add Dates should be avoided.

It should also be noted that new Scope Notes are occasionally added to older Descriptors (i.e., terms with earlier Add Dates). In cases where that may affect searching, an instructional statement is included in the new Scope Note:

> **Foundation Programs**   *JUL. 1966*
> SN Systems whereby state funds are used to supplement local or intermediate school district funds for elementary and secondary education—a "minimum foundation" of financial support is usually guaranteed regardless of the local district's ability to support education (Note: Prior to Mar80, this term was not scoped and was sometimes used to index "Philanthropic Foundations")

Descriptor Group Codes

Descriptor Group Codes are also provided for each term at its main alphabetical entry point. The three-digit number indicates the broad category to which that term belongs. The codes are useful for identifying other Descriptors that are conceptually related to the term, but that do not necessarily appear in the term's main display. (See p. xxxi for a complete list of the categories, and the Descriptor Group Display for lists of all Descriptors assigned within each category and having the same Group Code number.)

In the example below, the number 540 following "GC"

shows that SEX FAIRNESS is in the Descriptor Group 540, "Bias and Equity."

> **Sex Fairness**   *AUG. 1978*
> Postings: 2,580   GC: 540
> SN The correction of sex bias or discrimination
>   (Note: Use for descriptions of materials, procedures, activities, or programs that treat the sexes equitably)

Postings Note

As an additional aid to users, a Postings Note is provided for each Descriptor at its main alphabetical entry point. This notation appears above the Scope Note and indicates the number of times—as of October 2000—that the term was used as a Major or Minor Descriptor or Identifier in *RIE* and *CIJE*.

> **Equal Education**   *JUL. 1966*
> Postings: 10,765   GC: 540

Examination of the postings for a Descriptor may lead the user to check a term's NTs or RTs before the search strategy is formulated completely. For example, a term with 3,000 postings will not be searched easily manually, but one or more of its NTs could be. On the other hand, a term with only 15 postings might suggest that the searcher also consider including the term's RTs or even its BTs in the search strategy.

> NOTE: All terms in the ERIC *Thesaurus* have actually been used in indexing (either in their present form or a close variant form). Some terms showing zero or very low postings have replaced earlier obsolete terms, e.g., double-m PROGRAMMERS (15 postings) was added in March 1994 to replace the earlier single-m PROGRAMERS (150+ postings). Even though ERIC provides postings transfers from old to new in such situations, such transfers are not reflected in the ERIC database until general reloads are performed. The last such general reload was in December 1980. (See discussion under "Transferred Descriptors," p. xi. All Descriptors like the single-m PROGRAMERS that have been removed from the *Thesaurus* since December 1980 and that must still be considered in retrospective searching are listed there.)
>
> Postings counts for any Descriptor added to the *Thesaurus* after December 1980 may include the usage that term had as an earlier Identifier. For example, COLLEGIALITY, added as a Descriptor in August 1988, was previously an Identifier, and its postings count reflects its usage in both the Descriptor and Identifier fields. Also, postings counts can improperly reflect actual database content when a new Descriptor and a previously preferred Identifier form do not match, e.g., the 1993 Descriptor GEOGRAPHIC ISOLATION (128 postings) and the alternatively formatted Identifier ISOLATION (GEOGRAPHIC) (86 postings) preferred earlier. Identifier-to-Descriptor conversions are provided by ERIC, but, as with Descriptor-to-Descriptor transfers,

they are not actually reflected in the database until the next general reload. (See also discussion on p. xx.)

Invalid Descriptors

Occasionally, Descriptors have been added to the *Thesaurus* that, because of inherent ambiguity or subsequent indexing practices, have been used with such little consistency that their usefulness in retrieval has been diminished. Such Descriptors, when discovered, are generally deleted as usable terms in the *Thesaurus*. They are reentered as invalid or "dead" terms. Each Invalid Descriptor has two characteristics: a "life span" notation indicating the span of time that the term was actually used in indexing, and a Scope Note intended to indicate how the term was used and to lead indexers and searchers to more precise or meaningful terminology.

Language Instruction (1966 1980)

MAR. 1980

SN   Invalid Descriptor—used for both foreign and native language instruction—see "Second Language Instruction," "English Instruction," or "Native Language Instruction"

Structural Analysis (1966 1980)

MAR. 1980

SN   Invalid Descriptor—originally intended as a linguistics term but used indiscriminately—see "Structural Analysis (Linguistics)" and "Structural Analysis (Science)"—see also such Descriptors as "Cognitive Structures," "Chemical Analysis," "Literary Criticism," and "Group Structure," or such Identifiers as "Musical Analysis," "Structure of Knowledge," and "Structural Learning."

NOTE: Postings for all Invalid Descriptors still exist in the database, and Invalid Descriptors must often be coordinated with other Descriptors to achieve comprehensive searching. A list of ERIC's Invalid Descriptors is provided on pp. xii-xiii.

ROTATED DESCRIPTOR DISPLAY

The Rotated Display (see p. 359) provides an alphabetical index to all words found in Descriptors or their USE references in the *Thesaurus*. A single-word term will file in only one location; a two-word term will file in two locations, etc. Examples for the Descriptors LIFELONG LEARNING and CROSS CULTURAL STUDIES will illustrate:

LIFELONG LEARNING

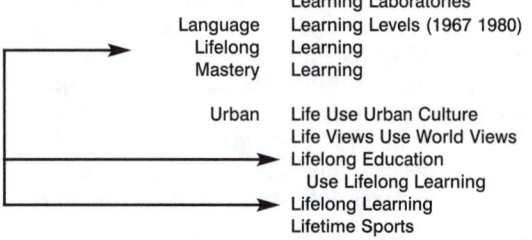

	Learning Laboratories
Language	Learning Levels (1967 1980)
Lifelong	Learning
Mastery	Learning
Urban	Life Use Urban Culture
	Life Views Use World Views
	Lifelong Education
	Use Lifelong Learning
	Lifelong Learning
	Lifetime Sports

CROSS CULTURAL STUDIES

	Cross Cultural
	Communication
	Use Intercultural
	Communication
	Cross Cultural Studies
	Cross Cultural Tests
	Use Culture Fair Tests
	Cross Cultural Training
	(Cross Database)
Interface Systems	Use Gateway Systems
	Cultural Pluralism
	Cultural Preservation
	Use Cultural Maintenance
Cross	Cultural Studies
Cross	Cultural Tests
	Use Culture Fair Tests
Cross	Cultural Training
Canadian	Studies
Case	Studies
Correlation	Studies
	Use Correlation
Cross Cultural	Studies
Cross Sectional	Studies
Unified	Studies Curriculum

The Rotated Descriptor Display is useful in determining all usages of a particular word in the *Thesaurus*, without respect to its position in a multiword Descriptor or USE reference. This Display tends to group related terms when they often may be separated in the main Alphabetical Display. This grouping aids indexers in more thoroughly examining the *Thesaurus* for the most specific Descriptors, helps searchers translate inquiries into the language of the system, and also helps Clearinghouse staff and lexicographers in structuring new Descriptors.

TWO-WAY HIERARCHICAL TERM DISPLAY

The Hierarchical Display (see p. 597) provides so-called "generic trees" for each Descriptor. That is, a Descriptor may have both Broader and Narrower Terms. The Hierarchical Display, therefore, depicts entire families of Descriptors related by class membership, providing complete two-way visibility of the broader-narrower relationships of all main (indexable) terms in the *Thesaurus*. Each generic tree is carried to its farthest extreme in both directions.

A sample generic tree for the term LANGUAGE SKILLS is shown below.

```
::Ability
:Skills
Language Skills
.Audiolingual Skills
..Listening Skills
..Speech Skills
.Communicative
  Competence (Languages)
..Threshold Level (Languages)
.Reading Skills
..Reading Comprehension
..Reading Rate
.Vocabulary Skills
.Writing Skills
```

The Broader Term SKILLS is identified by a colon; multiple colons indicate successively higher levels of BTs (ABILITY). Narrower Terms are identified by periods—AUDIOLINGUAL SKILLS, COMMUNICATIVE COMPETENCE (LANGUAGES), READING SKILLS, VOCABULARY SKILLS, and WRITING SKILLS. Multiple periods indicate successively lower level of NTs. Thus, for example, LISTENING SKILLS and SPEECH SKILLS are NTs to AUDIOLINGUAL SKILLS.

The Hierarchical Display serves as a valuable tool for indexers in their attempts to index documents to the most appropriate level of specificity and for searchers in developing comprehensive search strategies.

NOTE: Computer searching a Broader Term (BT) will not automatically retrieve citations posted by a Narrower Term (NT); searches requiring postings of both a BT and an NT would need to include both terms.

DESCRIPTOR GROUPS

The *Thesaurus of ERIC Descriptors*—like many similar vocabulary authorities—incorporates a system of broad categories into which all Descriptors are grouped. The purpose of these Descriptor Groups is to provide an easy access point, especially for users unfamiliar with the terms included in the *Thesaurus*. The Descriptor Groups, in a sense, offer a "table of contents" to the vocabulary. The Descriptor Group Code appears within the main entry of each term in the Alphabetical Display of the *Thesaurus* (see p. xxvii).

As part of the systemwide Vocabulary Improvement Project (1977 to 1980), the Descriptor Groups categories and the term assignments were revised. The current Descriptor Groups and their codes are listed below:

Groups Related to
LEARNING AND DEVELOPMENT
110   LEARNING AND PERCEPTION
120   INDIVIDUAL DEVELOPMENT AND
        CHARACTERISTICS

Groups Related to
PHYSICAL AND MENTAL CONDITIONS
210   HEALTH AND SAFETY
220   DISABILITIES
230   MENTAL HEALTH
240   COUNSELING

Groups Related to
EDUCATIONAL PROCESSES AND STRUCTURES
310   THE EDUCATIONAL PROCESS:
        CLASSROOM PERSPECTIVES
320   THE EDUCATIONAL PROCESS:
        SCHOOL PERSPECTIVES
330   THE EDUCATIONAL PROCESS:
        SOCIETAL PERSPECTIVES
340   EDUCATIONAL LEVELS, DEGREES,
        AND ORGANIZATIONS
350   CURRICULUM ORGANIZATION
360   STUDENTS, TEACHERS, SCHOOL
        PERSONNEL

Groups Related to
CURRICULUM AREAS
400   SUBJECTS OF INSTRUCTION
410   AGRICULTURE AND
        NATURAL RESOURCES
420   ARTS
430   HUMANITIES
440   LANGUAGES
450   LANGUAGE AND SPEECH
460   READING
470   PHYSICAL EDUCATION
        AND RECREATION
480   MATHEMATICS
490   SCIENCE AND TECHNOLOGY

Groups Related to
HUMAN SOCIETY
510   THE INDIVIDUAL IN SOCIAL CONTEXT
520   SOCIAL PROCESSES
        AND STRUCTURES
530   SOCIAL PROBLEMS
540   BIAS AND EQUITY
550   HUMAN GEOGRAPHY
560   PEOPLES AND CULTURES

Groups Related to
SOCIAL/ECONOMIC ENTERPRISE
610   GOVERNMENT AND POLITICS
620   ECONOMICS AND FINANCE
630   LABOR AND EMPLOYMENT
640   OCCUPATIONS
650   BUSINESS, COMMERCE, AND INDUSTRY

Groups Related to
INFORMATION AND COMMUNICATIONS
710   INFORMATION/COMMUNICATIONS
        SYSTEMS
720   COMMUNICATIONS MEDIA
730   PUBLICATION/DOCUMENT TYPES

Groups Related to
RESEARCH AND MEASUREMENT
810   RESEARCH AND THEORY
820   MEASUREMENT
830   TESTS AND SCALES

Groups Related to
FACILITIES AND EQUIPMENT
910   EQUIPMENT
920   FACILITIES

The Descriptors assigned to each of these groups are listed alphabetically within each group in the Descriptor Group Display (see p. 701).

Each term in the *Thesaurus* is assigned to one Descriptor Group and to only one. This principle of single-group assignment reflects guidelines established to determine the placement of Descriptors, which, because of the breadth of their scope, *could* be assigned to more than one group. Terms are assigned to groups based upon (1) the broadest application of the term in indexing or (2) the way the term has been used most frequently in indexing. Thus, terms that have been scoped to include subject areas outside of the field of education may be assigned to the "Groups Related" to EDUCATIONAL PROCESSES AND STRUCTURES because, in the ERIC database, the terms are used most frequently in this manner. These two guidelines also reflect the assignment of terms that were not entirely appropriate to any existing Descriptor Group.

ERIC NETWORK COMPONENTS

Educational Resources Information Center

The ERIC network of organizations comprises of the following major components:

- **ERIC Program Office**

    The central funding and monitoring unit within the U.S. Department of Education, Office of Educational Research and Improvement (OERI), National Library of Education (NLE). Responsible for overall management of the ERIC network.

    Educational Resources Information Center (ERIC)
    National Library of Education (NLE)
    Office of Educational Research and Improvement (OERI)
    U.S. Department of Education
    400 Maryland Avenue, SW
    Washington, DC 20202-5721
    Telephone: 202-401-3745
    Fax: 202-205-7759
    E-mail: . . . . .eric@ed.gov
    Web: . . . . .http://www.ed.gov

- **ERIC Clearinghouses**

    Sixteen contractors from the academic and not-for-profit sectors, each responsible for collecting the significant educational literature within their particular scope of interest area, e.g., career education, selecting the highest quality and most relevant material, processing (i.e., cataloging, indexing, abstracting) the selected items for input to the database, and synthesizing the literature and providing information analysis products (e.g., Digests) and various user services. (See list on p. xxxiii-xxxiv.)

- **Adjunct ERIC Clearinghouses**

    Various organizations that cooperate with ERIC Clearinghouses at no cost to ERIC to cover a particular specialized area of education in which they have a special interest, e.g., entrepreneurial education. (See list on p. xxxv.)

- **ERIC Support Components**

    Four components providing various specialized technical services in support of the ERIC Program Office, ERIC Clearinghouses, and each other: e.g., centralized database management and abstract journal production, document delivery and micrographics, outreach and user services, and commercial publishing (*Current Index to Journals in Education* [*CIJE*] and ERIC *Thesaurus*). (See list on p. xxxv.)

ERIC Clearinghouse on ADULT, CAREER, AND VOCATIONAL EDUCATION (CE)

Ohio State University
Center on Education and Training for Employment
1900 Kenny Road
Columbus, OH 43210-1090
Telephone: 614-292-7069; 800-848-4815
Fax: 614-292-1260
E-mail: . . . . .ericacve@postbox.acs.ohio-state.edu
Web: . . . . .http://ericacve.org

All levels of adult and continuing education, from basic literacy training through professional skill upgrading. The focus is upon factors contributing to the purposeful learning of adults in a variety of life situations usually related to adult roles (e.g., occupation, family, leisure time, citizenship, organizational relationships, retirement, and so forth).

ERIC Clearinghouse on ASSESSMENT AND EVALUATION (TM)

University of Maryland, College Park
1129 Shriver Lab
College Park, MD 20742-5701
Telephone: 301-405-7449; 800-464-ERIC (3742)
Fax: 301-405-8134
E-mail: . . . . .ericae@ericae.net
Web: . . . . .http://ericae.net

All aspects of tests and other measurement devices. The design and methodology of education-related research, measurement, and evaluation. The evaluation of educational programs and projects. The application of tests, measurement, and evaluation devices/instrumentation in education projects and programs. [Includes input from Adjunct ERIC Clearinghouse for the Test Collection.]

ERIC Clearinghouse for COMMUNITY COLLEGES (JC)

University of California at Los Angeles (UCLA)
405 Hilgard Avenue, 3051 Moore Hall
P.O. Box 951521
Los Angeles, CA 90024-1521
Telephone: 310-825-3931; 800-832-8256
Fax: 310-206-8095
E-mail: . . . . .ericcc@ucla.edu
Web: . . . . .http://www.gseis.ucla.edu/ERIC/eric.html

Development, administration, and evaluation of two-year public and private community and junior colleges, technical institutes, and two-year branch university campuses. Two-year college students, faculty, staff, curricula, programs, support services, libraries, and community services. Linkages between two-year colleges and business/industrial/community organizations. Articulation of two-year colleges with secondary and four-year postsecondary institutions. [Includes input from Adjunct ERIC Clearinghouse on Entrepreneurship Education.]

ERIC Clearinghouse on COUNSELING AND STUDENT SERVICES (CG)

University of North Carolina at Greensboro
School of Education
201 Ferguson Building, P.O. Box 26171
Greensboro, NC 27402-6171
Telephone: 336-334-4114; 800-414-9769
Fax: 336-334-4116
E-mail: . . . . .ericcass@uncg.edu
Web: . . . . .http://ericcass.uncg.edu

Preparation, practice, and supervision of counselors at all educational levels and in all educational settings. Theoretical development of counseling and guidance, as it pertains to education, including the nature of relevant human characteristics. Use and results of personnel practices and procedures. Group process (counseling, therapy, dynamics) and case work in education settings.

ERIC Clearinghouse on DISABILITIES AND GIFTED EDUCATION (EC)

Council for Exceptional Children (CEC)
1110 N. Glebe Road
Arlington, VA 22201-5704
Telephone: 703-264-9475; 800-328-0272
Fax: 703-620-2521
E-mail: . . . . .ericec@cec.sped.org
Web: . . . . .http://ericec.org

All aspects of the education and development of persons (of all ages) who have disabilities or who are gifted, including the delivery of all types of education-related services to these groups. Includes prevention, identification and assessment, intervention, and enrichment for these groups, in both regular and special education settings.

ERIC Clearinghouse on EDUCATIONAL MANAGEMENT (EA)

University of Oregon (Dept. 5207)
1787 Agate Street
Eugene, OR 97403-5207
Telephone: 541-346-5043; 800-438-8841
Fax: 541-346-2334
E-mail: . . . . .ppiele@oregon.uoregon.edu
Web: . . . . .http://eric.uoregon.edu

All aspects of the governance, leadership, administration, and structure of public and private educational organizations at the elementary and secondary levels.

ERIC Clearinghouse on ELEMENTARY AND EARLY CHILDHOOD EDUCATION (PS)

University of Illinois at Urbana-Champaign
Children's Research Center
51 Gerty Drive
Champaign, IL 61820-7469
Telephone: 217-333-1386; 800-583-4135
Fax: 217-333-3767
E-mail: . . . . .ericeece@uiuc.edu
Web: . . . . .http://ericeece.org

All aspects of the physical, cognitive, social, emotional, educational, and cultural development of children, from birth through early adolescence. Among the topics covered are: prenatal and infant development and care; parent education; home and school relationships; learning theory research and practice related to children's development; preparation of early childhood teachers and caregivers; and educational programs and community service for children. [Includes input from Adjunct ERIC Clearinghouse on Child Care.]

ERIC Clearinghouse on HIGHER EDUCATION (HE)

George Washington University
One Dupont Circle, NW, Suite 630
Washington, DC 20036-1183
Telephone: 202-296-2597; 800-773-ERIC (3742)
Fax: 202-452-1844
E-mail: . . . . .lcavell@eric-he.edu
Web: . . . . .http://www.eriche.org

All aspects of the conditions, programs, and problems at colleges and universities providing higher education (i.e., four-year degrees and beyond). This includes: governance and management; planning; finance; interinstitutional arrangements; business or industry programs leading to a degree; institutional research at the college/university level; Federal programs; legal issues and legislation; professional education (e.g., medicine, law, etc.) and professional continuing education. [Includes input from Adjunct ERIC Clearinghouse on Educational Opportunity.]

ERIC Clearinghouse on INFORMATION & TECHNOLOGY (IR)

Syracuse University
621 Skytop Road, Suite 160
Syracuse, NY 13244-5290
Telephone: 315-443-3640; 800-464-9107
Fax: 315-443-5448
E-mail: ....eric@ericir.syr.edu
Web: ....http://ericir.syr.edu/ithome
AskERIC (Question-answering service via Internet) .. askeric@askeric.org
AskERIC Web: ....http://www.askeric.org

Educational technology and library/information science at all academic levels and with all populations, including the preparation of professionals. The media and devices of educational communication, as they pertain to teaching and learning (in both conventional and distance education settings). The operation and management of libraries and information services. All aspects of information management and information technology related to education.

ERIC Clearinghouse on LANGUAGES AND LINGUISTICS (FL)

Center for Applied Linguistics (CAL)
4646 40th Street, NW
Washington, DC 20016-1859
Telephone: 202-362-0700; 800-276-9834
Fax: 202-363-7204
E-mail: ....eric@cal.org
Web: ....http://www.cal.org/ericcll

Languages and language sciences. All aspects of second language instruction and learning in all commonly and uncommonly taught languages, including English as a second language. Bilingualism and bilingual education. Cultural education in the context of second language learning, including intercultural communication, study abroad, and international educational exchange. All areas of linguistics, including theoretical and applied linguistics, sociolinguistics, and psycholinguistics. [Includes input from Adjunct ERIC Clearinghouse on ESL Literacy Education.]

ERIC Clearinghouse on READING, ENGLISH, AND COMMUNICATION (CS)

Indiana University
Smith Research Center
2805 East 10th Street, Suite 140
Bloomington, IN 47408-2698
Telephone: 812-855-5847; 800-759-4723
Fax: 812-856-5512
E-mail: ....ericcs@indiana.edu
Web: ....http://eric.indiana.edu

Reading and writing, English (as a first language), and communication skills (verbal and nonverbal), kindergarten through college. Includes family or intergenerational literacy. Research and instructional development in reading, writing, speaking, and listening. Identification, diagnosis, and remediation of reading problems. Speech communication (including forensics), mass communication (including journalism), interpersonal and small group interaction, oral interpretation, rhetorical and communication theory, and theater/drama. Preparation of instructional staff and related personnel in all the above areas.

ERIC Clearinghouse on RURAL EDUCATION AND SMALL SCHOOLS (RC)

Appalachia Educational Laboratory, Inc.
1031 Quarrier Street, Suite 607, P.O. Box 1348
Charleston, WV 25325-1348
Telephone: 304-347-0400; 800-624-9120
Fax: 304-347-0487
E-mail: ....ericrc@ael.org
Web: ....http://www.ael.org/eric

Curriculum and instructional programs and research/evaluation efforts that address the education of students in rural schools or districts, small schools wherever located, and schools or districts wherever located that serve American Indian and Alaskan natives, Mexican Americans, and migrants, or that have programs related to outdoor education. Includes the cultural, ethnic, linguistic, economic, and social conditions that affect these educational institutions and groups. Preparation programs, including related services that train education professionals to work in such contexts.

ERIC Clearinghouse for SCIENCE, MATHEMATICS, AND ENVIRONMENTAL EDUCATION (SE)

Ohio State University
1929 Kenny Road
Columbus, OH 43210-1080
Telephone: 614-292-6717; 800-276-0462
Fax: 614-292-0263
E-mail: ....ericse@osu.edu
Web: ....http://www.ericse.org

Science, mathematics, engineering/technology, and environmental education at all levels. The following topics when focused on any of the above broad scope areas: applications of learning theory; curriculum and instructional materials; teachers and teacher education; educational programs and projects; research and evaluative studies; applications of educational technology and media.

ERIC Clearinghouse for SOCIAL STUDIES/ SOCIAL SCIENCE EDUCATION (SO)

Indiana University
Social Studies Development Center
2805 East 10th Street, Suite 120
Bloomington, IN 47408-2698
Telephone: 812-855-3838; 800-266-3815
Fax: 812-855-0455
E-mail: ....ericso@indiana.edu
Web: ....http://www.indiana.edu/~ssdc/eric_chess.htm

All aspects of Social Studies and Social Science Education, including values education (and the social aspects of environmental education and sex education), international education, comparative education, and cross-cultural studies in all subject areas (K-12). Ethnic heritage, gender equity, aging, and social bias/discrimination topics as they pertain to education. Also covered are music, art, and architecture as related to the fine arts. [Includes input from Adjunct ERIC Clearinghouses for U.S.-Japan Studies, International Civic Education, and Service-Learning.]

ERIC Clearinghouse on TEACHING AND TEACHER EDUCATION (SP)

American Association of Colleges for Teacher Education (AACTE)
1307 New York Avenue, NW, Suite 300
Washington, DC 20005-4701
Telephone: 202-293-2450; 800-822-9229
Fax: 202-457-8095
E-mail: ....query@aacte.org
Web: ....http://www.ericsp.org

School personnel at all levels. Teacher recruitment, selection, licensing, certification, training, preservice and inservice preparation, evaluation, retention, and retirement. The theory, philosophy, and practice of teaching. Organization, administration, finance, and legal issues relating to teacher education programs and institutions. All aspects of health, physical, recreation, and dance education. [Includes input from Adjunct ERIC Clearinghouse on Clinical Schools.]

ERIC Clearinghouse on URBAN EDUCATION (UD)

Teachers College, Columbia University
Institute for Urban and Minority Education
Main Hall, Room 303, Box 40
525 West 120th Street
New York, NY 10027-6696
Telephone: 212-678-3433; 800-601-4868
Fax: 212-678-4012
E-mail: ....eric-cue@columbia.edu
Web: ....http://eric-web.tc.columbia.edu

The educational characteristics and experiences of the diverse racial, ethnic, social class, and linguistic populations in urban (and suburban) schools. Curriculum and instruction of students from these populations and the organization of their schools. The relationship of urban schools to their communities. The social and economic conditions that affect the education of urban populations, with particular attention to factors that place urban students at risk educationally, and ways that public and private sector policies can improve these conditions.

ADJUNCT AND AFFILIATE ERIC CLEARINGHOUSES

Adjunct ERIC CH on
Child Care
National Child Care Information Center
243 Church Street, NW, 2nd Floor
Vienna, VA 22180
Telephone:......................................800-616-2242
Fax:..800-716-2242
E-mail:...info@nccic.org
Web:..http://nccic.org

Adjunct ERIC CH on
Clinical Schools
American Assoc. of Colleges for
Teacher Education (AACTE)
1307 New York Avenue, NW, Suite 300
Washington, DC 20005-4701
Telephone:................202-293-2450; 800-822-9229
Fax:..202-457-8095
E-mail:...............................iabdalha@inet.ed.gov
Web: ....http://www.aacte.org/pro_dev_schools.htm

Adjunct ERIC CH on
Educational Opportunity
National TRIO Clearinghouse
Council for Opportunity in Education
1025 Vermont Avenue, NW, Suite 900
Washington, DC 20005
Telephone:....................................202-347-2218
Fax:..202-347-0786
E-mail:......................clearinghouse@hqcoe.org
Web:..http://www.trioprograms.org/clearinghouse

Adjunct ERIC CH on
Entrepreneurship Education
Center for Entrepreneurial Leadership
Ewing Marion Kauffman Foundation
4801 Rockhill Road
Kansas City, MO 64110-2046
Telephone:................310-206-9549; 888-423-5233
Fax:..310-206-8095
E-mail:...celcee@ucla.edu
Web:..................................http://www.celcee.edu

Adjunct ERIC CH for
ESL Literacy Education
National Clearinghouse for
Literacy Education (NCLE)
Center for Applied Linguistics (CAL)
4646 40th Street, NW
Washington, DC 20016-1859
Telephone:.......................202-362-0700, ext. 200
Fax:..202-363-7204
E-mail:...ncle@cal.org
Web: ....http://www.cal.org/ncle

Adjunct ERIC CH for
International Civic Education
Indiana University
Social Studies Development Center
2805 East 10th Street, Suite 120
Bloomington, IN 47408-2698
Telephone:..............812-855-3838; 800-266-3815
Fax:..812-855-0455
E-mail:.............................patrick@indiana.edu
Web: ....

Adjunct ERIC CH for
Service-Learning
University of Minnesota
College of Education and
Human Development
R-460 VoTech Building
1954 Buford Avenue
St. Paul, MN 55108-6197
Telephone:...........612-625-6276; 800-808-SERV
Fax:..612-625-6277
E-mail:..................................serve@tc.umn.edu
Web: ....http://umn.edu/~serve

Adjunct ERIC CH for the
Test Collection
Educational Testing Service (ETS)
Rosedale and Carter Roads
Princeton, NJ 08541
Telephone:....................................609-734-5689
Fax:..609-683-7186
E-mail:...library@ets.org
Web: ....http://ericae.net/testcol.htm

Adjunct ERIC CH for
United States-Japan Studies
Indiana University
Social Studies Development Center
2805 East 10th Street, Suite 120
Bloomington, IN 47408-2698
Telephone:............812-855-3838; 800-266-3815
Fax:..812-855-0455
E-mail:...............................japan@indiana.edu
Web:..................http://www.indiana.edu/~japan

❏ ❏ ❏ ❏ ❏

National Clearinghouse for
Educational Facilities
National Institute of Building Sciences
1090 Vermont Avenue, NW, Suite 700
Washington, DC 20005-4905
Telephone:............202-289-7800; 888-552-0624
Fax:..202-289-1092
E-mail:...ncef@nibs.org
Web: ....http://www.edfacilities.org

ERIC SUPPORT COMPONENTS

CENTRALIZED DATABASE MANAGEMENT
(and Abstract Journal Production)

ERIC Processing and Reference Facility
Computer Sciences Corporation
4483-A Forbes Boulevard
Lanham, MD 20706
Telephone: 301-552-4200; 800-799-ERIC (3742)
Fax: 301-552-4700
E-mail: . . . . ericfac@inet.ed.gov
Web: . . . . http://ericfacility.org.

OUTREACH AND USER SERVICES

ACCESS ERIC
Aspen Systems Corporation
2277 Research Boulevard, 6L
Rockville, MD 20850
Telephone: 301-519-5157; 800-LET-ERIC (538-3742)
Fax: 301-519-6760
E-mail: . . . . .accesseric@accesseric.org
Web: . . . . .http://www.accesseric.org

DOCUMENT DELIVERY AND MICROGRAPHICS

ERIC Document Reproduction Service (EDRS)
DynEDRS, Inc.
7420 Fullerton Road, Suite 110
Springfield, VA 22153-2852
Telephone: 703-440-1400; 800-443-ERIC (3742)
Fax: 703-440-1408
E-mail: . . . . .service@edrs.com
Web: . . . . .http://edrs.com

CIJE AND THESAURUS PUBLISHING

Oryx Press
An imprint of Greenwood Publishing Group, Inc.
88 Post Road West
Westport, CT 06881-5007
Telephone: .203-226-3571; 800-225-5800
Fax: 203-222-1502
E-mail: . . . . .customerservice@greenwood.com
Web: . . . . .http://www.oryxpress.com

Thesaurus of

ERIC℠
Educational Resources Information Center

Descriptors

14th Edition

Alphabetical Descriptor Display

The Alphabetical Descriptor Display is the primary arrangement of the *Thesaurus*. It is the only display containing the complete records of all *Thesaurus* terms. All valid Descriptors (main terms), invalid Descriptors (''dead'' terms), and USE references appear in this display interfiled alphabetically word by word.

Abbreviations   *JAN. 1969*
          Postings: 125   GC: 710
UF   Acronyms
RT   Mnemonics
          Orthographic Symbols
          Shorthand
          Written Language

Ability   *JUL. 1966*
          Postings: 1,240   GC: 120
SN   The degree of actual power present in an
          organism or system to perform a given
          physical or mental act (Note: Use a more
          specific term if possible)
NT   Academic Ability
          Cognitive Ability
          Competence
          Language Proficiency
          Leadership
          Nonverbal Ability
          Skills
          Spatial Ability
          Verbal Ability
RT   Ability Grouping
          Ability Identification
          Achievement
          Aptitude
          Aspiration
          Difficulty Level
          Disabilities
          Gifted
          Performance
          Productivity
          Qualifications
          Readiness
          Talent

Ability Grouping   *JUL. 1966*
          Postings: 1,192   GC: 310
SN   Selection or classification of students for
          schools, classes, or other educational
          programs based on differences in ability
          or achievement
BT   Homogeneous Grouping
RT   Ability
          Ability Identification
          Academic Ability
          Academic Achievement
          Advanced Placement
          Flexible Progression
          Instructional Program Divisions
          Nongraded Instructional Grouping
          Track System (Education)

Ability Identification   *JUL. 1966*
          Postings: 1,383   GC: 110
SN   Identification of an individual's actual
          power to perform various acts (Note: Do
          not confuse with "Talent Identification,"
          which frequently refers to innate apti-
          tudes or abilities, especially of the gifted)
BT   Identification
RT   Ability
          Ability Grouping
          Aptitude Tests
          Critical Incidents Method
          Disability Identification
          Early Identification
          Factor Analysis
          Intelligence Tests
          Probationary Period
          Skill Analysis
          Talent Identification

Able Students (1966 1978)
USE   Academically Gifted

Abnormal Psychology
USE   Psychopathology

Aboriginal People
USE   Indigenous Populations

Abortions   *SEP. 1970*
          Postings: 425   GC: 210
RT   Contraception
          Family Planning

          Gynecology
          Medical Services
          Obstetrics
          Pregnancy
          Surgery

Abreaction
USE   Catharsis

Absence (Employees)
USE   Employee Absenteeism

Absence (Students)
USE   Attendance

Absence (Teachers)
USE   Employee Absenteeism
AND   Teacher Attendance

Absolute Humidity
USE   Humidity

Absolute Pressure
USE   Pressure (Physics)

Abstract Bibliographies
USE   Annotated Bibliographies

Abstract Reasoning   *JUL. 1966*
          Postings: 1,889   GC: 110
SN   Process of reaching conclusions through
          the use of symbols or generalizations
          rather than on concrete factual informa-
          tion
UF   Abstraction Levels (1968 1980)
          Intellectualization (1970 1980)
NT   Generalization
BT   Cognitive Processes
RT   Comprehension
          Concept Formation
          Deduction
          Formal Operations
          Language Processing
          Logical Thinking
          Thinking Skills

Abstracting   *JUL. 1966*
          Postings: 265   GC: 710
BT   Documentation
          Writing (Composition)
RT   Abstracts
          Annotated Bibliographies
          Indexing
          Information Retrieval
          Library Technical Processes
          Technical Writing

Abstraction Levels (1968 1980)
USE   Abstract Reasoning

Abstraction Tests (1967 1980)
USE   Cognitive Tests

Abstracts   *JUL. 1966*
          Postings: 2,526   GC: 730
SN   (Note: Do not confuse with "Bibliographic
          Records")
UF   Annotations
BT   Reference Materials
RT   Abstracting
          Annotated Bibliographies
          Indexes

Abused Children
USE   Child Abuse

Abused Elderly
USE   Elder Abuse

Abused Women
USE   Battered Women

Academic Ability   *JUL. 1966*
          Postings: 2,458   GC: 120
SN   The degree of actual competence to per-
          form in scholastic or educational activi-
          ties (Note: For potential competence,
          use "Academic Aptitude"—for measured
          achievement, use "Academic Achieve-
          ment")
UF   Scholastic Ability
          Student Ability (1966 1980)
BT   Ability
RT   Ability Grouping
          Academic Achievement
          Academic Aptitude
          Academic Aspiration
          Academically Gifted
          Aptitude Treatment Interaction
          Cognitive Ability
          College Entrance Examinations
          High Risk Students
          Intelligence
          Scholarship
          Spatial Ability
          Student Characteristics
          Verbal Ability

Academic Accommodations (Disabilities)
                                                       JUL. 2000
          Postings: 210   GC: 220
SN   Modifications of services, programs, and
          facilities to help persons with disabilities
          access the general education curriculum
          and validly demonstrate learning
UF   Accommodations for Disabled (Educa-
          tional Settings)
BT   Accessibility (for Disabled)
RT   Access to Education
          Disabilities
          Educational Policy
          Equal Education
          Inclusive Schools
          Mainstreaming
          Regular and Special Education Rela-
          tionship

Academic Achievement   *JUL. 1966*
          Postings: 36,211   GC: 310
UF   Academic Performance (1966 1974)
          Academic Progress
          Academic Success
          Educational Achievement
          Educational Level
          Scholastic Achievement
          Student Achievement
NT   Educational Attainment
          Student Promotion
BT   Achievement
RT   Ability Grouping
          Academic Ability
          Academic Aptitude
          Academic Aspiration
          Academic Failure
          Academic Probation
          Academic Records
          Academic Standards
          Academically Gifted
          Achievement Gains
          Achievement Rating
          Advanced Placement
          Class Rank
          College Entrance Examinations
          Degree Requirements
          Educational Mobility
          Educationally Disadvantaged
          Excellence in Education
          Grades (Scholastic)
          Grading
          Graduation Requirements
          High Stakes Tests
          Instructional Effectiveness
          Intelligence
          Knowledge Level
          Learning Plateaus
          Learning Problems
          Mastery Learning
          Mastery Tests
          Mathematics Achievement

          Minimum Competency Testing
          Performance
          Performance Contracts
          Reading Achievement
          Report Cards
          Scholarship
          School Effectiveness
          Science Achievement
          Student Characteristics
          Student Evaluation
          Student Improvement
          Teacher Effectiveness
          Teacher Influence
          Writing Achievement

Academic Advising   *NOV. 1981*
          Postings: 1,138   GC: 240
SN   A decision-making process in which a
          student and academic adviser use the
          resources of a postsecondary education
          institution to analyze and coordinate learn-
          ing experiences consistent with the stu-
          dent's needs, abilities, interests, values,
          and goals (Note: Use "Educational Coun-
          seling" for academic advising at the sec-
          ondary school level)
BT   Educational Counseling
RT   College Credits
          College Curriculum
          Faculty Advisers
          Higher Education
          Postsecondary Education

Academic Alliances
USE   Partnerships in Education

Academic Aptitude   *JUL. 1966*
          Postings: 1,100   GC: 120
SN   An individual's potential ability to per-
          form in scholastic or educational activities
          (Note: For actual academic competence,
          use "Academic Ability"—for measured
          achievement, use "Academic Achieve-
          ment")
UF   Scholastic Potential
          Student Aptitude
BT   Aptitude
RT   Academic Ability
          Academic Achievement
          Academic Aspiration
          Academically Gifted
          Aptitude Treatment Interaction
          High Risk Students
          Intelligence
          Language Aptitude
          Mathematical Aptitude
          Student Characteristics
          Vocational Aptitude

Academic Aspiration   *JUL. 1966*
          Postings: 1,713   GC: 120
SN   Desire to reach a level of academic
          achievement
BT   Aspiration
RT   Academic Ability
          Academic Achievement
          Academic Aptitude
          College Bound Students
          College Choice
          Educational Mobility
          Learning Motivation
          Noncollege Bound Students
          Student Motivation
          Teacher Motivation

Academic Calendars
USE   School Schedules

Academic Curriculum
USE   Academic Education

Academic Deans   *MAR. 1980*
          Postings: 290   GC: 360
SN   Administrative officials in a college or
          other school who are responsible for the
          instructional program
UF   Chief Academic Officers

= Two or more Descriptors are used to represent this term.
The term's main entry shows the appropriate coordination.

Deans of Faculty
Deans of Instruction
BT Deans
RT Academic Education
    College Administration
    College Curriculum
    Deans of Students
    Instructional Leadership

Academic Departments
USE Departments

Academic Disciplines
USE Intellectual Disciplines

Academic Discourse   *AUG. 2000*
    Postings: 431   GC: 400
SN Presentation of ideas (usually in written form) in academic or scholarly contexts that exhibits conventional characteristics in form and expression—traditionally, such communication has been objective, analytical, and expository, and has generally advanced an argument for a particular thesis—can also refer to conventions of discourse followed within individual scholarly disciplines—is often addressed in writing instruction for college (and, in some cases, high school) students (Note: Do not confuse with "English for Academic Purposes," which involves English instruction for non-English speakers—see also the Identifier "Academic Language")
UF Academic Discourse Communities #
    Academic Writing
BT Language Styles
RT Academic Education
    Discourse Communities
    English for Academic Purposes
    Faculty Publishing
    Scholarly Communication
    Scholarly Writing
    Writing for Publication
    Writing Instruction

Academic Discourse Communities
USE Academic Discourse
AND Discourse Communities

Academic Education   *JUL. 1966*
    Postings: 1,869   GC: 400
SN Relating to college preparatory studies or liberal and classical studies in higher education, as contrasted with technical or vocational studies
UF Academic Curriculum
    Academic Subjects
BT Education
RT Academic Deans
    Academic Discourse
    College Preparation
    English for Academic Purposes
    General Education
    Humanities Instruction
    Intellectual Disciplines
    Liberal Arts
    Tech Prep

Academic Enrichment (1966 1980)
USE Enrichment

Academic Environment
USE Educational Environment

Academic Failure   *JUL. 1966*
    Postings: 1,284   GC: 310
UF Scholastic Failure
NT Reading Failure
BT Failure
RT Academic Achievement
    Academic Probation
    Dropouts
    Expulsion
    Grade Repetition
    High Risk Students

Learning Disabilities
Learning Problems
Low Achievement
Social Promotion
Student Promotion
Suspension
Underachievement

Academic Freedom   *JUL. 1966*
    Postings: 2,074   GC: 330
SN Right of teacher or student to be free from external or institutional coercion, censorship, or other forms of restrictive interference in academic matters
UF Teaching Freedom
BT Freedom
RT Censorship
    Civil Liberties
    College Environment
    Educational Environment
    Faculty College Relationship
    Freedom of Information
    Freedom of Speech
    Institutional Autonomy
    Intellectual Freedom
    Personal Autonomy
    Political Correctness
    Professional Autonomy
    Student Rights
    Teacher Rights
    Teacher Welfare
    Teaching Conditions

Academic Games
USE Educational Games

Academic Learning Time
USE Time on Task

Academic Libraries   *JAN. 1979*
    Postings: 5,406   GC: 710
SN Libraries forming part of, or associated with, institutions of higher education
NT College Libraries
BT Libraries
RT Archives
    Depository Libraries
    Learning Resources Centers
    Librarian Teacher Cooperation
    Research Libraries
    Special Libraries

Academic Malpractice
USE Educational Malpractice

Academic Performance (1966 1974)
USE Academic Achievement

Academic Persistence   *MAR. 1980*
    Postings: 2,773   GC: 310
SN Continuance of a student in school or college enrollment
BT Persistence
RT Attendance
    Dropout Research
    Dropouts
    School Holding Power
    Stopouts
    Student Attrition
    Time to Degree
    Withdrawal (Education)

Academic Planning
USE Educational Planning

Academic Probation   *JUL. 1966*
    Postings: 148   GC: 320
SN Trial period in which the student must improve academic achievement to avoid being dismissed
UF Scholastic Probation
BT Probationary Period
RT Academic Achievement
    Academic Failure
    Academic Standards

Expulsion
Grades (Scholastic)
Student School Relationship
Suspension

Academic Progress
USE Academic Achievement

Academic Promotion
USE Student Promotion

Academic Rank (Professional)   *JUL. 1966*
    Postings: 1,034   GC: 320
SN Professional position or standing among faculty members of an educational institution, usually expressed by official titles (professor, lecturer, instructor, etc.)
UF Faculty Rank
    Professorial Rank
BT Employment Level
RT Adjunct Faculty
    College Faculty
    Degrees (Academic)
    Faculty
    Faculty Promotion
    Nontenured Faculty
    Professors
    Seniority
    Teacher Employment Benefits
    Teacher Promotion
    Tenure
    Tenured Faculty

Academic Records   *JUL. 1966*
    Postings: 447   GC: 320
UF Transcripts (Academic)
BT Student Records
RT Academic Achievement
    College Credits
    Credits
    Grades (Scholastic)
    Profiles
    Registrars (School)
    Report Cards
    Student Evaluation

Academic Senates (Colleges)
USE College Governing Councils

Academic Standards   *JUL. 1966*
    Postings: 5,112   GC: 320
SN Criteria established by an educational institution to determine levels of student achievement
NT Graduation Requirements
BT Standards
RT Academic Achievement
    Academic Probation
    Accreditation (Institutions)
    Accrediting Agencies
    Admission (School)
    Admission Criteria
    Back to Basics
    Competency Based Education
    Competency Based Teacher Education
    Degree Requirements
    Educational Malpractice
    Excellence in Education
    Grade Inflation
    Grade Point Average
    Mastery Learning
    Mastery Tests
    Minimum Competency Testing
    National Standards
    Open Enrollment
    Outcome Based Education
    Pass Fail Grading
    Scholarly Journals
    Selective Admission
    Selective Colleges
    Social Promotion
    State Standards
    Test Score Decline

Academic Subjects
USE Academic Education

Academic Success
USE Academic Achievement

Academic Writing
USE Academic Discourse

Academically Disadvantaged
USE Educationally Disadvantaged

Academically Gifted   *JAN. 1978*
    Postings: 2,143   GC: 360
SN Persons with superior ability or aptitude for academic learning
UF Able Students (1966 1978)
    Gifted Students
    Superior Students (1966 1978)
BT Gifted
RT Academic Ability
    Academic Achievement
    Academic Aptitude
    Acceleration (Education)
    Advanced Placement
    Advanced Placement Programs
    Advanced Students
    Honors Curriculum
    Mainstreaming

Academically Handicapped (1966 1980)   *MAR. 1980*
    Postings: 172   GC: 220
SN Invalid Descriptor—used inconsistently in indexing—see such Descriptors as "Academic Ability," "Academic Aptitude," "Learning Disabilities," "Learning Problems," "Slow Learners," "Educationally Disadvantaged," etc.

Accelerated Courses (1966 1980)
USE Acceleration (Education)

Accelerated Programs (1966 1980)
USE Acceleration (Education)

Acceleration (Education)   *NOV. 1982*
    Postings: 552   GC: 310
SN The process of progressing through an educational program at a rate faster than that of the average student
UF Accelerated Courses (1966 1980)
    Accelerated Programs (1966 1980)
    Acceleration (1966 1982) (Education)
    Three Year Bachelors Degrees #
    Time Shortened Degree Programs
BT Flexible Progression
RT Academically Gifted
    Advanced Courses
    Advanced Placement
    Advanced Placement Programs
    Advanced Students
    Age Grade Placement
    Early Admission
    Honors Curriculum
    Student Placement
    Time to Degree
    Transitional Programs

Acceleration (Physics)   *AUG. 1982*
    Postings: 180   GC: 490
SN Change in velocity of an object with respect to time
UF Acceleration (1966 1982) (Physics)
    Deceleration
BT Motion
RT Fluid Mechanics
    Force
    Gravity (Physics)
    Kinetic Molecular Theory
    Kinetics
    Mechanics (Physics)
    Physics
    Quantum Mechanics
    Velocity
    Weight (Mass)

= Two or more Descriptors are used to represent this term.
The term's main entry shows the appropriate coordination.

Acceleration (1966 1982) (Education)
USE   Acceleration (Education)

Acceleration (1966 1982) (Physics)
USE   Acceleration (Physics)

Accents (Dialects)
USE   Dialects
AND   Pronunciation

Accents (Vocal Stress)
USE   Stress (Phonology)

Access to Education   SEP. 1977
        Postings: 7,281   GC: 330
SN   Accessibility of an education to a stu-
        dent, including access to appropriate
        educational institutions, materials, and
        personnel (Note: Do not confuse with
        "Accessibility (for Disabled)")
UF   Educational Access
BT   Educational Opportunities
RT   Academic Accommodations (Disabili-
          ties)
        Admission (School)
        Admission Criteria
        Attendance
        College Admission
        College Attendance
        Compulsory Education
        Distance Education
        Education
        Educational Demand
        Educational Discrimination
        Educational Finance
        Educational Supply
        Enrollment
        Equal Education
        Extension Education
        External Degree Programs
        Free Education
        Geographic Location
        Higher Education
        Inclusive Schools
        Intellectual Freedom
        Noncampus Colleges
        Nondiscriminatory Education
        Nontraditional Education
        Open Enrollment
        Open Universities
        Prior Learning
        School Location
        Special Education
        Student Costs
        Student Financial Aid

Access to Ideas
USE   Intellectual Freedom

Access to Information   AUG. 1986
        Postings: 4,021   GC: 710
SN   Means, processes, or rights related to
        obtaining or providing information—also,
        the degree of information availability
NT   Freedom of Information
RT   Information Industry
        Information Literacy
        Information Management
        Information Needs
        Information Policy
        Information Retrieval
        Information Seeking
        Information Services
        Information Sources
        Information Transfer
        Information Utilization
        Scholarly Communication
        Users (Information)

Accessibility (for Disabled)   MAR. 1980
        Postings: 1,425   GC: 220
SN   Characteristics of facilities, programs,
        and services that allow them to be en-
        tered or used by individuals despite vis-
        ual, hearing, mobility, or other impair-
        ments (Note: For physical access,
        coordinate with "Physical Mobility" or

        "Visually Impaired Mobility"—prior to
        Jun80, see also "Architectural Barriers")
UF   Barrier Free Environment (for Dis-
          abled)
NT   Academic Accommodations (Disabili-
          ties)
RT   Architecture
        Deaf Interpreting
        Design Requirements
        Disabilities
        Older Adults
        Physical Mobility
        Sensory Aids
        Structural Elements (Construction)

Accident Prevention   JUL. 1966
        Postings: 1,176   GC: 210
BT   Prevention
RT   Accidents
        Alarm Systems
        Risk Management
        Safety
        Safety Education
        Safety Equipment

Accidents   JUL. 1966
        Postings: 504   GC: 210
NT   School Accidents
        Traffic Accidents
RT   Accident Prevention
        Emergency Medical Technicians
        Emergency Squad Personnel
        Injuries
        Negligence
        Rescue
        Safety
        Safety Education

Accommodations for Disabled (Educational Settings)
USE   Academic Accommodations (Disabili-
          ties)

Accountability   APR. 1974
        Postings: 8,404   GC: 330
SN   Being held responsible and answerable
        for specified results or outcomes of an
        activity (over which one has authority)
UF   Educational Accountability (1970
          1980)
BT   Responsibility
RT   Audits (Verification)
        Charter Schools
        Codes of Ethics
        Competence
        Competency Based Education
        Competency Based Teacher Education
        Consumer Protection
        Contracts
        Cost Effectiveness
        Educational Malpractice
        Evaluation Criteria
        Evaluation Utilization
        High Stakes Tests
        Legal Responsibility
        Malpractice
        Management by Objectives
        Negligence
        Organizational Objectives
        Outcome Based Education
        Outcomes of Education
        Performance
        Productivity
        Program Effectiveness
        Program Validation
        Quality Control
        Relevance (Education)
        School Effectiveness
        Validated Programs

Accountants   JUL. 1966
        Postings: 102   GC: 640
NT   Certified Public Accountants
BT   Professional Personnel
RT   Accounting
        Farm Accounts
        Financial Services

Accounting   JUL. 1966
        Postings: 1,373   GC: 620
NT   Property Accounting
        School Accounting
BT   Technology
RT   Accountants
        Bookkeeping
        Budgeting
        Business Education
        Business Skills
        Certified Public Accountants
        Farm Accounts
        Financial Audits
        Financial Services
        Office Occupations Education
        Spreadsheets

Accreditation (Institutions)   JUL. 1966
        Postings: 3,103   GC: 330
BT   Certification
RT   Academic Standards
        Accrediting Agencies
        Eligibility
        Institutional Evaluation
        Quality Control
        Standards
        State Standards

Accrediting Agencies   MAR. 1980
        Postings: 862   GC: 330
SN   Agencies that establish operating stan-
        dards for educational or professional
        institutions and programs, determine the
        extent to which the standards are met,
        and publicly announce their findings
UF   Accrediting Associations
BT   Agencies
RT   Academic Standards
        Accreditation (Institutions)
        Agency Role
        Educational Quality
        Institutional Evaluation
        State Licensing Boards
        State Standards

Accrediting Associations
USE   Accrediting Agencies

Acculturation   JUL. 1966
        Postings: 2,973   GC: 560
SN   Absorption into any group of certain
        features of the culture
UF   Assimilation (Cultural)
RT   Biculturalism
        Cultural Pluralism
        Culture
        Immigrants
        Refugees
        Social Integration
        Subcultures

Acetylene Welding
USE   Welding

Achievement   JUL. 1966
        Postings: 2,842   GC: 120
SN   Level of attainment or proficiency in rela-
        tion to a standard measure of perform-
        ance, or, of success in bringing about a
        desired end (Note: Use a more specific
        term if possible)
UF   Achievement Level
        Achievement Prediction #
NT   Academic Achievement
        Black Achievement
        Graduation
        High Achievement
        Knowledge Level
        Low Achievement
        Mathematics Achievement
        Overachievement
        Reading Achievement
        Scholarship
        Science Achievement
        Underachievement
        Writing Achievement
RT   Ability
        Achievement Gains

        Achievement Need
        Achievement Rating
        Achievement Tests
        Aptitude
        Aspiration
        Competence
        Evaluation
        Expectation
        Failure
        Fear of Success
        Gifted
        Improvement
        Learning Plateaus
        Mastery Learning
        Mastery Tests
        Motivation
        National Competency Tests
        Performance
        Performance Factors
        Prerequisites
        Productivity
        Qualifications
        Recognition (Achievement)
        Self Efficacy
        Standards
        Success
        Talent

Achievement Comparison
USE   Achievement Rating

Achievement Gains   JUL. 1966
        Postings: 2,234   GC: 310
SN   Progress towards attaining a specified
        level of proficiency or bringing about a
        desired end
UF   Achievement Losses
BT   Improvement
RT   Academic Achievement
        Achievement
        Achievement Rating
        Achievement Tests
        Knowledge Level
        Mathematics Achievement
        Reading Achievement
        Science Achievement
        Success
        Writing Achievement

Achievement Incentives
USE   Incentives

Achievement Level
USE   Achievement

Achievement Losses
USE   Achievement Gains

Achievement Motivation
USE   Achievement Need

Achievement Need   JUL. 1966
        Postings: 796   GC: 120
SN   Forces that drive an individual to im-
        prove, succeed, or excel in things con-
        sidered both difficult and important (Note:
        Prior to Mar80, the instruction "Achieve-
        ment Motivation, USE Motivation" was
        carried in the Thesaurus)
UF   Achievement Motivation
BT   Motivation
        Psychological Needs
RT   Achievement
        Affiliation Need
        Aspiration
        Competition
        Failure
        Goal Orientation
        Self Motivation
        Status Need
        Success
        Type A Behavior
        Type B Behavior

Achievement Prediction
USE   Achievement

 # = Two or more Descriptors are used to represent this term.
The term's main entry shows the appropriate coordination.

AND   Prediction

Achievement Rating   *JUL. 1966*
         Postings: 939   GC: 820
SN   Judging individuals' or groups' levels of
         attainment or accomplishment and as-
         signing quantitative or qualitative values
         to them according to specified standards
         or procedures
UF   Achievement Comparison
NT   Grading
BT   Measurement
RT   Academic Achievement
         Achievement
         Achievement Gains
         Achievement Tests
         Awards
         Merit Rating
         Merit Scholarships
         Rating Scales
         Report Cards
         Student Evaluation

Achievement Tests   *JUL. 1966*
         Postings: 5,467   GC: 830
SN   Tests used to measure knowledge, abili-
         ties, understanding, or skills acquired
         from academic work (Note: Prior to
         Mar80, the instruction "Achievement Pre-
         diction, USE Achievement Tests" was
         carried in the Thesaurus)
UF   Proficiency Tests (Academic)
NT   Equivalency Tests
         Mastery Tests
         National Competency Tests
BT   Tests
RT   Achievement
         Achievement Gains
         Achievement Rating
         Aptitude Tests
         College Entrance Examinations
         Criterion Referenced Tests
         Educational Testing
         Essay Tests
         High Stakes Tests
         Language Tests
         Listening Comprehension Tests
         Mathematics Tests
         Norm Referenced Tests
         Open Book Tests
         Performance Based Assessment
         Performance Tests
         Reading Tests
         Science Tests
         Writing Tests

Acid Rain   *DEC. 1988*
         Postings: 107   GC: 410
SN   Precipitation (rain, snow, fog, etc.) con-
         taining destructive acid concentrations,
         caused when pollutants, chiefly oxides
         of sulfur and nitrogen, are chemically
         combined with water vapor in the atmos-
         phere
BT   Air Pollution
         Water Pollution
RT   Acids
         Meteorology
         Water Quality

Acids   *JUN. 1998*
         Postings: 159   GC: 490
BT   Matter
RT   Acid Rain
         Chemical Reactions
         Chemistry
         Inorganic Chemistry
         Organic Chemistry

Acoustic Barriers
USE   Acoustic Insulation

Acoustic Insulation   *NOV. 1969*
         Postings: 55   GC: 920
UF   Acoustic Barriers
         Anechoic Materials
         Insulation (Sound)
         Sound Barriers

         Sound Insulation
         Soundproofing
BT   Structural Elements (Construction)
RT   Acoustical Environment
         Acoustics
         Construction (Process)
         Construction Materials
         Noise (Sound)
         Thermal Insulation

Acoustic Phonetics   *JUL. 1966*
         Postings: 357   GC: 450
SN   Study of the physical properties of speech
         sounds during transmission and as they
         are heard by the listener (Note: Prior to
         Mar80, the use of this term was not
         restricted by a Scope Note)
BT   Phonetics
RT   Acoustics
         Artificial Speech
         Auditory Perception
         Consonants
         Distinctive Features (Language)
         Sound Spectrographs
         Speech

Acoustical Environment   *JUL. 1966*
         Postings: 280   GC: 920
UF   Sonic Environment
NT   Noise (Sound)
BT   Physical Environment
RT   Acoustic Insulation
         Acoustics
         Building Design
         Design Requirements
         Environmental Influences
         Human Factors Engineering
         Interior Design
         Music Facilities
         Theaters

Acoustics   *JUL. 1966*
         Postings: 649   GC: 490
SN   Science of sound—includes the study of
         the transmission of sound through vari-
         ous media or in various enclosures
UF   Sound
         Sound Transmission
         Sound Waves
NT   Psychoacoustics
BT   Sciences
RT   Acoustic Insulation
         Acoustic Phonetics
         Acoustical Environment
         Architecture
         Audio Equipment
         Auditory Stimuli
         Noise (Sound)
         Physics
         Sound Effects

Acquired Immune Deficiency Syndrome
                                          AUG. 1987
         Postings: 2,239   GC: 210
SN   Infectious, life-threatening virus that in-
         hibits the body's protective immune
         system—transmitted chiefly by sexual
         contact, the sharing of intravenous
         needles/syringes, or unscreened blood
         transfusions
UF   AIDS (Disease)
         HTLV 3
         Human Immunodeficiency Virus
         Human T Cell Lymphotropic Virus
            Type 3
BT   Communicable Diseases
         Viruses
RT   Physical Health

Acronyms
USE   Abbreviations

Acting   *JUL. 1966*
         Postings: 550   GC: 420
BT   Theater Arts
RT   Characterization
         Creative Dramatics
         Drama

         Dramatics
         Film Industry
         Film Production
         Film Study
         Opera
         Pantomime
         Readers Theater
         Rehearsals (Theater Arts)

Action Learning
USE   Experiential Learning

Action Programs (Community) (1966 1980)
USE   Community Action

Action Research   *JUL. 1966*
         Postings: 1,889   GC: 810
SN   Research designed to yield practical re-
         sults that are immediately applicable to a
         specific situation or problem (Note: As of
         Oct81, use as a minor Descriptor for
         examples of this kind of research—use
         as a major Descriptor only as the subject
         of a document)
UF   Participatory Action Research #
BT   Research
RT   Community Action
         Evaluation Methods
         Methods Research
         Operations Research
         Participatory Research
         Program Improvement
         Social Action
         Teacher Researchers
         Theory Practice Relationship

Activated Sludge
USE   Sludge

Active Learning   *NOV. 1994*
         Postings: 991   GC: 110
SN   Learning in which the learner is the prin-
         cipal driving force, with the instructor
         (if one is present) as facilitator of the
         process—among the many active learn-
         ing approaches are experiential
         learning, cooperative learning, problem-
         solving exercises, writing tasks, speak-
         ing activities, class discussion, case-
         study methods, simulations, role play-
         ing, peer teaching, fieldwork, indepen-
         dent study, library assignments, com-
         puter-assisted instruction, and homework
BT   Learning
RT   Activity Units
         Class Activities
         Cooperative Learning
         Discovery Learning
         Experiential Learning
         Independent Study
         Learner Controlled Instruction
         Learning Activities
         Problem Based Learning
         Student Participation

Activism   *JAN. 1969*
         Postings: 3,091   GC: 610
SN   Movements and procedures designed to
         force changes in rules and practices or
         to hasten social change
UF   Militancy
         Political Protest
         Student Protest
BT   Social Behavior
RT   Alienation
         Citizen Participation
         Civil Disobedience
         Demonstrations (Civil)
         Dissent
         Lobbying
         Participation
         Political Attitudes
         Revolution
         School Boycotts
         Social Action
         Social Attitudes
         Student Alienation
         Student College Relationship

         Student Rights
         Student Subcultures
         Terrorism

Activities   *JUL. 1966*
         Postings: 899   GC: 120
SN   Pursuits or experiences, usually requir-
         ing active participation, engaged in be-
         cause they are of intrinsic interest or lead
         to some goal sought by the participant
         (Note: Use a more specific term if possi-
         ble)
NT   Art Activities
         Creative Activities
         Cultural Activities
         Enrichment Activities
         Games
         Group Activities
         Health Activities
         Individual Activities
         Integrated Activities
         Learning Activities
         Lobbying
         Mathematics Activities
         Music Activities
         Outdoor Activities
         Physical Activities
         Play
         Recreational Activities
         Review (Reexamination)
         School Activities
         Science Activities
         Television Viewing
         Travel
RT   Activity Units
         Experience
         Interests
         Participation

Activity Learning (1968 1978)
USE   Experiential Learning

Activity Level (Motor Behavior)
USE   Physical Activity Level

Activity Units   *JUL. 1966*
         Postings: 761   GC: 350
SN   Units of study in which students partici-
         pate actively, usually in informal groups
UF   Experience Units
BT   Units of Study
RT   Active Learning
         Activities
         Cooperative Learning
         Discovery Learning
         Experiential Learning
         Learning Activities
         Resource Units

Ad Valorem Tax
USE   Property Taxes

Adages
USE   Proverbs

Adaptability (Personality)
USE   Adjustment (to Environment)
AND   Personality Traits

Adaptation Level Theory   *JUL. 1966*
         Postings: 94   GC: 810
SN   Theory that individuals judge the magni-
         tude of any stimuli (e.g., loudness, size,
         weight) by establishing subjective scales
         against which the stimuli are measured
BT   Behavior Theories
RT   Arousal Patterns
         Attention
         Cognitive Processes
         Individual Psychology
         Novelty (Stimulus Dimension)
         Perception

= Two or more Descriptors are used to represent this term.
The term's main entry shows the appropriate coordination.

Adapted Physical Education MAR. 1974
Postings: 467 GC: 220
SN Adaptation of regular physical education programs to meet the needs of disabled individuals
BT Physical Education
Special Education
RT Disabilities
Individualized Instruction
Physical Activities
Special Olympics

Adaptive Behavior
USE Adjustment (to Environment)

Adaptive Behavior (of Disabled) APR. 1982
Postings: 589 GC: 220
SN Ways in which disabled individuals meet the personal and social standards of their age or cultural groups
BT Adjustment (to Environment)
RT Coping
Daily Living Skills
Disabilities
Emotional Adjustment
Mental Disorders
Mental Retardation
Normalization (Disabilities)
Self Care Skills
Social Adjustment

Adaptive Equipment (Disabled)
USE Assistive Devices (for Disabled)

Adaptive Testing FEB. 1984
Postings: 489 GC: 820
SN Testing that involves selecting test items according to the examinee's ability as shown by responses to earlier test items
UF Computerized Adaptive Testing #
Computerized Tailored Testing #
Flexilevel Testing
Response Contingent Testing
Stradaptive Testing
Tailored Testing
BT Testing
RT Bayesian Statistics
Computer Assisted Testing
Individual Testing
Item Banks
Item Response Theory
Response Style (Tests)
Sequential Approach
Test Items

Addition OCT. 1968
Postings: 667 GC: 480
BT Arithmetic
RT Division
Multiplication
Subtraction

Additional Aid
USE Equalization Aid

Addresses
USE Speeches

Adhesives JUL. 1969
Postings: 26 GC: 910
UF Cements (Adhesives)
Glues
Pastes (Adhesives)
Sealants
Stickers
BT Supplies
RT Art Materials
Construction Materials
Finishing

Adjectives JUL. 1966
Postings: 522 GC: 450
BT Form Classes (Languages)
RT Adverbs
Morphology (Languages)

Semantic Differential
Sentence Structure
Syntax
Vocabulary

Adjunct Faculty AUG. 1986
Postings: 179 GC: 360
SN Temporary, part-time, or other auxiliary faculty of a school or college, usually with limited duties and benefits and often primarily employed outside of academia
UF Adjunct Professors
BT Faculty
RT Academic Rank (Professional)
College Faculty
Multiple Employment
Nontenured Faculty
Part Time Faculty
Specialists
Teachers

Adjunct Professors
USE Adjunct Faculty

Adjustment (to Environment) JUL. 1966
Postings: 6,413 GC: 230
SN A condition of harmonious relation to the environment, in which internal needs are satisfied and external demands are met (Note: For specificity on this aspect, use "Well Being")—also, the process of altering internal or external factors to attain this harmonious condition
UF Adaptability (Personality) #
Adaptive Behavior
Adjustment Problems (1966 1980)
Group Adjustment
Individual Adjustment
Maladjustment (1966 1980)
Personal Adjustment (1966 1980)
NT Adaptive Behavior (of Disabled)
Coping
Emotional Adjustment
Social Adjustment
Student Adjustment
Vocational Adjustment
BT Behavior
RT Adjustment Counselors
Attitude Change
Behavior Problems
Chronic Illness
Counseling
Ecology
Environment
Familiarity
Health
Individual Development
Intelligence
Life Events
Maturity (Individuals)
Mental Health
Orientation
Personality Problems
Psychoeducational Methods
Rehabilitation
Rehabilitation Counseling
Resilience (Personality)
Stress Management
Therapy
Well Being

Adjustment Counselors JUL. 1966
Postings: 54 GC: 240
BT Counselors
RT Adjustment (to Environment)
School Counselors
School Social Workers

Adjustment Problems (1966 1980)
USE Adjustment (to Environment)

Administration JUL. 1966
Postings: 4,897 GC: 320
SN Planning, organizing, directing, and controlling human or material resources to accomplish predetermined goals (Note: Use a more specific term if possible)

UF Management (1966 1980)
NT Building Operation
Business Administration
Construction Management
Crisis Management
Educational Administration
Energy Management
Enrollment Management
Farm Management
Home Management
Information Management
Institutional Administration
Management by Objectives
Middle Management
Money Management
Office Management
Personnel Management
Program Administration
Public Administration
Research Administration
Risk Management
Supervision
Time Management
Total Quality Management
BT Governance
RT Administrative Change
Administrative Organization
Administrative Policy
Administrative Principles
Administrative Problems
Administrator Responsibility
Administrator Role
Administrators
Budgeting
Committees
Coordination
Governing Boards
Management Information Systems
Management Systems
Management Teams
Managerial Occupations
Organization
Organizational Effectiveness
Participative Decision Making
Planning
Policy Formation
Quality Circles
Resource Allocation
Staff Utilization

Administrative Agencies (1966 1980)
MAR. 1980
Postings: 330 GC: 610
SN Invalid Descriptor—used inconsistently in indexing—see "Agencies" or "Public Agencies"

Administrative Change JUL. 1966
Postings: 717 GC: 320
SN Change in administrative personnel (reassignment, dismissal, etc.) or in the structure of an organization's administration
BT Change
RT Administration
Administrators
Change Strategies
Organizational Change
Organizational Development

Administrative Occupations
USE Managerial Occupations

Administrative Organization JUL. 1966
Postings: 4,388 GC: 320
SN The manner in which the authority, duties, and responsibilities of administrators, managers, or supervisors are structured—also, the structuring of an organization so that these duties, etc., can be carried out
NT Centralization
Decentralization
Departments
Management Teams
Participative Decision Making
BT Organization
RT Administration
Bureaucracy

Governance
Governing Boards
Informal Organization
Management Systems
Middle Management
Power Structure
School Organization

Administrative Personnel (1966 1980)
USE Administrators

Administrative Planning
USE Planning

Administrative Policy JUL. 1966
Postings: 3,624 GC: 320
SN Statement of an administrative body outlining the principles and practices to be followed with respect to specific matters—also, the fixed procedures and practices of administration
NT Board of Education Policy
BT Policy
RT Administration
Administrative Principles
Administrator Guides
Administrator Responsibility
Interdistrict Policies
Professional Autonomy

Administrative Principles AUG. 1968
Postings: 940 GC: 320
SN The assumptions, beliefs, values, or accepted practices that underlie administrative policy and activity (Note: Prior to Mar80, the use of this term was not restricted by a Scope Note)
BT Standards
RT Administration
Administrative Policy
Administrator Guides
Administrator Responsibility
Business Administration
Educational Principles
Supervisory Methods

Administrative Problems JUL. 1966
Postings: 1,707 GC: 320
SN (Note: Use a more precise term if possible)
BT Problems
RT Administration

Administrative Secretaries
USE Secretaries

Administrative Teams
USE Management Teams

Administrator Appraisal
USE Administrator Evaluation

Administrator Attitudes JUL. 1966
Postings: 7,192 GC: 320
SN Attitudes, opinions, or views held by administrators
UF Administrator Opinions
BT Attitudes
RT Administrator Behavior
Administrator Characteristics
Administrator Evaluation
Administrators
Employer Attitudes

Administrator Background (1967 1980)
USE Administrator Characteristics

Administrator Behavior MAY 1994
Postings: 202 GC: 320
SN Conduct of administrators in or out of job-related situations
NT Administrator Effectiveness
BT Behavior

= Two or more Descriptors are used to represent this term.
The term's main entry shows the appropriate coordination.

RT   Administrator Attitudes
      Administrator Characteristics
      Administrator Evaluation
      Administrator Role
      Administrators
      Leadership Styles

Administrator Characteristics   *JUL. 1966*
      Postings: 2,000   GC: 320
SN   Background and personal qualities of
      administrators (Note: Do not confuse
      with "Administrator Qualifications")
UF   Administrator Background (1967
      1980)
RT   Administrator Attitudes
      Administrator Behavior
      Administrator Evaluation
      Administrator Qualifications
      Administrator Selection
      Administrators
      Individual Characteristics

Administrator Education   *NOV. 1971*
      Postings: 3,696   GC: 400
SN   Preservice programs, usually offered by
      colleges or universities, designed to pre-
      pare individuals for administrative or
      managerial positions (Note: Prior to
      Mar80, this term was not restricted to
      preservice programs—see also "Man-
      agement Development")
UF   Administrator Preparation
      Management Education (1967 1980)
BT   Professional Education
RT   Administrator Qualifications
      Business Administration Education
      Management Development
      Public Administration Education
      Specialist in Education Degrees
      Supervisor Qualifications

Administrator Effectiveness   *DEC. 1988*
      Postings: 1,087   GC: 320
SN   Degree to which administrators are suc-
      cessful in satisfying their objectives, ob-
      ligations, or functions
BT   Administrator Behavior
RT   Administrator Evaluation
      Administrator Qualifications
      Administrator Role
      Administrators
      Educational Quality
      Excellence in Education
      Instructional Effectiveness
      Leadership Qualities
      Organizational Effectiveness
      School Effectiveness

Administrator Evaluation   *JUL. 1966*
      Postings: 1,325   GC: 320
SN   The evaluation or appraisal of adminis-
      trators or managers (Note: Prior to Mar80,
      the use of this term was not restricted by
      a Scope Note)
UF   Administrator Appraisal
BT   Personnel Evaluation
RT   Administrator Attitudes
      Administrator Behavior
      Administrator Characteristics
      Administrator Effectiveness
      Administrator Qualifications
      Administrator Selection
      Administrators
      Assessment Centers (Personnel)
      Faculty Evaluation

Administrator Guides   *JUL. 1966*
      Postings: 2,352   GC: 730
BT   Guides
RT   Administrative Policy
      Administrative Principles
      Administrator Responsibility
      Administrator Role
      Administrators
      Board Administrator Relationship
      Faculty Handbooks
      Guidelines
      Program Guides
      Teacher Administrator Relationship

Administrator Opinions
USE   Administrator Attitudes

Administrator Preparation
USE   Administrator Education

Administrator Qualifications   *JUL. 1966*
      Postings: 1,208   GC: 320
SN   The education, experience, and physical,
      social, and mental characteristics that
      determine an individual's fitness for an
      administrative position
BT   Qualifications
RT   Administrator Characteristics
      Administrator Education
      Administrator Effectiveness
      Administrator Evaluation
      Administrator Selection
      Administrators
      Employment Qualifications
      Leadership Qualities
      Supervisor Qualifications

Administrator Responsibility   *JUL. 1966*
      Postings: 3,750   GC: 320
BT   Responsibility
RT   Administration
      Administrative Policy
      Administrative Principles
      Administrator Guides
      Administrator Role
      Administrators
      Educational Responsibility
      Faculty Handbooks
      Faculty Workload
      Leadership Responsibility
      Teacher Responsibility

Administrator Role   *JUL. 1966*
      Postings: 9,819   GC: 320
SN   Functions and behaviors expected of or
      performed by persons in administrative
      positions
BT   Role
RT   Administration
      Administrator Behavior
      Administrator Effectiveness
      Administrator Guides
      Administrator Responsibility
      Administrators
      Faculty Handbooks

Administrator Selection   *JUL. 1966*
      Postings: 952   GC: 320
SN   Process of assessing and choosing can-
      didates for administrative positions
BT   Personnel Selection
RT   Administrator Characteristics
      Administrator Evaluation
      Administrator Qualifications
      Administrators
      Assessment Centers (Personnel)
      Faculty Recruitment
      Search Committees (Personnel)

Administrator Teacher Relationship
USE   Teacher Administrator Relationship

Administrator Training
USE   Management Development

Administrators   *MAR. 1980*
      Postings: 8,750   GC: 360
SN   Persons involved in planning, organiz-
      ing, directing, and controlling human or
      material resources to accomplish prede-
      termined goals
UF   Administrative Personnel (1966 1980)
      Business Officials (Industry)
      Chief Administrators (1967 1980)
      Community School Directors (1967
      1980) #
      Directors
      Management Personnel
      Managers
      School Administrators

NT   Admissions Officers
      Assistant Principals
      Beginning Principals
      Central Office Administrators
      Coordinators
      Deans
      Department Heads
      Library Administrators
      Medical Record Administrators
      Personnel Directors
      Presidents
      Principals
      Registrars (School)
      Research Directors
      School Business Officials
      Student Financial Aid Officers
      Superintendents
      Supervisors
      Trustees
      Vocational Directors
      Women Administrators
BT   Personnel
RT   Administration
      Administrative Change
      Administrator Attitudes
      Administrator Behavior
      Administrator Characteristics
      Administrator Effectiveness
      Administrator Evaluation
      Administrator Guides
      Administrator Qualifications
      Administrator Responsibility
      Administrator Role
      Administrator Selection
      Board Administrator Relationship
      Educational Administration
      Faculty
      Middle Management
      Professional Personnel
      Teacher Administrator Relationship

Admission (School)   *JUL. 1966*
      Postings: 1,131   GC: 320
UF   Matriculation
      School Admission
NT   College Admission
      Early Admission
      Open Enrollment
      Selective Admission
RT   Academic Standards
      Access to Education
      Admission Criteria
      Admissions Counseling
      Admissions Officers
      Competitive Selection
      Educational Supply
      Eligibility
      Enrollment
      Enrollment Management
      Late Registration
      Placement
      Portfolios (Background Materials)
      School Catalogs
      School Choice
      School Registration
      Schools
      Student Placement
      Student Recruitment
      Transitional Programs

Admission Criteria   *JUL. 1966*
      Postings: 3,896   GC: 320
UF   Student Selection
BT   Criteria
RT   Academic Standards
      Access to Education
      Admission (School)
      Admissions Officers
      College Applicants
      College Entrance Examinations
      Competitive Selection
      Early Admission
      Enrollment Influences
      Open Enrollment
      Prerequisites
      Prior Learning
      Residence Requirements
      School Catalogs
      Selective Admission
      Student Recruitment
      Transfer Policy

Admission Tests (Higher Education)
USE   College Entrance Examinations

Admission Tests (Occupational)
USE   Occupational Tests

Admissions Counseling   *MAR. 1980*
      Postings: 338   GC: 240
UF   Admissions Counselors (1973 1980)
BT   Educational Counseling
RT   Admission (School)
      Admissions Officers
      College Admission
      College Bound Students
      College Day
      College Preparation
      College School Cooperation
      Post High School Guidance
      Student Placement

Admissions Counselors (1973 1980)
USE   Admissions Counseling

Admissions Officers   *MAR. 1980*
      Postings: 235   GC: 360
SN   Administrative officials, usually at
      postsecondary institutions, with princi-
      pal responsibility for the recruitment,
      selection, and admission of students
BT   Administrators
      School Personnel
RT   Admission (School)
      Admission Criteria
      Admissions Counseling
      College Administration
      College Admission
      College Preparation
      Enrollment Management
      Enrollment Projections
      Middle Management
      Registrars (School)
      School Administration
      Student Personnel Workers
      Student Recruitment

Adolescence (1966 1980)
USE   Adolescents

Adolescent Attitudes   *AUG. 1999*
      Postings: 442   GC: 120
SN   Attitudes of, not toward, adolescents
BT   Attitudes
RT   Adolescent Behavior
      Adolescents
      Childhood Attitudes
      Student Attitudes
      Youth

Adolescent Behavior   *JUN. 2000*
      Postings: 257   GC: 120
SN   Behavior of adolescents (Note: Do not
      use for immature behavior by those older
      than adolescents)
BT   Behavior
RT   Adolescent Attitudes
      Adolescent Development
      Adolescents
      Affective Behavior
      Behavior Development
      Child Behavior
      Parent Child Relationship
      Social Behavior
      Student Behavior
      Youth

Adolescent Development   *MAR. 1980*
      Postings: 1,847   GC: 120
BT   Individual Development
RT   Adolescent Behavior
      Adolescents
      Developmental Stages
      Developmental Tasks
      Puberty
      Youth

= Two or more Descriptors are used to represent this term.
The term's main entry shows the appropriate coordination.

Adolescent Literature   *OCT. 1973*
Postings: 2,251   GC: 430
SN   Any reading material written primarily for, or read widely by, youth of secondary school age
BT   Literature
RT   Adolescents
     Childrens Literature
     Reading Materials

Adolescent Parents
USE   Early Parenthood

Adolescents   *JUL. 1966*
Postings: 22,669   GC: 120
SN   Approximately 13–17 years of age
UF   Adolescence (1966 1980)
     Teenagers (1966 1980)
BT   Age Groups
RT   Adolescent Attitudes
     Adolescent Behavior
     Adolescent Development
     Adolescent Literature
     Children
     Early Adolescents
     Early Parenthood
     High School Students
     Late Adolescents
     Parent Child Relationship
     Preadolescents
     Secondary School Students
     Youth

Adopted Children   *JUL. 1966*
Postings: 441   GC: 510
BT   Children
RT   Adoption
     Adoptive Parents
     Biological Parents
     Child Welfare
     Foster Children
     Foster Family
     Transracial Adoption

Adoption   *JUL. 1966*
Postings: 816   GC: 520
NT   Transracial Adoption
RT   Adopted Children
     Adoptive Parents
     Biological Parents
     Child Welfare
     Childlessness
     Foster Care
     Foster Family
     Kinship
     Placement

Adoption (Ideas)   *JUL. 1966*
Postings: 1,638   GC: 520
SN   Process of accepting new ideas or practices
RT   Attitude Change
     Change Strategies
     Diffusion (Communication)
     Discovery Processes
     Evaluation Utilization
     Information Utilization
     Innovation
     Linking Agents
     Pilot Projects
     Research Utilization
     Resistance to Change
     Theory Practice Relationship

Adoptive Parents   *APR. 1993*
Postings: 170   GC: 510
BT   Parents
RT   Adopted Children
     Adoption
     Biological Parents
     Foster Family
     Stepfamily
     Transracial Adoption

Adult Basic Education   *JUL. 1966*
Postings: 7,491   GC: 340
SN   Education provided for adults at the ele-

mentary level (through grade 8), usually with emphasis on communicative, computational, and social skills (Note: Also appears in the list of mandatory educational level Descriptors)
UF   Fundamental Education (Adults)
BT   Adult Education
     Elementary Education
RT   Adult Literacy
     Adult Reading Programs
     Basic Skills
     Functional Literacy
     High School Equivalency Programs
     Literacy Education
     Migrant Adult Education
     Primary Education
     Public School Adult Education
     Workplace Literacy

Adult Characteristics (1967 1980)
USE   Adults
AND   Individual Characteristics

Adult Children   *DEC. 1987*
Postings: 430   GC: 510
SN   Grown-up sons and daughters (approximately 18+ years of age)
UF   Adult Offspring
     Grown Children
BT   Adults
RT   Family (Sociological Unit)
     Family Caregivers
     Family Life
     Family Role
     Family Structure
     Parent Child Relationship

Adult Counseling   *JUL. 1966*
Postings: 660   GC: 240
BT   Counseling
RT   Adult Dropouts
     Adult Programs
     Adults
     Career Counseling
     Counselors

Adult Day Care   *MAR. 1978*
Postings: 165   GC: 220
SN   Care of disabled adults (includes frail elderly and those who are ill) during the day, in which health and social services are offered by professional and paraprofessional staff
BT   Social Services
RT   Adult Programs
     Adults
     Attendants
     Day Care
     Frail Elderly
     Home Health Aides
     Long Term Care
     Older Adults
     Visiting Homemakers

Adult Development   *JUL. 1966*
Postings: 1,597   GC: 120
SN   Physiological, psychological, and sociological growth or maturation occurring throughout an adult's lifetime
BT   Individual Development
RT   Adult Education
     Adult Learning
     Adults
     Aging (Individuals)
     Developmental Stages
     Developmental Tasks
     Educational Gerontology
     Gerontology
     Lifelong Learning
     Midlife Transitions
     Transformative Learning

Adult Dropouts   *JUL. 1966*
Postings: 168   GC: 510
SN   Adults who withdraw from an activity before its completion
BT   Adults
     Dropouts

RT   Adult Counseling
     Adult Education

Adult Education   *JUL. 1966*
Postings: 22,872   GC: 340
SN   Providing or coordinating purposeful learning activities for adults
UF   Adult Education Programs (1966 1980) #
     Further Education
NT   Adult Basic Education
     Adult Vocational Education
     Continuing Education
     Labor Education
     Migrant Adult Education
     Parent Education
     Preretirement Education
     Public School Adult Education
     Veterans Education
BT   Education
RT   Adult Development
     Adult Dropouts
     Adult Learning
     Adult Programs
     Adult Reading Programs
     Adult Students
     Adults
     Andragogy
     Community Education
     Continuing Education Centers
     Continuing Education Units
     Correctional Education
     Educational Gerontology
     Extension Education
     High School Equivalency Programs
     Lifelong Learning
     Noncredit Courses
     Nonschool Educational Programs
     Popular Education
     Postsecondary Education
     Professional Continuing Education
     Professional Education
     Refresher Courses
     Retraining
     Special Degree Programs
     Training Allowances
     Transformative Learning
     Womens Education

Adult Education Programs (1966 1980)
USE   Adult Education
AND   Adult Programs

Adult Educators   *JUL. 1966*
Postings: 1,714   GC: 360
SN   Teachers who specialize in adult education
BT   Teachers
RT   Extension Agents
     Instructor Coordinators
     Trainers

Adult Farmer Education   *JUL. 1966*
Postings: 328   GC: 410
SN   Vocational education in agriculture for adults aged 25 or over engaged in production agriculture (Note: For younger adults, use "Young Farmer Education")
BT   Adult Vocational Education
     Agricultural Education
RT   Farm Visits
     Farmers
     Rural Education
     Rural Extension
     Young Farmer Education

Adult Foster Care   *AUG. 1982*
Postings: 33   GC: 220
SN   Care of disabled adults (includes frail elderly and those who are ill) in private homes—caretakers are usually not close relatives and are paid an established fee for their services (Note: Do not confuse with "Residential Care")
UF   Foster Homes (1970 1982) (Adults)
BT   Social Services
RT   Adult Programs
     Adults
     Attendants

     Boarding Homes
     Deinstitutionalization (of Disabled)
     Foster Care
     Foster Family
     Frail Elderly
     Group Homes
     Home Health Aides
     Long Term Care
     Older Adults
     Visiting Homemakers

Adult Leaders (1967 1980)
USE   Leaders

Adult Learning   *JUL. 1966*
Postings: 3,295   GC: 110
BT   Learning
RT   Adult Development
     Adult Education
     Adult Programs
     Adult Students
     Adults
     Andragogy
     Lifelong Learning
     Transformative Learning

Adult Literacy   *JUL. 1970*
Postings: 4,924   GC: 460
UF   Illiterate Adults (1966 1980) #
BT   Literacy
RT   Adult Basic Education
     Adult Reading Programs
     Adults
     Family Literacy
     Functional Literacy
     Functional Reading
     Illiteracy
     Literacy Education
     Reading Skills
     Workplace Literacy
     Writing Skills

Adult Offspring
USE   Adult Children

Adult Programs   *JUL. 1966*
Postings: 3,275   GC: 340
SN   Programs for adults (Note: When appropriate, coordinate with an age-leveler, e.g., "Young Adults," "Middle Aged Adults," "Older Adults," or with a mandatory educational level Descriptor)
UF   Adult Education Programs (1966 1980) #
NT   Adult Reading Programs
     High School Equivalency Programs
BT   Programs
RT   Adult Counseling
     Adult Day Care
     Adult Education
     Adult Foster Care
     Adult Learning
     Adults
     Alumni Education
     Evening Programs

Adult Reading Programs   *JUL. 1966*
Postings: 830   GC: 460
BT   Adult Programs
     Reading Programs
RT   Adult Basic Education
     Adult Education
     Adult Literacy
     Correctional Education
     Functional Literacy
     Functional Reading
     High School Equivalency Programs
     Literacy Education
     Reading Instruction
     Speed Reading

Adult Runaways
USE   Runaways

= Two or more Descriptors are used to represent this term.
The term's main entry shows the appropriate coordination.

Adult Students   *JUL. 1966*
    Postings: 4,838   GC: 360
BT Adults
    Students
RT Adult Education
    Adult Learning
    Andragogy
    Continuing Education
    Evening Students
    Married Students
    Nontraditional Students
    Reentry Students
    Self Supporting Students
    Single Students
    Special Degree Programs
    Stopouts

Adult Vocational Education   *JUL. 1966*
    Postings: 1,894   GC: 400
SN Education for adults or out-of-school
    youth aged 16 or over engaged in or
    preparing to enter an occupation
NT Adult Farmer Education
    Young Farmer Education
BT Adult Education
    Vocational Education
RT Career Ladders
    Cooperative Education
    Industrial Training
    Job Training
    Public School Adult Education
    Retraining
    Trade and Industrial Education
    Vocational Rehabilitation

Adults   *JUL. 1966*
    Postings: 14,553   GC: 120
SN Approximately 18+ years of age
UF Adult Characteristics (1967 1980) #
NT Adult Children
    Adult Dropouts
    Adult Students
    Adults (30 to 45)
    Middle Aged Adults
    Older Adults
    Young Adults
BT Age Groups
RT Adult Counseling
    Adult Day Care
    Adult Development
    Adult Education
    Adult Foster Care
    Adult Learning
    Adult Literacy
    Adult Programs
    Parents

Adults (30 to 45)   *AUG. 1989*
    Postings: 24   GC: 120
SN Age group between ''Young Adults'' and
    ''Middle Aged Adults''—approximately
    30–45
BT Adults
RT Baby Boomers
    Middle Aged Adults
    Older Workers
    Young Adults

Advance Organizers   *MAR. 1977*
    Postings: 594   GC: 310
SN Preview questions and comments used
    to increase learners' comprehension and
    recall
BT Instructional Materials
RT Comprehension
    Directed Reading Activity
    Intentional Learning
    Learning
    Learning Activities
    Reading
    Reading Improvement
    Recall (Psychology)
    Retention (Psychology)
    Study Guides
    Study Skills
    Teaching Methods
    Verbal Learning

Advanced Courses   *MAR. 1980*
    Postings: 408   GC: 350
SN Courses beyond the introductory or ba-
    sic level
BT Courses
RT Acceleration (Education)
    Advanced Placement
    Advanced Placement Programs
    Advanced Students
    Elective Courses
    Introductory Courses
    Majors (Students)
    Required Courses

Advanced Credit Examinations
USE Equivalency Tests

Advanced Education
USE Higher Education

Advanced Nations
USE Developed Nations

Advanced Placement   *JUL. 1966*
    Postings: 431   GC: 320
SN Permitting students with academic credit
    or test scores beyond minimum require-
    ments to bypass coursework (Note: Prior
    to Mar80, this term was not restricted by
    a Scope Note—do not confuse with the
    more specific ''Advanced Placement Pro-
    grams'')
BT Placement
RT Ability Grouping
    Academic Achievement
    Academically Gifted
    Acceleration (Education)
    Advanced Courses
    Advanced Placement Programs
    Advanced Students
    College Entrance Examinations
    Equivalency Tests
    Honors Curriculum
    Prior Learning
    Student Placement

Advanced Placement Programs   *JUL. 1966*
    Postings: 404   GC: 320
SN Programs adopted in U.S. in 1956 under
    which high school students can take
    College Entrance Examination Board
    (CEEB) tests, receive college credit for
    acceptable scores, and be placed into
    sophomore-level college classes (Note:
    Prior to Mar80, the use of this term was
    not restricted by a Scope Note)
BT Programs
RT Academically Gifted
    Acceleration (Education)
    Advanced Courses
    Advanced Placement
    Advanced Students
    Articulation (Education)
    College Bound Students
    College Entrance Examinations
    College School Cooperation
    Educational Attainment
    Equivalency Tests

Advanced Programs (1966 1980)
                             MAR. 1980
    Postings: 97   GC: 320
SN Invalid Descriptor—used inconsistently
    in indexing—see such Descriptors as
    ''Acceleration (Education),'' ''Advanced
    Courses,'' ''Advanced Placement Pro-
    grams,'' etc.

Advanced Standing Examinations
USE Equivalency Tests

Advanced Students   *JUL. 1966*
    Postings: 374   GC: 360
SN Students studying a particular subject at
    an advanced level (Note: Do not confuse
    with ''Academically Gifted'')

    Students
RT Academically Gifted
    Acceleration (Education)
    Advanced Courses
    Advanced Placement
    Advanced Placement Programs

Advancement
USE Promotion (Occupational)

Advantaged   *MAR. 1980*
    Postings: 126   GC: 510
SN Individuals or groups who have high
    status in a particular society for reasons
    of race, sex, ethnicity, economics, lan-
    guage, geographic location, environment,
    education, etc.
UF Culturally Advantaged (1967 1980)
    Economically Advantaged
    Socially Advantaged
BT Groups
RT Affluent Youth
    Cultural Differences
    Disadvantaged
    Living Standards
    Middle Class
    Quality of Life
    Social Status
    Upper Class

Adventitious Impairments   *MAR. 1980*
    Postings: 122   GC: 220
SN Conditions resulting from illness or in-
    jury during the developmental or adult
    years
UF Adventitiously Handicapped (1975
    1980)
BT Disabilities
RT Congenital Impairments
    Diseases
    Injuries

Adventitiously Handicapped (1975 1980)
USE Adventitious Impairments

Adventure Education   *MAR. 1980*
    Postings: 945   GC: 400
SN Type of outdoor education that attempts
    to teach environmental awareness and
    build self-confidence through activities
    that involve risk or stress, such as rock
    climbing, survival training, etc.
UF Adventure Learning
BT Outdoor Education
RT Camping
    Discovery Learning
    Environmental Education
    Experiential Learning
    Field Experience Programs
    Field Trips
    Interdisciplinary Approach
    Outdoor Activities
    Outdoor Leadership
    Risk
    Self Concept
    Stress Management
    Trails
    Wilderness

Adventure Learning
USE Adventure Education

Adverbials
USE Adverbs

Adverbs   *JUL. 1966*
    Postings: 283   GC: 450
UF Adverbials
BT Form Classes (Languages)
RT Adjectives
    Morphology (Languages)
    Sentence Structure
    Syntax
    Verbs
    Vocabulary

Advertising   *MAR. 1980*
    Postings: 2,404   GC: 720
SN Persuasive presentation or promotion of
    ideas, goods, or services by means of
    mass communication
NT Television Commercials
BT Publicity
RT Commercial Art
    Consumer Protection
    Mass Media
    Merchandising
    Persuasive Discourse
    Political Campaigns
    Propaganda
    Salesmanship

Advertising Art
USE Commercial Art

Advisory Boards
USE Advisory Committees

Advisory Committees   *JUL. 1966*
    Postings: 2,779   GC: 320
UF Advisory Boards
BT Committees
RT Blue Ribbon Commissions
    Consultants
    Governing Boards
    Needs Assessment
    Participative Decision Making
    Planning Commissions
    Policy Formation
    Research Committees
    Search Committees (Personnel)
    Specialists

Advocacy   *NOV. 1981*
    Postings: 1,374   GC: 520
SN Full and active support for and represen-
    tation of an individual, group, cause, or
    idea
UF Citizen Advocacy
NT Child Advocacy
    Self Advocacy
RT Citizen Participation
    Empowerment
    Legal Aid
    Needs
    Services
    Social Action
    Social Behavior

Advocates (Law)
USE Lawyers

Aerobic Dance
USE Aerobics
AND Dance

Aerobics   *JUN. 1984*
    Postings: 198   GC: 470
SN Method of achieving physical condition-
    ing and fitness by stimulating heart (pulse
    rate) and lung (oxygen intake) activity
    through successively longer periods of
    vigorous exercise, thereby gradually ex-
    panding the capacity of the cardiovascu-
    lar and respiratory systems
UF Aerobic Dance #
BT Exercise
RT Cardiovascular System
    Heart Rate
    Physical Fitness

Aerospace Education   *APR. 1972*
    Postings: 608   GC: 490
UF Aerospace Science Education
NT Aviation Education
BT Education
RT Aerospace Technology
    Air Transportation
    Astronomy
    Aviation Technology
    Aviation Vocabulary
    Engineering Education

= Two or more Descriptors are used to represent this term.
The term's main entry shows the appropriate coordination.

Science Education
Space Sciences
Technical Education

Aerospace Industry   *JUL. 1966*
Postings: 176   GC: 650
BT   Manufacturing Industry
RT   Aerospace Technology
Air Transportation
Aviation Mechanics
Aviation Technology
Aviation Vocabulary
Electromechanical Technology

Aerospace Science Education
USE   Aerospace Education

Aerospace Sciences
USE   Aerospace Technology

Aerospace Technology   *JUL. 1966*
Postings: 549   GC: 490
UF   Aerospace Sciences
NT   Aviation Technology
BT   Technology
RT   Aerospace Education
Aerospace Industry
Air Traffic Control
Air Transportation
Aircraft Pilots
Astronomy
Engineering
Engineering Technology
Lunar Research
Physical Sciences
Satellites (Aerospace)
Space Exploration
Space Sciences

Aesthetic Education   *MAR. 1972*
Postings: 1,509   GC: 420
NT   Art Appreciation
Film Study
Music Appreciation
BT   Education
RT   Aesthetic Values
Aesthetics
Art Education
Cultural Enrichment
Dance Education
Music Education
Visual Literacy

Aesthetic Judgment
USE   Aesthetic Values
AND   Value Judgment

Aesthetic Values   *OCT. 1982*
Postings: 513   GC: 520
SN   Objective or subjective principles and
standards related to human preferences
among, or assessments of, artistic forms
and qualities (in music, literature, visual
arts, etc.) or objects and events in
nature—sometimes includes precepts of
non-perceptible (e.g., moral or intellec-
tual) beauty
UF   Aesthetic Judgment #
Beauty
Taste (Aesthetics)
BT   Values
RT   Aesthetic Education
Aesthetics
Art
Art Criticism
Art Expression
Cultural Context
Design Preferences
Perception
Sensory Experience
Social Values

Aesthetics   *NOV. 1994*
Postings: 209   GC: 430
SN   Branch of philosophy dealing with beauty,

artistic expression, and psychological
responses to beauty and art
UF   Esthetics
BT   Philosophy
RT   Aesthetic Education
Aesthetic Values
Art
Art Expression
Discipline Based Art Education
Fine Arts
Literature
Theater Arts
Visual Arts

Affection   *JUL. 1966*
Postings: 177   GC: 120
BT   Psychological Needs
RT   Affiliation Need
Emotional Experience
Interpersonal Attraction
Intimacy
Love

Affective Behavior   *FEB. 1969*
Postings: 3,971   GC: 120
SN   Behavior that involves or expresses emo-
tions, feelings, or sentiments
UF   Emotional Behavior
BT   Behavior
RT   Adolescent Behavior
Affective Measures
Affective Objectives
Attachment Behavior
Attitudes
Child Behavior
Desensitization
Emotional Development
Emotional Response
Extraversion Introversion
Guilt
Interests
Love
Moods
Prosocial Behavior
Psychological Patterns

Affective Education
USE   Humanistic Education

Affective Measures   *MAR. 1980*
Postings: 882   GC: 830
SN   Procedures or devices used to obtain
quantified descriptions of an individual's
feelings, emotional states, or disposi-
tions
UF   Affective Tests (1971 1980)
BT   Measures (Individuals)
RT   Affective Behavior
Affective Objectives
Association Measures
Attitude Measures
Emotional Adjustment
Emotional Development
Emotional Response
Forced Choice Technique
Interest Inventories
Personality Measures
Projective Measures
Self Concept Measures

Affective Objectives   *JUL. 1969*
Postings: 1,432   GC: 310
SN   Behavioral objectives which emphasize
changes in interest, attitudes, and val-
ues, or a degree of adjustment, accept-
ance, or rejection
BT   Behavioral Objectives
RT   Affective Behavior
Affective Measures
Cognitive Objectives
Emotional Development
Humanistic Education
Psychomotor Objectives

Affective Tests (1971 1980)
USE   Affective Measures

Affiliated Schools   *JUL. 1966*
Postings: 84   GC: 340
SN   Schools providing experiences for stu-
dent teachers or teacher interns, although
not integral parts of teacher education
institutions
UF   Cooperating Schools
BT   Schools
RT   College School Cooperation
Cooperating Teachers
Cooperative Education
Educational Cooperation
Elementary Schools
Field Experience Programs
Laboratory Schools
Preservice Teacher Education
Secondary Schools
Student Teaching
Teacher Education
Teaching Experience

Affiliation Need   *JUL. 1966*
Postings: 209   GC: 120
SN   Psychological drive for association with
others
NT   Peer Acceptance
BT   Psychological Needs
RT   Achievement Need
Affection
Dependency (Personality)
Status Need

Affirmative Action   *NOV. 1975*
Postings: 3,020   GC: 540
SN   Positive action taken to overcome
underrepresentation of women and mi-
nority groups in employment (including
career advancement programs) and in
the make-up of postsecondary student
bodies, as compared to the composition
of the area population
RT   College Admission
College Desegregation
Desegregation Methods
Desegregation Plans
Disability Discrimination
Disadvantaged
Educational Discrimination
Educational Opportunities
Employed Women
Employment Practices
Employment Services
Equal Education
Equal Opportunities (Jobs)
Ethnic Distribution
Faculty Integration
Minority Groups
Nondiscriminatory Education
Nontraditional Occupations
Personnel Integration
Personnel Policy
Personnel Selection
Quotas
Racial Balance
Racial Bias
Racial Composition
Racial Discrimination
Racial Integration
Racially Balanced Schools
Recruitment
Religious Discrimination
Reverse Discrimination
School Demography
Selective Admission
Sex Bias
Sex Discrimination
Sex Fairness
Teacher Integration
Tokenism

Affixes   *APR. 1990*
Postings: 22   GC: 450
SN   Morphemes attached to or inserted within
base or root words to form other words
with different meanings—includes pre-
fixes, infixes, and suffixes
NT   Prefixes (Grammar)
Suffixes
BT   Morphemes

RT   Form Classes (Languages)
Morphophonemics

Affluent Youth   *JUL. 1966*
Postings: 56   GC: 510
SN   (Note: Coordinate with an appropriate
age or educational level Descriptor)
BT   Youth
RT   Advantaged
Socioeconomic Status
Upper Class

African American Studies (1969 1977)
USE   Black Studies

African Americans
USE   Blacks

African Centered Perspective
USE   Afrocentrism

African Culture   *JUL. 1966*
Postings: 1,078   GC: 560
BT   Culture
RT   African History
African Literature
African Studies
Afrocentrism
Black Culture
Middle Eastern History
Middle Eastern Studies
Non Western Civilization
Tribes

African History   *JUL. 1969*
Postings: 569   GC: 430
BT   History
RT   African Culture
African Literature
African Studies
Afrocentrism
Black Culture
Black History
Black Literature
Black Studies
Middle Eastern History
Middle Eastern Studies
Non Western Civilization
Slavery
Tribes
World War I
World War II

African Languages   *JUL. 1966*
Postings: 458   GC: 440
NT   Akan
Bantu Languages
Basaa
Bini
Dyula
Ewe
Fulani
Ga
Gbaya
Igbo
Luo
Mandingo
Mende
Mossi
Nembe
Sango
Sara
Susu
Wolof
Yoruba
BT   Languages
RT   African Literature
African Studies
Language Classification

African Literature   *MAY 1970*
Postings: 212   GC: 430
BT   Literature
RT   African Culture
African History

= Two or more Descriptors are used to represent this term.
The term's main entry shows the appropriate coordination.

African Languages
Black Literature

African Studies   *AUG. 1988*
     Postings: 138   GC: 400
SN   Interdisciplinary instruction and research concerned with the continent of Africa and its inhabitants—generally encompasses sub-Saharan Africa, but may also include north Africa
BT   Area Studies
RT   African Culture
     African History
     African Languages
     Afrocentrism
     Apartheid
     Black Studies
     Foreign Culture
     Middle Eastern Studies
     Non Western Civilization

Africentrism
USE   Afrocentrism

Afrikaans   *MAY 1970*
     Postings: 58   GC: 440
BT   Indo European Languages
RT   Dutch

Afro Americans
USE   Blacks

Afro Asiatic Languages   *JUL. 1966*
     Postings: 26   GC: 440
NT   Berber Languages
     Chad Languages
     Semitic Languages
     Somali
BT   Languages

Afrocentrism   *AUG. 1999*
     Postings: 252   GC: 540
SN   Political and educational movement stressing African cultural values and the achievements of African civilizations, aimed at increasing confidence, identity, and unity among African-Americans and others of African descent
UF   African Centered Perspective
     Africentrism
RT   African Culture
     African History
     African Studies
     Black Culture
     Black History
     Black Studies
     Blacks
     Cultural Awareness
     Ethnicity
     Ethnocentrism
     Racial Identification
     Values

After School Activities (1967 1980)
USE   After School Programs

After School Centers   *JUL. 1966*
     Postings: 33   GC: 920
BT   Educational Facilities
RT   After School Education
     After School Programs
     Study Centers

After School Day Care (1978 1983)
USE   After School Programs
AND   School Age Day Care

After School Education   *JUL. 1966*
     Postings: 122   GC: 350
UF   After School Tutoring (1966 1980) #
BT   Education
RT   After School Centers
     After School Programs
     Compensatory Education

Extended School Day
Supplementary Education

After School Programs   *JUL. 1966*
     Postings: 672   GC: 350
UF   After School Activities (1967 1980)
     After School Day Care (1978 1983) #
BT   Programs
RT   After School Centers
     After School Education
     Enrichment Activities
     Extended School Day
     Extracurricular Activities
     School Activities
     School Age Day Care
     School Recreational Programs

After School Tutoring (1966 1980)
USE   After School Education
AND   Tutoring

Age   *JUL. 1966*
     Postings: 2,545   GC: 120
UF   Age Level
NT   Chronological Age
     Mental Age
     School Entrance Age
BT   Individual Characteristics
RT   Age Differences
     Age Grade Placement
     Age Groups
     Aging (Individuals)
     Aging in Academia
     Developmental Delays
     Developmental Stages
     Maturity (Individuals)

Age Differences   *JUL. 1966*
     Postings: 11,767   GC: 120
UF   Developmental Differences (Age Groups) #
BT   Individual Differences
RT   Age
     Age Groups
     Aging Education
     Andragogy
     Developmental Stages
     Developmentally Appropriate Practices
     Generation Gap
     Intergenerational Programs
     Mixed Age Grouping

Age Discrimination   *MAR. 1980*
     Postings: 597   GC: 540
SN   Discriminatory attitudes or practices on account of an individual's age
BT   Social Discrimination
RT   Aging (Individuals)
     Disability Discrimination
     Educational Discrimination
     Equal Education
     Equal Opportunities (Jobs)
     Mandatory Retirement
     Middle Aged Adults
     Older Adults
     Older Workers
     Racial Discrimination
     Retirement
     Reverse Discrimination
     Sex Discrimination
     Social Bias

Age Grade Placement   *JUL. 1966*
     Postings: 203   GC: 320
SN   Use of a student's age as the basis for assignment to a grade level or for school entrance—also, the relationship between age and grade level
UF   Age Grade Status
BT   Placement
RT   Acceleration (Education)
     Age
     Homogeneous Grouping
     Instructional Program Divisions
     Nongraded Instructional Grouping
     School Entrance Age
     School Readiness
     Social Promotion

Student Placement
Student Promotion

Age Grade Status
USE   Age Grade Placement

Age Groups   *JUL. 1966*
     Postings: 678   GC: 120
SN   (Note: See also list of age leveling Descriptors)
NT   Adolescents
     Adults
     Children
     Early Adolescents
     Late Adolescents
     Mixed Age Grouping
BT   Groups
RT   Age
     Age Differences
     Chronological Age
     Developmental Stages
     Intergenerational Programs
     Older Workers
     Peer Groups
     Youth

Age Level
USE   Age

Aged
USE   Older Adults

Agencies   *JUL. 1966*
     Postings: 853   GC: 610
SN   Organizations serving the public—also, administrative units of government (Note: Use a more specific term if possible)
NT   Accrediting Agencies
     Private Agencies
     Public Agencies
     Social Agencies
     Urban Renewal Agencies
     Voluntary Agencies
     Youth Agencies
BT   Organizations (Groups)
RT   Agency Cooperation
     Agency Role
     Government (Administrative Body)
     Nonprofit Organizations

Agency Cooperation   *MAR. 1980*
     Postings: 4,778   GC: 610
SN   Cooperation of agencies with each other or with other organizations, groups, etc.
UF   Interagency Cooperation (1967 1980)
     Interagency Coordination (1967 1980) #
     Interagency Planning (1966 1980) #
BT   Cooperation
RT   Agencies
     Cooperative Planning
     Educational Cooperation
     Institutional Cooperation
     Integrated Services
     Interdistrict Policies
     Regional Cooperation
     Research Coordinating Units
     Shared Resources and Services

Agency Function
USE   Agency Role

Agency Role   *JUL. 1966*
     Postings: 2,468   GC: 610
UF   Agency Function
BT   Institutional Role
RT   Accrediting Agencies
     Agencies
     Private Agencies
     Public Agencies
     Social Agencies
     State Agencies
     Urban Renewal Agencies
     Voluntary Agencies
     Welfare Agencies
     Youth Agencies

Agenda Setting   *DEC. 1989*
     Postings: 342   GC: 520
SN   The power of communication to shape and formulate opinion and direction through the choice of topics considered and/or the perspectives offered (Note: Do not confuse with the Identifier "Agenda Preparation (Meetings)")
RT   Audience Analysis
     Audience Response
     Bias
     Communication (Thought Transfer)
     Freedom of Information
     Information Dissemination
     Information Sources
     Mass Media
     Mass Media Effects
     Mass Media Role
     News Media
     News Reporting
     Persuasive Discourse
     Policy Formation
     Political Influences
     Press Opinion
     Public Opinion

Aggression   *JUL. 1966*
     Postings: 2,581   GC: 230
SN   Hostile actions or behavior (Note: For forceful behavior that is not hostile, see "Assertiveness")
BT   Antisocial Behavior
RT   Animal Behavior
     Assertiveness
     Bullying
     Catharsis
     Competition
     Crime
     Hostility
     Rape
     Terrorism
     Verbal Abuse
     Violence

Aging (Individuals)   *JUL. 1980*
     Postings: 2,307   GC: 120
SN   The physiological and psychological process of growing old
NT   Aging in Academia
BT   Individual Development
RT   Adult Development
     Age
     Age Discrimination
     Aging Education
     Developmental Stages
     Educational Gerontology
     Elder Abuse
     Frail Elderly
     Geriatrics
     Gerontology
     Independent Living
     Middle Aged Adults
     Midlife Transitions
     Older Adults
     Older Workers

Aging Education   *APR. 1982*
     Postings: 191   GC: 400
SN   Educational programs at all levels aimed at helping students gain a personal understanding of the process and problems of growing old (Note: Use "Educational Gerontology" for aging education as a professional field of study)
BT   Education
RT   Age Differences
     Aging (Individuals)
     Educational Gerontology

Aging in Academia   *AUG. 1986*
     Postings: 141   GC: 330
SN   The gradual aging of a particular academic staff or the general academic community due to demographics and work-life extensions, with implications for hiring, tenure, salary costs, etc.
UF   Aging Professoriate
     Graying of Faculty
BT   Aging (Individuals)

= Two or more Descriptors are used to represent this term.
The term's main entry shows the appropriate coordination.

RT Age
College Faculty
Faculty
Older Workers
Retirement
Seniority
Teacher Persistence
Teacher Retirement
Teachers
Tenure

Aging Professoriate
USE Aging in Academia

Agreements (Formal)
USE Contracts

Agribusiness   *JUL. 1971*
Postings: 635   GC: 410
SN All activities pertaining to manufacturing, processing, servicing, and distributing agricultural supplies and products
BT Business
RT Agricultural Education
Agricultural Engineering
Agricultural Machinery
Agricultural Occupations
Agricultural Production
Agricultural Supplies
Agricultural Trends
Agriculture
Distributive Education
Feed Industry
Field Crops
Meat Packing Industry
Off Farm Agricultural Occupations
Producer Services
Supervised Occupational Experience
(Agriculture)

Agricultural Agents
USE Extension Agents

Agricultural Chemical Occupations
    JUL. 1966
Postings: 88   GC: 410
BT Off Farm Agricultural Occupations
RT Agriculture
Chemical Engineering
Chemical Industry
Chemistry
Fertilizers
Herbicides
Insecticides
Pesticides

Agricultural Colleges   *JUL. 1966*
Postings: 161   GC: 340
BT Colleges
RT Agricultural Education
Agricultural Engineering
Agriculture
Experiment Stations
Land Grant Universities
State Colleges

Agricultural Education   *JUL. 1966*
Postings: 5,314   GC: 410
SN Formal preparation, at any level, for an agricultural occupation (Note: Prior to Mar80, this term was a narrower term of "Vocational Education")
UF Agricultural Education (Vocational) #
Vocational Agriculture (1967 1980) #
Vocational Agriculture Teachers (1967 1980) #
NT Adult Farmer Education
Supervised Occupational Experience
(Agriculture)
Young Farmer Education
BT Education
RT Agribusiness
Agricultural Colleges
Agricultural Engineering
Agricultural Occupations
Agricultural Personnel
Agricultural Production

Agricultural Skills
Agriculture
Extension Agents
Farm Management
Land Grant Universities
Natural Resources
Rural Extension
Technical Education
Vocational Education

Agricultural Education (Vocational)
USE Agricultural Education
AND Vocational Education

Agricultural Engineering   *JUL. 1966*
Postings: 385   GC: 410
SN Application of engineering principles to agriculture, including soil and water management, rural electrification, processing of agricultural products, and design and use of agricultural machinery
UF Agricultural Mechanics (Subject)
Farm Mechanics (Subject)
BT Engineering
RT Agribusiness
Agricultural Colleges
Agricultural Education
Agricultural Machinery
Agricultural Machinery Occupations
Agriculture
Assembly (Manufacturing)
Farm Management

Agricultural Extension
USE Rural Extension

Agricultural Labor Disputes (1966 1980)
USE Labor Demands

Agricultural Laborers   *JUL. 1966*
Postings: 529   GC: 410
SN Unskilled manual workers employed by farms, ranches, or other agricultural operations—may be regular, seasonal, local, migrant, full-time, or part-time
UF Agricultural Workers
NT Migrant Workers
Seasonal Laborers
BT Agricultural Personnel
Laborers
RT Agriculture
Braceros
Crew Leaders
Farm Labor
Sharecroppers

Agricultural Machinery   *JUL. 1966*
Postings: 212   GC: 410
BT Equipment
RT Agribusiness
Agricultural Engineering
Agricultural Machinery Occupations
Agriculture
Assembly (Manufacturing)
Diesel Engines
Engines
Fuels
Hydraulics
Machinery Industry
Tractors

Agricultural Machinery Occupations
    JUL. 1966
Postings: 104   GC: 410
UF Farm Mechanics (Occupation) (1967 1980)
BT Off Farm Agricultural Occupations
RT Agricultural Engineering
Agricultural Machinery
Agriculture
Machinery Industry
Mechanics (Process)

Agricultural Mechanics (Subject)
USE Agricultural Engineering

Agricultural Migrant Workers
USE Migrant Workers

Agricultural Migrants
USE Migrants

Agricultural Occupations   *JUL. 1966*
Postings: 460   GC: 410
NT Farm Occupations
Off Farm Agricultural Occupations
BT Occupations
RT Agribusiness
Agricultural Education
Agricultural Personnel
Agriculture
Farm Management
Farmers
Supervised Occupational Experience
(Agriculture)
Technical Occupations

Agricultural Personnel   *JUL. 1966*
Postings: 83   GC: 410
NT Agricultural Laborers
Agricultural Technicians
Farmers
BT Personnel
RT Agricultural Education
Agricultural Occupations
Agriculture
Animal Caretakers
Extension Agents
Farm Labor

Agricultural Production   *JUL. 1966*
Postings: 1,073   GC: 410
SN The provision of plant and animal commodities
UF Crop Production
Livestock Production
RT Agribusiness
Agricultural Education
Agricultural Supplies
Agricultural Trends
Agriculture
Agronomy
Biotechnology
Crop Processing Occupations
Farm Management
Farmers
Field Crops
Harvesting
Pesticides
Pests
Plant Growth

Agricultural Research Projects (1966 1981)
USE Research Projects

Agricultural Safety   *JUL. 1966*
Postings: 63   GC: 410
BT Safety
RT Agriculture
Safety Education

Agricultural Skills   *JUL. 1966*
Postings: 238   GC: 410
BT Skills
RT Agricultural Education
Agriculture
Practical Arts

Agricultural Supplies   *JUL. 1966*
Postings: 68   GC: 410
UF Farm Supplies
BT Supplies
RT Agribusiness
Agricultural Production
Agricultural Supply Occupations
Agriculture
Feed Industry
Feed Stores
Fertilizers
Herbicides
Insecticides
Pesticides

Agricultural Supply Occupations   *JUL. 1966*
Postings: 62   GC: 410
BT Off Farm Agricultural Occupations
RT Agricultural Supplies
Agriculture
Feed Industry
Sales Occupations
Sales Workers
Service Occupations

Agricultural Technicians   *JUL. 1966*
Postings: 95   GC: 410
SN Personnel who work in supporting or supplemental capacities with agricultural scientists, engineers, and other professionals, in agricultural production, processing, and distribution
BT Agricultural Personnel
Paraprofessional Personnel
RT Agriculture

Agricultural Trends   *JUL. 1966*
Postings: 269   GC: 410
RT Agribusiness
Agricultural Production
Agriculture
Trend Analysis

Agricultural Workers
USE Agricultural Laborers

Agriculture   *JUL. 1966*
Postings: 1,711   GC: 410
NT Agronomy
Animal Husbandry
Gardening
Harvesting
Horticulture
BT Technology
RT Agribusiness
Agricultural Chemical Occupations
Agricultural Colleges
Agricultural Education
Agricultural Engineering
Agricultural Laborers
Agricultural Machinery
Agricultural Machinery Occupations
Agricultural Occupations
Agricultural Personnel
Agricultural Production
Agricultural Safety
Agricultural Skills
Agricultural Supplies
Agricultural Supply Occupations
Agricultural Technicians
Agricultural Trends
Botany
Dairy Farmers
Entomology
Experiment Stations
Farm Management
Farm Occupations
Farm Visits
Farmers
Feed Industry
Fisheries
Food
Forestry
Genetics
Land Use
Natural Resources
Off Farm Agricultural Occupations
Ornithology
Part Time Farmers
Rural Sociology
Seasonal Employment
Sharecroppers
Supervised Occupational Experience
(Agriculture)
Tractors
Veterinary Medicine

Agronomy   *SEP. 1968*
Postings: 285   GC: 410
SN Branch of agriculture that deals with field crop production and soil management
UF Crop Planting #
BT Agriculture
RT Agricultural Production

= Two or more Descriptors are used to represent this term.
The term's main entry shows the appropriate coordination.

Crop Processing Occupations
Fertilizers
Field Crops
Grains (Food)
Harvesting
Herbicides
Insecticides
Land Use
Pesticides
Plant Growth
Plant Pathology
Plants (Botany)
Soil Conservation
Soil Science
Trees
Weeds

AIDS (Disease)
USE   Acquired Immune Deficiency
        Syndrome

Air Bags
USE   Restraints (Vehicle Safety)

Air Bases
USE   Military Air Facilities

Air Conditioning   JUL. 1966
        Postings: 377   GC: 920
BT   Climate Control
RT   Air Conditioning Equipment
        Air Flow
        Building Trades
        Fuel Consumption
        Heat Recovery
        Heating
        Humidity
        Refrigeration
        Temperature
        Thermal Environment
        Thermal Insulation
        Ventilation
        Windowless Rooms

Air Conditioning Equipment   JUL. 1966
        Postings: 121   GC: 910
BT   Equipment
RT   Air Conditioning
        Climate Control
        Fuel Consumption
        Heating
        Refrigeration Mechanics
        Sheet Metal Work
        Temperature
        Thermal Environment
        Ventilation

Air Conditioning Mechanics
USE   Refrigeration Mechanics

Air Flow   OCT. 1969
        Postings: 80   GC: 490
SN   Movement of air in or around a struc-
        ture, e.g., a building or vehicle (Note: Do
        not confuse with "Wind (Meteorology)")
RT   Air Conditioning
        Building Design
        Chimneys
        Heating
        Motion
        Refrigeration
        Temperature
        Ventilation

Air Force Bases
USE   Military Air Facilities

Air Inflated Structures (1972 1980)
USE   Air Structures

Air Pollution   MAR. 1980
        Postings: 1,203   GC: 410
UF   Air Pollution Control (1967 1980)
        Atmospheric Pollution

Smog
NT   Acid Rain
BT   Pollution
RT   Asbestos
        Chimneys
        Climate
        Climate Control
        Conservation (Environment)
        Ecology
        Environmental Education
        Environmental Standards
        Greenhouse Effect
        Urban Environment
        Ventilation
        Waste Disposal
        Wind (Meteorology)

Air Pollution Control (1967 1980)
USE   Air Pollution

Air Raid Shelters
USE   Fallout Shelters

Air Structures   SEP. 1968
        Postings: 64   GC: 920
SN   Buildings   or   shelters   that   are
        pneumatically inflated or that use in-
        flated structural elements
UF   Air Inflated Structures (1972 1980)
        Air Supported Structures (1972 1980)
        Hybrid Air Structures (1972 1980)
        Inflatable Structures
NT   Pneumatic Forms
BT   Facilities
RT   Buildings
        Encapsulated Facilities
        Prefabrication
        Relocatable Facilities

Air Supported Structures (1972 1980)
USE   Air Structures

Air Traffic Control   JAN. 1985
        Postings: 27   GC: 490
SN   Scheduling and monitoring the flow of
        air traffic at airports, during approaches,
        and en route
BT   Traffic Control
RT   Aerospace Technology
        Air Transportation
        Airports
        Aviation Education
        Aviation Technology
        Aviation Vocabulary
        Electronic Equipment
        Military Air Facilities
        Radar

Air Transportation   OCT. 1980
        Postings: 80   GC: 650
BT   Transportation
RT   Aerospace Education
        Aerospace Industry
        Aerospace Technology
        Air Traffic Control
        Aircraft Pilots
        Airports
        Aviation Education
        Aviation Technology

Airborne Field Trips (1968 1980)
USE   Field Trips

Airborne Television (1966 1980)
USE   Television

Aircraft Mechanics
USE   Aviation Mechanics

Aircraft Pilots   OCT. 1968
        Postings: 184   GC: 640
UF   Airline Pilots
        Airplane Pilots
        Commercial Pilots

Copilots
        Helicopter Pilots
BT   Personnel
RT   Aerospace Technology
        Air Transportation
        Aviation Education
        Aviation Technology
        Aviation Vocabulary

Airline Pilots
USE   Aircraft Pilots

Airplane Pilots
USE   Aircraft Pilots

Airports   FEB. 1971
        Postings: 42   GC: 920
BT   Facilities
RT   Air Traffic Control
        Air Transportation
        Aviation Education
        Aviation Technology
        Military Air Facilities

Akan   JUL. 1966
        Postings: 17   GC: 440
UF   Twi
BT   African Languages

Alarm Systems   MAR. 1978
        Postings: 169   GC: 910
SN   Methods and materials employed to
        sound or signal emergencies or impend-
        ing dangers
UF   Burglar Alarms
        Intrusion Detectors
        Security Systems (Alarms)
        Smoke Alarms
RT   Accident Prevention
        Civil Defense
        Closed Circuit Television
        Crime
        Crime Prevention
        Electrical Systems
        Electronic Equipment
        Emergency Programs
        Emergency Squad Personnel
        Fire Fighters
        Fire Protection
        Police
        Police Action
        Rescue
        Safety
        School Safety
        School Security
        Security Personnel

Alaska Natives   MAR. 1976
        Postings: 1,138   GC: 560
SN   Peoples indigenous to Alaska (Alaska's
        American Indians, Aleuts, and Eskimos)
BT   Ethnic Groups
        North Americans
RT   American Indians
        Athapascan Languages
        Canada Natives
        Eskimo Aleut Languages
        Eskimos
        Minority Groups
        Nonreservation American Indians
        Tribes

Albanian   JUL. 1966
        Postings: 43   GC: 440
BT   Indo European Languages

Alcohol Abuse   JUN. 1988
        Postings: 1,438   GC: 530
SN   Excessive or otherwise inappropriate in-
        gestion of alcoholic beverages, often
        causing risk or injury to health and im-
        paired social functioning (Note: If possi-
        ble, use the more specific term "Alcohol-
        ism")
UF   Alcohol Intoxication
        Drunkenness (Alcohol)

Problem Drinking
NT   Alcoholism
BT   Drinking
        Substance Abuse
RT   Alcohol Education
        Alcoholic Beverages
        Antisocial Behavior
        Driving While Intoxicated
        Drug Abuse
        Fetal Alcohol Syndrome

Alcohol Addiction
USE   Alcoholism

Alcohol Consumption
USE   Drinking

Alcohol Dependency
USE   Alcoholism

Alcohol Education   JUL. 1966
        Postings: 1,161   GC: 400
BT   Education
RT   Alcohol Abuse
        Alcoholic Beverages
        Alcoholism
        Drinking
        Drug Education
        Health Education

Alcohol Intoxication
USE   Alcohol Abuse

Alcohol Use
USE   Drinking

Alcoholic Beverages   FEB. 1974
        Postings: 497   GC: 210
RT   Alcohol Abuse
        Alcohol Education
        Alcoholism
        Drinking
        Drug Use

Alcoholism   MAY 1974
        Postings: 2,005   GC: 210
SN   Psychogenic or physiological depend-
        ence on alcohol
UF   Alcohol Addiction
        Alcohol Dependency
BT   Alcohol Abuse
        Diseases
RT   Alcohol Education
        Alcoholic Beverages
        Antisocial Behavior
        Drug Addiction
        Fetal Alcohol Syndrome
        Physical Health
        Special Health Problems

Aleut
USE   Eskimo Aleut Languages

Algebra   JUL. 1966
        Postings: 2,920   GC: 480
NT   Matrices
        Polynomials
        Vectors (Mathematics)
BT   Mathematics
RT   Analytic Geometry
        Equations (Mathematics)
        Modular Arithmetic
        Topology
        Transformations (Mathematics)

Algorisms
USE   Algorithms

Algorithms   JUL. 1966
        Postings: 1,803   GC: 480
UF   Algorisms
BT   Mathematical Applications

    Mathematical Logic
    Methods
RT Computation
    Mathematics
    Programming

Alien Culture
USE Foreign Culture

Alien Illegality
USE Undocumented Immigrants

Alienation   *MAR. 1980*
    Postings: 451   GC: 230
SN Estrangement from others, especially those from whom a relationship was expected, or from the prevalent values, goals, or trends of society (Note: Use a more specific term if possible)
NT Student Alienation
    Teacher Alienation
BT Psychological Patterns
RT Activism
    Anger
    Apathy
    Cultural Isolation
    Dropout Attitudes
    Emotional Adjustment
    Identification (Psychology)
    Interpersonal Relationship
    Loneliness
    Rejection (Psychology)
    Resentment
    Resistance (Psychology)
    Role Conflict
    Social Adjustment
    Social Attitudes
    Social Isolation
    Withdrawal (Psychology)

All Day Half Day Schedules
USE Full Day Half Day Schedules

Allegory   *JUN. 1969*
    Postings: 86   GC: 430
BT Figurative Language
RT Epics
    Fables
    Metaphors

Allergy   *JUL. 1966*
    Postings: 99   GC: 210
UF Hypersensitivity
BT Diseases
RT Asthma
    Physical Health
    Physiology
    Special Health Problems
    Toxicology

Allied Health Education
USE Allied Health Occupations Education

Allied Health Occupations   *MAR. 1980*
    Postings: 876   GC: 210
SN Professional, technical, and supportive occupations in patient services, administration, teaching, and research that support, complement, or supplement the functions of physicians, dentists, and registered nurses or other independent practitioners—also includes environmental health occupations
UF Allied Health Professions
    Allied Medical Occupations
    Health Related Professions
    Paramedical Occupations (1967 1980)
BT Health Occupations
RT Allied Health Occupations Education
    Allied Health Personnel
    Educational Gerontology
    Health
    Health Services
    Optometry
    Physical Therapy
    Practical Nursing

    Professional Occupations
    Respiratory Therapy
    Technical Occupations
    Therapeutic Recreation
    Therapy

Allied Health Occupations Education   *MAR. 1980*
    Postings: 3,731   GC: 210
SN Formal preparation for occupations in allied health at all levels (Note: Before Mar80, "Health Occupations Education" was displayed as a narrower term under "Vocational Education")
UF Allied Health Education
    Health Occupations Education (1967 1980)
    Health Occupations Education (Vocational) #
BT Education
RT Allied Health Occupations
    Allied Health Personnel
    Clinical Experience
    Clinical Teaching (Health Professions)
    Health Education
    Medical Education
    Medicine
    Professional Education
    Teaching Hospitals
    Technical Education
    Vocational Education

Allied Health Personnel   *MAR. 1980*
    Postings: 384   GC: 210
UF Audiologists (1968 1980) #
    Audiometrists (1967 1980) #
    Clinic Personnel (School) (1966 1980) #
    Paramedics
NT Dental Assistants
    Dental Hygienists
    Dental Technicians
    Dietitians
    Emergency Medical Technicians
    Environmental Technicians
    Home Health Aides
    Medical Assistants
    Medical Record Administrators
    Medical Record Technicians
    Medical Technologists
    Nurses Aides
    Occupational Therapy Assistants
    Optometrists
    Physical Therapy Aides
    Physicians Assistants
    Psychiatric Aides
    Radiologic Technologists
    Surgical Technicians
    Therapists
    Veterinary Assistants
BT Health Personnel
RT Allied Health Occupations
    Allied Health Occupations Education
    Attendants
    Paraprofessional Personnel
    Professional Personnel
    Scientific Personnel
    Visiting Homemakers

Allied Health Professions
USE Allied Health Occupations

Allied Medical Occupations
USE Allied Health Occupations

Allocation of Resources
USE Resource Allocation

Allomorphs (1967 1980)
USE Morphemes

Alphabetic Filing
USE Filing

Alphabetizing Skills   *JUL. 1966*
    Postings: 46   GC: 400
BT Basic Skills
RT Dictionaries
    Filing
    Spelling
    Word Study Skills

Alphabets   *JUL. 1966*
    Postings: 317   GC: 450
NT Cyrillic Alphabet
    Initial Teaching Alphabet
    Non Roman Scripts
    Phonemic Alphabets
RT Letters (Alphabet)
    Phonetic Transcription
    Romanization
    Written Language

Altaic Languages
USE Uralic Altaic Languages

Alternate Day Block Scheduling
USE Alternate Day Schedules
AND Block Scheduling

Alternate Day Schedules   *DEC. 1989*
    Postings: 20   GC: 320
SN Scheduling attendance on alternate days—frequently refers to kindergarten, preschool, or day care programs
UF Alternate Day Block Scheduling #
    Full Day Half Day Alternate Day #
BT Scheduling
RT Bilingual Education
    Day Care
    Full Day Half Day Schedules
    Kindergarten
    Preschool Education
    School Schedules
    Time Factors (Learning)

Alternative and Augmentative Communication
USE Augmentative and Alternative Communication

Alternative Assessment   *SEP. 2000*
    Postings: 827   GC: 820
SN Appraising knowledge or skills by means other than traditionally employed, objective tests, especially standardized multiple-choice tests
UF Alternative Evaluation (Individuals)
    Alternatives to Standardized Testing
NT Performance Based Assessment
BT Evaluation
RT Constructed Response
    Educational Assessment
    Evaluation Methods
    Informal Assessment
    Personnel Evaluation
    Portfolio Assessment
    Scoring Rubrics
    Self Evaluation (Individuals)
    Standardized Tests
    Student Evaluation
    Testing
    Writing Evaluation

Alternative Certification (Teaching)
USE Alternative Teacher Certification

Alternative Communication Systems (Disabled)
USE Augmentative and Alternative Communication

Alternative Education
USE Nontraditional Education

Alternative Energy Sources   *OCT. 1984*
    Postings: 227   GC: 490
SN Sources of energy other than conven-

tional fossil fuels (petroleum, coal, natural gas) or nuclear fission/fusion (Note: See also related Identifiers such as "Renewable Resources" and "Synthetic Fuels")
RT Electricity
    Energy
    Energy Conservation
    Energy Education
    Energy Management
    Energy Occupations
    Geothermal Energy
    Heat Recovery
    Natural Resources
    Power Technology
    Solar Energy
    Wind Energy

Alternative Evaluation (Individuals)
USE Alternative Assessment

Alternative Futures
USE Futures (of Society)

Alternative Life Styles
USE Life Style

Alternative Schools (1972 1980)
USE Nontraditional Education

Alternative Teacher Certification   *APR. 1990*
    Postings: 335   GC: 330
SN Departure from the traditional undergraduate route through college and university teacher education programs by which individuals become certified as teachers—differences may be in primary objective, program length, participants, or training design
UF Alternative Certification (Teaching)
BT Teacher Certification
RT Beginning Teachers
    Educational Certificates
    Extended Teacher Education Programs
    National Teacher Certification
    Nontraditional Education
    Professional Development Schools
    Special Degree Programs
    Teacher Education
    Teacher Education Curriculum
    Teacher Education Programs
    Teacher Interns
    Teacher Qualifications
    Teacher Recruitment
    Teacher Shortage

Alternatives to Standardized Testing
USE Alternative Assessment

Altruism   *APR. 1973*
    Postings: 459   GC: 120
SN Consideration for the welfare of others, sometimes in accordance with an ethical system
UF Humaneness
    Kindness
RT Cooperation
    Ethics
    Humanitarianism
    Interpersonal Relationship
    Love
    Prosocial Behavior
    Psychological Patterns
    Sharing Behavior
    Social Attitudes
    Social Exchange Theory
    Values

Alumni   *JAN. 1970*
    Postings: 1,030   GC: 360
SN Graduates or former students of a school, college, university, or educational program
NT Graduates
BT Groups

= Two or more Descriptors are used to represent this term.
The term's main entry shows the appropriate coordination.

RT   Alumni Associations
       Alumni Education
       Graduate Surveys
       Reunions

Alumni Associations   *MAR. 1980*
       Postings: 258   GC: 520
BT   Organizations (Groups)
RT   Alumni
       College Graduates
       Graduates
       Nonprofit Organizations

Alumni Colleges
USE   Alumni Education

Alumni Education   *NOV. 1968*
       Postings: 43   GC: 320
SN   Educational activities carried on by a college or university for the benefit of its graduates and former students—includes special seminars, courses, educational trips, postcollegiate professional instruction, etc.
UF   Alumni Colleges
BT   Education
RT   Adult Programs
       Alumni
       College Graduates
       College Programs
       Minicourses
       Professional Continuing Education
       Summer Programs
       Vacation Programs

Alzheimers Disease   *AUG. 1989*
       Postings: 285   GC: 220
SN   The most common form of dementia in middle-aged and older adults—characterized by severe, irreversible impairment of cognitive functions, such as thinking and memory, and by behavioral and personality changes
UF   Senile Dementia Alzheimers Type
BT   Diseases
RT   Frail Elderly
       Mental Disorders
       Neurological Impairments

Ambient Pressure
USE   Pressure (Physics)

Ambiguity   *APR. 1970*
       Postings: 452   GC: 430
BT   Figurative Language

Ambition
USE   Aspiration

Ambiversion
USE   Extraversion Introversion

Ambulance Attendants
USE   Emergency Medical Technicians

Amerasians
USE   Asian Americans

American Culture (1966 1980)   *MAR. 1980*
       Postings: 819   GC: 560
SN   Invalid Descriptor—used for North, South, Central American culture—see "North American Culture" or "Latin American Culture"

American Dream   *JAN. 1996*
       Postings: 68   GC: 520
SN   The ideals of freedom, equality, and opportunity traditionally held to be available to everyone in the U.S.—also, the popular belief that perseverance and hard work in the U.S. will bring forth happiness, success, and material well-being

BT   Democratic Values
RT   American Studies
       Cultural Context
       Equal Education
       Equal Opportunities (Jobs)
       North American Culture
       Quality of Life
       Social Mobility
       Social Values
       Work Ethic

American English (1968 1980)
USE   North American English

American Government (Course) (1966 1980)
USE   United States Government (Course)

American History (1966 1980)   *MAR. 1980*
       Postings: 870   GC: 430
SN   Invalid Descriptor—although Scope Note referred to North, South, and Central America, term used frequently for U.S. history—see "North American History," "Latin American History," or "United States History"

American Indian Culture   *MAY 1969*
       Postings: 2,487   GC: 560
BT   Culture
RT   American Indian History
       American Indian Languages
       American Indian Literature
       American Indian Studies
       American Indians
       Latin American Culture
       North American Culture
       Tribes

American Indian Education   *OCT. 1979*
       Postings: 2,991   GC: 330
SN   Formal and nonformal process of educating American Indians to their own and to the broader society (Note: Prior to Oct79, this concept was indexed under "American Indians")
UF   Indian Controlled Schools #
BT   Education
RT   American Indian Languages
       American Indian Studies
       American Indians
       Federal Indian Relationship
       Tribally Controlled Education
       Trust Responsibility (Government)

American Indian History   *JUN. 1983*
       Postings: 1,038   GC: 430
BT   History
RT   American Indian Culture
       American Indian Literature
       American Indian Reservations
       American Indian Studies
       American Indians
       Federal Indian Relationship
       Latin American History
       North American History
       Oral History
       Relocation
       Tribal Sovereignty
       Tribes

American Indian Languages   *JUL. 1966*
       Postings: 913   GC: 440
NT   Athapascan Languages
       Aymara
       Cherokee
       Choctaw
       Cree
       Dakota
       Guarani
       Mayan Languages
       Ojibwa
       Pomo
       Quechua
       Salish
       Uto Aztecan Languages
BT   Languages
RT   American Indian Culture

American Indian Education
American Indian Studies
American Indians
Eskimo Aleut Languages
Language Classification
Native Speakers

(continuation of American Indian Languages RT list:)
       American Indian Education
       American Indian Studies
       American Indians
       Eskimo Aleut Languages
       Language Classification
       Native Speakers

American Indian Literature   *OCT. 1979*
       Postings: 455   GC: 430
BT   Literature
RT   American Indian Culture
       American Indian History
       American Indian Studies
       American Indians
       Latin American Literature
       Legends
       Mythology
       North American Literature

American Indian Reservations   *MAR. 1980*
       Postings: 1,201   GC: 610
SN   Tracts of land, set aside by agreements between governments and Indian tribes, that are reserved for the exclusive use and occupancy of those tribes
UF   Reservations (Indian) (1971 1980)
BT   Political Divisions (Geographic)
RT   American Indian History
       American Indians
       Federal Indian Relationship
       Land Settlement
       Nonreservation American Indians
       Reservation American Indians
       Treaties
       Tribal Government
       Tribal Sovereignty
       Tribally Controlled Education
       Tribes
       Trust Responsibility (Government)

American Indian Studies   *OCT. 1979*
       Postings: 385   GC: 400
SN   Curriculum or subject area encompassing the culture, history, achievements, and contemporary concerns of American Indians
BT   Ethnic Studies
RT   American Indian Culture
       American Indian Education
       American Indian History
       American Indian Languages
       American Indian Literature
       American Indians
       American Studies
       Cultural Background
       Cultural Education
       Cultural Images
       Cultural Traits

American Indians   *JUL. 1966*
       Postings: 9,550   GC: 560
SN   Both North and South American Indians
NT   Cherokee (Tribe)
       Chippewa (Tribe)
       Choctaw (Tribe)
       Cree (Tribe)
       Iroquois (Tribe)
       Maya (People)
       Navajo (Nation)
       Nonreservation American Indians
       Pueblo (People)
       Reservation American Indians
       Sioux (Tribe)
       Tohono O Odham People
BT   Ethnic Groups
RT   Alaska Natives
       American Indian Culture
       American Indian Education
       American Indian History
       American Indian Languages
       American Indian Literature
       American Indian Reservations
       American Indian Studies
       Canada Natives
       Federal Indian Relationship
       Latin Americans
       Mexicans
       Minority Groups
       North Americans

(continuation:)
       Relocation
       Tribal Government
       Tribal Sovereignty
       Tribally Controlled Education
       Tribes
       Trust Responsibility (Government)

American Jews
USE   Jews

American Literature (1966 1980) (Latin America)
USE   Latin American Literature

American Literature (1966 1980) (United States)
USE   United States Literature

American Negroes
USE   Blacks

American Orientals
USE   Asian Americans

American Revolutionary War
USE   Revolutionary War (United States)

American Samoans
USE   Samoan Americans

American Sign Language   *SEP. 1982*
       Postings: 459   GC: 220
SN   Visual/gestural language used by the deaf community in the United States and parts of Canada—distinct from signed English, ASL has its own highly articulated linguistic system that makes use of the eyes, face, head, and body posture as well as the signer's hands
UF   Ameslan
BT   Languages
       Sign Language

American Studies   *APR. 1973*
       Postings: 317   GC: 400
SN   Interdisciplinary studies of the United States (Note: Prior to Mar80, this term was scoped to include studies of all of North America above Mexico)
BT   Area Studies
RT   American Dream
       American Indian Studies
       Black Studies
       North American Culture
       United States Government (Course)
       United States History
       United States Literature

Ameslan
USE   American Sign Language

Ametropia   *JUL. 1966*
       Postings: 5   GC: 220
UF   Error of Refraction
       Ocular Refractive Errors
       Refractive Errors
NT   Hyperopia
       Myopia
BT   Visual Impairments
RT   Vision
       Visual Acuity

Amharic   *JUL. 1966*
       Postings: 34   GC: 440
BT   Semitic Languages

Amish   *JUL. 1966*
       Postings: 85   GC: 560
BT   Protestants

= Two or more Descriptors are used to represent this term. The term's main entry shows the appropriate coordination.

Amputations   *MAR. 1980*
    Postings: 43   GC: 220
SN Loss of limbs or digits from the body
UF Amputees (1967 1980)
BT Physical Disabilities
RT Physical Therapy
    Prostheses
    Surgery

Amputees (1967 1980)
USE Amputations

Analog Computers   *JUL. 1966*
    Postings: 76   GC: 910
SN Computers that translate physical condi-
    tions (flow, temperature, pressure, etc.)
    into related mechanical or electrical quan-
    tities (length, voltage, current, etc.)—
    unlike digital computers, which count
    discrete quantities, analog computers
    measure continuous variables
BT Computers
RT Digital Computers

Analysis
USE Evaluation Methods

Analysis of Covariance   *DEC. 1970*
    Postings: 766   GC: 820
SN Statistical technique used to compare
    two or more groups with reference to
    one variable when differences on some
    other correlated variable may affect the
    comparison
UF Ancova
BT Statistical Analysis
RT Analysis of Variance
    Correlation
    Hypothesis Testing
    Predictor Variables
    Robustness (Statistics)
    Statistical Significance

Analysis of Variance   *JUL. 1966*
    Postings: 3,334   GC: 820
SN Statistical technique for determining if
    differences among the means of differ-
    ent groups of observations exceed what
    may be expected by chance
UF Anova
BT Statistical Analysis
RT Analysis of Covariance
    Generalizability Theory
    Hypothesis Testing
    Predictor Variables
    Robustness (Statistics)
    Statistical Significance

Analytic Geometry   *JUL. 1966*
    Postings: 219   GC: 480
UF Coordinate Geometry
BT Geometry
RT Algebra
    Calculus
    Plane Geometry
    Solid Geometry

Analytical Criticism (1969 1980)
                                 MAR. 1980
    Postings: 683   GC: 430
SN Invalid Descriptor—used indiscriminately
    for all types of analysis—see various
    "analysis" and "evaluation" Descriptors—
    for discussions of analytical criticism in
    a literary sense, use "Literary Criticism"

Anatomy   *JUL. 1966*
    Postings: 593   GC: 490
BT Biological Sciences
RT Biology
    Body Composition
    Brain
    Cardiovascular System
    Dissection
    Ears
    Embryology

    Evolution
    Eyes
    Human Body
    Medicine
    Muscular System
    Musculoskeletal System
    Neurology
    Pathology
    Physiology
    Scientific Research
    Skeletal System
    Surgery
    Zoology

Ancestral Lineage
USE Genealogy

Ancient History   *JUL. 1966*
    Postings: 529   GC: 430
BT History
RT Archaeology
    Biblical Literature
    Classical Literature
    Greek Civilization
    Greek Literature
    Latin Literature

Ancillary School Services   *MAR. 1980*
    Postings: 1,902   GC: 320
SN Noninstructional services offered by
    schools or educational programs (Note:
    Prior to Mar80, this concept was in-
    dexed under "Ancillary Services")
UF Auxiliary School Services
    School Services (1966 1980)
NT Mobile Educational Services
    Pupil Personnel Services
    School Health Services
    Student Personnel Services
BT Social Services
RT Counseling Services
    Day Care
    Education Service Centers
    Guidance Programs
    Integrated Services
    Library Services
    Lunch Programs
    Psychological Services
    School Age Day Care
    School Business Officials
    School Recreational Programs
    Schools
    Student Development
    Student Transportation

Ancillary Services (1967 1980)   *JUN. 1980*
    Postings: 633   GC: 520
SN Invalid Descriptor—see more precise
    Descriptors such as "Ancillary School
    Services," "Community Services," "So-
    cial Services," etc.

Ancova
USE Analysis of Covariance

Andragogy   *MAR. 1984*
    Postings: 385   GC: 310
SN The art and science of the facilitation of
    adult learning, distinguished from child-
    oriented "pedagogy" in terms of learner
    self-direction, application of knowledge
    and experience, learning readiness, ori-
    entation to the present, and problem-
    centeredness
UF Androgogy
RT Adult Education
    Adult Learning
    Adult Students
    Age Differences
    Educational Theories
    Learning Strategies
    Transformative Learning

Androgogy
USE Andragogy

Androgyny   *MAR. 1977*
    Postings: 510   GC: 120
SN Integration of male and female charac-
    teristics (roles, behaviors, personality
    traits, biological traits, etc.)
RT Femininity
    Individual Psychology
    Masculinity
    Sex Differences
    Sex Role
    Sexual Identity

Anechoic Materials
USE Acoustic Insulation

Anemia   *APR. 1973*
    Postings: 78   GC: 210
UF Iron Deficiency Anemia
NT Sickle Cell Anemia
BT Diseases
RT Lead Poisoning
    Nutrition
    Physical Health
    Prenatal Influences
    Special Health Problems

Anesthesiology   *JUL. 1966*
    Postings: 64   GC: 210
BT Medicine
RT Medical Services
    Pain
    Surgery

Anger   *AUG. 1986*
    Postings: 484   GC: 230
SN Strong displeasure
NT Hostility
BT Psychological Patterns
RT Alienation
    Anxiety
    Catharsis
    Depression (Psychology)
    Emotional Problems
    Helplessness
    Jealousy
    Loneliness
    Moods
    Rejection (Psychology)
    Resentment

Anglo Americans   *JUL. 1966*
    Postings: 935   GC: 560
SN Permanent residents of the Americas
    who are of English descent—commonly
    used in the U.S. as a label for the white
    and/or English-speaking majority, espe-
    cially in comparisons with minority eth-
    nic groups (Note: For specificity, coordi-
    nate with such Identifiers as "English
    Americans" and "British Americans"—
    use "Whites" or "White Students" for
    comparisons of whites with other groups)
UF Anglos
BT Ethnic Groups
    North Americans
RT Whites

Anglo Saxon
USE Old English

Anglos
USE Anglo Americans

Animal Behavior   *MAY 1969*
    Postings: 699   GC: 120
BT Behavior
RT Aggression
    Animal Facilities
    Animals
    Behavior Development
    Veterinary Medicine
    Zoology

Animal Biology
USE Zoology

Animal Caretakers   *JAN. 1969*
    Postings: 78   GC: 640
UF Animal Keepers
BT Semiskilled Workers
RT Agricultural Personnel
    Animal Facilities
    Animal Husbandry
    Animals
    Off Farm Agricultural Occupations
    Veterinary Assistants
    Veterinary Medicine

Animal Facilities   *SEP. 1969*
    Postings: 127   GC: 920
NT Zoos
BT Facilities
RT Animal Behavior
    Animal Caretakers
    Animal Husbandry
    Animals
    Laboratory Animals
    Laboratory Equipment
    Pets
    Wildlife Management

Animal Husbandry   *MAR. 1980*
    Postings: 463   GC: 410
SN Branch of agriculture concerned with the
    production and care of domestic animals
UF Animal Science (1967 1980)
    Livestock Technology
BT Agriculture
RT Animal Caretakers
    Animal Facilities
    Animals
    Dairy Farmers
    Farm Occupations
    Horses
    Laboratory Animals
    Livestock
    Meat Packing Industry
    Ornithology
    Veterinarians
    Veterinary Assistants
    Veterinary Medical Education
    Veterinary Medicine
    Zoology

Animal Keepers
USE Animal Caretakers

Animal Life
USE Animals

Animal Science (1967 1980)
USE Animal Husbandry

Animals   *AUG. 1980*
    Postings: 1,206   GC: 490
SN (Note: Use a more specific term if
    possible—prior to Aug80, the instruc-
    tion "Animal Life, USE Zoology" was
    carried in the Thesaurus)
UF Animal Life
NT Birds
    Dinosaurs
    Horses
    Laboratory Animals
    Livestock
    Pets
    Rats
RT Animal Behavior
    Animal Caretakers
    Animal Facilities
    Animal Husbandry
    Endangered Species
    Habitats
    Pests
    Protozoa
    Veterinary Medicine
    Wildlife
    Zoology

Animation   *MAY 1971*
    Postings: 296   GC: 720
SN Film or video techniques that bring move-
    ment to inanimate objects or drawings

= Two or more Descriptors are used to represent this term.
The term's main entry shows the appropriate coordination.

BT   Special Effects
RT   Cartoons
     Characterization
     Film Industry
     Film Production

Anishinabe (Tribe)
USE Chippewa (Tribe)

Annotated Bibliographies   *JUL. 1966*
     Postings: 11,588   GC: 730
UF   Abstract Bibliographies
BT   Bibliographies
RT   Abstracting
     Abstracts

Annotations
USE Abstracts

Annual Reports   *JUL. 1966*
     Postings: 2,739   GC: 730
SN   Includes data on progress, finance, material, personnel, instruction, etc.
BT   Reports
     Serials
RT   Yearbooks

Annuals
USE Yearbooks

Anomalies (1967 1980)
USE Congenital Impairments

Anorexia Nervosa   *OCT. 1983*
     Postings: 226   GC: 210
SN   Disorder characterized by prolonged refusal to eat, attended by serious psychological problems (e.g., intense fear of gaining weight) and leading to emaciation and nutritional deficiencies—most often seen in adolescent females
BT   Eating Disorders
RT   Bulimia
     Eating Habits
     Emotional Disturbances
     Nutrition
     Physical Health

Anova
USE Analysis of Variance

Answer Booklets
USE Answer Sheets

Answer Cards
USE Answer Sheets

Answer Keys   *JUL. 1966*
     Postings: 330   GC: 730
SN   Devices that display correct answers for particular tests
UF   Scoring Keys
RT   Answer Sheets
     Objective Tests
     Scoring
     Test Construction
     Test Manuals
     Test Scoring Machines
     Tests

Answer Sheets   *SEP. 1974*
     Postings: 65   GC: 730
SN   Separate forms, sheets, or cards on which examinees record their responses to tests or questionnaires
UF   Answer Booklets
     Answer Cards
RT   Answer Keys
     Questionnaires
     Scoring
     Test Construction
     Test Manuals

     Test Scoring Machines
     Tests

Anthologies   *JUL. 1966*
     Postings: 560   GC: 730
SN   Collections of selected writings or other materials, usually in one form, from one period, or on one subject
UF   Collected Readings
     Readings (Collections)
BT   Reference Materials
RT   Bibliographies
     Conference Proceedings
     Literature Reviews

Anthracite
USE Coal

Anthropological Linguistics   *OCT. 1977*
     Postings: 135   GC: 450
SN   Application of anthropological and linguistic techniques to the study of speech communities, particularly those with no writing system—attention is given to specific interrelationships in the concurrent and systematic development of culture and language
UF   Linguistic Anthropology
BT   Anthropology
     Linguistics
RT   Cultural Context
     Diachronic Linguistics
     Ethnography
     Ethnology
     Language Research
     Linguistic Theory
     Sociolinguistics
     Unwritten Languages

Anthropology   *JUL. 1966*
     Postings: 1,611   GC: 400
NT   Anthropological Linguistics
     Archaeology
     Educational Anthropology
     Ethnography
     Ethnology
BT   Social Sciences
RT   Area Studies
     Componential Analysis
     Cross Cultural Studies
     Cultural Pluralism
     Folk Culture
     Human Geography
     Material Culture
     Museums
     Primatology
     Race
     Social Science Research
     Social Scientists
     Social Studies
     Zoology

Anti Discrimination Legislation
USE Civil Rights Legislation

Anti Gay Bias
USE Homophobia

Anti Intellectualism   *JUL. 1966*
     Postings: 71   GC: 540
BT   Attitudes
RT   Fascism
     Negative Attitudes

Anti Poverty Programs
USE Poverty Programs

Anti Segregation Programs (1967 1980)
USE Racial Integration

Anti Semitism   *JUL. 1966*
     Postings: 268   GC: 540
RT   Ethnic Bias
     Ethnic Discrimination

     Ghettos
     Jews
     Nazism
     Religious Discrimination

Anti Social Behavior (1966 1980)
USE Antisocial Behavior

Antisocial Behavior   *MAR. 1980*
     Postings: 2,071   GC: 530
SN   Behavior that violates the normative rules, standards, understandings, or expectations of society
UF   Anti Social Behavior (1966 1980)
     Socially Deviant Behavior (1966 1980)
NT   Aggression
     Bullying
     Cheating
     Child Abuse
     Child Neglect
     Crime
     Driving While Intoxicated
     Elder Abuse
     Emotional Abuse
     Fraud
     Hazing
     Homicide
     Incest
     Sexual Abuse
     Sexual Harassment
     Stealing
     Terrorism
     Vandalism
     Verbal Abuse
     Violence
BT   Social Behavior
RT   Alcohol Abuse
     Alcoholism
     Behavior Disorders
     Behavior Problems
     Conflict
     Drug Abuse
     Drug Addiction
     Illegal Drug Use
     Lying
     Obscenity
     Prosocial Behavior
     Recidivism
     Self Destructive Behavior

Antithesis   *MAY 1969*
     Postings: 8   GC: 430
BT   Figurative Language
RT   Philosophy
     Poetry

Anxiety   *JUL. 1966*
     Postings: 4,095   GC: 230
NT   Communication Apprehension
     Computer Anxiety
     Mathematics Anxiety
     Separation Anxiety
     Test Anxiety
     Writing Apprehension
BT   Psychological Patterns
RT   Anger
     Catharsis
     Depression (Psychology)
     Desensitization
     Emotional Disturbances
     Emotional Problems
     Fear
     Guilt
     Homophobia
     Inhibition
     Jealousy
     Moods
     Nightmares
     Personality Traits
     Posttraumatic Stress Disorder
     Relaxation Training
     Resistance (Psychology)
     School Phobia
     Shyness

Apache   *APR. 1969*
     Postings: 16   GC: 440
SN   Athapascan language spoken by six culturally related tribes of the North Ameri-

can southwest (the Jicarilla, Mescalero, San Carlos, White Mountain, Chiricahua, and Kiowa Apache)
BT   Athapascan Languages

Apartheid   *AUG. 1989*
     Postings: 255   GC: 540
SN   Afrikaan word meaning "apartness," referring to the former system of racial segregation and political and economic discrimination officially practiced in the republic of South Africa (and the territory of Namibia) after the 1948 election victory of the Afrikaaner Nationalist Party (Note: Namibia achieved independence in Mar90, and South Africa abandoned the system under a new constitution and all-race elections in Apr94)
RT   African Studies
     Black Studies
     Civil Rights
     De Jure Segregation
     Racial Segregation
     Segregationist Organizations

Apathy   *AUG. 1978*
     Postings: 90   GC: 120
SN   Lack of feeling about, or interest in, things generally found stimulating or interesting
UF   Indifference
BT   Psychological Patterns
RT   Alienation
     Aspiration
     Emotional Problems
     Personality Problems

Aphasia   *JUL. 1966*
     Postings: 400   GC: 220
SN   Impairment of the ability to comprehend or produce the symbols of spoken or written language due to brain dysfunction, not to mental or intellectual deficiency
UF   Dysphasia
BT   Language Impairments
     Neurological Impairments
RT   Communication Disorders
     Dyslexia
     Echolalia
     Expressive Language
     Learning Disabilities
     Minimal Brain Dysfunction
     Perceptual Impairments
     Receptive Language
     Speech Impairments

Apparel Industry
USE Fashion Industry

Appetite Disorders
USE Eating Disorders

Appliance Repair   *SEP. 1981*
     Postings: 81   GC: 640
SN   Concerned with installation and maintenance of appliances, as well as their repair
UF   Appliance Repairers (1980 1981)
     Appliance Repairing (1968 1981)
     Appliance Service Technicians (1967 1980)
     Electrical Appliance Servicemen (1968 1980)
     Home Appliance Repair
BT   Repair
RT   Electrical Appliances
     Electrical Occupations
     Electricians
     Skilled Occupations

Appliance Repairers (1980 1981)
USE Appliance Repair

Appliance Repairing (1968 1981)
USE Appliance Repair

= Two or more Descriptors are used to represent this term.
The term's main entry shows the appropriate coordination.

Appliance Service Technicians (1967 1980)
USE   Appliance Repair

Appliances
USE   Equipment

Applied History
USE   Public History

Applied Linguistics   *JUL. 1966*
    Postings: 1,661   GC: 450
SN   Application of the findings of linguistic
     science to practical language problems,
     such as language teaching, lexicogra-
     phy, translation, speech therapy, etc.
BT   Linguistics
RT   English (Second Language)
     Nonstandard Dialects
     Second Language Instruction
     Structural Linguistics
     Substitution Drills
     Unwritten Languages

Applied Music   *JUL. 1966*
    Postings: 240   GC: 420
SN   Musical performance, or instruction in
     vocal or instrumental music
UF   Practical Music
BT   Music
RT   Bands (Music)
     Music Activities
     Music Education
     Orchestras
     Singing
     Vocal Music

Applied Reading (1966 1980)
USE   Reading

Applied Research
USE   Research

Applied Sciences
USE   Technology

Appraisal
USE   Evaluation

Apprenticeships   *JUL. 1966*
    Postings: 1,609   GC: 630
BT   On the Job Training
RT   Experiential Learning
     Field Experience Programs
     Industrial Training
     Inplant Programs
     Skilled Occupations
     Skilled Workers
     Trade and Industrial Education
     Trainees
     Vocational Education
     Work Experience Programs

Appropriate Technology   *AUG. 1986*
    Postings: 291   GC: 550
SN   Technology suited to the psychosocial
     and biophysical needs in a particular
     place and time
BT   Technology
RT   Development
     Environment
     Futures (of Society)
     Needs
     Quality of Life
     Science and Society
     Technical Assistance
     Technological Advancement
     Technological Literacy
     Technology Transfer
     World Affairs

Approved Programs (Validated)
USE   Validated Programs

Approximation (Mathematics)
USE   Estimation (Mathematics)

**Approximative Systems (Language
Learning)**
USE   Interlanguage

Aptitude   *JUL. 1966*
    Postings: 440   GC: 120
SN   The potential ability of an individual to
     perform an as yet unlearned task, skill,
     or act
NT   Academic Aptitude
     Language Aptitude
     Mathematical Aptitude
     Vocational Aptitude
RT   Ability
     Achievement
     Aptitude Tests
     Aspiration
     Cognitive Ability
     Expectation
     Gifted
     Learning
     Performance
     Qualifications
     Talent

Aptitude Tests   *JUL. 1966*
    Postings: 2,240   GC: 830
SN   Tests that are used to predict future
     performance, as well as tests that meas-
     ure those abilities which are not readily
     developed by formal training
UF   Talent Tests
NT   Reading Readiness Tests
     School Readiness Tests
BT   Tests
RT   Ability Identification
     Achievement Tests
     Aptitude
     College Entrance Examinations
     Intelligence Tests
     Interest Inventories
     Mathematics Tests
     Occupational Tests
     Performance Tests
     Predictive Measurement
     Screening Tests
     Talent Identification

Aptitude Treatment Interaction   *APR. 1980*
    Postings: 568   GC: 310
SN   Relationship between learner character-
     istics or traits and the characteristics of
     the learning task, learning situation,
     teacher, or teaching methods and mate-
     rials
UF   Trait Treatment Interaction
BT   Interaction
RT   Academic Ability
     Academic Aptitude
     Classroom Environment
     Cognitive Style
     Learning Processes
     Student Characteristics
     Student School Relationship
     Teacher Characteristics
     Teacher Student Relationship

Aquariums   *DEC. 1992*
    Postings: 66   GC: 920
SN   Tanks, bowls, or other containers in which
     aquatic organisms are housed and dis-
     played
BT   Facilities
RT   Educational Facilities
     Fisheries
     Nature Centers
     Parks
     Recreational Facilities
     Science Facilities
     Water
     Wildlife Management
     Zoos

Aquatic Sports   *JAN. 1985*
    Postings: 61   GC: 470
UF   Water Sports
NT   Diving
     Sailing
     Surfing
     Swimming
     Water Polo
     Waterskiing
BT   Athletics
RT   Swimming Pools
     Underwater Diving
     Water

Arab Americans
USE   Arabs
AND   North Americans

Arabic   *JUL. 1966*
    Postings: 703   GC: 440
BT   Semitic Languages
RT   Arabs

Arabs   *JAN. 1970*
    Postings: 377   GC: 560
UF   Arab Americans #
BT   Groups
RT   Arabic
     Ethnic Groups
     Islam
     Middle Eastern Studies
     Muslims
     Non Western Civilization

Arbitration   *MAR. 1969*
    Postings: 833   GC: 630
SN   The process by which the parties to a
     dispute submit their differences to the
     judgment of an impartial party appointed
     by mutual consent or statutory provision
UF   Mediation (Labor)
RT   Board of Education Policy
     Collective Bargaining
     Employer Employee Relationship
     Employment Problems
     Faculty College Relationship
     Grievance Procedures
     Labor Demands
     Labor Economics
     Labor Legislation
     Labor Problems
     Negotiation Agreements
     Negotiation Impasses
     Peer Mediation
     Sanctions
     Strikes
     Teacher Militancy
     Teacher Strikes
     Unions

Arc Welding
USE   Welding

Archaeology   *JUL. 1966*
    Postings: 508   GC: 400
BT   Anthropology
RT   Ancient History
     Ethnology
     Paleontology

Archery   *NOV. 1973*
    Postings: 37   GC: 470
BT   Athletics
RT   Lifetime Sports
     Olympic Games

Architects   *JUL. 1966*
    Postings: 417   GC: 420
BT   Professional Personnel
RT   Architectural Education
     Architecture
     Building Design
     Construction Industry

Architectural Barriers (1970 1980)   *JUN. 1980*
    Postings: 236   GC: 220
SN   Invalid Descriptor—coordinate other archi-
     tecture/facility terms with "Physical
     Mobility" or "Visually Impaired Mobil-
     ity"—also use "Accessibility (for Dis-
     abled)" if appropriate

Architectural Changes
USE   Building Design

Architectural Character   *JUL. 1966*
    Postings: 506   GC: 920
SN   Stylistic expression of verticality, scale,
     richness, variety and unity inherent to
     architectural tradition
UF   Architectural Style
     Architectural Tradition
RT   Architecture
     Building Design
     Campus Planning
     Educational Facilities Design
     Structural Elements (Construction)

Architectural Design
USE   Building Design

Architectural Drafting   *SEP. 1969*
    Postings: 98   GC: 640
SN   The art or practice of drawing architec-
     tural and structural features of any class
     of buildings and like structures—includes
     delineating design and details, and con-
     firming compliance with building codes
BT   Drafting
RT   Architectural Education
     Architectural Programming
     Architecture
     Building Plans
     Engineering Drawing

Architectural Education   *AUG. 1968*
    Postings: 272   GC: 400
BT   Professional Education
RT   Architects
     Architectural Drafting
     Architectural Research
     Architecture
     Art Education
     Technical Education

Architectural Elements (1968 1980)
USE   Structural Elements (Construction)

Architectural Programing (1968 1994)
USE   Architectural Programming

Architectural Programming   *MAR. 1994*
    Postings: 11   GC: 920
SN   The process of identification and sys-
     tematic organization of the functional,
     architectural, structural, mechanical, and
     aesthetic criteria that influence decision
     making for the design of a functional
     space, building, or facility
UF   Architectural Programing (1968 1994)
RT   Architectural Drafting
     Architectural Research
     Architecture
     Building Design
     Building Innovation
     Decision Making
     Design
     Design Requirements
     Educational Facilities Planning
     Facility Planning
     Systems Analysis

Architectural Research   *FEB. 1970*
    Postings: 154   GC: 810
SN   Basic, applied, and developmental re-
     search focusing on architectural theory,
     design, or education (Note: As of Oct81,
     use as a minor Descriptor for examples

= Two or more Descriptors are used to represent this term.
The term's main entry shows the appropriate coordination.

of this kind of research—use as a major Descriptor only as the subject of a document)
BT Research
RT Architectural Education
    Architectural Programming
    Architecture
    Behavioral Science Research
    Construction Materials
    Environmental Research
    Mechanical Equipment
    Physical Environment

Architectural Style
USE Architectural Character

Architectural Tradition
USE Architectural Character

Architecture   *JUL. 1966*
    Postings: 784   GC: 420
BT Visual Arts
RT Accessibility (for Disabled)
    Acoustics
    Architects
    Architectural Character
    Architectural Drafting
    Architectural Education
    Architectural Programming
    Architectural Research
    Art
    Building Design
    Built Environment
    Design
    Design Requirements
    Interior Design
    Lighting Design
    Neoclassicism
    Physical Mobility
    Postmodernism
    Spatial Relationship (Facilities)
    Structural Elements (Construction)

Archives   *JUL. 1966*
    Postings: 1,210   GC: 710
SN Repositories for public records or documents of historical importance concerning the activities of a nation, community, corporation, family, or historical figure—also includes the material preserved
BT Information Sources
RT Academic Libraries
    Government Libraries
    Libraries
    Library Collections
    Manuscripts
    National Libraries
    Public Libraries
    Records (Forms)
    Records Management
    State Libraries

Area   *OCT. 1983*
    Postings: 201   GC: 480
SN Two-dimensional space
UF Planar Area
    Surface Area
BT Geometric Concepts
    Space
RT Plane Geometry
    Polygons
    Volume (Mathematics)

Area Studies   *JUL. 1966*
    Postings: 2,072   GC: 400
SN Study of political or geographical area including history, geography, language, and general culture
NT African Studies
    American Studies
    Asian Studies
    Canadian Studies
    Middle Eastern Studies
BT Curriculum
RT Anthropology
    Cross Cultural Studies
    Cultural Awareness
    Developed Nations

    Developing Nations
    Ecology
    Economics
    Ethnic Studies
    Field Studies
    Geographic Regions
    Geography
    Global Education
    Greek Civilization
    History
    Human Geography
    Interdisciplinary Approach
    International Studies
    Middle Eastern History
    Non Western Civilization
    Political Science
    Regional Characteristics
    Regional Dialects
    Relocation
    Research
    Rural Sociology
    Social Science Research
    Social Sciences
    Sociology
    Urban Studies
    Western Civilization

Area Vocational Schools (1966 1980)
USE Regional Schools
AND Vocational Schools

Areas (Geographic)
USE Geographic Regions

Argumentation
USE Persuasive Discourse

Aristotelian Criticism (1969 1980)
    MAR. 1980
    Postings: 37   GC: 430
SN Invalid Descriptor—originally intended as a literary term, but used indiscriminately in indexing—for literary documents, see "Literary Criticism" and the Identifier "Aristotle"

Arithmetic   *JUL. 1966*
    Postings: 2,200   GC: 480
UF Arithmetic Curriculum (1966 1980) #
    Arithmetic Tests #
    Mental Arithmetic #
    Number Operations
    Remedial Arithmetic (1966 1980) #
NT Addition
    Division
    Modular Arithmetic
    Multiplication
    Subtraction
BT Mathematics
RT Computation
    Fractions
    Integers
    Mathematical Enrichment
    Number Concepts
    Numbers
    Numeracy
    Percentage
    Place Value
    Set Theory

Arithmetic Curriculum (1966 1980)
USE Arithmetic
AND Mathematics Curriculum

Arithmetic Systems
USE Number Systems

Arithmetic Tests
USE Arithmetic
AND Mathematics Tests

Armed Forces   *SEP. 1968*
    Postings: 774   GC: 610
UF Federal Troops (1966 1980)
BT Military Organizations

RT Disarmament
    Foreign Countries
    Guns
    Military Personnel
    Military Service
    National Defense
    War
    Weapons

Armenian   *JUL. 1966*
    Postings: 24   GC: 440
BT Indo European Languages

Arms (Weapons)
USE Weapons

Arms Control
USE Disarmament

Army Air Bases
USE Military Air Facilities

Arousal Patterns   *JUL. 1966*
    Postings: 410   GC: 110
BT Behavior Patterns
RT Adaptation Level Theory
    Attention
    Emotional Response
    Extraversion Introversion
    Habituation
    Novelty (Stimulus Dimension)
    Perception
    Stimulation
    Type A Behavior
    Type B Behavior

Art   *JUL. 1966*
    Postings: 2,336   GC: 420
SN Broad term for the processes and results of aesthetic expression (Note: See also the more precise Descriptors "Art Products," "Visual Arts," "Fine Arts," "Painting (Visual Arts)," etc.
NT Art Products
    Commercial Art
    Creative Art
RT Aesthetic Values
    Aesthetics
    Architecture
    Art Activities
    Art Appreciation
    Art Criticism
    Art Education
    Art Expression
    Art History
    Art Materials
    Art Teachers
    Art Therapy
    Artists
    Arts Centers
    Color
    Dance
    Design
    Drama
    Dramatics
    Fine Arts
    Literature
    Music
    Popular Culture
    Symmetry
    Theater Arts
    Visual Arts

Art Activities   *JUL. 1966*
    Postings: 2,855   GC: 420
SN Productive or appreciative participation in aesthetic experiences, including the use of such experiences generally in the school curriculum
BT Activities
RT Art
    Art Appreciation
    Art Education
    Art Materials
    Art Products
    Art Therapy
    Arts Centers

    Childrens Art
    Creative Activities
    Creative Art
    Cultural Activities
    Enrichment Activities
    Extracurricular Activities
    Fine Arts
    Handicrafts
    Recreational Activities
    Reggio Emilia Approach
    Visual Arts

Art Appreciation   *JUL. 1966*
    Postings: 1,112   GC: 420
BT Aesthetic Education
RT Art
    Art Activities
    Art Criticism
    Art History
    Audience Response
    Childrens Art
    Discipline Based Art Education
    Fine Arts
    Visual Literacy

Art Criticism   *DEC. 1989*
    Postings: 350   GC: 420
SN Description, interpretation, and evaluation of visual art works, e.g., painting, sculpture, architecture, photography, computer imagery, crafts—includes historical, recreative, and judicial analyses
BT Criticism
RT Aesthetic Values
    Art
    Art Appreciation
    Art Expression
    Art History
    Audience Response
    Critical Viewing
    Discipline Based Art Education
    Feminist Criticism
    Visual Arts

Art Education   *JUL. 1966*
    Postings: 6,876   GC: 420
SN Education concerned with one or more of the fine or applied arts, including studies and creative experiences
NT Discipline Based Art Education
    Studio Art
BT Education
RT Aesthetic Education
    Architectural Education
    Art
    Art Activities
    Art History
    Art Materials
    Art Teachers
    Childrens Art
    Commercial Art
    Fine Arts
    Visual Arts

Art Expression   *JUL. 1966*
    Postings: 1,245   GC: 420
SN Process of communicating thoughts or feelings aesthetically, as in painting, sculpture, music, etc.
RT Aesthetic Values
    Aesthetics
    Art
    Art Criticism
    Art Products
    Art Therapy
    Collage
    Creative Expression
    Creativity
    Expressionism
    Impressionism
    Literary Styles
    Modernism
    Motifs
    Naturalism
    Neoclassicism
    Postmodernism
    Realism
    Relief (Art)
    Romanticism

= Two or more Descriptors are used to represent this term. The term's main entry shows the appropriate coordination.

Self Expression
Studio Art
Surrealism
Symbolism

Art Galleries
USE   Arts Centers

Art History   *MAR. 1980*
Postings: 846   GC: 420
SN   Study of art expression through the ages,
including specific periods, artists, or
schools of art
BT   Intellectual History
RT   Art
Art Appreciation
Art Criticism
Art Education
Artists
Discipline Based Art Education
Fine Arts
Visual Arts

Art Making (Instruction)
USE   Studio Art

Art Materials   *JUL. 1966*
Postings: 859   GC: 420
RT   Adhesives
Art
Art Activities
Art Education
Childrens Art
Clay
Found Objects
Glass
Instructional Materials
Leather
Paper (Material)
Plastics
Studio Art
Supplies
Visual Arts

Art Production Curriculum
USE   Studio Art

Art Products   *JUL. 1966*
Postings: 991   GC: 420
SN   The final products of the creative proc-
ess involving the use of an art medium or
performance
BT   Art
RT   Art Activities
Art Expression
Art Therapy
Childrens Art
Collage
Copyrights
Handicrafts
Musical Composition
Painting (Visual Arts)
Photographs
Relief (Art)
Sculpture
Studio Art

Art Song   *JUL. 1966*
Postings: 25   GC: 420
SN   A song of serious artistic intent for one
voice written by a trained composer—as
opposed to a folk song
BT   Songs
RT   Singing

Art Studio Courses
USE   Studio Art

Art Teachers   *SEP. 1969*
Postings: 847   GC: 360
BT   Teachers
RT   Art
Art Education
Artists

Fine Arts
Visual Arts

Art Therapy   *JUN. 1977*
Postings: 367   GC: 230
SN   The therapeutic use of art forms (paint-
ing, sculpturing, drawing, etc.) in achiev-
ing self-expression and emotional re-
lease, usually in a context of remediation
or rehabilitation
BT   Therapy
RT   Art
Art Activities
Art Expression
Art Products
Creative Art
Educational Therapy
Music Therapy
Play Therapy
Psychotherapy
Self Expression
Therapeutic Recreation
Visual Arts

Articles (Grammar)
USE   Determiners (Languages)

Articles (Journals)
USE   Journal Articles

Articulation (Education)   *MAR. 1980*
Postings: 3,439   GC: 330
SN   Systematic coordination of course and/or
program content within and between edu-
cational institutions to facilitate the con-
tinuous and efficient progress of stu-
dents from grade to grade, school to
school, and from school to the working
world
UF   Articulation (Program) (1967 1980)
RT   Advanced Placement Programs
College School Cooperation
College Transfer Students
Curriculum Development
Developmental Continuity
Education
Educational Mobility
Educational Planning
Institutional Cooperation
Intercollegiate Cooperation
Program Content
Tech Prep
Transfer Policy
Transfer Programs
Transfer Rates (College)
Unified Studies Curriculum
Upper Division Colleges

Articulation (Program) (1967 1980)
USE   Articulation (Education)

Articulation (Speech)   *JUL. 1966*
Postings: 1,295   GC: 450
UF   Enunciation Improvement (1966
1980) #
Points of Articulation
BT   Speech
RT   Articulation Impairments
Diction
Language Rhythm
Phonetics
Speech Improvement
Speech Tests
Syllables
Vowels

Articulation Impairments   *MAR. 1980*
Postings: 284   GC: 220
SN   Disorders involving the substitution,
omission, distortion, and addition of
speech sounds that are uncharacteristic
of particular age groups (Note: Prior to
Mar80, this concept was indexed under
"Articulation (Speech)")
BT   Speech Impairments
RT   Articulation (Speech)
Cleft Palate

Speech
Speech Habits
Speech Improvement
Speech Tests
Speech Therapy
Stuttering
Visible Speech

Articulation Tests
USE   Speech Tests

Artificial Intelligence   *FEB. 1971*
Postings: 1,108   GC: 710
SN   Capability of a device to perform func-
tions normally associated with human
intelligence
NT   Expert Systems
RT   Bionics
Cognitive Processes
Cognitive Psychology
Computer Science
Computers
Cybernetics
Heuristics
Intelligence
Knowledge Representation
Logical Thinking
Natural Language Processing
Robotics

Artificial Languages   *JUL. 1973*
Postings: 87   GC: 440
SN   Languages created for international com-
munication, e.g., Esperanto, Interlingua,
Novial, Volapuk
UF   Constructed Languages
NT   Esperanto
BT   Language
RT   International Communication
International Trade Vocabulary
Language Universals
Programming Languages

Artificial Satellites
USE   Satellites (Aerospace)

Artificial Speech   *AUG. 1968*
Postings: 128   GC: 450
UF   Simulated Speech
Synthetic Speech
BT   Speech
RT   Acoustic Phonetics
Distinctive Features (Language)
Language
Phonology
Sound Spectrographs
Speech Synthesizers

Artisans
USE   Craft Workers

Artistic Talent
USE   Talent

Artists   *JUL. 1966*
Postings: 1,169   GC: 420
NT   Musicians
BT   Groups
RT   Art
Art History
Art Teachers
Fine Arts
Painting (Visual Arts)

Arts Centers   *JUL. 1966*
Postings: 326   GC: 920
UF   Art Galleries
Fine Arts Centers
BT   Resource Centers
RT   Art
Art Activities
Auditoriums
Cultural Centers
Drama Workshops
Educational Facilities

Fine Arts
Museums
Stages (Facilities)
Theaters

Asbestos   *NOV. 1982*
Postings: 147   GC: 410
SN   A variety of fibrous silicate minerals suit-
able for use where incombustible, non-
conductive, or chemically resistant ma-
terial is required
BT   Minerals
RT   Air Pollution
Construction Materials
Fire Protection
Geology
Hazardous Materials
Mining
Natural Resources
Physical Health

Asian American Students   *AUG. 2000*
Postings: 172   GC: 360
SN   Students of Asian heritage (descendants
of the indigenous peoples of East Asia
and Southeast Asia) who are citizens or
permanent residents of the United States
BT   Asian Americans
Students

Asian Americans   *AUG. 1974*
Postings: 2,491   GC: 560
SN   Citizens or permanent residents of the
United States who are descendants of
the indigenous peoples of east Asia
(China, Japan, Korea, Mongolia) and
Southeast Asia (Note: Prior to Mar80,
descendants of Pacific Islanders were
included in this Scope Note)
UF   Amerasians
American Orientals
Cambodian Americans #
Indochinese Americans #
Laotian Americans #
Oriental Americans
Vietnamese Americans #
NT   Asian American Students
Chinese Americans
Filipino Americans
Japanese Americans
Korean Americans
BT   North Americans
RT   Cambodians
Ethnic Groups
Hmong People
Indochinese
Laotians
Minority Groups
Pacific Americans
Vietnamese People

Asian History   *JUL. 1966*
Postings: 430   GC: 430
NT   Korean War
Vietnam War
BT   History
RT   Asian Studies
Middle Eastern History
Middle Eastern Studies
Non Western Civilization
World War I
World War II

Asian Music
USE   Oriental Music

Asian Studies   *MAR. 1973*
Postings: 691   GC: 400
SN   Studies, usually interdisciplinary in ap-
proach, of such geographic areas as
Asiatic Russia, Armenia, Azerbaijan,
Bangladesh, Bhutan, China, Georgia,
India, Indonesia, Japan, Kazakhstan,
Kirgizstan, Korea, Maldives, Mongolia,
Nepal, Pakistan, the Philippines, Sri Lanka,
Tajikistan, Turkmenistan, Uzbekistan, and
the Southeast Asian subcontinent
BT   Area Studies

= Two or more Descriptors are used to represent this term.
The term's main entry shows the appropriate coordination.

RT   Asian History
Burmese Culture
Chinese Culture
Foreign Culture
Indians
Islamic Culture
Japanese Culture
Korean Culture
Middle Eastern Studies
Non Western Civilization

Asphalts   *JAN. 1969*
Postings: 19   GC: 920
BT   Construction Materials
RT   Flooring
Road Construction
Roofing

Aspiration   *JUL. 1966*
Postings: 1,059   GC: 120
SN   Desire for the realization of ambitions, ideals, or accomplishments
UF   Ambition
Aspiration Level
Low Level Aspiration (1966 1980)
NT   Academic Aspiration
Occupational Aspiration
Parent Aspiration
RT   Ability
Achievement
Achievement Need
Apathy
Aptitude
Goal Orientation
Intention
Motivation
Objectives
Performance
Self Concept
Self Motivation
Student Educational Objectives

Aspiration Level
USE   Aspiration

Assembly (Manufacturing)   *JUL. 1966*
Postings: 122   GC: 650
BT   Manufacturing
RT   Agricultural Engineering
Agricultural Machinery
Computer Assisted Manufacturing
Equipment
Manufacturing Industry
Mass Production
Metal Working
Production Technicians
Sheet Metal Work

Assembly Programs   *JUL. 1966*
Postings: 60   GC: 350
BT   Programs
RT   Group Activities
Group Instruction
Meetings
School Activities
Student Participation

Assertive Training
USE   Assertiveness

Assertiveness   *MAR. 1977*
Postings: 836   GC: 120
SN   Bold, forceful expression of opinions or defense of one's interests
UF   Assertive Training
Assertiveness Training
BT   Behavior
RT   Aggression
Counseling Techniques
Individual Psychology
Inhibition
Interpersonal Communication
Personality Traits
Psychological Patterns
Self Advocacy
Self Esteem
Self Expression

Social Behavior
Socialization
Type A Behavior

Assertiveness Training
USE   Assertiveness

Assessed Valuation   *JUL. 1966*
Postings: 194   GC: 620
BT   Property Appraisal
RT   Building Obsolescence
Buildings
Estate Planning
Property Taxes
School Taxes
Taxes

Assessment
USE   Evaluation

Assessment Centers (Personnel)   *OCT. 1983*
Postings: 211   GC: 820
SN   Personnel evaluation centers using multiple assessment techniques for staff selection, promotion, or development—typically included are simulated work experiences and the use of multiple observers to appraise job-related behaviors
BT   Facilities
RT   Administrator Evaluation
Administrator Selection
Evaluation Methods
Job Performance
Job Placement
Management Development
Observation
Occupational Tests
Personnel Evaluation
Personnel Selection
Professional Development
Promotion (Occupational)
Simulation
Situational Tests

Assessment Instruments (Individuals)
USE   Measures (Individuals)

Assessment Rubrics
USE   Scoring Rubrics

Assignments   *JUL. 1966*
Postings: 1,097   GC: 310
SN   Learning tasks that are allotted to students or groups of students (Note: Prior to Mar80, the use of this term was not restricted by a Scope Note)
UF   Student Assignments
Textbook Assignments (1966 1980)
NT   Homework
Reading Assignments
Research Papers (Students)
Writing Assignments
BT   Instruction

Assimilation (Cultural)
USE   Acculturation

Assistance (Social Behavior)
USE   Helping Relationship

Assistant Principals   *JUL. 1974*
Postings: 248   GC: 360
UF   Vice Principals
BT   Administrators
School Personnel
RT   Beginning Principals
Principals
School Administration

Assistant Superintendent Role (1966 1980)   *JUN. 1980*
Postings: 15   GC: 360
SN   Invalid Descriptor—use "Superintendents" (Note: Occasionally used indiscriminately in the past for "assistant principal role"—see "Assistant Principals" for that concept)

Assistant Superintendents
USE   Superintendents

Assistantships   *OCT. 1980*
Postings: 51   GC: 620
SN   Financial aid in which college students, usually at the graduate level, are awarded assistant staff positions carrying stipends and, frequently, exemptions from fees
BT   Student Financial Aid
RT   Awards
Educational Finance
Eligibility
Fellowships
Grants
Internship Programs
Merit Scholarships
Professional Education
Research Assistants
Resident Assistants
Scholarship Funds
Student Costs
Student Employment
Teaching Assistants
Work Study Programs

Assistive Devices (for Disabled)   *APR. 1986*
Postings: 982   GC: 220
SN   Devices to aid the disabled to perform normal living or vocational tasks
UF   Adaptive Equipment (Disabled)
Self Help Devices (Disabled)
NT   Mobility Aids
Prostheses
BT   Equipment
RT   Biomedical Equipment
Communication Aids (for Disabled)
Disabilities
Normalization (Disabilities)
Sensory Aids

Associate Degrees   *JUL. 1966*
Postings: 1,372   GC: 340
SN   Degrees granted upon completion of an educational program of at least 2 but less than 4 academic years of college work, generally for completion of a curriculum of a 2-year institution—includes Associate in Arts, Associate in Science, and Associate in Applied Science degrees
UF   Two Plus Two Tech Prep Associate Degrees #
Two Year College Degrees
BT   Degrees (Academic)
RT   Bachelors Degrees
Community Colleges
Degree Requirements
Tech Prep
Technical Institutes
Two Year Colleges
Undergraduate Study

Association (Psychological) (1968 1980)
USE   Association (Psychology)

Association (Psychology)   *MAR. 1980*
Postings: 486   GC: 120
SN   Process or state of establishing functional relationships between new and previously known stimuli and/or responses, so that the presence of one tends to evoke the other(s)
UF   Association (Psychological) (1968 1980)
BT   Cognitive Processes
RT   Association Measures
Associative Learning
Behavior Chaining

Connected Discourse
Generalization
Learning Processes
Paired Associate Learning
Recognition (Psychology)
Serial Learning

Association Measures   *MAR. 1980*
Postings: 122   GC: 830
SN   Procedures or devices used to evaluate an individual's feelings, motives, or attitudes by requiring responses (usually spontaneous) to a set of verbal or pictorial stimuli (Note: Do not use for tests measuring paired associate learning)
UF   Association Tests (1968 1980)
BT   Projective Measures
RT   Affective Measures
Association (Psychology)
Associative Learning
Attitude Measures
Patterned Responses
Personality Assessment
Personality Measures
Psychological Evaluation
Verbal Stimuli
Visual Stimuli

Association Tests (1968 1980)
USE   Association Measures

Associations (Groups)
USE   Organizations (Groups)

Associative Learning   *JUL. 1966*
Postings: 838   GC: 110
SN   Learning that occurs through the establishment of functional relationships between new and previously known stimuli and/or responses
UF   Word Associations (Reading)
NT   Paired Associate Learning
BT   Learning
RT   Association (Psychology)
Association Measures
Aural Learning
Behavior Chaining
Learning Strategies
Nonverbal Learning
Serial Learning
Symbolic Learning
Visual Learning
Word Recognition

Asthma   *SEP. 1968*
Postings: 128   GC: 210
BT   Diseases
RT   Allergy
Physical Health
Physiology
Special Health Problems

Astronomy   *JUL. 1966*
Postings: 1,545   GC: 490
BT   Physical Sciences
RT   Aerospace Education
Aerospace Technology
Earth Science
Evolution
Lunar Research
Navigation
Planetariums
Scientific Research
Solar System
Space Exploration
Space Sciences
Spectroscopy
Stars

At Risk Persons   *APR. 1990*
Postings: 2,514   GC: 120
SN   Individuals or groups identified as possibly having or potentially developing a problem (physical, mental, educational, etc.) requiring further evaluation and/or intervention (Note: If possible, use the more specific term "High Risk Students")

= Two or more Descriptors are used to represent this term.
The term's main entry shows the appropriate coordination.

UF   High Risk Persons (1982 1990)
      Risk Populations
NT   High Risk Students
BT   Groups
RT   Developmental Delays
      Disabilities
      Disability Identification
      Early Identification
      Early Intervention
      Incidence
      Symptoms (Individual Disorders)

Athabascan Languages
USE Athapascan Languages

Athapascan Languages   *SEP. 1975*
      Postings: 139   GC: 440
UF   Athabascan Languages
NT   Apache
      Navajo
BT   American Indian Languages
RT   Alaska Natives

Athletes   *DEC. 1969*
      Postings: 1,505   GC: 470
BT   Groups
RT   Athletics
      Eligibility
      Sport Psychology
      Sports Medicine

Athletic Activities (1966 1974)
USE Athletics

Athletic Coaches   *MAR. 1971*
      Postings: 860   GC: 470
BT   Professional Personnel
RT   Athletics
      Physical Education
      Physical Education Teachers
      School Personnel
      Sport Psychology
      Sports Medicine

Athletic Equipment   *JUL. 1966*
      Postings: 291   GC: 910
BT   Equipment
RT   Athletics
      Educational Equipment
      Gymnasiums
      Physical Education
      Physical Education Facilities
      Physical Fitness
      Physical Recreation Programs
      Sports Medicine

Athletic Fields   *JUL. 1966*
      Postings: 98   GC: 470
BT   Facilities
RT   Athletics
      Field Houses
      Gymnasiums
      Parks
      Physical Education
      Physical Education Facilities
      Physical Recreation Programs
      Playgrounds
      Recreational Activities
      Recreational Facilities

Athletic Programs (1966 1980)
USE Athletics

Athletics   *JUL. 1966*
      Postings: 3,881   GC: 470
SN   Sports, games, or physical contests often engaged in competitively
UF   Athletic Activities (1966 1974)
      Athletic Programs (1966 1980)
      Sports
      Sports News #
      Sports Reporting #
NT   Aquatic Sports
      Archery
      Bowling

      College Athletics
      Extramural Athletics
      Fencing (Sport)
      Golf
      Gymnastics
      Handball
      Intramural Athletics
      Lifetime Sports
      Olympic Games
      Orienteering
      Racquet Sports
      Roller Skating
      Special Olympics
      Table Tennis
      Team Sports
      Track and Field
      Weightlifting
      Winter Sports
      Womens Athletics
      Wrestling
BT   Physical Activities
RT   Athletes
      Athletic Coaches
      Athletic Equipment
      Athletic Fields
      Bicycling
      Eligibility
      Exercise
      Extracurricular Activities
      Field Houses
      Games
      Gymnasiums
      Horseback Riding
      Jogging
      Locker Rooms
      News Reporting
      Outdoor Activities
      Physical Education
      Physical Education Facilities
      Physical Education Teachers
      Physical Fitness
      Physical Recreation Programs
      Playground Activities
      Recreational Activities
      Running
      Sport Psychology
      Sports Medicine
      Walking

Atlases   *JUL. 1966*
      Postings: 126   GC: 730
BT   Reference Materials
RT   Cartography
      Charts
      Geography
      Maps

Atmosphere (Social)
USE Social Environment

Atmospheric Pollution
USE Air Pollution

Atomic Bombs
USE Nuclear Weapons

Atomic Energy
USE Nuclear Energy

Atomic Physics
USE Nuclear Physics

Atomic Structure   *JUL. 1966*
      Postings: 453   GC: 490
RT   Atomic Theory
      Chemistry
      Crystallography
      Force
      Matter
      Molecular Structure
      Nuclear Physics
      Physical Chemistry
      Physical Sciences
      Physics
      Radiation Biology
      Radioisotopes
      Space

      Spectroscopy
      Stereochemistry
      Structural Analysis (Science)

Atomic Theory   *JUL. 1966*
      Postings: 313   GC: 490
BT   Theories
RT   Atomic Structure
      Force
      Matter
      Nuclear Energy
      Nuclear Physics
      Nuclear Warfare
      Nuclear Weapons
      Physics
      Radiation Biology
      Radioisotopes
      Space

Atomic Warfare
USE Nuclear Warfare

Attachment Behavior   *FEB. 1975*
      Postings: 1,335   GC: 120
SN   Behavior exhibited by an individual attracted (maintaining proximity) to and dependent on a specific person or object for emotional satisfaction
UF   Bonding (Behavior)
BT   Behavior
RT   Affective Behavior
      Behavior Development
      Caregiver Child Relationship
      Child Behavior
      Dependency (Personality)
      Emotional Development
      Emotional Response
      Exploratory Behavior
      Identification (Psychology)
      Infant Behavior
      Interpersonal Relationship
      Intimacy
      Love
      Parent Child Relationship
      Separation Anxiety

Attendance   *JUL. 1966*
      Postings: 1,962   GC: 320
UF   Absence (Students)
      Attendance Services (1968 1980) #
      Class Attendance (1966 1980)
      School Attendance
NT   Average Daily Attendance
      College Attendance
      Teacher Attendance
RT   Academic Persistence
      Access to Education
      Attendance Officers
      Attendance Patterns
      Attendance Records
      Auditing (Coursework)
      Dropouts
      Enrollment
      Expulsion
      Leaves of Absence
      No Shows
      Out of School Youth
      Participation
      Reentry Students
      School Attendance Legislation
      School Holding Power
      School Registration
      School Size
      Stopouts
      Students
      Suspension
      Transfer Policy
      Transfer Students
      Truancy
      Withdrawal (Education)

Attendance Officers   *JUL. 1966*
      Postings: 29   GC: 360
UF   Truant Officers #
BT   Pupil Personnel Workers
RT   Attendance
      Attendance Patterns
      Attendance Records

Attendance Patterns   *JUL. 1966*
      Postings: 781   GC: 320
RT   Attendance
      Attendance Officers
      Attendance Records
      Average Daily Attendance
      College Attendance
      Truancy

Attendance Records   *JUL. 1966*
      Postings: 149   GC: 320
BT   Records (Forms)
RT   Attendance
      Attendance Officers
      Attendance Patterns
      Average Daily Attendance

Attendance Services (1968 1980)
USE Attendance
AND Pupil Personnel Services

Attendant Training (1968 1980)
USE Attendants
AND Job Training

Attendants   *JUL. 1966*
      Postings: 220   GC: 640
SN   Individuals who attend or accompany others to give service
UF   Attendant Training (1968 1980) #
      Companions (Occupation) (1968 1980)
BT   Caregivers
      Service Workers
RT   Adult Day Care
      Adult Foster Care
      Allied Health Personnel
      Home Health Aides
      Household Workers
      Long Term Care
      Nurses Aides
      Occupational Home Economics
      Resident Advisers
      Residential Care

Attention   *JUL. 1966*
      Postings: 1,501   GC: 110
RT   Adaptation Level Theory
      Arousal Patterns
      Attention Control
      Attention Deficit Disorders
      Attention Span
      Audience Response
      Behavior
      Curiosity
      Habituation
      Listening
      Novelty (Stimulus Dimension)
      Perception
      Redundancy
      Time on Task

Attention Control   *JUL. 1966*
      Postings: 556   GC: 110
RT   Attention
      Meditation
      Motivation

Attention Deficit Disorders   *JUN. 1983*
      Postings: 1,006   GC: 220
SN   Developmentally inappropriate inattention and impulsivity
BT   Disabilities
RT   Attention
      Attention Span
      Behavior Disorders
      Emotional Disturbances
      Hyperactivity
      Learning Disabilities
      Neurological Impairments

Attention Span   *JUL. 1966*
      Postings: 590   GC: 120
BT   Psychological Characteristics
RT   Attention
      Attention Deficit Disorders

Conceptual Tempo
Hyperactivity
Motivation
Shift Studies

Attitude Change *MAR. 1980*
Postings: 8,058 GC: 120
UF Changing Attitudes (1966 1980)
BT Change
RT Adjustment (to Environment)
Adoption (Ideas)
Attitudes
Behavior Change
Change Agents
Change Strategies
Cognitive Restructuring
Consciousness Raising
Personality Change

Attitude Measures *MAR. 1980*
Postings: 4,109 GC: 830
SN Procedures or devices used to obtain
quantified descriptions of an individual's
predispositions to react to certain peo-
ple, objects, situations, ideas, etc.
UF Attitude Tests (1966 1980)
Opinion Scales
NT Likert Scales
Semantic Differential
BT Measures (Individuals)
RT Affective Measures
Association Measures
Attitudes
Beliefs
Forced Choice Technique
Interest Inventories
Opinions
Personality Measures
Questionnaires
Social Desirability
Surveys
Values

Attitude Tests (1966 1980)
USE Attitude Measures

Attitudes *JUL. 1966*
Postings: 9,025 GC: 120
SN Predispositions to react to certain per-
sons, objects, situations, ideas, etc., in
a particular manner—not always con-
sciously held (as are beliefs) nor read-
ily verbalized (as are opinions), they
are characterized as either affective or
valuative (Note: Use a more specific term
if possible)
NT Administrator Attitudes
Adolescent Attitudes
Anti Intellectualism
Attitudes toward Disabilities
Beliefs
Black Attitudes
Childhood Attitudes
Community Attitudes
Computer Attitudes
Counselor Attitudes
Design Preferences
Dropout Attitudes
Educational Attitudes
Employee Attitudes
Employer Attitudes
Family Attitudes
Language Attitudes
Librarian Attitudes
Majority Attitudes
Negative Attitudes
Opinions
Parent Attitudes
Political Attitudes
Program Attitudes
Racial Attitudes
Reading Attitudes
Regional Attitudes
Satisfaction
School Attitudes
Scientific Attitudes
Social Attitudes
Sportsmanship
Stereotypes

Student Attitudes
Student Teacher Attitudes
Teacher Attitudes
Trust (Psychology)
Work Attitudes
World Views
Writing Attitudes
RT Affective Behavior
Attitude Change
Attitude Measures
Behavior
Bias
Cognitive Dissonance
Cognitive Structures
Expectation
Human Dignity
Humanization
Intention
Interests
Moods
Objectivity
Psychological Patterns
Reputation
Response Style (Tests)
Self Fulfilling Prophecies
Semantic Differential

Attitudes toward Disabilities *JUN. 1999*
Postings: 657 GC: 220
SN Predispositions or opinions, of individu-
als or of societies, concerning people
with disabilities or concerning disabili-
ties (Note: See also the Identifier
"Ableism")
BT Attitudes
RT Disabilities
Disability Discrimination
Normalization (Disabilities)

Attorneys
USE Lawyers

Attractiveness (between Persons)
USE Interpersonal Attraction

Attribution Theory *OCT. 1976*
Postings: 1,953 GC: 810
SN Theory focusing on perceived causes of
behavior
UF Causal Attributions
BT Behavior Theories
RT Causal Models
Etiology
Intention
Locus of Control
Personality
Psychological Characteristics
Self Concept
Self Fulfilling Prophecies
Social Cognition

Attrition (Research Studies) *JUN. 1977*
Postings: 186 GC: 810
SN Reduction in size of the population sam-
ple during the period of time covered by
a longitudinal study (Note: Do not con-
fuse with "Student Attrition")
UF Mortality (Research Studies)
RT Control Groups
Dropouts
Experimental Groups
Longitudinal Studies
Matched Groups
Research
Research Design
Research Methodology
Research Problems
Sample Size
Sampling
Statistical Bias

Attrition (Students)
USE Student Attrition

Audience Analysis *OCT. 1983*
Postings: 722 GC: 810
SN Gathering and interpreting information

about the recipients of oral, written, or
visual communication
BT Evaluation Methods
RT Agenda Setting
Audience Awareness
Audience Participation
Audience Response
Audiences
Communication Research
Mass Media Effects
Media Research
Public Speaking
Writing (Composition)

Audience Awareness *AUG. 1988*
Postings: 1,278 GC: 430
SN The conceptions of the writer, speaker,
or performer concerning the recipients
of his/her communication
RT Audience Analysis
Audiences
Communication Skills
Narration
Rhetoric
Social Cognition
Writing Skills

Audience Participation *JUL. 1966*
Postings: 153 GC: 720
BT Participation
RT Audience Analysis
Audience Response
Audiences

Audience Response *AUG. 1988*
Postings: 822 GC: 110
SN Recipient reactions to, and interpreta-
tions of, oral, visual, or written commu-
nication (Note: If possible, use the more
specific term "Reader Response")
NT Reader Response
BT Responses
RT Agenda Setting
Art Appreciation
Art Criticism
Attention
Audience Analysis
Audience Participation
Audiences
Feedback
Film Criticism
Listening
Mass Media Effects
Mass Media Use
Music Appreciation
Public Opinion
Rhetorical Criticism
Speech Communication
Television Viewing
Visual Literacy

Audiences *AUG. 1968*
Postings: 1,404 GC: 720
UF Spectators
BT Groups
RT Audience Analysis
Audience Awareness
Audience Participation
Audience Response
Communication (Thought Transfer)
Drama
Listening Groups
Mass Instruction
Mass Media
Radio
Television Viewing
Theater Arts

Audio Active Compare Laboratories (1967 1980)
USE Language Laboratories

Audio Active Laboratories (1967 1980)
USE Language Laboratories

Audio Equipment *JUL. 1966*
Postings: 546 GC: 910
UF Central Sound Systems (1966 1980)
Sound Equipment
Sound Systems
NT Audiodisks
Audiotape Cassettes
Audiotape Recorders
Hearing Aids
Microphones
Sound Spectrographs
Speech Synthesizers
BT Equipment
RT Acoustics
Audiotape Recordings
Audiovisual Aids
Broadcast Reception Equipment
Language Laboratories
Noise (Sound)
Photographic Equipment
Projection Equipment
Radio
Sound Effects
Special Effects
Telephone Communications Systems
Video Equipment

Audio Passive Laboratories (1968 1980)
USE Language Laboratories

Audio Video Laboratories (1967 1980)
USE Audiovisual Centers

Audiodisc Recordings (1980 1986)
USE Audiodisks

Audiodisks *AUG. 1986*
Postings: 69 GC: 720
UF Audiodisc Recordings (1980 1986)
Language Records (Phonograph)
(1966 1980)
Phonograph Records (1966 1980)
BT Audio Equipment
Nonprint Media
RT Audiotape Recordings
Audiovisual Aids
Discographies
Optical Disks
Oral History
Programming (Broadcast)
Radio
Talking Books
Videodisks

Audiolingual Approaches
USE Audiolingual Methods

Audiolingual Methods *JUL. 1966*
Postings: 1,255 GC: 450
SN Foreign language teaching methods,
based on behaviorist theory, that em-
phasize the development of oral skills
through habit formation, fostered via
repetition and reinforcement
UF Audiolingual Approaches
BT Teaching Methods
RT Audiolingual Skills
Aural Learning
Conversational Language Courses
Grammar Translation Method
Interference (Language)
Second Language Instruction
Second Language Learning

Audiolingual Skills *JUL. 1966*
Postings: 620 GC: 450
UF Aural Oral Skills
NT Listening Skills
Speech Skills
BT Language Skills
RT Audiolingual Methods
Basic Skills
Communication Skills
Conversational Language Courses
Language Fluency

= Two or more Descriptors are used to represent this term.
The term's main entry shows the appropriate coordination.

Audiologists (1968 1980)
USE   Allied Health Personnel
AND   Audiology

Audiology   *JUL. 1966*
    Postings: 345   GC: 210
SN   Study of hearing and hearing impairments—includes assessment, therapy, and rehabilitation of hearing-impaired individuals
UF   Audiologists (1968 1980) #
     Audiometrists (1967 1980) #
BT   Medicine
RT   Auditory Evaluation
     Auditory Tests
     Cochlear Implants
     Ears
     Hearing (Physiology)
     Hearing Aids
     Hearing Conservation
     Hearing Impairments
     Hearing Therapy
     Speech and Hearing Clinics
     Speech Language Pathology

Audiometric Tests   *JUL. 1966*
    Postings: 128   GC: 830
SN   Tests assessing hearing acuity and range using an audiometer
BT   Auditory Tests
RT   Auditory Evaluation
     Hearing (Physiology)
     Hearing Impairments

Audiometrists (1967 1980)
USE   Allied Health Personnel
AND   Audiology

Audiotape Cartridges
USE   Audiotape Cassettes

Audiotape Cassette Recorders
USE   Audiotape Cassettes
AND   Audiotape Recorders

Audiotape Cassettes   *MAR. 1980*
    Postings: 195   GC: 720
UF   Audiotape Cartridges
     Audiotape Cassette Recorders #
BT   Audio Equipment
     Magnetic Tape Cassettes
RT   Audiotape Recorders
     Audiotape Recordings
     Videotape Cassettes
     Videotape Recordings

Audiotape Recorders   *MAR. 1980*
    Postings: 30   GC: 910
UF   Audiotape Cassette Recorders #
BT   Audio Equipment
     Tape Recorders
RT   Audiotape Cassettes
     Audiotape Recordings
     Audiovisual Aids
     Videotape Recorders

Audiotape Recordings   *JAN. 1979*
    Postings: 1,235   GC: 720
SN   Magnetic tapes on which electric signals are recorded and can be reproduced mechanically or electronically as sound—stored on open reels, cassettes, or cartridges
UF   Language Tapes
     Master Tapes (Audio) (1968 1980)
     Phonotape Recordings (1966 1978)
     Sound Tape Recordings
BT   Tape Recordings
RT   Audio Equipment
     Audiodisks
     Audiotape Cassettes
     Audiotape Recorders
     Audiovisual Aids
     Oral History
     Programming (Broadcast)
     Radio
     Sound Effects
     Talking Books
     Videotape Recordings

Audiovisual Aids   *JUL. 1966*
    Postings: 7,403   GC: 720
SN   Nonprint instructional materials and the equipment required for their display (Note: Prior to Mar80, the instruction "Nonprint Media, USE Audiovisual Aids" was carried in the Thesaurus—corresponds to Pubtype code 100—do not use except as the subject of a document)
UF   Audiovisual Equipment
     Audiovisual Materials
     Audiovisual Media
NT   Instructional Films
     Protocol Materials
BT   Educational Media
RT   Audio Equipment
     Audiodisks
     Audiotape Recorders
     Audiotape Recordings
     Audiovisual Centers
     Audiovisual Communications
     Audiovisual Coordinators
     Audiovisual Instruction
     Autoinstructional Aids
     Bulletin Boards
     Cartoons
     Chalkboards
     Courseware
     Display Aids
     Documentaries
     Educational Equipment
     Educational Technology
     Electromechanical Aids
     Electronic Equipment
     Filmstrips
     Instructional Materials
     Learning Resources Centers
     Mass Media
     Microphones
     Multimedia Materials
     Nonprint Media
     Optical Disks
     Photographic Equipment
     Photographs
     Programmed Instructional Materials
     Projection Equipment
     Screens (Displays)
     Sensory Aids
     Slides
     Talking Books
     Three Dimensional Aids
     Transparencies
     Video Equipment
     Videodisks
     Videotape Recorders
     Videotape Recordings
     Visual Aids

Audiovisual Centers   *JUL. 1966*
    Postings: 447   GC: 920
SN   Instructional areas with equipment for the storage and use of audiovisual aids
UF   Audio Video Laboratories (1967 1980)
BT   Educational Facilities
     Resource Centers
RT   Audiovisual Aids
     Audiovisual Communications
     Audiovisual Coordinators
     Learning Laboratories
     Learning Resources Centers

Audiovisual Communication (1967 1980)
USE   Audiovisual Communications

Audiovisual Communications   *MAR. 1980*
    Postings: 564   GC: 720
SN   Transmission of instructional information by audio and/or visual systems (Note: Prior to Mar80, "Audiovisual Communication" was not scoped and was occasionally used in noninstructional settings)
UF   Audiovisual Communication (1967 1980)
NT   Dial Access Information Systems

     Educational Radio
     Educational Television
     Loop Induction Systems
BT   Communications
RT   Audiovisual Aids
     Audiovisual Centers
     Audiovisual Instruction
     Educational Technology
     Media Selection

Audiovisual Coordinators   *FEB. 1969*
    Postings: 80   GC: 360
SN   Individuals at the school unit or district level who have responsibility for audiovisual materials and equipment
UF   Audiovisual Directors (1969 1980)
BT   Coordinators
     Media Specialists
     School Personnel
RT   Audiovisual Aids
     Audiovisual Centers
     Audiovisual Instruction

Audiovisual Directors (1969 1980)
USE   Audiovisual Coordinators

Audiovisual Education
USE   Audiovisual Instruction

Audiovisual Equipment
USE   Audiovisual Aids

Audiovisual Instruction   *JUL. 1966*
    Postings: 2,103   GC: 310
SN   Production, selection, and utilization of audiovisual aids in instruction
UF   Audiovisual Education
     Audiovisual Programs (1966 1980)
BT   Multimedia Instruction
RT   Audiovisual Aids
     Audiovisual Communications
     Audiovisual Coordinators
     Educational Radio
     Educational Television
     Instructional Films
     Intermode Differences
     Listening Groups
     Protocol Materials
     Repetitive Film Showings
     Telecourses

Audiovisual Materials
USE   Audiovisual Aids

Audiovisual Media
USE   Audiovisual Aids

Audiovisual Programs (1966 1980)
USE   Audiovisual Instruction

Auditing (Coursework)   *AUG. 1986*
    Postings: 2   GC: 320
SN   Attendance in classes or courses without receiving academic credit
RT   Attendance
     Continuing Education
     Continuing Education Units
     Courses
     Credits
     Enrollment
     Remedial Programs
     Student Interests

Audition (Physiology) (1967 1980)
USE   Hearing (Physiology)

Auditoriums   *JUL. 1966*
    Postings: 99   GC: 920
BT   Facilities
RT   Arts Centers
     Dramatics
     Educational Facilities
     Music Facilities

     Recreational Facilities
     Stages (Facilities)
     Theaters
     Windowless Rooms

Auditory Comprehension
USE   Listening Comprehension

Auditory Discrimination   *JUL. 1966*
    Postings: 912   GC: 110
SN   Ability to distinguish sounds of varying frequencies, intensities, and patterns
BT   Auditory Perception
RT   Auditory Stimuli
     Auditory Tests
     Auditory Training
     Aural Learning
     Discrimination Learning
     Psychoacoustics

Auditory Evaluation   *JUL. 1966*
    Postings: 286   GC: 820
SN   Determination of an individual's ability to hear and of any needed treatment
BT   Medical Evaluation
RT   Audiology
     Audiometric Tests
     Auditory Tests
     Hearing (Physiology)
     Hearing Impairments
     Hearing Therapy
     Speech and Hearing Clinics

Auditory Perception   *JUL. 1966*
    Postings: 1,797   GC: 110
SN   Ability to identify and assign meaning to sounds
NT   Auditory Discrimination
BT   Perception
RT   Acoustic Phonetics
     Auditory Stimuli
     Auditory Tests
     Auditory Training
     Aural Learning
     Echolocation
     Figural Aftereffects
     Hearing (Physiology)
     Language Processing
     Listening Comprehension
     Perception Tests
     Perceptual Impairments
     Psychoacoustics
     Sensory Experience

Auditory Stimuli   *MAR. 1980*
    Postings: 976   GC: 110
UF   Aural Stimuli (1966 1980)
BT   Stimuli
RT   Acoustics
     Auditory Discrimination
     Auditory Perception
     Echolocation
     Electrical Stimuli
     Hearing (Physiology)
     Listening
     Noise (Sound)
     Psychoacoustics
     Tactile Stimuli
     Verbal Stimuli
     Visual Stimuli

Auditory Tests   *JUL. 1966*
    Postings: 421   GC: 830
SN   Tests designed to assess hearing ability
UF   Auditory Visual Tests (1966 1980) #
     Hearing Tests
     Otological Tests
NT   Audiometric Tests
BT   Tests
RT   Audiology
     Auditory Discrimination
     Auditory Evaluation
     Auditory Perception
     Diagnostic Tests
     Ears
     Hearing (Physiology)
     Hearing Impairments
     Perception Tests

= Two or more Descriptors are used to represent this term.
The term's main entry shows the appropriate coordination.

Physical Examinations
Screening Tests

Auditory Training   *JUL. 1966*
Postings: 363   GC: 400
SN   Training in the recognition and interpre-
tation of common sounds, such as mu-
sical sounds or speech (Note: Use "Hear-
ing Therapy" for auditory training of the
hearing-impaired—prior to Mar80, the
use of this term was not restricted by a
Scope Note)
BT   Sensory Training
RT   Auditory Discrimination
Auditory Perception
Aural Learning
Hearing Therapy
Kodaly Method
Language Acquisition
Listening Comprehension
Perceptual Impairments
Sensory Integration
Suzuki Method

Auditory Visual Tests (1966 1980)
USE   Auditory Tests
AND   Vision Tests

Audits (Verification)   *AUG. 1986*
Postings: 154   GC: 820
SN   Verifications of legality, fidelity, efficiency,
or feasibility of procedures, operations,
transactions, or expenditures, often by
an independent person or agency
NT   Communication Audits
Energy Audits
Financial Audits
RT   Accountability
Compliance (Legal)
Evaluation Methods
Inspection
Measurement Techniques
Program Administration
Program Effectiveness
Quality Control
Recordkeeping
Standards

**Augmentative and Alternative
Communication**   *JUN. 1994*
Postings: 168   GC: 220
SN   Communication in which at least one
partner is a user of a visual, tactile, or
auditory system that either adds to or
replaces normal speech and/or writing
UF   Alternative and Augmentative Commu-
nication
Alternative Communication Systems
(Disabled)
Augmentative Communication Systems
NT   Manual Communication
Total Communication
BT   Communication (Thought Transfer)
RT   Communication Aids (for Disabled)
Communication Disorders
Language Impairments
Nonverbal Communication
Speech Impairments

Augmentative Communication Systems
USE   Augmentative and Alternative Communication

Aural Comprehension
USE   Listening Comprehension

Aural Language Learning
USE   Aural Learning
AND   Language Acquisition

Aural Learning   *JUL. 1966*
Postings: 512   GC: 110
SN   Learning through listening (Note: Do not
confuse with "Auditory Training")
UF   Aural Language Learning #
BT   Learning

RT   Associative Learning
Audiolingual Methods
Auditory Discrimination
Auditory Perception
Auditory Training
Learning Modalities
Listening Comprehension
Multisensory Learning
Phonics

Aural Oral Skills
USE   Audiolingual Skills

Aural Stimuli (1966 1980)
USE   Auditory Stimuli

Aurally Handicapped (1966 1980)
USE   Hearing Impairments

Australian Aboriginal Languages   *JUL. 1966*
Postings: 52   GC: 440
BT   Languages
RT   Australian Literature

Australian Literature   *JUN. 1970*
Postings: 29   GC: 430
BT   Literature
RT   Australian Aboriginal Languages

Austro Asiatic Languages   *JUL. 1966*
Postings: 21   GC: 440
NT   Cambodian
BT   Languages
RT   Sino Tibetan Languages

Austronesian Languages
USE   Malayo Polynesian Languages

Auteurism   *MAY 1976*
Postings: 52   GC: 430
SN   The consideration of films as embodi-
ments of the personalities of film direc-
tors
UF   Film Auteurism
RT   Creativity
Film Production
Film Production Specialists
Film Study
Films

Authentic Assessment
USE   Performance Based Assessment

Authoring Aids (Programing) (1983 1994)
USE   Authoring Aids (Programming)

Authoring Aids (Programming)   *MAR. 1994*
Postings: 267   GC: 730
SN   Guidelines and instructions to assist in
designing, writing, and editing of com-
puter software—such aids may them-
selves be software
UF   Authoring Aids (Programing) (1983
1994)
Authoring Languages #
Authoring Systems
RT   Computer Assisted Instruction
Computer Oriented Programs
Computer Software
Computer Software Development
Guidelines
Programming
Programming Languages

Authoring Languages
USE   Authoring Aids (Programming)
AND   Programming Languages

Authoring Systems
USE   Authoring Aids (Programming)

Authoritarianism   *DEC. 1969*
Postings: 467   GC: 120
RT   Dogmatism
Imperialism
Personal Autonomy
Political Attitudes
Political Science
Sociology
Totalitarianism

Authority Control (Information)   *APR. 1993*
Postings: 146   GC: 710
SN   The establishment and maintenance of
consistent forms of terms, as of names,
subjects, and titles, to be used as head-
ings in bibliographic records
UF   Authority Files
BT   Documentation
RT   Bibliographic Records
Cataloging
Indexing
Information Storage
Library Technical Processes
Subject Index Terms

Authority Files
USE   Authority Control (Information)

Authority Structure
USE   Power Structure

Authors   *SEP. 1969*
Postings: 2,940   GC: 430
UF   Writers
NT   Poets
BT   Groups
RT   Editors
Faculty Publishing
Literature
Manuscripts
Publications
Writing for Publication

Autism   *JUL. 1966*
Postings: 2,184   GC: 220
BT   Disabilities
RT   Behavior Disorders
Developmental Disabilities
Emotional Disturbances
Interpersonal Relationship
Personality Problems
Schizophrenia
Withdrawal (Psychology)

Auto Body Repairers   *MAR. 1980*
Postings: 138   GC: 640
UF   Auto Body Repairmen (1966 1980)
Body and Fender Repairers
BT   Skilled Workers
RT   Auto Mechanics
Motor Vehicles
Painting (Industrial Arts)
Repair

Auto Body Repairmen (1966 1980)
USE   Auto Body Repairers

Auto Mechanics   *JUL. 1966*
Postings: 877   GC: 640
UF   Auto Mechanics (Occupation) (1968
1980)
Automobile Mechanics
Diesel Mechanics
Truck Mechanics
BT   Mechanics (Process)
RT   Auto Body Repairers
Diesel Engines
Engines
Industrial Arts
Motor Vehicles
Power Technology
Skilled Occupations
Small Engine Mechanics
Technology Education

Auto Mechanics (Occupation) (1968 1980)
USE   Auto Mechanics

Auto Parts Clerks   *MAR. 1980*
Postings: 22   GC: 640
UF   Auto Parts Men (1968 1980)
BT   Sales Workers
RT   Motor Vehicles
Sales Occupations

Auto Parts Men (1968 1980)
USE   Auto Parts Clerks

Autobiographies   *JUL. 1966*
Postings: 705   GC: 730
SN   Accounts people write of their own lives
BT   Biographies
RT   Diaries
Personal Narratives

Autoinstructional Aids   *JUL. 1966*
Postings: 1,524   GC: 730
SN   Instructional materials, equipment, or
systems used, without the aid of a teacher,
in individual or individualized instruction
to present information and inform learn-
ers of their progress
UF   Self Instruction Aids
NT   Teaching Machines
BT   Educational Media
RT   Audiovisual Aids
Computer Assisted Instruction
Courseware
Educational Equipment
Electromechanical Aids
Electronic Classrooms
Independent Study
Individual Instruction
Individualized Instruction
Instructional Materials
Learner Controlled Instruction
Learning Laboratories
Programmed Instruction
Programmed Instructional Materials

Autoinstructional Laboratories (1967 1980)
USE   Learning Laboratories

Autoinstructional Methods (1966 1980)
USE   Programmed Instruction

Autoinstructional Programs (1966 1980)
USE   Programmed Instruction

Automatic Data Processing
USE   Data Processing

Automatic Indexing   *OCT. 1970*
Postings: 320   GC: 710
SN   Selection of keywords from a document
and construction of index entries using a
machine
UF   Computer Assisted Indexing
Machine Aided Indexing
BT   Indexing
RT   Automation
Computational Linguistics
Indexes
Machine Translation
Permuted Indexes

Automation   *JUL. 1966*
Postings: 1,514   GC: 490
SN   Investigation, design, development, and
application of methods of rendering proc-
esses automatic, self-moving, or self-
controlling
UF   Mechanization
NT   Library Automation
Office Automation
Robotics
BT   Technology
RT   Automatic Indexing
Computer Anxiety

= Two or more Descriptors are used to represent this term.
The term's main entry shows the appropriate coordination.

Computer Attitudes
Computer Science
Computers
Cybernetics
Data Processing
Electromechanical Technology
Electronic Control
Instrumentation
Job Simplification
Machine Translation
Man Machine Systems
Numerical Control
Obsolescence
Technological Advancement
Test Scoring Machines
Word Processing
Workstations

Automobile Mechanics
USE   Auto Mechanics

Auxiliary Laborers   *JUL. 1966*
    Postings: 7   GC: 630
UF   Auxiliary Workers
BT   Laborers

Auxiliary School Services
USE   Ancillary School Services

Auxiliary Workers
USE   Auxiliary Laborers

Average Daily Attendance   *JUL. 1966*
    Postings: 161   GC: 320
SN   Average of the number of students pres-
    ent at (as opposed to enrolled in) a
    school during the time it is in session
BT   Attendance
    Incidence
RT   Attendance Patterns
    Attendance Records
    Average Daily Membership
    School Attendance Legislation

Average Daily Enrollment (1968 1980)
USE   Average Daily Membership

Average Daily Membership   *MAR. 1980*
    Postings: 74   GC: 320
SN   Average of the number of students regis-
    tered or enrolled (as opposed to in at-
    tendance) in a school during the time it
    is in session
UF   Average Daily Enrollment (1968 1980)
BT   Enrollment Rate
RT   Average Daily Attendance
    Declining Enrollment
    Enrollment
    Enrollment Influences
    Enrollment Projections
    Enrollment Trends
    School Demography

Average Students (1967 1980)
USE   Students

Aviation Education   *DEC. 1989*
    Postings: 137   GC: 490
SN   Learning/teaching activities across all
    grade levels that focus on such topics as
    aircraft flight, airplane structure/mainte-
    nance/operation, avionics, air commerce/
    transportation, aerial safety/ground sup-
    port, and the effects of air travel on
    everyday life—includes both general and
    technical educational programs
BT   Aerospace Education
RT   Air Traffic Control
    Air Transportation
    Aircraft Pilots
    Airports
    Aviation Mechanics
    Aviation Technology
    Aviation Vocabulary
    Flight Training

Navigation
Science Education
Technical Education

Aviation Mechanics   *JUL. 1966*
    Postings: 139   GC: 640
UF   Aircraft Mechanics
BT   Aviation Technology
    Mechanics (Process)
RT   Aerospace Industry
    Aviation Education
    Aviation Vocabulary
    Engines
    Power Technology
    Skilled Occupations

Aviation Technology   *JUL. 1966*
    Postings: 352   GC: 490
NT   Aviation Mechanics
BT   Aerospace Technology
RT   Aerospace Education
    Aerospace Industry
    Air Traffic Control
    Air Transportation
    Aircraft Pilots
    Airports
    Aviation Education
    Aviation Vocabulary
    Navigation
    Technical Education

Aviation Vocabulary   *JUL. 1966*
    Postings: 38   GC: 450
BT   Vocabulary
RT   Aerospace Education
    Aerospace Industry
    Air Traffic Control
    Aircraft Pilots
    Aviation Education
    Aviation Mechanics
    Aviation Technology

Awards   *JUN. 1975*
    Postings: 1,062   GC: 520
SN   Verbal or material commendations, call-
    ing attention to activities, performances,
    or qualities
BT   Recognition (Achievement)
RT   Achievement Rating
    Assistantships
    Fellowships
    Grants
    Honor Societies
    Incentives
    Performance
    Praise
    Prestige
    Professional Recognition
    Rewards
    Sanctions
    Scholarships

Awareness
USE   Perception

Away from the Job Training
USE   Off the Job Training

Aymara   *SEP. 1968*
    Postings: 17   GC: 440
SN   Language of the South American Indians
    living in the southern part of the Titicaca
    plateau of the central Andes (a geo-
    graphic area roughly corresponding to
    Bolivia and Peru)
BT   American Indian Languages

Azerbaijani   *JUL. 1966*
    Postings: 7   GC: 440
BT   Turkic Languages

Baby Boomers   *AUG. 1989*
    Postings: 63   GC: 550
SN   Those born at a time when the popula-
    tion's birth rate is sharply increasing—

used most frequently for the post World
War II generation, especially those born
between 1946 and 1965
BT   Groups
RT   Adults (30 to 45)
    Birth Rate
    Middle Aged Adults
    Older Workers
    Population Growth
    Population Trends
    Socioeconomic Influences

Baccalaureate Degrees
USE   Bachelors Degrees

Bachelor of Arts Degrees
USE   Bachelors Degrees

Bachelor of Science Degrees
USE   Bachelors Degrees

Bachelors Degrees   *JUL. 1966*
    Postings: 1,624   GC: 340
UF   Baccalaureate Degrees
    Bachelor of Arts Degrees
    Bachelor of Science Degrees
    Three Year Bachelors Degrees #
BT   Degrees (Academic)
RT   Associate Degrees
    College Graduates
    Degree Requirements
    Doctoral Degrees
    External Degree Programs
    Masters Degrees
    Specialist in Education Degrees
    Undergraduate Study

Back to Basics   *SEP. 1982*
    Postings: 193   GC: 330
SN   Educational movement stressing basic
    skills, achievement, and accountability—
    begun in the early 1970s as a protest
    against school permissiveness and de-
    clining student performance
BT   Education
RT   Academic Standards
    Basic Skills
    Competency Based Education
    Conventional Instruction
    Educational Quality
    Minimum Competencies
    Traditional Schools

Background   *JUL. 1966*
    Postings: 599   GC: 120
SN   Sum of the regular and persistent in-
    fluences (experiences, conditions, cir-
    cumstances, events, etc.) contributing
    to the present development or character-
    istics of an individual, group, or organi-
    zation (Note: Use a more specific term if
    possible—do not confuse with "History")
NT   Cultural Background
    Educational Background
    Experience
    Parent Background
    Socioeconomic Background
    Teacher Background
RT   Biographical Inventories
    Credentials
    Environment
    History
    Individual Characteristics
    Individual Development
    Individual Differences
    Influences
    Opportunities
    Prerequisites
    Profiles
    Qualifications
    Reputation

Bacteria   *APR. 1990*
    Postings: 90   GC: 490
SN   Ubiquitous, prokaryotic microorganisms,
    variously involved in fermentation, pu-
    trefaction, infectious diseases, or nitro-

gen fixation—classified in the kingdom
Monera or, in earlier schemes, as Plantae
RT   Communicable Diseases
    Cytology
    Disease Control
    Diseases
    Epidemiology
    Fungi
    Hygiene
    Microbiology
    Monera
    Plants (Botany)
    Pollution
    Sanitation
    Viruses

Badminton   *JUN. 1984*
    Postings: 26   GC: 470
BT   Racquet Sports

Bahasa Indonesia
USE   Indonesian

Bakeries
USE   Bakery Industry

Bakery Industry   *JUN. 1977*
    Postings: 39   GC: 650
SN   Concerned with producing and market-
    ing baked goods (e.g., breads, cakes)
UF   Bakeries
BT   Industry
RT   Food
    Food Processing Occupations
    Food Service
    Occupational Home Economics

Ballads   *JAN. 1970*
    Postings: 40   GC: 430
BT   Literary Genres
    Lyric Poetry
    Songs
RT   Epics
    Odes
    Oral Tradition
    Sonnets

Ballet (1966 1980)
USE   Dance

Baltic Languages   *NOV. 1970*
    Postings: 17   GC: 440
NT   Latvian
    Lithuanian
BT   Indo European Languages
RT   Estonian

Baluchi   *JUL. 1966*
    Postings: 4   GC: 440
BT   Indo European Languages

Bands (Music)   *JUL. 1966*
    Postings: 322   GC: 420
UF   Marching Bands
RT   Applied Music
    Concerts
    Instrumentation and Orchestration
    Jazz
    Music
    Music Activities
    Music Techniques
    Musical Instruments
    Musicians
    Orchestras
    Popular Music
    Rock Music

Banking   *JUL. 1966*
    Postings: 641   GC: 620
UF   Banking Industry
BT   Industry
RT   Banking Vocabulary
    Business Education
    Capital

= Two or more Descriptors are used to represent this term.
The term's main entry shows the appropriate coordination.

Economics
Finance Occupations
Financial Services
Investment
Monetary Systems
Money Management
Student Loan Programs

Banking Industry
USE   Banking

Banking Vocabulary   *JUL. 1966*
Postings: 20   GC: 450
BT   Vocabulary
RT   Banking

Bantu Languages   *APR. 1970*
Postings: 94   GC: 440
NT   Bemba
Chinyanja
Ganda
Kirundi
Kituba
Lingala
Shona
Siswati
Swahili
BT   African Languages

Barbers   *JUL. 1966*
Postings: 32   GC: 640
BT   Service Workers

Barbiturates
USE   Sedatives

Bards
USE   Poets

Baroque Literature   *MAY 1970*
Postings: 15   GC: 430
SN   Literature of the late sixteenth to early
eighteenth centuries characterized by
elaborate, sometimes grotesque, orna-
mentation and complexity
BT   Literature
RT   Eighteenth Century Literature
Seventeenth Century Literature
Sixteenth Century Literature
World Literature

Barrier Free Environment (for Disabled)
USE   Accessibility (for Disabled)

Barristers
USE   Lawyers

Basaa   *JUN. 1971*
Postings: 3   GC: 440
BT   African Languages

Basal Reading   *MAR. 1980*
Postings: 893   GC: 460
SN   Instruction that develops reading skills
through the use of a series of reading
materials which are designed in sequen-
tial steps for successive levels of achieve-
ment (Note: Do not confuse with "Begin-
ning Reading")
BT   Reading
Reading Instruction
RT   Basic Vocabulary
Beginning Reading
Phonics
Reading Materials
Reading Programs
Sight Method
Sight Vocabulary

Baseball   *JUN. 1975*
Postings: 168   GC: 470
BT   Team Sports
RT   Softball

Bashfulness
USE   Shyness

Bashkir   *JUL. 1966*
Postings: 3   GC: 440
BT   Turkic Languages

Basic Business Education   *JUN. 1983*
Postings: 75   GC: 400
SN   Instruction or study in personal busi-
ness affairs—areas of concentration in-
clude legal knowledge, recordkeeping,
buying, and money management
UF   General Business Education
BT   Education
RT   Business Skills
Citizenship Education
Consumer Education
Daily Living Skills
Economics Education
Home Management
Money Management

Basic Language Patterns
USE   Language Patterns

Basic Reading (1967 1980)   *MAR. 1980*
Postings: 553   GC: 460
SN   Invalid Descriptor—used indiscriminately
in indexing—see such Descriptors as
"Basal Reading," "Beginning Reading,"
"Functional Reading," "Reading Readi-
ness," etc.

Basic Research
USE   Research

Basic Skills   *JUL. 1966*
Postings: 7,688   GC: 400
SN   Fundamental skills that are the basis
of later learning and achievement (Note:
Coordinate   with   subject-matter
Descriptors—do not confuse with "Mini-
mum Competencies")
UF   Fundamental Skills (School)
NT   Alphabetizing Skills
BT   Skills
RT   Adult Basic Education
Audiolingual Skills
Back to Basics
Basic Vocabulary
Basic Writing
Beginning Reading
Beginning Writing
Communication Skills
Developmental Studies Programs
Functional Literacy
Language Skills
Literacy
Literacy Education
Mathematics Skills
Minimum Competencies
Minimum Competency Testing
Numeracy
Reading Skills
Science Process Skills
Skill Development
Spatial Ability
Study Skills
Thinking Skills
Verbal Ability
Vocabulary Skills
Workplace Literacy
Writing Skills

Basic Vocabulary   *JUL. 1966*
Postings: 224   GC: 450
SN   Fundamental vocabulary considered es-
sential to effective comprehension and
expression (common to all fields and
subjects)
BT   Vocabulary
RT   Basal Reading
Basic Skills
Reading Comprehension
Reading Readiness
Sight Vocabulary

Vocabulary Skills
Word Lists

Basic Word Lists
USE   Word Lists

Basic Writing   *APR. 1990*
Postings: 494   GC: 400
SN   Developmental written composition or
remedial writing instruction concerned
with fundamental writing skills, includ-
ing grammar, punctuation, organization,
spelling, vocabulary, theme formulation,
and revision—also, basic writing for sec-
ond-language students (Note: Do not
confuse with basic writing for young
children, for which use "Beginning Writ-
ing")
UF   Developmental Writing
BT   Writing (Composition)
Writing Instruction
RT   Basic Skills
Developmental Studies Programs
Freshman Composition
Remedial Programs
Second Language Learning
Writing Apprehension
Writing Difficulties
Writing Laboratories
Writing Skills

Basketball   *FEB. 1978*
Postings: 217   GC: 470
BT   Team Sports
RT   Olympic Games

Basque   *JUL. 1966*
Postings: 61   GC: 440
UF   Euskara
BT   Languages

Bathrooms
USE   Toilet Facilities

Battered Women   *MAR. 1980*
Postings: 454   GC: 530
SN   Women who are victims of persistent
physical or emotional abuse by their
mates
UF   Abused Women
BT   Females
RT   Child Abuse
Elder Abuse
Emotional Abuse
Family Problems
Family Violence
Marital Instability
Rape
Sexual Abuse
Verbal Abuse
Victims of Crime
Violence

Batteries (Electric)
USE   Electric Batteries

Bayesian Statistics   *AUG. 1971*
Postings: 441   GC: 480
SN   Procedures that combine data from new
observations with prior observations or
estimates to derive new and more pre-
cise estimates
BT   Statistical Analysis
Statistics
RT   Adaptive Testing
Expectancy Tables
Hypothesis Testing
Nonparametric Statistics
Predictive Measurement
Probability
Statistical Inference
Statistical Significance

Beauticians
USE   Cosmetology

Beauty
USE   Aesthetic Values

Beauty Culture
USE   Cosmetology

Beauty Operators
USE   Cosmetology

Beginning Farmer Education
USE   Young Farmer Education

Beginning Principals   *AUG. 1997*
Postings: 101   GC: 360
SN   Certified administrators entering their ini-
tial career position as executive or ad-
ministrative officer of a school
UF   First Year Principals
BT   Administrators
School Personnel
RT   Assistant Principals
Instructional Leadership
Principals
School Administration
School Based Management
School Supervision

Beginning Reading   *JUL. 1966*
Postings: 3,621   GC: 460
SN   Initial activities, processes, or behaviors
involved in learning to read
BT   Reading
RT   Basal Reading
Basic Skills
Beginning Writing
Decoding (Reading)
Early Reading
Emergent Literacy
Initial Teaching Alphabet
Language Experience Approach
Phonics
Prereading Experience
Reading Readiness
Sight Method
Sight Vocabulary

Beginning Teacher Induction   *APR. 1990*
Postings: 768   GC: 320
SN   Structured processes or programs de-
signed to facilitate the initial inservice
teaching experience, usually involving
mentoring or peer support
UF   Entry Year Assistance (Teacher Induc-
tion)
BT   Teacher Orientation
RT   Beginning Teachers
College School Cooperation
Inservice Teacher Education
Internship Programs
Master Teachers
Mentors
Professional Development Schools
Teacher Certification
Teacher Interns
Teacher Supervision
Teaching Experience

Beginning Teachers   *JUL. 1966*
Postings: 2,715   GC: 360
SN   Certified teachers entering their first teach-
ing position
UF   First Year Teachers
BT   Teachers
RT   Alternative Teacher Certification
Beginning Teacher Induction
Master Teachers
Probationary Period
Teacher Certification
Teacher Employment

Beginning Workers
USE   Entry Workers

\# = Two or more Descriptors are used to represent this term.
The term's main entry shows the appropriate coordination.

Beginning Writing *AUG. 2000*
Postings: 176 GC: 400
SN Initial activities, processes, or behaviors involved in learning to write—usually applies to young children (Note: Do not confuse with "Basic Writing," which consists of instruction in fundamental skills, or "Freshman Composition," which is the instruction of first-year college students—see also the Identifier "Early Writing")
BT Writing (Composition)
RT Basic Skills
Beginning Reading
Childrens Writing
Emergent Literacy
Invented Spelling
Language Experience Approach
Writing Instruction
Writing Processes
Writing Readiness

Behavior *JUL. 1966*
Postings: 2,291 GC: 120
SN The aggregate of observable responses of an organism to internal and external stimuli (Note: Use a more specific term if possible)
UF Conduct (1966 1980)
NT Adjustment (to Environment)
Administrator Behavior
Adolescent Behavior
Affective Behavior
Animal Behavior
Assertiveness
Attachment Behavior
Child Behavior
Competition
Cooperation
Crying
Drinking
Drug Use
Exploratory Behavior
Group Behavior
Health Behavior
Hyperactivity
Imitation
Leadership Styles
Life Style
Modeling (Psychology)
Paranoid Behavior
Participation
Performance
Persistence
Physical Activity Level
Resistance (Psychology)
Response Style (Tests)
Responses
Self Control
Self Destructive Behavior
Smoking
Social Behavior
Spontaneous Behavior
Student Behavior
Substance Abuse
Teacher Behavior
Type A Behavior
Type B Behavior
RT Attention
Attitudes
Behavior Chaining
Behavior Change
Behavior Development
Behavior Disorders
Behavior Modification
Behavior Patterns
Behavior Problems
Behavior Rating Scales
Behavior Standards
Behavior Theories
Behavioral Objectives
Behavioral Sciences
Behaviorism
Counseling Theories
Ethology
Feedback
Human Dignity
Individual Power
Intention
Leadership
Motivation
Play

Protocol Materials
Psychology
Psychomotor Skills
Psychopathology
Self Congruence
Self Fulfilling Prophecies
Sleep
Sociology
Sportsmanship

Behavior Chaining *SEP. 1970*
Postings: 78 GC: 110
SN Process of learning a conditioned sequence of behaviors so that, when learned, the completion of one behavior provides a semiautomatic cue for the next, e.g., reciting a memorized poem (Note: Prior to Mar80, the Scope Note referred to "learning a behavior change")
UF Chain Reflexes (Behavior)
BT Learning Processes
RT Association (Psychology)
Associative Learning
Behavior
Behavior Modification
Contingency Management
Familiarity
Paired Associate Learning
Serial Learning

Behavior Change *JUL. 1966*
Postings: 8,481 GC: 120
SN Complete or partial alteration in the observable activities or responses of an organism (Note: Prior to Mar80, the Scope Note was restricted to changes "learned" by "persons")
BT Change
RT Attitude Change
Behavior
Behavior Development
Behavior Modification
Behavior Patterns
Behavioral Objectives
Change Strategies
Conditioning
Contingency Management
Habit Formation
Midlife Transitions
Modeling (Psychology)
Negative Practice
Nondirective Counseling
Personality Change

Behavior Development *JUL. 1966*
Postings: 1,389 GC: 120
NT Habit Formation
BT Individual Development
RT Adolescent Behavior
Animal Behavior
Attachment Behavior
Behavior
Behavior Change
Behaviorism
Bibliotherapy
Child Behavior
Developmental Delays
Developmental Psychology
Developmental Stages
Ethology
Exploratory Behavior
Nature Nurture Controversy
Object Manipulation
Pretend Play
Probationary Period
Self Actualization
Self Efficacy
Social Behavior

Behavior Disorders *JUN. 1983*
Postings: 2,347 GC: 230
SN Chronic or severe disorders of conduct, i.e., generally aberrant and unacceptable behaviors with or without serious underlying psychopathology (Note: Do not confuse with "Behavior Problems"—prior

to Jun83, "Behavior Problems" was not scoped and was frequently used for this concept)
BT Disabilities
RT Alcoholism
Antisocial Behavior
Attention Deficit Disorders
Autism
Behavior
Behavior Patterns
Behavior Problems
Clinical Psychology
Drug Addiction
Emotional Disturbances
Learning Problems
Mental Disorders
Neurological Impairments
Personality Problems
Problem Children
Psychiatry
Psychopathology
Recidivism
Self Destructive Behavior
Self Injurious Behavior
Suicide
Withdrawal (Psychology)

Behavior Modification *MAR. 1980*
Postings: 3,760 GC: 110
SN Alteration of behavior by the use of conditioning techniques (Note: Prior to Mar80, the instruction "Behavior Modification, USE Behavior Change" was carried in the Thesaurus)
UF Behavior Therapy
Behavioral Counseling (1967 1980)
Cognitive Behavior Modification #
NT Contingency Management
Desensitization
BT Conditioning
RT Behavior
Behavior Chaining
Behavior Change
Biofeedback
Classical Conditioning
Cognitive Restructuring
Counseling
Intervention
Operant Conditioning
Psychotherapy
Rational Emotive Therapy
Reality Therapy
Rehabilitation
Reinforcement
Self Control
Self Help Programs
Social Reinforcement
Special Education
Timeout
Token Economy
Transcendental Meditation

Behavior Patterns *JUL. 1966*
Postings: 9,099 GC: 120
SN Complex acts made up of distinguishable lesser acts
UF Patterned Behavior
NT Arousal Patterns
Reading Habits
Recidivism
Speech Habits
Study Habits
Type A Behavior
Type B Behavior
RT Behavior
Behavior Change
Behavior Disorders
Behavior Problems
Behavior Rating Scales
Behavioral Objectives
Coping
Deception
Ethology
Extraversion Introversion
Identification (Psychology)
Imitation
Pretend Play
Psychological Patterns
Sociobiology
Sportsmanship
Writing Processes

Behavior Problems *JUL. 1966*
Postings: 6,613 GC: 120
SN Transient or mild problems in conduct (Note: Do not confuse with "Behavior Disorders"—prior to Jun83, the use of this term was not restricted by a Scope Note)
UF Misbehavior (1966 1980)
BT Problems
RT Adjustment (to Environment)
Antisocial Behavior
Behavior
Behavior Disorders
Behavior Patterns
Discipline
Emotional Problems
Hyperactivity
Mental Disorders
Minimal Brain Dysfunction
Obedience
Paranoid Behavior
Personality Problems
Problem Children
Psychological Patterns
Psychopathology
Resistance (Psychology)
Self Control
Self Destructive Behavior
Student Problems
Withdrawal (Psychology)

Behavior Rating Scales *JUL. 1966*
Postings: 1,983 GC: 830
SN Devices used to observe and record the occurrence of specific behaviors (Note: Do not confuse with "Check Lists")
BT Rating Scales
RT Behavior
Behavior Patterns
Classroom Observation Techniques
Personality Assessment
Personality Measures
Precision Teaching
Student Evaluation

Behavior Standards *JUL. 1966*
Postings: 838 GC: 520
UF Normative Behavior
Social Norms #
NT Codes of Ethics
BT Standards
RT Behavior
Discipline Policy
Ideology
Loyalty Oaths
Probationary Period
Social Control

Behavior Theories *JUL. 1966*
Postings: 1,723 GC: 810
NT Adaptation Level Theory
Attribution Theory
Mediation Theory
BT Theories
RT Behavior
Counseling Theories
Personality Theories
Social Theories

Behavior Therapy
USE Behavior Modification

Behavioral Analysis
USE Behavioral Science Research

Behavioral Contracts
USE Performance Contracts

Behavioral Counseling (1967 1980)
USE Behavior Modification

Behavioral Objectives *JUL. 1966*
Postings: 10,883 GC: 310
SN Aims of instruction or any learning activity stated as actual performance criteria

---

= Two or more Descriptors are used to represent this term.
The term's main entry shows the appropriate coordination.

or as observable descriptions of measurable behavior
UF   Learning Objectives
     Performance Objectives
NT   Affective Objectives
     Cognitive Objectives
     Psychomotor Objectives
BT   Objectives
RT   Behavior
     Behavior Change
     Behavior Patterns
     Behaviorism
     Competency Based Education
     Competency Based Teacher Education
     Contingency Management
     Continuous Progress Plan
     Counseling Objectives
     Course Objectives
     Guidance Objectives
     Learning Modules
     Learning Strategies
     Mastery Learning
     Mastery Tests
     Outcome Based Education
     Performance Contracts
     Performance Technology
     Process Education
     Protocol Materials
     Student Behavior
     Student Centered Curriculum
     Training Objectives

Behavioral Science Research   *JUL. 1966*
     Postings: 5,183   GC: 810
SN   Basic, applied, and developmental research conducted to advance knowledge in the behavioral sciences (Note: As of Oct81, use as a minor Descriptor for examples of this kind of research—use as a major Descriptor only as the subject of a document)
UF   Behavioral Analysis
NT   Integration Studies
     Psychological Studies
BT   Research
RT   Architectural Research
     Behavioral Sciences
     Communication Research
     Educational Research
     Exceptional Child Research
     Interaction Process Analysis
     Language Universals
     Naturalistic Observation
     Organizational Development
     Social Science Research

Behavioral Sciences   *JUL. 1966*
     Postings: 897   GC: 400
UF   Behavioral Technology
NT   Ethology
     Psychology
     Sociobiology
     Sociology
BT   Sciences
RT   Behavior
     Behavioral Science Research
     Social Sciences

Behavioral Self Management
USE   Self Management

Behavioral Situation Films
USE   Protocol Materials

Behavioral Technology
USE   Behavioral Sciences

Behaviorism   *AUG. 1986*
     Postings: 315   GC: 120
SN   School of psychological thought, founded by J.B. Watson in 1913, concerned with the observable, tangible, objective facts of behavior, rather than with subjective phenomena such as thoughts, emotions, or impulses—contemporary behaviorism also emphasizes the study of mental states such as feelings and fantasies to

the extent that they can be directly observed and measured
UF   Behaviorist Psychology
BT   Psychology
RT   Behavior
     Behavior Development
     Behavioral Objectives
     Cognitive Psychology
     Conditioning
     Developmental Psychology
     Experimental Psychology
     Learning Theories
     Psychometrics
     Reinforcement
     Social Psychology

Behaviorist Psychology
USE   Behaviorism

Beliefs   *JUL. 1966*
     Postings: 2,912   GC: 120
SN   Ideas, doctrines, tenets, etc. That are accepted as true on grounds which are not immediately susceptible to rigorous proof
UF   Faith
BT   Attitudes
RT   Attitude Measures
     Credibility
     Dissent
     Dogmatism
     Ideology
     Opinions
     Religion
     Spirituality
     Trust (Psychology)
     Values
     World Views

Believability
USE   Credibility

Belorussian
USE   Bielorussian

Bemba   *AUG. 1969*
     Postings: 8   GC: 440
UF   Chibemba
     Icibemba
BT   Bantu Languages

Benchmarking   *FEB. 1998*
     Postings: 268   GC: 820
SN   Systematically measuring and comparing the operations and outcomes of organizations, systems, processes, etc., against agreed upon "best-in-class" frames of reference
BT   Evaluation Methods
RT   Comparative Analysis
     Educational Quality
     Performance
     Quality Control
     Standards

Benefit Cost Analysis
USE   Cost Effectiveness

Bengali   *JUL. 1966*
     Postings: 37   GC: 440
BT   Indo European Languages

Berber Languages   *AUG. 1968*
     Postings: 19   GC: 440
NT   Kabyle
     Riff
BT   Afro Asiatic Languages

Bereavement   *JUN. 1996*
     Postings: 182   GC: 510
SN   Deprivation or loss, especially or loved ones by death (Note: Prior to Jun96, this concept was frequently indexed by "Grief")

RT   Death
     Grief
     Widowed

Bias   *DEC. 1969*
     Postings: 2,210   GC: 540
SN   An inclination, or a lack of balance (Note: Use a more specific term if possible)
UF   Prejudice
NT   Social Bias
     Statistical Bias
     Test Bias
     Textbook Bias
RT   Agenda Setting
     Attitudes
     Egocentrism
     Mental Rigidity
     Objectivity

Bibles
USE   Biblical Literature

Biblical Literature   *JUL. 1966*
     Postings: 311   GC: 430
UF   Bibles
BT   Literature
RT   Ancient History
     Christianity
     Classical Literature
     Judaism
     Religion

Bibliocounseling
USE   Bibliotherapy

Bibliographic Citations (1969 1980)
USE   Citations (References)

Bibliographic Control
USE   Cataloging

Bibliographic Coupling   *AUG. 1968*
     Postings: 67   GC: 710
SN   Application of citation analysis in which documents are related by virtue of common bibliographic citations
BT   Citation Analysis
RT   Bibliographies
     Citation Indexes
     Citations (References)
     Relevance (Information Retrieval)

Bibliographic Databases   *DEC. 1987*
     Postings: 525   GC: 710
SN   Organized collections of machine-readable records that describe books, journal articles, reports, or other primary sources of information
BT   Databases
RT   Bibliographic Records
     Bibliographic Utilities
     Library Automation
     Library Catalogs
     Online Catalogs

Bibliographic Instruction
USE   Library Instruction

Bibliographic Records   *DEC. 1987*
     Postings: 335   GC: 720
SN   Records in a database or library catalog that describe a bibliographic item (book, film, etc.)—generally containing author, title, and publication information and often enhanced with abstracts and/or subject terms (Note: For references to other works within bibliographic items, use "Citations (References)," which, prior to Dec87, was sometimes used for "Bibliographic Records")
BT   Records (Forms)
RT   Authority Control (Information)
     Bibliographic Databases

Cataloging
Library Catalogs

Bibliographic References
USE   Citations (References)

Bibliographic Utilities   *APR. 1986*
     Postings: 288   GC: 710
SN   Online library networking organizations with large bibliographic databases that are shared by participating libraries for a variety of technical purposes, including cataloging, interlibrary loans, acquisitions, and authority file control (Note: See also such Identifiers as "OCLC," "Research Libraries Information Network," "Washington Library Network," and "University of Toronto Library Automation Systems")
BT   Library Networks
     Organizations (Groups)
RT   Bibliographic Databases
     Library Automation
     Library Technical Processes
     Online Systems
     Online Vendors

Bibliographies   *JUL. 1966*
     Postings: 9,879   GC: 720
SN   Descriptive lists of books or other printed materials, which are written by one author, during one period, on one subject, produced by one printer and/or publisher, or located in one place (Note: Corresponds to Pubtype code 131—do not use except as the subject of a document)
UF   Booklists (1967 1980)
     Literature Searches
NT   Annotated Bibliographies
BT   Reference Materials
RT   Anthologies
     Bibliographic Coupling
     Books
     Citation Analysis
     Citations (References)
     Discographies
     Filmographies
     Indexes
     Library Catalogs
     Literature Reviews
     State of the Art Reviews
     Union Catalogs

Bibliometrics   *AUG. 1986*
     Postings: 257   GC: 820
SN   The application of mathematical and statistical methods in the study of bodies of writings to reveal the historical development of subject fields and patterns of authorship, publication, and use
UF   Statistical Bibliography
NT   Citation Analysis
BT   Documentation
RT   Books
     Cataloging
     Classification
     Cluster Grouping
     Indexing
     Information Sources
     Information Utilization
     Library Collection Development
     Literature Reviews
     Periodicals
     Statistical Analysis

Bibliotherapy   *JUL. 1966*
     Postings: 468   GC: 230
SN   Use of selected reading and related materials for therapeutic purposes in physical medicine, mental health, and education
UF   Bibliocounseling
     Reading Therapy
BT   Therapy
RT   Behavior Development
     Psychotherapy
     Reading

= Two or more Descriptors are used to represent this term.
The term's main entry shows the appropriate coordination.

Bicultural Education
USE   Multicultural Education

Bicultural Training
USE   Cross Cultural Training

Biculturalism   *JUL. 1969*
         Postings: 1,438   GC: 560
BT   Cultural Pluralism
RT   Acculturation
         Bidialectalism
         Bilingualism
         Cross Cultural Studies
         Cross Cultural Training
         Cultural Awareness
         Cultural Background
         Cultural Context
         Cultural Differences
         Cultural Influences
         Cultural Interrelationships
         Culture
         Culture Conflict
         Culture Contact
         Ethnic Groups
         French Canadians
         Intercultural Communication
         Intercultural Programs
         Minority Groups
         Multicultural Education
         Sociocultural Patterns
         Spanish Speaking

Bicycling   *FEB. 1978*
         Postings: 121   GC: 470
BT   Physical Activities
RT   Athletics
         Olympic Games
         Outdoor Activities
         Recreational Activities

Bidialectalism   *OCT. 1983*
         Postings: 83   GC: 450
SN   Familiarity with and use of two dialects
         of the same language
RT   Biculturalism
         Bilingualism
         Black Dialects
         Code Switching (Language)
         Cross Cultural Studies
         Dialect Studies
         Dialects
         Diglossia
         Intercultural Communication
         Interference (Language)
         Language Usage
         Language Variation
         Minority Groups
         Mutual Intelligibility
         Native Language Instruction
         Native Speakers
         Nonstandard Dialects
         Psycholinguistics
         Regional Dialects
         Social Dialects
         Sociolinguistics

Bids   *FEB. 1970*
         Postings: 253   GC: 620
UF   Competitive Bidding
         Construction Bidding
RT   Contracts
         Educational Economics
         Educational Finance
         Expenditures
         Grantsmanship
         Program Proposals
         Proposal Writing
         Purchasing
         School Construction

Bielorussian   *JUL. 1966*
         Postings: 9   GC: 440
UF   Belorussian
         Byelorussian
BT   Slavic Languages

Bigotry
USE   Social Discrimination

Bikol   *SEP. 1968*
         Postings: 8   GC: 440
UF   Viracnon
BT   Indonesian Languages

Bilingual Education   *OCT. 1968*
         Postings: 7,319   GC: 330
SN   Encouragement of bilingualism through
         the teaching of regular school courses in
         both the national language and a second
         language (Note: Use a more precise term
         if possible)
BT   Education
RT   Alternate Day Schedules
         Bilingual Education Programs
         Bilingual Instructional Materials
         Bilingual Schools
         Bilingual Students
         Bilingual Teacher Aides
         Bilingual Teachers
         Bilingualism
         Educational Policy
         English (Second Language)
         Full Day Half Day Schedules
         Immersion Programs
         Intercultural Programs
         Language Dominance
         Language Enrichment
         Language Maintenance
         Language of Instruction
         Language Planning
         Limited English Speaking
         Mexican American Education
         Migrant Adult Education
         Migrant Education
         Multicultural Education
         Multicultural Textbooks
         Multilingualism
         Non English Speaking
         Official Languages
         Second Language Instruction
         Second Language Learning
         Second Languages

Bilingual Education Programs   *AUG. 1982*
         Postings: 1,347   GC: 450
SN   Activities that offer content area instruc-
         tion in two languages—appreciation of
         participants' cultural heritage is empha-
         sized, and native speakers of both lan-
         guages may be present—attention is
         given to developing the academic skills
         of minority students while they learn the
         language of the majority culture (Note:
         Do not confuse with "Second Language
         Programs")
BT   Programs
RT   Bilingual Education
         Bilingual Instructional Materials
         Bilingual Schools
         Bilingual Teacher Aides
         Bilingual Teachers
         Bilingualism
         English (Second Language)
         Intercultural Programs
         Language Maintenance
         Language of Instruction
         Limited English Speaking
         Native Language Instruction
         Native Speakers
         Non English Speaking
         Second Language Instruction
         Second Language Programs

Bilingual Instructional Materials   *AUG. 1982*
         Postings: 277   GC: 730
SN   Print and/or nonprint educational mate-
         rials developed specifically for use with
         students who need proficiency in two
         languages
BT   Instructional Materials
         Multilingual Materials
RT   Bilingual Education
         Bilingual Education Programs
         Bilingual Schools
         Bilingualism

         Language Maintenance
         Language of Instruction
         Multicultural Textbooks
         Native Language Instruction
         Second Language Instruction
         Second Language Learning
         Second Languages

Bilingual Materials
USE   Multilingual Materials

Bilingual Schools   *JUL. 1966*
         Postings: 293   GC: 340
BT   Schools
RT   Bilingual Education
         Bilingual Education Programs
         Bilingual Instructional Materials
         Bilingual Teacher Aides
         Bilingual Teachers
         Bilingualism

Bilingual Students   *JUL. 1966*
         Postings: 1,981   GC: 360
SN   Students who can communicate effec-
         tively in more than one language (Note:
         Do not confuse with "Limited English
         Speaking" or "Non English Speaking")
BT   Students
RT   Bilingual Education
         Bilingual Teacher Aides
         Bilingual Teachers
         Bilingualism
         Code Switching (Language)
         Immersion Programs
         Language Dominance
         Native Speakers
         Spanish Speaking

Bilingual Teacher Aides   *JUL. 1966*
         Postings: 115   GC: 360
SN   Teacher aides who can communicate
         effectively in more than one language
BT   Teacher Aides
RT   Bilingual Education
         Bilingual Education Programs
         Bilingual Schools
         Bilingual Students
         Bilingual Teachers
         Bilingualism
         English (Second Language)
         Language Dominance
         Limited English Speaking
         Native Speakers
         Non English Speaking
         School Aides
         Second Languages

Bilingual Teachers   *JUL. 1966*
         Postings: 646   GC: 360
SN   Teachers who can communicate effec-
         tively in more than one language
BT   Teachers
RT   Bilingual Education
         Bilingual Education Programs
         Bilingual Schools
         Bilingual Students
         Bilingual Teacher Aides
         Bilingualism
         English (Second Language)
         Language Dominance
         Limited English Speaking
         Native Speakers
         Non English Speaking
         Second Languages

Bilingualism   *JUL. 1966*
         Postings: 3,884   GC: 450
RT   Biculturalism
         Bidialectalism
         Bilingual Education
         Bilingual Education Programs
         Bilingual Instructional Materials
         Bilingual Schools
         Bilingual Students
         Bilingual Teacher Aides
         Bilingual Teachers
         Child Language
         Code Switching (Language)

         Cross Cultural Studies
         Cultural Pluralism
         Diglossia
         English (Second Language)
         English Only Movement
         French Canadians
         Immersion Programs
         Intercultural Communication
         Interference (Language)
         Language Dominance
         Language Maintenance
         Language Minorities
         Language Planning
         Language Proficiency
         Language Research
         Language Skill Attrition
         Languages
         Limited English Speaking
         Minority Groups
         Modern Languages
         Monolingualism
         Multicultural Education
         Multilingual Materials
         Multilingualism
         Native Speakers
         Psycholinguistics
         Second Language Learning
         Second Languages
         Sociolinguistics
         Spanish Speaking

Bini   *JUL. 1966*
         Postings: 8   GC: 440
BT   African Languages

Biochemical Effects
USE   Biochemistry

Biochemical Tests
USE   Biochemistry

Biochemistry   *AUG. 1968*
         Postings: 1,346   GC: 490
UF   Biochemical Effects
         Biochemical Tests
         Physiological Chemistry
BT   Biological Sciences
         Chemistry
RT   Biology
         Biomedicine
         Biotechnology
         Chromatography
         Cytology
         Enzymes
         Genetic Engineering
         Human Body
         Medicine
         Metabolism
         Molecular Biology
         Nucleic Acids
         Organic Chemistry
         Physical Sciences
         Physiology
         Plant Growth
         Rh Factors
         Toxicology

Biodiversity   *JUL. 2000*
         Postings: 79   GC: 490
SN   The variety of living organisms, encom-
         passing genetic differences within spe-
         cies to entire ecosystems
UF   Biological Diversity
         Diversity (Biology)
         Genetic Diversity
RT   Biological Sciences
         Conservation (Environment)
         Ecology
         Endangered Species
         Environmental Education
         Evolution
         Genetics
         Habitats
         Sustainable Development
         Wildlife

= Two or more Descriptors are used to represent this term.
The term's main entry shows the appropriate coordination.

Bioethics   *JAN. 1985*
       Postings: 111   GC: 430
SN   Discipline dealing with the moral and social implications of practices and developments in the biological sciences and medicine
BT   Ethics
RT   Biological Sciences
       Euthanasia
       Medicine
       Moral Values
       Social Biology

Biofeedback   *AUG. 1982*
       Postings: 202   GC: 490
SN   Auditory, visual, or other sensory feedback on physiological processes or states (e.g., heart rate, muscle tension, brain waves, skin temperature) in order to facilitate control of these normally involuntary functions
BT   Biological Sciences
       Feedback
RT   Behavior Modification
       Biology
       Biomechanics
       Bionics
       Cardiovascular System
       Conditioning
       Electroencephalography
       Health
       Human Body
       Metabolism
       Muscular System
       Physiology
       Psychophysiology
       Reinforcement
       Relaxation Training
       Self Control
       Self Help Programs
       Stimulation
       Transcendental Meditation

Biographical Inventories   *MAY 1971*
       Postings: 387   GC: 830
SN   Sets of questions used to gather information on an individual's background
UF   Biographical Profiles
BT   Measures (Individuals)
RT   Background
       Biographies
       Case Records
       Individual Characteristics
       Interest Inventories
       Profiles
       Questionnaires
       Surveys

Biographical Profiles
USE   Biographical Inventories

Biographies   *JUL. 1966*
       Postings: 2,423   GC: 730
SN   Written histories of people's lives (Note: Prior to Mar80, the instruction "Life Histories, USE Biographical Inventories" was carried in the Thesaurus)
UF   Hagiographies (1971 1980)
       Life Histories
NT   Autobiographies
BT   Literary Genres
       Nonfiction
RT   Biographical Inventories
       Personal Narratives

Biological Diversity
USE   Biodiversity

Biological Influences   *JUL. 1966*
       Postings: 829   GC: 120
NT   Rh Factors
BT   Influences
RT   Biology
       Environmental Influences
       Evolution
       Genetic Engineering
       Medicine
       Nature Nurture Controversy
       Perinatal Influences
       Prenatal Influences
       Sexual Identity

Biological Parents   *OCT. 1983*
       Postings: 149   GC: 510
SN   The genetic parents of a child, in contrast to adoptive, foster, and psychological parents or stepparents
UF   Birth Parents
       Natural Parents
BT   Parents
RT   Adopted Children
       Adoption
       Adoptive Parents
       Biology
       Foster Children
       Foster Family
       Genetics
       Stepfamily

Biological Sciences   *JUL. 1966*
       Postings: 2,175   GC: 490
UF   Life Sciences
NT   Anatomy
       Biochemistry
       Biofeedback
       Biology
       Biomedicine
       Biophysics
       Biotechnology
       Botany
       Cytology
       Ecology
       Embryology
       Ethology
       Genetics
       Mycology
       Physiology
       Sociobiology
       Zoology
BT   Natural Sciences
RT   Biodiversity
       Bioethics
       Conservation Education
       Environmental Education
       Human Body
       Wildlife

Biology   *JUL. 1966*
       Postings: 7,863   GC: 490
UF   Biology Instruction (1966 1980) #
       Human Biology
NT   Marine Biology
       Microbiology
       Molecular Biology
       Radiation Biology
       Social Biology
BT   Biological Sciences
RT   Anatomy
       Biochemistry
       Biofeedback
       Biological Influences
       Biological Parents
       Biomechanics
       Biomedicine
       Biophysics
       Biotechnology
       Botany
       Chromatography
       Cytology
       Dissection
       Ecology
       Embryology
       Enzymes
       Evolution
       Genetic Engineering
       Genetics
       Heredity
       Human Body
       Metabolism
       Mycology
       Nucleic Acids
       Physiology
       Pregnancy
       Race
       Radioisotopes
       Rh Factors
       Scientific Research
       Sex

Biology Instruction (1966 1980)
USE   Biology
AND   Science Instruction

Biomechanics   *MAR. 1978*
       Postings: 159   GC: 490
SN   Science of the action of forces, internal and external, on living things
BT   Biophysics
RT   Biofeedback
       Biology
       Bionics
       Exercise Physiology
       Force
       Human Body
       Human Factors Engineering
       Kinesthetic Perception
       Kinetics
       Motor Development
       Motor Reactions
       Movement Education
       Physical Activity Level
       Physiology
       Sports Medicine

Biomedical Equipment   *JUL. 1966*
       Postings: 133   GC: 910
BT   Equipment
RT   Assistive Devices (for Disabled)
       Electroencephalography
       Laboratory Equipment
       Measurement Equipment
       Medical Laboratory Assistants
       Medicine
       Surgery
       Wheelchairs

Biomedical Equipment Technicians
USE   Medical Laboratory Assistants

Biomedical Research
USE   Biomedicine

Biomedicine   *MAR. 1980*
       Postings: 266   GC: 210
SN   Branch of science concerned with the capacity of human beings to survive and function in specific environments
UF   Biomedical Research
BT   Biological Sciences
       Medicine
RT   Biochemistry
       Biology
       Biophysics
       Biotechnology
       Human Factors Engineering

Bionics   *AUG. 1971*
       Postings: 22   GC: 490
SN   Science which deals with the transformation of the functions of living systems into electronic, mechanical, or other analogs
UF   Intellectronics
NT   Robotics
BT   Biophysics
RT   Artificial Intelligence
       Biofeedback
       Biomechanics
       Cybernetics
       Human Factors Engineering
       Man Machine Systems

Biophysics   *AUG. 1968*
       Postings: 90   GC: 490
SN   Application of physical methods and principles to biological problems
NT   Biomechanics
       Bionics
BT   Biological Sciences
       Physics
RT   Biology
       Biomedicine

Soil Science
Zoology

Biotechnology   *DEC. 1992*
       Postings: 223   GC: 490
SN   The use of biological organisms, systems, or processes to make or modify products
BT   Biological Sciences
       Technology
RT   Agricultural Production
       Biochemistry
       Biology
       Biomedicine
       Chemical Engineering
       Cytology
       Enzymes
       Genetic Engineering
       Microbiology
       Molecular Biology
       Pharmacology
       Power Technology
       Technological Advancement
       Waste Disposal

Biracial Committees   *JUL. 1966*
       Postings: 11   GC: 540
BT   Committees
RT   Community Cooperation
       Racial Integration
       Racial Relations

Biracial Elementary Schools (1966 1980)
USE   School Desegregation

Biracial Persons
USE   Multiracial Persons

Biracial Schools (1966 1980)
USE   School Desegregation

Biracial Secondary Schools (1966 1980)
USE   School Desegregation

Bird Studies
USE   Ornithology

Birds   *DEC. 1992*
       Postings: 99   GC: 410
SN   Warm-blooded, egg-laying vertebrates of the class Aves, having feathers, wings, scaly legs, and a beak
BT   Animals
RT   Ornithology
       Wildlife

Birth   *OCT. 1977*
       Postings: 343   GC: 120
UF   Childbirth
       Labor (Childbirth)
       Parturition
RT   Birth Order
       Birth Rate
       Birth Weight
       Births to Single Women
       First Born
       Obstetrics
       Perinatal Influences
       Physiology
       Pregnancy
       Reproduction (Biology)
       Sex Education

Birth Control
USE   Contraception

Birth Defects
USE   Congenital Impairments

Diffusion (Physics)
Human Body
Physical Sciences
Physiology
Radiation Biology

= Two or more Descriptors are used to represent this term.
The term's main entry shows the appropriate coordination.

Birth Order
MAY 1969
Postings: 428   GC: 120
SN   (Note: For specificity, use the Descriptor "First Born"—see also the Identifiers "Second Born," "Middle Born," and "Last Born")
NT   First Born
BT   Family Structure
RT   Birth
     Family (Sociological Unit)
     Sibling Relationship

Birth Parents
USE   Biological Parents

Birth Rate
JUL. 1974
Postings: 787   GC: 550
SN   Ratio between the number of births and the number of individuals in a specified population
UF   Fertility Rate
     Natality
BT   Demography
     Incidence
RT   Baby Boomers
     Birth
     Births to Single Women
     Childlessness
     Contraception
     Family Planning
     Family Size
     Mortality Rate
     Overpopulation
     Population Distribution
     Population Growth
     Population Trends
     Pregnancy
     Reproduction (Biology)

Birth Weight
OCT. 1983
Postings: 377   GC: 120
SN   Body weight at time of birth
BT   Body Weight
RT   Birth
     Neonates
     Perinatal Influences
     Premature Infants
     Prenatal Influences

Births to Single Women
DEC. 1995
Postings: 161   GC: 520
UF   Illegitimacy
     Illegitimate Births (1967 1995)
     Nonmarital Childbirth
     Out of Wedlock Births
     Single Mother Births
     Unmarried Mother Births
RT   Birth
     Birth Rate
     Contraception
     Fatherless Family
     One Parent Family
     Parent Child Relationship
     Pregnancy
     Unwed Mothers

Bisexuality
JUN. 1998
Postings: 138   GC: 120
SN   Sexual responsiveness to both sexes
BT   Sexuality
RT   Homophobia
     Homosexuality
     Lesbianism
     Sexual Orientation

Bituminous Coal
USE   Coal

Black Achievement
JUL. 1977
Postings: 649   GC: 330
SN   Accomplishments by blacks in the areas of education, politics, social life, etc.
UF   Negro Achievement (1966 1977)
BT   Achievement
RT   Black Education
     Black Employment
     Black History

     Black Institutions
     Black Leadership
     Black Power
     Black Studies
     Blacks
     Educational Mobility
     Occupational Mobility
     Racial Factors
     Racial Integration
     Social Mobility

Black Americans
USE   Blacks

Black and White Films
USE   Films

Black Attitudes
JUL. 1977
Postings: 1,110   GC: 520
UF   Negro Attitudes (1966 1977)
BT   Attitudes
RT   Black Community
     Black Culture
     Black Power
     Blacks
     Racial Attitudes
     Racial Identification

Black Businesses
JUL. 1977
Postings: 93   GC: 650
UF   Negro Businesses (1967 1977)
BT   Business
RT   Black Employment
     Blacks

Black Children
USE   Black Youth

Black Colleges
JUL. 1977
Postings: 1,558   GC: 340
SN   Colleges whose enrollments are, or have traditionally been, predominantly black
UF   Historically Black Colleges
     Negro Colleges (1968 1977)
BT   Black Institutions
     Colleges
RT   Black Education
     Black Students
     Black Teachers
     Blacks
     College Segregation
     Developing Institutions

Black Community
AUG. 1968
Postings: 1,204   GC: 520
UF   Negro Community
BT   Community
RT   Black Attitudes
     Black Culture
     Black Institutions
     Black Power
     Black Studies
     Blacks
     Community Influence
     Ethnic Groups
     Socioeconomic Influences

Black Culture
JUL. 1977
Postings: 1,711   GC: 560
UF   Black Subculture
     Negro Culture (1966 1977)
BT   Culture
RT   African Culture
     African History
     Afrocentrism
     Black Attitudes
     Black Community
     Black Dialects
     Black Family
     Black History
     Black Influences
     Black Institutions
     Black Literature
     Black Studies
     Blacks
     Latin American Culture

     North American Culture
     Slavery

Black Dialects
JUL. 1977
Postings: 1,177   GC: 450
UF   Black English
     Ebonics
     Negro Dialects (1966 1977)
BT   Dialects
RT   Bidialectalism
     Black Culture
     Blacks
     Nonstandard Dialects
     Regional Dialects
     Social Dialects
     Urban Language

Black Education
JUL. 1977
Postings: 1,838   GC: 330
SN   Education of black people (Note: Do not confuse with "Black Studies")
UF   Negro Education (1966 1977)
BT   Education
RT   Black Achievement
     Black Colleges
     Black Institutions
     Black Students
     Black Studies
     Black Teachers
     Blacks
     Racially Balanced Schools
     School Desegregation
     School Segregation

Black Employment
JUL. 1977
Postings: 568   GC: 630
UF   Negro Employment (1966 1977)
BT   Employment
RT   Black Achievement
     Black Businesses
     Blacks

Black English
USE   Black Dialects

Black Family
OCT. 1983
Postings: 358   GC: 520
BT   Family (Sociological Unit)
RT   Black Culture
     Black Mothers
     Black Studies
     Blacks
     Extended Family
     Family Life
     Family Structure
     Kinship
     Slavery

Black History
JUL. 1977
Postings: 1,737   GC: 430
UF   Negro History (1966 1977)
BT   History
RT   African History
     Afrocentrism
     Black Achievement
     Black Culture
     Black Influences
     Black Literature
     Black Studies
     Blacks
     Latin American History
     North American History
     Racial Relations
     Racial Segregation
     Slavery
     United States History

Black Housing (1977 1980)
MAR. 1980
Postings: 59   GC: 550
SN   Invalid Descriptor—used inconsistently in indexing—see "Housing Discrimination," "Residential Patterns," or "Homeowners," in coordination with appropriate "black" term(s)

Black Influences
MAR. 1980
Postings: 578   GC: 520
SN   Influences of blacks on society (Note: The uses of "Negro Role" and "Black Role" were not restricted by scope notes)
UF   Black Role (1977 1980)
     Negro Role (1966 1977)
BT   Influences
RT   Black Culture
     Black History
     Black Leadership
     Black Organizations
     Black Power
     Black Studies
     Blacks
     Minority Group Influences

Black Institutions
JUL. 1977
Postings: 195   GC: 520
SN   Institutions whose ownership, leadership, and membership is primarily black (Note: Prior to Mar80, the use of this term was not restricted by a Scope Note)
UF   Negro Institutions (1966 1977)
NT   Black Colleges
BT   Institutions
RT   Black Achievement
     Black Community
     Black Culture
     Black Education
     Black Organizations
     Black Studies
     Blacks

Black Leadership
JUL. 1977
Postings: 588   GC: 540
UF   Negro Leadership (1966 1977)
BT   Leadership
RT   Black Achievement
     Black Influences
     Black Organizations
     Black Power
     Blacks
     Civil Rights
     Leadership Training

Black Literature
JUL. 1977
Postings: 1,037   GC: 430
UF   Negro Literature (1968 1977)
BT   Literature
RT   African History
     African Literature
     Black Culture
     Black History
     Black Studies
     Blacks
     Latin American Literature
     United States Literature

Black Mothers
JUL. 1977
Postings: 282   GC: 510
UF   Negro Mothers (1966 1977)
BT   Blacks
     Mothers
RT   Black Family

Black Nationalism
USE   Black Power

Black Organizations
JUL. 1977
Postings: 217   GC: 520
UF   Negro Organizations (1966 1977)
BT   Organizations (Groups)
RT   Black Influences
     Black Institutions
     Black Leadership
     Black Power
     Blacks
     Civil Rights

Black Population Trends
JUL. 1977
Postings: 155   GC: 550
UF   Negro Population Trends (1966 1977)
BT   Population Trends
RT   Blacks
     Ethnic Distribution
     Racial Distribution

= Two or more Descriptors are used to represent this term.
The term's main entry shows the appropriate coordination.

Black Power
AUG. 1968
Postings: 521　　GC: 540
- UF　Black Nationalism
- RT　Black Achievement
- 　　Black Attitudes
- 　　Black Community
- 　　Black Influences
- 　　Black Leadership
- 　　Black Organizations
- 　　Black Studies
- 　　Blacks
- 　　Civil Rights
- 　　Ethnicity
- 　　Group Unity
- 　　Nationalism
- 　　Political Power
- 　　Power Structure
- 　　Racial Identification
- 　　Racial Relations
- 　　Segregationist Organizations
- 　　Self Determination

Black Role (1977 1980)
- USE　Black Influences

Black Stereotypes
JUL. 1977
Postings: 414　　GC: 540
- SN　Unreflective, oversimplified, or unfounded beliefs based on the premise that all blacks are typified by, or conform to, an unvarying pattern of character, characteristics, etc. (Note: Prior to Mar80, this term was not restricted by a Scope Note)
- UF　Negro Stereotypes (1966 1977)
- BT　Ethnic Stereotypes
- RT　Blacks
- 　　Racial Attitudes
- 　　Racial Bias
- 　　Racial Differences
- 　　Racial Identification

Black Students
JUL. 1977
Postings: 7,257　　GC: 360
- UF　Negro Students (1966 1977)
- BT　Blacks
- 　　Students
- RT　Black Colleges
- 　　Black Education
- 　　Black Youth

Black Studies
JUL. 1977
Postings: 1,297　　GC: 400
- SN　Curriculum or subject area encompassing the history and contemporary social, political, and cultural situation of blacks
- UF　African American Studies (1969 1977)
- 　　Negro Studies
- BT　Ethnic Studies
- RT　African History
- 　　African Studies
- 　　Afrocentrism
- 　　American Studies
- 　　Apartheid
- 　　Black Achievement
- 　　Black Community
- 　　Black Culture
- 　　Black Education
- 　　Black Family
- 　　Black History
- 　　Black Influences
- 　　Black Institutions
- 　　Black Literature
- 　　Black Power
- 　　Blacks
- 　　Cultural Background
- 　　Cultural Education
- 　　Cultural Images
- 　　Cultural Traits
- 　　Multicultural Education
- 　　Racial Identification
- 　　Slavery
- 　　United States History

Black Subculture
- USE　Black Culture

Black Teachers
JUL. 1977
Postings: 690　　GC: 360
- UF　Negro Teachers (1966 1977)
- BT　Blacks
- 　　Teachers
- RT　Black Colleges
- 　　Black Education
- 　　Minority Group Teachers

Black White Relations
- USE　Racial Relations

Black Youth
JUL. 1977
Postings: 1,684　　GC: 510
- SN　(Note: Coordinate with an appropriate age or educational level Descriptor)
- UF　Black Children
- 　　Negro Youth (1966 1977)
- BT　Blacks
- 　　Youth
- RT　Black Students
- 　　Minority Group Children

Blackboards
- USE　Chalkboards

Blacks
JUL. 1977
Postings: 10,335　　GC: 560
- UF　African Americans
- 　　Afro Americans
- 　　American Negroes
- 　　Black Americans
- 　　Negroes (1966 1977)
- NT　Black Mothers
- 　　Black Students
- 　　Black Teachers
- 　　Black Youth
- BT　Groups
- RT　Afrocentrism
- 　　Black Achievement
- 　　Black Attitudes
- 　　Black Businesses
- 　　Black Colleges
- 　　Black Community
- 　　Black Culture
- 　　Black Dialects
- 　　Black Education
- 　　Black Employment
- 　　Black Family
- 　　Black History
- 　　Black Influences
- 　　Black Institutions
- 　　Black Leadership
- 　　Black Literature
- 　　Black Organizations
- 　　Black Population Trends
- 　　Black Power
- 　　Black Stereotypes
- 　　Black Studies
- 　　Ethnic Groups
- 　　Minority Groups
- 　　Race
- 　　Racial Relations

Blind Children (1966 1980)
- USE　Blindness

Blind (1966 1980)
- USE　Blindness

Blindness
MAR. 1980
Postings: 2,168　　GC: 220
- SN　Having no sight or such limited vision that hearing and touch are the chief means of perception and learning—legal blindness is usually defined as having central visual acuity of 20/200 or less in the better eye with correction or having a visual field no greater than 20 degrees
- UF　Blind (1966 1980)
- 　　Blind Children (1966 1980)
- BT　Visual Impairments
- RT　Braille
- 　　Deaf Blind
- 　　Echolocation
- 　　Low Vision Aids
- 　　Partial Vision

- 　　Raised Line Drawings
- 　　Tactile Adaptation
- 　　Talking Books
- 　　Vision
- 　　Visual Acuity

Block Grants
SEP. 1982
Postings: 332　　GC: 620
- SN　Financial assistance for broad ranges of activities and services, of which specific dispensations of allocated funds are made at the discretion of the grantee within the bounds of a statutory formula
- BT　Grants
- RT　Educational Finance
- 　　Federal Aid
- 　　Federal State Relationship
- 　　Government School Relationship
- 　　Institutional Autonomy
- 　　New Federalism
- 　　Revenue Sharing
- 　　School District Autonomy
- 　　State Aid

Block Scheduling
AUG. 1996
Postings: 193　　GC: 350
- SN　An instructional arrangement whereby part or all of the daily class schedule is organized into blocks of time longer than an hour, to facilitate flexibility and diversity in instructional activities (Note: Prior to Aug96, this concept was indexed as "Time Blocks")
- UF　Alternate Day Block Scheduling #
- 　　Block Time Teaching
- BT　School Schedules
- RT　Extended School Day
- 　　Flexible Scheduling
- 　　Time Blocks
- 　　Time Factors (Learning)

Block Time Teaching
- USE　Block Scheduling

Blood Circulation
JUN. 1969
Postings: 112　　GC: 210
- UF　Hemodynamics
- BT　Metabolism
- RT　Cardiovascular System
- 　　Heart Rate
- 　　Human Body
- 　　Hypertension
- 　　Physiology
- 　　Sickle Cell Anemia

Blood Donors
- USE　Tissue Donors

Blue Collar Occupations
JUL. 1966
Postings: 302　　GC: 640
- SN　Occupations that require manual labor— includes skilled, semiskilled, and unskilled occupations (Note: Use to distinguish from "White Collar Occupations")
- BT　Occupations
- RT　Building Trades
- 　　Semiskilled Occupations
- 　　Skilled Occupations
- 　　Trade and Industrial Education
- 　　Unskilled Occupations
- 　　White Collar Occupations
- 　　Working Class

Blue Ribbon Commissions
AUG. 1986
Postings: 112　　GC: 610
- SN　Panels of knowledgeable public leaders and informed private citizens appointed by government executives or legislative bodies for fixed durations to study and make recommendations on specific problems or topics
- BT　Organizations (Groups)
- RT　Advisory Committees
- 　　Change Agents
- 　　Consultants
- 　　Needs Assessment
- 　　Planning Commissions

- 　　Policy Formation
- 　　Political Issues
- 　　Statewide Planning

Blueprints
JUL. 1966
Postings: 137　　GC: 920
- BT　Building Plans
- RT　Building Design
- 　　Drafting
- 　　Engineering Drawing
- 　　Orthographic Projection

Board Administrator Relationship
JUL. 1966
Postings: 1,073　　GC: 330
- BT　Interpersonal Relationship
- RT　Administrator Guides
- 　　Administrators
- 　　Federal State Relationship
- 　　Governing Boards
- 　　Interprofessional Relationship
- 　　Politics of Education
- 　　School Administration
- 　　Student School Relationship
- 　　Teacher Administrator Relationship

Board Candidates
JUL. 1966
Postings: 140　　GC: 610
- BT　Groups
- RT　Boards of Education
- 　　Political Candidates
- 　　Trustees

Board of Education Members
- USE　Boards of Education

Board of Education Policy
JUL. 1966
Postings: 1,992　　GC: 330
- UF　School Board Policy
- 　　School District Policy
- BT　Administrative Policy
- RT　Arbitration
- 　　Boards of Education
- 　　Dress Codes
- 　　Educational Policy
- 　　Interdistrict Policies
- 　　Married Students
- 　　Negotiation Agreements
- 　　Negotiation Impasses
- 　　Politics of Education
- 　　Pregnant Students
- 　　School Closing
- 　　School District Autonomy
- 　　School Policy
- 　　Superintendents
- 　　Teacher Welfare

Board of Education Role
JUL. 1966
Postings: 1,443　　GC: 330
- UF　School Board Role
- BT　Role
- RT　Boards of Education
- 　　Role of Education
- 　　School District Autonomy

Board of Regents
- USE　Governing Boards

Board of Trustees
- USE　Governing Boards

Boarding Homes
JUL. 1966
Postings: 47　　GC: 920
- BT　Housing
- RT　Adult Foster Care
- 　　Boarding Schools
- 　　College Housing
- 　　Foster Care
- 　　Rehabilitation Centers
- 　　Residential Institutions

Boarding Schools
APR. 1970
Postings: 444　　GC: 340
- SN　Educational institutions at the elementa-

ry-secondary level in which students are in residence while enrolled in an instructional program (Note: See "Residential Schools" for boarding schools for disabled children)
NT   Residential Schools
BT   Residential Institutions
       Schools
RT   Boarding Homes
       Folk Schools
       Regional Schools
       Resident Advisers
       Residential Programs

Boards of Education   *JUL. 1966*
       Postings: 3,284   GC: 330
UF   Board of Education Members
       School Board Members
       School Boards
NT   State Boards of Education
BT   Governing Boards
RT   Board Candidates
       Board of Education Policy
       Board of Education Role
       Central Office Administrators
       County School Districts
       Intermediate Administrative Units
       Loyalty Oaths
       Public School Teachers
       School Administration
       School District Autonomy
       School Districts
       Schools
       Superintendents
       Trustees

Boat Operators   *MAR. 1980*
       Postings: 58   GC: 640
SN   (Note: May be used in a recreational as well as an occupational context)
UF   Boatmen (1967 1980)
       Motorboat Operators
BT   Semiskilled Workers
RT   Maritime Education
       Navigation
       Sailing
       Seafarers

Boatmen (1967 1980)
USE   Boat Operators

Body and Fender Repairers
USE   Auto Body Repairers

Body Attitude
USE   Human Posture

Body Care
USE   Hygiene

Body Composition   *AUG. 1988*
       Postings: 123   GC: 210
SN   The amounts of fat and nonfat tissue in the body, usually expressed as a ratio
UF   Body Density
       Body Fatness
       Body Mass
       Fat Ratio
       Lean Fat Ratio
       Percent Body Fat
NT   Obesity
BT   Physical Characteristics
RT   Anatomy
       Body Height
       Body Weight
       Dietetics
       Exercise Physiology
       Human Body
       Muscular Strength
       Physical Development
       Physical Fitness
       Physiology

Body Density
USE   Body Composition

Body Fatness
USE   Body Composition

Body Height   *JUN. 1969*
       Postings: 143   GC: 120
BT   Physical Characteristics
RT   Body Composition
       Human Body
       Physical Development

Body Image   *JUN. 1969*
       Postings: 597   GC: 120
SN   Conceptual representation of one's own body derived from internal and external sensations, emotions, and fantasies related to orientation, movement, and behavior
UF   Body Schema
       Physical Self Concept
BT   Self Concept
RT   Human Body
       Kinesthetic Perception
       Movement Education
       Personal Space
       Physical Attractiveness
       Puberty

Body Language   *JAN. 1973*
       Postings: 670   GC: 120
UF   Gestures (Nonverbal Communication)
       Kinesics
BT   Nonverbal Communication
RT   Eye Contact
       Eye Movements
       Facial Expressions
       Human Posture
       Interaction Process Analysis
       Movement Education
       Paralinguistics

Body Mass
USE   Body Composition

Body Schema
USE   Body Image

Body Weight   *JUN. 1969*
       Postings: 667   GC: 120
NT   Birth Weight
       Obesity
BT   Physical Characteristics
RT   Body Composition
       Eating Disorders
       Eating Habits
       Failure to Thrive
       Human Body
       Physical Development

Bogs
USE   Wetlands

Bomb Shelters
USE   Fallout Shelters

Bond Issues   *JUL. 1966*
       Postings: 345   GC: 620
RT   Educational Finance
       Local Issues
       Political Issues
       Voting

Bonding (Behavior)
USE   Attachment Behavior

Bone Arrangement
USE   Skeletal System

Book Buying
USE   Library Acquisition

Book Catalogs   *AUG. 1968*
       Postings: 110   GC: 710
SN   Literary catalogs in book form—individual catalog entries are photocopied or printed page by page
BT   Library Catalogs

Book Industry
USE   Publishing Industry

Book Lending
USE   Library Circulation

Book Reviews   *JUL. 1966*
       Postings: 2,264   GC: 730
BT   Publications
RT   Books
       Literary Criticism
       Literature Reviews
       Textbook Evaluation

Book Selection Aids
USE   Selection Tools

Book Thefts (1969 1980)
USE   Books
AND   Stealing

Bookkeeping   *JUL. 1966*
       Postings: 364   GC: 620
BT   Business Skills
RT   Accounting
       Clerical Occupations
       Financial Audits
       Financial Services
       Office Occupations
       Office Occupations Education
       Recordkeeping

Booklists (1967 1980)
USE   Bibliographies

Bookmobiles   *JAN. 1970*
       Postings: 147   GC: 910
SN   Large motor vehicles, specially equipped to carry books and other library materials, that serve as traveling libraries
UF   Mobile Libraries
BT   Library Equipment
       Service Vehicles
RT   Branch Libraries
       Library Extension
       Library Services
       Mobile Educational Services
       Outreach Programs

Books   *JUL. 1966*
       Postings: 5,548   GC: 720
SN   (Note: Corresponds to Pubtype code 010—do not use except as the subject of a document)
UF   Book Thefts (1969 1980) #
       Childrens Books (1966 1980) #
       Folklore Books (1966 1980) #
       Health Books (1966 1980) #
NT   Foreign Language Books
       High Interest Low Vocabulary Books
       Paperback Books
       Picture Books
       Textbooks
       Yearbooks
BT   Printed Materials
       Publications
RT   Bibliographies
       Bibliometrics
       Book Reviews
       Bookstores
       Literature
       Manuscripts
       Novels
       Reading Materials
       Serials
       Short Stories
       Talking Books

Bookshops
USE   Bookstores

Bookstores   *FEB. 2000*
       Postings: 140   GC: 920
SN   Commercial businesses where books are the primary items for sale (Note: See also the Identifiers "Booksellers" and "Book Dealers")
UF   Bookshops
       College Bookstores #
BT   Facilities
RT   Books
       College Stores
       Educational Facilities
       Merchandising
       Publishing Industry
       Retailing

Boom Town Areas
USE   Boomtowns

Boomtowns   *JUL. 1993*
       Postings: 48   GC: 550
SN   Towns that have experienced rapid growth and often transition from rural to urban-industrial life as a result of new economic activity, such as large-scale construction projects, new industry, or immigration (Note: Includes private, social, and public consequences of rapid community growth)
UF   Boom Town Areas
       Rapid Growth Communities
BT   Municipalities
RT   Community Change
       Community Development
       Community Size
       Economic Change
       Economic Development
       Economic Impact
       Employment Patterns
       Industrialization
       Migration
       Migration Patterns
       Population Growth
       Population Trends
       Rural Development
       Socioeconomic Influences
       Urbanization

Border Patrol Officers
USE   Immigration Inspectors

Borderline Mental Retardation
USE   Slow Learners

Bosnian
USE   Serbocroatian

Botany   *JUL. 1966*
       Postings: 950   GC: 490
UF   Plant Biology
BT   Biological Sciences
RT   Agriculture
       Biology
       Culturing Techniques
       Dissection
       Ecology
       Embryology
       Evolution
       Field Crops
       Floriculture
       Forestry
       Gardening
       Gardens
       Genetics
       Herbicides
       Horticulture
       Insecticides
       Landscaping
       Microbiology
       Mycology
       Photosynthesis
       Plant Growth
       Plant Identification
       Plant Pathology

= Two or more Descriptors are used to represent this term.
The term's main entry shows the appropriate coordination.

Plant Propagation
Plants (Botany)
Soil Science
Trees
Weeds
Wildlife

Bowling *APR. 1985*
Postings: 29 GC: 470
SN (Note: Do not confuse with the Identifiers "Lawn Bowling" and "Cricket (Sport)")
UF Tenpins
BT Athletics
RT Lifetime Sports

Boys
USE Males

Bracero Programs (1966 1980)
USE Braceros

Braceros *JUL. 1966*
Postings: 42 GC: 410
SN Mexican laborers permitted to enter the United States under immigration treaties to work for limited periods of time in agriculture or industry
UF Bracero Programs (1966 1980)
BT Foreign Workers
Mexicans
RT Agricultural Laborers
Migrant Employment
Migrant Workers
Migrants
Seasonal Employment
Seasonal Laborers

Brahmins (1967 1980)
USE Caste

Braille *JUL. 1966*
Postings: 542 GC: 220
BT Written Language
RT Blindness
Raised Line Drawings
Reading
Reading Instruction
Sensory Aids
Tactile Adaptation

Brain *SEP. 1997*
Postings: 216 GC: 210
UF Brain Research
RT Anatomy
Brain Hemisphere Functions
Cognitive Processes
Electroencephalography
Head Injuries
Human Body
Minimal Brain Dysfunction
Neurolinguistics
Neurological Impairments
Neurological Organization
Neurology
Neuropsychology

Brain Damage
USE Neurological Impairments

Brain Drain *FEB. 2000*
Postings: 71 GC: 550
SN Loss of highly skilled or educated persons from one country, region, institution, or job sector to another (for better pay, improved living conditions, expanded opportunities, etc.)
BT Migration
RT Employment Patterns
Immigration
Migration Patterns
Occupational Mobility
Population Trends
Relocation

Brain Hemisphere Functions *AUG. 1986*
Postings: 449 GC: 120
SN Specialized roles of the right and left halves of the brain
UF Cerebral Dominance (1967 1986)
Hemispheric Specialization (Brain)
BT Neurological Organization
RT Brain
Lateral Dominance
Neurology
Neuropsychology
Perceptual Development

Brain Research
USE Brain

Brainstorming *DEC. 1985*
Postings: 262 GC: 520
SN Activity or technique to encourage the creative generation of ideas—usually a group process, in which group members contribute suggestions in a spontaneous, noncritical manner
BT Creative Activities
RT Divergent Thinking
Group Discussion
Group Dynamics
Nominal Group Technique
Problem Solving
Spontaneous Behavior

Branch Campuses (Colleges)
USE Multicampus Colleges

Branch Libraries *NOV. 1969*
Postings: 145 GC: 710
SN Libraries other than the main or central one in a system
UF Satellite Libraries
BT Libraries
RT Bookmobiles
County Libraries
Library Networks
Public Libraries
Satellite Facilities
Special Libraries

Branching *JUL. 1966*
Postings: 190 GC: 710
SN An operation, frequently used in computer programming or programmed instruction, in which a choice is automatically made between two or more courses of action based on the result of some preceding operation, such as the answer to a question
UF Optional Branching (1966 1980)
BT Methods
RT Computer Oriented Programs
Fixed Sequence
Menu Driven Software
Programmed Instruction
Programming

Brass Instruments *MAY 2000*
Postings: 18 GC: 420
SN Musical wind instruments, such as trumpets, trombones, and tubas, made of brass or other metal tubing commonly curved two or more times, and having a cup-shaped mouthpiece at one end and a flared bell at the other
BT Wind Instruments
RT Music

Breadwinners
USE Heads of Households

Breakfast Programs *JUL. 1966*
Postings: 292 GC: 210
BT Health Programs
RT Dining Facilities
Food Handling Facilities
Food Standards
Hunger
Lunch Programs

Nutrition
School Health Services

Breastfeeding *APR. 1986*
Postings: 103 GC: 210
BT Nutrition
RT Infants

Brick Industry *AUG. 1970*
Postings: 5 GC: 650
BT Industry
RT Construction Industry
Manufacturing Industry

Brick Masonry
USE Bricklaying

Bricklayers (1968 1981)
USE Bricklaying

Bricklaying *JUL. 1966*
Postings: 61 GC: 640
UF Brick Masonry
Bricklayers (1968 1981)
BT Masonry
RT Building Trades
Skilled Occupations

British Infant Schools *DEC. 1985*
Postings: 39 GC: 340
SN Lower-division schools of the British primary system for children aged 5 to 7 or 8, often associated with an informal, open approach to teaching and student-selected learning activities (Note: Coordinate non-U.S., including British, applications with geographic Identifiers)
UF Infant Schools (British Primary System)
BT Schools
RT Elementary Schools
Open Education
Primary Education

British National Curriculum *SEP. 1994*
Postings: 575 GC: 350
SN A prescribed range of subjects to be studied by all British pupils between the ages of 5 and 16 (Note: Coordinate with Identifiers "England," "Wales," "Scotland," "Northern Ireland," and/or "United Kingdom" as appropriate)
BT National Curriculum
RT Core Curriculum

Broadcast Communications
USE Telecommunications

Broadcast Industry *JUL. 1966*
Postings: 1,454 GC: 650
BT Industry
RT Broadcast Journalism
Broadcast Television
Commercial Television
Copyrights
Film Industry
Information Industry
Mass Media
Mass Media Role
Programming (Broadcast)
Radio
Television
Television Curriculum

Broadcast Journalism *APR. 1990*
Postings: 220 GC: 720
SN The gathering, editing, and reporting of information and news for radio and television
UF News Broadcasting #
Radio Journalism
Television Journalism
BT Journalism
RT Broadcast Industry

Broadcast Television
Documentaries
Feature Stories
Mass Media Role
News Media
News Reporting
News Writing
Programming (Broadcast)
Radio
Television
Television Curriculum

Broadcast Reception Equipment *JUL. 1966*
Postings: 114 GC: 910
BT Electronic Equipment
RT Audio Equipment
Broadcast Television
Radio
Television
Television Studios
Video Equipment

Broadcast Scheduling
USE Programming (Broadcast)

Broadcast Television *JUL. 1966*
Postings: 787 GC: 720
SN System whereby television signals are transmitted through the air at preassigned frequencies and received by a general and geographically scattered audience simultaneously
UF Open Circuit Television (1966 1980)
BT Television
RT Broadcast Industry
Broadcast Journalism
Broadcast Reception Equipment

Brochures
USE Pamphlets

Brothers
USE Siblings

Bucolic Literature
USE Pastoral Literature

Buddhism *MAR. 1983*
Postings: 98 GC: 430
SN Religion based on the teachings of Gautama Buddha (India, 5th century B.C.)
BT Religion
RT Non Western Civilization
Philosophy
Religious Cultural Groups

Budget Allocations
USE Budgeting

Budget Cuts
USE Budgeting
AND Retrenchment

Budgeting *JUL. 1966*
Postings: 3,628 GC: 620
SN The process of determining estimates of proposed expenditures for a given period or purpose and the proposed means of financing them (Note: Prior to Mar80, this term was not restricted by a Scope Note and may have been confused with "Budgets," which are the actual estimates and means)
UF Budget Allocations
Budget Cuts #
NT Program Budgeting
BT Planning
RT Accounting
Administration
Budgets
Cost Estimates
Educational Finance
Expenditures
Financial Audits

= Two or more Descriptors are used to represent this term.
The term's main entry shows the appropriate coordination.

Money Management
Resource Allocation
Retrenchment
School Based Management

Budgets   *JUL. 1966*
    Postings: 2,284   GC: 620
SN Estimates of proposed expenditures for
    a given period or purpose and the pro-
    posed means of financing them (Note:
    Prior to Mar80, this term was not re-
    stricted by a Scope Note and may have
    been confused with "Budgeting," which
    is the process of creating budgets)
RT Budgeting
    Educational Finance
    Expenditures
    Income
    Operating Expenses
    Program Budgeting
    Resource Allocation
    School Budget Elections

Building Conversion   *JUL. 1966*
    Postings: 288   GC: 920
SN Modifying a building to make it suitable
    for a new use or purpose
BT Change
RT Building Innovation
    Building Obsolescence
    Buildings
    Construction (Process)
    Construction Costs
    Construction Needs
    Facility Expansion
    Facility Guidelines
    Facility Improvement
    Facility Requirements
    Facility Utilization Research
    Found Spaces
    School Expansion
    Space Utilization

Building Design   *JUL. 1966*
    Postings: 1,921   GC: 920
SN Conceiving and selecting the structure,
    elements, arrangement, materials, etc.,
    for a building—also, the plan or layout
    that results
UF Architectural Changes
    Architectural Design
NT Modular Building Design
BT Design
RT Acoustical Environment
    Air Flow
    Architects
    Architectural Character
    Architectural Programming
    Architecture
    Blueprints
    Building Innovation
    Building Plans
    Buildings
    Built Environment
    Color Planning
    Construction (Process)
    Construction Materials
    Design Build Approach
    Design Requirements
    Educational Facilities Design
    Facilities
    Facility Case Studies
    Facility Guidelines
    Facility Requirements
    Facility Utilization Research
    Fire Protection
    Flexible Lighting Design
    Interior Design
    Interior Space
    Life Cycle Costing
    Lighting Design
    Physical Mobility
    Space Utilization
    Spatial Relationship (Facilities)
    Structural Elements (Construction)
    Thermal Environment
    Visual Environment

Building Equipment (1966 1980)
USE Equipment

Building Improvement (1966 1980)
USE Facility Improvement

Building Innovation   *JUL. 1966*
    Postings: 348   GC: 920
SN Introduction of innovative approaches in
    the design and construction of new build-
    ings
BT Innovation
RT Architectural Programming
    Building Conversion
    Building Design
    Buildings
    Construction Materials
    Design Build Approach
    Encapsulated Facilities
    Facility Guidelines
    Facility Requirements
    Flexible Facilities
    Relocatable Facilities
    Systems Building
    Underground Facilities

Building Materials (1968 1980)
USE Construction Materials

Building Obsolescence   *JUL. 1966*
    Postings: 99   GC: 920
SN Decline of functional utility due to changes
    in style, practice, and technology, not
    including physical deterioration
BT Obsolescence
RT Assessed Valuation
    Building Conversion
    Buildings
    Facility Improvement
    Facility Utilization Research
    Property Appraisal
    Space Utilization

Building Operation   *JUL. 1966*
    Postings: 394   GC: 920
BT Administration
RT Building Trades
    Buildings
    Climate Control
    Energy Management
    Life Cycle Costing
    Operating Expenses
    School Maintenance

Building Plans   *DEC. 1969*
    Postings: 278   GC: 920
NT Blueprints
RT Architectural Drafting
    Building Design
    Buildings
    Design
    Design Build Approach
    Educational Facilities Design
    Educational Facilities Planning
    Facility Case Studies
    Facility Planning
    Facility Requirements
    Facility Utilization Research
    House Plan
    Life Cycle Costing
    Master Plans
    Planning
    Space Classification
    Space Utilization
    Spatial Relationship (Facilities)
    Specifications
    Systems Building

Building Programs
USE Construction Programs

Building Renovation
USE Facility Improvement

Building Systems   *DEC. 1976*
    Postings: 227   GC: 920
SN Assemblies of building subsystems and
    components (structural and mechani-
    cal), with instructions for putting them
    together—normally these components
    are mass-produced and used for specific
    generic projects in building construction
UF Component Building Systems (1968
    1976)
    Component Systems
NT Structural Building Systems
BT Structural Elements (Construction)
RT Buildings
    Construction (Process)
    Construction Programs
    Life Cycle Costing
    Modular Building Design
    Prefabrication
    Systems Building

Building Trades   *JUL. 1966*
    Postings: 681   GC: 640
UF Construction Occupations
    Structural Work Occupations
BT Occupations
RT Air Conditioning
    Blue Collar Occupations
    Bricklaying
    Building Operation
    Buildings
    Cabinetmaking
    Carpentry
    Construction (Process)
    Construction Industry
    Craft Workers
    Electricians
    Flooring
    Industrial Arts
    Masonry
    Operating Engineering
    Painting (Industrial Arts)
    Plumbing
    Roofing
    Semiskilled Occupations
    Skilled Occupations
    Trade and Industrial Education
    Woodworking

Buildings   *JUL. 1966*
    Postings: 252   GC: 920
NT School Buildings
BT Facilities
RT Air Structures
    Assessed Valuation
    Building Conversion
    Building Design
    Building Innovation
    Building Obsolescence
    Building Operation
    Building Plans
    Building Systems
    Building Trades
    Built Environment
    Ceilings
    Construction Costs
    Construction Industry
    Construction Materials
    Encapsulated Facilities
    Facility Improvement
    Facility Utilization Research
    Flooring
    Hotels
    Maintenance
    Material Culture
    Prefabrication
    Real Estate Occupations
    Repair
    Roofing
    Space Utilization
    Structural Building Systems
    Structural Elements (Construction)
    Systems Building
    Underground Facilities
    Visual Arts

Built Environment   *APR. 1990*
    Postings: 148   GC: 920
SN All buildings, monuments, roadways,

landscapes, etc., contributed by humans
to the natural physical environment
BT Physical Environment
RT Architecture
    Building Design
    Buildings
    Community Characteristics
    Design Requirements
    Environmental Influences
    Facilities
    Heritage Education
    Material Culture
    Site Development
    Structural Elements (Construction)
    Visual Environment

Bulgarian   *JUL. 1966*
    Postings: 42   GC: 440
BT Slavic Languages

Bulimarexia
USE Bulimia

Bulimia   *APR. 1986*
    Postings: 288   GC: 210
SN Disorder characterized by recurrent binge
    eating, usually followed by self-induced
    purging—attended by depressed moods
    and self-deprecating thoughts
UF Bulimarexia
BT Eating Disorders
RT Anorexia Nervosa
    Eating Habits
    Emotional Disturbances
    Nutrition
    Physical Health

Bulletin Boards   *JUL. 1966*
    Postings: 219   GC: 910
UF Tackboards
BT Visual Aids
RT Audiovisual Aids
    Chalkboards
    Educational Equipment

Bulletins   *APR. 1969*
    Postings: 291   GC: 730
BT Serials
RT Newsletters
    Newspapers
    Periodicals
    Program Descriptions
    Reports

Bullying   *JUL. 1998*
    Postings: 174   GC: 530
SN Cruelty and intimidation by teasing, taunt-
    ing, threatening, hitting, stealing, exclud-
    ing, ignoring, etc.
BT Antisocial Behavior
RT Aggression
    Violence

Bureaucracy   *JUL. 1966*
    Postings: 983   GC: 520
BT Organization
RT Administrative Organization
    Governmental Structure
    Public Sector

Burglar Alarms
USE Alarm Systems

Buriat   *JUL. 1966*
    Postings: 2   GC: 440
BT Mongolian Languages

Burmese   *JUL. 1966*
    Postings: 21   GC: 440
BT Sino Tibetan Languages
RT Burmese Culture

= Two or more Descriptors are used to represent this term.
The term's main entry shows the appropriate coordination.

Burmese Culture   *JUL. 1966*
     Postings: 19   GC: 560
BT   Culture
RT   Asian Studies
     Burmese
     Non Western Civilization

Burnout   *SEP. 1981*
     Postings: 474   GC: 230
SN   Negative feelings and/or behaviors resulting from unsuccessful attempts to cope with stress conditions—characterized by physical and emotional exhaustion, chronic negative attitudes, very low productivity, etc. (Note: If possible, use the more specific term "Teacher Burnout")
NT   Teacher Burnout
BT   Responses
RT   Coping
     Emotional Response
     Job Satisfaction
     Morale
     Motivation
     Negative Attitudes
     Organizational Climate
     Persistence
     Psychological Patterns
     Stress Variables

Burushaski   *JUL. 1966*
     Postings: 4   GC: 440
SN   Language of NW Kashmir, not known to be related to any other language
BT   Languages

Bus Drivers   *MAY 1994*
     Postings: 71   GC: 640
SN   (Note: For school bus drivers, coordinate with "School Buses")
UF   School Bus Drivers #
BT   Personnel
RT   Bus Transportation
     Driver Education
     School Buses

Bus Transportation   *JUL. 1966*
     Postings: 835   GC: 320
BT   Transportation
RT   Bus Drivers
     Busing
     Feeder Patterns
     School Buses
     Student Transportation

Buses
USE   Service Vehicles

Business   *JUL. 1966*
     Postings: 2,761   GC: 650
SN   Activities concerned with the production or exchange of goods or the rendering of financial or other services to the public for profit
UF   Commercial Enterprises
NT   Agribusiness
     Black Businesses
     Industry
     Small Businesses
RT   Business Administration
     Business Administration Education
     Business Communication
     Business Correspondence
     Business Cycles
     Business Education
     Business Responsibility
     Cooperatives
     Corporate Education
     Corporate Libraries
     Corporate Support
     Corporations
     Economic Impact
     Economics
     Entrepreneurship
     Exports
     Franchising
     Free Enterprise System
     Imports

     Insurance Companies
     International Trade
     Marketing
     Merchants
     Mergers
     Office Machines
     Office Occupations
     Organization Size (Groups)
     Ownership
     Private Sector
     Privatization
     Producer Services
     School Business Relationship
     Self Employment
     Vendors

Business Administration   *SEP. 1969*
     Postings: 1,718   GC: 650
SN   The organization and management of commercial enterprises (Note: Prior to Mar80, this term was scoped to mean the "subject" or "curriculum" of business administration—see also "Business Administration Education")
UF   Small Business Management #
BT   Administration
RT   Administrative Principles
     Business
     Business Administration Education
     Entrepreneurship
     Franchising
     Free Enterprise System
     Managerial Occupations
     Private Sector
     Public Administration
     Self Employment

Business Administration Education
                         MAR. 1980
     Postings: 1,839   GC: 400
SN   Professional study of the organization and management of commercial enterprises, usually at the baccalaureate level and above (Note: Do not confuse with "Business Education")
BT   Professional Education
RT   Administrator Education
     Business
     Business Administration
     Business Education
     Management Development
     Professional Training
     Public Administration Education

Business Communication   *DEC. 1974*
     Postings: 2,530   GC: 650
SN   Interchange of verbal and nonverbal messages in commercial or mercantile environments
UF   Commercial Communication
     Industrial Communication
NT   Business Correspondence
BT   Organizational Communication
RT   Business
     Business Education
     Business English
     International Communication
     International Trade Vocabulary
     Labor Relations

Business Correspondence   *JUL. 1966*
     Postings: 506   GC: 650
SN   Written communication between people or organizations engaged in business
UF   Business Letters
BT   Business Communication
     Verbal Communication
RT   Business
     Business English
     Dictation
     Letters (Correspondence)
     Office Occupations Education

Business Cycles   *JUL. 1966*
     Postings: 374   GC: 620
UF   Business Fluctuations
     Economic Cycles
     Economic Fluctuations
RT   Business

     Economic Climate
     Economic Factors
     Economic Progress
     Economics
     Inflation (Economics)
     Labor Economics
     Monetary Systems
     Supply and Demand

Business Education   *JUL. 1966*
     Postings: 5,850   GC: 400
SN   Formal preparation for occupations in business below the baccalaureate degree (Note: Do not confuse with "Basic Business Education" or "Business Administration Education"—if appropriate, use the more specific term "Office Occupations Education"—before Mar80, the use of this term was not restricted by a Scope Note)
UF   Business Subjects (1967 1980)
     Commercial Education
     Vocational Business Education
NT   Office Occupations Education
BT   Vocational Education
RT   Accounting
     Banking
     Business
     Business Administration Education
     Business Communication
     Business Education Facilities
     Business Education Teachers
     Business Skills
     Clerical Occupations
     Data Processing Occupations
     Distributive Education
     Economics Education
     Marketing
     Office Occupations

Business Education Facilities   *APR. 1970*
     Postings: 56   GC: 920
BT   Educational Facilities
RT   Business Education
     Classrooms
     Office Occupations Education

Business Education Teachers   *SEP. 1968*
     Postings: 482   GC: 360
UF   Business Teachers
BT   Vocational Education Teachers
RT   Business Education
     Office Occupations Education

Business English   *JUL. 1966*
     Postings: 363   GC: 400
BT   English
RT   Business Communication
     Business Correspondence
     Language Usage
     Office Occupations Education
     Technical Writing

Business Fluctuations
USE   Business Cycles

Business Games
USE   Management Games

Business Letters
USE   Business Correspondence

Business Machines
USE   Office Machines

Business Officials (Industry)
USE   Administrators

Business Officials (School)
USE   School Business Officials

Business Responsibility   *JUL. 1966*
     Postings: 709   GC: 650
SN   Obligations of the commercial business community
BT   Responsibility
RT   Business
     Corporate Support
     Leadership Responsibility
     Private Sector

Business School Relationship
USE   School Business Relationship

Business Skills   *JUL. 1966*
     Postings: 1,125   GC: 400
NT   Bookkeeping
     Keyboarding (Data Entry)
     Recordkeeping
     Typewriting
BT   Skills
RT   Accounting
     Basic Business Education
     Business Education
     Dictation
     Employment Qualifications
     Filing
     Job Skills
     Office Practice
     Practical Arts
     Proofreading
     Shorthand

Business Subjects (1967 1980)
USE   Business Education

Business Teachers
USE   Business Education Teachers

Busing   *MAR. 1980*
     Postings: 284   GC: 540
SN   Transporting students for the purpose of school desegregation (Note: Prior to Mar80, the instruction "Busing, USE Bus Transportation" was carried in the Thesaurus)
BT   Desegregation Methods
RT   Bus Transportation
     Desegregation Plans
     Feeder Patterns
     Magnet Schools
     Racial Composition
     Racial Integration
     Racially Balanced Schools
     School Buses
     School Desegregation

Butterfly Effect
USE   Chaos Theory

Byelorussian
USE   Bielorussian

Cabinetmakers
USE   Cabinetmaking

Cabinetmaking   *JUL. 1966*
     Postings: 36   GC: 640
SN   Cutting, shaping, assembling, and repairing prepared parts of complex wood products such as store fixtures, office equipment, and home furniture
UF   Cabinetmakers
     Millwork
BT   Construction (Process)
     Woodworking
RT   Building Trades
     Carpentry
     Industrial Arts
     Skilled Occupations

Cable Franchising   *DEC. 1989*
     Postings: 6   GC: 610
SN   Process by which a government unit selects and licenses a cable company to

---

= Two or more Descriptors are used to represent this term.
The term's main entry shows the appropriate coordination.

install, operate, and maintain a cable television service—includes the provisions of the resulting contract regarding fees, local programming, etc. (Note: See also "Franchising"—prior to Dec89, "Cable Franchising" was indexed as "Franchising")
UF   Franchising (Cable)
RT   Cable Television
     Community Programs
     Contracts
     Government Role

Cable Television   *JAN. 1970*
     Postings: 1,311   GC: 720
SN   System whereby distant television signals are brought to subscribers in a community via coaxial cable rather than being broadcast
UF   CATV
     Community Antennas (1966 1980)
BT   Television
RT   Cable Franchising
     Closed Circuit Television
     Interactive Television

CAD CAM
USE   Computer Assisted Design
AND   Computer Assisted Manufacturing

Cafeterias
USE   Dining Facilities

CAI
USE   Computer Assisted Instruction

Cakchiquel   *JUL. 1966*
     Postings: 3   GC: 440
SN   A Mayan language spoken by the Indian people of highland Guatemala
BT   Mayan Languages

Calculation (1966 1980)
USE   Computation

Calculators   *MAR. 1980*
     Postings: 1,327   GC: 910
SN   Electronic or mechanical devices for performing mathematical or arithmetic operations
UF   Electronic Calculators
     Hand Calculators
     Pocket Calculators
NT   Graphing Calculators
BT   Equipment
RT   Computation
     Computers
     Data Processing
     Electromechanical Aids
     Electronic Equipment
     Instrumentation
     Keyboarding (Data Entry)
     Mathematics
     Mechanical Equipment
     Office Machines
     Semiconductor Devices

Calculus   *JUL. 1966*
     Postings: 1,033   GC: 480
BT   Mathematics
RT   Analytic Geometry
     Differential Equations
     Functions (Mathematics)
     Limits (Mathematics)
     Trigonometry
     Vectors (Mathematics)

Calisthenics   *JUL. 1966*
     Postings: 33   GC: 470
BT   Exercise
RT   Gymnastics
     Muscular Strength
     Physical Fitness

Calligraphy
USE   Manuscript Writing (Handlettering)

Calorimeters   *JAN. 1970*
     Postings: 34   GC: 910
SN   Instruments that measure heat quantities generated or emitted by such processes as chemical reactions, changes of state, or formation of solutions
UF   Microcalorimeters
BT   Measurement Equipment
RT   Heat
     Thermodynamics

Cambodian   *AUG. 1968*
     Postings: 92   GC: 440
UF   Khmer (Language)
BT   Austro Asiatic Languages

Cambodian Americans
USE   Asian Americans
AND   Cambodians

Cambodians   *MAR. 1980*
     Postings: 160   GC: 560
UF   Cambodian Americans #
     Khmer (People)
BT   Indochinese
RT   Asian Americans
     Laotians
     Vietnamese People

Cameras
USE   Photographic Equipment

Camp Counselors (1968 1980)
USE   Camping

Camping   *JUL. 1966*
     Postings: 1,227   GC: 470
UF   Camp Counselors (1968 1980)
BT   Recreational Activities
RT   Adventure Education
     Day Camp Programs
     Outdoor Activities
     Resident Camp Programs
     Tourism
     Trails
     Wilderness

Campus Planning   *JUL. 1966*
     Postings: 783   GC: 920
SN   Grounds and facilities planning, usually at postsecondary institutions (Note: Prior to Mar80, this term was not scoped and was often confused with "College Planning")
BT   Educational Facilities Planning
RT   Architectural Character
     Campuses
     College Buildings
     College Environment
     College Planning
     Educational Facilities
     Educational Facilities Design
     Parking Facilities
     Physical Mobility
     School Buildings
     School Location
     Space Utilization

Campus Schools
USE   Laboratory Schools

Campus Security
USE   School Security

Campuses   *JUL. 1966*
     Postings: 311   GC: 920
BT   Educational Complexes
RT   Campus Planning
     College Buildings
     Colleges

Educational Parks
Multicampus Colleges
Multicampus Districts
School Buildings
School Security

Canada Natives   *AUG. 1977*
     Postings: 960   GC: 560
SN   Peoples indigenous to Canada (Canada's American Indians, Eskimos, or peoples whose ancestry is mixed with these groups)
NT   Metis (People)
BT   Ethnic Groups
     North Americans
RT   Alaska Natives
     American Indians
     Canadian Literature
     Canadian Studies
     Cree (Tribe)
     Eskimos
     Iroquois (Tribe)
     Minority Groups
     Tribes

Canadian Literature   *JUL. 1975*
     Postings: 127   GC: 430
UF   French Canadian Literature
BT   North American Literature
RT   Canada Natives
     Canadian Studies
     French Canadians

Canadian Studies   *JUN. 1993*
     Postings: 91   GC: 400
SN   Interdisciplinary instruction and research concerned with Canada and the Canadian provinces and territories
BT   Area Studies
RT   Canada Natives
     Canadian Literature
     Foreign Culture
     French Canadians
     North American Culture

Cancer   *OCT. 1979*
     Postings: 617   GC: 210
SN   Malignant and invasive growth or tumor
UF   Carcinogens
     Carcinoma
     Malignant Neoplasms
     Sarcoma
     Tumors (Malignant)
BT   Diseases
RT   Occupational Diseases
     Oncology
     Physical Health
     Radiologic Technologists
     Radiology
     Smoking
     Special Health Problems
     Surgery

Cannabis
USE   Marijuana

Canonical Correlation
USE   Multivariate Analysis

Cantonese   *JUL. 1966*
     Postings: 152   GC: 440
BT   Chinese

Capital   *JUL. 1966*
     Postings: 204   GC: 620
BT   Financial Support
RT   Banking
     Capital Outlay (for Fixed Assets)
     Educational Finance
     Endowment Funds
     Estate Planning
     Fund Raising
     Library Funding
     Money Management
     Ownership
     Private Financial Support

Resource Allocation
Scholarship Funds
School Funds
Trusts (Financial)

Capital Outlay (for Fixed Assets)   *JUL. 1966*
     Postings: 524   GC: 620
SN   Expenditure that results in acquisition of fixed assets or additions to fixed assets such as expenditure for land or existing buildings, improvement of grounds, construction or modification of buildings, or initial or additional equipment—includes installment or lease payments on such property
BT   Expenditures
RT   Capital
     Construction Costs
     Educational Finance
     Facility Improvement
     Facility Planning
     Land Acquisition

Capital Punishment   *AUG. 1998*
     Postings: 55   GC: 520
UF   Death Penalty
     Executions (Criminal Law)
BT   Punishment
RT   Criminal Law
     Death

Capitalism   *OCT. 1974*
     Postings: 690   GC: 610
NT   Free Enterprise System
BT   Social Systems
RT   Communism
     Democracy
     Economics
     Entrepreneurship
     Fascism
     Government (Administrative Body)
     Imperialism
     Marxism
     Political Science
     Socialism
     United States History
     Work Ethic

Capitalization (Alphabetic)   *JUL. 1966*
     Postings: 111   GC: 450
RT   Punctuation
     Sentence Structure
     Spelling
     Writing Skills
     Written Language

Captioned Media
USE   Captions

Captions   *DEC. 1974*
     Postings: 208   GC: 720
SN   Explanatory comments accompanying photographs, illustrations, etc.
UF   Captioned Media
     Cutlines
RT   Cartoons
     Films
     Illustrations
     Journalism
     Layout (Publications)
     Newspapers
     Photographs
     Photojournalism

Carcinogens
USE   Cancer

Carcinoma
USE   Cancer

Card Catalogs   *APR. 1980*
     Postings: 130   GC: 710
SN   Library catalogs made up of cards, with each card usually bearing a single entry
BT   Library Catalogs

= Two or more Descriptors are used to represent this term.
The term's main entry shows the appropriate coordination.

Cardiac (Person) (1968 1980)
USE　Heart Disorders

Cardiopulmonary Resuscitation　*APR. 1986*
Postings: 59　　　　　　GC: 210
SN　Procedure to restore normal breathing and heartbeat following cardiac arrest—may include mouth-to-mouth ventilation, external chest compression, and use of drugs
UF　CPR (Medicine)
BT　First Aid
RT　Cardiovascular System
　　Heart Disorders

Cardiovascular System　*JUN. 1969*
Postings: 734　　　　　　GC: 210
UF　Circulatory System
　　Vascular System
RT　Aerobics
　　Anatomy
　　Biofeedback
　　Blood Circulation
　　Cardiopulmonary Resuscitation
　　Exercise Physiology
　　Heart Disorders
　　Heart Rate
　　Human Body
　　Hypertension
　　Musculoskeletal System
　　Physiology
　　Zoology

Career Academies　*AUG. 1995*
Postings: 52　　　　　　GC: 350
SN　Schools-within-schools (usually high-school level) focusing on broadly defined career themes (health careers, electronics, etc.), with highly integrated academic and vocational curricula and active involvement of local employers
UF　High School Academies (Career Development)
　　Job Training Academies
　　Partnership Academies (School and Business)
　　Vocational Academies
BT　House Plan
　　Vocational Schools
RT　Career Education
　　Careers
　　Integrated Curriculum
　　Job Training
　　Vocational Education
　　Vocational High Schools

Career Awareness　*FEB. 1975*
Postings: 2,920　　　　　GC: 400
SN　Appreciation for and understanding of the variety of types of careers—often refers to the initial phase of career education appropriate to the elementary school
UF　Occupational Awareness
　　Vocational Awareness
BT　Career Development
RT　Career Choice
　　Career Education
　　Career Guidance
　　Career Planning
　　Careers
　　Occupations
　　School Guidance

Career Change　*JAN. 1969*
Postings: 1,388　　　　　GC: 120
UF　Employment Change
　　Job Change
　　Midcareer Change #
　　Vocational Change
　　Work Change
BT　Change
RT　Career Choice
　　Career Development
　　Career Planning
　　Careers
　　Dislocated Workers
　　Early Retirement
　　Education Work Relationship

Emerging Occupations
Employment Opportunities
Job Satisfaction
Job Search Methods
Labor Turnover
Midlife Transitions
Occupational Mobility
Persistence
Professional Development
Promotion (Occupational)
Vocational Adjustment

Career Choice　*JUL. 1966*
Postings: 7,955　　　　　GC: 120
UF　Career Objectives
　　Occupational Choice (1966 1980)
　　Vocational Choice
BT　Selection
RT　Career Awareness
　　Career Change
　　Career Development
　　Career Education
　　Career Exploration
　　Career Guidance
　　Career Information Systems
　　Career Planning
　　Careers
　　Decision Making
　　Education Work Relationship
　　Eligibility
　　Employment Opportunities
　　Interest Inventories
　　Nontraditional Occupations
　　Occupational Aspiration
　　Occupations
　　Prevocational Education
　　Reentry Workers
　　Vocational Aptitude
　　Vocational Interests
　　Vocational Maturity

Career Counseling　*MAR. 1980*
Postings: 5,497　　　　　GC: 240
SN　Counseling activities to assist clients in selecting appropriate career options
UF　Occupational Counseling
　　Vocational Counseling (1966 1980)
BT　Career Guidance
　　Counseling
RT　Adult Counseling
　　Career Development
　　Career Information Systems
　　Career Planning
　　Careers
　　Employment Counselors
　　Job Placement
　　Occupational Tests
　　Occupations
　　Outplacement Services (Employment)
　　Prevocational Education
　　Rehabilitation Counseling
　　Vocational Adjustment
　　Vocational Education
　　Vocational Interests
　　Vocational Training Centers

Career Development　*JAN. 1979*
Postings: 7,432　　　　　GC: 120
SN　The continuous process of making career decisions based on the individual's experiences and interactions (e.g., the child's first impression of the working world, the adolescent's consideration of vocational alternatives, or the adult's decision to change careers)
UF　Vocational Development (1967 1978)
NT　Career Awareness
　　Career Exploration
BT　Individual Development
RT　Career Change
　　Career Choice
　　Career Counseling
　　Career Education
　　Career Guidance
　　Career Planning
　　Careers
　　Education Work Relationship
　　Occupational Aspiration
　　Occupational Information
　　Occupations

Promotion (Occupational)
Vocational Interests
Vocational Maturity

Career Education　*OCT. 1971*
Postings: 11,170　　　　GC: 400
SN　A comprehensive educational program that focuses on individual career development, beginning with grade 1 or earlier and continuing through the adult years
BT　Education
RT　Career Academies
　　Career Awareness
　　Career Choice
　　Career Development
　　Career Exploration
　　Career Guidance
　　Career Information Systems
　　Career Planning
　　Careers
　　Cooperative Education
　　Education Work Relationship
　　Occupations
　　Prevocational Education
　　Relevance (Education)
　　School Business Relationship
　　Vocational Education
　　Work Experience Programs

Career Exploration　*SEP. 1975*
Postings: 2,742　　　　　GC: 400
SN　Investigating occupational interest areas often through real or simulated job experience—frequently found in career education programs for grades 6 through 10
UF　Occupational Exploration
BT　Career Development
RT　Career Choice
　　Career Education
　　Career Guidance
　　Career Information Systems
　　Career Planning
　　Careers
　　Occupations
　　Prevocational Education
　　School Guidance
　　Vocational Interests
　　Vocational Maturity
　　Work Experience
　　Work Experience Programs

Career Guidance　*MAR. 1980*
Postings: 4,715　　　　　GC: 240
SN　Spectrum of activities and programs designed to help people plan, choose, and succeed in their careers (Note: If applicable, use the more specific term "Career Counseling")
UF　Occupational Guidance (1966 1980)
　　Vocational Guidance
NT　Career Counseling
BT　Guidance
RT　Career Awareness
　　Career Choice
　　Career Development
　　Career Education
　　Career Exploration
　　Career Information Systems
　　Career Planning
　　Careers
　　Employment Potential
　　Job Placement
　　Occupations
　　Outplacement Services (Employment)
　　Post High School Guidance
　　School Guidance
　　Vocational Interests

Career Information Delivery Systems
USE　Career Information Systems

Career Information Systems　*DEC. 1989*
Postings: 208　　　　　　GC: 710
SN　Systems for collecting, organizing, and delivering information about occupations and relevant educational opportunities to support career planning, decision mak-

ing, and guidance, often with the assistance of computers
UF　Career Information Delivery Systems
　　Occupational Information Systems
BT　Information Systems
RT　Career Choice
　　Career Counseling
　　Career Education
　　Career Exploration
　　Career Guidance
　　Career Planning
　　Careers
　　Computer Oriented Programs
　　Decision Making
　　Education Work Relationship
　　Information Sources
　　Job Banks
　　Job Search Methods
　　Occupational Information
　　Occupations

Career Ladders　*MAY 1971*
Postings: 1,304　　　　　GC: 630
SN　Hierarchy of occupational progression, with training, from entry level position to higher levels in the same occupation
UF　Job Ladders
BT　Occupational Mobility
RT　Adult Vocational Education
　　Careers
　　Employment Level
　　Entry Workers
　　Inservice Education
　　Labor Force Development
　　Promotion (Occupational)
　　Training

Career Maturity
USE　Vocational Maturity

Career Objectives
USE　Career Choice

Career Opportunities (1966 1980)
　　　　　　　　　　　　MAR. 1980
Postings: 1,581　　　　　GC: 630
SN　Invalid Descriptor—used inconsistently in indexing—use "Careers," and, if appropriate, "Employment Opportunities"

Career Orientation
USE　Career Planning

Career Planning　*JUL. 1966*
Postings: 5,097　　　　　GC: 240
UF　Career Orientation
BT　Planning
RT　Career Awareness
　　Career Change
　　Career Choice
　　Career Counseling
　　Career Development
　　Career Education
　　Career Exploration
　　Career Guidance
　　Career Information Systems
　　Careers
　　Demand Occupations
　　Education Work Relationship
　　Goal Orientation
　　Job Search Methods
　　Prevocational Education
　　Vocational Aptitude

Careers　*JUL. 1966*
Postings: 1,550　　　　　GC: 630
SN　The progressively developing sequences of related occupational roles or work experiences through which individuals move during their working lives, often with increasing prestige and rewards—also, the intended sequence of such roles established by individuals as part of their life plans (Note: Prior to Mar80, the use of this term was not restricted by a Scope Note)
NT　Science Careers

= Two or more Descriptors are used to represent this term.
The term's main entry shows the appropriate coordination.

RT Career Academies
Career Awareness
Career Change
Career Choice
Career Counseling
Career Development
Career Education
Career Exploration
Career Guidance
Career Information Systems
Career Ladders
Career Planning
Dual Career Family
Education Work Relationship
Employment
Entrepreneurship
Family Work Relationship
Occupational Mobility
Occupations
Quality of Working Life
Self Actualization
Self Employment
Work Experience
Work Life Expectancy

Caregiver Child Relationship   *JUL. 1994*
Postings: 458   GC: 510
SN (Note: If appropriate, coordinate with "Teacher Student Relationship"—for documents/articles about parents and children, use the more precise term "Parent Child Relationship")
BT Interpersonal Relationship
RT Attachment Behavior
Caregiver Role
Caregiver Speech
Child Abuse
Child Behavior
Child Caregivers
Child Neglect
Child Rearing
Children
Day Care
Foster Care
Infant Care
Parent Child Relationship
Preschool Teachers
Teacher Student Relationship

Caregiver Role   *APR. 1993*
Postings: 324   GC: 510
BT Role
RT Caregiver Child Relationship
Caregivers
Child Caregivers
Family Caregivers
Family Role
Parent Role

Caregiver Speech   *APR. 1990*
Postings: 205   GC: 450
SN Speech of caregiver to care recipient, especially speech directed toward a child by a parent, teacher, etc. (Note: Coordinate with "Child Language" and "Parent Child Relationship" for parent-child conversation, also using "Mothers" and/or "Fathers" as appropriate—see also the Identifier "Baby Talk")
UF Motherese and Fatherese #
Parent Talk #
BT Speech
RT Caregiver Child Relationship
Caregivers
Child Caregivers
Child Language
Interpersonal Communication
Language Acquisition
Language Patterns
Linguistic Input
Oral Language
Parent Child Relationship
Psycholinguistics
Receptive Language

Caregivers   *DEC. 1987*
Postings: 523   GC: 510
SN Individuals who provide personal care to others—includes professionals,

nonprofessionals, family members, and friends (Note: Use a more specific term if possible)
NT Attendants
Child Caregivers
Family Caregivers
BT Groups
RT Caregiver Role
Caregiver Speech
Health Personnel
Helping Relationship
Social Support Groups

Caricatures (1966 1980)   *MAR. 1980*
Postings: 17   GC: 420
SN Invalid Descriptor—see the more precise terms "Cartoons" and "Characterization"

Carpenters (1969 1981)
USE Carpentry

Carpentry   *SEP. 1981*
Postings: 244   GC: 640
SN Building or repairing structures and fixtures made from wood or materials that can be worked like wood, e.g., plastic, fiber glass
UF Carpenters (1969 1981)
BT Construction (Process)
Woodworking
RT Building Trades
Cabinetmaking
Industrial Arts
Skilled Occupations

Carpet Layers
USE Floor Layers

Carpeting   *AUG. 1968*
Postings: 150   GC: 920
UF Carpets
BT Flooring
RT Construction Materials
Floor Layers

Carpets
USE Carpeting

Carrels   *JUL. 1966*
Postings: 72   GC: 910
UF Study Carrels
BT Study Facilities
RT Library Equipment

Cartography   *AUG. 1977*
Postings: 333   GC: 400
SN Science or art of making maps
UF Mapping (Cartography)
BT Graphic Arts
RT Atlases
Civil Engineering
Earth Science
Geographic Location
Geography
Locational Skills (Social Studies)
Map Skills
Maps
Topography

Cartoons   *JUL. 1966*
Postings: 466   GC: 720
BT Visual Aids
RT Animation
Audiovisual Aids
Captions
Childrens Television
Comics (Publications)
Film Study
Films
Freehand Drawing
Illustrations
Instructional Materials
Nonprint Media

Case (Grammar)   *MAY 1969*
Postings: 367   GC: 450
BT Linguistic Theory
RT Form Classes (Languages)
Grammar
Language Patterns
Language Universals
Syntax

Case Based Instruction
USE Case Method (Teaching Technique)

Case Method (Teaching Technique)   *DEC. 1997*
Postings: 404   GC: 310
SN The practice of using cases as a pedagogical tool in fields such as law, business, medicine, and education—cases may include real and imagined scenarios, critical incident analysis, case studies, vignettes, and anecdotal accounts
UF Case Based Instruction
Case Study Approach (Teaching)
BT Teaching Methods
RT Case Studies
Discussion (Teaching Technique)
Experiential Learning
Problem Based Learning

Case Records   *JUL. 1966*
Postings: 275   GC: 320
NT Medical Case Histories
BT Records (Forms)
RT Biographical Inventories
Case Studies
Caseworker Approach
Confidential Records
Disclosure
Profiles
Recordkeeping
Student Records

Case Studies   *APR. 1970*
Postings: 19,209   GC: 810
SN Detailed analyses, usually focusing on a particular problem of an individual, group, or organization (Note: Do not confuse with "Medical Case Histories"—as of Dec97, use "Case Method (Teaching Technique)" for case-based instruction—as of Oct81, use as a minor Descriptor for examples of this kind of research—use as a major Descriptor only as the subject of a document)
UF Case Studies (Education) (1966 1980)
NT Cross Sectional Studies
Facility Case Studies
Longitudinal Studies
BT Evaluation Methods
Research
RT Case Method (Teaching Technique)
Case Records
Counseling
Qualitative Research

Case Studies (Education) (1966 1980)
USE Case Studies

Case Study Approach (Teaching)
USE Case Method (Teaching Technique)

Caseworker Approach   *JUL. 1966*
Postings: 327   GC: 240
SN Techniques, strategies, and procedures used by caseworkers, counselors, social workers, etc. for working with individuals or groups—includes determining and solving problems, recordkeeping, and followup activities
BT Methods
RT Case Records
Caseworkers
Counseling Techniques
Field Interviews
Rehabilitation Counseling
Social Work

Caseworkers   *JUL. 1966*
Postings: 203   GC: 240
SN Social service personnel responsible for solving or mitigating the specific problems of individuals, families, etc.
NT Parole Officers
Probation Officers
Social Workers
BT Personnel
RT Caseworker Approach
Counselors
Guidance Personnel
Rehabilitation
School Social Workers
Social Work

Cassettes (Tape)
USE Magnetic Tape Cassettes

Caste   *NOV. 1972*
Postings: 53   GC: 540
SN A closed social stratum based on heredity that determines its members' prestige, occupation, place of residence, and social relationships
UF Brahmins (1967 1980)
BT Social Class
RT Religious Cultural Groups
Social Discrimination
Social Stratification

Cataloging   *JUL. 1966*
Postings: 2,529   GC: 710
UF Bibliographic Control
Library Cataloging
NT Machine Readable Cataloging
BT Documentation
RT Authority Control (Information)
Bibliographic Records
Bibliometrics
Classification
Dewey Decimal Classification
Filing
Indexing
Library Catalogs
Library of Congress Classification
Library Technical Processes
Subject Index Terms
Universal Decimal Classification

Catalogs   *JUL. 1966*
Postings: 1,157   GC: 710
SN (Note: Use a more specific term if possible—see also "Reference Materials" hierarchy for more precise terminology)
NT Library Catalogs
Online Catalogs
School Catalogs
BT Publications

Categorical Aid   *SEP. 1982*
Postings: 179   GC: 620
SN Financial assistance for specific, limited programs or services prescribed by law or administrative regulations
BT Financial Support
RT Educational Finance
Equalization Aid
Federal Aid
Grants
Legal Responsibility
Resource Allocation
Special Needs Students
State Aid
Tax Allocation

Categorization
USE Classification

Catharsis   *APR. 1969*
Postings: 83   GC: 230
SN Relaxation of emotional tension by expressive reaction
UF Abreaction
Psychocatharsis
BT Emotional Experience

= Two or more Descriptors are used to represent this term.
The term's main entry shows the appropriate coordination.

RT   Aggression
     Anger
     Anxiety
     Emotional Development
     Hostility
     Psychological Patterns
     Psychotherapy
     Self Expression
     Stress Management

Cathode Ray Tube Terminals
USE   Video Display Terminals

Catholic Educators   *JUL. 1966*
     Postings: 604   GC: 360
SN   Teachers in Catholic schools or in diocesan educational programs (Note: Prior to Mar80, the use of this term was not restricted by a Scope Note)
BT   Teachers
RT   Catholic Schools
     Catholics
     Church Related Colleges
     Church Workers
     Religious Education

Catholic Elementary Schools (1967 1980)
USE   Catholic Schools

Catholic High Schools (1967 1980)
USE   Catholic Schools

Catholic Parents (1966 1980)
USE   Catholics
AND   Parents

Catholic Schools   *JUL. 1966*
     Postings: 1,876   GC: 340
UF   Catholic Elementary Schools (1967 1980)
     Catholic High Schools (1967 1980)
BT   Parochial Schools
RT   Catholic Educators
     Church Related Colleges
     Lay Teachers
     Private Education
     Private School Aid
     Religious Education

Catholics   *JUL. 1966*
     Postings: 537   GC: 560
UF   Catholic Parents (1966 1980) #
BT   Religious Cultural Groups
RT   Catholic Educators
     Christianity
     Nuns
     Priests

CATV
USE   Cable Television

Caucasian Languages   *JUL. 1966*
     Postings: 13   GC: 440
SN   Languages spoken in the area of the Caucasus mountain range which do not belong to the Indo-European, Semitic, or Uralic-Altaic families
UF   Circassian
     Darghi
     Georgian
BT   Languages

Caucasian Race (1967 1980)
USE   Whites

Caucasian Students (1967 1980)
USE   White Students

Caucasians (1967 1980)
USE   Whites

Causal Attributions
USE   Attribution Theory

Causal Factors
USE   Influences

Causal Models   *APR. 1990*
     Postings: 356   GC: 820
SN   Theoretical frameworks for estimating and diagrammatically expressing plausible causality among variables
NT   Structural Equation Models
BT   Models
RT   Attribution Theory
     Correlation
     Estimation (Mathematics)
     Etiology
     Evaluation Methods
     Influences
     Mathematical Models
     Matrices
     Multiple Regression Analysis
     Path Analysis
     Predictor Variables
     Regression (Statistics)
     Research Design
     Research Methodology
     Statistical Inference
     Validity

CCTV
USE   Closed Circuit Television

CD Recordings
USE   Optical Disks

CD ROM
USE   Optical Data Disks

Cebuano   *JUL. 1966*
     Postings: 10   GC: 440
BT   Visayan
RT   Dialects

Ceilings   *JUL. 1966*
     Postings: 46   GC: 920
BT   Structural Elements (Construction)
RT   Buildings
     Construction (Process)

Cell Biology
USE   Cytology

Cell Theory (1966 1980)
USE   Cytology

Cellular Molecular Biology
USE   Cytology
AND   Molecular Biology

Cement Industry   *JUL. 1966*
     Postings: 47   GC: 650
UF   Concrete Industry
BT   Manufacturing Industry
RT   Chemical Engineering
     Construction Industry
     Construction Materials
     Prestressed Concrete

Cements (Adhesives)
USE   Adhesives

Censorship   *JUL. 1966*
     Postings: 2,187   GC: 520
RT   Academic Freedom
     Freedom
     Freedom of Information
     Freedom of Speech
     Information Policy
     Intellectual Freedom
     Moral Issues
     Moral Values

     Political Correctness
     Sanctions

Census Figures   *JUL. 1966*
     Postings: 1,568   GC: 730
BT   Statistical Data
RT   Cohort Analysis
     Community Size
     Demography
     Incidence
     Profiles
     Statistical Analysis

Centers of Interest (1966 1980)
USE   Learning Centers (Classroom)

Central American History
USE   Latin American History

Central American Literature
USE   Latin American Literature

Central Americans
USE   Latin Americans

Central Office Administrators   *FEB. 1998*
     Postings: 126   GC: 360
SN   School district administrators, responsible to the superintendent and board of education for such areas as curriculum, personnel, budget, assessment, student services, and community relations (occasionally may be interpreted to include the superintendent and board of education)
BT   Administrators
RT   Boards of Education
     School Administration
     School Districts
     School Personnel
     Superintendents

Central Sound Systems (1966 1980)
USE   Audio Equipment

Centralization   *JUL. 1966*
     Postings: 996   GC: 520
BT   Administrative Organization
RT   Decentralization
     Mergers
     Organizational Change
     School Organization

Centralized Schools
USE   Consolidated Schools

Centroid Method of Factor Analysis
USE   Factor Analysis

Ceramics   *SEP. 1968*
     Postings: 230   GC: 420
UF   Pottery
BT   Handicrafts
RT   Childrens Art
     Clay
     Design Crafts
     Glass
     Industrial Arts

Cerebral Dominance (1967 1986)
USE   Brain Hemisphere Functions

Cerebral Palsy   *JUL. 1966*
     Postings: 512   GC: 220
BT   Congenital Impairments
     Neurological Impairments
RT   Developmental Disabilities
     Mental Retardation
     Multiple Disabilities
     Speech Impairments

Certification   *JUL. 1966*
     Postings: 2,838   GC: 330
UF   Licensing
NT   Accreditation (Institutions)
     Counselor Certification
     Student Certification
     Teacher Certification
RT   Credentials
     Credits
     Educational Certificates
     Eligibility
     Equivalency Tests
     Experiential Learning
     High School Equivalency Programs
     Licensing Examinations (Professions)
     Mandatory Continuing Education
     Portfolios (Background Materials)
     Prior Learning
     Proprietary Schools
     Qualifications
     Quality Control
     Special Degree Programs
     Standards
     State Licensing Boards

Certified Nurses
USE   Nurses

Certified Public Accountants   *JUL. 1966*
     Postings: 52   GC: 640
BT   Accountants
RT   Accounting
     Financial Services

CEU
USE   Continuing Education Units

Chad Languages   *JUL. 1966*
     Postings: 9   GC: 440
NT   Hausa
BT   Afro Asiatic Languages
RT   Language Classification

Chain Reflexes (Behavior)
USE   Behavior Chaining

Chalkboards   *JUL. 1966*
     Postings: 71   GC: 910
UF   Blackboards
BT   Visual Aids
RT   Audiovisual Aids
     Bulletin Boards
     Educational Equipment

Chamorro   *FEB. 1975*
     Postings: 79   GC: 440
SN   Native language of Guam and the other Mariana Islands
BT   Malayo Polynesian Languages

Chancellors (Education)
USE   College Presidents

Chancroid
USE   Venereal Diseases

Change   *MAR. 1980*
     Postings: 1,713   GC: 520
SN   Act or process of altering, modifying, transforming, substituting, or otherwise making or becoming different—includes deviation from established character, condition, sequence, or direction (Note: Do not confuse with "Development," which refers to sequential, progressive changes—use a more specific term if possible)
NT   Administrative Change
     Attitude Change
     Behavior Change
     Building Conversion
     Career Change
     Climate Change
     Community Change

= Two or more Descriptors are used to represent this term.
The term's main entry shows the appropriate coordination.

Data Conversion
Economic Change
Educational Change
Life Events
Media Adaptation
Midlife Transitions
Organizational Change
Personality Change
Social Change
RT Change Agents
    Change Strategies
    Development
    History
    Influences
    Innovation
    Inventions
    Resistance to Change
    Revolution

Change Agents   *JUL. 1966*
    Postings: 4,458   GC: 330
SN Individuals or groups who attempt
    change, aid in its accomplishment, or
    help to cope with it (Note: Use a more
    specific term if possible)
NT Extension Agents
    Linking Agents
BT Groups
RT Attitude Change
    Blue Ribbon Commissions
    Change
    Change Strategies
    Community Change
    Community Leaders
    Consultants
    Educational Change
    Social Change

Change Strategies   *MAY 1974*
    Postings: 12,624   GC: 330
SN Methods used by those who would alter
    the practice of some organization, insti-
    tution, or other group to incorporate new
    knowledge, products, procedures, or val-
    ues toward improved service or results
BT Methods
RT Administrative Change
    Adoption (Ideas)
    Attitude Change
    Behavior Change
    Change
    Change Agents
    Community Change
    Consciousness Raising
    Economic Change
    Educational Change
    Educational Strategies
    Finance Reform
    Improvement
    Incentives
    Organizational Change
    Resistance to Change
    Social Change
    Strategic Planning

Changing Attitudes (1966 1980)
USE Attitude Change

Chaos Theory   *JAN. 1999*
    Postings: 180   GC: 810
SN Study of complex, replicated patterns in
    seemingly random phenomena
UF Butterfly Effect
BT Theories
RT Mathematical Models
    Physics
    Prediction
    Probability
    Social Theories
    Systems Approach

Character
USE Personality

Character Portrayal
USE Characterization

Character Recognition   *OCT. 1969*
    Postings: 91   GC: 710
SN Technology of using a machine to sense
    and encode written or printed characters
    into a machine language (Note: Prior to
    Mar80, the use of this term was not
    restricted by a Scope Note)
UF Magnetic Ink Character Recognition
    OCR #
    Optical Character Recognition #
BT Pattern Recognition
RT Information Processing
    Optical Scanners

Characterization   *JUL. 1977*
    Postings: 1,706   GC: 430
SN The creation and convincing representa-
    tion of human characters or personali-
    ties as in fiction or drama
UF Character Portrayal
    Characterization (Literature) (1969
    1977)
BT Literary Devices
RT Acting
    Animation
    Literary Styles

Characterization (Literature) (1969 1977)
USE Characterization

Charitable Trusts
USE Trusts (Financial)

Charter Schools   *OCT. 1995*
    Postings: 438   GC: 340
SN Public schools run by groups of parents,
    teachers, and administrators under con-
    tract with local or state school boards,
    and given broad freedom from regula-
    tions in exchange for the promise of
    such favorable outcomes as improved
    test scores, attendance rates, and drop-
    out rates
BT Public Schools
RT Accountability
    Institutional Autonomy
    Nontraditional Education

Charts   *JUL. 1966*
    Postings: 1,263   GC: 720
NT Experience Charts
    Flow Charts
BT Visual Aids
RT Atlases
    Diagrams
    Graphs
    Illustrations
    Instructional Materials
    Nonprint Media
    Precision Teaching
    Profiles
    Records (Forms)
    Tables (Data)

Cheating   *JUL. 1966*
    Postings: 491   GC: 530
BT Antisocial Behavior
RT Codes of Ethics
    Discipline Problems
    Fraud
    Honesty
    Lying
    Plagiarism

Check Lists   *JUL. 1966*
    Postings: 3,106   GC: 730
SN Lists from which items can be com-
    pared, scheduled, verified, or identified
BT Records (Forms)
RT Guidelines
    Indexes
    Informal Assessment
    Rating Scales

Chefs
USE Cooks

Chemical Analysis   *JAN. 1970*
    Postings: 1,331   GC: 490
UF Chemical Determination
    Composition Measurement
    Determination (Chemical)
BT Evaluation Methods
RT Chemical Engineering
    Chemical Reactions
    Chemistry
    Chromatography
    Metallurgy
    Mineralogy
    Spectroscopy
    Structural Analysis (Science)
    Water Treatment

Chemical Bonding   *JUL. 1966*
    Postings: 382   GC: 490
BT Chemical Reactions
RT Chemistry
    Crystallography
    Inorganic Chemistry
    Molecular Structure
    Organic Chemistry
    Physical Sciences
    Stereochemistry
    Structural Analysis (Science)

Chemical Dependency (Drugs)
USE Drug Addiction

Chemical Determination
USE Chemical Analysis

Chemical Engineering   *AUG. 1982*
    Postings: 521   GC: 490
SN Branch of engineering concerned with
    industrial chemical processes involved
    in converting raw materials into prod-
    ucts, and the design/operation of plants/
    equipment to accomplish this work
BT Engineering
RT Agricultural Chemical Occupations
    Biotechnology
    Cement Industry
    Chemical Analysis
    Chemical Industry
    Chemistry
    Electrochemistry
    Kinetics
    Manufacturing Industry
    Mass Production
    Petroleum Industry
    Physical Chemistry
    Polymers
    Power Technology
    Water Treatment

Chemical Equilibrium   *JAN. 1970*
    Postings: 342   GC: 490
SN Condition in which a chemical reaction is
    occurring at equal rates in its forward
    and reverse directions, so that concen-
    trations of the reacting substances do
    not change with time
UF Equilibrium Constants
RT Chemical Reactions
    Chemistry
    Electrochemistry
    Entropy
    Physical Chemistry
    Thermodynamics

Chemical Industry   *AUG. 1969*
    Postings: 445   GC: 650
BT Manufacturing Industry
RT Agricultural Chemical Occupations
    Chemical Engineering
    Chemical Technicians
    Chemistry
    Petroleum Industry

Chemical Nomenclature   *OCT. 1972*
    Postings: 207   GC: 490
BT Vocabulary
RT Chemistry
    Classification

Chemical Reactions   *JAN. 1970*
    Postings: 1,753   GC: 490
UF Chemical Synthesis
NT Chemical Bonding
    Oxidation
    Photochemical Reactions
RT Acids
    Chemical Analysis
    Chemical Equilibrium
    Chemistry
    Diffusion (Physics)
    Enzymes
    Inorganic Chemistry
    Molecular Structure
    Nucleic Acids
    Organic Chemistry
    Polymers

Chemical Synthesis
USE Chemical Reactions

Chemical Technicians   *JUL. 1966*
    Postings: 68   GC: 640
BT Paraprofessional Personnel
RT Chemical Industry
    Chemistry
    Environmental Technicians
    Metallurgical Technicians
    Nuclear Power Plant Technicians
    Scientific Personnel

Chemistry   *JUL. 1966*
    Postings: 10,838   GC: 490
UF Chemistry Instruction (1967 1980) #
    Chemistry Teachers (1967 1980) #
NT Biochemistry
    Geochemistry
    Inorganic Chemistry
    Organic Chemistry
    Physical Chemistry
    Stereochemistry
BT Physical Sciences
RT Acids
    Agricultural Chemical Occupations
    Atomic Structure
    Chemical Analysis
    Chemical Bonding
    Chemical Engineering
    Chemical Equilibrium
    Chemical Industry
    Chemical Nomenclature
    Chemical Reactions
    Chemical Technicians
    Chromatography
    Coordination Compounds
    Crystallography
    Earth Science
    Metallurgy
    Mineralogy
    Molecular Structure
    Oxidation
    Petrology
    Photochemical Reactions
    Polymers
    Radiation Biology
    Radioisotopes
    Scientific Research
    Soil Science
    Spectroscopy
    Water

Chemistry Instruction (1967 1980)
USE Chemistry
AND Science Instruction

Chemistry Teachers (1967 1980)
USE Chemistry
AND Science Teachers

Chemotherapy
USE Drug Therapy

Cheremis   *JUL. 1966*
    Postings: 2   GC: 440
BT Finno Ugric Languages

= Two or more Descriptors are used to represent this term.
The term's main entry shows the appropriate coordination.

Cherokee   APR. 1970
    Postings: 21   GC: 440
SN The Iroquoian language of the Cherokee
    tribe of American Indians
BT American Indian Languages
RT Cherokee (Tribe)

Cherokee (Tribe)   JAN. 1994
    Postings: 103   GC: 560
SN An American Indian people formerly in-
    habiting the southern Appalachian moun-
    tains from the western Carolinas and
    eastern Tennessee to northern Georgia,
    with present-day populations in north-
    east Oklahoma and western North Caro-
    lina (also, dispersed kin) (Note: For the
    Cherokee language, use "Cherokee"—
    for the geographic concept of Chero-
    kee lands, use the Identifier "Cherokee
    Nation")
BT American Indians
    Tribes
RT Cherokee

Chi Square   DEC. 1988
    Postings: 223   GC: 820
SN The sum of the squares of observed
    values minus expected values divided by
    the expected values—used in testing
    hypotheses concerning the discrepancy
    between observed and expected results
BT Statistical Analysis
RT Correlation
    Goodness of Fit
    Hypothesis Testing
    Mathematical Models
    Nonparametric Statistics
    Predictor Variables
    Statistical Significance

Chibemba
USE Bemba

Chief Academic Officers
USE Academic Deans

Chief Administrators (1967 1980)
USE Administrators

Child Abuse   JUL. 1966
    Postings: 4,611   GC: 530
UF Abused Children
    Child Sexual Abuse #
BT Antisocial Behavior
RT Battered Women
    Caregiver Child Relationship
    Child Health
    Child Neglect
    Child Welfare
    Children
    Emotional Abuse
    Family Problems
    Family Violence
    Missing Children
    Parent Child Relationship
    Sexual Abuse
    Verbal Abuse
    Victims of Crime
    Violence

Child Advocacy   MAR. 1974
    Postings: 1,601   GC: 520
SN Active mobilization of social, economic,
    and legal resources for the purpose of
    ensuring the individual child's basic rights
    and developmental needs (including those
    related to home, community, and school)
BT Advocacy
RT Child Health
    Child Welfare
    Childhood Needs
    Children
    Childrens Rights
    Helping Relationship
    Individual Power
    Legal Aid
    Self Advocacy

Child Behavior   APR. 1993
    Postings: 1,022   GC: 120
NT Infant Behavior
BT Behavior
RT Adolescent Behavior
    Affective Behavior
    Attachment Behavior
    Behavior Development
    Caregiver Child Relationship
    Child Development
    Child Psychology
    Child Responsibility
    Child Role
    Childhood Attitudes
    Children
    Childrens Rights
    Developmental Delays
    Developmental Stages
    Exploratory Behavior
    Familiarity
    Imitation
    Obedience
    Parent Child Relationship
    Play
    Self Control
    Separation Anxiety
    Social Behavior
    Student Behavior
    Toys

Child Care Centers (1967 1980)
USE Day Care Centers

Child Care Occupations   JUL. 1966
    Postings: 405   GC: 640
BT Service Occupations
RT Child Caregivers
    Child Development Specialists
    Day Care
    Day Care Centers
    Foster Care
    Home Economics Skills
    Infant Care
    Occupational Home Economics
    Parenting Skills

Child Care Workers (1967 1980)
USE Child Caregivers

Child Care (1966 1980)   MAR. 1980
    Postings: 898   GC: 520
SN Invalid Descriptor—see "Child Rearing"
    or "Day Care"

Child Caregivers   APR. 1980
    Postings: 2,745   GC: 640
SN Persons who take care of children—
    includes professionals, nonprofessionals,
    parents, and others (Note: For docu-
    ments/articles involving parents, use a
    more precise term such as "Parents,"
    "Mothers," "Fathers," or other "parent"
    term)
UF Child Care Workers (1967 1980)
BT Caregivers
RT Caregiver Child Relationship
    Caregiver Role
    Caregiver Speech
    Child Care Occupations
    Child Rearing
    Day Care
    Day Care Centers
    Day Care Effects
    Foster Care
    Infant Care
    Parents
    Preschool Teachers
    Sick Child Care
    Social Workers

Child Centered Curriculum
USE Student Centered Curriculum

Child Custody   OCT. 1983
    Postings: 367   GC: 520
SN Court-authorized arrangement for the pri-
    mary care of children

RT Child Rearing
    Child Support
    Child Welfare
    Children
    Divorce
    Family Problems
    One Parent Family
    Parent Child Relationship

Child Development   JUL. 1966
    Postings: 10,244   GC: 120
BT Individual Development
RT Child Behavior
    Child Development Centers
    Child Development Specialists
    Child Health
    Child Language
    Child Rearing
    Child Responsibility
    Children
    Delayed Speech
    Developmental Delays
    Developmental Stages
    Developmental Tasks
    Developmentally Appropriate Practices
    Failure to Thrive
    Family Environment
    Parenthood Education
    Piagetian Theory

Child Development Centers   JUL. 1966
    Postings: 259   GC: 920
SN Educational facilities for preschool child-
    ren, which also provide health and family
    services—originally used in connection
    with Project Head Start for centers in
    which cooperation of family, commu-
    nity, and professional staff contribute to
    the total development of the child
BT Educational Facilities
RT Child Development
    Child Development Specialists
    Day Care Centers
    Early Childhood Education
    Nursery Schools
    Preschool Children
    Preschool Education

Child Development Specialists   JUL. 1966
    Postings: 127   GC: 360
SN Persons whose professional training has
    prepared them to understand and work
    with the changes that take place in child-
    ren as they develop from birth to
    maturity—these specialists may work
    with other professionals,
    paraprofessionals, or parents, as well as
    with children
BT Specialists
RT Child Care Occupations
    Child Development
    Child Development Centers
    Child Psychology
    Children

Child Health   DEC. 1989
    Postings: 2,098   GC: 210
UF Child Health Care
BT Health
RT Child Abuse
    Child Advocacy
    Child Development
    Child Neglect
    Child Psychology
    Child Safety
    Child Welfare
    Childhood Needs
    Children
    Comprehensive School Health Educa-
    tion
    Dental Health
    Diseases
    Failure to Thrive
    Family Health
    Health Programs
    Health Related Fitness
    Health Services
    Hygiene
    Immunization Programs

    Infant Care
    Infant Mortality
    Mental Health
    Nutrition
    Pediatrics
    Perinatal Influences
    Physical Fitness
    Physical Health
    Prenatal Care
    Prenatal Influences
    Preventive Medicine
    Primary Health Care
    Public Health
    School Health Services
    Sick Child Care
    Special Health Problems
    Sudden Infant Death Syndrome

Child Health Care
USE Child Health

Child Labor   JUL. 1966
    Postings: 306   GC: 630
UF Child Labor Laws (1966 1974) #
    Child Labor Legislation (1966 1980) #
BT Labor
RT Child Welfare
    Children

Child Labor Laws (1966 1974)
USE Child Labor
AND Labor Legislation

Child Labor Legislation (1966 1980)
USE Child Labor
AND Labor Legislation

Child Language   NOV. 1968
    Postings: 3,887   GC: 450
SN (Note: See also the Identifier "Baby Talk")
BT Language
RT Bilingualism
    Caregiver Speech
    Child Development
    Children
    Childrens Writing
    Egocentrism
    Immersion Programs
    Invented Spelling
    Language Acquisition
    Language Arts
    Language Experience Approach
    Language Impairments
    Language Patterns
    Language Research
    Linguistic Input
    Monolingualism
    Oral Language
    Pronunciation
    Psycholinguistics
    Speech Habits
    Verbal Development

Child Neglect   MAR. 1980
    Postings: 1,489   GC: 530
SN Failure of parents or caretakers to pro-
    vide to children the care essential for
    normal development
UF Neglected Children (1977 1980)
BT Antisocial Behavior
    Negligence
RT Caregiver Child Relationship
    Child Abuse
    Child Health
    Child Rearing
    Child Welfare
    Children
    Emotional Abuse
    Failure to Thrive
    Family Problems
    Parent Child Relationship
    Victims of Crime

Child Parent Literacy
USE Family Literacy

= Two or more Descriptors are used to represent this term.
The term's main entry shows the appropriate coordination.

Child Parent Relationship
USE   Parent Child Relationship

Child Psychology   *JUL. 1966*
    Postings: 740   GC: 230
BT   Psychology
RT   Child Behavior
    Child Development Specialists
    Child Health
    Children
    Developmental Psychology
    Individual Psychology
    School Psychology

Child Rearing   *JUL. 1966*
    Postings: 4,351   GC: 520
SN   Care of children by parents, guardians,
    or other primary caregivers (Note: See
    also "Day Care"—prior to Mar80, "Child
    Care" was also a valid Descriptor)
UF   Home Child Care
    Parenting
RT   Caregiver Child Relationship
    Child Caregivers
    Child Custody
    Child Development
    Child Neglect
    Children
    Family Relationship
    Infant Care
    Parent Child Relationship
    Parenthood Education
    Parenting Skills
    Parents as Teachers

Child Responsibility   *JUL. 1966*
    Postings: 257   GC: 510
SN   Responsibility of, not for, a child (Note:
    Prior to Mar80, the use of this term was
    not restricted by a Scope Note)
BT   Responsibility
RT   Child Behavior
    Child Development
    Child Role
    Childhood Needs
    Children
    Childrens Rights
    Parent Responsibility
    Student Responsibility
    Teacher Responsibility

Child Restraints (Vehicle Safety)
USE   Child Safety
AND   Restraints (Vehicle Safety)

Child Role   *JUL. 1966*
    Postings: 171   GC: 510
BT   Role
RT   Child Behavior
    Child Responsibility
    Children
    Family Role

Child Safety   *JUL. 2000*
    Postings: 294   GC: 210
SN   Freedom from, or prevention of, harm or
    danger to children (Note: See also "Child
    Welfare" for the related notion of a state
    in which physical and/or psychological
    needs of children are satisfied)
UF   Child Restraints (Vehicle Safety) #
BT   Safety
RT   Child Health
    Child Welfare
    Restraints (Vehicle Safety)
    Safety Education
    School Safety
    Traffic Safety

Child Sexual Abuse
USE   Child Abuse
AND   Sexual Abuse

Child Support   *AUG. 1989*
    Postings: 262   GC: 620
SN   Money paid for the care of one's minor

child, especially payments to a former
spouse under a decree of divorce
BT   Financial Support
RT   Child Custody
    Child Welfare
    Children
    Divorce
    Family Financial Resources
    Family Income
    Legal Responsibility
    One Parent Family
    Parent Child Relationship
    Parent Responsibility

Child Welfare   *JUL. 1966*
    Postings: 3,353   GC: 520
BT   Well Being
RT   Adopted Children
    Adoption
    Child Abuse
    Child Advocacy
    Child Custody
    Child Health
    Child Labor
    Child Neglect
    Child Safety
    Child Support
    Childhood Needs
    Children
    Childrens Rights
    Early Parenthood
    Foster Care
    Foster Children
    Foster Family
    Juvenile Justice
    Latchkey Children
    Missing Children
    Runaways
    Student Welfare

Childbirth
USE   Birth

Childhood Attitudes   *JUL. 1966*
    Postings: 2,464   GC: 120
SN   Attitudes of, not toward, children (Note:
    Prior to Mar80, the use of this term was
    not restricted by a Scope Note)
UF   Childrens Attitudes
BT   Attitudes
RT   Adolescent Attitudes
    Child Behavior
    Childhood Interests
    Children
    Student Attitudes

Childhood Friendship (1966 1980)
USE   Friendship

Childhood Interests   *JUL. 1966*
    Postings: 613   GC: 120
SN   Objects, activities, persons, etc., that
    engage the attention of children
UF   Childrens Interests
BT   Interests
RT   Childhood Attitudes
    Children
    Student Interests

Childhood Needs   *JUL. 1966*
    Postings: 2,078   GC: 120
SN   Those experiences, attentions, etc., which
    are necessary for the physical, biologi-
    cal, intellectual, personal, and social de-
    velopment of children
UF   Childrens Needs
BT   Individual Needs
RT   Child Advocacy
    Child Health
    Child Responsibility
    Child Welfare
    Children
    Childrens Rights
    Family Needs
    Psychological Needs
    Student Needs

Childhood (1966 1980)
USE   Children

Childlessness   *JUN. 1988*
    Postings: 67   GC: 520
SN   Having no natural children (Note: If ap-
    propriate, coordinate with the Identifier
    "Voluntary Childlessness")
RT   Adoption
    Birth Rate
    Children
    Family Planning
    Family Relationship
    Family Size
    Family Structure
    Gynecology

Children   *JUL. 1966*
    Postings: 19,409   GC: 120
SN   Aged birth through approximately 12
    years
UF   Childhood (1966 1980)
NT   Adopted Children
    Foster Children
    Grandchildren
    Hospitalized Children
    Latchkey Children
    Migrant Children
    Minority Group Children
    Missing Children
    Preadolescents
    Problem Children
    Transient Children
    Young Children
BT   Age Groups
RT   Adolescents
    Caregiver Child Relationship
    Child Abuse
    Child Advocacy
    Child Behavior
    Child Custody
    Child Development
    Child Development Specialists
    Child Health
    Child Labor
    Child Language
    Child Neglect
    Child Psychology
    Child Rearing
    Child Responsibility
    Child Role
    Child Support
    Child Welfare
    Childhood Attitudes
    Childhood Interests
    Childhood Needs
    Childlessness
    Childrens Art
    Childrens Games
    Childrens Libraries
    Childrens Literature
    Childrens Rights
    Childrens Television
    Childrens Writing
    Dependents
    Elementary School Students
    Family (Sociological Unit)
    Family Life
    Family Problems
    Parent Child Relationship
    Parenting Skills
    Play
    Youth

Childrens Art   *JUN. 1977*
    Postings: 684   GC: 420
SN   The process and/or the results of child-
    ren's production of art objects or arti-
    facts
BT   Visual Arts
RT   Art Activities
    Art Appreciation
    Art Education
    Art Materials
    Art Products
    Ceramics
    Children
    Creative Art
    Freehand Drawing
    Handicrafts

    Painting (Visual Arts)
    Printmaking

Childrens Attitudes
USE   Childhood Attitudes

Childrens Books (1966 1980)
USE   Books
AND   Childrens Literature

Childrens Courts
USE   Juvenile Courts

Childrens Games   *JUL. 1966*
    Postings: 498   GC: 470
BT   Games
RT   Children
    Play
    Playground Activities
    Recess Breaks
    Toys

Childrens Interests
USE   Childhood Interests

Childrens Libraries   *AUG. 1989*
    Postings: 311   GC: 710
SN   Libraries or sections of libraries devoted
    to collections and services for children
BT   Libraries
RT   Children
    Childrens Literature
    Public Libraries
    School Libraries

Childrens Literature   *MAY 1974*
    Postings: 8,071   GC: 430
SN   Any reading material written primarily
    for, or read widely by, children from their
    early years to adolescence
UF   Childrens Books (1966 1980) #
BT   Literature
RT   Adolescent Literature
    Children
    Childrens Libraries
    Comics (Publications)
    Didacticism
    Fairy Tales
    Nursery Rhymes
    Picture Books
    Reading Materials

Childrens Needs
USE   Childhood Needs

Childrens Play
USE   Play

Childrens Rights   *MAR. 1983*
    Postings: 580   GC: 520
SN   Legal and human rights of children, per-
    taining to physical and psychological
    welfare in such areas as guardianship,
    custody, child abuse, and juvenile court
    proceedings
BT   Civil Liberties
RT   Child Advocacy
    Child Behavior
    Child Responsibility
    Child Welfare
    Childhood Needs
    Children
    Civil Rights
    Due Process
    Juvenile Courts
    Juvenile Justice
    Parent Rights
    Student Rights

Childrens Television   *DEC. 1976*
    Postings: 592   GC: 720
SN   Television programming designed for or
    aimed at children's interests

= Two or more Descriptors are used to represent this term.
The term's main entry shows the appropriate coordination.

BT   Television
RT   Cartoons
     Children

Childrens Writing   *MAY 1995*
     Postings: 581   GC: 400
SN   Writing by, not for, children (Note: See
     also the Identifier "Early Writing")
BT   Writing (Composition)
RT   Beginning Writing
     Child Language
     Children
     Creative Writing
     Emergent Literacy
     Invented Spelling
     Student Writing Models
     Writing Exercises
     Writing Instruction
     Writing Skills

Chimneys   *OCT. 1969*
     Postings: 12   GC: 920
UF   Exhaust Stacks
     Smokestacks
BT   Structural Elements (Construction)
RT   Air Flow
     Air Pollution
     Heat
     Heating
     Pollution
     Ventilation

Chinese   *JUL. 1966*
     Postings: 1,626   GC: 440
NT   Cantonese
     Foochow
     Mandarin Chinese
BT   Sino Tibetan Languages
RT   Chinese Americans
     Chinese Culture
     Ideography

Chinese Americans   *JUL. 1966*
     Postings: 696   GC: 560
BT   Asian Americans
     Ethnic Groups
RT   Chinese

Chinese Culture   *JUL. 1966*
     Postings: 772   GC: 560
BT   Culture
RT   Asian Studies
     Chinese
     Non Western Civilization

Chinyanja   *JUL. 1966*
     Postings: 7   GC: 440
UF   Cinyanja
     Nyanja
BT   Bantu Languages

Chippewa (Language)
USE Ojibwa

Chippewa (Tribe)   *JAN. 1994*
     Postings: 80   GC: 560
SN   An American Indian people of the area
     around Lake Huron and Lake Superior,
     and westward to Saskatchewan and Mon-
     tana (also, dispersed kin)—known pri-
     marily as Ojibwas in Canada (Chippewa
     is a corruption of Ojibwa)
UF   Anishinabe (Tribe)
     Ojibwa (Tribe)
     Ojibway (Tribe)
     Ojibwe (Tribe)
BT   American Indians
     Tribes
RT   Ojibwa

Chlorination (Water)
USE Water Treatment

Choctaw   *APR. 1970*
     Postings: 22   GC: 440
SN   The Muskogean language of the Choc-
     taw tribe of American Indians
BT   American Indian Languages
RT   Choctaw (Tribe)
     Mississippi Band of Choctaw (Tribe)

Choctaw (Tribe)   *JAN. 1994*
     Postings: 48   GC: 560
SN   An American Indian people originally of
     Mississippi and Alabama, and presently
     of eastern Mississippi and southeastern
     Oklahoma (also, dispersed kin)
NT   Mississippi Band of Choctaw (Tribe)
BT   American Indians
     Tribes
RT   Choctaw

Choirs
USE Singing

Choral Music   *OCT. 1968*
     Postings: 193   GC: 420
SN   Music intended for group singing
BT   Vocal Music
RT   Hymns
     Music Activities
     Music Education
     Music Techniques
     Musical Composition
     Singing

Choral Speaking   *JUL. 1966*
     Postings: 85   GC: 420
SN   Ensemble speaking often using various
     voice combinations and contrasts to bring
     out the meaning or tonal beauty of a
     passage of poetry or prose
BT   Theater Arts
RT   Literature
     Literature Appreciation
     Oral Interpretation
     Poetry
     Speech

Choreography
USE Dance

Choruses (1968 1980)
USE Singing

Christianity   *MAY 1969*
     Postings: 734   GC: 430
BT   Religion
RT   Biblical Literature
     Catholics
     Judaism
     Philosophy
     Protestants
     Religious Cultural Groups
     Western Civilization

Chromatography   *JUL. 1969*
     Postings: 341   GC: 490
SN   Method of separating and analyzing mix-
     tures of chemical substances
UF   Electrochromatography
BT   Laboratory Procedures
RT   Biochemistry
     Biology
     Chemical Analysis
     Chemistry

Chronic Illness   *JUN. 1988*
     Postings: 459   GC: 210
SN   Disease or ailment of long duration or
     frequent recurrence, and often of in-
     creasing severity
UF   Chronic Pain #
BT   Diseases
RT   Adjustment (to Environment)
     Frail Elderly
     Health
     Hospitalized Children

     Long Term Care
     Patient Education
     Severity (of Disability)
     Special Health Problems

Chronic Pain
USE Chronic Illness
AND Pain

Chronicles   *SEP. 1969*
     Postings: 94   GC: 430
SN   Historical, chronological accounts of
     events
BT   Literary Genres
     Nonfiction
RT   History
     Medieval Literature
     Poetry
     Renaissance Literature

Chronological Age   *APR. 1980*
     Postings: 142   GC: 120
SN   Actual physical age of the individual ex-
     pressed in terms of years and months
BT   Age
RT   Age Groups
     Mixed Age Grouping
     Physical Characteristics
     Physical Development

Church Action
USE Church Role

Church Migrant Projects (1966 1980)
USE Church Programs
AND Migrant Programs

Church Programs   *JUL. 1966*
     Postings: 334   GC: 520
UF   Church Migrant Projects (1966
     1980) #
     Church Projects
BT   Programs
RT   Church Related Colleges
     Church Role
     Church Workers
     Churches
     Migrant Programs
     Nonprofit Organizations
     Religion
     Religious Education

Church Projects
USE Church Programs

Church Related Colleges   *JUL. 1966*
     Postings: 1,018   GC: 340
UF   Denominational Colleges
     Sectarian Colleges
     Seminaries #
BT   Colleges
RT   Catholic Educators
     Catholic Schools
     Church Programs
     Parochial Schools
     Private Colleges
     Private Education
     Private School Aid
     Religious Education
     Religious Organizations
     Single Sex Colleges
     Small Colleges
     Theological Education

Church Responsibility   *JUL. 1966*
     Postings: 102   GC: 520
BT   Responsibility
RT   Churches
     Leadership Responsibility

Church Role   *JUL. 1966*
     Postings: 703   GC: 520
UF   Church Action
BT   Institutional Role

RT   Church Programs
     Churches
     Religion
     State Church Separation

Church State Separation
USE State Church Separation

Church Workers   *NOV. 1969*
     Postings: 86   GC: 520
UF   Parish Workers
BT   Personnel
RT   Catholic Educators
     Church Programs
     Churches
     Clergy
     Lay People
     Lay Teachers
     Nuns
     Priests
     Religion
     Religious Education

Churches   *JUL. 1966*
     Postings: 242   GC: 920
BT   Institutions
RT   Church Programs
     Church Responsibility
     Church Role
     Church Workers
     Mergers
     Nonprofit Organizations
     Priests
     Religion
     Religious Organizations
     State Church Separation
     Theological Education

Chuvash   *JUL. 1966*
     Postings: 3   GC: 440
BT   Turkic Languages

Cigarette Smoking
USE Smoking

Cinema
USE Films

Cinema Study
USE Film Study

Cinyanja
USE Chinyanja

Circassian
USE Caucasian Languages

Circuit Teachers
USE Itinerant Teachers

Circuits (Electronic)
USE Electric Circuits

Circulatory System
USE Cardiovascular System

Citation Analysis   *AUG. 1986*
     Postings: 359   GC: 810
SN   Bibliometric application in which a body
     of literature is separated and classified
     through interconnections of bibliographic
     citations
NT   Bibliographic Coupling
BT   Bibliometrics
RT   Bibliographies
     Citation Indexes
     Citations (References)
     Classification

= Two or more Descriptors are used to represent this term.
The term's main entry shows the appropriate coordination.

Citation Indexes   *JUL. 1966*
    Postings: 187   GC: 710
SN Indexing system for identifying later writ-
    ings that refer to (cite) earlier works
BT Indexes
RT Bibliographic Coupling
    Citation Analysis
    Citations (References)
    Indexing

Citations (Legal)
USE Law Enforcement

Citations (References)   *MAR. 1980*
    Postings: 1,480   GC: 730
SN References that identify works which
    have been used as authorities or from
    which passages have been quoted (Note:
    Do not confuse with "Bibliographic Rec-
    ords")
UF Bibliographic Citations (1969 1980)
    Bibliographic References
    Footnotes (Bibliographic)
BT Reference Materials
RT Bibliographic Coupling
    Bibliographies
    Citation Analysis
    Citation Indexes

Cities
USE Municipalities

Citizen Advocacy
USE Advocacy

Citizen Involvement
USE Citizen Participation

Citizen Participation   *JUL. 1966*
    Postings: 3,189   GC: 610
SN Political or social involvement in the
    community, government, or school in
    order to improve or maintain the status
    quo or to have impact on policy forma-
    tion and decision making
UF Citizen Involvement
    Civic Involvement
    Public Participation
BT Participation
RT Activism
    Advocacy
    Citizens Councils
    Citizenship
    Citizenship Education
    Citizenship Responsibility
    Civil Disobedience
    Community Action
    Community Change
    Community Control
    Community Cooperation
    Community Development
    Community Involvement
    Community Organizations
    Community Role
    Community Support
    Juries
    Participative Decision Making
    Participatory Research
    Political Campaigns
    Public Affairs Education
    Public Service
    Social Action
    Social Responsibility
    Student Projects
    Voting

Citizen Responsibility
USE Citizenship Responsibility

Citizen Role   *JUL. 1966*
    Postings: 432   GC: 610
BT Role
RT Citizenship
    Citizenship Education

Citizens Councils   *JUL. 1966*
    Postings: 171   GC: 610
BT Community Organizations
RT Citizen Participation

Citizenship   *JUL. 1966*
    Postings: 1,274   GC: 610
SN Status of being a member of a political
    community with the attendant rights,
    responsibilities, and privileges
UF Good Citizenship
BT Status
RT Citizen Participation
    Citizen Role
    Citizenship Education
    Citizenship Responsibility
    Civics
    Community Attitudes
    Foreign Nationals
    Immigration
    Political Attitudes
    Student Rights

Citizenship Education   *MAR. 1980*
    Postings: 3,713   GC: 400
SN Learning activities, curriculum, and/or
    educational programs, at any educational
    level, concerned with rights and respon-
    sibilities of citizenship—the purpose is
    to promote knowledge, skills, and atti-
    tudes conducive to effective participa-
    tion in civic life
BT Education
RT Basic Business Education
    Citizen Participation
    Citizen Role
    Citizenship
    Citizenship Responsibility
    Civics
    Critical Thinking
    Current Events
    Ethical Instruction
    Global Education
    Law Related Education
    Public Affairs Education
    Service Learning
    Values Education

Citizenship Responsibility   *JUL. 1966*
    Postings: 1,207   GC: 610
UF Citizen Responsibility
    Civic Responsibility
BT Social Responsibility
RT Citizen Participation
    Citizenship
    Citizenship Education
    Community Responsibility
    Humanitarianism
    Juries
    Leadership Responsibility
    Patriotism
    Public Affairs Education
    Voting

City Demography (1966 1980)
USE Urban Demography

City Government   *JUL. 1966*
    Postings: 489   GC: 610
UF Municipal Government
BT Local Government
RT City Officials
    Community
    Government Employees
    Government School Relationship
    Public Agencies
    School District Autonomy
    Urban Improvement
    Urban Planning
    Urban Programs

City Improvement (1966 1980)
USE Urban Improvement

City Officials   *JUL. 1966*
    Postings: 130   GC: 610
UF Elected City Officials

BT Public Officials
RT City Government
    County Officials
    Legislators

City Planning (1966 1980)
USE Urban Planning

City Problems (1966 1980)
USE Urban Problems

City Schools
USE Urban Schools

City Wide Commissions (1966 1980)
USE Planning Commissions
AND Urban Planning

City Wide Programs (1967 1980)
USE Urban Programs

Civic Belief (1966 1980)
USE Political Attitudes

Civic Groups
USE Community Organizations

Civic Involvement
USE Citizen Participation

Civic Organizations
USE Community Organizations

Civic Programs
USE Community Programs

Civic Relations
USE Community Relations

Civic Responsibility
USE Citizenship Responsibility

Civics   *JUL. 1966*
    Postings: 1,525   GC: 400
SN The social science dealing with the fun-
    damental philosophical, political, social,
    economic, and historical aspects of gov-
    ernment and citizenship
BT Social Sciences
RT Citizenship
    Citizenship Education
    Civil Law
    Government (Administrative Body)
    Law Related Education
    Political Science
    Social Studies
    United States Government (Course)

Civil Defense   *JUL. 1966*
    Postings: 116   GC: 610
RT Alarm Systems
    Community Programs
    Emergency Programs
    Fallout Shelters
    Military Science
    National Defense
    Natural Disasters
    Nuclear Warfare

Civil Disobedience   *NOV. 1969*
    Postings: 152   GC: 610
RT Activism
    Citizen Participation
    Civil Rights
    Civil Rights Legislation
    Demonstrations (Civil)
    Segregationist Organizations
    Torts

Civil Engineering   *JUL. 1966*
    Postings: 156   GC: 490
UF Highway Engineering
BT Engineering
RT Cartography
    Engineering Drawing
    Engineering Graphics
    Highway Engineering Aides
    Road Construction
    Structural Building Systems
    Water Treatment

Civil Law   *APR. 1990*
    Postings: 175   GC: 610
SN The body of rules established by a na-
    tion, state, city, etc., dealing with the
    private rights of its citizens as distin-
    guished from criminal matters—civil laws
    are enforced via court proceedings or
    lawsuits brought to protect rights and to
    prevent, or gain payment for, wrongs
BT Laws
RT Civics
    Civil Liberties
    Civil Rights
    Civil Rights Legislation
    Constitutional Law
    Consumer Protection
    Contracts
    Court Litigation
    Criminal Law
    Federal Regulation
    Government Role
    International Law
    Justice
    Law Related Education
    Legal Education (Professions)
    Legal Responsibility
    Privacy
    Public Policy
    School Law
    Torts

Civil Liberties   *NOV. 1969*
    Postings: 2,816   GC: 610
SN Freedom from arbitrary governmental,
    social, or personal interference with per-
    son, property, or opinion (Note: Prior to
    Mar80, the use of this term was not
    restricted by a Scope Note)
UF Human Rights
    Individual Rights
    Personal Liberty
NT Childrens Rights
    Civil Rights
    Due Process
    Freedom of Speech
    Parent Rights
    Student Rights
    Teacher Rights
RT Academic Freedom
    Civil Law
    Constitutional Law
    Democracy
    Freedom
    Freedom of Information
    Genocide
    Home Schooling
    Intellectual Freedom
    International Crimes
    Justice
    Laws
    Libel and Slander
    Privacy
    Search and Seizure
    Slavery

Civil Rights   *JUL. 1966*
    Postings: 4,094   GC: 540
SN Rights of all individuals to equality under
    the law, sometimes denied because of
    personal characteristics (e.g., race, sex,
    ethnic background)
UF Minority Rights
NT Equal Education
    Equal Opportunities (Jobs)
    Equal Protection
    Voting Rights
BT Civil Liberties
RT Apartheid

Black Leadership
Black Organizations
Black Power
Childrens Rights
Civil Disobedience
Civil Law
Civil Rights Legislation
Constitutional Law
Democracy
Demonstrations (Civil)
Due Process
Equal Facilities
Feminism
Freedom
Freedom of Speech
Freedom Schools
Justice
Minority Groups
Parent Rights
Racial Integration
Racial Segregation
Search and Seizure
Segregationist Organizations
Sex Discrimination
Slavery
Social Discrimination
Student Rights
Teacher Rights
Torts

Civil Rights Legislation *JUL. 1966*
Postings: 1,105 GC: 610
SN Legislation that aims to protect the constitutional rights of citizens, especially to rectify past discriminatory actions toward minority groups
UF Anti Discrimination Legislation
BT Legislation
RT Civil Disobedience
Civil Law
Civil Rights
Constitutional Law
Discriminatory Legislation
Equal Education
Equal Facilities
Equal Opportunities (Jobs)
Equal Protection
Laws
Minority Groups
Racial Integration
Social Discrimination

Civil Service Employees
USE Government Employees

Civil War
USE War

Civil War (United States) *JUL. 1966*
Postings: 332 GC: 430
SN War from 1861 to 1865 between the North (Union) and the South (Confederacy)
BT United States History
War
RT Reconstruction Era
Slavery

Class Activities *JUL. 1966*
Postings: 11,674 GC: 310
SN (Note: When possible, coordinate with terms that identify the activities)
UF Class Newspapers (1967 1980) #
Class Projects
Classroom Activities
Classroom Games (1966 1980) #
Classroom Participation (1966 1980) #
BT School Activities
RT Active Learning
Classes (Groups of Students)
Classroom Techniques
Dramatic Play
Field Trips
Learning Activities
Play

Class Attendance (1966 1980)
USE Attendance

Class Attitudes (1966 1980) *MAR. 1980*
Postings: 75 GC: 520
SN Invalid Descriptor—used for both social class attitudes and classroom attitudes—see more precise attitude terms—refer to "Attitudes" in the hierarchical display

Class Average (1966 1980) *MAR. 1980*
Postings: 28 GC: 310
SN Invalid Descriptor—for related concepts, see "Grade Point Average" or "Class Rank"

Class Desegregation
USE Classroom Desegregation

Class Discussion
USE Discussion (Teaching Technique)

Class Management (1966 1980)
USE Classroom Techniques

Class Newspapers (1967 1980)
USE Class Activities
AND Student Publications

Class Organization *JUL. 1966*
Postings: 1,015 GC: 310
SN The way in which a class or group of students is structured to facilitate instruction (includes student grouping, scheduling of classes and classroom activities, classroom and materials arrangement)
BT Organization
RT Classes (Groups of Students)
Classroom Design
Classroom Environment
Classroom Techniques
Cluster Grouping
Course Organization
Grouping (Instructional Purposes)
Open Plan Schools
School Organization
School Schedules
Self Contained Classrooms
Teaching Methods

Class Projects
USE Class Activities

Class Rank *MAR. 1980*
Postings: 156 GC: 310
SN Academic standing within a class (Note: Prior to Mar80, this concept may have been indexed under "Class Average")
UF Rank in Class
RT Academic Achievement
Classes (Groups of Students)
Competition
Grade Point Average
Grades (Scholastic)

Class Size *JUL. 1966*
Postings: 1,440 GC: 310
RT Classes (Groups of Students)
Classroom Environment
Crowding
Flexible Scheduling
Small Classes
Teacher Student Ratio

Class Status
USE Social Status

Classes (Groups of Students) *JUL. 1966*
Postings: 241 GC: 310
NT Multigraded Classes
Multilevel Classes (Second Language Instruction)
Nonauthoritarian Classes
Small Classes
Special Classes

BT Groups
RT Class Activities
Class Organization
Class Rank
Class Size
Classroom Communication
Classroom Desegregation
Classroom Environment
Classroom Observation Techniques
Classroom Techniques
Grouping (Instructional Purposes)

Classical Conditioning *DEC. 1970*
Postings: 81 GC: 110
SN A form of conditioning in which an arbitrary or neutral stimulus (e.g., the bell in Pavlov's experiment) comes to elicit a response (e.g., salivation) after it is repeatedly paired with reinforcement (e.g., food)
BT Conditioning
RT Behavior Modification
Operant Conditioning

Classical Greek
USE Greek

Classical Languages *JUL. 1966*
Postings: 468 GC: 440
NT Latin
Sanskrit
BT Languages
RT Classical Literature
College Second Language Programs
Greek
Latin Literature

Classical Literature *JUL. 1966*
Postings: 553 GC: 430
SN Literature of ancient Greece and Rome (Note: Do not use for outstanding or time-honored books generally, for which see "Classics (Literature)")
NT Latin Literature
BT Literature
RT Ancient History
Biblical Literature
Classical Languages
Epics
Greek Civilization
Greek Literature
Latin
Legends
Literary History
Mythology
Platonism
World Literature

Classical Mechanics
USE Mechanics (Physics)

Classics (Literature) *AUG. 1996*
Postings: 124 GC: 430
SN Literary works of demonstrably enduring appeal and quality (Note: Do not confuse with the literature of ancient Greece and Rome, for which use "Classical Literature"—see also the Identifiers "Great Books Curriculum" and "Junior Great Books Program")
UF Literary Classics
BT Literature
RT Literary History
Reading Materials

Classification *JUL. 1966*
Postings: 7,825 GC: 710
SN Ordering of related phenomena into categories, groups, families, or systems according to characteristics or attributes
UF Categorization
Grouping Procedures (1966 1980)
Sorting Procedures (1966 1980)
Taxonomy (1967 1980)
Typology (1967 1980)
NT Cluster Grouping
Codification

Coding
Dewey Decimal Classification
Discourse Modes
Grouping (Instructional Purposes)
Labeling (of Persons)
Language Classification
Library of Congress Classification
Space Classification
Universal Decimal Classification
BT Organization
RT Bibliometrics
Cataloging
Chemical Nomenclature
Citation Analysis
Cluster Analysis
Content Analysis
Data Analysis
Documentation
Groups
Identification
Indexing
Library Technical Processes
Relationship
Statistical Distributions

Classification Clerks
USE File Clerks

Classroom Activities
USE Class Activities

Classroom Arrangement (1966 1980)
USE Classroom Design

Classroom Climate
USE Classroom Environment

Classroom Communication *JUL. 1966*
Postings: 4,105 GC: 310
BT Communication (Thought Transfer)
RT Classes (Groups of Students)
Classroom Environment
Classroom Observation Techniques
Classroom Techniques
Dialog Journals
Nonverbal Communication
Student Behavior
Teacher Behavior
Teacher Student Relationship
Verbal Communication

Classroom Desegregation *MAR. 1980*
Postings: 213 GC: 540
SN Process of bringing students of different ethnic or racial groups into the same classroom
UF Class Desegregation
Classroom Integration (1967 1980)
Desegregated Classes
Integrated Classes
BT Social Integration
RT Classes (Groups of Students)
Heterogeneous Grouping
Racial Integration
School Desegregation

Classroom Design *JUL. 1966*
Postings: 1,021 GC: 920
SN Conceiving and selecting the structure, elements, arrangement, and materials that make up or are enclosed by a classroom—also, the plan or layout that results
UF Classroom Arrangement (1966 1980)
BT Design
RT Class Organization
Classroom Environment
Classroom Furniture
Classroom Research
Classrooms
Design Requirements
Educational Facilities Design
Flexible Facilities
Flexible Lighting Design
Glass Walls
Interior Design
Interior Space

= Two or more Descriptors are used to represent this term.
The term's main entry shows the appropriate coordination.

Multipurpose Classrooms
Open Plan Schools
Space Dividers
Space Utilization

Classroom Discipline
USE   Classroom Techniques
AND   Discipline

Classroom Environment   *JUL. 1966*
   Postings: 9,321   GC: 310
SN   Intellectual, social, physical, etc., conditions within or exogenous to a classroom that influence the learning situation
UF   Classroom Climate
    Classroom Situation
BT   Educational Environment
RT   Aptitude Treatment Interaction
    Class Organization
    Class Size
    Classes (Groups of Students)
    Classroom Communication
    Classroom Design
    Classroom Observation Techniques
    Classroom Techniques
    Classrooms
    College Environment
    Student Attitudes
    Teacher Attitudes
    Teacher Expectations of Students
    Teacher Student Relationship
    Teaching Conditions

Classroom Equipment
USE   Educational Equipment

Classroom Furniture   *JUL. 1966*
   Postings: 214   GC: 910
UF   Furniture (Classroom)
BT   Educational Equipment
    Furniture
RT   Classroom Design
    Classrooms
    Furniture Arrangement
    Furniture Design

Classroom Games (1966 1980)
USE   Class Activities
AND   Educational Games

Classroom Guidance Programs (1968 1980)
    MAR. 1980
   Postings: 102   GC: 240
SN   Invalid Descriptor—used inconsistently in indexing—see more precise terms "Counselor Teacher Cooperation," "Group Guidance," "Career Guidance," etc.

Classroom Integration (1967 1980)
USE   Classroom Desegregation

Classroom Libraries (1966 1980)
USE   Instructional Materials

Classroom Management
USE   Classroom Techniques

Classroom Materials (1966 1980)
USE   Instructional Materials

Classroom Methods
USE   Classroom Techniques

Classroom Observation Techniques
    MAR. 1969
   Postings: 3,239   GC: 820
SN   Procedures used to obtain quantified descriptions of teacher and student behavior and interaction in a classroom setting
BT   Measurement Techniques

RT   Behavior Rating Scales
    Classes (Groups of Students)
    Classroom Communication
    Classroom Environment
    Classroom Research
    Clinical Supervision (of Teachers)
    Content Analysis
    Interaction Process Analysis
    Lesson Observation Criteria
    Naturalistic Observation
    Observation
    Participant Observation
    Student Behavior
    Student Evaluation
    Teacher Behavior
    Teacher Evaluation

Classroom Participation (1966 1980)
USE   Class Activities
AND   Student Participation

Classroom Research   *JUL. 1966*
   Postings: 3,442   GC: 810
SN   Systematic investigations conducted in or about a classroom setting—includes studies of instructors, students, and facilities (Note: As of Oct81, use as a minor Descriptor for examples of this kind of research—use as a major Descriptor only as the subject of a document)
BT   Educational Research
RT   Classroom Design
    Classroom Observation Techniques
    Classrooms
    Teacher Researchers

Classroom Situation
USE   Classroom Environment

Classroom Techniques   *JUL. 1966*
   Postings: 16,384   GC: 310
SN   Techniques used in the classroom by those in authority (e.g., teachers, aides, administrators)—may either be directly educational or facilitate educational processes
UF   Class Management (1966 1980)
    Classroom Discipline #
    Classroom Management
    Classroom Methods
BT   Educational Methods
RT   Class Activities
    Class Organization
    Classes (Groups of Students)
    Classroom Communication
    Classroom Environment
    Classrooms
    Discipline
    Educational Diagnosis
    Educational Therapy
    Learning Strategies
    Prereferral Intervention
    Proctoring
    Teaching Methods

Classrooms   *JUL. 1966*
   Postings: 432   GC: 920
SN   Spaces designed or adapted for group instruction—includes general and special classrooms but excludes such large assembly rooms as auditoriums, lunch rooms, and gymnasiums
UF   Flexible Classrooms (1968 1980) #
NT   Electronic Classrooms
    Mobile Classrooms
    Multipurpose Classrooms
    Self Contained Classrooms
BT   Educational Facilities
RT   Business Education Facilities
    Classroom Design
    Classroom Environment
    Classroom Furniture
    Classroom Research
    Classroom Techniques
    Laboratories
    Music Facilities
    School Shops
    School Space
    Science Facilities

Clay   *OCT. 1994*
   Postings: 36   GC: 490
SN   Fine-grained soil material (consisting chiefly of hydrated silicates of aluminum) that is plastic when wet—has many uses in art and industry
UF   Clay Minerals
RT   Art Materials
    Ceramics
    Geology
    Sculpture
    Soil Science

Clay Minerals
USE   Clay

Clean Water
USE   Water Quality

Cleaning   *MAR. 1969*
   Postings: 225   GC: 210
NT   Dishwashing
BT   Sanitation
RT   Disease Control
    Equipment Maintenance
    Housekeepers
    Hygiene
    Maintenance
    Preservation
    School Maintenance

Clearinghouses   *JUL. 1966*
   Postings: 653   GC: 710
SN   Organizations that collect, process, maintain, and disseminate material, usually derived from current research, on a particular topic
BT   Information Centers

Cleft Lip (1967 1980)
USE   Cleft Palate

Cleft Palate   *JUL. 1966*
   Postings: 78   GC: 220
UF   Cleft Lip (1967 1980)
BT   Congenital Impairments
    Physical Disabilities
    Speech Impairments
RT   Articulation Impairments
    Speech Therapy

Clergy   *MAR. 1980*
   Postings: 421   GC: 640
UF   Clergymen (1968 1980)
    Ministers
    Parsons
    Preachers
NT   Priests
BT   Personnel
RT   Church Workers
    Lay People
    Nuns
    Religion
    Religious Cultural Groups
    Religious Education
    Religious Organizations
    Theological Education

Clergymen (1968 1980)
USE   Clergy

Clerical Occupations   *JUL. 1966*
   Postings: 492   GC: 640
SN   Occupations concerned with preparing, transcribing, systematizing, and preserving written communications and records, distributing information, or collecting accounts
BT   Occupations
RT   Bookkeeping
    Business Education
    Clerical Workers
    Data Processing Occupations
    Keyboarding (Data Entry)
    Office Occupations

Office Occupations Education
Office Practice
Recordkeeping
Shorthand
Typewriting
White Collar Occupations
Word Processing

Clerical Workers   *JUL. 1966*
   Postings: 311   GC: 640
NT   Court Reporters
    Examiners
    File Clerks
    Receptionists
    Secretaries
BT   Nonprofessional Personnel
RT   Clerical Occupations
    Employees

Clerk Stenographers
USE   Shorthand

Clerk Typists
USE   Typewriting

Clerkships (Medicine)
USE   Clinical Experience

Cliches   *SEP. 1970*
   Postings: 33   GC: 430
SN   Trite phrases or expressions
RT   Jargon
    Language Styles

Client Background (Human Services)
USE   Client Characteristics (Human Services)

Client Caseworkers (1966 1980)
USE   Social Workers

Client Centered Counseling
USE   Nondirective Counseling

Client Characteristics (Human Services)
    OCT. 1984
   Postings: 1,029   GC: 120
SN   Distinguishing traits or qualities of persons who engage the assistance of human service workers (counselors, psychologists, physicians, nurses, social workers, etc.)
UF   Client Background (Human Services)
RT   Counselor Client Relationship
    Help Seeking
    Human Services
    Individual Characteristics
    Participant Characteristics
    Patients

Client Counselor Ratio
USE   Counselor Client Ratio

Client Counselor Relationship
USE   Counselor Client Relationship

Climate   *MAR. 1980*
   Postings: 500   GC: 490
SN   The prevailing conditions of the physical environment, indoor or outdoor
UF   Climatic Factors (1969 1980)
BT   Physical Environment
RT   Air Pollution
    Climate Change
    Climate Control
    Diffusion (Physics)
    Earth Science
    Ecology
    Environment
    Environmental Influences
    Geographic Location
    Heat
    Humidity

= Two or more Descriptors are used to represent this term.
The term's main entry shows the appropriate coordination.

Light
Meteorology
Oceanography
Pollution
Solar Energy
Temperature
Thermal Environment
Water
Weather
Wind (Meteorology)

Climate Change   JAN. 1993
    Postings: 47
SN   Nonseasonal, semipermanent change in the physical environment of a region or the entirety of the earth including fluctuations in temperature, precipitation, solar radiation, gas and suspended particle concentrations, and ocean levels (Note: For worldwide climate change, coordinate with the Identifier "Global Change" or use the narrower term "Global Warming")
NT   Global Warming
BT   Change
RT   Climate
      Environmental Influences
      Meteorology
      Oceanography
      Physical Environment
      Temperature
      Thermal Environment
      Weather

Climate Control   JUL. 1966
    Postings: 396   GC: 490
UF   Hvac
NT   Air Conditioning
      Heat Recovery
      Heating
      Refrigeration
      Ventilation
RT   Air Conditioning Equipment
      Air Pollution
      Building Operation
      Climate
      Design Requirements
      Electrical Systems
      Energy Conservation
      Energy Management
      Environmental Influences
      Humidity
      Lighting
      Physical Environment
      Solar Energy
      Temperature
      Thermal Environment
      Thermal Insulation
      Weather
      Windowless Rooms
      Windows

Climatic Factors (1969 1980)
USE   Climate

Clinic Personnel (School) (1966 1980)
USE   Allied Health Personnel
AND   School Health Services

Clinical Diagnosis   JUL. 1966
    Postings: 3,189   GC: 210
SN   Identification of diseases or disorders and the prescription of treatment
UF   Diagnosis (Clinical)
BT   Identification
RT   Clinical Psychology
      Diagnostic Tests
      Disability Identification
      Early Identification
      Early Intervention
      Educational Diagnosis
      Etiology
      Internal Medicine
      Medical Case Histories
      Medical Evaluation
      Physical Examinations
      Severity (of Disability)
      Sports Medicine
      Symptoms (Individual Disorders)

Clinical Experience   SEP. 1968
    Postings: 1,978   GC: 210
SN   Practical experience in medical and health-related services that occurs as part of an educational program (Note: If possible, use the more precise term "Clinical Teaching (Health Professions)")
UF   Clerkships (Medicine)
      Clinical Learning Experience
      Externships (Medicine)
      Preceptorships (Medicine)
BT   Learning Experience
RT   Allied Health Occupations Education
      Clinical Teaching (Health Professions)
      Clinics
      Experiential Learning
      Field Experience Programs
      Graduate Medical Education
      Internship Programs
      Medical Education
      Medical School Faculty
      Pharmaceutical Education
      Practicum Supervision
      Practicums
      Problem Based Learning
      Student Experience
      Teaching Hospitals
      Work Experience Programs

Clinical Judgment (Medicine)
USE   Medical Evaluation

Clinical Judgment (Psychology)
USE   Psychological Evaluation

Clinical Learning Experience
USE   Clinical Experience

Clinical Professors (1967 1980) (Education)
USE   Student Teacher Supervisors

Clinical Professors (1967 1980) (Medicine)
USE   Medical School Faculty

Clinical Psychology   OCT. 1977
    Postings: 487   GC: 230
SN   Branch of psychology devoted to psychological methods of diagnosing and treating mental and emotional disorders, as well as research into the causes of these disorders and the effects of therapy
BT   Psychology
RT   Behavior Disorders
      Clinical Diagnosis
      Community Psychology
      Counseling Psychology
      Emotional Disturbances
      Experimental Psychology
      Mental Disorders
      Neuropsychology
      Personality Problems
      Psychiatry
      Psychological Evaluation
      Psychological Studies
      Psychological Testing
      Psychometrics
      Psychopathology
      Psychophysiology
      Psychotherapy
      Social Psychology

Clinical Schools (Teacher Education)
USE   Professional Development Schools

Clinical Services
USE   Clinics

Clinical Supervision (of Teachers)
           AUG. 1989
    Postings: 113   GC: 320
SN   A collegial model of teacher supervision and improvement that includes at least three phases— planning conference, classroom observation, and feedback conference
BT   Teacher Supervision
RT   Classroom Observation Techniques
      Instructional Improvement
      Lesson Observation Criteria
      Peer Evaluation
      Professional Development Schools
      Supervisory Methods
      Teacher Effectiveness
      Teacher Improvement

Clinical Teaching (Health Professions)
           SEP. 1981
    Postings: 388   GC: 210
SN   Instruction in the clinical setting where actual symptoms are studied and treatment is given
BT   Teaching Methods
RT   Allied Health Occupations Education
      Clinical Experience
      Medical Education
      Medical School Faculty
      Practicum Supervision
      Practicums
      Teaching Hospitals

Clinical Teaching (Individualized Instruction)
USE   Individualized Instruction

Clinics   JUL. 1966
    Postings: 685   GC: 920
UF   Clinical Services
      Preschool Clinics (1966 1980) #
      Rural Clinics (1966 1980) #
      Treatment Centers
NT   Dental Clinics
      Mental Health Clinics
      Mobile Clinics
      Psychoeducational Clinics
      Speech and Hearing Clinics
RT   Clinical Experience
      Facilities
      Health
      Health Facilities
      Hospitals
      Medical Services
      Meetings
      Services

Clock Arithmetic
USE   Modular Arithmetic

Clockmakers
USE   Watchmakers

Closed Circuit Television   JUL. 1966
    Postings: 638   GC: 720
SN   System whereby the transmission of television signals is limited to those audiences directly connected to the origination point by coaxial cable or microwave link—usually limited to a building, campus, etc.
UF   CCTV
BT   Television
RT   Alarm Systems
      Cable Television
      Educational Television
      Interactive Television

Closed Head Injuries
USE   Head Injuries

Closed Schools
USE   School Closing

Clothing   JUL. 1966
    Postings: 575   GC: 210
UF   Fashions (Clothing)
NT   School Uniforms
RT   Clothing Design
      Clothing Instruction
      Fashion Industry

Laundry Drycleaning Occupations
Material Culture
Needle Trades
Self Care Skills
Sewing Instruction
Sewing Machine Operators
Textiles Instruction

Clothing Design   JUL. 1966
    Postings: 153   GC: 420
UF   Costume Design
      Dress Design
BT   Design
RT   Clothing
      Clothing Instruction
      Design Crafts
      Fashion Industry
      Needle Trades
      Patternmaking

Clothing Industry
USE   Fashion Industry

Clothing Instruction   JUL. 1966
    Postings: 277   GC: 400
BT   Instruction
RT   Clothing
      Clothing Design
      Consumer Science
      Fashion Industry
      Home Economics
      Laundry Drycleaning Occupations
      Needle Trades
      Sewing Instruction
      Sewing Machine Operators
      Textiles Instruction

Cloze Procedure   JUL. 1966
    Postings: 1,164   GC: 460
SN   Completion exercises requiring the reader to insert missing words with the aid of surrounding context
UF   Cloze Techniques
BT   Methods
RT   Context Clues
      Informal Reading Inventories
      Language Skills
      Language Tests
      Readability
      Reading
      Reading Comprehension
      Reading Skills
      Reading Tests
      Substitution Drills
      Teaching Methods

Cloze Techniques
USE   Cloze Procedure

Clubs   JUL. 1966
    Postings: 256   GC: 520
UF   Homemakers Clubs (1966 1980) #
NT   Science Clubs
      Youth Clubs
BT   Groups
RT   Extracurricular Activities

Clues
USE   Cues

Cluster Analysis   MAR. 1971
    Postings: 710   GC: 820
SN   Systematic method of grouping measures or variables together according to their degree of similarity in a correlation matrix or table
BT   Multivariate Analysis
RT   Classification
      Cluster Grouping
      Correlation
      Factor Analysis
      Multidimensional Scaling

= Two or more Descriptors are used to represent this term.
The term's main entry shows the appropriate coordination.

Cluster Colleges — *FEB. 1971*
Postings: 74 — GC: 340
SN Colleges, in close physical proximity, that constitute a single institution, share facilities and services, and usually have a centralized administration—generally each college in the cluster focuses on one area of study (Note: Do not confuse with "Consortia"—prior to Mar80, this term was not restricted by a Scope Note)
BT Colleges
RT Consortia
    Educational Complexes
    Experimental Colleges
    House Plan
    Shared Facilities

Cluster Grouping — *JUL. 1966*
Postings: 651 — GC: 820
SN Classifying or selecting the items within a collection (of people, ideas, objects, etc.) on the basis of specified similarities (Note: Use a more precise term if possible)
BT Classification
RT Bibliometrics
    Class Organization
    Cluster Analysis
    Group Structure
    Homogeneous Grouping
    Judgment Analysis Technique
    Occupational Clusters
    Peer Institutions

CMI
USE Computer Managed Instruction

Co Op Programs
USE Cooperative Programs

Co Ops
USE Cooperatives

Coaching Teachers (1966 1974)
USE Tutors

Coal — *AUG. 1982*
Postings: 146 — GC: 410
SN Combustible solid of organic origin used as a fuel (Note: Use also for coal by-products such as coal gas, coal tar, cokeite, etc.)
UF Anthracite
    Bituminous Coal
    Coal Mining #
    Coal Resources
    Lignite
BT Fossil Fuels
    Natural Resources
RT Geology
    Mining
    Soil Science

Coal Mining
USE Coal
AND Mining

Coal Resources
USE Coal

Coast Guard Air Stations
USE Military Air Facilities

Cocaine — *DEC. 1989*
Postings: 217 — GC: 210
SN Narcotic alkaloid obtained from coca leaves—widely used systemically as a stimulant or euphoriant
UF Cocaine Prenatal Exposure #
NT Crack
BT Narcotics
RT Drug Abuse
    Drug Addiction
    Drug Legislation
    Drug Rehabilitation
    Drug Use
    Illegal Drug Use
    Stimulants

Cocaine Prenatal Exposure
USE Cocaine
AND Prenatal Drug Exposure

Cochlear Implants — *OCT. 1999*
Postings: 77 — GC: 220
SN Surgically inserted devices that convert sound reaching the cochlea into electrical impulses that are transmitted by wire to the auditory nerve—designed for persons with severe to profound hearing loss who receive little or no benefit from hearing aids
BT Prostheses
    Sensory Aids
RT Audiology
    Communication Aids (for Disabled)
    Deafness
    Hearing Aids
    Hearing Impairments
    Hearing Therapy

Cocounseling — *MAY 1970*
Postings: 84 — GC: 240
SN Two or more counselors working as a team with a single client or group of clients, usually at the same time but sometimes consecutively
UF Conjoint Counseling
    Team Counseling
BT Counseling
RT Teamwork

Cocurricular Activities (1966 1980)
USE Extracurricular Activities

Code Switching (Language) — *AUG. 1978*
Postings: 504 — GC: 450
SN The alternating use of languages, dialects, or language styles in the speech of an individual (e.g., the bilingual's use of two languages in speech)—may occur at the word, phrase, clause, or sentence level
UF Switching (Language)
RT Bidialectalism
    Bilingual Students
    Bilingualism
    Interference (Language)
    Language
    Language Patterns
    Language Usage
    Language Variation
    Linguistic Borrowing
    Linguistic Performance
    Morphology (Languages)
    Multilingualism
    Phonology
    Sociolinguistics
    Syntax
    Vocabulary

Codes (Logic)
USE Coding

Codes of Ethics — *JAN. 1978*
Postings: 996 — GC: 520
SN Standards of ethical conduct, violation of which may subject individuals to disciplinary action
UF Honor Codes
BT Behavior Standards
RT Accountability
    Cheating
    Codification
    Conflict of Interest
    Discipline
    Discipline Policy
    Ethics
    Faculty College Relationship
    Loyalty Oaths
    Lying
    Malpractice
    Moral Development
    Moral Values
    Plagiarism
    Stealing
    Student College Relationship

Codification — *JUL. 1966*
Postings: 323 — GC: 710
SN Process of collecting and arranging laws and standards according to a system
BT Classification
RT Codes of Ethics
    Documentation
    Laws
    Standards

Coding — *APR. 1990*
Postings: 355 — GC: 710
SN The process of using symbols or patterns of symbols to classify information, often for easy or rapid (sometimes secret) communication and transmission between or among persons and/or machines—also includes "decoding," i.e., changing coded symbols back to an original form (Note: Do not confuse with "Encoding (Psychology)")
UF Codes (Logic)
    Decoding (Information)
    Encoding (Information)
    Notation
    Symbolic Coding
BT Classification
RT Documentation
    Information Theory
    Matrices
    Numerical Control
    Programming

Coeducation — *MAY 1969*
Postings: 411 — GC: 330
BT Education
RT Heterogeneous Grouping
    Single Sex Colleges
    Single Sex Schools
    Womens Education

Cognitive Ability — *JUL. 1966*
Postings: 3,509 — GC: 120
SN (Note: Prior to Apr80, the instruction "Mental Ability, USE Intelligence" was carried in the Thesaurus)
UF Mental Ability
NT Thinking Skills
BT Ability
RT Academic Ability
    Aptitude
    Cognitive Development
    Cognitive Measurement
    Cognitive Psychology
    Cognitive Structures
    Cognitive Tests
    Encoding (Psychology)
    Epistemology
    Formal Operations
    Habituation
    Heuristics
    Intelligence
    Intuition
    Metacognition
    Productive Thinking
    Schemata (Cognition)
    Social Cognition
    Spatial Ability

Cognitive Behavior Modification
USE Behavior Modification
AND Cognitive Restructuring

Cognitive Development — *JUL. 1966*
Postings: 13,945 — GC: 120
SN Increasing complexity of awareness, including perceiving, conceiving, reasoning, and judging, through adaptation to the environment and assimilation of information (Note: Prior to Mar80, this term was not restricted by a Scope Note)
UF Mental Development (1966 1980)
NT Intellectual Development
    Perceptual Development
    Verbal Development
BT Individual Development
RT Cognitive Ability
    Cognitive Measurement
    Cognitive Objectives
    Cognitive Processes
    Cognitive Psychology
    Cognitive Structures
    Cognitive Style
    Cognitive Tests
    Concept Formation
    Constructivism (Learning)
    Developmental Delays
    Developmental Disabilities
    Developmental Psychology
    Developmental Stages
    Epistemology
    Learning Readiness
    Learning Strategies
    Piagetian Theory
    Schemata (Cognition)
    School Readiness
    Thinking Skills

Cognitive Dissonance — *AUG. 1986*
Postings: 127 — GC: 120
SN Psychological conflict resulting from incongruous attitudes or beliefs held simultaneously, or from inconsistency between attitudes and behavior
BT Psychological Patterns
RT Attitudes
    Cognitive Processes
    Cognitive Structures
    Congruence (Psychology)
    Motivation
    Socialization

Cognitive Mapping — *OCT. 1983*
Postings: 384 — GC: 110
SN Patterning by an individual of experiences and expectations to form perceptions of cause-effect or means-ends relationships
BT Learning Processes
RT Cognitive Structures
    Cognitive Style
    Concept Mapping
    Expectation
    Learning Modalities
    Perception
    Schemata (Cognition)
    Spatial Ability

Cognitive Measurement — *JUL. 1966*
Postings: 1,628 — GC: 820
SN The use of systematic procedures to obtain indications of individuals' cognitive ability, style, development, or other mental processes that are primarily cognitive rather than affective or psychomotor
BT Measurement
RT Cognitive Ability
    Cognitive Development
    Cognitive Objectives
    Cognitive Processes
    Cognitive Psychology
    Cognitive Structures
    Cognitive Style
    Cognitive Tests
    Intelligence Tests
    Psychometrics

Cognitive Modification
USE Cognitive Restructuring

Cognitive Objectives — *JUL. 1969*
Postings: 1,112 — GC: 310
SN Behavioral objectives that emphasize remembering or reproducing something which has presumably been learned, or that involve the solving of some intellectual task
BT Behavioral Objectives
RT Affective Objectives
    Cognitive Development

= Two or more Descriptors are used to represent this term.
The term's main entry shows the appropriate coordination.

Cognitive Measurement
Psychomotor Objectives

Cognitive Processes　　　　　　　　*JUL. 1966*
　　Postings: 19,571　　　　　　　　GC: 110
SN　Processes based on perception, intro-
　　spection, or memory through which an
　　individual obtains knowledge or concep-
　　tual understanding, e.g., perceiving, judg-
　　ing, abstracting, reasoning, imagining,
　　remembering, and anticipating (Note: Use
　　a more specific term if possible—see
　　displays of the narrower terms)
UF　Information Processes (Psychological)
　　Thinking Processes
　　Thought Processes (1966 1980)
NT　Abstract Reasoning
　　Association (Psychology)
　　Conflict Resolution
　　Consciousness Raising
　　Convergent Thinking
　　Creative Thinking
　　Critical Thinking
　　Decision Making
　　Encoding (Psychology)
　　Intuition
　　Language Processing
　　Learning Processes
　　Logical Thinking
　　Memory
　　Mental Computation
　　Metacognition
　　Perception
　　Problem Solving
　　Role Perception
　　Serial Ordering
　　Social Cognition
　　Visualization
RT　Adaptation Level Theory
　　Artificial Intelligence
　　Brain
　　Cognitive Development
　　Cognitive Dissonance
　　Cognitive Measurement
　　Cognitive Psychology
　　Cognitive Structures
　　Cognitive Style
　　Cognitive Tests
　　Compensation (Concept)
　　Comprehension
　　Conceptual Tempo
　　Conservation (Concept)
　　Context Effect
　　Epistemology
　　Field Dependence Independence
　　Formal Operations
　　Hermeneutics
　　Intelligence
　　Knowledge Representation
　　Learning
　　Learning Disabilities
　　Learning Strategies
　　Learning Theories
　　Mediation Theory
　　Object Permanence
　　Piagetian Theory
　　Protocol Analysis
　　Sensory Deprivation
　　Synthesis
　　Task Analysis
　　Thinking Skills

Cognitive Psychology　　　　　　*DEC. 1985*
　　Postings: 985　　　　　　　　　　GC: 110
SN　Branch of psychology concerned with
　　the nature and structure of complex
　　"knowledge processes" (e.g., recogniz-
　　ing, conceiving, judging, and reasoning)
　　and their effects on, or interactions with,
　　behavior—particularly identified with "in-
　　formation processing" models of human
　　cognition, usually simulated on comput-
　　ers
BT　Psychology
RT　Artificial Intelligence
　　Behaviorism
　　Cognitive Ability
　　Cognitive Development
　　Cognitive Measurement
　　Cognitive Processes
　　Cognitive Structures

Cognitive Style
Constructivism (Learning)
Epistemology
Experimental Psychology
Intelligence
Knowledge Representation
Neuropsychology
Piagetian Theory
Protocol Analysis
Psychological Studies
Psychometrics
Psychophysiology
Schemata (Cognition)

Cognitive Restructuring　　　　　*OCT. 1983*
　　Postings: 828　　　　　　　　　　GC: 110
SN　Use of counseling, therapy, or self-moni-
　　toring techniques to alter attitudes, con-
　　cepts, and/or expectations
UF　Cognitive Behavior Modification #
　　Cognitive Modification
　　Cognitive Therapy
RT　Attitude Change
　　Behavior Modification
　　Cognitive Structures
　　Counseling
　　Intervention
　　Learning Disabilities
　　Learning Theories
　　Psychoeducational Methods
　　Psychotherapy
　　Rational Emotive Therapy
　　Rehabilitation
　　Self Control

Cognitive Skills
USE　Thinking Skills

Cognitive Structures　　　　　　*OCT. 1983*
　　Postings: 1,458　　　　　　　　　GC: 110
SN　Frameworks or forms of thinking that
　　can change with age and experience
UF　Knowledge Structures
RT　Attitudes
　　Cognitive Ability
　　Cognitive Development
　　Cognitive Dissonance
　　Cognitive Mapping
　　Cognitive Measurement
　　Cognitive Processes
　　Cognitive Psychology
　　Cognitive Restructuring
　　Cognitive Style
　　Cognitive Tests
　　Concept Formation
　　Constructivism (Learning)
　　Epistemology
　　Expectation
　　Ideology
　　Intention
　　Interests
　　Knowledge Representation
　　Learning Processes
　　Misconceptions
　　Schemata (Cognition)
　　Self Efficacy

Cognitive Style　　　　　　　　　*OCT. 1976*
　　Postings: 5,946　　　　　　　　　GC: 110
SN　Information processing habits which rep-
　　resent the learner's typical modes of
　　perceiving, thinking, remembering, and
　　problem solving
UF　Learning Style
　　Perceptual Style
NT　Conceptual Tempo
　　Field Dependence Independence
BT　Psychological Characteristics
RT　Aptitude Treatment Interaction
　　Cognitive Development
　　Cognitive Mapping
　　Cognitive Measurement
　　Cognitive Processes
　　Cognitive Psychology
　　Cognitive Structures
　　Cognitive Tests
　　Encoding (Psychology)
　　Intuition
　　Learning Modalities

Learning Strategies
Multiple Intelligences
Personality Traits
Phenomenology
Schemata (Cognition)
Thinking Skills

Cognitive Tempo
USE　Conceptual Tempo

Cognitive Tests　　　　　　　　　*JUL. 1966*
　　Postings: 1,248　　　　　　　　　GC: 830
SN　Tests used to obtain indications of an
　　individual's cognitive style, development,
　　or other characteristics of cognitive func-
　　tioning (Note: Use a more specific term if
　　possible)
UF　Abstraction Tests (1967 1980)
NT　Intelligence Tests
　　Perception Tests
BT　Tests
RT　Cognitive Ability
　　Cognitive Development
　　Cognitive Measurement
　　Cognitive Processes
　　Cognitive Structures
　　Cognitive Style

Cognitive Theory
USE　Epistemology

Cognitive Therapy
USE　Cognitive Restructuring

Cohabitation　　　　　　　　　　*JUN. 1988*
　　Postings: 125　　　　　　　　　　GC: 520
SN　Refers primarily to unmarried couples
　　living together
BT　Interpersonal Relationship
RT　Family (Sociological Unit)
　　Family Life
　　Family Relationship
　　Life Style
　　Marital Status
　　Mate Selection
　　Sexuality

Coherence　　　　　　　　　　　*NOV. 1981*
　　Postings: 369　　　　　　　　　　GC: 450
SN　The presentation of thoughts or state-
　　ments so that the meaning is clear and
　　intelligible
BT　Rhetoric
RT　Cohesion (Written Composition)
　　Comprehension
　　Discourse Analysis
　　Language Processing
　　Outlining (Discourse)
　　Paragraphs
　　Semantics
　　Speech
　　Story Grammar
　　Verbal Communication
　　Writing (Composition)
　　Writing Evaluation

Cohesion (Written Composition)　*NOV. 1981*
　　Postings: 380　　　　　　　　　　GC: 450
SN　The combination of language usage and
　　stylistic choices to hold the parts of a
　　written discourse together as a unit
BT　Connected Discourse
RT　Coherence
　　Comprehension
　　Discourse Analysis
　　Language Usage
　　Paragraph Composition
　　Sentence Structure
　　Story Grammar
　　Syntax
　　Text Structure
　　Writing (Composition)
　　Writing Evaluation
　　Writing Skills

Cohort Analysis　　　　　　　　　*DEC. 1976*
　　Postings: 710　　　　　　　　　　GC: 820
SN　Group by group analytic treatment of
　　individuals having a statistical factor in
　　common to each group—group mem-
　　bers share a particular characteristic (e.g.,
　　born, married, etc., within a given year)
　　or a common experience (e.g., entering
　　a particular training phase at a given
　　time) (Note: As of Oct81, use as a major
　　Desc. only for document subject)
BT　Research
RT　Census Figures
　　Community Study
　　Cross Sectional Studies
　　Demography
　　Population Trends

Collaboration
USE　Cooperation

Collaborative Decision Making
USE　Participative Decision Making

Collaborative Teachers
USE　Teacher Collaboration

Collaborative Teaching
USE　Team Teaching

Collaboratives (Education)
USE　Partnerships in Education

Collage　　　　　　　　　　　　*OCT. 1994*
　　Postings: 45　　　　　　　　　　GC: 420
SN　Composition of various materials or ob-
　　jects, as for artistic and other creative
　　purposes
RT　Art Expression
　　Art Products
　　Found Objects
　　Visual Arts

Collected Readings
USE　Anthologies

Collection Development (Libraries)
USE　Library Collection Development

Collective Bargaining　　　　　　*JUL. 1966*
　　Postings: 4,077　　　　　　　　　GC: 630
SN　Negotiation on wages, hours, and other
　　conditions of employment between an
　　organization and its employees as repre-
　　sented by a union or an employee asso-
　　ciation
UF　Collective Negotiation (1967 1977)
　　Professional Negotiation
NT　Scope of Bargaining
RT　Arbitration
　　Employer Employee Relationship
　　Employment Problems
　　Faculty College Relationship
　　Grievance Procedures
　　Job Security
　　Labor Demands
　　Labor Legislation
　　Labor Problems
　　Labor Relations
　　Negotiation Agreements
　　Negotiation Impasses
　　Sanctions
　　Strikes
　　Teacher Discipline
　　Teacher Militancy
　　Teacher Rights
　　Teacher Strikes
　　Teacher Welfare
　　Unions

Collective Behavior
USE　Group Behavior

= Two or more Descriptors are used to represent this term.
The term's main entry shows the appropriate coordination.

Collective Decision Making
USE   Participative Decision Making

Collective Negotiation (1967 1977)
USE   Collective Bargaining

Collective Settlements   JUL. 1966
       Postings: 132   GC: 550
SN   Communities practicing common own-
       ership and cooperative living
UF   Communal Living #
       Communistic Settlements
BT   Community
RT   Communism
       Cooperatives
       Municipalities
       Neighborhoods
       Rural Areas
       Settlement Houses
       Socialism

College Administration   JUL. 1966
       Postings: 9,206   GC: 320
UF   University Administration (1967 1980)
BT   School Administration
RT   Academic Deans
       Admissions Officers
       College Governing Councils
       College Planning
       College Presidents
       Colleges
       Deans
       Governing Boards
       Registrars (School)

College Admission   JUL. 1966
       Postings: 3,452   GC: 320
BT   Admission (School)
RT   Access to Education
       Admissions Counseling
       Admissions Officers
       Affirmative Action
       College Applicants
       College Attendance
       College Bound Students
       College Choice
       College Entrance Examinations
       College Freshmen
       College School Cooperation
       Colleges
       Enrollment Management
       Higher Education
       Selective Admission
       Selective Colleges

College Applicants   MAR. 1980
       Postings: 1,046   GC: 360
SN   Individuals applying for admission to
       institutions of higher education—includes
       those accepted who do not attend as well
       as those not accepted
UF   Law School Applicants #
       Medical School Applicants #
       Student Application (1966 1980)
BT   Groups
RT   Admission Criteria
       College Admission
       College Bound Students
       College Choice
       College Freshmen
       Eligibility
       Financial Aid Applicants
       No Shows
       Portfolios (Background Materials)

College Athletics   AUG. 1986
       Postings: 737   GC: 470
UF   Intercollegiate Athletics #
BT   Athletics
RT   College Curriculum
       Colleges
       Extramural Athletics
       Intramural Athletics
       Physical Education

College Attendance   JUL. 1966
       Postings: 1,139   GC: 330
SN   Past or present attendance by students
       in an institution of higher education (Note:
       Use "Attendance" for the concept of
       college students' class attendance—prior
       to Mar80, this term was not restricted by
       a Scope Note)
BT   Attendance
RT   Access to Education
       Attendance Patterns
       College Admission
       College Bound Students
       College Transfer Students
       Colleges
       Enrollment
       Expulsion
       Higher Education
       School Holding Power
       School Registration
       Student Attrition
       Suspension
       Withdrawal (Education)

College Bookstores
USE   Bookstores
AND   College Stores

College Bound Students   JUL. 1966
       Postings: 2,471   GC: 360
SN   High school students planning to attend
       a degree-granting postsecondary insti-
       tution (Note: See also "Reentry Students"
       and "Nontraditional Students")
BT   High School Students
RT   Academic Aspiration
       Admissions Counseling
       Advanced Placement Programs
       College Admission
       College Applicants
       College Attendance
       College Choice
       College Day
       College Freshmen
       College Preparation
       College School Cooperation
       College Students
       High School Graduates
       High School Seniors
       Higher Education
       Noncollege Bound Students
       Paying for College

College Buildings   JUL. 1966
       Postings: 633   GC: 920
BT   School Buildings
RT   Campus Planning
       Campuses
       College Housing
       Colleges
       Dormitories
       Educational Equipment
       Educational Facilities Design
       Facility Utilization Research
       Living Learning Centers
       Space Utilization

College Catalogs
USE   School Catalogs

College Characteristics
USE   Institutional Characteristics

College Choice   AUG. 1968
       Postings: 1,647   GC: 330
BT   School Choice
RT   Academic Aspiration
       College Admission
       College Applicants
       College Bound Students
       College Day
       College Freshmen
       College Preparation
       Colleges
       Consumer Protection
       Decision Making
       Eligibility

College Closing
USE   School Closing

College Community Relationship
USE   School Community Relationship

College Cooperation (1966 1980)
USE   Intercollegiate Cooperation

College Costs (Financing for Individual Students)
USE   Paying for College

College Costs (Incurred by Students)
USE   Student Costs

College Counselors
USE   School Counselors

College Credits   JUL. 1966
       Postings: 1,291   GC: 340
SN   Units for expressing quantitatively the
       work completed by a student in a college
       course, in a program accepted by the
       college, or for prior learning accepted by
       the college
BT   Credits
RT   Academic Advising
       Academic Records
       College Curriculum
       Colleges
       Credit Courses
       Credit No Credit Grading
       Degree Requirements
       Experiential Learning
       Grades (Scholastic)
       Pass Fail Grading
       Prior Learning
       Special Degree Programs
       Transfer Policy
       Transfer Programs

College Curriculum   JUL. 1966
       Postings: 4,443   GC: 350
NT   College English
       College Mathematics
       College Science
       College Second Language Programs
       Education Courses
       Freshman Composition
       Postsecondary Education as a Field of
         Study
       Teacher Education Curriculum
BT   Curriculum
RT   Academic Advising
       Academic Deans
       College Athletics
       College Credits
       College Instruction
       College Outcomes Assessment
       Colleges
       Higher Education

College Day   JUL. 1966
       Postings: 31   GC: 330
SN   Event or program of activities during
       which high school students and their
       parents can meet with representatives of
       colleges and universities to learn about
       programs or services offered
UF   College Night
BT   Programs
RT   Admissions Counseling
       College Bound Students
       College Choice
       College School Cooperation
       Colleges

College Deans (1968 1980)
USE   Deans
AND   Higher Education

College Desegregation   MAR. 1980
       Postings: 384   GC: 540
SN   Process of bringing ethnically or racially
       mixed students into the same colleges or
       universities
UF   College Integration (1966 1980)
       Desegregated Colleges
       Integrated Colleges
BT   School Desegregation
RT   Affirmative Action
       Colleges
       Racial Integration

College Dropouts
USE   Dropouts

College English   MAR. 1980
       Postings: 1,476   GC: 400
SN   English curriculum at the college level
       (Note: For English as a second language
       at the college level, use "College Second
       Language Programs" and "English (Sec-
       ond Language)")
BT   College Curriculum
       English Curriculum
RT   English
       English Departments
       English Instruction
       Freshman Composition

College Enrollment
USE   Enrollment

College Entrance Examinations   JUL. 1966
       Postings: 2,201   GC: 830
SN   Aptitude, achievement, or other meas-
       ures used in connection with admissions
       programs for colleges, universities, or
       graduate or professional schools
UF   Admission Tests (Higher Education)
BT   Tests
RT   Academic Ability
       Academic Achievement
       Achievement Tests
       Admission Criteria
       Advanced Placement
       Advanced Placement Programs
       Aptitude Tests
       College Admission
       Colleges
       Graduate Study
       Predictive Measurement
       Professional Education
       Screening Tests
       Standardized Tests

College Environment   JUL. 1966
       Postings: 3,126   GC: 320
SN   Conditions, forces, or factors that affect
       institutions of higher education and/or
       the people associated with them
BT   Educational Environment
       Institutional Environment
RT   Academic Freedom
       Campus Planning
       Classroom Environment
       Colleges
       Deans of Students
       Faculty College Relationship
       Institutional Characteristics
       Residential Colleges
       Student College Relationship

College Faculty   JUL. 1966
       Postings: 18,228   GC: 360
SN   Academic staff members engaged in in-
       struction, research, administration, or
       related educational activities in a college
       or university
UF   College Teachers (1967 1980)
NT   College Presidents
       Counselor Educators
       Graduate School Faculty
       Professors
       Student Teacher Supervisors
       Teacher Educators
       Teaching Assistants
BT   Faculty

= Two or more Descriptors are used to represent this term.
The term's main entry shows the appropriate coordination.

RT   Academic Rank (Professional)
      Adjunct Faculty
      Aging in Academia
      College Governing Councils
      College Instruction
      Colleges
      Doctor of Arts Degrees
      Faculty College Relationship
      Faculty Development
      Faculty Handbooks
      Faculty Organizations
      Higher Education
      Nontenured Faculty
      Postsecondary Education as a Field of
          Study
      Student Personnel Workers
      Teachers
      Tenured Faculty
      Universities

College Freshmen   *JUL. 1966*
      Postings: 5,268   GC: 360
SN   First-year students at higher education,
      generally four-year, institutions (Note:
      Prior to Mar80, "Freshmen" was also a
      valid Descriptor)
UF   Freshmen (1967 1980) (First Year
          College Students)
BT   College Students
RT   College Admission
      College Applicants
      College Bound Students
      College Choice
      College Juniors
      College Seniors
      College Sophomores
      Colleges
      Freshman Composition
      Two Year College Students
      Undergraduate Students

College Governing Councils   *DEC. 1976*
      Postings: 283   GC: 320
SN   Organizations of faculty representatives,
      sometimes including administrators and
      students, that consider administrative,
      academic, or operational policies of the
      institution
UF   Academic Senates (Colleges)
      Faculty Senates (Colleges)
      University Senates
BT   Organizations (Groups)
RT   College Administration
      College Faculty
      College Planning
      Faculty College Relationship
      Faculty Organizations
      Governance
      Institutional Autonomy
      Participative Decision Making
      Policy Formation

College Graduates   *JUL. 1966*
      Postings: 2,979   GC: 360
SN   Individuals who have completed the re-
      quirements of a college or university
      program and have been awarded a de-
      gree
BT   Graduates
RT   Alumni Associations
      Alumni Education
      Bachelors Degrees
      College Outcomes Assessment
      College Seniors
      College Students
      Colleges
      Commencement Ceremonies
      Degrees (Academic)
      Graduate Students
      Graduate Study
      Graduation
      Undergraduate Students

**College High School Cooperation (1967
1980)**
USE   College School Cooperation

College Housing   *JUL. 1966*
      Postings: 783   GC: 920
SN   Living quarters (e.g., dormitories, apart-
      ments) for college or university students
      or staff, usually but not necessarily on
      campus
UF   Student Housing (College)
BT   Housing
RT   Boarding Homes
      College Buildings
      College Students
      Colleges
      Dormitories
      Living Learning Centers
      On Campus Students
      Resident Advisers
      Resident Assistants
      Residential Colleges

College Instruction   *JUL. 1966*
      Postings: 5,097   GC: 320
UF   College Teaching
BT   Instruction
RT   College Curriculum
      College Faculty
      Colleges
      Higher Education

College Integration (1966 1980)
USE   College Desegregation

College Juniors   *APR. 1990*
      Postings: 52   GC: 360
SN   Students in their third year of a four-year
      baccalaureate program
BT   College Students
RT   College Freshmen
      College Seniors
      College Sophomores
      College Transfer Students
      Colleges
      Undergraduate Students

College Language Programs (1967 1980)
                                            MAR. 1980
      Postings: 993   GC: 450
SN   Invalid Descriptor—used for both native
      and foreign language programs—see
      such Descriptors as "College Second
      Language Programs," "College English,"
      "Native Language Instruction," and "Eng-
      lish Teacher Education"

College Libraries   *JUL. 1966*
      Postings: 3,915   GC: 710
SN   Libraries established, maintained, and
      administered by institutions of higher
      education to meet the needs of their
      students and faculty
UF   Junior College Libraries (1966 1980) #
      University Libraries (1968 1980)
BT   Academic Libraries
RT   Colleges

College Majors (1968 1980)
USE   Majors (Students)

College Mathematics   *JUL. 1966*
      Postings: 3,049   GC: 480
BT   College Curriculum
      Mathematics Curriculum
RT   Elementary School Mathematics
      Mathematics
      Mathematics Education
      Mathematics Instruction
      Secondary School Mathematics

College Night
USE   College Day

College Outcomes Assessment   *APR. 1990*
      Postings: 1,305   GC: 330
SN   Formal or informal appraisal or judg-
      ment of two- or four-year college pro-
      grams or students in relation to

institutional or public expectations of
achievement or development—often but
not always measured against specific
objectives
UF   Outcomes Measurement (College)
BT   Educational Assessment
      Outcomes of Education
RT   College Curriculum
      College Graduates
      College Planning
      College Programs
      College Role
      College Students
      Colleges
      Institutional Evaluation
      Institutional Research
      Self Evaluation (Groups)
      Undergraduate Study

College Placement (1966 1980)
USE   Student Placement

College Planning   *JUL. 1966*
      Postings: 4,035   GC: 320
SN   Administrative planning at higher educa-
      tion institutions (Note: Prior to Mar80,
      this term was not scoped and was often
      confused with "Campus Planning")
BT   Educational Planning
RT   Campus Planning
      College Administration
      College Governing Councils
      College Outcomes Assessment
      College Role
      Colleges
      Environmental Scanning
      Institutional Research
      Intercollegiate Cooperation
      Mission Statements

College Preparation   *JUL. 1966*
      Postings: 1,692   GC: 330
BT   Secondary Education
RT   Academic Education
      Admissions Counseling
      Admissions Officers
      College Bound Students
      College Choice
      Colleges
      Developmental Studies Programs
      Educational Counseling
      Higher Education
      Post High School Guidance
      Tech Prep
      Transitional Programs

College Presidents   *MAR. 1980*
      Postings: 1,453   GC: 360
SN   Principal administrative officers respon-
      sible for the direction of all affairs and
      operations of a higher education institu-
      tion (Note: Prior to Mar80, "Presidents"
      was used for both college presidents and
      nonacademic presidents)
UF   Chancellors (Education)
BT   College Faculty
      Presidents
RT   College Administration
      Deans

College Programs   *JUL. 1966*
      Postings: 3,829   GC: 320
SN   Programs offered by institutions of higher
      education (Note: Use a more specific
      term if possible)
NT   Doctoral Programs
      External Degree Programs
      Masters Programs
BT   Programs
RT   Alumni Education
      College Outcomes Assessment
      Colleges
      Higher Education
      Special Degree Programs
      Student Personnel Workers

College Registrars
USE   Registrars (School)

College Registration
USE   School Registration

College Role   *JUL. 1966*
      Postings: 5,481   GC: 330
SN   Functions expected of or carried out by
      the college in society
BT   School Role
RT   College Outcomes Assessment
      College Planning
      Colleges
      Educational Responsibility
      Living Learning Centers
      Role of Education

College School Cooperation   *JUL. 1966*
      Postings: 4,999   GC: 330
SN   Cooperation between colleges, universi-
      ties, or professional schools and other
      kinds of schools (e.g., elementary, sec-
      ondary, vocational, technical, special edu-
      cation. . .) (Note: Use "Intercollegiate
      Cooperation" for cooperation between
      two or more colleges, etc.)
UF   College High School Cooperation
          (1967 1980)
      High School College Cooperation
      School College Cooperation
BT   Educational Cooperation
      Institutional Cooperation
RT   Admissions Counseling
      Advanced Placement Programs
      Affiliated Schools
      Articulation (Education)
      Beginning Teacher Induction
      College Admission
      College Bound Students
      College Day
      Colleges
      Intercollegiate Cooperation
      Laboratory Schools
      Partnerships in Education
      Professional Development Schools
      Schools
      Student Teachers
      Tech Prep

College Science   *JUL. 1966*
      Postings: 16,261   GC: 490
BT   College Curriculum
      Science Curriculum
RT   Elementary School Science
      Science Departments
      Science Education
      Science Instruction
      Secondary School Science

College Second Language Programs
                                            MAR. 1980
      Postings: 915   GC: 450
SN   (Note: Prior to Mar80, this concept was
      indexed under "College Language Pro-
      grams")
BT   College Curriculum
      Second Language Programs
RT   Classical Languages
      Modern Language Curriculum
      Second Language Instruction
      Second Language Learning

College Segregation   *JUL. 1966*
      Postings: 50   GC: 540
SN   Exclusion on the basis of race or ethnic
      status from admission to, or full partici-
      pation in, a college or university (Note:
      Prior to Mar80, the use of this term was
      not restricted by a Scope Note)
BT   School Segregation
RT   Black Colleges
      Colleges
      Racial Segregation

College Seniors   *MAR. 1980*
      Postings: 382   GC: 360
SN   Students in their last year of a
      baccalaureate program (Note: Prior to
      Mar80, this concept was indexed under

"Seniors," which also referred to high
school seniors)
UF   Seniors (1966 1980) (Last Year
      Undergraduates)
BT   College Students
RT   College Freshmen
      College Graduates
      College Juniors
      College Sophomores
      Colleges

College Sophomores   APR. 1990
      Postings: 85   GC: 360
SN   Students in their second year of a four-
      year baccalaureate program (or a two-
      year associate-degree program)
BT   College Students
RT   College Freshmen
      College Juniors
      College Seniors
      Colleges
      Two Year College Students
      Undergraduate Students

College Stores   APR. 1975
      Postings: 193   GC: 920
SN   Higher educational facilities that sell books
      and other merchandise for student needs
UF   College Bookstores #
BT   Facilities
RT   Bookstores
      Colleges
      Educational Facilities
      Merchandising
      Retailing
      Student Unions

College Student Relationship
USE   Student College Relationship

College Students   JUL. 1966
      Postings: 34,585   GC: 360
SN   Students attending an institution of higher
      education—includes all levels, 1st-year
      through postgraduate (Note: Coordinate
      with the appropriate mandatory educa-
      tional level Descriptor—if possible, use
      a more specific term)
UF   Middle Class College Students (1966
      1980) #
      University Students
NT   College Freshmen
      College Juniors
      College Seniors
      College Sophomores
      College Transfer Students
      Graduate Students
      In State Students
      On Campus Students
      Out of State Students
      Preservice Teachers
      Resident Assistants
      Two Year College Students
      Undergraduate Students
BT   Students
RT   College Bound Students
      College Graduates
      College Housing
      College Outcomes Assessment
      Colleges
      Degree Requirements
      Late Adolescents
      Nontraditional Students
      Paying for College
      Reentry Students
      Self Supporting Students
      Stopouts
      Student College Relationship
      Universities
      Young Adults

College Supervisors (1967 1980)
USE   Student Teacher Supervisors

College Teachers (1967 1980)
USE   College Faculty

College Teaching
USE   College Instruction

College Transfer Rates
USE   Transfer Rates (College)

College Transfer Students   MAR. 1980
      Postings: 1,478   GC: 360
SN   Students who have transferred or intend
      to transfer from one higher education
      institution or program to another to
      achieve more advanced or different edu-
      cational goals
BT   College Students
      Transfer Students
RT   Articulation (Education)
      College Attendance
      College Juniors
      Educational Mobility
      Enrollment
      Student Mobility
      Transfer Rates (College)
      Two Year College Students

College Unions
USE   Student Unions

College Work Study Programs
USE   Work Study Programs

Colleges   JUL. 1966
      Postings: 3,929   GC: 340
SN   Degree granting institutions of higher
      education (Note: Use a more specific
      term if possible—for specific aspects of
      colleges, use "school" terms if corre-
      sponding "college" terms are not avail-
      able)
UF   Higher Education Institutions
NT   Agricultural Colleges
      Black Colleges
      Church Related Colleges
      Cluster Colleges
      Commuter Colleges
      Dental Schools
      Developing Institutions
      Experimental Colleges
      Law Schools
      Library Schools
      Medical Schools
      Multicampus Colleges
      Noncampus Colleges
      Private Colleges
      Public Colleges
      Residential Colleges
      Selective Colleges
      Single Sex Colleges
      Small Colleges
      Two Year Colleges
      Universities
      Upper Division Colleges
BT   Schools
RT   Campuses
      College Administration
      College Admission
      College Athletics
      College Attendance
      College Buildings
      College Choice
      College Credits
      College Curriculum
      College Day
      College Desegregation
      College Entrance Examinations
      College Environment
      College Faculty
      College Freshmen
      College Graduates
      College Housing
      College Instruction
      College Juniors
      College Libraries
      College Outcomes Assessment
      College Planning
      College Preparation
      College Programs
      College Role
      College School Cooperation
      College Segregation

College Seniors
College Sophomores
College Stores
College Students
Extension Education
Faculty College Relationship
Faculty Handbooks
Higher Education
Intercollegiate Cooperation
Living Learning Centers
Nonprofit Organizations
Postsecondary Education
School Counseling
School Counselors
School Guidance
Student College Relationship
Undergraduate Study
University Presses

Colleges of Education
USE   Schools of Education

Collegial Models
USE   Collegiality

Collegiality   AUG. 1988
      Postings: 1,484   GC: 520
SN   Relationship among people within a pro-
      fession, field, organization, or office, char-
      acterized by trust, openness, concern,
      and cooperation
UF   Collegial Models
BT   Interpersonal Relationship
RT   Cooperation
      Employer Employee Relationship
      Interprofessional Relationship
      Leadership Qualities
      Mentors
      Organizational Climate
      Participative Decision Making
      Peer Relationship
      Professional Associations
      Professional Development
      Professional Isolation
      Quality of Working Life
      Staff Development
      Teacher Collaboration
      Teamwork
      Work Environment

Colloquial Standard Usage
USE   Standard Spoken Usage

Colloquiums (Meetings)
USE   Meetings

Colonial History (United States)   JUL. 1966
      Postings: 590   GC: 430
BT   United States History
RT   Colonialism
      Puritans
      Revolutionary War (United States)
      Slavery

Colonialism   SEP. 1968
      Postings: 677   GC: 610
BT   Imperialism
RT   Colonial History (United States)
      International Relations
      Nationalism
      Political Attitudes
      Political Divisions (Geographic)
      Revolutionary War (United States)

Colonization
USE   Land Settlement

Color   OCT. 1969
      Postings: 973   GC: 490
UF   Color Presentation (1969 1980)
      Color Television (1969 1980) #
      Hue
RT   Art
      Color Planning
      Contrast

Dimensional Preference
Light
Painting (Visual Arts)
Visual Environment
Visual Perception

Color Films
USE   Films

Color Planning   OCT. 1968
      Postings: 93   GC: 420
BT   Planning
RT   Building Design
      Color
      Interior Design
      Painting (Industrial Arts)
      Visual Arts
      Visual Environment

Color Presentation (1969 1980)
USE   Color

Color Television (1969 1980)
USE   Color
AND   Television

COM
USE   Computer Output Microfilm

Combat Instruments
USE   Weapons

Comedy   JUL. 1966
      Postings: 166   GC: 430
UF   Comedy of Manners
NT   Skits
BT   Drama
RT   Humor
      Literary Devices
      Literary Genres
      Scripts
      Tragedy

Comedy of Manners
USE   Comedy

Comics (Publications)   JUN. 1975
      Postings: 233   GC: 720
SN   Narrative series of drawings or pictures,
      usually accompanied by balloons giving
      conversation, which present humorous
      incidents or dramatic adventures—in-
      cludes comic strips and comic books
BT   Publications
RT   Cartoons
      Childrens Literature
      Fiction
      Humor
      Instructional Materials
      Newspapers
      Parody
      Satire
      Serials
      Visual Aids

Commencement Ceremonies   MAR. 1980
      Postings: 57   GC: 320
SN   Occasions at which formal recognition is
      given for a student's completion of a
      program of study, usually in the form of
      a certificate, degree, or diploma
UF   Graduate Ceremonies
BT   Recognition (Achievement)
RT   College Graduates
      Degrees (Academic)
      Graduation

Commercial Art   OCT. 1968
      Postings: 206   GC: 420
UF   Advertising Art
BT   Art
RT   Advertising
      Art Education

= Two or more Descriptors are used to represent this term.
The term's main entry shows the appropriate coordination.

Graphic Arts
Merchandising
Television Commercials
Visual Arts

Commercial Communication
USE   Business Communication

Commercial Correspondence Schools
USE   Correspondence Schools

Commercial Education
USE   Business Education

Commercial Enterprises
USE   Business

Commercial Pilots
USE   Aircraft Pilots

Commercial Search Services (Online)
USE   Online Vendors

Commercial Television   *JUL. 1966*
          Postings: 998   GC: 720
SN   Television system operating for profit
          and accepting paid advertising
BT   Television
RT   Broadcast Industry
          Public Television
          Television Commercials

Committees   *JUL. 1966*
          Postings: 1,240   GC: 520
NT   Advisory Committees
          Biracial Committees
          Research Committees
          Search Committees (Personnel)
RT   Administration
          Governing Boards
          Organizations (Groups)
          Planning

Common Fractions (1966 1980)
USE   Fractions

Communal Living
USE   Collective Settlements
AND   Group Experience

Communicable Diseases   *JUL. 1966*
          Postings: 677   GC: 210
UF   Contagious Diseases
          Infectious Diseases (1966 1974)
NT   Acquired Immune Deficiency
              Syndrome
          Rubella
          Venereal Diseases
BT   Diseases
RT   Bacteria
          Disease Control
          Immunization Programs
          Physical Health
          Public Health
          Sick Child Care
          Viruses

Communication (Thought Transfer)
                                                  JUL. 1966
          Postings: 9,884   GC: 520
SN   Transmission and reception of signals or
          meanings through a system of symbols
          (codes, gestures, language, etc.) com-
          mon to sender and receiver (Note: Use a
          more specific term if possible—prior to
          Mar80, the instruction "Communication
          Theory, USE Information Theory" was
          carried in the Thesaurus)
UF   Communication Theory
          Intercommunication (1966 1980)
NT   Augmentative and Alternative Commu-
              nication
          Classroom Communication

Computer Mediated Communication
Development Communication
Diffusion (Communication)
Discussion
Intercultural Communication
International Communication
Interpersonal Communication
Nonverbal Communication
Organizational Communication
Propaganda
Publicity
Scholarly Communication
Speech Communication
Verbal Communication
RT   Agenda Setting
          Audiences
          Communication Aids (for Disabled)
          Communication Apprehension
          Communication Disorders
          Communication Problems
          Communication Research
          Communication Skills
          Content Analysis
          Credibility
          Cybernetics
          Deaf Interpreting
          Deception
          Disclosure
          Discourse Communities
          Discourse Modes
          Expressive Language
          Familiarity
          Feedback
          Hermeneutics
          Inferences
          Information Dissemination
          Information Networks
          Information Seeking
          Information Theory
          Information Transfer
          Intention
          Interaction
          Intergroup Relations
          Interpreters
          Intimacy
          Jargon
          Language Arts
          Mutual Intelligibility
          Network Analysis
          Networks
          Persuasive Discourse
          Receptive Language
          Rhetorical Theory
          Social Networks

Communication Aids (for Disabled)
                                                  NOV. 1981
          Postings: 624   GC: 220
SN   Devices and materials that enable per-
          sons with communication disorders to
          communicate more normally
RT   Assistive Devices (for Disabled)
          Augmentative and Alternative Commu-
              nication
          Cochlear Implants
          Communication (Thought Transfer)
          Communication Disorders
          Hearing Aids
          Sensory Aids
          Total Communication

Communication Apprehension   *AUG. 1982*
          Postings: 628   GC: 120
SN   Fear or anxiety experienced by an indi-
          vidual in anticipation of and/or during
          the course of communication—usually
          oral—with another person or group (Note:
          Do not confuse with "Writing Apprehen-
          sion")
BT   Anxiety
RT   Communication (Thought Transfer)
          Communication Problems
          Shyness
          Speech Communication

Communication Audits   *AUG. 1986*
          Postings: 46   GC: 520
SN   Assessments of communication effec-
          tiveness within organizations, or between

organizations and external groups or the
public
BT   Audits (Verification)
RT   Institutional Advancement
          Network Analysis
          Organizational Communication
          Public Relations

Communication Disorders   *MAR. 1980*
          Postings: 809   GC: 220
SN   Impairments of an individual's ability to
          communicate due to disorders of hear-
          ing, speech, language, etc. (Note: Use a
          more precise term if possible, and do not
          confuse with "Communication Prob-
          lems," which are not the result of impair-
          ments)
BT   Disabilities
RT   Aphasia
          Augmentative and Alternative Commu-
              nication
          Communication (Thought Transfer)
          Communication Aids (for Disabled)
          Communication Problems
          Developmental Disabilities
          Hearing Impairments
          Language Impairments
          Learning Disabilities
          Speech Impairments
          Speech Language Pathology

Communication Problems   *JUL. 1966*
          Postings: 2,696   GC: 120
BT   Problems
RT   Communication (Thought Transfer)
          Communication Apprehension
          Communication Disorders
          Intercultural Communication
          International Communication
          Jargon
          Nonverbal Communication
          Verbal Abuse

Communication Research   *SEP. 1980*
          Postings: 6,759   GC: 810
SN   Investigation into the nature and func-
          tion of human communication, both ver-
          bal and nonverbal, in one-to-one or group
          settings (Note: Do not confuse with "Lan-
          guage Research")
UF   Speech Communication Research #
BT   Research
RT   Audience Analysis
          Behavioral Science Research
          Communication (Thought Transfer)
          Discourse Analysis
          Interaction Process Analysis
          Journalism Research
          Language Research
          Network Analysis
          Reading Research
          Social Science Research
          Writing Research

Communication Satellites (1967 1980)
USE   Communications Satellites

Communication Skills   *JUL. 1966*
          Postings: 10,705   GC: 400
UF   Conference Skills (Communication)
NT   Communicative Competence
              (Languages)
BT   Skills
RT   Audience Awareness
          Audiolingual Skills
          Basic Skills
          Communication (Thought Transfer)
          Credibility
          Daily Living Skills
          Deaf Interpreting
          Expressive Language
          Inferences
          Intimacy
          Language Skills
          Manual Communication
          Metacognition
          Nonverbal Communication
          Oral Communication Method
          Receptive Language

Social Cognition
Teaching Skills
Telephone Usage Instruction
Thinking Skills
Total Communication
Transactional Analysis
Verbal Ability
Verbal Communication

Communication Theory
USE   Communication (Thought Transfer)

Communications   *JUL. 1966*
          Postings: 3,244   GC: 710
SN   Science and technology of the transmis-
          sion and reception of information (Note:
          Prior to Mar80, the Thesaurus carried
          the instructions, "Communication Net-
          works, Services, or Systems, USE Tele-
          communication")
UF   Communications Networks
          Communications Services
          Communications Systems
          Mass Media Technology #
          Media Technology (1968 1980)
NT   Audiovisual Communications
          Telecommunications
BT   Technology
RT   Cybernetics
          Delivery Systems
          Distributive Education
          Hypermedia
          Information Industry
          Information Networks
          Information Processing
          Information Technology
          Information Theory
          Information Transfer
          Interactive Video
          Mass Media
          Multimedia Materials
          Network Analysis
          Networks
          Nonprint Media
          Printed Materials
          Propaganda
          Publications
          Publicity
          Social Networks
          Technology Education

Communications Media
USE   Mass Media

Communications Networks
USE   Communications

Communications Satellites   *MAR. 1980*
          Postings: 1,127   GC: 710
UF   Communication Satellites (1967 1980)
BT   Satellites (Aerospace)
          Telecommunications
RT   Distance Education
          Information Networks
          Interactive Television

Communications Services
USE   Communications

Communications Systems
USE   Communications

Communications Theory
USE   Information Theory

Communicative Competence (Languages)
                                                  AUG. 1976
          Postings: 2,904   GC: 450
SN   The ability to converse or correspond
          with a native speaker of the target lan-
          guage in a real-life situation, with em-
          phasis on communication of ideas rather
          than on correctness of language form
NT   Threshold Level (Languages)
BT   Communication Skills

= Two or more Descriptors are used to represent this term.
The term's main entry shows the appropriate coordination.

Language Skills
RT   Conversational Language Courses
      Dialogs (Language)
      Language Fluency
      Language Proficiency
      Linguistic Competence
      Linguistic Performance
      Notional Functional Syllabi
      Second Language Learning
      Speech Communication
      Verbal Communication

Communism   JUL. 1966
      Postings: 853   GC: 610
BT   Social Systems
RT   Capitalism
      Collective Settlements
      Democracy
      Economics
      Fascism
      Government (Administrative Body)
      Imperialism
      Marxism
      Political Science
      Socialism
      Totalitarianism

Communistic Settlements
USE   Collective Settlements

Community   JUL. 1966
      Postings: 840   GC: 520
SN   A social group linked by common inter-
      ests through residence in a specific lo-
      cality, or, whether or not in physical
      proximity, whose members perceive
      themselves as sharing a common ideol-
      ogy, interest, or other characteristic
NT   Black Community
      Collective Settlements
      Discourse Communities
      Municipalities
      Neighborhoods
      Planned Communities
RT   City Government
      Community Action
      Community Attitudes
      Community Based Instruction (Disa-
        bilities)
      Community Benefits
      Community Centers
      Community Change
      Community Characteristics
      Community Colleges
      Community Control
      Community Cooperation
      Community Coordination
      Community Development
      Community Education
      Community Health Services
      Community Influence
      Community Involvement
      Community Leaders
      Community Needs
      Community Organizations
      Community Planning
      Community Problems
      Community Programs
      Community Psychology
      Community Relations
      Community Resources
      Community Responsibility
      Community Role
      Community Satisfaction
      Community Schools
      Community Services
      Community Study
      Community Support
      Community Surveys
      Community Zoning
      Ethnic Distribution
      Group Unity
      Local Government
      Local Issues
      Place of Residence
      Police Community Relationship
      School Community Programs
      School Community Relationship
      Suburbs

Community Action   JUL. 1966
      Postings: 1,595   GC: 520
SN   Grass roots mobilization of local re-
      sources to meet community needs
UF   Action Programs (Community) (1966
        1980)
      Community Effort
BT   Social Action
RT   Action Research
      Citizen Participation
      Community
      Community Change
      Community Control
      Community Cooperation
      Community Development
      Community Involvement
      Community Needs
      Community Organizations
      Community Problems
      Community Responsibility
      Community Role
      Community Services
      Community Support
      Local Issues
      Self Help Programs
      Social Responsibility

Community Agencies (Public) (1966 1980)
USE   Public Agencies

Community Analysis
USE   Community Study

Community Antennas (1966 1980)
USE   Cable Television

Community Attitudes   JUL. 1966
      Postings: 2,090   GC: 520
NT   Community Satisfaction
BT   Attitudes
RT   Citizenship
      Community
      Community Characteristics
      Community Cooperation
      Community Involvement
      Community Relations
      Community Role
      Community Support
      Community Surveys
      Local Issues
      Political Attitudes
      Social Attitudes

Community Based Education
USE   Community Education

Community Based Instruction (Disabilities)
                                             JUN. 1994
      Postings: 74   GC: 220
SN   Systematic training of people with disa-
      bilities in functional skills within the natu-
      ral community setting where such skills
      are used, in order to ease/enhance tran-
      sitions to independent living, community
      participation, and employment
BT   Teaching Methods
RT   Community
      Daily Living Skills
      Experiential Learning
      Normalization (Disabilities)
      School Community Relationship
      Special Education
      Transitional Programs

Community Benefits   JUL. 1966
      Postings: 298   GC: 330
SN   Advantages derived by communities from
      their association with institutions, indus-
      tries, programs, etc. (Note: For advan-
      tages provided by communities, use such
      Descriptors as "Community Services,"
      "Community Programs," "Community
      Resources," etc.—prior to Mar80, the
      use of this term was not restricted by a
      Scope Note)
RT   Community
      Community Cooperation

Community Coordination
Community Development
Community Relations

Community Centers   MAR. 1980
      Postings: 395   GC: 920
SN   Facilities at which social, educational,
      recreational, and other activities are held
      for the benefit of the community (Note:
      Use of the original term, "Neighborhood
      Centers," was not restricted by a Scope
      Note)
UF   Community Rooms (1967 1980)
      Neighborhood Centers (1966 1980)
BT   Facilities
RT   Community
      Community Education
      Community Organizations
      Community Programs
      Community Recreation Programs
      Community Resources
      Community Services

Community Change   JUL. 1966
      Postings: 651   GC: 550
SN   Change in or of a community—may be
      either planned or unplanned, initiated in
      the community or by outside forces,
      toward or away from improvement
BT   Change
RT   Boomtowns
      Change Agents
      Change Strategies
      Citizen Participation
      Community
      Community Action
      Community Development
      Community Involvement
      Community Leaders
      Community Planning
      Culture Lag
      Economic Change
      Local Issues
      Social Change
      Urban Renewal

Community Characteristics   JUL. 1966
      Postings: 1,463   GC: 520
UF   Community Traits
NT   Community Size
RT   Built Environment
      Community
      Community Attitudes
      Community Cooperation
      Community Development
      Community Resources
      Community Surveys
      Counties
      Heritage Education
      Local History
      Local Issues
      Neighborhoods
      Place of Residence
      Regional Characteristics
      Urban Environment

Community Colleges   JUL. 1966
      Postings: 24,311   GC: 340
SN   Public, postsecondary institutions com-
      monly organized into 2-year programs
      and offering instruction adapted in con-
      tent, level, and schedule to the needs
      of the community in which they are
      located—usually offer a comprehensive
      curriculum with transfer, occupational,
      general education, and adult education
      components
BT   Public Colleges
      Two Year Colleges
RT   Associate Degrees
      Community
      Community Education
      Community Services
      Multicampus Colleges
      Multicampus Districts
      Postsecondary Education
      Public Education
      School Community Relationship
      State Colleges

Technical Institutes
Two Year College Students
Undergraduate Study

Community Committees
USE   Community Organizations

Community Compliance
USE   Community Cooperation

Community Consultant Programs (1966 1980)
USE   Consultation Programs

Community Consultants (1966 1980)
USE   Consultants

Community Control   AUG. 1969
      Postings: 860   GC: 330
SN   Control of community programs, insti-
      tutions, agencies, etc., by recognized
      groups within the community (e.g., mi-
      nority controlled schools, elitist versus
      pluralistic control, etc.)
BT   Governance
RT   Citizen Participation
      Community
      Community Action
      Community Involvement
      Community Schools
      Decentralization
      Ethnic Relations
      Government School Relationship
      Majority Attitudes
      Minority Group Influences
      Participative Decision Making
      Participatory Research
      Policy Formation
      Politics
      School Community Relationship
      School District Autonomy
      Self Determination
      Tribally Controlled Education

Community Cooperation   JUL. 1966
      Postings: 948   GC: 520
SN   Cooperation of a community as a whole
      (i.e., local government and constituents)
      in any activity or endeavor (Note: Do not
      confuse with "Community Coordina-
      tion"—prior to Mar80, this term was not
      restricted by a Scope Note)
UF   Community Compliance
BT   Cooperation
RT   Biracial Committees
      Citizen Participation
      Community
      Community Action
      Community Attitudes
      Community Benefits
      Community Characteristics
      Community Coordination
      Community Involvement
      Community Organizations
      Community Programs
      Community Psychology
      Community Relations
      Community Role
      Community Services
      Community Support
      Cooperative Planning
      Institutional Cooperation
      Police Community Relationship
      School Community Relationship

Community Coordination   JUL. 1966
      Postings: 390   GC: 520
SN   Process of bringing together the diverse
      elements of a community (people, groups,
      agencies, organizations) into a working
      whole (Note: Do not confuse with "Com-
      munity Cooperation"—prior to Mar80,
      this term was not restricted by a Scope
      Note)
UF   Community Coordinators (1966
        1980) #
BT   Coordination

= Two or more Descriptors are used to represent this term.
The term's main entry shows the appropriate coordination.

RT　Community
　　Community Benefits
　　Community Cooperation
　　Community Development
　　Community Education
　　Community Organizations
　　Community Planning
　　Community Problems
　　Community Programs
　　Community Psychology
　　Community Services
　　Local Issues
　　Police Community Relationship
　　School Community Relationship

Community Coordinators (1966 1980)
USE　Community Coordination
AND　Coordinators

Community Development　　　*JUL. 1966*
　　Postings: 2,933　　　　　　GC: 550
SN　Process by which communities and out-
　　side agencies plan, organize, or imple-
　　ment general improvements of commu-
　　nity resources, facilities, economic
　　conditions, etc.
BT　Development
RT　Boomtowns
　　Citizen Participation
　　Community
　　Community Action
　　Community Benefits
　　Community Change
　　Community Characteristics
　　Community Coordination
　　Community Education
　　Community Planning
　　Community Resources
　　Community Responsibility
　　Developing Nations
　　Economic Development
　　Living Standards
　　Modernization
　　Neighborhood Improvement
　　Quality of Life
　　Rural Development
　　Sustainable Development
　　Technical Assistance
　　Urban Improvement

Community Education　　　*JUL. 1966*
　　Postings: 2,679　　　　　　GC: 340
SN　Extending existing educational resources
　　(including those of schools, colleges,
　　and local organizations) into the com-
　　munity to serve all age groups and spe-
　　cial target groups not ordinarily served
　　by regular educational programs (Note:
　　Do not confuse with community-focused
　　place-based education, for which use the
　　Identifier "Place Based Education," co-
　　ordinated as appropriate with a second
　　Identifier "Sense of Community")
UF　Community Based Education
BT　Education
RT　Adult Education
　　Community
　　Community Centers
　　Community Colleges
　　Community Coordination
　　Community Development
　　Community Resources
　　Community Schools
　　Community Services
　　Continuing Education
　　Extension Education
　　Lifelong Learning
　　Nonschool Educational Programs
　　Outreach Programs
　　Popular Education

Community Effort
USE　Community Action

Community Enterprises
USE　Community Programs

Community Experience
USE　Experiential Learning

Community Health Services　　*JUL. 1966*
　　Postings: 1,088　　　　　　GC: 210
UF　Community Health Workers #
　　Community Mental Health Workers #
BT　Community Services
　　Health Services
RT　Community
　　Community Psychology
　　Home Health Aides
　　Home Visits
　　Immunization Programs
　　Long Term Care
　　Medical Care Evaluation
　　Prenatal Care
　　Public Health

Community Health Workers
USE　Community Health Services
AND　Health Personnel

Community Health (1966 1980)
USE　Public Health

Community History
USE　Local History

Community Influence　　　*JUL. 1966*
　　Postings: 638　　　　　　GC: 520
SN　The influence exerted by a community
　　(Note: Prior to Mar80, the use of this
　　term was not restricted by a Scope Note)
BT　Influences
RT　Black Community
　　Community
　　Community Involvement
　　Community Leaders
　　Community Role
　　Community Support

Community Information Centers
USE　Community Information Services

Community Information Services　*FEB. 1975*
　　Postings: 478　　　　　　GC: 710
SN　Those services of local libraries or other
　　community groups that provide direct
　　access or referral to nontraditional infor-
　　mation (e.g., unpublished materials, gov-
　　ernment agency information on public
　　services, broadcast information on cur-
　　rent topics, data for use in emergencies,
　　etc.)
UF　Community Information Centers
　　Information Services (Community)
　　Local Information Services
　　Referral Services (Community) #
NT　Hotlines (Public)
BT　Community Services
　　Information Services
RT　Information Centers
　　Public Libraries
　　Reference Services
　　Referral
　　Social Services

Community Involvement　　　*JUL. 1966*
　　Postings: 7,099　　　　　　GC: 330
SN　Involvement of a community in activities
　　or programs (Note: Do not confuse with
　　"Citizen Participation"—prior to Mar80,
　　the use of this term was not restricted by
　　a Scope Note)
UF　Community Participation
BT　Participation
RT　Citizen Participation
　　Community
　　Community Action
　　Community Attitudes
　　Community Change
　　Community Control
　　Community Cooperation
　　Community Influence
　　Community Role

Community Services
　　Community Support
　　Outreach Programs
　　Participatory Research
　　Partnerships in Education
　　Public Service

Community Leaders　　　*JUL. 1966*
　　Postings: 674　　　　　　GC: 520
BT　Groups
　　Leaders
RT　Change Agents
　　Community
　　Community Change
　　Community Influence
　　Leadership
　　Political Candidates
　　Public Officials

Community Legislation
USE　Local Legislation

Community Mental Health Workers
USE　Community Health Services
AND　Mental Health Workers

Community Migrant Projects (1966 1980)
USE　Community Programs
AND　Migrant Programs

Community Needs　　　*AUG. 1998*
　　Postings: 171　　　　　　GC: 520
SN　Necessary conditions for optimal func-
　　tion, development, or well-being of the
　　community
BT　Needs
RT　Community
　　Community Action
　　Community Programs
　　Community Resources
　　Community Satisfaction
　　Community Services
　　Community Surveys

Community Organizations　　*JUL. 1966*
　　Postings: 1,695　　　　　　GC: 520
UF　Civic Groups
　　Civic Organizations
　　Community Committees
　　Community Workers
NT　Citizens Councils
BT　Organizations (Groups)
RT　Citizen Participation
　　Community
　　Community Action
　　Community Centers
　　Community Cooperation
　　Community Coordination
　　Community Programs
　　Community Services
　　Cooperatives
　　National Organizations
　　Nongovernmental Organizations
　　Public Affairs Education
　　Social Organizations

Community Outreach
USE　Outreach Programs

Community Participation
USE　Community Involvement

Community Planning　　　*JUL. 1966*
　　Postings: 606　　　　　　GC: 550
BT　Planning
RT　Community
　　Community Change
　　Community Coordination
　　Community Development
　　Community Programs
　　Community Zoning
　　Facility Planning
　　Land Use
　　Planning Commissions
　　Urban Planning

Community Police Relationship
USE　Police Community Relationship

Community Problems　　　*JUL. 1966*
　　Postings: 592　　　　　　GC: 530
UF　Community Tensions
BT　Problems
RT　Community
　　Community Action
　　Community Coordination
　　Local Issues
　　Urban Problems

Community Programs　　　*JUL. 1966*
　　Postings: 3,993　　　　　　GC: 520
UF　Civic Programs
　　Community Enterprises
　　Community Migrant Projects (1966
　　　1980) #
　　Community Projects
　　Local Community Programs
NT　Community Recreation Programs
　　School Community Programs
BT　Programs
RT　Cable Franchising
　　Civil Defense
　　Community
　　Community Centers
　　Community Cooperation
　　Community Coordination
　　Community Needs
　　Community Organizations
　　Community Planning
　　Community Resources
　　Community Responsibility
　　County Programs
　　Crime Prevention
　　Deinstitutionalization (of Disabled)
　　Group Homes
　　Intergenerational Programs
　　Migrant Programs
　　Public Agencies
　　Public Service
　　Settlement Houses
　　Social Responsibility
　　Supported Employment
　　Youth Programs

Community Projects
USE　Community Programs

Community Psychology　　　*APR. 1986*
　　Postings: 49　　　　　　GC: 230
SN　The application of psychological meth-
　　ods (in collaboration with psychiatry,
　　sociology, social work, etc.) to problems
　　arising in a community and soluble only
　　through a community-wide approach—
　　attention is given to problems of mental
　　health, social welfare, group relation-
　　ships, education, social action, etc., in-
　　volving the well-being of all community
　　members
BT　Psychology
RT　Clinical Psychology
　　Community
　　Community Cooperation
　　Community Coordination
　　Community Health Services
　　Community Relations
　　Community Role
　　Community Services
　　Psychopathology
　　Social Psychology

**Community Recreation Legislation (1966
1978)**
USE　Local Legislation
AND　Recreation Legislation

Community Recreation Programs　*JUL. 1966*
　　Postings: 187　　　　　　GC: 470
BT　Community Programs
　　Recreational Programs
RT　Community Centers
　　Community Resources
　　Community Services

= Two or more Descriptors are used to represent this term.
The term's main entry shows the appropriate coordination.

Lifetime Sports
Recreational Facilities

Community Relations   *JUL. 1966*
     Postings: 656   GC: 520
UF   Civic Relations
BT   Relationship
RT   Community
     Community Attitudes
     Community Benefits
     Community Cooperation
     Community Psychology

Community Resources   *JUL. 1966*
     Postings: 2,487   GC: 520
SN   The financial, material, and/or human
     assets of a community
BT   Resources
RT   Community
     Community Centers
     Community Characteristics
     Community Development
     Community Education
     Community Needs
     Community Programs
     Community Recreation Programs
     Community Satisfaction
     Community Services
     Financial Support
     Human Resources
     Information Sources
     Material Culture
     Museums
     Natural Resources
     Parks
     Public Libraries
     Recreational Facilities

Community Responsibility   *JUL. 1966*
     Postings: 361   GC: 520
SN   Obligations, duties, or trusts given to or
     assumed by a community (Note: Do not
     confuse with "Community Role"—prior
     to Mar80, this term was not restricted by
     a Scope Note)
BT   Responsibility
RT   Citizenship Responsibility
     Community
     Community Action
     Community Development
     Community Programs
     Community Role
     Community Services
     Humanitarianism
     Neighborhood Improvement
     Social Responsibility
     Urban Improvement

Community Role   *JUL. 1966*
     Postings: 1,178   GC: 520
SN   Functions expected of or performed by a
     community
BT   Role
RT   Citizen Participation
     Community
     Community Action
     Community Attitudes
     Community Cooperation
     Community Influence
     Community Involvement
     Community Psychology
     Community Responsibility
     Community Services
     Community Support
     Institutional Role

Community Rooms (1967 1980)
USE   Community Centers

Community Satisfaction   *JUN. 1978*
     Postings: 157   GC: 520
SN   The extent to which individuals or groups
     are content with the quality of life in their
     immediate locale
BT   Community Attitudes
     Satisfaction
RT   Community
     Community Needs

Community Resources
Need Gratification
Quality of Life

Community School Directors (1967 1980)
USE   Administrators
AND   Community Schools

Community School Programs
USE   School Community Programs

Community School Relationship
USE   School Community Relationship

Community Schools   *JUL. 1966*
     Postings: 807   GC: 340
SN   Schools that are closely connected with
     the life of the community in which they
     are located, i.e., instruction and other
     school activities are intended to be rele-
     vant to most or all segments of the
     community's population
UF   Community School Directors (1967
     1980) #
BT   Schools
RT   Community
     Community Control
     Community Education
     Folk Schools
     Neighborhood Schools
     Nontraditional Education
     Outreach Programs
     Public School Adult Education
     School Community Relationship
     Shared Facilities
     Tribally Controlled Education

Community Service Learning
USE   Service Learning

Community Service Programs (1966 1980)
USE   Community Services

Community Services   *JUL. 1966*
     Postings: 3,868   GC: 520
SN   Includes educational, recreational, cul-
     tural, and social welfare services, and/or
     the provision of facilities for such activi-
     ties, offered for the benefit of the general
     public by community groups or agen-
     cies, often as an adjunct to their primary
     functions
UF   Community Service Programs (1966
     1980)
NT   Community Health Services
     Community Information Services
BT   Services
RT   Community
     Community Action
     Community Centers
     Community Colleges
     Community Cooperation
     Community Coordination
     Community Education
     Community Involvement
     Community Needs
     Community Organizations
     Community Psychology
     Community Recreation Programs
     Community Resources
     Community Responsibility
     Community Role
     Community Support
     Continuing Education
     Eligibility
     Local Government
     Outreach Programs
     Service Learning
     Social Services

Community Size   *NOV. 1968*
     Postings: 196   GC: 550
BT   Community Characteristics
RT   Boomtowns
     Census Figures
     Demography

Geographic Distribution
Overpopulation
Population Distribution
Population Growth
Population Trends
Small Towns
Urban Demography
Urban Population

Community Study   *JUL. 1966*
     Postings: 912   GC: 810
SN   Analysis of the work, amusements, read-
     ing, beliefs, and customs of a whole
     community in an effort to understand
     community life and problems (Note: As
     of Oct81, use as a minor Descriptor for
     examples of this kind of research—use
     as a major Descriptor only as the subject
     of a document)
UF   Community Analysis
BT   Research
RT   Cohort Analysis
     Community
     Local History

Community Support   *JUL. 1966*
     Postings: 1,168   GC: 330
SN   Support by the community of something
     (issue, program, policy, etc.)
RT   Citizen Participation
     Community
     Community Action
     Community Attitudes
     Community Cooperation
     Community Influence
     Community Involvement
     Community Role
     Community Services
     Local Issues
     Public Support
     School Support

Community Surveys   *JUL. 1966*
     Postings: 1,067   GC: 810
SN   Investigations of social conditions and
     resources, community attitudes, uses of
     community agencies, institutional prac-
     tices, etc., as they exist at a given time in
     a given community (Note: As of Oct81,
     use as a minor Descriptor for examples
     of this kind of survey—use as a major
     Descriptor only as the subject of a docu-
     ment)
BT   Surveys
RT   Community
     Community Attitudes
     Community Characteristics
     Community Needs
     Occupational Surveys

Community Tensions
USE   Community Problems

Community Traits
USE   Community Characteristics

Community Workers
USE   Community Organizations

Community Zoning   *JUL. 1966*
     Postings: 37   GC: 550
BT   Zoning
RT   Community
     Community Planning

Commuter Colleges   *MAR. 1980*
     Postings: 107   GC: 340
SN   Institutions of higher education that pri-
     marily serve commuting students
UF   Nonresidential Schools (1967 1980)
BT   Colleges
RT   Commuting Students
     Residential Colleges
     School Location
     Student Transportation

Commuting Students   *JUL. 1966*
     Postings: 290   GC: 360
SN   Students living off campus who travel to
     an institution for classes, study, and
     other activities
BT   Students
RT   Commuter Colleges
     On Campus Students
     Student Transportation

Compact Disks
USE   Optical Disks

Companion Animals
USE   Pets

Companions (Occupation) (1968 1980)
USE   Attendants

Company Libraries
USE   Corporate Libraries

Company Size (Industry)
USE   Organization Size (Groups)

Comparable Institutions
USE   Peer Institutions

Comparable Worth   *JAN. 1986*
     Postings: 212   GC: 540
SN   Principle of equal pay for work of com-
     parable value, i.e., equal pay for jobs
     that may have different duties but that
     require similar levels of skill, effort, and
     responsibility under similar working
     conditions—frequently advocated to re-
     dress sex-based pay inequities, i.e., be-
     tween comparable female- and male-
     dominated jobs (some analyses con-
     sider race/ethnicity among job types as
     well)
UF   Pay Equity
RT   Employed Women
     Employment Practices
     Equal Opportunities (Jobs)
     Nontraditional Occupations
     Personnel Policy
     Salary Wage Differentials

Comparative Analysis   *JUL. 1966*
     Postings: 32,837   GC: 820
SN   (Note: As of Oct81, use as a minor
     Descriptor to convey the use of this
     technique in a document—use as a ma-
     jor Descriptor only as the subject of a
     document)
UF   Comparative Evaluation
     Comparative Statistics (1966 1980) #
     Comparative Study
NT   Educational Status Comparison
     Error Analysis (Language)
BT   Evaluation Methods
RT   Benchmarking
     Comparative Testing
     Correlation
     Cross Cultural Studies
     Differences
     Etymology
     Glottochronology
     International Studies
     Language Classification
     Lexicology
     Meta Analysis
     Multiple Regression Analysis
     Multitrait Multimethod Techniques
     Multivariate Analysis
     National Norms
     Peer Institutions
     Surveys
     Synthesis
     Trend Analysis

Comparative Education   *JUL. 1966*
     Postings: 7,437   GC: 400
SN   Field of study dealing with the compari-

\# = Two or more Descriptors are used to represent this term.
The term's main entry shows the appropriate coordination.

son of educational theory and practice in different countries
BT   Education
RT   Cross Cultural Studies
      Educational Anthropology
      Foreign Culture
      Foundations of Education
      International Education
      International Educational Exchange
      Nonformal Education

Comparative Evaluation
USE   Comparative Analysis

Comparative Linguistics
USE   Contrastive Linguistics

Comparative Religion
USE   Religion Studies

Comparative Statistics (1966 1980)
USE   Comparative Analysis
AND   Statistical Analysis

Comparative Study
USE   Comparative Analysis

Comparative Testing   *JUL. 1966*
       Postings: 1,393   GC: 820
SN   Testing in which two or more individu-als, groups, or tests are compared
BT   Testing
RT   Comparative Analysis
      Concurrent Validity
      Differences
      National Norms
      Norm Referenced Tests
      Test Format
      Test Norms
      Test Reviews

Compensation (Concept)   *JAN. 1973*
       Postings: 32   GC: 110
SN   The principle that material undergoing a transformation in one dimension is ac-companied by a reciprocal change in another dimension—in developmental psychology, the recognition or under-standing of this principle
BT   Fundamental Concepts
RT   Cognitive Processes
      Concept Formation
      Conservation (Concept)
      Developmental Stages

Compensation (Remuneration)   *OCT. 1979*
       Postings: 1,013   GC: 630
SN   Total payment awarded, including wage or salary, fringe benefits, and perquisites
UF   Remuneration
BT   Expenditures
RT   Costs
      Fringe Benefits
      Income
      Professional Recognition
      Recognition (Achievement)
      Retirement Benefits
      Rewards
      Salaries
      Wages

Compensatory Development
USE   Compensatory Education

Compensatory Education   *JUL. 1966*
       Postings: 4,561   GC: 330
SN   Education that seeks to compensate for environmental and experiential deficits in relation to such areas as schooling, housing, employment, poverty, racism, and other social and cultural factors
UF   Compensatory Development
       Compensatory Education Programs (1966 1980)

Compensatory Opportunity
BT   Education
RT   After School Education
      Cultural Enrichment
      Developmental Studies Programs
      Early Intervention
      Educationally Disadvantaged
      Extended School Day
      High Risk Students
      Rehabilitation Programs
      Remedial Instruction
      Remedial Programs
      Study Centers
      Supplementary Education
      Transitional Programs

Compensatory Education Programs (1966 1980)
USE   Compensatory Education

Compensatory Opportunity
USE   Compensatory Education

Competence   *OCT. 1979*
       Postings: 4,087   GC: 120
SN   The individual's demonstrated capacity to perform, i.e., the possession of knowl-edge, skills, and personal characteristics needed to satisfy the special demands or requirements of a particular situation (Note: Prior to Oct79, the instruction "Competencies, USE Skills" was carried in the Thesaurus)
UF   Competency
NT   Interpersonal Competence
      Minimum Competencies
      Teacher Competencies
BT   Ability
RT   Accountability
      Achievement
      Competency Based Education
      Competency Based Teacher Education
      Job Performance
      Minimum Competency Testing
      Performance
      Performance Based Assessment
      Personnel Evaluation
      Skills
      Student Evaluation
      Teacher Competency Testing
      Vocational Evaluation

Competency
USE   Competence

Competency Based Education   *MAR. 1980*
       Postings: 6,865   GC: 330
SN   Educational system that emphasizes the specification, learning, and demonstra-tion of those competencies (knowledge, skills, behaviors) that are of central im-portance to a given task, activity, or career
UF   Consequence Based Education
      Criterion Referenced Education
      Output Oriented Education
      Performance Based Education (1974 1980)
      Proficiency Based Education
NT   Competency Based Teacher Education
BT   Education
RT   Academic Standards
      Accountability
      Back to Basics
      Behavioral Objectives
      Competence
      Individualized Instruction
      Minimum Competencies
      Minimum Competency Testing
      Outcome Based Education
      Performance
      Performance Based Assessment
      Student Certification

Competency Based Teacher Education
                                            MAR. 1980
       Postings: 2,887   GC: 400
SN   Educational system that stresses the ex-

plicit demonstration of specified per-formance as evidence of what a teacher should know and be able to do
UF   Consequence Based Teacher Education
      Criterion Referenced Teacher Educa-tion
      Output Oriented Teacher Education
      Performance Based Teacher Education (1972 1980)
      Proficiency Based Teacher Education
BT   Competency Based Education
      Teacher Education
RT   Academic Standards
      Accountability
      Behavioral Objectives
      Competence
      Extended Teacher Education Programs
      Individualized Instruction
      Performance
      Performance Based Assessment
      Teacher Competencies
      Teacher Competency Testing

Competition   *MAR. 1978*
       Postings: 2,806   GC: 520
SN   Rivalry between individuals or groups seeking the same object or goal
NT   Competitive Selection
BT   Behavior
RT   Achievement Need
      Aggression
      Class Rank
      Cooperation
      Free Enterprise System
      Goal Orientation
      Group Activities
      Intergroup Relations
      Interpersonal Relationship
      Performance
      Social Behavior
      Social Exchange Theory
      Supply and Demand
      Type A Behavior

Competitive Bidding
USE   Bids

Competitive Selection   *JUL. 1966*
       Postings: 543   GC: 330
BT   Competition
      Selection
RT   Admission (School)
      Admission Criteria
      Educational Opportunities
      Educational Supply
      Employment Opportunities
      Open Enrollment
      Personnel Selection
      Screening Tests
      Selective Admission

Complexity Level (1968 1979)
USE   Difficulty Level

Compliance (Legal)   *OCT. 1979*
       Postings: 3,571   GC: 610
SN   Conforming to laws or legal directives
BT   Compliance (Psychology)
RT   Audits (Verification)
      Court Judges
      Court Litigation
      Federal Regulation
      Law Enforcement
      Laws
      Legal Problems
      Legal Responsibility
      Legislation
      State Regulation

Compliance (Psychology)   *AUG. 1986*
       Postings: 272   GC: 120
SN   Yielding to desires, requests, dictates, instructions, regulations, standards, etc. (Note: Use a more specific term if possi-ble)
UF   Noncompliance (Psychology)
NT   Compliance (Legal)
      Obedience

BT   Cooperation
RT   Conformity
      Personality Traits
      Resistance (Psychology)
      Self Control
      Social Behavior
      Social Control
      Social Psychology
      Socialization

Component Building Systems (1968 1976)
USE   Building Systems

Component Systems
USE   Building Systems

Componential Analysis   *MAY 1969*
       Postings: 256   GC: 450
SN   Methodological procedure in linguistics and cognitive anthropology used to ex-plain, distinguish, or study the meaning of sounds, words, and sentences (in-cluding the concepts behind termino-logical choices of particular cultures) by specifying common components, fea-tures, or relationships (Note: Prior to Jun81, the use of this term was not restricted by a Scope Note)
BT   Evaluation Methods
RT   Anthropology
      Distinctive Features (Language)
      Lexicology
      Linguistic Theory
      Phonology
      Scientific Methodology
      Semantics
      Sound Spectrographs
      Structural Analysis (Linguistics)

Composition (Literary) (1966 1980)
USE   Writing (Composition)

Composition (Music)
USE   Musical Composition

Composition Measurement
USE   Chemical Analysis

Composition Processes (Literary)
USE   Writing Processes

Composition Skills (Literary) (1966 1980)
USE   Writing Skills

Comprehension   *JUL. 1966*
       Postings: 2,839   GC: 110
UF   Comprehension Development (1966 1980)
NT   Listening Comprehension
      Reading Comprehension
BT   Intelligence
RT   Abstract Reasoning
      Advance Organizers
      Cognitive Processes
      Coherence
      Cohesion (Written Composition)
      Concept Formation
      Cultural Literacy
      Difficulty Level
      Encoding (Psychology)
      Familiarity
      Inferences
      Intuition
      Knowledge Level
      Language Arts
      Language Processing
      Linguistic Competence
      Linguistic Input
      Metacognition
      Misconceptions
      Outlining (Discourse)
      Perception
      Reciprocal Teaching
      Schemata (Cognition)
      Scientific Literacy

= Two or more Descriptors are used to represent this term.
The term's main entry shows the appropriate coordination.

Technological Literacy
Thinking Skills

Comprehension Development (1966 1980)
USE   Comprehension

Comprehensive Districts (1967 1980)
USE   School Districts

Comprehensive High Schools (1967 1980)
USE   High Schools

Comprehensive Programs   *JUL. 1966*
        Postings: 483   GC: 320
SN   A full set of curricula including college
        preparatory, commercial, and vocational
        courses, usually implemented at the sec-
        ondary level (Note: Prior to Mar80, the
        use of this term was not restricted by a
        Scope Note)
BT   Programs
RT   Secondary Education

Comprehensive School Health Education
                                            NOV. 1995
        Postings: 324   GC: 400
SN   Sequential programs of health instruc-
        tion, health services, and healthful school
        environments that enable students in
        kindergarten through grade 12 to de-
        velop the awareness, knowledge, and
        skills needed for healthy behaviors—
        health areas covered include mental and
        emotional health, community and envi-
        ronmental health, consumer health, family
        life, growth and development, nutrition,
        personal health and fitness, safety and
        accident prevention, disease prevention
        and control, and substance use and abuse
UF   Comprehensive School Health Pro-
        grams
BT   Health Education
RT   Child Health
        Health Behavior
        Health Programs
        Health Promotion
        Integrated Services
        School Health Services

Comprehensive School Health Programs
USE   Comprehensive School Health Educa-
        tion

Comprehensive Services (School Linked)
USE   Integrated Services

Compressed Work Week
USE   Flexible Working Hours

Compulsory Attendance
USE   Compulsory Education

Compulsory Education   *MAR. 1980*
        Postings: 384   GC: 330
SN   Education that is legally required to be
        available to, and attended by, the school-
        age population
UF   Compulsory Attendance
        Mandatory Education
NT   Home Schooling
BT   Education
RT   Access to Education
        Educational Opportunities
        Educational Supply
        Educationally Disadvantaged
        Elementary Secondary Education
        Free Education
        Government School Relationship
        Public Education
        School Attendance Legislation
        Special Education

Compulsory Retirement
USE   Mandatory Retirement

Computation   *MAR. 1980*
        Postings: 2,046   GC: 480
SN   The act or method of calculating or esti-
        mating through the use of number op-
        erations and/or other mathematical proc-
        esses
UF   Calculation (1966 1980)
        Counting
NT   Estimation (Mathematics)
        Mental Computation
BT   Mathematical Applications
RT   Algorithms
        Arithmetic
        Calculators
        Mathematical Formulas
        Mathematics
        Mathematics Tests
        Measurement
        Numbers
        Numeracy
        Ratios (Mathematics)

Computational Linguistics   *JUL. 1966*
        Postings: 649   GC: 450
SN   Branch of linguistics concerned with the
        use of computers for the analysis and
        synthesis of language data—for exam-
        ple, in machine translation, word fre-
        quency counts, and speech recognition
        and synthesis (Note: Do not confuse
        with "Natural Language Processing")
NT   Machine Translation
BT   Linguistics
RT   Automatic Indexing
        Computer Science
        Language Processing
        Linguistic Theory
        Mathematical Linguistics
        Mathematical Logic
        Programming Languages
        Semantics
        Statistics
        Structural Analysis (Linguistics)
        Word Frequency

Computer Aided Design and Manufacturing
USE   Computer Assisted Design
AND   Computer Assisted Manufacturing

Computer Aided Instruction
USE   Computer Assisted Instruction

Computer Aided Instructional Management
USE   Computer Managed Instruction

Computer Anxiety   *JUL. 1993*
        Postings: 322   GC: 330
SN   Fear or mistrust of computers and com-
        puter technology—includes apprehen-
        sion about learning computer skills
UF   Computer Aversion
        Computerphobia
BT   Anxiety
RT   Automation
        Computer Attitudes
        Computer Literacy
        Computers
        Mathematics Anxiety
        School Phobia

Computer Applications
USE   Computer Oriented Programs

Computer Assisted Communication
USE   Computer Mediated Communication

Computer Assisted Design   *APR. 1990*
        Postings: 309   GC: 420
SN   Use of interactive computer systems to
        calculate, manipulate, display, evaluate,
        and modify design alternatives
UF   CAD CAM #
        Computer Aided Design and Manufac-
        turing #
        Computer Assisted Drafting #
BT   Design
RT   Computer Assisted Manufacturing
        Computer Graphics
        Computer Science
        Computer Simulation
        Computers
        Drafting
        Engineering Graphics
        Graphic Arts
        Interactive Video
        Technological Advancement

Computer Assisted Drafting
USE   Computer Assisted Design
AND   Drafting

Computer Assisted Indexing
USE   Automatic Indexing

Computer Assisted Instruction   *JUL. 1966*
        Postings: 20,167   GC: 310
SN   Interactive instructional technique in
        which a computer is used to present
        instructional material, monitor learning,
        and select additional instructional mate-
        rial in accordance with individual learner
        needs
UF   CAI
        Computer Aided Instruction
        Computer Assisted Learning
        Computer Based Instruction
        Computer Based Laboratories (1967
        1980) #
NT   Intelligent Tutoring Systems
BT   Computer Uses in Education
        Programmed Instruction
RT   Authoring Aids (Programming)
        Autoinstructional Aids
        Computer Centers
        Computer Games
        Computer Managed Instruction
        Computer Mediated Communication
        Computer Simulation
        Computers
        Courseware
        Educational Media
        Feedback
        Hypermedia
        Individualized Instruction
        Integrated Learning Systems
        Interactive Video
        Intermode Differences
        Learner Controlled Instruction
        Man Machine Systems
        Microworlds
        Programmed Instructional Materials
        Programmed Tutoring
        Teaching Machines

Computer Assisted Learning
USE   Computer Assisted Instruction

Computer Assisted Manufacturing
                                            APR. 1990
        Postings: 138   GC: 650
SN   Use of programmable automation (such
        as robots and numerical control sys-
        tems) to control the operations of manu-
        facturing machines and machine tools
UF   CAD CAM #
        Computer Aided Design and Manufac-
        turing #
BT   Manufacturing
RT   Assembly (Manufacturing)
        Computer Assisted Design
        Computer Science
        Computers
        Electronic Control
        Electronic Equipment
        Machine Tools
        Manufacturing Industry
        Numerical Control
        Robotics
        Technological Advancement

Computer Assisted Testing   *MAR. 1980*
        Postings: 1,655   GC: 820
SN   Use of computers in test administration
        or construction
UF   Computerized Adaptive Testing #
        Computerized Tailored Testing #
BT   Computer Uses in Education
        Testing
RT   Adaptive Testing
        Computer Science
        Computers
        Item Banks
        Test Construction
        Test Items
        Tests

Computer Attitudes   *JUL. 1993*
        Postings: 470   GC: 330
SN   Attitudes toward or about computers
        and computer use
BT   Attitudes
RT   Automation
        Computer Anxiety
        Computer Literacy
        Computers
        User Friendly Interface

Computer Auxiliary Equipment
USE   Computer Peripherals

Computer Aversion
USE   Computer Anxiety

Computer Based Communication
USE   Computer Mediated Communication

Computer Based Instruction
USE   Computer Assisted Instruction

Computer Based Instructional Management
USE   Computer Managed Instruction

**Computer Based Integrated Learning '
Systems**
USE   Integrated Learning Systems

Computer Based Laboratories (1967 1980)
USE   Computer Assisted Instruction
AND   Laboratories

Computer Based Message Systems
USE   Electronic Mail

Computer Based Microworlds
USE   Microworlds

Computer Based Reference Services
USE   Online Systems
AND   Reference Services

Computer Centers   *AUG. 1989*
        Postings: 281   GC: 920
SN   Locations housing computers, peripher-
        als, and software, ranging from micro-
        computer laboratories in single school-
        rooms to large mainframe installations
        offering a variety of data processing as-
        sistance and consultancy
UF   Data Processing Centers #
BT   Resource Centers
RT   Computer Assisted Instruction
        Computer Networks
        Computer Oriented Programs
        Computer System Design
        Computer Uses in Education
        Computers
        Data Processing
        Education Service Centers
        Information Centers
        Laboratories
        Learning Laboratories

 # = Two or more Descriptors are used to represent this term.
The term's main entry shows the appropriate coordination.

Computer Communication
USE　Computer Mediated Communication

Computer Conferencing
USE　Teleconferencing

Computer Display Design
USE　Screen Design (Computers)

Computer Displays
USE　Display Systems

Computer Games　　　　　　　　　DEC. 1987
　　　Postings: 389　　　　　　　　　GC: 720
SN　Games played on computers, as either
　　　educational tools or recreational pas-
　　　times (Note: Do not confuse with "Video
　　　Games" with built-in semiconductor chips
　　　or microprocessors that can be played
　　　independently of a computer)
BT　Games
RT　Computer Assisted Instruction
　　　Computer Simulation
　　　Computers
　　　Microcomputers
　　　Video Games

Computer Graphics　　　　　　　FEB. 1970
　　　Postings: 2,117　　　　　　　GC: 710
SN　Techniques for graphic or pictorial rep-
　　　resentation of information in a
　　　computer—representations may be in
　　　hardcopy or on display screens
UF　Drawing (Computerized)
BT　Graphic Arts
RT　Computer Assisted Design
　　　Computer Simulation
　　　Computers
　　　Desktop Publishing
　　　Display Systems
　　　Engineering Graphics
　　　Graphing Calculators
　　　Input Output Devices
　　　Photocomposition
　　　Screen Design (Computers)

Computer Interfaces　　　　　　NOV. 1994
　　　Postings: 501　　　　　　　　GC: 710
SN　Connecting links between computers,
　　　between computers and peripheral equip-
　　　ment, or between computers and users—
　　　hardware interfaces include plugs, sock-
　　　ets, and wires that carry electrical sig-
　　　nals, software interfaces are the lan-
　　　guages, codes, and messages used by
　　　programs to communicate with each
　　　other, and user interfaces are keyboards,
　　　mice, joy sticks, light pens, command
　　　languages, menus, display screens, and
　　　other devices used for interactive com-
　　　munication between users and comput-
　　　ers
UF　Interface Devices (Computers)
NT　User Friendly Interface
RT　Computer Networks
　　　Computer Peripherals
　　　Computer Software
　　　Computer System Design
　　　Computers
　　　Data Processing
　　　Gateway Systems
　　　Man Machine Systems
　　　Microcomputers
　　　Navigation (Information Systems)

Computer Keyboards
USE　Keyboarding (Data Entry)

Computer Languages
USE　Programming Languages

Computer Literacy　　　　　　　APR. 1982
　　　Postings: 3,729　　　　　　　GC: 330
SN　Awareness of or knowledge about com-
　　　puters (their capabilities, applications,

and limitations)—may include the ability
to interact with computers to solve prob-
lems
BT　Technological Literacy
RT　Computer Anxiety
　　　Computer Attitudes
　　　Computer Oriented Programs
　　　Computer Science Education
　　　Computer Uses in Education
　　　Computers
　　　Information Literacy
　　　Mathematical Logic
　　　Online Searching
　　　Programming
　　　Scientific Literacy
　　　Search Strategies

Computer Managed Instruction　JAN. 1979
　　　Postings: 1,293　　　　　　　GC: 310
SN　Use of a computer to maintain and ana-
　　　lyze data on learner performance and
　　　instructional progress as an aid to teach-
　　　ers in selecting learning activities
UF　CMI
　　　Computer Aided Instructional Manage-
　　　　ment
　　　Computer Based Instructional Manage-
　　　　ment
BT　Computer Uses in Education
　　　Information Systems
RT　Computer Assisted Instruction
　　　Computers
　　　Educational Media
　　　Integrated Learning Systems
　　　Intelligent Tutoring Systems
　　　Management Information Systems

Computer Mediated Communication
　　　　　　　　　　　　　　　　　AUG. 1994
　　　Postings: 1,829　　　　　　　GC: 710
SN　Interactive use of computers for elec-
　　　tronic mail, computer conferences, elec-
　　　tronic bulletin boards, and online jour-
　　　nals and databases (Note: See also the
　　　Identifier "Telematics")
UF　Computer Assisted Communication
　　　Computer Based Communication
　　　Computer Communication
NT　Electronic Mail
　　　Electronic Publishing
BT　Communication (Thought Transfer)
　　　Telecommunications
RT　Computer Assisted Instruction
　　　Computer Networks
　　　Computer Uses in Education
　　　Computers
　　　Decision Support Systems
　　　Distance Education
　　　Electronic Journals
　　　Electronic Libraries
　　　Electronic Text
　　　Information Networks
　　　Input Output Devices
　　　Internet
　　　Man Machine Systems
　　　Microcomputers
　　　Modems
　　　Online Systems
　　　Teleconferencing
　　　Videotex

Computer Microworlds
USE　Microworlds

Computer Networks　　　　　　AUG. 1986
　　　Postings: 3,545　　　　　　　GC: 710
SN　Interconnected computers and peripher-
　　　als, linked for resource sharing
NT　Integrated Learning Systems
　　　Internet
　　　Local Area Networks
BT　Networks
RT　Computer Centers
　　　Computer Interfaces
　　　Computer Mediated Communication
　　　Computer Oriented Programs
　　　Computer Peripherals
　　　Computer Science
　　　Computer System Design

Computer Uses in Education
Computers
Data Processing
Electronic Libraries
Information Networks
Man Machine Systems

Computer Oriented Programs　　JUL. 1966
　　　Postings: 7,295　　　　　　　GC: 320
SN　The application of computer technology
　　　to such tasks as instruction, documenta-
　　　tion, research, administration, etc. (Note:
　　　Use a more precise term if possible)
UF　Computer Applications
BT　Programs
RT　Authoring Aids (Programming)
　　　Branching
　　　Career Information Systems
　　　Computer Centers
　　　Computer Literacy
　　　Computer Networks
　　　Computer Simulation
　　　Computer System Design
　　　Computer Uses in Education
　　　Computers
　　　Concept Mapping
　　　Desktop Publishing
　　　Dial Access Information Systems
　　　Downloading
　　　Educational Technology
　　　Electronic Mail
　　　Flow Charts
　　　Graphing Calculators
　　　Information Technology
　　　Integrated Library Systems
　　　Keyboarding (Data Entry)
　　　Machine Readable Cataloging
　　　Man Machine Systems
　　　Management Information Systems
　　　Programmed Instruction
　　　Programming
　　　Selective Dissemination of Information
　　　Spreadsheets
　　　Technology Education
　　　Vendors
　　　Word Processing
　　　Workstations

Computer Output Microfilm　　FEB. 1970
　　　Postings: 149　　　　　　　　GC: 720
SN　Microfilm produced as direct computer
　　　output, without printout as intermediary
UF　COM
BT　Microfilm
RT　Computers
　　　Input Output Devices

Computer Peripherals　　　　　DEC. 1987
　　　Postings: 170　　　　　　　　GC: 910
SN　Any computer equipment other than the
　　　central processing unit, i.e., devices for
　　　input, output, storage, add-on memory,
　　　and other auxiliary functions
UF　Computer Auxiliary Equipment
NT　Computer Storage Devices
　　　Input Output Devices
　　　Modems
BT　Electronic Equipment
RT　Computer Interfaces
　　　Computer Networks
　　　Computer Selection
　　　Computer System Design
　　　Computers
　　　Data Processing
　　　Information Technology
　　　Microcomputers

Computer Printers　　　　　　JAN. 1988
　　　Postings: 96　　　　　　　　GC: 910
SN　Computer output devices that produce
　　　readable, hard-copy data on paper, film,
　　　etc.
BT　Input Output Devices
RT　Computer Terminals
　　　Printing

Computer Program Documentation
USE　Computer Software

Computer Programming
USE　Programming

Computer Programs (1966 1984)
USE　Computer Software

Computer Science　　　　　　JUL. 1966
　　　Postings: 2,291　　　　　　　GC: 710
SN　Study of the theory, design, analysis,
　　　and applications of computers and com-
　　　puter-based systems
NT　Programming
BT　Information Science
RT　Artificial Intelligence
　　　Automation
　　　Computational Linguistics
　　　Computer Assisted Design
　　　Computer Assisted Manufacturing
　　　Computer Assisted Testing
　　　Computer Networks
　　　Computer Science Education
　　　Computer System Design
　　　Computers
　　　Cybernetics
　　　Data Processing
　　　Electromechanical Technology
　　　Information Science Education
　　　Information Systems
　　　Information Theory
　　　Knowledge Representation
　　　Systems Analysis

Computer Science Education　　JUL. 1966
　　　Postings: 2,184　　　　　　　GC: 400
BT　Information Science Education
RT　Computer Literacy
　　　Computer Science
　　　Computer Uses in Education
　　　Computers
　　　Data Processing Occupations
　　　Information Science
　　　Programming
　　　Technical Education
　　　Technical Occupations

Computer Security　　　　　　NOV. 1994
　　　Postings: 254　　　　　　　　GC: 710
SN　Measures taken to protect computer sys-
　　　tems (hardware, software, and data files)
　　　from accidental or malicious damage or
　　　destruction and from unauthorized ac-
　　　cess (Note: See also the Identifiers "Com-
　　　puter Viruses" and "Data Security")
RT　Computers
　　　Crime
　　　Crime Prevention
　　　Privacy
　　　Safety
　　　School Security
　　　Security Personnel
　　　Stealing
　　　Vandalism

Computer Selection　　　　　　AUG. 1994
　　　Postings: 228　　　　　　　　GC: 710
SN　The process of evaluating and choosing
　　　computer hardware and/or systems
BT　Selection
RT　Computer Peripherals
　　　Computer Software Selection
　　　Computer System Design
　　　Computers
　　　Equipment Evaluation
　　　Microcomputers
　　　Purchasing
　　　Systems Development

Computer Simulation　　　　　OCT. 1983
　　　Postings: 2,345　　　　　　　GC: 310
SN　Computer-based representation of real
　　　situations or systems
NT　Virtual Reality
BT　Simulation
RT　Computer Assisted Design
　　　Computer Assisted Instruction
　　　Computer Games
　　　Computer Graphics
　　　Computer Oriented Programs

Computers
Decision Support Systems
Hypermedia
Markov Processes
Microworlds
Models
Monte Carlo Methods
Role Playing
Teaching Methods

Computer Software   JUN. 1984
Postings: 7,997   GC: 720
SN   Logical sequences of instructions used
to direct the actions of a computer sys-
tem, and accompanying documentation
(Note: Corresponds to Pubtype code 101
and should not be used except as the
subject of a document—this restriction
was not carried prior to Jun84 under the
former term "Computer Programs"—if
appropriate, use a more specific term)
UF   Computer Program Documentation
Computer Programs (1966 1984)
Software (Computers)
Text Editors #
NT   Courseware
Database Management Systems
Menu Driven Software
BT   Specifications
RT   Authoring Aids (Programming)
Computer Interfaces
Computer Software Development
Computer Software Evaluation
Computer Software Reviews
Computer Software Selection
Computer System Design
Computer Uses in Education
Computers
Copyrights
Data Processing
Decision Support Systems
Information Technology
Numerical Control
Programming
Programming Languages
Spreadsheets
User Friendly Interface
Virtual Reality

Computer Software Design
USE   Computer Software Development

Computer Software Development   APR. 1990
Postings: 1,234   GC: 710
SN   The process of designing, programming,
debugging, documenting, and upgrad-
ing computer software
UF   Computer Software Design
Computer Software Engineering
Computer Software Maintenance
Courseware Development #
Software Development (Computers)
NT   Programming
BT   Material Development
RT   Authoring Aids (Programming)
Computer Software
Computer Software Evaluation
Computer System Design
Courseware
Data Processing
Debugging (Computers)
Programming Languages
Systems Development

Computer Software Engineering
USE   Computer Software Development

Computer Software Evaluation   APR. 1990
Postings: 666   GC: 710
SN   Determining the efficacy, value, etc., of
computer software with respect to stated
objectives, standards, or criteria (Note:
Use as a major Descriptor only as the
subject of a document—do not confuse
with "Computer Software Reviews")
UF   Courseware Evaluation #
Software Evaluation (Computers)
BT   Evaluation
RT   Computer Software

Computer Software Development
Computer Software Reviews
Computer Software Selection
Courseware

Computer Software Maintenance
USE   Computer Software Development

Computer Software Reviews   AUG. 1986
Postings: 722   GC: 730
SN   Published critical appraisals of specific
computer software (Note: Do not con-
fuse with the software appraisal proc-
ess, for which see "Computer Software
Evaluation")
UF   Courseware Reviews #
Software Reviews (Computers)
BT   Publications
RT   Computer Software
Computer Software Evaluation
Computer Software Selection
Courseware

Computer Software Selection   APR. 1990
Postings: 332   GC: 710
SN   The process of choosing software for
acquisition
UF   Courseware Selection #
Software Selection (Computers)
BT   Media Selection
RT   Computer Selection
Computer Software
Computer Software Evaluation
Computer Software Reviews
Computer System Design
Courseware

Computer Storage Devices   JUL. 1966
Postings: 458   GC: 910
UF   Computer Tapes #
Memory Devices (Computers)
NT   Magnetic Disks
BT   Computer Peripherals
RT   Information Storage
Input Output Devices
Magnetic Tapes
Optical Disks

Computer System Design   JAN. 1988
Postings: 1,392   GC: 710
SN   The process of selecting, setting up, and
modifying a system of computer hard-
ware and software—also, the layout and
specifications of a computer system
UF   Computer System Development
NT   Screen Design (Computers)
BT   Design
RT   Computer Centers
Computer Interfaces
Computer Networks
Computer Oriented Programs
Computer Peripherals
Computer Science
Computer Selection
Computer Software
Computer Software Development
Computer Software Selection
Computer Uses in Education
Computers
Data Processing
Debugging (Computers)
Design Requirements
Information Systems
Man Machine Systems
Systems Development

Computer System Development
USE   Computer System Design

Computer Tapes
USE   Computer Storage Devices
AND   Magnetic Tapes

Computer Technology
USE   Computers

Computer Terminals   JAN. 1988
Postings: 24   GC: 910
SN   Input output devices, generally including
a keyboard and a display unit (video or
print), used to enter data into and receive
data from a computer (Note: Prior to
Jan88, the instruction "Computer Termi-
nals, USE Input Output Devices" was
carried in the Thesaurus)
NT   Video Display Terminals
BT   Input Output Devices
RT   Computer Printers
Workstations

Computer Uses in Education   AUG. 1986
Postings: 9,506   GC: 330
SN   The use of computers for instruction,
testing, student/pupil personnel services,
school administrative support services,
and other educational purposes (Note:
Use a more specific term if possible—
prior to Aug86, this concept was fre-
quently indexed by "Computer Oriented
Programs")
UF   Educational Computing
NT   Computer Assisted Instruction
Computer Assisted Testing
Computer Managed Instruction
Integrated Learning Systems
Microworlds
RT   Computer Centers
Computer Literacy
Computer Mediated Communication
Computer Networks
Computer Oriented Programs
Computer Science Education
Computer Software
Computer System Design
Computers
Educational Technology

Computer Workstations
USE   Workstations

Computerized Adaptive Testing
USE   Adaptive Testing
AND   Computer Assisted Testing

Computerized Tailored Testing
USE   Adaptive Testing
AND   Computer Assisted Testing

Computerphobia
USE   Computer Anxiety

Computers   JUL. 1966
Postings: 7,203   GC: 910
SN   Devices that solve problems by accept-
ing information, performing prescribed
operations on it, and supplying the re-
sults obtained—usually consist of units
for input, output, storage, control, and
arithmetic or logical operations (Note:
Use a more specific term if possible)
UF   Computer Technology
NT   Analog Computers
Digital Computers
Microcomputers
Minicomputers
BT   Electronic Equipment
RT   Artificial Intelligence
Automation
Calculators
Computer Anxiety
Computer Assisted Design
Computer Assisted Instruction
Computer Assisted Manufacturing
Computer Assisted Testing
Computer Attitudes
Computer Centers
Computer Games
Computer Graphics
Computer Interfaces
Computer Literacy
Computer Managed Instruction
Computer Mediated Communication
Computer Networks
Computer Oriented Programs

Computer Output Microfilm
Computer Peripherals
Computer Science
Computer Science Education
Computer Security
Computer Selection
Computer Simulation
Computer Software
Computer System Design
Computer Uses in Education
Cybernetics
Data Processing
Databases
Debugging (Computers)
Display Systems
Downloading
Electromechanical Aids
Electronic Publishing
Electronic Text
Expert Systems
Gateway Systems
Hypermedia
Information Industry
Information Systems
Information Technology
Input Output
Instrumentation
Knowledge Representation
Man Machine Systems
Multimedia Materials
Natural Language Processing
Online Systems
Online Vendors
Optical Data Disks
Optical Disks
Programming
Programming Languages
Screen Design (Computers)
Technological Advancement
Telecommunications
Time Sharing
User Friendly Interface
Videotex
Virtual Reality
Workstations

Concept Development
USE   Concept Formation

Concept Formation   JUL. 1966
Postings: 8,895   GC: 110
UF   Concept Development
Conceptual Distinctions
BT   Learning Processes
RT   Abstract Reasoning
Cognitive Development
Cognitive Structures
Compensation (Concept)
Comprehension
Concept Mapping
Concept Teaching
Conservation (Concept)
Constructivism (Learning)
Creative Thinking
Creativity
Developmental Stages
Discrimination Learning
Encoding (Psychology)
Epistemology
Fundamental Concepts
Generalization
Knowledge Representation
Misconceptions
Object Permanence
Piagetian Theory
Thinking Skills

Concept Mapping   NOV. 1996
Postings: 329   GC: 110
SN   The identification, organization, and
graphic depiction of relationships among
concepts in a knowledge domain—the
technique employs a node-link formalism in which domain key concepts are
circled, bracketed, etc., arranged
hierarchically (general to specific), then
interconnected by lines labeled with short
explanations
BT   Methods
RT   Cognitive Mapping

= Two or more Descriptors are used to represent this term.
The term's main entry shows the appropriate coordination.

Computer Oriented Programs
Concept Formation
Concept Teaching
Diagrams
Fundamental Concepts
Geographic Concepts
Knowledge Representation
Learning Strategies
Mathematical Concepts
Misconceptions
Problem Solving
Scientific Concepts
Teaching Methods

Concept Teaching *JUL. 1966*
Postings: 2,238 GC: 400
BT Instruction
RT Concept Formation
    Concept Mapping
    Fundamental Concepts
    Generalization
    Geographic Concepts

Conceptual Distinctions
USE Concept Formation

Conceptual Schemes (1967 1980)
                          MAR. 1980
Postings: 1,652 GC: 110
SN Invalid Descriptor—used indiscriminately
    for the organization of individuals' un-
    derstanding as well as the logical struc-
    ture of theories—see such Descriptors
    as "Models," "Schemata (Cognition),"
    "Concept Formation," "Cognitive Style,"
    etc.

Conceptual Tempo *JUL. 1972*
Postings: 544 GC: 110
SN An index of time spent in problem solv-
    ing sequences used to characterize the
    reflective/impulsive dimension of cogni-
    tive style
UF Cognitive Tempo
    Impulsivity
    Reflectivity
    Tempo (Cognition)
BT Cognitive Style
RT Attention Span
    Cognitive Processes
    Extraversion Introversion
    Reaction Time
    Time Factors (Learning)

Concerts *JUL. 1966*
Postings: 135 GC: 420
BT Music Activities
RT Bands (Music)
    Instrumentation and Orchestration
    Jazz
    Music
    Musicians
    Orchestras
    Rock Music
    Singing

Concordances (1967 1980)
USE Indexes

Concrete Industry
USE Cement Industry

Concurrent Validity *AUG. 1986*
Postings: 233 GC: 820
SN The extent to which a measure or some
    other factor approximates the results of
    another criterion available at the same
    time, e.g., the degree of correlation be-
    tween a new short-form test and a longer,
    more established measure of the same
    construct
UF Criterion Validity (Concurrent)
BT Validity
RT Comparative Testing
    Predictive Validity
    Scores

Test Validity
Testing

Conditioned Response (1967 1980)
USE Responses

Conditioned Stimulus (1966 1980)
USE Stimuli

Conditioning *DEC. 1970*
Postings: 616 GC: 110
SN Experimental procedures that attempt
    systematically to modify or control natu-
    ral behavior
UF Psychological Conditioning
NT Behavior Modification
    Classical Conditioning
    Operant Conditioning
RT Behavior Change
    Behaviorism
    Biofeedback
    Counseling Techniques
    Ethology
    Extinction (Psychology)
    Familiarity
    Learning Processes
    Learning Theories
    Meditation
    Psychology
    Reinforcement
    Responses
    Stimulation
    Stimuli

Conduct (1966 1980)
USE Behavior

Conference Papers *MAR. 1980*
Postings: 198 GC: 720
SN Individual papers presented at confer-
    ences (Note: The previous term "Confer-
    ence Reports" was not scoped and was
    frequently used for this concept—do
    not confuse with "Conference Proceed-
    ings"—corresponds to Pubtype code
    150—do not use except as the subject of
    a document)
BT Reports
RT Conferences
    Institutes (Training Programs)
    Meetings
    Speeches
    Workshops

Conference Proceedings *MAR. 1980*
Postings: 269 GC: 720
SN Collections of papers presented at con-
    ferences (Note: The previous term "Con-
    ference Reports" was not scoped and
    was frequently used for this concept—
    do not confuse with "Conference
    Papers"—corresponds to Pubtype code
    021—do not use except as the subject of
    a document)
BT Serials
RT Anthologies
    Conferences
    Institutes (Training Programs)
    Meetings
    Workshops

Conference Reports (1967 1980)
                          MAR. 1980
Postings: 4,824 GC: 730
SN Invalid Descriptor—used for both "Con-
    ference Proceedings" and "Conference
    Papers"—see the more precise terms

Conference Skills (Communication)
USE Communication Skills

Conferences *JUL. 1966*
Postings: 4,526 GC: 710
UF Symposia (1967 1980)
NT Parent Conferences

Parent Teacher Conferences
RT Conference Papers
    Conference Proceedings
    Continuing Education
    Institutes (Training Programs)
    Meetings
    Organizations (Groups)
    Teleconferencing
    Workshops

Confidence Testing *FEB. 1972*
Postings: 138 GC: 820
SN Testing technique that determines
    examinees' knowledge in objective or
    multiple choice tests by requiring them
    to indicate the degree of confidence they
    have in their answer (Note: Do not use
    for "confidence limits" or other statisti-
    cal measures—prior to Mar80, the use
    of this term was not restricted by a
    Scope Note)
BT Testing
RT Guessing (Tests)
    Knowledge Level
    Multiple Choice Tests
    Objective Tests
    Response Style (Tests)
    Scoring Formulas
    Test Interpretation
    Test Reliability
    Test Validity
    Testing Problems

Confidential Information
USE Confidentiality

Confidential Records *JUL. 1966*
Postings: 503 GC: 320
BT Records (Forms)
RT Case Records
    Confidentiality
    Disclosure
    Freedom of Information
    Privacy
    Student Records

Confidentiality *FEB. 1971*
Postings: 1,067 GC: 520
SN Protection of privileged information
UF Confidential Information
    Private Information
    Privileged Communication
BT Privacy
RT Confidential Records
    Counselor Role
    Disclosure
    Ethics
    Information Policy
    Interpersonal Communication

Conflict *JUL. 1966*
Postings: 2,507 GC: 530
NT Conflict of Interest
    Culture Conflict
    Religious Conflict
    Revolution
    Role Conflict
    War
RT Antisocial Behavior
    Conflict Resolution
    Controversial Issues (Course Content)
    Disarmament
    Dissent
    International Relations
    Resistance (Psychology)
    Social Problems

Conflict of Interest *AUG. 1986*
Postings: 290 GC: 520
SN Incompatibility or opposition among
    needs and responsibilities, especially be-
    tween private or personal interests and
    public or professional obligations
BT Conflict
RT Codes of Ethics
    Ethics
    Legal Responsibility
    Multiple Employment

Personnel Policy
Role Conflict

Conflict Resolution *JUL. 1966*
Postings: 4,403 GC: 520
NT Peer Mediation
BT Cognitive Processes
RT Conflict
    Crisis Management
    Decision Making
    International Law
    Interpersonal Communication
    Peace
    Problem Solving
    Revolution
    Social Cognition
    Social Control

Confluent Education
USE Humanistic Education

Conformity *JUL. 1966*
Postings: 555 GC: 520
BT Social Behavior
RT Compliance (Psychology)
    Congruence (Psychology)
    Identification (Psychology)
    Peer Groups
    Peer Influence
    Personality Traits
    Social Adjustment

Confucianism *MAR. 1983*
Postings: 67 GC: 430
SN Religion based on the teachings of Con-
    fucius (China, 5th century B.C.)
BT Religion
RT Non Western Civilization
    Philosophy
    Religious Cultural Groups

Congenital Impairments *MAR. 1980*
Postings: 671 GC: 220
SN Impairments present or originating at
    birth
UF Anomalies (1967 1980)
    Birth Defects
    Congenitally Handicapped (1975 1980)
NT Cerebral Palsy
    Cleft Palate
    Downs Syndrome
    Fetal Alcohol Syndrome
    Spina Bifida
BT Disabilities
RT Adventitious Impairments
    Genetics
    Heredity
    Perinatal Influences
    Prenatal Influences

Congenitally Handicapped (1975 1980)
USE Congenital Impairments

Congress Role
USE Government Role

Congressmen
USE Legislators

Congresswomen
USE Legislators

Congruence (Mathematics) *MAR. 1980*
Postings: 16 GC: 480
SN Property of geometric figures that can be
    made to coincide by a rigid transforma-
    tion
BT Geometric Concepts
RT Geometry
    Modular Arithmetic
    Symmetry
    Transformations (Mathematics)

= Two or more Descriptors are used to represent this term.
The term's main entry shows the appropriate coordination.

Congruence (Psychology)   *MAR. 1980*
    Postings: 467   GC: 230
SN In accord or agreement with others or
    oneself
NT Self Congruence
BT Psychological Patterns
RT Cognitive Dissonance
    Conformity
    Egocentrism
    Empathy
    Identification (Psychology)
    Interpersonal Attraction
    Locus of Control
    Personality Traits
    Self Fulfilling Prophecies

Congruence (1970 1980)   *MAR. 1980*
    Postings: 43   GC: 820
SN Invalid Descriptor—used for both mathe-
    matical and psychological congruence

Conjoint Counseling
USE Cocounseling

Conjunctions   *SEP. 1996*
    Postings: 61   GC: 450
SN Connective words, as "and," "but," "be-
    cause," "even though," that join words,
    phrases, clauses, or sentences (Note:
    See also the Identifier "Connectives
    (Grammar)")
BT Form Classes (Languages)
RT Function Words
    Morphology (Languages)
    Phrase Structure
    Sentence Structure
    Syntax

Connected Discourse   *AUG. 1968*
    Postings: 426   GC: 450
NT Cohesion (Written Composition)
RT Association (Psychology)
    Dialogs (Language)
    Discourse Analysis
    Language Patterns
    Paragraphs
    Prose
    Psycholinguistics
    Semantics
    Syntax
    Word Frequency

Consciousness Raising   *DEC. 1989*
    Postings: 968   GC: 510
SN The process of increasing knowledge
    and concerned awareness of social, po-
    litical, economic, and environmental re-
    alities and issues, and/or of one's own
    nature, beliefs, behavior, and power—
    often with the intent to effect change
BT Cognitive Processes
RT Attitude Change
    Change Strategies
    Critical Thinking
    Ethnicity
    Feminism
    Group Discussion
    Group Dynamics
    Humanistic Education
    Humanization
    Interpersonal Competence
    Language Attitudes
    Perspective Taking
    Political Attitudes
    Popular Education
    Self Concept
    Self Determination
    Sensitivity Training
    Social Attitudes
    Social Cognition
    Social Support Groups
    Socialization
    Values Clarification
    Womens Studies

Consequence Based Education
USE Competency Based Education

Consequence Based Teacher Education
USE Competency Based Teacher Education

Conservation (Concept)   *SEP. 1968*
    Postings: 998   GC: 110
SN The principle that mass, number, and
    volume do not vary despite transforma-
    tions in their form or embodiment (e.g.,
    a pound of clay is a pound of clay whether
    in the form of a ball or a sausage)—in
    developmental psychology, the recogni-
    tion or understanding of this phenomena
BT Fundamental Concepts
RT Cognitive Processes
    Compensation (Concept)
    Concept Formation
    Learning Processes
    Mathematical Concepts
    Scientific Concepts
    Serial Ordering

Conservation (Environment)   *JUL. 1974*
    Postings: 2,280   GC: 410
SN Preservation of the environment, includ-
    ing natural resources, from loss, waste,
    or harm
NT Energy Conservation
    Soil Conservation
RT Air Pollution
    Biodiversity
    Conservation Education
    Depleted Resources
    Ecological Factors
    Ecology
    Endangered Species
    Environment
    Environmental Education
    Forestry
    Fuel Consumption
    Mining
    National Parks
    Natural Resources
    Physical Environment
    Rainforests
    Recycling
    Sustainable Development
    Wastes
    Water Pollution
    Water Quality
    Water Resources
    Wetlands
    Wilderness
    Wildlife Management
    World Problems

Conservation Education   *JUL. 1966*
    Postings: 2,067   GC: 410
BT Environmental Education
RT Biological Sciences
    Conservation (Environment)
    Energy Conservation
    Energy Education
    Environmental Interpretation
    Fire Science Education
    Forestry
    Geography
    Natural Resources
    Outdoor Education
    Physical Sciences
    Rainforests
    Soil Conservation
    Trails
    Wetlands
    Wilderness

Conservatism   *JAN. 1985*
    Postings: 519   GC: 520
SN Philosophy or disposition that generally
    supports the preservation or reinstate-
    ment of traditional values and statuses in
    social or political affairs
RT Government Role
    Liberalism
    New Federalism
    Political Attitudes
    Political Socialization
    Social Values
    Traditionalism

Consistency
USE Reliability

Consolidated Schools   *AUG. 1969*
    Postings: 380   GC: 340
UF Centralized Schools
    School Consolidation
BT Schools
RT Mergers
    Regional Schools
    Rural Schools
    School Closing
    School District Reorganization
    School Districts
    School Zoning

Consonants   *JUL. 1966*
    Postings: 937   GC: 450
BT Phonemes
RT Acoustic Phonetics
    Distinctive Features (Language)
    Phonemic Alphabets
    Phonetics
    Syllables
    Vowels

Consortia   *JAN. 1970*
    Postings: 1,607   GC: 330
SN Associations of institutions (usually
    higher education or libraries) that share
    resources and/or students to strengthen
    programs or services and reduce costs
    (Note: Do not confuse with "Cluster Col-
    leges")
UF Consortiums
BT Organizations (Groups)
RT Cluster Colleges
    Cooperative Planning
    Cooperative Programs
    Coordination
    Dual Enrollment
    Educational Cooperation
    Institutional Cooperation
    Intercollegiate Cooperation
    Library Cooperation
    Library Networks
    Partnerships in Education
    Shared Resources and Services

Consortiums
USE Consortia

Constituent Structure
USE Phrase Structure

Constitutional History   *JUL. 1966*
    Postings: 722   GC: 430
BT History
RT Constitutional Law
    Federalism
    Government (Administrative Body)
    Government Role
    Governmental Structure
    Political Science
    United States Government (Course)
    United States History
    World History

Constitutional Law   *DEC. 1974*
    Postings: 2,125   GC: 610
BT Laws
RT Civil Law
    Civil Liberties
    Civil Rights
    Civil Rights Legislation
    Constitutional History
    Discriminatory Legislation
    Federalism
    Government (Administrative Body)
    Government Role
    Government School Relationship
    Governmental Structure
    Justice
    Law Related Education
    Legal Education (Professions)
    Libel and Slander
    Political Science

    Privacy
    Search and Seizure
    State Church Separation
    Torts
    United States Government (Course)

Construct Validity   *AUG. 1986*
    Postings: 751   GC: 820
SN The extent to which a test measures
    a hypothetical construct or trait (e.g.,
    creativity, analytical ability, persistence,
    mechanical competence, achievement
    motivation) that is the basis for test
    performance
BT Test Validity
RT Content Validity
    Factor Structure
    Testing

Constructed Languages
USE Artificial Languages

Constructed Response   *JUL. 1966*
    Postings: 181   GC: 110
SN Response that is created rather than
    selected from a set of alternative an-
    swers (Note: Prior to Mar80, the use of
    this term was not restricted by a Scope
    Note)
BT Responses
RT Alternative Assessment
    Essay Tests

Construction (Process)   *JUL. 1966*
    Postings: 862   GC: 920
SN Act of putting parts together to form a
    physical structure or facility (Note: Before
    Mar80, the scope note read "act of put-
    ting parts together")
NT Cabinetmaking
    Carpentry
    Masonry
    Prefabrication
    Road Construction
    School Construction
RT Acoustic Insulation
    Building Conversion
    Building Design
    Building Systems
    Building Trades
    Ceilings
    Construction Costs
    Construction Industry
    Construction Management
    Construction Materials
    Construction Needs
    Construction Programs
    Design Build Approach
    Facility Expansion
    Flooring
    Industrial Arts
    Roofing
    Site Development
    Structural Building Systems
    Structural Elements (Construction)
    Systems Building
    Technology Education
    Thermal Insulation
    Welding

Construction Bidding
USE Bids

Construction Costs   *JUL. 1966*
    Postings: 649   GC: 620
BT Costs
RT Building Conversion
    Buildings
    Capital Outlay (for Fixed Assets)
    Construction (Process)
    Construction Management
    Construction Materials
    Construction Needs
    Construction Programs
    Design Build Approach
    Facility Planning
    Life Cycle Costing

= Two or more Descriptors are used to represent this term.
The term's main entry shows the appropriate coordination.

Construction Industry   JUL. 1966
    Postings: 390   GC: 650
NT   Housing Industry
BT   Industry
RT   Architects
       Brick Industry
       Building Trades
       Buildings
       Cement Industry
       Construction (Process)

Construction Management   DEC. 1972
    Postings: 199   GC: 920
BT   Administration
RT   Construction (Process)
       Construction Costs
       Construction Programs
       Critical Path Method
       Design Build Approach
       Facility Planning
       Fast Track Scheduling
       Systems Building

Construction Materials   MAR. 1980
    Postings: 544   GC: 920
UF   Building Materials (1968 1980)
NT   Asphalts
       Prestressed Concrete
RT   Acoustic Insulation
       Adhesives
       Architectural Research
       Asbestos
       Building Design
       Building Innovation
       Buildings
       Carpeting
       Cement Industry
       Construction (Process)
       Construction Costs
       Construction Needs
       Doors
       Encapsulated Facilities
       Facilities
       Flooring
       Masonry
       Prefabrication
       Roofing
       School Buildings
       Structural Elements (Construction)
       Supplies
       Thermal Insulation

Construction Needs   JUL. 1966
    Postings: 193   GC: 920
BT   Needs
RT   Building Conversion
       Construction (Process)
       Construction Costs
       Construction Materials
       Construction Programs
       Facility Guidelines
       Facility Planning
       Facility Requirements
       Structural Elements (Construction)

Construction Occupations
USE   Building Trades

Construction Programs   JUL. 1966
    Postings: 422   GC: 920
UF   Building Programs
BT   Programs
RT   Building Systems
       Construction (Process)
       Construction Costs
       Construction Management
       Construction Needs
       Design Build Approach
       Educational Facilities Planning
       Facility Expansion
       Facility Inventory
       Facility Planning
       Facility Utilization Research
       Fast Track Scheduling
       Structural Building Systems
       Systems Building

Constructionism (Education)
USE   Constructivism (Learning)

Constructivism (Learning)   DEC. 1992
    Postings: 1,801   GC: 110
SN   Viewpoint in learning theory which holds that individuals acquire knowledge by building it from innate capabilities interacting with the environment (Note: See also the Identifier "Social Constructivism")
UF   Constructionism (Education)
BT   Learning Theories
RT   Cognitive Development
       Cognitive Psychology
       Cognitive Structures
       Concept Formation
       Developmental Psychology
       Epistemology
       Learning
       Postmodernism

Consultants   JUL. 1966
    Postings: 2,635   GC: 240
UF   Community Consultants (1966 1980)
NT   Medical Consultants
       Reading Consultants
       Science Consultants
BT   Personnel
RT   Advisory Committees
       Blue Ribbon Commissions
       Change Agents
       Consultation Programs
       Counselors
       Faculty
       Guidance Personnel
       Human Resources
       Professional Services
       Referral
       Resource Staff
       Resource Teachers
       School Psychologists
       Specialists
       Supervisors
       Technical Assistance
       Vendors

Consultation Programs   JUL. 1966
    Postings: 1,593   GC: 240
SN   Formal procedures whereby consulting services are provided by specialists (e.g., health workers, extension agents, counselors) to individuals or groups (e.g., teachers, students, administrators, parents, communities)
UF   Community Consultant Programs (1966 1980)
BT   Programs
RT   Consultants
       Counseling
       Counselor Teacher Cooperation
       Guidance
       Intermediate Administrative Units
       Intervention
       Prereferral Intervention
       Professional Services
       Referral
       Technical Assistance

Consumer Behavior
USE   Consumer Economics

Consumer Economics   JUL. 1966
    Postings: 1,484   GC: 620
SN   Economic principles and forces that affect the consumer and the interpretation of economic theories in terms of consumer interest as distinguished from producer interest
UF   Consumer Behavior
       Consumer Expenditures
       Family Economics
BT   Economics
RT   Consumer Education
       Consumer Protection
       Consumer Science
       Economic Impact
       Educational Economics
       Home Economics
       Home Management
       Merchandise Information
       Microeconomics
       Purchasing
       Supply and Demand

Consumer Education   AUG. 1968
    Postings: 2,771   GC: 400
SN   Study of intelligent and effective methods of buying and using goods and services, competent money management, and relationship of consumer to the economic system
NT   Consumer Science
BT   Education
RT   Basic Business Education
       Consumer Economics
       Consumer Protection
       Consumer Science
       Economics Education
       Energy Education
       Family Life Education
       Health Education
       Home Economics
       Home Economics Education
       Home Management
       Money Management
       Practical Arts
       Purchasing

Consumer Expenditures
USE   Consumer Economics

Consumer Protection   DEC. 1975
    Postings: 878   GC: 520
SN   Methods or processes intended to prevent the sale of unsafe or deceptively presented goods or services, or to assist the consumer to make informed decisions regarding purchase of goods or services
UF   Consumerism
RT   Accountability
       Advertising
       Civil Law
       College Choice
       Consumer Economics
       Consumer Education
       Deception
       Educational Quality
       Fraud
       Marketing
       Merchandise Information
       Purchasing
       Responsibility
       Safety

Consumer Science   JUL. 1966
    Postings: 168   GC: 400
SN   Those phases of science needed by or useful to the consumer including operation and repair of simple household equipment, effects of cleaning and other products, and preservation and care of food and clothing
UF   Household Science
BT   Consumer Education
       Technology
RT   Clothing Instruction
       Consumer Economics
       Consumer Education
       Foods Instruction
       Home Economics
       Housework
       Maintenance
       Repair

Consumerism
USE   Consumer Protection

Contagious Diseases
USE   Communicable Diseases

Contemporary History
USE   Modern History

Content Analysis   AUG. 1968
    Postings: 5,194   GC: 810
SN   Systematic, objective, and quantitative description of the manifest or latent content of print or nonprint communications
BT   Evaluation Methods
RT   Classification
       Classroom Observation Techniques
       Communication (Thought Transfer)
       Course Content
       Curriculum Research
       Data Analysis
       Difficulty Level
       Film Criticism
       Item Analysis
       Literary Criticism
       Readability Formulas
       Research Methodology
       Skill Analysis
       Task Analysis
       Test Content
       Textbook Content

Content Area Reading   MAR. 1980
    Postings: 2,995   GC: 460
SN   Instruction concerned with reading assignments—also, instructional material in such subject areas as social studies, mathematics, science, and English
UF   Content Reading (1967 1980)
       Reading in Content Areas
BT   Reading
       Reading Instruction
RT   Critical Reading
       Directed Reading Activity
       Functional Reading
       Readability
       Reading Assignments
       Reading Comprehension
       Reading Skills
       Study Skills

Content Area Writing   JUN. 1983
    Postings: 971   GC: 400
SN   Written composition or writing instruction for specific academic or vocational subject areas
NT   Writing Across the Curriculum
BT   Writing (Composition)
       Writing Instruction
RT   Literary Devices
       News Writing
       Research Papers (Students)
       Technical Writing
       Writing Exercises
       Writing Skills

Content Reading (1967 1980)
USE   Content Area Reading

Content Validity   AUG. 1986
    Postings: 236   GC: 820
SN   The extent to which a test adequately represents the subject-matter content or behavior to be measured—commonly used in evaluating achievement or proficiency tests
BT   Test Validity
RT   Construct Validity
       Item Analysis
       Test Content
       Test Items
       Testing

Context Clues   JUL. 1966
    Postings: 1,353   GC: 460
SN   Indications of the meaning of a word gained from the surrounding words, phrases, or sentences as well as the accompanying pictures (Note: Do not confuse with "Context Effect")
BT   Cues
RT   Cloze Procedure
       Decoding (Reading)
       Inferences
       Miscue Analysis
       Reading
       Reading Comprehension
       Structural Analysis (Linguistics)

Vocabulary Development
Vocabulary Skills
Word Recognition

Context Effect   *DEC. 1989*
Postings: 1,799   GC: 520
SN   The impact or consequences of an en-
compassing situation on the functions
and performance of something—in edu-
cation, the effects of situational variables
(e.g., physical setting, psychosocial con-
dition, expectations) on perception, cog-
nition, and experience (Note: Do not
confuse with "Context Clues")
UF   Contextual Effects
Situational Determinants
RT   Cognitive Processes
Cultural Context
Environment
Individual Development
Influences
Interpersonal Relationship
Learning Theories
Orientation
Performance Factors
Predictor Variables
Simulation
Systems Approach

Context Free Grammar   *JUL. 1966*
Postings: 26   GC: 450
BT   Transformational Generative Grammar
RT   Grammar
Machine Translation
Phrase Structure

Contextual Effects
USE   Context Effect

Contingency Contracts
USE   Contingency Management

Contingency Management   *FEB. 1975*
Postings: 871   GC: 110
SN   Systematic arrangement of reinforcing
events in order to strengthen or weaken
specific behavior
UF   Contingency Contracts
BT   Behavior Modification
RT   Behavior Chaining
Behavior Change
Behavioral Objectives
Extinction (Psychology)
Learning Processes
Motivation Techniques
Operant Conditioning
Performance Contracts
Reinforcement
Teaching Methods
Timeout
Token Economy

Continuation Education (1968 1980)
JUN. 1980
Postings: 126   GC: 330
SN   Invalid Descriptor—scoped to refer to
instruction for potential learners who
have rejected conventional schooling,
but used indiscriminately for "Continuing Education"—see "Continuation Students"

Continuation High Schools (1968 1980)
USE   Continuation Students

Continuation Students   *JUL. 1966*
Postings: 138   GC: 360
SN   Students enrolled in special continuation
education programs—continuation education enables youth and adults who
have previously dropped out of or otherwise rejected conventional schooling to
complete their formal education (Note:
Prior to Jun80, "Continuation Education" was also used to index this concept)

UF   Continuation High Schools (1968
1980)
BT   Students
RT   Delinquent Rehabilitation
Dropout Prevention
Dropout Programs
Dropouts
High School Equivalency Programs
High Schools
Late Registration
Nontraditional Education
Reentry Students
Rehabilitation Programs
Remedial Programs
Secondary Education
Special Education
Special Needs Students
Student Adjustment
Terminal Students
Transfer Students
Truancy
Vocational Education

Continuing Education   *APR. 1980*
Postings: 3,549   GC: 340
SN   Educational programs and services, usu-
ally on the postsecondary level, designed
to serve adults who seek particular learn-
ing experiences on a part-time or short
term basis for personal, academic, or
occupational development
NT   Mandatory Continuing Education
Professional Continuing Education
BT   Adult Education
RT   Adult Students
Auditing (Coursework)
Community Education
Community Services
Conferences
Continuing Education Centers
Continuing Education Units
Corporate Education
Correspondence Study
Distance Education
Evening Programs
Extension Education
Lifelong Learning
Noncredit Courses
Nontraditional Education
Outreach Programs
Postsecondary Education
Special Degree Programs
Staff Development
Womens Education

Continuing Education Centers   *JUL. 1966*
Postings: 314   GC: 920
BT   Educational Facilities
RT   Adult Education
Continuing Education
Extension Education
Living Learning Centers

Continuing Education Units   *FEB. 1976*
Postings: 155   GC: 340
SN   Uniform units of measurement reflecting
participation in organized continuing
(noncredit) education programs under
responsible sponsorship—designed to
provide a national standard for recogni-
tion of adult participation in post-degree
and non-degree education programs (one
unit equals ten contact hours)
UF   CEU
BT   Credits
RT   Adult Education
Auditing (Coursework)
Continuing Education
Credentials
Lifelong Learning
Noncredit Courses
Professional Continuing Education
Retraining
Student Certification
Units of Study

Continuity of Education
USE   Developmental Continuity

Continuous Guidance (1966 1980)
USE   Guidance

Continuous Learning (1967 1980)
USE   Lifelong Learning

Continuous Progress Plan   *JUL. 1966*
Postings: 267   GC: 350
SN   Curriculum organized so that students
can progress at their own rates through
a sequence of increasingly difficult
courses
BT   Curriculum
RT   Behavioral Objectives
Flexible Progression
Flexible Scheduling
Mixed Age Grouping
Nongraded Instructional Grouping

Contraception   *APR. 1969*
Postings: 1,001   GC: 210
UF   Birth Control
RT   Abortions
Birth Rate
Births to Single Women
Family Planning
Gynecology
Overpopulation
Pregnancy
Reproduction (Biology)
Sex Education

Contract Grading
USE   Grading
AND   Performance Contracts

Contract Salaries   *JUL. 1966*
Postings: 125   GC: 620
SN   Salaries stipulated by a formal agree-
ment limited by an expiration date
BT   Salaries
RT   Contracts
Teacher Salaries
Tenure

Contract Tribal Schools
USE   Tribally Controlled Education

Contracting Out (of Government Services)
USE   Privatization

Contractor Vehicles
USE   Service Vehicles

Contracts   *JUL. 1966*
Postings: 2,593   GC: 620
SN   Formal agreements between two or more
parties in which, for a benefit or to avoid
a penalty, one or more of the parties
agrees to do a certain thing
UF   Agreements (Formal)
NT   Performance Contracts
RT   Accountability
Bids
Cable Franchising
Civil Law
Contract Salaries
Faculty Workload
Franchising
Grantsmanship
Job Security
Labor Demands
Legal Responsibility
Negotiation Agreements
Ownership
Personnel Policy
Privatization
Probationary Period
Specifications
Teacher Dismissal
Teaching Load
Tenure

Contrast   *APR. 1970*
Postings: 44   GC: 420
SN   The perceived diversity of adjacent ele-
ments in the visual field
UF   Contrast Ratios
RT   Color
Light
Lighting
Lighting Design
Visual Discrimination

Contrast Ratios
USE   Contrast

Contrastive Language Analysis
USE   Contrastive Linguistics

Contrastive Linguistics   *JUL. 1966*
Postings: 1,882   GC: 450
SN   Study of the similarities and differences
between languages or dialects or be-
tween different periods in the historical
development of one language
UF   Comparative Linguistics
Contrastive Language Analysis
BT   Linguistics
RT   Cross Cultural Studies
Diachronic Linguistics
Error Analysis (Language)
Interference (Language)
Language Classification
Language Typology
Language Variation
Lexicology
Machine Translation
Mutual Intelligibility
Phoneme Grapheme Correspondence
Phonemics
Second Language Learning

Control Groups   *JUL. 1966*
Postings: 746   GC: 820
SN   Groups that match experimental groups
except that they are not exposed to the
experimental variables being studied—
differences arising between the groups
are then attributed to these variables
(Note: Use only for discussions of the
identification, selection, or treatment of
control groups)
BT   Groups
RT   Attrition (Research Studies)
Effect Size
Experimental Groups
Matched Groups
Participant Characteristics
Quasiexperimental Design
Research Design
Research Methodology
Sample Size
Sampling

Controlled Environment (1966 1980)
MAR. 1980
Postings: 262   GC: 920
SN   Invalid Descriptor—primarily used for
control of the physical environment, but
also used for manipulation of social or
psychological environments—use such
Descriptors as "Climate Control," "Physi-
cal Environment," "Social Environment,"
"Behavior Change," "Milieu Therapy,"
"Behavior Modification," etc.

Controversial Issues (Course Content)
OCT. 1980
Postings: 1,385   GC: 330
SN   Matters of public concern and contro-
versy that are taught, often through dis-
cussion, in social studies, current events,
science, and other classes (Note: For the
issues themselves as opposed to teach-
ing about them, use more precise terms)
RT   Conflict
Course Content
Critical Thinking
Current Events
Curriculum

= Two or more Descriptors are used to represent this term.
The term's main entry shows the appropriate coordination.

Dissent
Gender Issues
Moral Issues
Political Issues
Public Affairs Education
Social Change
Social Problems
Social Sciences
Social Studies
Values
World Problems

Convalescent Homes
USE   Nursing Homes

Conventional Instruction   *JUL. 1966*
    Postings: 1,306   GC: 310
UF   Traditional Instruction
BT   Teaching Methods
RT   Back to Basics
    Experimental Teaching
    Lecture Method
    Self Contained Classrooms
    Traditional Schools

Conventional Warfare
USE   War

Convergent Thinking   *NOV. 1968*
    Postings: 199   GC: 110
SN   Thought processes involved in search-
    ing for the one right, best, or conven-
    tional answer to a problem
BT   Cognitive Processes
RT   Critical Thinking
    Divergent Thinking
    Logical Thinking
    Problem Solving
    Productive Thinking
    Thinking Skills

Conversational Language Courses
                                           JUL. 1966
    Postings: 691   GC: 450
SN   Courses that develop conversational skills
    in a foreign language (Note: Prior to
    Mar80, this term was not scoped and
    was often misused to index "Conversa-
    tion")
BT   Courses
    Modern Language Curriculum
RT   Audiolingual Methods
    Audiolingual Skills
    Communicative Competence
    (Languages)
    Language Fluency
    Language Proficiency
    Languages
    Second Language Instruction
    Second Language Learning
    Second Language Programs
    Speech Communication
    Standard Spoken Usage

Conversion (Format)
USE   Data Conversion

Convicts
USE   Criminals

Cooking Instruction   *JUL. 1966*
    Postings: 393   GC: 400
BT   Instruction
RT   Cooks
    Foods Instruction
    Home Economics
    Nutrition Instruction
    Recipes (Food)

Cooks   *JUL. 1966*
    Postings: 110   GC: 640
UF   Chefs
BT   Service Workers
RT   Cooking Instruction
    Dietitians

Dining Facilities
Food
Food Service
Foods Instruction
Home Economics Skills
Nutrition Instruction
Occupational Home Economics
Recipes (Food)

Cooperating Schools
USE   Affiliated Schools

Cooperating Teachers   *JUL. 1966*
    Postings: 1,426   GC: 360
SN   Experienced elementary or secondary
    teachers employed to supervise student
    teachers or teacher interns in affiliated
    schools (Note: Do not confuse with the
    more general concept "Master Teach-
    ers" or with "Student Teacher Supervi-
    sors")
UF   Supervising Teachers
BT   Teachers
RT   Affiliated Schools
    Master Teachers
    Practicum Supervision
    Preservice Teacher Education
    Student Teacher Supervisors
    Student Teachers
    Student Teaching
    Teacher Education
    Teacher Educator Education
    Teacher Educators
    Teacher Interns
    Teacher Supervision

Cooperation   *MAR. 1978*
    Postings: 4,332   GC: 520
SN   Act of working together toward a com-
    mon goal (Note: Use a more specific
    term if possible)
UF   Collaboration
NT   Agency Cooperation
    Community Cooperation
    Compliance (Psychology)
    Educational Cooperation
    Institutional Cooperation
    International Cooperation
    Regional Cooperation
BT   Behavior
RT   Altruism
    Collegiality
    Competition
    Cooperative Learning
    Cooperative Planning
    Cooperative Programs
    Coordination
    Group Activities
    Group Unity
    Integrated Services
    Intergroup Relations
    Interpersonal Relationship
    Networks
    Prosocial Behavior
    Shared Resources and Services
    Sharing Behavior
    Social Behavior
    Social Exchange Theory
    Social Reinforcement
    Social Support Groups
    Teamwork
    Trust (Psychology)

Cooperative Activities
USE   Group Activities

Cooperative Education   *JUL. 1966*
    Postings: 2,237   GC: 400
SN   Work and school experiences under the
    direction of a teacher coordinator, ar-
    ranged between school and employer to
    complement each other toward an occu-
    pational goal—often more formally struc-
    tured and supervised than other work
    experience programs
UF   Cooperative Training
    Cooperative Work Experience Pro-
    grams
    Vocational Work Experience

BT   Vocational Education
RT   Adult Vocational Education
    Affiliated Schools
    Career Education
    Cooperative Programs
    Distributive Education
    Educational Cooperation
    Experiential Learning
    Field Experience Programs
    Instructor Coordinators
    Practicums
    School Business Relationship
    Supervised Occupational Experience
    (Agriculture)
    Work Experience
    Work Experience Programs

Cooperative Extension
USE   Extension Education

Cooperative Learning   *AUG. 1988*
    Postings: 4,709   GC: 310
SN   Learning situation in which students work
    together in small groups and receive
    rewards or recognition based on their
    group's performance
BT   Learning
RT   Active Learning
    Activity Units
    Cooperation
    Cooperative Planning
    Experiential Learning
    Group Activities
    Group Discussion
    Group Dynamics
    Grouping (Instructional Purposes)
    Humanistic Education
    Individualized Instruction
    Intergroup Relations
    Interpersonal Relationship
    Learning Activities
    Learning Centers (Classroom)
    Learning Strategies
    Mainstreaming
    Peer Teaching
    Problem Based Learning
    Reggio Emilia Approach
    Self Directed Groups
    Small Group Instruction
    Social Integration
    Socialization
    Student Participation
    Student Projects
    Team Training
    Teamwork

Cooperative Planning   *JUL. 1966*
    Postings: 3,584   GC: 520
SN   Process by which individuals or groups
    determine mutual objectives and the
    means for attaining them
UF   Interagency Planning (1966 1980) #
BT   Planning
RT   Agency Cooperation
    Community Cooperation
    Consortia
    Cooperation
    Cooperative Learning
    Counselor Teacher Cooperation
    Delphi Technique
    Educational Cooperation
    Institutional Cooperation
    Integrated Services
    Librarian Teacher Cooperation
    Nominal Group Technique
    Parent Teacher Cooperation
    Regional Cooperation
    School Community Relationship
    Shared Resources and Services
    Teacher Collaboration
    Team Teaching
    Teamwork

Cooperative Programs   *JUL. 1966*
    Postings: 6,896   GC: 330
SN   Programs conducted between or among
    independent institutions or organizations
    (Note: Prior to Mar80, the use of this
    term was not restricted by a Scope Note)

UF   Co Op Programs
    Program Coordination (1966 1980) #
BT   Programs
RT   Consortia
    Cooperation
    Cooperative Education
    Coordination
    Dual Enrollment
    Educational Cooperation
    Experiential Learning
    Institutional Cooperation
    Integrated Services
    Off the Job Training
    Partnerships in Education
    School Business Relationship
    School Community Relationship
    Shared Resources and Services
    Work Experience Programs
    Work Study Programs

Cooperative Teaching (1966 1980)
USE   Team Teaching

Cooperative Training
USE   Cooperative Education

Cooperative Work Experience Programs
USE   Cooperative Education

Cooperatives   *JUL. 1966*
    Postings: 244   GC: 650
SN   Economic enterprises wholly owned by
    their users
UF   Co Ops
BT   Organizations (Groups)
RT   Business
    Collective Settlements
    Community Organizations
    Economic Opportunities
    Industrial Structure
    Industry
    Marketing
    Ownership
    Participative Decision Making
    Purchasing

Coordinate Geometry
USE   Analytic Geometry

Coordinate Indexes   *JAN. 1969*
    Postings: 72   GC: 730
UF   Post Coordinate Indexes
    Uniterm Indexes
BT   Indexes
RT   Indexing
    Permuted Indexes
    Thesauri

Coordination   *JUL. 1966*
    Postings: 4,193   GC: 520
SN   Process of bringing about or organizing
    cooperative actions
UF   Educational Coordination (1967
    1980) #
    Interagency Coordination (1967
    1980) #
    Program Coordination (1966 1980) #
NT   Community Coordination
RT   Administration
    Consortia
    Cooperation
    Cooperative Programs
    Coordinators
    Managerial Occupations
    Networks
    Organization
    Partnerships in Education
    Planning
    Relationship
    Research Coordinating Units
    Scheduling
    Statewide Planning

Coordination (Psychomotor)
USE   Psychomotor Skills

= Two or more Descriptors are used to represent this term.
The term's main entry shows the appropriate coordination.

Coordination Compounds *JAN. 1970*
Postings: 52 GC: 490
SN Compounds with central atoms or ions and groups of ions or molecules surrounding them
RT Chemistry
Inorganic Chemistry
Molecular Structure
Organic Chemistry
Stereochemistry

Coordinator Trainers
USE Instructor Coordinators

Coordinators *JUL. 1966*
Postings: 370 GC: 360
SN Liaison agents between groups of people or organizations
UF Community Coordinators (1966 1980) #
NT Audiovisual Coordinators
Instructor Coordinators
BT Administrators
RT Coordination

Copilots
USE Aircraft Pilots

Coping *JAN. 1979*
Postings: 4,491 GC: 230
SN Contending with difficulties without altering purposes or goals
BT Adjustment (to Environment)
RT Adaptive Behavior (of Disabled)
Behavior Patterns
Burnout
Daily Living Skills
Decision Making
Defense Mechanisms
Goal Orientation
Individual Power
Life Events
Mental Health
Persistence
Problem Solving
Psychological Patterns
Resilience (Personality)
Stress Management
Well Being

Copyediting
USE Editing

Copyeditors
USE Editors

Copying (Reproduction)
USE Reprography

Copyrights *JUL. 1966*
Postings: 1,582 GC: 710
SN Exclusive privileges to publish, sell, or otherwise control works that can be reproduced, granted by governments to authors, composers, artists, publishers, etc., for a specified number of years
BT Intellectual Property
RT Art Products
Broadcast Industry
Computer Software
Downloading
Fair Use (Copyrights)
Federal Regulation
Film Industry
Films
Government Role
Legal Responsibility
National Libraries
Plagiarism
Programming (Broadcast)
Publications
Publishing Industry
Reprography

Core Courses (1966 1980)
USE Core Curriculum

Core Curriculum *JUL. 1966*
Postings: 2,236 GC: 350
SN Studies, activities, or courses that meet the common needs of students
UF Core Courses (1966 1980)
Teaching Core
BT Curriculum
RT British National Curriculum
General Science
Interdisciplinary Approach
Introductory Courses
Minimum Competencies
National Curriculum
Nonmajors
Relevance (Education)
Required Courses

Corn (Field Crop) (1968 1980)
USE Grains (Food)

Coronary Prone Behavior Pattern
USE Type A Behavior

Corporal Punishment *JUL. 1974*
Postings: 523 GC: 330
SN Disciplinary action involving infliction of physical pain upon one person by another
BT Punishment
RT Discipline
Discipline Policy
Negative Reinforcement

Corporate Colleges
USE Corporate Education

Corporate Education *AUG. 1986*
Postings: 893 GC: 330
SN Broad array of courses, curricula, and educational services offered by business and industry—may be completely in-house or offered cooperatively with an educational institution (Note: Do not confuse with "Industrial Training")
UF Corporate Colleges
BT Education
RT Business
Continuing Education
Corporations
Education Work Relationship
Industrial Training
Industry
Inplant Programs
Labor Force Development
Nonschool Educational Programs
Nontraditional Education
Postsecondary Education
Private Education
Professional Continuing Education
School Business Relationship

Corporate Giving
USE Corporate Support

Corporate Libraries *FEB. 2000*
Postings: 104 GC: 710
SN Special libraries located within business firms (Note: Do not confuse with the Identifier "Business Libraries," i.e., libraries that focus on business administration and other business subjects)
UF Company Libraries
Industrial Libraries
BT Special Libraries
RT Business
Corporations
Industry
Institutional Libraries

Corporate Support *AUG. 1986*
Postings: 723 GC: 620
SN Aid provided by business and industry

(e.g., money, equipment, materials, technical assistance)
UF Corporate Giving
RT Business
Business Responsibility
Corporations
Donors
Educational Finance
Industry
Partnerships in Education
Private Financial Support
School Business Relationship
School Support

Corporate Training
USE Industrial Training

Corporations *NOV. 1994*
Postings: 459 GC: 650
SN Businesses or other associations organized as legal entities, having rights and duties distinct from those of their individual members (Note: See also the Identifiers "Multinational Corporations" and "Transnational Corporations")
BT Organizations (Groups)
RT Business
Corporate Education
Corporate Libraries
Corporate Support
Industrial Structure
Industrial Training
Industry
Institutions
Mergers

Correctional Education *JUL. 1966*
Postings: 1,557 GC: 330
SN Educational programs provided for adults or youth in correctional institutions (Note: Prior to Mar80, the use of this term was not restricted by a Scope Note)
UF Prison Education
BT Education
RT Adult Education
Adult Reading Programs
Correctional Institutions
Correctional Rehabilitation
Criminals
Delinquent Rehabilitation
Human Services
Institutionalized Persons
Prison Libraries
Prisoners
Rehabilitation Programs
Released Time
Special Needs Students
Therapeutic Recreation
Vocational Rehabilitation

Correctional Institutions *MAR. 1980*
Postings: 1,342 GC: 920
UF Corrective Institutions (1966 1980)
Prisons
Training Schools (Juvenile Offenders)
BT Residential Institutions
RT Correctional Education
Correctional Rehabilitation
Crime
Criminals
Criminology
Delinquent Rehabilitation
Institutional Personnel
Institutionalized Persons
Prison Libraries
Prisoners
Sentencing

Correctional Rehabilitation *NOV. 1969*
Postings: 1,146 GC: 520
SN Activities designed to help prisoners and other offenders to lead useful lives
UF Corrections (Criminal Justice)
NT Delinquent Rehabilitation
BT Rehabilitation
RT Correctional Education
Correctional Institutions
Crime
Crime Prevention

Criminals
Criminology
Human Services
Parole Officers
Prisoners
Probation Officers
Probationary Period
Recidivism
Vocational Rehabilitation

Corrections (Criminal Justice)
USE Correctional Rehabilitation

Corrective Institutions (1966 1980)
USE Correctional Institutions

Corrective Reading *JUL. 1966*
Postings: 103 GC: 460
SN Reading instruction within a regular class for students with reading problems (Note: Do not confuse with "Remedial Reading")
BT Reading
Reading Instruction
RT Reading Difficulties
Remedial Reading

Correlation *JUL. 1966*
Postings: 5,504 GC: 820
SN Description of the degree of association or concomitant variation between two independently measured traits
UF Correlation Studies
Multiple Correlation
Part Correlation
Partial Correlation
Statistical Association Methods
BT Statistical Analysis
RT Analysis of Covariance
Causal Models
Chi Square
Cluster Analysis
Comparative Analysis
Factor Analysis
Input Output Analysis
Least Squares Statistics
Meta Analysis
Multidimensional Scaling
Multiple Regression Analysis
Multitrait Multimethod Techniques
Multivariate Analysis
Nonparametric Statistics
Oblique Rotation
Orthogonal Rotation
Path Analysis
Predictor Variables
Regression (Statistics)
Reliability
Scores
Statistical Inference
Statistics
Transformations (Mathematics)
Validity

Correlation Studies
USE Correlation

Correspondence (Letters)
USE Letters (Correspondence)

Correspondence Courses (1966 1980)
USE Correspondence Study

Correspondence Schools *JUL. 1966*
Postings: 149 GC: 340
UF Commercial Correspondence Schools
BT Schools
RT Correspondence Study
Distance Education
Extension Education
Part Time Students
Private Schools
Proprietary Schools

= Two or more Descriptors are used to represent this term.
The term's main entry shows the appropriate coordination.

Correspondence Study　　　　*JUL. 1966*
　　　Postings: 1,032　　　　　　　GC: 350
SN　Method of instruction with teacher student interaction by mail
UF　Correspondence Courses (1966 1980)
BT　Distance Education
RT　Continuing Education
　　　Correspondence Schools
　　　Home Study
　　　Independent Study
　　　Lifelong Learning
　　　Nontraditional Education

Corridors　　　　　　　　　　　*JUL. 1966*
　　　Postings: 27　　　　　　　　GC: 920
UF　Hallways
BT　Facilities
RT　School Space
　　　Windowless Rooms

Cosmetic Prostheses (1967 1980)
USE　Prostheses

Cosmetics Inspectors
USE　Food and Drug Inspectors

Cosmetologists (1969 1981)
USE　Cosmetology

Cosmetology　　　　　　　　　*JAN. 1969*
　　　Postings: 157　　　　　　　GC: 640
UF　Beauticians
　　　Beauty Culture
　　　Beauty Operators
　　　Cosmetologists (1969 1981)
BT　Technology
RT　Service Occupations

Cost Analysis
USE　Cost Effectiveness

Cost Benefit Analysis
USE　Cost Effectiveness

Cost Effectiveness　　　　　　*JUL. 1966*
　　　Postings: 9,801　　　　　　GC: 620
SN　Evaluation of the monetary gains and losses associated with various decisions, outcomes, or actions
UF　Benefit Cost Analysis
　　　Cost Analysis
　　　Cost Benefit Analysis
　　　Cost Effectiveness Analysis
　　　Cost Utility Analysis
BT　Evaluation Methods
RT　Accountability
　　　Cost Estimates
　　　Costs
　　　Econometrics
　　　Economic Impact
　　　Efficiency
　　　Expenditures
　　　Input Output Analysis
　　　Job Simplification
　　　Life Cycle Costing
　　　Operations Research
　　　Organizational Effectiveness
　　　Policy Analysis
　　　Program Effectiveness
　　　Resource Allocation
　　　Retrenchment
　　　Risk
　　　School Effectiveness
　　　Systems Analysis

Cost Effectiveness Analysis
USE　Cost Effectiveness

Cost Estimates　　　　　　　　*MAR. 1980*
　　　Postings: 896　　　　　　　GC: 620
UF　Estimated Costs (1966 1980)
BT　Costs
RT　Budgeting
　　　Cost Effectiveness

　　　Program Costs
　　　Unit Costs

Cost Indexes　　　　　　　　　*JUL. 1974*
　　　Postings: 360　　　　　　　GC: 620
SN　Measures of the difference in cost or price (prices of consumer goods, school costs, etc.) from that which existed during a designated base period
UF　Index Numbers (Costs)
　　　Price Indexes
RT　Costs
　　　Economic Change
　　　Economic Impact
　　　Economics
　　　Expenditures
　　　Inflation (Economics)
　　　Supply and Demand

Cost Utility Analysis
USE　Cost Effectiveness

Costs　　　　　　　　　　　　　*JUL. 1966*
　　　Postings: 5,591　　　　　　GC: 620
SN　Amount charged, but not necessarily paid, for something (Note: Do not confuse with "Expenditures"—prior to Mar80, the use of this term was not restricted by a Scope Note)
UF　Police Costs (1966 1980) #
NT　Construction Costs
　　　Cost Estimates
　　　Fees
　　　Health Care Costs
　　　Interest (Finance)
　　　Legal Costs
　　　Program Costs
　　　Student Costs
　　　Unit Costs
RT　Compensation (Remuneration)
　　　Cost Effectiveness
　　　Cost Indexes
　　　Economic Impact
　　　Educational Finance
　　　Expenditure per Student
　　　Expenditures
　　　Inflation (Economics)
　　　Library Expenditures
　　　Loan Repayment
　　　Operating Expenses
　　　Ownership
　　　Private Financial Support
　　　Retrenchment
　　　Salaries
　　　School District Spending
　　　Supply and Demand
　　　Wages

Costume Design
USE　Clothing Design

Cot Death
USE　Sudden Infant Death Syndrome

Cottage Parents
USE　Resident Advisers

Counseling　　　　　　　　　　*JUL. 1966*
　　　Postings: 5,437　　　　　　GC: 240
SN　Process of helping individuals and groups understand and cope with adjustment problems—involves giving advice, information, or encouragement, engaging in therapeutic discussions, or administering and interpreting tests (Note: "Counseling" is one aspect of the total process of "Guidance")
UF　Counseling Process
NT　Adult Counseling
　　　Career Counseling
　　　Cocounseling
　　　Educational Counseling
　　　Family Counseling
　　　Group Counseling
　　　Individual Counseling
　　　Marriage Counseling
　　　Nondirective Counseling

　　　Parent Counseling
　　　Peer Counseling
　　　Rehabilitation Counseling
　　　School Counseling
BT　Guidance
RT　Adjustment (to Environment)
　　　Behavior Modification
　　　Case Studies
　　　Cognitive Restructuring
　　　Consultation Programs
　　　Counseling Effectiveness
　　　Counseling Objectives
　　　Counseling Psychology
　　　Counseling Services
　　　Counseling Techniques
　　　Counseling Theories
　　　Counselor Client Relationship
　　　Counselors
　　　Crisis Intervention
　　　Guidance Centers
　　　Helping Relationship
　　　Intervention
　　　Microcounseling
　　　Ombudsmen
　　　Outcomes of Treatment
　　　Psychotherapy
　　　Referral
　　　Rehabilitation
　　　Social Support Groups
　　　Social Work
　　　Termination of Treatment
　　　Therapeutic Environment
　　　Wellness

Counseling Centers (1966 1977)
USE　Guidance Centers

Counseling Effectiveness　　　*JUL. 1966*
　　　Postings: 3,381　　　　　　GC: 240
RT　Counseling
　　　Counseling Objectives
　　　Counseling Techniques
　　　Counselor Performance
　　　Counselor Role
　　　Outcomes of Treatment

Counseling Goals (1966 1980)
USE　Counseling Objectives

Counseling Instructional Programs (1967 1980)　　　　　　　　*MAR. 1980*
　　　Postings: 94　　　　　　　GC: 240
SN　Invalid Descriptor—used for both counseling-instructional programs for students and counselor training—see such Descriptors as "Counselor Teacher Cooperation" and "Counselor Training"

Counseling Methods
USE　Counseling Techniques

Counseling Objectives　　　　*MAR. 1980*
　　　Postings: 967　　　　　　　GC: 240
SN　Aims or ends toward which the counseling process (one aspect of the total process of "guidance") is directed
UF　Counseling Goals (1966 1980)
BT　Guidance Objectives
RT　Behavioral Objectives
　　　Counseling
　　　Counseling Effectiveness

Counseling Process
USE　Counseling

Counseling Programs (1966 1980)
USE　Counseling Services

Counseling Psychology　　　　*JUN. 1993*
　　　Postings: 601　　　　　　　GC: 240
SN　Psychology relating to counseling—more specifically, psychology courses and learning experiences concerned with training counselors or counseling psychologists to assist persons to make adjust-

ments and choices, especially in regard to vocational, education, and personal matters
BT　Psychology
RT　Clinical Psychology
　　　Counseling
　　　Counseling Techniques
　　　Counseling Theories
　　　Counselor Client Relationship
　　　Counselor Educators
　　　Counselor Role
　　　Counselor Training
　　　Psychological Testing
　　　Psychotherapy

Counseling Services　　　　　*JUL. 1966*
　　　Postings: 4,409　　　　　　GC: 240
SN　Organized activities designed to help individuals or groups understand and cope with adjustment problems
UF　Counseling Programs (1966 1980)
　　　Evening Counseling Programs (1966 1980) #
BT　Human Services
RT　Ancillary School Services
　　　Counseling
　　　Counselor Characteristics
　　　Counselors
　　　Employee Assistance Programs
　　　Guidance Centers
　　　Hotlines (Public)
　　　Individualized Programs
　　　Outplacement Services (Employment)
　　　Outreach Programs
　　　Psychiatric Services
　　　Pupil Personnel Services
　　　Pupil Personnel Workers
　　　Student Personnel Services
　　　Student Personnel Workers

Counseling Techniques　　　　*MAR. 1980*
　　　Postings: 5,467　　　　　　GC: 240
SN　Methods, procedures, and approaches used by counselors in working with clients (Note: Prior to Mar80, the instruction "Counseling Techniques, USE Counseling" was carried in the Thesaurus)
UF　Counseling Methods
BT　Methods
RT　Assertiveness
　　　Caseworker Approach
　　　Conditioning
　　　Counseling
　　　Counseling Effectiveness
　　　Counseling Psychology
　　　Counseling Theories
　　　Counselor Client Relationship
　　　Counselor Role
　　　Desensitization
　　　Empathy
　　　Gestalt Therapy
　　　Interviews
　　　Intimacy
　　　Laboratory Training
　　　Microcounseling
　　　Modeling (Psychology)
　　　Rapport
　　　Reality Therapy
　　　Role Playing
　　　Self Disclosure (Individuals)
　　　Sensitivity Training
　　　Simulation
　　　Stress Management
　　　Transactional Analysis

Counseling Theories　　　　　*JUL. 1966*
　　　Postings: 1,445　　　　　　GC: 240
BT　Theories
RT　Behavior
　　　Behavior Theories
　　　Counseling
　　　Counseling Psychology
　　　Counseling Techniques
　　　Nondirective Counseling

Counselor Acceptance (1968 1980)
USE　Counselor Client Relationship

= Two or more Descriptors are used to represent this term.
The term's main entry shows the appropriate coordination.

Counselor Attitudes   *SEP. 1968*
Postings: 1,767   GC: 240
SN   Attitudes of, not toward, counselors
UF   Counselor Opinion
     Counselor Reaction
BT   Attitudes
RT   Counselor Characteristics
     Counselor Client Relationship
     Counselor Evaluation
     Counselor Performance
     Counselors

Counselor Background
USE   Counselor Characteristics

Counselor Certification   *JUL. 1966*
Postings: 227   GC: 240
UF   Counselor Licensing
BT   Certification
RT   Counselor Evaluation
     Counselor Qualifications
     Counselors

Counselor Characteristics   *JUL. 1966*
Postings: 1,193   GC: 240
SN   Physical and psychological characteristics of counselors, e.g., personality traits, values, experience, age, race, sex (Note: Do not confuse with "Counselor Qualifications")
UF   Counselor Background
RT   Counseling Services
     Counselor Attitudes
     Counselor Client Relationship
     Counselor Evaluation
     Counselor Performance
     Counselor Qualifications
     Counselor Role
     Counselor Selection
     Counselors
     Individual Characteristics

Counselor Client Ratio   *JUL. 1966*
Postings: 44   GC: 240
UF   Client Counselor Ratio
BT   Ratios (Mathematics)
RT   Counselors

Counselor Client Relationship   *MAR. 1980*
Postings: 2,170   GC: 240
UF   Client Counselor Relationship
     Counselor Acceptance (1968 1980)
BT   Interpersonal Relationship
RT   Client Characteristics (Human Services)
     Counseling
     Counseling Psychology
     Counseling Techniques
     Counselor Attitudes
     Counselor Characteristics
     Counselor Role
     Counselors
     Helping Relationship
     Physician Patient Relationship
     Therapeutic Environment

Counselor Education
USE   Counselor Training

Counselor Educators   *JUL. 1966*
Postings: 658   GC: 360
SN   Members of a college or university faculty who are primarily concerned with the preparation of counselors
BT   College Faculty
RT   Counseling Psychology
     Counselor Evaluation
     Counselor Training
     Practicum Supervision
     Professors

Counselor Evaluation   *JUL. 1966*
Postings: 751   GC: 240
SN   Process of judging counselor performance as related to established criteria
BT   Personnel Evaluation

RT   Counselor Attitudes
     Counselor Certification
     Counselor Characteristics
     Counselor Educators
     Counselor Performance
     Counselor Qualifications
     Counselor Selection
     Counselors

Counselor Functions (1967 1977)
USE   Counselor Role

Counselor Licensing
USE   Counselor Certification

Counselor Opinion
USE   Counselor Attitudes

Counselor Performance   *JUL. 1966*
Postings: 843   GC: 240
BT   Performance
RT   Counseling Effectiveness
     Counselor Attitudes
     Counselor Characteristics
     Counselor Evaluation
     Counselor Qualifications
     Counselor Role
     Counselors

Counselor Preparation
USE   Counselor Training

Counselor Qualifications   *JUL. 1966*
Postings: 449   GC: 240
SN   Abilities, aptitudes, or achievements that suit counselors for professional practice or employment, especially including the legal and educational requirements for counseling positions (Note: Do not confuse with "Counselor Characteristics")
BT   Qualifications
RT   Counselor Certification
     Counselor Characteristics
     Counselor Evaluation
     Counselor Performance
     Counselor Selection
     Counselors
     Employment Qualifications

Counselor Reaction
USE   Counselor Attitudes

Counselor Role   *JUL. 1966*
Postings: 5,552   GC: 240
UF   Counselor Functions (1967 1977)
BT   Role
RT   Confidentiality
     Counseling Effectiveness
     Counseling Psychology
     Counseling Techniques
     Counselor Characteristics
     Counselor Client Relationship
     Counselor Performance
     Counselors
     Staff Role

Counselor Selection   *NOV. 1969*
Postings: 125   GC: 240
SN   Selection of counselors for employment (Note: Prior to Mar80, this term was not scoped and was occasionally used for counselor selection of clients)
BT   Personnel Selection
RT   Counselor Characteristics
     Counselor Evaluation
     Counselor Qualifications
     Counselor Training
     Counselors

Counselor Teacher Cooperation   *MAR. 1980*
Postings: 270   GC: 240
UF   Teacher Counselor Cooperation
BT   Educational Cooperation
RT   Consultation Programs

Cooperative Planning
Diagnostic Teaching
Educational Diagnosis
Psychoeducational Methods
School Counseling
School Counselors
School Guidance
Teacher Guidance
Teachers

Counselor Training   *JUL. 1966*
Postings: 4,595   GC: 240
SN   Any formal or informal program that develops counseling skills of professionals or nonprofessionals
UF   Counselor Education
     Counselor Preparation
BT   Training
RT   Counseling Psychology
     Counselor Educators
     Counselor Selection
     Counselors
     Microcounseling
     Practicums

Counselors   *JUL. 1966*
Postings: 3,486   GC: 240
UF   Special Counselors (1966 1980) #
NT   Adjustment Counselors
     Employment Counselors
     School Counselors
BT   Guidance Personnel
RT   Adult Counseling
     Caseworkers
     Consultants
     Counseling
     Counseling Services
     Counselor Attitudes
     Counselor Certification
     Counselor Characteristics
     Counselor Client Ratio
     Counselor Client Relationship
     Counselor Evaluation
     Counselor Performance
     Counselor Qualifications
     Counselor Role
     Counselor Selection
     Counselor Training
     Mental Health Workers
     Parole Officers
     Probation Officers
     Psychologists
     Social Workers
     Specialists

Counties   *MAY 1993*
Postings: 284   GC: 550
SN   The principal, often geographically largest, areas into which states, territories, countries, etc., are divided for purposes of local government—in the U.S.A., administrative subdivisions of states
UF   County Government #
     County History #
NT   Low Income Counties
BT   Geographic Regions
RT   Community Characteristics
     County Libraries
     County Officials
     County Programs
     County School Districts
     Metropolitan Areas
     Municipalities

Counting
USE   Computation

County Extension Agents
USE   Extension Agents

County Government
USE   Counties
AND   Local Government

County History
USE   Counties
AND   Local History

County Libraries   *MAR. 1969*
Postings: 107   GC: 710
BT   Public Libraries
RT   Branch Libraries
     Counties
     Regional Libraries

County Norms
USE   Local Norms

County Officials   *JUL. 1966*
Postings: 86   GC: 610
BT   Public Officials
RT   City Officials
     Counties
     Extension Agents
     Legislators
     State Officials

County Programs   *JUL. 1970*
Postings: 254   GC: 610
BT   Programs
RT   Community Programs
     Counties
     Federal Programs
     Regional Programs
     State Programs

County School Districts   *MAR. 1980*
Postings: 260   GC: 340
SN   School systems that encompass the public schools (sometimes with specific exceptions) within a county
UF   County School Systems (1967 1980)
BT   School Districts
RT   Boards of Education
     Counties
     Rural Schools

County School Systems (1967 1980)
USE   County School Districts

Course Content   *JUL. 1966*
Postings: 11,613   GC: 310
SN   Subject matter or activities of a course of study
BT   Course Organization
RT   Content Analysis
     Controversial Issues (Course Content)
     Course Descriptions
     Course Objectives
     Curriculum
     Curriculum Development
     Curriculum Guides
     Elective Courses
     Program Content
     Program Validation
     Textbook Content
     Validated Programs

Course Descriptions   *JUL. 1966*
Postings: 9,544   GC: 730
SN   (Note: Prior to Mar80, the Thesaurus carried the instructions, "'Course Outlines' or 'Syllabus,' USE 'Curriculum Guides'")
UF   Course Outlines
     Syllabi
RT   Course Content
     Course Objectives
     Course Organization
     Courses
     Curriculum Guides
     Profiles
     School Catalogs

Course Enrichment
USE   Curriculum Enrichment

Course Evaluation   *JUL. 1966*
Postings: 3,290   GC: 310
BT   Evaluation
RT   Course Objectives
     Course Organization
     Course Selection (Students)

= Two or more Descriptors are used to represent this term.
The term's main entry shows the appropriate coordination.

Courses
- Curriculum Evaluation
- Instructional Effectiveness
- Instructional Material Evaluation
- Program Evaluation
- Program Validation
- Student Evaluation
- Student Evaluation of Teacher Performance
- Summative Evaluation
- Teacher Evaluation
- Validated Programs

Course Integrated Library Instruction
JAN. 1988
Postings: 432   GC: 400
- SN   Library instruction given as part of a course in another subject, i.e., English, history, etc.
- UF   Course Related Library Instruction
       Curriculum Integrated Library Instruction
       Integrated Library Instruction
- BT   Library Instruction
- RT   Librarian Teacher Cooperation

Course Objectives   JUL. 1966
Postings: 3,395   GC: 310
- BT   Objectives
- RT   Behavioral Objectives
       Course Content
       Course Descriptions
       Course Evaluation
       Courses

Course of Instruction
- USE   Course Organization

Course Organization   JUL. 1966
Postings: 2,401   GC: 310
- SN   General plan of instruction prepared by the teacher for use with particular groups of students for a specific period of time (Note: Use a more specific term if possible)
- UF   Course of Instruction
- NT   Course Content
- BT   Organization
- RT   Class Organization
       Course Descriptions
       Course Evaluation
       Courses
       Study Guides
       Teaching Methods

Course Outlines
- USE   Course Descriptions

Course Related Library Instruction
- USE   Course Integrated Library Instruction

Course Selection (Students)   AUG. 1986
Postings: 609   GC: 320
- SN   Student choice of an instructional class or course, or of a class/course cluster
- BT   Selection
- RT   Course Evaluation
       Courses
       Curriculum Design
       Decision Making
       Elective Courses
       Enrollment Influences
       Majors (Students)
       Nonmajors
       Relevance (Education)
       Required Courses
       Student Educational Objectives
       Student Interests
       Student Needs

Course Withdrawal
- USE   Withdrawal (Education)

Courses   JUL. 1966
Postings: 1,480   GC: 350
- SN   Educational units within the curriculum dealing systematically with a particular subject or discipline for a given period of time (Note: Use a more specific term if possible)
- NT   Advanced Courses
       Conversational Language Courses
       Credit Courses
       Education Courses
       Elective Courses
       Intensive Language Courses
       Introductory Courses
       Methods Courses
       Minicourses
       Noncredit Courses
       Practicums
       Refresher Courses
       Required Courses
       Telecourses
       United States Government (Course)
       Units of Study
- BT   Curriculum
- RT   Auditing (Coursework)
       Course Descriptions
       Course Evaluation
       Course Objectives
       Course Organization
       Course Selection (Students)
       Courseware
       Intellectual Disciplines

Courseware   JUN. 1984
Postings: 3,030   GC: 720
- SN   Computer software and accompanying documentation written for instructional applications (Note: Prior to Jun84, this concept was indexed by "Computer Programs," postings of which have since been merged to "Computer Software")
- UF   Courseware Development #
       Courseware Evaluation #
       Courseware Reviews #
       Courseware Selection #
       Instructional Software
- NT   Microworlds
- BT   Computer Software
       Instructional Materials
- RT   Audiovisual Aids
       Autoinstructional Aids
       Computer Assisted Instruction
       Computer Software Development
       Computer Software Evaluation
       Computer Software Reviews
       Computer Software Selection
       Courses
       Integrated Learning Systems
       Learner Controlled Instruction
       Programmed Instructional Materials
       Teaching Machines

Courseware Development
- USE   Computer Software Development
- AND   Courseware

Courseware Evaluation
- USE   Computer Software Evaluation
- AND   Courseware

Courseware Reviews
- USE   Computer Software Reviews
- AND   Courseware

Courseware Selection
- USE   Computer Software Selection
- AND   Courseware

Court Action
- USE   Court Litigation

Court Cases (1966 1980)
- USE   Court Litigation

Court Decisions
- USE   Court Litigation

Court Doctrine   JUL. 1966
Postings: 242   GC: 610
- BT   Standards
- RT   Courts
       Public Policy

Court Judges   AUG. 1980
Postings: 196   GC: 610
- SN   Public officials authorized to hear and decide cases in courts of law
- UF   Magistrates
- BT   Judges
       Public Officials
- RT   Compliance (Legal)
       Court Litigation
       Courts
       Hearings
       Justice
       Lawyers
       Legal Responsibility
       Legislators
       Sentencing

Court Litigation   JUL. 1966
Postings: 10,559   GC: 610
- SN   Legal action or process in a court
- UF   Court Action
       Court Cases (1966 1980)
       Court Decisions
       Federal Court Litigation (1966 1980) #
       Judicial Action
       Legal Decisions
       Legal Judgment
       Litigation
       State Court Litigation #
- NT   Desegregation Litigation
- RT   Civil Law
       Compliance (Legal)
       Court Judges
       Court Reporters
       Courts
       Educational Malpractice
       Evidence (Legal)
       Federal Courts
       Juries
       Juvenile Courts
       Laws
       Lawyers
       Legal Problems
       Legal Responsibility
       Libel and Slander
       Malpractice
       Negligence
       State Courts
       Torts

Court Reporters   JUL. 1966
Postings: 30   GC: 640
- SN   Workers involved in the recording (by stenotype) and transcription of legal proceedings
- BT   Clerical Workers
- RT   Court Litigation
       Courts
       Shorthand
       Typewriting

Court Role   JUL. 1966
Postings: 782   GC: 610
- UF   Judicial Role
- BT   Institutional Role
- RT   Courts
       Government Role

Courts   JUL. 1966
Postings: 454   GC: 610
- UF   Judicial System
- NT   Federal Courts
       Juvenile Courts
       State Courts
- BT   Institutions
- RT   Court Doctrine
       Court Judges
       Court Litigation
       Court Reporters
       Court Role
       Equal Protection
       Evidence (Legal)
       Hearings
       Juries
       Justice
       Laws
       Sentencing

Covert Response   JUL. 1966
Postings: 66   GC: 110
- BT   Responses
- RT   Overt Response

CPR (Medicine)
- USE   Cardiopulmonary Resuscitation

Crack   DEC. 1989
Postings: 76   GC: 210
- SN   Easily manufactured form of highly purified cocaine prepared with other ingredients for smoking, and known to be especially potent and addictive
- UF   Crack Babies #
- BT   Cocaine
- RT   Drug Abuse
       Drug Addiction
       Drug Legislation
       Drug Rehabilitation
       Drug Use
       Illegal Drug Use
       Stimulants

Crack Babies
- USE   Crack
- AND   Prenatal Drug Exposure

Craft Workers   APR. 1981
Postings: 139   GC: 640
- UF   Artisans
       Craftsmen (1970 1981)
- BT   Skilled Workers
- RT   Building Trades
       Design Crafts
       Handicrafts
       Industrial Arts
       Needle Trades

Crafts
- USE   Handicrafts

Crafts Rooms (1966 1980)
- USE   Educational Facilities
- AND   Handicrafts

Craftsmen (1970 1981)
- USE   Craft Workers

Creationism   MAY 1981
Postings: 386   GC: 430
- SN   Theory or belief that the universe and various forms of life were created by a transcendent god out of nothing—also, the theological doctrine that God creates a new human soul for each individual born
- UF   Scientific Creationism
       Special Creation Theory
- RT   Evolution
       Religion
       Religious Factors

Creative Ability (1968 1980)
- USE   Creativity

Creative Activities   JUL. 1966
Postings: 1,327   GC: 310
- NT   Brainstorming
       Creative Art
       Creative Expression
       Creative Writing
       Improvisation
- BT   Activities
- RT   Art Activities
       Creative Development
       Creativity

= Two or more Descriptors are used to represent this term.
The term's main entry shows the appropriate coordination.

Enrichment Activities
Handicrafts

Creative Art   *JUL. 1966*
Postings: 588   GC: 420
SN   Art involving original thought, imagination, structural ogranization, and personal expression or interpretation—also includes programs encouraging creative art
NT   Creative Dramatics
BT   Art
Creative Activities
RT   Art Activities
Art Therapy
Childrens Art
Freehand Drawing
Studio Art
Surrealism

Creative Development   *JUL. 1966*
Postings: 1,342   GC: 120
SN   Development of creative skills and aptitudes
BT   Individual Development
RT   Creative Activities
Creativity
Creativity Tests
Intellectual Development
Talent Development

Creative Dramatics   *JUL. 1966*
Postings: 698   GC: 420
SN   Activities where participants create informal, nonscripted plays using their own words and movements
BT   Creative Art
Dramatics
RT   Acting
Dramatic Play
Improvisation
Pantomime
Readers Theater
Skits

Creative Expression   *JUL. 1966*
Postings: 1,126   GC: 420
BT   Creative Activities
RT   Art Expression
Creativity
Creativity Tests
Dramatic Play
Improvisation
Self Expression

Creative Reading (1966 1980)   *MAR. 1980*
Postings: 106   GC: 460
SN   Invalid Descriptor—used inconsistently in indexing—see such Descriptors as "Oral Interpretation," "Critical Reading," "Creative Thinking," etc.

Creative Spelling
USE   Invented Spelling

Creative Teaching   *JUL. 1966*
Postings: 987   GC: 310
SN   Development and use of novel, original, or inventive teaching methods (Note: Refers to teaching that results from the teacher's creativity, not to teaching that is intended to develop the learner's creativity)
BT   Teaching Methods
RT   Creativity
Instructional Innovation

Creative Thinking   *JUL. 1966*
Postings: 2,141   GC: 110
NT   Divergent Thinking
Productive Thinking
BT   Cognitive Processes
RT   Concept Formation
Creativity
Creativity Tests
Discovery Processes

Heuristics
Imagination
Improvisation
Intuition
Inventions
Problem Solving
Thinking Skills
Transcendental Meditation
Visualization

Creative Thinking Tests
USE   Creativity Tests

Creative Writing   *JUL. 1966*
Postings: 2,990   GC: 400
SN   Writing characterized by originality, imaginativeness, and expressiveness
BT   Creative Activities
Writing (Composition)
RT   Childrens Writing
Descriptive Writing
Expository Writing
Free Writing
Heuristics
Journal Writing
Literary Devices
Playwriting
Poetry
Prose
Rhetorical Invention
Student Writing Models

Creativity   *JUL. 1966*
Postings: 4,955   GC: 120
SN   The attribute of constructive originality, often manifested in the ability to discover new solutions to problems or find new modes of artistic expression
UF   Creative Ability (1968 1980)
Originality (1966 1980)
NT   Imagination
BT   Psychological Characteristics
RT   Art Expression
Auteurism
Concept Formation
Creative Activities
Creative Development
Creative Expression
Creative Teaching
Creative Thinking
Creativity Research
Creativity Tests
Discovery Processes
Individualism
Intelligence
Inventions
Personality Traits
Rhetorical Invention
Self Expression
Talent

Creativity Measures
USE   Creativity Tests

Creativity Research   *JUL. 1966*
Postings: 519   GC: 810
SN   Basic, applied, and developmental research conducted to advance knowledge about constructive originality (Note: As of Oct81, use as a minor Descriptor for examples of this kind of research—use as a major Descriptor only as the subject of a document)
BT   Research
RT   Creativity
Creativity Tests

Creativity Tests   *MAR. 1971*
Postings: 391   GC: 830
SN   Tests used to indicate an individual's originality, inventiveness, or imagination
UF   Creative Thinking Tests
Creativity Measures
BT   Tests
RT   Creative Development
Creative Expression
Creative Thinking
Creativity

Creativity Research
Intelligence Tests
Projective Measures
Talent Identification

Credentials   *JUL. 1966*
Postings: 780   GC: 340
NT   Educational Certificates
Portfolios (Background Materials)
Resumes (Personal)
BT   Records (Forms)
RT   Background
Certification
Continuing Education Units
Degrees (Academic)
Equivalency Tests
Evaluation
Experience
Prerequisites
Qualifications
Reputation
Selection
Special Degree Programs
Standards

Credibility   *DEC. 1974*
Postings: 931   GC: 520
SN   Compatibility of a statement or situation with what is generally perceived as true or possible
UF   Believability
Source Credibility
Trustworthiness
BT   Relationship
RT   Beliefs
Communication (Thought Transfer)
Communication Skills
Deception
Ethics
Honesty
Integrity
Interpersonal Relationship
Opinions
Persuasive Discourse
Political Attitudes
Psychological Patterns
Public Opinion
Reputation
Trust (Psychology)
Values

Credit (Finance)   *AUG. 1968*
Postings: 576   GC: 620
RT   Debt (Financial)
Economics
Eligibility
Financial Aid Applicants
Financial Needs
Financial Services
Financial Support
Interest (Finance)
Investment
Loan Default
Loan Repayment
Merchandising
Money Management
Ownership
Paying for College
Student Loan Programs

Credit by Examination
USE   Equivalency Tests

Credit Courses   *JUL. 1966*
Postings: 596   GC: 350
BT   Courses
RT   College Credits
Credits
Grades (Scholastic)
Noncredit Courses

Credit No Credit Grading   *SEP. 1971*
Postings: 61   GC: 320
SN   Grading system in which a student's failure either is not recorded or is recorded as "no credit," which does not affect his or her grade point average, and

students who pass are given regular grades
UF   Pass No Credit Grading
Pass No Record Grading
BT   Grading
RT   College Credits
Credits
Cutting Scores
Grades (Scholastic)
Nongraded Student Evaluation
Pass Fail Grading

Credits   *JUL. 1966*
Postings: 543   GC: 340
SN   Units for expressing quantitatively the work completed by a student (Note: For postsecondary students, use "College Credits")
UF   Student Credit Hours
NT   College Credits
Continuing Education Units
RT   Academic Records
Auditing (Coursework)
Certification
Credit Courses
Credit No Credit Grading
Educational Certificates
Experiential Learning
Grades (Scholastic)
Graduation Requirements
Pass Fail Grading
Prerequisites
Prior Learning
Required Courses
Transfer Policy
Transfer Programs

Cree   *APR. 1969*
Postings: 43   GC: 440
SN   Algonquian language of the Cree tribe of American Indians
BT   American Indian Languages
RT   Cree (Tribe)

Cree (Tribe)   *JAN. 1994*
Postings: 57   GC: 560
SN   An American Indian people of subarctic Canada (British Columbia to Labrador) and the northern U.S. plains (Montana and North Dakota) (also, dispersed kin)
BT   American Indians
Tribes
RT   Canada Natives
Cree

Creoles   *JUL. 1966*
Postings: 334   GC: 440
SN   Mixed natural languages—composed of elements of different languages in areas of intensive language contact—that develop from pidgins and have native speakers
NT   Gullah
Haitian Creole
Mauritian Creole
Sierra Leone Creole
BT   Language Variation
Languages
RT   Linguistic Borrowing
Pidgins

Crew Leaders   *JUL. 1966*
Postings: 20   GC: 410
UF   Farm Foremen
BT   Supervisors
RT   Agricultural Laborers
Migrant Workers

Crib Death
USE   Sudden Infant Death Syndrome

Crime   *JUL. 1966*
Postings: 2,053   GC: 530
NT   Delinquency
International Crimes
BT   Antisocial Behavior
RT   Aggression

= Two or more Descriptors are used to represent this term.
The term's main entry shows the appropriate coordination.

Alarm Systems
Computer Security
Correctional Institutions
Correctional Rehabilitation
Crime Prevention
Criminal Law
Criminals
Criminology
Driving While Intoxicated
Drug Addiction
Evidence (Legal)
Family Violence
Fines (Penalties)
Fraud
Homicide
Illegal Drug Use
Incest
Juvenile Courts
Law Enforcement
Libel and Slander
Malpractice
Parole Officers
Police
Police Action
Polygraphs
Probation Officers
Rape
Resistance to Temptation
School Security
Search and Seizure
Security Personnel
Sentencing
Stealing
Terrorism
Vandalism
Victims of Crime
Violence

Crime Prevention   MAR. 1982
     Postings: 653   GC: 520
SN   Measures taken to forestall a delinquent or criminal act
NT   Delinquency Prevention
BT   Prevention
RT   Alarm Systems
     Community Programs
     Computer Security
     Correctional Rehabilitation
     Crime
     Criminal Law
     Criminals
     Law Enforcement
     Police
     Police Action
     Police Community Relationship
     Police School Relationship
     Resistance to Temptation
     School Security
     Security Personnel

Criminal Law   DEC. 1974
     Postings: 530   GC: 610
SN   Branch of jurisprudence that relates to crimes and their punishments
BT   Laws
RT   Capital Punishment
     Civil Law
     Crime
     Crime Prevention
     Criminals
     Criminology
     Law Enforcement
     Law Related Education
     Legal Education (Professions)
     Police
     Police Education
     Sentencing

Criminals   JUL. 1966
     Postings: 968   GC: 530
UF   Convicts
BT   Groups
RT   Correctional Education
     Correctional Institutions
     Correctional Rehabilitation
     Crime
     Crime Prevention
     Criminal Law
     Delinquency
     Prisoners

Recidivism
Sentencing

Criminology   MAY 1969
     Postings: 260   GC: 400
BT   Sociology
RT   Correctional Institutions
     Correctional Rehabilitation
     Crime
     Criminal Law
     Prisoners
     Social Psychology
     Sociologists

Crippled Children (1968 1980)
USE   Physical Disabilities

Crisis Intervention   MAR. 1980
     Postings: 1,001   GC: 230
SN   Techniques used to avert or deal with psychiatric or medical emergencies, as potential suicide, domestic violence, and drug overdose (Note: Prior to Aug99, this term was not restricted by a Scope Note)
UF   Crisis Therapy (1969 1980)
BT   Intervention
RT   Counseling
     Crisis Management
     Emergency Programs
     Hotlines (Public)
     Psychiatric Services
     Psychotherapy

Crisis Management   AUG. 1999
     Postings: 276   GC: 320
SN   Implementation of processes designed to prevent or alleviate crisis situations (e.g., violence, threats of violence, natural disasters, significant failures, scandals) in an organization, system, community, or environment (Note: Prior to Aug99, this concept was occasionally indexed "Crisis Intervention," which was not scoped)
BT   Administration
RT   Conflict Resolution
     Crisis Intervention
     Emergency Programs
     Organizational Communication
     Public Relations

Crisis Therapy (1969 1980)
USE   Crisis Intervention

Criteria   JUL. 1966
     Postings: 1,224   GC: 520
SN   Objective things, specifications, or requirements by reference to which judgments are made or confirmed
NT   Admission Criteria
     Evaluation Criteria
     Lesson Observation Criteria
BT   Standards
RT   Predictor Variables
     Prerequisites
     Quotas
     Specifications

Criterion Referenced Education
USE   Competency Based Education

Criterion Referenced Teacher Education
USE   Competency Based Teacher Education

Criterion Referenced Tests   SEP. 1970
     Postings: 2,552   GC: 830
SN   Tests in which the items are linked to explicitly stated objectives and where the scores are interpreted in terms of these objectives rather than a group norm
UF   Objective Referenced Tests
NT   Mastery Tests
BT   Tests
RT   Achievement Tests

Curriculum Based Assessment
Cutting Scores
Diagnostic Tests
Informal Reading Inventories
Item Banks
Measurement Techniques
Norm Referenced Tests
Performance Based Assessment
Performance Tests
Standardized Tests
Test Construction
Test Interpretation

Criterion Validity (Concurrent)
USE   Concurrent Validity

Criterion Validity (Predictive)
USE   Predictive Validity

Critical Analysis
USE   Criticism

Critical Evaluation
USE   Criticism

Critical Incidents Method   JUL. 1966
     Postings: 252   GC: 820
SN   Procedure used to gather examples of effective or ineffective behavior with respect to a designated activity to determine the requirements for its success
BT   Methods
RT   Ability Identification
     Evaluation Methods
     Job Analysis
     Observation
     Problem Solving
     Research Methodology
     Simulation
     Skill Analysis
     Task Analysis

Critical Path Method   JUL. 1966
     Postings: 181   GC: 320
SN   Technique used to coordinate and schedule the sequential activities of a project to complete it as efficiently and quickly as possible (Note: See also the Identifier "Program Evaluation and Review Technique"—prior to Mar80, the instruction "Path Analysis, USE Critical Path Method" was carried in the Thesaurus)
BT   Methods
RT   Construction Management
     Fast Track Scheduling
     Flow Charts
     Graphs
     Management Systems
     Operations Research
     Planning
     Scheduling
     Sequential Approach
     Systems Analysis

Critical Reading   JUL. 1966
     Postings: 1,463   GC: 460
SN   Reading carefully to thoroughly comprehend and evaluate what is read
BT   Reading
RT   Content Area Reading
     Inferences
     Literary Criticism
     Reading Comprehension

Critical Scores
USE   Cutting Scores

Critical Theory   APR. 1990
     Postings: 556   GC: 810
SN   An evaluative approach to social science research, associated with Germany's neo-Marxist "Frankfurt School" (1923–69), that aims to criticize as well as analyze society—opposing the political orthodoxy of modern communism, its goal is

to promote human emancipatory forces and to expose ideas and systems that impede them
BT   Social Science Research
     Theories
RT   Critical Thinking
     Educational Sociology
     Hermeneutics
     Humanization
     Marxian Analysis
     Phenomenology
     Postmodernism
     Social Change
     Social Theories
     Social Values
     Sociology

Critical Thinking   JUL. 1966
     Postings: 6,741   GC: 110
NT   Evaluative Thinking
BT   Cognitive Processes
RT   Citizenship Education
     Consciousness Raising
     Controversial Issues (Course Content)
     Convergent Thinking
     Critical Theory
     Decision Making
     Formal Operations
     Guided Design
     Heuristics
     Inferences
     Logical Thinking
     Problem Based Learning
     Problem Solving
     Productive Thinking
     Reflective Teaching
     Thinking Skills
     Transformative Learning

Critical Viewing   AUG. 1989
     Postings: 249   GC: 400
SN   Viewing carefully to comprehend and evaluate information presented by television, video recordings, and other visual media
RT   Art Criticism
     Film Criticism
     Inferences
     Television Viewing
     Visual Literacy

Criticism   APR. 1990
     Postings: 708   GC: 820
SN   Showing fault and/or worth in anything—frequently, the analysis, study, and evaluation of works of art or discourse (Note: Use a more specific term if possible)
UF   Critical Analysis
     Critical Evaluation
NT   Art Criticism
     Feminist Criticism
     Film Criticism
     Literary Criticism
RT   Evaluation
     Evaluation Methods
     Hermeneutics
     Humanities
     Learning Processes
     Praise
     Questioning Techniques
     Research
     Social Influences
     Value Judgment
     Verbal Abuse

Crop Harvesting
USE   Harvesting

Crop Planting
USE   Agronomy
AND   Horticulture

Crop Processing Occupations   JAN. 1969
     Postings: 33   GC: 410
UF   Grain Elevator Occupations
BT   Off Farm Agricultural Occupations
RT   Agricultural Production
     Agronomy

= Two or more Descriptors are used to represent this term.
The term's main entry shows the appropriate coordination.

Field Crops
Harvesting

Crop Production
USE   Agricultural Production

Cross Age Helping
USE   Cross Age Teaching

Cross Age Teaching   OCT. 1968
Postings: 657   GC: 310
SN   Utilization of older students from higher
grade levels to provide increased help
and attention for younger students at
lower grade levels
UF   Cross Age Helping
BT   Teaching Methods
RT   Interpersonal Relationship
Mixed Age Grouping
Peer Teaching
Remedial Instruction
Social Experience
Socialization
Tutorial Programs
Tutoring

Cross Categorical Education
USE   Noncategorical Education

Cross Cultural Communication
USE   Intercultural Communication

Cross Cultural Studies   AUG. 1969
Postings: 6,295   GC: 400
SN   Systematic efforts to compare sociologi-
cal, psychological, anthropological. . . as-
pects of two or more cultural groups,
either within the same country or in
different countries
UF   Cultural Comparisons
BT   Research
RT   Anthropology
Area Studies
Biculturalism
Bidialectalism
Bilingualism
Comparative Analysis
Comparative Education
Contrastive Linguistics
Cultural Background
Cultural Context
Cultural Differences
Cultural Education
Cultural Exchange
Cultural Influences
Cultural Interrelationships
Cultural Pluralism
Cultural Traits
Culture
Culture Conflict
Culture Contact
Culture Fair Tests
Ethnic Groups
Ethnic Relations
Ethnic Studies
Ethnicity
Ethnology
Folk Culture
Foreign Culture
Global Education
Human Geography
Intercultural Programs
Intergroup Relations
International Education
International Studies
Language Minorities
Migrants
Minority Groups
Multicultural Education
Multicultural Textbooks
Multilingualism
Religion Studies
Sociocultural Patterns
Sociology
Subcultures
Urban Culture

Cross Cultural Tests
USE   Culture Fair Tests

Cross Cultural Training   JUL. 1966
Postings: 1,900   GC: 400
SN   Training in communicative, behavioral,
and attitudinal skills required for suc-
cessful interaction with individuals of
other cultures—often used with person-
nel about to undertake overseas assign-
ments (Note: Prior to Jan79, "Cross
Cultural Training" was frequently used
for "Multicultural Education")
UF   Bicultural Training
Multicultural Training
Multiethnic Training
BT   Training
RT   Biculturalism
Cultural Awareness
Cultural Background
Cultural Differences
Cultural Education
Cultural Interrelationships
Cultural Pluralism
Culture
Culture Contact
Ethnic Relations
Exchange Programs
Foreign Culture
Indigenous Personnel
Intercultural Communication
Intercultural Programs
Interdisciplinary Approach
Intergroup Relations
International Communication
International Educational Exchange
International Relations
Multicultural Education
Social Integration
Sociocultural Patterns

Cross Eyes
USE   Strabismus

Cross Sectional Studies   APR. 1970
Postings: 346   GC: 810
SN   Studies that establish norms by assess-
ing large groups of people, practices, or
programs at a given time, as differenti-
ated from longitudinal studies of groups,
etc., at various times (Note: As of Oct81,
use as a minor Descriptor for examples
of this kind of research—use as a major
Descriptor only as the subject of a docu-
ment)
BT   Case Studies
RT   Cohort Analysis
Longitudinal Studies
Norms
Sampling

Crowding   MAR. 1982
Postings: 129   GC: 520
SN   Excessive number of individuals or enti-
ties in relation to available space
RT   Class Size
Ecological Factors
Environmental Influences
Environmental Standards
Overpopulation
Personal Space
Physical Environment
Physical Mobility
Proximity
Social Behavior
Space Utilization
Stress Variables
Urban Environment

Crude Oil
USE   Oil

Crude Scores
USE   Raw Scores

Crying   DEC. 1989
Postings: 116   GC: 120
SN   Sobbing or shedding tears
BT   Behavior
RT   Emotional Problems
Emotional Response
Infant Behavior
Nonverbal Communication
Personality Traits

Crystallography   AUG. 1982
Postings: 97   GC: 490
SN   The science of crystal structure and phe-
nomena
BT   Physical Sciences
RT   Atomic Structure
Chemical Bonding
Chemistry
Earth Science
Electronics
Geology
Matter
Metallurgy
Mineralogy
Molecular Structure
Optics
Petrology
Physical Chemistry
Physics
Radiology
Semiconductor Devices
Spectroscopy
Structural Analysis (Science)

Cuban Americans
USE   Cubans
AND   Hispanic Americans

Cubans   JUN. 1973
Postings: 343   GC: 560
UF   Cuban Americans #
BT   Latin Americans
RT   Ethnic Groups
Hispanic Americans
Spanish Speaking

Cubic Measure
USE   Volume (Mathematics)

Cue Cards
USE   Cues

Cued Speech   APR. 1969
Postings: 49   GC: 220
SN   Method of language learning for the deaf
utilizing manual configurations as a sup-
plement to lipreading
BT   Manual Communication
RT   Deaf Interpreting
Finger Spelling
Lipreading
Oral Communication Method
Speech
Visual Learning

Cues   OCT. 1968
Postings: 1,693   GC: 110
UF   Clues
Cue Cards
Prompts
NT   Context Clues
BT   Stimuli
RT   Dimensional Preference
Memory
Miscue Analysis
Mnemonics
Notetaking
Prompting
Recall (Psychology)
Retention (Psychology)

Cuing
USE   Prompting

Cultural Activities   JUL. 1966
Postings: 1,262   GC: 560
SN   Experiences, events, ceremonies, etc.,
that increase individuals' knowledge or
enjoyment of their own or another group's
cultural, social, intellectual, or artistic
heritage
UF   Cultural Events (1966 1980)
BT   Activities
RT   Art Activities
Cultural Awareness
Cultural Background
Cultural Education
Cultural Enrichment
Cultural Interrelationships
Cultural Literacy
Cultural Maintenance
Cultural Opportunities
Cultural Relevance
Culture
Dance
Enrichment Activities
Fine Arts
Holidays
Multicultural Education
Music Activities
Religion
Theater Arts
Visual Arts

Cultural Awareness   JUL. 1966
Postings: 9,333   GC: 560
UF   Cultural Understanding
RT   Afrocentrism
Area Studies
Biculturalism
Cross Cultural Training
Cultural Activities
Cultural Background
Cultural Images
Cultural Influences
Cultural Literacy
Cultural Maintenance
Cultural Opportunities
Cultural Pluralism
Culturally Relevant Education
Culture
Culture Conflict
Culture Contact
Ethnicity
Freedom Schools
Global Approach
Intercultural Communication
Intercultural Programs
Metalinguistics
Multicultural Education
Nationalism
Political Correctness
Religion Studies
Second Language Learning
Student Exchange Programs

Cultural Background   JUL. 1966
Postings: 3,999   GC: 560
SN   Collection of mores, folkways, and insti-
tutions that constitutes the social heri-
tage of an individual or group
UF   Cultural Heritage
Ethnic Heritage
BT   Background
RT   American Indian Studies
Biculturalism
Black Studies
Cross Cultural Studies
Cross Cultural Training
Cultural Activities
Cultural Awareness
Cultural Education
Cultural Maintenance
Cultural Pluralism
Cultural Relevance
Cultural Traits
Culture
Ethnic Groups
Ethnic Origins
Ethnic Studies
Ethnology
Heritage Education
Indigenous Populations
Multicultural Education
Non Western Civilization

= Two or more Descriptors are used to represent this term.
The term's main entry shows the appropriate coordination.

Western Civilization
World Views

Cultural Centers　　　　　　*JUL. 1966*
　　Postings: 211　　　　　　　GC: 920
BT　Resource Centers
RT　Arts Centers
　　Cultural Enrichment
　　Culture
　　Museums

Cultural Characteristics
USE　Cultural Traits

Cultural Comparisons
USE　Cross Cultural Studies

Cultural Context　　　　　　*JUL. 1966*
　　Postings: 5,304　　　　　　GC: 560
UF　Cultural Environment (1966 1980)
BT　Environment
RT　Aesthetic Values
　　American Dream
　　Anthropological Linguistics
　　Biculturalism
　　Context Effect
　　Cross Cultural Studies
　　Cultural Influences
　　Cultural Isolation
　　Cultural Literacy
　　Cultural Maintenance
　　Cultural Relevance
　　Cultural Traits
　　Culture
　　Culture Contact
　　Educational Anthropology
　　Ethnography
　　Ethnology
　　Ethnomathematics
　　Hermeneutics
　　Holidays
　　Multicultural Education
　　Non Western Civilization
　　Proverbs
　　Social Characteristics
　　Social Environment
　　Social History
　　Social Structure
　　Social Values
　　Sociocultural Patterns
　　Western Civilization

Cultural Differences　　　　*JUL. 1966*
　　Postings: 10,937　　　　　GC: 560
SN　(Note: Use a more precise term if possible)
UF　Diversity (Cultural) as an Observation
　　or a Fact
BT　Differences
RT　Advantaged
　　Biculturalism
　　Cross Cultural Studies
　　Cross Cultural Training
　　Cultural Interrelationships
　　Cultural Pluralism
　　Cultural Traits
　　Culture
　　Diversity (Faculty)
　　Diversity (Institutional)
　　Diversity (Student)
　　Ethnic Groups
　　Ethnic Relations
　　Ethnicity
　　Ethnocentrism
　　Individual Differences
　　Intercultural Communication
　　Intermarriage
　　Language Minorities
　　Minority Groups
　　Multicultural Education
　　Nature Nurture Controversy
　　Racial Attitudes
　　Racial Differences
　　Racial Relations
　　Rural Urban Differences
　　Social Bias
　　Social Differences
　　Subcultures

Cultural Disadvantagement (1966 1980)
USE　Disadvantaged

Cultural Education　　　　　*JUL. 1966*
　　Postings: 4,024　　　　　　GC: 400
SN　Education concerned with a group's cultural, social, intellectual, or artistic heritage
NT　Heritage Education
BT　Education
RT　American Indian Studies
　　Black Studies
　　Cross Cultural Studies
　　Cross Cultural Training
　　Cultural Activities
　　Cultural Background
　　Cultural Enrichment
　　Cultural Literacy
　　Cultural Maintenance
　　Culturally Relevant Education
　　Culture
　　Ethnic Groups
　　Ethnic Studies
　　Folk Culture
　　Folk Schools
　　Freedom Schools
　　Intercultural Programs
　　Multicultural Textbooks
　　Oral Tradition
　　Religion Studies
　　Social Studies

Cultural Enrichment　　　　*JUL. 1966*
　　Postings: 1,210　　　　　　GC: 310
BT　Enrichment
RT　Aesthetic Education
　　Compensatory Education
　　Cultural Activities
　　Cultural Centers
　　Cultural Education
　　Cultural Exchange
　　Cultural Literacy
　　Cultural Relevance
　　Culture
　　Fine Arts
　　Freedom Schools
　　Intercultural Programs

Cultural Environment (1966 1980)
USE　Cultural Context

Cultural Events (1966 1980)
USE　Cultural Activities

Cultural Exchange　　　　　*JUL. 1966*
　　Postings: 849　　　　　　　GC: 560
UF　Cultural Interaction
RT　Cross Cultural Studies
　　Cultural Enrichment
　　Cultural Influences
　　Culture
　　Culture Contact
　　Exchange Programs
　　Intercultural Communication
　　Intercultural Programs
　　International Educational Exchange

Cultural Factors (1966 1980)
USE　Cultural Influences

Cultural Geography
USE　Human Geography

Cultural Heritage
USE　Cultural Background

Cultural Images　　　　　　*JUL. 1966*
　　Postings: 971　　　　　　　GC: 540
RT　American Indian Studies
　　Black Studies
　　Cultural Awareness
　　Cultural Traits
　　Culture
　　Ethnic Groups
　　Ethnicity

Ethnocentrism
Stereotypes

Cultural Influences　　　　*MAR. 1980*
　　Postings: 7,990　　　　　　GC: 520
UF　Cultural Factors (1966 1980)
BT　Influences
RT　Biculturalism
　　Cross Cultural Studies
　　Cultural Awareness
　　Cultural Context
　　Cultural Exchange
　　Cultural Interrelationships
　　Cultural Literacy
　　Cultural Pluralism
　　Cultural Relevance
　　Cultural Traits
　　Culture
　　Culture Contact
　　Culture Lag
　　Ethnic Studies
　　Intercultural Programs
　　Language Role
　　Life Style
　　Linguistic Input
　　Minority Group Influences
　　Modernization
　　Nature Nurture Controversy
　　Racial Factors
　　Religious Factors
　　Social Influences
　　Sociocultural Patterns
　　Subcultures
　　Traditionalism
　　Work Ethic
　　World Views

Cultural Interaction
USE　Cultural Exchange

Cultural Interrelationships　*JUL. 1966*
　　Postings: 1,305　　　　　　GC: 560
BT　Relationship
RT　Biculturalism
　　Cross Cultural Studies
　　Cross Cultural Training
　　Cultural Activities
　　Cultural Differences
　　Cultural Influences
　　Cultural Pluralism
　　Cultural Traits
　　Culture
　　Ethnic Relations
　　Ethnology
　　Intercultural Communication
　　Intercultural Programs
　　Multicultural Education
　　Racial Relations
　　Social Influences
　　Social Integration
　　Sociocultural Patterns

Cultural Isolation　　　　　*JUL. 1966*
　　Postings: 254　　　　　　　GC: 560
SN　A subculture's relative lack of participation in, or communication with, the larger cultural system—can be internally or externally imposed
RT　Alienation
　　Cultural Context
　　Culture
　　Culture Conflict
　　Culture Contact
　　Culture Lag
　　Disadvantaged Environment
　　Geographic Isolation
　　Professional Isolation
　　Social Isolation
　　Subcultures

Cultural Lag
USE　Culture Lag

Cultural Literacy　　　　　*OCT. 1993*
　　Postings: 342　　　　　　　GC: 560
SN　Having sufficient common knowledge, i.e., educational background, experiences, basic skills, and training, to function

competently in a given society (the greater the level of comprehension of the given society's habits, attitudes, history, etc., the higher the level of cultural literacy)
RT　Comprehension
　　Cultural Activities
　　Cultural Awareness
　　Cultural Context
　　Cultural Education
　　Cultural Enrichment
　　Cultural Influences
　　Cultural Opportunities
　　Cultural Pluralism
　　Culture
　　Humanities
　　Knowledge Level
　　Literacy
　　Minimum Competencies
　　Multicultural Education
　　Socialization
　　Technological Literacy

Cultural Maintenance　　　*SEP. 1994*
　　Postings: 425　　　　　　　GC: 560
SN　The effort to sustain a culture by asserting its way of life (the ideology, life style, arts, language, etc.) and preserving its material embodiment (landscapes, architecture, and other artifacts)
UF　Cultural Preservation
　　Cultural Revitalization
RT　Cultural Activities
　　Cultural Awareness
　　Cultural Background
　　Cultural Context
　　Cultural Education
　　Culture
　　Ethnic Groups
　　Heritage Education
　　Language Maintenance
　　Multicultural Education
　　Sociocultural Patterns
　　Traditionalism

Cultural Opportunities　　　*JUL. 1966*
　　Postings: 124　　　　　　　GC: 540
SN　Circumstances or conditions that enable individuals or groups to attend or participate in cultural activities
BT　Opportunities
RT　Cultural Activities
　　Cultural Awareness
　　Cultural Literacy
　　Culture

Cultural Pluralism　　　　　*JUL. 1966*
　　Postings: 5,885　　　　　　GC: 520
UF　Diversity (Cultural) as a Value
　　Multiculturalism
NT　Biculturalism
RT　Acculturation
　　Anthropology
　　Bilingualism
　　Cross Cultural Studies
　　Cross Cultural Training
　　Cultural Awareness
　　Cultural Background
　　Cultural Differences
　　Cultural Influences
　　Cultural Interrelationships
　　Cultural Literacy
　　Culture
　　Culture Conflict
　　Culture Contact
　　Diversity (Faculty)
　　Diversity (Institutional)
　　Diversity (Student)
　　Ethnic Relations
　　Ethnicity
　　Ethnology
　　Intercultural Communication
　　Intercultural Programs
　　Language Minorities
　　Minority Groups
　　Multicultural Education
　　Multilingualism
　　Political Correctness
　　Postmodernism
　　Racial Relations

Sociocultural Patterns
United States History

Cultural Preservation
USE   Cultural Maintenance

Cultural Relevance   MAY 1995
        Postings: 191   GC: 560
SN   Applicability of materials, methods, or
        programs to one's own ethnicity, social
        status, gender, religion, home and com-
        munity environment, and/or personal ex-
        periences (Note: If possible, use the more
        specific term "Culturally Relevant Edu-
        cation")
UF   Relevance (Cultural)
NT   Culturally Relevant Education
RT   Cultural Activities
        Cultural Background
        Cultural Context
        Cultural Enrichment
        Cultural Influences
        Cultural Traits
        Culture

Cultural Revitalization
USE   Cultural Maintenance

Cultural Traits   JUL. 1966
        Postings: 1,488   GC: 560
UF   Cultural Characteristics
RT   American Indian Studies
        Black Studies
        Cross Cultural Studies
        Cultural Background
        Cultural Context
        Cultural Differences
        Cultural Images
        Cultural Influences
        Cultural Interrelationships
        Cultural Relevance
        Culture
        Ethnicity
        Ideology
        Oral Tradition
        Personal Space
        Place of Residence
        Racial Identification
        Regional Characteristics
        Social Characteristics
        Student Subcultures
        Subcultures

Cultural Understanding
USE   Cultural Awareness

Culturally Advantaged (1967 1980)
USE   Advantaged

Culturally Appropriate Education
USE   Culturally Relevant Education

Culturally Disadvantaged (1966 1980)
USE   Disadvantaged

Culturally Relevant Education   MAY 1995
        Postings: 391   GC: 330
SN   Educational practices and resources that
        reflect the culture, values, customs, and
        beliefs of students (i.e., help to connect
        what is to be learned with the students'
        own lives)
UF   Culturally Appropriate Education
        Culturally Responsive Education
        Culture Based Curriculum
BT   Cultural Relevance
        Education
        Relevance (Education)
RT   Cultural Awareness
        Cultural Education
        Culture Fair Tests
        Multicultural Education
        Student Centered Curriculum

Culturally Responsive Education
USE   Culturally Relevant Education

Culture   JUL. 1966
        Postings: 1,491   GC: 560
SN   Set of patterns, of and for behavior, that
        regulate interaction and enable mutual
        communication among a plurality of peo-
        ple, establishing them into a particular
        and distinct human group—occasion-
        ally used in the more limited sense of the
        intellectual and aesthetic products of cul-
        ture (Note: Use a more specific term if
        possible)
UF   Customs (Culture)
NT   African Culture
        American Indian Culture
        Black Culture
        Burmese Culture
        Chinese Culture
        Dutch Culture
        Folk Culture
        Foreign Culture
        Islamic Culture
        Japanese Culture
        Korean Culture
        Latin American Culture
        Material Culture
        Middle Class Culture
        Non Western Civilization
        North American Culture
        Oral Tradition
        Popular Culture
        School Culture
        Spanish Culture
        Subcultures
        Urban Culture
        Western Civilization
RT   Acculturation
        Biculturalism
        Cross Cultural Studies
        Cross Cultural Training
        Cultural Activities
        Cultural Awareness
        Cultural Background
        Cultural Centers
        Cultural Context
        Cultural Differences
        Cultural Education
        Cultural Enrichment
        Cultural Exchange
        Cultural Images
        Cultural Influences
        Cultural Interrelationships
        Cultural Isolation
        Cultural Literacy
        Cultural Maintenance
        Cultural Opportunities
        Cultural Pluralism
        Cultural Relevance
        Cultural Traits
        Culture Conflict
        Culture Contact
        Culture Lag
        Educational Anthropology
        Ethnic Groups
        Humanities
        Intellectual History
        Intercultural Communication
        Intercultural Programs
        Minority Groups
        Multicultural Education
        Nonformal Education
        Race
        Religious Cultural Groups
        Social History
        Sociocultural Patterns

Culture Based Curriculum
USE   Culturally Relevant Education

Culture Conflict   JUL. 1966
        Postings: 2,052   GC: 520
UF   Culture Shock
BT   Conflict
RT   Biculturalism
        Cross Cultural Studies
        Cultural Awareness
        Cultural Isolation
        Cultural Pluralism

Culture
Ethnicity
Ethnocentrism
Family School Relationship
Religious Conflict
Revolution
Social Differences
Social Environment
Values

Culture Contact   JUL. 1966
        Postings: 764   GC: 560
RT   Biculturalism
        Cross Cultural Studies
        Cross Cultural Training
        Cultural Awareness
        Cultural Context
        Cultural Exchange
        Cultural Influences
        Cultural Isolation
        Cultural Pluralism
        Culture
        Intercultural Communication
        Intercultural Programs
        Multicultural Education

Culture Fair Tests   MAR. 1980
        Postings: 562   GC: 540
SN   Tests designed to minimize the effects of
        the differing cultures or experiences of
        national, ethnic, sexual, or socioeconomic
        groups
UF   Cross Cultural Tests
        Culture Free Tests (1967 1980)
BT   Tests
RT   Cross Cultural Studies
        Culturally Relevant Education
        Ethnic Groups
        Item Bias
        Multicultural Education
        Nonverbal Tests
        Test Bias
        Test Construction
        Testing Problems

Culture Free Tests (1967 1980)
USE   Culture Fair Tests

Culture Lag   JUL. 1966
        Postings: 68   GC: 560
SN   Delay that occurs when one part of a
        culture changes more slowly than an-
        other part—also refers to the strain that
        results from this discrepancy
UF   Cultural Lag
RT   Community Change
        Cultural Influences
        Cultural Isolation
        Culture
        Developing Nations
        Economic Change
        Futures (of Society)
        Industrialization
        Modernization
        Social Change
        Sociocultural Patterns
        Technological Advancement
        Urbanization

Culture Shock
USE   Culture Conflict

Culturing Techniques   MAY 1969
        Postings: 140   GC: 490
SN   Cultivation of living cells or micro-or-
        ganisms in a controlled artificial environ-
        ment
BT   Laboratory Procedures
RT   Botany
        Cytology
        Genetic Engineering
        Microbiology
        Mycology
        Physiology
        Zoology

Curiosity   JUL. 1966
        Postings: 334   GC: 120
BT   Personality Traits
RT   Attention
        Exploratory Behavior
        Interests
        Motivation

Current Awareness Services
USE   Selective Dissemination of Information

Current Events   JUL. 1966
        Postings: 842   GC: 400
RT   Citizenship Education
        Controversial Issues (Course Content)
        Political Science
        Social Studies
        World Affairs

Curriculum   JUL. 1966
        Postings: 11,768   GC: 350
SN   Plan incorporating a structured series of
        intended learning outcomes and associ-
        ated learning experiences—generally or-
        ganized as a related combination or se-
        ries of courses (Note: Use a more specific
        term if possible)
UF   Curriculum Content
        Teaching Areas
NT   Area Studies
        College Curriculum
        Continuous Progress Plan
        Core Curriculum
        Courses
        Elementary School Curriculum
        English Curriculum
        Ethnic Studies
        Experimental Curriculum
        Fused Curriculum
        Home Economics
        Honors Curriculum
        Integrated Curriculum
        Mathematics Curriculum
        Military Science
        Modern Language Curriculum
        National Curriculum
        Preschool Curriculum
        Religion Studies
        Science Curriculum
        Secondary School Curriculum
        Shop Curriculum
        Social Studies
        Speech Curriculum
        Spiral Curriculum
        Student Centered Curriculum
        Television Curriculum
        Unified Studies Curriculum
        Urban Studies
        Womens Studies
RT   Controversial Issues (Course Content)
        Course Content
        Curriculum Based Assessment
        Curriculum Design
        Curriculum Development
        Curriculum Enrichment
        Curriculum Evaluation
        Curriculum Guides
        Curriculum Problems
        Curriculum Research
        Curriculum Study Centers
        Education
        Extracurricular Activities
        Hidden Curriculum
        Immersion Programs
        Instruction
        Intellectual Disciplines
        Language of Instruction
        Pretechnology Programs
        School Activities
        Specialization
        State Curriculum Guides
        Writing Across the Curriculum

Curriculum Adaptation
USE   Curriculum Development

Curriculum Based Assessment   OCT. 1993
        Postings: 349   GC: 310
SN   Direct and frequent measurement of stu-

 # = Two or more Descriptors are used to represent this term.
The term's main entry shows the appropriate coordination.

dent performance on the classroom curriculum in order to ascertain student instructional needs—used principally for instructional decision making, the approach also supports screening, placement, and monitoring in special education (Note: See also the Identifier "Curriculum Related Testing")
UF   Curriculum Based Measurement
    Curriculum Referenced Assessment
BT   Student Evaluation
RT   Criterion Referenced Tests
    Curriculum
    Curriculum Development
    Diagnostic Teaching
    Educational Testing
    Evaluation Methods
    Individualized Education Programs
    Individualized Instruction
    Informal Assessment
    Special Education

Curriculum Based Measurement
USE   Curriculum Based Assessment

Curriculum Content
USE   Curriculum

Curriculum Design   *JUL. 1966*
    Postings: 8,830   GC: 320
SN   Arrangement of the component parts of a curriculum (Note: Prior to Mar80, the use of this term was not restricted by a Scope Note)
BT   Design
RT   Course Selection (Students)
    Curriculum
    Curriculum Development
    Curriculum Research
    Educational Strategies
    Flexible Progression
    Horizontal Organization
    Instructional Design
    Instructional Development
    Interdisciplinary Approach
    Sequential Approach
    Student Centered Curriculum
    Thematic Approach
    Vertical Organization

Curriculum Development   *JUL. 1966*
    Postings: 42,160   GC: 320
SN   Activities such as conceptualizing, planning, implementing, field testing, and researching that are intended to produce new curricula or improve existing ones (Note: Prior to Mar80, the use of this term was not restricted by a Scope Note)
UF   Curriculum Adaptation
    Curriculum Improvement
    Curriculum Planning (1966 1980)
    Curriculum Reform
    Curriculum Reorganization
    Curriculum Revisions
BT   Educational Development
RT   Articulation (Education)
    Course Content
    Curriculum
    Curriculum Based Assessment
    Curriculum Design
    Curriculum Enrichment
    Curriculum Evaluation
    Curriculum Guides
    Curriculum Problems
    Curriculum Research
    Curriculum Study Centers
    Formative Evaluation
    Instructional Development
    Instructional Leadership
    Instructional Materials
    Material Development
    Media Adaptation
    Relevance (Education)
    School Supervision

Curriculum Enrichment   *JUL. 1966*
    Postings: 2,317   GC: 310
SN   Process of selectively modifying a curriculum by adding educational content

or new learning opportunities (e.g., out of school visits, special learning activities for gifted or deprived students, audiovisual presentations, etc.)
UF   Course Enrichment
BT   Enrichment
RT   Curriculum
    Curriculum Development

Curriculum Evaluation   *JUL. 1966*
    Postings: 5,736   GC: 320
SN   Determining the efficacy, value, etc., of a specific curriculum in terms of the validity of objectives, relevancy and sequence of content, and achievement of specified goals (Note: As of Oct81, use as a minor Descriptor for examples of this kind of evaluation—use as a major Descriptor only as the subject of a document)
UF   Curriculum Reevaluation
BT   Evaluation
RT   Course Evaluation
    Curriculum
    Curriculum Development
    Curriculum Research
    Educational Quality
    Excellence in Education
    Instructional Development
    Instructional Effectiveness
    Instructional Material Evaluation
    Program Evaluation
    Program Validation
    Relevance (Education)
    Summative Evaluation
    Validated Programs

Curriculum Guides   *JUL. 1966*
    Postings: 10,201   GC: 730
SN   (Note: Prior to Mar80, the Thesaurus carried the instructions, "'Course Outlines' or 'Syllabus,' USE 'Curriculum Guides'")
UF   FLES Guides (1967 1980) #
NT   State Curriculum Guides
BT   Guides
RT   Course Content
    Course Descriptions
    Curriculum
    Curriculum Development
    Curriculum Problems
    Learning Modules
    Lesson Plans
    Teaching Guides

Curriculum Improvement
USE   Curriculum Development

Curriculum Integrated Library Instruction
USE   Course Integrated Library Instruction

Curriculum Laboratories
USE   Curriculum Study Centers

Curriculum Materials
USE   Instructional Materials

Curriculum Planning (1966 1980)
USE   Curriculum Development

Curriculum Problems   *JUL. 1966*
    Postings: 1,012   GC: 320
BT   Problems
RT   Curriculum
    Curriculum Development
    Curriculum Guides

Curriculum Reevaluation
USE   Curriculum Evaluation

Curriculum Referenced Assessment
USE   Curriculum Based Assessment

Curriculum Reform
USE   Curriculum Development

Curriculum Relevance
USE   Relevance (Education)

Curriculum Reorganization
USE   Curriculum Development

Curriculum Research   *JUL. 1966*
    Postings: 1,827   GC: 810
SN   Systematic investigation, collection, and analysis of information about a structured series of learning outcomes and associated experiences (Note: As of Oct81, use as a minor Descriptor for examples of this kind of research—use as a major Descriptor only as the subject of a document)
BT   Educational Research
RT   Content Analysis
    Curriculum
    Curriculum Design
    Curriculum Development
    Curriculum Evaluation
    Curriculum Study Centers
    Institutional Research

Curriculum Resources
USE   Educational Resources

Curriculum Revisions
USE   Curriculum Development

Curriculum Study Centers   *JUL. 1966*
    Postings: 166   GC: 920
SN   Facilities where assistance (e.g., curriculum materials, audiovisual aids, curriculum research and development) is provided to educators in planning and preparing for instruction—may range from regional centers to units within schools
UF   Curriculum Laboratories
BT   Educational Facilities
    Resource Centers
RT   Curriculum
    Curriculum Development
    Curriculum Research
    Demonstration Centers
    Education Service Centers
    Research and Development Centers
    Research and Instruction Units
    Resource Units

Curriculum Vitae
USE   Resumes (Personal)

Cursive Writing   *JUL. 1966*
    Postings: 104   GC: 400
SN   Handwriting characterized by running or flowing lines, with strokes joined within the word
BT   Handwriting
RT   Manuscript Writing (Handlettering)

Custodial Mentally Handicapped (1968 1980)
USE   Severe Mental Retardation

Custodian Training   *JUL. 1966*
    Postings: 85   GC: 400
BT   Job Training
RT   School Maintenance

Customs (Culture)
USE   Culture

Cutaneous Sense (1968 1980)
USE   Tactual Perception

Cutlines
USE   Captions

Cutting Scores   *MAY 1972*
    Postings: 936   GC: 820
SN   A selected point on a score scale which divides individuals earning scores above and below it into two groups for some purpose
UF   Critical Scores
BT   Scores
RT   Credit No Credit Grading
    Criterion Referenced Tests
    Equated Scores
    Mastery Tests
    Pass Fail Grading
    Raw Scores
    Scoring Formulas
    True Scores

Cybernetics   *JUL. 1966*
    Postings: 357   GC: 710
SN   Comparative study of control and communication processes of organisms and machines
BT   Technology
RT   Artificial Intelligence
    Automation
    Bionics
    Communication (Thought Transfer)
    Communications
    Computer Science
    Computers
    Educational Technology
    Electronic Control
    Entropy
    Feedback
    Game Theory
    Human Factors Engineering
    Information Processing
    Information Science
    Information Technology
    Information Theory
    Input Output
    Instrumentation
    Man Machine Systems
    Numerical Control
    Pattern Recognition
    Robotics
    Systems Approach
    Technological Advancement

Cyesis
USE   Pregnancy

Cyrillic Alphabet   *JUL. 1966*
    Postings: 72   GC: 450
BT   Alphabets
RT   Non Roman Scripts
    Slavic Languages

Cystic Fibrosis   *OCT. 1998*
    Postings: 43   GC: 210
SN   Hereditary disease of the exocrine glands characterized by salty sweat and the overproduction of thick, sticky mucus that may obstruct passageways (including pancreatic and bile ducts, intestines, and bronchi)
BT   Diseases
RT   Genetics
    Physical Health
    Special Health Problems

Cytology   *SEP. 1968*
    Postings: 284   GC: 490
UF   Cell Biology
    Cell Theory (1966 1980)
    Cellular Molecular Biology #
BT   Biological Sciences
RT   Bacteria
    Biochemistry
    Biology
    Biotechnology
    Culturing Techniques
    Embryology
    Enzymes
    Evolution

= Two or more Descriptors are used to represent this term.
The term's main entry shows the appropriate coordination.

Genetic Engineering
Molecular Biology
Nucleic Acids
Physiology
Rh Factors
Viruses

Czech   *JUL. 1966*
    Postings: 81   GC: 440
BT   Slavic Languages
RT   Czech Literature

Czech Literature   *DEC. 1969*
    Postings: 5   GC: 430
BT   Literature
RT   Czech

Dactylology
USE   Finger Spelling

Dagur   *JUL. 1966*
    Postings: 2   GC: 440
BT   Mongolian Languages

Daily Living Skills   *MAR. 1974*
    Postings: 2,791   GC: 220
SN   Personal management and social skills
which are necessary for adequate functioning on an independent basis (Note: If applicable, use the more specific term "Self Care Skills")
UF   Fundamental Skills (Daily Living)
Independent Living Skills
Life Skills
Survival Skills (Daily Living)
NT   Self Care Skills
BT   Skills
RT   Adaptive Behavior (of Disabled)
Basic Business Education
Communication Skills
Community Based Instruction (Disabilities)
Coping
Decision Making Skills
Health
Home Economics Skills
Homemaking Skills
Independent Living
Interpersonal Competence
Job Skills
Language Skills
Normalization (Disabilities)
Practical Arts
Psychomotor Skills
Rehabilitation
Safety
Special Education
Telephone Usage Instruction
Travel Training
Visually Impaired Mobility

Dairy Farmers   *MAR. 1980*
    Postings: 88   GC: 410
UF   Dairymen (1966 1980)
BT   Farmers
RT   Agriculture
Animal Husbandry
Farm Occupations

Dairy Product Inspectors
USE   Food and Drug Inspectors

Dairymen (1966 1980)
USE   Dairy Farmers

Dakota   *MAR. 1994*
    Postings: 4   GC: 440
SN   The Siouan language of the Sioux tribe of American Indians (Note: Use "Sioux (Tribe)" for the Dakota people—use the Identifier "Siouan Languages" for the broad language family to which Dakota belongs)
NT   Lakota
BT   American Indian Languages

RT   Sioux (Tribe)

Dance   *JUL. 1966*
    Postings: 1,051   GC: 420
UF   Aerobic Dance #
Ballet (1966 1980)
Choreography
BT   Fine Arts
Physical Activities
RT   Art
Cultural Activities
Dance Education
Dance Therapy
Dramatics
Folk Culture
Movement Education
Music
Pantomime
Rehearsals (Theater Arts)
Theater Arts

Dance Education   *MAR. 1983*
    Postings: 290   GC: 420
SN   Any learning activities involving dance—may be integral to physical education or offered as a separate program of study
BT   Education
RT   Aesthetic Education
Dance
Fine Arts
Movement Education
Music Education
Physical Education

Dance Therapy   *FEB. 1978*
    Postings: 58   GC: 230
SN   The therapeutic use of rhythmical motor activity (folk dancing, ballroom dancing, exercising to music, etc.) as a bridge to mental or physical well-being
BT   Therapy
RT   Dance
Movement Education
Music Therapy
Physical Therapy
Play Therapy
Psychotherapy
Self Expression
Therapeutic Recreation

Dangerous Materials
USE   Hazardous Materials

Danish   *APR. 1990*
    Postings: 72   GC: 440
BT   Indo European Languages

Darghi
USE   Caucasian Languages

Data   *JUL. 1966*
    Postings: 479   GC: 710
SN   Information, often numerical and especially in a form suitable for processing by a computer or for other analysis
NT   Databases
Personal Data
Profiles
Scores
Statistical Data
RT   Data Analysis
Data Conversion
Data Processing
Diagrams
Measurement
Tables (Data)

Data Accumulation
USE   Data Collection

Data Analysis   *JUL. 1966*
    Postings: 7,763   GC: 820
SN   Preparation of factual information items for dissemination or further treatment

(includes compiling, verifying, ordering, classifying, and interpreting)
NT   Data Collection
Data Interpretation
Statistical Analysis
Trend Analysis
BT   Evaluation Methods
RT   Classification
Content Analysis
Data
Data Conversion
Data Processing
Hypothesis Testing
Research
Research Methodology

Data Banks
USE   Databases

Data Bases (1969 1981)
USE   Databases

Data Collection   *JUL. 1966*
    Postings: 7,416   GC: 810
SN   Generating or bringing together information that has been systematically observed, recorded, organized, categorized, or defined in such a way that logical processing and inferences may occur
UF   Data Accumulation
NT   Sampling
BT   Data Analysis
Information Processing
RT   Data Processing
Demography
Generalizability Theory
Observation
Questionnaires
Recordkeeping
Research
Research Methodology
Surveys
Testing
Worksheets

Data Conversion   *AUG. 1994*
    Postings: 62   GC: 710
SN   Process of moving data from one format to another, e.g., from tape to disk, from one computer to another, from one application to another on the same computer, from print to machine-readable form
UF   Conversion (Format)
NT   Retrospective Conversion (Library Catalogs)
BT   Change
RT   Data
Data Analysis
Data Processing
Electronic Publishing
Records Management

Data Dissemination
USE   Information Dissemination

Data Interpretation   *JAN. 1985*
    Postings: 760   GC: 820
SN   Explanation of the meaning, implications, or limitations of factual information
NT   Statistical Inference
Test Interpretation
BT   Data Analysis
RT   Evaluation
Evaluative Thinking
Experiments
Generalizability Theory
Hypothesis Testing
Inferences
Information Utilization
Interpretive Skills
Research
Research Methodology
Robustness (Statistics)
Statistical Analysis
Validity

Data Needs
USE   Information Needs

Data Processing   *JUL. 1966*
    Postings: 3,320   GC: 710
SN   Systematic handling, manipulation, and computation of information by machines
UF   Automatic Data Processing
Data Processing Centers #
Data Tabulation
Electronic Data Processing (1967 1980)
NT   Input Output
Natural Language Processing
Time Sharing
BT   Information Processing
RT   Automation
Calculators
Computer Centers
Computer Interfaces
Computer Networks
Computer Peripherals
Computer Science
Computer Software
Computer Software Development
Computer System Design
Computers
Data
Data Analysis
Data Collection
Data Conversion
Data Processing Occupations
Database Design
Database Management Systems
Databases
Downloading
Electromechanical Technology
Electronic Equipment
Electronic Text
Expert Systems
Hypermedia
Information Systems
Information Technology
Instrumentation
Machine Readable Cataloging
Machine Translation
Management Information Systems
Mechanical Equipment
Online Systems
Optical Data Disks
Programming
Programming Languages
User Friendly Interface
Worksheets
Workstations

Data Processing Centers
USE   Computer Centers
AND   Data Processing

Data Processing Occupations   *JUL. 1966*
    Postings: 149   GC: 640
BT   Occupations
RT   Business Education
Clerical Occupations
Computer Science Education
Data Processing
Electronic Technicians
Keyboarding (Data Entry)
Office Occupations
Professional Occupations
Semiskilled Occupations
Skilled Occupations
Technical Occupations
Trade and Industrial Education
White Collar Occupations

Data Sheets (1966 1980)
USE   Worksheets

Data Tabulation
USE   Data Processing

Database Design   *JAN. 1988*
    Postings: 282   GC: 710
SN   The process of planning and organizing the content and structure of a database—

\# = Two or more Descriptors are used to represent this term.
The term's main entry shows the appropriate coordination.

also, the specifications that result from this process
BT   Design
RT   Data Processing
     Database Management Systems
     Databases

Database Hosts
USE   Online Vendors

Database Management Systems   *APR. 1986*
     Postings: 619   GC: 710
SN   Software used to create, organize, se-
     cure, access, and update databases
UF   DBMS
     File Management Systems
BT   Computer Software
     Management Systems
RT   Data Processing
     Database Design
     Databases
     Information Management
     Information Retrieval
     Information Storage
     Integrated Library Systems
     Management Information Systems

Database Producers   *APR. 1986*
     Postings: 153   GC: 710
SN   Publishers, businesses, government
     agencies, or other organizations that cre-
     ate computer-readable information files,
     often for public access
BT   Organizations (Groups)
RT   Databases
     Information Industry
     Online Vendors
     Publishing Industry

Database Vendors
USE   Online Vendors

Databases   *APR. 1981*
     Postings: 6,686   GC: 710
SN   Collections of information items that are
     organized and stored in machine-read-
     able records and which are accessible
     and manipulable by computer through
     designated elements in the records
UF   Data Banks
     Data Bases (1969 1981)
     Machine Readable Data Files
NT   Bibliographic Databases
     Full Text Databases
     Numeric Databases
     Online Catalogs
BT   Data
     Information Sources
RT   Computers
     Data Processing
     Database Design
     Database Management Systems
     Database Producers
     Electronic Publishing
     Electronic Text
     Gateway Systems
     Hypermedia
     Information Retrieval
     Information Storage
     Job Banks
     Library Collections
     Online Vendors
     Research Tools
     Search Strategies

Dating (Social)   *JUL. 1966*
     Postings: 529   GC: 510
BT   Interpersonal Relationship
RT   Friendship
     Interpersonal Attraction
     Mate Selection
     Recreational Activities
     Social Life

Daughters   *SEP. 1981*
     Postings: 309   GC: 510
BT   Females

RT   Family (Sociological Unit)
     Family Environment
     Family Life
     Kinship
     Parent Child Relationship
     Parents
     Sons

Day Camp Programs   *JUL. 1966*
     Postings: 169   GC: 470
UF   Day Camps
BT   Recreational Programs
RT   Camping
     Resident Camp Programs
     Summer Programs

Day Camps
USE   Day Camp Programs

Day Care   *MAR. 1980*
     Postings: 5,444   GC: 520
SN   Care of children by persons other than
     their parents or guardians on a partial or
     full day basis (Note: See also "Child
     Rearing"—prior to Mar80, "Child Care"
     was also a valid Descriptor)
UF   Day Care Programs (1966 1980)
     Day Care Services (1967 1980)
NT   Employer Supported Day Care
     Family Day Care
     School Age Day Care
     Sick Child Care
BT   Social Services
RT   Adult Day Care
     Alternate Day Schedules
     Ancillary School Services
     Caregiver Child Relationship
     Child Care Occupations
     Child Caregivers
     Day Care Centers
     Day Care Effects
     Employed Parents
     Full Day Half Day Schedules
     Home Economics Education
     Infant Care
     Occupational Home Economics

Day Care Centers   *MAR. 1980*
     Postings: 2,428   GC: 920
SN   Professionally run facilities that care for
     groups of children on a partial or full day
     basis (Note: Prior to Mar80, the instruc-
     tion "Day Care Centers, USE Day Care
     Services" was carried in the Thesaurus)
UF   Child Care Centers (1967 1980)
     Migrant Child Care Centers (1966
          1980) #
BT   Facilities
RT   Child Care Occupations
     Child Caregivers
     Child Development Centers
     Day Care
     Day Care Effects
     Early Childhood Education
     Employer Supported Day Care
     Infant Care
     Nursery Schools
     Preschool Education
     School Age Day Care
     Sick Child Care

Day Care Effects   *JUL. 1993*
     Postings: 215   GC: 520
SN   Short- or long-term effects of day care
     placement on children's cognitive, so-
     cial, emotional, and physical develop-
     ment and on relations between parents
     and children—also includes broader so-
     cial consequences of day care attend-
     ance and availability
RT   Child Caregivers
     Day Care
     Day Care Centers
     Early Experience
     Infant Care
     Outcomes of Education

Day Care Programs (1966 1980)
USE   Day Care

Day Care Services (1967 1980)
USE   Day Care

Day Classes
USE   Day Programs

Day Programs   *JUL. 1966*
     Postings: 148   GC: 350
SN   Programs conducted during the daytime
     hours
UF   Day Classes
     Daytime Programs (1967 1980)
BT   Programs
RT   Day Schools
     Day Students
     Evening Programs
     Full Time Students

Day Release
USE   Released Time

Day Schools   *JUL. 1966*
     Postings: 143   GC: 340
SN   Schools attended by students during part
     of the day, as distinguished from schools
     where students are boarded and lodged
BT   Schools
RT   Day Programs
     Day Students

Day Students   *JUL. 1966*
     Postings: 116   GC: 360
BT   Students
RT   Day Programs
     Day Schools
     Evening Students
     Full Time Students

Daylight (1970 1980)
USE   Light

Daytime Programs (1967 1980)
USE   Day Programs

DBMS
USE   Database Management Systems

DDC (Classification)
USE   Dewey Decimal Classification

De Facto Segregation   *MAR. 1980*
     Postings: 244   GC: 540
UF   Defacto Segregation (1966 1980)
BT   Racial Segregation
RT   School Resegregation
     Tokenism

De Jure Segregation   *APR. 1980*
     Postings: 76   GC: 540
SN   Racial separation directly guaranteed by
     law
UF   Dejure Segregation (1966 1980)
     Legal Segregation (1966 1980)
BT   Racial Segregation
RT   Apartheid

Deaf Blind   *JUL. 1966*
     Postings: 673   GC: 220
BT   Multiple Disabilities
RT   Blindness
     Deafness
     Severe Disabilities

Deaf Children (1966 1980)
USE   Deafness

Deaf Education (1968 1980)
USE   Deafness

Deaf Interpreting   *JUL. 1966*
     Postings: 288   GC: 220
SN   Process of acting as interpreter to facili-
     tate communications between deaf and
     hearing persons
UF   Interpreting for the Deaf
BT   Translation
RT   Accessibility (for Disabled)
     Communication (Thought Transfer)
     Communication Skills
     Cued Speech
     Deafness
     Finger Spelling
     Interpreters
     Interpretive Skills
     Lipreading
     Manual Communication
     Sign Language

Deaf Research (1968 1980)
USE   Deafness

Deaf (1966 1980)
USE   Deafness

Deafness   *MAR. 1980*
     Postings: 4,474   GC: 220
SN   Deprivation of the functional use of the
     sense of hearing—usually a loss of more
     than 75 decibels
UF   Deaf (1966 1980)
     Deaf Children (1966 1980)
     Deaf Education (1968 1980)
     Deaf Research (1968 1980)
     Profoundly Hearing Impaired
BT   Hearing Impairments
RT   Cochlear Implants
     Deaf Blind
     Deaf Interpreting
     Hearing (Physiology)
     Manual Communication
     Oral Communication Method
     Partial Hearing
     Total Communication

Deans   *MAR. 1980*
     Postings: 629   GC: 360
SN   Administrative officials in a college or
     other school who are responsible for the
     academic program, student life, student
     services, etc. (Note: Use a more specific
     term if possible)
UF   College Deans (1968 1980) #
NT   Academic Deans
     Deans of Students
BT   Administrators
     Faculty
RT   College Administration
     College Presidents
     Middle Management
     School Administration

Deans of Faculty
USE   Academic Deans

Deans of Instruction
USE   Academic Deans

Deans of Men
USE   Deans of Students

Deans of Students   *MAR. 1980*
     Postings: 59   GC: 360
SN   Administrative officials in a college or
     other school who are responsible for all
     phases of student life, including student
     activities, personnel services, housing,
     employment, etc.
UF   Deans of Men
     Deans of Women
BT   Deans
RT   Academic Deans

= Two or more Descriptors are used to represent this term.
The term's main entry shows the appropriate coordination.

College Environment
Pupil Personnel Workers
Student Development
Student Personnel Workers
Student School Relationship
Student Welfare

Deans of Women
USE   Deans of Students

Death   MAR. 1969
      Postings: 2,463   GC: 120
UF   Death Education
      Mortality (Physiology)
      Thanatology
NT   Homicide
      Infant Mortality
      Suicide
RT   Bereavement
      Capital Punishment
      Euthanasia
      Hospices (Terminal Care)
      Mortality Rate
      Pathology
      Physiology
      Terminal Illness
      Widowed

Death Education
USE   Death

Death Penalty
USE   Capital Punishment

Death Rate
USE   Mortality Rate

Debate   JUL. 1966
      Postings: 1,276   GC: 400
UF   Presidential Debates (United States) #
BT   Language Arts
RT   Debate Format
      Persuasive Discourse
      Political Campaigns
      Political Candidates
      Public Speaking
      Social Problems
      Verbal Communication

Debate Format   AUG. 1988
      Postings: 121   GC: 450
SN   Structure or framework of formal de-
      bate, including order and duration of
      arguments
RT   Debate
      Persuasive Discourse
      Speech Instruction

Debate Judges
USE   Judges

Debt (Financial)   JUN. 1999
      Postings: 227   GC: 620
SN   Money owed by one party to another
      (Note: See also such Identifiers as "Ex-
      ternal Debt," "International Debt," and
      "National Debt")
RT   Credit (Finance)
      Economics
      Educational Finance
      Financial Problems
      Loan Default
      Loan Repayment
      Money Management
      Paying for College
      Student Loan Programs

Debugging (Computers)   APR. 1990
      Postings: 31   GC: 710
SN   Process of locating and correcting mis-
      takes in computer software and hard-
      ware
BT   Troubleshooting
RT   Computer Software Development

Computer System Design
Computers
Programming

Deceleration
USE   Acceleration (Physics)

Decentralization   JUL. 1966
      Postings: 2,140   GC: 520
SN   The dispersion or distribution of func-
      tions and powers from a central author-
      ity to a local, community, or individual
      office unit authority
UF   Decentralized Library Systems (1968
          1980) #
      Decentralized School Design (1966
          1980) #
BT   Administrative Organization
RT   Centralization
      Community Control
      Institutional Autonomy
      Networks
      New Federalism
      Organizational Change
      School Based Management
      School Organization
      School Restructuring

Decentralized Library Systems (1968 1980)
USE   Decentralization
AND   Library Networks

Decentralized School Design (1966 1980)
USE   Decentralization
AND   Educational Facilities Design

Deception   AUG. 1986
      Postings: 159   GC: 520
SN   Intentional or unintentional misrepresen-
      tation or delusion
NT   Fraud
      Lying
RT   Behavior Patterns
      Communication (Thought Transfer)
      Consumer Protection
      Credibility
      Propaganda

Decimal Classification (Dewey)
USE   Dewey Decimal Classification

Decimal Classification (Universal)
USE   Universal Decimal Classification

Decimal Fractions   JAN. 1969
      Postings: 366   GC: 480
UF   Decimals
BT   Fractions

Decimals
USE   Decimal Fractions

Decision Making   JUL. 1966
      Postings: 18,560   GC: 110
NT   Participative Decision Making
BT   Cognitive Processes
RT   Architectural Programming
      Career Choice
      Career Information Systems
      College Choice
      Conflict Resolution
      Coping
      Course Selection (Students)
      Critical Thinking
      Decision Making Skills
      Decision Support Systems
      Delphi Technique
      Discussion
      Empowerment
      Evaluation Utilization
      Evaluative Thinking
      Expert Systems
      Futures (of Society)
      Game Theory

Guided Design
Heuristics
Holistic Approach
Individual Power
Information Utilization
Judgment Analysis Technique
Management Games
Management Information Systems
Management Systems
Markov Processes
Nominal Group Technique
Personal Autonomy
Policy Analysis
Policy Formation
Problem Solving
Professional Autonomy
Psychology
Risk
School Based Management
School Choice
Systems Analysis
Systems Approach
Thinking Skills
Vocational Maturity

Decision Making Skills   JUL. 1966
      Postings: 2,105   GC: 110
BT   Skills
RT   Daily Living Skills
      Decision Making
      Decision Support Systems
      Problem Solving
      Thinking Skills

Decision Support Systems   NOV. 1994
      Postings: 172   GC: 710
SN   Computer-based decision-making and
      planning systems that enable users to
      predict the impact of decisions before
      they are made
UF   Group Decision Support Systems #
BT   Management Information Systems
RT   Computer Mediated Communication
      Computer Simulation
      Computer Software
      Decision Making
      Decision Making Skills
      Expert Systems
      Planning
      Prediction

Declining Enrollment   DEC. 1976
      Postings: 1,508   GC: 330
SN   Diminishing numbers of students in edu-
      cational institutions
BT   Enrollment Rate
RT   Average Daily Membership
      Educational Demand
      Educational Supply
      Enrollment
      Enrollment Influences
      Enrollment Management
      Enrollment Projections
      Enrollment Trends
      School Closing
      School Demography

Declining Scores
USE   Test Score Decline

Decoding (Information)
USE   Coding

Decoding (Reading)   DEC. 1972
      Postings: 1,257   GC: 460
SN   Acquisition of meaning from written lan-
      guage by trial and error process of
      graphophonic, semantic, and syntactic
      analyses
BT   Reading Processes
RT   Beginning Reading
      Context Clues
      Miscue Analysis
      Oral Reading
      Phoneme Grapheme Correspondence
      Phonics
      Reading
      Reading Comprehension

Reading Skills
Semantics
Structural Analysis (Linguistics)
Word Recognition

Deduction   MAR. 1980
      Postings: 550   GC: 110
SN   Logical thought process that attempts to
      reach conclusions by reasoning from
      general rules, principles, laws, or condi-
      tions to specific instances or cases
UF   Deductive Methods (1967 1980)
BT   Logical Thinking
RT   Abstract Reasoning
      Experiments
      Induction
      Learning Processes
      Research Methodology
      Scientific Methodology
      Thinking Skills
      Validity

Deductive Methods (1967 1980)
USE   Deduction

Deep Sea Diving
USE   Underwater Diving

Deep Structure   JUL. 1966
      Postings: 771   GC: 450
SN   Concept in transformational grammar
      referring to the abstract underlying form
      of a sentence that determines its mean-
      ing but is not necessarily represented in
      its oral or written expression
BT   Transformational Generative Grammar
RT   Grammar
      Linguistic Theory
      Linguistics
      Phrase Structure
      Semantics
      Sentence Diagraming
      Sentence Structure
      Surface Structure
      Syntax

Defacto Segregation (1966 1980)
USE   De Facto Segregation

Defamation of Character
USE   Libel and Slander

Defaulted Loans
USE   Loan Default

Defense Mechanisms   APR. 1990
      Postings: 121   GC: 230
SN   Intrapsychic strategies used by individu-
      als to avoid or confront unreasonable or
      undesirable impulses, feelings, or ideas
      (Note: For physiological or zoological
      defense mechanisms, use "Defense Reac-
      tions (Physiology)" or "Animal Defenses"
      as Identifiers)
NT   Denial (Psychology)
BT   Psychological Patterns
RT   Coping
      Emotional Adjustment
      Emotional Response
      Personality Traits
      Self Concept
      Self Control
      Social Adjustment

Deferred Tuition
USE   Income Contingent Loans

Definitions   DEC. 1969
      Postings: 7,037   GC: 710
RT   Dictionaries
      Etymology
      Glossaries
      Lexicography
      Lexicology

= Two or more Descriptors are used to represent this term.
The term's main entry shows the appropriate coordination.

Semantics
Vocabulary

Degree Completion Time
USE   Time to Degree

Degree Requirements   *JUL. 1966*
         Postings: 1,723   GC: 320
SN   Specifications of minimum courses,
         course distribution, and grades required
         for a higher education degree in a par-
         ticular field of study (Note: Use "Gradua-
         tion Requirements" for high school di-
         ploma requirements or general
         specifications for college graduation—
         prior to Mar80, the use of this term was
         not restricted by a Scope Note)
BT   Graduation Requirements
RT   Academic Achievement
         Academic Standards
         Associate Degrees
         Bachelors Degrees
         College Credits
         College Students
         Degrees (Academic)
         Doctor of Arts Degrees
         Doctoral Degrees
         Doctoral Programs
         External Degree Programs
         Graduate Study
         Majors (Students)
         Masters Degrees
         Masters Programs
         Nonmajors
         Nontraditional Education
         Required Courses
         School Catalogs
         Special Degree Programs
         Specialist in Education Degrees
         Time to Degree
         Undergraduate Study

Degrees (Academic)   *MAR. 1980*
         Postings: 2,489   GC: 340
UF   Degrees (Titles) (1966 1980)
         First Professional Degrees #
NT   Associate Degrees
         Bachelors Degrees
         Doctoral Degrees
         Masters Degrees
         Specialist in Education Degrees
RT   Academic Rank (Professional)
         College Graduates
         Commencement Ceremonies
         Credentials
         Degree Requirements
         Doctoral Dissertations
         External Degree Programs
         Higher Education
         Majors (Students)
         Qualifications
         Special Degree Programs
         Time to Degree

Degrees (Titles) (1966 1980)
USE   Degrees (Academic)

Dehumanization
USE   Humanization

Deinstitutionalization (of Disabled)
                                            AUG. 1980
         Postings: 526   GC: 220
SN   Processes and services that enable dis-
         abled persons to live outside of the con-
         fines of asylums, nursing homes, and
         other residential institutions
BT   Normalization (Disabilities)
RT   Adult Foster Care
         Community Programs
         Disabilities
         Group Homes
         Institutionalized Persons
         Rehabilitation
         Residential Programs

Dejure Segregation (1966 1980)
USE   De Jure Segregation

Delay of Gratification   *OCT. 1976*
         Postings: 111   GC: 120
SN   The self-imposed delay of reinforcement
         or voluntary deferment of reward
BT   Self Control
RT   Discipline
         Goal Orientation
         Locus of Control
         Need Gratification
         Psychological Needs
         Reinforcement
         Rewards
         Self Concept
         Self Motivation
         Self Reward

Delayed Development (Individuals)
USE   Developmental Delays

Delayed Speech   *MAR. 1980*
         Postings: 272   GC: 120
SN   Speech skill development that is below
         age level standards
UF   Retarded Speech Development (1968
         1980)
BT   Speech Impairments
RT   Child Development
         Developmental Delays
         Language Acquisition
         Speech Habits
         Speech Skills
         Speech Therapy

Delinquency   *JUL. 1966*
         Postings: 3,286   GC: 530
UF   Delinquent Behavior (1966 1983)
         Delinquent Identification (1966
         1980) #
         Delinquent Role (1966 1980)
         Delinquents (1966 1980)
         Juvenile Delinquency
BT   Crime
RT   Criminals
         Delinquency Causes
         Delinquency Prevention
         Delinquent Rehabilitation
         Group Homes
         Juvenile Courts
         Juvenile Gangs
         Juvenile Justice
         Law Enforcement
         Police School Relationship
         Recidivism
         Runaways
         Social Psychology
         Stealing
         Vandalism
         Violence
         Youth Problems

Delinquency Causes   *JUL. 1966*
         Postings: 323   GC: 530
RT   Delinquency
         Etiology

Delinquency Prevention   *JUL. 1966*
         Postings: 659   GC: 520
BT   Crime Prevention
RT   Delinquency
         Delinquent Rehabilitation
         Law Enforcement

Delinquent Behavior (1966 1983)
USE   Delinquency

Delinquent Identification (1966 1980)
USE   Delinquency
AND   Identification

Delinquent Rehabilitation   *JUL. 1966*
         Postings: 837   GC: 240
BT   Correctional Rehabilitation

RT   Continuation Students
         Correctional Education
         Correctional Institutions
         Delinquency
         Delinquency Prevention
         Juvenile Courts
         Probation Officers
         Probationary Period
         Recidivism

Delinquent Role (1966 1980)
USE   Delinquency

Delinquents (1966 1980)
USE   Delinquency

Delivery Systems   *MAY 1974*
         Postings: 8,144   GC: 520
SN   Organizational and administrative aspects
         of the provision of services
NT   Document Delivery
BT   Services
RT   Communications
         Information Dissemination
         Needs Assessment
         Outreach Programs
         Referral
         Resource Allocation

Delphi Technique   *APR. 1982*
         Postings: 527   GC: 820
SN   Method of synthesizing diverse opinions
         into a consensus (most frequently, among
         experts)—usually carried out by a series
         of questionnaires, the technique is char-
         acterized by minimal influence from so-
         cial pressures through anonymity, re-
         peated rounds of controlled feedback,
         and weighted responses
BT   Methods
RT   Cooperative Planning
         Decision Making
         Feedback
         Futures (of Society)
         Long Range Planning
         Maximum Likelihood Statistics
         Nominal Group Technique
         Operations Research
         Opinions
         Planning
         Policy Formation
         Prediction

Demand for Education
USE   Educational Demand

Demand Occupations   *APR. 1969*
         Postings: 484   GC: 640
SN   Occupations for which personnel are
         needed, at the present or in the projected
         future
NT   Emerging Occupations
BT   Occupations
RT   Career Planning
         Educational Demand
         Employment Opportunities
         Employment Patterns
         Employment Potential
         Employment Projections
         Labor Market
         Labor Needs
         Occupational Information
         Supply and Demand

Dementia Praecox
USE   Schizophrenia

Democracy   *JUL. 1966*
         Postings: 1,858   GC: 610
RT   Capitalism
         Civil Liberties
         Civil Rights
         Communism
         Democratic Values
         Free Enterprise System
         Freedom

         Freedom of Information
         Freedom of Speech
         Intellectual Freedom
         Personal Autonomy
         Self Determination
         Totalitarianism

Democratic Management
USE   Participative Decision Making

Democratic Values   *JUL. 1966*
         Postings: 2,410   GC: 610
NT   American Dream
BT   Values
RT   Democracy
         Freedom
         Political Attitudes
         Social Values

Demography   *JUL. 1966*
         Postings: 7,758   GC: 550
UF   National Demography (1966 1980)
         Population Research
NT   Birth Rate
         Employment Patterns
         Geographic Distribution
         Mortality Rate
         Population Distribution
         Population Growth
         Population Trends
         Racial Composition
         Residential Patterns
         School Demography
         Social Distribution
         Urban Demography
BT   Social Sciences
RT   Census Figures
         Cohort Analysis
         Community Size
         Data Collection
         Employment Projections
         Geographic Isolation
         Human Geography
         Incidence
         Industrialization
         Land Settlement
         Migration
         Migration Patterns
         Overpopulation
         Place of Residence
         Population Education
         Rural Population
         Social Science Research
         Social Scientists
         Sociocultural Patterns
         Sociology
         Topography
         Urbanization

Demonstration Centers   *JUL. 1966*
         Postings: 137   GC: 920
SN   Areas of educational facilities set up to
         solve specified educational problems
         through research and experimentation
         (Note: Prior to Mar80, the use of this
         term was not restricted by a Scope Note)
BT   Educational Facilities
RT   Curriculum Study Centers
         Demonstration Programs
         Demonstrations (Educational)
         Education Service Centers
         Educational Experiments
         Educational Research
         Laboratories

Demonstration Programs   *JUL. 1966*
         Postings: 5,500   GC: 330
UF   Demonstration Projects (1966 1980)
         Exemplary Programs
         Model Programs
BT   Programs
RT   Demonstration Centers
         Experimental Programs
         Field Tests
         Innovation
         Program Validation
         Validated Programs

= Two or more Descriptors are used to represent this term.
The term's main entry shows the appropriate coordination.

Demonstration Projects (1966 1980)
USE   Demonstration Programs

Demonstrations (Civil)   *JUL. 1966*
       Postings: 319   GC: 610
UF   Public Demonstrations
RT   Activism
       Civil Disobedience
       Civil Rights
       School Boycotts
       Student Rights
       Violence

Demonstrations (Educational)   *JUL. 1966*
       Postings: 1,679   GC: 310
SN   Teaching method in which explanations
       are given by example or experiment
NT   Demonstrations (Science)
BT   Teaching Methods
RT   Demonstration Centers
       Educational Experiments
       Laboratories
       Laboratory Procedures

Demonstrations (Science)   *MAY 1994*
       Postings: 456   GC: 490
SN   Descriptions or explanations of scientific
       phenomena by means of experiments,
       examples, specimens, or practical appli-
       cations
BT   Demonstrations (Educational)
RT   Hands on Science
       Laboratory Procedures
       Science Education
       Science Equipment
       Science Experiments
       Science Instruction
       Science Laboratories

Denial (Psychology)   *NOV. 1997*
       Postings: 82   GC: 230
SN   Refusal or inability to accept painful or
       difficult realities
BT   Defense Mechanisms
RT   Resistance (Psychology)

Denominational Colleges
USE   Church Related Colleges

Density (Matter)   *MAY 1998*
       Postings: 99   GC: 490
SN   Mass per unit volume of a substance
BT   Scientific Concepts
RT   Force
       Gravity (Physics)
       Matter
       Pressure (Physics)
       Space
       Weight (Mass)

Dental Assessment
USE   Dental Evaluation

Dental Assistants   *JUL. 1966*
       Postings: 178   GC: 210
SN   Personnel who assist dentists at chairside
       in dental operatory, perform reception
       and clerical functions, and carry out den-
       tal radiography and selected dental labo-
       ratory work
BT   Allied Health Personnel
RT   Dental Clinics
       Dental Evaluation
       Dental Hygienists
       Dental Technicians
       Dentistry

Dental Associations (1966 1980)
USE   Dentistry
AND   Professional Associations

Dental Clinics   *JUL. 1966*
       Postings: 44   GC: 210
BT   Clinics

RT   Dental Assistants
       Dental Evaluation
       Dental Health
       Dental Hygienists
       Dental Schools
       Dental Technicians
       Dentistry
       Dentists

Dental Evaluation   *JUL. 1966*
       Postings: 97   GC: 210
SN   Determination of an individual's dental
       health and of any needed treatment—
       also, the appraisal of dental procedures,
       programs, equipment, etc., according to
       professional standards
UF   Dental Assessment
BT   Medical Evaluation
RT   Dental Assistants
       Dental Clinics
       Dental Health
       Dental Hygienists
       Dental Technicians
       Dentistry
       Dentists

Dental Health   *JUL. 1966*
       Postings: 522   GC: 210
BT   Physical Health
RT   Child Health
       Dental Clinics
       Dental Evaluation
       Dental Hygienists
       Dentistry
       Fluoridation
       Hygiene

Dental Hygienists   *AUG. 1968*
       Postings: 212   GC: 210
SN   Licensed oral health clinicians and edu-
       cators who help the public develop and
       maintain optimum oral health—they may
       perform preventive, restorative, and thera-
       peutic services under the supervision of
       dentists
UF   Oral Hygienists
       Prophylacticians
BT   Allied Health Personnel
RT   Dental Assistants
       Dental Clinics
       Dental Evaluation
       Dental Health
       Dental Technicians
       Dentistry
       Hygiene

Dental Laboratory Technicians
USE   Dental Technicians

Dental School Faculty
USE   Dental Schools
AND   Medical School Faculty

Dental Schools   *JUL. 1966*
       Postings: 957   GC: 340
UF   Dental School Faculty #
       Schools of Dentistry
BT   Colleges
RT   Dental Clinics
       Dental Students
       Dentistry
       Dentists
       Medical Education
       Medical School Faculty
       Medical Schools
       Professional Education

Dental Sciences
USE   Dentistry

Dental Students   *OCT. 1982*
       Postings: 237   GC: 360
SN   Students enrolled in dental schools (Note:
       Excludes undergraduate students pre-
       paring for dental school)
BT   Graduate Students

RT   Dental Schools
       Dentistry
       Medical Students
       Professional Education

Dental Surgeons
USE   Dentists

Dental Technicians   *JUL. 1966*
       Postings: 73   GC: 210
SN   Personnel who construct complete and
       partial dentures, make orthodontic appli-
       ances, fix bridgework, crowns, and other
       dental restorations and appliances, as
       authorized by dentists
UF   Dental Laboratory Technicians
       Orthodontic Technicians
BT   Allied Health Personnel
RT   Dental Assistants
       Dental Clinics
       Dental Evaluation
       Dental Hygienists
       Dentistry
       Laboratory Technology

Dentistry   *JUL. 1966*
       Postings: 576   GC: 210
UF   Dental Associations (1966 1980) #
       Dental Sciences
       Orthodontics
BT   Medicine
RT   Dental Assistants
       Dental Clinics
       Dental Evaluation
       Dental Health
       Dental Hygienists
       Dental Schools
       Dental Students
       Dental Technicians
       Dentists
       Health
       Medical Services

Dentists   *AUG. 1968*
       Postings: 265   GC: 210
UF   Dental Surgeons
       Orthodontists
BT   Health Personnel
       Professional Personnel
RT   Dental Clinics
       Dental Evaluation
       Dental Schools
       Dentistry
       Medical Services

Deoxyribonucleic Acid
USE   DNA

Department Chairpersons
USE   Department Heads

Department Directors (School) (1966 1980)
USE   Department Heads

Department Heads   *MAR. 1980*
       Postings: 1,126   GC: 360
SN   Faculty members responsible for the co-
       ordination or administration of an aca-
       demic area of study (Note: Prior to Apr76,
       the instruction "Department Chairmen,
       USE Administrative Personnel" was car-
       ried in the Thesaurus)
UF   Department Chairpersons
       Department Directors (School) (1966
       1980)
BT   Administrators
       Faculty
RT   Departments
       Instructional Leadership
       Middle Management
       School Administration
       Teachers

Departmental Majors
USE   Majors (Students)

Departmental Teaching Plans (1968 1980)
USE   Departments

Departmentalization
USE   Departments

Departments   *SEP. 1969*
       Postings: 2,127   GC: 350
UF   Academic Departments
       Departmental Teaching Plans (1968
       1980)
       Departmentalization
NT   English Departments
       Science Departments
       State Departments of Education
BT   Administrative Organization
RT   Department Heads
       Intellectual Disciplines
       School Organization

Dependability
USE   Reliability

Dependency (Drugs)
USE   Drug Addiction

Dependency (Personality)   *APR. 1990*
       Postings: 133   GC: 120
SN   Reliance on other persons or things for
       comfort and support (Note: Do not use
       for drug or economic dependence, for
       which see "Drug Addiction" or the Iden-
       tifier "Dependency (Economics)")
BT   Personality Traits
RT   Affiliation Need
       Attachment Behavior
       Dependents
       Emotional Development
       Interpersonal Relationship
       Psychological Needs
       Social Development

Dependents   *JUL. 1966*
       Postings: 185   GC: 510
BT   Groups
RT   Children
       Dependency (Personality)
       Family Size
       Family Structure
       Older Adults

Depleted Resources   *JUL. 1966*
       Postings: 323   GC: 410
BT   Resources
RT   Conservation (Environment)
       Energy Conservation
       Fuel Consumption
       Natural Resources
       Physical Environment
       Recycling
       Soil Conservation
       Water Resources

Depository Libraries   *NOV. 1968*
       Postings: 403   GC: 710
SN   Libraries that receive public documents
       from national, provincial, or local gov-
       ernmental units with the provision that
       they will provide public access to the
       collections
BT   Libraries
RT   Academic Libraries
       Government (Administrative Body)
       Government Publications
       Law Libraries
       Public Libraries
       Research Libraries
       Special Libraries

Depressed Areas (Geographic) (1966 1980)
USE   Poverty Areas

= Two or more Descriptors are used to represent this term.
The term's main entry shows the appropriate coordination.

Depression (Psychology)   AUG. 1978
    Postings: 2,596   GC: 230
SN Emotional state of dejection and sad-
    ness, ranging from mild discouragement
    to utter despair
UF Despair
    Despondency
    Dysphoria
    Dysthymia
    Melancholia
BT Psychological Patterns
RT Anger
    Anxiety
    Emotional Disturbances
    Emotional Problems
    Fear
    Grief
    Guilt
    Helplessness
    Loneliness
    Moods
    Personality Problems
    Posttraumatic Stress Disorder
    Psychopathology
    Sadness

Deprivation
USE Disadvantaged Environment

Deprived
USE Disadvantaged

Deprived Children
USE Disadvantaged Youth

Deprived Environment
USE Disadvantaged Environment

Depth Perception   MAR. 1980
    Postings: 100   GC: 110
UF Stereopsis (1968 1980)
BT Visual Perception
RT Spatial Ability
    Vision

Dermal Sense
USE Tactual Perception

Descriptive Linguistics   JUL. 1966
    Postings: 1,452   GC: 450
SN Approach to linguistics that is concerned
    with the observation and description of a
    language at one point in time—describes
    language as it is actually used rather
    than prescribing how it should be used
    (Note: Prior to Mar80, the use of this
    term was not restricted by a Scope Note)
UF Synchronic Linguistics (1967 1980)
NT Grammar
    Semantics
BT Linguistics
RT Error Analysis (Language)
    Language Typology
    Linguistic Borrowing
    Phonemics
    Phonology
    Structural Analysis (Linguistics)
    Structural Grammar
    Tone Languages

Descriptive Writing   JUL. 1966
    Postings: 424   GC: 400
BT Writing (Composition)
RT Creative Writing
    Expository Writing
    Literary Devices
    Poetry
    Prose
    Student Writing Models

Descriptors
USE Subject Index Terms

Desegregated Classes
USE Classroom Desegregation

Desegregated Colleges
USE College Desegregation

Desegregated Schools
USE School Desegregation

Desegregation (Disabled Students)
USE Mainstreaming

Desegregation Effects   MAR. 1980
    Postings: 1,316   GC: 540
UF Desegregation Impact
    Integration Effects (1966 1980)
    Integration Impact
RT Integration Studies
    Racial Integration
    School Desegregation
    Social Integration

Desegregation Impact
USE Desegregation Effects

Desegregation Litigation   MAR. 1980
    Postings: 627   GC: 540
UF Integration Litigation (1966 1980)
BT Court Litigation
RT Racial Integration
    School Desegregation

Desegregation Methods   MAR. 1980
    Postings: 1,013   GC: 540
UF Integration Methods (1966 1980)
NT Busing
BT Methods
RT Affirmative Action
    Desegregation Plans
    Open Enrollment
    Racial Integration
    School Desegregation
    Selective Admission
    Social Integration

Desegregation Plans   MAR. 1980
    Postings: 707   GC: 540
UF Integration Plans (1966 1980)
BT Planning
RT Affirmative Action
    Busing
    Desegregation Methods
    Integration Readiness
    Racial Integration
    School Desegregation
    Social Integration
    Voluntary Desegregation

Desegregation Readiness
USE Integration Readiness

Desensitization   DEC. 1971
    Postings: 292   GC: 230
SN Planned exposure to anxiety producing
    stimuli in order to reduce illogical fears
UF Systematic Desensitization
BT Behavior Modification
RT Affective Behavior
    Anxiety
    Counseling Techniques
    Gestalt Therapy
    Relaxation Training
    Stimuli

Design   JUL. 1966
    Postings: 1,322   GC: 420
SN The process of conceiving and selecting
    the structure, elements, arrangement,
    materials, steps, or procedures of some
    activity or thing—also, the plan, layout,
    or mental scheme that results (Note: Use
    a more specific term if possible)
NT Building Design

Classroom Design
    Clothing Design
    Computer Assisted Design
    Computer System Design
    Curriculum Design
    Database Design
    Educational Facilities Design
    Furniture Design
    Instructional Design
    Interior Design
    Lighting Design
    Park Design
    Program Design
    Research Design
RT Architectural Programming
    Architecture
    Art
    Building Plans
    Design Crafts
    Design Preferences
    Design Requirements
    Designers
    Development
    Guidelines
    Mechanical Design Technicians
    Organization
    Planning
    Specifications

Design Build Approach   SEP. 1974
    Postings: 39   GC: 920
SN Entering into a single contract for design
    services and construction services
UF Design Construct Method
    Turnkey Building
BT Systems Building
RT Building Design
    Building Innovation
    Building Plans
    Construction (Process)
    Construction Costs
    Construction Management
    Construction Programs
    Facility Planning
    Fast Track Scheduling

Design Construct Method
USE Design Build Approach

Design Crafts   JUL. 1966
    Postings: 225   GC: 420
SN The artistic creation or decoration of a
    structure or material, either by hand or
    by machine
BT Visual Arts
RT Ceramics
    Clothing Design
    Craft Workers
    Design
    Furniture Design
    Handicrafts
    Industrial Arts
    Skilled Occupations

Design Needs (1968 1980)
USE Design Requirements

Design Preferences   JUL. 1966
    Postings: 403   GC: 420
BT Attitudes
RT Aesthetic Values
    Design
    Design Requirements
    Individual Needs
    Values

Design Requirements   MAR. 1980
    Postings: 2,042   GC: 920
SN Specifications that must be met for the
    designs of facilities or objects in order to
    satisfy the physical or psychological
    needs of users
UF Design Needs (1968 1980)
    Physical Design Needs (1968 1980)
    Psychological Design Needs (1968
    1980)
BT Specifications
RT Accessibility (for Disabled)

Acoustical Environment
    Architectural Programming
    Architecture
    Building Design
    Built Environment
    Classroom Design
    Climate Control
    Computer System Design
    Design
    Design Preferences
    Educational Facilities Design
    Educational Facilities Planning
    Facility Planning
    Facility Requirements
    Facility Utilization Research
    Flexible Facilities
    Furniture Design
    Human Factors Engineering
    Humanization
    Individual Needs
    Interior Design
    Interior Space
    Lighting Design
    Physical Environment
    Physical Mobility
    Privacy
    Psychological Needs
    Safety
    Sanitation
    Space Utilization
    Spatial Relationship (Facilities)
    Storage
    Technology Education
    Thermal Environment
    Visual Environment

Designers   JAN. 1969
    Postings: 153   GC: 640
BT Personnel
RT Design
    Drafting

Desktop Computers
USE Microcomputers

Desktop Publishing   AUG. 1989
    Postings: 291   GC: 710
SN The production of finished publications
    in one's home or office using a micro-
    computer, a peripheral high-resolution
    printer, and page-composition software
    that permits the integration of text, graph-
    ics, photography, and/or type sizes and
    styles
UF Personal Publishing
BT Production Techniques
RT Computer Graphics
    Computer Oriented Programs
    Electronic Publishing
    Microcomputers
    Publications

Desoxyribonucleic Acid
USE DNA

Despair
USE Depression (Psychology)

Despondency
USE Depression (Psychology)

Destiny Control
USE Self Determination

Determination (Chemical)
USE Chemical Analysis

Determiners (Languages)   JUL. 1966
    Postings: 232   GC: 450
UF Articles (Grammar)
BT Form Classes (Languages)
RT Function Words
    Morphology (Languages)
    Syntax

= Two or more Descriptors are used to represent this term.
The term's main entry shows the appropriate coordination.

Developed Nations   *JAN. 1969*
　　Postings: 2,575   GC: 610
UF　Advanced Nations
　　Economically Advanced Nations
　　Industrial Nations
BT　Geographic Regions
RT　Area Studies
　　Developing Nations
　　Development
　　Economic Development
　　Human Resources
　　Industrial Personnel
　　Industrial Structure
　　Industrialization
　　International Programs
　　International Relations
　　International Trade
　　Labor Economics
　　Labor Force
　　Living Standards
　　Modernization
　　National Programs
　　Productivity
　　Quality of Life
　　Sustainable Development
　　Technical Assistance
　　Technological Advancement
　　Technology
　　World Affairs

Developing Institutions   *MAR. 1980*
　　Postings: 114   GC: 340
SN　Smaller colleges and universities that,
　　for reasons beyond their control, are not
　　realizing their full potential, are strug-
　　gling for survival, and are isolated from
　　the mainstream of academic life—specifi-
　　cally, institutions affected by Title III of
　　the Higher Education Act of 1965
BT　Colleges
RT　Black Colleges
　　Equalization Aid
　　Federal Aid
　　Government School Relationship
　　Higher Education
　　Institutional Survival
　　Small Colleges

Developing Nations   *JUL. 1966*
　　Postings: 11,378   GC: 610
UF　Emerging Nations
　　Third World Countries
　　Underdeveloped Nations
BT　Geographic Regions
RT　Area Studies
　　Community Development
　　Culture Lag
　　Developed Nations
　　Development
　　Development Communication
　　Economic Development
　　Foreign Nationals
　　Human Resources
　　Industrialization
　　International Programs
　　International Relations
　　International Trade
　　Labor Economics
　　Living Standards
　　Modernization
　　National Programs
　　Nationalism
　　Nonformal Education
　　Productivity
　　Quality of Life
　　Revolution
　　Sustainable Development
　　Technical Assistance
　　Technological Advancement
　　World Affairs
　　World Problems

Development   *JUL. 1966*
　　Postings: 1,084   GC: 520
SN　Progression from earlier to later stages
　　of growth or organization—includes grad-
　　ual realization of potential, usually ac-
　　companied by advances in size, com-
　　plexity, efficiency, etc. (Note: Do not
　　confuse with "Change," which refers to

alterations, modifications, etc., that are
not sequential and progressive—use a
more specific term if possible)
NT　Community Development
　　Economic Development
　　Educational Development
　　Evolution
　　Facility Expansion
　　Individual Development
　　Industrialization
　　Job Development
　　Labor Force Development
　　Library Collection Development
　　Library Development
　　Material Development
　　Modernization
　　Organizational Development
　　Plant Growth
　　Population Growth
　　Program Development
　　Rural Development
　　Site Development
　　Student Development
　　Sustainable Development
　　Systems Development
　　Technological Advancement
　　Urbanization
　　Vocabulary Development
RT　Appropriate Technology
　　Change
　　Design
　　Developed Nations
　　Developing Nations
　　Development Communication
　　Developmental Continuity
　　Developmental Delays
　　Developmental Disabilities
　　Developmental Programs
　　Developmental Stages
　　Developmental Tasks
　　Developmentally Appropriate Practices
　　History
　　Improvement
　　Influences
　　Innovation
　　Planning
　　Research and Development
　　Research and Development Centers
　　Technology

Development Communication   *AUG. 1989*
　　Postings: 58   GC: 520
SN　Mass communication intended to pro-
　　mote social and material advancement
　　(greater equality, freedom, productivity,
　　etc.) of developing nations or among
　　poor peoples
BT　Communication (Thought Transfer)
RT　Developing Nations
　　Development
　　Developmental Programs
　　Mass Media

Developmental Continuity   *OCT. 1983*
　　Postings: 252   GC: 520
SN　Transitional continuity in human learn-
　　ing and development, e.g., between dif-
　　ferent elements and levels of schooling
UF　Continuity of Education
BT　Relationship
RT　Articulation (Education)
　　Development
　　Developmental Psychology
　　Developmental Stages
　　Epistemology
　　Experience
　　Humanization
　　Individual Development

Developmental Delays   *JUN. 1994*
　　Postings: 351   GC: 120
SN　Gaps between developmental (mental or
　　functional) age and chronological age—
　　serious delays may eventually be diag-
　　nosed as specific developmental disa-
　　bilities, while less severe delays may
　　catch up over time with normal develop-
　　ment and disappear (Note: See also the
　　Identifier "Language Delayed"—prior to

Jun94, "Developmental Disabilities" was
sometimes used to index this concept)
UF　Delayed Development (Individuals)
　　Developmentally Delayed
RT　Age
　　At Risk Persons
　　Behavior Development
　　Child Behavior
　　Child Development
　　Cognitive Development
　　Delayed Speech
　　Development
　　Developmental Disabilities
　　Developmental Stages
　　Disabilities
　　Early Intervention
　　Emotional Development
　　Individual Development
　　Individualized Family Service Plans
　　Motor Development
　　Personality Development
　　Physical Development
　　Readiness
　　Social Development
　　Special Education
　　Special Needs Students

Developmental Differences (Age Groups)
USE　Age Differences
AND　Individual Development

Developmental Disabilities   *JUN. 1977*
　　Postings: 2,268   GC: 220
SN　Category in federal legislation referring
　　to disabilities resulting from mental re-
　　tardation, cerebral palsy, epilepsy, au-
　　tism, or other neurological conditions
　　closely related to mental retardation that
　　originate before age 18 and are consid-
　　ered substantial impediments to normal
　　functioning
BT　Disabilities
RT　Autism
　　Cerebral Palsy
　　Cognitive Development
　　Communication Disorders
　　Development
　　Developmental Delays
　　Epilepsy
　　Learning Disabilities
　　Mental Retardation
　　Neurological Impairments

Developmental Guidance (1967 1980)
USE　Guidance

Developmental Patterns (Individuals)
USE　Individual Development

Developmental Programs   *JUL. 1966*
　　Postings: 1,655   GC: 520
SN　Programs promoting gradual growth of
　　persons or systems through progressive
　　advances in size, complexity, capacity,
　　or efficiency (Note: Coordinate with ap-
　　propriate "Development" term if possi-
　　ble)
NT　Developmental Studies Programs
BT　Programs
RT　Development
　　Development Communication
　　Economic Development
　　Educational Development
　　Individual Development
　　Labor Force Development
　　Library Development

Developmental Psychology   *JUL. 1966*
　　Postings: 1,850   GC: 230
BT　Psychology
RT　Behavior Development
　　Behaviorism
　　Child Psychology
　　Cognitive Development
　　Constructivism (Learning)
　　Developmental Continuity
　　Developmental Stages
　　Developmental Tasks

Emotional Development
Individual Development
Individual Psychology
Nature Nurture Controversy
Personality Development
Piagetian Theory
Sexual Identity

Developmental Reading (1966 1980)
　　　　　　　　　　　　　　　　　　　　　MAR. 1980
　　Postings: 466   GC: 460
SN　Invalid Descriptor—used for the devel-
　　opment of average or above average
　　readers' skills in elementary and second-
　　ary education and for the development of
　　below average readers' skills in higher
　　education—see "Reading Instruction" for
　　the former concept and "Remedial Read-
　　ing" for the latter

Developmental Stages   *OCT. 1976*
　　Postings: 4,932   GC: 120
SN　Natural or common divisions of the hu-
　　man developmental process, character-
　　ized by types of behavior (as in the oral
　　stage), by biological properties or mani-
　　festations (as in the embryonic stage), or
　　by mental processes (as in Piaget's "con-
　　crete operations" stage)
UF　Piagetian Stages #
　　Stage Theory
　　Stages of Development
RT　Adolescent Development
　　Adult Development
　　Age
　　Age Differences
　　Age Groups
　　Aging (Individuals)
　　Behavior Development
　　Child Behavior
　　Child Development
　　Cognitive Development
　　Compensation (Concept)
　　Concept Formation
　　Development
　　Developmental Continuity
　　Developmental Delays
　　Developmental Psychology
　　Developmental Tasks
　　Developmentally Appropriate Practices
　　Emotional Development
　　Epistemology
　　Formal Operations
　　Individual Development
　　Infant Behavior
　　Object Permanence
　　Physical Development
　　Piagetian Theory
　　Puberty

Developmental Studies Programs
　　　　　　　　　　　　　　　　　　　　　MAR. 1980
　　Postings: 939   GC: 310
SN　Comprehensive programs with both cog-
　　nitive and affective components designed
　　to develop the learning and academic
　　skills and the attitudes toward self and
　　others needed to enter and succeed at
　　postsecondary institutions (Note: Do not
　　confuse with "Developmental Programs,"
　　which prior to Mar80, was frequently
　　used for "Developmental Studies Pro-
　　grams")
BT　Developmental Programs
RT　Basic Skills
　　Basic Writing
　　College Preparation
　　Compensatory Education
　　Educationally Disadvantaged
　　High Risk Students
　　Individual Development
　　Remedial Programs
　　Skill Development
　　Transitional Programs

Developmental Tasks   *JUL. 1966*
　　Postings: 706   GC: 120
SN　Tasks that arise during different stages
　　of individual development, and whose

= Two or more Descriptors are used to represent this term.
The term's main entry shows the appropriate coordination.

successful completion is regarded by a society or culture as appropriate and necessary for acceptable functioning and subsequent development
UF   Piagetian Tasks #
RT   Adolescent Development
       Adult Development
       Child Development
       Development
       Developmental Psychology
       Developmental Stages
       Developmentally Appropriate Practices
       Readiness

Developmental Writing
USE   Basic Writing

Developmentally Appropriate Practices
                                                            APR. 2000
       Postings: 956   GC: 310
SN   Student-centered educational practices based on developmental needs (usually of young children) that are both age appropriate and individually appropriate—individuals' patterns of growth, personality, families, and culture are among the important elements of the latter dimension
UF   Developmentally Appropriate Programs
       Developmentally Inappropriate Education
BT   Educational Practices
RT   Age Differences
       Child Development
       Development
       Developmental Stages
       Developmental Tasks
       Early Childhood Education
       Educational Philosophy
       Individual Development
       Student Centered Curriculum
       Student Development
       Teaching Methods
       Young Children

Developmentally Appropriate Programs
USE   Developmentally Appropriate Practices

Developmentally Delayed
USE   Developmental Delays

Developmentally Inappropriate Education
USE   Developmentally Appropriate Practices

Dewey Decimal Classification   OCT. 1997
       Postings: 144   GC: 710
SN   Widely used hierarchical system for classifying library materials, devised by Melvil Dewey in 1873 and revised many times since then, that divides knowledge into ten 3-digit numeric subject classes, with further specification expressed by numerals following decimal notation
UF   DDC (Classification)
       Decimal Classification (Dewey)
BT   Classification
RT   Cataloging
       Indexing
       Information Retrieval
       Library Catalogs
       Library Collections
       Library Materials
       Library of Congress Classification
       Library Technical Processes
       Subject Index Terms
       Universal Decimal Classification

Diabetes   APR. 1969
       Postings: 281   GC: 210
BT   Diseases
RT   Physical Health
       Physiology
       Special Health Problems

Diachronic Linguistics   JUL. 1966
       Postings: 1,390   GC: 450
SN   Study of languages or linguistic features through the course of their historical development
UF   Historical Linguistics
       History of Language
       Language Evolution
       Language History
NT   Etymology
       Glottochronology
BT   Linguistics
RT   Anthropological Linguistics
       Contrastive Linguistics
       Language Classification
       Language Research
       Language Universals
       Language Variation
       Lexicology
       Linguistic Borrowing
       Middle English
       Morphology (Languages)
       Old English
       Onomastics
       Phonemics
       Phonology
       Structural Analysis (Linguistics)
       Structural Linguistics

Diacritical Marking   JUL. 1966
       Postings: 81   GC: 450
BT   Orthographic Symbols
RT   Graphemes
       Phonetic Transcription
       Phonetics
       Pronunciation
       Reading
       Spelling

Diagnosis
USE   Identification

Diagnosis (Clinical)
USE   Clinical Diagnosis

Diagnosis (Educational)
USE   Educational Diagnosis

Diagnostic Teaching   JUL. 1966
       Postings: 1,542   GC: 310
SN   Process of diagnosing student abilities, needs, and objectives and prescribing requisite learning activities
UF   Prescriptive Teaching
BT   Teaching Methods
RT   Counselor Teacher Cooperation
       Curriculum Based Assessment
       Diagnostic Tests
       Educational Diagnosis
       Educational Therapy
       Individualized Education Programs
       Individualized Instruction
       Informal Assessment
       Learning Problems
       Miscue Analysis
       Prereferral Intervention
       Psychoeducational Methods
       Remedial Instruction
       Special Education

Diagnostic Tests   JUL. 1966
       Postings: 2,317   GC: 830
SN   Tests used to identify the nature and source of an individual's educational, psychological, or medical difficulties or disabilities in order to facilitate correction or remediation
BT   Tests
RT   Auditory Tests
       Clinical Diagnosis
       Criterion Referenced Tests
       Diagnostic Teaching
       Disability Identification
       Early Identification
       Educational Diagnosis
       Identification
       Informal Reading Inventories
       Medical Evaluation

Personality Measures
Physical Examinations
Preschool Tests
Prognostic Tests
Projective Measures
Psychological Evaluation
Psychological Testing
Reading Readiness Tests
School Readiness Tests
Screening Tests
Vision Tests
Vocational Evaluation
Work Sample Tests

Diagrams   DEC. 1969
       Postings: 1,310   GC: 720
BT   Visual Aids
RT   Charts
       Concept Mapping
       Data
       Geometric Constructions
       Graphic Arts
       Illustrations
       Instructional Materials
       Mathematical Models
       Nonprint Media
       Records (Forms)
       Sentence Diagraming

Dial Access Information Systems
                                                            AUG. 1968
       Postings: 202   GC: 710
SN   Telecommunication systems in which users select (using a dial similar to a telephone dial) stored audio and/or video programs from remote locations
BT   Audiovisual Communications
       Information Systems
RT   Computer Oriented Programs
       Information Networks
       Language Laboratories
       Learning Laboratories
       Online Systems
       Telephone Communications Systems

Dialect Interference
USE   Dialects
AND   Interference (Language)

Dialect Studies   JUL. 1966
       Postings: 781   GC: 810
SN   Studies of the different ways in which the same language is spoken in different geographic regions or among different social classes (Note: As of Oct81, use as a minor Descriptor for examples of this kind of research—use as a major Descriptor only as the subject of a document)
BT   Language Research
       Sociolinguistics
RT   Bidialectalism
       Dialects
       Diglossia
       Etymology
       Language Variation

Dialectical Materialism
USE   Marxism

Dialects   JUL. 1966
       Postings: 1,102   GC: 450
SN   Special varieties within a language distinguished by differences in vocabulary, pronunciation, and grammar but not sufficiently different to be regarded as separate languages
UF   Accents (Dialects) #
       Dialect Interference #
NT   Black Dialects
       Nonstandard Dialects
       Regional Dialects
       Social Dialects
BT   Language Variation
       Languages
RT   Bidialectalism
       Cebuano
       Dialect Studies
       Diglossia

Foochow
Grammatical Acceptability
Idioms
Language
Language Classification
Language Standardization
Language Usage
Linguistics
Mutual Intelligibility
Native Speakers
North American English
Sociolinguistics

Dialog Journals   APR. 1990
       Postings: 217   GC: 310
SN   Logs or notebooks used by more than one person for exchanging experiences, ideas, or reflections—used most often in education as a means of sustained writing interaction between students and teachers at all educational levels and in second language and other types of instruction
UF   Dialogue Journals
BT   Diaries
RT   Classroom Communication
       Dialogs (Language)
       Interpersonal Communication
       Journal Writing
       Reading Writing Relationship
       Student Journals
       Teacher Student Relationship
       Teaching Methods
       Writing Exercises

Dialogs (Language)   APR. 1980
       Postings: 826   GC: 450
RT   Communicative Competence
          (Languages)
       Connected Discourse
       Dialog Journals
       Interpersonal Communication
       Language Fluency
       Language Patterns
       Language Proficiency
       Pattern Drills (Language)
       Second Language Instruction
       Speech Acts
       Speech Communication

Dialogs (Literary)   APR. 1980
       Postings: 338   GC: 430
UF   Dialogue (1969 1980)
BT   Literary Devices
RT   Drama

Dialogue Journals
USE   Dialog Journals

Dialogue (1969 1980)
USE   Dialogs (Literary)

Diaries   AUG. 1968
       Postings: 380   GC: 430
SN   Records, written daily or at frequent intervals, of the experiences, observations, attitudes, etc., of their authors (Note: Prior to Mar80, this term was not scoped and carried the instruction "Minutes (Records), USE Diaries")
NT   Dialog Journals
       Student Journals
BT   Literary Genres
       Nonfiction
RT   Autobiographies
       Journal Writing
       Literature
       Manuscripts
       Personal Narratives

Dictation   JUN. 1983
       Postings: 189   GC: 720
SN   Saying or reading aloud for transcription or machine recording—also, the resulting transcribed or recorded text
UF   Machine Dictation
BT   Verbal Communication

= Two or more Descriptors are used to represent this term.
The term's main entry shows the appropriate coordination.

RT Business Correspondence
    Business Skills
    Language Skills
    Second Language Learning
    Secretaries
    Shorthand

Dictatorship
USE Totalitarianism

Diction   JUL. 1966
    Postings: 76   GC: 450
RT Articulation (Speech)
    Language Fluency
    Language Patterns
    Pronunciation
    Speech
    Speech Tests

Dictionaries   JUL. 1966
    Postings: 1,269   GC: 720
SN (Note: Corresponds to Pubtype code
    134—do not use except as the subject of
    a document)
UF Lexicons
NT Glossaries
BT Reference Materials
RT Alphabetizing Skills
    Definitions
    Lexicography
    Lexicology
    Thesauri
    Word Lists

Dictionary Catalogs (1968 1980)
USE Library Catalogs

Didacticism   APR. 1970
    Postings: 101   GC: 430
SN Instructive qualities in literature, espe-
    cially concerning moral, ethical, or relig-
    ious matters
RT Childrens Literature
    Epics
    Fables
    Legends
    Literary Criticism

Diesel Engines   JUL. 1966
    Postings: 123   GC: 910
UF Diesel Fuel #
BT Engines
RT Agricultural Machinery
    Auto Mechanics
    Locomotive Engineers
    Motor Vehicles
    Small Engine Mechanics

Diesel Fuel
USE Diesel Engines
AND Fuels

Diesel Mechanics
USE Auto Mechanics

Dietary Technicians
USE Dietitians

Dietetic Aides
USE Dietitians

Dietetics   SEP. 1968
    Postings: 878   GC: 210
UF Diets
BT Medicine
RT Body Composition
    Dietitians
    Eating Habits
    Food
    Food Standards
    Nutrition
    Obesity

Dietitians   JUL. 1966
    Postings: 87   GC: 210
UF Dietary Technicians
    Dietetic Aides
BT Allied Health Personnel
RT Cooks
    Dietetics
    Food
    Food Service
    Food Standards
    Foods Instruction
    Home Economics Skills
    Nutrition
    Occupational Home Economics

Diets
USE Dietetics

Differences   JAN. 1978
    Postings: 665   GC: 520
SN Distinguishing elements or factors which
    differentiate one entity from another
    (Note: Use a more specific term if possi-
    ble)
UF Institutional Differences #
    Regional Differences #
NT Cultural Differences
    Individual Differences
    Intermode Differences
    Racial Differences
    Religious Differences
    Rural Urban Differences
    Salary Wage Differentials
    Social Differences
RT Comparative Analysis
    Comparative Testing
    Evaluation
    Specialization

Differential Equations   APR. 1990
    Postings: 68   GC: 480
SN Equations that express a relationship
    between mathematical functions and their
    derivatives
BT Equations (Mathematics)
RT Calculus

Differential Item Functioning
USE Item Bias

Differential Item Performance
USE Item Bias

Differential Psychology
USE Individual Psychology

Differentiated Staffs   MAY 1969
    Postings: 467   GC: 360
SN Staffs utilizing various levels of profes-
    sional and semiprofessional personnel
BT Personnel
RT Master Teachers
    Merit Pay
    Paraprofessional School Personnel
    Staff Utilization
    Teacher Interns
    Teachers

Difficulty Level   MAR. 1980
    Postings: 2,468   GC: 810
UF Complexity Level (1968 1979)
    Intricacy Level
    Item Difficulty #
    Task Difficulty
RT Ability
    Comprehension
    Content Analysis
    Item Analysis
    Performance
    Problems
    Readability Formulas
    Skill Analysis
    Skills
    Task Analysis

Diffusion (Communication)   SEP. 1982
    Postings: 348   GC: 710
SN Process by which an idea gets from its
    source or origin to its place of ultimate
    use
UF Diffusion (1967 1982) (Communica-
    tion)
BT Communication (Thought Transfer)
RT Adoption (Ideas)
    Information Dissemination
    Information Transfer
    Information Utilization
    Linking Agents
    Networks
    Research Utilization
    Technology Transfer
    Theory Practice Relationship
    Transfer of Training

Diffusion (Physics)   SEP. 1982
    Postings: 49   GC: 490
SN Spontaneous movement and scattering
    of particles (atoms, molecules, electrons,
    etc.)
UF Diffusion (1967 1982) (Physics)
BT Kinetics
RT Biophysics
    Chemical Reactions
    Climate
    Electronics
    Energy
    Kinetic Molecular Theory
    Matter
    Motion
    Optics
    Physics
    Thermodynamics

Diffusion (1967 1982) (Communication)
USE Diffusion (Communication)

Diffusion (1967 1982) (Physics)
USE Diffusion (Physics)

Diffusion (1967 1982) (Populations)
USE Population Distribution

Digital Computers   JUL. 1966
    Postings: 226   GC: 910
SN Computers that process discrete or dis-
    continuous data, performing sequences
    of arithmetic and logical operations
BT Computers
RT Analog Computers

Digital Libraries
USE Electronic Libraries

Digital Optical Data Disks
USE Optical Data Disks

Diglossia   JUL. 1966
    Postings: 194   GC: 450
SN Situation in which two (or more) lan-
    guages or language varieties are used
    for differing functions (e.g., vernacular
    and literary, colloquial and formal) within a
    single speech community
RT Bidialectalism
    Bilingualism
    Dialect Studies
    Dialects
    Language Classification
    Language Standardization
    Language Variation
    Multilingualism
    Mutual Intelligibility
    Nonstandard Dialects
    Social Dialects
    Sociolinguistics

Dimensional Preference   JUL. 1972
    Postings: 200   GC: 110
SN Cue response to color, form or size
BT Responses

RT Color
    Cues
    Learning Modalities
    Novelty (Stimulus Dimension)
    Patterned Responses
    Stimuli
    Tactual Perception
    Visual Perception

Dining Facilities   JUL. 1966
    Postings: 281   GC: 920
UF Cafeterias
    Restaurants
    Snack Bars
BT Facilities
RT Breakfast Programs
    Cooks
    Dishwashing
    Food Handling Facilities
    Food Service
    Hospitality Occupations
    Lunch Programs
    Waiters and Waitresses

Dinosaurs   DEC. 1992
    Postings: 98   GC: 490
SN Herbivorous or carnivorous reptiles of
    the extinct orders Saurischia and
    Ornithischia from the Mesozoic era
BT Animals
RT Paleontology

Diploma Requirements
USE Graduation Requirements

Diplomacy
USE International Relations

Diplomatic History   JUN. 1973
    Postings: 157   GC: 610
SN History of negotiations among nations,
    including the study of international alli-
    ances, treaties, and other agreements
BT History
RT Foreign Diplomats
    Foreign Policy
    International Education
    International Relations
    Political Science
    World Affairs
    World History

Diplomatic Policy
USE Foreign Policy

Direct Assessment
USE Performance Based Assessment

Directed Reading Activity   JUL. 1966
    Postings: 384   GC: 460
SN Teacher-guided reading activity—usu-
    ally includes the following steps: readi-
    ness, concept development, silent read-
    ing, discussion, and reinforcement of
    new skills and concepts (Note: Prior to
    Mar80, the use of this term was not
    restricted by a Scope Note)
BT Reading
    Reading Instruction
RT Advance Organizers
    Content Area Reading
    Learning Activities
    Reading Assignments
    Reading Comprehension

Direction Writing (1966 1980)   MAR. 1980
    Postings: 25   GC: 400
SN Invalid Descriptor—used inconsistently
    in indexing

Directories   JUL. 1966
    Postings: 2,301   GC: 720
SN Systematically arranged lists of persons
    or organizations, usually including

locational information (Note: Corresponds to Pubtype code 132—do not use except as the subject of a document)
BT   Reference Materials
RT   Guides
     Indexes

Directors
USE   Administrators

Directors of Research
USE   Research Directors

Disabilities   *MAR. 1980*
    Postings: 20,568   GC: 220
SN   Physical, mental, or sensory impairments that render major life activities more difficult (Note: Use a more specific term if possible)
UF   Disabled
     Handicapped (1966 1980)
     Handicaps
NT   Adventitious Impairments
     Attention Deficit Disorders
     Autism
     Behavior Disorders
     Communication Disorders
     Congenital Impairments
     Developmental Disabilities
     Diseases
     Hearing Impairments
     Injuries
     Language Impairments
     Learning Disabilities
     Low Incidence Disabilities
     Mental Disorders
     Mental Retardation
     Mild Disabilities
     Multiple Disabilities
     Perceptual Impairments
     Physical Disabilities
     Severe Disabilities
     Special Health Problems
     Speech Impairments
     Visual Impairments
RT   Ability
     Academic Accommodations (Disabilities)
     Accessibility (for Disabled)
     Adapted Physical Education
     Adaptive Behavior (of Disabled)
     Assistive Devices (for Disabled)
     At Risk Persons
     Attitudes toward Disabilities
     Deinstitutionalization (of Disabled)
     Developmental Delays
     Disability Discrimination
     Disability Identification
     Exceptional Child Research
     Frail Elderly
     Gifted Disabled
     Group Homes
     Health
     Inclusive Schools
     Individualized Family Service Plans
     Intervention
     Long Term Care
     Mainstreaming
     Normalization (Disabilities)
     Parents with Disabilities
     Patients
     Rehabilitation
     Residential Care
     Respite Care
     Self Advocacy
     Self Care Skills
     Severity (of Disability)
     Sheltered Workshops
     Special Education
     Special Education Teachers
     Special Needs Students
     Teachers with Disabilities
     Therapy

Disability Discrimination   *MAR. 1994*
    Postings: 138   GC: 540
SN   Restriction or denial of rights, privileges, and choice because of physical, mental, or sensory impairment

UF   Handicap Discrimination (1984 1994)
BT   Social Discrimination
RT   Affirmative Action
     Age Discrimination
     Attitudes toward Disabilities
     Disabilities
     Educational Discrimination
     Equal Education
     Equal Opportunities (Jobs)
     Normalization (Disabilities)
     Reverse Discrimination
     Social Bias

Disability Identification   *MAR. 1994*
    Postings: 886   GC: 220
UF   Handicap Detection (1966 1980)
     Handicap Identification (1980 1994)
BT   Identification
RT   Ability Identification
     At Risk Persons
     Clinical Diagnosis
     Diagnostic Tests
     Disabilities
     Early Identification
     Etiology
     Medical Evaluation
     Prereferral Intervention
     Referral
     Screening Tests
     Severity (of Disability)
     Symptoms (Individual Disorders)

Disabled
USE   Disabilities

Disabled Parents
USE   Parents with Disabilities

Disabled Teachers
USE   Teachers with Disabilities

Disadvantaged   *MAR. 1980*
    Postings: 5,590   GC: 540
SN   Individuals or groups who have low status in a particular society for reasons of race, sex, ethnicity, economics, language, geographic location, environment, education, disabilities, etc. (Note: Use a more specific term if possible)
UF   Cultural Disadvantagement (1966 1980)
     Culturally Disadvantaged (1966 1980)
     Deprived
     Disadvantaged Groups (1966 1980)
     Social Disadvantagement (1966 1980)
     Socially Disadvantaged (1966 1980)
     Underprivileged
NT   Disadvantaged Youth
     Economically Disadvantaged
     Educationally Disadvantaged
     Gifted Disadvantaged
BT   Groups
RT   Advantaged
     Affirmative Action
     Disadvantaged Environment
     Intervention
     Living Standards
     Lower Class
     Quality of Life
     Rehabilitation
     Social Status

Disadvantaged Children
USE   Disadvantaged Youth

Disadvantaged Environment   *JUL. 1966*
    Postings: 566   GC: 550
SN   An environment characterized by neglect, poverty, or social, cultural, racial, or linguistic isolation
UF   Deprivation
     Deprived Environment
     Disadvantagement
BT   Environment
RT   Cultural Isolation
     Disadvantaged
     Disadvantaged Schools

Educationally Disadvantaged
     Poverty
     Poverty Areas
     Slum Environment
     Social Isolation

Disadvantaged Groups (1966 1980)
USE   Disadvantaged

Disadvantaged Schools   *JUL. 1966*
    Postings: 205   GC: 340
SN   Schools whose programs, facilities, or resources do not meet the basic educational needs of their students (Note: Prior to Mar80, the use of this term was not restricted by a Scope Note)
BT   Schools
RT   Disadvantaged Environment
     Educationally Disadvantaged
     Equalization Aid
     Slum Schools

Disadvantaged Youth   *JUL. 1966*
    Postings: 9,108   GC: 540
SN   (Note: Coordinate with an appropriate age or educational level Descriptor)
UF   Deprived Children
     Disadvantaged Children
     Slum Children
BT   Disadvantaged
     Youth
RT   Lower Class Students

Disadvantagement
USE   Disadvantaged Environment

Disarmament   *APR. 1972*
    Postings: 376   GC: 610
UF   Arms Control
     Multilateral Disarmament
     Nuclear Control
     Unilateral Disarmament
RT   Armed Forces
     Conflict
     Gun Control
     International Relations
     Military Science
     National Defense
     Nuclear Warfare
     Nuclear Weapons
     Peace
     War
     Weapons
     World Problems

Disaster Readiness
USE   Emergency Programs

Disbursements (Money)
USE   Expenditures

Disciplinary Action
USE   Discipline

Discipline   *JUL. 1966*
    Postings: 3,969   GC: 330
UF   Classroom Discipline #
     Disciplinary Action
NT   Dismissal (Personnel)
     Expulsion
     Suspension
     Teacher Discipline
RT   Behavior Problems
     Classroom Techniques
     Codes of Ethics
     Corporal Punishment
     Delay of Gratification
     Discipline Policy
     Discipline Problems
     Obedience
     Proctoring
     Punishment
     Reality Therapy
     Sanctions
     Self Control

Discipline Based Art Education   *OCT. 1994*
    Postings: 270   GC: 420
SN   Art education that draws its content from the four foundational art disciplines of art production, art history, art criticism, and aesthetics, rather than emphasizing art production (studio experiences) alone
BT   Art Education
RT   Aesthetics
     Art Appreciation
     Art Criticism
     Art History
     Studio Art
     Visual Arts

Discipline Policy   *JUL. 1966*
    Postings: 1,811   GC: 330
BT   Policy
RT   Behavior Standards
     Codes of Ethics
     Corporal Punishment
     Discipline
     Dress Codes
     In Loco Parentis
     In School Suspension
     School Policy
     School Uniforms
     Student Rights

Discipline Problems   *JUL. 1966*
    Postings: 1,128   GC: 530
BT   Problems
RT   Cheating
     Discipline
     Lying
     Plagiarism
     Resistance (Psychology)
     Stealing
     Vandalism

Disclosure   *MAR. 1978*
    Postings: 749   GC: 710
SN   Communication of personal, organizational, or institutional information and records
UF   Public Disclosure
NT   Self Disclosure (Individuals)
RT   Case Records
     Communication (Thought Transfer)
     Confidential Records
     Confidentiality
     Freedom of Information
     Information Dissemination
     Information Policy
     Intellectual Freedom
     Privacy
     Student Records
     Student Rights

Discographies   *FEB. 1976*
    Postings: 81   GC: 730
SN   Organized lists of phonograph records
UF   Phonograph Record Lists
BT   Reference Materials
RT   Audiodisks
     Bibliographies
     Filmographies
     Indexes
     Library Catalogs
     Music
     Oral History

Discourse Analysis   *AUG. 1968*
    Postings: 5,603   GC: 450
BT   Structural Analysis (Linguistics)
RT   Coherence
     Cohesion (Written Composition)
     Communication Research
     Connected Discourse
     Discourse Communities
     Grammar
     Hermeneutics
     Language Research
     Morphology (Languages)
     Narration
     Paragraph Composition
     Pragmatics
     Rhetorical Theory
     Semantics

= Two or more Descriptors are used to represent this term.
The term's main entry shows the appropriate coordination.

Sentences
Speech Acts
Story Grammar
Syntax

Discourse Communities　　　*AUG. 2000*
　　Postings: 269　　　　　　GC: 520
SN　Groups in which expressions of thought, either written or spoken, share characteristics of vocabulary, communicative intent, subject matter, form of presentation, etc.
UF　Academic Discourse Communities #
　　Rhetorical Community
BT　Community
RT　Academic Discourse
　　Communication (Thought Transfer)
　　Discourse Analysis
　　Language Styles

Discourse Modes　　　　　*APR. 1990*
　　Postings: 423　　　　　　GC: 450
SN　Ways of organizing and classifying spoken or written discourse, such as by purpose, style, situation, and/or intended audience, e.g., poetic/technical, narrative/expository, informative/indicative, personal/formal
BT　Classification
RT　Communication (Thought Transfer)
　　Language Arts
　　Literary Devices
　　Mass Media
　　Rhetoric
　　Speech
　　Verbal Communication
　　Writing (Composition)

Discovery
USE　Discovery Processes

Discovery Learning　　　　*JUL. 1966*
　　Postings: 2,221　　　　　GC: 110
SN　Learning situation in which the principal content of what is to be learned is not given but must be independently discovered by the learner
UF　Exploratory Learning
BT　Learning
RT　Active Learning
　　Activity Units
　　Adventure Education
　　Discovery Processes
　　Experiential Learning
　　Heuristics
　　Independent Study
　　Inquiry
　　Learner Controlled Instruction
　　Learning Activities
　　Learning Centers (Classroom)
　　Learning Strategies
　　Montessori Method
　　Observational Learning
　　Open Education
　　Problem Based Learning
　　Questioning Techniques

Discovery Processes　　　*JUL. 1966*
　　Postings: 611　　　　　　GC: 110
SN　Behaviors (e.g., inquiry, exploration, experimentation, etc.) used by persons in ascertaining things not hitherto known, or known by them (Note: Compare "Inventions"—do not confuse with "Exploratory Behavior")
UF　Discovery
BT　Learning Processes
RT　Adoption (Ideas)
　　Creative Thinking
　　Creativity
　　Discovery Learning
　　Experience
　　Experiments
　　Innovation
　　Intellectual Property
　　Inventions
　　Perception
　　Productive Thinking
　　Research

Discriminant Analysis　　　*JUL. 1966*
　　Postings: 711　　　　　　GC: 820
SN　Statistical method for combining a set of measures, or score profiles, to obtain the maximum difference or discrimination between two or more groups
UF　Discriminant Function Analysis
　　Discriminatory Analysis
　　Multiple Discriminant Analysis
BT　Multivariate Analysis
RT　Factor Analysis
　　Item Analysis
　　Mathematical Models
　　Multidimensional Scaling
　　Multitrait Multimethod Techniques

Discriminant Function Analysis
USE　Discriminant Analysis

Discrimination (Social)
USE　Social Discrimination

Discrimination Learning　　　*JUL. 1966*
　　Postings: 1,374　　　　　GC: 110
SN　Learning to detect and respond to differences among stimuli
BT　Learning
RT　Auditory Discrimination
　　Concept Formation
　　Perception
　　Sensory Training
　　Shift Studies
　　Visual Discrimination

Discrimination Transfer
USE　Shift Studies

Discriminatory Analysis
USE　Discriminant Analysis

Discriminatory Attitudes (Social) (1966 1980)
USE　Social Bias

Discriminatory Legislation　　*JUL. 1966*
　　Postings: 324　　　　　　GC: 540
SN　Legislation that is biased against a particular group
UF　Legislative Discrimination
BT　Legislation
RT　Civil Rights Legislation
　　Constitutional Law
　　Laws
　　Legal Problems
　　Majority Attitudes
　　Social Bias
　　Social Discrimination

Discussion　　　　　　　*MAR. 1980*
　　Postings: 510　　　　　　GC: 720
SN　Oral, and sometimes written, exchange of opinions—usually to analyze, clarify, or reach conclusions about issues, questions, or problems
UF　Discussion Experience (1966 1980)
　　Discussion Programs (1966 1980)
NT　Group Discussion
BT　Communication (Thought Transfer)
RT　Decision Making
　　Discussion (Teaching Technique)
　　Discussion Groups
　　Interpersonal Communication
　　Interviews
　　Participation
　　Problem Solving
　　Speech Communication

Discussion (Teaching Technique)　*JUL. 1966*
　　Postings: 2,515　　　　　GC: 310
UF　Class Discussion
　　Discussion Guides #
BT　Teaching Methods
RT　Case Method (Teaching Technique)
　　Discussion
　　Discussion Groups

Lecture Method
Questioning Techniques
Reciprocal Teaching
Wait Time

Discussion Experience (1966 1980)
USE　Discussion

Discussion Groups　　　　*JUL. 1966*
　　Postings: 876　　　　　　GC: 310
SN　Groups that meet to discuss subjects of mutual interest (Note: Do not confuse with "Group Discussion")
NT　Focus Groups
　　Listening Groups
BT　Groups
RT　Discussion
　　Discussion (Teaching Technique)
　　Group Discussion
　　Listservs

Discussion Guides
USE　Discussion (Teaching Technique)
AND　Teaching Guides

Discussion Programs (1966 1980)
USE　Discussion

Disease Control　　　　　*JUL. 1966*
　　Postings: 1,147　　　　　GC: 210
NT　Fluoridation
RT　Bacteria
　　Cleaning
　　Communicable Diseases
　　Disease Incidence
　　Diseases
　　Dishwashing
　　Drinking Water
　　Epidemiology
　　Health
　　Health Education
　　Hygiene
　　Immunization Programs
　　Pesticides
　　Pests
　　Pollution
　　Preventive Medicine
　　Public Health
　　Sanitation
　　Sick Child Care
　　Symptoms (Individual Disorders)
　　Viruses
　　Water Treatment

Disease Incidence　　　　*MAR. 1980*
　　Postings: 255　　　　　　GC: 210
UF　Disease Rate (1967 1980)
BT　Incidence
RT　Disease Control
　　Diseases
　　Epidemiology
　　Low Incidence Disabilities
　　Mortality Rate
　　Public Health

Disease Rate (1967 1980)
USE　Disease Incidence

Diseases　　　　　　　　*JUL. 1966*
　　Postings: 1,490　　　　　GC: 210
SN　(Note: Use "Special Health Problems" for discussions of the effects (or potential effects) of particular diseases on individual learning and development—prior to Mar80, this term did not carry a Scope Note)
UF　Illnesses
　　Sicknesses
NT　Alcoholism
　　Allergy
　　Alzheimers Disease
　　Anemia
　　Asthma
　　Cancer
　　Chronic Illness
　　Communicable Diseases

Cystic Fibrosis
Diabetes
Drug Addiction
Eating Disorders
Failure to Thrive
Fetal Alcohol Syndrome
Hypertension
Obesity
Occupational Diseases
Otitis Media
Poisoning
Seizures
Terminal Illness
BT　Disabilities
RT　Adventitious Impairments
　　Bacteria
　　Child Health
　　Disease Control
　　Disease Incidence
　　Epidemiology
　　Gynecology
　　Health
　　Heart Disorders
　　Hygiene
　　Internal Medicine
　　Pain
　　Pathology
　　Patient Education
　　Perinatal Influences
　　Pests
　　Physical Health
　　Pollution
　　Prenatal Influences
　　Radiation Effects
　　Rehabilitation
　　Sick Child Care
　　Stress Variables
　　Surgery
　　Viruses

Disemployment
USE　Dislocated Workers

Dishonesty
USE　Honesty

Dishwashing　　　　　　*MAR. 1969*
　　Postings: 32　　　　　　GC: 210
BT　Cleaning
RT　Dining Facilities
　　Disease Control
　　Food Handling Facilities
　　Food Service
　　Hygiene
　　Sanitary Facilities

Disk Drives　　　　　　　*JAN. 1988*
　　Postings: 36　　　　　　GC: 910
SN　Input output devices that effect the necessary movements of disks or disk packs and that have read/write heads for accessing and recording data on the disks and communicating with the computer
BT　Input Output Devices
RT　Magnetic Disks
　　Optical Disks

Diskettes
USE　Floppy Disks

Dislocated Workers　　　　*MAR. 1984*
　　Postings: 616　　　　　　GC: 630
SN　Workers who have lost their jobs because of economic and technological changes in a business or industry, e.g., plant closings or relocation, increased competition, automation, or market fluctuations
UF　Disemployment
　　Displaced Workers
BT　Personnel
RT　Career Change
　　Dismissal (Personnel)
　　Employees
　　Employment
　　Employment Patterns
　　Employment Practices
　　Job Applicants

= Two or more Descriptors are used to represent this term.
The term's main entry shows the appropriate coordination.

　　Job Layoff
　　Job Search Methods
　　Job Skills
　　Labor Economics
　　Labor Force
　　Labor Market
　　Labor Turnover
　　Outplacement Services (Employment)
　　Reduction in Force
　　Retraining
　　Skill Obsolescence
　　Structural Unemployment
　　Technological Advancement
　　Unemployment

Dismissal (Personnel)　　　　MAR. 1980
　　　　Postings: 337　　　　GC: 630
SN　Termination of employment when initi-
　　ated by the employer (Note: If applicable,
　　use the more specific term "Teacher
　　Dismissal"—prior to Mar80, the instruc-
　　tion "Dismissal, USE Disqualification"
　　was carried in the Thesaurus)
UF　Personnel Discharge
　　Personnel Dismissal
NT　Teacher Dismissal
BT　Discipline
RT　Dislocated Workers
　　Disqualification
　　Employment Practices
　　Financial Exigency
　　Job Layoff
　　Outplacement Services (Employment)
　　Personnel Evaluation
　　Personnel Policy
　　Reduction in Force

Displaced Homemakers　　　　MAR. 1980
　　　　Postings: 355　　　　GC: 510
SN　Women over age 35 who have become
　　responsible for their own support due to
　　divorce, separation, or the death of their
　　husbands and who have been outside
　　the work force for an extended period of
　　time—they may face earning a living
　　with minimal skills and experience
BT　Females
RT　Divorce
　　Fatherless Family
　　Heads of Households
　　Homemakers
　　Job Applicants
　　Labor Market
　　Marital Instability
　　Mothers
　　Reentry Workers
　　Special Needs Students
　　Widowed

Displaced Workers
USE　Dislocated Workers

Display Aids　　　　MAR. 1980
　　　　Postings: 193　　　　GC: 720
SN　Materials and/or equipment used for vis-
　　ual displays
UF　Display Panels (1968 1980)
BT　Visual Aids
RT　Audiovisual Aids
　　Educational Equipment
　　Exhibits
　　Merchandising
　　Nonprint Media
　　Screens (Displays)
　　Three Dimensional Aids

Display Layout (Computers)
USE　Screen Design (Computers)

Display Panels (1968 1980)
USE　Display Aids

Display Systems　　　　JUL. 1966
　　　　Postings: 513　　　　GC: 710
SN　Combination hardware and software sys-
　　tems that present information visually
　　on console screens or similar devices

connected to computers (Note: Prior to
Mar80, this term was not scoped and
was sometimes used for audiovisual dis-
plays)
UF　Computer Displays
RT　Computer Graphics
　　Computers
　　Information Retrieval
　　Information Systems
　　Input Output Devices
　　Interactive Video
　　Man Machine Systems
　　Screen Design (Computers)
　　Video Display Terminals

Disposition (Individuals)
USE　Personality

Dispositional Characteristics
USE　Personality Traits

Disqualification　　　　JUL. 1966
　　　　Postings: 72　　　　GC: 520
SN　The act of making ineligible
UF　Ineligibility
RT　Dismissal (Personnel)
　　Eligibility
　　Expulsion
　　Qualifications
　　Suspension
　　Teacher Dismissal
　　Withdrawal (Education)

Dissection　　　　OCT. 1996
　　　　Postings: 86　　　　GC: 490
SN　Examining the structure of an animal or
　　plant by cutting it apart—frequently com-
　　puter-simulated, and may include hu-
　　man anatomical study (Note: For opera-
　　tive medical treatment, use "Surgery")
BT　Laboratory Procedures
RT　Anatomy
　　Biology
　　Botany
　　Zoology

Dissent　　　　APR. 1972
　　　　Postings: 490　　　　GC: 610
BT　Social Behavior
RT　Activism
　　Beliefs
　　Conflict
　　Controversial Issues (Course Content)
　　Opinions
　　Political Attitudes
　　Resistance (Psychology)
　　Revolution
　　Social Action
　　Social Attitudes
　　Values

Distance　　　　AUG. 1968
　　　　Postings: 315　　　　GC: 480
UF　Range (Distance)
RT　Geographic Location
　　Height
　　Intervals
　　Proximity
　　Relationship
　　School Location
　　Scientific Concepts
　　Space
　　Time
　　Topology
　　Transportation

Distance Education　　　　OCT. 1983
　　　　Postings: 5,709　　　　GC: 330
SN　Education via the communications me-
　　dia (correspondence, radio, television,
　　and others) with little or no classroom or
　　other face-to-face contact between stu-
　　dents and teachers
NT　Correspondence Study
BT　Education
RT　Access to Education
　　Communications Satellites

Computer Mediated Communication
Continuing Education
Correspondence Schools
Educational Radio
Educational Television
Extension Education
External Degree Programs
Geographic Isolation
Home Study
Independent Study
Interactive Television
Lifelong Learning
Mass Instruction
Nontraditional Education
Open Universities
Outreach Programs
Part Time Students
Telecommunications
Telecourses

Distinctive Features (Language)　　MAR. 1980
　　　　Postings: 584　　　　GC: 450
SN　Features that distinguish linguistic units
　　from one another—most commonly used
　　in phonology, where phonemes may be
　　defined in terms of such distinctive fea-
　　tures as voicing, point of articulation,
　　and manner of articulation
UF　Distinctive Features (1967 1980)
BT　Linguistics
RT　Acoustic Phonetics
　　Artificial Speech
　　Componential Analysis
　　Consonants
　　Language Universals
　　Phonemes
　　Phonetics
　　Phonology

Distinctive Features (1967 1980)
USE　Distinctive Features (Language)

Distractors (Tests)　　　　AUG. 1988
　　　　Postings: 87　　　　GC: 820
SN　Incorrect alternative answers used in
　　objective test items—also, incorrect
　　choices or extraneous information used
　　in test-like tasks
RT　Guessing (Tests)
　　Multiple Choice Tests
　　Objective Tests
　　Test Construction
　　Test Items
　　Test Validity
　　Testing
　　Tests

Distribution (Economics)
USE　Marketing

Distribution Free Statistics
USE　Nonparametric Statistics

Distributions (Statistics)
USE　Statistical Distributions

Distributive Education　　　　JUL. 1966
　　　　Postings: 1,259　　　　GC: 400
SN　Formal preparation for occupations in
　　the field of distribution and marketing
　　covering such activities as selling, buy-
　　ing, transporting, storing, promoting, fi-
　　nancing, marketing research, and man-
　　agement
UF　Retail Training
BT　Vocational Education
RT　Agribusiness
　　Business Education
　　Communications
　　Cooperative Education
　　Distributive Education Teachers
　　Food Service
　　Insurance Occupations
　　Manufacturing
　　Marketing
　　Merchandising
　　Office Occupations

Real Estate Occupations
Retailing
Sales Occupations
Salesmanship
Transportation
Utilities
Wholesaling

Distributive Education Teachers　　SEP. 1968
　　　　Postings: 68　　　　GC: 360
BT　Vocational Education Teachers
RT　Distributive Education

District Libraries
USE　Regional Libraries

District Norms
USE　Local Norms

Divergent Thinking　　　　NOV. 1968
　　　　Postings: 605　　　　GC: 110
SN　Creative, imaginative, and flexible think-
　　ing that results in a variety and abun-
　　dance of ideas or answers to a problem
BT　Creative Thinking
RT　Brainstorming
　　Convergent Thinking
　　Problem Solving
　　Productive Thinking
　　Thinking Skills

Diversity (Biology)
USE　Biodiversity

Diversity (Cultural) as a Value
USE　Cultural Pluralism

Diversity (Cultural) as an Observation or a Fact
USE　Cultural Differences

Diversity (Faculty)　　　　AUG. 1997
　　　　Postings: 263　　　　GC: 330
SN　Variation within a faculty population of
　　such characteristics as race, religion,
　　gender, cultural background, sexual ori-
　　entation, or socioeconomic class
RT　Cultural Differences
　　Cultural Pluralism
　　Diversity (Institutional)
　　Diversity (Student)
　　Ethnic Relations
　　Faculty
　　Faculty Integration
　　Minority Group Teachers
　　Minority Groups
　　Multicultural Education
　　Racial Relations
　　Teacher Characteristics
　　Teacher Integration

Diversity (Institutional)　　　　MAY 1993
　　　　Postings: 547　　　　GC: 330
SN　The multiplicity of variables that embody
　　an institution, including its policies and
　　programs, organization, reputation, and
　　staff/client population characteristics
BT　Institutional Characteristics
RT　Cultural Differences
　　Cultural Pluralism
　　Diversity (Faculty)
　　Diversity (Student)
　　Educational Quality
　　Governance
　　Institutional Autonomy
　　Institutional Environment
　　Institutional Evaluation
　　Institutional Mission
　　Institutional Research
　　Institutional Role
　　Intercultural Programs
　　Multicultural Education
　　Nontraditional Education
　　Organizational Climate
　　Organizational Theories

= Two or more Descriptors are used to represent this term.
The term's main entry shows the appropriate coordination.

School Choice
School Demography
School Organization
School Size
Student Characteristics

Diversity (Student)   *AUG. 1997*
  Postings: 2,078   GC: 330
SN Variation within a student population of
    such characteristics as race, religion,
    gender, cultural background, sexual ori-
    entation, or socioeconomic class
BT Student Characteristics
RT Cultural Differences
    Cultural Pluralism
    Diversity (Faculty)
    Diversity (Institutional)
    Ethnic Relations
    Minority Groups
    Multicultural Education
    Racial Relations
    Students

Divided Catalogs (1968 1980)
USE Library Catalogs

Diving   *JAN. 1985*
  Postings: 26   GC: 470
SN Plunging into water in a prescribed man-
    ner (Note: Do not confuse with "Under-
    water Diving")
UF Platform Diving
    Springboard Diving
    Tower Diving
BT Aquatic Sports
RT Olympic Games
    Swimming
    Swimming Pools

Division   *JUL. 1966*
  Postings: 429   GC: 480
BT Arithmetic
RT Addition
    Multiplication
    Subtraction

Divorce   *FEB. 1976*
  Postings: 1,924   GC: 520
SN The legal dissolution of a marriage
UF Divorced Persons
RT Child Custody
    Child Support
    Displaced Homemakers
    Family Problems
    Fatherless Family
    Marital Instability
    Marital Status
    Marriage
    Marriage Counseling
    Motherless Family
    One Parent Family
    Remarriage
    Spouses

Divorced Persons
USE Divorce

DNA   *OCT. 1982*
  Postings: 254   GC: 490
SN Any of the class of nucleic acids that
    contains deoxyribose, found chiefly in
    cell nuclei and associated with the trans-
    mission of genetic information
UF Deoxyribonucleic Acid
    Desoxyribonucleic Acid
    Recombinant DNA #
BT Nucleic Acids
RT Genetic Engineering
    Genetics

Doctor of Arts Degrees   *MAR. 1976*
  Postings: 52   GC: 340
SN Degrees emphasizing broad subject-mat-
    ter competence and teaching skills and
    designed for students entering careers
    as college teachers

BT Doctoral Degrees
RT College Faculty
    Degree Requirements
    Doctoral Programs
    Graduate Study

Doctor Patient Relationship
USE Physician Patient Relationship

Doctoral Degrees   *JUL. 1966*
  Postings: 1,820   GC: 340
NT Doctor of Arts Degrees
BT Degrees (Academic)
RT Bachelors Degrees
    Degree Requirements
    Doctoral Dissertations
    Doctoral Programs
    Graduate Study
    Masters Degrees
    Specialist in Education Degrees
    Teacher Educator Education

Doctoral Dissertations   *MAR. 1980*
  Postings: 5,051   GC: 720
SN Theses submitted in partial fulfillment of
    doctoral degree requirements (Note: Cor-
    responds to Pubtype code 041—do not
    use except as the subject of a document)
UF Doctoral Theses (1967 1980)
BT Theses
RT Degrees (Academic)
    Doctoral Degrees
    Doctoral Programs
    Graduate Study
    Practicum Papers

Doctoral Programs   *JUL. 1966*
  Postings: 1,852   GC: 340
SN Formal graduate programs in higher edu-
    cation institutions that culminate in the
    award of a doctoral degree, such as a
    PhD or EdD
BT College Programs
RT Degree Requirements
    Doctor of Arts Degrees
    Doctoral Degrees
    Doctoral Dissertations
    Graduate School Faculty
    Graduate Students
    Graduate Study
    Higher Education
    Masters Programs
    Postdoctoral Education
    Teacher Educator Education

Doctoral Theses (1967 1980)
USE Doctoral Dissertations

Document Delivery   *NOV. 1995*
  Postings: 280   GC: 710
SN Transmission of a print or electronic
    document, such as a journal article, from
    a vendor or library to the requestor—
    may be fee-based or free
BT Delivery Systems
    Information Dissemination
RT Facsimile Transmission
    Information Networks
    Information Retrieval
    Interlibrary Loans
    Library Services

Document Readers
USE Optical Scanners

Documentaries   *SEP. 1971*
  Postings: 314   GC: 720
SN Factual film, videotape, or audio record-
    ings of some real event or historic sub-
    ject
BT Nonprint Media
RT Audiovisual Aids
    Broadcast Journalism
    Educational Radio
    Educational Television
    Film Industry

    Film Study
    Films
    Instructional Films
    Tape Recordings

Documentation   *JUL. 1966*
  Postings: 1,299   GC: 710
SN Techniques used to collect, process, or-
    ganize, store, and retrieve documents
    (Note: Use "Computer Software" for com-
    puter program documentation)
NT Abstracting
    Authority Control (Information)
    Bibliometrics
    Cataloging
    Filing
    Indexing
BT Information Processing
RT Classification
    Codification
    Coding
    Information Dissemination
    Information Retrieval
    Information Storage
    Information Systems
    Special Libraries
    Technical Writing

Dogmatism   *JUL. 1966*
  Postings: 316   GC: 120
RT Authoritarianism
    Beliefs
    Ideology
    Opinions
    Personality Traits
    Totalitarianism

Domestic Violence (Family)
USE Family Violence

Domestics (1970 1980)
USE Household Workers

Dominican Americans
USE Dominicans
AND Hispanic Americans

Dominicans   *SEP. 1975*
  Postings: 48   GC: 560
SN Citizens of, or those who identify them-
    selves as bearers of the culture of, the
    Dominican Republic
UF Dominican Americans #
BT Latin Americans
RT Ethnic Groups
    Hispanic Americans
    Spanish Speaking

Donors   *OCT. 1982*
  Postings: 693   GC: 620
SN Individuals or organizations who donate
    money, land, or material goods to a
    cause, fund, or institution (Note: For
    donors of body organs, blood, etc., use
    "Tissue Donors")
UF Financial Donors
BT Groups
RT Corporate Support
    Endowment Funds
    Fund Raising
    Philanthropic Foundations
    Phonathons
    Private Financial Support
    Social Support Groups
    Trusts (Financial)

Doors   *JUL. 1969*
  Postings: 26   GC: 920
BT Structural Elements (Construction)
RT Construction Materials

Dormitories   *JUL. 1966*
  Postings: 813   GC: 920
UF Dormitory Living #
    Residence Halls

BT Housing
RT College Buildings
    College Housing
    Educational Facilities
    House Plan
    Living Learning Centers
    On Campus Students
    Resident Advisers
    Resident Assistants
    Residential Colleges

Dormitory Living
USE Dormitories
AND Group Experience

Double Employment
USE Multiple Employment

Double Sessions   *DEC. 1969*
  Postings: 21   GC: 350
SN School days consisting of separate ses-
    sions for two groups of students in the
    same instructional space, e.g., one room
    used by one fourth-grade class in the
    morning and by another fourth-grade
    class in the afternoon
UF Split Sessions
BT School Schedules
RT School Organization
    Space Utilization

Downloading   *APR. 1993*
  Postings: 72   GC: 710
SN The process of transferring or transmit-
    ting a file, program, software, data, char-
    acter sets, etc., from a distant to a nearby
    computer, from a larger to a smaller
    computer, or from a computer to a pe-
    ripheral device
BT Information Retrieval
RT Computer Oriented Programs
    Computers
    Copyrights
    Data Processing
    Fair Use (Copyrights)
    Information Systems
    Information Technology
    Information Transfer
    Online Searching
    Online Systems

Downs Anomaly
USE Downs Syndrome

Downs Syndrome   *JAN. 1978*
  Postings: 869   GC: 220
UF Downs Anomaly
    Mongolism (1968 1978)
BT Congenital Impairments
    Mental Retardation
RT Genetics
    Mild Mental Retardation
    Moderate Mental Retardation
    Neurological Impairments
    Physical Characteristics

Drafters (1980 1981)
USE Drafting

Drafting   *JUL. 1966*
  Postings: 694   GC: 640
SN Communication of ideas through draw-
    ings, sketches, charts, graphs, and maps
    according to mathematical rules of
    projection—also, the use of drafting in-
    struments in lettering, sketching, geo-
    metric construction, orthographic and
    pictorial drawings, working drawings,
    etc.
UF Computer Assisted Drafting #
    Drafters (1980 1981)
    Draftsmen (1968 1980)
    Drawing (Precision Draft)
NT Architectural Drafting
    Engineering Drawing
    Technical Illustration

= Two or more Descriptors are used to represent this term.
The term's main entry shows the appropriate coordination.

BT	Visual Arts
RT	Blueprints
	Computer Assisted Design
	Designers
	Graphic Arts
	Industrial Arts
	Orthographic Projection
	Technical Occupations
	Technology Education

Draftsmen (1968 1980)
USE　Drafting

Drama　　　　　　　　　　　　JUL. 1966
　　　Postings: 2,774　　　　　　　GC: 430
UF　Dramatic Unities (1970 1980)
　　Folk Drama (1969 1980) #
　　Outdoor Drama (1968 1980) #
　　Plays (Theatrical)
NT　Comedy
　　Scripts
　　Soap Operas
　　Tragedy
BT　Literature
　　Theater Arts
RT　Acting
　　Art
　　Audiences
　　Dialogs (Literary)
　　Dramatics
　　Fiction
　　Folk Culture
　　Literary Devices
　　Literary Genres
　　Literary Styles
　　Monologs
　　Oral Interpretation
　　Poetry
　　Prose
　　Rehearsals (Theater Arts)

Drama Workshops　　　　　　JUL. 1966
　　　Postings: 83　　　　　　　　GC: 420
BT　Workshops
RT　Arts Centers
　　Dramatics
　　Theaters

Dramatic Arts
USE　Dramatics

Dramatic Play　　　　　　　　JUL. 1966
　　　Postings: 718　　　　　　　　GC: 420
UF　Sociodramatic Play
BT　Role Playing
RT　Class Activities
　　Creative Dramatics
　　Creative Expression
　　Improvisation
　　Play
　　Pretend Play
　　Self Expression
　　Teaching Methods

Dramatic Unities (1970 1980)
USE　Drama

Dramatics　　　　　　　　　　JUL. 1966
　　　Postings: 1,103　　　　　　　GC: 420
SN　Activities in the creation, preparation,
　　and production of plays
UF　Dramatic Arts
NT　Creative Dramatics
BT　Theater Arts
RT　Acting
　　Art
　　Auditoriums
　　Dance
　　Drama
　　Drama Workshops
　　Improvisation
　　Language Arts
　　Pantomime
　　Playwriting
　　Prompting
　　Rehearsals (Theater Arts)

　　Skits
　　Theaters

Dravidian Languages　　　　JUL. 1966
　　　Postings: 32　　　　　　　　GC: 440
NT　Kannada
　　Malayalam
　　Tamil
　　Telugu
BT　Languages
RT　Language Classification
　　Native Speakers

Drawing (Computerized)
USE　Computer Graphics

Drawing (Freehand)
USE　Freehand Drawing

Drawing (Precision Draft)
USE　Drafting

Dreams　　　　　　　　　　　DEC. 1989
　　　Postings: 105　　　　　　　　GC: 230
SN　Thoughts, sensations, emotions, or im-
　　ages experienced during sleep
NT　Nightmares
RT　Emotional Experience
　　Fantasy
　　Imagination
　　Psychological Patterns
　　Sleep

Dress Codes　　　　　　　　OCT. 1971
　　　Postings: 200　　　　　　　　GC: 320
SN　Regulations governing personal dress
　　and appearance including clothing,
　　beards, hair, and cleanliness
BT　Standards
RT　Board of Education Policy
　　Discipline Policy
　　Due Process
　　Employment Practices
　　Personnel Policy
　　School Uniforms
　　Student Behavior
　　Student Rights
　　Student School Relationship

Dress Design
USE　Clothing Design

Drill Press Operators
USE　Machine Tool Operators

Drill Presses
USE　Machine Tools

Drills (Practice)　　　　　　MAR. 1980
　　　Postings: 675　　　　　　　　GC: 310
SN　Repetition of tasks or procedures
NT　Pattern Drills (Language)
BT　Teaching Methods
RT　Memorization
　　Rote Learning
　　Study

Drinking　　　　　　　　　　MAY 1974
　　　Postings: 2,154　　　　　　　GC: 210
SN　Consumption of alcoholic beverages
UF　Alcohol Consumption
　　Alcohol Use
　　Social Drinking
NT　Alcohol Abuse
BT　Behavior
RT　Alcohol Education
　　Alcoholic Beverages
　　Drug Use
　　Health Behavior
　　Health Education
　　Recreational Activities

Drinking Drivers
USE　Driving While Intoxicated

Drinking Water　　　　　　　NOV. 1982
　　　Postings: 92　　　　　　　　GC: 410
UF　Potable Water
BT　Water
RT　Disease Control
　　Fluoridation
　　Physical Health
　　Public Health
　　Utilities
　　Water Quality
　　Water Treatment

Driver Education　　　　　　JUL. 1966
　　　Postings: 527　　　　　　　　GC: 400
UF　Driver Training
BT　Education
RT　Bus Drivers
　　Traffic Safety

Driver Training
USE　Driver Education

Driveways　　　　　　　　　JAN. 1969
　　　Postings: 8　　　　　　　　GC: 920
BT　Facilities
RT　Parking Facilities
　　Traffic Circulation
　　Vehicular Traffic

Driving While Intoxicated　　AUG. 1989
　　　Postings: 126　　　　　　　　GC: 530
UF　Drinking Drivers
　　Drunk Driving
BT　Antisocial Behavior
RT　Alcohol Abuse
　　Crime
　　Drug Abuse
　　Traffic Accidents

Dropout Attitudes　　　　　　JUL. 1966
　　　Postings: 376　　　　　　　　GC: 330
SN　Attitudes of, not toward, dropouts (Note:
　　Prior to Mar80, the use of this term was
　　not restricted by a Scope Note)
BT　Attitudes
RT　Alienation
　　Dropout Characteristics
　　Dropouts
　　Student Alienation

Dropout Characteristics　　　JUL. 1966
　　　Postings: 1,296　　　　　　　GC: 330
UF　Dropout Identification (1966 1980)
RT　Dropout Attitudes
　　Dropout Prevention
　　Dropouts
　　Individual Characteristics
　　Participant Characteristics
　　Potential Dropouts

Dropout Employment
USE　Dropout Programs

Dropout Identification (1966 1980)
USE　Dropout Characteristics

Dropout Prevention　　　　　JUL. 1966
　　　Postings: 2,675　　　　　　　GC: 320
BT　Prevention
RT　Continuation Students
　　Dropout Characteristics
　　Dropout Programs
　　Dropout Research
　　Dropouts
　　Potential Dropouts

Dropout Problems (1966 1980)
USE　Dropouts

Dropout Programs　　　　　JUL. 1966
　　　Postings: 1,060　　　　　　　GC: 320
UF　Dropout Employment
　　Dropout Rehabilitation (1966 1980)
　　Dropout Teaching (1966 1980)
BT　Rehabilitation Programs
RT　Continuation Students
　　Dropout Prevention
　　Dropouts
　　High School Equivalency Programs

Dropout Rate　　　　　　　　JUL. 1966
　　　Postings: 1,470　　　　　　　GC: 330
BT　Incidence
RT　Dropout Research
　　Dropouts
　　Student Attrition

Dropout Rehabilitation (1966 1980)
USE　Dropout Programs

Dropout Research　　　　　　JUL. 1966
　　　Postings: 1,510　　　　　　　GC: 810
SN　Systematic investigations focusing on
　　the characteristics, motives, etc., of indi-
　　viduals who withdraw from an activity
　　before its completion (Note: As of Oct81,
　　use as a minor Descriptor for examples
　　of this kind of research—use as a major
　　Descriptor only as the subject of a docu-
　　ment)
BT　Research
RT　Academic Persistence
　　Dropout Prevention
　　Dropout Rate
　　Dropouts
　　Persistence
　　School Holding Power
　　Student Attrition
　　Withdrawal (Education)

Dropout Role (1966 1980)
USE　Dropouts

Dropout Teaching (1966 1980)
USE　Dropout Programs

Dropouts　　　　　　　　　　JUL. 1966
　　　Postings: 3,976　　　　　　　GC: 510
SN　Individuals who withdraw from an activ-
　　ity (e.g., educational program) before its
　　completion
UF　College Dropouts
　　Dropout Problems (1966 1980)
　　Dropout Role (1966 1980)
　　Early School Leavers
　　High School Dropouts
　　Rural Dropouts (1966 1981)
　　School Dropouts
　　Urban Dropouts (1966 1981)
NT　Adult Dropouts
BT　Groups
RT　Academic Failure
　　Academic Persistence
　　Attendance
　　Attrition (Research Studies)
　　Continuation Students
　　Dropout Attitudes
　　Dropout Characteristics
　　Dropout Prevention
　　Dropout Programs
　　Dropout Rate
　　Dropout Research
　　Enrollment
　　Expulsion
　　High School Equivalency Programs
　　No Shows
　　Out of School Youth
　　Persistence
　　Potential Dropouts
　　Reentry Students
　　Reentry Workers
　　Rehabilitation
　　Retraining
　　Runaways
　　School Holding Power
　　Special Needs Students
　　Stopouts

= Two or more Descriptors are used to represent this term.
The term's main entry shows the appropriate coordination.

Student Attrition
Truancy
Withdrawal (Education)

Drought   *NOV. 1995*
Postings: 17   GC: 410
SN   Climatic period(s) of extreme dryness, in
     which natural water supplies are insuffi-
     cient for plant life and other needs (Note:
     See also the Identifier "Desertification")
BT   Natural Disasters
     Weather
RT   Water
     Water Resources

Drowsiness
USE   Sleep

Drug Abuse   *JUL. 1966*
Postings: 4,247   GC: 530
SN   Excessive use or misuse of drugs, caus-
     ing physical, emotional, mental, or sen-
     sory injury or impairment (Note: If appli-
     cable, use the more specific term "Drug
     Addiction")
NT   Drug Addiction
BT   Drug Use
     Substance Abuse
RT   Alcohol Abuse
     Antisocial Behavior
     Cocaine
     Crack
     Driving While Intoxicated
     Drug Education
     Drug Legislation
     Drug Rehabilitation
     Drug Use Testing
     Heroin
     Illegal Drug Use
     Lysergic Acid Diethylamide
     Marijuana
     Narcotics
     Pharmacology
     Prenatal Drug Exposure
     Sedatives
     Stimulants

Drug Addiction   *JUL. 1966*
Postings: 972   GC: 530
UF   Chemical Dependency (Drugs)
     Dependency (Drugs)
     Narcotics Addiction
BT   Diseases
     Drug Abuse
RT   Alcoholism
     Antisocial Behavior
     Behavior Disorders
     Cocaine
     Crack
     Crime
     Drug Education
     Drug Legislation
     Drug Rehabilitation
     Heroin
     Illegal Drug Use
     Lysergic Acid Diethylamide
     Marijuana
     Narcotics
     Pharmacology
     Special Health Problems

Drug Education   *JAN. 1972*
Postings: 2,148   GC: 400
SN   Study of the varied aspects of drugs,
     their source, abuse, chemical composi-
     tion, and physical, personal, and social
     effects
BT   Education
RT   Alcohol Education
     Drug Abuse
     Drug Addiction
     Drug Rehabilitation
     Drug Use
     Health Education
     Narcotics
     Pharmaceutical Education

Drug Exposure in Utero
USE   Prenatal Drug Exposure

Drug Inspectors
USE   Food and Drug Inspectors

Drug Legislation   *JUL. 1966*
Postings: 302   GC: 610
BT   Public Health Legislation
RT   Cocaine
     Crack
     Drug Abuse
     Drug Addiction
     Heroin
     Illegal Drug Use
     Laws
     Marijuana
     Narcotics
     Pharmacy

Drug Rehabilitation   *MAR. 1980*
Postings: 539   GC: 210
SN   Process of restoring drug addicts or
     abusers to the best possible level of
     physical, mental, emotional, social, or
     vocational functioning (Note: Do not con-
     fuse with "Drug Therapy")
UF   Drug Withdrawal
     Withdrawal (Drugs)
BT   Rehabilitation
RT   Cocaine
     Crack
     Drug Abuse
     Drug Addiction
     Drug Education
     Heroin
     Narcotics
     Sedatives
     Stimulants

Drug Testing (Presence in Body)
USE   Drug Use Testing

Drug Therapy   *MAY 1969*
Postings: 1,380   GC: 210
SN   Treatment or prevention of diseases and
     other disorders by the administration of
     drugs (Note: Prior to Mar80, this term
     was not restricted by a Scope Note and
     was sometimes confused with "Drug
     Rehabilitation")
UF   Chemotherapy
BT   Therapy
RT   Drug Use
     Genetic Engineering
     Medical Services
     Pharmaceutical Education
     Pharmacy

Drug Use   *MAR. 1980*
Postings: 1,623   GC: 210
SN   Medicinal or nonmedicinal use of drugs
NT   Drug Abuse
     Illegal Drug Use
     Prenatal Drug Exposure
BT   Behavior
RT   Alcoholic Beverages
     Cocaine
     Crack
     Drinking
     Drug Education
     Drug Therapy
     Drug Use Testing
     Heroin
     Lysergic Acid Diethylamide
     Marijuana
     Narcotics
     Pharmacology
     Sedatives
     Stimulants

Drug Use Testing   *AUG. 1989*
Postings: 112   GC: 210
SN   Screening for drug use or abuse by the
     quantitative determination of drug me-
     tabolites in the blood, urine, tissue, etc.
UF   Drug Testing (Presence in Body)

BT   Evaluation Methods
RT   Drug Abuse
     Drug Use
     Illegal Drug Use
     Physical Examinations

Drug Withdrawal
USE   Drug Rehabilitation

Druggists
USE   Pharmacists

Drunk Driving
USE   Driving While Intoxicated

Drunkenness (Alcohol)
USE   Alcohol Abuse

Drycleaning Laundry Occupations
USE   Laundry Drycleaning Occupations

Dual Career Family   *OCT. 1982*
Postings: 337   GC: 510
SN   Family in which both partners or spouses
     pursue careers (i.e., long-term and
     developmentally sequential occupational
     activities outside of family life) (Note: Do
     not confuse with "Employed Parents")
BT   Family (Sociological Unit)
RT   Careers
     Employed Parents
     Employed Women
     Family Structure
     Family Work Relationship

Dual Earner Parents
USE   Employed Parents

Dual Enrollment   *AUG. 1968*
Postings: 120   GC: 330
SN   Enrollment of students in two schools at
     the same time
UF   Shared Time (Education)
     Split Time
BT   Enrollment
RT   Consortia
     Cooperative Programs
     Institutional Cooperation
     Shared Resources and Services

Due Process   *OCT. 1971*
Postings: 2,233   GC: 610
SN   A course of proceedings established in
     the law for the enforcement and protec-
     tion of private rights
UF   Procedural Due Process
BT   Civil Liberties
RT   Childrens Rights
     Civil Rights
     Dress Codes
     Equal Protection
     Financial Exigency
     Freedom of Speech
     Juries
     Justice
     Laws
     Parent Rights
     Search and Seizure
     Student Behavior
     Student Rights
     Student School Relationship
     Teacher Discipline
     Teacher Dismissal
     Teacher Rights

Dues
USE   Fees

Duplicating
USE   Reprography

Dusun   *JUL. 1966*
Postings: 1   GC: 440
BT   Indonesian Languages

Dutch   *JUL. 1966*
Postings: 327   GC: 440
BT   Indo European Languages
RT   Afrikaans

Dutch Culture   *JUL. 1966*
Postings: 18   GC: 560
BT   Culture

Dwellings
USE   Housing

Dyadic Communication
USE   Interpersonal Communication

Dyslexia   *JUL. 1966*
Postings: 1,035   GC: 220
SN   Impairment in the ability to read despite
     adequate intelligence and proper instruc-
     tion
BT   Language Impairments
RT   Aphasia
     Learning Disabilities
     Minimal Brain Dysfunction
     Neurological Impairments
     Perceptual Impairments
     Reading Difficulties
     Reading Failure
     Remedial Reading

Dysphasia
USE   Aphasia

Dysphonia
USE   Voice Disorders

Dysphoria
USE   Depression (Psychology)

Dysthymia
USE   Depression (Psychology)

Dyula   *JUL. 1966*
Postings: 5   GC: 440
BT   African Languages

E Zines
USE   Electronic Journals

Ear Infections (Middle Ear)
USE   Otitis Media

Early Admission   *JUL. 1966*
Postings: 203   GC: 320
BT   Admission (School)
RT   Acceleration (Education)
     Admission Criteria
     School Entrance Age
     School Readiness

Early Adolescence
USE   Early Adolescents

Early Adolescents   *JUL. 1994*
Postings: 488   GC: 120
SN   Age group between, and overlapping with,
     "Preadolescents" and "Adolescents"—
     approximately 11–15 years of age
UF   Early Adolescence
     Young Adolescents
BT   Age Groups
RT   Adolescents
     Junior High School Students
     Middle School Students
     Preadolescents

= Two or more Descriptors are used to represent this term.
The term's main entry shows the appropriate coordination.

Puberty
Youth

Early Childhood Education　　　*JUL. 1966*
　　　Postings: 17,624　　　GC: 340
SN　Activities and/or experiences that are intended to effect developmental changes in children, from birth through the primary units of elementary school (grades k-3) (Note: Also appears in the list of mandatory educational level Descriptors)
NT　Preschool Education
　　　Primary Education
BT　Education
RT　Child Development Centers
　　　Day Care Centers
　　　Developmentally Appropriate Practices
　　　Early Intervention
　　　Elementary Education
　　　Kindergarten
　　　Montessori Method
　　　Nursery Schools
　　　Reggio Emilia Approach
　　　Young Children

Early Childhood (1966 1980)
USE　Young Children

Early Detection
USE　Early Identification

Early Diagnosis
USE　Early Identification

Early Experience　　　*JUL. 1966*
　　　Postings: 1,075　　　GC: 120
SN　Experiences in infancy or early childhood that influence subsequent development
UF　Preschool Experience
BT　Experience
RT　Day Care Effects
　　　Early Intervention
　　　Early Reading
　　　Prereading Experience
　　　Young Children

Early Identification　　　*JUN. 1996*
　　　Postings: 238　　　GC: 820
SN　Diagnosis of an exceptionality (disability and/or giftedness), medical condition, or risk factor early in life or in the condition's early stages (Note: Prior to Jun96, the instruction "Early Detection, USE Identification" was carried in the Thesaurus)
UF　Early Detection
　　　Early Diagnosis
BT　Identification
RT　Ability Identification
　　　At Risk Persons
　　　Clinical Diagnosis
　　　Diagnostic Tests
　　　Disability Identification
　　　Early Intervention
　　　Educational Diagnosis
　　　Screening Tests
　　　Symptoms (Individual Disorders)
　　　Talent Identification

Early Intervention　　　*AUG. 1989*
　　　Postings: 3,086　　　GC: 520
SN　Intervention with individuals at risk for, or in the early stages of mental, physical, learning, or other disorders—usually refers to efforts targeted at young children (infancy through primary grades), sometimes including prenatal care
NT　Individualized Family Service Plans
BT　Intervention
RT　At Risk Persons
　　　Clinical Diagnosis
　　　Compensatory Education
　　　Developmental Delays
　　　Early Childhood Education
　　　Early Experience
　　　Early Identification

Educational Diagnosis
Prenatal Care
Prevention
Special Education
Special Needs Students
Symptoms (Individual Disorders)

Early Literacy
USE　Emergent Literacy

Early Parenthood　　　*NOV. 1982*
　　　Postings: 1,403　　　GC: 520
SN　Parenthood assumed before age 20
UF　Adolescent Parents
RT　Adolescents
　　　Child Welfare
　　　Family Planning
　　　Family Problems
　　　Family Relationship
　　　Parent Child Relationship
　　　Parents
　　　Pregnancy
　　　Youth Problems

Early Reading　　　*JUL. 1966*
　　　Postings: 597　　　GC: 460
SN　Reading by children before they reach school age
BT　Reading
RT　Beginning Reading
　　　Early Experience
　　　Emergent Literacy
　　　Prereading Experience
　　　Reading Readiness

Early Retirement　　　*MAR. 1984*
　　　Postings: 229　　　GC: 630
SN　Withdrawal from one's occupation or career at an earlier age or time than is mandatory or customary
BT　Retirement
RT　Career Change
　　　Employment Practices
　　　Fringe Benefits
　　　Mandatory Retirement
　　　Middle Aged Adults
　　　Midlife Transitions
　　　Older Workers
　　　Personnel Policy
　　　Reduction in Force
　　　Teacher Retirement
　　　Work Life Expectancy

Early School Leavers
USE　Dropouts

Ears　　　*JUL. 1966*
　　　Postings: 49　　　GC: 210
RT　Anatomy
　　　Audiology
　　　Auditory Tests
　　　Hearing (Physiology)
　　　Hearing Impairments
　　　Human Body
　　　Otitis Media

Earth Science　　　*JUL. 1966*
　　　Postings: 2,903　　　GC: 490
UF　Geoscience
NT　Geochemistry
　　　Geology
　　　Geophysics
　　　Hydrology
　　　Meteorology
　　　Oceanography
　　　Physical Geography
　　　Seismology
　　　Soil Science
BT　Physical Sciences
RT　Astronomy
　　　Cartography
　　　Chemistry
　　　Climate
　　　Crystallography
　　　Physical Environment
　　　Physics
　　　Planetariums

Plate Tectonics
Satellites (Aerospace)
Space Sciences
Topography
Water
Wind (Meteorology)

Earthquakes　　　*OCT. 1983*
　　　Postings: 147　　　GC: 490
RT　Motion
　　　Natural Disasters
　　　Plate Tectonics
　　　Seismology
　　　Volcanoes

Eastern Civilization
USE　Non Western Civilization

Eating Disorders　　　*JUN. 1993*
　　　Postings: 279　　　GC: 210
SN　Gross disturbances in eating patterns
UF　Appetite Disorders
NT　Anorexia Nervosa
　　　Bulimia
BT　Diseases
RT　Body Weight
　　　Eating Habits
　　　Nutrition
　　　Obesity
　　　Physical Health
　　　Psychological Patterns

Eating Habits　　　*JUL. 1966*
　　　Postings: 1,430　　　GC: 210
RT　Anorexia Nervosa
　　　Body Weight
　　　Bulimia
　　　Dietetics
　　　Eating Disorders
　　　Health Behavior
　　　Nutrition
　　　Obesity
　　　Physical Health
　　　Self Care Skills

Ebonics
USE　Black Dialects

Echolalia　　　*SEP. 1968*
　　　Postings: 65　　　GC: 230
SN　Involuntary and senseless repetition of words heard spoken by another person
UF　Echophasia
BT　Psychosis
RT　Aphasia
　　　Language Impairments
　　　Language Patterns
　　　Schizophrenia

Echolocation　　　*OCT. 1968*
　　　Postings: 17　　　GC: 220
SN　Ability of organisms to locate objects or to spatially orient themselves by means of reflected sound waves
RT　Auditory Perception
　　　Auditory Stimuli
　　　Blindness
　　　Psychoacoustics
　　　Spatial Ability
　　　Travel Training
　　　Visually Impaired Mobility

Echophasia
USE　Echolalia

Ecological Factors　　　*JUL. 1966*
　　　Postings: 966　　　GC: 410
BT　Influences
RT　Conservation (Environment)
　　　Crowding
　　　Ecology
　　　Energy Conservation
　　　Poisons
　　　Pollution
　　　Radiation Effects

Ecology　　　*JUL. 1966*
　　　Postings: 4,571　　　GC: 490
SN　Study of the interrelationships between organisms and their environment
UF　Ecosystems
BT　Biological Sciences
RT　Adjustment (to Environment)
　　　Air Pollution
　　　Area Studies
　　　Biodiversity
　　　Biology
　　　Botany
　　　Climate
　　　Conservation (Environment)
　　　Ecological Factors
　　　Energy Conservation
　　　Entropy
　　　Environment
　　　Environmental Education
　　　Environmental Standards
　　　Estuaries
　　　Ethology
　　　Evolution
　　　Habitats
　　　Human Geography
　　　Marine Biology
　　　Mycology
　　　Noise (Sound)
　　　Ocean Engineering
　　　Pests
　　　Photosynthesis
　　　Quality of Life
　　　Radiation Biology
　　　Rainforests
　　　Recycling
　　　Scientific Research
　　　Social Biology
　　　Soil Conservation
　　　Sustainable Development
　　　Waste Disposal
　　　Wastes
　　　Water
　　　Water Pollution
　　　Water Quality
　　　Weather
　　　Wetlands
　　　Wilderness
　　　Wind (Meteorology)
　　　Zoology

Econometrics　　　*OCT. 1994*
　　　Postings: 104　　　GC: 620
SN　Application of mathematical and statistical techniques to economic analyses
BT　Economics
RT　Cost Effectiveness
　　　Economic Impact
　　　Economic Research
　　　Educational Economics
　　　Labor Economics
　　　Macroeconomics
　　　Measurement Techniques
　　　Microeconomics
　　　Statistical Analysis

Economic Analysis
USE　Economic Research

Economic Change　　　*JUN. 1969*
　　　Postings: 1,974　　　GC: 620
BT　Change
RT　Boomtowns
　　　Change Strategies
　　　Community Change
　　　Cost Indexes
　　　Culture Lag
　　　Economic Climate
　　　Economic Development
　　　Economic Factors
　　　Economic Impact
　　　Economic Progress
　　　Economic Status
　　　Economics
　　　Finance Reform
　　　Institutional Survival
　　　Revolution
　　　Social Change
　　　Structural Unemployment
　　　Supply and Demand

Economic Climate   *JUL. 1966*
Postings: 1,118   GC: 620
NT   Inflation (Economics)
BT   Environment
RT   Business Cycles
     Economic Change
     Economic Impact
     Economic Opportunities
     Economics
     Quality of Life
     Supply and Demand

Economic Cycles
USE   Business Cycles

Economic Development   *JUL. 1966*
Postings: 5,193   GC: 620
NT   Economic Progress
BT   Development
RT   Boomtowns
     Community Development
     Developed Nations
     Developing Nations
     Developmental Programs
     Economic Change
     Economic Impact
     Economics
     Educational Economics
     Labor Force Development
     Sustainable Development

Economic Disadvantagement (1966 1980)
USE   Poverty

Economic Education (1971 1980)
USE   Economics Education

Economic Effects
USE   Economic Impact

Economic Factors   *JUL. 1966*
Postings: 6,971   GC: 620
UF   Economic Influences
     Poverty Factors #
BT   Influences
RT   Business Cycles
     Economic Change
     Economic Impact
     Economics
     Educational Demand
     Employment
     Employment Patterns
     Financial Exigency
     Fiscal Capacity
     Inflation (Economics)
     Labor Utilization
     Living Standards
     Marxian Analysis
     Ownership
     Productivity
     Socioeconomic Influences
     Supply and Demand

Economic Fluctuations
USE   Business Cycles

Economic Geography
USE   Human Geography

Economic Impact   *DEC. 1989*
Postings: 942   GC: 620
SN   Effect of an action, event, or other cir-
     cumstance (e.g., legislation, migration,
     commercial development, literacy, exist-
     ence of a school or college) on the
     economic well-being of an individual,
     enterprise, community, region, etc.
UF   Economic Effects
RT   Boomtowns
     Business
     Consumer Economics
     Cost Effectiveness
     Cost Indexes
     Costs
     Econometrics

Economic Change
Economic Climate
Economic Development
Economic Factors
Economic Opportunities
Economic Progress
Economic Research
Economic Status
Economics
Educational Economics
Employment
Expenditures
Finance Reform
Income
Inflation (Economics)
Investment
Labor Economics
Productivity
Rural Economics
School Business Relationship
School Community Relationship
Socioeconomic Influences
Taxes

Economic Influences
USE   Economic Factors

Economic Insecurity
USE   Poverty

Economic Opportunities   *JUL. 1966*
Postings: 614   GC: 540
SN   Circumstances or conditions that enable
     individuals or groups to improve their
     financial status
BT   Opportunities
RT   Cooperatives
     Economic Climate
     Economic Impact
     Economic Progress
     Economic Status
     Economics
     Employment Opportunities
     Entrepreneurship
     Franchising
     Ownership
     Self Employment
     Socioeconomic Influences

Economic Plight
USE   Poverty

Economic Progress   *JUL. 1966*
Postings: 527   GC: 620
BT   Economic Development
RT   Business Cycles
     Economic Change
     Economic Impact
     Economic Opportunities
     Economics
     Modernization
     Technology Transfer

Economic Research   *JUL. 1966*
Postings: 1,165   GC: 810
SN   Basic, applied, and developmental re-
     search conducted to advance knowledge
     in economics (Note: As of Oct81, use as
     a minor Descriptor for examples of this
     kind of research—use as a major Descrip-
     tor only as the subject of a document)
UF   Economic Analysis
BT   Social Science Research
RT   Econometrics
     Economic Impact
     Economics
     Input Output Analysis
     Labor Economics
     Linear Programming
     Macroeconomics
     Microeconomics

Economic Status   *JUL. 1966*
Postings: 1,040   GC: 510
NT   Poverty
BT   Status
RT   Economic Change

Economic Impact
Economic Opportunities
Economics
Income
Inflation (Economics)
Ownership
Quality of Life
Socioeconomic Status

Economic Support
USE   Financial Support

Economically Advanced Nations
USE   Developed Nations

Economically Advantaged
USE   Advantaged

Economically Depressed Areas
USE   Poverty Areas

Economically Deprived
USE   Economically Disadvantaged

Economically Disadvantaged   *JUL. 1966*
Postings: 4,768   GC: 540
UF   Economically Deprived
     Poor
     Poverty Stricken
BT   Disadvantaged
RT   Group Homes
     Homeless People
     Low Income Groups
     Poverty
     Special Needs Students
     Welfare Recipients

Economics   *JUL. 1966*
Postings: 3,948   GC: 620
UF   Economy
NT   Consumer Economics
     Econometrics
     Educational Economics
     Labor Economics
     Macroeconomics
     Microeconomics
     Rural Economics
BT   Social Sciences
RT   Area Studies
     Banking
     Business
     Business Cycles
     Capitalism
     Communism
     Cost Indexes
     Credit (Finance)
     Debt (Financial)
     Economic Change
     Economic Climate
     Economic Development
     Economic Factors
     Economic Impact
     Economic Opportunities
     Economic Progress
     Economic Research
     Economic Status
     Economics Education
     Efficiency
     Entrepreneurship
     Exports
     Fascism
     Finance Occupations
     Free Enterprise System
     Human Capital
     Imports
     Inflation (Economics)
     Interest (Finance)
     International Studies
     International Trade
     International Trade Vocabulary
     Investment
     Marxism
     Monetary Systems
     Ownership
     Private Sector
     Privatization
     Productivity

Public Sector
Retrenchment
Social History
Social Science Research
Social Scientists
Social Studies
Socialism
Socioeconomic Background
Socioeconomic Influences
Socioeconomic Status
Supply and Demand
Urban Studies

Economics Curriculum
USE   Economics Education

Economics Education   *MAR. 1980*
Postings: 2,992   GC: 400
UF   Economic Education (1971 1980)
     Economics Curriculum
     Economics Instruction
BT   Education
RT   Basic Business Education
     Business Education
     Consumer Education
     Economics
     Global Education
     Macroeconomics
     Microeconomics

Economics Instruction
USE   Economics Education

Economics of Education
USE   Educational Economics

Economy
USE   Economics

Ecosystems
USE   Ecology

Editing   *JUL. 1973*
Postings: 1,214   GC: 720
SN   To make suitable for publication or for
     public presentation by selecting, emend-
     ing, revising, and compiling
UF   Copyediting
RT   Editors
     Film Production
     Film Study
     Journalism
     Language Arts
     Language Styles
     News Media
     News Writing
     Proofreading
     Publications
     Quality Control
     Technical Writing
     Word Processing

Editorials   *OCT. 1972*
Postings: 587   GC: 720
BT   News Media
RT   Editors
     Journalism
     Journalism History
     Newspapers
     Opinions
     Periodicals
     Persuasive Discourse
     Press Opinion
     Publications

Editors   *AUG. 1986*
Postings: 443   GC: 710
SN   Persons who prepare materials, usually
     works of others, for publication or public
     presentation
UF   Copyeditors
BT   Personnel
RT   Authors
     Editing
     Editorials

= Two or more Descriptors are used to represent this term.
The term's main entry shows the appropriate coordination.

Layout (Publications)
Mass Media
News Media
Periodicals
Publications
Publishing Industry
Scholarly Journals
School Publications
Student Publications
Writing for Publication

Educable Mentally Handicapped (1966 1980)
USE   Mild Mental Retardation

Education   *JUL. 1966*
Postings: 3,426   GC: 330
SN   Process of imparting or obtaining knowl-
edge, attitudes, skills, or socially valued
qualities of character or behavior—in-
cludes the philosophy, purposes, pro-
grams, methods, organizational patterns,
etc., of the entire educational process as
most broadly conceived (Note: The most
general term—use a more specific term
if possible)
NT   Academic Education
Adult Education
Aerospace Education
Aesthetic Education
After School Education
Aging Education
Agricultural Education
Alcohol Education
Allied Health Occupations Education
Alumni Education
American Indian Education
Art Education
Back to Basics
Basic Business Education
Bilingual Education
Black Education
Career Education
Citizenship Education
Coeducation
Community Education
Comparative Education
Compensatory Education
Competency Based Education
Compulsory Education
Consumer Education
Corporate Education
Correctional Education
Cultural Education
Culturally Relevant Education
Dance Education
Distance Education
Driver Education
Drug Education
Early Childhood Education
Economics Education
Elementary Secondary Education
Energy Education
Environmental Education
Equal Education
Extension Education
Family Life Education
Free Education
General Education
Global Education
Health Education
Humanistic Education
Industrial Education
Informal Education
Inservice Education
Intergroup Education
Journalism Education
Law Related Education
Leisure Education
Literacy Education
Marine Education
Mathematics Education
Mexican American Education
Migrant Education
Music Education
Noncategorical Education
Nondiscriminatory Education
Nonformal Education
Nontraditional Education
Open Education
Outcome Based Education

Outdoor Education
Patient Education
Physical Education
Police Education
Popular Education
Population Education
Postsecondary Education
Private Education
Process Education
Professional Education
Progressive Education
Public Affairs Education
Public Education
Religious Education
Rural Education
Safety Education
Science Education
Special Education
Study Abroad
Supplementary Education
Technology Education
Terminal Education
Tribally Controlled Education
Urban Education
Values Education
Vocational Education
Womens Education
RT   Access to Education
Articulation (Education)
Curriculum
Education Courses
Education Majors
Education Service Centers
Education Work Relationship
Educational Attitudes
Educational Background
Educational Benefits
Educational Certificates
Educational Change
Educational Complexes
Educational Counseling
Educational Demand
Educational Development
Educational Discrimination
Educational Environment
Educational Equipment
Educational Experience
Educational Experiments
Educational Facilities
Educational Finance
Educational Improvement
Educational Innovation
Educational Legislation
Educational Malpractice
Educational Media
Educational Methods
Educational Mobility
Educational Needs
Educational Objectives
Educational Opportunities
Educational Planning
Educational Policy
Educational Practices
Educational Principles
Educational Quality
Educational Research
Educational Resources
Educational Responsibility
Educational Status Comparison
Educational Strategies
Educational Supply
Educational Technology
Educational Testing
Educational Theories
Educational Therapy
Educational Trends
Educationally Disadvantaged
Excellence in Education
Foundations of Education
Instruction
Learning
Outcomes of Education
Politics of Education
Regular and Special Education Rela-
tionship
Role of Education
Schools
Training

Education and Work
USE   Education Work Relationship

Education Courses   *FEB. 1969*
Postings: 813   GC: 400
BT   College Curriculum
Courses
RT   Education
Education Majors
Methods Courses
Postsecondary Education as a Field of
Study
Schools of Education
Teacher Education
Teacher Education Curriculum
Teacher Education Programs

Education Departments (School)
USE   Schools of Education

Education Majors   *JUL. 1966*
Postings: 1,764   GC: 360
BT   Majors (Students)
RT   Education
Education Courses
Postsecondary Education as a Field of
Study
Preservice Teachers
Schools of Education
Specialist in Education Degrees
Student Teachers
Teacher Education
Teacher Education Curriculum
Teacher Education Programs

Education Permanente
USE   Lifelong Learning

Education Role
USE   Role of Education

Education Service Centers   *JUL. 1966*
Postings: 486   GC: 920
SN   Multipurpose educational facilities that
provide cooperative services to school
districts within a region—typical serv-
ices include research, curriculum devel-
opment, instructional materials, inservice
training, data processing, legal and fi-
nancial advice, psychological programs,
and direct services to students
UF   Educational Service Centers
Supplementary Educational Centers
(1966 1980) #
BT   Educational Facilities
Resource Centers
RT   Ancillary School Services
Computer Centers
Curriculum Study Centers
Demonstration Centers
Education
Information Centers
Nature Centers
Regional Programs
Science Teaching Centers
Shared Resources and Services
Teacher Centers

Education Vouchers (1971 1980)
USE   Educational Vouchers

Education Work Relationship   *OCT. 1979*
Postings: 9,406   GC: 330
SN   Relationship between educational pro-
grams or courses of study and status or
opportunities (social, financial, etc.) in
the work force (Note: Do not confuse
with "Work Study Programs" or "School
Business Relationship")
UF   Education and Work
School to Work Transition
Work and Education
Work Education Relationship
BT   Relationship
RT   Career Change
Career Choice
Career Development
Career Education
Career Information Systems
Career Planning

Careers
Corporate Education
Education
Educational Benefits
Educational Demand
Educational Objectives
Educational Philosophy
Educational Status Comparison
Employment
Employment Opportunities
Employment Patterns
Employment Potential
Entrepreneurship
Liberal Arts
Occupations
Opportunities
Partnerships in Education
Promotion (Occupational)
Relevance (Education)
School Business Relationship
Student Educational Objectives
Technology
Vocational Followup

Educational Access
USE   Access to Education

Educational Accountability (1970 1980)
USE   Accountability

Educational Achievement
USE   Academic Achievement

Educational Administration   *JUL. 1966*
Postings: 8,746   GC: 320
SN   Planning, organizing, directing, and con-
trolling human or material resources in
an educational setting, and the study of
this process (Note: Use a more specific
term if possible)
UF   Educational Management
NT   School Administration
BT   Administration
RT   Administrators
Educational Finance
Educational Planning
Educational Policy
Politics of Education
Retrenchment
Trustees

Educational Advantages
USE   Educational Opportunities

Educational Alternatives (1974 1980)
USE   Nontraditional Education

Educational Anthropology   *JUN. 1973*
Postings: 530   GC: 400
SN   Application of anthropological concepts
and methods to the study of educational
institutions and processes
BT   Anthropology
Foundations of Education
RT   Comparative Education
Cultural Context
Culture
Educational History
Educational Principles
Educational Psychology
Educational Sociology
Educational Theories
Ethnography
Ethnology
Nonformal Education
Sociocultural Patterns

Educational Assessment   *JAN. 1974*
Postings: 11,570   GC: 810
SN   Determining and interpreting the attainment of educational objectives (nationwide, statewide, or locally) for use in
educational planning, development, policy formation, and resource allocation
(Note: Do not confuse with "Educational
Diagnosis" or "Testing")

= Two or more Descriptors are used to represent this term.
The term's main entry shows the appropriate coordination.

UF Educational Quality Assessment #
NT College Outcomes Assessment
BT Evaluation
RT Alternative Assessment
   Educational Needs
   Educational Objectives
   Educational Planning
   Educational Policy
   Effective Schools Research
   Evaluation Methods
   Formative Evaluation
   High Stakes Tests
   Input Output Analysis
   National Programs
   National Surveys
   Needs Assessment
   Outcomes of Education
   Program Effectiveness
   Program Evaluation
   Program Validation
   Public Policy
   Resource Allocation
   Role of Education
   School Effectiveness
   State Programs
   State Surveys
   Summative Evaluation
   Surveys
   Validated Programs

Educational Attainment   *MAR. 1980*
   Postings: 3,003   GC: 510
SN Years of successfully completed school-
   ing or the equivalent according to some
   accreditation standard (Note: Prior to
   Mar80, the instruction "Educational At-
   tainment, USE Academic Achievement"
   was carried in the Thesaurus)
BT Academic Achievement
RT Advanced Placement Programs
   Educational Experience
   Educational Status Comparison
   External Degree Programs
   Graduation
   High School Equivalency Programs
   Student Educational Objectives

Educational Attitudes   *JUL. 1966*
   Postings: 3,383   GC: 330
SN Attitudes toward or about education
BT Attitudes
RT Education
   Reading Attitudes
   Writing Attitudes

Educational Background   *JUL. 1966*
   Postings: 2,362   GC: 510
NT Educational Experience
BT Background
RT Education
   Educational Mobility
   Educational Opportunities
   Educational Status Comparison
   Employment Potential
   Knowledge Level
   Participant Characteristics

Educational Benefits   *JUL. 1966*
   Postings: 2,466   GC: 330
SN Individual benefits obtained from acqui-
   sition of education (Note: Prior to Mar80,
   the use of this term was restricted to
   benefits from advanced education)
BT Outcomes of Education
RT Education
   Education Work Relationship
   Educational Mobility
   Educational Status Comparison
   Employment Potential
   Higher Education
   Professional Recognition
   Rewards
   Socioeconomic Status
   Student Educational Objectives

Educational Certificates   *JUL. 1966*
   Postings: 716   GC: 340
BT Credentials
RT Alternative Teacher Certification

   Certification
   Credits
   Education
   Equivalency Tests
   High School Equivalency Programs
   National Teacher Certification
   Student Certification
   Teacher Certification

Educational Change   *JUL. 1966*
   Postings: 32,395   GC: 330
SN Alterations in the scope of the total edu-
   cational endeavor—includes modifica-
   tion of curriculum, teaching methods,
   enrollment patterns, etc. (Note: Prior to
   Mar80, the use of this term was not
   restricted by a Scope Note)
UF Educational Reform
BT Change
RT Change Agents
   Change Strategies
   Education
   Educational Development
   Educational Environment
   Educational Improvement
   Educational Innovation
   Educational Trends
   Excellence in Education
   School Restructuring
   Transitional Schools

Educational Choice
USE School Choice

Educational Complexes   *JUL. 1966*
   Postings: 84   GC: 920
SN Large aggregations of educational facili-
   ties (Note: Use a more specific term if
   possible)
NT Campuses
   Educational Parks
BT Educational Facilities
RT Cluster Colleges
   Education
   Educational Facilities Planning
   Facility Utilization Research
   House Plan
   School Buildings
   Site Analysis
   Site Development
   Space Utilization

Educational Computing
USE Computer Uses in Education

Educational Cooperation   *MAR. 1980*
   Postings: 4,080   GC: 330
SN Cooperation of educators or educational
   organizations, agencies, or institutions
   among themselves or with outside per-
   sons, organizations, agencies, or institu-
   tions (Note: Use a more specific term if
   possible)
UF Educational Coordination (1967
   1980) #
NT College School Cooperation
   Counselor Teacher Cooperation
   Intercollegiate Cooperation
   Librarian Teacher Cooperation
   Parent Teacher Cooperation
   Partnerships in Education
   Teacher Collaboration
BT Cooperation
RT Affiliated Schools
   Agency Cooperation
   Consortia
   Cooperative Education
   Cooperative Planning
   Cooperative Programs
   Educational Planning
   Inclusive Schools
   Institutional Cooperation
   Interschool Communication
   Regular and Special Education Rela-
   tionship
   Teacher Centers
   Team Teaching

Educational Coordination (1967 1980)
USE Coordination
AND Educational Cooperation

Educational Counseling   *JUL. 1966*
   Postings: 1,372   GC: 240
SN Assisting individuals to select a program
   of studies suited to their abilities, inter-
   ests, future plans, and general circum-
   stances
UF Educational Guidance (1966 1977)
NT Academic Advising
   Admissions Counseling
BT Counseling
RT College Preparation
   Education
   Educational Psychology
   Educational Therapy
   Faculty Advisers
   Faculty Workload
   Post High School Guidance
   School Counseling
   School Orientation
   Student Educational Objectives
   Student Placement

Educational Demand   *JUL. 1966*
   Postings: 1,744   GC: 330
SN Consumer demand for education
UF Demand for Education
RT Access to Education
   Declining Enrollment
   Demand Occupations
   Economic Factors
   Education
   Education Work Relationship
   Educational Economics
   Educational Needs
   Educational Opportunities
   Educational Supply
   Educational Trends
   Enrollment
   Enrollment Influences
   Equal Education
   Supply and Demand
   Teacher Supply and Demand

Educational Development   *DEC. 1969*
   Postings: 7,110   GC: 330
SN Growth, differentiation, or evolution of
   educational systems (Note: Do not con-
   fuse with "Student Development" or "Fac-
   ulty Development")
NT Curriculum Development
   Instructional Development
BT Development
RT Developmental Programs
   Education
   Educational Change
   Educational Improvement
   Educational Innovation
   Educational Mobility
   Educational Planning
   Educational Research
   Educational Technology
   Formative Evaluation
   Library Development
   Nontraditional Education
   Program Development
   Research and Development
   Research and Development Centers
   Systems Development

Educational Diagnosis   *JUL. 1966*
   Postings: 3,099   GC: 310
SN Identification of the nature and cause of
   learning disabilities, problems, or other
   conditions that may impede or promote
   school performance
UF Diagnosis (Educational)
NT Reading Diagnosis
BT Identification
RT Classroom Techniques
   Clinical Diagnosis
   Counselor Teacher Cooperation
   Diagnostic Teaching
   Diagnostic Tests
   Early Identification
   Early Intervention

   Educational Testing
   Educational Therapy
   Etiology
   Learning Disabilities
   Learning Problems
   Prereferral Intervention
   Psychoeducational Clinics
   Psychoeducational Methods
   Severity (of Disability)
   Student Evaluation
   Symptoms (Individual Disorders)
   Testing Programs
   Writing Evaluation

Educational Disadvantagement (1966 1980)
USE Educationally Disadvantaged

Educational Discrimination   *JUL. 1966*
   Postings: 1,043   GC: 540
NT School Segregation
BT Social Discrimination
RT Access to Education
   Affirmative Action
   Age Discrimination
   Disability Discrimination
   Education
   Educational Opportunities
   Equal Education
   Nondiscriminatory Education
   Racial Discrimination
   Reverse Discrimination
   Selective Admission
   Sex Discrimination

Educational Economics   *FEB. 1969*
   Postings: 2,843   GC: 620
UF Economics of Education
NT Educational Finance
BT Economics
   Foundations of Education
RT Bids
   Consumer Economics
   Econometrics
   Economic Development
   Economic Impact
   Educational Demand
   Educational Supply
   Educational Vouchers
   Efficiency
   Financial Exigency
   Financial Policy
   Financial Support
   Fiscal Capacity
   Fiscal Neutrality
   Human Capital
   Institutional Survival
   Instructional Student Costs
   Investment
   Microeconomics
   Privatization
   Productivity
   Resource Allocation
   School District Wealth
   School Support
   Student Costs

Educational Endowments
USE Endowment Funds

Educational Environment   *JUL. 1966*
   Postings: 10,592   GC: 320
SN Conditions, forces, or factors within or
   exogenous to an educational setting ca-
   pable of influencing the setting or those
   within it (Note: Use a more specific term
   if possible)
UF Academic Environment
   School Climate
   School Conditions (1966 1980)
   School Environment (1966 1980)
NT Classroom Environment
   College Environment
   Teaching Conditions
BT Environment
RT Academic Freedom
   Education
   Educational Change
   Educational Facilities
   Educational Facilities Design

= Two or more Descriptors are used to represent this term.
The term's main entry shows the appropriate coordination.

Educational Innovation
Educational Objectives
Educational Philosophy
Environmental Scanning
Hidden Curriculum
Institutional Environment
Instruction
Learning
Organizational Climate
Role of Education
School Culture
School Organization
School Role
Schools
Student Rights
Student School Relationship
Student Subcultures

Educational Equality (1966 1976)
USE Equal Education

Educational Equipment   JUL. 1966
Postings: 1,269   GC: 910
SN   Furnishings, machines, or other manu-
     factured accessories that are used in
     educational settings
UF   Classroom Equipment
NT   Classroom Furniture
BT   Equipment
RT   Athletic Equipment
     Audiovisual Aids
     Autoinstructional Aids
     Bulletin Boards
     Chalkboards
     College Buildings
     Display Aids
     Education
     Educational Facilities
     Educational Media
     Educational Resources
     Educational Technology
     Library Equipment
     Projection Equipment
     School Buildings
     Science Equipment

Educational Equity (Finance)   NOV. 1982
Postings: 1,230   GC: 620
SN   Equal distribution of financial inputs and
     costs of education, including revenues,
     expenditures, resources, services, tax
     burdens, and tax effort, based on stu-
     dent needs and taxpayers' ability to pay
UF   Equity (Educational Finance)
     Fiscal Equity (Education)
     School Finance Equity
     Tax Equity (Education)
RT   Educational Finance
     Equalization Aid
     Expenditure per Student
     Finance Reform
     Financial Needs
     Financial Policy
     Financial Problems
     Financial Support
     Fiscal Capacity
     Fiscal Neutrality
     Foundation Programs
     Nondiscriminatory Education
     Resource Allocation
     School District Spending
     School District Wealth
     School Support
     School Taxes
     Student Costs
     Tax Allocation
     Tax Effort
     Tax Rates

Educational Equity (Opportunities)
USE Equal Education

Educational Excellence
USE Educational Quality

Educational Excellence Movement (United States)
USE Excellence in Education

Educational Experience   JUL. 1966
Postings: 1,559   GC: 510
UF   School Experience
BT   Educational Background
     Experience
RT   Education
     Educational Attainment
     Educational Status Comparison
     Prior Learning
     Resumes (Personal)

Educational Experiments   JUL. 1966
Postings: 1,067   GC: 810
BT   Experiments
RT   Demonstration Centers
     Demonstrations (Educational)
     Education

Educational Facilities   JUL. 1966
Postings: 4,404   GC: 920
UF   Crafts Rooms (1966 1980) #
     School Facilities
     School Plants
     Teaching Facilities
NT   After School Centers
     Audiovisual Centers
     Business Education Facilities
     Child Development Centers
     Classrooms
     Continuing Education Centers
     Curriculum Study Centers
     Demonstration Centers
     Education Service Centers
     Educational Complexes
     Found Spaces
     Guidance Centers
     Learning Centers (Classroom)
     Learning Laboratories
     Learning Resources Centers
     Living Learning Centers
     Off Campus Facilities
     Physical Education Facilities
     Reading Centers
     School Buildings
     School Shops
     School Space
     Science Teaching Centers
     Skill Centers
     Student Unions
     Study Facilities
     Vocational Training Centers
     Writing Laboratories
BT   Facilities
RT   Aquariums
     Arts Centers
     Auditoriums
     Bookstores
     Campus Planning
     College Stores
     Dormitories
     Education
     Educational Environment
     Educational Equipment
     Educational Facilities Design
     Educational Facilities Planning
     Educational Resources
     Facility Guidelines
     Facility Inventory
     Facility Requirements
     Facility Utilization Research
     Museums
     Music Facilities
     Nature Centers
     Noncampus Colleges
     Parks
     Planetariums
     School Construction
     School Expansion
     Schools
     Structural Elements (Construction)
     Teaching Hospitals
     Theaters
     Zoos

Educational Facilities Design   MAR. 1980
Postings: 1,904   GC: 920
SN   Conceiving and selecting the structure,
     elements, arrangement, materials, etc.,
     for a school building or facility—also,
     the plan or layout that results

UF   Decentralized School Design (1966
     1980) #
     High School Design (1966 1980)
     School Architecture (1966 1980)
     School Design (1966 1980)
BT   Design
RT   Architectural Character
     Building Design
     Building Plans
     Campus Planning
     Classroom Design
     College Buildings
     Design Requirements
     Educational Environment
     Educational Facilities
     Educational Facilities Planning
     Flexible Facilities
     Life Cycle Costing
     Mobile Classrooms
     Modular Building Design
     Open Plan Schools
     Physical Mobility
     School Buildings
     School Construction
     School Size
     School Space
     Schools
     Site Development
     Site Selection
     Structural Elements (Construction)

Educational Facilities Improvement
                                   MAR. 1980
Postings: 1,352   GC: 920
UF   School Improvement (1966 1980)
     School Renovation
BT   Facility Improvement
RT   Educational Facilities Planning
     School Buildings
     School Expansion
     School Maintenance
     School Safety
     Schools

Educational Facilities Planning   MAR. 1980
Postings: 1,005   GC: 920
SN   Planning the facilities and grounds of
     educational institutions (Note: Prior to
     Mar80, this concept was indexed under
     "School Planning")
NT   Campus Planning
BT   Educational Planning
     Facility Planning
RT   Architectural Programming
     Building Plans
     Construction Programs
     Design Requirements
     Educational Complexes
     Educational Facilities
     Educational Facilities Design
     Educational Facilities Improvement
     Facility Guidelines
     Facility Requirements
     Facility Utilization Research
     Flexible Facilities
     Land Use
     Life Cycle Costing
     Physical Mobility
     School Buildings
     School Business Officials
     School Construction
     School Expansion
     School Safety
     School Size
     School Space
     Schools
     Site Analysis
     Site Development
     Site Selection
     Space Utilization
     Spatial Relationship (Facilities)
     Systems Building

Educational Finance   JUL. 1966
Postings: 18,254   GC: 620
SN   Any aspect of raising and spending reve-
     nue for educational purposes (Note: Use
     a more precise term if possible)
UF   Educational Support
     School Aid

School Finance
BT   Educational Economics
RT   Access to Education
     Assistantships
     Bids
     Block Grants
     Bond Issues
     Budgeting
     Budgets
     Capital
     Capital Outlay (for Fixed Assets)
     Categorical Aid
     Corporate Support
     Costs
     Debt (Financial)
     Education
     Educational Administration
     Educational Equity (Finance)
     Educational Planning
     Educational Vouchers
     Endowment Funds
     Equalization Aid
     Expenditure per Student
     Expenditures
     Federal Aid
     Fellowships
     Finance Reform
     Financial Exigency
     Financial Needs
     Financial Policy
     Financial Problems
     Financial Services
     Financial Support
     Fiscal Capacity
     Fiscal Neutrality
     Foundation Programs
     Full State Funding
     Fund Raising
     Grants
     Incentive Grants
     Inflation (Economics)
     Instructional Student Costs
     Loan Default
     Loan Repayment
     New Federalism
     Noninstructional Student Costs
     Paying for College
     Politics of Education
     Private Financial Support
     Private School Aid
     Property Taxes
     Proprietary Schools
     Purchasing
     Retrenchment
     Revenue Sharing
     Salary Wage Differentials
     Scholarship Funds
     Scholarships
     School Accounting
     School Budget Elections
     School Business Officials
     School District Spending
     School District Wealth
     School Funds
     School Support
     School Taxes
     State Aid
     State Federal Aid
     State School District Relationship
     Student Costs
     Student Financial Aid
     Student Financial Aid Officers
     Student Loan Programs
     Tax Allocation
     Tax Effort
     Training Allowances

Educational Foundations
USE Philanthropic Foundations

Educational Futures
USE Educational Trends
AND Futures (of Society)

Educational Games   JUL. 1966
Postings: 3,978   GC: 720
SN   Individual or group games that have
     cognitive, social, behavioral, and/or emo-
     tional, etc., dimensions which are re-
     lated to educational objectives (Note:

= Two or more Descriptors are used to represent this term.
The term's main entry shows the appropriate coordination.

Prior to Mar80, this term was not restricted by a Scope Note)
UF Academic Games
     Classroom Games (1966 1980) #
     Heuristic Games
NT Reading Games
BT Games
RT Instructional Materials
     Learning Activities
     Puzzles
     Simulation

Educational Gerontology   *AUG. 1976*
     Postings: 495   GC: 400
SN Study and practice of educational endeavors for the aged and aging, and preparation of persons to work with these groups (Note: Do not confuse with "Aging Education")
BT Gerontology
RT Adult Development
     Adult Education
     Aging (Individuals)
     Aging Education
     Allied Health Occupations
     Geriatrics
     Older Adults
     Preretirement Education
     Professional Education
     Retirement

Educational Goals
USE Educational Objectives

Educational Goals of Students
USE Student Educational Objectives

Educational Guidance (1966 1977)
USE Educational Counseling

Educational History   *JUL. 1966*
     Postings: 12,360   GC: 330
UF History of Education
NT Science Education History
BT Foundations of Education
     History
RT Educational Anthropology
     Educational Practices
     Educational Theories
     Educational Trends

Educational Improvement   *JUL. 1966*
     Postings: 12,057   GC: 330
SN Enhancing the value or quality of education (Note: Use a more specific term if possible)
NT Instructional Improvement
BT Improvement
RT Education
     Educational Change
     Educational Development
     Educational Innovation
     Educational Needs
     Educational Quality
     Excellence in Education
     Formative Evaluation
     Partnerships in Education
     Relevance (Education)
     Research and Instruction Units

Educational Inequality
USE Equal Education

Educational Innovation   *JUL. 1966*
     Postings: 10,931   GC: 330
SN Introduction of new ideas or practices into educational programs, systems, or structures (Note: Prior to Mar80, the use of this term was not restricted by a Scope Note—do not confuse with "Instructional Innovation")
NT Instructional Innovation
BT Innovation
RT Education
     Educational Change
     Educational Development

     Educational Environment
     Educational Improvement
     Educational Research
     Educational Technology
     Experimental Colleges
     Experimental Curriculum
     Experimental Schools
     Experimental Teaching
     Nontraditional Education
     Research and Development
     School Restructuring
     Theory Practice Relationship

Educational Institutions
USE Schools

Educational Interest (1967 1980)
USE Student Educational Objectives

Educational Legislation   *JUL. 1966*
     Postings: 6,548   GC: 330
NT School Attendance Legislation
BT Legislation
RT Education
     Government School Relationship
     Laws
     Politics of Education
     School Law

Educational Level
USE Academic Achievement

Educational Malpractice   *OCT. 1980*
     Postings: 185   GC: 330
SN Wrongful or negligent acts on the part of teachers or schools that result (or may result) in student detriments, especially including the failure of students to learn
UF Academic Malpractice
BT Malpractice
RT Academic Standards
     Accountability
     Court Litigation
     Education
     Educational Responsibility
     Laws
     Legal Problems
     Legal Responsibility
     Libel and Slander
     Negligence
     Torts

Educational Management
USE Educational Administration

Educational Materials
USE Instructional Materials

Educational Media   *MAR. 1980*
     Postings: 7,393   GC: 720
SN Equipment and materials used for communication in instruction (Note: Use a more specific term if possible)
UF Instructional Aids (1966 1980)
     Instructional Media (1967 1980)
     Mechanical Teaching Aids (1966 1980)
NT Audiovisual Aids
     Autoinstructional Aids
     Instructional Materials
RT Computer Assisted Instruction
     Computer Managed Instruction
     Education
     Educational Equipment
     Educational Resources
     Educational Technology
     Electronic Classrooms
     Hypermedia
     Intermode Differences
     Learning Laboratories
     Learning Resources Centers
     Mass Media
     Media Adaptation
     Media Research
     Media Selection
     Media Specialists

     Multimedia Instruction
     Multimedia Materials
     Nonprint Media
     Printed Materials
     Production Techniques
     Programmed Instruction
     Telephone Instruction
     Visual Aids

Educational Media Adaptation
USE Media Adaptation

Educational Media Selection
USE Media Selection

Educational Methods   *JUL. 1966*
     Postings: 1,806   GC: 310
SN (Note: Use a more specific term if instruction or training is the primary emphasis)
NT Classroom Techniques
     Educational Strategies
     Psychoeducational Methods
     Teaching Methods
BT Methods
RT Education
     Educational Practices
     Educational Technology
     Methods Research
     Nontraditional Education

Educational Mobility   *JUL. 1966*
     Postings: 317   GC: 330
SN Changes in an individual's or group's level of formal education, often resulting in improved social and economic status (Note: Use "Student Mobility" or "Faculty Mobility" for the geographic mobility of those groups—prior to Mar80, this term was not restricted by a Scope Note)
BT Mobility
RT Academic Achievement
     Academic Aspiration
     Articulation (Education)
     Black Achievement
     College Transfer Students
     Education
     Educational Background
     Educational Benefits
     Educational Development
     Educational Opportunities
     Educational Status Comparison
     Social Mobility
     Transfer Students

Educational Needs   *JUL. 1966*
     Postings: 17,347   GC: 330
SN Necessary knowledge, skills, or attitudes that may be obtained through learning experiences—also, the needs of educational systems (Note: Use a more precise term if possible)
BT Needs
RT Education
     Educational Assessment
     Educational Demand
     Educational Improvement
     Educational Objectives
     Educational Planning
     Educational Quality
     Educational Responsibility
     Educationally Disadvantaged
     Excellence in Education
     Nontraditional Education
     Relevance (Education)
     Special Education
     Special Needs Students

Educational Objectives   *JUL. 1966*
     Postings: 28,016   GC: 330
SN Objectives relating to the outcomes or organization of the educational process—includes goals proposed or established by educational authorities at all levels (Note: Prior to Mar80, this term was not scoped and was used for institutional and personal goals relating to education—

for these concepts, see other, more precise, "Objectives" Descriptors)
UF Educational Goals
     Educational Purposes
BT Objectives
RT Education
     Education Work Relationship
     Educational Assessment
     Educational Environment
     Educational Needs
     Educational Philosophy
     Educational Planning
     Educational Principles
     Educational Quality
     Educational Theories
     Excellence in Education
     Outcome Based Education
     Outcomes of Education
     Relevance (Education)
     Role of Education
     School Role

Educational Objectives of Students
USE Student Educational Objectives

Educational Opportunities   *JUL. 1966*
     Postings: 4,361   GC: 330
SN Circumstances or conditions that enable individuals or groups to improve their educational status
UF Educational Advantages
     Training Opportunities
NT Access to Education
BT Opportunities
RT Affirmative Action
     Competitive Selection
     Compulsory Education
     Education
     Educational Background
     Educational Demand
     Educational Discrimination
     Educational Mobility
     Educationally Disadvantaged
     Equal Education
     Nondiscriminatory Education
     Nontraditional Education
     Open Enrollment

Educational Outcomes
USE Outcomes of Education

Educational Parks   *JUL. 1966*
     Postings: 90   GC: 540
SN Complex of schools, usually ranging from kindergarten through high school or the two-year college, that draws students from a metropolitan area and is intended to minimize the effects of segregation (Note: Prior to Mar80, the use of this term was not restricted by a Scope Note)
BT Educational Complexes
RT Campuses
     Magnet Schools
     Neighborhood Schools
     Racial Integration
     School Desegregation

Educational Partnerships
USE Partnerships in Education

Educational Philosophy   *JUL. 1966*
     Postings: 12,417   GC: 330
UF School Philosophy
BT Foundations of Education
     Philosophy
RT Developmentally Appropriate Practices
     Education Work Relationship
     Educational Environment
     Educational Objectives
     Educational Principles
     Educational Theories
     Inclusive Schools
     Reflective Teaching
     School Restructuring
     Traditional Schools
     Transitional Schools

= Two or more Descriptors are used to represent this term.
The term's main entry shows the appropriate coordination.

Educational Planning JUL. 1966
 Postings: 12,249 GC: 330
SN Process of determining the objectives of education, educational institutions, or educational programs and the means (activities, procedures, resources, etc.) for attaining them (Note: Use a more specific term if possible)
UF Academic Planning
  Educational Plans
NT College Planning
  Educational Facilities Planning
BT Planning
RT Articulation (Education)
  Education
  Educational Administration
  Educational Assessment
  Educational Cooperation
  Educational Development
  Educational Finance
  Educational Needs
  Educational Objectives
  Educational Strategies
  Environmental Scanning
  Formative Evaluation
  Resource Allocation
  Strategic Planning

Educational Plans
USE Educational Planning

Educational Policy JUL. 1966
 Postings: 16,929 GC: 330
BT Policy
RT Academic Accommodations (Disabilities)
  Bilingual Education
  Board of Education Policy
  Education
  Educational Administration
  Educational Assessment
  Educational Principles
  Excellence in Education
  Language of Instruction
  Language Planning
  New Federalism
  Official Languages
  Politics of Education
  Regular and Special Education Relationship
  School District Autonomy
  School Policy
  School Restructuring
  Self Determination

Educational Politics
USE Politics of Education

Educational Practice (1967 1980)
USE Educational Practices

Educational Practices MAR. 1980
 Postings: 9,046 GC: 330
SN Customary operations in education, from the educational system as a whole to the individual classroom or teacher (Note: Use a more precise term if possible)
UF Educational Practice (1967 1980)
NT Developmentally Appropriate Practices
RT Education
  Educational History
  Educational Methods
  Educational Principles
  Educational Research
  Educational Trends
  Progressive Education
  Theory Practice Relationship

Educational Principles JUL. 1966
 Postings: 2,633 GC: 330
SN Values or assumptions that guide decisions concerning educational methods or objectives
BT Foundations of Education
  Standards
RT Administrative Principles
  Education
  Educational Anthropology

Educational Objectives
Educational Philosophy
Educational Policy
Educational Practices
Educational Psychology
Educational Research
Educational Theories
Nontraditional Education
Values

Educational Problems (1966 1980)
  MAR. 1980
 Postings: 3,890 GC: 330
SN Invalid Descriptor—used inconsistently in indexing—see more precise Descriptors relating to the particular problem

Educational Processes
USE Learning Processes

Educational Production Functions
USE Productivity

Educational Programs (1966 1980)
  MAR. 1980
 Postings: 8,324 GC: 320
SN Invalid Descriptor—used inconsistently in indexing—coordinate more specific Descriptors

Educational Psychology JUL. 1966
 Postings: 1,830 GC: 400
BT Foundations of Education
  Psychology
RT Educational Anthropology
  Educational Counseling
  Educational Principles
  Educational Sociology
  Educational Theories
  Intervention
  School Psychology
  Social Psychology

Educational Purposes
USE Educational Objectives

Educational Quality JUL. 1966
 Postings: 10,089 GC: 330
SN Degrees of excellence in meeting educational objectives (Note: Use a more precise term if possible)
UF Educational Excellence
  Educational Quality Assessment #
  Quality Education
RT Accrediting Agencies
  Administrator Effectiveness
  Back to Basics
  Benchmarking
  Consumer Protection
  Curriculum Evaluation
  Diversity (Institutional)
  Education
  Educational Improvement
  Educational Needs
  Educational Objectives
  Effective Schools Research
  Equal Education
  Excellence in Education
  Instructional Effectiveness
  Program Effectiveness
  Quality of Life
  School Effectiveness
  Teacher Effectiveness

Educational Quality Assessment
USE Educational Assessment
AND Educational Quality

Educational Radio JUL. 1966
 Postings: 1,111 GC: 720
UF Instructional Radio
BT Audiovisual Communications
  Radio
RT Audiovisual Instruction
  Distance Education

Documentaries
Educational Television
Listening Groups
Mass Instruction

Educational Reform
USE Educational Change

Educational Relevance
USE Relevance (Education)

Educational Research JUL. 1966
 Postings: 34,693 GC: 810
SN Basic, applied, and developmental research conducted to advance knowledge in the field of education or bearing on educational problems (Note: Use a more specific term if possible—as of Oct81, use as a minor Descriptor for examples of educational research—use as a major Descriptor only as the subject of a document)
NT Classroom Research
  Curriculum Research
  Effective Schools Research
  Reading Research
  Writing Research
BT Research
RT Behavioral Science Research
  Demonstration Centers
  Education
  Educational Development
  Educational Innovation
  Educational Practices
  Educational Principles
  Educational Researchers
  Educational Status Comparison
  Educational Testing
  Exceptional Child Research
  Experimental Curriculum
  Experimental Schools
  Experimental Teaching
  Field Studies
  Graduate Surveys
  Institutional Research
  Laboratory Schools
  Program Effectiveness
  Research and Development
  Research and Instruction Units
  Research Committees
  Research Coordinating Units
  School Statistics
  School Surveys
  Social Science Research
  Student Surveys
  Teacher Researchers
  Teacher Surveys
  Theory Practice Relationship

Educational Researchers JUL. 1966
 Postings: 977 GC: 360
UF Research Specialists (Education)
NT Teacher Researchers
BT Researchers
RT Educational Research
  Evaluators
  Research Directors

Educational Resources JUL. 1966
 Postings: 7,045 GC: 330
SN The equipment, facilities, materials, and personnel available for education (Note: Use a more precise term if possible)
UF Curriculum Resources
  Learning Resources
  Teaching Resources
NT Educational Supply
BT Resources
RT Education
  Educational Equipment
  Educational Facilities
  Educational Media
  Educational Technology
  Faculty
  Information Sources
  Instructional Materials

Educational Responsibility JUL. 1966
 Postings: 2,274 GC: 330
SN Obligations or duties to meet educational needs (Note: Use a more precise term if possible—prior to Mar80, the use of this term was not restricted by a Scope Note)
BT Responsibility
RT Administrator Responsibility
  College Role
  Education
  Educational Malpractice
  Educational Needs
  Noninstructional Responsibility
  Parent Responsibility
  Relevance (Education)
  Role of Education
  School Responsibility
  School Role
  Social Responsibility
  Student Responsibility
  Teacher Responsibility

Educational Retardation (1966 1980)
  MAR. 1980
 Postings: 52 GC: 220
SN Invalid Descriptor—used inconsistently in indexing—see such Descriptors as "Slow Learners," "Educationally Disadvantaged," "Learning Disabilities," "Learning Problems," "Academic Ability," etc.

Educational Service Centers
USE Education Service Centers

Educational Sociology JUL. 1966
 Postings: 1,159 GC: 400
UF Sociology of Education
BT Foundations of Education
  Sociology
RT Critical Theory
  Educational Anthropology
  Educational Psychology
  School Community Relationship
  Social Psychology
  Sociologists

Educational Specifications (1967 1980)
  MAR. 1980
 Postings: 455 GC: 320
SN Invalid Descriptor—used inconsistently in indexing—see such Descriptors as "Educational Facilities Design," "Facility Guidelines," "Curriculum Development," etc.

Educational Status Comparison JUL. 1966
 Postings: 748 GC: 510
SN Comparison of the level of education achieved by individuals or groups and their socioeconomic status
BT Comparative Analysis
RT Education
  Education Work Relationship
  Educational Attainment
  Educational Background
  Educational Benefits
  Educational Experience
  Educational Mobility
  Educational Research
  Educationally Disadvantaged
  Social Mobility
  Socioeconomic Status

Educational Strategies JUL. 1966
 Postings: 8,508 GC: 310
SN Overall plans for implementing instructional goals, methods, or techniques
UF Instructional Strategies
BT Educational Methods
RT Change Strategies
  Curriculum Design
  Education
  Educational Planning
  Instructional Design
  Instructional Development
  Learning Strategies

= Two or more Descriptors are used to represent this term.
The term's main entry shows the appropriate coordination.

Motivation Techniques
Strategic Planning
Teaching Methods

Educational Supply　　　　　*AUG. 1968*
　　Postings: 770　　　　　　　GC: 330
SN　Education provided to meet consumer
　　demand
UF　Supply of Education
BT　Educational Resources
RT　Access to Education
　　Admission (School)
　　Competitive Selection
　　Compulsory Education
　　Declining Enrollment
　　Education
　　Educational Demand
　　Educational Economics
　　Educational Trends
　　Enrollment
　　Enrollment Influences
　　Supply and Demand

Educational Support
USE　Educational Finance

Educational Surveys
USE　School Surveys

Educational Technology　　　*JUL. 1969*
　　Postings: 14,319　　　　　GC: 330
SN　Systematic identification, development,
　　organization, or utilization of educational
　　resources and/or the management of
　　these processes—occasionally used in a
　　more limited sense to describe the use of
　　equipment-oriented techniques or au-
　　diovisual aids in educational settings
UF　Instructional Technology (1966 1978)
NT　Instructional Systems
　　Performance Technology
BT　Technology
RT　Audiovisual Aids
　　Audiovisual Communications
　　Computer Oriented Programs
　　Computer Uses in Education
　　Cybernetics
　　Education
　　Educational Development
　　Educational Equipment
　　Educational Innovation
　　Educational Media
　　Educational Methods
　　Educational Resources
　　Information Technology
　　Instruction
　　Instructional Design
　　Instructional Development
　　Instructional Improvement
　　Instructional Innovation
　　Instructional Materials
　　Multimedia Instruction
　　Programmed Instruction

Educational Television　　　*JUL. 1966*
　　Postings: 6,033　　　　　　GC: 720
SN　Transmission of educational or informa-
　　tional programs or material by televi-
　　sion (Note: Use a more specific term if
　　possible—see also "Telecourses")
UF　ETV
　　Fixed Service Television (1969 1980)
　　Instructional Television (1966 1974)
　　Instructor Centered Television (1966
　　1980)
　　ITFS
　　ITV
　　Televised Instruction (1966 1974)
BT　Audiovisual Communications
　　Television
RT　Audiovisual Instruction
　　Closed Circuit Television
　　Distance Education
　　Documentaries
　　Educational Radio
　　Home Programs
　　Instructional Films
　　Interactive Television
　　Listening Groups

Mass Instruction
Public Television
Telecourses
Television Teachers

Educational Testing　　　　*JUL. 1966*
　　Postings: 2,829　　　　　　GC: 820
SN　Use of tests to assess the effect of edu-
　　cational programs and activities on stu-
　　dents (Note: Prior to Mar80, the use of
　　this term was not restricted by a Scope
　　Note)
UF　Student Testing (1966 1980)
BT　Testing
RT　Achievement Tests
　　Curriculum Based Assessment
　　Education
　　Educational Diagnosis
　　Educational Research
　　Grading
　　Performance Based Assessment
　　Precision Teaching
　　Prognostic Tests
　　Student Evaluation
　　Student Placement
　　Test Score Decline

Educational Theories　　　　*JUL. 1966*
　　Postings: 6,638　　　　　　GC: 810
BT　Foundations of Education
　　Theories
RT　Andragogy
　　Education
　　Educational Anthropology
　　Educational History
　　Educational Objectives
　　Educational Philosophy
　　Educational Principles
　　Educational Psychology
　　Hidden Curriculum
　　Nontraditional Education
　　Progressive Education

Educational Therapy　　　　*JUL. 1966*
　　Postings: 273　　　　　　　GC: 310
SN　Educational practices that contribute to
　　the treatment of students' organic or
　　functional disorders (e.g., remedial read-
　　ing instruction that improves self-es-
　　teem)
BT　Therapy
RT　Art Therapy
　　Classroom Techniques
　　Diagnostic Teaching
　　Education
　　Educational Counseling
　　Educational Diagnosis
　　Intervention
　　Music Therapy
　　Psychoeducational Clinics
　　Psychoeducational Methods
　　Reality Therapy
　　Rehabilitation
　　Remedial Programs
　　School Counseling
　　Therapeutic Environment

Educational Trends　　　　　*JUL. 1966*
　　Postings: 14,167　　　　　GC: 330
UF　Educational Futures #
RT　Education
　　Educational Change
　　Educational Demand
　　Educational History
　　Educational Practices
　　Educational Supply
　　Enrollment Trends
　　Reentry Students
　　School Statistics
　　Trend Analysis

Educational Vouchers　　　　*MAR. 1980*
　　Postings: 775　　　　　　　GC: 620
SN　Allocations of public funds to parents to
　　pay the costs of their children's educa-
　　tion in the public or private school of
　　their choice
UF　Education Vouchers (1971 1980)
　　Voucher Plans

BT　Grants
RT　Educational Economics
　　Educational Finance
　　Fellowships
　　Private School Aid
　　Scholarships
　　School Choice
　　Student Costs
　　Student Financial Aid
　　Tuition Grants

Educationally Deprived
USE　Educationally Disadvantaged

Educationally Disadvantaged　*JUL. 1966*
　　Postings: 4,665　　　　　　GC: 540
SN　Individuals or groups whose schooling
　　is judged to be qualitatively or quantita-
　　tively inferior as compared with what is
　　considered necessary for achievement
　　in a particular society
UF　Academically Disadvantaged
　　Educational Disadvantagement (1966
　　1980)
　　Educationally Deprived
　　Progressive Retardation (1966 1980)
　　(in School)
BT　Disadvantaged
RT　Academic Achievement
　　Compensatory Education
　　Compulsory Education
　　Developmental Studies Programs
　　Disadvantaged Environment
　　Disadvantaged Schools
　　Education
　　Educational Needs
　　Educational Opportunities
　　Educational Status Comparison
　　Equal Education
　　High Risk Students
　　Illiteracy
　　Individualized Education Programs
　　Learning Problems
　　Nontraditional Students
　　Open Enrollment
　　Remedial Programs
　　Slow Learners
　　Special Needs Students
　　Supplementary Education
　　Transitional Programs

Educationese
USE　Jargon

EEG
USE　Electroencephalography

Effect Size　　　　　　　　*OCT. 1983*
　　Postings: 436　　　　　　　GC: 820
SN　Statistical calculation of the magnitude
　　of a measurable effect, e.g., the mean
　　difference on a variable between experi-
　　mental and control groups divided by the
　　standard deviation on that variable of the
　　pooled groups or of the control group
　　alone
UF　Magnitude of Effect
BT　Statistical Analysis
RT　Control Groups
　　Experimental Groups
　　Experiments
　　Matched Groups
　　Mathematical Models
　　Meta Analysis
　　Predictor Variables
　　Research Design
　　Research Methodology
　　Sample Size
　　Statistical Significance
　　Statistics

Effective Schooling
USE　School Effectiveness

Effective Schools Research　　*APR. 1990*
　　Postings: 535　　　　　　　GC: 810
SN　Educational research focused on identi-

fying unusually effective schools, study-
ing the underlying attributes of their pro-
grams and personnel, and designing
techniques to operationalize these attrib-
utes in less effective schools (Note: Use
as a minor Descriptor for examples of
this kind of research—use as a major
Descriptor only as the subject of a docu-
ment)
BT　Educational Research
RT　Educational Assessment
　　Educational Quality
　　Excellence in Education
　　Institutional Research
　　Outcomes of Education
　　School Effectiveness
　　Schools

Effective Teaching (1966 1980)
USE　Teacher Effectiveness

Efficacy Expectation
USE　Self Efficacy

Efficiency　　　　　　　　　*JAN. 1974*
　　Postings: 1,919　　　　　　GC: 620
SN　Capacity to produce desired results with
　　a minimum expenditure of energy, time,
　　money, or materials
RT　Cost Effectiveness
　　Economics
　　Educational Economics
　　Evaluation Criteria
　　Job Simplification
　　Organizational Effectiveness
　　Performance
　　Productivity
　　Program Effectiveness
　　Resource Allocation
　　Time Management

EFL
USE　English (Second Language)

Egg Inspectors
USE　Food and Drug Inspectors

Ego
USE　Self Concept

Egocentrism　　　　　　　　*FEB. 1975*
　　Postings: 317　　　　　　　GC: 120
SN　State of mind characterized by preoccu-
　　pation with the self—often refers to the
　　Piagetian stage in mental development
　　when the child sees things only from his/
　　her own limited point of view
UF　Egotism
　　Self Bias
　　Self Centeredness
BT　Psychological Patterns
RT　Bias
　　Child Language
　　Congruence (Psychology)
　　Extraversion Introversion
　　Interpersonal Relationship
　　Personality Traits
　　Perspective Taking
　　Self Concept
　　Social Attitudes
　　Social Cognition
　　Social Development
　　Values

Egotism
USE　Egocentrism

Eidetic Imagery　　　　　　*MAR. 1980*
　　Postings: 57　　　　　　　　GC: 110
SN　Vividly clear, detailed imagery of some-
　　thing (usually visual) that has been pre-
　　viously perceived
UF　Eidetic Images (1967 1980)
　　Photographic Memory
BT　Memory

= Two or more Descriptors are used to represent this term.
The term's main entry shows the appropriate coordination.

RT　　Visualization

Eidetic Images (1967 1980)
USE　Eidetic Imagery

Eight Millimeter Projectors (1970 1980)
USE　Projection Equipment

Eighteenth Century Literature　　　*JUN. 1969*
　　　Postings: 172　　　　　　　　　　GC: 430
BT　　Literature
RT　　Baroque Literature
　　　Literary History
　　　Neoclassicism
　　　Romanticism

Elder Abuse　　　　　　　　　　　　*JUN. 1983*
　　　Postings: 107　　　　　　　　　　GC: 530
SN　　Physical, psychological, financial, and/or
　　　legal abuse of older persons by their
　　　relatives or caretakers
UF　　Abused Elderly
BT　　Antisocial Behavior
RT　　Aging (Individuals)
　　　Battered Women
　　　Emotional Abuse
　　　Family Problems
　　　Family Violence
　　　Middle Aged Adults
　　　Older Adults
　　　Parent Child Relationship
　　　Verbal Abuse
　　　Victims of Crime
　　　Violence

Elderly
USE　Older Adults

Eldest Siblings
USE　First Born

Elected City Officials
USE　City Officials

Election Campaigns
USE　Political Campaigns

Elections　　　　　　　　　　　　　*JUL. 1966*
　　　Postings: 923　　　　　　　　　　GC: 610
UF　　Presidential Elections (United States) #
NT　　School Budget Elections
BT　　Selection
RT　　Local Issues
　　　Political Campaigns
　　　Political Candidates
　　　Political Issues
　　　Political Science
　　　Politics
　　　Voter Registration
　　　Voting
　　　Voting Rights

Elective Courses　　　　　　　　　*JUN. 1977*
　　　Postings: 817　　　　　　　　　　GC: 350
SN　　Courses from which students may select
　　　on the basis of personal preference
UF　　Elective Subjects (1966 1977)
　　　Optional Courses
BT　　Courses
RT　　Advanced Courses
　　　Course Content
　　　Course Selection (Students)
　　　Majors (Students)
　　　Minicourses
　　　Noncredit Courses
　　　Required Courses
　　　Student Interests

Elective Reading (1966 1980)　　　*MAR. 1980*
　　　Postings: 40　　　　　　　　　　　GC: 460
SN　　Invalid Descriptor—used inconsistently
　　　in indexing—see "Independent Read-
　　　ing," "Recreational Reading," etc.

Elective Subjects (1966 1977)
USE　Elective Courses

Electric Batteries　　　　　　　　　*SEP. 1968*
　　　Postings: 108　　　　　　　　　　GC: 910
UF　　Batteries (Electric)
　　　Storage Batteries
BT　　Equipment
　　　Supplies
RT　　Electric Circuits
　　　Electricity
　　　Electrochemistry
　　　Electronics

Electric Circuits　　　　　　　　　　*SEP. 1968*
　　　Postings: 585　　　　　　　　　　GC: 910
UF　　Circuits (Electronic)
　　　Electronic Circuits
BT　　Equipment
RT　　Electric Batteries
　　　Electricity
　　　Electronics
　　　Microelectronics
　　　Potentiometers (Instruments)

Electric Motors　　　　　　　　　　*JUL. 1966*
　　　Postings: 101　　　　　　　　　　GC: 910
BT　　Engines
RT　　Electrical Appliances
　　　Electricity
　　　Motor Vehicles

Electric Systems
USE　Electrical Systems

Electric Utilities
USE　Utilities

**Electrical Appliance Servicemen (1968
1980)**
USE　Appliance Repair

Electrical Appliances　　　　　　　*JUL. 1966*
　　　Postings: 111　　　　　　　　　　GC: 910
BT　　Equipment
RT　　Appliance Repair
　　　Electric Motors
　　　Electricity
　　　Home Furnishings

Electrical Controls
USE　Electronic Control

Electrical Occupations　　　　　　　*JUL. 1966*
　　　Postings: 294　　　　　　　　　　GC: 640
UF　　Electromechanical Occupations #
BT　　Occupations
RT　　Appliance Repair
　　　Electricians
　　　Electricity
　　　Electromechanical Technology
　　　Electronic Technicians
　　　Electronics
　　　Energy Occupations
　　　Equipment Maintenance
　　　Semiskilled Occupations
　　　Skilled Occupations
　　　Trade and Industrial Education

Electrical Stimuli　　　　　　　　　*SEP. 1968*
　　　Postings: 65　　　　　　　　　　　GC: 110
BT　　Stimuli
RT　　Auditory Stimuli
　　　Electricity
　　　Pictorial Stimuli
　　　Tactile Stimuli
　　　Verbal Stimuli
　　　Visual Stimuli

Electrical Systems　　　　　　　　　*AUG. 1968*
　　　Postings: 409　　　　　　　　　　GC: 920
UF　　Electric Systems
RT　　Alarm Systems

Climate Control
Electricians
Electricity
Electronic Control
Electronics
Lighting
Utilities

Electrical Technicians
USE　Electronic Technicians

Electricians　　　　　　　　　　　　*AUG. 1968*
　　　Postings: 131　　　　　　　　　　GC: 640
BT　　Skilled Workers
RT　　Appliance Repair
　　　Building Trades
　　　Electrical Occupations
　　　Electrical Systems
　　　Electricity
　　　Electronic Technicians
　　　Electronics

Electricity　　　　　　　　　　　　　*JUL. 1966*
　　　Postings: 1,717　　　　　　　　　GC: 490
RT　　Alternative Energy Sources
　　　Electric Batteries
　　　Electric Circuits
　　　Electric Motors
　　　Electrical Appliances
　　　Electrical Occupations
　　　Electrical Stimuli
　　　Electrical Systems
　　　Electricians
　　　Electrochemistry
　　　Electromechanical Aids
　　　Electromechanical Technology
　　　Electronic Technicians
　　　Electronics
　　　Force
　　　Geothermal Energy
　　　Magnets
　　　Physics
　　　Potentiometers (Instruments)
　　　Power Technology
　　　Solar Energy
　　　Superconductors
　　　Transistors
　　　Wind Energy

Electrochemistry　　　　　　　　　　*DEC. 1992*
　　　Postings: 100　　　　　　　　　　GC: 490
SN　　Branch of physical chemistry dealing
　　　with the interconversion of electrical and
　　　chemical energy
BT　　Physical Chemistry
RT　　Chemical Engineering
　　　Chemical Equilibrium
　　　Electric Batteries
　　　Electricity
　　　Photochemical Reactions

Electrochromatography
USE　Chromatography

Electroencephalography　　　　　　*JUL. 1966*
　　　Postings: 184　　　　　　　　　　GC: 210
UF　　EEG
BT　　Medicine
RT　　Biofeedback
　　　Biomedical Equipment
　　　Brain
　　　Laboratory Technology
　　　Medical Evaluation
　　　Medical Services
　　　Neurology

Electromechanical Aids　　　　　　*JUL. 1966*
　　　Postings: 384　　　　　　　　　　GC: 910
BT　　Equipment
RT　　Audiovisual Aids
　　　Autoinstructional Aids
　　　Calculators
　　　Computers
　　　Electricity
　　　Electromechanical Technology
　　　Electronic Classrooms
　　　Electronic Equipment

Low Vision Aids
Mobility Aids
Prostheses
Sensory Aids

Electromechanical Occupations
USE　Electrical Occupations
AND　Electromechanical Technology

Electromechanical Technology　　　*JUL. 1966*
　　　Postings: 265　　　　　　　　　　GC: 490
SN　　Technology of mechanical devices, sys-
　　　tems, or processes that are
　　　electrostatically or electromagnetically ac-
　　　tuated or controlled
UF　　Electromechanical Occupations #
BT　　Technology
RT　　Aerospace Industry
　　　Automation
　　　Computer Science
　　　Data Processing
　　　Electrical Occupations
　　　Electricity
　　　Electromechanical Aids
　　　Electronic Control
　　　Electronics
　　　Electronics Industry
　　　Engineering
　　　Engineering Technology
　　　Horology
　　　Mechanical Design Technicians
　　　Microelectronics
　　　Robotics
　　　Technical Education

Electronic Aids
USE　Electronic Equipment

Electronic Bulletin Boards
USE　Electronic Mail

Electronic Calculators
USE　Calculators

Electronic Circuits
USE　Electric Circuits

Electronic Classroom Use (1966 1980)
USE　Electronic Classrooms

Electronic Classrooms　　　　　　　*JUL. 1966*
　　　Postings: 218　　　　　　　　　　GC: 920
SN　　Classrooms equipped with
　　　electromechanical aids, such as those
　　　used in language instruction
UF　　Electronic Classroom Use (1966 1980)
BT　　Classrooms
RT　　Autoinstructional Aids
　　　Educational Media
　　　Electromechanical Aids
　　　Electronic Equipment
　　　Language Laboratories
　　　Learning Laboratories
　　　Programmed Instruction

Electronic Communications Systems
USE　Telecommunications

Electronic Control　　　　　　　　　*JAN. 1969*
　　　Postings: 167　　　　　　　　　　GC: 490
SN　　Control of a machine or process by cir-
　　　cuits using electron tubes, transistors,
　　　magnetic amplifiers, or other devices
　　　having comparable functions
UF　　Electrical Controls
　　　Magnetic Amplifiers
　　　Static Controls
RT　　Automation
　　　Computer Assisted Manufacturing
　　　Cybernetics
　　　Electrical Systems
　　　Electromechanical Technology
　　　Electronic Equipment
　　　Electronics

Instrumentation
Microelectronics
Numerical Control
Robotics

Electronic Data Processing (1967 1980)
USE   Data Processing

Electronic Discussion Lists
USE   Listservs

Electronic Equipment   *JUL. 1966*
    Postings: 1,644   GC: 910
UF   Electronic Aids
NT   Broadcast Reception Equipment
     Computer Peripherals
     Computers
     Magnetic Tapes
     Microphones
     Optical Disks
     Polygraphs
     Radar
     Semiconductor Devices
     Sound Spectrographs
     Speech Synthesizers
     Tape Recorders
     Video Equipment
BT   Equipment
RT   Air Traffic Control
     Alarm Systems
     Audiovisual Aids
     Calculators
     Computer Assisted Manufacturing
     Data Processing
     Electromechanical Aids
     Electronic Classrooms
     Electronic Control
     Electronic Mail
     Electronic Publishing
     Electronics
     Electronics Industry
     Facsimile Transmission
     Instrumentation
     Loop Induction Systems
     Microelectronics
     Radio
     Telecommunications
     Teleconferencing
     Television
     Word Processing

Electronic Information Exchange
USE   Information Networks
AND   Telecommunications

Electronic Journals   *AUG. 1996*
    Postings: 259   GC: 720
SN   Periodicals, usually topical and moder-
     ated, that are published and dissemi-
     nated (sometimes on an irregular sched-
     ule) in the form of electronic text or
     hypertext on computer networks (such
     as the Internet) or other computerized
     media (e.g., CD-ROM)
UF   E Zines
     Electronic Magazines
     Online Journals
     Webzines
BT   Periodicals
RT   Computer Mediated Communication
     Electronic Publishing
     Electronic Text
     Full Text Databases
     Hypermedia
     Information Dissemination
     Information Networks
     Internet
     Online Systems
     Scholarly Communication
     Scholarly Journals

Electronic Libraries   *SEP. 1996*
    Postings: 587   GC: 710
SN   Services and collections of information
     made accessible through computer
     networks—includes services such as
     document delivery, end-user searching
     and training, network access, and online

catalog enhancements, and access to
collections of bibliographic and full-text
databases, electronic journals, and digital images
UF   Digital Libraries
     Virtual Libraries
BT   Libraries
RT   Computer Mediated Communication
     Computer Networks
     Electronic Publishing
     Electronic Text
     Information Technology
     Internet
     Library Automation
     Online Systems

Electronic Magazines
USE   Electronic Journals

Electronic Mail   *APR. 1986*
    Postings: 2,019   GC: 710
SN   The processing and delivery of printed
     messages (text or graphics) via telecom-
     munications terminals
UF   Computer Based Message Systems
     Electronic Bulletin Boards
NT   Listservs
BT   Computer Mediated Communication
RT   Computer Oriented Programs
     Electronic Equipment
     Electronic Text
     Facsimile Transmission
     Information Dissemination
     Information Networks
     Input Output Devices
     Internet
     Online Systems

Electronic Publishing   *APR. 1986*
    Postings: 1,043   GC: 710
SN   Use of computers, instead of traditional
     print media, to produce and distribute
     information
BT   Computer Mediated Communication
     Production Techniques
RT   Computers
     Data Conversion
     Databases
     Desktop Publishing
     Electronic Equipment
     Electronic Journals
     Electronic Libraries
     Electronic Text
     Full Text Databases
     Hypermedia
     Information Dissemination
     Information Networks
     Internet
     Publishing Industry
     Scholarly Communication
     Videotex

Electronic Spreadsheets
USE   Spreadsheets

Electronic Superhighway
USE   Internet

Electronic Technicians   *JUL. 1966*
    Postings: 308   GC: 640
UF   Electrical Technicians
BT   Paraprofessional Personnel
RT   Data Processing Occupations
     Electrical Occupations
     Electricians
     Electricity
     Electronics
     Engineering Technicians
     Instrumentation Technicians
     Medical Laboratory Assistants
     Nuclear Power Plant Technicians

Electronic Text   *AUG. 1994*
    Postings: 431   GC: 710
SN   Alphanumeric data (with or without graph-
     ics) that can be stored on, and manipu-
     lated by, computers

UF   Machine Readable Text
BT   Written Language
RT   Computer Mediated Communication
     Computers
     Data Processing
     Databases
     Electronic Journals
     Electronic Libraries
     Electronic Mail
     Electronic Publishing
     Information Technology
     Machine Readable Cataloging
     Online Systems
     Optical Data Disks
     Text Structure
     Videotex
     Word Processing

Electronics   *JUL. 1966*
    Postings: 1,333   GC: 490
NT   Microelectronics
BT   Physics
RT   Crystallography
     Diffusion (Physics)
     Electric Batteries
     Electric Circuits
     Electrical Occupations
     Electrical Systems
     Electricians
     Electricity
     Electromechanical Technology
     Electronic Control
     Electronic Equipment
     Electronic Technicians
     Electronics Industry
     Industrial Arts
     Instrumentation Technicians
     Lasers
     Magnets
     Optics
     Radar
     Robotics
     Technology Education
     Transistors

Electronics Industry   *JUL. 1966*
    Postings: 129   GC: 650
BT   Manufacturing Industry
RT   Electromechanical Technology
     Electronic Equipment
     Electronics
     Microelectronics
     Semiconductor Devices

Electrooptics (1968 1980)
USE   Optics

Elementary Education   *JUL. 1966*
    Postings: 62,735   GC: 340
SN   Education provided in kindergarten or
     grade 1 through grade 6, 7, or 8 (Note:
     Also appears in the list of mandatory
     educational level Descriptors)
UF   Elementary Grades (1966 1980)
NT   Adult Basic Education
     Primary Education
BT   Elementary Secondary Education
RT   Early Childhood Education
     Elementary School Curriculum
     Elementary School Students
     Elementary School Teachers
     Elementary Schools
     Grade 1
     Grade 2
     Grade 3
     Grade 4
     Grade 5
     Grade 6
     Grade 7
     Grade 8
     Intermediate Grades
     Kindergarten

Elementary Grades (1966 1980)
USE   Elementary Education

Elementary School Children
USE   Elementary School Students

Elementary School Counseling (1967 1980)
USE   School Counseling

Elementary School Counselors (1967 1980)
USE   School Counselors

Elementary School Curriculum   *AUG. 1968*
    Postings: 2,004   GC: 350
NT   Elementary School Mathematics
     Elementary School Science
     FLES
BT   Curriculum
RT   Elementary Education
     Elementary Schools
     Preschool Curriculum

Elementary School Guidance (1967 1980)
USE   School Guidance

Elementary School Libraries (1966 1980)
USE   School Libraries

Elementary School Mathematics   *JUL. 1966*
    Postings: 7,881   GC: 480
SN   Mathematics curriculum or instruction
     provided in kindergarten or grade 1
     through grade 6, 7, or 8
BT   Elementary School Curriculum
     Mathematics Curriculum
RT   College Mathematics
     Mathematics
     Mathematics Education
     Mathematics Instruction
     Modern Mathematics
     Secondary School Mathematics

Elementary School Role (1966 1980)
USE   School Role

Elementary School Science   *JUL. 1966*
    Postings: 7,923   GC: 490
UF   Elementary Science (1966 1980)
BT   Elementary School Curriculum
     Science Curriculum
RT   College Science
     Science Departments
     Science Education
     Science Instruction
     Secondary School Science

Elementary School Students   *JUL. 1966*
    Postings: 17,710   GC: 360
SN   (Note: Coordinate with the appropriate
     mandatory educational level Descriptor)
UF   Elementary School Children
BT   Students
RT   Children
     Elementary Education
     Elementary Schools
     Middle School Students

Elementary School Supervisors (1966 1980)
USE   School Supervision

Elementary School Teachers   *JUL. 1966*
    Postings: 6,891   GC: 360
BT   Teachers
RT   Elementary Education
     Elementary Schools
     Middle School Teachers
     Public School Teachers

Elementary Schools   *JUL. 1966*
    Postings: 3,527   GC: 340
BT   Schools
RT   Affiliated Schools
     British Infant Schools
     Elementary Education
     Elementary School Curriculum
     Elementary School Students
     Elementary School Teachers
     Laboratory Schools

= Two or more Descriptors are used to represent this term.
The term's main entry shows the appropriate coordination.

Multiunit Schools
Professional Development Schools

Elementary Science (1966 1980)
USE　Elementary School Science

Elementary Secondary Education　　*FEB. 1975*
　　　Postings: 147,432　　　　　　GC: 340
SN　Formal education provided in kindergarten or grade 1 through grade 12 (Note: Also appears in the list of mandatory educational level Descriptors)
NT　Elementary Education
　　　Secondary Education
BT　Education
RT　Compulsory Education

Eligibility　　　　　　　　　　　*AUG. 1978*
　　　Postings: 2,274　　　　　　　GC: 520
SN　Qualifying for certain benefits or services (e.g., student eligibility for financial aid, institutional eligibility for accreditation, family eligibility for welfare assistance, employee eligibility for retirement)
UF　Institutional Eligibility
　　　Student Eligibility
RT　Accreditation (Institutions)
　　　Admission (School)
　　　Assistantships
　　　Athletes
　　　Athletics
　　　Career Choice
　　　Certification
　　　College Applicants
　　　College Choice
　　　Community Services
　　　Credit (Finance)
　　　Disqualification
　　　Federal Aid
　　　Fellowships
　　　Financial Aid Applicants
　　　Financial Services
　　　Financial Support
　　　Grants
　　　Health Services
　　　Insurance
　　　Legal Aid
　　　Need Analysis (Student Financial Aid)
　　　Personnel Selection
　　　Prerequisites
　　　Scholarships
　　　School Choice
　　　Services
　　　Social Services
　　　Standards
　　　State Aid
　　　Status
　　　Student Financial Aid
　　　Student Loan Programs
　　　Welfare Recipients
　　　Welfare Services

Elite Colleges
USE　Selective Colleges

Elitism　　　　　　　　　　　　*AUG. 1986*
　　　Postings: 238　　　　　　　　GC: 520
SN　Rule or participation by a select subgroup
RT　Ideology
　　　Intergroup Relations
　　　Political Science
　　　Selective Colleges
　　　Social Stratification
　　　Sociology
　　　Values

Emancipated Students (1975 1980)
USE　Self Supporting Students

Embryology　　　　　　　　　　*MAY 1969*
　　　Postings: 74　　　　　　　　GC: 490
BT　Biological Sciences
RT　Anatomy
　　　Biology
　　　Botany
　　　Cytology

Evolution
Genetic Engineering
Genetics
Heredity
Medicine
Nucleic Acids
Pathology
Physiology
Plant Growth
Rh Factors
Zoology

Emergency Medical Technicians　*NOV. 1982*
　　　Postings: 86　　　　　　　　GC: 210
SN　Personnel trained to respond to medical emergencies, evaluate the nature of the emergency, provide aid or treatment according to a physician's orders, and transport victim(s) to medical facilities
UF　Ambulance Attendants
BT　Allied Health Personnel
　　　Emergency Squad Personnel
RT　Accidents
　　　First Aid
　　　Medical Assistants
　　　Medical Services
　　　Rescue

Emergency Programs　　　　　　*JUL. 1966*
　　　Postings: 631　　　　　　　GC: 320
UF　Disaster Readiness
BT　Programs
RT　Alarm Systems
　　　Civil Defense
　　　Crisis Intervention
　　　Crisis Management
　　　Natural Disasters
　　　Rescue
　　　Safety
　　　School Safety
　　　Terrorism

Emergency Squad Personnel　　　*JUL. 1966*
　　　Postings: 141　　　　　　　GC: 640
UF　Rescue Squad Personnel
NT　Emergency Medical Technicians
BT　Service Workers
RT　Accidents
　　　Alarm Systems
　　　Fire Fighters
　　　Police
　　　Rescue

Emergent Literacy　　　　　　　*MAR. 1996*
　　　Postings: 1,153　　　　　　GC: 460
SN　The early stages of learning to read and write—an increasing awareness of the print world, usually associated with young learners observing and experimenting with reading and writing processes (Note: In the 1980s, the emergent literacy perspective was a departure from the more traditional stage view of reading/writing readiness followed by formal learning)
UF　Early Literacy
BT　Literacy
RT　Beginning Reading
　　　Beginning Writing
　　　Childrens Writing
　　　Early Reading
　　　Family Literacy
　　　Invented Spelling
　　　Reading Instruction
　　　Writing Instruction

Emerging Nations
USE　Developing Nations

Emerging Occupations　　　　　*OCT. 1983*
　　　Postings: 219　　　　　　　GC: 640
SN　Occupations that are new or that consist of new combinations of existing skills and knowledge, and for which considerable demand exists or is projected
BT　Demand Occupations
RT　Career Change
　　　Futures (of Society)
　　　Industrialization

Job Development
Labor Force Development
Technological Advancement

Emotional Abuse　　　　　　　　*JUN. 1994*
　　　Postings: 91　　　　　　　　GC: 530
SN　Continual belittling, threatening, blaming, ignoring, rejecting, or otherwise inflicting of psychological pain
UF　Psychological Abuse
BT　Antisocial Behavior
RT　Battered Women
　　　Child Abuse
　　　Child Neglect
　　　Elder Abuse
　　　Emotional Disturbances
　　　Emotional Problems
　　　Family Problems
　　　Mental Health
　　　Psychological Patterns
　　　Sexual Harassment
　　　Verbal Abuse

Emotional Adjustment　　　　　*JUL. 1966*
　　　Postings: 2,355　　　　　　GC: 230
UF　Emotional Maladjustment (1966 1980)
BT　Adjustment (to Environment)
RT　Adaptive Behavior (of Disabled)
　　　Affective Measures
　　　Alienation
　　　Defense Mechanisms
　　　Emotional Disturbances
　　　Emotional Problems
　　　Morale
　　　Psychiatry
　　　Psychopathology
　　　Psychotherapy

Emotional Behavior
USE　Affective Behavior

Emotional Development　　　　　*JUL. 1966*
　　　Postings: 2,412　　　　　　GC: 120
BT　Individual Development
RT　Affective Behavior
　　　Affective Measures
　　　Affective Objectives
　　　Attachment Behavior
　　　Catharsis
　　　Dependency (Personality)
　　　Developmental Delays
　　　Developmental Psychology
　　　Developmental Stages
　　　Empathy
　　　Identification (Psychology)
　　　Learning Readiness
　　　Love
　　　Personality Development
　　　Perspective Taking
　　　Psychological Patterns
　　　School Readiness

Emotional Disturbances　　　　*MAR. 1980*
　　　Postings: 5,184　　　　　　GC: 230
SN　Persistent, serious emotional disorders and resulting behavior problems (Note: For lesser, transient emotional difficulties, see "Emotional Problems")
UF　Emotionally Disturbed (1966 1980)
　　　Emotionally Disturbed Children (1967 1980)
NT　Psychosomatic Disorders
BT　Mental Disorders
RT　Anorexia Nervosa
　　　Anxiety
　　　Attention Deficit Disorders
　　　Autism
　　　Behavior Disorders
　　　Bulimia
　　　Clinical Psychology
　　　Depression (Psychology)
　　　Emotional Abuse
　　　Emotional Adjustment
　　　Emotional Problems
　　　Helplessness
　　　Hyperactivity
　　　Mental Health
　　　Neurosis
　　　Personality Problems

Posttraumatic Stress Disorder
Psychiatry
Psychopathology
Psychosis
Psychotherapy
Rehabilitation
Schizophrenia
Self Injurious Behavior

Emotional Experience　　　　　*JUL. 1966*
　　　Postings: 804　　　　　　　GC: 120
NT　Catharsis
BT　Experience
RT　Affection
　　　Dreams
　　　Emotional Response
　　　Love
　　　Moods
　　　Psychological Patterns
　　　Security (Psychology)

Emotional Health
USE　Mental Health

Emotional Maladjustment (1966 1980)
USE　Emotional Adjustment

Emotional Needs
USE　Psychological Needs

Emotional Patterns
USE　Psychological Patterns

Emotional Problems　　　　　　*JUL. 1966*
　　　Postings: 1,837　　　　　　GC: 120
SN　Transient emotional difficulties, usually the result of a specific event or situation
BT　Problems
RT　Anger
　　　Anxiety
　　　Apathy
　　　Behavior Problems
　　　Crying
　　　Depression (Psychology)
　　　Emotional Abuse
　　　Emotional Adjustment
　　　Emotional Disturbances
　　　Fear
　　　Grief
　　　Guilt
　　　Helplessness
　　　Jealousy
　　　Learning Disabilities
　　　Loneliness
　　　Moods
　　　Nightmares
　　　Paranoid Behavior
　　　Personality Problems
　　　Psychological Patterns
　　　Psychopathology

Emotional Response　　　　　　*DEC. 1970*
　　　Postings: 2,703　　　　　　GC: 120
BT　Responses
RT　Affective Behavior
　　　Affective Measures
　　　Arousal Patterns
　　　Attachment Behavior
　　　Burnout
　　　Crying
　　　Defense Mechanisms
　　　Emotional Experience
　　　Interpersonal Attraction
　　　Moods
　　　Prosocial Behavior
　　　Psychological Patterns
　　　Separation Anxiety
　　　Spontaneous Behavior
　　　Stranger Reactions
　　　Violence

Emotional Security
USE　Security (Psychology)

= Two or more Descriptors are used to represent this term.
The term's main entry shows the appropriate coordination.

Emotionally Disturbed Children (1967 1980)
USE   Emotional Disturbances

Emotionally Disturbed (1966 1980)
USE   Emotional Disturbances

Empathy   JUL. 1966
       Postings: 1,387   GC: 120
BT   Psychological Patterns
RT   Congruence (Psychology)
       Counseling Techniques
       Emotional Development
       Identification (Psychology)
       Interpersonal Relationship
       Nondirective Counseling
       Perspective Taking
       Social Cognition

Employability
USE   Employment Potential

Employable Skills
USE   Employment Potential
AND   Job Skills

Employed Mothers
USE   Employed Parents
AND   Mothers

Employed Parents   MAR. 1980
       Postings: 1,267   GC: 510
SN   Parents engaged in remunerative work,
       usually away from the family household
       (Note: If appropriate, use the more pre-
       cise term "Dual Career Family")
UF   Dual Earner Parents
       Employed Mothers #
       Working Parents (1966 1980)
BT   Parents
RT   Day Care
       Dual Career Family
       Employed Women
       Employment
       Family Work Relationship
       Fathers
       Flexible Working Hours
       Labor Force
       Latchkey Children
       Mothers
       Personnel
       Reentry Workers

Employed Women   MAR. 1980
       Postings: 4,433   GC: 630
UF   Women Workers
       Working Women (1968 1980)
NT   Women Administrators
       Women Faculty
BT   Females
RT   Affirmative Action
       Comparable Worth
       Dual Career Family
       Employed Parents
       Employment
       Flexible Working Hours
       Labor Force
       Nontraditional Occupations
       Personnel
       Reentry Workers
       Sex Discrimination

Employee Absenteeism   DEC. 1989
       Postings: 54   GC: 630
SN   Absences of employees during regularly
       scheduled work hours
UF   Absence (Employees)
       Absence (Teachers) #
RT   Employees
       Employer Employee Relationship
       Employment Practices
       Job Satisfaction
       Labor Problems
       Leaves of Absence
       Organizational Climate
       Personnel Policy
       Substitute Teachers

       Teacher Attendance
       Work Environment
       Working Hours

Employee Assistance Programs   AUG. 1986
       Postings: 201   GC: 630
SN   Programs sponsored by employers to
       help employees remedy personal prob-
       lems affecting job performance (e.g.,
       alcohol rehabilitation, mental health as-
       sistance, financial counseling)
BT   Programs
RT   Counseling Services
       Employees
       Employer Employee Relationship
       Fringe Benefits
       Guidance Programs
       Mental Health Programs
       Personnel Policy
       Quality of Working Life

Employee Attitudes   JUL. 1966
       Postings: 2,284   GC: 630
SN   Attitudes of, not toward, employees
UF   Employee Opinions
       Employee Work Attitudes #
BT   Attitudes
RT   Employees
       Employer Employee Relationship
       Job Enrichment
       Job Security
       Vocational Maturity
       Work Attitudes

Employee Employer Relationship
USE   Employer Employee Relationship

Employee Evaluation
USE   Personnel Evaluation

Employee Fringe Benefits
USE   Fringe Benefits

Employee Opinions
USE   Employee Attitudes

Employee Performance
USE   Job Performance

Employee Relations
USE   Labor Relations

Employee Responsibility   JUL. 1966
       Postings: 263   GC: 630
SN   Responsibility assumed by, not for, em-
       ployees (Note: Prior to Mar80, this term
       was not scoped)
BT   Responsibility
RT   Employees
       Employer Employee Relationship
       Indemnity Bonds
       Probationary Period

Employee Work Attitudes
USE   Employee Attitudes
AND   Work Attitudes

Employees   JUL. 1966
       Postings: 1,052   GC: 630
NT   Entry Workers
BT   Personnel
RT   Clerical Workers
       Dislocated Workers
       Employee Absenteeism
       Employee Assistance Programs
       Employee Attitudes
       Employee Responsibility
       Employer Attitudes
       Employer Employee Relationship
       Employers
       Employment
       Employment Interviews
       Fringe Benefits

       Industrial Personnel
       Labor
       Laborers
       Older Workers
       Paraprofessional Personnel
       Personnel Needs
       Professional Personnel
       Reentry Workers
       Sales Workers
       Semiskilled Workers
       Seniority
       Service Workers
       Skilled Workers
       Teachers
       Tenure
       Unskilled Workers
       Working Class

Employer Attitudes   JUL. 1966
       Postings: 2,648   GC: 630
SN   Attitudes of, not toward, employers
UF   Employer Opinions
BT   Attitudes
RT   Administrator Attitudes
       Employees
       Employer Employee Relationship
       Employers

Employer Employee Relationship   JUL. 1966
       Postings: 3,691   GC: 630
UF   Employee Employer Relationship
BT   Interpersonal Relationship
RT   Arbitration
       Collective Bargaining
       Collegiality
       Employee Absenteeism
       Employee Assistance Programs
       Employee Attitudes
       Employee Responsibility
       Employees
       Employer Attitudes
       Employers
       Employment
       Faculty College Relationship
       Faculty Handbooks
       Faculty Workload
       Fringe Benefits
       Grievance Procedures
       Job Enrichment
       Job Satisfaction
       Job Security
       Labor Legislation
       Labor Relations
       Management by Objectives
       Organizational Development
       Participative Decision Making
       Personnel Management
       Probationary Period
       Quality Circles
       Quality of Working Life
       Released Time
       Seniority
       Teacher Administrator Relationship
       Tenure
       Total Quality Management
       Unions
       Vocational Adjustment
       Work Environment

Employer Opinions
USE   Employer Attitudes

Employer Sponsored Day Care
USE   Employer Supported Day Care

Employer Supported Day Care   AUG. 1982
       Postings: 287   GC: 630
SN   Child care services that are partially or
       fully financed and/or organized by em-
       ployers as a benefit to their employees—
       includes work-site centers, cooperative
       arrangements with the community, etc.
UF   Employer Sponsored Day Care
BT   Day Care
RT   Day Care Centers
       Family Day Care
       Fringe Benefits
       School Age Day Care
       Sick Child Care

Employers   JUL. 1966
       Postings: 608   GC: 630
BT   Groups
RT   Employees
       Employer Attitudes
       Employer Employee Relationship
       Employment
       Employment Interviews
       Industrial Personnel

Employment   JUL. 1966
       Postings: 3,920   GC: 630
SN   State or condition of engaging in remu-
       nerative work (Note: Use a more specific
       term if possible)
UF   Jobs (1966 1980)
       Work
NT   Black Employment
       Migrant Employment
       Multiple Employment
       Overseas Employment
       Part Time Employment
       Seasonal Employment
       Self Employment
       Student Employment
       Supported Employment
       Teacher Employment
       Temporary Employment
       Underemployment
       Youth Employment
RT   Careers
       Dislocated Workers
       Economic Factors
       Economic Impact
       Education Work Relationship
       Employed Parents
       Employed Women
       Employees
       Employer Employee Relationship
       Employers
       Employment Experience
       Employment Interviews
       Employment Level
       Employment Opportunities
       Employment Patterns
       Employment Potential
       Employment Practices
       Employment Problems
       Employment Programs
       Employment Projections
       Employment Qualifications
       Employment Services
       Employment Statistics
       Family Work Relationship
       Fringe Benefits
       Job Applicants
       Job Application
       Job Development
       Job Layoff
       Job Performance
       Job Placement
       Job Search Methods
       Job Security
       Job Training
       Labor
       Labor Economics
       Labor Force
       Labor Force Nonparticipants
       Labor Market
       Labor Utilization
       Occupational Information
       Occupational Safety and Health
       Occupational Surveys
       Occupations
       Older Workers
       Personnel
       Probationary Period
       Quality of Working Life
       Reentry Workers
       Seniority
       Tenure
       Work Attitudes
       Work Environment
       Working Hours

Employment Adjustment
USE   Vocational Adjustment

Employment Change
USE   Career Change

= Two or more Descriptors are used to represent this term.
The term's main entry shows the appropriate coordination.

Employment Counselors　　　*NOV. 1969*
　　　Postings: 403　　　GC: 630
BT　Counselors
RT　Career Counseling
　　Employment Opportunities
　　Employment Services
　　Outplacement Services (Employment)

Employment Discrimination
USE　Equal Opportunities (Jobs)

Employment Experience　　　*JUL. 1966*
　　　Postings: 948　　　GC: 630
SN　Experience gained through participation
　　in remunerative work (Note: Prior to
　　Mar80, the instruction "Job Experience,
　　USE Work Experience" was carried in
　　the Thesaurus)
UF　Job Experience
BT　Work Experience
RT　Employment
　　Employment Potential
　　Employment Qualifications
　　Entry Workers
　　Experiential Learning
　　Job Performance
　　Job Skills
　　Labor Market
　　Occupational Mobility
　　Personnel Data
　　Prior Learning
　　Resumes (Personal)
　　Seniority
　　Tenure

Employment Forecasts
USE　Employment Projections

Employment Interviews　　　*JUL. 1966*
　　　Postings: 1,387　　　GC: 630
UF　Job Interviews
BT　Interviews
RT　Employees
　　Employers
　　Employment
　　Employment Qualifications
　　Employment Services
　　Job Applicants
　　Job Application
　　Job Search Methods
　　Personnel Selection
　　Resumes (Personal)

Employment Level　　　*JUL. 1966*
　　　Postings: 1,808　　　GC: 630
SN　Employment rank, position, or status
　　achieved by an individual or group (Note:
　　For the labor force as a whole, use
　　"Employment Patterns"—prior to Mar80,
　　the use of this term was not restricted by
　　a Scope Note)
UF　Employment Status
　　Occupational Level
NT　Academic Rank (Professional)
　　Tenure
BT　Status
RT　Career Ladders
　　Employment
　　Employment Patterns
　　Entry Workers
　　Equal Opportunities (Jobs)
　　Full Time Equivalency
　　Full Time Faculty
　　Income
　　Job Skills
　　Part Time Faculty
　　Professional Recognition
　　Promotion (Occupational)
　　Reentry Workers
　　Self Employment
　　Seniority
　　Socioeconomic Status

Employment Market
USE　Labor Market

Employment Opportunities　　　*JUL. 1966*
　　　Postings: 7,164　　　GC: 630
SN　Available remunerative work, as well as
　　the outlook or trend in particular occupa-
　　tions or industries at a given time
UF　Job Opportunities
　　Job Vacancies
NT　Equal Opportunities (Jobs)
BT　Opportunities
RT　Career Change
　　Career Choice
　　Competitive Selection
　　Demand Occupations
　　Economic Opportunities
　　Education Work Relationship
　　Employment
　　Employment Counselors
　　Employment Patterns
　　Employment Programs
　　Employment Projections
　　Employment Services
　　Job Applicants
　　Job Application
　　Job Banks
　　Job Development
　　Job Search Methods
　　Job Skills
　　Labor Market
　　Labor Needs
　　Nontraditional Occupations
　　Occupational Mobility
　　Occupational Surveys
　　Occupations
　　Promotion (Occupational)
　　Recruitment
　　Reentry Workers
　　Youth Opportunities

Employment Patterns　　　*JUL. 1966*
　　　Postings: 6,532　　　GC: 630
UF　Employment Trends (1966 1980)
　　Job Holding Patterns
BT　Demography
RT　Boomtowns
　　Brain Drain
　　Demand Occupations
　　Dislocated Workers
　　Economic Factors
　　Education Work Relationship
　　Employment
　　Employment Level
　　Employment Opportunities
　　Employment Projections
　　Employment Statistics
　　Labor Economics
　　Labor Market
　　Labor Turnover
　　Migration Patterns
　　Nontraditional Occupations
　　Occupational Surveys
　　Older Workers
　　Quality of Working Life
　　Self Employment
　　Teacher Supply and Demand
　　Trend Analysis
　　Underemployment
　　Unemployment
　　Vocational Followup

Employment Potential　　　*JUL. 1966*
　　　Postings: 2,812　　　GC: 630
UF　Employability
　　Employable Skills #
　　Marketable Skills #
RT　Career Guidance
　　Demand Occupations
　　Education Work Relationship
　　Educational Background
　　Educational Benefits
　　Employment
　　Employment Experience
　　Employment Qualifications
　　Job Skills
　　Self Employment
　　Skill Obsolescence
　　Structural Unemployment
　　Supported Employment

Employment Practices　　　*JUL. 1966*
　　　Postings: 3,511　　　GC: 630
RT　Affirmative Action
　　Comparable Worth
　　Dislocated Workers
　　Dismissal (Personnel)
　　Dress Codes
　　Early Retirement
　　Employee Absenteeism
　　Employment
　　Job Layoff
　　Job Security
　　Job Sharing
　　Labor Legislation
　　Loyalty Oaths
　　Mandatory Retirement
　　Midlife Transitions
　　Occupational Segregation
　　Older Workers
　　Outplacement Services (Employment)
　　Personnel Integration
　　Personnel Management
　　Personnel Policy
　　Reduction in Force
　　Salary Wage Differentials
　　Scope of Bargaining
　　Seniority
　　Tenure

Employment Preparation
USE　Job Training

Employment Problems　　　*JUL. 1966*
　　　Postings: 1,435　　　GC: 630
BT　Problems
RT　Arbitration
　　Collective Bargaining
　　Employment
　　Job Development
　　Labor Problems
　　Negotiation Impasses
　　Underemployment
　　Unemployment

Employment Programs　　　*JUL. 1966*
　　　Postings: 2,529　　　GC: 630
BT　Programs
RT　Employment
　　Employment Opportunities
　　Employment Services

Employment Projections　　　*JUL. 1966*
　　　Postings: 1,596　　　GC: 730
UF　Employment Forecasts
BT　Prediction
RT　Demand Occupations
　　Demography
　　Employment
　　Employment Opportunities
　　Employment Patterns
　　Labor Market
　　Labor Needs

Employment Qualifications　　　*JUL. 1966*
　　　Postings: 3,363　　　GC: 630
BT　Qualifications
RT　Administrator Qualifications
　　Business Skills
　　Counselor Qualifications
　　Employment
　　Employment Experience
　　Employment Interviews
　　Employment Potential
　　Entry Workers
　　Home Economics Skills
　　Job Analysis
　　Job Applicants
　　Job Application
　　Job Search Methods
　　Job Skills
　　Loyalty Oaths
　　Mechanical Skills
　　Occupational Information
　　Occupational Tests
　　Office Occupations
　　Personnel Data
　　Personnel Evaluation
　　Promotion (Occupational)
　　Reentry Workers

Resumes (Personal)
Skill Obsolescence
Supervisor Qualifications
Teacher Qualifications
Tenure
Vocational Aptitude
Work Experience

Employment Referral Services
USE　Employment Services

Employment Satisfaction
USE　Job Satisfaction

Employment Security
USE　Job Security

Employment Services　　　*JUL. 1966*
　　　Postings: 1,257　　　GC: 630
UF　Employment Referral Services
　　Temporary Help Services #
NT　Outplacement Services (Employment)
BT　Human Services
RT　Affirmative Action
　　Employment
　　Employment Counselors
　　Employment Interviews
　　Employment Opportunities
　　Employment Programs
　　Job Applicants
　　Job Application
　　Job Banks
　　Job Placement
　　Job Search Methods

Employment Statistics　　　*JUL. 1966*
　　　Postings: 1,344　　　GC: 730
NT　Worker Days
BT　Statistical Data
RT　Employment
　　Employment Patterns
　　Labor Market
　　Statistical Analysis

Employment Status
USE　Employment Level

Employment Surveys
USE　Occupational Surveys

Employment Tests
USE　Occupational Tests

Employment Trends (1966 1980)
USE　Employment Patterns

Empowerment　　　*JUL. 1996*
　　　Postings: 1,478　　　GC: 520
SN　Promotion or attainment of autonomy
　　and freedom of choice for individuals
　　or groups (Note: Use a more specific
　　term if possible—see the Identifiers
　　"Community Empowerment," "Employee
　　Empowerment," and "Staff
　　Empowerment")
UF　Personal Empowerment
　　Self Empowerment
NT　Parent Empowerment
　　Student Empowerment
　　Teacher Empowerment
RT　Advocacy
　　Decision Making
　　Individual Power
　　Participative Decision Making
　　Personal Autonomy
　　Political Power
　　Power Structure
　　Professional Autonomy
　　Self Actualization
　　Self Determination

= Two or more Descriptors are used to represent this term.
The term's main entry shows the appropriate coordination.

Encapsulated Facilities   *SEP. 1974*
Postings: 14   GC: 920
SN   Environmentally controlled enclosures made of lightweight material to provide high mobility and flexibility—usually built at less cost than traditional structures
BT   Facilities
RT   Air Structures
     Building Innovation
     Buildings
     Construction Materials
     Flexible Facilities
     Prefabrication
     Relocatable Facilities

Encoding (Information)
USE   Coding

Encoding (Psychology)   *OCT. 1983*
Postings: 353   GC: 110
SN   The mental conversion of signals or information into stored nerve impulses— also, the psychological transformation of one message or image into another, e.g., writing into oral language, ideas into words
UF   Information Storage (Psychology)
     Recoding (Psychology)
BT   Cognitive Processes
RT   Cognitive Ability
     Cognitive Style
     Comprehension
     Concept Formation
     Epistemology
     Language Processing
     Learning Processes
     Learning Strategies
     Memory
     Perception
     Reaction Time
     Recall (Psychology)
     Recognition (Psychology)
     Responses
     Retention (Psychology)

Encyclopedias   *JUL. 1966*
Postings: 267   GC: 730
BT   Reference Materials

End Users (Information)
USE   Users (Information)

Endangered Species   *OCT. 1984*
Postings: 199   GC: 410
SN   Plants or animals in danger of extinction
BT   Wildlife
RT   Animals
     Biodiversity
     Conservation (Environment)
     Natural Resources
     Physical Environment
     Plant Pathology
     Plants (Botany)
     Wildlife Management

Endowed Scholarships
USE   Scholarships

Endowment Funds   *SEP. 1977*
Postings: 444   GC: 620
SN   Capital sums set aside as sources of income—the principal of each sum is usually left intact and invested, while the income may be expended
UF   Educational Endowments
BT   Financial Support
RT   Capital
     Donors
     Educational Finance
     Fund Raising
     Income
     Investment
     Library Funding
     Money Management
     Philanthropic Foundations
     School Funds

Trustees
Trusts (Financial)

Energy   *SEP. 1968*
Postings: 3,314   GC: 490
NT   Geothermal Energy
     Heat
     Radiation
     Wind Energy
BT   Scientific Concepts
RT   Alternative Energy Sources
     Diffusion (Physics)
     Energy Audits
     Energy Conservation
     Energy Education
     Energy Management
     Energy Occupations
     Entropy
     Fatigue (Biology)
     Force
     Fuels
     Kinetics
     Lasers
     Mechanics (Physics)
     Motion
     Optics
     Physics
     Power Technology
     Quantum Mechanics
     Relativity

Energy Audits   *AUG. 1986*
Postings: 57   GC: 410
SN   Verifications of energy efficiency of a structure, production process, or piece of equipment
BT   Audits (Verification)
RT   Energy
     Energy Conservation
     Energy Management
     Environmental Standards
     Fuel Consumption

Energy Conservation   *APR. 1974*
Postings: 2,390   GC: 410
SN   Preventing loss or waste of energy
NT   Heat Recovery
BT   Conservation (Environment)
RT   Alternative Energy Sources
     Climate Control
     Conservation Education
     Depleted Resources
     Ecological Factors
     Ecology
     Energy
     Energy Audits
     Energy Education
     Energy Management
     Energy Occupations
     Environmental Education
     Fuel Consumption
     Fuels
     Life Cycle Costing
     Motor Vehicles
     Natural Resources
     Thermal Insulation
     Underground Facilities
     Water Resources

Energy Education   *JAN. 1985*
Postings: 734   GC: 400
SN   Learning/teaching activities, often interdisciplinary in nature, that focus on such topics as energy resources, conversions, conservation, forms, uses, and issues— includes both general and technical educational programs
BT   Education
RT   Alternative Energy Sources
     Conservation Education
     Consumer Education
     Energy
     Energy Conservation
     Energy Occupations
     Environmental Education
     Fuels
     Science Education
     Technology Education
     Utilities

Energy Management   *JAN. 1986*
Postings: 214   GC: 410
SN   Planning, operating, and maintaining facilities and equipment for maximum energy efficiency—includes conserving energy and procuring more economical fuels
BT   Administration
RT   Alternative Energy Sources
     Building Operation
     Climate Control
     Energy
     Energy Audits
     Energy Conservation
     Environmental Standards
     Fuel Consumption
     Life Cycle Costing
     Thermal Insulation
     Utilities

Energy Occupations   *NOV. 1982*
Postings: 87   GC: 640
SN   Occupations related to the production, transfer, or use of energy
UF   Nuclear Energy Occupations #
BT   Occupations
RT   Alternative Energy Sources
     Electrical Occupations
     Energy
     Energy Conservation
     Energy Education
     Engineering Technology
     Fuels
     Nuclear Power Plant Technicians
     Petroleum Industry
     Power Technology
     Technical Occupations
     Utilities

Energy Technology
USE   Power Technology

Engaged Time (Learning)
USE   Time on Task

Engine Development Technicians
USE   Mechanical Design Technicians

Engineering   *JUL. 1966*
Postings: 2,427   GC: 490
NT   Agricultural Engineering
     Chemical Engineering
     Civil Engineering
     Ocean Engineering
     Operating Engineering
BT   Technology
RT   Aerospace Technology
     Electromechanical Technology
     Engineering Education
     Engineering Technicians
     Engineering Technology
     Engineers
     Highway Engineering Aides
     Manufacturing
     Microelectronics
     Mining
     Nuclear Technology
     Sciences
     Site Development

Engineering Aides
USE   Engineering Technicians

Engineering Drawing   *JUL. 1966*
Postings: 128   GC: 490
SN   Preparation of clear, complete, and accurate working plans and detail drawings from rough or detailed sketches or notes for engineering or manufacturing purposes, according to specified dimensions (Note: Prior to Sep81, the use of this term was not restricted by a Scope Note)
UF   Mechanical Drawing
BT   Drafting
     Engineering Graphics
RT   Architectural Drafting

Blueprints
Civil Engineering
Technical Illustration

Engineering Education   *JUL. 1966*
Postings: 4,921   GC: 490
BT   Professional Education
RT   Aerospace Education
     Engineering
     Engineering Technology
     Engineers
     Land Grant Universities
     Science Education
     Technical Education

Engineering Graphics   *JUL. 1966*
Postings: 134   GC: 490
SN   Technical functions including engineering drawing, problem solving or analytical graphics, and descriptive geometry— also, the illustrations resulting from these functions
NT   Engineering Drawing
BT   Graphic Arts
RT   Civil Engineering
     Computer Assisted Design
     Computer Graphics
     Orthographic Projection
     Signs

Engineering Technicians   *JUL. 1966*
Postings: 180   GC: 640
UF   Engineering Aides
NT   Highway Engineering Aides
BT   Paraprofessional Personnel
RT   Electronic Technicians
     Engineering
     Engineering Technology
     Mechanical Design Technicians
     Metallurgical Technicians
     Nuclear Power Plant Technicians
     Production Technicians

Engineering Technology   *JUN. 1969*
Postings: 531   GC: 490
BT   Technology
RT   Aerospace Technology
     Electromechanical Technology
     Energy Occupations
     Engineering
     Engineering Education
     Engineering Technicians
     Engineers
     Nuclear Technology
     Physical Sciences
     Power Technology
     Technical Education

Engineers   *JUL. 1966*
Postings: 1,322   GC: 640
BT   Professional Personnel
RT   Engineering
     Engineering Education
     Engineering Technology
     Mathematicians
     Scientific Personnel
     Scientists

Engines   *JUL. 1966*
Postings: 326   GC: 910
NT   Diesel Engines
     Electric Motors
BT   Equipment
RT   Agricultural Machinery
     Auto Mechanics
     Aviation Mechanics
     Fuels
     Hydraulics
     Kinetics
     Locomotive Engineers
     Lubricants
     Power Technology
     Small Engine Mechanics

English   *JUL. 1966*
Postings: 5,927   GC: 440
NT   Business English

= Two or more Descriptors are used to represent this term.
The term's main entry shows the appropriate coordination.

　　English (Second Language)
　　Middle English
　　North American English
　　Old English
　　Oral English
BT　Indo European Languages
RT　College English
　　English Curriculum
　　English Instruction
　　English Literature
　　English Only Movement
　　English Teacher Education
　　English Teachers
　　Linguistics
　　Welsh

English (Second Language)　　*JUL. 1966*
　　Postings: 18,722　　　　GC: 440
SN　English as a foreign or non-native language (i.e., English for non-English speakers)
UF　EFL
　　ESL
　　ESOL
　　TEFL
　　TENES
　　TESL
　　TESOL
NT　English for Special Purposes
BT　English
　　Second Languages
RT　Applied Linguistics
　　Bilingual Education
　　Bilingual Education Programs
　　Bilingual Teacher Aides
　　Bilingual Teachers
　　Bilingualism
　　English Only Movement
　　Family English Literacy
　　Immersion Programs
　　Language Dominance
　　Language of Instruction
　　Language Skills
　　Limited English Speaking
　　Linguistics
　　Mexican American Education
　　Migrant Adult Education
　　Migrant Education
　　Multilingualism
　　Non English Speaking
　　Second Language Instruction
　　Second Language Learning
　　Second Language Programs
　　Spanish Speaking

English Curriculum　　*JUL. 1966*
　　Postings: 4,038　　　　GC: 400
UF　English Programs (1966 1980)
NT　College English
　　World Literature
BT　Curriculum
RT　English
　　English Instruction
　　English Teachers
　　Language Arts

English Departments　　*JUN. 1969*
　　Postings: 907　　　　GC: 350
BT　Departments
RT　College English
　　English Teachers
　　Science Departments

English Education (1967 1980)　　*MAR. 1980*
　　Postings: 931　　　　GC: 400
SN　Invalid Descriptor—see the more precise terms "English Teacher Education," "English Instruction," and "English Curriculum"

English for Academic Purposes　　*DEC. 1985*
　　Postings: 384　　　　GC: 440
SN　English for non-English speakers who require specialized skills in the language in order to pursue studies at the college or college-preparatory level
BT　English for Special Purposes
RT　Academic Discourse
　　Academic Education

English for Science and Technology
　　　　　　　　　　　　DEC. 1985
　　Postings: 149　　　　GC: 440
SN　Specialized English for non-English speakers who are studying or working in scientific and technological fields
BT　English for Special Purposes
RT　Natural Sciences
　　Sciences
　　Technology

English for Special Purposes　　*OCT. 1974*
　　Postings: 791　　　　GC: 440
SN　English for non-English speakers who need a certain specialized knowledge of the language in their studies, profession, or trade
NT　English for Academic Purposes
　　English for Science and Technology
　　Vocational English (Second Language)
BT　English (Second Language)
　　Languages for Special Purposes
RT　Second Language Instruction
　　Second Language Learning

English Instruction　　*JUL. 1966*
　　Postings: 11,501　　　　GC: 400
SN　(Note: For instruction in English as a second language, coordinate "Second Language Instruction" and "English (Second Language)")
BT　Native Language Instruction
RT　College English
　　English
　　English Curriculum
　　English Teacher Education
　　English Teachers
　　Student Writing Models

English Literature　　*JUL. 1966*
　　Postings: 873　　　　GC: 430
NT　Old English Literature
BT　Literature
RT　English
　　United States Literature

English Neoclassic Literary Period (1968 1980)
　　　　　　　　　　　　MAR. 1980
　　Postings: 7　　　　GC: 430
SN　Invalid Descriptor—see such Descriptors as "English Literature," "Neoclassicism," "Seventeenth Century Literature," "Eighteenth Century Literature," etc.

English Only Movement　　*DEC. 1995*
　　Postings: 72　　　　GC: 440
SN　Efforts to make English the single official language of a government or other group (commonly, of the nation and states of the U.S.A.)
UF　Official English Movement
RT　Bilingualism
　　English
　　English (Second Language)
　　Language Attitudes
　　Monolingualism
　　Multilingualism
　　North American English
　　Official Languages

English Programs (1966 1980)
USE　English Curriculum

English Teacher Education　　*MAR. 1980*
　　Postings: 475　　　　GC: 400
SN　Teacher education in the field of English language arts (Note: Before Mar80, this concept was indexed by the term "English Education," usually in coordination with "Teacher Education" or one of its narrower terms)
BT　Teacher Education
RT　English
　　English Instruction
　　English Teachers

English Teachers　　*SEP. 1995*
　　Postings: 611　　　　GC: 360
SN　Teachers of English-language arts and letters (Note: May be coordinated with "English (Second Language)" for teachers of English as a second language)
BT　Language Teachers
RT　English
　　English Curriculum
　　English Departments
　　English Instruction
　　English Teacher Education

Enlargement Methods
USE　Magnification Methods

Enlisted Men (1967 1976)
USE　Enlisted Personnel

Enlisted Personnel　　*MAY 1976*
　　Postings: 382　　　　GC: 640
UF　Enlisted Men (1967 1976)
　　Enlisted Women
BT　Military Personnel
RT　Military Science
　　Military Service
　　Military Training
　　Veterans

Enlisted Women
USE　Enlisted Personnel

Enrichment　　*JUL. 1966*
　　Postings: 772　　　　GC: 310
UF　Academic Enrichment (1966 1980)
　　Enrichment Experience (1966 1980)
NT　Cultural Enrichment
　　Curriculum Enrichment
　　Job Enrichment
　　Language Enrichment
　　Mathematical Enrichment
RT　Enrichment Activities

Enrichment Activities　　*JUL. 1966*
　　Postings: 2,481　　　　GC: 310
SN　Supplementary or compensatory activities and programs
UF　Enrichment Programs (1966 1980)
BT　Activities
RT　After School Programs
　　Art Activities
　　Creative Activities
　　Cultural Activities
　　Enrichment
　　Exchange Programs
　　Extracurricular Activities
　　Improvement Programs
　　Music Activities
　　Supplementary Education
　　Weekend Programs

Enrichment Experience (1966 1980)
USE　Enrichment

Enrichment Programs (1966 1980)
USE　Enrichment Activities

Enrollment　　*JUL. 1966*
　　Postings: 6,185　　　　GC: 320
SN　The total number of individuals registered as participants in a program or activity (Note: For the act or process of enrolling in school, see "School Registration")
UF　College Enrollment
　　School Enrollment
　　Student Enrollment (1966 1977)
NT　Dual Enrollment
　　Language Enrollment
　　Student Attrition
RT　Access to Education
　　Admission (School)
　　Attendance
　　Auditing (Coursework)
　　Average Daily Membership
　　College Attendance
　　College Transfer Students
　　Declining Enrollment
　　Dropouts
　　Educational Demand
　　Educational Supply
　　Enrollment Influences
　　Enrollment Management
　　Enrollment Projections
　　Enrollment Rate
　　Enrollment Trends
　　Full Time Equivalency
　　Full Time Students
　　Group Membership
　　No Shows
　　Part Time Students
　　Participation
　　Registrars (School)
　　School District Size
　　School Entrance Age
　　School Registration
　　School Schedules
　　School Size
　　Stopouts
　　Student Recruitment
　　Students
　　Transfer Policy
　　Transfer Students

Enrollment Influences　　*JUL. 1966*
　　Postings: 2,188　　　　GC: 320
SN　Factors affecting enrollment
BT　Influences
RT　Admission Criteria
　　Average Daily Membership
　　Course Selection (Students)
　　Declining Enrollment
　　Educational Demand
　　Educational Supply
　　Enrollment
　　Enrollment Management
　　Enrollment Rate
　　Enrollment Trends

Enrollment Management　　*MAY 1993*
　　Postings: 252　　　　GC: 320
SN　A set of systematic, interrelated activities for controlling enrollment patterns—involves marketing, recruitment, admissions, pricing, and financial aid
BT　Administration
　　Management Systems
RT　Admission (School)
　　Admissions Officers
　　College Admission
　　Declining Enrollment
　　Enrollment
　　Enrollment Influences
　　Enrollment Projections
　　Enrollment Rate
　　Enrollment Trends
　　Institutional Advancement
　　Registrars (School)
　　School Holding Power
　　Student Attrition
　　Student Recruitment

Enrollment Projections　　*JUL. 1966*
　　Postings: 1,585　　　　GC: 730
BT　Prediction
RT　Admissions Officers
　　Average Daily Membership
　　Declining Enrollment
　　Enrollment
　　Enrollment Management
　　Enrollment Rate
　　Enrollment Trends
　　School Demography
　　School Statistics

Enrollment Rate　　*JUL. 1966*
　　Postings: 1,420　　　　GC: 330
NT　Average Daily Membership
　　Declining Enrollment
BT　Incidence
RT　Enrollment
　　Enrollment Influences
　　Enrollment Management
　　Enrollment Projections

= Two or more Descriptors are used to represent this term.
The term's main entry shows the appropriate coordination.

Enrollment Trends
Full Time Equivalency
Language Enrollment

Enrollment Trends   *JUL. 1966*
          Postings: 6,099   GC: 330
RT   Average Daily Membership
     Declining Enrollment
     Educational Trends
     Enrollment
     Enrollment Influences
     Enrollment Management
     Enrollment Projections
     Enrollment Rate
     Feeder Patterns
     Language Enrollment
     School Demography
     Trend Analysis

Enterprisers
USE   Entrepreneurship

Entomology   *JUL. 1966*
          Postings: 466   GC: 490
UF   Insect Studies
BT   Zoology
RT   Agriculture
     Horticulture
     Insecticides
     Pests

Entrepreneurs
USE   Entrepreneurship

Entrepreneurship   *OCT. 1982*
          Postings: 1,633   GC: 650
SN   Initiation, organization, promotion, and/or
     management of a business or enterprise
     with assumption of the risk of loss or
     failure
UF   Enterprisers
     Entrepreneurs
RT   Business
     Business Administration
     Capitalism
     Careers
     Economic Opportunities
     Economics
     Education Work Relationship
     Financial Support
     Franchising
     Free Enterprise System
     Merchants
     Occupations
     Risk
     Self Employment
     Small Businesses

Entropy   *DEC. 1988*
          Postings: 70   GC: 490
SN   The amount of disorder, or tendency
     toward randomness, in a physical or
     social system, e.g., the extent to which
     the energy in a thermodynamic system
     is unavailable for useful work, the dimin-
     ished capacity of human systems (over
     time) for adaptation or change, the de-
     gree of uncertainty in a message or
     signal
UF   Negentropy
BT   Scientific Concepts
RT   Chemical Equilibrium
     Cybernetics
     Ecology
     Energy
     Information Theory
     Mathematical Models
     Organization
     Social Change
     Systems Approach
     Thermodynamics

Entry Workers   *FEB. 1969*
          Postings: 1,200   GC: 630
UF   Beginning Workers
BT   Employees
RT   Career Ladders

Employment Experience
Employment Level
Employment Qualifications

Entry Year Assistance (Teacher Induction)
USE   Beginning Teacher Induction

Enunciation Improvement (1966 1980)
USE   Articulation (Speech)
AND   Speech Improvement

Environment   *JUL. 1966*
          Postings: 3,717   GC: 410
SN   Surrounding conditions, forces, or fac-
     tors potentially capable of influencing,
     modifying, or interacting with an organ-
     ism, material, or other entity (Note: Use a
     more specific term if possible)
NT   Cultural Context
     Disadvantaged Environment
     Economic Climate
     Educational Environment
     Family Environment
     Institutional Environment
     Organizational Climate
     Permissive Environment
     Physical Environment
     Rural Environment
     Simulated Environment
     Slum Environment
     Social Environment
     Suburban Environment
     Therapeutic Environment
     Urban Environment
     Work Environment
RT   Adjustment (to Environment)
     Appropriate Technology
     Background
     Climate
     Conservation (Environment)
     Context Effect
     Ecology
     Environmental Education
     Environmental Influences
     Environmental Research
     Humanization
     Influences
     Nature Nurture Controversy
     Place of Residence
     Regional Characteristics
     Resources
     Well Being

Environment Heredity Controversy
USE   Nature Nurture Controversy

Environmental Criteria (1967 1980)
USE   Environmental Standards

Environmental Education   *OCT. 1969*
          Postings: 13,014   GC: 410
NT   Conservation Education
     Environmental Interpretation
BT   Education
RT   Adventure Education
     Air Pollution
     Biodiversity
     Biological Sciences
     Conservation (Environment)
     Ecology
     Energy Conservation
     Energy Education
     Environment
     Forestry
     Global Education
     Marine Education
     Mining
     Natural Resources
     Outdoor Education
     Pollution
     Population Education
     Rainforests
     Science and Society
     Social Biology
     Soil Conservation
     Sustainable Development
     Water Pollution

Wetlands
Wilderness

Environmental Factors
USE   Environmental Influences

Environmental Influences   *JUL. 1966*
          Postings: 6,090   GC: 120
SN   Influences of the physical environment
     (Note: Prior to Mar80, this term was not
     scoped and was also used for influences
     of social, educational, cultural, etc., en-
     vironments—see also such Descriptors
     as "Biological Influences," "Nature Nur-
     ture Controversy," "Cultural Context,"
     "Family Environment," "Social Influ-
     ences," "Educational Environment," etc.)
UF   Environmental Factors
BT   Influences
RT   Acoustical Environment
     Biological Influences
     Built Environment
     Climate
     Climate Change
     Climate Control
     Crowding
     Environment
     Environmental Research
     Hazardous Materials
     Nature Nurture Controversy
     Physical Environment
     Pollution
     Radiation Effects
     Sanitation
     Thermal Environment
     Visual Environment
     Weather

Environmental Interpretation   *APR. 2000*
          Postings: 113   GC: 410
SN   Presentation of the ecological or scien-
     tific significance of a park or other natu-
     ral site—may take place in museums or
     other off-site locations
BT   Environmental Education
RT   Conservation Education
     Nature Centers
     Outdoor Education
     Parks

Environmental Research   *JUL. 1966*
          Postings: 923   GC: 810
SN   Study of the physical environment (Note:
     Prior to Mar80, the use of this term was
     restricted to research on the physical
     environment's relationship to humans—
     as of Oct81, use as a minor Descriptor
     for examples of this kind of research—
     use as a major Descriptor only as the
     subject of a document—see also "Envi-
     ronmental Influences" and "Social Sci-
     ence Research")
BT   Research
RT   Architectural Research
     Environment
     Environmental Influences
     Physical Environment
     Scientific Research
     Use Studies

Environmental Scanning   *MAY 1993*
          Postings: 170   GC: 330
SN   Assessing events and identifying trends,
     in the external environment, that portend
     challenges or opportunities—integral
     component of strategic planning
BT   Evaluation Methods
RT   College Planning
     Educational Environment
     Educational Planning
     Futures (of Society)
     Institutional Administration
     Institutional Environment
     Long Range Planning
     Prediction
     Strategic Planning
     Trend Analysis

Environmental Standards   *MAR. 1980*
          Postings: 870   GC: 610
SN   Laws, rules, or regulations relating to the
     quality of the physical environment
UF   Environmental Criteria (1967 1980)
BT   Standards
RT   Air Pollution
     Crowding
     Ecology
     Energy Audits
     Energy Management
     Hazardous Materials
     Labor Standards
     Living Standards
     Motor Vehicles
     Noise (Sound)
     Occupational Safety and Health
     Pests
     Physical Environment
     Poisons
     Pollution
     Public Health
     Quality of Life
     Waste Disposal
     Water Pollution
     Water Quality

Environmental Technicians   *MAR. 1969*
          Postings: 314   GC: 640
UF   Sanitary Inspectors
     Sanitary Technicians
BT   Allied Health Personnel
     Paraprofessional Personnel
RT   Chemical Technicians
     Sanitation
     Water Treatment

Environmental Therapy
USE   Milieu Therapy

Envy
USE   Jealousy

Enzymes   *OCT. 1982*
          Postings: 180   GC: 490
SN   Group of catalytic proteins produced by
     living cells that mediate and promote the
     chemical processes of life without them-
     selves being changed
RT   Biochemistry
     Biology
     Biotechnology
     Chemical Reactions
     Cytology
     Genetics
     Medicine
     Metabolism
     Molecular Biology
     Nucleic Acids
     Physiology

Epee Fencing
USE   Fencing (Sport)

Epics   *JUL. 1966*
          Postings: 123   GC: 430
SN   Narrative poems about events, settings,
     or (especially) characters of heroic pro-
     portions, frequently treating the early
     history of a tribe or nation
BT   Literary Genres
     Poetry
RT   Allegory
     Ballads
     Classical Literature
     Didacticism
     Legends
     Lyric Poetry
     Medieval Literature
     Mythology
     Poets
     World Literature

Epidemic Roseola
USE   Rubella

= Two or more Descriptors are used to represent this term.
The term's main entry shows the appropriate coordination.

Epidemiology   *AUG. 1986*
Postings: 393   GC: 210
SN   Science of the incidence, distribution, control, and contributing factors of epidemic illness or disease
BT   Medicine
RT   Bacteria
     Disease Control
     Disease Incidence
     Diseases
     Etiology
     Health
     Health Conditions
     Immunization Programs
     Medical Services
     Pathology
     Preventive Medicine
     Public Health
     Viruses

Epilepsy   *JUL. 1966*
Postings: 260   GC: 220
BT   Neurological Impairments
RT   Developmental Disabilities
     Minimal Brain Dysfunction
     Seizures

Episode Teaching (1967 1980)   *MAR. 1980*
Postings: 9   GC: 310
SN   Invalid Descriptor—previously used to index a method of introducing student teachers to teaching, as well as a technique for presenting material in social studies instruction

Epistemology   *OCT. 1980*
Postings: 2,298   GC: 110
SN   The study of how knowledge is acquired
UF   Cognitive Theory
BT   Philosophy
RT   Cognitive Ability
     Cognitive Development
     Cognitive Processes
     Cognitive Psychology
     Cognitive Structures
     Concept Formation
     Constructivism (Learning)
     Developmental Continuity
     Developmental Stages
     Encoding (Psychology)
     Hermeneutics
     Knowledge Level
     Learning
     Phenomenology
     Piagetian Theory
     Postmodernism
     Rhetorical Theory

Epistles (1970 1980)
USE   Letters (Correspondence)

Equal Education   *JUL. 1966*
Postings: 10,765   GC: 540
SN   System of education extending comparable opportunities to all individuals regardless of race, color, creed, age, sex, socioeconomic class, or ability
UF   Educational Equality (1966 1976)
     Educational Equity (Opportunities)
     Educational Inequality
     Equal Educational Opportunities
     Equality of Education
     Equity (Educational Opportunities)
     Universal Education (1968 1976)
BT   Civil Rights
     Education
RT   Academic Accommodations (Disabilities)
     Access to Education
     Affirmative Action
     Age Discrimination
     American Dream
     Civil Rights Legislation
     Disability Discrimination
     Educational Demand
     Educational Discrimination
     Educational Opportunities
     Educational Quality
     Educationally Disadvantaged

     Equal Facilities
     Excellence in Education
     Fiscal Neutrality
     Individualized Education Programs
     Nondiscriminatory Education
     Open Enrollment
     Outcome Based Education
     Racial Discrimination
     Reverse Discrimination
     Selective Admission
     Sex Discrimination
     Special Needs Students
     Tokenism

Equal Educational Opportunities
USE   Equal Education

Equal Employment
USE   Equal Opportunities (Jobs)

Equal Facilities   *JUL. 1966*
Postings: 140   GC: 540
SN   Facilities that are qualitatively equal without regard to the characteristics (e.g., sex, ethnicity, social class) of the groups that use or benefit from them (Note: Do not confuse with "Accessibility (for Disabled)")
UF   Equalized Facilities
BT   Facilities
RT   Civil Rights
     Civil Rights Legislation
     Equal Education
     Public Facilities
     Racial Discrimination
     Sex Discrimination
     Sex Fairness
     Social Discrimination

Equal Opportunities (Jobs)   *JUL. 1966*
Postings: 4,603   GC: 540
UF   Employment Discrimination
     Equal Employment
     Job Discrimination
NT   Occupational Segregation
BT   Civil Rights
     Employment Opportunities
RT   Affirmative Action
     Age Discrimination
     American Dream
     Civil Rights Legislation
     Comparable Worth
     Disability Discrimination
     Employment Level
     Equal Protection
     Faculty Integration
     Job Development
     Nontraditional Occupations
     Personnel Integration
     Racial Discrimination
     Reverse Discrimination
     Salary Wage Differentials
     Sex Discrimination
     Sex Fairness
     Teacher Integration
     Tokenism

Equal Pay
USE   Salary Wage Differentials

Equal Protection   *JUL. 1966*
Postings: 972   GC: 540
BT   Civil Rights
RT   Civil Rights Legislation
     Courts
     Due Process
     Equal Opportunities (Jobs)
     Justice
     Laws
     Married Students
     Pregnant Students
     Sex Fairness
     Student Rights

Equality of Education
USE   Equal Education

Equalization Aid   *JAN. 1969*
Postings: 926   GC: 620
SN   State and/or federal monies that are given in inverse proportion to local resources
UF   Additional Aid
BT   Financial Support
RT   Categorical Aid
     Developing Institutions
     Disadvantaged Schools
     Educational Equity (Finance)
     Educational Finance
     Expenditure per Student
     Federal Aid
     Finance Reform
     Fiscal Capacity
     Fiscal Neutrality
     Foundation Programs
     Full State Funding
     Grants
     Resource Allocation
     Revenue Sharing
     School District Wealth
     State Aid
     State Federal Aid
     Tax Effort

Equalized Facilities
USE   Equal Facilities

Equated Scores   *JUL. 1966*
Postings: 530   GC: 820
SN   Scores from different forms of the same test, or from different tests measuring the same trait, that are converted to a common score scale so that they can be treated as equivalent and directly compared
BT   Scores
RT   Cutting Scores
     Grade Equivalent Scores
     Item Response Theory
     Raw Scores
     Scaling
     Statistical Analysis
     Test Theory
     True Scores
     Weighted Scores

Equations (Mathematics)   *APR. 1982*
Postings: 1,172   GC: 480
SN   Statements of equality among mathematical entities
NT   Differential Equations
BT   Mathematical Formulas
RT   Algebra
     Functions (Mathematics)
     Mathematical Concepts
     Polynomials
     Relationship
     Structural Equation Models

Equilibrium Constants
USE   Chemical Equilibrium

Equipment   *JUL. 1966*
Postings: 1,815   GC: 910
SN   Any instrument, machine, apparatus, or set of articles used in an operation or activity without losing its original shape or appearance (Note: Use a more specific term if possible)
UF   Appliances
     Building Equipment (1966 1980)
NT   Agricultural Machinery
     Air Conditioning Equipment
     Assistive Devices (for Disabled)
     Athletic Equipment
     Audio Equipment
     Biomedical Equipment
     Calculators
     Educational Equipment
     Electric Batteries
     Electric Circuits
     Electrical Appliances
     Electromechanical Aids
     Electronic Equipment
     Engines
     Furniture
     Guns

     Hand Tools
     Home Furnishings
     Laboratory Equipment
     Library Equipment
     Machine Tools
     Measurement Equipment
     Mechanical Equipment
     Motor Vehicles
     Musical Instruments
     Office Machines
     Photographic Equipment
     Projection Equipment
     Safety Equipment
     Science Equipment
     Space Dividers
     Test Scoring Machines
     Vending Machines
RT   Assembly (Manufacturing)
     Equipment Evaluation
     Equipment Maintenance
     Equipment Manufacturers
     Equipment Standards
     Equipment Storage
     Equipment Utilization
     Facilities
     Facility Inventory
     Machinery Industry
     Maintenance
     Material Culture
     Resources
     Sanitary Facilities
     Supplies

Equipment Evaluation   *JUL. 1966*
Postings: 893   GC: 910
SN   Judging apparatus, furnishings, instruments, machinery, tools, or other devices in terms of established standards
UF   Field Check (1967 1980)
BT   Evaluation
RT   Computer Selection
     Equipment
     Equipment Standards
     Field Tests
     Inspection
     Life Cycle Costing

Equipment Inventory
USE   Facility Inventory

Equipment Maintenance   *JUL. 1966*
Postings: 1,223   GC: 910
UF   Equipment Repair
     Equipment Upkeep
BT   Maintenance
RT   Cleaning
     Electrical Occupations
     Equipment
     Equipment Storage
     Machine Repairers
     Repair
     School Maintenance
     Skilled Occupations
     Troubleshooting

Equipment Manufacturers   *JUL. 1966*
Postings: 290   GC: 650
BT   Personnel
RT   Equipment
     Equipment Standards
     Industry
     Manufacturing
     Manufacturing Industry

Equipment Purchasing
USE   Purchasing

Equipment Repair
USE   Equipment Maintenance

Equipment Standards   *JUL. 1966*
Postings: 528   GC: 910
SN   Specifications, requirements, and criteria for evaluating the construction and performance of apparatus, furnishings, instruments, machinery, tools, and other devices

---

\# = Two or more Descriptors are used to represent this term.
The term's main entry shows the appropriate coordination.

BT Standards
RT Equipment
    Equipment Evaluation
    Equipment Manufacturers
    Purchasing

Equipment Storage   *JUL. 1966*
    Postings: 99   GC: 910
BT Storage
RT Equipment
    Equipment Maintenance
    Facility Utilization Research
    Furniture
    Furniture Design
    Locker Rooms
    Space Utilization
    Warehouses

Equipment Upkeep
USE Equipment Maintenance

Equipment Utilization   *JUL. 1966*
    Postings: 1,356   GC: 910
RT Equipment
    Facility Inventory
    Operating Engineering

Equity (Educational Finance)
USE Educational Equity (Finance)

Equity (Educational Opportunities)
USE Equal Education

Equity (Impartiality)
USE Justice

Equivalency Tests   *AUG. 1968*
    Postings: 629   GC: 830
SN Tests to measure the extent to which
    previous schooling, knowledge, or ex-
    perience satisfies course or job require-
    ments (Note: See also the Identifier "Gen-
    eral Educational Development Tests"—
    prior to Sep77 and Mar80 respectively,
    the instructions "GED Tests, USE
    Equivalency Tests" and "Proficiency Ex-
    aminations, USE Equivalency Tests" were
    carried in the Thesaurus)
UF Advanced Credit Examinations
    Advanced Standing Examinations
    Credit by Examination
BT Achievement Tests
RT Advanced Placement
    Advanced Placement Programs
    Certification
    Credentials
    Educational Certificates
    Experiential Learning
    Grade Equivalent Scores
    High School Equivalency Programs
    Job Skills
    Licensing Examinations (Professions)
    Prior Learning
    Special Degree Programs
    Student Placement

Ergonomics
USE Human Factors Engineering

Error Analysis (Language)   *MAR. 1977*
    Postings: 1,343   GC: 450
SN In language teaching and testing, a tech-
    nique of measuring progress and of de-
    vising teaching methods by recording
    and classifying the mistakes made by
    students—in linguistics, the observation
    of errors in the speech process as a
    means of understanding the phonologi-
    cal and semantic components of lan-
    guage, interactional processes, and
    speakers' discourse strategies
BT Comparative Analysis
RT Contrastive Linguistics
    Descriptive Linguistics
    Error Correction

Error Patterns
Interference (Language)
Interlanguage
Language Patterns
Language Skills
Language Usage
Linguistic Difficulty (Inherent)
Phonetic Analysis
Phonology
Second Language Instruction
Second Language Learning
Semantics
Structural Analysis (Linguistics)
Syntax

Error Correction   *APR. 1990*
    Postings: 416   GC: 310
SN The correction of mistakes made by hu-
    mans or machines—in education, the
    rectification or remediation of student
    errors (in learning or performance), usu-
    ally by classroom teachers, but also by
    computers, other "instructors" (peers,
    parents, supervisors, etc.), or oneself
RT Error Analysis (Language)
    Error Patterns
    Evaluation
    Feedback
    Learning Processes
    Programmed Instruction
    Proofreading
    Quality Control
    Remedial Instruction
    Review (Reexamination)
    Revision (Written Composition)
    Troubleshooting

Error of Measurement   *MAR. 1980*
    Postings: 1,003   GC: 820
SN Difference between observed and true
    scores due to random errors introduced
    by the measuring instrument or admin-
    istering person, i.e., that portion of a
    score variance that can not be accounted
    for systematically (Note: Do not use for
    test bias errors)
UF Error Variance
    Measurement Error
    Standard Error of Estimate
    Standard Error of Measurement (1970
       1980)
BT Statistical Analysis
RT Generalizability Theory
    Interrater Reliability
    Least Squares Statistics
    Meta Analysis
    Multitrait Multimethod Techniques
    Predictor Variables
    Raw Scores
    Reliability
    Robustness (Statistics)
    Sampling
    Scores
    Scoring
    Statistical Bias
    Test Interpretation
    Test Norms
    Test Reliability
    Testing Problems
    True Scores

Error of Refraction
USE Ametropia

Error Patterns   *MAY 1970*
    Postings: 1,817   GC: 820
SN Systematically recurring errors
RT Error Analysis (Language)
    Error Correction
    Evaluation Methods
    Item Analysis
    Redundancy
    Reliability
    Research
    Statistical Bias
    Test Bias
    Testing

Error Variance
USE Error of Measurement

Escapees
USE Refugees

Eskimo Aleut Languages   *SEP. 1975*
    Postings: 160   GC: 440
UF Aleut
NT Inupiaq
    Yupik
BT Languages
RT Alaska Natives
    American Indian Languages
    Eskimos

Eskimos   *JUL. 1966*
    Postings: 672   GC: 560
UF Inuit (People)
BT Groups
RT Alaska Natives
    Canada Natives
    Eskimo Aleut Languages
    Ethnic Groups
    Minority Groups
    North Americans
    Trust Responsibility (Government)

ESL
USE English (Second Language)

ESOL
USE English (Second Language)

Esperanto   *AUG. 1989*
    Postings: 82   GC: 440
SN International language created in 1887
    by Polish philologist, Ludwig Zamenhof,
    based on approximately 1,000 word roots
    common to the Western European
    languages—a century after its creation,
    the language had 15,000 roots from
    which 150,000 words could be formed
BT Artificial Languages

Essay Tests   *JUL. 1966*
    Postings: 674   GC: 830
SN Tests in which respondents are asked to
    compose written statements, discussions,
    summaries, or descriptions that are to
    be used as measures of knowledge, un-
    derstanding, or writing proficiency
BT Verbal Tests
RT Achievement Tests
    Constructed Response
    Essays
    Objective Tests
    Writing Skills
    Writing Tests

Essays   *JUL. 1966*
    Postings: 1,664   GC: 430
SN Short analytic, interpretative, or critical
    literary compositions, usually in prose
BT Literary Genres
    Nonfiction
RT Essay Tests
    Expository Writing
    Opinion Papers
    Theses

Estate Planning   *SEP. 1969*
    Postings: 110   GC: 620
BT Planning
RT Assessed Valuation
    Capital
    Finance Occupations
    Financial Services
    Investment
    Money Management
    Ownership
    Property Accounting
    Property Appraisal
    Taxes
    Trustees

Trusts (Financial)
Wills

Esthetics
USE Aesthetics

Estimated Costs (1966 1980)
USE Cost Estimates

Estimation (Mathematics)   *APR. 1982*
    Postings: 2,004   GC: 480
SN Process of determining an approximate
    solution for numerical or measurement
    problems
UF Approximation (Mathematics)
BT Computation
RT Causal Models
    Mathematical Models
    Mathematics
    Measurement
    Mental Computation
    Monte Carlo Methods
    Prediction
    Predictive Measurement
    Probability
    Statistical Inference
    Statistics

Estonian   *JUL. 1966*
    Postings: 23   GC: 440
BT Finno Ugric Languages
RT Baltic Languages

Estuaries   *APR. 1985*
    Postings: 60   GC: 410
SN Mouths of rivers, and other semi-en-
    closed bodies of water, that are open to
    the sea and within which fresh and salt
    water are mixed by runoff and tides
RT Ecology
    Fisheries
    Habitats
    Marine Biology
    Marine Education
    Oceanography
    Rivers
    Water
    Water Resources
    Wetlands

Ethical Instruction   *NOV. 1969*
    Postings: 2,428   GC: 400
SN Instruction having to do with morality
    and good conduct
UF Moral Instruction
BT Instruction
RT Citizenship Education
    Ethics
    Moral Values
    Religious Education
    Sex Education
    Values Education

Ethical Values (1966 1980)
USE Moral Values

Ethics   *NOV. 1969*
    Postings: 5,849   GC: 430
UF Morals
NT Bioethics
    Work Ethic
BT Philosophy
RT Altruism
    Codes of Ethics
    Confidentiality
    Conflict of Interest
    Credibility
    Ethical Instruction
    Fraud
    Honesty
    Integrity
    Intellectual Freedom
    Moral Development
    Moral Values
    Plagiarism
    Political Correctness

= Two or more Descriptors are used to represent this term.
The term's main entry shows the appropriate coordination.

Privacy
Religious Education
Sex Education

Ethnic Bias　　　　　　　　　　*MAR. 1980*
　　　Postings: 506　　　　　　　　　GC: 540
SN　Prejudicial opinions about particular groups because of their ethnic origins (Note: Do not confuse with "Ethnic Discrimination," which refers to actions based on those attitudes)
BT　Social Bias
RT　Anti Semitism
　　Ethnic Discrimination
　　Ethnic Groups
　　Ethnic Relations
　　Ethnic Stereotypes
　　Ethnicity
　　Ethnocentrism
　　Racial Bias

Ethnic Community
USE　Ethnic Groups

Ethnic Consciousness
USE　Ethnicity

Ethnic Cultural Groups
USE　Ethnic Groups

Ethnic Discrimination　　　　　*MAR. 1980*
　　　Postings: 483　　　　　　　　　GC: 540
SN　Restriction or denial of rights, privileges, and choice because of ethnic origins (Note: Do not confuse with "Ethnic Bias")
BT　Social Discrimination
RT　Anti Semitism
　　Ethnic Bias
　　Ethnic Distribution
　　Ethnic Groups
　　Ethnic Relations
　　Ethnic Stereotypes
　　Ethnocentrism
　　Racial Discrimination
　　Religious Discrimination

Ethnic Distribution　　　　　　*JUL. 1966*
　　　Postings: 492　　　　　　　　　GC: 550
BT　Population Distribution
RT　Affirmative Action
　　Black Population Trends
　　Community
　　Ethnic Discrimination
　　Ethnic Groups
　　Ethnic Origins
　　Geographic Distribution
　　Incidence
　　Neighborhood Integration
　　Racial Distribution

Ethnic Group Studies
USE　Ethnic Studies

Ethnic Grouping (1966 1980)　　*MAR. 1980*
　　　Postings: 67　　　　　　　　　 GC: 550
SN　Invalid Descriptor—used inconsistently in indexing—see such Descriptors as "Ethnicity," "Ethnic Groups," "Ethnic Distribution," "Demography," "Classification," etc.

Ethnic Groups　　　　　　　　*JUL. 1966*
　　　Postings: 8,250　　　　　　　 GC: 560
SN　Subgroups within a larger cultural or social order that are distinguished from the majority and each other by their national, religious, linguistic, cultural, and sometimes racial background (Note: Do not confuse with "Minority Groups," which has the connotation of being the object of prejudice or discrimination— use a more specific term if possible)
UF　Ethnic Community
　　Ethnic Cultural Groups
　　Racial Cultural Groups

NT　Alaska Natives
　　American Indians
　　Anglo Americans
　　Canada Natives
　　Chinese Americans
　　Filipino Americans
　　French Canadians
　　Greek Americans
　　Hawaiians
　　Hmong People
　　Italian Americans
　　Japanese Americans
　　Korean Americans
　　Maori (People)
　　Mexican Americans
　　Polish Americans
　　Portuguese Americans
　　Samoan Americans
　　Spanish Americans
BT　Groups
RT　Arabs
　　Asian Americans
　　Biculturalism
　　Black Community
　　Blacks
　　Cross Cultural Studies
　　Cubans
　　Cultural Background
　　Cultural Differences
　　Cultural Education
　　Cultural Images
　　Cultural Maintenance
　　Culture
　　Culture Fair Tests
　　Dominicans
　　Eskimos
　　Ethnic Bias
　　Ethnic Discrimination
　　Ethnic Distribution
　　Ethnic Origins
　　Ethnic Status
　　Ethnic Stereotypes
　　Ethnic Studies
　　Ethnicity
　　Ethnography
　　Ethnology
　　Ethnomathematics
　　Foreign Culture
　　Ghettos
　　Haitians
　　Hispanic Americans
　　Indians
　　Indigenous Populations
　　Indochinese
　　Intercultural Programs
　　Jews
　　Language Minorities
　　Limited English Speaking
　　Mexicans
　　Minority Groups
　　Multicultural Education
　　Muslims
　　Nationalism
　　Native Language Instruction
　　Native Speakers
　　Non English Speaking
　　North Americans
　　Pacific Americans
　　Pacific Islanders
　　Puerto Ricans
　　Race
　　Religious Cultural Groups
　　Self Determination
　　Social Integration
　　Subcultures
　　Tribes

Ethnic Heritage
USE　Cultural Background

Ethnic Identification
USE　Ethnicity

Ethnic Integration
USE　Social Integration

Ethnic Origins　　　　　　　　*JUL. 1966*
　　　Postings: 340　　　　　　　　　GC: 560
RT　Cultural Background

Ethnic Distribution
Ethnic Groups
Ethnic Studies
Ethnicity
Ethnology
Genealogy
Regional Dialects

Ethnic Relations　　　　　　　*JUL. 1966*
　　　Postings: 777　　　　　　　　　GC: 540
SN　Contact and interaction between or among ethnic groups
BT　Intergroup Relations
RT　Community Control
　　Cross Cultural Studies
　　Cross Cultural Training
　　Cultural Differences
　　Cultural Interrelationships
　　Cultural Pluralism
　　Diversity (Faculty)
　　Diversity (Student)
　　Ethnic Bias
　　Ethnic Discrimination
　　Ethnic Status
　　Ethnicity
　　Ethnocentrism
　　Intercultural Communication
　　Interfaith Relations
　　Multicultural Education
　　Racial Relations
　　Religious Cultural Groups
　　Social Integration

Ethnic Status　　　　　　　　*JUL. 1966*
　　　Postings: 234　　　　　　　　　GC: 510
BT　Status
RT　Ethnic Groups
　　Ethnic Relations
　　Ethnicity

Ethnic Stereotypes　　　　　　*JUL. 1966*
　　　Postings: 1,012　　　　　　　　GC: 540
UF　Jewish Stereotypes (1966 1980) #
NT　Black Stereotypes
BT　Stereotypes
RT　Ethnic Bias
　　Ethnic Discrimination
　　Ethnic Groups
　　Ethnic Studies
　　Ethnicity
　　Racial Attitudes
　　Racial Differences
　　Racial Identification

Ethnic Studies　　　　　　　　*AUG. 1969*
　　　Postings: 1,655　　　　　　　　GC: 400
UF　Ethnic Group Studies
NT　American Indian Studies
　　Black Studies
BT　Curriculum
RT　Area Studies
　　Cross Cultural Studies
　　Cultural Background
　　Cultural Education
　　Cultural Influences
　　Ethnic Groups
　　Ethnic Origins
　　Ethnic Stereotypes
　　Ethnicity
　　Global Education
　　History
　　Integration Studies
　　Interdisciplinary Approach
　　Minority Groups
　　Religion Studies
　　Social Science Research
　　Social Sciences
　　Urban Studies

Ethnic Unity
USE　Group Unity

Ethnicity　　　　　　　　　　*OCT. 1977*
　　　Postings: 2,927　　　　　　　 GC: 120
SN　Identification with a specific kind of ethnic character, quality, or peculiarity— awareness of the ethnic character of oneself or others

UF　Ethnic Consciousness
　　Ethnic Identification
BT　Sociocultural Patterns
RT　Afrocentrism
　　Black Power
　　Consciousness Raising
　　Cross Cultural Studies
　　Cultural Awareness
　　Cultural Differences
　　Cultural Images
　　Cultural Pluralism
　　Cultural Traits
　　Culture Conflict
　　Ethnic Bias
　　Ethnic Groups
　　Ethnic Origins
　　Ethnic Relations
　　Ethnic Status
　　Ethnic Stereotypes
　　Ethnic Studies
　　Ethnocentrism
　　Group Unity
　　Identification (Psychology)
　　Minority Groups
　　Multicultural Education
　　Multiracial Persons
　　Nationalism
　　Psychological Patterns
　　Race
　　Racial Attitudes
　　Racial Identification
　　Religious Conflict
　　Self Concept
　　Socialization
　　Traditionalism
　　Transracial Adoption

Ethnocentrism　　　　　　　　*SEP. 1973*
　　　Postings: 704　　　　　　　　　GC: 540
SN　Habitual disposition to judge foreign peoples or groups by the standards and practices of one's own culture or ethnic group
RT　Afrocentrism
　　Cultural Differences
　　Cultural Images
　　Culture Conflict
　　Ethnic Bias
　　Ethnic Discrimination
　　Ethnic Relations
　　Ethnicity
　　Foreign Culture
　　Intergroup Relations
　　International Relations
　　Multicultural Education
　　Psychological Patterns
　　Racial Differences
　　Sociocultural Patterns
　　Stereotypes
　　Values

Ethnography　　　　　　　　　*JAN. 1979*
　　　Postings: 2,311　　　　　　　　GC: 400
SN　Descriptive study (i.e., observation and reporting) of human culture and societies
BT　Anthropology
RT　Anthropological Linguistics
　　Cultural Context
　　Educational Anthropology
　　Ethnic Groups
　　Ethnology
　　Ethnomathematics
　　Folk Culture
　　Kinship
　　Naturalistic Observation
　　Participant Observation
　　Qualitative Research
　　Social Science Research
　　Social Scientists
　　Sociocultural Patterns
　　Sociology

Ethnology　　　　　　　　　　*AUG. 1968*
　　　Postings: 422　　　　　　　　　GC: 400
SN　Historical, analytic, or comparative study of human culture and societies
NT　Ethnomathematics
BT　Anthropology
RT　Anthropological Linguistics

= Two or more Descriptors are used to represent this term.
The term's main entry shows the appropriate coordination.

Archaeology
Cross Cultural Studies
Cultural Background
Cultural Context
Cultural Interrelationships
Cultural Pluralism
Educational Anthropology
Ethnic Groups
Ethnic Origins
Ethnography
Folk Culture
Human Geography
Kinship
Social Science Research
Social Scientists
Sociocultural Patterns
Sociology

Ethnomathematics   *JUL. 2000*
Postings: 112   GC: 480
SN   Study of mathematical theories, con-
     cepts, or practices as affected by their
     sociocultural context—also the applica-
     tion of knowledge gained from such study,
     e.g., mathematics instruction for mem-
     bers of particular sociocultural groups
BT   Ethnology
     Mathematics
RT   Cultural Context
     Ethnic Groups
     Ethnography
     Mathematical Concepts
     Mathematics Education
     Mathematics History
     Mathematics Instruction
     Multicultural Education

Ethology   *MAR. 1983*
Postings: 85   GC: 490
SN   Study of the behavior of humans and
     other animals under natural conditions
     from both evolutionary/genetic and eco-
     logical/experiential perspectives
BT   Behavioral Sciences
     Biological Sciences
RT   Behavior
     Behavior Development
     Behavior Patterns
     Conditioning
     Ecology
     Evolution
     Naturalistic Observation
     Sociobiology
     Zoology

Etiology   *JUL. 1966*
Postings: 1,859   GC: 210
SN   Study of causes, origins, or reasons
BT   Technology
RT   Attribution Theory
     Causal Models
     Clinical Diagnosis
     Delinquency Causes
     Disability Identification
     Educational Diagnosis
     Epidemiology
     Identification
     Pathology

ETV
USE   Educational Television

Etymology   *JUL. 1966*
Postings: 375   GC: 450
NT   Onomastics
BT   Diachronic Linguistics
RT   Comparative Analysis
     Definitions
     Dialect Studies
     Glottochronology
     Language Classification
     Language Research
     Language Typology
     Languages
     Lexicography
     Lexicology
     North American English
     Semantics

European History   *JUL. 1966*
Postings: 934   GC: 430
BT   History
RT   Western Civilization
     World War I
     World War II

Euskara
USE   Basque

Euthanasia   *OCT. 1997*
Postings: 64   GC: 210
SN   Inducing the death of persons or animals
     suffering from incurable conditions or
     diseases (Note: Related Identifiers are
     "Assisted Suicide" and "Right to Die")
UF   Mercy Killing
RT   Bioethics
     Death
     Medical Services
     Terminal Illness

Evaluation   *JUL. 1966*
Postings: 10,679   GC: 820
SN   Appraising or judging persons, organi-
     zations, or things in relation to stated
     objectives, standards, or criteria (Note:
     Use a more specific term if possible—
     see also "Testing" and "Measurement")
UF   Appraisal
     Assessment
NT   Alternative Assessment
     Computer Software Evaluation
     Course Evaluation
     Curriculum Evaluation
     Educational Assessment
     Equipment Evaluation
     Formative Evaluation
     Holistic Evaluation
     Informal Assessment
     Institutional Evaluation
     Instructional Material Evaluation
     Medical Care Evaluation
     Medical Evaluation
     Needs Assessment
     Peer Evaluation
     Personnel Evaluation
     Portfolio Assessment
     Preschool Evaluation
     Program Evaluation
     Property Appraisal
     Psychological Evaluation
     Recognition (Achievement)
     Self Evaluation (Groups)
     Self Evaluation (Individuals)
     Student Evaluation
     Student Teacher Evaluation
     Summative Evaluation
     Vocational Evaluation
     Writing Evaluation
RT   Achievement
     Credentials
     Criticism
     Data Interpretation
     Differences
     Error Correction
     Evaluation Criteria
     Evaluation Methods
     Evaluation Needs
     Evaluation Problems
     Evaluation Research
     Evaluation Utilization
     Evaluative Thinking
     Evaluators
     Expectation
     Failure
     Inspection
     Judgment Analysis Technique
     Measurement
     Measures (Individuals)
     Objectives
     Observation
     Participant Satisfaction
     Performance Factors
     Prerequisites
     Quality of Life
     Research
     Research and Development
     Specifications
     Standards

Success
Testing
Tests
Troubleshooting
User Satisfaction (Information)
Validity

Evaluation Criteria   *JUL. 1966*
Postings: 13,953   GC: 820
SN   Specifications or standards that may be
     used to judge or appraise individuals,
     organizations, or things
NT   Reliability
     Validity
BT   Criteria
RT   Accountability
     Efficiency
     Evaluation
     Evaluation Methods
     Evaluation Needs
     Evaluation Problems
     Minimum Competencies
     Performance
     Performance Factors
     Productivity
     Scoring Rubrics
     Selection
     Specifications
     Values

Evaluation Designs
USE   Evaluation Methods

Evaluation Methods   *JUL. 1966*
Postings: 28,161   GC: 820
SN   Objective or subjective procedures used
     to obtain and organize information for
     appraisal in relation to stated objectives,
     standards, or criteria (Note: Prior to
     Mar80, this term was not restricted by a
     Scope Note)
UF   Analysis
     Evaluation Designs
     Evaluation Procedures
     Evaluation Techniques (1966 1974)
NT   Audience Analysis
     Benchmarking
     Case Studies
     Chemical Analysis
     Comparative Analysis
     Componential Analysis
     Content Analysis
     Cost Effectiveness
     Data Analysis
     Drug Use Testing
     Environmental Scanning
     Hypothesis Testing
     Input Output Analysis
     Inspection
     Interviews
     Job Analysis
     Life Cycle Costing
     Need Analysis (Student Financial Aid)
     Phonetic Analysis
     Policy Analysis
     Pretesting
     Quality Control
     Readability Formulas
     Scoring Rubrics
     Site Analysis
     Skill Analysis
     Structural Analysis (Linguistics)
     Structural Analysis (Science)
     Surveys
     Synthesis
     Task Analysis
BT   Methods
RT   Action Research
     Alternative Assessment
     Assessment Centers (Personnel)
     Audits (Verification)
     Causal Models
     Critical Incidents Method
     Criticism
     Curriculum Based Assessment
     Educational Assessment
     Error Patterns
     Evaluation
     Evaluation Criteria
     Evaluation Needs

Evaluation Problems
Evaluation Research
Evaluation Utilization
Informal Assessment
Interrater Reliability
Investigations
Measurement Techniques
Measures (Individuals)
Methods Research
Needs Assessment
Objectivity
Participant Observation
Performance Based Assessment
Portfolio Assessment
Portfolios (Background Materials)
Precision Teaching
Qualitative Research
Questionnaires
Relevance (Information Retrieval)
Research
Research Methodology
Sample Size
Sampling
Supervisory Methods
Triangulation
Use Studies

Evaluation Needs   *JUL. 1966*
Postings: 1,436   GC: 820
SN   Questions or problems that require
     evaluation (Note: Prior to Mar80, the use
     of this term was not restricted by a
     Scope Note)
BT   Needs
RT   Evaluation
     Evaluation Criteria
     Evaluation Methods
     Evaluation Problems
     Evaluation Utilization
     Information Needs
     Measurement Objectives
     Research Needs

Evaluation Problems   *JAN. 1986*
Postings: 1,044   GC: 820
SN   Difficulties associated with the method-
     ology, interpretation, or use of apprais-
     als of persons, organizations, or things
     (Note: Do not confuse with "Testing
     Problems" and "Research Problems")
BT   Problems
RT   Evaluation
     Evaluation Criteria
     Evaluation Methods
     Evaluation Needs
     Evaluation Research
     Evaluation Utilization
     Research Problems
     Testing Problems

Evaluation Procedures
USE   Evaluation Methods

Evaluation Research   *DEC. 1988*
Postings: 585   GC: 810
SN   Systematic investigation into the nature
     and process of evaluation, including meth-
     ods, practices, and utilization of results
     (Note: Do not confuse with evaluation
     conducted in an exhaustive or research-
     like manner, for which see "Evaluation")
UF   Evaluative Research
BT   Methods Research
RT   Evaluation
     Evaluation Methods
     Evaluation Problems
     Evaluation Utilization
     Evaluators
     Research Design
     Research Methodology

Evaluation Specialists
USE   Evaluators

Evaluation Techniques (1966 1974)
USE   Evaluation Methods

= Two or more Descriptors are used to represent this term.
The term's main entry shows the appropriate coordination.

Evaluation Utilization   MAR. 1983
Postings: 1,229   GC: 820
SN   The use of evaluative information in communication, learning, motivation, accountability, program improvement, decision making, or other processes
BT   Information Utilization
RT   Accountability
     Adoption (Ideas)
     Decision Making
     Evaluation
     Evaluation Methods
     Evaluation Needs
     Evaluation Problems
     Evaluation Research
     Formative Evaluation
     Research Utilization
     Summative Evaluation
     Test Use

Evaluative Research
USE   Evaluation Research

Evaluative Thinking   NOV. 1968
Postings: 1,140   GC: 110
SN   Process of determining or judging the appropriateness, efficacy, or value of something with respect to specified objectives or standards
UF   Judgmental Processes
NT   Value Judgment
BT   Critical Thinking
RT   Data Interpretation
     Decision Making
     Evaluation
     Judgment Analysis Technique
     Problem Solving
     Productive Thinking
     Thinking Skills

Evaluators   SEP. 1977
Postings: 1,160   GC: 360
SN   Individuals who collect information according to a design and use such information as a basis for judging either the absolute or relative value of programs, products, or personnel
UF   Evaluation Specialists
BT   Personnel
RT   Educational Researchers
     Evaluation
     Evaluation Research
     Interrater Reliability
     Researchers

Evening Classes (1967 1980)
USE   Evening Programs

Evening Colleges (1967 1980)
USE   Evening Programs

Evening Counseling Programs (1966 1980)
USE   Counseling Services
AND   Evening Programs

Evening Programs   JUL. 1966
Postings: 450   GC: 350
SN   Programs, usually educational, offered by institutions, businesses, or communities during the evening
UF   Evening Classes (1967 1980)
     Evening Colleges (1967 1980)
     Evening Counseling Programs (1966 1980) #
     Night Schools (1966 1980)
BT   Programs
RT   Adult Programs
     Continuing Education
     Day Programs
     Evening Students
     Extension Education
     High School Equivalency Programs
     Part Time Students

Evening Students   JUL. 1966
Postings: 202   GC: 360
BT   Students
RT   Adult Students
     Day Students
     Evening Programs
     Extension Education
     External Degree Programs
     Part Time Students

Evidence (Legal)   OCT. 1994
Postings: 49   GC: 610
SN   Material, such as testimony, records, or objects, used in forming conclusions or judgments in legal matters—often presented to courts or juries during trials
RT   Court Litigation
     Courts
     Crime
     Juries
     Law Enforcement
     Laws
     Legal Problems
     Legal Responsibility
     Search and Seizure

Evolution   SEP. 1968
Postings: 1,203   GC: 490
NT   Heredity
BT   Development
RT   Anatomy
     Astronomy
     Biodiversity
     Biological Influences
     Biology
     Botany
     Creationism
     Cytology
     Ecology
     Embryology
     Ethology
     Genetics
     Paleontology
     Physiology
     Sociobiology
     Zoology

Ewe   JUL. 1966
Postings: 9   GC: 440
BT   African Languages

Examinations
USE   Tests

Examiner Characteristics
USE   Examiners
AND   Experimenter Characteristics

Examiners   JAN. 1970
Postings: 279   GC: 640
SN   Individuals who administer tests
UF   Examiner Characteristics #
     Test Administrators
BT   Clerical Workers
RT   Experimenter Characteristics
     Familiarity
     Interrater Reliability
     Psychometrics
     Testing
     Tests

Excellence in Education   DEC. 1988
Postings: 1,558   GC: 330
SN   Educational reform movement in the United States directed at stemming declining academic performance and renewing a commitment to high-quality, effective schooling for all—begun in 1983 with the issuance of "A Nation at Risk," the final report of the National Commission on Excellence in Education, which focused attention and prompted widespread actions toward educational improvement
UF   Educational Excellence Movement (United States)
NT   School Restructuring

RT   Academic Achievement
     Academic Standards
     Administrator Effectiveness
     Curriculum Evaluation
     Education
     Educational Change
     Educational Improvement
     Educational Needs
     Educational Objectives
     Educational Policy
     Educational Quality
     Effective Schools Research
     Equal Education
     Instructional Effectiveness
     Instructional Improvement
     Instructional Leadership
     Minimum Competencies
     National Programs
     Outcomes of Education
     Program Effectiveness
     Program Improvement
     Relevance (Education)
     School Effectiveness
     School Support
     State Programs
     Student Development
     Student Improvement
     Student Needs
     Teacher Effectiveness
     Teacher Improvement

Exceptional (Atypical) (1966 1978)
USE   Exceptional Persons (1978 1994)

Exceptional Child Education (1968 1980)
           MAR. 1980
Postings: 5,836   GC: 220
SN   Invalid Descriptor—used inconsistently in indexing—see "Special Education"

Exceptional Child Research   JUL. 1966
Postings: 8,228   GC: 810
BT   Research
RT   Behavioral Science Research
     Disabilities
     Educational Research
     Gifted
     Medical Research
     Personality Studies
     Psychological Studies

Exceptional Child Services (1968 1980)
           MAR. 1980
Postings: 1,448   GC: 220
SN   Invalid Descriptor—used inconsistently in indexing—coordinate more specific Descriptors

Exceptional Children (1966 1978)
USE   Exceptional Persons (1978 1994)

Exceptional Persons (1978 1994)
           SEP. 1994
Postings: 1,048   GC: 120
SN   Invalid term—used inconsistently in indexing—see "Disabilities" and/or "Gifted"
UF   Exceptional (Atypical) (1966 1978)
     Exceptional Children (1966 1978)
     Exceptional Students (1966 1978)

Exceptional Students (1966 1978)
USE   Exceptional Persons (1978 1994)

Exchange Programs   JUL. 1966
Postings: 495   GC: 330
NT   Student Exchange Programs
     Teacher Exchange Programs
BT   Programs
RT   Cross Cultural Training
     Cultural Exchange
     Enrichment Activities
     Institutional Cooperation
     Intercultural Programs
     International Cooperation
     International Educational Exchange

Excursions (Instruction)
USE   Field Trips

Executions (Criminal Law)
USE   Capital Punishment

Executive Development
USE   Management Development

Executive Secretaries
USE   Secretaries

Exemplary Programs
USE   Demonstration Programs

Exercise   MAR. 1980
Postings: 807   GC: 470
SN   Bodily exertion to develop and maintain physical strength, skills, or fitness
UF   Muscular Exercise #
     Physical Exercise
NT   Aerobics
     Calisthenics
     Plyometrics
BT   Physical Activities
RT   Athletics
     Exercise Physiology
     Health Behavior
     Human Body
     Lifetime Sports
     Muscular Strength
     Muscular System
     Physical Fitness
     Psychomotor Skills

Exercise (Physiology) (1969 1980)
           MAR. 1980
Postings: 521   GC: 470
SN   Invalid Descriptor—see the more precise terms "Exercise" and "Exercise Physiology"

Exercise Physiology   MAR. 1980
Postings: 403   GC: 210
SN   Study of the physiological effects of bodily exertion
BT   Physiology
RT   Biomechanics
     Body Composition
     Cardiovascular System
     Exercise
     Fatigue (Biology)
     Medical Research
     Metabolism
     Motor Reactions
     Musculoskeletal System
     Physical Activity Level
     Physical Education
     Physical Health
     Sports Medicine
     Stress Variables

Exhaust Stacks
USE   Chimneys

Exhausting (1969 1980)
USE   Ventilation

Exhaustion
USE   Fatigue (Biology)

Exhibits   JUL. 1966
Postings: 870   GC: 720
SN   Thematic displays or shows for the public, as well as the collection of objects that is presented
UF   Expositions (1971 1980)
     Fairs
NT   Science Fairs
BT   Nonprint Media
RT   Display Aids
     Instructional Materials
     Museums

= Two or more Descriptors are used to represent this term.
The term's main entry shows the appropriate coordination.

Realia
Screens (Displays)
Three Dimensional Aids

Exiles
USE   Refugees

Existentialism   MAY 1969
      Postings: 356   GC: 430
BT   Philosophy
RT   Individualism
      Phenomenology
      Twentieth Century Literature

Exogamous Marriage
USE   Intermarriage

Expectancy
USE   Expectation

Expectancy Tables   JUL. 1966
      Postings: 103   GC: 480
BT   Tables (Data)
RT   Bayesian Statistics
      Expectation
      Predictive Measurement
      Predictive Validity
      Predictor Variables
      Probability
      Statistical Analysis
      Statistical Distributions
      Statistical Inference
      Statistics

Expectation   DEC. 1969
      Postings: 3,679   GC: 120
SN   Anticipation of future events, conditions,
      or trends, and the effects of that antici-
      pation
UF   Expectancy
NT   Self Fulfilling Prophecies
      Teacher Expectations of Students
      Work Life Expectancy
RT   Achievement
      Aptitude
      Attitudes
      Cognitive Mapping
      Cognitive Structures
      Evaluation
      Expectancy Tables
      Failure
      Intention
      Intuition
      Life Events
      Opinions
      Performance
      Prediction
      Predictive Validity
      Probability
      Reliability
      Self Efficacy
      Stereotypes
      Success
      Symptoms (Individual Disorders)

Expenditure per Student   SEP. 1968
      Postings: 1,853   GC: 620
SN   Average amount of expenses incurred
      per student by an institution for a desig-
      nated service for a given period of time
      (Note: Do not confuse with "Student
      Costs"—prior to Mar80, this term was
      not restricted by a Scope Note)
BT   Expenditures
RT   Costs
      Educational Equity (Finance)
      Educational Finance
      Equalization Aid
      Fiscal Neutrality
      Full State Funding
      Program Costs
      School District Spending
      School District Wealth
      School Statistics
      Student Costs

Expenditures   JUL. 1966
      Postings: 2,964   GC: 620
SN   Actual payments, or commitments to
      make future payments, for something
      received (Note: Do not confuse with
      "Costs"—prior to Mar80, the use of this
      term was not restricted by a Scope Note)
UF   Disbursements (Money)
      Expenses
      Initial Expenses (1966 1980)
      Minimum Initial Expenses
NT   Capital Outlay (for Fixed Assets)
      Compensation (Remuneration)
      Expenditure per Student
      Library Expenditures
      Merit Pay
      Operating Expenses
      Premium Pay
      Salaries
      School District Spending
      Wages
RT   Bids
      Budgeting
      Budgets
      Cost Effectiveness
      Cost Indexes
      Costs
      Economic Impact
      Educational Finance
      Financial Audits
      Resource Allocation
      Retrenchment
      Tax Rates

Expenses
USE   Expenditures

Experience   JUL. 1966
      Postings: 833   GC: 120
SN   The process of observing, encountering,
      or undergoing a set of circumstances or
      events from which knowledge, under-
      standing, skills, or attitudes are derived—
      also, the cumulative result of this proc-
      ess (Note: Use a more specific term if
      possible)
NT   Early Experience
      Educational Experience
      Emotional Experience
      Group Experience
      Intellectual Experience
      Learning Experience
      Life Events
      Prereading Experience
      Sensory Experience
      Social Experience
      Student Experience
      Teaching Experience
      Work Experience
BT   Background
RT   Activities
      Credentials
      Developmental Continuity
      Discovery Processes
      Experiential Learning
      Familiarity
      Lifelong Learning
      Participation
      Prior Learning
      Reminiscence
      Transfer Programs

Experience Based Education
USE   Experiential Learning

Experience Charts   JUL. 1966
      Postings: 27   GC: 310
SN   Charts prepared by the teacher and based
      upon some experience in which the stu-
      dents participate—often used in reading
      instruction and instruction of the dis-
      abled
BT   Charts
      Instructional Materials
RT   Experiential Learning
      Precision Teaching
      Reading Instruction
      Student Developed Materials
      Student Experience

Student Participation
Teacher Developed Materials

Experience Units
USE   Activity Units

Experienced Laborers (1966 1980)
USE   Laborers

Experiential Learning   JUN. 1978
      Postings: 8,774   GC: 310
SN   Learning by doing—includes knowledge
      and skills acquired outside of book/lec-
      ture learning situations through work,
      play, and other life experiences (Note:
      Do not confuse with "Learning Experi-
      ence")
UF   Action Learning
      Activity Learning (1968 1978)
      Community Experience
      Experience Based Education
      Hands on Learning
      Home Experience
      Prior Experiential Learning #
NT   Field Experience Programs
      Internship Programs
      Service Learning
BT   Learning
RT   Active Learning
      Activity Units
      Adventure Education
      Apprenticeships
      Case Method (Teaching Technique)
      Certification
      Clinical Experience
      College Credits
      Community Based Instruction (Disa-
        bilities)
      Cooperative Education
      Cooperative Learning
      Cooperative Programs
      Credits
      Discovery Learning
      Employment Experience
      Equivalency Tests
      Experience
      Experience Charts
      Farm Visits
      Field Instruction
      Field Trips
      Hands on Science
      High School Equivalency Programs
      Improvisation
      Informal Assessment
      Informal Education
      Laboratory Procedures
      Laboratory Schools
      Learning Activities
      Learning Centers (Classroom)
      Learning Experience
      Learning Strategies
      Lifelong Learning
      Living Learning Centers
      Manipulative Materials
      On the Job Training
      Outdoor Education
      Outdoor Leadership
      Physical Education
      Portfolios (Background Materials)
      Practical Arts
      Practicums
      Prior Learning
      Problem Based Learning
      Professional Education
      Reggio Emilia Approach
      Sensory Experience
      Simulation
      Social Experience
      Special Degree Programs
      Student Experience
      Student Journals
      Student Projects
      Teaching Experience
      Vocational Education
      Volunteer Training
      Work Experience
      Work Experience Programs

Experiment Stations   SEP. 1968
      Postings: 23   GC: 410
SN   Field stations at which experiments are
      conducted—usually maintained by a uni-
      versity and concerned with experiments
      in agriculture or other applied sciences
UF   Field Experiment Stations
BT   Facilities
RT   Agricultural Colleges
      Agriculture
      Experiments
      Extension Agents
      Research and Development Centers
      Research Projects
      Scientific Research

Experimental Colleges   NOV. 1969
      Postings: 256   GC: 340
SN   Higher education institutions character-
      ized by innovative curricula, learning ex-
      periences, teaching methods, etc.—also
      refers to institutions or programs set up
      by dissident students and faculty, espe-
      cially in the U.S. during the 1960s
UF   Free Universities
BT   Colleges
      Experimental Schools
RT   Cluster Colleges
      Educational Innovation
      Experimental Curriculum
      Experimental Programs
      Experimental Teaching
      Instructional Innovation
      Nontraditional Education
      Open Universities
      Relevance (Education)
      Student College Relationship
      Student Interests
      Student Participation

Experimental Curriculum   JUL. 1966
      Postings: 733   GC: 350
SN   Curriculum marked by new or innovative
      ideas, methods, or organization of sub-
      ject matter—often used in comparison
      with a standard curriculum to assess the
      relative effectiveness of each
BT   Curriculum
RT   Educational Innovation
      Educational Research
      Experimental Colleges
      Experimental Programs
      Experimental Schools
      Experimental Teaching
      Fused Curriculum
      Instructional Innovation
      Nontraditional Education
      Spiral Curriculum

Experimental Design
USE   Research Design

Experimental Extinction
USE   Extinction (Psychology)

Experimental Groups   JUL. 1966
      Postings: 720   GC: 820
SN   Subjects who are exposed to an experi-
      mental treatment or condition, and whose
      subsequent performance may be attrib-
      uted to that treatment or condition (Note:
      Use only for discussions of the identifi-
      cation, selection, or treatment of experi-
      mental groups)
BT   Groups
RT   Attrition (Research Studies)
      Control Groups
      Effect Size
      Matched Groups
      Participant Characteristics
      Quasiexperimental Design
      Research Design
      Research Methodology
      Sample Size
      Sampling

Experimental Procedures
USE   Research Methodology

= Two or more Descriptors are used to represent this term.
The term's main entry shows the appropriate coordination.

Experimental Programs   *JUL. 1966*
Postings: 2,198   GC: 320
BT   Programs
RT   Demonstration Programs
    Experimental Colleges
    Experimental Curriculum
    Experimental Schools
    Experimental Teaching
    Experiments
    Feasibility Studies
    Institutional Research
    Pilot Projects
    Research Projects

Experimental Psychology   *JUL. 1966*
Postings: 1,082   GC: 230
BT   Psychology
RT   Behaviorism
    Clinical Psychology
    Cognitive Psychology
    Experiments
    Laboratory Experiments
    Psychological Studies
    Research

Experimental Schools   *JUL. 1966*
Postings: 529   GC: 340
SN   Schools in which new teaching methods, new organizations of subject matter, personnel practices, and advanced educational theories and hypotheses are tested
UF   Project Schools
NT   Experimental Colleges
BT   Schools
RT   Educational Innovation
    Educational Research
    Experimental Curriculum
    Experimental Programs
    Experimental Teaching
    Free Schools
    Instructional Innovation
    Laboratory Schools
    Nontraditional Education
    Open Education
    Professional Development Schools
    Relevance (Education)
    Student Interests
    Student Participation
    Teaching Experience
    Transitional Schools

Experimental Teaching   *JUL. 1966*
Postings: 515   GC: 310
SN   Teaching that uses new or innovative ideas, methods, or devices (Note: Prior to Mar80, this term was a narrower term of "Educational Research")
BT   Teaching Methods
RT   Conventional Instruction
    Educational Innovation
    Educational Research
    Experimental Colleges
    Experimental Curriculum
    Experimental Programs
    Experimental Schools
    Instructional Innovation

Experimentation
USE   Experiments

Experimenter Bias
USE   Experimenter Characteristics

Experimenter Characteristics   *MAY 1976*
Postings: 307   GC: 810
SN   Distinguishing traits or qualities of an experimenter which may influence experimental results
UF   Examiner Characteristics #
    Experimenter Bias
    Researcher Characteristics #
RT   Examiners
    Experiments
    Individual Characteristics
    Interrater Reliability
    Research Methodology
    Research Problems

    Researchers
    Scientists
    Social Scientists
    Testing Problems

Experiments   *JUL. 1966*
Postings: 1,521   GC: 810
UF   Experimentation
NT   Educational Experiments
    Laboratory Experiments
    Science Experiments
RT   Data Interpretation
    Deduction
    Discovery Processes
    Effect Size
    Experiment Stations
    Experimental Programs
    Experimental Psychology
    Experimenter Characteristics
    Generalization
    Induction
    Innovation
    Inventions
    Investigations
    Observation
    Research
    Research Needs

Expert Systems   *AUG. 1986*
Postings: 705   GC: 710
SN   Computer systems capable of matching a database of factual information with a knowledge base of judgmental rules to answer questions, make decisions, or teach a skill
UF   Knowledge Based Systems
NT   Intelligent Tutoring Systems
BT   Artificial Intelligence
RT   Computers
    Data Processing
    Decision Making
    Decision Support Systems
    Information Systems
    Knowledge Representation
    Man Machine Systems
    Problem Solving

Exploratory Behavior   *MAR. 1983*
Postings: 132   GC: 120
SN   Movements made by organisms to acquaint themselves with their surroundings—commonly refers to infant/child behavior (Note: Do not confuse with "Discovery Processes")
BT   Behavior
RT   Attachment Behavior
    Behavior Development
    Child Behavior
    Curiosity
    Novelty (Stimulus Dimension)
    Perceptual Motor Coordination
    Spontaneous Behavior

Exploratory Learning
USE   Discovery Learning

Exports   *JUL. 1966*
Postings: 182   GC: 650
BT   International Trade
RT   Business
    Economics
    Imports
    International Relations
    International Trade Vocabulary

Exposition (Literary)
USE   Expository Writing

Expositions (1971 1980)
USE   Exhibits

Expository Writing   *NOV. 1968*
Postings: 1,200   GC: 400
SN   Form of written prose that deals with definitions, processes, generalizations, and the clarification of ideas and prin-

ciples, with the intent of presenting meanings in readily communicable and unemotive language
UF   Exposition (Literary)
BT   Writing (Composition)
RT   Creative Writing
    Descriptive Writing
    Essays
    Journal Writing
    Journalism
    Journalism Education
    News Reporting
    News Writing
    Prose
    Research Papers (Students)
    Rhetoric
    Student Writing Models
    Technical Writing
    Theses

Expressionism   *JUN. 1969*
Postings: 56   GC: 430
SN   Early 20th century movement in the creative arts that depicts the subjective emotions and responses of the artist/author to objects or events, often using distortion, exaggeration, or symbolism
RT   Art Expression
    Intellectual History
    Literary Styles
    Music
    Twentieth Century Literature

Expressive Language   *JUL. 1966*
Postings: 1,205   GC: 450
SN   The cognitive processing involved in the transmission of oral, symbolic, or written language (Note: Prior to Mar80, the use of this term was not restricted by a Scope Note)
BT   Language Processing
RT   Aphasia
    Communication (Thought Transfer)
    Communication Skills
    Language Acquisition
    Language Fluency
    Language Impairments
    Language Skills
    Language Styles
    Oral Language
    Psycholinguistics
    Receptive Language

Expulsion   *JUL. 1966*
Postings: 402   GC: 330
SN   Forced withdrawal from school
BT   Discipline
RT   Academic Failure
    Academic Probation
    Attendance
    College Attendance
    Disqualification
    Dropouts
    Out of School Youth
    School Attendance Legislation
    Student Attrition
    Suspension
    Withdrawal (Education)

Extemporization
USE   Improvisation

Extended Degree Programs (Teacher Education)
USE   Extended Teacher Education Programs

Extended Family   *JUN. 1977*
Postings: 376   GC: 520
SN   A form of family organization consisting of blood relatives and their several nuclear family units
BT   Family (Sociological Unit)
RT   Black Family
    Family Life
    Family Relationship
    Family Size
    Family Structure
    Genealogy

    Kinship
    Nuclear Family
    One Parent Family
    Stepfamily

Extended School Day   *JUL. 1966*
Postings: 242   GC: 350
SN   Plan that extends the time a school is open during the day, either before or after normal school hours—may be for academic, recreational, day care, or other purposes
UF   Staggered Sessions
BT   School Schedules
RT   After School Education
    After School Programs
    Block Scheduling
    Compensatory Education
    Extracurricular Activities
    Flexible Scheduling
    School Age Day Care
    School Recreational Programs
    Time Factors (Learning)

Extended School Year   *OCT. 1968*
Postings: 428   GC: 350
SN   Plan that mandates an increase in the number of days students must attend school (Note: Prior to Mar80, this term was not scoped and was often confused with "Year Round Schools")
BT   School Schedules
RT   Flexible Scheduling
    Quarter System
    Summer Schools
    Time Factors (Learning)
    Trimester System
    Year Round Schools

Extended Teacher Education Programs
    APR. 1990
Postings: 64   GC: 340
SN   Teacher education programs requiring more time to complete than traditional 4-year programs, e.g., 4-plus-1 internship, 4-plus-1 noneducation B.A. with education courses, 5-year masters-level initial certification
UF   Extended Degree Programs (Teacher Education)
    Five Year Teacher Preparation Programs
BT   Teacher Education Programs
RT   Alternative Teacher Certification
    Competency Based Teacher Education
    Graduate Study
    Internship Programs
    Masters Degrees
    Nontraditional Education
    Preservice Teacher Education
    Program Length
    Student Teaching
    Teacher Education
    Teacher Education Curriculum
    Teacher Interns
    Teaching Experience

Extended Universities
USE   Open Universities

Extension Agents   *JUL. 1966*
Postings: 752   GC: 410
UF   Agricultural Agents
    County Extension Agents
    Farm Agents
    Four H Club Agents
    Home Demonstration Agents
    Village Extension Agents
BT   Change Agents
    Government Employees
RT   Adult Educators
    Agricultural Education
    Agricultural Personnel
    County Officials
    Experiment Stations
    Home Economics Education
    Home Economics Teachers
    State Officials

= Two or more Descriptors are used to represent this term.
The term's main entry shows the appropriate coordination.

Extension Education   *JUL. 1966*
Postings: 3,264   GC: 350
SN   Instructional activities offered beyond the confines of regular classes in school or on campus in order to serve a wider clientele—may include evening classes, short courses, exhibits, telecourses, correspondence courses, seminars, and institutes
UF   Cooperative Extension
    Extension Services
    Extramural Departments
    Off Campus Education
    University Extension (1967 1980)
NT   External Degree Programs
    Library Extension
    Rural Extension
    Urban Extension
BT   Education
RT   Access to Education
    Adult Education
    Colleges
    Community Education
    Continuing Education
    Continuing Education Centers
    Correspondence Schools
    Distance Education
    Evening Programs
    Evening Students
    Higher Education
    Home Study
    Industrial Training
    Mobile Educational Services
    Noncampus Colleges
    Nontraditional Education
    Off Campus Facilities
    Open Universities
    Outreach Programs
    Part Time Students
    Professional Continuing Education
    Satellite Facilities
    Universities

Extension Services
USE   Extension Education

External Degree Programs   *AUG. 1972*
Postings: 961   GC: 350
SN   Higher education programs offering validated degrees to students who have studied outside the institution—e.g., programs offered by Nova University or University Without Walls
BT   College Programs
    Extension Education
RT   Access to Education
    Bachelors Degrees
    Degree Requirements
    Degrees (Academic)
    Distance Education
    Educational Attainment
    Evening Students
    High School Equivalency Programs
    Independent Study
    Noncampus Colleges
    Nontraditional Education
    Open Universities
    Part Time Students
    Special Degree Programs

Externships (Medicine)
USE   Clinical Experience

Extinction (Psychology)   *JUL. 1969*
Postings: 188   GC: 110
SN   Progressive reduction in conditioned response after prolonged repetition of the eliciting stimulus without reinforcement
UF   Experimental Extinction
BT   Learning Processes
RT   Conditioning
    Contingency Management
    Negative Reinforcement
    Retention (Psychology)
    Timeout

Extracurricular Activities   *MAR. 1980*
Postings: 2,364   GC: 470
SN   Activities, under the sponsorship or direction of a school, of the type for which participation generally is not required and credit generally is not awarded
UF   Cocurricular Activities (1966 1980)
    School Related Activities
    Student Activities (Extraclass)
BT   School Activities
RT   After School Programs
    Art Activities
    Athletics
    Clubs
    Curriculum
    Enrichment Activities
    Extended School Day
    Music Activities
    Recreational Activities
    School Newspapers
    School Recreational Programs
    Science Fairs
    Student Interests
    Student Organizations
    Student Projects
    Student Unions
    Student Volunteers
    Students
    Supplementary Education

Extradimensional Shift
USE   Shift Studies

Extrainstructional Duties
USE   Noninstructional Responsibility

Extramural Athletic Programs (1966 1980)
USE   Extramural Athletics

Extramural Athletics   *MAR. 1980*
Postings: 135   GC: 470
UF   Extramural Athletic Programs (1966 1980)
    Extramural Sports
    Interscholastic Athletics
BT   Athletics
RT   College Athletics
    Intramural Athletics
    School Recreational Programs

Extramural Departments
USE   Extension Education

Extramural Sports
USE   Extramural Athletics

Extrateaching Duties
USE   Noninstructional Responsibility

Extraterrestrial Exploration
USE   Space Exploration

Extraversion Introversion   *DEC. 1989*
Postings: 133   GC: 120
SN   Personality dimension described or measured in terms of direction of interest and attention outward or inward, ease or difficulty of social adjustment, and tendency toward open or secretive behavior
UF   Ambiversion
    Extroversion
    Introversion
BT   Personality Traits
RT   Affective Behavior
    Arousal Patterns
    Behavior Patterns
    Conceptual Tempo
    Egocentrism
    Field Dependence Independence
    Interpersonal Competence
    Interpersonal Relationship
    Locus of Control
    Perspective Taking
    Psychological Patterns
    Self Concept
    Shyness
    Social Adjustment
    Social Cognition
    Social Isolation

Extrinsic Motivation
USE   Incentives

Extroversion
USE   Extraversion Introversion

Eye Contact   *APR. 1985*
Postings: 110   GC: 120
SN   Direct eye-to-eye contact between individuals
BT   Nonverbal Communication
RT   Body Language
    Eye Fixations
    Eyes
    Facial Expressions
    Interaction Process Analysis
    Interpersonal Communication

Eye Fixations   *JUL. 1966*
Postings: 298   GC: 110
SN   Directing and focusing of the eye(s) toward an object or point so that the image falls on the retina(s)
BT   Eye Movements
RT   Eye Contact
    Reading Processes
    Strabismus
    Visual Perception

Eye Hand Coordination   *JUL. 1966*
Postings: 205   GC: 120
BT   Perceptual Motor Coordination
RT   Eye Movements
    Handedness
    Motor Development
    Object Manipulation
    Tactual Visual Tests

Eye Movements   *JUL. 1966*
Postings: 470   GC: 110
UF   Eye Regressions (1966 1980)
NT   Eye Fixations
BT   Motor Reactions
RT   Body Language
    Eye Hand Coordination
    Eye Voice Span
    Eyes
    Facial Expressions
    Pupillary Dilation
    Visual Impairments

Eye Regressions (1966 1980)
USE   Eye Movements

Eye Voice Span   *JUL. 1966*
Postings: 22   GC: 460
SN   During oral reading, the distance (measured in letters) between the word being spoken and the word on which the eyes are focused
BT   Perceptual Motor Coordination
RT   Eye Movements
    Oral Reading
    Reading Skills
    Speech Skills
    Visual Perception

Eyes   *AUG. 1968*
Postings: 194   GC: 210
RT   Anatomy
    Eye Contact
    Eye Movements
    Human Body
    Ophthalmology
    Optometrists
    Optometry
    Pupillary Dilation
    Vision
    Vision Tests
    Visual Impairments

Fables   *JUL. 1966*
Postings: 196   GC: 430
SN   Short fictional tales about supernatural or unusual incidents, usually told to teach a moral and frequently having animals or inanimate objects as characters
BT   Tales
RT   Allegory
    Didacticism
    Fairy Tales
    Fantasy
    Fiction
    Mythology

Fabrication
USE   Manufacturing

Facial Expressions   *APR. 1986*
Postings: 281   GC: 120
BT   Nonverbal Communication
RT   Body Language
    Eye Contact
    Eye Movements

Facilities   *JUL. 1966*
Postings: 1,399   GC: 920
SN   Any physical structures or spaces constructed, installed, or established to perform particular functions or to serve particular ends (Note: Use a more specific term if possible)
UF   Institutional Facilities (1967 1980)
    Physical Facilities (1966 1980)
NT   Air Structures
    Airports
    Animal Facilities
    Aquariums
    Assessment Centers (Personnel)
    Athletic Fields
    Auditoriums
    Bookstores
    Buildings
    College Stores
    Community Centers
    Corridors
    Day Care Centers
    Dining Facilities
    Driveways
    Educational Facilities
    Encapsulated Facilities
    Equal Facilities
    Experiment Stations
    Fallout Shelters
    Feed Stores
    Field Houses
    Fisheries
    Flexible Facilities
    Food Handling Facilities
    Food Stores
    Foundries
    Gardens
    Greenhouses
    Gymnasiums
    Health Facilities
    Housing
    Interior Space
    Laboratories
    Library Facilities
    Locker Rooms
    Military Air Facilities
    Museums
    Music Facilities
    Nuclear Power Plants
    Nurseries (Horticulture)
    Offices (Facilities)
    Parking Facilities
    Parks
    Planetariums
    Public Facilities
    Recreational Facilities
    Rehabilitation Centers
    Relocatable Facilities
    Research and Development Centers
    Resource Centers
    Sanitary Facilities
    Satellite Facilities
    Science Facilities
    Settlement Houses
    Shared Facilities
    Swimming Pools

= Two or more Descriptors are used to represent this term.
The term's main entry shows the appropriate coordination.

Television Studios
Theaters
Trails
Underground Facilities
Warehouses
Windowless Rooms
Workstations
RT Building Design
Built Environment
Clinics
Construction Materials
Equipment
Facility Expansion
Facility Guidelines
Facility Improvement
Facility Inventory
Facility Planning
Facility Requirements
Facility Utilization Research
Maintenance
Resources
Space Utilization
Structural Elements (Construction)

Facility Case Studies   *JUL. 1966*
Postings: 265   GC: 810
SN Gathering and organizing of all relevant material to enable analysis and explication of facilities (Note: As of Oct81, use as a minor Descriptor for examples of this kind of research—use as a major Descriptor only as the subject of a document)
BT Case Studies
RT Building Design
Building Plans
Facility Guidelines
Facility Inventory
Facility Planning
Facility Requirements
Facility Utilization Research
Site Analysis
Space Utilization

Facility Design
USE Facility Guidelines

Facility Expansion   *JUL. 1966*
Postings: 380   GC: 920
SN Adding to a facility or altering it to accommodate additional people, equipment, etc.
NT School Expansion
BT Development
RT Building Conversion
Construction (Process)
Construction Programs
Facilities
Facility Guidelines
Facility Improvement
Facility Planning
Facility Requirements
Facility Utilization Research
Found Spaces
Relocatable Facilities
Site Analysis
Site Development
Space Utilization

Facility Guidelines   *JUL. 1966*
Postings: 1,318   GC: 920
SN Written guidelines, specifications, standards, or criteria used in assessing physical facility requirements
UF Facility Design
Facility Specifications
Facility Standards
BT Guidelines
RT Building Conversion
Building Design
Building Innovation
Construction Needs
Educational Facilities
Educational Facilities Planning
Facilities
Facility Case Studies
Facility Expansion
Facility Improvement
Facility Inventory

Facility Planning
Facility Requirements
Facility Utilization Research
Life Cycle Costing
Master Plans
Site Analysis
Space Utilization

Facility Improvement   *JUL. 1966*
Postings: 932   GC: 920
SN Remedying deficiencies in existing facilities or bringing facilities up to higher standards
UF Building Improvement (1966 1980)
Building Renovation
NT Educational Facilities Improvement
BT Improvement
RT Building Conversion
Building Obsolescence
Buildings
Capital Outlay (for Fixed Assets)
Facilities
Facility Expansion
Facility Guidelines
Facility Requirements

Facility Inventory   *JUL. 1966*
Postings: 490   GC: 920
UF Equipment Inventory
Materials Inventory
Property Inventory
RT Construction Programs
Educational Facilities
Equipment
Equipment Utilization
Facilities
Facility Case Studies
Facility Guidelines
Facility Requirements
Facility Utilization Research
Property Accounting
Resources
Space Classification
Supplies

Facility Needs
USE Facility Requirements

Facility Planning   *MAY 1974*
Postings: 1,288   GC: 920
SN Process of determining the purposes of facilities and the means (activities, procedures, resources, etc.) for attaining them
NT Educational Facilities Planning
BT Planning
RT Architectural Programming
Building Plans
Capital Outlay (for Fixed Assets)
Community Planning
Construction Costs
Construction Management
Construction Needs
Construction Programs
Design Build Approach
Design Requirements
Facilities
Facility Case Studies
Facility Expansion
Facility Guidelines
Facility Requirements
Facility Utilization Research
Fast Track Scheduling
Found Spaces
Land Use
Life Cycle Costing
Master Plans
Relocatable Facilities
Shared Facilities
Site Analysis
Site Development
Site Selection
Space Utilization
Spatial Relationship (Facilities)
Systems Building
Underground Facilities
Urban Planning

Facility Requirements   *AUG. 1968*
Postings: 1,315   GC: 920
SN Any aspect of the physical plant determined necessary to accommodate various functions
UF Facility Needs
BT Specifications
RT Building Conversion
Building Design
Building Innovation
Building Plans
Construction Needs
Design Requirements
Educational Facilities
Educational Facilities Planning
Facilities
Facility Case Studies
Facility Expansion
Facility Guidelines
Facility Improvement
Facility Inventory
Facility Planning
Facility Utilization Research
Master Plans
Space Utilization
Storage

Facility Specifications
USE Facility Guidelines

Facility Standards
USE Facility Guidelines

Facility Utilization Research   *JUL. 1966*
Postings: 639   GC: 810
BT Use Studies
RT Building Conversion
Building Design
Building Obsolescence
Building Plans
Buildings
College Buildings
Construction Programs
Design Requirements
Educational Complexes
Educational Facilities
Educational Facilities Planning
Equipment Storage
Facilities
Facility Case Studies
Facility Expansion
Facility Guidelines
Facility Inventory
Facility Planning
Facility Requirements
School Buildings
School Expansion
School Space
Space Classification
Space Utilization
Spatial Relationship (Facilities)
Storage

Facsimile Communication Systems (1968 1980)
USE Facsimile Transmission

Facsimile Transmission   *JUL. 1966*
Postings: 224   GC: 710
UF Facsimile Communication Systems (1968 1980)
Fax
Telefacsimile
Telefax
BT Telecommunications
RT Document Delivery
Electronic Equipment
Electronic Mail
Information Networks
Information Transfer
Input Output Devices
Reprography
Telephone Communications Systems

Factor Analysis   *JUL. 1966*
Postings: 4,648   GC: 820
SN Mathematical methods used to explain the relationships observed among a large

number of descriptive variables in terms of a smaller number of underlying or inferred factors
UF Centroid Method of Factor Analysis
Maximum Likelihood Factor Analysis #
Principal Components Analysis
NT Oblique Rotation
Orthogonal Rotation
BT Multivariate Analysis
RT Ability Identification
Cluster Analysis
Correlation
Discriminant Analysis
Factor Structure
Goodness of Fit
Item Analysis
Least Squares Statistics
Maximum Likelihood Statistics
Multidimensional Scaling
Multitrait Multimethod Techniques
Path Analysis
Personality Assessment
Q Methodology
Research Methodology
Structural Equation Models
Test Construction
Test Validity
Testing
Transformations (Mathematics)
Trend Analysis

Factor Structure   *JUL. 1966*
Postings: 1,637   GC: 820
SN The end product of factor analysis when the interrelationships and relative positions of the underlying factors used in the analysis have been established
RT Construct Validity
Factor Analysis
Item Analysis
Oblique Rotation
Orthogonal Rotation
Test Interpretation
Test Validity

Factual Reading (1966 1980)   *MAR. 1980*
Postings: 55   GC: 460
SN Invalid Descriptor—used inconsistently in indexing—see "Functional Reading" and "Reading Comprehension"

Faculty   *JUL. 1966*
Postings: 1,690   GC: 360
SN Academic staff members engaged in instruction, research, administration, or related educational activities in a school, college, or university (Note: Use a more specific term if possible)
NT Adjunct Faculty
College Faculty
Deans
Department Heads
Faculty Advisers
Full Time Faculty
Nontenured Faculty
Part Time Faculty
Tenured Faculty
Women Faculty
BT Professional Personnel
School Personnel
RT Academic Rank (Professional)
Administrators
Aging in Academia
Consultants
Diversity (Faculty)
Educational Resources
Faculty Development
Faculty Evaluation
Faculty Fellowships
Faculty Handbooks
Faculty Integration
Faculty Mobility
Faculty Organizations
Faculty Promotion
Faculty Publishing
Faculty Recruitment
Faculty Workload
Ombudsmen
Teachers

= Two or more Descriptors are used to represent this term.
The term's main entry shows the appropriate coordination.

Faculty Advancement
USE   Faculty Promotion

Faculty Advisers   MAR. 1980
      Postings: 1,032   GC: 240
SN   Academic staff members assigned to
      counsel students in academic and some-
      times nonacademic matters
UF   Faculty Advisors (1967 1980)
      Faculty Counselors
BT   Faculty
RT   Academic Advising
      Educational Counseling
      Faculty Workload
      Foreign Student Advisers
      Pupil Personnel Workers
      School Counseling
      School Counselors
      Student Adjustment
      Student College Relationship
      Student Personnel Workers
      Student School Relationship

Faculty Advisors (1967 1980)
USE   Faculty Advisers

Faculty College Relationship   OCT. 1979
      Postings: 1,576   GC: 320
SN   The relationship between a college or
      university and its faculty
UF   Teacher College Relationship
BT   Relationship
RT   Academic Freedom
      Arbitration
      Codes of Ethics
      Collective Bargaining
      College Environment
      College Faculty
      College Governing Councils
      Colleges
      Employer Employee Relationship
      Faculty Handbooks
      Faculty Workload
      Negotiation Agreements
      Participative Decision Making
      Student College Relationship
      Teacher Administrator Relationship
      Teacher Discipline
      Teacher Rights
      Teacher Welfare
      Unions

Faculty Counselors
USE   Faculty Advisers

Faculty Desegregation
USE   Faculty Integration

Faculty Development   OCT. 1977
      Postings: 6,083   GC: 320
SN   Activities to encourage and enhance fac-
      ulty professional growth
UF   Faculty Growth
      Faculty Improvement
BT   Professional Development
      Staff Development
RT   College Faculty
      Faculty
      Faculty Evaluation
      Faculty Fellowships
      Faculty Handbooks
      Faculty Promotion
      Faculty Publishing
      Individual Development
      Inservice Education
      Inservice Teacher Education
      Organizational Development
      Professional Continuing Education
      Professional Development Schools
      Professional Training
      Sabbatical Leaves
      Teacher Evaluation
      Teacher Exchange Programs
      Teacher Improvement
      Teacher Promotion

Faculty Evaluation   JUL. 1966
      Postings: 1,926   GC: 320
SN   Judging the value or competence of ad-
      ministrative, instructional, or other aca-
      demic staff in schools, colleges, or uni-
      versities based on established criteria
      (Note: For documents/articles only in-
      volving instructional staff or administra-
      tors, use "Teacher Evaluation" or "Ad-
      ministrator Evaluation"—before Mar80,
      this term did not carry a Scope Note)
BT   Personnel Evaluation
RT   Administrator Evaluation
      Faculty
      Faculty Development
      Faculty Promotion
      Faculty Workload
      Teacher Evaluation

Faculty Fellowships   JUL. 1966
      Postings: 59   GC: 620
BT   Fellowships
RT   Faculty
      Faculty Development
      Sabbatical Leaves

Faculty Growth
USE   Faculty Development

Faculty Handbooks   AUG. 1978
      Postings: 311   GC: 730
SN   Guidelines developed and published by a
      school, college, or university that outline
      the duties of faculty members, their roles
      within the institution, procedures, and/or
      organizational information
BT   Guides
      School Publications
RT   Administrator Guides
      Administrator Responsibility
      Administrator Role
      College Faculty
      Colleges
      Employer Employee Relationship
      Faculty
      Faculty College Relationship
      Faculty Development
      Faculty Workload
      Schools
      Staff Orientation
      Staff Role
      Teacher Administrator Relationship
      Teacher Orientation
      Teacher Responsibility
      Teacher Role
      Teacher Student Relationship
      Teaching Conditions
      Universities

Faculty Improvement
USE   Faculty Development

Faculty Integration   JUL. 1966
      Postings: 275   GC: 540
SN   Process of balancing the racial, ethnic,
      or sexual composition of the instruc-
      tional, administrative, or other academic
      staff of schools, colleges, or universities
      (Note: For documents/articles involving
      only instructional staff, use "Teacher
      Integration"—prior to Mar80, this differ-
      entiation was not made)
UF   Faculty Desegregation
      Integrated Faculty
BT   Personnel Integration
RT   Affirmative Action
      Diversity (Faculty)
      Equal Opportunities (Jobs)
      Faculty
      Teacher Integration

Faculty Load
USE   Faculty Workload

Faculty Mobility   JUL. 1966
      Postings: 739   GC: 330
SN   (Note: If possible, use the more precise
      term "Teacher Transfer")
UF   Teacher Attrition
      Teacher Mobility
      Teacher Turnover
BT   Occupational Mobility
RT   Faculty
      Teacher Persistence
      Teacher Placement
      Teacher Transfer
      Teaching (Occupation)

Faculty Offices
USE   Offices (Facilities)

Faculty Organizations   JUL. 1966
      Postings: 402   GC: 320
SN   Associations or groups composed of
      instructional, administrative, and other
      academic staff, usually at the college or
      university level (Note: See also "Teacher
      Associations"—prior to Mar80, this term
      was not restricted by a Scope Note)
BT   Organizations (Groups)
RT   College Faculty
      College Governing Councils
      Faculty
      Faculty Workload
      Professional Associations
      Teacher Associations
      Unions

Faculty Promotion   JUL. 1966
      Postings: 1,153   GC: 320
SN   Advancement in position or rank of ad-
      ministrative, instructional, or other aca-
      demic staff in schools, colleges, or uni-
      versities (Note: For documents/articles
      relating to the advancement of instruc-
      tional staff only, use "Teacher Promo-
      tion"—prior to Mar80, this differentia-
      tion was not made)
UF   Faculty Advancement
BT   Promotion (Occupational)
RT   Academic Rank (Professional)
      Faculty
      Faculty Development
      Faculty Evaluation
      Faculty Publishing
      Faculty Workload
      Teacher Promotion
      Tenure

Faculty Publishing   AUG. 1986
      Postings: 852   GC: 720
SN   The production and issuance of schol-
      arly writings by academia
RT   Academic Discourse
      Authors
      Faculty
      Faculty Development
      Faculty Promotion
      Faculty Workload
      Productivity
      Publications
      Publish or Perish Issue
      Research
      Scholarly Journals
      Scholarly Writing
      University Presses
      Writing for Publication

Faculty Rank
USE   Academic Rank (Professional)

Faculty Recruitment   JUL. 1966
      Postings: 711   GC: 320
SN   Process of attracting qualified academic
      staff members to vacant positions (Note:
      For recuritment of instructional staff only,
      use "Teacher Recruitment"—prior to
      Mar80, this differentiation was not made)
BT   Recruitment
RT   Administrator Selection
      Faculty
      Teacher Recruitment

Faculty Senates (Colleges)
USE   College Governing Councils

Faculty Workload   OCT. 1976
      Postings: 1,417   GC: 320
SN   The sum of all activities that take the time
      of the teacher or other faculty member
      and that are related either directly or
      indirectly to professional duties, respon-
      sibilities, and interests (Note: Prior to
      Oct76, the instruction "Faculty Load, USE
      Teaching Load" was carried in the The-
      saurus)
UF   Faculty Load
NT   Teaching Load
RT   Administrator Responsibility
      Contracts
      Educational Counseling
      Employer Employee Relationship
      Faculty
      Faculty Advisers
      Faculty College Relationship
      Faculty Evaluation
      Faculty Handbooks
      Faculty Organizations
      Faculty Promotion
      Faculty Publishing
      Full Time Faculty
      Noninstructional Responsibility
      Parent Teacher Conferences
      Part Time Faculty
      Sabbatical Leaves
      School Counseling
      Staff Meetings
      Staff Utilization
      State Standards
      Teacher Administrator Relationship
      Teacher Evaluation
      Teacher Promotion
      Teacher Responsibility
      Teaching Conditions
      Working Hours

Failure   MAR. 1980
      Postings: 1,592   GC: 820
SN   Achievements or accomplishments that
      do not meet stated expectations, re-
      quirements, or standards
UF   Failure Factors (1966 1980)
NT   Academic Failure
BT   Performance
RT   Achievement
      Achievement Need
      Evaluation
      Expectation
      Fear of Success
      Goal Orientation
      Helplessness
      Low Achievement
      Motivation
      Objectives
      Outcomes of Education
      Standards
      Success
      Underachievement

Failure Factors (1966 1980)
USE   Failure

Failure to Thrive   APR. 1986
      Postings: 40   GC: 120
SN   Growth disorder of infants and children
      associated with nutritional and/or emo-
      tional deprivation—characterized by low
      weight gain and psychosocial retarda-
      tion
UF   Nonorganic Failure to Thrive
BT   Diseases
RT   Body Weight
      Child Development
      Child Health
      Child Neglect
      Infant Behavior
      Nutrition
      Parent Child Relationship
      Physical Health
      Psychosomatic Disorders

= Two or more Descriptors are used to represent this term.
The term's main entry shows the appropriate coordination.

Fair Dealing (Copyrights)
USE　Fair Use (Copyrights)

Fair Use (Copyrights)　　　　　APR. 1990
　　Postings: 219　　　　　　　GC: 710
SN　Limited legal copying of copyrighted ma-
　　terials without express authorization, such
　　as for classroom use or private study
UF　Fair Dealing (Copyrights)
RT　Copyrights
　　Downloading
　　Reprography

Fairs
USE　Exhibits

Fairy Tales　　　　　　　　APR. 1990
　　Postings: 230　　　　　　　GC: 430
SN　Fanciful narratives, usually for children
　　and often embodied in folklore, about
　　mysterious forces and supernatural be-
　　ings (as fairies, wizards, and goblins)
BT　Tales
RT　Childrens Literature
　　Fables
　　Fantasy
　　Fiction
　　Folk Culture
　　Legends
　　Mythology

Faith
USE　Beliefs

Fallout Shelters　　　　　　JUL. 1966
　　Postings: 35　　　　　　　　GC: 920
UF　Air Raid Shelters
　　Bomb Shelters
BT　Facilities
RT　Civil Defense
　　Radiation
　　Radiation Effects
　　Safety
　　Underground Facilities
　　Windowless Rooms

Fame
USE　Reputation

Familiarity　　　　　　　　DEC. 1989
　　Postings: 193　　　　　　　GC: 110
SN　Close acquaintance with or considerable
　　knowledge of a person, object, situation,
　　task, or stimulus (Note: See also re-
　　lated Identifiers such as "Expertise" and
　　"Knowledge")
RT　Adjustment (to Environment)
　　Behavior Chaining
　　Child Behavior
　　Communication (Thought Transfer)
　　Comprehension
　　Conditioning
　　Examiners
　　Experience
　　Habituation
　　Infant Behavior
　　Interpersonal Communication
　　Interpersonal Competence
　　Interpersonal Relationship
　　Intimacy
　　Knowledge Level
　　Language Processing
　　Novelty (Stimulus Dimension)
　　Orientation
　　Perception
　　Performance
　　Prior Learning
　　Reaction Time
　　Recall (Psychology)
　　Recognition (Psychology)
　　Retention (Psychology)
　　Schemata (Cognition)
　　Scholarship
　　Skills
　　Stranger Reactions

Family (Sociological Unit)　　JUL. 1966
　　Postings: 3,465　　　　　　GC: 520
SN　Group of individuals related by blood,
　　marriage, adoption, or cohabitation (Note:
　　Use a more specific term if possible)
UF　Households
NT　Black Family
　　Dual Career Family
　　Extended Family
　　Foster Family
　　Nuclear Family
　　One Parent Family
　　Rural Family
　　Stepfamily
BT　Groups
RT　Adult Children
　　Birth Order
　　Children
　　Cohabitation
　　Daughters
　　Family Attitudes
　　Family Characteristics
　　Family English Literacy
　　Family Environment
　　Family Financial Resources
　　Family Health
　　Family History
　　Family Income
　　Family Influence
　　Family Involvement
　　Family Life
　　Family Literacy
　　Family Mobility
　　Family Needs
　　Family Planning
　　Family Problems
　　Family Programs
　　Family Relationship
　　Family Role
　　Family School Relationship
　　Family Size
　　Family Status
　　Family Structure
　　Family Violence
　　Family Work Relationship
　　First Born
　　Genealogy
　　Grandparents
　　Heads of Households
　　Home Management
　　Homemakers
　　Kinship
　　Marriage
　　Parents
　　Reunions
　　Siblings
　　Sons
　　Spouses
　　Twins

Family Attitudes　　　　　　JUL. 1966
　　Postings: 755　　　　　　　GC: 510
BT　Attitudes
RT　Family (Sociological Unit)
　　Family Counseling
　　Parent Attitudes

Family Background (1966 1980)
USE　Family Characteristics

Family Breadwinners
USE　Heads of Households

Family Caregivers　　　　　DEC. 1988
　　Postings: 422　　　　　　　GC: 510
SN　Individuals providing personal care to
　　their relatives (or, on occasion, close
　　friends)—such care is usually informal
　　and in the home (frequently for elderly
　　parents)
BT　Caregivers
RT　Adult Children
　　Caregiver Role
　　Family Involvement
　　Family Problems
　　Family Role
　　Frail Elderly
　　Home Programs

　　Homebound
　　Long Term Care

Family Characteristics　　　JUL. 1966
　　Postings: 3,781　　　　　　GC: 510
SN　Family attributes such as size, structure,
　　socioeconomic status, health, ethnicity,
　　etc.
UF　Family Background (1966 1980)
RT　Family (Sociological Unit)
　　Family Financial Resources
　　Family History
　　Family Income
　　Family Relationship
　　Family Size
　　Family Status
　　Family Structure
　　Parent Background

Family Choice (Education)
USE　School Choice

Family Counseling　　　　　JUL. 1966
　　Postings: 2,153　　　　　　GC: 240
BT　Counseling
RT　Family Attitudes
　　Family Influence
　　Family Problems
　　Family Relationship
　　Group Counseling
　　Group Dynamics
　　Group Therapy
　　Hospices (Terminal Care)
　　Marriage Counseling
　　Milieu Therapy
　　Parent Counseling

Family Culture
USE　Family Life

Family Day Care　　　　　　FEB. 1975
　　Postings: 858　　　　　　　GC: 520
SN　Care of children, by persons other than
　　their parents or guardians, in private
　　homes
UF　Home Day Care
BT　Day Care
RT　Employer Supported Day Care
　　Family Environment
　　School Age Day Care
　　Sick Child Care

Family Economics
USE　Consumer Economics

Family English Literacy　　　MAY 1997
　　Postings: 28　　　　　　　　GC: 460
SN　English literacy for limited-English-pro-
　　ficient and non-English-speaking
　　families—family English literacy pro-
　　grams usually include adult literacy, pre-
　　school/school-age education, and par-
　　enting education (Note: Use only for
　　English as a Second Language
　　programs—otherwise, use "Family Lit-
　　eracy")
BT　Family Literacy
RT　English (Second Language)
　　Family (Sociological Unit)
　　Limited English Speaking
　　Literacy Education
　　Non English Speaking

Family Environment　　　　　JUL. 1966
　　Postings: 3,906　　　　　　GC: 510
UF　Home
　　Home Conditions
　　Home Environment
BT　Environment
RT　Child Development
　　Daughters
　　Family (Sociological Unit)
　　Family Day Care
　　Family Influence
　　Family Relationship
　　Grandparents

　　Home Furnishings
　　Home Management
　　Housework
　　Housing
　　Parents
　　Permissive Environment
　　Siblings
　　Sons

Family Financial Resources　　MAR. 1980
　　Postings: 534　　　　　　　GC: 620
SN　A family's immediate and/or possible
　　sources of revenue
UF　Family Resources (1966 1980)
BT　Resources
RT　Child Support
　　Family (Sociological Unit)
　　Family Characteristics
　　Family Income
　　Family Status
　　Parent Financial Contribution

Family Health　　　　　　　JUL. 1966
　　Postings: 447　　　　　　　GC: 210
BT　Health
RT　Child Health
　　Family (Sociological Unit)
　　Family Practice (Medicine)
　　Hygiene
　　Primary Health Care

Family History　　　　　　　JAN. 1985
　　Postings: 331　　　　　　　GC: 430
SN　History that identifies or traces the struc-
　　ture, size, membership, customs, eth-
　　nicity, migration, socioeconomic status,
　　biological characteristics, or lineal de-
　　scent of a family or families
NT　Genealogy
BT　History
RT　Family (Sociological Unit)
　　Family Characteristics
　　Family Life
　　Family Relationship
　　Kinship
　　Local History
　　Oral History
　　Social History

Family Income　　　　　　　JUL. 1966
　　Postings: 1,586　　　　　　GC: 620
BT　Income
RT　Child Support
　　Family (Sociological Unit)
　　Family Characteristics
　　Family Financial Resources
　　Family Status
　　Parent Financial Contribution

Family Influence　　　　　　JUL. 1966
　　Postings: 3,284　　　　　　GC: 510
UF　Home Influence
BT　Influences
RT　Family (Sociological Unit)
　　Family Counseling
　　Family Environment
　　Family Involvement
　　Family Role
　　Family Status
　　Parent Influence

Family Involvement　　　　　JUL. 1966
　　Postings: 1,847　　　　　　GC: 510
UF　Family Participation
BT　Participation
RT　Family (Sociological Unit)
　　Family Caregivers
　　Family Influence
　　Family Life Education
　　Family Role
　　Individualized Family Service Plans
　　Parent Participation

Family Job Relationship
USE　Family Work Relationship

= Two or more Descriptors are used to represent this term.
The term's main entry shows the appropriate coordination.

Family Life   *JUL. 1966*
    Postings: 3,427   GC: 510
UF   Family Culture
        Family Living
        Home Life
RT   Adult Children
        Black Family
        Children
        Cohabitation
        Daughters
        Extended Family
        Family (Sociological Unit)
        Family History
        Family Life Education
        Family Programs
        Family Work Relationship
        Grandparents
        Group Experience
        Homemakers
        Homemaking Skills
        Housework
        Marital Instability
        Marital Satisfaction
        Marriage
        Marriage Counseling
        Nuclear Family
        Parenthood Education
        Parents
        Siblings
        Sons
        Spouses
        Stepfamily

Family Life Education   *JUL. 1966*
    Postings: 1,290   GC: 400
UF   Home and Family Life Education
NT   Parenthood Education
        Sex Education
BT   Education
RT   Consumer Education
        Family Involvement
        Family Life
        Family Relationship
        Home Management

Family Literacy   *MAY 1997*
    Postings: 577   GC: 460
SN   Literacy for all family members—family
        literacy programs frequently combine
        adult literacy, preschool/school-age edu-
        cation, and parenting education (Note:
        Use the more specific term "Family Eng-
        lish Literacy" for English as a Second
        Language programs)
UF   Child Parent Literacy
        Parent Child Literacy
NT   Family English Literacy
BT   Literacy
RT   Adult Literacy
        Emergent Literacy
        Family (Sociological Unit)
        Family School Relationship
        Literacy Education
        Parents as Teachers

Family Living
USE   Family Life

Family Management (1966 1980)
USE   Home Management

Family Mobility   *JUL. 1966*
    Postings: 185   GC: 550
SN   Geographic movement of families (Note:
        For family social mobility, coordinate
        "Social Mobility" and appropriate "fam-
        ily" Descriptors—prior to Mar80, this
        term was not restricted by a Scope Note)
BT   Migration
RT   Family (Sociological Unit)
        Place of Residence
        Relocation
        Residential Patterns
        Student Mobility

Family Needs   *JUN. 1996*
    Postings: 340   GC: 520
SN   Conditions or factors necessary for opti-

mal function, development, or well-be-
ing of families
BT   Needs
RT   Childhood Needs
        Family (Sociological Unit)
        Family Problems
        Family Programs

Family Participation
USE   Family Involvement

Family Planning   *JUL. 1966*
    Postings: 1,125   GC: 210
SN   Voluntary regulation of the spacing and/or
        number of births in a family—includes
        programs or counseling to assist indi-
        viduals or couples with such planning
BT   Planning
RT   Abortions
        Birth Rate
        Childlessness
        Contraception
        Early Parenthood
        Family (Sociological Unit)
        Family Size
        Overpopulation
        Population Education
        Population Growth
        Population Trends
        Pregnancy
        Reproduction (Biology)

Family Practice (Medicine)   *MAR. 1980*
    Postings: 412   GC: 210
UF   General Practice (Medicine)
BT   Medicine
RT   Family Health
        Gynecology
        Internal Medicine
        Medical Services
        Obstetrics
        Pediatrics
        Primary Health Care

Family Problems   *JUL. 1966*
    Postings: 3,599   GC: 530
BT   Problems
RT   Battered Women
        Child Abuse
        Child Custody
        Child Neglect
        Children
        Divorce
        Early Parenthood
        Elder Abuse
        Emotional Abuse
        Family (Sociological Unit)
        Family Caregivers
        Family Counseling
        Family Needs
        Family Violence
        Frail Elderly
        Group Homes
        Hospices (Terminal Care)
        Long Term Care
        Marital Instability
        Marriage Counseling
        Missing Children
        Parents
        Problem Children
        Respite Care
        Runaways
        Sick Child Care
        Visiting Homemakers

Family Programs   *JUL. 1966*
    Postings: 2,646   GC: 520
SN   Plans or courses of action developed
        and/or implemented by governmental
        units or other organizations to provide
        supporting services and resources to
        families (Note: Prior to Sep81, the use of
        this term was not restricted by a Scope
        Note)
UF   Family Projects (1966 1980)
        Family Services Policy #
BT   Programs
RT   Family (Sociological Unit)
        Family Life

Family Needs
Individualized Family Service Plans
Integrated Services

Family Projects (1966 1980)
USE   Family Programs

Family Relationship   *JUL. 1966*
    Postings: 4,036   GC: 510
NT   Parent Child Relationship
        Sibling Relationship
BT   Interpersonal Relationship
RT   Child Rearing
        Childlessness
        Cohabitation
        Early Parenthood
        Extended Family
        Family (Sociological Unit)
        Family Characteristics
        Family Counseling
        Family Environment
        Family History
        Family Life Education
        Family Size
        Family Status
        Family Structure
        Housework
        Kinship
        Midlife Transitions
        Nuclear Family
        Parenthood Education
        Parenting Skills
        Significant Others
        Stepfamily

Family Resources (1966 1980)
USE   Family Financial Resources

Family Role   *JUL. 1966*
    Postings: 1,770   GC: 510
BT   Role
RT   Adult Children
        Caregiver Role
        Child Role
        Family (Sociological Unit)
        Family Caregivers
        Family Influence
        Family Involvement
        Parent Role

Family School Relationship   *JUL. 1966*
    Postings: 2,124   GC: 330
UF   Home School Relationship
        School Family Relationship
        School Home Relationship
NT   Parent School Relationship
BT   Relationship
RT   Culture Conflict
        Family (Sociological Unit)
        Family Literacy
        Integrated Services
        Partnerships in Education
        Politics of Education
        School Attitudes
        School Community Relationship
        School Involvement
        School Role
        Schools
        Student School Relationship

Family Services Policy
USE   Family Programs
AND   Public Policy

Family Size   *JUN. 1983*
    Postings: 338   GC: 520
RT   Birth Rate
        Childlessness
        Dependents
        Extended Family
        Family (Sociological Unit)
        Family Characteristics
        Family Planning
        Family Relationship
        Family Structure
        Housing
        Nuclear Family

One Parent Family
Population Growth
Population Trends
Siblings

Family Status   *JUL. 1966*
    Postings: 288   GC: 510
BT   Group Status
RT   Family (Sociological Unit)
        Family Characteristics
        Family Financial Resources
        Family Income
        Family Influence
        Family Relationship

Family Structure   *JUL. 1966*
    Postings: 2,232   GC: 520
SN   Organizational framework that determines
        family membership, and the functions
        and hierarchical position of family mem-
        bers
NT   Birth Order
BT   Group Structure
RT   Adult Children
        Black Family
        Childlessness
        Dependents
        Dual Career Family
        Extended Family
        Family (Sociological Unit)
        Family Characteristics
        Family Relationship
        Family Size
        Family Work Relationship
        Homemakers
        Kinship
        Nuclear Family
        One Parent Family
        Siblings
        Social Structure
        Stepfamily
        Unwed Mothers

Family Trees
USE   Genealogy

Family Unity
USE   Group Unity

Family Violence   *OCT. 1984*
    Postings: 700   GC: 530
SN   Injurious or abusive physical force among
        members of a family or household
UF   Domestic Violence (Family)
BT   Violence
RT   Battered Women
        Child Abuse
        Crime
        Elder Abuse
        Family (Sociological Unit)
        Family Problems
        Marital Instability
        Victims of Crime

Family Work Relationship   *MAY 1994*
    Postings: 419   GC: 520
SN   Effect of work on the family and/or effect
        of the family on work
UF   Family Job Relationship
        Job Family Relationship
        Work Family Relationship
BT   Relationship
RT   Careers
        Dual Career Family
        Employed Parents
        Employment
        Family (Sociological Unit)
        Family Life
        Family Structure
        Job Satisfaction
        Life Satisfaction
        Work Environment
        Work Ethic

Fantasy   *JUL. 1966*
    Postings: 759   GC: 120
RT   Dreams

= Two or more Descriptors are used to represent this term.
The term's main entry shows the appropriate coordination.

Fables
Fairy Tales
Fiction
Imagination
Pretend Play
Science Fiction

Fantasy Play
USE　Pretend Play

Farm Accounts　　　　　　　　　　　　JUL. 1966
　　　Postings: 90　　　　　　　　　　　GC: 410
BT　Records (Forms)
RT　Accountants
　　Accounting
　　Farm Management

Farm Agents
USE　Extension Agents

Farm Foremen
USE　Crew Leaders

Farm Labor　　　　　　　　　　　　　JUL. 1966
　　　Postings: 310　　　　　　　　　　GC: 410
SN　All labor involved in farm operations
　　(Note: For unskilled farm labor, coordi-
　　nate this term with "Agricultural Labor-
　　ers"—prior to Mar80, the Thesaurus
　　carried the instruction "Farm Laborers
　　or Farm Workers, USE Agricultural La-
　　borers")
UF　Farm Labor Legislation (1966 1980) #
　　Farm Labor Problems (1966 1980) #
　　Farm Labor Supply (1966 1980) #
BT　Labor
RT　Agricultural Laborers
　　Agricultural Personnel
　　Farm Occupations
　　Farmers
　　Rural Women

Farm Labor Legislation (1966 1980)
USE　Farm Labor
AND　Labor Legislation

Farm Labor Problems (1966 1980)
USE　Farm Labor
AND　Labor Problems

Farm Labor Supply (1966 1980)
USE　Farm Labor
AND　Labor Supply

Farm Management　　　　　　　　　JUL. 1966
　　　Postings: 532　　　　　　　　　　GC: 410
BT　Administration
RT　Agricultural Education
　　Agricultural Engineering
　　Agricultural Occupations
　　Agricultural Production
　　Agriculture
　　Farm Accounts
　　Farm Visits
　　Farmers

Farm Mechanics (Occupation) (1967 1980)
USE　Agricultural Machinery Occupations

Farm Mechanics (Subject)
USE　Agricultural Engineering

Farm Occupations　　　　　　　　　JUL. 1966
　　　Postings: 195　　　　　　　　　　GC: 410
BT　Agricultural Occupations
RT　Agriculture
　　Animal Husbandry
　　Dairy Farmers
　　Farm Labor
　　Farmers
　　Off Farm Agricultural Occupations
　　Part Time Farmers
　　Sharecroppers

Farm Operators
USE　Farmers

Farm Related Occupations
USE　Off Farm Agricultural Occupations

Farm Supplies
USE　Agricultural Supplies

Farm Visits　　　　　　　　　　　　AUG. 1968
　　　Postings: 63　　　　　　　　　　GC: 410
BT　Field Trips
RT　Adult Farmer Education
　　Agriculture
　　Experiential Learning
　　Farm Management
　　Farmers
　　Supervised Occupational Experience
　　　(Agriculture)
　　Young Farmer Education

Farm Women
USE　Rural Women

Farm Youth
USE　Rural Youth

Farmers　　　　　　　　　　　　　　JUL. 1966
　　　Postings: 977　　　　　　　　　　GC: 410
UF　Farm Operators
NT　Dairy Farmers
　　Part Time Farmers
　　Sharecroppers
BT　Agricultural Personnel
RT　Adult Farmer Education
　　Agricultural Occupations
　　Agricultural Production
　　Agriculture
　　Farm Labor
　　Farm Management
　　Farm Occupations
　　Farm Visits
　　Rural Farm Residents
　　Rural Women
　　Young Farmer Education

Farsi (Language)
USE　Persian

Farsightedness
USE　Hyperopia

Fascism　　　　　　　　　　　　　　MAR. 1982
　　　Postings: 37　　　　　　　　　　GC: 610
SN　A political philosophy or movement that
　　exalts nation and stands for a centralized
　　autocratic government, economic and
　　social regimentation, and suppression of
　　opposition
NT　Nazism
BT　Social Systems
RT　Anti Intellectualism
　　Capitalism
　　Communism
　　Economics
　　Government (Administrative Body)
　　Imperialism
　　Nationalism
　　Political Science
　　Socialism
　　Totalitarianism

Fashion Industry　　　　　　　　　JUN. 1977
　　　Postings: 252　　　　　　　　　　GC: 650
SN　Concerned with the design, production,
　　and marketing of clothing
UF　Apparel Industry
　　Clothing Industry
　　Garment Industry
BT　Industry
RT　Clothing
　　Clothing Design
　　Clothing Instruction
　　Needle Trades

Occupational Home Economics
Service Occupations
Sewing Instruction
Sewing Machine Operators
Textiles Instruction

Fashions (Clothing)
USE　Clothing

Fast Track Scheduling　　　　　　DEC. 1972
　　　Postings: 51　　　　　　　　　　GC: 920
SN　A construction management technique
　　in which design and construction proc-
　　ess activities are scheduled to overlap
　　rather than scheduled sequentially
BT　Scheduling
RT　Construction Management
　　Construction Programs
　　Critical Path Method
　　Design Build Approach
　　Facility Planning
　　Systems Building

Fat Ratio
USE　Body Composition

Father Absence
USE　Fatherless Family

Father Attitudes　　　　　　　　　AUG. 1982
　　　Postings: 147　　　　　　　　　　GC: 510
SN　Attitudes of, not toward, fathers
BT　Parent Attitudes
RT　Fathers
　　Mother Attitudes

Father Role
USE　Fathers
AND　Parent Role

Fatherless Family　　　　　　　　　JUL. 1966
　　　Postings: 474　　　　　　　　　　GC: 510
UF　Father Absence
BT　One Parent Family
RT　Births to Single Women
　　Displaced Homemakers
　　Divorce
　　Feminization of Poverty
　　Heads of Households
　　Motherless Family
　　Mothers
　　Unwed Mothers
　　Widowed

Fathers　　　　　　　　　　　　　　JUL. 1966
　　　Postings: 1,837　　　　　　　　　GC: 510
UF　Father Role #
　　Middle Class Fathers (1966 1980) #
BT　Males
　　Parents
RT　Employed Parents
　　Father Attitudes
　　Heads of Households
　　Motherless Family
　　One Parent Family
　　Parent Associations
　　Parent Child Relationship
　　Parent Influence
　　Parent Role

Fatigue (Biology)　　　　　　　　　APR. 1969
　　　Postings: 145　　　　　　　　　　GC: 210
UF　Exhaustion
　　Weariness
RT　Energy
　　Exercise Physiology
　　Health
　　Physical Fitness
　　Sensory Deprivation
　　Sleep
　　Symptoms (Individual Disorders)

Fax
USE　Facsimile Transmission

Fear　　　　　　　　　　　　　　　JUL. 1966
　　　Postings: 984　　　　　　　　　　GC: 230
NT　Fear of Success
　　School Phobia
BT　Psychological Patterns
RT　Anxiety
　　Depression (Psychology)
　　Emotional Problems
　　Helplessness
　　Homophobia
　　Neurosis
　　Nightmares
　　Paranoid Behavior
　　Withdrawal (Psychology)

Fear of Success　　　　　　　　　AUG. 1978
　　　Postings: 154　　　　　　　　　　GC: 230
SN　Need to refrain from maximally utilizing
　　one's abilities in achievement situations
　　because of expected negative conse-
　　quences
UF　Success Avoidance
BT　Fear
RT　Achievement
　　Failure
　　Goal Orientation
　　Inhibition
　　Low Achievement
　　Motivation
　　Self Motivation
　　Sex Role
　　Success
　　Underachievement

Feasibility Studies　　　　　　　　JUL. 1966
　　　Postings: 1,238　　　　　　　　　GC: 810
SN　Investigations or surveys to determine
　　the practicability of instituting a pro-
　　gram, course, larger study, or other pro-
　　posed activity (Note: As of Oct81, use as
　　a minor Descriptor for examples of this
　　kind of research—use as a major Descrip-
　　tor only as the subject of a document)
BT　Research
RT　Experimental Programs
　　Pilot Projects
　　Surveys

Feature Stories　　　　　　　　　APR. 1990
　　　Postings: 107　　　　　　　　　　GC: 720
SN　Prominent articles or reports in newspa-
　　pers, periodicals, or broadcast media,
　　usually providing background or analy-
　　sis of news, often presented in personal
　　style, and frequently of more lasting
　　interest than general news stories
RT　Broadcast Journalism
　　Journalism
　　New Journalism
　　News Media
　　News Reporting
　　News Writing
　　Newspapers
　　Periodicals

Federal Aid　　　　　　　　　　　JUL. 1966
　　　Postings: 10,076　　　　　　　　GC: 620
UF　Federal Grants
NT　Revenue Sharing
　　State Federal Aid
RT　Block Grants
　　Categorical Aid
　　Developing Institutions
　　Educational Finance
　　Eligibility
　　Equalization Aid
　　Federal Government
　　Federal Indian Relationship
　　Federal Programs
　　Federal Regulation
　　Finance Reform
　　Financial Support
　　Foundation Programs
　　Government School Relationship
　　Grantsmanship
　　Incentive Grants
　　Land Grant Universities
　　Library Funding
　　New Federalism

= Two or more Descriptors are used to represent this term.
The term's main entry shows the appropriate coordination.

Private School Aid
Public Support
School Funds
School Support
Technical Assistance
Training Allowances
Veterans Education

Federal Control
USE   Federal Regulation

Federal Court Litigation (1966 1980)
USE   Court Litigation
AND   Federal Courts

Federal Courts   *JUL. 1966*
       Postings: 1,238   GC: 610
UF   Federal Court Litigation (1966 1980) #
BT   Courts
RT   Court Litigation
       Federal Government
       Federal Legislation
       State Courts

Federal Government   *JUL. 1966*
       Postings: 5,808   GC: 610
UF   Federal Libraries #
BT   Government (Administrative Body)
RT   Federal Aid
       Federal Courts
       Federal Indian Relationship
       Federal Legislation
       Federal Programs
       Federal Regulation
       Federal State Relationship
       Federalism
       Government Employees
       Government School Relationship
       Military Organizations
       National Parks
       National Security
       New Federalism
       Presidential Campaigns (United States)
       Presidents of the United States
       Public Agencies
       State Church Separation
       Treaties
       Tribal Sovereignty
       Trust Responsibility (Government)

Federal Grants
USE   Federal Aid

Federal Indian Relationship   *OCT. 1979*
       Postings: 833   GC: 610
SN   Relationship between the United States
       government and the American Indians,
       including legal obligations to protect and
       enhance Indian trust resources and tribal
       self-government while providing eco-
       nomic and social programs necessary to
       a level comparable to non-Indian society
BT   Relationship
RT   American Indian Education
       American Indian History
       American Indian Reservations
       American Indians
       Federal Aid
       Federal Government
       Federal Programs
       Treaties
       Tribal Government
       Tribal Sovereignty
       Tribally Controlled Education
       Tribes
       Trust Responsibility (Government)

Federal Laws (1966 1974)
USE   Federal Legislation

Federal Legislation   *JUL. 1966*
       Postings: 13,948   GC: 610
UF   Federal Laws (1966 1974)
       Federal Recreation Legislation (1966
         1978) #
BT   Legislation

RT   Federal Courts
       Federal Government
       Federal Regulation
       Federalism
       Laws
       Legislators
       Local Legislation
       New Federalism
       Revenue Sharing
       State Legislation
       Treaties
       Tribal Sovereignty

Federal Libraries
USE   Federal Government
AND   Government Libraries

Federal Programs   *JUL. 1966*
       Postings: 11,485   GC: 610
SN   Programs sponsored by the federal gov-
       ernment (Note: Do not confuse with "Na-
       tional Programs"—prior to Mar80, the
       use of this term was not restricted by a
       Scope Note)
BT   Programs
RT   County Programs
       Federal Aid
       Federal Government
       Federal Indian Relationship
       Federal State Relationship
       Federalism
       Individualized Education Programs
       Individualized Family Service Plans
       National Programs
       New Federalism
       Public Agencies
       Public Policy
       State Programs
       Student Loan Programs

Federal Recreation Legislation (1966 1978)
USE   Federal Legislation
AND   Recreation Legislation

Federal Regulation   *SEP. 1977*
       Postings: 3,272   GC: 610
SN   Federal government control or influence
       based on legislation
UF   Federal Control
BT   Governance
RT   Civil Law
       Compliance (Legal)
       Copyrights
       Federal Aid
       Federal Government
       Federal Legislation
       Federal State Relationship
       Federalism
       Government Role
       Government School Relationship
       Institutional Autonomy
       Patents
       State Regulation

Federal State Aid
USE   State Federal Aid

Federal State Relationship   *JUL. 1966*
       Postings: 1,806   GC: 610
UF   State Federal Relationship
BT   Relationship
RT   Block Grants
       Board Administrator Relationship
       Federal Government
       Federal Programs
       Federal Regulation
       Federalism
       Government School Relationship
       New Federalism
       Revenue Sharing
       State Government
       State Regulation
       States Powers
       Statewide Planning

Federal Troops (1966 1980)
USE   Armed Forces

Federalism   *OCT. 1994*
       Postings: 79   GC: 610
SN   Principle of shared power between a
       central government and constituent unit
       governments—often prescribed by a writ-
       ten constitution (Note: See also the Iden-
       tifiers "Federalists" and "Federalist
       Papers")
NT   New Federalism
RT   Constitutional History
       Constitutional Law
       Federal Government
       Federal Legislation
       Federal Programs
       Federal Regulation
       Federal State Relationship
       Government (Administrative Body)
       Government Role
       Governmental Structure
       Political Attitudes
       Political Science
       States Powers
       United States History

Feed Industry   *JUL. 1966*
       Postings: 21   GC: 410
BT   Industry
RT   Agribusiness
       Agricultural Supplies
       Agricultural Supply Occupations
       Agriculture
       Feed Stores
       Food
       Food Processing Occupations
       Grains (Food)
       Off Farm Agricultural Occupations

Feed Stores   *JUL. 1966*
       Postings: 3   GC: 410
UF   Livestock Feed Stores
BT   Facilities
RT   Agricultural Supplies
       Feed Industry
       Merchandising

Feedback   *JUL. 1966*
       Postings: 5,925   GC: 710
SN   A response within a system that returns
       to the input a part of the output, thus
       influencing the continued activity or pro-
       ductivity of that system
UF   Knowledge of Results
NT   Biofeedback
BT   Interaction
RT   Audience Response
       Behavior
       Communication (Thought Transfer)
       Computer Assisted Instruction
       Cybernetics
       Delphi Technique
       Error Correction
       Guided Design
       Information Processing
       Learning Processes
       Man Machine Systems
       Motivation
       Performance
       Programmed Instruction
       Reinforcement
       Teacher Response

Feeder Patterns   *JUL. 1966*
       Postings: 46   GC: 330
SN   Routes or plans by which students are
       brought into a school jurisdiction
UF   Feeder Programs (1966 1980)
RT   Bus Transportation
       Busing
       Enrollment Trends
       Magnet Schools
       School Demography
       School District Reorganization

Feeder Programs (1966 1980)
USE   Feeder Patterns

Fees   *SEP. 1969*
       Postings: 976   GC: 620
UF   Dues
NT   Fines (Penalties)
       Tuition
BT   Costs
RT   Financial Support
       Library Funding
       Student Costs

Fellows (Medical)
USE   Graduate Medical Students

Fellowships   *JUL. 1966*
       Postings: 657   GC: 620
SN   Awards, usually in graduate education,
       given to assist students with the cost of
       study—may or may not require teaching
       or other special duties
NT   Faculty Fellowships
BT   Student Financial Aid
RT   Assistantships
       Awards
       Educational Finance
       Educational Vouchers
       Eligibility
       Grants
       Instructional Student Costs
       Noninstructional Student Costs
       Research Assistants
       Scholarship Funds
       Scholarships
       Student Costs
       Teaching Assistants

Female Homosexuality
USE   Lesbianism

Female Role
USE   Females
AND   Sex Role

Females   *JUL. 1966*
       Postings: 24,144   GC: 120
UF   Female Role #
       Girls
       Women
NT   Battered Women
       Daughters
       Displaced Homemakers
       Employed Women
       Mothers
       Nuns
       Pregnant Students
       Rural Women
BT   Groups
RT   Femininity
       Feminism
       Feminist Criticism
       Feminization of Poverty
       Gender Issues
       Gynecology
       Lesbianism
       Menstruation
       Obstetrics
       Sex
       Sex Differences
       Sex Role
       Sex Stereotypes
       Single Sex Colleges
       Single Sex Schools
       Sororities
       Spouses
       Womens Athletics
       Womens Education
       Womens Studies

Femininity   *JUN. 2000*
       Postings: 232   GC: 120
SN   The quality or condition of being
       feminine—may be considered to be de-
       termined or affected by biological, so-
       cial, or cultural factors
RT   Androgyny
       Females
       Feminism
       Gender Issues
       Masculinity

= Two or more Descriptors are used to represent this term.
The term's main entry shows the appropriate coordination.

Self Concept
Sex Differences
Sex Role
Sex Stereotypes
Sexual Identity

Feminism   NOV. 1970
Postings: 4,406   GC: 540
UF   Womens Liberation
     Womens Rights
RT   Civil Rights
     Consciousness Raising
     Females
     Femininity
     Feminist Criticism
     Gender Issues
     Life Style
     Sex Discrimination
     Sex Fairness
     Womens Studies

Feminist Criticism   SEP. 1996
Postings: 349   GC: 540
SN   Description, interpretation, and evalua-
     tion of literature, art, music, educational
     programs, etc., from a feminist perspec-
     tive (i.e., of female consciousness,
     women's rights, and the resistance to
     male domination)
BT   Criticism
RT   Art Criticism
     Females
     Feminism
     Film Criticism
     Gender Issues
     Literary Criticism
     Rhetorical Criticism
     Womens Studies

Feminization of Poverty   JUN. 1993
Postings: 74   GC: 530
SN   Trend towards disproportionately large
     numbers of women at or below poverty
     level
RT   Fatherless Family
     Females
     Poverty
     Sex Discrimination

Fencing (Sport)   JUN. 1984
Postings: 3   GC: 470
UF   Epee Fencing
BT   Athletics
RT   Olympic Games

Fenestration
USE   Windows

Fenno Ugric Languages
USE   Finno Ugric Languages

Fens
USE   Wetlands

Fertility Rate
USE   Birth Rate

Fertilizers   JUL. 1966
Postings: 98   GC: 410
RT   Agricultural Chemical Occupations
     Agricultural Supplies
     Agronomy
     Plant Growth
     Soil Science

Fetal Alcohol Syndrome   JAN. 1994
Postings: 128   GC: 220
SN   A medical condition resulting from ma-
     ternal alcohol abuse during pregnancy—
     it is characterized by growth deficiency
     (low weight or short length), facial and
     other physical abnormalities, and cen-
     tral nervous system impairments (e.g.,
     abnormal smallness of the head,

hyperactivity, motor problems, and cog-
nitive disabilities)
BT   Congenital Impairments
     Diseases
RT   Alcohol Abuse
     Alcoholism
     Mental Retardation
     Neurological Impairments
     Pregnancy
     Prenatal Drug Exposure
     Prenatal Influences

Fetal Care
USE   Prenatal Care

Fetal Drug Exposure
USE   Prenatal Drug Exposure

Fiction   JUL. 1966
Postings: 2,305   GC: 430
NT   Novels
     Science Fiction
     Short Stories
BT   Prose
RT   Comics (Publications)
     Drama
     Fables
     Fairy Tales
     Fantasy
     Humor
     Imagination
     Legends
     Literary Devices
     Literary Genres
     Nonfiction
     Poetry
     Tales

Field Check (1967 1980)
USE   Equipment Evaluation

Field Crops   SEP. 1968
Postings: 204   GC: 410
NT   Grains (Food)
     Tobacco
BT   Plants (Botany)
RT   Agribusiness
     Agricultural Production
     Agronomy
     Botany
     Crop Processing Occupations
     Harvesting
     Horticulture

Field Dependence
USE   Field Dependence Independence

Field Dependence Independence   OCT. 1983
Postings: 527   GC: 110
SN   Cognitive style or aspect of personality
     seen in the psychological perception of
     objects in a background field—field de-
     pendence refers to a tendency to experi-
     ence events globally, while field indepen-
     dence refers to a tendency to approach
     the environment in analytical terms
UF   Field Dependence
     Field Independence
BT   Cognitive Style
RT   Cognitive Processes
     Extraversion Introversion
     Locus of Control
     Perception Tests
     Personality Measures
     Visual Perception

Field Experience Programs   JUL. 1966
Postings: 3,045   GC: 350
SN   Practical experiential learning activities
     under institutional or organizational spon-
     sorship, usually away from the class-
     room or campus—associated most of-
     ten with grades 10–16, and characterized
     as less formal and concentrated than
     professional internship programs (Note:

Before Jun78, the use of this term was
not restricted by a Scope Note)
UF   Field Laboratory Experience
NT   Supervised Occupational Experience
     (Agriculture)
BT   Experiential Learning
     Programs
RT   Adventure Education
     Affiliated Schools
     Apprenticeships
     Clinical Experience
     Cooperative Education
     Field Instruction
     Field Trips
     Internship Programs
     Nontraditional Education
     On the Job Training
     Practicum Supervision
     Practicums
     Student Experience
     Student Teaching
     Teacher Centers
     Teaching Experience
     Work Experience Programs

Field Experiment Stations
USE   Experiment Stations

Field Hockey   DEC. 1975
Postings: 16   GC: 470
BT   Team Sports
RT   Olympic Games

Field Houses   JUL. 1966
Postings: 37   GC: 920
BT   Facilities
RT   Athletic Fields
     Athletics
     Gymnasiums
     Physical Education Facilities
     Physical Recreation Programs
     Recreational Facilities

Field Independence
USE   Field Dependence Independence

Field Instruction   JUL. 1966
Postings: 568   GC: 350
SN   Instruction that takes place outside the
     school and enables students to learn
     about something by taking an active part
     in it
UF   Field Teaching
BT   Instruction
RT   Experiential Learning
     Field Experience Programs
     Field Trips

Field Interviews   JUL. 1966
Postings: 353   GC: 810
BT   Interviews
RT   Caseworker Approach

Field Laboratory Experience
USE   Field Experience Programs

Field Properties (Mathematics)
USE   Properties (Mathematics)

Field Studies   JUL. 1966
Postings: 1,696   GC: 810
SN   Academic or other investigative studies
     undertaken in a natural setting, rather
     than in laboratories, classrooms, or other
     structured environments (Note: As of
     Oct81, use as a minor Descriptor for
     examples of this kind of research—use
     as a major Descriptor only as the subject
     of a document)
BT   Research
RT   Area Studies
     Educational Research
     Naturalistic Observation
     Qualitative Research
     Research Methodology

Field Teaching
USE   Field Instruction

Field Tests   MAR. 1980
Postings: 508   GC: 830
SN   On site evaluation of equipment, pro-
     grams, personnel, etc.
UF   On Site Tests
BT   Tests
RT   Demonstration Programs
     Equipment Evaluation
     Inspection
     Program Evaluation

Field Trips   JUL. 1966
Postings: 2,150   GC: 350
UF   Airborne Field Trips (1968 1980)
     Excursions (Instruction)
     Instructional Trips (1966 1980)
     Study Trips
NT   Farm Visits
RT   Adventure Education
     Class Activities
     Experiential Learning
     Field Experience Programs
     Field Instruction
     Outdoor Education
     Travel

Fifteenth Century Literature   MAY 1969
Postings: 12   GC: 430
BT   Literature
RT   Literary History
     Medieval Literature
     Renaissance Literature

Figural Aftereffects   JUN. 1969
Postings: 38   GC: 110
BT   Sensory Experience
RT   Auditory Perception
     Kinesthetic Perception
     Perception
     Psychophysiology
     Tactual Perception
     Visual Perception

Figurative Language   JUL. 1966
Postings: 593   GC: 430
UF   Figures of Speech
NT   Allegory
     Ambiguity
     Antithesis
     Imagery
     Irony
     Metaphors
     Puns
     Symbols (Literary)
BT   Language
     Literary Devices
RT   Literature
     Parody
     Satire

Figures of Speech
USE   Figurative Language

File Clerks   AUG. 1968
Postings: 18   GC: 640
UF   Classification Clerks
     Record Clerks
BT   Clerical Workers
RT   Filing
     Medical Record Technicians

File Management Systems
USE   Database Management Systems

Filing   JUL. 1969
Postings: 219   GC: 710
SN   Process of arranging materials in a use-
     ful order
UF   Alphabetic Filing
     Numeric Filing
BT   Documentation
RT   Alphabetizing Skills

= Two or more Descriptors are used to represent this term.
The term's main entry shows the appropriate coordination.

Business Skills
Cataloging
File Clerks
Indexing
Information Storage
Medical Record Technicians

Filing Systems
USE   Information Storage

Filipino Americans   SEP. 1968
        Postings: 229   GC: 560
BT   Asian Americans
        Ethnic Groups

Film (Cameras)
USE   Photographic Equipment

Film Auteurism
USE   Auteurism

Film Clips
USE   Filmstrips

Film Criticism   MAY 1976
        Postings: 371   GC: 430
SN   Act and art of analyzing and judging the
        quality of films
BT   Criticism
RT   Audience Response
        Content Analysis
        Critical Viewing
        Feminist Criticism
        Films
        Imagery
        Motifs
        Rhetorical Criticism

Film Industry   JUN. 1977
        Postings: 161   GC: 650
BT   Industry
RT   Acting
        Animation
        Broadcast Industry
        Copyrights
        Documentaries
        Film Production
        Film Production Specialists
        Films
        Information Industry
        Mass Media
        Mass Media Role
        Theater Arts
        Videotape Recordings

Film Libraries   JAN. 1971
        Postings: 229   GC: 710
UF   Videotape Libraries
BT   Special Libraries
RT   Filmographies
        Films
        Filmstrips
        Kinescope Recordings
        Videotape Recordings

Film Lists
USE   Filmographies

Film Loops
USE   Filmstrips

Film Production   JUL. 1966
        Postings: 987   GC: 720
UF   Filmmaking
BT   Production Techniques
        Visual Arts
RT   Acting
        Animation
        Auteurism
        Editing
        Film Industry
        Film Production Specialists
        Film Study

Films
Filmstrips
Photographic Equipment
Photography
Special Effects
Theater Arts
Videotape Recordings

Film Production Specialists JUL. 1966
        Postings: 154   GC: 720
UF   Filmmakers
BT   Specialists
RT   Auteurism
        Film Industry
        Film Production

Film Projectors
USE   Projection Equipment

Film Study   NOV. 1968
        Postings: 1,159   GC: 400
SN   Study of film (as an art form) and
        filmmaking (Note: For the use of film in
        teaching, see "Instructional Films"—prior
        to Mar80, this term was not restricted by
        a Scope Note)
UF   Cinema Study
        Screen Education
BT   Aesthetic Education
RT   Acting
        Auteurism
        Cartoons
        Documentaries
        Editing
        Film Production
        Filmographies
        Films
        Filmstrips
        Photography
        Repetitive Film Showings
        Special Effects
        Theater Arts
        Visual Literacy

Filmmakers
USE   Film Production Specialists

Filmmaking
USE   Film Production

Filmographies   MAY 1976
        Postings: 333   GC: 730
SN   Lists of films, sometimes including other
        media and/or commentary
UF   Film Lists
BT   Reference Materials
RT   Bibliographies
        Discographies
        Film Libraries
        Film Study
        Films
        Indexes
        Library Catalogs

Films   JUL. 1966
        Postings: 4,171   GC: 720
UF   Black and White Films
        Cinema
        Color Films
        Motion Pictures
        Silent Films
        Sound Films (1966 1980)
NT   Foreign Language Films
        Instructional Films
        Kinescope Recordings
        Single Concept Films
BT   Mass Media
        Nonprint Media
        Visual Aids
RT   Auteurism
        Captions
        Cartoons
        Copyrights
        Documentaries
        Film Criticism
        Film Industry
        Film Libraries

Film Production
Film Study
Filmographies
Filmstrips
Literary Styles
Photographs
Popular Culture
Repetitive Film Showings
Theater Arts
Transparencies
Videotape Recordings

Filmstrip Projectors   JUL. 1966
        Postings: 31   GC: 910
BT   Projection Equipment
RT   Filmstrips

Filmstrips   JUL. 1966
        Postings: 791   GC: 720
UF   Film Clips
        Film Loops
BT   Nonprint Media
        Visual Aids
RT   Audiovisual Aids
        Film Libraries
        Film Production
        Film Study
        Films
        Filmstrip Projectors
        Microfilm
        Single Concept Films
        Slides

Finance Occupations   SEP. 1968
        Postings: 145   GC: 640
BT   Occupations
RT   Banking
        Economics
        Estate Planning
        Financial Services
        Fund Raising
        Investment
        Money Management
        Office Occupations
        Trusts (Financial)

Finance Reform   DEC. 1974
        Postings: 1,475   GC: 620
SN   A change in income/revenue sources or
        in money management methods, de-
        signed to remove inequities or other
        faults in existing systems
UF   Tax Reform
BT   Improvement
RT   Change Strategies
        Economic Change
        Economic Impact
        Educational Equity (Finance)
        Educational Finance
        Equalization Aid
        Federal Aid
        Financial Policy
        Financial Problems
        Financial Support
        Fiscal Capacity
        Fiscal Neutrality
        Money Management
        State Aid
        Tax Effort
        Taxes

Financial Aid Applicants   MAR. 1980
        Postings: 443   GC: 360
SN   Individuals requesting financial support
UF   Loan Applicants
BT   Groups
RT   College Applicants
        Credit (Finance)
        Eligibility
        Financial Needs
        Financial Problems
        Financial Services
        Financial Support
        Grants
        Loan Repayment
        Paying for College
        Student Financial Aid

Financial Audits   AUG. 1986
        Postings: 256   GC: 620
SN   Verifications of the stated financial as-
        sets and liabilities of an individual or
        group
BT   Audits (Verification)
RT   Accounting
        Bookkeeping
        Budgeting
        Expenditures
        Financial Policy
        Financial Services
        Financial Support
        Fiscal Capacity
        Income
        Money Management

Financial Barriers
USE   Financial Problems

Financial Donors
USE   Donors

Financial Exigency   DEC. 1989
        Postings: 274   GC: 620
SN   A state of financial crisis—commonly, a
        judicially accepted condition permitting
        an educational institution to terminate
        programs and eliminate staff positions,
        including those of tenured faculty
UF   Fiscal Exigency
RT   Dismissal (Personnel)
        Due Process
        Economic Factors
        Educational Economics
        Educational Finance
        Financial Policy
        Financial Problems
        Fiscal Capacity
        Institutional Survival
        Job Layoff
        Legal Problems
        Legal Responsibility
        Personnel Policy
        Program Termination
        Reduction in Force
        Retrenchment
        Teacher Dismissal
        Tenure

Financial Management
USE   Money Management

Financial Needs   JUL. 1966
        Postings: 1,537   GC: 620
BT   Needs
RT   Credit (Finance)
        Educational Equity (Finance)
        Educational Finance
        Financial Aid Applicants
        Financial Support
        Fund Raising
        Income
        Loan Repayment
        Need Analysis (Student Financial Aid)
        Paying for College
        Purchasing
        Resource Allocation
        Self Supporting Students
        Student Loan Programs
        Tax Allocation

Financial Policy   JUL. 1966
        Postings: 2,477   GC: 620
UF   Fiscal Policy
BT   Policy
RT   Educational Economics
        Educational Equity (Finance)
        Educational Finance
        Finance Reform
        Financial Audits
        Financial Exigency
        Financial Support
        Fiscal Capacity
        Money Management
        New Federalism

= Two or more Descriptors are used to represent this term.
The term's main entry shows the appropriate coordination.

Financial Problems   JUL. 1966
    Postings: 3,056   GC: 620
UF   Financial Barriers
    Fiscal Strain
BT   Problems
RT   Debt (Financial)
    Educational Equity (Finance)
    Educational Finance
    Finance Reform
    Financial Aid Applicants
    Financial Exigency
    Fund Raising
    Income
    Inflation (Economics)
    Institutional Survival
    Loan Default
    Loan Repayment
    Paying for College
    Retrenchment

Financial Services   JUL. 1966
    Postings: 457   GC: 620
SN   Programs that offer aid with money management (Note: Use a more precise term if possible)
BT   Services
RT   Accountants
    Accounting
    Banking
    Bookkeeping
    Certified Public Accountants
    Credit (Finance)
    Educational Finance
    Eligibility
    Estate Planning
    Finance Occupations
    Financial Aid Applicants
    Financial Audits
    Financial Support
    Fund Raising
    Insurance
    Loan Repayment
    Money Management
    Ownership
    Student Loan Programs
    Trusts (Financial)

Financial Support   JUL. 1966
    Postings: 13,963   GC: 620
UF   Economic Support
    Financing
    Funding
NT   Capital
    Categorical Aid
    Child Support
    Endowment Funds
    Equalization Aid
    Full State Funding
    Grants
    Library Funding
    Private Financial Support
    Private School Aid
    Recreation Finances
    Revenue Sharing
    Scholarship Funds
    School Funds
    Student Financial Aid
    Tax Allocation
    Training Allowances
    Unemployment Insurance
    Workers Compensation
RT   Community Resources
    Credit (Finance)
    Educational Economics
    Educational Equity (Finance)
    Educational Finance
    Eligibility
    Entrepreneurship
    Federal Aid
    Fees
    Finance Reform
    Financial Aid Applicants
    Financial Audits
    Financial Needs
    Financial Policy
    Financial Services
    Foundation Programs
    Fund Raising
    Grantsmanship
    Income
    Insurance

    Investment
    Loan Repayment
    Need Analysis (Student Financial Aid)
    Paying for College
    Program Proposals
    Proposal Writing
    Public Support
    Research Opportunities
    Resources
    School District Wealth
    School Support
    State Aid
    State Federal Aid
    Student Financial Aid Officers
    Student Loan Programs
    Technical Assistance
    Trusts (Financial)
    Wills
    Work Study Programs

Financing
USE   Financial Support

Fine Arts   JUL. 1966
    Postings: 1,797   GC: 420
SN   Any of the arts for which aesthetic purposes are primary or uppermost
NT   Dance
    Music
    Theater Arts
    Visual Arts
BT   Humanities
RT   Aesthetics
    Art
    Art Activities
    Art Appreciation
    Art Education
    Art History
    Art Teachers
    Artists
    Arts Centers
    Cultural Activities
    Cultural Enrichment
    Dance Education
    Music Activities
    Music Appreciation
    Music Education
    Music Teachers
    Musicians

Fine Arts Centers
USE   Arts Centers

Fines (Penalties)   FEB. 1970
    Postings: 57   GC: 620
UF   Library Fines
BT   Fees
RT   Crime
    Incentives
    Law Enforcement
    Legal Responsibility
    Library Administration
    Library Circulation
    Sanctions

Finger Spelling   JUL. 1966
    Postings: 142   GC: 220
SN   Spelling by finger movements
UF   Dactylology
BT   Manual Communication
    Spelling
RT   Cued Speech
    Deaf Interpreting
    Sign Language
    Total Communication

Finishing   MAR. 1969
    Postings: 102   GC: 640
UF   Metal Finishing
    Surface Finishing
    Textile Finishing
    Wood Finishing
RT   Adhesives
    Metal Working
    Welding
    Woodworking

Finite Arithmetic
USE   Modular Arithmetic

Finnish   JUL. 1966
    Postings: 199   GC: 440
BT   Finno Ugric Languages

Finno Ugric Languages   JUL. 1966
    Postings: 20   GC: 440
UF   Fenno Ugric Languages
NT   Cheremis
    Estonian
    Finnish
    Hungarian
    Ostyak
    Vogul
BT   Uralic Altaic Languages

Fire Fighters   JUL. 1966
    Postings: 165   GC: 640
UF   Firemen
BT   Service Workers
RT   Alarm Systems
    Emergency Squad Personnel
    Fire Science Education

Fire Insurance   SEP. 1968
    Postings: 33   GC: 620
BT   Insurance
RT   Fire Protection
    Insurance Occupations

Fire Prevention
USE   Fire Protection

Fire Protection   JUL. 1966
    Postings: 489   GC: 210
UF   Fire Prevention
BT   Safety
RT   Alarm Systems
    Asbestos
    Building Design
    Fire Insurance
    Fire Science Education
    Preservation
    Prevention
    Safety Education
    School Safety

Fire Science Education   JUL. 1966
    Postings: 149   GC: 400
BT   Technical Education
RT   Conservation Education
    Fire Fighters
    Fire Protection
    Safety Education

Firearms
USE   Guns

Firearms Control
USE   Gun Control

Firemen
USE   Fire Fighters

First Aid   JUL. 1966
    Postings: 532   GC: 210
NT   Cardiopulmonary Resuscitation
BT   Medical Services
RT   Emergency Medical Technicians
    Health Education
    Health Facilities
    Injuries
    Rescue

First Born   APR. 1993
    Postings: 62   GC: 120
SN   Children or adults born first among siblings (Note: See also the Identifiers "Second Born," "Middle Born," and "Last Born")
UF   Eldest Siblings

    Firstborns
BT   Birth Order
    Siblings
RT   Birth
    Family (Sociological Unit)
    Sibling Relationship

First Professional Degrees
USE   Degrees (Academic)
AND Professional Education

First Year Principals
USE   Beginning Principals

First Year Teachers
USE   Beginning Teachers

Firstborns
USE   First Born

Fiscal Capacity   JUL. 1966
    Postings: 555   GC: 620
SN   Wealth of a government, institution, organization, or individual—also, the relative ability to obtain revenue
NT   School District Wealth
RT   Economic Factors
    Educational Economics
    Educational Equity (Finance)
    Educational Finance
    Equalization Aid
    Finance Reform
    Financial Audits
    Financial Exigency
    Financial Policy
    Fiscal Neutrality
    Inflation (Economics)
    Ownership
    Property Taxes
    Resource Allocation
    Tax Effort

Fiscal Equity (Education)
USE   Educational Equity (Finance)

Fiscal Exigency
USE   Financial Exigency

Fiscal Neutrality   MAY 1994
    Postings: 47   GC: 620
SN   Equity goal that the level of spending for public education may not be a function of local or school district wealth (Note: Occasionally refers as well to the notion of equal probability of college attendance across all incomes)
UF   Wealth Neutrality
RT   Educational Economics
    Educational Equity (Finance)
    Educational Finance
    Equal Education
    Equalization Aid
    Expenditure per Student
    Finance Reform
    Fiscal Capacity
    School District Spending
    School District Wealth
    School Support

Fiscal Policy
USE   Financial Policy

Fiscal Strain
USE   Financial Problems

Fish Inspectors
USE   Food and Drug Inspectors

Fish Studies
USE   Ichthyology

= Two or more Descriptors are used to represent this term.
The term's main entry shows the appropriate coordination.

Fisheries   *JUL. 1966*
   Postings: 193   GC: 410
BT   Facilities
RT   Agriculture
     Aquariums
     Estuaries
     Ichthyology
     Marine Biology
     Oceanography
     Wetlands

Five Year Teacher Preparation Programs
USE Extended Teacher Education Programs

Fixed Sequence   *JUL. 1966*
   Postings: 31   GC: 350
BT   Methods
RT   Branching
     Pacing
     Programmed Instruction
     Sequential Approach

Fixed Service Television (1969 1980)
USE Educational Television

FLES   *JUL. 1966*
   Postings: 991   GC: 450
UF   FLES Guides (1967 1980) #
     FLES Materials (1967 1980) #
     FLES Programs (1967 1980) #
     FLES Teachers (1967 1980) #
     Foreign Languages in the Elementary
       School
BT   Elementary School Curriculum
     Modern Language Curriculum
RT   Immersion Programs
     Languages
     Second Language Instruction
     Second Language Learning
     Second Language Programs
     Second Languages

FLES Guides (1967 1980)
USE Curriculum Guides
AND FLES

FLES Materials (1967 1980)
USE FLES
AND Instructional Materials

FLES Programs (1967 1980)
USE FLES
AND Second Language Programs

FLES Teachers (1967 1980)
USE FLES
AND Language Teachers

Flexible Classrooms (1968 1980)
USE Classrooms
AND Flexible Facilities

Flexible Disks
USE Floppy Disks

Flexible Facilities   *JUL. 1966*
   Postings: 688   GC: 920
SN   Facilities designed to be adaptable for
     more than one purpose or use
UF   Flexible Classrooms (1968 1980) #
BT   Facilities
RT   Building Innovation
     Classroom Design
     Design Requirements
     Educational Facilities Design
     Educational Facilities Planning
     Encapsulated Facilities
     Flexible Lighting Design
     Furniture Arrangement
     Interior Space
     Mobile Classrooms
     Movable Partitions
     Multipurpose Classrooms

     Open Plan Schools
     Relocatable Facilities
     School Space
     Shared Facilities
     Space Dividers
     Space Utilization
     Spatial Relationship (Facilities)
     Structural Elements (Construction)

Flexible Lighting Design   *JUL. 1966*
   Postings: 29   GC: 920
SN   Lighting unit arrangement as well as
     lighting fixture design that allows for
     flexible lighting requirements
BT   Lighting Design
RT   Building Design
     Classroom Design
     Flexible Facilities
     Lighting

Flexible Progression   *JUL. 1966*
   Postings: 210   GC: 350
SN   Advancement of students through an
     educational program at different rates,
     depending on their abilities, preferences,
     or other factors (Note: Prior to Mar80,
     the use of this term was not restricted by
     a Scope Note, and the instruction "Track
     System, USE Flexible Progression" was
     carried in the Thesaurus)
NT   Acceleration (Education)
RT   Ability Grouping
     Continuous Progress Plan
     Curriculum Design
     Nongraded Instructional Grouping
     Student Promotion

Flexible Schedules (1967 1980)   *JUN. 1980*
   Postings: 150   GC: 320
SN   Invalid Descriptor—used inconsistently
     in indexing for both school and job
     schedules—see "Flexible Scheduling"
     and "Flexible Working Hours" respec-
     tively for those concepts

Flexible Scheduling   *JUL. 1966*
   Postings: 888   GC: 320
SN   Responsive instructional scheduling that
     provides for team teaching, variations in
     student groupings within and among
     courses, and changes in the frequency
     and length of time courses meet (Note:
     Prior to Mar80, the use of this term was
     not restricted by a Scope Note)
UF   Modular Scheduling
     Schedule Modules (1968 1980)
BT   School Schedules
RT   Block Scheduling
     Class Size
     Continuous Progress Plan
     Extended School Day
     Extended School Year
     Grouping (Instructional Purposes)
     Instructional Development
     Instructional Innovation
     Team Teaching
     Time Blocks

Flexible Working Hours   *MAR. 1980*
   Postings: 253   GC: 630
SN   Scheduling method by which the time of
     arrival and departure from work, the
     number of hours worked per day, or the
     number of days worked per week may be
     varied, provided that a full complement
     of hours is worked
UF   Compressed Work Week
     Flextime
     Four Day Work Week
BT   Working Hours
RT   Employed Parents
     Employed Women
     Job Satisfaction
     Job Sharing
     Part Time Employment
     Partnership Teachers
     Released Time
     Work Environment

Flexilevel Testing
USE Adaptive Testing

Flextime
USE Flexible Working Hours

Flight Training   *JUL. 1966*
   Postings: 332   GC: 400
SN   Training of military or civilian aircraft
     personnel
UF   Pilot Training
BT   Training
RT   Aviation Education
     Job Training
     Military Training

Floods   *NOV. 1995*
   Postings: 47   GC: 490
SN   Bodies of water that overtop their natural
     or artificial confines and that cover areas
     not normally underwater
RT   Hydrology
     Natural Disasters
     Rivers
     Water
     Weather

Floor Covering
USE Flooring

Floor Installation
USE Flooring

Floor Layers   *JUL. 1966*
   Postings: 21   GC: 640
UF   Carpet Layers
BT   Skilled Workers
RT   Carpeting
     Flooring

Flooring   *JUL. 1966*
   Postings: 156   GC: 920
UF   Floor Covering
     Floor Installation
     Floors
     Resilient Floor Covering
NT   Carpeting
BT   Structural Elements (Construction)
RT   Asphalts
     Building Trades
     Buildings
     Construction (Process)
     Construction Materials
     Floor Layers

Floors
USE Flooring

Floppy Disks   *DEC. 1987*
   Postings: 57   GC: 720
SN   Computer storage devices in the form of
     small flexible magnetic disks enclosed in
     semirigid jackets—generally used with
     microcomputers
UF   Diskettes
     Flexible Disks
BT   Magnetic Disks

Floriculture   *JUL. 1966*
   Postings: 86   GC: 410
BT   Ornamental Horticulture
RT   Botany
     Gardening
     Landscaping
     Plant Identification
     Plant Pathology
     Plant Propagation

Flow Charts   *DEC. 1970*
   Postings: 1,105   GC: 720
SN   Diagrammatic representation of
     sequenced events or processes
BT   Charts

RT   Computer Oriented Programs
     Critical Path Method
     Graphs
     Planning
     Records (Forms)

Fluid Mechanics   *MAR. 1980*
   Postings: 134   GC: 490
SN   Science that deals with fluids, either at
     rest or in motion, and with pressures,
     velocities, and accelerations in fluids
UF   Fluid Power Education (1967 1980)
BT   Mechanics (Physics)
RT   Acceleration (Physics)
     Force
     Hydraulics
     Kinetics
     Motion
     Power Technology
     Pressure (Physics)
     Velocity

Fluid Power Education (1967 1980)
USE Fluid Mechanics

Fluid Pressure
USE Pressure (Physics)

Fluoridation   *AUG. 1982*
   Postings: 27   GC: 210
SN   Treatment of water and teeth with fluo-
     rides in order to reduce tooth decay
BT   Disease Control
RT   Dental Health
     Drinking Water
     Health Services
     Preventive Medicine
     Public Health
     Water Treatment

Focus Groups   *MAY 1996*
   Postings: 488   GC: 820
SN   Small, roundtable discussion groups
     charged with examining specific topics
     or problems (e.g., consumer preferences,
     product attributes, educational issues),
     including possible options or solutions—
     focus groups usually consist of 4–12
     participants, guided by moderators to
     keep the discussion flowing and to col-
     lect and report the results
UF   Focused Group Interviews
BT   Discussion Groups
RT   Group Discussion
     Interviews
     Marketing
     Qualitative Research
     Research Methodology
     Use Studies

Focused Group Interviews
USE Focus Groups

Folding Partitions
USE Movable Partitions

Folk Culture   *JUL. 1966*
   Postings: 2,211   GC: 560
SN   Traditional modes of behavior and ex-
     pression that are transmitted from gen-
     eration to generation (by firsthand inter-
     action) among a group or people
UF   Folk Drama (1969 1980) #
     Folklore
     Folklore Books (1966 1980) #
     Traditions (Culture)
BT   Culture
RT   Anthropology
     Cross Cultural Studies
     Cultural Education
     Dance
     Drama
     Ethnography
     Ethnology
     Fairy Tales
     Legends

 # = Two or more Descriptors are used to represent this term.
The term's main entry shows the appropriate coordination.

Literature
Material Culture
Music
Mythology
Nonformal Education
Nursery Rhymes
Oral Tradition
Poetry
Proverbs

Folk Drama (1969 1980)
USE   Drama
AND   Folk Culture

Folk Schools   *JUL. 1966*
       Postings: 113   GC: 340
SN   Schools, often residential, that are es-
       tablished with voluntary funds and con-
       cerned with the culture and lives of the
       people in the surrounding community
       (Note: Coordinate with geographic Iden-
       tifiers when possible—prior to Mar80,
       the use of this term was not restricted by
       a Scope Note)
BT   Schools
RT   Boarding Schools
       Community Schools
       Cultural Education
       Nontraditional Education

Folklore
USE   Folk Culture

Folklore Books (1966 1980)
USE   Books
AND   Folk Culture

Followup Programs
USE   Followup Studies

Followup Studies   *JUL. 1966*
       Postings: 4,693   GC: 810
SN   Studies that focus on the activities, prog-
       ress, attitudes, etc., of individuals or
       groups after some treatment or follow-
       ing their participation in a program, course
       of study, guidance process, etc. (Note:
       As of Oct81, use as a minor Descriptor
       for examples of this kind of study—use
       as a major Descriptor only as the subject
       of a document)
UF   Followup Programs
NT   Graduate Surveys
       Vocational Followup
BT   Longitudinal Studies
RT   Outcomes of Education

Foochow   *JUL. 1966*
       Postings: 6   GC: 440
BT   Chinese
RT   Dialects

Food   *JUL. 1966*
       Postings: 1,934   GC: 210
UF   Seafood (1968 1980)
NT   Grains (Food)
       Meat
RT   Agriculture
       Bakery Industry
       Cooks
       Dietetics
       Dietitians
       Feed Industry
       Food and Drug Inspectors
       Food Handling Facilities
       Food Processing Occupations
       Food Service
       Food Standards
       Food Stores
       Foods Instruction
       Gardening
       Gardens
       Hunger
       Meat Packing Industry
       Nutrition

Recipes (Food)
Vending Machines

Food and Drug Inspectors   *JAN. 1969*
       Postings: 36   GC: 640
UF   Cosmetics Inspectors
       Dairy Product Inspectors
       Drug Inspectors
       Egg Inspectors
       Fish Inspectors
       Food Inspectors
       Fruit and Vegetable Inspectors
       Meat Inspectors
       Peanut Inspectors
       Processed Foods Inspectors
BT   Government Employees
RT   Food
       Food Processing Occupations
       Food Service
       Food Standards
       Meat Packing Industry

Food Handling Facilities   *JUL. 1966*
       Postings: 210   GC: 920
SN   Equipment and space for storing, pre-
       paring, and serving food
BT   Facilities
RT   Breakfast Programs
       Dining Facilities
       Dishwashing
       Food
       Food Service
       Lunch Programs
       Vending Machines

Food Inspectors
USE   Food and Drug Inspectors

Food Markets
USE   Food Stores

Food Processing Occupations   *AUG. 1968*
       Postings: 144   GC: 640
BT   Off Farm Agricultural Occupations
RT   Bakery Industry
       Feed Industry
       Food
       Food and Drug Inspectors
       Meat Packing Industry

Food Service   *JUL. 1966*
       Postings: 1,475   GC: 210
UF   Food Service Industry (1967 1981)
       Food Service Occupations (1968
          1981)
       Food Service Workers (1968 1981)
BT   Human Services
RT   Bakery Industry
       Cooks
       Dietitians
       Dining Facilities
       Dishwashing
       Distributive Education
       Food
       Food and Drug Inspectors
       Food Handling Facilities
       Food Standards
       Food Stores
       Foods Instruction
       Home Economics Skills
       Hospitality Occupations
       Hygiene
       Occupational Home Economics
       Recipes (Food)
       Vending Machines
       Waiters and Waitresses

Food Service Industry (1967 1981)
USE   Food Service

Food Service Occupations (1968 1981)
USE   Food Service

Food Service Workers (1968 1981)
USE   Food Service

Food Standards   *JUL. 1966*
       Postings: 403   GC: 210
BT   Standards
RT   Breakfast Programs
       Dietetics
       Dietitians
       Food
       Food and Drug Inspectors
       Food Service
       Foods Instruction
       Lunch Programs
       Meat Packing Industry
       Nutrition

Food Stores   *AUG. 1968*
       Postings: 120   GC: 920
SN   Retail markets selling foodstuffs
UF   Food Markets
       Grocery Stores
       Supermarkets
BT   Facilities
RT   Food
       Food Service
       Meat
       Merchandising
       Retailing

Foods Instruction   *JUL. 1966*
       Postings: 661   GC: 400
BT   Instruction
RT   Consumer Science
       Cooking Instruction
       Cooks
       Dietitians
       Food
       Food Service
       Food Standards
       Home Economics
       Nutrition Instruction
       Recipes (Food)

Football   *DEC. 1975*
       Postings: 275   GC: 470
BT   Team Sports

Footnotes (Bibliographic)
USE   Citations (References)

Force   *OCT. 1968*
       Postings: 564   GC: 490
UF   Force (Physical)
BT   Scientific Concepts
RT   Acceleration (Physics)
       Atomic Structure
       Atomic Theory
       Biomechanics
       Density (Matter)
       Electricity
       Energy
       Fluid Mechanics
       Gravity (Physics)
       Kinetic Molecular Theory
       Kinetics
       Mechanics (Physics)
       Motion
       Nuclear Physics
       Physics
       Pressure (Physics)
       Quantum Mechanics
       Vectors (Mathematics)
       Weight (Mass)
       Wind Energy

Force (Physical)
USE   Force

Force Field Analysis   *JUL. 1966*
       Postings: 57   GC: 820
SN   Method of distinguishing factors in the
       psychological environment of individu-
       als or groups, based on Lewin's theory
BT   Psychological Studies
RT   Interdisciplinary Approach
       Research Methodology

Forced Choice Technique   *JUL. 1966*
       Postings: 125   GC: 820
SN   Procedure in which individuals are re-
       quired to choose among options that
       have equal acceptability but unequal
       validity—used to minimize the ability of
       individuals to give overly favorable re-
       sponses
BT   Measurement Techniques
RT   Affective Measures
       Attitude Measures
       Interest Inventories
       Personality Measures
       Q Methodology
       Rating Scales
       Response Style (Tests)
       Social Desirability
       Testing
       Tests

Forecast
USE   Prediction

Foreign Countries   *JUL. 1966*
       Postings: 82,334   GC: 610
SN   Countries other than the U.S. (Note: Coor-
       dinate with geographic Identifiers to in-
       dicate document subject—prior to Mar80,
       the use of this term was not restricted by
       a Scope Note)
BT   Geographic Regions
RT   Armed Forces
       Foreign Diplomats
       Foreign Policy
       International Education
       International Relations
       International Studies
       Overseas Employment

Foreign Culture   *JUL. 1966*
       Postings: 1,242   GC: 560
SN   Culture regarded as foreign from the
       perspective of the document or journal
       article (Note: Use major geographic Identi-
       fiers to identify the foreign culture, and
       minor geographic Identifiers to identify
       the native culture—prior to Mar80, this
       term was not restricted by a Scope Note
       and carried no special instruction)
UF   Alien Culture
BT   Culture
RT   African Studies
       Asian Studies
       Canadian Studies
       Comparative Education
       Cross Cultural Studies
       Cross Cultural Training
       Ethnic Groups
       Ethnocentrism
       Intercultural Communication
       International Education
       International Educational Exchange
       Middle Eastern Studies
       Multicultural Education
       Native Speakers

Foreign Diplomats   *JUL. 1966*
       Postings: 31   GC: 610
BT   Government Employees
RT   Diplomatic History
       Foreign Countries
       Foreign Policy
       Foreign Workers
       International Relations

Foreign Language Books   *JUL. 1966*
       Postings: 225   GC: 730
UF   Second Language Books
BT   Books
RT   Foreign Language Films
       Foreign Language Periodicals
       Languages
       Second Language Learning

Foreign Language Enrollment
USE   Language Enrollment

= Two or more Descriptors are used to represent this term.
The term's main entry shows the appropriate coordination.

Foreign Language Films   *JUL. 1966*
    Postings: 169   GC: 720
UF   Second Language Films
BT   Films
RT   Foreign Language Books
     Foreign Language Periodicals
     Languages
     Second Language Learning

Foreign Language Instruction
USE Second Language Instruction

Foreign Language Learning
USE Second Language Learning

Foreign Language Periodicals   *JUL. 1966*
    Postings: 180   GC: 730
UF   Second Language Periodicals
BT   Periodicals
RT   Foreign Language Books
     Foreign Language Films
     Languages
     Second Language Learning

Foreign Language Programs
USE Second Language Programs

Foreign Language Teachers
USE Language Teachers

Foreign Language Teaching
USE Second Language Instruction

Foreign Languages
USE Second Languages

Foreign Languages in the Elementary School
USE FLES

Foreign Medical Graduates   *OCT. 1979*
    Postings: 100   GC: 360
SN   Medical students or physicians, either U.S. or foreign nationals, who have graduated from non-U.S. medical schools (Note: Includes foreign graduate medical students transferring from non-U.S. to U.S. medical schools)
UF   Foreign Trained Physicians
BT   Graduates
     Physicians
RT   Foreign Students
     Graduate Medical Education
     Graduate Medical Students
     International Educational Exchange
     Medical Schools
     Medical Students
     Study Abroad

Foreign Nationals   *SEP. 1970*
    Postings: 339   GC: 520
SN   Citizens of countries other than those in which they reside
RT   Citizenship
     Developing Nations
     Foreign Students
     Foreign Workers
     Immigrants
     Indigenous Populations
     International Programs
     Migrants
     Refugees

Foreign Policy   *AUG. 1968*
    Postings: 1,190   GC: 610
UF   Diplomatic Policy
     International Policy
NT   Imperialism
BT   Policy
RT   Diplomatic History
     Foreign Countries
     Foreign Diplomats
     Immigration

     International Education
     International Law
     International Programs
     International Relations
     International Studies
     International Trade
     Nationalism
     Peace
     Political Science
     Self Determination
     World Affairs

Foreign Relations (1966 1976)
USE International Relations

Foreign Student Advisers   *DEC. 1969*
    Postings: 93   GC: 360
SN   Faculty or staff members who coordinate services provided to foreign students and counsel them in academic and personal matters, including problems with government regulations such as visas, work permits, etc.
BT   School Personnel
RT   Faculty Advisers
     Foreign Students
     Student Adjustment
     Student College Relationship
     Student Exchange Programs
     Student Personnel Workers

Foreign Students   *JUL. 1966*
    Postings: 2,759   GC: 360
UF   International Students
     Nonresident Students (1967 1980) (Foreign)
BT   Students
RT   Foreign Medical Graduates
     Foreign Nationals
     Foreign Student Advisers
     International Educational Exchange
     Student Exchange Programs

Foreign Trained Physicians
USE Foreign Medical Graduates

Foreign Workers   *JUL. 1966*
    Postings: 184   GC: 630
SN   Personnel working in other than their native countries
UF   Undocumented Workers #
NT   Braceros
BT   Personnel
RT   Foreign Diplomats
     Foreign Nationals
     Migrant Workers
     Refugees

Foremen
USE Supervisors

Forensics
USE Persuasive Discourse

Forester Aides
USE Forestry Aides

Forestry   *JUL. 1966*
    Postings: 569   GC: 410
BT   Technology
RT   Agriculture
     Botany
     Conservation (Environment)
     Conservation Education
     Environmental Education
     Forestry Aides
     Forestry Occupations
     Land Use
     Lumber Industry
     Natural Resources
     Nurseries (Horticulture)
     Rainforests
     Soil Conservation
     Soil Science

     Trees
     Wildlife Management

Forestry Aides   *JUL. 1966*
    Postings: 24   GC: 410
UF   Forester Aides
BT   Paraprofessional Personnel
RT   Forestry
     Forestry Occupations

Forestry Occupations   *MAY 1969*
    Postings: 109   GC: 410
BT   Occupations
RT   Forestry
     Forestry Aides
     Lumber Industry
     Off Farm Agricultural Occupations

Forgetting
USE Memory

Form Classes (Languages)   *JUL. 1966*
    Postings: 1,092   GC: 450
UF   Parts of Speech
NT   Adjectives
     Adverbs
     Conjunctions
     Determiners (Languages)
     Function Words
     Nouns
     Prepositions
     Pronouns
     Verbs
BT   Syntax
RT   Affixes
     Case (Grammar)
     Language Patterns
     Morphology (Languages)
     Phrase Structure
     Plurals
     Structural Grammar
     Tenses (Grammar)
     Traditional Grammar

Formal Criticism (1969 1980)   *MAR. 1980*
    Postings: 270   GC: 430
SN   Invalid Descriptor—originally intended as a literary term, but used indiscriminately in indexing

Formal Operations   *AUG. 1986*
    Postings: 224   GC: 110
SN   Fourth and final stage in Piaget's theory of intellectual development, beginning at approximately 12 years, in which abstraction and suppositional capacities are acquired
BT   Intelligence
RT   Abstract Reasoning
     Cognitive Ability
     Cognitive Processes
     Critical Thinking
     Developmental Stages
     Intellectual Development
     Logical Thinking
     Piagetian Theory

Formal Organizations
USE Organizations (Groups)

Format (Publications)
USE Layout (Publications)

Formative Evaluation   *JUN. 1971*
    Postings: 2,811   GC: 310
SN   Evaluation that is used to modify or improve products, programs, or activities and is based on feedback obtained during their planning and development
UF   Process Evaluation
BT   Evaluation
RT   Curriculum Development
     Educational Assessment
     Educational Development
     Educational Improvement

     Educational Planning
     Evaluation Utilization
     Material Development
     Pretesting
     Program Development
     Program Improvement
     Self Evaluation (Groups)
     Summative Evaluation
     Systems Development

Former Teachers (1967 1980)   *MAR. 1980*
    Postings: 13   GC: 360
SN   Invalid Descriptor—see such Descriptors as "Teacher Retirement," "Career Change," etc.

Fossil Fuels   *DEC. 1992*
    Postings: 29   GC: 410
SN   Hydrocarbon fuels derived from the remains of former life
UF   Fuel Oil #
     Heating Oils #
     Petroleum (Oil and Gas) #
NT   Coal
     Gasoline
     Natural Gas
BT   Fuels
     Natural Resources
RT   Oil
     Petroleum Industry

Fossils
USE Paleontology

Foster Care   *AUG. 1982*
    Postings: 818   GC: 520
SN   Care and rearing of children in private homes by persons other than the natural parents, with or without adoption
UF   Foster Homes (1970 1982) (Children)
BT   Social Services
RT   Adoption
     Adult Foster Care
     Boarding Homes
     Caregiver Child Relationship
     Child Care Occupations
     Child Caregivers
     Child Welfare
     Foster Children
     Foster Family
     Group Homes

Foster Children   *NOV. 1969*
    Postings: 604   GC: 510
BT   Children
RT   Adopted Children
     Biological Parents
     Child Welfare
     Foster Care
     Foster Family

Foster Family   *JUL. 1966*
    Postings: 516   GC: 510
UF   Foster Parents
BT   Family (Sociological Unit)
RT   Adopted Children
     Adoption
     Adoptive Parents
     Adult Foster Care
     Biological Parents
     Child Welfare
     Foster Care
     Foster Children
     Placement

Foster Homes (1970 1982) (Adults)
USE Adult Foster Care

Foster Homes (1970 1982) (Children)
USE Foster Care

Foster Parents
USE Foster Family

= Two or more Descriptors are used to represent this term.
The term's main entry shows the appropriate coordination.

Found Materials
USE Found Objects

Found Objects *OCT. 1994*
Postings: 3 GC: 420
SN Usually familiar and often freely available materials that are found, selected, and used in artwork, play activity, etc.
UF Found Materials
RT Art Materials
Collage
Visual Arts

Found Spaces *DEC. 1972*
Postings: 66 GC: 920
SN Spaces which do not resemble traditional school facilities but can easily be converted, e.g., hotels, supermarkets, residences, and enclosed or semi-enclosed outdoor areas adjacent to new or existing facilities
BT Educational Facilities
RT Building Conversion
Facility Expansion
Facility Planning
Site Development
Space Utilization

Foundation Courses (Introductory)
USE Introductory Courses

Foundation Courses (Required)
USE Required Courses

Foundation Programs *JUL. 1966*
Postings: 468 GC: 620
SN Systems whereby state funds are used to supplement local or intermediate school district funds for elementary and secondary education—a "minimum foundation" of financial support is usually guaranteed regardless of the local district's ability to support education (Note: Prior to Mar80, this term was not scoped and was sometimes used to index "Philanthropic Foundations")
BT Programs
State Aid
RT Educational Equity (Finance)
Educational Finance
Equalization Aid
Federal Aid
Financial Support
Incentive Grants
School Funds
School Support

Foundations (Institutions)
USE Philanthropic Foundations

Foundations of Education *MAY 1971*
Postings: 899 GC: 400
SN The philosophy, social forces, institutions, and human relations upon which the formal educational system is based
NT Educational Anthropology
Educational Economics
Educational History
Educational Philosophy
Educational Principles
Educational Psychology
Educational Sociology
Educational Theories
RT Comparative Education
Education
Knowledge Base for Teaching
Teacher Education Curriculum

Foundries *JUN. 1969*
Postings: 46 GC: 920
UF Iron Foundries
Steel Foundries
BT Facilities
RT Industrial Arts
Metal Industry
Metal Working

Four Day Work Week
USE Flexible Working Hours

Four H Club Agents
USE Extension Agents

Fractions *JUL. 1966*
Postings: 939 GC: 480
UF Common Fractions (1966 1980)
NT Decimal Fractions
BT Rational Numbers
RT Arithmetic
Reciprocals (Mathematics)

Frail Elderly *JUN. 1988*
Postings: 234 GC: 210
SN Elderly persons whose physical or mental abilities are so reduced that regular assistance is needed for daily living or social contacts
BT Older Adults
RT Adult Day Care
Adult Foster Care
Aging (Individuals)
Alzheimers Disease
Chronic Illness
Disabilities
Family Caregivers
Family Problems
Long Term Care
Old Old Adults
Patients
Personal Care Homes
Physical Mobility
Young Old Adults

Franchising *DEC. 1989*
Postings: 61 GC: 650
SN Process in which a firm or enterprise offers to another the right to conduct a business operation in keeping with established policies, procedures, and goals and using the offeror's trade name or trademark (Note: Do not confuse with "Cable Franchising," which, prior to Dec89, was indexed as "Franchising")
RT Business
Business Administration
Contracts
Economic Opportunities
Entrepreneurship
Industrial Structure
Industry
Investment
Marketing
Ownership
Retailing
Small Businesses

Franchising (Cable)
USE Cable Franchising

Fraternities *JUL. 1966*
Postings: 248 GC: 520
BT Organizations (Groups)
RT Honor Societies
National Organizations
Professional Associations
Social Organizations
Sororities
Student Organizations

Fraud *JUN. 1999*
Postings: 208 GC: 530
SN Deceit, trickery, or breach of confidence in order to gain unfair or dishonest advantage
BT Antisocial Behavior
Deception
RT Cheating
Consumer Protection
Crime
Ethics
Lying
Malpractice
Plagiarism
Stealing

Free Choice Transfer Programs *JUL. 1966*
Postings: 155 GC: 330
SN Transfer programs that allow students to attend the school of their choice
BT Transfer Programs
RT Open Enrollment
School Choice
Transfer Policy
Transfer Students

Free Education *OCT. 1980*
Postings: 42 GC: 330
SN Education that does not require the payment of tuition (Note: Do not confuse with "Free Schools")
BT Education
RT Access to Education
Compulsory Education
Open Universities
Private Education
Public Education
Tuition

Free Enterprise System *AUG. 1988*
Postings: 628 GC: 610
SN Economic system in which individuals, rather than the government, make decisions about the way goods and services are produced, distributed, and used
UF Free Market
Laissez Faire Economy
Market Economy
BT Capitalism
RT Business
Business Administration
Competition
Democracy
Economics
Entrepreneurship
Freedom
Private Financial Support
Private Sector
Privatization

Free Market
USE Free Enterprise System

Free Play
USE Play

Free Schools *MAR. 1980*
Postings: 90 GC: 340
SN Alternative schools offering a completely voluntaristic framework, including an unstructured curriculum and a spontaneous learning environment—students are free to select what to learn, with whom, when, and how—grades, competition, and comparisons between individuals are discarded (Note: Do not confuse with "Free Education" or "Freedom Schools")
BT Schools
RT Experimental Schools
Humanistic Education
Nongraded Student Evaluation
Nontraditional Education
Open Education
Progressive Education
Relevance (Education)
Student Interests
Student Rights

Free Translation
USE Translation

Free Universities
USE Experimental Colleges

Free Writing *APR. 1990*
Postings: 127 GC: 400
SN The free written expression of ideas without concern for spelling and correct usage—used, often with peer consultation, as a starting point for more structured writing
UF Freewrites

BT Writing (Composition)
RT Creative Writing
Journal Writing
Prewriting
Writing Exercises

Freedom *OCT. 1994*
Postings: 178 GC: 610
UF Liberty
NT Academic Freedom
Freedom of Information
Freedom of Speech
Intellectual Freedom
RT Censorship
Civil Liberties
Civil Rights
Democracy
Democratic Values
Free Enterprise System
Human Dignity
Individual Power
Individualism
Justice
Personal Autonomy
Political Attitudes
Privacy
Self Determination
Slavery
Social Values

Freedom of Information *AUG. 1986*
Postings: 351 GC: 610
SN Freedom from interference with the flow of information, especially unrestricted public access to government records and documents without compromising rights of privacy or endangering government security
UF Right to Know
BT Access to Information
Freedom
RT Academic Freedom
Agenda Setting
Censorship
Civil Liberties
Confidential Records
Democracy
Disclosure
Freedom of Speech
Government Publications
Information Dissemination
Intellectual Freedom
Journalism
Laws
News Media
Privacy

Freedom of Speech *JUL. 1966*
Postings: 2,331 GC: 610
UF Freedom of the Press
BT Civil Liberties
Freedom
RT Academic Freedom
Censorship
Civil Rights
Democracy
Due Process
Freedom of Information
Intellectual Freedom
Journalism
Libel and Slander
News Media
Political Correctness
Press Opinion
Student Rights
Teacher Rights

Freedom of the Press
USE Freedom of Speech

Freedom of Thought
USE Intellectual Freedom

Freedom Schools *JUL. 1966*
Postings: 35 GC: 340
SN Schools or classes outside the regular school system, organized to teach minority group children about their cultural

heritage or, on occasion, when strikes or other problems prevent these children from attending the public schools (Note: Do not confuse with "Free Schools")
- BT Schools
- RT Civil Rights
  Cultural Awareness
  Cultural Education
  Cultural Enrichment
  Nontraditional Education

Freedom to Read
USE Intellectual Freedom

Freehand Drawing *AUG. 1968*
Postings: 904 GC: 420
- UF Drawing (Freehand)
- BT Visual Arts
- RT Cartoons
  Childrens Art
  Creative Art
  Painting (Visual Arts)

Freewrites
USE Free Writing

French *JUL. 1966*
Postings: 7,173 GC: 440
- BT Romance Languages
- RT French Canadians
  French Literature

French Canadian Literature
USE Canadian Literature

French Canadians *DEC. 1989*
Postings: 160 GC: 560
- SN A major ethnic component of contemporary Canadian society dating back to 17th-century settlement (New France), whose language and culture are officially preserved, along with those of English-speaking Canadians, by the federal government of Canada (Note: For U.S. citizens of French-Canadian descent, coordinate with the Identifier "Franco Americans")
- BT Ethnic Groups
  North Americans
- RT Biculturalism
  Bilingualism
  Canadian Literature
  Canadian Studies
  French
  Language Maintenance
  Minority Groups

French Literature *APR. 1969*
Postings: 499 GC: 430
- BT Literature
- RT French

Frequency Distributions
USE Statistical Distributions

Freshman Composition *AUG. 1986*
Postings: 1,079 GC: 400
- SN Writing instruction intended for first-year college students
- BT College Curriculum
  Writing (Composition)
  Writing Instruction
- RT Basic Writing
  College English
  College Freshmen

Freshmen (1967 1980) (First Year College Students)
USE College Freshmen

Freshmen (1967 1980) (Grade 9)
USE High School Freshmen

Friendship *JUL. 1966*
Postings: 1,559 GC: 510
- UF Childhood Friendship (1966 1980)
- BT Interpersonal Relationship
- RT Dating (Social)
  Love
  Peer Relationship
  Popularity
  Prosocial Behavior
  Significant Others
  Social Development
  Social Life

Fringe Benefits *JUL. 1966*
Postings: 1,805 GC: 630
- UF Employee Fringe Benefits
  Perquisites (Employment)
- RT Compensation (Remuneration)
  Early Retirement
  Employee Assistance Programs
  Employees
  Employer Employee Relationship
  Employer Supported Day Care
  Employment
  Health Insurance
  Labor Relations
  Leaves of Absence
  Personnel Policy
  Preretirement Education
  Retirement Benefits
  Salaries
  Scope of Bargaining
  Teacher Employment Benefits
  Unemployment Insurance
  Vacations
  Wages

Front End Systems (Computers)
USE Gateway Systems

Fruit and Vegetable Inspectors
USE Food and Drug Inspectors

FTE
USE Full Time Equivalency

Fuel Consumption *SEP. 1968*
Postings: 557 GC: 410
- RT Air Conditioning
  Air Conditioning Equipment
  Conservation (Environment)
  Depleted Resources
  Energy Audits
  Energy Conservation
  Energy Management
  Fuels
  Heat Recovery
  Heating
  Temperature
  Thermal Environment
  Ventilation

Fuel Oil
USE Fossil Fuels
AND Oil

Fuels *JUL. 1966*
Postings: 717 GC: 410
- UF Diesel Fuel #
- NT Fossil Fuels
- RT Agricultural Machinery
  Energy
  Energy Conservation
  Energy Education
  Energy Occupations
  Engines
  Fuel Consumption
  Heat
  Heating
  Kinetics
  Minerals
  Mining
  Motor Vehicles
  Power Technology
  Utilities

Ful
USE Fulani

Fula
USE Fulani

Fulani *JUL. 1966*
Postings: 14 GC: 440
- UF Ful
  Fula
  Fulfulde
  Peul
  Pheul
- BT African Languages

Fulfulde
USE Fulani

Full Day Half Day Alternate Day
USE Alternate Day Schedules
AND Full Day Half Day Schedules

Full Day Half Day Schedules *DEC. 1989*
Postings: 92 GC: 320
- SN Scheduling in full or half day sessions— usually refers to kindergarten, preschool, or day care attendance
- UF All Day Half Day Schedules
  Full Day Half Day Alternate Day #
  Half Day Schedules
- BT Scheduling
- RT Alternate Day Schedules
  Bilingual Education
  Day Care
  Kindergarten
  Preschool Education
  School Schedules
  Time Factors (Learning)

Full Inclusion
USE Inclusive Schools

Full Service Schools (Human Services)
USE Integrated Services

Full State Funding *JAN. 1973*
Postings: 263 GC: 620
- SN Financial support provided wholly by a state government
- BT Financial Support
  State Aid
- RT Educational Finance
  Equalization Aid
  Expenditure per Student
  Government School Relationship
  Institutional Autonomy
  School District Autonomy
  School District Spending
  School Support
  School Taxes
  State Federal Aid
  Tax Allocation

Full Text Databases *JAN. 1988*
Postings: 230 GC: 710
- SN Machine-readable files containing the complete texts of journal articles, newspaper items, legal documents, encyclopedias, or other works
- BT Databases
- RT Electronic Journals
  Electronic Publishing

Full Time Equivalency *MAR. 1980*
Postings: 385 GC: 320
- SN Part-time status (as of students, personnel, etc.) expressed as a percentage of corresponding full-time status
- UF FTE
- BT Status
- RT Employment Level
  Enrollment
  Enrollment Rate
  Full Time Faculty

Full Time Students
Measurement
Part Time Employment
Part Time Faculty
Part Time Students

Full Time Faculty *OCT. 1979*
Postings: 669 GC: 360
- SN Faculty members considered by the institution to be carrying a full workload
- UF Full Time Teachers
- BT Faculty
- RT Employment Level
  Faculty Workload
  Full Time Equivalency
  Part Time Faculty
  Teacher Employment
  Teachers
  Teaching Load
  Tenured Faculty
  Working Hours

Full Time Students *OCT. 1979*
Postings: 764 GC: 360
- SN Students carrying a full credit load as defined by the institution
- BT Students
- RT Day Programs
  Day Students
  Enrollment
  Full Time Equivalency
  On Campus Students
  Part Time Students

Full Time Teachers
USE Full Time Faculty

Function Words *JUL. 1966*
Postings: 235 GC: 450
- SN Words that have grammatical, but little or no lexical meaning, as "in," "the," "or"
- UF Functors
- BT Form Classes (Languages)
- RT Conjunctions
  Determiners (Languages)
  Morphology (Languages)
  Prepositions
  Sentence Structure
  Structural Grammar
  Surface Structure
  Syntax
  Tagmemic Analysis

Functional Illiteracy (1968 1980)
USE Functional Literacy

Functional Literacy *MAR. 1980*
Postings: 1,182 GC: 460
- SN Ability to read and write at the level necessary to participate effectively in society
- UF Functional Illiteracy (1968 1980)
  Survival Literacy
- NT Functional Reading
- BT Literacy
- RT Adult Basic Education
  Adult Literacy
  Adult Reading Programs
  Basic Skills
  Literacy Education
  Minimum Competencies
  Reading Skills
  Workplace Literacy
  Writing Skills

Functional Notional Syllabi
USE Notional Functional Syllabi

Functional Reading *JUL. 1966*
Postings: 286 GC: 460
- SN Ability to read nonacademic, nonfiction materials such as bus schedules, tax forms, recipes, street signs, insurance forms, and job-related items
- UF Survival Reading Skills

= Two or more Descriptors are used to represent this term.
The term's main entry shows the appropriate coordination.

BT Functional Literacy
Reading
RT Adult Literacy
Adult Reading Programs
Content Area Reading
Literacy Education
Reading Skills

Functional Systems Theory
USE Systems Analysis

Functions (Mathematics) *APR. 1982*
Postings: 709 GC: 480
SN Mathematical associations in which a variable is so related to another that for each value assumed by one there is a value determined for the other
UF Mappings (Mathematics)
BT Mathematical Formulas
RT Calculus
Equations (Mathematics)
Limits (Mathematics)
Logarithms
Mathematical Concepts
Polynomials
Statistical Distributions
Transformations (Mathematics)
Vectors (Mathematics)

Functions (Sociology)
USE Role

Functors
USE Function Words

Fund Raising *FEB. 1978*
Postings: 2,157 GC: 620
SN Identifying, soliciting, acquiring, and cultivating financial resources (Note: Prior to Feb78, the instruction "Fund Raising, USE Financial Support" was carried in the Thesaurus)
NT Grantsmanship
RT Capital
Donors
Educational Finance
Endowment Funds
Finance Occupations
Financial Needs
Financial Problems
Financial Services
Financial Support
Income
Institutional Advancement
Investment
Library Funding
Phonathons
Political Campaigns
Private Financial Support
Program Proposals
Proposal Writing
Scholarship Funds
School Funds
Trusts (Financial)

Fundamental Concepts *JUL. 1966*
Postings: 1,103 GC: 110
SN Elementary or essential ideas and constructs
NT Compensation (Concept)
Conservation (Concept)
Object Permanence
RT Concept Formation
Concept Mapping
Concept Teaching
Geographic Concepts
Mathematical Concepts
Scientific Concepts

Fundamental Education (Adults)
USE Adult Basic Education

Fundamental Skills (Daily Living)
USE Daily Living Skills

Fundamental Skills (School)
USE Basic Skills

Funding
USE Financial Support

Fungi *APR. 1990*
Postings: 42 GC: 490
SN Nucleated, sporebearing organisms devoid of chlorophyll—classified as a separate kingdom or as a division of plantae
RT Bacteria
Mycology
Pesticides
Plants (Botany)

Furniture *JUL. 1966*
Postings: 150 GC: 910
NT Classroom Furniture
BT Equipment
RT Equipment Storage
Furniture Arrangement
Furniture Design
Furniture Industry
Home Furnishings

Furniture (Classroom)
USE Classroom Furniture

Furniture Arrangement *JUL. 1966*
Postings: 133 GC: 920
BT Organization
RT Classroom Furniture
Flexible Facilities
Furniture
Furniture Design
Home Furnishings
Interior Design
Interior Space
Space Utilization

Furniture Design *JUL. 1966*
Postings: 121 GC: 420
BT Design
RT Classroom Furniture
Design Crafts
Design Requirements
Equipment Storage
Furniture
Furniture Arrangement
Furniture Industry
Lumber Industry

Furniture Industry *AUG. 1969*
Postings: 18 GC: 650
BT Manufacturing Industry
RT Furniture
Furniture Design
Home Furnishings
Lumber Industry
Woodworking

Further Education
USE Adult Education

Fused Curriculum *JUL. 1966*
Postings: 603 GC: 350
SN Curriculum that combines two or more subjects and studies their interrelationship (e.g., a high school course that combines the study of literature and history)
BT Curriculum
RT Experimental Curriculum
Integrated Curriculum
Interdisciplinary Approach
Unified Studies Curriculum

Future Studies
USE Futures (of Society)

Futures (of Society) *JUN. 1973*
Postings: 16,075 GC: 520
UF Alternative Futures
Educational Futures #
Future Studies
Futurism
Futuristics
Futurology
RT Appropriate Technology
Culture Lag
Decision Making
Delphi Technique
Emerging Occupations
Environmental Scanning
Long Range Planning
Planning
Prediction
Public Policy
Relevance (Education)
Revolution
Science and Society
Social Change
Social Indicators
Strategic Planning
Technological Advancement
Trend Analysis
Values
World Affairs

Futures Planning
USE Long Range Planning

Futurism
USE Futures (of Society)

Futuristics
USE Futures (of Society)

Futurology
USE Futures (of Society)

G Scores
USE Grade Equivalent Scores

Ga *JUL. 1966*
Postings: 6 GC: 440
BT African Languages

Gaelic (Irish)
USE Irish

Gaelic (Scottish)
USE Scots Gaelic

Game Theory *JUL. 1966*
Postings: 506 GC: 810
BT Operations Research
Theories
RT Cybernetics
Decision Making
Heuristics
Management Games
Mathematical Logic
Mathematical Models
Monte Carlo Methods
Probability
Problem Solving
Risk
Simulation
Statistics

Gamekeeping
USE Wildlife Management

Games *JUL. 1966*
Postings: 2,231 GC: 470
NT Childrens Games
Computer Games
Educational Games
Management Games
Olympic Games
Puzzles
Video Games

BT Activities
RT Athletics
Play
Recreational Activities
Toys

Ganda *JUL. 1966*
Postings: 11 GC: 440
UF Luganda
BT Bantu Languages

Garbage
USE Solid Wastes

Gardeners
USE Gardening
AND Grounds Keepers

Gardening *SEP. 2000*
Postings: 203 GC: 410
SN The laying out and care of a plot of ground devoted partially or wholly to the growing of plants such as flowers, herbs, or vegetables
UF Gardeners #
BT Agriculture
RT Botany
Floriculture
Food
Gardens
Horticulture
Landscaping
Ornamental Horticulture
Plant Growth
Plant Propagation
Plants (Botany)
Weeds

Gardens *SEP. 2000*
Postings: 65 GC: 410
SN Plots of ground where herbs, fruits, flowers, vegetables, or other plants are cultivated—includes "water gardens," built about streams or pools, often with aquatic plants
BT Facilities
RT Botany
Food
Gardening
Greenhouses
Nurseries (Horticulture)
Parks
Plant Growth
Plants (Botany)

Garment Industry
USE Fashion Industry

Gas Utilities
USE Utilities

Gas Welding
USE Welding

Gasoline *DEC. 1992*
Postings: 5 GC: 410
SN Mixture of liquid hydrocarbons used chiefly to fuel spark-ignited internal combustion engines
BT Fossil Fuels
RT Motor Vehicles
Oil
Petroleum Industry

Gateway Systems *AUG. 1989*
Postings: 141 GC: 710
SN Intermediary computer systems that simplify access to and use of other computer systems, networks, and bulletin boards, sometimes including unified access and switching across multiple databank hosts
UF Front End Systems (Computers)
Interface Systems (Cross Database)

= Two or more Descriptors are used to represent this term.
The term's main entry shows the appropriate coordination.

RT   Computer Interfaces
Computers
Databases
Information Systems
Man Machine Systems
Menu Driven Software
Online Searching
Online Systems
User Needs (Information)

Gauges
USE   Measurement Equipment

Gbaya   *JUL. 1966*
   Postings: 3   GC: 440
UF   Gbeya
BT   African Languages

Gbeya
USE   Gbaya

GED Programs
USE   High School Equivalency Programs

Gender (Sex)
USE   Sex

Gender Bias
USE   Sex Bias

Gender Differences (Sex)
USE   Sex Differences

Gender Discrimination
USE   Sex Discrimination

Gender Identity (Sex)
USE   Sexual Identity

Gender Issues   *JUN. 2000*
   Postings: 730   GC: 520
SN   Points of discussion or controversy pertaining to aspects of the male or female sex, especially in relation to societal or cultural conceptions of masculine and feminine roles or traits (Note: Use a more precise term if possible—do not confuse with the Identifier "Gender (Language)")
RT   Controversial Issues (Course Content)
Females
Femininity
Feminism
Feminist Criticism
Males
Masculinity
Sex
Sex Bias
Sex Differences
Sex Discrimination
Sex Fairness
Sex Role
Sex Stereotypes
Sexism in Language
Sexual Identity
Sexuality
Womens Education
Womens Studies

Gender Role (Sex)
USE   Sex Role

Gender Stereotypes
USE   Sex Stereotypes

Genealogy   *JAN. 1985*
   Postings: 151   GC: 430
SN   History or account of lineal descent from an ancestor or ancestors
UF   Ancestral Lineage
Family Trees
BT   Family History

RT   Ethnic Origins
Extended Family
Family (Sociological Unit)
Information Sources
Kinship

General and Special Education Relationship
USE   Regular and Special Education Relationship

General Business Education
USE   Basic Business Education

General Education   *JUL. 1966*
   Postings: 3,584   GC: 400
SN   Integrated learning experiences structured across subject disciplines to provide the set of skills and knowledge needed to function in society
UF   General High Schools (1966 1980)
Liberal Education
BT   Education
RT   Academic Education
Liberal Arts
Technology Education

General Educational Development Programs
USE   High School Equivalency Programs

General High Schools (1966 1980)
USE   General Education

General Mathematics   *DEC. 1992*
   Postings: 52   GC: 480
SN   Mathematics courses, frequently of an introductory or remedial nature, that emphasize everyday computational operations and usually include practical applications—most commonly conducted for noncollege-bound secondary school students
BT   Mathematics Curriculum
RT   Mathematical Applications
Mathematics
Mathematics Education
Mathematics Instruction
Remedial Mathematics

General Mechanics
USE   Mechanics (Process)

General Methods Courses
USE   Methods Courses

General Practice (Medicine)
USE   Family Practice (Medicine)

General Science   *JUL. 1966*
   Postings: 664   GC: 490
SN   Science courses, frequently introductory, that include such components as physical, biological, space, and earth sciences
BT   Science Curriculum
RT   Core Curriculum
Science Education
Science Instruction

General Semantics
USE   Semantics

General Shop
USE   Shop Curriculum

Generalizability Theory   *OCT. 1983*
   Postings: 295   GC: 810
SN   Statistical model for interpreting variance components associated with a specified universe of conditions

BT   Theories
RT   Analysis of Variance
Data Collection
Data Interpretation
Error of Measurement
Interrater Reliability
Mathematical Models
Measurement
Multivariate Analysis
Reliability
Research Design
Sample Size
Sampling
Scores
Statistical Analysis
Statistical Data
Statistical Distributions
Statistical Inference
Test Interpretation
Test Reliability
Test Theory
True Scores

Generalization   *JUN. 1969*
   Postings: 1,701   GC: 110
SN   Process of drawing inferences or forming general conclusions from a number of specific instances—also, the tendency to make the same response to new but similar stimuli
NT   Stimulus Generalization
BT   Abstract Reasoning
Learning Processes
RT   Association (Psychology)
Concept Formation
Concept Teaching
Experiments
Induction
Inferences
Learning Theories
Mediation Theory
Patterned Responses
Research Methodology
Scientific Methodology
Theories
Transfer of Training
Validity

Generation Gap   *APR. 1970*
   Postings: 371   GC: 530
RT   Age Differences
Intergenerational Programs
Parent Child Relationship
Student Alienation
Youth Problems

Generative Grammar   *OCT. 1968*
   Postings: 356   GC: 450
SN   A grammar, or system of rules, designed to generate (i.e., produce or predict) all of and only the well-formed (i.e., "grammatical") sentences of a language
NT   Transformational Generative Grammar
BT   Linguistic Theory
RT   Generative Phonology
Grammar
Sentence Structure
Syntax

Generative Phonology   *SEP. 1974*
   Postings: 116   GC: 450
SN   Theory or system of rules which describes or predicts well-formed phonological outputs, and is used to express the ability of speakers to produce the sounds of their native language
BT   Linguistic Theory
Phonology
RT   Generative Grammar
Phonemics
Phonetics

Generative Transformational Grammar
USE   Transformational Generative Grammar

Genetic Diversity
USE   Biodiversity

Genetic Engineering   *OCT. 1982*
   Postings: 202   GC: 490
SN   Human manipulation of genetic material to effect biological change
UF   Recombinant DNA #
BT   Genetics
Technology
RT   Biochemistry
Biological Influences
Biology
Biotechnology
Culturing Techniques
Cytology
DNA
Drug Therapy
Embryology
Medicine
Microbiology
Molecular Biology
Nucleic Acids
Radiation Biology
Radiology
Reproduction (Biology)
Scientific Research

Genetics   *JUL. 1966*
   Postings: 1,993   GC: 490
SN   Biological science which deals with the phenomena of heredity and the variation between parents and offspring
NT   Genetic Engineering
BT   Biological Sciences
RT   Agriculture
Biodiversity
Biological Parents
Biology
Botany
Congenital Impairments
Cystic Fibrosis
DNA
Downs Syndrome
Embryology
Enzymes
Evolution
Heredity
Medicine
Microbiology
Molecular Biology
Nature Nurture Controversy
Nucleic Acids
Prenatal Influences
Radiation Biology
Radioisotopes
Reproduction (Biology)
Rh Factors
Sickle Cell Anemia
Sociobiology
Zoology

Genocide   *FEB. 2000*
   Postings: 114   GC: 610
SN   Deliberate systematic measures, often overtly or tacitly supported by a government, intended to exterminate a racial, political, or cultural group of people—usually refers to mass murder and other physical harm but may include destruction of language, religion, or culture (Note: See also the Identifier "Holocaust")
BT   International Crimes
RT   Civil Liberties
Homicide
Minority Groups
Nazism
War

Geochemistry   *DEC. 1992*
   Postings: 29   GC: 490
SN   Study of the chemistry of the earth (or a celestial body)
BT   Chemistry
Earth Science
RT   Geology
Geophysics
Metallurgy
Mineralogy
Physical Chemistry

= Two or more Descriptors are used to represent this term.
The term's main entry shows the appropriate coordination.

Geographic Concepts　　　　*JUL. 1966*
　　Postings: 824　　　　　　　GC: 400
SN　Abstract ideas related to geography that
　　are usually emphasized in instruction
　　(i.e., mobility, population distribution,
　　demographic variation, spatial distribu-
　　tion, microclimate, energy flow, etc.)
RT　Concept Mapping
　　Concept Teaching
　　Fundamental Concepts
　　Geography
　　Geography Instruction

Geographic Dialects
USE　Regional Dialects

Geographic Distribution　　*JUL. 1966*
　　Postings: 984　　　　　　　GC: 550
BT　Demography
RT　Community Size
　　Ethnic Distribution
　　Geography
　　Human Geography
　　Incidence
　　Physical Geography
　　Population Distribution
　　Racial Distribution
　　School District Size
　　Teacher Distribution

Geographic Isolation　　　*MAY 1993*
　　Postings: 128　　　　　　　GC: 550
SN　A condition characterized by remote-
　　ness, relative inaccessibility, and spar-
　　sity or small size of population (Note:
　　Prior to May93, the Identifier "Isolation
　　(Geographic)" was used to index this
　　concept—see also the current Identifier
　　"School District Isolation")
RT　Cultural Isolation
　　Demography
　　Distance Education
　　Geographic Location
　　Geography
　　Professional Isolation
　　Rural Areas
　　Rural Environment
　　Rural Population
　　Rural Schools
　　Social Isolation

Geographic Location　　　*JUL. 1966*
　　Postings: 840　　　　　　　GC: 550
RT　Access to Education
　　Cartography
　　Climate
　　Distance
　　Geographic Isolation
　　Geography
　　Physical Geography
　　Place of Residence
　　Proximity
　　Relocation
　　School Location
　　Site Analysis
　　Topography

Geographic Mobility (1980 1980)
USE　Migration

Geographic Regions　　　*JUL. 1966*
　　Postings: 1,213　　　　　　GC: 550
UF　Areas (Geographic)
NT　Counties
　　Developed Nations
　　Developing Nations
　　Foreign Countries
　　Low Income States
　　Metropolitan Areas
　　Nonmetropolitan Areas
　　Physical Divisions (Geographic)
　　Political Divisions (Geographic)
　　Poverty Areas
　　Rural Areas
　　Urban Areas
RT　Area Studies
　　Geography
　　Physical Geography

Place of Residence
Regional Attitudes
Regional Characteristics
Regional Dialects
Regional Schools
School Districts

Geography　　　　　　　*JUL. 1966*
　　Postings: 2,629　　　　　　GC: 400
NT　Human Geography
　　Physical Geography
　　World Geography
BT　Social Sciences
RT　Area Studies
　　Atlases
　　Cartography
　　Conservation Education
　　Geographic Concepts
　　Geographic Distribution
　　Geographic Isolation
　　Geographic Location
　　Geographic Regions
　　Geography Instruction
　　Map Skills
　　Maps
　　Oceanography
　　Physical Divisions (Geographic)
　　Political Divisions (Geographic)
　　Social Science Research
　　Social Scientists
　　Social Studies
　　Topography

Geography Instruction　　*JUL. 1966*
　　Postings: 2,771　　　　　　GC: 400
BT　Instruction
RT　Geographic Concepts
　　Geography

Geology　　　　　　　　*JUL. 1966*
　　Postings: 1,898　　　　　　GC: 490
NT　Mineralogy
　　Paleontology
　　Petrology
BT　Earth Science
RT　Asbestos
　　Clay
　　Coal
　　Crystallography
　　Geochemistry
　　Geophysics
　　Geothermal Energy
　　Groundwater
　　Hydrology
　　Minerals
　　Mining
　　Natural Gas
　　Oceanography
　　Oil
　　Physical Geography
　　Plate Tectonics
　　Scientific Research
　　Seismology
　　Soil Science
　　Volcanoes

Geometric Concepts　　　*JUL. 1966*
　　Postings: 2,138　　　　　　GC: 480
NT　Area
　　Congruence (Mathematics)
　　Orthographic Projection
　　Polygons
　　Vectors (Mathematics)
　　Volume (Mathematics)
BT　Mathematical Concepts
RT　Geometric Constructions
　　Geometry
　　Patternmaking
　　Patterns in Mathematics
　　Properties (Mathematics)
　　Symmetry

Geometric Constructions　　*APR. 1982*
　　Postings: 348　　　　　　　GC: 480
SN　Diagrams and other forms that illustrate
　　geometric relationships, figures, or pat-
　　terns
BT　Visual Aids
RT　Diagrams

Geometric Concepts
Geometry
Mathematics Materials
Polygons

Geometrical Optics
USE　Optics

Geometrodynamics
USE　Relativity

Geometry　　　　　　　*JUL. 1966*
　　Postings: 2,583　　　　　　GC: 480
NT　Analytic Geometry
　　Plane Geometry
　　Solid Geometry
　　Topology
BT　Mathematics
RT　Congruence (Mathematics)
　　Geometric Concepts
　　Geometric Constructions
　　Symmetry
　　Transformations (Mathematics)
　　Vectors (Mathematics)

Geophysics　　　　　　*DEC. 1969*
　　Postings: 162　　　　　　　GC: 490
NT　Plate Tectonics
BT　Earth Science
RT　Geochemistry
　　Geology
　　Geothermal Energy
　　Gravity (Physics)
　　Hydrology
　　Mineralogy
　　Mining
　　Petrology
　　Physics
　　Seismology
　　Wind Energy

Georgian
USE　Caucasian Languages

Geoscience
USE　Earth Science

Geothermal Energy　　　*OCT. 1984*
　　Postings: 41　　　　　　　GC: 490
SN　Power derived from the earth's heat
BT　Energy
RT　Alternative Energy Sources
　　Electricity
　　Geology
　　Geophysics
　　Groundwater
　　Heat
　　Power Technology
　　Water Resources

Geriatrics　　　　　　　*AUG. 1968*
　　Postings: 704　　　　　　　GC: 210
SN　Branch of medicine dealing with the physi-
　　ology and pathology of old age
BT　Medicine
RT　Aging (Individuals)
　　Educational Gerontology
　　Gerontology
　　Medical Services
　　Older Adults

German　　　　　　　　*JUL. 1966*
　　Postings: 3,077　　　　　　GC: 440
NT　Yiddish
BT　Indo European Languages
RT　German Literature

German Literature　　　*APR. 1969*
　　Postings: 334　　　　　　　GC: 430
BT　Literature
RT　German

German Measles
USE　Rubella

Gerontology　　　　　　*AUG. 1976*
　　Postings: 1,715　　　　　　GC: 400
SN　Scientific study of aging and problems of
　　the aged
NT　Educational Gerontology
BT　Social Sciences
RT　Adult Development
　　Aging (Individuals)
　　Geriatrics
　　Older Adults
　　Retirement
　　Social Science Research
　　Social Scientists

Gestalt Therapy　　　　*JAN. 1985*
　　Postings: 92　　　　　　　GC: 230
SN　Form of psychotherapy focusing on the
　　totality of the individual's current func-
　　tioning and relationships rather than on
　　past experiences or developmental
　　history—individual or group techniques
　　are designed to elicit spontaneous feel-
　　ings and self-awareness
BT　Holistic Approach
　　Psychotherapy
RT　Counseling Techniques
　　Desensitization
　　Laboratory Training
　　Phenomenology
　　Self Actualization
　　Self Concept

Gestation
USE　Pregnancy

Gestures (Deaf Communication)
USE　Sign Language

Gestures (Nonverbal Communication)
USE　Body Language

Ghettos　　　　　　　　*JUL. 1966*
　　Postings: 421　　　　　　　GC: 550
SN　Residential areas, usually within cities,
　　in which members of a particular racial
　　or cultural group live, primarily because
　　of social, economic, or legal factors (Note:
　　Prior to Mar80, this term was not scoped
　　and was often used synonymously with
　　"Slums")
RT　Anti Semitism
　　Ethnic Groups
　　Housing Discrimination
　　Inner City
　　Jews
　　Racial Discrimination
　　Racial Segregation
　　Slums
　　Social Discrimination
　　Subcultures
　　Urban Population

Gifted　　　　　　　　*JUL. 1966*
　　Postings: 7,604　　　　　　GC: 120
UF　Gifted Children
　　Gifted Teachers
　　Gifted Youth
　　Mentally Advanced Children
NT　Academically Gifted
　　Gifted Disabled
　　Gifted Disadvantaged
BT　Groups
RT　Ability
　　Achievement
　　Aptitude
　　Exceptional Child Research
　　Special Education
　　Special Education Teachers
　　Talent

Gifted Children
USE　Gifted

= Two or more Descriptors are used to represent this term.
The term's main entry shows the appropriate coordination.

Gifted Disabled   OCT. 1983
   Postings: 213   GC: 220
SN   Persons of superior ability or potential
      who also have physical, sensory, emo-
      tional, or behavioral disabilities
UF   Gifted Handicapped
BT   Gifted
RT   Disabilities
      Gifted Disadvantaged

Gifted Disadvantaged   OCT. 1983
   Postings: 197   GC: 540
SN   Persons of superior ability or potential
      who are also economically, education-
      ally, or socially disadvantaged
BT   Disadvantaged
      Gifted
RT   Gifted Disabled

Gifted Handicapped
USE   Gifted Disabled

Gifted Students
USE   Academically Gifted

Gifted Teachers
USE   Gifted

Gifted Youth
USE   Gifted

Girls
USE   Females

Girls Clubs (1966 1980)
USE   Youth Clubs

Glare   APR. 1969
   Postings: 39   GC: 920
RT   Light
      Lighting
      Lighting Design
      Luminescence
      Visual Environment
      Windows

Glass   JUL. 1966
   Postings: 54   GC: 910
RT   Art Materials
      Ceramics
      Glaziers
      Industrial Arts

Glass Installers
USE   Glaziers

Glass Walls   JUL. 1966
   Postings: 22   GC: 920
SN   Walls consisting largely of windows
UF   Window Walls
BT   Structural Elements (Construction)
RT   Classroom Design
      Windows

Glaziers   JUL. 1966
   Postings: 11   GC: 640
UF   Glass Installers
BT   Skilled Workers
RT   Glass

Glee Clubs
USE   Singing

Global Approach   OCT. 1974
   Postings: 5,453   GC: 310
SN   Approach to social, cultural, scientific,
      and humanistic questions involving an
      orientation to the world as a single inter-
      acting system (Note: Do not confuse
      with outlooks or philosophies of life, for
      which see "World Views")

UF   Global Perspectives
      International Approach
      Worldmindedness
      Worldwide Approach
NT   Global Education
BT   Holistic Approach
RT   Cultural Awareness
      Group Unity
      Intercultural Programs
      Interdisciplinary Approach
      International Cooperation
      International Relations
      Social Sciences
      World Affairs
      World Problems

Global Education   NOV. 1994
   Postings: 950   GC: 400
SN   Learning/teaching activities across all
      grade levels that focus on the inter-
      relatedness of peoples, cultures, and
      nations—subfields include world geog-
      raphy, world history, and international
      relations
UF   Global Studies Education
      World Studies Education
NT   International Education
BT   Education
      Global Approach
RT   Area Studies
      Citizenship Education
      Cross Cultural Studies
      Economics Education
      Environmental Education
      Ethnic Studies
      Multicultural Education
      Peace
      World Geography
      World History

Global Perspectives
USE   Global Approach

Global Studies Education
USE   Global Education

Global Warming   JAN. 1993
   Postings: 84   GC: 490
SN   Gradual increases in the earth's average
      temperatures (Note: If appropriate, use
      the more specific term "Greenhouse
      Effect")
NT   Greenhouse Effect
BT   Climate Change
RT   Heat
      Temperature
      World Problems

Glossaries   JUL. 1966
   Postings: 1,146   GC: 730
SN   Dictionaries of special or technical terms
      with limited subject scope
BT   Dictionaries
RT   Definitions
      Lexicography
      Thesauri
      Vocabulary

Glottochronology   JUL. 1966
   Postings: 11   GC: 450
SN   A technique for estimating by statistical
      comparison of vocabulary samples the
      time during which two or more lan-
      guages have evolved separately from a
      common source
BT   Diachronic Linguistics
RT   Comparative Analysis
      Etymology
      Language Classification
      Language Research
      Languages
      Lexicography
      Lexicology
      Linguistics
      Vocabulary

Glues
USE   Adhesives

Goal Attainment
USE   Success

Goal Orientation   JUL. 1966
   Postings: 2,450   GC: 120
SN   Psychological disposition toward achiev-
      ing one's objectives
BT   Orientation
RT   Achievement Need
      Aspiration
      Career Planning
      Competition
      Coping
      Delay of Gratification
      Failure
      Fear of Success
      Motivation
      Need Gratification
      Objectives
      Personality Assessment
      Psychological Characteristics
      Psychological Needs
      Self Motivation
      Student Educational Objectives
      Success
      Type A Behavior
      Type B Behavior
      Values Clarification
      Work Ethic

Goals
USE   Objectives

Golf   JUN. 1975
   Postings: 64   GC: 470
BT   Athletics
RT   Lifetime Sports

Gonorrhea
USE   Venereal Diseases

Good Citizenship
USE   Citizenship

Goodness of Fit   NOV. 1970
   Postings: 777   GC: 820
SN   Statistical estimate of the extent to which
      a score distribution, or other numerical
      series of observations, differs signifi-
      cantly from the numerical values pre-
      dicted by a mathematical model (i.e., an
      estimation of how well the theory fits the
      data)
BT   Statistical Analysis
RT   Chi Square
      Factor Analysis
      Mathematical Models
      Maximum Likelihood Statistics
      Robustness (Statistics)
      Statistical Significance
      Statistics

Governance   JUL. 1966
   Postings: 5,212   GC: 330
SN   The policy-making, objective-setting, and
      exercise of authority in an organization,
      institution, or agency—includes admin-
      istrative or management functions to the
      extent that they relate to the execution of
      policy and authority
NT   Administration
      Community Control
      Federal Regulation
      State Regulation
RT   Administrative Organization
      College Governing Councils
      Diversity (Institutional)
      Governing Boards
      Government (Administrative Body)
      Government School Relationship
      Institutional Autonomy
      Policy Formation
      Politics

      Professional Autonomy
      School District Autonomy
      Tribal Sovereignty
      Trustees

Governing Boards   JUL. 1966
   Postings: 1,992   GC: 330
SN   Group charged with the responsibility
      for some degree of control over manag-
      ing the affairs of public or private institu-
      tions
UF   Board of Regents
      Board of Trustees
NT   Boards of Education
BT   Organizations (Groups)
RT   Administration
      Administrative Organization
      Advisory Committees
      Board Administrator Relationship
      College Administration
      Committees
      Governance
      Institutional Administration
      Policy Formation
      School Administration
      State Departments of Education
      Trustees

Government (Administrative Body)
                                                             JUL. 1966
   Postings: 1,040   GC: 610
NT   Federal Government
      Local Government
      State Government
      Student Government
      Tribal Government
BT   Organizations (Groups)
RT   Agencies
      Capitalism
      Civics
      Communism
      Constitutional History
      Constitutional Law
      Depository Libraries
      Fascism
      Federalism
      Governance
      Government Employees
      Government Libraries
      Government Publications
      Government Role
      Government School Relationship
      Governmental Structure
      Hearings
      Legislation
      Loyalty Oaths
      Nonprofit Organizations
      Police
      Political Affiliation
      Political Campaigns
      Political Candidates
      Political Parties
      Politics
      Producer Services
      Public Administration
      Public Administration Education
      Public Agencies
      Public Service Occupations
      Socialism
      Totalitarianism
      United States Government (Course)

Government Agencies
USE   Public Agencies

Government Documents
USE   Government Publications

Government Employees   JUL. 1966
   Postings: 1,417   GC: 610
UF   Civil Service Employees
      Public Employees
NT   Extension Agents
      Food and Drug Inspectors
      Foreign Diplomats
      Immigration Inspectors
      Military Personnel
      Police
      Public Officials

= Two or more Descriptors are used to represent this term.
The term's main entry shows the appropriate coordination.

Public School Teachers
BT Personnel
RT City Government
Federal Government
Government (Administrative Body)
Governmental Structure
Local Government
Public Sector
Public Service Occupations
Service Workers
State Government

Government Functions
USE Government Role

Government Libraries
JUL. 1966
Postings: 262
GC: 710
SN Special libraries maintained out of government funds (Note: Use a more specific term if possible)
UF Federal Libraries #
NT National Libraries
State Libraries
BT Special Libraries
RT Archives
Depository Libraries
Government (Administrative Body)
Law Libraries

Government Policy
USE Public Policy

Government Publications
NOV. 1968
Postings: 1,763
GC: 730
SN Publications that are funded, prepared, and/or distributed by national, state, or local government units
UF Government Documents
Public Documents
BT Publications
RT Depository Libraries
Freedom of Information
Government (Administrative Body)

Government Role
JUL. 1966
Postings: 12,662
GC: 610
UF Congress Role
Government Functions
BT Role
RT Cable Franchising
Civil Law
Conservatism
Constitutional History
Constitutional Law
Copyrights
Court Role
Federal Regulation
Federalism
Government (Administrative Body)
Government School Relationship
Institutional Autonomy
Institutional Role
Liberalism
National Parks
National Security
New Federalism
Patents
Privatization
Public Agencies
Public Policy
Public Sector
Revenue Sharing
School District Autonomy
State Action
State Regulation
Tribal Sovereignty
Trust Responsibility (Government)

Government School Relationship
SEP. 1977
Postings: 5,683
GC: 330
SN Any interaction of an educational institution or school district with a local, provincial, or central government
UF School Government Relationship
NT State School District Relationship
BT Relationship
RT Block Grants
City Government

Community Control
Compulsory Education
Constitutional Law
Developing Institutions
Educational Legislation
Federal Aid
Federal Government
Federal Regulation
Federal State Relationship
Full State Funding
Governance
Government (Administrative Body)
Government Role
Institutional Autonomy
Local Government
National Competency Tests
National Curriculum
Partnerships in Education
Politics of Education
Private School Aid
Privatization
Public Policy
Public Service
School Administration
School Attitudes
School District Autonomy
School Involvement
School Role
Schools
State Aid
State Government
State Regulation
Student Records
Tribally Controlled Education

Government Sector
USE Public Sector

Government Structure
USE Governmental Structure

Governmental Structure
JUL. 1966
Postings: 550
GC: 610
UF Government Structure
BT Group Structure
RT Bureaucracy
Constitutional History
Constitutional Law
Federalism
Government (Administrative Body)
Government Employees
Public Administration Education
Social Structure

Grade 1
JUL. 1966
Postings: 4,323
GC: 340
BT Instructional Program Divisions
RT Elementary Education
Primary Education

Grade 10
JUL. 1966
Postings: 1,735
GC: 340
BT Instructional Program Divisions
RT High Schools
Secondary Education

Grade 11
JUL. 1966
Postings: 1,543
GC: 340
BT Instructional Program Divisions
RT High Schools
Secondary Education

Grade 12
JUL. 1966
Postings: 1,780
GC: 340
BT Instructional Program Divisions
RT High School Seniors
High Schools
Secondary Education

Grade 13 (1970 1980)
USE Postsecondary Education

Grade 14 (1970 1980)
USE Postsecondary Education

Grade 2
JUL. 1966
Postings: 2,810
GC: 340
BT Instructional Program Divisions
RT Elementary Education
Primary Education

Grade 3
JUL. 1966
Postings: 3,318
GC: 340
BT Instructional Program Divisions
RT Elementary Education
Primary Education

Grade 4
JUL. 1966
Postings: 4,095
GC: 340
BT Instructional Program Divisions
RT Elementary Education
Intermediate Grades

Grade 5
JUL. 1966
Postings: 4,247
GC: 340
BT Instructional Program Divisions
RT Elementary Education
Intermediate Grades
Middle Schools

Grade 6
JUL. 1966
Postings: 4,275
GC: 340
BT Instructional Program Divisions
RT Elementary Education
Intermediate Grades
Middle Schools

Grade 7
JUL. 1966
Postings: 3,049
GC: 340
BT Instructional Program Divisions
RT Elementary Education
Junior High Schools
Middle Schools
Secondary Education

Grade 8
JUL. 1966
Postings: 3,904
GC: 340
BT Instructional Program Divisions
RT Elementary Education
Junior High Schools
Middle Schools
Secondary Education

Grade 9
JUL. 1966
Postings: 2,465
GC: 340
BT Instructional Program Divisions
RT High School Freshmen
High Schools
Junior High Schools
Middle Schools
Secondary Education

Grade a Year Integration (1966 1980)
USE School Desegregation

Grade Average
USE Grade Point Average

Grade Cards
USE Report Cards

Grade Charts (1966 1980)
MAR. 1980
Postings: 6
GC: 310
SN Invalid Descriptor—used for curriculum charts that are organized by instructional program "grades," or for student skill charts that either record scholastic "grades" or student progression through several instructional program "grades"

Grade Equivalent Scales (1967 1980)
USE Grade Equivalent Scores

Grade Equivalent Scores
NOV. 1970
Postings: 173
GC: 820
SN Ability or achievement scores that have been converted to the grade level norm—

usually expressed in years and tenths, e.g., 6.4 means sixth grade, fourth month (Note: Do not use for readability level of written material)
UF G Scores
Grade Equivalent Scales (1967 1980)
Grade Scores
BT Scores
RT Equated Scores
Equivalency Tests
High School Equivalency Programs
Measurement
Measurement Techniques
Norm Referenced Tests
Raw Scores
Student Certification
Test Norms
Testing
Weighted Scores

Grade Inflation
OCT. 1979
Postings: 172
GC: 320
SN A continuous rise in the proportion of higher scholastic grades awarded, often associated with a perceived laxity in academic standards
UF Inflated Grades
BT Grades (Scholastic)
RT Academic Standards
Grade Point Average
Grading
Scoring

Grade Levels
USE Instructional Program Divisions

Grade Organization (1966 1980)
USE Instructional Program Divisions

Grade Point Average
JUL. 1966
Postings: 2,558
GC: 820
SN A measure of scholastic achievement in several subjects or courses obtained by dividing the sum of the total grade points by the total number of hours of course work (Note: Prior to Mar80, the instruction "Grade Average, USE Class Average" was carried in the Thesaurus)
UF Grade Average
Quality Point Ratio
BT Grades (Scholastic)
RT Academic Standards
Class Rank
Grade Inflation
Grade Prediction

Grade Prediction
JUL. 1966
Postings: 515
GC: 820
SN Estimation of future achievement, expressed in scholastic grades or marks, on the basis of past and current information
BT Prediction
RT Grade Point Average
Grades (Scholastic)
Grading
Predictive Measurement

Grade Repetition
JUL. 1966
Postings: 631
GC: 320
SN Repeating a grade level in school because of deficient achievement
UF Retention (in Grade)
RT Academic Failure
Low Achievement
Social Promotion
Student Promotion
Underachievement

Grade Scores
USE Grade Equivalent Scores

Grades (Program Divisions)
USE Instructional Program Divisions

Grades (Scholastic)   JUL. 1966
Postings: 2,207   GC: 310
UF   Marks (Scholastic)
NT   Grade Inflation
      Grade Point Average
RT   Academic Achievement
      Academic Probation
      Academic Records
      Class Rank
      College Credits
      Credit Courses
      Credit No Credit Grading
      Credits
      Grade Prediction
      Grading
      Graduation Requirements
      Pass Fail Grading
      Report Cards
      Scores
      Student Evaluation

Grading   JUL. 1966
Postings: 2,763   GC: 310
SN   Process of rating an individual's or
      group's performance, achievement, or
      less frequently, behavior, using specifi-
      cally established scales of values
UF   Contract Grading #
      Marking (Scholastic)
NT   Credit No Credit Grading
      Pass Fail Grading
BT   Achievement Rating
RT   Academic Achievement
      Educational Testing
      Grade Inflation
      Grade Prediction
      Grades (Scholastic)
      Holistic Evaluation
      Informal Assessment
      Report Cards
      Scoring
      Scoring Rubrics
      Student Evaluation
      Summative Evaluation
      Teacher Student Relationship
      Writing Evaluation

Graduate Ceremonies
USE   Commencement Ceremonies

Graduate Education
USE   Graduate Study

Graduate Medical Education   AUG. 1976
Postings: 807   GC: 210
SN   Medical education beyond the under-
      graduate medical school and the attain-
      ment of the professional degree, leading
      to eligibility for certification in a specialty
UF   Internships (Medical)
      Residency Programs (Medical)
BT   Graduate Study
      Medical Education
RT   Clinical Experience
      Foreign Medical Graduates
      Graduate Medical Students
      Medical School Faculty
      Medical Schools
      Medicine
      Physicians
      Teaching Hospitals

Graduate Medical Students   AUG. 1976
Postings: 580   GC: 360
SN   Medical school graduates preparing for
      professional certification as specialists,
      usually in teaching hospitals
UF   Fellows (Medical)
      Interns (Medical)
      Physicians in Training
      Residents (Medical)
BT   Medical Students
RT   Foreign Medical Graduates
      Graduate Medical Education
      Hospital Personnel
      Medical Schools
      Physicians

Graduate Professors (1966 1980)
USE   Graduate School Faculty

Graduate School Faculty   MAR. 1980
Postings: 247   GC: 360
SN   Academic staff members engaged in in-
      struction, research, administration, or
      related educational activities in a gradu-
      ate school of a college or university
      (Note: Do not confuse with "Teaching
      Assistants")
UF   Graduate Professors (1966 1980)
NT   Medical School Faculty
BT   College Faculty
RT   Doctoral Programs
      Graduate Study
      Masters Programs

Graduate Students   JUL. 1966
Postings: 5,443   GC: 360
NT   Dental Students
      Law Students
      Medical Students
BT   College Students
RT   College Graduates
      Doctoral Programs
      Graduate Study
      Graduates
      Higher Education
      Masters Programs
      Research Assistants
      Teaching Assistants

Graduate Study   JUL. 1966
Postings: 8,439   GC: 340
UF   Graduate Education
      Graduate Training
NT   Graduate Medical Education
      Postsecondary Education as a Field of
      Study
BT   Higher Education
RT   College Entrance Examinations
      College Graduates
      Degree Requirements
      Doctor of Arts Degrees
      Doctoral Degrees
      Doctoral Dissertations
      Doctoral Programs
      Extended Teacher Education Programs
      Graduate School Faculty
      Graduate Students
      Masters Degrees
      Masters Programs
      Masters Theses
      Postdoctoral Education
      Professional Education
      Undergraduate Study
      Universities
      Upper Division Colleges

Graduate Surveys   JUL. 1966
Postings: 2,887   GC: 810
SN   Followup studies of students who have
      graduated (Note: As of Oct81, use as a
      minor Descriptor for examples of this
      kind of study—use as a major Descrip-
      tor only as the subject of a document)
BT   Followup Studies
      Surveys
RT   Alumni
      Educational Research
      Graduates
      School Surveys
      Student Surveys
      Vocational Followup

Graduate Training
USE   Graduate Study

Graduates   JUL. 1966
Postings: 402   GC: 360
SN   Individuals who have satisfactorily com-
      pleted the requirements of an educa-
      tional program and have been awarded a
      certificate, diploma, or degree
NT   College Graduates
      Foreign Medical Graduates
      High School Graduates

BT   Alumni
RT   Alumni Associations
      Graduate Students
      Graduate Surveys

Graduation   JUL. 1966
Postings: 487   GC: 320
SN   The process of receiving a diploma or
      degree for completing a phase of formal
      education (Note: Do not confuse with
      "Commencement Ceremonies"—use a
      more precise term if possible)
BT   Achievement
RT   College Graduates
      Commencement Ceremonies
      Educational Attainment
      Graduation Requirements
      High School Graduates
      Recognition (Achievement)

Graduation Requirements   JUL. 1966
Postings: 1,506   GC: 320
SN   Educational and other specifications or
      minimum competencies of a program,
      school, college, or university that a stu-
      dent must satisfactorily complete to
      graduate (often stated in terms of se-
      mester hours, credits, residence require-
      ments, or minimum grades)
UF   Diploma Requirements
NT   Degree Requirements
BT   Academic Standards
RT   Academic Achievement
      Credits
      Grades (Scholastic)
      Graduation
      Required Courses
      Residence Requirements
      School Catalogs

Grain Elevator Occupations
USE   Crop Processing Occupations

Grain Marketing
USE   Grains (Food)

Grain Processing
USE   Grains (Food)

Grain Production
USE   Grains (Food)

Grains (Food)   FEB. 1970
Postings: 103   GC: 410
UF   Corn (Field Crop) (1968 1980)
      Grain Marketing
      Grain Processing
      Grain Production
BT   Field Crops
      Food
RT   Agronomy
      Feed Industry

Grammar   JUL. 1966
Postings: 7,568   GC: 450
NT   Morphology (Languages)
      Syntax
BT   Descriptive Linguistics
RT   Case (Grammar)
      Context Free Grammar
      Deep Structure
      Discourse Analysis
      Generative Grammar
      Grammar Translation Method
      Grammatical Acceptability
      Idioms
      Kernel Sentences
      Sentence Diagraming
      Sentence Structure
      Sentences
      Structural Grammar
      Surface Structure
      Tagmemic Analysis
      Traditional Grammar
      Writing Skills

Grammar Translation Method   JUL. 1966
Postings: 163   GC: 450
SN   Traditional foreign language teaching
      method that emphasizes grammatical
      rules and their application to translation—
      emphasis is on reading and writing rather
      than oral communication
BT   Teaching Methods
RT   Audiolingual Methods
      Grammar
      Second Language Instruction
      Translation

Grammatical Acceptability   APR. 1980
Postings: 165   GC: 450
SN   The judgment of a speaker of a language
      concerning the acceptability or gram-
      matical "correctness" of a given utter-
      ance or structure in that language
BT   Language Attitudes
RT   Dialects
      Grammar
      Language Usage
      Language Variation
      Psycholinguistics
      Sociolinguistics

Grandchildren   DEC. 1970
Postings: 104   GC: 510
UF   Granddaughters
      Grandsons
BT   Children

Granddaughters
USE   Grandchildren

Grandfathers
USE   Grandparents

Grandmothers
USE   Grandparents

Grandparents   DEC. 1970
Postings: 427   GC: 510
UF   Grandfathers
      Grandmothers
BT   Parents
RT   Family (Sociological Unit)
      Family Environment
      Family Life
      Older Adults

Grandsons
USE   Grandchildren

Grant Proposals
USE   Grants
AND   Program Proposals

Grants   JUL. 1966
Postings: 3,482   GC: 620
SN   Funds given by a foundation, govern-
      ment, institution, or other organization,
      usually for a specific purpose (Note:
      Prior to Mar80, this term was not re-
      stricted to pecuniary bestowments)
UF   Grant Proposals #
      Subsidies
NT   Block Grants
      Educational Vouchers
      Incentive Grants
      Tuition Grants
BT   Financial Support
RT   Assistantships
      Awards
      Categorical Aid
      Educational Finance
      Eligibility
      Equalization Aid
      Fellowships
      Financial Aid Applicants
      Grantsmanship
      Library Funding
      Philanthropic Foundations
      Revenue Sharing

= Two or more Descriptors are used to represent this term.
The term's main entry shows the appropriate coordination.

Scholarships
Student Costs
Student Financial Aid
Training Allowances

Grantsmanship   *MAR. 1980*
    Postings: 500   GC: 620
SN   Skills and procedures for applying for external funding
BT   Fund Raising
RT   Bids
     Contracts
     Federal Aid
     Financial Support
     Grants
     Private Financial Support
     Program Proposals
     Proposal Writing
     Research Opportunities
     State Aid

Grapheme Phoneme Correspondence
USE   Phoneme Grapheme Correspondence

Graphemes   *JUL. 1966*
    Postings: 221   GC: 450
BT   Written Language
RT   Diacritical Marking
     Letters (Alphabet)
     Orthographic Symbols
     Phoneme Grapheme Correspondence
     Phonemes
     Phonetics
     Romanization
     Spelling
     Structural Analysis (Linguistics)

Graphic Arts   *JUL. 1966*
    Postings: 1,062   GC: 420
NT   Cartography
     Computer Graphics
     Engineering Graphics
     Layout (Publications)
     Printing
BT   Visual Arts
RT   Commercial Art
     Computer Assisted Design
     Diagrams
     Drafting
     Industrial Arts
     Orthographic Projection
     Photocomposition
     Printmaking
     Sign Painters
     Signs
     Technical Illustration
     Technology Education

Graphing Calculators   *JUN. 1997*
    Postings: 136   GC: 910
SN   Calculators capable of producing animated graphing sequences based on mathematical formulas (Note: Prior to Jun97, the Identifier "Graphing Utilities" was commonly used to index this concept)
BT   Calculators
RT   Computer Graphics
     Computer Oriented Programs
     Graphs
     Mathematics

Graphs   *JUL. 1966*
    Postings: 2,447   GC: 720
BT   Visual Aids
RT   Charts
     Critical Path Method
     Flow Charts
     Graphing Calculators
     Illustrations
     Instructional Materials
     Nonprint Media
     Records (Forms)
     Tables (Data)
     Topology

Gravitation
USE   Gravity (Physics)

Gravity (Physics)   *OCT. 1982*
    Postings: 153   GC: 490
SN   Mutual attraction among all bodies in the universe, dependent on their respective masses, distance apart, and speed of motion relative to each other
UF   Gravitation
BT   Scientific Concepts
RT   Acceleration (Physics)
     Density (Matter)
     Force
     Geophysics
     Kinetic Molecular Theory
     Kinetics
     Mechanics (Physics)
     Motion
     Physical Environment
     Physics
     Pressure (Physics)
     Relativity
     Space
     Weight (Mass)

Graying of Faculty
USE   Aging in Academia

Grease
USE   Lubricants

Greek   *JUL. 1966*
    Postings: 398   GC: 440
UF   Classical Greek
     Modern Greek
BT   Indo European Languages
RT   Classical Languages
     Greek Civilization
     Greek Literature

Greek Americans   *OCT. 1980*
    Postings: 49   GC: 560
BT   Ethnic Groups
     North Americans
RT   Minority Groups

Greek Civilization   *JUL. 1966*
    Postings: 189   GC: 430
SN   Studies of modern or ancient Greece
RT   Ancient History
     Area Studies
     Classical Literature
     Greek
     Greek Literature
     Western Civilization
     World History

Greek Literature   *JUL. 1970*
    Postings: 150   GC: 430
SN   Classical and modern Greek literature
BT   Literature
RT   Ancient History
     Classical Literature
     Greek
     Greek Civilization

Greenhouse Effect   *JAN. 1993*
    Postings: 76   GC: 410
SN   Global warming caused by atmospheric gases and particulates that trap heat and radiate it back to earth—of concern is possible runaway warming due to buildups of carbon dioxide and other gases through fossil fuel burning and deforestation
BT   Global Warming
RT   Air Pollution
     Solar Energy

Greenhouse Workers
USE   Nursery Workers (Horticulture)

Greenhouses   *JUL. 1966*
    Postings: 94   GC: 410
UF   Hothouses
BT   Facilities
RT   Gardens
     Nurseries (Horticulture)
     Ornamental Horticulture
     Plant Growth

Greenlandic
USE   Inupiaq

Gregariousness
USE   Interpersonal Competence

Grief   *SEP. 1977*
    Postings: 886   GC: 230
SN   Emotional state of intense sadness associated with external loss or deprivation
UF   Mourning
BT   Sadness
RT   Bereavement
     Depression (Psychology)
     Emotional Problems

Grievance Procedures   *JUL. 1966*
    Postings: 1,227   GC: 630
BT   Methods
RT   Arbitration
     Collective Bargaining
     Employer Employee Relationship
     Interpersonal Communication
     Labor Demands
     Negotiation Agreements
     Negotiation Impasses
     Ombudsmen
     Peer Mediation

Grinding Machines
USE   Machine Tools

Grocery Stores
USE   Food Stores

Gross Scores
USE   Raw Scores

Ground Water Supplies
USE   Groundwater

Grounds Caretakers
USE   Grounds Keepers

Grounds Keepers   *JUL. 1966*
    Postings: 81   GC: 410
UF   Gardeners #
     Grounds Caretakers
     Yard Workers (Horticulture)
BT   Semiskilled Workers
RT   Landscaping
     Ornamental Horticulture Occupations
     Plant Propagation
     Turf Management

Groundwater   *APR. 1990*
    Postings: 60   GC: 410
SN   Water beneath the surface of the ground
UF   Ground Water Supplies
     Underground Water
BT   Water
     Water Resources
RT   Geology
     Geothermal Energy
     Hydrology
     Physical Geography
     Soil Conservation
     Water Pollution
     Water Quality

Group Activities   *JUL. 1966*
    Postings: 2,231   GC: 310
UF   Cooperative Activities
BT   Activities

RT   Assembly Programs
     Competition
     Cooperation
     Cooperative Learning
     Group Experience
     Groups
     Participation
     Self Directed Groups

Group Adjustment
USE   Adjustment (to Environment)

Group Behavior   *JUL. 1966*
    Postings: 1,367   GC: 520
SN   Behavior of a group as a whole, as well as the behavior of an individual as influenced by his or her membership in a group
UF   Collective Behavior
NT   Teamwork
BT   Behavior
RT   Group Dynamics
     Group Membership
     Groups
     Social Behavior
     Sociometric Techniques

Group Cohesiveness
USE   Group Unity

Group Counseling   *JUL. 1966*
    Postings: 2,136   GC: 240
SN   Using the dynamics of a group in a counselor-structured situation to increase counselees' self-understanding and adjustment
BT   Counseling
     Group Guidance
RT   Family Counseling
     Group Discussion
     Group Dynamics
     Group Therapy
     Groups
     Individual Counseling

Group Decision Support Systems
USE   Decision Support Systems
AND   Group Dynamics

Group Discussion   *JUL. 1966*
    Postings: 2,163   GC: 310
SN   Discussion in groups
BT   Discussion
RT   Brainstorming
     Consciousness Raising
     Cooperative Learning
     Discussion Groups
     Focus Groups
     Group Counseling
     Group Dynamics
     Group Guidance
     Groups
     Guided Design
     Interpersonal Communication
     Nominal Group Technique
     Peer Groups

Group Dynamics   *JUL. 1966*
    Postings: 6,323   GC: 520
SN   Formation and functioning of human groups—includes both the interaction within and among groups
UF   Group Decision Support Systems #
     Group Interaction
     Group Pressures
     Group Processes
     Group Relations (1966 1980)
BT   Interaction
RT   Brainstorming
     Consciousness Raising
     Cooperative Learning
     Family Counseling
     Group Behavior
     Group Counseling
     Group Discussion
     Group Experience
     Group Guidance

= Two or more Descriptors are used to represent this term.
The term's main entry shows the appropriate coordination.

Group Instruction
Group Membership
Group Structure
Groups
Humanistic Education
Informal Leadership
Interaction Process Analysis
Interpersonal Communication
Nominal Group Technique
Organizational Communication
Outdoor Leadership
Peer Influence
Role Playing
Self Directed Groups
Sensitivity Training
Social Psychology
Sociometric Techniques
Speech Communication
Transactional Analysis

Group Experience   *JUL. 1966*
    Postings: 1,095   GC: 520
SN Experience of a group as a whole, as well
    as the experience of an individual result-
    ing from his or her membership in a
    group
UF Communal Living #
    Dormitory Living #
    Group Living (1966 1977)
BT Experience
RT Family Life
    Group Activities
    Group Dynamics
    Group Homes
    Group Membership
    Groups
    Human Relations
    Living Learning Centers
    Normalization (Disabilities)
    Residential Programs
    Self Directed Groups

Group Guidance   *JUL. 1966*
    Postings: 393   GC: 240
SN Guidance carried on in groups to assist
    members to develop realistic and satis-
    fying goals, plans, and activities
NT Group Counseling
BT Guidance
RT Group Discussion
    Group Dynamics
    Group Instruction
    Group Therapy
    Groups

Group Homes   *AUG. 1980*
    Postings: 494   GC: 220
SN Nonconfining residential facilities pro-
    viding professional supervision in a group
    living arrangement for either adults or
    juveniles, usually those who are unable
    to function independently—intended to
    reproduce as closely as possible the
    circumstances of family life, and at mini-
    mum providing access to community
    activities and resources (Note: Do not
    confuse with "Personal Care Homes")
UF Halfway Houses #
BT Housing
RT Adult Foster Care
    Community Programs
    Deinstitutionalization (of Disabled)
    Delinquency
    Disabilities
    Economically Disadvantaged
    Family Problems
    Foster Care
    Group Experience
    Groups
    Normalization (Disabilities)
    Personal Care Homes
    Rehabilitation Centers
    Resident Advisers
    Social Services

Group Instruction   *JUL. 1966*
    Postings: 1,093   GC: 310
NT Large Group Instruction
    Small Group Instruction

BT Instruction
RT Assembly Programs
    Group Dynamics
    Group Guidance
    Grouping (Instructional Purposes)
    Groups
    Individual Instruction
    Individualized Instruction
    Listening Groups

Group Intelligence Testing (1966 1980)
USE Group Testing
AND Intelligence Tests

Group Intelligence Tests (1966 1980)
USE Group Testing
AND Intelligence Tests

Group Interaction
USE Group Dynamics

Group Interests
USE Interests

Group Living (1966 1977)
USE Group Experience

Group Membership   *JUL. 1966*
    Postings: 910   GC: 510
NT Political Affiliation
RT Enrollment
    Group Behavior
    Group Dynamics
    Group Experience
    Groups
    Participant Characteristics
    Social Stratification

Group Norms (1968 1980)   *MAR. 1980*
    Postings: 343   GC: 520
SN Invalid Descriptor—used inconsistently
    in indexing—see such Descriptors as
    "Norms," "Standards," or "Behavior Stan-
    dards"

Group Pacing
USE Pacing

Group Pressures
USE Group Dynamics

Group Processes
USE Group Dynamics

Group Reading (1966 1980)   *MAR. 1980*
    Postings: 52   GC: 460
SN Invalid Descriptor—used indiscriminately
    in indexing—see such Descriptors as
    "Reading," "Choral Speaking," and
    "Grouping (Instructional Purposes)"

Group Relations (1966 1980)
USE Group Dynamics

Group Status   *JUL. 1966*
    Postings: 236   GC: 520
SN Status of a group (Note: Prior to Mar80,
    this term was not scoped and was used
    to index both the status of a group and
    the status of individuals within a group)
NT Family Status
BT Status
RT Group Structure
    Group Unity
    Groups
    Reference Groups
    Social Stratification

Group Structure   *JUL. 1966*
    Postings: 641   GC: 520
NT Family Structure

    Governmental Structure
BT Organization
RT Cluster Grouping
    Group Dynamics
    Group Status
    Groups
    Interaction Process Analysis
    Power Structure
    Social Structure
    Social Systems
    Sociometric Techniques

Group Testing   *MAR. 1980*
    Postings: 392   GC: 820
SN Process of administering tests to groups
UF Group Intelligence Testing (1966
    1980) #
    Group Intelligence Tests (1966
    1980) #
    Group Tests (1966 1980)
BT Testing
RT Groups
    Individual Testing

Group Tests (1966 1980)
USE Group Testing

Group Therapy   *JUL. 1966*
    Postings: 1,194   GC: 230
BT Therapy
RT Family Counseling
    Group Counseling
    Group Guidance
    Groups
    Milieu Therapy
    Psychotherapy
    Sensitivity Training
    Transactional Analysis

Group Unity   *AUG. 1968*
    Postings: 907   GC: 520
SN Cohesiveness of groups of people, fami-
    lies, tribes and nations
UF Ethnic Unity
    Family Unity
    Group Cohesiveness
    Unification
BT Interpersonal Relationship
RT Black Power
    Community
    Cooperation
    Ethnicity
    Global Approach
    Group Status
    Groups
    Ideology
    Morale
    Nationalism
    Patriotism
    Trust (Psychology)

Group Values
USE Social Values

Grouping (Instructional Purposes)
                                   JUL. 1966
    Postings: 2,319   GC: 310
SN Organization or classification of students
    according to specified criteria for in-
    structional purposes
UF Student Grouping (1966 1980)
NT Heterogeneous Grouping
    Homogeneous Grouping
    Nongraded Instructional Grouping
BT Classification
RT Class Organization
    Classes (Groups of Students)
    Cooperative Learning
    Flexible Scheduling
    Group Instruction
    Groups
    Instructional Program Divisions
    Labeling (of Persons)
    Special Education
    Student Placement
    Transitional Programs
    Tutorial Programs

Grouping Procedures (1966 1980)
USE Classification

Groups   *JUL. 1966*
    Postings: 601   GC: 520
NT Advantaged
    Age Groups
    Alumni
    Arabs
    Artists
    At Risk Persons
    Athletes
    Audiences
    Authors
    Baby Boomers
    Blacks
    Board Candidates
    Caregivers
    Change Agents
    Classes (Groups of Students)
    Clubs
    College Applicants
    Community Leaders
    Control Groups
    Criminals
    Dependents
    Disadvantaged
    Discussion Groups
    Donors
    Dropouts
    Employers
    Eskimos
    Ethnic Groups
    Experimental Groups
    Family (Sociological Unit)
    Females
    Financial Aid Applicants
    Gifted
    Heads of Households
    Homeless People
    Homemakers
    Homeowners
    Indians
    Indigenous Populations
    Indochinese
    Institutionalized Persons
    Job Applicants
    Judges
    Juries
    Juvenile Gangs
    Labor Force Nonparticipants
    Landlords
    Language Minorities
    Latin Americans
    Lay People
    Leaders
    Left Handed Writer
    Limited English Speaking
    Low Income Groups
    Males
    Matched Groups
    Migrants
    Minority Groups
    Multiracial Persons
    Native Speakers
    No Shows
    Non English Speaking
    North Americans
    Organizations (Groups)
    Pacific Islanders
    Parents
    Patients
    Peer Groups
    Personnel
    Political Candidates
    Potential Dropouts
    Quality Circles
    Recreationists
    Reference Groups
    Religious Cultural Groups
    Research and Instruction Units
    Role Models
    Runaways
    Rural Population
    Seafarers
    Self Directed Groups
    Siblings
    Slow Learners
    Social Class
    Social Support Groups
    Spouses
    Stopouts

= Two or more Descriptors are used to represent this term.
The term's main entry shows the appropriate coordination.

Students
Tissue Donors
Trainees
Tribes
Union Members
Urban Population
Users (Information)
Vendors
Veterans
Victims of Crime
Volunteers
Welfare Recipients
Whites
Widowed
Youth
Youth Leaders
RT Classification
    Group Activities
    Group Behavior
    Group Counseling
    Group Discussion
    Group Dynamics
    Group Experience
    Group Guidance
    Group Homes
    Group Instruction
    Group Membership
    Group Status
    Group Structure
    Group Testing
    Group Therapy
    Group Unity
    Grouping (Instructional Purposes)
    Interaction Process Analysis
    Labeling (of Persons)
    Social Psychology
    Sociometric Techniques

Grown Children
USE Adult Children

Growth Motivation
USE Self Actualization

Growth Patterns (1966 1980)   *MAR. 1980*
    Postings: 371   GC: 520
SN Invalid Descriptor—used inconsistently in indexing—see the displays and hierarchies of "Development" and "Change," as well as more precise Descriptors such as "Employment Patterns," "Population Growth," "Trend Analysis," etc.

Guarani   *MAR. 1971*
    Postings: 21   GC: 440
SN Native language spoken by the Tupi Guaranian Indians of Bolivia, Paraguay, and southern Brazil
UF Mbya Guarani
    Tupi Guarani
BT American Indian Languages

Guaranteed Income   *AUG. 1968*
    Postings: 89   GC: 620
UF Negative Income Tax
BT Income
RT Minimum Wage
    Salaries
    Wages

Guards (Border Patrol)
USE Immigration Inspectors

Guards (Security)
USE Security Personnel

Guerrilla Warfare
USE War

Guessing (Tests)   *NOV. 1970*
    Postings: 376   GC: 820
SN Responding to test items without certainty of the correct answers
BT Response Style (Tests)
RT Confidence Testing

Distractors (Tests)
Multiple Choice Tests
Objective Tests
Raw Scores
Scoring Formulas
Test Coaching
Test Interpretation
Test Reliability
Test Wiseness
Testing
Testing Problems
Tests
True Scores

Guidance   *JUL. 1966*
    Postings: 994   GC: 240
SN Process of assisting individuals and groups to develop realistic and satisfying goals, plans, and activities (Note: "Counseling" is one aspect of the total process of "Guidance")
UF Continuous Guidance (1966 1980)
    Developmental Guidance (1967 1980)
NT Career Guidance
    Counseling
    Group Guidance
    Post High School Guidance
    School Guidance
    Teacher Guidance
RT Consultation Programs
    Guidance Centers
    Guidance Objectives
    Guidance Personnel
    Guidance Programs

Guidance Centers   *JUL. 1966*
    Postings: 534   GC: 240
UF Counseling Centers (1966 1977)
    Guidance Facilities (1967 1977)
BT Educational Facilities
RT Counseling
    Counseling Services
    Guidance
    Guidance Programs

Guidance Counseling (1966 1980)
USE School Counseling

Guidance Counselors
USE School Counselors

Guidance Facilities (1967 1977)
USE Guidance Centers

Guidance Functions (1968 1980)
USE Guidance Objectives

Guidance Goals
USE Guidance Objectives

Guidance Objectives   *JUL. 1966*
    Postings: 600   GC: 240
SN Aims or ends toward which the guidance process is directed (Note: If appropriate, use the more specific term "Counseling Objectives")
UF Guidance Functions (1968 1980)
    Guidance Goals
NT Counseling Objectives
BT Objectives
RT Behavioral Objectives
    Guidance
    Guidance Programs

Guidance Personnel   *JUL. 1966*
    Postings: 484   GC: 240
SN Professionals engaged in assisting individuals and groups to develop realistic and satisfying plans, goals, and activities (Note: Prior to Mar80, the instruction "Guidance Workers, USE Counselors" was carried in the Thesaurus)
UF Guidance Specialists #
NT Counselors
BT Personnel

RT Caseworkers
    Consultants
    Guidance
    Guidance Programs
    Instructor Coordinators
    Parole Officers
    Probation Officers
    Pupil Personnel Workers
    Social Workers
    Student Personnel Workers

Guidance Programs   *JUL. 1966*
    Postings: 2,077   GC: 240
SN Ongoing activities designed to assist individuals and groups develop realistic and satisfying goals, plans, and activities
UF Guidance Services (1966 1980)
BT Programs
RT Ancillary School Services
    Employee Assistance Programs
    Guidance
    Guidance Centers
    Guidance Objectives
    Guidance Personnel
    Individualized Programs
    Outreach Programs
    Pupil Personnel Services
    Rehabilitation Programs
    Student Personnel Services

Guidance Services (1966 1980)
USE Guidance Programs

Guidance Specialists
USE Guidance Personnel
AND Specialists

Guidebooks
USE Guides

Guided Design   *APR. 1990*
    Postings: 49   GC: 310
SN Reasoning-centered instructional method developed by Charles E. Wales and Robert A. Stager that uses small-group techniques and a prepared outline of decision-making steps to guide students through the process of resolving open-ended problems
BT Teaching Methods
RT Critical Thinking
    Decision Making
    Feedback
    Group Discussion
    Individualized Instruction
    Problem Solving
    Programmed Instruction
    Small Group Instruction

Guidelines   *JUL. 1966*
    Postings: 14,439   GC: 730
NT Facility Guidelines
RT Administrator Guides
    Authoring Aids (Programming)
    Check Lists
    Design
    Guides
    Objectives
    Planning
    Specifications

Guides   *JUL. 1966*
    Postings: 5,994   GC: 720
SN (Note: Corresponds to Pubtype code 050—do not use except as the subject of a document)
UF Guidebooks
    Handbooks
    Health Activities Handbooks (1966 1980) #
    Health Guides (1966 1980) #
    Manuals (1966 1980)
NT Administrator Guides
    Curriculum Guides
    Faculty Handbooks
    Laboratory Manuals
    Leaders Guides

    Library Guides
    Program Guides
    Study Guides
    Teaching Guides
    Test Manuals
BT Reference Materials
RT Directories
    Guidelines
    Orientation Materials
    Parent Materials

Guilt   *MAY 1993*
    Postings: 138   GC: 230
SN Emotional state produced by the knowledge of having committed a real or imagined ethical, moral, or religious offense—less commonly in educational literature, the fact of having committed a violation of law and, possibly, being liable for the penalties associated with that violation (Note: See related Identifiers "Shame" and "Self Blame")
RT Affective Behavior
    Anxiety
    Depression (Psychology)
    Emotional Problems
    Legal Responsibility
    Psychological Patterns
    Responsibility
    Sexuality

Gujarati   *JUL. 1966*
    Postings: 13   GC: 440
UF Gujerati
BT Indo European Languages

Gujerati
USE Gujarati

Gullah   *FEB. 1970*
    Postings: 21   GC: 440
BT Creoles

Gun Control   *SEP. 1998*
    Postings: 50   GC: 210
SN The regulation of the manufacture, transport, sale, ownership, and use of firearms
UF Firearms Control
RT Disarmament
    Guns

Guns   *SEP. 1998*
    Postings: 176   GC: 910
SN Weapons using an explosive, usually gunpowder, to hurl bullets or other projectiles (Note: Do not use for the Identifier "Toy Guns")
UF Firearms
    Small Arms
BT Equipment
    Weapons
RT Armed Forces
    Gun Control
    Marksmanship
    Safety
    School Safety
    Violence

Gymnasiums   *JUL. 1966*
    Postings: 127   GC: 920
BT Facilities
RT Athletic Equipment
    Athletic Fields
    Athletics
    Field Houses
    Physical Education Facilities
    Physical Recreation Programs
    Recreational Facilities

Gymnastics   *FEB. 1978*
    Postings: 142   GC: 470
NT Tumbling
BT Athletics
RT Calisthenics
    Olympic Games

= Two or more Descriptors are used to represent this term.
The term's main entry shows the appropriate coordination.

Gynecology OCT. 1977
Postings: 122 GC: 210
SN Branch of medicine dealing with the diseases, hygiene, and reproduction function of females
BT Medicine
RT Abortions
Childlessness
Contraception
Diseases
Family Practice (Medicine)
Females
Medical Services
Menstruation
Obstetrics
Pregnancy
Reproduction (Biology)

Habit Formation JUL. 1966
Postings: 301 GC: 110
BT Behavior Development
RT Behavior Change
Listening Habits
Personality
Reading Habits
Self Care Skills
Speech Habits

Habitats JAN. 1993
Postings: 173 GC: 410
SN Places where animals or plants live (Note: For human habitats, use "Housing," "Place of Residence," "Residential Patterns," etc.)
RT Animals
Biodiversity
Ecology
Estuaries
Natural Resources
Physical Environment
Plants (Botany)
Rainforests
Wetlands
Wildlife
Wildlife Management

Habituation OCT. 1984
Postings: 131 GC: 110
SN Progressive decrease in responsiveness to repetitive stimuli (Note: For drug habituation, use "Drug Abuse" or "Drug Addiction")
BT Learning Processes
RT Arousal Patterns
Attention
Cognitive Ability
Familiarity
Novelty (Stimulus Dimension)
Perception
Redundancy
Retention (Psychology)
Sensory Experience

Hagiographies (1971 1980)
USE Biographies

Haiku APR. 1970
Postings: 74 GC: 430
UF Hokku
BT Literary Genres
Poetry
RT Imagery

Haitian Creole JUL. 1966
Postings: 123 GC: 440
BT Creoles

Haitians OCT. 1980
Postings: 234 GC: 560
SN Peoples of Haiti or Haitian descent
BT Latin Americans
RT Ethnic Groups

Half Day Schedules
USE Full Day Half Day Schedules

Half Reversal Shift
USE Shift Studies

Halfway Houses
USE Group Homes
AND Rehabilitation Centers

Hallways
USE Corridors

Hand Calculators
USE Calculators

Hand Tools JUL. 1966
Postings: 378 GC: 910
BT Equipment
RT Machine Tools
Metal Working
Shop Curriculum
Woodworking

Handball APR. 1985
Postings: 3 GC: 470
SN Singles or doubles game played by striking a small rubber ball against a wall or walls with the hands (Note: Do not confuse with "Team Handball")
BT Athletics
RT Racquetball

Handbooks
USE Guides

Handedness APR. 1990
Postings: 89 GC: 120
SN Dominant or preferred use of either the right or left hand
NT Left Handed Writer
BT Lateral Dominance
RT Eye Hand Coordination
Handwriting
Object Manipulation

Handicap Detection (1966 1980)
USE Disability Identification

Handicap Discrimination (1984 1994)
USE Disability Discrimination

Handicap Identification (1980 1994)
USE Disability Identification

Handicapped Children (1966 1980)
MAR. 1980
Postings: 5,973 GC: 220
SN Invalid Descriptor—coordinate specific Descriptors from the "Disabilities" display with appropriate age-level or mandatory educational level Descriptors (Note: In Mar80, the postings of "Blind, Crippled, Deaf, Homebound, Neurotic, Psychotic, and Retarded Children" were transferred here, as well as to the appropriate "Disabilities" terms)

Handicapped Students (1967 1980)
MAR. 1980
Postings: 1,224 GC: 220
SN Invalid Descriptor—coordinate specific Descriptors from the "Disabilities" display with appropriate "student," age-level, or mandatory educational level Descriptors

Handicapped (1966 1980)
USE Disabilities

Handicaps
USE Disabilities

Handicrafts JUL. 1966
Postings: 735 GC: 420
SN Creative activities of making articles by hand, often with the aid of simple tools or machines—also, the handiworks resulting from such activities
UF Crafts
Crafts Rooms (1966 1980) #
NT Ceramics
BT Visual Arts
RT Art Activities
Art Products
Childrens Art
Craft Workers
Creative Activities
Design Crafts
Leather
Metal Working
Plastics
School Shops
Skilled Occupations
Woodworking

Hands on Learning
USE Experiential Learning

Hands on Science DEC. 1995
Postings: 1,113 GC: 490
SN Science activities and programs that require active personal participation
RT Demonstrations (Science)
Experiential Learning
Manipulative Materials
Science Activities
Science Curriculum
Science Education
Science Fairs
Science Process Skills
Science Programs

Handwriting JUL. 1966
Postings: 600 GC: 400
UF Handwriting Development (1966 1980) #
Handwriting Instruction (1966 1983) #
Handwriting Materials (1966 1983) #
Handwriting Readiness (1966 1983) #
Handwriting Skills (1966 1983) #
NT Cursive Writing
Manuscript Writing (Handlettering)
BT Language Arts
RT Handedness
Left Handed Writer
Writing (Composition)
Writing Ability
Writing Difficulties
Writing Evaluation
Writing Exercises
Writing Improvement
Writing Instruction
Writing Readiness
Writing Research
Writing Skills

Handwriting Development (1966 1980)
USE Handwriting
AND Writing Skills

Handwriting Instruction (1966 1983)
USE Handwriting
AND Writing Instruction

Handwriting Materials (1966 1983)
USE Handwriting
AND Instructional Materials

Handwriting Readiness (1966 1983)
USE Handwriting
AND Writing Readiness

Handwriting Skills (1966 1983)
USE Handwriting
AND Writing Skills

Hangul
USE Korean

Hanja
USE Korean

Hankul
USE Korean

Happiness DEC. 1994
Postings: 145 GC: 120
SN State of psychological well-being characterized by dominantly agreeable emotions ranging from contentment to intense joy
UF Joy
BT Psychological Patterns
RT Humor
Moods
Satisfaction
Well Being

Haptic Perception (1967 1980)
USE Tactual Perception

Hard of Hearing (1967 1980)
USE Partial Hearing

Harmony (Music) OCT. 1994
Postings: 17 GC: 420
SN The simultaneous occurrence of musical notes or tones
BT Music
RT Melody
Music Techniques
Musical Composition

Harvesting JUL. 1966
Postings: 68 GC: 410
UF Crop Harvesting
BT Agriculture
RT Agricultural Production
Agronomy
Crop Processing Occupations
Field Crops
Horticulture
Plants (Botany)

Hashish
USE Marijuana

Hausa JUL. 1966
Postings: 57 GC: 440
BT Chad Languages

Hawaiian AUG. 1969
Postings: 58 GC: 440
BT Malayo Polynesian Languages
RT Hawaiians

Hawaiians MAR. 1976
Postings: 237 GC: 560
SN Polynesian or part-Polynesian people indigenous to the Hawaiian Islands
BT Ethnic Groups
Pacific Americans
RT Hawaiian

Hazardous Materials OCT. 1984
Postings: 710 GC: 210
SN Ignitable, corrosive, infectious, reactive, or toxic materials that pose a present or potential threat to living things
UF Dangerous Materials
Hazardous Wastes #
NT Poisons
RT Asbestos
Environmental Influences
Environmental Standards
Laboratory Safety
Occupational Safety and Health
Physical Environment
Physical Health

= Two or more Descriptors are used to represent this term.
The term's main entry shows the appropriate coordination.

Pollution
Public Health
Radiation
Safety
Sanitation
School Safety
Wastes

Hazardous Wastes
USE   Hazardous Materials
AND   Wastes

Hazing   SEP. 2000
      Postings: 39   GC: 530
SN   Subjecting people to humiliation or abuse
      as part of an initiation process
BT   Antisocial Behavior
RT   Violence

Head Banging
USE   Self Injurious Behavior

Head Injuries   APR. 1990
      Postings: 286   GC: 220
SN   Injuries to the head, especially those
      causing disabilities—medical/social con-
      cerns range from coma to the return to
      community life
UF   Closed Head Injuries
      Traumatic Brain Injury #
BT   Injuries
RT   Brain
      Neurological Impairments

Head Librarians
USE   Library Directors

Headlines   DEC. 1974
      Postings: 113   GC: 720
SN   Titles of news articles or newscasts
RT   Journalism
      Layout (Publications)
      News Media
      News Reporting
      News Writing
      Newspapers

Heads of Households   NOV. 1969
      Postings: 316   GC: 510
UF   Breadwinners
      Family Breadwinners
      Household Heads
BT   Groups
RT   Displaced Homemakers
      Family (Sociological Unit)
      Fatherless Family
      Fathers
      Motherless Family
      Mothers
      One Parent Family
      Parents

Health   JUL. 1966
      Postings: 3,070   GC: 210
NT   Child Health
      Family Health
      Mental Health
      Occupational Safety and Health
      Physical Health
      Public Health
      Wellness
RT   Adjustment (to Environment)
      Allied Health Occupations
      Biofeedback
      Chronic Illness
      Clinics
      Daily Living Skills
      Dentistry
      Disabilities
      Disease Control
      Diseases
      Epidemiology
      Fatigue (Biology)
      Health Activities
      Health Behavior
      Health Care Costs

Health Conditions
Health Education
Health Facilities
Health Insurance
Health Maintenance Organizations
Health Materials
Health Needs
Health Occupations
Health Personnel
Health Programs
Health Promotion
Health Services
Human Body
Hygiene
Injuries
Medical Evaluation
Medicine
Nutrition
Pain
Patient Education
Perinatal Influences
Pests
Pollution
Prenatal Care
Prenatal Influences
Primary Health Care
Radiation Effects
Safety
Sanitation
Self Care Skills
Severity (of Disability)
Sleep
Special Health Problems
Stress Variables
Symptoms (Individual Disorders)
Terminal Illness
Ventilation
Water Quality
Water Treatment

Health Activities   JUL. 1966
      Postings: 314   GC: 210
NT   Health Promotion
BT   Activities
RT   Health
      Health Behavior
      Health Education
      Health Materials
      Physical Activities

Health Activities Handbooks (1966 1980)
USE   Guides
AND   Health Materials

Health Behavior   JUN. 2000
      Postings: 486   GC: 120
SN   Actions, practices, or habits that have an
      impact on health
BT   Behavior
RT   Comprehensive School Health Educa-
      tion
      Drinking
      Eating Habits
      Exercise
      Health
      Health Activities
      Health Education
      Health Promotion
      Health Related Fitness
      Nutrition
      Physical Activity Level
      Prevention
      Sexuality
      Smoking
      Stress Management
      Substance Abuse
      Tobacco

Health Books (1966 1980)
USE   Books
AND   Health Materials

Health Care Costs   JUN. 1988
      Postings: 345   GC: 620
UF   Health Costs
      Medical Costs #
BT   Costs
RT   Health

Health Insurance
Health Services

Health Care Evaluation
USE   Medical Care Evaluation

Health Conditions   JUL. 1966
      Postings: 438   GC: 210
RT   Epidemiology
      Health
      Sanitary Facilities

Health Costs
USE   Health Care Costs

Health Education   JUL. 1966
      Postings: 7,517   GC: 400
SN   Educational activities that promote un-
      derstanding, attitudes, and practices con-
      sistent with individual, family, and com-
      munity health needs (Note: For study
      and training in the health/health-related
      occupations, use "Medical Education"
      or "Allied Health Occupations Educa-
      tion")
NT   Comprehensive School Health Educa-
      tion
BT   Education
RT   Alcohol Education
      Allied Health Occupations Education
      Consumer Education
      Disease Control
      Drinking
      Drug Education
      First Aid
      Health
      Health Activities
      Health Behavior
      Health Materials
      Health Programs
      Health Promotion
      Health Related Fitness
      Human Body
      Hygiene
      Nutrition Instruction
      Oral Rehydration Therapy
      Patient Education
      Smoking
      Stress Management
      Substance Abuse
      Tobacco
      Venereal Diseases
      Wellness

Health Facilities   JUL. 1966
      Postings: 549   GC: 210
UF   Infirmaries
NT   Nursing Homes
BT   Facilities
RT   Clinics
      First Aid
      Health
      Health Maintenance Organizations
      Health Needs
      Health Services
      Hospices (Terminal Care)
      Hospitals
      Long Term Care
      Medical Care Evaluation
      Medical Services
      Public Facilities
      Sanitary Facilities

Health Guides (1966 1980)
USE   Guides
AND   Health Materials

Health Insurance   JUL. 1966
      Postings: 863   GC: 620
BT   Insurance
RT   Fringe Benefits
      Health
      Health Care Costs
      Health Maintenance Organizations
      Health Services
      Insurance Occupations
      Teacher Employment Benefits

Unemployment Insurance
Workers Compensation

Health Maintenance Organizations
                                              NOV. 1995
      Postings: 213   GC: 210
SN   Prepaid comprehensive medical service
      systems (Note: See also the Identifier
      "Social Health Maintenance Organiza-
      tions")
UF   HMOs
      Managed Care (HMOs)
BT   Organizations (Groups)
RT   Health
      Health Facilities
      Health Insurance
      Health Promotion
      Health Services
      Medical Services

Health Materials   MAR. 1980
      Postings: 401   GC: 730
UF   Health Activities Handbooks (1966
      1980) #
      Health Books (1966 1980) #
      Health Guides (1966 1980) #
RT   Health
      Health Activities
      Health Education
      Instructional Materials
      Resource Materials
      Science Materials

Health Needs   JUL. 1966
      Postings: 1,834   GC: 210
BT   Needs
RT   Health
      Health Facilities
      Health Related Fitness
      Health Services

Health Occupations   JUL. 1966
      Postings: 1,040   GC: 210
NT   Allied Health Occupations
BT   Occupations
RT   Health
      Health Personnel
      Health Services
      Medical Associations
      Medical Education
      Medicine
      Professional Occupations
      Technical Occupations

Health Occupations Centers (1968 1980)
                                              MAR. 1980
      Postings: 38   GC: 210
SN   Invalid Descriptor—used inconsistently
      in indexing—for "Health Education Cen-
      ters," coordinate "Allied Health Occupa-
      tions Education," "Medical Education,"
      etc., with appropriate "Facilities" Descrip-
      tors

Health Occupations Education (Vocational)
USE   Allied Health Occupations Education
AND   Vocational Education

Health Occupations Education (1967 1980)
USE   Allied Health Occupations Education

Health Occupations Personnel
USE   Health Personnel

Health Personnel   JUL. 1966
      Postings: 1,871   GC: 210
UF   Community Health Workers #
      Health Occupations Personnel
      Health Service Personnel
      Health Service Workers
      Health Workers
NT   Allied Health Personnel
      Dentists
      Hospital Personnel
      Medical Consultants

= Two or more Descriptors are used to represent this term.
The term's main entry shows the appropriate coordination.

Mental Health Workers
Nurses
Pharmacists
Physicians
Psychologists
Veterinarians
BT Personnel
RT Caregivers
Health
Health Occupations
Health Services
Medical Education
Medical Evaluation
Medical Libraries
Paraprofessional Personnel
Professional Personnel
Pupil Personnel Workers
Scientific Personnel
Student Personnel Workers

Health Programs   *JUL. 1966*
Postings: 1,736   GC: 210
NT Breakfast Programs
Immunization Programs
Lunch Programs
Mental Health Programs
BT Programs
RT Child Health
Comprehensive School Health Education
Health
Health Education
Health Promotion
Health Services
Outreach Programs

Health Promotion   *JUN. 1988*
Postings: 2,074   GC: 210
SN Activities that encourage and support optimum physical and mental states or conditions
UF Preventive Health
BT Health Activities
RT Comprehensive School Health Education
Health
Health Behavior
Health Education
Health Maintenance Organizations
Health Programs
Health Related Fitness
Health Services
Physical Education
Prevention
Preventive Medicine
Well Being
Wellness

Health Related Fitness   *NOV. 1994*
Postings: 147   GC: 210
SN Physical fitness related to basic functional health, in contrast to "skill-related" physical fitness or the ability to perform in sports
BT Physical Fitness
RT Child Health
Health Behavior
Health Education
Health Needs
Health Promotion
Physical Education
Physical Fitness Tests

Health Related Professions
USE Allied Health Occupations

Health Sciences Libraries
USE Medical Libraries

Health Service Personnel
USE Health Personnel

Health Service Workers
USE Health Personnel

Health Services   *JUL. 1966*
Postings: 4,194   GC: 210
NT Community Health Services
Hospices (Terminal Care)
Long Term Care
Medical Services
Migrant Health Services
Prenatal Care
School Health Services
BT Human Services
RT Allied Health Occupations
Child Health
Eligibility
Fluoridation
Health
Health Care Costs
Health Facilities
Health Insurance
Health Maintenance Organizations
Health Needs
Health Occupations
Health Personnel
Health Programs
Health Promotion
Hospitals
Integrated Services
Medical Care Evaluation
Medical Libraries
Optometry
Oral Rehydration Therapy

Health Workers
USE Health Personnel

Hearing (Physiology)   *MAR. 1980*
Postings: 255   GC: 110
SN Sense or act of hearing
UF Audition (Physiology) (1967 1980)
RT Audiology
Audiometric Tests
Auditory Evaluation
Auditory Perception
Auditory Stimuli
Auditory Tests
Deafness
Ears
Hearing Aids
Hearing Impairments
Hearing Therapy
Partial Hearing
Psychoacoustics

Hearing Aids   *JUL. 1966*
Postings: 305   GC: 220
BT Audio Equipment
Sensory Aids
RT Audiology
Cochlear Implants
Communication Aids (for Disabled)
Hearing (Physiology)
Hearing Impairments
Hearing Therapy
Loop Induction Systems
Partial Hearing
Total Communication

Hearing Clinics (1968 1980)
USE Speech and Hearing Clinics

Hearing Conservation   *JUL. 1966*
Postings: 56   GC: 210
SN Activities (such as the wearing of ear protectors in loud industrial settings) designed to prevent hearing loss
BT Prevention
RT Audiology
Hearing Impairments
Noise (Sound)
Occupational Diseases

Hearing Impairments   *MAR. 1980*
Postings: 5,420   GC: 220
SN Mild to total hearing losses
UF Aurally Handicapped (1966 1980)
Hearing Loss (1967 1980)
NT Deafness
Partial Hearing
BT Disabilities

RT Audiology
Audiometric Tests
Auditory Evaluation
Auditory Tests
Cochlear Implants
Communication Disorders
Ears
Hearing (Physiology)
Hearing Aids
Hearing Conservation
Hearing Therapy
Language Impairments
Learning Problems
Loop Induction Systems
Manual Communication
Oral Communication Method
Otitis Media
Sensory Aids
Speech and Hearing Clinics
Speech Impairments
Total Communication
Visible Speech

Hearing Loss (1967 1980)
USE Hearing Impairments

Hearing Rehabilitation
USE Hearing Therapy

Hearing Tests
USE Auditory Tests

Hearing Therapists (1967 1980)
USE Hearing Therapy
AND Therapists

Hearing Therapy   *JUL. 1966*
Postings: 147   GC: 220
SN Treatment of the hearing impaired to improve hearing skills and make maximum use of residual hearing (Note: Do not confuse with "Auditory Training"—prior to Mar80, the use of this term was not restricted by a Scope Note)
UF Hearing Rehabilitation
Hearing Therapists (1967 1980) #
BT Therapy
RT Audiology
Auditory Evaluation
Auditory Training
Cochlear Implants
Hearing (Physiology)
Hearing Aids
Hearing Impairments
Lipreading
Manual Communication
Oral Communication Method
Speech and Hearing Clinics
Total Communication

Hearings   *SEP. 1977*
Postings: 2,172   GC: 610
SN Sessions in which witnesses are heard and testimony is recorded (Note: For U.S. Congressional hearings, coordinate "Hearings" with such Identifiers as "Congress," "Congress 95th," etc.)
UF Public Hearings
RT Court Judges
Courts
Government (Administrative Body)
Laws
Legislation
Meetings

Heart Disorders   *MAR. 1980*
Postings: 377   GC: 210
UF Cardiac (Person) (1968 1980)
BT Physical Disabilities
RT Cardiopulmonary Resuscitation
Cardiovascular System
Diseases
Heart Rate
Physical Health
Special Health Problems
Type A Behavior
Type B Behavior

Heart Rate   *JUN. 1969*
Postings: 430   GC: 210
UF Pulse Rate
BT Metabolism
RT Aerobics
Blood Circulation
Cardiovascular System
Heart Disorders
Human Body
Hypertension
Physical Fitness
Physical Health
Physiology

Heat   *JUL. 1966*
Postings: 477   GC: 490
BT Energy
RT Calorimeters
Chimneys
Climate
Fuels
Geothermal Energy
Global Warming
Kinetic Molecular Theory
Kinetics
Solar Energy
Temperature
Thermodynamics

Heat Equations
USE Thermodynamics

Heat Recovery   *OCT. 1976*
Postings: 123   GC: 910
SN Transfer of excess heat generated by people, lighting, equipment, and other sources into either heating or cooling systems as required
BT Climate Control
Energy Conservation
RT Air Conditioning
Alternative Energy Sources
Fuel Consumption
Heating
Refrigeration
Thermal Environment
Ventilation

Heating   *JUL. 1966*
Postings: 672   GC: 920
UF Solar Heating #
BT Climate Control
RT Air Conditioning
Air Conditioning Equipment
Air Flow
Chimneys
Fuel Consumption
Fuels
Heat Recovery
Humidity
Temperature
Thermal Environment
Thermal Insulation
Utilities
Ventilation

Heating Oils
USE Fossil Fuels
AND Oil

Hebrew   *JUL. 1966*
Postings: 423   GC: 440
BT Semitic Languages

Height   *JUN. 1969*
Postings: 23   GC: 490
SN (Note: For living organisms, use "Body Height")
BT Scientific Concepts
RT Distance
Mathematics
Proximity

Helicopter Pilots
USE Aircraft Pilots

= Two or more Descriptors are used to represent this term.
The term's main entry shows the appropriate coordination.

Help Giving
USE   Helping Relationship

Help Seeking   *DEC. 1988*
     Postings: 230   GC: 520
SN   Searching for and requesting assistance from others through formal or informal mechanisms (Note: Do not confuse with "Information Seeking")
BT   Social Behavior
RT   Client Characteristics (Human Services)
     Helping Relationship
     Problem Solving
     Self Motivation

Helping Behavior
USE   Helping Relationship

Helping Relationship   *NOV. 1970*
     Postings: 3,272   GC: 240
SN   Relationship characterized by the provision of assistance—helping behavior may be one-sided or reciprocal
UF   Assistance (Social Behavior)
     Help Giving
     Helping Behavior
BT   Interpersonal Relationship
RT   Caregivers
     Child Advocacy
     Counseling
     Counselor Client Relationship
     Help Seeking
     Individual Counseling
     Intervention
     Outcomes of Treatment
     Peer Counseling
     Physician Patient Relationship
     Sharing Behavior
     Social Support Groups
     Supported Employment
     Termination of Treatment
     Therapy

Helplessness   *SEP. 1981*
     Postings: 281   GC: 230
SN   Being or feeling powerless to control or cope with events
UF   Learned Helplessness
RT   Anger
     Depression (Psychology)
     Emotional Disturbances
     Emotional Problems
     Failure
     Fear
     Inhibition
     Paranoid Behavior
     Psychological Patterns

Hemispheric Specialization (Brain)
USE   Brain Hemisphere Functions

Hemodynamics
USE   Blood Circulation

Herbicides   *JUL. 1966*
     Postings: 110   GC: 410
BT   Pesticides
RT   Agricultural Chemical Occupations
     Agricultural Supplies
     Agronomy
     Botany
     Horticulture
     Insecticides
     Plant Growth
     Plant Pathology
     Weeds

Heredity   *JUL. 1966*
     Postings: 760   GC: 490
SN   The transmission of developmental potentialities from one generation of living things to the next and following generations through the natural process of reproduction
BT   Evolution

RT   Biology
     Congenital Impairments
     Embryology
     Genetics
     Nature Nurture Controversy
     Nucleic Acids
     Prenatal Influences
     Reproduction (Biology)

Heredity Environment Controversy
USE   Nature Nurture Controversy

Heritage Education   *APR. 1990*
     Postings: 307   GC: 400
SN   Education that uses resources from the material culture and built environment to enrich learning and instill a preservation ethic—studies of historic sites, landscapes, structures, and objects are integrated into existing curriculum units in the liberal and fine arts and sciences
BT   Cultural Education
RT   Built Environment
     Community Characteristics
     Cultural Background
     Cultural Maintenance
     Historic Sites
     Historical Interpretation
     Interdisciplinary Approach
     Local History
     Material Culture

Hermeneutics   *APR. 1990*
     Postings: 316   GC: 810
SN   Philosophy or methodology dealing with interpretation and understanding, originally of textual materials (mainly sacred scriptures)—contemporary applications may search for meaning in any human act or creation
BT   Methods
     Philosophy
RT   Cognitive Processes
     Communication (Thought Transfer)
     Critical Theory
     Criticism
     Cultural Context
     Discourse Analysis
     Epistemology
     Historical Interpretation
     Historiography
     Inquiry
     Interpretive Skills
     Phenomenology
     Research Methodology
     Semiotics

Heroin   *DEC. 1989*
     Postings: 47   GC: 210
SN   Highly addictive narcotic prepared from morphine
BT   Narcotics
RT   Drug Abuse
     Drug Addiction
     Drug Legislation
     Drug Rehabilitation
     Drug Use
     Illegal Drug Use

Heterogeneous Grouping   *JUL. 1966*
     Postings: 723   GC: 310
SN   Organization or classification of students according to specified criteria for the purpose of forming instructional groups with a high degree of dissimilarity
BT   Grouping (Instructional Purposes)
RT   Classroom Desegregation
     Coeducation
     Homogeneous Grouping
     Mainstreaming
     Mixed Age Grouping
     Multicultural Education
     Multigraded Classes
     Multilevel Classes (Second Language Instruction)

Heterophoria (1968 1974)
USE   Strabismus

Heterotropia (1968 1974)
USE   Strabismus

Heuristic Games
USE   Educational Games

Heuristics   *OCT. 1983*
     Postings: 769   GC: 810
SN   Learning or problem-solving processes, neither wholly rule-governed nor trial and error, in which one tries each of several plausible approaches and evaluates progress toward a satisfactory conclusion after each attempt
BT   Methods
RT   Artificial Intelligence
     Cognitive Ability
     Creative Thinking
     Creative Writing
     Critical Thinking
     Decision Making
     Discovery Learning
     Game Theory
     Inquiry
     Learning Processes
     Learning Strategies
     Logical Thinking
     Mathematical Models
     Problem Solving
     Simulation

Hidden Curriculum   *JUN. 1983*
     Postings: 365   GC: 330
SN   Unstated norms, values, and beliefs that are transmitted to students through the underlying educational structure
RT   Curriculum
     Educational Environment
     Educational Theories
     Incidental Learning
     Socialization
     Student Development
     Student School Relationship
     Values

Hierarchy
USE   Vertical Organization

High Achievement   *MAR. 1980*
     Postings: 978   GC: 120
UF   High Achievers (1966 1980)
BT   Achievement
RT   Low Achievement
     Overachievement
     Success

High Achievers (1966 1980)
USE   High Achievement

High Blood Pressure
USE   Hypertension

High Interest Low Vocabulary Books
                              JUL. 1966
     Postings: 254   GC: 720
SN   Books designed to interest learners whose reading abilities are below age or grade level
BT   Books
RT   Instructional Materials
     Readability
     Reading Materials
     Remedial Reading
     Supplementary Reading Materials

High Risk Persons (1982 1990)
USE   At Risk Persons

High Risk Students   *MAR. 1980*
     Postings: 6,188   GC: 360
SN   Students, with normal intelligence, whose academic background or prior performance may cause them to be perceived as candidates for future academic failure or

early withdrawal (Note: Prior to Mar80, this concept was occasionally indexed under "Educationally Disadvantaged")
BT   At Risk Persons
     Students
RT   Academic Ability
     Academic Aptitude
     Academic Failure
     Compensatory Education
     Developmental Studies Programs
     Educationally Disadvantaged
     Nontraditional Students
     Open Enrollment
     Potential Dropouts
     Prereferral Intervention
     Remedial Programs
     Special Needs Students
     Transitional Programs

High School Academies (Career Development)
USE   Career Academies

High School College Cooperation
USE   College School Cooperation

High School Curriculum (1967 1980)
USE   Secondary School Curriculum

High School Design (1966 1980)
USE   Educational Facilities Design

High School Dropouts
USE   Dropouts

High School Equivalency Programs
                              FEB. 1975
     Postings: 1,156   GC: 340
SN   Adult educational activities concerned with the preparation for and the taking of tests which lead to a high school equivalency certificate, e.g., General Educational Development programs (Note: Also appears in the list of mandatory educational level Descriptors)
UF   GED Programs
     General Educational Development Programs
BT   Adult Programs
RT   Adult Basic Education
     Adult Education
     Adult Reading Programs
     Certification
     Continuation Students
     Dropout Programs
     Dropouts
     Educational Attainment
     Educational Certificates
     Equivalency Tests
     Evening Programs
     Experiential Learning
     External Degree Programs
     Grade Equivalent Scores
     High School Graduates
     Nontraditional Education
     Public School Adult Education
     Secondary Education
     Student Certification

High School Freshmen   *MAR. 1980*
     Postings: 173   GC: 360
SN   Students in their first year of high school (Note: Prior to Mar80, "Freshmen" was also a valid Descriptor—for curriculum or classroom-based materials, use "Grade 9" or "Grade 10")
UF   Freshmen (1967 1980) (Grade 9)
BT   High School Students
RT   Grade 9
     High School Seniors
     High Schools

High School Graduates   *JUL. 1966*
     Postings: 2,115   GC: 360
BT   Graduates
RT   College Bound Students

= Two or more Descriptors are used to represent this term.
The term's main entry shows the appropriate coordination.

Graduation
High School Equivalency Programs
High School Seniors
High School Students
High Schools
Post High School Guidance

High School Libraries
USE   School Libraries

High School Organization (1966 1980)
USE   School Organization

High School Role (1966 1980)
USE   School Role

High School Seniors   MAR. 1980
    Postings: 1,288   GC: 360
SN Students in their last year of high school
    (Note: Prior to Mar80, "Seniors" was
    also a valid Descriptor—for curriculum
    or classroom-based materials, use "Grade
    12")
UF Seniors (1966 1980) (Grade 12)
BT High School Students
RT College Bound Students
    Grade 12
    High School Freshmen
    High School Graduates
    Noncollege Bound Students

High School Students   JUL. 1966
    Postings: 11,957   GC: 360
SN Students in grade 9 or 10 through grade
    12 (Note: Coordinate with the appropri-
    ate mandatory educational level Descrip-
    tor)
UF Senior High School Students
NT College Bound Students
    High School Freshmen
    High School Seniors
    Noncollege Bound Students
BT Secondary School Students
RT Adolescents
    High School Graduates
    High Schools
    Junior High School Students
    Middle School Students
    Reentry Students

High School Supervisors (1966 1980)
USE   School Supervision

High School Teachers
USE   Secondary School Teachers

High Schools   JUL. 1966
    Postings: 26,079   GC: 340
SN Providing formal education in grades 9
    or 10 through 12 (Note: Also appears in
    the list of mandatory educational level
    Descriptors)
UF Comprehensive High Schools (1967
    1980)
    Precollege Level
    Senior High Schools (1966 1980)
NT Vocational High Schools
BT Secondary Schools
RT Continuation Students
    Grade 10
    Grade 11
    Grade 12
    Grade 9
    High School Freshmen
    High School Graduates
    High School Students
    Junior High Schools
    Middle Schools
    Post High School Guidance
    Secondary Education
    Secondary School Curriculum

High Stakes Tests   JUL. 2000
    Postings: 136   GC: 830
SN Tests whose results are the chief deter-

minants of significant consequences for
individuals (e.g., graduation, grade promotion, or tracking) or institutions (e.g.,
accreditation, funding, or ranking)
BT Tests
RT Academic Achievement
    Accountability
    Achievement Tests
    Educational Assessment
    Standardized Tests
    Test Use

High Technology
USE   Technological Advancement

Higher Education   JUL. 1966
    Postings: 216,007   GC: 340
SN All education beyond the secondary level
    leading to a formal degree (Note: Also
    appears in the list of mandatory educa-
    tional level Descriptors)
UF Advanced Education
    College Deans (1968 1980) #
    Private Higher Education #
    Public Higher Education #
NT Graduate Study
    Postdoctoral Education
    Undergraduate Study
BT Postsecondary Education
RT Academic Advising
    Access to Education
    College Admission
    College Attendance
    College Bound Students
    College Curriculum
    College Instruction
    College Preparation
    College Programs
    Colleges
    Degrees (Academic)
    Developing Institutions
    Doctoral Programs
    Educational Benefits
    Extension Education
    Graduate Students
    Masters Programs
    Nontraditional Students
    Postsecondary Education as a Field of
    Study
    Undergraduate Students
    Universities

Higher Education as a Field of Study
USE   Postsecondary Education as a Field of
      Study

Higher Education Institutions
USE   Colleges

Higher Order Skills
USE   Thinking Skills

Highway Construction
USE   Road Construction

Highway Engineering
USE   Civil Engineering

Highway Engineering Aides   JUL. 1966
    Postings: 10   GC: 640
BT Engineering Technicians
RT Civil Engineering
    Engineering
    Road Construction

Hindi   JUL. 1966
    Postings: 145   GC: 440
BT Indo European Languages
RT Urdu

Hiring (Personnel)
USE   Personnel Selection

Hispanic American Culture   MAR. 1980
    Postings: 430   GC: 560
SN Culture of the residents or citizens of the
    United States who are of Hispanic heri-
    tage
UF Mexican American Culture #
BT North American Culture
RT Hispanic American Literature
    Hispanic Americans
    Latin American Culture
    Mexican American Culture
    Portuguese Americans
    Spanish Americans
    Spanish Culture

Hispanic American Literature   MAR. 1980
    Postings: 419   GC: 430
SN Literature of Spanish- or Portuguese-
    speaking people in the United States
    (Note: For Hispanic literature outside the
    United States, see "Spanish Literature"
    or "Latin American Literature")
UF Spanish American Literature (1969
    1980)
NT Mexican American Literature
BT United States Literature
RT Hispanic American Culture
    Hispanic Americans
    Latin American Literature
    Spanish Americans
    Spanish Speaking

Hispanic American Students   JUN. 2000
    Postings: 540   GC: 360
SN Students of Hispanic heritage who are
    citizens or permanent residents of the
    United States
BT Hispanic Americans
    Students

Hispanic Americans   MAR. 1980
    Postings: 5,664   GC: 560
SN Citizens or permanent residents of the
    United States who are of Hispanic heri-
    tage (Note: Use a more specific term if
    possible)
UF Cuban Americans #
    Dominican Americans #
NT Hispanic American Students
    Mexican Americans
    Portuguese Americans
    Spanish Americans
BT North Americans
RT Cubans
    Dominicans
    Ethnic Groups
    Hispanic American Culture
    Hispanic American Literature
    Latin American History
    Latin Americans
    Minority Groups
    Puerto Ricans
    Spanish Speaking

Historians   NOV. 1996
    Postings: 193   GC: 640
SN Scholars or writers of chronological ac-
    counts of human events
BT Social Scientists
RT Historiography
    History
    Researchers
    Social Science Research

Historic Sites   APR. 2000
    Postings: 138   GC: 920
SN Locations having historical significance
UF Historical Sites
RT Heritage Education
    Historical Interpretation
    History
    Museums
    Parks

Historical Criticism (1969 1980)
                                                  MAR. 1980
    Postings: 251   GC: 430
SN Invalid Descriptor—originally intended

as a literary term, but used indiscriminately in indexing—see "Literary Criticism" and appropriate "History" term(s)
for this concept—see also "Literary History" or "Historiography"

Historical Geography
USE   Human Geography

Historical Interpretation   APR. 2000
    Postings: 103   GC: 430
SN Explanation of historical events, sub-
    jects, or sites
RT Heritage Education
    Hermeneutics
    Historic Sites
    Historiography
    History
    History Instruction
    Parks

Historical Linguistics
USE   Diachronic Linguistics

Historical Reviews (1966 1980)
USE   History

Historical Sites
USE   Historic Sites

Historically Black Colleges
USE   Black Colleges

Historiography   APR. 1974
    Postings: 1,185   GC: 430
SN Study of the principles and methodology
    of historical writing, including study of
    the trends in historical interpretation
BT History
RT Hermeneutics
    Historians
    Historical Interpretation
    History Instruction
    Intellectual History
    Journalism History
    Oral History
    Primary Sources
    Public History
    Social History
    Social Science Research

History   JUL. 1966
    Postings: 8,500   GC: 430
SN The most general term for the study of
    the past—also used for historical re-
    views or discussions of various top-
    ics (Note: Use a more specific term if
    possible—prior to Mar80, this term did
    not carry a Scope Note)
UF Historical Reviews (1966 1980)
NT African History
    American Indian History
    Ancient History
    Asian History
    Black History
    Constitutional History
    Diplomatic History
    Educational History
    European History
    Family History
    Historiography
    Intellectual History
    Journalism History
    Latin American History
    Local History
    Mathematics History
    Medieval History
    Middle Eastern History
    Modern History
    North American History
    Oral History
    Public History
    Science History
    Social History
    World History
BT Humanities

= Two or more Descriptors are used to represent this term.
The term's main entry shows the appropriate coordination.

Social Sciences
RT Area Studies
Background
Change
Chronicles
Development
Ethnic Studies
Historians
Historic Sites
Historical Interpretation
History Instruction
History Textbooks
Literature
Museums
Non Western Civilization
Peace
Primary Sources
Religion Studies
Revolution
Social Science Research
Social Scientists
Social Studies
War
Western Civilization

History Curriculum
USE History Instruction

History Education
USE History Instruction

History Instruction JUL. 1966
Postings: 4,781 GC: 430
UF History Curriculum
History Education
BT Humanities Instruction
RT Historical Interpretation
Historiography
History
History Textbooks

History of Education
USE Educational History

History of Language
USE Diachronic Linguistics

History Textbooks JUL. 1966
Postings: 310 GC: 730
BT Textbooks
RT History
History Instruction

Hmong AUG. 1989
Postings: 51 GC: 440
SN Miao-Yao language of southern China
and Southeast Asia
UF Meo
Miao
Mong
BT Sino Tibetan Languages
RT Hmong People

Hmong People AUG. 1989
Postings: 159 GC: 560
SN Ethnic group from the mountains of
southeastern China and adjacent areas
of Laos, Vietnam, and Thailand—many
became refugees at the end of the Viet-
nam War
UF Meos
Miaos
BT Ethnic Groups
RT Asian Americans
Hmong
Laotians
Vietnamese People

HMOs
USE Health Maintenance Organizations

Hobbies JUL. 1966
Postings: 122 GC: 470
BT Recreational Activities

RT Individual Activities
Interests

Hokku
USE Haiku

Holding Power (of Schools)
USE School Holding Power

Holidays OCT. 1984
Postings: 299 GC: 520
SN Days set aside for commemorating his-
torical, cultural, religious, or other spe-
cial events—often marked by cessation
of ordinary work or school activity (Note:
If appropriate, use the more specific
term "Religious Holidays")
NT Religious Holidays
RT Cultural Activities
Cultural Context
Leaves of Absence
Leisure Time
Social History
Vacations

Holistic Approach APR. 1982
Postings: 1,790 GC: 810
SN Techniques and/or philosophies that con-
sider an entity or phenomenon in totality,
rather than as an aggregate of constitu-
ent parts
UF Whole Person Approach
Wholistic Approach
NT Gestalt Therapy
Global Approach
Systems Approach
Whole Language Approach
BT Methods
RT Decision Making
Holistic Evaluation
Humanization
Integrated Activities
Interdisciplinary Approach
Philosophy
Planning
Research Methodology
Scientific Methodology

Holistic Evaluation JUN. 1981
Postings: 510 GC: 820
SN Determination of the overall quality of a
piece of work or an endeavor by consid-
ering various aspects or components of
the work without marking or tallying
them
BT Evaluation
RT Grading
Holistic Approach
Program Evaluation
Scaling
Scoring
Student Evaluation
Writing Evaluation

Holography NOV. 1971
Postings: 87 GC: 720
SN A technique for producing three-dimen-
sional images by wavefront reconstruc-
tion
BT Photography
RT Lasers
Three Dimensional Aids

Holy Days
USE Religious Holidays

Home
USE Family Environment

Home and Family Life Education
USE Family Life Education

Home Appliance Repair
USE Appliance Repair

Home Attendants
USE Home Health Aides

Home Child Care
USE Child Rearing

Home Conditions
USE Family Environment

Home Day Care
USE Family Day Care

Home Demonstration Agents
USE Extension Agents

Home Economics JUL. 1966
Postings: 1,832 GC: 400
SN Study, below the postsecondary level, of
home management—includes budget-
ing, child care, nutrition, cooking, sew-
ing, etc. (Note: Do not confuse with
"Home Economics Education")
UF Homemaking Education (1967 1980)
BT Curriculum
RT Clothing Instruction
Consumer Economics
Consumer Education
Consumer Science
Cooking Instruction
Foods Instruction
Home Economics Education
Home Economics Skills
Home Economics Teachers
Home Management
Homemakers
Homemaking Skills
Nutrition Instruction
Occupational Home Economics
Sewing Instruction
Textiles Instruction

Home Economics Education JUL. 1966
Postings: 1,247 GC: 400
SN Instruction offered at the college or gradu-
ate-school level for professional careers
requiring home economics knowledge
and skills (Note: Prior to Mar80, this
term was not scoped and was often used
for elementary, secondary, or vocational
courses—for these concepts, see "Home
Economics" or "Occupational Home
Economics")
BT Professional Education
RT Consumer Education
Day Care
Extension Agents
Home Economics
Home Economics Skills
Home Economics Teachers
Homemaking Skills
Occupational Home Economics

Home Economics Skills JUL. 1966
Postings: 224 GC: 400
SN Abilities in such areas as clothing, nutri-
tion, household work, food service, etc.
(Note: Do not confuse with "Homemaking
Skills")
BT Skills
RT Child Care Occupations
Cooks
Daily Living Skills
Dietitians
Employment Qualifications
Food Service
Home Economics
Home Economics Education
Homemaking Skills
Household Workers
Housekeepers
Housework
Housing Management Aides
Job Skills
Laundry Drycleaning Occupations
Needle Trades
Occupational Home Economics
Visiting Homemakers

Home Economics Teachers JUL. 1966
Postings: 313 GC: 360
BT Teachers
RT Extension Agents
Home Economics
Home Economics Education
Occupational Home Economics
Vocational Education Teachers

Home Environment
USE Family Environment

Home Experience
USE Experiential Learning

Home Furnishings JUL. 1966
Postings: 138 GC: 910
BT Equipment
RT Electrical Appliances
Family Environment
Furniture
Furniture Arrangement
Furniture Industry
Housing

Home Health Aides MAY 1971
Postings: 166 GC: 210
SN Workers who, under professional super-
vision, provide routine health/personal
care and housekeeping services in homes
of disabled, ill, or elderly clients
UF Home Attendants
BT Allied Health Personnel
Household Workers
RT Adult Day Care
Adult Foster Care
Attendants
Community Health Services
Home Programs
Hospices (Terminal Care)
Long Term Care
Nurses Aides
Public Health
Visiting Homemakers

Home Influence
USE Family Influence

Home Instruction JUL. 1966
Postings: 448 GC: 350
SN Instruction provided in the home, by
educational personnel, for children with
special needs (usually homebound or
preschool) or their parents (Note: Do
not confuse with "Home Schooling" or
"Home Study")
BT Instruction
RT Home Programs
Home Visits
Homebound
Individual Instruction
Itinerant Teachers
Parents as Teachers
Preschool Education
Telephone Instruction

Home Life
USE Family Life

Home Management JUL. 1966
Postings: 660 GC: 400
SN Utilization of human and physical re-
sources to maximize individual and fa-
milial development within the home
UF Family Management (1966 1980)
BT Administration
RT Basic Business Education
Consumer Economics
Consumer Education
Family (Sociological Unit)
Family Environment
Family Life Education
Home Economics
Homemakers
Homemaking Skills
Housework

= Two or more Descriptors are used to represent this term.
The term's main entry shows the appropriate coordination.

Housing
Money Management
Private Sector
Visiting Homemakers

Home Programs JUL. 1966
Postings: 1,008 GC: 330
SN Planned activities or procedures (e.g., educational, health, counseling) that take place in the home
BT Programs
RT Educational Television
Family Caregivers
Home Health Aides
Home Instruction
Home Schooling
Home Study
Home Visits
Homebound
Hospices (Terminal Care)
Long Term Care
Videotex
Visiting Homemakers

Home School Relationship
USE Family School Relationship

Home Schooling OCT. 1982
Postings: 364 GC: 330
SN Provision of compulsory education in the home as an alternative to traditional public/private schooling—often motivated by parental desire to exclude their children from the traditional school environment (Note: Do not confuse with "Home Instruction" or "Home Study")
BT Compulsory Education
RT Civil Liberties
Home Programs
Nontraditional Education
Parent Student Relationship
Parents
Parents as Teachers
Private Education
School Attendance Legislation

Home Study JUL. 1966
Postings: 483 GC: 310
SN Studying done at home outside school hours, including work on school assignments, community projects, or individual problems (Note: Do not confuse with "Home Instruction" or "Home Schooling")
NT Homework
BT Study
RT Correspondence Study
Distance Education
Extension Education
Home Programs
Independent Study
Nontraditional Education
Parents as Teachers

Home Visits JUL. 1966
Postings: 797 GC: 330
BT Methods
RT Community Health Services
Home Instruction
Home Programs
Parent Teacher Cooperation
Parents
Students
Teachers
Visiting Homemakers

Homebound JUL. 1966
Postings: 170 GC: 220
SN Individuals who are confined to their homes due to illness or disability
UF Homebound Children (1966 1980)
RT Family Caregivers
Home Instruction
Home Programs
Itinerant Teachers
Special Education
Telephone Instruction

Homebound Children (1966 1980)
USE Homebound

Homebound Teachers (1966 1980)
USE Itinerant Teachers

Homeless People JAN. 1986
Postings: 1,066 GC: 530
SN Individuals or families without permanent or fixed residences, typically living in abandoned buildings, public places, or the streets and, at times, seeking temporary shelter with public or private charities
UF Homelessness
Street People
BT Groups
RT Economically Disadvantaged
Housing Needs
Poverty
Runaways

Homelessness
USE Homeless People

Homemakers MAR. 1980
Postings: 397 GC: 640
SN Men or women who carry major responsibilities for household or family management
UF Househusbands
Housewives (1968 1980)
BT Groups
RT Displaced Homemakers
Family (Sociological Unit)
Family Life
Family Structure
Home Economics
Home Management
Homemaking Skills
Housework
Spouses

Homemakers Clubs (1966 1980)
USE Clubs
AND Homemaking Skills

Homemaking Education (1967 1980)
USE Home Economics

Homemaking Skills JUL. 1966
Postings: 391 GC: 400
SN Ability to create, manage, and maintain a home environment (Note: Do not confuse with "Home Economics Skills")
UF Homemakers Clubs (1966 1980) #
BT Skills
RT Daily Living Skills
Family Life
Home Economics
Home Economics Education
Home Economics Skills
Home Management
Homemakers
Housework
Practical Arts

Homeowners MAR. 1980
Postings: 79 GC: 510
SN People who own houses and, generally, live in them
BT Groups
RT Housing
Landlords
Ownership

Homes for the Aged
USE Personal Care Homes

Homework JUL. 1966
Postings: 1,092 GC: 310
BT Assignments
Home Study

Homicide APR. 1990
Postings: 241 GC: 530
SN Killing of one human being by another
UF Murder
BT Antisocial Behavior
Death
RT Crime
Genocide
Suicide
Victims of Crime
Violence

Homogeneous Grouping JUL. 1966
Postings: 378 GC: 310
SN Organization or classification of students according to specified criteria for the purpose of forming instructional groups with a high degree of similarity
NT Ability Grouping
BT Grouping (Instructional Purposes)
RT Age Grade Placement
Cluster Grouping
Heterogeneous Grouping
Single Sex Colleges
Single Sex Schools

Homonegativism
USE Homophobia

Homophobia JUN. 1993
Postings: 301 GC: 540
SN Fear of or antipathy toward homosexuality and homosexuals
UF Anti Gay Bias
Homonegativism
BT Social Bias
RT Anxiety
Bisexuality
Fear
Homosexuality
Lesbianism
Sexual Orientation

Homosexuality JAN. 1974
Postings: 1,288 GC: 120
SN Sexual attraction and/or intercourse between members of the same sex (Note: Use a more specific term if possible)
NT Lesbianism
BT Sexuality
RT Bisexuality
Homophobia
Sexual Orientation

Honesty NOV. 1997
Postings: 106 GC: 120
SN Truthfulness—freedom from deceit or fraud
UF Dishonesty
Truthfulness
RT Cheating
Credibility
Ethics
Integrity
Lying
Trust (Psychology)
Values

Honor Codes
USE Codes of Ethics

Honor Societies JUL. 1966
Postings: 53 GC: 330
BT Organizations (Groups)
RT Awards
Fraternities
Honors Curriculum
National Organizations
Sororities

Honors Classes (1966 1980)
USE Honors Curriculum

Honors Courses
USE Honors Curriculum

Honors Curriculum JUL. 1966
Postings: 440 GC: 310
UF Honors Classes (1966 1980)
Honors Courses
BT Curriculum
RT Academically Gifted
Acceleration (Education)
Advanced Placement
Honor Societies
Independent Study

Hopi MAR. 1971
Postings: 22 GC: 440
SN The Uto-Aztecan language spoken by the Hopi tribe of American Indians
BT Uto Aztecan Languages
RT Hopi (Tribe)

Hopi (Tribe) JAN. 1994
Postings: 84 GC: 560
SN An American Indian people of northeastern Arizona (and dispersed kin)
UF Moqui (Tribe)
BT Pueblo (People)
Tribes
RT Hopi

Horizontal Organization JUL. 1966
Postings: 73 GC: 520
BT Organization
RT Curriculum Design
Pyramid Organization
Vertical Organization

Horologists
USE Watchmakers

Horology JAN. 1969
Postings: 10 GC: 490
BT Technology
RT Electromechanical Technology
Instrumentation
Motion
Skilled Occupations
Technical Education
Time
Watchmakers

Horseback Riding FEB. 1978
Postings: 37 GC: 470
BT Physical Activities
RT Athletics
Horses
Outdoor Activities
Recreational Activities

Horses JUL. 1966
Postings: 50 GC: 410
BT Animals
RT Animal Husbandry
Horseback Riding
Livestock

Horticulture JUL. 1966
Postings: 454 GC: 410
UF Crop Planting #
Planting (1966 1980)
Transplanting (1968 1980)
NT Ornamental Horticulture
BT Agriculture
RT Botany
Entomology
Field Crops
Gardening
Harvesting
Herbicides
Nurseries (Horticulture)
Ornithology
Plant Growth
Plant Identification
Plant Propagation
Plants (Botany)

= Two or more Descriptors are used to represent this term.
The term's main entry shows the appropriate coordination.

Hospices (Terminal Care)   AUG. 1986
    Postings: 44   GC: 210
SN Multidisciplinary programs or facilities offering care and comfort to dying patients and their families
BT Health Services
RT Death
    Family Counseling
    Family Problems
    Health Facilities
    Home Health Aides
    Home Programs
    Hospitals
    Medical Services
    Nursing Homes
    Social Services
    Terminal Illness
    Visiting Homemakers

Hospital Attendants
USE Nurses Aides

Hospital Libraries   APR. 1980
    Postings: 41   GC: 710
SN Libraries provided for use by hospital patients and sometimes the staff
BT Institutional Libraries
RT Hospitals
    Psychiatric Hospitals

Hospital Personnel   JUL. 1966
    Postings: 374   GC: 210
BT Health Personnel
RT Graduate Medical Students
    Institutional Personnel
    Medical Services
    Nurses
    Physicians
    Psychiatrists

Hospital Record Administrators
USE Medical Record Administrators

Hospital Record Technicians
USE Medical Record Technicians

Hospital Schools   JUL. 1966
    Postings: 46   GC: 340
SN Schools in hospitals for formal instruction of hospitalized children (Note: Do not confuse with "Teaching Hospitals" or "Patient Education"—prior to Oct79, this term was not scoped)
BT Institutional Schools
RT Hospitalized Children
    Hospitals
    Itinerant Teachers

Hospitality Occupations   NOV. 1982
    Postings: 287   GC: 640
SN Customer/guest service occupations in restaurants, hotels, motels, amusement and recreation facilities, and the tourism industry
BT Service Occupations
RT Dining Facilities
    Food Service
    Hotels
    Parks
    Recreation
    Recreational Facilities
    Tourism

Hospitalized Children   JUL. 1966
    Postings: 413   GC: 210
BT Children
    Patients
RT Chronic Illness
    Hospital Schools
    Itinerant Teachers
    Sick Child Care

Hospitals   JUL. 1966
    Postings: 1,142   GC: 210
UF Sanatoriums

NT Psychiatric Hospitals
    Teaching Hospitals
BT Institutions
RT Clinics
    Health Facilities
    Health Services
    Hospices (Terminal Care)
    Hospital Libraries
    Hospital Schools
    Long Term Care
    Medical Services
    Nonprofit Organizations
    Nursing Homes
    Patients
    Surgery

Hostility   JUL. 1966
    Postings: 386   GC: 230
SN Enmity or animosity, frequently marked by aggressiveness
BT Anger
RT Aggression
    Catharsis
    Paranoid Behavior
    Resentment

Hotels   JUL. 1966
    Postings: 209   GC: 920
UF Inns
    Motels
    Tourist Courts
BT Housing
RT Buildings
    Hospitality Occupations
    Tourism

Hothouses
USE Greenhouses

Hotlines (Public)   MAR. 1980
    Postings: 140   GC: 240
SN Telephone services that provide information, assistance, or crisis counseling (Note: Prior to Mar80, the instruction "Hot Lines (Public), USE Community Information Services" was carried in the Thesaurus)
UF Telephone Crisis Services
BT Community Information Services
RT Counseling Services
    Crisis Intervention
    Information Needs
    Information Sources
    Outreach Programs

Hours of Work
USE Working Hours

House Plan   JUL. 1966
    Postings: 131   GC: 350
SN The organization of a school or college into smaller units or communities, each having its own program, services, or facilities
UF Schools within a School Plan
NT Career Academies
BT School Organization
RT Building Plans
    Cluster Colleges
    Dormitories
    Educational Complexes

Household Chores
USE Housework

Household Heads
USE Heads of Households

Household Occupations
USE Household Workers
AND Service Occupations

Household Science
USE Consumer Science

Household Workers   MAR. 1980
    Postings: 103   GC: 640
SN Employees working in private homes
UF Domestics (1970 1980)
    Household Occupations #
    Maids (1968 1980)
NT Home Health Aides
BT Service Workers
RT Attendants
    Home Economics Skills
    Housekeepers
    Housework

Households
USE Family (Sociological Unit)

Househusbands
USE Homemakers

Housekeepers   MAR. 1980
    Postings: 104   GC: 640
SN Workers who perform or supervise activities to maintain cleanliness and orderliness in private homes, hotels, restaurants, hospitals, or other institutions
UF Housekeeping Aides
BT Service Workers
RT Cleaning
    Home Economics Skills
    Household Workers
    Housework
    Occupational Home Economics
    Visiting Homemakers

Housekeeping (Households)
USE Housework

Housekeeping Aides
USE Housekeepers

Houseparents
USE Resident Advisers

Housewives (1968 1980)
USE Homemakers

Housework   NOV. 1996
    Postings: 99   GC: 640
SN Tasks, including cleaning, food preparation, and doing laundry, that are necessary for the maintenance of a household (Note: See also the Identifier "Division of Labor (Household)")
UF Household Chores
    Housekeeping (Households)
RT Consumer Science
    Family Environment
    Family Life
    Family Relationship
    Home Economics Skills
    Home Management
    Homemakers
    Homemaking Skills
    Household Workers
    Housekeepers

Housing   JUL. 1966
    Postings: 1,846   GC: 920
SN Buildings or other shelters in which people live—also, the provision of such shelters (Note: Use a more specific term if possible)
UF Dwellings
    Living Quarters
    Local Housing Authorities (1966 1980)
NT Boarding Homes
    College Housing
    Dormitories
    Group Homes
    Hotels
    Low Rent Housing
    Middle Income Housing
    Migrant Housing
    Suburban Housing
    Teacher Housing

BT Facilities
RT Family Environment
    Family Size
    Home Furnishings
    Home Management
    Homeowners
    Housing Deficiencies
    Housing Discrimination
    Housing Industry
    Housing Management Aides
    Housing Needs
    Housing Opportunities
    Human Services
    Landlords
    Place of Residence
    Planned Communities
    Real Estate Occupations
    Rehabilitation Centers
    Residential Institutions
    Residential Patterns
    Residential Programs

Housing Deficiencies   JUL. 1966
    Postings: 193   GC: 530
RT Housing
    Housing Needs
    Neighborhood Improvement
    Urban Renewal

Housing Discrimination   JUL. 1966
    Postings: 255   GC: 540
BT Social Discrimination
RT Ghettos
    Housing
    Housing Opportunities
    Neighborhood Integration
    Racial Segregation
    Reverse Discrimination

Housing Industry   JUL. 1966
    Postings: 73   GC: 650
BT Construction Industry
RT Housing
    Housing Opportunities
    Real Estate Occupations

Housing Management Aides   AUG. 1968
    Postings: 8   GC: 640
SN Persons who aid public or private housing residents concerning regulations, relocations, etc., in addition to providing records for owners or managers
BT Paraprofessional Personnel
    Service Workers
RT Home Economics Skills
    Housing
    Occupational Home Economics
    Public Housing
    Real Estate Occupations
    Welfare Services

Housing Needs   JUL. 1966
    Postings: 619   GC: 920
BT Needs
RT Homeless People
    Housing
    Housing Deficiencies
    Neighborhood Improvement

Housing Opportunities   JUL. 1966
    Postings: 190   GC: 540
BT Opportunities
RT Housing
    Housing Discrimination
    Housing Industry
    Neighborhood Integration

Housing Patterns (1966 1980)
USE Residential Patterns

HTLV 3
USE Acquired Immune Deficiency Syndrome

= Two or more Descriptors are used to represent this term.
The term's main entry shows the appropriate coordination.

Hue
USE   Color

Human Biology
USE   Biology

Human Body   JUL. 1966
      Postings: 998   GC: 210
RT   Anatomy
      Biochemistry
      Biofeedback
      Biological Sciences
      Biology
      Biomechanics
      Biophysics
      Blood Circulation
      Body Composition
      Body Height
      Body Image
      Body Weight
      Brain
      Cardiovascular System
      Ears
      Exercise
      Eyes
      Health
      Health Education
      Heart Rate
      Human Posture
      Hygiene
      Medicine
      Metabolism
      Movement Education
      Muscular System
      Musculoskeletal System
      Physical Activity Level
      Physiology
      Skeletal System

Human Capital   JUL. 1966
      Postings: 907   GC: 620
SN   Investment in the education and skills of
      a nation's population (Note: Do not con-
      fuse with "Human Resources")
BT   Investment
RT   Economics
      Educational Economics
      Human Resources
      Labor Force
      Labor Supply
      Population Education
      Productivity

Human Development (1966 1980)
                                                  MAR. 1980
      Postings: 1,144   GC: 520
SN   Invalid Descriptor—used inconsistently
      in indexing—use more specific Descrip-
      tors, i.e., NTs of "Individual Develop-
      ment," "Evolution," "History," etc.

Human Dignity   JUL. 1966
      Postings: 438   GC: 540
UF   Individual Dignity
RT   Attitudes
      Behavior
      Freedom
      Humanism
      Humanitarianism
      Humanization
      Individual Needs
      Individualism
      Self Esteem

Human Engineering (1967 1980)
USE   Human Factors Engineering

Human Factors Engineering   MAR. 1980
      Postings: 620   GC: 490
SN   Area of knowledge dealing with the capa-
      bilities and limitations of human per-
      formance in relation to the design or
      modification of machines, jobs, and other
      aspects of a person's environment
UF   Ergonomics
      Human Engineering (1967 1980)
RT   Acoustical Environment

      Biomechanics
      Biomedicine
      Bionics
      Cybernetics
      Design Requirements
      Lighting
      Man Machine Systems
      Performance Technology
      Physical Environment
      Quality of Life
      Quality of Working Life
      Thermal Environment
      Work Environment

Human Geography   AUG. 1971
      Postings: 1,078   GC: 550
SN   Study of the distribution of human groups
      and the interaction of these groups with
      their physical environment
UF   Cultural Geography
      Economic Geography
      Historical Geography
      Political Geography
      Social Geography
      Urban Geography
BT   Geography
RT   Anthropology
      Area Studies
      Cross Cultural Studies
      Demography
      Ecology
      Ethnology
      Geographic Distribution
      Political Science
      Population Distribution
      Population Trends
      Racial Distribution
      Social Systems
      Urban Studies

Human Immunodeficiency Virus
USE   Acquired Immune Deficiency
      Syndrome

Human Living (1966 1980)   MAR. 1980
      Postings: 187   GC: 520
SN   Invalid Descriptor—used inconsistently
      in indexing—see such Descriptors as
      "Life Style," "Quality of Life," "Living
      Standards," "Ecology," etc.

Human Performance Technology
USE   Performance Technology

Human Posture   JUL. 1966
      Postings: 149   GC: 210
UF   Body Attitude
      Posture Development
      Posture Patterns
RT   Body Language
      Human Body
      Musculoskeletal System

Human Relations   JUL. 1966
      Postings: 2,335   GC: 520
SN   Patterns of interaction between and
      among people that persist over time and
      cause common expectations and influ-
      ences
UF   Human Relations Units (1966 1980) #
NT   Intergroup Relations
      Peace
      Slavery
BT   Relationship
RT   Group Experience
      Human Relations Programs
      Humanistic Education
      Humanization
      Interaction
      Intergroup Education
      Interpersonal Relationship
      Laboratory Training
      Rapport
      Social Integration
      Sociocultural Patterns

Human Relations Organizations (1966 1980)
USE   Human Relations Programs

Human Relations Programs   JUL. 1966
      Postings: 266   GC: 540
UF   Human Relations Organizations (1966
      1980)
BT   Programs
RT   Human Relations

Human Relations Training
USE   Sensitivity Training

Human Relations Units (1966 1980)
USE   Human Relations
AND   Units of Study

Human Resources   JUL. 1966
      Postings: 2,238   GC: 520
SN   People who can be drawn upon for their
      knowledge, skills, or productive capaci-
      ties (Note: Do not confuse with "Human
      Capital")
NT   Labor Force
      Labor Supply
BT   Resources
RT   Community Resources
      Consultants
      Developed Nations
      Developing Nations
      Human Capital
      Information Sources
      Labor
      Personnel
      Technical Assistance

Human Resources Development (Labor)
USE   Labor Force Development

Human Rights
USE   Civil Liberties

Human Services   MAR. 1969
      Postings: 2,401   GC: 520
SN   Fields of public service in which human
      interaction is part of the provision of the
      services
NT   Counseling Services
      Employment Services
      Food Service
      Health Services
      Integrated Services
      Psychological Services
      Social Services
BT   Services
RT   Client Characteristics (Human Serv-
      ices)
      Correctional Education
      Correctional Rehabilitation
      Housing
      Intervention
      Law Enforcement
      Public Relations
      Rehabilitation Programs
      Residential Programs
      Social Support Groups

Human Sexuality
USE   Sexuality

Human T Cell Lymphotropic Virus Type 3
USE   Acquired Immune Deficiency
      Syndrome

Humaneness
USE   Altruism

Humanism   JUL. 1969
      Postings: 1,302   GC: 430
SN   A philosophy that asserts the dignity and
      worth of man
BT   Philosophy
RT   Human Dignity

      Humanistic Education
      Individualism
      Literature
      Poetry
      Renaissance Literature

Humanistic Education   NOV. 1974
      Postings: 2,894   GC: 400
SN   Educational system designed to achieve
      affective outcomes or psychological
      growth—learning activities in math, so-
      cial studies, English, and so on, are
      oriented toward improving self-aware-
      ness and mutual understanding among
      people
UF   Affective Education
      Confluent Education
      Psychological Education
BT   Education
RT   Affective Objectives
      Consciousness Raising
      Cooperative Learning
      Free Schools
      Group Dynamics
      Human Relations
      Humanism
      Humanization
      Individualized Instruction
      Interpersonal Competence
      Laboratory Training
      Learning Centers (Classroom)
      Liberalism
      Multicultural Education
      Open Education
      Progressive Education
      Psychoeducational Methods
      Self Actualization
      Self Concept
      Sensitivity Training
      Values
      Values Education

Humanitarianism   MAR. 1980
      Postings: 119   GC: 520
SN   Theory or actual promotion of human
      welfare and social reform, often by phil-
      anthropic or charitable means
BT   Sociocultural Patterns
RT   Altruism
      Citizenship Responsibility
      Community Responsibility
      Human Dignity
      Political Attitudes
      Social Action
      Social Responsibility
      Social Services
      Social Support Groups
      Social Values
      Welfare Services

Humanities   JUL. 1966
      Postings: 2,642   GC: 430
NT   Fine Arts
      History
      Literature
      Philosophy
BT   Liberal Arts
RT   Criticism
      Cultural Literacy
      Culture
      Humanities Instruction
      Religion

Humanities Instruction   JUL. 1966
      Postings: 1,179   GC: 430
NT   History Instruction
      Native Language Instruction
      Second Language Instruction
BT   Instruction
RT   Academic Education
      Humanities

Humanization   DEC. 1972
      Postings: 814   GC: 520
SN   The process of changing the environ-
      ment (attitudes, structures, relationships)
      to be more humane and better adapted
      to human needs
UF   Dehumanization

= Two or more Descriptors are used to represent this term.
The term's main entry shows the appropriate coordination.

RT   Attitudes
      Consciousness Raising
      Critical Theory
      Design Requirements
      Developmental Continuity
      Environment
      Holistic Approach
      Human Dignity
      Human Relations
      Humanistic Education
      Liberalism
      Life Style
      Milieu Therapy
      Open Education
      Psychological Needs
      Quality of Life

Humid Areas
USE   Humidity

Humidity   *APR. 1970*
      Postings: 53   GC: 490
UF   Absolute Humidity
      Humid Areas
      Relative Humidity
RT   Air Conditioning
      Climate
      Climate Control
      Heating
      Meteorology
      Temperature
      Thermal Environment
      Water

Humor   *NOV. 1969*
      Postings: 1,140   GC: 430
RT   Comedy
      Comics (Publications)
      Fiction
      Happiness
      Literary Devices
      Literary Genres
      Literature
      Personality Traits

Hungarian   *JUL. 1966*
      Postings: 93   GC: 440
BT   Finno Ugric Languages

Hunger   *NOV. 1969*
      Postings: 439   GC: 210
RT   Breakfast Programs
      Food
      Lunch Programs
      Nutrition
      Poverty
      World Problems

Hurricanes   *NOV. 1995*
      Postings: 40   GC: 490
SN   Tropical cyclones with high-speed winds equaling or exceeding 64 knots (73 mph)
UF   Tropical Cyclones
      Typhoons
BT   Weather
RT   Natural Disasters
      Tornadoes
      Wind (Meteorology)

Husbands
USE   Spouses

Hvac
USE   Climate Control

Hybrid Air Structures (1972 1980)
USE   Air Structures

Hydraulics   *JUL. 1966*
      Postings: 120   GC: 490
BT   Technology
RT   Agricultural Machinery
      Engines
      Fluid Mechanics

      Hydrology
      Kinetics
      Water

Hydrology   *JAN. 1993*
      Postings: 59   GC: 490
SN   Study of the occurrence, circulation, distribution, and properties of the waters of the earth and its atmosphere
BT   Earth Science
RT   Floods
      Geology
      Geophysics
      Groundwater
      Hydraulics
      Marine Education
      Ocean Engineering
      Oceanography
      Physical Geography
      Rivers
      Soil Science
      Water
      Water Pollution
      Water Quality
      Water Resources
      Water Treatment

Hygiene   *JUL. 1966*
      Postings: 750   GC: 210
UF   Body Care
      Personal Grooming
      Personal Health
RT   Bacteria
      Child Health
      Cleaning
      Dental Health
      Dental Hygienists
      Disease Control
      Diseases
      Dishwashing
      Family Health
      Food Service
      Health
      Health Education
      Human Body
      Medicine
      Mental Health
      Occupational Safety and Health
      Physical Health
      Physiology
      Preventive Medicine
      Public Health
      Sanitary Facilities
      Sanitation
      Self Care Skills
      Special Health Problems
      Toilet Training
      Viruses

Hymns   *JUL. 1970*
      Postings: 18   GC: 420
BT   Literary Genres
      Lyric Poetry
      Songs
RT   Choral Music
      Religion
      Singing

Hyperactivity   *JUL. 1966*
      Postings: 1,458   GC: 220
SN   Behavior characterized by overactivity, restlessness, distractibility, and short attention span
UF   Hyperkinesis
BT   Behavior
RT   Attention Deficit Disorders
      Attention Span
      Behavior Problems
      Emotional Disturbances
      Learning Disabilities
      Minimal Brain Dysfunction
      Neurological Impairments
      Perceptual Impairments
      Physical Activity Level

Hyperkinesis
USE   Hyperactivity

Hypermedia   *APR. 1990*
      Postings: 1,813   GC: 720
SN   Computerized compilations of information units (text, sound, graphics, animation, and/or video) interconnected by logical nonlinear linkages that enable users to follow optional paths through the material—also, the systems used to create and display this information
UF   Hypertext
RT   Communications
      Computer Assisted Instruction
      Computer Simulation
      Computers
      Data Processing
      Databases
      Educational Media
      Electronic Journals
      Electronic Publishing
      Information Systems
      Interactive Video
      Multimedia Instruction
      Multimedia Materials
      Navigation (Information Systems)
      Nonprint Media
      World Wide Web

Hyperopia   *JUL. 1966*
      Postings: 1   GC: 220
UF   Farsightedness
BT   Ametropia
RT   Myopia
      Vision
      Visual Acuity

Hypersensitivity
USE   Allergy

Hypertension   *NOV. 1975*
      Postings: 187   GC: 210
UF   High Blood Pressure
BT   Diseases
RT   Blood Circulation
      Cardiovascular System
      Heart Rate
      Physical Health
      Relaxation Training
      Special Health Problems
      Stress Variables
      Type A Behavior

Hypertext
USE   Hypermedia

Hypnosis   *JUL. 1966*
      Postings: 204   GC: 230
RT   Meditation
      Psychotherapy
      Relaxation Training
      Suggestopedia

Hypnotics
USE   Sedatives

Hypothesis Testing   *JUL. 1966*
      Postings: 3,056   GC: 820
SN   Processes by which hypotheses are accepted or rejected (Note: Prior to Mar80, the use of this term was not restricted by a Scope Note)
BT   Evaluation Methods
RT   Analysis of Covariance
      Analysis of Variance
      Bayesian Statistics
      Chi Square
      Data Analysis
      Data Interpretation
      Markov Processes
      Mathematical Models
      Meta Analysis
      Monte Carlo Methods
      Research Design
      Scientific Methodology
      Statistical Analysis
      Statistical Inference
      Statistical Significance
      Theories

Ibo (1967 1993)
USE   Igbo

ICAI
USE   Intelligent Tutoring Systems

Ice Hockey   *APR. 1985*
      Postings: 34   GC: 470
BT   Team Sports
      Winter Sports
RT   Olympic Games

Ice Skating   *FEB. 1978*
      Postings: 19   GC: 470
BT   Winter Sports
RT   Olympic Games

Ichthyology   *AUG. 1982*
      Postings: 82   GC: 490
UF   Fish Studies
BT   Zoology
RT   Fisheries
      Marine Biology
      Oceanography

Icibemba
USE   Bemba

Identification   *JUL. 1966*
      Postings: 3,228   GC: 820
SN   Recognition of the attributes by which an individual, condition, thing, etc., can be classified
UF   Delinquent Identification (1966 1980) #
      Diagnosis
NT   Ability Identification
      Clinical Diagnosis
      Disability Identification
      Early Identification
      Educational Diagnosis
      Plant Identification
      Racial Identification
      Talent Identification
RT   Classification
      Diagnostic Tests
      Etiology
      Labeling (of Persons)
      Recognition (Psychology)
      Screening Tests
      Troubleshooting

Identification (Psychological) (1968 1980)
USE   Identification (Psychology)

Identification (Psychology)   *MAR. 1980*
      Postings: 2,134   GC: 120
SN   Process or state of imitating or merging emotionally with someone or something
UF   Identification (Psychological) (1968 1980)
      Introjection
BT   Psychological Patterns
RT   Alienation
      Attachment Behavior
      Behavior Patterns
      Conformity
      Congruence (Psychology)
      Emotional Development
      Empathy
      Ethnicity
      Imitation
      Modeling (Psychology)
      Observational Learning
      Perspective Taking
      Racial Identification
      Reference Groups
      Role Models
      Role Perception
      Role Theory
      Self Actualization
      Self Concept
      Self Concept Measures
      Sexual Identity
      Significant Others

= Two or more Descriptors are used to represent this term.
The term's main entry shows the appropriate coordination.

Identification Tests (1966 1980)
USE   Tests

Ideography   AUG. 1973
Postings: 194   GC: 450
SN   System of writing using pictures or symbolic characters instead of letters or syllable signs
BT   Written Language
RT   Chinese
    Language Patterns
    Non Roman Scripts
    Symbolic Language

Ideology   AUG. 1986
Postings: 1,135   GC: 520
SN   The body of ideas reflecting the social needs and aspirations of an individual, group, class, or culture
RT   Behavior Standards
    Beliefs
    Cognitive Structures
    Cultural Traits
    Dogmatism
    Elitism
    Group Unity
    Political Attitudes
    Political Correctness
    Public Opinion
    Social Action
    Social Attitudes
    Social Systems
    Social Theories
    Social Values
    Socialization
    Sociocultural Patterns
    Sociology
    Values
    World Views

Idiomatic Expressions
USE   Idioms

Idioms   JUL. 1966
Postings: 468   GC: 450
UF   Idiomatic Expressions
BT   Language Patterns
RT   Dialects
    Grammar
    Languages
    North American English
    Proverbs
    Regional Dialects
    Structural Analysis (Linguistics)

Igbo   JUL. 1966
Postings: 21   GC: 440
SN   A Kwa language of Nigeria
UF   Ibo (1967 1993)
BT   African Languages

Ill Child Care
USE   Sick Child Care

Illegal Aliens
USE   Undocumented Immigrants

Illegal Drug Use   MAR. 1980
Postings: 512   GC: 530
BT   Drug Use
RT   Antisocial Behavior
    Cocaine
    Crack
    Crime
    Drug Abuse
    Drug Addiction
    Drug Legislation
    Drug Use Testing
    Heroin
    Lysergic Acid Diethylamide
    Marijuana
    Narcotics
    Prenatal Drug Exposure

Illegal Immigrants (1976 1984)
USE   Undocumented Immigrants

Illegitimacy
USE   Births to Single Women

Illegitimate Births (1967 1995)
USE   Births to Single Women

Illiteracy   JUL. 1966
Postings: 1,530   GC: 460
UF   Illiterate Adults (1966 1980) #
RT   Adult Literacy
    Educationally Disadvantaged
    Literacy

Illiterate Adults (1966 1980)
USE   Adult Literacy
AND   Illiteracy

Illnesses
USE   Diseases

Illocutionary Acts
USE   Speech Acts

Illumination Levels (1968 1980)
USE   Lighting

Illustrations   JUL. 1966
Postings: 2,170   GC: 720
BT   Visual Aids
RT   Captions
    Cartoons
    Charts
    Diagrams
    Graphs
    Instructional Materials
    Maps
    Nonprint Media
    Photographs
    Photojournalism
    Picture Books
    Raised Line Drawings
    Technical Illustration

Imagery   JUN. 1969
Postings: 1,312   GC: 430
BT   Figurative Language
RT   Film Criticism
    Haiku
    Metaphors
    Sonnets
    Symbols (Literary)

Imagination   JUL. 1966
Postings: 1,096   GC: 120
SN   The ability to form a mental image of qualities, objects, situations, relationships, etc., that are not apparent to the senses (Note: Prior to Mar80, the use of this term was not restricted by a Scope Note)
BT   Creativity
RT   Creative Thinking
    Dreams
    Fantasy
    Fiction
    Intuition
    Pretend Play
    Surrealism

Imitation   JUL. 1966
Postings: 888   GC: 110
SN   Copying, whether consciously or not, the appearance, mannerisms, speech, behavior, or actions of others
BT   Behavior
RT   Behavior Patterns
    Child Behavior
    Identification (Psychology)
    Modeling (Psychology)
    Observational Learning

    Pretend Play
    Role Models
    Socialization

Imitative Learning
USE   Observational Learning

Immaturity (1966 1980)
USE   Maturity (Individuals)

Immersion Programs   AUG. 1977
Postings: 1,154   GC: 450
SN   Educational programs in which all curriculum materials are taught in a second language, generally at the elementary level and almost always within the context of a first language school
BT   Second Language Programs
RT   Bilingual Education
    Bilingual Students
    Bilingualism
    Child Language
    Curriculum
    English (Second Language)
    FLES
    Language of Instruction
    Language Planning
    Modern Languages
    Native Speakers
    Second Language Instruction
    Second Language Learning
    Second Languages
    Sociolinguistics

Immigrant Illegality
USE   Undocumented Immigrants

Immigrants   JUL. 1966
Postings: 4,915   GC: 510
NT   Undocumented Immigrants
BT   Migrants
RT   Acculturation
    Foreign Nationals
    Immigration
    Migration
    Refugees
    Transient Children

Immigration   SEP. 1994
Postings: 443   GC: 550
SN   The process in which people move to and permanently settle in a country other than their native one (Note: For legal and other aspects, see also "Immigration" Identifiers)
BT   Migration
RT   Brain Drain
    Citizenship
    Foreign Policy
    Immigrants
    Immigration Inspectors
    International Relations
    Land Settlement
    Migrants
    Migration Patterns
    Place of Residence
    Population Distribution
    Population Trends
    Refugees
    Undocumented Immigrants

Immigration Inspectors   JUL. 1969
Postings: 20   GC: 640
UF   Border Patrol Officers
    Guards (Border Patrol)
BT   Government Employees
RT   Immigration
    Law Enforcement
    Migrants
    Police
    Undocumented Immigrants

Immunization Programs   JUL. 1966
Postings: 246   GC: 210
BT   Health Programs
RT   Child Health

    Communicable Diseases
    Community Health Services
    Disease Control
    Epidemiology
    Internal Medicine
    Preventive Medicine

Impairment Severity
USE   Severity (of Disability)

Impasse Resolution
USE   Negotiation Impasses

Imperative Mood
USE   Verbs

Imperialism   NOV. 1969
Postings: 178   GC: 610
NT   Colonialism
BT   Foreign Policy
RT   Authoritarianism
    Capitalism
    Communism
    Fascism
    Nationalism
    Political Attitudes
    Political Divisions (Geographic)
    Political Power
    Socialism
    World Problems

Imports   AUG. 1988
Postings: 43   GC: 650
BT   International Trade
RT   Business
    Economics
    Exports
    International Relations
    International Trade Vocabulary

Impressionism   JUL. 1970
Postings: 25   GC: 430
SN   Artistic style of the late 19th and early 20th centuries associated primarily with painting that seeks to capture the effects of light on canvas with short brush strokes—extended to literature and music, it seeks to evoke moods and impressions rather than to convey precise details of reality
RT   Art Expression
    Intellectual History
    Literary Styles
    Music
    Nineteenth Century Literature
    Twentieth Century Literature

Impressionistic Criticism (1969 1980)   MAR. 1980
Postings: 199   GC: 430
SN   Invalid Descriptor—originally intended as a literary term, but used indiscriminately in indexing—see "Literary Criticism" and "Reader Response"

Improvement   JUL. 1966
Postings: 493   GC: 520
SN   Remedying deficiencies in existing conditions or bringing satisfactory conditions to a higher level of excellence (Note: Use a more specific term if possible)
UF   Renovation
    Upgrading
NT   Achievement Gains
    Educational Improvement
    Facility Improvement
    Finance Reform
    Neighborhood Improvement
    Program Improvement
    Reading Improvement
    Speech Improvement
    Student Improvement
    Teacher Improvement
    Urban Improvement
    Writing Improvement
RT   Achievement

= Two or more Descriptors are used to represent this term.
The term's main entry shows the appropriate coordination.

Change Strategies
Development
Improvement Programs
Innovation
Pretests Posttests
Satisfaction
Success

Improvement Programs   *JUL. 1966*
    Postings: 1,078   GC: 320
SN Systematic plans to upgrade and in-
    crease effectiveness of skills, conditions,
    methods, curricula, facilities, persons,
    etc.
NT Self Help Programs
BT Programs
RT Enrichment Activities
    Improvement
    Inservice Education
    Performance Technology
    Professional Training
    Refresher Courses

Improvisation   *APR. 1990*
    Postings: 205   GC: 420
SN The act of extemporaneous composi-
    tion, arrangement, performance, or in-
    vention
UF Extemporization
BT Creative Activities
RT Creative Dramatics
    Creative Expression
    Creative Thinking
    Dramatic Play
    Dramatics
    Experiential Learning
    Jazz
    Musical Composition
    Role Playing

Impulse Control
USE Self Control

Impulsivity
USE Conceptual Tempo

In Loco Parentis   *APR. 1993*
    Postings: 62   GC: 330
SN A legal doctrine charging schools and
    higher education institutions with the
    authority and responsibility to supervise,
    regulate, care for, and protect students
    "in the place of the parent"
UF Loco Parentis
RT Discipline Policy
    Legal Responsibility
    Parent School Relationship
    School Law
    School Responsibility
    School Role
    Student Behavior
    Student College Relationship
    Student Rights
    Student School Relationship

In School Suspension   *AUG. 1986*
    Postings: 92   GC: 320
SN Practice in which a student who has
    been temporarily removed from classes
    for disciplinary reasons is required to
    participate in a special program within
    the school, which stresses behavior
    change and may incorporate instruc-
    tional and counseling activities as well
BT Suspension
RT Discipline Policy
    Intervention
    Special Classes
    Study Centers

In State Students   *MAR. 1980*
    Postings: 412   GC: 360
SN College students who are legal residents
    of the state or province in which they
    attend school
UF Resident Students (1967 1980) (in
    State)

BT College Students
RT Place of Residence
    Residence Requirements
    Tuition

Inadequate Employment
USE Underemployment

Incentive Grants   *JUL. 1966*
    Postings: 181   GC: 620
SN Grants intended to encourage recipients
    to perform or produce in a specified way
    or according to a specified schedule
BT Grants
RT Educational Finance
    Federal Aid
    Foundation Programs
    State Aid

Incentive Systems (1967 1980)
USE Incentives

Incentives   *MAR. 1980*
    Postings: 1,891   GC: 520
SN External factors motivating or inciting
    the individual to action or effort (Note:
    Prior to Mar80, the instruction "Incen-
    tives, USE Motivation" was carried in the
    Thesaurus)
UF Achievement Incentives
    Extrinsic Motivation
    Incentive Systems (1967 1980)
RT Awards
    Change Strategies
    Fines (Penalties)
    Merit Pay
    Motivation
    Motivation Techniques
    Positive Reinforcement
    Praise
    Recognition (Achievement)
    Rewards
    Sanctions
    Self Motivation
    Self Reward
    Token Economy

Incest   *JUN. 1983*
    Postings: 276   GC: 530
SN Sexual activity between persons of closer
    kinship than law or social custom allows
UF Incest Taboo
BT Antisocial Behavior
RT Crime
    Rape
    Sexual Abuse
    Sexuality
    Victims of Crime

Incest Taboo
USE Incest

Incidence   *JUL. 1966*
    Postings: 2,618   GC: 480
SN Frequency with which a condition or
    event occurs within a given time and
    population
UF Prevalence
NT Average Daily Attendance
    Birth Rate
    Disease Incidence
    Dropout Rate
    Enrollment Rate
    Low Incidence Disabilities
    Mortality Rate
    Transfer Rates (College)
RT At Risk Persons
    Census Figures
    Demography
    Ethnic Distribution
    Geographic Distribution
    Longitudinal Studies
    Population Distribution
    Probability
    Racial Distribution
    Ratios (Mathematics)

Social Distribution
Teacher Distribution

Incidental Learning   *JUL. 1966*
    Postings: 339   GC: 110
BT Learning
RT Hidden Curriculum
    Intentional Learning
    Observational Learning
    Test Wiseness

Inclusion (Education)
USE Inclusive Schools

Inclusive Education
USE Inclusive Schools

Inclusive Schools   *DEC. 1994*
    Postings: 2,172   GC: 340
SN Educational institutions/programs in
    which students with disabilities and other
    special needs are integrated fully into
    regular curricular and noncurricular ac-
    tivities—"inclusion" means successfully
    educating all students (whether with or
    without disabilities, disadvantages, etc.)
    together in the same schools and class-
    rooms, while celebrating the resulting
    diversity, including various abilities and
    cultures
UF Full Inclusion
    Inclusion (Education)
    Inclusive Education
BT Schools
RT Academic Accommodations (Disabili-
    ties)
    Access to Education
    Disabilities
    Educational Cooperation
    Educational Philosophy
    Individualized Education Programs
    Mainstreaming
    Normalization (Disabilities)
    Regular and Special Education Rela-
    tionship
    Social Integration
    Special Education
    Special Needs Students

Income   *JUL. 1966*
    Postings: 4,463   GC: 620
UF Income Patterns
    Revenue
NT Family Income
    Guaranteed Income
    Interest (Finance)
    Low Income
    Merit Pay
    Premium Pay
    Salaries
    Wages
RT Budgets
    Compensation (Remuneration)
    Economic Impact
    Economic Status
    Employment Level
    Endowment Funds
    Financial Audits
    Financial Needs
    Financial Problems
    Financial Support
    Fund Raising
    Income Contingent Loans
    Inflation (Economics)
    Middle Income Housing
    Money Management
    Overtime
    Retirement Benefits
    School District Wealth
    Social Class
    Socioeconomic Status
    Trusts (Financial)

Income Contingent Loans   *AUG. 1976*
    Postings: 74   GC: 620
SN Loans for which repayment is based on a
    percentage of future annual income
UF Deferred Tuition

Tuition Postponement
BT Student Financial Aid
RT Income
    Loan Repayment
    Student Loan Programs

Income Patterns
USE Income

Indemnity Bonds   *SEP. 1968*
    Postings: 13   GC: 620
RT Employee Responsibility
    Insurance
    Legal Responsibility

Independent Colleges
USE Private Colleges

Independent Learning
USE Independent Study

Independent Living   *AUG. 1989*
    Postings: 601   GC: 120
SN Capacity to function in one's environ-
    ment without supervision or aid (Note:
    Do not confuse with, or use for, the more
    precise concept "Daily Living Skills")
RT Aging (Individuals)
    Daily Living Skills
    Maturity (Individuals)
    Normalization (Disabilities)
    Personal Autonomy
    Rehabilitation
    Self Management

Independent Living Skills
USE Daily Living Skills

Independent Reading   *JUL. 1966*
    Postings: 431   GC: 460
SN Reading that a student does without
    assistance from a teacher, usually at his
    or her own option
BT Reading
RT Independent Study
    Individualized Reading
    Intellectual Freedom
    Reading Interests
    Recreational Reading
    Supplementary Reading Materials

Independent Schools
USE Private Schools

Independent Students (Self Supporting)
USE Self Supporting Students

Independent Study   *JUL. 1966*
    Postings: 4,098   GC: 310
SN Individual study, usually self-initiated,
    that may be directed or assisted by in-
    structional staff during periodic con-
    sultations (Note: Do not confuse with
    "Individual Instruction")
UF Independent Learning
    Individual Study (1966 1980)
    Self Directed Learning
    Self Instruction
    Self Teaching
BT Study
RT Active Learning
    Autoinstructional Aids
    Correspondence Study
    Discovery Learning
    Distance Education
    External Degree Programs
    Home Study
    Honors Curriculum
    Independent Reading
    Individual Instruction
    Intellectual Freedom
    Learner Controlled Instruction
    Learning Laboratories
    Learning Modules

= Two or more Descriptors are used to represent this term.
The term's main entry shows the appropriate coordination.

Lifelong Learning
Open Education
Pacing
Personal Autonomy
Self Management
Student Projects
Student Research
Study Guides

Independent Variables
USE   Predictor Variables

Index Numbers (Costs)
USE   Cost Indexes

Index Terms
USE   Subject Index Terms

Indexes   MAR. 1980
       Postings: 2,428   GC: 730
SN   Systematic guides to information, con-
       sisting of lists of logically arranged items
       with references that show where the
       items are located (Note: Do not use for
       "Cost Indexes")
UF   Concordances (1967 1980)
       Indexes (Locaters) (1967 1980)
NT   Citation Indexes
       Coordinate Indexes
       Permuted Indexes
BT   Reference Materials
RT   Abstracts
       Automatic Indexing
       Bibliographies
       Check Lists
       Directories
       Discographies
       Filmographies
       Indexing
       Information Retrieval
       Information Utilization
       Keywords
       Library Catalogs
       Subject Index Terms
       Thesauri

Indexes (Locaters) (1967 1980)
USE   Indexes

Indexing   JUL. 1966
       Postings: 1,367   GC: 710
SN   Assignment of index terms to documents
       or objects in order to later retrieve or
       locate these documents or objects ac-
       cording to the selected concepts desig-
       nated by the index terms (Note: Do not
       use for "Cost Indexes")
UF   Subject Access
NT   Automatic Indexing
BT   Documentation
RT   Abstracting
       Authority Control (Information)
       Bibliometrics
       Cataloging
       Citation Indexes
       Classification
       Coordinate Indexes
       Dewey Decimal Classification
       Filing
       Indexes
       Information Retrieval
       Library of Congress Classification
       Library Technical Processes
       Permuted Indexes
       Search Strategies
       Subject Index Terms
       Thesauri
       Universal Decimal Classification

Indian Controlled Schools
USE   American Indian Education
AND   Tribally Controlled Education

Indians   JUL. 1966
       Postings: 363   GC: 560
SN   Natives of India or of the East Indies

BT   Groups
RT   Asian Studies
       Ethnic Groups

Indicative Mood
USE   Verbs

Indifference
USE   Apathy

Indigenous Personnel   JUL. 1966
       Postings: 168   GC: 630
SN   Workers who share a common back-
       ground or culture with the people they
       represent or serve
BT   Personnel
RT   Cross Cultural Training
       Outreach Programs

Indigenous Populations   MAR. 1980
       Postings: 889   GC: 550
SN   People born in a specific region, country,
       etc., or whose ancestry is connected
       therewith (Note: When appropriate, co-
       ordinate with geographic Identifier(s),
       e.g., "Australia (Northern Territory)")
UF   Aboriginal People
       Natives
BT   Groups
RT   Cultural Background
       Ethnic Groups
       Foreign Nationals
       Race

Individual Activities   JUL. 1966
       Postings: 251   GC: 310
BT   Activities
RT   Hobbies
       Lifetime Sports

Individual Adjustment
USE   Adjustment (to Environment)

Individual Autonomy
USE   Personal Autonomy

Individual Characteristics   JUL. 1966
       Postings: 6,215   GC: 120
SN   Physical and psychological characteris-
       tics of a single individual, or a single
       group of individuals, within any species
       (Note: Prior to Mar80, the use of this
       term was restricted to humans, and the
       instruction "Personality Traits, USE Indi-
       vidual Characteristics" was carried in the
       Thesaurus)
UF   Adult Characteristics (1967 1980) #
NT   Age
       Maturity (Individuals)
       Physical Characteristics
       Psychological Characteristics
RT   Administrator Characteristics
       Background
       Biographical Inventories
       Client Characteristics (Human Serv-
          ices)
       Counselor Characteristics
       Dropout Characteristics
       Experimenter Characteristics
       Individual Development
       Individual Differences
       Participant Characteristics
       Reputation
       Social Characteristics
       Student Characteristics
       Teacher Characteristics

Individual Counseling   JUL. 1966
       Postings: 529   GC: 240
SN   Counseling that is direct, active, per-

sonal, and focused on increasing the
individual client's self-understanding and
adjustment (Note: Do not confuse with
"Nondirective Counseling")
BT   Counseling
RT   Group Counseling
       Helping Relationship
       Parent Counseling

Individual Development   JUL. 1966
       Postings: 8,056   GC: 120
SN   Growth or maturation in the individuals
       of a species due to aging, learning, or
       experience (Note: Prior to Mar80, the
       use of this term was not restricted by a
       Scope Note—use a more specific term if
       possible)
UF   Developmental Differences (Age
          Groups) #
       Developmental Patterns (Individuals)
       Personal Development
       Personal Growth (1967 1980)
       Self Growth
NT   Adolescent Development
       Adult Development
       Aging (Individuals)
       Behavior Development
       Career Development
       Child Development
       Cognitive Development
       Creative Development
       Emotional Development
       Moral Development
       Personality Development
       Physical Development
       Skill Development
       Social Development
       Talent Development
BT   Development
RT   Adjustment (to Environment)
       Background
       Context Effect
       Developmental Continuity
       Developmental Delays
       Developmental Programs
       Developmental Psychology
       Developmental Stages
       Developmental Studies Programs
       Developmentally Appropriate Practices
       Faculty Development
       Individual Characteristics
       Individual Differences
       Individual Psychology
       Learning
       Life Events
       Maturity (Individuals)
       Maturity Tests
       Nature Nurture Controversy
       Professional Development
       Readiness
       Self Actualization
       Self Help Programs
       Student Development

Individual Differences   JUL. 1966
       Postings: 5,776   GC: 120
SN   Differences in personality, attitudes,
       physiology, learning or perceptual proc-
       esses, etc., that account for variation in
       performance or behavior
NT   Age Differences
       Intelligence Differences
       Sex Differences
BT   Differences
RT   Background
       Cultural Differences
       Individual Characteristics
       Individual Development
       Nature Nurture Controversy
       Racial Differences
       Religious Differences
       Social Differences

Individual Dignity
USE   Human Dignity

Individual Family Service Plans
USE   Individualized Family Service Plans

Individual Instruction   JUL. 1966
       Postings: 1,489   GC: 310
SN   Instruction of individuals (i.e., not group
       instruction) (Note: Do not confuse with
       "Independent Study" or "Individualized
       Instruction")
NT   Tutoring
BT   Instruction
RT   Autoinstructional Aids
       Group Instruction
       Home Instruction
       Independent Study
       Individual Needs
       Individualized Instruction
       Itinerant Teachers
       Teaching Methods
       Telephone Instruction
       Tutorial Programs

Individual Needs   JUL. 1966
       Postings: 2,708   GC: 120
UF   Special Needs (Individuals)
NT   Childhood Needs
       Psychological Needs
BT   Needs
RT   Design Preferences
       Design Requirements
       Human Dignity
       Individual Instruction
       Individualized Education Programs
       Individualized Instruction
       Individualized Programs
       Need Gratification
       Special Education
       Special Needs Students
       Special Programs
       Student Needs
       Well Being

Individual Power   JUL. 1966
       Postings: 1,445   GC: 120
SN   Feeling of power to effect changes in
       one's social and physical surroundings
       by decision making
UF   Individual Volition
       Volition
RT   Behavior
       Child Advocacy
       Coping
       Decision Making
       Empowerment
       Freedom
       Individualism
       Life Satisfaction
       Locus of Control
       Mental Health
       Personal Autonomy
       Psychological Patterns
       Self Actualization
       Self Advocacy
       Self Control
       Self Determination
       Self Efficacy
       Self Expression

Individual Psychology   JUL. 1966
       Postings: 625   GC: 230
SN   Branch of psychology whose theory and
       practice stress the unique wholeness of
       the individual and regard the purposive
       striving of the psyche as the motive force
       of human development—also sometimes
       used to refer to the study of individual
       differences
UF   Differential Psychology
BT   Psychology
RT   Adaptation Level Theory
       Androgyny
       Assertiveness
       Child Psychology
       Developmental Psychology
       Individual Development
       Life Style
       Personal Autonomy
       Personality
       Psychological Characteristics
       Psychological Needs

= Two or more Descriptors are used to represent this term.
The term's main entry shows the appropriate coordination.

Psychotherapy
Self Actualization

Individual Reading (1966 1980)
　　　　　　　　　　　　　　　　　MAR. 1980
　　　Postings: 68　　　　　　　　GC: 460
SN　Invalid Descriptor—used inconsistently
　　　in indexing—see such Descriptors as
　　　"Individualized Reading," "Independent
　　　Reading," and "Recreational Reading"

Individual Rights
USE　Civil Liberties

Individual Study (1966 1980)
USE　Independent Study

Individual Testing　　　　　　　MAR. 1980
　　　Postings: 311　　　　　　　GC: 820
SN　Process of administering tests to indi-
　　　viduals (i.e., not in a group setting)
UF　Individual Tests (1966 1980)
BT　Testing
RT　Adaptive Testing
　　　Group Testing

Individual Tests (1966 1980)
USE　Individual Testing

Individual Volition
USE　Individual Power

Individualism　　　　　　　　　OCT. 1969
　　　Postings: 697　　　　　　　GC: 430
SN　A theory or policy having primary regard
　　　for the liberty, rights, or independent
　　　actions of individuals
RT　Creativity
　　　Existentialism
　　　Freedom
　　　Human Dignity
　　　Humanism
　　　Individual Power
　　　Intellectual Freedom
　　　Personal Autonomy
　　　Phenomenology
　　　Philosophy
　　　Self Actualization
　　　Self Determination
　　　Self Expression
　　　Social Development
　　　Social Values

Individualized Curriculum (1966 1980)
USE　Individualized Instruction

Individualized Education
USE　Individualized Instruction

Individualized Education Programs
　　　　　　　　　　　　　　　　　OCT. 1980
　　　Postings: 1,979　　　　　　GC: 330
SN　Educational programs for individual stu-
　　　dents, each geared to the particular stu-
　　　dent's needs and conducted in accord-
　　　ance with a written plan agreed on
　　　between the student (and/or parents)
　　　and school officials—IEPs were origi-
　　　nally conceived for use in educating dis-
　　　abled children and were gradually ex-
　　　panded to include all special needs groups
BT　Special Programs
RT　Curriculum Based Assessment
　　　Diagnostic Teaching
　　　Educationally Disadvantaged
　　　Equal Education
　　　Federal Programs
　　　Inclusive Schools
　　　Individual Needs
　　　Individualized Family Service Plans
　　　Individualized Instruction
　　　Mainstreaming
　　　Nontraditional Education
　　　Resource Room Programs

Special Education
Special Needs Students

Individualized Family Service Plans
　　　　　　　　　　　　　　　　　JUN. 1994
　　　Postings: 167　　　　　　　GC: 220
SN　Early intervention programs developed
　　　by multidisciplinary teams of health care
　　　and educational practitioners and the
　　　families of young children who have
　　　physical or mental disabilities or are at
　　　risk for such disabilities—each program
　　　or "plan" is written to provide for the
　　　individual child's developmental needs,
　　　the family's needs related to enhancing
　　　the child's development, and the early
　　　intervention services required
UF　Individual Family Service Plans
BT　Early Intervention
　　　Special Programs
RT　Developmental Delays
　　　Disabilities
　　　Family Involvement
　　　Family Programs
　　　Federal Programs
　　　Individualized Education Programs
　　　Individualized Instruction
　　　Individualized Programs
　　　Parent Participation

Individualized Instruction　　　JAN. 1969
　　　Postings: 11,108　　　　　GC: 310
SN　Adapting instruction to individual needs
　　　within the group (Note: Do not confuse
　　　with "Independent Study" or "Individual
　　　Instruction")
UF　Clinical Teaching (Individualized
　　　　Instruction)
　　　Individualized Curriculum (1966 1980)
　　　Individualized Education
　　　Personalized Instruction
　　　Self Paced Instruction #
BT　Teaching Methods
RT　Adapted Physical Education
　　　Autoinstructional Aids
　　　Competency Based Education
　　　Competency Based Teacher Education
　　　Computer Assisted Instruction
　　　Cooperative Learning
　　　Curriculum Based Assessment
　　　Diagnostic Teaching
　　　Group Instruction
　　　Guided Design
　　　Humanistic Education
　　　Individual Instruction
　　　Individual Needs
　　　Individualized Education Programs
　　　Individualized Family Service Plans
　　　Individualized Programs
　　　Individualized Reading
　　　Learner Controlled Instruction
　　　Learning Centers (Classroom)
　　　Learning Laboratories
　　　Learning Modules
　　　Mass Instruction
　　　Montessori Method
　　　Multilevel Classes (Second Language
　　　　Instruction)
　　　Pacing
　　　Prereferral Intervention
　　　Programmed Instruction
　　　Small Group Instruction
　　　Special Education
　　　Special Needs Students

Individualized Programs　　　　JUL. 1966
　　　Postings: 2,261　　　　　　GC: 310
SN　Noneducational programs (e.g., thera-
　　　peutic, work-related, medicinal) adapted
　　　to meet individualized needs within a
　　　group (Note: Prior to Mar80, the use
　　　of this term was not restricted to
　　　noneducational programs—see also "In-
　　　dividualized Instruction," "Individualized
　　　Reading," and "Individualized Education
　　　Programs")
BT　Programs
RT　Counseling Services
　　　Guidance Programs
　　　Individual Needs

Individualized Family Service Plans
Individualized Instruction
Individualized Reading
Rehabilitation Programs
Sheltered Workshops
Special Programs
Supported Employment

Individualized Reading　　　　　JUL. 1966
　　　Postings: 604　　　　　　　GC: 460
SN　Type of reading instruction that empha-
　　　sizes self-pacing and student selection
　　　of reading materials
BT　Reading
　　　Reading Instruction
RT　Independent Reading
　　　Individualized Instruction
　　　Individualized Programs
　　　Pacing
　　　Reading Assignments
　　　Reading Centers
　　　Reading Interests
　　　Reading Programs

Indo European Languages　　　JUL. 1966
　　　Postings: 193　　　　　　　GC: 440
NT　Afrikaans
　　　Albanian
　　　Armenian
　　　Baltic Languages
　　　Baluchi
　　　Bengali
　　　Danish
　　　Dutch
　　　English
　　　German
　　　Greek
　　　Gujarati
　　　Hindi
　　　Irish
　　　Kashmiri
　　　Kurdish
　　　Marathi
　　　Nepali
　　　Norwegian
　　　Ossetic
　　　Pashto
　　　Persian
　　　Punjabi
　　　Romance Languages
　　　Scots Gaelic
　　　Singhalese
　　　Slavic Languages
　　　Swedish
　　　Tajik
　　　Urdu
　　　Welsh
BT　Languages
RT　Language Classification
　　　Middle English
　　　Native Speakers
　　　Old English

Indochinese　　　　　　　　　　MAR. 1976
　　　Postings: 416　　　　　　　GC: 560
UF　Indochinese Americans #
NT　Cambodians
　　　Laotians
　　　Vietnamese People
BT　Groups
RT　Asian Americans
　　　Ethnic Groups

Indochinese Americans
USE　Asian Americans
AND　Indochinese

Indonesian　　　　　　　　　　　JUL. 1966
　　　Postings: 115　　　　　　　GC: 440
UF　Bahasa Indonesia
BT　Indonesian Languages

Indonesian Languages　　　　　JUL. 1966
　　　Postings: 58　　　　　　　GC: 440
NT　Bikol
　　　Dusun
　　　Indonesian
　　　Javanese

Malagasy
Malay
Maranao
Tagalog
Visayan
BT　Malayo Polynesian Languages

Induction　　　　　　　　　　　MAR. 1980
　　　Postings: 851　　　　　　　GC: 110
SN　Logical thought process that attempts to
　　　reach conclusions by reasoning from
　　　specific instances or cases to general
　　　rules, principles, laws, or conditions
UF　Inductive Methods (1967 1980)
BT　Logical Thinking
RT　Deduction
　　　Experiments
　　　Generalization
　　　Learning Processes
　　　Research Methodology
　　　Scientific Methodology
　　　Thinking Skills
　　　Validity

Inductive Methods (1967 1980)
USE　Induction

Industrial and Organizational Psychology
USE　Industrial Psychology

Industrial Arts　　　　　　　　　JUL. 1966
　　　Postings: 2,497　　　　　　GC: 400
SN　(Note: Since the mid-1980's, most in-
　　　dustrial arts programs have become tech-
　　　nology education programs—see the
　　　Descriptor "Technology Education")
UF　Industrial Crafts
NT　Painting (Industrial Arts)
RT　Auto Mechanics
　　　Building Trades
　　　Cabinetmaking
　　　Carpentry
　　　Ceramics
　　　Construction (Process)
　　　Craft Workers
　　　Design Crafts
　　　Drafting
　　　Electronics
　　　Foundries
　　　Glass
　　　Graphic Arts
　　　Industrial Arts Teachers
　　　Industrial Education
　　　Industry
　　　Laboratory Procedures
　　　Leather
　　　Manufacturing
　　　Metal Working
　　　Needle Trades
　　　Patternmaking
　　　Plastics
　　　Power Technology
　　　Practical Arts
　　　Printing
　　　Robotics
　　　School Shops
　　　Shop Curriculum
　　　Small Engine Mechanics
　　　Technology Education
　　　Trade and Industrial Education
　　　Vocational Education
　　　Woodworking

Industrial Arts Shops
USE　School Shops

Industrial Arts Teachers　　　　JUL. 1966
　　　Postings: 270　　　　　　　GC: 360
BT　Teachers
RT　Industrial Arts
　　　Industrial Education
　　　Technology Education
　　　Trade and Industrial Teachers
　　　Vocational Education Teachers

Industrial Communication
USE　Business Communication

= Two or more Descriptors are used to represent this term.
The term's main entry shows the appropriate coordination.

Industrial Crafts
USE   Industrial Arts

Industrial Education   *JUL. 1966*
Postings: 1,512   GC: 400
SN   All types of education related to industry
including industrial arts and education
for occupations in industry at all levels
(Note: Use a more precise term if possible)
BT   Education
RT   Industrial Arts
Industrial Arts Teachers
Industrial Training
Industry
Labor Education
Technical Education
Technology Education
Trade and Industrial Education
Trade and Industrial Teachers
Vocational Education

Industrial Libraries
USE   Corporate Libraries

Industrial Nations
USE   Developed Nations

Industrial Personnel   *JUL. 1966*
Postings: 397   GC: 640
BT   Personnel
RT   Developed Nations
Employees
Employers
Industry
Laborers
Trade and Industrial Education

Industrial Psychology   *AUG. 1986*
Postings: 103   GC: 230
SN   Application of psychological knowledge
and methods to the study of human
behavior in the workplace, often with the
goals of increasing organizational effi-
ciency and enhancing the quality of work-
ing life
UF   Industrial and Organizational
Psychology
Occupational Psychology
Organizational Psychology (Work Envi-
ronment)
BT   Psychology
RT   Job Satisfaction
Labor Relations
Occupations
Organizational Climate
Organizational Development
Personnel
Personnel Management
Quality of Working Life
Social Psychology
Vocational Adjustment
Work Environment

Industrial Relations (1969 1980)
USE   Labor Relations

Industrial Robotics
USE   Robotics

Industrial Structure   *JUL. 1966*
Postings: 288   GC: 650
BT   Organization
RT   Cooperatives
Corporations
Developed Nations
Franchising
Industrialization
Industry
Mergers
Middle Management
Organization Size (Groups)
Organizational Development
Ownership
Social Structure
Structural Unemployment
Vertical Organization

Industrial Technology Education
USE   Technology Education

Industrial Technology (1969 1980)
USE   Industry
AND   Technology

Industrial Training   *JUL. 1966*
Postings: 1,717   GC: 400
SN   Technical and skills training conducted
by industrial organizations for their em-
ployees (Note: Do not confuse with "Cor-
porate Education")
UF   Corporate Training
BT   Training
RT   Adult Vocational Education
Apprenticeships
Corporate Education
Corporations
Extension Education
Industrial Education
Inplant Programs
Inservice Education
Job Training
Labor Education
Labor Force Development
Management Development
Off the Job Training
On the Job Training
Performance Technology
Professional Development
Professional Training
Released Time
Staff Development
Trade and Industrial Education
Trainees
Trainers
Training Allowances

Industrial X Ray Operators
USE   Radiographers

Industrialization   *JUL. 1966*
Postings: 994   GC: 650
BT   Development
RT   Boomtowns
Culture Lag
Demography
Developed Nations
Developing Nations
Emerging Occupations
Industrial Structure
Industry
Modernization
Revolution
Socioeconomic Influences
Technological Advancement
Technological Literacy
Technology
Technology Transfer
Urbanization

Industry   *JUL. 1966*
Postings: 4,182   GC: 650
SN   Productive enterprises, especially manu-
facturing or certain service enterprises
such as transportation and communi-
cations, which employ relatively large
amounts of capital and labor
UF   Industrial Technology (1969 1980) #
NT   Bakery Industry
Banking
Brick Industry
Broadcast Industry
Construction Industry
Fashion Industry
Feed Industry
Film Industry
Information Industry
Insurance Companies
Lumber Industry
Manufacturing Industry
Meat Packing Industry
Petroleum Industry
Publishing Industry

Telephone Communications Industry
Tourism
BT   Business
RT   Cooperatives
Corporate Education
Corporate Libraries
Corporate Support
Corporations
Equipment Manufacturers
Franchising
Industrial Arts
Industrial Education
Industrial Personnel
Industrial Structure
Industrialization
Mergers
Office Machines
Organization Size (Groups)
Organizations (Groups)
Producer Services
Production Techniques
School Business Relationship
Technology
Technology Education

Industry School Relationship
USE   School Business Relationship

Ineligibility
USE   Disqualification

Inequalities (1970 1980)   *JUN. 1980*
Postings: 82   GC: 540
SN   Invalid Descriptor—used inconsistently
in indexing—for mathematical inequalities, use "Inequality (Mathematics)"—
for educational inequalities, use "Equal
Education"—for social or economic inequalities, see "Disadvantaged" or Descriptors relating to social, racial, sex, or
ethnic bias or discrimination

Inequality (Mathematics)   *MAR. 1980*
Postings: 24   GC: 480
SN   Mathematical expression or proposition
concerning the difference in size between two quantities (Note: For educational or socioeconomic inequality, refer
to Scope Note of "Inequalities (1970
1980)")
BT   Mathematical Concepts

Infancy (1966 1980)
USE   Infants

Infant Behavior   *JUL. 1966*
Postings: 1,741   GC: 120
BT   Child Behavior
RT   Attachment Behavior
Crying
Developmental Stages
Failure to Thrive
Familiarity
Infant Care
Infants
Neonates
Separation Anxiety
Stranger Reactions

Infant Care   *JUL. 1994*
Postings: 269   GC: 520
SN   Nurturant care to meet the physical, men-
tal, emotional, and social needs of young
children from birth to about 24 months
of age—encompasses a variety of care
settings, such as day care centers, fam-
ily day care homes, the child's own home,
foster homes, hospitals, and other es-
tablishments
RT   Caregiver Child Relationship
Child Care Occupations
Child Caregivers
Child Health
Child Rearing
Day Care
Day Care Centers
Day Care Effects

Infant Behavior
Infant Mortality
Infants
Neonates
Parent Child Relationship
Parenting Skills
Pediatrics
Premature Infants

Infant Death Rate
USE   Infant Mortality
AND   Mortality Rate

Infant Mortality   *AUG. 1970*
Postings: 449   GC: 210
UF   Infant Death Rate #
NT   Sudden Infant Death Syndrome
BT   Death
RT   Child Health
Infant Care
Infants
Mortality Rate
Neonates
Premature Infants
Prenatal Care

Infant Schools (British Primary System)
USE   British Infant Schools

Infants   *JUL. 1966*
Postings: 7,414   GC: 120
SN   Aged birth to approximately 24 months
UF   Infancy (1966 1980)
NT   Neonates
Premature Infants
BT   Young Children
RT   Breastfeeding
Infant Behavior
Infant Care
Infant Mortality
Sudden Infant Death Syndrome
Toddlers

Infectious Diseases (1966 1974)
USE   Communicable Diseases

Inferences   *JAN. 1985*
Postings: 641   GC: 110
SN   Judgments or conclusions derived from
premises or evidence (Note: See also
such Identifiers as "Causal Inferences,"
"Transitive Inferences," and "Social Infer-
ences")
NT   Statistical Inference
RT   Communication (Thought Transfer)
Communication Skills
Comprehension
Context Clues
Critical Reading
Critical Thinking
Critical Viewing
Data Interpretation
Generalization
Language Skills
Learning Strategies
Logical Thinking
Perception
Reading Skills

Inferential Statistics
USE   Statistical Inference
AND   Statistics

Infirmaries
USE   Health Facilities

Inflatable Structures
USE   Air Structures

Inflated Grades
USE   Grade Inflation

= Two or more Descriptors are used to represent this term.
The term's main entry shows the appropriate coordination.

Inflation (Economics)　　　JUL. 1977
Postings: 551　　　　　GC: 620
SN　Disproportionate increase in the quantity of money or credit, or both, relative to goods and services available for purchase
BT　Economic Climate
RT　Business Cycles
　　Cost Indexes
　　Costs
　　Economic Factors
　　Economic Impact
　　Economic Status
　　Economics
　　Educational Finance
　　Financial Problems
　　Fiscal Capacity
　　Income
　　Interest (Finance)
　　Monetary Systems
　　Money Management
　　Poverty
　　Productivity
　　Supply and Demand

Influences　　　MAR. 1980
Postings: 2,046　　　　GC: 520
SN　Factors directly or indirectly affecting the condition (behavior, development, etc.) of an organism or entity, that alter some situation, or determine some result (Note: Use a more specific term if possible)
UF　Causal Factors
NT　Biological Influences
　　Black Influences
　　Community Influence
　　Cultural Influences
　　Ecological Factors
　　Economic Factors
　　Enrollment Influences
　　Environmental Influences
　　Family Influence
　　Minority Group Influences
　　Parent Influence
　　Peer Influence
　　Performance Factors
　　Perinatal Influences
　　Political Influences
　　Prenatal Influences
　　Racial Factors
　　Religious Factors
　　Social Influences
　　Socioeconomic Influences
　　Teacher Influence
　　Time Factors (Learning)
RT　Background
　　Causal Models
　　Change
　　Context Effect
　　Development
　　Environment
　　Opportunities
　　Relationship
　　Role

Informal Assessment　　　JUN. 1977
Postings: 795　　　　GC: 820
SN　Appraisal of an individual's or group's status or growth by means other than standardized instruments
BT　Evaluation
RT　Alternative Assessment
　　Check Lists
　　Curriculum Based Assessment
　　Diagnostic Teaching
　　Evaluation Methods
　　Experiential Learning
　　Grading
　　Informal Reading Inventories
　　Nongraded Student Evaluation
　　Personnel Evaluation
　　Portfolio Assessment
　　Portfolios (Background Materials)
　　Prereferral Intervention
　　Rating Scales
　　Student Evaluation
　　Testing

Informal Conversational Usage
USE　Standard Spoken Usage

Informal Education　　　JAN. 1999
Postings: 432　　　　GC: 330
SN　Casual and continuous learning from life experiences outside organized formal or nonformal education (Note: Do not confuse with "Nonschool Educational Programs" or "Nonformal Education")
BT　Education
RT　Experiential Learning
　　Lifelong Learning
　　Nonformal Education
　　Prior Learning

Informal Leadership　　　JUL. 1966
Postings: 83　　　　GC: 520
SN　Guidance or direction provided by individuals or groups whose authority is not officially derived
BT　Leadership
RT　Group Dynamics
　　Informal Organization
　　Instructional Leadership
　　Interpersonal Relationship
　　Peer Influence

Informal Organization　　　JUL. 1966
Postings: 219　　　　GC: 520
SN　An informal network of communication and interaction among groups (e.g., employees, supervisors, members, etc.) within a formal organization (Note: Prior to Mar80, the use of this term was not restricted by a Scope Note)
BT　Organization
RT　Administrative Organization
　　Informal Leadership
　　Organizational Climate
　　Organizations (Groups)
　　Power Structure
　　Social Exchange Theory

Informal Reading Inventories　　　MAR. 1980
Postings: 397　　　　GC: 830
SN　Use of observation or informal procedures to diagnose or evaluate reading proficiency or reading problems
UF　Informal Reading Inventory (1968 1980)
BT　Reading Tests
RT　Cloze Procedure
　　Criterion Referenced Tests
　　Diagnostic Tests
　　Informal Assessment
　　Reading
　　Reading Comprehension
　　Reading Diagnosis

Informal Reading Inventory (1968 1980)
USE　Informal Reading Inventories

Informatics
USE　Information Science

Information and Referral Services
USE　Information Services
AND　Referral

Information Brokers
USE　Information Scientists

Information Centers　　　JUL. 1966
Postings: 1,559　　　　GC: 710
SN　Facilities or programs that provide a variety of information services
NT　Clearinghouses
BT　Information Sources
　　Resource Centers
RT　Community Information Services
　　Computer Centers
　　Education Service Centers
　　Information Dissemination
　　Information Networks
　　Information Services
　　Library Services

Information Dissemination　　　JUL. 1966
Postings: 8,904　　　　GC: 710
SN　Distribution of information from a storage point to users
UF　Data Dissemination
NT　Document Delivery
　　Propaganda
　　Publicity
　　Selective Dissemination of Information
BT　Information Services
RT　Agenda Setting
　　Communication (Thought Transfer)
　　Delivery Systems
　　Diffusion (Communication)
　　Disclosure
　　Documentation
　　Electronic Journals
　　Electronic Mail
　　Electronic Publishing
　　Freedom of Information
　　Information Centers
　　Information Networks
　　Information Policy
　　Information Processing
　　Information Storage
　　Information Systems
　　Information Technology
　　Information Theory
　　Information Transfer
　　Information Utilization
　　Internet
　　Library Circulation
　　Library Extension
　　Linking Agents
　　Mass Media
　　Mass Media Role
　　Online Vendors
　　Publishing Industry
　　Reference Services
　　Referral
　　Technology Transfer

Information Flow
USE　Information Transfer

Information Industry　　　AUG. 1994
Postings: 299　　　　GC: 650
SN　All enterprise involved in providing access to information, whether via traditional print media, electronic technologies, or otherwise
BT　Industry
RT　Access to Information
　　Broadcast Industry
　　Communications
　　Computers
　　Database Producers
　　Film Industry
　　Information Networks
　　Information Science
　　Information Scientists
　　Information Services
　　Information Sources
　　Mass Media
　　Mass Media Role
　　Online Vendors
　　Publishing Industry
　　Reprography
　　Telephone Communications Industry

Information Literacy　　　DEC. 1992
Postings: 583　　　　GC: 330
SN　The ability to access, evaluate, and use information from a variety of sources (Note: Use the more generic term "Information Skills," if appropriate)
BT　Literacy
RT　Access to Information
　　Computer Literacy
　　Information Seeking
　　Information Skills
　　Information Utilization
　　Librarian Teacher Cooperation
　　Library Instruction
　　Library Skills
　　Online Searching
　　Scientific Literacy
　　Search Strategies
　　Technological Literacy
　　Users (Information)

Information Management　　　AUG. 1989
Postings: 1,051　　　　GC: 710
SN　Management of the acquisition, organization, storage, retrieval, and dissemination of information—can combine such traditional organizational functions as data processing, telecommunications, records control, and user services
UF　Information Resources Management
　　IRM
NT　Records Management
BT　Administration
RT　Access to Information
　　Database Management Systems
　　Information Needs
　　Information Policy
　　Information Science
　　Information Services
　　Information Systems
　　Information Technology
　　Information Transfer
　　Information Utilization
　　Library Administration
　　Management Information Systems

Information Needs　　　JUL. 1966
Postings: 4,170　　　　GC: 710
UF　Data Needs
BT　Needs
RT　Access to Information
　　Evaluation Needs
　　Hotlines (Public)
　　Information Management
　　Information Networks
　　Information Seeking
　　Information Services
　　Information Sources
　　Information Systems
　　Information Utilization
　　Online Searching
　　Research Needs
　　Search Intermediaries
　　Search Strategies
　　Selective Dissemination of Information
　　User Needs (Information)

Information Networks　　　FEB. 1969
Postings: 4,676　　　　GC: 710
SN　Interconnected or interrelated communication channels, linked for the transmission or exchange of information
UF　Electronic Information Exchange #
NT　Internet
　　Library Networks
BT　Networks
RT　Communication (Thought Transfer)
　　Communications
　　Communications Satellites
　　Computer Mediated Communication
　　Computer Networks
　　Dial Access Information Systems
　　Document Delivery
　　Electronic Journals
　　Electronic Mail
　　Electronic Publishing
　　Facsimile Transmission
　　Information Centers
　　Information Dissemination
　　Information Industry
　　Information Needs
　　Information Services
　　Information Systems
　　Information Technology
　　Information Theory
　　Information Transfer
　　Interactive Television
　　Social Networks
　　Teleconferencing
　　Videotex

Information Policy　　　AUG. 1994
Postings: 579　　　　GC: 710
SN　Governing principles that serve as guidelines or rules for decision-making and action in the area of information
NT　Library Policy
BT　Policy
RT　Access to Information
　　Censorship
　　Confidentiality

= Two or more Descriptors are used to represent this term.
The term's main entry shows the appropriate coordination.

Disclosure
Information Dissemination
Information Management
Information Services
Information Systems
Information Technology
Privacy
Users (Information)

Information Processes (Psychological)
USE   Cognitive Processes

Information Processing   *JUL. 1966*
        Postings: 3,140   GC: 710
SN   Acquisition, storage, and manipulation
        of information so that it appears in a
        useful form (Note: Prior to Mar80, this
        term was not scoped and was some-
        times used instead of "Cognitive Proc-
        esses" or "Data Processing" for
        psychological or machine processing of
        information—use a more specific term if
        possible)
NT   Data Collection
        Data Processing
        Documentation
        Information Retrieval
        Information Storage
        Word Processing
BT   Information Services
RT   Character Recognition
        Communications
        Cybernetics
        Feedback
        Information Dissemination
        Information Science
        Information Science Education
        Information Systems
        Information Technology
        Information Theory
        Information Transfer
        Knowledge Representation
        Library Technical Processes
        Pattern Recognition

Information Professionals
USE   Information Scientists

Information Resources Management
USE   Information Management

Information Retrieval   *JUL. 1966*
        Postings: 6,349   GC: 710
SN   Techniques used to recover specific in-
        formation from large quantities of stored
        data
NT   Downloading
        Online Searching
BT   Information Processing
RT   Abstracting
        Access to Information
        Database Management Systems
        Databases
        Dewey Decimal Classification
        Display Systems
        Document Delivery
        Documentation
        Indexes
        Indexing
        Information Science
        Information Seeking
        Information Systems
        Information Theory
        Library of Congress Classification
        Natural Language Processing
        Navigation (Information Systems)
        Relevance (Information Retrieval)
        Search Intermediaries
        Search Strategies
        Selective Dissemination of Information
        Thesauri
        Universal Decimal Classification
        User Needs (Information)
        User Satisfaction (Information)

Information Science   *JUL. 1966*
        Postings: 2,138   GC: 710
SN   Study of the properties of information,

i.e., its generation, transformation, com-
munication, transfer, storage, and use
UF   Informatics
NT   Computer Science
        Library Science
BT   Sciences
RT   Computer Science Education
        Cybernetics
        Information Industry
        Information Management
        Information Processing
        Information Retrieval
        Information Science Education
        Information Scientists
        Information Services
        Information Skills
        Information Systems
        Information Technology
        Information Theory
        Information Utilization
        Knowledge Representation
        Library Associations
        Library Education
        Library Schools

Information Science Education   *APR. 1990*
        Postings: 327   GC: 400
SN   Education concerned with the handling
        of information, comprising such infor-
        mation-oriented fields of study as com-
        puter and communications science,
        librarianship, and information
        management—levels of study encom-
        pass basic education for the profession,
        advanced education and research, and
        continuing professional education
NT   Computer Science Education
        Library Education
BT   Professional Education
RT   Computer Science
        Information Processing
        Information Science
        Information Scientists
        Information Technology
        Library Schools
        Library Science
        Professional Training
        Vocational Education

Information Scientists   *JUL. 1971*
        Postings: 581   GC: 710
SN   Individuals who observe, measure, and
        describe the behavior of information, as
        well as those who organize information
        and provide services for its use
UF   Information Brokers
        Information Professionals
        Information Specialists
NT   Librarians
        Search Intermediaries
BT   Professional Personnel
RT   Information Industry
        Information Science
        Information Science Education
        Library Associations

Information Seeking   *AUG. 1968*
        Postings: 2,131   GC: 110
NT   Search Strategies
RT   Access to Information
        Communication (Thought Transfer)
        Information Literacy
        Information Needs
        Information Retrieval
        Information Services
        Information Skills
        Information Sources
        Information Systems
        Information Utilization
        Inquiry
        Librarian Teacher Cooperation
        Library Instruction
        Problem Solving
        User Needs (Information)
        Users (Information)

Information Services   *JUL. 1966*
        Postings: 4,471   GC: 710
SN   The activities (e.g., information selec-

tion, collection, organization, and dis-
semination), programs, and facilities by
which information is made available for
use
UF   Information and Referral Services #
NT   Community Information Services
        Information Dissemination
        Information Processing
        Library Services
        Reference Services
        Videotex
BT   Services
RT   Access to Information
        Information Centers
        Information Industry
        Information Management
        Information Needs
        Information Networks
        Information Policy
        Information Science
        Information Seeking
        Information Skills
        Information Sources
        Information Systems
        Information Utilization
        Libraries
        Online Vendors
        Scientific and Technical Information
        User Needs (Information)
        User Satisfaction (Information)
        Users (Information)
        Vendors

Information Services (Community)
USE   Community Information Services

Information Skills   *SEP. 1994*
        Postings: 395   GC: 710
SN   Basic to expert-level informational abili-
        ties, involved in finding information, and
        reading, analyzing, interpreting, apply-
        ing, maintaining, and communicating it
        skillfully and appropriately (Note: Do not
        confuse with "Information Literacy")
NT   Library Skills
BT   Skills
RT   Information Literacy
        Information Science
        Information Seeking
        Information Services
        Research Skills
        Study Skills

Information Sources   *JUL. 1966*
        Postings: 6,571   GC: 710
SN   Persons, places, or things from which
        information is derived
NT   Archives
        Databases
        Information Centers
        Libraries
        Primary Sources
RT   Access to Information
        Agenda Setting
        Bibliometrics
        Career Information Systems
        Community Resources
        Educational Resources
        Genealogy
        Hotlines (Public)
        Human Resources
        Information Industry
        Information Needs
        Information Seeking
        Information Services
        Information Transfer
        Information Utilization
        Internet
        Journalism
        Mass Media
        Online Systems
        Research Tools
        Scientific and Technical Information
        Use Studies

Information Specialists
USE   Information Scientists

Information Storage   *JUL. 1966*
        Postings: 2,016   GC: 710
UF   Filing Systems
BT   Information Processing
        Storage
RT   Authority Control (Information)
        Computer Storage Devices
        Database Management Systems
        Databases
        Documentation
        Filing
        Information Dissemination
        Information Systems
        Magnetic Tapes
        Microfiche
        Microfilm
        Microforms
        Natural Language Processing
        Optical Disks
        Recordkeeping
        Records (Forms)
        Records Management
        Search Strategies

Information Storage (Psychology)
USE   Encoding (Psychology)

Information Superhighway
USE   Internet

Information Systems   *JUL. 1966*
        Postings: 5,771   GC: 710
SN   Procedures, operations, and functions
        devoted to processing information within
        an organization (Note: Use a more spe-
        cific term if possible)
NT   Career Information Systems
        Computer Managed Instruction
        Dial Access Information Systems
        Integrated Learning Systems
        Integrated Library Systems
        Management Information Systems
RT   Computer Science
        Computer System Design
        Computers
        Data Processing
        Display Systems
        Documentation
        Downloading
        Expert Systems
        Gateway Systems
        Hypermedia
        Information Dissemination
        Information Management
        Information Needs
        Information Networks
        Information Policy
        Information Processing
        Information Retrieval
        Information Science
        Information Seeking
        Information Services
        Information Storage
        Information Technology
        Information Theory
        Information Utilization
        Keyboarding (Data Entry)
        Management Systems
        Navigation (Information Systems)
        Online Systems
        Optical Data Disks
        Organizational Communication
        Search Strategies
        Users (Information)
        Word Processing
        Workstations

Information Technology   *AUG. 1986*
        Postings: 4,964   GC: 710
SN   The application of modern communica-
        tion and computing technologies to the
        creation, management, and use of infor-
        mation
BT   Technology
RT   Communications
        Computer Oriented Programs
        Computer Peripherals
        Computer Software
        Computers

Cybernetics
Data Processing
Downloading
Educational Technology
Electronic Libraries
Electronic Text
Information Dissemination
Information Management
Information Networks
Information Policy
Information Processing
Information Science
Information Science Education
Information Systems
Library Automation
Library Technical Processes
Office Automation
Reprography
Telecommunications
Vendors

Information Theory *JUL. 1966*
Postings: 1,075 GC: 810
SN   Mathematical theory concerned with the rate and accuracy of information transmission within a system as affected by the number and width of channels, distortion, noise, etc. (Note: Prior to Mar80, the instruction "Communication Theory, USE Information Theory" was carried in the Thesaurus)
UF   Communications Theory
BT   Theories
RT   Coding
Communication (Thought Transfer)
Communications
Computer Science
Cybernetics
Entropy
Information Dissemination
Information Networks
Information Processing
Information Retrieval
Information Science
Information Systems
Information Transfer
Input Output
Mathematical Models
Operations Research
Systems Analysis
Systems Approach

Information Transfer *AUG. 1986*
Postings: 539 GC: 710
SN   The process or result of moving information from one point to another
UF   Information Flow
RT   Access to Information
Communication (Thought Transfer)
Communications
Diffusion (Communication)
Downloading
Facsimile Transmission
Information Dissemination
Information Management
Information Networks
Information Processing
Information Sources
Information Theory
Information Utilization
Linking Agents
Reprography
Technology Transfer

Information User Needs
USE   User Needs (Information)

Information User Satisfaction
USE   User Satisfaction (Information)

Information Users
USE   Users (Information)

Information Utilities (Online)
USE   Online Vendors

Information Utilization *JUL. 1966*
Postings: 3,040 GC: 710
NT   Evaluation Utilization
Research Utilization
RT   Access to Information
Adoption (Ideas)
Bibliometrics
Data Interpretation
Decision Making
Diffusion (Communication)
Indexes
Information Dissemination
Information Literacy
Information Management
Information Needs
Information Science
Information Seeking
Information Services
Information Sources
Information Systems
Information Transfer
Linking Agents
Mass Media Use
Problem Solving
Search Strategies
Surveys
Technology Transfer
Use Studies
Users (Information)

Inhalation Therapists (1969 1985)
USE   Respiratory Therapy
AND   Therapists

Inhibition *JUL. 1966*
Postings: 392 GC: 120
SN   Condition in which action or mental function is arrested or blocked, either by internal or external influences
UF   Proactive Inhibition
Reactive Inhibition
Retroactive Inhibition
RT   Anxiety
Assertiveness
Fear of Success
Helplessness
Psychological Patterns
Self Control
Shyness
Socialization

Initial Expenses (1966 1980)
USE   Expenditures

Initial Teaching Alphabet *JUL. 1966*
Postings: 255 GC: 460
SN   A 44-character orthography used in beginning reading instruction in which each character represents one English phoneme
UF   ITA
BT   Alphabets
RT   Beginning Reading
Orthographic Symbols
Phonics
Reading
Reading Instruction

Injuries *JUL. 1966*
Postings: 1,160 GC: 210
NT   Head Injuries
BT   Disabilities
RT   Accidents
Adventitious Impairments
First Aid
Health
Medical Services
Pain
Rehabilitation
Safety
Special Health Problems
Sports Medicine

Inmates
USE   Prisoners

Inner City *JUL. 1966*
Postings: 1,852 GC: 550
SN   Central section of a city which is usually older and more densely populated
BT   Urban Areas
RT   Ghettos
Slums
Urban Demography

Inner City Education
USE   Urban Education

Inner Speech (Subvocal) *JUL. 1966*
Postings: 107 GC: 450
UF   Silent Speech
BT   Speech
RT   Reading
Silent Reading

Innovation *JUL. 1966*
Postings: 2,398 GC: 520
SN   The introduction of new ideas, methods, devices, etc. (Note: Use a more specific term if possible)
NT   Building Innovation
Educational Innovation
RT   Adoption (Ideas)
Change
Demonstration Programs
Development
Discovery Processes
Experiments
Improvement
Inventions
Linking Agents
Modernization
Research
Research and Development
Resistance to Change
Technological Literacy
Technology Transfer
Theory Practice Relationship

Inns
USE   Hotels

Inorganic Chemistry *AUG. 1982*
Postings: 250 GC: 490
SN   Study of chemical reactions and properties of all elements and their compounds other than hydrocarbons
BT   Chemistry
RT   Acids
Chemical Bonding
Chemical Reactions
Coordination Compounds
Metallurgy
Mineralogy
Radioisotopes

Inplant Programs *JUL. 1966*
Postings: 544 GC: 630
SN   Educational or training programs carried on within business or industrial establishments
BT   Programs
RT   Apprenticeships
Corporate Education
Industrial Training
Inservice Education
Labor Education
Nonschool Educational Programs
Off the Job Training
On the Job Training
Staff Development

Input Devices
USE   Input Output Devices

Input Evaluation
USE   Input Output Analysis

Input Output *JUL. 1966*
Postings: 257 GC: 710
SN   Process of transmitting information from an external source to the computer or from the computer to an external source
NT   Keyboarding (Data Entry)
BT   Data Processing
RT   Computers
Cybernetics
Information Theory
Input Output Devices
Time Sharing

Input Output Analysis *JUL. 1966*
Postings: 496 GC: 620
SN   Detailed analysis of the relationship between the products of an economy, system, or program and the resources required to produce them (Note: Prior to Mar80, the use of this term was not restricted by a Scope Note)
UF   Input Evaluation
BT   Evaluation Methods
RT   Correlation
Cost Effectiveness
Economic Research
Educational Assessment
Program Evaluation
Resource Allocation
Systems Analysis

Input Output Devices *SEP. 1968*
Postings: 871 GC: 910
SN   Equipment used to communicate with a computer, i.e., those units designed to accept data and produce the results in forms readable by humans or other processing units
UF   Input Devices
Output Devices
NT   Computer Printers
Computer Terminals
Disk Drives
Optical Scanners
BT   Computer Peripherals
RT   Computer Graphics
Computer Mediated Communication
Computer Output Microfilm
Computer Storage Devices
Display Systems
Electronic Mail
Facsimile Transmission
Input Output
Keyboarding (Data Entry)
Magnetic Tapes
Modems
Online Systems
Optical Disks
Speech Synthesizers
Word Processing

Inquiry *MAR. 1980*
Postings: 2,873 GC: 810
SN   Method or process of seeking knowledge, understanding, or information (Note: Prior to Mar80, the instruction "Inquiry, USE Questioning Techniques" was carried in the Thesaurus)
UF   Inquiry Training (1967 1980)
BT   Methods
RT   Discovery Learning
Hermeneutics
Heuristics
Information Seeking
Interviews
Learning Processes
Learning Strategies
Questioning Techniques
Research Methodology
Scientific Attitudes
Surveys

Inquiry Training (1967 1980)
USE   Inquiry

Insect Studies
USE   Entomology

Insecticides *JUL. 1966*
Postings: 109 GC: 410
BT   Pesticides

RT   Agricultural Chemical Occupations
     Agricultural Supplies
     Agronomy
     Botany
     Entomology
     Herbicides
     Plant Growth

Insecurity (1966 1980)
USE   Security (Psychology)

Inservice Courses (1966 1980)
USE   Inservice Education

Inservice Education   *JUL. 1966*
     Postings: 5,824   GC: 630
SN   Courses or programs designed to pro-
     vide employee/staff growth in job-re-
     lated competencies or skills, often spon-
     sored by employers, usually at the
     professional level (Note: If applicable,
     use the more specific term "Inservice
     Teacher Education")
UF   Inservice Courses (1966 1980)
     Inservice Education Programs
     Inservice Programs (1966 1980)
     Inservice Teaching (1966 1980) #
NT   Inservice Teacher Education
BT   Education
RT   Career Ladders
     Faculty Development
     Improvement Programs
     Industrial Training
     Inplant Programs
     Institutes (Training Programs)
     Management Development
     Minicourses
     Off the Job Training
     On the Job Training
     Professional Continuing Education
     Professional Development
     Professional Training
     Refresher Courses
     Retraining
     Staff Development

Inservice Education Programs
USE   Inservice Education

Inservice Programs (1966 1980)
USE   Inservice Education

Inservice Teacher Education   *JUL. 1966*
     Postings: 16,098   GC: 320
UF   Inservice Teacher Training
BT   Inservice Education
     Teacher Education
RT   Beginning Teacher Induction
     Faculty Development
     Institutes (Training Programs)
     Internship Programs
     Preservice Teacher Education
     Professional Development Schools
     Professional Training
     School Visitation
     Teacher Centers
     Teacher Educator Education
     Teacher Improvement
     Teacher Interns
     Teacher Workshops

Inservice Teacher Training
USE   Inservice Teacher Education

Inservice Teaching Experience
USE   Teaching Experience

Inservice Teaching (1966 1980)
USE   Inservice Education
AND   Teaching (Occupation)

Inspection   *JUL. 1966*
     Postings: 305   GC: 650
SN   Official examination or review

BT   Evaluation Methods
RT   Audits (Verification)
     Equipment Evaluation
     Evaluation
     Field Tests
     Observation
     Quality Control
     Standards

Institute Type Courses (1966 1980)
USE   Institutes (Training Programs)

Institutes (Training Programs)   *JUL. 1966*
     Postings: 2,097   GC: 350
SN   Programs of training designed to pro-
     vide advanced study in a subject field,
     usually more intensive than conventions
     or conferences but less elaborate than
     workshops
UF   Institute Type Courses (1966 1980)
     Science Institutes (1967 1980) #
     Summer Institutes (1967 1980) #
BT   Programs
RT   Conference Papers
     Conference Proceedings
     Conferences
     Inservice Education
     Inservice Teacher Education
     Meetings
     Minicourses
     Off the Job Training
     Professional Continuing Education
     Professional Training
     Seminars
     Teacher Centers
     Teacher Education
     Training Methods
     Workshops

Institution Libraries (1969 1980)
USE   Institutional Libraries

Institutional Administration   *JUL. 1966*
     Postings: 571   GC: 320
SN   Planning, organizing, directing, and con-
     trolling human or material resources in
     public service organizations, e.g., schools,
     churches, hospitals, prisons, etc.
NT   Library Administration
     School Administration
BT   Administration
RT   Environmental Scanning
     Governing Boards
     Institutional Autonomy
     Institutional Mission
     Institutions
     Retrenchment
     Strategic Planning

Institutional Advancement   *OCT. 1982*
     Postings: 947   GC: 720
SN   Interpretation and promotion of an insti-
     tution to its various constituencies—
     includes fund raising, internal and exter-
     nal communications, government rela-
     tions, and public relations
BT   Publicity
RT   Communication Audits
     Enrollment Management
     Fund Raising
     Institutions
     Lobbying
     Marketing
     Mission Statements
     Organizational Communication
     Public Relations

Institutional Assessment
USE   Institutional Evaluation

Institutional Autonomy   *SEP. 1977*
     Postings: 1,053   GC: 330
SN   Freedom of an institution to act without
     external control
NT   School Based Management
RT   Academic Freedom
     Block Grants

     Charter Schools
     College Governing Councils
     Decentralization
     Diversity (Institutional)
     Federal Regulation
     Full State Funding
     Governance
     Government Role
     Government School Relationship
     Institutional Administration
     Institutions
     Intellectual Freedom
     Professional Autonomy
     School District Autonomy
     Self Determination
     State Regulation

Institutional Characteristics   *JUN. 1978*
     Postings: 4,454   GC: 320
SN   Descriptive features of an institution,
     such as funding, size, demographics,
     and governance
UF   College Characteristics
     Institutional Differences #
     School Characteristics
     University Characteristics
NT   Diversity (Institutional)
     School Size
RT   College Environment
     Institutional Environment
     Institutional Evaluation
     Institutions
     Organization Size (Groups)
     Peer Institutions
     Reputation
     School Demography
     School Organization
     Schools

Institutional Cooperation   *MAR. 1980*
     Postings: 3,447   GC: 330
SN   Cooperation of institutions with each other
     or with other organizations, groups, etc.
UF   Interinstitutional Cooperation (1968
     1980)
NT   College School Cooperation
     Intercollegiate Cooperation
     Library Cooperation
BT   Cooperation
RT   Agency Cooperation
     Articulation (Education)
     Community Cooperation
     Consortia
     Cooperative Planning
     Cooperative Programs
     Dual Enrollment
     Educational Cooperation
     Exchange Programs
     Institutional Survival
     Institutions
     Integrated Services
     Interdistrict Policies
     International Cooperation
     Interschool Communication
     Partnerships in Education
     Peer Institutions
     Regional Cooperation
     Research Coordinating Units
     Shared Facilities
     Shared Resources and Services
     Statewide Planning
     Teacher Centers

Institutional Differences
USE   Differences
AND   Institutional Characteristics

Institutional Eligibility
USE   Eligibility

Institutional Environment   *JUL. 1966*
     Postings: 820   GC: 320
SN   Conditions, forces, or factors that affect
     institutions (Note: Use a more specific
     term if possible)
NT   College Environment
BT   Environment
RT   Diversity (Institutional)
     Educational Environment

     Environmental Scanning
     Institutional Characteristics
     Institutional Mission
     Institutions
     Organizational Climate

Institutional Evaluation   *OCT. 1979*
     Postings: 1,617   GC: 320
SN   Formal or informal assessment of an
     institution from without, often for ac-
     creditation purposes (Note: Do not con-
     fuse with "Institutional Research" or "Self
     Evaluation (Groups)")
UF   Institutional Assessment
BT   Evaluation
RT   Accreditation (Institutions)
     Accrediting Agencies
     College Outcomes Assessment
     Diversity (Institutional)
     Institutional Characteristics
     Institutional Research
     Institutions
     Program Evaluation
     Self Evaluation (Groups)
     Summative Evaluation

Institutional Facilities (1967 1980)
USE   Facilities

Institutional Function
USE   Institutional Role

Institutional Goals
USE   Organizational Objectives

Institutional Libraries   *APR. 1980*
     Postings: 209   GC: 710
SN   (Note: Coordinate with another term to
     identify type of institution)
UF   Institution Libraries (1969 1980)
NT   Hospital Libraries
     Prison Libraries
BT   Special Libraries
RT   Corporate Libraries
     Institutions

Institutional Mission   *AUG. 1986*
     Postings: 1,771   GC: 320
SN   The purpose(s) for which a particular
     institution is established and around
     which policies of the institution evolve
     (Note: Prior to Aug86, the Thesaurus
     carried the instruction "Institutional Mis-
     sion, USE Institutional Role")
BT   Organizational Objectives
RT   Diversity (Institutional)
     Institutional Administration
     Institutional Environment
     Institutional Role
     Institutions
     Mission Statements
     Public Policy
     School Policy

Institutional Objectives
USE   Organizational Objectives

Institutional Personnel   *JUL. 1966*
     Postings: 219   GC: 520
BT   Personnel
RT   Correctional Institutions
     Hospital Personnel
     Institutions

Institutional Research   *JUL. 1966*
     Postings: 4,113   GC: 810
SN   Research on an institution, usually to
     provide greater understanding of its op-
     erations (Note: As of Oct81, use as a
     minor Descriptor for examples of this
     kind of research—use as a major Descrip-
     tor only as the subject of a document)
BT   Research
RT   College Outcomes Assessment
     College Planning

= Two or more Descriptors are used to represent this term.
The term's main entry shows the appropriate coordination.

Curriculum Research
Diversity (Institutional)
Educational Research
Effective Schools Research
Experimental Programs
Institutional Evaluation
Institutions
Media Research
Peer Institutions
Research Directors
Self Evaluation (Groups)
Use Studies

Institutional Role   MAY 1969
Postings: 2,115   GC: 330
SN   Function performed by or expected of an
     institution
UF   Institutional Function
NT   Agency Role
     Church Role
     Court Role
     Library Role
     School Role
BT   Role
RT   Community Role
     Diversity (Institutional)
     Government Role
     Institutional Mission
     Institutional Survival
     Institutions
     Leadership
     Research
     Responsibility
     Services

Institutional Schools   JUL. 1966
Postings: 81   GC: 340
SN   Schools that are part of larger residen-
     tial institutions such as hospitals or
     correctional institutions (Note: Prior to
     Mar80, the use of this term was not
     restricted by a Scope Note)
NT   Hospital Schools
BT   Special Schools
RT   Institutions
     Residential Schools

Institutional Self Study
USE Self Evaluation (Groups)

Institutional Survival   AUG. 1986
Postings: 329   GC: 330
SN   Continuance of an institution as a viable
     entity, as opposed to closure or merger
RT   Developing Institutions
     Economic Change
     Educational Economics
     Financial Exigency
     Financial Problems
     Institutional Cooperation
     Institutional Role
     Institutions
     Retrenchment
     School Closing
     School Support
     Small Schools
     Social Change

Institutionalized (Persons) (1967 1976)
USE Institutionalized Persons

Institutionalized Persons   MAY 1976
Postings: 2,189   GC: 220
UF   Institutionalized (Persons) (1967
     1976)
NT   Prisoners
BT   Groups
RT   Correctional Education
     Correctional Institutions
     Deinstitutionalization (of Disabled)
     Mental Disorders
     Patients
     Residential Programs
     Severe Disabilities

Institutions   JUL. 1966
Postings: 599   GC: 520
SN   Established organizations, usually of a
     public nature, that are dedicated to an
     educational, economic, political, relig-
     ious, charitable, or other social purpose—
     includes foundations, societies, corpo-
     rations, etc. (Note: Use a more specific
     term if possible)
UF   Social Institutions (Organizations)
NT   Black Institutions
     Churches
     Courts
     Hospitals
     Libraries
     Peer Institutions
     Philanthropic Foundations
     Residential Institutions
     Schools
RT   Corporations
     Institutional Administration
     Institutional Advancement
     Institutional Autonomy
     Institutional Characteristics
     Institutional Cooperation
     Institutional Environment
     Institutional Evaluation
     Institutional Libraries
     Institutional Mission
     Institutional Personnel
     Institutional Research
     Institutional Role
     Institutional Schools
     Institutional Survival
     Nonprofit Organizations
     Organizational Objectives
     Organizations (Groups)
     Rehabilitation Centers
     Religious Organizations
     Resources

Instruction   JUL. 1966
Postings: 12,313   GC: 310
SN   Process by which knowledge, attitudes,
     or skills are deliberately conveyed—
     includes the total instructional process,
     from planning and implementation
     through evaluation and feedback (Note:
     Use a more specific term if possible—
     for standard approaches, see "Teaching
     Methods")
UF   Pedagogy
     Teaching (Process)
NT   Assignments
     Clothing Instruction
     College Instruction
     Concept Teaching
     Cooking Instruction
     Ethical Instruction
     Field Instruction
     Foods Instruction
     Geography Instruction
     Group Instruction
     Home Instruction
     Humanities Instruction
     Individual Instruction
     Library Instruction
     Mass Instruction
     Mathematics Instruction
     Nutrition Instruction
     Reading Instruction
     Remedial Instruction
     Science Instruction
     Sewing Instruction
     Speech Instruction
     Spelling Instruction
     Telephone Usage Instruction
     Test Coaching
     Textiles Instruction
     Writing Instruction
RT   Curriculum
     Education
     Educational Environment
     Educational Technology
     Instructional Design
     Instructional Development
     Instructional Effectiveness
     Instructional Improvement
     Instructional Innovation
     Instructional Leadership
     Instructional Materials
     Instructional Systems

Laboratory Procedures
Language of Instruction
Learning
School Supervision
Teaching Methods
Teaching Models

Instructional Aids (1966 1980)
USE Educational Media

Instructional Alternatives
USE Nontraditional Education

Instructional Design   JUL. 1966
Postings: 6,193   GC: 310
SN   Analysis and prescription of optimal in-
     structional methods (Note: Prior to
     Apr80, the use of this term was not
     restricted by a Scope Note)
BT   Design
RT   Curriculum Design
     Educational Strategies
     Educational Technology
     Instruction
     Instructional Development
     Instructional Improvement
     Instructional Innovation

Instructional Development   MAR. 1980
Postings: 3,015   GC: 310
SN   Systematic approach to design, produc-
     tion, evaluation, and utilization of in-
     structional systems and programs, in-
     cluding the management of these
     components
UF   Instructional Planning
BT   Educational Development
RT   Curriculum Design
     Curriculum Development
     Curriculum Evaluation
     Educational Strategies
     Educational Technology
     Flexible Scheduling
     Instruction
     Instructional Design
     Instructional Improvement
     Instructional Innovation
     Instructional Leadership
     Instructional Material Evaluation
     Instructional Systems

Instructional Effectiveness   AUG. 1986
Postings: 9,481   GC: 310
SN   Degree to which instructional materials
     or programs are successful in accom-
     plishing their objectives
RT   Academic Achievement
     Administrator Effectiveness
     Course Evaluation
     Curriculum Evaluation
     Educational Quality
     Excellence in Education
     Instruction
     Instructional Improvement
     Instructional Innovation
     Instructional Leadership
     Instructional Material Evaluation
     Instructional Materials
     Outcomes of Education
     Program Effectiveness
     School Effectiveness
     Teacher Effectiveness
     Teaching Methods

Instructional Films   JUL. 1966
Postings: 1,206   GC: 720
BT   Audiovisual Aids
     Films
     Instructional Materials
RT   Audiovisual Instruction
     Documentaries
     Educational Television
     Programmed Instructional Materials
     Protocol Materials
     Single Concept Films
     Teaching Methods

Instructional Improvement   JUL. 1966
Postings: 7,475   GC: 310
SN   Enhancing the value or quality of instruc-
     tion
BT   Educational Improvement
RT   Clinical Supervision (of Teachers)
     Educational Technology
     Excellence in Education
     Instruction
     Instructional Design
     Instructional Development
     Instructional Effectiveness
     Instructional Innovation
     Instructional Leadership
     Research and Instruction Units
     School Supervision
     Student Evaluation of Teacher Per-
     formance
     Teacher Effectiveness
     Teacher Improvement

Instructional Innovation   JUL. 1966
Postings: 5,977   GC: 310
SN   Introduction of new teaching ideas, meth-
     ods, or devices (Note: Do not confuse
     with "Educational Innovation")
UF   Teaching Innovations
BT   Educational Innovation
RT   Creative Teaching
     Educational Technology
     Experimental Colleges
     Experimental Curriculum
     Experimental Schools
     Experimental Teaching
     Flexible Scheduling
     Instruction
     Instructional Design
     Instructional Development
     Instructional Effectiveness
     Instructional Improvement
     Instructional Leadership
     Multiunit Schools
     Nontraditional Education
     Spiral Curriculum
     Teacher Effectiveness

Instructional Language
USE Language of Instruction

Instructional Leadership   AUG. 1986
Postings: 1,599   GC: 320
SN   Providing direction, coordination, and
     resources for the improvement of cur-
     riculum and instruction
BT   Leadership
RT   Academic Deans
     Beginning Principals
     Curriculum Development
     Department Heads
     Excellence in Education
     Informal Leadership
     Instruction
     Instructional Development
     Instructional Effectiveness
     Instructional Improvement
     Instructional Innovation
     Leadership Responsibility
     Leadership Training
     Principals
     School Administration
     School Supervision
     Superintendents
     Teacher Administrator Relationship
     Teaching Methods

Instructional Material Adaptation
USE Media Adaptation

Instructional Material Development
USE Material Development

Instructional Material Evaluation
                                          JUN. 1984
Postings: 869   GC: 310
SN   Determining the efficacy, value, etc., of
     any type of instructional material with
     respect to stated objectives, standards,
     or criteria (Note: Use as a minor Descrip-

= Two or more Descriptors are used to represent this term.
The term's main entry shows the appropriate coordination.

tor for examples of this kind of eval-
uation—use as a major Descriptor only
as the subject of a document)
NT   Textbook Evaluation
BT   Evaluation
RT   Course Evaluation
     Curriculum Evaluation
     Instructional Development
     Instructional Effectiveness
     Instructional Materials
     Material Development
     Media Adaptation
     Media Selection
     Program Evaluation

Instructional Material Selection
USE   Media Selection

Instructional Materials   *JUL. 1966*
     Postings: 38,487   GC: 730
SN   Print and/or nonprint materials used in
     instruction
UF   Classroom Libraries (1966 1980)
     Classroom Materials (1966 1980)
     Curriculum Materials
     Educational Materials
     FLES Materials (1967 1980) #
     Handwriting Materials (1966 1983) #
     Teaching Materials
NT   Advance Organizers
     Bilingual Instructional Materials
     Courseware
     Experience Charts
     Instructional Films
     Laboratory Manuals
     Learning Modules
     Manipulative Materials
     Problem Sets
     Programmed Instructional Materials
     Protocol Materials
     Student Developed Materials
     Study Guides
     Teacher Developed Materials
     Textbooks
     Workbooks
BT   Educational Media
RT   Art Materials
     Audiovisual Aids
     Autoinstructional Aids
     Cartoons
     Charts
     Comics (Publications)
     Curriculum Development
     Diagrams
     Educational Games
     Educational Resources
     Educational Technology
     Exhibits
     Graphs
     Health Materials
     High Interest Low Vocabulary Books
     Illustrations
     Instruction
     Instructional Effectiveness
     Instructional Material Evaluation
     Large Type Materials
     Learning Resources Centers
     Library Materials
     Maps
     Material Development
     Mathematics Materials
     Microforms
     Orientation Materials
     Printed Materials
     Publications
     Reading Materials
     Realia
     Recipes (Food)
     Reference Materials
     Resource Materials
     Science Course Improvement Projects
     Science Materials
     Signs
     Supplementary Reading Materials
     Teaching Guides
     Telegraphic Materials
     Tests
     Toys
     Visual Aids

Instructional Materials Centers (1966 1980)
USE   Learning Resources Centers

Instructional Media (1967 1980)
USE   Educational Media

Instructional Methods
USE   Teaching Methods

Instructional Outcomes
USE   Outcomes of Education

Instructional Planning
USE   Instructional Development

Instructional Program Divisions   *JUL. 1966*
     Postings: 1,067   GC: 340
SN   Divisions marked by the use of grade
     levels or other groupings to structure the
     formal educational process
UF   Grade Levels
     Grade Organization (1966 1980)
     Grades (Program Divisions)
     Six Three Three Organization
NT   Grade 1
     Grade 10
     Grade 11
     Grade 12
     Grade 2
     Grade 3
     Grade 4
     Grade 5
     Grade 6
     Grade 7
     Grade 8
     Grade 9
     Intermediate Grades
     Kindergarten
RT   Ability Grouping
     Age Grade Placement
     Grouping (Instructional Purposes)
     Multigraded Classes
     Nongraded Instructional Grouping
     School Organization
     Student Promotion

Instructional Programs (1966 1980)
                                              MAR. 1980
     Postings: 1,595   GC: 310
SN   Invalid Descriptor—used inconsistently
     in indexing—coordinate more specific
     Descriptors

Instructional Radio
USE   Educational Radio

Instructional Software
USE   Courseware

Instructional Staff (1966 1980)
USE   Teachers

Instructional Strategies
USE   Educational Strategies

Instructional Student Costs   *DEC. 1975*
     Postings: 197   GC: 620
SN   Costs incurred by students specifically
     for instruction, e.g., tuition, laboratory
     fees (Note: Use "Noninstructional Stu-
     dent Costs" for student costs not di-
     rectly related to instruction, such as trans-
     portation expenses and room and board)
NT   Tuition
BT   Student Costs
RT   Educational Economics
     Educational Finance
     Fellowships
     Noninstructional Student Costs
     Operating Expenses
     Program Costs
     Scholarships
     Student Financial Aid

     Student Loan Programs
     Tuition Grants

Instructional Systems   *MAR. 1971*
     Postings: 1,293   GC: 310
SN   Combination, arrangement, and manage-
     ment of instructional components to solve
     problems or achieve other educational
     objectives
BT   Educational Technology
RT   Instruction
     Instructional Development
     Performance Technology
     Systems Analysis
     Systems Approach

Instructional Teams
USE   Team Teaching

Instructional Technology (1966 1978)
USE   Educational Technology

Instructional Television (1966 1974)
USE   Educational Television

Instructional Trips (1966 1980)
USE   Field Trips

Instructionally Effective Schools
USE   School Effectiveness

Instructor Centered Television (1966 1980)
USE   Educational Television

Instructor Coordinators   *JUL. 1966*
     Postings: 316   GC: 360
SN   Teachers responsible for coordinating
     students' education and on-the-job ac-
     tivities
UF   Coordinator Trainers
     Teacher Coordinators
BT   Coordinators
     Teachers
RT   Adult Educators
     Cooperative Education
     Guidance Personnel
     School Guidance
     Vocational Education Teachers

Instructor Manuals
USE   Teaching Guides

Instructors
USE   Teachers

Instrumental Conditioning
USE   Operant Conditioning

Instrumentation   *JUL. 1966*
     Postings: 902   GC: 910
SN   Use of physical instruments or instru-
     ment systems for detection, observa-
     tion, measurement, communication, con-
     trol, etc.
NT   Visible Speech
RT   Automation
     Calculators
     Computers
     Cybernetics
     Data Processing
     Electronic Control
     Electronic Equipment
     Horology
     Instrumentation Technicians
     Measurement Equipment
     Polygraphs
     Sound Spectrographs
     Test Scoring Machines
     Transistors

Instrumentation and Orchestration
                                              OCT. 1994
     Postings: 38   GC: 420
SN   Study or use of the various musical
     instruments—includes organizing instru-
     mental groups, e.g., orchestras or bands,
     and composing instrumental music
UF   Orchestration (Music)
BT   Music Activities
RT   Bands (Music)
     Concerts
     Music
     Music Techniques
     Music Theory
     Musical Composition
     Musical Instruments
     Orchestras

Instrumentation Technicians   *JUL. 1966*
     Postings: 60   GC: 640
BT   Paraprofessional Personnel
RT   Electronic Technicians
     Electronics
     Instrumentation

Insulation (Heat)
USE   Thermal Insulation

Insulation (Sound)
USE   Acoustic Insulation

Insurance   *MAR. 1980*
     Postings: 834   GC: 620
SN   Method of pooling or shifting probable
     losses among a group to reduce eco-
     nomic risk
UF   Insurance Programs (1968 1980)
NT   Fire Insurance
     Health Insurance
     Unemployment Insurance
     Workers Compensation
BT   Methods
RT   Eligibility
     Financial Services
     Financial Support
     Indemnity Bonds
     Insurance Companies
     Insurance Occupations
     Ownership
     Property Appraisal
     Retirement Benefits
     Risk
     Risk Management

Insurance Companies   *JUL. 1966*
     Postings: 178   GC: 650
UF   Insurance Industry
BT   Industry
RT   Business
     Insurance
     Insurance Occupations

Insurance Industry
USE   Insurance Companies

Insurance Occupations   *SEP. 1968*
     Postings: 63   GC: 640
BT   Occupations
RT   Distributive Education
     Fire Insurance
     Health Insurance
     Insurance
     Insurance Companies
     Sales Occupations
     Unemployment Insurance

Insurance Programs (1968 1980)
USE   Insurance

Integers   *FEB. 1970*
     Postings: 146   GC: 480
NT   Prime Numbers
     Whole Numbers
BT   Rational Numbers
RT   Arithmetic

= Two or more Descriptors are used to represent this term.
The term's main entry shows the appropriate coordination.

Integrated Activities *JUL. 1966*
Postings: 2,632   GC: 310
SN Systematic organization of units into a meaningful pattern (Note: Use a more specific term if possible—prior to Mar80, the instruction "Integrated Learning, USE Integrated Curriculum" was carried in the Thesaurus)
UF Integrated Learning #
Integrated Teaching Method #
NT Integrated Curriculum
BT Activities
RT Holistic Approach
Integrated Learning Systems
Integrated Services
Interdisciplinary Approach
Living Learning Centers
Systems Analysis
Teaching Methods

Integrated Automated Library Systems
USE Integrated Library Systems

Integrated Classes
USE Classroom Desegregation

Integrated Colleges
USE College Desegregation

Integrated Curriculum *JUL. 1966*
Postings: 4,533   GC: 350
SN Systematic organization of curriculum content and parts into a meaningful pattern
UF Integrated Education
BT Curriculum
Integrated Activities
RT Career Academies
Fused Curriculum
Tech Prep
Unified Studies Curriculum

Integrated Education
USE Integrated Curriculum

Integrated Faculty
USE Faculty Integration

Integrated Instructional Systems (Computers)
USE Integrated Learning Systems

Integrated Learning
USE Integrated Activities
AND Learning Activities

Integrated Learning Systems *AUG. 1994*
Postings: 228   GC: 710
SN Networked computers running broad-based curriculum software and a management system that tracks students' progress
UF Computer Based Integrated Learning Systems
Integrated Instructional Systems (Computers)
BT Computer Networks
Computer Uses in Education
Information Systems
RT Computer Assisted Instruction
Computer Managed Instruction
Courseware
Integrated Activities
Microcomputers
Minicomputers
Multimedia Instruction

Integrated Library Instruction
USE Course Integrated Library Instruction

Integrated Library Systems *AUG. 1989*
Postings: 251   GC: 710
SN Online library computer systems that

provide both technical support and public access
UF Integrated Automated Library Systems
Turnkey Systems (Libraries)
BT Information Systems
Online Systems
RT Computer Oriented Programs
Database Management Systems
Libraries
Library Automation
Library Circulation
Library Technical Processes
Machine Readable Cataloging
Online Catalogs

Integrated Neighborhoods
USE Neighborhood Integration

Integrated Public Facilities (1966 1980)
USE Public Facilities
AND Racial Integration

Integrated Schools
USE School Desegregation

Integrated Services *DEC. 1994*
Postings: 776   GC: 330
SN Collaboration among the education, health, and social service sectors to provide a school-based or school-linked comprehensive, coordinated continuum of preventive and prescriptive student and family services—usually for persons considered to be at-risk
UF Comprehensive Services (School Linked)
Full Service Schools (Human Services)
School Based Interagency Services
School Linked Services
BT Human Services
RT Agency Cooperation
Ancillary School Services
Comprehensive School Health Education
Cooperation
Cooperative Planning
Cooperative Programs
Family Programs
Family School Relationship
Health Services
Institutional Cooperation
Integrated Activities
Parent School Relationship
School Community Programs
School Community Relationship
School Health Services
Social Services
Student School Relationship

Integrated Teaching Method
USE Integrated Activities
AND Teaching Methods

Integration (Disabled Students)
USE Mainstreaming

Integration (Racial)
USE Racial Integration

Integration (Social)
USE Social Integration

Integration Effects (1966 1980)
USE Desegregation Effects

Integration Impact
USE Desegregation Effects

Integration Litigation (1966 1980)
USE Desegregation Litigation

Integration Methods (1966 1980)
USE Desegregation Methods

Integration Plans (1966 1980)
USE Desegregation Plans

Integration Readiness *JUL. 1966*
Postings: 127   GC: 540
SN Preparedness of individuals or groups to accept their own desegregation/integration with other ethnic or racial groups
UF Desegregation Readiness
BT Readiness
RT Desegregation Plans
Integration Studies
Neighborhood Integration
Racial Attitudes
Racial Integration
School Desegregation
Social Integration

Integration Studies *JUL. 1966*
Postings: 316   GC: 810
BT Behavioral Science Research
RT Desegregation Effects
Ethnic Studies
Integration Readiness
Racial Integration

Integrative Analysis
USE Meta Analysis

Integrity *JUL. 1966*
Postings: 414   GC: 120
RT Credibility
Ethics
Honesty
Moral Development
Moral Values
Reputation

Intellectronics
USE Bionics

Intellectual Development *JUL. 1966*
Postings: 2,693   GC: 120
SN Increasing complexity or growth of reasoning and thought processes (Note: Prior to Mar80, the use of this term was not restricted by a Scope Note)
BT Cognitive Development
RT Creative Development
Formal Operations
Intellectual Experience
Intellectual Freedom
Intelligence
Intelligence Differences
Intelligence Tests
Mental Age
Mental Rigidity
Piagetian Theory

Intellectual Disciplines *JUL. 1966*
Postings: 3,394   GC: 350
SN Areas of knowledge or instruction
UF Academic Disciplines
Subject Disciplines
RT Academic Education
Courses
Curriculum
Departments
Majors (Students)

Intellectual Experience *JUL. 1966*
Postings: 177   GC: 110
BT Experience
RT Intellectual Development
Intelligence

Intellectual Freedom *OCT. 1983*
Postings: 633   GC: 330
SN The absence of external coercion, censorship, or other forms of restrictive interference on the exercise of thought
UF Access to Ideas
Freedom of Thought
Freedom to Read
BT Freedom

RT Academic Freedom
Access to Education
Censorship
Civil Liberties
Democracy
Disclosure
Ethics
Freedom of Information
Freedom of Speech
Independent Reading
Independent Study
Individualism
Institutional Autonomy
Intellectual Development
Personal Autonomy
Privacy
Professional Autonomy
Public Libraries
State Church Separation

Intellectual History *AUG. 1977*
Postings: 520   GC: 430
SN Branch of history that deals with the evolution of ideas, how these ideas were influenced by various factors, and what happens to these ideas or thoughts among people in a given society
NT Art History
Literary History
BT History
RT Culture
Expressionism
Historiography
Impressionism
Rhetorical Theory
Social History

Intellectual Property *MAR. 1980*
Postings: 483   GC: 710
SN Expressions or results of mental activity (especially such things as literary, artistic, or scholarly creations, research designs, etc.) for which one has a legal right to own, use, reproduce, or sell
UF Ownership of Ideas
NT Copyrights
Patents
BT Ownership
RT Discovery Processes
Inventions
Legal Responsibility
Plagiarism
Research Utilization

Intellectualization (1970 1980)
USE Abstract Reasoning

Intelligence *JUL. 1966*
Postings: 3,679   GC: 120
UF Intelligence Factors (1966 1980)
Intelligence Level (1966 1980)
National Intelligence Norm (1966 1980) #
NT Comprehension
Formal Operations
Mental Age
Multiple Intelligences
BT Psychological Characteristics
RT Academic Ability
Academic Achievement
Academic Aptitude
Adjustment (to Environment)
Artificial Intelligence
Cognitive Ability
Cognitive Processes
Cognitive Psychology
Creativity
Intellectual Development
Intellectual Experience
Intelligence Differences
Intelligence Quotient
Intelligence Tests
Mental Retardation
Nature Nurture Controversy

Intelligence Age
USE Mental Age

= Two or more Descriptors are used to represent this term.
The term's main entry shows the appropriate coordination.

Intelligence Differences   *JUL. 1966*
     Postings: 997   GC: 120
BT   Individual Differences
RT   Intellectual Development
      Intelligence
      Intelligence Quotient
      Intelligence Tests
      Mental Age
      Multiple Intelligences
      Nature Nurture Controversy

Intelligence Factors (1966 1980)
USE   Intelligence

Intelligence Level (1966 1980)
USE   Intelligence

Intelligence Measures
USE   Intelligence Tests

Intelligence Quotient   *JUL. 1966*
     Postings: 1,992   GC: 820
UF   IQ
BT   Ratios (Mathematics)
RT   Intelligence
      Intelligence Differences
      Intelligence Tests
      Mental Age
      Talent Identification

Intelligence Tests   *JUL. 1966*
     Postings: 3,538   GC: 830
SN   Measures used to indicate an individual's cognitive ability to adjust to the environment, i.e., the ability to learn, deal with new situations, or solve problems
UF   Group Intelligence Testing (1966 1980) #
      Group Intelligence Tests (1966 1980) #
      Intelligence Measures
BT   Cognitive Tests
RT   Ability Identification
      Aptitude Tests
      Cognitive Measurement
      Creativity Tests
      Intellectual Development
      Intelligence
      Intelligence Differences
      Intelligence Quotient
      Mental Age
      Multiple Intelligences
      Psychological Testing
      Talent Identification

Intelligent CAI Systems
USE   Intelligent Tutoring Systems

Intelligent Computer Assisted Instruction
USE   Intelligent Tutoring Systems

Intelligent Tutoring Systems   *SEP. 1994*
     Postings: 269   GC: 310
SN   Computer-assisted instructional systems employing the principles of artificial intelligence to carry on dialogs with students and use student responses to assess learning
UF   ICAI
      Intelligent CAI Systems
      Intelligent Computer Assisted Instruction
BT   Computer Assisted Instruction
      Expert Systems
RT   Computer Managed Instruction
      Interactive Video
      Programmed Tutoring
      Tutorial Programs

Intelligent Video
USE   Interactive Video

Intensive Language Courses   *JUL. 1966*
     Postings: 769   GC: 450
SN   Foreign language courses that involve more contact hours per day than conventional courses offer—the work of two or more conventional courses is completed within one intensive course
BT   Courses
      Modern Language Curriculum
RT   Language Proficiency
      Languages
      Second Language Instruction
      Second Language Learning
      Second Language Programs

Intention   *DEC. 1989*
     Postings: 267   GC: 120
SN   Attitude or activity directed toward a conclusion or result (Note: See also such Identifiers as "Collective Intent," "Communicative Intention," "Legislative Intent," and "Unconscious Intention")
RT   Aspiration
      Attitudes
      Attribution Theory
      Behavior
      Cognitive Structures
      Communication (Thought Transfer)
      Expectation
      Intentional Learning
      Moral Development
      Motivation
      Objectives
      Policy Formation
      Social Cognition
      Verbal Development

Intentional Learning   *OCT. 1970*
     Postings: 151   GC: 110
SN   Purposive learning according to a predetermined pattern
BT   Learning
RT   Advance Organizers
      Incidental Learning
      Intention
      Learner Controlled Instruction
      Learning Motivation
      Learning Processes
      Learning Strategies
      Observational Learning
      Test Wiseness

Interaction   *JUL. 1966*
     Postings: 5,775   GC: 510
SN   Mutual or reciprocal action and response between two or more persons, systems, or other entities (Note: Use a more specific term if possible—prior to Mar80, the instruction "Interaction Analysis, USE Interaction Process Analysis" was carried in the Thesaurus)
UF   Interaction Analysis
NT   Aptitude Treatment Interaction
      Feedback
      Group Dynamics
BT   Relationship
RT   Communication (Thought Transfer)
      Human Relations
      Interaction Process Analysis
      Intergroup Relations
      Interpersonal Relationship
      Man Machine Systems
      Participation
      Statistical Analysis

Interaction Analysis
USE   Interaction

Interaction Process Analysis   *JUL. 1966*
     Postings: 4,586   GC: 820
SN   Method of studying social groups wherein all explicit interactions in small face-to-face groups are carefully recorded according to a systematic classification and analyzed (Note: Prior to Mar80, the use of this term was not restricted by a Scope Note)
BT   Research Methodology
RT   Behavioral Science Research

      Body Language
      Classroom Observation Techniques
      Communication Research
      Eye Contact
      Group Dynamics
      Group Structure
      Groups
      Interaction
      Interpersonal Relationship
      Naturalistic Observation
      Paralinguistics
      Self Directed Groups
      Social Behavior
      Social Integration
      Sociometric Techniques

Interactive Cable Television
USE   Interactive Television

Interactive Satellite Television
USE   Interactive Television

Interactive Searching (Online)
USE   Online Searching

Interactive Systems (Online)
USE   Online Systems

Interactive Television   *SEP. 1994*
     Postings: 273   GC: 720
SN   Two-way television systems that allow interaction between the viewer and whatever is on the screen—used in education, teleconferencing, telebanking, teleshopping, electronic opinion polling, etc.
UF   Interactive Cable Television
      Interactive Satellite Television
      Two Way Television
BT   Television
RT   Cable Television
      Closed Circuit Television
      Communications Satellites
      Distance Education
      Educational Television
      Information Networks
      Interactive Video
      Teleconferencing
      Telecourses
      Videotex

Interactive Video   *APR. 1986*
     Postings: 1,454   GC: 710
SN   Online video computing systems capable of rapid, accept-and-react communications with human operators
UF   Intelligent Video
BT   Online Systems
RT   Communications
      Computer Assisted Design
      Computer Assisted Instruction
      Display Systems
      Hypermedia
      Intelligent Tutoring Systems
      Interactive Television
      Learner Controlled Instruction
      Menu Driven Software
      Optical Data Disks
      Optical Disks
      Video Display Terminals
      Video Equipment
      Videodisks
      Videotape Cassettes
      Videotape Recordings

Interagency Cooperation (1967 1980)
USE   Agency Cooperation

Interagency Coordination (1967 1980)
USE   Agency Cooperation
AND   Coordination

Interagency Planning (1966 1980)
USE   Agency Cooperation
AND   Cooperative Planning

Intercollegiate Athletics
USE   College Athletics
AND   Intercollegiate Cooperation

Intercollegiate Cooperation   *MAR. 1980*
     Postings: 1,636   GC: 330
SN   Cooperation between or among colleges, universities, or professional schools
UF   College Cooperation (1966 1980)
      Intercollegiate Athletics #
      Intercollegiate Programs (1967 1980)
BT   Educational Cooperation
      Institutional Cooperation
RT   Articulation (Education)
      College Planning
      College School Cooperation
      Colleges
      Consortia

Intercollegiate Programs (1967 1980)
USE   Intercollegiate Cooperation

Intercommunication (1966 1980)
USE   Communication (Thought Transfer)

Intercultural Communication   *AUG. 1982*
     Postings: 2,089   GC: 330
SN   Verbal and nonverbal communication among people of different cultures
UF   Cross Cultural Communication
BT   Communication (Thought Transfer)
RT   Biculturalism
      Bidialectalism
      Bilingualism
      Communication Problems
      Cross Cultural Training
      Cultural Awareness
      Cultural Differences
      Cultural Exchange
      Cultural Interrelationships
      Cultural Pluralism
      Culture
      Culture Contact
      Ethnic Relations
      Foreign Culture
      Intercultural Programs
      International Communication
      Multicultural Education
      Multilingual Materials
      Multilingualism
      Speech Communication

Intercultural Education
USE   Multicultural Education

Intercultural Programs   *JUL. 1966*
     Postings: 787   GC: 560
BT   Programs
RT   Biculturalism
      Bilingual Education
      Bilingual Education Programs
      Cross Cultural Studies
      Cross Cultural Training
      Cultural Awareness
      Cultural Education
      Cultural Enrichment
      Cultural Exchange
      Cultural Influences
      Cultural Interrelationships
      Cultural Pluralism
      Culture
      Culture Contact
      Diversity (Institutional)
      Ethnic Groups
      Exchange Programs
      Global Approach
      Intercultural Communication
      Interdisciplinary Approach
      Intergroup Education
      International Programs
      International Studies
      Multicultural Education

Interdimensional Shift
USE   Shift Studies

 # = Two or more Descriptors are used to represent this term.
The term's main entry shows the appropriate coordination.

Interdisciplinary Approach   *JUL. 1966*
     Postings: 14,466   GC: 310
SN   Participation or cooperation of two or more disciplines
UF   Multidisciplinary Approach
BT   Methods
RT   Adventure Education
     Area Studies
     Core Curriculum
     Cross Cultural Training
     Curriculum Design
     Ethnic Studies
     Force Field Analysis
     Fused Curriculum
     Global Approach
     Heritage Education
     Holistic Approach
     Integrated Activities
     Intercultural Programs
     International Studies
     Multicultural Education
     Nonmajors
     Outdoor Education
     Religion Studies
     Science and Society
     Thematic Approach
     Unified Studies Curriculum
     Urban Studies
     Writing Across the Curriculum

Interdistrict Policies   *JUL. 1966*
     Postings: 87   GC: 330
SN   Policies that have been cooperatively determined by two or more school districts
BT   Policy
RT   Administrative Policy
     Agency Cooperation
     Board of Education Policy
     Institutional Cooperation
     School Districts
     School Policy

Interest (Finance)   *NOV. 1981*
     Postings: 144   GC: 620
SN   The price paid for the use of money over time
UF   Interest (1967 1981)
BT   Costs
     Income
RT   Credit (Finance)
     Economics
     Inflation (Economics)
     Investment
     Loan Repayment
     Monetary Systems

Interest Centers (Classroom)
USE   Learning Centers (Classroom)

Interest Inventories   *MAR. 1980*
     Postings: 1,190   GC: 830
SN   Measures designed to reveal the objects and activities that are of interest to, preferred, liked, or disliked by an individual (Note: Do not confuse with "Attitude Measures")
UF   Interest Scales (1966 1980)
     Interest Tests (1966 1980)
BT   Measures (Individuals)
RT   Affective Measures
     Aptitude Tests
     Attitude Measures
     Biographical Inventories
     Career Choice
     Forced Choice Technique
     Interest Research
     Interests
     Occupational Tests
     Opinions
     Personality Measures
     Predictive Measurement
     Predictive Validity
     Predictor Variables
     Profiles
     Prognostic Tests

Interest Research   *JUL. 1966*
     Postings: 278   GC: 810
SN   Systematic investigation of those activities, avocations, objects, etc., that have special worth or significance to individuals or groups (Note: As of Oct81, use as a minor Descriptor for examples of this kind of research—use as a major Descriptor only as the subject of a document)
BT   Psychological Studies
RT   Interest Inventories
     Interests

Interest Scales (1966 1980)
USE   Interest Inventories

Interest Tests (1966 1980)
USE   Interest Inventories

Interest (1967 1981)
USE   Interest (Finance)

Interests   *JUL. 1966*
     Postings: 778   GC: 120
SN   Activities, avocations, objects, etc., that have special worth or significance for individuals or groups and are given special attention (Note: Use a more specific term if possible)
UF   Group Interests
     Personal Interests (1966 1980)
NT   Childhood Interests
     Reading Interests
     Science Interests
     Student Interests
     Vocational Interests
RT   Activities
     Affective Behavior
     Attitudes
     Cognitive Structures
     Curiosity
     Hobbies
     Interest Inventories
     Interest Research
     Motivation
     Participation

Interface Devices (Computers)
USE   Computer Interfaces

Interface Systems (Cross Database)
USE   Gateway Systems

Interfaith Relations   *JUL. 1966*
     Postings: 83   GC: 520
BT   Intergroup Relations
RT   Ethnic Relations
     Religion
     Religious Conflict
     Religious Cultural Groups
     Religious Differences
     Religious Discrimination
     Social Integration

Interference (Language Learning) (1968 1980)
USE   Interference (Language)

Interference (Language)   *MAR. 1980*
     Postings: 1,062   GC: 450
SN   The negative effect of carrying over features of pronunciation, grammar, or vocabulary from one language or dialect to another
UF   Dialect Interference #
     Interference (Language Learning) (1968 1980)
     Linguistic Difficulty (Contrastive)
BT   Language Processing
RT   Audiolingual Methods
     Bidialectalism
     Bilingualism
     Code Switching (Language)
     Contrastive Linguistics
     Error Analysis (Language)

     Interlanguage
     Language Dominance
     Learning Processes
     Multilingualism
     Psycholinguistics
     Second Language Learning

Intergenerational Programs   *APR. 1986*
     Postings: 612   GC: 520
SN   Programs that provide interaction among generational age groups, usually between older adults and younger persons
BT   Programs
RT   Age Differences
     Age Groups
     Community Programs
     Generation Gap
     Mixed Age Grouping
     Older Adults
     Older Workers

Intergovernmental Organizations
USE   International Organizations

Intergroup Education   *JUL. 1966*
     Postings: 221   GC: 330
SN   Learning activities, curriculum, and/or educational programs, at any educational level, concerned with improving human relations and increasing intercultural and intergroup understanding
NT   Multicultural Education
BT   Education
RT   Human Relations
     Intercultural Programs
     Intergroup Relations
     Multicultural Textbooks
     Social Integration

Intergroup Relations   *JUL. 1966*
     Postings: 1,203   GC: 520
NT   Ethnic Relations
     Interfaith Relations
     Racial Relations
BT   Human Relations
RT   Communication (Thought Transfer)
     Competition
     Cooperation
     Cooperative Learning
     Cross Cultural Studies
     Cross Cultural Training
     Elitism
     Ethnocentrism
     Interaction
     Intergroup Education
     Intermarriage
     Multicultural Education
     Political Correctness
     Social Bias
     Social Discrimination
     Social Integration
     Social Mobility
     Social Networks
     Sociometric Techniques

Interinstitutional Cooperation (1968 1980)
USE   Institutional Cooperation

Interior Decoration
USE   Interior Design

Interior Design   *JAN. 1970*
     Postings: 411   GC: 420
UF   Interior Decoration
BT   Design
RT   Acoustical Environment
     Architecture
     Building Design
     Classroom Design
     Color Planning
     Design Requirements
     Furniture Arrangement
     Interior Space
     Lighting Design
     Offices (Facilities)
     Painting (Industrial Arts)
     Physical Environment

     Space Classification
     Spatial Relationship (Facilities)
     Thermal Environment

Interior Monologues
USE   Monologs

Interior Space   *JUL. 1966*
     Postings: 274   GC: 920
SN   Area available within a building
BT   Facilities
RT   Building Design
     Classroom Design
     Design Requirements
     Flexible Facilities
     Furniture Arrangement
     Interior Design
     Offices (Facilities)
     Open Plan Schools
     Physical Environment
     School Space
     Space Classification
     Space Utilization
     Storage

Interjudge Agreement
USE   Interrater Reliability

Interlanguage   *JUL. 1980*
     Postings: 601   GC: 450
SN   A learner's systematic, internally structured, and autonomous version of a target language—this system evolves, is governed by rules, and defines the developing linguistic competence of the learner
UF   Approximative Systems (Language Learning)
BT   Language
RT   Error Analysis (Language)
     Interference (Language)
     Learning Processes
     Linguistic Competence
     Linguistic Performance
     Psycholinguistics
     Second Language Learning

Interlibrary Loans   *JUL. 1966*
     Postings: 1,210   GC: 710
BT   Library Circulation
RT   Document Delivery
     Library Cooperation
     Library Networks
     Shared Library Resources
     Union Catalogs

Intermarriage   *JUL. 1966*
     Postings: 119   GC: 520
SN   Marriage between members of different racial, social, or religious groups
UF   Exogamous Marriage
BT   Marriage
RT   Cultural Differences
     Intergroup Relations
     Mate Selection
     Multiracial Persons
     Racial Differences
     Religious Differences
     Social Differences

Intermediate Administrative Units   *JUL. 1966*
     Postings: 222   GC: 340
SN   Administrative units smaller than the state that exist to provide consulting, advisory, administrative, or statistical services to local school districts, and/or to exercise regulatory functions over local districts
UF   Intermediate School Districts
     Intermediate Service Districts
RT   Boards of Education
     Consultation Programs
     Professional Services
     Regional Cooperation
     School District Reorganization

     # = Two or more Descriptors are used to represent this term.
     The term's main entry shows the appropriate coordination.

School Districts
State School District Relationship

Intermediate Grades   JUL. 1966
Postings: 12,843   GC: 340
SN   Includes the middle and/or upper elementary grades, but usually 4, 5, and 6 (Note: Also appears in the list of mandatory educational level Descriptors)
BT   Instructional Program Divisions
RT   Elementary Education
Grade 4
Grade 5
Grade 6
Middle Schools
Preadolescents

Intermediate School Districts
USE   Intermediate Administrative Units

Intermediate Service Districts
USE   Intermediate Administrative Units

Intermode Differences   JUL. 1966
Postings: 1,095   GC: 310
SN   Variations among instructional materials or modes of presentation
BT   Differences
RT   Audiovisual Instruction
Computer Assisted Instruction
Educational Media
Learning Modalities
Media Adaptation
Multimedia Instruction
Programmed Instruction
Teaching Methods

Intern Teachers
USE   Teacher Interns

Internal External Locus of Control
USE   Locus of Control

Internal Immigrants
USE   Migrants

Internal Medicine   OCT. 1979
Postings: 244   GC: 210
SN   Branch of medicine dealing with the diagnosis and nonsurgical treatment of diseases
BT   Medicine
RT   Clinical Diagnosis
Diseases
Family Practice (Medicine)
Immunization Programs
Medical Services
Oncology
Primary Health Care

Internal Review (Organizations)
USE   Self Evaluation (Groups)

Internal Scaling (1966 1980)
USE   Scaling

Internation Behavior
USE   International Relations

International Approach
USE   Global Approach

International Communication   APR. 1990
Postings: 406   GC: 330
SN   Flow of communication among nations or international bodies
BT   Communication (Thought Transfer)
RT   Artificial Languages
Business Communication
Communication Problems
Cross Cultural Training
Intercultural Communication

International Cooperation
International Relations
International Trade Vocabulary
Multilingual Materials
Multilingualism
World Affairs

International Cooperation   JUN. 1983
Postings: 2,048   GC: 520
SN   Cooperation between or among nations or international bodies
BT   Cooperation
RT   Exchange Programs
Global Approach
Institutional Cooperation
International Communication
International Education
International Educational Exchange
International Law
International Organizations
International Programs
International Relations
International Trade
International Trade Vocabulary
World Affairs
World Problems

International Crimes   APR. 1972
Postings: 130   GC: 530
SN   Crimes such as piracy, illicit trade in narcotics, or slave trading that are in violation of international law
UF   War Crimes
NT   Genocide
BT   Crime
RT   Civil Liberties
International Law
Laws
Nazism
Slavery
Terrorism
War

International Education   JUL. 1966
Postings: 4,064   GC: 400
SN   Study of educational, social, political, economic, and environmental forces of international relations, with special emphasis on the role and potentialities of educational forces
BT   Global Education
RT   Comparative Education
Cross Cultural Studies
Diplomatic History
Foreign Countries
Foreign Culture
Foreign Policy
International Cooperation
International Educational Exchange
International Law
International Organizations
International Programs
International Relations
International Studies
International Trade
International Trade Vocabulary
Peace

International Educational Exchange
APR. 1976
Postings: 2,049   GC: 330
SN   Exchange among nations of instructional materials, techniques, students, teachers, and technicians for purposes of sharing knowledge and furthering international understanding
RT   Comparative Education
Cross Cultural Training
Cultural Exchange
Exchange Programs
Foreign Culture
Foreign Medical Graduates
Foreign Students
International Cooperation
International Education
International Organizations
International Programs
International Relations
International Trade

Student Exchange Programs
Study Abroad
Teacher Exchange Programs
Technical Assistance

International Law   APR. 1972
Postings: 320   GC: 610
UF   International Legal Analysis
International Torts
Law of Nations
BT   Laws
RT   Civil Law
Conflict Resolution
Foreign Policy
International Cooperation
International Crimes
International Education
International Organizations
International Relations
International Studies
Law Related Education
Legal Education (Professions)
Political Science
Treaties
War
World Affairs

International Legal Analysis
USE   International Law

International Organizations   JUL. 1966
Postings: 2,382   GC: 610
UF   Intergovernmental Organizations
BT   Organizations (Groups)
RT   International Cooperation
International Education
International Educational Exchange
International Law
International Programs
International Relations
International Studies
National Organizations
Nongovernmental Organizations
Peace
Professional Associations

International Peace
USE   Peace

International Policy
USE   Foreign Policy

International Politics
USE   International Relations

International Programs   JUL. 1966
Postings: 3,148   GC: 610
SN   Programs sponsored by governments, institutions, or private organizations that involve more than one country
UF   International Technical Assistance #
BT   Programs
RT   Developed Nations
Developing Nations
Foreign Nationals
Foreign Policy
Intercultural Programs
International Cooperation
International Education
International Educational Exchange
International Organizations
International Relations
International Trade
Olympic Games
Technical Assistance

International Relations   AUG. 1976
Postings: 3,208   GC: 610
SN   Relations among political units of national rank—also, a field of study (often considered as a branch of political science) dealing primarily with foreign policies, the organization and function of governmental agencies concerned with foreign policy, and the factors (as geog-

raphy and economics) underlying foreign policy
UF   Diplomacy
Foreign Relations (1966 1976)
Internation Behavior
International Politics
BT   Relationship
RT   Colonialism
Conflict
Cross Cultural Training
Developed Nations
Developing Nations
Diplomatic History
Disarmament
Ethnocentrism
Exports
Foreign Countries
Foreign Diplomats
Foreign Policy
Global Approach
Immigration
Imports
International Communication
International Cooperation
International Education
International Educational Exchange
International Law
International Organizations
International Programs
International Studies
International Trade
National Security
Nationalism
Peace
Political Science
Treaties
War
World Affairs

International Students
USE   Foreign Students

International Studies   AUG. 1976
Postings: 1,323   GC: 400
SN   Multidisciplinary field of inquiry concerned with analyzing social phenomena that occur within, between, and transcending nationally organized politics—commonly identified subfields are "international politics," "foreign policy," "international law," "international organization," "international economics," and "comparative area studies"
BT   Social Sciences
RT   Area Studies
Comparative Analysis
Cross Cultural Studies
Economics
Foreign Countries
Foreign Policy
Intercultural Programs
Interdisciplinary Approach
International Education
International Law
International Organizations
International Relations
Multilingual Materials
Political Science
Politics
Social Science Research
Social Scientists

International Technical Assistance
USE   International Programs
AND   Technical Assistance

International Torts
USE   International Law

International Trade   JUN. 1983
Postings: 1,064   GC: 650
SN   Exchange of goods and services among nations
NT   Exports
Imports
RT   Business
Developed Nations
Developing Nations
Economics

= Two or more Descriptors are used to represent this term.
The term's main entry shows the appropriate coordination.

Foreign Policy
International Cooperation
International Education
International Educational Exchange
International Programs
International Relations
International Trade Vocabulary
Marketing
Monetary Systems
Structural Unemployment
Supply and Demand
World Affairs

International Trade Vocabulary   *JUL. 1966*
Postings: 58   GC: 450
SN   Words and terms used frequently in in-
     ternational trade—more specifically, the
     vocabulary needed for participation in
     the multilingual environment of interna-
     tional trade
BT   Vocabulary
RT   Artificial Languages
     Business Communication
     Economics
     Exports
     Imports
     International Communication
     International Cooperation
     International Education
     International Trade
     Professional Training

International War
USE   War

Internet   *FEB. 1996*
Postings: 4,583   GC: 710
SN   The international network of computer
     networks interconnected by routers or
     gateways and using the standard TCP/IP
     telecommunications protocol to transfer
     data such as electronic mail—the Internet
     connects millions of users among indus-
     try, education, government, research,
     commerce, and private households (Note:
     See also the Identifier "National Infor-
     mation Infrastructure" for documents
     related to the U.S. government's federal
     NII/Internet policy initiative)
UF   Electronic Superhighway
     Information Superhighway
NT   World Wide Web
BT   Computer Networks
     Information Networks
RT   Computer Mediated Communication
     Electronic Journals
     Electronic Libraries
     Electronic Mail
     Electronic Publishing
     Information Dissemination
     Information Sources
     Listservs
     Microcomputers
     Online Systems

Internet Discussion Lists
USE   Listservs

Interns (Medical)
USE   Graduate Medical Students

Internship Programs   *JUL. 1966*
Postings: 2,498   GC: 350
SN   Programs offering supervised practical
     experience for advanced students or re-
     cent graduates in professional fields
     (Note: Use "Graduate Medical Educa-
     tion" for graduate medical internship or
     residency programs)
BT   Experiential Learning
     Programs
RT   Assistantships
     Beginning Teacher Induction
     Clinical Experience
     Extended Teacher Education Programs
     Field Experience Programs
     Inservice Teacher Education
     On the Job Training

Practicum Supervision
Practicums
Professional Education
Student Experience
Teacher Interns
Teaching Experience

Internships (Medical)
USE   Graduate Medical Education

Interobserver Reliability
USE   Interrater Reliability

Interpersonal Attraction   *AUG. 1978*
Postings: 507   GC: 510
SN   Perceived personal qualities (physical,
     mental, emotional, and social) drawing
     persons to one another
UF   Attractiveness (between Persons)
NT   Physical Attractiveness
BT   Interpersonal Relationship
RT   Affection
     Congruence (Psychology)
     Dating (Social)
     Emotional Response
     Interpersonal Communication
     Love
     Psychological Characteristics
     Rapport
     Social Life

Interpersonal Communication   *NOV. 1982*
Postings: 6,113   GC: 510
SN   The interpersonal sharing of opinions,
     interests, and feelings—includes verbal
     and nonverbal exchanges between two
     or more persons, in which participants
     are actively involved as both senders and
     receivers
UF   Dyadic Communication
BT   Communication (Thought Transfer)
RT   Assertiveness
     Caregiver Speech
     Confidentiality
     Conflict Resolution
     Dialog Journals
     Dialogs (Language)
     Discussion
     Eye Contact
     Familiarity
     Grievance Procedures
     Group Discussion
     Group Dynamics
     Interpersonal Attraction
     Interpersonal Competence
     Interpersonal Relationship
     Interviews
     Letters (Correspondence)
     Peer Mediation
     Rapport
     Self Disclosure (Individuals)
     Self Expression
     Shyness
     Social Cognition
     Speech Communication
     Standard Spoken Usage

Interpersonal Competence   *JUL. 1966*
Postings: 9,146   GC: 120
UF   Gregariousness
     Interpersonal Skills
     Perceptiveness (between Persons) #
     Sociability
     Social Awareness
     Social Competence
     Social Skills
BT   Competence
RT   Consciousness Raising
     Daily Living Skills
     Extraversion Introversion
     Familiarity
     Humanistic Education
     Interpersonal Communication
     Interpersonal Relationship
     Laboratory Training
     Maturity (Individuals)
     Personality Traits
     Popularity
     Prosocial Behavior

Reality Therapy
Sensitivity Training
Shyness
Skills
Social Adjustment
Social Attitudes
Social Behavior
Social Characteristics
Social Cognition
Social Development
Social Experience
Socialization
Teamwork
Transactional Analysis

Interpersonal Perception
USE   Social Cognition

Interpersonal Problems (1966 1980)
USE   Interpersonal Relationship

Interpersonal Relationship   *JUL. 1966*
Postings: 10,991   GC: 510
UF   Interpersonal Problems (1966 1980)
     Personal Relationship (1966 1974)
     Social Interaction
NT   Board Administrator Relationship
     Caregiver Child Relationship
     Cohabitation
     Collegiality
     Counselor Client Relationship
     Dating (Social)
     Employer Employee Relationship
     Family Relationship
     Friendship
     Group Unity
     Helping Relationship
     Interpersonal Attraction
     Interprofessional Relationship
     Kinship
     Marriage
     Peer Relationship
     Physician Patient Relationship
     Rapport
     Significant Others
     Teacher Administrator Relationship
     Teacher Student Relationship
BT   Relationship
RT   Alienation
     Altruism
     Attachment Behavior
     Autism
     Competition
     Context Effect
     Cooperation
     Cooperative Learning
     Credibility
     Cross Age Teaching
     Dependency (Personality)
     Egocentrism
     Empathy
     Extraversion Introversion
     Familiarity
     Human Relations
     Informal Leadership
     Interaction
     Interaction Process Analysis
     Interpersonal Communication
     Interpersonal Competence
     Intimacy
     Jealousy
     Love
     Mentors
     Personal Autonomy
     Perspective Taking
     Privacy
     Professional Autonomy
     Reference Groups
     Rejection (Psychology)
     Sexual Identity
     Sexual Orientation
     Sharing Behavior
     Social Cognition
     Social Exchange Theory
     Social Integration
     Social Life
     Social Mobility
     Social Networks
     Sociometric Techniques

Teamwork
Trust (Psychology)

Interpersonal Skills
USE   Interpersonal Competence

Interpreters   *JUL. 1966*
Postings: 416   GC: 640
UF   Translators
BT   Personnel
RT   Communication (Thought Transfer)
     Deaf Interpreting
     Language Skills
     Speech Communication
     Speech Skills
     Translation

Interpreting for the Deaf
USE   Deaf Interpreting

Interpretive Reading (1966 1980)
MAR. 1980
Postings: 291   GC: 460
SN   Invalid Descriptor—used to index items
     on reading comprehension, oral reading,
     and listening comprehension—see such
     Descriptors as "Comprehension," "Oral
     Interpretation," and "Critical Reading"

Interpretive Skills   *JUL. 1966*
Postings: 529   GC: 450
BT   Skills
RT   Data Interpretation
     Deaf Interpreting
     Hermeneutics
     Language Skills
     Thinking Skills
     Translation

Interprofessional Relationship   *JUL. 1966*
Postings: 2,284   GC: 520
BT   Interpersonal Relationship
RT   Board Administrator Relationship
     Collegiality
     Mentors
     Peer Evaluation
     Professional Autonomy
     Professional Isolation
     Professional Services
     Teacher Administrator Relationship
     Teamwork

Interracial Adoption
USE   Transracial Adoption

Interracial Offspring
USE   Multiracial Persons

Interracial Relations
USE   Racial Relations

Interrater Reliability   *MAR. 1983*
Postings: 831   GC: 820
SN   The degree of agreement among raters
     or observers in evaluating subjects' be-
     havior/performance or other specific en-
     tity/event
UF   Interjudge Agreement
     Interobserver Reliability
     Interscorer Reliability
BT   Reliability
RT   Error of Measurement
     Evaluation Methods
     Evaluators
     Examiners
     Experimenter Characteristics
     Generalizability Theory
     Judges
     Measurement Techniques
     Observation
     Rating Scales
     Scores
     Scoring
     Test Reliability

= Two or more Descriptors are used to represent this term.
The term's main entry shows the appropriate coordination.

Testing Problems
True Scores

Interscholastic Athletics
USE   Extramural Athletics

Interschool Communication   *JUL. 1966*
      Postings: 172   GC: 330
BT   Organizational Communication
RT   Educational Cooperation
      Institutional Cooperation
      Schools

Interschool Visits
USE   School Visitation

Interscorer Reliability
USE   Interrater Reliability

Intersensory Integration
USE   Sensory Integration

Intersession School Programs
USE   Vacation Programs

Interstate Programs   *JUL. 1966*
      Postings: 199   GC: 610
BT   Programs
RT   State Programs

Interstate Workers (1966 1980) (Migrants)
USE   Migrant Workers

Interval Pacing (1967 1980)
USE   Pacing

Intervals   *JUL. 1969*
      Postings: 89   GC: 490
RT   Distance
      Proximity
      Scheduling
      Scientific Concepts
      Space
      Time

Intervention   *AUG. 1968*
      Postings: 11,153   GC: 520
SN   Action performed to direct or influence
      behavior (Note: If possible, use "Cri-
      sis Intervention," "Early Intervention,"
      "Prereferral Intervention," or other, more
      precise terminology)
NT   Crisis Intervention
      Early Intervention
      Prereferral Intervention
RT   Behavior Modification
      Cognitive Restructuring
      Consultation Programs
      Counseling
      Disabilities
      Disadvantaged
      Educational Psychology
      Educational Therapy
      Helping Relationship
      Human Services
      In School Suspension
      Medical Services
      Outreach Programs
      Prognostic Tests
      Psychoeducational Methods
      Psychology
      Rehabilitation
      Resource Room Programs
      Special Education
      Therapy

Interviewing
USE   Interviews

Interviews   *JUL. 1966*
      Postings: 11,301   GC: 810
UF   Interviewing

Question Answer Interviews (1966
      1980)
NT   Employment Interviews
      Field Interviews
BT   Evaluation Methods
RT   Counseling Techniques
      Discussion
      Focus Groups
      Inquiry
      Interpersonal Communication
      Measures (Individuals)
      Oral History
      Personal Narratives
      Qualitative Research
      Questioning Techniques
      Speech Communication
      Surveys
      Telephone Surveys

Intimacy   *JUN. 1988*
      Postings: 447   GC: 120
SN   Especially close association or familiar-
      ity (usually interpersonal, often affec-
      tionate or loving)
BT   Relationship
RT   Affection
      Attachment Behavior
      Communication (Thought Transfer)
      Communication Skills
      Counseling Techniques
      Familiarity
      Interpersonal Relationship
      Love
      Psychological Patterns
      Self Disclosure (Individuals)
      Sexuality

Intonation   *JUL. 1966*
      Postings: 747   GC: 450
SN   Melodic pattern produced by the varia-
      tion in pitch of the voice during speech
UF   Intonation Contours
      Suprasegmental Morphemes
BT   Suprasegmentals
RT   Morphology (Languages)
      Paralinguistics
      Phonemes
      Phonology
      Sentences
      Stress (Phonology)
      Structural Analysis (Linguistics)
      Syllables
      Tone Languages

Intonation Contours
USE   Intonation

Intramural Athletic Programs (1966 1980)
USE   Intramural Athletics

Intramural Athletics   *MAR. 1980*
      Postings: 190   GC: 470
UF   Intramural Athletic Programs (1966
      1980)
      Intramural Sports
BT   Athletics
RT   College Athletics
      Extramural Athletics
      School Recreational Programs

Intramural Sports
USE   Intramural Athletics

Intricacy Level
USE   Difficulty Level

Intrinsic Motivation
USE   Self Motivation

Introductory Courses   *MAR. 1980*
      Postings: 1,819   GC: 350
SN   Preliminary or basic courses that are
      frequently intended to provide an over-
      view of a topic or to lay the foundation

for advanced courses in the same sub-
      ject
UF   Foundation Courses (Introductory)
      Survey Courses
BT   Courses
RT   Advanced Courses
      Core Curriculum
      Minicourses
      Nonmajors
      Required Courses

Introjection
USE   Identification (Psychology)

Introversion
USE   Extraversion Introversion

Intrusion Detectors
USE   Alarm Systems

Intuition   *OCT. 1983*
      Postings: 290   GC: 110
SN   Knowing or understanding without con-
      scious use of reasoning
BT   Cognitive Processes
RT   Cognitive Ability
      Cognitive Style
      Comprehension
      Creative Thinking
      Expectation
      Imagination
      Learning Processes
      Mathematical Applications
      Perception
      Problem Solving
      Spontaneous Behavior
      Thinking Skills

Inuit
USE   Inupiaq

Inuit (People)
USE   Eskimos

Inuktitut
USE   Inupiaq

Inupiaq   *APR. 1990*
      Postings: 43   GC: 440
SN   Multidialectal Eskimo language of north-
      ernmost North America, from Greenland
      and eastern Canada to northern Alaska
UF   Greenlandic
      Inuit
      Inuktitut
      Inupiat
      Inupik
      Netsilik
      Numamiut
      Taremiut
BT   Eskimo Aleut Languages

Inupiat
USE   Inupiaq

Inupik
USE   Inupiaq

Invalids
USE   Patients

Invasion of Privacy
USE   Privacy

Invented Spelling   *APR. 1990*
      Postings: 142   GC: 400
SN   Spelling based on how a word sounds,
      and used when the writer does not know
      the conventional spelling of a word
UF   Creative Spelling
      Inventive Spelling
BT   Spelling

RT   Beginning Writing
      Child Language
      Childrens Writing
      Emergent Literacy
      Language Experience Approach
      Phoneme Grapheme Correspondence
      Phonics
      Phonology
      Reading Writing Relationship
      Spelling Instruction
      Writing Exercises

Inventions   *MAR. 1978*
      Postings: 246   GC: 490
SN   Original products or processes (things
      not previously existing) developed by
      creative thought or experimentation (Note:
      For "discoveries," see the Descriptor
      "Discovery Processes")
RT   Change
      Creative Thinking
      Creativity
      Discovery Processes
      Experiments
      Innovation
      Intellectual Property
      Patents
      Problem Solving
      Productive Thinking
      Research
      Technological Advancement
      Technology
      Technology Transfer

Inventive Spelling
USE   Invented Spelling

Inventories (Measurement)
USE   Measures (Individuals)

Investigations   *JUL. 1966*
      Postings: 811   GC: 810
BT   Research
RT   Evaluation Methods
      Experiments
      Surveys

Investment   *JUL. 1966*
      Postings: 1,053   GC: 620
NT   Human Capital
RT   Banking
      Credit (Finance)
      Economic Impact
      Economics
      Educational Economics
      Endowment Funds
      Estate Planning
      Finance Occupations
      Financial Support
      Franchising
      Fund Raising
      Interest (Finance)
      Ownership
      Productivity
      Trusts (Financial)

IQ
USE   Intelligence Quotient

Iris Reflex
USE   Pupillary Dilation

Irish   *APR. 1990*
      Postings: 66   GC: 440
SN   The Celtic language of Ireland in its his-
      torical or modern form (Note: Do not use
      for Irish English—see the Identifier "Eng-
      lish (Irish)" for that concept)
UF   Gaelic (Irish)
BT   Indo European Languages

IRM
USE   Information Management

= Two or more Descriptors are used to represent this term.
The term's main entry shows the appropriate coordination.

Iron Deficiency Anemia
USE   Anemia

Iron Foundries
USE   Foundries

Irony   *JUL. 1969*
       Postings: 123   GC: 430
UF   Sarcasm
BT   Figurative Language
RT   Literary Styles

Iroquois (Tribe)   *MAR. 1994*
       Postings: 45   GC: 560
SN   An American Indian people comprising
       the Iroquois six nations (Cayuga,
       Mohawk, Oneida, Onondaga, Seneca, and
       Tuscarora)—originally centered in New
       York, present-day Iroquois live primarily
       in New York, Wisconsin, Oklahoma,
       Ontario, and Quebec
BT   American Indians
       Tribes
RT   Canada Natives

IRT LTT Measurement Theory
USE   Item Response Theory

Isiswati
USE   Siswati

Islam   *JUN. 1999*
       Postings: 142   GC: 430
SN   Religion that professes belief in Allah as
       the sole deity and in Muhammad as the
       prophet of Allah
BT   Religion
RT   Arabs
       Islamic Culture
       Muslims
       Philosophy
       Religious Cultural Groups

Islamic Culture   *AUG. 1968*
       Postings: 297   GC: 560
BT   Culture
RT   Asian Studies
       Islam
       Middle Eastern Studies
       Muslims
       Religion

Isolation (Perceptual)
USE   Sensory Deprivation

ITA
USE   Initial Teaching Alphabet

Italian   *JUL. 1966*
       Postings: 687   GC: 440
BT   Romance Languages
RT   Italian Literature

Italian Americans   *JUL. 1966*
       Postings: 179   GC: 560
BT   Ethnic Groups
       North Americans
RT   Minority Groups

Italian Literature   *JUN. 1969*
       Postings: 125   GC: 430
BT   Literature
RT   Italian

Item Analysis   *JUL. 1966*
       Postings: 2,172   GC: 820
SN   Determining the difficulty, discriminability,
       internal consistency, reliability, and va-
       lidity of items in a test, questionnaire, or
       rating scale
BT   Statistical Analysis
RT   Content Analysis

Content Validity
Difficulty Level
Discriminant Analysis
Error Patterns
Factor Analysis
Factor Structure
Item Bias
Item Response Theory
Multitrait Multimethod Techniques
Q Methodology
Standardized Tests
Test Construction
Test Items
Test Reliability
Test Theory
Test Validity
Testing
Tests
Weighted Scores

Item Banks   *OCT. 1972*
       Postings: 654   GC: 830
SN   Collections of test items classified ac-
       cording to objectives, subtests, difficulty,
       grade level, content, etc., which may be
       used to construct tests to meet the user's
       specifications
UF   Item Pools
RT   Adaptive Testing
       Computer Assisted Testing
       Criterion Referenced Tests
       Item Sampling
       Problem Sets
       Test Construction
       Test Items
       Test Manuals
       Testing
       Tests

Item Bias   *APR. 1990*
       Postings: 297   GC: 540
SN   Differential interactions between content
       of test items and group membership of
       examinees
UF   Differential Item Functioning
       Differential Item Performance
BT   Test Bias
RT   Culture Fair Tests
       Item Analysis
       Item Response Theory
       Social Bias
       Statistical Bias
       Test Construction
       Test Interpretation
       Test Items
       Test Validity
       Testing
       Testing Problems
       Tests

Item Characteristic Curve Theory
USE   Item Response Theory

Item Difficulty
USE   Difficulty Level
AND   Test Items

Item Pools
USE   Item Banks

Item Response Theory   *APR. 1990*
       Postings: 927   GC: 810
SN   The study of test and item scores based
       on assumptions concerning the mathe-
       matical relationship between abilities (or
       other hypothesized traits) and item re-
       sponses (Note: "Item Response Theory"
       includes both the "Rasch Model" and
       the "Birnbaum Models"—see those Iden-
       tifiers)
UF   IRT LTT Measurement Theory
       Item Characteristic Curve Theory
       Latent Trait Theory (1980 1990)
BT   Test Theory
RT   Adaptive Testing
       Equated Scores
       Item Analysis
       Item Bias

Mathematical Models
Psychometrics
Scores
Scoring
Test Construction
Test Interpretation
Test Items
Test Reliability
Test Validity
Testing
Tests

Item Sampling   *OCT. 1970*
       Postings: 234   GC: 820
SN   Estimation of total test score statistics
       (mean and variance) by administering
       random subsets of test items to ran-
       domly selected students
UF   Matrix Sampling
       Multiple Matrix Sampling
BT   Sampling
RT   Item Banks
       Measurement Techniques
       National Norms
       Statistical Analysis
       Test Construction
       Test Items
       Test Norms

Item Types
USE   Test Format

ITFS
USE   Educational Television

Itinerant Clinics (1966 1980)
USE   Mobile Clinics

Itinerant Teachers   *JUL. 1966*
       Postings: 195   GC: 360
SN   Teachers who travel from school to
       school, or to homes and hospitals, to
       teach students with special needs (Note:
       Prior to Mar80, the Thesaurus carried
       the instruction "Visiting Teachers, USE
       School Social Workers")
UF   Circuit Teachers
       Homebound Teachers (1966 1980)
       Traveling Teachers
       Visiting Teachers
BT   Teachers
RT   Home Instruction
       Homebound
       Hospital Schools
       Hospitalized Children
       Individual Instruction
       Mainstreaming
       Mobile Clinics
       Mobile Educational Services
       Resource Room Programs
       Resource Teachers
       Special Education
       Special Education Teachers
       Specialists

ITV
USE   Educational Television

Jail Inmates
USE   Prisoners

JAN Technique
USE   Judgment Analysis Technique

Japanese   *JUL. 1966*
       Postings: 1,383   GC: 440
NT   Okinawan
BT   Languages
RT   Japanese Culture

Japanese American Culture   *JUL. 1966*
       Postings: 100   GC: 560
BT   Japanese Culture
       North American Culture

RT   Japanese Americans

Japanese Americans   *SEP. 1968*
       Postings: 413   GC: 560
BT   Asian Americans
       Ethnic Groups
RT   Japanese American Culture

Japanese Culture   *MAR. 1996*
       Postings: 164   GC: 560
NT   Japanese American Culture
BT   Culture
RT   Asian Studies
       Japanese
       Non Western Civilization

Jargon   *APR. 1990*
       Postings: 145   GC: 450
SN   Uncommon words and expressions, of-
       ten peculiar to a specialty, trade, or group,
       and hard to understand by outsiders
       (Note: See also Identifiers "Bureaucratic
       Language," "Doublespeak,"
       "Euphemism," "Malapropisms," and
       "Plain English Movement")
UF   Educationese
BT   Vocabulary
RT   Cliches
       Communication (Thought Transfer)
       Communication Problems
       Language Patterns
       Language Styles
       Language Usage
       Language Variation
       Mutual Intelligibility
       Technical Writing

Javanese   *JUL. 1966*
       Postings: 13   GC: 440
BT   Indonesian Languages

Jazz   *APR. 1969*
       Postings: 170   GC: 420
UF   Ragtime Music
       Swing Music
BT   Music
RT   Bands (Music)
       Concerts
       Improvisation
       Music Techniques
       Musical Composition
       North American Culture
       Popular Music

Jealousy   *MAR. 1982*
       Postings: 33   GC: 230
SN   Intolerance or wariness of rivalry or
       faithlessness
UF   Envy
BT   Psychological Patterns
RT   Anger
       Anxiety
       Emotional Problems
       Interpersonal Relationship
       Negative Attitudes
       Personality Traits
       Resentment

Jewish Stereotypes (1966 1980)
USE   Ethnic Stereotypes
AND   Jews

Jews   *JUL. 1966*
       Postings: 925   GC: 560
UF   American Jews
       Jewish Stereotypes (1966 1980) #
BT   Religious Cultural Groups
RT   Anti Semitism
       Ethnic Groups
       Ghettos
       Judaism
       Middle Eastern Studies
       Minority Groups

= Two or more Descriptors are used to represent this term.
The term's main entry shows the appropriate coordination.

Job Adjustment
USE   Vocational Adjustment

Job Analysis   *JUL. 1966*
       Postings: 2,485   GC: 630
SN   Process of determining the aspects of a
       particular job or the tasks performed
       within an occupational area (Note: For
       the product of such an analysis, use
       "Occupational Information"—do not con-
       fuse with "Task Analysis," this term's
       former NT—before Mar80, the use of
       this term was not restricted by a Scope
       Note)
UF   Job Content Analysis
       Occupational Analysis
BT   Evaluation Methods
RT   Critical Incidents Method
       Employment Qualifications
       Job Development
       Job Enrichment
       Job Performance
       Job Simplification
       Job Skills
       Occupational Clusters
       Occupational Information
       Skill Analysis
       Task Analysis

Job Applicants   *JUL. 1966*
       Postings: 1,540   GC: 630
UF   Job Seekers
BT   Groups
RT   Dislocated Workers
       Displaced Homemakers
       Employment
       Employment Interviews
       Employment Opportunities
       Employment Qualifications
       Employment Services
       Job Application
       Job Placement
       Job Search Methods
       Portfolios (Background Materials)
       Resumes (Personal)

Job Application   *JUL. 1966*
       Postings: 918   GC: 630
RT   Employment
       Employment Interviews
       Employment Opportunities
       Employment Qualifications
       Employment Services
       Job Applicants
       Job Placement
       Job Search Methods
       Portfolios (Background Materials)
       Reentry Workers
       Resumes (Personal)

Job Banks   *APR. 1990*
       Postings: 20   GC: 710
SN   Data files or agencies for matching per-
       sons seeking work with suitable job open-
       ings
RT   Career Information Systems
       Databases
       Employment Opportunities
       Employment Services
       Job Placement

Job Behaviors
USE   Job Skills

Job Change
USE   Career Change

Job Clusters
USE   Occupational Clusters

Job Conditions
USE   Work Environment

Job Content
USE   Occupational Information

Job Content Analysis
USE   Job Analysis

Job Creation
USE   Job Development

Job Descriptions
USE   Occupational Information

Job Design
USE   Job Development

Job Development   *JAN. 1969*
       Postings: 1,299   GC: 630
SN   (Note: Prior to Mar80, the instruction
       "Job Redesign, USE Work Simplifica-
       tion" was carried in the Thesaurus)
UF   Job Creation
       Job Design
       Job Redesign
       Job Restructuring
NT   Job Enrichment
       Job Simplification
BT   Development
RT   Emerging Occupations
       Employment
       Employment Opportunities
       Employment Problems
       Equal Opportunities (Jobs)
       Job Analysis
       Labor Force Development
       Occupational Information
       Organizational Development
       Promotion (Occupational)
       Scope of Bargaining

Job Discrimination
USE   Equal Opportunities (Jobs)

Job Elimination
USE   Job Layoff

Job Enrichment   *FEB. 1976*
       Postings: 206   GC: 630
SN   Redesign of a job to provide more mean-
       ingful job content, thus increasing em-
       ployee/staff responsibility, satisfaction,
       and motivation
UF   Work Enrichment
BT   Enrichment
       Job Development
RT   Employee Attitudes
       Employer Employee Relationship
       Job Analysis
       Job Satisfaction
       Organizational Development
       Quality of Working Life
       Vocational Adjustment
       Work Attitudes
       Work Environment

Job Experience
USE   Employment Experience

Job Families
USE   Occupational Clusters

Job Family Relationship
USE   Family Work Relationship

Job Holding Patterns
USE   Employment Patterns

Job Interviews
USE   Employment Interviews

Job Ladders
USE   Career Ladders

Job Layoff   *JUL. 1966*
       Postings: 617   GC: 630
SN   Temporary or indefinite ending of jobs
       by employers
UF   Job Elimination
BT   Reduction in Force
RT   Dislocated Workers
       Dismissal (Personnel)
       Employment
       Employment Practices
       Financial Exigency
       Labor Market
       Labor Turnover
       Outplacement Services (Employment)
       Personnel Policy
       Seniority
       Structural Unemployment
       Tenure
       Unemployment

Job Literacy
USE   Workplace Literacy

Job Loss Services
USE   Outplacement Services (Employment)

Job Market (1966 1980)
USE   Labor Market

Job Mobility
USE   Occupational Mobility

Job Opportunities
USE   Employment Opportunities

Job Performance   *MAR. 1980*
       Postings: 2,155   GC: 630
SN   Accomplishment of work-related tasks
       or skills by an employee or trainee—may
       refer to specific skills or to overall
       performance—also use for factors asso-
       ciated with success or failure in job
       situations (Note: Prior to Mar80, the
       instruction "Job Performance, USE Task
       Performance" was carried in the The-
       saurus)
UF   Employee Performance
BT   Performance
RT   Assessment Centers (Personnel)
       Competence
       Employment
       Employment Experience
       Job Analysis
       Job Skills
       Occupational Tests
       Performance Technology
       Personnel Evaluation
       Promotion (Occupational)
       Vocational Evaluation
       Work Sample Tests

Job Placement   *JUL. 1966*
       Postings: 3,496   GC: 630
UF   Student Job Placement #
       Vocational Placement
NT   Teacher Placement
BT   Placement
RT   Assessment Centers (Personnel)
       Career Counseling
       Career Guidance
       Employment
       Employment Services
       Job Applicants
       Job Application
       Job Banks
       Job Search Methods
       Outplacement Services (Employment)
       Personnel Evaluation
       Prior Learning
       Reentry Workers
       Student Employment
       Supported Employment
       Transfer Programs
       Vocational Education

Job Redesign
USE   Job Development

Job Related Literacy
USE   Workplace Literacy

Job Restructuring
USE   Job Development

Job Safety
USE   Occupational Safety and Health

Job Sample Tests
USE   Work Sample Tests

Job Samples
USE   Work Sample Tests

Job Satisfaction   *JUL. 1966*
       Postings: 5,187   GC: 630
UF   Employment Satisfaction
       Occupational Satisfaction
       Vocational Satisfaction
       Work Satisfaction
BT   Satisfaction
       Work Attitudes
RT   Burnout
       Career Change
       Employee Absenteeism
       Employer Employee Relationship
       Family Work Relationship
       Flexible Working Hours
       Industrial Psychology
       Job Enrichment
       Life Satisfaction
       Need Gratification
       Organizational Climate
       Organizational Development
       Quality of Working Life
       Self Actualization
       Vocational Adjustment
       Work Environment
       Work Ethic

Job Search Methods   *DEC. 1976*
       Postings: 1,817   GC: 630
SN   Procedures preceding job application
       whereby employment opportunities are
       determined
BT   Methods
RT   Career Change
       Career Information Systems
       Career Planning
       Dislocated Workers
       Employment
       Employment Interviews
       Employment Opportunities
       Employment Qualifications
       Employment Services
       Job Applicants
       Job Application
       Job Placement
       Labor Market
       Occupational Surveys
       Reentry Workers
       Resumes (Personal)
       Unemployment

Job Security   *FEB. 2000*
       Postings: 69   GC: 630
SN   The assurance or belief that one's em-
       ployment in a particular job will continue
UF   Employment Security
RT   Collective Bargaining
       Contracts
       Employee Attitudes
       Employer Employee Relationship
       Employment
       Employment Practices
       Personnel Policy
       Security (Psychology)
       Tenure
       Work Environment

= Two or more Descriptors are used to represent this term.
The term's main entry shows the appropriate coordination.

Job Seekers
USE   Job Applicants

Job Segregation
USE   Occupational Segregation

Job Sharing   NOV. 1982
      Postings: 115   GC: 630
SN   Division of available work or work hours
      among eligible employees, providing part-
      time employment options—sometimes
      used as an alternative to layoffs
UF   Work Sharing
BT   Part Time Employment
RT   Employment Practices
      Flexible Working Hours
      Labor Market
      Labor Utilization
      Partnership Teachers
      Personnel Policy
      Underemployment

Job Simplification   MAR. 1980
      Postings: 111   GC: 630
SN   Redesign of a job to improve production
      and efficiency
UF   Work Simplification (1968 1980)
BT   Job Development
RT   Automation
      Cost Effectiveness
      Efficiency
      Job Analysis
      Labor Utilization
      Productivity

Job Skills   JUL. 1966
      Postings: 10,137   GC: 630
UF   Employable Skills #
      Job Behaviors
      Marketable Skills #
      Vocational Skills
BT   Skills
RT   Business Skills
      Daily Living Skills
      Dislocated Workers
      Employment Experience
      Employment Level
      Employment Opportunities
      Employment Potential
      Employment Qualifications
      Equivalency Tests
      Home Economics Skills
      Job Analysis
      Job Performance
      Job Training
      Lifting
      Mechanical Skills
      Merit Rating
      Minimum Competencies
      Occupational Tests
      Personnel Evaluation
      Professional Training
      Promotion (Occupational)
      Reentry Workers
      Salesmanship
      Skill Obsolescence
      Skilled Occupations
      Skilled Workers
      Structural Unemployment
      Teaching Skills
      Vocational Education
      Vocational English (Second Language)
      Vocational Evaluation
      Work Sample Tests
      Workplace Literacy

Job Specifications
USE   Occupational Information

Job Tenure (1967 1978)
USE   Tenure

Job Training   JUL. 1966
      Postings: 8,563   GC: 630
SN   (Note: Prior to Mar80, the instruction
      "Occupational Training, USE Vocational

Education" was carried in the Thesau-
rus)
UF   Attendant Training (1968 1980) #
      Employment Preparation
      Occupational Training
NT   Custodian Training
      Off the Job Training
      On the Job Training
BT   Training
RT   Adult Vocational Education
      Career Academies
      Employment
      Flight Training
      Industrial Training
      Job Skills
      Labor Force Development
      Occupations
      Office Occupations
      Performance Technology
      Retraining
      Scope of Bargaining
      Sheltered Workshops
      Supervisory Training
      Trainees
      Training Allowances
      Vocational Education
      Vocational Training Centers
      Work Experience Programs

Job Training Academies
USE   Career Academies

Job Vacancies
USE   Employment Opportunities

Job Vacancy Surveys
USE   Occupational Surveys

Jobs (1966 1980)
USE   Employment

Jogging   FEB. 1978
      Postings: 59   GC: 470
SN   The exercise of running at a slow, regu-
      lar pace, often alternately with walking
BT   Running
RT   Athletics

Joint Occupancy
USE   Shared Facilities

Journal Articles   JUN. 1996
      Postings: 286   GC: 720
SN   Works of prose, complete in themselves,
      that are published with other such works
      in periodicals (Note: Corresponds to
      Pubtype code 080—do not use except
      as the subject of a document)
UF   Articles (Journals)
      Magazine Articles
      Periodical Articles
BT   Publications
RT   Periodicals
      Scholarly Journals
      Scholarly Writing

Journal Writing   AUG. 1988
      Postings: 1,206   GC: 400
SN   Writing done regularly in logs or note-
      books to gather thoughts or ideas, some-
      times for later use in more formal writing
      (Note: Use "Writing for Publication" for
      journal article writing)
BT   Writing (Composition)
RT   Creative Writing
      Dialog Journals
      Diaries
      Expository Writing
      Free Writing
      Personal Narratives
      Prewriting
      Self Expression
      Student Journals
      Student Writing Models
      Writing Across the Curriculum
      Writing Exercises

Journalism   JUL. 1966
      Postings: 4,303   GC: 720
SN   Preparation and dissemination of infor-
      mation on current affairs
NT   Broadcast Journalism
      New Journalism
      News Reporting
      News Writing
      Photojournalism
      Scholastic Journalism
BT   Technology
RT   Captions
      Editing
      Editorials
      Expository Writing
      Feature Stories
      Freedom of Information
      Freedom of Speech
      Headlines
      Information Sources
      Journalism Education
      Journalism History
      Journalism Research
      Layout (Publications)
      Literature
      Mass Media
      Mass Media Role
      News Media
      Newspapers
      Periodicals
      Photography
      Press Opinion
      Publications
      Serials
      Writing for Publication

Journalism Education   MAR. 1977
      Postings: 2,529   GC: 400
SN   Preparing students to pursue careers or
      work in journalism as writers, reporters,
      broadcasters, technicians, and teachers
BT   Education
RT   Expository Writing
      Journalism
      Journalism History
      Journalism Research
      Language Arts
      Mass Media
      News Media
      Newspapers
      Periodicals
      Publications
      Radio
      Scholastic Journalism
      School Publications
      Serials
      Student Publications
      Television
      Television Curriculum
      Writing Instruction

Journalism History   AUG. 1988
      Postings: 343   GC: 430
BT   History
RT   Editorials
      Historiography
      Journalism
      Journalism Education
      Journalism Research
      Literary History
      News Media
      Newspapers
      Periodicals
      Press Opinion
      Publications
      Social History

Journalism Research   SEP. 1995
      Postings: 610   GC: 810
SN   Basic, applied, and developmental re-
      search conducted to advance knowledge
      about journalism (Note: Use as a minor
      Descriptor for examples of this kind of
      research—use as a major Descriptor
      only as the subject of a document)
BT   Media Research
RT   Communication Research
      Journalism
      Journalism Education
      Journalism History

      Reading Research
      Writing Research

Journals
USE   Periodicals

Journey Workers
USE   Skilled Workers

Joy
USE   Happiness

Judaism   MAY 1969
      Postings: 324   GC: 430
BT   Religion
RT   Biblical Literature
      Christianity
      Jews
      Philosophy
      Religious Cultural Groups
      Western Civilization

Judges   MAR. 1980
      Postings: 302   GC: 640
SN   Persons selected or appointed to decide
      in competitions or contests (Note: If
      possible, use the more specific term
      "Court Judges")
UF   Debate Judges
NT   Court Judges
BT   Groups
RT   Interrater Reliability
      Justice
      Professional Personnel

Judgment Analysis Technique   OCT. 1982
      Postings: 24   GC: 820
SN   A statistical process combining a multi-
      ple regression approach with a hierar-
      chical grouping procedure to identify
      and describe evaluation policies and
      strategies within groups of decision mak-
      ers
UF   JAN Technique
BT   Statistical Analysis
RT   Cluster Grouping
      Decision Making
      Evaluation
      Evaluative Thinking
      Multiple Regression Analysis
      Operations Research
      Policy Formation
      Sociometric Techniques

Judgmental Processes
USE   Evaluative Thinking

Judicial Action
USE   Court Litigation

Judicial Role
USE   Court Role

Judicial System
USE   Courts

Junior College Libraries (1966 1980)
USE   College Libraries
AND   Two Year Colleges

Junior College Students (1969 1980)
USE   Two Year College Students

Junior Colleges (1966 1980)
USE   Two Year Colleges

Junior High School Role (1966 1980)
USE   School Role

= Two or more Descriptors are used to represent this term.
The term's main entry shows the appropriate coordination.

Junior High School Students   *JUL. 1966*
Postings: 4,060   GC: 360
SN   (Note: Coordinate with the appropriate mandatory educational level Descriptor)
BT   Secondary School Students
RT   Early Adolescents
High School Students
Junior High Schools
Middle School Students

Junior High School Teachers
USE   Secondary School Teachers

Junior High Schools   *JUL. 1966*
Postings: 13,534   GC: 340
SN   Providing formal education in grades 7, 8, and 9—less commonly 7 and 8, or 8 and 9 (Note: Also appears in the list of mandatory educational level Descriptors)
BT   Secondary Schools
RT   Grade 7
Grade 8
Grade 9
High Schools
Junior High School Students
Middle Schools
Secondary Education

Juries   *DEC. 1989*
Postings: 99   GC: 610
SN   Bodies of persons impaneled to render verdicts, usually in real or simulated courts of law
UF   Trial by Jury
BT   Groups
RT   Citizen Participation
Citizenship Responsibility
Court Litigation
Courts
Due Process
Evidence (Legal)
Justice
Sentencing

Justice   *DEC. 1974*
Postings: 1,357   GC: 610
SN   Fair and equitable treatment—includes the maintenance or administration of what is just
UF   Equity (Impartiality)
NT   Juvenile Justice
RT   Civil Law
Civil Liberties
Civil Rights
Constitutional Law
Court Judges
Courts
Due Process
Equal Protection
Freedom
Judges
Juries
Laws
Sex Fairness
Social Attitudes
Social Problems
Social Values
Torts
Values

Juvenile Courts   *AUG. 1968*
Postings: 565   GC: 610
UF   Childrens Courts
BT   Courts
RT   Childrens Rights
Court Litigation
Crime
Delinquency
Delinquent Rehabilitation
Juvenile Justice
Youth Problems

Juvenile Delinquency
USE   Delinquency

Juvenile Gangs   *JUL. 1966*
Postings: 359   GC: 530
BT   Groups
RT   Delinquency
Juvenile Justice
Peer Groups
Youth Clubs

Juvenile Justice   *APR. 1990*
Postings: 466   GC: 610
SN   Laws, legal programs, and judicial institutions dealing with delinquent and exploited children and youth (from under 16 to under 21 in the U.S., depending on the state)
UF   Juvenile Justice System
BT   Justice
RT   Child Welfare
Childrens Rights
Delinquency
Juvenile Courts
Juvenile Gangs
Law Related Education
Laws
Youth Problems

Juvenile Justice System
USE   Juvenile Justice

Juvenile Runaways
USE   Runaways

Kabyle   *JUL. 1966*
Postings: 3   GC: 440
BT   Berber Languages

Kannada   *JUL. 1966*
Postings: 23   GC: 440
BT   Dravidian Languages

Kashmiri   *JUL. 1966*
Postings: 9   GC: 440
BT   Indo European Languages

Kechua
USE   Quechua

Kernel Sentences   *JUL. 1966*
Postings: 95   GC: 450
BT   Sentences
Transformational Generative Grammar
RT   Grammar
Phonology
Phrase Structure
Sentence Combining
Sentence Structure
Syntax

Key Word Access Points
USE   Keywords

Key Word in Context
USE   Permuted Indexes

Keyboarding (Data Entry)   *AUG. 1986*
Postings: 329   GC: 710
SN   Act of using an alphanumeric keyboard to prepare computer-readable data or to communicate directly with a computer
UF   Computer Keyboards
Keypunching
BT   Business Skills
Input Output
RT   Calculators
Clerical Occupations
Computer Oriented Programs
Data Processing Occupations
Information Systems
Input Output Devices
Office Machines
Office Occupations
Office Occupations Education
Typewriting
Word Processing

Keypunching
USE   Keyboarding (Data Entry)

Keywords   *SEP. 1996*
Postings: 140   GC: 450
SN   In information science, words and phrases in an abstract, title, text, etc., of a work that identify its significant content (Note: Keywords are usually the uncontrolled or "natural-language" vocabulary—do not confuse with controlled subject headings, for which use "Subject Index Terms")—in learning and language development, words and phrases of prime importance to a particular task/activity, frequently associated with one another or with pictorial images for easy remembrance (Note: See also more precise Identifiers "Keyword Mnemonics," "Keyword Method (Language Learning)," and "Keyword Method (Second Language Learning)")
UF   Key Word Access Points
BT   Vocabulary
RT   Indexes
Mnemonics
Subject Index Terms
Word Lists

Khalkha
USE   Mongolian

Khmer (Language)
USE   Cambodian

Khmer (People)
USE   Cambodians

Kikongo Ya Leta
USE   Kituba

Kindergarten   *JUL. 1966*
Postings: 3,998   GC: 340
BT   Instructional Program Divisions
RT   Alternate Day Schedules
Early Childhood Education
Elementary Education
Full Day Half Day Schedules
Kindergarten Children
Preschool Education
Primary Education

Kindergarten Children   *JUL. 1966*
Postings: 3,223   GC: 120
BT   Young Children
RT   Kindergarten
Preschool Children

Kindergarten Teachers
USE   Preschool Teachers

Kindness
USE   Altruism

Kinescope Recordings   *JUL. 1966*
Postings: 30   GC: 720
UF   Kinescopes
BT   Films
RT   Film Libraries
Television
Videotape Recordings

Kinescopes
USE   Kinescope Recordings

Kinesics
USE   Body Language

Kinesthesia
USE   Kinesthetic Perception

Kinesthesis
USE   Kinesthetic Perception

Kinesthetic Memory
USE   Kinesthetic Perception

Kinesthetic Methods   *JUL. 1966*
Postings: 167   GC: 110
BT   Teaching Methods
RT   Kinesthetic Perception
Paralinguistics
Reading Instruction
Speech Instruction

Kinesthetic Perception   *AUG. 1968*
Postings: 343   GC: 110
SN   Sense perception of movement, weight, resistance, and position
UF   Kinesthesia
Kinesthesis
Kinesthetic Memory
Muscle Sense
BT   Perception
RT   Biomechanics
Body Image
Figural Aftereffects
Kinesthetic Methods
Learning Modalities
Manipulative Materials
Musculoskeletal System
Perception Tests
Perceptual Motor Learning
Personal Space
Tactual Perception

Kinetic Molecular Theory   *JUL. 1966*
Postings: 157   GC: 490
BT   Theories
RT   Acceleration (Physics)
Diffusion (Physics)
Force
Gravity (Physics)
Heat
Kinetics
Mechanics (Physics)
Molecular Structure
Motion
Physics

Kinetics   *JUL. 1966*
Postings: 611   GC: 490
SN   Branch of science that deals with the effects of forces upon the motions of material bodies or with changes in physical or chemical systems
UF   Power Transfer Systems
NT   Diffusion (Physics)
BT   Mechanics (Physics)
RT   Acceleration (Physics)
Biomechanics
Chemical Engineering
Energy
Engines
Fluid Mechanics
Force
Fuels
Gravity (Physics)
Heat
Hydraulics
Kinetic Molecular Theory
Motion
Relativity
Velocity
Wind Energy

Kinship   *OCT. 1983*
Postings: 209   GC: 520
SN   Socially recognized relationship based on real or supposed common descent, or such rituals as marriage and adoption
UF   Kinship Role
BT   Interpersonal Relationship
RT   Adoption
Black Family

= Two or more Descriptors are used to represent this term.
The term's main entry shows the appropriate coordination.

Daughters
Ethnography
Ethnology
Extended Family
Family (Sociological Unit)
Family History
Family Relationship
Family Structure
Genealogy
Kinship Terminology
Marriage
Nuclear Family
Parents
Remarriage
Siblings
Sociocultural Patterns
Sons
Spouses
Stepfamily

Kinship Role
USE Kinship

Kinship Terminology   *OCT. 1983*
    Postings: 12   GC: 450
SN Vocabulary representing kinship ties, e.g., "husband"/"wife"/"spouse," "father"/ "mother"/"parent," "father-in-law"/"mother-in-law," "uncle"/"aunt," "cousin"
BT Vocabulary
RT Kinship
    Language Patterns
    Sociolinguistics

Kirghiz (1968 1998)
USE Kyrgyz

Kirgiz
USE Kyrgyz

Kirundi   *JUL. 1966*
    Postings: 6   GC: 440
UF Rundi
BT Bantu Languages

Kiswahili
USE Swahili

Kituba   *JUL. 1966*
    Postings: 7   GC: 440
UF Kikongo Ya Leta
    Munukutaba
BT Bantu Languages

Knowledge Base for Teaching   *NOV. 1994*
    Postings: 1,060   GC: 310
SN Variable construct of skills and information considered desirable and important for prospective and experienced teachers to know—categories include: subject content knowledge, general pedagogical knowledge, curriculum knowledge, pedagogical content knowledge, knowledge of learners and their characteristics, knowledge of educational contexts, and knowledge of educational purposes and values (Note: Do not confuse with "Teacher Competencies" or the Identifier "Teacher Knowledge")
UF Teacher Education Knowledge Base
    Teacher Knowledge Base
    Teaching Knowledge Base
RT Foundations of Education
    Knowledge Level
    Pedagogical Content Knowledge
    Teacher Certification
    Teacher Competencies
    Teacher Education
    Teacher Education Curriculum
    Teacher Education Programs
    Teacher Effectiveness
    Teacher Qualifications
    Teaching (Occupation)
    Teaching Experience
    Teaching Skills

Knowledge Based Systems
USE Expert Systems

Knowledge Level   *JUL. 1966*
    Postings: 4,924   GC: 120
SN Extent of knowledge attained
BT Achievement
RT Academic Achievement
    Achievement Gains
    Comprehension
    Confidence Testing
    Cultural Literacy
    Educational Background
    Epistemology
    Familiarity
    Knowledge Base for Teaching
    Learning
    Learning Plateaus
    Pedagogical Content Knowledge
    Performance
    Scholarship

Knowledge of Results
USE Feedback

Knowledge Representation   *AUG. 1994*
    Postings: 475   GC: 810
SN The encoding of knowledge in biological systems or computers (Note: See also such Identifiers as "Knowledge Bases" and "Knowledge Engineering")
RT Artificial Intelligence
    Cognitive Processes
    Cognitive Psychology
    Cognitive Structures
    Computer Science
    Computers
    Concept Formation
    Concept Mapping
    Expert Systems
    Information Processing
    Information Science
    Natural Language Processing

Knowledge Structures
USE Cognitive Structures

Kodaly Method   *AUG. 1988*
    Postings: 42   GC: 420
SN System of music education for children that includes singing, ear training, solfeggio, rhythmic movement, and improvisation—developed by Hungarian composer, Zoltan Kodaly, to achieve the goal of music literacy
BT Music Education
    Teaching Methods
RT Auditory Training
    Movement Education
    Music Reading
    Music Techniques
    Orff Method
    Singing

Korean   *JUL. 1966*
    Postings: 308   GC: 440
UF Hangul
    Hanja
    Hankul
BT Languages
RT Korean Culture

Korean Americans   *SEP. 1968*
    Postings: 253   GC: 560
BT Asian Americans
    Ethnic Groups
RT Korean Culture

Korean Culture   *JUL. 1966*
    Postings: 109   GC: 560
BT Culture
RT Asian Studies
    Korean
    Korean Americans
    Non Western Civilization

Korean War   *APR. 1990*
    Postings: 26   GC: 430
SN War from 1950 to 1953 between North Korea, aided by Communist China, and South Korea, aided by the U.S. and other United Nations members
BT Asian History
    War
RT United States History
    Vietnam War
    World War II

Krio
USE Sierra Leone Creole

Kurdish   *JUL. 1966*
    Postings: 14   GC: 440
BT Indo European Languages

KWIC Indexes
USE Permuted Indexes

KWOC Indexes
USE Permuted Indexes

Kyrghyz
USE Kyrgyz

Kyrgyz   *APR. 1998*
    Postings: 4   GC: 440
UF Kirghiz (1968 1998)
    Kirgiz
    Kyrghyz
BT Turkic Languages

Labeling (of Persons)   *SEP. 1975*
    Postings: 1,285   GC: 540
SN Designating a special or complex condition of an individual or group by a simplistic word or phrase which may connote status, and perhaps, stigma
BT Classification
RT Grouping (Instructional Purposes)
    Groups
    Identification
    Noncategorical Education
    Normalization (Disabilities)
    Self Fulfilling Prophecies
    Social Bias
    Special Education
    Stereotypes

Labor   *JUL. 1966*
    Postings: 177   GC: 630
SN Human activity that provides the goods and services in an economy—also, the services performed by workers for wages as distinguished from those rendered by entrepreneurs for profits (Note: Use for general works and theory—use a more specific term if possible)
NT Child Labor
    Farm Labor
RT Employees
    Employment
    Human Resources
    Labor Conditions
    Labor Demands
    Labor Economics
    Labor Force
    Labor Legislation
    Labor Market
    Labor Needs
    Labor Problems
    Labor Relations
    Labor Standards
    Labor Supply
    Labor Utilization
    Laborers

Labor (Childbirth)
USE Birth

Labor Camps (1966 1980) (Migrants)
USE Migrant Housing

Labor Conditions   *JUL. 1966*
    Postings: 278   GC: 630
RT Labor
    Labor Demands
    Labor Economics
    Labor Legislation
    Labor Needs
    Labor Problems
    Labor Relations
    Labor Standards
    Laborers
    Quality of Working Life
    Work Environment

Labor Demands   *JUL. 1966*
    Postings: 298   GC: 630
SN Demands of labor (Note: Do not confuse with "Labor Needs")
UF Agricultural Labor Disputes (1966 1980)
RT Arbitration
    Collective Bargaining
    Contracts
    Grievance Procedures
    Labor
    Labor Conditions
    Labor Economics
    Labor Legislation
    Labor Problems
    Labor Standards
    Negotiation Impasses
    Sanctions
    Strikes
    Unions

Labor Economics   *JUL. 1966*
    Postings: 776   GC: 620
BT Economics
RT Arbitration
    Business Cycles
    Developed Nations
    Developing Nations
    Dislocated Workers
    Econometrics
    Economic Impact
    Economic Research
    Employment
    Employment Patterns
    Labor
    Labor Conditions
    Labor Demands
    Labor Force
    Labor Force Development
    Labor Market
    Labor Needs
    Labor Relations
    Labor Supply
    Labor Utilization
    Marxism
    Microeconomics
    Negotiation Impasses
    Structural Unemployment
    Unemployment

Labor Education   *JUL. 1966*
    Postings: 858   GC: 630
SN Education and training of workers often sponsored by labor unions and sometimes in cooperation with educational institutions
UF Workers Education
BT Adult Education
RT Industrial Education
    Industrial Training
    Inplant Programs
    Labor Force
    Nonschool Educational Programs
    Off the Job Training
    Unions

Labor Force   *JUL. 1966*
    Postings: 2,263   GC: 630
SN (Note: Prior to Mar80, the instruction "Work Force, USE Laborers" was carried in the Thesaurus)
UF Manpower

Work Force
BT   Human Resources
RT   Developed Nations
      Dislocated Workers
      Employed Parents
      Employed Women
      Employment
      Human Capital
      Labor
      Labor Economics
      Labor Education
      Labor Force Nonparticipants
      Labor Market
      Labor Needs
      Labor Supply
      Labor Turnover
      Labor Utilization
      Laborers
      Occupational Surveys
      Older Workers
      Organization Size (Groups)
      Reentry Workers
      Strikes
      Unions
      Working Class

Labor Force Development   MAR. 1980
      Postings: 5,469   GC: 630
UF   Human Resources Development (La-
      bor)
      Manpower Development (1966 1980)
NT   Management Development
      Professional Development
      Staff Development
BT   Development
RT   Career Ladders
      Corporate Education
      Developmental Programs
      Economic Development
      Emerging Occupations
      Industrial Training
      Job Development
      Job Training
      Labor Economics
      Labor Needs
      Labor Utilization
      Performance Technology
      Retraining
      Technical Assistance
      Training Allowances
      Vocational Education
      Work Experience Programs

Labor Force Nonparticipants   JUL. 1966
      Postings: 299   GC: 630
SN   Persons neither employed nor looking
      for employment
BT   Groups
RT   Employment
      Labor Force
      Labor Supply
      Labor Utilization
      Retirement
      Unemployment
      Work Attitudes

Labor Force Surveys
USE   Occupational Surveys

Labor Laws (1966 1974)
USE   Labor Legislation

Labor Legislation   JUL. 1966
      Postings: 1,006   GC: 610
UF   Child Labor Laws (1966 1974) #
      Child Labor Legislation (1966 1980) #
      Farm Labor Legislation (1966 1980) #
      Labor Laws (1966 1974)
BT   Legislation
RT   Arbitration
      Collective Bargaining
      Employer Employee Relationship
      Employment Practices
      Labor
      Labor Conditions
      Labor Demands
      Labor Standards
      Laborers
      Laws

Negotiation Impasses
Unions

Labor Market   JUL. 1966
      Postings: 4,484   GC: 630
UF   Employment Market
      Job Market (1966 1980)
NT   Teacher Supply and Demand
RT   Demand Occupations
      Dislocated Workers
      Displaced Homemakers
      Employment
      Employment Experience
      Employment Opportunities
      Employment Patterns
      Employment Projections
      Employment Statistics
      Job Layoff
      Job Search Methods
      Job Sharing
      Labor
      Labor Economics
      Labor Force
      Labor Needs
      Labor Supply
      Labor Turnover
      Laborers
      Occupational Segregation
      Occupational Surveys
      Personnel Selection
      Reduction in Force
      Reentry Workers
      Structural Unemployment
      Supply and Demand
      Teacher Employment
      Underemployment
      Unemployment

Labor Mobility
USE   Occupational Mobility

Labor Needs   MAR. 1980
      Postings: 3,408   GC: 630
SN   Demands for labor in the economy as a
      whole or in particular sectors or indus-
      tries (Note: Do not confuse with "Labor
      Demands")
UF   Manpower Needs (1968 1980)
NT   Personnel Needs
BT   Needs
RT   Demand Occupations
      Employment Opportunities
      Employment Projections
      Labor
      Labor Conditions
      Labor Economics
      Labor Force
      Labor Force Development
      Labor Market
      Labor Utilization
      Promotion (Occupational)
      Supply and Demand

Labor Problems   JUL. 1966
      Postings: 486   GC: 630
UF   Farm Labor Problems (1966 1980) #
BT   Problems
RT   Arbitration
      Collective Bargaining
      Employee Absenteeism
      Employment Problems
      Labor
      Labor Conditions
      Labor Demands
      Labor Turnover
      Laborers
      Negotiation Impasses
      Relocation
      Seniority
      Strikes
      Teacher Strikes
      Tenure

Labor Relations   MAR. 1980
      Postings: 1,377   GC: 630
SN   All of the relationships that grow out of
      the fact of employment
UF   Employee Relations
      Industrial Relations (1969 1980)

BT   Relationship
RT   Business Communication
      Collective Bargaining
      Employer Employee Relationship
      Fringe Benefits
      Industrial Psychology
      Labor
      Labor Conditions
      Labor Economics
      Personnel
      Public Relations
      Quality of Working Life
      Unions

Labor Standards   JUL. 1966
      Postings: 182   GC: 630
SN   Standards for acceptable employment
      conditions, e.g., working hours, wage
      rates, safety and health conditions (Note:
      Prior to Mar80, the use of this term was
      not restricted by a Scope Note)
UF   Occupational Safety and Health Stan-
      dards #
BT   Standards
RT   Environmental Standards
      Labor
      Labor Conditions
      Labor Demands
      Labor Legislation
      Laborers

Labor Supply   SEP. 1968
      Postings: 1,097   GC: 630
UF   Farm Labor Supply (1966 1980) #
      Supply of Labor
BT   Human Resources
RT   Human Capital
      Labor
      Labor Economics
      Labor Force
      Labor Force Nonparticipants
      Labor Market
      Labor Turnover
      Labor Utilization
      Occupational Surveys
      Supply and Demand
      Working Class

Labor Turnover   JUL. 1966
      Postings: 1,003   GC: 630
UF   Retention (of Employees)
RT   Career Change
      Dislocated Workers
      Employment Patterns
      Job Layoff
      Labor Force
      Labor Market
      Labor Problems
      Labor Supply
      Occupational Mobility
      Reduction in Force
      Relocation
      Stopouts
      Teacher Persistence
      Tenure

Labor Unions (1966 1980)
USE   Unions

Labor Utilization   MAR. 1980
      Postings: 1,756   GC: 630
UF   Manpower Utilization (1966 1980)
NT   Staff Utilization
RT   Economic Factors
      Employment
      Job Sharing
      Job Simplification
      Labor
      Labor Economics
      Labor Force
      Labor Force Development
      Labor Force Nonparticipants
      Labor Needs
      Labor Supply
      Reduction in Force
      Relocation
      Underemployment
      Unemployment

Use Studies
Worker Days

Laboratories   JUL. 1966
      Postings: 1,107   GC: 920
SN   Facilities specifically designed and
      equipped for experimentation, demon-
      stration, observation, practice, or research
      in a field of study (Note: Use a more
      specific term if possible)
UF   Computer Based Laboratories (1967
      1980) #
NT   Learning Laboratories
      Mobile Laboratories
      Regional Laboratories
      Science Laboratories
      Writing Laboratories
BT   Facilities
RT   Classrooms
      Computer Centers
      Demonstration Centers
      Demonstrations (Educational)
      Laboratory Animals
      Laboratory Equipment
      Laboratory Experiments
      Laboratory Manuals
      Laboratory Procedures
      Laboratory Safety
      Laboratory Technology

Laboratory Animals   AUG. 1980
      Postings: 194   GC: 490
BT   Animals
RT   Animal Facilities
      Animal Husbandry
      Laboratories
      Laboratory Experiments
      Laboratory Procedures
      Medical Research
      Rats
      Zoology

Laboratory Equipment   JUL. 1966
      Postings: 1,946   GC: 910
UF   Language Laboratory Equipment (1966
      1980) #
NT   Microscopes
BT   Equipment
RT   Animal Facilities
      Biomedical Equipment
      Laboratories
      Laboratory Procedures
      Measurement Equipment
      Science Equipment

Laboratory Experiments   JUL. 1966
      Postings: 2,744   GC: 490
BT   Experiments
RT   Experimental Psychology
      Laboratories
      Laboratory Animals
      Laboratory Procedures
      Science Experiments

Laboratory Manuals   JUL. 1966
      Postings: 268   GC: 730
BT   Guides
      Instructional Materials
RT   Laboratories
      Laboratory Procedures
      Laboratory Safety
      Textbooks
      Workbooks

Laboratory Preschools
USE   Laboratory Schools
AND   Preschool Education

Laboratory Procedures   JUL. 1966
      Postings: 3,518   GC: 490
SN   Procedures used in the laboratory
NT   Chromatography
      Culturing Techniques
      Dissection
BT   Methods
RT   Demonstrations (Educational)
      Demonstrations (Science)

= Two or more Descriptors are used to represent this term.
The term's main entry shows the appropriate coordination.

Experiential Learning
Industrial Arts
Instruction
Laboratories
Laboratory Animals
Laboratory Equipment
Laboratory Experiments
Laboratory Manuals
Laboratory Safety
Laboratory Technology
Science Activities
Science Experiments
Science Projects
Simulation
Teaching Methods

Laboratory Safety *JUL. 1966*
Postings: 668 GC: 210
BT Safety
RT Hazardous Materials
Laboratories
Laboratory Manuals
Laboratory Procedures
Laboratory Technology
Radiation
Radiation Effects
Safety Education
School Safety

Laboratory Schools *JUL. 1966*
Postings: 309 GC: 340
SN Schools of preschool, elementary, or
secondary grades attached to universi-
ties or colleges for purposes of research
and teacher training
UF Campus Schools
Laboratory Preschools #
University Schools
BT Schools
RT Affiliated Schools
College School Cooperation
Educational Research
Elementary Schools
Experiential Learning
Experimental Schools
Laboratory Training
Preschool Education
Professional Development Schools
Schools of Education
Secondary Schools
Teacher Education
Teaching Experience

Laboratory Techniques (1967 1980)
JUN. 1980
Postings: 962 GC: 490
SN Invalid Descriptor—used inconsistently
in indexing—use "Laboratory Training"
for human relations laboratory
techniques—otherwise, use "Laboratory
Procedures"

Laboratory Technology *JUL. 1966*
Postings: 137 GC: 490
BT Technology
RT Dental Technicians
Electroencephalography
Laboratories
Laboratory Procedures
Laboratory Safety
Medical Laboratory Assistants

Laboratory Training *JUL. 1966*
Postings: 518 GC: 240
SN Method of training designed to facilitate
self insight, process awareness, inter-
personal competence, and dynamics of
change
BT Training
RT Counseling Techniques
Gestalt Therapy
Human Relations
Humanistic Education
Interpersonal Competence
Laboratory Schools
Microteaching
Practicum Supervision
Practicums
Protocol Materials

Resistance to Change
Sensitivity Training
Simulation
Teacher Centers
Teacher Education
Teaching Experience
Trainers
Transactional Analysis

Laborers *JUL. 1966*
Postings: 174 GC: 630
UF Experienced Laborers (1966 1980)
NT Agricultural Laborers
Auxiliary Laborers
BT Unskilled Workers
RT Employees
Industrial Personnel
Labor
Labor Conditions
Labor Force
Labor Legislation
Labor Market
Labor Problems
Labor Standards

Lacrosse *FEB. 1978*
Postings: 22 GC: 470
BT Team Sports

Laissez Faire Economy
USE Free Enterprise System

Lakhota
USE Lakota

Lakota *MAR. 1994*
Postings: 3 GC: 440
SN The Siouan language of the Lakota tribe
of American Indians
UF Lakhota
Teton Dakota
BT Dakota
RT Lakota (Tribe)
Oglala Sioux (Tribe)

Lakota (Tribe) *MAR. 1994*
Postings: 46 GC: 560
SN Largest and westernmost of the Sioux
peoples, principally in South Dakota, Mon-
tana, and Manitoba (and dispersed kin)
UF Teton Sioux (Tribe)
NT Oglala Sioux (Tribe)
BT Sioux (Tribe)
RT Lakota

Land Acquisition *JAN. 1972*
Postings: 180 GC: 920
RT Capital Outlay (for Fixed Assets)
Land Settlement
Land Use
Ownership
Site Development
Site Selection

Land Colonization
USE Land Settlement

Land Grant Colleges
USE Land Grant Universities

Land Grant Universities *JUL. 1966*
Postings: 498 GC: 340
SN Universities that have received grants of
land from the federal government, espe-
cially those made in accordance with the
Morrill Act of 1862, originally to promote
study in practical subjects like engineer-
ing and agriculture but now usually ex-
panded to include a wide range of disci-
plines
UF Land Grant Colleges
BT Universities
RT Agricultural Colleges
Agricultural Education

Engineering Education
Federal Aid
Rural Extension
State Colleges
State Universities

Land Settlement *JAN. 1970*
Postings: 475 GC: 550
UF Colonization
Land Colonization
Resettlement
Settlement Patterns
NT Rural Resettlement
BT Land Use
RT American Indian Reservations
Demography
Immigration
Land Acquisition
Nomads
Place of Residence
Population Trends
Refugees
Relocation
Wilderness

Land Use *JUL. 1966*
Postings: 1,439 GC: 550
NT Land Settlement
Soil Conservation
RT Agriculture
Agronomy
Community Planning
Educational Facilities Planning
Facility Planning
Forestry
Land Acquisition
Landlords
Mining
Parks
Rainforests
Real Estate
Road Construction
Soil Science
Turf Management
Underground Facilities
Urban Planning
Use Studies
Wetlands
Wilderness
Zoning

Landladies
USE Landlords

Landlords *SEP. 1968*
Postings: 56 GC: 640
UF Landladies
BT Groups
RT Homeowners
Housing
Land Use
Real Estate
Real Estate Occupations

Landscaping *JUL. 1966*
Postings: 288 GC: 410
BT Ornamental Horticulture
RT Botany
Floriculture
Gardening
Grounds Keepers
Plant Identification
Site Development
Trails
Turf Management

Language *JUL. 1966*
Postings: 1,632 GC: 450
SN Systematic means of communicating
ideas and feelings through the use of
signs, gestures, words, and/or auditory
symbols (Note: For natural languages
and language families, see "Languages")
NT Artificial Languages
Child Language
Figurative Language
Interlanguage
Language of Instruction

Language Universals
Languages for Special Purposes
Official Languages
Oral Language
Programming Languages
Second Languages
Sign Language
Symbolic Language
Tone Languages
Uncommonly Taught Languages
Unwritten Languages
Urban Language
Written Language
RT Artificial Speech
Code Switching (Language)
Dialects
Language Acquisition
Language Arts
Language Attitudes
Language Enrichment
Language Impairments
Language Patterns
Language Planning
Language Processing
Language Proficiency
Language Research
Language Rhythm
Language Role
Language Skill Attrition
Language Skills
Language Styles
Language Tests
Language Universals
Language Usage
Language Variation
Languages
Linguistics
Onomastics
Semiotics
Social Dialects
Speech
Speech Communication
Verbal Communication
Word Frequency
Word Order

Language Ability (1966 1980) *MAR. 1980*
Postings: 768 GC: 450
SN Invalid Descriptor—used inconsistently
in indexing—see such Descriptors as
"Language Aptitude," "Language Profi-
ciency," "Language Skills," etc.

Language Acquisition *MAR. 1980*
Postings: 10,953 GC: 120
SN Development in the individual of his/her
native language (Note: Do not use for
"Second Language Learning"—prior to
Mar80, the Thesaurus carried the in-
struction "Language Acquisition, USE
Language Development"—"Language
Development" did not carry a Scope
Note)
UF Aural Language Learning #
Language Development (1966 1980)
Visual Language Learning #
BT Verbal Development
RT Auditory Training
Caregiver Speech
Child Language
Delayed Speech
Expressive Language
Language
Language Aptitude
Language Enrichment
Language Fluency
Language Impairments
Language Processing
Language Skill Attrition
Language Skills
Language Universals
Linguistic Competence
Linguistic Difficulty (Inherent)
Linguistic Input
Linguistic Performance
Metalinguistics
Oral Language
Psycholinguistics
Receptive Language
Verbal Learning
Written Language

= Two or more Descriptors are used to represent this term.
The term's main entry shows the appropriate coordination.

Language Aids (1966 1980) *JUN. 1980*
Postings: 112 GC: 450
SN Invalid Descriptor—used for both "Native Language Instruction" and "Second Language Instruction"—see those Descriptors as well as "Educational Media"

Language and Area Centers (1968 1980) *MAR. 1980*
Postings: 42 GC: 920
SN Invalid Descriptor—see such Descriptors as "Area Studies," "Resource Centers," "Second Language Programs," "Second Language Instruction," etc.

Language Aptitude *MAR. 1980*
Postings: 183 GC: 450
BT Aptitude
RT Academic Aptitude
   Language Acquisition
   Language Fluency
   Language Proficiency
   Language Skills
   Language Tests
   Second Language Learning
   Verbal Ability

Language Arts *JUL. 1966*
Postings: 8,441 GC: 450
NT Debate
   Handwriting
   Listening
   Outlining (Discourse)
   Reading
   Rhetoric
   Speech
   Spelling
   Story Telling
   Writing (Composition)
RT Child Language
   Communication (Thought Transfer)
   Comprehension
   Discourse Modes
   Dramatics
   Editing
   English Curriculum
   Journalism Education
   Language
   Language Experience Approach
   Language Skills
   Lexicology
   Literature
   Reading Writing Relationship
   Self Expression
   Speech Communication
   Speech Curriculum
   Translation
   Verbal Ability
   Verbal Communication
   Vocabulary
   Whole Language Approach

Language Attitudes *MAR. 1976*
Postings: 2,384 GC: 450
SN Reactions, beliefs, or values about language and language use
NT Grammatical Acceptability
BT Attitudes
RT Consciousness Raising
   English Only Movement
   Language
   Language Planning
   Language Role
   Language Usage
   Metalinguistics
   Psycholinguistics
   Sexism in Language
   Social Attitudes
   Sociolinguistics

Language Attrition (Skills)
USE Language Skill Attrition

Language Awareness
USE Metalinguistics

Language Classification *JUL. 1966*
Postings: 350 GC: 450
SN Arrangement of languages into groups on the basis of historical development, structural features (see "Language Typology"), or geographic location
NT Language Typology
BT Classification
RT African Languages
   American Indian Languages
   Chad Languages
   Comparative Analysis
   Contrastive Linguistics
   Diachronic Linguistics
   Dialects
   Diglossia
   Dravidian Languages
   Etymology
   Glottochronology
   Indo European Languages
   Language Research
   Language Styles
   Languages
   Malayo Polynesian Languages
   Mutual Intelligibility
   North American English
   Regional Dialects
   Sino Tibetan Languages
   Slavic Languages
   Urban Language

Language Development (1966 1980)
USE Language Acquisition

Language Disabilities
USE Language Impairments

Language Dominance *AUG. 1978*
Postings: 352 GC: 450
SN The bilingual or multilingual individual's greater command of one of the languages in his/her repertoire
RT Bilingual Education
   Bilingual Students
   Bilingual Teacher Aides
   Bilingual Teachers
   Bilingualism
   English (Second Language)
   Interference (Language)
   Language of Instruction
   Language Proficiency
   Language Skills
   Language Tests
   Language Usage
   Languages
   Limited English Speaking
   Multilingualism
   Non English Speaking
   Second Languages

Language Enrichment *JUL. 1966*
Postings: 636 GC: 450
UF Language Experience
BT Enrichment
RT Bilingual Education
   Language
   Language Acquisition
   Languages
   Linguistic Input
   Second Language Instruction
   Second Language Learning
   Whole Language Approach

Language Enrollment *JUL. 1966*
Postings: 508 GC: 320
SN Enrollment of students in foreign or second language courses or programs (prior to Mar80, the use of this term was not restricted by a Scope Note)
UF Foreign Language Enrollment
   Second Language Enrollment
BT Enrollment
RT Enrollment Rate
   Enrollment Trends
   Languages
   Second Language Instruction
   Second Language Programs

Language Evolution
USE Diachronic Linguistics

Language Experience
USE Language Enrichment

Language Experience Approach *JUL. 1966*
Postings: 1,007 GC: 450
SN An approach to teaching reading and language arts that uses words and stories from the student's own language and experience
BT Teaching Methods
RT Beginning Reading
   Beginning Writing
   Child Language
   Invented Spelling
   Language Arts
   Narration
   Reading Comprehension
   Reading Instruction
   Reading Programs
   Student Developed Materials
   Whole Language Approach

Language Fluency *JUL. 1966*
Postings: 809 GC: 450
SN Ability to speak a language easily, smoothly, and readily (Note: Prior to Mar80, the use of this term was not restricted by a Scope Note)
BT Language Proficiency
RT Audiolingual Skills
   Communicative Competence (Languages)
   Conversational Language Courses
   Dialogs (Language)
   Diction
   Expressive Language
   Language Acquisition
   Language Aptitude
   Language Skills
   Languages
   Second Language Learning
   Speech Skills

Language Guides (1966 1980) *JUN. 1980*
Postings: 154 GC: 730
SN Invalid Descriptor—used for both "Native Language Instruction" and "Second Language Instruction"—see those Descriptors as well as "Curriculum Guides," "Dictionaries," etc.

Language Handicapped (1967 1980)
USE Language Impairments

Language Handicaps (1966 1994)
USE Language Impairments

Language History
USE Diachronic Linguistics

Language Impairments *MAR. 1994*
Postings: 688 GC: 220
SN Receptive or expressive language disabilities (Note: Use "Learning Disabilities" if the disability is being considered in an educational setting—use "Speech Impairments" for disorders of the peripheral speech mechanisms)
UF Language Disabilities
   Language Handicapped (1967 1980)
   Language Handicaps (1966 1994)
NT Aphasia
   Dyslexia
BT Disabilities
RT Augmentative and Alternative Communication
   Child Language
   Communication Disorders
   Echolalia
   Expressive Language
   Hearing Impairments
   Language
   Language Acquisition
   Learning Disabilities
   Neurolinguistics
   Neurological Impairments
   Perceptual Impairments
   Reading Difficulties
   Receptive Language
   Speech Impairments
   Speech Language Pathology
   Writing Difficulties

Language Input
USE Linguistic Input

Language Instruction (1966 1980) *MAR. 1980*
Postings: 12,547 GC: 450
SN Invalid Descriptor—used for both foreign and native language instruction—see "Second Language Instruction," "English Instruction," or "Native Language Instruction"

Language Laboratories *JUL. 1966*
Postings: 1,165 GC: 920
UF Audio Active Compare Laboratories (1967 1980)
   Audio Active Laboratories (1967 1980)
   Audio Passive Laboratories (1968 1980)
   Language Laboratory Equipment (1966 1980) #
   Language Laboratory Use (1966 1980)
BT Learning Laboratories
RT Audio Equipment
   Dial Access Information Systems
   Electronic Classrooms
   Languages
   Programmed Instruction
   Second Language Instruction
   Second Language Programs
   Writing Laboratories

Language Laboratory Equipment (1966 1980)
USE Laboratory Equipment
AND Language Laboratories

Language Laboratory Use (1966 1980)
USE Language Laboratories

Language Learning (Foreign)
USE Second Language Learning

Language Learning Levels (1967 1980) *MAR. 1980*
Postings: 659 GC: 450
SN Invalid Descriptor—used for levels of achievement in both native and foreign language—see "Second Language Learning" or "Language Acquisition"

Language Loss (Skills)
USE Language Skill Attrition

Language Maintenance *OCT. 1977*
Postings: 998 GC: 450
SN The maintenance of a given language rather than its displacement by another language (includes maintaining the languages of cultural minority groups through family practices, rituals, concerted educational endeavors with society at large, etc.)
RT Bilingual Education
   Bilingual Education Programs
   Bilingual Instructional Materials
   Bilingualism
   Cultural Maintenance
   French Canadians
   Language Minorities
   Language of Instruction
   Language Planning
   Language Role
   Language Skill Attrition
   Language Usage

= Two or more Descriptors are used to represent this term.
The term's main entry shows the appropriate coordination.

Languages
Multilingualism
Sociolinguistics

Language Minorities   *AUG. 1996*
Postings: 688   GC: 450
SN   Groups whose native language is not the
      dominant language of the larger society
      (Note: "Limited English Speaking" may
      be more appropriate for documents deal-
      ing with English-as-a-Second-Language
      instruction)
UF   Linguistic Minorities
      Minority Language Groups
BT   Groups
RT   Bilingualism
      Cross Cultural Studies
      Cultural Differences
      Cultural Pluralism
      Ethnic Groups
      Language Maintenance
      Languages
      Limited English Speaking
      Minority Groups
      Non English Speaking
      Sociolinguistics

Language of Instruction   *MAR. 1976*
Postings: 1,314   GC: 450
SN   Language in which curriculum subjects
      are presented
UF   Instructional Language
      Medium of Instruction (Language)
      Teaching Language
BT   Language
RT   Bilingual Education
      Bilingual Education Programs
      Bilingual Instructional Materials
      Curriculum
      Educational Policy
      English (Second Language)
      Immersion Programs
      Instruction
      Language Dominance
      Language Maintenance
      Language Planning
      Language Usage
      Languages
      Native Speakers
      Official Languages
      Second Language Instruction
      Second Language Learning
      Second Languages
      Sociolinguistics

Language Patterns   *JUL. 1966*
Postings: 5,103   GC: 450
UF   Basic Language Patterns
      Linguistic Patterns (1966 1980)
NT   Idioms
      Language Rhythm
      Paragraphs
      Phoneme Grapheme Correspondence
RT   Caregiver Speech
      Case (Grammar)
      Child Language
      Code Switching (Language)
      Connected Discourse
      Dialogs (Language)
      Diction
      Echolalia
      Error Analysis (Language)
      Form Classes (Languages)
      Ideography
      Jargon
      Kinship Terminology
      Language
      Language Styles
      Language Typology
      Language Universals
      Language Usage
      Languages
      Lexicology
      Linguistic Borrowing
      Linguistics
      Morphology (Languages)
      Native Speakers
      North American English
      Phonemics
      Pragmatics

Pronouns
Semantics
Semiotics
Sentence Combining
Sentence Diagraming
Sexism in Language
Speech Acts
Speech Communication
Speech Habits
Speech Skills
Standard Spoken Usage
Syntax
Tagmemic Analysis
Urban Language
Verbal Abuse
Verbal Communication
Word Order

Language Planning   *AUG. 1969*
Postings: 1,016   GC: 450
SN   Planned language change directed to-
      ward improving the utility of a language
      or increasing its use in a given country or
      region
NT   Language Standardization
BT   Planning
      Sociolinguistics
RT   Bilingual Education
      Bilingualism
      Educational Policy
      Immersion Programs
      Language
      Language Attitudes
      Language Maintenance
      Language of Instruction
      Language Usage
      Languages
      Multilingualism
      National Norms
      National Programs
      Official Languages
      Second Languages
      Sociolinguistics

Language Processing   *AUG. 1978*
Postings: 2,840   GC: 450
SN   The cognitive processing of spoken or
      written language, ranging from the con-
      struction of spoken or written messages
      to the abstraction of meaning from
      language—includes the computerized
      simulation of these processes (Note: For
      the concept of using ordinary language
      to communicate with computers, use
      "Natural Language Processing")
NT   Expressive Language
      Interference (Language)
      Reading Processes
      Receptive Language
BT   Cognitive Processes
RT   Abstract Reasoning
      Auditory Perception
      Coherence
      Comprehension
      Computational Linguistics
      Encoding (Psychology)
      Familiarity
      Language
      Language Acquisition
      Language Research
      Language Skills
      Language Usage
      Learning Processes
      Learning Strategies
      Linguistic Difficulty (Inherent)
      Linguistic Performance
      Linguistic Theory
      Linguistics
      Listening
      Metalinguistics
      Neurolinguistics
      Psycholinguistics
      Reading
      Speech Communication
      Structural Analysis (Linguistics)
      Verbal Communication
      Verbal Stimuli
      Visual Perception
      Writing (Composition)
      Writing Processes

Language Proficiency   *JUL. 1966*
Postings: 4,536   GC: 450
SN   Degree or level of accuracy and fluency
      of language use for communication
UF   Proficiency Tests (Language) #
NT   Language Fluency
      Threshold Level (Languages)
BT   Ability
RT   Bilingualism
      Communicative Competence
        (Languages)
      Conversational Language Courses
      Dialogs (Language)
      Intensive Language Courses
      Language
      Language Aptitude
      Language Dominance
      Language Skill Attrition
      Language Skills
      Language Tests
      Languages
      Limited English Speaking
      Linguistic Competence
      Linguistic Input
      Linguistic Performance
      Multilevel Classes (Second Language
        Instruction)
      Second Language Instruction
      Second Language Learning

Language Programs (1966 1980)
                                 MAR. 1980
Postings: 1,806   GC: 450
SN   Invalid Descriptor—used for both native
      and foreign language programs—see
      such Descriptors as "Second Language
      Programs," "English Instruction," and
      "Native Language Instruction"

**Language Records (Phonograph) (1966
1980)**
USE   Audiodisks

Language Research   *JUL. 1966*
Postings: 10,238   GC: 810
SN   Study of either the acquisition of spoken/
      written language or the elements of lan-
      guage as defined by linguistics, e.g.,
      phonology, morphology, syntax, lexicon
      (Note: Do not confuse with "Communi-
      cation Research"—as of Oct81, use as a
      minor Descriptor for examples of this
      kind of research—use as a major Descrip-
      tor only as the subject of a document)
UF   Linguistic Research
NT   Dialect Studies
BT   Research
RT   Anthropological Linguistics
      Bilingualism
      Child Language
      Communication Research
      Diachronic Linguistics
      Discourse Analysis
      Etymology
      Glottochronology
      Language
      Language Classification
      Language Processing
      Language Role
      Language Universals
      Languages
      Linguistics
      Onomastics
      Phonetic Analysis
      Sociolinguistics
      Speech Compression
      Structural Analysis (Linguistics)
      Tagmemic Analysis
      Unwritten Languages
      Urban Language

Language Rhythm   *SEP. 1968*
Postings: 405   GC: 450
SN   Regular or intermittent pattern in the
      flow of spoken or written language
UF   Rhythm (Language)
BT   Language Patterns
RT   Articulation (Speech)
      Language

Language Styles
Oral Language
Poetry
Prose
Rhyme
Speech Communication
Speech Habits
Speech Skills
Written Language

Language Role   *JUL. 1966*
Postings: 3,191   GC: 450
BT   Role
RT   Cultural Influences
      Language
      Language Attitudes
      Language Maintenance
      Language Research
      Social Dialects
      Social Influences
      Sociolinguistics

Language Skill Attrition   *JAN. 1985*
Postings: 132   GC: 450
SN   The loss of native or second language
      skills due to discontinued use (Note: Do
      not confuse with "Language Impair-
      ments")
UF   Language Attrition (Skills)
      Language Loss (Skills)
RT   Bilingualism
      Language
      Language Acquisition
      Language Maintenance
      Language Proficiency
      Language Skills
      Language Usage
      Multilingualism
      Psycholinguistics
      Retention (Psychology)
      Second Language Learning
      Sociolinguistics

Language Skills   *JUL. 1966*
Postings: 7,252   GC: 450
NT   Audiolingual Skills
      Communicative Competence
        (Languages)
      Reading Skills
      Vocabulary Skills
      Writing Skills
BT   Skills
RT   Basic Skills
      Cloze Procedure
      Communication Skills
      Daily Living Skills
      Dictation
      English (Second Language)
      Error Analysis (Language)
      Expressive Language
      Inferences
      Interpreters
      Interpretive Skills
      Language
      Language Acquisition
      Language Aptitude
      Language Arts
      Language Dominance
      Language Fluency
      Language Processing
      Language Proficiency
      Language Skill Attrition
      Language Tests
      Languages
      Linguistic Competence
      Linguistic Performance
      Listening Comprehension
      Metalinguistics
      Monolingualism
      Psycholinguistics
      Receptive Language
      Second Language Learning
      Sentence Combining
      Thinking Skills
      Translation
      Verbal Ability
      Whole Language Approach
      Word Study Skills

= Two or more Descriptors are used to represent this term.
The term's main entry shows the appropriate coordination.

Language Standardization   *JUL. 1966*
          Postings: 485   GC: 450
SN   The official acceptance by at least some
          groups within a speech community of
          certain general patterns of pronuncia-
          tion, grammar, orthography, and/or vo-
          cabulary
BT   Language Planning
RT   Dialects
          Diglossia
          Languages
          National Norms
          National Programs
          Native Language Instruction
          Official Languages
          Romanization
          Sociolinguistics
          Standard Spoken Usage

Language Styles   *JUL. 1966*
          Postings: 2,082   GC: 450
SN   Optional variants in sounds, structures,
          and vocabulary of a language which are
          characteristic of different users, situa-
          tions, or literary types
UF   Linguistic Styles
NT   Academic Discourse
BT   Language Usage
          Language Variation
RT   Cliches
          Discourse Communities
          Editing
          Expressive Language
          Jargon
          Language
          Language Classification
          Language Patterns
          Language Rhythm
          Literary Devices
          Native Speakers
          Speech Skills
          Standard Spoken Usage
          Writing Skills

Language Tapes
USE   Audiotape Recordings

Language Teachers   *JUL. 1966*
          Postings: 3,265   GC: 360
UF   FLES Teachers (1967 1980) #
          Foreign Language Teachers
          Second Language Teachers
NT   English Teachers
BT   Teachers
RT   Languages
          Native Language Instruction
          Reading Teachers
          Second Language Instruction
          Writing Teachers

Language Tests   *JUL. 1966*
          Postings: 3,894   GC: 830
SN   Tests to measure proficiency, diagnose
          strengths and weaknesses, or predict
          future performance in a native or foreign
          language (Note: For foreign language
          tests, coordinate this term with "Second
          Language Learning," and, when appro-
          priate, the language)
UF   Proficiency Tests (Language) #
BT   Verbal Tests
RT   Achievement Tests
          Cloze Procedure
          Language
          Language Aptitude
          Language Dominance
          Language Proficiency
          Language Skills
          Languages
          Listening Comprehension Tests
          Reading Tests
          Second Language Learning
          Speech Tests
          Writing Skills
          Writing Tests

Language Typology   *JUL. 1966*
          Postings: 285   GC: 450
SN   Classification of languages on the basis

of similarities and differences in their
structural features—phonology, grammar, and vocabulary, including semantic
meaning in specific contexts
BT   Language Classification
RT   Contrastive Linguistics
          Descriptive Linguistics
          Etymology
          Language Patterns
          Language Universals
          Morphology (Languages)
          Phonemes
          Phonology
          Syntax
          Tone Languages

Language Universals   *AUG. 1968*
          Postings: 674   GC: 450
SN   Characteristics assumed to be common
          to all languages
UF   Linguistic Universals
BT   Language
RT   Artificial Languages
          Behavioral Science Research
          Case (Grammar)
          Diachronic Linguistics
          Distinctive Features (Language)
          Language
          Language Acquisition
          Language Patterns
          Language Research
          Language Typology
          Languages
          Linguistic Difficulty (Inherent)
          Linguistic Theory
          Negative Forms (Language)
          Structural Analysis (Linguistics)

Language Usage   *JUL. 1966*
          Postings: 7,251   GC: 450
NT   Language Styles
          Sexism in Language
          Standard Spoken Usage
RT   Bidialectalism
          Business English
          Code Switching (Language)
          Cohesion (Written Composition)
          Dialects
          Error Analysis (Language)
          Grammatical Acceptability
          Jargon
          Language
          Language Attitudes
          Language Dominance
          Language Maintenance
          Language of Instruction
          Language Patterns
          Language Planning
          Language Processing
          Language Skill Attrition
          Language Variation
          Languages
          Linguistic Borrowing
          Linguistics
          Miscue Analysis
          Native Language Instruction
          Native Speakers
          North American English
          Obscenity
          Oral Language
          Pragmatics
          Sociolinguistics
          Speech Habits
          Urban Language
          Verbal Abuse
          Written Language

Language Variation   *JUN. 1975*
          Postings: 1,849   GC: 450
SN   Differences in systems of a language
          that result from historical, geographic,
          social, or functional changes
NT   Creoles
          Dialects
          Language Styles
          Linguistic Borrowing
          Pidgins
BT   Sociolinguistics
RT   Bidialectalism
          Code Switching (Language)

          Contrastive Linguistics
          Diachronic Linguistics
          Dialect Studies
          Diglossia
          Grammatical Acceptability
          Jargon
          Language
          Language Usage
          Urban Language

Languages   *JUL. 1966*
          Postings: 568   GC: 440
SN   (Note: Use a more specific term if possi-
          ble)
NT   African Languages
          Afro Asiatic Languages
          American Indian Languages
          American Sign Language
          Australian Aboriginal Languages
          Austro Asiatic Languages
          Basque
          Burushaski
          Caucasian Languages
          Classical Languages
          Creoles
          Dialects
          Dravidian Languages
          Eskimo Aleut Languages
          Indo European Languages
          Japanese
          Korean
          Malayo Polynesian Languages
          Modern Languages
          Pidgins
          Sino Tibetan Languages
          Uralic Altaic Languages
          Vietnamese
RT   Bilingualism
          Conversational Language Courses
          Etymology
          FLES
          Foreign Language Books
          Foreign Language Films
          Foreign Language Periodicals
          Glottochronology
          Idioms
          Intensive Language Courses
          Language
          Language Classification
          Language Dominance
          Language Enrichment
          Language Enrollment
          Language Fluency
          Language Laboratories
          Language Maintenance
          Language Minorities
          Language of Instruction
          Language Patterns
          Language Planning
          Language Proficiency
          Language Research
          Language Skills
          Language Standardization
          Language Teachers
          Language Tests
          Language Universals
          Language Usage
          Languages for Special Purposes
          Middle English
          Monolingualism
          Multilevel Classes (Second Language
              Instruction)
          Multilingual Materials
          Multilingualism
          Mutual Intelligibility
          Natural Language Processing
          Notional Functional Syllabi
          Old English
          Second Language Instruction
          Word Frequency
          Word Order

Languages for Special Purposes
                                      APR. 1975
          Postings: 765   GC: 440
SN   Languages taught to or learned by non-
          native speakers who need a certain spe-
          cialized foreign language capability in
          their studies, profession, or trade
NT   English for Special Purposes
BT   Language

          RT   Languages
          Second Language Instruction
          Second Language Learning

Lao   *JUL. 1966*
          Postings: 69   GC: 440
UF   Laotian
BT   Sino Tibetan Languages

Laotian
USE   Lao

Laotian Americans
USE   Asian Americans
AND   Laotians

Laotians   *MAR. 1980*
          Postings: 136   GC: 560
UF   Laotian Americans #
BT   Indochinese
RT   Asian Americans
          Cambodians
          Hmong People
          Vietnamese People

Lap Belts
USE   Restraints (Vehicle Safety)

Laps
USE   Learning Modules

Large Cities
USE   Urban Areas

Large Group Instruction   *JUL. 1966*
          Postings: 397   GC: 310
SN   Teaching of students in large classroom
          situations (Note: Do not confuse with
          "Mass Instruction")
BT   Group Instruction
RT   Mass Instruction
          Small Group Instruction
          Teaching Methods

Large Scale Production
USE   Mass Production

Large Type Books
USE   Large Type Materials

Large Type Materials   *JUL. 1966*
          Postings: 125   GC: 220
UF   Large Type Books
BT   Reading Materials
RT   Instructional Materials
          Low Vision Aids
          Magnification Methods
          Partial Vision
          Reading Instruction
          Sensory Aids

Laser Disks
USE   Optical Disks

Laser Oscillators
USE   Lasers

Lasers   *DEC. 1969*
          Postings: 351   GC: 490
UF   Laser Oscillators
          Light Amplifiers (Lasers)
          Optical Masers
RT   Electronics
          Energy
          Holography
          Light
          Optical Data Disks
          Optical Disks
          Optics
          Physics
          Radiation

= Two or more Descriptors are used to represent this term.
The term's main entry shows the appropriate coordination.

Science Equipment
Semiconductor Devices
Spectroscopy

Latchkey Children   *APR. 1986*
Postings: 236   GC: 510
SN   Children left alone or unsupervised before or after the school day
BT   Children
RT   Child Welfare
     Employed Parents
     School Age Day Care

Late Adolescence
USE   Late Adolescents

Late Adolescents   *JUL. 1994*
Postings: 154   GC: 120
SN   Age group between, and overlapping with, "Adolescents" and "Young Adults"—approximately 16–23 years of age
UF   Late Adolescence
     Older Adolescents
BT   Age Groups
RT   Adolescents
     College Students
     Young Adults
     Youth

Late Registration   *AUG. 1980*
Postings: 23   GC: 320
SN   Enrolling after the school semester, quarter, etc., has begun (Note: For the age of students when they enter school, see "School Entrance Age")
BT   School Registration
RT   Admission (School)
     Continuation Students

Latent Trait Theory (1980 1990)
USE   Item Response Theory

Lateral Dominance   *JUL. 1966*
Postings: 443   GC: 120
SN   Consistent preference for the use of the muscles and limbs on one side of the body, generally thought to be the result of the dominance of one hemisphere of the brain over the other
UF   Left Right Preference
NT   Handedness
BT   Physical Characteristics
RT   Brain Hemisphere Functions
     Motor Development
     Neurological Organization
     Physical Development
     Psychomotor Skills

Lathes
USE   Machine Tools

Latin   *JUL. 1966*
Postings: 786   GC: 440
BT   Classical Languages
     Romance Languages
RT   Classical Literature
     Latin Literature

Latin American Culture   *JUL. 1966*
Postings: 720   GC: 560
SN   Culture of the Caribbean Islands, Mexico, Central and South America, including the culture of non-Hispanic peoples in that area—e.g., Jamaicans, Haitians, Guyanese, etc.
NT   Luso Brazilian Culture
     Puerto Rican Culture
BT   Culture
RT   American Indian Culture
     Black Culture
     Hispanic American Culture
     Latin American History
     Latin American Literature
     Latin Americans

Latin American History   *MAR. 1980*
Postings: 284   GC: 430
SN   History of the Caribbean Islands, Mexico, Central and South America, including the history of non-Hispanic peoples in that area—e.g., Jamaicans, Haitians, Guyanese, etc.
UF   Central American History
     South American History
BT   History
RT   American Indian History
     Black History
     Hispanic Americans
     Latin American Culture
     Latin American Literature
     Latin Americans
     Western Civilization

Latin American Literature   *MAR. 1980*
Postings: 120   GC: 430
SN   Literature of Mexico, Central and South America, and the Caribbean countries (Note: See also the Identifier "Mexican Literature"—prior to Mar80, the instruction "Mexican Literature, USE Spanish American Literature" was carried in the Thesaurus)
UF   American Literature (1966 1980) (Latin America)
     Central American Literature
     South American Literature
BT   Literature
RT   American Indian Literature
     Black Literature
     Hispanic American Literature
     Latin American Culture
     Latin American History
     Latin Americans
     Mexican American Literature

Latin Americans   *MAR. 1980*
Postings: 421   GC: 560
SN   Indigenous peoples, permanent residents, or citizens of the Caribbean Islands, Mexico, Central and South America, including non-Hispanic peoples in that area—e.g., Jamaicans, Haitians, Guyanese, etc.
UF   Central Americans
     South Americans
NT   Cubans
     Dominicans
     Haitians
     Maya (People)
     Mexicans
     Puerto Ricans
BT   Groups
RT   American Indians
     Hispanic Americans
     Latin American Culture
     Latin American History
     Latin American Literature

Latin Literature   *JUL. 1970*
Postings: 125   GC: 430
UF   Roman Literature
BT   Classical Literature
RT   Ancient History
     Classical Languages
     Latin

Latvian   *NOV. 1970*
Postings: 11   GC: 440
BT   Baltic Languages

Laundry Drycleaning Occupations   *MAR. 1980*
Postings: 35   GC: 640
UF   Drycleaning Laundry Occupations
BT   Service Occupations
RT   Clothing
     Clothing Instruction
     Home Economics Skills
     Needle Trades
     Occupational Home Economics

Spanish Culture
Western Civilization

Semiskilled Occupations
Textiles Instruction

Law Enforcement   *JUL. 1966*
Postings: 1,387   GC: 610
UF   Citations (Legal)
NT   Police Action
     Sentencing
RT   Compliance (Legal)
     Crime
     Crime Prevention
     Criminal Law
     Delinquency
     Delinquency Prevention
     Evidence (Legal)
     Fines (Penalties)
     Human Services
     Immigration Inspectors
     Laws
     National Security
     Police
     School Security
     Security Personnel
     Social Control

Law Enforcement Officers
USE   Police

Law Libraries   *JUL. 1966*
Postings: 202   GC: 710
SN   Libraries consisting of law-related materials and providing services to those interested in legal practices
UF   Legislative Reference Libraries (1968 1980)
BT   Special Libraries
RT   Depository Libraries
     Government Libraries
     Law Schools
     Laws
     Research Libraries

Law of Nations
USE   International Law

Law of Primacy
USE   Primacy Effect

Law Related Education   *AUG. 1986*
Postings: 1,239   GC: 400
SN   Learning activities, often at grades k-12 but sometimes at postsecondary levels, concerned with law and legal systems (Note: Do not confuse with "Legal Education (Professions)"—prior to Aug86, this concept was indexed by "Legal Education")
BT   Education
RT   Citizenship Education
     Civics
     Civil Law
     Constitutional Law
     Criminal Law
     International Law
     Juvenile Justice
     Laws
     Police Education
     Social Studies

Law School Applicants
USE   College Applicants
AND   Law Schools

Law School Education
USE   Legal Education (Professions)

Law Schools   *JUL. 1966*
Postings: 731   GC: 340
SN   Schools or colleges, usually affiliated with universities, that prepare students who have completed baccalaureate programs to be attorneys—typical degrees granted include Doctor of Jurisprudence, Doctor of Law, and Master of Law
UF   Law School Applicants #

BT   Colleges
RT   Law Libraries
     Law Students
     Lawyers
     Legal Education (Professions)
     Professional Education

Law Students   *MAR. 1980*
Postings: 246   GC: 360
SN   Students enrolled in law schools and pursuing a professional education for preparation as attorneys
BT   Graduate Students
RT   Law Schools
     Lawyers
     Legal Education (Professions)
     Professional Education

Lawmakers
USE   Legislators

Lawn Maintenance
USE   Turf Management

Laws   *JUL. 1966*
Postings: 2,291   GC: 610
SN   Rules of conduct or action established by authority, society, or custom
NT   Civil Law
     Constitutional Law
     Criminal Law
     International Law
     School Law
BT   Standards
RT   Civil Liberties
     Civil Rights Legislation
     Codification
     Compliance (Legal)
     Court Litigation
     Courts
     Discriminatory Legislation
     Drug Legislation
     Due Process
     Educational Legislation
     Educational Malpractice
     Equal Protection
     Evidence (Legal)
     Federal Legislation
     Freedom of Information
     Hearings
     International Crimes
     Justice
     Juvenile Justice
     Labor Legislation
     Law Enforcement
     Law Libraries
     Law Related Education
     Lawyers
     Legal Education (Professions)
     Legal Responsibility
     Legislation
     Libel and Slander
     Local Legislation
     Malpractice
     Minimum Wage Legislation
     Negligence
     Ownership
     Privacy
     Public Health Legislation
     Recreation Legislation
     Sanctions
     School Attendance Legislation
     State Legislation
     Torts

Lawyers   *JAN. 1969*
Postings: 942   GC: 640
UF   Advocates (Law)
     Attorneys
     Barristers
     Solicitors (Law)
BT   Professional Personnel
RT   Court Judges
     Court Litigation
     Law Schools
     Law Students
     Laws
     Legal Aid
     Legal Assistants

= Two or more Descriptors are used to represent this term.
The term's main entry shows the appropriate coordination.

Legal Education (Professions)
Legal Problems

Lay People   *MAR. 1980*
Postings: 134   GC: 520
SN   People lacking special training or knowl-
edge in a given field—also refers to
members of the laity as opposed to the
clergy
UF   Laymen (1966 1980)
    Nonspecialists
NT   Lay Teachers
BT   Groups
RT   Church Workers
    Clergy
    Professional Personnel

Lay Teachers   *JUL. 1966*
Postings: 76   GC: 360
BT   Lay People
    Teachers
RT   Catholic Schools
    Church Workers
    Parochial Schools
    Religious Education

Laymen (1966 1980)
USE   Lay People

Layout (Publications)   *JUL. 1973*
Postings: 940   GC: 720
UF   Format (Publications)
BT   Graphic Arts
RT   Captions
    Editors
    Headlines
    Journalism
    Newspapers
    Photography
    Photojournalism
    Printed Materials
    Printing
    Publications

Lc Classification
USE   Library of Congress Classification

Lea
USE   School Districts

Lead Lecture Plan (1966 1980)
USE   Lecture Method

Lead Poisoning   *APR. 1973*
Postings: 189   GC: 210
BT   Poisoning
RT   Anemia
    Neurological Impairments
    Occupational Diseases
    Physical Health
    Pollution
    Special Health Problems

Leader Participation (1966 1980)
USE   Leadership

Leaderless Groups
USE   Self Directed Groups

Leaders   *MAR. 1980*
Postings: 748   GC: 510
UF   Adult Leaders (1967 1980)
    Team Leader (Teaching) (1966
    1980) #
NT   Community Leaders
    Youth Leaders
BT   Groups
RT   Leaders Guides
    Leadership
    Leadership Qualities
    Leadership Responsibility
    Leadership Styles

Leadership Training
Supervisors

Leaders Guides   *JUL. 1966*
Postings: 456   GC: 730
BT   Guides
RT   Leaders
    Leadership
    Leadership Training

Leadership   *JUL. 1966*
Postings: 5,824   GC: 520
UF   Leader Participation (1966 1980)
NT   Black Leadership
    Informal Leadership
    Instructional Leadership
    Outdoor Leadership
    Student Leadership
BT   Ability
RT   Behavior
    Community Leaders
    Institutional Role
    Leaders
    Leaders Guides
    Leadership Qualities
    Leadership Responsibility
    Leadership Training
    Middle Management
    Nonauthoritarian Classes
    Supervision

Leadership Qualities   *JUL. 1966*
Postings: 2,609   GC: 520
RT   Administrator Effectiveness
    Administrator Qualifications
    Collegiality
    Leaders
    Leadership
    Leadership Responsibility
    Leadership Training
    Prestige

Leadership Responsibility   *JUL. 1966*
Postings: 2,087   GC: 520
BT   Responsibility
RT   Administrator Responsibility
    Business Responsibility
    Church Responsibility
    Citizenship Responsibility
    Instructional Leadership
    Leaders
    Leadership
    Leadership Qualities
    School Responsibility
    Social Responsibility
    Teacher Responsibility

Leadership Styles   *JUL. 1966*
Postings: 2,166   GC: 520
BT   Behavior
RT   Administrator Behavior
    Leaders
    Supervisory Methods
    Teaching Styles

Leadership Training   *JUL. 1966*
Postings: 3,661   GC: 400
BT   Training
RT   Black Leadership
    Instructional Leadership
    Leaders
    Leaders Guides
    Leadership
    Leadership Qualities
    Management Development
    Outdoor Leadership
    Student Leadership
    Supervisory Training
    Trainers
    Youth Leaders

Leaflets
USE   Pamphlets

Lean Fat Ratio
USE   Body Composition

Learned Helplessness
USE   Helplessness

Learner Autonomy
USE   Personal Autonomy

Learner Control
USE   Learner Controlled Instruction

Learner Controlled Instruction   *APR. 1990*
Postings: 717   GC: 310
SN   Instruction in which the individual learner
has considerable influence over what is
taught, how it is taught, and the pace of
instruction—often used in relation to
student interaction with courseware
UF   Learner Control
    Student Controlled Learning
BT   Teaching Methods
RT   Active Learning
    Autoinstructional Aids
    Computer Assisted Instruction
    Courseware
    Discovery Learning
    Independent Study
    Individualized Instruction
    Intentional Learning
    Interactive Video
    Learning Laboratories
    Pacing
    Personal Autonomy
    Programmed Instruction
    Programmed Instructional Materials
    Student Role
    Teaching Machines

Learner Outcomes
USE   Outcomes of Education

Learning   *JUL. 1966*
Postings: 5,427   GC: 110
SN   Process of acquiring knowledge, atti-
tudes, or skills from study, instruction,
or experience (Note: Use a more specific
term if possible)
UF   Learning Characteristics (1968 1980)
NT   Active Learning
    Adult Learning
    Associative Learning
    Aural Learning
    Cooperative Learning
    Discovery Learning
    Discrimination Learning
    Experiential Learning
    Incidental Learning
    Intentional Learning
    Lifelong Learning
    Mastery Learning
    Multisensory Learning
    Nonverbal Learning
    Observational Learning
    Prior Learning
    Problem Based Learning
    Rote Learning
    Second Language Learning
    Sequential Learning
    Serial Learning
    Symbolic Learning
    Transfer of Training
    Transformative Learning
    Verbal Learning
    Visual Learning
RT   Advance Organizers
    Aptitude
    Cognitive Processes
    Constructivism (Learning)
    Education
    Educational Environment
    Epistemology
    Individual Development
    Instruction
    Knowledge Level
    Learning Activities
    Learning Experience
    Learning Modalities
    Learning Modules
    Learning Motivation
    Learning Plateaus
    Learning Problems

Learning Processes
Learning Readiness
Learning Strategies
Learning Theories
Mnemonics
Nature Nurture Controversy
Recall (Psychology)
Schemata (Cognition)
Scholarship
Time Factors (Learning)

Learning Activities   *JUL. 1966*
Postings: 26,959   GC: 310
SN   Activities engaged in by the learner for
the purpose of acquiring certain skills,
concepts, or knowledge, whether guided
by an instructor or not (Note: Do not
confuse with mental process terms, e.g.,
"Cognitive Processes" or "Learning Proc-
esses")
UF   Integrated Learning #
NT   Study
BT   Activities
RT   Active Learning
    Activity Units
    Advance Organizers
    Class Activities
    Cooperative Learning
    Directed Reading Activity
    Discovery Learning
    Educational Games
    Experiential Learning
    Learning
    Learning Experience
    Learning Modules
    Learning Strategies
    Negative Practice
    Observational Learning
    Problem Based Learning
    Problem Sets
    School Activities
    Time on Task

Learning Activity Packages
USE   Learning Modules

Learning Activity Packets
USE   Learning Modules

Learning Centers (Classroom)   *MAR. 1980*
Postings: 520   GC: 310
SN   Areas arranged by teachers (usually within
the classroom) in which materials are
provided so that individuals or very small
groups can explore a topic without direct
instruction from the teacher (Note: Prior
to Mar80, the instruction "Learning Centers, USE Learning Laboratories" was
carried in the Thesaurus)
UF   Centers of Interest (1966 1980)
    Interest Centers (Classroom)
    Learning Stations (Classroom)
BT   Educational Facilities
    Resource Centers
RT   Cooperative Learning
    Discovery Learning
    Experiential Learning
    Humanistic Education
    Individualized Instruction
    Open Education
    Writing Laboratories

Learning Characteristics (1968 1980)
USE   Learning

Learning Contracts
USE   Performance Contracts

Learning Cycles
USE   Learning Processes

Learning Difficulties (1966 1980)
USE   Learning Problems

= Two or more Descriptors are used to represent this term.
The term's main entry shows the appropriate coordination.

Learning Disabilities — JUL. 1966
Postings: 12,229 — GC: 220
SN Category in federal legislation referring to disorders involved in understanding or using language, manifested in imperfect ability to listen, think, speak, read, write, spell, or do mathematical calculations (Note: Use "Language Impairments" if the disability is being considered in a non-educational setting—do not confuse with "Learning Problems")
UF Specific Learning Disabilities
BT Disabilities
RT Academic Failure
Aphasia
Attention Deficit Disorders
Cognitive Processes
Cognitive Restructuring
Communication Disorders
Developmental Disabilities
Dyslexia
Educational Diagnosis
Emotional Problems
Hyperactivity
Language Impairments
Learning Problems
Minimal Brain Dysfunction
Neurological Impairments
Perceptual Impairments
Reading Difficulties
Recall (Psychology)
Recognition (Psychology)
Remedial Reading
Writing Difficulties

Learning Experience — JUL. 1966
Postings: 2,430 — GC: 110
SN Any experience that results in learning (Note: Prior to Jun78, this term was frequently used for "Experiential Learning")
NT Clinical Experience
BT Experience
RT Experiential Learning
Learning
Learning Activities
Learning Readiness
Mnemonics
Prior Learning

Learning Kits
USE Learning Modules

Learning Laboratories — JUL. 1966
Postings: 1,232 — GC: 920
SN Facilities with programmed or autoinstructional materials and the equipment required for their display—used primarily for independent study or individualized instruction (Note: Prior to Mar80, the instruction "Learning Centers, USE Learning Laboratories" was carried in the Thesaurus)
UF Autoinstructional Laboratories (1967 1980)
NT Language Laboratories
BT Educational Facilities
Laboratories
RT Audiovisual Centers
Autoinstructional Aids
Computer Centers
Dial Access Information Systems
Educational Media
Electronic Classrooms
Independent Study
Individualized Instruction
Learner Controlled Instruction
Learning Resources Centers
Programmed Instruction
Reading Centers
Skill Centers
Writing Laboratories

Learning Maturation Controversy
USE Nature Nurture Controversy

Learning Modalities — OCT. 1971
Postings: 943 — GC: 110
SN The sense modalities used in learning—

for example, information may be processed visually, aurally, or tactually
RT Aural Learning
Cognitive Mapping
Cognitive Style
Dimensional Preference
Intermode Differences
Kinesthetic Perception
Learning
Learning Processes
Learning Strategies
Multisensory Learning
Nonverbal Learning
Perceptual Development
Perceptual Motor Learning
Sensory Experience
Tactual Perception
Teaching Methods
Thinking Skills
Verbal Learning
Visual Learning

Learning Modules — OCT. 1976
Postings: 5,447 — GC: 730
SN Packets of subject-related teaching materials containing objectives, directions for use, and test items
UF Laps
Learning Activity Packages
Learning Activity Packets
Learning Kits
Learning Packages
Modular Learning
BT Instructional Materials
RT Behavioral Objectives
Curriculum Guides
Independent Study
Individualized Instruction
Learning
Learning Activities
Learning Strategies
Minicourses
Programmed Instructional Materials
Resource Units
Teaching Guides
Teaching Methods
Units of Study

Learning Motivation — JUL. 1966
Postings: 2,496 — GC: 110
BT Motivation
RT Academic Aspiration
Intentional Learning
Learning
Learning Readiness
Learning Strategies
Reading Motivation
Self Motivation
Student Motivation

Learning Objectives
USE Behavioral Objectives

Learning Packages
USE Learning Modules

Learning Plateaus — JUL. 1966
Postings: 60 — GC: 110
SN Time periods during which there is no evidence of learning progress (Note: Prior to Mar80, the use of this term was not restricted by a Scope Note)
RT Academic Achievement
Achievement
Knowledge Level
Learning
Learning Processes
Learning Theories
Psychological Characteristics
Skill Development
Student Improvement

Learning Problems — MAR. 1980
Postings: 2,221 — GC: 110
SN Category in federal legislation referring to problems encountered in the process of learning—may be the result of visual, hearing, or motor impairments, men-

tal retardation, behavioral disorders, or health impairments, or of cultural, environmental, or economic disadvantage (Note: Do not confuse with "Learning Disabilities")
UF Learning Difficulties (1966 1980)
BT Problems
RT Academic Achievement
Academic Failure
Behavior Disorders
Diagnostic Teaching
Educational Diagnosis
Educationally Disadvantaged
Hearing Impairments
Learning
Learning Disabilities
Learning Readiness
Low Achievement
Mental Retardation
Motor Development
Prereferral Intervention
Reading Difficulties
Remedial Instruction
Remedial Reading
Slow Learners
Special Health Problems
Student Problems
Underachievement
Visual Impairments
Writing Difficulties

Learning Processes — JUL. 1966
Postings: 12,670 — GC: 110
UF Educational Processes
Learning Cycles
NT Behavior Chaining
Cognitive Mapping
Concept Formation
Discovery Processes
Extinction (Psychology)
Generalization
Habituation
Memorization
Primacy Effect
BT Cognitive Processes
RT Aptitude Treatment Interaction
Association (Psychology)
Cognitive Structures
Conditioning
Conservation (Concept)
Contingency Management
Criticism
Deduction
Encoding (Psychology)
Error Correction
Feedback
Heuristics
Induction
Inquiry
Intentional Learning
Interference (Language)
Interlanguage
Intuition
Language Processing
Learning
Learning Modalities
Learning Plateaus
Learning Readiness
Learning Strategies
Learning Theories
Mediation Theory
Memory
Mental Computation
Metacognition
Misconceptions
Mnemonics
Multiple Intelligences
Observational Learning
Psychoeducational Methods
Questioning Techniques
Recall (Psychology)
Recognition (Psychology)
Shift Studies
Thinking Skills
Transformative Learning

Learning Readiness — JUL. 1966
Postings: 828 — GC: 120
SN State or condition of an individual that makes it possible for him or her to engage profitably in a given learning

activity—learning readiness depends on such factors as past experiences, cognitive development, affective factors, and motivation as well as on the instructional methods and materials to be used
BT Readiness
RT Cognitive Development
Emotional Development
Learning
Learning Experience
Learning Motivation
Learning Problems
Learning Processes
Mastery Learning
Reading Readiness
School Entrance Age
School Readiness
Writing Readiness

Learning Reinforcement
USE Reinforcement

Learning Resources
USE Educational Resources

Learning Resources Centers — MAR. 1980
Postings: 3,765 — GC: 710
SN Areas within schools that provide services and equipment for the use of an integrated collection of print and nonprint materials (Note: Do not confuse with "Learning Laboratories" or "Learning Centers (Classroom)")
UF Instructional Materials Centers (1966 1980)
LRC
School Media Centers
BT Educational Facilities
Resource Centers
RT Academic Libraries
Audiovisual Aids
Audiovisual Centers
Educational Media
Instructional Materials
Learning Laboratories
Librarian Teacher Cooperation
Media Specialists
Resource Materials
School Libraries

Learning Specialists (1966 1980)
USE Specialists

Learning Stations (Classroom)
USE Learning Centers (Classroom)

Learning Strategies — OCT. 1983
Postings: 8,588 — GC: 110
SN Rules, principles, and procedures used to facilitate learning, frequently applicable to a variety of specific learning tasks (Note: For self-discovered, self-selected learning strategies, coordinate with "Cognitive Style")
UF Learning to Learn
NT Reading Strategies
BT Methods
RT Andragogy
Associative Learning
Behavioral Objectives
Classroom Techniques
Cognitive Development
Cognitive Processes
Cognitive Style
Concept Mapping
Cooperative Learning
Discovery Learning
Educational Strategies
Encoding (Psychology)
Experiential Learning
Heuristics
Inferences
Inquiry
Intentional Learning
Language Processing
Learning
Learning Activities
Learning Modalities

Learning Modules
Learning Motivation
Learning Processes
Mastery Learning
Memory
Metacognition
Mnemonics
Observational Learning
Pacing
Problem Based Learning
Problem Solving
Prompting
Psychoeducational Methods
Sequential Learning
Simulation
Skill Development
Study Skills
Task Analysis
Teaching Methods
Thinking Skills
Transfer of Training
Wait Time
Writing Strategies

Learning Style
USE   Cognitive Style

Learning Theories   *JUL. 1966*
       Postings: 7,984   GC: 810
UF   Transformation Theory (Adult Learn-
        ing) #
NT   Constructivism (Learning)
BT   Theories
RT   Behaviorism
      Cognitive Processes
      Cognitive Restructuring
      Conditioning
      Context Effect
      Generalization
      Learning
      Learning Plateaus
      Learning Processes
      Mnemonics
      Multiple Intelligences
      Paired Associate Learning
      Piagetian Theory
      Primacy Effect
      Rote Learning
      Schemata (Cognition)
      Self Efficacy
      Serial Learning
      Transformative Learning

Learning to Learn
USE   Learning Strategies

Least Restrictive Environment (Disabled)
USE   Mainstreaming

Least Squares Statistics   *OCT. 1980*
       Postings: 289   GC: 820
SN   Statistics that are designed to provide
      estimates that minimize the probability
      of large errors by minimizing the sum
      of squared errors (the "least squares
      method" fits a curve to a given set of
      data such that the sum of the squares of
      the distances from each point of the data
      to the fitted curve is a minimum)
BT   Statistical Analysis
      Statistics
RT   Correlation
      Error of Measurement
      Factor Analysis
      Predictive Measurement
      Probability
      Regression (Statistics)
      Statistical Significance

Leather   *MAR. 1980*
       Postings: 17   GC: 910
SN   (Note: Prior to Mar80, the instruction
      "Leather Crafts, USE Handicrafts" was
      carried in the Thesaurus)
UF   Leather Crafts
RT   Art Materials
      Handicrafts

Industrial Arts
Patternmaking

Leather Crafts
USE   Leather

Leave of Absence (1968 1980)
USE   Leaves of Absence

Leaves of Absence   *MAR. 1980*
       Postings: 717   GC: 630
SN   Authorized absences from duty or em-
      ployment
UF   Leave of Absence (1968 1980)
NT   Sabbatical Leaves
RT   Attendance
      Employee Absenteeism
      Fringe Benefits
      Holidays
      Personnel Policy
      Reentry Workers
      Released Time
      Scope of Bargaining
      Stopouts
      Teacher Employment Benefits
      Vacations

Lecture Method   *MAR. 1980*
       Postings: 1,651   GC: 310
SN   Teaching method in which information is
      presented orally to a class with a mini-
      mal amount of class participation
UF   Lead Lecture Plan (1966 1980)
      Lecture (1966 1980)
BT   Teaching Methods
RT   Conventional Instruction
      Discussion (Teaching Technique)
      Speeches

Lecture (1966 1980)
USE   Lecture Method

Left Handed Writer   *JUL. 1966*
       Postings: 81   GC: 120
BT   Groups
      Handedness
RT   Handwriting

Left Right Preference
USE   Lateral Dominance

Legal Aid   *JUL. 1966*
       Postings: 398   GC: 520
UF   Legal Aid Projects (1966 1980)
      Legal Services
RT   Advocacy
      Child Advocacy
      Eligibility
      Lawyers
      Legal Assistants
      Legal Costs
      Legal Problems

Legal Aid Projects (1966 1980)
USE   Legal Aid

Legal Assistants   *DEC. 1976*
       Postings: 77   GC: 640
SN   Trained paraprofessionals who, under a
      lawyer's supervision or on legal authori-
      zation, perform certain legal activities
      traditionally carried out only by lawyers
UF   Paralegal Education #
      Paralegals
BT   Paraprofessional Personnel
RT   Lawyers
      Legal Aid
      Legal Education (Professions)
      Legal Problems

Legal Costs   *JUL. 1966*
       Postings: 52   GC: 620
BT   Costs

RT   Legal Aid

Legal Decisions
USE   Court Litigation

Legal Education (Professions)   *AUG. 1986*
       Postings: 487   GC: 400
SN   Programs of academic study within a
      law school or other postsecondary insti-
      tution that prepare students to enter the
      legal profession as attorneys or paralegals
      (Note: Do not confuse with "Law Related
      Education"—prior to Aug86, this con-
      cept was indexed by "Legal Education"
      and "Professional Education")
UF   Law School Education
      Paralegal Education #
BT   Professional Education
RT   Civil Law
      Constitutional Law
      Criminal Law
      International Law
      Law Schools
      Law Students
      Laws
      Lawyers
      Legal Assistants

Legal Education (1977 1986)   *AUG. 1986*
       Postings: 1,584   GC: 400
SN   Invalid Descriptor—see "Law Related
      Education" and "Legal Education (Pro-
      fessions)"—(Note: Includes the former
      postings of "Law Instruction," merged
      here in Jun77)

Legal Judgment
USE   Court Litigation

Legal Problems   *JUL. 1966*
       Postings: 4,017   GC: 610
BT   Problems
RT   Compliance (Legal)
      Court Litigation
      Discriminatory Legislation
      Educational Malpractice
      Evidence (Legal)
      Financial Exigency
      Lawyers
      Legal Aid
      Legal Assistants
      Legal Responsibility
      Libel and Slander
      Loan Default
      Malpractice
      Negligence
      Torts

Legal Responsibility   *JUL. 1966*
       Postings: 5,184   GC: 610
UF   Liability (Responsibility)
NT   Trust Responsibility (Government)
BT   Responsibility
RT   Accountability
      Categorical Aid
      Child Support
      Civil Law
      Compliance (Legal)
      Conflict of Interest
      Contracts
      Copyrights
      Court Judges
      Court Litigation
      Educational Malpractice
      Evidence (Legal)
      Financial Exigency
      Fines (Penalties)
      Guilt
      In Loco Parentis
      Indemnity Bonds
      Intellectual Property
      Laws
      Legal Problems
      Libel and Slander
      Licensing Examinations (Professions)
      Loan Repayment
      Malpractice
      Negligence

Ownership
Patents
Risk Management
Torts
Treaties

Legal Secretaries
USE   Secretaries

Legal Segregation (1966 1980)
USE   De Jure Segregation

Legal Services
USE   Legal Aid

Legends   *JUL. 1966*
       Postings: 551   GC: 430
BT   Literary Genres
      Literature
RT   American Indian Literature
      Classical Literature
      Didacticism
      Epics
      Fairy Tales
      Fiction
      Folk Culture
      Medieval Literature
      Metaphors
      Mythology
      Oral Tradition

Legislation   *JUL. 1966*
       Postings: 2,537   GC: 610
SN   The enactments of, or matters under
      consideration by, a legislative body (Note:
      Use a more specific term if possible)
NT   Civil Rights Legislation
      Discriminatory Legislation
      Educational Legislation
      Federal Legislation
      Labor Legislation
      Local Legislation
      Minimum Wage Legislation
      Public Health Legislation
      Recreation Legislation
      State Legislation
RT   Compliance (Legal)
      Government (Administrative Body)
      Hearings
      Laws
      Legislators
      Lobbying
      Policy Formation
      Political Issues
      Politics
      Public Policy

Legislative Discrimination
USE   Discriminatory Legislation

Legislative Reference Libraries (1968 1980)
USE   Law Libraries

Legislators   *JUL. 1969*
       Postings: 771   GC: 610
UF   Congressmen
      Congresswomen
      Lawmakers
      Representatives
      Senators
BT   Public Officials
RT   City Officials
      County Officials
      Court Judges
      Federal Legislation
      Legislation
      Lobbying
      Local Legislation
      State Legislation
      State Officials

Leisure
USE   Leisure Time

= Two or more Descriptors are used to represent this term.
The term's main entry shows the appropriate coordination.

Leisure Counseling
USE Leisure Education

Leisure Education   *OCT. 1983*
  Postings: 227   GC: 400
SN Organized activities intended to help in-
  dividuals or groups use non-work time
  in a manner conducive to physical and
  mental well-being
UF Leisure Counseling
BT Education
RT Leisure Time
  Recreation
  Recreationists

Leisure Time   *JUL. 1966*
  Postings: 1,939   GC: 470
UF Leisure
RT Holidays
  Leisure Education
  Recreation
  Recreational Activities
  Recreationists
  Vacations
  Work Ethic

Leisure Time Reading
USE Recreational Reading

Leitmotifs
USE Motifs

Leitmotivs
USE Motifs

Lesbianism   *MAR. 1980*
  Postings: 451   GC: 120
UF Female Homosexuality
BT Homosexuality
RT Bisexuality
  Females
  Homophobia
  Sexual Orientation

Less Commonly Taught Languages
USE Uncommonly Taught Languages

Lesson Notes
USE Lesson Plans

Lesson Observation Criteria *JUL. 1966*
  Postings: 212   GC: 820
SN Rules or standards used by observers to
  evaluate teachers' lessons and class-
  room performances
BT Criteria
RT Classroom Observation Techniques
  Clinical Supervision (of Teachers)
  Lesson Plans
  Observation
  Student Teaching
  Teacher Evaluation

Lesson Plans   *JUL. 1966*
  Postings: 6,215   GC: 730
UF Lesson Notes
RT Curriculum Guides
  Lesson Observation Criteria
  Planning
  Units of Study

Lesson Units
USE Units of Study

Letter Sound Correspondence
USE Phoneme Grapheme Correspondence

Letters (Alphabet)   *MAR. 1971*
  Postings: 509   GC: 450
BT Orthographic Symbols
RT Alphabets
  Graphemes

Literacy
Phonemes

Letters (Correspondence)   *AUG. 1968*
  Postings: 1,050   GC: 720
UF Correspondence (Letters)
  Epistles (1970 1980)
BT Verbal Communication
RT Business Correspondence
  Interpersonal Communication
  Literature
  Manuscripts
  Writing (Composition)

Lexicography   *JUL. 1966*
  Postings: 413   GC: 710
SN The writing or compilation of dictionar-
  ies or thesauri (Note: Do not confuse
  with "Lexicology")
BT Technology
RT Definitions
  Dictionaries
  Etymology
  Glossaries
  Glottochronology
  Lexicology
  Thesauri
  Vocabulary Development

Lexicology   *JUL. 1966*
  Postings: 757   GC: 710
SN Study of the vocabulary or words of a
  language (Note: Do not confuse with
  "Lexicography")
BT Semantics
RT Comparative Analysis
  Componential Analysis
  Contrastive Linguistics
  Definitions
  Diachronic Linguistics
  Dictionaries
  Etymology
  Glottochronology
  Language Arts
  Language Patterns
  Lexicography
  Linguistic Borrowing
  Morphology (Languages)
  Onomastics
  Vocabulary

Lexicons
USE Dictionaries

Liability (Responsibility)
USE Legal Responsibility

Libel and Slander   *DEC. 1989*
  Postings: 68   GC: 530
SN Any oral or printed false statements (in-
  cluding photographs or pictures) that
  injure another's reputation—also, the act
  of uttering, publishing, or broadcasting
  such statements
UF Defamation of Character
  Slander
RT Civil Liberties
  Constitutional Law
  Court Litigation
  Crime
  Educational Malpractice
  Freedom of Speech
  Laws
  Legal Problems
  Legal Responsibility
  Lying
  Malpractice
  Privacy
  Torts
  Verbal Abuse
  Victims of Crime

Liberal Arts   *JUL. 1966*
  Postings: 3,521   GC: 400
UF Liberal Arts Majors (1967 1980) #
NT Humanities
  Mathematics

Sciences
RT Academic Education
  Education Work Relationship
  General Education
  Technology

Liberal Arts Majors (1967 1980)
USE Liberal Arts
AND Majors (Students)

Liberal Education
USE General Education

Liberalism   *JAN. 1985*
  Postings: 349   GC: 520
SN Philosophy or disposition that seeks to
  use social and political institutions to
  foster human development and well-
  being—originally advocated freedom
  from government encroachment, but cur-
  rently endorses government interven-
  tion when necessary to ensure individual
  welfare
RT Conservatism
  Government Role
  Humanistic Education
  Humanization
  Political Attitudes
  Political Socialization
  Social Values

Liberty
USE Freedom

Librarian Attitudes   *APR. 1990*
  Postings: 344   GC: 710
SN Attitudes, opinions, or views held by
  librarians
BT Attitudes
RT Librarians

Librarian Teacher Cooperation *SEP. 1994*
  Postings: 432   GC: 710
SN Cooperative interaction between librari-
  ans and teachers
UF Teacher Librarian Cooperation
BT Educational Cooperation
RT Academic Libraries
  Cooperative Planning
  Course Integrated Library Instruction
  Information Literacy
  Information Seeking
  Learning Resources Centers
  Librarians
  Library Instruction
  Library Services
  Media Specialists
  School Libraries
  Teachers

Librarians   *JUL. 1966*
  Postings: 5,104   GC: 710
UF Library Specialists
  Reference Librarians #
BT Information Scientists
  Library Personnel
RT Librarian Attitudes
  Librarian Teacher Cooperation
  Libraries
  Library Administrators
  Library Associations
  Library Directors
  Library Education
  Library Schools
  Library Science
  Library Technicians
  Media Specialists
  Search Intermediaries

Librarianship
USE Library Science

Libraries   *JUL. 1966*
  Postings: 3,234   GC: 710
SN Institutions housing collections of sys-

tematically acquired and organized in-
formation resources, and usually provid-
ing assistance to users (Note: Use a
more specific term if possible)
NT Academic Libraries
  Branch Libraries
  Childrens Libraries
  Depository Libraries
  Electronic Libraries
  Public Libraries
  Research Libraries
  School Libraries
  Special Libraries
BT Information Sources
  Institutions
RT Archives
  Information Services
  Integrated Library Systems
  Librarians
  Library Administration
  Library Administrators
  Library Automation
  Library Catalogs
  Library Collection Development
  Library Collections
  Library Cooperation
  Library Development
  Library Directors
  Library Equipment
  Library Expenditures
  Library Extension
  Library Facilities
  Library Funding
  Library Guides
  Library Instruction
  Library Materials
  Library Networks
  Library Personnel
  Library Planning
  Library Policy
  Library Research
  Library Role
  Library Science
  Library Services
  Library Skills
  Library Standards
  Library Statistics
  Library Surveys
  Library Technical Processes
  Library Technicians
  Resource Centers
  Shared Library Resources
  Users (Information)
  Weeding (Library)

Library Acquisition   *JUL. 1966*
  Postings: 1,533   GC: 710
SN Process of acquiring library materials by
  purchase, gift, or exchange, as well as
  the development and maintenance of
  essential records of these acquisitions
UF Book Buying
NT Library Material Selection
BT Library Technical Processes
RT Library Collection Development
  Library Materials
  Nonprint Media
  Publications
  Purchasing

Library Administration   *SEP. 1975*
  Postings: 2,693   GC: 710
SN Planning, organizing, directing, and con-
  trolling human or material resources
  within a library or library network
UF Library Management
BT Institutional Administration
RT Fines (Penalties)
  Information Management
  Libraries
  Library Administrators
  Library Collection Development
  Library Development
  Library Directors
  Library Expenditures
  Library Funding
  Library Planning
  Library Policy
  Library Role
  Library Services

= Two or more Descriptors are used to represent this term.
The term's main entry shows the appropriate coordination.

Library Standards
Library Technical Processes

Library Administrators   *AUG. 1996*
Postings: 43   GC: 710
SN   Library personnel whose responsibilities
     may include managing library staff, evalu-
     ating programs, planning and managing
     budgets, developing collections, and plan-
     ning library services (Note: Prior to
     Aug96, the instruction "Library Admin-
     istrators, USE Library Administration"
     was carried in the Thesaurus)
NT   Library Directors
BT   Administrators
     Library Personnel
RT   Librarians
     Libraries
     Library Administration

Library Aides
USE   Library Technicians

Library Aids
USE   Library Equipment

Library Associations   *JUL. 1966*
Postings: 1,412   GC: 520
SN   Groups of librarians organized on a lo-
     cal, district, state, national, or interna-
     tional basis for consideration of and ac-
     tion on professional matters
UF   Library Organizations
BT   Professional Associations
RT   Information Science
     Information Scientists
     Librarians
     Library Development
     Library Science

Library Automation   *AUG. 1971*
Postings: 3,577   GC: 710
SN   Application of computers and related
     equipment to the processing of data in
     libraries
UF   Library Mechanization
NT   Retrospective Conversion (Library
          Catalogs)
BT   Automation
RT   Bibliographic Databases
     Bibliographic Utilities
     Electronic Libraries
     Information Technology
     Integrated Library Systems
     Libraries
     Library Development
     Library Equipment
     Library Technical Processes

Library Cataloging
USE   Cataloging

Library Catalogs   *MAR. 1980*
Postings: 1,217   GC: 710
SN   Lists of library materials arranged in
     some definite order, which record, de-
     scribe, and index the resources of collec-
     tions, libraries, or groups of libraries
     (Note: Prior to Mar80, "Catalogs" was
     used to index this concept)
UF   Dictionary Catalogs (1968 1980)
     Divided Catalogs (1968 1980)
NT   Book Catalogs
     Card Catalogs
     Union Catalogs
BT   Catalogs
     Reference Materials
RT   Bibliographic Databases
     Bibliographic Records
     Bibliographies
     Cataloging
     Dewey Decimal Classification
     Discographies
     Filmographies
     Indexes
     Libraries
     Library Materials

Library of Congress Classification
Online Catalogs
Retrospective Conversion (Library
     Catalogs)
Subject Index Terms
Universal Decimal Classification

Library Circulation   *JUL. 1966*
Postings: 1,205   GC: 710
UF   Book Lending
     Library Loans
NT   Interlibrary Loans
BT   Library Services
RT   Fines (Penalties)
     Information Dissemination
     Integrated Library Systems
     Library Materials

Library Clerks
USE   Library Technicians

Library Clients
USE   Users (Information)

Library Collection Development   *APR. 1985*
Postings: 1,572   GC: 710
SN   Activities related to building, maintain-
     ing, evaluating, and expanding library
     collections—includes user needs assess-
     ment, budget management, selection pol-
     icy formation, resource sharing, and
     weeding (Note: Prior to Apr85, the in-
     struction "Collection Development (Li-
     braries), USE Library Acquisition" was
     carried in the Thesaurus)
UF   Collection Development (Libraries)
NT   Weeding (Library)
BT   Development
RT   Bibliometrics
     Libraries
     Library Acquisition
     Library Administration
     Library Collections
     Library Development
     Library Expenditures
     Library Material Selection
     Library Materials
     Library Planning
     Library Policy
     Library Research
     Library Standards
     Selection Tools
     User Needs (Information)

Library Collections   *JUL. 1966*
Postings: 3,989   GC: 710
SN   Libraries' organized holdings on particu-
     lar subjects
UF   Library Holdings
BT   Library Materials
RT   Archives
     Databases
     Dewey Decimal Classification
     Libraries
     Library Collection Development
     Library of Congress Classification
     Manuscripts
     Nonprint Media
     Publications
     Universal Decimal Classification
     Weeding (Library)

Library Cooperation   *JUL. 1966*
Postings: 2,260   GC: 710
BT   Institutional Cooperation
RT   Consortia
     Interlibrary Loans
     Libraries
     Library Networks
     Library Services
     Shared Library Resources
     Union Catalogs

Library Development   *APR. 1990*
Postings: 930   GC: 710
SN   The process of planning, organizing, and
     implementing growth or improvements

in library facilities, resources, services,
etc.—often refers to libraries in a particular country, state, or other geographic
area
BT   Development
RT   Developmental Programs
     Educational Development
     Libraries
     Library Administration
     Library Associations
     Library Automation
     Library Collection Development
     Library Facilities
     Library Funding
     Library Networks
     Library Planning
     Library Policy
     Library Research
     Library Services
     Library Standards
     Shared Library Resources

Library Directors   *AUG. 1996*
Postings: 122   GC: 710
SN   Chief executive officers of libraries or
     library systems responsible for overall
     direction and coordination of library serv-
     ices, resources, and programs
UF   Head Librarians
BT   Library Administrators
RT   Librarians
     Libraries
     Library Administration

Library Education   *JUL. 1966*
Postings: 2,629   GC: 400
SN   Education or training of library person-
     nel, including professionals and
     paraprofessionals, usually at the
     postsecondary level (Note: Do not con-
     fuse with "Library Instruction")
BT   Information Science Education
RT   Information Science
     Librarians
     Library Personnel
     Library Schools
     Library Science
     Library Technicians

Library Employees
USE   Library Personnel

Library Equipment   *JUL. 1966*
Postings: 519   GC: 910
SN   (Note: Prior to Mar80, the instruction
     "Library Aids, USE Library Facilities"
     was carried in the Thesaurus)
UF   Library Aids
NT   Bookmobiles
BT   Equipment
RT   Carrels
     Educational Equipment
     Libraries
     Library Automation
     Library Expenditures
     Library Facilities
     Library Materials

Library Expenditures   *JUL. 1966*
Postings: 1,284   GC: 620
BT   Expenditures
RT   Costs
     Libraries
     Library Administration
     Library Collection Development
     Library Equipment
     Library Facilities
     Library Funding
     Library Materials
     Library Policy
     Library Services
     Library Technical Processes
     Operating Expenses

Library Extension   *JUL. 1966*
Postings: 321   GC: 710
SN   Provision of special activities within

and/or outside libraries to draw attention
to and promote their services
BT   Extension Education
     Library Services
RT   Bookmobiles
     Information Dissemination
     Libraries
     Public Relations
     Publicity

Library Facilities   *JUL. 1966*
Postings: 1,562   GC: 920
SN   Structures or spaces that are constructed,
     installed, or established to serve speci-
     fied library functions
BT   Facilities
RT   Libraries
     Library Development
     Library Equipment
     Library Expenditures
     Library Guides
     Library Planning
     Study Facilities

Library Finance
USE   Library Funding

Library Fines
USE   Fines (Penalties)

Library Funding   *JUL. 1994*
Postings: 668   GC: 620
SN   The means, including both the sources
     and the processes of securing the funds,
     by which libraries pay for their operating
     expenses
UF   Library Finance
BT   Financial Support
RT   Capital
     Endowment Funds
     Federal Aid
     Fees
     Fund Raising
     Grants
     Libraries
     Library Administration
     Library Development
     Library Expenditures
     Library Planning
     Philanthropic Foundations
     State Aid

Library Guides   *JUL. 1966*
Postings: 403   GC: 730
SN   Handbooks designed to acquaint users
     with the functions, resources, and facili-
     ties of particular libraries
UF   Library Handbooks
BT   Guides
RT   Libraries
     Library Facilities
     Library Instruction
     Library Materials
     Library Policy
     Library Role
     Library Services

Library Handbooks
USE   Library Guides

Library Holdings
USE   Library Collections

Library Instruction   *JUL. 1966*
Postings: 2,420   GC: 400
SN   Training of patrons in the workings and
     use of the library (Note: Do not confuse
     with "Library Education"—prior to Mar80,
     the use of this term was not restricted by
     a Scope Note)
UF   Bibliographic Instruction
     Library Orientation
NT   Course Integrated Library Instruction
BT   Instruction
RT   Information Literacy
     Information Seeking

= Two or more Descriptors are used to represent this term.
The term's main entry shows the appropriate coordination.

Librarian Teacher Cooperation
Libraries
Library Guides
Library Skills
Orientation Materials
Users (Information)

Library Loans
USE　Library Circulation

Library Management
USE　Library Administration

Library Material Selection　　　　　*JUL. 1966*
　　　Postings: 1,533　　　　　　　　　GC: 710
SN　Professional choice of library materials
　　from a number of alternatives on the
　　basis of specified criteria
BT　Library Acquisition
　　Media Selection
RT　Library Collection Development
　　Library Materials
　　Nonprint Media
　　Publications
　　Reading Material Selection

Library Materials　　　　　　　　　*JUL. 1966*
　　　Postings: 2,838　　　　　　　　　GC: 710
SN　Books, periodicals, pamphlets, reports,
　　microforms, maps, records, tapes, and
　　other materials that are acquired by li-
　　braries (Note: Use a more specific term if
　　possible)
UF　Library Reference Materials #
NT　Library Collections
RT　Dewey Decimal Classification
　　Instructional Materials
　　Libraries
　　Library Acquisition
　　Library Catalogs
　　Library Circulation
　　Library Collection Development
　　Library Equipment
　　Library Expenditures
　　Library Guides
　　Library Material Selection
　　Library of Congress Classification
　　Library Planning
　　Library Services
　　Library Technical Processes
　　Nonprint Media
　　Printed Materials
　　Publications
　　Reference Materials
　　Research Tools
　　Resource Materials
　　Universal Decimal Classification
　　User Needs (Information)
　　User Satisfaction (Information)

Library Mechanization
USE　Library Automation

Library Networks　　　　　　　　　*JAN. 1969*
　　　Postings: 2,571　　　　　　　　　GC: 710
SN　Formal associations of two or more li-
　　braries, established to increase resources,
　　improve services, and reduce costs
UF　Decentralized Library Systems (1968
　　　1980) #
　　Library Systems
NT　Bibliographic Utilities
BT　Information Networks
RT　Branch Libraries
　　Consortia
　　Interlibrary Loans
　　Libraries
　　Library Cooperation
　　Library Development
　　Library Planning
　　Library Services
　　Public Libraries
　　Shared Library Resources
　　Union Catalogs

Library of Congress Classification
　　　　　　　　　　　　　　　　　　　APR. 1998
　　　Postings: 117　　　　　　　　　　GC: 710
SN　Library material classification system,
　　designed for large collections and used
　　widely by academic libraries, that repre-
　　sents knowledge by a mixed notation of
　　letters and numbers—developed initially
　　in 1897 for the U.S. Library of Congress
UF　Lc Classification
BT　Classification
RT　Cataloging
　　Dewey Decimal Classification
　　Indexing
　　Information Retrieval
　　Library Catalogs
　　Library Collections
　　Library Materials
　　Library Technical Processes
　　Subject Index Terms
　　Universal Decimal Classification

Library Organizations
USE　Library Associations

Library Orientation
USE　Library Instruction

Library Patrons
USE　Users (Information)

Library Personnel　　　　　　　　*MAR. 1980*
　　　Postings: 1,827　　　　　　　　　GC: 710
SN　Professional, paraprofessional, and
　　nonprofessional library employees (Note:
　　Use a more specific term if possible)
UF　Library Employees
NT　Librarians
　　Library Administrators
　　Library Technicians
BT　Personnel
RT　Libraries
　　Library Education
　　Library Policy
　　Library Services
　　Library Standards

Library Planning　　　　　　　　　*FEB. 1969*
　　　Postings: 3,108　　　　　　　　　GC: 710
SN　Formulation of plans for achieving li-
　　brary objectives
BT　Planning
RT　Libraries
　　Library Administration
　　Library Collection Development
　　Library Development
　　Library Facilities
　　Library Funding
　　Library Materials
　　Library Networks
　　Library Policy
　　Library Research
　　Library Role
　　Library Science
　　Library Services
　　Library Standards
　　Mission Statements

Library Policy　　　　　　　　　　*NOV. 1994*
　　　Postings: 451　　　　　　　　　　GC: 710
SN　Governing principles that serve as guide-
　　lines or rules for decision-making and
　　action in libraries
BT　Information Policy
RT　Libraries
　　Library Administration
　　Library Collection Development
　　Library Development
　　Library Expenditures
　　Library Guides
　　Library Personnel
　　Library Planning
　　Library Role
　　Library Services
　　Library Standards

Library Programs (1966 1980)
USE　Library Services

Library Reference Materials
USE　Library Materials
AND　Reference Materials

Library Reference Services (1968 1980)
USE　Library Services
AND　Reference Services

Library Research　　　　　　　　　*JUL. 1966*
　　　Postings: 1,753　　　　　　　　　GC: 810
SN　Research about libraries (Note: For re-
　　search in libraries, coordinate "Informa-
　　tion Seeking" with "Libraries" or a more
　　specific "Library" term—prior to Mar80,
　　this term was not restricted by a Scope
　　Note—as of Oct81, use as a minor
　　Descriptor for examples of this kind of
　　research—use as a major Descriptor
　　only as the subject of a document)
BT　Research
RT　Libraries
　　Library Collection Development
　　Library Development
　　Library Planning
　　Library Science
　　Library Statistics
　　Library Surveys
　　Use Studies

Library Role　　　　　　　　　　　*FEB. 1975*
　　　Postings: 3,351　　　　　　　　　GC: 710
SN　Functions expected of or carried out by
　　libraries
BT　Institutional Role
RT　Libraries
　　Library Administration
　　Library Guides
　　Library Planning
　　Library Policy
　　Library Services
　　Library Standards

Library Schools　　　　　　　　　*JUL. 1966*
　　　Postings: 1,136　　　　　　　　　GC: 340
SN　Professional schools, departments, or
　　divisions organized and maintained by
　　an institution of higher education for the
　　preparation of students in professional
　　librarianship
BT　Colleges
RT　Information Science
　　Information Science Education
　　Librarians
　　Library Education
　　Library Science
　　Professional Education

Library Science　　　　　　　　　*JUL. 1966*
　　　Postings: 1,727　　　　　　　　　GC: 710
SN　Study and profession of the administra-
　　tion of libraries and their contents—
　　includes the procedures by which librar-
　　ies recognize, acquire, organize, dissemi-
　　nate, and utilize information
UF　Librarianship
BT　Information Science
RT　Information Science Education
　　Librarians
　　Libraries
　　Library Associations
　　Library Education
　　Library Planning
　　Library Research
　　Library Schools
　　Library Services

Library Services　　　　　　　　　*JUL. 1966*
　　　Postings: 10,530　　　　　　　　GC: 710
SN　Acquiring, selecting, evaluating, organ-
　　izing, and disseminating information in
　　libraries
UF　Library Programs (1966 1980)
　　Library Reference Services (1968
　　　1980) #

NT　Library Circulation
　　Library Extension
　　Library Technical Processes
BT　Information Services
RT　Ancillary School Services
　　Bookmobiles
　　Document Delivery
　　Information Centers
　　Librarian Teacher Cooperation
　　Libraries
　　Library Administration
　　Library Cooperation
　　Library Development
　　Library Expenditures
　　Library Guides
　　Library Materials
　　Library Networks
　　Library Personnel
　　Library Planning
　　Library Policy
　　Library Role
　　Library Science
　　Library Standards
　　Library Surveys
　　Outreach Programs
　　Reference Services
　　Selective Dissemination of Information
　　User Needs (Information)
　　User Satisfaction (Information)
　　Users (Information)
　　Vendors

Library Skills　　　　　　　　　　*JUL. 1966*
　　　Postings: 1,431　　　　　　　　　GC: 710
SN　Competency in the use of a library
BT　Information Skills
RT　Information Literacy
　　Libraries
　　Library Instruction
　　Users (Information)

Library Specialists
USE　Librarians

Library Standards　　　　　　　　*JUL. 1966*
　　　Postings: 1,046　　　　　　　　　GC: 710
SN　Criteria by which the quality of library
　　services, operations, personnel, facili-
　　ties, equipment, etc., are judged
BT　Standards
RT　Libraries
　　Library Administration
　　Library Collection Development
　　Library Development
　　Library Personnel
　　Library Planning
　　Library Policy
　　Library Role
　　Library Services
　　Library Statistics
　　Library Surveys

Library Statistics　　　　　　　　*APR. 1985*
　　　Postings: 860　　　　　　　　　　GC: 730
BT　Statistical Data
RT　Libraries
　　Library Research
　　Library Standards
　　Library Surveys
　　Statistical Analysis

Library Surveys　　　　　　　　　*JUL. 1966*
　　　Postings: 2,781　　　　　　　　　GC: 810
BT　Surveys
RT　Libraries
　　Library Research
　　Library Services
　　Library Standards
　　Library Statistics
　　Use Studies
　　User Needs (Information)
　　User Satisfaction (Information)

Library Systems
USE　Library Networks

= Two or more Descriptors are used to represent this term.
The term's main entry shows the appropriate coordination.

Library Technical Assistants
USE   Library Technicians

Library Technical Processes   JUL. 1966
Postings: 2,034   GC: 710
SN   Acquisition, preparation, and organization of library materials for use
UF   Technical Processes (Libraries)
Technical Services (Libraries)
NT   Library Acquisition
BT   Library Services
RT   Abstracting
Authority Control (Information)
Bibliographic Utilities
Cataloging
Classification
Dewey Decimal Classification
Indexing
Information Processing
Information Technology
Integrated Library Systems
Libraries
Library Administration
Library Automation
Library Expenditures
Library Materials
Library of Congress Classification
Retrospective Conversion (Library Catalogs)
Universal Decimal Classification
Weeding (Library)

Library Technicians   JUL. 1966
Postings: 364   GC: 710
SN   Paraprofessional or nonprofessional library and information personnel, proficient in one or more functional areas, who provide support to professional librarians
UF   Library Aides
Library Clerks
Library Technical Assistants
NT   Medical Record Technicians
BT   Library Personnel
RT   Librarians
Libraries
Library Education
Paraprofessional Personnel

Library User Needs
USE   User Needs (Information)

Library User Satisfaction
USE   User Satisfaction (Information)

Library Users
USE   Users (Information)

Licensed Nurses
USE   Nurses

Licensing
USE   Certification

Licensing Examinations (Professions)
                                         AUG. 1986
Postings: 527   GC: 830
SN   Legally required qualifying examinations (as from a state) that individuals must pass before obtaining a license to practice a profession
BT   Tests
RT   Certification
Equivalency Tests
Legal Responsibility
Mastery Tests
Occupational Tests
Predictive Measurement
Professional Education
Standardized Tests
State Licensing Boards
Teacher Competency Testing

Lie Detectors
USE   Polygraphs

Life Costs (Facilities and Equipment)
USE   Life Cycle Costing

Life Cycle Costing   OCT. 1976
Postings: 106   GC: 620
SN   Calculation of initial facility or equipment costs, plus operation and maintenance expenses (including energy and replacement costs) for life expectancy of the facility or equipment
UF   Life Costs (Facilities and Equipment)
BT   Evaluation Methods
RT   Building Design
Building Operation
Building Plans
Building Systems
Construction Costs
Cost Effectiveness
Educational Facilities Design
Educational Facilities Planning
Energy Conservation
Energy Management
Equipment Evaluation
Facility Guidelines
Facility Planning
Maintenance
Operating Expenses
School Construction

Life Events   AUG. 1989
Postings: 882   GC: 120
SN   All significant changes in a person's life, e.g., marriage, childbirth, divorce, hospitalization, bereavement, unemployment
BT   Change
Experience
RT   Adjustment (to Environment)
Coping
Expectation
Individual Development
Life Satisfaction
Life Style
Midlife Transitions
Self Actualization
Stress Variables
Well Being

Life Histories
USE   Biographies

Life Quality
USE   Quality of Life

Life Satisfaction   MAR. 1982
Postings: 984   GC: 230
SN   Contentment with life, particularly in regard to the fulfillment of one's needs and expectations
BT   Satisfaction
RT   Family Work Relationship
Individual Power
Job Satisfaction
Life Events
Marital Satisfaction
Mental Health
Need Gratification
Quality of Life
Quality of Working Life
Reminiscence
Self Actualization
Social Indicators
Values
Well Being

Life Sciences
USE   Biological Sciences

Life Skills
USE   Daily Living Skills

Life Span Education
USE   Lifelong Learning

Life Style   OCT. 1973
Postings: 2,309   GC: 520
SN   Manner of living chosen as a personal response to the social and cultural milieu
UF   Alternative Life Styles
BT   Behavior
RT   Cohabitation
Cultural Influences
Feminism
Humanization
Individual Psychology
Life Events
Personal Autonomy
Role Theory
Social History
Sociocultural Patterns
Wellness
World Views

Life Views
USE   World Views

Lifelong Education
USE   Lifelong Learning

Lifelong Learning   MAR. 1980
Postings: 3,812   GC: 340
SN   Process by which individuals consciously acquire formal or informal education throughout their life spans for personal development or career advancement
UF   Continuing Learning (1967 1980)
Education Permanente
Life Span Education
Lifelong Education
Permanent Education
Recurrent Education
BT   Learning
RT   Adult Development
Adult Education
Adult Learning
Community Education
Continuing Education
Continuing Education Units
Correspondence Study
Distance Education
Experience
Experiential Learning
Independent Study
Informal Education
Nonformal Education
Professional Continuing Education
Self Help Programs
Student Educational Objectives
Transformative Learning

Lifetime Sports   DEC. 1975
Postings: 193   GC: 470
SN   Sports where participation can be carried on throughout one's lifetime—generally includes (but is not necessarily limited to) a variety of individual and dual sports for which facilities are widely available, and body contact is limited or unnecessary
BT   Athletics
RT   Archery
Bowling
Community Recreation Programs
Exercise
Golf
Individual Activities
Recreational Activities
Swimming
Tennis
Track and Field

Lifting   JUL. 1966
Postings: 25   GC: 630
SN   Act of raising or elevating a weighted object
NT   Weightlifting
BT   Physical Activities
RT   Job Skills

Light   SEP. 1968
Postings: 837   GC: 490
SN   (Note: Use "Lighting" for the illumina-

tion of facilities or the process of creating artificial light—prior to Apr80, this differentiation was not made)
UF   Daylight (1970 1980)
Light Radiation
Optical Spectrum
Visible Radiation
Visible Spectrum
BT   Radiation
RT   Climate
Color
Contrast
Glare
Lasers
Lighting
Luminescence
Optics
Photosynthesis
Physics
Relativity
Solar Energy
Spectroscopy
Stars
Visual Environment

Light Amplifiers (Lasers)
USE   Lasers

Light Radiation
USE   Light

Lighted Playgrounds (1966 1980)
USE   Playgrounds

Lighting   JUL. 1966
Postings: 664   GC: 920
UF   Illumination Levels (1968 1980)
Lights (1966 1980)
Outdoor Lighting (1971 1980)
NT   Television Lighting
RT   Climate Control
Contrast
Electrical Systems
Flexible Lighting Design
Glare
Human Factors Engineering
Light
Lighting Design
Luminescence
Optics
Utilities
Visual Environment
Windowless Rooms
Windows

Lighting Design   APR. 1970
Postings: 188   GC: 920
NT   Flexible Lighting Design
BT   Design
RT   Architecture
Building Design
Contrast
Design Requirements
Glare
Interior Design
Lighting
Windowless Rooms

Lights (1966 1980)
USE   Lighting

Lignite
USE   Coal

Likert Scales   DEC. 1988
Postings: 335   GC: 830
SN   Measures in which subjects rate a series of attitudinal statements on a continuum, e.g., strongly agree, agree, undecided, disagree, strongly disagree—from a procedure originally developed by Rensis Likert
UF   Summated Rating Scales
BT   Attitude Measures
Rating Scales

Limited English Proficient
USE   Limited English Speaking

Limited English Speaking   AUG. 1982
      Postings: 3,919   GC: 450
SN   Individuals who know English as a for-
      eign language but without sufficient pro-
      ficiency to participate fully in an English-
      speaking society
UF   Limited English Proficient
BT   Groups
RT   Bilingual Education
      Bilingual Education Programs
      Bilingual Teacher Aides
      Bilingual Teachers
      Bilingualism
      English (Second Language)
      Ethnic Groups
      Family English Literacy
      Language Dominance
      Language Minorities
      Language Proficiency
      Minority Groups
      Native Speakers
      Non English Speaking
      Second Language Learning
      Spanish Speaking
      Special Needs Students

Limits (Mathematics)   JUN. 1997
      Postings: 40   GC: 480
SN   The minimum and maximum points of
      variable x—also, the values approximated
      by a function f(x) as the independent
      variable x approaches a specific value,
      usually associated with calculus
BT   Mathematical Concepts
RT   Calculus
      Functions (Mathematics)
      Number Concepts

Linear Programing (1966 1994)
USE   Linear Programming

Linear Programming   MAR. 1994
      Postings: 21   GC: 480
SN   Technique, often used in operations re-
      search or business and economic plan-
      ning, to solve problems involving many
      variables where a best value or set of
      values is to be found (e.g., determining
      the blend of gasoline that yields the
      highest octane at the minimum cost)
UF   Linear Programing (1966 1994)
BT   Mathematical Applications
RT   Economic Research
      Management Systems
      Mathematical Models
      Monte Carlo Methods
      Operations Research

Linear Regression
USE   Regression (Statistics)

Linear Structural Equation Models
USE   Structural Equation Models

Lingala   JUL. 1966
      Postings: 9   GC: 440
UF   Mangala
BT   Bantu Languages

Linguistic Anthropology
USE   Anthropological Linguistics

Linguistic Awareness
USE   Metalinguistics

Linguistic Borrowing   OCT. 1976
      Postings: 490   GC: 450
SN   Process whereby one language absorbs
      words and expressions, and possibly
      sounds and grammatical forms, from

another language and adapts them to its
own use
UF   Loan Words
      Phonological Borrowing
      Syntactic Borrowing
      Word Borrowing
BT   Language Variation
RT   Code Switching (Language)
      Creoles
      Descriptive Linguistics
      Diachronic Linguistics
      Language Patterns
      Language Usage
      Lexicology
      Linguistics
      Morphology (Languages)
      Phonology
      Pidgins
      Sociolinguistics
      Syntax
      Vocabulary

Linguistic Competence   MAR. 1969
      Postings: 966   GC: 450
SN   Concept in Chomskyan theory referring
      to the intuitive knowledge of the rules of
      a language that enables native speaker-
      hearers to understand and produce sen-
      tences they have never heard or uttered
      before (Note: Prior to Mar80, the use of
      this term was not restricted by a Scope
      Note)
BT   Linguistic Theory
RT   Communicative Competence
      (Languages)
      Comprehension
      Interlanguage
      Language Acquisition
      Language Proficiency
      Language Skills
      Linguistic Performance
      Linguistics
      Psycholinguistics
      Verbal Ability

Linguistic Difficulty (Contrastive)
USE   Interference (Language)

Linguistic Difficulty (Inherent)   SEP. 1974
      Postings: 103   GC: 450
SN   Universal difficulty (or ease) in articulat-
      ing, auditing, or processing particular
      linguistic units and unit sequences
RT   Error Analysis (Language)
      Language Acquisition
      Language Processing
      Language Universals
      Linguistic Theory
      Linguistics
      Native Speakers
      Psycholinguistics

Linguistic Input   APR. 1990
      Postings: 129   GC: 450
SN   All words, contexts, and other forms of
      language to which a learner is exposed,
      relative to acquired proficiency in first or
      second languages
UF   Language Input
RT   Caregiver Speech
      Child Language
      Comprehension
      Cultural Influences
      Language Acquisition
      Language Enrichment
      Language Proficiency
      Linguistic Theory
      Linguistics
      Psycholinguistics
      Receptive Language
      Second Language Learning
      Verbal Ability

Linguistic Minorities
USE   Language Minorities

Linguistic Patterns (1966 1980)
USE   Language Patterns

Linguistic Performance   MAR. 1969
      Postings: 699   GC: 450
SN   Concept in Chomskyan theory referring
      to the actual production and comprehen-
      sion of oral or written language—reflects
      linguistic competence but is also af-
      fected by situational variables such as
      fatigue and distraction (Note: Prior to
      Mar80, the use of this term was not
      restricted by a Scope Note)
BT   Linguistic Theory
RT   Code Switching (Language)
      Communicative Competence
      (Languages)
      Interlanguage
      Language Acquisition
      Language Processing
      Language Proficiency
      Language Skills
      Linguistic Competence
      Linguistics
      Psycholinguistics
      Verbal Ability

Linguistic Research
USE   Language Research

Linguistic Styles
USE   Language Styles

Linguistic Theory   JUL. 1966
      Postings: 5,542   GC: 450
UF   Transformation Theory (Language)
      (1967 1980) #
NT   Case (Grammar)
      Generative Grammar
      Generative Phonology
      Linguistic Competence
      Linguistic Performance
      Semiotics
      Structural Grammar
      Traditional Grammar
BT   Theories
RT   Anthropological Linguistics
      Componential Analysis
      Computational Linguistics
      Deep Structure
      Language Processing
      Language Universals
      Linguistic Difficulty (Inherent)
      Linguistic Input
      Linguistics
      Metalinguistics
      Neurolinguistics
      Psycholinguistics
      Rhetorical Theory
      Sociolinguistics
      Surface Structure

Linguistic Universals
USE   Language Universals

Linguistics   JUL. 1966
      Postings: 3,065   GC: 450
SN   The study of language—this term is used
      primarily for material dealing with the
      field of linguistics as a whole (Note: Use
      a more specific term if possible—prior
      to Mar80, the use of this term was not
      restricted by a Scope Note)
UF   Philology
NT   Anthropological Linguistics
      Applied Linguistics
      Computational Linguistics
      Contrastive Linguistics
      Descriptive Linguistics
      Diachronic Linguistics
      Distinctive Features (Language)
      Mathematical Linguistics
      Metalinguistics
      Neurolinguistics
      Paralinguistics
      Phonology
      Psycholinguistics
      Sociolinguistics
      Structural Linguistics
RT   Deep Structure
      Dialects
      English

English (Second Language)
Glottochronology
Language
Language Patterns
Language Processing
Language Research
Language Usage
Linguistic Borrowing
Linguistic Competence
Linguistic Difficulty (Inherent)
Linguistic Input
Linguistic Performance
Linguistic Theory
Middle English
Miscue Analysis
North American English
Old English
Onomastics
Phoneme Grapheme Correspondence
Phonemics
Semiotics
Sentence Diagraming
Social Dialects
Speech
Speech Communication
Structural Analysis (Linguistics)
Surface Structure
Traditional Grammar
Verbal Communication

Linking Agents   OCT. 1980
      Postings: 712   GC: 330
SN   Individuals or groups who attempt change
      by connecting knowledge and related
      resources to practitioners—the linker's
      role often includes providing necessary
      support for adoption/adaptation of new
      ideas or developments
BT   Change Agents
RT   Adoption (Ideas)
      Diffusion (Communication)
      Information Dissemination
      Information Transfer
      Information Utilization
      Innovation
      Networks
      Outreach Programs
      Research and Development
      Research and Development Centers
      Research Utilization
      Resource Allocation
      Technical Assistance
      Technology Transfer
      Theory Practice Relationship

Lipreading   JUL. 1966
      Postings: 246   GC: 220
UF   Speech Reading
BT   Oral Communication Method
RT   Cued Speech
      Deaf Interpreting
      Hearing Therapy
      Total Communication

Lisrel Type Models
USE   Structural Equation Models

Listening   JUL. 1966
      Postings: 990   GC: 310
BT   Language Arts
RT   Attention
      Audience Response
      Auditory Stimuli
      Language Processing
      Listening Comprehension
      Listening Habits
      Listening Skills
      Speech Communication

Listening Comprehension   JUL. 1966
      Postings: 2,860   GC: 110
UF   Auditory Comprehension
      Aural Comprehension
BT   Comprehension
RT   Auditory Perception
      Auditory Training
      Aural Learning
      Language Skills
      Listening

Listening Comprehension Tests
Listening Habits
Listening Skills
Oral Interpretation
Receptive Language

Listening Comprehension Tests   *MAR. 1980*
    Postings: 291   GC: 830
SN Tests of aural comprehension either in native or foreign language
UF Listening Tests (1970 1980)
BT Verbal Tests
RT Achievement Tests
     Language Tests
     Listening Comprehension
     Listening Skills

Listening Groups   *JUL. 1966*
    Postings: 62   GC: 310
SN Organized groups that meet to hear radio or television programs and discuss the subjects presented
BT Discussion Groups
RT Audiences
     Audiovisual Instruction
     Educational Radio
     Educational Television
     Group Instruction
     Mass Instruction

Listening Habits   *JUL. 1966*
    Postings: 244   GC: 120
RT Habit Formation
     Listening
     Listening Comprehension
     Listening Skills

Listening Skills   *JUL. 1966*
    Postings: 2,740   GC: 120
SN Skills involved in literal, evaluative, and critical listening
BT Audiolingual Skills
RT Listening
     Listening Comprehension
     Listening Comprehension Tests
     Listening Habits
     Thinking Skills

Listening Tests (1970 1980)
USE Listening Comprehension Tests

Listservs   *NOV. 1998*
    Postings: 291   GC: 710
SN Electronic mailing lists that serve specific purposes or areas of interest and that automatically distribute messages from subscribers to all other subscribers
UF Electronic Discussion Lists
     Internet Discussion Lists
     Mailing List Servers
BT Electronic Mail
RT Discussion Groups
     Internet
     Scholarly Communication

Literacy   *JUL. 1966*
    Postings: 4,892   GC: 460
SN Ability to read and write—also, communication with written or printed symbols (i.e., reading and writing)
UF Literacy Skills
NT Adult Literacy
     Emergent Literacy
     Family Literacy
     Functional Literacy
     Information Literacy
     Reading
     Scientific Literacy
     Workplace Literacy
     Writing (Composition)
RT Basic Skills
     Cultural Literacy
     Illiteracy
     Letters (Alphabet)
     Literacy Education
     Metalinguistics
     Numeracy

Reading Skills
Reading Writing Relationship
Writing Skills

Literacy Classes (1966 1980)
USE Literacy Education

Literacy Education   *JUL. 1966*
    Postings: 6,940   GC: 460
SN Teaching of reading, writing and social skills to prepare persons to function at the fifth grade level
UF Literacy Classes (1966 1980)
BT Education
RT Adult Basic Education
     Adult Literacy
     Adult Reading Programs
     Basic Skills
     Family English Literacy
     Family Literacy
     Functional Literacy
     Functional Reading
     Literacy
     Minimum Competencies
     Popular Education
     Reading Instruction
     Reading Skills
     Workplace Literacy
     Writing Skills

Literacy Skills
USE Literacy

Literary Analysis (1968 1980)
USE Literary Criticism

Literary Classics
USE Classics (Literature)

Literary Conventions (1968 1980)
USE Literary Devices

Literary Criticism   *JUL. 1966*
    Postings: 4,928   GC: 430
SN Analysis, interpretation, or evaluation of literature—often includes the examination of literary contexts, types, themes, trends, history, or principles (Note: Do not confuse with "Writing Evaluation"—prior to Mar80, the use of this term was not restricted by a Scope Note)
UF Literary Analysis (1968 1980)
NT Rhetorical Criticism
BT Criticism
RT Book Reviews
     Content Analysis
     Critical Reading
     Didacticism
     Feminist Criticism
     Literary Devices
     Literary Genres
     Literary History
     Literary Styles
     Literature
     Reader Response

Literary Devices   *MAR. 1980*
    Postings: 902   GC: 430
SN Modes or techniques of expression, usually, but not always, literary
UF Literary Conventions (1968 1980)
NT Characterization
     Dialogs (Literary)
     Figurative Language
     Monologs
     Motifs
     Narration
RT Comedy
     Content Area Writing
     Creative Writing
     Descriptive Writing
     Discourse Modes
     Drama
     Fiction
     Humor
     Language Styles

Literary Criticism
Literary Genres
Literary Styles
Literature
Nonfiction
Parallelism (Literary)
Playwriting
Rhetoric
Symbols (Literary)
Tragedy
Writing (Composition)

Literary Discrimination (1966 1980)   *MAR. 1980*
    Postings: 131   GC: 430
SN Invalid Descriptor—use "Literary Criticism," "Reading Comprehension," "Critical Reading," etc.

Literary Genres   *JUL. 1966*
    Postings: 862   GC: 430
SN Divisions of literature into categories or classes that group works by form or type, such as biographies, essays, or poetry, rather than by movements such as Naturalism, Realism, or Romanticism
NT Ballads
     Biographies
     Chronicles
     Diaries
     Epics
     Essays
     Haiku
     Hymns
     Legends
     Novels
     Odes
     Parody
     Satire
     Scripts
     Short Stories
     Skits
     Sonnets
     Tales
RT Comedy
     Drama
     Fiction
     Humor
     Literary Criticism
     Literary Devices
     Literary History
     Literary Styles
     Literature
     Nonfiction
     Poetry
     Prose
     Tragedy
     World Literature

Literary History   *JUL. 1966*
    Postings: 718   GC: 430
SN Study of literary trends and movements, as well as the development of various branches or genres of literature (e.g., Australian literary history, history of the Polish novel, etc.)
BT Intellectual History
RT Classical Literature
     Classics (Literature)
     Eighteenth Century Literature
     Fifteenth Century Literature
     Journalism History
     Literary Criticism
     Literary Genres
     Literary Styles
     Literature
     Nineteenth Century Literature
     Old English Literature
     Seventeenth Century Literature
     Sixteenth Century Literature
     Twentieth Century Literature
     World Literature

Literary Influences (1969 1980)   *MAR. 1980*
    Postings: 374   GC: 430
SN Invalid Descriptor—used inconsistently in indexing—see such Descriptors as "Literature," "Literary Styles," "Figura-

tive Language," "Literary Criticism," "Literary History," etc.

Literary Mood (1970 1980)   *MAR. 1980*
    Postings: 44   GC: 430
SN Invalid Descriptor—used inconsistently in indexing—see such Descriptors as "Literature," "Literary Criticism," "Literary Devices," "Figurative Language," etc.

Literary Perspective (1969 1980)   *MAR. 1980*
    Postings: 319   GC: 430
SN Invalid Descriptor—see such Descriptors as "Literature," "Literary Devices," "Literary Criticism," "Literary Styles," "Figurative Language," etc.

Literary Styles   *JUL. 1969*
    Postings: 1,198   GC: 430
SN Aspects of written language that distinguish and characterize individual writers, literary movements, or literary periods
RT Art Expression
     Characterization
     Drama
     Expressionism
     Films
     Impressionism
     Irony
     Literary Criticism
     Literary Devices
     Literary Genres
     Literary History
     Literature
     Modernism
     Music
     Mysticism
     Naturalism
     Neoclassicism
     Nonfiction
     Parody
     Poetry
     Postmodernism
     Prose
     Realism
     Romanticism
     Satire
     Surrealism
     Symbolism
     Writing (Composition)

Literature   *JUL. 1966*
    Postings: 4,948   GC: 430
NT Adolescent Literature
     African Literature
     American Indian Literature
     Australian Literature
     Baroque Literature
     Biblical Literature
     Black Literature
     Childrens Literature
     Classical Literature
     Classics (Literature)
     Czech Literature
     Drama
     Eighteenth Century Literature
     English Literature
     Fifteenth Century Literature
     French Literature
     German Literature
     Greek Literature
     Italian Literature
     Latin American Literature
     Legends
     Medieval Literature
     Nineteenth Century Literature
     North American Literature
     Pastoral Literature
     Poetry
     Polish Literature
     Prose
     Renaissance Literature
     Russian Literature
     Seventeenth Century Literature
     Sixteenth Century Literature
     Spanish Literature
     Twentieth Century Literature

= Two or more Descriptors are used to represent this term.
The term's main entry shows the appropriate coordination.

Victorian Literature
BT   Humanities
RT   Aesthetics
      Art
      Authors
      Books
      Choral Speaking
      Diaries
      Figurative Language
      Folk Culture
      History
      Humanism
      Humor
      Journalism
      Language Arts
      Letters (Correspondence)
      Literary Criticism
      Literary Devices
      Literary Genres
      Literary History
      Literary Styles
      Literature Appreciation
      Literature Reviews
      Local Color Writing
      Mythology
      Philosophy
      Poets
      Popular Culture
      Rhetorical Criticism
      Symbols (Literary)
      Whole Language Approach
      World Literature

Literature Appreciation   JUL. 1966
      Postings: 5,987   GC: 400
UF   Reading Enjoyment
RT   Choral Speaking
      Literature
      Metalinguistics
      Oral Interpretation
      Reader Response
      Reading Motivation
      Recreational Reading
      Whole Language Approach

Literature Guides (1966 1980)   MAR. 1980
      Postings: 187   GC: 730
SN   Invalid Descriptor—used indiscriminately
      in indexing—see such Descriptors as
      "Bibliographies," "Literature Reviews,"
      etc.

Literature Programs (1966 1980)
                                     MAR. 1980
      Postings: 330   GC: 400
SN   Invalid Descriptor—coordinate "Litera-
      ture" or its narrower terms with such
      Descriptors as "English Curriculum,"
      "Reading Programs," "Second Language
      Programs," etc.

Literature Reviews   JUL. 1966
      Postings: 14,924   GC: 730
SN   Surveys of the materials published on a
      topic (Note: Prior to Mar80, "Research
      Reviews (Publications)" was also a valid
      Descriptor)
UF   Literature Surveys
      Reviews of the Literature
BT   Publications
RT   Anthologies
      Bibliographies
      Bibliometrics
      Book Reviews
      Literature
      Meta Analysis
      Research
      Research Methodology
      Research Tools
      State of the Art Reviews
      Surveys

Literature Searches
USE   Bibliographies

Literature Surveys
USE   Literature Reviews

Lithuanian   NOV. 1970
      Postings: 14   GC: 440
BT   Baltic Languages

Litigation
USE   Court Litigation

Litter
USE   Solid Wastes

Livestock   AUG. 1969
      Postings: 176   GC: 410
BT   Animals
RT   Animal Husbandry
      Horses
      Veterinary Medicine

Livestock Feed Stores
USE   Feed Stores

Livestock Production
USE   Agricultural Production

Livestock Technology
USE   Animal Husbandry

Living Learning Centers   MAR. 1980
      Postings: 53   GC: 920
SN   Residential facilities of a higher educa-
      tion institution designed to enhance stu-
      dents' educational experiences by ena-
      bling them to integrate their academic
      activities with their ordinary living activi-
      ties (Note: Prior to Mar80, this concept
      may have been indexed under "Residen-
      tial Colleges")
BT   Educational Facilities
RT   College Buildings
      College Housing
      College Role
      Colleges
      Continuing Education Centers
      Dormitories
      Experiential Learning
      Group Experience
      Integrated Activities
      On Campus Students
      Peer Relationship
      Relevance (Education)
      Residential Colleges

Living Quarters
USE   Housing

Living Standards   JUL. 1966
      Postings: 515   GC: 520
BT   Standards
RT   Advantaged
      Community Development
      Developed Nations
      Developing Nations
      Disadvantaged
      Economic Factors
      Environmental Standards
      Quality of Life
      Social Indicators

Loan Applicants
USE   Financial Aid Applicants

Loan Default   APR. 1990
      Postings: 196   GC: 620
SN   Failure to repay financial debts or credits
UF   Defaulted Loans
BT   Loan Repayment
RT   Credit (Finance)
      Debt (Financial)
      Educational Finance
      Financial Problems
      Legal Problems
      Student Loan Programs

Loan Repayment   FEB. 1978
      Postings: 600   GC: 620
SN   Repayment of financial debts or credits
      (Note: If possible, use the more specific
      term "Loan Default")
NT   Loan Default
RT   Costs
      Credit (Finance)
      Debt (Financial)
      Educational Finance
      Financial Aid Applicants
      Financial Needs
      Financial Problems
      Financial Services
      Financial Support
      Income Contingent Loans
      Interest (Finance)
      Legal Responsibility
      Money Management
      Paying for College
      Student Financial Aid
      Student Loan Programs
      Student Responsibility

Loan Words
USE   Linguistic Borrowing

Lobbying   MAR. 1980
      Postings: 569   GC: 610
SN   Conducting activities to influence public
      officials, especially members of a legis-
      lative body, on legislation
UF   Political Advocacy
BT   Activities
RT   Activism
      Institutional Advancement
      Legislation
      Legislators
      Political Influences
      Political Issues
      Political Power
      Politics
      Position Papers
      Public Officials

Local Area Networks   AUG. 1986
      Postings: 379   GC: 710
SN   Interconnected computer equipment and
      peripherals contained within a small geo-
      graphic area, typically a single building
      or plant
BT   Computer Networks
RT   Microcomputers
      Minicomputers
      Office Automation
      Office Machines
      Office Management
      Workstations

Local Autonomy (of Schools)
USE   School District Autonomy

Local Color Writing   MAY 1969
      Postings: 76   GC: 430
SN   Composition that emphasizes the speech,
      dress, mannerisms, habits, or peculiari-
      ties of particular places or regions
BT   Writing (Composition)
RT   Literature
      Poetry

Local Community Programs
USE   Community Programs

Local Control (of Schools)
USE   School District Autonomy

Local Education Agencies
USE   School Districts

Local Education Authorities
USE   School Districts

Local Government   SEP. 1971
      Postings: 1,374   GC: 610
UF   County Government #
NT   City Government
BT   Government (Administrative Body)
RT   Community
      Community Services
      Government Employees
      Government School Relationship
      Local Legislation
      Municipalities
      Public Agencies
      Revenue Sharing
      School District Autonomy
      School Districts
      Tribal Government
      Tribal Sovereignty

Local History   NOV. 1974
      Postings: 1,169   GC: 430
SN   History associated with a neighborhood,
      town, county, or other specific subdivi-
      sion of a larger geopolitical region
UF   Community History
      County History #
BT   History
RT   Community Characteristics
      Community Study
      Family History
      Heritage Education
      Local Issues
      Oral History
      Social History
      State History

Local Housing Authorities (1966 1980)
USE   Housing

Local Information Services
USE   Community Information Services

Local Issues   JUL. 1966
      Postings: 711   GC: 610
SN   Matters of concern to a particular com-
      munity, neighborhood, or locality
RT   Bond Issues
      Community
      Community Action
      Community Attitudes
      Community Change
      Community Characteristics
      Community Coordination
      Community Problems
      Community Support
      Elections
      Local History
      Local Legislation
      Political Issues
      Voting

Local Legislation   JAN. 1979
      Postings: 93   GC: 610
SN   Ordinances and regulations relating to a
      particular locality within a state or prov-
      ince
UF   Community Legislation
      Community Recreation Legislation
          (1966 1978) #
      Local Recreation Legislation (1966
          1978) #
BT   Legislation
RT   Federal Legislation
      Laws
      Legislators
      Local Government
      Local Issues
      State Legislation

Local Norms   MAR. 1980
      Postings: 164   GC: 820
SN   Statistical description of the typical per-
      formance, behavior, achievement, func-
      tion, etc., of a particular locality (e.g.,
      school, school district, community, cor-
      poration, etc.) (Note: Use only for nu-
      merical data and not for subjectively
      described standards)
UF   County Norms

= Two or more Descriptors are used to represent this term.
The term's main entry shows the appropriate coordination.

District Norms
School District Norms
BT   Norms
RT   National Norms
State Norms

Local Recreation Legislation (1966 1978)
USE   Local Legislation
AND   Recreation Legislation

Local Unions (1966 1980)
USE   Unions

Locational Skills (Social Studies)
                                          JUL. 1966
Postings: 245   GC: 400
SN   Ability to locate physical features and
political or cultural boundaries of the
earth
BT   Skills
RT   Cartography
Map Skills
Maps
Social Studies
Study Skills

Locker Rooms   *JUL. 1966*
Postings: 26   GC: 920
BT   Facilities
RT   Athletics
Equipment Storage
Physical Education Facilities
Sanitary Facilities

Loco Parentis
USE   In Loco Parentis

Locomotive Engineers   *JUL. 1966*
Postings: 4   GC: 640
BT   Skilled Workers
RT   Diesel Engines
Engines
Mechanics (Process)

Locus of Control   *JAN. 1973*
Postings: 2,891   GC: 120
SN   Personality construct referring to an in-
dividual's perception of the locus of events
as determined internally by his/her own
behavior vs. fate, luck, or external forces
UF   Internal External Locus of Control
BT   Personality Traits
RT   Attribution Theory
Congruence (Psychology)
Delay of Gratification
Extraversion Introversion
Field Dependence Independence
Individual Power
Personal Autonomy
Self Concept

Logarithms   *OCT. 1984*
Postings: 76   GC: 480
SN   Exponents that indicate the power to
which base numbers are raised to pro-
duce given numbers
BT   Numbers
RT   Functions (Mathematics)

Logic   *JUL. 1966*
Postings: 1,013   GC: 400
NT   Mathematical Logic
BT   Philosophy
RT   Logical Thinking
Paradox
Validity

Logical Thinking   *JUL. 1966*
Postings: 2,174   GC: 110
SN   Process of reasoning from premise to
conclusion
NT   Deduction
Induction
BT   Cognitive Processes

RT   Abstract Reasoning
Artificial Intelligence
Convergent Thinking
Critical Thinking
Formal Operations
Heuristics
Inferences
Logic
Piagetian Theory
Problem Solving
Thinking Skills

Loneliness   *AUG. 1980*
Postings: 340   GC: 230
SN   Unhappiness caused by a lack of friends
or companions
BT   Sadness
RT   Alienation
Anger
Depression (Psychology)
Emotional Problems
Moods
Social Isolation

Long Range Planning   *OCT. 1979*
Postings: 2,924   GC: 330
SN   Systematic planning based on assump-
tions about situations and needs beyond
a 1-year period
UF   Futures Planning
Long Term Planning
BT   Planning
RT   Delphi Technique
Environmental Scanning
Futures (of Society)
Management Systems
Master Plans
Operations Research
Planning Commissions
Prediction
Strategic Planning
Trend Analysis

Long Term Care   *AUG. 1989*
Postings: 369   GC: 210
SN   Medical and social care given to indi-
viduals with chronic impairments
BT   Health Services
RT   Adult Day Care
Adult Foster Care
Attendants
Chronic Illness
Community Health Services
Disabilities
Family Caregivers
Family Problems
Frail Elderly
Health Facilities
Home Health Aides
Home Programs
Hospitals
Medical Services
Nursing Homes
Personal Care Homes
Residential Care
Social Services
Visiting Homemakers

Long Term Memory   *NOV. 1981*
Postings: 277   GC: 110
SN   Process of recalling information or performing appropriately a long time after
instruction or presentation of material—
characterized by slow decay and a large
volume of remembered material (in contrast to "Short Term Memory")
BT   Memory
RT   Short Term Memory

Long Term Planning
USE   Long Range Planning

Longitudinal Studies   *JUL. 1966*
Postings: 9,233   GC: 810
NT   Followup Studies
BT   Case Studies
RT   Attrition (Research Studies)
Cross Sectional Studies

Incidence
Outcomes of Education
Sampling
Trend Analysis

Look Guess Method
USE   Sight Method

Look Say Method
USE   Sight Method

Loop Induction Systems   *MAY 1969*
Postings: 12   GC: 220
SN   Electronic system consisting of micro-
phone, amplifier, and a loop of wire
circling the room—sound is transmitted
to students through coils in their hearing
aids
BT   Audiovisual Communications
RT   Electronic Equipment
Hearing Aids
Hearing Impairments
Sensory Aids

Love   *DEC. 1989*
Postings: 176   GC: 120
SN   A complex emotion comprising attach-
ment, tenderness, affection, and con-
cern for the well-being of another person
or persons—may be reflected affectively,
cognitively, behaviorally, verbally, physi-
cally, or in fantasy
RT   Affection
Affective Behavior
Altruism
Attachment Behavior
Emotional Development
Emotional Experience
Friendship
Interpersonal Attraction
Interpersonal Relationship
Intimacy
Marital Satisfaction
Mate Selection
Need Gratification
Parent Child Relationship
Prosocial Behavior
Psychological Needs
Psychological Patterns
Rapport
Sexuality
Trust (Psychology)

Low Ability Students (1967 1980)
                                          MAR. 1980
Postings: 440   GC: 360
SN   Invalid Descriptor—see "Academic Ability," "Slow Learners," "Learning Problems," "Low Achievement," "Educationally Disadvantaged," etc.

Low Achievement   *MAR. 1980*
Postings: 2,374   GC: 120
UF   Low Achievement Factors (1966 1980)
Low Achievers (1966 1980)
BT   Achievement
RT   Academic Failure
Failure
Fear of Success
Grade Repetition
High Achievement
Learning Problems
Social Promotion
Underachievement

Low Achievement Factors (1966 1980)
USE   Low Achievement

Low Achievers (1966 1980)
USE   Low Achievement

Low Incidence Disabilities   *APR. 1990*
Postings: 33   GC: 220
SN   Infrequently occurring disabilities among
demographic groups, necessitating spe-

cial or unusual arrangements for acces-
sible treatment and services
BT   Disabilities
Incidence
RT   Disease Incidence

Low Income   *JUL. 1966*
Postings: 779   GC: 620
BT   Income
RT   Low Income Counties
Low Income Groups
Low Income States
Lower Class
Poverty
Poverty Programs
Underemployment

Low Income Counties   *JUL. 1966*
Postings: 103   GC: 550
BT   Counties
RT   Low Income
Low Income Groups
Low Income States
Poverty Areas

Low Income Groups   *JUL. 1966*
Postings: 3,477   GC: 520
BT   Groups
RT   Economically Disadvantaged
Low Income
Low Income Counties
Low Income States
Lower Class
Poverty
Welfare Recipients

Low Income States   *JUL. 1966*
Postings: 28   GC: 550
BT   Geographic Regions
RT   Low Income
Low Income Counties
Low Income Groups
Poverty Areas

Low Level Aspiration (1966 1980)
USE   Aspiration

Low Motivation (1966 1980)
USE   Motivation

Low Rent Housing   *JUL. 1966*
Postings: 129   GC: 550
NT   Public Housing
BT   Housing

Low Vision Aids   *JUN. 1977*
Postings: 118   GC: 220
SN   Lenses or devices other than conven-
tional eyeglasses used to improve visual
functioning in the partially sighted
BT   Sensory Aids
RT   Blindness
Electromechanical Aids
Large Type Materials
Magnification Methods
Mobility Aids
Partial Vision
Vision
Visual Impairments

Lower Class   *JUL. 1966*
Postings: 587   GC: 520
UF   Lower Class Males (1966 1980) #
BT   Social Class
RT   Disadvantaged
Low Income
Low Income Groups
Lower Class Parents
Lower Class Students
Lower Middle Class
Middle Class
Poverty
Upper Class
Working Class

= Two or more Descriptors are used to represent this term.
The term's main entry shows the appropriate coordination.

Lower Class Males (1966 1980)
USE　Lower Class
AND　Males

Lower Class Parents　　　　　　*JUL. 1966*
　　　Postings: 94　　　　　　　　　GC: 510
BT　Parents
RT　Lower Class

Lower Class Students　　　　　　*JUL. 1966*
　　　Postings: 347　　　　　　　　GC: 360
BT　Students
RT　Disadvantaged Youth
　　　Lower Class
　　　Middle Class Students

Lower Middle Class　　　　　　*JUL. 1966*
　　　Postings: 57　　　　　　　　　GC: 520
BT　Social Class
RT　Lower Class
　　　Middle Class
　　　Upper Class
　　　Working Class

Loyalty Oaths　　　　　　　　*APR. 1969*
　　　Postings: 32　　　　　　　　　GC: 630
RT　Behavior Standards
　　　Boards of Education
　　　Codes of Ethics
　　　Employment Practices
　　　Employment Qualifications
　　　Government (Administrative Body)
　　　Patriotism
　　　Personnel Policy

Lozanov Method
USE　Suggestopedia

LRC
USE　Learning Resources Centers

LSD
USE　Lysergic Acid Diethylamide

Lubricants　　　　　　　　　*JUL. 1966*
　　　Postings: 30　　　　　　　　　GC: 910
UF　Grease
　　　Motor Oil #
RT　Engines
　　　Oil
　　　Petroleum Industry

Luganda
USE　Ganda

Lumber Industry　　　　　　　*JUL. 1966*
　　　Postings: 146　　　　　　　　GC: 410
UF　Lumbering
　　　Timber Based Industry
BT　Industry
RT　Forestry
　　　Forestry Occupations
　　　Furniture Design
　　　Furniture Industry
　　　Woodworking

Lumbering
USE　Lumber Industry

Luminescence　　　　　　　　*JAN. 1970*
　　　Postings: 59　　　　　　　　　GC: 490
UF　Photometric Brightness
RT　Glare
　　　Light
　　　Lighting
　　　Physics
　　　Radiation

Lunar Exploration
USE　Lunar Research

Lunar Research　　　　　　　*APR. 1972*
　　　Postings: 96　　　　　　　　　GC: 810
SN　Scientific activities designed to provide
　　　information about the origin, structure,
　　　and properties of the moon
UF　Lunar Exploration
BT　Space Exploration
RT ·　Aerospace Technology
　　　Astronomy
　　　Planetariums
　　　Satellites (Aerospace)
　　　Space Sciences

Lunch Programs　　　　　　　*JUL. 1966*
　　　Postings: 736　　　　　　　　GC: 210
BT　Health Programs
RT　Ancillary School Services
　　　Breakfast Programs
　　　Dining Facilities
　　　Food Handling Facilities
　　　Food Standards
　　　Hunger
　　　Nutrition
　　　School Health Services

Luo　　　　　　　　　　　　*JUL. 1970*
　　　Postings: 9　　　　　　　　　GC: 440
BT　African Languages

Luso Brazilian Culture　　　　　*JUL. 1966*
　　　Postings: 25　　　　　　　　　GC: 560
SN　Aspects of Portuguese influence reflected
　　　in Brazilian culture
BT　Latin American Culture

Lying　　　　　　　　　　　*AUG. 1986*
　　　Postings: 84　　　　　　　　　GC: 530
SN　The deliberate conveyance of falsehood
BT　Deception
　　　Social Behavior
RT　Antisocial Behavior
　　　Cheating
　　　Codes of Ethics
　　　Discipline Problems
　　　Fraud
　　　Honesty
　　　Libel and Slander
　　　Polygraphs

Lyric Poetry　　　　　　　　*JUN. 1969*
　　　Postings: 168　　　　　　　　GC: 430
NT　Ballads
　　　Hymns
　　　Odes
　　　Sonnets
BT　Poetry
RT　Epics
　　　Poets
　　　Songs

Lyric Poets
USE　Poets

Lysergic Acid Diethylamide　　　*JUL. 1966*
　　　Postings: 116　　　　　　　　GC: 210
UF　LSD
RT　Drug Abuse
　　　Drug Addiction
　　　Drug Use
　　　Illegal Drug Use

Machine Aided Indexing
USE　Automatic Indexing

Machine Dictation
USE　Dictation

Machine Readable Cataloging　　*AUG. 1986*
　　　Postings: 258　　　　　　　　GC: 710
SN　(Note: For the Library of Congress for-
　　　mat and program, see Identifiers "MARC"
　　　and "MARC II")
BT　Cataloging
RT　Computer Oriented Programs

　　　Data Processing
　　　Electronic Text
　　　Integrated Library Systems
　　　Online Catalogs
　　　Retrospective Conversion (Library
　　　　Catalogs)

Machine Readable Data Files
USE　Databases

Machine Readable Text
USE　Electronic Text

Machine Repairers　　　　　　*MAR. 1980*
　　　Postings: 122　　　　　　　　GC: 640
UF　Machine Repairmen (1968 1980)
　　　Machinery Maintenance Workers
　　　Maintenance Machinists
　　　Shop Mechanics
BT　Machinists
RT　Equipment Maintenance
　　　Mechanics (Process)
　　　Repair
　　　Service Workers

Machine Repairmen (1968 1980)
USE　Machine Repairers

Machine Tool Operators　　　　*JUL. 1966*
　　　Postings: 237　　　　　　　　GC: 640
SN　Workers who operate power-driven tools
　　　used for shaping, cutting, turning, bor-
　　　ing, drilling, grinding, or polishing (Note:
　　　Prior to Sep81, the use of this term was
　　　not restricted by a Scope Note)
UF　Drill Press Operators
　　　Production Machine Operators
　　　Punch Press Operators
　　　Sheet Metal Machine Operators #
BT　Machinists
RT　Machine Tools
　　　Manufacturing Industry
　　　Sheet Metal Work
　　　Tool and Die Makers

Machine Tools　　　　　　　*AUG. 1968*
　　　Postings: 368　　　　　　　　GC: 910
UF　Drill Presses
　　　Grinding Machines
　　　Lathes
　　　Milling Machines
　　　Punch Presses
　　　Shapers
BT　Equipment
RT　Computer Assisted Manufacturing
　　　Hand Tools
　　　Machine Tool Operators
　　　Machinery Industry
　　　Machinists
　　　Manufacturing Industry
　　　Mechanics (Process)
　　　Metal Working
　　　Numerical Control
　　　Tool and Die Makers

Machine Translation　　　　　*JUL. 1966*
　　　Postings: 224　　　　　　　　GC: 710
SN　Translation of text from one language to
　　　another by computer
UF　Mechanical Translation
BT　Computational Linguistics
　　　Translation
RT　Automatic Indexing
　　　Automation
　　　Context Free Grammar
　　　Contrastive Linguistics
　　　Data Processing
　　　Structural Analysis (Linguistics)
　　　Word Processing

Machinery Industry　　　　　　*JUL. 1966*
　　　Postings: 66　　　　　　　　　GC: 650
SN　Manufacturers of machinery and equip-
　　　ment other than electrical or transporta-
　　　tion eqipment
UF　Machinery Manufacturing Industry

BT　Manufacturing Industry
RT　Agricultural Machinery
　　　Agricultural Machinery Occupations
　　　Equipment
　　　Machine Tools
　　　Machinists
　　　Mechanical Equipment
　　　Tool and Die Makers

Machinery Maintenance Workers
USE　Machine Repairers

Machinery Manufacturing Industry
USE　Machinery Industry

Machinists　　　　　　　　　*AUG. 1968*
　　　Postings: 188　　　　　　　　GC: 640
SN　Workers who make, operate, or repair
　　　machines
NT　Machine Repairers
　　　Machine Tool Operators
　　　Tool and Die Makers
BT　Skilled Workers
RT　Machine Tools
　　　Machinery Industry
　　　Mechanics (Process)
　　　Metal Working

Macroeconomics　　　　　　*OCT. 1994*
　　　Postings: 150　　　　　　　　GC: 620
SN　Study of the overall aspects and work-
　　　ings of large economic systems, as of a
　　　nation
BT　Economics
RT　Econometrics
　　　Economic Research
　　　Economics Education
　　　Microeconomics

Magazine Articles
USE　Journal Articles

Magazines
USE　Periodicals

Magistrates
USE　Court Judges

Magnet Centers
USE　Magnet Schools

Magnet Schools　　　　　　　*OCT. 1979*
　　　Postings: 799　　　　　　　　GC: 340
SN　Schools offering special courses not avail-
　　　able in the regular school curriculum and
　　　designed to attract students on a volun-
　　　tary basis from all parts of a school
　　　district without reference to the usual
　　　attendance zone rules—often used to
　　　aid in school desegregation
UF　Magnet Centers
BT　Schools
RT　Busing
　　　Educational Parks
　　　Feeder Patterns
　　　Nontraditional Education
　　　School Desegregation
　　　Urban Schools
　　　Voluntary Desegregation

Magnetic Amplifiers
USE　Electronic Control

Magnetic Disks　　　　　　　*DEC. 1987*
　　　Postings: 12　　　　　　　　　GC: 720
SN　Computer storage devices in the form of
　　　flat circular plates coated on one or both
　　　sides with magnetic material on which
　　　information may be recorded and stored
　　　for future use
NT　Floppy Disks
BT　Computer Storage Devices

= Two or more Descriptors are used to represent this term.
The term's main entry shows the appropriate coordination.

RT   Disk Drives
      Videodisks

Magnetic Ink Character Recognition
USE   Character Recognition

Magnetic Tape Cartridges
USE   Magnetic Tape Cassettes

Magnetic Tape Cassette Recorders (1970 1980)
USE   Magnetic Tape Cassettes
AND   Tape Recorders

Magnetic Tape Cassettes   SEP. 1970
      Postings: 234   GC: 720
UF   Cassettes (Tape)
      Magnetic Tape Cartridges
      Magnetic Tape Cassette Recorders
         (1970 1980) #
NT   Audiotape Cassettes
      Videotape Cassettes
BT   Magnetic Tapes
RT   Tape Recorders
      Tape Recordings

Magnetic Tapes   JAN. 1969
      Postings: 145   GC: 720
SN   Tapes coated on one or both sides with a
      magnetic oxide, on which data are stored
      by the selective polarization of portions
      of the surfaces—used for recording video,
      audio, or computer data (Note: Use a
      more specific term if possible)
UF   Computer Tapes #
NT   Magnetic Tape Cassettes
BT   Electronic Equipment
      Supplies
RT   Computer Storage Devices
      Information Storage
      Input Output Devices
      Tape Recorders
      Tape Recordings

Magnets   SEP. 1968
      Postings: 302   GC: 490
UF   Permanent Magnets
RT   Electricity
      Electronics
      Physics

Magnification Methods   JUL. 1966
      Postings: 39   GC: 720
UF   Enlargement Methods
BT   Methods
RT   Large Type Materials
      Low Vision Aids
      Microform Readers
      Microscopes
      Photography
      Projection Equipment
      Reprography
      Sensory Aids
      Tactile Adaptation

Magnitude of Effect
USE   Effect Size

Maids (1968 1980)
USE   Household Workers

Mail Surveys   AUG. 1988
      Postings: 501   GC: 810
SN   Includes postal and electronic mail sur-
      veys (Note: Use as a minor Descriptor
      for examples of this kind of survey—use
      as a major Descriptor only as the subject
      of a document)
BT   Surveys
RT   Questionnaires
      Research Methodology
      Telephone Surveys

Mailing List Servers
USE   Listservs

Mainstreaming   JUN. 1978
      Postings: 7,626   GC: 220
SN   Progressively including and maintaining
      exceptional students (disabled or gifted)
      in classes and schools with regular or
      normal students, with steps taken to see
      that special needs are satisfied within
      this arrangement
UF   Desegregation (Disabled Students)
      Integration (Disabled Students)
      Least Restrictive Environment (Dis-
         abled)
      Regular Class Placement (1968 1978)
BT   Placement
RT   Academic Accommodations (Disabili-
         ties)
      Academically Gifted
      Cooperative Learning
      Disabilities
      Heterogeneous Grouping
      Inclusive Schools
      Individualized Education Programs
      Itinerant Teachers
      Normalization (Disabilities)
      Prereferral Intervention
      Regular and Special Education Rela-
         tionship
      Resource Room Programs
      Resource Teachers
      Special Education
      Student Placement
      Transitional Programs

Maintenance   JUL. 1966
      Postings: 993   GC: 920
SN   Preservation or continuance of a condi-
      tion
NT   Equipment Maintenance
      Preservation
      Repair
      School Maintenance
RT   Buildings
      Cleaning
      Consumer Science
      Equipment
      Facilities
      Life Cycle Costing
      Obsolescence
      Supplies
      Troubleshooting

Maintenance Machinists
USE   Machine Repairers

Maintenance Vehicles
USE   Service Vehicles

Majority Attitudes   JUL. 1966
      Postings: 405   GC: 520
BT   Attitudes
RT   Community Control
      Discriminatory Legislation
      Minority Groups
      Public Opinion
      Public Support
      Reputation

Majority Culture
USE   Middle Class Culture

Majors (Students)   MAR. 1980
      Postings: 3,198   GC: 320
UF   College Majors (1968 1980)
      Departmental Majors
      Liberal Arts Majors (1967 1980) #
NT   Education Majors
BT   Students
RT   Advanced Courses
      Course Selection (Students)
      Degree Requirements
      Degrees (Academic)
      Elective Courses
      Intellectual Disciplines
      Nonmajors

Required Courses
Specialization

Make Believe Play
USE   Pretend Play

Maladjusted Students
USE   Student Adjustment

Maladjustment (1966 1980)
USE   Adjustment (to Environment)

Malagasy   JUL. 1966
      Postings: 11   GC: 440
BT   Indonesian Languages

Malay   JUL. 1966
      Postings: 83   GC: 440
BT   Indonesian Languages

Malayalam   SEP. 1969
      Postings: 8   GC: 440
BT   Dravidian Languages

Malayo Polynesian Languages   JUL. 1966
      Postings: 140   GC: 440
UF   Austronesian Languages
NT   Chamorro
      Hawaiian
      Indonesian Languages
      Maori
      Melanesian Languages
      Samoan
BT   Languages
RT   Language Classification
      Native Speakers

Male Role
USE   Males
AND   Sex Role

Males   JUL. 1966
      Postings: 10,845   GC: 120
UF   Boys
      Lower Class Males (1966 1980) #
      Male Role #
      Men
NT   Fathers
      Sons
BT   Groups
RT   Gender Issues
      Masculinity
      Sex
      Sex Differences
      Sex Role
      Sex Stereotypes
      Single Sex Colleges
      Single Sex Schools
      Spouses

Malignant Neoplasms
USE   Cancer

Malnutrition
USE   Nutrition

Malpractice   OCT. 1980
      Postings: 112   GC: 530
SN   Wrongful or negligent treatment of cli-
      ents by professional personnel that re-
      sults (or may result) in damage, injury,
      or loss (Note: Coordinate with such
      Descriptors as "Medical Services," "Psy-
      chological Services," etc., as appropri-
      ate, or use the more specific Descriptor
      "Educational Malpractice"—for malprac-
      tice of lawyers, court judges, etc., use
      the Identifier "Legal Malpractice")
NT   Educational Malpractice
RT   Accountability
      Codes of Ethics
      Court Litigation
      Crime

Fraud
Laws
Legal Problems
Legal Responsibility
Libel and Slander
Negligence
Professional Services
Torts
Victims of Crime

Man Days (1968 1980)
USE   Worker Days

Man Machine Dialogs
USE   Man Machine Systems

Man Machine Interface
USE   Man Machine Systems

Man Machine Systems   AUG. 1968
      Postings: 1,639   GC: 710
SN   Interactive organizations of individuals
      and machines (usually computers) that
      regulate and control events as single
      systems
UF   Man Machine Dialogs
      Man Machine Interface
NT   User Friendly Interface
RT   Automation
      Bionics
      Computer Assisted Instruction
      Computer Interfaces
      Computer Mediated Communication
      Computer Networks
      Computer Oriented Programs
      Computer System Design
      Computers
      Cybernetics
      Display Systems
      Expert Systems
      Feedback
      Gateway Systems
      Human Factors Engineering
      Interaction
      Management Information Systems
      Natural Language Processing
      Navigation (Information Systems)
      Online Systems
      Robotics
      Systems Development
      Virtual Reality
      Workstations

Managed Care (HMOs)
USE   Health Maintenance Organizations

Management by Objectives   JUL. 1974
      Postings: 728   GC: 320
SN   Method of combining performance ap-
      praisal with the process of developing
      and refining organizational goals—
      involves mutual goal setting between
      manager and subordinate, during which
      specific performance or measurement
      criteria are spelled out and agreed upon
BT   Administration
      Management Systems
RT   Accountability
      Employer Employee Relationship
      Objectives
      Organizational Development
      Organizational Objectives
      Performance
      Performance Contracts
      Personnel Evaluation

Management Development   JUL. 1966
      Postings: 3,845   GC: 320
SN   Inservice programs designed to increase
      the supervisory and managerial skills of
      administrators, managers, and manage-
      ment trainees (Note: Use "Administrator
      Education" for formal preservice educa-
      tion programs—prior to Mar80, this term
      was not restricted to inservice programs)
UF   Administrator Training
      Executive Development

= Two or more Descriptors are used to represent this term.
The term's main entry shows the appropriate coordination.

Management Training
BT Labor Force Development
RT Administrator Education
    Assessment Centers (Personnel)
    Business Administration Education
    Industrial Training
    Inservice Education
    Leadership Training
    Off the Job Training
    Professional Continuing Education
    Professional Development
    Professional Training
    Public Administration Education
    Staff Development
    Supervisory Training

Management Education (1967 1980)
USE Administrator Education

Management Games   *JUL. 1966*
    Postings: 418   GC: 310
UF Business Games
BT Games
    Training Methods
RT Decision Making
    Game Theory
    Management Systems
    Problem Solving
    Simulated Environment
    Simulation

Management Information Systems
                  JUL. 1971
    Postings: 2,376   GC: 710
SN Communications systems that are de-
    signed to furnish management and su-
    pervisory personnel with information
    needed for decision making
UF MIS
NT Decision Support Systems
BT Information Systems
    Management Systems
RT Administration
    Computer Managed Instruction
    Computer Oriented Programs
    Data Processing
    Database Management Systems
    Decision Making
    Information Management
    Man Machine Systems

Management Personnel
USE Administrators

Management Systems   *OCT. 1969*
    Postings: 2,420   GC: 320
SN A general term indicating that a systems
    approach has been used in dealing with
    management concerns (Note: Use a more
    specific term if possible—prior to Mar80,
    the use of this term was not restricted by
    a Scope Note)
NT Database Management Systems
    Enrollment Management
    Management by Objectives
    Management Information Systems
    Total Quality Management
RT Administration
    Administrative Organization
    Critical Path Method
    Decision Making
    Information Systems
    Linear Programming
    Long Range Planning
    Management Games
    Operations Research
    Organizational Communication
    Performance Technology
    Problem Solving
    Simulation
    Strategic Planning
    Systems Analysis
    Systems Approach
    Systems Development

Management Teams   *MAR. 1980*
    Postings: 533   GC: 320
UF Administrative Teams

Team Administration (1967 1980)
    Team Management
BT Administrative Organization
RT Administration
    Organizational Development
    Participative Decision Making
    Power Structure
    Quality Circles
    Teamwork
    Total Quality Management

Management Training
USE Management Development

Management (1966 1980)
USE Administration

Managerial Occupations   *JUL. 1966*
    Postings: 591   GC: 640
UF Administrative Occupations
BT Occupations
RT Administration
    Business Administration
    Coordination
    Professional Occupations
    White Collar Occupations

Managers
USE Administrators

Manchu   *MAR. 1971*
    Postings: 3   GC: 440
BT Uralic Altaic Languages

Mandarin Chinese   *JUL. 1966*
    Postings: 373   GC: 440
UF Putonghua
BT Chinese

Mandatory Continuing Education   *MAY 1997*
    Postings: 53   GC: 340
SN Education required by regulation or law
    for occupational and professional devel-
    opment, e.g., for work licensure or certi-
    fication
BT Continuing Education
RT Certification
    Professional Continuing Education
    Required Courses

Mandatory Courses
USE Required Courses

Mandatory Education
USE Compulsory Education

Mandatory Retirement   *JUN. 1996*
    Postings: 79   GC: 630
SN Forced retirement upon reaching a maxi-
    mum age—this age can be set through
    statute, court ruling, or contract
UF Compulsory Retirement
BT Retirement
RT Age Discrimination
    Early Retirement
    Employment Practices
    Older Adults
    Older Workers
    Personnel Policy
    Teacher Retirement

Mandingo   *JUL. 1966*
    Postings: 14   GC: 440
BT African Languages

Mangala
USE Lingala

Manipulative Materials   *JUL. 1966*
    Postings: 1,291   GC: 720
SN Instructional materials that are designed
    to be touched or handled by students

and which develop their muscles, per-
ceptual skills, psychomotor skills, etc.
UF Tactile Materials
BT Instructional Materials
RT Experiential Learning
    Hands on Science
    Kinesthetic Perception
    Montessori Method
    Object Manipulation
    Perceptual Motor Learning
    Psychomotor Skills
    Sensory Aids
    Tactile Stimuli
    Tactual Perception

Manpower
USE Labor Force

Manpower Development (1966 1980)
USE Labor Force Development

Manpower Needs (1968 1980)
USE Labor Needs

Manpower Utilization (1966 1980)
USE Labor Utilization

Manual Communication   *JUL. 1966*
    Postings: 448   GC: 220
SN A form of communication with and among
    the deaf in which sign language and
    finger spelling are substituted for speech
UF Signed English
NT Cued Speech
    Finger Spelling
    Sign Language
BT Augmentative and Alternative Commu-
    nication
RT Communication Skills
    Deaf Interpreting
    Deafness
    Hearing Impairments
    Hearing Therapy
    Oral Communication Method
    Total Communication

Manuals (1966 1980)
USE Guides

Manufacturing   *JUL. 1966*
    Postings: 620   GC: 650
UF Fabrication
    Manufacturing Methods
    Manufacturing Techniques
NT Assembly (Manufacturing)
    Computer Assisted Manufacturing
    Mass Production
BT Technology
RT Distributive Education
    Engineering
    Equipment Manufacturers
    Industrial Arts
    Manufacturing Industry
    Production Technicians
    Technology Education

Manufacturing Industry   *JUL. 1966*
    Postings: 744   GC: 650
NT Aerospace Industry
    Cement Industry
    Chemical Industry
    Electronics Industry
    Furniture Industry
    Machinery Industry
    Metal Industry
BT Industry
RT Assembly (Manufacturing)
    Brick Industry
    Chemical Engineering
    Computer Assisted Manufacturing
    Equipment Manufacturers
    Machine Tool Operators
    Machine Tools
    Manufacturing
    Mechanical Design Technicians
    Production Technicians

Manufacturing Methods
USE Manufacturing

Manufacturing Techniques
USE Manufacturing

Manuscript Writing (Handlettering)
                  JUL. 1966
    Postings: 130   GC: 420
SN Handwriting based on adaptations of the
    printed letter forms
UF Calligraphy
    Printscript
    Uncial Script
BT Handwriting
RT Cursive Writing
    Manuscripts

Manuscripts   *JUN. 2000*
    Postings: 87   GC: 730
SN Typewritten or handwritten versions of
    books or other works, especially the
    authors' own copies—the form of writ-
    ten works submitted for publication
BT Printed Materials
RT Archives
    Authors
    Books
    Diaries
    Letters (Correspondence)
    Library Collections
    Manuscript Writing (Handlettering)
    Primary Sources
    Publications
    Writing (Composition)

Maori   *SEP. 1996*
    Postings: 22   GC: 440
SN Language of the indigenous Polynesian
    people of New Zealand
BT Malayo Polynesian Languages
RT Maori (People)

Maori (People)   *SEP. 1996*
    Postings: 144   GC: 560
SN Indigenous Polynesian people of New
    Zealand
BT Ethnic Groups
    Pacific Islanders
RT Maori
    Minority Groups

Map Reading Skills
USE Map Skills

Map Skills   *JUL. 1966*
    Postings: 972   GC: 400
UF Map Reading Skills
BT Skills
RT Cartography
    Geography
    Locational Skills (Social Studies)
    Maps

Mapping (Cartography)
USE Cartography

Mappings (Mathematics)
USE Functions (Mathematics)

Maps   *JUL. 1966*
    Postings: 1,359   GC: 720
BT Visual Aids
RT Atlases
    Cartography
    Geography
    Illustrations
    Instructional Materials
    Locational Skills (Social Studies)
    Map Skills
    Nonprint Media
    Relief (Art)
    Topography

= Two or more Descriptors are used to represent this term.
The term's main entry shows the appropriate coordination.

Maranao   JUL. 1966
   Postings: 2
BT   Indonesian Languages

Marathi   JUL. 1966
   Postings: 27   GC: 440
BT   Indo European Languages

Marching Bands
USE   Bands (Music)

Marihuana (1969 1986)
USE   Marijuana

Marijuana   AUG. 1986
   Postings: 227   GC: 210
UF   Cannabis
   Hashish
   Marihuana (1969 1986)
BT   Narcotics
RT   Drug Abuse
   Drug Addiction
   Drug Legislation
   Drug Use
   Illegal Drug Use

Marine Biology   JUL. 1966
   Postings: 770   GC: 490
BT   Biology
RT   Ecology
   Estuaries
   Fisheries
   Ichthyology
   Marine Education
   Marine Technicians
   Ocean Engineering
   Oceanography
   Radiation Biology
   Wetlands

Marine Corps Air Stations
USE   Military Air Facilities

Marine Education   OCT. 1983
   Postings: 441   GC: 400
SN   Interdisciplinary group of learning/teach-
   ing activities concerning the earth's wa-
   ters and seas (Note: Use a more precise
   term if possible)
UF   Marine Science Education
NT   Maritime Education
BT   Education
RT   Environmental Education
   Estuaries
   Hydrology
   Marine Biology
   Oceanography
   Science Education
   Underwater Diving
   Water
   Wetlands

Marine Science Education
USE   Marine Education

Marine Technicians   JUL. 1966
   Postings: 90   GC: 640
BT   Paraprofessional Personnel
RT   Marine Biology
   Oceanography
   Scientific Personnel
   Seafarers
   Underwater Diving

Mariners
USE   Seafarers

Marital Counseling
USE   Marriage Counseling

Marital Instability   JUL. 1966
   Postings: 957   GC: 530
RT   Battered Women

   Displaced Homemakers
   Divorce
   Family Life
   Family Problems
   Family Violence
   Marriage
   Marriage Counseling
   One Parent Family

Marital Satisfaction   OCT. 1983
   Postings: 732   GC: 510
SN   Level of contentment with one's married
   life
BT   Satisfaction
RT   Family Life
   Life Satisfaction
   Love
   Marriage
   Marriage Counseling
   Need Gratification
   Self Actualization

Marital Status   AUG. 1974
   Postings: 1,303   GC: 510
BT   Status
RT   Cohabitation
   Divorce
   Marriage
   Married Students
   Single Students
   Spouses
   Widowed

Maritime Education   FEB. 1984
   Postings: 43   GC: 490
SN   Learning/teaching activities concerned
   with building, operating, and navigating
   boats, ships, and other floating struc-
   tures, as well as related harbor and dock
   technology
BT   Marine Education
RT   Boat Operators
   Oceanography
   Sailing
   Seafarers
   Water

Market Economy
USE   Free Enterprise System

Marketable Skills
USE   Employment Potential
AND   Job Skills

Marketing   JUL. 1966
   Postings: 4,310   GC: 650
SN   An aggregate of functions involved in the
   transfer of goods from producer to con-
   sumer
UF   Distribution (Economics)
NT   Merchandising
   Retailing
   Salesmanship
   Wholesaling
BT   Technology
RT   Business
   Business Education
   Consumer Protection
   Cooperatives
   Distributive Education
   Focus Groups
   Franchising
   Institutional Advancement
   International Trade
   Merchandise Information
   Merchants
   Rail Transportation
   Strategic Planning
   Supply and Demand
   Technology Transfer
   Vendors

Marking (Scholastic)
USE   Grading

Markov Chains
USE   Markov Processes

Markov Processes   DEC. 1988
   Postings: 101   GC: 480
SN   Probabilistic simulations in which future
   events are determined completely by pres-
   ent and immediately preceding events,
   and not on anything occurring earlier—
   derived from the model developed by
   Russian mathematician A.A. Markov
UF   Markov Chains
BT   Simulation
RT   Computer Simulation
   Decision Making
   Hypothesis Testing
   Mathematical Models
   Matrices
   Planning
   Prediction
   Predictive Measurement
   Probability
   Research Methodology
   Scientific Methodology
   Statistical Analysis

Marks (Scholastic)
USE   Grades (Scholastic)

Marksmanship   JUL. 1966
   Postings: 18   GC: 400
BT   Psychomotor Skills
RT   Guns
   Military Science

Marriage   JUL. 1966
   Postings: 2,017   GC: 520
NT   Intermarriage
   Remarriage
BT   Interpersonal Relationship
RT   Divorce
   Family (Sociological Unit)
   Family Life
   Kinship
   Marital Instability
   Marital Satisfaction
   Marital Status
   Marriage Counseling
   Married Students
   Mate Selection
   Spouses

Marriage Counseling   APR. 1970
   Postings: 903   GC: 240
UF   Marital Counseling
BT   Counseling
RT   Divorce
   Family Counseling
   Family Life
   Family Problems
   Marital Instability
   Marital Satisfaction
   Marriage

Married Persons
USE   Spouses

Married Students   AUG. 1974
   Postings: 164   GC: 360
BT   Students
RT   Adult Students
   Board of Education Policy
   Equal Protection
   Marital Status
   Marriage
   Self Supporting Students
   Single Students
   Spouses
   Student Rights

Marshes
USE   Wetlands

Marxian Analysis   MAR. 1984
   Postings: 199   GC: 810
SN   Application of Marxist concepts, princi-
   ples, and models in any field (e.g., edu-
   cational or historical or literary criticism)
UF   Marxist Criticism
BT   Methods
RT   Critical Theory
   Economic Factors
   Marxism
   Social Change
   Social Science Research
   Social Stratification
   Sociology

Marxism   MAR. 1984
   Postings: 367   GC: 610
SN   Body of social, economic, and political
   thought originating with Karl Marx and
   Friedrich Engels—distinguished by the
   labor theory of value, the principles of
   dialectical materialism and economic de-
   terminism, and the doctrine of revolu-
   tionary change leading to a classless
   society
UF   Dialectical Materialism
BT   Philosophy
RT   Capitalism
   Communism
   Economics
   Labor Economics
   Marxian Analysis
   Political Attitudes
   Political Power
   Political Science
   Revolution
   Social Class
   Socialism
   Sociology
   Twentieth Century Literature
   Working Class

Marxist Criticism
USE   Marxian Analysis

Masculinity   JUN. 2000
   Postings: 316   GC: 120
SN   The quality or condition of being
   masculine—may be considered to be
   determined or affected by biological, so-
   cial, or cultural factors
RT   Androgyny
   Femininity
   Gender Issues
   Males
   Self Concept
   Sex Differences
   Sex Role
   Sex Stereotypes
   Sexual Identity

Masonry   SEP. 1969
   Postings: 112   GC: 920
SN   Building or working with stone or brick
UF   Masons (Trade)
NT   Bricklaying
BT   Construction (Process)
   Technology
RT   Building Trades
   Construction Materials
   Prefabrication
   Prestressed Concrete
   Skilled Occupations
   Structural Building Systems

Masons (Trade)
USE   Masonry

Mass Communications
USE   Mass Media

Mass Culture
USE   Popular Culture

= Two or more Descriptors are used to represent this term.
The term's main entry shows the appropriate coordination.

Mass Instruction JUL. 1966
Postings: 231 GC: 350
SN Large-scale activities aimed at dissemi-
nating information to or influencing the
opinion of the general public (Note: Prior
to Mar80, the use of this term was not
restricted by a Scope Note)
BT Instruction
RT Audiences
Distance Education
Educational Radio
Educational Television
Individualized Instruction
Large Group Instruction
Listening Groups
Mass Media
Mass Media Role
Public Opinion
Teaching Methods

Mass Media JUL. 1966
Postings: 6,160 GC: 720
SN Systems or instruments of communica-
tion intended to reach general and geo-
graphically dispersed audiences simul-
taneously
UF Communications Media
Mass Communications
Mass Media Technology #
NT Films
News Media
Radio
Television
RT Advertising
Agenda Setting
Audiences
Audiovisual Aids
Broadcast Industry
Communications
Development Communication
Discourse Modes
Editors
Educational Media
Film Industry
Information Dissemination
Information Industry
Information Sources
Journalism
Journalism Education
Mass Instruction
Mass Media Effects
Mass Media Role
Mass Media Use
Media Research
Multimedia Materials
Nonprint Media
Political Campaigns
Popular Culture
Press Opinion
Printed Materials
Propaganda
Publications
Publicity
Publishing Industry
Television Commercials

Mass Media Effects AUG. 1982
Postings: 2,042 GC: 520
SN The impact or consequences of mass
media on social structures, laws, and/or
human behavior
RT Agenda Setting
Audience Analysis
Audience Response
Mass Media
Mass Media Role
Mass Media Use
Media Research
Public Opinion

Mass Media Role AUG. 1988
Postings: 1,221 GC: 520
SN Functions or tasks expected of or per-
formed by the mass media in society,
e.g., news, education, entertainment,
propaganda
UF Media Role (Mass Media)
Press Role #
Television Role #
BT Role

RT Agenda Setting
Broadcast Industry
Broadcast Journalism
Film Industry
Information Dissemination
Information Industry
Journalism
Mass Instruction
Mass Media
Mass Media Effects
Media Research
News Reporting
Press Opinion
Publishing Industry
Social Influences

Mass Media Technology
USE Communications
AND Mass Media

Mass Media Use AUG. 1988
Postings: 581 GC: 720
SN The manner, purpose, frequency, etc., of
audience use of the electronic or printed
mass media
UF Media Use (Mass Media)
News Use #
Television Use #
RT Audience Response
Information Utilization
Mass Media
Mass Media Effects
Media Adaptation
Media Selection
Public Opinion
Recreational Activities
Socialization
Television Viewing
Use Studies

Mass Production SEP. 1969
Postings: 73 GC: 650
UF Large Scale Production
BT Manufacturing
RT Assembly (Manufacturing)
Chemical Engineering
Production Technicians
Production Techniques

Massed Negative Reinforcement
USE Negative Reinforcement

Master of Arts Degrees
USE Masters Degrees

Master of Arts in College Teaching
USE Masters Degrees

Master of Arts in Teaching
USE Masters Degrees

Master of Science Degrees
USE Masters Degrees

Master of Science in Teaching
USE Masters Degrees

Master Plans JUL. 1966
Postings: 1,000 GC: 730
RT Building Plans
Facility Guidelines
Facility Planning
Facility Requirements
Long Range Planning
Mission Statements
Planning
Planning Commissions
Policy Formation
Specifications
Statewide Planning
Strategic Planning

Master Tapes (Audio) (1968 1980)
USE Audiotape Recordings

Master Teachers JUL. 1966
Postings: 447 GC: 360
SN Elementary or secondary school teach-
ers who, because of advance profes-
sional preparation and teaching
experience, are qualified to assist in the
preparation of student teachers or teacher
interns, to give guidance to inexperi-
enced teachers, or to coordinate and
lead teams of teachers (Note: Do not
confuse with the more precise term "Co-
operating Teachers")
UF Senior Teacher Role (1966 1980) #
BT Teachers
RT Beginning Teacher Induction
Beginning Teachers
Cooperating Teachers
Differentiated Staffs
Merit Pay
Student Teachers
Student Teaching
Teacher Education
Teacher Educator Education
Teacher Educators
Teacher Interns
Team Teaching

Masters Degrees JUL. 1966
Postings: 1,445 GC: 340
UF Master of Arts Degrees
Master of Arts in College Teaching
Master of Arts in Teaching
Master of Science Degrees
Master of Science in Teaching
BT Degrees (Academic)
RT Bachelors Degrees
Degree Requirements
Doctoral Degrees
Extended Teacher Education Programs
Graduate Study
Masters Programs
Masters Theses
Specialist in Education Degrees
Teacher Educator Education

Masters Programs MAR. 1980
Postings: 968 GC: 340
SN Formal graduate programs in higher edu-
cation institutions that culminate in the
award of a master's degree
BT College Programs
RT Degree Requirements
Doctoral Programs
Graduate School Faculty
Graduate Students
Graduate Study
Higher Education
Masters Degrees
Masters Theses

Masters Theses JUL. 1966
Postings: 866 GC: 720
SN Written reports of some extensiveness
submitted in partial fulfillment of mas-
ter's degree requirements (Note: Corre-
sponds to Pubtype code 042—do not
use except as the subject of a document)
BT Theses
RT Graduate Study
Masters Degrees
Masters Programs
Practicum Papers

Mastery Learning DEC. 1976
Postings: 1,140 GC: 310
SN Strategy characterized by: the definition
of learning objectives and expected
achievement level, a design that permits
as many students as possible to achieve
objectives to specified level, and the
assignment of grades based on achievement of objectives at specified level
BT Learning
RT Academic Achievement
Academic Standards
Achievement

Behavioral Objectives
Learning Readiness
Learning Strategies
Mastery Tests
Minimum Competencies
Objectives
Outcome Based Education
Pacing
Performance
Skill Development
Skills

Mastery Tests DEC. 1976
Postings: 473 GC: 830
SN Tests used to place individuals into two
distinct groups: those who have clearly
reached a predetermined standard of
competency and those who have not
BT Achievement Tests
Criterion Referenced Tests
RT Academic Achievement
Academic Standards
Achievement
Behavioral Objectives
Cutting Scores
Licensing Examinations (Professions)
Mastery Learning
Minimum Competency Testing
National Competency Tests
Performance
Skill Development
Skills

Matched Groups JUL. 1966
Postings: 120 GC: 820
SN Groups, used in experiments, who are
equivalent in all necessary respects so
that any differences arising among them
can be attributed to experimental treat-
ments
BT Groups
RT Attrition (Research Studies)
Control Groups
Effect Size
Experimental Groups
Participant Characteristics
Quasiexperimental Design
Research Design
Research Methodology
Sampling
Statistical Bias

Matching Tests
USE Objective Tests

Mate Selection MAR. 1977
Postings: 174 GC: 510
SN Process of choosing a partner for mar-
riage or cohabitation
BT Selection
RT Cohabitation
Dating (Social)
Intermarriage
Love
Marriage
Social Development

Material Adaptation
USE Media Adaptation

Material Culture APR. 1990
Postings: 192 GC: 560
SN The inventory of physical objects and
artifacts made and used by a human
group, e.g., tools, ornaments, art, archi-
tecture, recreational and religious ob-
jects, items for communication and trans-
portation
BT Culture
RT Anthropology
Buildings
Built Environment
Clothing
Community Resources
Equipment
Folk Culture
Heritage Education
Middle Class Culture

= Two or more Descriptors are used to represent this term.
The term's main entry shows the appropriate coordination.

Museums
Popular Culture
Realia
Technological Advancement
Visual Arts

Material Development   JUL. 1966
Postings: 4,630   GC: 310
UF   Instructional Material Development
     Material Research
NT   Computer Software Development
     Test Construction
BT   Development
RT   Curriculum Development
     Formative Evaluation
     Instructional Material Evaluation
     Instructional Materials
     Media Adaptation
     Pretesting
     Programming (Broadcast)
     Student Developed Materials
     Teacher Developed Materials

Material Research
USE   Material Development

Material Selection
USE   Media Selection

Material Sources
USE   Resource Materials

Materials Inventory
USE   Facility Inventory

Mathematical Applications   JUL. 1966
Postings: 3,004   GC: 480
UF   Practical Mathematics (1966 1980)
NT   Algorithms
     Computation
     Linear Programming
     Mathematical Formulas
     Word Problems (Mathematics)
RT   General Mathematics
     Intuition
     Mathematical Models
     Mathematics
     Mathematics Activities
     Mathematics Skills
     Problem Sets
     Problem Solving

Mathematical Aptitude   JAN. 1993
Postings: 186   GC: 480
SN   Natural capacity or inclination for skillful
     performance of mathematical tasks
UF   Mathematics Aptitude
     Quantitative Aptitude
BT   Aptitude
RT   Academic Aptitude
     Mathematics
     Mathematics Achievement
     Mathematics Skills
     Mathematics Tests

Mathematical Concepts   JUL. 1966
Postings: 3,502   GC: 480
NT   Geometric Concepts
     Inequality (Mathematics)
     Limits (Mathematics)
     Number Concepts
     Patterns in Mathematics
     Properties (Mathematics)
RT   Concept Mapping
     Conservation (Concept)
     Equations (Mathematics)
     Ethnomathematics
     Functions (Mathematics)
     Fundamental Concepts
     Mathematical Models
     Mathematics
     Mathematics Skills
     Mathematics Tests
     Misconceptions
     Nonparametric Statistics
     Percentage

Polynomials
Probability
Proof (Mathematics)
Quotas
Ratios (Mathematics)
Reciprocals (Mathematics)
Transformations (Mathematics)
Trigonometry

Mathematical Enrichment   JUL. 1966
Postings: 1,422   GC: 480
SN   Experiences which replace, supplement,
     or extend normally offered mathematics
     instruction
BT   Enrichment
RT   Arithmetic
     Mathematics
     Mathematics Activities
     Mathematics Instruction
     Mathematics Materials
     Trigonometry

Mathematical Experience (1966 1980)
                        MAR. 1980
Postings: 107   GC: 480
SN   Invalid Descriptor—used inconsistently
     in indexing—see more precise "mathe-
     matics" Descriptors

Mathematical Expressions
USE   Mathematical Formulas

Mathematical Formulas   AUG. 1978
Postings: 1,076   GC: 480
SN   Equations or rules relating mathematical
     objects or quantities
UF   Mathematical Expressions
     Mathematical Sentences
NT   Equations (Mathematics)
     Functions (Mathematics)
     Polynomials
BT   Mathematical Applications
     Mathematical Logic
RT   Computation
     Mathematical Models
     Mathematics
     Symbols (Mathematics)

Mathematical Linguistics   JUL. 1966
Postings: 143   GC: 450
UF   Statistical Linguistics
BT   Linguistics
RT   Computational Linguistics
     Mathematics
     Word Frequency

Mathematical Literacy
USE   Numeracy

Mathematical Logic   JUL. 1966
Postings: 474   GC: 480
UF   Symbolic Logic
NT   Algorithms
     Mathematical Formulas
     Proof (Mathematics)
     Set Theory
BT   Logic
RT   Computational Linguistics
     Computer Literacy
     Game Theory
     Mathematics
     Mathematics Skills
     Matrices
     Statistics

Mathematical Models   JUL. 1966
Postings: 4,989   GC: 730
BT   Models
RT   Causal Models
     Chaos Theory
     Chi Square
     Diagrams
     Discriminant Analysis
     Effect Size
     Entropy
     Estimation (Mathematics)

Game Theory
Generalizability Theory
Goodness of Fit
Heuristics
Hypothesis Testing
Information Theory
Item Response Theory
Linear Programming
Markov Processes
Mathematical Applications
Mathematical Concepts
Mathematical Formulas
Mathematics
Measurement
Monte Carlo Methods
Multitrait Multimethod Techniques
Multivariate Analysis
Operations Research
Proof (Mathematics)
Robustness (Statistics)
Scaling
Statistics
Structural Equation Models
Test Theory

Mathematical Patterns
USE   Patterns in Mathematics

Mathematical Sentences
USE   Mathematical Formulas

Mathematical Statistics
USE   Statistics

Mathematical Vocabulary   JUL. 1966
Postings: 315   GC: 480
BT   Vocabulary
RT   Mathematics
     Trigonometry

Mathematicians   SEP. 1968
Postings: 295   GC: 640
BT   Professional Personnel
     Scientific Personnel
RT   Engineers
     Mathematics
     Mathematics History
     Mathematics Teachers
     Systems Analysts

Mathematics   JUL. 1966
Postings: 6,325   GC: 480
NT   Algebra
     Arithmetic
     Calculus
     Ethnomathematics
     Geometry
     Probability
     Statistics
     Technical Mathematics
     Trigonometry
BT   Liberal Arts
RT   Algorithms
     Calculators
     College Mathematics
     Computation
     Elementary School Mathematics
     Estimation (Mathematics)
     General Mathematics
     Graphing Calculators
     Height
     Mathematical Applications
     Mathematical Aptitude
     Mathematical Concepts
     Mathematical Enrichment
     Mathematical Formulas
     Mathematical Linguistics
     Mathematical Logic
     Mathematical Models
     Mathematical Vocabulary
     Mathematicians
     Mathematics Achievement
     Mathematics Activities
     Mathematics Anxiety
     Mathematics Curriculum
     Mathematics Education
     Mathematics History
     Mathematics Instruction

Mathematics Materials
Mathematics Skills
Mathematics Teachers
Mathematics Tests
Mental Computation
Modern Mathematics
Number Systems
Numbers
Numeracy
Proof (Mathematics)
Quantum Mechanics
Remedial Mathematics
Sciences
Secondary School Mathematics
Symbols (Mathematics)
Word Problems (Mathematics)

Mathematics Achievement   SEP. 1981
Postings: 3,306   GC: 480
SN   Level of attainment in any or all mathe-
     matics skills, usually estimated by per-
     formance on a test
BT   Achievement
RT   Academic Achievement
     Achievement Gains
     Mathematical Aptitude
     Mathematics
     Mathematics Skills
     Mathematics Tests

Mathematics Activities   AUG. 1997
Postings: 1,007   GC: 480
SN   Methods of mathematics instruction that
     usually involve some participation by
     students—may include projects outside
     the school
BT   Activities
RT   Mathematical Applications
     Mathematical Enrichment
     Mathematics
     Mathematics Curriculum
     Mathematics Education
     Mathematics Instruction
     Mathematics Materials

Mathematics Anxiety   MAR. 1980
Postings: 623   GC: 480
UF   Mathematics Avoidance
     Mathophobia
BT   Anxiety
RT   Computer Anxiety
     Mathematics
     School Phobia

Mathematics Aptitude
USE   Mathematical Aptitude

Mathematics Avoidance
USE   Mathematics Anxiety

Mathematics Curriculum   JUL. 1966
Postings: 3,745   GC: 480
UF   Arithmetic Curriculum (1966 1980) #
NT   College Mathematics
     Elementary School Mathematics
     General Mathematics
     Modern Mathematics
     Secondary School Mathematics
BT   Curriculum
RT   Mathematics
     Mathematics Activities
     Mathematics Instruction

Mathematics Education   JUL. 1966
Postings: 15,842   GC: 480
BT   Education
RT   College Mathematics
     Elementary School Mathematics
     Ethnomathematics
     General Mathematics
     Mathematics
     Mathematics Activities
     Mathematics History
     Mathematics Instruction
     Secondary School Mathematics

= Two or more Descriptors are used to represent this term.
The term's main entry shows the appropriate coordination.

Mathematics History   FEB. 1997
Postings: 227   GC: 480
SN   Study of mathematical sciences and activities through the ages, including specific periods, geographic areas, branches, and mathematicians
BT   History
RT   Ethnomathematics
Mathematicians
Mathematics
Mathematics Education

Mathematics Instruction   JUL. 1966
Postings: 14,731   GC: 480
NT   Remedial Mathematics
BT   Instruction
RT   College Mathematics
Elementary School Mathematics
Ethnomathematics
General Mathematics
Mathematical Enrichment
Mathematics
Mathematics Activities
Mathematics Curriculum
Mathematics Education
Mathematics Materials
Mathematics Teachers
Secondary School Mathematics

Mathematics Materials   JUL. 1966
Postings: 1,173   GC: 730
RT   Geometric Constructions
Instructional Materials
Mathematical Enrichment
Mathematics
Mathematics Activities
Mathematics Instruction

Mathematics Skills   MAR. 1983
Postings: 2,575   GC: 480
SN   Complex behaviors developed through practice in order to complete mathematical tasks (Note: Use for documents whose specific focus is on the acquisition and/or use of mathematics skills—do not use as an automatic adjunct to "Mathematics Curriculum," "Mathematics Education," etc.)
BT   Skills
RT   Basic Skills
Mathematical Applications
Mathematical Aptitude
Mathematical Concepts
Mathematical Logic
Mathematics
Mathematics Achievement
Mathematics Tests
Measurement
Minimum Competencies
Numbers
Numeracy
Science Process Skills
Thinking Skills

Mathematics Teachers   JUL. 1966
Postings: 1,567   GC: 360
BT   Teachers
RT   Mathematicians
Mathematics
Mathematics Instruction

Mathematics Tests   DEC. 1985
Postings: 1,304   GC: 830
SN   Tests of ability, achievement, or aptitude in arithmetic or other aspects of mathematics
UF   Arithmetic Tests #
Number Skills Tests
Quantitative Tests (1980 1985) (Mathematics)
BT   Tests
RT   Achievement Tests
Aptitude Tests
Computation
Mathematical Aptitude
Mathematical Concepts
Mathematics
Mathematics Achievement
Mathematics Skills

Number Concepts
Numbers
Verbal Tests
Word Problems (Mathematics)

Mathophobia
USE   Mathematics Anxiety

Matrices   JUN. 1973
Postings: 1,021   GC: 480
BT   Algebra
RT   Causal Models
Coding
Markov Processes
Mathematical Logic
Multitrait Multimethod Techniques
Oblique Rotation
Orthogonal Rotation
Spreadsheets
Statistical Analysis
Vectors (Mathematics)

Matriculation
USE   Admission (School)

Matrix Sampling
USE   Item Sampling

Matter   JUL. 1966
Postings: 243   GC: 490
NT   Acids
Minerals
Polymers
Sludge
Wastes
Water
RT   Atomic Structure
Atomic Theory
Crystallography
Density (Matter)
Diffusion (Physics)
Nuclear Physics
Physical Chemistry
Physics
Quantum Mechanics
Radioisotopes
Relativity
Weight (Mass)

Maturation Learning Controversy
USE   Nature Nurture Controversy

Maturation (1967 1980)   MAR. 1980
Postings: 584   GC: 120
SN   Invalid Descriptor—see "Development," "Individual Development," and "Maturity (Individuals)"

Maturity (Individuals)   MAR. 1980
Postings: 563   GC: 120
SN   Full growth or development of the individual (Note: Prior to Mar80, "Maturation" was a valid Descriptor—see "Individual Development" or other "development" terms for the process of maturing)
UF   Immaturity (1966 1980)
Social Immaturity (1966 1980)
Social Maturity (1966 1980)
NT   Vocational Maturity
BT   Individual Characteristics
RT   Adjustment (to Environment)
Age
Independent Living
Individual Development
Interpersonal Competence
Maturity Tests
Personality Traits
Physical Characteristics
Psychological Characteristics
Self Care Skills
Self Control

Maturity Tests   JUL. 1966
Postings: 126   GC: 830
SN   Measures of social, emotional, behav

ioral, or physiological development of individuals from infancy through adulthood
BT   Tests
RT   Individual Development
Maturity (Individuals)
Occupational Tests
Personality Measures
Preschool Tests
School Readiness Tests
Vocational Maturity

Mauritian Creole   JUN. 1971
Postings: 4   GC: 440
BT   Creoles

Maximum Likelihood Factor Analysis
USE   Factor Analysis
AND   Maximum Likelihood Statistics

Maximum Likelihood Statistics   OCT. 1980
Postings: 481   GC: 820
SN   Statistics that are designed to provide estimates that maximize the probability of zero, or negligible, error (that is, estimates most likely to be correct)
UF   Maximum Likelihood Factor Analysis #
BT   Statistical Analysis
Statistics
RT   Delphi Technique
Factor Analysis
Goodness of Fit
Predictive Measurement
Probability
Sampling
Statistical Significance

Maya (People)   AUG. 1997
Postings: 56   GC: 560
SN   Indigenous people of Guatemala, Belize, southern Mexico, and the Yucatan Peninsula (Note: See also the Identifier "Mayan Civilization")
UF   Mayans
BT   American Indians
Latin Americans
RT   Mayan Languages

Mayan Languages   DEC. 1970
Postings: 48   GC: 440
NT   Cakchiquel
Quiche
Tzeltal
Tzotzil
Yucatec
BT   American Indian Languages
RT   Maya (People)

Mayans
USE   Maya (People)

Mbya Guarani
USE   Guarani

Measurement   JUL. 1966
Postings: 3,748   GC: 820
SN   Process of obtaining a numerical description of the extent to which persons, organizations, or things possess specified characteristics (Note: See also "Testing" and "Evaluation")
NT   Achievement Rating
Cognitive Measurement
Merit Rating
Predictive Measurement
Scoring
RT   Computation
Data
Estimation (Mathematics)
Evaluation
Full Time Equivalency
Generalizability Theory
Grade Equivalent Scores
Mathematical Models
Mathematics Skills
Measurement Objectives

Measurement Techniques
Measures (Individuals)
Mental Computation
Metric System
Norms
Observation
Proof (Mathematics)
Scores
Standards
Statistical Analysis
Statistical Data
Testing
Tests

Measurement Equipment   MAR. 1980
Postings: 357   GC: 910
UF   Gauges
Meters
NT   Calorimeters
Polygraphs
Potentiometers (Instruments)
Sound Spectrographs
BT   Equipment
RT   Biomedical Equipment
Instrumentation
Laboratory Equipment
Science Equipment

Measurement Error
USE   Error of Measurement

Measurement Goals (1966 1980)
USE   Measurement Objectives

Measurement Instruments (1966 1980)   MAR. 1980
Postings: 3,412   GC: 910
SN   Invalid Descriptor—used for equipment as well as mental measures—see the displays of "Measurement Equipment" and "Measures (Individuals)" or "Measurement Techniques" respectively for these concepts

Measurement Objectives   MAR. 1980
Postings: 642   GC: 820
SN   Aims or ends toward which measurement efforts are directed, including desired improvements in the technology of quantification
UF   Measurement Goals (1966 1980)
BT   Objectives
RT   Evaluation Needs
Measurement
Research Needs
Testing

Measurement Techniques   JUL. 1966
Postings: 7,593   GC: 820
SN   Procedures used to systematically obtain quantified descriptions of the extent to which persons, organizations, or things possess specific characteristics (Note: Prior to Mar80, the use of this term was not restricted by a Scope Note)
NT   Classroom Observation Techniques
Forced Choice Technique
Q Methodology
Scaling
Scoring Formulas
Sociometric Techniques
Testing
BT   Methods
RT   Audits (Verification)
Criterion Referenced Tests
Econometrics
Evaluation Methods
Grade Equivalent Scores
Interrater Reliability
Item Sampling
Measurement
Measures (Individuals)
Monte Carlo Methods
Multitrait Multimethod Techniques
Rating Scales
Readability Formulas
Research Methodology
Sample Size

= Two or more Descriptors are used to represent this term.
The term's main entry shows the appropriate coordination.

Sampling
Scientific Methodology

Measures (Individuals) *MAR. 1980*
Postings: 2,074 GC: 830
SN Procedures, devices, or sets of items that are used to estimate or rate the characteristics of individuals, e.g., their abilities, attitudes, opinions, or mental traits (Note: Use a more specific term if possible)
UF Assessment Instruments (Individuals)
Inventories (Measurement)
Scales
NT Affective Measures
Attitude Measures
Biographical Inventories
Interest Inventories
Personality Measures
Projective Measures
Questionnaires
Rating Scales
Tests
RT Evaluation
Evaluation Methods
Interviews
Measurement
Measurement Techniques
Surveys

Meat *FEB. 1970*
Postings: 53 GC: 410
BT Food
RT Food Stores
Meat Packing Industry

Meat Inspectors
USE Food and Drug Inspectors

Meat Packing Industry *JUL. 1966*
Postings: 57 GC: 650
BT Industry
RT Agribusiness
Animal Husbandry
Food
Food and Drug Inspectors
Food Processing Occupations
Food Standards
Meat

Mechanical Design Technicians *AUG. 1968*
Postings: 30 GC: 640
UF Engine Development Technicians
Mechanical Engineering Assistants
Propulsion Development Technicians
BT Paraprofessional Personnel
RT Design
Electromechanical Technology
Engineering Technicians
Manufacturing Industry
Mechanics (Process)

Mechanical Devices
USE Mechanical Equipment

Mechanical Drawing
USE Engineering Drawing

Mechanical Engineering Assistants
USE Mechanical Design Technicians

Mechanical Equipment *NOV. 1968*
Postings: 263 GC: 910
SN Machinery or tools which automatically perform operations in controlling or producing a physical change in environment or in accomplishment of a given task
UF Mechanical Devices
BT Equipment
RT Architectural Research
Calculators
Data Processing
Machinery Industry
Mechanical Skills
Word Processing

Mechanical Skills *JUL. 1966*
Postings: 159 GC: 400
BT Skills
RT Employment Qualifications
Job Skills
Mechanical Equipment
Mechanics (Process)
Trade and Industrial Education

Mechanical Teaching Aids (1966 1980)
USE Educational Media

Mechanical Translation
USE Machine Translation

Mechanics (Physics) *MAR. 1973*
Postings: 1,167 GC: 490
SN The science that deals with the effects of energy and force on the equilibrium, deformation, or motion of solid, liquid, and gaseous bodies—includes both classical (Newtonian) and modern (atomic-level) mechanics
UF Classical Mechanics
NT Fluid Mechanics
Kinetics
Quantum Mechanics
BT Physics
RT Acceleration (Physics)
Energy
Force
Gravity (Physics)
Kinetic Molecular Theory
Motion
Pressure (Physics)
Relativity
Velocity

Mechanics (Process) *JUL. 1966*
Postings: 221 GC: 640
SN Assembly, operation, and repair of machines (Note: Prior to Mar80, the use of this term was not restricted by a Scope Note)
UF General Mechanics
NT Auto Mechanics
Aviation Mechanics
Refrigeration Mechanics
Small Engine Mechanics
BT Technology
RT Agricultural Machinery Occupations
Locomotive Engineers
Machine Repairers
Machine Tools
Machinists
Mechanical Design Technicians
Mechanical Skills
Nuclear Power Plant Technicians

Mechanization
USE Automation

Media Adaptation *JAN. 1985*
Postings: 342 GC: 720
SN Modification of existing information and materials to meet alternative needs
UF Educational Media Adaptation
Instructional Material Adaptation
Material Adaptation
NT Tactile Adaptation
BT Change
RT Curriculum Development
Educational Media
Instructional Material Evaluation
Intermode Differences
Mass Media Use
Material Development
Media Selection
Media Specialists

Media Research *JUL. 1966*
Postings: 4,403 GC: 810
SN Systematic investigations of the use, characteristics, and effects of print and nonprint media (Note: As of Oct81, use as a minor Descriptor for examples of this kind of research—use as a major

Descriptor only as the subject of a document)
NT Journalism Research
Television Research
Textbook Research
BT Research
RT Audience Analysis
Educational Media
Institutional Research
Mass Media
Mass Media Effects
Mass Media Role
Media Specialists
Use Studies

Media Role (Mass Media)
USE Mass Media Role

Media Selection *AUG. 1971*
Postings: 2,203 GC: 720
SN Choice of the most appropriate material or channel of communication
UF Educational Media Selection
Instructional Material Selection
Material Selection
NT Computer Software Selection
Library Material Selection
Reading Material Selection
Textbook Selection
BT Selection
RT Audiovisual Communications
Educational Media
Instructional Material Evaluation
Mass Media Use
Media Adaptation
Media Specialists
Multimedia Instruction
Nonprint Media

Media Specialists *JUL. 1966*
Postings: 1,936 GC: 720
SN Persons who specialize in the development, organization, and application of various types of educational media
NT Audiovisual Coordinators
BT Specialists
RT Educational Media
Learning Resources Centers
Librarian Teacher Cooperation
Librarians
Media Adaptation
Media Research
Media Selection
Multimedia Instruction
School Libraries

Media Technology (1968 1980)
USE Communications

Media Use (Mass Media)
USE Mass Media Use

Mediation (Labor)
USE Arbitration

Mediation Theory *JUL. 1966*
Postings: 440 GC: 810
SN Theory that stimuli do not directly initiate behavior but rather activate intervening processes that initiate the behavior
BT Behavior Theories
RT Cognitive Processes
Generalization
Learning Processes
Recall (Psychology)
Retention (Psychology)
Shift Studies
Stimulus Generalization
Verbal Learning

Medical Assistance
USE Medical Services

Medical Assistants *JUL. 1969*
Postings: 173 GC: 210
NT Medical Laboratory Assistants
BT Allied Health Personnel
RT Emergency Medical Technicians
Medical Services
Nurses Aides
Secretaries

Medical Associations *JUL. 1966*
Postings: 56 GC: 520
BT Professional Associations
RT Health Occupations
Medicine
Nurses
Pharmacists
Physicians
Psychiatrists

Medical Audit
USE Medical Care Evaluation

Medical Care
USE Medical Services

Medical Care Evaluation *DEC. 1976*
Postings: 473 GC: 210
SN Judgment of the amount, quality, and appropriateness of the services and facilities provided for sick and injured persons, and also of the quality of preventive medical care
UF Health Care Evaluation
Medical Audit
Patient Care Evaluation
BT Evaluation
RT Community Health Services
Health Facilities
Health Services
Medical Evaluation
Medical Services
Medicine
Outcomes of Treatment
Physician Patient Relationship
Primary Health Care

Medical Case Histories *JUL. 1966*
Postings: 517 GC: 210
BT Case Records
RT Clinical Diagnosis
Medical Evaluation
Medical Record Administrators
Medical Record Technicians
Medical Research
Medical Services
Medicine
Patients
Profiles

Medical Consultants *JUL. 1966*
Postings: 56 GC: 210
BT Consultants
Health Personnel
RT Medical Services
Physicians
Psychiatrists

Medical Costs
USE Health Care Costs
AND Medical Services

Medical Doctors
USE Physicians

Medical Education *AUG. 1969*
Postings: 6,358 GC: 210
SN Professional education and training concerned with the health of individuals or the care and treatment of patients—presented by or under the supervision of physicians, dentists, nurses, etc. (Note: Do not confuse with "Health Education")
NT Graduate Medical Education
Nursing Education
Pharmaceutical Education

= Two or more Descriptors are used to represent this term.
The term's main entry shows the appropriate coordination.

Veterinary Medical Education
BT   Professional Education
RT   Allied Health Occupations Education
     Clinical Experience
     Clinical Teaching (Health Professions)
     Dental Schools
     Health Occupations
     Health Personnel
     Medical School Faculty
     Medical Schools
     Medical Students
     Medicine
     Premedical Students
     Problem Based Learning
     Teaching Hospitals

Medical Evaluation   *JUL. 1966*
     Postings: 955   GC: 210
SN   Determination of an individual's health
     and of any needed treatment—also, the
     judgment of the efficacy of a program,
     procedure, etc., from a medical or phar-
     macological perspective
UF   Clinical Judgment (Medicine)
NT   Auditory Evaluation
     Dental Evaluation
     Physical Examinations
     Speech Evaluation
BT   Evaluation
RT   Clinical Diagnosis
     Diagnostic Tests
     Disability Identification
     Electroencephalography
     Health
     Health Personnel
     Medical Care Evaluation
     Medical Case Histories
     Medical Services
     Medicine
     Patients
     Physician Patient Relationship
     Symptoms (Individual Disorders)

Medical Laboratory Assistants   *JUL. 1966*
     Postings: 129   GC: 210
UF   Biomedical Equipment Technicians
     Medical Technicians
BT   Medical Assistants
RT   Biomedical Equipment
     Electronic Technicians
     Laboratory Technology
     Medical Technologists

Medical Laboratory Technologists
USE   Medical Technologists

Medical Libraries   *JUL. 1966*
     Postings: 511   GC: 710
SN   Libraries devoted to information and re-
     lated services in the science and practice
     of medicine
UF   Health Sciences Libraries
BT   Special Libraries
RT   Health Personnel
     Health Services
     Medical Research
     Medical Schools
     Medicine
     Research Libraries
     Science Libraries

Medical Record Administrators   *MAR. 1980*
     Postings: 29   GC: 210
SN   Individuals who plan, develop, and ad-
     minister medical record systems for hos-
     pitals, clinics, health centers, etc. (Note:
     For librarians in medical libraries, coor-
     dinate "Librarians" and "Medical Librar-
     ies"—for librarians who are directly in-
     volved in patient care, use the Identifier
     "Clinical Medical Librarians")
UF   Hospital Record Administrators
     Medical Record Librarians (1969
        1980)
BT   Administrators
     Allied Health Personnel
RT   Medical Case Histories
     Medical Record Technicians

Medical Record Clerks
USE   Medical Record Technicians

Medical Record Librarians (1969 1980)
USE   Medical Record Administrators

Medical Record Technicians   *AUG. 1968*
     Postings: 57   GC: 210
SN   Individuals who compile and maintain
     medical records of hospital, clinic, or
     health center patients
UF   Hospital Record Technicians
     Medical Record Clerks
BT   Allied Health Personnel
     Library Technicians
RT   File Clerks
     Filing
     Medical Case Histories
     Medical Record Administrators
     Recordkeeping

Medical Research   *JUL. 1966*
     Postings: 1,137   GC: 810
SN   Basic, applied, and developmental re-
     search conducted to advance knowledge
     in medicine (Note: As of Oct81, use as a
     minor Descriptor for examples of this
     kind of research—use as a major Descrip-
     tor only as the subject of a document)
BT   Research
RT   Exceptional Child Research
     Exercise Physiology
     Laboratory Animals
     Medical Case Histories
     Medical Libraries
     Medical Services
     Medicine
     Nursing Research
     Scientific Research

Medical School Applicants
USE   College Applicants
AND   Medical Schools

Medical School Faculty   *MAR. 1980*
     Postings: 666   GC: 360
SN   Persons instructing in medical or dental
     programs, including field supervisors of
     related clinical experience programs (e.g.,
     externships or preceptorships)
UF   Clinical Professors (1967 1980)
        (Medicine)
     Dental School Faculty #
BT   Graduate School Faculty
RT   Clinical Experience
     Clinical Teaching (Health Professions)
     Dental Schools
     Graduate Medical Education
     Medical Education
     Medical Schools
     Practicum Supervision

Medical Schools   *JUL. 1966*
     Postings: 1,868   GC: 340
SN   Schools or colleges of medicine, usually
     professional schools of universities, that
     prepare students who have completed
     baccalaureate programs to be physicians
     and award Doctor of Medicine (M.D.)
     degrees
UF   Medical School Applicants #
     Schools of Medicine
BT   Colleges
RT   Dental Schools
     Foreign Medical Graduates
     Graduate Medical Education
     Graduate Medical Students
     Medical Education
     Medical Libraries
     Medical School Faculty
     Medical Students
     Medicine
     Professional Education
     Teaching Hospitals

Medical Sciences
USE   Medicine

Medical Secretaries
USE   Secretaries

Medical Services   *JUL. 1966*
     Postings: 4,163   GC: 210
UF   Medical Assistance
     Medical Care
     Medical Costs #
     Medical Treatment (1967 1980)
NT   First Aid
     Psychiatric Services
BT   Health Services
RT   Abortions
     Anesthesiology
     Clinics
     Dentistry
     Dentists
     Drug Therapy
     Electroencephalography
     Emergency Medical Technicians
     Epidemiology
     Euthanasia
     Family Practice (Medicine)
     Geriatrics
     Gynecology
     Health Facilities
     Health Maintenance Organizations
     Hospices (Terminal Care)
     Hospital Personnel
     Hospitals
     Injuries
     Internal Medicine
     Intervention
     Long Term Care
     Medical Assistants
     Medical Care Evaluation
     Medical Case Histories
     Medical Consultants
     Medical Evaluation
     Medical Research
     Medical Technologists
     Medicine
     Nurses
     Nursing
     Nursing Homes
     Obstetrics
     Occupational Therapy
     Oncology
     Ophthalmology
     Oral Rehydration Therapy
     Osteopathy
     Outcomes of Treatment
     Patients
     Pediatrics
     Pharmacists
     Pharmacy
     Physical Therapy
     Physician Patient Relationship
     Physicians
     Physicians Assistants
     Podiatry
     Prenatal Care
     Preventive Medicine
     Primary Health Care
     Professional Services
     Prognostic Tests
     Psychiatrists
     Psychiatry
     Rehabilitation
     Respiratory Therapy
     Sick Child Care
     Speech Therapy
     Sports Medicine
     Surgery
     Surgical Technicians
     Termination of Treatment
     Therapy
     Tissue Donors
     Toxicology
     Veterinary Medicine

Medical Students   *JUL. 1966*
     Postings: 2,171   GC: 360
SN   Students enrolled in medical schools
     (Note: For undergraduates preparing for
     medical school, use "Premedical Stu-
     dents"—prior to Oct81, the use of this
     term was not restricted by a Scope Note)
NT   Graduate Medical Students
BT   Graduate Students
RT   Dental Students

Foreign Medical Graduates
     Medical Education
     Medical Schools
     Premedical Students
     Professional Education

Medical Technicians
USE   Medical Laboratory Assistants

Medical Technologists   *MAY 1969*
     Postings: 182   GC: 210
SN   Personnel responsible for performing
     chemical, microscopic, serologic,
     hematologic, immunohematologic, para-
     sitic, and bacteriologic tests to provide
     data for use in treatment and diagnosis
     of disease—may supervise medical labo-
     ratory technicians/assistants
UF   Medical Laboratory Technologists
BT   Allied Health Personnel
RT   Medical Laboratory Assistants
     Medical Services

Medical Treatment (1967 1980)
USE   Medical Services

Medical Vocabulary   *JUL. 1966*
     Postings: 173   GC: 210
BT   Vocabulary
RT   Medicine
     Physicians
     Professional Training

Medicine   *AUG. 1969*
     Postings: 1,320   GC: 210
UF   Medical Sciences
     Paramedical Sciences
NT   Anesthesiology
     Audiology
     Biomedicine
     Dentistry
     Dietetics
     Electroencephalography
     Epidemiology
     Family Practice (Medicine)
     Geriatrics
     Gynecology
     Internal Medicine
     Neurology
     Nursing
     Obstetrics
     Oncology
     Ophthalmology
     Osteopathy
     Pathology
     Pediatrics
     Pharmacology
     Pharmacy
     Podiatry
     Preventive Medicine
     Primary Health Care
     Psychiatry
     Sports Medicine
     Surgery
     Toxicology
     Veterinary Medicine
BT   Technology
RT   Allied Health Occupations Education
     Anatomy
     Biochemistry
     Bioethics
     Biological Influences
     Biomedical Equipment
     Embryology
     Enzymes
     Genetic Engineering
     Genetics
     Graduate Medical Education
     Health
     Health Occupations
     Human Body
     Hygiene
     Medical Associations
     Medical Care Evaluation
     Medical Case Histories
     Medical Education
     Medical Evaluation
     Medical Libraries
     Medical Research

= Two or more Descriptors are used to represent this term.
The term's main entry shows the appropriate coordination.

Medical Schools
Medical Services
Medical Vocabulary
Microbiology
Nurse Practitioners
Physical Health
Physicians
Physiology
Radiation Biology
Radiology
Therapy

Medieval History   *JUL. 1966*
           Postings: 200   GC: 430
BT   History
RT   Medieval Literature

Medieval Literature   *JUN. 1969*
           Postings: 165   GC: 430
SN   Literature of the Middle Ages (about 500 to 1500 A.D.)
UF   Medieval Romance (1969 1980)
BT   Literature
RT   Chronicles
      Epics
      Fifteenth Century Literature
      Legends
      Medieval History
      Middle English
      Mythology
      World Literature

Medieval Romance (1969 1980)
USE   Medieval Literature

Meditation   *OCT. 1982*
           Postings: 109   GC: 110
SN   Integration of ideas, feelings, and attitudes through focused concentration or sustained reflection, often as a devotional act
NT   Transcendental Meditation
BT   Metacognition
RT   Attention Control
      Conditioning
      Hypnosis
      Psychophysiology
      Psychotherapy
      Religion
      School Prayer
      Self Congruence
      Sensory Experience
      Suggestopedia

Medium of Instruction (Language)
USE   Language of Instruction

Meetings   *JUL. 1966*
           Postings: 1,254   GC: 520
UF   Colloquiums (Meetings)
      Planning Meetings (1966 1980)
NT   Reunions
      Seminars
      Staff Meetings
RT   Assembly Programs
      Clinics
      Conference Papers
      Conference Proceedings
      Conferences
      Hearings
      Institutes (Training Programs)
      Workshops

Melancholia
USE   Depression (Psychology)

Melancholy
USE   Sadness

Melanesian Languages   *JAN. 1970*
           Postings: 4   GC: 440
BT   Malayo Polynesian Languages

Melody   *OCT. 1994*
           Postings: 49   GC: 420
SN   A succession of single musical tones in some rhythmic scheme or pattern
BT   Music
RT   Harmony (Music)
      Musical Composition
      Rhythm (Music)

Memorization   *MAR. 1980*
           Postings: 604   GC: 110
SN   Process of committing to memory
UF   Memorizing (1967 1980)
BT   Learning Processes
RT   Drills (Practice)
      Memory
      Mnemonics
      Primacy Effect
      Recall (Psychology)
      Retention (Psychology)
      Rote Learning
      Serial Learning
      Verbal Learning
      Visualization

Memorizing (1967 1980)
USE   Memorization

Memory   *JUL. 1966*
           Postings: 6,133   GC: 110
UF   Forgetting
      Remembering
NT   Eidetic Imagery
      Long Term Memory
      Recall (Psychology)
      Recognition (Psychology)
      Retention (Psychology)
      Short Term Memory
BT   Cognitive Processes
RT   Cues
      Encoding (Psychology)
      Learning Processes
      Learning Strategies
      Memorization
      Metacognition
      Mnemonics
      Visualization

Memory Devices (Computers)
USE   Computer Storage Devices

Men
USE   Males

Mende   *JUL. 1966*
           Postings: 11   GC: 440
BT   African Languages

Meningomyelocele
USE   Spina Bifida

Menses
USE   Menstruation

Menstruation   *AUG. 1988*
           Postings: 103   GC: 210
SN   Cyclic discharge of blood and tissues from the uterus, normally occurring between puberty and menopause except during pregnancy (Note: See also Identifiers "Menarche," "Menopause," "Menstrual Disorders," "Premenstrual Syndrome," and "Toxic Shock Syndrome")
UF   Menses
RT   Females
      Gynecology
      Physical Development
      Physical Health
      Physiology
      Puberty
      Reproduction (Biology)
      Sex Education

Mental Ability
USE   Cognitive Ability

Mental Age   *APR. 1980*
           Postings: 92   GC: 120
SN   The individual's intelligence level expressed as equivalent to the chronological age at which the average person attains that level
UF   Intelligence Age
BT   Age
      Intelligence
RT   Intellectual Development
      Intelligence Differences
      Intelligence Quotient
      Intelligence Tests

Mental Arithmetic
USE   Arithmetic
AND   Mental Computation

Mental Computation   *APR. 2000*
           Postings: 129   GC: 480
SN   Performance of mathematical operations in the head, i.e., without aid of pencil and paper, or calculator
UF   Mental Arithmetic #
      Mental Mathematics
BT   Cognitive Processes
      Computation
RT   Estimation (Mathematics)
      Learning Processes
      Mathematics
      Measurement
      Thinking Skills

Mental Development (1966 1980)
USE   Cognitive Development

Mental Disorders   *MAR. 1980*
           Postings: 1,966   GC: 230
SN   General term for any emotional or organic mental impairments (Note: Do not confuse with "Mental Retardation," and, use a more specific term if possible)
UF   Mental Illness (1966 1980)
NT   Emotional Disturbances
      Neurosis
      Psychosis
BT   Disabilities
RT   Adaptive Behavior (of Disabled)
      Alzheimers Disease
      Behavior Disorders
      Behavior Problems
      Clinical Psychology
      Institutionalized Persons
      Mental Health
      Neurological Impairments
      Personality Problems
      Physical Disabilities
      Psychiatric Hospitals
      Psychiatric Services
      Psychiatry
      Psychopathology
      Psychotherapy
      Self Destructive Behavior

Mental Health   *JUL. 1966*
           Postings: 3,899   GC: 230
SN   Relatively enduring state of adjustment in which people have feelings of well-being, are realizing their abilities, and coping with everyday demands without excessive stress—also includes efforts to maintain and promote this state to prevent mental disorders
UF   Emotional Health
      Mental Hygiene
BT   Health
RT   Adjustment (to Environment)
      Child Health
      Coping
      Emotional Abuse
      Emotional Disturbances
      Hygiene
      Individual Power
      Life Satisfaction
      Mental Disorders

Mental Health Clinics
Mental Health Programs
Mental Health Workers
Morale
Neurology
Neuropsychology
Neurosis
Psychiatric Services
Psychiatry
Psychological Services
Psychosis
Psychotherapy
Public Health
Self Actualization
Wellness

Mental Health Clinics   *JUL. 1966*
           Postings: 427   GC: 230
BT   Clinics
RT   Mental Health
      Psychiatric Hospitals
      Psychoeducational Clinics
      Rehabilitation Centers
      Therapeutic Environment

Mental Health Programs   *JUL. 1966*
           Postings: 1,749   GC: 230
UF   Mental Health Resources
BT   Health Programs
RT   Employee Assistance Programs
      Mental Health
      Psychiatric Services
      Rehabilitation Programs
      Residential Programs

Mental Health Resources
USE   Mental Health Programs

Mental Health Workers   *APR. 1990*
           Postings: 223   GC: 230
SN   All types/levels of mental health practitioners—professional counselors/therapists, paraprofessionals, technicians, aides, etc.
UF   Community Mental Health Workers #
NT   Psychiatric Aides
      Psychiatrists
      School Psychologists
BT   Health Personnel
RT   Counselors
      Mental Health
      Psychologists
      Social Workers

Mental Hygiene
USE   Mental Health

Mental Illness (1966 1980)
USE   Mental Disorders

Mental Mathematics
USE   Mental Computation

Mental Retardation   *JUL. 1966*
           Postings: 10,620   GC: 220
SN   Intellectual functioning that is two or more standard deviations below the mean (usually below 70 IQ range), concurrent with deficits in adaptive behavior, and manifested during the developmental period (Note: Use a more specific term if possible)
UF   Mentally Handicapped (1966 1980)
      Retardation (1966 1980)
      Retarded Children (1966 1980)
NT   Downs Syndrome
      Mild Mental Retardation
      Moderate Mental Retardation
      Severe Mental Retardation
BT   Disabilities
RT   Adaptive Behavior (of Disabled)
      Cerebral Palsy
      Developmental Disabilities
      Fetal Alcohol Syndrome
      Intelligence
      Learning Problems

= Two or more Descriptors are used to represent this term.
The term's main entry shows the appropriate coordination.

Neurological Impairments
Special Health Problems
Special Olympics

Mental Rigidity   *JUL. 1966*
Postings: 73   GC: 120
BT   Personality Traits
RT   Bias
      Intellectual Development

Mental Tests (1966 1980)
USE   Psychological Testing

Mentally Advanced Children
USE   Gifted

Mentally Handicapped (1966 1980)
USE   Mental Retardation

Mentors   *MAR. 1980*
Postings: 3,359   GC: 520
SN   Trusted and experienced supervisors or
      advisers who have personal and direct
      interest in the development and/or edu-
      cation of younger or less experienced
      individuals, usually in professional edu-
      cation or professional occupations
BT   Role Models
RT   Beginning Teacher Induction
      Collegiality
      Interpersonal Relationship
      Interprofessional Relationship
      Modeling (Psychology)
      Professional Development
      Significant Others
      Teacher Student Relationship

Menu Driven Software   *APR. 1986*
Postings: 163   GC: 720
SN   User-friendly software that presents lists
      of options at various stages of a program
      sequence—from each list, a selection is
      made to initiate subsequent actions
BT   Computer Software
RT   Branching
      Gateway Systems
      Interactive Video
      Online Systems
      User Friendly Interface
      Users (Information)
      Videotex
      Word Processing

Meo
USE   Hmong

Meos
USE   Hmong People

Merchandise Information   *JUL. 1966*
Postings: 724   GC: 650
SN   Literature or labels identifying product
      value, regulation, service, and care for
      the consumer and the trade
UF   Product Information
      Product Labels
RT   Consumer Economics
      Consumer Protection
      Marketing
      Merchandising
      Salesmanship

Merchandising   *JUL. 1966*
Postings: 659   GC: 650
SN   Sales promotion as a comprehensive
      function including market research, ad-
      vertising, and selling
UF   Sales Promotion
BT   Marketing
RT   Advertising
      Bookstores
      College Stores
      Commercial Art
      Credit (Finance)

Display Aids
Distributive Education
Feed Stores
Food Stores
Merchandise Information
Merchants
Retailing
Sales Occupations
Salesmanship
Television Commercials

Merchants   *APR. 1969*
Postings: 65   GC: 640
BT   Personnel
      Vendors
RT   Business
      Entrepreneurship
      Marketing
      Merchandising
      Retailing
      Sales Occupations
      Sales Workers
      Wholesaling

Mercy Killing
USE   Euthanasia

Mergers   *JUL. 1969*
Postings: 295   GC: 520
SN   Combination of two or more organiza-
      tions or institutions
BT   Organizational Change
RT   Business
      Centralization
      Churches
      Consolidated Schools
      Corporations
      Industrial Structure
      Industry
      Organization
      Organization Size (Groups)
      Organizations (Groups)
      School Closing

Merit Pay   *OCT. 1972*
Postings: 573   GC: 630
BT   Expenditures
      Income
RT   Differentiated Staffs
      Incentives
      Master Teachers
      Merit Rating
      Personnel Policy
      Premium Pay
      Recognition (Achievement)
      Salaries
      Salary Wage Differentials
      Teacher Employment
      Wages

Merit Rating   *MAR. 1980*
Postings: 173   GC: 320
SN   Periodic evaluation of individual efficiency
      as a basis for compensation and/or pro-
      motion
UF   Merit Rating Programs (1967 1980)
BT   Measurement
RT   Achievement Rating
      Job Skills
      Merit Pay
      Peer Evaluation
      Personnel Evaluation
      Recognition (Achievement)
      Rewards

Merit Rating Programs (1967 1980)
USE   Merit Rating

Merit Scholarships   *AUG. 1986*
Postings: 55   GC: 620
SN   Financial aid awards given to students in
      recognition of academic, athletic, or ar-
      tistic achievement (Note: See also Identi-
      fiers "National Merit Scholarship Pro-
      gram" and "National Merit Scholars")
NT   No Need Scholarships
BT   Scholarships

RT   Achievement Rating
      Assistantships
      Recognition (Achievement)
      Scholarship Funds
      Tuition Grants

Meta Analysis   *OCT. 1983*
Postings: 1,274   GC: 820
SN   Statistical analysis of the summary find-
      ings of many empirical studies
UF   Integrative Analysis
BT   Statistical Analysis
RT   Comparative Analysis
      Correlation
      Effect Size
      Error of Measurement
      Hypothesis Testing
      Literature Reviews
      Research
      Research Methodology
      Statistical Data
      Synthesis

Meta Knowledge
USE   Metacognition

Metabolism   *NOV. 1969*
Postings: 244   GC: 210
NT   Blood Circulation
      Heart Rate
RT   Biochemistry
      Biofeedback
      Biology
      Enzymes
      Exercise Physiology
      Human Body
      Photosynthesis
      Physiology

Metacognition   *OCT. 1980*
Postings: 2,304   GC: 110
SN   Knowledge or beliefs about factors af-
      fecting one's own cognitive activities—
      also, reflection on or monitoring of one's
      own cognitive processes, such as mem-
      ory or comprehension
UF   Meta Knowledge
      Metamemory
NT   Meditation
BT   Cognitive Processes
RT   Cognitive Ability
      Communication Skills
      Comprehension
      Learning Processes
      Learning Strategies
      Memory
      Metalinguistics
      Self Control
      Self Efficacy
      Self Evaluation (Individuals)
      Self Motivation
      Social Cognition
      Study Skills
      Thinking Skills

Metal Finishing
USE   Finishing

Metal Forming Occupations
USE   Metal Working

Metal Industry   *DEC. 1969*
Postings: 154   GC: 650
UF   Steel Industry (1967 1980)
BT   Manufacturing Industry
RT   Foundries
      Metal Working
      Metallurgical Technicians
      Metallurgy
      Metals

Metal Trades
USE   Metal Working

Metal Working   *MAR. 1980*
Postings: 374   GC: 640
UF   Metal Forming Occupations
      Metal Trades
      Metal Working Occupations (1968
      1980)
NT   Sheet Metal Work
BT   Technology
RT   Assembly (Manufacturing)
      Finishing
      Foundries
      Hand Tools
      Handicrafts
      Industrial Arts
      Machine Tools
      Machinists
      Metal Industry
      Metals
      Patternmaking
      Semiskilled Occupations
      Shop Curriculum
      Skilled Occupations
      Technology Education
      Tool and Die Makers
      Visual Arts
      Welding

Metal Working Occupations (1968 1980)
USE   Metal Working

Metalinguistics   *APR. 1990*
Postings: 367   GC: 450
SN   Branch of linguistics concerned with
      knowledge about, and the capacity to
      express the dimensions of, language
      properties, structures, and relationships
      with culture
UF   Language Awareness
      Linguistic Awareness
BT   Linguistics
RT   Cultural Awareness
      Language Acquisition
      Language Attitudes
      Language Processing
      Language Skills
      Linguistic Theory
      Literacy
      Literature Appreciation
      Metacognition
      Psycholinguistics
      Reading Writing Relationship
      Second Language Learning

Metallurgical Technicians   *JUL. 1966*
Postings: 10   GC: 640
BT   Paraprofessional Personnel
RT   Chemical Technicians
      Engineering Technicians
      Metal Industry
      Metallurgy
      Physics
      Radiographers
      Scientific Personnel

Metallurgy   *MAY 1969*
Postings: 118   GC: 490
BT   Technology
RT   Chemical Analysis
      Chemistry
      Crystallography
      Geochemistry
      Inorganic Chemistry
      Metal Industry
      Metallurgical Technicians
      Metals
      Mineralogy
      Physics

Metals   *SEP. 1969*
Postings: 369   GC: 490
RT   Metal Industry
      Metal Working
      Metallurgy
      Minerals
      Mining

Metamemory
USE   Metacognition

= Two or more Descriptors are used to represent this term.
The term's main entry shows the appropriate coordination.

Metaphors   *MAY 1969*
    Postings: 1,598   GC: 430
BT Figurative Language
RT Allegory
    Imagery
    Legends
    Sonnets
    Symbols (Literary)

Meteorology   *JUL. 1966*
    Postings: 492   GC: 490
BT Earth Science
RT Acid Rain
    Climate
    Climate Change
    Humidity
    Physics
    Solar Energy
    Temperature
    Thermal Environment
    Water
    Weather
    Wind (Meteorology)

Meters
USE Measurement Equipment

Methodology (1966 1974)
USE Methods

Methods   *JUL. 1966*
    Postings: 2,260   GC: 810
SN Systematic approaches to the conduct of an operation or process—includes steps of procedure, application of techniques, systems of reasoning or analysis, and the modes of inquiry employed by a science or discipline (Note: Use a more specific term if possible)
UF Methodology (1966 1974)
    Procedures
    Techniques (1966 1974)
NT Algorithms
    Branching
    Caseworker Approach
    Change Strategies
    Cloze Procedure
    Concept Mapping
    Counseling Techniques
    Critical Incidents Method
    Critical Path Method
    Delphi Technique
    Desegregation Methods
    Educational Methods
    Evaluation Methods
    Fixed Sequence
    Grievance Procedures
    Hermeneutics
    Heuristics
    Holistic Approach
    Home Visits
    Inquiry
    Insurance
    Interdisciplinary Approach
    Job Search Methods
    Laboratory Procedures
    Learning Strategies
    Magnification Methods
    Marxian Analysis
    Measurement Techniques
    Motivation Techniques
    Music Techniques
    Network Analysis
    Nominal Group Technique
    Pacing
    Production Techniques
    Prompting
    Questioning Techniques
    Research Methodology
    Sequential Approach
    Simulation
    Supervisory Methods
    Systems Analysis
    Troubleshooting
    Writing Strategies
RT Methods Courses
    Methods Research
    Methods Teachers

Methods Courses   *JUL. 1966*
    Postings: 1,626   GC: 400
SN Courses in standard classroom procedures that may be used in teaching any subject
UF General Methods Courses
    Special Methods Courses
BT Courses
    Teacher Education Curriculum
RT Education Courses
    Methods
    Methods Research
    Methods Teachers
    Student Teaching
    Teacher Education
    Teacher Education Programs

Methods Research   *JUL. 1966*
    Postings: 794   GC: 810
SN Systematic investigation of the procedures, materials, tools, and/or equipment used to perform a task (Note: As of Oct81, use as a minor Descriptor for examples of this kind of research—use as a major Descriptor only as the subject of a document)
NT Evaluation Research
BT Research
RT Action Research
    Educational Methods
    Evaluation Methods
    Methods
    Methods Courses
    Program Effectiveness
    Research Methodology
    Teaching Methods
    Theory Practice Relationship

Methods Teachers   *JUL. 1966*
    Postings: 74   GC: 360
SN Teacher educators who provide instruction in how to teach a particular subject or general classroom procedures that may be used in teaching any subject
BT Teacher Educators
RT Methods
    Methods Courses
    Teacher Education

Metis (People)   *JAN. 1994*
    Postings: 100   GC: 560
SN People in Canada and adjacent areas of the U.S. who are of mixed Native American and European ancestry
BT Canada Natives

Metric System   *OCT. 1971*
    Postings: 1,061   GC: 480
UF Metrication
    SI Units
BT Standards
RT Measurement

Metrication
USE Metric System

Metropolitan Areas   *JUL. 1966*
    Postings: 788   GC: 550
SN Geographic areas consisting of a large population nucleus (i.e., a city), as well as the surrounding areas that are linked to the center by social, economic, or political considerations
NT Suburbs
BT Geographic Regions
RT Counties
    Municipalities
    Neighborhoods
    Nonmetropolitan Areas
    Urban Areas
    Urban Demography

Mexican American Culture
USE Hispanic American Culture
AND Mexican Americans

Mexican American Education   *MAR. 1980*
    Postings: 483   GC: 330
SN Education for Mexican Americans (Note: Prior to Mar80, this concept was indexed under "Mexican Americans")
BT Education
RT Bilingual Education
    English (Second Language)
    Mexican Americans
    Multicultural Education

Mexican American History   *JUL. 1966*
    Postings: 275   GC: 430
SN History of the Mexican American people and of the United States' relations with Mexico (Note: Do not use to index "Mexican History")
BT United States History
RT Mexican American Literature
    Mexican Americans
    Mexicans
    Modern History

Mexican American Literature   *MAR. 1980*
    Postings: 74   GC: 430
BT Hispanic American Literature
RT Latin American Literature
    Mexican American History
    Mexican Americans
    Spanish Speaking

Mexican Americans   *JUL. 1966*
    Postings: 5,133   GC: 560
UF Mexican American Culture #
BT Ethnic Groups
    Hispanic Americans
RT Hispanic American Culture
    Mexican American Education
    Mexican American History
    Mexican American Literature
    Mexicans
    Spanish Americans
    Spanish Speaking

Mexicans   *JUL. 1972*
    Postings: 488   GC: 560
SN Citizens of Mexico
NT Braceros
BT Latin Americans
RT American Indians
    Ethnic Groups
    Mexican American History
    Mexican Americans
    Spanish Speaking

Miao
USE Hmong

Miaos
USE Hmong People

Microbiology   *AUG. 1968*
    Postings: 566   GC: 490
BT Biology
RT Bacteria
    Biotechnology
    Botany
    Culturing Techniques
    Genetic Engineering
    Genetics
    Medicine
    Monera
    Mycology
    Pests
    Physiology
    Protists
    Protozoa
    Viruses
    Zoology

Microcalorimeters
USE Calorimeters

Microcomputers   *MAR. 1980*
    Postings: 9,750   GC: 910
SN Physically the smallest computer and distinguished from other computers by size rather than capacity—often incorporated into other devices, e.g., electronic calculators, videodisc recorders, to perform specific logical and control functions—component parts are usually contained on a single circuit board composed of LSI (large-scale integration) semiconductor chips
UF Desktop Computers
    Microprocessors
    Personal Computers
    Pocket Computers
    Portable Computers
BT Computers
RT Computer Games
    Computer Interfaces
    Computer Mediated Communication
    Computer Peripherals
    Computer Selection
    Desktop Publishing
    Integrated Learning Systems
    Internet
    Local Area Networks
    Microelectronics
    Minicomputers
    Online Systems
    Workstations

Microcounseling   *NOV. 1968*
    Postings: 122   GC: 240
SN Method of counselor training in which simulated counseling sessions (often videotaped) are used to analyze trainees' specific counseling skills and behaviors
BT Training Methods
RT Counseling
    Counseling Techniques
    Counselor Training
    Microteaching
    Practicums
    Videotape Recordings

Microeconomics   *OCT. 1994*
    Postings: 142   GC: 620
SN Study of some portion of an economy such as individuals, a household, a company, an industry, or a sector
BT Economics
RT Consumer Economics
    Econometrics
    Economic Research
    Economics Education
    Educational Economics
    Labor Economics
    Macroeconomics
    Rural Economics

Microelectronics   *DEC. 1989*
    Postings: 72   GC: 490
SN Electronics concerned with the design and manufacture of chips, integrated circuits, and other miniaturized electronic components
UF Microminiature Electronics
    Miniaturized Electronics
BT Electronics
RT Electric Circuits
    Electromechanical Technology
    Electronic Control
    Electronic Equipment
    Electronics Industry
    Engineering
    Microcomputers
    Semiconductor Devices
    Superconductors
    Telecommunications
    Transistors

Microfiche   *JUL. 1966*
    Postings: 449   GC: 720
SN Sheet of photographic negative film that contains microimages of pages, drawings, etc., in an array of frames, and, at the top, a catalog entry or title that is readable with the naked eye

---

\# = Two or more Descriptors are used to represent this term.
The term's main entry shows the appropriate coordination.

UF Ultramicrofiche
BT Microforms
RT Information Storage
     Microfilm

Microfilm *JUL. 1966*
    Postings: 316   GC: 720
NT Computer Output Microfilm
BT Microforms
RT Filmstrips
     Information Storage
     Microfiche

Microfilming
USE Microreproduction

Microform Reader Printers (1971 1980)
USE Microform Readers

Microform Readers *JAN. 1971*
    Postings: 109   GC: 910
UF Microform Reader Printers (1971
     1980)
BT Projection Equipment
RT Magnification Methods
     Microforms
     Microreproduction

Microforms *SEP. 1969*
    Postings: 583   GC: 720
UF Microimages
     Microtexts
NT Microfiche
     Microfilm
BT Visual Aids
RT Information Storage
     Instructional Materials
     Microform Readers
     Microreproduction
     Reprography

Micrographics
USE Microreproduction

Microimages
USE Microforms

Microminiature Electronics
USE Microelectronics

Microphones *JUL. 1966*
    Postings: 37   GC: 910
BT Audio Equipment
     Electronic Equipment
RT Audiovisual Aids

Microphotography
USE Microreproduction

Microprocessors
USE Microcomputers

Microreproduction *SEP. 1971*
    Postings: 218   GC: 720
SN Production of copy by photographic or
     other means in sizes too small to be read
     without magnification
UF Microfilming
     Micrographics
     Microphotography
BT Reprography
RT Microform Readers
     Microforms

Microscopes *JUL. 1966*
    Postings: 158   GC: 910
BT Laboratory Equipment
RT Magnification Methods

Microteaching *JUL. 1966*
    Postings: 849   GC: 310
SN Method of teacher training in which simu-
     lated teaching sessions (often videotaped)
     are used to develop and analyze trainees'
     specific teaching skills and behaviors
BT Training Methods
RT Laboratory Training
     Microcounseling
     Protocol Materials
     Student Teachers
     Student Teaching
     Teacher Education
     Teaching Experience
     Teaching Skills
     Videotape Recordings

Microtexts
USE Microforms

Microwave Relay Systems (1971 1980)
USE Telecommunications

Microworlds *AUG. 1994*
    Postings: 87   GC: 720
SN Computer-based learning tools that pro-
     vide exploration and manipulation within
     analogical representations of some as-
     pect of the natural world
UF Computer Based Microworlds
     Computer Microworlds
BT Computer Uses in Education
     Courseware
RT Computer Assisted Instruction
     Computer Simulation

Midcareer Change
USE Career Change
AND Midlife Transitions

Middle Aged Adults *MAR. 1980*
    Postings: 1,162   GC: 120
SN Approximately 45–64 years of age
UF Middle Aged (1966 1980)
     Midlife
BT Adults
RT Adults (30 to 45)
     Age Discrimination
     Aging (Individuals)
     Baby Boomers
     Early Retirement
     Elder Abuse
     Midlife Transitions
     Older Adults
     Older Workers
     Preretirement Education
     Young Old Adults

Middle Aged (1966 1980)
USE Middle Aged Adults

Middle Class *JUL. 1966*
    Postings: 801   GC: 520
BT Social Class
RT Advantaged
     Lower Class
     Lower Middle Class
     Middle Class Culture
     Middle Class Parents
     Middle Class Standards
     Middle Class Students
     Upper Class
     Working Class

Middle Class College Students (1966 1980)
USE College Students
AND Middle Class Students

Middle Class Culture *JUL. 1966*
    Postings: 161   GC: 560
UF Majority Culture
BT Culture
RT Material Culture
     Middle Class
     Middle Class Standards

Middle Class Fathers (1966 1980)
USE Fathers
AND Middle Class Parents

Middle Class Mothers (1966 1980)
USE Middle Class Parents
AND Mothers

Middle Class Norm (1966 1980)
USE Middle Class Standards

Middle Class Parents *JUL. 1966*
    Postings: 142   GC: 510
UF Middle Class Fathers (1966 1980) #
     Middle Class Mothers (1966 1980) #
BT Parents
RT Middle Class

Middle Class Standards *MAR. 1980*
    Postings: 292   GC: 520
UF Middle Class Norm (1966 1980)
     Middle Class Values (1966 1980)
BT Standards
RT Middle Class
     Middle Class Culture

Middle Class Students *MAR. 1980*
    Postings: 136   GC: 360
UF Middle Class College Students (1966
     1980) #
BT Students
RT Lower Class Students
     Middle Class

Middle Class Values (1966 1980)
USE Middle Class Standards

Middle Ear Disease
USE Otitis Media

Middle Eastern History *JUN. 1969*
    Postings: 125   GC: 430
SN History of all or part of the geographic
     area that includes Afghanistan, Cyprus,
     Egypt, Iran, Iraq, Israel, Jordan, Lebanon,
     Libya, Sudan, Syria, Turkey, and the
     Arabian peninsula
UF Near Eastern History
BT History
RT African Culture
     African History
     Area Studies
     Asian History
     Middle Eastern Studies
     Non Western Civilization

Middle Eastern Studies *JUN. 1973*
    Postings: 214   GC: 400
SN Studies, usually interdisciplinary in ap-
     proach, of all or part of the geographic
     area that includes Afghanistan, Cyprus,
     Egypt, Iran, Iraq, Israel, Jordan, Lebanon,
     Libya, Sudan, Syria, Turkey, and the
     Arabian peninsula
BT Area Studies
RT African Culture
     African History
     African Studies
     Arabs
     Asian History
     Asian Studies
     Foreign Culture
     Islamic Culture
     Jews
     Middle Eastern History
     Non Western Civilization

Middle English *MAY 1969*
    Postings: 27   GC: 440
BT English
RT Diachronic Linguistics
     Indo European Languages
     Languages
     Linguistics

     Medieval Literature
     Welsh

Middle Income Housing *JUL. 1966*
    Postings: 19   GC: 550
BT Housing
RT Income

Middle Level Management
USE Middle Management

Middle Management *JUN. 1978*
    Postings: 257   GC: 630
SN The intermediate level of management,
     excluding top-level management on the
     one hand and first-level supervision on
     the other
UF Middle Level Management
     Midmanagement
BT Administration
RT Administrative Organization
     Administrators
     Admissions Officers
     Deans
     Department Heads
     Industrial Structure
     Leadership
     Power Structure
     School Business Officials
     Student Financial Aid Officers

Middle School Students *JUL. 1999*
    Postings: 1,385   GC: 360
SN (Note: Coordinate with the appropriate
     mandatory educational level Descriptor)
BT Students
RT Early Adolescents
     Elementary School Students
     High School Students
     Junior High School Students
     Middle Schools
     Preadolescents

Middle School Teachers *JUL. 1999*
    Postings: 149   GC: 360
BT Teachers
RT Elementary School Teachers
     Middle Schools
     Public School Teachers
     Secondary School Teachers

Middle Schools *JUL. 1966*
    Postings: 9,058   GC: 340
SN Various combinations of grades 5 through
     9—mainly 6–8, but also 5–7, 5–8, 7–8,
     or 7–9 (Note: Added Jul99 to list of
     mandatory educational level Descrip-
     tors—indexed with levelers "Inter-
     mediate Grades" and/or "Junior High
     Schools" prior to that time)
BT Schools
RT Grade 5
     Grade 6
     Grade 7
     Grade 8
     Grade 9
     High Schools
     Intermediate Grades
     Junior High Schools
     Middle School Students
     Middle School Teachers

Midlife
USE Middle Aged Adults

Midlife Transitions *JUN. 1981*
    Postings: 369   GC: 120
SN Physical, occupational, social, or psy-
     chological changes occurring among mid-
     dle aged adults
UF Midcareer Change #
BT Change
RT Adult Development
     Aging (Individuals)
     Behavior Change
     Career Change

= Two or more Descriptors are used to represent this term.
The term's main entry shows the appropriate coordination.

Early Retirement
Employment Practices
Family Relationship
Life Events
Middle Aged Adults
Physical Health
Preretirement Education
Psychological Characteristics
Self Actualization
Social Development

Midmanagement
USE   Middle Management

Midtwentieth Century Literature
USE   Twentieth Century Literature

Midwifery
USE   Obstetrics

Migrant Adult Education   *JUL. 1966*
        Postings: 100   GC: 330
SN   Learning activities and experiences pro-
       vided by a school district, etc., to
       migratory workers and/or their families—
       includes postsecondary, adult, and vo-
       cational education
BT   Adult Education
RT   Adult Basic Education
       Bilingual Education
       English (Second Language)
       Migrant Education
       Migrant Problems
       Migrant Programs
       Migrant Workers
       Migrant Youth
       Migrants

Migrant Adults
USE   Migrants

Migrant Child Care Centers (1966 1980)
USE   Day Care Centers
AND   Migrant Children

Migrant Child Education (1967 1980)
USE   Migrant Education

Migrant Children   *JUL. 1966*
        Postings: 762   GC: 510
SN   Children who travel with their families
       from one temporary residence to an-
       other so that one or more family mem-
       bers might secure temporary or sea-
       sonal employment (Note: Do not confuse
       with "Transient Children")
UF   Migrant Child Care Centers (1966
       1980) #
       Migratory Children
BT   Children
       Migrants
RT   Migrant Education
       Migrant Youth
       Student Mobility
       Transfer Students

Migrant Education   *JUL. 1966*
        Postings: 1,817   GC: 330
SN   Formal supplementary learning activities
       and experiences provided by a school
       district, etc., to the children of migratory
       workers from early childhood through
       grade 12
UF   Migrant Child Education (1967 1980)
       Migrant Schools (1966 1980)
BT   Education
RT   Bilingual Education
       English (Second Language)
       Migrant Adult Education
       Migrant Children
       Migrant Problems
       Migrant Programs
       Migrant Youth
       Migration
       Mobile Educational Services

Multicultural Education
Student Mobility
Supplementary Education

Migrant Employment   *JUL. 1966*
        Postings: 120   GC: 630
BT   Employment
RT   Braceros
       Migrant Problems
       Migrant Programs
       Migrants
       Seasonal Employment
       Seasonal Laborers

Migrant Health Services   *JUL. 1966*
        Postings: 254   GC: 210
BT   Health Services
RT   Migrant Problems
       Migrant Programs
       Migrants

Migrant Housing   *JUL. 1966*
        Postings: 126   GC: 920
SN   Dwellings for migratory workers and their
       families—includes the immediate sur-
       roundings, and related services or facili-
       ties
UF   Labor Camps (1966 1980) (Migrants)
BT   Housing
RT   Migrant Problems
       Migrant Programs
       Migrants

Migrant Population
USE   Migrants

Migrant Problems   *JUL. 1966*
        Postings: 317   GC: 530
SN   Problems of migrants
BT   Problems
RT   Migrant Adult Education
       Migrant Education
       Migrant Employment
       Migrant Health Services
       Migrant Housing
       Migrant Programs
       Migrant Welfare Services
       Migrant Workers
       Migrants

Migrant Programs   *MAR. 1980*
        Postings: 438   GC: 520
SN   Projects or programs for or by migrant
       workers and their families designed to
       further their social or economic
       progress—often include educational,
       medical, or occupational assistance
UF   Church Migrant Projects (1966
       1980) #
       Community Migrant Projects (1966
       1980) #
       Migrant Projects
       Migrant Worker Projects (1966
       1980) #
BT   Programs
RT   Church Programs
       Community Programs
       Migrant Adult Education
       Migrant Education
       Migrant Employment
       Migrant Health Services
       Migrant Housing
       Migrant Problems
       Migrant Welfare Services
       Migrants
       Outreach Programs

Migrant Projects
USE   Migrant Programs

Migrant Schools (1966 1980)
USE   Migrant Education

Migrant Transportation (1966 1980)
USE   Migrants

AND   Transportation

Migrant Welfare Services   *JUL. 1966*
        Postings: 85   GC: 520
BT   Welfare Services
RT   Migrant Problems
       Migrant Programs
       Migrants

Migrant Worker Projects (1966 1980)
USE   Migrant Programs
AND   Migrant Workers

Migrant Workers   *JUL. 1966*
        Postings: 758   GC: 630
UF   Agricultural Migrant Workers
       Interstate Workers (1966 1980) (Mi-
       grants)
       Migrant Worker Projects (1966
       1980) #
       Migratory Agricultural Workers
BT   Agricultural Laborers
       Migrants
RT   Braceros
       Crew Leaders
       Foreign Workers
       Migrant Adult Education
       Migrant Problems
       Migrant Youth
       Seasonal Employment
       Seasonal Laborers

Migrant Youth   *JUL. 1966*
        Postings: 311   GC: 510
SN   Young persons, approximately 12 to 21
       years of age, who travel alone or with
       their families from one temporary resi-
       dence to another so that they, or other
       family members, might secure tempo-
       rary or seasonal employment (Note: Coor-
       dinate with an appropriate age or educa-
       tional level Descriptor)
BT   Migrants
       Youth
RT   Migrant Adult Education
       Migrant Children
       Migrant Education
       Migrant Workers
       Rural Youth
       Student Mobility
       Transfer Students

Migrants   *JUL. 1966*
        Postings: 702   GC: 510
SN   Persons who move from place to place
UF   Agricultural Migrants
       Internal Immigrants
       Migrant Adults
       Migrant Population
       Migrant Transportation (1966 1980) #
       Native Migrants
NT   Immigrants
       Migrant Children
       Migrant Workers
       Migrant Youth
       Nomads
       Refugees
       Transient Children
BT   Groups
RT   Braceros
       Cross Cultural Studies
       Foreign Nationals
       Immigration
       Immigration Inspectors
       Migrant Adult Education
       Migrant Employment
       Migrant Health Services
       Migrant Housing
       Migrant Problems
       Migrant Programs
       Migrant Welfare Services
       Migration
       Migration Patterns
       Occupational Mobility
       Relocation
       Special Needs Students

Migration   *JUL. 1966*
        Postings: 977   GC: 550
SN   Demographic movements of individuals
       or groups
UF   Geographic Mobility (1980 1980)
       Northward Movement
       Population Movements
       Population Shifts
       White Flight #
NT   Brain Drain
       Family Mobility
       Immigration
       Migration Patterns
       Relocation
       Rural to Urban Migration
       Student Mobility
       Urban to Rural Migration
       Urban to Suburban Migration
BT   Mobility
RT   Boomtowns
       Demography
       Immigrants
       Migrant Education
       Migrants
       Nomads
       Occupational Mobility
       Place of Residence
       Population Distribution
       Population Trends
       Refugees
       Residential Patterns
       Transient Children
       Undocumented Immigrants

Migration Patterns   *JUL. 1966*
        Postings: 1,048   GC: 550
SN   Specific migration which constitutes an
       identifiable or even predictable move-
       ment of people
UF   Migration Trends
BT   Migration
RT   Boomtowns
       Brain Drain
       Demography
       Employment Patterns
       Immigration
       Migrants
       Population Distribution
       Population Trends
       Relocation
       Residential Patterns
       Rural to Urban Migration
       Trend Analysis
       Urban to Rural Migration
       Urban to Suburban Migration

Migration Trends
USE   Migration Patterns

Migratory Agricultural Workers
USE   Migrant Workers

Migratory Children
USE   Migrant Children

Mild Disabilities   *MAR. 1980*
        Postings: 1,000   GC: 220
SN   Impairments that are sufficiently mild so
       that generally normal functioning is pos-
       sible when appropriate medical, educa-
       tional, or other special services are pro-
       vided
NT   Mild Mental Retardation
       Minimal Brain Dysfunction
BT   Disabilities
RT   Partial Hearing
       Severe Disabilities
       Severity (of Disability)

Mild Mental Retardation   *MAR. 1980*
        Postings: 3,303   GC: 220
SN   Intellectual functioning that ranges two
       to three standard deviations below the
       mean (usually 55–69 IQ range), concur-
       rent with adaptive deficiencies—mildly
       or educable retarded individuals are able
       to acquire functional academic skills
       through special education and adults

= Two or more Descriptors are used to represent this term.
The term's main entry shows the appropriate coordination.

can usually maintain themselves at least semi-independently in a community
UF   Educable Mentally Handicapped (1966 1980)
BT   Mental Retardation
     Mild Disabilities
RT   Downs Syndrome
     Moderate Mental Retardation
     Residential Schools
     Severe Mental Retardation
     Slow Learners

Milieu Therapy   JUL. 1966
     Postings: 121   GC: 230
SN   Treatment that modifies a person's life circumstances or immediate environment (Note: Mental institutions or rehabilitation centers that use milieu therapy are often called therapeutic communities, and, prior to Mar80, this concept was usually indexed under "Therapeutic Environment")
UF   Environmental Therapy
     Situational Therapy
     Therapeutic Communities
BT   Psychotherapy
RT   Family Counseling
     Group Therapy
     Humanization
     Psychiatric Hospitals
     Rehabilitation Centers
     Therapeutic Environment

Militancy
USE Activism

Military Air Facilities   AUG. 1969
     Postings: 65   GC: 920
UF   Air Bases
     Air Force Bases
     Army Air Bases
     Coast Guard Air Stations
     Marine Corps Air Stations
     Naval Air Stations
BT   Facilities
RT   Air Traffic Control
     Airports
     Military Science
     Military Service
     Military Training

Military Organizations   MAR. 1969
     Postings: 253   GC: 610
NT   Armed Forces
BT   Organizations (Groups)
RT   Federal Government
     Military Personnel
     National Defense

Military Personnel   JUL. 1966
     Postings: 1,827   GC: 640
NT   Enlisted Personnel
     Officer Personnel
BT   Government Employees
RT   Armed Forces
     Military Organizations
     Military Science
     Military Service
     Military Training
     National Defense
     Seafarers
     Veterans
     Veterans Education

Military Schools   JAN. 1969
     Postings: 252   GC: 340
BT   Schools
RT   Military Science
     Military Training

Military Science   JUL. 1966
     Postings: 226   GC: 400
BT   Curriculum
RT   Civil Defense
     Disarmament
     Enlisted Personnel
     Marksmanship

Military Air Facilities
Military Personnel
Military Schools
Military Service
Military Training
National Defense
Nuclear Warfare
Officer Personnel
Political Science
War
Weapons

Military Service   JUL. 1966
     Postings: 614   GC: 640
RT   Armed Forces
     Enlisted Personnel
     Military Air Facilities
     Military Personnel
     Military Science
     Military Training
     Officer Personnel
     Veterans

Military Training   JUL. 1966
     Postings: 2,064   GC: 400
BT   Training
RT   Enlisted Personnel
     Flight Training
     Military Air Facilities
     Military Personnel
     Military Schools
     Military Science
     Military Service
     National Defense
     Officer Personnel
     Weapons

Milling Machines
USE Machine Tools

Millwork
USE Cabinetmaking

Mime
USE Pantomime

Mineral Oil
USE Oil

Mineralogy   OCT. 1984
     Postings: 93   GC: 490
SN   Science dealing with minerals, including their distribution, identification, and properties
BT   Geology
RT   Chemical Analysis
     Chemistry
     Crystallography
     Geochemistry
     Geophysics
     Inorganic Chemistry
     Metallurgy
     Minerals
     Petrology
     Physical Geography
     Soil Science

Minerals   OCT. 1984
     Postings: 113   GC: 410
SN   Solid homogeneous chemical elements or compounds, usually with characteristic crystalline properties, that result from inorganic processes of nature
NT   Asbestos
BT   Matter
RT   Fuels
     Geology
     Metals
     Mineralogy
     Mining
     Natural Resources

Miniaturized Electronics
USE Microelectronics

Minicomputers   MAR. 1980
     Postings: 239   GC: 910
SN   Compact, low cost (relative to mainframes), general purpose computers capable of either stand-alone operation or attachment to other computers
BT   Computers
RT   Integrated Learning Systems
     Local Area Networks
     Microcomputers
     Online Systems

Minicourses   MAR. 1980
     Postings: 700   GC: 350
SN   Courses at any educational level that are of relatively short duration (e.g., shorter than a school's regular academic term or session) and intended to achieve certain limited objectives
UF   Short Courses (1970 1980)
BT   Courses
RT   Alumni Education
     Elective Courses
     Inservice Education
     Institutes (Training Programs)
     Introductory Courses
     Learning Modules
     Noncredit Courses
     Professional Continuing Education
     Refresher Courses
     Seminars
     Summer Programs
     Supplementary Education
     Workshops

Minimal Brain Dysfunction   MAR. 1980
     Postings: 380   GC: 220
SN   Mild neurological abnormality that causes learning and/or motor difficulties
UF   Minimally Brain Injured (1966 1980)
BT   Mild Disabilities
     Neurological Impairments
RT   Aphasia
     Behavior Problems
     Brain
     Dyslexia
     Epilepsy
     Hyperactivity
     Learning Disabilities

Minimal Competencies
USE Minimum Competencies

Minimal Competency Testing
USE Minimum Competency Testing

Minimally Brain Injured (1966 1980)
USE Minimal Brain Dysfunction

Minimum Competencies   MAR. 1980
     Postings: 1,110   GC: 330
SN   Skills that are deemed essential for a given age, grade, or performance level
UF   Minimal Competencies
BT   Competence
     Skills
RT   Back to Basics
     Basic Skills
     Competency Based Education
     Core Curriculum
     Cultural Literacy
     Evaluation Criteria
     Excellence in Education
     Functional Literacy
     Job Skills
     Literacy Education
     Mastery Learning
     Mathematics Skills
     Minimum Competency Testing
     Performance
     Reading Skills
     Teacher Competencies
     Writing Skills

Minimum Competency Testing   JAN. 1979
     Postings: 1,719   GC: 820
SN   Measurement of the attainment of skills

deemed essential for a particular level of education
UF   Minimal Competency Testing
BT   Testing
RT   Academic Achievement
     Academic Standards
     Basic Skills
     Competence
     Competency Based Education
     Mastery Tests
     Minimum Competencies
     National Competency Tests
     Student Certification
     Teacher Competency Testing
     Test Score Decline

Minimum Initial Expenses
USE Expenditures

Minimum Operating Expenses
USE Operating Expenses

Minimum Wage   JUL. 1966
     Postings: 116   GC: 630
BT   Wages
RT   Guaranteed Income
     Minimum Wage Legislation

Minimum Wage Laws (1966 1974)
USE Minimum Wage Legislation

Minimum Wage Legislation   JUL. 1966
     Postings: 76   GC: 610
UF   Minimum Wage Laws (1966 1974)
BT   Legislation
RT   Laws
     Minimum Wage
     Wages

Mining   SEP. 1982
     Postings: 215   GC: 410
SN   Process or business involved in extracting ore, coal, precious stones, etc., from the earth
UF   Coal Mining #
BT   Technology
RT   Asbestos
     Coal
     Conservation (Environment)
     Engineering
     Environmental Education
     Fuels
     Geology
     Geophysics
     Land Use
     Metals
     Minerals
     Natural Resources
     Ventilation

Ministers
USE Clergy

Minnesingers
USE Poets

Minority Culture
USE Minority Groups

Minority Group Children   JUL. 1966
     Postings: 2,542   GC: 510
BT   Children
RT   Black Youth
     Minority Groups

Minority Group Influences   MAR. 1980
     Postings: 346   GC: 520
SN   Influences of minority groups on other groups or society as a whole
UF   Minority Role (1966 1980)
BT   Influences
RT   Black Influences
     Community Control

= Two or more Descriptors are used to represent this term.
The term's main entry shows the appropriate coordination.

Cultural Influences
Minority Groups
Racial Factors
Social Influences
Sociocultural Patterns

Minority Group Teachers　　　*JUL. 1966*
　　Postings: 831　　　　GC: 360
SN　Teachers who are members of minority groups
BT　Teachers
RT　Black Teachers
　　Diversity (Faculty)
　　Minority Groups

Minority Groups　　　*JUL. 1966*
　　Postings: 16,616　　　GC: 520
SN　Subgroups within a larger society that are distinguished from the majority and each other by race, national heritage, or sometimes by religious or cultural affiliation (Note: Unlike "Ethnic Groups," "Minority Groups" also have the connotation of being objects of prejudice or discrimination)
UF　Minority Culture
　　Population Minorities
BT　Groups
RT　Affirmative Action
　　Alaska Natives
　　American Indians
　　Asian Americans
　　Biculturalism
　　Bidialectalism
　　Bilingualism
　　Blacks
　　Canada Natives
　　Civil Rights
　　Civil Rights Legislation
　　Cross Cultural Studies
　　Cultural Differences
　　Cultural Pluralism
　　Culture
　　Diversity (Faculty)
　　Diversity (Student)
　　Eskimos
　　Ethnic Groups
　　Ethnic Studies
　　Ethnicity
　　French Canadians
　　Genocide
　　Greek Americans
　　Hispanic Americans
　　Italian Americans
　　Jews
　　Language Minorities
　　Limited English Speaking
　　Majority Attitudes
　　Maori (People)
　　Minority Group Children
　　Minority Group Influences
　　Minority Group Teachers
　　Multicultural Education
　　Multiracial Persons
　　Non English Speaking
　　Pacific Americans
　　Polish Americans
　　Race
　　Religious Cultural Groups
　　Self Determination
　　Slavery
　　Social Bias
　　Social Discrimination
　　Spanish Americans
　　Subcultures

Minority Language Groups
USE　Language Minorities

Minority Rights
USE　Civil Rights

Minority Role (1966 1980)
USE　Minority Group Influences

Miosis
USE　Myopia

MIS
USE　Management Information Systems

Misassignment of Teachers　　*APR. 1990*
　　Postings: 9　　　　GC: 320
SN　Assignment of teachers to subjects or grades for which they have neither been certified nor prepared
UF　Misplaced Teachers
RT　Teacher Distribution
　　Teacher Placement
　　Teacher Qualifications
　　Teacher Shortage
　　Teachers

Misbehavior (1966 1980)
USE　Behavior Problems

Misconceptions　　　*AUG. 1986*
　　Postings: 1,941　　　GC: 110
SN　Ideas or interpretations that are inaccurate or that contradict scientific knowledge
UF　Mistaken Conceptions
RT　Cognitive Structures
　　Comprehension
　　Concept Formation
　　Concept Mapping
　　Learning Processes
　　Mathematical Concepts
　　Scientific Concepts

Miscue Analysis　　　*FEB. 1974*
　　Postings: 456　　　GC: 460
SN　Examination and interpretation of observed responses in oral reading which do not match expected responses, as a technique for measuring the learner's control of the reading process
UF　Miscue Taxonomy
BT　Reading Diagnosis
RT　Context Clues
　　Cues
　　Decoding (Reading)
　　Diagnostic Teaching
　　Language Usage
　　Linguistics
　　Oral Reading
　　Phoneme Grapheme Correspondence
　　Phonetic Analysis
　　Reading
　　Reading Instruction
　　Reading Processes
　　Structural Analysis (Linguistics)

Miscue Taxonomy
USE　Miscue Analysis

Misplaced Teachers
USE　Misassignment of Teachers

Missing Children　　　*AUG. 1988*
　　Postings: 19　　　GC: 530
BT　Children
RT　Child Abuse
　　Child Welfare
　　Family Problems
　　Runaways
　　Victims of Crime

Mission Statements　　　*AUG. 1986*
　　Postings: 613　　　GC: 730
SN　Written statements of institutional purpose—each statement reflects the official purpose(s) of a particular institution as developed or approved by the founders or governing body
BT　Position Papers
RT　College Planning
　　Institutional Advancement
　　Institutional Mission
　　Library Planning
　　Master Plans
　　Policy Formation
　　Strategic Planning

Mississippi Band of Choctaw (Tribe)
　　　　　　　　　　　　JAN. 1994
　　Postings: 19　　　GC: 560
SN　American Indians of east central Mississippi who are descendants of Choctaw not removed to the Indian Territory (Oklahoma) in the 1830's
BT　Choctaw (Tribe)
RT　Choctaw

Mistaken Conceptions
USE　Misconceptions

Mixed Age Grouping　　　*JUL. 1994*
　　Postings: 248　　　GC: 310
SN　Grouping children or students so that the chronological age span is greater than one year—the primary purpose is to maximize age-group interaction and cooperation (Note: Do not confuse with "Nongraded Instructional Grouping" or "Multigraded Classes," both typically including various ages, but not necessarily for the purpose of age-group mixing)
UF　Multiage Grouping
BT　Age Groups
RT　Age Differences
　　Chronological Age
　　Continuous Progress Plan
　　Cross Age Teaching
　　Heterogeneous Grouping
　　Intergenerational Programs
　　Multigraded Classes
　　Multiunit Schools
　　Nongraded Instructional Grouping

Mixed Race Persons
USE　Multiracial Persons

Mnemonics　　　*JUL. 1966*
　　Postings: 609　　　GC: 110
SN　Techniques for improving memory
RT　Abbreviations
　　Cues
　　Keywords
　　Learning
　　Learning Experience
　　Learning Processes
　　Learning Strategies
　　Learning Theories
　　Memorization
　　Memory
　　Notetaking
　　Recall (Psychology)
　　Retention (Psychology)
　　Suggestopedia

Mobile Classrooms　　　*AUG. 1968*
　　Postings: 159　　　GC: 920
SN　Readily movable vehicles, or attachments to vehicles, that are used as classrooms
BT　Classrooms
RT　Educational Facilities Design
　　Flexible Facilities
　　Mobile Educational Services
　　Relocatable Facilities
　　School Expansion
　　Transportation

Mobile Clinics　　　*MAR. 1980*
　　Postings: 16　　　GC: 920
UF　Itinerant Clinics (1966 1980)
BT　Clinics
RT　Itinerant Teachers
　　Mobile Laboratories
　　Outreach Programs
　　Relocatable Facilities

Mobile Educational Services　　*JUL. 1966*
　　Postings: 277　　　GC: 330
BT　Ancillary School Services
RT　Bookmobiles
　　Extension Education
　　Itinerant Teachers
　　Migrant Education
　　Mobile Classrooms

Outreach Programs
Special Education

Mobile Laboratories　　　*JUL. 1966*
　　Postings: 72　　　GC: 920
BT　Laboratories
RT　Mobile Clinics
　　Relocatable Facilities

Mobile Libraries
USE　Bookmobiles

Mobility　　　*JUL. 1966*
　　Postings: 345　　　GC: 550
SN　Geographic, physical, or social movement of people (Note: Use a more specific term if possible—prior to Mar80, this term was not restricted by a Scope Note)
NT　Educational Mobility
　　Migration
　　Occupational Mobility
　　Physical Mobility
　　Social Mobility

Mobility Aids　　　*JUL. 1966*
　　Postings: 252　　　GC: 220
SN　Devices that assist disabled persons to move freely within their environment
NT　Wheelchairs
BT　Assistive Devices (for Disabled)
RT　Electromechanical Aids
　　Low Vision Aids
　　Physical Disabilities
　　Physical Mobility
　　Prostheses
　　Travel Training
　　Visual Impairments
　　Visually Impaired Mobility

Model Programs
USE　Demonstration Programs

Modeling (Psychological) (1977 1980)
USE　Modeling (Psychology)

Modeling (Psychology)　　　*MAR. 1980*
　　Postings: 1,093　　　GC: 120
SN　Process in which salient characteristics of an agent or model are acquired by an observer
UF　Modeling (Psychological) (1977 1980)
BT　Behavior
RT　Behavior Change
　　Counseling Techniques
　　Identification (Psychology)
　　Imitation
　　Mentors
　　Observational Learning
　　Role Models
　　Significant Others
　　Socialization

Models　　　*JUL. 1966*
　　Postings: 40,767　　　GC: 730
SN　Representations of objects, principles, processes, or ideas—often used for imitation or emulation
UF　Paradigms
　　Theoretical Models
NT　Causal Models
　　Mathematical Models
　　Role Models
　　Student Writing Models
　　Teaching Models
BT　Simulation
RT　Computer Simulation
　　Network Analysis
　　Operations Research
　　Research Design
　　Research Methodology
　　Research Tools
　　Schematic Studies
　　Standards
　　Systems Analysis
　　Systems Approach

= Two or more Descriptors are used to represent this term.
The term's main entry shows the appropriate coordination.

Theories
Theory Practice Relationship
Three Dimensional Aids

Modems JAN. 1988
Postings: 104 GC: 910
SN Devices that convert computer output to signals that can be transmitted over communications lines and that restore the signals to their original form at the receiving end
UF Modulator Demodulators
BT Computer Peripherals
RT Computer Mediated Communication
Input Output Devices
Online Systems
Telephone Communications Systems

Moderate Mental Retardation MAR. 1980
Postings: 1,640 GC: 220
SN Intellectual functioning that ranges three to four standard deviations below the mean (usually 40–54 IQ range), concurrent with adaptive deficiencies—moderately or trainable retarded individuals can learn self-help, communication, social, or simple vocational skills but only limited academic skills
UF Trainable Mentally Handicapped (1967 1980)
BT Mental Retardation
RT Downs Syndrome
Mild Mental Retardation
Residential Schools
Severe Mental Retardation

Modern Greek
USE Greek

Modern History JUL. 1966
Postings: 593 GC: 430
SN History of recent centuries—usually thought of as beginning with the Renaissance and extending to the present
UF Contemporary History
BT History
RT Mexican American History
Nuclear Warfare
Oral History
United States History

Modern Language Curriculum JUL. 1966
Postings: 829 GC: 450
NT Conversational Language Courses
FLES
Intensive Language Courses
Notional Functional Syllabi
BT Curriculum
RT College Second Language Programs
Modern Languages
Multilevel Classes (Second Language Instruction)
Second Language Learning
Second Language Programs

Modern Languages JUL. 1966
Postings: 2,192 GC: 440
BT Languages
RT Bilingualism
Immersion Programs
Modern Language Curriculum
Multilingual Materials
Multilingualism
Second Language Learning

Modern Mathematics JUL. 1966
Postings: 297 GC: 480
SN Curricular innovations in precollege mathematics
UF New Mathematics
BT Mathematics Curriculum
RT Elementary School Mathematics
Mathematics
Secondary School Mathematics

Modern Science (1966 1980)
USE Sciences

Modernism MAY 1969
Postings: 278 GC: 430
SN Reflection, in religion and the creative arts, of a deliberate break with the past and a search for new forms of expression
RT Art Expression
Literary Styles
Music
Nineteenth Century Literature
Philosophy
Postmodernism
Religion
Twentieth Century Literature

Modernization MAR. 1982
Postings: 453 GC: 520
SN Process of change in a society or social institution in which the most recent ways, ideas, or styles are adapted or acquired
BT Development
Social Change
RT Community Development
Cultural Influences
Culture Lag
Developed Nations
Developing Nations
Economic Progress
Industrialization
Innovation
Rural Development
Socioeconomic Influences
Technological Advancement
Technology Transfer
Traditionalism
Urbanization

Modular Arithmetic JAN. 1993
Postings: 67 GC: 480
SN An arithmetic of a finite rather than an infinite set of numbers—the maximum integer (n) selected is known as the modulus, and the arithmetic is referred to as "arithmetic modulo n"—any number greater than n is expressed as the remainder left after its division by n—sometimes called "clock arithmetic," because the clock provides an example (e.g., n=12)
UF Clock Arithmetic
Finite Arithmetic
BT Arithmetic
Number Concepts
RT Algebra
Congruence (Mathematics)
Numbers

Modular Building Design JUL. 1966
Postings: 139 GC: 920
SN Orderly planning so arranged as to make logical and extensive use of a repetitive module or dimension of one foot or more
UF Modular Drafting
BT Building Design
RT Building Systems
Educational Facilities Design
School Construction
Systems Building

Modular Drafting
USE Modular Building Design

Modular Learning
USE Learning Modules

Modular Scheduling
USE Flexible Scheduling

Modulator Demodulators
USE Modems

Mole
USE Mossi

Molecular Biology JAN. 1993
Postings: 74 GC: 490
SN Science dealing with the structure and function of the molecules (e.g., proteins, nucleic acids, enzymes) that make up living organisms
UF Cellular Molecular Biology #
BT Biology
RT Biochemistry
Biotechnology
Cytology
Enzymes
Genetic Engineering
Genetics
Molecular Structure
Nucleic Acids
Physiology
Rh Factors
Viruses

Molecular Structure OCT. 1972
Postings: 617 GC: 490
RT Atomic Structure
Chemical Bonding
Chemical Reactions
Chemistry
Coordination Compounds
Crystallography
Kinetic Molecular Theory
Molecular Biology
Physical Chemistry
Physical Sciences
Physics
Polymers
Spectroscopy
Stereochemistry
Structural Analysis (Science)

Monera APR. 1990
Postings: 7 GC: 490
SN The biological kingdom of single-celled, prokaryotic organisms, including bacteria and blue green algae—classified by some schemes as a division of Plantae
RT Bacteria
Microbiology
Protists

Monetary Systems MAR. 1980
Postings: 243 GC: 620
SN Policies and practices affecting the money of nations
UF Money Systems (1966 1980)
RT Banking
Business Cycles
Economics
Inflation (Economics)
Interest (Finance)
International Trade

Money Management JUL. 1966
Postings: 2,697 GC: 620
UF Financial Management
BT Administration
RT Banking
Basic Business Education
Budgeting
Capital
Consumer Education
Credit (Finance)
Debt (Financial)
Endowment Funds
Estate Planning
Finance Occupations
Finance Reform
Financial Audits
Financial Policy
Financial Services
Home Management
Income
Inflation (Economics)
Loan Repayment
Paying for College
Risk Management
School Funds

Tax Rates
Trusts (Financial)

Money Systems (1966 1980)
USE Monetary Systems

Mong
USE Hmong

Mongol
USE Mongolian

Mongolian JUL. 1966
Postings: 16 GC: 440
UF Khalkha
Mongol
BT Mongolian Languages

Mongolian Languages JUL. 1966
Postings: 6 GC: 440
NT Buriat
Dagur
Mongolian
BT Uralic Altaic Languages

Mongolism (1968 1978)
USE Downs Syndrome

Monolingualism JAN. 1973
Postings: 264 GC: 450
RT Bilingualism
Child Language
English Only Movement
Language Skills
Languages
Multilingualism
Native Speakers
Sociolinguistics

Monologs OCT. 1980
Postings: 45 GC: 430
UF Interior Monologues
Monologues (1970 1980)
Soliloquies
BT Literary Devices
RT Drama
Personal Narratives
Poetry
Speech

Monologues (1970 1980)
USE Monologs

Monte Carlo Methods MAR. 1984
Postings: 529 GC: 820
SN Statistical simulation techniques using random numbers to derive probabilistic approximations to the solutions of problems—used especially for complex problems with many variables or interrelationships
BT Simulation
RT Computer Simulation
Estimation (Mathematics)
Game Theory
Hypothesis Testing
Linear Programming
Mathematical Models
Measurement Techniques
Operations Research
Predictor Variables
Probability
Problem Solving
Research Methodology
Sampling
Statistical Analysis
Statistical Distributions
Statistical Studies
Statistics

Montessori Method DEC. 1985
Postings: 451 GC: 310
SN Child-centered approach to teaching, de-

= Two or more Descriptors are used to represent this term.
The term's main entry shows the appropriate coordination.

veloped by Maria Montessori and most often used in the early childhood years, that features a wide range of graded, self-motivational techniques and materials specially designed to provide sensorimotor pathways to higher learning

BT   Teaching Methods
RT   Discovery Learning
     Early Childhood Education
     Individualized Instruction
     Manipulative Materials
     Sensory Experience
     Student Centered Curriculum

Moods   *APR. 1990*
     Postings: 220   GC: 230
SN   Temporary, often fluctuating, feelings and emotions
BT   Psychological Patterns
RT   Affective Behavior
     Anger
     Anxiety
     Attitudes
     Depression (Psychology)
     Emotional Experience
     Emotional Problems
     Emotional Response
     Happiness
     Loneliness
     Morale
     Personality Traits
     Sadness

Moonlighting
USE   Multiple Employment

Moqui (Tribe)
USE   Hopi (Tribe)

Moral Criticism (1969 1980)   *MAR. 1980*
     Postings: 188   GC: 430
SN   Invalid Descriptor—originally intended as a literary term, but used indiscriminately in indexing—see "Literary Criticism," and "Moral Issues" or "Moral Values"

Moral Development   *NOV. 1972*
     Postings: 3,085   GC: 120
SN   Developmental processes in the formation of moral reasoning and judgments
BT   Individual Development
RT   Codes of Ethics
     Ethics
     Integrity
     Intention
     Moral Values
     Personality Development
     Social Cognition
     Values

Moral Instruction
USE   Ethical Instruction

Moral Issues   *JUL. 1966*
     Postings: 1,337   GC: 520
RT   Censorship
     Controversial Issues (Course Content)
     Moral Values
     Obscenity
     Plagiarism

Moral Judgment
USE   Moral Values
AND   Value Judgment

Moral Values   *JUL. 1966*
     Postings: 5,121   GC: 520
SN   Principles and standards which determine the extent to which human action or conduct is right or wrong
UF   Ethical Values (1966 1980)
     Moral Judgment #
BT   Values

RT   Bioethics
     Censorship
     Codes of Ethics
     Ethical Instruction
     Ethics
     Integrity
     Moral Development
     Moral Issues
     Social Values
     Work Ethic

Morale   *JUL. 1966*
     Postings: 522   GC: 230
NT   Teacher Morale
BT   Psychological Patterns
RT   Burnout
     Emotional Adjustment
     Group Unity
     Mental Health
     Moods
     Motivation
     Need Gratification
     Organizational Climate
     Peer Acceptance
     Recognition (Achievement)
     Self Actualization
     Self Concept
     Sportsmanship
     Teamwork

Morals
USE   Ethics

More
USE   Mossi

Morphemes   *JUL. 1966*
     Postings: 454   GC: 450
SN   Smallest units of meaning in a language (e.g., a word is composed of one or more morphemes)
UF   Allomorphs (1967 1980)
NT   Affixes
     Negative Forms (Language)
     Plurals
     Tenses (Grammar)
BT   Morphology (Languages)
RT   Morphophonemics
     Phonemes
     Syntax

Morphemics
USE   Morphology (Languages)

Morphology (Languages)   *JUL. 1966*
     Postings: 2,352   GC: 450
SN   Study of the forms and formation of words
UF   Morphemics
NT   Morphemes
     Morphophonemics
BT   Grammar
RT   Adjectives
     Adverbs
     Code Switching (Language)
     Conjunctions
     Determiners (Languages)
     Diachronic Linguistics
     Discourse Analysis
     Form Classes (Languages)
     Function Words
     Intonation
     Language Patterns
     Language Typology
     Lexicology
     Linguistic Borrowing
     Nouns
     Phonology
     Prepositions
     Pronouns
     Suprasegmentals
     Surface Structure
     Syntax
     Traditional Grammar
     Verbs

Morphophonemics   *JUL. 1966*
     Postings: 269   GC: 450
SN   Study of the phonemic aspects of morphemes
BT   Morphology (Languages)
RT   Affixes
     Morphemes
     Negative Forms (Language)
     Phonemes
     Phonemics
     Phonetics
     Phonology
     Stress (Phonology)
     Suprasegmentals
     Surface Structure
     Tone Languages

Mortality (Physiology)
USE   Death

Mortality (Research Studies)
USE   Attrition (Research Studies)

Mortality Rate   *JUN. 1988*
     Postings: 349   GC: 550
SN   Ratio between the number of deaths and the number of individuals in a specified population
UF   Death Rate
     Infant Death Rate #
BT   Demography
     Incidence
RT   Birth Rate
     Death
     Disease Incidence
     Infant Mortality
     Population Distribution
     Population Trends

Moslems
USE   Muslims

Mossi   *JUL. 1966*
     Postings: 4   GC: 440
UF   Mole
     More
BT   African Languages

Motels
USE   Hotels

Mother Absence
USE   Motherless Family

Mother Attitudes   *JUL. 1966*
     Postings: 983   GC: 510
SN   Attitudes of, not toward, mothers
BT   Parent Attitudes
RT   Father Attitudes
     Mothers

Mother Goose Rhymes
USE   Nursery Rhymes

Mother Role
USE   Mothers
AND   Parent Role

Motherese and Fatherese
USE   Caregiver Speech
AND   Parent Child Relationship

Motherhood
USE   Mothers

Motherless Family   *MAR. 1980*
     Postings: 27   GC: 510
UF   Mother Absence
BT   One Parent Family
RT   Divorce
     Fatherless Family
     Fathers

     Heads of Households
     Widowed

Mothers   *JUL. 1966*
     Postings: 6,411   GC: 510
UF   Employed Mothers #
     Middle Class Mothers (1966 1980) #
     Mother Role #
     Motherhood
NT   Black Mothers
     Unwed Mothers
BT   Females
     Parents
RT   Displaced Homemakers
     Employed Parents
     Fatherless Family
     Heads of Households
     Mother Attitudes
     One Parent Family
     Parent Associations
     Parent Child Relationship
     Parent Influence
     Parent Role

Motifs   *MAY 1969*
     Postings: 307   GC: 430
SN   Recurrent thematic or unifying elements in literary works—also found in art (prevailing designs or repeated patterns) and music (recurring melodic or rhythmic phrases)
UF   Leitmotifs
     Leitmotivs
BT   Literary Devices
RT   Art Expression
     Film Criticism
     Symbols (Literary)

Motion   *SEP. 1968*
     Postings: 1,311   GC: 490
UF   Movement
NT   Acceleration (Physics)
     Velocity
BT   Scientific Concepts
RT   Air Flow
     Diffusion (Physics)
     Earthquakes
     Energy
     Fluid Mechanics
     Force
     Gravity (Physics)
     Horology
     Kinetic Molecular Theory
     Kinetics
     Mechanics (Physics)
     Physics
     Quantum Mechanics
     Relativity
     Vectors (Mathematics)
     Wind (Meteorology)

Motion Pictures
USE   Films

Motivation   *JUL. 1966*
     Postings: 6,304   GC: 120
SN   Forces that initiate, direct, and sustain individual or group behavior in order to satisfy a need or attain a goal
UF   Low Motivation (1966 1980)
NT   Achievement Need
     Learning Motivation
     Reading Motivation
     Self Motivation
     Student Motivation
     Teacher Motivation
RT   Achievement
     Aspiration
     Attention Control
     Attention Span
     Behavior
     Burnout
     Cognitive Dissonance
     Curiosity
     Failure
     Fear of Success
     Feedback
     Goal Orientation
     Incentives

= Two or more Descriptors are used to represent this term.
The term's main entry shows the appropriate coordination.

Intention
Interests
Morale
Motivation Techniques
Needs
Pacing
Performance
Praise
Professional Recognition
Readiness
Reinforcement
Rewards
Satisfaction
Self Fulfilling Prophecies
Sportsmanship
Stimulation
Stimuli
Success
Work Ethic

Motivation Techniques   *JUL. 1966*
    Postings: 2,324   GC: 310
SN   Techniques used to prompt an individual or group to act in a specified way
BT   Methods
RT   Contingency Management
    Educational Strategies
    Incentives
    Motivation
    Performance Contracts
    Persuasive Discourse
    Prewriting
    Self Directed Groups

Motor Ability
USE   Psychomotor Skills

Motor Development   *AUG. 1968*
    Postings: 1,845   GC: 120
BT   Physical Development
RT   Biomechanics
    Developmental Delays
    Eye Hand Coordination
    Lateral Dominance
    Learning Problems
    Motor Reactions
    Movement Education
    Musculoskeletal System
    Neurological Impairments
    Neurological Organization
    Object Manipulation
    Perceptual Motor Coordination
    Perceptual Motor Learning
    Physical Activity Level
    Psychomotor Objectives
    Psychomotor Skills
    Skill Development

Motor Oil
USE   Lubricants
AND   Oil

Motor Reactions   *JUL. 1969*
    Postings: 542   GC: 120
UF   Muscular Activities
    Muscular Extensions
    Muscular Flexions
NT   Eye Movements
    Pupillary Dilation
BT   Responses
RT   Biomechanics
    Exercise Physiology
    Motor Development
    Muscular Strength
    Muscular System
    Osteopathy
    Physical Activity Level
    Physiology
    Plyometrics
    Psychomotor Skills
    Reaction Time
    Sports Medicine

Motor Skills
USE   Psychomotor Skills

Motor Vehicles   *JUL. 1966*
    Postings: 650   GC: 910
NT   Service Vehicles
    Tractors
BT   Equipment
RT   Auto Body Repairers
    Auto Mechanics
    Auto Parts Clerks
    Diesel Engines
    Electric Motors
    Energy Conservation
    Environmental Standards
    Fuels
    Gasoline
    Parking Controls
    Parking Facilities
    Traffic Circulation
    Traffic Control
    Traffic Safety
    Transportation
    Travel
    Vehicular Traffic

Motorboat Operators
USE   Boat Operators

Mourning
USE   Grief

Movable Partitions   *JUL. 1966*
    Postings: 61   GC: 920
SN   Interior walls that can be readily moved
UF   Folding Partitions
BT   Space Dividers
RT   Flexible Facilities
    Prefabrication

Movement
USE   Motion

Movement Education   *FEB. 1978*
    Postings: 698   GC: 470
SN   Developing and applying coordinated and rhythmical body movements in learning situations
BT   Physical Education
RT   Biomechanics
    Body Image
    Body Language
    Dance
    Dance Education
    Dance Therapy
    Human Body
    Kodaly Method
    Motor Development
    Orff Method
    Pantomime
    Perceptual Motor Coordination
    Perceptual Motor Learning
    Physical Activities
    Psychomotor Objectives
    Psychomotor Skills
    Self Expression

MTMM Methodology
USE   Multitrait Multimethod Techniques

Mulattoes
USE   Multiracial Persons

Multiage Grouping
USE   Mixed Age Grouping

Multicampus Colleges   *FEB. 1978*
    Postings: 402   GC: 340
SN   Higher education institutions, including universities, which have multiple (two or more) locations
UF   Branch Campuses (Colleges)
BT   Colleges
RT   Campuses
    Community Colleges
    Multicampus Districts
    State Colleges
    State Universities

Two Year Colleges
Universities

Multicampus Districts   *JUL. 1966*
    Postings: 328   GC: 340
SN   Community or junior college districts that contain more than one campus (Note: Prior to Mar80, the use of this term was not restricted by a Scope Note)
BT   School Districts
RT   Campuses
    Community Colleges
    Multicampus Colleges
    School Location
    Two Year Colleges
    Zoning

Multichannel Programing (1966 1980)
USE   Programming (Broadcast)

Multicultural Education   *JAN. 1979*
    Postings: 7,793   GC: 540
SN   Education involving two or more ethnic groups and designed to help participants clarify their own ethnic identity and appreciate that of others, reduce prejudice and stereotyping, and promote cultural pluralism and equal participation (Note: Do not confuse with "Cross Cultural Training," which, prior to Jan79, was frequently used for "Multicultural Education")
UF   Bicultural Education
    Intercultural Education
    Multiethnic Education
BT   Intergroup Education
RT   Biculturalism
    Bilingual Education
    Bilingualism
    Black Studies
    Cross Cultural Studies
    Cross Cultural Training
    Cultural Activities
    Cultural Awareness
    Cultural Background
    Cultural Context
    Cultural Differences
    Cultural Interrelationships
    Cultural Literacy
    Cultural Maintenance
    Cultural Pluralism
    Culturally Relevant Education
    Culture
    Culture Contact
    Culture Fair Tests
    Diversity (Faculty)
    Diversity (Institutional)
    Diversity (Student)
    Ethnic Groups
    Ethnic Relations
    Ethnicity
    Ethnocentrism
    Ethnomathematics
    Foreign Culture
    Global Education
    Heterogeneous Grouping
    Humanistic Education
    Intercultural Communication
    Intercultural Programs
    Interdisciplinary Approach
    Intergroup Relations
    Mexican American Education
    Migrant Education
    Minority Groups
    Multicultural Textbooks
    Multilingualism
    Political Correctness
    Social Integration

Multicultural Textbooks   *AUG. 1968*
    Postings: 166   GC: 540
BT   Textbooks
RT   Bilingual Education
    Bilingual Instructional Materials
    Cross Cultural Studies
    Cultural Education
    Intergroup Education
    Multicultural Education

Textbook Bias
Textbook Content

Multicultural Training
USE   Cross Cultural Training

Multiculturalism
USE   Cultural Pluralism

Multidimensional Scaling   *AUG. 1972*
    Postings: 603   GC: 820
SN   Procedures used to analyze judgments, usually about the similarities and differences among a set of items, to determine the number of independent factors which underlie the judgments
BT   Multivariate Analysis
    Scaling
RT   Cluster Analysis
    Correlation
    Discriminant Analysis
    Factor Analysis
    Semantic Differential
    Sociometric Techniques

Multidisciplinary Approach
USE   Interdisciplinary Approach

Multiethnic Education
USE   Multicultural Education

Multiethnic Training
USE   Cross Cultural Training

Multigraded Classes   *JUL. 1966*
    Postings: 224   GC: 310
SN   Classes composed of students in two or more grades (Note: Do not confuse with "Nongraded Instructional Grouping")
BT   Classes (Groups of Students)
RT   Heterogeneous Grouping
    Instructional Program Divisions
    Mixed Age Grouping
    Multilevel Classes (Second Language Instruction)
    Nongraded Instructional Grouping

Multilateral Disarmament
USE   Disarmament

Multilevel Classes (Second Language Instruction)   *OCT. 1983*
    Postings: 56   GC: 450
SN   Second language classes composed of students with a wide range of proficiency in the language being taught
BT   Classes (Groups of Students)
RT   Heterogeneous Grouping
    Individualized Instruction
    Language Proficiency
    Languages
    Modern Language Curriculum
    Multigraded Classes
    Second Language Instruction
    Second Language Learning
    Second Language Programs

Multilingual Materials   *NOV. 1982*
    Postings: 136   GC: 720
SN   Print and/or nonprint materials whose contents include equivalent or near-equivalent information in two or more languages (Note: Corresponds to Pubtype 171—do not use except as the subject of a document)
UF   Bilingual Materials
NT   Bilingual Instructional Materials
RT   Bilingualism
    Intercultural Communication
    International Communication
    International Studies
    Languages
    Modern Languages
    Multilingualism

= Two or more Descriptors are used to represent this term.
The term's main entry shows the appropriate coordination.

Reference Materials
Resource Materials
Second Language Learning
Vocabulary

Multilingualism　　　　　　*JUL. 1966*
Postings: 880　　　　　　GC: 450
UF　Plurilingualism
RT　Bilingual Education
　　Bilingualism
　　Code Switching (Language)
　　Cross Cultural Studies
　　Cultural Pluralism
　　Diglossia
　　English (Second Language)
　　English Only Movement
　　Intercultural Communication
　　Interference (Language)
　　International Communication
　　Language Dominance
　　Language Maintenance
　　Language Planning
　　Language Skill Attrition
　　Languages
　　Modern Languages
　　Monolingualism
　　Multicultural Education
　　Multilingual Materials
　　Psycholinguistics
　　Sociolinguistics

Multilithing
USE　Reprography

Multimedia Instruction　　　*JUL. 1966*
Postings: 3,248　　　　　GC: 310
SN　The integration of more than one me-
　　dium in a presentation or module of
　　instruction
NT　Audiovisual Instruction
BT　Teaching Methods
RT　Educational Media
　　Educational Technology
　　Hypermedia
　　Integrated Learning Systems
　　Intermode Differences
　　Media Selection
　　Media Specialists
　　Multimedia Materials

Multimedia Materials　　　　*DEC. 1994*
Postings: 1,429　　　　　GC: 720
SN　Materials, frequently computer applica-
　　tions, that combine some or all of text,
　　sound, graphics, animation, and video
　　into integrated packages
RT　Audiovisual Aids
　　Communications
　　Computers
　　Educational Media
　　Hypermedia
　　Mass Media
　　Multimedia Instruction
　　Nonprint Media
　　Virtual Reality
　　World Wide Web

Multiple Choice Tests　　　　*JUL. 1966*
Postings: 1,967　　　　　GC: 830
SN　Tests in which two or more answers are
　　offered as alternative responses for each
　　item
BT　Objective Tests
RT　Confidence Testing
　　Distractors (Tests)
　　Guessing (Tests)
　　Scoring Formulas

Multiple Correlation
USE　Correlation

Multiple Disabilities　　　　*MAR. 1980*
Postings: 1,985　　　　　GC: 220
SN　Concomitant impairments, the combina-
　　tion of which causes adjustment and
　　educational problems
UF　Multiply Handicapped (1967 1980)

NT　Deaf Blind
BT　Disabilities
RT　Cerebral Palsy
　　Severe Disabilities
　　Spina Bifida

Multiple Discriminant Analysis
USE　Discriminant Analysis

Multiple Employment　　　　*JAN. 1969*
Postings: 122　　　　　　GC: 630
UF　Double Employment
　　Moonlighting
　　Multiple Jobholding
　　Secondary Employment
BT　Employment
RT　Adjunct Faculty
　　Conflict of Interest
　　Part Time Employment
　　Seasonal Employment

Multiple Intelligences　　　*AUG. 1998*
Postings: 498　　　　　　GC: 120
SN　Theory or view of human intellect, origi-
　　nated in 1983 by Howard Gardner, that
　　every individual has at least seven differ-
　　ent autonomous intelligences, i.e., lin-
　　guistic, logical-mathematical, spatial,
　　bodily-kinesthetic, musical, interpersonal,
　　and intrapersonal—more recently, an
　　eighth intelligence (naturalist) has been
　　recognized, and a ninth (existential) is
　　being considered
BT　Intelligence
RT　Cognitive Style
　　Intelligence Differences
　　Intelligence Tests
　　Learning Processes
　　Learning Theories

Multiple Jobholding
USE　Multiple Employment

Multiple Matrix Sampling
USE　Item Sampling

Multiple Regression Analysis　　*OCT. 1970*
Postings: 1,706　　　　　GC: 820
SN　Prediction of a criterion score, or de-
　　pendent variable, from a weighted com-
　　bination of scores for two or more inde-
　　pendent variables
BT　Regression (Statistics)
RT　Causal Models
　　Comparative Analysis
　　Correlation
　　Judgment Analysis Technique
　　Path Analysis
　　Predictive Measurement
　　Predictor Variables
　　Statistics
　　Suppressor Variables
　　Validity
　　Weighted Scores

Multiplication　　　　　　*OCT. 1968*
Postings: 588　　　　　　GC: 480
BT　Arithmetic
RT　Addition
　　Division
　　Subtraction

Multiply Handicapped (1967 1980)
USE　Multiple Disabilities

Multipurpose Classrooms　　　*JUL. 1966*
Postings: 55　　　　　　GC: 920
SN　Classrooms designed for more than one
　　use, such as for a discussion area and
　　laboratory
BT　Classrooms
RT　Classroom Design
　　Flexible Facilities
　　Open Plan Schools

School Space
Stages (Facilities)

Multiracial Persons　　　　*AUG. 2000*
Postings: 112　　　　　　GC: 560
SN　Individuals of mixed racial ancestry (Note:
　　See also the Identifier "Multiracial Fam-
　　ily")
UF　Biracial Persons
　　Interracial Offspring
　　Mixed Race Persons
　　Mulattoes
　　Racially Mixed Persons
BT　Groups
RT　Ethnicity
　　Intermarriage
　　Minority Groups
　　Race
　　Racial Differences
　　Racial Factors
　　Racial Identification
　　Racial Relations

Multisensory Learning　　　　*JUL. 1966*
Postings: 428　　　　　　GC: 110
SN　Learning that involves the processing of
　　stimuli through two or more senses (e.g.,
　　through hearing as well as seeing)
BT　Learning
RT　Aural Learning
　　Learning Modalities
　　Perceptual Motor Learning
　　Sensory Integration
　　Sensory Training
　　Visual Learning

Multitrait Multimethod Techniques
　　　　　　　　　　　　APR. 1985
Postings: 165　　　　　　GC: 820
SN　Experimental validation designs requir-
　　ing the assessment of two or more traits,
　　each by two or more methods—the pur-
　　pose is to provide a dual approach in
　　which different methods of measuring
　　the same trait should have high correla-
　　tions (convergent validity), and different
　　traits measured with the same method
　　should have low correlations with the
　　trait of interest (discriminant validity)
UF　MTMM Methodology
BT　Research Methodology
RT　Comparative Analysis
　　Correlation
　　Discriminant Analysis
　　Error of Measurement
　　Factor Analysis
　　Item Analysis
　　Mathematical Models
　　Matrices
　　Measurement Techniques
　　Rating Scales
　　Test Validity
　　Testing

Multiunit Schools　　　　　*SEP. 1971*
Postings: 126　　　　　　GC: 340
SN　Schools featuring nongraded (rather than
　　age-graded) classroom units for instruc-
　　tion and research, building-level com-
　　mittees for instructional improvement,
　　and system-wide committees for policy
　　making (Note: Do not confuse with
　　"Multicampus Colleges"—see also the
　　Identifier "Individually Guided Education")
BT　Schools
RT　Elementary Schools
　　Instructional Innovation
　　Mixed Age Grouping
　　Nongraded Instructional Grouping
　　Research and Instruction Units
　　School Organization
　　Team Teaching

Multivariate Analysis　　　　*MAR. 1980*
Postings: 1,127　　　　　GC: 820
SN　Study of the relationships among three
　　or more variables that are either depend-
　　ent or neither dependent nor independ-
　　ent (Note: Do not confuse with "Multiple

Regression Analysis"—prior to Mar80,
the instruction "Multivariate Analysis,
USE Statistical Analysis" was carried in
the Thesaurus)
UF　Canonical Correlation
　　Multivariate Analysis of Variance
　　Multivariate Statistics
NT　Cluster Analysis
　　Discriminant Analysis
　　Factor Analysis
　　Multidimensional Scaling
　　Path Analysis
BT　Statistical Analysis
RT　Comparative Analysis
　　Correlation
　　Generalizability Theory
　　Mathematical Models
　　Robustness (Statistics)
　　Sampling

Multivariate Analysis of Variance
USE　Multivariate Analysis

Multivariate Statistics
USE　Multivariate Analysis

Municipal Government
USE　City Government

Municipalities　　　　　　*JUL. 1966*
Postings: 347　　　　　　GC: 550
SN　Towns, cities, or other districts having
　　powers of local self-government pro-
　　vided by specific charter or state statute
UF　Cities
　　Towns
NT　Boomtowns
　　Small Towns
BT　Community
　　Urban Areas
RT　Collective Settlements
　　Counties
　　Local Government
　　Metropolitan Areas
　　Suburbs

Munukutaba
USE　Kituba

Murder
USE　Homicide

Muscle Sense
USE　Kinesthetic Perception

Muscles
USE　Muscular System

Muscular Activities
USE　Motor Reactions

Muscular Exercise
USE　Exercise
AND　Muscular System

Muscular Extensions
USE　Motor Reactions

Muscular Flexions
USE　Motor Reactions

Muscular Strength　　　　　*JUN. 1969*
Postings: 399　　　　　　GC: 120
UF　Physical Strength
　　Strength (Biology)
BT　Physical Characteristics
RT　Body Composition
　　Calisthenics
　　Exercise
　　Motor Reactions
　　Muscular System
　　Physical Development

= Two or more Descriptors are used to represent this term.
The term's main entry shows the appropriate coordination.

	Physical Education		
	Physical Fitness		
	Plyometrics		
	Weightlifting		

Muscular System   *APR. 1990*
Postings: 34   GC: 210
UF   Muscles
    Muscular Exercise #
BT   Musculoskeletal System
RT   Anatomy
    Biofeedback
    Exercise
    Human Body
    Motor Reactions
    Muscular Strength
    Physiology
    Skeletal System

Musculoskeletal System   *APR. 1990*
Postings: 47   GC: 210
UF   Skeletomuscular System
NT   Muscular System
    Skeletal System
RT   Anatomy
    Cardiovascular System
    Exercise Physiology
    Human Body
    Human Posture
    Kinesthetic Perception
    Motor Development
    Osteopathy
    Physiology
    Zoology

Museums   *JUL. 1966*
Postings: 1,501   GC: 920
BT   Facilities
RT   Anthropology
    Arts Centers
    Community Resources
    Cultural Centers
    Educational Facilities
    Exhibits
    Historic Sites
    History
    Material Culture
    Realia
    Recreational Facilities
    Resource Centers
    Science Teaching Centers

Music   *JUL. 1966*
Postings: 2,887   GC: 420
NT   Applied Music
    Harmony (Music)
    Jazz
    Melody
    Oriental Music
    Popular Music
    Rock Music
    Vocal Music
BT   Fine Arts
RT   Art
    Bands (Music)
    Brass Instruments
    Concerts
    Dance
    Discographies
    Expressionism
    Folk Culture
    Impressionism
    Instrumentation and Orchestration
    Literary Styles
    Modernism
    Music Activities
    Music Appreciation
    Music Education
    Music Facilities
    Music Reading
    Music Teachers
    Music Techniques
    Music Theory
    Music Therapy
    Musical Composition
    Musical Instruments
    Musicians
    Neoclassicism
    Opera

    Orchestras
    Popular Culture
    Rehearsals (Theater Arts)
    Rhythm (Music)
    Romanticism
    String Instruments
    Suggestopedia
    Tempo (Music)
    Wind Instruments
    Woodwind Instruments

Music Activities   *JUL. 1966*
Postings: 1,484   GC: 420
NT   Concerts
    Instrumentation and Orchestration
    Singing
BT   Activities
RT   Applied Music
    Bands (Music)
    Choral Music
    Cultural Activities
    Enrichment Activities
    Extracurricular Activities
    Fine Arts
    Music
    Music Appreciation
    Music Education
    Music Facilities
    Music Techniques
    Music Therapy
    Musical Composition
    Orchestras
    Popular Music
    Recreational Activities
    Rhythm (Music)
    Songs
    Vocal Music

Music Appreciation   *JUN. 1969*
Postings: 713   GC: 420
BT   Aesthetic Education
RT   Audience Response
    Fine Arts
    Music
    Music Activities
    Music Education

Music Education   *JUL. 1966*
Postings: 4,336   GC: 420
NT   Kodaly Method
    Orff Method
    Suzuki Method
BT   Education
RT   Aesthetic Education
    Applied Music
    Choral Music
    Dance Education
    Fine Arts
    Music
    Music Activities
    Music Appreciation
    Music Teachers
    Music Techniques
    Musicians
    Orchestras
    Rhythm (Music)
    Songs
    Vocal Music

Music Facilities   *OCT. 1968*
Postings: 83   GC: 920
BT   Facilities
RT   Acoustical Environment
    Auditoriums
    Classrooms
    Educational Facilities
    Music
    Music Activities
    Stages (Facilities)
    Theaters

Music Reading   *JUL. 1966*
Postings: 189   GC: 420
UF   Score Reading
    Sight Playing
    Sight Singing
BT   Reading
RT   Kodaly Method
    Music

Music Teachers   *APR. 1970*
Postings: 802   GC: 360
BT   Teachers
RT   Fine Arts
    Music
    Music Education

Music Techniques   *JUL. 1966*
Postings: 615   GC: 420
SN   Technical skills used to produce musical results, either vocally or on instruments
BT   Methods
RT   Bands (Music)
    Choral Music
    Harmony (Music)
    Instrumentation and Orchestration
    Jazz
    Kodaly Method
    Music
    Music Activities
    Music Education
    Musical Composition
    Musical Instruments
    Musicians
    Orchestras
    Orff Method
    Rhythm (Music)
    Rock Music
    Songs
    Suzuki Method
    Vocal Music

Music Theory   *JUL. 1966*
Postings: 253   GC: 420
BT   Theories
RT   Instrumentation and Orchestration
    Music
    Musical Composition

Music Therapy   *JUN. 1977*
Postings: 132   GC: 230
SN   The therapeutic use of musical forms (concerts, music appreciation sessions, group singing, individual performance, etc.) in achieving self-awareness, self-esteem, and emotional release, usually in a context of remediation or rehabilitation
BT   Therapy
RT   Art Therapy
    Dance Therapy
    Educational Therapy
    Music
    Music Activities
    Play Therapy
    Psychotherapy
    Self Expression
    Therapeutic Recreation

Musical Composition   *OCT. 1969*
Postings: 556   GC: 420
SN   A written piece of music, or the act of creating a musical composition
UF   Composition (Music)
RT   Art Products
    Choral Music
    Harmony (Music)
    Improvisation
    Instrumentation and Orchestration
    Jazz
    Melody
    Music
    Music Activities
    Music Techniques
    Music Theory
    Opera
    Oriental Music
    Popular Music
    Rhythm (Music)
    Rock Music
    Songs
    Vocal Music

Musical Instruments   *OCT. 1969*
Postings: 568   GC: 420
NT   String Instruments
    Wind Instruments
BT   Equipment
RT   Bands (Music)

    Instrumentation and Orchestration
    Music
    Music Techniques
    Musicians
    Orchestras
    Orff Method
    Suzuki Method

Musicians   *JUL. 1969*
Postings: 452   GC: 420
BT   Artists
RT   Bands (Music)
    Concerts
    Fine Arts
    Music
    Music Education
    Music Techniques
    Musical Instruments
    Orchestras

Muslims   *JUN. 1999*
Postings: 122   GC: 560
SN   Persons who accept the creed and teachings of Islam (Note: Do not confuse with Identifiers "Black Muslims" and alternate "Nation of Islam")
UF   Moslems
BT   Religious Cultural Groups
RT   Arabs
    Ethnic Groups
    Islam
    Islamic Culture

Mutual Intelligibility   *JUL. 1966*
Postings: 145   GC: 450
RT   Bidialectalism
    Communication (Thought Transfer)
    Contrastive Linguistics
    Dialects
    Diglossia
    Jargon
    Language Classification
    Languages
    Sociolinguistics
    Speech Acts
    Verbal Communication

Mycology   *APR. 1990*
Postings: 8   GC: 490
SN   The scientific study of fungi
BT   Biological Sciences
RT   Biology
    Botany
    Culturing Techniques
    Ecology
    Fungi
    Microbiology

Myelocele
USE   Spina Bifida

Myelomeningocele
USE   Spina Bifida

Myopia   *JUL. 1966*
Postings: 6   GC: 220
UF   Miosis
    Myosis
    Nearsightedness
BT   Ametropia
RT   Hyperopia
    Vision
    Visual Acuity

Myosis
USE   Myopia

Mysticism   *JUL. 1970*
Postings: 96   GC: 430
SN   Theory of knowing or communing with God or the ultimate reality using a human faculty that transcends intellect
RT   Literary Styles
    Philosophy

= Two or more Descriptors are used to represent this term.
The term's main entry shows the appropriate coordination.

Religion
Spirituality

Mythic Criticism (1969 1980)   *MAR. 1980*
Postings: 75   GC: 430
SN   Invalid Descriptor—originally intended as a literary term, but used indiscriminately in indexing—see "Literary Criticism" and the Identifiers "Frye (Northrop)" or "Archetypes"—see also "Mythology"

Mythology   *JUL. 1966*
Postings: 932   GC: 430
UF   Myths
RT   American Indian Literature
    Classical Literature
    Epics
    Fables
    Fairy Tales
    Folk Culture
    Legends
    Literature
    Medieval Literature
    Oral Tradition
    Symbols (Literary)

Myths
USE   Mythology

N C Systems
USE   Numerical Control

Narcotics   *JUL. 1966*
Postings: 357   GC: 210
NT   Cocaine
    Heroin
    Marijuana
    Sedatives
RT   Drug Abuse
    Drug Addiction
    Drug Education
    Drug Legislation
    Drug Rehabilitation
    Drug Use
    Illegal Drug Use
    Stimulants

Narcotics Addiction
USE   Drug Addiction

Narration   *APR. 1970*
Postings: 1,044   GC: 430
BT   Literary Devices
RT   Audience Awareness
    Discourse Analysis
    Language Experience Approach
    Personal Narratives
    Story Grammar
    Story Telling
    Writing (Composition)

Natality
USE   Birth Rate

National Achievement Tests
USE   National Competency Tests

National Certification (Teaching)
USE   National Teacher Certification

National Competency Tests   *JUL. 1966*
Postings: 1,042   GC: 830
SN   Tests used to establish national norms and/or standards for achievement
UF   National Achievement Tests
    National Tests (of Achievement)
BT   Achievement Tests
RT   Achievement
    Government School Relationship
    Mastery Tests
    Minimum Competency Testing
    National Curriculum

National Norms
National Standards
National Surveys
National Teacher Certification
Norm Referenced Tests
Skills
Standardized Tests
Teacher Competency Testing

National Curriculum   *SEP. 1994*
Postings: 327   GC: 350
SN   Any curriculum adopted by a particular country that students of given ages or academic levels take in order to advance or graduate—may be voluntary or required (Note: If appropriate, use the more specific term "British National Curriculum")
NT   British National Curriculum
BT   Curriculum
RT   Core Curriculum
    Government School Relationship
    National Competency Tests
    National Programs
    National Standards
    Relevance (Education)

National Defense   *SEP. 1968*
Postings: 405   GC: 610
SN   Mobilization of a nation's military/civilian forces and other resources to deter war, to provide protection from aggression or enemy attack, and to wage war
BT   National Security
RT   Armed Forces
    Civil Defense
    Disarmament
    Military Organizations
    Military Personnel
    Military Science
    Military Training
    Peace
    War

National Demography (1966 1980)
USE   Demography

National Intelligence Norm (1966 1980)
USE   Intelligence
AND   National Norms

National Languages
USE   Official Languages

National Libraries   *MAR. 1969*
Postings: 655   GC: 710
SN   Libraries, maintained out of government funds, that serve the nation as a whole—functions may include collecting and preserving the country's publications, compiling union catalogs and national bibliographies, or acting as a national bibliographic center
BT   Government Libraries
RT   Archives
    Copyrights
    Union Catalogs

National Norms   *JUL. 1966*
Postings: 793   GC: 820
SN   Statistical description of the typical performance, behavior, form, function, etc., of a nation (Note: Use only for numerical data and not for subjectively described standards—prior to Mar80, the use of this term was not restricted by a Scope Note)
UF   National Intelligence Norm (1966 1980) #
BT   Norms
RT   Comparative Analysis
    Comparative Testing
    Item Sampling
    Language Planning
    Language Standardization
    Local Norms
    National Competency Tests

National Surveys
Norm Referenced Tests
State Norms

National Organizations   *JUL. 1966*
Postings: 1,374   GC: 520
BT   Organizations (Groups)
RT   Community Organizations
    Fraternities
    Honor Societies
    International Organizations
    National Programs
    Professional Associations
    Sororities

National Parks   *SEP. 1996*
Postings: 64   GC: 920
SN   Areas of scenic, historical, scientific, or ecological importance protected and preserved by a national government for public enjoyment or study
BT   Parks
RT   Conservation (Environment)
    Federal Government
    Government Role
    National Programs
    Natural Resources

National Programs   *JUL. 1966*
Postings: 4,037   GC: 610
SN   Privately or publicly sponsored nationwide programs (Note: Do not confuse with "Federal Programs"—prior to Mar80, the use of this term was not restricted by a Scope Note)
BT   Programs
RT   Developed Nations
    Developing Nations
    Educational Assessment
    Excellence in Education
    Federal Programs
    Language Planning
    Language Standardization
    National Curriculum
    National Organizations
    National Parks
    National Security
    National Standards
    National Surveys
    Nationalism
    Public Policy

National Security   *OCT. 1983*
Postings: 237   GC: 610
SN   Policies and programs undertaken by a nation to protect itself (i.e., its people, institutions, resources, communications, interests, etc.)—encompasses economic, scientific, and military aspects of security
NT   National Defense
RT   Federal Government
    Government Role
    International Relations
    Law Enforcement
    National Programs
    Safety

National Skill Standards
USE   National Standards

National Socialism
USE   Nazism

National Standards   *NOV. 1997*
Postings: 725   GC: 610
SN   Guidelines, requirements, and other specifications that are enacted and administered, publicly or privately, at the national level (Note: See also Identifiers for specific national educational standards, cross-indexed under "National Standards. . ." in the Identifier Authority List)
UF   National Skill Standards
BT   Standards
RT   Academic Standards
    National Competency Tests

National Curriculum
National Programs
National Teacher Certification
State Standards

National Surveys   *JUL. 1966*
Postings: 12,012   GC: 810
SN   Nationwide investigations of a field to determine current practices, trends, and/or norms (Note: As of Oct81, use as a minor Descriptor for examples of this kind of survey—use as a major Descriptor only as the subject of a document)
BT   Surveys
RT   Educational Assessment
    National Competency Tests
    National Norms
    National Programs
    State Surveys

National Teacher Certification   *DEC. 1995*
Postings: 22   GC: 820
SN   Use of nationwide competency assessment and testing to certify teachers (Note: Do not confuse with the Identifier "National Teacher Examinations," which is a specific test series published by the Educational Testing Service)
UF   National Certification (Teaching)
BT   Teacher Certification
RT   Alternative Teacher Certification
    Educational Certificates
    National Competency Tests
    National Standards
    Teacher Competency Testing
    Teacher Education
    Teacher Education Curriculum
    Teacher Qualifications

National Tests (of Achievement)
USE   National Competency Tests

Nationalism   *JUL. 1966*
Postings: 846   GC: 610
NT   Patriotism
RT   Black Power
    Colonialism
    Cultural Awareness
    Developing Nations
    Ethnic Groups
    Ethnicity
    Fascism
    Foreign Policy
    Group Unity
    Imperialism
    International Relations
    National Programs
    Political Attitudes
    Political Divisions (Geographic)
    Self Determination

Native Informants
USE   Native Speakers

Native Language Instruction   *MAR. 1980*
Postings: 1,209   GC: 450
SN   Teaching languages to native speakers of those languages (Note: For English, use "English Instruction" except when emphasis is explicitly on teaching standard English to speakers of nonstandard English dialects—in those cases, coordinate "Native Language Instruction" and "English Instruction")
NT   English Instruction
BT   Humanities Instruction
RT   Bidialectalism
    Bilingual Education Programs
    Bilingual Instructional Materials
    Ethnic Groups
    Language Standardization
    Language Teachers
    Language Usage
    Native Speakers
    Nonstandard Dialects
    Spanish Speaking

= Two or more Descriptors are used to represent this term.
The term's main entry shows the appropriate coordination.

Native Migrants
USE   Migrants

Native Speakers   *JUL. 1969*
      Postings: 1,398   GC: 450
SN   (Note: Used primarily to index material
      involving the use of native informants in
      linguistic studies and the use of native
      speakers in the teaching of a foreign
      language)
UF   Native Informants
NT   Spanish Speaking
BT   Groups
RT   American Indian Languages
      Bidialectalism
      Bilingual Education Programs
      Bilingual Students
      Bilingual Teacher Aides
      Bilingual Teachers
      Bilingualism
      Dialects
      Dravidian Languages
      Ethnic Groups
      Foreign Culture
      Immersion Programs
      Indo European Languages
      Language of Instruction
      Language Patterns
      Language Styles
      Language Usage
      Limited English Speaking
      Linguistic Difficulty (Inherent)
      Malayo Polynesian Languages
      Monolingualism
      Native Language Instruction
      Non English Speaking
      Official Languages
      Regional Dialects
      Second Language Instruction
      Second Language Programs
      Second Languages
      Sino Tibetan Languages
      Slavic Languages
      Sociolinguistics
      Speech Habits

Natives
USE   Indigenous Populations

Natural Disasters   *JUN. 1983*
      Postings: 254   GC: 210
SN   Calamitous occurrences produced by
      natural forces, often widespread and gen-
      erally resulting in distress, loss, or mate-
      rial damage
NT   Drought
RT   Civil Defense
      Earthquakes
      Emergency Programs
      Floods
      Hurricanes
      Safety
      Tornadoes
      Volcanoes
      Weather

Natural Gas   *DEC. 1992*
      Postings: 10   GC: 410
SN   A combustible mixture of hydrocarbon
      gases, usually found in sedimentary rocks
      and in association with petroleum de-
      posits
BT   Fossil Fuels
RT   Geology
      Oil
      Petroleum Industry
      Utilities

Natural Language Processing   *AUG. 1994*
      Postings: 146   GC: 710
SN   Human communication with computers
      using natural languages, such as English
      and Japanese, rather than programming
      languages, such as Basic and Pascal
      (Note: Do not confuse with "Computa-
      tional Linguistics"—for other applica-
      tions, see the Identifiers "Natural Lan-
      guage" and "Natural Languages")

UF   Natural Language Understanding Sys-
      tems
BT   Data Processing
RT   Artificial Intelligence
      Computers
      Information Retrieval
      Information Storage
      Knowledge Representation
      Languages
      Man Machine Systems

Natural Language Understanding Systems
USE   Natural Language Processing

Natural Parents
USE   Biological Parents

Natural Resources   *JUL. 1966*
      Postings: 4,348   GC: 410
NT   Coal
      Fossil Fuels
      Oil
      Water Resources
BT   Resources
RT   Agricultural Education
      Agriculture
      Alternative Energy Sources
      Asbestos
      Community Resources
      Conservation (Environment)
      Conservation Education
      Depleted Resources
      Endangered Species
      Energy Conservation
      Environmental Education
      Forestry
      Habitats
      Minerals
      Mining
      National Parks
      Parks
      Physical Environment
      Recycling
      Soil Conservation
      Sustainable Development
      Wilderness
      Wildlife

Natural Sciences   *JUL. 1966*
      Postings: 772   GC: 490
NT   Biological Sciences
      Physical Sciences
BT   Sciences
RT   English for Science and Technology
      Nature Centers
      Scientific and Technical Information
      Scientific Enterprise

Naturalism   *MAY 1969*
      Postings: 108   GC: 430
SN   In philosophy and theology, the notion
      that the human mind is part of the mate-
      rial world, including the doctrine that
      moral values can be empirically discov-
      ered and verified—in literature and the
      arts, the environmental and evolutionary
      view of life that finds expression in at-
      tempts to make art reflect (by accurate
      representation, depiction, etc.) the ob-
      jective reality of nature
RT   Art Expression
      Literary Styles
      Nineteenth Century Literature
      Philosophy
      Religion
      Twentieth Century Literature

Naturalistic Observation   *OCT. 1984*
      Postings: 561   GC: 820
SN   Observation of behaviors and events in
      natural settings without experimental ma-
      nipulation or other interference
BT   Observation
RT   Behavioral Science Research
      Classroom Observation Techniques
      Ethnography
      Ethology
      Field Studies

      Interaction Process Analysis
      Participant Observation
      Qualitative Research
      Research Methodology
      Scientific Methodology
      Sociometric Techniques
      Triangulation

Nature Centers   *JUL. 1966*
      Postings: 264   GC: 920
BT   Resource Centers
RT   Aquariums
      Education Service Centers
      Educational Facilities
      Environmental Interpretation
      Natural Sciences
      Parks
      Science Teaching Centers

Nature Nurture Controversy   *MAY 1974*
      Postings: 697   GC: 120
SN   Argument concerning the relative influ-
      ences of hereditary and environmental
      factors in determining behavior patterns
UF   Environment Heredity Controversy
      Heredity Environment Controversy
      Learning Maturation Controversy
      Maturation Learning Controversy
RT   Behavior Development
      Biological Influences
      Cultural Differences
      Cultural Influences
      Developmental Psychology
      Environment
      Environmental Influences
      Genetics
      Heredity
      Individual Development
      Individual Differences
      Intelligence
      Intelligence Differences
      Learning
      Prenatal Influences
      Race
      Racial Differences
      Social Bias
      Sociobiology

Nature of Science
USE   Scientific Principles

Nature Trails
USE   Trails

Navaho (1967 1978)
USE   Navajo

Navajo   *JUN. 1978*
      Postings: 352   GC: 440
SN   Athapascan language spoken by the Dine
      or Navajo Indians of Arizona, Utah, and
      northern New Mexico
UF   Navaho (1967 1978)
BT   Athapascan Languages
RT   Navajo (Nation)

Navajo (Nation)   *MAR. 1994*
      Postings: 654   GC: 560
SN   The largest American Indian tribe—
      centered on the Navajo Reservation in
      northeast Arizona and adjacent areas of
      New Mexico and Utah
BT   American Indians
      Tribes
RT   Navajo

Naval Air Stations
USE   Military Air Facilities

Navigation   *JUL. 1966*
      Postings: 176   GC: 490
SN   Managed point-to-point movement in any
      environment or medium (Note: If ap-
      propriate, use the more specific terms
      "Orienteering" for the sport of cross-

      country navigation and "Navigation (In-
      formation Systems)" for movement
      among or within Internet sites and other
      locations on computers)
NT   Navigation (Information Systems)
      Orienteering
RT   Astronomy
      Aviation Education
      Aviation Technology
      Boat Operators
      Radar
      Seafarers
      Space Sciences
      Vectors (Mathematics)

Navigation (Information Systems)
                                             JAN. 1997
      Postings: 266   GC: 710
SN   The process of finding one's way around
      the contents of a database or hypermedia-
      based program—navigability is a chief
      goal of those who design computer sys-
      tems, human-computer interfaces, and
      hypermedia links, and also a leading
      criterion for those who evaluate them
BT   Navigation
RT   Computer Interfaces
      Hypermedia
      Information Retrieval
      Information Systems
      Man Machine Systems

Nazism   *MAR. 1982*
      Postings: 240   GC: 610
SN   The body of fascist political and eco-
      nomic doctrines based on principles of
      totalitarian government, state control of
      industry, and racist nationalism—first
      brought to power in 1933 in the Third
      German Reich
UF   National Socialism
      Neo Nazism
BT   Fascism
      Totalitarianism
RT   Anti Semitism
      Genocide
      International Crimes
      Segregationist Organizations

Near Eastern History
USE   Middle Eastern History

Nearsightedness
USE   Myopia

Need Analysis (Student Financial Aid)
                                             OCT. 1979
      Postings: 364   GC: 620
SN   Process of evaluating the resources of a
      student to determine his/her need or
      eligibility for financial aid
BT   Evaluation Methods
RT   Eligibility
      Financial Needs
      Financial Support
      Needs Assessment
      No Need Scholarships
      Parent Financial Contribution
      Paying for College
      Self Supporting Students
      Student Costs
      Student Financial Aid
      Student Loan Programs
      Student Needs

Need Gratification   *JUL. 1966*
      Postings: 440   GC: 120
SN   Satisfaction of basic needs
UF   Need Reduction
RT   Community Satisfaction
      Delay of Gratification
      Goal Orientation
      Individual Needs
      Job Satisfaction
      Life Satisfaction
      Love
      Marital Satisfaction
      Morale

= Two or more Descriptors are used to represent this term.
The term's main entry shows the appropriate coordination.

Needs
Psychological Needs
Satisfaction
Self Actualization

Need Reduction
USE   Need Gratification

Needle Trades   JUL. 1966
Postings: 139   GC: 640
UF   Seamstresses (1968 1980)
      Tailors
BT   Occupations
RT   Clothing
      Clothing Design
      Clothing Instruction
      Craft Workers
      Fashion Industry
      Home Economics Skills
      Industrial Arts
      Laundry Drycleaning Occupations
      Occupational Home Economics
      Patternmaking
      Semiskilled Occupations
      Sewing Instruction
      Sewing Machine Operators

Needs   JUL. 1966
Postings: 806   GC: 520
SN   Conditions or factors necessary for opti-
      mal function, development, or well-be-
      ing, the lack of which may impair effi-
      ciency or trigger action toward fulfillment
      (Note: Use a more specific term if possi-
      ble)
NT   Community Needs
      Construction Needs
      Educational Needs
      Evaluation Needs
      Family Needs
      Financial Needs
      Health Needs
      Housing Needs
      Individual Needs
      Information Needs
      Labor Needs
      Research Needs
      Student Needs
      User Needs (Information)
RT   Advocacy
      Appropriate Technology
      Motivation
      Need Gratification
      Needs Assessment
      Objectives
      Resources
      Satisfaction

Needs Assessment   FEB. 1976
Postings: 11,927   GC: 810
SN   Identifying needs and deciding on priori-
      ties among them
UF   Priority Determination
BT   Evaluation
RT   Advisory Committees
      Blue Ribbon Commissions
      Delivery Systems
      Educational Assessment
      Evaluation Methods
      Need Analysis (Student Financial Aid)
      Needs
      Nominal Group Technique
      Objectives
      Planning
      Policy Formation
      Position Papers
      Resource Allocation
      Self Evaluation (Groups)
      Surveys
      Systems Analysis
      Testing

Negative Attitudes   JUL. 1966
Postings: 1,336   GC: 540
BT   Attitudes
RT   Anti Intellectualism
      Burnout
      Jealousy
      Resentment

Resistance (Psychology)
Social Bias

Negative Forms (Language)   AUG. 1968
Postings: 280   GC: 450
SN   The structures of a language that signify
      negation
BT   Morphemes
RT   Language Universals
      Morphophonemics
      Semantics
      Tagmemic Analysis

Negative Income Tax
USE   Guaranteed Income

Negative Practice   JUL. 1966
Postings: 22   GC: 310
SN   Systematic repetition of erroneous re-
      sponses to emphasize differences be-
      tween appropriate and inappropriate per-
      formance
BT   Teaching Methods
RT   Behavior Change
      Learning Activities
      Negative Reinforcement

Negative Reinforcement   JUL. 1966
Postings: 346   GC: 110
SN   Conditioning technique whereby the re-
      moval of an aversive stimulus increases
      the probability that a specified behavior
      will occur (Note: Do not confuse with
      "Punishment" or "Extinction (Psychol-
      ogy)")
UF   Massed Negative Reinforcement
      Spaced Negative Reinforcement
BT   Reinforcement
RT   Corporal Punishment
      Extinction (Psychology)
      Negative Practice
      Positive Reinforcement
      Punishment
      Social Reinforcement

Negentropy
USE   Entropy

Neglected Children (1977 1980)
USE   Child Neglect

Neglected Languages
USE   Uncommonly Taught Languages

Negligence   OCT. 1994
Postings: 128   GC: 530
SN   Failure to do what a reasonable, careful,
      conscientious person is expected to do
NT   Child Neglect
RT   Accidents
      Accountability
      Court Litigation
      Educational Malpractice
      Laws
      Legal Problems
      Legal Responsibility
      Malpractice
      Responsibility
      Torts

Negotiation Agreements   NOV. 1968
Postings: 815   GC: 630
SN   Documents containing a clause which
      recognizes one or more organizations as
      representative of employees on employ-
      ment issues
RT   Arbitration
      Board of Education Policy
      Collective Bargaining
      Contracts
      Faculty College Relationship
      Grievance Procedures
      Negotiation Impasses
      Public School Teachers

Teacher Strikes
Unions

Negotiation Impasses   APR. 1969
Postings: 324   GC: 630
UF   Impasse Resolution
RT   Arbitration
      Board of Education Policy
      Collective Bargaining
      Employment Problems
      Grievance Procedures
      Labor Demands
      Labor Economics
      Labor Legislation
      Labor Problems
      Negotiation Agreements
      Sanctions
      Strikes
      Teacher Militancy
      Teacher Strikes
      Unions

Negro Achievement (1966 1977)
USE   Black Achievement

Negro Attitudes (1966 1977)
USE   Black Attitudes

Negro Businesses (1967 1977)
USE   Black Businesses

Negro Colleges (1968 1977)
USE   Black Colleges

Negro Community
USE   Black Community

Negro Culture (1966 1977)
USE   Black Culture

Negro Dialects (1966 1977)
USE   Black Dialects

Negro Education (1966 1977)
USE   Black Education

Negro Employment (1966 1977)
USE   Black Employment

Negro History (1966 1977)
USE   Black History

Negro Housing (1966 1977)   MAR. 1980
Postings: 19   GC: 550
SN   Invalid Descriptor—postings transferred
      to "Black Housing," which was invali-
      dated Mar80—see "Housing Discrimi-
      nation," "Residential Patterns," or
      "Homeowners" in coordination with ap-
      propriate "Black" Descriptor(s)

Negro Institutions (1966 1977)
USE   Black Institutions

Negro Leadership (1966 1977)
USE   Black Leadership

Negro Literature (1968 1977)
USE   Black Literature

Negro Mothers (1966 1977)
USE   Black Mothers

Negro Organizations (1966 1977)
USE   Black Organizations

Negro Population Trends (1966 1977)
USE   Black Population Trends

Negro Role (1966 1977)
USE   Black Influences

Negro Stereotypes (1966 1977)
USE   Black Stereotypes

Negro Students (1966 1977)
USE   Black Students

Negro Studies
USE   Black Studies

Negro Teachers (1966 1977)
USE   Black Teachers

Negro Youth (1966 1977)
USE   Black Youth

Negroes (1966 1977)
USE   Blacks

Neighborhood Centers (1966 1980)
USE   Community Centers

Neighborhood Improvement   JUL. 1966
Postings: 198   GC: 550
BT   Improvement
RT   Community Development
      Community Responsibility
      Housing Deficiencies
      Housing Needs
      Neighborhoods
      Social Responsibility
      Urban Improvement
      Urban Renewal

Neighborhood Integration   JUL. 1966
Postings: 181   GC: 540
UF   Integrated Neighborhoods
      Residential Desegregation
BT   Social Integration
RT   Ethnic Distribution
      Housing Discrimination
      Housing Opportunities
      Integration Readiness
      Neighborhoods
      Racial Composition
      Racial Distribution
      Racial Integration
      Residential Patterns
      Tokenism

Neighborhood School Policy (1966 1980)
USE   Neighborhood Schools
AND   School Policy

Neighborhood Schools   JUL. 1966
Postings: 237   GC: 340
SN   Schools in which most or all of the
      student population comes from the im-
      mediate geographic area in which the
      school is located
UF   Neighborhood School Policy (1966
      1980) #
BT   Schools
RT   Community Schools
      Educational Parks
      Neighborhoods
      School Desegregation

Neighborhood Settlements
USE   Settlement Houses

Neighborhood (1966 1980)
USE   Neighborhoods

= Two or more Descriptors are used to represent this term.
The term's main entry shows the appropriate coordination.

Neighborhoods   MAR. 1980
    Postings: 506   GC: 550
SN Small sections or districts within larger communities, usually marked by distinctive physical or human features (e.g., age, architecture, or social characteristics of the residents) that provide a sense of local identity
UF Neighborhood (1966 1980)
BT Community
RT Collective Settlements
    Community Characteristics
    Metropolitan Areas
    Neighborhood Improvement
    Neighborhood Integration
    Neighborhood Schools
    Place of Residence
    Residential Patterns
    Suburbs

Nembe   FEB. 1970
    Postings: 3   GC: 440
BT African Languages

Neo Nazism
USE Nazism

Neoclassicism   JUL. 1971
    Postings: 14   GC: 430
SN A style of artistic expression based on or felt to be based on the classical style
RT Architecture
    Art Expression
    Eighteenth Century Literature
    Literary Styles
    Music
    Seventeenth Century Literature

Neonates   JUN. 1977
    Postings: 610   GC: 120
SN Aged birth to approximately 1 month (Note: Added Mar89 to list of age leveling Descriptors—prior to that, this concept was frequently indexed by "Infants")
UF Newborn Infants
BT Infants
RT Birth Weight
    Infant Behavior
    Infant Care
    Infant Mortality
    Pediatrics
    Premature Infants

Neopsychoanalysis
USE Psychiatry

Nepali   JUL. 1966
    Postings: 27   GC: 440
BT Indo European Languages

Netsilik
USE Inupiaq

Network Analysis   NOV. 1982
    Postings: 144   GC: 820
SN Examination of the interactive communication patterns among individuals, groups, and/or organizations (Note: Do not confuse with "Systems Analysis" or "Critical Path Method")
BT Methods
RT Communication (Thought Transfer)
    Communication Audits
    Communication Research
    Communications
    Models
    Networks
    Research Methodology
    Systems Analysis

Networks   JUL. 1966
    Postings: 1,694   GC: 710
SN Series of points interconnected by communication channels (Note: Use more specific term if possible)

NT Computer Networks
    Information Networks
    Social Networks
RT Communication (Thought Transfer)
    Communications
    Cooperation
    Coordination
    Decentralization
    Diffusion (Communication)
    Linking Agents
    Network Analysis
    Radio
    Telecommunications
    Television

Neurolinguistics   JUN. 1972
    Postings: 384   GC: 450
SN Study of the biological foundations of language and the brain mechanisms underlying its acquisition and use
BT Linguistics
RT Brain
    Language Impairments
    Language Processing
    Linguistic Theory
    Neurological Impairments
    Neurological Organization
    Neurology
    Neuropsychology
    Psycholinguistics

Neurological Defects (1966 1980)
USE Neurological Impairments

Neurological Impairments   MAR. 1980
    Postings: 1,719   GC: 220
SN Organic disorders of the brain or nervous system
UF Brain Damage
    Neurological Defects (1966 1980)
    Neurologically Handicapped (1966 1980)
    Paraplegia
    Quadriplegia (1969 1980)
    Tetraplegia
    Traumatic Brain Injury #
NT Aphasia
    Cerebral Palsy
    Epilepsy
    Minimal Brain Dysfunction
BT Physical Disabilities
RT Alzheimers Disease
    Attention Deficit Disorders
    Behavior Disorders
    Brain
    Developmental Disabilities
    Downs Syndrome
    Dyslexia
    Fetal Alcohol Syndrome
    Head Injuries
    Hyperactivity
    Language Impairments
    Lead Poisoning
    Learning Disabilities
    Mental Disorders
    Mental Retardation
    Motor Development
    Neurolinguistics
    Neurological Organization
    Neurology
    Neuropsychology
    Perceptual Impairments
    Psychomotor Skills
    Seizures
    Spina Bifida

Neurological Organization   JUL. 1966
    Postings: 840   GC: 210
NT Brain Hemisphere Functions
BT Physical Characteristics
RT Brain
    Lateral Dominance
    Motor Development
    Neurolinguistics
    Neurological Impairments
    Neurology
    Neuropsychology
    Perception
    Perceptual Development

    Physical Development
    Physiology
    Psychomotor Skills
    Stimulation

Neurologically Handicapped (1966 1980)
USE Neurological Impairments

Neurology   JUL. 1966
    Postings: 793   GC: 210
BT Medicine
RT Anatomy
    Brain
    Brain Hemisphere Functions
    Electroencephalography
    Mental Health
    Neurolinguistics
    Neurological Impairments
    Neurological Organization
    Neuropsychology
    Pathology
    Physiology

Neuropsychology   APR. 1990
    Postings: 412   GC: 230
SN Study of the relationship between the nervous system and behavior
BT Psychology
RT Brain
    Brain Hemisphere Functions
    Clinical Psychology
    Cognitive Psychology
    Mental Health
    Neurolinguistics
    Neurological Impairments
    Neurological Organization
    Neurology
    Perception
    Psychiatry
    Psychological Testing
    Psychomotor Skills
    Psychophysiology
    Sensory Integration

Neurosis   JUL. 1966
    Postings: 260   GC: 230
UF Neurotic Children (1966 1980)
NT Posttraumatic Stress Disorder
BT Mental Disorders
RT Emotional Disturbances
    Fear
    Mental Health
    Personality Problems
    Psychosomatic Disorders
    School Phobia

Neurotic Children (1966 1980)
USE Neurosis

New Federalism   DEC. 1989
    Postings: 86   GC: 610
SN A trend in late 20th century U.S. conservative political thought toward federal decentralization and more active state governments
BT Federalism
RT Block Grants
    Conservatism
    Decentralization
    Educational Finance
    Educational Policy
    Federal Aid
    Federal Government
    Federal Legislation
    Federal Programs
    Federal State Relationship
    Financial Policy
    Government Role
    Politics
    Revenue Sharing
    Social Services
    State Aid
    States Powers

New Journalism   DEC. 1974
    Postings: 65   GC: 430
SN Reporting which combines traditional

journalism techniques with such devices of fiction writing as: scene by scene reconstruction of settings, recording of dialogue, use of third person point-of-view, and extensive recording of external characteristics of individual characters—emphasis is on capturing the "concrete reality" or "immediacy" of cultural phenomena
BT Journalism
RT Feature Stories
    News Media
    News Writing
    Newspapers
    Nonfiction
    Publications

New Mathematics
USE Modern Mathematics

Newborn Infants
USE Neonates

News Broadcasting
USE Broadcast Journalism
AND News Reporting

News Media   JUL. 1966
    Postings: 2,641   GC: 720
UF News Use #
    Press
    Press Role #
    Sports News #
NT Editorials
    Newspapers
BT Mass Media
RT Agenda Setting
    Broadcast Journalism
    Editing
    Editors
    Feature Stories
    Freedom of Information
    Freedom of Speech
    Headlines
    Journalism
    Journalism Education
    Journalism History
    New Journalism
    News Reporting
    News Writing
    Photojournalism
    Press Opinion
    Radio
    Television

News Reporting   JAN. 1974
    Postings: 2,931   GC: 720
UF News Broadcasting #
    Sports Reporting #
BT Journalism
RT Agenda Setting
    Athletics
    Broadcast Journalism
    Expository Writing
    Feature Stories
    Headlines
    Mass Media Role
    News Media
    News Writing
    Photojournalism
    Reports

News Use
USE Mass Media Use
AND News Media

News Writing   JUL. 1977
    Postings: 825   GC: 720
SN Writing about events and activities for dissemination through newspapers, news broadcasts, or the news services
BT Journalism
    Writing (Composition)
RT Broadcast Journalism
    Content Area Writing
    Editing
    Expository Writing

= Two or more Descriptors are used to represent this term.
The term's main entry shows the appropriate coordination.

Feature Stories
Headlines
New Journalism
News Media
News Reporting
Writing for Publication

Newsletters *JUL. 1966*
Postings: 1,189 GC: 730
BT Newspapers
RT Bulletins

Newspapers *JUL. 1966*
Postings: 3,677 GC: 720
NT Newsletters
School Newspapers
BT News Media
Serials
RT Bulletins
Captions
Comics (Publications)
Editorials
Feature Stories
Headlines
Journalism
Journalism Education
Journalism History
Layout (Publications)
New Journalism
Photojournalism
Printed Materials
Reading Materials

Night Schools (1966 1980)
USE Evening Programs

Nightmares *DEC. 1989*
Postings: 13 GC: 230
SN Dreams that arouse intense fear and
distress
BT Dreams
RT Anxiety
Emotional Problems
Fear
Sleep

Nineteenth Century Literature *MAY 1969*
Postings: 532 GC: 430
BT Literature
RT Impressionism
Literary History
Modernism
Naturalism
Romanticism
Symbolism
Victorian Literature

No Need Scholarships *AUG. 1986*
Postings: 25 GC: 620
SN Scholarship awards based on merit re-
gardless of financial need
BT Merit Scholarships
RT Need Analysis (Student Financial Aid)
Scholarship Funds

No Shows *AUG. 1986*
Postings: 32 GC: 520
SN Individuals who arrange to be some-
where (e.g., attending a meeting, begin-
ning a course of study, enrolling in col-
lege) but who fail to appear
BT Groups
RT Attendance
College Applicants
Dropouts
Enrollment

Noise (Sound) *OCT. 1982*
Postings: 270 GC: 490
UF Noise Control
Noise Levels
Noise Pollution
Noise Testing
Volume (Sound)
BT Acoustical Environment
RT Acoustic Insulation

Acoustics
Audio Equipment
Auditory Stimuli
Ecology
Environmental Standards
Hearing Conservation
Pollution
Psychoacoustics
Sound Effects

Noise Control
USE Noise (Sound)

Noise Levels
USE Noise (Sound)

Noise Pollution
USE Noise (Sound)

Noise Testing
USE Noise (Sound)

Nomads *JAN. 1970*
Postings: 55 GC: 560
UF Pastoral Peoples
Transhumance
BT Migrants
RT Land Settlement
Migration
Transient Children
Tribes

Nominal Group Technique *APR. 1990*
Postings: 96 GC: 820
SN Method of achieving consensus in group
meetings, involving silent generation of
ideas, round-robin listing, individual rank-
ing, and tabulation to produce a set of
recommendations in priority order—
designed to prevent individual domina-
tion and ensure balanced participation
BT Methods
RT Brainstorming
Cooperative Planning
Decision Making
Delphi Technique
Group Discussion
Group Dynamics
Needs Assessment
Participative Decision Making

Nominals (1967 1980)
USE Nouns

Non English Speaking *JUL. 1966*
Postings: 846 GC: 450
BT Groups
RT Bilingual Education
Bilingual Education Programs
Bilingual Teacher Aides
Bilingual Teachers
English (Second Language)
Ethnic Groups
Family English Literacy
Language Dominance
Language Minorities
Limited English Speaking
Minority Groups
Native Speakers
Spanish Speaking

Non Latin Alphabets
USE Non Roman Scripts

Non Roman Scripts *AUG. 1989*
Postings: 42 GC: 450
SN Language signs and characters that are
not included in the Roman alphabet, e.g.,
Arabic letters, Chinese ideograms
UF Non Latin Alphabets
Nonroman Alphabets
BT Alphabets
RT Cyrillic Alphabet

Ideography
Romanization

Non Western Civilization *SEP. 1968*
Postings: 1,013 GC: 560
SN Includes Asia and Africa
UF Eastern Civilization
Oriental Civilization
South Asian Civilization
BT Culture
RT African Culture
African History
African Studies
Arabs
Area Studies
Asian History
Asian Studies
Buddhism
Burmese Culture
Chinese Culture
Confucianism
Cultural Background
Cultural Context
History
Japanese Culture
Korean Culture
Middle Eastern History
Middle Eastern Studies
Religion Studies
Sociocultural Patterns
Taoism
World History

Nonauthoritarian Classes *JUL. 1966*
Postings: 31 GC: 310
BT Classes (Groups of Students)
RT Leadership
Permissive Environment

Nonbook Materials
USE Nonprint Media

Noncampus Colleges *OCT. 1977*
Postings: 71 GC: 340
SN Postsecondary institutions which dis-
pense with the fixed campus in favor of
rented, borrowed, or mobile facilities in
many locations
BT Colleges
RT Access to Education
Educational Facilities
Extension Education
External Degree Programs
Nontraditional Education
Outreach Programs
Postsecondary Education

Noncategorical Education *APR. 1990*
Postings: 32 GC: 330
SN Educational programs or philosophies
that refrain from diagnostic labels, e.g.,
"impaired," "learning disabled," "nor-
mal"
UF Cross Categorical Education
BT Education
RT Labeling (of Persons)
Special Education
Special Education Teachers

Noncollege Bound Students *MAR. 1980*
Postings: 430 GC: 360
SN Students not planning on attending an
institution of higher education
UF Noncollege Preparatory Students
(1967 1980)
BT High School Students
RT Academic Aspiration
College Bound Students
High School Seniors
Vocational Education

**Noncollege Preparatory Students (1967
1980)**
USE Noncollege Bound Students

Noncompliance (Psychology)
USE Compliance (Psychology)

Noncredit Courses *JUL. 1966*
Postings: 540 GC: 350
BT Courses
RT Adult Education
Continuing Education
Continuing Education Units
Credit Courses
Elective Courses
Minicourses
Student Interests

Nondirective Counseling *JUL. 1966*
Postings: 215 GC: 240
SN Counseling procedure in which the coun-
selor is empathetic and does not evalu-
ate or direct (but may clarify) clients'
remarks, thus assisting them to accept
responsibility for their own problem-solv-
ing
UF Client Centered Counseling
BT Counseling
RT Behavior Change
Counseling Theories
Empathy

Nondiscriminatory Education *JUL. 1966*
Postings: 647 GC: 540
BT Education
RT Access to Education
Affirmative Action
Educational Discrimination
Educational Equity (Finance)
Educational Opportunities
Equal Education
Sex Fairness

Nondiscursive Measures
USE Visual Measures

Nonfarm Agricultural Occupations
USE Off Farm Agricultural Occupations

Nonfiction *SEP. 1974*
Postings: 721 GC: 430
NT Biographies
Chronicles
Diaries
Essays
BT Prose
RT Fiction
Literary Devices
Literary Genres
Literary Styles
New Journalism

Nonformal Education *JUL. 1973*
Postings: 1,519 GC: 330
SN Organized education without formal
schooling or institutionalization in which
knowledge, skills, and values are taught
by relatives, peers, or other community
members (Note: Do not confuse with
"Nonschool Educational Programs" or
"Informal Education")
BT Education
RT Comparative Education
Culture
Developing Nations
Educational Anthropology
Folk Culture
Informal Education
Lifelong Learning
Nontraditional Education
Socialization
Tribes

Nongovernmental Organizations *SEP. 1999*
Postings: 156 GC: 520
SN Private sector organizations, typically nonprofit, voluntary, and international in
scope, that carry out a variety of social
development or public interest functions
BT Organizations (Groups)

= Two or more Descriptors are used to represent this term.
The term's main entry shows the appropriate coordination.

RT　Community Organizations
　　International Organizations
　　Nonprofit Organizations
　　Private Agencies
　　Social Agencies
　　Voluntary Agencies

Nongraded Classes (1966 1980)
USE　Nongraded Instructional Grouping

Nongraded Instructional Grouping
　　　　　　　　　　　　　　　MAR. 1980
　　Postings: 716　　　　　　　GC: 350
SN　Grouping students according to such
　　characteristics as academic achievement,
　　mental and physical ability, or emotional
　　development rather than by age or grade
　　level (Note: Some of the former
　　"nongraded/ungraded" Descriptors
　　merged with this term were occasionally
　　used to index "Nongraded Student Evalua-
　　tion")
UF　Nongraded Classes (1966 1980)
　　Nongraded Primary System (1966
　　　1980)
　　Nongraded System (1966 1980)
　　Ungraded Classes (1966 1980)
　　Ungraded Curriculum (1966 1980)
　　Ungraded Elementary Programs (1966
　　　1980)
　　Ungraded Primary Programs (1966
　　　1980)
　　Ungraded Programs (1966 1980)
　　Ungraded Schools (1966 1980)
BT　Grouping (Instructional Purposes)
RT　Ability Grouping
　　Age Grade Placement
　　Continuous Progress Plan
　　Flexible Progression
　　Instructional Program Divisions
　　Mixed Age Grouping
　　Multigraded Classes
　　Multiunit Schools
　　Open Education

Nongraded Primary System (1966 1980)
USE　Nongraded Instructional Grouping

Nongraded Student Evaluation　MAR. 1980
　　Postings: 52　　　　　　　　GC: 320
SN　Evaluation of student progress or achieve-
　　ment without the use of letter grades
　　or other summary ratings—provides
　　feedback about a student's specific
　　strengths and weaknesses rather than
　　summarizing his or her overall perform-
　　ance (Note: Some of the former
　　"nongraded/ungraded" Descriptors
　　merged with "Nongraded Instructional
　　Grouping" were occasionally used to
　　index this concept)
BT　Student Evaluation
RT　Credit No Credit Grading
　　Free Schools
　　Informal Assessment
　　Pass Fail Grading

Nongraded System (1966 1980)
USE　Nongraded Instructional Grouping

Noninstructional Responsibility　JUL. 1966
　　Postings: 452　　　　　　　GC: 320
SN　Duties assumed by, or assigned to, teach-
　　ers that are outside of their regular teach-
　　ing responsibilities (e.g., lunchroom duty,
　　advising, community involvement)
UF　Extrainstructional Duties
　　Extrateaching Duties
　　Nonteaching Duties
BT　Teacher Responsibility
RT　Educational Responsibility
　　Faculty Workload
　　School Responsibility
　　Teacher Role
　　Teachers

Noninstructional Student Costs　DEC. 1975
　　Postings: 108　　　　　　　GC: 620
SN　Costs met by students that are not in-
　　structional costs (tuition, etc.) but are
　　necessary in the pursuit of an education—
　　includes room and board, transportation
　　expenses, book costs, personal expenses,
　　foregone income, etc.
BT　Student Costs
RT　Educational Finance
　　Fellowships
　　Instructional Student Costs
　　Scholarships
　　Student Financial Aid
　　Student Loan Programs

Nonmajors　　　　　　　　　　MAR. 1980
　　Postings: 357　　　　　　　GC: 360
BT　Students
RT　Core Curriculum
　　Course Selection (Students)
　　Degree Requirements
　　Interdisciplinary Approach
　　Introductory Courses
　　Majors (Students)

Nonmarital Childbirth
USE　Births to Single Women

Nonmetropolitan Areas　　　SEP. 1994
　　Postings: 154　　　　　　　GC: 550
SN　Geographic areas outside of cities and
　　suburbs
BT　Geographic Regions
RT　Metropolitan Areas
　　Rural Areas
　　Small Towns

Nonorganic Failure to Thrive
USE　Failure to Thrive

Nonparametric Statistics　　NOV. 1970
　　Postings: 320　　　　　　　GC: 480
SN　Forms of descriptive or sampling statis-
　　tics applied to data when no assump-
　　tions can be made about the distribu-
　　tions involved
UF　Distribution Free Statistics
BT　Statistics
RT　Bayesian Statistics
　　Chi Square
　　Correlation
　　Mathematical Concepts
　　Statistical Analysis
　　Statistical Studies

Nonprint Media　　　　　　　MAR. 1980
　　Postings: 758　　　　　　　GC: 720
SN　Materials used in communication that
　　are not in the print medium nor textual or
　　book-like in nature (Note: Use "Audio-
　　visual Aids" for instructional nonprint
　　media—prior to Mar80, this concept was
　　indexed under "Audiovisual Aids")
UF　Nonbook Materials
NT　Audiodisks
　　Documentaries
　　Exhibits
　　Films
　　Filmstrips
　　Optical Disks
　　Realia
　　Tape Recordings
　　Transparencies
　　Videodisks
RT　Audiovisual Aids
　　Cartoons
　　Charts
　　Communications
　　Diagrams
　　Display Aids
　　Educational Media
　　Graphs
　　Hypermedia
　　Illustrations
　　Library Acquisition
　　Library Collections
　　Library Material Selection

　　Library Materials
　　Maps
　　Mass Media
　　Media Selection
　　Multimedia Materials
　　Photographs
　　Printed Materials
　　Publications
　　Resource Materials
　　Talking Books
　　Visual Aids

Nonprofessional Personnel　JUL. 1966
　　Postings: 765　　　　　　　GC: 630
NT　Clerical Workers
　　Sales Workers
　　Semiskilled Workers
　　Service Workers
　　Skilled Workers
　　Unskilled Workers
BT　Personnel
RT　Paraprofessional Personnel
　　Professional Personnel

Nonprofit Organizations　　JAN. 1978
　　Postings: 781　　　　　　　GC: 520
SN　Organizations not designed primarily to
　　pay dividends on invested capital (Note:
　　Prior to Dec77, the instruction "Non-
　　profit Organizations, USE Voluntary Agen-
　　cies" was carried in the Thesaurus)
BT　Organizations (Groups)
RT　Agencies
　　Alumni Associations
　　Church Programs
　　Churches
　　Colleges
　　Government (Administrative Body)
　　Hospitals
　　Institutions
　　Nongovernmental Organizations
　　Philanthropic Foundations
　　Religious Organizations
　　Schools
　　Settlement Houses
　　Universities

Nonpublic Agencies
USE　Private Agencies

Nonpublic Education
USE　Private Education

Nonpublic School Aid (1972 1980)
USE　Private School Aid

Nonpublic Schools
USE　Private Schools

Nonpublic Sector
USE　Private Sector

Nonreservation American Indians
　　　　　　　　　　　　　　　OCT. 1972
　　Postings: 179　　　　　　　GC: 560
SN　American Indians living off reservations
　　who remain on the tribal census roll or
　　who maintain their Indian identity
UF　Off Reservation American Indians
NT　Rural American Indians
　　Urban American Indians
BT　American Indians
RT　Alaska Natives
　　American Indian Reservations
　　Relocation
　　Reservation American Indians

Nonresident Farmers
USE　Part Time Farmers

Nonresident Students (1967 1980) (Foreign)
USE　Foreign Students

Nonresident Students (1967 1980) (Out of District)
USE　Residence Requirements

Nonresident Students (1967 1980) (Out of State)
USE　Out of State Students

Nonresidential Schools (1967 1980)
USE　Commuter Colleges

Nonreversal Shift
USE　Shift Studies

Nonroman Alphabets
USE　Non Roman Scripts

Nonschool Educational Programs
　　　　　　　　　　　　　　　MAR. 1980
　　Postings: 298　　　　　　　GC: 330
SN　Programs with formal educational in-
　　tent offered by institutions or organi-
　　zations other than schools, e.g., busi-
　　nesses, churches, community agencies,
　　etc. (Note: Do not confuse with "Home
　　Schooling" or "Nonformal Education")
BT　Programs
RT　Adult Education
　　Community Education
　　Corporate Education
　　Inplant Programs
　　Labor Education

Nonsexist Language
USE　Sexism in Language

Nonspecialists
USE　Lay People

Nonstandard Dialects　　　　JUL. 1966
　　Postings: 1,190　　　　　　GC: 450
SN　Varieties of a language that differ in
　　pronunciation, grammar, or vocabulary
　　from recognized standards
BT　Dialects
RT　Applied Linguistics
　　Bidialectalism
　　Black Dialects
　　Diglossia
　　Native Language Instruction
　　Oral Language
　　Regional Dialects
　　Social Dialects
　　Sociolinguistics
　　Standard Spoken Usage
　　Urban Language

Nonteaching Duties
USE　Noninstructional Responsibility

Nontenured Faculty　　　　　FEB. 1984
　　Postings: 191　　　　　　　GC: 360
SN　Academic staff who have not received
　　tenure (permanence of position) at their
　　school or institution—includes those
　　awaiting tenured appointments and those
　　who are ineligible for tenure
UF　Nontenured Teachers
　　Untenured Faculty
BT　Faculty
RT　Academic Rank (Professional)
　　Adjunct Faculty
　　College Faculty
　　Part Time Faculty
　　Probationary Period
　　Teachers
　　Tenure
　　Tenured Faculty

Nontenured Teachers
USE　Nontenured Faculty

= Two or more Descriptors are used to represent this term.
The term's main entry shows the appropriate coordination.

Nontraditional Careers
USE   Nontraditional Occupations

Nontraditional Education   MAR. 1980
      Postings: 6,507   GC: 330
SN   Educational programs that are offered as
      alternatives within or without the formal
      educational system and provide innova-
      tive and flexible instruction, curriculum,
      grading systems, or degree requirements
UF   Alternative Education
      Alternative Schools (1972 1980)
      Educational Alternatives (1974 1980)
      Instructional Alternatives
      Teaching Alternatives
      Training Alternatives
BT   Education
RT   Access to Education
      Alternative Teacher Certification
      Charter Schools
      Community Schools
      Continuation Students
      Continuing Education
      Corporate Education
      Correspondence Study
      Degree Requirements
      Distance Education
      Diversity (Institutional)
      Educational Development
      Educational Innovation
      Educational Methods
      Educational Needs
      Educational Opportunities
      Educational Principles
      Educational Theories
      Experimental Colleges
      Experimental Curriculum
      Experimental Schools
      Extended Teacher Education Programs
      Extension Education
      External Degree Programs
      Field Experience Programs
      Folk Schools
      Free Schools
      Freedom Schools
      High School Equivalency Programs
      Home Schooling
      Home Study
      Individualized Education Programs
      Instructional Innovation
      Magnet Schools
      Noncampus Colleges
      Nonformal Education
      Nontraditional Students
      Open Education
      Open Universities
      Prior Learning
      Reentry Students
      Relevance (Education)
      School Choice
      Special Degree Programs
      Traditional Schools
      Transitional Schools

Nontraditional Occupations   OCT. 1979
      Postings: 1,248   GC: 540
SN   Occupations in which, historically, cer-
      tain   groups   have   been
      underrepresented—usually applies to the
      sexes (e.g., men in nursing, women in
      auto mechanics)
UF   Nontraditional Careers
BT   Occupations
RT   Affirmative Action
      Career Choice
      Comparable Worth
      Employed Women
      Employment Opportunities
      Employment Patterns
      Equal Opportunities (Jobs)
      Occupational Aspiration
      Occupational Segregation
      Personnel Integration
      Sex Fairness
      Special Needs Students
      Work Attitudes

Nontraditional Students   JUN. 1977
      Postings: 2,288   GC: 360
SN   Adults beyond traditional school age (be-

yond the mid-twenties), ethnic minorities, women with dependent children,
underprepared students, and other special groups who have historically been
underrepresented in postsecondary education
BT   Students
RT   Adult Students
      College Students
      Educationally Disadvantaged
      High Risk Students
      Higher Education
      Nontraditional Education
      Open Enrollment
      Postsecondary Education
      Prior Learning
      Reentry Students
      Special Degree Programs
      Special Needs Students

Nonverbal Ability   JUL. 1966
      Postings: 231   GC: 120
SN   Ability in such nonlanguage areas as
      music, psychomotor skills, mathemat-
      ics, and spatial relations (Note: Use "Non-
      verbal Communication" for nonverbal
      communicative skills—prior to Mar80,
      the use of this term was not restricted by
      a Scope Note)
BT   Ability
RT   Nonverbal Communication
      Nonverbal Learning
      Nonverbal Tests
      Verbal Ability

Nonverbal Communication   MAR. 1969
      Postings: 2,719   GC: 120
SN   Communication through nonverbal sym-
      bols, i.e., facial expression, body move-
      ment, spatial relationships, and nonver-
      bal vocal cues
NT   Body Language
      Eye Contact
      Facial Expressions
BT   Communication (Thought Transfer)
RT   Augmentative and Alternative Commu-
         nication
      Classroom Communication
      Communication Problems
      Communication Skills
      Crying
      Nonverbal Ability
      Nonverbal Learning
      Paralinguistics
      Personal Space
      Speech Communication
      Verbal Communication
      Visual Literacy

Nonverbal Learning   JUL. 1966
      Postings: 242   GC: 110
SN   Learning that does not involve the use of
      language
NT   Perceptual Motor Learning
BT   Learning
RT   Associative Learning
      Learning Modalities
      Nonverbal Ability
      Nonverbal Communication
      Nonverbal Tests
      Psychomotor Skills
      Verbal Learning
      Visual Learning

Nonverbal Tests   JAN. 1969
      Postings: 271   GC: 830
SN   Tests which minimize or do not require
      the use of speech or language by exam-
      iner or subject—items may consist of
      symbols, figures, numbers, or pictures,
      but not words
NT   Visual Measures
BT   Tests
RT   Culture Fair Tests
      Nonverbal Ability
      Nonverbal Learning
      Performance Tests
      Preschool Tests
      Verbal Tests

Norm Referenced Measures
USE   Norm Referenced Tests

Norm Referenced Tests   SEP. 1970
      Postings: 1,003   GC: 830
SN   Tests used to describe an individual's
      performance in relation to the perform-
      ance of others on the same test (Note:
      Do not confuse with "Standardized Tests"
      or "Objective Tests," which are often
      norm-referenced)
UF   Norm Referenced Measures
BT   Tests
RT   Achievement Tests
      Comparative Testing
      Criterion Referenced Tests
      Grade Equivalent Scores
      National Competency Tests
      National Norms
      Standardized Tests
      Test Interpretation
      Test Norms

Normalization (Disabilities)   MAR. 1994
      Postings: 200   GC: 220
SN   Use of culturally normative means (pat-
      terns and conditions of everyday life) to
      facilitate adjustment and functioning by
      the disabled
UF   Normalization (Handicapped) (1974
         1994)
NT   Deinstitutionalization (of Disabled)
RT   Adaptive Behavior (of Disabled)
      Assistive Devices (for Disabled)
      Attitudes toward Disabilities
      Community Based Instruction (Disa-
         bilities)
      Daily Living Skills
      Disabilities
      Disability Discrimination
      Group Experience
      Group Homes
      Inclusive Schools
      Independent Living
      Labeling (of Persons)
      Mainstreaming
      Rehabilitation
      Special Education
      Supported Employment

Normalization (Handicapped) (1974 1994)
USE   Normalization (Disabilities)

Normative Behavior
USE   Behavior Standards

Norms   OCT. 1970
      Postings: 1,228   GC: 820
SN   Statistical description of the typical per-
      formance, behavior, form, function, etc.,
      of a given population (Note: Use only for
      numerical data and not for subjectively
      described standards)
NT   Local Norms
      National Norms
      State Norms
      Test Norms
BT   Statistical Data
RT   Cross Sectional Studies
      Measurement
      Participant Characteristics
      Sampling
      Scaling
      Standards
      Statistical Analysis
      Statistical Distributions
      Values

North American Culture   MAR. 1980
      Postings: 296   GC: 560
SN   Culture of the United States and Canada
NT   Hispanic American Culture
      Japanese American Culture
BT   Culture
RT   American Dream
      American Indian Culture
      American Studies
      Black Culture

Canadian Studies
Jazz
North American History
North American Literature
North Americans
Western Civilization

North American English   MAR. 1980
      Postings: 662   GC: 450
SN   English as used in the United States and
      Canada—differs from British or other
      varieties of English principally in certain
      features of vocabulary, pronunciation,
      grammar, and spelling
UF   American English (1968 1980)
BT   English
RT   Dialects
      English Only Movement
      Etymology
      Idioms
      Language Classification
      Language Patterns
      Language Usage
      Linguistics
      North American Literature
      Regional Dialects
      Speech Habits
      Standard Spoken Usage

North American History   MAR. 1980
      Postings: 341   GC: 430
SN   History of the geographic area that in-
      cludes the United States and Canada
NT   United States History
BT   History
RT   American Indian History
      Black History
      North American Culture
      North American Literature
      North Americans
      Western Civilization

North American Literature   MAR. 1980
      Postings: 42   GC: 430
SN   Literature of the United States and Cana-
      da
NT   Canadian Literature
      United States Literature
BT   Literature
RT   American Indian Literature
      North American Culture
      North American English
      North American History
      North Americans

North Americans   MAR. 1980
      Postings: 131   GC: 560
SN   Indigenous peoples, permanent residents,
      or citizens of the United States and Cana-
      da
UF   Arab Americans #
NT   Alaska Natives
      Anglo Americans
      Asian Americans
      Canada Natives
      French Canadians
      Greek Americans
      Hispanic Americans
      Italian Americans
      Pacific Americans
      Polish Americans
BT   Groups
RT   American Indians
      Eskimos
      Ethnic Groups
      North American Culture
      North American History
      North American Literature

Northern Attitudes (1968 1980)
USE   Regional Attitudes

Northern Schools (1966 1980)   MAR. 1980
      Postings: 87   GC: 340
SN   Invalid Descriptor—coordinate appropri-
      ate "school" or "education" Descriptors
      with the Identifier "United States (North)"

= Two or more Descriptors are used to represent this term.
The term's main entry shows the appropriate coordination.

Northward Movement
USE   Migration

Norwegian   *JUL. 1966*
      Postings: 68   GC: 440
BT   Indo European Languages

Notation
USE   Coding

Notetaking   *OCT. 1982*
      Postings: 480   GC: 310
SN   Making a brief written record to aid the
      memory
BT   Writing (Composition)
RT   Cues
      Mnemonics
      Outlining (Discourse)
      Prewriting
      Study Skills
      Writing Across the Curriculum
      Writing Skills

Notional Functional Syllabi   *OCT. 1980*
      Postings: 220   GC: 450
SN   Foreign language course curricula based
      upon the learner's communicative needs
      and organized according to the content
      of what is to be communicated rather
      than the grammatical form of the lan-
      guage or specific situational requirements
UF   Functional Notional Syllabi
BT   Modern Language Curriculum
RT   Communicative Competence
         (Languages)
      Languages
      Second Language Instruction
      Second Language Learning
      Second Language Programs

Nouns   *APR. 1980*
      Postings: 1,166   GC: 450
SN   Words that name a subject of discourse
UF   Nominals (1967 1980)
BT   Form Classes (Languages)
RT   Morphology (Languages)
      Phrase Structure
      Sentence Structure
      Syntax
      Vocabulary

Novella
USE   Novels

Novels   *JUL. 1966*
      Postings: 2,136   GC: 430
UF   Novella
      Sociological Novels (1969 1980)
BT   Fiction
      Literary Genres
RT   Books

Novelty (Stimulus Dimension)   *MAR. 1978*
      Postings: 207   GC: 110
SN   A stimulus dimension which reflects the
      quality or state of being new or unfamil-
      iar to an individual
RT   Adaptation Level Theory
      Arousal Patterns
      Attention
      Dimensional Preference
      Exploratory Behavior
      Familiarity
      Habituation
      Perception
      Redundancy
      Sensory Experience
      Stimuli

Nuclear Arms
USE   Nuclear Weapons

Nuclear Control
USE   Disarmament

Nuclear Energy   *OCT. 1980*
      Postings: 378   GC: 490
SN   Power derived from the fission (split-
      ting) of the nuclei of heavy elements
      such as uranium, or the fusion of light
      elements such as the hydrogen isotopes
      deuterium and tritium
UF   Atomic Energy
      Nuclear Energy Occupations #
BT   Radiation
RT   Atomic Theory
      Nuclear Physics
      Nuclear Power Plant Technicians
      Nuclear Power Plants
      Nuclear Technology
      Nuclear Warfare
      Nuclear Weapons
      Radiation Biology
      Radiation Effects
      Radioisotopes

Nuclear Energy Occupations
USE   Energy Occupations
AND   Nuclear Energy

Nuclear Family   *JUN. 1977*
      Postings: 354   GC: 520
SN   A family group consisting of father,
      mother, and children
UF   Traditional Family Unit
      Two Parent Family
BT   Family (Sociological Unit)
RT   Extended Family
      Family Life
      Family Relationship
      Family Size
      Family Structure
      Kinship
      One Parent Family
      Stepfamily

Nuclear Medicine
USE   Radiology

Nuclear Medicine Technologists
USE   Radiologic Technologists

Nuclear Physics   *JUL. 1966*
      Postings: 656   GC: 490
UF   Atomic Physics
BT   Physics
RT   Atomic Structure
      Atomic Theory
      Force
      Matter
      Nuclear Energy
      Nuclear Power Plant Technicians
      Nuclear Power Plants
      Nuclear Technology
      Nuclear Warfare
      Nuclear Weapons
      Quantum Mechanics
      Radiation
      Radiation Biology
      Radiation Effects
      Radioisotopes
      Scientific Research
      Thermodynamics

Nuclear Power Plant Technicians
                                                 AUG. 1982
      Postings: 88   GC: 640
BT   Paraprofessional Personnel
RT   Chemical Technicians
      Electronic Technicians
      Energy Occupations
      Engineering Technicians
      Mechanics (Process)
      Nuclear Energy
      Nuclear Physics
      Nuclear Power Plants
      Nuclear Technology
      Scientific Personnel

Nuclear Power Plants   *AUG. 1982*
      Postings: 177   GC: 920
SN   Facilities in which nuclear energy is con-
      verted into heat to provide electric power
BT   Facilities
RT   Nuclear Energy
      Nuclear Physics
      Nuclear Power Plant Technicians
      Nuclear Technology
      Utilities

Nuclear Technology   *OCT. 1982*
      Postings: 241   GC: 490
SN   Application and use of nuclear fission or
      fusion processes
BT   Power Technology
RT   Engineering
      Engineering Technology
      Nuclear Energy
      Nuclear Physics
      Nuclear Power Plant Technicians
      Nuclear Power Plants
      Nuclear Warfare
      Nuclear Weapons
      Physical Sciences
      Radiation
      Radiation Biology
      Radiation Effects
      Radiographers
      Radioisotopes
      Radiologic Technologists
      Radiology
      Technical Education

Nuclear Warfare   *NOV. 1969*
      Postings: 621   GC: 610
UF   Atomic Warfare
BT   War
RT   Atomic Theory
      Civil Defense
      Disarmament
      Military Science
      Modern History
      Nuclear Energy
      Nuclear Physics
      Nuclear Technology
      Nuclear Weapons
      Radiation Effects
      World Problems

Nuclear Weapons   *JAN. 1999*
      Postings: 150   GC: 490
UF   Atomic Bombs
      Nuclear Arms
BT   Weapons
RT   Atomic Theory
      Disarmament
      Nuclear Energy
      Nuclear Physics
      Nuclear Technology
      Nuclear Warfare

Nucleic Acids   *OCT. 1982*
      Postings: 38   GC: 490
SN   Large chainlike molecules containing ni-
      trogen, sugar, and phosphoric acid that
      are found in all living organisms and in
      viruses—they are important in the trans-
      ference of genetic characteristics and in
      synthesizing protein
NT   DNA
      RNA
RT   Biochemistry
      Biology
      Chemical Reactions
      Cytology
      Embryology
      Enzymes
      Genetic Engineering
      Genetics
      Heredity
      Molecular Biology
      Physiology
      Polymers
      Reproduction (Biology)

Numamiut
USE   Inupiaq

Number Concepts   *JUL. 1966*
      Postings: 3,235   GC: 480
NT   Modular Arithmetic
      Place Value
BT   Mathematical Concepts
RT   Arithmetic
      Limits (Mathematics)
      Mathematics Tests
      Numbers
      Numeracy
      Patterns in Mathematics
      Properties (Mathematics)

Number Operations
USE   Arithmetic

Number Skills Tests
USE   Mathematics Tests

Number Systems   *JUL. 1966*
      Postings: 441   GC: 480
UF   Arithmetic Systems
BT   Numbers
RT   Mathematics

Number Use
USE   Numbers

Numbers   *JUL. 1966*
      Postings: 646   GC: 480
UF   Number Use
NT   Logarithms
      Number Systems
      Rational Numbers
      Reciprocals (Mathematics)
BT   Symbols (Mathematics)
RT   Arithmetic
      Computation
      Mathematics
      Mathematics Skills
      Mathematics Tests
      Modular Arithmetic
      Number Concepts
      Numeracy
      Numeric Databases
      Place Value
      Spreadsheets
      Statistics

Numeracy   *FEB. 1993*
      Postings: 496   GC: 480
SN   Familiarity with the use of numbers, or
      basic competence in mathematics
UF   Mathematical Literacy
      Quantitative Literacy
RT   Arithmetic
      Basic Skills
      Computation
      Literacy
      Mathematics
      Mathematics Skills
      Number Concepts
      Numbers

Numeric Databases   *JAN. 1988*
      Postings: 33   GC: 710
SN   Machine-readable files primarily consist-
      ing of statistical or other quantitative
      data, often with user manipulability
BT   Databases
RT   Numbers
      Statistical Data

Numeric Filing
USE   Filing

Numerical Control   *JUL. 1966*
      Postings: 117   GC: 710
SN   Technique involving coded, numerical
      instructions for the automatic control
      and performance of a machine tool
UF   N C Systems
RT   Automation
      Coding
      Computer Assisted Manufacturing

= Two or more Descriptors are used to represent this term.
The term's main entry shows the appropriate coordination.

Computer Software
Cybernetics
Electronic Control
Machine Tools

Nun Teachers (1966 1980)
USE Nuns

Nuns   JUL. 1966
     Postings: 69   GC: 640
UF   Nun Teachers (1966 1980)
BT   Females
RT   Catholics
     Church Workers
     Clergy
     Religion
     Religious Cultural Groups
     Theological Education

Nurse Practitioners   NOV. 1982
     Postings: 141   GC: 210
SN   Registered nurses who have additional
     training and certification in a specialized
     field and who perform highly indepen-
     dent roles in clinical care and teaching of
     patients
UF   School Nurse Practitioners #
BT   Nurses
RT   Medicine
     Patient Education
     Physicians Assistants

Nurseries (Horticulture)   SEP. 1968
     Postings: 77   GC: 410
BT   Facilities
RT   Forestry
     Gardens
     Greenhouses
     Horticulture
     Nursery Workers (Horticulture)
     Ornamental Horticulture

Nursery Rhymes   DEC. 1995
     Postings: 54   GC: 430
SN   Short rhymed poems or songs for child-
     ren that often tell a story
UF   Mother Goose Rhymes
BT   Poetry
RT   Childrens Literature
     Folk Culture
     Rhyme
     Songs

Nursery Schools   JUL. 1966
     Postings: 665   GC: 340
SN   Schools for preschool children, usually
     2 1/2 to 5 1/2 years of age—nursery
     school programs are either part-day or
     part-week and may be operated as a
     service by public schools, or for profit by
     other agencies or individuals
BT   Schools
RT   Child Development Centers
     Day Care Centers
     Early Childhood Education
     Preschool Education

Nursery Workers (Horticulture)   JUL. 1966
     Postings: 49   GC: 410
UF   Greenhouse Workers
BT   Semiskilled Workers
RT   Nurseries (Horticulture)
     Ornamental Horticulture Occupations
     Plant Propagation

Nurses   JUL. 1966
     Postings: 1,940   GC: 210
SN   (Note: If applicable, use the more spe-
     cific terms "School Nurses" and/or
     "Nurse Practitioners")
UF   Certified Nurses
     Licensed Nurses
     Practical Nurses (1967 1981) #
     Professional Nurses
     Registered Nurses
     Teacher Nurses (1966 1980)

NT   Nurse Practitioners
     School Nurses
BT   Health Personnel
     Professional Personnel
RT   Hospital Personnel
     Medical Associations
     Medical Services
     Nurses Aides
     Nursing
     Nursing Education
     Nursing Research

Nurses Aides   JUL. 1966
     Postings: 305   GC: 210
UF   Hospital Attendants
     Nursing Aides
     Nursing Assistants
     Rest Home Aides
BT   Allied Health Personnel
RT   Attendants
     Home Health Aides
     Medical Assistants
     Nurses
     Nursing
     Psychiatric Aides

Nursing   JUL. 1966
     Postings: 1,533   GC: 210
NT   Practical Nursing
BT   Medicine
RT   Medical Services
     Nurses
     Nurses Aides
     Nursing Education
     Nursing Homes
     Nursing Research

Nursing Aides
USE Nurses Aides

Nursing Assistants
USE Nurses Aides

Nursing Education   MAR. 1980
     Postings: 2,936   GC: 210
SN   Formal instruction in nursing offered by
     a school, college, or university, often
     affiliated with a hospital—includes 2-
     year, 3-year, 4-year, and graduate pro-
     grams (Note: Prior to Mar80, this con-
     cept was frequently indexed under "Nurs-
     ing")
BT   Medical Education
RT   Nurses
     Nursing
     Nursing Research
     Pharmaceutical Education
     Teaching Hospitals

Nursing Homes   JUL. 1966
     Postings: 784   GC: 920
SN   Resident facilities providing skilled nurs-
     ing care as their primary and predomi-
     nant function
UF   Convalescent Homes
BT   Health Facilities
     Residential Institutions
RT   Hospices (Terminal Care)
     Hospitals
     Long Term Care
     Medical Services
     Nursing
     Personal Care Homes
     Practical Nursing
     Residential Care

Nursing Research   DEC. 1989
     Postings: 98   GC: 810
SN   Basic, applied, and developmental re-
     search conducted to advance knowledge
     in nursing (Note: Use as a minor Descrip-
     tor for examples of this kind of research—
     use as a major Descriptor only as the
     subject of a document)
BT   Research
RT   Medical Research
     Nurses

Nursing
Nursing Education
Scientific Research

Nutrient Deficiencies
USE Nutrition

Nutrition   JUL. 1966
     Postings: 3,668   GC: 210
UF   Malnutrition
     Nutrient Deficiencies
     Nutritional Deficiencies
NT   Breastfeeding
RT   Anemia
     Anorexia Nervosa
     Breakfast Programs
     Bulimia
     Child Health
     Dietetics
     Dietitians
     Eating Disorders
     Eating Habits
     Failure to Thrive
     Food
     Food Standards
     Health
     Health Behavior
     Hunger
     Lunch Programs
     Nutrition Instruction
     Obesity
     Physical Health
     Physiology
     Recipes (Food)
     Vending Machines

Nutrition Instruction   JUL. 1966
     Postings: 1,572   GC: 400
BT   Instruction
RT   Cooking Instruction
     Cooks
     Foods Instruction
     Health Education
     Home Economics
     Nutrition
     Recipes (Food)

Nutritional Deficiencies
USE Nutrition

Nyanja
USE Chinyanja

OBE
USE Outcome Based Education

Obedience   AUG. 1986
     Postings: 66   GC: 110
SN   Compliance with the demands or re-
     quests of persons in authority
BT   Compliance (Psychology)
     Social Behavior
RT   Behavior Problems
     Child Behavior
     Discipline
     Problem Children

Obesity   OCT. 1980
     Postings: 399   GC: 210
SN   Body condition characterized by a disfig-
     uring excess of weight or fat
UF   Overweight (Excessive Body Fat)
BT   Body Composition
     Body Weight
     Diseases
RT   Dietetics
     Eating Disorders
     Eating Habits
     Nutrition
     Physical Health

Object Concept
USE Object Permanence

Object Manipulation   JUL. 1966
     Postings: 195   GC: 310
BT   Psychomotor Skills
RT   Behavior Development
     Eye Hand Coordination
     Handedness
     Manipulative Materials
     Motor Development
     Perceptual Motor Coordination
     Skill Analysis
     Tactual Perception

Object Permanence   OCT. 1980
     Postings: 114   GC: 110
SN   The knowledge that objects continue to
     exist even when one is not perceiving
     them
UF   Object Concept
BT   Fundamental Concepts
RT   Cognitive Processes
     Concept Formation
     Developmental Stages

Objective Referenced Tests
USE Criterion Referenced Tests

Objective Tests   JUL. 1966
     Postings: 710   GC: 830
SN   Tests that have predetermined lists of
     correct answers so that subjective opin-
     ions or judgments are eliminated in scor-
     ing (Note: Do not confuse with "Stand-
     ardized Tests")
UF   Matching Tests
     Objectively Scored Tests
     True False Tests
NT   Multiple Choice Tests
BT   Tests
RT   Answer Keys
     Confidence Testing
     Distractors (Tests)
     Essay Tests
     Guessing (Tests)
     Projective Measures
     Scoring
     Scoring Formulas
     Standardized Tests
     Test Bias

Objectively Scored Tests
USE Objective Tests

Objectives   JUL. 1966
     Postings: 4,318   GC: 520
SN   Aims or ends toward which effort is
     directed (Note: Use a more specific term
     if possible)
UF   Goals
NT   Behavioral Objectives
     Course Objectives
     Educational Objectives
     Guidance Objectives
     Measurement Objectives
     Organizational Objectives
     Student Educational Objectives
     Training Objectives
RT   Aspiration
     Evaluation
     Failure
     Goal Orientation
     Guidelines
     Intention
     Management by Objectives
     Mastery Learning
     Needs
     Needs Assessment
     Performance
     Quotas
     Standards
     Success
     Task Analysis

Objectivity   APR. 2000
     Postings: 220   GC: 110
SN   The idea that facts or conditions may be
     perceived or reported without distortion
     by feelings or biases, and therefore may
     be verified (Note: See also such Identifi-

= Two or more Descriptors are used to represent this term.
The term's main entry shows the appropriate coordination.

ers as "Journalistic Objectivity," "Specific Objectivity")
RT Attitudes
   Bias
   Evaluation Methods
   Personality Traits
   Philosophy
   Realism
   Value Judgment

Oblique Rotation NOV. 1970
Postings: 102 GC: 820
SN Method for transforming the results of a factor analysis that permits the factors to be correlated
BT Factor Analysis
RT Correlation
   Factor Structure
   Matrices
   Orthogonal Rotation
   Transformations (Mathematics)

Obscenity OCT. 1983
Postings: 139 GC: 530
SN Character or quality of any act, expression, idea, etc., that offends one's sensibility
RT Antisocial Behavior
   Language Usage
   Moral Issues
   Pornography
   Verbal Abuse

Observation JUL. 1966
Postings: 3,057 GC: 820
SN Directed or intentional examination of persons, situations, or things to obtain information—includes the quantified values by which observed facts are represented
NT Naturalistic Observation
   Participant Observation
   School Visitation
RT Assessment Centers (Personnel)
   Classroom Observation Techniques
   Critical Incidents Method
   Data Collection
   Evaluation
   Experiments
   Inspection
   Interrater Reliability
   Lesson Observation Criteria
   Measurement
   Observational Learning
   Performance
   Research
   Research Methodology

Observational Learning NOV. 1972
Postings: 706 GC: 110
SN Learning resulting from the observation of a model or event
UF Imitative Learning
BT Learning
RT Discovery Learning
   Identification (Psychology)
   Imitation
   Incidental Learning
   Intentional Learning
   Learning Activities
   Learning Processes
   Learning Strategies
   Modeling (Psychology)
   Observation
   Role Models

Obsolescence JAN. 1969
Postings: 153 GC: 490
SN Condition of being no longer useful or in fashion, usually because of outmoded design or hard wear
NT Building Obsolescence
   Skill Obsolescence
RT Automation
   Maintenance
   Preservation
   Repair
   Technological Advancement
   Time

Obstetrics OCT. 1979
Postings: 135 GC: 210
SN Branch of medicine concerned with pregnancy and childbirth
UF Midwifery
BT Medicine
RT Abortions
   Birth
   Family Practice (Medicine)
   Females
   Gynecology
   Medical Services
   Perinatal Influences
   Pregnancy
   Prenatal Care
   Prenatal Influences
   Reproduction (Biology)
   Rh Factors

Obtained Scores
USE Raw Scores

Occidental Civilization
USE Western Civilization

Occupational Adjustment
USE Vocational Adjustment

Occupational Analysis
USE Job Analysis

Occupational Aspiration SEP. 1968
Postings: 2,596 GC: 120
SN Desire for, or expectation of, personal occupational accomplishment
UF Occupational Aspiration Level
   Vocational Aspiration
BT Aspiration
RT Career Choice
   Career Development
   Nontraditional Occupations
   Occupations
   Promotion (Occupational)
   Vocational Interests
   Vocational Maturity
   Work Attitudes
   Work Ethic

Occupational Aspiration Level
USE Occupational Aspiration

Occupational Awareness
USE Career Awareness

Occupational Choice (1966 1980)
USE Career Choice

Occupational Clusters JUL. 1966
Postings: 1,340 GC: 640
SN Occupations grouped together on the basis of similar job requirements or worker characteristics
UF Job Clusters
   Job Families
   Occupational Families
RT Cluster Grouping
   Job Analysis
   Occupations

Occupational Counseling
USE Career Counseling

Occupational Diseases JUL. 1966
Postings: 96 GC: 210
BT Diseases
RT Cancer
   Hearing Conservation
   Lead Poisoning
   Occupational Safety and Health
   Occupations
   Physical Health

Occupational Exploration
USE Career Exploration

Occupational Families
USE Occupational Clusters

Occupational Followup
USE Vocational Followup

Occupational Guidance (1966 1980)
USE Career Guidance

Occupational Health
USE Occupational Safety and Health

Occupational Home Economics JUL. 1966
Postings: 894 GC: 400
SN Formal preparation for occupations using home economics knowledge and skills—below the baccalaureate level (Note: For the baccalaureate level and above, use "Home Economics Education")
BT Vocational Education
RT Attendants
   Bakery Industry
   Child Care Occupations
   Cooks
   Day Care
   Dietitians
   Fashion Industry
   Food Service
   Home Economics
   Home Economics Education
   Home Economics Skills
   Home Economics Teachers
   Housekeepers
   Housing Management Aides
   Laundry Drycleaning Occupations
   Needle Trades
   Sewing Machine Operators
   Visiting Homemakers

Occupational Information JUL. 1966
Postings: 6,576 GC: 630
SN Descriptive information about the functions and characteristics of specific occupations—may include duties, working conditions, requirements, methods of entry and advancement, rewards, and/or supply and demand
UF Job Content
   Job Descriptions
   Job Specifications
RT Career Development
   Career Information Systems
   Demand Occupations
   Employment
   Employment Qualifications
   Job Analysis
   Job Development
   Occupations

Occupational Information Systems
USE Career Information Systems

Occupational Level
USE Employment Level

Occupational Literacy
USE Workplace Literacy

Occupational Mobility JUL. 1966
Postings: 1,692 GC: 630
UF Job Mobility
   Labor Mobility
   Occupational Succession
NT Career Ladders
   Faculty Mobility
   Teacher Transfer
BT Mobility
RT Black Achievement
   Brain Drain
   Career Change

Careers
Employment Experience
Employment Opportunities
Labor Turnover
Migrants
Migration
Overseas Employment
Persistence
Population Trends
Promotion (Occupational)
Relocation
Social Mobility
Tenure
Vocational Adjustment

Occupational Psychology
USE Industrial Psychology

Occupational Safety and Health AUG. 1982
Postings: 783 GC: 210
SN Area of activities concerned with promoting comfortable, safe employment conditions, including the prevention of workplace accidents and diseases
UF Job Safety
   Occupational Health
   Occupational Safety and Health Standards #
BT Health
   Safety
RT Employment
   Environmental Standards
   Hazardous Materials
   Hygiene
   Occupational Diseases
   Occupations
   Public Health
   Safety Education
   Work Environment

Occupational Safety and Health Standards
USE Labor Standards
AND Occupational Safety and Health

Occupational Satisfaction
USE Job Satisfaction

Occupational Segregation OCT. 1999
Postings: 109 GC: 540
SN Concentration of one gender or of a particular racial, ethnic, or other group in an occupation or job classification (Note: For occupational sex segregation, coordinate with the Identifier "Sex Segregation")
UF Job Segregation
BT Equal Opportunities (Jobs)
RT Employment Practices
   Labor Market
   Nontraditional Occupations
   Occupations
   Personnel Policy
   Racial Segregation
   Salary Wage Differentials
   Sex Discrimination
   Social Discrimination

Occupational Succession
USE Occupational Mobility

Occupational Surveys JUL. 1966
Postings: 2,409 GC: 810
SN Investigations to gather pertinent information about industries or occupations in an area, about occupational opportunities or trends on regional or national levels, or about the need for training in an occupational area (Note: As of Oct81, use as a minor Descriptor for examples of this kind of survey—use as a major Descriptor only as the subject of a document)
UF Employment Surveys
   Job Vacancy Surveys
   Labor Force Surveys
BT Surveys
RT Community Surveys

= Two or more Descriptors are used to represent this term.
The term's main entry shows the appropriate coordination.

Employment
Employment Opportunities
Employment Patterns
Job Search Methods
Labor Force
Labor Market
Labor Supply
Occupations

Occupational Tests   *JUL. 1966*
     Postings: 882   GC: 830
SN   Tests designed to predict job perform-
     ance by recording specific abilities and
     interests that correspond with those of
     persons successfully engaging in the
     particular field of work (Note: For occu-
     pational interest inventories, use "Inter-
     est Inventories")
UF   Admission Tests (Occupational)
     Employment Tests
     Personnel Tests
     Vocational Tests
NT   Work Sample Tests
BT   Tests
RT   Aptitude Tests
     Assessment Centers (Personnel)
     Career Counseling
     Employment Qualifications
     Interest Inventories
     Job Performance
     Job Skills
     Licensing Examinations (Professions)
     Maturity Tests
     Performance Tests
     Personnel Evaluation
     Predictive Measurement
     Vocational Aptitude
     Vocational Evaluation
     Vocational Interests

Occupational Therapists   *JUL. 1966*
     Postings: 181   GC: 230
BT   Therapists
RT   Occupational Therapy
     Occupational Therapy Assistants

Occupational Therapy   *JUL. 1966*
     Postings: 478   GC: 230
SN   Purposeful, often medically prescribed,
     work-related activities using manual, crea-
     tive, or industrial arts to treat physical
     and psychiatric disorders or disabilities,
     and frequently serving to promote voca-
     tional skills
BT   Therapy
RT   Medical Services
     Occupational Therapists
     Occupational Therapy Assistants
     Physical Therapy
     Psychotherapy
     Rehabilitation
     Therapeutic Recreation

Occupational Therapy Assistants   *JUL. 1969*
     Postings: 35   GC: 230
BT   Allied Health Personnel
RT   Occupational Therapists
     Occupational Therapy

Occupational Training
USE   Job Training

Occupations   *JUL. 1966*
     Postings: 1,587   GC: 640
SN   General categories of job or work spe-
     cializations, as characterized by duties,
     skill levels, status, pay, responsibility
     levels, or other distinguishing factors
     (Note: Use a more specific term if possi-
     ble)
UF   Vocations
NT   Agricultural Occupations
     Blue Collar Occupations
     Building Trades
     Clerical Occupations

Data Processing Occupations
Demand Occupations
Electrical Occupations
Energy Occupations
Finance Occupations
Forestry Occupations
Health Occupations
Insurance Occupations
Managerial Occupations
Needle Trades
Nontraditional Occupations
Office Occupations
Professional Occupations
Public Service Occupations
Real Estate Occupations
Sales Occupations
Semiskilled Occupations
Service Occupations
Skilled Occupations
Technical Occupations
Unskilled Occupations
White Collar Occupations
RT   Career Awareness
     Career Choice
     Career Counseling
     Career Development
     Career Education
     Career Exploration
     Career Guidance
     Career Information Systems
     Careers
     Education Work Relationship
     Employment
     Employment Opportunities
     Entrepreneurship
     Industrial Psychology
     Job Training
     Occupational Aspiration
     Occupational Clusters
     Occupational Diseases
     Occupational Information
     Occupational Safety and Health
     Occupational Segregation
     Occupational Surveys
     Quality of Working Life
     Retraining
     Specialization
     Vocational Education
     Work Environment
     Work Life Expectancy

Ocean Engineering   *FEB. 1970*
     Postings: 99   GC: 490
SN   Application of engineering technology to
     problems in oceans, seas, and large bod-
     ies of fresh water
BT   Engineering
RT   Ecology
     Hydrology
     Marine Biology
     Oceanography
     Water

Oceanography   *MAR. 1980*
     Postings: 1,082   GC: 490
SN   Science that deals with the oceans and
     other large bodies of water, including
     their exploration, preservation, use, and
     interactions with air, dry land, and all life
     forms
UF   Oceanology (1966 1980)
BT   Earth Science
RT   Climate
     Climate Change
     Estuaries
     Fisheries
     Geography
     Geology
     Hydrology
     Ichthyology
     Marine Biology
     Marine Technicians
     Maritime Education
     Ocean Engineering
     Physical Geography
     Plate Tectonics
     Seafarers
     Underwater Diving
     Water
     Wetlands

Oceanology (1966 1980)
USE   Oceanography

OCR
USE   Character Recognition
AND   Optical Scanners

Ocular Refractive Errors
USE   Ametropia

Odes   *SEP. 1969*
     Postings: 4   GC: 430
BT   Literary Genres
     Lyric Poetry
RT   Ballads
     Pastoral Literature
     Sonnets

Off Campus Education
USE   Extension Education

Off Campus Facilities   *JUL. 1966*
     Postings: 262   GC: 920
SN   Those facilities located some distance
     away from the educational institutions to
     which they are related
BT   Educational Facilities
RT   Extension Education
     Outreach Programs
     Satellite Facilities
     Shared Facilities

Off Campus Student Teaching
USE   Student Teaching

Off Farm Agricultural Occupations
          JUL. 1966
     Postings: 312   GC: 410
UF   Farm Related Occupations
     Nonfarm Agricultural Occupations
NT   Agricultural Chemical Occupations
     Agricultural Machinery Occupations
     Agricultural Supply Occupations
     Crop Processing Occupations
     Food Processing Occupations
     Ornamental Horticulture Occupations
BT   Agricultural Occupations
RT   Agribusiness
     Agriculture
     Animal Caretakers
     Farm Occupations
     Feed Industry
     Forestry Occupations

Off Reservation American Indians
USE   Nonreservation American Indians

Off Site Training
USE   Off the Job Training

Off the Job Training   *JUL. 1966*
     Postings: 201   GC: 630
SN   Conducted in a company school or ar-
     ranged with technical schools, universi-
     ties, or professional agencies
UF   Away from the Job Training
     Off Site Training
BT   Job Training
RT   Cooperative Programs
     Industrial Training
     Inplant Programs
     Inservice Education
     Institutes (Training Programs)
     Labor Education
     Management Development
     On the Job Training
     Released Time
     Skill Centers
     Staff Development
     Vocational Training Centers

Office Automation   *JAN. 1988*
     Postings: 249   GC: 650
SN   Application of computer and communi-
     cations technologies to office functions
     and tasks
BT   Automation
RT   Information Technology
     Local Area Networks
     Office Machines
     Office Management
     Office Occupations
     Word Processing

Office Communication
USE   Organizational Communication

Office Education
USE   Office Occupations Education

Office Machines   *JUL. 1966*
     Postings: 396   GC: 910
UF   Business Machines
BT   Equipment
RT   Business
     Calculators
     Industry
     Keyboarding (Data Entry)
     Local Area Networks
     Office Automation
     Office Management
     Office Practice
     Typewriting
     Word Processing

Office Management   *JUL. 1966*
     Postings: 382   GC: 650
BT   Administration
RT   Local Area Networks
     Office Automation
     Office Machines
     Office Occupations
     Office Occupations Education
     Office Practice
     Personnel
     Personnel Management
     Records (Forms)
     Records Management

Office Occupations   *JUL. 1966*
     Postings: 449   GC: 640
SN   Occupations associated with the man-
     agement and operation of offices
BT   Occupations
RT   Bookkeeping
     Business
     Business Education
     Clerical Occupations
     Data Processing Occupations
     Distributive Education
     Employment Qualifications
     Finance Occupations
     Job Training
     Keyboarding (Data Entry)
     Office Automation
     Office Management
     Office Occupations Education
     Office Practice
     Recordkeeping
     Shorthand
     Typewriting
     White Collar Occupations
     Word Processing

Office Occupations Education   *JUL. 1966*
     Postings: 1,677   GC: 400
SN   Formal preparation for occupations re-
     lated to the facilitating functions of the
     office—such functions include a variety
     of activities such as recording and re-
     trieval of data, supervision and coordina-
     tion of office activities, internal and ex-
     ternal communication, and the reporting
     of information (Note: Before Mar80, the
     use of this term was not restricted by a
     Scope Note)
UF   Office Education
BT   Business Education
RT   Accounting

= Two or more Descriptors are used to represent this term.
The term's main entry shows the appropriate coordination.

Bookkeeping
Business Correspondence
Business Education Facilities
Business Education Teachers
Business English
Clerical Occupations
Keyboarding (Data Entry)
Office Management
Office Occupations
Office Practice
Recordkeeping
Shorthand
Typewriting
Word Processing

Office Practice   *JUL. 1966*
Postings: 392   GC: 400
BT   Practicums
RT   Business Skills
     Clerical Occupations
     Office Machines
     Office Management
     Office Occupations
     Office Occupations Education
     Simulation

Office Supplies
USE   Supplies

Officer Personnel   *JUL. 1966*
Postings: 264   GC: 640
BT   Military Personnel
RT   Military Science
     Military Service
     Military Training
     Veterans

Offices (Facilities)   *OCT. 1968*
Postings: 142   GC: 920
UF   Faculty Offices
     Staff Offices
BT   Facilities
RT   Interior Design
     Interior Space
     School Space
     Space Classification

Official English Movement
USE   English Only Movement

Official Languages   *JUL. 1966*
Postings: 784   GC: 450
SN   Languages authorized or prescribed by
     law—usually for official or public pur-
     poses such as government activity, busi-
     ness, and education
UF   National Languages
BT   Language
RT   Bilingual Education
     Educational Policy
     English Only Movement
     Language of Instruction
     Language Planning
     Language Standardization
     Native Speakers
     Sociolinguistics

Oglala Sioux (Tribe)   *MAR. 1994*
Postings: 35   GC: 560
SN   American Indian people constituting a
     subdivision of the Lakotas and located
     mainly in southwestern South Dakota
     (includes dispersed kin)
BT   Lakota (Tribe)
RT   Lakota

Oil   *DEC. 1992*
Postings: 56   GC: 410
SN   Any viscous, combustible, water-immis-
     cible liquid composed principally of hy-
     drocarbons and obtained from the
     ground (Note: For "Vegetable Oils" and "Animal
     Oils," use those Identifiers)
UF   Crude Oil
     Fuel Oil #
     Heating Oils #

Mineral Oil
Motor Oil #
Petroleum (Oil and Gas) #
Petroleum (Oil)
BT   Natural Resources
RT   Fossil Fuels
     Gasoline
     Geology
     Lubricants
     Natural Gas
     Petroleum Industry
     Soil Science

Ojibwa   *JAN. 1971*
Postings: 32   GC: 440
SN   Algonquian language spoken by North
     American Indians known as Chippewas
     in the U.S. and Ojibwas in Canada, and
     by Ottawas, Algonquins, and others (Note:
     Use Identifiers for dialects "Ottawa,"
     "Algonquin," etc.)
UF   Chippewa (Language)
BT   American Indian Languages
RT   Chippewa (Tribe)

Ojibwa (Tribe)
USE   Chippewa (Tribe)

Ojibway (Tribe)
USE   Chippewa (Tribe)

Ojibwe (Tribe)
USE   Chippewa (Tribe)

Okinawan   *JUL. 1966*
Postings: 3   GC: 440
BT   Japanese

Old Age
USE   Older Adults

Old English   *MAY 1969*
Postings: 54   GC: 440
UF   Anglo Saxon
BT   English
RT   Diachronic Linguistics
     Indo European Languages
     Languages
     Linguistics
     Old English Literature
     Welsh

Old English Literature   *APR. 1970*
Postings: 29   GC: 430
BT   English Literature
RT   Literary History
     Old English

Old Old Adults   *AUG. 1989*
Postings: 72   GC: 120
SN   Approximately 75+ years of age
BT   Older Adults
RT   Frail Elderly
     Young Old Adults

Older Adolescents
USE   Late Adolescents

Older Adults   *JUL. 1966*
Postings: 9,809   GC: 120
SN   Approximately 65+ years of age
UF   Aged
     Elderly
     Old Age
     Senior Citizens (1967 1980)
NT   Frail Elderly
     Old Old Adults
     Young Old Adults
BT   Adults
RT   Accessibility (for Disabled)
     Adult Day Care
     Adult Foster Care
     Age Discrimination

Aging (Individuals)
Dependents
Educational Gerontology
Elder Abuse
Geriatrics
Gerontology
Grandparents
Intergenerational Programs
Mandatory Retirement
Middle Aged Adults
Older Workers
Personal Care Homes
Physical Mobility
Preretirement Education
Retirement

Older Workers   *JUL. 1997*
Postings: 172   GC: 630
SN   Personnel, aged 40+, employed full- or
     part-time (Note: For specificity, coor-
     dinate with appropriate age-level
     Descriptors—"40+" in definition is per
     Age Discrimination in Employment Act
     of 1967 (U.S.))
BT   Personnel
RT   Adults (30 to 45)
     Age Discrimination
     Age Groups
     Aging (Individuals)
     Aging in Academia
     Baby Boomers
     Early Retirement
     Employees
     Employment
     Employment Patterns
     Employment Practices
     Intergenerational Programs
     Labor Force
     Mandatory Retirement
     Middle Aged Adults
     Older Adults
     Personnel Policy
     Preretirement Education
     Retirement
     Teacher Retirement

Olympic Games   *AUG. 1989*
Postings: 133   GC: 470
SN   International program of sports compe-
     tition held in a different country every 4
     years (summer and winter games alter-
     nate in even-numbered years)—the mod-
     ern Olympic games, first held in 1896,
     are a revival of similar quadrennial con-
     tests held in ancient Greece (Note: Do
     not confuse with "Special Olympics")
UF   Summer Olympic Games
     Winter Olympic Games #
BT   Athletics
     Games
RT   Archery
     Basketball
     Bicycling
     Diving
     Fencing (Sport)
     Field Hockey
     Gymnastics
     Ice Hockey
     Ice Skating
     International Programs
     Skiing
     Soccer
     Special Olympics
     Swimming
     Table Tennis
     Team Handball
     Track and Field
     Volleyball
     Water Polo
     Weightlifting
     Womens Athletics
     Wrestling

Ombudsmen   *NOV. 1969*
Postings: 141   GC: 360
SN   Officials designated to hear and investi-
     gate complaints by single parties against
     institutions or organizations
BT   Personnel
RT   Counseling

Faculty
Grievance Procedures
Pupil Personnel Workers
Student College Relationship
Student Personnel Workers
Student Rights
Student School Relationship
Student Welfare

On Campus Students   *MAR. 1980*
Postings: 176   GC: 360
SN   College students living on campus (Note:
     Prior to Mar80, this concept was some-
     times indexed under "Resident Students,"
     which did not carry a Scope Note)
BT   College Students
RT   College Housing
     Commuting Students
     Dormitories
     Full Time Students
     Living Learning Centers
     Resident Assistants
     Residential Colleges

On Line Systems (1971 1980)
USE   Online Systems

On Site Tests
USE   Field Tests

On the Job Training   *JUL. 1966*
Postings: 2,137   GC: 630
NT   Apprenticeships
BT   Job Training
RT   Experiential Learning
     Field Experience Programs
     Industrial Training
     Inplant Programs
     Inservice Education
     Internship Programs
     Off the Job Training
     Staff Development
     Trade and Industrial Education
     Work Experience Programs

Oncology   *OCT. 1979*
Postings: 56   GC: 210
SN   Branch of medicine dealing with tumors
BT   Medicine
RT   Cancer
     Internal Medicine
     Medical Services
     Pathology
     Surgery

One Parent Family   *JUL. 1966*
Postings: 1,821   GC: 510
SN   (Note: Use a more specific term if possi-
     ble)
UF   Parent Absence
     Single Parent Family
NT   Fatherless Family
     Motherless Family
BT   Family (Sociological Unit)
RT   Births to Single Women
     Child Custody
     Child Support
     Divorce
     Extended Family
     Family Size
     Family Structure
     Fathers
     Heads of Households
     Marital Instability
     Mothers
     Nuclear Family
     Parents
     Runaways
     Widowed

One Room Schools
USE   One Teacher Schools

One Teacher Schools   *JUL. 1966*
Postings: 187   GC: 340
UF   One Room Schools

= Two or more Descriptors are used to represent this term.
The term's main entry shows the appropriate coordination.

BT   Small Schools
RT   Rural Schools
      Teachers

Online Catalogs   *AUG. 1986*
      Postings: 1,127   GC: 710
SN   Machine-readable catalogs that can be accessed through interactive communications terminals
UF   Online Public Access Catalogs
BT   Catalogs
      Databases
      Online Systems
RT   Bibliographic Databases
      Integrated Library Systems
      Library Catalogs
      Machine Readable Cataloging
      Retrospective Conversion (Library Catalogs)

Online Information Retrieval
USE   Online Searching

Online Journals
USE   Electronic Journals

Online Public Access Catalogs
USE   Online Catalogs

Online Reference Services
USE   Online Systems
AND   Reference Services

Online Searching   *APR. 1985*
      Postings: 2,207   GC: 710
SN   Use of an interactive communications terminal to access and retrieve information stored in a computer (Note: Prior to Apr85, this concept was indexed under "Online Systems" and "Information Retrieval")
UF   Interactive Searching (Online)
      Online Information Retrieval
BT   Information Retrieval
RT   Computer Literacy
      Downloading
      Gateway Systems
      Information Literacy
      Information Needs
      Online Systems
      Online Vendors
      Reference Services
      Relevance (Information Retrieval)
      Search Intermediaries
      Search Strategies
      Selective Dissemination of Information
      User Needs (Information)

Online Systems   *MAR. 1980*
      Postings: 5,646   GC: 710
SN   Computer systems in which peripheral devices, which may include remote terminals, are in direct and continuing communication with the central processor
UF   Computer Based Reference Services #
      Interactive Systems (Online)
      On Line Systems (1971 1980)
      Online Reference Services #
NT   Integrated Library Systems
      Interactive Video
      Online Catalogs
RT   Bibliographic Utilities
      Computer Mediated Communication
      Computers
      Data Processing
      Dial Access Information Systems
      Downloading
      Electronic Journals
      Electronic Libraries
      Electronic Mail
      Electronic Text
      Gateway Systems
      Information Sources
      Information Systems
      Input Output Devices
      Internet
      Man Machine Systems

      Menu Driven Software
      Microcomputers
      Minicomputers
      Modems
      Online Searching
      Online Vendors
      Teleconferencing
      Time Sharing
      Videotex
      Word Processing

Online Vendors   *APR. 1986*
      Postings: 447   GC: 710
SN   Organizations that maintain databases and related software on their computer systems and sell online retrieval time to clients at multiple remote locations (Note: See also such Identifiers as "DIALOG," "BRS Information Technologies," and "ORBIT")
UF   Commercial Search Services (Online)
      Database Hosts
      Database Vendors
      Information Utilities (Online)
BT   Organizations (Groups)
      Vendors
RT   Bibliographic Utilities
      Computers
      Database Producers
      Databases
      Information Dissemination
      Information Industry
      Information Services
      Online Searching
      Online Systems

Onomastics   *AUG. 1968*
      Postings: 53   GC: 450
UF   Onomatology
BT   Etymology
RT   Diachronic Linguistics
      Language
      Language Research
      Lexicology
      Linguistics

Onomatology
USE   Onomastics

Opaque Projectors   *JUL. 1966*
      Postings: 17   GC: 910
BT   Projection Equipment

Open Admission
USE   Open Enrollment

Open Area Schools
USE   Open Plan Schools

Open Book Tests   *JUL. 1974*
      Postings: 25   GC: 830
SN   Examinations during which individuals may consult textbooks, reference books, or notes, the purpose being to emphasize command of knowledge as distinguished from recall of factual information
BT   Tests
RT   Achievement Tests

Open Circuit Television (1966 1980)
USE   Broadcast Television

Open Education   *JAN. 1972*
      Postings: 1,971   GC: 350
SN   An approach to teaching and learning emphasizing the student's right to make decisions and that views the teacher as facilitator of learning rather than as transmitter of knowledge—it may include such characteristics as vertical grouping, cross-age teaching, independent study, individualized rates of progression, open plan schools, and unstructured time and curriculum

UF   Open Schools
BT   Education
RT   British Infant Schools
      Discovery Learning
      Experimental Schools
      Free Schools
      Humanistic Education
      Humanization
      Independent Study
      Learning Centers (Classroom)
      Nongraded Instructional Grouping
      Nontraditional Education
      Open Plan Schools
      Personal Autonomy
      Progressive Education
      Self Contained Classrooms
      Self Directed Groups
      Student Centered Curriculum
      Transitional Schools

Open Enrollment   *JUL. 1966*
      Postings: 830   GC: 330
SN   Admissions policy (usually at college level) of accepting candidates regardless of their grade point average and sometimes (usually at elementary or secondary level) regardless of their place of residence
UF   Open Admission
BT   Admission (School)
RT   Academic Standards
      Access to Education
      Admission Criteria
      Competitive Selection
      Desegregation Methods
      Educational Opportunities
      Educationally Disadvantaged
      Equal Education
      Free Choice Transfer Programs
      High Risk Students
      Nontraditional Students
      Open Universities
      Selective Admission

Open Plan Schools   *FEB. 1970*
      Postings: 677   GC: 920
SN   Schools without interior walls
UF   Open Area Schools
BT   Schools
RT   Class Organization
      Classroom Design
      Educational Facilities Design
      Flexible Facilities
      Interior Space
      Multipurpose Classrooms
      Open Education
      School Buildings
      School Space
      Team Teaching

Open Schools
USE   Open Education

Open Universities   *MAR. 1980*
      Postings: 744   GC: 340
SN   Higher education institutions with liberal admission policies that feature external degree programs and often use nontraditional delivery systems (telecourses, etc.)—e.g., Open University of the United Kingdom, University of Mid-America (Note: Before Mar80, the Thesaurus carried the instruction "Open University, USE External Degree Programs")
UF   Extended Universities
      Universities without Walls
BT   Universities
RT   Access to Education
      Distance Education
      Experimental Colleges
      Extension Education
      External Degree Programs
      Free Education
      Nontraditional Education
      Open Enrollment
      Outreach Programs

Opera   *JUL. 1966*
      Postings: 134   GC: 420
BT   Theater Arts
RT   Acting
      Music
      Musical Composition
      Vocal Music

Operant Conditioning   *JUL. 1966*
      Postings: 1,115   GC: 110
SN   Form of conditioning in which reinforcement (e.g., food) is contingent upon the occurrence of the response (e.g., a hungry animal pressing a lever)
UF   Instrumental Conditioning
NT   Verbal Operant Conditioning
BT   Conditioning
RT   Behavior Modification
      Classical Conditioning
      Contingency Management
      Reinforcement
      Timeout
      Token Economy

Operating Engineering   *JUL. 1966*
      Postings: 35   GC: 640
SN   Onsite operation of power construction equipment to excavate and grade earth, erect structural and reinforcing steel, pour concrete, etc.
BT   Engineering
RT   Building Trades
      Equipment Utilization
      Technical Occupations

Operating Expenses   *JUL. 1966*
      Postings: 1,049   GC: 620
UF   Minimum Operating Expenses
BT   Expenditures
RT   Budgets
      Building Operation
      Costs
      Instructional Student Costs
      Library Expenditures
      Life Cycle Costing
      Resource Allocation
      Salaries
      Wages

Operating Room Technicians
USE   Surgical Technicians

Operations (Surgery)
USE   Surgery

Operations Analysis
USE   Operations Research

Operations Research   *JUL. 1966*
      Postings: 637   GC: 810
SN   The application of scientific and especially mathematical methods to the analysis of operating procedures in an organization or system (Note: As of Oct81, use as a minor Descriptor for examples of this kind of research—use as a major Descriptor only as the subject of a document)
UF   Operations Analysis
NT   Game Theory
BT   Research
RT   Action Research
      Cost Effectiveness
      Critical Path Method
      Delphi Technique
      Information Theory
      Judgment Analysis Technique
      Linear Programming
      Long Range Planning
      Management Systems
      Mathematical Models
      Models
      Monte Carlo Methods
      Planning
      Quality Control
      Search Strategies

= Two or more Descriptors are used to represent this term. The term's main entry shows the appropriate coordination.

Strategic Planning
Troubleshooting

Ophthalmology   *JUL. 1966*
      Postings: 93   GC: 210
BT   Medicine
RT   Eyes
      Medical Services
      Optometry
      Vision
      Vision Tests
      Visual Acuity
      Visual Impairments

Opinion Papers   *MAR. 1980*
      Postings: 335   GC: 730
SN   Statements of personal viewpoints
BT   Reports
RT   Essays
      Opinions
      Personal Narratives
      Position Papers

Opinion Scales
USE   Attitude Measures

Opinions   *JUL. 1966*
      Postings: 3,283   GC: 120
SN   Judgments or conclusions based on evi-
      dence that is insufficient to produce cer-
      tainty
NT   Press Opinion
      Public Opinion
BT   Attitudes
RT   Attitude Measures
      Beliefs
      Credibility
      Delphi Technique
      Dissent
      Dogmatism
      Editorials
      Expectation
      Interest Inventories
      Opinion Papers
      Questionnaires
      Reputation
      Surveys

Opportunities   *JUL. 1966*
      Postings: 131   GC: 540
SN   Circumstances or conditions that make
      possible any actions leading to
      betterment—includes the absence of bar-
      riers that prevent such possibilities (Note:
      Use a more specific term if possible)
NT   Cultural Opportunities
      Economic Opportunities
      Educational Opportunities
      Employment Opportunities
      Housing Opportunities
      Research Opportunities
      Youth Opportunities
RT   Background
      Education Work Relationship
      Influences

Opportunity Classes (1966 1980)
USE   Special Classes

Optical Character Recognition
USE   Character Recognition
AND   Optical Scanners

Optical Data Disks   *AUG. 1986*
      Postings: 1,657   GC: 720
SN   Optical disks formatted for storage and
      retrieval of text, i.e., computer-readable
      alphanumeric data (with or without ac-
      companying graphics and/or sound)
UF   CD ROM
      Digital Optical Data Disks
BT   Optical Disks
RT   Computers
      Data Processing
      Electronic Text
      Information Systems

Interactive Video
Lasers

Optical Disks   *AUG. 1986*
      Postings: 306   GC: 720
SN   Information storage devices, typically
      made of plastic, on which high-density
      audio and/or video images are recorded
      and read by laser beams
UF   CD Recordings
      Compact Disks
      Laser Disks
      Optical Videodisks #
NT   Optical Data Disks
BT   Electronic Equipment
      Nonprint Media
RT   Audiodisks
      Audiovisual Aids
      Computer Storage Devices
      Computers
      Disk Drives
      Information Storage
      Input Output Devices
      Interactive Video
      Lasers
      Optics
      Programming (Broadcast)
      Videodisks

Optical Masers
USE   Lasers

Optical Scanners   *SEP. 1968*
      Postings: 156   GC: 910
UF   Document Readers
      OCR #
      Optical Character Recognition #
      Page Readers
      Visual Scanners
BT   Input Output Devices
RT   Character Recognition
      Optics
      Test Scoring Machines

Optical Spectrum
USE   Light

Optical Videodisks
USE   Optical Disks
AND   Videodisks

Optics   *DEC. 1969*
      Postings: 818   GC: 490
UF   Electrooptics (1968 1980)
      Geometrical Optics
      Physical Optics
BT   Physics
RT   Crystallography
      Diffusion (Physics)
      Electronics
      Energy
      Lasers
      Light
      Lighting
      Optical Disks
      Optical Scanners
      Radiation
      Relativity
      Spectroscopy

Optional Branching (1966 1980)
USE   Branching

Optional Courses
USE   Elective Courses

Optometrists   *JUL. 1966*
      Postings: 88   GC: 210
BT   Allied Health Personnel
      Professional Personnel
RT   Eyes
      Optometry
      Vision
      Vision Tests

Optometry   *OCT. 1979*
      Postings: 321   GC: 210
SN   The practice or profession of testing the
      eyes for defects in vision in order to
      prescribe corrective lenses
BT   Technology
RT   Allied Health Occupations
      Eyes
      Health Services
      Ophthalmology
      Optometrists
      Vision
      Vision Tests
      Visual Acuity
      Visual Impairments

Oral Communication Method   *JUL. 1977*
      Postings: 208   GC: 220
SN   The use of vocal communication (lip-
      reading and talking), as opposed to man-
      ual communication (sign language or
      finger spelling), in teaching the hearing
      impaired
NT   Lipreading
BT   Teaching Methods
RT   Communication Skills
      Cued Speech
      Deafness
      Hearing Impairments
      Hearing Therapy
      Manual Communication
      Partial Hearing
      Speech Communication
      Total Communication
      Verbal Communication

Oral Communication (1966 1977)
USE   Speech Communication

Oral English   *JUL. 1966*
      Postings: 288   GC: 450
BT   English
RT   Speech Communication
      Standard Spoken Usage

Oral Expression (1966 1977)
USE   Speech Communication

Oral Facility
USE   Speech Skills

Oral History   *FEB. 1976*
      Postings: 934   GC: 430
SN   History via recordings and transcripts of
      speech
BT   History
RT   American Indian History
      Audiodisks
      Audiotape Recordings
      Discographies
      Family History
      Historiography
      Interviews
      Local History
      Modern History
      Oral Tradition
      Primary Sources
      Public History
      Social History
      Speech Communication

Oral Hygienists
USE   Dental Hygienists

Oral Interpretation   *MAR. 1980*
      Postings: 422   GC: 420
SN   The oral interpretation and presentation
      of a work of literature to an audience
      (Note: Prior to Mar80, the instruction
      "Oral Interpretation, USE Interpretive
      Reading" was carried in the Thesaurus)
BT   Speech Communication
RT   Choral Speaking
      Drama
      Listening Comprehension
      Literature Appreciation

Oral Reading
Readers Theater
Reading Aloud to Others
Reading Comprehension
Speech Instruction

Oral Language   *APR. 1980*
      Postings: 2,867   GC: 450
SN   Spoken aspect of language that can be
      heard, interpreted, and understood (Note:
      Do not confuse with the behavioral con-
      cept of "Speech Communication")
BT   Language
RT   Caregiver Speech
      Child Language
      Expressive Language
      Language Acquisition
      Language Rhythm
      Language Usage
      Nonstandard Dialects
      Rhyme
      Second Language Learning
      Speech
      Speech Communication
      Standard Spoken Usage
      Verbal Communication
      Written Language

Oral Reading   *JUL. 1966*
      Postings: 1,485   GC: 460
SN   The act of reading aloud, often used to
      develop or test reading skills (Note: Use
      "Reading Aloud to Others" when the
      purpose of oral reading is to inform or
      entertain a listener or group of listeners)
BT   Reading
RT   Decoding (Reading)
      Eye Voice Span
      Miscue Analysis
      Oral Interpretation
      Reading Aloud to Others
      Reading Instruction
      Silent Reading

Oral Rehydration Therapy   *AUG. 1988*
      Postings: 12   GC: 210
SN   Use of a special drink of sugar and salt in
      water to reverse or prevent dehydration
      caused by acute diarrhea
BT   Therapy
RT   Health Education
      Health Services
      Medical Services
      Preventive Medicine

Oral Skills
USE   Speech Skills

Oral Tradition   *JUL. 1993*
      Postings: 307   GC: 560
SN   Aspects of a society's culture (e.g., his-
      tory, literature, cultural character) that
      are passed by mouth from generation to
      generation in ritual drama, songs, po-
      etry, narratives, games, oratory, etc.,
      rather than by written accounts
BT   Culture
RT   Ballads
      Cultural Education
      Cultural Traits
      Folk Culture
      Legends
      Mythology
      Oral History
      Socialization
      Speech Communication
      Story Telling

Orbiting Satellites
USE   Satellites (Aerospace)

Orchestras   *AUG. 1968*
      Postings: 171   GC: 420
UF   Repertory Orchestras
      Symphony Orchestras
RT   Applied Music
      Bands (Music)

= Two or more Descriptors are used to represent this term.
The term's main entry shows the appropriate coordination.

Concerts
Instrumentation and Orchestration
Music
Music Activities
Music Education
Music Techniques
Musical Instruments
Musicians
Theater Arts

Orchestration (Music)
USE Instrumentation and Orchestration

Orff Method AUG. 1989
Postings: 39 GC: 420
SN System of music education for children
that combines music with motion and
incorporates the use of simple, mostly
percussion, instruments—developed by
German composer, Carl Orff
UF Orff Schulwerk Approach
BT Music Education
Teaching Methods
RT Kodaly Method
Movement Education
Music Techniques
Musical Instruments
Singing

Orff Schulwerk Approach
USE Orff Method

Organ Donors
USE Tissue Donors

Organic Chemistry OCT. 1968
Postings: 1,149 GC: 490
SN Study of chemical reactions and proper-
ties of the organic compounds (hydro-
carbons)
BT Chemistry
RT Acids
Biochemistry
Chemical Bonding
Chemical Reactions
Coordination Compounds
Polymers
Radiation Biology

Organic Curriculum
USE Student Centered Curriculum

Organization JUL. 1966
Postings: 2,957 GC: 520
SN The structure or framework of formal
and functional relations that unites the
parts of a system into a coherent whole—
also, the process by which such a struc-
ture is identified and established (Note:
Use a more specific term if possible)
UF Structural Arrangement
NT Administrative Organization
Bureaucracy
Class Organization
Classification
Course Organization
Furniture Arrangement
Group Structure
Horizontal Organization
Industrial Structure
Informal Organization
Power Structure
Pyramid Organization
School District Reorganization
School Organization
Social Structure
Vertical Organization
RT Administration
Coordination
Design
Entropy
Mergers
Organizational Theories
Organizations (Groups)
Planning

Organization Size (Groups) JUL. 1966
Postings: 291 GC: 320
SN Size of an organization as measured by
the dimensions of its physical plant or by
the number of employees or members
UF Company Size (Industry)
NT School District Size
RT Business
Industrial Structure
Industry
Institutional Characteristics
Labor Force
Mergers
Organizations (Groups)
Small Businesses

Organizational Change JUL. 1966
Postings: 4,719 GC: 320
SN Any alteration in the form, nature, con-
tent, future course, etc., of an organiza-
tion (Note: Use a more precise term if
possible)
NT Mergers
BT Change
RT Administrative Change
Centralization
Change Strategies
Decentralization
Organizational Development
Organizations (Groups)
School Restructuring

Organizational Climate JUL. 1966
Postings: 4,244 GC: 320
SN Properties, procedures, conditions, etc.,
of an organization that influence or inter-
act with its members
BT Environment
RT Burnout
Collegiality
Diversity (Institutional)
Educational Environment
Employee Absenteeism
Industrial Psychology
Informal Organization
Institutional Environment
Job Satisfaction
Morale
Organizational Development
Organizations (Groups)
Power Structure
Quality of Working Life
Work Environment

Organizational Communication DEC. 1974
Postings: 3,443 GC: 320
SN Exchange of thoughts, messages, etc.,
within and between organizations (groups
of people)—includes exchanges between
specific organizations and the general
public
UF Office Communication
NT Business Communication
Interschool Communication
BT Communication (Thought Transfer)
RT Communication Audits
Crisis Management
Group Dynamics
Information Systems
Institutional Advancement
Management Systems
Organizations (Groups)
Public Relations

Organizational Development APR. 1973
Postings: 3,357 GC: 320
SN The application of behavioral technology
to organizations by attempting to inte-
grate individual needs for growth and
development with organizational goals
and objectives
BT Development
RT Administrative Change
Behavioral Science Research
Employer Employee Relationship
Faculty Development
Industrial Psychology
Industrial Structure
Job Development

Job Enrichment
Job Satisfaction
Management by Objectives
Management Teams
Organizational Change
Organizational Climate
Organizational Objectives
Organizations (Groups)
Participative Decision Making
Performance Technology
Power Structure
Program Administration
Quality Circles
Quality of Working Life
School Restructuring
Social Exchange Theory
Staff Development
Systems Development
Teamwork
Total Quality Management
Work Environment

Organizational Effectiveness JUL. 1974
Postings: 2,459 GC: 320
SN Degree to which organizations (groups
of people) are successful in satisfying
their objectives or functions
NT School Effectiveness
RT Administration
Administrator Effectiveness
Cost Effectiveness
Efficiency
Organizational Theories
Organizations (Groups)
Productivity
Program Effectiveness
Self Evaluation (Groups)
Success
Systems Analysis

Organizational Goals
USE Organizational Objectives

Organizational Objectives MAR. 1980
Postings: 2,095 GC: 320
SN Short- or long-term goals of organiza-
tions or institutions for management,
operations, functional outcomes, etc.
(Note: Prior to Mar80, the term "Educa-
tional Objectives" was frequently used
for the objectives of educational institu-
tions)
UF Institutional Goals
Institutional Objectives
Organizational Goals
NT Institutional Mission
BT Objectives
RT Accountability
Institutions
Management by Objectives
Organizational Development
Organizations (Groups)
Planning

Organizational Plans
USE Planning

Organizational Psychology (Work Environment)
USE Industrial Psychology

Organizational Self Study
USE Self Evaluation (Groups)

Organizational Theories JUL. 1974
Postings: 1,910 GC: 810
SN Ideas or hypotheses relating to the form
and structure of organizations (groups
of people), describing how such organi-
zations do operate or should operate
BT Social Theories
RT Diversity (Institutional)
Organization
Organizational Effectiveness
Organizations (Groups)
Social Exchange Theory

Organizations (Groups) JUL. 1966
Postings: 3,503 GC: 520
UF Associations (Groups)
Formal Organizations
NT Agencies
Alumni Associations
Bibliographic Utilities
Black Organizations
Blue Ribbon Commissions
College Governing Councils
Community Organizations
Consortia
Cooperatives
Corporations
Database Producers
Faculty Organizations
Fraternities
Governing Boards
Government (Administrative Body)
Health Maintenance Organizations
Honor Societies
International Organizations
Military Organizations
National Organizations
Nongovernmental Organizations
Nonprofit Organizations
Online Vendors
Parent Associations
Political Parties
Professional Associations
Religious Organizations
Research Coordinating Units
School Districts
Segregationist Organizations
Social Organizations
Sororities
Student Organizations
Unions
BT Groups
RT Committees
Conferences
Industry
Informal Organization
Institutions
Mergers
Organization
Organization Size (Groups)
Organizational Change
Organizational Climate
Organizational Communication
Organizational Development
Organizational Effectiveness
Organizational Objectives
Organizational Theories
Resources
Social Exchange Theory
Vendors

Oriental Americans
USE Asian Americans

Oriental Civilization
USE Non Western Civilization

Oriental Music JUL. 1966
Postings: 22 GC: 420
SN Music of China, Japan, Indochina,
Polynesia, India, Arabia, and North Afri-
ca
UF Asian Music
BT Music
RT Musical Composition

Orientation JUL. 1966
Postings: 911 GC: 120
SN Awareness or the process of becoming
aware of one's position or direction in
relation to persons, situations, expecta-
tions, or the physical environment (Note:
Use a more specific term if possible)
NT Goal Orientation
School Orientation
Sexual Orientation
Staff Orientation
Teacher Orientation
RT Adjustment (to Environment)
Context Effect
Familiarity
Orientation Materials

= Two or more Descriptors are used to represent this term.
The term's main entry shows the appropriate coordination.

Orientation Materials   *JUL. 1966*
Postings: 378   GC: 730
RT   Guides
     Instructional Materials
     Library Instruction
     Orientation
     Resource Materials

Orienteering   *FEB. 1978*
Postings: 71   GC: 470
SN   The act or sport of cross-country navigation using a map and compass as guides—emphasis is on determining, then taking, the shortest and quickest way to a specified destination
BT   Athletics
     Navigation
RT   Trails

Original Scores
USE   Raw Scores

Original Sources
USE   Primary Sources

Originality (1966 1980)
USE   Creativity

Ornamental Horticulture   *JUL. 1966*
Postings: 227   GC: 410
NT   Floriculture
     Landscaping
     Turf Management
BT   Horticulture
RT   Gardening
     Greenhouses
     Nurseries (Horticulture)
     Ornamental Horticulture Occupations
     Plant Growth
     Plant Identification
     Plant Propagation
     Trees

Ornamental Horticulture Occupation (1967 1976)
USE   Ornamental Horticulture Occupations

Ornamental Horticulture Occupations   *MAY 1976*
Postings: 95   GC: 410
UF   Ornamental Horticulture Occupation (1967 1976)
BT   Off Farm Agricultural Occupations
RT   Grounds Keepers
     Nursery Workers (Horticulture)
     Ornamental Horticulture

Ornithology   *MAR. 1982*
Postings: 110   GC: 490
UF   Bird Studies
BT   Zoology
RT   Agriculture
     Animal Husbandry
     Birds
     Horticulture

Orthodontic Technicians
USE   Dental Technicians

Orthodontics
USE   Dentistry

Orthodontists
USE   Dentists

Orthogonal Projection (1967 1980)
USE   Orthographic Projection

Orthogonal Rotation   *NOV. 1970*
Postings: 160   GC: 820
SN   Method for processing the results of a factor analysis so that the factors will not be correlated
BT   Factor Analysis
RT   Correlation
     Factor Structure
     Matrices
     Oblique Rotation
     Transformations (Mathematics)

Orthographic Projection   *MAR. 1980*
Postings: 67   GC: 480
SN   Projection in which the projecting lines are perpendicular to the plane of projection
UF   Orthogonal Projection (1967 1980)
BT   Geometric Concepts
RT   Blueprints
     Drafting
     Engineering Graphics
     Graphic Arts
     Technical Illustration

Orthographic Symbols   *JUL. 1966*
Postings: 548   GC: 450
NT   Diacritical Marking
     Letters (Alphabet)
     Phonetic Transcription
BT   Written Language
RT   Abbreviations
     Graphemes
     Initial Teaching Alphabet
     Romanization
     Spelling

Orthopedically Handicapped (1968 1980)
USE   Physical Disabilities

Ossetic   *JUL. 1966*
Postings: 3   GC: 440
BT   Indo European Languages

Osteopathy   *OCT. 1979*
Postings: 60   GC: 210
SN   Medical study or practice of restoring or preserving health chiefly by manipulation of the skeleton and muscles
BT   Medicine
RT   Medical Services
     Motor Reactions
     Musculoskeletal System
     Physical Therapy

Ostyak   *JUL. 1966*
Postings: 3   GC: 440
BT   Finno Ugric Languages

Otitis Media   *NOV. 1996*
Postings: 81   GC: 210
SN   Infection, and/or collection of fluid, in the middle ear, occurring most often in infants and young children—may cause hearing loss in recurrent or long-standing cases
UF   Ear Infections (Middle Ear)
     Middle Ear Disease
BT   Diseases
RT   Ears
     Hearing Impairments

Otological Tests
USE   Auditory Tests

Out of School Youth   *JUL. 1966*
Postings: 434   GC: 510
SN   Children of compulsory school age who have been excused from attending school, or adolescents over 16 years of age who are out of school legally (Note: Coordinate with an appropriate age or educational level Descriptor)
BT   Youth
RT   Attendance
     Dropouts
     Expulsion
     Suspension
     Withdrawal (Education)

Out of State Students   *MAR. 1980*
Postings: 380   GC: 360
SN   College students who are legal residents of a state or province other than the one in which they attend school
UF   Nonresident Students (1967 1980) (Out of State)
BT   College Students
RT   Place of Residence
     Residence Requirements
     Tuition

Out of Wedlock Births
USE   Births to Single Women

Outcome Based Education   *AUG. 1995*
Postings: 385   GC: 330
SN   The effort, often by a state or local education agency, to organize all the features of schooling (including aims, curriculum, instruction, and assessment) so as to produce specifically delineated results (often including noncognitive as well as cognitive results) and generally with the expectation that all students will demonstrate such results
UF   OBE
     Outcomes Based Education
     Results Based Education
BT   Education
RT   Academic Standards
     Accountability
     Behavioral Objectives
     Competency Based Education
     Educational Objectives
     Equal Education
     Mastery Learning
     Outcomes of Education

Outcomes Based Education
USE   Outcome Based Education

Outcomes Measurement (College)
USE   College Outcomes Assessment

Outcomes of Education   *MAR. 1980*
Postings: 9,948   GC: 330
SN   Results or consequences of education (Note: Use only for materials indicating actual results attained—for discussions of desired results, use "Educational Objectives," "Student Educational Objectives," etc.)
UF   Educational Outcomes
     Instructional Outcomes
     Learner Outcomes
     Results of Education
     Student Outcomes
NT   College Outcomes Assessment
     Educational Benefits
RT   Accountability
     Day Care Effects
     Education
     Educational Assessment
     Educational Objectives
     Effective Schools Research
     Excellence in Education
     Failure
     Followup Studies
     Instructional Effectiveness
     Longitudinal Studies
     Outcome Based Education
     Program Effectiveness
     Program Evaluation
     Role of Education
     School Effectiveness
     Student Development
     Student Educational Objectives
     Success

Outcomes of Treatment   *AUG. 1986*
Postings: 1,771   GC: 210
SN   Results or consequences of personal health treatment (medical, psychological, etc.)
RT   Counseling
     Counseling Effectiveness
     Helping Relationship
     Medical Care Evaluation
     Medical Services
     Termination of Treatment
     Therapy

Outdoor Activities   *MAR. 1980*
Postings: 1,060   GC: 470
SN   Activities taking place in the open air (Note: If applicable, use the more precise term "Outdoor Education")
UF   Outdoor Drama (1968 1980) #
     Outdoor Theaters (1968 1980) #
BT   Activities
RT   Adventure Education
     Athletics
     Bicycling
     Camping
     Horseback Riding
     Outdoor Education
     Outdoor Leadership
     Playground Activities
     Recess Breaks
     Recreational Activities
     Tourism
     Travel
     Wilderness

Outdoor Drama (1968 1980)
USE   Drama
AND   Outdoor Activities

Outdoor Education   *JUL. 1966*
Postings: 4,019   GC: 400
SN   Utilization of the outdoor environment to promote experiential learning and enrich the curriculum
NT   Adventure Education
BT   Education
RT   Conservation Education
     Environmental Education
     Environmental Interpretation
     Experiential Learning
     Field Trips
     Interdisciplinary Approach
     Outdoor Activities
     Outdoor Leadership
     Rural Education
     Summer Programs
     Trails
     Wilderness

Outdoor Leadership   *AUG. 1998*
Postings: 198   GC: 470
SN   Management or direction of groups in the outdoors—includes planning and conducting outdoor group activities, evaluating risks and safety concerns, influencing group dynamics, and facilitating participant reflection on the experience
BT   Leadership
RT   Adventure Education
     Experiential Learning
     Group Dynamics
     Leadership Training
     Outdoor Activities
     Outdoor Education

Outdoor Lighting (1971 1980)
USE   Lighting

Outdoor Theaters (1968 1980)
USE   Outdoor Activities
AND   Theaters

Outer Space Research
USE   Space Exploration

Outlining (Discourse)   *JAN. 1985*
Postings: 116   GC: 310
SN   The sequential enumeration in condensed

= Two or more Descriptors are used to represent this term.
The term's main entry shows the appropriate coordination.

form of the main ideas and supporting details of written or spoken material
BT Language Arts
RT Coherence
     Comprehension
     Notetaking
     Prewriting
     Speech Communication
     Study Skills
     Writing (Composition)
     Writing Skills

Outlooks on Life
USE World Views

Outplacement Services (Employment)
                       OCT. 1983
     Postings: 119   GC: 630
SN Services designed to help terminated employees deal with the stress of job loss, engage in job/career planning, and secure re-employment
UF Job Loss Services
BT Employment Services
RT Career Counseling
     Career Guidance
     Counseling Services
     Dislocated Workers
     Dismissal (Personnel)
     Employment Counselors
     Employment Practices
     Job Layoff
     Job Placement
     Personnel Policy
     Reduction in Force

Output Devices
USE Input Output Devices

Output Oriented Education
USE Competency Based Education

Output Oriented Teacher Education
USE Competency Based Teacher Education

Outreach Counseling
USE Outreach Programs

Outreach Programs   *MAY 1974*
     Postings: 2,851   GC: 330
SN Efforts to increase the availability and utilization of services, especially through direct intervention and interaction with the target population
UF Community Outreach
     Outreach Counseling
BT Programs
RT Bookmobiles
     Community Education
     Community Involvement
     Community Schools
     Community Services
     Continuing Education
     Counseling Services
     Delivery Systems
     Distance Education
     Extension Education
     Guidance Programs
     Health Programs
     Hotlines (Public)
     Indigenous Personnel
     Intervention
     Library Services
     Linking Agents
     Migrant Programs
     Mobile Clinics
     Mobile Educational Services
     Noncampus Colleges
     Off Campus Facilities
     Open Universities
     Recreational Programs
     Rehabilitation Programs
     School Community Programs
     Use Studies

Overachievement   *MAR. 1980*
     Postings: 61   GC: 120
SN Achievement beyond expectations
UF Overachievers (1966 1980)
BT Achievement
RT High Achievement
     Success
     Underachievement

Overachievers (1966 1980)
USE Overachievement

Overhead Projectors   *JUL. 1966*
     Postings: 314   GC: 910
UF Overhead Transparency Projectors
     Transparency Projectors
BT Projection Equipment

Overhead Television (1966 1980)
USE Television

Overhead Transparencies
USE Transparencies

Overhead Transparency Projectors
USE Overhead Projectors

Overpopulation   *JUL. 1966*
     Postings: 306   GC: 550
RT Birth Rate
     Community Size
     Contraception
     Crowding
     Demography
     Family Planning
     Population Distribution
     Population Growth
     Population Trends

Overseas Employment   *AUG. 1968*
     Postings: 233   GC: 630
UF Working Abroad
     Working Overseas
BT Employment
RT Foreign Countries
     Occupational Mobility

Overt Response   *JUL. 1966*
     Postings: 128   GC: 110
BT Responses
RT Covert Response

Overtime   *JUL. 1966*
     Postings: 45   GC: 630
RT Income
     Payroll Records
     Personnel Policy
     Premium Pay
     Salary Wage Differentials
     Scope of Bargaining
     Wages
     Working Hours

Overweight (Excessive Body Fat)
USE Obesity

Ownership   *AUG. 1986*
     Postings: 290   GC: 620
SN Legal possession of material or intellectual property
NT Intellectual Property
     Real Estate
RT Business
     Capital
     Contracts
     Cooperatives
     Costs
     Credit (Finance)
     Economic Factors
     Economic Opportunities
     Economic Status
     Economics
     Estate Planning
     Financial Services
     Fiscal Capacity
     Franchising
     Homeowners
     Industrial Structure
     Insurance
     Investment
     Land Acquisition
     Laws
     Legal Responsibility
     Private Sector
     Productivity
     Property Appraisal
     Public Sector
     Purchasing
     Resources
     Socioeconomic Status
     Stealing
     Taxes
     Trusts (Financial)

Ownership of Ideas
USE Intellectual Property

Oxidation   *JAN. 1970*
     Postings: 148   GC: 490
BT Chemical Reactions
RT Chemistry

Oxygen Inhalation Therapy
USE Respiratory Therapy

Pacific Americans   *SEP. 1982*
     Postings: 237   GC: 560
SN Citizens or permanent residents of the United States who are descendants of the indigenous peoples of Micronesia, Polynesia, and Melanesia
NT Hawaiians
     Samoan Americans
BT North Americans
     Pacific Islanders
RT Asian Americans
     Ethnic Groups
     Minority Groups

Pacific Islanders   *JAN. 1996*
     Postings: 64   GC: 560
SN Indigenous peoples of Micronesia, Polynesia, and Melanesia, and their descendants (Note: Use a more specific term, if appropriate—see also the geographic Identifiers "Pacific Islands" and "Oceania")
NT Maori (People)
     Pacific Americans
BT Groups
RT Ethnic Groups

Pacing   *JUL. 1966*
     Postings: 794   GC: 310
SN Act of directing the performance of individuals or groups by indicating the speed to be achieved
UF Group Pacing
     Interval Pacing (1967 1980)
     Self Paced Instruction #
     Self Pacing
BT Methods
RT Fixed Sequence
     Independent Study
     Individualized Instruction
     Individualized Reading
     Learner Controlled Instruction
     Learning Strategies
     Mastery Learning
     Motivation
     Programmed Instruction
     Sequential Approach
     Sequential Learning
     Teaching Machines
     Teaching Methods
     Time Factors (Learning)
     Time Management

Page Readers
USE Optical Scanners

Pain   *APR. 1990*
     Postings: 173   GC: 210
SN Distress and suffering caused by injury or disease of the body (Note: See also Identifiers "Low Back Pain," "Pain Control," and "Pain Tolerance"—do not use for emotional pain, for which see the Identifier "Emotional Distress")
UF Chronic Pain #
RT Anesthesiology
     Diseases
     Health
     Injuries
     Physical Disabilities
     Physical Health
     Sensory Experience
     Special Health Problems
     Symptoms (Individual Disorders)

Painting (Industrial Arts)   *MAR. 1980*
     Postings: 78   GC: 640
SN Act of or training for automotive painting, construction and maintenance painting, or interior decoration painting (Note: Prior to Mar80, this concept was indexed under "Painting")
UF Painting (1966 1980) (Industrial)
BT Industrial Arts
RT Auto Body Repairers
     Building Trades
     Color Planning
     Interior Design
     Sign Painters
     Skilled Occupations

Painting (Visual Arts)   *MAR. 1980*
     Postings: 707   GC: 420
SN Act or result of producing two-dimensional works in a variety of media such as oils, water color, tempera, casein, synthetics, or mixed media (Note: Prior to Mar80, this concept was indexed under "Painting")
UF Painting (1966 1980) (Artistic)
BT Visual Arts
RT Art Products
     Artists
     Childrens Art
     Color
     Freehand Drawing

Painting (1966 1980) (Artistic)
USE Painting (Visual Arts)

Painting (1966 1980) (Industrial)
USE Painting (Industrial Arts)

Paired Associate Learning   *JUL. 1966*
     Postings: 829   GC: 110
SN Learning in which items (words, designs, etc.) are presented in pairs—learning and retention are then measured by presenting the first element and asking the subject to respond with the second
BT Associative Learning
RT Association (Psychology)
     Behavior Chaining
     Learning Theories
     Patterned Responses
     Perception
     Recall (Psychology)
     Serial Learning

Palaeontology
USE Paleontology

Paleontology   *JUL. 1966*
     Postings: 301   GC: 490
UF Fossils
     Palaeontology
BT Geology
RT Archaeology
     Dinosaurs
     Evolution
     Zoology

= Two or more Descriptors are used to represent this term.
The term's main entry shows the appropriate coordination.

Pamphlets   *JUL. 1969*
    Postings: 391   GC: 730
UF   Brochures
     Leaflets
BT   Printed Materials
     Publications

Panjabi (1967 1994)
USE   Punjabi

Pantomime   *JUN. 1970*
    Postings: 118   GC: 420
UF   Mime
BT   Theater Arts
RT   Acting
     Creative Dramatics
     Dance
     Dramatics
     Movement Education
     Skits

Papago   *JUL. 1966*
    Postings: 24   GC: 440
SN   The Uto-Aztecan language of the Tohono
     O'Odham nation of American Indians—
     related to Pima, the two languages are
     sometimes referred to collectively as
     O'Odham, the Papago and Pima word for
     "people")
BT   Uto Aztecan Languages
RT   Tohono O Odham People

Papago (Tribe)
USE   Tohono O Odham People

Paper (Material)   *SEP. 1968*
    Postings: 225   GC: 910
RT   Art Materials
     Printed Materials
     Printing
     Supplies

Paperback Books   *JUL. 1966*
    Postings: 323   GC: 720
UF   Soft Cover Books
BT   Books

Paradigms
USE   Models

Paradox   *MAY 1971*
    Postings: 117   GC: 430
RT   Logic
     Philosophy

Paragraph Composition   *JUL. 1966*
    Postings: 315   GC: 400
BT   Writing (Composition)
RT   Cohesion (Written Composition)
     Discourse Analysis
     Paragraphs
     Writing Skills

Paragraphs   *NOV. 1968*
    Postings: 165   GC: 450
NT   Sentences
BT   Language Patterns
RT   Coherence
     Connected Discourse
     Paragraph Composition
     Parallelism (Literary)
     Traditional Grammar
     Writing (Composition)

Paralanguage
USE   Paralinguistics

Paralegal Education
USE   Legal Assistants
AND   Legal Education (Professions)

Paralegals
USE   Legal Assistants

Paralinguistics   *JUL. 1966*
    Postings: 276   GC: 450
SN   Study of those aspects of speech com-
     munication that do not pertain to lin-
     guistic structure or content, e.g., vocal
     qualifiers, intonation, and body language
UF   Paralanguage
BT   Linguistics
RT   Body Language
     Interaction Process Analysis
     Intonation
     Kinesthetic Methods
     Nonverbal Communication
     Speech Communication
     Speech Habits
     Stress (Phonology)
     Suprasegmentals

Parallelism (Literary)   *APR. 1970*
    Postings: 21   GC: 430
SN   Similarity of meaning or of structural
     arrangement in parts of a sentence, sen-
     tences, paragraphs, or larger units of
     writing
BT   Writing (Composition)
RT   Literary Devices
     Paragraphs
     Poetry
     Sentence Structure
     Writing Skills

Paramedical Occupations (1967 1980)
USE   Allied Health Occupations

Paramedical Sciences
USE   Medicine

Paramedics
USE   Allied Health Personnel

Paranoid Behavior   *NOV. 1972*
    Postings: 45   GC: 230
SN   Behavior characterized by suspicious-
     ness or delusions of persecution or gran-
     deur
BT   Behavior
RT   Behavior Problems
     Emotional Problems
     Fear
     Helplessness
     Hostility
     Personality Problems
     Psychological Patterns
     Psychosis
     Schizophrenia

Paraplegia
USE   Neurological Impairments

Paraprofessional Personnel   *FEB. 1976*
    Postings: 1,521   GC: 630
SN   Persons engaged to work with profes-
     sionals in secondary or supplementary
     capacities
UF   Subprofessionals (1967 1977)
     Technicians
NT   Agricultural Technicians
     Chemical Technicians
     Electronic Technicians
     Engineering Technicians
     Environmental Technicians
     Forestry Aides
     Housing Management Aides
     Instrumentation Technicians
     Legal Assistants
     Marine Technicians
     Mechanical Design Technicians
     Metallurgical Technicians
     Nuclear Power Plant Technicians
     Paraprofessional School Personnel
     Production Technicians
     Radiographers
     Veterinary Assistants

     Visiting Homemakers
BT   Personnel
RT   Allied Health Personnel
     Employees
     Health Personnel
     Library Technicians
     Nonprofessional Personnel
     Professional Personnel
     Research Assistants
     Technical Education
     Technical Occupations
     Vocational Education

Paraprofessional School Personnel
                                                 JAN. 1969
    Postings: 1,322   GC: 360
SN   Persons engaged to work with school
     professional staffs in secondary or sup-
     plemental capacities (Note: Use a more
     specific term if possible)
NT   School Aides
     Teacher Aides
BT   Paraprofessional Personnel
     School Personnel
RT   Differentiated Staffs
     Student Teachers
     Teacher Interns
     Volunteers

Parent Absence
USE   One Parent Family

Parent as a Teacher
USE   Parents as Teachers

Parent Aspiration   *MAR. 1980*
    Postings: 378   GC: 510
SN   Level of achievement or quality of per-
     formance that parents desire for their
     children (Note: The use of "Parental Aspi-
     ration" was not restricted by a Scope
     Note)
UF   Parental Aspiration (1966 1980)
BT   Aspiration
RT   Parent Attitudes
     Parent Child Relationship
     Parent Influence
     Parent Role
     Parents

Parent Associations   *SEP. 1968*
    Postings: 370   GC: 330
BT   Organizations (Groups)
RT   Fathers
     Mothers
     Parent Participation
     Parent Responsibility
     Parents

Parent Attitudes   *JUL. 1966*
    Postings: 8,164   GC: 510
SN   Attitudes of, not toward, parents (Note:
     Prior to Apr80, the use of this term was
     not restricted by a Scope Note)
UF   Parent Opinions
     Parent Reaction (1966 1980)
NT   Father Attitudes
     Mother Attitudes
BT   Attitudes
RT   Family Attitudes
     Parent Aspiration
     Parent Background
     Parent Counseling
     Parent Grievances
     Parents

Parent Background   *MAR. 1980*
    Postings: 844   GC: 510
UF   Parental Background (1966 1980)
BT   Background
RT   Family Characteristics
     Parent Attitudes
     Parent Child Relationship
     Parent School Relationship
     Parents

Parent Behavior
USE   Parent Child Relationship

Parent Child Interaction
USE   Parent Child Relationship

Parent Child Literacy
USE   Family Literacy

Parent Child Relationship   *JUL. 1966*
    Postings: 13,166   GC: 510
SN   (Note: If appropriate, use the more spe-
     cific term "Parent Student Relationship")
UF   Child Parent Relationship
     Motherese and Fatherese #
     Parent Behavior
     Parent Child Interaction
     Parent Talk #
NT   Parent Student Relationship
BT   Family Relationship
RT   Adolescent Behavior
     Adolescents
     Adult Children
     Attachment Behavior
     Births to Single Women
     Caregiver Child Relationship
     Caregiver Speech
     Child Abuse
     Child Behavior
     Child Custody
     Child Neglect
     Child Rearing
     Child Support
     Children
     Daughters
     Early Parenthood
     Elder Abuse
     Failure to Thrive
     Fathers
     Generation Gap
     Infant Care
     Love
     Mothers
     Parent Aspiration
     Parent Background
     Parent Counseling
     Parent Education
     Parent Influence
     Parent Role
     Parenthood Education
     Parenting Skills
     Parents
     Parents as Teachers
     Sons

Parent Conferences   *JUL. 1966*
    Postings: 142   GC: 330
UF   Parent Forums
     Parent Study Groups
BT   Conferences
RT   Parent Education
     Parent Participation
     Parent Responsibility
     Parent Workshops
     Parents

Parent Counseling   *JUL. 1966*
    Postings: 720   GC: 240
SN   Counseling of parents
BT   Counseling
RT   Family Counseling
     Individual Counseling
     Parent Attitudes
     Parent Child Relationship
     Parent Participation
     Parent School Relationship
     Parent Teacher Conferences
     Parent Teacher Cooperation
     Parents

Parent Education   *JUL. 1966*
    Postings: 4,477   GC: 330
SN   Instruction or information directed to-
     ward parents on effective parenting (Note:
     Do not confuse with "Parenthood Edu-
     cation"—prior to Mar80, the use of this
     term was not restricted by a Scope Note)
BT   Adult Education

= Two or more Descriptors are used to represent this term.
The term's main entry shows the appropriate coordination.

RT   Parent Child Relationship
     Parent Conferences
     Parent Materials
     Parent Role
     Parent School Relationship
     Parent Teacher Conferences
     Parent Teacher Cooperation
     Parent Workshops
     Parenting Skills
     Parents

Parent Empowerment   *JUL. 1996*
     Postings: 123   GC: 520
SN   Promotion or attainment of autonomy
     and freedom of choice for parents
BT   Empowerment
RT   Parent Participation
     Parent Rights
     Parent Role
     Parents

Parent Financial Contribution   *MAR. 1980*
     Postings: 392   GC: 620
SN   Partial or complete financial support of a
     student's educational expenses by a par-
     ent
UF   Parental Financial Contribution (1978
     1980)
BT   Student Financial Aid
RT   Family Financial Resources
     Family Income
     Need Analysis (Student Financial Aid)
     Parent Responsibility
     Parents
     Paying for College
     Self Supporting Students
     Student Costs
     Student Loan Programs
     Tax Credits

Parent Forums
USE   Parent Conferences

Parent Grievances   *MAR. 1980*
     Postings: 174   GC: 330
UF   Parental Grievances (1967 1980)
RT   Parent Attitudes
     Parent School Relationship
     Parents

Parent Influence   *JUL. 1966*
     Postings: 3,426   GC: 510
BT   Influences
RT   Family Influence
     Fathers
     Mothers
     Parent Aspiration
     Parent Child Relationship
     Parent Participation
     Parent Role
     Parents
     Parents as Teachers

Parent Involvement
USE   Parent Participation

Parent Materials   *OCT. 1982*
     Postings: 666   GC: 730
SN   Print and/or nonprint materials intended
     primarily for parents (or prospective par-
     ents)
UF   Parenting Materials
RT   Guides
     Parent Education
     Parenthood Education
     Parenting Skills
     Parents
     Resource Materials

Parent Opinions
USE   Parent Attitudes

Parent Participation   *JUL. 1966*
     Postings: 12,531   GC: 330
UF   Parent Involvement

BT   Participation
RT   Family Involvement
     Individualized Family Service Plans
     Parent Associations
     Parent Conferences
     Parent Counseling
     Parent Empowerment
     Parent Influence
     Parent Role
     Parent School Relationship
     Parent Teacher Conferences
     Parents
     Parents as Teachers
     Partnerships in Education
     Reggio Emilia Approach

Parent Reaction (1966 1980)
USE   Parent Attitudes

Parent Responsibility   *JUL. 1966*
     Postings: 1,270   GC: 510
UF   Parental Obligations
BT   Responsibility
RT   Child Responsibility
     Child Support
     Educational Responsibility
     Parent Associations
     Parent Conferences
     Parent Financial Contribution
     Parent Rights
     Parents

Parent Rights   *OCT. 1983*
     Postings: 427   GC: 520
SN   Rights of parents, either legal or granted
     by custom, in areas involving their child-
     ren
BT   Civil Liberties
RT   Childrens Rights
     Civil Rights
     Due Process
     Parent Empowerment
     Parent Responsibility
     Parents

Parent Role   *JUL. 1966*
     Postings: 6,405   GC: 510
UF   Father Role #
     Mother Role #
NT   Parents as Teachers
BT   Role
RT   Caregiver Role
     Family Role
     Fathers
     Mothers
     Parent Aspiration
     Parent Child Relationship
     Parent Education
     Parent Empowerment
     Parent Influence
     Parent Participation
     Parenthood Education
     Parenting Skills
     Parents
     Student Role

Parent School Relationship   *JUL. 1966*
     Postings: 5,641   GC: 330
UF   School Parent Relationship
BT   Family School Relationship
RT   In Loco Parentis
     Integrated Services
     Parent Background
     Parent Counseling
     Parent Education
     Parent Grievances
     Parent Participation
     Parent Student Relationship
     Parent Teacher Conferences
     Parent Teacher Cooperation
     Parents
     Parents as Teachers
     Partnerships in Education
     Politics of Education
     School Attitudes
     School Community Relationship
     School Involvement
     School Role

     Schools
     Student School Relationship

Parent Skills
USE   Parenting Skills

Parent Student Conferences (1967 1980)
USE   Parent Teacher Conferences

Parent Student Relationship   *JUL. 1966*
     Postings: 1,774   GC: 330
SN   Relationship between parent and child
     that focuses on the child's role as stu-
     dent (Note: Prior to Mar80, the use of
     this term was not restricted by a Scope
     Note)
UF   Student Parent Relationship
BT   Parent Child Relationship
RT   Home Schooling
     Parent School Relationship
     Parent Teacher Conferences
     Parents
     Parents as Teachers
     Self Supporting Students
     Student School Relationship
     Students

Parent Study Groups
USE   Parent Conferences

Parent Talk
USE   Caregiver Speech
AND   Parent Child Relationship

Parent Teacher Conferences   *JUL. 1966*
     Postings: 678   GC: 330
UF   Parent Student Conferences (1967
     1980)
     Teacher Parent Conferences
BT   Conferences
RT   Faculty Workload
     Parent Counseling
     Parent Education
     Parent Participation
     Parent School Relationship
     Parent Student Relationship
     Parent Teacher Cooperation
     Parents
     Teachers

Parent Teacher Cooperation   *JUL. 1966*
     Postings: 2,602   GC: 330
UF   Teacher Parent Cooperation
BT   Educational Cooperation
RT   Cooperative Planning
     Home Visits
     Parent Counseling
     Parent Education
     Parent School Relationship
     Parent Teacher Conferences
     Parents
     Parents as Teachers
     Partnerships in Education
     Teachers

Parent Workshops   *JUL. 1966*
     Postings: 390   GC: 330
BT   Workshops
RT   Parent Conferences
     Parent Education
     Parents

Parental Aspiration (1966 1980)
USE   Parent Aspiration

Parental Background (1966 1980)
USE   Parent Background

Parental Financial Contribution (1978 1980)
USE   Parent Financial Contribution

Parental Grievances (1967 1980)
USE   Parent Grievances

Parental Obligations
USE   Parent Responsibility

Parenthood Education   *JUL. 1973*
     Postings: 654   GC: 400
SN   Programs designed to help children and
     adolescents prepare for effective parent-
     hood by learning about child develop-
     ment and the role of parents, and by
     working closely with young children
BT   Family Life Education
RT   Child Development
     Child Rearing
     Family Life
     Family Relationship
     Parent Child Relationship
     Parent Materials
     Parent Role
     Parenting Skills
     Parents

Parenting
USE   Child Rearing

Parenting Materials
USE   Parent Materials

Parenting Skills   *OCT. 1984*
     Postings: 1,296   GC: 120
SN   Child rearing skills used by parents or
     other primary caregivers
UF   Parent Skills
BT   Skills
RT   Child Care Occupations
     Child Rearing
     Children
     Family Relationship
     Infant Care
     Parent Child Relationship
     Parent Education
     Parent Materials
     Parent Role
     Parenthood Education
     Parents
     Parents as Teachers

Parents   *JUL. 1966*
     Postings: 3,438   GC: 510
UF   Catholic Parents (1966 1980) #
NT   Adoptive Parents
     Biological Parents
     Employed Parents
     Fathers
     Grandparents
     Lower Class Parents
     Middle Class Parents
     Mothers
     Parents as Teachers
     Parents with Disabilities
BT   Groups
RT   Adults
     Child Caregivers
     Daughters
     Early Parenthood
     Family (Sociological Unit)
     Family Environment
     Family Life
     Family Problems
     Heads of Households
     Home Schooling
     Home Visits
     Kinship
     One Parent Family
     Parent Aspiration
     Parent Associations
     Parent Attitudes
     Parent Background
     Parent Child Relationship
     Parent Conferences
     Parent Counseling
     Parent Education
     Parent Empowerment
     Parent Financial Contribution
     Parent Grievances
     Parent Influence
     Parent Materials
     Parent Participation
     Parent Responsibility
     Parent Rights

= Two or more Descriptors are used to represent this term.
The term's main entry shows the appropriate coordination.

Parent Role
Parent School Relationship
Parent Student Relationship
Parent Teacher Conferences
Parent Teacher Cooperation
Parent Workshops
Parenthood Education
Parenting Skills
Sons
Spouses

Parents as Teachers   DEC. 1989
     Postings: 1,016   GC: 330
SN   Parents assuming either formal or informal roles as teachers of their children at home and/or school—covers the range of involvement from full-time compulsory "Home Schooling" to occasional help with homework
UF   Parent as a Teacher
BT   Parent Role
       Parents
RT   Child Rearing
       Family Literacy
       Home Instruction
       Home Schooling
       Home Study
       Parent Child Relationship
       Parent Influence
       Parent Participation
       Parent School Relationship
       Parent Student Relationship
       Parent Teacher Cooperation
       Parenting Skills
       Prereading Experience

Parents with Disabilities   APR. 1996
     Postings: 51   GC: 220
SN   Parents who have a disability or impairment of any type
UF   Disabled Parents
BT   Parents
RT   Disabilities

Parish Workers
USE   Church Workers

Park Design   JUL. 1966
     Postings: 96   GC: 920
BT   Design
RT   Parks
       Recreational Facilities
       Trails

Parking Areas (1966 1980)
USE   Parking Facilities

Parking Controls   OCT. 1968
     Postings: 30   GC: 920
UF   Parking Meters (1968 1980)
       Parking Permits
       Parking Regulations
RT   Motor Vehicles
       Parking Facilities
       Traffic Circulation
       Traffic Control
       Vehicular Traffic

Parking Facilities   OCT. 1968
     Postings: 118   GC: 920
SN   On and off street surface areas, and above and/or below ground structures for storage of vehicles
UF   Parking Areas (1966 1980)
       Parking Garages
       Parking Lots
       Parking Ramps
       Street Parking Areas
BT   Facilities
RT   Campus Planning
       Driveways
       Motor Vehicles
       Parking Controls
       Traffic Circulation
       Traffic Control
       Vehicular Traffic

Parking Garages
USE   Parking Facilities

Parking Lots
USE   Parking Facilities

Parking Meters (1968 1980)
USE   Parking Controls

Parking Permits
USE   Parking Controls

Parking Ramps
USE   Parking Facilities

Parking Regulations
USE   Parking Controls

Parks   JUL. 1966
     Postings: 662   GC: 920
NT   National Parks
BT   Facilities
RT   Aquariums
       Athletic Fields
       Community Resources
       Educational Facilities
       Environmental Interpretation
       Gardens
       Historic Sites
       Historical Interpretation
       Hospitality Occupations
       Land Use
       Natural Resources
       Nature Centers
       Park Design
       Physical Education Facilities
       Recreational Facilities
       Trails
       Zoos

Parliamentary Procedures   JUL. 1971
     Postings: 127   GC: 610
SN   The rules, precedents, or agreed upon conventions governing the proceedings of deliberative assemblies and other organizations
BT   Standards

Parochial School Aid (1972 1980)
USE   Parochial Schools
AND   Private School Aid

Parochial Schools   JUL. 1966
     Postings: 914   GC: 340
UF   Parochial School Aid (1972 1980) #
NT   Catholic Schools
BT   Private Schools
RT   Church Related Colleges
       Lay Teachers
       Private Education
       Private School Aid
       Religious Education

Parody   JUN. 1969
     Postings: 102   GC: 430
BT   Literary Genres
RT   Comics (Publications)
       Figurative Language
       Literary Styles
       Satire

Parole Officers   JUL. 1966
     Postings: 50   GC: 640
BT   Caseworkers
RT   Correctional Rehabilitation
       Counselors
       Crime
       Guidance Personnel
       Police
       Probation Officers
       Social Workers

Parsons
USE   Clergy

Part Correlation
USE   Correlation

Part Time Employment   MAR. 1980
     Postings: 760   GC: 630
UF   Part Time Jobs (1966 1980)
       Part Time Work
NT   Job Sharing
BT   Employment
RT   Flexible Working Hours
       Full Time Equivalency
       Multiple Employment
       Part Time Faculty
       Part Time Farmers
       Student Employment
       Temporary Employment
       Underemployment
       Work Study Programs
       Working Hours
       Youth Employment

Part Time Faculty   MAR. 1980
     Postings: 1,102   GC: 360
UF   Part Time Teachers (1967 1980)
       Part Time Teaching (1967 1980)
NT   Partnership Teachers
BT   Faculty
RT   Adjunct Faculty
       Employment Level
       Faculty Workload
       Full Time Equivalency
       Full Time Faculty
       Nontenured Faculty
       Part Time Employment
       Substitute Teachers
       Teacher Employment
       Teachers
       Teaching Load
       Working Hours

Part Time Farmers   JUL. 1966
     Postings: 38   GC: 410
UF   Nonresident Farmers
BT   Farmers
RT   Agriculture
       Farm Occupations
       Part Time Employment

Part Time Jobs (1966 1980)
USE   Part Time Employment

Part Time Students   JUL. 1966
     Postings: 1,359   GC: 360
BT   Students
RT   Correspondence Schools
       Distance Education
       Enrollment
       Evening Programs
       Evening Students
       Extension Education
       External Degree Programs
       Full Time Equivalency
       Full Time Students

Part Time Teachers (1967 1980)
USE   Part Time Faculty

Part Time Teaching (1967 1980)
USE   Part Time Faculty

Part Time Work
USE   Part Time Employment

Partial Correlation
USE   Correlation

Partial Hearing   MAR. 1980
     Postings: 522   GC: 220
SN   Mild to moderate hearing impairment—usually a loss of less than 75 decibels

UF   Hard of Hearing (1967 1980)
BT   Hearing Impairments
RT   Deafness
       Hearing (Physiology)
       Hearing Aids
       Mild Disabilities
       Oral Communication Method
       Total Communication

Partial Vision   MAR. 1980
     Postings: 477   GC: 220
SN   Severe visual impairment requiring special aid for perception of printed material and/or mobility—legally defined as having central visual acuity between 20/200 and 20/70 in the better eye with correction
UF   Partially Sighted (1967 1980)
BT   Visual Impairments
RT   Blindness
       Large Type Materials
       Low Vision Aids
       Special Education
       Talking Books
       Vision
       Visual Acuity

Partially Sighted (1967 1980)
USE   Partial Vision

Participant Characteristics   JUL. 1966
     Postings: 1,779   GC: 330
RT   Client Characteristics (Human Services)
       Control Groups
       Dropout Characteristics
       Educational Background
       Experimental Groups
       Group Membership
       Individual Characteristics
       Matched Groups
       Norms
       Participation
       Research Design
       Sampling

Participant Involvement (1967 1980)
USE   Participation

Participant Observation   OCT. 1984
     Postings: 366   GC: 820
SN   Observation in which the investigator participates in the situation being studied
BT   Observation
RT   Classroom Observation Techniques
       Ethnography
       Evaluation Methods
       Naturalistic Observation
       Participation
       Qualitative Research
       Research Methodology
       Social Science Research

Participant Satisfaction   JUL. 1966
     Postings: 3,446   GC: 310
SN   An individual's assessment of the degree to which an experience meets his or her needs or expectations
BT   Satisfaction
RT   Evaluation
       Participation
       Summative Evaluation

Participation   JUL. 1966
     Postings: 2,816   GC: 120
SN   Sharing or taking part in an activity (Note: Use a more specific term if possible)
UF   Participant Involvement (1967 1980)
NT   Audience Participation
       Citizen Participation
       Community Involvement
       Family Involvement
       Parent Participation
       School Involvement
       Student Participation
       Teacher Participation

= Two or more Descriptors are used to represent this term.
The term's main entry shows the appropriate coordination.

BT   Behavior
RT   Activism
        Activities
        Attendance
        Discussion
        Enrollment
        Experience
        Group Activities
        Interaction
        Interests
        Participant Characteristics
        Participant Observation
        Participant Satisfaction
        Participative Decision Making
        Participatory Research
        Performance

Participative Decision Making   *AUG. 1982*
        Postings: 3,441   GC: 320
SN   Formal involvement of people besides
        administrators (e.g., staff, students, work-
        ers, or community members) in the gov-
        ernance, management, or policy-making
        processes of an institution or organiza-
        tion of which they are a part—the extent
        of participation can vary from advising to
        power-sharing
UF   Collaborative Decision Making
        Collective Decision Making
        Democratic Management
        Participative Management
        Participative Problem Solving #
BT   Administrative Organization
        Decision Making
RT   Administration
        Advisory Committees
        Citizen Participation
        College Governing Councils
        Collegiality
        Community Control
        Cooperatives
        Employer Employee Relationship
        Empowerment
        Faculty College Relationship
        Management Teams
        Nominal Group Technique
        Organizational Development
        Participation
        Participatory Research
        Policy Formation
        Power Structure
        Quality Circles
        School Based Management
        School Community Relationship
        School Restructuring
        Student Participation
        Student School Relationship
        Teacher Administrator Relationship
        Teacher Participation
        Teamwork
        Total Quality Management

Participative Management
USE   Participative Decision Making

Participative Problem Solving
USE   Participative Decision Making
AND   Problem Solving

Participatory Action Research
USE   Action Research
AND   Participatory Research

Participatory Research   *DEC. 1989*
        Postings: 340   GC: 810
SN   Social research in which the persons
        being studied are also fully involved in
        the research design and analysis (Note:
        Use as a minor Descriptor for examples
        of this kind of research—use as a major
        Descriptor only as the subject of a
        document—do not use for "Participa-
        tion Research," i.e., research about par-
        ticipation)
UF   Participatory Action Research #
BT   Research
RT   Action Research
        Citizen Participation
        Community Control

        Community Involvement
        Participation
        Participative Decision Making
        Political Power
        Research Methodology
        Social Action
        Social Change
        Theory Practice Relationship

Partners in Education Projects
USE   Partnerships in Education

Partnership Academies (School and Business)
USE   Career Academies

Partnership Teachers   *JUL. 1966*
        Postings: 19   GC: 360
SN   Two part-time teachers hired as one full-
        time teacher
BT   Part Time Faculty
RT   Flexible Working Hours
        Job Sharing

Partnerships in Education   *JUL. 1993*
        Postings: 3,814   GC: 330
SN   Collaborative arrangements and endeav-
        ors between and among schools and
        other entities (corporate enterprises, com-
        munity agencies, student/parent/citizen
        groups, colleges, other schools, indi-
        viduals, etc.) designed to share resources,
        achieve common goals, and foster edu-
        cational achievement, improvement, and
        reform (Note: See also the Identifiers
        "Coalitions" and "Teacher Partnerships")
UF   Academic Alliances
        Collaboratives (Education)
        Educational Partnerships
        Partners in Education Projects
BT   Educational Cooperation
RT   College School Cooperation
        Community Involvement
        Consortia
        Cooperative Programs
        Coordination
        Corporate Support
        Education Work Relationship
        Educational Improvement
        Family School Relationship
        Government School Relationship
        Institutional Cooperation
        Parent Participation
        Parent School Relationship
        Parent Teacher Cooperation
        School Business Relationship
        School Community Programs
        School Community Relationship
        School Restructuring
        Shared Resources and Services

Parts of Speech
USE   Form Classes (Languages)

Parturition
USE   Birth

Pashto   *JUL. 1966*
        Postings: 40   GC: 440
UF   Pashtu
        Pushto
        Pushtu
BT   Indo European Languages

Pashtu
USE   Pashto

Pass Fail Grading   *JUL. 1966*
        Postings: 267   GC: 320
SN   Grading system in which students re-
        ceive marks of "pass" or "fail" rather
        than the more conventional letter grades
BT   Grading
RT   Academic Standards
        College Credits

        Credit No Credit Grading
        Credits
        Cutting Scores
        Grades (Scholastic)
        Nongraded Student Evaluation
        Scoring

Pass No Credit Grading
USE   Credit No Credit Grading

Pass No Record Grading
USE   Credit No Credit Grading

Pastes (Adhesives)
USE   Adhesives

Pastoral Literature   *JUL. 1969*
        Postings: 21   GC: 430
UF   Bucolic Literature
BT   Literature
RT   Odes
        Poetry

Pastoral Peoples
USE   Nomads

Patents   *AUG. 1968*
        Postings: 262   GC: 610
SN   Government grants that give people or
        companies sole rights to make, use, or
        sell new inventions for a specified num-
        ber of years
BT   Intellectual Property
RT   Federal Regulation
        Government Role
        Inventions
        Legal Responsibility
        Technology Transfer

Path Analysis   *MAR. 1980*
        Postings: 502   GC: 820
SN   Method of multivariate analysis used to
        evaluate hypothesized causal relation-
        ships among the traits represented in a
        study (Note: Prior to Mar80, the instruc-
        tion "Path Analysis, USE Critical Path
        Method" was carried in the Thesaurus)
BT   Multivariate Analysis
RT   Causal Models
        Correlation
        Factor Analysis
        Multiple Regression Analysis
        Predictor Variables
        Structural Equation Models
        Suppressor Variables
        Validity

Pathogenesis
USE   Pathology

Pathology   *JUL. 1966*
        Postings: 246   GC: 210
UF   Pathogenesis
NT   Plant Pathology
        Psychopathology
        Speech Language Pathology
BT   Medicine
RT   Anatomy
        Death
        Diseases
        Embryology
        Epidemiology
        Etiology
        Neurology
        Oncology
        Physiology
        Psychophysiology
        Toxicology
        Zoology

Pathways
USE   Trails

Patient Care Evaluation
USE   Medical Care Evaluation

Patient Education   *MAR. 1980*
        Postings: 389   GC: 210
SN   Teaching patients about disease man-
        agement, health care, physician serv-
        ices, etc. (Note: Do not confuse with the
        more general Descriptor "Health Educa-
        tion")
BT   Education
RT   Chronic Illness
        Diseases
        Health
        Health Education
        Nurse Practitioners
        Patients
        Physician Patient Relationship
        Preventive Medicine
        Primary Health Care

Patient Physician Relationship
USE   Physician Patient Relationship

Patients   *MAR. 1980*
        Postings: 2,230   GC: 210
SN   Persons who are ill or ailing, usually
        awaiting or undergoing medical treat-
        ment
UF   Invalids
        Patients (Persons) (1968 1980)
NT   Hospitalized Children
BT   Groups
RT   Client Characteristics (Human Serv-
        ices)
        Disabilities
        Frail Elderly
        Hospitals
        Institutionalized Persons
        Medical Case Histories
        Medical Evaluation
        Medical Services
        Patient Education
        Physician Patient Relationship
        Rehabilitation
        Surgery

Patients (Persons) (1968 1980)
USE   Patients

Patriotism   *MAR. 1982*
        Postings: 125   GC: 610
SN   Love for or devotion to one's country
BT   Nationalism
RT   Citizenship Responsibility
        Group Unity
        Loyalty Oaths
        Political Socialization

Pattern Drills (Language)   *JUL. 1966*
        Postings: 1,085   GC: 450
NT   Substitution Drills
BT   Drills (Practice)
RT   Dialogs (Language)
        Patterned Responses
        Second Language Instruction

Pattern Recognition   *OCT. 1969*
        Postings: 690   GC: 710
NT   Character Recognition
BT   Recognition (Psychology)
RT   Cybernetics
        Information Processing
        Perception
        Reading
        Serial Ordering

Patterned Behavior
USE   Behavior Patterns

Patterned Responses   *JUL. 1966*
        Postings: 225   GC: 110
SN   Using various organizations of stimuli to
        cue desired responses
UF   Stimulus Synthesis

= Two or more Descriptors are used to represent this term.
The term's main entry shows the appropriate coordination.

BT   Responses
RT   Association Measures
     Dimensional Preference
     Generalization
     Paired Associate Learning
     Pattern Drills (Language)
     Perception
     Stimulus Generalization

Patternmaking   *JUL. 1966*
     Postings: 86   GC: 640
SN   (Note: Do not use for the study of numerical patterns—see the Identifier "Number Sequences" for that concept)
RT   Clothing Design
     Geometric Concepts
     Industrial Arts
     Leather
     Metal Working
     Needle Trades
     Plastics
     Skilled Occupations
     Visual Arts
     Woodworking

Patterns in Mathematics   *AUG. 1999*
     Postings: 450   GC: 480
SN   Numerical and geometrical configurations of natural or human origin (Note: See also the Identifier "Number Sequences")
UF   Mathematical Patterns
BT   Mathematical Concepts
RT   Geometric Concepts
     Number Concepts

Pay Equity
USE   Comparable Worth

Paying for College   *APR. 1990*
     Postings: 799   GC: 620
SN   The ways and means of financing an individual's higher education, whether a two-year, four-year, graduate-level, or nondegree program (Note: Prior to Apr90, "Student Costs" or its narrower terms were frequently used to index this concept)
UF   College Costs (Financing for Individual Students)
RT   College Bound Students
     College Students
     Credit (Finance)
     Debt (Financial)
     Educational Finance
     Financial Aid Applicants
     Financial Needs
     Financial Problems
     Financial Support
     Loan Repayment
     Money Management
     Need Analysis (Student Financial Aid)
     Parent Financial Contribution
     Student Costs
     Student Employment
     Student Financial Aid
     Student Financial Aid Officers
     Student Loan Programs
     Work Study Programs

Payroll Records   *JUL. 1966*
     Postings: 84   GC: 630
UF   Wage Statements (1966 1980)
BT   Records (Forms)
RT   Overtime
     Premium Pay
     Salaries
     Wages

Peace   *APR. 1972*
     Postings: 1,344   GC: 610
UF   International Peace
     World Peace
BT   Human Relations
RT   Conflict Resolution
     Disarmament
     Foreign Policy
     Global Education

     History
     International Education
     International Organizations
     International Relations
     National Defense
     Prosocial Behavior
     Treaties
     War
     World Affairs

Peanut Inspectors
USE   Food and Drug Inspectors

Pedagogical Content Knowledge   *MAR. 1998*
     Postings: 224   GC: 310
SN   An integration of teacher understanding that combines content (subject matter), pedagogy (instructional methods), and learner characteristics
RT   Knowledge Base for Teaching
     Knowledge Level
     Teacher Effectiveness
     Teaching Methods
     Teaching Skills

Pedagogy
USE   Instruction

Pedestrian Circulation
USE   Pedestrian Traffic

Pedestrian Traffic   *OCT. 1968*
     Postings: 100   GC: 920
UF   Pedestrian Circulation
RT   Traffic Circulation
     Traffic Control
     Vehicular Traffic
     Walking

Pediatrics   *MAR. 1980*
     Postings: 478   GC: 210
SN   Branch of medicine dealing with the development, care, and diseases of children
UF   Pediatrics Training (1966 1980)
BT   Medicine
RT   Child Health
     Family Practice (Medicine)
     Infant Care
     Medical Services
     Neonates
     Primary Health Care

Pediatrics Training (1966 1980)
USE   Pediatrics

Peer Acceptance   *JUL. 1966*
     Postings: 1,471   GC: 510
BT   Affiliation Need
RT   Morale
     Peer Evaluation
     Peer Groups
     Peer Influence
     Peer Relationship
     Popularity

Peer Counseling   *AUG. 1973*
     Postings: 772   GC: 240
SN   Performance of limited counselor functions, under counselor supervision, by person of approximate age of counselee
BT   Counseling
RT   Helping Relationship
     Peer Influence
     Peer Mediation
     Peer Relationship

Peer Evaluation   *DEC. 1976*
     Postings: 2,052   GC: 320
SN   Evaluation by one's peers
UF   Peer Review
BT   Evaluation
RT   Clinical Supervision (of Teachers)
     Interprofessional Relationship

     Merit Rating
     Peer Acceptance
     Peer Influence
     Peer Relationship
     Personnel Evaluation
     Sociometric Techniques
     Student Evaluation

Peer Groups   *JUL. 1966*
     Postings: 1,158   GC: 520
BT   Groups
RT   Age Groups
     Conformity
     Group Discussion
     Juvenile Gangs
     Peer Acceptance
     Peer Influence
     Peer Relationship
     Social Values

Peer Influence   *FEB. 1978*
     Postings: 2,106   GC: 510
SN   Pressure, either planned or unplanned, exerted by peers to influence personal behavior
UF   Peer Pressure
BT   Influences
RT   Conformity
     Group Dynamics
     Informal Leadership
     Peer Acceptance
     Peer Counseling
     Peer Evaluation
     Peer Groups
     Peer Mediation
     Peer Relationship
     Peer Teaching
     Resistance to Temptation
     Socialization

Peer Institutions   *AUG. 1986*
     Postings: 79   GC: 320
SN   Institutions with comparable characteristics, e.g., mission, governance, size (Note: Do not confuse or coordinate with other "peer" Descriptors, all of which refer to people)
UF   Comparable Institutions
BT   Institutions
RT   Cluster Grouping
     Comparative Analysis
     Institutional Characteristics
     Institutional Cooperation
     Institutional Research

Peer Mediation   *JUN. 2000*
     Postings: 144   GC: 520
SN   The use of peers (e.g., students, teachers) to promote reconciliation, settlement, or compromise between conflicting parties
UF   Student Mediation
BT   Conflict Resolution
RT   Arbitration
     Grievance Procedures
     Interpersonal Communication
     Peer Counseling
     Peer Influence
     Peer Relationship

Peer Pressure
USE   Peer Influence

Peer Relationship   *JUL. 1966*
     Postings: 6,065   GC: 510
BT   Interpersonal Relationship
RT   Collegiality
     Friendship
     Living Learning Centers
     Peer Acceptance
     Peer Counseling
     Peer Evaluation
     Peer Groups
     Peer Influence
     Peer Mediation
     Peer Teaching
     Popularity
     Teamwork

Peer Review
USE   Peer Evaluation

Peer Teaching   *JUL. 1966*
     Postings: 2,437   GC: 310
UF   Peer Tutoring #
BT   Teaching Methods
RT   Cooperative Learning
     Cross Age Teaching
     Peer Influence
     Peer Relationship
     Reciprocal Teaching
     Tutorial Programs
     Tutoring

Peer Tutoring
USE   Peer Teaching
AND   Tutoring

Pensions
USE   Retirement Benefits

People Days
USE   Worker Days

Peoples Education
USE   Popular Education

Percent
USE   Percentage

Percent Body Fat
USE   Body Composition

Percentage   *JAN. 1969*
     Postings: 200   GC: 480
UF   Percent
BT   Ratios (Mathematics)
RT   Arithmetic
     Mathematical Concepts

Perception   *JUL. 1966*
     Postings: 4,536   GC: 110
SN   The process of becoming aware of objects, qualities, or relations via the sense organs—involves the reception, processing, and interpretation of sensory impressions (Note: Use a more specific term if possible—do not confuse with "Attitudes" or "Opinions")
UF   Awareness
NT   Auditory Perception
     Kinesthetic Perception
     Tactual Perception
     Visual Perception
BT   Cognitive Processes
RT   Adaptation Level Theory
     Aesthetic Values
     Arousal Patterns
     Attention
     Cognitive Mapping
     Comprehension
     Discovery Processes
     Discrimination Learning
     Encoding (Psychology)
     Familiarity
     Figural Aftereffects
     Habituation
     Inferences
     Intuition
     Neurological Organization
     Neuropsychology
     Novelty (Stimulus Dimension)
     Paired Associate Learning
     Pattern Recognition
     Patterned Responses
     Perception Tests
     Perceptual Development
     Perceptual Impairments
     Perceptual Motor Coordination
     Phenomenology
     Physiology
     Recognition (Psychology)
     Sensory Deprivation
     Sensory Experience

= Two or more Descriptors are used to represent this term.
The term's main entry shows the appropriate coordination.

Sensory Integration
Spatial Ability
Stimuli

Perception (between Persons)
USE   Social Cognition

Perception Tests   *JUL. 1966*
      Postings: 577   GC: 830
SN   Measures used to indicate an individ-
      ual's awareness, organization, and un-
      derstanding of sensory impressions
      (Note: Do not confuse with "Physical
      Examinations")
NT   Tactual Visual Tests
BT   Cognitive Tests
RT   Auditory Perception
      Auditory Tests
      Field Dependence Independence
      Kinesthetic Perception
      Perception
      Perceptual Development
      Tactual Perception
      Vision Tests
      Visual Literacy
      Visual Perception

Perceptiveness (between Persons)
USE   Interpersonal Competence
AND   Social Cognition

Perceptual Deprivation
USE   Sensory Deprivation

Perceptual Development   *JUL. 1966*
      Postings: 2,013   GC: 120
SN   Stages or growth in organizing and un-
      derstanding sensory impressions, i.e.,
      the process of recognizing, identifying,
      or becoming aware of objects, qualities,
      or relations
BT   Cognitive Development
RT   Brain Hemisphere Functions
      Learning Modalities
      Neurological Organization
      Perception
      Perception Tests
      Perceptual Impairments
      Perceptual Motor Coordination
      Perceptual Motor Learning
      Physical Development
      Psychomotor Skills
      Sensory Integration
      Sensory Training
      Spatial Ability
      Visual Literacy

Perceptual Handicaps (1980 1994)
USE   Perceptual Impairments

Perceptual Impairments   *MAR. 1994*
      Postings: 56   GC: 220
SN   Impairments of the ability to recognize
      and interpret information that is received
      through the senses
UF   Perceptual Handicaps (1980 1994)
      Perceptually Handicapped (1966 1980)
BT   Disabilities
RT   Aphasia
      Auditory Perception
      Auditory Training
      Dyslexia
      Hyperactivity
      Language Impairments
      Learning Disabilities
      Neurological Impairments
      Perception
      Perceptual Development
      Perceptual Motor Coordination
      Perceptual Motor Learning
      Recall (Psychology)
      Recognition (Psychology)
      Sensory Experience
      Sensory Integration
      Visual Literacy
      Visual Perception

Perceptual Motor Coordination   *JUL. 1966*
      Postings: 832   GC: 120
NT   Eye Hand Coordination
      Eye Voice Span
BT   Psychomotor Skills
RT   Exploratory Behavior
      Motor Development
      Movement Education
      Object Manipulation
      Perception
      Perceptual Development
      Perceptual Impairments
      Perceptual Motor Learning
      Reaction Time
      Tactual Visual Tests

Perceptual Motor Learning   *JUL. 1966*
      Postings: 916   GC: 110
SN   Learning that involves the perceptual
      processing of nonverbal stimuli
UF   Sensory Motor Learning
BT   Nonverbal Learning
RT   Kinesthetic Perception
      Learning Modalities
      Manipulative Materials
      Motor Development
      Movement Education
      Multisensory Learning
      Perceptual Development
      Perceptual Impairments
      Perceptual Motor Coordination
      Psychomotor Skills
      Sensory Integration
      Sensory Training
      Tactual Visual Tests

Perceptual Style
USE   Cognitive Style

Perceptually Handicapped (1966 1980)
USE   Perceptual Impairments

Performance   *JUL. 1966*
      Postings: 2,939   GC: 120
SN   Execution or accomplishment of an in-
      tended action or goal
NT   Counselor Performance
      Failure
      Job Performance
      Success
BT   Behavior
RT   Ability
      Academic Achievement
      Accountability
      Achievement
      Aptitude
      Aspiration
      Awards
      Benchmarking
      Competence
      Competency Based Education
      Competency Based Teacher Education
      Competition
      Difficulty Level
      Efficiency
      Evaluation Criteria
      Expectation
      Familiarity
      Feedback
      Knowledge Level
      Management by Objectives
      Mastery Learning
      Mastery Tests
      Minimum Competencies
      Motivation
      Objectives
      Observation
      Participation
      Performance Based Assessment
      Performance Factors
      Performance Technology
      Performance Tests
      Qualifications
      Quality Control
      Relevance (Information Retrieval)
      Reliability
      Scoring Rubrics
      Time Management
      Time on Task

Performance Appraisal (Personnel)
USE   Personnel Evaluation

**Performance Assessment (Higher Order
Learning)**
USE   Performance Based Assessment

**Performance Assessment (Skilled Bodily
Movements)**
USE   Performance Tests

Performance Based Assessment   *APR. 1996*
      Postings: 2,137   GC: 820
SN   Evaluation of achievement, learning, etc.,
      that requires direct demonstration of
      knowledge and skills via the construc-
      tion of responses, and for which scoring
      can be based on the processes of the
      response construction as well as the
      final product—typically, performance-
      based assessments are designed to elicit
      and strengthen examinees' critical-think-
      ing skills, problem-solving strategies, self-
      evaluation skills, and other higher-order
      thinking skills (Note: Do not confuse
      with "Performance Tests," whose usage
      is restricted to evaluations of manual
      manipulations and body movements)
UF   Authentic Assessment
      Direct Assessment
      Performance Assessment (Higher Or-
         der Learning)
      Performance Based Evaluation
BT   Alternative Assessment
RT   Achievement Tests
      Competence
      Competency Based Education
      Competency Based Teacher Education
      Criterion Referenced Tests
      Educational Testing
      Evaluation Methods
      Performance
      Performance Factors
      Personnel Evaluation
      Portfolio Assessment
      Scoring Rubrics
      Student Evaluation
      Teacher Competency Testing

Performance Based Education (1974 1980)
USE   Competency Based Education

Performance Based Evaluation
USE   Performance Based Assessment

**Performance Based Teacher Education
(1972 1980)**
USE   Competency Based Teacher Education

Performance Contracts   *JAN. 1971*
      Postings: 1,100   GC: 310
SN   Agreements to achieve specified objec-
      tives within established time frames with
      reward or payment dependent upon the
      level of performance
UF   Behavioral Contracts
      Contract Grading #
      Learning Contracts
      Student Learning Contracts
BT   Contracts
RT   Academic Achievement
      Behavioral Objectives
      Contingency Management
      Management by Objectives
      Motivation Techniques

Performance Criteria (1968 1980)
                                             JUN. 1980
      Postings: 2,165   GC: 820
SN   Invalid Descriptor—used inconsistently
      in indexing—see "Evaluation Criteria"
      and "Specifications"

Performance Factors   *JUL. 1966*
      Postings: 6,969   GC: 310
SN   Influences, conditions, or characteris-
      tics related to the accomplishment of a
      goal or task by a person, organization,
      program, or system
BT   Influences
RT   Achievement
      Context Effect
      Evaluation
      Evaluation Criteria
      Performance
      Performance Based Assessment
      Performance Technology
      Predictor Variables

Performance Objectives
USE   Behavioral Objectives

Performance Specifications (1969 1980)
                                             JUN. 1980
      Postings: 684   GC: 820
SN   Invalid Descriptor—used inconsistently
      in indexing—see such Descriptors as
      "Equipment Standards," "Facility Require-
      ments," and "Performance Factors"

Performance Technology   *AUG. 1994*
      Postings: 213   GC: 330
SN   Systematic design, analysis, selection,
      implementation, and evaluation of prod-
      ucts and activities to influence human
      and organizational performance
UF   Human Performance Technology
BT   Educational Technology
RT   Behavioral Objectives
      Human Factors Engineering
      Improvement Programs
      Industrial Training
      Instructional Systems
      Job Performance
      Job Training
      Labor Force Development
      Management Systems
      Organizational Development
      Performance
      Performance Factors
      Productivity
      Systems Development
      Training
      Training Objectives
      Work Environment

Performance Tests   *JUL. 1966*
      Postings: 1,267   GC: 830
SN   Tests that require the manipulation of
      objects or skilled bodily movements
      (Note: Do not confuse with "Nonver-
      bal Tests," which minimize the use of
      language but may not emphasize the
      manipulation of objects or skilled
      movement—prior to Mar80, the use of
      this term was not restricted by a Scope
      Note—use "Performance Based Assess-
      ment" for "higher-order" performance
      testing)
UF   Performance Assessment (Skilled Bod-
         ily Movements)
BT   Tests
RT   Achievement Tests
      Aptitude Tests
      Criterion Referenced Tests
      Nonverbal Tests
      Occupational Tests
      Performance
      Physical Fitness Tests
      Situational Tests
      Work Sample Tests

Performing Arts
USE   Theater Arts

Performing Arts Centers
USE   Theaters

= Two or more Descriptors are used to represent this term.
The term's main entry shows the appropriate coordination.

Perinatal Influences *SEP. 1975*
Postings: 291 GC: 120
SN Factors occurring at the time of birth and affecting the physical or mental development of an individual
BT Influences
RT Biological Influences
Birth
Birth Weight
Child Health
Congenital Impairments
Diseases
Health
Obstetrics
Pregnancy
Premature Infants
Prenatal Influences
Rh Factors

Periodical Articles
USE Journal Articles

Periodicals *JUL. 1966*
Postings: 4,158 GC: 730
UF Journals
Magazines
NT Electronic Journals
Foreign Language Periodicals
Scholarly Journals
BT Serials
RT Bibliometrics
Bulletins
Editorials
Editors
Feature Stories
Journal Articles
Journalism
Journalism Education
Journalism History
Printed Materials
Reading Materials
Writing for Publication

Permanent Education
USE Lifelong Learning

Permanent Magnets
USE Magnets

Permissive Environment *JUL. 1966*
Postings: 98 GC: 510
BT Environment
RT Family Environment
Nonauthoritarian Classes

Permuted Indexes *JUL. 1966*
Postings: 110 GC: 730
SN Indexes based on the cyclic permutation of words, with each substantive word being brought to a predetermined position and alphabetized
UF Key Word in Context
KWIC Indexes
KWOC Indexes
Title Word Indexes
BT Indexes
RT Automatic Indexing
Coordinate Indexes
Indexing

Perquisites (Employment)
USE Fringe Benefits

Perseverance
USE Persistence

Persian *JUL. 1966*
Postings: 127 GC: 440
UF Farsi (Language)
BT Indo European Languages

Persistence *JUL. 1966*
Postings: 763 GC: 120
SN Continuance of an individual in an endeavor or activity
UF Perseverance
NT Academic Persistence
Teacher Persistence
BT Behavior
RT Burnout
Career Change
Coping
Dropout Research
Dropouts
Occupational Mobility
Personality Traits
Resilience (Personality)
Stopouts
Time on Task

Person Days
USE Worker Days

Person Perception
USE Social Cognition

Personal Accounts (Narratives)
USE Personal Narratives

Personal Adjustment (1966 1980)
USE Adjustment (to Environment)

Personal Autonomy *NOV. 1982*
Postings: 1,466 GC: 510
SN Individual independence, self-determination, and freedom from external restraint or authority
UF Individual Autonomy
Learner Autonomy
RT Academic Freedom
Authoritarianism
Decision Making
Democracy
Empowerment
Freedom
Independent Living
Independent Study
Individual Power
Individual Psychology
Individualism
Intellectual Freedom
Interpersonal Relationship
Learner Controlled Instruction
Life Style
Locus of Control
Open Education
Personality
Power Structure
Professional Autonomy
Psychological Needs
Resistance (Psychology)
Role Theory
Self Actualization
Self Control
Self Determination
Self Motivation
Sociology

Personal Care Homes *AUG. 1968*
Postings: 108 GC: 920
SN Residential facilities, usually for older adults, providing personal services such as assistance in mobilization, bathing, dressing, etc., as opposed to highly skilled care given in facilities like nursing homes
UF Homes for the Aged
Rest Homes
BT Residential Institutions
RT Frail Elderly
Group Homes
Long Term Care
Nursing Homes
Older Adults
Residential Care
Respite Care

Personal Computers
USE Microcomputers

Personal Development
USE Individual Development

Personal Empowerment
USE Empowerment

Personal Grooming
USE Hygiene

Personal Growth (1967 1980)
USE Individual Development

Personal Health
USE Hygiene

Personal Interests (1966 1980)
USE Interests

Personal Liberty
USE Civil Liberties

Personal Narratives *SEP. 1982*
Postings: 2,961 GC: 730
SN Verbal accounts, usually in the first person, of an individual's experiences, thoughts, and feelings
UF Personal Accounts (Narratives)
BT Reports
RT Autobiographies
Biographies
Diaries
Interviews
Journal Writing
Monologs
Narration
Opinion Papers
Reminiscence
Speeches
Student Journals

Personal Publishing
USE Desktop Publishing

Personal Relationship (1966 1974)
USE Interpersonal Relationship

Personal Space *MAR. 1980*
Postings: 218 GC: 120
SN Individuals' sense of physical space required for psychological comfort—may vary greatly from culture to culture and within cultures (Note: Do not confuse with "Spatial Ability")
UF Proxemics
BT Psychological Needs
RT Body Image
Crowding
Cultural Traits
Kinesthetic Perception
Nonverbal Communication

Personal Values (1966 1980)
USE Values

Personality *JUL. 1966*
Postings: 2,228 GC: 120
SN The dynamic, integrated pattern of motivational and temperamental or emotional qualities that distinguishes the individual (Note: For specific personality attributes, see "Personality Traits")
UF Character
Disposition (Individuals)
Temperament
RT Attribution Theory
Habit Formation
Individual Psychology
Personal Autonomy
Personality Assessment
Personality Change
Personality Development
Personality Measures
Personality Problems

Personality Studies
Personality Theories
Personality Traits
Phenomenology
Self Concept
Self Motivation

Personality Assessment *JUL. 1966*
Postings: 2,130 GC: 820
SN Evaluation of the patterns of enduring traits that characterize a particular individual's motivation, temperament, or behavior
UF Personality Rating
BT Psychological Evaluation
RT Association Measures
Behavior Rating Scales
Factor Analysis
Goal Orientation
Personality
Personality Development
Personality Measures
Personality Studies
Projective Measures
Q Methodology
Type A Behavior
Type B Behavior

Personality Change *JUL. 1966*
Postings: 279 GC: 120
SN Complete or partial alteration in personality (Note: Prior to Mar80, the use of this term was not restricted by a Scope Note)
BT Change
RT Attitude Change
Behavior Change
Personality
Personality Development

Personality Development *JUL. 1966*
Postings: 1,431 GC: 120
SN Progressive organization of the psychological traits unique to an individual, occurring as the result of maturation and learning from birth through adulthood (Note: Do not confuse with "Personality Change," which refers to a shift in the direction of this development)
BT Individual Development
RT Developmental Delays
Developmental Psychology
Emotional Development
Moral Development
Personality
Personality Assessment
Personality Change
Personality Measures
Personality Problems
Self Actualization
Social Development

Personality Measures *MAR. 1980*
Postings: 2,051 GC: 830
SN Procedures or devices used to obtain quantified descriptions of an individual's motivational and temperamental traits or behavior patterns
UF Personality Tests (1968 1980)
NT Self Concept Measures
BT Measures (Individuals)
RT Affective Measures
Association Measures
Attitude Measures
Behavior Rating Scales
Diagnostic Tests
Field Dependence Independence
Forced Choice Technique
Interest Inventories
Maturity Tests
Personality
Personality Assessment
Personality Development
Personality Studies
Personality Theories
Personality Traits
Psychological Evaluation
Psychological Testing
Q Methodology

= Two or more Descriptors are used to represent this term.
The term's main entry shows the appropriate coordination.

Semantic Differential
Social Desirability

Personality Problems   *JUL. 1966*
    Postings: 461   GC: 230
BT   Problems
RT   Adjustment (to Environment)
    Apathy
    Autism
    Behavior Disorders
    Behavior Problems
    Clinical Psychology
    Depression (Psychology)
    Emotional Disturbances
    Emotional Problems
    Mental Disorders
    Neurosis
    Paranoid Behavior
    Personality
    Personality Development
    Problem Children
    Psychiatry
    Psychopathology
    Self Destructive Behavior

Personality Rating
USE   Personality Assessment

Personality Studies   *JUL. 1966*
    Postings: 860   GC: 810
SN   Studies of the components of personal-
    ity and their causal factors (Note: As of
    Oct81, use as a minor Descriptor for
    examples of this kind of research—use
    as a major Descriptor only as the subject
    of a document)
BT   Psychological Studies
RT   Exceptional Child Research
    Personality
    Personality Assessment
    Personality Measures
    Teaching Styles

Personality Tests (1968 1980)
USE   Personality Measures

Personality Theories   *JUL. 1966*
    Postings: 1,078   GC: 810
BT   Theories
RT   Behavior Theories
    Personality
    Personality Measures

Personality Traits   *MAR. 1980*
    Postings: 4,157   GC: 120
SN   Specific motivational, temperamental, or
    emotional attributes that contribute to
    the total personality (Note: Prior to Mar80,
    the instruction "Personality Traits, USE
    Individual Characteristics" was carried
    in the Thesaurus)
UF   Adaptability (Personality) #
    Dispositional Characteristics
NT   Curiosity
    Dependency (Personality)
    Extraversion Introversion
    Locus of Control
    Mental Rigidity
    Resilience (Personality)
    Shyness
BT   Psychological Characteristics
RT   Anxiety
    Assertiveness
    Cognitive Style
    Compliance (Psychology)
    Conformity
    Congruence (Psychology)
    Creativity
    Crying
    Defense Mechanisms
    Dogmatism
    Egocentrism
    Humor
    Interpersonal Competence
    Jealousy
    Maturity (Individuals)
    Moods
    Objectivity

Persistence
Personality
Personality Measures
Resistance (Psychology)
Self Control
Self Esteem
Sexuality

Personalized Instruction
USE   Individualized Instruction

Personnel   *JUL. 1966*
    Postings: 875   GC: 630
NT   Administrators
    Agricultural Personnel
    Aircraft Pilots
    Bus Drivers
    Caseworkers
    Church Workers
    Clergy
    Consultants
    Designers
    Differentiated Staffs
    Dislocated Workers
    Editors
    Employees
    Equipment Manufacturers
    Evaluators
    Foreign Workers
    Government Employees
    Guidance Personnel
    Health Personnel
    Indigenous Personnel
    Industrial Personnel
    Institutional Personnel
    Interpreters
    Library Personnel
    Merchants
    Nonprofessional Personnel
    Older Workers
    Ombudsmen
    Paraprofessional Personnel
    Professional Personnel
    Programmers
    Reentry Workers
    Research Assistants
    Resident Advisers
    Resource Staff
    School Personnel
    Scientific Personnel
    Security Personnel
    Specialists
    Systems Analysts
    Trainers
BT   Groups
RT   Employed Parents
    Employed Women
    Employment
    Human Resources
    Industrial Psychology
    Labor Relations
    Office Management
    Personnel Data
    Personnel Directors
    Personnel Evaluation
    Personnel Integration
    Personnel Management
    Personnel Needs
    Personnel Policy
    Personnel Selection
    Recruitment
    Staff Development
    Staff Meetings
    Staff Orientation
    Staff Role
    Staff Utilization

Personnel Administrators
USE   Personnel Directors

Personnel Data   *JUL. 1966*
    Postings: 426   GC: 630
BT   Data
RT   Employment Experience
    Employment Qualifications
    Personnel

Profiles
Resumes (Personal)
Seniority
Tenure

Personnel Development
USE   Staff Development

Personnel Directors   *OCT. 1968*
    Postings: 239   GC: 640
UF   Personnel Administrators
    Personnel Managers
    School Personnel Directors #
BT   Administrators
RT   Personnel
    Personnel Management
    Personnel Policy
    Personnel Selection
    School Personnel

Personnel Discharge
USE   Dismissal (Personnel)

Personnel Dismissal
USE   Dismissal (Personnel)

Personnel Evaluation   *JUL. 1966*
    Postings: 2,419   GC: 630
SN   Judging employee value, competence,
    productivity, work quality, etc., using
    previously established objectives or stan-
    dards, for decisions concerning selec-
    tion, classification, placement, promo-
    tion, merit salary increases, etc. (Note:
    Do not confuse with "Vocational Evalua-
    tion")
UF   Employee Evaluation
    Performance Appraisal (Personnel)
    Staff Evaluation
    Worker Evaluation
NT   Administrator Evaluation
    Counselor Evaluation
    Faculty Evaluation
    Teacher Evaluation
BT   Evaluation
RT   Alternative Assessment
    Assessment Centers (Personnel)
    Competence
    Dismissal (Personnel)
    Employment Qualifications
    Informal Assessment
    Job Performance
    Job Placement
    Job Skills
    Management by Objectives
    Merit Rating
    Occupational Tests
    Peer Evaluation
    Performance Based Assessment
    Personnel
    Personnel Management
    Personnel Selection
    Portfolios (Background Materials)
    Promotion (Occupational)
    Vocational Evaluation

Personnel Integration   *JUL. 1966*
    Postings: 124   GC: 540
SN   Process of balancing the racial, ethnic,
    or sexual composition of the employees
    or staff of an organization, business, or
    institution (Note: Use a more specific
    term if possible)
NT   Faculty Integration
    Teacher Integration
BT   Social Integration
RT   Affirmative Action
    Employment Practices
    Equal Opportunities (Jobs)
    Nontraditional Occupations
    Personnel
    Personnel Policy
    Racial Integration
    Sex Fairness
    Tokenism

Personnel Management   *FEB. 1970*
    Postings: 2,104   GC: 630
SN   Recruitment, selection, development, su-
    pervision, dismissal, etc., of employees
BT   Administration
RT   Employer Employee Relationship
    Employment Practices
    Industrial Psychology
    Office Management
    Personnel
    Personnel Directors
    Personnel Evaluation
    Personnel Needs
    Personnel Policy
    Personnel Selection
    Staff Utilization

Personnel Managers
USE   Personnel Directors

Personnel Needs   *JUL. 1966*
    Postings: 1,025   GC: 630
SN   Requirements for staff
BT   Labor Needs
RT   Employees
    Personnel
    Personnel Management
    Personnel Policy
    Personnel Selection
    Recruitment
    Resource Staff

Personnel Policy   *JUL. 1966*
    Postings: 3,358   GC: 630
SN   Governing principles that serve as guide-
    lines or rules for decision-making and
    action concerning employees
BT   Policy
RT   Affirmative Action
    Comparable Worth
    Conflict of Interest
    Contracts
    Dismissal (Personnel)
    Dress Codes
    Early Retirement
    Employee Absenteeism
    Employee Assistance Programs
    Employment Practices
    Financial Exigency
    Fringe Benefits
    Job Layoff
    Job Security
    Job Sharing
    Leaves of Absence
    Loyalty Oaths
    Mandatory Retirement
    Merit Pay
    Occupational Segregation
    Older Workers
    Outplacement Services (Employment)
    Overtime
    Personnel
    Personnel Directors
    Personnel Integration
    Personnel Management
    Personnel Needs
    Personnel Selection
    Premium Pay
    Reduction in Force
    Released Time
    Retirement Benefits
    Salary Wage Differentials
    Scope of Bargaining
    Seniority
    Tenure

Personnel Recruitment
USE   Recruitment

Personnel Role
USE   Staff Role

Personnel Selection   *JUL. 1966*
    Postings: 2,291   GC: 630
UF   Hiring (Personnel)
NT   Administrator Selection
    Counselor Selection
    Teacher Selection

= Two or more Descriptors are used to represent this term.
The term's main entry shows the appropriate coordination.

BT   Selection
RT   Affirmative Action
       Assessment Centers (Personnel)
       Competitive Selection
       Eligibility
       Employment Interviews
       Labor Market
       Personnel
       Personnel Directors
       Personnel Evaluation
       Personnel Management
       Personnel Needs
       Personnel Policy
       Portfolios (Background Materials)
       Recruitment
       Resumes (Personal)
       Search Committees (Personnel)

Personnel Tests
USE   Occupational Tests

Perspective Taking   *OCT. 1977*
       Postings: 991   GC: 120
SN   Perceiving physical, social, or emotional
       situations from a point of view other than
       one's own (Note: Do not confuse with
       "Role Playing")
UF   Role Taking
RT   Consciousness Raising
       Egocentrism
       Emotional Development
       Empathy
       Extraversion Introversion
       Identification (Psychology)
       Interpersonal Relationship
       Psychological Patterns
       Role Perception
       Role Playing
       Self Concept
       Social Cognition
       Social Development

Perspective Transformation
USE   Transformative Learning

Persuasive Discourse   *APR. 1970*
       Postings: 3,992   GC: 450
SN   Oral or written effort to win others over
       to an opinion or action
UF   Argumentation
       Forensics
BT   Rhetoric
RT   Advertising
       Agenda Setting
       Communication (Thought Transfer)
       Credibility
       Debate
       Debate Format
       Editorials
       Motivation Techniques
       Political Campaigns
       Propaganda
       Public Speaking
       Resistance (Psychology)
       Rhetorical Criticism
       Rhetorical Invention
       Rhetorical Theory
       Salesmanship
       Speech
       Speech Communication
       Speeches
       Verbal Communication
       Writing (Composition)

Pest Control
USE   Pests

Pesticides   *JUL. 1966*
       Postings: 630   GC: 410
UF   Rodenticides (1968 1980)
NT   Herbicides
       Insecticides
BT   Poisons
RT   Agricultural Chemical Occupations
       Agricultural Production
       Agricultural Supplies
       Agronomy
       Disease Control

       Fungi
       Pests
       Rats

Pests   *AUG. 1982*
       Postings: 127   GC: 410
SN   Annoying or detrimental animals and
       plants
UF   Pest Control
RT   Agricultural Production
       Animals
       Disease Control
       Diseases
       Ecology
       Entomology
       Environmental Standards
       Health
       Microbiology
       Pesticides
       Physical Health
       Plants (Botany)
       Rats
       Sanitation
       Weeds

Petrography
USE   Petrology

Petroleum (Oil and Gas)
USE   Fossil Fuels
AND   Oil

Petroleum (Oil)
USE   Oil

Petroleum Industry   *JUN. 1970*
       Postings: 235   GC: 650
BT   Industry
RT   Chemical Engineering
       Chemical Industry
       Energy Occupations
       Fossil Fuels
       Gasoline
       Lubricants
       Natural Gas
       Oil

Petrology   *JAN. 1993*
       Postings: 47   GC: 490
SN   The branch of geology concerned with
       the origin, occurrence, structure, classi-
       fication, and history of rocks
UF   Petrography
       Rock Studies
BT   Geology
RT   Chemistry
       Crystallography
       Geophysics
       Mineralogy
       Physical Geography
       Soil Science

Pets   *MAR. 1996*
       Postings: 116   GC: 490
SN   Animals kept for pleasure and compan-
       ionship (Note: Coordinate with individ-
       ual animals as appropriate, e.g., Descrip-
       tors "Birds," "Horses" or Identifiers
       "Cats," "Dogs")
UF   Companion Animals
BT   Animals
RT   Animal Facilities
       Veterinary Medicine

Peul
USE   Fulani

Pharmaceutical Education   *AUG. 1977*
       Postings: 1,132   GC: 210
SN   Formal study of the art and science of
       preparing and dispensing drugs and medi-
       cine
BT   Medical Education
RT   Clinical Experience
       Drug Education

       Drug Therapy
       Nursing Education
       Pharmacists
       Pharmacy

Pharmacists   *AUG. 1968*
       Postings: 393   GC: 210
UF   Druggists
BT   Health Personnel
       Professional Personnel
RT   Medical Associations
       Medical Services
       Pharmaceutical Education
       Pharmacy

Pharmacology   *SEP. 1980*
       Postings: 301   GC: 210
SN   The science of the nature and properties
       of drugs, particularly their actions or
       effects (Note: See also "Pharmacy")
BT   Medicine
RT   Biotechnology
       Drug Abuse
       Drug Addiction
       Drug Use
       Pharmacy
       Toxicology

Pharmacy   *DEC. 1976*
       Postings: 408   GC: 210
SN   The art or practice of preparing, preserv-
       ing, compounding, and dispensing drugs
       (Note: See also "Pharmacology")
BT   Medicine
RT   Drug Legislation
       Drug Therapy
       Medical Services
       Pharmaceutical Education
       Pharmacists
       Pharmacology

Phenomenology   *OCT. 1984*
       Postings: 338   GC: 430
SN   Study of reality in terms of individual
       perceptions or conscious experiences at
       any moment, without external interpre-
       tation and judgment
BT   Philosophy
RT   Cognitive Style
       Critical Theory
       Epistemology
       Existentialism
       Gestalt Therapy
       Hermeneutics
       Individualism
       Perception
       Personality
       Psychological Characteristics
       Self Concept
       Socialization

Pheul
USE   Fulani

Philanthropic Foundations   *MAR. 1980*
       Postings: 855   GC: 620
SN   Trusts or corporations created for chari-
       table purposes that provide grants of
       funds to finance research, services, fa-
       cilities, equipment, or library resources
       (Note: Prior to Mar80, this concept was
       often indexed under "Foundation Pro-
       grams," which was not scoped)
UF   Educational Foundations
       Foundations (Institutions)
BT   Institutions
RT   Donors
       Endowment Funds
       Grants
       Library Funding
       Nonprofit Organizations
       Private Financial Support
       Trusts (Financial)

Philanthropy
USE   Private Financial Support

Philology
USE   Linguistics

Philosophy   *JUL. 1966*
       Postings: 3,241   GC: 430
SN   Critical examination of the grounds for
       fundamental beliefs and analysis of the
       basic concepts, doctrines, or practices
       that express such beliefs
NT   Aesthetics
       Educational Philosophy
       Epistemology
       Ethics
       Existentialism
       Hermeneutics
       Humanism
       Logic
       Marxism
       Phenomenology
       Platonism
       Semiotics
       World Views
BT   Humanities
RT   Antithesis
       Buddhism
       Christianity
       Confucianism
       Holistic Approach
       Individualism
       Islam
       Judaism
       Literature
       Modernism
       Mysticism
       Naturalism
       Objectivity
       Paradox
       Postmodernism
       Realism
       Religion
       Romanticism
       Spirituality
       Taoism
       Traditionalism

Philosophy of Life
USE   World Views

Phonathons   *MAY 1998*
       Postings: 42   GC: 620
SN   Fund raising or other solicitation activi-
       ties using the telephone
UF   Telephone Solicitation Programs
RT   Donors
       Fund Raising
       Private Financial Support
       Telephone Communications Systems

Phoneme Grapheme Correspondence
                                    JUL. 1973
       Postings: 614   GC: 450
SN   Relationship between speech sound (pho-
       neme) and written symbol (grapheme)
UF   Grapheme Phoneme Correspondence
       Letter Sound Correspondence
BT   Language Patterns
RT   Contrastive Linguistics
       Decoding (Reading)
       Graphemes
       Invented Spelling
       Linguistics
       Miscue Analysis
       Phonemes
       Phonemics
       Phonics
       Phonology
       Reading
       Spelling
       Written Language

Phonemes   *JUL. 1966*
       Postings: 1,013   GC: 450
SN   The smallest units of speech that distin-
       guish one utterance from another in a
       given language—for example, "p" in "pat"
       and "b" in "bat" represent two English
       phonemes—"p" in "pat" and "p" in
       "spat" represent the same phoneme,
       despite their difference in sound, be-

cause this difference is never the only distinguishing feature between two words in English
UF   Phonological Units (1966 1980)
NT   Consonants
      Vowels
BT   Phonemics
RT   Distinctive Features (Language)
      Graphemes
      Intonation
      Language Typology
      Letters (Alphabet)
      Morphemes
      Morphophonemics
      Phoneme Grapheme Correspondence
      Phonemic Alphabets
      Phonics
      Phonology
      Suprasegmentals
      Syllables

Phonemic Alphabets   *JUL. 1966*
     Postings: 85   GC: 450
BT   Alphabets
RT   Consonants
      Phonemes
      Phonemics
      Phonics

Phonemics   *JUL. 1966*
     Postings: 438   GC: 450
SN   The study of phonemes
NT   Phonemes
BT   Phonology
RT   Contrastive Linguistics
      Descriptive Linguistics
      Diachronic Linguistics
      Generative Phonology
      Language Patterns
      Linguistics
      Morphophonemics
      Phoneme Grapheme Correspondence
      Phonemic Alphabets
      Phonetics
      Speech

Phonetic Analysis   *JUL. 1966*
     Postings: 277   GC: 450
BT   Evaluation Methods
RT   Error Analysis (Language)
      Language Research
      Miscue Analysis
      Phonetics
      Phonics

Phonetic Transcription   *JUL. 1966*
     Postings: 184   GC: 450
SN   Representation of speech sounds in phonetic symbols
BT   Orthographic Symbols
RT   Alphabets
      Diacritical Marking
      Phonetics
      Phonology
      Written Language

Phonetics   *JUL. 1966*
     Postings: 1,343   GC: 450
SN   Study and classification of speech sounds, including their production, transmission, and perception
NT   Acoustic Phonetics
      Phonics
BT   Phonology
RT   Articulation (Speech)
      Consonants
      Diacritical Marking
      Distinctive Features (Language)
      Generative Phonology
      Graphemes
      Morphophonemics
      Phonemics
      Phonetic Analysis
      Phonetic Transcription
      Speech
      Stress (Phonology)
      Vowels

Phonic Method
USE   Phonics

Phonics   *JUL. 1966*
     Postings: 1,494   GC: 460
SN   The study of sound-letter relationships in reading and spelling, and the use of this knowledge in recognizing and pronouncing words
UF   Phonic Method
BT   Phonetics
RT   Aural Learning
      Basal Reading
      Beginning Reading
      Decoding (Reading)
      Initial Teaching Alphabet
      Invented Spelling
      Phoneme Grapheme Correspondence
      Phonemes
      Phonemic Alphabets
      Phonetic Analysis
      Phonology
      Reading Instruction
      Reading Skills
      Spelling
      Word Study Skills

Phonograph Record Lists
USE   Discographies

Phonograph Records (1966 1980)
USE   Audiodisks

Phonological Borrowing
USE   Linguistic Borrowing

Phonological Units (1966 1980)
USE   Phonemes

Phonology   *JUL. 1966*
     Postings: 3,750   GC: 450
SN   Study of the ways in which speech sounds form systems and patterns in language
NT   Generative Phonology
      Phonemics
      Phonetics
      Suprasegmentals
      Syllables
BT   Linguistics
RT   Artificial Speech
      Code Switching (Language)
      Componential Analysis
      Descriptive Linguistics
      Diachronic Linguistics
      Distinctive Features (Language)
      Error Analysis (Language)
      Intonation
      Invented Spelling
      Kernel Sentences
      Language Typology
      Linguistic Borrowing
      Morphology (Languages)
      Morphophonemics
      Phoneme Grapheme Correspondence
      Phonemes
      Phonetic Transcription
      Phonics
      Rhyme
      Sound Spectrographs
      Speech
      Stress (Phonology)
      Surface Structure
      Vowels

Phonotape Recordings (1966 1978)
USE   Audiotape Recordings

Photochemical Reactions   *JAN. 1970*
     Postings: 115   GC: 490
SN   Chemical reactions influenced or initiated by light
UF   Photochemistry
NT   Photosynthesis
BT   Chemical Reactions
RT   Chemistry
      Electrochemistry

Photochemistry
USE   Photochemical Reactions

Photocomposition   *OCT. 1969*
     Postings: 150   GC: 710
SN   Automatic selection and projection onto photographic film of alphabetic characters, figures, punctuation marks, and other symbols in the correct sequence to produce readable text ready for the various printing processes (Note: Before Mar80, the use of this term was not restricted by a Scope Note)
BT   Production Techniques
RT   Computer Graphics
      Graphic Arts
      Photography
      Printing
      Publications
      Reprography

Photocopying
USE   Reprography

Photographic Equipment   *AUG. 1971*
     Postings: 352   GC: 910
UF   Cameras
      Film (Cameras)
BT   Equipment
      Visual Aids
RT   Audio Equipment
      Audiovisual Aids
      Film Production
      Photography
      Projection Equipment
      Video Equipment

Photographic Memory
USE   Eidetic Imagery

Photographs   *JUL. 1966*
     Postings: 1,249   GC: 720
BT   Visual Aids
RT   Art Products
      Audiovisual Aids
      Captions
      Films
      Illustrations
      Nonprint Media
      Photography
      Photojournalism

Photography   *JUL. 1966*
     Postings: 1,424   GC: 420
SN   Art or process of producing images on sensitized surfaces by the action of light or other radiant energy
NT   Holography
BT   Visual Arts
RT   Film Production
      Film Study
      Journalism
      Layout (Publications)
      Magnification Methods
      Photocomposition
      Photographic Equipment
      Photographs
      Photojournalism
      Production Techniques
      Reprography
      Special Effects

Photojournalism   *DEC. 1985*
     Postings: 216   GC: 720
SN   The art or profession of using still photography or other pictorial copy as the primary means of presenting information on current affairs
UF   Pictorial Journalism
BT   Journalism
RT   Captions
      Illustrations
      Layout (Publications)
      News Media
      News Reporting
      Newspapers
      Photographs

Photography
Publications

Photometric Brightness
USE   Luminescence

Photoreproduction
USE   Reprography

Photosynthesis   *AUG. 1970*
     Postings: 125   GC: 490
BT   Photochemical Reactions
RT   Botany
      Ecology
      Light
      Metabolism
      Plant Growth
      Plants (Botany)

Phrase Structure   *JUL. 1966*
     Postings: 833   GC: 450
UF   Constituent Structure
BT   Syntax
RT   Conjunctions
      Context Free Grammar
      Deep Structure
      Form Classes (Languages)
      Kernel Sentences
      Nouns
      Prepositions
      Pronouns
      Suprasegmentals
      Surface Structure
      Transformational Generative Grammar
      Word Order

Physical Activities   *JUL. 1966*
     Postings: 1,431   GC: 470
NT   Athletics
      Bicycling
      Dance
      Exercise
      Horseback Riding
      Lifting
      Running
      Underwater Diving
      Walking
BT   Activities
RT   Adapted Physical Education
      Health Activities
      Movement Education
      Physical Education
      Physical Recreation Programs
      Playground Activities
      Recreational Activities

Physical Activity Level   *MAR. 1978*
     Postings: 558   GC: 120
SN   Extent of motor behavior manifested by an individual or group
UF   Activity Level (Motor Behavior)
BT   Behavior
RT   Biomechanics
      Exercise Physiology
      Health Behavior
      Human Body
      Hyperactivity
      Motor Development
      Motor Reactions
      Physical Development
      Physiology

Physical Attractiveness   *JUN. 1988*
     Postings: 201   GC: 120
SN   (Note: See also the Identifier "Facial Attractiveness")
BT   Interpersonal Attraction
RT   Body Image
      Physical Characteristics

Physical Characteristics   *JUL. 1966*
     Postings: 832   GC: 120
NT   Body Composition
      Body Height
      Body Weight
      Lateral Dominance

\# = Two or more Descriptors are used to represent this term.
The term's main entry shows the appropriate coordination.

Muscular Strength
Neurological Organization
Race
Sex
BT   Individual Characteristics
RT   Chronological Age
Downs Syndrome
Maturity (Individuals)
Physical Attractiveness
Physical Development
Physical Disabilities
Physical Health
Puberty
Racial Differences
Sex Differences

Physical Chemistry   *APR. 1990*
Postings: 100   GC: 490
SN   Study of the relationship between the physical properties of substances and their chemical properties
NT   Electrochemistry
BT   Chemistry
RT   Atomic Structure
Chemical Engineering
Chemical Equilibrium
Crystallography
Geochemistry
Matter
Molecular Structure
Physics
Spectroscopy
Stereochemistry
Thermodynamics

Physical Conditioning
USE   Physical Fitness

Physical Design Needs (1968 1980)
USE   Design Requirements

Physical Development   *JUL. 1966*
Postings: 1,109   GC: 120
NT   Motor Development
BT   Individual Development
RT   Body Composition
Body Height
Body Weight
Chronological Age
Developmental Delays
Developmental Stages
Lateral Dominance
Menstruation
Muscular Strength
Neurological Organization
Perceptual Development
Physical Activity Level
Physical Characteristics
Physical Disabilities
Physical Health
Prenatal Influences
Puberty
School Readiness

Physical Disabilities   *MAR. 1980*
Postings: 3,485   GC: 220
SN   Disorders that result in significantly reduced bodily function, mobility, or endurance (Note: Avoid misindexing "Hearing Impairments" or "Visual Impairments" with this term)
UF   Crippled Children (1968 1980)
Orthopedically Handicapped (1968 1980)
Physical Handicaps (1966 1980)
Physically Handicapped (1966 1980)
NT   Amputations
Cleft Palate
Heart Disorders
Neurological Impairments
BT   Disabilities
RT   Mental Disorders
Mobility Aids
Pain
Physical Characteristics
Physical Development
Physical Health
Physical Mobility
Physical Therapy

Prostheses
Rehabilitation
Special Health Problems
Travel Training
Wheelchairs

Physical Divisions (Geographic)   *JUL. 1966*
Postings: 56   GC: 550
BT   Geographic Regions
RT   Geography
Physical Environment
Physical Geography
Political Divisions (Geographic)

Physical Education   *JUL. 1966*
Postings: 5,308   GC: 470
NT   Adapted Physical Education
Movement Education
BT   Education
RT   Athletic Coaches
Athletic Equipment
Athletic Fields
Athletics
College Athletics
Dance Education
Exercise Physiology
Experiential Learning
Health Promotion
Health Related Fitness
Muscular Strength
Physical Activities
Physical Education Facilities
Physical Education Teachers
Physical Fitness
Physical Fitness Tests
Physical Recreation Programs
Recreational Activities
Running
School Health Services
Sport Psychology
Sports Medicine
Sportsmanship
Womens Athletics

Physical Education Facilities   *JUL. 1966*
Postings: 347   GC: 920
BT   Educational Facilities
RT   Athletic Equipment
Athletic Fields
Athletics
Field Houses
Gymnasiums
Locker Rooms
Parks
Physical Education
Playgrounds
Recreational Facilities
Swimming Pools

Physical Education Teachers   *NOV. 1982*
Postings: 713   GC: 360
UF   Physical Educators
BT   Teachers
RT   Athletic Coaches
Athletics
Physical Education

Physical Educators
USE   Physical Education Teachers

Physical Environment   *JUL. 1966*
Postings: 1,788   GC: 920
NT   Acoustical Environment
Built Environment
Climate
Thermal Environment
Visual Environment
Wilderness
BT   Environment
RT   Architectural Research
Climate Change
Climate Control
Conservation (Environment)
Crowding
Depleted Resources
Design Requirements
Earth Science
Endangered Species

Environmental Influences
Environmental Research
Environmental Standards
Gravity (Physics)
Habitats
Hazardous Materials
Human Factors Engineering
Interior Design
Interior Space
Natural Resources
Physical Divisions (Geographic)
Poisons
Pollution
Pressure (Physics)
Quality of Life
Radiation
Sanitation
Sustainable Development
Water
Water Quality
Weather
Wildlife
Wind (Meteorology)

Physical Examinations   *JUL. 1966*
Postings: 332   GC: 210
SN   Medical inspections of individuals to determine their physical condition, including the detection of present or potential dysfunction
UF   Physical Tests
BT   Medical Evaluation
RT   Auditory Tests
Clinical Diagnosis
Diagnostic Tests
Drug Use Testing
Physical Fitness Tests
Physical Health
Screening Tests
Vision Tests

Physical Exercise
USE   Exercise

Physical Facilities (1966 1980)
USE   Facilities

Physical Fitness   *JUL. 1966*
Postings: 2,160   GC: 210
UF   Physical Conditioning
Physical Performance
NT   Health Related Fitness
BT   Physical Health
RT   Aerobics
Athletic Equipment
Athletics
Body Composition
Calisthenics
Child Health
Exercise
Fatigue (Biology)
Heart Rate
Muscular Strength
Physical Education
Physical Fitness Tests
Physical Recreation Programs
Plyometrics
Running
Sport Psychology
Sports Medicine
Walking
Wellness

Physical Fitness Tests   *JUN. 1993*
Postings: 42   GC: 830
SN   Tests designed to measure one or more health-related fitness components, such as cardiorespiratory capacity, body composition, muscular strength and endurance, and low back/hamstring flexibility
BT   Tests
RT   Health Related Fitness
Performance Tests
Physical Education
Physical Examinations
Physical Fitness

Physical Geography   *JUL. 1966*
Postings: 597   GC: 490
BT   Earth Science
Geography
RT   Geographic Distribution
Geographic Location
Geographic Regions
Geology
Groundwater
Hydrology
Mineralogy
Oceanography
Petrology
Physical Divisions (Geographic)
Plate Tectonics
Rivers
Seismology
Volcanoes
Water
Wind (Meteorology)

Physical Handicaps (1966 1980)
USE   Physical Disabilities

Physical Health   *JUL. 1966*
Postings: 1,981   GC: 210
NT   Dental Health
Physical Fitness
BT   Health
RT   Acquired Immune Deficiency Syndrome
Alcoholism
Allergy
Anemia
Anorexia Nervosa
Asbestos
Asthma
Bulimia
Cancer
Child Health
Communicable Diseases
Cystic Fibrosis
Diabetes
Diseases
Drinking Water
Eating Disorders
Eating Habits
Exercise Physiology
Failure to Thrive
Hazardous Materials
Heart Disorders
Heart Rate
Hygiene
Hypertension
Lead Poisoning
Medicine
Menstruation
Midlife Transitions
Nutrition
Obesity
Occupational Diseases
Pain
Pests
Physical Characteristics
Physical Development
Physical Disabilities
Physical Examinations
Physical Therapy
Poisoning
Pollution
Psychosomatic Disorders
Public Health
Rubella
Sanitary Facilities
Sanitation
Seizures
Sickle Cell Anemia
Smoking
Special Health Problems
Substance Abuse
Sudden Infant Death Syndrome
Surgery
Tissue Donors
Venereal Diseases
Ventilation
Wellness

Physical Mobility   *MAR. 1980*
Postings: 260   GC: 220
SN   Individual's ability to move within his or

= Two or more Descriptors are used to represent this term.
The term's main entry shows the appropriate coordination.

her immediate environment (Note: For demographic or geographic mobility, use "Migration"—prior to Mar80, "Architectural Barriers" was frequently used to index this concept)
NT   Visually Impaired Mobility
BT   Mobility
RT   Accessibility (for Disabled)
     Architecture
     Building Design
     Campus Planning
     Crowding
     Design Requirements
     Educational Facilities Design
     Educational Facilities Planning
     Frail Elderly
     Mobility Aids
     Older Adults
     Physical Disabilities
     Space Utilization
     Structural Elements (Construction)
     Travel Training
     Walking
     Wheelchairs

Physical Optics
USE   Optics

Physical Performance
USE   Physical Fitness

Physical Pressure
USE   Pressure (Physics)

Physical Recreation Programs   *JUL. 1966*
     Postings: 228   GC: 470
BT   Recreational Programs
RT   Athletic Equipment
     Athletic Fields
     Athletics
     Field Houses
     Gymnasiums
     Physical Activities
     Physical Education
     Physical Fitness
     Playground Activities
     School Health Services
     Sports Medicine

Physical Sciences   *JUL. 1966*
     Postings: 2,991   GC: 490
NT   Astronomy
     Chemistry
     Crystallography
     Earth Science
     Physics
     Spectroscopy
BT   Natural Sciences
RT   Aerospace Technology
     Atomic Structure
     Biochemistry
     Biophysics
     Chemical Bonding
     Conservation Education
     Engineering Technology
     Molecular Structure
     Nuclear Technology
     Radiation Biology
     Space Sciences

Physical Self Concept
USE   Body Image

Physical Strength
USE   Muscular Strength

Physical Tests
USE   Physical Examinations

Physical Therapists   *JUL. 1966*
     Postings: 94   GC: 210
BT   Therapists
RT   Physical Therapy
     Physical Therapy Aides

Physical Therapy   *JUL. 1966*
     Postings: 373   GC: 210
SN   Treatment of disability, injury, or disease through such means as exercise, massage, body manipulation, heat, light, water, etc.
BT   Therapy
RT   Allied Health Occupations
     Amputations
     Dance Therapy
     Medical Services
     Occupational Therapy
     Osteopathy
     Physical Disabilities
     Physical Health
     Physical Therapists
     Physical Therapy Aides
     Rehabilitation
     Respiratory Therapy
     Sports Medicine
     Therapeutic Recreation

Physical Therapy Aides   *JUL. 1969*
     Postings: 54   GC: 210
UF   Physical Therapy Attendants
BT   Allied Health Personnel
RT   Physical Therapists
     Physical Therapy

Physical Therapy Attendants
USE   Physical Therapy Aides

Physically Handicapped (1966 1980)
USE   Physical Disabilities

Physician Patient Relationship   *OCT. 1979*
     Postings: 755   GC: 210
SN   Relationship between physicians and persons in their care that affects mutual trust and understanding
UF   Doctor Patient Relationship
     Patient Physician Relationship
BT   Interpersonal Relationship
RT   Counselor Client Relationship
     Helping Relationship
     Medical Care Evaluation
     Medical Evaluation
     Medical Services
     Patient Education
     Patients
     Physicians
     Psychiatric Services
     Psychiatrists
     Therapeutic Environment

Physicians   *JUL. 1966*
     Postings: 2,480   GC: 210
UF   Medical Doctors
     Preceptors (Medicine) #
NT   Foreign Medical Graduates
     Psychiatrists
BT   Health Personnel
     Professional Personnel
RT   Graduate Medical Education
     Graduate Medical Students
     Hospital Personnel
     Medical Associations
     Medical Consultants
     Medical Services
     Medical Vocabulary
     Medicine
     Physician Patient Relationship
     Physicians Assistants

Physicians Assistants   *APR. 1972*
     Postings: 164   GC: 210
SN   Highly trained paraprofessionals who, under physicians' supervision, perform many health care activities usually carried out only by physicians
BT   Allied Health Personnel
RT   Medical Services
     Nurse Practitioners
     Physicians

Physicians in Training
USE   Graduate Medical Students

Physics   *JUL. 1966*
     Postings: 9,743   GC: 490
UF   Physics Curriculum (1966 1980) #
     Physics Experiments (1966 1980) #
     Physics Instruction (1966 1980) #
     Physics Teachers (1967 1980) #
NT   Biophysics
     Electronics
     Mechanics (Physics)
     Nuclear Physics
     Optics
     Thermodynamics
BT   Physical Sciences
RT   Acceleration (Physics)
     Acoustics
     Atomic Structure
     Atomic Theory
     Chaos Theory
     Crystallography
     Diffusion (Physics)
     Earth Science
     Electricity
     Energy
     Force
     Geophysics
     Gravity (Physics)
     Kinetic Molecular Theory
     Lasers
     Light
     Luminescence
     Magnets
     Matter
     Metallurgical Technicians
     Metallurgy
     Meteorology
     Molecular Structure
     Motion
     Physical Chemistry
     Pressure (Physics)
     Radiation
     Radiation Biology
     Radioisotopes
     Radiology
     Relativity
     Scientific Research
     Spectroscopy
     Vectors (Mathematics)
     Velocity

Physics Curriculum (1966 1980)
USE   Physics
AND   Science Curriculum

Physics Experiments (1966 1980)
USE   Physics
AND   Science Experiments

Physics Instruction (1966 1980)
USE   Physics
AND   Science Instruction

Physics Teachers (1967 1980)
USE   Physics
AND   Science Teachers

Physiological Chemistry
USE   Biochemistry

Physiological Psychology
USE   Psychophysiology

Physiology   *JUL. 1966*
     Postings: 2,047   GC: 490
NT   Exercise Physiology
     Psychophysiology
BT   Biological Sciences
RT   Allergy
     Anatomy
     Asthma
     Biochemistry
     Biofeedback
     Biology
     Biomechanics
     Biophysics
     Birth
     Blood Circulation
     Body Composition
     Cardiovascular System
     Culturing Techniques
     Cytology
     Death
     Diabetes
     Embryology
     Enzymes
     Evolution
     Heart Rate
     Human Body
     Hygiene
     Medicine
     Menstruation
     Metabolism
     Microbiology
     Molecular Biology
     Motor Reactions
     Muscular System
     Musculoskeletal System
     Neurological Organization
     Neurology
     Nucleic Acids
     Nutrition
     Pathology
     Perception
     Physical Activity Level
     Puberty
     Radiation Biology
     Relaxation Training
     Rh Factors
     Scientific Research
     Sedatives
     Sensory Deprivation
     Skeletal System
     Stimulants
     Stress Variables
     Toxicology
     Zoology

Piagetian Stages
USE   Developmental Stages
AND   Piagetian Theory

Piagetian Tasks
USE   Developmental Tasks
AND   Piagetian Theory

Piagetian Theory   *APR. 1986*
     Postings: 1,225   GC: 810
SN   Theory of children's intellectual development (postulated by Swiss developmental psychologist Jean Piaget) that describes a universal sequence of four distinct mental stages—sensorimotor, preoperational thought, concrete operations, and formal operations—through which children progress from birth to maturity
UF   Piagetian Stages #
     Piagetian Tasks #
BT   Theories
RT   Child Development
     Cognitive Development
     Cognitive Processes
     Cognitive Psychology
     Concept Formation
     Developmental Psychology
     Developmental Stages
     Epistemology
     Formal Operations
     Intellectual Development
     Learning Theories
     Logical Thinking

Pictorial Journalism
USE   Photojournalism

Pictorial Stimuli   *JUL. 1966*
     Postings: 1,374   GC: 110
BT   Visual Stimuli
RT   Electrical Stimuli
     Projective Measures
     Tachistoscopes
     Visual Learning
     Visual Measures

Pictorial Tests
USE   Visual Measures

= Two or more Descriptors are used to represent this term.
The term's main entry shows the appropriate coordination.

Picture Books   *SEP. 1980*
Postings: 916   GC: 720
SN   Books (usually but not necessarily for children) in which illustrations are essential to the presentation, either coordinated closely with the text or used alone without text
BT   Books
RT   Childrens Literature
     Illustrations

Pidgins   *JUL. 1966*
Postings: 192   GC: 440
SN   Simplified forms of speech, usually mixtures of two or more languages, that have rudimentary grammar and vocabulary and are used for communication between groups speaking different languages
BT   Language Variation
     Languages
RT   Creoles
     Linguistic Borrowing

Pilipino
USE   Tagalog

Pilot Programs
USE   Pilot Projects

Pilot Projects   *JUL. 1966*
Postings: 3,324   GC: 810
SN   Organized exploratory or trial undertakings conducted as preparation for larger, more involved programs (Note: As of Oct81, use as a minor Descriptor for examples of pilot projects—use as a major Descriptor only as the subject of a document)
UF   Pilot Programs
BT   Programs
RT   Adoption (Ideas)
     Experimental Programs
     Feasibility Studies
     Research
     Research Methodology

Pilot Training
USE   Flight Training

Ping Pong
USE   Table Tennis

Pipe Fitting
USE   Plumbing

Place of Residence   *JAN. 1978*
Postings: 825   GC: 550
SN   Locality of habitation including both site (geographic region) and type (housing)
UF   Residential Location
RT   Community
     Community Characteristics
     Cultural Traits
     Demography
     Environment
     Family Mobility
     Geographic Location
     Geographic Regions
     Housing
     Immigration
     In State Students
     Land Settlement
     Migration
     Neighborhoods
     Out of State Students
     Population Distribution
     Relocation
     Residence Requirements
     Residential Patterns
     Rural Urban Differences
     Social Characteristics

Place Value   *AUG. 1986*
Postings: 89   GC: 480
SN   The value of a position in a number, e.g., the decimal 37 has three tens and seven ones
BT   Number Concepts
RT   Arithmetic
     Numbers

Placement   *JUL. 1966*
Postings: 988   GC: 520
NT   Advanced Placement
     Age Grade Placement
     Job Placement
     Mainstreaming
     Student Placement
RT   Admission (School)
     Adoption
     Foster Family
     Referral
     Screening Tests

Plagiarism   *JAN. 1969*
Postings: 277   GC: 530
BT   Stealing
RT   Cheating
     Codes of Ethics
     Copyrights
     Discipline Problems
     Ethics
     Fraud
     Intellectual Property
     Moral Issues
     Writing (Composition)

Planar Area
USE   Area

Plane Geometry   *JUL. 1966*
Postings: 115   GC: 480
NT   Polygons
BT   Geometry
RT   Analytic Geometry
     Area
     Solid Geometry

Planetariums   *AUG. 1968*
Postings: 125   GC: 920
BT   Facilities
RT   Astronomy
     Earth Science
     Educational Facilities
     Lunar Research
     Recreational Facilities
     Science Facilities
     Science Laboratories
     Science Teaching Centers
     Scientific Research
     Solar System
     Space Exploration
     Space Sciences
     Stars

Planetary Exploration
USE   Space Exploration

Planned Communities   *MAR. 1980*
Postings: 52   GC: 550
UF   Planned Community (1966 1980)
BT   Community
RT   Housing
     Planning
     Urban Renewal

Planned Community (1966 1980)
USE   Planned Communities

Planning   *JUL. 1966*
Postings: 5,197   GC: 110
SN   The process of determining objectives and the means (activities, procedures, resources, etc.) for attaining them (Note: Use a more specific term if possible)
UF   Administrative Planning
     Organizational Plans

NT   Budgeting
     Career Planning
     Color Planning
     Community Planning
     Cooperative Planning
     Desegregation Plans
     Educational Planning
     Estate Planning
     Facility Planning
     Family Planning
     Language Planning
     Library Planning
     Long Range Planning
     Policy Formation
     Regional Planning
     Scheduling
     Social Planning
     Statewide Planning
     Strategic Planning
     Urban Planning
RT   Administration
     Building Plans
     Committees
     Coordination
     Critical Path Method
     Decision Support Systems
     Delphi Technique
     Design
     Development
     Flow Charts
     Futures (of Society)
     Guidelines
     Holistic Approach
     Lesson Plans
     Markov Processes
     Master Plans
     Needs Assessment
     Operations Research
     Organization
     Organizational Objectives
     Planned Communities
     Planning Commissions
     Specifications
     Systems Approach
     Time Management
     Zoning

Planning Commissions   *JUL. 1966*
Postings: 281   GC: 610
SN   Elected or appointed committees that formulate courses of action based on community, state, or national needs
UF   City Wide Commissions (1966 1980) #
BT   Public Agencies
RT   Advisory Committees
     Blue Ribbon Commissions
     Community Planning
     Long Range Planning
     Master Plans
     Planning
     Regional Planning
     Social Planning
     Statewide Planning
     Strategic Planning
     Urban Planning

Planning Meetings (1966 1980)
USE   Meetings

Plant Biology
USE   Botany

Plant Diseases
USE   Plant Pathology

Plant Growth   *JUL. 1966*
Postings: 407   GC: 410
BT   Development
RT   Agricultural Production
     Agronomy
     Biochemistry
     Botany
     Embryology
     Fertilizers
     Gardening
     Gardens
     Greenhouses
     Herbicides

     Horticulture
     Insecticides
     Ornamental Horticulture
     Photosynthesis
     Plant Pathology
     Plants (Botany)
     Wildlife

Plant Identification   *JUL. 1966*
Postings: 222   GC: 410
BT   Identification
RT   Botany
     Floriculture
     Horticulture
     Landscaping
     Ornamental Horticulture
     Plants (Botany)

Plant Life
USE   Plants (Botany)

Plant Pathology   *JUL. 1966*
Postings: 89   GC: 410
UF   Plant Diseases
BT   Pathology
RT   Agronomy
     Botany
     Endangered Species
     Floriculture
     Herbicides
     Plant Growth
     Plants (Botany)

Plant Propagation   *JUL. 1966*
Postings: 162   GC: 410
RT   Botany
     Floriculture
     Gardening
     Grounds Keepers
     Horticulture
     Nursery Workers (Horticulture)
     Ornamental Horticulture
     Plants (Botany)

Plant Science (1967 1980)   *MAR. 1980*
Postings: 208   GC: 410
SN   Invalid Descriptor—used for both "Agronomy" and "Botany"—see those Descriptors for the concepts

Plantae
USE   Plants (Botany)

Planting (1966 1980)
USE   Horticulture

Plants (Botany)   *APR. 1990*
Postings: 422   GC: 490
SN   Nucleated multicellular organisms that contain chlorophyll and have rigid cell walls—some classifications include bacteria, unicellular algae, and/or fungi (Note: Use a more specific term if possible)
UF   Plant Life
     Plantae
NT   Field Crops
     Trees
     Weeds
RT   Agronomy
     Bacteria
     Botany
     Endangered Species
     Fungi
     Gardening
     Gardens
     Habitats
     Harvesting
     Horticulture
     Pests
     Photosynthesis
     Plant Growth
     Plant Identification
     Plant Pathology
     Plant Propagation
     Wildlife

Plastics   JUL. 1966
          Postings: 204   GC: 910
RT   Art Materials
     Handicrafts
     Industrial Arts
     Patternmaking
     Polymers

Plate Tectonics   OCT. 1984
          Postings: 150   GC: 490
SN   Branch of geophysics and seismology
     concerned with continental movements,
     based on the theory that the earth's
     surface is composed of vast crustal blocks
     that float across the mantle, with seismic
     activity and volcanism occurring prima-
     rily along the periphery of these blocks
BT   Geophysics
     Seismology
RT   Earth Science
     Earthquakes
     Geology
     Oceanography
     Physical Geography
     Volcanoes

Platform Diving
USE   Diving

Platonic Criticism (1970 1980)   MAR. 1980
          Postings: 9   GC: 430
SN   Invalid Descriptor—originally intended
     as a literary term, but used indiscrimi-
     nately in indexing—see "Literary Criti-
     cism" and the Identifier "Plato of Ath-
     ens" for literary documents

Platonism   SEP. 1969
          Postings: 50   GC: 430
SN   Philosophical theory characterized by the
     view that abstract universals (such as
     "truth" and "beauty") exist apart from
     the material world, which is but their
     pale and fleeting reflection, and that
     through reason the human mind has the
     capacity to understand them (Note: Also
     see the Identifier "Plato of Athens")
BT   Philosophy
RT   Classical Literature
     Romanticism

Play   JAN. 1971
          Postings: 3,397   GC: 470
SN   Pleasurable activity carried on for its
     own sake
UF   Childrens Play
     Free Play
NT   Pretend Play
BT   Activities
RT   Behavior
     Child Behavior
     Children
     Childrens Games
     Class Activities
     Dramatic Play
     Games
     Play Therapy
     Playground Activities
     Recess Breaks
     Recreational Activities
     Toys

Play Therapy   JUL. 1966
          Postings: 284   GC: 230
UF   Therapeutic Play
BT   Therapeutic Recreation
RT   Art Therapy
     Dance Therapy
     Music Therapy
     Play

Playground Activities   JUL. 1966
          Postings: 263   GC: 470
BT   Recreational Activities
RT   Athletics
     Childrens Games
     Outdoor Activities

     Physical Activities
     Physical Recreation Programs
     Play
     Recess Breaks

Playgrounds   JUL. 1966
          Postings: 554   GC: 920
UF   Lighted Playgrounds (1966 1980)
BT   Recreational Facilities
RT   Athletic Fields
     Physical Education Facilities
     Trails

Plays (Theatrical)
USE   Drama

Playwriting   AUG. 1968
          Postings: 322   GC: 430
BT   Writing (Composition)
RT   Creative Writing
     Dramatics
     Literary Devices
     Scripts
     Theater Arts

Plumbing   JUL. 1966
          Postings: 209   GC: 640
UF   Pipe Fitting
BT   Technology
RT   Building Trades
     Sanitary Facilities

Pluralization
USE   Plurals

Plurals   SEP. 1968
          Postings: 123   GC: 450
SN   Grammatical forms used to denote more
     than one
UF   Pluralization
BT   Morphemes
RT   Form Classes (Languages)
     Spelling

Plurilingualism
USE   Multilingualism

Plyometrics   DEC. 1989
          Postings: 1   GC: 470
SN   Exercises to develop eccentric contrac-
     tion (muscle stretching)—includes depth
     jumping, hopping, skipping, and leaping
     activities, all done with rapid, explosive
     movements
BT   Exercise
RT   Motor Reactions
     Muscular Strength
     Physical Fitness

Pneumatic Forms   AUG. 1972
          Postings: 4   GC: 920
SN   Structures used as forms for placing
     concrete, reinforced and/or foam plastic
     materials
BT   Air Structures

Pocket Calculators
USE   Calculators

Pocket Computers
USE   Microcomputers

Podiatry   OCT. 1979
          Postings: 85   GC: 210
SN   Medical treatment or study of foot disor-
     ders
BT   Medicine
RT   Medical Services

Poetry   JUL. 1966
          Postings: 4,811   GC: 430
UF   Prosody (Literary)

     Versification (1969 1980)
NT   Epics
     Haiku
     Lyric Poetry
     Nursery Rhymes
BT   Literature
RT   Antithesis
     Choral Speaking
     Chronicles
     Creative Writing
     Descriptive Writing
     Drama
     Fiction
     Folk Culture
     Humanism
     Language Rhythm
     Literary Genres
     Literary Styles
     Local Color Writing
     Monologs
     Parallelism (Literary)
     Pastoral Literature
     Poets
     Prose
     Puns
     Rhyme
     Tales
     Tragedy
     Writing (Composition)

Poets   JUN. 1969
          Postings: 458   GC: 430
UF   Bards
     Lyric Poets
     Minnesingers
     Troubadours
BT   Authors
RT   Epics
     Literature
     Lyric Poetry
     Poetry

Points of Articulation
USE   Articulation (Speech)

Poisoning   MAR. 1980
          Postings: 116   GC: 210
NT   Lead Poisoning
BT   Diseases
RT   Physical Health
     Poisons
     Pollution
     Radiation Effects
     Safety
     Special Health Problems
     Substance Abuse
     Toxicology

Poisons   SEP. 1982
          Postings: 157   GC: 210
SN   Chemical or organic substances that can
     cause injury to health or destroy life
UF   Toxic Substances
     Toxins
NT   Pesticides
BT   Hazardous Materials
RT   Ecological Factors
     Environmental Standards
     Physical Environment
     Poisoning
     Pollution
     Public Health
     Toxicology
     Wastes

Police   JUL. 1966
          Postings: 771   GC: 640
UF   Law Enforcement Officers
     Police Costs (1966 1980) #
     State Police (1966 1980)
BT   Government Employees
RT   Alarm Systems
     Crime
     Crime Prevention
     Criminal Law
     Emergency Squad Personnel
     Government (Administrative Body)
     Immigration Inspectors
     Law Enforcement

     Parole Officers
     Police Action
     Police Community Relationship
     Police Education
     Police School Relationship
     Security Personnel

Police Action   JUL. 1966
          Postings: 243   GC: 610
NT   Search and Seizure
BT   Law Enforcement
RT   Alarm Systems
     Crime
     Crime Prevention
     Police
     Police Community Relationship
     Police Education
     Police School Relationship
     School Security

Police Community Relationship   JUL. 1966
          Postings: 248   GC: 520
UF   Community Police Relationship
BT   Relationship
RT   Community
     Community Cooperation
     Community Coordination
     Crime Prevention
     Police
     Police Action
     Police School Relationship

Police Costs (1966 1980)
USE   Costs
AND   Police

Police Education   MAR. 1980
          Postings: 196   GC: 400
SN   Education that prepares individuals for
     entrance into police work or gives added
     instruction or training to employed law-
     enforcement officers
UF   Police Seminars (1966 1980)
BT   Education
RT   Criminal Law
     Law Related Education
     Police
     Police Action

Police School Liaison
USE   Police School Relationship

Police School Relationship   JUL. 1966
          Postings: 306   GC: 330
UF   Police School Liaison
     School Police Relationship
BT   Relationship
RT   Crime Prevention
     Delinquency
     Police
     Police Action
     Police Community Relationship
     School Attitudes
     School Security
     Schools
     Search and Seizure

Police Seminars (1966 1980)
USE   Police Education

Policy   JUL. 1966
          Postings: 1,655   GC: 330
SN   Governing principles that serve as guide-
     lines or rules for decision making and
     action in a given area (Note: Use a more
     specific term if possible)
NT   Administrative Policy
     Discipline Policy
     Educational Policy
     Financial Policy
     Foreign Policy
     Information Policy
     Interdistrict Policies
     Personnel Policy
     Public Policy
     School Policy

= Two or more Descriptors are used to represent this term.
The term's main entry shows the appropriate coordination.

Transfer Policy
RT Policy Analysis
     Policy Formation
     Standards

Policy Analysis   *OCT. 1993*
     Postings: 486   GC: 820
SN Systematic study of the nature, ration-
     ale, cost, impact, effectiveness,
     implications, etc., of existing or alterna-
     tive policies, using the theories and
     methodologies of relevant social science
     disciplines (Note: Use as a minor Descrip-
     tor for examples of this kind of study—
     use as a major Descriptor only as the
     subject of a document)
BT Evaluation Methods
RT Cost Effectiveness
     Decision Making
     Policy
     Policy Formation
     Politics
     Position Papers
     Social Science Research
     Systems Analysis
     Trend Analysis

Policy Formation   *JUL. 1966*
     Postings: 13,253   GC: 330
SN Act of establishing principles to serve as
     guidelines for decision making and ac-
     tion
BT Planning
RT Administration
     Advisory Committees
     Agenda Setting
     Blue Ribbon Commissions
     College Governing Councils
     Community Control
     Decision Making
     Delphi Technique
     Governance
     Governing Boards
     Intention
     Judgment Analysis Technique
     Legislation
     Master Plans
     Mission Statements
     Needs Assessment
     Participative Decision Making
     Policy
     Policy Analysis
     Politics
     Position Papers
     Self Evaluation (Groups)
     Strategic Planning

Policy Statements
USE Position Papers

Polish   *JUL. 1966*
     Postings: 191   GC: 440
BT Slavic Languages
RT Polish Literature

Polish Americans   *MAR. 1972*
     Postings: 78   GC: 560
BT Ethnic Groups
     North Americans
RT Minority Groups

Polish Literature   *DEC. 1969*
     Postings: 13   GC: 430
BT Literature
RT Polish

Political Advocacy
USE Lobbying

Political Affiliation   *JUL. 1966*
     Postings: 294   GC: 610
BT Group Membership

RT Government (Administrative Body)
     Political Attitudes
     Political Candidates
     Political Issues
     Political Parties
     Political Socialization
     Politics

Political Attitudes   *JUL. 1966*
     Postings: 3,729   GC: 610
SN Beliefs, opinions, attitudes, or values
     toward governmental actions, affairs, or
     practices
UF Civic Belief (1966 1980)
BT Attitudes
RT Activism
     Authoritarianism
     Citizenship
     Colonialism
     Community Attitudes
     Consciousness Raising
     Conservatism
     Credibility
     Democratic Values
     Dissent
     Federalism
     Freedom
     Humanitarianism
     Ideology
     Imperialism
     Liberalism
     Marxism
     Nationalism
     Political Affiliation
     Political Campaigns
     Political Parties
     Political Socialization
     Politics
     Public Opinion
     Refugees
     Regional Attitudes
     Social Attitudes
     Social Values
     Terrorism
     Totalitarianism
     Values
     Voting

Political Campaigns   *DEC. 1985*
     Postings: 382   GC: 610
SN Competitive efforts to win support of the
     voting public for candidates or ballot
     propositions
UF Election Campaigns
NT Presidential Campaigns (United States)
BT Politics
RT Advertising
     Citizen Participation
     Debate
     Elections
     Fund Raising
     Government (Administrative Body)
     Mass Media
     Persuasive Discourse
     Political Attitudes
     Political Candidates
     Political Influences
     Political Issues
     Voting

Political Candidates   *DEC. 1985*
     Postings: 235   GC: 610
SN Persons seeking election or appointment
     to public office
UF Political Nominees
     Presidential Candidates (United
          States) #
BT Groups
RT Board Candidates
     Community Leaders
     Debate
     Elections
     Government (Administrative Body)
     Political Affiliation
     Political Campaigns
     Political Issues
     Political Parties
     Politics
     Public Officials
     Voting

Political Correctness   *JUN. 1996*
     Postings: 162   GC: 540
SN The attempt in communication or other
     activity to be inoffensive and inclusive—
     may lead to censorship and intolerance
     in some cases, and is regarded with
     derision by many (Note: See also the
     Identifiers "Speech Codes" and "Hate
     Speech")
UF Politically Correct Communication
RT Academic Freedom
     Censorship
     Cultural Awareness
     Cultural Pluralism
     Ethics
     Freedom of Speech
     Ideology
     Intergroup Relations
     Multicultural Education
     Politics
     Values

Political Divisions (Geographic)   *JUL. 1966*
     Postings: 155   GC: 610
NT American Indian Reservations
BT Geographic Regions
RT Colonialism
     Geography
     Imperialism
     Nationalism
     Physical Divisions (Geographic)
     Treaties

Political Geography
USE Human Geography

Political Influences   *JUL. 1966*
     Postings: 5,573   GC: 610
SN Factors directly or indirectly affecting
     political beliefs and/or behavior (Note:
     Prior to Mar80, the instruction "Political
     Pressures, USE Political Power" was
     carried in the Thesaurus)
BT Influences
RT Agenda Setting
     Lobbying
     Political Campaigns
     Political Issues
     Political Power
     Political Socialization
     Politics
     Social Action
     Social Change
     Socioeconomic Influences

Political Issues   *JUL. 1966*
     Postings: 3,932   GC: 610
RT Blue Ribbon Commissions
     Bond Issues
     Controversial Issues (Course Content)
     Elections
     Legislation
     Lobbying
     Local Issues
     Political Affiliation
     Political Campaigns
     Political Candidates
     Political Influences
     Political Parties
     Political Power
     Politics
     Politics of Education
     Public Affairs Education
     Social Action
     Social Problems
     Voting

Political Nominees
USE Political Candidates

Political Parties   *APR. 1990*
     Postings: 137   GC: 610
SN Groups of people with some measure of
     ideological agreement who organize to
     win elections, operate governments, and
     determine public policy
BT Organizations (Groups)
RT Government (Administrative Body)

     Political Affiliation
     Political Attitudes
     Political Candidates
     Political Issues
     Politics
     Voting

Political Power   *JUL. 1966*
     Postings: 1,787   GC: 610
SN Political control or authority over others
     (Note: Prior to Mar80, this term was not
     restricted by a Scope Note)
RT Black Power
     Empowerment
     Imperialism
     Lobbying
     Marxism
     Participatory Research
     Political Influences
     Political Issues
     Politics
     Power Structure
     Totalitarianism

Political Protest
USE Activism

Political Reform
USE Social Action

Political Refugees
USE Refugees

Political Science   *JUL. 1966*
     Postings: 2,506   GC: 400
BT Social Sciences
RT Area Studies
     Authoritarianism
     Capitalism
     Civics
     Communism
     Constitutional History
     Constitutional Law
     Current Events
     Diplomatic History
     Elections
     Elitism
     Fascism
     Federalism
     Foreign Policy
     Human Geography
     International Law
     International Relations
     International Studies
     Marxism
     Military Science
     Political Socialization
     Politics
     Public Administration
     Public Administration Education
     Public Affairs Education
     Revolution
     Social Science Research
     Social Scientists
     Social Studies
     Socialism
     Totalitarianism
     United States Government (Course)

Political Socialization   *JUL. 1966*
     Postings: 1,650   GC: 520
SN Process by which political norms are
     transmitted through various social agents,
     e.g., school, parents, peer group, mass
     media, etc.
UF Politicalization
BT Socialization
RT Conservatism
     Liberalism
     Patriotism
     Political Affiliation
     Political Attitudes
     Political Influences
     Political Science
     Social Attitudes
     Social Change
     Social Influences

= Two or more Descriptors are used to represent this term.
The term's main entry shows the appropriate coordination.

Politicalization
USE   Political Socialization

Politically Correct Communication
USE   Political Correctness

Politics   OCT. 1971
Postings: 3,408   GC: 610
SN   Activities concerned with guiding or influencing governmental policy, including winning and holding control over a governing body
NT   Political Campaigns
Politics of Education
RT   Community Control
Elections
Governance
Government (Administrative Body)
International Studies
Legislation
Lobbying
New Federalism
Policy Analysis
Policy Formation
Political Affiliation
Political Attitudes
Political Candidates
Political Correctness
Political Influences
Political Issues
Political Parties
Political Power
Political Science
Public Policy
Voting

Politics of Education   JUN. 1983
Postings: 4,809   GC: 330
SN   Political aspects of governance and decision making within educational systems and institutions, and political activities related to education in general
UF   Educational Politics
BT   Politics
RT   Board Administrator Relationship
Board of Education Policy
Education
Educational Administration
Educational Finance
Educational Legislation
Educational Policy
Family School Relationship
Government School Relationship
Parent School Relationship
Political Issues
School Community Relationship
School Law
School Policy
School Role
Teacher Administrator Relationship

Pollution   JUL. 1969
Postings: 2,655   GC: 410
NT   Air Pollution
Water Pollution
RT   Bacteria
Chimneys
Climate
Disease Control
Diseases
Ecological Factors
Environmental Education
Environmental Influences
Environmental Standards
Hazardous Materials
Health
Lead Poisoning
Noise (Sound)
Physical Environment
Physical Health
Poisoning
Poisons
Public Health
Radiation Effects
Recycling
Solid Wastes
Urban Environment
Viruses
Waste Disposal

Waste Water
Wastes

Polygons   JUL. 1993
Postings: 108   GC: 480
SN   Closed plane (two-dimensional) figures formed by the line segments that connect three or more points not in a straight line (Note: See also specific Identifiers, e.g., "Triangles," "Quadrilaterals")
BT   Geometric Concepts
Plane Geometry
RT   Area
Geometric Constructions

Polygraphs   JUL. 1966
Postings: 34   GC: 910
UF   Lie Detectors
BT   Electronic Equipment
Measurement Equipment
RT   Crime
Instrumentation
Lying

Polymers   AUG. 1986
Postings: 134   GC: 490
SN   Natural or synthetic substances of usually high molecular weight formed by the union of relatively light and simple molecules
BT   Matter
RT   Chemical Engineering
Chemical Reactions
Chemistry
Molecular Structure
Nucleic Acids
Organic Chemistry
Plastics

Polynomials   APR. 1990
Postings: 90   GC: 480
SN   Mathematical expressions of the sums of two or more algebraic terms—specifically, the sums of finite numbers of terms each composed of a positive power of a variable multiplied by a constant
BT   Algebra
Mathematical Formulas
RT   Equations (Mathematics)
Functions (Mathematics)
Mathematical Concepts

Pomo   APR. 1970
Postings: 6   GC: 440
BT   American Indian Languages

Poor
USE   Economically Disadvantaged

Pop Culture
USE   Popular Culture

Pop Music
USE   Popular Music

Popular Culture   SEP. 1977
Postings: 1,445   GC: 720
SN   Artistic and commercial expressions which reach a majority of the people through mass media, mass production, or transportation
UF   Mass Culture
Pop Culture
BT   Culture
RT   Art
Films
Literature
Mass Media
Material Culture
Music
Popular Music
Publications
Radio
Recreational Activities
Television

Popular Education   FEB. 1997
Postings: 128   GC: 330
SN   Education that encourages learners to critically examine their day-to-day lives and collectively take action to change social conditions and systems (frequently associated with Paulo Freire's critical pedagogy and participatory literacy campaigns)
UF   Peoples Education
BT   Education
RT   Adult Education
Community Education
Consciousness Raising
Literacy Education
Social Action
Social Change

Popular Music   JAN. 1996
Postings: 99   GC: 420
SN   Music enjoyed by the general public and commonly disseminated via the mass media (Note: Prior to Jan96, this concept was frequently indexed by "Popular Culture" coordinated with "Music" terms)
UF   Pop Music
BT   Music
RT   Bands (Music)
Jazz
Music Activities
Musical Composition
Popular Culture
Rock Music
Vocal Music

Popularity   AUG. 1986
Postings: 226   GC: 520
SN   Being commonly admired, approved, or sought after—especially, the likability of individuals concurred among friends, associates, or acquaintances
RT   Friendship
Interpersonal Competence
Peer Acceptance
Peer Relationship
Prestige
Social Desirability
Social Life
Social Status

Population Changes
USE   Population Trends

Population Distribution   JUL. 1966
Postings: 1,070   GC: 550
UF   Diffusion (1967 1982) (Populations)
NT   Ethnic Distribution
Racial Distribution
BT   Demography
RT   Birth Rate
Community Size
Geographic Distribution
Human Geography
Immigration
Incidence
Migration
Migration Patterns
Mortality Rate
Overpopulation
Place of Residence
Population Growth
Population Trends
Racial Composition
Relocation
Residential Patterns
Rural Population
Rural to Urban Migration
Urban Population
Urban to Rural Migration
Urban to Suburban Migration

Population Education   FEB. 1972
Postings: 819   GC: 400
SN   Transmission of knowledge about population processes and characteristics, the causes of population change and the consequences of that change for the individual and society
BT   Education

RT   Demography
Environmental Education
Family Planning
Human Capital

Population Growth   JUL. 1966
Postings: 1,563   GC: 550
SN   Increase in the number of individuals in a given area (world, nation, or local region) due to either natural reproduction or resettlement
BT   Demography
Development
RT   Baby Boomers
Birth Rate
Boomtowns
Community Size
Family Planning
Family Size
Overpopulation
Population Distribution
Population Trends
Rural Population
Social Influences
Urban Population
Urbanization

Population Minorities
USE   Minority Groups

Population Movements
USE   Migration

Population Research
USE   Demography

Population Shifts
USE   Migration

Population Trends   JUL. 1966
Postings: 3,209   GC: 550
UF   Population Changes
NT   Black Population Trends
BT   Demography
RT   Baby Boomers
Birth Rate
Boomtowns
Brain Drain
Cohort Analysis
Community Size
Family Planning
Family Size
Human Geography
Immigration
Land Settlement
Migration
Migration Patterns
Mortality Rate
Occupational Mobility
Overpopulation
Population Distribution
Population Growth
Relocation
Residential Patterns
Rural Population
Rural to Urban Migration
Structural Unemployment
Trend Analysis
Urban Population
Urban to Rural Migration
Urban to Suburban Migration

Pornography   OCT. 1983
Postings: 185   GC: 720
SN   Visual, written, or oral communication intended explicitly to promote sexual excitement—pornography is often distinguished from erotic material in general by its exclusively prurient intent, its lack of redeeming artistic/literary value, and its commercial motivation
RT   Obscenity
Sexuality

Portable Computers
USE   Microcomputers

= Two or more Descriptors are used to represent this term.
The term's main entry shows the appropriate coordination.

Portable Facilities
USE   Relocatable Facilities

Portfolio Assessment   *DEC. 1994*
        Postings: 1,056   GC: 310
SN   Systematic collection of a student's work
       samples, records of observation, test
       results, etc., over a period of time for the
       purpose of evaluating student growth
       and achievement—used occasionally with
       populations other than students (Note:
       Prior to Dec94, "Portfolios (Background
       Materials)" was used, usually with "Stu-
       dent Evaluation," to index this concept)
BT   Evaluation
RT   Alternative Assessment
       Evaluation Methods
       Informal Assessment
       Performance Based Assessment
       Portfolios (Background Materials)
       Self Evaluation (Individuals)
       Student Evaluation
       Student Records
       Writing Evaluation

Portfolios (Background Materials)
                                  JUN. 1978
        Postings: 1,484   GC: 330
SN   Collections of records, letters of refer-
       ence, work samples, etc., documenting
       skills, capabilities, and past experiences
BT   Credentials
RT   Admission (School)
       Certification
       College Applicants
       Evaluation Methods
       Experiential Learning
       Informal Assessment
       Job Applicants
       Job Application
       Personnel Evaluation
       Personnel Selection
       Portfolio Assessment
       Profiles
       Qualifications
       Resumes (Personal)
       Student Evaluation
       Student Records

Portuguese   *JUL. 1966*
        Postings: 439   GC: 440
BT   Romance Languages

Portuguese Americans   *MAR. 1976*
        Postings: 40   GC: 560
BT   Ethnic Groups
       Hispanic Americans
RT   Hispanic American Culture

Position Papers   *MAR. 1980*
        Postings: 1,481   GC: 730
SN   Statements of official or organizational
       viewpoints, often recommending a par-
       ticular course of action
UF   Policy Statements
NT   Mission Statements
BT   Reports
RT   Lobbying
       Needs Assessment
       Opinion Papers
       Policy Analysis
       Policy Formation

Positive Reinforcement   *JUL. 1966*
        Postings: 1,619   GC: 110
BT   Reinforcement
RT   Incentives
       Negative Reinforcement
       Praise
       Self Reward
       Social Reinforcement

Post Coordinate Indexes
USE   Coordinate Indexes

Post Doctoral Education (1967 1980)
USE   Postdoctoral Education

Post High School Education
USE   Postsecondary Education

Post High School Guidance   *JUL. 1966*
        Postings: 152   GC: 240
SN   Guidance services for in- or out-of-school
       youth, designed to help them with future
       plans for postsecondary education, or
       for employment
BT   Guidance
RT   Admissions Counseling
       Career Guidance
       College Preparation
       Educational Counseling
       High School Graduates
       High Schools
       Postsecondary Education
       School Counseling

Post Modernism
USE   Postmodernism

Post Secondary Education (1967 1978)
USE   Postsecondary Education

Post Testing (1966 1980)
USE   Pretests Posttests

Post Traumatic Stress Syndrome
USE   Posttraumatic Stress Disorder

Postdoctoral Education   *MAR. 1980*
        Postings: 285   GC: 340
SN   Research and study beyond the doctoral
       degree, usually on special projects
UF   Post Doctoral Education (1967 1980)
BT   Higher Education
RT   Doctoral Programs
       Graduate Study
       Professional Education
       Research
       Specialization

Postmodernism   *JUL. 2000*
        Postings: 686   GC: 430
SN   A cultural, philosophical, or stylistic re-
       action to or successor of modernism,
       beginning from about 1960—the
       postmodern period or approach is char-
       acterized by a relativistic or pluralistic
       sense that truth or reality is dependent
       on specific context or individual per-
       spective
UF   Post Modernism
RT   Architecture
       Art Expression
       Constructivism (Learning)
       Critical Theory
       Cultural Pluralism
       Epistemology
       Literary Styles
       Modernism
       Philosophy
       Twentieth Century Literature

Postsecondary Education   *JAN. 1979*
        Postings: 27,527   GC: 340
SN   All education beyond the secondary
       level—includes learning activities and
       experiences beyond the compulsory
       school attendance age with the excep-
       tion of adult basic education and high
       school equivalency programs (Note:
       Appears in the list of mandatory educa-
       tional level Descriptors—before Apr75,
       restricted to education beyond grade 12
       and less than the baccalaureate level)
UF   Grade 13 (1970 1980)
       Grade 14 (1970 1980)
       Post High School Education
       Post Secondary Education (1967
        1978)

Postsecondary Instructional Level
       Tertiary Education
NT   Higher Education
BT   Education
RT   Academic Advising
       Adult Education
       Colleges
       Community Colleges
       Continuing Education
       Corporate Education
       Noncampus Colleges
       Nontraditional Students
       Post High School Guidance
       Postsecondary Education as a Field of
        Study
       Pretechnology Programs
       Student Financial Aid
       Technical Education
       Technical Institutes
       Two Year Colleges
       Universities
       Vocational Education
       Vocational Schools
       Womens Education

**Postsecondary Education as a Field of
Study**   *JAN. 1979*
        Postings: 349   GC: 400
SN   The formal examination or study of
       postsecondary education—leads to a
       masters or doctoral degree in higher/
       postsecondary education with concen-
       trations in college research, administra-
       tion, teaching, etc., (originally added
       to the Thesaurus in Jul77 with
       "Postsecondary" as two words)
UF   Higher Education as a Field of Study
BT   College Curriculum
       Graduate Study
RT   College Faculty
       Education Courses
       Education Majors
       Higher Education
       Postsecondary Education
       Professional Education
       Schools of Education
       Teacher Educator Education
       Teacher Educators

Postsecondary Instructional Level
USE   Postsecondary Education

Posttraumatic Neurosis
USE   Posttraumatic Stress Disorder

Posttraumatic Stress Disorder *OCT. 1995*
        Postings: 246   GC: 230
SN   Acute or chronic delayed reaction to
       highly stressing events such as military
       combat, sexual assault, childhood abuse,
       natural disasters, unexpected deaths, and
       life-threatening accidents—symptoms in-
       clude anxiety, depression, intrusive rec-
       ollections, and emotional detachment
UF   Post Traumatic Stress Syndrome
       Posttraumatic Neurosis
       PTSD
BT   Neurosis
RT   Anxiety
       Depression (Psychology)
       Emotional Disturbances
       Stress Variables

Posture Development
USE   Human Posture

Posture Patterns
USE   Human Posture

Potable Water
USE   Drinking Water

Potential Dropouts   *JUL. 1966*
        Postings: 798   GC: 360
BT   Groups
RT   Dropout Characteristics

       Dropout Prevention
       Dropouts
       High Risk Students
       Special Needs Students

Potentiometers (Instruments) *JAN. 1970*
        Postings: 13   GC: 910
SN   Instruments used to measure electro-
       motive forces
BT   Measurement Equipment
RT   Electric Circuits
       Electricity

Pottery
USE   Ceramics

Potty Training
USE   Toilet Training

Poverty   *MAR. 1980*
        Postings: 4,877   GC: 530
SN   Lack of means to acquire material needs
       or comforts
UF   Economic Disadvantagement (1966
        1980)
       Economic Insecurity
       Economic Plight
       Poverty Factors #
       Poverty Research (1970 1980)
BT   Economic Status
RT   Disadvantaged Environment
       Economically Disadvantaged
       Feminization of Poverty
       Homeless People
       Hunger
       Inflation (Economics)
       Low Income
       Low Income Groups
       Lower Class
       Poverty Areas
       Poverty Programs
       Slums
       Underemployment
       Unemployment

Poverty Areas   *MAR. 1980*
        Postings: 678   GC: 550
SN   Geographic areas or regions that are
       characterized by economic hardship
UF   Depressed Areas (Geographic) (1966
        1980)
       Economically Depressed Areas
NT   Slums
BT   Geographic Regions
RT   Disadvantaged Environment
       Low Income Counties
       Low Income States
       Poverty

Poverty Factors
USE   Economic Factors
AND   Poverty

Poverty Programs   *JUL. 1966*
        Postings: 772   GC: 620
UF   Anti Poverty Programs
BT   Programs
RT   Low Income
       Poverty
       Welfare Services

Poverty Research (1970 1980)
USE   Poverty

Poverty Stricken
USE   Economically Disadvantaged

Power Mechanics (1969 1980)
USE   Power Technology

Power Structure   *JUL. 1966*
        Postings: 4,063   GC: 520
UF   Authority Structure

= Two or more Descriptors are used to represent this term.
The term's main entry shows the appropriate coordination.

BT   Organization
RT   Administrative Organization
     Black Power
     Empowerment
     Group Structure
     Informal Organization
     Management Teams
     Middle Management
     Organizational Climate
     Organizational Development
     Participative Decision Making
     Personal Autonomy
     Political Power
     Professional Autonomy
     Social Control
     Social Exchange Theory
     Social Structure

Power Technology   *MAR. 1980*
     Postings: 527   GC: 490
SN   Study and/or application of energy transfer or generation processes
UF   Energy Technology
     Power Mechanics (1969 1980)
NT   Nuclear Technology
BT   Technology
RT   Alternative Energy Sources
     Auto Mechanics
     Aviation Mechanics
     Biotechnology
     Chemical Engineering
     Electricity
     Energy
     Energy Occupations
     Engineering Technology
     Engines
     Fluid Mechanics
     Fuels
     Geothermal Energy
     Industrial Arts
     Small Engine Mechanics
     Solar Energy
     Technology Education
     Utilities
     Wind Energy

Power Transfer Systems
USE   Kinetics

Practical Arts   *JUL. 1966*
     Postings: 132   GC: 400
SN   Functional curricula usually employing a performance based method of learning and generally associated with the subject areas of business education, home economics, industrial arts, and health and recreation—emphasizes preparation for everyday life rather than vocational training
RT   Agricultural Skills
     Business Skills
     Consumer Education
     Daily Living Skills
     Experiential Learning
     Homemaking Skills
     Industrial Arts
     Practical Nursing

Practical Mathematics (1966 1980)
USE   Mathematical Applications

Practical Music
USE   Applied Music

Practical Nurses (1967 1981)
USE   Nurses
AND   Practical Nursing

Practical Nursing   *JUL. 1966*
     Postings: 232   GC: 210
UF   Practical Nurses (1967 1981) #
     Vocational Nursing
BT   Nursing
RT   Allied Health Occupations
     Nursing Homes
     Practical Arts

Practice Teaching
USE   Student Teaching

Practicum Papers   *MAR. 1980*
     Postings: 16   GC: 720
SN   Written presentations used to satisfy academic degree requirements for practicums (Note: Corresponds to Pubtype code 043—do not use except as the subject of a document)
BT   Reports
RT   Doctoral Dissertations
     Masters Theses
     Practicums

Practicum Supervision   *JAN. 1969*
     Postings: 584   GC: 310
UF   Preceptors (Medicine) #
BT   Supervision
RT   Clinical Experience
     Clinical Teaching (Health Professions)
     Cooperating Teachers
     Counselor Educators
     Field Experience Programs
     Internship Programs
     Laboratory Training
     Medical School Faculty
     Practicums
     Student Teacher Supervisors
     Student Teaching
     Teacher Supervision

Practicums   *JUL. 1966*
     Postings: 1,502   GC: 350
SN   Supervised academic exercises consisting of study and practical work
NT   Office Practice
BT   Courses
RT   Clinical Experience
     Clinical Teaching (Health Professions)
     Cooperative Education
     Counselor Training
     Experiential Learning
     Field Experience Programs
     Internship Programs
     Laboratory Training
     Microcounseling
     Practicum Papers
     Practicum Supervision
     Student Teaching

Pragmatics   *AUG. 1977*
     Postings: 1,099   GC: 450
SN   The study of the aspects of meaning in language that are related to the use of language in a natural context
BT   Semiotics
RT   Discourse Analysis
     Language Patterns
     Language Usage
     Semantics
     Sociolinguistics
     Speech Acts
     Syntax

Praise   *APR. 1993*
     Postings: 118   GC: 110
SN   Expression of approval or favorable judgment
RT   Awards
     Criticism
     Incentives
     Motivation
     Positive Reinforcement
     Psychological Needs
     Recognition (Achievement)
     Rewards
     Value Judgment

Prayer in Schools
USE   School Prayer

Preachers
USE   Clergy

Preadolescence
USE   Preadolescents

Preadolescents   *NOV. 1982*
     Postings: 1,438   GC: 120
SN   Approximately 9–12 years of age
UF   Preadolescence
BT   Children
RT   Adolescents
     Early Adolescents
     Intermediate Grades
     Middle School Students
     Youth

Preceptors (Medicine)
USE   Physicians
AND   Practicum Supervision

Preceptorships (Medicine)
USE   Clinical Experience

Precision Ratio
USE   Relevance (Information Retrieval)

Precision Teaching   *SEP. 1971*
     Postings: 114   GC: 310
SN   Teaching method, based on behavior modification, that uses daily measurement and charting procedures as reinforcement for learning
BT   Teaching Methods
RT   Behavior Rating Scales
     Charts
     Educational Testing
     Evaluation Methods
     Experience Charts
     Profiles
     Student Evaluation

Precollege Level
USE   High Schools

Prediction   *JUL. 1966*
     Postings: 4,242   GC: 820
SN   Process or act of foretelling future events, conditions, outcomes, or trends on the basis of current information
UF   Achievement Prediction #
     Forecast
NT   Employment Projections
     Enrollment Projections
     Grade Prediction
RT   Chaos Theory
     Decision Support Systems
     Delphi Technique
     Environmental Scanning
     Estimation (Mathematics)
     Expectation
     Futures (of Society)
     Long Range Planning
     Markov Processes
     Predictive Measurement
     Probability
     Regression (Statistics)
     Reliability
     Risk
     Self Fulfilling Prophecies
     Social Indicators
     Strategic Planning

Predictive Ability (Testing) (1966 1980)
USE   Predictive Measurement

Predictive Measurement   *JUL. 1966*
     Postings: 3,078   GC: 820
SN   Use of tests, inventories, or other measures to determine or estimate future events, conditions, outcomes, or trends
UF   Predictive Ability (Testing) (1966 1980)
BT   Measurement
RT   Aptitude Tests
     Bayesian Statistics
     College Entrance Examinations
     Estimation (Mathematics)

     Expectancy Tables
     Grade Prediction
     Interest Inventories
     Least Squares Statistics
     Licensing Examinations (Professions)
     Markov Processes
     Maximum Likelihood Statistics
     Multiple Regression Analysis
     Occupational Tests
     Prediction
     Predictive Validity
     Predictor Variables
     Probability
     Prognostic Tests
     Regression (Statistics)
     Robustness (Statistics)
     Sampling
     Statistics
     Suppressor Variables
     Test Use
     Test Validity
     Testing

Predictive Validity   *JUL. 1966*
     Postings: 2,950   GC: 820
SN   Degree to which a variable, such as test scores, grades, ratings, or some other factor, correlates with some future performance or variable
UF   Criterion Validity (Predictive)
BT   Validity
RT   Concurrent Validity
     Expectancy Tables
     Expectation
     Interest Inventories
     Predictive Measurement
     Predictor Variables
     Scores
     Test Validity
     Testing

Predictive Variables
USE   Predictor Variables

Predictor Variables   *SEP. 1970*
     Postings: 8,178   GC: 820
SN   Scores or measurements that are used to predict outcomes or to make estimates of other measures—in research, they describe the characteristics of the sample that are expected to affect the outcome
UF   Independent Variables
     Predictive Variables
     Predictors
     Regressors
NT   Suppressor Variables
RT   Analysis of Covariance
     Analysis of Variance
     Causal Models
     Chi Square
     Context Effect
     Correlation
     Criteria
     Effect Size
     Error of Measurement
     Expectancy Tables
     Interest Inventories
     Monte Carlo Methods
     Multiple Regression Analysis
     Path Analysis
     Performance Factors
     Predictive Measurement
     Predictive Validity
     Probability
     Prognostic Tests
     Research Design
     Statistical Analysis
     Symptoms (Individual Disorders)
     Test Validity

Predictors
USE   Predictor Variables

Prefabrication   *JUL. 1966*
     Postings: 94   GC: 920
BT   Construction (Process)
RT   Air Structures
     Building Systems

= Two or more Descriptors are used to represent this term.
The term's main entry shows the appropriate coordination.

Buildings
Construction Materials
Encapsulated Facilities
Masonry
Movable Partitions
Prestressed Concrete
Relocatable Facilities
School Construction
Structural Building Systems
Structural Elements (Construction)

Preferential Admission
USE   Selective Admission

Prefixes (Grammar)   APR. 1990
       Postings: 23   GC: 450
BT   Affixes
RT   Structural Analysis (Linguistics)
       Suffixes

Pregnancy   JUL. 1966
       Postings: 1,846   GC: 120
UF   Cyesis
       Gestation
RT   Abortions
       Biology
       Birth
       Birth Rate
       Births to Single Women
       Contraception
       Early Parenthood
       Family Planning
       Fetal Alcohol Syndrome
       Gynecology
       Obstetrics
       Perinatal Influences
       Pregnant Students
       Premature Infants
       Prenatal Care
       Prenatal Drug Exposure
       Prenatal Influences
       Reproduction (Biology)
       Rh Factors
       Unwed Mothers

Pregnant Students   DEC. 1972
       Postings: 588   GC: 360
BT   Females
       Students
RT   Board of Education Policy
       Equal Protection
       Pregnancy
       Special Needs Students
       Student Rights
       Unwed Mothers

Prejudice
USE   Bias

Prekindergarten
USE   Preschool Education

Prekindergarten Classes
USE   Preschool Education

Prekindergarten Teachers
USE   Preschool Teachers

Premature Birth
USE   Premature Infants

Premature Infants   JUL. 1966
       Postings: 407   GC: 120
UF   Premature Birth
BT   Infants
RT   Birth Weight
       Infant Care
       Infant Mortality
       Neonates
       Perinatal Influences
       Pregnancy

Premedical Students   OCT. 1982
       Postings: 64   GC: 360
SN   Undergraduates preparing for medical
       school
BT   Undergraduate Students
RT   Medical Education
       Medical Students
       Professional Education

Premium Pay   JUL. 1966
       Postings: 40   GC: 630
SN   A sum in addition to regular compensa-
       tion paid due to unusual circumstances
       such as overtime, holiday work, hazard-
       ous or unpleasant work, or superior em-
       ployee productivity or skill
BT   Expenditures
       Income
RT   Merit Pay
       Overtime
       Payroll Records
       Personnel Policy
       Salaries
       Salary Wage Differentials
       Scope of Bargaining
       Wages

Prenatal Care   APR. 1993
       Postings: 254   GC: 210
SN   Medical, educational, and social services
       provided or obtained during pregnancy
UF   Fetal Care
BT   Health Services
RT   Child Health
       Community Health Services
       Early Intervention
       Health
       Infant Mortality
       Medical Services
       Obstetrics
       Pregnancy
       Prenatal Influences
       Preventive Medicine
       Primary Health Care

Prenatal Drug Exposure   OCT. 1996
       Postings: 48   GC: 210
SN   Maternal drug use during pregnancy—
       also, a medical condition in infants and
       children resulting from such use
UF   Cocaine Prenatal Exposure #
       Crack Babies #
       Drug Exposure in Utero
       Fetal Drug Exposure
       Prenatal Exposure to Drugs
BT   Drug Use
       Prenatal Influences
RT   Drug Abuse
       Fetal Alcohol Syndrome
       Illegal Drug Use
       Pregnancy

Prenatal Exposure to Drugs
USE   Prenatal Drug Exposure

Prenatal Influences   AUG. 1968
       Postings: 766   GC: 120
SN   Factors occurring between conception
       and birth and affecting the physical or
       mental development of an individual
       (Note: Use the more precise "Prenatal
       Care" or the narrower "Prenatal Drug
       Exposure," if appropriate)
NT   Prenatal Drug Exposure
BT   Influences
RT   Anemia
       Biological Influences
       Birth Weight
       Child Health
       Congenital Impairments
       Diseases
       Fetal Alcohol Syndrome
       Genetics
       Health
       Heredity
       Nature Nurture Controversy
       Obstetrics
       Perinatal Influences
       Physical Development

Pregnancy
Prenatal Care
Rh Factors
Rubella
Substance Abuse

Prepositions   JAN. 1985
       Postings: 155   GC: 450
BT   Form Classes (Languages)
RT   Function Words
       Morphology (Languages)
       Phrase Structure
       Sentence Structure
       Syntax

Prereading Experience   JUL. 1966
       Postings: 503   GC: 460
SN   Preschool incidental learning that pre-
       pares children for reading (Note: Use
       "Reading   Readiness"   for   formal
       prereading training—prior to Sep80, the
       use of this term was not restricted by a
       Scope Note)
BT   Experience
RT   Beginning Reading
       Early Experience
       Early Reading
       Parents as Teachers
       Reading Readiness

Prereferral Assessment
USE   Prereferral Intervention

Prereferral Intervention   OCT. 1993
       Postings: 116   GC: 310
SN   Activities designed to increase class-
       room teachers' capacity to instruct and
       manage   difficult-to-teach   students,
       thereby reducing unnecessary and inap-
       propriate special education referrals—
       often "brokered" by one or more sup-
       port staff, such as a special educator or
       school psychologist
UF   Prereferral Assessment
BT   Intervention
RT   Classroom Techniques
       Consultation Programs
       Diagnostic Teaching
       Disability Identification
       Educational Diagnosis
       High Risk Students
       Individualized Instruction
       Informal Assessment
       Learning Problems
       Mainstreaming
       Prevention
       Referral
       Regular and Special Education Rela-
       tionship
       Special Education
       Special Needs Students
       Student Evaluation

Prerequisite Courses
USE   Prerequisites
AND   Required Courses

Prerequisites   SEP. 1982
       Postings: 199   GC: 520
SN   Knowledge, achievements, or other char-
       acteristics or circumstances required be-
       fore proceeding on a given course of
       action
UF   Prerequisite Courses #
RT   Achievement
       Admission Criteria
       Background
       Credentials
       Credits
       Criteria
       Eligibility
       Evaluation
       Prior Learning
       Qualifications
       Selection
       Standards
       Status

Preretirement Education   NOV. 1982
       Postings: 124   GC: 400
SN   Courses, counseling, and other activities
       designed to help individuals make the
       psychological, physical, and financial ad-
       justments to retirement
UF   Preretirement Programs
BT   Adult Education
RT   Educational Gerontology
       Fringe Benefits
       Middle Aged Adults
       Midlife Transitions
       Older Adults
       Older Workers
       Retirement

Preretirement Programs
USE   Preretirement Education

Preschool Children   JUL. 1966
       Postings: 10,855   GC: 120
SN   Approximately 2–5 years of age
UF   Preschoolers
BT   Young Children
RT   Child Development Centers
       Kindergarten Children
       Preschool Education
       Toddlers

Preschool Clinics (1966 1980)
USE   Clinics
AND   Preschool Education

Preschool Curriculum   JUL. 1966
       Postings: 845   GC: 350
BT   Curriculum
RT   Elementary School Curriculum
       Preschool Education

Preschool Education   JUL. 1966
       Postings: 15,354   GC: 340
SN   Activities and/or experiences that are
       intended to effect developmental changes
       in children, from birth to entrance in
       kindergarten (or grade 1 when kinder-
       garten is not attended) (Note: Also ap-
       pears in the list of mandatory educa-
       tional level Descriptors)
UF   Laboratory Preschools #
       Prekindergarten
       Prekindergarten Classes
       Preschool Clinics (1966 1980) #
       Preschool Programs (1966 1980)
       Preschool Workshops (1966 1980) #
       Reggio Emilia Preschools #
BT   Early Childhood Education
RT   Alternate Day Schedules
       Child Development Centers
       Day Care Centers
       Full Day Half Day Schedules
       Home Instruction
       Kindergarten
       Laboratory Schools
       Nursery Schools
       Preschool Children
       Preschool Curriculum
       Preschool Evaluation
       Preschool Teachers
       Preschool Tests

Preschool Evaluation   JUL. 1966
       Postings: 288   GC: 320
SN   Evaluation of preschool programs, not
       preschool children (Note: Prior to Mar80,
       this term was not restricted by a Scope
       Note—for evaluation of preschool child-
       ren, see "Identification," "Disability Identi-
       fication," "Screening Tests," "Diagnos-
       tic Tests," etc.)
BT   Evaluation
RT   Preschool Education

Preschool Experience
USE   Early Experience

= Two or more Descriptors are used to represent this term.
The term's main entry shows the appropriate coordination.

Preschool Learning (1966 1980)
MAR. 1980
Postings: 304   GC: 110
SN   Invalid Descriptor—see more appropriate "preschool" and "learning" Descriptors

Preschool Programs (1966 1980)
USE   Preschool Education

Preschool Teachers
JUL. 1966
Postings: 1,592   GC: 360
UF   Kindergarten Teachers
Prekindergarten Teachers
BT   Teachers
RT   Caregiver Child Relationship
Child Caregivers
Preschool Education

Preschool Tests
JUL. 1966
Postings: 329   GC: 830
BT   Tests
RT   Diagnostic Tests
Maturity Tests
Nonverbal Tests
Preschool Education
Prognostic Tests
Reading Readiness Tests
School Readiness Tests
Screening Tests

Preschool Workshops (1966 1980)
USE   Preschool Education
AND   Workshops

Preschoolers
USE   Preschool Children

Prescriptive Teaching
USE   Diagnostic Teaching

Presentation Methods
USE   Teaching Methods

Preservation
SEP. 1968
Postings: 1,155   GC: 490
SN   Prevention of deterioration of stored commodities, structural members, materials, etc.
BT   Maintenance
RT   Cleaning
Fire Protection
Obsolescence
Prevention
Records Management
Repair

Preservice Education (1966 1980)
USE   Preservice Teacher Education

Preservice Teacher Education
MAR. 1980
Postings: 14,328   GC: 400
UF   Preservice Education (1966 1980)
NT   Student Teaching
BT   Teacher Education
RT   Affiliated Schools
Cooperating Teachers
Extended Teacher Education Programs
Inservice Teacher Education
Preservice Teachers
Professional Development Schools
Student Teacher Supervisors
Student Teachers
Teacher Education Curriculum
Teacher Education Programs
Teacher Educator Education

Preservice Teachers
AUG. 1998
Postings: 947   GC: 360
SN   Students in a teacher education program, at a college or university, preparing for professional-level teaching positions (Note: Prior to Aug98, this concept

was sometimes indexed by "Student Teachers" or "Education Majors")
UF   Prospective Teachers
NT   Student Teachers
BT   College Students
RT   Education Majors
Preservice Teacher Education
Schools of Education
Teacher Education Curriculum
Teacher Education Programs
Teachers

Preservice Teaching Experience
USE   Teaching Experience

Presidential Campaigns (United States)
DEC. 1985
Postings: 259   GC: 610
SN   Competitive efforts of rival candidates for the office of the President of the United States
UF   Presidential Candidates (United States) #
Presidential Debates (United States) #
Presidential Elections (United States) #
BT   Political Campaigns
RT   Federal Government
Presidents of the United States
United States History

Presidential Candidates (United States)
USE   Political Candidates
AND   Presidential Campaigns (United States)

Presidential Debates (United States)
USE   Debate
AND   Presidential Campaigns (United States)

Presidential Elections (United States)
USE   Elections
AND   Presidential Campaigns (United States)

Presidents
JUL. 1966
Postings: 719   GC: 640
SN   Individuals appointed or elected to preside over an organized body of people, e.g., republic, assembly, organization, etc. (Note: Use a more specific term if possible)
UF   Women Presidents #
NT   College Presidents
Presidents of the United States
BT   Administrators

Presidents of the United States
AUG. 1986
Postings: 316   GC: 610
SN   Individuals serving (past or present) as the chief executive officer of the United States government
BT   Presidents
RT   Federal Government
Presidential Campaigns (United States)
United States History

Press
USE   News Media

Press Opinion
JUL. 1966
Postings: 718   GC: 610
BT   Opinions
RT   Agenda Setting
Editorials
Freedom of Speech
Journalism
Journalism History
Mass Media
Mass Media Role
News Media
Public Opinion

Press Role
USE   Mass Media Role
AND   News Media

Pressure (Physics)
MAR. 1980
Postings: 119   GC: 490
SN   Physical force applied to an object or surface (Note: The previous Descriptor "Pressure" was not scoped and was occasionally used for emotional or psychological pressure)
UF   Absolute Pressure
Ambient Pressure
Fluid Pressure
Physical Pressure
BT   Scientific Concepts
RT   Density (Matter)
Fluid Mechanics
Force
Gravity (Physics)
Mechanics (Physics)
Physical Environment
Physics
Weight (Mass)

Pressure (1970 1980)
JUN. 1980
Postings: 43   GC: 490
SN   Invalid Descriptor—originally intended as a physical science term but used inconsistently for social pressure, psychological stress, etc., as well as physical pressure—see such Descriptors as "Pressure (Physics)," "Political Influences," "Social Influences," and "Stress Variables"

Prestige
JUN. 1983
Postings: 175   GC: 520
SN   High esteem or regard accorded to an individual, group, institution, role/occupation, etc.
BT   Reputation
RT   Awards
Leadership Qualities
Popularity
Professional Recognition
Selective Colleges
Social Status
Status Need

Prestressed Concrete
SEP. 1968
Postings: 19   GC: 920
UF   Pretensioned Concrete
BT   Construction Materials
RT   Cement Industry
Masonry
Prefabrication
Structural Building Systems

Pretechnology Programs
JUL. 1966
Postings: 35   GC: 400
SN   Special curriculum to prepare individuals for technical education
BT   Programs
RT   Curriculum
Postsecondary Education
Secondary Education
Technical Education

Pretend Play
MAY 1976
Postings: 585   GC: 120
SN   Play involving fantasy or make believe
UF   Fantasy Play
Make Believe Play
Symbolic Play
BT   Play
RT   Behavior Development
Behavior Patterns
Dramatic Play
Fantasy
Imagination
Imitation
Role Playing

Pretensioned Concrete
USE   Prestressed Concrete

Pretesting
JUL. 1966
Postings: 400   GC: 820
SN   Preliminary trying out of something (e.g., measures, equipment, instructional ma-

terials) to ensure that it has the desired characteristics (Note: Do not confuse with "Pretests Posttests"—prior to Mar80, the use of this term was not restricted by a Scope Note)
BT   Evaluation Methods
RT   Formative Evaluation
Material Development
Quality Control
Test Construction

Pretests Posttests
MAR. 1980
Postings: 2,666   GC: 830
SN   Measures used before and after a treatment, program, course, etc., to determine its effectiveness (Note: The previous Descriptors "Pretests" and "Post Testing" were not restricted by Scope Notes—do not confuse with "Pretesting")
UF   Post Testing (1966 1980)
Pretests (1966 1980)
BT   Tests
RT   Improvement
Program Effectiveness
Research Design
Testing

Pretests (1966 1980)
USE   Pretests Posttests

Prevalence
USE   Incidence

Prevention
JUL. 1966
Postings: 6,783   GC: 520
UF   Preventive Measures
NT   Accident Prevention
Crime Prevention
Dropout Prevention
Hearing Conservation
RT   Early Intervention
Fire Protection
Health Behavior
Health Promotion
Prereferral Intervention
Preservation
Preventive Medicine
Risk Management

Preventive Health
USE   Health Promotion

Preventive Measures
USE   Prevention

Preventive Medicine
JUL. 1966
Postings: 798   GC: 210
SN   Medical science that deals with prevention of diseases
BT   Medicine
RT   Child Health
Disease Control
Epidemiology
Fluoridation
Health Promotion
Hygiene
Immunization Programs
Medical Services
Oral Rehydration Therapy
Patient Education
Prenatal Care
Prevention
Public Health
Sports Medicine

Previous Learning
USE   Prior Learning

Prevocational Education
JUL. 1966
Postings: 854   GC: 400
SN   Orientation and counseling, usually at the junior high/middle school level, designed to assist students in determining the occupational areas for which they might best prepare—may include train-

= Two or more Descriptors are used to represent this term.
The term's main entry shows the appropriate coordination.

ing in work habits and skills applicable to a variety of jobs (i.e., following directions, punctuality, etc.) (Note: Prior to Mar80, the use of this term was not restricted by a Scope Note)
UF   Prevocational Training
BT   Vocational Education
RT   Career Choice
     Career Counseling
     Career Education
     Career Exploration
     Career Planning
     Technical Education
     Vocational Aptitude

Prevocational Training
USE   Prevocational Education

Prewriting   *JUN. 1981*
     Postings: 465   GC: 400
SN   All activities that precede the first draft of a written work—includes planning, outlining, notetaking, oral discussion, use of visual aids, etc. (Note: Do not confuse with "Writing Readiness")
BT   Writing Processes
RT   Free Writing
     Journal Writing
     Motivation Techniques
     Notetaking
     Outlining (Discourse)
     Process Approach (Writing)
     Rhetorical Invention
     Writing (Composition)
     Writing Exercises
     Writing Instruction
     Writing Readiness
     Writing Skills

Price Indexes
USE   Cost Indexes

Priests   *JUL. 1966*
     Postings: 92   GC: 640
BT   Clergy
RT   Catholics
     Church Workers
     Churches
     Religion
     Religious Cultural Groups
     Theological Education

Primacy Effect   *DEC. 1970*
     Postings: 48   GC: 110
SN   Learning process in which earlier items of a series are more readily learned and favored in recall
UF   Law of Primacy
BT   Learning Processes
RT   Learning Theories
     Memorization
     Recall (Psychology)
     Retention (Psychology)
     Rote Learning
     Serial Learning

Primary Education   *JUL. 1966*
     Postings: 14,985   GC: 340
SN   Education provided in kindergarten through grade 3 (Note: Also appears in the list of mandatory educational level Descriptors)
UF   Primary Grades (1966 1980)
BT   Early Childhood Education
     Elementary Education
RT   Adult Basic Education
     British Infant Schools
     Grade 1
     Grade 2
     Grade 3
     Kindergarten

Primary Grades (1966 1980)
USE   Primary Education

Primary Health Care   *DEC. 1974*
     Postings: 823   GC: 210
SN   First contact health care, including longitudinal responsibility for the patient and coordination of all aspects of the patient's care
BT   Medicine
RT   Child Health
     Family Health
     Family Practice (Medicine)
     Health
     Internal Medicine
     Medical Care Evaluation
     Medical Services
     Patient Education
     Pediatrics
     Prenatal Care

Primary Sources   *MAY 1974*
     Postings: 1,337   GC: 720
SN   Persons, places, or things that provide firsthand information about something
UF   Original Sources
BT   Information Sources
RT   Historiography
     History
     Manuscripts
     Oral History
     Research Tools
     Resource Materials

Primatology   *SEP. 1968*
     Postings: 56   GC: 490
BT   Zoology
RT   Anthropology

Prime Numbers   *FEB. 1970*
     Postings: 110   GC: 480
BT   Integers

Principal Components Analysis
USE   Factor Analysis

Principals   *JUL. 1966*
     Postings: 8,512   GC: 360
UF   School Principals
BT   Administrators
     School Personnel
RT   Assistant Principals
     Beginning Principals
     Instructional Leadership
     School Administration
     School Based Management
     School Supervision

Print Making Arts
USE   Printmaking

Print Media (Materials)
USE   Printed Materials

Printed Materials   *DEC. 1994*
     Postings: 672   GC: 720
SN   Communication media making use of paper or a similar substance to inscribe text, illustrations, etc.
UF   Print Media (Materials)
     Printed Text
NT   Books
     Manuscripts
     Pamphlets
RT   Communications
     Educational Media
     Instructional Materials
     Layout (Publications)
     Library Materials
     Mass Media
     Newspapers
     Nonprint Media
     Paper (Material)
     Periodicals
     Printing
     Publications
     Publishing Industry
     Reference Materials
     Resource Materials

Printed Text
USE   Printed Materials

Printing   *JUL. 1966*
     Postings: 685   GC: 640
BT   Graphic Arts
RT   Computer Printers
     Industrial Arts
     Layout (Publications)
     Paper (Material)
     Photocomposition
     Printed Materials
     Publications
     Publishing Industry
     Reprography
     Signs
     Textbook Publication
     Typewriting
     Written Language

Printmaking   *OCT. 1994*
     Postings: 56   GC: 420
SN   The process of making a picture or design from an impression of an engraved metal plate, wooden block, silkscreen stencil, lithographic stone, photographic negative, etc.
UF   Print Making Arts
BT   Visual Arts
RT   Childrens Art
     Graphic Arts

Printscript
USE   Manuscript Writing (Handlettering)

Prior Experiential Learning
USE   Experiential Learning
AND   Prior Learning

Prior Knowledge
USE   Prior Learning

Prior Learning   *OCT. 1979*
     Postings: 1,729   GC: 110
SN   Formal or informal learning taking place before entrance into a specific program—often assessed to determine awarding of credit for knowledge already attained (prior learning may include experiential learning)
UF   Previous Learning
     Prior Experiential Learning #
     Prior Knowledge
BT   Learning
RT   Access to Education
     Admission Criteria
     Advanced Placement
     Certification
     College Credits
     Credits
     Educational Experience
     Employment Experience
     Equivalency Tests
     Experience
     Experiential Learning
     Familiarity
     Informal Education
     Job Placement
     Learning Experience
     Nontraditional Education
     Nontraditional Students
     Prerequisites
     Special Degree Programs
     Student Experience
     Student Placement
     Transfer Policy
     Transfer Programs
     Transfer Students
     Work Experience

Priority Determination
USE   Needs Assessment

Prison Education
USE   Correctional Education

Prison Libraries   *APR. 1980*
     Postings: 69   GC: 710
SN   Libraries in prisons provided primarily for use by the inmates
BT   Institutional Libraries
RT   Correctional Education
     Correctional Institutions
     Prisoners

Prison Sentences
USE   Sentencing

Prisoners   *JUL. 1966*
     Postings: 1,635   GC: 530
UF   Inmates
     Jail Inmates
BT   Institutionalized Persons
RT   Correctional Education
     Correctional Institutions
     Correctional Rehabilitation
     Criminals
     Criminology
     Prison Libraries
     Sentencing

Prisons
USE   Correctional Institutions

Privacy   *OCT. 1977*
     Postings: 975   GC: 520
SN   Condition whereby individuals or their properties are free from unwarranted scrutiny
UF   Invasion of Privacy
NT   Confidentiality
BT   Relationship
RT   Civil Law
     Civil Liberties
     Computer Security
     Confidential Records
     Constitutional Law
     Design Requirements
     Disclosure
     Ethics
     Freedom
     Freedom of Information
     Information Policy
     Intellectual Freedom
     Interpersonal Relationship
     Laws
     Libel and Slander

Private Agencies   *JUL. 1966*
     Postings: 587   GC: 520
UF   Nonpublic Agencies
BT   Agencies
RT   Agency Role
     Nongovernmental Organizations
     Private Sector
     Public Agencies
     Voluntary Agencies

Private Colleges   *SEP. 1968*
     Postings: 3,922   GC: 340
SN   Degree-granting institutions of higher education which are privately funded and controlled
UF   Independent Colleges
     Private Junior Colleges #
     Private Universities
BT   Colleges
     Private Schools
RT   Church Related Colleges
     Private Education
     Private Financial Support
     Public Colleges
     Selective Colleges
     Single Sex Colleges
     Small Colleges

Private Education   *MAR. 1980*
     Postings: 659   GC: 340
SN   Education primarily supported by nonpublic funds
UF   Nonpublic Education
     Private Higher Education #
BT   Education

= Two or more Descriptors are used to represent this term.
The term's main entry shows the appropriate coordination.

RT Catholic Schools
    Church Related Colleges
    Corporate Education
    Free Education
    Home Schooling
    Parochial Schools
    Private Colleges
    Private School Aid
    Private Schools
    Private Sector
    Proprietary Schools
    Public Education

Private Financial Support   *JUL. 1966*
    Postings: 1,958   GC: 620
SN Financial aid received from private sources (Note: Do not confuse with "Private School Aid")
UF Philanthropy
BT Financial Support
RT Capital
    Corporate Support
    Costs
    Donors
    Educational Finance
    Free Enterprise System
    Fund Raising
    Grantsmanship
    Philanthropic Foundations
    Phonathons
    Private Colleges
    Proprietary Schools
    Public Support
    School Business Relationship

Private Higher Education
USE Higher Education
AND Private Education

Private Information
USE Confidentiality

Private Junior Colleges
USE Private Colleges
AND Two Year Colleges

Private School Aid   *MAR. 1980*
    Postings: 589   GC: 620
SN Public or private financial support given to private, religious, or other nonpublic schools, colleges, or universities (Note: Do not confuse with "Private Financial Support")
UF Nonpublic School Aid (1972 1980)
    Parochial School Aid (1972 1980) #
BT Financial Support
    School Support
RT Catholic Schools
    Church Related Colleges
    Educational Finance
    Educational Vouchers
    Federal Aid
    Government School Relationship
    Parochial Schools
    Private Education
    Private Schools
    School Choice
    School Funds
    School Taxes
    Shared Resources and Services
    State Aid
    State Church Separation

Private Schools   *JUL. 1966*
    Postings: 3,481   GC: 340
UF Independent Schools
    Nonpublic Schools
NT Parochial Schools
    Private Colleges
    Proprietary Schools
BT Schools
RT Correspondence Schools
    Private Education
    Private School Aid
    Single Sex Schools

Private Sector   *APR. 1990*
    Postings: 874   GC: 620
SN The segment of an economy that is privately owned and operated, including private businesses and households but excluding government agencies and government-owned corporations
UF Nonpublic Sector
RT Business
    Business Administration
    Business Responsibility
    Economics
    Free Enterprise System
    Home Management
    Ownership
    Private Agencies
    Private Education
    Privatization
    Public Sector

Private Universities
USE Private Colleges

Privatization   *APR. 1990*
    Postings: 560   GC: 620
SN The transfer of government assets and services to the private sector—also, the practice by government agencies of hiring private contractors to perform agency functions
UF Contracting Out (of Government Services)
RT Business
    Contracts
    Economics
    Educational Economics
    Free Enterprise System
    Government Role
    Government School Relationship
    Private Sector
    Public Agencies
    Public Policy
    School Business Relationship

Privileged Communication
USE Confidentiality

Proactive Inhibition
USE Inhibition

Probability   *JUL. 1966*
    Postings: 1,880   GC: 480
UF Probability Theory (1967 1980)
BT Mathematics
RT Bayesian Statistics
    Chaos Theory
    Estimation (Mathematics)
    Expectancy Tables
    Expectation
    Game Theory
    Incidence
    Least Squares Statistics
    Markov Processes
    Mathematical Concepts
    Maximum Likelihood Statistics
    Monte Carlo Methods
    Prediction
    Predictive Measurement
    Predictor Variables
    Reliability
    Risk
    Sample Size
    Sampling
    Statistical Analysis
    Statistical Distributions
    Statistical Inference
    Statistical Significance
    Statistics

Probability Theory (1967 1980)
USE Probability

Probation Officers   *JUL. 1966*
    Postings: 91   GC: 640
BT Caseworkers
RT Correctional Rehabilitation
    Counselors

Crime
Delinquent Rehabilitation
Guidance Personnel
Parole Officers
School Guidance
Social Workers

Probationary Period   *SEP. 1968*
    Postings: 239   GC: 630
SN Period in which a person must prove his/her ability to fulfill certain conditions as to achievement, behavior, or job assignment
UF Probationary Teachers
NT Academic Probation
RT Ability Identification
    Beginning Teachers
    Behavior Development
    Behavior Standards
    Contracts
    Correctional Rehabilitation
    Delinquent Rehabilitation
    Employee Responsibility
    Employer Employee Relationship
    Employment
    Nontenured Faculty
    Promotion (Occupational)
    Student School Relationship
    Tenure

Probationary Teachers
USE Probationary Period

Problem Based Learning   *NOV. 1999*
    Postings: 547   GC: 310
SN Any educational process that engages students to collaboratively investigate and resolve one or more ill-structured (open-ended) real-world problems
UF Problem Centered Curriculum
    Problem Oriented Instruction
BT Learning
RT Active Learning
    Case Method (Teaching Technique)
    Clinical Experience
    Cooperative Learning
    Critical Thinking
    Discovery Learning
    Experiential Learning
    Learning Activities
    Learning Strategies
    Medical Education
    Problem Solving
    Problems

Problem Centered Curriculum
USE Problem Based Learning

Problem Children   *JUL. 1966*
    Postings: 514   GC: 230
BT Children
RT Behavior Disorders
    Behavior Problems
    Family Problems
    Obedience
    Personality Problems
    Problems

Problem Drinking
USE Alcohol Abuse

Problem Oriented Instruction
USE Problem Based Learning

Problem Sets   *JUL. 1966*
    Postings: 557   GC: 830
SN Tasks, exercises, or test questions dealing with a specified educational subject or content area
BT Instructional Materials
RT Item Banks
    Learning Activities
    Mathematical Applications
    Problem Solving
    Test Items
    Test Manuals

Testing
Tests
Workbooks

Problem Solving   *JUL. 1966*
    Postings: 22,246   GC: 110
UF Participative Problem Solving #
BT Cognitive Processes
RT Brainstorming
    Concept Mapping
    Conflict Resolution
    Convergent Thinking
    Coping
    Creative Thinking
    Critical Incidents Method
    Critical Thinking
    Decision Making
    Decision Making Skills
    Discussion
    Divergent Thinking
    Evaluative Thinking
    Expert Systems
    Game Theory
    Guided Design
    Help Seeking
    Heuristics
    Information Seeking
    Information Utilization
    Intuition
    Inventions
    Learning Strategies
    Logical Thinking
    Management Games
    Management Systems
    Mathematical Applications
    Monte Carlo Methods
    Problem Based Learning
    Problem Sets
    Problems
    Productive Thinking
    Protocol Analysis
    Research Methodology
    Scientific Attitudes
    Scientific Methodology
    Systems Analysis
    Systems Approach
    Test Wiseness
    Thinking Skills
    Troubleshooting

Problems   *JUL. 1966*
    Postings: 2,611   GC: 530
SN Difficulties or obstacles not easily overcome (Note: Use a more specific term if possible)
NT Administrative Problems
    Behavior Problems
    Communication Problems
    Community Problems
    Curriculum Problems
    Discipline Problems
    Emotional Problems
    Employment Problems
    Evaluation Problems
    Family Problems
    Financial Problems
    Labor Problems
    Learning Problems
    Legal Problems
    Migrant Problems
    Personality Problems
    Reading Difficulties
    Research Problems
    Social Problems
    Student Problems
    Suburban Problems
    Testing Problems
    Urban Problems
    World Problems
    Writing Difficulties
    Youth Problems
RT Difficulty Level
    Problem Based Learning
    Problem Children
    Problem Solving

Procedural Due Process
USE Due Process

= Two or more Descriptors are used to represent this term.
The term's main entry shows the appropriate coordination.

Procedures
USE   Methods

Process Approach (Writing)   *AUG. 2000*
         Postings: 524   GC: 400
SN   Method of teaching writing, often in a
         workshop atmosphere, in which students
         are guided through all aspects of the
         writing process—students brainstorm
         topics, produce drafts, confer about their
         writing, revise, edit, and make their writ-
         ing available to others (i.e., "publish")
UF   Process Writing
         Writing as Process
         Writing Process Approach
BT   Writing Instruction
RT   Prewriting
         Revision (Written Composition)
         Writing (Composition)
         Writing Assignments
         Writing Improvement
         Writing Processes
         Writing Skills
         Writing Strategies
         Writing Workshops

Process Education   *AUG. 1974*
         Postings: 1,055   GC: 310
SN   Educational system which emphasizes
         the learning and demonstration of
         generalizable process skills (e.g., obser-
         vation, classification, measurement, pre-
         diction, communication, and inference)
BT   Education
RT   Behavioral Objectives
         Science Process Skills
         Skill Development
         Skills

Process Evaluation
USE   Formative Evaluation

Process Writing
USE   Process Approach (Writing)

Processed Foods Inspectors
USE   Food and Drug Inspectors

Procreation
USE   Reproduction (Biology)

Proctoring   *JUL. 1966*
         Postings: 52   GC: 310
SN   Acting with delegated authority to main-
         tain security, supervise, or discipline stu-
         dents in such school activities as exami-
         nations or study halls, generally by
         persons who are not teachers
BT   Supervision
RT   Classroom Techniques
         Discipline
         School Aides
         Study
         Teacher Aides
         Teaching Assistants
         Testing

Producer Services   *JUL. 1966*
         Postings: 59   GC: 650
SN   Business, professional, and government
         services provided to the business com-
         munity rather than the individual con-
         sumer, including maintenance,
         administrative, policy making, regula-
         tory, financial, etc.
BT   Services
RT   Agribusiness
         Business
         Government (Administrative Body)
         Industry
         Service Occupations

Product Evaluation
USE   Summative Evaluation

Product Information
USE   Merchandise Information

Product Labels
USE   Merchandise Information

Production Functions
USE   Productivity

Production Machine Operators
USE   Machine Tool Operators

Production Technicians   *AUG. 1968*
         Postings: 71   GC: 640
BT   Paraprofessional Personnel
RT   Assembly (Manufacturing)
         Engineering Technicians
         Manufacturing
         Manufacturing Industry
         Mass Production

Production Techniques   *JUL. 1966*
         Postings: 2,164   GC: 720
SN   Techniques for creating finished prod-
         ucts, such as films, radio and television
         programs, publications, etc.
NT   Desktop Publishing
         Electronic Publishing
         Film Production
         Photocomposition
         Special Effects
         Television Lighting
         Textbook Publication
BT   Methods
RT   Educational Media
         Industry
         Mass Production
         Photography
         Radio
         Television
         Television Curriculum
         Theater Arts

Productive Living (1967 1980)
USE   Quality of Life

Productive Thinking   *JUL. 1966*
         Postings: 469   GC: 110
SN   Creative thinking that results in some-
         thing new (Note: Prior to Mar80, the use
         of this term was not restricted by a
         Scope Note)
BT   Creative Thinking
RT   Cognitive Ability
         Convergent Thinking
         Critical Thinking
         Discovery Processes
         Divergent Thinking
         Evaluative Thinking
         Inventions
         Problem Solving
         Productivity
         Thinking Skills

Productivity   *JUL. 1966*
         Postings: 3,726   GC: 620
UF   Educational Production Functions
         Production Functions
RT   Ability
         Accountability
         Achievement
         Developed Nations
         Developing Nations
         Economic Factors
         Economic Impact
         Economics
         Educational Economics
         Efficiency
         Evaluation Criteria
         Faculty Publishing
         Human Capital
         Inflation (Economics)
         Investment
         Job Simplification
         Organizational Effectiveness
         Ownership

Performance Technology
Productive Thinking
Program Effectiveness
Quality of Life
Quality of Working Life
Research and Development
Retrenchment
Supply and Demand
Worker Days

Professional Associations   *JUL. 1966*
         Postings: 4,794   GC: 520
UF   Dental Associations (1966 1980) #
NT   Library Associations
         Medical Associations
         Teacher Associations
BT   Organizations (Groups)
RT   Collegiality
         Faculty Organizations
         Fraternities
         International Organizations
         National Organizations
         Sororities

Professional Autonomy   *NOV. 1982*
         Postings: 728   GC: 330
SN   Freedom of professionals or groups of
         professionals to function independently
UF   Teacher Autonomy
RT   Academic Freedom
         Administrative Policy
         Decision Making
         Empowerment
         Governance
         Institutional Autonomy
         Intellectual Freedom
         Interpersonal Relationship
         Interprofessional Relationship
         Personal Autonomy
         Power Structure
         Professional Personnel
         Professional Services
         School District Autonomy
         School Restructuring
         Self Determination
         Teacher Empowerment
         Teacher Welfare
         Teaching Conditions
         Work Attitudes
         Work Environment

Professional Continuing Education
                                          JUL. 1966
         Postings: 3,573   GC: 340
SN   Education of adults in professional fields
         for occupational updating and
         improvement—usually consists of short-
         term, intensive, specialized learning ex-
         periences often categorized by general
         field of specialization
BT   Continuing Education
         Professional Education
RT   Adult Education
         Alumni Education
         Continuing Education Units
         Corporate Education
         Extension Education
         Faculty Development
         Inservice Education
         Institutes (Training Programs)
         Lifelong Learning
         Management Development
         Mandatory Continuing Education
         Minicourses
         Professional Development
         Refresher Courses
         Sabbatical Leaves
         Teacher Centers
         Womens Education

Professional Development   *OCT. 1979*
         Postings: 8,120   GC: 630
SN   Activities to enhance professional career
         growth
UF   Professional Growth
NT   Faculty Development
BT   Labor Force Development
RT   Assessment Centers (Personnel)
         Career Change

Collegiality
Individual Development
Industrial Training
Inservice Education
Management Development
Mentors
Professional Continuing Education
Professional Development Schools
Professional Education
Professional Isolation
Professional Personnel
Professional Recognition
Professional Training
Sabbatical Leaves
Staff Development
Teacher Improvement
Writing for Publication

Professional Development Schools
                                          NOV. 1994
         Postings: 525   GC: 340
SN   Designated elementary or secondary
         schools that operate programs, gener-
         ally characterized by college/school dis-
         trict collaboration, in three areas—teacher
         education and development, research and
         experimentation, and improvement of
         teaching and student learning (Note: See
         also related Identifiers such as "Partner
         Schools," "Centers of Pedagogy," "Pro-
         fessional Development Centers," and
         "Teacher Education Academies")
UF   Clinical Schools (Teacher Education)
         Professional Practice Schools
BT   Schools
RT   Alternative Teacher Certification
         Beginning Teacher Induction
         Clinical Supervision (of Teachers)
         College School Cooperation
         Elementary Schools
         Experimental Schools
         Faculty Development
         Inservice Teacher Education
         Laboratory Schools
         Preservice Teacher Education
         Professional Development
         Secondary Schools
         Student Teaching
         Teacher Education

Professional Education   *JUL. 1966*
         Postings: 7,826   GC: 340
SN   Programs of academic study that pre-
         pare students to enter or advance in
         professional fields (Note: Prior to Mar80,
         this term was not differentiated from
         "Professional Training," which is more
         short term and job-specific)
UF   First Professional Degrees #
NT   Administrator Education
         Architectural Education
         Business Administration Education
         Engineering Education
         Home Economics Education
         Information Science Education
         Legal Education (Professions)
         Medical Education
         Professional Continuing Education
         Public Administration Education
         Teacher Education
         Theological Education
BT   Education
RT   Adult Education
         Allied Health Occupations Education
         Assistantships
         College Entrance Examinations
         Dental Schools
         Dental Students
         Educational Gerontology
         Experiential Learning
         Graduate Study
         Internship Programs
         Law Schools
         Law Students
         Library Schools
         Licensing Examinations (Professions)
         Medical Schools
         Medical Students
         Postdoctoral Education
         Postsecondary Education as a Field of
            Study

= Two or more Descriptors are used to represent this term.
The term's main entry shows the appropriate coordination.

Premedical Students
Professional Development
Professional Occupations
Professional Personnel
Professional Training
Sabbatical Leaves
State Licensing Boards
State Universities

Professional Growth
USE Professional Development

Professional Isolation   *MAY 1993*
Postings: 91   GC: 520
SN   A condition of professional individuals
     or groups characterized by lack of com-
     munication or interaction with colleagues,
     the relevant professional community, or
     related professional organizations (Note:
     Prior to May93, the Identifier "Isolation
     (Professional)" was used to index this
     concept—see also the current Identifier
     "Teacher Isolation")
RT   Collegiality
     Cultural Isolation
     Geographic Isolation
     Interprofessional Relationship
     Professional Development
     Professional Personnel
     Social Isolation
     Teaching Conditions
     Work Environment

Professional Negotiation
USE Collective Bargaining

Professional Nurses
USE Nurses

Professional Occupations   *JUL. 1966*
Postings: 1,324   GC: 640
NT   Teaching (Occupation)
BT   Occupations
RT   Allied Health Occupations
     Data Processing Occupations
     Health Occupations
     Managerial Occupations
     Professional Education
     Professional Personnel
     Professional Training
     Technology
     White Collar Occupations

Professional Personnel   *JUL. 1966*
Postings: 3,015   GC: 630
UF   Professional Staff
NT   Accountants
     Architects
     Athletic Coaches
     Dentists
     Engineers
     Faculty
     Information Scientists
     Lawyers
     Mathematicians
     Nurses
     Optometrists
     Pharmacists
     Physicians
     Psychologists
     Research Directors
     Researchers
     Scientists
     Social Scientists
     Social Workers
     Teachers
     Therapists
     Veterinarians
BT   Personnel
RT   Administrators
     Allied Health Personnel
     Employees
     Health Personnel
     Judges
     Lay People
     Nonprofessional Personnel
     Paraprofessional Personnel
     Professional Autonomy

Professional Development
Professional Education
Professional Isolation
Professional Occupations
Professional Recognition
Professional Services
Professional Training

Professional Practice Schools
USE Professional Development Schools

Professional Recognition   *JUL. 1966*
Postings: 2,586   GC: 520
SN   Expressed or implied acknowledgment
     of one's professional efforts, qualities,
     and/or training
UF   Professional Status
BT   Recognition (Achievement)
RT   Awards
     Compensation (Remuneration)
     Educational Benefits
     Employment Level
     Motivation
     Prestige
     Professional Development
     Professional Personnel
     Rewards
     Status
     Status Need
     Teacher Militancy
     Teacher Morale
     Teacher Welfare

Professional Services   *JUL. 1966*
Postings: 622   GC: 520
BT   Services
RT   Consultants
     Consultation Programs
     Intermediate Administrative Units
     Interprofessional Relationship
     Malpractice
     Medical Services
     Professional Autonomy
     Professional Personnel
     Referral
     Social Services

Professional Staff
USE Professional Personnel

Professional Standards
USE Standards

Professional Status
USE Professional Recognition

Professional Training   *JUL. 1966*
Postings: 2,955   GC: 330
SN   Special instruction to develop skills
     needed to improve job performance of
     professional personnel—usually short
     term and job-specific (Note: Prior to
     Mar80, this term was not differentiated
     from "Professional Education," which is
     the longer-term academic preparation
     needed to enter or advance in profes-
     sional fields)
BT   Training
RT   Business Administration Education
     Faculty Development
     Improvement Programs
     Industrial Training
     Information Science Education
     Inservice Education
     Inservice Teacher Education
     Institutes (Training Programs)
     International Trade Vocabulary
     Job Skills
     Management Development
     Medical Vocabulary
     Professional Development
     Professional Education
     Professional Occupations
     Professional Personnel

Professorial Rank
USE Academic Rank (Professional)

Professors   *JUL. 1966*
Postings: 1,013   GC: 360
SN   Teachers who have attained the high-
     est academic rank possible in higher
     education institutions (Note: Use "Col-
     lege Faculty" for associate or assistant
     professors—prior to Mar80, the use of
     this term was not restricted by a Scope
     Note)
BT   College Faculty
RT   Academic Rank (Professional)
     Counselor Educators
     Student Teacher Supervisors
     Teacher Educators
     Tenured Faculty

Proficiency Based Education
USE Competency Based Education

Proficiency Based Teacher Education
USE Competency Based Teacher Education

Proficiency Tests (Academic)
USE Achievement Tests

Proficiency Tests (Language)
USE Language Proficiency
AND Language Tests

Profile Evaluation (1966 1980)
USE Profiles

Profiles   *MAR. 1980*
Postings: 1,820   GC: 730
SN   Summary descriptions, often presented
     in diagrams or charts, that indicate the
     significant features of an individual, group,
     process, etc.
UF   Profile Evaluation (1966 1980)
BT   Data
RT   Academic Records
     Background
     Biographical Inventories
     Case Records
     Census Figures
     Charts
     Course Descriptions
     Interest Inventories
     Medical Case Histories
     Personnel Data
     Portfolios (Background Materials)
     Precision Teaching
     Program Descriptions
     Report Cards
     Resumes (Personal)
     Student Records

Profound Disabilities
USE Severe Disabilities

Profoundly Hearing Impaired
USE Deafness

Profoundly Mentally Retarded
USE Severe Mental Retardation

Prognoses
USE Prognostic Tests

Prognostic Tests   *JUL. 1966*
Postings: 157   GC: 830
SN   Tests used to predict the outcome of
     educational, medical, or psychological
     programs or treatments (Note: Prior to
     Mar80, this term was not scoped and
     was often used for "Aptitude Tests")
UF   Prognoses
BT   Tests
RT   Diagnostic Tests
     Educational Testing

Interest Inventories
Intervention
Medical Services
Predictive Measurement
Predictor Variables
Preschool Tests
Psychological Testing
Reading Readiness Tests
Rehabilitation Programs
School Readiness Tests
Screening Tests
Special Education

Program Administration   *JUL. 1966*
Postings: 6,398   GC: 320
BT   Administration
RT   Audits (Verification)
     Organizational Development
     Program Development
     Program Implementation
     Program Improvement
     Programs
     Research Administration
     Retrenchment
     Strategic Planning

Program Approval (Validation)
USE Program Validation

Program Attitudes   *JUL. 1966*
Postings: 975   GC: 320
SN   Attitudes toward or about programs
BT   Attitudes
RT   Program Evaluation
     Programs

Program Budgeting   *JUL. 1966*
Postings: 1,274   GC: 620
SN   Construction of budget estimates based
     on particular programs or functions, to
     help decision makers allocate funds for
     specific activities or objectives
BT   Budgeting
RT   Budgets
     Program Costs
     Program Implementation
     Programs

Program Content   *JUL. 1966*
Postings: 3,129   GC: 320
SN   Activities or subject matter of an educa-
     tional program
RT   Articulation (Education)
     Course Content
     Program Design
     Program Validation
     Programs
     Validated Programs

Program Coordination (1966 1980)
USE Cooperative Programs
AND Coordination

Program Costs   *JUL. 1966*
Postings: 3,249   GC: 620
BT   Costs
RT   Cost Estimates
     Expenditure per Student
     Instructional Student Costs
     Program Budgeting
     Program Evaluation
     Program Proposals
     Programs
     Unit Costs

Program Descriptions   *JUL. 1966*
Postings: 36,077   GC: 730
RT   Bulletins
     Profiles
     Program Evaluation
     Program Guides
     Program Proposals
     Programs
     Reports
     School Catalogs

= Two or more Descriptors are used to represent this term.
The term's main entry shows the appropriate coordination.

Program Design   *JUL. 1966*
        Postings: 6,026   GC: 320
SN   The arrangement or underlying scheme
        of a program that governs its functioning
        or development (Note: Do not confuse
        with "Program Development" or "Pro-
        gram Implementation"—prior to Mar80,
        the use of this term was not restricted by
        a Scope Note)
BT   Design
RT   Program Content
        Program Development
        Program Implementation
        Program Length
        Program Proposals
        Programs

Program Development   *JUL. 1966*
        Postings: 31,570   GC: 320
SN   Process of formulating a scheme, devis-
        ing procedures, or planning activities
        with regard to specific program objec-
        tives (Note: Do not confuse with "Pro-
        gram Design" or "Program Implementa-
        tion"—prior to Mar80, the use of this
        term was not restricted by a Scope Note)
UF   Program Planning (1966 1980)
BT   Development
RT   Educational Development
        Formative Evaluation
        Program Administration
        Program Design
        Program Effectiveness
        Program Evaluation
        Program Implementation
        Program Improvement
        Programs
        Systems Development

Program Discontinuance
USE   Program Termination

Program Effectiveness   *JUL. 1966*
        Postings: 22,634   GC: 320
SN   Degree to which programs are success-
        ful in accomplishing their objectives or
        in otherwise making changes
RT   Accountability
        Audits (Verification)
        Cost Effectiveness
        Educational Assessment
        Educational Quality
        Educational Research
        Efficiency
        Excellence in Education
        Instructional Effectiveness
        Methods Research
        Organizational Effectiveness
        Outcomes of Education
        Pretests Posttests
        Productivity
        Program Development
        Program Evaluation
        Program Validation
        Programs
        Quality Control
        School Effectiveness
        Success
        Summative Evaluation
        Validated Programs

Program Elimination
USE   Program Termination

Program Evaluation   *JUL. 1966*
        Postings: 39,464   GC: 320
SN   Judging the feasibility, efficacy, value,
        etc., of a program in relation to stated
        objectives, standards, or criteria
BT   Evaluation
RT   Course Evaluation
        Curriculum Evaluation
        Educational Assessment
        Field Tests
        Holistic Evaluation
        Input Output Analysis
        Institutional Evaluation
        Instructional Material Evaluation
        Outcomes of Education

        Program Attitudes
        Program Costs
        Program Descriptions
        Program Development
        Program Effectiveness
        Program Improvement
        Program Termination
        Program Validation
        Programs
        Self Evaluation (Groups)
        Summative Evaluation
        Validated Programs

Program Guides   *JUL. 1966*
        Postings: 1,753   GC: 730
BT   Guides
RT   Administrator Guides
        Program Descriptions
        Programs

Program Implementation   *MAR. 1980*
        Postings: 12,122   GC: 320
SN   Carrying out, by concrete measures, pro-
        gram plans and designs (Note: Prior to
        Mar80, the instruction "Program Imple-
        mentation, USE Program Development"
        was carried in the Thesaurus)
RT   Program Administration
        Program Budgeting
        Program Design
        Program Development
        Programs

Program Improvement   *JUL. 1966*
        Postings: 5,420   GC: 320
BT   Improvement
RT   Action Research
        Excellence in Education
        Formative Evaluation
        Program Administration
        Program Development
        Program Evaluation
        Programs

Program Length   *JUL. 1966*
        Postings: 493   GC: 350
SN   Length or duration of an educational
        program
RT   Extended Teacher Education Programs
        Program Design
        Program Termination
        Programs
        Scheduling
        Time Factors (Learning)
        Time to Degree

Program Phaseout
USE   Program Termination

Program Planning (1966 1980)
USE   Program Development

Program Proposals   *JUL. 1966*
        Postings: 1,529   GC: 730
UF   Grant Proposals #
        Project Proposals
NT   Research Proposals
RT   Bids
        Financial Support
        Fund Raising
        Grantsmanship
        Program Costs
        Program Descriptions
        Program Design
        Programs
        Proposal Writing
        Research Projects
        Specifications

Program Termination   *AUG. 1986*
        Postings: 248   GC: 320
SN   Discontinuance of a program or project
        due to funding, evaluation, or other deci-
        sions
UF   Program Discontinuance
        Program Elimination

        Program Phaseout
        Termination of Programs
RT   Financial Exigency
        Program Evaluation
        Program Length
        Program Validation
        Programs
        Reduction in Force
        Retrenchment
        School Closing

Program Validation   *MAR. 1977*
        Postings: 449   GC: 330
SN   The process of approving a program
        according to specified procedures that
        indicate attainment of the claims of the
        sponsors—unlike "evaluation," "valida-
        tion" connotes testing and documenta-
        tion by impartial experts of successful
        uses of the program, usually with the
        implication that it can be successfully
        replicated (Note: For the results of vali-
        dation, see "Validated Programs")
UF   Program Approval (Validation)
RT   Accountability
        Course Content
        Course Evaluation
        Curriculum Evaluation
        Demonstration Programs
        Educational Assessment
        Program Content
        Program Effectiveness
        Program Evaluation
        Program Termination
        Programs
        Summative Evaluation
        Validated Programs
        Validity

Programed Instruction (1966 1994)
USE   Programmed Instruction

**Programed Instructional Materials (1980
1994)**
USE   Programmed Instructional Materials

Programed Materials (1966 1980)
USE   Programmed Instructional Materials

Programed Texts (1966 1980)
USE   Programmed Instructional Materials
AND   Textbooks

Programed Tutoring (1967 1994)
USE   Programmed Tutoring

Programed Units (1966 1980)
USE   Programmed Instruction
AND   Units of Study

Programers (1967 1994)
USE   Programmers

Programing (Broadcast) (1971 1994)
USE   Programming (Broadcast)

Programing Languages (1969 1994)
USE   Programming Languages

Programing Problems (1966 1980)
                                        MAR. 1980
        Postings: 107   GC: 710
SN   Invalid Descriptor—used for various
        types of programing, e.g., computer,
        television, educational, etc.—coordinate
        specific "problem" and "programming"
        Descriptors

Programing (1966 1994)
USE   Programming

Programmed Instruction   *MAR. 1994*
        Postings: 51   GC: 310
SN   Instruction in which learners progress at
        their own rate using workbooks, text-
        books, or electromechanical devices that
        provide information in discrete steps,
        test learning at each step, and provide
        immediate feedback about achievement
UF   Autoinstructional Methods (1966
            1980)
        Autoinstructional Programs (1966
            1980)
        Programed Instruction (1966 1994)
        Programed Units (1966 1980) #
        Programmed Learning
        Programmed Self Instruction
NT   Computer Assisted Instruction
        Programmed Tutoring
BT   Teaching Methods
RT   Autoinstructional Aids
        Branching
        Computer Oriented Programs
        Educational Media
        Educational Technology
        Electronic Classrooms
        Error Correction
        Feedback
        Fixed Sequence
        Guided Design
        Individualized Instruction
        Intermode Differences
        Language Laboratories
        Learner Controlled Instruction
        Learning Laboratories
        Pacing
        Programmed Instructional Materials
        Prompting
        Sequential Approach
        Sequential Learning
        Teaching Machines

Programmed Instructional Materials
                                        MAR. 1994
        Postings: 58   GC: 730
SN   Materials prepared specifically to em-
        ploy programmed instruction techniques
UF   Programed Instructional Materials
            (1980 1994)
        Programed Materials (1966 1980)
        Programed Texts (1966 1980) #
        Self Instruction Materials
BT   Instructional Materials
RT   Audiovisual Aids
        Autoinstructional Aids
        Computer Assisted Instruction
        Courseware
        Instructional Films
        Learner Controlled Instruction
        Learning Modules
        Programmed Instruction
        Programmed Tutoring
        Study Guides
        Teaching Machines
        Textbooks
        Workbooks

Programmed Learning
USE   Programmed Instruction

Programmed Self Instruction
USE   Programmed Instruction

Programmed Tutoring   *MAR. 1994*
        Postings: 43   GC: 310
UF   Programed Tutoring (1967 1994)
BT   Programmed Instruction
        Tutoring
RT   Computer Assisted Instruction
        Intelligent Tutoring Systems
        Programmed Instructional Materials

Programmers   *MAR. 1994*
        Postings: 15   GC: 710
UF   Programers (1967 1994)
BT   Personnel
RT   Programming
        Programming Languages
        Systems Analysts

= Two or more Descriptors are used to represent this term.
The term's main entry shows the appropriate coordination.

Programming MAR. 1994
Postings: 256 GC: 710
SN Putting together a logical sequence of instructions to direct the actions of a computer system (Note: Prior to Mar80, this term, in the form "Programing," was not restricted by a Scope Note)
UF Computer Programming
  Programing (1966 1994)
BT Computer Science
  Computer Software Development
RT Algorithms
  Authoring Aids (Programming)
  Branching
  Coding
  Computer Literacy
  Computer Oriented Programs
  Computer Science Education
  Computer Software
  Computers
  Data Processing
  Debugging (Computers)
  Programmers
  Programming Languages

Programming (Broadcast) MAR. 1994
Postings: 334 GC: 720
SN Scheduling, planning, or constructing programs for broadcast media—the aggregate of programs presented
UF Broadcast Scheduling
  Multichannel Programing (1966 1980)
  Programing (Broadcast) (1971 1994)
  Radio Programming
  Television Programming
  Viewing Time (1968 1980)
RT Audiodisks
  Audiotape Recordings
  Broadcast Industry
  Broadcast Journalism
  Copyrights
  Material Development
  Optical Disks
  Radio
  Scheduling
  Serials
  Soap Operas
  Television
  Television Commercials
  Television Curriculum
  Television Research
  Television Studios
  Television Viewing
  Videodisks
  Videotape Recordings

Programming Languages MAR. 1994
Postings: 143 GC: 710
UF Authoring Languages #
  Computer Languages
  Programing Languages (1969 1994)
BT Language
RT Artificial Languages
  Authoring Aids (Programming)
  Computational Linguistics
  Computer Software
  Computer Software Development
  Computers
  Data Processing
  Programmers
  Programming

Programs JUL. 1966
Postings: 616 GC: 520
SN Schedules or plans of procedure under which a series of intended activities is directed toward desired results (Note: Use a more specific term if possbile)
NT Adult Programs
  Advanced Placement Programs
  After School Programs
  Assembly Programs
  Bilingual Education Programs
  Church Programs
  College Day
  College Programs
  Community Programs
  Comprehensive Programs
  Computer Oriented Programs
  Construction Programs

Consultation Programs
Cooperative Programs
County Programs
Day Programs
Demonstration Programs
Developmental Programs
Emergency Programs
Employee Assistance Programs
Employment Programs
Evening Programs
Exchange Programs
Experimental Programs
Family Programs
Federal Programs
Field Experience Programs
Foundation Programs
Guidance Programs
Health Programs
Home Programs
Human Relations Programs
Improvement Programs
Individualized Programs
Inplant Programs
Institutes (Training Programs)
Intercultural Programs
Intergenerational Programs
International Programs
Internship Programs
Interstate Programs
Migrant Programs
National Programs
Nonschool Educational Programs
Outreach Programs
Pilot Projects
Poverty Programs
Pretechnology Programs
Reading Programs
Recreational Programs
Regional Programs
Rehabilitation Programs
Remedial Programs
Research Projects
Residential Programs
Science Course Improvement Projects
Science Programs
Second Language Programs
Special Programs
State Programs
Student Loan Programs
Summer Programs
Teacher Education Programs
Testing Programs
Transfer Programs
Transitional Programs
Tutorial Programs
Urban Programs
Vacation Programs
Validated Programs
Weekend Programs
Work Experience Programs
Work Study Programs
Youth Programs
RT Program Administration
  Program Attitudes
  Program Budgeting
  Program Content
  Program Costs
  Program Descriptions
  Program Design
  Program Development
  Program Effectiveness
  Program Evaluation
  Program Guides
  Program Implementation
  Program Improvement
  Program Length
  Program Proposals
  Program Termination
  Program Validation

Progressive Education JUL. 1966
Postings: 592 GC: 310
SN An educational movement beginning in the last two decades of the 19th century that based its protest against formalism on the philosophy of John Dewey—basic tenets are commitment to democratic ideals, creative and purposeful activity, receptivity to student needs, and interaction with the community
BT Education
RT Educational Practices

Educational Theories
Free Schools
Humanistic Education
Open Education

Progressive Relaxation (1967 1980)
USE Relaxation Training

Progressive Retardation (1966 1980) (in School)
USE Educationally Disadvantaged

Project Applications (1967 1980) JUN. 1980
Postings: 219 GC: 730
SN Invalid Descriptor—used inconsistently in indexing—see "Program Proposals" and "Program Descriptions"

Project Methods
USE Student Projects
AND Teaching Methods

Project Proposals
USE Program Proposals

Project Schools
USE Experimental Schools

Project Training Methods (1968 1980)
USE Student Projects
AND Teaching Methods

Projection Equipment JUL. 1966
Postings: 398 GC: 910
UF Eight Millimeter Projectors (1970 1980)
  Film Projectors
  Projectors
  Sixteen Millimeter Projectors (1966 1980)
  Slide Projectors
NT Filmstrip Projectors
  Microform Readers
  Opaque Projectors
  Overhead Projectors
  Tachistoscopes
BT Equipment
  Visual Aids
RT Audio Equipment
  Audiovisual Aids
  Educational Equipment
  Magnification Methods
  Photographic Equipment
  Screens (Displays)

Projective Measures MAR. 1980
Postings: 350 GC: 830
SN Procedures or devices used to infer an individual's personality traits, propensities, attitudes, or feelings through responses to vague, ambiguous, or unstructured stimuli
UF Projective Tests (1968 1980)
NT Association Measures
BT Measures (Individuals)
RT Affective Measures
  Creativity Tests
  Diagnostic Tests
  Objective Tests
  Personality Assessment
  Pictorial Stimuli
  Psychological Evaluation
  Visual Measures

Projective Tests (1968 1980)
USE Projective Measures

Projectors
USE Projection Equipment

Projects (1966 1980) MAR. 1980
Postings: 903 GC: 810
SN Invalid Descriptor—see "Programs" and its hierarchy (i.e., narrower terms "Research Projects," "Pilot Projects," etc.)

Proletariat
USE Working Class

Promotion (Occupational) FEB. 1970
Postings: 1,289 GC: 630
UF Advancement
  Salary Raises
NT Faculty Promotion
  Teacher Promotion
RT Assessment Centers (Personnel)
  Career Change
  Career Development
  Career Ladders
  Education Work Relationship
  Employment Level
  Employment Opportunities
  Employment Qualifications
  Job Development
  Job Performance
  Job Skills
  Labor Needs
  Occupational Aspiration
  Occupational Mobility
  Personnel Evaluation
  Probationary Period
  Publish or Perish Issue
  Salaries
  Scope of Bargaining
  Seniority
  Tenure

Prompting JUL. 1966
Postings: 427 GC: 310
SN Providing directional aid through the use of hints, reminders, or cues
UF Cuing
BT Methods
RT Cues
  Dramatics
  Learning Strategies
  Programmed Instruction
  Teaching Methods

Prompts
USE Cues

Pronominals
USE Pronouns

Pronouns JUL. 1966
Postings: 732 GC: 450
UF Pronominals
BT Form Classes (Languages)
RT Language Patterns
  Morphology (Languages)
  Phrase Structure
  Sentence Structure
  Syntax

Pronunciation JUL. 1966
Postings: 1,481 GC: 450
UF Accents (Dialects) #
BT Speech
RT Child Language
  Diacritical Marking
  Diction
  Pronunciation Instruction
  Speech Tests
  Word Lists

Pronunciation Instruction JUL. 1966
Postings: 727 GC: 450
BT Speech Instruction
RT Pronunciation

Proof (Mathematics) APR. 1982
Postings: 645 GC: 480
SN The validity of mathematical statements—also, the sequences of steps, statements,

= Two or more Descriptors are used to represent this term.
The term's main entry shows the appropriate coordination.

or demonstrations that lead to valid
mathematical conclusions
BT   Mathematical Logic
      Validity
RT   Mathematical Concepts
      Mathematical Models
      Mathematics
      Measurement
      Research Methodology
      Robustness (Statistics)
      Test Theory

Proofreading   AUG. 1989
      Postings: 145   GC: 720
SN   Reading typescript or printed copy, of-
      ten against a preceding draft, to find and
      mark errors
RT   Business Skills
      Editing
      Error Correction
      Reading
      Writing Skills

Propaganda   JUL. 1966
      Postings: 569   GC: 720
BT   Communication (Thought Transfer)
      Information Dissemination
RT   Advertising
      Communications
      Deception
      Mass Media
      Persuasive Discourse
      Public Opinion

Properties (Mathematics)   APR. 1990
      Postings: 107   GC: 480
SN   General characteristics of a set of num-
      bers, e.g., closure, commutativity,
      associativity, distributivity, identity ele-
      ments, inverses
UF   Field Properties (Mathematics)
BT   Mathematical Concepts
RT   Geometric Concepts
      Number Concepts

Property Accounting   OCT. 1968
      Postings: 106   GC: 620
UF   Property Control
      Property Control Systems
BT   Accounting
RT   Estate Planning
      Facility Inventory
      Property Taxes
      Trusts (Financial)
      Wills

Property Appraisal   OCT. 1968
      Postings: 129   GC: 620
UF   Real Estate Appraisal
NT   Assessed Valuation
BT   Evaluation
RT   Building Obsolescence
      Estate Planning
      Insurance
      Ownership
      Property Taxes
      Real Estate
      Taxes
      Trusts (Financial)
      Wills

Property Control
USE   Property Accounting

Property Control Systems
USE   Property Accounting

Property Inventory
USE   Facility Inventory

Property Taxes   JUL. 1972
      Postings: 720   GC: 620
UF   Ad Valorem Tax
BT   Taxes
RT   Assessed Valuation

      Educational Finance
      Fiscal Capacity
      Property Accounting
      Property Appraisal
      School District Wealth
      School Taxes
      Tax Rates

Prophylacticians
USE   Dental Hygienists

Proportion (Mathematics)
USE   Ratios (Mathematics)

Proposal Writing   MAR. 1980
      Postings: 426   GC: 330
SN   Process of preparing a statement of goals
      and procedures as part of an application
      for a grant or contract award
BT   Writing (Composition)
RT   Bids
      Financial Support
      Fund Raising
      Grantsmanship
      Program Proposals
      Research Proposals
      Technical Writing

Proprietary Schools   JUL. 1966
      Postings: 634   GC: 340
SN   Private schools conducted for profit (Note:
      See also the Identifier "Profit Making
      Schools")
UF   Specialty Schools
BT   Private Schools
RT   Certification
      Correspondence Schools
      Educational Finance
      Private Education
      Private Financial Support
      Small Colleges
      Student Costs

Propulsion Development Technicians
USE   Mechanical Design Technicians

Prose   JUL. 1966
      Postings: 931   GC: 430
NT   Fiction
      Nonfiction
BT   Literature
RT   Connected Discourse
      Creative Writing
      Descriptive Writing
      Drama
      Expository Writing
      Language Rhythm
      Literary Genres
      Literary Styles
      Poetry
      Tragedy
      Writing (Composition)

Prosocial Behavior   MAY 1976
      Postings: 1,060   GC: 120
SN   Socially valued or positive social actions
      which are generally supportive of others
      within the existing social system
NT   Sharing Behavior
BT   Social Behavior
RT   Affective Behavior
      Altruism
      Antisocial Behavior
      Cooperation
      Emotional Response
      Friendship
      Interpersonal Competence
      Love
      Peace

Prosodic Features (Speech)
USE   Suprasegmentals

Prosody (Literary)
USE   Poetry

Prospective Teachers
USE   Preservice Teachers

Prostheses   JUL. 1966
      Postings: 102   GC: 220
SN   Artificial devices designed to replace ab-
      sent body parts
UF   Cosmetic Prostheses (1967 1980)
NT   Cochlear Implants
BT   Assistive Devices (for Disabled)
RT   Amputations
      Electromechanical Aids
      Mobility Aids
      Physical Disabilities

Protestant Ethic
USE   Work Ethic

Protestants   JUL. 1966
      Postings: 179   GC: 560
NT   Amish
      Puritans
BT   Religious Cultural Groups
RT   Christianity

Protista
USE   Protists

Protists   APR. 1990
      Postings: 3   GC: 490
SN   The biological kingdom of single-celled,
      eukaryotic organisms—sometimes in-
      terpreted more broadly to include all
      simple organisms traditionally classified
      as plants or animals
UF   Protista
      Protoctista
RT   Microbiology
      Monera
      Protozoa

Protocol Analysis   DEC. 1985
      Postings: 462   GC: 810
SN   Procedure for determining and examin-
      ing sequences of activities (protocols)
      used to perform a task, in order to char-
      acterize the cognitive/psychological proc-
      esses involved—protocols may list mo-
      tor behaviors, eye movements, subjects'
      self-reports of their thoughts, etc.
UF   Thinking Aloud Protocols
BT   Research Methodology
RT   Cognitive Processes
      Cognitive Psychology
      Problem Solving
      Skill Analysis
      Writing Processes

Protocol Materials   JAN. 1970
      Postings: 177   GC: 720
SN   Audio and video recordings of behavior
      which the preservice and inservice teacher
      education student can observe and ana-
      lyze
UF   Behavioral Situation Films
      Teacher Training Films
BT   Audiovisual Aids
      Instructional Materials
RT   Audiovisual Instruction
      Behavior
      Behavioral Objectives
      Instructional Films
      Laboratory Training
      Microteaching
      Sensitivity Training
      Teacher Behavior
      Teacher Education
      Videodisks
      Videotape Recordings

Protoctista
USE   Protists

Protozoa   APR. 1990
      Postings: 11   GC: 490
SN   Microscopic, single-celled organisms re-
      garded either as simple animals or mem-
      bers of the kingdom "Protista"
RT   Animals
      Microbiology
      Protists

Proverbs   MAR. 1969
      Postings: 168   GC: 430
UF   Adages
RT   Cultural Context
      Folk Culture
      Idioms

Provincial Aid
USE   State Aid

Provincial Government
USE   State Government

Provincial Libraries
USE   State Libraries

Provincial Regulation
USE   State Regulation

Provincial Surveys
USE   State Surveys

Proxemics
USE   Personal Space

Proximity   AUG. 1977
      Postings: 171   GC: 490
SN   Relative nearness in time, place, rela-
      tionship, etc. (Note: Prior to Aug77, the
      instruction "Proximity, USE Distance"
      was carried in the Thesaurus)
RT   Crowding
      Distance
      Geographic Location
      Height
      Intervals
      Relationship
      School Location
      Space
      Time
      Topology
      Transportation

Psychiatric Aides   JAN. 1969
      Postings: 55   GC: 230
SN   Persons who assist in the care and treat-
      ment of mentally ill patients in psychiat-
      ric facilities, working under the direction
      of nursing and medical staff
UF   Psychiatric Technicians
BT   Allied Health Personnel
      Mental Health Workers
RT   Nurses Aides
      Psychiatric Hospitals

Psychiatric Hospitals   JUL. 1966
      Postings: 441   GC: 230
BT   Hospitals
RT   Hospital Libraries
      Mental Disorders
      Mental Health Clinics
      Milieu Therapy
      Psychiatric Aides
      Psychiatrists
      Residential Institutions
      Therapeutic Environment

Psychiatric Services   JUL. 1966
      Postings: 656   GC: 230
BT   Medical Services
RT   Counseling Services
      Crisis Intervention
      Mental Disorders
      Mental Health

= Two or more Descriptors are used to represent this term.
The term's main entry shows the appropriate coordination.

Mental Health Programs
Physician Patient Relationship
Psychiatrists
Psychiatry
Psychological Services
Psychotherapy

Psychiatric Technicians
USE   Psychiatric Aides

Psychiatrists   *JUL. 1966*
Postings: 220   GC: 230
BT   Mental Health Workers
Physicians
RT   Hospital Personnel
Medical Associations
Medical Consultants
Medical Services
Physician Patient Relationship
Psychiatric Hospitals
Psychiatric Services
Psychiatry
Psychologists

Psychiatry   *SEP. 1968*
Postings: 873   GC: 230
SN   Prevention, diagnosis, and therapy of
emotional illness
UF   Neopsychoanalysis
Psychoanalysis
BT   Medicine
RT   Behavior Disorders
Clinical Psychology
Emotional Adjustment
Emotional Disturbances
Medical Services
Mental Disorders
Mental Health
Neuropsychology
Personality Problems
Psychiatric Services
Psychiatrists
Psychology
Psychotherapy

Psychoacoustics   *JUL. 1966*
Postings: 66   GC: 490
SN   Discipline dealing with the physics of
sound as it relates to audition—includes
study of the physiology of the ear and
psychology of hearing
BT   Acoustics
Psychology
RT   Auditory Discrimination
Auditory Perception
Auditory Stimuli
Echolocation
Hearing (Physiology)
Noise (Sound)

Psychoanalysis
USE   Psychiatry

Psychocatharsis
USE   Catharsis

Psychoeducational Clinics   *JUL. 1966*
Postings: 71   GC: 230
SN   Concerned primarily with behavior prob-
lems of school children related to the
school environment
BT   Clinics
RT   Educational Diagnosis
Educational Therapy
Mental Health Clinics
Psychoeducational Methods
Psychological Services

Psychoeducational Methods   *MAR. 1980*
Postings: 903   GC: 310
SN   Use of psychological principles and pro-
cedures to facilitate learning, in general,
and adjustment in educational settings
UF   Psychoeducational Processes (1966
1980)
BT   Educational Methods

RT   Adjustment (to Environment)
Cognitive Restructuring
Counselor Teacher Cooperation
Diagnostic Teaching
Educational Diagnosis
Educational Therapy
Humanistic Education
Intervention
Learning Processes
Learning Strategies
Psychoeducational Clinics
Psychological Services
School Psychology
Suggestopedia
Token Economy
Transcendental Meditation

Psychoeducational Processes (1966 1980)
USE   Psychoeducational Methods

Psycholinguistics   *JUL. 1966*
Postings: 3,701   GC: 450
SN   Study of the psychological processes
involved in language production and com-
prehension, including such aspects of
language behavior as acquisition and
processing
BT   Linguistics
RT   Bidialectalism
Bilingualism
Caregiver Speech
Child Language
Connected Discourse
Expressive Language
Grammatical Acceptability
Interference (Language)
Interlanguage
Language Acquisition
Language Attitudes
Language Processing
Language Skill Attrition
Language Skills
Linguistic Competence
Linguistic Difficulty (Inherent)
Linguistic Input
Linguistic Performance
Linguistic Theory
Metalinguistics
Multilingualism
Neurolinguistics
Psychology
Receptive Language
Sociolinguistics
Verbal Operant Conditioning

Psychological Abuse
USE   Emotional Abuse

Psychological Characteristics   *JUL. 1966*
Postings: 2,737   GC: 120
NT   Attention Span
Cognitive Style
Creativity
Intelligence
Personality Traits
Schemata (Cognition)
BT   Individual Characteristics
RT   Attribution Theory
Goal Orientation
Individual Psychology
Interpersonal Attraction
Learning Plateaus
Maturity (Individuals)
Midlife Transitions
Phenomenology
Psychological Evaluation
Psychological Needs
Psychological Patterns
Psychological Testing
Psychology
Role Conflict
Self Congruence
Sexual Identity
Type A Behavior
Type B Behavior

Psychological Conditioning
USE   Conditioning

Psychological Design Needs (1968 1980)
USE   Design Requirements

Psychological Education
USE   Humanistic Education

Psychological Evaluation   *JUL. 1966*
Postings: 1,256   GC: 230
SN   Evaluation of an individual's cognitive,
conative, or affective traits or conditions
UF   Clinical Judgment (Psychology)
NT   Personality Assessment
BT   Evaluation
RT   Association Measures
Clinical Psychology
Diagnostic Tests
Personality Measures
Projective Measures
Psychological Characteristics
Psychological Patterns
Psychological Services
Psychological Testing
Psychometrics
School Psychologists
School Psychology
Symptoms (Individual Disorders)

Psychological Needs   *JUL. 1966*
Postings: 1,907   GC: 120
UF   Emotional Needs
NT   Achievement Need
Affection
Affiliation Need
Personal Space
Security (Psychology)
Self Actualization
Status Need
BT   Individual Needs
RT   Childhood Needs
Delay of Gratification
Dependency (Personality)
Design Requirements
Goal Orientation
Humanization
Individual Psychology
Love
Need Gratification
Personal Autonomy
Praise
Psychological Characteristics
Psychological Services
Spatial Relationship (Facilities)
Student Needs

Psychological Patterns   *JUL. 1966*
Postings: 3,531   GC: 120
UF   Emotional Patterns
NT   Alienation
Anger
Anxiety
Apathy
Cognitive Dissonance
Congruence (Psychology)
Defense Mechanisms
Depression (Psychology)
Egocentrism
Empathy
Fear
Happiness
Identification (Psychology)
Jealousy
Moods
Morale
Rejection (Psychology)
Resentment
Resistance (Psychology)
Sadness
Withdrawal (Psychology)
RT   Affective Behavior
Altruism
Assertiveness
Attitudes
Behavior Patterns
Behavior Problems
Burnout
Catharsis
Coping
Credibility
Dreams

Eating Disorders
Emotional Abuse
Emotional Development
Emotional Experience
Emotional Problems
Emotional Response
Ethnicity
Ethnocentrism
Extraversion Introversion
Guilt
Helplessness
Individual Power
Inhibition
Intimacy
Love
Paranoid Behavior
Perspective Taking
Psychological Characteristics
Psychological Evaluation
Psychological Services
Psychological Testing
Psychosomatic Disorders
Responses
Role Conflict
Self Destructive Behavior
Sharing Behavior
Sleep
Social Behavior
Stress Variables
Teaching Styles
Trust (Psychology)
Well Being

Psychological Research
USE   Psychological Studies

Psychological Services   *JUL. 1966*
Postings: 888   GC: 230
UF   Sociopsychological Services (1967
1980) #
BT   Human Services
RT   Ancillary School Services
Mental Health
Psychiatric Services
Psychoeducational Clinics
Psychoeducational Methods
Psychological Evaluation
Psychological Needs
Psychological Patterns
Psychological Studies
Psychological Testing
Psychologists
Psychometrics
Psychotherapy
School Psychology

Psychological Studies   *JUL. 1966*
Postings: 4,635   GC: 810
SN   Basic, applied, and developmental stud-
ies conducted to advance knowledge in
psychology (Note: Use a more specific
term if possible—as of Oct81, use as a
minor Descriptor for examples of this
kind of research—use as a major Descrip-
tor only as the subject of a document)
UF   Psychological Research
NT   Force Field Analysis
Interest Research
Personality Studies
BT   Behavioral Science Research
RT   Clinical Psychology
Cognitive Psychology
Exceptional Child Research
Experimental Psychology
Psychological Services
Psychology
Social Science Research

Psychological Testing   *JUL. 1966*
Postings: 2,023   GC: 820
SN   Use of tests to assess individuals' or
groups' interaction with their environment (Note: Prior to Mar80, the use of
this term was not restricted by a Scope
Note, and the instruction "Mental Measurement, USE Cognitive Measurement"
was carried in the Thesaurus—use a
more precise term if possible)
UF   Mental Tests (1966 1980)

= Two or more Descriptors are used to represent this term.
The term's main entry shows the appropriate coordination.

Psychological Tests (1966 1980)
BT Testing
RT Clinical Psychology
Counseling Psychology
Diagnostic Tests
Intelligence Tests
Neuropsychology
Personality Measures
Prognostic Tests
Psychological Characteristics
Psychological Evaluation
Psychological Patterns
Psychological Services
Psychologists
Psychology
Psychometrics
School Psychology

Psychological Tests (1966 1980)
USE Psychological Testing

Psychologists   JUL. 1966
Postings: 1,189   GC: 230
NT School Psychologists
BT Health Personnel
Professional Personnel
RT Counselors
Mental Health Workers
Psychiatrists
Psychological Services
Psychological Testing
Psychology
Researchers
Social Scientists

Psychology   JUL. 1966
Postings: 4,546   GC: 230
NT Behaviorism
Child Psychology
Clinical Psychology
Cognitive Psychology
Community Psychology
Counseling Psychology
Developmental Psychology
Educational Psychology
Experimental Psychology
Individual Psychology
Industrial Psychology
Neuropsychology
Psychoacoustics
Psychometrics
Psychopathology
Psychophysiology
School Psychology
Social Psychology
Sport Psychology
BT Behavioral Sciences
RT Behavior
Conditioning
Decision Making
Intervention
Psychiatry
Psycholinguistics
Psychological Characteristics
Psychological Studies
Psychological Testing
Psychologists
Psychosomatic Disorders
Sensory Deprivation
Social Science Research
Social Sciences
Verbal Operant Conditioning

Psychometrics   JUL. 1966
Postings: 2,129   GC: 230
SN The development of psychological meas-
uring devices and the analysis of derived
data or scores
UF Psychometrists (1967 1980)
BT Psychology
RT Behaviorism
Clinical Psychology
Cognitive Measurement
Cognitive Psychology
Examiners
Item Response Theory
Psychological Evaluation
Psychological Services
Psychological Testing

School Psychologists
School Psychology
Statistical Analysis
Test Interpretation
Test Theory

Psychometrists (1967 1980)
USE Psychometrics

Psychomotor Objectives   JUL. 1969
Postings: 197   GC: 310
SN Behavioral objectives which emphasize
muscular or motor skills, manipulation
of materials or objects, or an act which
requires neuromuscular coordination
BT Behavioral Objectives
RT Affective Objectives
Cognitive Objectives
Motor Development
Movement Education
Psychomotor Skills

Psychomotor Skills   JUL. 1966
Postings: 2,349   GC: 120
SN Ability to manipulate and control limb
and body movements
UF Coordination (Psychomotor)
Motor Ability
Motor Skills
NT Marksmanship
Object Manipulation
Perceptual Motor Coordination
BT Skills
RT Behavior
Daily Living Skills
Exercise
Lateral Dominance
Manipulative Materials
Motor Development
Motor Reactions
Movement Education
Neurological Impairments
Neurological Organization
Neuropsychology
Nonverbal Learning
Perceptual Development
Perceptual Motor Learning
Psychomotor Objectives
Serial Ordering
Skill Analysis
Spatial Ability

Psychopathology   AUG. 1968
Postings: 1,261   GC: 230
SN Pathology of mental and emotional ill-
ness
UF Abnormal Psychology
BT Pathology
Psychology
RT Behavior
Behavior Disorders
Behavior Problems
Clinical Psychology
Community Psychology
Depression (Psychology)
Emotional Adjustment
Emotional Disturbances
Emotional Problems
Mental Disorders
Personality Problems
Psychophysiology
Psychosomatic Disorders
Self Injurious Behavior
Social Psychology
Suicide

Psychophysiology   AUG. 1968
Postings: 353   GC: 230
UF Physiological Psychology
BT Physiology
Psychology
RT Biofeedback
Clinical Psychology
Cognitive Psychology
Figural Aftereffects
Meditation
Neuropsychology
Pathology
Psychopathology

Psychosomatic Disorders
Stimuli

Psychosis   JUL. 1966
Postings: 330   GC: 230
UF Psychotic Children (1966 1980)
NT Echolalia
Schizophrenia
BT Mental Disorders
Severe Disabilities
RT Emotional Disturbances
Mental Health
Paranoid Behavior

Psychosomatic Diseases (1968 1980)
USE Psychosomatic Disorders

Psychosomatic Disorders   MAR. 1980
Postings: 122   GC: 230
UF Psychosomatic Diseases (1968 1980)
BT Emotional Disturbances
RT Failure to Thrive
Neurosis
Physical Health
Psychological Patterns
Psychology
Psychopathology
Psychophysiology

Psychotherapy   JUL. 1966
Postings: 2,889   GC: 230
SN Psychological treatment of mental, emo-
tional, or behavioral disorders and mal-
adjustments by specially trained medical
or nonmedical professionals in personal
or group consultation sessions
NT Gestalt Therapy
Milieu Therapy
Rational Emotive Therapy
Reality Therapy
Relaxation Training
Transactional Analysis
BT Therapy
RT Art Therapy
Behavior Modification
Bibliotherapy
Catharsis
Clinical Psychology
Cognitive Restructuring
Counseling
Counseling Psychology
Crisis Intervention
Dance Therapy
Emotional Adjustment
Emotional Disturbances
Group Therapy
Hypnosis
Individual Psychology
Meditation
Mental Disorders
Mental Health
Music Therapy
Occupational Therapy
Psychiatric Services
Psychiatry
Psychological Services
Rehabilitation
Role Playing
Self Congruence
Therapeutic Environment
Therapeutic Recreation
Therapists

Psychotic Children (1966 1980)
USE Psychosis

PTSD
USE Posttraumatic Stress Disorder

Puberty   DEC. 1995
Postings: 150   GC: 120
SN Period of life at which the individual
reaches sexual maturity and is capable
of reproduction (Note: See also the Iden-
tifier "Puberty Rites")
RT Adolescent Development
Body Image

Developmental Stages
Early Adolescents
Menstruation
Physical Characteristics
Physical Development
Physiology
Reproduction (Biology)
Sex Education

Public Accommodations
USE Public Facilities

Public Administration   MAR. 1980
Postings: 328   GC: 610
SN The organization and management of
government or community affairs (Note:
See also "Public Administration Educa-
tion")
BT Administration
RT Business Administration
Government (Administrative Body)
Political Science
Public Administration Education
Public Sector

Public Administration Education   JUL. 1966
Postings: 275   GC: 400
SN Professional study of the organization
and management of government or com-
munity affairs, usually at the baccalaureate
level or above (Note: Prior to Mar80, the
use of this term was not restricted by a
Scope Note)
BT Professional Education
RT Administrator Education
Business Administration Education
Government (Administrative Body)
Governmental Structure
Management Development
Political Science
Public Administration
Public Affairs Education
Public Service Occupations

Public Affairs Education   JUL. 1966
Postings: 651   GC: 400
SN Education designed to develop public
understanding of domestic and interna-
tional issues
BT Education
RT Citizen Participation
Citizenship Education
Citizenship Responsibility
Community Organizations
Controversial Issues (Course Content)
Political Issues
Political Science
Public Administration Education
Public Opinion
Public Service
Social Problems

Public Agencies   MAR. 1980
Postings: 2,579   GC: 610
UF Community Agencies (Public) (1966
1980)
Government Agencies
NT Planning Commissions
State Agencies
BT Agencies
RT Agency Role
City Government
Community Programs
Federal Government
Federal Programs
Government (Administrative Body)
Government Role
Local Government
Private Agencies
Privatization
Public Policy
Public Sector
Public Service Occupations
Social Agencies
Urban Renewal Agencies
Welfare Agencies

= Two or more Descriptors are used to represent this term.
The term's main entry shows the appropriate coordination.

Public Colleges AUG. 1986
Postings: 1,834　　GC: 340
SN Degree-granting two- or four-year institutions of higher education funded by and accountable to a state, county, or municipality (Note: This concept was previously indexed under "Higher Education" or "Two Year Colleges," and "Public Education")
NT Community Colleges
State Colleges
BT Colleges
RT Private Colleges
Public Education

Public Demonstrations
USE Demonstrations (Civil)

Public Disclosure
USE Disclosure

Public Documents
USE Government Publications

Public Education JUL. 1966
Postings: 4,142　　GC: 340
SN Education supported in part or entirely by taxation (Note: Coordinate with the appropriate mandatory educational level Descriptor)
UF Public Higher Education #
NT Public School Adult Education
BT Education
RT Community Colleges
Compulsory Education
Free Education
Private Education
Public Colleges
Public School Teachers
Public Schools
Public Sector
School Districts
State Boards of Education
State Colleges
State Departments of Education
State Schools
State Universities

Public Employees
USE Government Employees

Public Facilities JUL. 1966
Postings: 245　　GC: 920
UF Integrated Public Facilities (1966 1980) #
Public Accommodations
Segregated Public Facilities (1966 1980) #
NT Public Libraries
BT Facilities
RT Equal Facilities
Health Facilities
Toilet Facilities
Transportation

Public Health JUL. 1966
Postings: 2,488　　GC: 210
UF Community Health (1966 1980)
BT Health
RT Child Health
Communicable Diseases
Community Health Services
Disease Control
Disease Incidence
Drinking Water
Environmental Standards
Epidemiology
Fluoridation
Hazardous Materials
Home Health Aides
Hygiene
Mental Health
Occupational Safety and Health
Physical Health
Poisons
Pollution
Preventive Medicine

Public Health Legislation
Radiation Effects
Sanitation
Water Treatment

Public Health Laws (1966 1974)
USE Public Health Legislation

Public Health Legislation NOV. 1974
Postings: 189　　GC: 610
UF Public Health Laws (1966 1974)
NT Drug Legislation
BT Legislation
RT Laws
Public Health

Public Hearings
USE Hearings

Public Higher Education
USE Higher Education
AND Public Education

Public History APR. 2000
Postings: 15　　GC: 430
SN History as experienced in public settings, e.g., archives, museums, public policy organizations, historical societies, and the media—includes historical work and study in such settings
UF Applied History
BT History
RT Historiography
Oral History
Social History

Public Housing JUL. 1966
Postings: 170　　GC: 550
UF Public Housing Residents (1966 1980)
BT Low Rent Housing
RT Housing Management Aides
Urban Renewal
Welfare Services

Public Housing Residents (1966 1980)
USE Public Housing

Public Image
USE Public Opinion

Public Libraries JUL. 1966
Postings: 5,523　　GC: 710
SN Libraries freely available to all, that serve residents of a community, district, or region and receive all or part of their financial support from public funds
NT County Libraries
Regional Libraries
BT Libraries
Public Facilities
RT Archives
Branch Libraries
Childrens Libraries
Community Information Services
Community Resources
Depository Libraries
Intellectual Freedom
Library Networks
Research Libraries
Special Libraries

Public Officials JUL. 1966
Postings: 356　　GC: 610
NT City Officials
County Officials
Court Judges
Legislators
State Officials
BT Government Employees
RT Community Leaders
Lobbying
Political Candidates

Public Opinion JUL. 1966
Postings: 4,424　　GC: 610
UF Public Image
BT Opinions
RT Agenda Setting
Audience Response
Credibility
Ideology
Majority Attitudes
Mass Instruction
Mass Media Effects
Mass Media Use
Political Attitudes
Press Opinion
Propaganda
Public Affairs Education
Public Support
Questionnaires
Social Attitudes
Surveys
Voting

Public Participation
USE Citizen Participation

Public Policy JUL. 1966
Postings: 12,258　　GC: 610
SN Governing principles that serve as guidelines or rules for decision-making and action as embodied in legislative and judicial enactments
UF Family Services Policy #
Government Policy
BT Policy
RT Civil Law
Court Doctrine
Educational Assessment
Federal Programs
Futures (of Society)
Government Role
Government School Relationship
Institutional Mission
Legislation
National Programs
Politics
Privatization
Public Agencies
Public Sector
Public Service
Revenue Sharing
Self Determination
Taxes

Public Relations JUL. 1966
Postings: 5,061　　GC: 330
BT Relationship
RT Communication Audits
Crisis Management
Human Services
Institutional Advancement
Labor Relations
Library Extension
Organizational Communication
Public Service
Public Support
Publicity
School Community Relationship

Public School Adult Education JUL. 1966
Postings: 205　　GC: 340
BT Adult Education
Public Education
RT Adult Basic Education
Adult Vocational Education
Community Schools
High School Equivalency Programs

Public School Systems (1966 1980)
USE Public Schools
AND School Districts

Public School Teachers NOV. 1968
Postings: 739　　GC: 360
BT Government Employees
Teachers
RT Boards of Education
Elementary School Teachers
Middle School Teachers

Negotiation Agreements
Public Education
Public Schools
Secondary School Teachers

Public Schools JUL. 1966
Postings: 13,609　　GC: 340
SN (Note: Coordinate with the appropriate mandatory educational level Descriptor)
UF Public School Systems (1966 1980) #
NT Charter Schools
BT Schools
RT Public Education
Public School Teachers
School Districts
State Schools

Public Sector APR. 1990
Postings: 430　　GC: 620
SN The segment of an economy that is publicly owned and operated, including all government agencies and government-owned enterprises but excluding private businesses and households
UF Government Sector
RT Bureaucracy
Economics
Government Employees
Government Role
Ownership
Private Sector
Public Administration
Public Agencies
Public Education
Public Policy

Public Service AUG. 1986
Postings: 829　　GC: 330
SN Extension or voluntary service with government, community, or charitable organizations, including activity of educational institutions and personnel made available to the public outside the context of regular instruction and research programs (Note: For public service employment, use "Public Service Occupations")
RT Citizen Participation
Community Involvement
Community Programs
Government School Relationship
Public Affairs Education
Public Policy
Public Relations
Public Support
School Community Relationship
Service Learning
Services
Social Responsibility
Volunteers

Public Service Occupations SEP. 1973
Postings: 378　　GC: 640
SN Employment necessary to accomplish the mission of local, county, state, federal, or other government, except for military service
BT Occupations
RT Government (Administrative Body)
Government Employees
Public Administration Education
Public Agencies
Service Occupations

Public Speaking JUL. 1966
Postings: 1,317　　GC: 400
BT Speech Communication
RT Audience Analysis
Debate
Persuasive Discourse
Rhetorical Invention
Speech
Speeches

Public Support JUL. 1966
Postings: 1,117　　GC: 610
SN Moral or financial support supplied by the public or its funds (Note: Use "School

= Two or more Descriptors are used to represent this term.
The term's main entry shows the appropriate coordination.

Support" for support of educational institutions—prior to Mar80, the use of
this term was not restricted by a Scope
Note)
RT Community Support
    Federal Aid
    Financial Support
    Majority Attitudes
    Private Financial Support
    Public Opinion
    Public Relations
    Public Service
    School Support
    State Aid

Public Television   *JUL. 1966*
    Postings: 851   GC: 720
SN Non-commercial television, publicly
    owned and operated, that is dedicated to
    educational, cultural, and public-service
    programs
BT Television
RT Commercial Television
    Educational Television

Public Utilities
USE Utilities

Public Welfare Assistance
USE Welfare Services

Publications   *JUL. 1966*
    Postings: 3,231   GC: 720
NT Book Reviews
    Books
    Catalogs
    Comics (Publications)
    Computer Software Reviews
    Government Publications
    Journal Articles
    Literature Reviews
    Pamphlets
    Reference Materials
    Reports
    School Publications
    Serials
    State of the Art Reviews
    Test Reviews
RT Authors
    Communications
    Copyrights
    Desktop Publishing
    Editing
    Editorials
    Editors
    Faculty Publishing
    Instructional Materials
    Journalism
    Journalism Education
    Journalism History
    Layout (Publications)
    Library Acquisition
    Library Collections
    Library Material Selection
    Library Materials
    Manuscripts
    Mass Media
    New Journalism
    Nonprint Media
    Photocomposition
    Photojournalism
    Popular Culture
    Printed Materials
    Printing
    Publish or Perish Issue
    Publishing Industry
    Reading Materials
    Resource Materials
    University Presses
    Writing for Publication

Publicity   *MAR. 1980*
    Postings: 1,323   GC: 720
SN Activities and/or materials used to dis-
    seminate information to gain public no-
    tice
NT Advertising
    Institutional Advancement
BT Communication (Thought Transfer)

RT Communications
    Library Extension
    Mass Media
    Public Relations

Publicize (1968 1980)   *MAR. 1980*
    Postings: 1,228   GC: 720
SN Invalid Descriptor—see such Descrip-
    tors as "Publicity," "Advertising," "Mer-
    chandising," "Propaganda," etc.

Publish or Perish Issue   *AUG. 1986*
    Postings: 147   GC: 320
SN Controversial practice among some pro-
    fessions of linking scholarly writing to
    career advancement and remuneration
RT Faculty Publishing
    Promotion (Occupational)
    Publications
    Writing for Publication

Publishing Houses
USE Publishing Industry

Publishing Industry   *JUL. 1966*
    Postings: 2,412   GC: 650
UF Book Industry
    Publishing Houses
NT University Presses
BT Industry
RT Bookstores
    Copyrights
    Database Producers
    Editors
    Electronic Publishing
    Information Dissemination
    Information Industry
    Mass Media
    Mass Media Role
    Printed Materials
    Printing
    Publications
    Reprography
    Textbook Publication
    Writing for Publication

Pueblo (People)   *JAN. 1994*
    Postings: 114   GC: 560
SN Culturally similar American Indians of
    the southwestern United States and north-
    ern Mexico who have traditionally lived
    in permanent stone or adobe dwellings
    in compact villages—includes Zuni, Hopi,
    Tanoan, and Keresan groups
NT Hopi (Tribe)
    Zuni (Tribe)
BT American Indians

Puerto Rican Culture   *JUL. 1966*
    Postings: 277   GC: 560
BT Latin American Culture
RT Puerto Ricans

Puerto Ricans   *JUL. 1966*
    Postings: 1,546   GC: 560
SN Includes Puerto Ricans in Puerto Rico
    and the United States (Note: For the
    latter group, coordinate "Puerto Ricans"
    and "Hispanic Americans")
BT Latin Americans
RT Ethnic Groups
    Hispanic Americans
    Puerto Rican Culture
    Spanish Speaking
    Trust Responsibility (Government)

Pulse Rate
USE Heart Rate

Punch Press Operators
USE Machine Tool Operators

Punch Presses
USE Machine Tools

Punctuation   *JUL. 1966*
    Postings: 442   GC: 450
BT Written Language
RT Capitalization (Alphabetic)
    Sentence Structure
    Spelling
    Writing Skills

Punishment   *JAN. 1973*
    Postings: 805   GC: 520
NT Capital Punishment
    Corporal Punishment
BT Reinforcement
RT Discipline
    Negative Reinforcement
    Sanctions
    Sentencing

Punjabi   *JUL. 1994*
    Postings: 16   GC: 440
UF Panjabi (1967 1994)
BT Indo European Languages

Puns   *JUL. 1970*
    Postings: 37   GC: 430
BT Figurative Language
RT Poetry

Pupil Personnel Services   *NOV. 1969*
    Postings: 1,086   GC: 240
SN Supportive, non-instructional services to
    elementary and secondary pupils in a
    school setting
UF Attendance Services (1968 1980) #
BT Ancillary School Services
RT Counseling Services
    Guidance Programs
    Pupil Personnel Workers
    School Counseling
    School Guidance
    School Health Services
    School Orientation
    School Psychology
    Student Personnel Services
    Student Placement

Pupil Personnel Workers   *NOV. 1969*
    Postings: 333   GC: 240
SN Professional personnel who provide sup-
    portive, non-instructional services to ele-
    mentary and secondary pupils in a school
    setting
NT Attendance Officers
BT School Personnel
RT Counseling Services
    Deans of Students
    Faculty Advisers
    Guidance Personnel
    Health Personnel
    Ombudsmen
    Pupil Personnel Services
    Resident Advisers
    School Counselors
    School Psychologists
    School Social Workers
    Student Personnel Workers

Pupillary Dilation   *SEP. 1968*
    Postings: 22   GC: 110
UF Iris Reflex
    Pupillary Reflex
    Pupillary Response
BT Motor Reactions
RT Eye Movements
    Eyes

Pupillary Reflex
USE Pupillary Dilation

Pupillary Response
USE Pupillary Dilation

Pupils
USE Students

Puppet Shows
USE Puppetry

Puppetry   *APR. 1972*
    Postings: 283   GC: 420
UF Puppet Shows
    Puppets
BT Theater Arts

Puppets
USE Puppetry

Purchasing   *JUL. 1966*
    Postings: 1,602   GC: 620
UF Equipment Purchasing
RT Bids
    Computer Selection
    Consumer Economics
    Consumer Education
    Consumer Protection
    Cooperatives
    Educational Finance
    Equipment Standards
    Financial Needs
    Library Acquisition
    Ownership
    Selection Tools
    Specifications
    Supply and Demand

Puritan Ethic
USE Work Ethic

Puritans   *NOV. 1969*
    Postings: 46   GC: 560
BT Protestants
RT Colonial History (United States)

Pushto
USE Pashto

Pushtu
USE Pashto

Putonghua
USE Mandarin Chinese

Puzzles   *JUL. 1966*
    Postings: 524   GC: 730
BT Games
RT Educational Games
    Toys

Pygmalion Effect
USE Self Fulfilling Prophecies

Pyramid Organization   *JUL. 1966*
    Postings: 30   GC: 520
BT Organization
RT Horizontal Organization
    Vertical Organization

Q Analysis
USE Q Methodology

Q Methodology   *MAR. 1980*
    Postings: 245   GC: 820
SN Any of several statistical procedures,
    used primarily in personality assessment,
    in which the data are analyzed as though
    the persons in the study were them-
    selves the measuring instruments and
    the tests or items were the subjects
UF Q Analysis
    Q Sort (1967 1980)
    Q Technique
BT Measurement Techniques
RT Factor Analysis

= Two or more Descriptors are used to represent this term.
The term's main entry shows the appropriate coordination.

Forced Choice Technique
Item Analysis
Personality Assessment
Personality Measures
Rating Scales
Self Concept Measures
Statistical Analysis
Testing

Q Sort (1967 1980)
USE   Q Methodology

Q Technique
USE   Q Methodology

Quadriplegia (1969 1980)
USE   Neurological Impairments

Qualifications   JUL. 1966
          Postings: 437   GC: 630
SN   Abilities, aptitudes, achievements, or
          other personal characteristics that suit
          an individual to particular positions or
          tasks
NT   Administrator Qualifications
          Counselor Qualifications
          Employment Qualifications
          Supervisor Qualifications
          Teacher Qualifications
BT   Standards
RT   Ability
          Achievement
          Aptitude
          Background
          Certification
          Credentials
          Degrees (Academic)
          Disqualification
          Performance
          Portfolios (Background Materials)
          Prerequisites
          Reputation
          Resumes (Personal)
          Skills

Qualitative Research   DEC. 1985
          Postings: 2,635   GC: 810
SN   Research providing detailed narrative de-
          scriptions and explanations of phenom-
          ena investigated, with lesser emphasis
          given to numerical quantifications—
          methods used to collect qualitative data
          include ethnographic practices such as
          observing and interviewing (Note: Use
          as a minor Descriptor for examples of
          this kind of research—use as a major
          Descriptor only as the subject of a docu-
          ment)
BT   Research
RT   Case Studies
          Ethnography
          Evaluation Methods
          Field Studies
          Focus Groups
          Interviews
          Naturalistic Observation
          Participant Observation
          Research Methodology
          Social Science Research
          Triangulation

Quality Circles   APR. 1986
          Postings: 240   GC: 320
SN   Voluntary groups of individuals within
          an organization who meet regularly to
          identify, analyze, and solve work-related
          problems, with the goal of improving
          quality and productivity
BT   Groups
RT   Administration
          Employer Employee Relationship
          Management Teams
          Organizational Development
          Participative Decision Making
          Quality Control
          Total Quality Management

Quality Control   JUL. 1966
          Postings: 2,340   GC: 650
SN   Techniques, such as inspection and regu-
          lation, that are used to ensure a uniform
          quality of performance or product
BT   Evaluation Methods
RT   Accountability
          Accreditation (Institutions)
          Audits (Verification)
          Benchmarking
          Certification
          Editing
          Error Correction
          Inspection
          Operations Research
          Performance
          Pretesting
          Program Effectiveness
          Quality Circles
          Reliability
          Standards
          Total Quality Management

Quality Education
USE   Educational Quality

Quality of Life   SEP. 1977
          Postings: 2,968   GC: 520
SN   Any combination of objective standards
          and subjective attitudes, both other- and
          self-imposed, by which individuals and
          groups assess their life situations
UF   Life Quality
          Productive Living (1967 1980)
NT   Quality of Working Life
          Well Being
RT   Advantaged
          American Dream
          Appropriate Technology
          Community Development
          Community Satisfaction
          Developed Nations
          Developing Nations
          Disadvantaged
          Ecology
          Economic Climate
          Economic Status
          Educational Quality
          Environmental Standards
          Evaluation
          Human Factors Engineering
          Humanization
          Life Satisfaction
          Living Standards
          Physical Environment
          Productivity
          Science and Society
          Social Class
          Social Environment
          Social Indicators
          Social Problems
          Social Status
          Social Values
          Socioeconomic Status
          Technology
          Values

Quality of Working Life   APR. 1986
          Postings: 862   GC: 630
SN   Phenomenological construct of working
          environments including such extrinsic
          aspects as pay, benefits, security, safety,
          production, and efficiency, and such in-
          trinsic aspects as variety and challenge,
          responsibility, meaningful contribution,
          and recognition
BT   Quality of Life
RT   Careers
          Collegiality
          Employee Assistance Programs
          Employer Employee Relationship
          Employment
          Employment Patterns
          Human Factors Engineering
          Industrial Psychology
          Job Enrichment
          Job Satisfaction
          Labor Conditions
          Labor Relations
          Life Satisfaction

Occupations
Organizational Climate
Organizational Development
Productivity
Technology
Unions
Work Environment
Work Ethic

Quality Point Ratio
USE   Grade Point Average

Quantitative Aptitude
USE   Mathematical Aptitude

Quantitative Literacy
USE   Numeracy

Quantitative Research (Statistics)
USE   Statistical Analysis

**Quantitative Tests (1980 1985)
(Mathematics)**
USE   Mathematics Tests

Quantum Mechanics   JUL. 1966
          Postings: 468   GC: 490
BT   Mechanics (Physics)
RT   Acceleration (Physics)
          Energy
          Force
          Mathematics
          Matter
          Motion
          Nuclear Physics
          Relativity
          Space

Quarter System   JUL. 1966
          Postings: 156   GC: 350
SN   Division of the academic year into four
          equal terms
BT   School Schedules
RT   Extended School Year
          Semester System
          Trimester System
          Year Round Schools

Quasiexperimental Design   MAR. 1980
          Postings: 127   GC: 810
SN   Plan or organization of research that is
          conducted in settings where normal ex-
          perimental controls are not, or cannot
          be, applied
BT   Research Design
RT   Control Groups
          Experimental Groups
          Matched Groups
          Research
          Research Methodology
          Sampling
          Scientific Methodology

Quechua   JUL. 1966
          Postings: 85   GC: 440
UF   Kechua
BT   American Indian Languages

Question Answer Interviews (1966 1980)
USE   Interviews

Questioning Techniques   JUL. 1966
          Postings: 3,791   GC: 310
SN   Methods used for constructing and pre-
          senting questions in order to promote
          effective discussions and learning or to
          elicit information
BT   Methods
RT   Criticism
          Discovery Learning
          Discussion (Teaching Technique)
          Inquiry
          Interviews

Learning Processes
Questionnaires
Reciprocal Teaching
Teaching Methods
Test Format
Wait Time

Questionnaires   JUL. 1966
          Postings: 19,818   GC: 830
SN   Structured sets of questions on speci-
          fied subjects that are used to gather
          information, attitudes, or opinions
BT   Measures (Individuals)
RT   Answer Sheets
          Attitude Measures
          Biographical Inventories
          Data Collection
          Evaluation Methods
          Mail Surveys
          Opinions
          Public Opinion
          Questioning Techniques
          Research
          Response Rates (Questionnaires)
          Scoring
          Surveys
          Telephone Surveys

Quiche   DEC. 1970
          Postings: 16   GC: 440
BT   Mayan Languages
RT   Yucatec

Quizzes
USE   Tests

Quotas   JAN. 1978
          Postings: 166   GC: 540
SN   Numbers or percentages to be met for a
          specific objective
RT   Affirmative Action
          Criteria
          Mathematical Concepts
          Objectives
          Ratios (Mathematics)
          Selective Admission
          Standards

R and D
USE   Research and Development

R D and E
USE   Research and Development

Race   JUL. 1966
          Postings: 831   GC: 120
SN   Concept used to describe people who
          are united or classified together on the
          basis of genetically transmitted physical
          similarities deriving from their common
          descent, and who are also frequently
          thought to share cultural and social traits
BT   Physical Characteristics
RT   Anthropology
          Biology
          Blacks
          Culture
          Ethnic Groups
          Ethnicity
          Indigenous Populations
          Minority Groups
          Multiracial Persons
          Nature Nurture Controversy
          Racial Attitudes
          Racial Balance
          Racial Bias
          Racial Composition
          Racial Differences
          Racial Discrimination
          Racial Distribution
          Racial Factors
          Racial Identification
          Racial Integration
          Racial Relations
          Racial Segregation
          Transracial Adoption
          Whites

= Two or more Descriptors are used to represent this term.
The term's main entry shows the appropriate coordination.

Race Influences (1966 1980)
USE   Racial Factors

Race Relations (1966 1980)
USE   Racial Relations

Racial Attitudes   JUL. 1966
       Postings: 2,188   GC: 540
SN   Attitudes about race or particular racial
       groups (Note: Prior to Mar80, this term
       was not restricted by a Scope Note)
BT   Attitudes
RT   Black Attitudes
       Black Stereotypes
       Cultural Differences
       Ethnic Stereotypes
       Ethnicity
       Integration Readiness
       Race
       Racial Differences
       Racial Discrimination
       Racial Identification
       Racial Relations
       School Desegregation

Racial Balance   JUL. 1966
       Postings: 516   GC: 540
SN   Racial composition of a spatial unit or
       institution, either directly proportional to
       the racial composition of the society, or
       meeting other standards set as desirable
       for that particular situation
UF   Racial Imbalance
BT   Racial Composition
RT   Affirmative Action
       Race
       Racial Factors
       Racial Integration
       Racial Relations
       Racial Segregation
       Racially Balanced Schools
       Teacher Distribution
       Tokenism

Racial Bias   MAR. 1980
       Postings: 2,465   GC: 540
SN   Prejudicial opinions about particular
       groups because of their race (Note: Prior
       to Mar80, the instruction "Racial Bias,
       USE Racial Discrimination" was carried
       in the Thesaurus)
UF   Racial Prejudice
BT   Social Bias
RT   Affirmative Action
       Black Stereotypes
       Ethnic Bias
       Race
       Racial Differences
       Racial Discrimination
       Racial Identification
       Racial Relations

Racial Characteristics (1966 1980)
                                        MAR. 1980
       Postings: 164   GC: 540
SN   Invalid Descriptor—see such Descrip-
       tors as "Race" and "Racial Differences"
       or coordinate specific populations (e.g.,
       "Blacks," "Whites," etc.) with specific
       characteristics (e.g., "Psychological Char-
       acteristics," "Physical Characteristics,"
       etc.)

Racial Composition   JUL. 1966
       Postings: 864   GC: 550
SN   Proportional representation of racial
       groups within an institutional or spatial
       entity, e.g., school, town, district, etc.
       (Note: Do not confuse with "Racial Dis-
       tribution," the dispersal of groups among
       entities—prior to Mar80, the use of this
       term was not restricted by a Scope Note)
NT   Racial Balance
BT   Demography
RT   Affirmative Action
       Busing
       Neighborhood Integration
       Population Distribution

       Race
       Racial Distribution
       Racial Factors
       Racial Integration
       Racial Relations
       Residential Patterns
       School Desegregation
       Tokenism

Racial Cultural Groups
USE   Ethnic Groups

Racial Differences   JUL. 1966
       Postings: 5,415   GC: 510
BT   Differences
RT   Black Stereotypes
       Cultural Differences
       Ethnic Stereotypes
       Ethnocentrism
       Individual Differences
       Intermarriage
       Multiracial Persons
       Nature Nurture Controversy
       Physical Characteristics
       Race
       Racial Attitudes
       Racial Bias
       Racial Factors
       Racial Identification
       Social Differences

Racial Discrimination   JUL. 1966
       Postings: 5,044   GC: 540
SN   Restriction or denial of rights, privileges,
       and choice because of race (Note: Do not
       confuse with "Racial Bias")
NT   Racial Segregation
BT   Social Discrimination
RT   Affirmative Action
       Age Discrimination
       Educational Discrimination
       Equal Education
       Equal Facilities
       Equal Opportunities (Jobs)
       Ethnic Discrimination
       Ghettos
       Race
       Racial Attitudes
       Racial Bias
       Racial Relations
       Reverse Discrimination
       Segregationist Organizations
       Selective Admission
       Slavery

Racial Distribution   JUL. 1966
       Postings: 507   GC: 550
SN   Dispersal of racial groups among geo-
       graphic, spatial, or institutional units
       (Note: Do not confuse with "Racial Com-
       position," the proportional representa-
       tion of these groups within units—prior
       to Mar80, the use of this term was not
       restricted by a Scope Note)
BT   Population Distribution
RT   Black Population Trends
       Ethnic Distribution
       Geographic Distribution
       Human Geography
       Incidence
       Neighborhood Integration
       Race
       Racial Composition
       Residential Patterns

Racial Factors   JUL. 1966
       Postings: 1,671   GC: 540
UF   Race Influences (1966 1980)
BT   Influences
RT   Black Achievement
       Cultural Influences
       Minority Group Influences
       Multiracial Persons
       Race
       Racial Balance
       Racial Composition
       Racial Differences
       Racial Identification
       Racial Relations

Racial Identification   MAR. 1980
       Postings: 951   GC: 540
SN   Classification of oneself or another per-
       son or group as a member of a particular
       race (Note: Prior to Mar80, the instruc-
       tion "Racial Self Identification, USE Self
       Concept" was carried in the Thesaurus)
UF   Racial Identity
       Racial Recognition (1966 1980)
       Racial Self Identification
BT   Identification
RT   Afrocentrism
       Black Attitudes
       Black Power
       Black Stereotypes
       Black Studies
       Cultural Traits
       Ethnic Stereotypes
       Ethnicity
       Identification (Psychology)
       Multiracial Persons
       Race
       Racial Attitudes
       Racial Bias
       Racial Differences
       Racial Factors
       Self Concept
       Transracial Adoption

Racial Identity
USE   Racial Identification

Racial Imbalance
USE   Racial Balance

Racial Integration   JUL. 1966
       Postings: 1,705   GC: 540
UF   Anti Segregation Programs (1967
          1980)
       Integrated Public Facilities (1966
          1980) #
       Integration (Racial)
       Urban Desegregation
BT   Social Integration
RT   Affirmative Action
       Biracial Committees
       Black Achievement
       Busing
       Civil Rights
       Civil Rights Legislation
       Classroom Desegregation
       College Desegregation
       Desegregation Effects
       Desegregation Litigation
       Desegregation Methods
       Desegregation Plans
       Educational Parks
       Integration Readiness
       Integration Studies
       Neighborhood Integration
       Personnel Integration
       Race
       Racial Balance
       Racial Composition
       Racial Relations
       Racial Segregation
       Racially Balanced Schools
       School Desegregation
       Tokenism
       Voluntary Desegregation

Racial Interaction
USE   Racial Relations

Racial Prejudice
USE   Racial Bias

Racial Recognition (1966 1980)
USE   Racial Identification

Racial Relations   MAR. 1980
       Postings: 3,303   GC: 540
SN   Contact and interaction between/among
       racial groups
UF   Black White Relations
       Interracial Relations
       Race Relations (1966 1980)

       Racial Interaction
       White Black Relations
BT   Intergroup Relations
RT   Biracial Committees
       Black History
       Black Power
       Blacks
       Cultural Differences
       Cultural Interrelationships
       Cultural Pluralism
       Diversity (Faculty)
       Diversity (Student)
       Ethnic Relations
       Multiracial Persons
       Race
       Racial Attitudes
       Racial Balance
       Racial Bias
       Racial Composition
       Racial Discrimination
       Racial Factors
       Racial Integration
       Racial Segregation
       Whites

Racial Segregation   JUL. 1966
       Postings: 981   GC: 540
UF   Segregated Public Facilities (1966
          1980) #
       Segregation (Racial)
NT   De Facto Segregation
       De Jure Segregation
BT   Racial Discrimination
RT   Apartheid
       Black History
       Civil Rights
       College Segregation
       Ghettos
       Housing Discrimination
       Occupational Segregation
       Race
       Racial Balance
       Racial Integration
       Racial Relations
       Racially Balanced Schools
       School Resegregation
       School Segregation
       Segregationist Organizations

Racial Self Identification
USE   Racial Identification

Racially Balanced Schools   JUL. 1966
       Postings: 247   GC: 540
BT   Schools
RT   Affirmative Action
       Black Education
       Busing
       Racial Balance
       Racial Integration
       Racial Segregation
       School Desegregation
       Transfer Students

Racially Mixed Persons
USE   Multiracial Persons

Racism (1966 1980)   MAR. 1980
       Postings: 875   GC: 540
SN   Invalid Descriptor—used for both ac-
       tions and attitudes—see such Descrip-
       tors as "Racial Discrimination" and "Ra-
       cial Bias"

Racket Sports
USE   Racquet Sports

Racquet Sports   JUN. 1984
       Postings: 10   GC: 470
UF   Racket Sports
NT   Badminton
       Racquetball
       Squash (Game)
       Tennis
BT   Athletics
RT   Table Tennis

= Two or more Descriptors are used to represent this term.
The term's main entry shows the appropriate coordination.

Racquetball　　　　　　　　*JUN. 1984*
　　Postings: 19　　　　　　　GC: 470
BT　Racquet Sports
RT　Handball

Radar　　　　　　　　　　*AUG. 1968*
　　Postings: 41　　　　　　　GC: 910
BT　Electronic Equipment
RT　Air Traffic Control
　　Electronics
　　Navigation
　　Telecommunications

Radiation　　　　　　　　*JUL. 1966*
　　Postings: 680　　　　　　GC: 490
SN　Process of energy emission
NT　Light
　　Nuclear Energy
　　Solar Energy
BT　Energy
RT　Fallout Shelters
　　Hazardous Materials
　　Laboratory Safety
　　Lasers
　　Luminescence
　　Nuclear Physics
　　Nuclear Technology
　　Optics
　　Physical Environment
　　Physics
　　Radiation Biology
　　Radiation Effects
　　Radioisotopes
　　Radiology
　　Safety
　　Spectroscopy
　　Waste Disposal

Radiation Biology　　　　*JUL. 1966*
　　Postings: 61　　　　　　　GC: 490
SN　Study of the effects of radiation on liv-
　　ing organisms (Note: Use "Radiology"
　　for materials concerning the application
　　of radiation in medical diagnosis and
　　treatment—prior to Mar80, this term did
　　not carry a Scope Note)
UF　Radiobiology
BT　Biology
RT　Atomic Structure
　　Atomic Theory
　　Biophysics
　　Chemistry
　　Ecology
　　Genetic Engineering
　　Genetics
　　Marine Biology
　　Medicine
　　Nuclear Energy
　　Nuclear Physics
　　Nuclear Technology
　　Organic Chemistry
　　Physical Sciences
　　Physics
　　Physiology
　　Radiation
　　Radiology
　　Toxicology

Radiation Damage
USE　Radiation Effects

Radiation Effects　　　　*AUG. 1968*
　　Postings: 225　　　　　　GC: 490
SN　Changes in the properties of liquids,
　　gases, and solids caused by radiation
　　(e.g., gamma rays, X-rays, neutrons)
UF　Radiation Damage
RT　Diseases
　　Ecological Factors
　　Environmental Influences
　　Fallout Shelters
　　Health
　　Laboratory Safety
　　Nuclear Energy
　　Nuclear Physics
　　Nuclear Technology
　　Nuclear Warfare
　　Poisoning
　　Pollution

　　Public Health
　　Radiation
　　Radioisotopes
　　Radiology
　　Safety
　　Solar Energy

Radiation Therapy
USE　Radiology

Radiation Therapy Technologists
USE　Radiologic Technologists

Radio　　　　　　　　　　*JUL. 1966*
　　Postings: 1,918　　　　　GC: 720
UF　Radio Technology (1967 1980)
NT　Educational Radio
BT　Mass Media
　　Telecommunications
RT　Audiences
　　Audio Equipment
　　Audiodisks
　　Audiotape Recordings
　　Broadcast Industry
　　Broadcast Journalism
　　Broadcast Reception Equipment
　　Electronic Equipment
　　Journalism Education
　　Networks
　　News Media
　　Popular Culture
　　Production Techniques
　　Programming (Broadcast)
　　Soap Operas
　　Television
　　Television Radio Repairers

Radio Journalism
USE　Broadcast Journalism

Radio Programming
USE　Programming (Broadcast)

Radio Technology (1967 1980)
USE　Radio

Radio Television Repairers
USE　Television Radio Repairers

Radiobiology
USE　Radiation Biology

Radiographers　　　　　　*JUL. 1966*
　　Postings: 30　　　　　　　GC: 640
UF　Industrial X Ray Operators
BT　Paraprofessional Personnel
RT　Metallurgical Technicians
　　Nuclear Technology
　　Radiologic Technologists

Radioisotopes　　　　　　*JUL. 1966*
　　Postings: 150　　　　　　GC: 490
RT　Atomic Structure
　　Atomic Theory
　　Biology
　　Chemistry
　　Genetics
　　Inorganic Chemistry
　　Matter
　　Nuclear Energy
　　Nuclear Physics
　　Nuclear Technology
　　Physics
　　Radiation
　　Radiation Effects
　　Radiology

Radiologic Technologists　*AUG. 1969*
　　Postings: 107　　　　　　GC: 210
SN　Personnel responsible for applying Roent-
　　gen rays and radioactive substances to
　　patients for diagnostic and therapeutic
　　purposes

UF　Nuclear Medicine Technologists
　　Radiation Therapy Technologists
　　X Ray Technologists
BT　Allied Health Personnel
RT　Cancer
　　Nuclear Technology
　　Radiographers
　　Radiology

Radiology　　　　　　　　*JUN. 1969*
　　Postings: 169　　　　　　GC: 210
SN　Use of radiation in medical diagnosis
　　and treatment (Note: For documents con-
　　cerning the effects of radiation on living
　　organisms, use "Radiation Biology")
UF　Nuclear Medicine
　　Radiation Therapy
　　X Rays (Medicine)
BT　Technology
RT　Cancer
　　Crystallography
　　Genetic Engineering
　　Medicine
　　Nuclear Technology
　　Physics
　　Radiation
　　Radiation Biology
　　Radiation Effects
　　Radioisotopes
　　Radiologic Technologists

Ragtime Music
USE　Jazz

Rail Transportation　　　*APR. 1970*
　　Postings: 93　　　　　　　GC: 650
UF　Railroads
　　Railways
BT　Transportation
RT　Marketing

Railroads
USE　Rail Transportation

Railways
USE　Rail Transportation

Rain Forest Preserves
USE　Rainforests

Rainforests　　　　　　　*APR. 1995*
　　Postings: 28　　　　　　　GC: 410
SN　Woodlands of dense, mainly broad-leaved
　　evergreen trees in areas of high annual
　　rainfall (Note: Coordinate with Identifiers
　　"Deforestation," "Tropics," etc., as ap-
　　propriate)
UF　Rain Forest Preserves
　　Temperate Rainforests
　　Tropical Rainforests
RT　Conservation (Environment)
　　Conservation Education
　　Ecology
　　Environmental Education
　　Forestry
　　Habitats
　　Land Use
　　Trees
　　Wildlife Management

Raised Line Drawings　　*JUL. 1966*
　　Postings: 27　　　　　　　GC: 220
BT　Sensory Aids
　　Visual Aids
RT　Blindness
　　Braille
　　Illustrations
　　Tactile Adaptation

Range (Distance)
USE　Distance

Rank in Class
USE　Class Rank

Rape　　　　　　　　　　*SEP. 1975*
　　Postings: 631　　　　　　GC: 530
UF　Statutory Rape
BT　Sexual Abuse
RT　Aggression
　　Battered Women
　　Crime
　　Incest
　　Sexual Harassment
　　Sexuality
　　Victims of Crime
　　Violence

Rapid Growth Communities
USE　Boomtowns

Rapid Reading (1966 1980)
USE　Speed Reading

Rapport　　　　　　　　　*JUL. 1966*
　　Postings: 207　　　　　　GC: 510
BT　Interpersonal Relationship
RT　Counseling Techniques
　　Human Relations
　　Interpersonal Attraction
　　Interpersonal Communication
　　Love
　　Trust (Psychology)

Rate Tests
USE　Timed Tests

Rating Scales　　　　　　*JUL. 1966*
　　Postings: 4,308　　　　　GC: 830
SN　Forms for recording the estimated mag-
　　nitude of a trait or quality (Note: Do not
　　confuse with "Check Lists"—use a more
　　specific term if possible)
NT　Behavior Rating Scales
　　Likert Scales
　　Semantic Differential
BT　Measures (Individuals)
RT　Achievement Rating
　　Check Lists
　　Forced Choice Technique
　　Informal Assessment
　　Interrater Reliability
　　Measurement Techniques
　　Multitrait Multimethod Techniques
　　Q Methodology
　　Scaling

Rational Emotive Therapy　*MAR. 1980*
　　Postings: 194　　　　　　GC: 230
SN　Cognitive-behavior therapy based on the
　　premise that individuals' emotional dis-
　　turbances stem from irrational belief
　　systems—uses empirical method to com-
　　bat irrationality so individuals become
　　more realistic
UF　Rational Therapy (1968 1980)
BT　Psychotherapy
RT　Behavior Modification
　　Cognitive Restructuring

Rational Numbers　　　　*FEB. 1970*
　　Postings: 192　　　　　　GC: 480
NT　Fractions
　　Integers
BT　Numbers
RT　Reciprocals (Mathematics)

Rational Therapy (1968 1980)
USE　Rational Emotive Therapy

Ratios (Mathematics)　　*JAN. 1969*
　　Postings: 484　　　　　　GC: 480
UF　Proportion (Mathematics)
NT　Counselor Client Ratio
　　Intelligence Quotient
　　Percentage
　　Relevance (Information Retrieval)
　　Response Rates (Questionnaires)
　　Tax Rates
　　Teacher Student Ratio

= Two or more Descriptors are used to represent this term.
The term's main entry shows the appropriate coordination.

RT Computation
     Incidence
     Mathematical Concepts
     Quotas
     Relationship

Rats   *JUL. 1966*
     Postings: 93   GC: 490
BT Animals
RT Laboratory Animals
     Pesticides
     Pests

Raw Scores   *OCT. 1970*
     Postings: 198   GC: 820
SN Scores expressed in their original form
     without statistical treatment, such as the
     number of correct answers on a test
UF Crude Scores
     Gross Scores
     Obtained Scores
     Original Scores
BT Scores
RT Cutting Scores
     Equated Scores
     Error of Measurement
     Grade Equivalent Scores
     Guessing (Tests)
     Scoring Formulas
     Statistical Data
     True Scores
     Weighted Scores

Reaction Time   *SEP. 1969*
     Postings: 1,111   GC: 120
UF Response Latency
     Response Time
RT Conceptual Tempo
     Encoding (Psychology)
     Familiarity
     Motor Reactions
     Perceptual Motor Coordination
     Response Style (Tests)
     Responses
     Time Factors (Learning)

Reactive Behavior (1966 1980)
USE Responses

Reactive Inhibition
USE Inhibition

Readability   *JUL. 1966*
     Postings: 1,680   GC: 460
SN The quality of reading matter that makes
     it interesting and understandable to those
     for whom it is written (Note: Prior to
     Jun80, "Reading Difficulty" and "Read-
     ing Level" were occasionally used to
     index this concept)
RT Cloze Procedure
     Content Area Reading
     High Interest Low Vocabulary Books
     Readability Formulas
     Reader Text Relationship
     Reading
     Reading Comprehension
     Reading Instruction
     Reading Rate
     Story Grammar
     Telegraphic Materials
     Text Structure
     Textbook Evaluation

Readability Formulas   *MAR. 1977*
     Postings: 431   GC: 460
SN Devices, indexes, or methods for deter-
     mining the level of difficulty of written
     material based on the vocabulary, sen-
     tence length and structure, and other
     factors
BT Evaluation Methods
RT Content Analysis
     Difficulty Level
     Measurement Techniques
     Readability
     Reading

     Reading Comprehension
     Textbook Evaluation

Reader Response   *OCT. 1983*
     Postings: 1,862   GC: 110
SN Readers' reactions to written work, in-
     cluding the way these reactions shape
     interpretation
BT Audience Response
RT Literary Criticism
     Literature Appreciation
     Reader Text Relationship
     Reading
     Reading Comprehension
     Reading Habits
     Reading Interests
     Reading Processes
     Reading Rate
     Reading Skills

Reader Text Relationship   *DEC. 1985*
     Postings: 1,449   GC: 460
SN The character or quality of the reader's
     involvement or connection with the ma-
     terial being read
BT Relationship
RT Readability
     Reader Response
     Reading
     Reading Comprehension
     Reading Materials
     Reading Processes
     Reading Writing Relationship
     Story Grammar
     Text Structure

Readers (Materials)
USE Reading Materials

Readers Theater   *DEC. 1970*
     Postings: 178   GC: 420
BT Theater Arts
RT Acting
     Creative Dramatics
     Oral Interpretation

Readiness   *JUL. 1966*
     Postings: 525   GC: 120
SN Preparedness to respond or react
UF Readiness (Mental) (1966 1980)
NT Integration Readiness
     Learning Readiness
     Reading Readiness
     School Readiness
     Writing Readiness
RT Ability
     Developmental Delays
     Developmental Tasks
     Individual Development
     Motivation
     Schemata (Cognition)

Readiness (Mental) (1966 1980)
USE Readiness

Reading   *JUL. 1966*
     Postings: 3,913   GC: 460
SN (Note: Use a more specific term if possi-
     ble)
UF Applied Reading (1966 1980)
NT Basal Reading
     Beginning Reading
     Content Area Reading
     Corrective Reading
     Critical Reading
     Directed Reading Activity
     Early Reading
     Functional Reading
     Independent Reading
     Individualized Reading
     Music Reading
     Oral Reading
     Reading Aloud to Others
     Recreational Reading
     Remedial Reading
     Silent Reading
     Speed Reading

     Story Reading
     Sustained Silent Reading
BT Language Arts
     Literacy
RT Advance Organizers
     Bibliotherapy
     Braille
     Cloze Procedure
     Context Clues
     Decoding (Reading)
     Diacritical Marking
     Informal Reading Inventories
     Initial Teaching Alphabet
     Inner Speech (Subvocal)
     Language Processing
     Miscue Analysis
     Pattern Recognition
     Phoneme Grapheme Correspondence
     Proofreading
     Readability
     Readability Formulas
     Reader Response
     Reader Text Relationship
     Reading Ability
     Reading Achievement
     Reading Assignments
     Reading Attitudes
     Reading Centers
     Reading Comprehension
     Reading Consultants
     Reading Diagnosis
     Reading Difficulties
     Reading Failure
     Reading Games
     Reading Habits
     Reading Improvement
     Reading Instruction
     Reading Interests
     Reading Material Selection
     Reading Materials
     Reading Motivation
     Reading Processes
     Reading Programs
     Reading Rate
     Reading Readiness
     Reading Readiness Tests
     Reading Research
     Reading Skills
     Reading Strategies
     Reading Teachers
     Reading Tests
     Reading Writing Relationship
     Tachistoscopes
     Verbal Communication
     Vocabulary
     Writing (Composition)

Reading Ability   *JUL. 1966*
     Postings: 2,915   GC: 460
NT Reading Skills
BT Verbal Ability
RT Reading
     Reading Achievement
     Reading Attitudes
     Reading Difficulties
     Reading Readiness

Reading Achievement   *JUL. 1966*
     Postings: 5,951   GC: 460
SN Level of attainment in any or all reading
     skills, usually estimated by performance
     on a test (Note: Prior to Jun80, "Reading
     Level" was occasionally used to index
     this concept)
BT Achievement
RT Academic Achievement
     Achievement Gains
     Reading
     Reading Ability
     Reading Attitudes
     Reading Diagnosis
     Reading Failure
     Reading Improvement
     Reading Skills
     Reading Tests

Reading Aloud to Others   *SEP. 1980*
     Postings: 1,221   GC: 460
SN Reading aloud for the sake of the lis-
     tener's well-being (e.g., to inform or

     entertain the listener or audience, to
     develop his/her/their appreciation of lit-
     erature or reading readiness, etc.) (Note:
     Use "Oral Reading" when the purpose of
     reading aloud is to develop or diagnose
     the reader's language skills)
BT Reading
RT Oral Interpretation
     Oral Reading
     Reading Attitudes
     Story Reading
     Story Telling

Reading Assignments   *JUL. 1966*
     Postings: 312   GC: 460
BT Assignments
RT Content Area Reading
     Directed Reading Activity
     Individualized Reading
     Reading
     Reading Instruction
     Reading Materials
     Reading Programs

Reading Attitudes   *MAR. 1980*
     Postings: 1,715   GC: 460
SN Attitudes toward reading
BT Attitudes
RT Educational Attitudes
     Reading
     Reading Ability
     Reading Achievement
     Reading Aloud to Others
     Reading Habits
     Reading Interests
     Reading Motivation

Reading Centers   *JUL. 1966*
     Postings: 487   GC: 460
SN Facilities staffed by reading specialists
     or instructors that offer reading diagno-
     sis and individualized instruction, as well
     as remedial, developmental, or acceler-
     ated reading programs
UF Reading Clinics (1966 1980)
     Reading Laboratories
     Remedial Reading Clinics (1966
       1980) #
BT Educational Facilities
     Resource Centers
RT Individualized Reading
     Learning Laboratories
     Reading
     Reading Diagnosis
     Reading Improvement
     Reading Programs
     Reading Skills
     Remedial Reading

Reading Clinics (1966 1980)
USE Reading Centers

Reading Comprehension   *JUL. 1966*
     Postings: 10,880   GC: 460
BT Comprehension
     Reading Skills
RT Basic Vocabulary
     Cloze Procedure
     Content Area Reading
     Context Clues
     Critical Reading
     Decoding (Reading)
     Directed Reading Activity
     Informal Reading Inventories
     Language Experience Approach
     Oral Interpretation
     Readability
     Readability Formulas
     Reader Response
     Reader Text Relationship
     Reading
     Reading Habits
     Reading Processes
     Reading Rate
     Reading Strategies
     Reading Tests
     Receptive Language
     Reciprocal Teaching
     Story Grammar

Telegraphic Materials
Text Structure
Word Recognition

Reading Consultants — *JUL. 1966*
Postings: 357 — GC: 360
UF Reading Specialists
BT Consultants
RT Reading
Reading Instruction
Reading Teachers
Resource Teachers

Reading Development (1966 1980) — *MAR. 1980*
Postings: 1,213 — GC: 460
SN Invalid Descriptor—used inconsistently in indexing—see more precise "Reading" Descriptors

Reading Diagnosis — *JUL. 1966*
Postings: 1,728 — GC: 460
NT Miscue Analysis
BT Educational Diagnosis
RT Informal Reading Inventories
Reading
Reading Achievement
Reading Centers
Reading Difficulties
Reading Readiness Tests
Reading Tests
Remedial Reading

Reading Difficulties — *MAR. 1980*
Postings: 3,234 — GC: 460
SN Problems in reading, caused either by disabilities associated with psychological processes or by such factors as physical or sensory impairments, cultural background, low ability, etc. (Note: Do not use for "Readability"—the previous term "Reading Difficulty" was not scoped and was often confused with "Readability")
UF Reading Disabilities
Reading Problems
Retarded Readers (1966 1980)
BT Problems
RT Corrective Reading
Dyslexia
Language Impairments
Learning Disabilities
Learning Problems
Reading
Reading Ability
Reading Diagnosis
Reading Failure
Remedial Reading

Reading Difficulty (1966 1980) — *JUN. 1980*
Postings: 1,686 — GC: 460
SN Invalid Descriptor—used for both the reading problems of students and the reading level of materials—see "Reading Difficulties" and "Readability" respectively for these concepts

Reading Disabilities
USE Reading Difficulties

Reading Enjoyment
USE Literature Appreciation

Reading Failure — *JUL. 1966*
Postings: 330 — GC: 460
SN Lack of achievement or accomplishment in reading
BT Academic Failure
RT Dyslexia
Reading
Reading Achievement
Reading Difficulties

Reading Gain
USE Reading Improvement

Reading Games — *JUL. 1966*
Postings: 302 — GC: 460
BT Educational Games
RT Reading
Reading Instruction
Reading Materials

Reading Habits — *JUL. 1966*
Postings: 1,561 — GC: 460
BT Behavior Patterns
RT Habit Formation
Reader Response
Reading
Reading Attitudes
Reading Comprehension
Reading Interests
Reading Motivation
Reading Skills
Recreational Reading
Silent Reading
Study Habits
Sustained Silent Reading

Reading Improvement — *JUL. 1966*
Postings: 3,869 — GC: 460
SN Process of becoming a better reader (Note: Prior to Mar80, the instruction "Reading Gain, USE Reading Achievement" was carried in the Thesaurus)
UF Reading Gain
BT Improvement
RT Advance Organizers
Reading
Reading Achievement
Reading Centers
Reading Rate
Reading Skills
Reading Strategies

Reading in Content Areas
USE Content Area Reading

Reading Instruction — *JUL. 1966*
Postings: 18,931 — GC: 460
NT Basal Reading
Content Area Reading
Corrective Reading
Directed Reading Activity
Individualized Reading
Remedial Reading
Sustained Silent Reading
BT Instruction
RT Adult Reading Programs
Braille
Emergent Literacy
Experience Charts
Initial Teaching Alphabet
Kinesthetic Methods
Language Experience Approach
Large Type Materials
Literacy Education
Miscue Analysis
Oral Reading
Phonics
Readability
Reading
Reading Assignments
Reading Consultants
Reading Games
Reading Material Selection
Reading Motivation
Reading Readiness
Reading Skills
Reading Strategies
Reading Teachers
Sight Method
Sight Vocabulary
Silent Reading
Story Grammar
Structural Analysis (Linguistics)
Whole Language Approach

Reading Interests — *JUL. 1966*
Postings: 2,101 — GC: 460
BT Interests
RT Independent Reading
Individualized Reading
Reader Response
Reading

Reading Attitudes
Reading Habits
Reading Material Selection
Reading Motivation
Recreational Reading

Reading Laboratories
USE Reading Centers

Reading Level (1966 1980) — *JUN. 1980*
Postings: 647 — GC: 460
SN Invalid Descriptor—used for both the reading level of people and the readability level of materials—see "Reading Achievement" and "Readability" respectively for these concepts

Reading Material Selection — *JUL. 1966*
Postings: 2,665 — GC: 460
BT Media Selection
RT Library Material Selection
Reading
Reading Instruction
Reading Interests
Reading Materials
Recreational Reading
Supplementary Reading Materials
Textbook Selection

Reading Materials — *JUL. 1966*
Postings: 6,349 — GC: 730
UF Readers (Materials)
NT Large Type Materials
Supplementary Reading Materials
Telegraphic Materials
RT Adolescent Literature
Basal Reading
Books
Childrens Literature
Classics (Literature)
High Interest Low Vocabulary Books
Instructional Materials
Newspapers
Periodicals
Publications
Reader Text Relationship
Reading
Reading Assignments
Reading Games
Reading Material Selection
Science Materials
Talking Books
Textbooks

Reading Motivation — *NOV. 1995*
Postings: 727 — GC: 460
SN The arousal, direction, and sustaining of reading interest and activity for work, school, pleasure, or other purpose
BT Motivation
RT Learning Motivation
Literature Appreciation
Reading
Reading Attitudes
Reading Habits
Reading Instruction
Reading Interests
Reading Strategies
Student Motivation

Reading Problems
USE Reading Difficulties

Reading Processes — *JUL. 1966*
Postings: 3,728 — GC: 460
NT Decoding (Reading)
BT Language Processing
RT Eye Fixations
Miscue Analysis
Reader Response
Reader Text Relationship
Reading
Reading Comprehension
Reading Skills
Reading Strategies
Reading Writing Relationship
Receptive Language

Reading Programs — *JUL. 1966*
Postings: 5,321 — GC: 460
NT Adult Reading Programs
BT Programs
RT Basal Reading
Individualized Reading
Language Experience Approach
Reading
Reading Assignments
Reading Centers

Reading Rate — *JUL. 1977*
Postings: 860 — GC: 460
SN The speed at which an individual can read and comprehend what is read
UF Reading Speed (1966 1977)
BT Reading Skills
RT Readability
Reader Response
Reading
Reading Comprehension
Reading Improvement
Reading Tests
Silent Reading
Speed Reading
Telegraphic Materials

Reading Readiness — *JUL. 1966*
Postings: 1,775 — GC: 460
SN Act of preparing, or degree of preparedness, for formal reading instruction or any other reading activity or task
BT Readiness
RT Basic Vocabulary
Beginning Reading
Early Reading
Learning Readiness
Prereading Experience
Reading
Reading Ability
Reading Instruction
Reading Readiness Tests
School Readiness

Reading Readiness Tests — *JUL. 1966*
Postings: 198 — GC: 830
BT Aptitude Tests
RT Diagnostic Tests
Preschool Tests
Prognostic Tests
Reading
Reading Diagnosis
Reading Readiness
Reading Tests
School Readiness Tests
Screening Tests

Reading Research — *JUL. 1966*
Postings: 12,986 — GC: 810
SN Basic, applied, and developmental research conducted to advance knowledge about reading (Note: As of Oct81, use as a minor Descriptor for examples of this kind of research—use as a major Descriptor only as the subject of a document)
BT Educational Research
RT Communication Research
Journalism Research
Reading
Tachistoscopes

Reading Skills — *JUL. 1966*
Postings: 10,158 — GC: 460
SN Complex behaviors developed through practice in order to read proficiently
NT Reading Comprehension
Reading Rate
BT Language Skills
Reading Ability
RT Adult Literacy
Basic Skills
Cloze Procedure
Content Area Reading
Decoding (Reading)
Eye Voice Span
Functional Literacy
Functional Reading
Inferences
Literacy

= Two or more Descriptors are used to represent this term.
The term's main entry shows the appropriate coordination.

Literacy Education
Minimum Competencies
Phonics
Reader Response
Reading
Reading Achievement
Reading Centers
Reading Habits
Reading Improvement
Reading Instruction
Reading Processes
Reading Strategies
Reading Tests
Thinking Skills
Vocabulary Skills
Word Recognition
Word Study Skills

Reading Specialists
USE   Reading Consultants

Reading Speed (1966 1977)
USE   Reading Rate

Reading Strategies   OCT. 1983
      Postings: 2,509   GC: 460
SN   Plans or methods that can be used or
      taught to facilitate reading proficiency
BT   Learning Strategies
RT   Reading
      Reading Comprehension
      Reading Improvement
      Reading Instruction
      Reading Motivation
      Reading Processes
      Reading Skills

Reading Teachers   MAR. 1980
      Postings: 686   GC: 360
BT   Teachers
RT   Language Teachers
      Reading
      Reading Consultants
      Reading Instruction

Reading Tests   JUL. 1966
      Postings: 3,128   GC: 830
NT   Informal Reading Inventories
BT   Verbal Tests
RT   Achievement Tests
      Cloze Procedure
      Language Tests
      Reading
      Reading Achievement
      Reading Comprehension
      Reading Diagnosis
      Reading Rate
      Reading Readiness Tests
      Reading Skills

Reading Therapy
USE   Bibliotherapy

Reading Writing Relationship DEC. 1985
      Postings: 1,704   GC: 460
SN   The inherent interaction between the skills
      or processes of reading and writing
BT   Relationship
RT   Dialog Journals
      Invented Spelling
      Language Arts
      Literacy
      Metalinguistics
      Reader Text Relationship
      Reading
      Reading Processes
      Story Grammar
      Text Structure
      Whole Language Approach
      Writing (Composition)
      Writing Processes

Readings (Collections)
USE   Anthologies

Real Estate   AUG. 1968
      Postings: 211   GC: 650
BT   Ownership
RT   Land Use
      Landlords
      Property Appraisal
      Real Estate Occupations
      School Location
      Site Selection
      Zoning

Real Estate Appraisal
USE   Property Appraisal

Real Estate Occupations   SEP. 1968
      Postings: 66   GC: 640
BT   Occupations
RT   Buildings
      Distributive Education
      Housing
      Housing Industry
      Housing Management Aides
      Landlords
      Real Estate
      Sales Occupations

Realia   JUL. 1966
      Postings: 179   GC: 720
SN   Tangible objects, specimens, or artifacts
      that are not copies, representations, or
      models
BT   Nonprint Media
RT   Exhibits
      Instructional Materials
      Material Culture
      Museums
      Science Fairs
      Three Dimensional Aids

Realism   MAY 1969
      Postings: 445   GC: 430
SN   In philosophy, the theory that objects of
      sense perception or cognition are real
      and exist independently of their being
      known—in the creative arts, representa-
      tion of ordinary life without idealization
RT   Art Expression
      Literary Styles
      Objectivity
      Philosophy
      Twentieth Century Literature

Reality Therapy   AUG. 1986
      Postings: 78   GC: 230
SN   Psychotherapeutic approach in which rec-
      ognition of irresponsibility (reality) and
      respect for oneself and for others are the
      keys to responsible, acceptable behavior
BT   Psychotherapy
RT   Behavior Modification
      Counseling Techniques
      Discipline
      Educational Therapy
      Interpersonal Competence
      Self Actualization
      Self Concept
      Social Reinforcement

Reasoning Skills
USE   Thinking Skills

Recall (Psychological) (1967 1980)
USE   Recall (Psychology)

Recall (Psychology)   MAR. 1980
      Postings: 5,068   GC: 110
SN   The process whereby a representation of
      past experience is elicited and/or repro-
      duced (Note: See also "Recognition (Psy-
      chology)")
UF   Recall (Psychological) (1967 1980)
NT   Reminiscence
BT   Memory
RT   Advance Organizers
      Cues
      Encoding (Psychology)

Familiarity
Learning
Learning Disabilities
Learning Processes
Mediation Theory
Memorization
Mnemonics
Paired Associate Learning
Perceptual Impairments
Primacy Effect
Recognition (Psychology)
Retention (Psychology)
Schemata (Cognition)
Visualization

Recall Ratio
USE   Relevance (Information Retrieval)

Receptionists   AUG. 1970
      Postings: 35   GC: 640
BT   Clerical Workers

Receptive Communication
USE   Receptive Language

Receptive Language   JUL. 1966
      Postings: 648   GC: 450
SN   The cognitive processing involved in com-
      prehending oral, symbolic, or written
      language (Note: Prior to Mar80, the use
      of this term was not restricted by a
      Scope Note)
UF   Receptive Communication
BT   Language Processing
RT   Aphasia
      Caregiver Speech
      Communication (Thought Transfer)
      Communication Skills
      Expressive Language
      Language Acquisition
      Language Impairments
      Language Skills
      Linguistic Input
      Listening Comprehension
      Psycholinguistics
      Reading Comprehension
      Reading Processes

Recess Breaks   NOV. 1994
      Postings: 27   GC: 470
SN   Periods of rest during the schoolday, in
      which children may engage in recrea-
      tional activities
RT   Childrens Games
      Outdoor Activities
      Play
      Playground Activities
      Recreational Activities
      School Recreational Programs

Recidivism   SEP. 1970
      Postings: 475   GC: 530
SN   Tendency to relapse into previous crimi-
      nal or delinquent behavior habits
BT   Behavior Patterns
RT   Antisocial Behavior
      Behavior Disorders
      Correctional Rehabilitation
      Criminals
      Delinquency
      Delinquent Rehabilitation

Recipes (Food)   SEP. 1996
      Postings: 118   GC: 720
SN   Instructions and ingredients for prepar-
      ing food dishes
RT   Cooking Instruction
      Cooks
      Food
      Food Service
      Foods Instruction
      Instructional Materials
      Nutrition
      Nutrition Instruction

Reciprocal Teaching   APR. 1993
      Postings: 100   GC: 310
SN   An instructional technique in which a
      teacher and student, or a tutor and tutee,
      take turns with the role of teaching—
      frequently used for improving reading
      comprehension
BT   Teaching Methods
RT   Comprehension
      Discussion (Teaching Technique)
      Peer Teaching
      Questioning Techniques
      Reading Comprehension

Reciprocals (Mathematics)   JAN. 1969
      Postings: 10   GC: 480
BT   Numbers
RT   Fractions
      Mathematical Concepts
      Rational Numbers

Recoding (Psychology)
USE   Encoding (Psychology)

Recognition (Achievement)   MAR. 1980
      Postings: 545   GC: 520
SN   Acknowledgement of achievement or
      merit (Note: Prior to Mar80, this concept
      was indexed under "Recognition")
NT   Awards
      Commencement Ceremonies
      Professional Recognition
BT   Evaluation
RT   Achievement
      Compensation (Remuneration)
      Graduation
      Incentives
      Merit Pay
      Merit Rating
      Merit Scholarships
      Morale
      Praise
      Reputation
      Rewards
      Scholarship
      Status
      Status Need

Recognition (Psychology)   MAR. 1980
      Postings: 602   GC: 110
SN   Awareness that an object, word, sen-
      tence, person, etc., has been known or
      experienced before—one form of remem-
      bering (Note: Prior to Mar80, this con-
      cept was indexed under "Recognition"—
      see also "Recall (Psychology)")
NT   Pattern Recognition
      Word Recognition
BT   Memory
RT   Association (Psychology)
      Encoding (Psychology)
      Familiarity
      Identification
      Learning Disabilities
      Learning Processes
      Perception
      Perceptual Impairments
      Recall (Psychology)
      Retention (Psychology)
      Tachistoscopes

Recognition (1967 1980)   MAR. 1980
      Postings: 509   GC: 510
SN   Invalid Descriptor—used for both the
      psychological process of recognition and
      recognition of achievement—see "Rec-
      ognition (Psychology)" and "Recognition
      (Achievement)" respectively for these
      concepts

Recombinant DNA
USE   DNA
AND   Genetic Engineering

Reconstruction Era   JUL. 1966
      Postings: 126   GC: 430
SN   The period following the U.S. Civil War

= Two or more Descriptors are used to represent this term.
The term's main entry shows the appropriate coordination.

(1865–1877) during which the Confederate states were reorganized by the Federal government and brought back into the Union
BT United States History
RT Civil War (United States)

Record Clerks
USE File Clerks

Recordkeeping   JUL. 1966
Postings: 2,309   GC: 320
BT Business Skills
RT Audits (Verification)
Bookkeeping
Case Records
Clerical Occupations
Data Collection
Information Storage
Medical Record Technicians
Office Occupations
Office Occupations Education
Records (Forms)
Records Management
Reports

Records (Forms)   JUL. 1966
Postings: 2,714   GC: 730
NT Attendance Records
Bibliographic Records
Case Records
Check Lists
Confidential Records
Credentials
Farm Accounts
Payroll Records
Student Records
Wills
Worksheets
RT Archives
Charts
Diagrams
Flow Charts
Graphs
Information Storage
Office Management
Recordkeeping
Records Management
Reports

Records Management   AUG. 1989
Postings: 365   GC: 710
SN Management of the creation, use, handling, control, maintenance, and disposition of records in an office, organization, or household
BT Information Management
RT Archives
Data Conversion
Information Storage
Office Management
Preservation
Recordkeeping
Records (Forms)
Registrars (School)
Reports

Recreation   JUL. 1966
Postings: 1,400   GC: 470
NT Therapeutic Recreation
RT Hospitality Occupations
Leisure Education
Leisure Time
Recreation Finances
Recreation Legislation
Recreational Activities
Recreational Facilities
Recreational Programs
Recreationists
Vacations

Recreation Finances   JUL. 1966
Postings: 110   GC: 620
SN Funding for or operating expenses of recreational activities, especially those supported by a local, state, or federal government (Note: For school athletic programs, coordinate "Athletic

Programs" with "Educational Finance" or "School Funds")
BT Financial Support
RT Recreation
Recreational Facilities

Recreation Legislation   JUL. 1966
Postings: 97   GC: 610
UF Community Recreation Legislation (1966 1978) #
Federal Recreation Legislation (1966 1978) #
Local Recreation Legislation (1966 1978) #
State Recreation Legislation (1966 1978) #
BT Legislation
RT Laws
Recreation

Recreation Therapy
USE Therapeutic Recreation

Recreational Activities   JUL. 1966
Postings: 2,089   GC: 470
NT Camping
Hobbies
Playground Activities
Recreational Reading
BT Activities
RT Art Activities
Athletic Fields
Athletics
Bicycling
Dating (Social)
Drinking
Extracurricular Activities
Games
Horseback Riding
Leisure Time
Lifetime Sports
Mass Media Use
Music Activities
Outdoor Activities
Physical Activities
Physical Education
Play
Popular Culture
Recess Breaks
Recreation
Recreationists
School Recreational Programs
Seafarers
Singing
Special Olympics
Swimming
Therapeutic Recreation
Tourism
Travel
Underwater Diving
Wildlife Management
Womens Athletics

Recreational Facilities   JUL. 1966
Postings: 900   GC: 920
NT Playgrounds
BT Facilities
RT Aquariums
Athletic Fields
Auditoriums
Community Recreation Programs
Community Resources
Field Houses
Gymnasiums
Hospitality Occupations
Museums
Park Design
Parks
Physical Education Facilities
Planetariums
Recreation
Recreation Finances
Recreationists
Student Unions
Swimming Pools
Theaters
Trails
Windowless Rooms
Zoos

Recreational Programs   JUL. 1966
Postings: 717   GC: 470
UF Social Recreation Programs (1966 1980)
NT Community Recreation Programs
Day Camp Programs
Physical Recreation Programs
Resident Camp Programs
School Recreational Programs
BT Programs
RT Outreach Programs
Recreation
Recreationists
Summer Programs

Recreational Reading   JUL. 1966
Postings: 1,052   GC: 460
SN Reading that is done for relaxation or amusement, or to satisfy interests unrelated to educational or vocational obligations
UF Leisure Time Reading
BT Reading
Recreational Activities
RT Independent Reading
Literature Appreciation
Reading Habits
Reading Interests
Reading Material Selection
Supplementary Reading Materials

Recreationists   NOV. 1971
Postings: 134   GC: 470
SN Persons taking or seeking recreation
BT Groups
RT Leisure Education
Leisure Time
Recreation
Recreational Activities
Recreational Facilities
Recreational Programs
Vacations

Recruitment   JUL. 1966
Postings: 2,547   GC: 630
UF Personnel Recruitment
NT Faculty Recruitment
Student Recruitment
Teacher Recruitment
RT Affirmative Action
Employment Opportunities
Personnel
Personnel Needs
Personnel Selection
Selection

Recurrent Education
USE Lifelong Learning

Recycling   OCT. 1971
Postings: 615   GC: 410
SN Processing and reuse of materials instead of discarding them as waste
BT Waste Disposal
RT Conservation (Environment)
Depleted Resources
Ecology
Natural Resources
Pollution
Solid Wastes
Waste Water
Wastes
Water Treatment

Redevelopment Areas
USE Urban Renewal

Reduction in Force   MAR. 1977
Postings: 509   GC: 630
SN Reduction in the total number of people employed by an organization—includes such methods as laying off personnel, creating early retirement options, transferring personnel, and not filling openings created through normal staff attrition (Note: Prior to Mar77, the instruction

"Reduction in Force USE Job Layoff" was carried in the Thesaurus)
NT Job Layoff
RT Dislocated Workers
Dismissal (Personnel)
Early Retirement
Employment Practices
Financial Exigency
Labor Market
Labor Turnover
Labor Utilization
Outplacement Services (Employment)
Personnel Policy
Program Termination
Retrenchment
Seniority
Teacher Dismissal
Tenure
Unemployment

Redundancy   JUL. 1966
Postings: 190   GC: 310
RT Attention
Error Patterns
Habituation
Novelty (Stimulus Dimension)
Repetitive Film Showings
Retention (Psychology)
Stimuli

Reentry Students   MAR. 1980
Postings: 718   GC: 360
SN Individuals who return to an educational system, program, or institution following an extended absence
BT Students
RT Adult Students
Attendance
College Students
Continuation Students
Dropouts
Educational Trends
High School Students
Nontraditional Education
Nontraditional Students
Refresher Courses
Special Needs Students
Stopouts

Reentry Workers   MAR. 1980
Postings: 238   GC: 630
SN Individuals who return to employment following an extended absence
BT Personnel
RT Career Choice
Displaced Homemakers
Dropouts
Employed Parents
Employed Women
Employees
Employment
Employment Level
Employment Opportunities
Employment Qualifications
Job Application
Job Placement
Job Search Methods
Job Skills
Labor Force
Labor Market
Leaves of Absence
Retraining
Stopouts
Work Experience

Reference Books (1966 1980)
USE Reference Materials

Reference Groups   SEP. 1981
Postings: 119   GC: 110
SN Real or theoretical groups (social, ethnic, family, etc.) that serve as sources for identification, motivation, aspiration, attitudes, behavior, or modes of living (Note: Do not confuse with "Role Models" or the Identifier "Reference Individuals," both referring to individuals rather than groups, the former emulated

= Two or more Descriptors are used to represent this term.
The term's main entry shows the appropriate coordination.

in one or a few roles and the latter emulated in many roles)
BT   Groups
RT   Group Status
      Identification (Psychology)
      Interpersonal Relationship
      Self Concept
      Social Psychology
      Social Support Groups
      Socialization

Reference Librarians
USE   Librarians
AND   Reference Services

Reference Materials   *JUL. 1966*
       Postings: 3,940   GC: 720
SN   Materials compiled to supply definite pieces of information of varying extent, and intended to be referred to for brief consultations (Note: Corresponds to Pubtype code 130—do not use except as the subject of a document)
UF   Library Reference Materials #
       Reference Books (1966 1980)
NT   Abstracts
       Anthologies
       Atlases
       Bibliographies
       Citations (References)
       Dictionaries
       Directories
       Discographies
       Encyclopedias
       Filmographies
       Guides
       Indexes
       Library Catalogs
       Thesauri
       Yearbooks
BT   Publications
RT   Instructional Materials
       Library Materials
       Multilingual Materials
       Printed Materials
       Reference Services
       Research Tools
       Resource Materials
       Selection Tools

Reference Services   *APR. 1980*
       Postings: 2,540   GC: 710
SN   Activities designed to make information available to users—includes direct, personal aid to users by library or information personnel
UF   Computer Based Reference Services #
       Library Reference Services (1968 1980) #
       Online Reference Services #
       Reference Librarians #
BT   Information Services
RT   Community Information Services
       Information Dissemination
       Library Services
       Online Searching
       Reference Materials
       Search Intermediaries
       Search Strategies
       User Needs (Information)

Referral   *JUL. 1966*
       Postings: 1,717   GC: 240
SN   Process of referring an individual or group to an appropriate agency, service, or specialist
UF   Information and Referral Services #
       Referral Services (Community) #
RT   Community Information Services
       Consultants
       Consultation Programs
       Counseling
       Delivery Systems
       Disability Identification
       Information Dissemination
       Placement
       Prereferral Intervention
       Professional Services

Regular and Special Education Relationship
       Resource Room Programs
       Specialists
       Student Placement

Referral Services (Community)
USE   Community Information Services
AND   Referral

Reflective Teaching   *NOV. 1994*
       Postings: 1,202   GC: 310
SN   Thinking about and critically analyzing one's own teaching in order to improve teaching practice
RT   Critical Thinking
       Educational Philosophy
       Self Evaluation (Individuals)
       Teacher Education
       Teacher Effectiveness
       Teacher Improvement
       Teacher Researchers
       Teaching Experience

Reflectivity
USE   Conceptual Tempo

Refractive Errors
USE   Ametropia

Refresher Courses   *SEP. 1968*
       Postings: 157   GC: 350
BT   Courses
RT   Adult Education
       Improvement Programs
       Inservice Education
       Minicourses
       Professional Continuing Education
       Reentry Students
       Remedial Instruction
       Retraining
       Review (Reexamination)
       Supplementary Education

Refresher Training
USE   Retraining

Refrigeration   *JUL. 1966*
       Postings: 98   GC: 920
BT   Climate Control
RT   Air Conditioning
       Air Flow
       Heat Recovery
       Refrigeration Mechanics
       Temperature
       Thermal Insulation

Refrigeration Mechanics   *JUL. 1966*
       Postings: 74   GC: 640
UF   Air Conditioning Mechanics
BT   Mechanics (Process)
RT   Air Conditioning Equipment
       Refrigeration
       Skilled Occupations

Refugees   *MAY 1969*
       Postings: 1,508   GC: 510
UF   Escapees
       Exiles
       Political Refugees
BT   Migrants
RT   Acculturation
       Foreign Nationals
       Foreign Workers
       Immigrants
       Immigration
       Land Settlement
       Migration
       Political Attitudes
       Relocation
       Safety
       Undocumented Immigrants

Refuse
USE   Wastes

Regents
USE   Trustees

Reggio Emilia Approach   *FEB. 2000*
       Postings: 84   GC: 310
SN   An approach to early childhood education originating in the municipal preprimary schools of Reggio Emilia, Italy, characteristics of which include emphasis on children's symbolic representations (including drawing, sculpture, dramatic play, and writing), documentation of the children's experiences in long-term projects, and extensive involvement of parents and the community
UF   Reggio Emilia Preschools #
BT   Teaching Methods
RT   Art Activities
       Cooperative Learning
       Early Childhood Education
       Experiential Learning
       Parent Participation
       Student Centered Curriculum
       Student Projects

Reggio Emilia Preschools
USE   Preschool Education
AND   Reggio Emilia Approach

Regional Attitudes   *MAR. 1980*
       Postings: 255   GC: 550
SN   Attitudes representative of a particular region (Note: Use in coordination with appropriate Identifiers, e.g., "United States (North)," "United States (South)," etc.)
UF   Northern Attitudes (1968 1980)
       Southern Attitudes (1966 1980)
BT   Attitudes
RT   Geographic Regions
       Political Attitudes
       Regional Characteristics
       Rural Urban Differences
       Social Attitudes

Regional Characteristics   *JAN. 1978*
       Postings: 1,038   GC: 550
SN   Those identifying qualities or traits which constitute the essential nature of a geographic area's people and resources
UF   Regional Differences #
NT   Regional Dialects
RT   Area Studies
       Community Characteristics
       Cultural Traits
       Environment
       Geographic Regions
       Regional Attitudes
       Regional Cooperation
       Regional Laboratories
       Regional Libraries
       Regional Planning
       Regional Programs
       Regional Schools
       Rural Urban Differences
       Social Characteristics

Regional Cooperation   *JUL. 1966*
       Postings: 884   GC: 330
BT   Cooperation
RT   Agency Cooperation
       Cooperative Planning
       Institutional Cooperation
       Intermediate Administrative Units
       Regional Characteristics
       Regional Libraries
       Regional Programs

Regional Dialects   *AUG. 1968*
       Postings: 906   GC: 450
SN   Special varieties within a language, defined by the geographical origin of its speakers
UF   Geographic Dialects

BT   Dialects
       Regional Characteristics
RT   Area Studies
       Bidialectalism
       Black Dialects
       Ethnic Origins
       Geographic Regions
       Idioms
       Language Classification
       Native Speakers
       Nonstandard Dialects
       North American English
       Social Dialects
       Speech Habits

Regional Differences
USE   Differences
AND   Regional Characteristics

Regional Laboratories   *JUL. 1966*
       Postings: 182   GC: 920
BT   Laboratories
RT   Regional Characteristics
       Regional Programs

Regional Libraries   *MAR. 1969*
       Postings: 257   GC: 710
SN   Public libraries, supported in whole or in part by federal, state, or provincial funds, that serve several communities and/or counties
UF   District Libraries
BT   Public Libraries
RT   County Libraries
       Regional Characteristics
       Regional Cooperation
       Regional Programs

Regional Planning   *JUL. 1966*
       Postings: 1,066   GC: 330
BT   Planning
RT   Planning Commissions
       Regional Characteristics
       Regional Programs
       Social Planning
       Statewide Planning
       Urban Planning

Regional Programs   *JUL. 1966*
       Postings: 1,326   GC: 520
BT   Programs
RT   County Programs
       Education Service Centers
       Regional Characteristics
       Regional Cooperation
       Regional Laboratories
       Regional Libraries
       Regional Planning
       Regional Schools

Regional Schools   *JUL. 1966*
       Postings: 513   GC: 340
SN   Schools, often providing special services, that serve a wider geographic area than the usual school district
UF   Area Vocational Schools (1966 1980) #
BT   Schools
RT   Boarding Schools
       Consolidated Schools
       Geographic Regions
       Regional Characteristics
       Regional Programs
       Special Schools

Registered Nurses
USE   Nurses

Registrars (School)   *MAR. 1980*
       Postings: 85   GC: 360
SN   Administrative officials, usually at postsecondary institutions, who have principal responsibility for student enrollment and records
UF   College Registrars
BT   Administrators

= Two or more Descriptors are used to represent this term.
The term's main entry shows the appropriate coordination.

School Personnel
RT   Academic Records
     Admissions Officers
     College Administration
     Enrollment
     Enrollment Management
     Records Management
     School Administration
     School Registration
     Student Personnel Workers
     Student Records

Registration in School
USE   School Registration

Regression (Statistics)   *APR. 1980*
     Postings: 1,358   GC: 480
SN   The effect of imperfect correlation in the relationship between two sets of measurements, i.e., the tendency for predicted scores to lie closer to the mean than do the scores used to predict them—also, the statistical technique used when one or more measures are used to predict or make a least squares estimate of scores on another measure
UF   Linear Regression
     Regression Effects
NT   Multiple Regression Analysis
BT   Statistical Analysis
RT   Causal Models
     Correlation
     Least Squares Statistics
     Prediction
     Predictive Measurement
     Robustness (Statistics)
     Statistical Inference
     Statistics
     Validity

Regression Effects
USE   Regression (Statistics)

Regressors
USE   Predictor Variables

Regular and Special Education Relationship
     AUG. 1989
     Postings: 1,435   GC: 330
UF   General and Special Education Relationship
     Special and Regular Education Relationship
     Special Education Regular Education Cooperation
     Special Regular Education Interface
BT   Relationship
RT   Academic Accommodations (Disabilities)
     Education
     Educational Cooperation
     Educational Policy
     Inclusive Schools
     Mainstreaming
     Prereferral Intervention
     Referral
     Special Education
     Special Needs Students
     Teacher Collaboration

Regular Class Placement (1968 1978)
USE   Mainstreaming

Rehabilitation   *JUL. 1966*
     Postings: 1,919   GC: 240
SN   Process of restoring individuals, through education and/or therapy, to the best possible level of physical, mental, emotional, social, or vocational functioning
UF   Student Rehabilitation (1966 1980)
NT   Correctional Rehabilitation
     Drug Rehabilitation
     Vocational Rehabilitation
RT   Adjustment (to Environment)
     Behavior Modification
     Caseworkers
     Cognitive Restructuring

Counseling
Daily Living Skills
Deinstitutionalization (of Disabled)
Disabilities
Disadvantaged
Diseases
Dropouts
Educational Therapy
Emotional Disturbances
Independent Living
Injuries
Intervention
Medical Services
Normalization (Disabilities)
Occupational Therapy
Patients
Physical Disabilities
Physical Therapy
Psychotherapy
Rehabilitation Centers
Rehabilitation Counseling
Rehabilitation Programs
Retraining
Social Support Groups
Social Work
Special Education
Supported Employment
Therapeutic Environment
Therapeutic Recreation
Therapy
Victims of Crime

Rehabilitation Centers   *JUL. 1966*
     Postings: 300   GC: 920
UF   Halfway Houses #
BT   Facilities
RT   Boarding Homes
     Group Homes
     Housing
     Institutions
     Mental Health Clinics
     Milieu Therapy
     Rehabilitation
     Rehabilitation Counseling
     Residential Institutions
     Residential Schools
     Sheltered Workshops
     Therapeutic Environment
     Vocational Training Centers

Rehabilitation Counseling   *JUL. 1966*
     Postings: 1,165   GC: 240
BT   Counseling
RT   Adjustment (to Environment)
     Career Counseling
     Caseworker Approach
     Rehabilitation
     Rehabilitation Centers
     Rehabilitation Programs
     Sheltered Workshops

Rehabilitation Programs   *JUL. 1966*
     Postings: 1,507   GC: 240
NT   Dropout Programs
BT   Programs
RT   Compensatory Education
     Continuation Students
     Correctional Education
     Guidance Programs
     Human Services
     Individualized Programs
     Mental Health Programs
     Outreach Programs
     Prognostic Tests
     Rehabilitation
     Rehabilitation Counseling
     Residential Programs
     Self Help Programs
     Sheltered Workshops

Rehearsals (Theater Arts)   *FEB. 2000*
     Postings: 50   GC: 420
SN   Practice sessions generally under the instruction of a conductor or director in preparation for a public performance
BT   Theater Arts
RT   Acting
     Dance
     Drama

Dramatics
Music

Reinforcement   *JUL. 1966*
     Postings: 3,525   GC: 110
UF   Learning Reinforcement
     Reinforcement Theory
     Reinforcers (1966 1980)
NT   Negative Reinforcement
     Positive Reinforcement
     Punishment
     Rewards
     Social Reinforcement
     Timeout
     Token Economy
RT   Behavior Modification
     Behaviorism
     Biofeedback
     Conditioning
     Contingency Management
     Delay of Gratification
     Feedback
     Motivation
     Operant Conditioning
     Teacher Response
     Teaching Methods

Reinforcement Theory
USE   Reinforcement

Reinforcers (1966 1980)
USE   Reinforcement

Rejection (Psychology)   *MAR. 1980*
     Postings: 260   GC: 230
UF   Rejection (1966 1980)
BT   Psychological Patterns
RT   Alienation
     Anger
     Interpersonal Relationship
     Resentment
     Resistance (Psychology)
     Withdrawal (Psychology)

Rejection (1966 1980)
USE   Rejection (Psychology)

Relationship   *JUL. 1966*
     Postings: 1,064   GC: 520
SN   Type or mode of association between or among physical or conceptual entities, e.g., people, institutions, objects, ideas, processes (Note: Use a more specific term if possible—do not confuse with "Correlation"—prior to Mar80, the use of this term was not restricted by a Scope Note)
NT   Community Relations
     Credibility
     Cultural Interrelationships
     Developmental Continuity
     Education Work Relationship
     Faculty College Relationship
     Family School Relationship
     Family Work Relationship
     Federal Indian Relationship
     Federal State Relationship
     Government School Relationship
     Human Relations
     Interaction
     International Relations
     Interpersonal Relationship
     Intimacy
     Labor Relations
     Police Community Relationship
     Police School Relationship
     Privacy
     Public Relations
     Reader Text Relationship
     Reading Writing Relationship
     Regular and Special Education Relationship
     School Business Relationship
     School Community Relationship
     Science and Society
     Spatial Relationship (Facilities)
     State Church Separation
     Student School Relationship

Supply and Demand
Theory Practice Relationship
RT   Classification
     Coordination
     Distance
     Equations (Mathematics)
     Influences
     Proximity
     Ratios (Mathematics)
     Role
     Schematic Studies

Relative Humidity
USE   Humidity

Relativity   *OCT. 1968*
     Postings: 257   GC: 490
UF   Geometrodynamics
     Space Time Continuum
BT   Scientific Concepts
     Theories
RT   Energy
     Gravity (Physics)
     Kinetics
     Light
     Matter
     Mechanics (Physics)
     Motion
     Optics
     Physics
     Quantum Mechanics
     Space
     Time

Relaxation Training   *MAR. 1980*
     Postings: 641   GC: 230
SN   Training that emphasizes the acquisition of skills and techniques for managing and reducing stress, anxiety, and tension
UF   Progressive Relaxation (1967 1980)
BT   Psychotherapy
RT   Anxiety
     Biofeedback
     Desensitization
     Hypertension
     Hypnosis
     Physiology
     Stress Management
     Suggestopedia
     Transcendental Meditation

Released Time   *JUL. 1966*
     Postings: 342   GC: 630
SN   Time granted to students, employees, or institutionalized persons to pursue special activities
UF   Day Release
     Study Release Programs
     Work Release
RT   Correctional Education
     Employer Employee Relationship
     Flexible Working Hours
     Industrial Training
     Leaves of Absence
     Off the Job Training
     Personnel Policy
     Religious Education
     Sabbatical Leaves
     School Schedules
     Scope of Bargaining

Relevance (Cultural)
USE   Cultural Relevance

Relevance (Education)   *JUL. 1969*
     Postings: 8,095   GC: 330
SN   Applicability of what is taught by schools to the needs and interests of students and society
UF   Curriculum Relevance
     Educational Relevance
NT   Culturally Relevant Education
RT   Accountability
     Career Education
     Core Curriculum
     Course Selection (Students)
     Curriculum Development

= Two or more Descriptors are used to represent this term.
The term's main entry shows the appropriate coordination.

Curriculum Evaluation
Education Work Relationship
Educational Improvement
Educational Needs
Educational Objectives
Educational Responsibility
Excellence in Education
Experimental Colleges
Experimental Schools
Free Schools
Futures (of Society)
Living Learning Centers
National Curriculum
Nontraditional Education
Student Educational Objectives
Student Interests
Student Needs
Student School Relationship
Vocational Education

Relevance (Information Retrieval)

JUN. 1969
Postings: 974   GC: 710
SN   The number of retrieved documents
       judged relevant in proportion to the num-
       ber of documents returned in response
       to a query
UF   Precision Ratio
       Recall Ratio
BT   Ratios (Mathematics)
RT   Bibliographic Coupling
       Evaluation Methods
       Information Retrieval
       Online Searching
       Performance
       Reliability
       Search Strategies
       Systems Analysis
       User Needs (Information)
       User Satisfaction (Information)

Reliability

JUL. 1966
Postings: 2,251   GC: 820
SN   Extent to which something is consistent,
       dependable, and stable over repeated
       trials (Note: If applicable, use the more
       specific terms "Test Reliability" and/or
       "Interrater Reliability")
UF   Consistency
       Dependability
NT   Interrater Reliability
       Test Reliability
BT   Evaluation Criteria
RT   Correlation
       Error of Measurement
       Error Patterns
       Expectation
       Generalizability Theory
       Performance
       Prediction
       Probability
       Quality Control
       Relevance (Information Retrieval)
       Risk
       Robustness (Statistics)
       Sample Size
       Statistical Analysis
       Statistical Data
       Statistical Distributions
       True Scores
       Validity
       Weighted Scores

Relief (Art)

OCT. 1994
Postings: 7   GC: 420
SN   The projection of carved, molded, or
       modeled figures and forms from fixed
       backgrounds, as in sculpture, or such
       projection that is apparent only, as in
       painting
RT   Art Expression
       Art Products
       Maps
       Sculpture
       Visual Arts

Relief Teachers

USE   Substitute Teachers

Religion

JUL. 1966
Postings: 2,758   GC: 430
NT   Buddhism
       Christianity
       Confucianism
       Islam
       Judaism
       Taoism
RT   Beliefs
       Biblical Literature
       Church Programs
       Church Role
       Church Workers
       Churches
       Clergy
       Creationism
       Cultural Activities
       Humanities
       Hymns
       Interfaith Relations
       Islamic Culture
       Meditation
       Modernism
       Mysticism
       Naturalism
       Nuns
       Philosophy
       Priests
       Religion Studies
       Religious Conflict
       Religious Cultural Groups
       Religious Differences
       Religious Discrimination
       Religious Education
       Religious Factors
       Religious Holidays
       Religious Organizations
       School Prayer
       Spirituality
       State Church Separation
       Theological Education
       Traditionalism

Religion Studies

APR. 1990
Postings: 269   GC: 430
SN   Studies at any academic level about re-
       ligion and its influence on civilizations
       of the past and present in a
       nondenominational or global context
       (Note: Prior to Apr90, this concept was
       frequently indexed by "Religious Educa-
       tion")
UF   Comparative Religion
       Religious Studies
BT   Curriculum
RT   Cross Cultural Studies
       Cultural Awareness
       Cultural Education
       Ethnic Studies
       History
       Interdisciplinary Approach
       Non Western Civilization
       Religion
       Religious Cultural Groups
       Religious Differences
       Social Sciences
       Social Studies
       Western Civilization

Religious Agencies (1966 1980)

USE   Religious Organizations

Religious Conflict

JUL. 1966
Postings: 264   GC: 540
BT   Conflict
RT   Culture Conflict
       Ethnicity
       Interfaith Relations
       Religion
       Religious Cultural Groups
       Religious Discrimination
       Religious Factors

Religious Cultural Groups

JUL. 1966
Postings: 886   GC: 560
UF   Religious Groups
NT   Catholics
       Jews
       Muslims

Protestants
BT   Groups
RT   Buddhism
       Caste
       Christianity
       Clergy
       Confucianism
       Culture
       Ethnic Groups
       Ethnic Relations
       Interfaith Relations
       Islam
       Judaism
       Minority Groups
       Nuns
       Priests
       Religion
       Religion Studies
       Religious Conflict
       Religious Organizations
       Taoism

Religious Differences

JUL. 1966
Postings: 392   GC: 510
BT   Differences
RT   Individual Differences
       Interfaith Relations
       Intermarriage
       Religion
       Religion Studies
       Religious Factors

Religious Discrimination

JUL. 1966
Postings: 279   GC: 540
BT   Social Discrimination
RT   Affirmative Action
       Anti Semitism
       Ethnic Discrimination
       Interfaith Relations
       Religion
       Religious Conflict
       Religious Factors
       Reverse Discrimination
       Social Bias

Religious Education

JUL. 1966
Postings: 1,894   GC: 400
SN   Instruction in religion at any level not
       leading to a degree in theology (Note:
       Prior to Mar80, this term was not re-
       stricted by a Scope Note—for classes or
       courses in comparative religion, use "Re-
       ligion Studies"—for formal education
       for careers in religion, including the clergy,
       use "Theological Education")
BT   Education
RT   Catholic Educators
       Catholic Schools
       Church Programs
       Church Related Colleges
       Church Workers
       Clergy
       Ethical Instruction
       Ethics
       Lay Teachers
       Parochial Schools
       Released Time
       Religion
       Theological Education

Religious Factors

JUL. 1966
Postings: 1,915   GC: 520
BT   Influences
RT   Creationism
       Cultural Influences
       Religion
       Religious Conflict
       Religious Differences
       Religious Discrimination
       School Prayer
       Spirituality

Religious Groups

USE   Religious Cultural Groups

Religious Holidays

OCT. 1984
Postings: 58   GC: 520
UF   Holy Days

BT   Holidays
RT   Religion
       State Church Separation

Religious Organizations

JUL. 1966
Postings: 459   GC: 520
UF   Religious Agencies (1966 1980)
BT   Organizations (Groups)
RT   Church Related Colleges
       Churches
       Clergy
       Institutions
       Nonprofit Organizations
       Religion
       Religious Cultural Groups
       Voluntary Agencies

Religious Studies

USE   Religion Studies

Relocatable Facilities

DEC. 1972
Postings: 83   GC: 920
UF   Portable Facilities
       Temporary Facilities
BT   Facilities
RT   Air Structures
       Building Innovation
       Encapsulated Facilities
       Facility Expansion
       Facility Planning
       Flexible Facilities
       Mobile Classrooms
       Mobile Clinics
       Mobile Laboratories
       Prefabrication

Relocation

JUL. 1966
Postings: 835   GC: 550
SN   The voluntary or forced removal of an
       individual or group and establishment in
       a new place
NT   Rural Resettlement
BT   Migration
RT   American Indian History
       American Indians
       Area Studies
       Brain Drain
       Family Mobility
       Geographic Location
       Labor Problems
       Labor Turnover
       Labor Utilization
       Land Settlement
       Migrants
       Migration Patterns
       Nonreservation American Indians
       Occupational Mobility
       Place of Residence
       Population Distribution
       Population Trends
       Refugees
       Residential Patterns
       Rural to Urban Migration
       Transfer Policy
       Transfer Programs
       Urban to Rural Migration
       Urban to Suburban Migration

Remarriage

OCT. 1982
Postings: 242   GC: 520
SN   The act or state of marriage following
       widow(er)hood or divorce
BT   Marriage
RT   Divorce
       Kinship
       Stepfamily
       Widowed

Remedial Arithmetic (1966 1980)

USE   Arithmetic
AND   Remedial Mathematics

Remedial Courses (1966 1980)

USE   Remedial Instruction

= Two or more Descriptors are used to represent this term.
The term's main entry shows the appropriate coordination.

Remedial Education
USE   Remedial Instruction

Remedial Education Programs
USE   Remedial Programs

Remedial Instruction   *JUL. 1966*
          Postings: 3,478   GC: 310
UF   Remedial Courses (1966 1980)
          Remedial Education
          Remediation
NT   Remedial Mathematics
          Remedial Reading
BT   Instruction
RT   Compensatory Education
          Cross Age Teaching
          Diagnostic Teaching
          Error Correction
          Learning Problems
          Refresher Courses
          Remedial Programs
          Remedial Teachers
          Review (Reexamination)
          Transitional Programs
          Tutorial Programs
          Tutoring

Remedial Mathematics   *JUL. 1966*
          Postings: 900   GC: 480
UF   Remedial Arithmetic (1966 1980) #
BT   Mathematics Instruction
          Remedial Instruction
RT   General Mathematics
          Mathematics
          Remedial Programs

Remedial Programs   *JUL. 1966*
          Postings: 2,898   GC: 310
SN   Programs designed to develop specific
          cognitive skills (usually in the language
          arts and mathematics) from a deficient
          level to one appropriate to the educa-
          tional level and aspirations of the student
UF   Remedial Education Programs
          Remedial Reading Programs (1966
          1980) #
BT   Programs
RT   Auditing (Coursework)
          Basic Writing
          Compensatory Education
          Continuation Students
          Developmental Studies Programs
          Educational Therapy
          Educationally Disadvantaged
          High Risk Students
          Remedial Instruction
          Remedial Mathematics
          Remedial Reading
          Summer Programs
          Supplementary Education
          Transitional Programs

Remedial Reading   *JUL. 1966*
          Postings: 3,532   GC: 460
SN   Diagnosis and tutoring of students with
          reading difficulties, usually by a special
          teacher of reading
UF   Remedial Reading Clinics (1966
          1980) #
          Remedial Reading Programs (1966
          1980) #
BT   Reading
          Reading Instruction
          Remedial Instruction
RT   Corrective Reading
          Dyslexia
          High Interest Low Vocabulary Books
          Learning Disabilities
          Learning Problems
          Reading Centers
          Reading Diagnosis
          Reading Difficulties
          Remedial Programs

Remedial Reading Clinics (1966 1980)
USE   Reading Centers
AND   Remedial Reading

Remedial Reading Programs (1966 1980)
USE   Remedial Programs
AND   Remedial Reading

Remedial Teachers   *JUL. 1966*
          Postings: 100   GC: 360
BT   Teachers
RT   Remedial Instruction

Remediation
USE   Remedial Instruction

Remembering
USE   Memory

Reminiscence   *APR. 1990*
          Postings: 199   GC: 110
SN   Thinking or telling about one's life
BT   Recall (Psychology)
RT   Experience
          Life Satisfaction
          Personal Narratives
          Self Evaluation (Individuals)

Remuneration
USE   Compensation (Remuneration)

Renaissance Literature   *JUN. 1969*
          Postings: 125   GC: 430
SN   European literature written during the
          Renaissance (roughly from the fourteenth
          to the seventeenth centuries) and usu-
          ally characterized by a humanistic em-
          phasis
BT   Literature
RT   Chronicles
          Fifteenth Century Literature
          Humanism
          Seventeenth Century Literature
          Sixteenth Century Literature
          Sonnets
          World Literature

Renovation
USE   Improvement

Repair   *JUL. 1966*
          Postings: 412   GC: 640
NT   Appliance Repair
BT   Maintenance
RT   Auto Body Repairers
          Buildings
          Consumer Science
          Equipment Maintenance
          Machine Repairers
          Obsolescence
          Preservation
          Television Radio Repairers
          Troubleshooting

Repertory Catalogs
USE   Union Catalogs

Repertory Orchestras
USE   Orchestras

Repetitive Film Showings   *JUL. 1966*
          Postings: 44   GC: 310
RT   Audiovisual Instruction
          Film Study
          Films
          Redundancy

Report Cards   *JUL. 1966*
          Postings: 247   GC: 330
UF   Grade Cards
BT   Student Records
RT   Academic Achievement
          Academic Records
          Achievement Rating
          Grades (Scholastic)
          Grading

          Profiles
          Student Evaluation

Report Writing
USE   Technical Writing

Reports   *MAY 1969*
          Postings: 1,517   GC: 720
SN   (Note: Corresponds to Pubtype code
          140—do not use except as the subject of
          a document)
NT   Annual Reports
          Conference Papers
          Opinion Papers
          Personal Narratives
          Position Papers
          Practicum Papers
          Research Reports
          Theses
BT   Publications
RT   Bulletins
          News Reporting
          Program Descriptions
          Recordkeeping
          Records (Forms)
          Records Management

Representatives
USE   Legislators

Reproduction (Biology)   *AUG. 1970*
          Postings: 349   GC: 490
UF   Procreation
RT   Birth
          Birth Rate
          Contraception
          Family Planning
          Genetic Engineering
          Genetics
          Gynecology
          Heredity
          Menstruation
          Nucleic Acids
          Obstetrics
          Pregnancy
          Puberty
          Rh Factors

Reproduction (Copying)
USE   Reprography

Reprography   *OCT. 1970*
          Postings: 655   GC: 710
SN   Class of processes whose purpose is to
          replicate by optical or photomechanical
          means previously created graphic or
          coded messages
UF   Copying (Reproduction)
          Duplicating
          Multilithing
          Photocopying
          Photoreproduction
          Reproduction (Copying)
          Xerography
NT   Microreproduction
BT   Technology
RT   Copyrights
          Facsimile Transmission
          Fair Use (Copyrights)
          Information Industry
          Information Technology
          Information Transfer
          Magnification Methods
          Microforms
          Photocomposition
          Photography
          Printing
          Publishing Industry

Reputation   *MAR. 1980*
          Postings: 492   GC: 520
SN   General estimation in which an individ-
          ual, organization, or thing is held
UF   Fame
NT   Prestige
RT   Attitudes
          Background

          Credentials
          Credibility
          Individual Characteristics
          Institutional Characteristics
          Integrity
          Majority Attitudes
          Opinions
          Qualifications
          Recognition (Achievement)
          Status

Required Courses   *SEP. 1982*
          Postings: 640   GC: 350
SN   Courses required by an institution or
          administrative body for certification, ad-
          mission, graduation, etc. (Note: From
          Mar80 to Sep82, the Thesaurus carried
          the instruction "Required Courses, USE
          Core Curriculum"—prior to Mar80, the
          instruction read ". . . USE Core Courses")
UF   Foundation Courses (Required)
          Mandatory Courses
          Prerequisite Courses #
BT   Courses
RT   Advanced Courses
          Core Curriculum
          Course Selection (Students)
          Credits
          Degree Requirements
          Elective Courses
          Graduation Requirements
          Introductory Courses
          Majors (Students)
          Mandatory Continuing Education

Rescue   *JUL. 1966*
          Postings: 157   GC: 210
RT   Accidents
          Alarm Systems
          Emergency Medical Technicians
          Emergency Programs
          Emergency Squad Personnel
          First Aid
          Safety
          Safety Education

Rescue Squad Personnel
USE   Emergency Squad Personnel

Research   *JUL. 1966*
          Postings: 12,365   GC: 810
SN   Systematic investigation, collection, and
          analysis of data to reach conclusions,
          estimate effects, or test hypotheses (Note:
          Use a more specific term if possible)
UF   Applied Research
          Basic Research
NT   Action Research
          Architectural Research
          Behavioral Science Research
          Case Studies
          Cohort Analysis
          Communication Research
          Community Study
          Creativity Research
          Cross Cultural Studies
          Dropout Research
          Educational Research
          Environmental Research
          Exceptional Child Research
          Feasibility Studies
          Field Studies
          Institutional Research
          Investigations
          Language Research
          Library Research
          Media Research
          Medical Research
          Methods Research
          Nursing Research
          Operations Research
          Participatory Research
          Qualitative Research
          Schematic Studies
          Scientific Research
          Social Science Research
          Statistical Studies
          Student Research
          Use Studies

= Two or more Descriptors are used to represent this term.
The term's main entry shows the appropriate coordination.

RT   Area Studies
      Attrition (Research Studies)
      Criticism
      Data Analysis
      Data Collection
      Data Interpretation
      Discovery Processes
      Error Patterns
      Evaluation
      Evaluation Methods
      Experimental Psychology
      Experiments
      Faculty Publishing
      Innovation
      Institutional Role
      Inventions
      Literature Reviews
      Meta Analysis
      Observation
      Pilot Projects
      Postdoctoral Education
      Quasiexperimental Design
      Questionnaires
      Research Administration
      Research and Development
      Research and Development Centers
      Research Assistants
      Research Committees
      Research Design
      Research Directors
      Research Libraries
      Research Methodology
      Research Opportunities
      Research Problems
      Research Projects
      Research Proposals
      Research Reports
      Research Skills
      Research Tools
      Research Universities
      Research Utilization
      Researchers
      Response Rates (Questionnaires)
      Sciences
      Statistical Analysis
      Surveys
      Technology
      Technology Transfer
      Theories
      Theory Practice Relationship
      Theses
      Urban Studies

Research Administration   *AUG. 1986*
      Postings: 650   GC: 810
UF   Research Management
BT   Administration
RT   Program Administration
      Research
      Research and Development Centers
      Research Committees
      Research Coordinating Units
      Research Directors
      Research Projects
      Research Utilization

Research and Development   *OCT. 1983*
      Postings: 2,515   GC: 810
SN   Includes basic research, applied research, and the resultant development of new products, processes, services, or programs—evaluation and dissemination may be important collateral functions
UF   R and D
      R D and E
      Research Practice Relationship #
RT   Development
      Educational Development
      Educational Innovation
      Educational Research
      Evaluation
      Innovation
      Linking Agents
      Productivity
      Research
      Research and Development Centers
      Research Projects
      Research Utilization
      Science Programs
      Scientific Research

      Social Science Research
      Technological Advancement
      Technology
      Technology Transfer
      Theory Practice Relationship

Research and Development Centers
                           JUL. 1966
      Postings: 1,634   GC: 920
BT   Facilities
RT   Curriculum Study Centers
      Development
      Educational Development
      Experiment Stations
      Linking Agents
      Research
      Research Administration
      Research and Development
      Research and Instruction Units
      Research Assistants
      Research Directors
      Research Projects
      Research Universities
      Researchers
      Technology Transfer

Research and Instruction Units   *JUL. 1966*
      Postings: 110   GC: 340
SN   Organizational units of local schools or school districts that are concerned with the improvement of teaching methods
BT   Groups
RT   Curriculum Study Centers
      Educational Improvement
      Educational Research
      Instructional Improvement
      Multiunit Schools
      Research and Development Centers
      Research Coordinating Units
      Research Projects
      School Cadres

Research Apprenticeships (1967 1981)
USE   Research Assistants

Research Approaches
USE   Research Methodology

Research Assistants   *OCT. 1980*
      Postings: 99   GC: 640
UF   Research Apprenticeships (1967 1981)
BT   Personnel
RT   Assistantships
      Fellowships
      Graduate Students
      Paraprofessional Personnel
      Research
      Research and Development Centers
      Research Opportunities
      Research Projects
      Research Skills
      Researchers
      Student Research
      Teaching Assistants

Research Committees   *JUL. 1966*
      Postings: 143   GC: 810
BT   Committees
RT   Advisory Committees
      Educational Research
      Research
      Research Administration
      Research Projects

Research Coordinating Units   *JUL. 1966*
      Postings: 322   GC: 340
SN   Centers that stimulate and coordinate research among state departments of education, universities, local school districts, and other groups with an interest in vocational and technical education
BT   Organizations (Groups)

RT   Agency Cooperation
      Coordination
      Educational Research
      Institutional Cooperation
      Research Administration
      Research and Instruction Units
      Research Directors
      Research Projects
      Technical Education
      Vocational Education

Research Criteria (1967 1980)   *MAR. 1980*
      Postings: 453   GC: 810
SN   Invalid Descriptor—used inconsistently in indexing—see such Descriptors as "Research Methodology," "Needs Assessment," and "Evaluation Criteria"

Research Design   *JUL. 1966*
      Postings: 5,144   GC: 810
SN   The underlying plan or organization of a research project or study that determines its scope and approach—also, the process of planning and organizing research activities (Note: For documents/articles dealing with research methods or experimental procedures, use "Research Methodology")
UF   Experimental Design
      Research Planning
NT   Quasiexperimental Design
BT   Design
RT   Attrition (Research Studies)
      Causal Models
      Control Groups
      Effect Size
      Evaluation Research
      Experimental Groups
      Generalizability Theory
      Hypothesis Testing
      Matched Groups
      Models
      Participant Characteristics
      Predictor Variables
      Pretests Posttests
      Research
      Research Methodology
      Research Needs
      Research Problems
      Research Proposals
      Robustness (Statistics)
      Sample Size
      Sampling
      Scientific Methodology
      Search Strategies
      Statistical Significance

Research Directors   *JUL. 1966*
      Postings: 145   GC: 640
UF   Directors of Research
BT   Administrators
      Professional Personnel
RT   Educational Researchers
      Institutional Research
      Research
      Research Administration
      Research and Development Centers
      Research Coordinating Units
      Research Projects
      Researchers

Research Libraries   *JAN. 1969*
      Postings: 1,452   GC: 710
SN   Libraries consisting of specialized materials and providing facilities for undertaking exhaustive research
BT   Libraries
RT   Academic Libraries
      Depository Libraries
      Law Libraries
      Medical Libraries
      Public Libraries
      Research
      Research Universities
      Science Libraries
      Special Libraries

Research Limitations
USE   Research Problems

Research Management
USE   Research Administration

Research Methodology   *JUL. 1966*
      Postings: 22,916   GC: 810
SN   Procedures used in making systematic observations or otherwise obtaining data, evidence, or information as part of a research project or study (Note: Do not confuse with "Research Design," which refers to the planning and organization of such procedures)
UF   Experimental Procedures
      Research Approaches
      Social Science Methodology #
NT   Interaction Process Analysis
      Multitrait Multimethod Techniques
      Protocol Analysis
      Scientific Methodology
      Triangulation
BT   Methods
RT   Attrition (Research Studies)
      Causal Models
      Content Analysis
      Control Groups
      Critical Incidents Method
      Data Analysis
      Data Collection
      Data Interpretation
      Deduction
      Effect Size
      Evaluation Methods
      Evaluation Research
      Experimental Groups
      Experimenter Characteristics
      Factor Analysis
      Field Studies
      Focus Groups
      Force Field Analysis
      Generalization
      Hermeneutics
      Holistic Approach
      Induction
      Inquiry
      Literature Reviews
      Mail Surveys
      Markov Processes
      Matched Groups
      Measurement Techniques
      Meta Analysis
      Methods Research
      Models
      Monte Carlo Methods
      Naturalistic Observation
      Network Analysis
      Observation
      Participant Observation
      Participatory Research
      Pilot Projects
      Problem Solving
      Proof (Mathematics)
      Qualitative Research
      Quasiexperimental Design
      Research
      Research Design
      Research Needs
      Research Problems
      Research Skills
      Researchers
      Statistical Analysis
      Telephone Surveys

Research Needs   *JUL. 1966*
      Postings: 9,756   GC: 810
SN   Questions or problems that require research (Note: Prior to Mar80, the use of this term was not restricted by a Scope Note—see also "Research Methodology," "Research Opportunities," and "Research Problems")
BT   Needs
RT   Evaluation Needs
      Experiments
      Information Needs
      Measurement Objectives
      Research Design
      Research Methodology
      Research Opportunities
      Research Problems
      Research Proposals

= Two or more Descriptors are used to represent this term.
The term's main entry shows the appropriate coordination.

Research Opportunities   *JUL. 1966*
Postings: 1,035   GC: 810
SN   State of affairs or set of circumstances favorable for research
BT   Opportunities
RT   Financial Support
    Grantsmanship
    Research
    Research Assistants
    Research Needs
    Researchers
    Student Research

Research Papers (Students)   *JAN. 1985*
Postings: 621   GC: 310
SN   Extended written exercises required of students, usually involving collection of primary or secondary data through research, and careful documentation and organization (Note: Do not confuse with "Theses" or "Practicum Papers")
UF   Term Papers
BT   Assignments
RT   Content Area Writing
    Expository Writing
    Student Research
    Writing Across the Curriculum
    Writing Assignments

Research Planning
USE   Research Design

Research Practice Relationship
USE   Research and Development
AND   Theory Practice Relationship

Research Problems   *JUL. 1966*
Postings: 6,676   GC: 810
SN   Factors leading to difficulties or bias in the design, performance, management, or interpretation of research (Note: Prior to Mar80, the use of this term was not restricted by a Scope Note)
UF   Research Limitations
BT   Problems
RT   Attrition (Research Studies)
    Evaluation Problems
    Experimenter Characteristics
    Research
    Research Design
    Research Methodology
    Research Needs
    Sample Size
    Statistical Analysis

Research Programs
USE   Research Projects

Research Projects   *JUL. 1966*
Postings: 11,700   GC: 810
SN   (Note: Coordinate with another term for specificity (e.g., another program/project term in the "Programs" hierarchy))
UF   Agricultural Research Projects (1966 1981)
    Research Programs
BT   Programs
RT   Experiment Stations
    Experimental Programs
    Program Proposals
    Research
    Research Administration
    Research and Development
    Research and Development Centers
    Research and Instruction Units
    Research Assistants
    Research Committees
    Research Coordinating Units
    Research Directors
    Research Proposals
    Research Reports
    Research Universities
    Research Utilization
    Researchers

Research Proposals   *JUL. 1966*
Postings: 591   GC: 810
SN   (Note: As of Oct81, use as a minor Descriptor for examples of research proposals—use as a major Descriptor only as the subject of a document)
BT   Program Proposals
RT   Proposal Writing
    Research
    Research Design
    Research Needs
    Research Projects

Research Reports   *MAR. 1980*
Postings: 3,945   GC: 720
SN   Reports of research projects or programs (Note: Prior to Mar80, the instruction "Studies, USE Research" was carried in the Thesaurus—corresponds to Pubtype code 143—do not use except as the subject of a document)
UF   Research Studies
    Scientific Reports
    Technical Reports (1968 1980)
BT   Reports
RT   Research
    Research Projects
    Scholarly Writing
    Technical Writing

Research Reviews (Publications) (1966 1980)   *MAR. 1980*
Postings: 3,254   GC: 730
SN   Invalid Descriptor—used inconsistently in indexing—see such Descriptors as "Literature Reviews," "Bibliographies," "State of the Art Reviews," "Research Reports," etc.

Research Skills   *JUL. 1966*
Postings: 1,707   GC: 810
BT   Skills
RT   Information Skills
    Research
    Research Assistants
    Research Methodology
    Research Tools
    Researchers
    Scholarship
    Student Research
    Thinking Skills

Research Specialists (Education)
USE   Educational Researchers

Research Studies
USE   Research Reports

Research Tools   *JUL. 1966*
Postings: 1,526   GC: 810
RT   Databases
    Information Sources
    Library Materials
    Literature Reviews
    Models
    Primary Sources
    Reference Materials
    Research
    Research Skills
    Resource Materials
    Scholarly Journals

Research Universities   *AUG. 1986*
Postings: 862   GC: 340
SN   Universities that typically include a graduate school and research and development centers, and are known for their sponsored research activities
BT   Universities
RT   Research
    Research and Development Centers
    Research Libraries
    Research Projects
    State Universities

Research Utilization   *JUL. 1966*
Postings: 4,267   GC: 810
BT   Information Utilization
RT   Adoption (Ideas)
    Diffusion (Communication)
    Evaluation Utilization
    Intellectual Property
    Linking Agents
    Research
    Research Administration
    Research and Development
    Research Projects
    Technology
    Technology Transfer
    Theory Practice Relationship
    Use Studies

Researcher Characteristics
USE   Experimenter Characteristics
AND   Researchers

Researchers   *JUL. 1966*
Postings: 2,225   GC: 640
UF   Researcher Characteristics #
NT   Educational Researchers
BT   Professional Personnel
RT   Evaluators
    Experimenter Characteristics
    Historians
    Psychologists
    Research
    Research and Development Centers
    Research Assistants
    Research Directors
    Research Methodology
    Research Opportunities
    Research Projects
    Research Skills
    Scholarship
    Scientists
    Social Scientists
    Sociologists
    Systems Analysts

Resegregated Schools
USE   School Resegregation

Resentment   *JUL. 1966*
Postings: 39   GC: 120
BT   Psychological Patterns
RT   Alienation
    Anger
    Hostility
    Jealousy
    Negative Attitudes
    Rejection (Psychology)

Reservation American Indians   *MAR. 1980*
Postings: 271   GC: 560
SN   American Indians residing on trust or restricted Indian land
BT   American Indians
RT   American Indian Reservations
    Nonreservation American Indians

Reservations (Indian) (1971 1980)
USE   American Indian Reservations

Resettlement
USE   Land Settlement

Residence Factors
USE   Residence Requirements

Residence Halls
USE   Dormitories

Residence Requirements   *JUL. 1966*
Postings: 204   GC: 330
SN   Policies or laws requiring habitation in a particular place for a specified period of time—includes those related to welfare, voting, tuition, degree requirements, etc.
UF   Nonresident Students (1967 1980) (Out of District)
    Residence Factors
    Resident Students (1967 1980) (in District)
BT   Standards
RT   Admission Criteria
    Graduation Requirements
    In State Students
    Out of State Students
    Place of Residence
    Selective Admission
    Voting

Residency Programs (Medical)
USE   Graduate Medical Education

Resident Advisers   *JUN. 1983*
Postings: 46   GC: 360
SN   Personnel who live with and coordinate the activities of residents of boarding schools, dormitories, college fraternity or sorority houses, care and treatment institutions, children's homes, group homes, or similar establishments
UF   Cottage Parents
    Houseparents
    Resident Supervisors
NT   Resident Assistants
BT   Personnel
RT   Attendants
    Boarding Schools
    College Housing
    Dormitories
    Group Homes
    Pupil Personnel Workers
    Residential Care
    Residential Colleges
    Residential Institutions
    Residential Programs
    Residential Schools
    Service Workers
    Student Personnel Workers

Resident Assistants   *JUL. 1966*
Postings: 219   GC: 360
SN   Students employed by a college or university to help manage a dormitory or residence hall by maintaining an interpersonal relationship with hall residents
BT   College Students
    Resident Advisers
RT   Assistantships
    College Housing
    Dormitories
    On Campus Students
    Residential Colleges
    Student Personnel Workers

Resident Camp Programs   *JUL. 1966*
Postings: 585   GC: 470
BT   Recreational Programs
    Residential Programs
RT   Camping
    Day Camp Programs
    Summer Programs

Resident Students (1967 1980) (in District)
USE   Residence Requirements

Resident Students (1967 1980) (in State)
USE   In State Students

Resident Supervisors
USE   Resident Advisers

Residential Care   *JUL. 1966*
Postings: 554   GC: 220
SN   Assistance provided by trained personnel to individuals in residential institutions (Note: For care in private homes, see "Foster Care" and "Adult Foster Care"—prior to Mar80, the use of this term was not restricted by a Scope Note)
RT   Attendants
    Disabilities

= Two or more Descriptors are used to represent this term.
The term's main entry shows the appropriate coordination.

Long Term Care
Nursing Homes
Personal Care Homes
Resident Advisers
Residential Institutions
Residential Programs
Residential Schools
Respite Care
Severe Mental Retardation

Residential Centers (1967 1980)
USE　Residential Institutions

Residential Colleges　　　　　　　*SEP. 1969*
　　　Postings: 201　　　　　　　　　GC: 340
SN　Colleges that provide living quarters for their students (Note: The Scope Note carried by this term prior to Mar80 caused it to be confused with "Living Learning Centers")
BT　Colleges
　　　Residential Institutions
RT　College Environment
　　　College Housing
　　　Commuter Colleges
　　　Dormitories
　　　Living Learning Centers
　　　On Campus Students
　　　Resident Advisers
　　　Resident Assistants

Residential Desegregation
USE　Neighborhood Integration

Residential Institutions　　　　　　*MAR. 1980*
　　　Postings: 570　　　　　　　　　GC: 920
SN　Facilities that provide health, educational, welfare, or rehabilitative services to their residents
UF　Residential Centers (1967 1980)
NT　Boarding Schools
　　　Correctional Institutions
　　　Nursing Homes
　　　Personal Care Homes
　　　Residential Colleges
BT　Institutions
RT　Boarding Homes
　　　Housing
　　　Psychiatric Hospitals
　　　Rehabilitation Centers
　　　Resident Advisers
　　　Residential Care
　　　Residential Programs

Residential Location
USE　Place of Residence

Residential Patterns　　　　　　　*JUL. 1966*
　　　Postings: 993　　　　　　　　　GC: 550
UF　Housing Patterns (1966 1980)
BT　Demography
RT　Family Mobility
　　　Housing
　　　Migration
　　　Migration Patterns
　　　Neighborhood Integration
　　　Neighborhoods
　　　Place of Residence
　　　Population Distribution
　　　Population Trends
　　　Racial Composition
　　　Racial Distribution
　　　Relocation
　　　Rural to Urban Migration
　　　School Demography
　　　Trend Analysis
　　　Urban to Rural Migration
　　　Urban to Suburban Migration

Residential Programs　　　　　　　*JUL. 1966*
　　　Postings: 1,451　　　　　　　　GC: 350
NT　Resident Camp Programs
BT　Programs
RT　Boarding Schools
　　　Deinstitutionalization (of Disabled)
　　　Group Experience
　　　Housing

Human Services
Institutionalized Persons
Mental Health Programs
Rehabilitation Programs
Resident Advisers
Residential Care
Residential Institutions
Residential Schools

Residential Schools　　　　　　　*JUL. 1966*
　　　Postings: 559　　　　　　　　　GC: 340
SN　Boarding schools for atypical children of school age
BT　Boarding Schools
　　　Special Schools
RT　Institutional Schools
　　　Mild Mental Retardation
　　　Moderate Mental Retardation
　　　Rehabilitation Centers
　　　Resident Advisers
　　　Residential Care
　　　Residential Programs

Residents (Medical)
USE　Graduate Medical Students

Resilience (Personality)　　　　　*SEP. 1997*
　　　Postings: 342　　　　　　　　　GC: 120
SN　The ability to withstand and move beyond difficult life situations
BT　Personality Traits
RT　Adjustment (to Environment)
　　　Coping
　　　Persistence
　　　Self Esteem
　　　Stress Management

Resilient Floor Covering
USE　Flooring

Resistance (Psychology)　　　　　*APR. 1990*
　　　Postings: 308　　　　　　　　　GC: 120
SN　Act or capacity of opposing, withstanding, avoiding, or striving against unwanted or undesirable revelations, conditions, actions, or events (Note: Use a more specific term if possible)
NT　Resistance to Change
　　　Resistance to Temptation
BT　Behavior
　　　Psychological Patterns
RT　Alienation
　　　Anxiety
　　　Behavior Problems
　　　Compliance (Psychology)
　　　Conflict
　　　Denial (Psychology)
　　　Discipline Problems
　　　Dissent
　　　Negative Attitudes
　　　Personal Autonomy
　　　Personality Traits
　　　Persuasive Discourse
　　　Rejection (Psychology)
　　　Social Behavior
　　　Social Psychology

Resistance to Change　　　　　　*APR. 1990*
　　　Postings: 875　　　　　　　　　GC: 120
BT　Resistance (Psychology)
RT　Adoption (Ideas)
　　　Change
　　　Change Strategies
　　　Innovation
　　　Laboratory Training
　　　Traditionalism

Resistance to Temptation　　　　　*APR. 1990*
　　　Postings: 63　　　　　　　　　GC: 120
SN　Refraining from desires or advantages that are wrong or unwise
BT　Resistance (Psychology)
RT　Crime
　　　Crime Prevention
　　　Peer Influence
　　　Risk
　　　Self Control

Resource Allocation　　　　　　　*MAR. 1980*
　　　Postings: 6,035　　　　　　　　GC: 620
SN　The setting apart, assigning, or allotting of money, materials, personnel, or services for a particular purpose
UF　Allocation of Resources
　　　Resource Allocations (1966 1980)
RT　Administration
　　　Budgeting
　　　Budgets
　　　Capital
　　　Categorical Aid
　　　Cost Effectiveness
　　　Delivery Systems
　　　Educational Assessment
　　　Educational Economics
　　　Educational Equity (Finance)
　　　Educational Planning
　　　Efficiency
　　　Equalization Aid
　　　Expenditures
　　　Financial Needs
　　　Fiscal Capacity
　　　Input Output Analysis
　　　Linking Agents
　　　Needs Assessment
　　　Operating Expenses
　　　Resources
　　　Tax Allocation
　　　Trusts (Financial)
　　　Wills

Resource Allocations (1966 1980)
USE　Resource Allocation

Resource Centers　　　　　　　　*JUL. 1966*
　　　Postings: 1,514　　　　　　　　GC: 920
SN　Indoor or outdoor areas that offer a variety of resources (e.g., supplies, materials, information, equipment, etc.) designed to assist individuals with specific needs (Note: Use a more specific term if possible)
NT　Arts Centers
　　　Audiovisual Centers
　　　Computer Centers
　　　Cultural Centers
　　　Curriculum Study Centers
　　　Education Service Centers
　　　Information Centers
　　　Learning Centers (Classroom)
　　　Learning Resources Centers
　　　Nature Centers
　　　Reading Centers
　　　Teacher Centers
BT　Facilities
RT　Libraries
　　　Museums
　　　Resource Materials
　　　Resources

Resource Guides (1966 1980)
USE　Resource Materials

Resource Materials　　　　　　　*JUL. 1966*
　　　Postings: 13,821　　　　　　　GC: 730
SN　Print and/or nonprint materials collected and organized for a particular topic
UF　Material Sources
　　　Resource Guides (1966 1980)
NT　Resource Units
RT　Health Materials
　　　Instructional Materials
　　　Learning Resources Centers
　　　Library Materials
　　　Multilingual Materials
　　　Nonprint Media
　　　Orientation Materials
　　　Parent Materials
　　　Primary Sources
　　　Printed Materials
　　　Publications
　　　Reference Materials
　　　Research Tools
　　　Resource Centers
　　　Resources

Resource Room Programs　　　　　*OCT. 1977*
　　　Postings: 565　　　　　　　　　GC: 310
SN　Part-time programs in which specially trained teachers assist students who, because of their special needs, have been referred by their regular classroom teachers
BT　Special Programs
RT　Individualized Education Programs
　　　Intervention
　　　Itinerant Teachers
　　　Mainstreaming
　　　Referral
　　　Resource Teachers
　　　Special Classes
　　　Special Education
　　　Special Education Teachers
　　　Special Needs Students
　　　Transitional Programs

Resource Sharing
USE　Shared Resources and Services

Resource Staff　　　　　　　　　*MAR. 1980*
　　　Postings: 289　　　　　　　　　GC: 360
SN　Personnel with special skills or knowledge who supplement or assist regular staff members
UF　Resource Staff Role (1966 1980)
BT　Personnel
RT　Consultants
　　　Personnel Needs
　　　Resource Teachers
　　　Resources
　　　Specialists

Resource Staff Role (1966 1980)
USE　Resource Staff

Resource Teachers　　　　　　　*JUL. 1966*
　　　Postings: 546　　　　　　　　　GC: 360
SN　Teachers with special competencies who supplement regular course offerings or assist other teachers to develop teaching plans and materials
BT　Teachers
RT　Consultants
　　　Itinerant Teachers
　　　Mainstreaming
　　　Reading Consultants
　　　Resource Room Programs
　　　Resource Staff
　　　Resources
　　　Science Consultants
　　　Special Education Teachers
　　　Specialists

Resource Units　　　　　　　　　*JUL. 1966*
　　　Postings: 730　　　　　　　　　GC: 310
SN　Collections of learning and teaching activities, procedures, materials, and references on specific topics that are assembled for the use of teachers in developing their courses
BT　Resource Materials
RT　Activity Units
　　　Curriculum Study Centers
　　　Learning Modules
　　　Resources
　　　Teaching Guides
　　　Units of Study

Resources　　　　　　　　　　　*JUL. 1966*
　　　Postings: 1,595　　　　　　　　GC: 520
SN　Available means or assets, including sources of assistance, supply, or support (Note: Use a more specific term if possible)
NT　Community Resources
　　　Depleted Resources
　　　Educational Resources
　　　Family Financial Resources
　　　Human Resources
　　　Natural Resources
　　　Shared Resources and Services
　　　Supplies
RT　Environment
　　　Equipment

Facilities
Facility Inventory
Financial Support
Institutions
Needs
Organizations (Groups)
Ownership
Resource Allocation
Resource Centers
Resource Materials
Resource Staff
Resource Teachers
Resource Units
Services
Use Studies
Wastes

Respiratory Therapy   *JAN. 1985*
      Postings: 47   GC: 210
SN   Diagnosis and treatment of
      cardiopulmonary deficiencies or abnor-
      malities through the use of breathing
      methods and apparatus, and the admin-
      istration of gases and aerosols
UF   Inhalation Therapists (1969 1985) #
      Oxygen Inhalation Therapy
BT   Therapy
RT   Allied Health Occupations
      Medical Services
      Physical Therapy

Respite Care   *MAR. 1974*
      Postings: 222   GC: 220
SN   Short-term care of the disabled, in or
      outside the home, to provide family relief
RT   Disabilities
      Family Problems
      Personal Care Homes
      Residential Care
      Visiting Homemakers

Response Bias (Tests)
USE   Response Style (Tests)

Response Contingent Testing
USE   Adaptive Testing

Response Latency
USE   Reaction Time

Response Mode (1967 1980)
USE   Responses

Response Rates (Questionnaires)
                                         AUG. 1989
      Postings: 189   GC: 810
SN   Ratios of completed to distributed ques-
      tionnaires
UF   Return Rates (Questionnaires)
BT   Ratios (Mathematics)
RT   Questionnaires
      Research
      Responses
      Surveys

Response Set (Tests)
USE   Response Style (Tests)

Response Style (Tests)   *FEB. 1971*
      Postings: 929   GC: 820
SN   Test-taking behavior that is influenced
      by the individual's attitudes or tenden-
      cies and which may distort the meaning
      of the test score, e.g., a tendency to
      answer "yes" regardless of item content
UF   Response Bias (Tests)
      Response Set (Tests)
NT   Guessing (Tests)
BT   Behavior
RT   Adaptive Testing
      Attitudes
      Confidence Testing
      Forced Choice Technique
      Reaction Time
      Responses

Social Desirability
Stress Variables
Test Format
Test Validity
Test Wiseness
Testing Problems
Tests

Response Time
USE   Reaction Time

Responses   *MAR. 1980*
      Postings: 5,406   GC: 120
UF   Conditioned Response (1967 1980)
      Reactive Behavior (1966 1980)
      Response Mode (1967 1980)
      Stimulus Behavior (1966 1980)
NT   Audience Response
      Burnout
      Constructed Response
      Covert Response
      Dimensional Preference
      Emotional Response
      Motor Reactions
      Overt Response
      Patterned Responses
      Stranger Reactions
      Student Reaction
      Teacher Response
BT   Behavior
RT   Conditioning
      Encoding (Psychology)
      Psychological Patterns
      Reaction Time
      Response Rates (Questionnaires)
      Response Style (Tests)
      Schemata (Cognition)
      Shift Studies
      Situational Tests
      Social Desirability
      Stimuli
      Test Format
      Wait Time
      Well Being

Responsibility   *JUL. 1966*
      Postings: 1,250   GC: 520
SN   The process or act of fulfilling a duty,
      obligation, burden, or trust (Note: Use a
      more specific term if possible)
NT   Accountability
      Administrator Responsibility
      Business Responsibility
      Child Responsibility
      Church Responsibility
      Community Responsibility
      Educational Responsibility
      Employee Responsibility
      Leadership Responsibility
      Legal Responsibility
      Parent Responsibility
      School Responsibility
      Social Responsibility
      Student Responsibility
      Teacher Responsibility
RT   Consumer Protection
      Guilt
      Institutional Role
      Negligence
      Risk Management
      Role

Rest Home Aides
USE   Nurses Aides

Rest Homes
USE   Personal Care Homes

Restaurants
USE   Dining Facilities

Restraints (Vehicle Safety)   *AUG. 1986*
      Postings: 64   GC: 910
SN   Devices installed in vehicles to restrict
      bodily movements and prevent injuries
UF   Air Bags
      Child Restraints (Vehicle Safety) #

Lap Belts
Seat Belts
BT   Safety Equipment
RT   Child Safety
      Traffic Safety

Restrictive Admission
USE   Selective Admission

Restrictive Transfer Programs (1966 1980)
USE   Transfer Programs

Restrooms
USE   Toilet Facilities

Restructuring of Schools (United States)
USE   School Restructuring

Results Based Education
USE   Outcome Based Education

Results of Education
USE   Outcomes of Education

Resumes (Personal)   *JAN. 1985*
      Postings: 333   GC: 630
SN   Summaries of individual experience and
      qualifications, typically submitted as part
      of the job application process
UF   Curriculum Vitae
      Vitae
BT   Credentials
RT   Educational Experience
      Employment Experience
      Employment Interviews
      Employment Qualifications
      Job Applicants
      Job Application
      Job Search Methods
      Personnel Data
      Personnel Selection
      Portfolios (Background Materials)
      Profiles
      Qualifications

Retail Training
USE   Distributive Education

Retailing   *AUG. 1968*
      Postings: 442   GC: 650
BT   Marketing
RT   Bookstores
      College Stores
      Distributive Education
      Food Stores
      Franchising
      Merchandising
      Merchants
      Sales Occupations
      Salesmanship
      Wholesaling

Retardation (1966 1980)
USE   Mental Retardation

Retarded Children (1966 1980)
USE   Mental Retardation

Retarded Readers (1966 1980)
USE   Reading Difficulties

Retarded Speech Development (1968 1980)
USE   Delayed Speech

Retention (in Grade)
USE   Grade Repetition

Retention (in School)
USE   School Holding Power

Retention (of Employees)
USE   Labor Turnover

Retention (Psychology)   *MAR. 1980*
      Postings: 2,505   GC: 110
SN   That aspect of memory that involves
      either short- or long-term holding of
      information (Note: For the concept of
      "retention of personnel, teachers, stu-
      dents, etc.," see such Descriptors as
      "Employment Practices," "Teacher Per-
      sistence," and "School Holding Power")
UF   Retention (1966 1980)
      Retention Studies (1966 1980)
BT   Memory
RT   Advance Organizers
      Cues
      Encoding (Psychology)
      Extinction (Psychology)
      Familiarity
      Habituation
      Language Skill Attrition
      Mediation Theory
      Memorization
      Mnemonics
      Primacy Effect
      Recall (Psychology)
      Recognition (Psychology)
      Redundancy
      Rote Learning
      Schemata (Cognition)
      Visualization

Retention Studies (1966 1980)
USE   Retention (Psychology)

Retention (1966 1980)
USE   Retention (Psychology)

Retired Teachers
USE   Teacher Retirement

Retirement   *JUL. 1966*
      Postings: 1,573   GC: 630
NT   Early Retirement
      Mandatory Retirement
      Teacher Retirement
BT   Status
RT   Age Discrimination
      Aging in Academia
      Educational Gerontology
      Gerontology
      Labor Force Nonparticipants
      Older Adults
      Older Workers
      Preretirement Education
      Retirement Benefits

Retirement Benefits   *MAR. 1980*
      Postings: 619   GC: 630
SN   Money or other compensation given to
      employees who have left a job due to age
      or disability or who have rendered a
      specified number of years of service—
      also, the investment plans for such com-
      pensation
UF   Pensions
RT   Compensation (Remuneration)
      Fringe Benefits
      Income
      Insurance
      Personnel Policy
      Retirement
      Salaries
      Scope of Bargaining
      Wages

Retraining   *JUL. 1966*
      Postings: 1,348   GC: 630
UF   Refresher Training
      Vocational Retraining (1966 1980)
BT   Training
RT   Adult Education
      Adult Vocational Education
      Continuing Education Units
      Dislocated Workers
      Dropouts

= Two or more Descriptors are used to represent this term.
The term's main entry shows the appropriate coordination.

Inservice Education
Job Training
Labor Force Development
Occupations
Reentry Workers
Refresher Courses
Rehabilitation
Review (Reexamination)
Skill Development
Skill Obsolescence
Special Needs Students
Supplementary Education

Retrenchment   *AUG. 1977*
Postings: 2,025   GC: 620
SN   Reduction of costs or efforts, usually as
     an economic necessity
UF   Budget Cuts #
RT   Budgeting
     Cost Effectiveness
     Costs
     Economics
     Educational Administration
     Educational Finance
     Expenditures
     Financial Exigency
     Financial Problems
     Institutional Administration
     Institutional Survival
     Productivity
     Program Administration
     Program Termination
     Reduction in Force

Retroactive Inhibition
USE   Inhibition

Retrospective Conversion (Library Catalogs)
                                         AUG. 1994
Postings: 121   GC: 710
SN   Partial or complete conversion of exist-
     ing manual library files to machine-read-
     able form
BT   Data Conversion
     Library Automation
RT   Library Catalogs
     Library Technical Processes
     Machine Readable Cataloging
     Online Catalogs

Return Rates (Questionnaires)
USE   Response Rates (Questionnaires)

Reunions   *JUN. 2000*
Postings: 78   GC: 520
SN   The coming together of relatives, friends,
     or associates after periods of separation
BT   Meetings
RT   Alumni
     Family (Sociological Unit)
     Separation Anxiety

Revenue
USE   Income

Revenue Sharing   *JUL. 1973*
Postings: 221   GC: 620
SN   Practice of returning a percentage of
     federal tax money to states and localities
     for locally directed and controlled public
     service programs—includes functional
     grants for education and other major
     purposes (special) as well as unrestricted
     grants (general)
BT   Federal Aid
     Financial Support
RT   Block Grants
     Educational Finance
     Equalization Aid
     Federal Legislation
     Federal State Relationship
     Government Role

Grants
Local Government
New Federalism
Public Policy
School District Autonomy
Tax Allocation

Reversal Shift
USE   Shift Studies

Reverse Discrimination   *DEC. 1976*
Postings: 269   GC: 540
SN   Preferential treatment of groups of peo-
     ple who had previously been discrimi-
     nated against, to the exclusion of other
     groups
BT   Social Discrimination
RT   Affirmative Action
     Age Discrimination
     Disability Discrimination
     Educational Discrimination
     Equal Education
     Equal Opportunities (Jobs)
     Housing Discrimination
     Racial Discrimination
     Religious Discrimination
     Selective Admission
     Sex Discrimination

Review (Reexamination)   *JUL. 1966*
Postings: 455   GC: 110
SN   Study of material studied before (Note:
     Do not confuse with "Evaluation")
BT   Activities
RT   Error Correction
     Refresher Courses
     Remedial Instruction
     Retraining
     Study
     Study Guides
     Test Coaching
     Tutoring

Reviews of the Literature
USE   Literature Reviews

Revision (Written Composition)   *AUG. 1982*
Postings: 1,140   GC: 400
SN   The process of reformulating, correct-
     ing, and/or rewriting textual materials
UF   Rewriting
BT   Writing Processes
RT   Error Correction
     Process Approach (Writing)
     Writing (Composition)
     Writing Assignments
     Writing Skills

Revolution   *JUL. 1973*
Postings: 367   GC: 610
SN   The attempt to make radical changes to
     one or more political, social, or techno-
     logical systems that would be qualita-
     tively different from and destructive to
     the traditional values, norms, and prac-
     tices of such systems
BT   Conflict
RT   Activism
     Change
     Conflict Resolution
     Culture Conflict
     Developing Nations
     Dissent
     Economic Change
     Futures (of Society)
     History
     Industrialization
     Marxism
     Political Science
     Social Action
     Social Change
     Technological Advancement
     Terrorism
     Violence
     War
     World Problems

Revolutionary War (United States)
                                         MAY 1970
Postings: 327   GC: 430
SN   War from 1775 to 1783 between Great
     Britain and its American colonies
UF   American Revolutionary War
BT   United States History
     War
RT   Colonial History (United States)
     Colonialism

Rewards   *JUL. 1966*
Postings: 1,837   GC: 520
NT   Self Reward
BT   Reinforcement
RT   Awards
     Compensation (Remuneration)
     Delay of Gratification
     Educational Benefits
     Incentives
     Merit Rating
     Motivation
     Praise
     Professional Recognition
     Recognition (Achievement)
     Sanctions
     Social Exchange Theory
     Social Reinforcement
     Token Economy

Rewriting
USE   Revision (Written Composition)

Rezoning   *JUL. 1966*
Postings: 22   GC: 610
UF   Rezoning Districts
BT   Zoning
RT   School District Reorganization
     School Districts

Rezoning Districts
USE   Rezoning

Rh Factors   *SEP. 1969*
Postings: 7   GC: 210
BT   Biological Influences
RT   Biochemistry
     Biology
     Cytology
     Embryology
     Genetics
     Molecular Biology
     Obstetrics
     Perinatal Influences
     Physiology
     Pregnancy
     Prenatal Influences
     Reproduction (Biology)

Rhetoric   *JUL. 1966*
Postings: 3,169   GC: 430
SN   Art of speaking or writing effectively
NT   Coherence
     Persuasive Discourse
     Rhetorical Invention
BT   Language Arts
RT   Audience Awareness
     Discourse Modes
     Expository Writing
     Literary Devices
     Rhetorical Criticism
     Rhetorical Theory
     Speech
     Verbal Communication
     Writing (Composition)

Rhetorical Community
USE   Discourse Communities

Rhetorical Criticism   *FEB. 1971*
Postings: 1,521   GC: 430
SN   Criticism of rhetorical and persuasive
     discourse
BT   Literary Criticism
RT   Audience Response
     Feminist Criticism

Film Criticism
Literature
Persuasive Discourse
Rhetoric
Rhetorical Theory

Rhetorical Invention   *DEC. 1985*
Postings: 337   GC: 430
SN   Creativity or originality in speaking or
     writing—also, the process of choosing
     ideas appropriate to the subject, audi-
     ence, and occasion for either oral or
     written presentation
BT   Rhetoric
RT   Creative Writing
     Creativity
     Persuasive Discourse
     Prewriting
     Public Speaking
     Rhetorical Theory
     Speech
     Speech Communication
     Speeches
     Writing (Composition)
     Writing Skills

Rhetorical Theory   *APR. 1990*
Postings: 704   GC: 430
SN   Theory focusing on perceptual, linguis-
     tic, and cognitive aspects of rhetorical
     experiences and behavior, including philo-
     sophical, historical, and cultural under-
     pinnings
BT   Theories
RT   Communication (Thought Transfer)
     Discourse Analysis
     Epistemology
     Intellectual History
     Linguistic Theory
     Persuasive Discourse
     Rhetoric
     Rhetorical Criticism
     Rhetorical Invention
     Speech Communication
     Verbal Communication

Rhyme   *MAY 1997*
Postings: 98   GC: 430
SN   Correspondence of sounds among words
     or lines of verse
UF   Rime (Sound)
RT   Language Rhythm
     Nursery Rhymes
     Oral Language
     Phonology
     Poetry
     Vocal Music

Rhythm (Language)
USE   Language Rhythm

Rhythm (Music)   *OCT. 1994*
Postings: 60   GC: 420
SN   The aspect of music concerned with
     time, comprising such elements as me-
     ter, beat, accent, measures or bars, and
     tempo
NT   Tempo (Music)
RT   Melody
     Music
     Music Activities
     Music Education
     Music Techniques
     Musical Composition

Ribonucleic Acid
USE   RNA

Riff   *JUL. 1966*
Postings: 1   GC: 440
BT   Berber Languages

Right to Know
USE   Freedom of Information

= Two or more Descriptors are used to represent this term.
The term's main entry shows the appropriate coordination.

Rime (Sound)
USE   Rhyme

Risk   *JUL. 1966*
        Postings: 1,664   GC: 210
RT   Adventure Education
        Cost Effectiveness
        Decision Making
        Entrepreneurship
        Game Theory
        Insurance
        Prediction
        Probability
        Reliability
        Resistance to Temptation
        Risk Management

Risk Management   *SEP. 1994*
        Postings: 415   GC: 320
SN   Technique or profession of minimizing
        and preventing loss or harm to a busi-
        ness, institution, group, or individual, as
        through safety measures, the use of
        insurance, etc. (Note: see also related
        Identifiers "Risk Assessment" and "Risk
        Reduction")
BT   Administration
RT   Accident Prevention
        Insurance
        Legal Responsibility
        Money Management
        Prevention
        Responsibility
        Risk
        Safety

Risk Populations
USE   At Risk Persons

River Pollution
USE   Water Pollution

Rivers   *JUN. 2000*
        Postings: 149   GC: 410
SN   Streams of water that flow in a definite
        channel toward an ocean, a lake, or
        another body of water
UF   Streams
BT   Water Resources
RT   Estuaries
        Floods
        Hydrology
        Physical Geography
        Water
        Water Pollution
        Water Quality
        Wetlands

RNA   *OCT. 1982*
        Postings: 39   GC: 490
SN   Any of the class of nucleic acids that
        contains ribose, found chiefly in cell
        cytoplasm and associated with the con-
        trol of cellular chemical activity
UF   Ribonucleic Acid
BT   Nucleic Acids

Road Construction   *MAR. 1969*
        Postings: 93   GC: 920
UF   Highway Construction
BT   Construction (Process)
RT   Asphalts
        Civil Engineering
        Highway Engineering Aides
        Land Use
        Traffic Circulation
        Transportation
        Urban Planning

Road Signs
USE   Signs

Robotics   *MAR. 1984*
        Postings: 329   GC: 490
SN   Study, design, and use of robots, me-

chanical devices that can be programmed
to perform tasks of manipulation and
locomotion under automatic control
UF   Industrial Robotics
        Robots
BT   Automation
        Bionics
RT   Artificial Intelligence
        Computer Assisted Manufacturing
        Cybernetics
        Electromechanical Technology
        Electronic Control
        Electronics
        Industrial Arts
        Man Machine Systems
        Technology Education

Robots
USE   Robotics

Robustness (Statistics)   *APR. 1990*
        Postings: 136   GC: 820
SN   The degree to which statistical methods
        or models are resistant to violations of
        assumptions and such errors as bias
        and outliner distortion
BT   Statistical Analysis
RT   Analysis of Covariance
        Analysis of Variance
        Data Interpretation
        Error of Measurement
        Goodness of Fit
        Mathematical Models
        Multivariate Analysis
        Predictive Measurement
        Proof (Mathematics)
        Regression (Statistics)
        Reliability
        Research Design
        Statistical Inference
        Statistical Significance
        Statistics
        Test Interpretation
        Test Reliability
        Test Validity
        Validity
        Weighted Scores

Rock Music   *AUG. 1989*
        Postings: 120   GC: 420
BT   Music
RT   Bands (Music)
        Concerts
        Music Techniques
        Musical Composition
        Popular Music
        Vocal Music

Rock Studies
USE   Petrology

Rodenticides (1968 1980)
USE   Pesticides

Role   *JUN. 1994*
        Postings: 234   GC: 520
SN   Functions or tasks expected of or per-
        formed by individuals, groups, or things
        (Note: Use a more specific term if possi-
        ble)
UF   Functions (Sociology)
        Social Role
NT   Administrator Role
        Board of Education Role
        Caregiver Role
        Child Role
        Citizen Role
        Community Role
        Counselor Role
        Family Role
        Government Role
        Institutional Role
        Language Role
        Mass Media Role
        Parent Role
        Role of Education
        Sex Role
        Staff Role

        Student Role
        Teacher Role
RT   Influences
        Relationship
        Responsibility
        Role Conflict
        Role Models
        Role Perception
        Role Playing
        Role Theory
        Status

Role Conflict   *JUL. 1966*
        Postings: 1,655   GC: 120
SN   Incompatibility between multiple roles
        taken by an individual or between group
        and individual roles
BT   Conflict
RT   Alienation
        Conflict of Interest
        Psychological Characteristics
        Psychological Patterns
        Role
        Role Theory
        Socialization

Role Models   *MAY 1973*
        Postings: 2,323   GC: 110
SN   Individuals (real or theoretical) chosen
        for emulation in one or a selected few of
        their roles (Note: Do not confuse with
        "Reference Groups")
NT   Mentors
BT   Groups
        Models
RT   Identification (Psychology)
        Imitation
        Modeling (Psychology)
        Observational Learning
        Role
        Significant Others

Role of Education   *JAN. 1985*
        Postings: 2,466   GC: 330
SN   Functions of education, real or expected,
        in regard to the individual and the society
        at large (Note: Use a more precise term if
        possible)
UF   Education Role
BT   Role
RT   Board of Education Role
        College Role
        Education
        Educational Assessment
        Educational Environment
        Educational Objectives
        Educational Responsibility
        Outcomes of Education
        School Role
        Sociocultural Patterns
        Student Role
        Teacher Role

Role Perception   *JUL. 1966*
        Postings: 5,179   GC: 510
SN   Awareness of behavior patterns or func-
        tions expected of individuals or groups
BT   Cognitive Processes
RT   Identification (Psychology)
        Perspective Taking
        Role
        Role Playing
        Role Theory
        Self Actualization
        Social Cognition
        Stereotypes

Role Playing   *JUL. 1966*
        Postings: 3,255   GC: 240
UF   Sociodrama (1966 1980)
NT   Dramatic Play
BT   Simulation
RT   Computer Simulation
        Counseling Techniques
        Group Dynamics
        Improvisation
        Perspective Taking
        Pretend Play
        Psychotherapy

        Role
        Role Perception
        Teaching Methods

Role Taking
USE   Perspective Taking

Role Theory   *JUL. 1966*
        Postings: 859   GC: 810
BT   Theories
RT   Identification (Psychology)
        Life Style
        Personal Autonomy
        Role
        Role Conflict
        Role Perception
        Self Actualization
        Social Stratification
        Social Theories
        Student School Relationship

Roller Skating   *FEB. 1978*
        Postings: 8   GC: 470
BT   Athletics

Roman Literature
USE   Latin Literature

Romance Languages   *JUL. 1966*
        Postings: 184   GC: 440
NT   French
        Italian
        Latin
        Portuguese
        Romanian
        Spanish
BT   Indo European Languages
RT   Welsh

Romanian   *NOV. 1994*
        Postings: 9   GC: 440
SN   (Note: this Descriptor was returned to its
        original 1969–80 "Ro. . ." spelling—
        preferred spelling 1980–94 was
        "Ru. . .")
UF   Roumanian
        Rumanian (1980 1994)
BT   Romance Languages

Romanization   *JUL. 1966*
        Postings: 131   GC: 450
SN   The transliteration of another system of
        writing into the Roman alphabet
RT   Alphabets
        Graphemes
        Language Standardization
        Non Roman Scripts
        Orthographic Symbols
        Written Language

Romanticism   *JUN. 1969*
        Postings: 215   GC: 430
SN   Eighteenth and nineteenth century move-
        ment, style, and sensibility, originating
        as a reaction to the neoclassic focus on
        reason and intellect, and characterized
        by an emphasis on imagination, emo-
        tions, spontaneity, idealism, and indi-
        vidualism
RT   Art Expression
        Eighteenth Century Literature
        Literary Styles
        Nineteenth Century Literature
        Philosophy
        Platonism

Roof Installation
USE   Roofing

Roofers (1968 1981)
USE   Roofing
AND   Skilled Workers

= Two or more Descriptors are used to represent this term.
The term's main entry shows the appropriate coordination.

Roofing · JUL. 1966
· Postings: 176 · GC: 920
UF · Roof Installation
· Roofers (1968 1981) #
· Roofs
BT · Structural Elements (Construction)
RT · Asphalts
· Building Trades
· Buildings
· Construction (Process)
· Construction Materials
· Skilled Occupations

Roofs
USE · Roofing

Room Dividers
USE · Space Dividers

Rotation Plans · JUL. 1966
· Postings: 35 · GC: 320
RT · Team Teaching

Rote Learning · JUL. 1966
· Postings: 226 · GC: 110
BT · Learning
RT · Drills (Practice)
· Learning Theories
· Memorization
· Primacy Effect
· Retention (Psychology)
· Serial Learning

Roumanian
USE · Romanian

Rubella · APR. 1969
· Postings: 102 · GC: 210
UF · Epidemic Roseola
· German Measles
BT · Communicable Diseases
· Viruses
RT · Physical Health
· Prenatal Influences

Rubrics (Scoring Guides)
USE · Scoring Rubrics

Rumanian (1980 1994)
USE · Romanian

Runaways · AUG. 1978
· Postings: 287 · GC: 530
SN · Persons who leave home without notice,
· and stay away for indefinite periods of
· time
UF · Adult Runaways
· Juvenile Runaways
BT · Groups
RT · Child Welfare
· Delinquency
· Dropouts
· Family Problems
· Homeless People
· Missing Children
· One Parent Family
· Truancy
· Youth Problems

Rundi
USE · Kirundi

Running · SEP. 1968
· Postings: 249 · GC: 470
NT · Jogging
BT · Physical Activities
RT · Athletics
· Physical Education
· Physical Fitness
· Track and Field
· Walking

Rural American Indians · MAR. 1980
· Postings: 28 · GC: 560
SN · American Indians who reside in rural
· areas and may live near (but not on)
· reservations
BT · Nonreservation American Indians
· Rural Population
RT · Rural Areas
· Urban American Indians

Rural Areas · JUL. 1966
· Postings: 6,164 · GC: 550
UF · Rural Clinics (1966 1980) #
BT · Geographic Regions
RT · Collective Settlements
· Geographic Isolation
· Nonmetropolitan Areas
· Rural American Indians
· Rural Development
· Rural Economics
· Rural Education
· Rural Environment
· Rural Extension
· Rural Population
· Rural Resettlement
· Rural Schools
· Rural Sociology
· Rural to Urban Migration
· Rural Urban Differences
· Rural Women
· Small Towns
· Urban to Rural Migration

Rural Clinics (1966 1980)
USE · Clinics
AND · Rural Areas

Rural Development · JUL. 1966
· Postings: 2,150 · GC: 550
BT · Development
RT · Boomtowns
· Community Development
· Modernization
· Rural Areas
· Rural Economics
· Rural Environment
· Rural Sociology

Rural Dropouts (1966 1981)
USE · Dropouts

Rural Economics · JUL. 1966
· Postings: 566 · GC: 620
BT · Economics
RT · Economic Impact
· Microeconomics
· Rural Areas
· Rural Development
· Rural Environment
· Rural Sociology

Rural Education · JUL. 1966
· Postings: 4,837 · GC: 330
BT · Education
RT · Adult Farmer Education
· Outdoor Education
· Rural Areas
· Rural Environment
· Rural Extension
· Rural Schools
· Rural Sociology
· Young Farmer Education

Rural Environment · JUL. 1966
· Postings: 656 · GC: 550
BT · Environment
RT · Geographic Isolation
· Rural Areas
· Rural Development
· Rural Economics
· Rural Education
· Rural Extension
· Rural Family
· Rural Population
· Rural Resettlement
· Rural Sociology
· Rural to Urban Migration

Small Towns
· Urban to Rural Migration

Rural Extension · JUL. 1966
· Postings: 748 · GC: 350
SN · Extension work in rural settings
UF · Agricultural Extension
BT · Extension Education
RT · Adult Farmer Education
· Agricultural Education
· Land Grant Universities
· Rural Areas
· Rural Education
· Rural Environment
· Young Farmer Education

Rural Family · JUL. 1966
· Postings: 352 · GC: 510
BT · Family (Sociological Unit)
· Rural Population
RT · Rural Environment
· Rural Sociology
· Rural Women

Rural Farm Residents · SEP. 1968
· Postings: 345 · GC: 410
SN · Persons living in nonmetropolitan areas
· on land which is gainfully worked as an
· agricultural enterprise
BT · Rural Population
RT · Farmers
· Rural Nonfarm Residents
· Rural Women
· Sharecroppers

Rural Inhabitants
USE · Rural Population

Rural Nonfarm Residents · AUG. 1977
· Postings: 67 · GC: 510
SN · Persons living in nonmetropolitan areas
· on land which is not worked as an agri-
· cultural enterprise
BT · Rural Population
RT · Rural Farm Residents
· Rural Women

Rural Population · JUL. 1966
· Postings: 1,647 · GC: 550
UF · Rural Inhabitants
NT · Rural American Indians
· Rural Family
· Rural Farm Residents
· Rural Nonfarm Residents
· Rural Women
· Rural Youth
BT · Groups
RT · Demography
· Geographic Isolation
· Population Distribution
· Population Growth
· Population Trends
· Rural Areas
· Rural Environment
· Rural Resettlement
· Rural Sociology
· Rural to Urban Migration
· Rural Urban Differences
· Urban to Rural Migration

Rural Resettlement · JUL. 1966
· Postings: 70 · GC: 550
BT · Land Settlement
· Relocation
RT · Rural Areas
· Rural Environment
· Rural Population
· Rural Sociology
· Urban to Rural Migration

Rural School Systems (1966 1980)
USE · Rural Schools
AND · School Districts

Rural Schools · JUL. 1966
· Postings: 3,929 · GC: 340
UF · Rural School Systems (1966 1980) #
BT · Schools
RT · Consolidated Schools
· County School Districts
· Geographic Isolation
· One Teacher Schools
· Rural Areas
· Rural Education
· Small Schools

Rural Sociology · DEC. 1989
· Postings: 164 · GC: 520
SN · The study of rural communities and rural
· life in both agricultural and industrialized
· societies
BT · Sociology
RT · Agriculture
· Area Studies
· Rural Areas
· Rural Development
· Rural Economics
· Rural Education
· Rural Environment
· Rural Family
· Rural Population
· Rural Resettlement
· Rural to Urban Migration
· Rural Urban Differences
· Social Science Research
· Sociologists
· Urban to Rural Migration
· Urbanization

Rural to Urban Migration · OCT. 1976
· Postings: 489 · GC: 550
SN · Population movement from rural areas
· to urban areas for purpose of relocation
UF · Urban Immigration (1966 1976)
BT · Migration
RT · Migration Patterns
· Population Distribution
· Population Trends
· Relocation
· Residential Patterns
· Rural Areas
· Rural Environment
· Rural Population
· Rural Sociology
· Urban Areas
· Urban Demography
· Urban Population
· Urban to Rural Migration
· Urbanization

Rural Urban Differences · JUL. 1966
· Postings: 2,360 · GC: 550
UF · Urban Rural Differences
BT · Differences
RT · Cultural Differences
· Place of Residence
· Regional Attitudes
· Regional Characteristics
· Rural Areas
· Rural Population
· Rural Sociology
· Social Differences
· Urban Areas
· Urban Culture
· Urban Language
· Urban Population

Rural Women · SEP. 1994
· Postings: 114 · GC: 510
SN · Women living in rural areas or having
· strong social or economic ties to rural
· life
UF · Farm Women
BT · Females
· Rural Population
RT · Farm Labor
· Farmers
· Rural Areas
· Rural Family
· Rural Farm Residents
· Rural Nonfarm Residents

= Two or more Descriptors are used to represent this term.
The term's main entry shows the appropriate coordination.

Rural Youth JUL. 1966
Postings: 1,213 GC: 510
SN (Note: Coordinate with an appropriate age or educational level Descriptor)
UF Farm Youth
BT Rural Population
    Youth
RT Migrant Youth

Russian JUL. 1966
Postings: 1,218 GC: 440
BT Slavic Languages
RT Russian Literature

Russian Literature DEC. 1969
Postings: 159 GC: 430
BT Literature
RT Russian

Sabbatical Leaves JUL. 1966
Postings: 260 GC: 630
BT Leaves of Absence
RT Faculty Development
    Faculty Fellowships
    Faculty Workload
    Professional Continuing Education
    Professional Development
    Professional Education
    Released Time
    Teacher Attendance
    Teacher Employment Benefits
    Teacher Improvement

Sadness DEC. 1994
Postings: 69 GC: 120
SN Psychological state associated with unhappiness or sorrow
UF Melancholy
NT Grief
    Loneliness
BT Psychological Patterns
RT Depression (Psychology)
    Moods

Safety JUL. 1966
Postings: 3,454 GC: 210
UF Safety Provisions
NT Agricultural Safety
    Child Safety
    Fire Protection
    Laboratory Safety
    Occupational Safety and Health
    School Safety
    Traffic Safety
RT Accident Prevention
    Accidents
    Alarm Systems
    Computer Security
    Consumer Protection
    Daily Living Skills
    Design Requirements
    Emergency Programs
    Fallout Shelters
    Guns
    Hazardous Materials
    Health
    Injuries
    National Security
    Natural Disasters
    Poisoning
    Radiation
    Radiation Effects
    Refugees
    Rescue
    Risk Management
    Safety Education
    Safety Equipment
    Security Personnel
    Traffic Accidents
    Weapons

Safety Education JUL. 1966
Postings: 1,721 GC: 400
BT Education
RT Accident Prevention
    Accidents
    Agricultural Safety
    Child Safety

Fire Protection
Fire Science Education
Laboratory Safety
Occupational Safety and Health
Rescue
Safety
Safety Equipment
School Safety
Traffic Accidents
Traffic Safety

Safety Equipment AUG. 1968
Postings: 380 GC: 910
UF Safety Glasses
NT Restraints (Vehicle Safety)
BT Equipment
RT Accident Prevention
    Safety
    Safety Education

Safety Glasses
USE Safety Equipment

Safety Provisions
USE Safety

Sailing JAN. 1985
Postings: 35 GC: 470
BT Aquatic Sports
RT Boat Operators
    Maritime Education
    Seafarers

Salaries JUL. 1966
Postings: 3,062 GC: 630
SN Earnings paid at fixed intervals (week, month, year) rather than at hourly rates, and usually for professional, technical, and executive services (Note: Do not confuse with "Wages"—prior to Mar80, the use of this term was not restricted by a Scope Note)
NT Contract Salaries
    Teacher Salaries
BT Expenditures
    Income
RT Compensation (Remuneration)
    Costs
    Fringe Benefits
    Guaranteed Income
    Merit Pay
    Operating Expenses
    Payroll Records
    Premium Pay
    Promotion (Occupational)
    Retirement Benefits
    Salary Wage Differentials
    Scope of Bargaining
    Wages

Salary Differentials (1968 1980)
USE Salary Wage Differentials

Salary Raises
USE Promotion (Occupational)

Salary Wage Differentials MAR. 1980
Postings: 2,275 GC: 620
UF Equal Pay
    Salary Differentials (1968 1980)
    Wage Salary Differentials
BT Differences
RT Comparable Worth
    Educational Finance
    Employment Practices
    Equal Opportunities (Jobs)
    Merit Pay
    Occupational Segregation
    Overtime
    Personnel Policy
    Premium Pay
    Salaries
    Scope of Bargaining
    Wages

Sales Clerks
USE Sales Workers

Sales Occupations JUL. 1966
Postings: 290 GC: 640
BT Occupations
RT Agricultural Supply Occupations
    Auto Parts Clerks
    Distributive Education
    Insurance Occupations
    Merchandising
    Merchants
    Real Estate Occupations
    Retailing
    Sales Workers
    Salesmanship
    Service Occupations
    Vendors
    White Collar Occupations

Sales Promotion
USE Merchandising

Sales Workers JUL. 1966
Postings: 185 GC: 640
UF Sales Clerks
NT Auto Parts Clerks
BT Nonprofessional Personnel
RT Agricultural Supply Occupations
    Employees
    Merchants
    Sales Occupations
    Salesmanship
    Service Workers
    Vendors

Salesmanship JUL. 1966
Postings: 517 GC: 650
BT Marketing
    Skills
RT Advertising
    Distributive Education
    Job Skills
    Merchandise Information
    Merchandising
    Persuasive Discourse
    Retailing
    Sales Occupations
    Sales Workers
    Wholesaling

Salish JUL. 1970
Postings: 30 GC: 440
BT American Indian Languages

Salt Marshes
USE Wetlands

Samoan JAN. 1970
Postings: 42 GC: 440
BT Malayo Polynesian Languages
RT Samoan Americans

Samoan Americans MAR. 1976
Postings: 49 GC: 560
SN Polynesian or part-Polynesian people indigenous to the Samoan Islands
UF American Samoans
BT Ethnic Groups
    Pacific Americans
RT Samoan
    Trust Responsibility (Government)

Samoyed Languages JUL. 1966
Postings: 3 GC: 440
NT Yurak
BT Uralic Altaic Languages

Sample Size MAR. 1983
Postings: 720 GC: 820
SN The number of subjects (or items) selected to represent a population in a research or evaluation study
RT Attrition (Research Studies)

Control Groups
Effect Size
Evaluation Methods
Experimental Groups
Generalizability Theory
Measurement Techniques
Probability
Reliability
Research Design
Research Problems
Sampling
Statistical Analysis
Statistical Bias
Surveys

Sampling JUL. 1966
Postings: 2,295 GC: 820
SN Selecting a representative part of a population to draw inferences about the characteristics of the whole population
NT Item Sampling
BT Data Collection
    Statistics
RT Attrition (Research Studies)
    Control Groups
    Cross Sectional Studies
    Error of Measurement
    Evaluation Methods
    Experimental Groups
    Generalizability Theory
    Longitudinal Studies
    Matched Groups
    Maximum Likelihood Statistics
    Measurement Techniques
    Monte Carlo Methods
    Multivariate Analysis
    Norms
    Participant Characteristics
    Predictive Measurement
    Probability
    Quasiexperimental Design
    Research Design
    Sample Size
    Statistical Analysis
    Statistical Bias
    Statistical Inference
    Statistical Studies
    Statistical Surveys
    Surveys

Sanatoriums
USE Hospitals

Sanctions JUL. 1966
Postings: 258 GC: 520
SN Mechanisms of social control that punish deviancy or reward conformance with regard to specified standards
RT Arbitration
    Awards
    Censorship
    Collective Bargaining
    Discipline
    Fines (Penalties)
    Incentives
    Labor Demands
    Laws
    Negotiation Impasses
    Punishment
    Rewards
    Social Control
    Standards
    Teacher Militancy
    Teacher Strikes

Sango JUL. 1966
Postings: 10 GC: 440
BT African Languages

Sanitary Facilities JUL. 1966
Postings: 89 GC: 920
SN Equipment and building areas for keeping buildings clean and/or facilities for personal cleanliness
NT Toilet Facilities
BT Facilities
RT Dishwashing
    Equipment
    Health Conditions

= Two or more Descriptors are used to represent this term.
The term's main entry shows the appropriate coordination.

Health Facilities
Hygiene
Locker Rooms
Physical Health
Plumbing
Sanitation
Utilities
Waste Disposal

Sanitary Inspectors
USE   Environmental Technicians

Sanitary Technicians
USE   Environmental Technicians

Sanitation   *JUL. 1966*
       Postings: 522   GC: 210
UF   Sanitation Improvement (1966 1980)
NT   Cleaning
       Waste Disposal
RT   Bacteria
       Design Requirements
       Disease Control
       Environmental Influences
       Environmental Technicians
       Hazardous Materials
       Health
       Hygiene
       Pests
       Physical Environment
       Physical Health
       Public Health
       Sanitary Facilities
       Utilities
       Viruses
       Water Treatment

Sanitation Improvement (1966 1980)
USE   Sanitation

Sanskrit   *AUG. 1968*
       Postings: 26   GC: 440
BT   Classical Languages

Sara   *JUL. 1966*
       Postings: 6   GC: 440
BT   African Languages

Sarcasm
USE   Irony

Sarcoma
USE   Cancer

Satellite Facilities   *MAR. 1980*
       Postings: 75   GC: 920
SN   Subsidiary facilities that may be some
       distance from the facility or institution to
       which they are administratively related
BT   Facilities
RT   Branch Libraries
       Extension Education
       Off Campus Facilities

Satellite Laboratories (1966 1980)
USE   Satellites (Aerospace)

Satellite Libraries
USE   Branch Libraries

Satellites (Aerospace)   *MAR. 1980*
       Postings: 183   GC: 490
SN   (Note: If applicable, use the more spe-
       cific term "Communications Satellites")
UF   Artificial Satellites
       Orbiting Satellites
       Satellite Laboratories (1966 1980)
NT   Communications Satellites
RT   Aerospace Technology
       Earth Science
       Lunar Research
       Solar System

Space Exploration
Space Sciences

Satire   *JUL. 1966*
       Postings: 237   GC: 430
BT   Literary Genres
RT   Comics (Publications)
       Figurative Language
       Literary Styles
       Parody

Satisfaction   *APR. 1990*
       Postings: 481   GC: 120
SN   Disposition or state of mind achieved by
       the gratification of needs, motives, and
       expectations (Note: Use a more specific
       term if possible)
NT   Community Satisfaction
       Job Satisfaction
       Life Satisfaction
       Marital Satisfaction
       Participant Satisfaction
       User Satisfaction (Information)
BT   Attitudes
RT   Happiness
       Improvement
       Motivation
       Need Gratification
       Needs
       Success
       Values
       Well Being

Scales
USE   Measures (Individuals)

Scaling   *MAR. 1980*
       Postings: 543   GC: 820
SN   Arranging objects in a definite order by
       assigning values to them along a prede-
       termined continuum
UF   Internal Scaling (1966 1980)
NT   Multidimensional Scaling
BT   Measurement Techniques
RT   Equated Scores
       Holistic Evaluation
       Mathematical Models
       Norms
       Rating Scales
       Scoring
       Statistical Analysis
       Test Construction
       Testing

Schedule Modules (1968 1980)
USE   Flexible Scheduling

Scheduling   *JUL. 1966*
       Postings: 1,713   GC: 320
UF   Timetables
NT   Alternate Day Schedules
       Fast Track Scheduling
       Full Day Half Day Schedules
       School Schedules
       Working Hours
BT   Planning
RT   Coordination
       Critical Path Method
       Intervals
       Program Length
       Programming (Broadcast)
       Time Blocks
       Time Factors (Learning)
       Time Management

Schemata (Cognition)   *NOV. 1982*
       Postings: 1,111   GC: 110
SN   Mental images and concepts that pro-
       vide a cognitive framework by which the
       individual perceives, understands, and
       responds to stimuli
BT   Psychological Characteristics
RT   Cognitive Ability
       Cognitive Development
       Cognitive Mapping
       Cognitive Psychology
       Cognitive Structures

Cognitive Style
Comprehension
Familiarity
Learning
Learning Theories
Readiness
Recall (Psychology)
Responses
Retention (Psychology)

Schematic Studies   *JUL. 1966*
       Postings: 105   GC: 810
SN   Studies employing models or represen-
       tations that manifest the significant rela-
       tionships between concepts (Note: As of
       Oct81, use as a minor Descriptor for
       examples of this kind of research—use
       as a major Descriptor only as the subject
       of a document—prior to Oct81, this term
       did not carry a Scope Note)
BT   Research
RT   Models
       Relationship
       Systems Approach

Schizophrenia   *JUL. 1966*
       Postings: 627   GC: 230
UF   Dementia Praecox
BT   Psychosis
RT   Autism
       Echolalia
       Emotional Disturbances
       Paranoid Behavior

Scholarly Communication   *AUG. 2000*
       Postings: 145   GC: 720
SN   Exchange of ideas or information be-
       tween scholars—may occur through any
       medium and encompasses the spectrum
       from formal publication to informal dis-
       cussion
UF   Scholarly Information Exchange
BT   Communication (Thought Transfer)
       Scholarship
RT   Academic Discourse
       Access to Information
       Electronic Journals
       Electronic Publishing
       Listservs
       Scholarly Journals
       Scholarly Writing
       Scientific and Technical Information

Scholarly Information Exchange
USE   Scholarly Communication

Scholarly Journals   *JUL. 1966*
       Postings: 2,345   GC: 720
BT   Periodicals
RT   Academic Standards
       Editors
       Electronic Journals
       Faculty Publishing
       Journal Articles
       Research Tools
       Scholarly Communication
       Scholarly Writing
       Scholarship
       Writing for Publication

Scholarly Writing   *AUG. 2000*
       Postings: 168   GC: 720
SN   Formal written presentation of research
       or ideas by scholars (Note: Prior to Aug00,
       as an unscoped Identifier, this term was
       used broadly to index such concepts as
       "Faculty Publishing," "Writing for Publi-
       cation," "Academic Discourse," and
       "Scholarly Communication")
BT   Scholarship
       Writing (Composition)
RT   Academic Discourse
       Faculty Publishing
       Journal Articles
       Research Reports
       Scholarly Communication
       Scholarly Journals
       Writing for Publication

Scholarship   *MAR. 1980*
       Postings: 1,681   GC: 330
SN   Comprehensive mastery of an area of
       knowledge—also, the methods and at-
       tainments of scholars
NT   Scholarly Communication
       Scholarly Writing
BT   Achievement
RT   Academic Ability
       Academic Achievement
       Familiarity
       Knowledge Level
       Learning
       Recognition (Achievement)
       Research Skills
       Researchers
       Scholarly Journals
       Scientists
       Social Scientists
       Study

Scholarship Funds   *JUL. 1966*
       Postings: 174   GC: 620
SN   Revenue made available for scholarships
BT   Financial Support
RT   Assistantships
       Capital
       Educational Finance
       Fellowships
       Fund Raising
       Merit Scholarships
       No Need Scholarships
       Scholarships
       Student Costs
       Student Financial Aid
       Tuition Grants

Scholarship Loans (1966 1980)
USE   Scholarships
AND   Student Loan Programs

Scholarships   *JUL. 1966*
       Postings: 1,089   GC: 620
SN   Awards, usually of money or reduced
       tuition, given to students primarily in
       recognition of achievement or potential
       but also for other specific characteristics
       such as financial need, residence, or
       academic interest
UF   Endowed Scholarships
       Scholarship Loans (1966 1980) #
NT   Merit Scholarships
       Tuition Grants
BT   Student Financial Aid
RT   Awards
       Educational Finance
       Educational Vouchers
       Eligibility
       Fellowships
       Grants
       Instructional Student Costs
       Noninstructional Student Costs
       Scholarship Funds
       Student Costs

Scholastic Ability
USE   Academic Ability

Scholastic Achievement
USE   Academic Achievement

Scholastic Failure
USE   Academic Failure

Scholastic Journalism   *JUL. 2000*
       Postings: 218   GC: 720
SN   School-sponsored journalistic endeav-
       ors, e.g., production of newspapers, year-
       books, electronic periodicals, Web sites,
       or broadcast news programs
BT   Journalism
RT   Journalism Education
       School Newspapers
       School Publications
       Student Publications
       Writing for Publication
       Yearbooks

= Two or more Descriptors are used to represent this term.
The term's main entry shows the appropriate coordination.

Scholastic Potential
USE   Academic Aptitude

Scholastic Probation
USE   Academic Probation

School Accidents   *JUL. 1966*
      Postings: 109   GC: 210
BT   Accidents
RT   School Safety
      Schools

School Accounting   *JUL. 1966*
      Postings: 578   GC: 620
BT   Accounting
RT   Educational Finance
      School Administration
      School Based Management
      School Business Officials
      Schools

School Activities   *JUL. 1966*
      Postings: 791   GC: 320
UF   School Programs
NT   Class Activities
      Extracurricular Activities
      Student Projects
BT   Activities
RT   After School Programs
      Assembly Programs
      Curriculum
      Learning Activities
      School Recreational Programs
      Schools

School Adjustment
USE   Student Adjustment

School Administration   *JUL. 1966*
      Postings: 3,453   GC: 320
SN   Planning, organizing, directing, and con-
      trolling human or material resources
      within a school, college, or university
NT   College Administration
      School Based Management
BT   Educational Administration
      Institutional Administration
RT   Admissions Officers
      Assistant Principals
      Beginning Principals
      Board Administrator Relationship
      Boards of Education
      Central Office Administrators
      Deans
      Department Heads
      Governing Boards
      Government School Relationship
      Instructional Leadership
      Principals
      Registrars (School)
      School Accounting
      School Business Officials
      School Culture
      School District Autonomy
      School Law
      School Policy
      School Responsibility
      School Supervision
      Schools
      Student Government
      Student School Relationship
      Superintendents
      Teacher Administrator Relationship

School Administrators
USE   Administrators

School Admission
USE   Admission (School)

School Age Day Care   *OCT. 1983*
      Postings: 440   GC: 520
SN   Care of school-age children (usually 5–13
      years of age) before or after the school
      day

UF   After School Day Care (1978 1983) #
BT   Day Care
RT   After School Programs
      Ancillary School Services
      Day Care Centers
      Employer Supported Day Care
      Extended School Day
      Family Day Care
      Latchkey Children

School Aid
USE   Educational Finance

School Aides   *JUL. 1966*
      Postings: 173   GC: 360
SN   Paraprofessional school personnel who
      work under the guidance of school pro-
      fessionals, assisting in noninstructional
      areas—e.g., playground monitors (Note:
      Prior to Mar80, this term was not scoped
      and was often confused with "Teacher
      Aides," who assist in the instructional
      process)
BT   Paraprofessional School Personnel
RT   Bilingual Teacher Aides
      Proctoring
      Teacher Aides
      Volunteers

School Architecture (1966 1980)
USE   Educational Facilities Design

School Attendance
USE   Attendance

School Attendance Laws (1966 1974)
USE   School Attendance Legislation

School Attendance Legislation   *NOV. 1974*
      Postings: 263   GC: 330
UF   School Attendance Laws (1966 1974)
BT   Educational Legislation
      State Legislation
RT   Attendance
      Average Daily Attendance
      Compulsory Education
      Expulsion
      Home Schooling
      Laws
      School Policy
      Suspension

School Attitudes   *JUL. 1966*
      Postings: 988   GC: 330
SN   Attitudes toward or about schools
BT   Attitudes
RT   Family School Relationship
      Government School Relationship
      Parent School Relationship
      Police School Relationship
      School Community Relationship
      Schools
      Student School Relationship

School Based Interagency Services
USE   Integrated Services

School Based Management   *SEP. 1982*
      Postings: 1,662   GC: 320
SN   Administrative system in which an indi-
      vidual school exercises autonomous de-
      cision making on budgets, curriculum,
      and personnel within policy guidelines
      set by its governing board
UF   School Site Management
      Site Based Management (Schools)
BT   Institutional Autonomy
      School Administration
RT   Beginning Principals
      Budgeting
      Decentralization
      Decision Making
      Participative Decision Making
      Principals
      School Accounting

School Organization
School Policy
School Restructuring
School Supervision
Schools

School Board Members
USE   Boards of Education

School Board Policy
USE   Board of Education Policy

School Board Role
USE   Board of Education Role

School Boards
USE   Boards of Education

School Boundaries
USE   School Districts

School Boycotts   *JUL. 1966*
      Postings: 39   GC: 540
RT   Activism
      Demonstrations (Civil)
      School Resegregation
      School Segregation
      Schools
      Strikes
      Student Rights
      Teacher Strikes

School Budget Elections   *JUL. 1966*
      Postings: 186   GC: 620
BT   Elections
RT   Budgets
      Educational Finance
      School Funds
      School Support

School Buildings   *JUL. 1966*
      Postings: 1,173   GC: 920
NT   College Buildings
BT   Buildings
      Educational Facilities
RT   Campus Planning
      Campuses
      Construction Materials
      Educational Complexes
      Educational Equipment
      Educational Facilities Design
      Educational Facilities Improvement
      Educational Facilities Planning
      Facility Utilization Research
      Open Plan Schools
      School Construction
      School Expansion
      School Shops
      Schools
      Space Utilization

School Bus Drivers
USE   Bus Drivers
AND   School Buses

School Buses   *AUG. 1968*
      Postings: 441   GC: 910
UF   School Bus Drivers #
BT   Service Vehicles
RT   Bus Drivers
      Bus Transportation
      Busing
      Student Transportation

School Business Officials   *MAR. 1980*
      Postings: 486   GC: 360
SN   Administrative officers responsible for
      the direction of business and financial
      affairs of an educational institution—
      functions supervised include account-
      ing, purchasing, facility and property
      maintenance, personnel services, etc.
UF   Business Officials (School)

BT   Administrators
      School Personnel
RT   Ancillary School Services
      Educational Facilities Planning
      Educational Finance
      Middle Management
      School Accounting
      School Administration
      Student Financial Aid Officers

School Business Relationship   *MAR. 1980*
      Postings: 8,644   GC: 330
UF   Business School Relationship
      Industry School Relationship
      School Industry Relationship (1967
          1980)
BT   Relationship
RT   Business
      Career Education
      Cooperative Education
      Cooperative Programs
      Corporate Education
      Corporate Support
      Economic Impact
      Education Work Relationship
      Industry
      Partnerships in Education
      Private Financial Support
      Privatization
      School Community Relationship
      School Involvement
      School Support
      Schools
      Vocational Education
      Work Experience Programs

School Cadres   *MAR. 1969*
      Postings: 51   GC: 360
SN   Groups of school personnel previously
      coordinated in training to work together
      and to train others
BT   School Personnel
RT   Research and Instruction Units
      Staff Utilization
      Team Teaching
      Team Training

School Calendars (1967 1980)
USE   School Schedules

School Catalogs   *MAR. 1980*
      Postings: 146   GC: 320
SN   Publications issued by schools to pro-
      vide information on their courses, fac-
      ulty, facilities, etc. (Note: Prior to Mar80,
      "Catalogs" was used to index this con-
      cept)
UF   College Catalogs
BT   Catalogs
      School Publications
RT   Admission (School)
      Admission Criteria
      Course Descriptions
      Degree Requirements
      Graduation Requirements
      Program Descriptions
      Schools
      Student Recruitment

School Characteristics
USE   Institutional Characteristics

School Choice   *MAR. 1982*
      Postings: 1,614   GC: 330
SN   Individualized selection of public or pri-
      vate schools, alternative programs, or
      different school systems, sometimes
      made possible with little or no added
      financial cost through tax credits, vouch-
      ers, magnet schools, open enrollment,
      or other arrangements
UF   Educational Choice
      Family Choice (Education)
NT   College Choice
BT   Selection
RT   Admission (School)
      Decision Making
      Diversity (Institutional)

= Two or more Descriptors are used to represent this term.
The term's main entry shows the appropriate coordination.

Educational Vouchers
Eligibility
Free Choice Transfer Programs
Nontraditional Education
Private School Aid
School Restructuring
Tax Credits
Tuition

School Climate
USE   Educational Environment

School Closing   *JUL. 1966*
Postings: 600   GC: 330
SN   Permanent closing of schools
UF   Closed Schools
College Closing
RT   Board of Education Policy
Consolidated Schools
Declining Enrollment
Institutional Survival
Mergers
Program Termination
Schools
Student Attrition

School College Cooperation
USE   College School Cooperation

School Community Communication
USE   School Community Relationship

School Community Cooperation (1966 1980)
USE   School Community Relationship

School Community Coordination
USE   School Community Relationship

School Community Interaction
USE   School Community Relationship

School Community Programs   *JUL. 1966*
Postings: 1,565   GC: 330
SN   Programs sponsored jointly by an edu-
cational institution and the surrounding
community
UF   Community School Programs
BT   Community Programs
RT   Community
Integrated Services
Outreach Programs
Partnerships in Education
School Community Relationship
School Involvement
Schools
Service Learning

School Community Relationship   *JUL. 1966*
Postings: 12,836   GC: 330
SN   Formal or informal interactions between
an educational institution and the sur-
rounding community
UF   College Community Relationship
Community School Relationship
School Community Communication
School Community Cooperation (1966
1980)
School Community Coordination
School Community Interaction
BT   Relationship
RT   Community
Community Based Instruction (Disa-
bilities)
Community Colleges
Community Control
Community Cooperation
Community Coordination
Community Schools
Cooperative Planning
Cooperative Programs
Economic Impact
Educational Sociology
Family School Relationship
Integrated Services
Parent School Relationship

Participative Decision Making
Partnerships in Education
Politics of Education
Public Relations
Public Service
School Attitudes
School Business Relationship
School Community Programs
School Involvement
School Role
School Support
Schools
Service Learning
Tribally Controlled Education

School Conditions (1966 1980)
USE   Educational Environment

School Consolidation
USE   Consolidated Schools

School Construction   *JUL. 1966*
Postings: 956   GC: 320
BT   Construction (Process)
RT   Bids
Educational Facilities
Educational Facilities Design
Educational Facilities Planning
Life Cycle Costing
Modular Building Design
Prefabrication
School Buildings
School Expansion
Schools
Sheet Metal Work

School Counseling   *MAR. 1980*
Postings: 2,809   GC: 240
SN   Assistance given to students by the school
or college in order to help them un-
derstand and cope with adjustment
problems—includes the administration
and interpretation of tests (Note: Do not
confuse with "Educational Counseling"
or "Academic Advising")
UF   Elementary School Counseling (1967
1980)
Guidance Counseling (1966 1980)
Secondary School Counseling
BT   Counseling
School Guidance
RT   Colleges
Counselor Teacher Cooperation
Educational Counseling
Educational Therapy
Faculty Advisers
Faculty Workload
Post High School Guidance
Pupil Personnel Services
School Counselors
School Guidance
School Orientation
School Psychologists
School Psychology
School Social Workers
Schools
Student Development
Student Personnel Services

School Counselors   *MAR. 1980*
Postings: 2,589   GC: 240
SN   (Note: Prior to Mar80, the instruction
"Guidance Counselors, USE Counselors"
was carried in the Thesaurus)
UF   College Counselors
Elementary School Counselors (1967
1980)
Guidance Counselors
Secondary School Counselors (1967
1980)
BT   Counselors
School Personnel
RT   Adjustment Counselors
Colleges
Counselor Teacher Cooperation
Faculty Advisers
Pupil Personnel Workers
School Counseling
School Guidance

School Psychologists
School Social Workers
Schools
Student Personnel Workers

School Culture   *FEB. 1996*
Postings: 916   GC: 560
SN   Patterns of meaning or activity (norms,
values, beliefs, relationships, rituals, tra-
ditions, myths, etc.) shared in varying
degrees by members of a school com-
munity
BT   Culture
RT   Educational Environment
School Administration
School Effectiveness
School Organization
School Role
Schools
Student Subcultures

School Demography   *JUL. 1966*
Postings: 1,583   GC: 330
NT   Teacher Distribution
BT   Demography
RT   Affirmative Action
Average Daily Membership
Declining Enrollment
Diversity (Institutional)
Enrollment Projections
Enrollment Trends
Feeder Patterns
Institutional Characteristics
Residential Patterns
School Desegregation
School District Size
School Location
School Size
School Statistics
Schools
Student Attrition
Students

School Desegregation   *MAR. 1980*
Postings: 4,426   GC: 540
SN   Process of bringing students of different
ethnic or racial groups into the same
school
UF   Biracial Elementary Schools (1966
1980)
Biracial Schools (1966 1980)
Biracial Secondary Schools (1966
1980)
Desegregated Schools
Grade a Year Integration (1966 1980)
Integrated Schools
School Integration (1966 1980)
NT   College Desegregation
BT   Social Integration
RT   Black Education
Busing
Classroom Desegregation
Desegregation Effects
Desegregation Litigation
Desegregation Methods
Desegregation Plans
Educational Parks
Integration Readiness
Magnet Schools
Neighborhood Schools
Racial Attitudes
Racial Composition
Racial Integration
Racially Balanced Schools
School Demography
School Resegregation
Schools
Tokenism
Transfer Students
Voluntary Desegregation

School Design (1966 1980)
USE   Educational Facilities Design

School District Autonomy   *DEC. 1968*
Postings: 1,093   GC: 330
SN   Area of control granted a school district
or its officials through expressed or implied state authority

UF   Local Autonomy (of Schools)
Local Control (of Schools)
RT   Block Grants
Board of Education Policy
Board of Education Role
Boards of Education
City Government
Community Control
Educational Policy
Full State Funding
Governance
Government Role
Government School Relationship
Institutional Autonomy
Local Government
Professional Autonomy
Revenue Sharing
School Administration
School Districts
School Restructuring
Self Determination
State Government
State Regulation
State School District Relationship

School District Norms
USE   Local Norms

School District Policy
USE   Board of Education Policy

School District Reorganization   *MAR. 1980*
Postings: 425   GC: 330
SN   The changing of boundary lines of local
or intermediate basic administrative units,
the merging of existing districts, or the
creation of new districts
UF   School Redistricting (1966 1980)
BT   Organization
RT   Consolidated Schools
Feeder Patterns
Intermediate Administrative Units
Rezoning
School District Size
School Districts
School Location
School Zoning
Schools

School District Size   *JUN. 1983*
Postings: 369   GC: 330
SN   Size of a school district as measured by
its land area or number of students or
staff
BT   Organization Size (Groups)
RT   Enrollment
Geographic Distribution
School Demography
School District Reorganization
School Districts
School Personnel
School Size
School Statistics

School District Spending   *JUL. 1966*
Postings: 1,385   GC: 620
BT   Expenditures
RT   Costs
Educational Equity (Finance)
Educational Finance
Expenditure per Student
Fiscal Neutrality
Full State Funding
School District Wealth
School Districts
State School District Relationship

School District Wealth   *OCT. 1993*
Postings: 180   GC: 620
SN   Primary measure of a school district's
ability to pay the costs of education—
calculated variously by states, etc., based
on property tax revenues, per student
expenditures, median family income, and
other indicators
BT   Fiscal Capacity
RT   Educational Economics
Educational Equity (Finance)

= Two or more Descriptors are used to represent this term.
The term's main entry shows the appropriate coordination.

Educational Finance
Equalization Aid
Expenditure per Student
Financial Support
Fiscal Neutrality
Income
Property Taxes
School District Spending
School Districts
School Funds
School Support
School Taxes
State School District Relationship
Tax Effort

School Districts   *JUL. 1966*
    Postings: 11,326   GC: 340
SN   Local administrative units that operate schools or contract for school services in specific geographic areas
UF   Comprehensive Districts (1967 1980)
     Lea
     Local Education Agencies
     Local Education Authorities
     Public School Systems (1966 1980) #
     Rural School Systems (1966 1980) #
     School Boundaries
     School Systems (1966 1980)
NT   County School Districts
     Multicampus Districts
BT   Organizations (Groups)
RT   Boards of Education
     Central Office Administrators
     Consolidated Schools
     Geographic Regions
     Interdistrict Policies
     Intermediate Administrative Units
     Local Government
     Public Education
     Public Schools
     Rezoning
     School District Autonomy
     School District Reorganization
     School District Size
     School District Spending
     School District Wealth
     School Location
     Schools
     State School District Relationship
     Superintendents
     Zoning

School Dropouts
USE   Dropouts

School Effectiveness   *AUG. 1982*
    Postings: 4,377   GC: 320
SN   Degrees to which schools are successful in accomplishing their educational objectives or fulfilling their administrative, instructional, or service functions
UF   Effective Schooling
     Instructionally Effective Schools
BT   Organizational Effectiveness
RT   Academic Achievement
     Accountability
     Administrator Effectiveness
     Cost Effectiveness
     Educational Assessment
     Educational Quality
     Effective Schools Research
     Excellence in Education
     Instructional Effectiveness
     Outcomes of Education
     Program Effectiveness
     School Culture
     School Restructuring
     School Role
     Schools
     Student Development
     Teacher Effectiveness

School Employees
USE   School Personnel

School Enrollment
USE   Enrollment

School Entrance Age   *MAR. 1980*
    Postings: 217   GC: 330
SN   Age of students when they enroll in school (Note: See "Late Registration" for students who enroll after the school term has begun)
BT   Age
RT   Age Grade Placement
     Early Admission
     Enrollment
     Learning Readiness
     School Readiness
     School Readiness Tests
     Student Placement

School Environment (1966 1980)
USE   Educational Environment

School Expansion   *JUL. 1966*
    Postings: 244   GC: 320
SN   Increase in the number or size of school facilities
BT   Facility Expansion
RT   Building Conversion
     Educational Facilities
     Educational Facilities Improvement
     Educational Facilities Planning
     Facility Utilization Research
     Mobile Classrooms
     School Buildings
     School Construction
     School Size
     Schools
     Site Analysis
     Site Development
     Site Selection
     Space Utilization

School Experience
USE   Educational Experience

School Facilities
USE   Educational Facilities

School Family Relationship
USE   Family School Relationship

School Finance
USE   Educational Finance

School Finance Equity
USE   Educational Equity (Finance)

School Funds   *JUL. 1966*
    Postings: 1,237   GC: 620
SN   Money available for school use
BT   Financial Support
RT   Capital
     Educational Finance
     Endowment Funds
     Federal Aid
     Foundation Programs
     Fund Raising
     Money Management
     Private School Aid
     School Budget Elections
     School District Wealth
     School Support
     School Taxes
     Schools
     State Aid

School Government Relationship
USE   Government School Relationship

School Guidance   *MAR. 1980*
    Postings: 811   GC: 240
SN   Assistance given to students by the school or college to help them develop realistic and satisfying goals, plans, and activities (Note: Do not confuse with "Educational Counseling")
UF   Elementary School Guidance (1967 1980)

Secondary School Guidance
NT   School Counseling
BT   Guidance
RT   Career Awareness
     Career Exploration
     Career Guidance
     Colleges
     Counselor Teacher Cooperation
     Instructor Coordinators
     Probation Officers
     Pupil Personnel Services
     School Counseling
     School Counselors
     Schools
     Student Development
     Student Personnel Services
     Teacher Guidance

School Health Services   *JUL. 1966*
    Postings: 1,251   GC: 210
UF   Clinic Personnel (School) (1966 1980) #
BT   Ancillary School Services
     Health Services
RT   Breakfast Programs
     Child Health
     Comprehensive School Health Education
     Integrated Services
     Lunch Programs
     Physical Education
     Physical Recreation Programs
     Pupil Personnel Services
     School Nurses
     Sick Child Care
     Sports Medicine
     Student Personnel Services

School Holding Power   *JUL. 1966*
    Postings: 3,399   GC: 320
UF   Holding Power (of Schools)
     Retention (in School)
RT   Academic Persistence
     Attendance
     College Attendance
     Dropout Research
     Dropouts
     Enrollment Management
     Stopouts
     Student Attrition
     Students
     Truancy
     Withdrawal (Education)

School Home Relationship
USE   Family School Relationship

School Improvement (1966 1980)
USE   Educational Facilities Improvement

School Industry Relationship (1967 1980)
USE   School Business Relationship

School Integration (1966 1980)
USE   School Desegregation

School Involvement   *JUL. 1966*
    Postings: 406   GC: 330
SN   Involvement of schools or school representatives in activities or programs (Note: Prior to Mar80, this term was not scoped and was sometimes used for the involvement of individuals or groups in schools)
UF   School Participation
BT   Participation
RT   Family School Relationship
     Government School Relationship
     Parent School Relationship
     School Business Relationship
     School Community Programs
     School Community Relationship
     School Role
     Schools
     Teacher Participation
     Theory Practice Relationship

School Law   *JUL. 1966*
    Postings: 1,979   GC: 330
SN   That branch of law (constitutional, statutory, or common) that relates to public and private schools, school districts, and institutions of higher education
BT   Laws
RT   Civil Law
     Educational Legislation
     In Loco Parentis
     Politics of Education
     School Administration
     School Policy
     School Security
     Schools
     Search and Seizure
     Student Rights
     Teacher Rights

School Libraries   *JUL. 1966*
    Postings: 4,213   GC: 710
UF   Elementary School Libraries (1966 1980)
     High School Libraries
     Secondary School Libraries
BT   Libraries
RT   Childrens Libraries
     Learning Resources Centers
     Librarian Teacher Cooperation
     Media Specialists
     Schools

School Linked Services
USE   Integrated Services

School Location   *JUL. 1966*
    Postings: 442   GC: 330
UF   School Sites
RT   Access to Education
     Campus Planning
     Commuter Colleges
     Distance
     Geographic Location
     Multicampus Districts
     Proximity
     Real Estate
     School Demography
     School District Reorganization
     School Districts
     School Zoning
     Schools
     Site Analysis

School Maintenance   *JUL. 1966*
    Postings: 786   GC: 320
BT   Maintenance
RT   Building Operation
     Cleaning
     Custodian Training
     Educational Facilities Improvement
     Equipment Maintenance
     Schools

School Media Centers
USE   Learning Resources Centers

School Newspapers   *JUL. 1966*
    Postings: 1,097   GC: 720
BT   Newspapers
     School Publications
RT   Extracurricular Activities
     Scholastic Journalism
     Student Publications

School Nurse Practitioners
USE   Nurse Practitioners
AND   School Nurses

School Nurses   *JUL. 1966*
    Postings: 372   GC: 360
UF   School Nurse Practitioners #
BT   Nurses
     School Personnel
RT   School Health Services

= Two or more Descriptors are used to represent this term.
The term's main entry shows the appropriate coordination.

School Officials
USE   School Personnel

School Organization   *JUL. 1966*
Postings: 3,549   GC: 320
SN   (Note: Do not confuse with "School District Reorganization")
UF   High School Organization (1966 1980)
School Reorganization
NT   House Plan
School Restructuring
BT   Organization
RT   Administrative Organization
Centralization
Class Organization
Decentralization
Departments
Diversity (Institutional)
Double Sessions
Educational Environment
Institutional Characteristics
Instructional Program Divisions
Multiunit Schools
School Based Management
School Culture
School Schedules
Schools
Traditional Schools
Transitional Schools

School Orientation   *JUL. 1966*
Postings: 728   GC: 320
SN   Process of making new students aware
of a school's environment, rules, traditions, educational offerings, etc.
BT   Orientation
RT   Educational Counseling
Pupil Personnel Services
School Counseling
Schools
Student Adjustment
Student Personnel Services
Student School Relationship
Teacher Orientation

School Parent Relationship
USE   Parent School Relationship

School Participation
USE   School Involvement

School Personnel   *JUL. 1966*
Postings: 2,987   GC: 360
UF   School Employees
School Officials
School Personnel Directors #
NT   Admissions Officers
Assistant Principals
Audiovisual Coordinators
Beginning Principals
Faculty
Foreign Student Advisers
Paraprofessional School Personnel
Principals
Pupil Personnel Workers
Registrars (School)
School Business Officials
School Cadres
School Counselors
School Nurses
School Psychologists
School Secretaries
School Social Workers
Student Financial Aid Officers
Student Personnel Workers
BT   Personnel
RT   Athletic Coaches
Central Office Administrators
Personnel Directors
School District Size
School Size
Schools
Security Personnel
Superintendents
Teachers

School Personnel Directors
USE   Personnel Directors

AND   School Personnel

School Philosophy
USE   Educational Philosophy

School Phobia   *JUL. 1966*
Postings: 127   GC: 230
UF   Schoolsickness
BT   Fear
RT   Anxiety
Computer Anxiety
Mathematics Anxiety
Neurosis
Separation Anxiety
Student School Relationship
Test Anxiety
Writing Apprehension

School Planning (1966 1980)   *JUN. 1980*
Postings: 734   GC: 330
SN   Invalid Descriptor—use "Educational Facilities Planning" or, if appropriate, the broader term "Educational Planning"

School Plants
USE   Educational Facilities

School Police Relationship
USE   Police School Relationship

School Policy   *JUL. 1966*
Postings: 2,886   GC: 320
UF   Neighborhood School Policy (1966 1980) #
BT   Policy
RT   Board of Education Policy
Discipline Policy
Educational Policy
Institutional Mission
Interdistrict Policies
Politics of Education
School Administration
School Attendance Legislation
School Based Management
School Law
School Role
School Uniforms
Schools
Teacher Administrator Relationship
Transfer Policy

School Prayer   *AUG. 1988*
Postings: 122   GC: 330
SN   Individual or group prayer in a public or private school setting
UF   Prayer in Schools
RT   Meditation
Religion
Religious Factors
Schools
State Church Separation

School Principals
USE   Principals

School Programs
USE   School Activities

School Psychologists   *JUL. 1966*
Postings: 1,953   GC: 360
BT   Mental Health Workers
Psychologists
School Personnel
RT   Consultants
Psychological Evaluation
Psychometrics
Pupil Personnel Workers
School Counseling
School Counselors
School Psychology
Student Personnel Workers

School Psychology   *MAY 2000*
Postings: 107   GC: 230
SN   Application to the school setting of psychological knowledge and methods regarding cognitive, affective, or social development—includes activities such as assessment, diagnosis, consultation, and treatment—may refer to the practice or the study of school psychology (Note: Prior to May00, this term was frequently indexed by "School Psychologists")
BT   Psychology
RT   Child Psychology
Educational Psychology
Psychoeducational Methods
Psychological Evaluation
Psychological Services
Psychological Testing
Psychometrics
Pupil Personnel Services
School Counseling
School Psychologists
Student Development
Student Personnel Services

School Publications   *JUL. 1966*
Postings: 577   GC: 720
NT   Faculty Handbooks
School Catalogs
School Newspapers
Student Publications
BT   Publications
RT   Editors
Journalism Education
Scholastic Journalism
Schools
Student Developed Materials
Teacher Developed Materials
Writing for Publication
Yearbooks

School Readiness   *MAR. 1980*
Postings: 1,024   GC: 120
SN   Cognitive, physical, and psychosocial maturity prerequisite to learning in a school setting
BT   Readiness
RT   Age Grade Placement
Cognitive Development
Early Admission
Emotional Development
Learning Readiness
Physical Development
Reading Readiness
School Entrance Age
School Readiness Tests
Student Placement
Writing Readiness

School Readiness Tests   *FEB. 1971*
Postings: 228   GC: 830
BT   Aptitude Tests
RT   Diagnostic Tests
Maturity Tests
Preschool Tests
Prognostic Tests
Reading Readiness Tests
School Entrance Age
School Readiness
Screening Tests

School Recreational Programs   *JUL. 1966*
Postings: 87   GC: 470
BT   Recreational Programs
RT   After School Programs
Ancillary School Services
Extended School Day
Extracurricular Activities
Extramural Athletics
Intramural Athletics
Recess Breaks
Recreational Activities
School Activities
Schools

School Redistricting (1966 1980)
USE   School District Reorganization

School Registration   *JUL. 1966*
Postings: 367   GC: 320
UF   College Registration
Registration in School
NT   Late Registration
RT   Admission (School)
Attendance
College Attendance
Enrollment
Registrars (School)
Schools

School Related Activities
USE   Extracurricular Activities

School Renovation
USE   Educational Facilities Improvement

School Reorganization
USE   School Organization

School Resegregation   *OCT. 1979*
Postings: 126   GC: 540
SN   Reversion to segregation in schools that had been desegregated
UF   Resegregated Schools
BT   School Segregation
RT   De Facto Segregation
Racial Segregation
School Boycotts
School Desegregation

School Responsibility   *JUL. 1966*
Postings: 2,343   GC: 330
BT   Responsibility
RT   Educational Responsibility
In Loco Parentis
Leadership Responsibility
Noninstructional Responsibility
School Administration
School Role
Schools
Student Responsibility
Teacher Responsibility

School Restructuring   *APR. 1990*
Postings: 3,063   GC: 330
SN   A "second wave" reform strategy of the U.S. "Excellence in Education" movement, based on the premise that the organization of schools must be changed in order to stem widespread academic failure and to meet higher standards demanded by society—bureaucratic decentralization is the core component, whether in the form of school based management, a choice plan, or some variation on privatization
UF   Restructuring of Schools (United States)
BT   Excellence in Education
School Organization
RT   Decentralization
Educational Change
Educational Innovation
Educational Philosophy
Educational Policy
Organizational Change
Organizational Development
Participative Decision Making
Partnerships in Education
Professional Autonomy
School Based Management
School Choice
School District Autonomy
School Effectiveness
Transitional Schools

School Role   *JUL. 1966*
Postings: 4,667   GC: 330
SN   Functions expected of or performed by an educational institution
UF   Elementary School Role (1966 1980)
High School Role (1966 1980)
Junior High School Role (1966 1980)
NT   College Role
BT   Institutional Role

= Two or more Descriptors are used to represent this term.
The term's main entry shows the appropriate coordination.

RT   Educational Environment
      Educational Objectives
      Educational Responsibility
      Family School Relationship
      Government School Relationship
      In Loco Parentis
      Parent School Relationship
      Politics of Education
      Role of Education
      School Community Relationship
      School Culture
      School Effectiveness
      School Involvement
      School Policy
      School Responsibility
      Schools
      Student Development

School Safety   *JUL. 1966*
      Postings: 1,576   GC: 320
NT   School Security
BT   Safety
RT   Alarm Systems
      Child Safety
      Educational Facilities Improvement
      Educational Facilities Planning
      Emergency Programs
      Fire Protection
      Guns
      Hazardous Materials
      Laboratory Safety
      Safety Education
      School Accidents
      Schools
      Security Personnel
      Weapons

School Schedules   *JUL. 1966*
      Postings: 1,324   GC: 350
SN   Plans by which students and teachers
      are assigned to rooms and classes, the
      school day is divided into class periods,
      or the school year is organized into ses-
      sions and vacations (Note: Use a more
      specific term if possible)
UF   Academic Calendars
      School Calendars (1967 1980)
      Timetables (School)
NT   Block Scheduling
      Double Sessions
      Extended School Day
      Extended School Year
      Flexible Scheduling
      Quarter System
      Semester System
      Trimester System
BT   Scheduling
RT   Alternate Day Schedules
      Class Organization
      Enrollment
      Full Day Half Day Schedules
      Released Time
      School Organization
      Schools
      Time Blocks
      Vacation Programs
      Year Round Schools

School Secretaries   *JUL. 1966*
      Postings: 46   GC: 360
BT   School Personnel
      Secretaries

School Security   *MAR. 1978*
      Postings: 866   GC: 320
SN   Physical protection of school property,
      school personnel, and students from
      hostile acts or influences
UF   Campus Security
BT   School Safety
RT   Alarm Systems
      Campuses
      Computer Security
      Crime
      Crime Prevention
      Law Enforcement
      Police Action
      Police School Relationship
      School Law

      School Vandalism
      Schools
      Security Personnel
      Stealing
      Violence

School Segregation   *JUL. 1966*
      Postings: 647   GC: 540
SN   Exclusion on the basis of race or ethnic
      status from particular schools, or the
      assignment of different racial or ethnic
      groups to separate schools
NT   College Segregation
      School Resegregation
BT   Educational Discrimination
RT   Black Education
      Racial Segregation
      School Boycotts
      Schools

School Services (1966 1980)
USE   Ancillary School Services

School Shops   *JUL. 1966*
      Postings: 344   GC: 320
UF   Industrial Arts Shops
      Shop Rooms
BT   Educational Facilities
RT   Classrooms
      Handicrafts
      Industrial Arts
      School Buildings
      Shop Curriculum
      Technical Education
      Trade and Industrial Education

School Site Management
USE   School Based Management

School Sites
USE   School Location

School Size   *JUL. 1966*
      Postings: 1,144   GC: 320
SN   Size of a school as measured by the
      dimensions of its physical plant or by the
      number of students or staff
BT   Institutional Characteristics
RT   Attendance
      Diversity (Institutional)
      Educational Facilities Design
      Educational Facilities Planning
      Enrollment
      School Demography
      School District Size
      School Expansion
      School Personnel
      School Space
      School Statistics
      Schools
      Small Schools

School Social Workers   *JUL. 1966*
      Postings: 294   GC: 360
BT   School Personnel
      Social Workers
RT   Adjustment Counselors
      Caseworkers
      Pupil Personnel Workers
      School Counseling
      School Counselors
      Social Work
      Student Personnel Workers

School Space   *JUL. 1966*
      Postings: 310   GC: 320
BT   Educational Facilities
RT   Classrooms
      Corridors
      Educational Facilities Design
      Educational Facilities Planning
      Facility Utilization Research
      Flexible Facilities
      Interior Space
      Multipurpose Classrooms
      Offices (Facilities)

      Open Plan Schools
      School Size
      Schools
      Space Dividers
      Space Utilization
      Spatial Relationship (Facilities)

School Statistics   *JUL. 1966*
      Postings: 1,748   GC: 730
BT   Statistical Data
RT   Educational Research
      Educational Trends
      Enrollment Projections
      Expenditure per Student
      School Demography
      School District Size
      School Size
      School Surveys
      Schools
      Statistical Analysis
      Teacher Distribution

School Student Relationship
USE   Student School Relationship

School Study Centers (1966 1980)
USE   Study Centers

School Superintendents (1966 1980)
USE   Superintendents

School Supervision   *JUL. 1966*
      Postings: 448   GC: 320
SN   Professional activities concerned with
      the development, maintenance, and im-
      provement of a school's instructional
      program, especially its curriculum and
      teaching personnel
UF   Elementary School Supervisors (1966
      1980)
      High School Supervisors (1966 1980)
BT   Supervision
RT   Beginning Principals
      Curriculum Development
      Instruction
      Instructional Improvement
      Instructional Leadership
      Principals
      School Administration
      School Based Management
      Schools
      Teacher Supervision

School Supplies
USE   Supplies

School Support   *JUL. 1966*
      Postings: 1,285   GC: 620
SN   Moral or financial support supplied for
      the operation and maintenance of educa-
      tional institutions (Note: Prior to Mar80,
      the use of this term was not restricted by
      a Scope Note)
NT   Private School Aid
RT   Community Support
      Corporate Support
      Educational Economics
      Educational Equity (Finance)
      Educational Finance
      Excellence in Education
      Federal Aid
      Financial Support
      Fiscal Neutrality
      Foundation Programs
      Full State Funding
      Institutional Survival
      Public Support
      School Budget Elections
      School Business Relationship
      School Community Relationship
      School District Wealth
      School Funds
      School Taxes
      Schools
      State Aid

School Surveys   *JUL. 1966*
      Postings: 5,384   GC: 810
SN   Studies of schools, colleges, school sys-
      tems, or any parts thereof (Note: As of
      Oct81, use a minor Descriptor for
      examples of this kind of survey—use as
      a major Descriptor only as the subject of
      a document—prior to Oct81, this term
      did not carry a Scope Note)
UF   Educational Surveys
BT   Surveys
RT   Educational Research
      Graduate Surveys
      School Statistics
      Schools
      Student Surveys
      Teacher Surveys

School Systems (1966 1980)
USE   School Districts

School Taxes   *JUL. 1966*
      Postings: 842   GC: 620
BT   Taxes
RT   Assessed Valuation
      Educational Equity (Finance)
      Educational Finance
      Full State Funding
      Private School Aid
      Property Taxes
      School District Wealth
      School Funds
      School Support
      Schools
      Tax Rates

School to Work Transition
USE   Education Work Relationship

School Transportation
USE   Student Transportation

School Truancy
USE   Truancy

School Uniforms   *JUL. 2000*
      Postings: 47   GC: 320
SN   Standardized clothing for regular school
      attendance worn in conformity with
      school policy (Note: Excludes uniforms
      for special activities such as band, ath-
      letics, or ROTC—see also the Identifier
      "Uniforms")
BT   Clothing
RT   Discipline Policy
      Dress Codes
      School Policy
      Student Behavior
      Student Rights

School Vandalism   *JUL. 1966*
      Postings: 438   GC: 530
BT   Vandalism
RT   School Security
      Schools
      Security Personnel

School Visitation   *JUL. 1966*
      Postings: 171   GC: 330
SN   Approved interschool visitation by teach-
      ers or administrators to observe teach-
      ing methods or equipment
UF   Interschool Visits
      School Visits
BT   Observation
RT   Inservice Teacher Education

School Visits
USE   School Visitation

School Zoning   *JUL. 1966*
      Postings: 81   GC: 330
BT   Zoning
RT   Consolidated Schools

= Two or more Descriptors are used to represent this term.
The term's main entry shows the appropriate coordination.

School District Reorganization
School Location
Schools
Site Selection

Schools JUL. 1966
Postings: 1,064 GC: 340
SN Educational institutions at all levels (Note: Use a more specific term if possible)
UF Educational Institutions
NT Affiliated Schools
Bilingual Schools
Boarding Schools
British Infant Schools
Colleges
Community Schools
Consolidated Schools
Correspondence Schools
Day Schools
Disadvantaged Schools
Elementary Schools
Experimental Schools
Folk Schools
Free Schools
Freedom Schools
Inclusive Schools
Laboratory Schools
Magnet Schools
Middle Schools
Military Schools
Multiunit Schools
Neighborhood Schools
Nursery Schools
Open Plan Schools
Private Schools
Professional Development Schools
Public Schools
Racially Balanced Schools
Regional Schools
Rural Schools
Schools of Education
Secondary Schools
Single Sex Schools
Slum Schools
Small Schools
Special Schools
State Schools
Suburban Schools
Summer Schools
Traditional Schools
Transitional Schools
Urban Schools
Vocational Schools
Year Round Schools
BT Institutions
RT Admission (School)
Ancillary School Services
Boards of Education
College School Cooperation
Education
Educational Environment
Educational Facilities
Educational Facilities Design
Educational Facilities Improvement
Educational Facilities Planning
Effective Schools Research
Faculty Handbooks
Family School Relationship
Government School Relationship
Institutional Characteristics
Interschool Communication
Nonprofit Organizations
Parent School Relationship
Police School Relationship
School Accidents
School Accounting
School Activities
School Administration
School Attitudes
School Based Management
School Boycotts
School Buildings
School Business Relationship
School Catalogs
School Closing
School Community Programs
School Community Relationship
School Construction
School Counseling
School Counselors
School Culture
School Demography

School Desegregation
School District Reorganization
School Districts
School Effectiveness
School Expansion
School Funds
School Guidance
School Involvement
School Law
School Libraries
School Location
School Maintenance
School Organization
School Orientation
School Personnel
School Policy
School Prayer
School Publications
School Recreational Programs
School Registration
School Responsibility
School Role
School Safety
School Schedules
School Security
School Segregation
School Size
School Space
School Statistics
School Supervision
School Support
School Surveys
School Taxes
School Vandalism
School Zoning
Student School Relationship

Schools of Dentistry
USE Dental Schools

Schools of Education NOV. 1970
Postings: 2,089 GC: 340
SN Institutions, either independent or within a college or university, that train educational personnel at the undergraduate or graduate level
UF Colleges of Education
Education Departments (School)
Teachers Colleges (1966 1980)
BT Schools
RT Education Courses
Education Majors
Laboratory Schools
Postsecondary Education as a Field of Study
Preservice Teachers
Specialist in Education Degrees
Student Teachers
Teacher Education
Teacher Education Curriculum
Teacher Educator Education
Teacher Educators

Schools of Medicine
USE Medical Schools

Schools within a School Plan
USE House Plan

Schoolsickness
USE School Phobia

Science
USE Sciences

Science Achievement MAR. 2000
Postings: 298 GC: 490
SN Level of attainment in any or all science skills, usually estimated by performance on a test
BT Achievement
RT Academic Achievement

Achievement Gains
Science Process Skills
Science Tests
Sciences

Science Activities JUL. 1966
Postings: 11,129 GC: 490
SN Methods of science instruction that usually involve some participation by students—may include projects outside the school
NT Science Fairs
Science Projects
BT Activities
RT Hands on Science
Laboratory Procedures
Science Clubs
Science Curriculum
Science Education
Science Experiments
Science Instruction
Science Interests
Science Process Skills
Science Programs
Sciences

Science and Society AUG. 1986
Postings: 3,025 GC: 490
SN Interrelationships between scientific/technical developments and social activities—includes learning/teaching materials and programs dealing with these relationships
UF Science Technology and Society
Sts (Science Technology Society)
BT Relationship
RT Appropriate Technology
Environmental Education
Futures (of Society)
Interdisciplinary Approach
Quality of Life
Science Curriculum
Science Education
Sciences
Scientific Enterprise
Scientific Literacy
Social Change
Social Influences
Social Problems
Technological Advancement
Technological Literacy
Technology
Technology Education
Technology Transfer

Science and Technology Libraries
USE Science Libraries

Science Careers JUL. 1966
Postings: 882 GC: 490
BT Careers
RT Science Consultants
Science Education
Science Interests
Science Teachers
Sciences
Scientific Personnel
Scientists

Science Clubs JUL. 1966
Postings: 47 GC: 320
BT Clubs
RT Science Activities
Science Education
Science Interests

Science Consultants JUL. 1966
Postings: 56 GC: 640
BT Consultants
Scientific Personnel
RT Resource Teachers
Science Careers
Science Supervision
Science Teachers

Science Course Improvement Project (1967 1980)
USE Science Course Improvement Projects

Science Course Improvement Projects MAR. 1980
Postings: 1,205 GC: 490
SN Planned self-contained undertakings in the sciences in which instructional techniques and curriculum materials are developed (Note: Coordinate specific project titles as Identifiers, e.g., "Biological Sciences Curriculum Study," "Physical Science Study Committee")
UF Science Course Improvement Project (1967 1980)
BT Programs
RT Instructional Materials
Science Curriculum
Science Education
Science Instruction
Teaching Methods

Science Courses (1966 1980)
USE Science Curriculum

Science Curriculum JUL. 1966
Postings: 6,273 GC: 490
UF Physics Curriculum (1966 1980) #
Science Courses (1966 1980)
Science Units (1966 1980) #
NT College Science
Elementary School Science
General Science
Secondary School Science
BT Curriculum
RT Hands on Science
Science Activities
Science and Society
Science Course Improvement Projects
Science Education
Science Instruction
Science Process Skills
Science Programs
Sciences
Summer Science Programs

Science Departments JUL. 1966
Postings: 169 GC: 350
BT Departments
RT College Science
Elementary School Science
English Departments
Science Teachers
Secondary School Science

Science Education JUL. 1966
Postings: 41,365 GC: 490
BT Education
RT Aerospace Education
Aviation Education
College Science
Demonstrations (Science)
Elementary School Science
Energy Education
Engineering Education
General Science
Hands on Science
Marine Education
Science Activities
Science and Society
Science Careers
Science Clubs
Science Course Improvement Projects
Science Curriculum
Science Education History
Science Experiments
Science Facilities
Science Instruction
Science Process Skills
Science Programs
Science Projects
Science Teachers
Science Teaching Centers
Sciences
Scientific Literacy
Scientific Methodology
Secondary School Science
Technical Education

= Two or more Descriptors are used to represent this term.
The term's main entry shows the appropriate coordination.

Technological Literacy
Technology Education

Science Education History *JUL. 1966*
Postings: 348 GC: 490
BT Educational History
RT Science Education
Science History

Science Equipment *JUL. 1966*
Postings: 2,413 GC: 910
SN Hardware used for instruction or other activities in science (Note: For scientific measurement apparatus, coordinate with "Measurement Equipment")
BT Equipment
RT Demonstrations (Science)
Educational Equipment
Laboratory Equipment
Lasers
Measurement Equipment
Science Experiments
Science Facilities
Science Laboratories
Science Materials
Sciences

Science Experiments *JUL. 1966*
Postings: 3,981 GC: 490
SN Laboratory-based scientific investigations
UF Physics Experiments (1966 1980) #
BT Experiments
RT Demonstrations (Science)
Laboratory Experiments
Laboratory Procedures
Science Activities
Science Education
Science Equipment
Science Laboratories
Science Process Skills
Science Projects
Sciences

Science Facilities *JUL. 1966*
Postings: 398 GC: 920
SN Physical structures or spaces constructed, installed, or established for use in science (Note: Use a more specific term if possible)
NT Science Laboratories
Science Teaching Centers
BT Facilities
RT Aquariums
Classrooms
Planetariums
Science Education
Science Equipment
Science Libraries

Science Fairs *JUL. 1966*
Postings: 240 GC: 490
BT Exhibits
Science Activities
RT Extracurricular Activities
Hands on Science
Realia
Science Projects

Science Fiction *DEC. 1969*
Postings: 435 GC: 430
BT Fiction
RT Fantasy

Science History *JUL. 1966*
Postings: 1,956 GC: 490
BT History
RT Science Education History
Sciences
Scientific Research
Scientists

Science Information
USE Scientific and Technical Information

Science Institutes (1967 1980)
USE Institutes (Training Programs)
AND Science Programs

Science Instruction *JUL. 1966*
Postings: 15,129 GC: 490
UF Biology Instruction (1966 1980) #
Chemistry Instruction (1967 1980) #
Physics Instruction (1966 1980) #
BT Instruction
RT College Science
Demonstrations (Science)
Elementary School Science
General Science
Science Activities
Science Course Improvement Projects
Science Curriculum
Science Education
Science Process Skills
Science Programs
Science Teachers
Science Tests
Sciences
Secondary School Science
Summer Science Programs

Science Interests *MAR. 1980*
Postings: 534 GC: 490
UF Student Science Interests (1967 1980)
BT Interests
RT Science Activities
Science Careers
Science Clubs
Science Tests
Sciences
Scientific Research

Science Laboratories *JUL. 1966*
Postings: 971 GC: 920
SN Facilities specifically designed and equipped for scientific experiments, demonstrations, observations, practice, or research
BT Laboratories
Science Facilities
RT Demonstrations (Science)
Planetariums
Science Equipment
Science Experiments
Sciences

Science Libraries *AUG. 1994*
Postings: 49 GC: 710
SN Libraries, library departments, library branches, etc., devoted to one or more scientific or technical areas
UF Science and Technology Libraries
Technical Libraries
BT Special Libraries
RT Medical Libraries
Research Libraries
Science Facilities
Science Materials
Science Programs
Sciences
Scientific and Technical Information
Technology

Science Materials *JUL. 1966*
Postings: 2,301 GC: 730
RT Health Materials
Instructional Materials
Reading Materials
Science Equipment
Science Libraries
Scientific and Technical Information

Science Process Skills *MAY 1994*
Postings: 675 GC: 490
SN Broadly transferable intellectual skills, appropriate to all scientific endeavors—includes basic process skills (e.g., observing, inferring, measuring, communicating, classifying, predicting, using time-space relations, using numbers) and integrated process skills (e.g., controlling variables, defining operationally, formulating hypotheses, interpreting data, ex-
perimenting, formulating models) (Note: See also the Identifier "Science a Process Approach" for a curriculum espousing the learning and use of these skills)
BT Skills
RT Basic Skills
Hands on Science
Mathematics Skills
Process Education
Science Achievement
Science Activities
Science Curriculum
Science Education
Science Experiments
Science Instruction
Science Tests
Sciences
Scientific Concepts
Scientific Literacy
Scientific Methodology
Thinking Skills

Science Programs *JUL. 1966*
Postings: 1,530 GC: 490
UF Science Institutes (1967 1980) #
Technological Programs
NT Summer Science Programs
BT Programs
RT Hands on Science
Research and Development
Science Activities
Science Curriculum
Science Education
Science Instruction
Science Libraries
Sciences
Technical Assistance
Technological Advancement
Technology

Science Projects *JUL. 1966*
Postings: 772 GC: 490
BT Science Activities
RT Laboratory Procedures
Science Education
Science Experiments
Science Fairs
Sciences
Student Projects
Summer Science Programs

Science Supervision *JUL. 1966*
Postings: 65 GC: 320
BT Supervision
RT Science Consultants

Science Teachers *JUL. 1966*
Postings: 3,002 GC: 360
UF Chemistry Teachers (1967 1980) #
Physics Teachers (1967 1980) #
BT Teachers
RT Science Careers
Science Consultants
Science Departments
Science Education
Science Instruction

Science Teaching Centers *JUL. 1966*
Postings: 190 GC: 920
BT Educational Facilities
Science Facilities
RT Education Service Centers
Museums
Nature Centers
Planetariums
Science Education

Science Technology and Society
USE Science and Society

Science Tests *JUL. 1966*
Postings: 944 GC: 830
BT Tests
RT Achievement Tests
Science Achievement
Science Instruction
Science Interests

Science Process Skills
Sciences
Scientific Literacy

Science Units (1966 1980)
USE Science Curriculum
AND Units of Study

Sciences *JUL. 1966*
Postings: 4,068 GC: 490
SN Sciences other than the applied sciences
UF Modern Science (1966 1980)
Science
NT Acoustics
Behavioral Sciences
Information Science
Natural Sciences
Social Sciences
Space Sciences
BT Liberal Arts
RT Engineering
English for Science and Technology
Mathematics
Research
Science Achievement
Science Activities
Science and Society
Science Careers
Science Curriculum
Science Education
Science Equipment
Science Experiments
Science History
Science Instruction
Science Interests
Science Laboratories
Science Libraries
Science Process Skills
Science Programs
Science Projects
Science Tests
Scientific and Technical Information
Scientific Attitudes
Scientific Concepts
Scientific Enterprise
Scientific Methodology
Scientific Principles
Technology

Scientific and Technical Information
APR. 1985
Postings: 1,344 GC: 490
SN The body of information resulting from the study and technological application of natural scientific phenomena (Note: Use only when such information is the subject—do not use to classify items as scientific and/or technical)
UF Science Information
Scientific Information
Technical Information
Technological Information
RT Information Services
Information Sources
Natural Sciences
Scholarly Communication
Science Libraries
Science Materials
Sciences
Scientific Concepts
Scientific Literacy
Scientific Research
Technical Assistance
Technological Literacy
Technology
Technology Transfer

Scientific Attitudes *JUL. 1966*
Postings: 861 GC: 490
BT Attitudes
RT Inquiry
Problem Solving
Sciences
Scientific Enterprise
Scientific Methodology

Scientific Concepts *JUL. 1966*
Postings: 4,019 GC: 490
NT Density (Matter)

Energy
Entropy
Force
Gravity (Physics)
Height
Motion
Pressure (Physics)
Relativity
Space
Time
Weight (Mass)
RT Concept Mapping
Conservation (Concept)
Distance
Fundamental Concepts
Intervals
Misconceptions
Science Process Skills
Sciences
Scientific and Technical Information
Scientific Literacy
Scientific Methodology
Scientific Principles
Technology

Scientific Creationism
USE Creationism

Scientific Enterprise   JUL. 1966
Postings: 903   GC: 490
SN Totality of systematic activity of the sci-
ences as an institution involving proc-
esses, attitudes, ethics, and interrela-
tionships of science with other institutions
RT Natural Sciences
Science and Society
Sciences
Scientific Attitudes
Scientific Principles

Scientific Information
USE Scientific and Technical Information

Scientific Literacy   JUL. 1966
Postings: 1,501   GC: 490
SN Comprehension of scientific concepts,
processes, values, and ethics, and their
relation to technology and society
BT Literacy
RT Comprehension
Computer Literacy
Information Literacy
Science and Society
Science Education
Science Process Skills
Science Tests
Scientific and Technical Information
Scientific Concepts
Scientific Principles
Technological Literacy

Scientific Manpower (1967 1980)
USE Scientific Personnel

Scientific Methodology   JUL. 1966
Postings: 1,881   GC: 490
SN Research methodology adapted to the
requirements of the various scientific
disciplines
UF Scientific Methods
BT Research Methodology
RT Componential Analysis
Deduction
Generalization
Holistic Approach
Hypothesis Testing
Induction
Markov Processes
Measurement Techniques
Naturalistic Observation
Problem Solving
Quasiexperimental Design
Research Design
Science Education
Science Process Skills
Sciences
Scientific Attitudes
Scientific Concepts

Scientific Research
Theories

Scientific Methods
USE Scientific Methodology

Scientific Personnel   JUL. 1966
Postings: 629   GC: 490
UF Scientific Manpower (1967 1980)
NT Mathematicians
Science Consultants
Scientists
BT Personnel
RT Allied Health Personnel
Chemical Technicians
Engineers
Health Personnel
Marine Technicians
Metallurgical Technicians
Nuclear Power Plant Technicians
Science Careers

Scientific Principles   JUL. 1966
Postings: 878   GC: 490
UF Nature of Science
BT Standards
RT Sciences
Scientific Concepts
Scientific Enterprise
Scientific Literacy

Scientific Reports
USE Research Reports

Scientific Research   JUL. 1966
Postings: 3,895   GC: 810
SN Research conducted to advance knowl-
edge in a scientific field (Note: As of
Oct81, use as a minor Descriptor for
examples of this kind of research—use
as a major Descriptor only as the subject
of a document)
NT Space Exploration
BT Research
RT Anatomy
Astronomy
Biology
Chemistry
Ecology
Environmental Research
Experiment Stations
Genetic Engineering
Geology
Medical Research
Nuclear Physics
Nursing Research
Physics
Physiology
Planetariums
Research and Development
Science History
Science Interests
Scientific and Technical Information
Scientific Methodology

Scientists   JUL. 1966
Postings: 2,378   GC: 640
BT Professional Personnel
Scientific Personnel
RT Engineers
Experimenter Characteristics
Researchers
Scholarship
Science Careers
Science History
Social Scientists

Scope of Bargaining   OCT. 1980
Postings: 88   GC: 630
SN The topics and issues accepted or con-
tested as appropriate for consideration
in collective bargaining
BT Collective Bargaining
RT Employment Practices
Fringe Benefits
Job Development
Job Training

Leaves of Absence
Overtime
Personnel Policy
Premium Pay
Promotion (Occupational)
Released Time
Retirement Benefits
Salaries
Salary Wage Differentials
Vacations
Wages
Work Environment
Working Hours

Score Reading
USE Music Reading

Score Theory
USE Test Theory

Scores   OCT. 1970
Postings: 3,988   GC: 820
SN Results, usually in numerical form, of a
test or measure
UF Test Scores
NT Cutting Scores
Equated Scores
Grade Equivalent Scores
Raw Scores
True Scores
Weighted Scores
BT Data
RT Concurrent Validity
Correlation
Error of Measurement
Generalizability Theory
Grades (Scholastic)
Interrater Reliability
Item Response Theory
Measurement
Predictive Validity
Scoring
Scoring Formulas
Standards
Statistical Analysis
Statistical Distributions
Test Anxiety
Test Interpretation
Test Items
Test Norms
Test Reliability
Test Results
Test Score Decline
Test Scoring Machines
Test Theory
Test Use
Test Validity
Test Wiseness
Testing
Tests

Scoring   JUL. 1966
Postings: 2,182   GC: 820
SN Process of systematically assigning val-
ues (usually numerical, but also includ-
ing letter marks and verbal comments)
to the results of tests, questionnaires,
etc.
BT Measurement
RT Answer Keys
Answer Sheets
Error of Measurement
Grade Inflation
Grading
Holistic Evaluation
Interrater Reliability
Item Response Theory
Objective Tests
Pass Fail Grading
Questionnaires
Scaling
Scores
Scoring Formulas
Scoring Rubrics
Test Items
Test Manuals
Test Scoring Machines
Test Theory
Testing

Testing Problems
Tests

Scoring Formulas   JAN. 1971
Postings: 426   GC: 820
SN Formulas by which tests, especially ob-
jective tests, are scored
BT Measurement Techniques
RT Confidence Testing
Cutting Scores
Guessing (Tests)
Multiple Choice Tests
Objective Tests
Raw Scores
Scores
Scoring
Test Interpretation
Test Manuals
Test Wiseness
Weighted Scores

Scoring Keys
USE Answer Keys

Scoring Rubrics   JUN. 2000
Postings: 143   GC: 820
SN Evaluation tools, usually grids, that list
the criteria for a task or performance,
and articulate gradations of quality for
each criterion
UF Assessment Rubrics
Rubrics (Scoring Guides)
BT Evaluation Methods
RT Alternative Assessment
Evaluation Criteria
Grading
Performance
Performance Based Assessment
Scoring
Self Evaluation (Individuals)
Student Evaluation
Teacher Evaluation
Writing Evaluation

Scots Gaelic   APR. 1990
Postings: 14   GC: 440
SN The Celtic language native to the Hebrides
and the highlands of Scotland
UF Gaelic (Scottish)
BT Indo European Languages

Screen Design (Computers)   AUG. 1994
Postings: 223   GC: 710
SN The arrangement of the elements on
a computer screen—includes the con-
text, amount, and density of information
presented and the manner of presenta-
tion, e.g., capitals vs. lower case, in-
terlinear spacing, line length, row or
columnal format, etc. (Note: Prior to
Aug94, "Screen Format" was the pre-
ferred Identifier for this concept)
UF Computer Display Design
Display Layout (Computers)
Screen Format
BT Computer System Design
RT Computer Graphics
Computers
Display Systems
Screens (Displays)
Video Display Terminals

Screen Education
USE Film Study

Screen Format
USE Screen Design (Computers)

Screening Tests   JUL. 1966
Postings: 2,786   GC: 830
SN Tests used to identify individuals who
are likely to benefit from, or have diffi-
culty in, some program or treatment, or
who should be examined in greater depth
BT Tests
RT Aptitude Tests

= Two or more Descriptors are used to represent this term.
The term's main entry shows the appropriate coordination.

Auditory Tests
College Entrance Examinations
Competitive Selection
Diagnostic Tests
Disability Identification
Early Identification
Identification
Physical Examinations
Placement
Preschool Tests
Prognostic Tests
Reading Readiness Tests
School Readiness Tests
Vision Tests

Screens (Displays)   MAY 1971
Postings: 119   GC: 910
SN   Surfaces on which images are projected
     or formed
BT   Visual Aids
RT   Audiovisual Aids
     Display Aids
     Exhibits
     Projection Equipment
     Screen Design (Computers)

Scripts   SEP. 1969
Postings: 511   GC: 730
SN   The written texts (with directions) of
     stage plays, screenplays, or radio or
     television broadcasts
BT   Drama
     Literary Genres
RT   Comedy
     Playwriting
     Soap Operas
     Tragedy

Scuba Diving
USE Underwater Diving

Sculpture   JUL. 1966
Postings: 428   GC: 420
BT   Visual Arts
RT   Art Products
     Clay
     Relief (Art)
     Welding

SDI
USE Selective Dissemination of Information

Seafarers   MAR. 1980
Postings: 104   GC: 640
SN   Those engaged in travel on the seas,
     either as an occupational or recreational
     pursuit
UF   Mariners
     Seamen (1969 1980)
BT   Groups
RT   Boat Operators
     Marine Technicians
     Maritime Education
     Military Personnel
     Navigation
     Oceanography
     Recreational Activities
     Sailing
     Semiskilled Workers

Seafood (1968 1980)
USE Food

Sealants
USE Adhesives

Seamen (1969 1980)
USE Seafarers

Seamstresses (1968 1980)
USE Needle Trades

Search and Seizure   NOV. 1971
Postings: 320   GC: 610
BT   Police Action
RT   Civil Liberties
     Civil Rights
     Constitutional Law
     Crime
     Due Process
     Evidence (Legal)
     Police School Relationship
     School Law
     Student Rights
     Student School Relationship

Search Committees (Personnel)   AUG. 1986
Postings: 109   GC: 320
SN   Committees appointed or elected to iden-
     tify and select personnel for professional
     positions
UF   Selection Committees (Personnel)
BT   Committees
RT   Administrator Selection
     Advisory Committees
     Personnel Selection

Search Intermediaries   AUG. 1994
Postings: 130   GC: 710
SN   Individuals trained in database search-
     ing who perform online or other searches
     for requesters
BT   Information Scientists
RT   Information Needs
     Information Retrieval
     Librarians
     Online Searching
     Reference Services
     Search Strategies
     User Needs (Information)

Search Strategies   AUG. 1968
Postings: 2,704   GC: 710
SN   Comprehensive plans for finding in-
     formation—includes defining the infor-
     mation need, and determining the form
     in which it is needed, if it exists, where it
     is located, how it is organized, and how
     to retrieve it
BT   Information Seeking
RT   Computer Literacy
     Databases
     Indexing
     Information Literacy
     Information Needs
     Information Retrieval
     Information Storage
     Information Systems
     Information Utilization
     Online Searching
     Operations Research
     Reference Services
     Relevance (Information Retrieval)
     Research Design
     Search Intermediaries
     User Needs (Information)

Seasonal Employment   JUL. 1966
Postings: 127   GC: 630
UF   Seasonal Labor (1966 1980)
BT   Employment
RT   Agriculture
     Braceros
     Migrant Employment
     Migrant Workers
     Multiple Employment
     Seasonal Laborers
     Student Employment
     Temporary Employment
     Underemployment
     Youth Employment

Seasonal Labor (1966 1980)
USE Seasonal Employment

Seasonal Laborers   JUL. 1966
Postings: 157   GC: 630
BT   Agricultural Laborers
RT   Braceros
     Migrant Employment
     Migrant Workers
     Seasonal Employment
     Sharecroppers

Seat Belts
USE Restraints (Vehicle Safety)

Second Language Books
USE Foreign Language Books

Second Language Enrollment
USE Language Enrollment

Second Language Films
USE Foreign Language Films

Second Language Instruction   MAR. 1980
Postings: 15,122   GC: 450
SN   Instruction in a language that is not
     native to the learner (Note: Prior to Mar80,
     this concept was indexed under "Lan-
     guage Instruction")
UF   Foreign Language Instruction
     Foreign Language Teaching
     State Foreign Language Supervisors
       (1967 1980) #
BT   Humanities Instruction
RT   Applied Linguistics
     Audiolingual Methods
     Bilingual Education
     Bilingual Education Programs
     Bilingual Instructional Materials
     College Second Language Programs
     Conversational Language Courses
     Dialogs (Language)
     English (Second Language)
     English for Special Purposes
     Error Analysis (Language)
     FLES
     Grammar Translation Method
     Immersion Programs
     Intensive Language Courses
     Language Enrichment
     Language Enrollment
     Language Laboratories
     Language of Instruction
     Language Proficiency
     Language Teachers
     Languages
     Languages for Special Purposes
     Multilevel Classes (Second Language
       Instruction)
     Native Speakers
     Notional Functional Syllabi
     Pattern Drills (Language)
     Second Language Learning
     Second Language Programs
     Second Languages
     Suggestopedia
     Whole Language Approach

Second Language Learning   JUL. 1966
Postings: 17,975   GC: 450
UF   Foreign Language Learning
     Language Learning (Foreign)
BT   Learning
RT   Audiolingual Methods
     Basic Writing
     Bilingual Education
     Bilingual Instructional Materials
     Bilingualism
     College Second Language Programs
     Communicative Competence
       (Languages)
     Contrastive Linguistics
     Conversational Language Courses
     Cultural Awareness
     Dictation
     English (Second Language)
     English for Special Purposes
     Error Analysis (Language)
     FLES
     Foreign Language Books
     Foreign Language Films
     Foreign Language Periodicals
     Immersion Programs
     Intensive Language Courses
     Interference (Language)

Interlanguage
Language Aptitude
Language Enrichment
Language Fluency
Language of Instruction
Language Proficiency
Language Skill Attrition
Language Skills
Language Tests
Languages for Special Purposes
Limited English Speaking
Linguistic Input
Metalinguistics
Modern Language Curriculum
Modern Languages
Multilevel Classes (Second Language
  Instruction)
Multilingual Materials
Notional Functional Syllabi
Oral Language
Second Language Instruction
Second Language Programs
Second Languages
Threshold Level (Languages)
Unwritten Languages

Second Language Periodicals
USE Foreign Language Periodicals

Second Language Programs   MAR. 1980
Postings: 1,542   GC: 450
SN   (Note: Do not use for instructional ma-
     terials that refer to themselves as
     programs—prior to Mar80, this con-
     cept was indexed under "Language Pro-
     grams")
UF   FLES Programs (1967 1980) #
     Foreign Language Programs
NT   College Second Language Programs
     Immersion Programs
BT   Programs
RT   Bilingual Education Programs
     Conversational Language Courses
     English (Second Language)
     FLES
     Intensive Language Courses
     Language Enrollment
     Language Laboratories
     Modern Language Curriculum
     Multilevel Classes (Second Language
       Instruction)
     Native Speakers
     Notional Functional Syllabi
     Second Language Instruction
     Second Language Learning
     Second Languages

Second Language Teachers
USE Language Teachers

Second Languages   JUL. 1966
Postings: 2,306   GC: 450
SN   Any languages other than one's native or
     mother tongue, usually learned by for-
     mal language instruction (Note: Prior to
     Mar80, the instruction "Foreign Lan-
     guages, USE Languages" was carried in
     the Thesaurus)
UF   Foreign Languages
NT   English (Second Language)
BT   Language
RT   Bilingual Education
     Bilingual Instructional Materials
     Bilingual Teacher Aides
     Bilingual Teachers
     Bilingualism
     FLES
     Immersion Programs
     Language Dominance
     Language of Instruction
     Language Planning
     Native Speakers
     Second Language Instruction
     Second Language Learning
     Second Language Programs

Secondary Education   JUL. 1966
Postings: 76,961   GC: 340
SN   Education provided in grade 7, 8, or 9

= Two or more Descriptors are used to represent this term.
The term's main entry shows the appropriate coordination.

through grade 12 (Note: Also appears in the list of mandatory educational level Descriptors)
UF Secondary Grades (1966 1980)
NT College Preparation
BT Elementary Secondary Education
RT Comprehensive Programs
    Continuation Students
    Grade 10
    Grade 11
    Grade 12
    Grade 7
    Grade 8
    Grade 9
    High School Equivalency Programs
    High Schools
    Junior High Schools
    Pretechnology Programs
    Secondary School Curriculum
    Secondary School Students
    Secondary School Teachers
    Secondary Schools
    Vocational Education

Secondary Employment
USE Multiple Employment

Secondary Grades (1966 1980)
USE Secondary Education

Secondary School Counseling
USE School Counseling

Secondary School Counselors (1967 1980)
USE School Counselors

Secondary School Curriculum   *MAR. 1980*
    Postings: 2,271   GC: 350
UF High School Curriculum (1967 1980)
NT Secondary School Mathematics
    Secondary School Science
BT Curriculum
RT High Schools
    Secondary Education
    Secondary Schools

Secondary School Guidance
USE School Guidance

Secondary School Libraries
USE School Libraries

Secondary School Mathematics   *JUL. 1966*
    Postings: 7,473   GC: 480
BT Mathematics Curriculum
    Secondary School Curriculum
RT College Mathematics
    Elementary School Mathematics
    Mathematics
    Mathematics Education
    Mathematics Instruction
    Modern Mathematics

Secondary School Science   *JUL. 1966*
    Postings: 14,981   GC: 490
BT Science Curriculum
    Secondary School Curriculum
RT College Science
    Elementary School Science
    Science Departments
    Science Education
    Science Instruction

Secondary School Students   *JUL. 1966*
    Postings: 5,646   GC: 360
SN (Note: Coordinate with the appropriate mandatory educational level Descriptor)
NT High School Students
    Junior High School Students
BT Students
RT Adolescents
    Secondary Education
    Secondary Schools

Secondary School Teachers   *JUL. 1966*
    Postings: 4,801   GC: 360
UF High School Teachers
    Junior High School Teachers
BT Teachers
RT Middle School Teachers
    Public School Teachers
    Secondary Education
    Secondary Schools

Secondary Schools   *JUL. 1966*
    Postings: 3,206   GC: 340
NT High Schools
    Junior High Schools
BT Schools
RT Affiliated Schools
    Laboratory Schools
    Professional Development Schools
    Secondary Education
    Secondary School Curriculum
    Secondary School Students
    Secondary School Teachers
    Vocational Schools

Secretaries   *JUL. 1966*
    Postings: 525   GC: 640
UF Administrative Secretaries
    Executive Secretaries
    Legal Secretaries
    Medical Secretaries
NT School Secretaries
BT Clerical Workers
RT Dictation
    Medical Assistants
    Shorthand
    Typewriting
    Word Processing

Sectarian Colleges
USE Church Related Colleges

Security (Psychology)   *MAR. 1978*
    Postings: 294   GC: 230
SN Being or feeling free from risk or uncertainty (Note: The Descriptor "Security," without the parenthetical qualifier, was used from 1967 to Mar78)
UF Emotional Security
    Insecurity (1966 1980)
BT Psychological Needs
RT Emotional Experience
    Job Security
    Trust (Psychology)

Security Personnel   *MAR. 1978*
    Postings: 150   GC: 640
SN Persons employed by an institution or organization to provide physical protection from hostile acts or influences
UF Guards (Security)
BT Personnel
RT Alarm Systems
    Computer Security
    Crime
    Crime Prevention
    Law Enforcement
    Police
    Safety
    School Personnel
    School Safety
    School Security
    School Vandalism
    Stealing
    Vandalism

Security Systems (Alarms)
USE Alarm Systems

Security (1967 1978)   *MAR. 1978*
    Postings: 247   GC: 210
SN Invalid Descriptor—use a more precise Descriptor such as "Security (Psychology)," "School Security," "Computer Security," or "National Security," or use an Identifier such as "Building Security"

Sedatives   *APR. 1969*
    Postings: 92   GC: 210
UF Barbiturates
    Hypnotics
    Tranquilizing Drugs
BT Narcotics
RT Drug Abuse
    Drug Rehabilitation
    Drug Use
    Physiology
    Sensory Experience

Segregated Public Facilities (1966 1980)
USE Public Facilities
AND Racial Segregation

Segregation (Racial)
USE Racial Segregation

Segregationist Groups
USE Segregationist Organizations

Segregationist Organizations   *JUL. 1966*
    Postings: 19   GC: 540
SN Organizations whose purpose is to prevent desegregation/integration of certain ethnic or racial groups in a community or society
UF Segregationist Groups
BT Organizations (Groups)
RT Apartheid
    Black Power
    Civil Disobedience
    Civil Rights
    Nazism
    Racial Discrimination
    Racial Segregation
    Social Discrimination

Seismology   *SEP. 1969*
    Postings: 121   GC: 490
NT Plate Tectonics
BT Earth Science
RT Earthquakes
    Geology
    Geophysics
    Physical Geography
    Soil Science

Seizures   *JUL. 1966*
    Postings: 142   GC: 220
BT Diseases
RT Epilepsy
    Neurological Impairments
    Physical Health
    Special Health Problems

Selection   *JUL. 1966*
    Postings: 1,476   GC: 110
SN The process of choosing from among a number of alternatives, usually on the basis of fitness, excellence, or other criteria (Note: Use a more specific term if possible)
NT Career Choice
    Competitive Selection
    Computer Selection
    Course Selection (Students)
    Elections
    Mate Selection
    Media Selection
    Personnel Selection
    School Choice
    Site Selection
    Test Selection
RT Credentials
    Evaluation Criteria
    Prerequisites
    Recruitment
    Selection Tools

Selection Committees (Personnel)
USE Search Committees (Personnel)

Selection Tools   *NOV. 1994*
    Postings: 142   GC: 710
SN Items used to assist in selection activities, e.g., choosing reading materials, acquiring merchandise—most commonly refers to selection tools used by librarians, including such items as bibliographies, reviews, subject lists, and core collection lists
UF Book Selection Aids
RT Library Collection Development
    Purchasing
    Reference Materials
    Selection

Selective Admission   *OCT. 1979*
    Postings: 535   GC: 320
SN Process by which an institution, or a program area within the institution, selects students for admission from an applicant pool, considering such factors as academic background, race, sex, or geographic origin (Note: If appropriate, use the more precise term "Selective Colleges")
UF Preferential Admission
    Restrictive Admission
    Special Admission
BT Admission (School)
RT Academic Standards
    Admission Criteria
    Affirmative Action
    College Admission
    Competitive Selection
    Desegregation Methods
    Educational Discrimination
    Equal Education
    Open Enrollment
    Quotas
    Racial Discrimination
    Residence Requirements
    Reverse Discrimination
    Sex Discrimination

Selective Colleges   *OCT. 1983*
    Postings: 202   GC: 340
SN Colleges with especially high academic standards
UF Elite Colleges
BT Colleges
RT Academic Standards
    College Admission
    Elitism
    Prestige
    Private Colleges

Selective Dissemination of Information   *JUN. 1981*
    Postings: 203   GC: 710
SN An information service, usually computer-based, that periodically distributes copies or notices of current documents to its users—such distribution is often based on the users' own statements (sometimes called "interest profiles") of what they need
UF Current Awareness Services
    SDI
BT Information Dissemination
RT Computer Oriented Programs
    Information Needs
    Information Retrieval
    Library Services
    Online Searching
    User Needs (Information)

Self Abuse
USE Self Destructive Behavior

Self Actualization   *JUL. 1966*
    Postings: 3,621   GC: 120
SN The belief in or the process of developing the actuality of one's idealized image
UF Growth Motivation
    Self Development
    Self Realization
    Self Utilization
BT Psychological Needs
RT Behavior Development

= Two or more Descriptors are used to represent this term.
The term's main entry shows the appropriate coordination.

Careers
Empowerment
Gestalt Therapy
Humanistic Education
Identification (Psychology)
Individual Development
Individual Power
Individual Psychology
Individualism
Job Satisfaction
Life Events
Life Satisfaction
Marital Satisfaction
Mental Health
Midlife Transitions
Morale
Need Gratification
Personal Autonomy
Personality Development
Reality Therapy
Role Perception
Role Theory
Self Concept
Self Concept Measures
Self Congruence
Self Determination
Self Efficacy
Self Evaluation (Individuals)
Self Help Programs
Self Motivation
Social Psychology
Values Clarification

Self Advocacy   *JAN. 1997*
    Postings: 136   GC: 120
SN The process of exercising, defending,
    and promoting one's rights—most often
    refers to people with disabilities speak-
    ing and acting on behalf of themselves
BT Advocacy
RT Assertiveness
    Child Advocacy
    Disabilities
    Individual Power
    Self Determination
    Self Help Programs

Self Appraisal
USE Self Evaluation (Individuals)

Self Assessment
USE Self Evaluation (Individuals)

Self Attitude Tests
USE Self Concept Measures

Self Bias
USE Egocentrism

Self Care Skills   *JUL. 1966*
    Postings: 906   GC: 220
SN Ability to feed, dress, and groom oneself
BT Daily Living Skills
RT Adaptive Behavior (of Disabled)
    Clothing
    Disabilities
    Eating Habits
    Habit Formation
    Health
    Hygiene
    Maturity (Individuals)
    Toilet Training

Self Centeredness
USE Egocentrism

Self Concept   *JUL. 1966*
    Postings: 14,526   GC: 230
SN Individuals' perceptions of themselves
UF Ego
    Self Image
    Self Knowledge
    Self Understanding
NT Body Image
    Self Congruence
    Self Esteem

RT Adventure Education
    Aspiration
    Attribution Theory
    Consciousness Raising
    Defense Mechanisms
    Delay of Gratification
    Egocentrism
    Ethnicity
    Extraversion Introversion
    Femininity
    Gestalt Therapy
    Humanistic Education
    Identification (Psychology)
    Locus of Control
    Masculinity
    Morale
    Personality
    Perspective Taking
    Phenomenology
    Racial Identification
    Reality Therapy
    Reference Groups
    Self Actualization
    Self Concept Measures
    Self Disclosure (Individuals)
    Self Evaluation (Individuals)
    Self Motivation
    Sexual Identity
    Significant Others
    Social Cognition

Self Concept Measures   *MAR. 1980*
    Postings: 897   GC: 830
UF Self Attitude Tests
    Self Concept Tests (1971 1980)
BT Personality Measures
RT Affective Measures
    Identification (Psychology)
    Q Methodology
    Self Actualization
    Self Concept
    Self Congruence
    Self Esteem
    Self Evaluation (Individuals)

Self Concept Tests (1971 1980)
USE Self Concept Measures

Self Confidence
USE Self Esteem

Self Congruence   *JUL. 1966*
    Postings: 199   GC: 230
SN Conscious integration of an experience
    to become a part of the self
BT Congruence (Psychology)
    Self Concept
RT Behavior
    Meditation
    Psychological Characteristics
    Psychotherapy
    Self Actualization
    Self Concept Measures

Self Contained Classrooms   *JUL. 1966*
    Postings: 167   GC: 310
SN Classes having the same teacher or team
    of teachers for all or most of the daily
    session (Note: Prior to Mar80, the in-
    struction "Traditional Classrooms, USE
    Traditional Schools" was carried in the
    Thesaurus)
UF Traditional Classrooms
BT Classrooms
RT Class Organization
    Conventional Instruction
    Open Education
    Traditional Schools

Self Control   *JUL. 1966*
    Postings: 1,689   GC: 120
UF Impulse Control
    Self Discipline
    Self Restraint
NT Delay of Gratification
    Self Management
BT Behavior
RT Behavior Modification

    Behavior Problems
    Biofeedback
    Child Behavior
    Cognitive Restructuring
    Compliance (Psychology)
    Defense Mechanisms
    Discipline
    Individual Power
    Inhibition
    Maturity (Individuals)
    Metacognition
    Personal Autonomy
    Personality Traits
    Resistance to Temptation
    Self Destructive Behavior
    Self Determination
    Self Efficacy
    Self Motivation
    Sportsmanship

Self Destructive Behavior   *AUG. 1986*
    Postings: 254   GC: 230
SN Acting or tending to harm or destroy
    oneself (Note: For self-infliction of physi-
    cal injury, use "Self Injurious Behavior")
UF Self Abuse
NT Self Injurious Behavior
    Suicide
BT Behavior
RT Antisocial Behavior
    Behavior Disorders
    Behavior Problems
    Mental Disorders
    Personality Problems
    Psychological Patterns
    Self Control
    Substance Abuse

Self Determination   *MAR. 1978*
    Postings: 1,064   GC: 610
SN The right, power, opportunity, etc., of
    both individuals and peoples to deter-
    mine their own destinies (Note: Prior to
    Mar78, the instruction "Self Determina-
    tion, USE Individual Power" was carried
    in the Thesaurus)
UF Destiny Control
    Self Government
NT Tribal Sovereignty
RT Black Power
    Community Control
    Consciousness Raising
    Democracy
    Educational Policy
    Empowerment
    Ethnic Groups
    Foreign Policy
    Freedom
    Individual Power
    Individualism
    Institutional Autonomy
    Minority Groups
    Nationalism
    Personal Autonomy
    Professional Autonomy
    Public Policy
    School District Autonomy
    Self Actualization
    Self Advocacy
    Self Control
    Self Directed Groups
    Self Help Programs
    Trust Responsibility (Government)

Self Development
USE Self Actualization

Self Directed Classrooms (1966 1980)
                                 JUN. 1980
    Postings: 198   GC: 310
SN Invalid Descriptor—used inconsistently
    in indexing—see the more precise
    Descriptors "Open Education," "Inde-
    pendent Study," "Individualized Instruc-
    tion," and "Student Projects"

Self Directed Groups   *JUL. 1966*
    Postings: 448   GC: 520
SN Groups with a passive leader or without

    a specified leader in which all members
    mutually agree on group goals and pro-
    cedures
UF Leaderless Groups
    Self Guided Groups
BT Groups
RT Cooperative Learning
    Group Activities
    Group Dynamics
    Group Experience
    Interaction Process Analysis
    Motivation Techniques
    Open Education
    Self Determination
    Self Management

Self Directed Learning
USE Independent Study

Self Discipline
USE Self Control

Self Disclosure (Individuals)   *OCT. 1983*
    Postings: 382   GC: 120
SN Revealing information about oneself to
    others
BT Disclosure
RT Counseling Techniques
    Interpersonal Communication
    Intimacy
    Self Concept
    Self Expression

Self Efficacy   *JUN. 1988*
    Postings: 1,442   GC: 120
SN Belief or expectation about one's own
    ability to perform a given task success-
    fully
UF Efficacy Expectation
BT Self Esteem
RT Achievement
    Behavior Development
    Cognitive Structures
    Expectation
    Individual Power
    Learning Theories
    Metacognition
    Self Actualization
    Self Control
    Self Motivation

Self Employment   *DEC. 1989*
    Postings: 278   GC: 630
SN State of earning income from one's own
    business, trade, or profession rather than
    receiving salary or wages from an em-
    ployer
BT Employment
RT Business
    Business Administration
    Careers
    Economic Opportunities
    Employment Level
    Employment Patterns
    Employment Potential
    Entrepreneurship
    Small Businesses

Self Empowerment
USE Empowerment

Self Esteem   *JUL. 1966*
    Postings: 6,989   GC: 120
SN Individuals' value judgments of them-
    selves
UF Self Confidence
NT Self Efficacy
BT Self Concept
RT Assertiveness
    Human Dignity
    Personality Traits
    Resilience (Personality)
    Self Concept Measures
    Self Evaluation (Individuals)

    # = Two or more Descriptors are used to represent this term.
    The term's main entry shows the appropriate coordination.

Self Evaluation (Groups)   MAR. 1980
      Postings: 2,061   GC: 810
SN   Assessment of an institution, organiza-
      tion, program, etc., by its members or
      sponsors (Note: Prior to Mar80, the in-
      struction "Institutional Self Study, USE
      Institutional Research" was carried in
      the Thesaurus—this concept was also
      sometimes indexed under "Self Evalua-
      tion")
UF   Institutional Self Study
      Internal Review (Organizations)
      Organizational Self Study
BT   Evaluation
RT   College Outcomes Assessment
      Formative Evaluation
      Institutional Evaluation
      Institutional Research
      Needs Assessment
      Organizational Effectiveness
      Policy Formation
      Program Evaluation
      Summative Evaluation

Self Evaluation (Individuals)   MAR. 1980
      Postings: 5,726   GC: 120
SN   Individuals' assessment of themselves
UF   Self Appraisal
      Self Assessment
BT   Evaluation
RT   Alternative Assessment
      Metacognition
      Portfolio Assessment
      Reflective Teaching
      Reminiscence
      Scoring Rubrics
      Self Actualization
      Self Concept
      Self Concept Measures
      Self Esteem
      Sensitivity Training
      Transactional Analysis

Self Evaluation (1966 1980)   MAR. 1980
      Postings: 2,492   GC: 820
SN   Invalid Descriptor—used for personal,
      organizational, or program self eval-
      uation—see "Self Evaluation (Individu-
      als)" and "Self Evaluation (Groups)" re-
      spectively for these concepts

Self Expression   JUL. 1966
      Postings: 1,308   GC: 120
RT   Art Expression
      Art Therapy
      Assertiveness
      Catharsis
      Creative Expression
      Creativity
      Dance Therapy
      Dramatic Play
      Individual Power
      Individualism
      Interpersonal Communication
      Journal Writing
      Language Arts
      Movement Education
      Music Therapy
      Self Disclosure (Individuals)
      Transactional Analysis

Self Fulfilling Prophecies   DEC. 1989
      Postings: 104   GC: 120
SN   Expectations and predictions that serve
      to bring about their own fulfillment, e.g.,
      prophecies of success or failure often
      encourage or inhibit behaviors that influ-
      ence or even decide outcomes
UF   Pygmalion Effect
BT   Expectation
RT   Attitudes
      Attribution Theory
      Behavior
      Congruence (Psychology)
      Labeling (of Persons)
      Motivation
      Prediction
      Social Psychology
      Social Reinforcement

      Stereotypes
      Teacher Expectations of Students

Self Government
USE   Self Determination

Self Growth
USE   Individual Development

Self Guided Groups
USE   Self Directed Groups

Self Help Devices (Disabled)
USE   Assistive Devices (for Disabled)

Self Help Programs   JUL. 1966
      Postings: 874   GC: 520
SN   Programs in which communities, groups,
      or individuals help themselves
BT   Improvement Programs
RT   Behavior Modification
      Biofeedback
      Community Action
      Individual Development
      Lifelong Learning
      Rehabilitation Programs
      Self Actualization
      Self Advocacy
      Self Determination
      Self Management

Self Image
USE   Self Concept

Self Injurious Behavior   OCT. 1993
      Postings: 205   GC: 230
SN   Self-infliction of physical injury, through
      such behaviors as head banging, bit-
      ing, scratching, hair pulling, punching,
      pinching, and gouging—may occur
      among normal populations, but with
      greater frequency, severity, and chronicity
      among the developmentally disabled
UF   Head Banging
      Self Mutilation (1977 1993)
BT   Self Destructive Behavior
RT   Behavior Disorders
      Emotional Disturbances
      Psychopathology
      Suicide
      Violence

Self Instruction
USE   Independent Study

Self Instruction Aids
USE   Autoinstructional Aids

Self Instruction Materials
USE   Programmed Instructional Materials

Self Knowledge
USE   Self Concept

Self Management   OCT. 1993
      Postings: 540   GC: 120
SN   Deliberate use of learned strategies to
      maintain or modify one's own attitudes
      and actions—such strategies include goal
      setting, self-monitoring, self-correcting,
      and self-solicitation of feedback
UF   Behavioral Self Management
BT   Self Control
RT   Independent Living
      Independent Study
      Self Directed Groups
      Self Help Programs
      Self Reward
      Stress Management
      Time Management

Self Motivation   AUG. 1989
      Postings: 352   GC: 120
SN   Need or desire that arises from within
      the individual and causes action toward
      some goal—doing, or not doing, some-
      thing simply because one wants to, irre-
      spective of external stimuli
UF   Intrinsic Motivation
BT   Motivation
RT   Achievement Need
      Aspiration
      Delay of Gratification
      Fear of Success
      Goal Orientation
      Help Seeking
      Incentives
      Learning Motivation
      Metacognition
      Personal Autonomy
      Personality
      Self Actualization
      Self Concept
      Self Control
      Self Efficacy
      Self Reward

Self Mutilation (1977 1993)
USE   Self Injurious Behavior

Self Paced Instruction
USE   Individualized Instruction
AND   Pacing

Self Pacing
USE   Pacing

Self Pacing Machines (1966 1980)
USE   Teaching Machines

Self Realization
USE   Self Actualization

Self Restraint
USE   Self Control

Self Reward   JUL. 1966
      Postings: 158   GC: 120
BT   Rewards
RT   Delay of Gratification
      Incentives
      Positive Reinforcement
      Self Management
      Self Motivation
      Social Exchange Theory

Self Supporting Students   MAR. 1980
      Postings: 139   GC: 360
SN   Students who are legally (or perhaps
      financially) independent of their parents
      or former guardians
UF   Emancipated Students (1975 1980)
      Independent Students (Self Support-
      ing)
BT   Students
RT   Adult Students
      College Students
      Financial Needs
      Married Students
      Need Analysis (Student Financial Aid)
      Parent Financial Contribution
      Parent Student Relationship
      Student College Relationship
      Student Costs
      Student Loan Programs
      Student Rights
      Student School Relationship

Self Teaching
USE   Independent Study

Self Understanding
USE   Self Concept

Self Utilization
USE   Self Actualization

Semantic Differential   OCT. 1972
      Postings: 457   GC: 830
SN   Method of measuring attitudes, values,
      or the connotative meaning of words
      through the use of pairs of bipolar adjec-
      tives
BT   Attitude Measures
      Rating Scales
RT   Adjectives
      Attitudes
      Multidimensional Scaling
      Personality Measures
      Values

Semantics   JUL. 1966
      Postings: 5,774   GC: 450
SN   Study of meanings in language and of
      changes in those meanings
UF   General Semantics
      Word Meaning
NT   Lexicology
BT   Descriptive Linguistics
      Semiotics
RT   Coherence
      Componential Analysis
      Computational Linguistics
      Connected Discourse
      Decoding (Reading)
      Deep Structure
      Definitions
      Discourse Analysis
      Error Analysis (Language)
      Etymology
      Language Patterns
      Negative Forms (Language)
      Pragmatics
      Syntax

Semester Division (1966 1980)
USE   Semester System

Semester System   MAR. 1980
      Postings: 114   GC: 350
SN   Division of the academic year into two
      equal terms
UF   Semester Division (1966 1980)
BT   School Schedules
RT   Quarter System
      Trimester System

Semiconductor Devices   JAN. 1970
      Postings: 103   GC: 910
NT   Transistors
BT   Electronic Equipment
RT   Calculators
      Crystallography
      Electronics Industry
      Lasers
      Microelectronics
      Superconductors

Seminaries
USE   Church Related Colleges
AND   Theological Education

Seminars   JUL. 1966
      Postings: 2,163   GC: 350
UF   Student Seminars (1966 1980)
BT   Meetings
RT   Institutes (Training Programs)
      Minicourses
      Workshops

Semiology
USE   Semiotics

Semiotics   JUL. 1966
      Postings: 577   GC: 450
SN   The general philosophical theory of signs
      and symbols, dealing especially with their
      function in languages, and including
      syntactics, semantics, and pragmatics

= Two or more Descriptors are used to represent this term.
The term's main entry shows the appropriate coordination.

(Note: Prior to Mar80, the use of this term was not restricted by a Scope Note.)
UF Semiology
NT Pragmatics
    Semantics
BT Linguistic Theory
    Philosophy
RT Hermeneutics
    Language
    Language Patterns
    Linguistics
    Symbolic Language
    Syntax
    Verbal Communication
    Visual Literacy

Semiskilled Occupations   *JUL. 1966*
    Postings: 81   GC: 640
SN Occupations requiring skill in a limited range of activities and demanding less independent judgment, training, and experience than skilled occupations require
BT Occupations
RT Blue Collar Occupations
    Building Trades
    Data Processing Occupations
    Electrical Occupations
    Laundry Drycleaning Occupations
    Metal Working
    Needle Trades
    Semiskilled Workers
    Skilled Occupations
    Technical Occupations
    Trade and Industrial Education
    Unskilled Occupations

Semiskilled Workers   *JUL. 1966*
    Postings: 71   GC: 630
SN Operators/operatives possessing skill in a limited range of activities that demand less training, experience, and independent judgment than is required of skilled workers
NT Animal Caretakers
    Boat Operators
    Grounds Keepers
    Nursery Workers (Horticulture)
    Sewing Machine Operators
BT Nonprofessional Personnel
RT Employees
    Seafarers
    Semiskilled Occupations
    Skilled Workers
    Trade and Industrial Education
    Unskilled Workers
    Working Class

Semitic Languages   *JUL. 1966*
    Postings: 86   GC: 440
NT Amharic
    Arabic
    Hebrew
BT Afro Asiatic Languages

Senators
USE Legislators

Senile Dementia Alzheimers Type
USE Alzheimers Disease

Senior Citizens (1967 1980)
USE Older Adults

Senior High School Students
USE High School Students

Senior High Schools (1966 1980)
USE High Schools

Senior Teacher Role (1966 1980)
USE Master Teachers
AND Teacher Role

Seniority   *JAN. 1978*
    Postings: 167   GC: 630
SN Priority in status or rank derived from age or length of service
BT Status
RT Academic Rank (Professional)
    Aging in Academia
    Employees
    Employer Employee Relationship
    Employment
    Employment Experience
    Employment Level
    Employment Practices
    Job Layoff
    Labor Problems
    Personnel Data
    Personnel Policy
    Promotion (Occupational)
    Reduction in Force
    Tenure

Seniors (1966 1980) (Grade 12)
USE High School Seniors

Seniors (1966 1980) (Last Year Undergraduates)
USE College Seniors

Sensitivity Training   *JUL. 1966*
    Postings: 1,134   GC: 240
SN Technique in which group dynamics are used to increase participants' awareness of themselves, their interpersonal relationships, the group process, and larger social systems
UF Human Relations Training
    T Groups (1967 1980)
BT Training
RT Consciousness Raising
    Counseling Techniques
    Group Dynamics
    Group Therapy
    Humanistic Education
    Interpersonal Competence
    Laboratory Training
    Protocol Materials
    Self Evaluation (Individuals)

Sensory Aids   *JUL. 1966*
    Postings: 500   GC: 220
SN Devices and materials used to extend the functioning of the senses, most often including materials adapted for the visually or hearing impaired—also includes materials that have been translated from one sensory mode to another
NT Cochlear Implants
    Hearing Aids
    Low Vision Aids
    Raised Line Drawings
    Talking Books
RT Accessibility (for Disabled)
    Assistive Devices (for Disabled)
    Audiovisual Aids
    Braille
    Communication Aids (for Disabled)
    Electromechanical Aids
    Hearing Impairments
    Large Type Materials
    Loop Induction Systems
    Magnification Methods
    Manipulative Materials
    Sensory Training
    Tactile Adaptation
    Visual Impairments

Sensory Deprivation   *JUL. 1966*
    Postings: 117   GC: 110
UF Isolation (Perceptual)
    Perceptual Deprivation
BT Sensory Experience
RT Cognitive Processes
    Fatigue (Biology)
    Perception
    Physiology
    Psychology

Sensory Experience   *JUL. 1966*
    Postings: 944   GC: 110
NT Figural Aftereffects
    Sensory Deprivation
BT Experience
RT Aesthetic Values
    Auditory Perception
    Experiential Learning
    Habituation
    Learning Modalities
    Meditation
    Montessori Method
    Novelty (Stimulus Dimension)
    Pain
    Perception
    Perceptual Impairments
    Sedatives
    Sensory Integration
    Sensory Training
    Stimulants
    Stimuli
    Tactual Perception
    Visual Perception

Sensory Integration   *AUG. 1968*
    Postings: 452   GC: 110
SN The coordination of two or more perceptual modes (e.g., visual and tactile) while attending to a single phenomenon
UF Intersensory Integration
RT Auditory Training
    Multisensory Learning
    Neuropsychology
    Perception
    Perceptual Development
    Perceptual Impairments
    Perceptual Motor Learning
    Sensory Experience
    Sensory Training

Sensory Motor Learning
USE Perceptual Motor Learning

Sensory Training   *JUL. 1966*
    Postings: 376   GC: 400
NT Auditory Training
BT Training
RT Discrimination Learning
    Multisensory Learning
    Perceptual Development
    Perceptual Motor Learning
    Sensory Aids
    Sensory Experience
    Sensory Integration
    Tactual Perception
    Visual Discrimination
    Visual Perception

Sentence Combining   *JUN. 1977*
    Postings: 303   GC: 450
SN Combining a set of kernel sentences into a single complex or compound statement
UF Transformational Sentence Combining
BT Transformational Generative Grammar
RT Kernel Sentences
    Language Patterns
    Language Skills
    Sentence Structure
    Sentences
    Syntax
    Writing Exercises
    Writing Skills

Sentence Diagraming   *JUL. 1966*
    Postings: 65   GC: 450
RT Deep Structure
    Diagrams
    Grammar
    Language Patterns
    Linguistics
    Sentence Structure
    Sentences
    Structural Analysis (Linguistics)
    Surface Structure
    Syntax

Sentence Structure   *JUL. 1966*
    Postings: 3,257   GC: 450
BT Syntax
RT Adjectives
    Adverbs
    Capitalization (Alphabetic)
    Cohesion (Written Composition)
    Conjunctions
    Deep Structure
    Function Words
    Generative Grammar
    Grammar
    Kernel Sentences
    Nouns
    Parallelism (Literary)
    Prepositions
    Pronouns
    Punctuation
    Sentence Combining
    Sentence Diagraming
    Sentences
    Structural Analysis (Linguistics)
    Structural Grammar
    Structural Linguistics
    Suprasegmentals
    Surface Structure
    Tenses (Grammar)
    Text Structure
    Traditional Grammar
    Verbs
    Word Order

Sentences   *JUL. 1966*
    Postings: 904   GC: 450
SN Grammatically complete units of one or more words
NT Kernel Sentences
BT Paragraphs
RT Discourse Analysis
    Grammar
    Intonation
    Sentence Combining
    Sentence Diagraming
    Sentence Structure
    Syntax
    Writing (Composition)

Sentencing   *SEP. 1982*
    Postings: 129   GC: 520
SN Kind and duration of punishment for convicted offenses as specified by a court or judge
UF Prison Sentences
BT Law Enforcement
RT Correctional Institutions
    Court Judges
    Courts
    Crime
    Criminal Law
    Criminals
    Juries
    Prisoners
    Punishment

Separation Anxiety   *OCT. 1983*
    Postings: 232   GC: 230
SN Fear or distress occasioned by the threat or actuality of separation from significant persons or familiar surroundings—most frequently observed among young children when removed from a parent or parent substitute
BT Anxiety
RT Attachment Behavior
    Child Behavior
    Emotional Response
    Infant Behavior
    Reunions
    School Phobia

Sequential Approach   *JUL. 1966*
    Postings: 1,072   GC: 310
UF Sequential Programs (1966 1980)
    Sequential Reading Programs (1966 1980)
BT Methods
RT Adaptive Testing
    Critical Path Method
    Curriculum Design

= Two or more Descriptors are used to represent this term.
The term's main entry shows the appropriate coordination.

Fixed Sequence
Pacing
Programmed Instruction
Sequential Learning
Spiral Curriculum
Teaching Methods

Sequential Learning   *JUL. 1966*
   Postings: 769   GC: 110
SN   A learning situation in which one task is generally completed prior to the presentation of another, with each task building on the prior learning (Note: Consider the use of "Serial Learning" when the situation involves the learning of a single ordered set of responses, often through rote learning)
BT   Learning
RT   Learning Strategies
     Pacing
     Programmed Instruction
     Sequential Approach
     Serial Learning

Sequential Programs (1966 1980)
USE   Sequential Approach

Sequential Reading Programs (1966 1980)
USE   Sequential Approach

Serbocroatian   *JUL. 1966*
   Postings: 116   GC: 440
SN   (Note: See also Identifiers "Croatian" and "Serbian")
UF   Bosnian
BT   Slavic Languages

Serial Association
USE   Serial Learning

Serial Learning   *NOV. 1969*
   Postings: 236   GC: 110
SN   Learning to make a series of responses in a prescribed order (Note: Do not confuse with "Sequential Learning")
UF   Serial Association
     Serial Method
BT   Learning
RT   Association (Psychology)
     Associative Learning
     Behavior Chaining
     Learning Theories
     Memorization
     Paired Associate Learning
     Primacy Effect
     Rote Learning
     Sequential Learning

Serial Method
USE   Serial Learning

Serial Ordering   *JUL. 1966*
   Postings: 283   GC: 110
SN   Process of arranging items successively according to a definite principle, e.g., temporal, spatial, logical, qualitative, quantitative, etc.
BT   Cognitive Processes
RT   Conservation (Concept)
     Pattern Recognition
     Psychomotor Skills

Serials   *AUG. 1968*
   Postings: 635   GC: 720
SN   Materials issued in successive parts, usually at regular intervals and intended to be continued indefinitely (Note: Corresponds to Pubtype code 022—do not use except as the subject of a document)
NT   Annual Reports
     Bulletins
     Conference Proceedings
     Newspapers
     Periodicals
     Yearbooks

BT   Publications
RT   Books
     Comics (Publications)
     Journalism
     Journalism Education
     Programming (Broadcast)
     Soap Operas

Service Education (1966 1980)
USE   Vocational Education

Service Industry
USE   Service Occupations

Service Learning   *MAR. 1996*
   Postings: 859   GC: 330
SN   Learning through community service (or public service in a wider sphere), usually integrated with regular instruction in school or college (Note: See also related Identifiers "Community Service," "Youth Community Service," and "National Service")
UF   Community Service Learning
BT   Experiential Learning
RT   Citizenship Education
     Community Services
     Public Service
     School Community Programs
     School Community Relationship
     Services
     Student Participation
     Student Volunteers
     Volunteer Training

Service Occupations   *JUL. 1966*
   Postings: 688   GC: 640
SN   Occupations providing services in such areas as food and beverage preparation, lodging, barbering and cosmetology, amusements and recreation, apparel and furnishings, protection, building cleaning and maintenance, and miscellaneous private household and personal services
UF   Household Occupations #
     Service Industry
NT   Child Care Occupations
     Hospitality Occupations
     Laundry Drycleaning Occupations
BT   Occupations
RT   Agricultural Supply Occupations
     Cosmetology
     Fashion Industry
     Producer Services
     Public Service Occupations
     Sales Occupations
     Service Workers
     Services
     Trade and Industrial Education

Service Vehicles   *OCT. 1968*
   Postings: 45   GC: 910
SN   Motor vehicles used to provide accommodation and activities required by the public, as public transportation, freight transportation, and maintenance or repair services
UF   Buses
     Contractor Vehicles
     Maintenance Vehicles
NT   Bookmobiles
     School Buses
BT   Motor Vehicles
RT   Services
     Traffic Circulation
     Vehicular Traffic

Service Workers   *JUL. 1966*
   Postings: 147   GC: 640
SN   Personnel providing services in such areas as food and beverage preparation, lodging, barbering and cosmetology, amusements and recreation, apparel and furnishings, protection, building cleaning and maintenance, and miscellaneous private household and personal services
NT   Attendants
     Barbers

     Cooks
     Emergency Squad Personnel
     Fire Fighters
     Household Workers
     Housekeepers
     Housing Management Aides
     Waiters and Waitresses
BT   Nonprofessional Personnel
RT   Employees
     Government Employees
     Machine Repairers
     Resident Advisers
     Sales Workers
     Service Occupations
     Services
     Television Radio Repairers
     Trade and Industrial Education
     Vocational Education

Services   *JUL. 1966*
   Postings: 1,879   GC: 520
SN   Organized functions designed to meet individual or public needs, or to support some other organized function or activity (Note: Use a more specific term if possible)
UF   Special Services (1966 1980)
     Support Systems (Services)
NT   Community Services
     Delivery Systems
     Financial Services
     Human Services
     Information Services
     Producer Services
     Professional Services
     Shared Resources and Services
RT   Advocacy
     Clinics
     Eligibility
     Institutional Role
     Public Service
     Resources
     Service Learning
     Service Occupations
     Service Vehicles
     Service Workers
     Utilities

Set Theory   *JUL. 1966*
   Postings: 316   GC: 480
BT   Mathematical Logic
     Theories
RT   Arithmetic

Settlement Houses   *JUL. 1966*
   Postings: 16   GC: 920
UF   Neighborhood Settlements
     University Settlements
BT   Facilities
RT   Collective Settlements
     Community Programs
     Nonprofit Organizations
     Welfare Services

Settlement Patterns
USE   Land Settlement

Seventeenth Century Literature   *JUN. 1969*
   Postings: 150   GC: 430
BT   Literature
RT   Baroque Literature
     Literary History
     Neoclassicism
     Renaissance Literature

Severe Disabilities   *MAR. 1980*
   Postings: 2,642   GC: 220
SN   Extreme disabilities that make functioning and achievement unusually difficult—generally, rehabilitation services must go beyond those provided by traditional regular or special education programs
UF   Profound Disabilities
     Severely Handicapped (1975 1980)
NT   Psychosis
     Severe Mental Retardation
BT   Disabilities
RT   Deaf Blind

     Institutionalized Persons
     Mild Disabilities
     Multiple Disabilities
     Severity (of Disability)

Severe Mental Retardation   *MAR. 1980*
   Postings: 1,682   GC: 220
SN   Intellectual functioning that is more than four standard deviations below the mean (usually below 40 IQ range), concurrent with adaptive deficiencies—severely retarded individuals require continual supervision and care
UF   Custodial Mentally Handicapped (1968 1980)
     Profoundly Mentally Retarded
BT   Mental Retardation
     Severe Disabilities
RT   Mild Mental Retardation
     Moderate Mental Retardation
     Residential Care

Severely Handicapped (1975 1980)
USE   Severe Disabilities

Severity (of Disability)   *JUN. 1994*
   Postings: 223   GC: 220
SN   Extent of a mental, physical, or sensory impairment, from mild to severe (Note: Prior to Jun94, "Impairment Severity" was the preferred Identifier for this concept)
UF   Impairment Severity
RT   Chronic Illness
     Clinical Diagnosis
     Disabilities
     Disability Identification
     Educational Diagnosis
     Health
     Mild Disabilities
     Severe Disabilities

Sewage
USE   Waste Water

Sewing Instruction   *JUL. 1966*
   Postings: 194   GC: 400
BT   Instruction
RT   Clothing
     Clothing Instruction
     Fashion Industry
     Home Economics
     Needle Trades
     Sewing Machine Operators

Sewing Machine Operators   *JUL. 1966*
   Postings: 70   GC: 640
BT   Semiskilled Workers
RT   Clothing
     Clothing Instruction
     Fashion Industry
     Needle Trades
     Occupational Home Economics
     Sewing Instruction

Sex   *MAR. 1980*
   Postings: 694   GC: 120
SN   Concept used to describe the physiological traits that distinguish the males and females of a species (Note: Use a more precise term if possible—for sexual behavior, see "Sexuality")
UF   Gender (Sex)
BT   Physical Characteristics
RT   Biology
     Females
     Gender Issues
     Males
     Sex Bias
     Sex Discrimination
     Sex Education
     Sex Fairness
     Sex Role
     Sex Stereotypes
     Sexuality

= Two or more Descriptors are used to represent this term.
The term's main entry shows the appropriate coordination.

Sex (Characteristics) (1966 1980)
MAR. 1980
Postings: 647　　GC: 120
SN　Invalid Descriptor—see such Descriptors as "Sexuality," "Sex," and "Sex Differences" or coordinate "Males" or "Females" with specific characteristics, e.g., "Physical Characteristics," "Psychological Characteristics," etc.

Sex Bias
MAR. 1980
Postings: 3,772　　GC: 540
SN　Prejudicial attitudes toward people because of their sex, including the conscious or unconscious expression of these attitudes in writing, speaking, etc. (Note: Prior to Mar80, the instruction "Sex Bias, USE Sex Discrimination" was carried in the Thesaurus)
UF　Gender Bias
　　Sex Prejudice
　　Sexism
NT　Sexism in Language
BT　Social Bias
RT　Affirmative Action
　　Gender Issues
　　Sex
　　Sex Discrimination
　　Sex Stereotypes

Sex Differences
JUL. 1966
Postings: 24,325　　GC: 120
UF　Gender Differences (Sex)
BT　Individual Differences
RT　Androgyny
　　Females
　　Femininity
　　Gender Issues
　　Males
　　Masculinity
　　Physical Characteristics
　　Sex Discrimination
　　Sex Fairness
　　Sex Role
　　Sex Stereotypes
　　Sexual Identity
　　Sexuality

Sex Discrimination
MAR. 1972
Postings: 6,189　　GC: 540
SN　Restriction or denial of rights, privileges, and choice because of one's sex (Note: Do not confuse with "Sex Bias")
UF　Gender Discrimination
NT　Sexual Harassment
BT　Social Discrimination
RT　Affirmative Action
　　Age Discrimination
　　Civil Rights
　　Educational Discrimination
　　Employed Women
　　Equal Education
　　Equal Facilities
　　Equal Opportunities (Jobs)
　　Feminism
　　Feminization of Poverty
　　Gender Issues
　　Occupational Segregation
　　Reverse Discrimination
　　Selective Admission
　　Sex
　　Sex Bias
　　Sex Differences
　　Sex Role
　　Sex Stereotypes

Sex Education
JUL. 1966
Postings: 2,148　　GC: 400
BT　Family Life Education
RT　Birth
　　Contraception
　　Ethical Instruction
　　Ethics
　　Menstruation
　　Puberty
　　Sex
　　Sexuality
　　Venereal Diseases

Sex Fairness
AUG. 1978
Postings: 2,580　　GC: 540
SN　The correction of sex bias or discrimination (Note: Use for descriptions of materials, procedures, activities, or programs that treat the sexes equitably)
RT　Affirmative Action
　　Equal Facilities
　　Equal Opportunities (Jobs)
　　Equal Protection
　　Feminism
　　Gender Issues
　　Justice
　　Nondiscriminatory Education
　　Nontraditional Occupations
　　Personnel Integration
　　Sex
　　Sex Differences
　　Tokenism

Sex Prejudice
USE　Sex Bias

Sex Role
MAY 1974
Postings: 7,001　　GC: 510
SN　Pattern of attitudes and behavior that in any society is deemed appropriate to one sex rather than the other
UF　Female Role #
　　Gender Role (Sex)
　　Male Role #
BT　Role
RT　Androgyny
　　Fear of Success
　　Females
　　Femininity
　　Gender Issues
　　Males
　　Masculinity
　　Sex
　　Sex Differences
　　Sex Discrimination
　　Sex Stereotypes
　　Sexual Identity
　　Sexual Orientation

Sex Stereotypes
JUL. 1974
Postings: 5,114　　GC: 540
SN　Rigid or biased attitudes in which persons are ascribed certain traits because of their sex
UF　Gender Stereotypes
BT　Stereotypes
RT　Females
　　Femininity
　　Gender Issues
　　Males
　　Masculinity
　　Sex
　　Sex Bias
　　Sex Differences
　　Sex Discrimination
　　Sex Role
　　Sexism in Language
　　Sexual Identity

Sexism
USE　Sex Bias

Sexism in Language
APR. 1990
Postings: 126　　GC: 450
SN　Forms of language that instill and perpetuate (or avoid) sex role stereotyping (Note: Prior to Apr90, this concept was indexed by "Language Usage" and "Sex Bias")
UF　Nonsexist Language
　　Sexist Language
BT　Language Usage
　　Sex Bias
RT　Gender Issues
　　Language Attitudes
　　Language Patterns
　　Sex Stereotypes

Sexist Language
USE　Sexism in Language

Sexual Abuse
OCT. 1983
Postings: 2,255　　GC: 530
SN　Physical sexual advances or contact by force or without legally recognized consent
UF　Child Sexual Abuse #
　　Sexual Assault
NT　Rape
BT　Antisocial Behavior
RT　Battered Women
　　Child Abuse
　　Incest
　　Sexual Harassment
　　Sexuality
　　Victims of Crime

Sexual Assault
USE　Sexual Abuse

Sexual Behavior
USE　Sexuality

Sexual Harassment
OCT. 1982
Postings: 950　　GC: 530
SN　Unsolicited and unwelcome sexual behavior by any individual that interferes with work, study, or everyday life and creates an intimidating, hostile, or offensive environment
BT　Antisocial Behavior
　　Sex Discrimination
RT　Emotional Abuse
　　Rape
　　Sexual Abuse
　　Sexuality
　　Verbal Abuse

Sexual Identity
AUG. 1986
Postings: 587　　GC: 120
SN　Awareness of individuals (oneself or others) as male or female
UF　Gender Identity (Sex)
RT　Androgyny
　　Biological Influences
　　Developmental Psychology
　　Femininity
　　Gender Issues
　　Identification (Psychology)
　　Interpersonal Relationship
　　Masculinity
　　Psychological Characteristics
　　Self Concept
　　Sex Differences
　　Sex Role
　　Sex Stereotypes
　　Sexual Orientation
　　Sexuality
　　Social Development

Sexual Orientation
AUG. 2000
Postings: 163　　GC: 120
SN　The direction of one's psychosexual interest toward members of the same sex, the opposite sex, or both sexes
UF　Sexual Preference
BT　Orientation
RT　Bisexuality
　　Homophobia
　　Homosexuality
　　Interpersonal Relationship
　　Lesbianism
　　Sex Role
　　Sexual Identity
　　Sexuality

Sexual Preference
USE　Sexual Orientation

Sexuality
APR. 1969
Postings: 3,830　　GC: 120
UF　Human Sexuality
　　Sexual Behavior
NT　Bisexuality
　　Homosexuality
RT　Cohabitation
　　Gender Issues
　　Guilt
　　Health Behavior
　　Incest
　　Intimacy
　　Love
　　Personality Traits
　　Pornography
　　Rape
　　Sex
　　Sex Differences
　　Sex Education
　　Sexual Abuse
　　Sexual Harassment
　　Sexual Identity
　　Sexual Orientation

Shade Trees
USE　Trees

Shadow Plays
USE　Theater Arts

Shapers
USE　Machine Tools

Sharecroppers
JUL. 1966
Postings: 25　　GC: 410
BT　Farmers
RT　Agricultural Laborers
　　Agriculture
　　Farm Occupations
　　Rural Farm Residents
　　Seasonal Laborers

Shared Facilities
MAY 1974
Postings: 427　　GC: 920
SN　Facilities used by two or more distinct groups, institutions, organizations, etc., whether for the same function or for different functions
UF　Joint Occupancy
BT　Facilities
　　Shared Resources and Services
RT　Cluster Colleges
　　Community Schools
　　Facility Planning
　　Flexible Facilities
　　Institutional Cooperation
　　Off Campus Facilities

Shared Library Resources
AUG. 1986
Postings: 507　　GC: 710
SN　Personnel, equipment, materials, etc., shared among libraries
BT　Shared Resources and Services
RT　Interlibrary Loans
　　Libraries
　　Library Cooperation
　　Library Development
　　Library Networks
　　Union Catalogs
　　User Needs (Information)

Shared Resources and Services
AUG. 1986
Postings: 876　　GC: 330
SN　Personnel, facilities, equipment, materials, and other resources and services shared among persons and/or organizations
UF　Resource Sharing
　　Shared Services (1974 1986)
NT　Shared Facilities
　　Shared Library Resources
BT　Resources
　　Services
RT　Agency Cooperation
　　Consortia
　　Cooperation
　　Cooperative Planning
　　Cooperative Programs
　　Dual Enrollment
　　Education Service Centers
　　Institutional Cooperation
　　Partnerships in Education
　　Private School Aid
　　Specialists

= Two or more Descriptors are used to represent this term.
The term's main entry shows the appropriate coordination.

Shared Services (1974 1986)
USE　Shared Resources and Services

Shared Time (Computers)
USE　Time Sharing

Shared Time (Education)
USE　Dual Enrollment

Sharing Behavior　　　　　　　　*AUG. 1989*
　　Postings: 155　　　　　　　　　GC: 120
SN　To have, use, exercise, experience, occupy, or engage in something in common with another or others
BT　Prosocial Behavior
RT　Altruism
　　Cooperation
　　Helping Relationship
　　Interpersonal Relationship
　　Psychological Patterns

Sheet Metal Machine Operators
USE　Machine Tool Operators
AND　Sheet Metal Work

Sheet Metal Work　　　　　　　　*JUL. 1966*
　　Postings: 104　　　　　　　　　GC: 640
UF　Sheet Metal Machine Operators #
　　Sheet Metal Workers (1967 1981)
BT　Metal Working
RT　Air Conditioning Equipment
　　Assembly (Manufacturing)
　　Machine Tool Operators
　　School Construction
　　Skilled Occupations

Sheet Metal Workers (1967 1981)
USE　Sheet Metal Work

Sheltered Workshops　　　　　　*JUL. 1966*
　　Postings: 417　　　　　　　　　GC: 220
SN　Places where disabled persons are provided work experience with a view toward making them vocationally independent
BT　Workshops
RT　Disabilities
　　Individualized Programs
　　Job Training
　　Rehabilitation Centers
　　Rehabilitation Counseling
　　Rehabilitation Programs
　　Supported Employment
　　Vocational Rehabilitation
　　Vocational Training Centers
　　Work Experience Programs

Shift Studies　　　　　　　　　*DEC. 1970*
　　Postings: 129　　　　　　　　　GC: 810
SN　Studies that investigate factors in the ability of subjects to discriminate between different dimensions of a stimulus or situation and to shift their responses according to these dimensions
UF　Discrimination Transfer
　　Extradimensional Shift
　　Half Reversal Shift
　　Interdimensional Shift
　　Nonreversal Shift
　　Reversal Shift
RT　Attention Span
　　Discrimination Learning
　　Learning Processes
　　Mediation Theory
　　Responses

Shona　　　　　　　　　　　*JUL. 1966*
　　Postings: 11　　　　　　　　　GC: 440
BT　Bantu Languages

Shop Curriculum　　　　　　　*JUL. 1966*
　　Postings: 242　　　　　　　　　GC: 400
UF　General Shop
BT　Curriculum

RT　Hand Tools
　　Industrial Arts
　　Metal Working
　　School Shops
　　Woodworking

Shop Mechanics
USE　Machine Repairers

Shop Rooms
USE　School Shops

Short Courses (1970 1980)
USE　Minicourses

Short Stories　　　　　　　　　*JUL. 1966*
　　Postings: 830　　　　　　　　　GC: 430
BT　Fiction
　　Literary Genres
RT　Books
　　Tales

Short Term Memory　　　　　　*NOV. 1981*
　　Postings: 456　　　　　　　　　GC: 110
SN　Process of recalling information or performing appropriately soon after instruction or presentation of material—characterized by rapid decay and a limited volume of remembered material (in contrast to "Long Term Memory")
BT　Memory
RT　Long Term Memory

Shorthand　　　　　　　　　　*MAR. 1980*
　　Postings: 518　　　　　　　　　GC: 400
UF　Clerk Stenographers
　　Stenographers (1966 1981)
　　Stenography (1967 1980)
BT　Written Language
RT　Abbreviations
　　Business Skills
　　Clerical Occupations
　　Court Reporters
　　Dictation
　　Office Occupations
　　Office Occupations Education
　　Secretaries
　　Symbolic Language
　　Typewriting

Shyness　　　　　　　　　　　*APR. 1990*
　　Postings: 155　　　　　　　　　GC: 120
SN　Personality trait characterized by reserved, diffident, reticent, or timid behavior
UF　Bashfulness
　　Timidity
BT　Personality Traits
RT　Anxiety
　　Communication Apprehension
　　Extraversion Introversion
　　Inhibition
　　Interpersonal Communication
　　Interpersonal Competence
　　Social Isolation

SI Units
USE　Metric System

Sibling Relationship　　　　　　*AUG. 1988*
　　Postings: 310　　　　　　　　　GC: 510
BT　Family Relationship
RT　Birth Order
　　First Born
　　Siblings
　　Twins

Siblings　　　　　　　　　　　*JUL. 1966*
　　Postings: 1,079　　　　　　　　GC: 510
UF　Brothers
　　Sisters
NT　First Born
　　Twins
BT　Groups

RT　Family (Sociological Unit)
　　Family Environment
　　Family Life
　　Family Size
　　Family Structure
　　Kinship
　　Sibling Relationship

Sick Child Care　　　　　　　　*JUL. 1993*
　　Postings: 61　　　　　　　　　GC: 210
SN　Day care alternatives for children who are ill and already involved in regular day care or school programs, including care in isolated areas of the child's own day care center/school, separate sick child care centers, family day care homes open to sick children, and the child's own home by home health personnel or known adults (including parents under family leave policies or otherwise)
UF　Ill Child Care
BT　Day Care
RT　Child Caregivers
　　Child Health
　　Communicable Diseases
　　Day Care Centers
　　Disease Control
　　Diseases
　　Employer Supported Day Care
　　Family Day Care
　　Family Problems
　　Hospitalized Children
　　Medical Services
　　School Health Services

Sickle Cell Anemia　　　　　　*OCT. 1983*
　　Postings: 36　　　　　　　　　GC: 210
SN　An inherited condition, chiefly among black people, in which the red blood cells have an abnormal, crescent shape
UF　Sickle Cell Trait
BT　Anemia
RT　Blood Circulation
　　Genetics
　　Physical Health

Sickle Cell Trait
USE　Sickle Cell Anemia

Sicknesses
USE　Diseases

SIDS
USE　Sudden Infant Death Syndrome

Sierra Leone Creole　　　　　　*JUL. 1966*
　　Postings: 7　　　　　　　　　GC: 440
UF　Krio
　　Sierra Leone Krio
BT　Creoles

Sierra Leone Krio
USE　Sierra Leone Creole

Sight
USE　Vision

Sight Method　　　　　　　　　*JUL. 1966*
　　Postings: 167　　　　　　　　　GC: 460
SN　Method of teaching reading based on recognition and pronunciation of whole words
UF　Look Guess Method
　　Look Say Method
　　Whole Word Reading Approach
　　Word Method (Reading)
BT　Teaching Methods
RT　Basal Reading
　　Beginning Reading
　　Reading Instruction
　　Sight Vocabulary
　　Word Recognition

Sight Playing
USE　Music Reading

Sight Singing
USE　Music Reading

Sight Vocabulary　　　　　　　*JUL. 1966*
　　Postings: 373　　　　　　　　　GC: 460
SN　The words that one immediately recognizes while reading
BT　Vocabulary
RT　Basal Reading
　　Basic Vocabulary
　　Beginning Reading
　　Reading Instruction
　　Sight Method
　　Word Lists
　　Word Recognition

Sightseeing Industry
USE　Tourism

Sign Language　　　　　　　　　*JUL. 1966*
　　Postings: 1,097　　　　　　　　GC: 220
SN　Type of manual communication method used by the deaf in which gestures function as words—it has its own morphology, semantics, and syntax
UF　Gestures (Deaf Communication)
NT　American Sign Language
BT　Language
　　Manual Communication
RT　Deaf Interpreting
　　Finger Spelling
　　Total Communication

Sign Painters　　　　　　　　　*FEB. 1969*
　　Postings: 6　　　　　　　　　GC: 640
UF　Sign Writers
BT　Skilled Workers
RT　Graphic Arts
　　Painting (Industrial Arts)
　　Signs

Sign Writers
USE　Sign Painters

Signal Services
USE　Telecommunications

Signboards
USE　Signs

Signed English
USE　Manual Communication

Significance Measures
USE　Statistical Significance

Significant Others　　　　　　　*JUN. 1983*
　　Postings: 217　　　　　　　　　GC: 510
SN　Those individuals in a person's immediate environment (past or present) who are/were particularly influential in the formation, support, or modification of that person's values, attitudes, and self-concept
BT　Interpersonal Relationship
RT　Family Relationship
　　Friendship
　　Identification (Psychology)
　　Mentors
　　Modeling (Psychology)
　　Role Models
　　Self Concept
　　Socialization

Signs　　　　　　　　　　　　*NOV. 1968*
　　Postings: 161　　　　　　　　　GC: 720
UF　Road Signs
　　Signboards
　　Traffic Signs (1968 1980) #
BT　Visual Aids

 # = Two or more Descriptors are used to represent this term.
The term's main entry shows the appropriate coordination.

RT   Engineering Graphics
Graphic Arts
Instructional Materials
Printing
Sign Painters
Traffic Control

Silent Films
USE   Films

Silent Reading   *JUL. 1966*
Postings: 392   GC: 460
BT   Reading
RT   Inner Speech (Subvocal)
Oral Reading
Reading Habits
Reading Instruction
Reading Rate
Speed Reading
Sustained Silent Reading

Silent Speech
USE   Inner Speech (Subvocal)

Similarity Transformations
USE   Transformations (Mathematics)

Simulated Environment   *JUL. 1966*
Postings: 345   GC: 310
BT   Environment
RT   Management Games
Simulation

Simulated Speech
USE   Artificial Speech

Simulated Studies
USE   Simulation

Simulation   *JUL. 1966*
Postings: 7,071   GC: 310
SN   Duplication of the essential characteristics of a task or situation
UF   Simulated Studies
Simulators (1967 1980)
NT   Computer Simulation
Markov Processes
Models
Monte Carlo Methods
Role Playing
BT   Methods
RT   Assessment Centers (Personnel)
Context Effect
Counseling Techniques
Critical Incidents Method
Educational Games
Experiential Learning
Game Theory
Heuristics
Laboratory Procedures
Laboratory Training
Learning Strategies
Management Games
Management Systems
Office Practice
Simulated Environment
Situational Tests
Teaching Methods

Simulators (1967 1980)
USE   Simulation

Singhalese   *JUL. 1966*
Postings: 31   GC: 440
UF   Sinhalese
BT   Indo European Languages

Singing   *JUL. 1966*
Postings: 536   GC: 420
UF   Choirs
Choruses (1968 1980)
Glee Clubs
Vocal Ensembles

BT   Music Activities
RT   Applied Music
Art Song
Choral Music
Concerts
Hymns
Kodaly Method
Orff Method
Recreational Activities
Songs
Vocal Music

Single Concept Films   *JUL. 1966*
Postings: 96   GC: 720
BT   Films
RT   Filmstrips
Instructional Films

Single Mother Births
USE   Births to Single Women

Single Parent Family
USE   One Parent Family

Single Sex Colleges   *OCT. 1979*
Postings: 260   GC: 340
SN   Colleges or universities with little or no enrollment of one sex
BT   Colleges
Single Sex Schools
RT   Church Related Colleges
Coeducation
Females
Homogeneous Grouping
Males
Private Colleges
Womens Education

Single Sex Schools   *OCT. 1979*
Postings: 225   GC: 340
SN   Educational institutions with little or no enrollment of one sex (Note: If possible, use the more specific term "Single Sex Colleges")
NT   Single Sex Colleges
BT   Schools
RT   Coeducation
Females
Homogeneous Grouping
Males
Private Schools
Womens Education

Single Students   *JUL. 1966*
Postings: 38   GC: 360
UF   Unmarried Students
BT   Students
RT   Adult Students
Marital Status
Married Students

Sinhalese
USE   Singhalese

Sino Tibetan Languages   *JUL. 1966*
Postings: 105   GC: 440
NT   Burmese
Chinese
Hmong
Lao
Thai
Tibetan
BT   Languages
RT   Austro Asiatic Languages
Language Classification
Native Speakers

Sioux (Tribe)   *MAR. 1994*
Postings: 108   GC: 560
SN   An American Indian people mainly of the upper Mississippi area and the Great Plains (and dispersed kin) (Note: Use "Dakota" for the Sioux language—use the Identifier "Siouan Languages" for

the broad language family to which Dakota belongs)
NT   Lakota (Tribe)
BT   American Indians
Tribes
RT   Dakota

Sisters
USE   Siblings

Siswati   *MAR. 1971*
Postings: 8   GC: 440
UF   Isiswati
Swazi
BT   Bantu Languages

Site Analysis   *AUG. 1968*
Postings: 329   GC: 920
BT   Evaluation Methods
RT   Educational Complexes
Educational Facilities Planning
Facility Case Studies
Facility Expansion
Facility Guidelines
Facility Planning
Geographic Location
School Expansion
School Location
Site Development
Site Selection

Site Based Management (Schools)
USE   School Based Management

Site Development   *JUL. 1966*
Postings: 364   GC: 920
SN   Process of planning, engineering, and landscaping a plot of ground
BT   Development
RT   Built Environment
Construction (Process)
Educational Complexes
Educational Facilities Design
Educational Facilities Planning
Engineering
Facility Expansion
Facility Planning
Found Spaces
Land Acquisition
Landscaping
School Expansion
Site Analysis
Site Selection

Site Selection   *JUL. 1966*
Postings: 437   GC: 920
BT   Selection
RT   Educational Facilities Design
Educational Facilities Planning
Facility Planning
Land Acquisition
Real Estate
School Expansion
School Zoning
Site Analysis
Site Development

Situation Reaction Tests
USE   Situational Tests

Situation Response Tests
USE   Situational Tests

Situational Determinants
USE   Context Effect

Situational Tests   *NOV. 1968*
Postings: 278   GC: 830
SN   Measures of an individual's behavior in realistic or simulated situations which call for actual adaptive responses
UF   Situation Reaction Tests
Situation Response Tests
BT   Tests

RT   Assessment Centers (Personnel)
Performance Tests
Responses
Simulation
Vocational Evaluation
Work Sample Tests

Situational Therapy
USE   Milieu Therapy

Six Three Three Organization
USE   Instructional Program Divisions

Sixteen Millimeter Projectors (1966 1980)
USE   Projection Equipment

Sixteenth Century Literature   *APR. 1970*
Postings: 75   GC: 430
BT   Literature
RT   Baroque Literature
Literary History
Renaissance Literature

Skeletal System   *APR. 1990*
Postings: 31   GC: 210
SN   (Note: See also the Identifier "Bones")
UF   Bone Arrangement
BT   Musculoskeletal System
RT   Anatomy
Human Body
Muscular System
Physiology

Skeletomuscular System
USE   Musculoskeletal System

Skiing   *FEB. 1978*
Postings: 54   GC: 470
SN   Excludes waterskiing
UF   Snowskiing
BT   Winter Sports
RT   Olympic Games

Skill Analysis   *JUL. 1966*
Postings: 967   GC: 820
SN   Study and detailed description of the mental and/or physical behaviors that are needed for learning or the satisfactory completion of an activity
BT   Evaluation Methods
RT   Ability Identification
Content Analysis
Critical Incidents Method
Difficulty Level
Job Analysis
Object Manipulation
Protocol Analysis
Psychomotor Skills
Skill Development
Skill Obsolescence
Skills
Systems Analysis
Task Analysis
Test Construction

Skill Centers   *JUL. 1966*
Postings: 123   GC: 920
BT   Educational Facilities
RT   Learning Laboratories
Off the Job Training
Skill Development
Skills

Skill Development   *JUL. 1966*
Postings: 12,972   GC: 120
BT   Individual Development
RT   Basic Skills
Developmental Studies Programs
Learning Plateaus
Learning Strategies
Mastery Learning
Mastery Tests
Motor Development
Process Education

Retraining
Skill Analysis
Skill Centers
Skills
Talent Development
Thinking Skills
Training
Training Methods
Transfer of Training

Skill Obsolescence   *NOV. 1968*
          Postings: 177   GC: 630
BT   Obsolescence
RT   Dislocated Workers
      Employment Potential
      Employment Qualifications
      Job Skills
      Retraining
      Skill Analysis
      Structural Unemployment
      Vocational Adjustment

Skilled Labor (1966 1980)
USE   Skilled Workers

Skilled Occupations   *JUL. 1966*
          Postings: 574   GC: 640
SN   Occupations requiring a high degree of
      skill, usually in a wide range of related
      activities performed with a minimum of
      direction and supervision, and secured
      through a combination of job instruc-
      tion, trade instruction, and work experi-
      ence such as apprenticeships or coop-
      erative industrial programs
BT   Occupations
RT   Appliance Repair
      Apprenticeships
      Auto Mechanics
      Aviation Mechanics
      Blue Collar Occupations
      Bricklaying
      Building Trades
      Cabinetmaking
      Carpentry
      Data Processing Occupations
      Design Crafts
      Electrical Occupations
      Equipment Maintenance
      Handicrafts
      Horology
      Job Skills
      Masonry
      Metal Working
      Painting (Industrial Arts)
      Patternmaking
      Refrigeration Mechanics
      Roofing
      Semiskilled Occupations
      Sheet Metal Work
      Skilled Workers
      Small Engine Mechanics
      Technical Occupations
      Technology
      Trade and Industrial Education
      Unskilled Occupations
      Welding
      Woodworking

Skilled Workers   *JUL. 1966*
          Postings: 409   GC: 630
SN   Workers qualified in a particular occupa-
      tion, trade, or craft requiring a high de-
      gree of skill, usually in a wide range of
      related activities performed with a mini-
      mum of direction and supervision—have
      usually had a combination of job instruc-
      tion, trade instruction, and work experi-
      ence such as apprenticeships or coop-
      erative industrial programs
UF   Journey Workers
      Roofers (1968 1981) #
      Skilled Labor (1966 1980)
NT   Auto Body Repairers
      Craft Workers
      Electricians
      Floor Layers
      Glaziers
      Locomotive Engineers

Machinists
Sign Painters
Television Radio Repairers
Watchmakers
BT   Nonprofessional Personnel
RT   Apprenticeships
      Employees
      Job Skills
      Semiskilled Workers
      Skilled Occupations
      Trade and Industrial Education
      Unskilled Workers
      Working Class

Skills   *JUL. 1966*
          Postings: 922   GC: 120
SN   Complex mental and/or physical behav-
      iors that require practice to be performed
      proficiently (Note: Use a more specific
      term if possible)
NT   Agricultural Skills
      Basic Skills
      Business Skills
      Communication Skills
      Daily Living Skills
      Decision Making Skills
      Home Economics Skills
      Homemaking Skills
      Information Skills
      Interpretive Skills
      Job Skills
      Language Skills
      Locational Skills (Social Studies)
      Map Skills
      Mathematics Skills
      Mechanical Skills
      Minimum Competencies
      Parenting Skills
      Psychomotor Skills
      Research Skills
      Salesmanship
      Science Process Skills
      Study Skills
      Teaching Skills
      Thinking Skills
      Visual Literacy
BT   Ability
RT   Competence
      Difficulty Level
      Familiarity
      Interpersonal Competence
      Mastery Learning
      Mastery Tests
      National Competency Tests
      Process Education
      Qualifications
      Skill Analysis
      Skill Centers
      Skill Development

Skimming (Reading)
USE   Speed Reading

Skin Diving
USE   Underwater Diving

Skits   *JUL. 1966*
          Postings: 129   GC: 420
BT   Comedy
      Literary Genres
RT   Creative Dramatics
      Dramatics
      Pantomime
      Theater Arts

Slander
USE   Libel and Slander

Slavery   *JUL. 1966*
          Postings: 623   GC: 520
BT   Human Relations
RT   African History
      Black Culture
      Black Family
      Black History
      Black Studies
      Civil Liberties
      Civil Rights

Civil War (United States)
Colonial History (United States)
Freedom
International Crimes
Minority Groups
Racial Discrimination
World History

Slavic Languages   *JUL. 1966*
          Postings: 257   GC: 440
NT   Bielorussian
      Bulgarian
      Czech
      Polish
      Russian
      Serbocroatian
      Slovenian
      Ukrainian
BT   Indo European Languages
RT   Cyrillic Alphabet
      Language Classification
      Native Speakers

Sleep   *NOV. 1969*
          Postings: 258   GC: 210
UF   Drowsiness
RT   Behavior
      Dreams
      Fatigue (Biology)
      Health
      Nightmares
      Psychological Patterns

Slide Projectors
USE   Projection Equipment

Slides   *JAN. 1969*
          Postings: 882   GC: 720
SN   Mounted transparencies, either film or
      glass, intended for projection or viewing
      by transmitted light
BT   Transparencies
RT   Audiovisual Aids
      Filmstrips

Slovene
USE   Slovenian

Slovenian   *OCT. 1969*
          Postings: 30   GC: 440
UF   Slovene
BT   Slavic Languages

Slow Learners   *JUL. 1966*
          Postings: 667   GC: 220
SN   Individuals who have between average
      and mentally deficient intelligence (IQ
      usually between 70 and 85) and whose
      social behavior is less than age level
      standards
UF   Borderline Mental Retardation
BT   Groups
RT   Educationally Disadvantaged
      Learning Problems
      Mild Mental Retardation

Sludge   *AUG. 1982*
          Postings: 92   GC: 410
SN   Deposits of mud, slushy sediment, or
      residual semiliquid waste
UF   Activated Sludge
BT   Matter
RT   Solid Wastes
      Waste Water
      Wastes
      Water
      Water Pollution
      Water Treatment

Slum Children
USE   Disadvantaged Youth

Slum Conditions (1966 1980)
USE   Slum Environment

Slum Environment   *JUL. 1966*
          Postings: 60   GC: 550
UF   Slum Conditions (1966 1980)
BT   Environment
RT   Disadvantaged Environment
      Slums
      Urban Environment

Slum Schools   *JUL. 1966*
          Postings: 89   GC: 340
SN   Schools located in slum areas
BT   Schools
RT   Disadvantaged Schools
      Slums
      Urban Schools

Slums   *JUL. 1966*
          Postings: 139   GC: 550
SN   Residential areas, usually urban, charac-
      terized by deteriorated buildings, high
      population density, and generally poor
      living conditions (Note: Prior to Mar80,
      this term was often used synonymously
      with "Ghettos")
UF   Urban Slums (1966 1980)
BT   Poverty Areas
RT   Ghettos
      Inner City
      Poverty
      Slum Environment
      Slum Schools
      Urban Areas
      Urban Renewal

Small Arms
USE   Guns

Small Business Management
USE   Business Administration
AND   Small Businesses

Small Businesses   *NOV. 1982*
          Postings: 1,237   GC: 650
SN   Independently owned, for-profit enter-
      prises with a small number of employees
      (usually not exceeding 500 for manufac-
      turing or 100 for non-manufacturing)—
      precise designation varies according to
      product or service offered
UF   Small Business Management #
BT   Business
RT   Entrepreneurship
      Franchising
      Organization Size (Groups)
      Self Employment

Small Classes   *JUL. 1966*
          Postings: 188   GC: 310
BT   Classes (Groups of Students)
RT   Class Size
      Special Classes

Small Colleges   *JAN. 1978*
          Postings: 768   GC: 340
SN   Colleges with less than 2500 students
BT   Colleges
      Small Schools
RT   Church Related Colleges
      Developing Institutions
      Private Colleges
      Proprietary Schools

Small Engine Mechanics   *MAR. 1984*
          Postings: 98   GC: 640
SN   Assembly, operation, and repair of recip-
      rocating internal-combustion engines
      used on lawnmowers, garden tractors,
      chain saws, and other portable power
      equipment—small engines are generally
      air-cooled and under 20 horsepower
BT   Mechanics (Process)
RT   Auto Mechanics
      Diesel Engines
      Engines
      Industrial Arts
      Power Technology

= Two or more Descriptors are used to represent this term.
The term's main entry shows the appropriate coordination.

Skilled Occupations
Technology Education

Small Group Instruction JUL. 1966
Postings: 1,850 GC: 310
BT Group Instruction
RT Cooperative Learning
Guided Design
Individualized Instruction
Large Group Instruction
Teaching Methods
Team Training

Small Schools JUL. 1966
Postings: 1,906 GC: 340
SN Although designation is relative to lo-
cale, small schools usually do not ex-
ceed 750 students, grades k-12
NT One Teacher Schools
Small Colleges
BT Schools
RT Institutional Survival
Rural Schools
School Size

Small Towns JUL. 1993
Postings: 225 GC: 550
SN Small settlements of both residences
and businesses, often acting as trade
and service centers for surrounding rural areas—largely urban in character,
small towns are generally distinguished
by such qualities as ready access to local
political figures and a close-knit sense of
community, rather than defined by population size (frequently 2,500–10,000, but
can be to 25,000 or higher)
BT Municipalities
RT Community Size
Nonmetropolitan Areas
Rural Areas
Rural Environment

Smog
USE Air Pollution

Smoke Alarms
USE Alarm Systems

Smokestacks
USE Chimneys

Smoking APR. 1969
Postings: 1,437 GC: 210
UF Cigarette Smoking
BT Behavior
RT Cancer
Health Behavior
Health Education
Physical Health
Stimulants
Substance Abuse
Tobacco

Snack Bars
USE Dining Facilities

Snowskiing
USE Skiing

Soap Operas DEC. 1989
Postings: 95 GC: 720
SN Serial melodramas—customarily appear-
ing on broadcast television or radio,
historically sponsored by "soap" com-
panies, and usually scheduled during the
day (Note: For prime-time soap operas,
coordinate with the Identifier "Prime Time
Television")
BT Drama
RT Programming (Broadcast)
Radio
Scripts
Serials

Television
Television Viewing

Soccer DEC. 1975
Postings: 82 GC: 470
BT Team Sports
RT Olympic Games

Sociability
USE Interpersonal Competence

Social Action NOV. 1969
Postings: 2,156 GC: 520
UF Political Reform
Social Reform
NT Community Action
RT Action Research
Activism
Advocacy
Citizen Participation
Dissent
Humanitarianism
Ideology
Participatory Research
Political Influences
Political Issues
Popular Education
Revolution
Social Attitudes
Social Change
Social Responsibility

Social Adjustment JUL. 1966
Postings: 1,964 GC: 230
UF Socially Maladjusted (1966 1980)
BT Adjustment (to Environment)
Social Behavior
RT Adaptive Behavior (of Disabled)
Alienation
Conformity
Defense Mechanisms
Extraversion Introversion
Interpersonal Competence
Social Development
Social Influences
Social Isolation
Social Problems

Social Agencies JUL. 1966
Postings: 649 GC: 520
SN Nonprofit, voluntary, and/or tax-sup-
ported service organizations
NT Welfare Agencies
BT Agencies
RT Agency Role
Nongovernmental Organizations
Public Agencies
Social Services
Social Support Groups
Social Work
Social Workers
Voluntary Agencies

Social Attitudes JUL. 1966
Postings: 4,979 GC: 510
SN Attitudes of individuals or groups with
respect to social objects or phenomena
such as persons, races, institutions, or
traits
NT Social Bias
Social Desirability
BT Attitudes
RT Activism
Alienation
Altruism
Community Attitudes
Consciousness Raising
Dissent
Egocentrism
Ideology
Interpersonal Competence
Justice
Language Attitudes
Political Attitudes
Political Socialization
Public Opinion
Regional Attitudes
Social Action

Social Change
Social Characteristics
Social Cognition
Social Development
Social Differences
Social Environment
Social Influences
Social Problems
Social Values
Traditionalism

Social Awareness
USE Interpersonal Competence

Social Background JUL. 1966
Postings: 299 GC: 510
NT Social Experience
BT Socioeconomic Background
RT Social Class
Social Influences

Social Behavior DEC. 1970
Postings: 3,747 GC: 120
SN Behavior influenced or controlled by other
persons or by organized society
UF Social Norms #
NT Activism
Antisocial Behavior
Conformity
Dissent
Help Seeking
Lying
Obedience
Prosocial Behavior
Social Adjustment
BT Behavior
RT Adolescent Behavior
Advocacy
Assertiveness
Behavior Development
Child Behavior
Competition
Compliance (Psychology)
Cooperation
Crowding
Group Behavior
Interaction Process Analysis
Interpersonal Competence
Psychological Patterns
Resistance (Psychology)
Social Control
Social Desirability
Social Influences
Social Networks
Sociobiology
Sociology
Sociometric Techniques
Stranger Reactions
Transactional Analysis

Social Bias MAR. 1980
Postings: 2,210 GC: 540
SN Prejudicial attitudes toward particular
groups, races, sexes, or religions, in-
cluding the conscious or unconscious
expression of these attitudes in writing,
speaking, etc. (Note: Do not confuse
with various "Discrimination" terms,
which refer to the actions based on those
attitudes)
UF Discriminatory Attitudes (Social) (1966
1980)
NT Ethnic Bias
Homophobia
Racial Bias
Sex Bias
BT Bias
Social Attitudes
RT Age Discrimination
Cultural Differences
Disability Discrimination
Discriminatory Legislation
Intergroup Relations
Item Bias
Labeling (of Persons)
Minority Groups
Nature Nurture Controversy
Negative Attitudes
Religious Discrimination

Social Desirability
Social Discrimination
Stereotypes
Test Bias

Social Biology OCT. 1983
Postings: 41 GC: 490
SN The study of the application of biology to
social problems, from food production,
pollution, overpopulation, etc., to the
long-range goals of social and ecological
planning (Note: Do not confuse with
"Sociobiology")
BT Biology
RT Bioethics
Ecology
Environmental Education
Social Change
Sociology

Social Change JUL. 1966
Postings: 10,326 GC: 520
SN Evolution or change at the societal, rather
than individual, level, possibly involving
the restructuring of political and/or eco-
nomic relations (Note: Prior to Mar80,
the use of this term was not restricted by
a Scope Note)
UF Social Reconstruction
Societal Change
NT Modernization
BT Change
RT Change Agents
Change Strategies
Community Change
Controversial Issues (Course Content)
Critical Theory
Culture Lag
Economic Change
Entropy
Futures (of Society)
Institutional Survival
Marxian Analysis
Participatory Research
Political Influences
Political Socialization
Popular Education
Revolution
Science and Society
Social Action
Social Attitudes
Social Biology
Social History
Social Indicators
Social Influences
Social Integration
Social Problems
Social Theories
Social Values
Sociocultural Patterns
Traditionalism

Social Characteristics JUL. 1966
Postings: 596 GC: 510
SN Criteria used to rate members of a social
class
RT Cultural Context
Cultural Traits
Individual Characteristics
Interpersonal Competence
Place of Residence
Regional Characteristics
Social Attitudes
Social Class
Social Differences
Social Environment
Social Indicators
Social Influences
Social Values
Sociology

Social Class JUL. 1966
Postings: 1,998 GC: 520
NT Caste
Lower Class
Lower Middle Class
Middle Class
Upper Class
Working Class

= Two or more Descriptors are used to represent this term.
The term's main entry shows the appropriate coordination.

BT   Groups
RT   Income
      Marxism
      Quality of Life
      Social Background
      Social Characteristics
      Social Dialects
      Social Differences
      Social Distribution
      Social Integration
      Social Status
      Social Stratification
      Social Structure
      Socioeconomic Status
      Status
      Subcultures

Social Class Differences
USE   Social Differences

Social Class Integration
USE   Social Integration

Social Climate
USE   Social Environment

Social Cognition   *OCT. 1980*
      Postings: 2,135   GC: 110
SN   Conceptions about interpersonal and so-
      cial phenomena (e.g., persons, the self,
      motives, feelings, relations, social rules,
      societal institutions)—also, cognitive
      processes and skills used in social inter-
      action (e.g., communication skills, per-
      spective taking, empathy)
UF   Interpersonal Perception
      Perception (between Persons)
      Perceptiveness (between Persons) #
      Person Perception
      Social Perception
BT   Cognitive Processes
RT   Attribution Theory
      Audience Awareness
      Cognitive Ability
      Communication Skills
      Conflict Resolution
      Consciousness Raising
      Egocentrism
      Empathy
      Extraversion Introversion
      Intention
      Interpersonal Communication
      Interpersonal Competence
      Interpersonal Relationship
      Metacognition
      Moral Development
      Perspective Taking
      Role Perception
      Self Concept
      Social Attitudes
      Social Development
      Social Theories
      Transactional Analysis

Social Competence
USE   Interpersonal Competence

Social Context
USE   Social Environment

Social Control   *JUN. 1983*
      Postings: 499   GC: 510
SN   Use of sanctions and laws by societies to
      circumscribe individual action
RT   Behavior Standards
      Compliance (Psychology)
      Conflict Resolution
      Law Enforcement
      Power Structure
      Sanctions
      Social Behavior
      Social Environment
      Social Influences
      Social Problems
      Social Reinforcement
      Social Structure
      Socialization

Social Desirability   *AUG. 1986*
      Postings: 197   GC: 520
SN   Perceived social acceptability, frequently
      manifested in response biases on inven-
      tories or surveys (i.e., the tendency to
      give socially favorable, or sometimes
      unfavorable, answers)
BT   Social Attitudes
RT   Attitude Measures
      Forced Choice Technique
      Personality Measures
      Popularity
      Response Style (Tests)
      Responses
      Social Behavior
      Social Bias
      Social Influences

Social Development   *JUL. 1966*
      Postings: 5,061   GC: 120
SN   Pattern or process of change exhibited
      by individuals resulting from their inter-
      action with other individuals, social insti-
      tutions, social customs, etc. (Note: Do
      not confuse with "Social Change"—prior
      to Mar80, the use of this term was not
      restricted by a Scope Note)
BT   Individual Development
RT   Dependency (Personality)
      Developmental Delays
      Egocentrism
      Friendship
      Individualism
      Interpersonal Competence
      Mate Selection
      Midlife Transitions
      Personality Development
      Perspective Taking
      Sexual Identity
      Social Adjustment
      Social Attitudes
      Social Cognition
      Social Differences
      Social Environment
      Social Experience
      Social Influences
      Social Life
      Socialization

Social Dialects   *JUL. 1966*
      Postings: 470   GC: 450
SN   Special varieties within a language, de-
      fined by the social environment of its
      speakers
BT   Dialects
RT   Bidialectalism
      Black Dialects
      Diglossia
      Language
      Language Role
      Linguistics
      Nonstandard Dialects
      Regional Dialects
      Social Class
      Standard Spoken Usage
      Urban Language

Social Differences   *JUL. 1966*
      Postings: 1,464   GC: 510
UF   Social Class Differences
BT   Differences
RT   Cultural Differences
      Culture Conflict
      Individual Differences
      Intermarriage
      Racial Differences
      Rural Urban Differences
      Social Attitudes
      Social Characteristics
      Social Class
      Social Development
      Social Environment
      Social Integration
      Social Values

Social Disadvantagement (1966 1980)
USE   Disadvantaged

Social Discrimination   *JUL. 1966*
      Postings: 1,768   GC: 540
SN   Unfavorable treatment of individuals or
      groups on arbitrary grounds (Note: Do
      not confuse with various "Bias" terms,
      which refer to prejudicial attitudes that
      may lead to such treatment)
UF   Bigotry
      Discrimination (Social)
NT   Age Discrimination
      Disability Discrimination
      Educational Discrimination
      Ethnic Discrimination
      Housing Discrimination
      Racial Discrimination
      Religious Discrimination
      Reverse Discrimination
      Sex Discrimination
RT   Caste
      Civil Rights
      Civil Rights Legislation
      Discriminatory Legislation
      Equal Facilities
      Ghettos
      Intergroup Relations
      Minority Groups
      Occupational Segregation
      Segregationist Organizations
      Social Bias
      Social Integration
      Test Bias

Social Distribution   *JUL. 1966*
      Postings: 64   GC: 550
SN   Description of the distribution of indi-
      viduals or groups with reference to their
      social status
BT   Demography
RT   Incidence
      Social Class
      Social Mobility
      Social Status
      Social Stratification

Social Drinking
USE   Drinking

Social Environment   *JUL. 1966*
      Postings: 2,438   GC: 510
SN   Aggregate of social factors or conditions
      that influence individuals or groups
UF   Atmosphere (Social)
      Social Climate
      Social Context
NT   Social Isolation
BT   Environment
RT   Cultural Context
      Culture Conflict
      Quality of Life
      Social Attitudes
      Social Characteristics
      Social Control
      Social Development
      Social Differences
      Social History
      Social Indicators
      Social Influences
      Social Integration
      Social Theories
      Social Values
      Sociocultural Patterns
      Subcultures
      Work Environment

Social Exchange Theory   *JUL. 1966*
      Postings: 269   GC: 810
SN   Social interactions conceptualized as eco-
      nomic transactions, with social behavior
      oriented toward expected returns (either
      material or psychic)
BT   Social Theories
RT   Altruism
      Competition
      Cooperation
      Informal Organization
      Interpersonal Relationship
      Organizational Development
      Organizational Theories
      Organizations (Groups)

      Power Structure
      Rewards
      Self Reward

Social Experience   *JUL. 1966*
      Postings: 372   GC: 510
BT   Experience
      Social Background
RT   Cross Age Teaching
      Experiential Learning
      Interpersonal Competence
      Social Development
      Social Influences

Social Factors (1968 1980)
USE   Social Influences

Social Geography
USE   Human Geography

Social History   *APR. 1975*
      Postings: 2,148   GC: 430
SN   History that concentrates on the socio-
      cultural aspects of the life, customs,
      trends, and institutions/organizations of
      a people
BT   History
RT   Cultural Context
      Culture
      Economics
      Family History
      Historiography
      Holidays
      Intellectual History
      Journalism History
      Life Style
      Local History
      Oral History
      Public History
      Social Change
      Social Environment
      Sociocultural Patterns
      Socioeconomic Influences
      Sociology
      Traditionalism

Social Immaturity (1966 1980)
USE   Maturity (Individuals)

Social Indicators   *OCT. 1976*
      Postings: 680   GC: 520
SN   Output-oriented measures of individuals
      and groups that reflect quality of life
BT   Statistical Data
RT   Futures (of Society)
      Life Satisfaction
      Living Standards
      Prediction
      Quality of Life
      Social Change
      Social Characteristics
      Social Environment
      Social Problems
      Social Science Research
      Sociocultural Patterns
      Socioeconomic Influences
      Trend Analysis

Social Influences   *JUL. 1966*
      Postings: 8,712   GC: 510
SN   Social factors or circumstances that af-
      fect or alter some condition or situation
      (Note: Use a more precise term if possi-
      ble)
UF   Social Factors (1968 1980)
      Social Pressure
BT   Influences
RT   Criticism
      Cultural Influences
      Cultural Interrelationships
      Language Role
      Mass Media Role
      Minority Group Influences
      Political Socialization
      Population Growth
      Science and Society
      Social Adjustment

= Two or more Descriptors are used to represent this term.
The term's main entry shows the appropriate coordination.

Social Attitudes
Social Background
Social Behavior
Social Change
Social Characteristics
Social Control
Social Desirability
Social Development
Social Environment
Social Experience
Social Integration
Social Status
Social Stratification
Social Theories
Social Values
Sociocultural Patterns
Socioeconomic Influences
Sociology
Subcultures

Social Institutions (Organizations)
USE   Institutions

Social Institutions (Social Patterns)
USE   Sociocultural Patterns

Social Integration   *DEC. 1968*
        Postings: 2,648   GC: 540
SN   Process of uniting the diverse groups of
        a society into a cohesive and harmoni-
        ous whole
UF   Ethnic Integration
        Integration (Social)
        Social Class Integration
NT   Classroom Desegregation
        Neighborhood Integration
        Personnel Integration
        Racial Integration
        School Desegregation
        Voluntary Desegregation
RT   Acculturation
        Cooperative Learning
        Cross Cultural Training
        Cultural Interrelationships
        Desegregation Effects
        Desegregation Methods
        Desegregation Plans
        Ethnic Groups
        Ethnic Relations
        Human Relations
        Inclusive Schools
        Integration Readiness
        Interaction Process Analysis
        Interfaith Relations
        Intergroup Education
        Intergroup Relations
        Interpersonal Relationship
        Multicultural Education
        Social Change
        Social Class
        Social Differences
        Social Discrimination
        Social Environment
        Social Influences
        Social Networks
        Social Problems
        Social Systems
        Tokenism

Social Interaction
USE   Interpersonal Relationship

Social Isolation   *JUL. 1966*
        Postings: 709   GC: 530
BT   Social Environment
RT   Alienation
        Cultural Isolation
        Disadvantaged Environment
        Extraversion Introversion
        Geographic Isolation
        Loneliness
        Professional Isolation
        Shyness
        Social Adjustment
        Social Psychology

Social Issues
USE   Social Problems

Social Learning
USE   Socialization

Social Life   *JUL. 1966*
        Postings: 397   GC: 520
RT   Dating (Social)
        Friendship
        Interpersonal Attraction
        Interpersonal Relationship
        Popularity
        Social Development

Social Maturity (1966 1980)
USE   Maturity (Individuals)

Social Mobility   *JUL. 1966*
        Postings: 848   GC: 520
SN   Change in the social status of individuals
        or groups
UF   Social Opportunities (1966 1980)
        Social Restrictions
BT   Mobility
RT   American Dream
        Black Achievement
        Educational Mobility
        Educational Status Comparison
        Intergroup Relations
        Interpersonal Relationship
        Occupational Mobility
        Social Distribution
        Social Status
        Socioeconomic Status

Social Networks   *NOV. 1982*
        Postings: 925   GC: 710
SN   Series of communication linkages relat-
        ing groups, organizations, or persons in
        social situations—can be interpersonal,
        economic, political, action-based, or role-
        based links
BT   Networks
RT   Communication (Thought Transfer)
        Communications
        Information Networks
        Intergroup Relations
        Interpersonal Relationship
        Social Behavior
        Social Integration
        Social Services
        Social Structure
        Social Support Groups
        Social Systems
        Social Theories
        Sociometric Techniques

Social Norms
USE   Behavior Standards
AND   Social Behavior

Social Opportunities (1966 1980)
USE   Social Mobility

Social Organizations   *JUL. 1966*
        Postings: 222   GC: 520
SN   Organizations whose primary purpose is
        encouraging social activities and inter-
        action (Note: Do not confuse with "So-
        cial Agencies"—prior to Mar80, the use
        of this term was not restricted by a
        Scope Note)
BT   Organizations (Groups)
RT   Community Organizations
        Fraternities
        Sororities
        Student Unions

Social Perception
USE   Social Cognition

Social Planning   *JUL. 1966*
        Postings: 321   GC: 610
BT   Planning
RT   Planning Commissions
        Regional Planning
        Urban Planning

Social Pressure
USE   Social Influences

Social Problems   *JUL. 1966*
        Postings: 6,143   GC: 530
UF   Social Issues
BT   Problems
RT   Conflict
        Controversial Issues (Course Content)
        Debate
        Justice
        Political Issues
        Public Affairs Education
        Quality of Life
        Science and Society
        Social Adjustment
        Social Attitudes
        Social Change
        Social Control
        Social Indicators
        Social Integration
        Social Studies
        Sociology
        Values

Social Promotion   *FEB. 2000*
        Postings: 61   GC: 320
SN   Process of passing students on to the
        next level or grade based on age or social
        maturity rather than academic accom-
        plishment
BT   Student Promotion
RT   Academic Failure
        Academic Standards
        Age Grade Placement
        Grade Repetition
        Low Achievement
        Underachievement

Social Psychology   *JUL. 1966*
        Postings: 1,766   GC: 230
SN   The study of the way the personality,
        attitudes, and motivations of individuals
        reciprocally influence and are influenced
        by the structure, dynamics, and behavior
        of the social groups with which they
        interact
BT   Psychology
        Sociology
RT   Behaviorism
        Clinical Psychology
        Community Psychology
        Compliance (Psychology)
        Criminology
        Delinquency
        Educational Psychology
        Educational Sociology
        Group Dynamics
        Groups
        Industrial Psychology
        Psychopathology
        Reference Groups
        Resistance (Psychology)
        Self Actualization
        Self Fulfilling Prophecies
        Social Isolation
        Social Reinforcement

Social Reconstruction
USE   Social Change

Social Recreation Programs (1966 1980)
USE   Recreational Programs

Social Reform
USE   Social Action

Social Reinforcement   *AUG. 1969*
        Postings: 580   GC: 110
BT   Reinforcement
RT   Behavior Modification
        Cooperation
        Negative Reinforcement
        Positive Reinforcement
        Reality Therapy
        Rewards
        Self Fulfilling Prophecies

Social Control
Social Psychology
Sociology

Social Relations (1966 1980)   *MAR. 1980*
        Postings: 1,589   GC: 520
SN   Invalid Descriptor—used to index both
        interpersonal and group relations—see
        such Descriptors as "Interpersonal Re-
        lationship," "Intergroup Relations,"
        "Group Dynamics," "Human Relations,"
        etc.

Social Responsibility   *JUN. 1969*
        Postings: 2,167   GC: 510
NT   Citizenship Responsibility
BT   Responsibility
RT   Citizen Participation
        Community Action
        Community Programs
        Community Responsibility
        Educational Responsibility
        Humanitarianism
        Leadership Responsibility
        Neighborhood Improvement
        Public Service
        Social Action
        Social Services
        Social Support Groups
        Urban Improvement
        Welfare Services

Social Restrictions
USE   Social Mobility

Social Role
USE   Role

Social Science Methodology
USE   Research Methodology
AND   Social Science Research

Social Science Research   *SEP. 1975*
        Postings: 4,636   GC: 810
SN   Basic, applied, and developmental re-
        search conducted to advance knowledge
        in the social sciences (Note: As of Oct81,
        use as a minor Descriptor for examples
        of this kind of research—use as a major
        Descriptor only as the subject of a docu-
        ment)
UF   Social Science Methodology #
        Sociological Studies #
NT   Critical Theory
        Economic Research
BT   Research
RT   Anthropology
        Area Studies
        Behavioral Science Research
        Communication Research
        Demography
        Economics
        Educational Research
        Ethnic Studies
        Ethnography
        Ethnology
        Geography
        Gerontology
        Historians
        Historiography
        History
        International Studies
        Marxian Analysis
        Participant Observation
        Policy Analysis
        Political Science
        Psychological Studies
        Psychology
        Qualitative Research
        Research and Development
        Rural Sociology
        Social Indicators
        Social Sciences
        Social Scientists
        Social Studies
        Sociologists
        Sociology
        Urban Studies

= Two or more Descriptors are used to represent this term.
The term's main entry shows the appropriate coordination.

Social Sciences   *JUL. 1966*
Postings: 4,354   GC: 400
NT   Anthropology
    Civics
    Demography
    Economics
    Geography
    Gerontology
    History
    International Studies
    Political Science
    Social Studies
    Sociology
    Topography
BT   Sciences
RT   Area Studies
    Behavioral Sciences
    Controversial Issues (Course Content)
    Ethnic Studies
    Global Approach
    Psychology
    Religion Studies
    Social Science Research
    Social Scientists
    Sociobiology
    Urban Studies

Social Scientists   *SEP. 1982*
Postings: 285   GC: 640
NT   Historians
    Sociologists
BT   Professional Personnel
RT   Anthropology
    Demography
    Economics
    Ethnography
    Ethnology
    Experimenter Characteristics
    Geography
    Gerontology
    History
    International Studies
    Political Science
    Psychologists
    Researchers
    Scholarship
    Scientists
    Social Science Research
    Social Sciences
    Sociology
    Topography

Social Services   *JUL. 1966*
Postings: 4,273   GC: 520
SN   Organized assistance provided by public or private agencies and organizations to the members of a society
UF   Sociopsychological Services (1967 1980) #
NT   Adult Day Care
    Adult Foster Care
    Ancillary School Services
    Day Care
    Foster Care
    Social Work
    Welfare Services
BT   Human Services
RT   Community Information Services
    Community Services
    Eligibility
    Group Homes
    Hospices (Terminal Care)
    Humanitarianism
    Integrated Services
    Long Term Care
    New Federalism
    Professional Services
    Social Agencies
    Social Networks
    Social Responsibility
    Social Support Groups
    Visiting Homemakers

Social Skills
USE   Interpersonal Competence

Social Status   *JUL. 1966*
Postings: 1,372   GC: 510
UF   Class Status

BT   Status
RT   Advantaged
    Disadvantaged
    Popularity
    Prestige
    Quality of Life
    Social Class
    Social Distribution
    Social Influences
    Social Mobility
    Social Structure
    Socioeconomic Status
    Status Need

Social Stratification   *OCT. 1972*
Postings: 772   GC: 520
BT   Social Structure
RT   Caste
    Elitism
    Group Membership
    Group Status
    Marxian Analysis
    Role Theory
    Social Class
    Social Distribution
    Social Influences
    Social Systems
    Status

Social Structure   *JUL. 1966*
Postings: 1,504   GC: 520
NT   Social Stratification
BT   Organization
RT   Cultural Context
    Family Structure
    Governmental Structure
    Group Structure
    Industrial Structure
    Power Structure
    Social Class
    Social Control
    Social Networks
    Social Status
    Social Systems
    Social Theories
    Sociocultural Patterns

Social Studies   *JUL. 1966*
Postings: 20,729   GC: 400
SN   Social studies consist of adaptations of knowledge from the social sciences for teaching purposes at the elementary and secondary levels of education
UF   Social Studies Units (1966 1980) #
BT   Curriculum
    Social Sciences
RT   Anthropology
    Civics
    Controversial Issues (Course Content)
    Cultural Education
    Current Events
    Economics
    Geography
    History
    Law Related Education
    Locational Skills (Social Studies)
    Political Science
    Religion Studies
    Social Problems
    Social Science Research
    United States Government (Course)
    World Affairs

Social Studies Units (1966 1980)
USE   Social Studies
AND   Units of Study

Social Support Groups   *SEP. 1982*
Postings: 3,138   GC: 240
SN   Persons (incl. individuals), organizations, or institutions that provide physical, emotional, spiritual, psychic, or intellectual maintenance and sustenance
UF   Support Groups (Human Services)
    Support Networks (Personal Assistance)
BT   Groups
RT   Caregivers
    Consciousness Raising

    Cooperation
    Counseling
    Donors
    Helping Relationship
    Human Services
    Humanitarianism
    Reference Groups
    Rehabilitation
    Social Agencies
    Social Networks
    Social Responsibility
    Social Services
    Social Work
    Social Workers

Social Systems   *JUL. 1966*
Postings: 849   GC: 520
NT   Capitalism
    Communism
    Fascism
    Socialism
RT   Group Structure
    Human Geography
    Ideology
    Social Integration
    Social Networks
    Social Stratification
    Social Structure
    Social Theories
    Sociocultural Patterns

Social Theories   *OCT. 1982*
Postings: 941   GC: 810
SN   Theories about the structure, organization, and functioning of human societies
NT   Organizational Theories
    Social Exchange Theory
BT   Theories
RT   Behavior Theories
    Chaos Theory
    Critical Theory
    Ideology
    Role Theory
    Social Change
    Social Cognition
    Social Environment
    Social Influences
    Social Networks
    Social Structure
    Social Systems
    Socialization
    Sociocultural Patterns
    Socioeconomic Influences
    Sociology

Social Trends
USE   Sociocultural Patterns

Social Values   *JUL. 1966*
Postings: 4,818   GC: 520
SN   Principles and standards of human interaction within a given group that are regarded by members of that group as being worthy, important, or significant
UF   Group Values
BT   Values
RT   Aesthetic Values
    American Dream
    Conservatism
    Critical Theory
    Cultural Context
    Democratic Values
    Freedom
    Humanitarianism
    Ideology
    Individualism
    Justice
    Liberalism
    Moral Values
    Peer Groups
    Political Attitudes
    Quality of Life
    Social Attitudes
    Social Change
    Social Characteristics
    Social Differences
    Social Environment
    Social Influences
    Work Ethic

Social Welfare (1966 1980)   *MAR. 1980*
Postings: 316   GC: 520
SN   Invalid Descriptor—used for well-being and various types of social services—use "Well Being" for former concept, "Welfare Services" for organized assistance to the disadvantaged, and "Social Services" or other appropriate terms for social services provided to the general population

Social Work   *JUL. 1966*
Postings: 2,312   GC: 640
SN   Activities and services designed to improve social conditions affecting communities, families, or individuals
BT   Social Services
RT   Caseworker Approach
    Caseworkers
    Counseling
    Rehabilitation
    School Social Workers
    Social Agencies
    Social Support Groups
    Social Workers
    Welfare Agencies
    Welfare Services

Social Workers   *JUL. 1966*
Postings: 1,725   GC: 640
UF   Client Caseworkers (1966 1980)
NT   School Social Workers
BT   Caseworkers
    Professional Personnel
RT   Child Caregivers
    Counselors
    Guidance Personnel
    Mental Health Workers
    Parole Officers
    Probation Officers
    Social Agencies
    Social Support Groups
    Social Work
    Welfare Agencies

Socialism   *OCT. 1974*
Postings: 474   GC: 610
BT   Social Systems
RT   Capitalism
    Collective Settlements
    Communism
    Economics
    Fascism
    Government (Administrative Body)
    Imperialism
    Marxism
    Political Science

Socialization   *JUL. 1966*
Postings: 6,059   GC: 120
UF   Social Learning
NT   Political Socialization
RT   Assertiveness
    Cognitive Dissonance
    Compliance (Psychology)
    Consciousness Raising
    Cooperative Learning
    Cross Age Teaching
    Cultural Literacy
    Ethnicity
    Hidden Curriculum
    Ideology
    Imitation
    Inhibition
    Interpersonal Competence
    Mass Media Use
    Modeling (Psychology)
    Nonformal Education
    Oral Tradition
    Peer Influence
    Phenomenology
    Reference Groups
    Role Conflict
    Significant Others
    Social Control
    Social Development
    Social Theories
    Subcultures

\# = Two or more Descriptors are used to represent this term.
The term's main entry shows the appropriate coordination.

Socially Advantaged
USE   Advantaged

Socially Deviant Behavior (1966 1980)
USE   Antisocial Behavior

Socially Disadvantaged (1966 1980)
USE   Disadvantaged

Socially Maladjusted (1966 1980)
USE   Social Adjustment

Societal Change
USE   Social Change

Sociobiology   *OCT. 1983*
        Postings: 86   GC: 490
SN   The study of the biological basis of social
        behavior, especially as such behavior is
        transmitted genetically (Note: Do not
        confuse with "Social Biology")
BT   Behavioral Sciences
        Biological Sciences
RT   Behavior Patterns
        Ethology
        Evolution
        Genetics
        Nature Nurture Controversy
        Social Behavior
        Social Sciences
        Zoology

Sociocultural Patterns   *JUL. 1966*
        Postings: 4,585   GC: 520
UF   Social Institutions (Social Patterns)
        Social Trends
NT   Ethnicity
        Humanitarianism
RT   Biculturalism
        Cross Cultural Studies
        Cross Cultural Training
        Cultural Context
        Cultural Influences
        Cultural Interrelationships
        Cultural Maintenance
        Cultural Pluralism
        Culture
        Culture Lag
        Demography
        Educational Anthropology
        Ethnocentrism
        Ethnography
        Ethnology
        Human Relations
        Ideology
        Kinship
        Life Style
        Minority Group Influences
        Non Western Civilization
        Role of Education
        Social Change
        Social Environment
        Social History
        Social Indicators
        Social Influences
        Social Structure
        Social Systems
        Social Theories
        Sociolinguistics
        Sociology
        Traditionalism
        Trend Analysis
        Western Civilization

Sociodrama (1966 1980)
USE   Role Playing

Sociodramatic Play
USE   Dramatic Play

Socioeconomic Background   *JUL. 1966*
        Postings: 1,236   GC: 510
NT   Social Background
BT   Background

RT   Economics
        Socioeconomic Influences

Socioeconomic Influences   *JUL. 1966*
        Postings: 5,300   GC: 510
BT   Influences
RT   Baby Boomers
        Black Community
        Boomtowns
        Economic Factors
        Economic Impact
        Economic Opportunities
        Economics
        Industrialization
        Modernization
        Political Influences
        Social History
        Social Indicators
        Social Influences
        Social Theories
        Socioeconomic Background
        Socioeconomic Status
        Supply and Demand
        Traditionalism

Socioeconomic Level
USE   Socioeconomic Status

Socioeconomic Status   *JUL. 1966*
        Postings: 5,976   GC: 510
UF   Socioeconomic Level
BT   Status
RT   Affluent Youth
        Economic Status
        Economics
        Educational Benefits
        Educational Status Comparison
        Employment Level
        Income
        Ownership
        Quality of Life
        Social Class
        Social Mobility
        Social Status
        Socioeconomic Influences
        Sociolinguistics

Sociograms
USE   Sociometric Techniques

Sociolinguistics   *JUL. 1966*
        Postings: 3,771   GC: 450
SN   The study of language in society—more
        specifically, the study of language varie-
        ties, their functions, and their speakers
NT   Dialect Studies
        Language Planning
        Language Variation
BT   Linguistics
RT   Anthropological Linguistics
        Bidialectalism
        Bilingualism
        Code Switching (Language)
        Dialects
        Diglossia
        Grammatical Acceptability
        Immersion Programs
        Kinship Terminology
        Language Attitudes
        Language Maintenance
        Language Minorities
        Language of Instruction
        Language Planning
        Language Research
        Language Role
        Language Skill Attrition
        Language Standardization
        Language Usage
        Linguistic Borrowing
        Linguistic Theory
        Monolingualism
        Multilingualism
        Mutual Intelligibility
        Native Speakers
        Nonstandard Dialects
        Official Languages
        Pragmatics
        Psycholinguistics
        Sociocultural Patterns

        Socioeconomic Status
        Sociology
        Standard Spoken Usage
        Urban Language

Sociological Novels (1969 1980)
USE   Novels

Sociological Studies
USE   Social Science Research
AND   Sociology

Sociologists   *FEB. 1996*
        Postings: 58   GC: 640
SN   Scholars who systematically study and
        critique the development, structure, func-
        tioning, and dilemmas of human society
BT   Social Scientists
RT   Criminology
        Educational Sociology
        Researchers
        Rural Sociology
        Social Science Research
        Sociology

Sociology   *JUL. 1966*
        Postings: 3,282   GC: 400
UF   Sociological Studies #
NT   Criminology
        Educational Sociology
        Rural Sociology
        Social Psychology
BT   Behavioral Sciences
        Social Sciences
RT   Area Studies
        Authoritarianism
        Behavior
        Critical Theory
        Cross Cultural Studies
        Demography
        Elitism
        Ethnography
        Ethnology
        Ideology
        Marxian Analysis
        Marxism
        Personal Autonomy
        Social Behavior
        Social Biology
        Social Characteristics
        Social History
        Social Influences
        Social Problems
        Social Reinforcement
        Social Science Research
        Social Scientists
        Social Theories
        Sociocultural Patterns
        Sociolinguistics
        Sociologists

Sociology of Education
USE   Educational Sociology

Sociometric Techniques   *JUL. 1966*
        Postings: 660   GC: 820
SN   Procedures used to identify the prefer-
        ences, likes, or dislikes of the members
        of a group with respect to each other, as
        well as to identify various patterns of
        group structure or interaction
UF   Sociograms
BT   Measurement Techniques
RT   Group Behavior
        Group Dynamics
        Group Structure
        Groups
        Interaction Process Analysis
        Intergroup Relations
        Interpersonal Relationship
        Judgment Analysis Technique
        Multidimensional Scaling
        Naturalistic Observation
        Peer Evaluation
        Social Behavior
        Social Networks

Sociopsychological Services (1967 1980)
USE   Psychological Services
AND   Social Services

Soft Cover Books
USE   Paperback Books

Softball   *DEC. 1975*
        Postings: 49   GC: 470
BT   Team Sports
RT   Baseball

Software (Computers)
USE   Computer Software

Software Development (Computers)
USE   Computer Software Development

Software Evaluation (Computers)
USE   Computer Software Evaluation

Software Reviews (Computers)
USE   Computer Software Reviews

Software Selection (Computers)
USE   Computer Software Selection

Soil Conservation   *JUL. 1966*
        Postings: 277   GC: 410
BT   Conservation (Environment)
        Land Use
RT   Agronomy
        Conservation Education
        Depleted Resources
        Ecology
        Environmental Education
        Forestry
        Groundwater
        Natural Resources
        Soil Science
        Water
        Wetlands
        Wind (Meteorology)

Soil Science   *JUL. 1966*
        Postings: 404   GC: 410
BT   Earth Science
RT   Agronomy
        Biology
        Botany
        Chemistry
        Clay
        Coal
        Fertilizers
        Forestry
        Geology
        Hydrology
        Land Use
        Mineralogy
        Oil
        Petrology
        Seismology
        Soil Conservation

Solar Energy   *JUN. 1983*
        Postings: 198   GC: 490
SN   Light and heat radiation of the sun—also
        the energy collected as heat or converted
        to electricity from this source
UF   Solar Heating #
        Solar Radiation (1968 1983)
        Solar Radiation Energy
BT   Radiation
RT   Alternative Energy Sources
        Climate
        Climate Control
        Electricity
        Greenhouse Effect
        Heat
        Light
        Meteorology
        Power Technology
        Radiation Effects
        Temperature

= Two or more Descriptors are used to represent this term.
The term's main entry shows the appropriate coordination.

Thermal Environment
Wind (Meteorology)

Solar Heating
USE   Heating
AND   Solar Energy

Solar Radiation Energy
USE   Solar Energy

Solar Radiation (1968 1983)
USE   Solar Energy

Solar System   JAN. 1993
       Postings: 109   GC: 490
SN   The sun and all the celestial bodies that
       revolve around it (including the planets
       and their moons, the asteroids, comets,
       and meteoroids)
RT   Astronomy
       Planetariums
       Satellites (Aerospace)
       Space Exploration
       Space Sciences
       Stars

Solicitors (Law)
USE   Lawyers

Solid Geometry   JUL. 1966
       Postings: 96   GC: 480
BT   Geometry
RT   Analytic Geometry
       Plane Geometry
       Volume (Mathematics)

Solid Wastes   AUG. 1982
       Postings: 232   GC: 410
SN   Unwanted solid or semisolid materials
       discarded by farms, businesses, com-
       munities, or individuals (Note: Use "Waste
       Water" for sewage)
UF   Garbage
       Litter
       Trash
BT   Wastes
RT   Pollution
       Recycling
       Sludge
       Waste Disposal
       Waste Water
       Water Treatment

Soliloquies
USE   Monologs

Somali   JUL. 1966
       Postings: 19   GC: 440
BT   Afro Asiatic Languages

Songs   AUG. 1986
       Postings: 390   GC: 420
NT   Art Song
       Ballads
       Hymns
BT   Vocal Music
RT   Lyric Poetry
       Music Activities
       Music Education
       Music Techniques
       Musical Composition
       Nursery Rhymes
       Singing

Sonic Environment
USE   Acoustical Environment

Sonnets   JAN. 1970
       Postings: 24   GC: 430
SN   Lyric poems of fourteen lines following
       one of several definite rhyme schemes
BT   Literary Genres
       Lyric Poetry

RT   Ballads
       Imagery
       Metaphors
       Odes
       Renaissance Literature

Sons   SEP. 1981
       Postings: 140   GC: 510
BT   Males
RT   Daughters
       Family (Sociological Unit)
       Family Environment
       Family Life
       Kinship
       Parent Child Relationship
       Parents

Sororities   JAN. 1978
       Postings: 157   GC: 520
SN   Groups of women associated through
       social, scholastic, or professional inter-
       ests
BT   Organizations (Groups)
RT   Females
       Fraternities
       Honor Societies
       National Organizations
       Professional Associations
       Social Organizations
       Student Organizations
       Womens Education

Sorting Procedures (1966 1980)
USE   Classification

Sound
USE   Acoustics

Sound Barriers
USE   Acoustic Insulation

Sound Effects   JUL. 1966
       Postings: 116   GC: 720
BT   Special Effects
RT   Acoustics
       Audio Equipment
       Audiotape Recordings
       Noise (Sound)

Sound Equipment
USE   Audio Equipment

Sound Films (1966 1980)
USE   Films

Sound Insulation
USE   Acoustic Insulation

Sound Spectrographs   MAR. 1980
       Postings: 198   GC: 910
SN   Electronic instruments used in acoustic
       phonetics to record the frequency, am-
       plitude, and duration of sound waves
       produced by speech (Note: Prior to
       Mar80, "Spectrograms" was used for
       this concept)
UF   Spectrograms (1967 1980)
       Spectrographs (Sound)
BT   Audio Equipment
       Electronic Equipment
       Measurement Equipment
RT   Acoustic Phonetics
       Artificial Speech
       Componential Analysis
       Instrumentation
       Phonology
       Speech
       Speech Therapy
       Visible Speech

Sound Systems
USE   Audio Equipment

Sound Tape Recordings
USE   Audiotape Recordings

Sound Tracks (1966 1980)   MAR. 1980
       Postings: 43   GC: 720
SN   Invalid Descriptor—see other appropri-
       ate "film," "audio," and "sound" Descrip-
       tors

Sound Transmission
USE   Acoustics

Sound Waves
USE   Acoustics

Soundproofing
USE   Acoustic Insulation

Source Credibility
USE   Credibility

South American History
USE   Latin American History

South American Literature
USE   Latin American Literature

South Americans
USE   Latin Americans

South Asian Civilization
USE   Non Western Civilization

Southern Attitudes (1966 1980)
USE   Regional Attitudes

Southern Citizens (1966 1980)   MAR. 1980
       Postings: 17   GC: 610
SN   Invalid Descriptor—coordinate the Iden-
       tifier "United States (South)" with ap-
       propriate population Descriptors

Southern Community (1966 1980)
                                          MAR. 1980
       Postings: 51   GC: 520
SN   Invalid Descriptor—coordinate the Iden-
       tifier "United States (South)" with ap-
       propriate "community" Descriptors

Southern Schools (1966 1980)   MAR. 1980
       Postings: 262   GC: 340
SN   Invalid Descriptor—coordinate the Iden-
       tifier "United States (South)" with ap-
       propriate "school" and "education"
       Descriptors

Space   JUL. 1966
       Postings: 262   GC: 490
SN   Area or volume between specified
       boundaries (Note: Do not confuse with
       "Personal Space" or "Space Sciences"—
       prior to Mar80, the use of this term was
       not restricted by a Scope Note)
NT   Area
       Volume (Mathematics)
BT   Scientific Concepts
RT   Atomic Structure
       Atomic Theory
       Density (Matter)
       Distance
       Gravity (Physics)
       Intervals
       Proximity
       Quantum Mechanics
       Relativity
       Time

Space Classification   AUG. 1968
       Postings: 153   GC: 920
SN   Categorization of areas in a given facility
       generally by function or purpose
BT   Classification
RT   Building Plans
       Facility Inventory
       Facility Utilization Research
       Interior Design
       Interior Space
       Offices (Facilities)
       Space Utilization
       Spatial Relationship (Facilities)

Space Dividers   JUL. 1966
       Postings: 41   GC: 920
SN   Vertical surface or structure used for
       separating areas within larger rooms
UF   Room Dividers
NT   Movable Partitions
BT   Equipment
       Structural Elements (Construction)
RT   Classroom Design
       Flexible Facilities
       School Space
       Space Utilization

Space Exploration   MAR. 1980
       Postings: 343   GC: 490
SN   Scientific investigations of areas beyond
       the earth's atmosphere (Note: Use "Lu-
       nar Research" for studies referring to
       the earth's moon)
UF   Extraterrestrial Exploration
       Outer Space Research
       Planetary Exploration
NT   Lunar Research
BT   Scientific Research
RT   Aerospace Technology
       Astronomy
       Planetariums
       Satellites (Aerospace)
       Solar System
       Space Sciences
       Stars

Space Orientation (1968 1980)   MAR. 1980
       Postings: 329   GC: 120
SN   Invalid Descriptor—used inconsistently
       in indexing—see the Descriptors "Per-
       sonal Space" and "Spatial Ability"

Space Sciences   MAY 1972
       Postings: 1,022   GC: 490
BT   Sciences
RT   Aerospace Education
       Aerospace Technology
       Astronomy
       Earth Science
       Lunar Research
       Navigation
       Physical Sciences
       Planetariums
       Satellites (Aerospace)
       Solar System
       Space Exploration
       Stars

Space Time Continuum
USE   Relativity

Space Utilization   JUL. 1966
       Postings: 1,568   GC: 920
RT   Building Conversion
       Building Design
       Building Obsolescence
       Building Plans
       Buildings
       Campus Planning
       Classroom Design
       College Buildings
       Crowding
       Design Requirements
       Double Sessions
       Educational Complexes
       Educational Facilities Planning
       Equipment Storage
       Facilities

= Two or more Descriptors are used to represent this term.
The term's main entry shows the appropriate coordination.

Facility Case Studies
Facility Expansion
Facility Guidelines
Facility Planning
Facility Requirements
Facility Utilization Research
Flexible Facilities
Found Spaces
Furniture Arrangement
Interior Space
Physical Mobility
School Buildings
School Expansion
School Space
Space Classification
Space Dividers
Spatial Relationship (Facilities)
Storage
Underground Facilities

Spaced Negative Reinforcement
USE   Negative Reinforcement

Spanish   *JUL. 1966*
      Postings: 5,315   GC: 440
BT   Romance Languages
RT   Spanish Literature
      Spanish Speaking

Spanish American Literature (1969 1980)
USE   Hispanic American Literature

Spanish Americans   *JUL. 1966*
      Postings: 687   GC: 560
SN   Citizens or permanent residents of the
      United States who are of Spanish de-
      scent (Note: For other Hispanic peoples
      in the United States see "Hispanic Ameri-
      cans"—for those in the Caribbean or
      South America see "Latin Americans"—
      prior to Mar80, this term was not re-
      stricted by a Scope Note)
BT   Ethnic Groups
      Hispanic Americans
RT   Hispanic American Culture
      Hispanic American Literature
      Mexican Americans
      Minority Groups
      Spanish Speaking

Spanish Culture   *JUL. 1966*
      Postings: 301   GC: 560
SN   Culture of Spain (Note: For cultures of
      other Spanish-speaking peoples, see
      "Latin American Culture" or "Hispanic
      American Culture"—prior to Mar80, the
      use of this term was not restricted by a
      Scope Note)
BT   Culture
RT   Hispanic American Culture
      Latin American Culture
      Spanish Literature
      Spanish Speaking

Spanish Literature   *MAY 1969*
      Postings: 596   GC: 430
SN   Literature of Spain (Note: For other lit-
      erature in Spanish, see "Latin American
      Literature," "Mexican American Litera-
      ture," or "Hispanic American Litera-
      ture"—prior to Mar80, the use of this
      term was not restricted by a Scope Note)
BT   Literature
RT   Spanish
      Spanish Culture

Spanish Speaking   *JUL. 1966*
      Postings: 4,341   GC: 450
BT   Native Speakers
RT   Biculturalism
      Bilingual Students
      Bilingualism
      Cubans
      Dominicans
      English (Second Language)
      Hispanic American Literature
      Hispanic Americans

Limited English Speaking
Mexican American Literature
Mexican Americans
Mexicans
Native Language Instruction
Non English Speaking
Puerto Ricans
Spanish
Spanish Americans
Spanish Culture

Spatial Ability   *MAR. 1981*
      Postings: 1,569   GC: 120
SN   Ability to perceive or solve problems
      associated with relationships between
      objects or figures, including position,
      direction, size, form, and distance (Note:
      Prior to mid-1980, this concept was
      indexed under "Space Orientation" and
      "Spatial Relationship"—do not confuse
      with "Personal Space")
UF   Spatial Perception (1980 1981)
      Visuospatial Ability
BT   Ability
RT   Academic Ability
      Basic Skills
      Cognitive Ability
      Cognitive Mapping
      Depth Perception
      Echolocation
      Perception
      Perceptual Development
      Psychomotor Skills
      Visual Measures
      Visualization
      Visually Impaired Mobility

Spatial Perception (1980 1981)
USE   Spatial Ability

Spatial Relationship (Facilities)
                                     MAR. 1980
      Postings: 56   GC: 920
SN   Functional interconnections among ar-
      eas of buildings
BT   Relationship
RT   Architecture
      Building Design
      Building Plans
      Design Requirements
      Educational Facilities Planning
      Facility Planning
      Facility Utilization Research
      Flexible Facilities
      Interior Design
      Psychological Needs
      School Space
      Space Classification
      Space Utilization

Spatial Relationship (1966 1980)
                                     MAR. 1980
      Postings: 255   GC: 920
SN   Invalid Descriptor—used for both the
      spatial relationship among areas of a
      facility and the spatial orientation of indi-
      viduals—see the Descriptors "Spatial
      Relationship (Facilities)," "Spatial Abil-
      ity," and "Personal Space" for these
      concepts

Speaking Activities (1966 1980)
USE   Speech Communication

Speaking Skills
USE   Speech Skills

Speaking (1966 1980)
USE   Speech Communication

Special Admission
USE   Selective Admission

Special and Regular Education Relationship
USE   Regular and Special Education Rela-
      tionship

Special Classes   *JUL. 1966*
      Postings: 1,027   GC: 310
UF   Opportunity Classes (1966 1980)
BT   Classes (Groups of Students)
RT   In School Suspension
      Resource Room Programs
      Small Classes
      Special Education
      Special Education Teachers
      Special Schools
      Transitional Programs

Special Counselors (1966 1980)
USE   Counselors
AND   Specialists

Special Creation Theory
USE   Creationism

Special Degree Programs   *AUG. 1968*
      Postings: 383   GC: 340
SN   Postsecondary-level programs geared to
      the needs of adult students, taking into
      account previous experience or self-edu-
      cation rather than traditional college
      credits—may include external degree pro-
      grams
BT   Special Programs
RT   Adult Education
      Adult Students
      Alternative Teacher Certification
      Certification
      College Credits
      College Programs
      Continuing Education
      Credentials
      Degree Requirements
      Degrees (Academic)
      Equivalency Tests
      Experiential Learning
      External Degree Programs
      Nontraditional Education
      Nontraditional Students
      Prior Learning

Special Education   *JUL. 1966*
      Postings: 10,794   GC: 220
SN   Educational programs and services for
      disabled and/or gifted individuals who
      have intellectually, physically, emotion-
      ally, or socially different characteristics
      from those who can be taught through
      normal methods or materials (Note: Use
      a more specific term if possible)
NT   Adapted Physical Education
BT   Education
RT   Access to Education
      Behavior Modification
      Community Based Instruction (Disa-
         bilities)
      Compulsory Education
      Continuation Students
      Curriculum Based Assessment
      Daily Living Skills
      Developmental Delays
      Diagnostic Teaching
      Disabilities
      Early Intervention
      Educational Needs
      Gifted
      Grouping (Instructional Purposes)
      Homebound
      Inclusive Schools
      Individual Needs
      Individualized Education Programs
      Individualized Instruction
      Intervention
      Itinerant Teachers
      Labeling (of Persons)
      Mainstreaming
      Mobile Educational Services
      Noncategorical Education
      Normalization (Disabilities)
      Partial Vision
      Prereferral Intervention

Prognostic Tests
Regular and Special Education Rela-
   tionship
Rehabilitation
Resource Room Programs
Special Classes
Special Education Teachers
Special Programs
Special Schools
Specialists
Therapeutic Recreation
Therapy

Special Education Regular Education Cooperation
USE   Regular and Special Education Rela-
      tionship

Special Education Teachers   *JUL. 1966*
      Postings: 2,751   GC: 220
BT   Teachers
RT   Disabilities
      Gifted
      Itinerant Teachers
      Noncategorical Education
      Resource Room Programs
      Resource Teachers
      Special Classes
      Special Education
      Special Schools

Special Effects   *AUG. 1971*
      Postings: 115   GC: 720
SN   The use of electrical or mechanical de-
      vices or of photographic techniques to
      simulate audio and visual backgrounds
NT   Animation
      Sound Effects
BT   Production Techniques
RT   Audio Equipment
      Film Production
      Film Study
      Photography
      Tape Recordings
      Television
      Theater Arts
      Video Equipment

Special Health Problems   *JUL. 1966*
      Postings: 1,646   GC: 210
SN   Category in federal legislation referring
      to conditions that interfere with learning
      and development but are not classified
      under physical, visual, hearing, mental,
      or learning disabilities—usually involve
      limited strength, vitality, or alertness
BT   Disabilities
RT   Alcoholism
      Allergy
      Anemia
      Asthma
      Cancer
      Child Health
      Chronic Illness
      Cystic Fibrosis
      Diabetes
      Drug Addiction
      Health
      Heart Disorders
      Hygiene
      Hypertension
      Injuries
      Lead Poisoning
      Learning Problems
      Mental Retardation
      Pain
      Physical Disabilities
      Physical Health
      Poisoning
      Seizures
      Terminal Illness

Special Libraries   *JUL. 1966*
      Postings: 1,640   GC: 710
SN   Libraries consisting of materials on a
      specialized topic (e.g., music libraries)
      or in a non-print form (e.g., film librar-
      ies), or serving a specialized clientele

= Two or more Descriptors are used to represent this term.
The term's main entry shows the appropriate coordination.

(e.g., corporate, non-profit, or govern-
ment-agency libraries)
NT Corporate Libraries
    Film Libraries
    Government Libraries
    Institutional Libraries
    Law Libraries
    Medical Libraries
    Science Libraries
BT Libraries
RT Academic Libraries
    Branch Libraries
    Depository Libraries
    Documentation
    Public Libraries
    Research Libraries

Special Methods Courses
USE Methods Courses

Special Needs (Individuals)
USE Individual Needs

Special Needs Students   DEC. 1989
     Postings: 2,723   GC: 360
SN   Broad legislative category referring to all
     students identified as needing special
     assistance to achieve educational equity,
     e.g., the disabled, the disadvantaged,
     those seeking nontraditional careers, lim-
     ited English speakers—first appeared in
     U.S. "Voc-Ed" legislation of the mid-
     1970s (Note: Do not use for special
     education students—see "Special Edu-
     cation")
BT   Students
RT   Categorical Aid
     Continuation Students
     Correctional Education
     Developmental Delays
     Disabilities
     Displaced Homemakers
     Dropouts
     Early Intervention
     Economically Disadvantaged
     Educational Needs
     Educationally Disadvantaged
     Equal Education
     High Risk Students
     Inclusive Schools
     Individual Needs
     Individualized Education Programs
     Individualized Instruction
     Limited English Speaking
     Migrants
     Nontraditional Occupations
     Nontraditional Students
     Potential Dropouts
     Pregnant Students
     Prereferral Intervention
     Reentry Students
     Regular and Special Education Rela-
       tionship
     Resource Room Programs
     Retraining
     Student Needs
     Vocational Education

Special Olympics   AUG. 1989
     Postings: 41   GC: 220
SN   Fitness and athletic contests, modeled
     on the Olympic games, for mentally re-
     tarded children and adults
BT   Athletics
RT   Adapted Physical Education
     Mental Retardation
     Olympic Games
     Recreational Activities

Special Personnel
USE Specialists

Special Programs   JUL. 1966
     Postings: 1,608   GC: 320
SN   Planned activities that take account of
     individual mental and physical differ-
     ences
NT   Individualized Education Programs

Individualized Family Service Plans
Resource Room Programs
Special Degree Programs
BT   Programs
RT   Individual Needs
     Individualized Programs
     Special Education

Special Regular Education Interface
USE Regular and Special Education Rela-
       tionship

Special Schools   JUL. 1966
     Postings: 862   GC: 340
SN   Schools established for the purpose of
     caring for the educational needs of atypi-
     cal children (Note: Prior to Mar80, the
     use of this term was not restricted by a
     Scope Note)
UF   Special Service Schools
NT   Institutional Schools
     Residential Schools
BT   Schools
RT   Regional Schools
     Special Classes
     Special Education
     Special Education Teachers

Special Service Schools
USE Special Schools

Special Services (1966 1980)
USE Services

Special Teachers
USE Specialists

Special Zoning   JUL. 1966
     Postings: 8   GC: 610
BT   Zoning

Specialist in Education Degrees   JUL. 1966
     Postings: 51   GC: 340
SN   Degrees awarded upon completion of
     two-year programs at postbaccalaureate
     level for training school administrators
BT   Degrees (Academic)
RT   Administrator Education
     Bachelors Degrees
     Degree Requirements
     Doctoral Degrees
     Education Majors
     Masters Degrees
     Schools of Education
     Teacher Educator Education
     Teacher Educators

Specialists   JUL. 1966
     Postings: 845   GC: 360
UF   Guidance Specialists #
     Learning Specialists (1966 1980)
     Special Counselors (1966 1980) #
     Special Personnel
     Special Teachers
NT   Child Development Specialists
     Film Production Specialists
     Media Specialists
BT   Personnel
RT   Adjunct Faculty
     Advisory Committees
     Consultants
     Counselors
     Itinerant Teachers
     Referral
     Resource Staff
     Resource Teachers
     Shared Resources and Services
     Special Education
     Specialization
     Teachers

Specialization   JUL. 1966
     Postings: 1,398   GC: 120
SN   Concentration of interest and effort, or
     restriction of function, to a particular

aspect of some larger area of endeavor
(such as a field of study, occupation,
etc.)—also, the process of progressive
differentiation of functions
RT   Curriculum
     Differences
     Majors (Students)
     Occupations
     Postdoctoral Education
     Specialists

Specialty Schools
USE Proprietary Schools

Specific Learning Disabilities
USE Learning Disabilities

Specifications   SEP. 1968
     Postings: 551   GC: 720
SN   Detailed written statements of character-
     istics or requirements (Note: Use a more
     specific term if possible)
NT   Computer Software
     Design Requirements
     Facility Requirements
BT   Standards
RT   Building Plans
     Contracts
     Criteria
     Design
     Evaluation
     Evaluation Criteria
     Guidelines
     Master Plans
     Planning
     Program Proposals
     Purchasing

Spectator Traffic Control
USE Traffic Control

Spectators
USE Audiences

Spectrograms (1967 1980)
USE Sound Spectrographs

Spectrographs (Sound)
USE Sound Spectrographs

Spectroscopy   MAR. 1980
     Postings: 515   GC: 490
SN   Production, measurement, and analy-
     sis of spectra, especially electromagnetic
     radiation (Note: Prior to Mar80,
     "Spectrograms" was sometimes used
     for this concept)
BT   Physical Sciences
RT   Astronomy
     Atomic Structure
     Chemical Analysis
     Chemistry
     Crystallography
     Lasers
     Light
     Molecular Structure
     Optics
     Physical Chemistry
     Physics
     Radiation
     Structural Analysis (Science)

Speech   JUL. 1966
     Postings: 1,448   GC: 450
SN   (Note: Use a more specific term if possi-
     ble)
NT   Articulation (Speech)
     Artificial Speech
     Caregiver Speech
     Inner Speech (Subvocal)
     Pronunciation
     Speech Acts
     Speech Compression
BT   Language Arts
RT   Acoustic Phonetics

Articulation Impairments
Choral Speaking
Coherence
Cued Speech
Diction
Discourse Modes
Language
Linguistics
Monologs
Oral Language
Persuasive Discourse
Phonemics
Phonetics
Phonology
Public Speaking
Rhetoric
Rhetorical Invention
Sound Spectrographs
Speech and Hearing Clinics
Speech Communication
Speech Curriculum
Speech Evaluation
Speech Habits
Speech Impairments
Speech Improvement
Speech Instruction
Speech Language Pathology
Speech Skills
Speech Synthesizers
Speech Tests
Speech Therapy
Verbal Communication
Visible Speech
Voice Disorders
Word Frequency

Speech Acts   MAR. 1983
     Postings: 543   GC: 450
SN   Minimal units of meaningful communi-
     cation (from single words to sentences)
     that are conceptualized and produced in
     terms of particular functions (i.e., to
     question, command, warn, request, in-
     form, explain, convince, compliment,
     apologize, promise, etc.)
UF   Illocutionary Acts
BT   Speech
RT   Dialogs (Language)
     Discourse Analysis
     Language Patterns
     Mutual Intelligibility
     Pragmatics

Speech and Hearing Clinics   MAR. 1980
     Postings: 66   GC: 920
UF   Hearing Clinics (1968 1980)
     Speech Clinics (1968 1980)
BT   Clinics
RT   Audiology
     Auditory Evaluation
     Hearing Impairments
     Hearing Therapy
     Speech
     Speech Evaluation
     Speech Impairments
     Speech Therapy

Speech and Language Pathology
USE Speech Language Pathology

Speech Clinics (1968 1980)
USE Speech and Hearing Clinics

Speech Communication   JUL. 1977
     Postings: 8,734   GC: 450
SN   Human interaction in which oral mes-
     sages are exchanged through verbal and
     nonverbal symbols (Note: Do not con-
     fuse with the linguistics concept of "Oral
     Language")
UF   Oral Communication (1966 1977)
     Oral Expression (1966 1977)
     Speaking (1966 1980)
     Speaking Activities (1966 1980)
     Speech Communication Curriculum #
     Speech Communication Research #
NT   Oral Interpretation
     Public Speaking
BT   Communication (Thought Transfer)

= Two or more Descriptors are used to represent this term.
The term's main entry shows the appropriate coordination.

RT Audience Response
    Communication Apprehension
    Communicative Competence
      (Languages)
    Conversational Language Courses
    Dialogs (Language)
    Discussion
    Group Dynamics
    Intercultural Communication
    Interpersonal Communication
    Interpreters
    Interviews
    Language
    Language Arts
    Language Patterns
    Language Processing
    Language Rhythm
    Linguistics
    Listening
    Nonverbal Communication
    Oral Communication Method
    Oral English
    Oral History
    Oral Language
    Oral Tradition
    Outlining (Discourse)
    Paralinguistics
    Persuasive Discourse
    Rhetorical Invention
    Rhetorical Theory
    Speech
    Speech Curriculum
    Speech Instruction
    Speeches
    Standard Spoken Usage
    Theater Arts
    Verbal Communication

Speech Communication Curriculum
USE Speech Communication
AND Speech Curriculum

Speech Communication Research
USE Communication Research
AND Speech Communication

Speech Compression   *JUL. 1966*
     Postings: 151   GC: 450
SN   Separating and transmitting voice com-
     municated words at accelerated rates
BT   Speech
RT   Language Research

Speech Curriculum   *JUL. 1966*
     Postings: 664   GC: 450
SN   (Note: Usually used for curriculum at the
     secondary and postsecondary levels—
     for lower levels, consider "Language Arts"
     and other "Speech" Descriptors)
UF   Speech Communication Curriculum #
BT   Curriculum
RT   Language Arts
     Speech
     Speech Communication
     Speech Instruction
     Speech Skills

Speech Education (1966 1980)   *MAR. 1980*
     Postings: 365   GC: 450
SN   Invalid Descriptor—see the more pre-
     cise Descriptors "Speech Curriculum,"
     "Speech Instruction," and "Speech Ther-
     apy"

Speech Evaluation   *JUL. 1966*
     Postings: 560   GC: 450
SN   Determination of an individual's speak-
     ing ability and of any needed treatment
BT   Medical Evaluation
RT   Speech
     Speech and Hearing Clinics
     Speech Impairments
     Speech Language Pathology
     Speech Tests
     Speech Therapy

Speech Habits   *JUL. 1966*
     Postings: 603   GC: 450
BT   Behavior Patterns
RT   Articulation Impairments
     Child Language
     Delayed Speech
     Habit Formation
     Language Patterns
     Language Rhythm
     Language Usage
     Native Speakers
     North American English
     Paralinguistics
     Regional Dialects
     Speech
     Stuttering

Speech Handicapped (1967 1980)
USE Speech Impairments

Speech Handicaps (1966 1994)
USE Speech Impairments

Speech Impairments   *MAR. 1994*
     Postings: 288   GC: 220
SN   Defects and disturbances that interfere
     with oral communication
UF   Speech Handicapped (1967 1980)
     Speech Handicaps (1966 1994)
NT   Articulation Impairments
     Cleft Palate
     Delayed Speech
     Stuttering
     Voice Disorders
BT   Disabilities
RT   Aphasia
     Augmentative and Alternative Commu-
       nication
     Cerebral Palsy
     Communication Disorders
     Hearing Impairments
     Language Impairments
     Speech
     Speech and Hearing Clinics
     Speech Evaluation
     Speech Improvement
     Speech Language Pathology
     Speech Tests
     Speech Therapy

Speech Improvement   *JUL. 1966*
     Postings: 420   GC: 450
SN   Enhancement of adequate or socially cor-
     rect speech—includes articulation,
     rhythm, and intonation
UF   Enunciation Improvement (1966
       1980) #
BT   Improvement
RT   Articulation (Speech)
     Articulation Impairments
     Speech
     Speech Impairments
     Speech Instruction
     Speech Language Pathology
     Speech Tests
     Speech Therapy
     Stuttering

Speech Instruction   *JUL. 1966*
     Postings: 1,227   GC: 450
SN   Instruction concerned with the devel-
     opment of oral communication skills—
     includes various aspects of oral com-
     munication such as discussion, conver-
     sation, debate, interpretative reading, and
     drama (Note: Do not confuse with
     "Speech Therapy")
NT   Pronunciation Instruction
BT   Instruction
RT   Debate Format
     Kinesthetic Methods
     Oral Interpretation
     Speech
     Speech Communication
     Speech Curriculum
     Speech Improvement
     Speech Skills
     Speech Therapy

Speech Language Pathology   *JUN. 1994*
     Postings: 219   GC: 220
SN   The science and practice of screening,
     assessing, diagnosing, rehabilitating, and
     preventing disorders of speech, language,
     and related communication functions
UF   Speech and Language Pathology
     Speech Pathology (1967 1994)
BT   Pathology
RT   Audiology
     Communication Disorders
     Language Impairments
     Speech
     Speech Evaluation
     Speech Impairments
     Speech Improvement
     Speech Therapy

Speech Pathology (1967 1994)
USE Speech Language Pathology

Speech Reading
USE Lipreading

Speech Skills   *JUL. 1966*
     Postings: 2,873   GC: 450
SN   Skills that aid in the production of spoken
     language
UF   Oral Facility
     Oral Skills
     Speaking Skills
BT   Audiolingual Skills
RT   Delayed Speech
     Eye Voice Span
     Interpreters
     Language Fluency
     Language Patterns
     Language Rhythm
     Language Styles
     Speech
     Speech Curriculum
     Speech Instruction
     Speech Tests
     Speech Therapy
     Stuttering
     Total Communication
     Verbal Ability

Speech Synthesizers   *JAN. 1988*
     Postings: 138   GC: 910
SN   Devices that simulate the human voice
UF   Text to Speech Synthesizers
     Voice Synthesizers
BT   Audio Equipment
     Electronic Equipment
RT   Artificial Speech
     Input Output Devices
     Speech

Speech Tests   *JUL. 1966*
     Postings: 201   GC: 830
SN   Tests of the ability to enunciate, pro-
     nounce, and communicate orally
UF   Articulation Tests
BT   Verbal Tests
RT   Articulation (Speech)
     Articulation Impairments
     Diction
     Language Tests
     Pronunciation
     Speech
     Speech Evaluation
     Speech Impairments
     Speech Improvement
     Speech Skills
     Speech Therapy

Speech Therapists (1966 1980)
USE Speech Therapy
AND Therapists

Speech Therapy   *JUL. 1966*
     Postings: 1,374   GC: 220
SN   Treatment of speech disorders (Note: Do
     not confuse with "Speech Instruction")
UF   Speech Therapists (1966 1980) #
BT   Therapy

RT   Articulation Impairments
     Cleft Palate
     Delayed Speech
     Medical Services
     Sound Spectrographs
     Speech
     Speech and Hearing Clinics
     Speech Evaluation
     Speech Impairments
     Speech Improvement
     Speech Instruction
     Speech Language Pathology
     Speech Skills
     Speech Tests
     Stuttering
     Visible Speech
     Voice Disorders

Speeches   *JUL. 1966*
     Postings: 4,306   GC: 720
SN   (Note: Corresponds to Pubtype code
     150—do not use except as the subject of
     a document)
UF   Addresses
     Talks
RT   Conference Papers
     Lecture Method
     Personal Narratives
     Persuasive Discourse
     Public Speaking
     Rhetorical Invention
     Speech Communication

Speed Reading   *JUL. 1966*
     Postings: 184   GC: 460
SN   Rapidity in reading, including skimming
     and scanning
UF   Rapid Reading (1966 1980)
     Skimming (Reading)
BT   Reading
RT   Adult Reading Programs
     Reading Rate
     Silent Reading

Speed Tests
USE Timed Tests

Spelling   *JUL. 1966*
     Postings: 2,516   GC: 400
NT   Finger Spelling
     Invented Spelling
BT   Language Arts
RT   Alphabetizing Skills
     Capitalization (Alphabetic)
     Diacritical Marking
     Graphemes
     Orthographic Symbols
     Phoneme Grapheme Correspondence
     Phonics
     Plurals
     Punctuation
     Spelling Instruction
     Word Lists
     Writing (Composition)
     Writing Skills

Spelling Instruction   *JUL. 1966*
     Postings: 1,208   GC: 400
BT   Instruction
RT   Invented Spelling
     Spelling

Sperm Donors
USE Tissue Donors

Spina Bifida   *AUG. 1989*
     Postings: 67   GC: 220
SN   Congenital defect in which part of the
     vertebral column is absent—may be ac-
     companied by hernial protrusion of the
     spinal cord or its membranes and asso-
     ciated paralysis, hydrocephalus, or other
     neurological problems
UF   Meningomyelocele
     Myelocele
     Myelomeningocele
BT   Congenital Impairments

= Two or more Descriptors are used to represent this term.
The term's main entry shows the appropriate coordination.

RT   Multiple Disabilities
       Neurological Impairments

Spiral Curriculum   JUL. 1966
       Postings: 138   GC: 350
SN   Curriculum in which students repeat the
       study of a subject at different grade
       levels, each time at a higher level of
       difficulty and in greater depth
BT   Curriculum
RT   Experimental Curriculum
       Instructional Innovation
       Sequential Approach

Spirituality   MAY 1999
       Postings: 395   GC: 430
SN   Openness to an existence or superior
       being beyond ordinary sensory and in-
       tellectual experience, i.e., to a transcen-
       dent or supernatural reality or creative
       spirit
RT   Beliefs
       Mysticism
       Philosophy
       Religion
       Religious Factors
       Values

Split Sessions
USE   Double Sessions

Split Time
USE   Dual Enrollment

Spontaneous Behavior   JUL. 1966
       Postings: 207   GC: 120
BT   Behavior
RT   Brainstorming
       Emotional Response
       Exploratory Behavior
       Intuition

Sport Medicine
USE   Sports Medicine

Sport Psychology   NOV. 1982
       Postings: 172   GC: 230
SN   Study of the affective and behavioral
       aspects of individuals involved in athletic
       activities and competition
UF   Sports Psychology
BT   Psychology
RT   Athletes
       Athletic Coaches
       Athletics
       Physical Education
       Physical Fitness
       Sports Medicine
       Sportsmanship

Sports
USE   Athletics

Sports Medicine   AUG. 1988
       Postings: 248   GC: 210
SN   Branch of medicine concerned with the
       effects of sports and exercise on health
       and fitness and with the prevention and
       treatment of athletic injuries
UF   Sport Medicine
BT   Medicine
RT   Athletes
       Athletic Coaches
       Athletic Equipment
       Athletics
       Biomechanics
       Clinical Diagnosis
       Exercise Physiology
       Injuries
       Medical Services
       Motor Reactions
       Physical Education
       Physical Fitness
       Physical Recreation Programs
       Physical Therapy

       Preventive Medicine
       School Health Services
       Sport Psychology

Sports News
USE   Athletics
AND   News Media

Sports Psychology
USE   Sport Psychology

Sports Reporting
USE   Athletics
AND   News Reporting

Sportsmanship   JUL. 1969
       Postings: 168   GC: 470
BT   Attitudes
RT   Behavior
       Behavior Patterns
       Morale
       Motivation
       Physical Education
       Self Control
       Sport Psychology
       Teamwork
       Values

Spouses   OCT. 1979
       Postings: 1,679   GC: 510
UF   Husbands
       Married Persons
       Wives
BT   Groups
RT   Divorce
       Family (Sociological Unit)
       Family Life
       Females
       Homemakers
       Kinship
       Males
       Marital Status
       Marriage
       Married Students
       Parents
       Widowed

Spreadsheets   AUG. 1989
       Postings: 569   GC: 710
SN   Software or paper worksheets for ar-
       ranging numbers and other variables in
       columns and rows—microcomputer soft-
       ware packages (for accounting, financial
       planning, etc.) offer automatic recalcula-
       tion whenever a value is changed
UF   Electronic Spreadsheets
BT   Worksheets
RT   Accounting
       Computer Oriented Programs
       Computer Software
       Matrices
       Numbers
       Tables (Data)

Springboard Diving
USE   Diving

Squash (Game)   FEB. 1978
       Postings: 17   GC: 470
SN   Includes squash rackets and squash ten-
       nis
BT   Racquet Sports
RT   Tennis

Staff Days
USE   Worker Days

Staff Development   MAR. 1980
       Postings: 9,022   GC: 320
SN   Employer-sponsored activities, or provi-
       sions such as release time and tuition
       grants, through which existing person-
       nel renew or acquire skills, knowledge,

       and attitudes related to job or personal
       development
UF   Personnel Development
       Staff Improvement (1966 1980)
NT   Faculty Development
BT   Labor Force Development
RT   Collegiality
       Continuing Education
       Industrial Training
       Inplant Programs
       Inservice Education
       Management Development
       Off the Job Training
       On the Job Training
       Organizational Development
       Personnel
       Professional Development
       Staff Orientation

Staff Evaluation
USE   Personnel Evaluation

Staff Improvement (1966 1980)
USE   Staff Development

Staff Meetings   JUL. 1966
       Postings: 122   GC: 320
BT   Meetings
RT   Faculty Workload
       Personnel

Staff Offices
USE   Offices (Facilities)

Staff Orientation   JUL. 1966
       Postings: 420   GC: 320
SN   The process or programs an organiza-
       tion uses to make its personnel aware of
       policies or duties
BT   Orientation
RT   Faculty Handbooks
       Personnel
       Staff Development
       Teacher Orientation

Staff Role   JUL. 1966
       Postings: 1,984   GC: 320
UF   Personnel Role
BT   Role
RT   Counselor Role
       Faculty Handbooks
       Personnel
       Teacher Role

Staff Utilization   JUL. 1966
       Postings: 1,499   GC: 320
BT   Labor Utilization
RT   Administration
       Differentiated Staffs
       Faculty Workload
       Personnel
       Personnel Management
       School Cadres

Stage Theory
USE   Developmental Stages

Stages (Facilities)   MAR. 1980
       Postings: 69   GC: 920
SN   Platforms raised above floor level in thea-
       ters, lecture halls, classrooms, etc.
UF   Stages (1969 1980)
BT   Structural Elements (Construction)
RT   Arts Centers
       Auditoriums
       Multipurpose Classrooms
       Music Facilities
       Theaters

Stages of Development
USE   Developmental Stages

Stages (1969 1980)
USE   Stages (Facilities)

Staggered Sessions
USE   Extended School Day

Stammering
USE   Stuttering

Standard Error of Estimate
USE   Error of Measurement

Standard Error of Measurement (1970 1980)
USE   Error of Measurement

Standard Spoken Usage   JUL. 1966
       Postings: 1,893   GC: 450
SN   Customary use or employment of lan-
       guage, words, expressions, etc., by na-
       tive speakers in nonformal situations
UF   Colloquial Standard Usage
       Informal Conversational Usage
BT   Language Usage
RT   Conversational Language Courses
       Interpersonal Communication
       Language Patterns
       Language Standardization
       Language Styles
       Nonstandard Dialects
       North American English
       Oral English
       Oral Language
       Social Dialects
       Sociolinguistics
       Speech Communication

Standardized Tests   JUL. 1966
       Postings: 5,778   GC: 830
SN   Tests for which content has been se-
       lected and checked empirically, norms
       have been established, uniform methods
       of administering have been developed,
       and which may be scored with a rela-
       tively high degree of objectivity
BT   Tests
RT   Alternative Assessment
       College Entrance Examinations
       Criterion Referenced Tests
       High Stakes Tests
       Item Analysis
       Licensing Examinations (Professions)
       National Competency Tests
       Norm Referenced Tests
       Objective Tests
       Test Norms
       Test Score Decline
       Testing Programs

Standards   JUL. 1966
       Postings: 8,188   GC: 520
SN   Rules, principles, or criteria by which
       levels or degrees of adequacy, accepta-
       bility, quantity, quality, or value are meas-
       ured or judged (Note: Use a more spe-
       cific term if possible)
UF   Professional Standards
NT   Academic Standards
       Administrative Principles
       Behavior Standards
       Court Doctrine
       Criteria
       Dress Codes
       Educational Principles
       Environmental Standards
       Equipment Standards
       Food Standards
       Labor Standards
       Laws
       Library Standards
       Living Standards
       Metric System
       Middle Class Standards
       National Standards
       Parliamentary Procedures
       Qualifications
       Residence Requirements
       Scientific Principles

\# = Two or more Descriptors are used to represent this term.
The term's main entry shows the appropriate coordination.

Specifications
State Standards
Textbook Standards
RT   Accreditation (Institutions)
Achievement
Audits (Verification)
Benchmarking
Certification
Codification
Credentials
Eligibility
Evaluation
Failure
Inspection
Measurement
Models
Norms
Objectives
Policy
Prerequisites
Quality Control
Quotas
Sanctions
Scores
Success
Teaching Models
Values

Stars   JAN. 1993
Postings: 70   GC: 490
SN   Self-luminous celestial bodies of hot gas
held together by gravity—their energy is
produced by nuclear-fusion reactions
RT   Astronomy
Light
Planetariums
Solar System
Space Exploration
Space Sciences

State Action   JUL. 1966
Postings: 1,590   GC: 610
RT   Government Role
State Aid
State Departments of Education
State Government
State Legislation
State Programs
State Regulation

State Agencies   JUL. 1966
Postings: 1,900   GC: 610
NT   State Departments of Education
State Licensing Boards
BT   Public Agencies
RT   Agency Role
State Boards of Education
State Government
State Libraries
State Officials
State Programs
Statewide Planning
Urban Renewal Agencies
Welfare Agencies

State Aid   JUL. 1966
Postings: 5,096   GC: 620
UF   Provincial Aid
State Assistance
State Financial Aid
State Support
NT   Foundation Programs
Full State Funding
State Federal Aid
RT   Block Grants
Categorical Aid
Educational Finance
Eligibility
Equalization Aid
Finance Reform
Financial Support
Government School Relationship
Grantsmanship
Incentive Grants
Library Funding
New Federalism
Private School Aid
Public Support
School Funds

School Support
State Action
State Government
State Programs
State Regulation
State School District Relationship
State Schools
State Standards
Training Allowances

State Assistance
USE   State Aid

State Boards of Education   JUL. 1969
Postings: 1,356   GC: 330
SN   Groups of appointed or elected officials
who are responsible for the manage-
ment and direction of public education in
a state (Note: Do not confuse with "State
Departments of Education")
UF   State Committees on Education
State School Boards
BT   Boards of Education
RT   Public Education
State Agencies
State Curriculum Guides
State Departments of Education
State School District Relationship
State Standards

State Boards of Licensing
USE   State Licensing Boards

State Church Separation   JUL. 1966
Postings: 897   GC: 610
UF   Church State Separation
BT   Relationship
RT   Church Role
Churches
Constitutional Law
Federal Government
Intellectual Freedom
Private School Aid
Religion
Religious Holidays
School Prayer
State Government

State Colleges   JUL. 1966
Postings: 3,043   GC: 340
SN   Degree-granting institutions of higher
education that are funded and controlled
by a state
NT   State Universities
BT   Public Colleges
State Schools
RT   Agricultural Colleges
Community Colleges
Land Grant Universities
Multicampus Colleges
Public Education
Two Year Colleges

State Committees on Education
USE   State Boards of Education

State Court Litigation
USE   Court Litigation
AND   State Courts

State Courts   MAR. 1980
Postings: 454   GC: 610
UF   State Court Litigation #
State Supreme Courts
BT   Courts
RT   Court Litigation
Federal Courts
State Government
State Legislation

State Curriculum Bulletins
USE   State Curriculum Guides

State Curriculum Guides   JUL. 1966
Postings: 2,731   GC: 730
UF   State Curriculum Bulletins
State Syllabi
BT   Curriculum Guides
RT   Curriculum
State Boards of Education
State Departments of Education
State Programs
State Standards
Statewide Planning

State Departments of Education   JUL. 1966
Postings: 2,714   GC: 330
SN   Organizations, composed of the chief
state school officer and staff, that carry
out work delegated to them by law (Note:
Do not confuse with "State Boards of
Education")
UF   State Education Agencies
BT   Departments
State Agencies
RT   Governing Boards
Public Education
State Action
State Boards of Education
State Curriculum Guides
State Programs
State School District Relationship

State Education Agencies
USE   State Departments of Education

State Federal Aid   JUL. 1966
Postings: 1,354   GC: 620
SN   Joint financial or other support by fed-
eral and state governments
UF   Federal State Aid
State Federal Support (1966 1977)
BT   Federal Aid
State Aid
RT   Educational Finance
Equalization Aid
Financial Support
Full State Funding

State Federal Relationship
USE   Federal State Relationship

State Federal Support (1966 1977)
USE   State Federal Aid

State Financial Aid
USE   State Aid

**State Foreign Language Supervisors (1967
1980)**
USE   Second Language Instruction
AND   State Supervisors

State Government   JUL. 1966
Postings: 2,895   GC: 610
UF   Provincial Government
State Government Programs #
BT   Government (Administrative Body)
RT   Federal State Relationship
Government Employees
Government School Relationship
School District Autonomy
State Action
State Agencies
State Aid
State Church Separation
State Courts
State History
State Legislation
State Officials
State Programs
State Regulation
State School District Relationship
States Powers

State Government Programs
USE   State Government
AND   State Programs

State History   AUG. 1977
Postings: 674   GC: 430
SN   History associated with individual states
within the United States
BT   United States History
RT   Local History
State Government

State Laws (1966 1974)
USE   State Legislation

State Legislation   JUL. 1966
Postings: 7,182   GC: 610
UF   State Laws (1966 1974)
State Recreation Legislation (1966
1978) #
NT   School Attendance Legislation
BT   Legislation
RT   Federal Legislation
Laws
Legislators
Local Legislation
State Action
State Courts
State Government
State Regulation
State Standards

State Libraries   JUL. 1966
Postings: 905   GC: 710
SN   Government libraries, maintained by state
funds, that preserve state records and
publications for use by state officials and
citizens
UF   Provincial Libraries
BT   Government Libraries
RT   Archives
State Agencies

State Licensing Boards   JUL. 1966
Postings: 479   GC: 610
SN   Agencies that authorize the practice of a
profession or operation of a business in
a state after determining that established
standards and requirements have been
met
UF   State Boards of Licensing
BT   State Agencies
RT   Accrediting Agencies
Certification
Licensing Examinations (Professions)
Professional Education
State Standards
Testing Programs

State Norms   MAR. 1980
Postings: 330   GC: 820
SN   Statistical description of the typical per-
formance, behavior, form, function, etc.,
of a particular state or province (Note:
Use only for numerical data and not for
subjectively described standards)
BT   Norms
RT   Local Norms
National Norms
State Surveys

State of the Art Reviews   MAY 1972
Postings: 6,578   GC: 730
SN   Exhaustive, systematic, and often critical
reviews of the published or unpublished
material on a topic
BT   Publications
RT   Bibliographies
Literature Reviews
Surveys

State Officials   JUL. 1966
Postings: 331   GC: 610
NT   State Supervisors
BT   Public Officials
RT   County Officials
Extension Agents
Legislators
State Agencies
State Government

= Two or more Descriptors are used to represent this term.
The term's main entry shows the appropriate coordination.

State Planning
USE   Statewide Planning

State Police (1966 1980)
USE   Police

State Programs   *JUL. 1966*
          Postings: 13,170   GC: 610
UF   State Government Programs #
          Statewide Programs
BT   Programs
RT   County Programs
          Educational Assessment
          Excellence in Education
          Federal Programs
          Interstate Programs
          State Action
          State Agencies
          State Aid
          State Curriculum Guides
          State Departments of Education
          State Government
          State Surveys
          Statewide Planning

State Recreation Legislation (1966 1978)
USE   Recreation Legislation
AND   State Legislation

State Regulation   *JUL. 1994*
          Postings: 511   GC: 610
SN   State/provincial government control or
          influence based on legislation
UF   Provincial Regulation
BT   Governance
RT   Compliance (Legal)
          Federal Regulation
          Federal State Relationship
          Government Role
          Government School Relationship
          Institutional Autonomy
          School District Autonomy
          State Action
          State Aid
          State Government
          State Legislation
          State School District Relationship
          State Schools
          State Standards

State School Boards
USE   State Boards of Education

State School District Relationship
                                                JUL. 1966
          Postings: 2,070   GC: 330
SN   Interaction or dealings between a state
          or provincial government and local school
          districts
BT   Government School Relationship
RT   Educational Finance
          Intermediate Administrative Units
          School District Autonomy
          School District Spending
          School District Wealth
          School Districts
          State Aid
          State Boards of Education
          State Departments of Education
          State Government
          State Regulation
          State Standards
          Statewide Planning

State Schools   *JUL. 1966*
          Postings: 247   GC: 340
SN   Educational institutions primarily sup-
          ported and controlled by provincial or
          central governments, especially schools
          providing special services not duplicated
          locally, e.g., teachers colleges, schools
          for the blind, armed forces dependents
          schools
NT   State Colleges
BT   Schools
RT   Public Education
          Public Schools

          State Aid
          State Regulation

State Standards   *JUL. 1966*
          Postings: 4,849   GC: 610
BT   Standards
RT   Academic Standards
          Accreditation (Institutions)
          Accrediting Agencies
          Faculty Workload
          National Standards
          State Aid
          State Boards of Education
          State Curriculum Guides
          State Legislation
          State Licensing Boards
          State Regulation
          State School District Relationship

State Supervisors   *JUL. 1966*
          Postings: 195   GC: 360
UF   State Foreign Language Supervisors
          (1967 1980) #
BT   State Officials
          Supervisors
RT   Teacher Supervision

State Support
USE   State Aid

State Supreme Courts
USE   State Courts

State Surveys   *JUL. 1966*
          Postings: 7,013   GC: 810
SN   Statewide investigations of a field to
          determine current practices, trends,
          and/or norms (Note: As of Oct81, use as
          a minor Descriptor for examples of this
          kind of survey—use as a major Descrip-
          tor only as the subject of a document)
UF   Provincial Surveys
BT   Surveys
RT   Educational Assessment
          National Surveys
          State Norms
          State Programs
          Statewide Planning

State Syllabi
USE   State Curriculum Guides

State Universities   *JUL. 1966*
          Postings: 4,565   GC: 340
SN   Degree-granting institutions of higher
          education, funded and controlled by the
          state, that typically include a liberal arts
          undergraduate college, a graduate school,
          and two or more undergraduate and
          graduate professional schools
BT   State Colleges
          Universities
RT   Land Grant Universities
          Multicampus Colleges
          Professional Education
          Public Education
          Research Universities

States Powers   *JUL. 1966*
          Postings: 138   GC: 610
UF   States Rights
RT   Federal State Relationship
          Federalism
          New Federalism
          State Government

States Rights
USE   States Powers

Statewide Coordination
USE   Statewide Planning

Statewide Planning   *OCT. 1970*
          Postings: 6,278   GC: 330
UF   State Planning
          Statewide Coordination
BT   Planning
RT   Blue Ribbon Commissions
          Coordination
          Federal State Relationship
          Institutional Cooperation
          Master Plans
          Planning Commissions
          Regional Planning
          State Agencies
          State Curriculum Guides
          State Programs
          State School District Relationship
          State Surveys

Statewide Programs
USE   State Programs

Static Controls
USE   Electronic Control

Statistical Analysis   *JUL. 1966*
          Postings: 10,420   GC: 820
SN   Application of statistical processes and
          theory to the compilation, presentation,
          discussion, and interpretation of numeri-
          cal data (Note: Use a more specific term
          if possible)
UF   Comparative Statistics (1966 1980) #
          Quantitative Research (Statistics)
          Statistical Methods
          Statistical Processes
NT   Analysis of Covariance
          Analysis of Variance
          Bayesian Statistics
          Chi Square
          Correlation
          Effect Size
          Error of Measurement
          Goodness of Fit
          Item Analysis
          Judgment Analysis Technique
          Least Squares Statistics
          Maximum Likelihood Statistics
          Meta Analysis
          Multivariate Analysis
          Regression (Statistics)
          Robustness (Statistics)
          Statistical Distributions
          Statistical Inference
          Statistical Significance
BT   Data Analysis
RT   Bibliometrics
          Census Figures
          Data Interpretation
          Econometrics
          Employment Statistics
          Equated Scores
          Expectancy Tables
          Generalizability Theory
          Hypothesis Testing
          Interaction
          Item Sampling
          Library Statistics
          Markov Processes
          Matrices
          Measurement
          Monte Carlo Methods
          Nonparametric Statistics
          Norms
          Predictor Variables
          Probability
          Psychometrics
          Q Methodology
          Reliability
          Research
          Research Methodology
          Research Problems
          Sample Size
          Sampling
          Scaling
          School Statistics
          Scores
          Statistical Bias
          Statistical Data
          Statistical Studies
          Statistics

          Test Theory
          Trend Analysis
          Triangulation
          Validity

Statistical Association Methods
USE   Correlation

Statistical Bias   *AUG. 1971*
          Postings: 590   GC: 820
SN   Characteristics of an experimental or sam-
          pling design, or the mathematical treat-
          ment of data, that systematically affects
          the results of a study so as to produce
          incorrect, unjustified, or inappropriate
          inferences or conclusions
BT   Bias
RT   Attrition (Research Studies)
          Error of Measurement
          Error Patterns
          Item Bias
          Matched Groups
          Sample Size
          Sampling
          Statistical Analysis
          Statistics
          Test Bias

Statistical Bibliography
USE   Bibliometrics

Statistical Data   *JUL. 1966*
          Postings: 6,644   GC: 820
SN   (Note: Corresponds to Pubtype code
          110—do not use except as the subject of
          a document)
NT   Census Figures
          Employment Statistics
          Library Statistics
          Norms
          School Statistics
          Social Indicators
BT   Data
RT   Generalizability Theory
          Measurement
          Meta Analysis
          Numeric Databases
          Raw Scores
          Reliability
          Statistical Analysis
          Statistical Distributions
          Statistical Inference
          Statistical Studies
          Statistical Surveys
          Statistics
          Tests
          Trend Analysis
          True Scores
          Validity

Statistical Distributions   *OCT. 1980*
          Postings: 622   GC: 480
SN   Tables or graphs of observed, predicted,
          or theoretical data indicating either the
          probability or the number of instances to
          be found along successive intervals of
          an ordered scale—also, the mathemati-
          cal functions of distributions
UF   Distributions (Statistics)
          Frequency Distributions
BT   Statistical Analysis
          Statistics
RT   Classification
          Expectancy Tables
          Functions (Mathematics)
          Generalizability Theory
          Monte Carlo Methods
          Norms
          Probability
          Reliability
          Scores
          Statistical Data
          Validity

Statistical Inference   *JAN. 1986*
          Postings: 150   GC: 480
SN   The computation or prediction of statis-

= Two or more Descriptors are used to represent this term.
The term's main entry shows the appropriate coordination.

tics for a collective or whole (population) on the basis of a sample
UF   Inferential Statistics #
BT   Data Interpretation
     Inferences
     Statistical Analysis
RT   Bayesian Statistics
     Causal Models
     Correlation
     Estimation (Mathematics)
     Expectancy Tables
     Generalizability Theory
     Hypothesis Testing
     Probability
     Regression (Statistics)
     Robustness (Statistics)
     Sampling
     Statistical Data
     Statistical Significance
     Statistics

Statistical Linguistics
USE   Mathematical Linguistics

Statistical Methods
USE   Statistical Analysis

Statistical Processes
USE   Statistical Analysis

Statistical Significance   *MAR. 1980*
    Postings: 829   GC: 820
SN   Property of having low probability of occurrence on the basis of chance alone (in this sense, "significance" means neither "bigness" nor "importance"—usually, the odds have to be at least 20 to 1 and preferably 100 to 1 against pure chance for significance to be claimed)
UF   Significance Measures
     Tests of Significance (1966 1980)
BT   Statistical Analysis
RT   Analysis of Covariance
     Analysis of Variance
     Bayesian Statistics
     Chi Square
     Effect Size
     Goodness of Fit
     Hypothesis Testing
     Least Squares Statistics
     Maximum Likelihood Statistics
     Probability
     Research Design
     Robustness (Statistics)
     Statistical Inference
     Statistics

Statistical Studies   *JUL. 1966*
    Postings: 1,296   GC: 810
SN   Studies designed to investigate, evaluate, or improve statistical techniques (Note: As of Oct81, use as a minor Descriptor for examples of this kind of research—use as a major Descriptor only as the subject of a document—prior to Oct81, this term did not carry a Scope Note—do not confuse with "Statistical Surveys")
BT   Research
RT   Monte Carlo Methods
     Nonparametric Statistics
     Sampling
     Statistical Analysis
     Statistical Data
     Statistical Surveys

Statistical Surveys   *JUL. 1966*
    Postings: 1,243   GC: 810
SN   Investigations that employ statistical techniques or gather statistical data to discover current practices, trends, and/or norms (Note: As of Oct81, use as a minor Descriptor for examples of this kind of survey—use as a major Descriptor only as the subject of a document—do not confuse with "Statistical Studies")
BT   Surveys

RT   Sampling
     Statistical Data
     Statistical Studies

Statistical Theory
USE   Statistics

Statistics   *JUL. 1966*
    Postings: 2,355   GC: 480
SN   Branch of mathematics dealing with collections of quantitative data (Note: Prior to Mar80, the instructions "Mathematical Statistics and Statistical Theory, USE Statistical Analysis" were carried in the Thesaurus—do not confuse with "Statistical Data" or "Test Results")
UF   Inferential Statistics #
     Mathematical Statistics
     Statistical Theory
NT   Bayesian Statistics
     Least Squares Statistics
     Maximum Likelihood Statistics
     Nonparametric Statistics
     Sampling
     Statistical Distributions
BT   Mathematics
RT   Computational Linguistics
     Correlation
     Effect Size
     Estimation (Mathematics)
     Expectancy Tables
     Game Theory
     Goodness of Fit
     Mathematical Logic
     Mathematical Models
     Monte Carlo Methods
     Multiple Regression Analysis
     Numbers
     Predictive Measurement
     Probability
     Regression (Statistics)
     Robustness (Statistics)
     Statistical Analysis
     Statistical Bias
     Statistical Data
     Statistical Inference
     Statistical Significance

Status   *JUL. 1966*
    Postings: 871   GC: 520
NT   Citizenship
     Economic Status
     Employment Level
     Ethnic Status
     Full Time Equivalency
     Group Status
     Marital Status
     Retirement
     Seniority
     Social Status
     Socioeconomic Status
RT   Eligibility
     Prerequisites
     Professional Recognition
     Recognition (Achievement)
     Reputation
     Role
     Social Class
     Social Stratification
     Status Need

Status Need   *JUL. 1966*
    Postings: 196   GC: 120
SN   Psychological need for recognition
BT   Psychological Needs
RT   Achievement Need
     Affiliation Need
     Prestige
     Professional Recognition
     Recognition (Achievement)
     Social Status
     Status

Statutory Rape
USE   Rape

Stealing   *JUN. 1969*
    Postings: 285   GC: 530
UF   Book Thefts (1969 1980) #
     Thefts
NT   Plagiarism
BT   Antisocial Behavior
RT   Codes of Ethics
     Computer Security
     Crime
     Delinquency
     Discipline Problems
     Fraud
     Ownership
     School Security
     Security Personnel
     Victims of Crime

Steel Foundries
USE   Foundries

Steel Industry (1967 1980)
USE   Metal Industry

Stenographers (1966 1981)
USE   Shorthand

Stenography (1967 1980)
USE   Shorthand

Step in Step out Students
USE   Stopouts

Stepfamily   *MAR. 1982*
    Postings: 285   GC: 520
SN   Persons related as a result of the remarriage of a parent (Note: For specificity, coordinate with other terms—for example, with "Parent Child Relationship" (for stepparenting), with "Fathers" (for stepfathers), and so on)
BT   Family (Sociological Unit)
RT   Adoptive Parents
     Biological Parents
     Extended Family
     Family Life
     Family Relationship
     Family Structure
     Kinship
     Nuclear Family
     Remarriage

Stereochemistry   *APR. 1990*
    Postings: 40   GC: 490
SN   Study of the relationship of arrangements of atoms to chemical properties
BT   Chemistry
RT   Atomic Structure
     Chemical Bonding
     Coordination Compounds
     Molecular Structure
     Physical Chemistry

Stereopsis (1968 1980)
USE   Depth Perception

Stereotypes   *JUL. 1966*
    Postings: 2,444   GC: 540
NT   Ethnic Stereotypes
     Sex Stereotypes
     Teacher Stereotypes
BT   Attitudes
RT   Cultural Images
     Ethnocentrism
     Expectation
     Labeling (of Persons)
     Role Perception
     Self Fulfilling Prophecies
     Social Bias

Stickers
USE   Adhesives

Stimulants   *SEP. 1968*
    Postings: 206   GC: 210
BT   Stimuli
RT   Cocaine
     Crack
     Drug Abuse
     Drug Rehabilitation
     Drug Use
     Narcotics
     Physiology
     Sensory Experience
     Smoking
     Tobacco

Stimulation   *FEB. 1971*
    Postings: 568   GC: 110
SN   Arousal or excitation of an organism—technically, the arousal of neural impulses, but also used more generally for the elicitation of physical, cognitive, or emotional responses
RT   Arousal Patterns
     Biofeedback
     Conditioning
     Motivation
     Neurological Organization
     Stimuli

Stimuli   *JUN. 1969*
    Postings: 821   GC: 110
UF   Conditioned Stimulus (1966 1980)
     Stimulus Characteristics
NT   Auditory Stimuli
     Cues
     Electrical Stimuli
     Stimulants
     Tactile Stimuli
     Verbal Stimuli
     Visual Stimuli
RT   Conditioning
     Desensitization
     Dimensional Preference
     Motivation
     Novelty (Stimulus Dimension)
     Perception
     Psychophysiology
     Redundancy
     Responses
     Sensory Experience
     Stimulation
     Stimulus Generalization

Stimulus Behavior (1966 1980)
USE   Responses

Stimulus Characteristics
USE   Stimuli

Stimulus Devices (1966 1980)   *MAR. 1980*
    Postings: 200   GC: 910
SN   Invalid Descriptor—used for both mechanical devices and techniques of generating student interest—use "Stimuli" and "Stimulation" respectively for these concepts

Stimulus Generalization   *JUL. 1966*
    Postings: 188   GC: 110
SN   Process by which a response originally conditioned by a given stimulus may subsequently be elicited by other similar stimuli
BT   Generalization
RT   Mediation Theory
     Patterned Responses
     Stimuli

Stimulus Synthesis
USE   Patterned Responses

Stockpiles
USE   Supplies

= Two or more Descriptors are used to represent this term.
The term's main entry shows the appropriate coordination.

Stopouts   AUG. 1986
Postings: 136   GC: 510
SN   Individuals who briefly interrupt their education, vocation, etc., to pursue other activities (Note: Do not confuse with "Reentry Students/Workers")
UF   Step in Step out Students
BT   Groups
RT   Academic Persistence
     Adult Students
     Attendance
     College Students
     Dropouts
     Enrollment
     Labor Turnover
     Leaves of Absence
     Persistence
     Reentry Students
     Reentry Workers
     School Holding Power

Storage   OCT. 1969
Postings: 231   GC: 920
NT   Equipment Storage
     Information Storage
RT   Design Requirements
     Facility Requirements
     Facility Utilization Research
     Interior Space
     Space Utilization
     Warehouses

Storage Batteries
USE   Electric Batteries

Story Grammar   AUG. 1986
Postings: 319   GC: 460
SN   Order or structure of elements in a textual passage, representing the meaning intended by the author and used to explain and predict the comprehension and/or recall of readers—analogous to nouns, verbs, and other elements of traditional sentence grammar, story grammar's elements are such things as settings, episodes, and events
UF   Story Structure
RT   Coherence
     Cohesion (Written Composition)
     Discourse Analysis
     Narration
     Readability
     Reader Text Relationship
     Reading Comprehension
     Reading Instruction
     Reading Writing Relationship
     Story Reading
     Story Telling
     Text Structure
     Writing (Composition)
     Writing Instruction
     Writing Skills

Story Problems (Mathematics)
USE   Word Problems (Mathematics)

Story Reading   JUL. 1966
Postings: 825   GC: 460
BT   Reading
RT   Reading Aloud to Others
     Story Grammar
     Story Telling

Story Structure
USE   Story Grammar

Story Telling   JUL. 1966
Postings: 2,027   GC: 720
BT   Language Arts
RT   Narration
     Oral Tradition
     Reading Aloud to Others
     Story Grammar
     Story Reading

Strabismus   MAY 1974
Postings: 18   GC: 220
SN   Lack of coordination of eye muscles so that the two eyes do not focus on the same point
UF   Cross Eyes
     Heterophoria (1968 1974)
     Heterotropia (1968 1974)
     Walleyes
BT   Visual Impairments
RT   Eye Fixations
     Vision
     Visual Acuity

Stradaptive Testing
USE   Adaptive Testing

Stranger Reactions   FEB. 1975
Postings: 259   GC: 120
SN   Reactions to strangers (positive, negative, or mixed in character)—often refers to infant behavior patterns but may be used with any age group
UF   Xenophobia
BT   Responses
RT   Emotional Response
     Familiarity
     Infant Behavior
     Social Behavior

Strategic Management
USE   Strategic Planning

Strategic Planning   FEB. 1993
Postings: 2,212   GC: 330
SN   Process of continuous planning for change, which assesses an organization's or program's internal and external environment, analyzes the implications of relevant trends, and identifies effective strategies for achieving a desired future state
UF   Strategic Management
BT   Planning
RT   Change Strategies
     Educational Planning
     Educational Strategies
     Environmental Scanning
     Futures (of Society)
     Institutional Administration
     Long Range Planning
     Management Systems
     Marketing
     Master Plans
     Mission Statements
     Operations Research
     Planning Commissions
     Policy Formation
     Prediction
     Program Administration
     Systems Analysis
     Trend Analysis

Stream Pollution
USE   Water Pollution

Streams
USE   Rivers

Street Layouts
USE   Traffic Circulation

Street Parking Areas
USE   Parking Facilities

Street People
USE   Homeless People

Strength (Biology)
USE   Muscular Strength

Stress (Phonology)   MAR. 1976
Postings: 364   GC: 450
UF   Accents (Vocal Stress)
BT   Suprasegmentals
RT   Intonation
     Morphophonemics
     Paralinguistics
     Phonetics
     Phonology
     Structural Analysis (Linguistics)
     Syllables

Stress Management   OCT. 1983
Postings: 1,898   GC: 230
SN   Techniques to handle psychological and/or physical tensions and their causes
RT   Adjustment (to Environment)
     Adventure Education
     Catharsis
     Coping
     Counseling Techniques
     Health Behavior
     Health Education
     Relaxation Training
     Resilience (Personality)
     Self Management
     Stress Variables
     Symptoms (Individual Disorders)
     Wellness

Stress Variables   JUL. 1966
Postings: 5,578   GC: 230
SN   Causes and consequences of psychological and physiological strain
RT   Burnout
     Crowding
     Diseases
     Exercise Physiology
     Health
     Hypertension
     Life Events
     Physiology
     Posttraumatic Stress Disorder
     Psychological Patterns
     Response Style (Tests)
     Stress Management
     Type A Behavior
     Type B Behavior

Strikes   JUL. 1966
Postings: 289   GC: 630
NT   Teacher Strikes
RT   Arbitration
     Collective Bargaining
     Labor Demands
     Labor Force
     Labor Problems
     Negotiation Impasses
     School Boycotts
     Unions

String Instruments   AUG. 1999
Postings: 50   GC: 420
SN   Musical instruments, ordinarily the violin family (violin, viola, cello, double bass) but occasionally also the guitar, lute, harp, etc., in which tone is produced with strings stretched on a frame and bowed or plucked by hand—excludes keyboard instruments, such as the piano or harpsichord, with strings struck or plucked mechanically (Note: See also more precise Identifiers "Violins," "Violin Instruction," "Guitars," etc.)
UF   Stringed Instruments
BT   Musical Instruments
RT   Music

Stringed Instruments
USE   String Instruments

Structural Analysis (Linguistics)   MAR. 1980
Postings: 1,165   GC: 450
SN   (Note: Prior to Mar80, this concept was indexed under "Structural Analysis")
NT   Discourse Analysis
     Tagmemic Analysis
BT   Evaluation Methods
RT   Componential Analysis
     Computational Linguistics
     Context Clues
     Decoding (Reading)
     Descriptive Linguistics
     Diachronic Linguistics
     Error Analysis (Language)
     Graphemes
     Idioms
     Intonation
     Language Processing
     Language Research
     Language Universals
     Linguistics
     Machine Translation
     Miscue Analysis
     Prefixes (Grammar)
     Reading Instruction
     Sentence Diagraming
     Sentence Structure
     Stress (Phonology)
     Suffixes
     Suprasegmentals
     Syllables
     Text Structure
     Word Order

Structural Analysis (Science)   MAR. 1980
Postings: 153   GC: 490
SN   (Note: Prior to Mar80, this concept was indexed under "Structural Analysis")
BT   Evaluation Methods
RT   Atomic Structure
     Chemical Analysis
     Chemical Bonding
     Crystallography
     Molecular Structure
     Spectroscopy

Structural Analysis (1966 1980)   MAR. 1980
Postings: 1,471   GC: 450
SN   Invalid Descriptor—originally intended as a linguistics term but used indiscriminately—see "Structural Analysis (Linguistics)" and "Structural Analysis (Science)"—see also such Descriptors as "Cognitive Structures," "Chemical Analysis," "Literary Criticism," and "Group Structure," or such Identifiers as "Musical Analysis," "Structure of Knowledge," and "Structural Learning"

Structural Arrangement
USE   Organization

Structural Building Systems   JUL. 1966
Postings: 127   GC: 920
SN   Combination of such structural members and methods as foundations, post and beam, vaults, or lift-slabs to form the structural frame or shell of a building
BT   Building Systems
RT   Buildings
     Civil Engineering
     Construction (Process)
     Construction Programs
     Masonry
     Prefabrication
     Prestressed Concrete
     Systems Building

Structural Elements (Construction)   MAR. 1980
Postings: 351   GC: 920
SN   Structural, dimensional, functional, or aesthetic components of constructed entities (e.g., buildings, facilities, vehicles)
UF   Architectural Elements (1968 1980)
NT   Acoustic Insulation
     Building Systems
     Ceilings
     Chimneys
     Doors
     Flooring
     Glass Walls
     Roofing
     Space Dividers
     Stages (Facilities)
     Thermal Insulation

= Two or more Descriptors are used to represent this term.
The term's main entry shows the appropriate coordination.

Windows
RT Accessibility (for Disabled)
    Architectural Character
    Architecture
    Building Design
    Buildings
    Built Environment
    Construction (Process)
    Construction Materials
    Construction Needs
    Educational Facilities
    Educational Facilities Design
    Facilities
    Flexible Facilities
    Physical Mobility
    Prefabrication
    Systems Building

Structural Equation Models   APR. 1990
        Postings: 329   GC: 820
SN Causal models for simultaneously in-
    terrelating various observed measures
    or structural indicators with a latent or
    underlying variable (Note: See also the
    Identifiers "LISREL Analysis" and
    "LISREL Computer Program")
UF Linear Structural Equation Models
    Lisrel Type Models
BT Causal Models
RT Equations (Mathematics)
    Factor Analysis
    Mathematical Models
    Path Analysis

Structural Grammar   JUL. 1966
        Postings: 420   GC: 450
BT Linguistic Theory
RT Descriptive Linguistics
    Form Classes (Languages)
    Function Words
    Grammar
    Sentence Structure
    Structural Linguistics
    Syntax
    Tagmemic Analysis
    Traditional Grammar

Structural Linguistics   JUL. 1966
        Postings: 505   GC: 450
BT Linguistics
RT Applied Linguistics
    Diachronic Linguistics
    Sentence Structure
    Structural Grammar

Structural Unemployment   AUG. 1986
        Postings: 99   GC: 630
SN Unemployment resulting from structural
    changes in an economy (and conse-
    quent mismatches between jobs and
    skills), caused by technological devel-
    opments, population shifts, industry
    relocations, modified consumer patterns,
    altered government policies, etc.—may
    often be inherent and persistent in dy-
    namic market economies
UF Technological Unemployment
BT Unemployment
RT Dislocated Workers
    Economic Change
    Employment Potential
    Industrial Structure
    International Trade
    Job Layoff
    Job Skills
    Labor Economics
    Labor Market
    Population Trends
    Skill Obsolescence
    Technological Advancement
    Underemployment

Structural Work Occupations
USE Building Trades

Sts (Science Technology Society)
USE Science and Society

Student Ability (1966 1980)
USE Academic Ability

Student Achievement
USE Academic Achievement

Student Activities (Extraclass)
USE Extracurricular Activities

Student Adjustment   JUL. 1966
        Postings: 2,323   GC: 320
SN (Note: Prior to Mar80, the Thesaurus
    carried the instruction "Maladjusted Stu-
    dents, USE Maladjustment")
UF Maladjusted Students
    School Adjustment
    Student Maladjustment
BT Adjustment (to Environment)
    Student Behavior
RT Continuation Students
    Faculty Advisers
    Foreign Student Advisers
    School Orientation
    Student Alienation
    Student Characteristics
    Students

Student Affairs Services
USE Student Personnel Services

Student Affairs Workers
USE Student Personnel Workers

Student Aid
USE Student Financial Aid

Student Alienation   JUL. 1966
        Postings: 994   GC: 320
BT Alienation
RT Activism
    Dropout Attitudes
    Generation Gap
    Student Adjustment
    Student Attitudes
    Student Behavior
    Student Characteristics
    Student Subcultures
    Students

Student Application (1966 1980)
USE College Applicants

Student Appraisal
USE Student Evaluation

Student Aptitude
USE Academic Aptitude

Student Assignments
USE Assignments

Student Attitudes   JUL. 1966
        Postings: 37,482   GC: 320
SN Attitudes of, not toward, students (Note:
    Prior to Apr80, the use of this term was
    not restricted by a Scope Note)
UF Student Opinion (1966 1980)
BT Attitudes
RT Adolescent Attitudes
    Childhood Attitudes
    Classroom Environment
    Student Alienation
    Student Behavior
    Student Characteristics
    Student Evaluation of Teacher Per-
      formance
    Student Interests
    Student Motivation
    Student Reaction
    Student Role
    Student Subcultures
    Student Surveys

Student Teacher Attitudes
    Students

Student Attrition   MAR. 1980
        Postings: 1,552   GC: 320
SN Reduction in a school's student popula-
    tion as a result of transfers or dropouts
    (Note: Do not confuse with the research
    methodology term "Attrition (Research
    Studies)")
UF Attrition (Students)
BT Enrollment
RT Academic Persistence
    College Attendance
    Dropout Rate
    Dropout Research
    Dropouts
    Enrollment Management
    Expulsion
    School Closing
    School Demography
    School Holding Power
    Students
    Withdrawal (Education)

Student Behavior   JUL. 1966
        Postings: 9,078   GC: 310
NT Student Adjustment
    Student Participation
    Student Reaction
BT Behavior
RT Adolescent Behavior
    Behavioral Objectives
    Child Behavior
    Classroom Communication
    Classroom Observation Techniques
    Dress Codes
    Due Process
    In Loco Parentis
    School Uniforms
    Student Alienation
    Student Attitudes
    Student Characteristics
    Student Evaluation
    Student Rights
    Student Role
    Student Subcultures
    Students
    Time on Task

Student Centered Curriculum   MAY 1971
        Postings: 2,030   GC: 310
SN Systematic group of courses or sequence
    of subjects that utilizes student experi-
    ences, backgrounds, and interests
UF Child Centered Curriculum
    Organic Curriculum
BT Curriculum
RT Behavioral Objectives
    Culturally Relevant Education
    Curriculum Design
    Developmentally Appropriate Practices
    Montessori Method
    Open Education
    Reggio Emilia Approach
    Student Characteristics
    Student Interests
    Students

Student Centers
USE Student Unions

Student Certification   JUL. 1966
        Postings: 561   GC: 330
SN Evidence that a student meets the stan-
    dards of performance required for em-
    ployment or further training (Note: Prior
    to Mar80, the use of this term was not
    restricted by a Scope Note)
BT Certification
RT Competency Based Education
    Continuing Education Units
    Educational Certificates
    Grade Equivalent Scores
    High School Equivalency Programs
    Minimum Competency Testing
    Student Evaluation
    Students

Student Characteristics   JUL. 1966
        Postings: 16,381   GC: 320
NT Diversity (Student)
RT Academic Ability
    Academic Achievement
    Academic Aptitude
    Aptitude Treatment Interaction
    Diversity (Institutional)
    Individual Characteristics
    Student Adjustment
    Student Alienation
    Student Attitudes
    Student Behavior
    Student Centered Curriculum
    Student Development
    Student Evaluation
    Student Experience
    Student Interests
    Student Motivation
    Student Needs
    Student Participation
    Student Reaction
    Student Responsibility
    Student Role
    Student Subcultures
    Student Surveys
    Students

Student College Relationship   JUL. 1966
        Postings: 2,613   GC: 320
SN The relationship between a college and
    its students
UF College Student Relationship
BT Student School Relationship
RT Activism
    Codes of Ethics
    College Environment
    College Students
    Colleges
    Experimental Colleges
    Faculty Advisers
    Faculty College Relationship
    Foreign Student Advisers
    In Loco Parentis
    Ombudsmen
    Self Supporting Students
    Student Needs
    Student Welfare
    Teacher Student Relationship

Student Controlled Learning
USE Learner Controlled Instruction

Student Costs   JUL. 1966
        Postings: 1,893   GC: 620
SN Amount of money required by a student
    for expenses such as tuition, fees, room
    and board, books and supplies, clothes,
    travel, recreation, and incidentals (Note:
    Use a more specific term if possible—do
    not confuse with "Expenditure per Stu-
    dent"—prior to Mar80, this term did not
    carry a Scope Note)
UF College Costs (Incurred by Students)
NT Instructional Student Costs
    Noninstructional Student Costs
BT Costs
RT Access to Education
    Assistantships
    Educational Economics
    Educational Equity (Finance)
    Educational Finance
    Educational Vouchers
    Expenditure per Student
    Fees
    Fellowships
    Grants
    Need Analysis (Student Financial Aid)
    Parent Financial Contribution
    Paying for College
    Proprietary Schools
    Scholarship Funds
    Scholarships
    Self Supporting Students
    Student Financial Aid
    Student Loan Programs
    Students
    Tuition

= Two or more Descriptors are used to represent this term.
The term's main entry shows the appropriate coordination.

Student Councils
USE   Student Government

Student Credit Hours
USE   Credits

Student Developed Materials   *JUL. 1966*
Postings: 1,180   GC: 720
SN   Instructional materials prepared by students
NT   Student Writing Models
BT   Instructional Materials
RT   Experience Charts
     Language Experience Approach
     Material Development
     School Publications
     Student Participation
     Student Projects
     Student Publications
     Student Research
     Students
     Teacher Developed Materials

Student Development   *JUL. 1966*
Postings: 5,645   GC: 310
SN   The aspects of an individual's development that are influenced by his or her schooling
BT   Development
RT   Ancillary School Services
     Deans of Students
     Developmentally Appropriate Practices
     Excellence in Education
     Hidden Curriculum
     Individual Development
     Outcomes of Education
     School Counseling
     School Effectiveness
     School Guidance
     School Psychology
     School Role
     Student Characteristics
     Student Educational Objectives
     Student Improvement
     Students

Student Distribution (1966 1980)
                 JUN. 1980
Postings: 98   GC: 330
SN   Invalid Descriptor—used indiscriminately in indexing—see such Descriptors as "School Demography," "Geographic Distribution," and "Test Norms"

Student Educational Objectives   *MAR. 1980*
Postings: 3,954   GC: 330
SN   Short- or long-term goals held by or for students with regard to their educational attainment—includes degree or credit objectives, the reasons for participating in a particular educational program, etc. (Note: Prior to Mar80, "Educational Objectives" was frequently used for this concept)
UF   Educational Goals of Students
     Educational Interest (1967 1980)
     Educational Objectives of Students
BT   Objectives
RT   Aspiration
     Course Selection (Students)
     Education Work Relationship
     Educational Attainment
     Educational Benefits
     Educational Counseling
     Goal Orientation
     Lifelong Learning
     Outcomes of Education
     Relevance (Education)
     Student Development
     Student Interests
     Student Needs
     Students

Student Eligibility
USE   Eligibility

Student Employment   *JUL. 1966*
Postings: 1,045   GC: 630
UF   Student Job Placement #
BT   Employment
RT   Assistantships
     Job Placement
     Part Time Employment
     Paying for College
     Seasonal Employment
     Student Financial Aid
     Student Personnel Services
     Students
     Work Study Programs

Student Empowerment   *JUL. 1996*
Postings: 456   GC: 330
SN   Promotion or attainment of autonomy and freedom of choice for students
BT   Empowerment
RT   Student Leadership
     Student Participation
     Student Rights
     Student Role
     Students

Student Engaged Time
USE   Time on Task

Student Enrollment (1966 1977)
USE   Enrollment

Student Evaluation   *JUL. 1966*
Postings: 20,565   GC: 320
SN   Judging student performance or behavior as related to established criteria (Note: Before May76, the use of this term was not restricted by a Scope Note)
UF   Student Appraisal
NT   Curriculum Based Assessment
     Nongraded Student Evaluation
BT   Evaluation
RT   Academic Achievement
     Academic Records
     Achievement Rating
     Alternative Assessment
     Behavior Rating Scales
     Classroom Observation Techniques
     Competence
     Course Evaluation
     Educational Diagnosis
     Educational Testing
     Grades (Scholastic)
     Grading
     Holistic Evaluation
     Informal Assessment
     Peer Evaluation
     Performance Based Assessment
     Portfolio Assessment
     Portfolios (Background Materials)
     Precision Teaching
     Prereferral Intervention
     Report Cards
     Scoring Rubrics
     Student Behavior
     Student Certification
     Student Characteristics
     Student Improvement
     Student Records
     Student Teacher Evaluation
     Students
     Teacher Expectations of Students
     Vocational Evaluation
     Writing Evaluation

Student Evaluation of Teacher Performance
                 MAY 1976
Postings: 2,308   GC: 320
SN   Student involvement in judging, rating, or assessing the quality of teacher performance or competence
BT   Teacher Evaluation
RT   Course Evaluation
     Instructional Improvement
     Student Attitudes
     Student Reaction
     Summative Evaluation
     Teacher Effectiveness
     Teacher Improvement
     Teacher Student Relationship

Student Exchange Programs   *JUL. 1966*
Postings: 608   GC: 330
BT   Exchange Programs
RT   Cultural Awareness
     Foreign Student Advisers
     Foreign Students
     International Educational Exchange
     Students
     Study Abroad

Student Experience   *JUL. 1966*
Postings: 2,678   GC: 310
BT   Experience
RT   Clinical Experience
     Experience Charts
     Experiential Learning
     Field Experience Programs
     Internship Programs
     Prior Learning
     Student Characteristics
     Student Journals
     Student Projects
     Students
     Work Experience Programs

Student Financial Aid   *MAR. 1976*
Postings: 4,912   GC: 620
UF   Student Aid
NT   Assistantships
     Fellowships
     Income Contingent Loans
     Parent Financial Contribution
     Scholarships
BT   Financial Support
RT   Access to Education
     Educational Finance
     Educational Vouchers
     Eligibility
     Financial Aid Applicants
     Grants
     Instructional Student Costs
     Loan Repayment
     Need Analysis (Student Financial Aid)
     Noninstructional Student Costs
     Paying for College
     Postsecondary Education
     Scholarship Funds
     Student Costs
     Student Employment
     Student Financial Aid Officers
     Student Loan Programs
     Student Needs
     Student Personnel Services
     Students
     Tax Credits
     Tuition
     Veterans Education
     Work Study Programs

Student Financial Aid Officers   *MAR. 1980*
Postings: 140   GC: 360
SN   Administrative personnel, usually at postsecondary institutions, who are responsible for assisting students with applications for grants, loans, scholarships, etc., and who maintain appropriate financial aid records
BT   Administrators
     School Personnel
RT   Educational Finance
     Financial Support
     Middle Management
     Paying for College
     School Business Officials
     Student Financial Aid
     Student Loan Programs
     Student Personnel Workers

Student Government   *JUL. 1971*
Postings: 240   GC: 320
SN   Organized group(s) of student representatives participating in the governance of a school, with authority delegated by the school administration—applies to all levels of education
UF   Student Councils
BT   Government (Administrative Body)
     Student Organizations
RT   School Administration

Student Leadership
     Student Participation
     Student Responsibility
     Student Role
     Student School Relationship
     Students

Student Grouping (1966 1980)
USE   Grouping (Instructional Purposes)

Student Housing (College)
USE   College Housing

Student Improvement   *JUL. 1966*
Postings: 1,675   GC: 310
BT   Improvement
RT   Academic Achievement
     Excellence in Education
     Learning Plateaus
     Student Development
     Student Evaluation
     Students

Student Interests   *JUL. 1966*
Postings: 3,681   GC: 310
BT   Interests
RT   Auditing (Coursework)
     Childhood Interests
     Course Selection (Students)
     Elective Courses
     Experimental Colleges
     Experimental Schools
     Extracurricular Activities
     Free Schools
     Noncredit Courses
     Relevance (Education)
     Student Attitudes
     Student Centered Curriculum
     Student Characteristics
     Student Educational Objectives
     Student Motivation
     Student Surveys
     Students

Student Job Placement
USE   Job Placement
AND   Student Employment

Student Journals   *AUG. 1988*
Postings: 834   GC: 310
SN   Logs or notebooks in which students regularly record their experiences, ideas, or reflections, often for later revision, and usually not for formal grading by a teacher
UF   Student Logs
     Student Notebooks (Diaries)
BT   Diaries
RT   Dialog Journals
     Experiential Learning
     Journal Writing
     Personal Narratives
     Student Experience
     Student Reaction
     Student Research
     Students
     Writing Across the Curriculum
     Writing Exercises
     Writing Skills

Student Leadership   *JUL. 1966*
Postings: 512   GC: 330
BT   Leadership
RT   Leadership Training
     Student Empowerment
     Student Government
     Student Responsibility
     Students

Student Learning Contracts
USE   Performance Contracts

Student Loading Areas (1968 1980)
USE   Student Transportation

= Two or more Descriptors are used to represent this term.
The term's main entry shows the appropriate coordination.

Student Loan Programs *AUG. 1968*
Postings: 1,767 GC: 620
UF Scholarship Loans (1966 1980) #
BT Programs
RT Banking
Credit (Finance)
Debt (Financial)
Educational Finance
Eligibility
Federal Programs
Financial Needs
Financial Services
Financial Support
Income Contingent Loans
Instructional Student Costs
Loan Default
Loan Repayment
Need Analysis (Student Financial Aid)
Noninstructional Student Costs
Parent Financial Contribution
Paying for College
Self Supporting Students
Student Costs
Student Financial Aid
Student Financial Aid Officers
Tuition

Student Logs
USE Student Journals

Student Maladjustment
USE Student Adjustment

Student Mediation
USE Peer Mediation

Student Mobility *JUL. 1966*
Postings: 666 GC: 330
SN Geographic mobility of students from
one region or school district to another
(Note: Do not confuse with "Educational
Mobility"—prior to Mar80, the use of
this term was not restricted by a Scope
Note)
BT Migration
RT College Transfer Students
Family Mobility
Migrant Children
Migrant Education
Migrant Youth
Student Recruitment
Students
Transfer Students
Transient Children

Student Motivation *JUL. 1966*
Postings: 10,840 GC: 310
BT Motivation
RT Academic Aspiration
Learning Motivation
Reading Motivation
Student Attitudes
Student Characteristics
Student Interests
Students
Teacher Influence

Student Needs *JUL. 1966*
Postings: 10,200 GC: 320
BT Needs
RT Childhood Needs
Course Selection (Students)
Excellence in Education
Individual Needs
Need Analysis (Student Financial Aid)
Psychological Needs
Relevance (Education)
Special Needs Students
Student Characteristics
Student College Relationship
Student Educational Objectives
Student Financial Aid
Student School Relationship
Student Surveys
Students

Student Notebooks (Diaries)
USE Student Journals

Student Opinion (1966 1980)
USE Student Attitudes

Student Organizations *JUL. 1966*
Postings: 1,396 GC: 320
NT Student Government
Student Unions
BT Organizations (Groups)
RT Extracurricular Activities
Fraternities
Sororities
Student Participation
Student Volunteers
Students

Student Outcomes
USE Outcomes of Education

Student Parent Relationship
USE Parent Student Relationship

Student Participation *JUL. 1966*
Postings: 8,233 GC: 310
SN Involvement of students in school or
nonschool activities
UF Classroom Participation (1966 1980) #
BT Participation
Student Behavior
RT Active Learning
Assembly Programs
Cooperative Learning
Experience Charts
Experimental Colleges
Experimental Schools
Participative Decision Making
Service Learning
Student Characteristics
Student Developed Materials
Student Empowerment
Student Government
Student Organizations
Student Projects
Student Research
Student Responsibility
Student Volunteers
Students

Student Personnel Programs (1967 1980)
USE Student Personnel Services

Student Personnel Services *JUL. 1966*
Postings: 4,120 GC: 240
SN Supportive, non-instructional services to
college or university students in a school
setting
UF Student Affairs Services
Student Personnel Programs (1967
1980)
Student Personnel Work (1967 1980)
BT Ancillary School Services
RT Counseling Services
Guidance Programs
Pupil Personnel Services
School Counseling
School Guidance
School Health Services
School Orientation
School Psychology
Student Employment
Student Financial Aid
Student Personnel Workers
Student Placement
Student Welfare

Student Personnel Work (1967 1980)
USE Student Personnel Services

Student Personnel Workers *NOV. 1969*
Postings: 1,138 GC: 240
SN Professional personnel who provide sup-
portive, non-instructional services to col-
lege or university students in a school
setting
UF Student Affairs Workers
BT School Personnel
RT Admissions Officers
College Faculty
College Programs
Counseling Services
Deans of Students
Faculty Advisers
Foreign Student Advisers
Guidance Personnel
Health Personnel
Ombudsmen
Pupil Personnel Workers
Registrars (School)
Resident Advisers
Resident Assistants
School Counselors
School Psychologists
School Social Workers
Student Financial Aid Officers
Student Personnel Services
Student Welfare

Student Placement *JUL. 1966*
Postings: 5,330 GC: 320
SN Assignment of students to schools or
academic classes and programs accord-
ing to their background, readiness, abili-
ties, and goals (Note: Do not use for
"Student Job Placement"—prior to
Mar80, the use of this term was not
restricted by a Scope Note)
UF College Placement (1966 1980)
BT Placement
RT Acceleration (Education)
Admission (School)
Admissions Counseling
Advanced Placement
Age Grade Placement
Educational Counseling
Educational Testing
Equivalency Tests
Grouping (Instructional Purposes)
Mainstreaming
Prior Learning
Pupil Personnel Services
Referral
School Entrance Age
School Readiness
Student Personnel Services
Student Promotion
Students
Track System (Education)
Transfer Programs
Transitional Programs

Student Problems *JUL. 1966*
Postings: 1,636 GC: 330
SN (Note: Use a more precise term if possi-
ble)
BT Problems
RT Behavior Problems
Learning Problems
Students

Student Projects *JUL. 1966*
Postings: 4,193 GC: 310
UF Project Methods #
Project Training Methods (1968
1980) #
BT School Activities
RT Citizen Participation
Cooperative Learning
Experiential Learning
Extracurricular Activities
Independent Study
Reggio Emilia Approach
Science Projects
Student Developed Materials
Student Experience
Student Participation
Student Publications
Student Research
Student Volunteers
Students

Student Promotion *JUL. 1966*
Postings: 424 GC: 320
SN Process by which a student is passed to
the next higher instruction or grade level
UF Academic Promotion
NT Social Promotion
BT Academic Achievement
RT Academic Failure
Age Grade Placement
Flexible Progression
Grade Repetition
Instructional Program Divisions
Student Placement
Students
Transitional Programs

Student Protest
USE Activism

Student Publications *JUL. 1971*
Postings: 1,784 GC: 720
SN Publications prepared by students (Note:
Prior to Mar80, this term was also used
for publications for students)
UF Class Newspapers (1967 1980) #
BT School Publications
RT Editors
Journalism Education
Scholastic Journalism
School Newspapers
Student Developed Materials
Student Projects
Student Research
Students
Writing for Publication
Yearbooks

Student Reaction *JUL. 1966*
Postings: 3,554 GC: 310
UF Student Responses
BT Responses
Student Behavior
RT Student Attitudes
Student Characteristics
Student Evaluation of Teacher Per-
formance
Student Journals
Student Surveys
Students

Student Records *JUL. 1966*
Postings: 1,544 GC: 320
NT Academic Records
Report Cards
BT Records (Forms)
RT Case Records
Confidential Records
Disclosure
Government School Relationship
Portfolio Assessment
Portfolios (Background Materials)
Profiles
Registrars (School)
Student Evaluation
Student Rights
Students

Student Recruitment *FEB. 1976*
Postings: 3,403 GC: 320
SN Activity designed to encourage students
or potential students to enroll in a par-
ticular program, course, or class, or at a
particular institution
BT Recruitment
RT Admission (School)
Admission Criteria
Admissions Officers
Enrollment
Enrollment Management
School Catalogs
Student Mobility
Students

Student Rehabilitation (1966 1980)
USE Rehabilitation

 # = Two or more Descriptors are used to represent this term.
The term's main entry shows the appropriate coordination.

Student Research   *JUL. 1966*
    Postings: 2,025   GC: 810
SN   Research by, not about, students (Note: Prior to Mar80, the use of this term was not restricted by a Scope Note)
BT   Research
RT   Independent Study
    Research Assistants
    Research Opportunities
    Research Papers (Students)
    Research Skills
    Student Developed Materials
    Student Journals
    Student Participation
    Student Projects
    Student Publications
    Students

Student Responses
USE   Student Reaction

Student Responsibility   *NOV. 1972*
    Postings: 1,489   GC: 330
SN   Responsibility of, not for, the student
BT   Responsibility
RT   Child Responsibility
    Educational Responsibility
    Loan Repayment
    School Responsibility
    Student Characteristics
    Student Government
    Student Leadership
    Student Participation
    Student Rights
    Student Role
    Student School Relationship
    Students

Student Rights   *SEP. 1971*
    Postings: 2,975   GC: 330
SN   The guarantee of protection of students against improper institutional actions or decisions in such areas as academic freedom, due process, disclosure of records, discrimination, or violation of civil liberties or citizenship rights
BT   Civil Liberties
RT   Academic Freedom
    Activism
    Childrens Rights
    Citizenship
    Civil Rights
    Demonstrations (Civil)
    Discipline Policy
    Disclosure
    Dress Codes
    Due Process
    Educational Environment
    Equal Protection
    Free Schools
    Freedom of Speech
    In Loco Parentis
    Married Students
    Ombudsmen
    Pregnant Students
    School Boycotts
    School Law
    School Uniforms
    Search and Seizure
    Self Supporting Students
    Student Behavior
    Student Empowerment
    Student Records
    Student Responsibility
    Student School Relationship
    Students

Student Role   *AUG. 1968*
    Postings: 1,963   GC: 320
BT   Role
RT   Learner Controlled Instruction
    Parent Role
    Role of Education
    Student Attitudes
    Student Behavior
    Student Characteristics
    Student Empowerment
    Student Government
    Student Responsibility

Student School Relationship
    Students
    Teacher Role

Student School Relationship   *JUL. 1966*
    Postings: 2,925   GC: 320
SN   The relationship between a school (e.g., nursery, elementary, secondary, vocational) and its students (Note: If applicable, use the more specific term "Student College Relationship")
UF   School Student Relationship
NT   Student College Relationship
BT   Relationship
RT   Academic Probation
    Aptitude Treatment Interaction
    Board Administrator Relationship
    Deans of Students
    Dress Codes
    Due Process
    Educational Environment
    Faculty Advisers
    Family School Relationship
    Hidden Curriculum
    In Loco Parentis
    Integrated Services
    Ombudsmen
    Parent School Relationship
    Parent Student Relationship
    Participative Decision Making
    Probationary Period
    Relevance (Education)
    Role Theory
    School Administration
    School Attitudes
    School Orientation
    School Phobia
    Schools
    Search and Seizure
    Self Supporting Students
    Student Government
    Student Needs
    Student Responsibility
    Student Rights
    Student Role
    Student Subcultures
    Students
    Teacher Student Relationship

Student Science Interests (1967 1980)
USE   Science Interests

Student Selection
USE   Admission Criteria

Student Seminars (1966 1980)
USE   Seminars

Student Subcultures   *JUL. 1966*
    Postings: 313   GC: 330
SN   Student groups exhibiting characteristic patterns of behavior or subscribing to identifiable value systems that differ from those of other groups within the educational environment
BT   Subcultures
RT   Activism
    Cultural Traits
    Educational Environment
    School Culture
    Student Alienation
    Student Attitudes
    Student Behavior
    Student Characteristics
    Student School Relationship
    Students

Student Surveys   *AUG. 1994*
    Postings: 1,220   GC: 810
SN   Studies in which data are gathered from students on their attitudes, interests, activities, characteristics, etc. (Note: Use as a minor Descriptor for examples of this kind of survey—use as a major Descriptor only as the subject of a document)
BT   Surveys
RT   Educational Research

Graduate Surveys
    School Surveys
    Student Attitudes
    Student Characteristics
    Student Interests
    Student Needs
    Student Reaction
    Students

Student Teacher Attitudes   *JUN. 1984*
    Postings: 773   GC: 320
SN   Attitudes of, not toward, student teachers
BT   Attitudes
RT   Student Attitudes
    Student Teacher Evaluation
    Student Teachers
    Student Teaching
    Teacher Attitudes
    Teaching Conditions

Student Teacher Evaluation   *DEC. 1985*
    Postings: 298   GC: 320
SN   Judging performances of student teachers based on established criteria
BT   Evaluation
RT   Student Evaluation
    Student Teacher Attitudes
    Student Teacher Supervisors
    Student Teachers
    Student Teaching
    Teacher Evaluation
    Teaching Skills

Student Teacher Interaction
USE   Teacher Student Relationship

Student Teacher Ratio (1966 1984)
USE   Teacher Student Ratio

Student Teacher Relationship (1966 1984)
USE   Teacher Student Relationship

Student Teacher Supervisors   *MAR. 1980*
    Postings: 1,131   GC: 360
SN   College faculty members who oversee student teachers (Note: Do not confuse with "Cooperating Teachers")
UF   Clinical Professors (1967 1980) (Education)
    College Supervisors (1967 1980)
BT   College Faculty
    Supervisors
RT   Cooperating Teachers
    Practicum Supervision
    Preservice Teacher Education
    Professors
    Student Teacher Evaluation
    Student Teachers
    Student Teaching
    Teacher Education
    Teacher Educators
    Teacher Supervision

Student Teachers   *JUL. 1966*
    Postings: 3,957   GC: 360
SN   Persons enrolled in a school of education who are assigned to assist a regular teacher in a real-school situation
BT   Preservice Teachers
    Teachers
RT   College School Cooperation
    Cooperating Teachers
    Education Majors
    Master Teachers
    Microteaching
    Paraprofessional School Personnel
    Preservice Teacher Education
    Schools of Education
    Student Teacher Attitudes
    Student Teacher Evaluation
    Student Teacher Supervisors
    Student Teaching
    Teacher Education
    Teacher Interns
    Teacher Supervision

Student Teaching   *JUL. 1966*
    Postings: 2,759   GC: 320
UF   Off Campus Student Teaching
    Practice Teaching
BT   Preservice Teacher Education
RT   Affiliated Schools
    Cooperating Teachers
    Extended Teacher Education Programs
    Field Experience Programs
    Lesson Observation Criteria
    Master Teachers
    Methods Courses
    Microteaching
    Practicum Supervision
    Practicums
    Professional Development Schools
    Student Teacher Attitudes
    Student Teacher Evaluation
    Student Teacher Supervisors
    Student Teachers
    Students
    Teacher Centers
    Teaching Experience

Student Testing (1966 1980)
USE   Educational Testing

Student Transfers
USE   Transfer Students

Student Transportation   *JUL. 1966*
    Postings: 923   GC: 320
SN   The movement of school students from residence to school and return by means of any conveyance, usually a bus, at public expense
UF   School Transportation
    Student Loading Areas (1968 1980)
BT   Transportation
RT   Ancillary School Services
    Bus Transportation
    Commuter Colleges
    Commuting Students
    School Buses
    Students
    Traffic Circulation

Student Travel
USE   Travel

Student Unions   *JUL. 1966*
    Postings: 232   GC: 920
SN   Organizations and facilities planned for the community life of students
UF   College Unions
    Student Centers
BT   Educational Facilities
    Student Organizations
RT   College Stores
    Extracurricular Activities
    Recreational Facilities
    Social Organizations

Student Violence
USE   Violence

Student Volunteers   *JUL. 1966*
    Postings: 504   GC: 360
BT   Students
    Volunteers
RT   Extracurricular Activities
    Service Learning
    Student Organizations
    Student Participation
    Student Projects
    Youth Programs

Student Welfare   *JUL. 1966*
    Postings: 379   GC: 240
SN   Social, economic, or emotional well-being of students
BT   Well Being
RT   Child Welfare
    Deans of Students
    Ombudsmen
    Student College Relationship

= Two or more Descriptors are used to represent this term. The term's main entry shows the appropriate coordination.

Student Personnel Services
Student Personnel Workers
Students

Student Writing Models   AUG. 1968
      Postings: 909   GC: 720
SN   Written work by students that is used to
      discuss composition, rhetoric, grammar,
      or usage principles
BT   Models
      Student Developed Materials
RT   Childrens Writing
      Creative Writing
      Descriptive Writing
      English Instruction
      Expository Writing
      Journal Writing
      Writing (Composition)
      Writing Instruction
      Writing Skills

Students   JUL. 1966
      Postings: 2,730   GC: 360
SN   (Note: Use a more specific term if possi-
      ble)
UF   Average Students (1967 1980)
      Pupils
NT   Adult Students
      Advanced Students
      Asian American Students
      Bilingual Students
      Black Students
      College Students
      Commuting Students
      Continuation Students
      Day Students
      Elementary School Students
      Evening Students
      Foreign Students
      Full Time Students
      High Risk Students
      Hispanic American Students
      Lower Class Students
      Majors (Students)
      Married Students
      Middle Class Students
      Middle School Students
      Nonmajors
      Nontraditional Students
      Part Time Students
      Pregnant Students
      Reentry Students
      Secondary School Students
      Self Supporting Students
      Single Students
      Special Needs Students
      Student Volunteers
      Terminal Students
      Transfer Students
      White Students
BT   Groups
RT   Attendance
      Diversity (Student)
      Enrollment
      Extracurricular Activities
      Home Visits
      Parent Student Relationship
      School Demography
      School Holding Power
      Student Adjustment
      Student Alienation
      Student Attitudes
      Student Attrition
      Student Behavior
      Student Centered Curriculum
      Student Certification
      Student Characteristics
      Student Costs
      Student Developed Materials
      Student Development
      Student Educational Objectives
      Student Employment
      Student Empowerment
      Student Evaluation
      Student Exchange Programs
      Student Experience
      Student Financial Aid
      Student Government
      Student Improvement
      Student Interests
      Student Journals

Student Leadership
Student Mobility
Student Motivation
Student Needs
Student Organizations
Student Participation
Student Placement
Student Problems
Student Projects
Student Promotion
Student Publications
Student Reaction
Student Records
Student Recruitment
Student Research
Student Responsibility
Student Rights
Student Role
Student School Relationship
Student Subcultures
Student Surveys
Student Teaching
Student Transportation
Student Welfare
Teacher Expectations of Students
Teacher Student Ratio
Teacher Student Relationship
Trainees
Truancy

Studio Art   OCT. 1994
      Postings: 69   GC: 420
SN   Instruction and study concerned with
      the practice of drawing, painting, sculp-
      ture, printmaking, and other visual arts
UF   Art Making (Instruction)
      Art Production Curriculum
      Art Studio Courses
BT   Art Education
RT   Art Expression
      Art Materials
      Art Products
      Creative Art
      Discipline Based Art Education
      Visual Arts

Studio Floor Plans (1966 1980)   MAR. 1980
      Postings: 28   GC: 920
SN   Invalid Descriptor—used inconsistently
      in indexing—see such Descriptors as
      "Building Plans," "Building Design,"
      "Educational Facilities Design," "Class-
      room Design," "Television Studios," etc.

Study   JUL. 1966
      Postings: 139   GC: 310
SN   Application of the mind to the acquisition
      of knowledge (Note: Prior to Mar80, this
      term did not carry a Scope Note and
      was occasionally used to represent a
      Pubtype—see Pubtype 143 for this us-
      age)
UF   Study Hours
NT   Home Study
      Independent Study
BT   Learning Activities
RT   Drills (Practice)
      Proctoring
      Review (Reexamination)
      Scholarship
      Study Centers
      Study Facilities
      Study Guides
      Study Habits
      Study Skills
      Time on Task

Study Abroad   JUL. 1966
      Postings: 1,359   GC: 350
BT   Education
RT   Foreign Medical Graduates
      International Educational Exchange
      Student Exchange Programs
      Tourism
      Travel

Study Carrels
USE   Carrels

Study Centers   JUL. 1966
      Postings: 169   GC: 920
UF   School Study Centers (1966 1980)
      Study Halls
BT   Study Facilities
RT   After School Centers
      Compensatory Education
      In School Suspension
      Study

Study Facilities   JUL. 1966
      Postings: 100   GC: 920
NT   Carrels
      Study Centers
BT   Educational Facilities
RT   Library Facilities
      Study

Study Guides   JUL. 1966
      Postings: 1,183   GC: 730
BT   Guides
      Instructional Materials
RT   Advance Organizers
      Course Organization
      Independent Study
      Programmed Instructional Materials
      Review (Reexamination)
      Study
      Study Habits
      Study Skills

Study Habits   JUL. 1966
      Postings: 1,101   GC: 310
BT   Behavior Patterns
RT   Reading Habits
      Study
      Study Guides
      Study Skills
      Word Study Skills

Study Halls
USE   Study Centers

Study Hours
USE   Study

Study Release Programs
USE   Released Time

Study Skills   JUL. 1966
      Postings: 3,157   GC: 310
NT   Word Study Skills
BT   Skills
RT   Advance Organizers
      Basic Skills
      Content Area Reading
      Information Skills
      Learning Strategies
      Locational Skills (Social Studies)
      Metacognition
      Notetaking
      Outlining (Discourse)
      Study
      Study Guides
      Study Habits
      Thinking Skills

Study Trips
USE   Field Trips

Stunts and Tumbling
USE   Tumbling

Stuttering   JUL. 1966
      Postings: 573   GC: 220
SN   Disorder of speech rhythm or fluency
      characterized by repetition or prolonga-
      tion of speech sounds, interjection of
      superfluous speech elements, or silent
      intervals
UF   Stammering
BT   Speech Impairments
RT   Articulation Impairments
      Speech Habits

Speech Improvement
Speech Skills
Speech Therapy

Subculture (1967 1980)
USE   Subcultures

Subcultures   MAR. 1980
      Postings: 481   GC: 560
SN   Ethnic, regional, economic, or social
      groups exhibiting characteristic patterns
      of behavior sufficient to distinguish them
      from the larger society to which they
      belong
UF   Subculture (1967 1980)
NT   Student Subcultures
BT   Culture
RT   Acculturation
      Cross Cultural Studies
      Cultural Differences
      Cultural Influences
      Cultural Isolation
      Cultural Traits
      Ethnic Groups
      Ghettos
      Minority Groups
      Social Class
      Social Environment
      Social Influences
      Socialization

Subemployment (1968 1980)
USE   Underemployment

Subject Access
USE   Indexing

Subject Disciplines
USE   Intellectual Disciplines

Subject Headings
USE   Subject Index Terms

Subject Index Terms   JUL. 1969
      Postings: 1,332   GC: 710
UF   Descriptors
      Index Terms
      Subject Headings
      Uniterms
BT   Vocabulary
RT   Authority Control (Information)
      Cataloging
      Dewey Decimal Classification
      Indexes
      Indexing
      Keywords
      Library Catalogs
      Library of Congress Classification
      Thesauri
      Universal Decimal Classification

Subjunctive Mood
USE   Verbs

Subprofessionals (1967 1977)
USE   Paraprofessional Personnel

Subsidies
USE   Grants

Substance Abuse   JUN. 1988
      Postings: 2,030   GC: 530
SN   Excessive or otherwise inappropriate in-
      gestion of alcohol, drugs, tobacco, or
      other chemical or organic substances,
      often impairing physiological and/or psy-
      chological functions
NT   Alcohol Abuse
      Drug Abuse
BT   Behavior
RT   Health Behavior
      Health Education
      Physical Health

= Two or more Descriptors are used to represent this term.
The term's main entry shows the appropriate coordination.

Poisoning
Prenatal Influences
Self Destructive Behavior
Smoking
Tobacco

Substitute Teachers   OCT. 1969
Postings: 225   GC: 360
UF Relief Teachers
BT Teachers
RT Employee Absenteeism
Part Time Faculty
Teacher Attendance
Teacher Employment

Substitution Drills   JUL. 1966
Postings: 95   GC: 310
BT Pattern Drills (Language)
RT Applied Linguistics
Cloze Procedure
Teaching Methods

Subtraction   JUL. 1966
Postings: 584   GC: 480
BT Arithmetic
RT Addition
Division
Multiplication

Suburban Environment   JUL. 1966
Postings: 103   GC: 550
BT Environment
RT Suburban Housing
Suburban Problems
Suburban Schools
Suburban Youth
Suburbs

Suburban Housing   JUL. 1966
Postings: 49   GC: 550
BT Housing
RT Suburban Environment
Suburban Problems
Suburbs

Suburban Problems   JUL. 1966
Postings: 33   GC: 550
BT Problems
RT Suburban Environment
Suburban Housing
Suburban Schools
Suburban Youth
Suburbs

Suburban Schools   JUL. 1966
Postings: 685   GC: 340
BT Schools
RT Suburban Environment
Suburban Problems
Suburbs

Suburban Youth   JUL. 1966
Postings: 128   GC: 510
SN (Note: Coordinate with an appropriate age or educational level Descriptor)
BT Youth
RT Suburban Environment
Suburban Problems
Suburbs

Suburbs   JUL. 1966
Postings: 204   GC: 550
BT Metropolitan Areas
RT Community
Municipalities
Neighborhoods
Suburban Environment
Suburban Housing
Suburban Problems
Suburban Schools
Suburban Youth
Urban to Suburban Migration

Success   MAR. 1980
Postings: 5,125   GC: 820
SN Attainment of a goal or desired outcome
UF Goal Attainment
Success Factors (1968 1980)
BT Performance
RT Achievement
Achievement Gains
Achievement Need
Evaluation
Expectation
Failure
Fear of Success
Goal Orientation
High Achievement
Improvement
Motivation
Objectives
Organizational Effectiveness
Outcomes of Education
Overachievement
Program Effectiveness
Satisfaction
Standards

Success Avoidance
USE Fear of Success

Success Factors (1968 1980)
USE Success

Sudden Infant Death Syndrome   OCT. 1999
Postings: 49   GC: 210
SN The sudden and unexpected death of an apparently healthy infant, occurring almost always during sleep, that cannot be explained by postmortem studies
UF Cot Death
Crib Death
SIDS
BT Infant Mortality
RT Child Health
Infants
Physical Health

Suffixes   JAN. 1969
Postings: 214   GC: 450
BT Affixes
RT Prefixes (Grammar)
Structural Analysis (Linguistics)

Suggestopedia   JAN. 1985
Postings: 158   GC: 110
SN Method of teaching, developed by Georgi Lozanov, in which relaxed concentration is combined with synchronized music and rhythmic presentation to tap the unconscious reserves of the mind and thereby accelerate learning—originally applied in language courses, but since expanded to a variety of learning tasks
UF Lozanov Method
BT Teaching Methods
RT Hypnosis
Meditation
Mnemonics
Music
Psychoeducational Methods
Relaxation Training
Second Language Instruction

Suicide   FEB. 1969
Postings: 1,977   GC: 230
BT Death
Self Destructive Behavior
RT Behavior Disorders
Homicide
Psychopathology
Self Injurious Behavior

Summated Rating Scales
USE Likert Scales

Summative Evaluation   JUN. 1971
Postings: 1,883   GC: 310
SN Evaluation at the conclusion of an activity or plan to determine its effectiveness
UF Product Evaluation
BT Evaluation
RT Course Evaluation
Curriculum Evaluation
Educational Assessment
Evaluation Utilization
Formative Evaluation
Grading
Institutional Evaluation
Participant Satisfaction
Program Effectiveness
Program Evaluation
Program Validation
Self Evaluation (Groups)
Student Evaluation of Teacher Performance
Validated Programs

Summer Institutes (1967 1980)
USE Institutes (Training Programs)
AND Summer Programs

Summer Olympic Games
USE Olympic Games

Summer Programs   JUL. 1966
Postings: 3,679   GC: 350
SN Programs scheduled during the summer months
UF Summer Institutes (1967 1980) #
Summer Workshops (1966 1980) #
NT Summer Science Programs
BT Programs
RT Alumni Education
Day Camp Programs
Minicourses
Outdoor Education
Recreational Programs
Remedial Programs
Resident Camp Programs
Summer Schools
Vacation Programs

Summer Schools   JUL. 1966
Postings: 478   GC: 350
UF Summer Session
BT Schools
RT Extended School Year
Summer Programs
Supplementary Education
Transitional Programs
Year Round Schools

Summer Science Programs   JUL. 1966
Postings: 197   GC: 490
BT Science Programs
Summer Programs
RT Science Curriculum
Science Instruction
Science Projects

Summer Session
USE Summer Schools

Summer Workshops (1966 1980)
USE Summer Programs
AND Workshops

Superconductors   JAN. 1970
Postings: 21   GC: 910
RT Electricity
Microelectronics
Semiconductor Devices

Superintendent Role (1966 1980)
USE Superintendents

Superintendents   JUL. 1966
Postings: 2,722   GC: 360
SN Administrators who coordinate and direct the operation of an institution, organization, or department—in education, the administrators at the district, city, county, or state level who direct and coordinate the activities of school systems in accordance with school board standards
UF Assistant Superintendents
School Superintendents (1966 1980)
Superintendent Role (1966 1980)
BT Administrators
RT Board of Education Policy
Boards of Education
Central Office Administrators
Instructional Leadership
School Administration
School Districts
School Personnel

Superior Students (1966 1978)
USE Academically Gifted

Supermarkets
USE Food Stores

Supervised Farm Practice (1966 1990)
USE Supervised Occupational Experience (Agriculture)

Supervised Occupational Experience (Agriculture)   APR. 1990
Postings: 63   GC: 410
SN Planned practical activities conducted outside of class in which students develop and apply agricultural knowledge and skills in a learning environment closely related to the real conditions of agricultural occupations
UF Supervised Farm Practice (1966 1990)
BT Agricultural Education
Field Experience Programs
RT Agribusiness
Agricultural Occupations
Agriculture
Cooperative Education
Farm Visits
Work Experience Programs

Supervising Teachers
USE Cooperating Teachers

Supervision   JUL. 1966
Postings: 1,852   GC: 630
SN The process or function of directing and evaluating activities in progress, and of providing leadership and guidance to the employees or staff involved (Note: Use a more specific term if possible)
UF Supervisory Activities (1968 1980)
NT Practicum Supervision
Proctoring
School Supervision
Science Supervision
Teacher Supervision
BT Administration
RT Leadership
Supervisors
Supervisory Methods

Supervisor Qualifications   JUL. 1966
Postings: 250   GC: 630
BT Qualifications
RT Administrator Education
Administrator Qualifications
Employment Qualifications
Supervisors
Supervisory Training

Supervisor Training
USE Supervisory Training

Supervisors   JUL. 1966
Postings: 1,468   GC: 640
UF Foremen
NT Crew Leaders

= Two or more Descriptors are used to represent this term.
The term's main entry shows the appropriate coordination.

State Supervisors
Student Teacher Supervisors
BT   Administrators
RT   Consultants
Leaders
Supervision
Supervisor Qualifications
Supervisory Methods
Supervisory Training

Supervisory Activities (1968 1980)
USE Supervision

Supervisory Methods   *JUL. 1966*
Postings: 1,294   GC: 630
SN   Approaches or techniques for directing or overseeing individuals or work in progress—may include evaluation
BT   Methods
RT   Administrative Principles
Clinical Supervision (of Teachers)
Evaluation Methods
Leadership Styles
Supervision
Supervisors
Supervisory Training

Supervisory Training   *JUL. 1966*
Postings: 1,095   GC: 400
UF   Supervisor Training
BT   Training
RT   Job Training
Leadership Training
Management Development
Supervisor Qualifications
Supervisors
Supervisory Methods

Supplementary Education   *JUL. 1966*
Postings: 628   GC: 350
SN   Education provided outside of school hours either to reinforce and support the regular school program or to compensate for educational disadvantages (Note: Prior to Mar80, this term was not restricted by a Scope Note—see also "Compensatory Education," "Remedial Programs," etc.)
UF   Supplementary Educational Centers (1966 1980) #
BT   Education
RT   After School Education
Compensatory Education
Educationally Disadvantaged
Enrichment Activities
Extracurricular Activities
Migrant Education
Minicourses
Refresher Courses
Remedial Programs
Retraining
Summer Schools
Transitional Programs

Supplementary Educational Centers (1966 1980)
USE Education Service Centers
AND Supplementary Education

Supplementary Reading Materials
JUL. 1966
Postings: 1,173   GC: 460
SN   Books, magazines, or fugitive materials, aside from basal texts, used to enrich instructional materials or to furnish additional practice in reading
UF   Supplementary Textbooks (1967 1980) #
BT   Reading Materials
RT   High Interest Low Vocabulary Books
Independent Reading
Instructional Materials
Reading Material Selection
Recreational Reading

Supplementary Textbooks (1967 1980)
USE Supplementary Reading Materials

AND   Textbooks

Supplies   *AUG. 1968*
Postings: 216   GC: 910
SN   Material items that are expended or consumed through use—includes property other than land, buildings, furniture, or equipment
UF   Office Supplies
School Supplies
Stockpiles
NT   Adhesives
Agricultural Supplies
Electric Batteries
Magnetic Tapes
BT   Resources
RT   Art Materials
Construction Materials
Equipment
Facility Inventory
Maintenance
Paper (Material)
Vendors

Supply and Demand   *DEC. 1989*
Postings: 367   GC: 620
SN   Relationship between quantities of goods and services offered in the marketplace and quantities that consumers are prepared to buy—also, the impact of that relationship on market availability and price
NT   Teacher Supply and Demand
BT   Relationship
RT   Business Cycles
Competition
Consumer Economics
Cost Indexes
Costs
Demand Occupations
Economic Change
Economic Climate
Economic Factors
Economics
Educational Demand
Educational Supply
Inflation (Economics)
International Trade
Labor Market
Labor Needs
Labor Supply
Marketing
Productivity
Purchasing
Socioeconomic Influences

Supply of Education
USE Educational Supply

Supply of Labor
USE Labor Supply

Support Groups (Human Services)
USE Social Support Groups

Support Networks (Personal Assistance)
USE Social Support Groups

Support Systems (Services)
USE Services

Supported Competitive Employment
USE Supported Employment

Supported Employment   *APR. 1990*
Postings: 405   GC: 630
SN   Paid employment in a normal work environment for special needs individuals who receive the ongoing support and services (e.g., transportation) necessary to maintain that employment
UF   Supported Competitive Employment
Supported Work Programs
BT   Employment
RT   Community Programs

Employment Potential
Helping Relationship
Individualized Programs
Job Placement
Normalization (Disabilities)
Rehabilitation
Sheltered Workshops
Vocational Rehabilitation
Work Experience Programs

Supported Work Programs
USE Supported Employment

Suppressor Variables   *JAN. 1971*
Postings: 31   GC: 820
SN   Predictor variables that have negligible correlation with a criterion, but which improve the prediction of a test battery or other group of predictor measures because of their correlation with another predictor in the battery
BT   Predictor Variables
RT   Multiple Regression Analysis
Path Analysis
Predictive Measurement

Suprasegmental Morphemes
USE Intonation

Suprasegmental Phonemes
USE Suprasegmentals

Suprasegmentals   *NOV. 1968*
Postings: 514   GC: 450
UF   Prosodic Features (Speech)
Suprasegmental Phonemes
NT   Intonation
Stress (Phonology)
BT   Phonology
RT   Morphology (Languages)
Morphophonemics
Paralinguistics
Phonemes
Phrase Structure
Sentence Structure
Structural Analysis (Linguistics)

Supreme Court Litigation (1966 1980)
MAR. 1980
Postings: 1,015   GC: 610
SN   Invalid Descriptor—used for litigation from both state supreme courts and the U.S. Supreme Court—coordinate "Court Litigation" with "State Courts" or the Identifier "Supreme Court" respectively for these concepts

Supreme Courts (1966 1980)   *MAR. 1980*
Postings: 74   GC: 610
SN   Invalid Descriptor—used for both state supreme courts and the U.S. Supreme Court—use "State Courts" or the Identifier "Supreme Court" respectively for these concepts

Surface Area
USE Area

Surface Finishing
USE Finishing

Surface Structure   *JUL. 1966*
Postings: 670   GC: 450
SN   Concept in transformational grammar referring to the form of a sentence as it is actually seen, heard, or spoken—in contrast to its deep structure
BT   Transformational Generative Grammar
RT   Deep Structure
Function Words
Grammar
Linguistic Theory
Linguistics
Morphology (Languages)

Morphophonemics
Phonology
Phrase Structure
Sentence Diagraming
Sentence Structure
Syntax

Surfing   *JAN. 1985*
Postings: 6   GC: 470
BT   Aquatic Sports

Surgery   *OCT. 1977*
Postings: 249   GC: 210
SN   Branch of medicine which treats trauma and diseases wholly or in part by manual and operative procedures
UF   Operations (Surgery)
BT   Medicine
RT   Abortions
Amputations
Anatomy
Anesthesiology
Biomedical Equipment
Cancer
Diseases
Hospitals
Medical Services
Oncology
Patients
Physical Health
Surgical Technicians

Surgical Technicians   *JUL. 1966*
Postings: 40   GC: 210
SN   Technical assistants on a surgical team who arrange supplies and instruments in the operating room, maintain antiseptic conditions, prepare patients for surgery, and assist surgeons during the operation
UF   Operating Room Technicians
BT   Allied Health Personnel
RT   Medical Services
Surgery

Surrealism   *APR. 1969*
Postings: 57   GC: 430
SN   Early 20th century movement, style, or sensibility in the arts emphasizing the unrestrained expression of the subconscious through such devices as automatic (stream of consciousness) writing and the abnormal juxtaposition of natural objects shown in unnatural states
RT   Art Expression
Creative Art
Imagination
Literary Styles
Symbols (Literary)
Twentieth Century Literature

Survey Courses
USE Introductory Courses

Surveys   *JUL. 1966*
Postings: 18,635   GC: 810
NT   Community Surveys
Graduate Surveys
Library Surveys
Mail Surveys
National Surveys
Occupational Surveys
School Surveys
State Surveys
Statistical Surveys
Student Surveys
Teacher Surveys
Telephone Surveys
Television Surveys
BT   Evaluation Methods
RT   Attitude Measures
Biographical Inventories
Comparative Analysis
Data Collection
Educational Assessment
Feasibility Studies
Information Utilization
Inquiry

= Two or more Descriptors are used to represent this term.
The term's main entry shows the appropriate coordination.

Interviews
Investigations
Literature Reviews
Measures (Individuals)
Needs Assessment
Opinions
Public Opinion
Questionnaires
Research
Response Rates (Questionnaires)
Sample Size
Sampling
State of the Art Reviews
Test Reviews
Trend Analysis

Survival Literacy
USE　Functional Literacy

Survival Reading Skills
USE　Functional Reading

Survival Skills (Daily Living)
USE　Daily Living Skills

Suspension　　　　　　　　　　　*NOV. 1969*
　　　Postings: 707　　　　　　　　　　GC: 330
SN　Temporary, forced withdrawal from the
　　　regular school program
NT　In School Suspension
BT　Discipline
RT　Academic Failure
　　　Academic Probation
　　　Attendance
　　　College Attendance
　　　Disqualification
　　　Expulsion
　　　Out of School Youth
　　　School Attendance Legislation
　　　Withdrawal (Education)

Sustainable Development　　　*NOV. 1994*
　　　Postings: 354　　　　　　　　　　GC: 410
SN　Development that meets the needs of the
　　　present without compromising the abil-
　　　ity of future generations to meet their
　　　own needs (i.e., development that nur-
　　　tures the economy and improves the
　　　quality of life without undermining the
　　　natural resources and environmental in-
　　　tegrity on which they depend) (Note: See
　　　also the Identifier "Sustainable Agricul-
　　　ture")
BT　Development
RT　Biodiversity
　　　Community Development
　　　Conservation (Environment)
　　　Developed Nations
　　　Developing Nations
　　　Ecology
　　　Economic Development
　　　Environmental Education
　　　Natural Resources
　　　Physical Environment

Sustained Silent Reading　　　*MAR. 1980*
　　　Postings: 152　　　　　　　　　　GC: 460
SN　An instructional practice in which a pe-
　　　riod of time is set aside for everyone in a
　　　class or school to read silently
BT　Reading
　　　Reading Instruction
RT　Reading Habits
　　　Silent Reading

Susu　　　　　　　　　　　　　　　　*JUL. 1966*
　　　Postings: 4　　　　　　　　　　　　GC: 440
BT　African Languages

Suzuki Method　　　　　　　　　*AUG. 1989*
　　　Postings: 26　　　　　　　　　　　GC: 420
SN　Method developed by Japanese music
　　　educator, Shinichi Suzuki, for teaching
　　　the violin and other musical instruments
　　　by ear—students usually begin as
　　　preschoolers

BT　Music Education
　　　Teaching Methods
RT　Auditory Training
　　　Music Techniques
　　　Musical Instruments

Swahili　　　　　　　　　　　　　　*JUL. 1966*
　　　Postings: 128　　　　　　　　　　GC: 440
UF　Kiswahili
BT　Bantu Languages

Swamps
USE　Wetlands

Swazi
USE　Siswati

Swedish　　　　　　　　　　　　　　*MAR. 1978*
　　　Postings: 189　　　　　　　　　　GC: 440
BT　Indo European Languages

Swimming　　　　　　　　　　　　*APR. 1970*
　　　Postings: 257　　　　　　　　　　GC: 470
BT　Aquatic Sports
RT　Diving
　　　Lifetime Sports
　　　Olympic Games
　　　Recreational Activities
　　　Swimming Pools
　　　Water Polo

Swimming Pools　　　　　　　　*SEP. 1968*
　　　Postings: 123　　　　　　　　　　GC: 920
BT　Facilities
RT　Aquatic Sports
　　　Diving
　　　Physical Education Facilities
　　　Recreational Facilities
　　　Swimming

Swing Music
USE　Jazz

Switching (Language)
USE　Code Switching (Language)

Syllabi
USE　Course Descriptions

Syllables　　　　　　　　　　　　　*JUL. 1966*
　　　Postings: 733　　　　　　　　　　GC: 450
BT　Phonology
RT　Articulation (Speech)
　　　Consonants
　　　Intonation
　　　Phonemes
　　　Stress (Phonology)
　　　Structural Analysis (Linguistics)
　　　Vowels

Symbolic Coding
USE　Coding

Symbolic Language　　　　　　*JUL. 1966*
　　　Postings: 312　　　　　　　　　　GC: 450
BT　Language
RT　Ideography
　　　Semiotics
　　　Shorthand

Symbolic Learning　　　　　　　*JUL. 1966*
　　　Postings: 346　　　　　　　　　　GC: 110
BT　Learning
RT　Associative Learning
　　　Visual Learning
　　　Word Recognition

Symbolic Logic
USE　Mathematical Logic

Symbolic Play
USE　Pretend Play

Symbolism　　　　　　　　　　　　*JUN. 1969*
　　　Postings: 595　　　　　　　　　　GC: 430
SN　In a broad sense, the use of one object to
　　　represent or suggest another—in art and
　　　literature, a movement beginning in the
　　　late nineteenth century involving the se-
　　　rious and extensive use of symbols
RT　Art Expression
　　　Literary Styles
　　　Nineteenth Century Literature
　　　Symbols (Literary)
　　　Twentieth Century Literature

Symbols (Literary)　　　　　　　*JUL. 1966*
　　　Postings: 396　　　　　　　　　　GC: 430
BT　Figurative Language
RT　Imagery
　　　Literary Devices
　　　Literature
　　　Metaphors
　　　Motifs
　　　Mythology
　　　Surrealism
　　　Symbolism

Symbols (Mathematics)　　　　*JAN. 1969*
　　　Postings: 302　　　　　　　　　　GC: 480
NT　Numbers
RT　Mathematical Formulas
　　　Mathematics

Symmetry　　　　　　　　　　　　　*JUL. 1966*
　　　Postings: 224　　　　　　　　　　GC: 480
RT　Art
　　　Congruence (Mathematics)
　　　Geometric Concepts
　　　Geometry

Symphony Orchestras
USE　Orchestras

Symposia (1967 1980)
USE　Conferences

Symptoms (Individual Disorders)　*APR. 1990*
　　　Postings: 704　　　　　　　　　　GC: 210
SN　Premonitory signs of physical, mental,
　　　behavioral, or learning dysfunction within
　　　individuals
RT　At Risk Persons
　　　Clinical Diagnosis
　　　Disability Identification
　　　Disease Control
　　　Early Identification
　　　Early Intervention
　　　Educational Diagnosis
　　　Expectation
　　　Fatigue (Biology)
　　　Health
　　　Medical Evaluation
　　　Pain
　　　Predictor Variables
　　　Psychological Evaluation
　　　Stress Management

Synchronic Linguistics (1967 1980)
USE　Descriptive Linguistics

Syntactic Borrowing
USE　Linguistic Borrowing

Syntax　　　　　　　　　　　　　　　*JUL. 1966*
　　　Postings: 5,563　　　　　　　　　GC: 450
UF　Valence (Language)
NT　Form Classes (Languages)
　　　Phrase Structure
　　　Sentence Structure
BT　Grammar
RT　Adjectives
　　　Adverbs
　　　Case (Grammar)

Code Switching (Language)
Cohesion (Written Composition)
Conjunctions
Connected Discourse
Deep Structure
Determiners (Languages)
Discourse Analysis
Error Analysis (Language)
Function Words
Generative Grammar
Kernel Sentences
Language Patterns
Language Typology
Linguistic Borrowing
Morphemes
Morphology (Languages)
Nouns
Pragmatics
Prepositions
Pronouns
Semantics
Semiotics
Sentence Combining
Sentence Diagraming
Sentences
Structural Grammar
Surface Structure
Tenses (Grammar)
Text Structure
Traditional Grammar
Transformational Generative Grammar
Verbs
Word Order

Synthesis　　　　　　　　　　　　　*JUL. 1966*
　　　Postings: 507　　　　　　　　　　GC: 820
SN　Combination of separate elements to form
　　　a coherent whole (Note: Use as a major
　　　Descriptor for discussions of synthesis
　　　as a process—use as a minor Descriptor
　　　for documents that are a synthesis of
　　　ideas, etc.—prior to Mar80, this term
　　　did not carry a Scope Note)
BT　Evaluation Methods
RT　Cognitive Processes
　　　Comparative Analysis
　　　Meta Analysis

Synthetic Speech
USE　Artificial Speech

Syphilis
USE　Venereal Diseases

Systematic Desensitization
USE　Desensitization

Systems Analysis　　　　　　　　*JUL. 1966*
　　　Postings: 1,966　　　　　　　　　GC: 820
SN　Examination of the interrelated elements
　　　of any organization, structure, proce-
　　　dure, etc., to improve the functioning of
　　　the system as a whole
UF　Functional Systems Theory
BT　Methods
RT　Architectural Programming
　　　Computer Science
　　　Cost Effectiveness
　　　Critical Path Method
　　　Decision Making
　　　Information Theory
　　　Input Output Analysis
　　　Instructional Systems
　　　Integrated Activities
　　　Management Systems
　　　Models
　　　Needs Assessment
　　　Network Analysis
　　　Organizational Effectiveness
　　　Policy Analysis
　　　Problem Solving
　　　Relevance (Information Retrieval)
　　　Skill Analysis
　　　Strategic Planning
　　　Systems Analysts
　　　Systems Approach
　　　Systems Development

Systems Analysts   *JAN. 1969*
     Postings: 55   GC: 640
BT   Personnel
RT   Mathematicians
     Programmers
     Researchers
     Systems Analysis
     Systems Development

Systems Approach   *JUL. 1966*
     Postings: 4,947   GC: 320
SN   Overall, macroscopic way of looking at
     organizations, structures, procedures,
     etc., and their context—involves a con-
     cern for the whole rather than the con-
     stituent parts
UF   Systems Theory
NT   Systems Building
BT   Holistic Approach
RT   Chaos Theory
     Context Effect
     Cybernetics
     Decision Making
     Entropy
     Information Theory
     Instructional Systems
     Management Systems
     Models
     Planning
     Problem Solving
     Schematic Studies
     Systems Analysis

Systems Building   *DEC. 1976*
     Postings: 39   GC: 920
SN   Use of the systems approach in facilities
     construction to organize planning, fi-
     nancing, manufacturing, and evaluation
     under single or highly coordinated man-
     agement (Note: Do not confuse with
     "Systems Development")
NT   Design Build Approach
BT   Systems Approach
RT   Building Innovation
     Building Plans
     Building Systems
     Buildings
     Construction (Process)
     Construction Management
     Construction Programs
     Educational Facilities Planning
     Facility Planning
     Fast Track Scheduling
     Modular Building Design
     Structural Building Systems
     Structural Elements (Construction)

Systems Concepts (1966 1980)   *MAR. 1980*
     Postings: 322   GC: 320
SN   Invalid Descriptor—used indiscriminately
     in indexing

Systems Development   *JUL. 1966*
     Postings: 1,899   GC: 320
SN   Planning, designing, constructing, or ex-
     panding an assembly of components or
     concepts that will interact as an organ-
     ized whole and be more effective in meet-
     ing particular goals
BT   Development
RT   Computer Selection
     Computer Software Development
     Computer System Design
     Educational Development
     Formative Evaluation
     Man Machine Systems
     Management Systems
     Organizational Development
     Performance Technology
     Program Development
     Systems Analysis
     Systems Analysts
     Technological Advancement

Systems Theory
USE   Systems Approach

T Groups (1967 1980)
USE   Sensitivity Training

Table Tennis   *APR. 1985*
     Postings: 6   GC: 470
UF   Ping Pong
BT   Athletics
RT   Olympic Games
     Racquet Sports

Tables (Data)   *JUL. 1966*
     Postings: 21,088   GC: 730
NT   Expectancy Tables
BT   Visual Aids
RT   Charts
     Data
     Graphs
     Spreadsheets

Tachistoscopes   *JUL. 1966*
     Postings: 109   GC: 910
SN   Apparatus that project visual stimuli (e.g.,
     pictures, letters, words. . .) for very brief
     and accurately timed intervals
BT   Projection Equipment
RT   Pictorial Stimuli
     Reading
     Reading Research
     Recognition (Psychology)
     Visual Stimuli

Tackboards
USE   Bulletin Boards

Tactile Adaptation   *JUL. 1966*
     Postings: 177   GC: 220
SN   The conversion of educational materials
     for use with the instruction of the blind
BT   Media Adaptation
RT   Blindness
     Braille
     Magnification Methods
     Raised Line Drawings
     Sensory Aids
     Tactile Stimuli
     Tactual Perception
     Tactual Visual Tests

Tactile Materials
USE   Manipulative Materials

Tactile Stimuli   *JAN. 1988*
     Postings: 107   GC: 110
UF   Tactual Stimuli
BT   Stimuli
RT   Auditory Stimuli
     Electrical Stimuli
     Manipulative Materials
     Tactile Adaptation
     Tactual Perception
     Visual Stimuli

Tactual Perception   *JUL. 1966*
     Postings: 547   GC: 110
SN   Ability to interpret sensory stimuli that
     are experienced through the skin
UF   Cutaneous Sense (1968 1980)
     Dermal Sense
     Haptic Perception (1967 1980)
BT   Perception
RT   Dimensional Preference
     Figural Aftereffects
     Kinesthetic Perception
     Learning Modalities
     Manipulative Materials
     Object Manipulation
     Perception Tests
     Sensory Experience
     Sensory Training
     Tactile Adaptation
     Tactile Stimuli
     Tactual Visual Tests

Tactual Stimuli
USE   Tactile Stimuli

Tactual Visual Tests   *JUL. 1966*
     Postings: 32   GC: 830
SN   Tests used to indicate tactual-visual per-
     ception and coordination
BT   Perception Tests
RT   Eye Hand Coordination
     Perceptual Motor Coordination
     Perceptual Motor Learning
     Tactile Adaptation
     Tactual Perception
     Vision Tests
     Visual Perception

Tadjik Persian
USE   Tajik

Tagalog   *JUL. 1966*
     Postings: 102   GC: 440
UF   Pilipino
BT   Indonesian Languages

Tagmemic Analysis   *JUL. 1966*
     Postings: 117   GC: 450
BT   Structural Analysis (Linguistics)
RT   Function Words
     Grammar
     Language Patterns
     Language Research
     Negative Forms (Language)
     Structural Grammar

Tailored Testing
USE   Adaptive Testing

Tailors
USE   Needle Trades

Tajik   *JUL. 1966*
     Postings: 5   GC: 440
UF   Tadjik Persian
BT   Indo European Languages

Talent   *JUL. 1966*
     Postings: 1,994   GC: 120
SN   Superior ability or aptitude, such as in
     the arts or athletics—distinguished from
     "Aptitude" by usually being actual rather
     than potential, and from "Ability" by
     usually being innate rather than acquired
UF   Artistic Talent
     Talented Students (1966 1980)
RT   Ability
     Achievement
     Aptitude
     Creativity
     Gifted
     Talent Development
     Talent Identification
     Vocational Aptitude

Talent Development   *JUL. 1966*
     Postings: 522   GC: 120
UF   Talent Preservation
BT   Individual Development
RT   Creative Development
     Skill Development
     Talent

Talent Identification   *JUL. 1966*
     Postings: 1,070   GC: 820
SN   Identification of superior and usually in-
     nate aptitudes or abilities, such as in the
     arts or athletics (Note: Do not confuse
     with "Ability Identification")
BT   Identification
RT   Ability Identification
     Aptitude Tests
     Creativity Tests
     Early Identification
     Intelligence Quotient
     Intelligence Tests
     Talent

Talent Preservation
USE   Talent Development

Talent Tests
USE   Aptitude Tests

Talent Utilization (1966 1980)   *MAR. 1980*
     Postings: 58   GC: 520
SN   Invalid Descriptor—used inconsistently
     in indexing—see such Descriptors as
     "Talent," "Self Actualization," "Staff Utili-
     zation," etc.

Talented Students (1966 1980)
USE   Talent

Tales   *JUN. 1969*
     Postings: 215   GC: 430
SN   Simple narratives, in prose or verse
NT   Fables
     Fairy Tales
BT   Literary Genres
RT   Fiction
     Poetry
     Short Stories

Talking Books   *JUL. 1966*
     Postings: 173   GC: 720
SN   Phonograph records or tape recordings
     of books, articles, or other publications,
     usually for the blind
BT   Sensory Aids
RT   Audiodisks
     Audiotape Recordings
     Audiovisual Aids
     Blindness
     Books
     Nonprint Media
     Partial Vision
     Reading Materials

Talks
USE   Speeches

Tamil   *JUL. 1966*
     Postings: 56   GC: 440
BT   Dravidian Languages

Taoism   *MAR. 1983*
     Postings: 47   GC: 430
SN   Religion based on the teachings of Lao-
     Tse (China, 6th century B.C.)
BT   Religion
RT   Non Western Civilization
     Philosophy
     Religious Cultural Groups

Tape Recorders   *JUL. 1966*
     Postings: 302   GC: 910
UF   Magnetic Tape Cassette Recorders
     (1970 1980) #
NT   Audiotape Recorders
     Videotape Recorders
BT   Electronic Equipment
RT   Magnetic Tape Cassettes
     Magnetic Tapes
     Tape Recordings

Tape Recordings   *JUL. 1966*
     Postings: 1,399   GC: 720
SN   Magnetic tapes on which audio or video
     signals are recorded—stored on open
     reels, cassettes, or cartridges (Note: Use
     a more specific term if possible)
NT   Audiotape Recordings
     Videotape Recordings
BT   Nonprint Media
RT   Documentaries
     Magnetic Tape Cassettes
     Magnetic Tapes
     Special Effects
     Tape Recorders

\# = Two or more Descriptors are used to represent this term.
The term's main entry shows the appropriate coordination.

Taremiut
USE   Inupiaq

Task Analysis   JUL. 1966
     Postings: 2,865   GC: 820
SN   Process of identifying all the things that must be done to satisfactorily complete an activity (Note: Prior to Mar80, this term was not scoped and was frequently used for "Job Analysis"—do not confuse with "Content Analysis" or "Skill Analysis")
BT   Evaluation Methods
RT   Cognitive Processes
     Content Analysis
     Critical Incidents Method
     Difficulty Level
     Job Analysis
     Learning Strategies
     Objectives
     Skill Analysis
     Test Construction

Task Difficulty
USE   Difficulty Level

Task Performance (1966 1980)   MAR. 1980
     Postings: 3,056   GC: 310
SN   Invalid Descriptor—used indiscriminately in indexing—see "Performance," "Job Performance," etc.

Taste (Aesthetics)
USE   Aesthetic Values

Tatar   JUL. 1966
     Postings: 2   GC: 440
BT   Turkic Languages

Tax Allocation   JUL. 1966
     Postings: 1,008   GC: 620
SN   Extent to which taxes are apportioned to finance a particular constituency
UF   Tax Support (1966 1980)
BT   Financial Support
RT   Categorical Aid
     Educational Equity (Finance)
     Educational Finance
     Financial Needs
     Full State Funding
     Resource Allocation
     Revenue Sharing
     Tax Effort
     Tax Rates
     Taxes

Tax Credits   MAR. 1980
     Postings: 384   GC: 620
SN   Sums subtracted from total tax liability
UF   Tuition Tax Credits #
RT   Parent Financial Contribution
     School Choice
     Student Financial Aid
     Tax Deductions
     Tax Rates
     Taxes
     Tuition

Tax Deductions   NOV. 1982
     Postings: 133   GC: 620
SN   Sums subtracted from taxable income
RT   Tax Credits
     Tax Rates
     Taxes

Tax Effort   JUL. 1966
     Postings: 455   GC: 620
SN   The measure of a community's or society's willingness to tax itself
RT   Educational Equity (Finance)
     Educational Finance
     Equalization Aid
     Finance Reform
     Fiscal Capacity
     School District Wealth

     Tax Allocation
     Tax Rates
     Taxes

Tax Equity (Education)
USE   Educational Equity (Finance)

Tax Rates   JUL. 1966
     Postings: 436   GC: 620
BT   Ratios (Mathematics)
RT   Educational Equity (Finance)
     Expenditures
     Money Management
     Property Taxes
     School Taxes
     Tax Allocation
     Tax Credits
     Tax Deductions
     Tax Effort
     Taxes

Tax Reform
USE   Finance Reform

Tax Support (1966 1980)
USE   Tax Allocation

Taxes   JUL. 1966
     Postings: 1,257   GC: 620
NT   Property Taxes
     School Taxes
RT   Assessed Valuation
     Economic Impact
     Estate Planning
     Finance Reform
     Ownership
     Property Appraisal
     Public Policy
     Tax Allocation
     Tax Credits
     Tax Deductions
     Tax Effort
     Tax Rates

Taxonomy (1967 1980)
USE   Classification

Teacher Administrator Relationship   JUL. 1966
     Postings: 4,075   GC: 320
UF   Administrator Teacher Relationship
BT   Interpersonal Relationship
RT   Administrator Guides
     Administrators
     Board Administrator Relationship
     Employer Employee Relationship
     Faculty College Relationship
     Faculty Handbooks
     Faculty Workload
     Instructional Leadership
     Interprofessional Relationship
     Participative Decision Making
     Politics of Education
     School Administration
     School Policy
     Teacher Discipline
     Teacher Evaluation
     Teacher Militancy
     Teacher Morale
     Teacher Rights
     Teacher Supervision
     Teacher Welfare
     Teachers
     Teaching Load

Teacher Advancement
USE   Teacher Promotion

Teacher Aides   JUL. 1966
     Postings: 1,385   GC: 360
SN   Paraprofessional school personnel who assist k-12 teachers in the instructional process (Note: For higher education aides, use "Teaching Assistants"—prior to Mar80, this term was not scoped and

was often confused with "School Aides," who assist in noninstructional areas)
NT   Bilingual Teacher Aides
BT   Paraprofessional School Personnel
RT   Proctoring
     School Aides
     Teachers
     Volunteers

Teacher Alienation   JUL. 1966
     Postings: 237   GC: 320
BT   Alienation
RT   Teacher Attitudes
     Teacher Behavior
     Teacher Burnout
     Teacher Militancy
     Teacher Morale
     Teachers

Teacher Associations   JUL. 1966
     Postings: 1,499   GC: 330
SN   Organizations composed of teachers, usually but not always at the elementary/secondary school level (Note: See "Faculty Organizations" for most higher education organizations as well as those that include administrative staff—prior to Mar80, the use of this term was not restricted by a Scope Note)
UF   Teacher Organizations
BT   Professional Associations
RT   Faculty Organizations
     Teacher Militancy
     Teacher Strikes
     Teacher Welfare
     Teachers
     Teaching (Occupation)
     Teaching Load
     Unions

Teacher Attendance   JUL. 1966
     Postings: 102   GC: 320
SN   Teachers' presence for classroom and other assigned duties (Note: Use "Teacher Participation" for attendance at unassigned functions)
UF   Absence (Teachers) #
BT   Attendance
RT   Employee Absenteeism
     Sabbatical Leaves
     Substitute Teachers
     Teacher Behavior
     Teacher Discipline
     Teacher Dismissal
     Teachers

Teacher Attitudes   JUL. 1966
     Postings: 28,999   GC: 320
SN   Attitudes of, not toward, teachers (Note: Prior to Mar80, the use of this term was not restricted by a Scope Note, and the instruction "Teacher Reaction, USE Teacher Attitudes" was carried in the Thesaurus)
UF   Teacher Opinions
BT   Attitudes
RT   Classroom Environment
     Student Teacher Attitudes
     Teacher Alienation
     Teacher Behavior
     Teacher Characteristics
     Teacher Evaluation
     Teacher Expectations of Students
     Teacher Morale
     Teacher Response
     Teacher Surveys
     Teachers
     Teaching Conditions

Teacher Attrition
USE   Faculty Mobility

Teacher Autonomy
USE   Professional Autonomy

Teacher Background   JUL. 1966
     Postings: 1,116   GC: 320
SN   Aspects of a teacher's personal history that have influenced his or her personal and professional development (Note: Do not confuse with "Teaching Experience")
BT   Background
RT   Teacher Characteristics
     Teacher Education
     Teacher Employment
     Teacher Evaluation
     Teacher Qualifications
     Teacher Recruitment
     Teacher Selection
     Teachers
     Teaching Experience

Teacher Behavior   JUL. 1966
     Postings: 8,127   GC: 310
SN   Conduct of teachers in or out of job-related situations
NT   Teacher Collaboration
     Teacher Effectiveness
     Teacher Militancy
     Teacher Participation
     Teacher Persistence
     Teacher Response
BT   Behavior
RT   Classroom Communication
     Classroom Observation Techniques
     Protocol Materials
     Teacher Alienation
     Teacher Attendance
     Teacher Attitudes
     Teacher Characteristics
     Teacher Evaluation
     Teacher Influence
     Teacher Motivation
     Teacher Role
     Teachers
     Teaching Styles

Teacher Burnout   OCT. 1981
     Postings: 730   GC: 320
SN   Teachers' syndrome caused by inability to cope with stressful occupational conditions—characterized by low morale, low productivity, high absenteeism, and high job turnover
BT   Burnout
RT   Teacher Alienation
     Teacher Morale
     Teacher Motivation
     Teacher Persistence
     Teacher Response
     Teachers
     Teaching Conditions

Teacher Centers   SEP. 1973
     Postings: 760   GC: 920
SN   Interinstitutional centers (school/college/community) offering teacher-oriented professional development programs, at preservice/inservice levels, of educational demonstrations, experimental teaching, laboratory experiences, and other participatory learning activities
UF   Teacher Education Centers
     University Training Centers
BT   Resource Centers
RT   Education Service Centers
     Educational Cooperation
     Field Experience Programs
     Inservice Teacher Education
     Institutes (Training Programs)
     Institutional Cooperation
     Laboratory Training
     Professional Continuing Education
     Student Teaching
     Teacher Education
     Teacher Workshops
     Teachers
     Teaching Experience

Teacher Certificates (1967 1980)
USE   Teacher Certification

= Two or more Descriptors are used to represent this term. The term's main entry shows the appropriate coordination.

Teacher Certification JUL. 1966
Postings: 3,725 GC: 330
UF Teacher Certificates (1967 1980)
Teaching Certificates
NT Alternative Teacher Certification
National Teacher Certification
BT Certification
RT Beginning Teacher Induction
Beginning Teachers
Educational Certificates
Knowledge Base for Teaching
Teacher Competencies
Teacher Competency Testing
Teacher Education
Teacher Education Curriculum
Teacher Employment
Teacher Evaluation
Teacher Qualifications
Teachers
Teaching (Occupation)

Teacher Characteristics JUL. 1966
Postings: 6,506 GC: 320
NT Teaching Styles
RT Aptitude Treatment Interaction
Diversity (Faculty)
Individual Characteristics
Teacher Attitudes
Teacher Background
Teacher Behavior
Teacher Competencies
Teacher Evaluation
Teacher Expectations of Students
Teacher Qualifications
Teacher Role
Teacher Selection
Teacher Stereotypes
Teacher Surveys
Teachers

Teacher Collaboration MAY 1996
Postings: 1,133 GC: 320
SN An interactive process that enables teach-
ers with diverse expertise to work to-
gether as equals and engage in shared
decision making toward mutually de-
fined goals
UF Collaborative Teachers
Teacher Cooperation
BT Educational Cooperation
Teacher Behavior
RT Collegiality
Cooperative Planning
Regular and Special Education Rela-
tionship
Teachers
Team Teaching
Teamwork

Teacher College Relationship
USE Faculty College Relationship

Teacher Competencies JUN. 1993
Postings: 813 GC: 310
SN Explicit, demonstrable knowledge and
skills necessary for performing the role
of teacher (Note: If possible, use the
more precise terms "Competency Based
Teacher Education" and/or "Teacher Com-
petency Testing")
BT Competence
RT Competency Based Teacher Education
Knowledge Base for Teaching
Minimum Competencies
Teacher Certification
Teacher Characteristics
Teacher Competency Testing
Teacher Effectiveness
Teacher Evaluation
Teacher Qualifications
Teacher Role
Teacher Selection
Teachers
Teaching Skills

Teacher Competency Testing JUN. 1993
Postings: 121 GC: 820
SN Measurement of the ability of teachers or
would-be teachers to demonstrate spe-

cific, predetermined, and desirable peda-
gogical techniques or subject-matter
knowledge
UF Teacher Testing (for Competency)
BT Testing
RT Competence
Competency Based Teacher Education
Licensing Examinations (Professions)
Minimum Competency Testing
National Competency Tests
National Teacher Certification
Performance Based Assessment
Teacher Certification
Teacher Competencies
Teacher Evaluation
Teachers

Teacher Cooperation
USE Teacher Collaboration

Teacher Coordinators
USE Instructor Coordinators

Teacher Counselor Cooperation
USE Counselor Teacher Cooperation

Teacher Desegregation
USE Teacher Integration

Teacher Developed Materials JUL. 1966
Postings: 3,278 GC: 730
SN Instructional materials prepared by teach-
ers
NT Teacher Made Tests
BT Instructional Materials
RT Experience Charts
Material Development
School Publications
Student Developed Materials
Teachers
Teaching Load

Teacher Directed Practice
USE Teacher Guidance

Teacher Discipline JAN. 1973
Postings: 140 GC: 320
SN Discipline of, not by, teachers
NT Teacher Dismissal
BT Discipline
RT Collective Bargaining
Due Process
Faculty College Relationship
Teacher Administrator Relationship
Teacher Attendance
Teacher Employment
Teacher Evaluation
Teacher Militancy
Teacher Responsibility
Teacher Rights
Teacher Strikes
Teachers

Teacher Dismissal JAN. 1973
Postings: 831 GC: 320
SN Dismissal of, not by, the teacher
BT Dismissal (Personnel)
Teacher Discipline
RT Contracts
Disqualification
Due Process
Financial Exigency
Reduction in Force
Teacher Attendance
Teacher Evaluation
Teacher Responsibility
Teachers

Teacher Distribution JUL. 1966
Postings: 188 GC: 330
SN The apportionment of teachers among
schools over a geographic area (with
regard to race, teacher quality, student/
staff ratios, etc.)
BT School Demography

RT Geographic Distribution
Incidence
Misassignment of Teachers
Racial Balance
School Statistics
Teacher Placement
Teacher Student Ratio
Teachers

Teacher Education JUL. 1966
Postings: 28,179 GC: 400
UF Teacher Preparation
Teacher Training
NT Competency Based Teacher Education
English Teacher Education
Inservice Teacher Education
Preservice Teacher Education
Teacher Educator Education
BT Professional Education
RT Affiliated Schools
Alternative Teacher Certification
Cooperating Teachers
Education Courses
Education Majors
Extended Teacher Education Programs
Institutes (Training Programs)
Knowledge Base for Teaching
Laboratory Schools
Laboratory Training
Master Teachers
Methods Courses
Methods Teachers
Microteaching
National Teacher Certification
Professional Development Schools
Protocol Materials
Reflective Teaching
Schools of Education
Student Teacher Supervisors
Student Teachers
Teacher Background
Teacher Centers
Teacher Certification
Teacher Education Programs
Teacher Educators
Teacher Qualifications
Teacher Supervision
Teachers
Teaching (Occupation)
Teaching Experience

Teacher Education Centers
USE Teacher Centers

Teacher Education Curriculum JUL. 1966
Postings: 3,546 GC: 400
NT Methods Courses
BT College Curriculum
RT Alternative Teacher Certification
Education Courses
Education Majors
Extended Teacher Education Programs
Foundations of Education
Knowledge Base for Teaching
National Teacher Certification
Preservice Teacher Education
Preservice Teachers
Schools of Education
Teacher Certification
Teacher Education Programs
Teacher Qualifications
Teachers

Teacher Education Knowledge Base
USE Knowledge Base for Teaching

Teacher Education Programs MAR. 1980
Postings: 4,089 GC: 400
UF Teacher Programs (1966 1980)
NT Extended Teacher Education Programs
BT Programs
RT Alternative Teacher Certification
Education Courses
Education Majors
Knowledge Base for Teaching
Methods Courses
Preservice Teacher Education
Preservice Teachers
Teacher Education

Teacher Education Curriculum
Teacher Workshops
Teachers

Teacher Educator Education SEP. 1969
Postings: 565 GC: 400
BT Teacher Education
RT Cooperating Teachers
Doctoral Degrees
Doctoral Programs
Inservice Teacher Education
Master Teachers
Masters Degrees
Postsecondary Education as a Field of
Study
Preservice Teacher Education
Schools of Education
Specialist in Education Degrees
Teacher Educators

Teacher Educators JUL. 1966
Postings: 2,198 GC: 360
UF Teacher Trainers
NT Methods Teachers
BT College Faculty
RT Cooperating Teachers
Master Teachers
Postsecondary Education as a Field of
Study
Professors
Schools of Education
Specialist in Education Degrees
Student Teacher Supervisors
Teacher Education
Teacher Educator Education

Teacher Effectiveness MAR. 1980
Postings: 12,222 GC: 310
SN Degree to which teachers are successful
in satisfying their objectives, obligations,
or functions
UF Effective Teaching (1966 1980)
Teacher Quality
Teaching Quality (1966 1980)
BT Teacher Behavior
RT Academic Achievement
Clinical Supervision (of Teachers)
Educational Quality
Excellence in Education
Instructional Effectiveness
Instructional Improvement
Instructional Innovation
Knowledge Base for Teaching
Pedagogical Content Knowledge
Reflective Teaching
School Effectiveness
Student Evaluation of Teacher Per-
formance
Teacher Competencies
Teacher Evaluation
Teacher Influence
Teacher Role
Teachers
Teaching (Occupation)
Teaching Models
Teaching Skills
Teaching Styles

Teacher Employment JUL. 1966
Postings: 1,350 GC: 630
BT Employment
RT Beginning Teachers
Full Time Faculty
Labor Market
Merit Pay
Part Time Faculty
Substitute Teachers
Teacher Background
Teacher Certification
Teacher Discipline
Teacher Employment Benefits
Teacher Exchange Programs
Teacher Persistence
Teacher Placement
Teacher Recruitment
Teacher Salaries
Teacher Selection
Teacher Shortage
Teacher Supply and Demand

Teachers
Teaching (Occupation)
Teaching Experience
Tenure

Teacher Employment Benefits   *MAR. 1980*
Postings: 455   GC: 630
UF   Teaching Benefits (1966 1980)
RT   Academic Rank (Professional)
Fringe Benefits
Health Insurance
Leaves of Absence
Sabbatical Leaves
Teacher Employment
Teacher Promotion
Teacher Retirement
Teacher Salaries
Teacher Welfare
Teachers
Teaching (Occupation)
Tenure
Unemployment Insurance
Workers Compensation

Teacher Empowerment   *JUL. 1996*
Postings: 296   GC: 330
SN   Promotion or attainment of autonomy
and freedom of choice for teachers
BT   Empowerment
RT   Professional Autonomy
Teacher Participation
Teacher Rights
Teacher Role
Teachers

Teacher Evaluation   *JUL. 1966*
Postings: 6,636   GC: 320
SN   Judging teacher performance based on
established criteria
UF   Teacher Rating (1966 1977)
NT   Student Evaluation of Teacher Per-
formance
BT   Personnel Evaluation
RT   Classroom Observation Techniques
Course Evaluation
Faculty Development
Faculty Evaluation
Faculty Workload
Lesson Observation Criteria
Scoring Rubrics
Student Teacher Evaluation
Teacher Administrator Relationship
Teacher Attitudes
Teacher Background
Teacher Behavior
Teacher Certification
Teacher Characteristics
Teacher Competencies
Teacher Competency Testing
Teacher Discipline
Teacher Dismissal
Teacher Effectiveness
Teacher Improvement
Teacher Promotion
Teacher Qualifications
Teacher Selection
Teacher Student Relationship
Teacher Supervision
Teachers
Teaching Load
Teaching Skills

Teacher Exchange Programs   *JUL. 1966*
Postings: 390   GC: 330
SN   Includes domestic and international
teacher exchange programs
BT   Exchange Programs
RT   Faculty Development
International Educational Exchange
Teacher Employment
Teachers

Teacher Expectations of Students
AUG. 1988
Postings: 1,128   GC: 310
SN   Teacher anticipation of student behavior
or achievement based on preconcep-
tions and such intervening cues as students' test scores, physical appearance,

speech patterns, etc.—also, the effects
of that anticipation
BT   Expectation
RT   Classroom Environment
Self Fulfilling Prophecies
Student Evaluation
Students
Teacher Attitudes
Teacher Characteristics
Teacher Influence
Teacher Response
Teacher Student Relationship
Teachers

Teacher Experience (1966 1974)
USE   Teaching Experience

Teacher Guidance   *JUL. 1966*
Postings: 386   GC: 240
SN   Guidance provided by teachers (Note:
Prior to Mar80, this term was not scoped
and was sometimes used to index guid-
ance given to teachers)
UF   Teacher Directed Practice
BT   Guidance
RT   Counselor Teacher Cooperation
School Guidance
Teacher Student Relationship
Teachers

Teacher Guides
USE   Teaching Guides

Teacher Housing   *JUL. 1966*
Postings: 31   GC: 920
SN   Living quarters of teachers (Note: Prior
to Mar80, the use of this term was not
restricted by a Scope Note)
BT   Housing
RT   Teachers

Teacher Improvement   *JUL. 1966*
Postings: 5,681   GC: 310
BT   Improvement
RT   Clinical Supervision (of Teachers)
Excellence in Education
Faculty Development
Inservice Teacher Education
Instructional Improvement
Professional Development
Reflective Teaching
Sabbatical Leaves
Student Evaluation of Teacher Per-
formance
Teacher Evaluation
Teachers

Teacher Induction
USE   Teacher Orientation

Teacher Influence   *JUL. 1966*
Postings: 2,642   GC: 310
BT   Influences
RT   Academic Achievement
Student Motivation
Teacher Behavior
Teacher Effectiveness
Teacher Expectations of Students
Teacher Participation
Teacher Role
Teacher Student Relationship
Teachers
Teaching Styles

Teacher Integration   *JUL. 1966*
Postings: 103   GC: 540
SN   Process of balancing the racial, ethnic,
or sexual composition of the instruc-
tional staff of a school, college, or uni-
versity
UF   Teacher Desegregation
BT   Personnel Integration
RT   Affirmative Action
Diversity (Faculty)
Equal Opportunities (Jobs)

Faculty Integration
Teachers

Teacher Interns   *JUL. 1966*
Postings: 547   GC: 360
SN   Advanced students or recent graduates
accruing college credits while teaching
under supervision, usually paid a small
salary (Note: Do not confuse with "Stu-
dent Teachers")
UF   Intern Teachers
Urban Teaching Interns #
BT   Teachers
RT   Alternative Teacher Certification
Beginning Teacher Induction
Cooperating Teachers
Differentiated Staffs
Extended Teacher Education Programs
Inservice Teacher Education
Internship Programs
Master Teachers
Paraprofessional School Personnel
Student Teachers

Teacher Knowledge Base
USE   Knowledge Base for Teaching

Teacher Librarian Cooperation
USE   Librarian Teacher Cooperation

Teacher Load
USE   Teaching Load

Teacher Made Tests   *OCT. 1980*
Postings: 308   GC: 830
SN   Tests and other measures that are
planned, assembled, written, or otherwise prepared by teachers for use with
particular groups of students (Note: For
specificity, coordinate with other terms
in the "Tests" and "Measures (Individuals)" hierarchies)
BT   Teacher Developed Materials
Tests
RT   Teachers
Test Construction

Teacher Militancy   *JAN. 1969*
Postings: 444   GC: 330
BT   Teacher Behavior
RT   Arbitration
Collective Bargaining
Negotiation Impasses
Professional Recognition
Sanctions
Teacher Administrator Relationship
Teacher Alienation
Teacher Associations
Teacher Discipline
Teacher Morale
Teacher Strikes
Teacher Welfare
Teachers

Teacher Mobility
USE   Faculty Mobility

Teacher Morale   *JUL. 1966*
Postings: 1,338   GC: 320
BT   Morale
RT   Professional Recognition
Teacher Administrator Relationship
Teacher Alienation
Teacher Attitudes
Teacher Burnout
Teacher Militancy
Teacher Motivation
Teacher Welfare
Teachers
Teaching Conditions

Teacher Motivation   *JUL. 1966*
Postings: 1,262   GC: 310
BT   Motivation
RT   Academic Aspiration

Teacher Behavior
Teacher Burnout
Teacher Morale
Teachers

Teacher Nurses (1966 1980)
USE   Nurses

Teacher Opinions
USE   Teacher Attitudes

Teacher Organizations
USE   Teacher Associations

Teacher Orientation   *JUL. 1966*
Postings: 756   GC: 320
SN   The process of acquainting teachers with
the policies, rules, traditions, and educa-
tional offerings of a school
UF   Teacher Induction
NT   Beginning Teacher Induction
BT   Orientation
RT   Faculty Handbooks
School Orientation
Staff Orientation
Teacher Supervision
Teachers

Teacher Parent Conferences
USE   Parent Teacher Conferences

Teacher Parent Cooperation
USE   Parent Teacher Cooperation

Teacher Participation   *JUL. 1966*
Postings: 2,763   GC: 320
SN   (Note: Use "Teacher Attendance" for pres-
ence for teaching assignments)
BT   Participation
Teacher Behavior
RT   Participative Decision Making
School Involvement
Teacher Empowerment
Teacher Influence
Teachers

Teacher Persistence   *JUL. 1966*
Postings: 670   GC: 330
SN   One's active continuance as a teacher by
reason of personal choice
UF   Teaching Persistence
BT   Persistence
Teacher Behavior
RT   Aging in Academia
Faculty Mobility
Labor Turnover
Teacher Burnout
Teacher Employment
Teacher Recruitment
Teacher Shortage
Teachers
Teaching (Occupation)

Teacher Placement   *JUL. 1966*
Postings: 403   GC: 330
SN   Process by which teachers obtain teach-
ing positions (Note: Do not confuse with
"Teacher Distribution"—prior to Mar80,
the use of this term was not restricted by
a Scope Note)
BT   Job Placement
RT   Faculty Mobility
Misassignment of Teachers
Teacher Distribution
Teacher Employment
Teacher Recruitment
Teacher Selection
Teacher Supply and Demand
Teacher Transfer
Teachers

Teacher Preparation
USE   Teacher Education

= Two or more Descriptors are used to represent this term.
The term's main entry shows the appropriate coordination.

Teacher Programs (1966 1980)
USE　Teacher Education Programs

Teacher Promotion　　　　　　　　*JUL. 1966*
　Postings: 377　　　　　　　　　GC: 320
SN　Advancement in rank or position of a
　　teacher
UF　Teacher Advancement
BT　Promotion (Occupational)
RT　Academic Rank (Professional)
　　Faculty Development
　　Faculty Promotion
　　Faculty Workload
　　Teacher Employment Benefits
　　Teacher Evaluation
　　Teachers
　　Teaching (Occupation)
　　Teaching Load
　　Tenure

Teacher Qualifications　　　　　　*JUL. 1966*
　Postings: 4,267　　　　　　　　GC: 320
SN　One's education, experience, and physi-
　　cal, social, and mental characteristics
　　that determine fitness for a teaching
　　position
BT　Qualifications
RT　Alternative Teacher Certification
　　Employment Qualifications
　　Knowledge Base for Teaching
　　Misassignment of Teachers
　　National Teacher Certification
　　Teacher Background
　　Teacher Certification
　　Teacher Characteristics
　　Teacher Competencies
　　Teacher Education
　　Teacher Education Curriculum
　　Teacher Evaluation
　　Teacher Selection
　　Teachers
　　Teaching (Occupation)
　　Teaching Experience

Teacher Quality
USE　Teacher Effectiveness

Teacher Rating (1966 1977)
USE　Teacher Evaluation

Teacher Reaction
USE　Teacher Response

Teacher Recruitment　　　　　　*JUL. 1966*
　Postings: 1,803　　　　　　　　GC: 320
SN　Process of attracting candidates to the
　　teaching profession or finding teachers
　　to fill teaching vacancies
BT　Recruitment
RT　Alternative Teacher Certification
　　Faculty Recruitment
　　Teacher Background
　　Teacher Employment
　　Teacher Persistence
　　Teacher Placement
　　Teacher Selection
　　Teacher Shortage
　　Teacher Supply and Demand
　　Teachers
　　Teaching Conditions

Teacher Researchers　　　　　　*NOV. 1997*
　Postings: 673　　　　　　　　　GC: 360
SN　Teachers who engage in educational re-
　　search, generally to improve their own
　　classroom practices
UF　Teachers as Researchers
BT　Educational Researchers
　　Teachers
RT　Action Research
　　Classroom Research
　　Educational Research
　　Reflective Teaching
　　Teacher Role
　　Theory Practice Relationship

Teacher Response　　　　　　　*JUL. 1966*
　Postings: 2,100　　　　　　　　GC: 310
SN　Teacher reaction to instructional and/or
　　classroom situations (Note: Prior to
　　Mar80, the instruction "Teacher Reac-
　　tion, USE Teacher Attitudes" was carried
　　in the Thesaurus)
UF　Teacher Reaction
BT　Responses
　　Teacher Behavior
RT　Feedback
　　Reinforcement
　　Teacher Attitudes
　　Teacher Burnout
　　Teacher Expectations of Students
　　Teacher Student Relationship
　　Teacher Surveys
　　Teachers
　　Teaching Styles

Teacher Responsibility　　　　　*JUL. 1966*
　Postings: 4,007　　　　　　　　GC: 320
NT　Noninstructional Responsibility
BT　Responsibility
RT　Administrator Responsibility
　　Child Responsibility
　　Educational Responsibility
　　Faculty Handbooks
　　Faculty Workload
　　Leadership Responsibility
　　School Responsibility
　　Teacher Discipline
　　Teacher Dismissal
　　Teacher Rights
　　Teachers
　　Teaching (Occupation)
　　Teaching Load

Teacher Retirement　　　　　　*JUL. 1966*
　Postings: 729　　　　　　　　　GC: 630
UF　Retired Teachers
BT　Retirement
RT　Aging in Academia
　　Early Retirement
　　Mandatory Retirement
　　Older Workers
　　Teacher Employment Benefits
　　Teachers

Teacher Rights　　　　　　　　*JUN. 1983*
　Postings: 454　　　　　　　　　GC: 330
SN　Legal, procedural, and human rights of
　　teachers
BT　Civil Liberties
RT　Academic Freedom
　　Civil Rights
　　Collective Bargaining
　　Due Process
　　Faculty College Relationship
　　Freedom of Speech
　　School Law
　　Teacher Administrator Relationship
　　Teacher Discipline
　　Teacher Empowerment
　　Teacher Responsibility
　　Teacher Welfare
　　Teachers
　　Teaching (Occupation)
　　Tenure

Teacher Role　　　　　　　　　*JUL. 1966*
　Postings: 20,023　　　　　　　GC: 320
UF　Senior Teacher Role (1966 1980) #
BT　Role
RT　Faculty Handbooks
　　Noninstructional Responsibility
　　Role of Education
　　Staff Role
　　Student Role
　　Teacher Behavior
　　Teacher Characteristics
　　Teacher Competencies
　　Teacher Effectiveness
　　Teacher Empowerment
　　Teacher Influence
　　Teacher Researchers
　　Teacher Stereotypes
　　Teachers

Teacher Salaries　　　　　　　*JUL. 1966*
　Postings: 3,837　　　　　　　　GC: 620
BT　Salaries
RT　Contract Salaries
　　Teacher Employment
　　Teacher Employment Benefits
　　Teachers
　　Teaching (Occupation)

Teacher Selection　　　　　　　*JUL. 1966*
　Postings: 1,080　　　　　　　　GC: 320
SN　Process of assessing and choosing can-
　　didates for teaching positions
BT　Personnel Selection
RT　Teacher Background
　　Teacher Characteristics
　　Teacher Competencies
　　Teacher Employment
　　Teacher Evaluation
　　Teacher Placement
　　Teacher Qualifications
　　Teacher Recruitment
　　Teacher Supply and Demand
　　Teachers
　　Teaching Experience

Teacher Seminars (1966 1980)
USE　Teacher Workshops

Teacher Shortage　　　　　　　*JUL. 1966*
　Postings: 992　　　　　　　　　GC: 630
BT　Teacher Supply and Demand
RT　Alternative Teacher Certification
　　Misassignment of Teachers
　　Teacher Employment
　　Teacher Persistence
　　Teacher Recruitment
　　Teachers

Teacher Skills
USE　Teaching Skills

Teacher Stereotypes　　　　　　*JUL. 1966*
　Postings: 116　　　　　　　　　GC: 540
SN　Standardized and biased conceptions of
　　the attributes of teachers (Note: For teach-
　　ers' stereotyped attitudes use "Teacher
　　Attitudes"—prior to Mar80, the use of
　　this term was not restricted by a Scope
　　Note)
BT　Stereotypes
RT　Teacher Characteristics
　　Teacher Role
　　Teachers
　　Teaching (Occupation)

Teacher Strikes　　　　　　　　*JUL. 1966*
　Postings: 583　　　　　　　　　GC: 630
BT　Strikes
RT　Arbitration
　　Collective Bargaining
　　Labor Problems
　　Negotiation Agreements
　　Negotiation Impasses
　　Sanctions
　　School Boycotts
　　Teacher Associations
　　Teacher Discipline
　　Teacher Militancy
　　Teacher Welfare
　　Teachers
　　Unions

Teacher Student Interaction
USE　Teacher Student Relationship

Teacher Student Ratio　　　　　*DEC. 1984*
　Postings: 620　　　　　　　　　GC: 320
UF　Student Teacher Ratio (1966 1984)
BT　Ratios (Mathematics)
RT　Class Size
　　Students

Teaching (Occupation)
Teaching Styles

Teacher Student Relationship　　*DEC. 1984*
　Postings: 10,125　　　　　　　GC: 310
UF　Student Teacher Interaction
　　Student Teacher Relationship (1966
　　1984)
　　Teacher Student Interaction
BT　Interpersonal Relationship
RT　Aptitude Treatment Interaction
　　Caregiver Child Relationship
　　Classroom Communication
　　Classroom Environment
　　Dialog Journals
　　Faculty Handbooks
　　Grading
　　Mentors
　　Student College Relationship
　　Student Evaluation of Teacher Per-
　　　formance
　　Student School Relationship
　　Students
　　Teacher Evaluation
　　Teacher Expectations of Students
　　Teacher Guidance
　　Teacher Influence
　　Teacher Response
　　Teachers

Teacher Supervision　　　　　　*JUL. 1966*
　Postings: 1,483　　　　　　　　GC: 320
SN　Supervision of preservice and inservice
　　teachers
NT　Clinical Supervision (of Teachers)
BT　Supervision
RT　Beginning Teacher Induction
　　Cooperating Teachers
　　Practicum Supervision
　　School Supervision
　　State Supervisors
　　Student Teacher Supervisors
　　Student Teachers
　　Teacher Administrator Relationship
　　Teacher Education
　　Teacher Evaluation
　　Teacher Orientation
　　Teachers

Teacher Supply and Demand　　*JUL. 1966*
　Postings: 1,674　　　　　　　　GC: 630
NT　Teacher Shortage
BT　Labor Market
　　Supply and Demand
RT　Educational Demand
　　Employment Patterns
　　Teacher Employment
　　Teacher Placement
　　Teacher Recruitment
　　Teacher Selection
　　Teachers
　　Teaching (Occupation)

Teacher Surveys　　　　　　　*OCT. 1997*
　Postings: 623　　　　　　　　　GC: 810
SN　Studies in which data are gathered from
　　teachers on their attitudes, interests, ac-
　　tivities, characteristics, etc. (Note: Use
　　as a minor Descriptor for examples of
　　this kind of survey—use as a major
　　Descriptor only as the subject of a docu-
　　ment)
BT　Surveys
RT　Educational Research
　　School Surveys
　　Teacher Attitudes
　　Teacher Characteristics
　　Teacher Response
　　Teachers

Teacher Testing (for Competency)
USE　Teacher Competency Testing

Teacher Trainers
USE　Teacher Educators

Teacher Distribution
Teachers

= Two or more Descriptors are used to represent this term.
The term's main entry shows the appropriate coordination.

Teacher Training
USE   Teacher Education

Teacher Training Films
USE   Protocol Materials

Teacher Transfer   *JUL. 1966*
       Postings: 145   GC: 330
BT   Occupational Mobility
RT   Faculty Mobility
       Teacher Placement
       Teachers
       Transfer Policy
       Transfer Programs

Teacher Travel
USE   Travel

Teacher Turnover
USE   Faculty Mobility

Teacher Unions
USE   Unions

Teacher Wait Time
USE   Wait Time

Teacher Welfare   *NOV. 1968*
       Postings: 671   GC: 330
SN   Status and advancement of interests of
       teachers and the teaching profession
BT   Well Being
RT   Academic Freedom
       Board of Education Policy
       Collective Bargaining
       Faculty College Relationship
       Professional Autonomy
       Professional Recognition
       Teacher Administrator Relationship
       Teacher Associations
       Teacher Employment Benefits
       Teacher Militancy
       Teacher Morale
       Teacher Rights
       Teacher Strikes
       Teachers
       Teaching (Occupation)
       Teaching Conditions
       Teaching Load

Teacher Workshops   *JUL. 1966*
       Postings: 2,869   GC: 350
UF   Teacher Seminars (1966 1980)
BT   Workshops
RT   Inservice Teacher Education
       Teacher Centers
       Teacher Education Programs
       Teachers

Teachers   *JUL. 1966*
       Postings: 6,878   GC: 360
SN   (Note: See "Faculty" for other specific
       terminology related to "Teachers")
UF   Instructional Staff (1966 1980)
       Instructors
NT   Adult Educators
       Art Teachers
       Beginning Teachers
       Bilingual Teachers
       Black Teachers
       Catholic Educators
       Cooperating Teachers
       Elementary School Teachers
       Home Economics Teachers
       Industrial Arts Teachers
       Instructor Coordinators
       Itinerant Teachers
       Language Teachers
       Lay Teachers
       Master Teachers
       Mathematics Teachers
       Middle School Teachers
       Minority Group Teachers
       Music Teachers
       Physical Education Teachers

       Preschool Teachers
       Public School Teachers
       Reading Teachers
       Remedial Teachers
       Resource Teachers
       Science Teachers
       Secondary School Teachers
       Special Education Teachers
       Student Teachers
       Substitute Teachers
       Teacher Interns
       Teacher Researchers
       Teachers with Disabilities
       Television Teachers
       Tutors
       Vocational Education Teachers
       Writing Teachers
BT   Professional Personnel
RT   Adjunct Faculty
       Aging in Academia
       College Faculty
       Counselor Teacher Cooperation
       Department Heads
       Differentiated Staffs
       Employees
       Faculty
       Full Time Faculty
       Home Visits
       Librarian Teacher Cooperation
       Misassignment of Teachers
       Noninstructional Responsibility
       Nontenured Faculty
       One Teacher Schools
       Parent Teacher Conferences
       Parent Teacher Cooperation
       Part Time Faculty
       Preservice Teachers
       School Personnel
       Specialists
       Teacher Administrator Relationship
       Teacher Aides
       Teacher Alienation
       Teacher Associations
       Teacher Attendance
       Teacher Attitudes
       Teacher Background
       Teacher Behavior
       Teacher Burnout
       Teacher Centers
       Teacher Certification
       Teacher Characteristics
       Teacher Collaboration
       Teacher Competencies
       Teacher Competency Testing
       Teacher Developed Materials
       Teacher Discipline
       Teacher Dismissal
       Teacher Distribution
       Teacher Education
       Teacher Education Curriculum
       Teacher Education Programs
       Teacher Effectiveness
       Teacher Employment
       Teacher Employment Benefits
       Teacher Empowerment
       Teacher Evaluation
       Teacher Exchange Programs
       Teacher Expectations of Students
       Teacher Guidance
       Teacher Housing
       Teacher Improvement
       Teacher Influence
       Teacher Integration
       Teacher Made Tests
       Teacher Militancy
       Teacher Morale
       Teacher Motivation
       Teacher Orientation
       Teacher Participation
       Teacher Persistence
       Teacher Placement
       Teacher Promotion
       Teacher Qualifications
       Teacher Recruitment
       Teacher Response
       Teacher Responsibility
       Teacher Retirement
       Teacher Rights
       Teacher Role
       Teacher Salaries
       Teacher Selection
       Teacher Shortage
       Teacher Stereotypes

       Teacher Strikes
       Teacher Student Ratio
       Teacher Student Relationship
       Teacher Supervision
       Teacher Supply and Demand
       Teacher Surveys
       Teacher Transfer
       Teacher Welfare
       Teacher Workshops
       Teaching (Occupation)
       Teaching Experience
       Tenured Faculty
       Trainers

Teachers as Researchers
USE   Teacher Researchers

Teachers Colleges (1966 1980)
USE   Schools of Education

Teachers with Disabilities   *APR. 1996*
       Postings: 16   GC: 220
SN   Teachers who have a disability or impair-
       ment of any type.
UF   Disabled Teachers
BT   Teachers
RT   Disabilities

Teaching (Occupation)   *MAR. 1980*
       Postings: 2,585   GC: 640
SN   The profession of teaching, including its
       occupational conditions and attributes,
       interprofessional and societal relations,
       career lines, etc. (Note: For "the teaching
       process," see "Instruction")
UF   Inservice Teaching (1966 1980) #
       Teaching Profession
NT   Team Teaching
       Urban Teaching
BT   Professional Occupations
RT   Faculty Mobility
       Knowledge Base for Teaching
       Teacher Associations
       Teacher Certification
       Teacher Education
       Teacher Effectiveness
       Teacher Employment
       Teacher Employment Benefits
       Teacher Persistence
       Teacher Promotion
       Teacher Qualifications
       Teacher Responsibility
       Teacher Rights
       Teacher Role
       Teacher Salaries
       Teacher Stereotypes
       Teacher Supply and Demand
       Teacher Welfare
       Teachers
       Teaching Conditions
       Teaching Experience
       Teaching Load
       Tenure

Teaching (Process)
USE   Instruction

Teaching Alternatives
USE   Nontraditional Education

Teaching Areas
USE   Curriculum

Teaching Assignment (1966 1980)
                                            MAR. 1980
       Postings: 92   GC: 320
SN   Invalid Descriptor—used indiscriminately
       in indexing—see the more precise terms
       "Teacher Placement" and "Teaching
       Load"—see also "Teacher Role,"
       "Teacher Responsibility," "Noninstruc-
       tional Responsibility," and "Teach-
       ing (Occupation)" (Note: Prior to
       Mar80, the Thesaurus carried the in-
       struction "Teacher Assignment, USE
       Teacher Placement")

Teaching Assistants   *JUL. 1966*
       Postings: 1,097   GC: 360
SN   Persons, usually graduate students, who
       assist as instructors at the college level
       (Note: For k-12 assistants, use "Teacher
       Aides")
BT   College Faculty
RT   Assistantships
       Fellowships
       Graduate Students
       Proctoring
       Research Assistants

Teaching Benefits (1966 1980)
USE   Teacher Employment Benefits

Teaching Certificates
USE   Teacher Certification

Teaching Conditions   *JUL. 1966*
       Postings: 1,756   GC: 310
BT   Educational Environment
       Work Environment
RT   Academic Freedom
       Classroom Environment
       Faculty Handbooks
       Faculty Workload
       Professional Autonomy
       Professional Isolation
       Student Teacher Attitudes
       Teacher Attitudes
       Teacher Burnout
       Teacher Morale
       Teacher Recruitment
       Teacher Welfare
       Teaching (Occupation)

Teaching Core
USE   Core Curriculum

Teaching Experience   *NOV. 1969*
       Postings: 3,540   GC: 310
SN   Actual and simulated experiences of
       preservice and inservice teachers
UF   Inservice Teaching Experience
       Preservice Teaching Experience
       Teacher Experience (1966 1974)
BT   Experience
RT   Affiliated Schools
       Beginning Teacher Induction
       Experiential Learning
       Experimental Schools
       Extended Teacher Education Programs
       Field Experience Programs
       Internship Programs
       Knowledge Base for Teaching
       Laboratory Schools
       Laboratory Training
       Microteaching
       Reflective Teaching
       Student Teaching
       Teacher Background
       Teacher Centers
       Teacher Education
       Teacher Employment
       Teacher Qualifications
       Teacher Selection
       Teachers
       Teaching (Occupation)

Teaching Facilities
USE   Educational Facilities

Teaching Freedom
USE   Academic Freedom

Teaching Guides   *JUL. 1966*
       Postings: 10,637   GC: 730
SN   Manuals containing presentation meth-
       ods for, and further information on, a
       topic—usually for use with a specific
       text
UF   Discussion Guides #
       Instructor Manuals
       Teacher Guides
BT   Guides

= Two or more Descriptors are used to represent this term.
The term's main entry shows the appropriate coordination.

RT   Curriculum Guides
      Instructional Materials
      Learning Modules
      Resource Units
      Teaching Methods
      Textbooks

Teaching Hospitals   OCT. 1979
      Postings: 442   GC: 340
SN   Hospitals where formal medical training
      takes place, usually affiliated with nurs-
      ing or medical schools (Note: Do not
      confuse with "Hospital Schools" or "Pa-
      tient Education")
UF   University Teaching Hospitals
BT   Hospitals
RT   Allied Health Occupations Education
      Clinical Experience
      Clinical Teaching (Health Professions)
      Educational Facilities
      Graduate Medical Education
      Medical Education
      Medical Schools
      Nursing Education

Teaching Innovations
USE   Instructional Innovation

Teaching Knowledge Base
USE   Knowledge Base for Teaching

Teaching Language
USE   Language of Instruction

Teaching Load   JUL. 1966
      Postings: 711   GC: 320
UF   Teacher Load
BT   Faculty Workload
RT   Contracts
      Full Time Faculty
      Part Time Faculty
      Teacher Administrator Relationship
      Teacher Associations
      Teacher Developed Materials
      Teacher Evaluation
      Teacher Promotion
      Teacher Responsibility
      Teacher Welfare
      Teaching (Occupation)
      Working Hours

Teaching Machines   JUL. 1966
      Postings: 658   GC: 910
SN   Devices that mechanically, electrically,
      and/or electronically present instructional
      programs at a rate controlled by the
      learners' responses
UF   Self Pacing Machines (1966 1980)
BT   Autoinstructional Aids
RT   Computer Assisted Instruction
      Courseware
      Learner Controlled Instruction
      Pacing
      Programmed Instruction
      Programmed Instructional Materials
      Teaching Methods
      Time Factors (Learning)

Teaching Materials
USE   Instructional Materials

Teaching Methods   JUL. 1966
      Postings: 82,243   GC: 310
SN   Ways of presenting instructional materi-
      als or conducting instructional activi-
      ties (Note: Use a more specific term if
      possible—for the instructional process
      in general, see "Instruction"—for the
      individual teacher's manner of teaching,
      see "Teaching Styles")
UF   Instructional Methods
      Integrated Teaching Method #
      Presentation Methods
      Project Methods #
      Project Training Methods (1968
        1980) #

      Teaching Practices
      Teaching Procedures (1966 1980)
      Teaching Systems
      Teaching Techniques (1966 1980)
NT   Audiolingual Methods
      Case Method (Teaching Technique)
      Clinical Teaching (Health Professions)
      Community Based Instruction (Disa-
        bilities)
      Conventional Instruction
      Creative Teaching
      Cross Age Teaching
      Demonstrations (Educational)
      Diagnostic Teaching
      Discussion (Teaching Technique)
      Drills (Practice)
      Experimental Teaching
      Grammar Translation Method
      Guided Design
      Individualized Instruction
      Kinesthetic Methods
      Kodaly Method
      Language Experience Approach
      Learner Controlled Instruction
      Lecture Method
      Montessori Method
      Multimedia Instruction
      Negative Practice
      Oral Communication Method
      Orff Method
      Peer Teaching
      Precision Teaching
      Programmed Instruction
      Reciprocal Teaching
      Reggio Emilia Approach
      Sight Method
      Suggestopedia
      Suzuki Method
      Telephone Instruction
      Thematic Approach
      Training Methods
      Whole Language Approach
BT   Educational Methods
RT   Advance Organizers
      Class Organization
      Classroom Techniques
      Cloze Procedure
      Computer Simulation
      Concept Mapping
      Contingency Management
      Course Organization
      Developmentally Appropriate Practices
      Dialog Journals
      Dramatic Play
      Educational Strategies
      Individual Instruction
      Instruction
      Instructional Effectiveness
      Instructional Films
      Instructional Leadership
      Integrated Activities
      Intermode Differences
      Laboratory Procedures
      Large Group Instruction
      Learning Modalities
      Learning Modules
      Learning Strategies
      Mass Instruction
      Methods Research
      Pacing
      Pedagogical Content Knowledge
      Prompting
      Questioning Techniques
      Reinforcement
      Role Playing
      Science Course Improvement Projects
      Sequential Approach
      Simulation
      Small Group Instruction
      Substitution Drills
      Teaching Guides
      Teaching Machines
      Teaching Models
      Theory Practice Relationship
      Tutorial Programs
      Wait Time
      Writing Across the Curriculum

Teaching Models   JUL. 1966
      Postings: 2,251   GC: 310
SN   Standards of teaching behaviors identi-

      fied as desirable for given teaching situa-
      tions
BT   Models
RT   Instruction
      Standards
      Teacher Effectiveness
      Teaching Methods

Teaching Persistence
USE   Teacher Persistence

Teaching Practices
USE   Teaching Methods

Teaching Procedures (1966 1980)
USE   Teaching Methods

Teaching Profession
USE   Teaching (Occupation)

Teaching Programs (1966 1980)
                                    MAR. 1980
      Postings: 226   GC: 320
SN   Invalid Descriptor—used indiscriminately
      in indexing—see "Instruction" and
      "Teacher Education Programs"

Teaching Quality (1966 1980)
USE   Teacher Effectiveness

Teaching Resources
USE   Educational Resources

Teaching Skills   JUL. 1966
      Postings: 3,870   GC: 310
UF   Teacher Skills
BT   Skills
RT   Communication Skills
      Job Skills
      Knowledge Base for Teaching
      Microteaching
      Pedagogical Content Knowledge
      Student Teacher Evaluation
      Teacher Competencies
      Teacher Effectiveness
      Teacher Evaluation

Teaching Styles   JUL. 1966
      Postings: 2,700   GC: 310
SN   Individual teachers' distinctive or char-
      acteristic manners of teaching
BT   Teacher Characteristics
RT   Leadership Styles
      Personality Studies
      Psychological Patterns
      Teacher Behavior
      Teacher Effectiveness
      Teacher Influence
      Teacher Response
      Teacher Role

Teaching Systems
USE   Teaching Methods

Teaching Techniques (1966 1980)
USE   Teaching Methods

Teaching (1966 1980)   JUN. 1980
      Postings: 1,038   GC: 310
SN   Invalid Descriptor—used inconsistently
      in indexing—see "Instruction," "Teach-
      ing (Occupation)," and "Teaching Meth-
      ods"

Team Administration (1967 1980)
USE   Management Teams

Team Counseling
USE   Cocounseling

Team Handball   APR. 1985
      Postings: 2   GC: 470
SN   Team sport played on a rectangular floor
      (court) whose object is to dribble and
      pass an inflated ball with the hands so as
      to throw it into a netted, floor-level end
      goal
BT   Team Sports
RT   Olympic Games

Team Leader (Teaching) (1966 1980)
USE   Leaders
AND   Team Teaching

Team Management
USE   Management Teams

Team Sports   JUN. 1984
      Postings: 139   GC: 470
NT   Baseball
      Basketball
      Field Hockey
      Football
      Ice Hockey
      Lacrosse
      Soccer
      Softball
      Team Handball
      Volleyball
      Water Polo
BT   Athletics
RT   Team Training
      Teamwork

Team Teaching   JUL. 1966
      Postings: 2,467   GC: 310
UF   Collaborative Teaching
      Cooperative Teaching (1966 1980)
      Instructional Teams
      Team Leader (Teaching) (1966
        1980) #
BT   Teaching (Occupation)
RT   Cooperative Planning
      Educational Cooperation
      Flexible Scheduling
      Master Teachers
      Multiunit Schools
      Open Plan Schools
      Rotation Plans
      School Cadres
      Teacher Collaboration
      Team Training
      Teamwork

Team Training   NOV. 1969
      Postings: 564   GC: 310
SN   Training individuals in teams or to work
      as teams
BT   Training
RT   Cooperative Learning
      School Cadres
      Small Group Instruction
      Team Sports
      Team Teaching
      Teamwork

Teamwork   JAN. 1969
      Postings: 4,092   GC: 520
BT   Group Behavior
RT   Cocounseling
      Collegiality
      Cooperation
      Cooperative Learning
      Cooperative Planning
      Interpersonal Competence
      Interpersonal Relationship
      Interprofessional Relationship
      Management Teams
      Morale
      Organizational Development
      Participative Decision Making
      Peer Relationship
      Sportsmanship
      Teacher Collaboration
      Team Sports
      Team Teaching
      Team Training

= Two or more Descriptors are used to represent this term.
The term's main entry shows the appropriate coordination.

Theory Practice Relationship
Total Quality Management

Tech Prep   *MAR. 1995*
Postings: 607   GC: 400
SN   Sequential programs of study that integrate preparation for technical careers with academic education in a highly structured and closely articulated secondary and postsecondary curriculum, leading to a minimum of an associate degree or 2-year certificate in a specific career field
UF   Two Plus Two Tech Prep
     Two Plus Two Tech Prep Associate Degrees #
BT   Technical Education
RT   Academic Education
     Articulation (Education)
     Associate Degrees
     College Preparation
     College School Cooperation
     Integrated Curriculum
     Technical Occupations

Technical Assistance   *JUL. 1966*
Postings: 2,034   GC: 610
SN   Technical, scientific, or economic assistance given by governments, institutions, or private organizations to assist in the development of human and material resources—includes domestic and foreign programs
UF   International Technical Assistance #
RT   Appropriate Technology
     Community Development
     Consultants
     Consultation Programs
     Developed Nations
     Developing Nations
     Federal Aid
     Financial Support
     Human Resources
     International Educational Exchange
     International Programs
     Labor Force Development
     Linking Agents
     Science Programs
     Scientific and Technical Information
     Technological Advancement
     Technology Transfer

Technical Education   *JUL. 1966*
Postings: 6,503   GC: 610
SN   Formal preparation for occupations between the skilled trades and the professions—usually at the postsecondary level and including the underlying sciences and supporting mathematics as well as methods, skills, materials, and processes of a specialized field of technology required for such positions as technicians, engineering aides, and production specialists
UF   Technical Instruction
NT   Fire Science Education
     Tech Prep
BT   Vocational Education
RT   Aerospace Education
     Agricultural Education
     Allied Health Occupations Education
     Architectural Education
     Aviation Education
     Aviation Technology
     Computer Science Education
     Electromechanical Technology
     Engineering Education
     Engineering Technology
     Horology
     Industrial Education
     Nuclear Technology
     Paraprofessional Personnel
     Postsecondary Education
     Pretechnology Programs
     Prevocational Education
     Research Coordinating Units
     School Shops
     Science Education
     Technical Institutes
     Technical Mathematics
     Technical Occupations

Technological Literacy
Technology
Technology Education
Trade and Industrial Education
Two Year Colleges
Vocational Education Teachers

Technical Education Directors
USE   Vocational Directors

Technical High Schools
USE   Vocational High Schools

Technical Illustration   *MAY 1969*
Postings: 125   GC: 720
SN   Process of laying out and drawing illustrations for reproduction in reference works, brochures, and technical manuals
BT   Drafting
RT   Engineering Drawing
     Graphic Arts
     Illustrations
     Orthographic Projection

Technical Information
USE   Scientific and Technical Information

Technical Institutes   *JUL. 1966*
Postings: 1,884   GC: 340
SN   Postsecondary schools offering training in occupations at a level between the skilled trades and the professions
BT   Two Year Colleges
RT   Associate Degrees
     Community Colleges
     Postsecondary Education
     Technical Education
     Two Year College Students
     Vocational Education

Technical Instruction
USE   Technical Education

Technical Libraries
USE   Science Libraries

Technical Mathematics   *JUL. 1966*
Postings: 109   GC: 480
SN   Mathematics needed in technical occupations such as electronics
BT   Mathematics
RT   Technical Education
     Technical Occupations

Technical Occupations   *JUL. 1966*
Postings: 864   GC: 640
SN   Occupations between the skilled trades and the professions such as technicians, technologists, engineering aides, paraprofessionals, and production specialists—usually requiring postsecondary education in the underlying sciences and mathematics as well as the specialized technology
BT   Occupations
RT   Agricultural Occupations
     Allied Health Occupations
     Computer Science Education
     Data Processing Occupations
     Drafting
     Energy Occupations
     Health Occupations
     Operating Engineering
     Paraprofessional Personnel
     Semiskilled Occupations
     Skilled Occupations
     Tech Prep
     Technical Education
     Technical Mathematics
     Technology
     Trade and Industrial Education
     White Collar Occupations

Technical Processes (Libraries)
USE   Library Technical Processes

Technical Reports (1968 1980)
USE   Research Reports

Technical Schools
USE   Vocational Schools

Technical Services (Libraries)
USE   Library Technical Processes

Technical Writing   *JUL. 1966*
Postings: 3,253   GC: 720
SN   Writing, often specialized or concerned with practical applications, that is employed for scientific, engineering, business, or other technical purposes
UF   Report Writing
BT   Writing (Composition)
RT   Abstracting
     Business English
     Content Area Writing
     Documentation
     Editing
     Expository Writing
     Jargon
     Proposal Writing
     Research Reports
     Textbook Preparation
     Writing for Publication

Technicians
USE   Paraprofessional Personnel

Techniques (1966 1974)
USE   Methods

Technological Advancement   *JUL. 1966*
Postings: 11,409   GC: 490
UF   High Technology
BT   Development
RT   Appropriate Technology
     Automation
     Biotechnology
     Computer Assisted Design
     Computer Assisted Manufacturing
     Computers
     Culture Lag
     Cybernetics
     Developed Nations
     Developing Nations
     Dislocated Workers
     Emerging Occupations
     Futures (of Society)
     Industrialization
     Inventions
     Material Culture
     Modernization
     Obsolescence
     Research and Development
     Revolution
     Science and Society
     Science Programs
     Structural Unemployment
     Systems Development
     Technical Assistance
     Technological Literacy
     Technology
     Technology Education
     Technology Transfer

Technological Education
USE   Technology Education

Technological Information
USE   Scientific and Technical Information

Technological Literacy   *SEP. 1982*
Postings: 1,004   GC: 490
SN   Comprehension of technological innovation and the impact of technology on society—may include the ability to se-

lect and use specific innovations appropriate to one's interests and needs
NT   Computer Literacy
RT   Appropriate Technology
     Comprehension
     Cultural Literacy
     Industrialization
     Information Literacy
     Innovation
     Science and Society
     Science Education
     Scientific and Technical Information
     Scientific Literacy
     Technical Education
     Technological Advancement
     Technology
     Technology Education
     Technology Transfer

Technological Programs
USE   Science Programs

Technological Unemployment
USE   Structural Unemployment

Technology   *JUL. 1966*
Postings: 6,386   GC: 490
UF   Applied Sciences
     Industrial Technology (1969 1980) #
NT   Accounting
     Aerospace Technology
     Agriculture
     Appropriate Technology
     Automation
     Biotechnology
     Communications
     Consumer Science
     Cosmetology
     Cybernetics
     Educational Technology
     Electromechanical Technology
     Engineering
     Engineering Technology
     Etiology
     Forestry
     Genetic Engineering
     Horology
     Hydraulics
     Information Technology
     Journalism
     Laboratory Technology
     Lexicography
     Manufacturing
     Marketing
     Masonry
     Mechanics (Process)
     Medicine
     Metal Working
     Metallurgy
     Mining
     Optometry
     Plumbing
     Power Technology
     Radiology
     Reprography
     Water Treatment
     Welding
     Wildlife Management
     Woodworking
RT   Developed Nations
     Development
     Education Work Relationship
     English for Science and Technology
     Industrialization
     Industry
     Inventions
     Liberal Arts
     Professional Occupations
     Quality of Life
     Quality of Working Life
     Research
     Research and Development
     Research Utilization
     Science and Society
     Science Libraries
     Science Programs
     Sciences
     Scientific and Technical Information
     Scientific Concepts
     Skilled Occupations

= Two or more Descriptors are used to represent this term.
The term's main entry shows the appropriate coordination.

Technical Education
Technical Occupations
Technological Advancement
Technological Literacy
Technology Education
Technology Transfer
Trade and Industrial Education
Vocational Education

Technology Education   *FEB. 1993*
　　Postings: 1,580   GC: 490
SN　General education programs concerned
　　with the study of technology, the use of
　　technical means and processes to solve
　　problems, and the impact of technology
　　on individuals and society (Note: Since
　　the mid-1980s, "Technology Education"
　　has become the preferred name for "In-
　　dustrial Arts" programs)
UF　Industrial Technology Education
　　Technological Education
BT　Education
RT　Auto Mechanics
　　Communications
　　Computer Oriented Programs
　　Construction (Process)
　　Design Requirements
　　Drafting
　　Electronics
　　Energy Education
　　General Education
　　Graphic Arts
　　Industrial Arts
　　Industrial Arts Teachers
　　Industrial Education
　　Industry
　　Manufacturing
　　Metal Working
　　Power Technology
　　Robotics
　　Science and Society
　　Science Education
　　Small Engine Mechanics
　　Technical Education
　　Technological Advancement
　　Technological Literacy
　　Technology
　　Trade and Industrial Education
　　Transportation
　　Woodworking

Technology Transfer   *MAR. 1978*
　　Postings: 1,156   GC: 490
SN　Transfer of research results, technologi-
　　cal developments, or knowledge from an
　　original application to other settings
RT　Appropriate Technology
　　Diffusion (Communication)
　　Economic Progress
　　Industrialization
　　Information Dissemination
　　Information Transfer
　　Information Utilization
　　Innovation
　　Inventions
　　Linking Agents
　　Marketing
　　Modernization
　　Patents
　　Research
　　Research and Development
　　Research and Development Centers
　　Research Utilization
　　Science and Society
　　Scientific and Technical Information
　　Technical Assistance
　　Technological Advancement
　　Technological Literacy
　　Technology
　　Use Studies

Teenagers (1966 1980)
USE　Adolescents

TEFL
USE　English (Second Language)

Telecommunication (1970 1980)
USE　Telecommunications

Telecommunications   *MAR. 1980*
　　Postings: 5,415   GC: 710
SN　Long-distance communications using
　　electromagnetic systems—includes wire
　　(e.g., telephone or telegraph) and broad-
　　cast transmission (e.g., radio, television,
　　or satellite) (Note: Prior to Mar80, the
　　Thesaurus carried the instruction "Com-
　　munication Networks, Services, or Sys-
　　tems, USE Telecommunication")
UF　Broadcast Communications
　　Electronic Communications Systems
　　Electronic Information Exchange #
　　Microwave Relay Systems (1971
　　　1980)
　　Signal Services
　　Telecommunication (1970 1980)
　　Wire Communications
　　Wireless Communications
NT　Communications Satellites
　　Computer Mediated Communication
　　Facsimile Transmission
　　Radio
　　Teleconferencing
　　Telephone Communications Systems
　　Television
　　Videotex
BT　Communications
RT　Computers
　　Distance Education
　　Electronic Equipment
　　Information Technology
　　Microelectronics
　　Networks
　　Radar
　　Television Studios

Teleconferencing   *OCT. 1979*
　　Postings: 1,208   GC: 710
SN　Conducting conferences between per-
　　sons remote from one another by means
　　of a telecommunications system
UF　Computer Conferencing
BT　Telecommunications
RT　Computer Mediated Communication
　　Conferences
　　Electronic Equipment
　　Information Networks
　　Interactive Television
　　Online Systems
　　Telephone Communications Systems
　　Television

Telecourses   *JUL. 1966*
　　Postings: 829   GC: 350
SN　Sequences of lessons offered over tele-
　　vision for credit or auditing purposes
　　(Note: For courses on the subject of
　　television, use "Television Curriculum"—
　　prior to Mar80, this term did not carry a
　　Scope Note)
BT　Courses
RT　Audiovisual Instruction
　　Distance Education
　　Educational Television
　　Interactive Television
　　Television Teachers

Telefacsimile
USE　Facsimile Transmission

Telefax
USE　Facsimile Transmission

Telegraphic Materials   *FEB. 1969*
　　Postings: 10   GC: 720
SN　Highly abbreviated and condensed tex-
　　tual materials retaining all essential in-
　　formation
BT　Reading Materials
RT　Instructional Materials
　　Readability
　　Reading Comprehension
　　Reading Rate

Telegu
USE　Telugu

**Telephone Communication Systems (1967
1980)**
USE　Telephone Communications Systems

Telephone Communications Industry
                                                            JUL. 1966
　　Postings: 155   GC: 650
BT　Industry
RT　Information Industry
　　Telephone Communications Systems
　　Utilities

Telephone Communications Systems
                                                            MAR. 1980
　　Postings: 862   GC: 710
UF　Telephone Communication Systems
　　　(1967 1980)
　　Telephones
BT　Telecommunications
RT　Audio Equipment
　　Dial Access Information Systems
　　Facsimile Transmission
　　Modems
　　Phonathons
　　Teleconferencing
　　Telephone Communications Industry
　　Telephone Instruction
　　Telephone Surveys
　　Telephone Usage Instruction
　　Videotex

Telephone Crisis Services
USE　Hotlines (Public)

Telephone Instruction   *JUL. 1966*
　　Postings: 243   GC: 350
SN　Special education by use of the tele-
　　phone (Note: Do not confuse with "Tele-
　　phone Usage Instruction")
BT　Teaching Methods
RT　Educational Media
　　Home Instruction
　　Homebound
　　Individual Instruction
　　Telephone Communications Systems

Telephone Solicitation Programs
USE　Phonathons

Telephone Surveys   *AUG. 1989*
　　Postings: 388   GC: 810
SN　(Note: Use as a minor Descriptor for
　　examples of this kind of survey—use as
　　a major Descriptor only as the subject of
　　a document)
BT　Surveys
RT　Interviews
　　Mail Surveys
　　Questionnaires
　　Research Methodology
　　Telephone Communications Systems

Telephone Usage Instruction   *MAR. 1980*
　　Postings: 149   GC: 400
SN　Instruction in the use of the telephone
　　(Note: Prior to Mar80, this concept was
　　occasionally indexed under "Telephone
　　Instruction")
BT　Instruction
RT　Communication Skills
　　Daily Living Skills
　　Telephone Communications Systems

Telephones
USE　Telephone Communications Systems

Teletext
USE　Videotex

Televised Instruction (1966 1974)
USE　Educational Television

Television   *JUL. 1966*
　　Postings: 4,295   GC: 720
SN　System whereby visual images, with or
　　without accompanying sound, are con-
　　verted into electromagnetic waves and
　　transmitted to distant receivers where
　　they are reconverted into moving visible
　　images (Note: Prior to Mar80, the The-
　　saurus carried the instruction "Televi-
　　sion Technology, USE Media Technol-
　　ogy")
UF　Airborne Television (1966 1980)
　　Color Television (1969 1980) #
　　Overhead Television (1966 1980)
　　Television Role #
　　Television Technology
　　TV
NT　Broadcast Television
　　Cable Television
　　Childrens Television
　　Closed Circuit Television
　　Commercial Television
　　Educational Television
　　Interactive Television
　　Public Television
BT　Mass Media
　　Telecommunications
RT　Broadcast Industry
　　Broadcast Journalism
　　Broadcast Reception Equipment
　　Electronic Equipment
　　Journalism Education
　　Kinescope Recordings
　　Networks
　　News Media
　　Popular Culture
　　Production Techniques
　　Programming (Broadcast)
　　Radio
　　Soap Operas
　　Special Effects
　　Teleconferencing
　　Television Commercials
　　Television Curriculum
　　Television Lighting
　　Television Radio Repairers
　　Television Research
　　Television Studios
　　Television Surveys
　　Television Teachers
　　Television Viewing
　　Video Equipment
　　Video Games
　　Videodisks
　　Videotape Recordings
　　Videotex

Television Commercials   *JUL. 1966*
　　Postings: 737   GC: 720
BT　Advertising
RT　Commercial Art
　　Commercial Television
　　Mass Media
　　Merchandising
　　Programming (Broadcast)
　　Television
　　Television Viewing

Television Curriculum   *JUL. 1966*
　　Postings: 392   GC: 400
SN　Curriculum concerned with television,
　　television production, etc. (Note: For
　　courses taught on television, use
　　"Telecourses"—prior to Mar80, this term
　　did not carry a Scope Note)
BT　Curriculum
RT　Broadcast Industry
　　Broadcast Journalism
　　Journalism Education
　　Production Techniques
　　Programming (Broadcast)
　　Television
　　Television Teachers

Television Equipment
USE　Video Equipment

Television Journalism
USE　Broadcast Journalism

= Two or more Descriptors are used to represent this term.
The term's main entry shows the appropriate coordination.

Television Lecturers
USE   Television Teachers

Television Lighting   *JUL. 1966*
        Postings: 64   GC: 910
UF   Television Lights (1966 1980)
BT   Lighting
        Production Techniques
RT   Television
        Television Studios

Television Lights (1966 1980)
USE   Television Lighting

Television Programming
USE   Programming (Broadcast)

Television Radio Repairers   *MAR. 1980*
        Postings: 53   GC: 640
UF   Radio Television Repairers
        Television Repairmen (1968 1980)
BT   Skilled Workers
RT   Radio
        Repair
        Service Workers
        Television

Television Repairmen (1968 1980)
USE   Television Radio Repairers

Television Research   *JUL. 1966*
        Postings: 2,719   GC: 810
SN   Basic, applied, and developmental re-
        search conducted to further knowledge
        about program content, impact, and use
        of television (Note: As of Oct81, use as a
        minor Descriptor for examples of this
        kind of research—use as a major Descrip-
        tor only as the subject of a document)
BT   Media Research
RT   Programming (Broadcast)
        Television
        Television Surveys
        Television Viewing

Television Role
USE   Mass Media Role
AND   Television

Television Studios   *MAR. 1980*
        Postings: 44   GC: 920
UF   Video Production Centers
BT   Facilities
RT   Broadcast Reception Equipment
        Programming (Broadcast)
        Telecommunications
        Television
        Television Lighting
        Video Equipment

Television Surveys   *JUL. 1966*
        Postings: 419   GC: 810
SN   Investigations of television viewership,
        viewing behavior, availability, etc., con-
        ducted to determine current status,
        trends, and/or norms—includes surveys
        of television viewers and producers (Note:
        As of Oct81, use as a minor Descriptor
        for examples of this kind of survey—use
        as a major Descriptor only as the subject
        of a document)
BT   Surveys
RT   Television
        Television Research

Television Teachers   *JUL. 1966*
        Postings: 182   GC: 360
SN   Teachers who provide instruction through
        the medium of television—also, at the
        college level, instructors in the field of
        television production and techniques
UF   Television Lecturers
BT   Teachers
RT   Educational Television

Telecourses
Television
Television Curriculum

Television Technology
USE   Television

Television Use
USE   Mass Media Use
AND   Television Viewing

Television Viewing   *JUL. 1966*
        Postings: 3,404   GC: 720
SN   Act of viewing television programs
UF   Television Use #
BT   Activities
RT   Audience Response
        Audiences
        Critical Viewing
        Mass Media Use
        Programming (Broadcast)
        Soap Operas
        Television
        Television Commercials
        Television Research
        Visual Literacy
        Visual Stimuli

Telugu   *JUL. 1966*
        Postings: 14   GC: 440
UF   Telegu
BT   Dravidian Languages

Temperament
USE   Personality

Temperate Rainforests
USE   Rainforests

Temperature   *JUL. 1966*
        Postings: 447   GC: 490
RT   Air Conditioning
        Air Conditioning Equipment
        Air Flow
        Climate
        Climate Change
        Climate Control
        Fuel Consumption
        Global Warming
        Heat
        Heating
        Humidity
        Meteorology
        Refrigeration
        Solar Energy
        Thermal Environment
        Thermal Insulation
        Ventilation
        Wind (Meteorology)

Tempo (Cognition)
USE   Conceptual Tempo

Tempo (Music)   *OCT. 1994*
        Postings: 19   GC: 420
SN   The rate of speed at which a musical
        composition is performed
BT   Rhythm (Music)
RT   Music

Temporal Perspective
USE   Time Perspective

Temporary Employment   *JUL. 1999*
        Postings: 111   GC: 630
SN   Work arrangement in which it is under-
        stood that the job is of limited duration
        (Note: See also the Identifier "Tempo-
        rary Faculty")
UF   Temporary Help Services #
BT   Employment
RT   Part Time Employment
        Seasonal Employment

Temporary Facilities
USE   Relocatable Facilities

Temporary Help Services
USE   Employment Services
AND   Temporary Employment

TENES
USE   English (Second Language)

TENL (1968 1980)   *MAR. 1980*
        Postings: 204   GC: 450
SN   Invalid Descriptor—coordinate "Nonstan-
        dard Dialects" with such Descriptors as
        "English Instruction," "Teaching Meth-
        ods," "Reading Instruction," "English
        Curriculum," "Writing (Composition),"
        etc.

Tennis   *JUN. 1975*
        Postings: 130   GC: 470
BT   Racquet Sports
RT   Lifetime Sports
        Squash (Game)

Tenpins
USE   Bowling

Tenses (Grammar)   *OCT. 1983*
        Postings: 331   GC: 450
SN   Grammatical constructions, such as verb
        inflections, for specifying time and dura-
        tion
BT   Morphemes
RT   Form Classes (Languages)
        Sentence Structure
        Syntax
        Time Perspective
        Verbs

Tenure   *JUL. 1966*
        Postings: 2,838   GC: 630
SN   Status of a person in a position or occu-
        pation (i.e., length of service, terms of
        employment, or permanence of posi-
        tion)
UF   Job Tenure (1967 1978)
BT   Employment Level
RT   Academic Rank (Professional)
        Aging in Academia
        Contract Salaries
        Contracts
        Employees
        Employer Employee Relationship
        Employment
        Employment Experience
        Employment Practices
        Employment Qualifications
        Faculty Promotion
        Financial Exigency
        Job Layoff
        Job Security
        Labor Problems
        Labor Turnover
        Nontenured Faculty
        Occupational Mobility
        Personnel Data
        Personnel Policy
        Probationary Period
        Promotion (Occupational)
        Reduction in Force
        Seniority
        Teacher Employment
        Teacher Employment Benefits
        Teacher Promotion
        Teacher Rights
        Teaching (Occupation)
        Tenured Faculty
        Work Life Expectancy

Tenured Faculty   *OCT. 1983*
        Postings: 332   GC: 360
SN   Academic staff who have been granted
        tenure (permanence of position) by their
        school or institution
UF   Tenured Teachers

BT   Faculty
RT   Academic Rank (Professional)
        College Faculty
        Full Time Faculty
        Nontenured Faculty
        Professors
        Teachers
        Tenure

Tenured Teachers
USE   Tenured Faculty

Term Papers
USE   Research Papers (Students)

Terminal Education   *JUL. 1966*
        Postings: 49   GC: 340
SN   Includes secondary and postsecondary
        curricula designed to be complete in
        themselves for students who may not
        continue their formal education—at the
        2-year college level, frequently applies to
        programs that do not lead to transfer to
        4-year institutions
BT   Education
RT   Terminal Students
        Transfer Programs

Terminal Illness   *AUG. 1989*
        Postings: 216   GC: 210
BT   Diseases
RT   Death
        Euthanasia
        Health
        Hospices (Terminal Care)
        Special Health Problems

Terminal Students   *JUL. 1966*
        Postings: 100   GC: 360
SN   Secondary school students whose edu-
        cational goals extend no further than
        high school graduation or students at
        the postsecondary level enrolled in pro-
        grams that do not lead to 4-year degrees
BT   Students
RT   Continuation Students
        Terminal Education
        Two Year College Students

Termination of Programs
USE   Program Termination

Termination of Treatment   *OCT. 1983*
        Postings: 117   GC: 210
SN   The ending of personal health treatment
        (medical, psychological, etc.)
RT   Counseling
        Helping Relationship
        Medical Services
        Outcomes of Treatment
        Therapy

Terminology
USE   Vocabulary

Terrorism   *OCT. 1984*
        Postings: 135   GC: 610
SN   Threat or use of violence against a popu-
        lation or government to achieve social or
        political ends
BT   Antisocial Behavior
RT   Activism
        Aggression
        Crime
        Emergency Programs
        International Crimes
        Political Attitudes
        Revolution
        Violence
        War

Tertiary Education
USE   Postsecondary Education

= Two or more Descriptors are used to represent this term.
The term's main entry shows the appropriate coordination.

TESL
USE   English (Second Language)

TESOL
USE   English (Second Language)

Test Abuse
USE   Test Use

Test Administration
USE   Testing

Test Administrators
USE   Examiners

Test Analysis
USE   Test Theory

Test Anxiety   MAR. 1980
        Postings: 635   GC: 310
SN   Distress or uneasiness over test taking,
        often affecting test performance
BT   Anxiety
RT   School Phobia
        Scores
        Test Wiseness
        Testing
        Testing Problems
        Tests

Test Bias   MAR. 1971
        Postings: 2,041   GC: 540
SN   Unfairness in the construction, content,
        administration, or interpretation of tests,
        either for or against various groups such
        as minorities, the disabled, women, or
        socioeconomic classes
NT   Item Bias
BT   Bias
RT   Culture Fair Tests
        Error Patterns
        Objective Tests
        Social Bias
        Social Discrimination
        Statistical Bias
        Test Coaching
        Test Construction
        Test Interpretation
        Test Items
        Test Results
        Test Selection
        Test Use
        Test Validity
        Test Wiseness
        Testing
        Testing Problems
        Tests

Test Books
USE   Tests

Test Characteristics (Physical)
USE   Test Format

Test Coaching   MAR. 1980
        Postings: 499   GC: 310
SN   Activities designed to prepare individu-
        als, in a relatively short time, for taking
        tests and maximizing the scores ob-
        tained
BT   Instruction
RT   Guessing (Tests)
        Review (Reexamination)
        Test Bias
        Test Results
        Test Validity
        Test Wiseness
        Testing
        Testing Problems
        Tests
        Tutoring

Test Construction   JUL. 1966
        Postings: 8,843   GC: 820
SN   Planning, assembling, writing, editing,
        or otherwise preparing a test or other
        individual measure for administration
UF   Test Design
BT   Material Development
RT   Answer Keys
        Answer Sheets
        Computer Assisted Testing
        Criterion Referenced Tests
        Culture Fair Tests
        Distractors (Tests)
        Factor Analysis
        Item Analysis
        Item Banks
        Item Bias
        Item Response Theory
        Item Sampling
        Pretesting
        Scaling
        Skill Analysis
        Task Analysis
        Teacher Made Tests
        Test Bias
        Test Content
        Test Format
        Test Items
        Test Length
        Test Manuals
        Test Reliability
        Test Theory
        Test Validity
        Testing
        Testing Problems
        Tests

Test Content   APR. 1990
        Postings: 319   GC: 820
SN   The subject matter, items, instructions,
        and any other parts of a test
RT   Content Analysis
        Content Validity
        Test Construction
        Test Format
        Test Items
        Test Length
        Test Reviews
        Test Selection
        Testing
        Tests

Test Design
USE   Test Construction

Test Format   APR. 1980
        Postings: 1,489   GC: 820
SN   Types of test items and the responses
        they require (multiple choice, essay, com-
        puter assisted, cloze, etc.)—also, the
        arrangement of items on the test form
        (e.g., arranging items in order of in-
        creasing difficulty)
UF   Item Types
        Test Characteristics (Physical)
        Test Type
RT   Comparative Testing
        Questioning Techniques
        Response Style (Tests)
        Responses
        Test Construction
        Test Content
        Test Items
        Test Length
        Test Manuals
        Testing
        Tests

Test Interpretation   JUL. 1966
        Postings: 3,406   GC: 820
SN   Explanation of the meaning, or descrip-
        tion of the uses and limitations of, a test
        score or group of test scores
BT   Data Interpretation
RT   Confidence Testing
        Criterion Referenced Tests
        Error of Measurement
        Factor Structure
        Generalizability Theory

Guessing (Tests)
        Item Bias
        Item Response Theory
        Norm Referenced Tests
        Psychometrics
        Robustness (Statistics)
        Scores
        Scoring Formulas
        Test Bias
        Test Items
        Test Manuals
        Test Norms
        Test Reliability
        Test Results
        Test Score Decline
        Test Theory
        Test Use
        Test Validity
        Testing
        Tests

Test Items   MAR. 1977
        Postings: 3,708   GC: 820
SN   Questions, problems, exercises, or other
        units of a test that elicit responses which
        can be scored separately and related to
        the skills the test is measuring as a
        whole
UF   Item Difficulty #
RT   Adaptive Testing
        Computer Assisted Testing
        Content Validity
        Distractors (Tests)
        Item Analysis
        Item Banks
        Item Bias
        Item Response Theory
        Item Sampling
        Problem Sets
        Scores
        Scoring
        Test Bias
        Test Construction
        Test Content
        Test Format
        Test Interpretation
        Test Length
        Test Manuals
        Test Reliability
        Test Theory
        Test Validity
        Testing
        Tests

Test Length   OCT. 1983
        Postings: 265   GC: 820
SN   The number of items in a test—also, the
        amount of time required to administer
        and/or complete a test
RT   Test Construction
        Test Content
        Test Format
        Test Items
        Test Reliability
        Testing
        Tests
        Timed Tests

Test Manuals   MAR. 1983
        Postings: 245   GC: 730
SN   Guides provided for use with tests, in-
        cluding descriptive information, direc-
        tions for administration/scoring/interpre-
        tation, normative data, and/or related
        information, such as construction pro-
        cedures (Note: Use as major term for
        document subject, as minor term for
        document type—do not use for "Test
        Taking Manuals," for which see "Study
        Guides" and "Test Wiseness")
BT   Guides
RT   Answer Keys
        Answer Sheets
        Item Banks
        Problem Sets
        Scoring
        Scoring Formulas
        Test Construction
        Test Format
        Test Interpretation

Test Items
        Test Norms
        Test Results
        Test Use
        Testing
        Testing Problems
        Testing Programs
        Tests

Test Norms   MAR. 1980
        Postings: 545   GC: 820
SN   Statistical descriptions, such as score
        distributions, expressing the character-
        istic performance of a specified group or
        population with respect to a particular
        measure
BT   Norms
RT   Comparative Testing
        Error of Measurement
        Grade Equivalent Scores
        Item Sampling
        Norm Referenced Tests
        Scores
        Standardized Tests
        Test Interpretation
        Test Manuals
        Test Results
        Test Score Decline
        Testing
        Testing Programs
        Tests

Test Reliability   JUL. 1966
        Postings: 7,204   GC: 820
SN   Accuracy, consistency, and stability of
        the results from a test or other measure-
        ment technique for a given population
        (Note: Prior to Mar80, "Reliability" was
        not restricted by a Scope Note, and
        many items indexed by "Reliability"
        should have been indexed with "Test
        Reliability")
BT   Reliability
RT   Confidence Testing
        Error of Measurement
        Generalizability Theory
        Guessing (Tests)
        Interrater Reliability
        Item Analysis
        Item Response Theory
        Robustness (Statistics)
        Scores
        Test Construction
        Test Interpretation
        Test Items
        Test Length
        Test Results
        Test Reviews
        Test Selection
        Test Theory
        Test Validity
        Testing
        Testing Problems
        Tests
        True Scores

Test Results   JUL. 1966
        Postings: 4,896   GC: 820
SN   Decisions, judgments, and other activi-
        ties based on the outcome of testing
        (Note: Do not confuse with "Scores"—
        prior to Mar80, the use of this term was
        not restricted by a Scope Note)
RT   Scores
        Test Bias
        Test Coaching
        Test Interpretation
        Test Manuals
        Test Norms
        Test Reliability
        Test Score Decline
        Test Use
        Test Validity
        Testing
        Tests

Test Reviews   JAN. 1971
        Postings: 742   GC: 730
BT   Publications

\# = Two or more Descriptors are used to represent this term.
The term's main entry shows the appropriate coordination.

RT   Comparative Testing
      Surveys
      Test Content
      Test Reliability
      Test Selection
      Test Validity
      Testing
      Tests

Test Score Decline   *AUG. 1988*
      Postings: 151   GC: 330
SN   Decreasing scores of groups of test tak-
      ers or a decrease in the average score of
      all examinees
UF   Declining Scores
RT   Academic Standards
      Educational Testing
      Minimum Competency Testing
      Scores
      Standardized Tests
      Test Interpretation
      Test Norms
      Test Results
      Test Validity
      Testing
      Testing Problems
      Tests

Test Scores
USE   Scores

Test Scoring Machines   *JUL. 1966*
      Postings: 115   GC: 910
BT   Equipment
RT   Answer Keys
      Answer Sheets
      Automation
      Instrumentation
      Optical Scanners
      Scores
      Scoring
      Testing
      Tests

Test Selection   *JUL. 1966*
      Postings: 832   GC: 820
BT   Selection
RT   Test Bias
      Test Content
      Test Reliability
      Test Reviews
      Test Use
      Test Validity
      Testing
      Testing Problems
      Tests

Test Taking Skills
USE   Test Wiseness

Test Taking Strategies
USE   Test Wiseness

Test Theory   *APR. 1980*
      Postings: 689   GC: 810
SN   The study and analysis of the relation-
      ships between the characteristics of tests
      (and test items) and test scores and
      score distributions (including such char-
      acteristics as reliability and validity)
UF   Score Theory
      Test Analysis
NT   Item Response Theory
BT   Theories
RT   Equated Scores
      Generalizability Theory
      Item Analysis
      Mathematical Models
      Proof (Mathematics)
      Psychometrics
      Scores
      Scoring
      Statistical Analysis
      Test Construction
      Test Interpretation
      Test Items
      Test Reliability

      Test Validity
      Testing
      Tests

Test Type
USE   Test Format

Test Use   *NOV. 1981*
      Postings: 3,116   GC: 820
SN   The uses of tests and test results
UF   Test Abuse
RT   Evaluation Utilization
      High Stakes Tests
      Predictive Measurement
      Scores
      Test Bias
      Test Interpretation
      Test Manuals
      Test Results
      Test Selection
      Test Validity
      Testing
      Testing Problems
      Tests

Test Validity   *JUL. 1966*
      Postings: 11,224   GC: 820
SN   Extent to which a test, inventory, rating
      scale, questionnaire, etc., is an effective
      index of what it is used or intended to
      measure (Note: Prior to Mar80, "Valid-
      ity" was not restricted by a Scope Note,
      and many items indexed by "Validity"
      should have been indexed with "Test
      Validity")
NT   Construct Validity
      Content Validity
BT   Validity
RT   Concurrent Validity
      Confidence Testing
      Distractors (Tests)
      Factor Analysis
      Factor Structure
      Item Analysis
      Item Bias
      Item Response Theory
      Multitrait Multimethod Techniques
      Predictive Measurement
      Predictive Validity
      Predictor Variables
      Response Style (Tests)
      Robustness (Statistics)
      Scores
      Test Bias
      Test Coaching
      Test Construction
      Test Interpretation
      Test Items
      Test Reliability
      Test Results
      Test Reviews
      Test Score Decline
      Test Selection
      Test Theory
      Test Use
      Test Wiseness
      Testing
      Testing Problems
      Tests

Test Wiseness   *FEB. 1971*
      Postings: 1,113   GC: 310
SN   Skills and strategies, unrelated to the
      traits a test is intended to measure, that
      may increase test takers' scores—may
      include the effects of coaching or experi-
      ence in taking tests
UF   Test Taking Skills
      Test Taking Strategies
RT   Guessing (Tests)
      Incidental Learning
      Intentional Learning
      Problem Solving
      Response Style (Tests)
      Scores
      Scoring Formulas
      Test Anxiety
      Test Bias
      Test Coaching

      Test Validity
      Testing
      Testing Problems
      Tests

Testing   *JUL. 1966*
      Postings: 7,924   GC: 820
SN   Gathering and processing information
      about individuals' ability, skill, under-
      standing, or knowledge under controlled
      conditions (Note: See also "Evaluation"
      and "Measurement")
UF   Test Administration
      Testing Methods
      Testing Techniques
NT   Adaptive Testing
      Comparative Testing
      Computer Assisted Testing
      Confidence Testing
      Educational Testing
      Group Testing
      Individual Testing
      Minimum Competency Testing
      Psychological Testing
      Teacher Competency Testing
BT   Measurement Techniques
RT   Alternative Assessment
      Concurrent Validity
      Construct Validity
      Content Validity
      Data Collection
      Distractors (Tests)
      Error Patterns
      Evaluation
      Examiners
      Factor Analysis
      Forced Choice Technique
      Grade Equivalent Scores
      Guessing (Tests)
      Informal Assessment
      Item Analysis
      Item Banks
      Item Bias
      Item Response Theory
      Measurement
      Measurement Objectives
      Multitrait Multimethod Techniques
      Needs Assessment
      Predictive Measurement
      Predictive Validity
      Pretests Posttests
      Problem Sets
      Proctoring
      Q Methodology
      Scaling
      Scores
      Scoring
      Test Anxiety
      Test Bias
      Test Coaching
      Test Construction
      Test Content
      Test Format
      Test Interpretation
      Test Items
      Test Length
      Test Manuals
      Test Norms
      Test Reliability
      Test Results
      Test Reviews
      Test Score Decline
      Test Scoring Machines
      Test Selection
      Test Theory
      Test Use
      Test Validity
      Test Wiseness
      Testing Problems
      Testing Programs
      Tests
      Timed Tests

Testing Methods
USE   Testing

Testing Problems   *JUL. 1966*
      Postings: 4,072   GC: 820
SN   Difficulties associated with the selection,

      administration, scoring, or interpreta-
      tion of tests or other individual measures
BT   Problems
RT   Confidence Testing
      Culture Fair Tests
      Error of Measurement
      Evaluation Problems
      Experimenter Characteristics
      Guessing (Tests)
      Interrater Reliability
      Item Bias
      Response Style (Tests)
      Scoring
      Test Anxiety
      Test Bias
      Test Coaching
      Test Construction
      Test Manuals
      Test Reliability
      Test Score Decline
      Test Selection
      Test Use
      Test Validity
      Test Wiseness
      Testing
      Tests

Testing Programs   *JUL. 1966*
      Postings: 3,258   GC: 820
SN   Organized plans and activities for select-
      ing, administering, scoring, and inter-
      preting measures of individual abilities,
      traits, interests, and attitudes
BT   Programs
RT   Educational Diagnosis
      Standardized Tests
      State Licensing Boards
      Test Manuals
      Test Norms
      Testing
      Tests

Testing Techniques
USE   Testing

Tests   *JUL. 1966*
      Postings: 4,521   GC: 830
SN   Devices, procedures, or sets of items
      that are used to measure ability, skill,
      understanding, knowledge, or achieve-
      ment (Note: Use a more specific term if
      possible—this broad term corresponds
      to Pubtype code 160 and should not be
      used except as the subject of a docu-
      ment)
UF   Examinations
      Identification Tests (1966 1980)
      Quizzes
      Test Books
NT   Achievement Tests
      Aptitude Tests
      Auditory Tests
      Cognitive Tests
      College Entrance Examinations
      Creativity Tests
      Criterion Referenced Tests
      Culture Fair Tests
      Diagnostic Tests
      Field Tests
      High Stakes Tests
      Licensing Examinations (Professions)
      Mathematics Tests
      Maturity Tests
      Nonverbal Tests
      Norm Referenced Tests
      Objective Tests
      Occupational Tests
      Open Book Tests
      Performance Tests
      Physical Fitness Tests
      Preschool Tests
      Pretests Posttests
      Prognostic Tests
      Science Tests
      Screening Tests
      Situational Tests
      Standardized Tests
      Teacher Made Tests
      Timed Tests
      Verbal Tests

= Two or more Descriptors are used to represent this term.
The term's main entry shows the appropriate coordination.

Vision Tests
BT   Measures (Individuals)
RT   Answer Keys
    Answer Sheets
    Computer Assisted Testing
    Distractors (Tests)
    Evaluation
    Examiners
    Forced Choice Technique
    Guessing (Tests)
    Instructional Materials
    Item Analysis
    Item Banks
    Item Bias
    Item Response Theory
    Measurement
    Problem Sets
    Response Style (Tests)
    Scores
    Scoring
    Statistical Data
    Test Anxiety
    Test Bias
    Test Coaching
    Test Construction
    Test Content
    Test Format
    Test Interpretation
    Test Items
    Test Length
    Test Manuals
    Test Norms
    Test Reliability
    Test Results
    Test Reviews
    Test Score Decline
    Test Scoring Machines
    Test Selection
    Test Theory
    Test Use
    Test Validity
    Test Wiseness
    Testing
    Testing Problems
    Testing Programs

Tests of Significance (1966 1980)
USE   Statistical Significance

Teton Dakota
USE   Lakota

Teton Sioux (Tribe)
USE   Lakota (Tribe)

Tetraplegia
USE   Neurological Impairments

Text Editing
USE   Word Processing

Text Editors
USE   Computer Software
AND   Word Processing

Text Processing
USE   Word Processing

Text Structure   *AUG. 1988*
    Postings: 932   GC: 460
SN   Arrangement and connectivity of the ideas
    in a textual passage in terms of for-
    mat, order, density, repetitiveness,
    elaborateness, etc., as related to com-
    prehension and/or recall
RT   Cohesion (Written Composition)
    Electronic Text
    Readability
    Reader Text Relationship
    Reading Comprehension
    Reading Writing Relationship
    Sentence Structure
    Story Grammar
    Structural Analysis (Linguistics)
    Syntax
    Writing Skills

Text to Speech Synthesizers
USE   Speech Synthesizers

Textbook Assignments (1966 1980)
USE   Assignments

Textbook Bias   *JUL. 1966*
    Postings: 841   GC: 540
BT   Bias
RT   Multicultural Textbooks
    Textbook Content
    Textbook Evaluation
    Textbook Preparation
    Textbook Research
    Textbook Selection
    Textbooks

Textbook Content   *JUL. 1966*
    Postings: 2,715   GC: 310
RT   Content Analysis
    Course Content
    Multicultural Textbooks
    Textbook Bias
    Textbook Evaluation
    Textbook Preparation
    Textbook Research
    Textbook Selection
    Textbook Standards
    Textbooks

Textbook Development
USE   Textbook Preparation

Textbook Evaluation   *JUL. 1966*
    Postings: 2,411   GC: 320
SN   Determining the efficacy, value, etc., of
    textbooks with respect to stated objec-
    tives, standards, or criteria (Note: As of
    Oct81, use as a minor Descriptor for
    examples of this kind of evaluation—use
    as a major Descriptor only as the subject
    of a document)
BT   Instructional Material Evaluation
RT   Book Reviews
    Readability
    Readability Formulas
    Textbook Bias
    Textbook Content
    Textbook Research
    Textbook Selection
    Textbook Standards
    Textbooks

Textbook Preparation   *JUL. 1966*
    Postings: 573   GC: 720
UF   Textbook Development
    Textbook Writing
RT   Technical Writing
    Textbook Bias
    Textbook Content
    Textbook Publication
    Textbook Research
    Textbook Standards
    Textbooks

Textbook Production
USE   Textbook Publication

Textbook Publication   *MAR. 1980*
    Postings: 202   GC: 720
SN   Act or process of publishing a textbook
UF   Textbook Production
    Textbook Publishing
BT   Production Techniques
RT   Printing
    Publishing Industry
    Textbook Preparation
    Textbooks

Textbook Publications (1966 1980)   *JUN. 1980*
    Postings: 111   GC: 730
SN   Invalid Descriptor—see the more pre-
    cise Descriptors "Textbooks" and "Text-
    book Publication"

Textbook Publishing
USE   Textbook Publication

Textbook Research   *JUL. 1966*
    Postings: 880   GC: 810
SN   Systematic investigation of the design,
    content, biases, impact, etc., of text-
    books (Note: As of Oct81, use as a minor
    Descriptor for examples of this kind of
    research—use as a major Descriptor
    only as the subject of a document—do
    not confuse with "Textbook Evaluation")
BT   Media Research
RT   Textbook Bias
    Textbook Content
    Textbook Evaluation
    Textbook Preparation
    Textbooks

Textbook Selection   *JUL. 1966*
    Postings: 1,119   GC: 320
BT   Media Selection
RT   Reading Material Selection
    Textbook Bias
    Textbook Content
    Textbook Evaluation
    Textbook Standards
    Textbooks

Textbook Standards   *JUL. 1966*
    Postings: 321   GC: 330
BT   Standards
RT   Textbook Content
    Textbook Evaluation
    Textbook Preparation
    Textbook Selection
    Textbooks

Textbook Writing
USE   Textbook Preparation

Textbooks   *JUL. 1966*
    Postings: 6,116   GC: 730
UF   Programed Texts (1966 1980) #
    Supplementary Textbooks (1967
      1980) #
NT   History Textbooks
    Multicultural Textbooks
BT   Books
    Instructional Materials
RT   Laboratory Manuals
    Programmed Instructional Materials
    Reading Materials
    Teaching Guides
    Textbook Bias
    Textbook Content
    Textbook Evaluation
    Textbook Preparation
    Textbook Publication
    Textbook Research
    Textbook Selection
    Textbook Standards
    Workbooks

Textile Finishing
USE   Finishing

Textiles Instruction   *JUL. 1966*
    Postings: 250   GC: 400
BT   Instruction
RT   Clothing
    Clothing Instruction
    Fashion Industry
    Home Economics
    Laundry Drycleaning Occupations

Textual Criticism (1969 1980)   *MAR. 1980*
    Postings: 176   GC: 430
SN   Invalid Descriptor—originally intended
    as a literary term, but used indiscrimi-
    nately in indexing—see "Literary Criti-
    cism," "Evaluation," "Evaluation Meth-
    ods," etc.

Thai   *JUL. 1966*
    Postings: 166   GC: 440
BT   Sino Tibetan Languages

Thanatology
USE   Death

Theater
USE   Theater Arts

Theater Arts   *JUL. 1966*
    Postings: 2,545   GC: 420
UF   Performing Arts
    Shadow Plays
    Theater
NT   Acting
    Choral Speaking
    Drama
    Dramatics
    Opera
    Pantomime
    Puppetry
    Readers Theater
    Rehearsals (Theater Arts)
BT   Fine Arts
RT   Aesthetics
    Art
    Audiences
    Cultural Activities
    Dance
    Film Industry
    Film Production
    Film Study
    Films
    Orchestras
    Playwriting
    Production Techniques
    Skits
    Special Effects
    Speech Communication
    Theaters

Theaters   *JUL. 1966*
    Postings: 236   GC: 920
UF   Outdoor Theaters (1968 1980) #
    Performing Arts Centers
BT   Facilities
RT   Acoustical Environment
    Arts Centers
    Auditoriums
    Drama Workshops
    Dramatics
    Educational Facilities
    Music Facilities
    Recreational Facilities
    Stages (Facilities)
    Theater Arts

Thefts
USE   Stealing

Thematic Approach   *DEC. 1969*
    Postings: 1,521   GC: 310
SN   Teaching approach that organizes sub-
    ject matter around unifying themes
BT   Teaching Methods
RT   Curriculum Design
    Interdisciplinary Approach

Theme Writing
USE   Writing (Composition)

Theological Education   *JUL. 1966*
    Postings: 339   GC: 400
SN   Formal education in a higher education
    institution in preparation for careers in
    religion, including the clergy (Note: Prior
    to Mar80, this term was not restricted by
    a Scope Note)
UF   Seminaries #
BT   Professional Education
RT   Church Related Colleges
    Churches
    Clergy
    Nuns
    Priests

= Two or more Descriptors are used to represent this term.
The term's main entry shows the appropriate coordination.

Religion
Religious Education

Theoretical Criticism (1969 1980)
                                        MAR. 1980
Postings: 205   GC: 430
SN   Invalid Descriptor—originally intended
     as a literary term, but used indiscrimi-
     nately in indexing—see "Literary Criti-
     cism," "Standards," "Theories," "Evalua-
     tion," etc.

Theoretical Models
USE   Models

Theories   *JUL. 1966*
Postings: 6,041   GC: 810
SN   Generalizations or principles, supported
     by substantial evidence but not conclu-
     sively established, proposed as explana-
     tions of observed phenomena or of the
     relations in a given body of facts (Note:
     Use a more specific term if possible)
NT   Atomic Theory
     Behavior Theories
     Chaos Theory
     Counseling Theories
     Critical Theory
     Educational Theories
     Game Theory
     Generalizability Theory
     Information Theory
     Kinetic Molecular Theory
     Learning Theories
     Linguistic Theory
     Music Theory
     Personality Theories
     Piagetian Theory
     Relativity
     Rhetorical Theory
     Role Theory
     Set Theory
     Social Theories
     Test Theory
RT   Generalization
     Hypothesis Testing
     Models
     Research
     Scientific Methodology
     Theory Practice Relationship

Theory Practice Relationship   *DEC. 1985*
Postings: 7,257   GC: 810
SN   The association between knowledge/un-
     derstanding and action/application
UF   Research Practice Relationship #
BT   Relationship
RT   Action Research
     Adoption (Ideas)
     Diffusion (Communication)
     Educational Innovation
     Educational Practices
     Educational Research
     Innovation
     Linking Agents
     Methods Research
     Models
     Participatory Research
     Research
     Research and Development
     Research Utilization
     School Involvement
     Teacher Researchers
     Teaching Methods
     Teamwork
     Theories

Therapeutic Communities
USE   Milieu Therapy

Therapeutic Environment   *JUL. 1966*
Postings: 735   GC: 230
SN   Surrounding conditions, forces, or fac-
     tors that facilitate the process of therapy
BT   Environment
RT   Counseling
     Counselor Client Relationship
     Educational Therapy

Mental Health Clinics
Milieu Therapy
Physician Patient Relationship
Psychiatric Hospitals
Psychotherapy
Rehabilitation
Rehabilitation Centers
Therapy
Token Economy

Therapeutic Play
USE   Play Therapy

Therapeutic Recreation   *JUN. 1983*
Postings: 186   GC: 230
SN   Recreation services and activities de-
     signed to treat or rehabilitate individuals
     with certain physical, emotional, and/or
     social problems (e.g., the disabled, in-
     firm, or incarcerated)
UF   Recreation Therapy
NT   Play Therapy
BT   Recreation
     Therapy
RT   Allied Health Occupations
     Art Therapy
     Correctional Education
     Dance Therapy
     Music Therapy
     Occupational Therapy
     Physical Therapy
     Psychotherapy
     Recreational Activities
     Rehabilitation
     Special Education

Therapeutics
USE   Therapy

Therapists   *JUL. 1966*
Postings: 1,289   GC: 640
UF   Hearing Therapists (1967 1980) #
     Inhalation Therapists (1969 1985) #
     Speech Therapists (1966 1980) #
NT   Occupational Therapists
     Physical Therapists
BT   Allied Health Personnel
     Professional Personnel
RT   Psychotherapy
     Therapy

Therapy   *AUG. 1969*
Postings: 2,008   GC: 210
UF   Therapeutics
NT   Art Therapy
     Bibliotherapy
     Dance Therapy
     Drug Therapy
     Educational Therapy
     Group Therapy
     Hearing Therapy
     Music Therapy
     Occupational Therapy
     Oral Rehydration Therapy
     Physical Therapy
     Psychotherapy
     Respiratory Therapy
     Speech Therapy
     Therapeutic Recreation
RT   Adjustment (to Environment)
     Allied Health Occupations
     Disabilities
     Helping Relationship
     Intervention
     Medical Services
     Medicine
     Outcomes of Treatment
     Rehabilitation
     Special Education
     Termination of Treatment
     Therapeutic Environment
     Therapists

Thermal Environment   *JUL. 1966*
Postings: 333   GC: 920
SN   Related to the combined effects of radi-
     ant temperature, air temperature, hu-
     midity, and air velocity

BT   Physical Environment
RT   Air Conditioning
     Air Conditioning Equipment
     Building Design
     Climate
     Climate Change
     Climate Control
     Design Requirements
     Environmental Influences
     Fuel Consumption
     Heat Recovery
     Heating
     Human Factors Engineering
     Humidity
     Interior Design
     Meteorology
     Solar Energy
     Temperature
     Thermal Insulation
     Thermodynamics
     Ventilation
     Water
     Weather
     Wind (Meteorology)

Thermal Insulation   *MAY 1994*
Postings: 7   GC: 920
SN   Prevention of transfer of heat (by con-
     duction, convection, or radiation) from a
     hot area to a cold
UF   Insulation (Heat)
BT   Structural Elements (Construction)
RT   Acoustic Insulation
     Air Conditioning
     Climate Control
     Construction (Process)
     Construction Materials
     Energy Conservation
     Energy Management
     Heating
     Refrigeration
     Temperature
     Thermal Environment
     Thermodynamics

Thermodynamics   *AUG. 1968*
Postings: 655   GC: 490
UF   Heat Equations
     Thermomechanics
     Thermophysics
     Thermoscience
BT   Physics
RT   Calorimeters
     Chemical Equilibrium
     Diffusion (Physics)
     Entropy
     Heat
     Nuclear Physics
     Physical Chemistry
     Thermal Environment
     Thermal Insulation

Thermomechanics
USE   Thermodynamics

Thermophysics
USE   Thermodynamics

Thermoscience
USE   Thermodynamics

Thesauri   *JUL. 1966*
Postings: 546   GC: 730
BT   Reference Materials
RT   Coordinate Indexes
     Dictionaries
     Glossaries
     Indexes
     Indexing
     Information Retrieval
     Lexicography
     Subject Index Terms
     Vocabulary

Theses   *MAR. 1980*
Postings: 89   GC: 720
SN   Propositions that are advanced and de-

fended by argument, and which may be
based on original research and used to
satisfy academic degree requirements
(Note: Corresponds to Pubtype code
040—do not use except as the subject of
a document)
NT   Doctoral Dissertations
     Masters Theses
BT   Reports
RT   Essays
     Expository Writing
     Research

Thinking Aloud Protocols
USE   Protocol Analysis

Thinking Processes
USE   Cognitive Processes

Thinking Skills   *APR. 1990*
Postings: 4,972   GC: 110
SN   Interrelated, generally "higher-order" cog-
     nitive skills that enable human beings to
     comprehend experiences and informa-
     tion, apply knowledge, express complex
     concepts, make decisions, criticize and
     revise unsuitable constructs, and solve
     problems—used frequently for a cogni-
     tive approach to learning that views ex-
     plicit "thinking skills" at the teachable
     level
UF   Cognitive Skills
     Higher Order Skills
     Reasoning Skills
BT   Cognitive Ability
     Skills
RT   Abstract Reasoning
     Basic Skills
     Cognitive Development
     Cognitive Processes
     Cognitive Style
     Communication Skills
     Comprehension
     Concept Formation
     Convergent Thinking
     Creative Thinking
     Critical Thinking
     Decision Making
     Decision Making Skills
     Deduction
     Divergent Thinking
     Evaluative Thinking
     Induction
     Interpretive Skills
     Intuition
     Language Skills
     Learning Modalities
     Learning Processes
     Learning Strategies
     Listening Skills
     Logical Thinking
     Mathematics Skills
     Mental Computation
     Metacognition
     Problem Solving
     Productive Thinking
     Reading Skills
     Research Skills
     Science Process Skills
     Skill Development
     Study Skills
     Visualization
     Writing Skills

Third World Countries
USE   Developing Nations

Thought Processes (1966 1980)
USE   Cognitive Processes

Three Dimensional Aids   *JUL. 1966*
Postings: 206   GC: 720
BT   Visual Aids
RT   Audiovisual Aids
     Display Aids
     Exhibits
     Holography

= Two or more Descriptors are used to represent this term.
The term's main entry shows the appropriate coordination.

Models
Realia

Three Year Bachelors Degrees
USE   Acceleration (Education)
AND   Bachelors Degrees

Threshold Level (Languages)   OCT. 1980
      Postings: 32   GC: 450
SN   The minimum level of foreign language
      proficiency needed for learners to com-
      municate in most everyday situations,
      including situations for which they have
      not been specifically trained—emphasis
      is on oral skills and listening com-
      prehension—objectives for reading and
      writing skills are narrowly restricted
BT   Communicative Competence
      (Languages)
      Language Proficiency
RT   Second Language Learning

Tibetan   JUL. 1966
      Postings: 14   GC: 440
BT   Sino Tibetan Languages

Timber Based Industry
USE   Lumber Industry

Time   JUL. 1966
      Postings: 1,296   GC: 490
NT   Time Blocks
BT   Scientific Concepts
RT   Distance
      Horology
      Intervals
      Obsolescence
      Proximity
      Relativity
      Space
      Time Factors (Learning)
      Time Management
      Timed Tests

Time Allocation
USE   Time Management

Time Blocks   JUL. 1966
      Postings: 343   GC: 350
SN   (Note: Prior to Aug96, this concept was a
      narrower term of "School Schedules,"
      and its usage generally was reserved for
      that context—"Block Scheduling" has
      replaced it in the "School Schedules"
      hierarchy)
BT   Time
RT   Block Scheduling
      Flexible Scheduling
      Scheduling
      School Schedules
      Time Factors (Learning)

Time Estimation
USE   Time Management

Time Factors (Learning)   JUL. 1966
      Postings: 2,833   GC: 110
BT   Influences
RT   Alternate Day Schedules
      Block Scheduling
      Conceptual Tempo
      Extended School Day
      Extended School Year
      Full Day Half Day Schedules
      Learning
      Pacing
      Program Length
      Reaction Time
      Scheduling
      Teaching Machines
      Time
      Time Blocks
      Time Management
      Time on Task
      Time Perspective

Time to Degree
Wait Time

Time Management   JUN. 1983
      Postings: 1,749   GC: 310
SN   Use or allocation of time by individuals
      or groups—can include strategies for
      estimating and budgeting time to im-
      prove effectiveness
UF   Time Allocation
      Time Estimation
      Time Use Data
      Time Utilization
BT   Administration
RT   Efficiency
      Pacing
      Performance
      Planning
      Scheduling
      Self Management
      Time
      Time Factors (Learning)
      Time on Task
      Time Perspective
      Timed Tests

Time on Task   NOV. 1981
      Postings: 1,282   GC: 310
SN   The period of time during which a stu-
      dent is actively engaged in a learning
      activity (Note: Prior to Oct81, this con-
      cept was frequently indexed under "Time
      Factors (Learning)")
UF   Academic Learning Time
      Engaged Time (Learning)
      Student Engaged Time
RT   Attention
      Learning Activities
      Performance
      Persistence
      Student Behavior
      Study
      Time Factors (Learning)
      Time Management

Time Perspective   JUL. 1966
      Postings: 746   GC: 110
UF   Temporal Perspective
RT   Tenses (Grammar)
      Time Factors (Learning)
      Time Management

Time Sharing   JUL. 1966
      Postings: 323   GC: 710
SN   Computing technique in which numer-
      ous terminal devices can utilize a central
      computer concurrently for input, proc-
      essing, and output functions
UF   Shared Time (Computers)
BT   Data Processing
RT   Computers
      Input Output
      Online Systems

Time Shortened Degree Programs
USE   Acceleration (Education)

Time to Degree   APR. 1998
      Postings: 141   GC: 350
SN   Total length of time between original
      enrollment to completion of all require-
      ments for a postsecondary degree
UF   Degree Completion Time
RT   Academic Persistence
      Acceleration (Education)
      Degree Requirements
      Degrees (Academic)
      Program Length
      Time Factors (Learning)

Time Use Data
USE   Time Management

Time Utilization
USE   Time Management

Timed Tests   JUL. 1966
      Postings: 268   GC: 830
SN   Tests that must be completed within a
      given period of time, usually scored on
      the basis of the number of items com-
      pleted correctly
UF   Rate Tests
      Speed Tests
BT   Tests
RT   Test Length
      Testing
      Time
      Time Management

Timeout   OCT. 1972
      Postings: 158   GC: 110
SN   Period of time in which no positive rein-
      forcers are available, e.g., isolation in a
      small room
BT   Reinforcement
RT   Behavior Modification
      Contingency Management
      Extinction (Psychology)
      Operant Conditioning

Timetables
USE   Scheduling

Timetables (School)
USE   School Schedules

Timidity
USE   Shyness

Tissue Donors   OCT. 1982
      Postings: 21   GC: 210
SN   Individuals who donate blood, sperm,
      organs, etc., for medical and health use
UF   Blood Donors
      Organ Donors
      Sperm Donors
BT   Groups
RT   Medical Services
      Physical Health

Title Word Indexes
USE   Permuted Indexes

Tobacco   JUL. 1966
      Postings: 477   GC: 210
BT   Field Crops
RT   Health Behavior
      Health Education
      Smoking
      Stimulants
      Substance Abuse

Toddlers   OCT. 1984
      Postings: 2,193   GC: 120
SN   Approximately 1–3 years of age
BT   Young Children
RT   Infants
      Preschool Children

Tohono O Odham People   DEC. 1995
      Postings: 3   GC: 560
SN   A desert-dwelling American Indian peo-
      ple of southern Arizona and the province
      of Sonora in northwest Mexico (also,
      dispersed kin)
UF   Papago (Tribe)
BT   American Indians
      Tribes
RT   Papago

Toilet Facilities   APR. 1970
      Postings: 43   GC: 920
UF   Bathrooms
      Restrooms
      Washrooms
BT   Sanitary Facilities
RT   Public Facilities
      Toilet Training

Toilet Learning
USE   Toilet Training

Toilet Training   OCT. 1999
      Postings: 74   GC: 210
SN   Process of teaching a child or disabled
      individual to control bladder and bowel
      functions and use the toilet
UF   Potty Training
      Toilet Learning
BT   Training
RT   Hygiene
      Self Care Skills
      Toilet Facilities

Token Economy   OCT. 1982
      Postings: 171   GC: 110
SN   Planned reinforcement programs in which
      individuals earn tokens or points for
      performing desired behaviors—these to-
      kens or points can then be exchanged for
      a variety of rewards or privileges
BT   Reinforcement
RT   Behavior Modification
      Contingency Management
      Incentives
      Operant Conditioning
      Psychoeducational Methods
      Rewards
      Therapeutic Environment

Token Integration (1966 1980)
USE   Tokenism

Tokenism   MAR. 1980
      Postings: 91   GC: 540
SN   Superficial efforts or symbolic gestures
      toward complying with desegregation or
      equal opportunity laws, rulings, or guide-
      lines
UF   Token Integration (1966 1980)
RT   Affirmative Action
      De Facto Segregation
      Equal Education
      Equal Opportunities (Jobs)
      Neighborhood Integration
      Personnel Integration
      Racial Balance
      Racial Composition
      Racial Integration
      School Desegregation
      Sex Fairness
      Social Integration

Tone Languages   JUL. 1966
      Postings: 227   GC: 450
SN   Languages in which tone or pitch pat-
      terns form part of the structure of words
      rather than sentences (Note: See African
      and Sino-Tibetan language families for
      specific languages)
BT   Language
RT   Descriptive Linguistics
      Intonation
      Language Typology
      Morphophonemics

Tool and Die Makers   AUG. 1969
      Postings: 45   GC: 640
SN   Workers responsible for constructing,
      repairing, maintaining, and calibrating
      machine-shop tools, jigs and fixtures,
      gauges, and metal-forming dies
BT   Machinists
RT   Machine Tool Operators
      Machine Tools
      Machinery Industry
      Metal Working

Topography   MAR. 1980
      Postings: 126   GC: 480
SN   Science of compiling detailed descrip-
      tions of areas, especially graphic repre-
      sentations of physical configurations
      which include features of both natural
      and human origin
BT   Social Sciences

= Two or more Descriptors are used to represent this term.
The term's main entry shows the appropriate coordination.

RT　Cartography
　　Demography
　　Earth Science
　　Geographic Location
　　Geography
　　Maps
　　Social Scientists

Topology　　　　　　　　　　　　　*OCT. 1968*
　　Postings: 147　　　　　　　　　　GC: 480
SN　Study of the properties of geometric
　　forms that remain constant under such
　　transformations as bending or stretch-
　　ing
BT　Geometry
RT　Algebra
　　Distance
　　Graphs
　　Proximity
　　Vectors (Mathematics)

Tornadoes　　　　　　　　　　　　*NOV. 1995*
　　Postings: 31　　　　　　　　　　GC: 490
SN　Violently rotating storms, usually visible
　　as funnel clouds, with wind speeds of
　　100–200 mph and causing considerable
　　destruction when touching ground—
　　most common in the U.S. and Australia
BT　Weather
RT　Hurricanes
　　Natural Disasters
　　Wind (Meteorology)

Torts　　　　　　　　　　　　　　*JAN. 1978*
　　Postings: 364　　　　　　　　　　GC: 610
SN　Private or civil wrongs, not including
　　breach of contract, for which perpetra-
　　tors may be legally prosecuted and in-
　　jured parties may be compensated
RT　Civil Disobedience
　　Civil Law
　　Civil Rights
　　Constitutional Law
　　Court Litigation
　　Educational Malpractice
　　Justice
　　Laws
　　Legal Problems
　　Legal Responsibility
　　Libel and Slander
　　Malpractice
　　Negligence

Total Communication　　　　　　　*JUL. 1977*
　　Postings: 260　　　　　　　　　　GC: 220
SN　Use of all available forms of communica-
　　tion, i.e., aural, manual, and oral, to
　　develop language competence and en-
　　sure effective communication—usually
　　with and among the hearing impaired
BT　Augmentative and Alternative Commu-
　　nication
RT　Communication Aids (for Disabled)
　　Communication Skills
　　Deafness
　　Finger Spelling
　　Hearing Aids
　　Hearing Impairments
　　Hearing Therapy
　　Lipreading
　　Manual Communication
　　Oral Communication Method
　　Partial Hearing
　　Sign Language
　　Speech Skills
　　Verbal Communication

Total Quality Management　　　　　*MAY 1994*
　　Postings: 869　　　　　　　　　　GC: 320
SN　Management approach to long-term suc-
　　cess through customer satisfaction
　　(based on concepts developed by W.
　　Edwards Deming and Joseph M. Juran)—
　　TQM involves all members of an organi-
　　zation in continuously improving proc-
　　esses, products, and services
UF　TQM
BT　Administration
　　Management Systems

RT　Employer Employee Relationship
　　Management Teams
　　Organizational Development
　　Participative Decision Making
　　Quality Circles
　　Quality Control
　　Teamwork

Totalitarianism　　　　　　　　　*OCT. 1974*
　　Postings: 98　　　　　　　　　　GC: 610
UF　Dictatorship
NT　Nazism
RT　Authoritarianism
　　Communism
　　Democracy
　　Dogmatism
　　Fascism
　　Government (Administrative Body)
　　Political Attitudes
　　Political Power
　　Political Science

Tourism　　　　　　　　　　　　*NOV. 1969*
　　Postings: 491　　　　　　　　　　GC: 650
UF　Sightseeing Industry
　　Tourist Industry
BT　Industry
RT　Camping
　　Hospitality Occupations
　　Hotels
　　Outdoor Activities
　　Recreational Activities
　　Study Abroad
　　Transportation
　　Travel

Tourist Courts
USE　Hotels

Tourist Industry
USE　Tourism

Tower Diving
USE　Diving

Towns
USE　Municipalities

Toxic Substances
USE　Poisons

Toxicology　　　　　　　　　　　*SEP. 1982*
　　Postings: 103　　　　　　　　　　GC: 210
SN　Science dealing with the nature, effects,
　　and detection of poisonous substances
　　and methods of treatment for poison
　　intake
BT　Medicine
RT　Allergy
　　Biochemistry
　　Medical Services
　　Pathology
　　Pharmacology
　　Physiology
　　Poisoning
　　Poisons
　　Radiation Biology

Toxins
USE　Poisons

Toys　　　　　　　　　　　　　　*JUL. 1966*
　　Postings: 836　　　　　　　　　　GC: 470
RT　Child Behavior
　　Childrens Games
　　Games
　　Instructional Materials
　　Play
　　Puzzles
　　Video Games

TQM
USE　Total Quality Management

Track and Field　　　　　　　　　*DEC. 1975*
　　Postings: 90　　　　　　　　　　GC: 470
BT　Athletics
RT　Lifetime Sports
　　Olympic Games
　　Running

Track System (Education)　　　　　*MAR. 1980*
　　Postings: 671　　　　　　　　　　GC: 330
SN　System whereby students of the same
　　chronological age or grade level are as-
　　signed to different classes, programs, or
　　schools (e.g., college preparatory pro-
　　grams vs. vocational programs) on the
　　basis of perceived ability, achievement
　　level, career/vocational choice, etc. (Note:
　　Prior to Mar80, the term "Flexible Pro-
　　gression" was used for this concept)
RT　Ability Grouping
　　Student Placement

Tracking (1968 1980)　　　　　　*JUN. 1980*
　　Postings: 65　　　　　　　　　　GC: 330
SN　Invalid Descriptor—used indiscriminately
　　in indexing—see more precise Descrip-
　　tors "Track System (Education)," "Per-
　　ceptual Motor Coordination," and
　　"Psychomotor Skills," as well as the
　　Identifier "Tracking (Science)"

Tractors　　　　　　　　　　　　*JUL. 1966*
　　Postings: 57　　　　　　　　　　GC: 410
BT　Motor Vehicles
RT　Agricultural Machinery
　　Agriculture

Trade and Industrial Education　　　*JUL. 1966*
　　Postings: 3,085　　　　　　　　　GC: 400
SN　Formal preparation for a wide range of
　　trades and occupations in industry at the
　　semiskilled, skilled, or supervisory lev-
　　els
UF　Vocational Industrial Education
BT　Vocational Education
RT　Adult Vocational Education
　　Apprenticeships
　　Blue Collar Occupations
　　Building Trades
　　Data Processing Occupations
　　Electrical Occupations
　　Industrial Arts
　　Industrial Education
　　Industrial Personnel
　　Industrial Training
　　Mechanical Skills
　　On the Job Training
　　School Shops
　　Semiskilled Occupations
　　Semiskilled Workers
　　Service Occupations
　　Service Workers
　　Skilled Occupations
　　Skilled Workers
　　Technical Education
　　Technical Occupations
　　Technology
　　Technology Education
　　Trade and Industrial Teachers
　　Two Year Colleges

Trade and Industrial Teachers　　　*JUL. 1966*
　　Postings: 192　　　　　　　　　　GC: 360
BT　Vocational Education Teachers
RT　Industrial Arts Teachers
　　Industrial Education
　　Trade and Industrial Education

Trade Unions
USE　Unions

Traditional Classrooms
USE　Self Contained Classrooms

Traditional Family Unit
USE　Nuclear Family

Traditional Grammar　　　　　　　*JUL. 1966*
　　Postings: 285　　　　　　　　　　GC: 450
BT　Linguistic Theory
RT　Form Classes (Languages)
　　Grammar
　　Linguistics
　　Morphology (Languages)
　　Paragraphs
　　Sentence Structure
　　Structural Grammar
　　Syntax
　　Transformational Generative Grammar

Traditional Instruction
USE　Conventional Instruction

Traditional Schools　　　　　　　*JUL. 1966*
　　Postings: 400　　　　　　　　　　GC: 340
SN　Schools characterized by a conventional,
　　non-innovative approach to education
BT　Schools
RT　Back to Basics
　　Conventional Instruction
　　Educational Philosophy
　　Nontraditional Education
　　School Organization
　　Self Contained Classrooms
　　Transitional Schools

Traditionalism　　　　　　　　　*JUN. 1983*
　　Postings: 498　　　　　　　　　　GC: 520
SN　Disposition to accept or adhere to the
　　values, practices, and institutions of past
　　generations
RT　Conservatism
　　Cultural Influences
　　Cultural Maintenance
　　Ethnicity
　　Modernization
　　Philosophy
　　Religion
　　Resistance to Change
　　Social Attitudes
　　Social Change
　　Social History
　　Sociocultural Patterns
　　Socioeconomic Influences
　　Values

Traditions (Culture)
USE　Folk Culture

Traffic Accidents　　　　　　　　*JUL. 1966*
　　Postings: 257　　　　　　　　　　GC: 210
BT　Accidents
RT　Driving While Intoxicated
　　Safety
　　Safety Education
　　Traffic Control
　　Traffic Safety

Traffic Circulation　　　　　　　*OCT. 1968*
　　Postings: 128　　　　　　　　　　GC: 920
UF　Street Layouts
　　Traffic Flow
　　Traffic Patterns (1968 1980)
RT　Driveways
　　Motor Vehicles
　　Parking Controls
　　Parking Facilities
　　Pedestrian Traffic
　　Road Construction
　　Service Vehicles
　　Student Transportation
　　Traffic Control
　　Vehicular Traffic

Traffic Control　　　　　　　　　*OCT. 1968*
　　Postings: 183　　　　　　　　　　GC: 920
UF　Spectator Traffic Control
　　Traffic Regulations (1968 1980)
　　Traffic Signs (1968 1980) #
NT　Air Traffic Control
RT　Motor Vehicles
　　Parking Controls
　　Parking Facilities
　　Pedestrian Traffic

= Two or more Descriptors are used to represent this term.
The term's main entry shows the appropriate coordination.

Signs
Traffic Accidents
Traffic Circulation
Traffic Safety
Transportation
Vehicular Traffic

Traffic Flow
USE   Traffic Circulation

Traffic Patterns (1968 1980)
USE   Traffic Circulation

Traffic Regulations (1968 1980)
USE   Traffic Control

Traffic Safety   *JUL. 1966*
     Postings: 664   GC: 210
BT   Safety
RT   Child Safety
     Driver Education
     Motor Vehicles
     Restraints (Vehicle Safety)
     Safety Education
     Traffic Accidents
     Traffic Control

Traffic Signs (1968 1980)
USE   Signs
AND   Traffic Control

Tragedy   *JUL. 1966*
     Postings: 123   GC: 430
BT   Drama
RT   Comedy
     Literary Devices
     Literary Genres
     Poetry
     Prose
     Scripts

Trails   *NOV. 1969*
     Postings: 162   GC: 920
UF   Nature Trails
     Pathways
BT   Facilities
RT   Adventure Education
     Camping
     Conservation Education
     Landscaping
     Orienteering
     Outdoor Education
     Park Design
     Parks
     Playgrounds
     Recreational Facilities
     Walking

Trainable Mentally Handicapped (1967 1980)
USE   Moderate Mental Retardation

Trainees   *JUL. 1966*
     Postings: 446   GC: 630
SN   Participants in vocational, administra-
     tive, or technical training programs for
     purpose of developing job related skills
BT   Groups
RT   Apprenticeships
     Industrial Training
     Job Training
     Students
     Training
     Training Methods
     Work Experience Programs

Trainers   *JUL. 1966*
     Postings: 1,048   GC: 630
SN   Persons who direct the practice of skills
     toward immediate improvement in some
     art or task
BT   Personnel
RT   Adult Educators
     Industrial Training

Laboratory Training
Leadership Training
Teachers
Training
Training Methods

Training   *JUL. 1966*
     Postings: 5,851   GC: 330
SN   Instructional process aimed at the acqui-
     sition of defined skills relating to particu-
     lar functions or activities (Note: Use a
     more specific term if possible)
NT   Counselor Training
     Cross Cultural Training
     Flight Training
     Industrial Training
     Job Training
     Laboratory Training
     Leadership Training
     Military Training
     Professional Training
     Retraining
     Sensitivity Training
     Sensory Training
     Supervisory Training
     Team Training
     Toilet Training
     Travel Training
     Volunteer Training
RT   Career Ladders
     Education
     Performance Technology
     Skill Development
     Trainees
     Trainers
     Training Allowances
     Training Methods
     Training Objectives
     Transfer of Training

Training Allowances   *JUL. 1966*
     Postings: 171   GC: 620
BT   Financial Support
RT   Adult Education
     Educational Finance
     Federal Aid
     Grants
     Industrial Training
     Job Training
     Labor Force Development
     State Aid
     Training
     Tuition Grants
     Veterans Education

Training Alternatives
USE   Nontraditional Education

Training Goals
USE   Training Objectives

Training Laboratories (1967 1980)
                                                      MAR. 1980
     Postings: 159   GC: 920
SN   Invalid Descriptor used inconsistently
     —coordinate "Laboratories" or its nar-
     rower terms with specific "training"
     Descriptors (e.g., "Sensitivity Training,"
     "Job Training," "Leadership Training,"
     "Laboratory Training," etc.)

Training Methods   *MAR. 1980*
     Postings: 6,961   GC: 310
SN   Standard procedures or approaches de-
     signed to help individuals or groups ac-
     quire the skills needed for specific activi-
     ties or functions
UF   Training Techniques (1967 1980)
NT   Management Games
     Microcounseling
     Microteaching
BT   Teaching Methods
RT   Institutes (Training Programs)
     Skill Development
     Trainees
     Trainers
     Training
     Training Objectives

Work Experience Programs
Workshops

Training Objectives   *JUL. 1966*
     Postings: 1,723   GC: 310
UF   Training Goals
BT   Objectives
RT   Behavioral Objectives
     Performance Technology
     Training
     Training Methods

Training Opportunities
USE   Educational Opportunities

Training Schools (Juvenile Offenders)
USE   Correctional Institutions

Training Techniques (1967 1980)
USE   Training Methods

Trait Treatment Interaction
USE   Aptitude Treatment Interaction

Tranquilizing Drugs
USE   Sedatives

Transactional Analysis   *APR. 1982*
     Postings: 133   GC: 240
SN   Psychotherapeutic approach that postu-
     lates three ego states (adult, parent, and
     child) from which all human interaction
     or communication emanates—the ap-
     proach maintains that awareness or
     knowledge of the three states leads to
     more constructive interpersonal relations
BT   Psychotherapy
RT   Communication Skills
     Counseling Techniques
     Group Dynamics
     Group Therapy
     Interpersonal Competence
     Laboratory Training
     Self Evaluation (Individuals)
     Self Expression
     Social Behavior
     Social Cognition

Transcendental Meditation   *OCT. 1982*
     Postings: 46   GC: 110
SN   A meditative technique, developed by
     Maharishi Mahesh Yogi, using the repe-
     tition of a specific sound (mantra) to
     induce a state of mental neutrality (ab-
     sence of extraneous thought) and mysti-
     cal insight
BT   Meditation
RT   Behavior Modification
     Biofeedback
     Creative Thinking
     Psychoeducational Methods
     Relaxation Training

Transcripts (Academic)
USE   Academic Records

Transfer of Learning
USE   Transfer of Training

Transfer of Training   *JUL. 1966*
     Postings: 2,794   GC: 110
SN   The influence that an existing habit, skill,
     or idea exerts on the acquisition, per-
     formance, or relearning of another simi-
     lar characteristic
UF   Transfer of Learning
BT   Learning
RT   Diffusion (Communication)
     Generalization
     Learning Strategies
     Skill Development
     Training

Transfer Policy   *JUL. 1966*
     Postings: 809   GC: 330
SN   A formal plan or set of principles regard-
     ing the transfer of individuals from one
     institution or program to another and the
     granting of credit for past experience
BT   Policy
RT   Admission Criteria
     Articulation (Education)
     Attendance
     College Credits
     Credits
     Enrollment
     Free Choice Transfer Programs
     Prior Learning
     Relocation
     School Policy
     Teacher Transfer
     Transfer Programs
     Transfer Rates (College)
     Transfer Students

Transfer Programs   *JUL. 1966*
     Postings: 759   GC: 330
SN   Programs that yield credit to new stu-
     dents or employees for prior learning
     and/or experience
UF   Restrictive Transfer Programs (1966
     1980)
NT   Free Choice Transfer Programs
BT   Programs
RT   Articulation (Education)
     College Credits
     Credits
     Experience
     Job Placement
     Prior Learning
     Relocation
     Student Placement
     Teacher Transfer
     Terminal Education
     Transfer Policy
     Transfer Rates (College)
     Transfer Students

Transfer Rates (College)   *JAN. 1998*
     Postings: 155   GC: 330
SN   Percentages of students who have trans-
     ferred from one institution of higher edu-
     cation to another (calculation varies, de-
     pending on the definition of transfer
     utilized)
UF   College Transfer Rates
BT   Incidence
RT   Articulation (Education)
     College Transfer Students
     Transfer Policy
     Transfer Programs
     Two Year Colleges

Transfer Students   *JUL. 1966*
     Postings: 1,258   GC: 360
SN   Students transferring from one school
     or educational program to another (Note:
     If applicable, use the more specific term
     "College Transfer Students")
UF   Student Transfers
NT   College Transfer Students
BT   Students
RT   Attendance
     Continuation Students
     Educational Mobility
     Enrollment
     Free Choice Transfer Programs
     Migrant Children
     Migrant Youth
     Prior Learning
     Racially Balanced Schools
     School Desegregation
     Student Mobility
     Transfer Policy
     Transfer Programs
     Transient Children

Transfers (1966 1980)   *MAR. 1980*
     Postings: 119   GC: 320
SN   Invalid Descriptor—see "Relocation" and
     other "Transfer" Descriptors

= Two or more Descriptors are used to represent this term.
The term's main entry shows the appropriate coordination.

Transformation Generative Grammar (1968 1980)
USE   Transformational Generative Grammar

Transformation Theory (Adult Learning)
USE   Learning Theories
AND   Transformative Learning

Transformation Theory (Language) (1967 1980)
USE   Linguistic Theory
AND   Transformational Generative Grammar

Transformational Generative Grammar
                                                    MAR. 1980
         Postings: 1,425   GC: 450
SN   A generative grammar consisting of syn-
     tactic, phonological, and semantic com-
     ponents in which transformational rules
     are used to relate the surface structures
     and deep structures of sentences (Note:
     Prior to Mar80, the use of this term was
     not restricted by a Scope Note)
UF   Generative Transformational Grammar
     Transformation Generative Grammar
       (1968 1980)
     Transformation Theory (Language)
       (1967 1980) #
     Transformational Grammar
     Transformations (Language) (1967
       1980)
NT   Context Free Grammar
     Deep Structure
     Kernel Sentences
     Sentence Combining
     Surface Structure
BT   Generative Grammar
RT   Phrase Structure
     Syntax
     Traditional Grammar

Transformational Geometry
USE   Transformations (Mathematics)

Transformational Grammar
USE   Transformational Generative Grammar

Transformational Sentence Combining
USE   Sentence Combining

Transformations (Adult Learning)
USE   Transformative Learning

Transformations (Language) (1967 1980)
USE   Transformational Generative Grammar

Transformations (Mathematics)   FEB. 1970
         Postings: 304   GC: 480
SN   Substitution of one mathematical con-
     figuration or expression by another in
     accord with a mathematical rule
UF   Similarity Transformations
     Transformational Geometry
RT   Algebra
     Congruence (Mathematics)
     Correlation
     Factor Analysis
     Functions (Mathematics)
     Geometry
     Mathematical Concepts
     Oblique Rotation
     Orthogonal Rotation

Transformative Learning   JUN. 2000
         Postings: 96   GC: 110
SN   Learning by reflecting critically on one's
     own experiences, assumptions, beliefs,
     feelings, and mental perspectives in or-
     der to construe new or revised inter-
     pretations—often associated with adult
     learning
UF   Perspective Transformation
     Transformation Theory (Adult Learn-
       ing) #

Transformations (Adult Learning)
BT   Learning
RT   Adult Development
     Adult Education
     Adult Learning
     Andragogy
     Critical Thinking
     Learning Processes
     Learning Theories
     Lifelong Learning

Transhumance
USE   Nomads

Transient Children   JUL. 1966
         Postings: 117   GC: 510
SN   Children who move frequently with their
     families from one semi-permanent loca-
     tion to another—includes children of
     military personnel, construction work-
     ers, gypsies, etc. (Note: Do not confuse
     with "Migrant Children")
BT   Children
     Migrants
RT   Immigrants
     Migration
     Nomads
     Student Mobility
     Transfer Students

Transistors   SEP. 1969
         Postings: 51   GC: 910
BT   Semiconductor Devices
RT   Electricity
     Electronics
     Instrumentation
     Microelectronics

Transitional Classes (1966 1981)
USE   Transitional Programs

Transitional Programs   NOV. 1981
         Postings: 2,710   GC: 340
SN   Special classes, courses, or other pro-
     grams designed to prepare individuals to
     move from one grade, school, or activity
     to the next
UF   Transitional Classes (1966 1981)
BT   Programs
RT   Acceleration (Education)
     Admission (School)
     College Preparation
     Community Based Instruction (Disa-
       bilities)
     Compensatory Education
     Developmental Studies Programs
     Educationally Disadvantaged
     Grouping (Instructional Purposes)
     High Risk Students
     Mainstreaming
     Remedial Instruction
     Remedial Programs
     Resource Room Programs
     Special Classes
     Student Placement
     Student Promotion
     Summer Schools
     Supplementary Education

Transitional Schools   JUL. 1966
         Postings: 31   GC: 340
SN   Schools undergoing administrative, pro-
     cedural, or philosophical change
BT   Schools
RT   Educational Change
     Educational Philosophy
     Experimental Schools
     Nontraditional Education
     Open Education
     School Organization
     School Restructuring
     Traditional Schools

Translation   JUL. 1966
         Postings: 1,933   GC: 450
SN   One language to another
UF   Free Translation

NT   Deaf Interpreting
     Machine Translation
RT   Grammar Translation Method
     Interpreters
     Interpretive Skills
     Language Arts
     Language Skills

Translators
USE   Interpreters

Transparencies   JUL. 1966
         Postings: 875   GC: 720
SN   Visual materials that are viewed using
     transmitted light
UF   Overhead Transparencies
NT   Slides
BT   Nonprint Media
     Visual Aids
RT   Audiovisual Aids
     Films

Transparency Projectors
USE   Overhead Projectors

Transplanting (1968 1980)
USE   Horticulture

Transportation   JUL. 1966
         Postings: 1,579   GC: 650
UF   Migrant Transportation (1966 1980) #
NT   Air Transportation
     Bus Transportation
     Rail Transportation
     Student Transportation
RT   Distance
     Distributive Education
     Mobile Classrooms
     Motor Vehicles
     Proximity
     Public Facilities
     Road Construction
     Technology Education
     Tourism
     Traffic Control
     Travel
     Vehicular Traffic

Transracial Adoption   AUG. 1988
         Postings: 74   GC: 520
UF   Interracial Adoption
BT   Adoption
RT   Adopted Children
     Adoptive Parents
     Ethnicity
     Race
     Racial Identification

Trash
USE   Solid Wastes

Traumatic Brain Injury
USE   Head Injuries
AND   Neurological Impairments

Travel   JUL. 1969
         Postings: 883   GC: 550
UF   Student Travel
     Teacher Travel
BT   Activities
RT   Field Trips
     Motor Vehicles
     Outdoor Activities
     Recreational Activities
     Study Abroad
     Tourism
     Transportation
     Travel Training

Travel Training   JUL. 1966
         Postings: 213   GC: 220
SN   Process of teaching a disabled person to
     move freely in his/her environment
BT   Training

RT   Daily Living Skills
     Echolocation
     Mobility Aids
     Physical Disabilities
     Physical Mobility
     Travel
     Visual Impairments
     Visually Impaired Mobility
     Walking

Traveling Teachers
USE   Itinerant Teachers

Treaties   JUL. 1973
         Postings: 435   GC: 610
SN   Negotiated agreements between two or
     more political authorities (e.g., states,
     sovereign nations)
RT   American Indian Reservations
     Federal Government
     Federal Indian Relationship
     Federal Legislation
     International Law
     International Relations
     Legal Responsibility
     Peace
     Political Divisions (Geographic)
     Tribal Sovereignty
     Trust Responsibility (Government)
     War

Treatment Centers
USE   Clinics

Trees   JUL. 1966
         Postings: 320   GC: 410
UF   Shade Trees
BT   Plants (Botany)
RT   Agronomy
     Botany
     Forestry
     Ornamental Horticulture
     Rainforests
     Wildlife

Trend Analysis   NOV. 1970
         Postings: 11,039   GC: 820
SN   Use of a series of measurements of a
     variable, taken over a period of time, to
     determine a direction of change
BT   Data Analysis
RT   Agricultural Trends
     Comparative Analysis
     Educational Trends
     Employment Patterns
     Enrollment Trends
     Environmental Scanning
     Factor Analysis
     Futures (of Society)
     Long Range Planning
     Longitudinal Studies
     Migration Patterns
     Policy Analysis
     Population Trends
     Residential Patterns
     Social Indicators
     Sociocultural Patterns
     Statistical Analysis
     Statistical Data
     Strategic Planning
     Surveys

Trial by Jury
USE   Juries

Triangulation   AUG. 1994
         Postings: 68   GC: 820
SN   A research technique for increasing the
     validity of one's results by using multiple
     and diverse (at least three) collection
     methods or data sources, e.g., using
     both qualitative and quantitative meas-
     ures or obtaining perspectives from sev-
     eral different groups—also, occasionally
     refers to a procedure used in survey-
     ing and navigation to determine dis-
     tance (Note: Do not use for family trian-

= Two or more Descriptors are used to represent this term.
The term's main entry shows the appropriate coordination.

gulation—see the Identifier "Family Triangles" for that concept)
BT   Research Methodology
RT   Evaluation Methods
     Naturalistic Observation
     Qualitative Research
     Statistical Analysis
     Validity

Tribal Colleges
USE   Tribally Controlled Education

Tribal Government   *SEP. 1994*
     Postings: 171   GC: 610
SN   Includes the modern government(s) of
     American Indian tribes and Canada/Alaska
     native villages, as well as traditional/
     contemporary political institutions of tribal
     societies in general
BT   Government (Administrative Body)
RT   American Indian Reservations
     American Indians
     Federal Indian Relationship
     Local Government
     Tribal Sovereignty
     Tribally Controlled Education
     Tribes

Tribal Schools
USE   Tribally Controlled Education

Tribal Societies
USE   Tribes

Tribal Sovereignty   *OCT. 1979*
     Postings: 417   GC: 610
SN   The authority or right of tribal entities to
     exercise decision-making power and
     choice regarding their political, social,
     and cultural patterns
BT   Self Determination
RT   American Indian History
     American Indian Reservations
     American Indians
     Federal Government
     Federal Indian Relationship
     Federal Legislation
     Governance
     Government Role
     Local Government
     Treaties
     Tribal Government
     Tribally Controlled Education
     Tribes
     Trust Responsibility (Government)

Tribally Controlled Education   *MAY 1993*
     Postings: 365   GC: 340
SN   Educational ideologies, philosophies,
     theories, and practices specified by a
     native tribal government or other forms
     of native sovereignty, as well as educa-
     tional institutions managed by such au-
     thorities
UF   Contract Tribal Schools
     Indian Controlled Schools #
     Tribal Colleges
     Tribal Schools
BT   Education
RT   American Indian Education
     American Indian Reservations
     American Indians
     Community Control
     Community Schools
     Federal Indian Relationship
     Government School Relationship
     School Community Relationship
     Tribal Government
     Tribal Sovereignty
     Tribes

Tribes   *JAN. 1970*
     Postings: 1,603   GC: 560
UF   Tribal Societies
NT   Cherokee (Tribe)
     Chippewa (Tribe)
     Choctaw (Tribe)

Cree (Tribe)
Hopi (Tribe)
Iroquois (Tribe)
Navajo (Nation)
Sioux (Tribe)
Tohono O Odham People
Zuni (Tribe)
BT   Groups
RT   African Culture
     African History
     Alaska Natives
     American Indian Culture
     American Indian History
     American Indian Reservations
     American Indians
     Canada Natives
     Ethnic Groups
     Federal Indian Relationship
     Nomads
     Nonformal Education
     Tribal Government
     Tribal Sovereignty
     Tribally Controlled Education
     Trust Responsibility (Government)

Trigonometry   *JUN. 1969*
     Postings: 456   GC: 480
BT   Mathematics
RT   Calculus
     Mathematical Concepts
     Mathematical Enrichment
     Mathematical Vocabulary

Trimester Schedules (1966 1980)
USE   Trimester System

Trimester System   *MAR. 1980*
     Postings: 104   GC: 350
SN   Division of the academic year into three
     terms, usually but not always equal in
     length
UF   Trimester Schedules (1966 1980)
BT   School Schedules
RT   Extended School Year
     Quarter System
     Semester System
     Year Round Schools

Tropical Cyclones
USE   Hurricanes

Tropical Rainforests
USE   Rainforests

Troubadours
USE   Poets

Troubleshooting   *APR. 1990*
     Postings: 174   GC: 640
SN   Process of systematically diagnosing and
     correcting operational problems, e.g.,
     mechanical or technological malfunctions,
     environmental mishaps, workplace dis-
     ruptions, social impasses
NT   Debugging (Computers)
BT   Methods
RT   Equipment Maintenance
     Error Correction
     Evaluation
     Identification
     Maintenance
     Operations Research
     Problem Solving
     Repair

Truancy   *JUL. 1966*
     Postings: 402   GC: 330
UF   School Truancy
     Truant Officers #
RT   Attendance
     Attendance Patterns
     Continuation Students
     Dropouts
     Runaways
     School Holding Power
     Students

Truant Officers
USE   Attendance Officers
AND   Truancy

Truck Mechanics
USE   Auto Mechanics

True False Tests
USE   Objective Tests

True Measure
USE   True Scores

True Scores   *OCT. 1970*
     Postings: 287   GC: 820
SN   Value of an observation or measure which
     is free from error, the mean of an infinite
     number of observations
UF   True Measure
BT   Scores
RT   Cutting Scores
     Equated Scores
     Error of Measurement
     Generalizability Theory
     Guessing (Tests)
     Interrater Reliability
     Raw Scores
     Reliability
     Statistical Data
     Test Reliability

Trust (Psychology)   *DEC. 1985*
     Postings: 321   GC: 120
SN   Assured reliance in the character, ability,
     strength, or truth of some person, group,
     institution, idea, or thing
BT   Attitudes
RT   Beliefs
     Cooperation
     Credibility
     Group Unity
     Honesty
     Interpersonal Relationship
     Love
     Psychological Patterns
     Rapport
     Security (Psychology)

Trust Funds
USE   Trusts (Financial)

Trust Responsibility (Government)
                                         OCT. 1979
     Postings: 172   GC: 610
SN   A central government's legal responsi-
     bility to safeguard the interests of peo-
     ples under its jurisdiction, especially the
     inhabitants of territories that are not yet
     fully self-governing nations or states
BT   Legal Responsibility
RT   American Indian Education
     American Indian Reservations
     American Indians
     Eskimos
     Federal Government
     Federal Indian Relationship
     Government Role
     Puerto Ricans
     Samoan Americans
     Self Determination
     Treaties
     Tribal Sovereignty
     Tribes

Trustees   *JUL. 1966*
     Postings: 1,363   GC: 360
SN   Members of governing boards
UF   Regents
BT   Administrators
RT   Board Candidates
     Boards of Education
     Educational Administration
     Endowment Funds
     Estate Planning
     Governance

Governing Boards
Trusts (Financial)

Trusts (Financial)   *SEP. 1969*
     Postings: 199   GC: 620
SN   Property or finances held by one party
     for the benefit of another
UF   Charitable Trusts
     Trust Funds
RT   Capital
     Donors
     Endowment Funds
     Estate Planning
     Finance Occupations
     Financial Services
     Financial Support
     Fund Raising
     Income
     Investment
     Money Management
     Ownership
     Philanthropic Foundations
     Property Accounting
     Property Appraisal
     Resource Allocation
     Trustees
     Wills

Trustworthiness
USE   Credibility

Truthfulness
USE   Honesty

Tuition   *JUL. 1966*
     Postings: 2,063   GC: 620
UF   Tuition Tax Credits #
BT   Fees
     Instructional Student Costs
RT   Free Education
     In State Students
     Out of State Students
     School Choice
     Student Costs
     Student Financial Aid
     Student Loan Programs
     Tax Credits
     Tuition Grants

Tuition Grants   *JUL. 1966*
     Postings: 321   GC: 620
SN   Grants awarded solely for tuition ex-
     penses
BT   Grants
     Scholarships
RT   Educational Vouchers
     Instructional Student Costs
     Merit Scholarships
     Scholarship Funds
     Training Allowances
     Tuition

Tuition Postponement
USE   Income Contingent Loans

Tuition Tax Credits
USE   Tax Credits
AND   Tuition

Tumbling   *JUL. 1966*
     Postings: 19   GC: 470
UF   Stunts and Tumbling
BT   Gymnastics

Tumors (Malignant)
USE   Cancer

Tupi Guarani
USE   Guarani

Turf Management   *JUL. 1966*
     Postings: 138   GC: 410
UF   Lawn Maintenance

= Two or more Descriptors are used to represent this term.
The term's main entry shows the appropriate coordination.

BT Ornamental Horticulture
RT Grounds Keepers
    Land Use
    Landscaping

Turkic Languages   *JUL. 1966*
    Postings: 25   GC: 440
NT Azerbaijani
    Bashkir
    Chuvash
    Kyrgyz
    Tatar
    Turkish
    Uzbek
    Yakut
BT Uralic Altaic Languages

Turkish   *JUL. 1966*
    Postings: 138   GC: 440
BT Turkic Languages

Turnkey Building
USE Design Build Approach

Turnkey Systems (Libraries)
USE Integrated Library Systems

Tutorial Instruction
USE Tutoring

Tutorial Plans
USE Tutorial Programs

Tutorial Programs   *JUL. 1966*
    Postings: 1,858   GC: 310
SN Programs, established by educational
    institutions, to tutor selected students
    (Note: Prior to Mar80, this term was not
    scoped and was occasionally used for
    programs to train tutors)
UF Tutorial Plans
    Tutorial Services
BT Programs
RT Cross Age Teaching
    Grouping (Instructional Purposes)
    Individual Instruction
    Intelligent Tutoring Systems
    Peer Teaching
    Remedial Instruction
    Teaching Methods
    Tutoring
    Tutors

Tutorial Services
USE Tutorial Programs

Tutoring   *JUL. 1966*
    Postings: 2,867   GC: 310
SN Instruction provided to a learner, or small
    group of learners, by direct interaction
    with a professional teacher, a peer, or
    another individual with appropriate train-
    ing or experience
UF After School Tutoring (1966 1980) #
    Peer Tutoring #
    Tutorial Instruction
NT Programmed Tutoring
BT Individual Instruction
RT Cross Age Teaching
    Peer Teaching
    Remedial Instruction
    Review (Reexamination)
    Test Coaching
    Tutorial Programs
    Tutors

Tutors   *NOV. 1974*
    Postings: 1,014   GC: 360
SN Persons engaged, often privately, to in-
    struct an individual or small group in
    a particular subject (Note: Use "Col-
    lege Faculty" for British postsecondary
    tutors—prior to Mar80, this term did not
    carry a Scope Note)

UF Coaching Teachers (1966 1974)
BT Teachers
RT Tutorial Programs
    Tutoring

TV
USE Television

Twentieth Century Literature   *JUL. 1966*
    Postings: 1,267   GC: 430
UF Midtwentieth Century Literature
BT Literature
RT Existentialism
    Expressionism
    Impressionism
    Literary History
    Marxism
    Modernism
    Naturalism
    Postmodernism
    Realism
    Surrealism
    Symbolism

Twi
USE Akan

Twins   *JUL. 1966*
    Postings: 320   GC: 120
BT Siblings
RT Family (Sociological Unit)
    Sibling Relationship

Two Parent Family
USE Nuclear Family

Two Plus Two Tech Prep
USE Tech Prep

Two Plus Two Tech Prep Associate Degrees
USE Associate Degrees
AND Tech Prep

Two Way Television
USE Interactive Television

Two Year College Degrees
USE Associate Degrees

Two Year College Students   *MAR. 1980*
    Postings: 4,586   GC: 360
SN (Note: Coordinate with the appropriate
    mandatory educational level Descriptor)
UF Junior College Students (1969 1980)
BT College Students
RT College Freshmen
    College Sophomores
    College Transfer Students
    Community Colleges
    Technical Institutes
    Terminal Students
    Two Year Colleges
    Undergraduate Students
    Undergraduate Study

Two Year Colleges   *MAR. 1980*
    Postings: 27,663   GC: 340
SN Public or private postsecondary institu-
    tions providing at least 2, but less than 4,
    years of academic and/or occupational
    education (Note: Also appears in the list
    of mandatory educational level Descrip-
    tors)
UF Junior College Libraries (1966 1980) #
    Junior Colleges (1966 1980)
    Private Junior Colleges #
NT Community Colleges
    Technical Institutes
BT Colleges
RT Associate Degrees
    Multicampus Colleges
    Multicampus Districts
    Postsecondary Education

    State Colleges
    Technical Education
    Trade and Industrial Education
    Transfer Rates (College)
    Two Year College Students
    Undergraduate Study
    Upper Division Colleges

Type A Behavior   *APR. 1990*
    Postings: 130   GC: 120
SN Pattern of behavior characterized by com-
    petitiveness, a sense of urgency, impa-
    tience, perfectionism, and assertiveness,
    and possibly associated with an increased
    risk of heart disease
UF Coronary Prone Behavior Pattern
BT Behavior
    Behavior Patterns
RT Achievement Need
    Arousal Patterns
    Assertiveness
    Competition
    Goal Orientation
    Heart Disorders
    Hypertension
    Personality Assessment
    Psychological Characteristics
    Stress Variables
    Type B Behavior

Type B Behavior   *APR. 1990*
    Postings: 39   GC: 120
SN Pattern of behavior characterized by an
    unhurried, patient, tolerant manner, an
    ability to relax easily, and amiability, and
    possibly associated with a decreased
    risk of heart disease
BT Behavior
    Behavior Patterns
RT Achievement Need
    Arousal Patterns
    Goal Orientation
    Heart Disorders
    Personality Assessment
    Psychological Characteristics
    Stress Variables
    Type A Behavior

Typewriting   *JUL. 1966*
    Postings: 903   GC: 400
UF Clerk Typists
    Typing
    Typists (1967 1981)
BT Business Skills
RT Clerical Occupations
    Court Reporters
    Keyboarding (Data Entry)
    Office Machines
    Office Occupations
    Office Occupations Education
    Printing
    Secretaries
    Shorthand
    Word Processing

Typhoons
USE Hurricanes

Typing
USE Typewriting

Typists (1967 1981)
USE Typewriting

Typology (1967 1980)
USE Classification

Tzeltal   *JUN. 1969*
    Postings: 9   GC: 440
UF Tzendal
BT Mayan Languages

Tzendal
USE Tzeltal

Tzotzil   *DEC. 1969*
    Postings: 9   GC: 440
BT Mayan Languages

UDC (Classification)
USE Universal Decimal Classification

Ukrainian   *JUL. 1966*
    Postings: 67   GC: 440
BT Slavic Languages

Ultramicrofiche
USE Microfiche

Uncial Script
USE Manuscript Writing (Handlettering)

Uncommonly Taught Languages   *JUL. 1966*
    Postings: 3,637   GC: 450
SN Languages not generally offered for in-
    struction in the United States educa-
    tional system (Note: Also see the specific
    language, e.g., Turkish, or the language
    family, e.g., Uralic Altaic languages)
UF Less Commonly Taught Languages
    Neglected Languages
BT Language
RT Unwritten Languages

Unconventional Warfare
USE War

Underachievement   *MAR. 1980*
    Postings: 1,418   GC: 120
UF Underachievers (1966 1979)
BT Achievement
RT Academic Failure
    Failure
    Fear of Success
    Grade Repetition
    Learning Problems
    Low Achievement
    Overachievement
    Social Promotion

Underachievers (1966 1979)
USE Underachievement

Underdeveloped Nations
USE Developing Nations

Underemployed (1969 1980)
USE Underemployment

Underemployment   *MAR. 1980*
    Postings: 498   GC: 630
SN Employment that is less than the number
    of hours employees want to work or
    below their demonstrated skills or earn-
    ing levels
UF Inadequate Employment
    Subemployment (1968 1980)
    Underemployed (1969 1980)
BT Employment
RT Employment Patterns
    Employment Problems
    Job Sharing
    Labor Market
    Labor Utilization
    Low Income
    Part Time Employment
    Poverty
    Seasonal Employment
    Structural Unemployment
    Unemployment

Undergraduate Education
USE Undergraduate Study

Undergraduate Students   *APR. 1975*
    Postings: 4,866   GC: 360
SN College or university students who are

engaged in studies leading to the bachelor's degree
NT Premedical Students
BT College Students
RT College Freshmen
    College Graduates
    College Juniors
    College Sophomores
    Higher Education
    Two Year College Students
    Undergraduate Study

Undergraduate Study JUL. 1966
    Postings: 6,309 GC: 340
SN Study in an institution of higher education that precedes the bachelor's or first professional degree
UF Undergraduate Education
    Undergraduate Training
BT Higher Education
RT Associate Degrees
    Bachelors Degrees
    College Outcomes Assessment
    Colleges
    Community Colleges
    Degree Requirements
    Graduate Study
    Two Year College Students
    Two Year Colleges
    Undergraduate Students
    Universities

Undergraduate Training
USE Undergraduate Study

Underground Facilities JAN. 1979
    Postings: 43 GC: 920
SN Buildings, rooms, passageways, etc., that are below the surface of the ground
BT Facilities
RT Building Innovation
    Buildings
    Energy Conservation
    Facility Planning
    Fallout Shelters
    Land Use
    Space Utilization
    Windowless Rooms

Underground Water
USE Groundwater

Underprivileged
USE Disadvantaged

Underwater Diving JAN. 1985
    Postings: 17 GC: 470
UF Deep Sea Diving
    Scuba Diving
    Skin Diving
BT Physical Activities
RT Aquatic Sports
    Marine Education
    Marine Technicians
    Oceanography
    Recreational Activities

Undocumented Immigrants FEB. 1984
    Postings: 231 GC: 510
SN Persons residing in a foreign country without proper authorization, having entered that country by unlawful means or having violated the provisions of their visas
UF Alien Illegality
    Illegal Aliens
    Illegal Immigrants (1976 1984)
    Immigrant Illegality
    Undocumented Workers #
BT Immigrants
RT Immigration
    Immigration Inspectors
    Migration
    Refugees

Undocumented Workers
USE Foreign Workers
AND Undocumented Immigrants

Unemployed (1967 1980)
USE Unemployment

Unemployment JUL. 1966
    Postings: 3,940 GC: 630
UF Unemployed (1967 1980)
NT Structural Unemployment
RT Dislocated Workers
    Employment Patterns
    Employment Problems
    Job Layoff
    Job Search Methods
    Labor Economics
    Labor Force Nonparticipants
    Labor Market
    Labor Utilization
    Poverty
    Reduction in Force
    Underemployment
    Unemployment Insurance

Unemployment Insurance JUL. 1966
    Postings: 213 GC: 630
BT Financial Support
    Insurance
RT Fringe Benefits
    Health Insurance
    Insurance Occupations
    Teacher Employment Benefits
    Unemployment
    Workers Compensation

Ungraded Classes (1966 1980)
USE Nongraded Instructional Grouping

Ungraded Curriculum (1966 1980)
USE Nongraded Instructional Grouping

Ungraded Elementary Programs (1966 1980)
USE Nongraded Instructional Grouping

Ungraded Primary Programs (1966 1980)
USE Nongraded Instructional Grouping

Ungraded Programs (1966 1980)
USE Nongraded Instructional Grouping

Ungraded Schools (1966 1980)
USE Nongraded Instructional Grouping

Unification
USE Group Unity

Unified Studies Curriculum MAR. 1980
    Postings: 252 GC: 350
SN Curriculum designed to integrate an educational program by eliminating the traditional boundaries between fields of study and presenting them as one unified subject
UF Unified Studies Programs (1966 1980)
BT Curriculum
RT Articulation (Education)
    Fused Curriculum
    Integrated Curriculum
    Interdisciplinary Approach

Unified Studies Programs (1966 1980)
USE Unified Studies Curriculum

Unilateral Disarmament
USE Disarmament

Union Catalogs NOV. 1968
    Postings: 434 GC: 710
SN Author and/or subject catalogs of the

holdings of a group of libraries—can cover their entire collections or be limited by subject or type of material
UF Repertory Catalogs
BT Library Catalogs
RT Bibliographies
    Interlibrary Loans
    Library Cooperation
    Library Networks
    National Libraries
    Shared Library Resources

Union Members JUL. 1966
    Postings: 231 GC: 630
BT Groups
RT Unions

Unions JUL. 1966
    Postings: 3,990 GC: 630
SN Employee organizations whose major objective is to represent their members' interests in negotiations with employers (Note: Prior to Mar80, the use of this term was not restricted by a Scope Note)
UF Labor Unions (1966 1980)
    Local Unions (1966 1980)
    Teacher Unions
    Trade Unions
BT Organizations (Groups)
RT Arbitration
    Collective Bargaining
    Employer Employee Relationship
    Faculty College Relationship
    Faculty Organizations
    Labor Demands
    Labor Education
    Labor Force
    Labor Legislation
    Labor Relations
    Negotiation Agreements
    Negotiation Impasses
    Quality of Working Life
    Strikes
    Teacher Associations
    Teacher Strikes
    Union Members
    Work Environment

Unit Costs JUL. 1966
    Postings: 299 GC: 620
BT Costs
RT Cost Estimates
    Program Costs

Unit Plan (1966 1980) APR. 1980
    Postings: 822 GC: 350
SN Invalid Descriptor—used inconsistently in indexing—see such Descriptors as "Activity Units," "Learning Modules," "Lesson Plans," "Resource Units," "Units of Study," etc.

United States Government (Course) MAR. 1980
    Postings: 798 GC: 400
UF American Government (Course) (1966 1980)
BT Courses
RT American Studies
    Civics
    Constitutional History
    Constitutional Law
    Government (Administrative Body)
    Political Science
    Social Studies

United States History JUL. 1966
    Postings: 6,749 GC: 430
SN (Note: Prior to Mar80, "American History" was occasionally used for this concept)
NT Civil War (United States)
    Colonial History (United States)
    Mexican American History
    Reconstruction Era
    Revolutionary War (United States)
    State History
BT North American History

RT American Studies
    Black History
    Black Studies
    Capitalism
    Constitutional History
    Cultural Pluralism
    Federalism
    Korean War
    Modern History
    Presidential Campaigns (United States)
    Presidents of the United States
    United States Literature
    Vietnam War
    Womens Studies
    World War I
    World War II

United States Literature MAR. 1980
    Postings: 1,064 GC: 430
UF American Literature (1966 1980) (United States)
NT Hispanic American Literature
BT North American Literature
RT American Studies
    Black Literature
    English Literature
    United States History

Uniterm Indexes
USE Coordinate Indexes

Uniterms
USE Subject Index Terms

Units of Study JUL. 1977
    Postings: 7,503 GC: 350
SN Subdivisions of instruction within a course, textbook, or subject field
UF Human Relations Units (1966 1980) #
    Lesson Units
    Programed Units (1966 1980) #
    Science Units (1966 1980) #
    Social Studies Units (1966 1980) #
    Units of Study (Subject Fields) (1966 1977)
NT Activity Units
BT Courses
RT Continuing Education Units
    Learning Modules
    Lesson Plans
    Resource Units

Units of Study (Subject Fields) (1966 1977)
USE Units of Study

Universal Decimal Classification APR. 1998
    Postings: 46 GC: 710
SN Elaborate system for classifying library materials that divides the total field of knowledge into 10 main branches, with increased specialization provided by further subdivisions of 10 and additional auxiliary notations of special signs and numbers—devised in 1895 as an expansion of the Dewey Decimal Classification, and revised continually since then
UF Decimal Classification (Universal)
    UDC (Classification)
BT Classification
RT Cataloging
    Dewey Decimal Classification
    Indexing
    Information Retrieval
    Library Catalogs
    Library Collections
    Library Materials
    Library of Congress Classification
    Library Technical Processes
    Subject Index Terms

Universal Education (1968 1976)
USE Equal Education

Universities JUL. 1966
    Postings: 8,602 GC: 340
SN Degree-granting institutions of higher

= Two or more Descriptors are used to represent this term.
The term's main entry shows the appropriate coordination.

education that typically include a liberal arts undergraduate college, a graduate school, and two or more undergraduate and graduate professional schools (Note: For specific aspects, use a "College" term where a corresponding "University" term is not available)
NT   Land Grant Universities
     Open Universities
     Research Universities
     State Universities
     Urban Universities
BT   Colleges
RT   College Faculty
     College Students
     Extension Education
     Faculty Handbooks
     Graduate Study
     Higher Education
     Multicampus Colleges
     Nonprofit Organizations
     Postsecondary Education
     Undergraduate Study
     University Presses
     Upper Division Colleges

Universities without Walls
USE Open Universities

University Administration (1967 1980)
USE College Administration

University Characteristics
USE Institutional Characteristics

University Extension (1967 1980)
USE Extension Education

University Libraries (1968 1980)
USE College Libraries

University Presses   *OCT. 1998*
     Postings: 53   GC: 650
SN   Publishing houses associated with higher education institutions and often specializing in scholarly or creative works
BT   Publishing Industry
RT   Colleges
     Faculty Publishing
     Publications
     Universities

University Schools
USE Laboratory Schools

University Senates
USE College Governing Councils

University Settlements
USE Settlement Houses

University Students
USE College Students

University Teaching Hospitals
USE Teaching Hospitals

University Training Centers
USE Teacher Centers

Unmarried Mother Births
USE Births to Single Women

Unmarried Students
USE Single Students

Unskilled Labor (1966 1980)
USE Unskilled Workers

Unskilled Occupations   *JUL. 1966*
     Postings: 52   GC: 640
SN   Occupations requiring little or no training or experience
BT   Occupations
RT   Blue Collar Occupations
     Semiskilled Occupations
     Skilled Occupations
     Unskilled Workers

Unskilled Workers   *JUL. 1966*
     Postings: 237   GC: 630
SN   Manual workers whose tasks require little or no training or experience
UF   Unskilled Labor (1966 1980)
NT   Laborers
BT   Nonprofessional Personnel
RT   Employees
     Semiskilled Workers
     Skilled Workers
     Unskilled Occupations
     Working Class

Untenured Faculty
USE Nontenured Faculty

Unwed Mothers   *JUL. 1966*
     Postings: 498   GC: 510
BT   Mothers
RT   Births to Single Women
     Family Structure
     Fatherless Family
     Pregnancy
     Pregnant Students

Unwritten Language (1968 1980)
                  APR. 1980
     Postings: 33   GC: 450
SN   Invalid Descriptor—used inconsistently in indexing—see "Oral Language" or "Unwritten Languages"

Unwritten Languages   *APR. 1980*
     Postings: 14   GC: 450
SN   Languages without a native system of writing
BT   Language
RT   Anthropological Linguistics
     Applied Linguistics
     Language Research
     Second Language Learning
     Uncommonly Taught Languages
     Written Language

Upgrading
USE Improvement

Upper Class   *JUL. 1966*
     Postings: 119   GC: 520
BT   Social Class
RT   Advantaged
     Affluent Youth
     Lower Class
     Lower Middle Class
     Middle Class

Upper Division Colleges   *MAY 1972*
     Postings: 129   GC: 340
SN   Colleges offering junior, senior, and graduate level courses only
BT   Colleges
RT   Articulation (Education)
     Graduate Study
     Two Year Colleges
     Universities

Uralic Altaic Languages   *JUL. 1966*
     Postings: 21   GC: 440
UF   Altaic Languages
NT   Finno Ugric Languages
     Manchu
     Mongolian Languages
     Samoyed Languages
     Turkic Languages
BT   Languages

Urban American Indians   *MAR. 1980*
     Postings: 165   GC: 560
SN   American Indians who reside in or near urban centers
BT   Nonreservation American Indians
     Urban Population
RT   Rural American Indians
     Urban Areas

Urban Areas   *JUL. 1966*
     Postings: 3,041   GC: 550
SN   Geographic areas that are heavily populated and often industrialized
UF   Large Cities
NT   Inner City
     Municipalities
BT   Geographic Regions
RT   Metropolitan Areas
     Rural to Urban Migration
     Rural Urban Differences
     Slums
     Urban American Indians
     Urban Culture
     Urban Demography
     Urban Education
     Urban Environment
     Urban Extension
     Urban Language
     Urban Population
     Urban Renewal
     Urban Renewal Agencies
     Urban Schools
     Urban Studies
     Urban Teaching
     Urban to Rural Migration
     Urban to Suburban Migration
     Urban Universities
     Urbanization

Urban Culture   *JUL. 1966*
     Postings: 441   GC: 560
UF   Urban Life
BT   Culture
RT   Cross Cultural Studies
     Rural Urban Differences
     Urban Areas
     Urban Environment
     Urban Language
     Urban Studies

Urban Demography   *MAR. 1980*
     Postings: 342   GC: 550
UF   City Demography (1966 1980)
BT   Demography
RT   Community Size
     Inner City
     Metropolitan Areas
     Rural to Urban Migration
     Urban Areas
     Urban Population
     Urban Renewal
     Urban to Rural Migration
     Urban to Suburban Migration

Urban Desegregation
USE Racial Integration

Urban Dropouts (1966 1981)
USE Dropouts

Urban Education   *JUL. 1966*
     Postings: 3,837   GC: 330
SN   Schooling that takes place in urban (and sometimes metropolitan) areas
UF   Inner City Education
BT   Education
RT   Urban Areas
     Urban Extension
     Urban Schools
     Urban Teaching
     Urban Universities

Urban Environment   *JUL. 1966*
     Postings: 1,387   GC: 550
BT   Environment
RT   Air Pollution
     Community Characteristics

     Crowding
     Pollution
     Slum Environment
     Urban Areas
     Urban Culture
     Urban Improvement
     Urban Language
     Urban Planning
     Urban Population
     Urban Problems
     Urban Renewal
     Urbanization
     Water Pollution

Urban Extension   *JUL. 1966*
     Postings: 103   GC: 350
SN   Extension work in urban settings
BT   Extension Education
RT   Urban Areas
     Urban Education
     Urban Universities

Urban Geography
USE Human Geography

Urban Immigration (1966 1976)
USE Rural to Urban Migration

Urban Improvement   *MAR. 1980*
     Postings: 239   GC: 550
SN   The betterment of services, environment, or other factors affecting the quality of life in an urban area
UF   City Improvement (1966 1980)
NT   Urban Renewal
BT   Improvement
RT   City Government
     Community Development
     Community Responsibility
     Neighborhood Improvement
     Social Responsibility
     Urban Environment
     Urban Planning
     Urban Programs

Urban Language   *JUL. 1966*
     Postings: 107   GC: 450
BT   Language
RT   Black Dialects
     Language Classification
     Language Patterns
     Language Research
     Language Usage
     Language Variation
     Nonstandard Dialects
     Rural Urban Differences
     Social Dialects
     Sociolinguistics
     Urban Areas
     Urban Culture
     Urban Environment

Urban Life
USE Urban Culture

Urban Planning   *MAR. 1980*
     Postings: 666   GC: 550
UF   City Planning (1966 1980)
     City Wide Commissions (1966 1980) #
BT   Planning
RT   City Government
     Community Planning
     Facility Planning
     Land Use
     Planning Commissions
     Regional Planning
     Road Construction
     Social Planning
     Urban Environment
     Urban Improvement
     Urban Programs
     Urban Renewal
     Urban Studies
     Urbanization

= Two or more Descriptors are used to represent this term.
The term's main entry shows the appropriate coordination.

Urban Population   *JUL. 1966*
    Postings: 693   GC: 550
NT   Urban American Indians
    Urban Youth
BT   Groups
RT   Community Size
    Ghettos
    Population Distribution
    Population Growth
    Population Trends
    Rural to Urban Migration
    Rural Urban Differences
    Urban Areas
    Urban Demography
    Urban Environment
    Urban to Rural Migration
    Urban to Suburban Migration
    Urbanization

Urban Problems   *MAR. 1980*
    Postings: 1,604   GC: 530
UF   City Problems (1966 1980)
BT   Problems
RT   Community Problems
    Urban Environment

Urban Programs   *MAR. 1980*
    Postings: 308   GC: 520
UF   City Wide Programs (1967 1980)
BT   Programs
RT   City Government
    Urban Improvement
    Urban Planning

Urban Renewal   *JUL. 1966*
    Postings: 319   GC: 550
SN   The systematic rebuilding of decaying urban areas, including federal, state, or municipal programs directed at such rebuilding
UF   Redevelopment Areas
BT   Urban Improvement
RT   Community Change
    Housing Deficiencies
    Neighborhood Improvement
    Planned Communities
    Public Housing
    Slums
    Urban Areas
    Urban Demography
    Urban Environment
    Urban Planning
    Urban Renewal Agencies

Urban Renewal Agencies   *JUL. 1966*
    Postings: 15   GC: 610
BT   Agencies
RT   Agency Role
    Public Agencies
    State Agencies
    Urban Areas
    Urban Renewal

Urban Rural Differences
USE Rural Urban Differences

Urban Schools   *JUL. 1966*
    Postings: 6,938   GC: 340
UF   City Schools
NT   Urban Universities
BT   Schools
RT   Magnet Schools
    Slum Schools
    Urban Areas
    Urban Education

Urban Slums (1966 1980)
USE Slums

Urban Studies   *OCT. 1970*
    Postings: 551   GC: 400
BT   Curriculum
RT   Area Studies
    Economics
    Ethnic Studies
    Human Geography

    Interdisciplinary Approach
    Research
    Social Science Research
    Social Sciences
    Urban Areas
    Urban Culture
    Urban Planning

Urban Teaching   *JUL. 1966*
    Postings: 472   GC: 330
UF   Urban Teaching Interns #
BT   Teaching (Occupation)
RT   Urban Areas
    Urban Education

Urban Teaching Interns
USE Teacher Interns
AND Urban Teaching

Urban to Rural Migration   *OCT. 1976*
    Postings: 240   GC: 550
SN   Population movement from urban areas to rural areas for purpose of relocation
BT   Migration
RT   Migration Patterns
    Population Distribution
    Population Trends
    Relocation
    Residential Patterns
    Rural Areas
    Rural Environment
    Rural Population
    Rural Resettlement
    Rural Sociology
    Rural to Urban Migration
    Urban Areas
    Urban Demography
    Urban Population
    Urban to Suburban Migration

Urban to Suburban Migration   *OCT. 1976*
    Postings: 173   GC: 550
SN   Population movement from urban areas to suburban areas for purpose of relocation
BT   Migration
RT   Migration Patterns
    Population Distribution
    Population Trends
    Relocation
    Residential Patterns
    Suburbs
    Urban Areas
    Urban Demography
    Urban Population
    Urban to Rural Migration

Urban Universities   *JUL. 1966*
    Postings: 705   GC: 340
SN   Universities located in and serving an urban community, but not necessarily maintained by a municipality
BT   Universities
    Urban Schools
RT   Urban Areas
    Urban Education
    Urban Extension

Urban Youth   *JUL. 1966*
    Postings: 2,092   GC: 510
SN   (Note: Coordinate with an appropriate age or educational level Descriptor)
BT   Urban Population
    Youth

Urbanization   *JUL. 1966*
    Postings: 609   GC: 550
BT   Development
RT   Boomtowns
    Culture Lag
    Demography
    Industrialization
    Modernization
    Population Growth
    Rural Sociology
    Rural to Urban Migration
    Urban Areas

    Urban Environment
    Urban Planning
    Urban Population

Urdu   *JUL. 1966*
    Postings: 77   GC: 440
BT   Indo European Languages
RT   Hindi

Use Studies   *AUG. 1968*
    Postings: 4,395   GC: 810
SN   Studies of the use of resources (information, human resources, natural resources, facilities, organizations, institutions, etc.) (Note: As of Oct81, use as a minor Descriptor for examples of this kind of research—use as a major Descriptor only as the subject of a document)
UF   User Studies
NT   Facility Utilization Research
BT   Research
RT   Environmental Research
    Evaluation Methods
    Focus Groups
    Information Sources
    Information Utilization
    Institutional Research
    Labor Utilization
    Land Use
    Library Research
    Library Surveys
    Mass Media Use
    Media Research
    Outreach Programs
    Research Utilization
    Resources
    Technology Transfer
    Users (Information)

User Friendly Interface   *SEP. 1994*
    Postings: 50   GC: 710
SN   Any connection or link to a computer system that is easy to learn and use (Note: Prior to Sep94, the Identifier "User Cordial Interface" was used to index this concept)
BT   Computer Interfaces
    Man Machine Systems
RT   Computer Attitudes
    Computer Software
    Computers
    Data Processing
    Menu Driven Software
    User Satisfaction (Information)
    Users (Information)

User Needs (Information)   *AUG. 1986*
    Postings: 2,934   GC: 710
SN   The needs of users (or prospective users) related to information or library systems and services
UF   Information User Needs
    Library User Needs
BT   Needs
RT   Gateway Systems
    Information Needs
    Information Retrieval
    Information Seeking
    Information Services
    Library Collection Development
    Library Materials
    Library Services
    Library Surveys
    Online Searching
    Reference Services
    Relevance (Information Retrieval)
    Search Intermediaries
    Search Strategies
    Selective Dissemination of Information
    Shared Library Resources
    User Satisfaction (Information)
    Users (Information)

User Satisfaction (Information)   *JAN. 1979*
    Postings: 1,310   GC: 710
SN   Users' assessment of the degree to which information or library services meet their needs (Note: Prior to Jan79, "Participant

    Satisfaction" was sometimes used to index this concept)
UF   Information User Satisfaction
    Library User Satisfaction
BT   Satisfaction
RT   Evaluation
    Information Retrieval
    Information Services
    Library Materials
    Library Services
    Library Surveys
    Relevance (Information Retrieval)
    User Friendly Interface
    User Needs (Information)
    Users (Information)

User Studies
USE Use Studies

Users (Information)   *AUG. 1986*
    Postings: 2,153   GC: 710
SN   Users of information or library resources and services
UF   End Users (Information)
    Information Users
    Library Clients
    Library Patrons
    Library Users
BT   Groups
RT   Access to Information
    Information Literacy
    Information Policy
    Information Seeking
    Information Services
    Information Systems
    Information Utilization
    Libraries
    Library Instruction
    Library Services
    Library Skills
    Menu Driven Software
    Use Studies
    User Friendly Interface
    User Needs (Information)
    User Satisfaction (Information)

Utilities   *APR. 1969*
    Postings: 583   GC: 920
UF   Electric Utilities
    Gas Utilities
    Public Utilities
    Water Utilities
    Water Works #
RT   Distributive Education
    Drinking Water
    Electrical Systems
    Energy Education
    Energy Management
    Energy Occupations
    Fuels
    Heating
    Lighting
    Natural Gas
    Nuclear Power Plants
    Power Technology
    Sanitary Facilities
    Sanitation
    Services
    Telephone Communications Industry
    Water Resources
    Water Treatment

Uto Aztecan Languages   *JUL. 1966*
    Postings: 26   GC: 440
NT   Hopi
    Papago
BT   American Indian Languages

Uzbek   *JUL. 1966*
    Postings: 12   GC: 440
BT   Turkic Languages

Vacation Programs   *JUL. 1966*
    Postings: 70   GC: 350
SN   Programs scheduled for times when schools are not normally in session
UF   Intersession School Programs
BT   Programs

= Two or more Descriptors are used to represent this term.
The term's main entry shows the appropriate coordination.

RT Alumni Education
   School Schedules
   Summer Programs
   Vacations
   Year Round Schools

Vacations MAR. 1980
   Postings: 133 GC: 630
SN Periods of time devoted to rest and re-laxation (Note: Prior to Mar80, the in-struction "Vacations, USE Leave of Absence" was carried in the Thesaurus)
RT Fringe Benefits
   Holidays
   Leaves of Absence
   Leisure Time
   Recreation
   Recreationists
   Scope of Bargaining
   Vacation Programs

Valence (Language)
USE Syntax

Validated Programs JAN. 1979
   Postings: 519 GC: 320
SN Programs that have been approved ac-cording to specified procedures, indicat-ing attainment of the claims of the spon-sors (Note: For the relationship between evaluation and validation, see "Program Validation")
UF Approved Programs (Validated)
BT Programs
RT Accountability
   Course Content
   Course Evaluation
   Curriculum Evaluation
   Demonstration Programs
   Educational Assessment
   Program Content
   Program Effectiveness
   Program Evaluation
   Program Validation
   Summative Evaluation
   Validity

Validity AUG. 1968
   Postings: 3,073 GC: 820
SN In logic, the quality of being founded on truth, fact, or law or the attribute of an argument that conforms with logical laws—in common usage, the extent to which something does what it is used or intended to do (Note: Use "Test Validity" for validity of tests, inventories, scales, etc.—prior to Mar80, this term was not scoped)
NT Concurrent Validity
   Predictive Validity
   Proof (Mathematics)
   Test Validity
BT Evaluation Criteria
RT Causal Models
   Correlation
   Data Interpretation
   Deduction
   Evaluation
   Generalization
   Induction
   Logic
   Multiple Regression Analysis
   Path Analysis
   Program Validation
   Regression (Statistics)
   Reliability
   Robustness (Statistics)
   Statistical Analysis
   Statistical Data
   Statistical Distributions
   Triangulation
   Validated Programs
   Weighted Scores

Value Judgment OCT. 1982
   Postings: 685 GC: 110
SN Estimating the merit or goodness of something (person, object, situation, act)

relative to one's attitudes, needs, and desires
UF Aesthetic Judgment #
   Moral Judgment #
BT Evaluative Thinking
RT Criticism
   Objectivity
   Praise
   Values

Values JUL. 1966
   Postings: 9,763 GC: 520
SN Principles and standards that determine the degree of worth or merit of an object or act
UF Personal Values (1966 1980)
NT Aesthetic Values
   Democratic Values
   Moral Values
   Social Values
RT Afrocentrism
   Altruism
   Attitude Measures
   Beliefs
   Controversial Issues (Course Content)
   Credibility
   Culture Conflict
   Design Preferences
   Dissent
   Educational Principles
   Egocentrism
   Elitism
   Ethnocentrism
   Evaluation Criteria
   Futures (of Society)
   Hidden Curriculum
   Honesty
   Humanistic Education
   Ideology
   Justice
   Life Satisfaction
   Moral Development
   Norms
   Political Attitudes
   Political Correctness
   Quality of Life
   Satisfaction
   Semantic Differential
   Social Problems
   Spirituality
   Sportsmanship
   Standards
   Traditionalism
   Value Judgment
   Values Clarification
   Values Education
   World Views

Values Clarification MAR. 1980
   Postings: 983 GC: 400
SN Teaching and helping people to become aware of their values and to act upon them
RT Consciousness Raising
   Goal Orientation
   Self Actualization
   Values
   Values Education

Values Education MAR. 1980
   Postings: 2,054 GC: 400
SN The attempt to teach about values or to develop certain values in other people in school or non-school settings
BT Education
RT Citizenship Education
   Ethical Instruction
   Humanistic Education
   Values
   Values Clarification

Vandalism SEP. 1969
   Postings: 207 GC: 530
NT School Vandalism
BT Antisocial Behavior
RT Computer Security
   Crime
   Delinquency
   Discipline Problems

   Security Personnel
   Victims of Crime

Vascular System
USE Cardiovascular System

Vectors (Mathematics) AUG. 1982
   Postings: 174 GC: 480
SN Quantities having magnitude (represented by length of line segments) and direction (represented by orientation of the line segments in space)
BT Algebra
   Geometric Concepts
RT Calculus
   Force
   Functions (Mathematics)
   Geometry
   Matrices
   Motion
   Navigation
   Physics
   Topology

Vehicular Circulation
USE Vehicular Traffic

Vehicular Traffic OCT. 1968
   Postings: 120 GC: 920
UF Vehicular Circulation
RT Driveways
   Motor Vehicles
   Parking Controls
   Parking Facilities
   Pedestrian Traffic
   Service Vehicles
   Traffic Circulation
   Traffic Control
   Transportation

Velocity MAY 1998
   Postings: 137 GC: 490
SN Rate of motion in a specified direction (Note: See also the Identifiers "Angular Velocity" (rate of rotational motion) and "Nerve Conduction Velocity")
BT Motion
RT Acceleration (Physics)
   Fluid Mechanics
   Kinetics
   Mechanics (Physics)
   Physics

Vending Machines JUL. 1966
   Postings: 29 GC: 910
BT Equipment
RT Food
   Food Handling Facilities
   Food Service
   Nutrition
   Vendors

Vendors AUG. 1994
   Postings: 639 GC: 640
SN Organizations or individuals that market and sell materials and/or services
NT Merchants
   Online Vendors
BT Groups
RT Business
   Computer Oriented Programs
   Consultants
   Information Services
   Information Technology
   Library Services
   Marketing
   Organizations (Groups)
   Sales Occupations
   Sales Workers
   Supplies
   Vending Machines

Venereal Diseases JAN. 1974
   Postings: 258 GC: 210
UF Chancroid
   Gonorrhea

   Syphilis
BT Communicable Diseases
RT Health Education
   Physical Health
   Sex Education

Ventilation JUL. 1966
   Postings: 267 GC: 920
UF Exhausting (1969 1980)
BT Climate Control
RT Air Conditioning
   Air Conditioning Equipment
   Air Flow
   Air Pollution
   Chimneys
   Fuel Consumption
   Health
   Heat Recovery
   Heating
   Mining
   Physical Health
   Temperature
   Thermal Environment
   Windowless Rooms
   Windows

Verbal Ability JUL. 1966
   Postings: 1,823 GC: 450
SN Facility in the use and comprehension of words
NT Reading Ability
   Writing Ability
BT Ability
RT Academic Ability
   Basic Skills
   Communication Skills
   Language Aptitude
   Language Arts
   Language Skills
   Linguistic Competence
   Linguistic Input
   Linguistic Performance
   Nonverbal Ability
   Speech Skills
   Verbal Development
   Verbal Learning
   Verbal Operant Conditioning
   Verbal Tests

Verbal Abuse SEP. 1994
   Postings: 77 GC: 530
SN Insulting, intimidating, or excessively criti-cal statements (oral or written)
BT Antisocial Behavior
   Verbal Communication
RT Aggression
   Battered Women
   Child Abuse
   Communication Problems
   Criticism
   Elder Abuse
   Emotional Abuse
   Language Patterns
   Language Usage
   Libel and Slander
   Obscenity
   Sexual Harassment

Verbal Communication JUL. 1966
   Postings: 4,178 GC: 450
SN Transferring ideas and information through spoken or written words
UF Verbal Interaction
NT Business Correspondence
   Dictation
   Letters (Correspondence)
   Verbal Abuse
BT Communication (Thought Transfer)
RT Classroom Communication
   Coherence
   Communication Skills
   Communicative Competence (Languages)
   Debate
   Discourse Modes
   Language
   Language Arts
   Language Patterns
   Language Processing

Linguistics
Mutual Intelligibility
Nonverbal Communication
Oral Communication Method
Oral Language
Persuasive Discourse
Reading
Rhetoric
Rhetorical Theory
Semiotics
Speech
Speech Communication
Total Communication
Writing (Composition)

Verbal Development   *JUL. 1966*
     Postings: 925   GC: 450
SN   Growth in ability to use and comprehend words in either oral or written form
NT   Language Acquisition
BT   Cognitive Development
RT   Child Language
     Intention
     Verbal Ability
     Verbal Learning
     Verbal Stimuli
     Vocabulary Development

Verbal Interaction
USE   Verbal Communication

Verbal Learning   *JUL. 1966*
     Postings: 1,360   GC: 110
SN   Learning that involves the use of language, ranging from learning to associate two nonsense syllables to learning to solve complex problems presented in verbal terms
BT   Learning
RT   Advance Organizers
     Language Acquisition
     Learning Modalities
     Mediation Theory
     Memorization
     Nonverbal Learning
     Verbal Ability
     Verbal Development
     Verbal Stimuli

Verbal Operant Conditioning   *JUL. 1966*
     Postings: 209   GC: 110
BT   Operant Conditioning
RT   Psycholinguistics
     Psychology
     Verbal Ability

Verbal Stimuli   *JUL. 1966*
     Postings: 741   GC: 110
BT   Stimuli
RT   Association Measures
     Auditory Stimuli
     Electrical Stimuli
     Language Processing
     Verbal Development
     Verbal Learning
     Visual Stimuli
     Word Recognition

Verbal Tests   *JUL. 1966*
     Postings: 603   GC: 830
SN   Tests of verbal ability, or any tests requiring written or spoken language in administering, responding, or both
NT   Essay Tests
     Language Tests
     Listening Comprehension Tests
     Reading Tests
     Speech Tests
     Writing Tests
BT   Tests
RT   Mathematics Tests
     Nonverbal Tests
     Verbal Ability

Verbs   *JUL. 1966*
     Postings: 2,687   GC: 450
UF   Imperative Mood

     Indicative Mood
     Subjunctive Mood
BT   Form Classes (Languages)
RT   Adverbs
     Morphology (Languages)
     Sentence Structure
     Syntax
     Tenses (Grammar)
     Vocabulary

Versification (1969 1980)
USE   Poetry

Vertical Organization   *JUL. 1966*
     Postings: 379   GC: 520
SN   Organization involving several successive grades or different levels within a system (e.g., vertical monopolies, vertical labor unions, vertical sequences for organizing curriculum content)
UF   Hierarchy
BT   Organization
RT   Curriculum Design
     Horizontal Organization
     Industrial Structure
     Pyramid Organization

Veterans   *JAN. 1970*
     Postings: 594   GC: 510
NT   Vietnam Veterans
BT   Groups
RT   Enlisted Personnel
     Military Personnel
     Military Service
     Officer Personnel
     Veterans Education

Veterans Education   *JUL. 1966*
     Postings: 344   GC: 330
BT   Adult Education
RT   Federal Aid
     Military Personnel
     Student Financial Aid
     Training Allowances
     Veterans
     Vietnam Veterans

Veterinarians   *MAR. 1980*
     Postings: 45   GC: 640
SN   Persons qualified and authorized to treat diseases and injuries of animals
BT   Health Personnel
     Professional Personnel
RT   Animal Husbandry
     Veterinary Assistants
     Veterinary Medical Education
     Veterinary Medicine

Veterinary Assistants   *JUL. 1966*
     Postings: 33   GC: 640
UF   Veterinary Hospital Attendants
BT   Allied Health Personnel
     Paraprofessional Personnel
RT   Animal Caretakers
     Animal Husbandry
     Veterinarians
     Veterinary Medicine

Veterinary Hospital Attendants
USE   Veterinary Assistants

Veterinary Medical Education   *MAR. 1980*
     Postings: 110   GC: 400
SN   Professional education and training in prevention, cure, and alleviation of diseases or injuries of animals
BT   Medical Education
RT   Animal Husbandry
     Veterinarians
     Veterinary Medicine

Veterinary Medicine   *JUL. 1966*
     Postings: 264   GC: 410
BT   Medicine
RT   Agriculture

     Animal Behavior
     Animal Caretakers
     Animal Husbandry
     Animals
     Livestock
     Medical Services
     Pets
     Veterinarians
     Veterinary Assistants
     Veterinary Medical Education

Vice Principals
USE   Assistant Principals

Victims of Crime   *MAR. 1981*
     Postings: 1,196   GC: 510
SN   Individuals suffering death, physical or mental distress, or loss of property, as the result of an actual or attempted criminal offense committed by another person
BT   Groups
RT   Battered Women
     Child Abuse
     Child Neglect
     Crime
     Elder Abuse
     Family Violence
     Homicide
     Incest
     Libel and Slander
     Malpractice
     Missing Children
     Rape
     Rehabilitation
     Sexual Abuse
     Stealing
     Vandalism
     Violence

Victorian Literature   *MAY 1969*
     Postings: 48   GC: 430
SN   Literature written during the reign of Queen Victoria (1837–1901)
BT   Literature
RT   Nineteenth Century Literature
     World Literature

Video Cassette Systems (1971 1980)
USE   Videotape Cassettes

Video Display Terminals   *JAN. 1988*
     Postings: 77   GC: 910
UF   Cathode Ray Tube Terminals
     Visual Display Units
BT   Computer Terminals
RT   Display Systems
     Interactive Video
     Screen Design (Computers)
     Videotex
     Word Processing

Video Equipment   *AUG. 1971*
     Postings: 1,296   GC: 910
SN   Equipment used in the reproduction, recording, and/or transmission of visual images for television use
UF   Television Equipment
     Video Systems
NT   Videodisks
     Videotape Cassettes
     Videotape Recorders
BT   Electronic Equipment
     Visual Aids
RT   Audio Equipment
     Audiovisual Aids
     Broadcast Reception Equipment
     Interactive Video
     Photographic Equipment
     Special Effects
     Television
     Television Studios
     Video Games
     Videotape Recordings
     Videotex

Video Games   *DEC. 1988*
     Postings: 109   GC: 720
SN   Games played by manipulating graphics on a television screen or other video display, usually by means of hand controllers (joysticks, buttons, etc.)—includes microchip-controlled video arcade games and hand-held toys (Note: Coordinate with "Computer Games" for cassette-type or similar games requiring access to a computer)
UF   Videogames (Electronic)
BT   Games
RT   Computer Games
     Television
     Toys
     Video Equipment

Video Production Centers
USE   Television Studios

Video Systems
USE   Video Equipment

Video Tape Recordings (1966 1978)
USE   Videotape Recordings

Videodisc Recordings (1979 1986)
USE   Videodisks

Videodisks   *AUG. 1986*
     Postings: 695   GC: 720
SN   Magnetic, capacitive, or optical (laser) disks on which are recorded video signals (with or without accompanying sound) for play back on a television monitor or screen
UF   Optical Videodisks #
     Videodisc Recordings (1979 1986)
BT   Nonprint Media
     Video Equipment
RT   Audiodisks
     Audiovisual Aids
     Interactive Video
     Magnetic Disks
     Optical Disks
     Programming (Broadcast)
     Protocol Materials
     Television
     Videotape Recordings

Videogames (Electronic)
USE   Video Games

Videotape Cartridges
USE   Videotape Cassettes

Videotape Cassette Recorders
USE   Videotape Cassettes
AND   Videotape Recorders

Videotape Cassettes   *MAR. 1980*
     Postings: 619   GC: 720
UF   Video Cassette Systems (1971 1980)
     Videotape Cartridges
     Videotape Cassette Recorders #
BT   Magnetic Tape Cassettes
     Video Equipment
RT   Audiotape Cassettes
     Interactive Video
     Videotape Recorders
     Videotape Recordings

Videotape Libraries
USE   Film Libraries

Videotape Recorders   *MAR. 1980*
     Postings: 147   GC: 910
UF   Videotape Cassette Recorders #
BT   Tape Recorders
     Video Equipment
RT   Audiotape Recorders
     Audiovisual Aids

= Two or more Descriptors are used to represent this term.
The term's main entry shows the appropriate coordination.

      Videotape Cassettes
      Videotape Recordings

Videotape Recordings   *JAN. 1979*
      Postings: 5,491   GC: 720
SN   Magnetic tapes on which video signals (with or without accompanying sound) are recorded for television use—stored on open reels, cassettes, or cartridges
UF   Video Tape Recordings (1966 1978)
BT   Tape Recordings
      Visual Aids
RT   Audiotape Cassettes
      Audiotape Recordings
      Audiovisual Aids
      Film Industry
      Film Libraries
      Film Production
      Films
      Interactive Video
      Kinescope Recordings
      Microcounseling
      Microteaching
      Programming (Broadcast)
      Protocol Materials
      Television
      Video Equipment
      Videodisks
      Videotape Cassettes
      Videotape Recorders

Videotex   *MAR. 1982*
      Postings: 329   GC: 710
SN   Electronic information services that use adapted telephone and television sets—includes "Teletext" which broadcasts information to television sets and "Viewdata" which links computers to television sets by telephone lines
UF   Teletext
      Videotext
      Viewdata
BT   Information Services
      Telecommunications
RT   Computer Mediated Communication
      Computers
      Electronic Publishing
      Electronic Text
      Home Programs
      Information Networks
      Interactive Television
      Menu Driven Software
      Online Systems
      Telephone Communications Systems
      Television
      Video Display Terminals
      Video Equipment

Videotext
USE   Videotex

Vietnam Veterans   *DEC. 1989*
      Postings: 126   GC: 510
BT   Veterans
RT   Veterans Education
      Vietnam War

Vietnam War   *APR. 1990*
      Postings: 274   GC: 430
SN   War from 1955 to 1975 between South Vietnam (aided by the U.S., South Korea, Australia, the Philippines, Thailand, and New Zealand) and the Vietcong guerrillas and North Vietnam
BT   Asian History
      War
RT   Korean War
      United States History
      Vietnam Veterans
      World War II

Vietnamese   *JUL. 1966*
      Postings: 341   GC: 440
BT   Languages
RT   Vietnamese People

Vietnamese Americans
USE   Asian Americans
AND   Vietnamese People

Vietnamese People   *MAR. 1980*
      Postings: 391   GC: 560
UF   Vietnamese Americans #
BT   Indochinese
RT   Asian Americans
      Cambodians
      Hmong People
      Laotians
      Vietnamese

Viewdata
USE   Videotex

Viewing Time (1968 1980)
USE   Programming (Broadcast)

Village Extension Agents
USE   Extension Agents

Violence   *JUL. 1966*
      Postings: 4,456   GC: 530
UF   Student Violence
NT   Family Violence
BT   Antisocial Behavior
RT   Aggression
      Battered Women
      Bullying
      Child Abuse
      Crime
      Delinquency
      Demonstrations (Civil)
      Elder Abuse
      Emotional Response
      Guns
      Hazing
      Homicide
      Rape
      Revolution
      School Security
      Self Injurious Behavior
      Terrorism
      Victims of Crime
      War
      Weapons

Viracnon
USE   Bikol

Virtual Libraries
USE   Electronic Libraries

Virtual Reality   *AUG. 1996*
      Postings: 277   GC: 720
SN   Computer-generated simulations of three-dimensional environments, intended to seem real, with which users interact using combinations of sensing and interface devices and software
BT   Computer Simulation
RT   Computer Software
      Computers
      Man Machine Systems
      Multimedia Materials

Viruses   *APR. 1990*
      Postings: 52   GC: 490
SN   Parasitic particles capable of independent metabolism and reproduction within living cells
NT   Acquired Immune Deficiency Syndrome
      Rubella
RT   Bacteria
      Communicable Diseases
      Cytology
      Disease Control
      Diseases
      Epidemiology
      Hygiene
      Microbiology
      Molecular Biology
      Pollution
      Sanitation

Visayan   *JUL. 1966*
      Postings: 2   GC: 440
NT   Cebuano
BT   Indonesian Languages

Visible Radiation
USE   Light

Visible Spectrum
USE   Light

Visible Speech   *SEP. 1968*
      Postings: 38   GC: 220
SN   Translation of speech into a readable form—sound waves are transformed into electrical impulses which are then transformed into flashes of light and photographed (Note: Prior to Mar80, the use of this term was not restricted by a Scope Note)
BT   Instrumentation
RT   Articulation Impairments
      Hearing Impairments
      Sound Spectrographs
      Speech
      Speech Therapy
      Visual Learning

Vision   *JUL. 1966*
      Postings: 363   GC: 110
UF   Sight
RT   Ametropia
      Blindness
      Depth Perception
      Eyes
      Hyperopia
      Low Vision Aids
      Myopia
      Ophthalmology
      Optometrists
      Optometry
      Partial Vision
      Strabismus
      Vision Tests
      Visual Acuity
      Visual Discrimination
      Visual Environment
      Visual Impairments
      Visual Learning
      Visual Perception
      Visual Stimuli

Vision Tests   *JUL. 1966*
      Postings: 299   GC: 830
SN   Tests designed to assess visual ability
UF   Auditory Visual Tests (1966 1980) #
BT   Tests
RT   Diagnostic Tests
      Eyes
      Ophthalmology
      Optometrists
      Optometry
      Perception Tests
      Physical Examinations
      Screening Tests
      Tactual Visual Tests
      Vision
      Visual Acuity
      Visual Discrimination
      Visual Impairments
      Visual Perception

Visiting Homemakers   *JUL. 1966*
      Postings: 70   GC: 640
SN   Trained paraprofessionals who provide homemaking and/or basic health care services to the disabled, ill, or elderly
BT   Paraprofessional Personnel
RT   Adult Day Care
      Adult Foster Care
      Allied Health Personnel
      Family Problems
      Home Economics Skills
      Home Health Aides
      Home Management
      Home Programs
      Home Visits
      Hospices (Terminal Care)
      Housekeepers
      Long Term Care
      Occupational Home Economics
      Respite Care
      Social Services

Visiting Teachers
USE   Itinerant Teachers

Visual Acuity   *JUL. 1966*
      Postings: 212   GC: 110
SN   Clearness or keenness of vision as measured by the individual's ability to distinguish visual details
BT   Visual Perception
RT   Ametropia
      Blindness
      Hyperopia
      Myopia
      Ophthalmology
      Optometry
      Partial Vision
      Strabismus
      Vision
      Vision Tests
      Visual Discrimination
      Visual Impairments

Visual Aids   *APR. 1972*
      Postings: 2,092   GC: 720
UF   Visual Equipment
      Visual Materials
      Visual Media
NT   Bulletin Boards
      Cartoons
      Chalkboards
      Charts
      Diagrams
      Display Aids
      Films
      Filmstrips
      Geometric Constructions
      Graphs
      Illustrations
      Maps
      Microforms
      Photographic Equipment
      Photographs
      Projection Equipment
      Raised Line Drawings
      Screens (Displays)
      Signs
      Tables (Data)
      Three Dimensional Aids
      Transparencies
      Video Equipment
      Videotape Recordings
RT   Audiovisual Aids
      Comics (Publications)
      Educational Media
      Instructional Materials
      Nonprint Media
      Visual Literacy
      Visual Stimuli

Visual Arts   *JUL. 1966*
      Postings: 1,873   GC: 420
NT   Architecture
      Childrens Art
      Design Crafts
      Drafting
      Film Production
      Freehand Drawing
      Graphic Arts
      Handicrafts
      Painting (Visual Arts)
      Photography
      Printmaking
      Sculpture
BT   Fine Arts
RT   Aesthetics
      Art
      Art Activities
      Art Criticism
      Art Education

= Two or more Descriptors are used to represent this term.
The term's main entry shows the appropriate coordination.

Art History
Art Materials
Art Teachers
Art Therapy
Buildings
Collage
Color Planning
Commercial Art
Cultural Activities
Discipline Based Art Education
Found Objects
Material Culture
Metal Working
Patternmaking
Relief (Art)
Studio Art
Woodworking

Visual Discrimination   *JUL. 1966*
              Postings: 958   GC: 110
SN   Ability to recognize and identify visual
           shapes, forms, and patterns
BT   Visual Perception
RT   Contrast
           Discrimination Learning
           Sensory Training
           Vision
           Vision Tests
           Visual Acuity
           Visual Environment
           Visual Learning
           Visual Literacy
           Visual Stimuli

Visual Display Units
USE   Video Display Terminals

Visual Environment   *JUL. 1966*
              Postings: 207   GC: 920
BT   Physical Environment
RT   Building Design
           Built Environment
           Color
           Color Planning
           Design Requirements
           Environmental Influences
           Glare
           Light
           Lighting
           Vision
           Visual Discrimination

Visual Equipment
USE   Visual Aids

Visual Impairments   *MAR. 1980*
              Postings: 3,834   GC: 220
SN   Visual losses that interfere with normal
           functioning and performance and range
           from mild to total
UF   Visually Handicapped (1966 1980)
NT   Ametropia
           Blindness
           Partial Vision
           Strabismus
BT   Disabilities
RT   Eye Movements
           Eyes
           Learning Problems
           Low Vision Aids
           Mobility Aids
           Ophthalmology
           Optometry
           Sensory Aids
           Travel Training
           Vision
           Vision Tests
           Visual Acuity
           Visually Impaired Mobility

Visual Language Learning
USE   Language Acquisition
AND   Visual Learning

Visual Learning   *JUL. 1966*
              Postings: 1,607   GC: 110
SN   Learning that involves the processing of
           visual stimuli
UF   Visual Language Learning #
BT   Learning
RT   Associative Learning
           Cued Speech
           Learning Modalities
           Multisensory Learning
           Nonverbal Learning
           Pictorial Stimuli
           Symbolic Learning
           Visible Speech
           Vision
           Visual Discrimination
           Visual Literacy
           Visual Perception
           Visual Stimuli

Visual Literacy   *MAR. 1972*
              Postings: 1,019   GC: 110
SN   A group of competencies that allows
           humans to discriminate and interpret the
           visible action, objects, and/or symbols,
           natural or constructed, that they encoun-
           ter in the environment (e.g., television,
           films, paintings, etc.)
BT   Skills
RT   Aesthetic Education
           Art Appreciation
           Audience Response
           Critical Viewing
           Film Study
           Nonverbal Communication
           Perception Tests
           Perceptual Development
           Perceptual Impairments
           Semiotics
           Television Viewing
           Visual Aids
           Visual Discrimination
           Visual Learning
           Visual Measures
           Visual Perception
           Visual Stimuli

Visual Materials
USE   Visual Aids

Visual Measures   *JUL. 1966*
              Postings: 397   GC: 830
SN   Tests in which the items are presented in
           pictures, patterns, diagrams, graphic fig-
           ures, or other visual displays with a
           minimum of verbal or numerical material
           (Note: Do not confuse with "Vision Tests")
UF   Nondiscursive Measures
           Pictorial Tests
BT   Nonverbal Tests
RT   Pictorial Stimuli
           Projective Measures
           Spatial Ability
           Visual Literacy
           Visual Stimuli

Visual Media
USE   Visual Aids

Visual Perception   *JUL. 1966*
              Postings: 3,376   GC: 110
SN   Ability to interpret what is seen
NT   Depth Perception
           Visual Acuity
           Visual Discrimination
BT   Perception
RT   Color
           Dimensional Preference
           Eye Fixations
           Eye Voice Span
           Field Dependence Independence
           Figural Aftereffects
           Language Processing
           Perception Tests
           Perceptual Impairments
           Sensory Experience
           Sensory Training
           Tactual Visual Tests
           Vision

Vision Tests
Visual Learning
Visual Literacy
Visual Stimuli
Visualization

Visual Scanners
USE   Optical Scanners

Visual Stimuli   *JUL. 1966*
              Postings: 2,454   GC: 110
NT   Pictorial Stimuli
BT   Stimuli
RT   Association Measures
           Auditory Stimuli
           Electrical Stimuli
           Tachistoscopes
           Tactile Stimuli
           Television Viewing
           Verbal Stimuli
           Vision
           Visual Aids
           Visual Discrimination
           Visual Learning
           Visual Literacy
           Visual Measures
           Visual Perception

Visualization   *JUL. 1966*
              Postings: 981   GC: 110
SN   Act or power of forming mentally visual
           images of objects not present to the eye
BT   Cognitive Processes
RT   Creative Thinking
           Eidetic Imagery
           Memorization
           Memory
           Recall (Psychology)
           Retention (Psychology)
           Spatial Ability
           Thinking Skills
           Visual Perception

Visually Handicapped Mobility (1967 1994)
USE   Visually Impaired Mobility

Visually Handicapped Orientation (1967 1980)
USE   Visually Impaired Mobility

Visually Handicapped (1966 1980)
USE   Visual Impairments

Visually Impaired Mobility   *MAR. 1994*
              Postings: 92   GC: 220
UF   Visually Handicapped Mobility (1967 1994)
           Visually Handicapped Orientation (1967 1980)
BT   Physical Mobility
RT   Daily Living Skills
           Echolocation
           Mobility Aids
           Spatial Ability
           Travel Training
           Visual Impairments

Visuospatial Ability
USE   Spatial Ability

Vitae
USE   Resumes (Personal)

Vocabulary   *JUL. 1966*
              Postings: 4,908   GC: 450
SN   (Note: Use a more specific term if
           possible—this broad term corresponds
           to Pubtype code 134 and should not be
           used except as the subject of a docu-
           ment)
UF   Terminology
NT   Aviation Vocabulary
           Banking Vocabulary
           Basic Vocabulary

Chemical Nomenclature
International Trade Vocabulary
Jargon
Keywords
Kinship Terminology
Mathematical Vocabulary
Medical Vocabulary
Sight Vocabulary
Subject Index Terms
Word Lists
RT   Adjectives
           Adverbs
           Code Switching (Language)
           Definitions
           Glossaries
           Glottochronology
           Language Arts
           Lexicology
           Linguistic Borrowing
           Multilingual Materials
           Nouns
           Reading
           Thesauri
           Verbs
           Vocabulary Development
           Vocabulary Skills
           Word Frequency

Vocabulary Building
USE   Vocabulary Development

Vocabulary Development   *JUL. 1966*
              Postings: 5,089   GC: 450
UF   Vocabulary Building
BT   Development
RT   Context Clues
           Lexicography
           Verbal Development
           Vocabulary

Vocabulary Skills   *JUL. 1966*
              Postings: 1,165   GC: 450
BT   Language Skills
RT   Basic Skills
           Basic Vocabulary
           Context Clues
           Reading Skills
           Vocabulary

Vocal Ensembles
USE   Singing

Vocal Music   *OCT. 1968*
              Postings: 381   GC: 420
SN   Musical compositions written for voices,
           either solo or chorus
NT   Choral Music
           Songs
BT   Music
RT   Applied Music
           Music Activities
           Music Education
           Music Techniques
           Musical Composition
           Opera
           Popular Music
           Rhyme
           Rock Music
           Singing

Vocational Academies
USE   Career Academies

Vocational Adjustment   *JUL. 1966*
              Postings: 1,673   GC: 630
UF   Employment Adjustment
           Job Adjustment
           Occupational Adjustment
           Work Adjustment
BT   Adjustment (to Environment)
RT   Career Change
           Career Counseling
           Employer Employee Relationship
           Industrial Psychology
           Job Enrichment
           Job Satisfaction
           Occupational Mobility

= Two or more Descriptors are used to represent this term.
The term's main entry shows the appropriate coordination.

Skill Obsolescence
Vocational Education
Vocational Evaluation
Vocational Maturity
Vocational Training Centers
Work Attitudes
Work Experience Programs

Vocational Agriculture Teachers (1967 1980)
USE Agricultural Education
AND Vocational Education Teachers

Vocational Agriculture (1967 1980)
USE Agricultural Education
AND Vocational Education

Vocational Aptitude   AUG. 1968
        Postings: 544   GC: 120
SN An individual's potential capacity or suita-
        bility for a vocation or occupation
UF Vocational Talents
BT Aptitude
RT Academic Aptitude
        Career Choice
        Career Planning
        Employment Qualifications
        Occupational Tests
        Prevocational Education
        Talent
        Vocational Evaluation

Vocational Aspiration
USE Occupational Aspiration

Vocational Assessment
USE Vocational Evaluation

Vocational Awareness
USE Career Awareness

Vocational Business Education
USE Business Education

Vocational Change
USE Career Change

Vocational Choice
USE Career Choice

Vocational Counseling (1966 1980)
USE Career Counseling

Vocational Development (1967 1978)
USE Career Development

Vocational Directors   JUL. 1966
        Postings: 363   GC: 360
SN Administrators of vocational education
        programs
UF Technical Education Directors
        Vocational Education Directors
BT Administrators
RT Vocational Education

Vocational Education   JUL. 1966
        Postings: 29,484   GC: 400
SN Formal preparation for semiskilled, skilled,
        technical, or paraprofessional occupa-
        tions usually below the baccalaureate
        degree (Note: Coordinate with the man-
        datory level term "Secondary Education,"
        unless another educational level is
        specified—if possible, use a more spe-
        cific Descriptor)
UF Agricultural Education (Vocational) #
        Health Occupations Education (Voca-
                tional) #
        Service Education (1966 1980)
        Vocational Agriculture (1967 1980) #
        Vocational Training
NT Adult Vocational Education

Business Education
Cooperative Education
Distributive Education
Occupational Home Economics
Prevocational Education
Technical Education
Trade and Industrial Education
BT Education
RT Agricultural Education
        Allied Health Occupations Education
        Apprenticeships
        Career Academies
        Career Counseling
        Career Education
        Continuation Students
        Experiential Learning
        Industrial Arts
        Industrial Education
        Information Science Education
        Job Placement
        Job Skills
        Job Training
        Labor Force Development
        Noncollege Bound Students
        Occupations
        Paraprofessional Personnel
        Postsecondary Education
        Relevance (Education)
        Research Coordinating Units
        School Business Relationship
        Secondary Education
        Service Workers
        Special Needs Students
        Technical Institutes
        Technology
        Vocational Adjustment
        Vocational Directors
        Vocational Education Teachers
        Vocational English (Second Language)
        Vocational Interests
        Vocational Rehabilitation
        Vocational Schools
        Vocational Training Centers
        Work Experience Programs

Vocational Education Directors
USE Vocational Directors

Vocational Education Teachers   JUL. 1966
        Postings: 2,506   GC: 360
UF Vocational Agriculture Teachers (1967
                1980) #
NT Business Education Teachers
        Distributive Education Teachers
        Trade and Industrial Teachers
BT Teachers
RT Home Economics Teachers
        Industrial Arts Teachers
        Instructor Coordinators
        Technical Education
        Vocational Education

Vocational English (Second Language)
                                        DEC. 1985
        Postings: 274   GC: 440
SN Specialized English for non-English speak-
        ers preparing for or working in skilled,
        semiskilled, paraprofessional, or techni-
        cal occupations
BT English for Special Purposes
RT Job Skills
        Vocational Education

Vocational Evaluation   NOV. 1982
        Postings: 692   GC: 820
SN Systematic use of real or simulated work
        experiences and/or other measures to
        assess vocational aptitude, skill, and ca-
        pacity to perform adequately in a par-
        ticular work environment—commonly ad-
        ministered for the disabled and
        disadvantaged, but may also be applica-
        ble to other populations (Note: Do not
        confuse with "Personnel Evaluation")
UF Vocational Assessment
        Work Evaluation (Performance)
        Work Performance Evaluation
BT Evaluation
RT Competence

Diagnostic Tests
Job Performance
Job Skills
Occupational Tests
Personnel Evaluation
Situational Tests
Student Evaluation
Vocational Adjustment
Vocational Aptitude
Vocational Rehabilitation
Work Sample Tests

Vocational Followup   JUL. 1966
        Postings: 1,376   GC: 810
SN Investigating the employment-related ac-
        tivities, progress, or attitudes of indi-
        viduals or groups following their partici-
        pation in a program, course of study,
        guidance process, etc. (Note: As of Oct81,
        use as a minor Descriptor for examples
        of this kind of study—use as a major
        Descriptor only as the subject of a docu-
        ment)
UF Occupational Followup
BT Followup Studies
RT Education Work Relationship
        Employment Patterns
        Graduate Surveys

Vocational Guidance
USE Career Guidance

Vocational High Schools   JUL. 1966
        Postings: 223   GC: 340
UF Technical High Schools
BT High Schools
        Vocational Schools
RT Career Academies

Vocational Industrial Education
USE Trade and Industrial Education

Vocational Interests   JUL. 1966
        Postings: 1,971   GC: 120
BT Interests
RT Career Choice
        Career Counseling
        Career Development
        Career Exploration
        Career Guidance
        Occupational Aspiration
        Occupational Tests
        Vocational Education

Vocational Maturity   OCT. 1973
        Postings: 658   GC: 120
SN Degree of an individual's skill in making
        decisions concerning his/her vocation at
        a given life stage
UF Career Maturity
BT Maturity (Individuals)
RT Career Choice
        Career Development
        Career Exploration
        Decision Making
        Employee Attitudes
        Maturity Tests
        Occupational Aspiration
        Vocational Adjustment
        Work Attitudes

Vocational Nursing
USE Practical Nursing

Vocational Placement
USE Job Placement

Vocational Rehabilitation   JUL. 1966
        Postings: 2,596   GC: 630
SN Process of developing, restoring, or pre-
        serving the ability to engage in suitable
        employment through such services as
        diagnosis, guidance, counseling, physi-
        cal restoration, education, training, and
        placement

BT Rehabilitation
RT Adult Vocational Education
        Correctional Education
        Correctional Rehabilitation
        Sheltered Workshops
        Supported Employment
        Vocational Education
        Vocational Evaluation
        Vocational Training Centers
        Work Sample Tests

Vocational Retraining (1966 1980)
USE Retraining

Vocational Satisfaction
USE Job Satisfaction

Vocational Schools   JUL. 1966
        Postings: 1,312   GC: 340
UF Area Vocational Schools (1966
                1980) #
        Technical Schools
NT Career Academies
        Vocational High Schools
BT Schools
RT Postsecondary Education
        Secondary Schools
        Vocational Education
        Vocational Training Centers

Vocational Skills
USE Job Skills

Vocational Talents
USE Vocational Aptitude

Vocational Tests
USE Occupational Tests

Vocational Training
USE Vocational Education

Vocational Training Centers   JUL. 1966
        Postings: 440   GC: 920
BT Educational Facilities
RT Career Counseling
        Job Training
        Off the Job Training
        Rehabilitation Centers
        Sheltered Workshops
        Vocational Adjustment
        Vocational Education
        Vocational Rehabilitation
        Vocational Schools

Vocational Work Experience
USE Cooperative Education

Vocations
USE Occupations

Vocoids
USE Vowels

Vogul   JUL. 1966
        Postings: 2   GC: 440
BT Finno Ugric Languages

Voice Disorders   JUL. 1966
        Postings: 239   GC: 220
SN Abnormal vocal quality, pitch, and inten-
        sity caused by pathology or misuse of
        the larynx
UF Dysphonia
BT Speech Impairments
RT Speech
        Speech Therapy

Voice Synthesizers
USE Speech Synthesizers

= Two or more Descriptors are used to represent this term.
The term's main entry shows the appropriate coordination.

Volcanoes   NOV. 1994
    Postings: 62   GC: 490
SN   Vents in the crust of a planet or moon through which lava, steam, ash, etc., are expelled either continuously or at irregular intervals—also, the mountains or hills formed by emissions from such vents
UF   Volcanology
RT   Earthquakes
    Geology
    Natural Disasters
    Physical Geography
    Plate Tectonics

Volcanology
USE   Volcanoes

Volition
USE   Individual Power

Volleyball   DEC. 1975
    Postings: 78   GC: 470
BT   Team Sports
RT   Olympic Games

Volume (Mathematics)   OCT. 1983
    Postings: 107   GC: 480
SN   Three-dimensional space
UF   Cubic Measure
BT   Geometric Concepts
    Space
RT   Area
    Solid Geometry
    Weight (Mass)

Volume (Sound)
USE   Noise (Sound)

Voluntary Agencies   JUL. 1966
    Postings: 974   GC: 520
UF   Voluntary Associations
    Voluntary Organizations
BT   Agencies
RT   Agency Role
    Nongovernmental Organizations
    Private Agencies
    Religious Organizations
    Social Agencies
    Volunteers
    Youth Agencies

Voluntary Associations
USE   Voluntary Agencies

Voluntary Desegregation   MAR. 1980
    Postings: 197   GC: 540
SN   Desegregation initiated on a voluntary basis, i.e., without a court order or other legal mandate
UF   Voluntary Integration (1966 1980)
BT   Social Integration
RT   Desegregation Plans
    Magnet Schools
    Racial Integration
    School Desegregation

Voluntary Integration (1966 1980)
USE   Voluntary Desegregation

Voluntary Organizations
USE   Voluntary Agencies

Volunteer Training   JUL. 1966
    Postings: 1,199   GC: 400
SN   The training of volunteers (Note: For training by volunteers, coordinate "Volunteers" and "Trainers"—prior to Mar83, the use of this term was not restricted by a Scope Note)
BT   Training
RT   Experiential Learning
    Service Learning

Volunteers
Work Experience

Volunteers   JUL. 1966
    Postings: 3,537   GC: 630
NT   Student Volunteers
BT   Groups
RT   Paraprofessional School Personnel
    Public Service
    School Aides
    Teacher Aides
    Voluntary Agencies
    Volunteer Training

Voter Registration   JUL. 1966
    Postings: 154   GC: 610
RT   Elections
    Voting
    Voting Rights

Voting   JUL. 1966
    Postings: 874   GC: 610
RT   Bond Issues
    Citizen Participation
    Citizenship Responsibility
    Elections
    Local Issues
    Political Attitudes
    Political Campaigns
    Political Candidates
    Political Issues
    Political Parties
    Politics
    Public Opinion
    Residence Requirements
    Voter Registration
    Voting Rights

Voting Rights   JUL. 1966
    Postings: 213   GC: 610
BT   Civil Rights
RT   Elections
    Voter Registration
    Voting

Voucher Plans
USE   Educational Vouchers

Vowels   JUL. 1966
    Postings: 1,024   GC: 450
UF   Vocoids
BT   Phonemes
RT   Articulation (Speech)
    Consonants
    Phonetics
    Phonology
    Syllables

Wage Salary Differentials
USE   Salary Wage Differentials

Wage Statements (1966 1980)
USE   Payroll Records

Wages   JUL. 1966
    Postings: 1,476   GC: 630
SN   Earnings paid at hourly rates or on a piecework basis (Note: Do not confuse with "Salaries"—prior to Mar80, the use of this term was not restricted by a Scope Note)
NT   Minimum Wage
BT   Expenditures
    Income
RT   Compensation (Remuneration)
    Costs
    Fringe Benefits
    Guaranteed Income
    Merit Pay
    Minimum Wage Legislation
    Operating Expenses
    Overtime
    Payroll Records
    Premium Pay
    Retirement Benefits

Salaries
Salary Wage Differentials
Scope of Bargaining

Wait Time   FEB. 1993
    Postings: 71   GC: 310
SN   The duration of pauses separating utterances in a conversation, e.g., the time a teacher waits after asking a question and after receiving a response (Note: Use the Identifiers "Time Lag" for broader contexts and "Time Delay" for response prompting and fading with the disabled—see also the generic Identifier "Waiting")
UF   Teacher Wait Time
RT   Discussion (Teaching Technique)
    Learning Strategies
    Questioning Techniques
    Responses
    Teaching Methods
    Time Factors (Learning)

Waiters and Waitresses   AUG. 1986
    Postings: 21   GC: 640
BT   Service Workers
RT   Dining Facilities
    Food Service

Walking   JUL. 1997
    Postings: 70   GC: 470
SN   (Note: See also the Identifier "Hiking")
BT   Physical Activities
RT   Athletics
    Pedestrian Traffic
    Physical Fitness
    Physical Mobility
    Running
    Trails
    Travel Training

Walleyes
USE   Strabismus

War   APR. 1972
    Postings: 1,208   GC: 610
UF   Civil War
    Conventional Warfare
    Guerrilla Warfare
    International War
    Unconventional Warfare
NT   Civil War (United States)
    Korean War
    Nuclear Warfare
    Revolutionary War (United States)
    Vietnam War
    World War I
    World War II
BT   Conflict
RT   Armed Forces
    Disarmament
    Genocide
    History
    International Crimes
    International Law
    International Relations
    Military Science
    National Defense
    Peace
    Revolution
    Terrorism
    Treaties
    Violence
    Weapons
    World Problems

War Crimes
USE   International Crimes

Warehouses   JUL. 1966
    Postings: 29   GC: 920
BT   Facilities
RT   Equipment Storage
    Storage

Washrooms
USE   Toilet Facilities

Waste Disposal   JUL. 1972
    Postings: 1,129   GC: 410
SN   Act or process of discarding or throwing away unneeded or excess material including solids, oils, gases, chemicals, and liquids
UF   Waste Management
NT   Recycling
BT   Sanitation
RT   Air Pollution
    Biotechnology
    Ecology
    Environmental Standards
    Pollution
    Radiation
    Sanitary Facilities
    Solid Wastes
    Waste Water
    Wastes
    Water Pollution

Waste Management
USE   Waste Disposal

Waste Water   AUG. 1982
    Postings: 166   GC: 410
SN   Used water carrying suspended or dissolved solids from farms, industries, businesses, or homes
UF   Sewage
    Waste Water Treatment #
BT   Wastes
    Water
RT   Pollution
    Recycling
    Sludge
    Solid Wastes
    Waste Disposal
    Water Pollution
    Water Treatment

Waste Water Treatment
USE   Waste Water
AND   Water Treatment

Wastes   JUL. 1972
    Postings: 532   GC: 410
SN   Unneeded, discarded, or excess material including solids, oils, gases, chemicals, and liquids
UF   Hazardous Wastes #
    Refuse
NT   Solid Wastes
    Waste Water
BT   Matter
RT   Conservation (Environment)
    Ecology
    Hazardous Materials
    Poisons
    Pollution
    Recycling
    Resources
    Sludge
    Waste Disposal

Watch Repairers
USE   Watchmakers

Watchmakers   JAN. 1969
    Postings: 9   GC: 640
UF   Clockmakers
    Horologists
    Watch Repairers
BT   Skilled Workers
RT   Horology

Water   AUG. 1982
    Postings: 474   GC: 490
SN   Odorless, colorless, tasteless liquid in the proportion of two atoms of hydrogen to one atom of oxygen (Note: Prior to Aug82, "Water Resources" was occasionally used for this concept)
NT   Drinking Water
    Groundwater
    Waste Water
BT   Matter

= Two or more Descriptors are used to represent this term.
The term's main entry shows the appropriate coordination.

RT   Aquariums
      Aquatic Sports
      Chemistry
      Climate
      Drought
      Earth Science
      Ecology
      Estuaries
      Floods
      Humidity
      Hydraulics
      Hydrology
      Marine Education
      Maritime Education
      Meteorology
      Ocean Engineering
      Oceanography
      Physical Environment
      Physical Geography
      Rivers
      Sludge
      Soil Conservation
      Thermal Environment
      Water Pollution
      Water Quality
      Water Resources
      Water Treatment
      Weather
      Wetlands

Water Pollution   MAR. 1980
      Postings: 1,365   GC: 410
UF   River Pollution
      Stream Pollution
      Water Pollution Control (1969 1980)
NT   Acid Rain
BT   Pollution
RT   Conservation (Environment)
      Ecology
      Environmental Education
      Environmental Standards
      Groundwater
      Hydrology
      Rivers
      Sludge
      Urban Environment
      Waste Disposal
      Waste Water
      Water
      Water Quality
      Water Resources
      Water Treatment

Water Pollution Control (1969 1980)
USE   Water Pollution

Water Polo   JAN. 1985
      Postings: 5   GC: 470
BT   Aquatic Sports
      Team Sports
RT   Olympic Games
      Swimming

Water Purification
USE   Water Treatment

Water Quality   AUG. 1982
      Postings: 457   GC: 410
SN   Biological, chemical, and physical char-
      acteristics of water that influence its
      healthy and fruitful use
UF   Clean Water
RT   Acid Rain
      Conservation (Environment)
      Drinking Water
      Ecology
      Environmental Standards
      Groundwater
      Health
      Hydrology
      Physical Environment
      Rivers
      Water
      Water Pollution
      Water Resources
      Water Treatment

Water Resources   JUL. 1966
      Postings: 1,553   GC: 410
SN   All sources and supplies of water such
      as rivers, lakes, streams, reservoirs, and
      ground water (Note: Prior to Aug82, the
      use of this term was not restricted by a
      Scope Note)
UF   Water Supply
NT   Groundwater
      Rivers
BT   Natural Resources
RT   Conservation (Environment)
      Depleted Resources
      Drought
      Energy Conservation
      Estuaries
      Geothermal Energy
      Hydrology
      Utilities
      Water
      Water Pollution
      Water Quality
      Water Treatment
      Wetlands

Water Softening
USE   Water Treatment

Water Sports
USE   Aquatic Sports

Water Supply
USE   Water Resources

Water Treatment   AUG. 1982
      Postings: 333   GC: 490
SN   Purification or other treatment of water
      for drinking, etc.
UF   Chlorination (Water)
      Waste Water Treatment #
      Water Purification
      Water Softening
      Water Works #
BT   Technology
RT   Chemical Analysis
      Chemical Engineering
      Civil Engineering
      Disease Control
      Drinking Water
      Environmental Technicians
      Fluoridation
      Health
      Hydrology
      Public Health
      Recycling
      Sanitation
      Sludge
      Solid Wastes
      Utilities
      Waste Water
      Water
      Water Pollution
      Water Quality
      Water Resources

Water Utilities
USE   Utilities

Water Works
USE   Utilities
AND   Water Treatment

Waterskiing   FEB. 1978
      Postings: 5   GC: 470
BT   Aquatic Sports

Wealth Neutrality
USE   Fiscal Neutrality

Weapons   JAN. 1999
      Postings: 126   GC: 210
SN   Instruments, devices, or techniques used
      to attack or to counter an attack
UF   Arms (Weapons)
      Combat Instruments

NT   Guns
      Nuclear Weapons
RT   Armed Forces
      Disarmament
      Military Science
      Military Training
      Safety
      School Safety
      Violence
      War

Weariness
USE   Fatigue (Biology)

Weather   MAR. 1980
      Postings: 411   GC: 490
SN   State of atmospheric conditions at any
      one place and time
NT   Drought
      Hurricanes
      Tornadoes
RT   Climate
      Climate Change
      Climate Control
      Ecology
      Environmental Influences
      Floods
      Meteorology
      Natural Disasters
      Physical Environment
      Thermal Environment
      Water
      Wind (Meteorology)

Web (The)
USE   World Wide Web

Webzines
USE   Electronic Journals

Weeding (Library)   AUG. 1994
      Postings: 87   GC: 710
SN   Practice of discarding or transferring to
      storage excess copies, rarely used books,
      and materials considered no longer use-
      ful in the library
BT   Library Collection Development
RT   Libraries
      Library Collections
      Library Technical Processes

Weeds   JUL. 1966
      Postings: 100   GC: 410
BT   Plants (Botany)
RT   Agronomy
      Botany
      Gardening
      Herbicides
      Pests
      Wildlife

Weekend Programs   JUL. 1966
      Postings: 184   GC: 350
BT   Programs
RT   Enrichment Activities

Weight (Mass)   OCT. 1980
      Postings: 121   GC: 490
SN   (Note: For living organisms, use "Body
      Weight")
BT   Scientific Concepts
RT   Acceleration (Physics)
      Density (Matter)
      Force
      Gravity (Physics)
      Matter
      Pressure (Physics)
      Volume (Mathematics)

Weight Training
USE   Weightlifting

Weight (1968 1980)   JUN. 1980
      Postings: 56   GC: 820
SN   Invalid Descriptor—used inconsistently
      in indexing—for inorganic physical ob-
      jects, use "Weight (Mass)"—for living
      organisms, use "Body Weight"—for
      scores, use "Weighted Scores"—for data
      other than scores, use the Identifier
      "Weighted Data"

Weighted Scores   MAY 1971
      Postings: 229   GC: 820
SN   Scores in which the components are
      modified by different multipliers to re-
      flect their relative importance—may be
      applied to test items, tests, grades, or
      other measures or ratings
BT   Scores
RT   Equated Scores
      Grade Equivalent Scores
      Item Analysis
      Multiple Regression Analysis
      Raw Scores
      Reliability
      Robustness (Statistics)
      Scoring Formulas
      Validity

Weightlifting   FEB. 1978
      Postings: 75   GC: 470
SN   The lifting of standard weights in a pre-
      scribed manner, as a competitive event
      or conditioning exercise
UF   Weight Training
BT   Athletics
      Lifting
RT   Muscular Strength
      Olympic Games

Welders (1968 1981)
USE   Welding

Welding   JUL. 1966
      Postings: 404   GC: 640
UF   Acetylene Welding
      Arc Welding
      Gas Welding
      Welders (1968 1981)
BT   Technology
RT   Construction (Process)
      Finishing
      Metal Working
      Sculpture
      Skilled Occupations

Welfare Agencies   JUL. 1966
      Postings: 345   GC: 520
SN   Agencies that provide welfare services
      (Note: Prior to Mar80, the use of this
      term was not restricted by a Scope Note)
BT   Social Agencies
RT   Agency Role
      Public Agencies
      Social Work
      Social Workers
      State Agencies
      Welfare Services
      Youth Agencies

Welfare Problems (1966 1980)
USE   Welfare Services

Welfare Recipients   JUL. 1966
      Postings: 1,322   GC: 510
SN   Individuals or groups who receive wel-
      fare services
BT   Groups
RT   Economically Disadvantaged
      Eligibility
      Low Income Groups
      Welfare Services

Welfare Services   JUL. 1966
      Postings: 1,853   GC: 520
SN   Organized public or private assistance
      provided to financially needy individuals

= Two or more Descriptors are used to represent this term.
The term's main entry shows the appropriate coordination.

or their families (Note: Prior to Mar80, this concept may have been indexed under "Welfare" or "Social Welfare")
UF   Public Welfare Assistance
     Welfare Problems (1966 1980)
NT   Migrant Welfare Services
BT   Social Services
RT   Eligibility
     Housing Management Aides
     Humanitarianism
     Poverty Programs
     Public Housing
     Settlement Houses
     Social Responsibility
     Social Work
     Welfare Agencies
     Welfare Recipients

Welfare (1966 1980)   MAR. 1980
     Postings: 238   GC: 520
SN   Invalid Descriptor—used for well-being and various types of social services—use "Well Being" for former concept, "Welfare Services" for organized assistance to the disadvantaged, and "Social Services" or other appropriate terms for social services provided to the general population

Well Being   MAR. 1982
     Postings: 1,905   GC: 120
SN   Condition of existence, or state of awareness, in which physical and/or psychological needs are satisfied
NT   Child Welfare
     Student Welfare
     Teacher Welfare
     Wellness
BT   Quality of Life
RT   Adjustment (to Environment)
     Coping
     Environment
     Happiness
     Health Promotion
     Individual Needs
     Life Events
     Life Satisfaction
     Psychological Patterns
     Responses
     Satisfaction

Wellness   APR. 2000
     Postings: 233   GC: 120
SN   Condition of physical and psychological well-being attained through deliberate pursuit of a healthy lifestyle (Note: Prior to Apr00, the instruction "Wellness Programs, USE Health Promotion" was carried in the Thesaurus)
UF   Wellness Programs
BT   Health
     Well Being
RT   Counseling
     Health Education
     Health Promotion
     Life Style
     Mental Health
     Physical Fitness
     Physical Health
     Stress Management

Wellness Programs
USE Wellness

Welsh   SEP. 1975
     Postings: 99   GC: 440
SN   The Celtic language native to Wales
BT   Indo European Languages
RT   English
     Middle English
     Old English
     Romance Languages

Weltanschauungen
USE World Views

Western Civilization   SEP. 1968
     Postings: 861   GC: 560
SN   Includes Europe and the Western Hemisphere from the time of the Roman Empire through the present
UF   Occidental Civilization
BT   Culture
RT   Area Studies
     Christianity
     Cultural Background
     Cultural Context
     European History
     Greek Civilization
     History
     Judaism
     Latin American Culture
     Latin American History
     North American Culture
     North American History
     Religion Studies
     Sociocultural Patterns
     World History

Wetlands   JAN. 1993
     Postings: 111   GC: 410
SN   Low areas with shallow water or water-soaked soils (e.g., freshwater marshes, saltwater marshes, swamps, mud flats, bogs)
UF   Bogs
     Fens
     Marshes
     Salt Marshes
     Swamps
RT   Conservation (Environment)
     Conservation Education
     Ecology
     Environmental Education
     Estuaries
     Fisheries
     Habitats
     Land Use
     Marine Biology
     Marine Education
     Oceanography
     Rivers
     Soil Conservation
     Water
     Water Resources
     Wildlife Management

Wheel Chairs (1970 1981)
USE Wheelchairs

Wheelchairs   NOV. 1981
     Postings: 133   GC: 220
UF   Wheel Chairs (1970 1981)
BT   Mobility Aids
RT   Biomedical Equipment
     Physical Disabilities
     Physical Mobility

White Black Relations
USE Racial Relations

White Collar Occupations   JUL. 1966
     Postings: 179   GC: 640
SN   Occupations requiring office, clerical, administrative, sales, professional, or technical work (Note: Use to distinguish from "Blue Collar Occupations")
BT   Occupations
RT   Blue Collar Occupations
     Clerical Occupations
     Data Processing Occupations
     Managerial Occupations
     Office Occupations
     Professional Occupations
     Sales Occupations
     Technical Occupations
     Working Class

White Ethnics
USE Whites

White Flight
USE Migration

AND Whites

White Students   MAR. 1980
     Postings: 2,151   GC: 360
UF   Caucasian Students (1967 1980)
BT   Students
     Whites

Whites   MAR. 1980
     Postings: 3,749   GC: 560
UF   Caucasian Race (1967 1980)
     Caucasians (1967 1980)
     White Ethnics
     White Flight #
NT   White Students
BT   Groups
RT   Anglo Americans
     Race
     Racial Relations

Whole Language Approach   APR. 1990
     Postings: 1,767   GC: 450
SN   Method of integrating language arts "across the curriculum" that uses the real literature of various age groups and subject fields to promote literacy (i.e., reading, writing, speaking, listening, as well as thinking, skills)
BT   Holistic Approach
     Teaching Methods
RT   Language Arts
     Language Enrichment
     Language Experience Approach
     Language Skills
     Literature
     Literature Appreciation
     Reading Instruction
     Reading Writing Relationship
     Second Language Instruction
     Writing Instruction

Whole Numbers   JUL. 1966
     Postings: 300   GC: 480
BT   Integers

Whole Person Approach
USE Holistic Approach

Whole Word Reading Approach
USE Sight Method

Wholesaling   AUG. 1968
     Postings: 62   GC: 650
BT   Marketing
RT   Distributive Education
     Merchants
     Retailing
     Salesmanship

Wholistic Approach
USE Holistic Approach

Widowed   NOV. 1975
     Postings: 288   GC: 510
SN   Widows and widowers
BT   Groups
RT   Bereavement
     Death
     Displaced Homemakers
     Fatherless Family
     Marital Status
     Motherless Family
     One Parent Family
     Remarriage
     Spouses

Wilderness   SEP. 1994
     Postings: 170   GC: 410
SN   An environmental condition that is characterized by a naturally developed life community undisturbed by human activity, often featuring remoteness, ruggedness, and sometimes potential dangers (Note: Coordinate with "Outdoor Activi-

ties" or "Outdoor Education" for experience or education relating to wilderness)
BT   Physical Environment
RT   Adventure Education
     Camping
     Conservation (Environment)
     Conservation Education
     Ecology
     Environmental Education
     Land Settlement
     Land Use
     Natural Resources
     Outdoor Activities
     Outdoor Education
     Wildlife

Wildlife   AUG. 1980
     Postings: 617   GC: 410
SN   Animals and/or plants living in a natural (undomesticated or uncultivated) state
NT   Endangered Species
RT   Animals
     Biodiversity
     Biological Sciences
     Birds
     Botany
     Habitats
     Natural Resources
     Physical Environment
     Plant Growth
     Plants (Botany)
     Trees
     Weeds
     Wilderness
     Wildlife Management
     Zoology

Wildlife Management   SEP. 1968
     Postings: 395   GC: 410
UF   Gamekeeping
BT   Technology
RT   Animal Facilities
     Aquariums
     Conservation (Environment)
     Endangered Species
     Forestry
     Habitats
     Rainforests
     Recreational Activities
     Wetlands
     Wildlife
     Zoos

Wills   SEP. 1969
     Postings: 53   GC: 620
BT   Records (Forms)
RT   Estate Planning
     Financial Support
     Property Accounting
     Property Appraisal
     Resource Allocation
     Trusts (Financial)

Wind (Meteorology)   AUG. 1982
     Postings: 68   GC: 490
SN   The natural motion of air (Note: Do not confuse with "Air Flow")
RT   Air Pollution
     Climate
     Earth Science
     Ecology
     Hurricanes
     Meteorology
     Motion
     Physical Environment
     Physical Geography
     Soil Conservation
     Solar Energy
     Temperature
     Thermal Environment
     Tornadoes
     Weather
     Wind Energy

Wind Energy   AUG. 1982
     Postings: 58   GC: 490
SN   Power derived from the force of wind
BT   Energy
RT   Alternative Energy Sources

= Two or more Descriptors are used to represent this term.
The term's main entry shows the appropriate coordination.

Electricity
Force
Geophysics
Kinetics
Power Technology
Wind (Meteorology)

Wind Instruments   *AUG. 2000*
    Postings: 14   GC: 420
SN   Musical instruments played by causing the air in the instrument to vibrate by blowing into or across the air tube
NT   Brass Instruments
    Woodwind Instruments
BT   Musical Instruments
RT   Music

Window Walls
USE   Glass Walls

Windowless Rooms   *JUL. 1966*
    Postings: 37   GC: 920
SN   Any area in a building closed to exterior environment
BT   Facilities
RT   Air Conditioning
    Auditoriums
    Climate Control
    Corridors
    Fallout Shelters
    Lighting
    Lighting Design
    Recreational Facilities
    Underground Facilities
    Ventilation

Windows   *APR. 1970*
    Postings: 74   GC: 920
UF   Fenestration
BT   Structural Elements (Construction)
RT   Climate Control
    Glare
    Glass Walls
    Lighting
    Ventilation

Winter Olympic Games
USE   Olympic Games
AND   Winter Sports

Winter Sports   *AUG. 1989*
    Postings: 6   GC: 470
SN   Sports played or competed on ice or snow
UF   Winter Olympic Games #
NT   Ice Hockey
    Ice Skating
    Skiing
BT   Athletics

Wire Communications
USE   Telecommunications

Wireless Communications
USE   Telecommunications

Withdrawal (Drugs)
USE   Drug Rehabilitation

Withdrawal (Education)   *MAR. 1980*
    Postings: 816   GC: 330
SN   Termination of class, grade, or school due to transfer, completion of school work, dropping out, or death
UF   Course Withdrawal
    Withdrawal (1966 1980)
RT   Academic Persistence
    Attendance
    College Attendance
    Disqualification
    Dropout Research
    Dropouts
    Expulsion
    Out of School Youth

School Holding Power
Student Attrition
Suspension

Withdrawal (Psychology)   *MAR. 1980*
    Postings: 273   GC: 230
UF   Withdrawal Tendencies (Psychology) (1966 1980)
BT   Psychological Patterns
RT   Alienation
    Autism
    Behavior Disorders
    Behavior Problems
    Fear
    Rejection (Psychology)

Withdrawal Tendencies (Psychology) (1966 1980)
USE   Withdrawal (Psychology)

Withdrawal (1966 1980)
USE   Withdrawal (Education)

Wives
USE   Spouses

Wolof   *JUL. 1966*
    Postings: 18   GC: 440
BT   African Languages

Women
USE   Females

Women Administrators   *APR. 1990*
    Postings: 581   GC: 360
SN   Female managers, directors, and executives in education, business, government, or other organized activity
UF   Women Directors
    Women Managers
    Women Presidents #
BT   Administrators
    Employed Women
RT   Women Faculty

Women Directors
USE   Women Administrators

Women Faculty   *SEP. 1980*
    Postings: 1,404   GC: 360
SN   Female academic staff members engaged in instruction, research, administration, or related educational activities
UF   Women Professors (1966 1980)
    Women Teachers (1967 1980)
BT   Employed Women
    Faculty
RT   Women Administrators

Women Managers
USE   Women Administrators

Women Presidents
USE   Presidents
AND   Women Administrators

Women Professors (1966 1980)
USE   Women Faculty

Women Teachers (1967 1980)
USE   Women Faculty

Women Workers
USE   Employed Women

Womens Athletics   *NOV. 1973*
    Postings: 575   GC: 470
BT   Athletics
RT   Females
    Olympic Games

Physical Education
Recreational Activities
Womens Education

Womens Education   *JUL. 1966*
    Postings: 3,922   GC: 330
SN   Education of females (Note: Do not confuse with "Womens Studies")
BT   Education
RT   Adult Education
    Coeducation
    Continuing Education
    Females
    Gender Issues
    Postsecondary Education
    Professional Continuing Education
    Single Sex Colleges
    Single Sex Schools
    Sororities
    Womens Athletics
    Womens Studies

Womens Liberation
USE   Feminism

Womens Rights
USE   Feminism

Womens Studies   *OCT. 1972*
    Postings: 2,249   GC: 400
SN   Curriculum or subject area encompassing the history and contemporary social, political, and cultural situation of women
BT   Curriculum
RT   Consciousness Raising
    Females
    Feminism
    Feminist Criticism
    Gender Issues
    United States History
    Womens Education

Wood Finishing
USE   Finishing

Woodwind Instruments   *AUG. 2000*
    Postings: 7   GC: 420
SN   Musical wind instruments, such as clarinets, flutes, saxophones, oboes, and bassoons, made of wood or metal tubing in which sound is produced by the vibration of one or two reeds in the mouthpiece or the passing of air over a mouth hole
BT   Wind Instruments
RT   Music

Woodworking   *JUL. 1966*
    Postings: 277   GC: 640
SN   Construction, finishing, and reclaiming of wood articles or structures—also, an area of study relating to industries producing or using lumber
NT   Cabinetmaking
    Carpentry
BT   Technology
RT   Building Trades
    Finishing
    Furniture Industry
    Hand Tools
    Handicrafts
    Industrial Arts
    Lumber Industry
    Patternmaking
    Shop Curriculum
    Skilled Occupations
    Technology Education
    Visual Arts

Word Associations (Reading)
USE   Associative Learning

Word Borrowing
USE   Linguistic Borrowing

Word Frequency   *JUL. 1966*
    Postings: 631   GC: 450
RT   Computational Linguistics
    Connected Discourse
    Language
    Languages
    Mathematical Linguistics
    Speech
    Vocabulary
    Word Recognition
    Written Language

Word Lists   *JUL. 1966*
    Postings: 1,471   GC: 730
SN   Lists of words usually used in teaching to develop students' reading, spelling, or pronunciation skills
UF   Basic Word Lists
BT   Vocabulary
RT   Basic Vocabulary
    Dictionaries
    Keywords
    Pronunciation
    Sight Vocabulary
    Spelling

Word Meaning
USE   Semantics

Word Method (Reading)
USE   Sight Method

Word Order   *OCT. 1998*
    Postings: 187   GC: 450
SN   The arrangement of words in a phrase, clause, or sentence—the sequence in which words are placed according to the conventions of a given language
RT   Language
    Language Patterns
    Languages
    Phrase Structure
    Sentence Structure
    Structural Analysis (Linguistics)
    Syntax

Word Problems (Mathematics)   *JAN. 1986*
    Postings: 632   GC: 480
SN   Mathematical problems expressed in narrative form—answered by conversion of the circumstances to equivalent computations or equations, which can be solved arithmetically, algebraically, or with symbolic logic
UF   Story Problems (Mathematics)
BT   Mathematical Applications
RT   Mathematics
    Mathematics Tests

Word Processing   *APR. 1982*
    Postings: 2,284   GC: 710
SN   The automated composition, manipulation, and production of text and textual documents using specialized text-editing equipment (Note: For psychological/cognitive word processing, use "Word Recognition")
UF   Text Editing
    Text Editors #
    Text Processing
BT   Information Processing
RT   Automation
    Clerical Occupations
    Computer Oriented Programs
    Editing
    Electronic Equipment
    Electronic Text
    Information Systems
    Input Output Devices
    Keyboarding (Data Entry)
    Machine Translation
    Mechanical Equipment
    Menu Driven Software
    Office Automation
    Office Machines
    Office Occupations
    Office Occupations Education
    Online Systems

= Two or more Descriptors are used to represent this term.
The term's main entry shows the appropriate coordination.

Secretaries
Typewriting
Video Display Terminals

Word Recognition   *JUL. 1966*
  Postings: 3,083   GC: 460
BT   Recognition (Psychology)
RT   Associative Learning
    Context Clues
    Decoding (Reading)
    Reading Comprehension
    Reading Skills
    Sight Method
    Sight Vocabulary
    Symbolic Learning
    Verbal Stimuli
    Word Frequency
    Word Study Skills

Word Study Skills   *JUL. 1966*
  Postings: 630   GC: 460
BT   Study Skills
RT   Alphabetizing Skills
    Language Skills
    Phonics
    Reading Skills
    Study Habits
    Word Recognition

Work
USE   Employment

Work Adjustment
USE   Vocational Adjustment

Work and Education
USE   Education Work Relationship

Work Attitudes   *JUL. 1966*
  Postings: 4,228   GC: 630
SN   Attitude of persons who are either employed, unemployed, or preparing for employment toward a particular job, employment in general, or a particular aspect of employment
UF   Employee Work Attitudes #
NT   Job Satisfaction
BT   Attitudes
RT   Employee Attitudes
    Employment
    Job Enrichment
    Labor Force Nonparticipants
    Nontraditional Occupations
    Occupational Aspiration
    Professional Autonomy
    Vocational Adjustment
    Vocational Maturity
    Work Ethic
    Work Experience

Work Change
USE   Career Change

Work Education Programs
USE   Work Study Programs

Work Education Relationship
USE   Education Work Relationship

Work Enrichment
USE   Job Enrichment

Work Environment   *JUL. 1966*
  Postings: 4,627   GC: 630
UF   Job Conditions
    Working Conditions
NT   Teaching Conditions
BT   Environment
RT   Collegiality
    Employee Absenteeism
    Employer Employee Relationship
    Employment
    Family Work Relationship

Flexible Working Hours
Human Factors Engineering
Industrial Psychology
Job Enrichment
Job Satisfaction
Job Security
Labor Conditions
Occupational Safety and Health
Occupations
Organizational Climate
Organizational Development
Performance Technology
Professional Autonomy
Professional Isolation
Quality of Working Life
Scope of Bargaining
Social Environment
Unions
Work Ethic

Work Ethic   *DEC. 1989*
  Postings: 260   GC: 520
SN   A set of values or beliefs concerning the place of work in one's life—traditionally, the view of work as a moral obligation
UF   Protestant Ethic
    Puritan Ethic
BT   Ethics
RT   American Dream
    Capitalism
    Cultural Influences
    Family Work Relationship
    Goal Orientation
    Job Satisfaction
    Leisure Time
    Moral Values
    Motivation
    Occupational Aspiration
    Quality of Working Life
    Social Values
    Work Attitudes
    Work Environment

Work Evaluation (Performance)
USE   Vocational Evaluation

Work Experience   *JUL. 1966*
  Postings: 1,784   GC: 630
NT   Employment Experience
BT   Experience
RT   Career Exploration
    Careers
    Cooperative Education
    Employment Qualifications
    Experiential Learning
    Prior Learning
    Reentry Workers
    Volunteer Training
    Work Attitudes
    Work Experience Programs

Work Experience Programs   *JUL. 1966*
  Postings: 2,713   GC: 350
SN   On-the-job experiences to increase the employability of participants—included are a variety of federal job training, vocational, career education, and corrections programs often less structured than cooperative education programs (Note: Do not confuse with "Work Study Programs"—before Mar80, the use of this term was not restricted by a Scope Note)
BT   Programs
RT   Apprenticeships
    Career Education
    Career Exploration
    Clinical Experience
    Cooperative Education
    Cooperative Programs
    Experiential Learning
    Field Experience Programs
    Job Training
    Labor Force Development
    On the Job Training
    School Business Relationship
    Sheltered Workshops
    Student Experience
    Supervised Occupational Experience
    (Agriculture)

Supported Employment
Trainees
Training Methods
Vocational Adjustment
Vocational Education
Work Experience

Work Family Relationship
USE   Family Work Relationship

Work Force
USE   Labor Force

Work Life Expectancy   *JUL. 1966*
  Postings: 127   GC: 630
BT   Expectation
RT   Careers
    Early Retirement
    Occupations
    Tenure

Work Performance Evaluation
USE   Vocational Evaluation

Work Release
USE   Released Time

Work Sample Tests   *DEC. 1976*
  Postings: 168   GC: 830
SN   Use of job tasks, either real or simulated, to ascertain the possession of needed skills for specific jobs and as diagnostic tools in the evaluation of vocational rehabilitation clients
UF   Job Sample Tests
    Job Samples
    Work Samples
BT   Occupational Tests
RT   Diagnostic Tests
    Job Performance
    Job Skills
    Performance Tests
    Situational Tests
    Vocational Evaluation
    Vocational Rehabilitation

Work Samples
USE   Work Sample Tests

Work Satisfaction
USE   Job Satisfaction

Work Sharing
USE   Job Sharing

Work Simplification (1968 1980)
USE   Job Simplification

Work Stations (Home or Office)
USE   Workstations

Work Study
USE   Work Study Programs

Work Study Programs   *JUL. 1966*
  Postings: 942   GC: 620
SN   Programs, generally federally funded, providing part-time employment to students who need financial aid to begin or continue their education—usually at the postsecondary level and different from "work experience programs" in that "work study" emphasizes financial aid and not employment experience (Note: Prior to Mar80, the Scope Note did not make this distinction)
UF   College Work Study Programs
    Work Education Programs
    Work Study
BT   Programs
RT   Assistantships
    Cooperative Programs

Financial Support
Part Time Employment
Paying for College
Student Employment
Student Financial Aid

Workbooks   *JUL. 1966*
  Postings: 1,361   GC: 730
BT   Instructional Materials
RT   Laboratory Manuals
    Problem Sets
    Programmed Instructional Materials
    Textbooks

Workday
USE   Working Hours

Worker Days   *MAR. 1980*
  Postings: 39   GC: 630
SN   Hypothetical estimate of productivity based on single units or days, each representing the average amount of work one person can complete during one normal working day
UF   Man Days (1968 1980)
    People Days
    Person Days
    Staff Days
BT   Employment Statistics
RT   Labor Utilization
    Productivity
    Working Hours

Worker Evaluation
USE   Personnel Evaluation

Workers Compensation   *MAR. 1980*
  Postings: 136   GC: 630
UF   Workmans Compensation (1966 1980)
BT   Financial Support
    Insurance
RT   Health Insurance
    Teacher Employment Benefits
    Unemployment Insurance

Workers Education
USE   Labor Education

Working Abroad
USE   Overseas Employment

Working Class   *SEP. 1982*
  Postings: 343   GC: 520
UF   Proletariat
BT   Social Class
RT   Blue Collar Occupations
    Employees
    Labor Force
    Labor Supply
    Lower Class
    Lower Middle Class
    Marxism
    Middle Class
    Semiskilled Workers
    Skilled Workers
    Unskilled Workers
    White Collar Occupations

Working Conditions
USE   Work Environment

Working Hours   *JUL. 1966*
  Postings: 607   GC: 630
UF   Hours of Work
    Workday
    Workweek
NT   Flexible Working Hours
BT   Scheduling
RT   Employee Absenteeism
    Employment
    Faculty Workload
    Full Time Faculty
    Overtime
    Part Time Employment

= Two or more Descriptors are used to represent this term.
The term's main entry shows the appropriate coordination.

Part Time Faculty
Scope of Bargaining
Teaching Load
Worker Days

Working Overseas
USE   Overseas Employment

Working Parents (1966 1980)
USE   Employed Parents

Working Women (1968 1980)
USE   Employed Women

Workmans Compensation (1966 1980)
USE   Workers Compensation

Workplace Literacy   FEB. 1996
     Postings: 1,514   GC: 460
SN   Reading, writing, computation, and communication skills performed in the context of job tasks
UF   Job Literacy
     Job Related Literacy
     Occupational Literacy
BT   Literacy
RT   Adult Basic Education
     Adult Literacy
     Basic Skills
     Functional Literacy
     Job Skills
     Literacy Education

Worksheets   JUL. 1966
     Postings: 1,743   GC: 730
SN   Forms designed for the rapid and efficient recording and processing of information (Note: Prior to Mar80, the use of this term was not restricted by a Scope Note)
UF   Data Sheets (1966 1980)
NT   Spreadsheets
BT   Records (Forms)
RT   Data Collection
     Data Processing

Workshops   JUL. 1966
     Postings: 6,404   GC: 350
SN   Programs in which individuals with common interests and problems meet, often with experts, to exchange information and learn needed skills or techniques
UF   Preschool Workshops (1966 1980) #
     Summer Workshops (1966 1980) #
NT   Drama Workshops
     Parent Workshops
     Sheltered Workshops
     Teacher Workshops
     Writing Workshops
RT   Conference Papers
     Conference Proceedings
     Conferences
     Institutes (Training Programs)
     Meetings
     Minicourses
     Seminars
     Training Methods

Workstations   AUG. 1994
     Postings: 298   GC: 920
SN   Individual work areas equipped for performing a particular type of task—usually refers to terminals or microcomputers in a local area network, or to stand-alone microcomputer configurations that may include such peripherals as printers and optical/video disk systems
UF   Computer Workstations
     Work Stations (Home or Office)
BT   Facilities
RT   Automation
     Computer Oriented Programs
     Computer Terminals

Computers
Data Processing
Information Systems
Local Area Networks
Man Machine Systems
Microcomputers

Workweek
USE   Working Hours

World Affairs   JUL. 1966
     Postings: 1,634   GC: 610
RT   Appropriate Technology
     Current Events
     Developed Nations
     Developing Nations
     Diplomatic History
     Foreign Policy
     Futures (of Society)
     Global Approach
     International Communication
     International Cooperation
     International Law
     International Relations
     International Trade
     Peace
     Social Studies
     World History
     World Problems

World Geography   JUL. 1966
     Postings: 206   GC: 400
BT   Geography
RT   Global Education

World History   JUL. 1966
     Postings: 1,255   GC: 430
NT   World War I
     World War II
BT   History
RT   Constitutional History
     Diplomatic History
     Global Education
     Greek Civilization
     Non Western Civilization
     Slavery
     Western Civilization
     World Affairs

World Literature   APR. 1970
     Postings: 257   GC: 430
BT   English Curriculum
RT   Baroque Literature
     Classical Literature
     Epics
     Literary Genres
     Literary History
     Literature
     Medieval Literature
     Renaissance Literature
     Victorian Literature

World Peace
USE   Peace

World Problems   JUL. 1966
     Postings: 2,091   GC: 530
BT   Problems
RT   Conservation (Environment)
     Controversial Issues (Course Content)
     Developing Nations
     Disarmament
     Global Approach
     Global Warming
     Hunger
     Imperialism
     International Cooperation
     Nuclear Warfare
     Revolution
     War
     World Affairs

World Studies Education
USE   Global Education

World Views   JUL. 1998
     Postings: 418   GC: 110
SN   Comprehensive belief/value systems held by individuals or groups—fundamental frameworks for perceiving and interpreting life and the universe (Note: Do not confuse with international or whole-world orientations and undertakings, for which see "Global Approach")
UF   Life Views
     Outlooks on Life
     Philosophy of Life
     Weltanschauungen
     Worldviews
BT   Attitudes
     Philosophy
RT   Beliefs
     Cultural Background
     Cultural Influences
     Ideology
     Life Style
     Values

World War I   APR. 1990
     Postings: 159   GC: 430
SN   War from 1914 to 1918 between the Central Powers and the Allies
BT   War
     World History
RT   African History
     Asian History
     European History
     United States History
     World War II

World War II   APR. 1990
     Postings: 603   GC: 430
SN   War from 1939 to 1945 between the Axis Powers and the Allies
BT   War
     World History
RT   African History
     Asian History
     European History
     Korean War
     United States History
     Vietnam War
     World War I

World Wide Web   JUN. 1996
     Postings: 2,997   GC: 710
SN   A hypertext-based information system for disseminating and retrieving text or multimedia files via the Internet—the files can be accessed with a browser program installed on the user's computer
UF   Web (The)
     Worldwide Web Service
     WWW
BT   Internet
RT   Hypermedia
     Multimedia Materials

Worldmindedness
USE   Global Approach

Worldviews
USE   World Views

Worldwide Approach
USE   Global Approach

Worldwide Web Service
USE   World Wide Web

Wrestling   FEB. 1978
     Postings: 37   GC: 470
BT   Athletics
RT   Olympic Games

Writers
USE   Authors

Writing (Composition)   MAR. 1980
     Postings: 10,828   GC: 400
SN   Organization and expression of ideas or information using written language (Note: Use a more specific term if possible)
UF   Composition (Literary) (1966 1980)
     Theme Writing
     Writing (1966 1980)
     Writing Development
NT   Abstracting
     Basic Writing
     Beginning Writing
     Childrens Writing
     Content Area Writing
     Creative Writing
     Descriptive Writing
     Expository Writing
     Free Writing
     Freshman Composition
     Journal Writing
     Local Color Writing
     News Writing
     Notetaking
     Paragraph Composition
     Parallelism (Literary)
     Playwriting
     Proposal Writing
     Scholarly Writing
     Technical Writing
     Writing for Publication
BT   Language Arts
     Literacy
RT   Audience Analysis
     Coherence
     Cohesion (Written Composition)
     Discourse Modes
     Handwriting
     Language Processing
     Letters (Correspondence)
     Literary Devices
     Literary Styles
     Manuscripts
     Narration
     Outlining (Discourse)
     Paragraphs
     Persuasive Discourse
     Plagiarism
     Poetry
     Prewriting
     Process Approach (Writing)
     Prose
     Reading
     Reading Writing Relationship
     Revision (Written Composition)
     Rhetoric
     Rhetorical Invention
     Sentences
     Spelling
     Story Grammar
     Student Writing Models
     Verbal Communication
     Writing Ability
     Writing Achievement
     Writing Apprehension
     Writing Assignments
     Writing Attitudes
     Writing Difficulties
     Writing Evaluation
     Writing Exercises
     Writing Improvement
     Writing Instruction
     Writing Laboratories
     Writing Processes
     Writing Readiness
     Writing Research
     Writing Skills
     Writing Strategies
     Writing Teachers
     Writing Tests
     Writing Workshops
     Written Language

Writing Ability   APR. 1990
     Postings: 205   GC: 400
NT   Writing Skills
BT   Verbal Ability
RT   Handwriting
     Writing (Composition)
     Writing Achievement
     Writing Attitudes

Writing Difficulties
Writing Readiness

Writing Achievement   *APR. 1990*
Postings: 400   GC: 120
SN   Level of attainment in any or all writing
       skills, usually estimated by performance
       on a test
BT   Achievement
RT   Academic Achievement
       Achievement Gains
       Writing (Composition)
       Writing Ability
       Writing Attitudes
       Writing Evaluation
       Writing Improvement
       Writing Skills
       Writing Tests

Writing Across the Curriculum   *DEC. 1987*
Postings: 1,171   GC: 400
SN   Educational movement or strategy that
       advocates the incorporation of writing
       into all classes and disciplines, to help
       students improve their writing and use
       writing as a learning tool
BT   Content Area Writing
RT   Curriculum
       Interdisciplinary Approach
       Journal Writing
       Notetaking
       Research Papers (Students)
       Student Journals
       Teaching Methods
       Writing Exercises
       Writing Improvement
       Writing Laboratories

Writing Apprehension   *NOV. 1982*
Postings: 334   GC: 120
SN   Fear or anxiety experienced in anticipa-
       tion of and/or during the writing/compo-
       sition process
BT   Anxiety
RT   Basic Writing
       School Phobia
       Writing (Composition)
       Writing Attitudes
       Writing Difficulties
       Writing Instruction
       Writing Readiness

Writing as Process
USE   Process Approach (Writing)

Writing Assignments   *APR. 1990*
Postings: 1,754   GC: 310
SN   Writing exercises allotted by teachers to
       students or groups of students
BT   Assignments
       Writing Exercises
RT   Process Approach (Writing)
       Research Papers (Students)
       Revision (Written Composition)
       Writing (Composition)
       Writing Evaluation
       Writing Instruction

Writing Attitudes   *APR. 1990*
Postings: 637   GC: 120
SN   Attitudes toward writing
BT   Attitudes
RT   Educational Attitudes
       Writing (Composition)
       Writing Ability
       Writing Achievement
       Writing Apprehension

Writing Centers
USE   Writing Laboratories

Writing Development
USE   Writing (Composition)

Writing Difficulties   *JUN. 1983*
Postings: 503   GC: 120
SN   Problems in writing/composition, caused
       by intrinsic or extrinsic disadvantage,
       e.g., disability, unfavorable environment,
       etc.
BT   Problems
RT   Basic Writing
       Handwriting
       Language Impairments
       Learning Disabilities
       Learning Problems
       Writing (Composition)
       Writing Ability
       Writing Apprehension

Writing Evaluation   *JUN. 1981*
Postings: 2,857   GC: 820
SN   Objective or subjective activities and pro-
       grams for describing, appraising, or judg-
       ing writing skills (Note: For specific writ-
       ing examinations and inventories, use
       "Writing Tests"—do not confuse with
       "Literary Criticism")
BT   Evaluation
RT   Alternative Assessment
       Coherence
       Cohesion (Written Composition)
       Educational Diagnosis
       Grading
       Handwriting
       Holistic Evaluation
       Portfolio Assessment
       Scoring Rubrics
       Student Evaluation
       Writing (Composition)
       Writing Achievement
       Writing Assignments
       Writing Skills
       Writing Tests
       Written Language

Writing Exercises   *JUL. 1966*
Postings: 2,842   GC: 310
SN   Activities designed to aid students in
       attaining proficiency in handwriting or
       composition
NT   Writing Assignments
RT   Childrens Writing
       Content Area Writing
       Dialog Journals
       Free Writing
       Handwriting
       Invented Spelling
       Journal Writing
       Prewriting
       Sentence Combining
       Student Journals
       Writing (Composition)
       Writing Across the Curriculum
       Writing Improvement
       Writing Skills
       Writing Strategies

Writing for Publication   *OCT. 1983*
Postings: 1,643   GC: 720
SN   Writing intended for acceptance by a
       publisher
BT   Writing (Composition)
RT   Academic Discourse
       Authors
       Editors
       Faculty Publishing
       Journalism
       News Writing
       Periodicals
       Professional Development
       Publications
       Publish or Perish Issue
       Publishing Industry
       Scholarly Journals
       Scholarly Writing
       Scholastic Journalism
       School Publications
       Student Publications
       Technical Writing

Writing Improvement   *JUN. 1983*
Postings: 2,386   GC: 400
SN   Process of becoming a better writer
BT   Improvement
RT   Handwriting
       Process Approach (Writing)
       Writing (Composition)
       Writing Achievement
       Writing Across the Curriculum
       Writing Exercises
       Writing Instruction
       Writing Laboratories
       Writing Processes
       Writing Skills
       Writing Strategies
       Writing Workshops

Writing Instruction   *MAR. 1980*
Postings: 13,328   GC: 400
SN   Instruction in written composition, gram-
       mar, and style, or in handwriting
UF   Handwriting Instruction (1966 1983) #
NT   Basic Writing
       Content Area Writing
       Freshman Composition
       Process Approach (Writing)
BT   Instruction
RT   Academic Discourse
       Beginning Writing
       Childrens Writing
       Emergent Literacy
       Handwriting
       Journalism Education
       Prewriting
       Story Grammar
       Student Writing Models
       Whole Language Approach
       Writing (Composition)
       Writing Apprehension
       Writing Assignments
       Writing Improvement
       Writing Readiness
       Writing Skills
       Writing Strategies
       Writing Teachers
       Writing Workshops

Writing Laboratories   *DEC. 1985*
Postings: 533   GC: 920
SN   Facilities specifically designed for devel-
       oping and improving writing/composi-
       tion skills, ranging from areas within
       classrooms to separate, specially staffed
       centers
UF   Writing Centers
BT   Educational Facilities
       Laboratories
RT   Basic Writing
       Language Laboratories
       Learning Centers (Classroom)
       Learning Laboratories
       Writing (Composition)
       Writing Across the Curriculum
       Writing Improvement
       Writing Skills
       Writing Workshops

Writing Process Approach
USE   Process Approach (Writing)

Writing Processes   *OCT. 1980*
Postings: 4,457   GC: 400
SN   Series of thoughts and behaviors in-
       volved in planning, writing, and/or revis-
       ing written compositions
UF   Composition Processes (Literary)
NT   Prewriting
       Revision (Written Composition)
RT   Beginning Writing
       Behavior Patterns
       Language Processing
       Process Approach (Writing)
       Protocol Analysis
       Reading Writing Relationship
       Writing (Composition)
       Writing Improvement
       Writing Skills
       Writing Strategies

Writing Readiness   *NOV. 1981*
Postings: 269   GC: 120
SN   Degree of preparedness for instruction
       in handwriting or formal composition
       (Note: Do not confuse with "Prewriting")
UF   Handwriting Readiness (1966 1983) #
BT   Readiness
RT   Beginning Writing
       Handwriting
       Learning Readiness
       Prewriting
       School Readiness
       Writing (Composition)
       Writing Ability
       Writing Apprehension
       Writing Instruction

Writing Research   *OCT. 1980*
Postings: 3,762   GC: 810
BT   Educational Research
RT   Communication Research
       Handwriting
       Journalism Research
       Writing (Composition)

Writing Skills   *JUL. 1966*
Postings: 10,840   GC: 400
SN   Skills that enable an individual to write
       lucidly, coherently, and grammatically,
       or to handwrite legibly with ease and
       speed
UF   Composition Skills (Literary) (1966
       1980)
       Handwriting Development (1966
       1980) #
       Handwriting Skills (1966 1983) #
BT   Language Skills
       Writing Ability
RT   Adult Literacy
       Audience Awareness
       Basic Skills
       Basic Writing
       Capitalization (Alphabetic)
       Childrens Writing
       Cohesion (Written Composition)
       Content Area Writing
       Essay Tests
       Functional Literacy
       Grammar
       Handwriting
       Language Styles
       Language Tests
       Literacy
       Literacy Education
       Minimum Competencies
       Notetaking
       Outlining (Discourse)
       Paragraph Composition
       Parallelism (Literary)
       Prewriting
       Process Approach (Writing)
       Proofreading
       Punctuation
       Revision (Written Composition)
       Rhetorical Invention
       Sentence Combining
       Spelling
       Story Grammar
       Student Journals
       Student Writing Models
       Text Structure
       Thinking Skills
       Writing (Composition)
       Writing Achievement
       Writing Evaluation
       Writing Exercises
       Writing Improvement
       Writing Instruction
       Writing Laboratories
       Writing Processes
       Writing Strategies
       Writing Tests
       Writing Workshops

Writing Strategies   *APR. 1990*
Postings: 942   GC: 400
SN   Plans or methods for facilitating writing
       proficiency and productivity
BT   Methods
RT   Learning Strategies

= Two or more Descriptors are used to represent this term.
The term's main entry shows the appropriate coordination.

Process Approach (Writing)
Writing (Composition)
Writing Exercises
Writing Improvement
Writing Instruction
Writing Processes
Writing Skills

Writing Systems
USE   Written Language

Writing Teachers   APR. 1990
Postings: 370   GC: 360
BT   Teachers
RT   Language Teachers
Writing (Composition)
Writing Instruction

Writing Tests   APR. 1990
Postings: 353   GC: 830
SN   Specific measures/instruments used to
assess writing skills and achievement
(Note: For the processes of writing as-
sessment, use "Writing Evaluation")
BT   Verbal Tests
RT   Achievement Tests
Essay Tests
Language Tests
Writing (Composition)
Writing Achievement
Writing Evaluation
Writing Skills

Writing Workshops   APR. 1990
Postings: 378   GC: 350
SN   Programs for students, teachers, em-
ployees, etc., providing practical or spe-
cialized training in writing skills and tech-
niques
BT   Workshops
RT   Process Approach (Writing)
Writing (Composition)
Writing Improvement
Writing Instruction
Writing Laboratories
Writing Skills

Writing (1966 1980)
USE   Writing (Composition)

Written Language   JUL. 1966
Postings: 2,406   GC: 450
SN   Systems of standardized visual signs
and symbols used to convey meaning
UF   Writing Systems
NT   Braille
Electronic Text
Graphemes
Ideography
Orthographic Symbols
Punctuation
Shorthand
BT   Language
RT   Abbreviations
Alphabets
Capitalization (Alphabetic)
Language Acquisition
Language Rhythm
Language Usage
Oral Language
Phoneme Grapheme Correspondence
Phonetic Transcription
Printing
Romanization
Unwritten Languages
Word Frequency
Writing (Composition)
Writing Evaluation

WWW
USE   World Wide Web

X Ray Technologists
USE   Radiologic Technologists

X Rays (Medicine)
USE   Radiology

Xenophobia
USE   Stranger Reactions

Xerography
USE   Reprography

Yakut   JUL. 1966
Postings: 3   GC: 440
BT   Turkic Languages

Yard Workers (Horticulture)
USE   Grounds Keepers

Year Round Schools   JUL. 1966
Postings: 546   GC: 350
SN   Schools that operate year-round but have
not increased the number of days stu-
dents must attend (Note: Prior to Mar80,
this term was not scoped and was often
confused with "Extended School Year")
BT   Schools
RT   Extended School Year
Quarter System
School Schedules
Summer Schools
Trimester System
Vacation Programs

Yearbooks   MAR. 1969
Postings: 787   GC: 730
SN   Annually published volumes that contain
current information or review the events
of a year in brief descriptive, statistical,
or pictorial form (Note: For "student
yearbooks," coordinate "Yearbooks" with
"Student Publications" or "School Pub-
lications")
UF   Annuals
BT   Books
Reference Materials
Serials
RT   Annual Reports
Scholastic Journalism
School Publications
Student Publications

Yiddish   JUL. 1966
Postings: 42   GC: 440
BT   German

Yoruba   JUL. 1966
Postings: 57   GC: 440
BT   African Languages

Young Adolescents
USE   Early Adolescents

Young Adults   JUL. 1966
Postings: 4,245   GC: 120
SN   Approximately 18–30 years of age
BT   Adults
RT   Adults (30 to 45)
College Students
Late Adolescents
Young Farmer Education
Youth

Young Children   MAR. 1980
Postings: 8,771   GC: 120
SN   Aged birth through approximately 8 years
UF   Early Childhood (1966 1980)
NT   Infants
Kindergarten Children
Preschool Children
Toddlers
BT   Children
RT   Developmentally Appropriate Practices
Early Childhood Education
Early Experience

Young Farmer Education   JUL. 1966
Postings: 154   GC: 410
SN   Vocational education in agriculture for
adults not more than 25 years of age
who are not otherwise enrolled in school
(Note: For adults 25 and over, use "Adult
Farmer Education")
UF   Beginning Farmer Education
BT   Adult Vocational Education
Agricultural Education
RT   Adult Farmer Education
Farm Visits
Farmers
Rural Education
Rural Extension
Young Adults

Young Old Adults   AUG. 1989
Postings: 34   GC: 120
SN   Approximately 65–75 years of age
BT   Older Adults
RT   Frail Elderly
Middle Aged Adults
Old Old Adults

Youth   JUL. 1966
Postings: 2,222   GC: 120
SN   Individuals or time of life between child-
hood and maturity (Note: Use a more
specific term if possible and an age or
educational level Descriptor)
NT   Affluent Youth
Black Youth
Disadvantaged Youth
Migrant Youth
Out of School Youth
Rural Youth
Suburban Youth
Urban Youth
BT   Groups
RT   Adolescent Attitudes
Adolescent Behavior
Adolescent Development
Adolescents
Age Groups
Children
Early Adolescents
Late Adolescents
Preadolescents
Young Adults
Youth Agencies
Youth Clubs
Youth Employment
Youth Leaders
Youth Opportunities
Youth Problems
Youth Programs

Youth Agencies   JUL. 1966
Postings: 243   GC: 520
BT   Agencies
RT   Agency Role
Voluntary Agencies
Welfare Agencies
Youth

Youth Clubs   JUL. 1966
Postings: 452   GC: 520
UF   Girls Clubs (1966 1980)
BT   Clubs
RT   Juvenile Gangs
Youth
Youth Leaders

Youth Employment   JUL. 1966
Postings: 1,599   GC: 630
UF   Youth Mobilization
BT   Employment
RT   Part Time Employment
Seasonal Employment
Youth
Youth Opportunities
Youth Programs

Youth Leaders   JUL. 1966
Postings: 232   GC: 510
SN   Young people who lead (Note: Coordi-

nate with an appropriate age or educa-
tional level Descriptor)
BT   Groups
Leaders
RT   Leadership Training
Youth
Youth Clubs

Youth Mobilization
USE   Youth Employment

Youth Opportunities   JUL. 1966
Postings: 389   GC: 540
BT   Opportunities
RT   Employment Opportunities
Youth
Youth Employment
Youth Programs

Youth Problems   JUL. 1966
Postings: 2,309   GC: 530
BT   Problems
RT   Delinquency
Early Parenthood
Generation Gap
Juvenile Courts
Juvenile Justice
Runaways
Youth

Youth Programs   JUL. 1966
Postings: 2,487   GC: 520
SN   Programs for adolescents and/or young
adults (Note: Also use an age or educa-
tional level Descriptor)
BT   Programs
RT   Community Programs
Student Volunteers
Youth
Youth Employment
Youth Opportunities

Yucatec   DEC. 1970
Postings: 1   GC: 440
BT   Mayan Languages
RT   Quiche

Yupik   APR. 1990
Postings: 44   GC: 440
SN   Eskimo language family (also Yup'ik) of
Alaska's southwest coasts, river deltas,
and islands, as well as the eastern tip of
Siberia—includes four mutually unintel-
ligible dialects, i.e., "Central Alaskan
Yupik," "Pacific Gulf Yupik," "St. Law-
rence Island Yupik," and "Sirenik"
BT   Eskimo Aleut Languages

Yurak   JUL. 1966
Postings: 3   GC: 440
BT   Samoyed Languages

Zoning   JUL. 1966
Postings: 102   GC: 610
NT   Community Zoning
Rezoning
School Zoning
Special Zoning
RT   Land Use
Multicampus Districts
Planning
Real Estate
School Districts

Zoology   AUG. 1968
Postings: 629   GC: 490
UF   Animal Biology
NT   Entomology
Ichthyology
Ornithology
Primatology
BT   Biological Sciences
RT   Anatomy
Animal Behavior
Animal Husbandry

= Two or more Descriptors are used to represent this term.
The term's main entry shows the appropriate coordination.

Animals
Anthropology
Biology
Cardiovascular System
Culturing Techniques
Dissection
Ecology
Embryology
Ethology
Evolution

Genetics
Laboratory Animals
Microbiology
Musculoskeletal System
Paleontology
Pathology
Physiology
Sociobiology
Wildlife

Zoos   *JUL. 1966*
    Postings: 166   GC: 920
BT Animal Facilities
RT Aquariums
    Educational Facilities
    Parks
    Recreational Facilities
    Wildlife Management

Zuni (Tribe)   *JAN. 1994*
    Postings: 3   GC: 560
SN An American Indian people of western
    New Mexico (and dispersed kin) (Note:
    Use the Identifiers "Zuni" for the Zuni
    language and "Zuni (Pueblo)" for the
    Zuni reservation in New Mexico)
BT Pueblo (People)
    Tribes

= Two or more Descriptors are used to represent this term.
The term's main entry shows the appropriate coordination.

Rotated Descriptor Display

The Rotated Descriptor Display is a permuted alphabetical index of *all words* that form *Thesaurus* terms, whether Descriptors or USE references. Each separate word is considered as a filing unit, and a term appears in as many locations in this display as it contains separate words. Subfiling under any one file point is performed first on the basis of the words to the right of the file point and second on the basis of the words to the left of the file point. The word order within the term itself is not altered.

Grade	1
Grade	10
Grade	11
Grade	12
Seniors (1966 1980) (Grade	12) Use High School Seniors
Grade	13 (1970 1980) Use Postsecondary Education
Grade	14 (1970 1980) Use Postsecondary Education
Grade	2
Grade	3
HTLV	3 Use Acquired Immune Deficiency Syndrome
Human T Cell Lymphotropic Virus Type	3 Use Acquired Immune Deficiency Syndrome
Adults	(30 to 45)
Grade	4
Adults (30 to	45)
Grade	5
Grade	6
Grade	7
Grade	8
Freshmen (1967 1980) (Grade	9) Use High School Freshmen
Grade	9
Type	A Behavior
Diversity (Cultural) as an Observation or	a Fact Use Cultural Differences
Higher Education as	a Field of Study Use Postsecondary Education as a Field of Study
Postsecondary Education as	a Field of Study
Schools within	a School Plan Use House Plan
Parent as	a Teacher Use Parents as Teachers
Diversity (Cultural) as	a Value Use Cultural Pluralism
Grade	a Year Integration (1966 1980) Use School Desegregation
	Abbreviations
	Ability
Academic	Ability
Cognitive	Ability
Creative	Ability (1968 1980) Use Creativity
	Ability Grouping
	Ability Identification
Language	Ability (1966 1980)
Mental	Ability Use Cognitive Ability
Motor	Ability Use Psychomotor Skills
Nonverbal	Ability
Reading	Ability
Scholastic	Ability Use Academic Ability
Spatial	Ability
Student	Ability (1966 1980) Use Academic Ability
Low	Ability Students (1967 1980)
Predictive	Ability (Testing) (1966 1980) Use Predictive Measurement
Verbal	Ability
Visuospatial	Ability Use Spatial Ability
Writing	Ability
	Able Students (1966 1978) Use Academically Gifted
	Abnormal Psychology Use Psychopathology
Australian	Aboriginal Languages
	Aboriginal People Use Indigenous Populations
	Abortions
	Abreaction Use Catharsis
Study	Abroad
Working	Abroad Use Overseas Employment
	Absence (Employees) Use Employee Absenteeism
Father	Absence Use Fatherless Family
Leave of	Absence (1968 1980) Use Leaves of Absence
Leaves of	Absence
Mother	Absence Use Motherless Family
Parent	Absence Use One Parent Family
	Absence (Students) Use Attendance
	Absence (Teachers) Use Employee Absenteeism and Teacher Attendance
Employee	Absenteeism
	Absolute Humidity Use Humidity
	Absolute Pressure Use Pressure (Physics)
	Abstract Bibliographies Use Annotated Bibliographies
	Abstract Reasoning
	Abstracting
	Abstraction Levels (1968 1980) Use Abstract Reasoning
	Abstraction Tests (1967 1980) Use Cognitive Tests
	Abstracts
Alcohol	Abuse
Child	Abuse
Child Sexual	Abuse Use Child Abuse and Sexual Abuse
Drug	Abuse
Elder	Abuse
Emotional	Abuse
Psychological	Abuse Use Emotional Abuse
Self	Abuse Use Self Destructive Behavior
Sexual	Abuse
Substance	Abuse
Test	Abuse Use Test Use
Verbal	Abuse
	Abused Children Use Child Abuse
	Abused Elderly Use Elder Abuse
	Abused Women Use Battered Women
Aging in	Academia
	Academic Ability
	Academic Accommodations (Disabilities)
	Academic Achievement
	Academic Advising

Academic Alliances   Use Partnerships in Education
Academic Aptitude
Academic Aspiration
Academic Calendars   Use School Schedules
Academic Curriculum   Use Academic Education
Academic Deans
Degrees   (Academic)
Academic Departments   Use Departments
Academic Disciplines   Use Intellectual Disciplines
Academic Discourse
Academic Discourse Communities   Use Academic Discourse and Discourse Communities
Academic Education
Academic Enrichment (1966 1980)   Use Enrichment
Academic Environment   Use Educational Environment
Academic Failure
Academic Freedom
Academic Games   Use Educational Games
Academic Learning Time   Use Time on Task
Academic Libraries
Academic Malpractice   Use Educational Malpractice
Chief   Academic Officers   Use Academic Deans
Academic Performance (1966 1974)   Use Academic Achievement
Academic Persistence
Academic Planning   Use Educational Planning
Academic Probation
Proficiency Tests   (Academic)   Use Achievement Tests
Academic Progress   Use Academic Achievement
Academic Promotion   Use Student Promotion
English for   Academic Purposes
Academic Rank (Professional)
Academic Records
Academic Senates (Colleges)   Use College Governing Councils
Academic Standards
Academic Subjects   Use Academic Education
Academic Success   Use Academic Achievement
Transcripts   (Academic)   Use Academic Records
Academic Writing   Use Academic Discourse
Academically Disadvantaged   Use Educationally Disadvantaged
Academically Gifted
Academically Handicapped (1966 1980)
Career   Academies
High School   Academies (Career Development)   Use Career Academies
Job Training   Academies   Use Career Academies
Partnership   Academies (School and Business)   Use Career Academies
Vocational   Academies   Use Career Academies
Accelerated Courses (1966 1980)   Use Acceleration (Education)
Accelerated Programs (1966 1980)   Use Acceleration (Education)
Acceleration (1966 1982) (Education)   Use Acceleration (Education)
Acceleration (Education)
Acceleration (1966 1982) (Physics)   Use Acceleration (Physics)
Acceleration (Physics)
Accents (Dialects)   Use Dialects and Pronunciation
Accents (Vocal Stress)   Use Stress (Phonology)
Grammatical   Acceptability
Counselor   Acceptance (1968 1980)   Use Counselor Client Relationship
Peer   Acceptance
Online Public   Access Catalogs   Use Online Catalogs
Educational   Access   Use Access to Education
Dial   Access Information Systems
Key Word   Access Points   Use Keywords
Subject   Access   Use Indexing
Access to Education
Access to Ideas   Use Intellectual Freedom
Access to Information
Accessibility (for Disabled)
Accident Prevention
Accidents
School   Accidents
Traffic   Accidents
Academic   Accommodations (Disabilities)
Accommodations for Disabled (Educational Settings)   Use Academic Accommodations (Disabilities)
Public   Accommodations   Use Public Facilities
Accountability
Educational   Accountability (1970 1980)   Use Accountability
Accountants
Certified Public   Accountants
Accounting
Property   Accounting
School   Accounting
Farm   Accounts
Personal   Accounts (Narratives)   Use Personal Narratives
Accreditation (Institutions)
Accrediting Agencies
Accrediting Associations   Use Accrediting Agencies
Acculturation
Data   Accumulation   Use Data Collection
Acetylene Welding   Use Welding
Achievement
Academic   Achievement
Black   Achievement
Achievement Comparison   Use Achievement Rating
Educational   Achievement   Use Academic Achievement
Low   Achievement Factors (1966 1980)   Use Low Achievement

```
                       Achievement Gains
              High     Achievement
                       Achievement Incentives    Use Incentives
                       Achievement Level    Use Achievement
                       Achievement Losses    Use Achievement Gains
               Low     Achievement
        Mathematics    Achievement
                       Achievement Motivation    Use Achievement Need
   National Tests (of  Achievement)    Use National Competency Tests
                       Achievement Need
             Negro     Achievement (1966 1977)    Use Black Achievement
                       Achievement Prediction    Use Achievement and Prediction
                       Achievement Rating
           Reading     Achievement
       Recognition     (Achievement)
        Scholastic     Achievement    Use Academic Achievement
           Science     Achievement
           Student     Achievement    Use Academic Achievement
                       Achievement Tests
          National     Achievement Tests    Use National Competency Tests
           Writing     Achievement
              High     Achievers (1966 1980)    Use High Achievement
               Low     Achievers (1966 1980)    Use Low Achievement
   Deoxyribonucleic    Acid    Use DNA
  Desoxyribonucleic    Acid    Use DNA
           Lysergic    Acid Diethylamide
                       Acid Rain
        Ribonucleic    Acid    Use RNA
                       Acids
            Nucleic    Acids
                       Acoustic Barriers    Use Acoustic Insulation
                       Acoustic Insulation
                       Acoustic Phonetics
                       Acoustical Environment
                       Acoustics
                       Acquired Immune Deficiency Syndrome
              Land     Acquisition
          Language     Acquisition
           Library     Acquisition
                       Acronyms    Use Abbreviations
           Writing     Across the Curriculum
                       Acting
       Affirmative     Action
            Church     Action    Use Church Role
         Community     Action
             Court     Action    Use Court Litigation
       Disciplinary    Action    Use Discipline
           Judicial    Action    Use Court Litigation
                       Action Learning    Use Experiential Learning
            Police     Action
                       Action Programs (Community) (1966 1980)    Use Community Action
                       Action Research
     Participatory     Action Research    Use Action Research and Participatory Research
            Social     Action
             State     Action
                       Activated Sludge    Use Sludge
             Audio     Active Compare Laboratories (1967 1980)    Use Language Laboratories
             Audio     Active Laboratories (1967 1980)    Use Language Laboratories
                       Active Learning
                       Activism
                       Activities
       After School    Activities (1967 1980)    Use After School Programs
               Art     Activities
           Athletic    Activities (1966 1974)    Use Athletics
             Class     Activities
         Classroom     Activities    Use Class Activities
        Cocurricular   Activities (1966 1980)    Use Extracurricular Activities
        Cooperative    Activities    Use Group Activities
          Creative     Activities
          Cultural     Activities
        Enrichment     Activities
           Student     Activities (Extraclass)    Use Extracurricular Activities
      Extracurricular  Activities
             Group     Activities
            Health     Activities Handbooks (1966 1980)    Use Guides and Health Materials
            Health     Activities
        Individual     Activities
         Integrated    Activities
          Learning     Activities
        Mathematics    Activities
          Muscular     Activities    Use Motor Reactions
             Music     Activities
           Outdoor     Activities
          Physical     Activities
        Playground     Activities
       Recreational    Activities
            School     Activities
       School Related  Activities    Use Extracurricular Activities
           Science     Activities
          Speaking     Activities (1966 1980)    Use Speech Communication
        Supervisory    Activities (1968 1980)    Use Supervision
    Directed Reading   Activity
                       Activity Learning (1968 1978)    Use Experiential Learning
```

	Activity Level (Motor Behavior) Use Physical Activity Level
Physical	Activity Level
Learning	Activity Packages Use Learning Modules
Learning	Activity Packets Use Learning Modules
	Activity Units
Illocutionary	Acts Use Speech Acts
Speech	Acts
Self	Actualization
Visual	Acuity
	Ad Valorem Tax Use Property Taxes
	Adages Use Proverbs
	Adaptability (Personality) Use Adjustment (to Environment) and Personality Traits
Curriculum	Adaptation Use Curriculum Development
Educational Media	Adaptation Use Media Adaptation
Instructional Material	Adaptation Use Media Adaptation
	Adaptation Level Theory
Material	Adaptation Use Media Adaptation
Media	Adaptation
Tactile	Adaptation
	Adapted Physical Education
	Adaptive Behavior Use Adjustment (to Environment)
	Adaptive Behavior (of Disabled)
	Adaptive Equipment (Disabled) Use Assistive Devices (for Disabled)
	Adaptive Testing
Computerized	Adaptive Testing Use Adaptive Testing and Computer Assisted Testing
Alcohol	Addiction Use Alcoholism
Drug	Addiction
Narcotics	Addiction Use Drug Addiction
	Addition
	Additional Aid Use Equalization Aid
	Addresses Use Speeches
	Adhesives
Cements	(Adhesives) Use Adhesives
Pastes	(Adhesives) Use Adhesives
	Adjectives
	Adjunct Faculty
	Adjunct Professors Use Adjunct Faculty
	Adjustment Counselors
Emotional	Adjustment
Employment	Adjustment Use Vocational Adjustment
Group	Adjustment Use Adjustment (to Environment)
Individual	Adjustment Use Adjustment (to Environment)
Job	Adjustment Use Vocational Adjustment
Occupational	Adjustment Use Vocational Adjustment
Personal	Adjustment (1966 1980) Use Adjustment (to Environment)
	Adjustment Problems (1966 1980) Use Adjustment (to Environment)
School	Adjustment Use Student Adjustment
Social	Adjustment
Student	Adjustment
	Adjustment (to Environment)
Vocational	Adjustment
Work	Adjustment Use Vocational Adjustment
	Administration
Business	Administration
College	Administration
Business	Administration Education
Public	Administration Education
Educational	Administration
Institutional	Administration
Library	Administration
Program	Administration
Public	Administration
Research	Administration
School	Administration
Team	Administration (1967 1980) Use Management Teams
Test	Administration Use Testing
University	Administration (1967 1980) Use College Administration
	Administrative Agencies (1966 1980)
Government	(Administrative Body)
	Administrative Change
	Administrative Occupations Use Managerial Occupations
	Administrative Organization
	Administrative Personnel (1966 1980) Use Administrators
	Administrative Planning Use Planning
	Administrative Policy
	Administrative Principles
	Administrative Problems
	Administrative Secretaries Use Secretaries
	Administrative Teams Use Management Teams
Intermediate	Administrative Units
	Administrator Appraisal Use Administrator Evaluation
	Administrator Attitudes
	Administrator Background (1967 1980) Use Administrator Characteristics
	Administrator Behavior
	Administrator Characteristics
	Administrator Education
	Administrator Effectiveness
	Administrator Evaluation
	Administrator Guides
	Administrator Opinions Use Administrator Attitudes
	Administrator Preparation Use Administrator Education
	Administrator Qualifications
Board	Administrator Relationship

Teacher	Administrator Relationship
	Administrator Responsibility
	Administrator Role
	Administrator Selection
	Administrator Teacher Relationship Use Teacher Administrator Relationship
	Administrator Training Use Management Development
	Administrators
Central Office	Administrators
Chief	Administrators (1967 1980) Use Administrators
Hospital Record	Administrators Use Medical Record Administrators
Library	Administrators
Medical Record	Administrators
Personnel	Administrators Use Personnel Directors
School	Administrators Use Administrators
Test	Administrators Use Examiners
Women	Administrators
College	Admission
	Admission Criteria
Early	Admission
Open	Admission Use Open Enrollment
Preferential	Admission Use Selective Admission
Restrictive	Admission Use Selective Admission
	Admission (School)
School	Admission Use Admission (School)
Selective	Admission
Special	Admission Use Selective Admission
	Admission Tests (Higher Education) Use College Entrance Examinations
	Admission Tests (Occupational) Use Occupational Tests
	Admissions Counseling
	Admissions Counselors (1973 1980) Use Admissions Counseling
	Admissions Officers
	Adolescence (1966 1980) Use Adolescents
Early	Adolescence Use Early Adolescents
Late	Adolescence Use Late Adolescents
	Adolescent Attitudes
	Adolescent Behavior
	Adolescent Development
	Adolescent Literature
	Adolescent Parents Use Early Parenthood
	Adolescents
Early	Adolescents
Late	Adolescents
Older	Adolescents Use Late Adolescents
Young	Adolescents Use Early Adolescents
	Adopted Children
	Adoption
	Adoption (Ideas)
Interracial	Adoption Use Transracial Adoption
Transracial	Adoption
	Adoptive Parents
	Adult Basic Education
	Adult Characteristics (1967 1980) Use Adults and Individual Characteristics
	Adult Children
	Adult Counseling
	Adult Day Care
	Adult Development
	Adult Dropouts
	Adult Education
Migrant	Adult Education
	Adult Education Programs (1966 1980) Use Adult Education and Adult Programs
Public School	Adult Education
	Adult Educators
	Adult Farmer Education
	Adult Foster Care
	Adult Leaders (1967 1980) Use Leaders
	Adult Learning
Transformation Theory	(Adult Learning) Use Learning Theories and Transformative Learning
Transformations	(Adult Learning) Use Transformative Learning
	Adult Literacy
	Adult Offspring Use Adult Children
	Adult Programs
	Adult Reading Programs
	Adult Runaways Use Runaways
	Adult Students
	Adult Vocational Education
	Adults
	Adults (30 to 45)
Foster Homes (1970 1982)	(Adults) Use Adult Foster Care
Fundamental Education	(Adults) Use Adult Basic Education
Illiterate	Adults (1966 1980) Use Adult Literacy and Illiteracy
Middle Aged	Adults
Migrant	Adults Use Migrants
Old Old	Adults
Older	Adults
Young	Adults
Young Old	Adults
	Advance Organizers
Mentally	Advanced Children Use Gifted
	Advanced Courses
	Advanced Credit Examinations Use Equivalency Tests
	Advanced Education Use Higher Education
	Advanced Nations Use Developed Nations
Economically	Advanced Nations Use Developed Nations

	Advanced Placement
	Advanced Placement Programs
	Advanced Programs (1966 1980)
	Advanced Standing Examinations Use Equivalency Tests
	Advanced Students
	Advancement Use Promotion (Occupational)
Faculty	Advancement Use Faculty Promotion
Institutional	Advancement
Teacher	Advancement Use Teacher Promotion
Technological	Advancement
	Advantaged
Culturally	Advantaged (1967 1980) Use Advantaged
Economically	Advantaged Use Advantaged
Socially	Advantaged Use Advantaged
Educational	Advantages Use Educational Opportunities
	Adventitious Impairments
	Adventitiously Handicapped (1975 1980) Use Adventitious Impairments
	Adventure Education
	Adventure Learning Use Adventure Education
	Adverbials Use Adverbs
	Adverbs
	Advertising
	Advertising Art Use Commercial Art
Faculty	Advisers
Foreign Student	Advisers
Resident	Advisers
Academic	Advising
Faculty	Advisors (1967 1980) Use Faculty Advisers
	Advisory Boards Use Advisory Committees
	Advisory Committees
	Advocacy
Child	Advocacy
Citizen	Advocacy Use Advocacy
Political	Advocacy Use Lobbying
Self	Advocacy
	Advocates (Law) Use Lawyers
	Aerobic Dance Use Aerobics and Dance
	Aerobics
	Aerospace Education
	Aerospace Industry
Satellites	(Aerospace)
	Aerospace Science Education Use Aerospace Education
	Aerospace Sciences Use Aerospace Technology
	Aerospace Technology
	Aesthetic Education
	Aesthetic Judgment Use Aesthetic Values and Value Judgment
	Aesthetic Values
	Aesthetics
Taste	(Aesthetics) Use Aesthetic Values
Public	Affairs Education
Student	Affairs Services Use Student Personnel Services
Student	Affairs Workers Use Student Personnel Workers
World	Affairs
	Affection
	Affective Behavior
	Affective Education Use Humanistic Education
	Affective Measures
	Affective Objectives
	Affective Tests (1971 1980) Use Affective Measures
	Affiliated Schools
	Affiliation Need
Political	Affiliation
	Affirmative Action
	Affixes
	Affluent Youth
	African American Studies (1969 1977) Use Black Studies
	African Americans Use Blacks
	African Centered Perspective Use Afrocentrism
	African Culture
	African History
	African Languages
	African Literature
	African Studies
	Africentrism Use Afrocentrism
	Afrikaans
	Afro Americans Use Blacks
	Afro Asiatic Languages
	Afrocentrism
	After School Activities (1967 1980) Use After School Programs
	After School Centers
	After School Day Care (1978 1983) Use After School Programs and School Age Day Care
	After School Education
	After School Programs
	After School Tutoring (1966 1980) Use After School Education and Tutoring
Figural	Aftereffects
	Age
Chronological	Age
School	Age Day Care
	Age Differences
	Age Discrimination
	Age Grade Placement
	Age Grade Status Use Age Grade Placement
Mixed	Age Grouping

Age Groups
Developmental Differences (Age Groups)   Use Age Differences and Individual Development
Cross Age Helping   Use Cross Age Teaching
Intelligence Age   Use Mental Age
Age Level   Use Age
Mental Age
Old Age   Use Older Adults
School Entrance Age
Cross Age Teaching
Aged   Use Older Adults
Middle Aged Adults
Homes for the Aged   Use Personal Care Homes
Middle Aged (1966 1980)   Use Middle Aged Adults
Agencies
Accrediting Agencies
Administrative Agencies (1966 1980)
Government Agencies   Use Public Agencies
Local Education Agencies   Use School Districts
Nonpublic Agencies   Use Private Agencies
Private Agencies
Public Agencies
Community Agencies (Public) (1966 1980)   Use Public Agencies
Religious Agencies (1966 1980)   Use Religious Organizations
Social Agencies
State Agencies
State Education Agencies   Use State Departments of Education
Urban Renewal Agencies
Voluntary Agencies
Welfare Agencies
Youth Agencies
Agency Cooperation
Agency Function   Use Agency Role
Agency Role
Agenda Setting
Agricultural Agents   Use Extension Agents
Change Agents
County Extension Agents   Use Extension Agents
Extension Agents
Farm Agents   Use Extension Agents
Four H Club Agents   Use Extension Agents
Home Demonstration Agents   Use Extension Agents
Linking Agents
Village Extension Agents   Use Extension Agents
Aggression
Aging Education
Aging in Academia
Aging (Individuals)
Aging Professoriate   Use Aging in Academia
Interjudge Agreement   Use Interrater Reliability
Agreements (Formal)   Use Contracts
Negotiation Agreements
Agribusiness
Agricultural Agents   Use Extension Agents
Agricultural Chemical Occupations
Agricultural Colleges
Agricultural Education
Agricultural Education (Vocational)   Use Agricultural Education and Vocational Education
Agricultural Engineering
Agricultural Extension   Use Rural Extension
Agricultural Labor Disputes (1966 1980)   Use Labor Demands
Agricultural Laborers
Agricultural Machinery
Agricultural Machinery Occupations
Agricultural Mechanics (Subject)   Use Agricultural Engineering
Agricultural Migrant Workers   Use Migrant Workers
Agricultural Migrants   Use Migrants
Agricultural Occupations
Nonfarm Agricultural Occupations   Use Off Farm Agricultural Occupations
Off Farm Agricultural Occupations
Agricultural Personnel
Agricultural Production
Agricultural Research Projects (1966 1981)   Use Research Projects
Agricultural Safety
Agricultural Skills
Agricultural Supplies
Agricultural Supply Occupations
Agricultural Technicians
Agricultural Trends
Agricultural Workers   Use Agricultural Laborers
Migratory Agricultural Workers   Use Migrant Workers
Agriculture
Supervised Occupational Experience (Agriculture)
Vocational Agriculture Teachers (1967 1980)   Use Agricultural Education and Vocational Education Teachers
Vocational Agriculture (1967 1980)   Use Agricultural Education and Vocational Education
Agronomy
Additional Aid   Use Equalization Aid
Financial Aid Applicants
Categorical Aid
Equalization Aid
Federal Aid
Federal State Aid   Use State Federal Aid
First Aid
Legal Aid

Need Analysis (Student Financial   Aid)
Nonpublic School   Aid (1972 1980)   Use Private School Aid
Student Financial   Aid Officers
Parochial School   Aid (1972 1980)   Use Parochial Schools and Private School Aid
Private School   Aid
Legal   Aid Projects (1966 1980)   Use Legal Aid
Provincial   Aid   Use State Aid
School   Aid   Use Educational Finance
State   Aid
State Federal   Aid
State Financial   Aid   Use State Aid
Student   Aid   Use Student Financial Aid
Student Financial   Aid
Computer   Aided Design and Manufacturing   Use Computer Assisted Design and Computer Assisted Manufacturing
Machine   Aided Indexing   Use Automatic Indexing
Computer   Aided Instruction   Use Computer Assisted Instruction
Computer   Aided Instructional Management   Use Computer Managed Instruction
Bilingual Teacher   Aides
Dietetic   Aides   Use Dietitians
Engineering   Aides   Use Engineering Technicians
Forester   Aides   Use Forestry Aides
Forestry   Aides
Highway Engineering   Aides
Home Health   Aides
Housekeeping   Aides   Use Housekeepers
Housing Management   Aides
Library   Aides   Use Library Technicians
Nurses   Aides
Nursing   Aides   Use Nurses Aides
Physical Therapy   Aides
Psychiatric   Aides
Rest Home   Aides   Use Nurses Aides
School   Aides
Teacher   Aides
Audiovisual   Aids
Autoinstructional   Aids
Book Selection   Aids   Use Selection Tools
AIDS (Disease)   Use Acquired Immune Deficiency Syndrome
Display   Aids
Electromechanical   Aids
Electronic   Aids   Use Electronic Equipment
Communication   Aids (for Disabled)
Hearing   Aids
Instructional   Aids (1966 1980)   Use Educational Media
Language   Aids (1966 1980)
Library   Aids   Use Library Equipment
Low Vision   Aids
Mechanical Teaching   Aids (1966 1980)   Use Educational Media
Mobility   Aids
Authoring   Aids (Programing) (1983 1994)   Use Authoring Aids (Programming)
Authoring   Aids (Programming)
Self Instruction   Aids   Use Autoinstructional Aids
Sensory   Aids
Three Dimensional   Aids
Visual   Aids
Air Bags   Use Restraints (Vehicle Safety)
Air Bases   Use Military Air Facilities
Army   Air Bases   Use Military Air Facilities
Air Conditioning
Air Conditioning Equipment
Air Conditioning Mechanics   Use Refrigeration Mechanics
Military   Air Facilities
Air Flow
Air Force Bases   Use Military Air Facilities
Air Inflated Structures (1972 1980)   Use Air Structures
Air Pollution
Air Pollution Control (1967 1980)   Use Air Pollution
Air Raid Shelters   Use Fallout Shelters
Coast Guard   Air Stations   Use Military Air Facilities
Marine Corps   Air Stations   Use Military Air Facilities
Naval   Air Stations   Use Military Air Facilities
Air Structures
Hybrid   Air Structures (1972 1980)   Use Air Structures
Air Supported Structures (1972 1980)   Use Air Structures
Air Traffic Control
Air Transportation
Airborne Field Trips (1968 1980)   Use Field Trips
Airborne Television (1966 1980)   Use Television
Aircraft Mechanics   Use Aviation Mechanics
Aircraft Pilots
Airline Pilots   Use Aircraft Pilots
Airplane Pilots   Use Aircraft Pilots
Airports
Akan
Alarm Systems
Burglar   Alarms   Use Alarm Systems
Security Systems   (Alarms)   Use Alarm Systems
Smoke   Alarms   Use Alarm Systems
Alaska Natives
Albanian
Alcohol Abuse
Alcohol Addiction   Use Alcoholism
Alcohol Consumption   Use Drinking

	Alcohol Dependency Use Alcoholism
Drunkenness	(Alcohol) Use Alcohol Abuse
	Alcohol Education
	Alcohol Intoxication Use Alcohol Abuse
Fetal	Alcohol Syndrome
	Alcohol Use Use Drinking
	Alcoholic Beverages
	Alcoholism
	Aleut Use Eskimo Aleut Languages
Eskimo	Aleut Languages
	Algebra
	Algorisms Use Algorithms
	Algorithms
	Alien Culture Use Foreign Culture
	Alien Illegality Use Undocumented Immigrants
	Alienation
Student	Alienation
Teacher	Alienation
Illegal	Aliens Use Undocumented Immigrants
	All Day Half Day Schedules Use Full Day Half Day Schedules
	Allegory
	Allergy
Academic	Alliances Use Partnerships in Education
	Allied Health Education Use Allied Health Occupations Education
	Allied Health Occupations
	Allied Health Occupations Education
	Allied Health Personnel
	Allied Health Professions Use Allied Health Occupations
	Allied Medical Occupations Use Allied Health Occupations
	Allocation of Resources Use Resource Allocation
Resource	Allocation
Tax	Allocation
Time	Allocation Use Time Management
Budget	Allocations Use Budgeting
Resource	Allocations (1966 1980) Use Resource Allocation
	Allomorphs (1967 1980) Use Morphemes
Training	Allowances
Thinking	Aloud Protocols Use Protocol Analysis
Reading	Aloud to Others
Cyrillic	Alphabet
Initial Teaching	Alphabet
Letters	(Alphabet)
Capitalization	(Alphabetic)
	Alphabetic Filing Use Filing
	Alphabetizing Skills
	Alphabets
Non Latin	Alphabets Use Non Roman Scripts
Nonroman	Alphabets Use Non Roman Scripts
Phonemic	Alphabets
	Altaic Languages Use Uralic Altaic Languages
Uralic	Altaic Languages
	Alternate Day Block Scheduling Use Alternate Day Schedules and Block Scheduling
Full Day Half Day	Alternate Day Use Alternate Day Schedules and Full Day Half Day Schedules
	Alternate Day Schedules
	Alternative and Augmentative Communication Use Augmentative and Alternative Communication
	Alternative Assessment
	Alternative Certification (Teaching) Use Alternative Teacher Certification
Augmentative and	Alternative Communication
	Alternative Communication Systems (Disabled) Use Augmentative and Alternative Communication
	Alternative Education Use Nontraditional Education
	Alternative Energy Sources
	Alternative Evaluation (Individuals) Use Alternative Assessment
	Alternative Futures Use Futures (of Society)
	Alternative Life Styles Use Life Style
	Alternative Schools (1972 1980) Use Nontraditional Education
	Alternative Teacher Certification
Educational	Alternatives (1974 1980) Use Nontraditional Education
Instructional	Alternatives Use Nontraditional Education
Teaching	Alternatives Use Nontraditional Education
	Alternatives to Standardized Testing Use Alternative Assessment
Training	Alternatives Use Nontraditional Education
	Altruism
	Alumni
	Alumni Associations
	Alumni Colleges Use Alumni Education
	Alumni Education
	Alzheimers Disease
Senile Dementia	Alzheimers Type Use Alzheimers Disease
	Ambient Pressure Use Pressure (Physics)
	Ambiguity
	Ambition Use Aspiration
	Ambiversion Use Extraversion Introversion
	Ambulance Attendants Use Emergency Medical Technicians
	Amerasians Use Asian Americans
American Literature (1966 1980) (Latin	America) Use Latin American Literature
	American Culture (1966 1980)
Hispanic	American Culture
Japanese	American Culture
Latin	American Culture
Mexican	American Culture Use Hispanic American Culture and Mexican Americans
North	American Culture
	American Dream
Mexican	American Education

	American English (1968 1980)	Use North American English
North	American English	
	American Government (Course) (1966 1980)	Use United States Government (Course)
	American History (1966 1980)	
Central	American History	Use Latin American History
Latin	American History	
Mexican	American History	
North	American History	
South	American History	Use Latin American History
	American Indian Culture	
	American Indian Education	
	American Indian History	
	American Indian Languages	
	American Indian Literature	
	American Indian Reservations	
	American Indian Studies	
	American Indians	
Nonreservation	American Indians	
Off Reservation	American Indians	Use Nonreservation American Indians
Reservation	American Indians	
Rural	American Indians	
Urban	American Indians	
	American Jews	Use Jews
Central	American Literature	Use Latin American Literature
Hispanic	American Literature	
Latin	American Literature	
	American Literature (1966 1980) (Latin America)	Use Latin American Literature
Mexican	American Literature	
North	American Literature	
South	American Literature	Use Latin American Literature
Spanish	American Literature (1969 1980)	Use Hispanic American Literature
	American Literature (1966 1980) (United States)	Use United States Literature
	American Negroes	Use Blacks
	American Orientals	Use Asian Americans
	American Revolutionary War	Use Revolutionary War (United States)
	American Samoans	Use Samoan Americans
	American Sign Language	
Asian	American Students	
Hispanic	American Students	
	American Studies	
African	American Studies (1969 1977)	Use Black Studies
African	Americans	Use Blacks
Afro	Americans	Use Blacks
Anglo	Americans	
Arab	Americans	Use Arabs and North Americans
Asian	Americans	
Black	Americans	Use Blacks
Cambodian	Americans	Use Asian Americans and Cambodians
Central	Americans	Use Latin Americans
Chinese	Americans	
Cuban	Americans	Use Cubans and Hispanic Americans
Dominican	Americans	Use Dominicans and Hispanic Americans
Filipino	Americans	
Greek	Americans	
Hispanic	Americans	
Indochinese	Americans	Use Asian Americans and Indochinese
Italian	Americans	
Japanese	Americans	
Korean	Americans	
Laotian	Americans	Use Asian Americans and Laotians
Latin	Americans	
Mexican	Americans	
North	Americans	
Oriental	Americans	Use Asian Americans
Pacific	Americans	
Polish	Americans	
Portuguese	Americans	
Samoan	Americans	
South	Americans	Use Latin Americans
Spanish	Americans	
Vietnamese	Americans	Use Asian Americans and Vietnamese People
	Ameslan	Use American Sign Language
	Ametropia	
	Amharic	
	Amish	
Light	Amplifiers (Lasers)	Use Lasers
Magnetic	Amplifiers	Use Electronic Control
	Amputations	
	Amputees (1967 1980)	Use Amputations
Diversity (Cultural) as	an Observation or a Fact	Use Cultural Differences
	Analog Computers	
	Analysis	Use Evaluation Methods
Audience	Analysis	
Behavioral	Analysis	Use Behavioral Science Research
Benefit Cost	Analysis	Use Cost Effectiveness
Centroid Method of Factor	Analysis	Use Factor Analysis
Chemical	Analysis	
Citation	Analysis	
Cluster	Analysis	
Cohort	Analysis	
Community	Analysis	Use Community Study
Comparative	Analysis	
Componential	Analysis	

Content	Analysis	
Contrastive Language	Analysis	Use Contrastive Linguistics
Cost	Analysis	Use Cost Effectiveness
Cost Benefit	Analysis	Use Cost Effectiveness
Cost Effectiveness	Analysis	Use Cost Effectiveness
Cost Utility	Analysis	Use Cost Effectiveness
Critical	Analysis	Use Criticism
Data	Analysis	
Discourse	Analysis	
Discriminant	Analysis	
Discriminant Function	Analysis	Use Discriminant Analysis
Discriminatory	Analysis	Use Discriminant Analysis
Economic	Analysis	Use Economic Research
Factor	Analysis	
Force Field	Analysis	
Input Output	Analysis	
Integrative	Analysis	Use Meta Analysis
Interaction	Analysis	Use Interaction
Interaction Process	Analysis	
International Legal	Analysis	Use International Law
Item	Analysis	
Job	Analysis	
Job Content	Analysis	Use Job Analysis
Error	Analysis (Language)	
Structural	Analysis (Linguistics)	
Literary	Analysis (1968 1980)	Use Literary Criticism
Marxian	Analysis	
Maximum Likelihood Factor	Analysis	Use Factor Analysis and Maximum Likelihood Statistics
Meta	Analysis	
Miscue	Analysis	
Multiple Discriminant	Analysis	Use Discriminant Analysis
Multiple Regression	Analysis	
Multivariate	Analysis	
Network	Analysis	
Occupational	Analysis	Use Job Analysis
	Analysis of Covariance	
	Analysis of Variance	
Multivariate	Analysis of Variance	Use Multivariate Analysis
Operations	Analysis	Use Operations Research
Path	Analysis	
Phonetic	Analysis	
Policy	Analysis	
Principal Components	Analysis	Use Factor Analysis
Protocol	Analysis	
Q	Analysis	Use Q Methodology
Structural	Analysis (Science)	
Site	Analysis	
Skill	Analysis	
Statistical	Analysis	
Structural	Analysis (1966 1980)	
Need	Analysis (Student Financial Aid)	
Systems	Analysis	
Tagmemic	Analysis	
Task	Analysis	
Judgment	Analysis Technique	
Test	Analysis	Use Test Theory
Transactional	Analysis	
Trend	Analysis	
Systems	Analysts	
	Analytic Geometry	
	Analytical Criticism (1969 1980)	
	Anatomy	
	Ancestral Lineage	Use Genealogy
	Ancient History	
	Ancillary School Services	
	Ancillary Services (1967 1980)	
	Ancova	Use Analysis of Covariance
Augmentative	and Alternative Communication	
Language	and Area Centers (1968 1980)	
Alternative	and Augmentative Communication	Use Augmentative and Alternative Communication
Partnership Academies (School	and Business)	Use Career Academies
R	and D	Use Research and Development
Supply	and Demand	
Teacher Supply	and Demand	
Research	and Development Centers	
Research	and Development	
Tool	and Die Makers	
Food	and Drug Inspectors	
R D	and E	Use Research and Development
Work	and Education	Use Education Work Relationship
Life Costs (Facilities	and Equipment)	Use Life Cycle Costing
Home	and Family Life Education	Use Family Life Education
Motherese	and Fatherese	Use Caregiver Speech and Parent Child Relationship
Body	and Fender Repairers	Use Auto Body Repairers
Track	and Field	
Petroleum (Oil	and Gas)	Use Fossil Fuels and Oil
Occupational Safety	and Health	
Occupational Safety	and Health Standards	Use Labor Standards and Occupational Safety and Health
Speech	and Hearing Clinics	
Trade	and Industrial Education	
Trade	and Industrial Teachers	
Research	and Instruction Units	
Speech	and Language Pathology	Use Speech Language Pathology

Computer Aided Design	and Manufacturing Use Computer Assisted Design and Computer Assisted Manufacturing
Instrumentation	and Orchestration
Industrial	and Organizational Psychology Use Industrial Psychology
Information	and Referral Services Use Information Services and Referral
Special	and Regular Education Relationship Use Regular and Special Education Relationship
Search	and Seizure
Shared Resources	and Services
Libel	and Slander
Science	and Society
Science Technology	and Society Use Science and Society
General	and Special Education Relationship Use Regular and Special Education Relationship
Regular	and Special Education Relationship
Scientific	and Technical Information
English for Science	and Technology
Science	and Technology Libraries Use Science Libraries
Stunts	and Tumbling Use Tumbling
Fruit	and Vegetable Inspectors Use Food and Drug Inspectors
Waiters	and Waitresses
Black	and White Films Use Films
Education	and Work Use Education Work Relationship
	Andragogy
	Androgogy Use Andragogy
	Androgyny
	Anechoic Materials Use Acoustic Insulation
	Anemia
Iron Deficiency	Anemia Use Anemia
Sickle Cell	Anemia
	Anesthesiology
	Anger
	Anglo Americans
	Anglo Saxon Use Old English
	Anglos Use Anglo Americans
	Animal Behavior
	Animal Biology Use Zoology
	Animal Caretakers
	Animal Facilities
	Animal Husbandry
	Animal Keepers Use Animal Caretakers
	Animal Life Use Animals
	Animal Science (1967 1980) Use Animal Husbandry
	Animals
Companion	Animals Use Pets
Laboratory	Animals
	Animation
	Anishinabe (Tribe) Use Chippewa (Tribe)
	Annotated Bibliographies
	Annotations Use Abstracts
	Annual Reports
	Annuals Use Yearbooks
	Anomalies (1967 1980) Use Congenital Impairments
Downs	Anomaly Use Downs Syndrome
	Anorexia Nervosa
	Anova Use Analysis of Variance
	Answer Booklets Use Answer Sheets
	Answer Cards Use Answer Sheets
Question	Answer Interviews (1966 1980) Use Interviews
	Answer Keys
	Answer Sheets
Community	Antennas (1966 1980) Use Cable Television
	Anthologies
	Anthracite Use Coal
	Anthropological Linguistics
	Anthropology
Educational	Anthropology
Linguistic	Anthropology Use Anthropological Linguistics
	Anti Discrimination Legislation Use Civil Rights Legislation
	Anti Gay Bias Use Homophobia
	Anti Intellectualism
	Anti Poverty Programs Use Poverty Programs
	Anti Segregation Programs (1967 1980) Use Racial Integration
	Anti Semitism
	Anti Social Behavior (1966 1980) Use Antisocial Behavior
	Antisocial Behavior
	Antithesis
	Anxiety
Computer	Anxiety
Mathematics	Anxiety
Separation	Anxiety
Test	Anxiety
	Apache
	Apartheid
	Apathy
	Aphasia
	Apparel Industry Use Fashion Industry
	Appetite Disorders Use Eating Disorders
	Appliance Repair
Home	Appliance Repair Use Appliance Repair
	Appliance Repairers (1980 1981) Use Appliance Repair
	Appliance Repairing (1968 1981) Use Appliance Repair
	Appliance Service Technicians (1967 1980) Use Appliance Repair
Electrical	Appliance Servicemen (1968 1980) Use Appliance Repair
	Appliances Use Equipment
Electrical	Appliances

College	Applicants
Financial Aid	Applicants
Job	Applicants
Law School	Applicants Use College Applicants and Law Schools
Loan	Applicants Use Financial Aid Applicants
Medical School	Applicants Use College Applicants and Medical Schools
Job	Application
Student	Application (1966 1980) Use College Applicants
Computer	Applications Use Computer Oriented Programs
Mathematical	Applications
Project	Applications (1967 1980)
	Applied History Use Public History
	Applied Linguistics
	Applied Music
	Applied Reading (1966 1980) Use Reading
	Applied Research Use Research
	Applied Sciences Use Technology
	Appraisal Use Evaluation
Administrator	Appraisal Use Administrator Evaluation
Performance	Appraisal (Personnel) Use Personnel Evaluation
Property	Appraisal
Real Estate	Appraisal Use Property Appraisal
Self	Appraisal Use Self Evaluation (Individuals)
Student	Appraisal Use Student Evaluation
Art	Appreciation
Literature	Appreciation
Music	Appreciation
Communication	Apprehension
Writing	Apprehension
	Apprenticeships
Research	Apprenticeships (1967 1981) Use Research Assistants
Caseworker	Approach
Design Build	Approach
Global	Approach
Holistic	Approach
Interdisciplinary	Approach
International	Approach Use Global Approach
Language Experience	Approach
Multidisciplinary	Approach Use Interdisciplinary Approach
Orff Schulwerk	Approach Use Orff Method
Reggio Emilia	Approach
Sequential	Approach
Systems	Approach
Case Study	Approach (Teaching) Use Case Method (Teaching Technique)
Thematic	Approach
Whole Language	Approach
Whole Person	Approach Use Holistic Approach
Whole Word Reading	Approach Use Sight Method
Wholistic	Approach Use Holistic Approach
Worldwide	Approach Use Global Approach
Process	Approach (Writing)
Writing Process	Approach Use Process Approach (Writing)
Audiolingual	Approaches Use Audiolingual Methods
Research	Approaches Use Research Methodology
Culturally	Appropriate Education Use Culturally Relevant Education
Developmentally	Appropriate Practices
Developmentally	Appropriate Programs Use Developmentally Appropriate Practices
	Appropriate Technology
Program	Approval (Validation) Use Program Validation
	Approved Programs (Validated) Use Validated Programs
	Approximation (Mathematics) Use Estimation (Mathematics)
	Approximative Systems (Language Learning) Use Interlanguage
	Aptitude
Academic	Aptitude
Language	Aptitude
Mathematical	Aptitude
Mathematics	Aptitude Use Mathematical Aptitude
Quantitative	Aptitude Use Mathematical Aptitude
Student	Aptitude Use Academic Aptitude
	Aptitude Tests
	Aptitude Treatment Interaction
Vocational	Aptitude
	Aquariums
	Aquatic Sports
	Arab Americans Use Arabs and North Americans
	Arabic
	Arabs
	Arbitration
	Arc Welding Use Welding
	Archaeology
	Archery
	Architects
	Architectural Barriers (1970 1980)
	Architectural Changes Use Building Design
	Architectural Character
	Architectural Design Use Building Design
	Architectural Drafting
	Architectural Education
	Architectural Elements (1968 1980) Use Structural Elements (Construction)
	Architectural Programing (1968 1994) Use Architectural Programming
	Architectural Programming
	Architectural Research
	Architectural Style Use Architectural Character

	Architectural Tradition Use Architectural Character
	Architecture
School	Architecture (1966 1980) Use Educational Facilities Design
	Archives
	Area
Language and	Area Centers (1968 1980)
Local	Area Networks
Planar	Area Use Area
Content	Area Reading
Open	Area Schools Use Open Plan Schools
	Area Studies
Surface	Area Use Area
	Area Vocational Schools (1966 1980) Use Regional Schools and Vocational Schools
Content	Area Writing
Boom Town	Areas Use Boomtowns
Economically Depressed	Areas Use Poverty Areas
	Areas (Geographic) Use Geographic Regions
Depressed	Areas (Geographic) (1966 1980) Use Poverty Areas
Humid	Areas Use Humidity
Metropolitan	Areas
Nonmetropolitan	Areas
Parking	Areas (1966 1980) Use Parking Facilities
Poverty	Areas
Reading in Content	Areas Use Content Area Reading
Redevelopment	Areas Use Urban Renewal
Rural	Areas
Street Parking	Areas Use Parking Facilities
Student Loading	Areas (1968 1980) Use Student Transportation
Teaching	Areas Use Curriculum
Urban	Areas
	Argumentation Use Persuasive Discourse
	Aristotelian Criticism (1969 1980)
	Arithmetic
Clock	Arithmetic Use Modular Arithmetic
	Arithmetic Curriculum (1966 1980) Use Arithmetic and Mathematics Curriculum
Finite	Arithmetic Use Modular Arithmetic
Mental	Arithmetic Use Arithmetic and Mental Computation
Modular	Arithmetic
Remedial	Arithmetic (1966 1980) Use Arithmetic and Remedial Mathematics
	Arithmetic Systems Use Number Systems
	Arithmetic Tests Use Arithmetic and Mathematics Tests
	Armed Forces
	Armenian
	Arms Control Use Disarmament
Nuclear	Arms Use Nuclear Weapons
Small	Arms Use Guns
	Arms (Weapons) Use Weapons
	Army Air Bases Use Military Air Facilities
	Arousal Patterns
Bone	Arrangement Use Skeletal System
Classroom	Arrangement (1966 1980) Use Classroom Design
Furniture	Arrangement
Structural	Arrangement Use Organization
	Art
	Art Activities
Advertising	Art Use Commercial Art
	Art Appreciation
Childrens	Art
Commercial	Art
Creative	Art
	Art Criticism
	Art Education
Discipline Based	Art Education
	Art Expression
	Art Galleries Use Arts Centers
	Art History
	Art Making (Instruction) Use Studio Art
	Art Materials
	Art Production Curriculum Use Studio Art
	Art Products
Relief	(Art)
State of the	Art Reviews
	Art Song
Studio	Art
	Art Studio Courses Use Studio Art
	Art Teachers
	Art Therapy
	Articles (Grammar) Use Determiners (Languages)
Journal	Articles
	Articles (Journals) Use Journal Articles
Magazine	Articles Use Journal Articles
Periodical	Articles Use Journal Articles
	Articulation (Education)
	Articulation Impairments
Points of	Articulation Use Articulation (Speech)
	Articulation (Program) (1967 1980) Use Articulation (Education)
	Articulation (Speech)
	Articulation Tests Use Speech Tests
	Artificial Intelligence
	Artificial Languages
	Artificial Satellites Use Satellites (Aerospace)
	Artificial Speech
	Artisans Use Craft Workers

```
        Painting (1966 1980)  (Artistic)   Use Painting (Visual Arts)
                              Artistic Talent   Use Talent
                              Artists
                              Arts Centers
                       Fine  Arts Centers   Use Arts Centers
                 Performing  Arts Centers   Use Theaters
                Bachelor of  Arts Degrees   Use Bachelors Degrees
                  Doctor of  Arts Degrees
                  Master of  Arts Degrees   Use Masters Degrees
                   Dramatic  Arts   Use Dramatics
                       Fine  Arts
                    Graphic  Arts
                  Master of  Arts in College Teaching   Use Masters Degrees
                  Master of  Arts in Teaching   Use Masters Degrees
                 Industrial  Arts
                   Language  Arts
                    Liberal  Arts
                    Liberal  Arts Majors (1967 1980)   Use Liberal Arts and Majors (Students)
       Painting (Industrial  Arts)
          Painting (Visual  Arts)
                 Performing  Arts   Use Theater Arts
                  Practical  Arts
              Print Making   Arts   Use Printmaking
        Rehearsals (Theater  Arts)
                 Industrial  Arts Shops   Use School Shops
                 Industrial  Arts Teachers
                    Theater  Arts
                     Visual  Arts
            Higher Education  as a Field of Study   Use Postsecondary Education as a Field of Study
     Postsecondary Education  as a Field of Study
                     Parent  as a Teacher   Use Parents as Teachers
          Diversity (Cultural)  as a Value   Use Cultural Pluralism
          Diversity (Cultural)  as an Observation or a Fact   Use Cultural Differences
                    Writing  as Process   Use Process Approach (Writing)
                   Teachers  as Researchers   Use Teacher Researchers
                    Parents  as Teachers
                              Asbestos
                              Asian American Students
                              Asian Americans
                      South  Asian Civilization   Use Non Western Civilization
                              Asian History
                              Asian Music   Use Oriental Music
                              Asian Studies
                       Afro  Asiatic Languages
                     Austro  Asiatic Languages
                              Asphalts
                              Aspiration
                   Academic  Aspiration
                              Aspiration Level   Use Aspiration
               Occupational  Aspiration Level   Use Occupational Aspiration
                  Low Level  Aspiration (1966 1980)   Use Aspiration
               Occupational  Aspiration
                     Parent  Aspiration
                   Parental  Aspiration (1966 1980)   Use Parent Aspiration
                 Vocational  Aspiration   Use Occupational Aspiration
                     Sexual  Assault   Use Sexual Abuse
                              Assembly (Manufacturing)
                              Assembly Programs
                              Assertive Training   Use Assertiveness
                              Assertiveness
                              Assertiveness Training   Use Assertiveness
                              Assessed Valuation
                              Assessment   Use Evaluation
                Alternative  Assessment
                  Authentic  Assessment   Use Performance Based Assessment
                              Assessment Centers (Personnel)
          College Outcomes  Assessment
            Curriculum Based  Assessment
        Curriculum Referenced  Assessment   Use Curriculum Based Assessment
                     Dental  Assessment   Use Dental Evaluation
                     Direct  Assessment   Use Performance Based Assessment
                Educational  Assessment
          Educational Quality  Assessment   Use Educational Assessment and Educational Quality
                Performance  Assessment (Higher Order Learning)   Use Performance Based Assessment
                   Informal  Assessment
              Institutional  Assessment   Use Institutional Evaluation
                              Assessment Instruments (Individuals)   Use Measures (Individuals)
                      Needs  Assessment
         Performance Based  Assessment
                Personality  Assessment
                  Portfolio  Assessment
                 Prereferral  Assessment   Use Prereferral Intervention
                              Assessment Rubrics   Use Scoring Rubrics
                       Self  Assessment   Use Self Evaluation (Individuals)
                Performance  Assessment (Skilled Bodily Movements)   Use Performance Tests
                 Vocational  Assessment   Use Vocational Evaluation
        Capital Outlay (for Fixed  Assets)
                   Teaching  Assignment (1966 1980)
                              Assignments
                    Reading  Assignments
                    Student  Assignments   Use Assignments
                   Textbook  Assignments (1966 1980)   Use Assignments
                    Writing  Assignments
```

	Assimilation (Cultural) Use Acculturation
International Technical	Assistance Use International Programs and Technical Assistance
Medical	Assistance Use Medical Services
Employee	Assistance Programs
Public Welfare	Assistance Use Welfare Services
	Assistance (Social Behavior) Use Helping Relationship
State	Assistance Use State Aid
Support Networks (Personal	Assistance) Use Social Support Groups
Entry Year	Assistance (Teacher Induction) Use Beginning Teacher Induction
Technical	Assistance
	Assistant Principals
	Assistant Superintendent Role (1966 1980)
	Assistant Superintendents Use Superintendents
Dental	Assistants
Legal	Assistants
Library Technical	Assistants Use Library Technicians
Mechanical Engineering	Assistants Use Mechanical Design Technicians
Medical	Assistants
Medical Laboratory	Assistants
Nursing	Assistants Use Nurses Aides
Occupational Therapy	Assistants
Physicians	Assistants
Research	Assistants
Resident	Assistants
Teaching	Assistants
Veterinary	Assistants
	Assistantships
Computer	Assisted Communication Use Computer Mediated Communication
Computer	Assisted Design
Computer	Assisted Drafting Use Computer Assisted Design and Drafting
Computer	Assisted Indexing Use Automatic Indexing
Computer	Assisted Instruction
Intelligent Computer	Assisted Instruction Use Intelligent Tutoring Systems
Computer	Assisted Learning Use Computer Assisted Instruction
Computer	Assisted Manufacturing
Computer	Assisted Testing
	Assistive Devices (for Disabled)
	Associate Degrees
Two Plus Two Tech Prep	Associate Degrees Use Associate Degrees and Tech Prep
Paired	Associate Learning
	Association Measures
Statistical	Association Methods Use Correlation
	Association (Psychological) (1968 1980) Use Association (Psychology)
	Association (Psychology)
Serial	Association Use Serial Learning
	Association Tests (1968 1980) Use Association Measures
Accrediting	Associations Use Accrediting Agencies
Alumni	Associations
Dental	Associations (1966 1980) Use Dentistry and Professional Associations
	Associations (Groups) Use Organizations (Groups)
Library	Associations
Medical	Associations
Parent	Associations
Professional	Associations
Word	Associations (Reading) Use Associative Learning
Teacher	Associations
Voluntary	Associations Use Voluntary Agencies
	Associative Learning
	Asthma
	Astronomy
	At Risk Persons
	Athabascan Languages Use Athapascan Languages
	Athapascan Languages
	Athletes
	Athletic Activities (1966 1974) Use Athletics
	Athletic Coaches
	Athletic Equipment
	Athletic Fields
	Athletic Programs (1966 1980) Use Athletics
Extramural	Athletic Programs (1966 1980) Use Extramural Athletics
Intramural	Athletic Programs (1966 1980) Use Intramural Athletics
	Athletics
College	Athletics
Extramural	Athletics
Intercollegiate	Athletics Use College Athletics and Intercollegiate Cooperation
Interscholastic	Athletics Use Extramural Athletics
Intramural	Athletics
Womens	Athletics
	Atlases
	Atmosphere (Social) Use Social Environment
	Atmospheric Pollution Use Air Pollution
	Atomic Bombs Use Nuclear Weapons
	Atomic Energy Use Nuclear Energy
	Atomic Physics Use Nuclear Physics
	Atomic Structure
	Atomic Theory
	Atomic Warfare Use Nuclear Warfare
	Attachment Behavior
Educational	Attainment
Goal	Attainment Use Success
	Attendance
Average Daily	Attendance
Class	Attendance (1966 1980) Use Attendance

College	Attendance
Compulsory	Attendance Use Compulsory Education
School	Attendance Laws (1966 1974) Use School Attendance Legislation
School	Attendance Legislation
	Attendance Officers
	Attendance Patterns
	Attendance Records
School	Attendance Use Attendance
	Attendance Services (1968 1980) Use Attendance and Pupil Personnel Services
Teacher	Attendance
	Attendant Training (1968 1980) Use Attendants and Job Training
	Attendants
Ambulance	Attendants Use Emergency Medical Technicians
Home	Attendants Use Home Health Aides
Hospital	Attendants Use Nurses Aides
Physical Therapy	Attendants Use Physical Therapy Aides
Veterinary Hospital	Attendants Use Veterinary Assistants
	Attention
	Attention Control
	Attention Deficit Disorders
	Attention Span
Body	Attitude Use Human Posture
	Attitude Change
	Attitude Measures
	Attitude Tests (1966 1980) Use Attitude Measures
Self	Attitude Tests Use Self Concept Measures
	Attitudes
Administrator	Attitudes
Adolescent	Attitudes
Black	Attitudes
Changing	Attitudes (1966 1980) Use Attitude Change
Childhood	Attitudes
Childrens	Attitudes Use Childhood Attitudes
Class	Attitudes (1966 1980)
Community	Attitudes
Computer	Attitudes
Counselor	Attitudes
Dropout	Attitudes
Educational	Attitudes
Employee	Attitudes
Employee Work	Attitudes Use Employee Attitudes and Work Attitudes
Employer	Attitudes
Family	Attitudes
Father	Attitudes
Language	Attitudes
Librarian	Attitudes
Majority	Attitudes
Mother	Attitudes
Negative	Attitudes
Negro	Attitudes (1966 1977) Use Black Attitudes
Northern	Attitudes (1968 1980) Use Regional Attitudes
Parent	Attitudes
Political	Attitudes
Program	Attitudes
Racial	Attitudes
Reading	Attitudes
Regional	Attitudes
School	Attitudes
Scientific	Attitudes
Social	Attitudes
Discriminatory	Attitudes (Social) (1966 1980) Use Social Bias
Southern	Attitudes (1966 1980) Use Regional Attitudes
Student	Attitudes
Student Teacher	Attitudes
Teacher	Attitudes
	Attitudes toward Disabilities
Work	Attitudes
Writing	Attitudes
	Attorneys Use Lawyers
Interpersonal	Attraction
	Attractiveness (between Persons) Use Interpersonal Attraction
Physical	Attractiveness
	Attribution Theory
Causal	Attributions Use Attribution Theory
Language Skill	Attrition
	Attrition (Research Studies)
Language	Attrition (Skills) Use Language Skill Attrition
Student	Attrition
	Attrition (Students) Use Student Attrition
Teacher	Attrition Use Faculty Mobility
Exceptional	(Atypical) (1966 1978) Use Exceptional Persons (1978 1994)
	Audience Analysis
	Audience Awareness
	Audience Participation
	Audience Response
	Audiences
	Audio Active Compare Laboratories (1967 1980) Use Language Laboratories
	Audio Active Laboratories (1967 1980) Use Language Laboratories
	Audio Equipment
Master Tapes	(Audio) (1968 1980) Use Audiotape Recordings
	Audio Passive Laboratories (1968 1980) Use Language Laboratories
	Audio Video Laboratories (1967 1980) Use Audiovisual Centers
	Audiodisc Recordings (1980 1986) Use Audiodisks

Audiodisks
Audiolingual Approaches   Use Audiolingual Methods
Audiolingual Methods
Audiolingual Skills
Audiologists (1968 1980)   Use Allied Health Personnel and Audiology
Audiology
Audiometric Tests
Audiometrists (1967 1980)   Use Allied Health Personnel and Audiology
Audiotape Cartridges   Use Audiotape Cassettes
Audiotape Cassette Recorders   Use Audiotape Cassettes and Audiotape Recorders
Audiotape Cassettes
Audiotape Recorders
Audiotape Recordings
Audiovisual Aids
Audiovisual Centers
Audiovisual Communication (1967 1980)   Use Audiovisual Communications
Audiovisual Communications
Audiovisual Coordinators
Audiovisual Directors (1969 1980)   Use Audiovisual Coordinators
Audiovisual Education   Use Audiovisual Instruction
Audiovisual Equipment   Use Audiovisual Aids
Audiovisual Instruction
Audiovisual Materials   Use Audiovisual Aids
Audiovisual Media   Use Audiovisual Aids
Audiovisual Programs (1966 1980)   Use Audiovisual Instruction
Medical   Audit   Use Medical Care Evaluation
Auditing (Coursework)
Audition (Physiology) (1967 1980)   Use Hearing (Physiology)
Auditoriums
Auditory Comprehension   Use Listening Comprehension
Auditory Discrimination
Auditory Evaluation
Auditory Perception
Auditory Stimuli
Auditory Tests
Auditory Training
Auditory Visual Tests (1966 1980)   Use Auditory Tests and Vision Tests
Communication   Audits
Energy   Audits
Financial   Audits
Audits (Verification)
Augmentative and Alternative Communication
Alternative and   Augmentative Communication   Use Augmentative and Alternative Communication
Augmentative Communication Systems   Use Augmentative and Alternative Communication
Aural Comprehension   Use Listening Comprehension
Aural Language Learning   Use Aural Learning and Language Acquisition
Aural Learning
Aural Oral Skills   Use Audiolingual Skills
Aural Stimuli (1966 1980)   Use Auditory Stimuli
Aurally Handicapped (1966 1980)   Use Hearing Impairments
Australian Aboriginal Languages
Australian Literature
Austro Asiatic Languages
Austronesian Languages   Use Malayo Polynesian Languages
Auteurism
Film   Auteurism   Use Auteurism
Authentic Assessment   Use Performance Based Assessment
Authoring Aids (Programing) (1983 1994)   Use Authoring Aids (Programming)
Authoring Aids (Programming)
Authoring Languages   Use Authoring Aids (Programming) and Programming Languages
Authoring Systems   Use Authoring Aids (Programming)
Authoritarianism
Local Education   Authorities   Use School Districts
Local Housing   Authorities (1966 1980)   Use Housing
Authority Control (Information)
Authority Files   Use Authority Control (Information)
Authority Structure   Use Power Structure
Authors
Autism
Auto Body Repairers
Auto Body Repairmen (1966 1980)   Use Auto Body Repairers
Auto Mechanics
Auto Mechanics (Occupation) (1968 1980)   Use Auto Mechanics
Auto Parts Clerks
Auto Parts Men (1968 1980)   Use Auto Parts Clerks
Autobiographies
Autoinstructional Aids
Autoinstructional Laboratories (1967 1980)   Use Learning Laboratories
Autoinstructional Methods (1966 1980)   Use Programmed Instruction
Autoinstructional Programs (1966 1980)   Use Programmed Instruction
Integrated   Automated Library Systems   Use Integrated Library Systems
Automatic Data Processing   Use Data Processing
Automatic Indexing
Automation
Library   Automation
Office   Automation
Automobile Mechanics   Use Auto Mechanics
Individual   Autonomy   Use Personal Autonomy
Institutional   Autonomy
Learner   Autonomy   Use Personal Autonomy
Local   Autonomy (of Schools)   Use School District Autonomy
Personal   Autonomy
Professional   Autonomy

School District	Autonomy
Teacher	Autonomy Use Professional Autonomy
Computer	Auxiliary Equipment Use Computer Peripherals
	Auxiliary Laborers
	Auxiliary School Services Use Ancillary School Services
	Auxiliary Workers Use Auxiliary Laborers
Class	Average (1966 1980)
	Average Daily Attendance
	Average Daily Enrollment (1968 1980) Use Average Daily Membership
	Average Daily Membership
Grade	Average Use Grade Point Average
Grade Point	Average
	Average Students (1967 1980) Use Students
Computer	Aversion Use Computer Anxiety
	Aviation Education
	Aviation Mechanics
	Aviation Technology
	Aviation Vocabulary
Mathematics	Avoidance Use Mathematics Anxiety
Success	Avoidance Use Fear of Success
	Awards
	Awareness Use Perception
Audience	Awareness
Career	Awareness
Cultural	Awareness
Language	Awareness Use Metalinguistics
Linguistic	Awareness Use Metalinguistics
Occupational	Awareness Use Career Awareness
Current	Awareness Services Use Selective Dissemination of Information
Social	Awareness Use Interpersonal Competence
Vocational	Awareness Use Career Awareness
	Away from the Job Training Use Off the Job Training
	Aymara
	Azerbaijani
Uto	Aztecan Languages
Type	B Behavior
Crack	Babies Use Crack and Prenatal Drug Exposure
	Baby Boomers
	Baccalaureate Degrees Use Bachelors Degrees
	Bachelor of Arts Degrees Use Bachelors Degrees
	Bachelor of Science Degrees Use Bachelors Degrees
	Bachelors Degrees
Three Year	Bachelors Degrees Use Acceleration (Education) and Bachelors Degrees
	Back to Basics
	Background
Administrator	Background (1967 1980) Use Administrator Characteristics
Counselor	Background Use Counselor Characteristics
Cultural	Background
Educational	Background
Family	Background (1966 1980) Use Family Characteristics
Client	Background (Human Services) Use Client Characteristics (Human Services)
Portfolios	(Background Materials)
Parent	Background
Parental	Background (1966 1980) Use Parent Background
Social	Background
Socioeconomic	Background
Teacher	Background
	Bacteria
	Badminton
Air	Bags Use Restraints (Vehicle Safety)
	Bahasa Indonesia Use Indonesian
	Bakeries Use Bakery Industry
	Bakery Industry
Racial	Balance
Racially	Balanced Schools
	Ballads
	Ballet (1966 1980) Use Dance
	Baltic Languages
	Baluchi
Mississippi	Band of Choctaw (Tribe)
Marching	Bands Use Bands (Music)
	Bands (Music)
Head	Banging Use Self Injurious Behavior
	Banking
	Banking Industry Use Banking
	Banking Vocabulary
Data	Banks Use Databases
Item	Banks
Job	Banks
	Bantu Languages
	Barbers
	Barbiturates Use Sedatives
	Bards Use Poets
Collective	Bargaining
Scope of	Bargaining
	Baroque Literature
	Barrier Free Environment (for Disabled) Use Accessibility (for Disabled)
Acoustic	Barriers Use Acoustic Insulation
Architectural	Barriers (1970 1980)
Financial	Barriers Use Financial Problems
Sound	Barriers Use Acoustic Insulation
	Barristers Use Lawyers
Snack	Bars Use Dining Facilities

	Basaa
	Basal Reading
Knowledge	Base for Teaching
Teacher Education Knowledge	Base Use Knowledge Base for Teaching
Teacher Knowledge	Base Use Knowledge Base for Teaching
Teaching Knowledge	Base Use Knowledge Base for Teaching
	Baseball
Discipline	Based Art Education
Curriculum	Based Assessment
Performance	Based Assessment
Computer	Based Communication Use Computer Mediated Communication
Culture	Based Curriculum Use Culturally Relevant Education
Community	Based Education Use Community Education
Competency	Based Education
Consequence	Based Education Use Competency Based Education
Experience	Based Education Use Experiential Learning
Outcome	Based Education
Outcomes	Based Education Use Outcome Based Education
Performance	Based Education (1974 1980) Use Competency Based Education
Proficiency	Based Education Use Competency Based Education
Results	Based Education Use Outcome Based Education
Performance	Based Evaluation Use Performance Based Assessment
Timber	Based Industry Use Lumber Industry
Case	Based Instruction Use Case Method (Teaching Technique)
Computer	Based Instruction Use Computer Assisted Instruction
Community	Based Instruction (Disabilities)
Computer	Based Instructional Management Use Computer Managed Instruction
Computer	Based Integrated Learning Systems Use Integrated Learning Systems
School	Based Interagency Services Use Integrated Services
Computer	Based Laboratories (1967 1980) Use Computer Assisted Instruction and Laboratories
Problem	Based Learning
School	Based Management
Site	Based Management (Schools) Use School Based Management
Curriculum	Based Measurement Use Curriculum Based Assessment
Computer	Based Message Systems Use Electronic Mail
Computer	Based Microworlds Use Microworlds
Computer	Based Reference Services Use Online Systems and Reference Services
Knowledge	Based Systems Use Expert Systems
Competency	Based Teacher Education
Consequence	Based Teacher Education Use Competency Based Teacher Education
Performance	Based Teacher Education (1972 1980) Use Competency Based Teacher Education
Proficiency	Based Teacher Education Use Competency Based Teacher Education
Air	Bases Use Military Air Facilities
Air Force	Bases Use Military Air Facilities
Army Air	Bases Use Military Air Facilities
Data	Bases (1969 1981) Use Databases
	Bashfulness Use Shyness
	Bashkir
	Basic Business Education
Adult	Basic Education
	Basic Language Patterns Use Language Patterns
	Basic Reading (1967 1980)
	Basic Research Use Research
	Basic Skills
	Basic Vocabulary
	Basic Word Lists Use Word Lists
	Basic Writing
Back to	Basics
	Basketball
	Basque
	Bathrooms Use Toilet Facilities
	Battered Women
	Batteries (Electric) Use Electric Batteries
Electric	Batteries
Storage	Batteries Use Electric Batteries
	Bayesian Statistics
	Beauticians Use Cosmetology
	Beauty Use Aesthetic Values
	Beauty Culture Use Cosmetology
	Beauty Operators Use Cosmetology
	Beginning Farmer Education Use Young Farmer Education
	Beginning Principals
	Beginning Reading
	Beginning Teacher Induction
	Beginning Teachers
	Beginning Workers Use Entry Workers
	Beginning Writing
	Behavior
Activity Level (Motor	Behavior) Use Physical Activity Level
Adaptive	Behavior Use Adjustment (to Environment)
Administrator	Behavior
Adolescent	Behavior
Affective	Behavior
Animal	Behavior
Anti Social	Behavior (1966 1980) Use Antisocial Behavior
Antisocial	Behavior
Assistance (Social	Behavior) Use Helping Relationship
Attachment	Behavior
Bonding	(Behavior) Use Attachment Behavior
Chain Reflexes	(Behavior) Use Behavior Chaining
	Behavior Chaining
	Behavior Change
Child	Behavior

Collective Behavior   Use Group Behavior
Consumer Behavior   Use Consumer Economics
Delinquent Behavior (1966 1983)   Use Delinquency
Behavior Development
Behavior Disorders
Emotional Behavior   Use Affective Behavior
Exploratory Behavior
Group Behavior
Health Behavior
Helping Behavior   Use Helping Relationship
Infant Behavior
Internation Behavior   Use International Relations
Behavior Modification
Cognitive Behavior Modification   Use Behavior Modification and Cognitive Restructuring
Normative Behavior   Use Behavior Standards
Adaptive Behavior (of Disabled)
Paranoid Behavior
Parent Behavior   Use Parent Child Relationship
Coronary Prone Behavior Pattern   Use Type A Behavior
Patterned Behavior   Use Behavior Patterns
Behavior Patterns
Behavior Problems
Prosocial Behavior
Behavior Rating Scales
Reactive Behavior (1966 1980)   Use Responses
Self Destructive Behavior
Self Injurious Behavior
Sexual Behavior   Use Sexuality
Sharing Behavior
Social Behavior
Socially Deviant Behavior (1966 1980)   Use Antisocial Behavior
Spontaneous Behavior
Behavior Standards
Stimulus Behavior (1966 1980)   Use Responses
Student Behavior
Teacher Behavior
Behavior Theories
Behavior Therapy   Use Behavior Modification
Type A Behavior
Type B Behavior
Behavioral Analysis   Use Behavioral Science Research
Behavioral Contracts   Use Performance Contracts
Behavioral Counseling (1967 1980)   Use Behavior Modification
Behavioral Objectives
Behavioral Science Research
Behavioral Sciences
Behavioral Self Management   Use Self Management
Behavioral Situation Films   Use Protocol Materials
Behavioral Technology   Use Behavioral Sciences
Behaviorism
Behaviorist Psychology   Use Behaviorism
Job Behaviors   Use Job Skills
Well Being
Civic Belief (1966 1980)   Use Political Attitudes
Beliefs
Believability   Use Credibility
Make Believe Play   Use Pretend Play
Belorussian   Use Bielorussian
Lap Belts   Use Restraints (Vehicle Safety)
Seat Belts   Use Restraints (Vehicle Safety)
Bemba
Benchmarking
Cost Benefit Analysis   Use Cost Effectiveness
Benefit Cost Analysis   Use Cost Effectiveness
Community Benefits
Educational Benefits
Employee Fringe Benefits   Use Fringe Benefits
Fringe Benefits
Retirement Benefits
Teacher Employment Benefits
Teaching Benefits (1966 1980)   Use Teacher Employment Benefits
Bengali
Berber Languages
Bereavement
Attractiveness (between Persons)   Use Interpersonal Attraction
Perception (between Persons)   Use Social Cognition
Perceptiveness (between Persons)   Use Interpersonal Competence and Social Cognition
Alcoholic Beverages
Bias
Anti Gay Bias   Use Homophobia
Ethnic Bias
Experimenter Bias   Use Experimenter Characteristics
Gender Bias   Use Sex Bias
Item Bias
Racial Bias
Self Bias   Use Egocentrism
Sex Bias
Social Bias
Statistical Bias
Test Bias
Response Bias (Tests)   Use Response Style (Tests)
Textbook Bias
Bibles   Use Biblical Literature

	Biblical Literature
	Bibliocounseling Use Bibliotherapy
	Bibliographic Citations (1969 1980) Use Citations (References)
	Bibliographic Control Use Cataloging
	Bibliographic Coupling
	Bibliographic Databases
Footnotes	(Bibliographic) Use Citations (References)
	Bibliographic Instruction Use Library Instruction
	Bibliographic Records
	Bibliographic References Use Citations (References)
	Bibliographic Utilities
	Bibliographies
Abstract	Bibliographies Use Annotated Bibliographies
Annotated	Bibliographies
Statistical	Bibliography Use Bibliometrics
	Bibliometrics
	Bibliotherapy
	Bicultural Education Use Multicultural Education
	Bicultural Training Use Cross Cultural Training
	Biculturalism
	Bicycling
Competitive	Bidding Use Bids
Construction	Bidding Use Bids
	Bidialectalism
	Bids
	Bielorussian
Spina	Bifida
	Bigotry Use Social Discrimination
	Bikol
	Bilingual Education
	Bilingual Education Programs
	Bilingual Instructional Materials
	Bilingual Materials Use Multilingual Materials
	Bilingual Schools
	Bilingual Students
	Bilingual Teacher Aides
	Bilingual Teachers
	Bilingualism
	Bini
	Biochemical Effects Use Biochemistry
	Biochemical Tests Use Biochemistry
	Biochemistry
	Biodiversity
	Bioethics
	Biofeedback
	Biographical Inventories
	Biographical Profiles Use Biographical Inventories
	Biographies
	Biological Diversity Use Biodiversity
	Biological Influences
	Biological Parents
	Biological Sciences
	Biology
Animal	Biology Use Zoology
Cell	Biology Use Cytology
Cellular Molecular	Biology Use Cytology and Molecular Biology
Diversity	(Biology) Use Biodiversity
Fatigue	(Biology)
Human	Biology Use Biology
	Biology Instruction (1966 1980) Use Biology and Science Instruction
Marine	Biology
Molecular	Biology
Plant	Biology Use Botany
Radiation	Biology
Reproduction	(Biology)
Social	Biology
Strength	(Biology) Use Muscular Strength
	Biomechanics
	Biomedical Equipment
	Biomedical Equipment Technicians Use Medical Laboratory Assistants
	Biomedical Research Use Biomedicine
	Biomedicine
	Bionics
	Biophysics
	Biotechnology
	Biracial Committees
	Biracial Elementary Schools (1966 1980) Use School Desegregation
	Biracial Persons Use Multiracial Persons
	Biracial Schools (1966 1980) Use School Desegregation
	Biracial Secondary Schools (1966 1980) Use School Desegregation
	Bird Studies Use Ornithology
	Birds
	Birth
	Birth Control Use Contraception
	Birth Defects Use Congenital Impairments
	Birth Order
	Birth Parents Use Biological Parents
Premature	Birth Use Premature Infants
	Birth Rate
	Birth Weight
Illegitimate	Births (1967 1995) Use Births to Single Women
Out of Wedlock	Births Use Births to Single Women
Single Mother	Births Use Births to Single Women

```
                               Births to Single Women
          Unmarried Mother     Births    Use Births to Single Women
                               Bisexuality
                               Bituminous Coal    Use Coal
                               Black Achievement
                               Black Americans    Use Blacks
                               Black and White Films    Use Films
                               Black Attitudes
                               Black Businesses
                               Black Children    Use Black Youth
                               Black Colleges
              Historically     Black Colleges    Use Black Colleges
                               Black Community
                               Black Culture
                               Black Dialects
                               Black Education
                               Black Employment
                               Black English    Use Black Dialects
                               Black Family
                               Black History
                               Black Housing (1977 1980)
                               Black Influences
                               Black Institutions
                               Black Leadership
                               Black Literature
                               Black Mothers
                               Black Nationalism    Use Black Power
                               Black Organizations
                               Black Population Trends
                               Black Power
                     White     Black Relations    Use Racial Relations
                               Black Role (1977 1980)    Use Black Influences
                               Black Stereotypes
                               Black Students
                               Black Studies
                               Black Subculture    Use Black Culture
                               Black Teachers
                               Black White Relations    Use Racial Relations
                               Black Youth
                               Blackboards    Use Chalkboards
                               Blacks
                               Blind (1966 1980)    Use Blindness
                               Blind Children (1966 1980)    Use Blindness
                      Deaf     Blind
                               Blindness
                               Block Grants
                               Block Scheduling
             Alternate Day     Block Scheduling    Use Alternate Day Schedules and Block Scheduling
                               Block Time Teaching    Use Block Scheduling
                      Time     Blocks
                               Blood Circulation
                               Blood Donors    Use Tissue Donors
                      High     Blood Pressure    Use Hypertension
                               Blue Collar Occupations
                               Blue Ribbon Commissions
                               Blueprints
                               Board Administrator Relationship
                               Board Candidates
                    School     Board Members    Use Boards of Education
                               Board of Education Members    Use Boards of Education
                               Board of Education Policy
                               Board of Education Role
                               Board of Regents    Use Governing Boards
                               Board of Trustees    Use Governing Boards
                    School     Board Policy    Use Board of Education Policy
                    School     Board Role    Use Board of Education Role
                               Boarding Homes
                               Boarding Schools
                  Advisory     Boards    Use Advisory Committees
                   Bulletin    Boards
       Electronic Bulletin     Boards    Use Electronic Mail
                 Governing     Boards
                               Boards of Education
                     State     Boards of Education
                     State     Boards of Licensing    Use State Licensing Boards
                    School     Boards    Use Boards of Education
            State Licensing    Boards
             State School      Boards    Use State Boards of Education
                               Boat Operators
                               Boatmen (1967 1980)    Use Boat Operators
  Performance Assessment (Skilled  Bodily Movements)    Use Performance Tests
                               Body and Fender Repairers    Use Auto Body Repairers
                               Body Attitude    Use Human Posture
                               Body Care    Use Hygiene
                               Body Composition
                               Body Density    Use Body Composition
     Drug Testing (Presence in  Body)    Use Drug Use Testing
       Overweight (Excessive    Body Fat)    Use Obesity
                   Percent     Body Fat    Use Body Composition
                               Body Fatness    Use Body Composition
   Government (Administrative    Body)
                               Body Height
                     Human     Body
```

	Body Image
	Body Language
	Body Mass Use Body Composition
Auto	Body Repairers
Auto	Body Repairmen (1966 1980) Use Auto Body Repairers
	Body Schema Use Body Image
	Body Weight
	Bogs Use Wetlands
	Bomb Shelters Use Fallout Shelters
Atomic	Bombs Use Nuclear Weapons
	Bond Issues
	Bonding (Behavior) Use Attachment Behavior
Chemical	Bonding
Indemnity	Bonds
	Bone Arrangement Use Skeletal System
	Book Buying Use Library Acquisition
	Book Catalogs
	Book Industry Use Publishing Industry
	Book Lending Use Library Circulation
	Book Reviews
	Book Selection Aids Use Selection Tools
Open	Book Tests
	Book Thefts (1969 1980) Use Books and Stealing
	Bookkeeping
Answer	Booklets Use Answer Sheets
	Booklists (1967 1980) Use Bibliographies
	Bookmobiles
	Books
Childrens	Books (1966 1980) Use Books and Childrens Literature
Folklore	Books (1966 1980) Use Books and Folk Culture
Foreign Language	Books
Health	Books (1966 1980) Use Books and Health Materials
High Interest Low Vocabulary	Books
Large Type	Books Use Large Type Materials
Paperback	Books
Picture	Books
Reference	Books (1966 1980) Use Reference Materials
Second Language	Books Use Foreign Language Books
Soft Cover	Books Use Paperback Books
Talking	Books
Test	Books Use Tests
	Bookshops Use Bookstores
	Bookstores
College	Bookstores Use Bookstores and College Stores
	Boom Town Areas Use Boomtowns
Baby	Boomers
	Boomtowns
Guards	(Border Patrol) Use Immigration Inspectors
	Border Patrol Officers Use Immigration Inspectors
	Borderline Mental Retardation Use Slow Learners
First	Born
Linguistic	Borrowing
Phonological	Borrowing Use Linguistic Borrowing
Syntactic	Borrowing Use Linguistic Borrowing
Word	Borrowing Use Linguistic Borrowing
	Bosnian Use Serbocroatian
	Botany
Plants	(Botany)
College	Bound Students
Noncollege	Bound Students
School	Boundaries Use School Districts
	Bowling
School	Boycotts
	Boys Use Males
	Bracero Programs (1966 1980) Use Braceros
	Braceros
	Brahmins (1967 1980) Use Caste
	Braille
	Brain
	Brain Damage Use Neurological Impairments
	Brain Drain
Minimal	Brain Dysfunction
	Brain Hemisphere Functions
Hemispheric Specialization	(Brain) Use Brain Hemisphere Functions
Minimally	Brain Injured (1966 1980) Use Minimal Brain Dysfunction
Traumatic	Brain Injury Use Head Injuries and Neurological Impairments
	Brain Research Use Brain
	Brainstorming
	Branch Campuses (Colleges) Use Multicampus Colleges
	Branch Libraries
	Branching
Optional	Branching (1966 1980) Use Branching
	Brass Instruments
Luso	Brazilian Culture
	Breadwinners Use Heads of Households
Family	Breadwinners Use Heads of Households
	Breakfast Programs
Recess	Breaks
	Breastfeeding
	Brick Industry
	Brick Masonry Use Bricklaying
	Bricklayers (1968 1981) Use Bricklaying
	Bricklaying

Photometric	Brightness Use Luminescence
	British Infant Schools
	British National Curriculum
Infant Schools	(British Primary System) Use British Infant Schools
	Broadcast Communications Use Telecommunications
	Broadcast Industry
	Broadcast Journalism
Programing	(Broadcast) (1971 1994) Use Programming (Broadcast)
Programming	(Broadcast)
	Broadcast Reception Equipment
	Broadcast Scheduling Use Programming (Broadcast)
	Broadcast Television
News	Broadcasting Use Broadcast Journalism and News Reporting
	Brochures Use Pamphlets
Information	Brokers Use Information Scientists
	Brothers Use Siblings
	Bucolic Literature Use Pastoral Literature
	Buddhism
	Budget Allocations Use Budgeting
	Budget Cuts Use Budgeting and Retrenchment
School	Budget Elections
	Budgeting
Program	Budgeting
	Budgets
Design	Build Approach
	Building Conversion
	Building Design
Modular	Building Design
	Building Equipment (1966 1980) Use Equipment
	Building Improvement (1966 1980) Use Facility Improvement
	Building Innovation
	Building Materials (1968 1980) Use Construction Materials
	Building Obsolescence
	Building Operation
	Building Plans
	Building Programs Use Construction Programs
	Building Renovation Use Facility Improvement
	Building Systems
Systems	Building
Component	Building Systems (1968 1976) Use Building Systems
Structural	Building Systems
	Building Trades
Turnkey	Building Use Design Build Approach
Vocabulary	Building Use Vocabulary Development
	Buildings
College	Buildings
School	Buildings
	Built Environment
	Bulgarian
	Bulimarexia Use Bulimia
	Bulimia
	Bulletin Boards
Electronic	Bulletin Boards Use Electronic Mail
	Bulletins
State Curriculum	Bulletins Use State Curriculum Guides
	Bullying
	Bureaucracy
	Burglar Alarms Use Alarm Systems
	Buriat
	Burmese
	Burmese Culture
	Burnout
Teacher	Burnout
	Burushaski
	Bus Drivers
School	Bus Drivers Use Bus Drivers and School Buses
	Bus Transportation
	Buses Use Service Vehicles
School	Buses
	Business
	Business Administration
	Business Administration Education
	Business Communication
	Business Correspondence
	Business Cycles
	Business Education
Basic	Business Education
	Business Education Facilities
General	Business Education Use Basic Business Education
	Business Education Teachers
Vocational	Business Education Use Business Education
	Business English
	Business Fluctuations Use Business Cycles
	Business Games Use Management Games
	Business Letters Use Business Correspondence
	Business Machines Use Office Machines
Small	Business Management Use Business Administration and Small Businesses
	Business Officials (Industry) Use Administrators
	Business Officials (School) Use School Business Officials
School	Business Officials
Partnership Academies (School and	Business) Use Career Academies
School	Business Relationship
	Business Responsibility

	Business School Relationship Use School Business Relationship
	Business Skills
	Business Subjects (1967 1980) Use Business Education
	Business Teachers Use Business Education Teachers
Black	Businesses
Negro	Businesses (1967 1977) Use Black Businesses
Small	Businesses
	Busing
	Butterfly Effect Use Chaos Theory
Book	Buying Use Library Acquisition
Credit	by Examination Use Equivalency Tests
Trial	by Jury Use Juries
Management	by Objectives
College Costs (Incurred	by Students) Use Student Costs
	Byelorussian Use Bielorussian
N	C Systems Use Numerical Control
	Cabinetmakers Use Cabinetmaking
	Cabinetmaking
	Cable Franchising
Franchising	(Cable) Use Cable Franchising
	Cable Television
Interactive	Cable Television Use Interactive Television
	CAD CAM Use Computer Assisted Design and Computer Assisted Manufacturing
School	Cadres
	Cafeterias Use Dining Facilities
	CAI Use Computer Assisted Instruction
Intelligent	CAI Systems Use Intelligent Tutoring Systems
	Cakchiquel
	Calculation (1966 1980) Use Computation
	Calculators
Electronic	Calculators Use Calculators
Graphing	Calculators
Hand	Calculators Use Calculators
Pocket	Calculators Use Calculators
	Calculus
Academic	Calendars Use School Schedules
School	Calendars (1967 1980) Use School Schedules
	Calisthenics
	Calligraphy Use Manuscript Writing (Handlettering)
	Calorimeters
CAD	CAM Use Computer Assisted Design and Computer Assisted Manufacturing
	Cambodian
	Cambodian Americans Use Asian Americans and Cambodians
	Cambodians
	Cameras Use Photographic Equipment
Film	(Cameras) Use Photographic Equipment
	Camp Counselors (1968 1980) Use Camping
Day	Camp Programs
Resident	Camp Programs
Election	Campaigns Use Political Campaigns
Political	Campaigns
Presidential	Campaigns (United States)
	Camping
Day	Camps Use Day Camp Programs
Labor	Camps (1966 1980) (Migrants) Use Migrant Housing
Off	Campus Education Use Extension Education
Off	Campus Facilities
	Campus Planning
	Campus Schools Use Laboratory Schools
	Campus Security Use School Security
Off	Campus Student Teaching Use Student Teaching
On	Campus Students
	Campuses
Branch	Campuses (Colleges) Use Multicampus Colleges
	Canada Natives
	Canadian Literature
French	Canadian Literature Use Canadian Literature
	Canadian Studies
French	Canadians
	Cancer
Board	Candidates
Political	Candidates
Presidential	Candidates (United States) Use Political Candidates and Presidential Campaigns (United States)
	Cannabis Use Marijuana
	Canonical Correlation Use Multivariate Analysis
	Cantonese
Fiscal	Capacity
	Capital
Human	Capital
	Capital Outlay (for Fixed Assets)
	Capital Punishment
	Capitalism
	Capitalization (Alphabetic)
	Captioned Media Use Captions
	Captions
	Carcinogens Use Cancer
	Carcinoma Use Cancer
	Card Catalogs
	Cardiac (Person) (1968 1980) Use Heart Disorders
	Cardiopulmonary Resuscitation
	Cardiovascular System
Answer	Cards Use Answer Sheets
Cue	Cards Use Cues

Grade   Cards   Use Report Cards
Report   Cards
Adult Day   Care
Adult Foster   Care
After School Day   Care (1978 1983)   Use After School Programs and School Age Day Care
Body   Care   Use Hygiene
Child   Care Centers (1967 1980)   Use Day Care Centers
Day   Care Centers
Migrant Child   Care Centers (1966 1980)   Use Day Care Centers and Migrant Children
Child   Care (1966 1980)
Child Health   Care   Use Child Health
Health   Care Costs
Day   Care
Day   Care Effects
Employer Sponsored Day   Care   Use Employer Supported Day Care
Employer Supported Day   Care
Health   Care Evaluation   Use Medical Care Evaluation
Medical   Care Evaluation
Patient   Care Evaluation   Use Medical Care Evaluation
Family Day   Care
Fetal   Care   Use Prenatal Care
Foster   Care
Managed   Care (HMOs)   Use Health Maintenance Organizations
Home Child   Care   Use Child Rearing
Home Day   Care   Use Family Day Care
Personal   Care Homes
Hospices (Terminal   Care)
Ill Child   Care   Use Sick Child Care
Infant   Care
Long Term   Care
Medical   Care   Use Medical Services
Child   Care Occupations
Prenatal   Care
Primary Health   Care
Day   Care Programs (1966 1980)   Use Day Care
Residential   Care
Respite   Care
School Age Day   Care
Day   Care Services (1967 1980)   Use Day Care
Sick Child   Care
Self   Care Skills
Child   Care Workers (1967 1980)   Use Child Caregivers
Career Academies
Career Awareness
Career Change
Career Choice
Career Counseling
Career Development
High School Academies   (Career Development)   Use Career Academies
Career Education
Career Exploration
Dual   Career Family
Career Guidance
Career Information Delivery Systems   Use Career Information Systems
Career Information Systems
Career Ladders
Career Maturity   Use Vocational Maturity
Career Objectives   Use Career Choice
Career Opportunities (1966 1980)
Career Orientation   Use Career Planning
Career Planning
Careers
Nontraditional   Careers   Use Nontraditional Occupations
Science   Careers
Caregiver Child Relationship
Caregiver Role
Caregiver Speech
Caregivers
Child   Caregivers
Family   Caregivers
Animal   Caretakers
Grounds   Caretakers   Use Grounds Keepers
Caricatures (1966 1980)
Monte   Carlo Methods
Carpenters (1969 1981)   Use Carpentry
Carpentry
Carpet Layers   Use Floor Layers
Carpeting
Carpets   Use Carpeting
Carrels
Study   Carrels   Use Carrels
Cartography
Mapping   (Cartography)   Use Cartography
Cartoons
Audiotape   Cartridges   Use Audiotape Cassettes
Magnetic Tape   Cartridges   Use Magnetic Tape Cassettes
Videotape   Cartridges   Use Videotape Cassettes
Case Based Instruction   Use Case Method (Teaching Technique)
Case (Grammar)
Medical   Case Histories
Case Method (Teaching Technique)
Case Records
Case Studies

Case Studies (Education) (1966 1980)   Use Case Studies
Facility   Case Studies
Case Study Approach (Teaching)   Use Case Method (Teaching Technique)
Court   Cases (1966 1980)   Use Court Litigation
Caseworker Approach
Caseworkers
Client   Caseworkers (1966 1980)   Use Social Workers
Audiotape   Cassette Recorders   Use Audiotape Cassettes and Audiotape Recorders
Magnetic Tape   Cassette Recorders (1970 1980)   Use Magnetic Tape Cassettes and Tape Recorders
Videotape   Cassette Recorders   Use Videotape Cassettes and Videotape Recorders
Video   Cassette Systems (1971 1980)   Use Videotape Cassettes
Audiotape   Cassettes
Magnetic Tape   Cassettes
Cassettes (Tape)   Use Magnetic Tape Cassettes
Videotape   Cassettes
Caste
Cataloging
Library   Cataloging   Use Cataloging
Machine Readable   Cataloging
Catalogs
Book   Catalogs
Card   Catalogs
College   Catalogs   Use School Catalogs
Dictionary   Catalogs (1968 1980)   Use Library Catalogs
Divided   Catalogs (1968 1980)   Use Library Catalogs
Library   Catalogs
Online   Catalogs
Online Public Access   Catalogs   Use Online Catalogs
Repertory   Catalogs   Use Union Catalogs
Retrospective Conversion (Library   Catalogs)
School   Catalogs
Union   Catalogs
Categorical Aid
Cross   Categorical Education   Use Noncategorical Education
Categorization   Use Classification
Catharsis
Cathode Ray Tube Terminals   Use Video Display Terminals
Catholic Educators
Catholic Elementary Schools (1967 1980)   Use Catholic Schools
Catholic High Schools (1967 1980)   Use Catholic Schools
Catholic Parents (1966 1980)   Use Catholics and Parents
Catholic Schools
Catholics
CATV   Use Cable Television
Caucasian Languages
Caucasian Race (1967 1980)   Use Whites
Caucasian Students (1967 1980)   Use White Students
Caucasians (1967 1980)   Use Whites
Causal Attributions   Use Attribution Theory
Causal Factors   Use Influences
Causal Models
Delinquency   Causes
CCTV   Use Closed Circuit Television
CD Recordings   Use Optical Disks
CD ROM   Use Optical Data Disks
Cebuano
Ceilings
Sickle   Cell Anemia
Cell Biology   Use Cytology
Human T   Cell Lymphotropic Virus Type 3   Use Acquired Immune Deficiency Syndrome
Cell Theory (1966 1980)   Use Cytology
Sickle   Cell Trait   Use Sickle Cell Anemia
Cellular Molecular Biology   Use Cytology and Molecular Biology
Cement Industry
Cements (Adhesives)   Use Adhesives
Censorship
Census Figures
Client   Centered Counseling   Use Nondirective Counseling
Child   Centered Curriculum   Use Student Centered Curriculum
Problem   Centered Curriculum   Use Problem Based Learning
Student   Centered Curriculum
African   Centered Perspective   Use Afrocentrism
Instructor   Centered Television (1966 1980)   Use Educational Television
Self   Centeredness   Use Egocentrism
After School   Centers
Arts   Centers
Audiovisual   Centers
Child Care   Centers (1967 1980)   Use Day Care Centers
Child Development   Centers
Interest   Centers (Classroom)   Use Learning Centers (Classroom)
Learning   Centers (Classroom)
Community   Centers
Community Information   Centers   Use Community Information Services
Computer   Centers
Continuing Education   Centers
Counseling   Centers (1966 1977)   Use Guidance Centers
Cultural   Centers
Curriculum Study   Centers
Data Processing   Centers   Use Computer Centers and Data Processing
Day Care   Centers
Demonstration   Centers
Education Service   Centers
Educational Service   Centers   Use Education Service Centers

Fine Arts Centers   Use Arts Centers
Guidance Centers
Health Occupations Centers (1968 1980)
Information Centers
Instructional Materials Centers (1966 1980)   Use Learning Resources Centers
Language and Area Centers (1968 1980)
Learning Resources Centers
Living Learning Centers
Magnet Centers   Use Magnet Schools
Migrant Child Care Centers (1966 1980)   Use Day Care Centers and Migrant Children
Nature Centers
Neighborhood Centers (1966 1980)   Use Community Centers
Centers of Interest (1966 1980)   Use Learning Centers (Classroom)
Performing Arts Centers   Use Theaters
Assessment Centers (Personnel)
Reading Centers
Rehabilitation Centers
Research and Development Centers
Residential Centers (1967 1980)   Use Residential Institutions
Resource Centers
School Media Centers   Use Learning Resources Centers
School Study Centers (1966 1980)   Use Study Centers
Science Teaching Centers
Skill Centers
Student Centers   Use Student Unions
Study Centers
Supplementary Educational Centers (1966 1980)   Use Education Service Centers and Supplementary Education
Teacher Centers
Teacher Education Centers   Use Teacher Centers
Treatment Centers   Use Clinics
University Training Centers   Use Teacher Centers
Video Production Centers   Use Television Studios
Vocational Training Centers
Writing Centers   Use Writing Laboratories
Central American History   Use Latin American History
Central American Literature   Use Latin American Literature
Central Americans   Use Latin Americans
Central Office Administrators
Central Sound Systems (1966 1980)   Use Audio Equipment
Centralization
Centralized Schools   Use Consolidated Schools
Centroid Method of Factor Analysis   Use Factor Analysis
Eighteenth Century Literature
Fifteenth Century Literature
Midtwentieth Century Literature   Use Twentieth Century Literature
Nineteenth Century Literature
Seventeenth Century Literature
Sixteenth Century Literature
Twentieth Century Literature
Ceramics
Cerebral Dominance (1967 1986)   Use Brain Hemisphere Functions
Cerebral Palsy
Commencement Ceremonies
Graduate Ceremonies   Use Commencement Ceremonies
Educational Certificates
Teacher Certificates (1967 1980)   Use Teacher Certification
Teaching Certificates   Use Teacher Certification
Certification
Alternative Teacher Certification
Counselor Certification
National Teacher Certification
Student Certification
Teacher Certification
Alternative Certification (Teaching)   Use Alternative Teacher Certification
National Certification (Teaching)   Use National Teacher Certification
Certified Nurses   Use Nurses
Certified Public Accountants
CEU   Use Continuing Education Units
Chad Languages
Chain Reflexes (Behavior)   Use Behavior Chaining
Behavior Chaining
Markov Chains   Use Markov Processes
Department Chairpersons   Use Department Heads
Wheel Chairs (1970 1981)   Use Wheelchairs
Chalkboards
Chamorro
Chancellors (Education)   Use College Presidents
Chancroid   Use Venereal Diseases
Change
Administrative Change
Change Agents
Attitude Change
Behavior Change
Career Change
Climate Change
Community Change
Economic Change
Educational Change
Employment Change   Use Career Change
Job Change   Use Career Change
Midcareer Change   Use Career Change and Midlife Transitions
Organizational Change
Personality Change

Resistance to	Change
Social	Change
Societal	Change Use Social Change
	Change Strategies
Vocational	Change Use Career Change
Work	Change Use Career Change
Architectural	Changes Use Building Design
Population	Changes Use Population Trends
	Changing Attitudes (1966 1980) Use Attitude Change
	Chaos Theory
	Character Use Personality
Architectural	Character
Defamation of	Character Use Libel and Slander
	Character Portrayal Use Characterization
	Character Recognition
Magnetic Ink	Character Recognition Use Character Recognition
Optical	Character Recognition Use Character Recognition and Optical Scanners
Item	Characteristic Curve Theory Use Item Response Theory
Administrator	Characteristics
Adult	Characteristics (1967 1980) Use Adults and Individual Characteristics
College	Characteristics Use Institutional Characteristics
Community	Characteristics
Counselor	Characteristics
Cultural	Characteristics Use Cultural Traits
Dispositional	Characteristics Use Personality Traits
Dropout	Characteristics
Examiner	Characteristics Use Examiners and Experimenter Characteristics
Experimenter	Characteristics
Family	Characteristics
Client	Characteristics (Human Services)
Individual	Characteristics
Institutional	Characteristics
Learning	Characteristics (1968 1980) Use Learning
Participant	Characteristics
Physical	Characteristics
Test	Characteristics (Physical) Use Test Format
Psychological	Characteristics
Racial	Characteristics (1966 1980)
Regional	Characteristics
Researcher	Characteristics Use Experimenter Characteristics and Researchers
School	Characteristics Use Institutional Characteristics
Sex	(Characteristics) (1966 1980)
Social	Characteristics
Stimulus	Characteristics Use Stimuli
Student	Characteristics
Teacher	Characteristics
University	Characteristics Use Institutional Characteristics
	Characterization
	Characterization (Literature) (1969 1977) Use Characterization
	Charitable Trusts Use Trusts (Financial)
	Charter Schools
	Charts
Experience	Charts
Flow	Charts
Grade	Charts (1966 1980)
	Cheating
Field	Check (1967 1980) Use Equipment Evaluation
	Check Lists
	Chefs Use Cooks
	Chemical Analysis
	Chemical Bonding
	Chemical Dependency (Drugs) Use Drug Addiction
	Chemical Determination Use Chemical Analysis
Determination	(Chemical) Use Chemical Analysis
	Chemical Engineering
	Chemical Equilibrium
	Chemical Industry
	Chemical Nomenclature
Agricultural	Chemical Occupations
	Chemical Reactions
	Chemical Synthesis Use Chemical Reactions
	Chemical Technicians
	Chemistry
Inorganic	Chemistry
	Chemistry Instruction (1967 1980) Use Chemistry and Science Instruction
Organic	Chemistry
Physical	Chemistry
Physiological	Chemistry Use Biochemistry
	Chemistry Teachers (1967 1980) Use Chemistry and Science Teachers
	Chemotherapy Use Drug Therapy
	Cheremis
	Cherokee
	Cherokee (Tribe)
	Chi Square
	Chibemba Use Bemba
	Chief Academic Officers Use Academic Deans
	Chief Administrators (1967 1980) Use Administrators
	Child Abuse
	Child Advocacy
	Child Behavior
	Child Care (1966 1980)
	Child Care Centers (1967 1980) Use Day Care Centers
Migrant	Child Care Centers (1966 1980) Use Day Care Centers and Migrant Children

Home	Child Care Use Child Rearing
Ill	Child Care Use Sick Child Care
	Child Care Occupations
Sick	Child Care
	Child Care Workers (1967 1980) Use Child Caregivers
	Child Caregivers
	Child Centered Curriculum Use Student Centered Curriculum
	Child Custody
	Child Development
	Child Development Centers
	Child Development Specialists
Exceptional	Child Education (1968 1980)
Migrant	Child Education (1967 1980) Use Migrant Education
	Child Health
	Child Health Care Use Child Health
Parent	Child Interaction Use Parent Child Relationship
	Child Labor
	Child Labor Laws (1966 1974) Use Child Labor and Labor Legislation
	Child Labor Legislation (1966 1980) Use Child Labor and Labor Legislation
	Child Language
Parent	Child Literacy Use Family Literacy
	Child Neglect
	Child Parent Literacy Use Family Literacy
	Child Parent Relationship Use Parent Child Relationship
	Child Psychology
	Child Rearing
Caregiver	Child Relationship
Parent	Child Relationship
Exceptional	Child Research
	Child Responsibility
	Child Restraints (Vehicle Safety) Use Child Safety and Restraints (Vehicle Safety)
	Child Role
	Child Safety
Exceptional	Child Services (1968 1980)
	Child Sexual Abuse Use Child Abuse and Sexual Abuse
	Child Support
	Child Welfare
	Childbirth Use Birth
Labor	(Childbirth) Use Birth
Nonmarital	Childbirth Use Births to Single Women
	Childhood (1966 1980) Use Children
	Childhood Attitudes
Early	Childhood (1966 1980) Use Young Children
Early	Childhood Education
	Childhood Friendship (1966 1980) Use Friendship
	Childhood Interests
	Childhood Needs
	Childlessness
	Children
Abused	Children Use Child Abuse
Adopted	Children
Adult	Children
Black	Children Use Black Youth
Blind	Children (1966 1980) Use Blindness
Crippled	Children (1968 1980) Use Physical Disabilities
Deaf	Children (1966 1980) Use Deafness
Deprived	Children Use Disadvantaged Youth
Disadvantaged	Children Use Disadvantaged Youth
Elementary School	Children Use Elementary School Students
Emotionally Disturbed	Children (1967 1980) Use Emotional Disturbances
Exceptional	Children (1966 1978) Use Exceptional Persons (1978 1994)
Foster	Children
Foster Homes (1970 1982)	(Children) Use Foster Care
Gifted	Children Use Gifted
Grown	Children Use Adult Children
Handicapped	Children (1966 1980)
Homebound	Children (1966 1980) Use Homebound
Hospitalized	Children
Kindergarten	Children
Latchkey	Children
Mentally Advanced	Children Use Gifted
Migrant	Children
Migratory	Children Use Migrant Children
Minority Group	Children
Missing	Children
Neglected	Children (1977 1980) Use Child Neglect
Neurotic	Children (1966 1980) Use Neurosis
Preschool	Children
Problem	Children
Psychotic	Children (1966 1980) Use Psychosis
Retarded	Children (1966 1980) Use Mental Retardation
Slum	Children Use Disadvantaged Youth
Transient	Children
Young	Children
	Childrens Art
	Childrens Attitudes Use Childhood Attitudes
	Childrens Books (1966 1980) Use Books and Childrens Literature
	Childrens Courts Use Juvenile Courts
	Childrens Games
	Childrens Interests Use Childhood Interests
	Childrens Libraries
	Childrens Literature
	Childrens Needs Use Childhood Needs

	Childrens Play Use Play
	Childrens Rights
	Childrens Television
	Childrens Writing
	Chimneys
	Chinese
	Chinese Americans
	Chinese Culture
Mandarin	Chinese
	Chinyanja
	Chippewa (Language) Use Ojibwa
	Chippewa (Tribe)
	Chlorination (Water) Use Water Treatment
	Choctaw
	Choctaw (Tribe)
Mississippi Band of	Choctaw (Tribe)
Career	Choice
College	Choice
Family	Choice (Education) Use School Choice
Educational	Choice Use School Choice
Occupational	Choice (1966 1980) Use Career Choice
School	Choice
Forced	Choice Technique
Multiple	Choice Tests
Free	Choice Transfer Programs
Vocational	Choice Use Career Choice
	Choirs Use Singing
	Choral Music
	Choral Speaking
	Choreography Use Dance
Household	Chores Use Housework
	Choruses (1968 1980) Use Singing
	Christianity
	Chromatography
	Chronic Illness
	Chronic Pain Use Chronic Illness and Pain
	Chronicles
	Chronological Age
	Church Action Use Church Role
	Church Migrant Projects (1966 1980) Use Church Programs and Migrant Programs
	Church Programs
	Church Projects Use Church Programs
	Church Related Colleges
	Church Responsibility
	Church Role
State	Church Separation
	Church State Separation Use State Church Separation
	Church Workers
	Churches
	Chuvash
	Cigarette Smoking Use Smoking
	Cinema Use Films
	Cinema Study Use Film Study
	Cinyanja Use Chinyanja
	Circassian Use Caucasian Languages
Quality	Circles
	Circuit Teachers Use Itinerant Teachers
Closed	Circuit Television
Open	Circuit Television (1966 1980) Use Broadcast Television
Electric	Circuits
	Circuits (Electronic) Use Electric Circuits
Electronic	Circuits Use Electric Circuits
Blood	Circulation
Library	Circulation
Pedestrian	Circulation Use Pedestrian Traffic
Traffic	Circulation
Vehicular	Circulation Use Vehicular Traffic
	Circulatory System Use Cardiovascular System
	Citation Analysis
	Citation Indexes
Bibliographic	Citations (1969 1980) Use Citations (References)
	Citations (Legal) Use Law Enforcement
	Citations (References)
	Cities Use Municipalities
Large	Cities Use Urban Areas
	Citizen Advocacy Use Advocacy
	Citizen Involvement Use Citizen Participation
	Citizen Participation
	Citizen Responsibility Use Citizenship Responsibility
	Citizen Role
	Citizens Councils
Senior	Citizens (1967 1980) Use Older Adults
Southern	Citizens (1966 1980)
	Citizenship
	Citizenship Education
Good	Citizenship Use Citizenship
	Citizenship Responsibility
	City Demography (1966 1980) Use Urban Demography
Inner	City Education Use Urban Education
	City Government
	City Improvement (1966 1980) Use Urban Improvement
Inner	City
	City Officials

```
              Elected  City Officials   Use City Officials
                       City Planning (1966 1980)   Use Urban Planning
                       City Problems (1966 1980)   Use Urban Problems
                       City Schools   Use Urban Schools
                       City Wide Commissions (1966 1980)   Use Planning Commissions and Urban Planning
                       City Wide Programs (1967 1980)   Use Urban Programs
                       Civic Belief (1966 1980)   Use Political Attitudes
                       Civic Groups   Use Community Organizations
                       Civic Involvement   Use Citizen Participation
                       Civic Organizations   Use Community Organizations
                       Civic Programs   Use Community Programs
                       Civic Relations   Use Community Relations
                       Civic Responsibility   Use Citizenship Responsibility
                       Civics
                       Civil Defense
        Demonstrations (Civil)
                       Civil Disobedience
                       Civil Engineering
                       Civil Law
                       Civil Liberties
                       Civil Rights
                       Civil Rights Legislation
                       Civil Service Employees   Use Government Employees
                       Civil War   Use War
                       Civil War (United States)
               Eastern Civilization   Use Non Western Civilization
                 Greek Civilization
           Non Western Civilization
             Occidental Civilization   Use Western Civilization
               Oriental Civilization   Use Non Western Civilization
            South Asian Civilization   Use Non Western Civilization
               Western Civilization
                Values Clarification
                       Class Activities
                       Class Attendance (1966 1980)   Use Attendance
                       Class Attitudes (1966 1980)
                       Class Average (1966 1980)
                Middle Class College Students (1966 1980)   Use College Students and Middle Class Students
                Middle Class Culture
                       Class Desegregation   Use Classroom Desegregation
                Social Class Differences   Use Social Differences
                       Class Discussion   Use Discussion (Teaching Technique)
                Middle Class Fathers (1966 1980)   Use Fathers and Middle Class Parents
                Social Class Integration   Use Social Integration
                 Lower Class
          Lower Middle Class
                 Lower Class Males (1966 1980)   Use Lower Class and Males
                       Class Management (1966 1980)   Use Classroom Techniques
                Middle Class
                Middle Class Mothers (1966 1980)   Use Middle Class Parents and Mothers
                       Class Newspapers (1967 1980)   Use Class Activities and Student Publications
                Middle Class Norm (1966 1980)   Use Middle Class Standards
                       Class Organization
                 Lower Class Parents
                Middle Class Parents
               Regular Class Placement (1968 1978)   Use Mainstreaming
                       Class Projects   Use Class Activities
                       Class Rank
               Rank in Class   Use Class Rank
                       Class Size
                Social Class
                Middle Class Standards
                       Class Status   Use Social Status
                 Lower Class Students
                Middle Class Students
                 Upper Class
                Middle Class Values (1966 1980)   Use Middle Class Standards
               Working Class
                   Day Classes   Use Day Programs
          Desegregated Classes   Use Classroom Desegregation
               Evening Classes (1967 1980)   Use Evening Programs
                       Classes (Groups of Students)
                Honors Classes (1966 1980)   Use Honors Curriculum
             Integrated Classes   Use Classroom Desegregation
                  Form Classes (Languages)
              Literacy Classes (1966 1980)   Use Literacy Education
            Multigraded Classes
        Nonauthoritarian Classes
             Nongraded Classes (1966 1980)   Use Nongraded Instructional Grouping
           Opportunity Classes (1966 1980)   Use Special Classes
         Prekindergarten Classes   Use Preschool Education
             Multilevel Classes (Second Language Instruction)
                 Small Classes
               Special Classes
            Transitional Classes (1966 1981)   Use Transitional Programs
              Ungraded Classes (1966 1980)   Use Nongraded Instructional Grouping
                       Classical Conditioning
                       Classical Greek   Use Greek
                       Classical Languages
                       Classical Literature
                       Classical Mechanics   Use Mechanics (Physics)
               Literary Classics   Use Classics (Literature)
                       Classics (Literature)
```

	Classification
	Classification Clerks Use File Clerks
DDC	(Classification) Use Dewey Decimal Classification
Dewey Decimal	Classification
Decimal	Classification (Dewey) Use Dewey Decimal Classification
Language	Classification
Lc	Classification Use Library of Congress Classification
Library of Congress	Classification
Space	Classification
UDC	(Classification) Use Universal Decimal Classification
Universal Decimal	Classification
Decimal	Classification (Universal) Use Universal Decimal Classification
	Classroom Activities Use Class Activities
	Classroom Arrangement (1966 1980) Use Classroom Design
	Classroom Climate Use Classroom Environment
	Classroom Communication
	Classroom Desegregation
	Classroom Design
	Classroom Discipline Use Classroom Techniques and Discipline
	Classroom Environment
	Classroom Equipment Use Educational Equipment
	Classroom Furniture
Furniture	(Classroom) Use Classroom Furniture
	Classroom Games (1966 1980) Use Class Activities and Educational Games
	Classroom Guidance Programs (1968 1980)
	Classroom Integration (1967 1980) Use Classroom Desegregation
Interest Centers	(Classroom) Use Learning Centers (Classroom)
Learning Centers	(Classroom)
Learning Stations	(Classroom) Use Learning Centers (Classroom)
	Classroom Libraries (1966 1980) Use Instructional Materials
	Classroom Management Use Classroom Techniques
	Classroom Materials (1966 1980) Use Instructional Materials
	Classroom Methods Use Classroom Techniques
	Classroom Observation Techniques
	Classroom Participation (1966 1980) Use Class Activities and Student Participation
	Classroom Research
	Classroom Situation Use Classroom Environment
	Classroom Techniques
Electronic	Classroom Use (1966 1980) Use Electronic Classrooms
	Classrooms
Electronic	Classrooms
Flexible	Classrooms (1968 1980) Use Classrooms and Flexible Facilities
Mobile	Classrooms
Multipurpose	Classrooms
Self Contained	Classrooms
Self Directed	Classrooms (1966 1980)
Traditional	Classrooms Use Self Contained Classrooms
	Clay
	Clay Minerals Use Clay
	Clean Water Use Water Quality
	Cleaning
	Clearinghouses
	Cleft Lip (1967 1980) Use Cleft Palate
	Cleft Palate
	Clergy
	Clergymen (1968 1980) Use Clergy
	Clerical Occupations
	Clerical Workers
	Clerk Stenographers Use Shorthand
	Clerk Typists Use Typewriting
Auto Parts	Clerks
Classification	Clerks Use File Clerks
File	Clerks
Library	Clerks Use Library Technicians
Medical Record	Clerks Use Medical Record Technicians
Record	Clerks Use File Clerks
Sales	Clerks Use Sales Workers
	Clerkships (Medicine) Use Clinical Experience
	Cliches
	Client Background (Human Services) Use Client Characteristics (Human Services)
	Client Caseworkers (1966 1980) Use Social Workers
	Client Centered Counseling Use Nondirective Counseling
	Client Characteristics (Human Services)
	Client Counselor Ratio Use Counselor Client Ratio
	Client Counselor Relationship Use Counselor Client Relationship
Counselor	Client Ratio
Counselor	Client Relationship
Library	Clients Use Users (Information)
	Climate
	Climate Change
Classroom	Climate Use Classroom Environment
	Climate Control
Economic	Climate
Organizational	Climate
School	Climate Use Educational Environment
Social	Climate Use Social Environment
	Climatic Factors (1969 1980) Use Climate
	Clinic Personnel (School) (1966 1980) Use Allied Health Personnel and School Health Services
	Clinical Diagnosis
Diagnosis	(Clinical) Use Clinical Diagnosis
	Clinical Experience
	Clinical Judgment (Medicine) Use Medical Evaluation
	Clinical Judgment (Psychology) Use Psychological Evaluation

```
                        Clinical Learning Experience   Use Clinical Experience
                        Clinical Professors (1967 1980) (Education)   Use Student Teacher Supervisors
                        Clinical Professors (1967 1980) (Medicine)   Use Medical School Faculty
                        Clinical Psychology
                        Clinical Schools (Teacher Education)   Use Professional Development Schools
                        Clinical Services   Use Clinics
                        Clinical Supervision (of Teachers)
                        Clinical Teaching (Health Professions)
                        Clinical Teaching (Individualized Instruction)   Use Individualized Instruction
                        Clinics
           Dental       Clinics
          Hearing       Clinics (1968 1980)   Use Speech and Hearing Clinics
         Itinerant      Clinics (1966 1980)   Use Mobile Clinics
     Mental Health      Clinics
           Mobile       Clinics
         Preschool      Clinics (1966 1980)   Use Clinics and Preschool Education
  Psychoeducational     Clinics
          Reading       Clinics (1966 1980)   Use Reading Centers
  Remedial Reading      Clinics (1966 1980)   Use Reading Centers and Remedial Reading
            Rural       Clinics (1966 1980)   Use Clinics and Rural Areas
           Speech       Clinics (1968 1980)   Use Speech and Hearing Clinics
 Speech and Hearing     Clinics
            Film        Clips   Use Filmstrips
                        Clock Arithmetic   Use Modular Arithmetic
                        Clockmakers   Use Watchmakers
                        Closed Circuit Television
                        Closed Head Injuries   Use Head Injuries
                        Closed Schools   Use School Closing
          College       Closing   Use School Closing
           School       Closing
                        Clothing
                        Clothing Design
         Fashions       (Clothing)   Use Clothing
                        Clothing Industry   Use Fashion Industry
                        Clothing Instruction
                        Cloze Procedure
                        Cloze Techniques   Use Cloze Procedure
          Four H        Club Agents   Use Extension Agents
                        Clubs
            Girls       Clubs (1966 1980)   Use Youth Clubs
            Glee        Clubs   Use Singing
      Homemakers        Clubs (1966 1980)   Use Clubs and Homemaking Skills
          Science       Clubs
           Youth        Clubs
                        Clues   Use Cues
          Context       Clues
                        Cluster Analysis
                        Cluster Colleges
                        Cluster Grouping
             Job        Clusters   Use Occupational Clusters
      Occupational      Clusters
                        CMI   Use Computer Managed Instruction
                        Co Op Programs   Use Cooperative Programs
                        Co Ops   Use Cooperatives
         Athletic       Coaches
                        Coaching Teachers (1966 1974)   Use Tutors
            Test        Coaching
                        Coal
      Bituminous        Coal   Use Coal
                        Coal Mining   Use Coal and Mining
                        Coal Resources   Use Coal
                        Coast Guard Air Stations   Use Military Air Facilities
                        Cocaine
                        Cocaine Prenatal Exposure   Use Cocaine and Prenatal Drug Exposure
                        Cochlear Implants
                        Cocounseling
                        Cocurricular Activities (1966 1980)   Use Extracurricular Activities
                        Code Switching (Language)
           Dress        Codes
           Honor        Codes   Use Codes of Ethics
                        Codes (Logic)   Use Coding
                        Codes of Ethics
                        Codification
                        Coding
         Symbolic       Coding   Use Coding
                        Coeducation
         Schemata       (Cognition)
          Social        Cognition
          Tempo         (Cognition)   Use Conceptual Tempo
                        Cognitive Ability
                        Cognitive Behavior Modification   Use Behavior Modification and Cognitive Restructuring
                        Cognitive Development
                        Cognitive Dissonance
                        Cognitive Mapping
                        Cognitive Measurement
                        Cognitive Modification   Use Cognitive Restructuring
                        Cognitive Objectives
                        Cognitive Processes
                        Cognitive Psychology
                        Cognitive Restructuring
                        Cognitive Skills   Use Thinking Skills
                        Cognitive Structures
                        Cognitive Style
```

Cognitive Tempo   Use Conceptual Tempo
Cognitive Tests
Cognitive Theory   Use Epistemology
Cognitive Therapy   Use Cognitive Restructuring
Cohabitation
Coherence
Cohesion (Written Composition)
Group   Cohesiveness   Use Group Unity
Cohort Analysis
Collaboration   Use Cooperation
Teacher   Collaboration
Collaborative Decision Making   Use Participative Decision Making
Collaborative Teachers   Use Teacher Collaboration
Collaborative Teaching   Use Team Teaching
Collaboratives (Education)   Use Partnerships in Education
Collage
Blue   Collar Occupations
White   Collar Occupations
Collected Readings   Use Anthologies
Data   Collection
Collection Development (Libraries)   Use Library Collection Development
Library   Collection Development
Library   Collections
Readings   (Collections)   Use Anthologies
Collective Bargaining
Collective Behavior   Use Group Behavior
Collective Decision Making   Use Participative Decision Making
Collective Negotiation (1967 1977)   Use Collective Bargaining
Collective Settlements
College Administration
College Admission
College Applicants
College Athletics
College Attendance
College Bookstores   Use Bookstores and College Stores
College Bound Students
College Buildings
College Catalogs   Use School Catalogs
College Characteristics   Use Institutional Characteristics
College Choice
College Closing   Use School Closing
College Community Relationship   Use School Community Relationship
College Cooperation (1966 1980)   Use Intercollegiate Cooperation
High School   College Cooperation   Use College School Cooperation
School   College Cooperation   Use College School Cooperation
College Costs (Financing for Individual Students)   Use Paying for College
College Costs (Incurred by Students)   Use Student Costs
College Counselors   Use School Counselors
College Credits
College Curriculum
College Day
College Deans (1968 1980)   Use Deans and Higher Education
Two Year   College Degrees   Use Associate Degrees
College Desegregation
College Dropouts   Use Dropouts
College English
College Enrollment   Use Enrollment
College Entrance Examinations
College Environment
College Faculty
College Freshmen
College Governing Councils
College Graduates
College High School Cooperation (1967 1980)   Use College School Cooperation
College Housing
College Instruction
College Integration (1966 1980)   Use College Desegregation
College Juniors
College Language Programs (1967 1980)
College Libraries
Junior   College Libraries (1966 1980)   Use College Libraries and Two Year Colleges
College Majors (1968 1980)   Use Majors (Students)
College Mathematics
College Night   Use College Day
College Outcomes Assessment
Outcomes Measurement   (College)   Use College Outcomes Assessment
Paying for   College
College Placement (1966 1980)   Use Student Placement
College Planning
College Preparation
College Presidents
College Programs
College Registrars   Use Registrars (School)
College Registration   Use School Registration
Faculty   College Relationship
Student   College Relationship
Teacher   College Relationship   Use Faculty College Relationship
College Role
College School Cooperation
College Science
College Second Language Programs
College Segregation
College Seniors

	College Sophomores
	College Stores
Student Housing	(College) Use College Housing
	College Student Relationship Use Student College Relationship
	College Students
Freshmen (1967 1980) (First Year	College Students) Use College Freshmen
Junior	College Students (1969 1980) Use Two Year College Students
Middle Class	College Students (1966 1980) Use College Students and Middle Class Students
Two Year	College Students
	College Supervisors (1967 1980) Use Student Teacher Supervisors
	College Teachers (1967 1980) Use College Faculty
	College Teaching Use College Instruction
Master of Arts in	College Teaching Use Masters Degrees
	College Transfer Rates Use Transfer Rates (College)
Transfer Rates	(College)
	College Transfer Students
	College Unions Use Student Unions
	College Work Study Programs Use Work Study Programs
	Colleges
Academic Senates	(Colleges) Use College Governing Councils
Agricultural	Colleges
Alumni	Colleges Use Alumni Education
Black	Colleges
Branch Campuses	(Colleges) Use Multicampus Colleges
Church Related	Colleges
Cluster	Colleges
Community	Colleges
Commuter	Colleges
Corporate	Colleges Use Corporate Education
Denominational	Colleges Use Church Related Colleges
Desegregated	Colleges Use College Desegregation
Elite	Colleges Use Selective Colleges
Evening	Colleges (1967 1980) Use Evening Programs
Experimental	Colleges
Faculty Senates	(Colleges) Use College Governing Councils
Historically Black	Colleges Use Black Colleges
Independent	Colleges Use Private Colleges
Integrated	Colleges Use College Desegregation
Junior	Colleges (1966 1980) Use Two Year Colleges
Land Grant	Colleges Use Land Grant Universities
Multicampus	Colleges
Negro	Colleges (1968 1977) Use Black Colleges
Noncampus	Colleges
	Colleges of Education Use Schools of Education
Private	Colleges
Private Junior	Colleges Use Private Colleges and Two Year Colleges
Public	Colleges
Residential	Colleges
Sectarian	Colleges Use Church Related Colleges
Selective	Colleges
Single Sex	Colleges
Small	Colleges
State	Colleges
Teachers	Colleges (1966 1980) Use Schools of Education
Tribal	Colleges Use Tribally Controlled Education
Two Year	Colleges
Upper Division	Colleges
	Collegial Models Use Collegiality
	Collegiality
	Colloquial Standard Usage Use Standard Spoken Usage
	Colloquiums (Meetings) Use Meetings
	Colonial History (United States)
	Colonialism
	Colonization Use Land Settlement
Land	Colonization Use Land Settlement
	Color
	Color Films Use Films
	Color Planning
	Color Presentation (1969 1980) Use Color
	Color Television (1969 1980) Use Color and Television
Local	Color Writing
	COM Use Computer Output Microfilm
	Combat Instruments Use Weapons
Sentence	Combining
Transformational Sentence	Combining Use Sentence Combining
	Comedy
	Comedy of Manners Use Comedy
	Comics (Publications)
	Commencement Ceremonies
	Commercial Art
	Commercial Communication Use Business Communication
	Commercial Correspondence Schools Use Correspondence Schools
	Commercial Education Use Business Education
	Commercial Enterprises Use Business
	Commercial Pilots Use Aircraft Pilots
	Commercial Search Services (Online) Use Online Vendors
	Commercial Television
Television	Commercials
Blue Ribbon	Commissions
City Wide	Commissions (1966 1980) Use Planning Commissions and Urban Planning
Planning	Commissions
	Committees
Advisory	Committees

Biracial Committees
Community Committees   Use Community Organizations
State Committees on Education   Use State Boards of Education
Search Committees (Personnel)
Selection Committees (Personnel)   Use Search Committees (Personnel)
Research Committees
Common Fractions (1966 1980)   Use Fractions
Less Commonly Taught Languages   Use Uncommonly Taught Languages
Communal Living   Use Collective Settlements and Group Experience
Communicable Diseases
Communication Aids (for Disabled)
Alternative and Augmentative Communication   Use Augmentative and Alternative Communication
Communication Apprehension
Audiovisual Communication (1967 1980)   Use Audiovisual Communications
Communication Audits
Augmentative and Alternative Communication
Business Communication
Classroom Communication
Commercial Communication   Use Business Communication
Computer Communication   Use Computer Mediated Communication
Computer Assisted Communication   Use Computer Mediated Communication
Computer Based Communication   Use Computer Mediated Communication
Computer Mediated Communication
Conference Skills (Communication)   Use Communication Skills
Cross Cultural Communication   Use Intercultural Communication
Speech Communication Curriculum   Use Speech Communication and Speech Curriculum
Development Communication
Diffusion (1967 1982) (Communication)   Use Diffusion (Communication)
Diffusion (Communication)
Communication Disorders
Dyadic Communication   Use Interpersonal Communication
Gestures (Deaf Communication)   Use Sign Language
Gestures (Nonverbal Communication)   Use Body Language
Industrial Communication   Use Business Communication
Intercultural Communication
International Communication
Interpersonal Communication
Interschool Communication
Manual Communication
Oral Communication Method
Nonverbal Communication
Office Communication   Use Organizational Communication
Oral Communication (1966 1977)   Use Speech Communication
Organizational Communication
Politically Correct Communication   Use Political Correctness
Privileged Communication   Use Confidentiality
Communication Problems
Receptive Communication   Use Receptive Language
Communication Research
Speech Communication Research   Use Communication Research and Speech Communication
Communication Satellites (1967 1980)   Use Communications Satellites
Scholarly Communication
School Community Communication   Use School Community Relationship
Communication Skills
Speech Communication
Augmentative Communication Systems   Use Augmentative and Alternative Communication
Alternative Communication Systems (Disabled)   Use Augmentative and Alternative Communication
Facsimile Communication Systems (1968 1980)   Use Facsimile Transmission
Telephone Communication Systems (1967 1980)   Use Telephone Communications Systems
Communication Theory   Use Communication (Thought Transfer)
Communication (Thought Transfer)
Total Communication
Verbal Communication
Communications
Audiovisual Communications
Broadcast Communications   Use Telecommunications
Telephone Communications Industry
Mass Communications   Use Mass Media
Communications Media   Use Mass Media
Communications Networks   Use Communications
Communications Satellites
Communications Services   Use Communications
Communications Systems   Use Communications
Electronic Communications Systems   Use Telecommunications
Telephone Communications Systems
Communications Theory   Use Information Theory
Wire Communications   Use Telecommunications
Wireless Communications   Use Telecommunications
Communicative Competence (Languages)
Communism
Communistic Settlements   Use Collective Settlements
Academic Discourse Communities   Use Academic Discourse and Discourse Communities
Discourse Communities
Planned Communities
Rapid Growth Communities   Use Boomtowns
Therapeutic Communities   Use Milieu Therapy
Community
Community Action
Action Programs (Community) (1966 1980)   Use Community Action
Community Agencies (Public) (1966 1980)   Use Public Agencies
Community Analysis   Use Community Study
Community Antennas (1966 1980)   Use Cable Television
Community Attitudes

Community Based Education   Use Community Education
Community Based Instruction (Disabilities)
Community Benefits
Black   Community
Community Centers
Community Change
Community Characteristics
Community Colleges
Community Committees   Use Community Organizations
School   Community Communication   Use School Community Relationship
Community Compliance   Use Community Cooperation
Community Consultant Programs (1966 1980)   Use Consultation Programs
Community Consultants (1966 1980)   Use Consultants
Community Control
Community Cooperation
School   Community Cooperation (1966 1980)   Use School Community Relationship
Community Coordination
School   Community Coordination   Use School Community Relationship
Community Coordinators (1966 1980)   Use Community Coordination and Coordinators
Community Development
Community Education
Community Effort   Use Community Action
Community Enterprises   Use Community Programs
Ethnic   Community   Use Ethnic Groups
Community Experience   Use Experiential Learning
Community Health (1966 1980)   Use Public Health
Community Health Services
Community Health Workers   Use Community Health Services and Health Personnel
Community History   Use Local History
Community Influence
Community Information Centers   Use Community Information Services
Community Information Services
Information Services   (Community)   Use Community Information Services
School   Community Interaction   Use School Community Relationship
Community Involvement
Community Leaders
Community Legislation   Use Local Legislation
Community Mental Health Workers   Use Community Health Services and Mental Health Workers
Community Migrant Projects (1966 1980)   Use Community Programs and Migrant Programs
Community Needs
Negro   Community   Use Black Community
Community Organizations
Community Outreach   Use Outreach Programs
Community Participation   Use Community Involvement
Planned   Community (1966 1980)   Use Planned Communities
Community Planning
Community Police Relationship   Use Police Community Relationship
Community Problems
Community Programs
Local   Community Programs   Use Community Programs
School   Community Programs
Community Projects   Use Community Programs
Community Psychology
Community Recreation Legislation (1966 1978)   Use Local Legislation and Recreation Legislation
Community Recreation Programs
Referral Services   (Community)   Use Community Information Services and Referral
Community Relations
College   Community Relationship   Use School Community Relationship
Police   Community Relationship
School   Community Relationship
Community Resources
Community Responsibility
Rhetorical   Community   Use Discourse Communities
Community Role
Community Rooms (1967 1980)   Use Community Centers
Community Satisfaction
Community School Directors (1967 1980)   Use Administrators and Community Schools
Community School Programs   Use School Community Programs
Community School Relationship   Use School Community Relationship
Community Schools
Community Service Learning   Use Service Learning
Community Service Programs (1966 1980)   Use Community Services
Community Services
Community Size
Southern   Community (1966 1980)
Community Study
Community Support
Community Surveys
Community Tensions   Use Community Problems
Community Traits   Use Community Characteristics
Community Workers   Use Community Organizations
Community Zoning
Commuter Colleges
Commuting Students
Compact Disks   Use Optical Disks
Insurance   Companies
Companion Animals   Use Pets
Companions (Occupation) (1968 1980)   Use Attendants
Company Libraries   Use Corporate Libraries
Company Size (Industry)   Use Organization Size (Groups)
Comparable Institutions   Use Peer Institutions
Comparable Worth
Comparative Analysis

Comparative Education
Comparative Evaluation   Use Comparative Analysis
Comparative Linguistics   Use Contrastive Linguistics
Comparative Religion   Use Religion Studies
Comparative Statistics (1966 1980)   Use Comparative Analysis and Statistical Analysis
Comparative Study   Use Comparative Analysis
Comparative Testing
Audio Active   Compare Laboratories (1967 1980)   Use Language Laboratories
Achievement   Comparison   Use Achievement Rating
Educational Status   Comparison
Cultural   Comparisons   Use Cross Cultural Studies
Compensation (Concept)
Compensation (Remuneration)
Workers   Compensation
Workmans   Compensation (1966 1980)   Use Workers Compensation
Compensatory Development   Use Compensatory Education
Compensatory Education
Compensatory Education Programs (1966 1980)   Use Compensatory Education
Compensatory Opportunity   Use Compensatory Education
Competence
Interpersonal   Competence
Communicative   Competence (Languages)
Linguistic   Competence
Social   Competence   Use Interpersonal Competence
Minimal   Competencies   Use Minimum Competencies
Minimum   Competencies
Teacher   Competencies
Competency   Use Competence
Competency Based Education
Competency Based Teacher Education
Teacher Testing (for   Competency)   Use Teacher Competency Testing
Minimal   Competency Testing   Use Minimum Competency Testing
Minimum   Competency Testing
Teacher   Competency Testing
National   Competency Tests
Competition
Competitive Bidding   Use Bids
Supported   Competitive Employment   Use Supported Employment
Competitive Selection
Degree   Completion Time   Use Time to Degree
Educational   Complexes
Complexity Level (1968 1979)   Use Difficulty Level
Community   Compliance   Use Community Cooperation
Compliance (Legal)
Compliance (Psychology)
Component Building Systems (1968 1976)   Use Building Systems
Component Systems   Use Building Systems
Componential Analysis
Principal   Components Analysis   Use Factor Analysis
Body   Composition
Cohesion (Written   Composition)
Freshman   Composition
Composition (Literary) (1966 1980)   Use Writing (Composition)
Composition Measurement   Use Chemical Analysis
Composition (Music)   Use Musical Composition
Musical   Composition
Paragraph   Composition
Composition Processes (Literary)   Use Writing Processes
Racial   Composition
Revision (Written   Composition)
Composition Skills (Literary) (1966 1980)   Use Writing Skills
Writing   (Composition)
Coordination   Compounds
Comprehension
Auditory   Comprehension   Use Listening Comprehension
Aural   Comprehension   Use Listening Comprehension
Comprehension Development (1966 1980)   Use Comprehension
Listening   Comprehension
Reading   Comprehension
Listening   Comprehension Tests
Comprehensive Districts (1967 1980)   Use School Districts
Comprehensive High Schools (1967 1980)   Use High Schools
Comprehensive Programs
Comprehensive School Health Education
Comprehensive School Health Programs   Use Comprehensive School Health Education
Comprehensive Services (School Linked)   Use Integrated Services
Compressed Work Week   Use Flexible Working Hours
Speech   Compression
Compulsory Attendance   Use Compulsory Education
Compulsory Education
Compulsory Retirement   Use Mandatory Retirement
Computation
Mental   Computation
Computational Linguistics
Computer Aided Design and Manufacturing   Use Computer Assisted Design and Computer Assisted Manufacturing
Computer Aided Instruction   Use Computer Assisted Instruction
Computer Aided Instructional Management   Use Computer Managed Instruction
Computer Anxiety
Computer Applications   Use Computer Oriented Programs
Computer Assisted Communication   Use Computer Mediated Communication
Computer Assisted Design
Computer Assisted Drafting   Use Computer Assisted Design and Drafting
Computer Assisted Indexing   Use Automatic Indexing

Self	Concept
	Concept Teaching
Self	Concept Tests (1971 1980) Use Self Concept Measures
Mistaken	Conceptions Use Misconceptions
Fundamental	Concepts
Geographic	Concepts
Geometric	Concepts
Mathematical	Concepts
Number	Concepts
Scientific	Concepts
Systems	Concepts (1966 1980)
	Conceptual Distinctions Use Concept Formation
	Conceptual Schemes (1967 1980)
	Conceptual Tempo
	Concerts
	Concordances (1967 1980) Use Indexes
	Concrete Industry Use Cement Industry
Prestressed	Concrete
Pretensioned	Concrete Use Prestressed Concrete
Criterion Validity	(Concurrent) Use Concurrent Validity
	Concurrent Validity
	Conditioned Response (1967 1980) Use Responses
	Conditioned Stimulus (1966 1980) Use Stimuli
	Conditioning
Air	Conditioning
Classical	Conditioning
Air	Conditioning Equipment
Instrumental	Conditioning Use Operant Conditioning
Air	Conditioning Mechanics Use Refrigeration Mechanics
Operant	Conditioning
Physical	Conditioning Use Physical Fitness
Psychological	Conditioning Use Conditioning
Verbal Operant	Conditioning
Health	Conditions
Home	Conditions Use Family Environment
Job	Conditions Use Work Environment
Labor	Conditions
School	Conditions (1966 1980) Use Educational Environment
Slum	Conditions (1966 1980) Use Slum Environment
Teaching	Conditions
Working	Conditions Use Work Environment
	Conduct (1966 1980) Use Behavior
	Conference Papers
	Conference Proceedings
	Conference Reports (1967 1980)
	Conference Skills (Communication) Use Communication Skills
	Conferences
Parent	Conferences
Parent Student	Conferences (1967 1980) Use Parent Teacher Conferences
Parent Teacher	Conferences
Teacher Parent	Conferences Use Parent Teacher Conferences
Computer	Conferencing Use Teleconferencing
Self	Confidence Use Self Esteem
	Confidence Testing
	Confidential Information Use Confidentiality
	Confidential Records
	Confidentiality
	Conflict
Culture	Conflict
	Conflict of Interest
Religious	Conflict
	Conflict Resolution
Role	Conflict
	Confluent Education Use Humanistic Education
	Conformity
	Confucianism
	Congenital Impairments
	Congenitally Handicapped (1975 1980) Use Congenital Impairments
Library of	Congress Classification
	Congress Role Use Government Role
	Congressmen Use Legislators
	Congresswomen Use Legislators
	Congruence (1970 1980)
	Congruence (Mathematics)
	Congruence (Psychology)
Self	Congruence
	Conjoint Counseling Use Cocounseling
	Conjunctions
	Connected Discourse
Ethnic	Consciousness Use Ethnicity
	Consciousness Raising
	Consequence Based Education Use Competency Based Education
	Consequence Based Teacher Education Use Competency Based Teacher Education
	Conservation (Concept)
	Conservation Education
Energy	Conservation
	Conservation (Environment)
Hearing	Conservation
Soil	Conservation
	Conservatism
	Consistency Use Reliability
	Consolidated Schools
School	Consolidation Use Consolidated Schools

```
                        Consonants
                        Consortia
                        Consortiums    Use Consortia
        Equilibrium     Constants    Use Chemical Equilibrium
                        Constituent Structure    Use Phrase Structure
                        Constitutional History
                        Constitutional Law
        Design          Construct Method    Use Design Build Approach
                        Construct Validity
                        Constructed Languages    Use Artificial Languages
                        Constructed Response
                        Construction Bidding    Use Bids
                        Construction Costs
        Highway         Construction    Use Road Construction
                        Construction Industry
                        Construction Management
                        Construction Materials
                        Construction Needs
                        Construction Occupations    Use Building Trades
                        Construction (Process)
                        Construction Programs
        Road            Construction
        School          Construction
Structural Elements     (Construction)
        Test            Construction
                        Constructionism (Education)    Use Constructivism (Learning)
        Geometric       Constructions
                        Constructivism (Learning)
        Community       Consultant Programs (1966 1980)    Use Consultation Programs
                        Consultants
        Community       Consultants (1966 1980)    Use Consultants
        Medical         Consultants
        Reading         Consultants
        Science         Consultants
                        Consultation Programs
                        Consumer Behavior    Use Consumer Economics
                        Consumer Economics
                        Consumer Education
                        Consumer Expenditures    Use Consumer Economics
                        Consumer Protection
                        Consumer Science
                        Consumerism    Use Consumer Protection
        Alcohol         Consumption    Use Drinking
        Fuel            Consumption
        Culture         Contact
        Eye             Contact
                        Contagious Diseases    Use Communicable Diseases
        Self            Contained Classrooms
                        Contemporary History    Use Modern History
                        Content Analysis
        Job             Content Analysis    Use Job Analysis
                        Content Area Reading
                        Content Area Writing
        Reading in      Content Areas    Use Content Area Reading
Controversial Issues (Course  Content)
        Course          Content
        Curriculum      Content    Use Curriculum
        Job             Content    Use Occupational Information
        Pedagogical     Content Knowledge
        Program         Content
                        Content Reading (1967 1980)    Use Content Area Reading
        Test            Content
        Textbook        Content
                        Content Validity
                        Context Clues
        Cultural        Context
                        Context Effect
                        Context Free Grammar
        Key Word in     Context    Use Permuted Indexes
        Social          Context    Use Social Environment
                        Contextual Effects    Use Context Effect
                        Contingency Contracts    Use Contingency Management
                        Contingency Management
        Income          Contingent Loans
        Response        Contingent Testing    Use Adaptive Testing
                        Continuation Education (1968 1980)
                        Continuation High Schools (1968 1980)    Use Continuation Students
                        Continuation Students
                        Continuing Education
                        Continuing Education Centers
        Mandatory       Continuing Education
        Professional    Continuing Education
                        Continuing Education Units
        Developmental   Continuity
                        Continuity of Education    Use Developmental Continuity
                        Continuous Guidance (1966 1980)    Use Guidance
                        Continuous Learning (1967 1980)    Use Lifelong Learning
                        Continuous Progress Plan
        Space Time      Continuum    Use Relativity
        Intonation      Contours    Use Intonation
                        Contraception
                        Contract Grading    Use Grading and Performance Contracts
                        Contract Salaries
```

	Contract Tribal Schools	Use Tribally Controlled Education
	Contracting Out (of Government Services)	Use Privatization
	Contractor Vehicles	Use Service Vehicles
	Contracts	
Behavioral	Contracts	Use Performance Contracts
Contingency	Contracts	Use Contingency Management
Learning	Contracts	Use Performance Contracts
Performance	Contracts	
Student Learning	Contracts	Use Performance Contracts
	Contrast	
	Contrast Ratios	Use Contrast
	Contrastive Language Analysis	Use Contrastive Linguistics
Linguistic Difficulty	(Contrastive)	Use Interference (Language)
	Contrastive Linguistics	
Parent Financial	Contribution	
Parental Financial	Contribution (1978 1980)	Use Parent Financial Contribution
Air Pollution	Control (1967 1980)	Use Air Pollution
Air Traffic	Control	
Arms	Control	Use Disarmament
Attention	Control	
Bibliographic	Control	Use Cataloging
Birth	Control	Use Contraception
Climate	Control	
Community	Control	
Destiny	Control	Use Self Determination
Disease	Control	
Electronic	Control	
Federal	Control	Use Federal Regulation
Firearms	Control	Use Gun Control
	Control Groups	
Gun	Control	
Impulse	Control	Use Self Control
Authority	Control (Information)	
Internal External Locus of	Control	Use Locus of Control
Learner	Control	Use Learner Controlled Instruction
Locus of	Control	
Noise	Control	Use Noise (Sound)
Nuclear	Control	Use Disarmament
Numerical	Control	
Local	Control (of Schools)	Use School District Autonomy
Pest	Control	Use Pests
Property	Control	Use Property Accounting
Quality	Control	
Self	Control	
Social	Control	
Spectator Traffic	Control	Use Traffic Control
Property	Control Systems	Use Property Accounting
Traffic	Control	
Water Pollution	Control (1969 1980)	Use Water Pollution
Tribally	Controlled Education	
	Controlled Environment (1966 1980)	
Learner	Controlled Instruction	
Student	Controlled Learning	Use Learner Controlled Instruction
Indian	Controlled Schools	Use American Indian Education and Tribally Controlled Education
Electrical	Controls	Use Electronic Control
Parking	Controls	
Static	Controls	Use Electronic Control
	Controversial Issues (Course Content)	
Environment Heredity	Controversy	Use Nature Nurture Controversy
Heredity Environment	Controversy	Use Nature Nurture Controversy
Learning Maturation	Controversy	Use Nature Nurture Controversy
Maturation Learning	Controversy	Use Nature Nurture Controversy
Nature Nurture	Controversy	
	Convalescent Homes	Use Nursing Homes
	Conventional Instruction	
	Conventional Warfare	Use War
Literary	Conventions (1968 1980)	Use Literary Devices
	Convergent Thinking	
	Conversational Language Courses	
Informal	Conversational Usage	Use Standard Spoken Usage
Building	Conversion	
Data	Conversion	
	Conversion (Format)	Use Data Conversion
Retrospective	Conversion (Library Catalogs)	
	Convicts	Use Criminals
	Cooking Instruction	
	Cooks	
	Cooperating Schools	Use Affiliated Schools
	Cooperating Teachers	
	Cooperation	
Agency	Cooperation	
College	Cooperation (1966 1980)	Use Intercollegiate Cooperation
College High School	Cooperation (1967 1980)	Use College School Cooperation
College School	Cooperation	
Community	Cooperation	
Counselor Teacher	Cooperation	
Educational	Cooperation	
High School College	Cooperation	Use College School Cooperation
Institutional	Cooperation	
Interagency	Cooperation (1967 1980)	Use Agency Cooperation
Intercollegiate	Cooperation	
Interinstitutional	Cooperation (1968 1980)	Use Institutional Cooperation
International	Cooperation	

Librarian Teacher Cooperation
Library Cooperation
Parent Teacher Cooperation
Regional Cooperation
School College Cooperation   Use College School Cooperation
School Community Cooperation (1966 1980)   Use School Community Relationship
Special Education Regular Education Cooperation   Use Regular and Special Education Relationship
Teacher Cooperation   Use Teacher Collaboration
Teacher Counselor Cooperation   Use Counselor Teacher Cooperation
Teacher Librarian Cooperation   Use Librarian Teacher Cooperation
Teacher Parent Cooperation   Use Parent Teacher Cooperation
Cooperative Activities   Use Group Activities
Cooperative Education
Cooperative Extension   Use Extension Education
Cooperative Learning
Cooperative Planning
Cooperative Programs
Cooperative Teaching (1966 1980)   Use Team Teaching
Cooperative Training   Use Cooperative Education
Cooperative Work Experience Programs   Use Cooperative Education
Cooperatives
Coordinate Geometry   Use Analytic Geometry
Coordinate Indexes
Post Coordinate Indexes   Use Coordinate Indexes
Research Coordinating Units
Coordination
Community Coordination
Coordination Compounds
Educational Coordination (1967 1980)   Use Coordination and Educational Cooperation
Eye Hand Coordination
Interagency Coordination (1967 1980)   Use Agency Cooperation and Coordination
Perceptual Motor Coordination
Program Coordination (1966 1980)   Use Cooperative Programs and Coordination
Coordination (Psychomotor)   Use Psychomotor Skills
School Community Coordination   Use School Community Relationship
Statewide Coordination   Use Statewide Planning
Coordinator Trainers   Use Instructor Coordinators
Coordinators
Audiovisual Coordinators
Community Coordinators (1966 1980)   Use Community Coordination and Coordinators
Instructor Coordinators
Teacher Coordinators   Use Instructor Coordinators
Copilots   Use Aircraft Pilots
Coping
Copyediting   Use Editing
Copyeditors   Use Editors
Copying (Reproduction)   Use Reprography
Reproduction (Copying)   Use Reprography
Copyrights
Fair Dealing (Copyrights)   Use Fair Use (Copyrights)
Fair Use (Copyrights)
Core Courses (1966 1980)   Use Core Curriculum
Core Curriculum
Teaching Core   Use Core Curriculum
Corn (Field Crop) (1968 1980)   Use Grains (Food)
Coronary Prone Behavior Pattern   Use Type A Behavior
Corporal Punishment
Corporate Colleges   Use Corporate Education
Corporate Education
Corporate Giving   Use Corporate Support
Corporate Libraries
Corporate Support
Corporate Training   Use Industrial Training
Corporations
Marine Corps Air Stations   Use Military Air Facilities
Politically Correct Communication   Use Political Correctness
Error Correction
Correctional Education
Correctional Institutions
Correctional Rehabilitation
Corrections (Criminal Justice)   Use Correctional Rehabilitation
Corrective Institutions (1966 1980)   Use Correctional Institutions
Corrective Reading
Political Correctness
Correlation
Canonical Correlation   Use Multivariate Analysis
Multiple Correlation   Use Correlation
Part Correlation   Use Correlation
Partial Correlation   Use Correlation
Correlation Studies   Use Correlation
Business Correspondence
Correspondence Courses (1966 1980)   Use Correspondence Study
Grapheme Phoneme Correspondence   Use Phoneme Grapheme Correspondence
Letter Sound Correspondence   Use Phoneme Grapheme Correspondence
Correspondence (Letters)   Use Letters (Correspondence)
Letters (Correspondence)
Phoneme Grapheme Correspondence
Correspondence Schools
Commercial Correspondence Schools   Use Correspondence Schools
Correspondence Study
Corridors
Cosmetic Prostheses (1967 1980)   Use Prostheses
Cosmetics Inspectors   Use Food and Drug Inspectors

	Cosmetologists (1969 1981) Use Cosmetology
	Cosmetology
	Cost Analysis Use Cost Effectiveness
Benefit	Cost Analysis Use Cost Effectiveness
	Cost Benefit Analysis Use Cost Effectiveness
	Cost Effectiveness
	Cost Effectiveness Analysis Use Cost Effectiveness
	Cost Estimates
	Cost Indexes
	Cost Utility Analysis Use Cost Effectiveness
Life Cycle	Costing
	Costs
Construction	Costs
Estimated	Costs (1966 1980) Use Cost Estimates
Life	Costs (Facilities and Equipment) Use Life Cycle Costing
College	Costs (Financing for Individual Students) Use Paying for College
Health	Costs Use Health Care Costs
Health Care	Costs
College	Costs (Incurred by Students) Use Student Costs
Index Numbers	(Costs) Use Cost Indexes
Instructional Student	Costs
Legal	Costs
Medical	Costs Use Health Care Costs and Medical Services
Noninstructional Student	Costs
Police	Costs (1966 1980) Use Costs and Police
Program	Costs
Student	Costs
Unit	Costs
	Costume Design Use Clothing Design
	Cot Death Use Sudden Infant Death Syndrome
	Cottage Parents Use Resident Advisers
Citizens	Councils
College Governing	Councils
Student	Councils Use Student Government
	Counseling
Admissions	Counseling
Adult	Counseling
Behavioral	Counseling (1967 1980) Use Behavior Modification
Career	Counseling
	Counseling Centers (1966 1977) Use Guidance Centers
Client Centered	Counseling Use Nondirective Counseling
Conjoint	Counseling Use Cocounseling
Educational	Counseling
	Counseling Effectiveness
Elementary School	Counseling (1967 1980) Use School Counseling
Family	Counseling
	Counseling Goals (1966 1980) Use Counseling Objectives
Group	Counseling
Guidance	Counseling (1966 1980) Use School Counseling
Individual	Counseling
	Counseling Instructional Programs (1967 1980)
Leisure	Counseling Use Leisure Education
Marital	Counseling Use Marriage Counseling
Marriage	Counseling
	Counseling Methods Use Counseling Techniques
Nondirective	Counseling
	Counseling Objectives
Occupational	Counseling Use Career Counseling
Outreach	Counseling Use Outreach Programs
Parent	Counseling
Peer	Counseling
	Counseling Process Use Counseling
	Counseling Programs (1966 1980) Use Counseling Services
Evening	Counseling Programs (1966 1980) Use Counseling Services and Evening Programs
	Counseling Psychology
Rehabilitation	Counseling
School	Counseling
Secondary School	Counseling Use School Counseling
	Counseling Services
Team	Counseling Use Cocounseling
	Counseling Techniques
	Counseling Theories
Vocational	Counseling (1966 1980) Use Career Counseling
	Counselor Acceptance (1968 1980) Use Counselor Client Relationship
	Counselor Attitudes
	Counselor Background Use Counselor Characteristics
	Counselor Certification
	Counselor Characteristics
	Counselor Client Ratio
	Counselor Client Relationship
Teacher	Counselor Cooperation Use Counselor Teacher Cooperation
	Counselor Education Use Counselor Training
	Counselor Educators
	Counselor Evaluation
	Counselor Functions (1967 1977) Use Counselor Role
	Counselor Licensing Use Counselor Certification
	Counselor Opinion Use Counselor Attitudes
	Counselor Performance
	Counselor Preparation Use Counselor Training
	Counselor Qualifications
Client	Counselor Ratio Use Counselor Client Ratio
	Counselor Reaction Use Counselor Attitudes
Client	Counselor Relationship Use Counselor Client Relationship

	Counselor Role
	Counselor Selection
	Counselor Teacher Cooperation
	Counselor Training
	Counselors
Adjustment	Counselors
Admissions	Counselors (1973 1980) Use Admissions Counseling
Camp	Counselors (1968 1980) Use Camping
College	Counselors Use School Counselors
Elementary School	Counselors (1967 1980) Use School Counselors
Employment	Counselors
Faculty	Counselors Use Faculty Advisers
Guidance	Counselors Use School Counselors
School	Counselors
Secondary School	Counselors (1967 1980) Use School Counselors
Special	Counselors (1966 1980) Use Counselors and Specialists
	Counties
Low Income	Counties
	Counting Use Computation
Foreign	Countries
Third World	Countries Use Developing Nations
	County Extension Agents Use Extension Agents
	County Government Use Counties and Local Government
	County History Use Counties and Local History
	County Libraries
	County Norms Use Local Norms
	County Officials
	County Programs
	County School Districts
	County School Systems (1967 1980) Use County School Districts
Bibliographic	Coupling
American Government	(Course) (1966 1980) Use United States Government (Course)
	Course Content
Controversial Issues	(Course Content)
	Course Descriptions
	Course Enrichment Use Curriculum Enrichment
	Course Evaluation
Science	Course Improvement Project (1967 1980) Use Science Course Improvement Projects
Science	Course Improvement Projects
	Course Integrated Library Instruction
	Course Objectives
	Course of Instruction Use Course Organization
	Course Organization
	Course Outlines Use Course Descriptions
	Course Related Library Instruction Use Course Integrated Library Instruction
	Course Selection (Students)
United States Government	(Course)
	Course Withdrawal Use Withdrawal (Education)
	Courses
Accelerated	Courses (1966 1980) Use Acceleration (Education)
Advanced	Courses
Art Studio	Courses Use Studio Art
Conversational Language	Courses
Core	Courses (1966 1980) Use Core Curriculum
Correspondence	Courses (1966 1980) Use Correspondence Study
Credit	Courses
Education	Courses
Elective	Courses
General Methods	Courses Use Methods Courses
Honors	Courses Use Honors Curriculum
Inservice	Courses (1966 1980) Use Inservice Education
Institute Type	Courses (1966 1980) Use Institutes (Training Programs)
Intensive Language	Courses
Introductory	Courses
Foundation	Courses (Introductory) Use Introductory Courses
Mandatory	Courses Use Required Courses
Methods	Courses
Noncredit	Courses
Optional	Courses Use Elective Courses
Prerequisite	Courses Use Prerequisites and Required Courses
Refresher	Courses
Remedial	Courses (1966 1980) Use Remedial Instruction
Required	Courses
Foundation	Courses (Required) Use Required Courses
Science	Courses (1966 1980) Use Science Curriculum
Short	Courses (1970 1980) Use Minicourses
Special Methods	Courses Use Methods Courses
Survey	Courses Use Introductory Courses
	Courseware
	Courseware Development Use Computer Software Development and Courseware
	Courseware Evaluation Use Computer Software Evaluation and Courseware
	Courseware Reviews Use Computer Software Reviews and Courseware
	Courseware Selection Use Computer Software Selection and Courseware
Auditing	(Coursework)
	Court Action Use Court Litigation
	Court Cases (1966 1980) Use Court Litigation
	Court Decisions Use Court Litigation
	Court Doctrine
	Court Judges
	Court Litigation
Federal	Court Litigation (1966 1980) Use Court Litigation and Federal Courts
State	Court Litigation Use Court Litigation and State Courts
Supreme	Court Litigation (1966 1980)

	Court Reporters
	Court Role
	Courts
Childrens	Courts Use Juvenile Courts
Federal	Courts
Juvenile	Courts
State	Courts
State Supreme	Courts Use State Courts
Supreme	Courts (1966 1980)
Tourist	Courts Use Hotels
Analysis of	Covariance
Soft	Cover Books Use Paperback Books
Floor	Covering Use Flooring
Resilient Floor	Covering Use Flooring
	Covert Response
	CPR (Medicine) Use Cardiopulmonary Resuscitation
	Crack
	Crack Babies Use Crack and Prenatal Drug Exposure
	Craft Workers
	Crafts Use Handicrafts
Design	Crafts
Industrial	Crafts Use Industrial Arts
Leather	Crafts Use Leather
	Crafts Rooms (1966 1980) Use Educational Facilities and Handicrafts
	Craftsmen (1970 1981) Use Craft Workers
Job	Creation Use Job Development
Special	Creation Theory Use Creationism
	Creationism
Scientific	Creationism Use Creationism
	Creative Ability (1968 1980) Use Creativity
	Creative Activities
	Creative Art
	Creative Development
	Creative Dramatics
	Creative Expression
	Creative Reading (1966 1980)
	Creative Spelling Use Invented Spelling
	Creative Teaching
	Creative Thinking
	Creative Thinking Tests Use Creativity Tests
	Creative Writing
	Creativity
	Creativity Measures Use Creativity Tests
	Creativity Research
	Creativity Tests
	Credentials
	Credibility
Source	Credibility Use Credibility
	Credit by Examination Use Equivalency Tests
	Credit Courses
Advanced	Credit Examinations Use Equivalency Tests
	Credit (Finance)
Credit No	Credit Grading
Pass No	Credit Grading Use Credit No Credit Grading
Student	Credit Hours Use Credits
	Credit No Credit Grading
	Credits
College	Credits
Tax	Credits
Tuition Tax	Credits Use Tax Credits and Tuition
	Cree
	Cree (Tribe)
Haitian	Creole
Mauritian	Creole
Sierra Leone	Creole
	Creoles
	Crew Leaders
	Crib Death Use Sudden Infant Death Syndrome
	Crime
	Crime Prevention
Victims of	Crime
International	Crimes
War	Crimes Use International Crimes
Corrections	(Criminal Justice) Use Correctional Rehabilitation
	Criminal Law
Executions	(Criminal Law) Use Capital Punishment
	Criminals
	Criminology
	Crippled Children (1968 1980) Use Physical Disabilities
	Crisis Intervention
	Crisis Management
Telephone	Crisis Services Use Hotlines (Public)
	Crisis Therapy (1969 1980) Use Crisis Intervention
	Criteria
Admission	Criteria
Environmental	Criteria (1967 1980) Use Environmental Standards
Evaluation	Criteria
Lesson Observation	Criteria
Performance	Criteria (1968 1980)
Research	Criteria (1967 1980)
	Criterion Referenced Education Use Competency Based Education
	Criterion Referenced Teacher Education Use Competency Based Teacher Education
	Criterion Referenced Tests

Criterion Validity (Concurrent)   Use Concurrent Validity
Criterion Validity (Predictive)   Use Predictive Validity
Critical Analysis   Use Criticism
Critical Evaluation   Use Criticism
Critical Incidents Method
Critical Path Method
Critical Reading
Critical Scores   Use Cutting Scores
Critical Theory
Critical Thinking
Critical Viewing
Criticism
Analytical   Criticism (1969 1980)
Aristotelian   Criticism (1969 1980)
Art   Criticism
Feminist   Criticism
Film   Criticism
Formal   Criticism (1969 1980)
Historical   Criticism (1969 1980)
Impressionistic   Criticism (1969 1980)
Literary   Criticism
Marxist   Criticism   Use Marxian Analysis
Moral   Criticism (1969 1980)
Mythic   Criticism (1969 1980)
Platonic   Criticism (1970 1980)
Rhetorical   Criticism
Textual   Criticism (1969 1980)
Theoretical   Criticism (1969 1980)
Corn (Field   Crop) (1968 1980)   Use Grains (Food)
Crop Harvesting   Use Harvesting
Crop Planting   Use Agronomy and Horticulture
Crop Processing Occupations
Crop Production   Use Agricultural Production
Field   Crops
Cross Age Helping   Use Cross Age Teaching
Cross Age Teaching
Cross Categorical Education   Use Noncategorical Education
Cross Cultural Communication   Use Intercultural Communication
Cross Cultural Studies
Cross Cultural Tests   Use Culture Fair Tests
Cross Cultural Training
Interface Systems   (Cross Database)   Use Gateway Systems
Cross Eyes   Use Strabismus
Cross Sectional Studies
Crowding
Crude Oil   Use Oil
Crude Scores   Use Raw Scores
Crying
Crystallography
Cuban Americans   Use Cubans and Hispanic Americans
Cubans
Cubic Measure   Use Volume (Mathematics)
Cue Cards   Use Cues
Cued Speech
Cues
Cuing   Use Prompting
Cultural Activities
Diversity   (Cultural) as a Value   Use Cultural Pluralism
Diversity   (Cultural) as an Observation or a Fact   Use Cultural Differences
Assimilation   (Cultural)   Use Acculturation
Cultural Awareness
Cultural Background
Cultural Centers
Cultural Characteristics   Use Cultural Traits
Cross   Cultural Communication   Use Intercultural Communication
Cultural Comparisons   Use Cross Cultural Studies
Cultural Context
Cultural Differences
Cultural Disadvantagement (1966 1980)   Use Disadvantaged
Cultural Education
Cultural Enrichment
Cultural Environment (1966 1980)   Use Cultural Context
Cultural Events (1966 1980)   Use Cultural Activities
Cultural Exchange
Cultural Factors (1966 1980)   Use Cultural Influences
Cultural Geography   Use Human Geography
Ethnic   Cultural Groups   Use Ethnic Groups
Racial   Cultural Groups   Use Ethnic Groups
Religious   Cultural Groups
Cultural Heritage   Use Cultural Background
Cultural Images
Cultural Influences
Cultural Interaction   Use Cultural Exchange
Cultural Interrelationships
Cultural Isolation
Cultural Lag   Use Culture Lag
Cultural Literacy
Cultural Maintenance
Cultural Opportunities
Cultural Pluralism
Cultural Preservation   Use Cultural Maintenance
Cultural Relevance
Relevance   (Cultural)   Use Cultural Relevance

	Cultural Revitalization	Use Cultural Maintenance
Cross	Cultural Studies	
Cross	Cultural Tests	Use Culture Fair Tests
Cross	Cultural Training	
	Cultural Traits	
	Cultural Understanding	Use Cultural Awareness
	Culturally Advantaged (1967 1980)	Use Advantaged
	Culturally Appropriate Education	Use Culturally Relevant Education
	Culturally Disadvantaged (1966 1980)	Use Disadvantaged
	Culturally Relevant Education	
	Culturally Responsive Education	Use Culturally Relevant Education
	Culture	
African	Culture	
Alien	Culture	Use Foreign Culture
American	Culture (1966 1980)	
American Indian	Culture	
	Culture Based Curriculum	Use Culturally Relevant Education
Beauty	Culture	Use Cosmetology
Black	Culture	
Burmese	Culture	
Chinese	Culture	
	Culture Conflict	
	Culture Contact	
Customs	(Culture)	Use Culture
Dutch	Culture	
	Culture Fair Tests	
Family	Culture	Use Family Life
Folk	Culture	
Foreign	Culture	
	Culture Free Tests (1967 1980)	Use Culture Fair Tests
Hispanic American	Culture	
Islamic	Culture	
Japanese	Culture	
Japanese American	Culture	
Korean	Culture	
	Culture Lag	
Latin American	Culture	
Luso Brazilian	Culture	
Majority	Culture	Use Middle Class Culture
Mass	Culture	Use Popular Culture
Material	Culture	
Mexican American	Culture	Use Hispanic American Culture and Mexican Americans
Middle Class	Culture	
Minority	Culture	Use Minority Groups
Negro	Culture (1966 1977)	Use Black Culture
North American	Culture	
Pop	Culture	Use Popular Culture
Popular	Culture	
Puerto Rican	Culture	
School	Culture	
	Culture Shock	Use Culture Conflict
Spanish	Culture	
Traditions	(Culture)	Use Folk Culture
Urban	Culture	
	Culturing Techniques	
	Curiosity	
	Current Awareness Services	Use Selective Dissemination of Information
	Current Events	
	Curriculum	
Academic	Curriculum	Use Academic Education
	Curriculum Adaptation	Use Curriculum Development
Arithmetic	Curriculum (1966 1980)	Use Arithmetic and Mathematics Curriculum
Art Production	Curriculum	Use Studio Art
	Curriculum Based Assessment	
	Curriculum Based Measurement	Use Curriculum Based Assessment
British National	Curriculum	
State	Curriculum Bulletins	Use State Curriculum Guides
Child Centered	Curriculum	Use Student Centered Curriculum
College	Curriculum	
	Curriculum Content	Use Curriculum
Core	Curriculum	
Culture Based	Curriculum	Use Culturally Relevant Education
	Curriculum Design	
	Curriculum Development	
Economics	Curriculum	Use Economics Education
Elementary School	Curriculum	
English	Curriculum	
	Curriculum Enrichment	
	Curriculum Evaluation	
Experimental	Curriculum	
Fused	Curriculum	
	Curriculum Guides	
State	Curriculum Guides	
Hidden	Curriculum	
High School	Curriculum (1967 1980)	Use Secondary School Curriculum
History	Curriculum	Use History Instruction
Honors	Curriculum	
	Curriculum Improvement	Use Curriculum Development
Individualized	Curriculum (1966 1980)	Use Individualized Instruction
Integrated	Curriculum	
	Curriculum Integrated Library Instruction	Use Course Integrated Library Instruction
	Curriculum Laboratories	Use Curriculum Study Centers
	Curriculum Materials	Use Instructional Materials

Mathematics Curriculum
Modern Language Curriculum
National Curriculum
Organic Curriculum   Use Student Centered Curriculum
Physics Curriculum (1966 1980)   Use Physics and Science Curriculum
Curriculum Planning (1966 1980)   Use Curriculum Development
Preschool Curriculum
Problem Centered Curriculum   Use Problem Based Learning
Curriculum Problems
Curriculum Reevaluation   Use Curriculum Evaluation
Curriculum Referenced Assessment   Use Curriculum Based Assessment
Curriculum Reform   Use Curriculum Development
Curriculum Relevance   Use Relevance (Education)
Curriculum Reorganization   Use Curriculum Development
Curriculum Research
Curriculum Resources   Use Educational Resources
Curriculum Revisions   Use Curriculum Development
Science Curriculum
Secondary School Curriculum
Shop Curriculum
Speech Curriculum
Speech Communication Curriculum   Use Speech Communication and Speech Curriculum
Spiral Curriculum
Student Centered Curriculum
Curriculum Study Centers
Teacher Education Curriculum
Television Curriculum
Ungraded Curriculum (1966 1980)   Use Nongraded Instructional Grouping
Unified Studies Curriculum
Curriculum Vitae   Use Resumes (Personal)
Writing Across the Curriculum
Cursive Writing
Item Characteristic Curve Theory   Use Item Response Theory
Custodial Mentally Handicapped (1968 1980)   Use Severe Mental Retardation
Custodian Training
Child Custody
Customs (Culture)   Use Culture
Cutaneous Sense (1968 1980)   Use Tactual Perception
Cutlines   Use Captions
Budget Cuts   Use Budgeting and Retrenchment
Cutting Scores
Cybernetics
Life Cycle Costing
Business Cycles
Economic Cycles   Use Business Cycles
Learning Cycles   Use Learning Processes
Tropical Cyclones   Use Hurricanes
Cyesis   Use Pregnancy
Cyrillic Alphabet
Cystic Fibrosis
Cytology
Czech
Czech Literature
R D and E   Use Research and Development
R and D   Use Research and Development
Dactylology   Use Finger Spelling
Dagur
Average Daily Attendance
Average Daily Enrollment (1968 1980)   Use Average Daily Membership
Fundamental Skills (Daily Living)   Use Daily Living Skills
Daily Living Skills
Survival Skills (Daily Living)   Use Daily Living Skills
Average Daily Membership
Dairy Farmers
Dairy Product Inspectors   Use Food and Drug Inspectors
Dairymen (1966 1980)   Use Dairy Farmers
Dakota
Teton Dakota   Use Lakota
Brain Damage   Use Neurological Impairments
Radiation Damage   Use Radiation Effects
Dance
Aerobic Dance   Use Aerobics and Dance
Dance Education
Dance Therapy
Dangerous Materials   Use Hazardous Materials
Danish
Darghi   Use Caucasian Languages
Data
Data Accumulation   Use Data Collection
Data Analysis
Data Banks   Use Databases
Data Bases (1969 1981)   Use Databases
Data Collection
Data Conversion
Digital Optical Data Disks   Use Optical Data Disks
Optical Data Disks
Data Dissemination   Use Information Dissemination
Keyboarding (Data Entry)
Machine Readable Data Files   Use Databases
Data Interpretation
Data Needs   Use Information Needs
Personnel Data
Data Processing

Automatic	Data Processing Use Data Processing
	Data Processing Centers Use Computer Centers and Data Processing
Electronic	Data Processing (1967 1980) Use Data Processing
	Data Processing Occupations
	Data Sheets (1966 1980) Use Worksheets
Statistical	Data
Tables	(Data)
	Data Tabulation Use Data Processing
Time Use	Data Use Time Management
	Database Design
	Database Hosts Use Online Vendors
Interface Systems (Cross	Database) Use Gateway Systems
	Database Management Systems
	Database Producers
	Database Vendors Use Online Vendors
	Databases
Bibliographic	Databases
Full Text	Databases
Numeric	Databases
	Dating (Social)
	Daughters
Full Day Half	Day Alternate Day Use Alternate Day Schedules and Full Day Half Day Schedules
Alternate	Day Block Scheduling Use Alternate Day Schedules and Block Scheduling
	Day Camp Programs
	Day Camps Use Day Camp Programs
	Day Care
Adult	Day Care
After School	Day Care (1978 1983) Use After School Programs and School Age Day Care
	Day Care Centers
	Day Care Effects
Employer Sponsored	Day Care Use Employer Supported Day Care
Employer Supported	Day Care
Family	Day Care
Home	Day Care Use Family Day Care
	Day Care Programs (1966 1980) Use Day Care
School Age	Day Care
	Day Care Services (1967 1980) Use Day Care
	Day Classes Use Day Programs
College	Day
Extended School	Day
Full Day Half Day Alternate	Day Use Alternate Day Schedules and Full Day Half Day Schedules
Full	Day Half Day Alternate Day Use Alternate Day Schedules and Full Day Half Day Schedules
All	Day Half Day Schedules Use Full Day Half Day Schedules
Full	Day Half Day Schedules
	Day Programs
	Day Release Use Released Time
All Day Half	Day Schedules Use Full Day Half Day Schedules
Alternate	Day Schedules
Full Day Half	Day Schedules
Half	Day Schedules Use Full Day Half Day Schedules
	Day Schools
	Day Students
Four	Day Work Week Use Flexible Working Hours
	Daylight (1970 1980) Use Light
Holy	Days Use Religious Holidays
Man	Days (1968 1980) Use Worker Days
People	Days Use Worker Days
Person	Days Use Worker Days
Staff	Days Use Worker Days
Worker	Days
	Daytime Programs (1967 1980) Use Day Programs
	DBMS Use Database Management Systems
	DDC (Classification) Use Dewey Decimal Classification
	De Facto Segregation
	De Jure Segregation
	Deaf (1966 1980) Use Deafness
	Deaf Blind
	Deaf Children (1966 1980) Use Deafness
Gestures	(Deaf Communication) Use Sign Language
	Deaf Education (1968 1980) Use Deafness
	Deaf Interpreting
Interpreting for the	Deaf Use Deaf Interpreting
	Deaf Research (1968 1980) Use Deafness
	Deafness
Fair	Dealing (Copyrights) Use Fair Use (Copyrights)
	Deans
Academic	Deans
College	Deans (1968 1980) Use Deans and Higher Education
	Deans of Faculty Use Academic Deans
	Deans of Instruction Use Academic Deans
	Deans of Men Use Deans of Students
	Deans of Students
	Deans of Women Use Deans of Students
	Death
Cot	Death Use Sudden Infant Death Syndrome
Crib	Death Use Sudden Infant Death Syndrome
	Death Education Use Death
	Death Penalty Use Capital Punishment
	Death Rate Use Mortality Rate
Infant	Death Rate Use Infant Mortality and Mortality Rate
Sudden Infant	Death Syndrome
	Debate
	Debate Format

Debate Judges   Use Judges
Presidential   Debates (United States)   Use Debate and Presidential Campaigns (United States)
Debt (Financial)
Debugging (Computers)
Deceleration   Use Acceleration (Physics)
Decentralization
Decentralized Library Systems (1968 1980)   Use Decentralization and Library Networks
Decentralized School Design (1966 1980)   Use Decentralization and Educational Facilities Design
Deception
Decimal Classification (Dewey)   Use Dewey Decimal Classification
Dewey   Decimal Classification
Decimal Classification (Universal)   Use Universal Decimal Classification
Universal   Decimal Classification
Decimal Fractions
Decimals   Use Decimal Fractions
Decision Making
Collaborative   Decision Making   Use Participative Decision Making
Collective   Decision Making   Use Participative Decision Making
Participative   Decision Making
Decision Making Skills
Decision Support Systems
Group   Decision Support Systems   Use Decision Support Systems and Group Dynamics
Court   Decisions   Use Court Litigation
Legal   Decisions   Use Court Litigation
Test Score   Decline
Declining Enrollment
Declining Scores   Use Test Score Decline
Decoding (Information)   Use Coding
Decoding (Reading)
Interior   Decoration   Use Interior Design
Deduction
Tax   Deductions
Deductive Methods (1967 1980)   Use Deduction
Deep Sea Diving   Use Underwater Diving
Deep Structure
Defacto Segregation (1966 1980)   Use De Facto Segregation
Defamation of Character   Use Libel and Slander
Loan   Default
Defaulted Loans   Use Loan Default
Birth   Defects   Use Congenital Impairments
Neurological   Defects (1966 1980)   Use Neurological Impairments
Civil   Defense
Defense Mechanisms
National   Defense
Deferred Tuition   Use Income Contingent Loans
Housing   Deficiencies
Nutrient   Deficiencies   Use Nutrition
Nutritional   Deficiencies   Use Nutrition
Iron   Deficiency Anemia   Use Anemia
Acquired Immune   Deficiency Syndrome
Attention   Deficit Disorders
Definitions
Degree Completion Time   Use Time to Degree
External   Degree Programs
Special   Degree Programs
Extended   Degree Programs (Teacher Education)   Use Extended Teacher Education Programs
Time Shortened   Degree Programs   Use Acceleration (Education)
Degree Requirements
Time to   Degree
Degrees (Academic)
Associate   Degrees
Baccalaureate   Degrees   Use Bachelors Degrees
Bachelor of Arts   Degrees   Use Bachelors Degrees
Bachelor of Science   Degrees   Use Bachelors Degrees
Bachelors   Degrees
Doctor of Arts   Degrees
Doctoral   Degrees
First Professional   Degrees   Use Degrees (Academic) and Professional Education
Master of Arts   Degrees   Use Masters Degrees
Master of Science   Degrees   Use Masters Degrees
Masters   Degrees
Specialist in Education   Degrees
Three Year Bachelors   Degrees   Use Acceleration (Education) and Bachelors Degrees
Degrees (Titles) (1966 1980)   Use Degrees (Academic)
Two Plus Two Tech Prep Associate   Degrees   Use Associate Degrees and Tech Prep
Two Year College   Degrees   Use Associate Degrees
Dehumanization   Use Humanization
Deinstitutionalization (of Disabled)
Dejure Segregation (1966 1980)   Use De Jure Segregation
Delay of Gratification
Delayed Development (Individuals)   Use Developmental Delays
Developmentally   Delayed   Use Developmental Delays
Delayed Speech
Developmental   Delays
Delinquency
Delinquency Causes
Juvenile   Delinquency   Use Delinquency
Delinquency Prevention
Delinquent Behavior (1966 1983)   Use Delinquency
Delinquent Identification (1966 1980)   Use Delinquency and Identification
Delinquent Rehabilitation
Delinquent Role (1966 1980)   Use Delinquency
Delinquents (1966 1980)   Use Delinquency

Document Delivery
Delivery Systems
Career Information Delivery Systems   Use Career Information Systems
Delphi Technique
Educational Demand
Demand for Education   Use Educational Demand
Demand Occupations
Supply and Demand
Teacher Supply and Demand
Labor Demands
Senile Dementia Alzheimers Type   Use Alzheimers Disease
Dementia Praecox   Use Schizophrenia
Democracy
Democratic Management   Use Participative Decision Making
Democratic Values
Modulator Demodulators   Use Modems
Demography
City Demography (1966 1980)   Use Urban Demography
National Demography (1966 1980)   Use Demography
School Demography
Urban Demography
Home Demonstration Agents   Use Extension Agents
Demonstration Centers
Demonstration Programs
Demonstration Projects (1966 1980)   Use Demonstration Programs
Demonstrations (Civil)
Demonstrations (Educational)
Public Demonstrations   Use Demonstrations (Civil)
Demonstrations (Science)
Denial (Psychology)
Denominational Colleges   Use Church Related Colleges
Body Density   Use Body Composition
Density (Matter)
Dental Assessment   Use Dental Evaluation
Dental Assistants
Dental Associations (1966 1980)   Use Dentistry and Professional Associations
Dental Clinics
Dental Evaluation
Dental Health
Dental Hygienists
Dental Laboratory Technicians   Use Dental Technicians
Dental School Faculty   Use Dental Schools and Medical School Faculty
Dental Schools
Dental Sciences   Use Dentistry
Dental Students
Dental Surgeons   Use Dentists
Dental Technicians
Dentistry
Schools of Dentistry   Use Dental Schools
Dentists
Deoxyribonucleic Acid   Use DNA
Department Chairpersons   Use Department Heads
Department Directors (School) (1966 1980)   Use Department Heads
Department Heads
Departmental Majors   Use Majors (Students)
Departmental Teaching Plans (1968 1980)   Use Departments
Departmentalization   Use Departments
Departments
Academic Departments   Use Departments
English Departments
Extramural Departments   Use Extension Education
State Departments of Education
Education Departments (School)   Use Schools of Education
Science Departments
Dependability   Use Reliability
Field Dependence   Use Field Dependence Independence
Field Dependence Independence
Alcohol Dependency   Use Alcoholism
Dependency (Drugs)   Use Drug Addiction
Chemical Dependency (Drugs)   Use Drug Addiction
Dependency (Personality)
Dependents
Depleted Resources
Depository Libraries
Economically Depressed Areas   Use Poverty Areas
Depressed Areas (Geographic) (1966 1980)   Use Poverty Areas
Depression (Psychology)
Deprivation   Use Disadvantaged Environment
Perceptual Deprivation   Use Sensory Deprivation
Sensory Deprivation
Deprived   Use Disadvantaged
Deprived Children   Use Disadvantaged Youth
Economically Deprived   Use Economically Disadvantaged
Educationally Deprived   Use Educationally Disadvantaged
Deprived Environment   Use Disadvantaged Environment
Depth Perception
Dermal Sense   Use Tactual Perception
Course Descriptions
Job Descriptions   Use Occupational Information
Program Descriptions
Descriptive Linguistics
Descriptive Writing
Descriptors   Use Subject Index Terms

Desegregated Classes   Use Classroom Desegregation
Desegregated Colleges   Use College Desegregation
Desegregated Schools   Use School Desegregation
Class   Desegregation   Use Classroom Desegregation
Classroom   Desegregation
College   Desegregation
Desegregation (Disabled Students)   Use Mainstreaming
Desegregation Effects
Faculty   Desegregation   Use Faculty Integration
Desegregation Impact   Use Desegregation Effects
Desegregation Litigation
Desegregation Methods
Desegregation Plans
Desegregation Readiness   Use Integration Readiness
Residential   Desegregation   Use Neighborhood Integration
School   Desegregation
Teacher   Desegregation   Use Teacher Integration
Urban   Desegregation   Use Racial Integration
Voluntary   Desegregation
Desensitization
Systematic   Desensitization   Use Desensitization
Design
Computer Aided   Design and Manufacturing   Use Computer Assisted Design and Computer Assisted Manufacturing
Architectural   Design   Use Building Design
Design Build Approach
Building   Design
Classroom   Design
Clothing   Design
Computer Assisted   Design
Computer Display   Design   Use Screen Design (Computers)
Computer Software   Design   Use Computer Software Development
Computer System   Design
Screen   Design (Computers)
Design Construct Method   Use Design Build Approach
Costume   Design   Use Clothing Design
Design Crafts
Curriculum   Design
Database   Design
Decentralized School   Design (1966 1980)   Use Decentralization and Educational Facilities Design
Dress   Design   Use Clothing Design
Educational Facilities   Design
Experimental   Design   Use Research Design
Facility   Design   Use Facility Guidelines
Flexible Lighting   Design
Furniture   Design
Guided   Design
High School   Design (1966 1980)   Use Educational Facilities Design
Instructional   Design
Interior   Design
Job   Design   Use Job Development
Lighting   Design
Modular Building   Design
Design Needs (1968 1980)   Use Design Requirements
Physical   Design Needs (1968 1980)   Use Design Requirements
Psychological   Design Needs (1968 1980)   Use Design Requirements
Park   Design
Design Preferences
Program   Design
Quasiexperimental   Design
Design Requirements
Research   Design
School   Design (1966 1980)   Use Educational Facilities Design
Mechanical   Design Technicians
Test   Design   Use Test Construction
Designers
Evaluation   Designs   Use Evaluation Methods
Social   Desirability
Desktop Computers   Use Microcomputers
Desktop Publishing
Desoxyribonucleic Acid   Use DNA
Despair   Use Depression (Psychology)
Despondency   Use Depression (Psychology)
Destiny Control   Use Self Determination
Self   Destructive Behavior
Early   Detection   Use Early Identification
Handicap   Detection (1966 1980)   Use Disability Identification
Intrusion   Detectors   Use Alarm Systems
Lie   Detectors   Use Polygraphs
Situational   Determinants   Use Context Effect
Determination (Chemical)   Use Chemical Analysis
Chemical   Determination   Use Chemical Analysis
Priority   Determination   Use Needs Assessment
Self   Determination
Determiners (Languages)
Student   Developed Materials
Teacher   Developed Materials
Developed Nations
Developing Institutions
Developing Nations
Development
Adolescent   Development
Adult   Development
Behavior   Development

Career	Development
Child	Development Centers
Research and	Development Centers
Child	Development
Cognitive	Development
	Development Communication
Community	Development
Compensatory	Development Use Compensatory Education
Comprehension	Development (1966 1980) Use Comprehension
Computer Software	Development
Computer System	Development Use Computer System Design
Software	Development (Computers) Use Computer Software Development
Concept	Development Use Concept Formation
Courseware	Development Use Computer Software Development and Courseware
Creative	Development
Curriculum	Development
Economic	Development
Educational	Development
Emotional	Development
Executive	Development Use Management Development
Faculty	Development
Handwriting	Development (1966 1980) Use Handwriting and Writing Skills
High School Academies (Career	Development) Use Career Academies
Human	Development (1966 1980)
Individual	Development
Delayed	Development (Individuals) Use Developmental Delays
Instructional	Development
Instructional Material	Development Use Material Development
Intellectual	Development
Job	Development
Labor Force	Development
Human Resources	Development (Labor) Use Labor Force Development
Language	Development (1966 1980) Use Language Acquisition
Collection	Development (Libraries) Use Library Collection Development
Library	Development
Library Collection	Development
Management	Development
Manpower	Development (1966 1980) Use Labor Force Development
Material	Development
Mental	Development (1966 1980) Use Cognitive Development
Moral	Development
Motor	Development
Organizational	Development
Perceptual	Development
Personal	Development Use Individual Development
Personality	Development
Personnel	Development Use Staff Development
Physical	Development
Posture	Development Use Human Posture
Professional	Development
Program	Development
General Educational	Development Programs Use High School Equivalency Programs
Reading	Development (1966 1980)
Research and	Development
Retarded Speech	Development (1968 1980) Use Delayed Speech
Rural	Development
Professional	Development Schools
Self	Development Use Self Actualization
Site	Development
Skill	Development
Social	Development
Child	Development Specialists
Staff	Development
Stages of	Development Use Developmental Stages
Student	Development
Sustainable	Development
Systems	Development
Talent	Development
Engine	Development Technicians Use Mechanical Design Technicians
Propulsion	Development Technicians Use Mechanical Design Technicians
Textbook	Development Use Textbook Preparation
Verbal	Development
Vocabulary	Development
Vocational	Development (1967 1978) Use Career Development
Writing	Development Use Writing (Composition)
	Developmental Continuity
	Developmental Delays
	Developmental Differences (Age Groups) Use Age Differences and Individual Development
	Developmental Disabilities
	Developmental Guidance (1967 1980) Use Guidance
	Developmental Patterns (Individuals) Use Individual Development
	Developmental Programs
	Developmental Psychology
	Developmental Reading (1966 1980)
	Developmental Stages
	Developmental Studies Programs
	Developmental Tasks
	Developmental Writing Use Basic Writing
	Developmentally Appropriate Practices
	Developmentally Appropriate Programs Use Developmentally Appropriate Practices
	Developmentally Delayed Use Developmental Delays
	Developmentally Inappropriate Education Use Developmentally Appropriate Practices
Socially	Deviant Behavior (1966 1980) Use Antisocial Behavior

```
       Computer Storage  Devices
                Interface  Devices (Computers)   Use Computer Interfaces
                 Memory  Devices (Computers)   Use Computer Storage Devices
               Self Help  Devices (Disabled)   Use Assistive Devices (for Disabled)
               Assistive  Devices (for Disabled)
                  Input  Devices   Use Input Output Devices
           Input Output  Devices
                Literary  Devices
             Mechanical  Devices   Use Mechanical Equipment
                 Output  Devices   Use Input Output Devices
         Semiconductor  Devices
               Stimulus  Devices (1966 1980)
                         Dewey Decimal Classification
  Decimal Classification  (Dewey)   Use Dewey Decimal Classification
                         Diabetes
                         Diachronic Linguistics
                         Diacritical Marking
                         Diagnosis   Use Identification
                         Diagnosis (Clinical)   Use Clinical Diagnosis
                Clinical  Diagnosis
                  Early  Diagnosis   Use Early Identification
                         Diagnosis (Educational)   Use Educational Diagnosis
            Educational  Diagnosis
                Reading  Diagnosis
                         Diagnostic Teaching
                         Diagnostic Tests
               Sentence  Diagraming
                         Diagrams
                         Dial Access Information Systems
                         Dialect Interference   Use Dialects and Interference (Language)
                         Dialect Studies
                         Dialectical Materialism   Use Marxism
                         Dialects
                 Accents  (Dialects)   Use Dialects and Pronunciation
                  Black  Dialects
              Geographic  Dialects   Use Regional Dialects
                  Negro  Dialects (1966 1977)   Use Black Dialects
            Nonstandard  Dialects
               Regional  Dialects
                 Social  Dialects
                         Dialog Journals
                         Dialogs (Language)
                         Dialogs (Literary)
             Man Machine  Dialogs   Use Man Machine Systems
                         Dialogue (1969 1980)   Use Dialogs (Literary)
                         Dialogue Journals   Use Dialog Journals
                         Diaries
        Student Notebooks  (Diaries)   Use Student Journals
                         Dictation
                Machine  Dictation   Use Dictation
                         Dictatorship   Use Totalitarianism
                         Diction
                         Dictionaries
                         Dictionary Catalogs (1968 1980)   Use Library Catalogs
                         Didacticism
                Tool and  Die Makers
                         Diesel Engines
                         Diesel Fuel   Use Diesel Engines and Fuels
                         Diesel Mechanics   Use Auto Mechanics
                         Dietary Technicians   Use Dietitians
                         Dietetic Aides   Use Dietitians
                         Dietetics
            Lysergic Acid  Diethylamide
                         Dietitians
                         Diets   Use Dietetics
                         Differences
                   Age  Differences
           Developmental  Differences (Age Groups)   Use Age Differences and Individual Development
                Cultural  Differences
              Individual  Differences
            Institutional  Differences   Use Differences and Institutional Characteristics
             Intelligence  Differences
              Intermode  Differences
                 Racial  Differences
               Regional  Differences   Use Differences and Regional Characteristics
               Religious  Differences
             Rural Urban  Differences
                   Sex  Differences
                Gender  Differences (Sex)   Use Sex Differences
                 Social  Differences
            Social Class  Differences   Use Social Differences
             Urban Rural  Differences   Use Rural Urban Differences
                         Differential Equations
                         Differential Item Functioning   Use Item Bias
                         Differential Item Performance   Use Item Bias
                         Differential Psychology   Use Individual Psychology
               Semantic  Differential
                 Salary  Differentials (1968 1980)   Use Salary Wage Differentials
            Salary Wage  Differentials
             Wage Salary  Differentials   Use Salary Wage Differentials
                         Differentiated Staffs
               Learning  Difficulties (1966 1980)   Use Learning Problems
                Reading  Difficulties
```

Writing Difficulties
Linguistic Difficulty (Contrastive)   Use Interference (Language)
Linguistic Difficulty (Inherent)
Item Difficulty   Use Difficulty Level and Test Items
Difficulty Level
Reading Difficulty (1966 1980)
Task Difficulty   Use Difficulty Level
Diffusion (1967 1982) (Communication)   Use Diffusion (Communication)
Diffusion (Communication)
Diffusion (1967 1982) (Physics)   Use Diffusion (Physics)
Diffusion (Physics)
Diffusion (1967 1982) (Populations)   Use Population Distribution
Digital Computers
Digital Libraries   Use Electronic Libraries
Digital Optical Data Disks   Use Optical Data Disks
Diglossia
Human Dignity
Individual Dignity   Use Human Dignity
Pupillary Dilation
Novelty (Stimulus Dimension)
Three Dimensional Aids
Dimensional Preference
Dining Facilities
Dinosaurs
Diploma Requirements   Use Graduation Requirements
Diplomacy   Use International Relations
Diplomatic History
Diplomatic Policy   Use Foreign Policy
Foreign Diplomats
Direct Assessment   Use Performance Based Assessment
Self Directed Classrooms (1966 1980)
Self Directed Groups
Self Directed Learning   Use Independent Study
Teacher Directed Practice   Use Teacher Guidance
Directed Reading Activity
Direction Writing (1966 1980)
Directories
Directors   Use Administrators
Audiovisual Directors (1969 1980)   Use Audiovisual Coordinators
Community School Directors (1967 1980)   Use Administrators and Community Schools
Library Directors
Directors of Research   Use Research Directors
Personnel Directors
Research Directors
Department Directors (School) (1966 1980)   Use Department Heads
School Personnel Directors   Use Personnel Directors and School Personnel
Technical Education Directors   Use Vocational Directors
Vocational Directors
Vocational Education Directors   Use Vocational Directors
Women Directors   Use Women Administrators
Disabilities
Academic Accommodations (Disabilities)
Attitudes toward Disabilities
Community Based Instruction (Disabilities)
Developmental Disabilities
Language Disabilities   Use Language Impairments
Learning Disabilities
Low Incidence Disabilities
Mild Disabilities
Multiple Disabilities
Normalization (Disabilities)
Parents with Disabilities
Physical Disabilities
Profound Disabilities   Use Severe Disabilities
Reading Disabilities   Use Reading Difficulties
Severe Disabilities
Specific Learning Disabilities   Use Learning Disabilities
Teachers with Disabilities
Disability Discrimination
Disability Identification
Severity (of Disability)
Disabled   Use Disabilities
Accessibility (for Disabled)
Adaptive Behavior (of Disabled)
Adaptive Equipment (Disabled)   Use Assistive Devices (for Disabled)
Alternative Communication Systems (Disabled)   Use Augmentative and Alternative Communication
Assistive Devices (for Disabled)
Barrier Free Environment (for Disabled)   Use Accessibility (for Disabled)
Communication Aids (for Disabled)
Deinstitutionalization (of Disabled)
Accommodations for Disabled (Educational Settings)   Use Academic Accommodations (Disabilities)
Gifted Disabled
Least Restrictive Environment (Disabled)   Use Mainstreaming
Disabled Parents   Use Parents with Disabilities
Self Help Devices (Disabled)   Use Assistive Devices (for Disabled)
Desegregation (Disabled Students)   Use Mainstreaming
Integration (Disabled Students)   Use Mainstreaming
Disabled Teachers   Use Teachers with Disabilities
Disadvantaged
Academically Disadvantaged   Use Educationally Disadvantaged
Disadvantaged Children   Use Disadvantaged Youth
Culturally Disadvantaged (1966 1980)   Use Disadvantaged
Economically Disadvantaged

Educationally Disadvantaged
Disadvantaged Environment
Gifted Disadvantaged
Disadvantaged Groups (1966 1980)   Use Disadvantaged
Disadvantaged Schools
Socially Disadvantaged (1966 1980)   Use Disadvantaged
Disadvantaged Youth
Disadvantagement   Use Disadvantaged Environment
Cultural Disadvantagement (1966 1980)   Use Disadvantaged
Economic Disadvantagement (1966 1980)   Use Poverty
Educational Disadvantagement (1966 1980)   Use Educationally Disadvantaged
Social Disadvantagement (1966 1980)   Use Disadvantaged
Disarmament
Multilateral Disarmament   Use Disarmament
Unilateral Disarmament   Use Disarmament
Disaster Readiness   Use Emergency Programs
Natural Disasters
Disbursements (Money)   Use Expenditures
Personnel Discharge   Use Dismissal (Personnel)
Disciplinary Action   Use Discipline
Discipline
Discipline Based Art Education
Classroom Discipline   Use Classroom Techniques and Discipline
Discipline Policy
Discipline Problems
Self Discipline   Use Self Control
Teacher Discipline
Academic Disciplines   Use Intellectual Disciplines
Intellectual Disciplines
Subject Disciplines   Use Intellectual Disciplines
Disclosure
Self Disclosure (Individuals)
Public Disclosure   Use Disclosure
Discographies
Program Discontinuance   Use Program Termination
Academic Discourse
Discourse Analysis
Discourse Communities
Academic Discourse Communities   Use Academic Discourse and Discourse Communities
Connected Discourse
Discourse Modes
Outlining (Discourse)
Persuasive Discourse
Discovery   Use Discovery Processes
Discovery Learning
Discovery Processes
Discriminant Analysis
Multiple Discriminant Analysis   Use Discriminant Analysis
Discriminant Function Analysis   Use Discriminant Analysis
Age Discrimination
Auditory Discrimination
Disability Discrimination
Educational Discrimination
Employment Discrimination   Use Equal Opportunities (Jobs)
Ethnic Discrimination
Gender Discrimination   Use Sex Discrimination
Handicap Discrimination (1984 1994)   Use Disability Discrimination
Housing Discrimination
Job Discrimination   Use Equal Opportunities (Jobs)
Discrimination Learning
Anti Discrimination Legislation   Use Civil Rights Legislation
Legislative Discrimination   Use Discriminatory Legislation
Literary Discrimination (1966 1980)
Racial Discrimination
Religious Discrimination
Reverse Discrimination
Sex Discrimination
Discrimination (Social)   Use Social Discrimination
Social Discrimination
Discrimination Transfer   Use Shift Studies
Visual Discrimination
Discriminatory Analysis   Use Discriminant Analysis
Discriminatory Attitudes (Social) (1966 1980)   Use Social Bias
Discriminatory Legislation
Discussion
Class Discussion   Use Discussion (Teaching Technique)
Discussion Experience (1966 1980)   Use Discussion
Group Discussion
Discussion Groups
Discussion Guides   Use Discussion (Teaching Technique) and Teaching Guides
Electronic Discussion Lists   Use Listservs
Internet Discussion Lists   Use Listservs
Discussion Programs (1966 1980)   Use Discussion
Discussion (Teaching Technique)
AIDS (Disease)   Use Acquired Immune Deficiency Syndrome
Alzheimers Disease
Disease Control
Disease Incidence
Middle Ear Disease   Use Otitis Media
Disease Rate (1967 1980)   Use Disease Incidence
Diseases
Communicable Diseases
Contagious Diseases   Use Communicable Diseases

```
           Infectious  Diseases (1966 1974)   Use Communicable Diseases
         Occupational  Diseases
                Plant  Diseases   Use Plant Pathology
         Psychosomatic  Diseases (1968 1980)   Use Psychosomatic Disorders
             Venereal  Diseases
                       Disemployment   Use Dislocated Workers
                       Dishonesty   Use Honesty
                       Dishwashing
                       Disk Drives
                       Diskettes   Use Floppy Disks
              Compact  Disks   Use Optical Disks
   Digital Optical Data  Disks   Use Optical Data Disks
             Flexible  Disks   Use Floppy Disks
               Floppy  Disks
                Laser  Disks   Use Optical Disks
             Magnetic  Disks
              Optical  Disks
         Optical Data  Disks
                       Dislocated Workers
                       Dismissal (Personnel)
            Personnel  Dismissal   Use Dismissal (Personnel)
              Teacher  Dismissal
                Civil  Disobedience
   Posttraumatic Stress  Disorder
             Appetite  Disorders   Use Eating Disorders
     Attention Deficit  Disorders
             Behavior  Disorders
        Communication  Disorders
               Eating  Disorders
                Heart  Disorders
               Mental  Disorders
         Psychosomatic  Disorders
  Symptoms (Individual  Disorders)
                Voice  Disorders
                       Displaced Homemakers
                       Displaced Workers   Use Dislocated Workers
                       Display Aids
             Computer  Display Design   Use Screen Design (Computers)
                       Display Layout (Computers)   Use Screen Design (Computers)
                       Display Panels (1968 1980)   Use Display Aids
                       Display Systems
                Video  Display Terminals
               Visual  Display Units   Use Video Display Terminals
             Computer  Displays   Use Display Systems
              Screens  (Displays)
                Waste  Disposal
                       Disposition (Individuals)   Use Personality
                       Dispositional Characteristics   Use Personality Traits
    Agricultural Labor  Disputes (1966 1980)   Use Labor Demands
                       Disqualification
                       Dissection
                 Data  Dissemination   Use Information Dissemination
          Information  Dissemination
            Selective  Dissemination of Information
                       Dissent
             Doctoral  Dissertations
            Cognitive  Dissonance
                       Distance
                       Distance Education
                Range  (Distance)   Use Distance
           Conceptual  Distinctions   Use Concept Formation
                       Distinctive Features (1967 1980)   Use Distinctive Features (Language)
                       Distinctive Features (Language)
                       Distractors (Tests)
                       Distribution (Economics)   Use Marketing
               Ethnic  Distribution
                       Distribution Free Statistics   Use Nonparametric Statistics
           Geographic  Distribution
           Population  Distribution
               Racial  Distribution
               Social  Distribution
              Student  Distribution (1966 1980)
              Teacher  Distribution
            Frequency  Distributions   Use Statistical Distributions
           Statistical  Distributions
                       Distributions (Statistics)   Use Statistical Distributions
                       Distributive Education
                       Distributive Education Teachers
               School  District Autonomy
                       District Libraries   Use Regional Libraries
  Nonresident Students (1967 1980) (Out of  District)   Use Residence Requirements
                       District Norms   Use Local Norms
               School  District Norms   Use Local Norms
               School  District Policy   Use Board of Education Policy
         State School  District Relationship
               School  District Reorganization
  Resident Students (1967 1980) (in  District)   Use Residence Requirements
               School  District Size
               School  District Spending
               School  District Wealth
        Comprehensive  Districts (1967 1980)   Use School Districts
         County School  Districts
   Intermediate School  Districts   Use Intermediate Administrative Units
```

Intermediate Service	Districts Use Intermediate Administrative Units
Multicampus	Districts
Rezoning	Districts Use Rezoning
School	Districts
Emotional	Disturbances
Emotionally	Disturbed Children (1967 1980) Use Emotional Disturbances
Emotionally	Disturbed (1966 1980) Use Emotional Disturbances
	Divergent Thinking
Biological	Diversity Use Biodiversity
	Diversity (Biology) Use Biodiversity
	Diversity (Cultural) as a Value Use Cultural Pluralism
	Diversity (Cultural) as an Observation or a Fact Use Cultural Differences
	Diversity (Faculty)
Genetic	Diversity Use Biodiversity
	Diversity (Institutional)
	Diversity (Student)
	Divided Catalogs (1968 1980) Use Library Catalogs
Room	Dividers Use Space Dividers
Space	Dividers
	Diving
Deep Sea	Diving Use Underwater Diving
Platform	Diving Use Diving
Scuba	Diving Use Underwater Diving
Skin	Diving Use Underwater Diving
Springboard	Diving Use Diving
Tower	Diving Use Diving
Underwater	Diving
	Division
Upper	Division Colleges
Semester	Division (1966 1980) Use Semester System
Physical	Divisions (Geographic)
Political	Divisions (Geographic)
Grades (Program	Divisions) Use Instructional Program Divisions
Instructional Program	Divisions
	Divorce
	Divorced Persons Use Divorce
	DNA
Recombinant	DNA Use DNA and Genetic Engineering
	Doctor of Arts Degrees
	Doctor Patient Relationship Use Physician Patient Relationship
	Doctoral Degrees
	Doctoral Dissertations
Post	Doctoral Education (1967 1980) Use Postdoctoral Education
	Doctoral Programs
	Doctoral Theses (1967 1980) Use Doctoral Dissertations
Medical	Doctors Use Physicians
Court	Doctrine
	Document Delivery
	Document Readers Use Optical Scanners
	Documentaries
	Documentation
Computer Program	Documentation Use Computer Software
Government	Documents Use Government Publications
Public	Documents Use Government Publications
	Dogmatism
	Domestic Violence (Family) Use Family Violence
	Domestics (1970 1980) Use Household Workers
Cerebral	Dominance (1967 1986) Use Brain Hemisphere Functions
Language	Dominance
Lateral	Dominance
	Dominican Americans Use Dominicans and Hispanic Americans
	Dominicans
	Donors
Blood	Donors Use Tissue Donors
Financial	Donors Use Donors
Organ	Donors Use Tissue Donors
Sperm	Donors Use Tissue Donors
Tissue	Donors
	Doors
	Dormitories
	Dormitory Living Use Dormitories and Group Experience
	Double Employment Use Multiple Employment
	Double Sessions
	Downloading
	Downs Anomaly Use Downs Syndrome
	Downs Syndrome
Drawing (Precision	Draft) Use Drafting
	Drafters (1980 1981) Use Drafting
	Drafting
Architectural	Drafting
Computer Assisted	Drafting Use Computer Assisted Design and Drafting
Modular	Drafting Use Modular Building Design
	Draftsmen (1968 1980) Use Drafting
Brain	Drain
	Drama
Folk	Drama (1969 1980) Use Drama and Folk Culture
Outdoor	Drama (1968 1980) Use Drama and Outdoor Activities
	Drama Workshops
	Dramatic Arts Use Dramatics
	Dramatic Play
	Dramatic Unities (1970 1980) Use Drama
	Dramatics
Creative	Dramatics

```
                        Dravidian Languages
                        Drawing (Computerized)   Use Computer Graphics
            Engineering Drawing
                        Drawing (Freehand)   Use Freehand Drawing
               Freehand Drawing
             Mechanical Drawing   Use Engineering Drawing
                        Drawing (Precision Draft)   Use Drafting
            Raised Line Drawings
               American Dream
                        Dreams
                        Dress Codes
                        Dress Design   Use Clothing Design
                        Drill Press Operators   Use Machine Tool Operators
                        Drill Presses   Use Machine Tools
                Pattern Drills (Language)
                        Drills (Practice)
           Substitution Drills
                        Drinking
                        Drinking Drivers   Use Driving While Intoxicated
                Problem Drinking   Use Alcohol Abuse
                 Social Drinking   Use Drinking
                        Drinking Water
                   Menu Driven Software
                        Driver Education
                        Driver Training   Use Driver Education
                    Bus Drivers
               Drinking Drivers   Use Driving While Intoxicated
             School Bus Drivers   Use Bus Drivers and School Buses
                   Disk Drives
                        Driveways
                  Drunk Driving   Use Driving While Intoxicated
                        Driving While Intoxicated
                        Dropout Attitudes
                        Dropout Characteristics
                        Dropout Employment   Use Dropout Programs
                        Dropout Identification (1966 1980)   Use Dropout Characteristics
                        Dropout Prevention
                        Dropout Problems (1966 1980)   Use Dropouts
                        Dropout Programs
                        Dropout Rate
                        Dropout Rehabilitation (1966 1980)   Use Dropout Programs
                        Dropout Research
                        Dropout Role (1966 1980)   Use Dropouts
                        Dropout Teaching (1966 1980)   Use Dropout Programs
                        Dropouts
                  Adult Dropouts
                College Dropouts   Use Dropouts
            High School Dropouts   Use Dropouts
              Potential Dropouts
                  Rural Dropouts (1966 1981)   Use Dropouts
                 School Dropouts   Use Dropouts
                  Urban Dropouts (1966 1981)   Use Dropouts
                        Drought
                        Drowsiness   Use Sleep
                        Drug Abuse
                        Drug Addiction
                        Drug Education
                  Fetal Drug Exposure   Use Prenatal Drug Exposure
                        Drug Exposure in Utero   Use Prenatal Drug Exposure
               Prenatal Drug Exposure
                        Drug Inspectors   Use Food and Drug Inspectors
               Food and Drug Inspectors
                        Drug Legislation
                        Drug Rehabilitation
                        Drug Testing (Presence in Body)   Use Drug Use Testing
                        Drug Therapy
                        Drug Use
                Illegal Drug Use
                        Drug Use Testing
                        Drug Withdrawal   Use Drug Rehabilitation
                        Druggists   Use Pharmacists
    Chemical Dependency (Drugs)   Use Drug Addiction
            Dependency (Drugs)   Use Drug Addiction
   Prenatal Exposure to Drugs   Use Prenatal Drug Exposure
           Tranquilizing Drugs   Use Sedatives
             Withdrawal (Drugs)   Use Drug Rehabilitation
                        Drunk Driving   Use Driving While Intoxicated
                        Drunkenness (Alcohol)   Use Alcohol Abuse
                        Drycleaning Laundry Occupations   Use Laundry Drycleaning Occupations
                Laundry Drycleaning Occupations
                        Dual Career Family
                        Dual Earner Parents   Use Employed Parents
                        Dual Enrollment
                        Due Process
             Procedural Due Process   Use Due Process
                        Dues   Use Fees
                        Duplicating   Use Reprography
                        Dusun
                        Dutch
                        Dutch Culture
       Extrainstructional Duties   Use Noninstructional Responsibility
           Extrateaching Duties   Use Noninstructional Responsibility
             Nonteaching Duties   Use Noninstructional Responsibility
```

Dwellings   Use Housing
Dyadic Communication   Use Interpersonal Communication
Group Dynamics
Minimal Brain Dysfunction
Dyslexia
Dysphasia   Use Aphasia
Dysphonia   Use Voice Disorders
Dysphoria   Use Depression (Psychology)
Dysthymia   Use Depression (Psychology)
Dyula
R D and E   Use Research and Development
E Zines   Use Electronic Journals
Middle Ear Disease   Use Otitis Media
Ear Infections (Middle Ear)   Use Otitis Media
Ear Infections (Middle Ear)   Use Otitis Media
Early Admission
Early Adolescence   Use Early Adolescents
Early Adolescents
Early Childhood (1966 1980)   Use Young Children
Early Childhood Education
Early Detection   Use Early Identification
Early Diagnosis   Use Early Identification
Early Experience
Early Identification
Early Intervention
Early Literacy   Use Emergent Literacy
Early Parenthood
Early Reading
Early Retirement
Early School Leavers   Use Dropouts
Dual Earner Parents   Use Employed Parents
Ears
Earth Science
Earthquakes
Eastern Civilization   Use Non Western Civilization
Middle Eastern History
Near Eastern History   Use Middle Eastern History
Middle Eastern Studies
Eating Disorders
Eating Habits
Ebonics   Use Black Dialects
Echolalia
Echolocation
Echophasia   Use Echolalia
Ecological Factors
Ecology
Econometrics
Economic Analysis   Use Economic Research
Economic Change
Economic Climate
Economic Cycles   Use Business Cycles
Economic Development
Economic Disadvantagement (1966 1980)   Use Poverty
Economic Education (1971 1980)   Use Economics Education
Economic Effects   Use Economic Impact
Economic Factors
Economic Fluctuations   Use Business Cycles
Economic Geography   Use Human Geography
Economic Impact
Economic Influences   Use Economic Factors
Economic Insecurity   Use Poverty
Economic Opportunities
Economic Plight   Use Poverty
Economic Progress
Economic Research
Economic Status
Economic Support   Use Financial Support
Economically Advanced Nations   Use Developed Nations
Economically Advantaged   Use Advantaged
Economically Depressed Areas   Use Poverty Areas
Economically Deprived   Use Economically Disadvantaged
Economically Disadvantaged
Economics
Consumer Economics
Economics Curriculum   Use Economics Education
Distribution (Economics)   Use Marketing
Economics Education
Home Economics Education
Educational Economics
Family Economics   Use Consumer Economics
Home Economics
Inflation (Economics)
Economics Instruction   Use Economics Education
Labor Economics
Occupational Home Economics
Economics of Education   Use Educational Economics
Rural Economics
Home Economics Skills
Home Economics Teachers
Economy   Use Economics
Laissez Faire Economy   Use Free Enterprise System
Market Economy   Use Free Enterprise System
Token Economy

Ecosystems   Use Ecology
Editing
Text   Editing   Use Word Processing
Editorials
Editors
Text   Editors   Use Computer Software and Word Processing
Educable Mentally Handicapped (1966 1980)   Use Mild Mental Retardation
Education
Academic   Education
Acceleration (1966 1982)   (Education)   Use Acceleration (Education)
Acceleration   (Education)
Access to   Education
Adapted Physical   Education
Administrator   Education
Admission Tests (Higher   Education)   Use College Entrance Examinations
Adult   Education
Adult Basic   Education
Adult Farmer   Education
Adult Vocational   Education
Fundamental   Education (Adults)   Use Adult Basic Education
Advanced   Education   Use Higher Education
Adventure   Education
Aerospace   Education
Aerospace Science   Education   Use Aerospace Education
Aesthetic   Education
Affective   Education   Use Humanistic Education
After School   Education
Local   Education Agencies   Use School Districts
State   Education Agencies   Use State Departments of Education
Aging   Education
Agricultural   Education
Alcohol   Education
Allied Health   Education   Use Allied Health Occupations Education
Allied Health Occupations   Education
Alternative   Education   Use Nontraditional Education
Alumni   Education
American Indian   Education
Education and Work   Use Education Work Relationship
Architectural   Education
Art   Education
Articulation   (Education)
Higher   Education as a Field of Study   Use Postsecondary Education as a Field of Study
Postsecondary   Education as a Field of Study
Audiovisual   Education   Use Audiovisual Instruction
Local   Education Authorities   Use School Districts
Aviation   Education
Basic Business   Education
Beginning Farmer   Education   Use Young Farmer Education
Bicultural   Education   Use Multicultural Education
Bilingual   Education
Black   Education
Boards of   Education
Business   Education
Business Administration   Education
Career   Education
Case Studies   (Education) (1966 1980)   Use Case Studies
Continuing   Education Centers
Teacher   Education Centers   Use Teacher Centers
Chancellors   (Education)   Use College Presidents
Citizenship   Education
Clinical Professors (1967 1980)   (Education)   Use Student Teacher Supervisors
Clinical Schools (Teacher   Education)   Use Professional Development Schools
Collaboratives   (Education)   Use Partnerships in Education
Colleges of   Education   Use Schools of Education
Commercial   Education   Use Business Education
Community   Education
Community Based   Education   Use Community Education
Comparative   Education
Compensatory   Education
Competency Based   Education
Competency Based Teacher   Education
Comprehensive School Health   Education
Compulsory   Education
Computer Science   Education
Computer Uses in   Education
Confluent   Education   Use Humanistic Education
Consequence Based   Education   Use Competency Based Education
Consequence Based Teacher   Education   Use Competency Based Teacher Education
Conservation   Education
Constructionism   (Education)   Use Constructivism (Learning)
Consumer   Education
Continuation   Education (1968 1980)
Continuing   Education
Continuity of   Education   Use Developmental Continuity
Special Education Regular   Education Cooperation   Use Regular and Special Education Relationship
Cooperative   Education
Corporate   Education
Correctional   Education
Counselor   Education   Use Counselor Training
Education Courses
Criterion Referenced   Education   Use Competency Based Education
Criterion Referenced Teacher   Education   Use Competency Based Teacher Education
Cross Categorical   Education   Use Noncategorical Education

```
                        Cultural   Education
          Culturally Appropriate   Education    Use Culturally Relevant Education
             Culturally Relevant   Education
           Culturally Responsive   Education    Use Culturally Relevant Education
                        Teacher    Education Curriculum
                          Dance    Education
                           Deaf    Education (1968 1980)    Use Deafness
                          Death    Education    Use Death
                   Specialist in   Education Degrees
                    Demand for     Education    Use Educational Demand
                                   Education Departments (School)    Use Schools of Education
     Developmentally Inappropriate  Education    Use Developmentally Appropriate Practices
                       Technical    Education Directors    Use Vocational Directors
                      Vocational    Education Directors    Use Vocational Directors
            Discipline Based Art    Education
                       Distance    Education
                    Distributive    Education
                         Driver    Education
                           Drug    Education
                Early Childhood    Education
                       Economic    Education (1971 1980)    Use Economics Education
                      Economics    Education
                   Economics of    Education    Use Educational Economics
                     Elementary    Education
            Elementary Secondary    Education
                         Energy    Education
                    Engineering    Education
                        English    Education (1967 1980)
                 English Teacher   Education
                  Environmental    Education
                          Equal    Education
                     Equality of   Education    Use Equal Education
                   Excellence in   Education
                Exceptional Child  Education (1968 1980)
                Experience Based   Education    Use Experiential Learning
 Extended Degree Programs (Teacher Education)    Use Extended Teacher Education Programs
                       Extension   Education
                       Business    Education Facilities
                       Physical    Education Facilities
                   Family Choice   (Education)    Use School Choice
                    Family Life    Education
                   Fire Science    Education
                   Fiscal Equity   (Education)    Use Educational Equity (Finance)
                    Fluid Power    Education (1967 1980)    Use Fluid Mechanics
                  Foundations of   Education
                           Free    Education
                        Further    Education    Use Adult Education
                        General    Education
                General Business   Education    Use Basic Business Education
                         Global    Education
                 Global Studies    Education    Use Global Education
                       Graduate    Education    Use Graduate Study
               Graduate Medical    Education
                         Health    Education
              Health Occupations   Education (1967 1980)    Use Allied Health Occupations Education
                       Heritage    Education
                         Higher    Education
                        History    Education    Use History Instruction
                     History of    Education    Use Educational History
                        Science    Education History
            Home and Family Life   Education    Use Family Life Education
                Home Economics     Education
                    Homemaking     Education (1967 1980)    Use Home Economics
                     Humanistic    Education
                      Inclusion    (Education)    Use Inclusive Schools
                      Inclusive    Education    Use Inclusive Schools
                  Individualized    Education    Use Individualized Instruction
                      Industrial   Education
             Industrial Technology Education    Use Technology Education
                        Informal   Education
            Information Science    Education
                     Inner City    Education    Use Urban Education
                       Inservice   Education
              Inservice Teacher    Education
                         Higher    Education Institutions    Use Colleges
                     Integrated    Education    Use Integrated Curriculum
                   Intercultural   Education    Use Multicultural Education
               Special Regular    Education Interface    Use Regular and Special Education Relationship
                      Intergroup   Education
                 International     Education
                     Journalism    Education
                        Teacher    Education Knowledge Base    Use Knowledge Base for Teaching
                          Labor    Education
                    Law Related    Education
                     Law School    Education    Use Legal Education (Professions)
                          Legal    Education (1977 1986)
                        Leisure    Education
                        Liberal    Education    Use General Education
                        Library    Education
                      Life Span    Education    Use Lifelong Learning
                       Lifelong    Education    Use Lifelong Learning
                        Literacy    Education
                                   Education Majors
```

Management	Education (1967 1980)	Use Administrator Education
Mandatory	Education	Use Compulsory Education
Mandatory Continuing	Education	
Marine	Education	
Marine Science	Education	Use Marine Education
Maritime	Education	
Mathematics	Education	
Medical	Education	
Board of	Education Members	Use Boards of Education
Mexican American	Education	
Migrant	Education	
Migrant Adult	Education	
Migrant Child	Education (1967 1980)	Use Migrant Education
Movement	Education	
Multicultural	Education	
Multiethnic	Education	Use Multicultural Education
Music	Education	
Negro	Education (1966 1977)	Use Black Education
Noncategorical	Education	
Nondiscriminatory	Education	
Nonformal	Education	
Nonpublic	Education	Use Private Education
Nontraditional	Education	
Nursing	Education	
Off Campus	Education	Use Extension Education
Office	Education	Use Office Occupations Education
Office Occupations	Education	
Open	Education	
Outcome Based	Education	
Outcomes Based	Education	Use Outcome Based Education
Outcomes of	Education	
Outdoor	Education	
Output Oriented	Education	Use Competency Based Education
Output Oriented Teacher	Education	Use Competency Based Teacher Education
Paralegal	Education	Use Legal Assistants and Legal Education (Professions)
Parent	Education	
Parenthood	Education	
Partnerships in	Education	
Patient	Education	
Peoples	Education	Use Popular Education
Performance Based	Education (1974 1980)	Use Competency Based Education
Performance Based Teacher	Education (1972 1980)	Use Competency Based Teacher Education
Permanent	Education	Use Lifelong Learning
	Education Permanente	Use Lifelong Learning
Pharmaceutical	Education	
Physical	Education	
Police	Education	
Board of	Education Policy	
Politics of	Education	
Popular	Education	
Population	Education	
Post Doctoral	Education (1967 1980)	Use Postdoctoral Education
Post High School	Education	Use Postsecondary Education
Post Secondary	Education (1967 1978)	Use Postsecondary Education
Postdoctoral	Education	
Postsecondary	Education	
Preretirement	Education	
Preschool	Education	
Preservice	Education (1966 1980)	Use Preservice Teacher Education
Preservice Teacher	Education	
Prevocational	Education	
Primary	Education	
Prison	Education	Use Correctional Education
Private	Education	
Private Higher	Education	Use Higher Education and Private Education
Process	Education	
Professional	Education	
Professional Continuing	Education	
Legal	Education (Professions)	
Proficiency Based	Education	Use Competency Based Education
Proficiency Based Teacher	Education	Use Competency Based Teacher Education
Adult	Education Programs (1966 1980)	Use Adult Education and Adult Programs
Bilingual	Education Programs	
Compensatory	Education Programs (1966 1980)	Use Compensatory Education
Extended Teacher	Education Programs	
Individualized	Education Programs	
Inservice	Education Programs	Use Inservice Education
Remedial	Education Programs	Use Remedial Programs
Teacher	Education Programs	
Work	Education Programs	Use Work Study Programs
Progressive	Education	
Partners in	Education Projects	Use Partnerships in Education
Psychological	Education	Use Humanistic Education
Public	Education	
Public Administration	Education	
Public Affairs	Education	
Public Higher	Education	Use Higher Education and Public Education
Public School Adult	Education	
Quality	Education	Use Educational Quality
Recurrent	Education	Use Lifelong Learning
Special	Education Regular Education Cooperation	Use Regular and Special Education Relationship
General and Special	Education Relationship	Use Regular and Special Education Relationship
Regular and Special	Education Relationship	

Special and Regular Education Relationship   Use Regular and Special Education Relationship
              Work Education Relationship   Use Education Work Relationship
          Relevance (Education)
          Religious Education
           Remedial Education   Use Remedial Instruction
Research Specialists (Education)   Use Educational Researchers
       Results Based Education   Use Outcome Based Education
         Results of Education   Use Outcomes of Education
                     Education Role   Use Role of Education
           Board of Education Role
            Role of Education
              Rural Education
             Safety Education
          Schools of Education
            Science Education
             Screen Education   Use Film Study
          Secondary Education
            Service Education (1966 1980)   Use Vocational Education
                     Education Service Centers
                Sex Education
         Shared Time (Education)   Use Dual Enrollment
        Sociology of Education   Use Educational Sociology
            Special Education
             Speech Education (1966 1980)
     State Boards of Education
  State Committees on Education   Use State Boards of Education
State Departments of Education
      Supplementary Education
          Supply of Education   Use Educational Supply
         Tax Equity (Education)   Use Educational Equity (Finance)
            Teacher Education
    Teacher Educator Education
           Business Education Teachers
        Distributive Education Teachers
           Physical Education Teachers
            Special Education Teachers
         Vocational Education Teachers
          Technical Education
       Technological Education   Use Technology Education
         Technology Education
           Terminal Education
            Tertiary Education   Use Postsecondary Education
        Theological Education
        Track System (Education)
Trade and Industrial Education
   Tribally Controlled Education
      Undergraduate Education   Use Undergraduate Study
         Continuing Education Units
          Universal Education (1968 1976)   Use Equal Education
              Urban Education
             Values Education
           Veterans Education
  Veterinary Medical Education
         Vocational Education
        Agricultural Education (Vocational)   Use Agricultural Education and Vocational Education
 Vocational Business Education   Use Business Education
  Health Occupations Education (Vocational)   Use Allied Health Occupations Education and Vocational Education
 Vocational Industrial Education   Use Trade and Industrial Education
                     Education Vouchers (1971 1980)   Use Educational Vouchers
         Withdrawal (Education)
            Womens Education
           Work and Education   Use Education Work Relationship
                     Education Work Relationship
            Workers Education   Use Labor Education
       World Studies Education   Use Global Education
       Young Farmer Education
                     Educational Access   Use Access to Education
                     Educational Accountability (1970 1980)   Use Accountability
                     Educational Achievement   Use Academic Achievement
                     Educational Administration
                     Educational Advantages   Use Educational Opportunities
                     Educational Alternatives (1974 1980)   Use Nontraditional Education
                     Educational Anthropology
                     Educational Assessment
                     Educational Attainment
                     Educational Attitudes
                     Educational Background
                     Educational Benefits
      Supplementary Educational Centers (1966 1980)   Use Education Service Centers and Supplementary Education
                     Educational Certificates
                     Educational Change
                     Educational Choice   Use School Choice
                     Educational Complexes
                     Educational Computing   Use Computer Uses in Education
                     Educational Cooperation
                     Educational Coordination (1967 1980)   Use Coordination and Educational Cooperation
                     Educational Counseling
                     Educational Demand
      Demonstrations (Educational)
                     Educational Development
            General Educational Development Programs   Use High School Equivalency Programs
                     Educational Diagnosis
          Diagnosis (Educational)   Use Educational Diagnosis

Educational Disadvantagement (1966 1980)   Use Educationally Disadvantaged
Educational Discrimination
Educational Economics
Educational Endowments   Use Endowment Funds
Educational Environment
Educational Equality (1966 1976)   Use Equal Education
Educational Equipment
Educational Equity (Finance)
Educational Equity (Opportunities)   Use Equal Education
Educational Excellence   Use Educational Quality
Educational Excellence Movement (United States)   Use Excellence in Education
International   Educational Exchange
Educational Experience
Educational Experiments
Educational Facilities
Educational Facilities Design
Educational Facilities Improvement
Educational Facilities Planning
Educational Finance
Equity   (Educational Finance)   Use Educational Equity (Finance)
Educational Foundations   Use Philanthropic Foundations
Educational Futures   Use Educational Trends and Futures (of Society)
Educational Games
Educational Gerontology
Educational Goals   Use Educational Objectives
Educational Goals of Students   Use Student Educational Objectives
Educational Guidance (1966 1977)   Use Educational Counseling
Educational History
Educational Improvement
Educational Inequality   Use Equal Education
Educational Innovation
Educational Institutions   Use Schools
Educational Interest (1967 1980)   Use Student Educational Objectives
Educational Legislation
Educational Level   Use Academic Achievement
Educational Malpractice
Educational Management   Use Educational Administration
Educational Materials   Use Instructional Materials
Educational Media
Educational Media Adaptation   Use Media Adaptation
Educational Media Selection   Use Media Selection
Educational Methods
Educational Mobility
Educational Needs
Educational Objectives
Educational Objectives of Students   Use Student Educational Objectives
Student   Educational Objectives
Educational Opportunities
Equal   Educational Opportunities   Use Equal Education
Equity   (Educational Opportunities)   Use Equal Education
Educational Outcomes   Use Outcomes of Education
Educational Parks
Educational Partnerships   Use Partnerships in Education
Educational Philosophy
Educational Planning
Educational Plans   Use Educational Planning
Educational Policy
Educational Politics   Use Politics of Education
Educational Practice (1967 1980)   Use Educational Practices
Educational Practices
Educational Principles
Educational Problems (1966 1980)
Educational Processes   Use Learning Processes
Educational Production Functions   Use Productivity
Educational Programs (1966 1980)
Nonschool   Educational Programs
Educational Psychology
Educational Purposes   Use Educational Objectives
Educational Quality
Educational Quality Assessment   Use Educational Assessment and Educational Quality
Educational Radio
Educational Reform   Use Educational Change
Educational Relevance   Use Relevance (Education)
Educational Research
Educational Researchers
Educational Resources
Educational Responsibility
Educational Retardation (1966 1980)
Educational Service Centers   Use Education Service Centers
Mobile   Educational Services
Accommodations for Disabled   (Educational Settings)   Use Academic Accommodations (Disabilities)
Educational Sociology
Educational Specifications (1967 1980)
Educational Status Comparison
Educational Strategies
Educational Supply
Educational Support   Use Educational Finance
Educational Surveys   Use School Surveys
Educational Technology
Educational Television
Educational Testing
Educational Theories
Educational Therapy

Educational Trends
Educational Vouchers
Educationally Deprived   Use Educationally Disadvantaged
Educationally Disadvantaged
Educationese   Use Jargon
Teacher   Educator Education
Adult   Educators
Catholic   Educators
Counselor   Educators
Physical   Educators   Use Physical Education Teachers
Teacher   Educators
EEG   Use Electroencephalography
Butterfly   Effect   Use Chaos Theory
Context   Effect
Greenhouse   Effect
Magnitude of   Effect   Use Effect Size
Primacy   Effect
Pygmalion   Effect   Use Self Fulfilling Prophecies
Effect Size
Effective Schooling   Use School Effectiveness
Instructionally   Effective Schools   Use School Effectiveness
Effective Schools Research
Effective Teaching (1966 1980)   Use Teacher Effectiveness
Administrator   Effectiveness
Cost   Effectiveness Analysis   Use Cost Effectiveness
Cost   Effectiveness
Counseling   Effectiveness
Instructional   Effectiveness
Organizational   Effectiveness
Program   Effectiveness
School   Effectiveness
Teacher   Effectiveness
Biochemical   Effects   Use Biochemistry
Contextual   Effects   Use Context Effect
Day Care   Effects
Desegregation   Effects
. Economic   Effects   Use Economic Impact
Integration   Effects (1966 1980)   Use Desegregation Effects
Mass Media   Effects
Radiation   Effects
Regression   Effects   Use Regression (Statistics)
Sound   Effects
Special   Effects
Efficacy Expectation   Use Self Efficacy
Self   Efficacy
Efficiency
Community   Effort   Use Community Action
Tax   Effort
EFL   Use English (Second Language)
Egg Inspectors   Use Food and Drug Inspectors
Ego   Use Self Concept
Egocentrism
Egotism   Use Egocentrism
Eidetic Imagery
Eidetic Images (1967 1980)   Use Eidetic Imagery
Eight Millimeter Projectors (1970 1980)   Use Projection Equipment
Eighteenth Century Literature
Elder Abuse
Elderly   Use Older Adults
Abused   Elderly   Use Elder Abuse
Frail   Elderly
Eldest Siblings   Use First Born
Elected City Officials   Use City Officials
Election Campaigns   Use Political Campaigns
Elections
School Budget   Elections
Presidential   Elections (United States)   Use Elections and Presidential Campaigns (United States)
Elective Courses
Elective Reading (1966 1980)
Elective Subjects (1966 1977)   Use Elective Courses
Electric Batteries
Batteries   (Electric)   Use Electric Batteries
Electric Circuits
Electric Motors
Electric Systems   Use Electrical Systems
Electric Utilities   Use Utilities
Electrical Appliance Servicemen (1968 1980)   Use Appliance Repair
Electrical Appliances
Electrical Controls   Use Electronic Control
Electrical Occupations
Electrical Stimuli
Electrical Systems
Electrical Technicians   Use Electronic Technicians
Electricians
Electricity
Electrochemistry
Electrochromatography   Use Chromatography
Electroencephalography
Electromechanical Aids
Electromechanical Occupations   Use Electrical Occupations and Electromechanical Technology
Electromechanical Technology
Electronic Aids   Use Electronic Equipment
Electronic Bulletin Boards   Use Electronic Mail

Electronic Calculators   Use Calculators
Electronic Circuits   Use Electric Circuits
Circuits   (Electronic)   Use Electric Circuits
Electronic Classroom Use (1966 1980)   Use Electronic Classrooms
Electronic Classrooms
Electronic Communications Systems   Use Telecommunications
Electronic Control
Electronic Data Processing (1967 1980)   Use Data Processing
Electronic Discussion Lists   Use Listservs
Electronic Equipment
Electronic Information Exchange   Use Information Networks and Telecommunications
Electronic Journals
Electronic Libraries
Electronic Magazines   Use Electronic Journals
Electronic Mail
Electronic Publishing
Electronic Spreadsheets   Use Spreadsheets
Electronic Superhighway   Use Internet
Electronic Technicians
Electronic Text
Videogames   (Electronic)   Use Video Games
Electronics
Electronics Industry
Microminiature   Electronics   Use Microelectronics
Miniaturized   Electronics   Use Microelectronics
Electrooptics (1968 1980)   Use Optics
Elementary Education
Elementary Grades (1966 1980)   Use Elementary Education
Ungraded   Elementary Programs (1966 1980)   Use Nongraded Instructional Grouping
Elementary School Children   Use Elementary School Students
Elementary School Counseling (1967 1980)   Use School Counseling
Elementary School Counselors (1967 1980)   Use School Counselors
Elementary School Curriculum
Foreign Languages in the   Elementary School   Use FLES
Elementary School Guidance (1967 1980)   Use School Guidance
Elementary School Libraries (1966 1980)   Use School Libraries
Elementary School Mathematics
Elementary School Role (1966 1980)   Use School Role
Elementary School Science
Elementary School Students
Elementary School Supervisors (1966 1980)   Use School Supervision
Elementary School Teachers
Elementary Schools
Biracial   Elementary Schools (1966 1980)   Use School Desegregation
Catholic   Elementary Schools (1967 1980)   Use Catholic Schools
Elementary Science (1966 1980)   Use Elementary School Science
Elementary Secondary Education
Architectural   Elements (1968 1980)   Use Structural Elements (Construction)
Structural   Elements (Construction)
Grain   Elevator Occupations   Use Crop Processing Occupations
Eligibility
Institutional   Eligibility   Use Eligibility
Student   Eligibility   Use Eligibility
Job   Elimination   Use Job Layoff
Program   Elimination   Use Program Termination
Elite Colleges   Use Selective Colleges
Elitism
Emancipated Students (1975 1980)   Use Self Supporting Students
Embryology
Emergency Medical Technicians
Emergency Programs
Emergency Squad Personnel
Emergent Literacy
Emerging Nations   Use Developing Nations
Emerging Occupations
Reggio   Emilia Approach
Reggio   Emilia Preschools   Use Preschool Education and Reggio Emilia Approach
Emotional Abuse
Emotional Adjustment
Emotional Behavior   Use Affective Behavior
Emotional Development
Emotional Disturbances
Emotional Experience
Emotional Health   Use Mental Health
Emotional Maladjustment (1966 1980)   Use Emotional Adjustment
Emotional Needs   Use Psychological Needs
Emotional Patterns   Use Psychological Patterns
Emotional Problems
Emotional Response
Emotional Security   Use Security (Psychology)
Emotionally Disturbed (1966 1980)   Use Emotional Disturbances
Emotionally Disturbed Children (1967 1980)   Use Emotional Disturbances
Rational   Emotive Therapy
Empathy
Employability   Use Employment Potential
Employable Skills   Use Employment Potential and Job Skills
Employed Mothers   Use Employed Parents and Mothers
Employed Parents
Employed Women
Employee Absenteeism
Employee Assistance Programs
Employee Attitudes
Employee Employer Relationship   Use Employer Employee Relationship

Employee Evaluation   Use Personnel Evaluation
Employee Fringe Benefits   Use Fringe Benefits
Employee Opinions   Use Employee Attitudes
Employee Performance   Use Job Performance
Employee Relations   Use Labor Relations
Employer   Employee Relationship
Employee Responsibility
Employee Work Attitudes   Use Employee Attitudes and Work Attitudes
Employees
Absence   (Employees)   Use Employee Absenteeism
Civil Service   Employees   Use Government Employees
Government   Employees
Library   Employees   Use Library Personnel
Public   Employees   Use Government Employees
Retention (of   Employees)   Use Labor Turnover
School   Employees   Use School Personnel
Employer Attitudes
Employer Employee Relationship
Employer Opinions   Use Employer Attitudes
Employee   Employer Relationship   Use Employer Employee Relationship
Employer Sponsored Day Care   Use Employer Supported Day Care
Employer Supported Day Care
Employers
Employment
Employment Adjustment   Use Vocational Adjustment
Teacher   Employment Benefits
Black   Employment
Employment Change   Use Career Change
Employment Counselors
Employment Discrimination   Use Equal Opportunities (Jobs)
Double   Employment   Use Multiple Employment
Dropout   Employment   Use Dropout Programs
Equal   Employment   Use Equal Opportunities (Jobs)
Employment Experience
Employment Forecasts   Use Employment Projections
Inadequate   Employment   Use Underemployment
Employment Interviews
Employment Level
Employment Market   Use Labor Market
Migrant   Employment
Multiple   Employment
Negro   Employment (1966 1977)   Use Black Employment
Employment Opportunities
Outplacement Services   (Employment)
Overseas   Employment
Part Time   Employment
Employment Patterns
Perquisites   (Employment)   Use Fringe Benefits
Employment Potential
Employment Practices
Employment Preparation   Use Job Training
Employment Problems
Employment Programs
Employment Projections
Employment Qualifications
Employment Referral Services   Use Employment Services
Employment Satisfaction   Use Job Satisfaction
Seasonal   Employment
Secondary   Employment   Use Multiple Employment
Employment Security   Use Job Security
Self   Employment
Employment Services
Employment Statistics
Employment Status   Use Employment Level
Student   Employment
Supported   Employment
Supported Competitive   Employment   Use Supported Employment
Employment Surveys   Use Occupational Surveys
Teacher   Employment
Temporary   Employment
Employment Tests   Use Occupational Tests
Employment Trends (1966 1980)   Use Employment Patterns
Youth   Employment
Empowerment
Parent   Empowerment
Personal   Empowerment   Use Empowerment
Self   Empowerment   Use Empowerment
Student   Empowerment
Teacher   Empowerment
Encapsulated Facilities
Encoding (Information)   Use Coding
Encoding (Psychology)
Encyclopedias
Front   End Systems (Computers)   Use Gateway Systems
End Users (Information)   Use Users (Information)
Endangered Species
Endowed Scholarships   Use Scholarships
Endowment Funds
Educational   Endowments   Use Endowment Funds
Energy
Atomic   Energy   Use Nuclear Energy
Energy Audits
Energy Conservation

	Energy Education
Geothermal	Energy
	Energy Management
Nuclear	Energy
	Energy Occupations
Nuclear	Energy Occupations Use Energy Occupations and Nuclear Energy
Solar	Energy
Solar Radiation	Energy Use Solar Energy
Alternative	Energy Sources
	Energy Technology Use Power Technology
Wind	Energy
Law	Enforcement
Law	Enforcement Officers Use Police
	Engaged Time (Learning) Use Time on Task
Student	Engaged Time Use Time on Task
	Engine Development Technicians Use Mechanical Design Technicians
Small	Engine Mechanics
	Engineering
Agricultural	Engineering
	Engineering Aides Use Engineering Technicians
Highway	Engineering Aides
Mechanical	Engineering Assistants Use Mechanical Design Technicians
Chemical	Engineering
Civil	Engineering
Computer Software	Engineering Use Computer Software Development
	Engineering Drawing
	Engineering Education
Genetic	Engineering
	Engineering Graphics
Highway	Engineering Use Civil Engineering
Human	Engineering (1967 1980) Use Human Factors Engineering
Human Factors	Engineering
Ocean	Engineering
Operating	Engineering
	Engineering Technicians
	Engineering Technology
	Engineers
Locomotive	Engineers
	Engines
Diesel	Engines
	English
American	English (1968 1980) Use North American English
Black	English Use Black Dialects
Business	English
College	English
	English Curriculum
	English Departments
	English Education (1967 1980)
	English for Academic Purposes
	English for Science and Technology
	English for Special Purposes
	English Instruction
Family	English Literacy
	English Literature
Old	English Literature
Middle	English
Official	English Movement Use English Only Movement
	English Neoclassic Literary Period (1968 1980)
North American	English
Old	English
	English Only Movement
Oral	English
Limited	English Proficient Use Limited English Speaking
	English Programs (1966 1980) Use English Curriculum
	English (Second Language)
Vocational	English (Second Language)
Signed	English Use Manual Communication
Limited	English Speaking
Non	English Speaking
	English Teacher Education
	English Teachers
Reading	Enjoyment Use Literature Appreciation
	Enlargement Methods Use Magnification Methods
	Enlisted Men (1967 1976) Use Enlisted Personnel
	Enlisted Personnel
	Enlisted Women Use Enlisted Personnel
	Enrichment
Academic	Enrichment (1966 1980) Use Enrichment
	Enrichment Activities
Course	Enrichment Use Curriculum Enrichment
Cultural	Enrichment
Curriculum	Enrichment
	Enrichment Experience (1966 1980) Use Enrichment
Job	Enrichment
Language	Enrichment
Mathematical	Enrichment
	Enrichment Programs (1966 1980) Use Enrichment Activities
Work	Enrichment Use Job Enrichment
	Enrollment
Average Daily	Enrollment (1968 1980) Use Average Daily Membership
College	Enrollment Use Enrollment
Declining	Enrollment
Dual	Enrollment

Foreign Language Enrollment   Use Language Enrollment
Enrollment Influences
Language Enrollment
Enrollment Management
Open Enrollment
Enrollment Projections
Enrollment Rate
School Enrollment   Use Enrollment
Second Language Enrollment   Use Language Enrollment
Student Enrollment (1966 1977)   Use Enrollment
Enrollment Trends
Vocal Ensembles   Use Singing
Scientific Enterprise
Free Enterprise System
Enterprisers   Use Entrepreneurship
Commercial Enterprises   Use Business
Community Enterprises   Use Community Programs
Entomology
School Entrance Age
College Entrance Examinations
Entrepreneurs   Use Entrepreneurship
Entrepreneurship
Entropy
Keyboarding (Data Entry)
Entry Workers
Entry Year Assistance (Teacher Induction)   Use Beginning Teacher Induction
Enunciation Improvement (1966 1980)   Use Articulation (Speech) and Speech Improvement
Environment
Academic Environment   Use Educational Environment
Acoustical Environment
Adjustment (to Environment)
Built Environment
Classroom Environment
College Environment
Conservation (Environment)
Controlled Environment (1966 1980)
Heredity Environment Controversy   Use Nature Nurture Controversy
Cultural Environment (1966 1980)   Use Cultural Context
Deprived Environment   Use Disadvantaged Environment
Least Restrictive Environment (Disabled)   Use Mainstreaming
Disadvantaged Environment
Educational Environment
Family Environment
Barrier Free Environment (for Disabled)   Use Accessibility (for Disabled)
Environment Heredity Controversy   Use Nature Nurture Controversy
Home Environment   Use Family Environment
Institutional Environment
Organizational Psychology (Work Environment)   Use Industrial Psychology
Permissive Environment
Physical Environment
Rural Environment
School Environment (1966 1980)   Use Educational Environment
Simulated Environment
Slum Environment
Social Environment
Sonic Environment   Use Acoustical Environment
Suburban Environment
Therapeutic Environment
Thermal Environment
Urban Environment
Visual Environment
Work Environment
Environmental Criteria (1967 1980)   Use Environmental Standards
Environmental Education
Environmental Factors   Use Environmental Influences
Environmental Influences
Environmental Interpretation
Environmental Research
Environmental Scanning
Environmental Standards
Environmental Technicians
Environmental Therapy   Use Milieu Therapy
Envy   Use Jealousy
Enzymes
Epee Fencing   Use Fencing (Sport)
Epics
Epidemic Roseola   Use Rubella
Epidemiology
Epilepsy
Episode Teaching (1967 1980)
Epistemology
Epistles (1970 1980)   Use Letters (Correspondence)
Equal Education
Equal Educational Opportunities   Use Equal Education
Equal Employment   Use Equal Opportunities (Jobs)
Equal Facilities
Equal Opportunities (Jobs)
Equal Pay   Use Salary Wage Differentials
Equal Protection
Educational Equality (1966 1976)   Use Equal Education
Equality of Education   Use Equal Education
Equalization Aid
Equalized Facilities   Use Equal Facilities

	Equated Scores
Linear Structural	Equation Models Use Structural Equation Models
Structural	Equation Models
Differential	Equations
Heat	Equations Use Thermodynamics
	Equations (Mathematics)
Chemical	Equilibrium
	Equilibrium Constants Use Chemical Equilibrium
	Equipment
Air Conditioning	Equipment
Athletic	Equipment
Audio	Equipment
Audiovisual	Equipment Use Audiovisual Aids
Biomedical	Equipment
Broadcast Reception	Equipment
Building	Equipment (1966 1980) Use Equipment
Classroom	Equipment Use Educational Equipment
Computer Auxiliary	Equipment Use Computer Peripherals
Adaptive	Equipment (Disabled) Use Assistive Devices (for Disabled)
Educational	Equipment
Electronic	Equipment
	Equipment Evaluation
	Equipment Inventory Use Facility Inventory
Laboratory	Equipment
Language Laboratory	Equipment (1966 1980) Use Laboratory Equipment and Language Laboratories
Library	Equipment
Life Costs (Facilities and	Equipment) Use Life Cycle Costing
	Equipment Maintenance
	Equipment Manufacturers
Measurement	Equipment
Mechanical	Equipment
Photographic	Equipment
Projection	Equipment
	Equipment Purchasing Use Purchasing
	Equipment Repair Use Equipment Maintenance
Safety	Equipment
Science	Equipment
Sound	Equipment Use Audio Equipment
	Equipment Standards
	Equipment Storage
Biomedical	Equipment Technicians Use Medical Laboratory Assistants
Television	Equipment Use Video Equipment
	Equipment Upkeep Use Equipment Maintenance
	Equipment Utilization
Video	Equipment
Visual	Equipment Use Visual Aids
Fiscal	Equity (Education) Use Educational Equity (Finance)
Tax	Equity (Education) Use Educational Equity (Finance)
	Equity (Educational Finance) Use Educational Equity (Finance)
	Equity (Educational Opportunities) Use Equal Education
Educational	Equity (Finance)
	Equity (Impartiality) Use Justice
Educational	Equity (Opportunities) Use Equal Education
Pay	Equity Use Comparable Worth
School Finance	Equity Use Educational Equity (Finance)
Full Time	Equivalency
High School	Equivalency Programs
	Equivalency Tests
Grade	Equivalent Scales (1967 1980) Use Grade Equivalent Scores
Grade	Equivalent Scores
Reconstruction	Era
	Ergonomics Use Human Factors Engineering
	Error Analysis (Language)
	Error Correction
Measurement	Error Use Error of Measurement
Standard	Error of Estimate Use Error of Measurement
	Error of Measurement
Standard	Error of Measurement (1970 1980) Use Error of Measurement
	Error of Refraction Use Ametropia
	Error Patterns
	Error Variance Use Error of Measurement
Ocular Refractive	Errors Use Ametropia
Refractive	Errors Use Ametropia
	Escapees Use Refugees
	Eskimo Aleut Languages
	Eskimos
	ESL Use English (Second Language)
	ESOL Use English (Second Language)
	Esperanto
	Essay Tests
	Essays
Real	Estate Appraisal Use Property Appraisal
Real	Estate Occupations
	Estate Planning
Real	Estate
Self	Esteem
	Esthetics Use Aesthetics
Standard Error of	Estimate Use Error of Measurement
	Estimated Costs (1966 1980) Use Cost Estimates
Cost	Estimates
	Estimation (Mathematics)
Time	Estimation Use Time Management
	Estonian

```
                          Estuaries
              Protestant  Ethic    Use Work Ethic
                 Puritan  Ethic    Use Work Ethic
                    Work  Ethic
                          Ethical Instruction
                          Ethical Values (1966 1980)    Use Moral Values
                          Ethics
                Codes of  Ethics
                          Ethnic Bias
                          Ethnic Community   Use Ethnic Groups
                          Ethnic Consciousness    Use Ethnicity
                          Ethnic Cultural Groups    Use Ethnic Groups
                          Ethnic Discrimination
                          Ethnic Distribution
                          Ethnic Group Studies    Use Ethnic Studies
                          Ethnic Grouping (1966 1980)
                          Ethnic Groups
                          Ethnic Heritage    Use Cultural Background
                          Ethnic Identification    Use Ethnicity
                          Ethnic Integration    Use Social Integration
                          Ethnic Origins
                          Ethnic Relations
                          Ethnic Status
                          Ethnic Stereotypes
                          Ethnic Studies
                          Ethnic Unity    Use Group Unity
                          Ethnicity
                   White  Ethnics    Use Whites
                          Ethnocentrism
                          Ethnography
                          Ethnology
                          Ethnomathematics
                          Ethology
                          Etiology
                          ETV    Use Educational Television
                          Etymology
                          European History
                    Indo  European Languages
                          Euskara    Use Basque
                          Euthanasia
                          Evaluation
            Administrator  Evaluation
                 Auditory  Evaluation
              Comparative  Evaluation    Use Comparative Analysis
         Computer Software  Evaluation
                 Software  Evaluation (Computers)    Use Computer Software Evaluation
                Counselor  Evaluation
                  Course   Evaluation
               Courseware  Evaluation    Use Computer Software Evaluation and Courseware
                          Evaluation Criteria
                 Critical  Evaluation    Use Criticism
               Curriculum  Evaluation
                   Dental  Evaluation
                          Evaluation Designs    Use Evaluation Methods
                Employee  Evaluation    Use Personnel Evaluation
                Equipment  Evaluation
                  Faculty  Evaluation
                Formative  Evaluation
                    Self  Evaluation (Groups)
             Health Care  Evaluation    Use Medical Care Evaluation
                 Holistic  Evaluation
             Alternative  Evaluation (Individuals)    Use Alternative Assessment
                    Self  Evaluation (Individuals)
                   Input  Evaluation    Use Input Output Analysis
            Institutional  Evaluation
     Instructional Material  Evaluation
                 Medical  Evaluation
            Medical Care  Evaluation
                          Evaluation Methods
                          Evaluation Needs
        Nongraded Student  Evaluation
                 Student  Evaluation of Teacher Performance
             Patient Care  Evaluation    Use Medical Care Evaluation
                    Peer  Evaluation
       Performance Based  Evaluation    Use Performance Based Assessment
                    Work  Evaluation (Performance)    Use Vocational Evaluation
               Personnel  Evaluation
                Preschool  Evaluation
                          Evaluation Problems
                          Evaluation Procedures    Use Evaluation Methods
                 Process  Evaluation    Use Formative Evaluation
                 Product  Evaluation    Use Summative Evaluation
                  Profile  Evaluation (1966 1980)    Use Profiles
                 Program  Evaluation
            Psychological  Evaluation
                          Evaluation Research
                    Self  Evaluation (1966 1980)
                          Evaluation Specialists    Use Evaluators
                  Speech  Evaluation
                   Staff  Evaluation    Use Personnel Evaluation
                 Student  Evaluation
         Student Teacher  Evaluation
               Summative  Evaluation
```

Teacher	Evaluation
	Evaluation Techniques (1966 1974) Use Evaluation Methods
Textbook	Evaluation
	Evaluation Utilization
Vocational	Evaluation
Work Performance	Evaluation Use Vocational Evaluation
Worker	Evaluation Use Personnel Evaluation
Writing	Evaluation
	Evaluative Research Use Evaluation Research
	Evaluative Thinking
	Evaluators
	Evening Classes (1967 1980) Use Evening Programs
	Evening Colleges (1967 1980) Use Evening Programs
	Evening Counseling Programs (1966 1980) Use Counseling Services and Evening Programs
	Evening Programs
	Evening Students
Cultural	Events (1966 1980) Use Cultural Activities
Current	Events
Life	Events
	Evidence (Legal)
	Evolution
Language	Evolution Use Diachronic Linguistics
	Ewe
Credit by	Examination Use Equivalency Tests
	Examinations Use Tests
Advanced Credit	Examinations Use Equivalency Tests
Advanced Standing	Examinations Use Equivalency Tests
College Entrance	Examinations
Physical	Examinations
Licensing	Examinations (Professions)
	Examiner Characteristics Use Examiners and Experimenter Characteristics
	Examiners
Educational	Excellence Use Educational Quality
	Excellence in Education
Educational	Excellence Movement (United States) Use Excellence in Education
	Exceptional (Atypical) (1966 1978) Use Exceptional Persons (1978 1994)
	Exceptional Child Education (1968 1980)
	Exceptional Child Research
	Exceptional Child Services (1968 1980)
	Exceptional Children (1966 1978) Use Exceptional Persons (1978 1994)
	Exceptional Persons (1978 1994)
	Exceptional Students (1966 1978) Use Exceptional Persons (1978 1994)
Overweight	(Excessive Body Fat) Use Obesity
Cultural	Exchange
Electronic Information	Exchange Use Information Networks and Telecommunications
International Educational	Exchange
	Exchange Programs
Student	Exchange Programs
Teacher	Exchange Programs
Scholarly Information	Exchange Use Scholarly Communication
Social	Exchange Theory
	Excursions (Instruction) Use Field Trips
	Executions (Criminal Law) Use Capital Punishment
	Executive Development Use Management Development
	Executive Secretaries Use Secretaries
	Exemplary Programs Use Demonstration Programs
	Exercise
Muscular	Exercise Use Exercise and Muscular System
Physical	Exercise Use Exercise
	Exercise (Physiology) (1969 1980)
	Exercise Physiology
Writing	Exercises
	Exhaust Stacks Use Chimneys
	Exhausting (1969 1980) Use Ventilation
	Exhaustion Use Fatigue (Biology)
	Exhibits
Financial	Exigency
Fiscal	Exigency Use Financial Exigency
	Exiles Use Refugees
	Existentialism
	Exogamous Marriage Use Intermarriage
Facility	Expansion
School	Expansion
	Expectancy Use Expectation
	Expectancy Tables
Work Life	Expectancy
	Expectation
Efficacy	Expectation Use Self Efficacy
Teacher	Expectations of Students
	Expenditure per Student
	Expenditures
Consumer	Expenditures Use Consumer Economics
Library	Expenditures
	Expenses Use Expenditures
Initial	Expenses (1966 1980) Use Expenditures
Minimum Initial	Expenses Use Expenditures
Minimum Operating	Expenses Use Operating Expenses
Operating	Expenses
	Experience
Supervised Occupational	Experience (Agriculture)
Language	Experience Approach
	Experience Based Education Use Experiential Learning
	Experience Charts

Clinical Experience
Clinical Learning Experience   Use Clinical Experience
Community Experience   Use Experiential Learning
Discussion Experience (1966 1980)   Use Discussion
Early Experience
Educational Experience
Emotional Experience
Employment Experience
Enrichment Experience (1966 1980)   Use Enrichment
Field Laboratory Experience   Use Field Experience Programs
Group Experience
Home Experience   Use Experiential Learning
Inservice Teaching Experience   Use Teaching Experience
Intellectual Experience
Job Experience   Use Employment Experience
Language Experience   Use Language Enrichment
Learning Experience
Mathematical Experience (1966 1980)
Prereading Experience
Preschool Experience   Use Early Experience
Preservice Teaching Experience   Use Teaching Experience
Cooperative Work Experience Programs   Use Cooperative Education
Field Experience Programs
Work Experience Programs
School Experience   Use Educational Experience
Sensory Experience
Social Experience
Student Experience
Teacher Experience (1966 1974)   Use Teaching Experience
Teaching Experience
Experience Units   Use Activity Units
Vocational Work Experience   Use Cooperative Education
Work Experience
Experienced Laborers (1966 1980)   Use Laborers
Experiential Learning
Prior Experiential Learning   Use Experiential Learning and Prior Learning
Experiment Stations
Field Experiment Stations   Use Experiment Stations
Experimental Colleges
Experimental Curriculum
Experimental Design   Use Research Design
Experimental Extinction   Use Extinction (Psychology)
Experimental Groups
Experimental Procedures   Use Research Methodology
Experimental Programs
Experimental Psychology
Experimental Schools
Experimental Teaching
Experimentation   Use Experiments
Experimenter Bias   Use Experimenter Characteristics
Experimenter Characteristics
Experiments
Educational Experiments
Laboratory Experiments
Physics Experiments (1966 1980)   Use Physics and Science Experiments
Science Experiments
Expert Systems
Career Exploration
Extraterrestrial Exploration   Use Space Exploration
Lunar Exploration   Use Lunar Research
Occupational Exploration   Use Career Exploration
Planetary Exploration   Use Space Exploration
Space Exploration
Exploratory Behavior
Exploratory Learning   Use Discovery Learning
Exports
Exposition (Literary)   Use Expository Writing
Expositions (1971 1980)   Use Exhibits
Expository Writing
Cocaine Prenatal Exposure   Use Cocaine and Prenatal Drug Exposure
Fetal Drug Exposure   Use Prenatal Drug Exposure
Drug Exposure in Utero   Use Prenatal Drug Exposure
Prenatal Drug Exposure
Prenatal Exposure to Drugs   Use Prenatal Drug Exposure
Art Expression
Creative Expression
Oral Expression (1966 1977)   Use Speech Communication
Self Expression
Expressionism
Facial Expressions
Idiomatic Expressions   Use Idioms
Mathematical Expressions   Use Mathematical Formulas
Expressive Language
Expulsion
Extemporization   Use Improvisation
Extended Degree Programs (Teacher Education)   Use Extended Teacher Education Programs
Extended Family
Extended School Day
Extended School Year
Extended Teacher Education Programs
Extended Universities   Use Open Universities
Extension Agents
County Extension Agents   Use Extension Agents

Village	Extension Agents Use Extension Agents
Agricultural	Extension Use Rural Extension
Cooperative	Extension Use Extension Education
	Extension Education
Library	Extension
Rural	Extension
	Extension Services Use Extension Education
University	Extension (1967 1980) Use Extension Education
Urban	Extension
Muscular	Extensions Use Motor Reactions
	External Degree Programs
Internal	External Locus of Control Use Locus of Control
	Externships (Medicine) Use Clinical Experience
Experimental	Extinction Use Extinction (Psychology)
	Extinction (Psychology)
Student Activities	(Extraclass) Use Extracurricular Activities
	Extracurricular Activities
	Extradimensional Shift Use Shift Studies
	Extrainstructional Duties Use Noninstructional Responsibility
	Extramural Athletic Programs (1966 1980) Use Extramural Athletics
	Extramural Athletics
	Extramural Departments Use Extension Education
	Extramural Sports Use Extramural Athletics
	Extrateaching Duties Use Noninstructional Responsibility
	Extraterrestrial Exploration Use Space Exploration
	Extraversion Introversion
	Extrinsic Motivation Use Incentives
	Extroversion Use Extraversion Introversion
	Eye Contact
	Eye Fixations
	Eye Hand Coordination
	Eye Movements
	Eye Regressions (1966 1980) Use Eye Movements
	Eye Voice Span
	Eyes
Cross	Eyes Use Strabismus
	Fables
	Fabrication Use Manufacturing
	Facial Expressions
	Facilities
Life Costs	(Facilities and Equipment) Use Life Cycle Costing
Animal	Facilities
Business Education	Facilities
Educational	Facilities Design
Dining	Facilities
Educational	Facilities
Encapsulated	Facilities
Equal	Facilities
Equalized	Facilities Use Equal Facilities
Flexible	Facilities
Food Handling	Facilities
Guidance	Facilities (1967 1977) Use Guidance Centers
Health	Facilities
Educational	Facilities Improvement
Institutional	Facilities (1967 1980) Use Facilities
Integrated Public	Facilities (1966 1980) Use Public Facilities and Racial Integration
Library	Facilities
Military Air	Facilities
Music	Facilities
Off Campus	Facilities
Offices	(Facilities)
Parking	Facilities
Physical	Facilities (1966 1980) Use Facilities
Physical Education	Facilities
Educational	Facilities Planning
Portable	Facilities Use Relocatable Facilities
Public	Facilities
Recreational	Facilities
Relocatable	Facilities
Sanitary	Facilities
Satellite	Facilities
School	Facilities Use Educational Facilities
Science	Facilities
Segregated Public	Facilities (1966 1980) Use Public Facilities and Racial Segregation
Shared	Facilities
Spatial Relationship	(Facilities)
Stages	(Facilities)
Study	Facilities
Teaching	Facilities Use Educational Facilities
Temporary	Facilities Use Relocatable Facilities
Toilet	Facilities
Underground	Facilities
	Facility Case Studies
	Facility Design Use Facility Guidelines
	Facility Expansion
	Facility Guidelines
	Facility Improvement
	Facility Inventory
	Facility Needs Use Facility Requirements
Oral	Facility Use Speech Skills
	Facility Planning
	Facility Requirements
	Facility Specifications Use Facility Guidelines

Facility Standards   Use Facility Guidelines
Facility Utilization Research
Facsimile Communication Systems (1968 1980)   Use Facsimile Transmission
Facsimile Transmission
Diversity (Cultural) as an Observation or a   Fact   Use Cultural Differences
De   Facto Segregation
Factor Analysis
Centroid Method of   Factor Analysis   Use Factor Analysis
Maximum Likelihood   Factor Analysis   Use Factor Analysis and Maximum Likelihood Statistics
Factor Structure
Causal   Factors   Use Influences
Climatic   Factors (1969 1980)   Use Climate
Cultural   Factors (1966 1980)   Use Cultural Influences
Ecological   Factors
Economic   Factors
Human   Factors Engineering
Environmental   Factors   Use Environmental Influences
Failure   Factors (1966 1980)   Use Failure
Intelligence   Factors (1966 1980)   Use Intelligence
Time   Factors (Learning)
Low Achievement   Factors (1966 1980)   Use Low Achievement
Performance   Factors
Poverty   Factors   Use Economic Factors and Poverty
Racial   Factors
Religious   Factors
Residence   Factors   Use Residence Requirements
Rh   Factors
Social   Factors (1968 1980)   Use Social Influences
Success   Factors (1968 1980)   Use Success
Factual Reading (1966 1980)
Faculty
Adjunct   Faculty
Faculty Advancement   Use Faculty Promotion
Faculty Advisers
Faculty Advisors (1967 1980)   Use Faculty Advisers
College   Faculty
Faculty College Relationship
Faculty Counselors   Use Faculty Advisers
Deans of   Faculty   Use Academic Deans
Dental School   Faculty   Use Dental Schools and Medical School Faculty
Faculty Desegregation   Use Faculty Integration
Faculty Development
Diversity   (Faculty)
Faculty Evaluation
Faculty Fellowships
Full Time   Faculty
Graduate School   Faculty
Graying of   Faculty   Use Aging in Academia
Faculty Growth   Use Faculty Development
Faculty Handbooks
Faculty Improvement   Use Faculty Development
Integrated   Faculty   Use Faculty Integration
Faculty Integration
Faculty Load   Use Faculty Workload
Medical School   Faculty
Faculty Mobility
Nontenured   Faculty
Faculty Offices   Use Offices (Facilities)
Faculty Organizations
Part Time   Faculty
Faculty Promotion
Faculty Publishing
Faculty Rank   Use Academic Rank (Professional)
Faculty Recruitment
Faculty Senates (Colleges)   Use College Governing Councils
Tenured   Faculty
Untenured   Faculty   Use Nontenured Faculty
Women   Faculty
Faculty Workload
Pass   Fail Grading
Failure
Academic   Failure
Failure Factors (1966 1980)   Use Failure
Reading   Failure
Scholastic   Failure   Use Academic Failure
Failure to Thrive
Nonorganic   Failure to Thrive   Use Failure to Thrive
Fair Dealing (Copyrights)   Use Fair Use (Copyrights)
Culture   Fair Tests
Fair Use (Copyrights)
Laissez   Faire Economy   Use Free Enterprise System
Sex   Fairness
Fairs   Use Exhibits
Science   Fairs
Fairy Tales
Faith   Use Beliefs
Fallout Shelters
True   False Tests   Use Objective Tests
Fame   Use Reputation
Familiarity
Job   Families   Use Occupational Clusters
Occupational   Families   Use Occupational Clusters
Family Attitudes

<pre>
                   Family Background (1966 1980)   Use Family Characteristics
            Black Family
                   Family Breadwinners   Use Heads of Households
                   Family Caregivers
                   Family Characteristics
                   Family Choice (Education)   Use School Choice
                   Family Counseling
                   Family Culture   Use Family Life
                   Family Day Care
 Domestic Violence (Family)   Use Family Violence
       Dual Career Family
                   Family Economics   Use Consumer Economics
                   Family English Literacy
                   Family Environment
         Extended Family
        Fatherless Family
                   Family Financial Resources
            Foster Family
                   Family Health
                   Family History
                   Family Income
                   Family Influence
                   Family Involvement
                   Family Job Relationship   Use Family Work Relationship
                   Family Life
                   Family Life Education
        Home and Family Life Education   Use Family Life Education
                   Family Literacy
                   Family Living   Use Family Life
                   Family Management (1966 1980)   Use Home Management
                   Family Mobility
        Motherless Family
                   Family Needs
           Nuclear Family
        One Parent Family
                   Family Participation   Use Family Involvement
                   Family Planning
                   Family Practice (Medicine)
                   Family Problems
                   Family Programs
                   Family Projects (1966 1980)   Use Family Programs
                   Family Relationship
              Job Family Relationship   Use Family Work Relationship
           School Family Relationship   Use Family School Relationship
             Work Family Relationship   Use Family Work Relationship
                   Family Resources (1966 1980)   Use Family Financial Resources
                   Family Role
            Rural Family
                   Family School Relationship
        Individual Family Service Plans   Use Individualized Family Service Plans
     Individualized Family Service Plans
                   Family Services Policy   Use Family Programs and Public Policy
     Single Parent Family   Use One Parent Family
                   Family Size
                   Family (Sociological Unit)
                   Family Status
                   Family Structure
                   Family Trees   Use Genealogy
       Two Parent Family   Use Nuclear Family
       Traditional Family Unit   Use Nuclear Family
                   Family Unity   Use Group Unity
                   Family Violence
                   Family Work Relationship
                   Fantasy
                   Fantasy Play   Use Pretend Play
                   Farm Accounts
                   Farm Agents   Use Extension Agents
              Off Farm Agricultural Occupations
                   Farm Foremen   Use Crew Leaders
                   Farm Labor
                   Farm Labor Legislation (1966 1980)   Use Farm Labor and Labor Legislation
                   Farm Labor Problems (1966 1980)   Use Farm Labor and Labor Problems
                   Farm Labor Supply (1966 1980)   Use Farm Labor and Labor Supply
                   Farm Management
                   Farm Mechanics (Occupation) (1967 1980)   Use Agricultural Machinery Occupations
                   Farm Mechanics (Subject)   Use Agricultural Engineering
                   Farm Occupations
                   Farm Operators   Use Farmers
        Supervised Farm Practice (1966 1990)   Use Supervised Occupational Experience (Agriculture)
                   Farm Related Occupations   Use Off Farm Agricultural Occupations
            Rural Farm Residents
                   Farm Supplies   Use Agricultural Supplies
                   Farm Visits
                   Farm Women   Use Rural Women
                   Farm Youth   Use Rural Youth
            Adult Farmer Education
        Beginning Farmer Education   Use Young Farmer Education
            Young Farmer Education
                   Farmers
            Dairy Farmers
      Nonresident Farmers   Use Part Time Farmers
         Part Time Farmers
                   Farsi (Language)   Use Persian
</pre>

Farsightedness   Use Hyperopia
Fascism
Fashion Industry
Fashions (Clothing)   Use Clothing
Fast Track Scheduling
Overweight (Excessive Body   Fat)   Use Obesity
Percent Body   Fat   Use Body Composition
Fat Ratio   Use Body Composition
Lean   Fat Ratio   Use Body Composition
Father Absence   Use Fatherless Family
Father Attitudes
Father Role   Use Fathers and Parent Role
Motherese and   Fatherese   Use Caregiver Speech and Parent Child Relationship
Fatherless Family
Fathers
Middle Class   Fathers (1966 1980)   Use Fathers and Middle Class Parents
Fatigue (Biology)
Body   Fatness   Use Body Composition
Fax   Use Facsimile Transmission
Fear
Fear of Success
Feasibility Studies
Feature Stories
Distinctive   Features (1967 1980)   Use Distinctive Features (Language)
Distinctive   Features (Language)
Prosodic   Features (Speech)   Use Suprasegmentals
Federal Aid
State   Federal Aid
Federal Control   Use Federal Regulation
Federal Court Litigation (1966 1980)   Use Court Litigation and Federal Courts
Federal Courts
Federal Government
Federal Grants   Use Federal Aid
Federal Indian Relationship
Federal Laws (1966 1974)   Use Federal Legislation
Federal Legislation
Federal Libraries   Use Federal Government and Government Libraries
Federal Programs
Federal Recreation Legislation (1966 1978)   Use Federal Legislation and Recreation Legislation
Federal Regulation
State   Federal Relationship   Use Federal State Relationship
Federal State Aid   Use State Federal Aid
Federal State Relationship
State   Federal Support (1966 1977)   Use State Federal Aid
Federal Troops (1966 1980)   Use Armed Forces
Federalism
New   Federalism
Feed Industry
Feed Stores
Livestock   Feed Stores   Use Feed Stores
Feedback
Feeder Patterns
Feeder Programs (1966 1980)   Use Feeder Patterns
Fees
Fellows (Medical)   Use Graduate Medical Students
Fellowships
Faculty   Fellowships
Female Homosexuality   Use Lesbianism
Female Role   Use Females and Sex Role
Females
Femininity
Feminism
Feminist Criticism
Feminization of Poverty
Epee   Fencing   Use Fencing (Sport)
Fencing (Sport)
Body and   Fender Repairers   Use Auto Body Repairers
Fenestration   Use Windows
Fenno Ugric Languages   Use Finno Ugric Languages
Fens   Use Wetlands
Fertility Rate   Use Birth Rate
Fertilizers
Fetal Alcohol Syndrome
Fetal Care   Use Prenatal Care
Fetal Drug Exposure   Use Prenatal Drug Exposure
Cystic   Fibrosis
Fiction
Science   Fiction
Force   Field Analysis
Field Check (1967 1980)   Use Equipment Evaluation
Corn   (Field Crop) (1968 1980)   Use Grains (Food)
Field Crops
Field Dependence   Use Field Dependence Independence
Field Dependence Independence
Field Experience Programs
Field Experiment Stations   Use Experiment Stations
Field Hockey
Field Houses
Field Independence   Use Field Dependence Independence
Field Instruction
Field Interviews
Field Laboratory Experience   Use Field Experience Programs
Higher Education as a   Field of Study   Use Postsecondary Education as a Field of Study

Postsecondary Education as a	Field of Study
	Field Properties (Mathematics) Use Properties (Mathematics)
	Field Studies
	Field Teaching Use Field Instruction
	Field Tests
Track and	Field
	Field Trips
Airborne	Field Trips (1968 1980) Use Field Trips
Athletic	Fields
Units of Study (Subject	Fields) (1966 1977) Use Units of Study
	Fifteenth Century Literature
Fire	Fighters
	Figural Aftereffects
	Figurative Language
Census	Figures
	Figures of Speech Use Figurative Language
	File Clerks
	File Management Systems Use Database Management Systems
Authority	Files Use Authority Control (Information)
Machine Readable Data	Files Use Databases
	Filing
Alphabetic	Filing Use Filing
Numeric	Filing Use Filing
	Filing Systems Use Information Storage
	Filipino Americans
	Film Auteurism Use Auteurism
	Film (Cameras) Use Photographic Equipment
	Film Clips Use Filmstrips
	Film Criticism
	Film Industry
	Film Libraries
	Film Lists Use Filmographies
	Film Loops Use Filmstrips
	Film Production
	Film Production Specialists
	Film Projectors Use Projection Equipment
Repetitive	Film Showings
	Film Study
	Filmmakers Use Film Production Specialists
	Filmmaking Use Film Production
	Filmographies
	Films
Behavioral Situation	Films Use Protocol Materials
Black and White	Films Use Films
Color	Films Use Films
Foreign Language	Films
Instructional	Films
Second Language	Films Use Foreign Language Films
Silent	Films Use Films
Single Concept	Films
Sound	Films (1966 1980) Use Films
Teacher Training	Films Use Protocol Materials
	Filmstrip Projectors
	Filmstrips
Credit	(Finance)
Educational	Finance
Educational Equity	(Finance)
Equity (Educational	Finance) Use Educational Equity (Finance)
School	Finance Equity Use Educational Equity (Finance)
Interest	(Finance)
Library	Finance Use Library Funding
	Finance Occupations
	Finance Reform
School	Finance Use Educational Finance
Recreation	Finances
	Financial Aid Applicants
Need Analysis (Student	Financial Aid)
Student	Financial Aid Officers
State	Financial Aid Use State Aid
Student	Financial Aid
	Financial Audits
	Financial Barriers Use Financial Problems
Parent	Financial Contribution
Parental	Financial Contribution (1978 1980) Use Parent Financial Contribution
Debt	(Financial)
	Financial Donors Use Donors
	Financial Exigency
	Financial Management Use Money Management
	Financial Needs
	Financial Policy
	Financial Problems
Family	Financial Resources
	Financial Services
	Financial Support
Private	Financial Support
Trusts	(Financial)
	Financing Use Financial Support
College Costs	(Financing for Individual Students) Use Paying for College
	Fine Arts
	Fine Arts Centers Use Arts Centers
Library	Fines Use Fines (Penalties)
	Fines (Penalties)
	Finger Spelling

	Finishing
Metal	Finishing Use Finishing
Surface	Finishing Use Finishing
Textile	Finishing Use Finishing
Wood	Finishing Use Finishing
	Finite Arithmetic Use Modular Arithmetic
	Finnish
	Finno Ugric Languages
	Fire Fighters
	Fire Insurance
	Fire Prevention Use Fire Protection
	Fire Protection
	Fire Science Education
	Firearms Use Guns
	Firearms Control Use Gun Control
	Firemen Use Fire Fighters
	First Aid
	First Born
	First Professional Degrees Use Degrees (Academic) and Professional Education
Freshmen (1967 1980)	(First Year College Students) Use College Freshmen
	First Year Principals Use Beginning Principals
	First Year Teachers Use Beginning Teachers
	Firstborns Use First Born
	Fiscal Capacity
	Fiscal Equity (Education) Use Educational Equity (Finance)
	Fiscal Exigency Use Financial Exigency
	Fiscal Neutrality
	Fiscal Policy Use Financial Policy
	Fiscal Strain Use Financial Problems
	Fish Inspectors Use Food and Drug Inspectors
	Fish Studies Use Ichthyology
	Fisheries
Goodness of	Fit
Health Related	Fitness
Physical	Fitness
Physical	Fitness Tests
Pipe	Fitting Use Plumbing
	Five Year Teacher Preparation Programs Use Extended Teacher Education Programs
Eye	Fixations
Capital Outlay (for	Fixed Assets)
	Fixed Sequence
	Fixed Service Television (1969 1980) Use Educational Television
	FLES
	FLES Guides (1967 1980) Use Curriculum Guides and FLES
	FLES Materials (1967 1980) Use FLES and Instructional Materials
	FLES Programs (1967 1980) Use FLES and Second Language Programs
	FLES Teachers (1967 1980) Use FLES and Language Teachers
	Flexible Classrooms (1968 1980) Use Classrooms and Flexible Facilities
	Flexible Disks Use Floppy Disks
	Flexible Facilities
	Flexible Lighting Design
	Flexible Progression
	Flexible Schedules (1967 1980)
	Flexible Scheduling
	Flexible Working Hours
	Flexilevel Testing Use Adaptive Testing
Muscular	Flexions Use Motor Reactions
	Flextime Use Flexible Working Hours
	Flight Training
White	Flight Use Migration and Whites
	Floods
	Floor Covering Use Flooring
Resilient	Floor Covering Use Flooring
	Floor Installation Use Flooring
	Floor Layers
Studio	Floor Plans (1966 1980)
	Flooring
	Floors Use Flooring
	Floppy Disks
	Floriculture
Air	Flow
	Flow Charts
Information	Flow Use Information Transfer
Traffic	Flow Use Traffic Circulation
Business	Fluctuations Use Business Cycles
Economic	Fluctuations Use Business Cycles
Language	Fluency
	Fluid Mechanics
	Fluid Power Education (1967 1980) Use Fluid Mechanics
	Fluid Pressure Use Pressure (Physics)
	Fluoridation
	Focus Groups
	Focused Group Interviews Use Focus Groups
	Folding Partitions Use Movable Partitions
	Folk Culture
	Folk Drama (1969 1980) Use Drama and Folk Culture
	Folk Schools
	Folklore Use Folk Culture
	Folklore Books (1966 1980) Use Books and Folk Culture
Occupational	Followup Use Vocational Followup
	Followup Programs Use Followup Studies
	Followup Studies
Vocational	Followup

	Foochow
	Food
	Food and Drug Inspectors
Grains	(Food)
	Food Handling Facilities
	Food Inspectors Use Food and Drug Inspectors
	Food Markets Use Food Stores
	Food Processing Occupations
Recipes	(Food)
	Food Service
	Food Service Industry (1967 1981) Use Food Service
	Food Service Occupations (1968 1981) Use Food Service
	Food Service Workers (1968 1981) Use Food Service
	Food Standards
	Food Stores
Processed	Foods Inspectors Use Food and Drug Inspectors
	Foods Instruction
	Football
	Footnotes (Bibliographic) Use Citations (References)
English	for Academic Purposes
Paying	for College
Teacher Testing	(for Competency) Use Teacher Competency Testing
Accessibility	(for Disabled)
Assistive Devices	(for Disabled)
Barrier Free Environment	(for Disabled) Use Accessibility (for Disabled)
Communication Aids	(for Disabled)
Accommodations	for Disabled (Educational Settings) Use Academic Accommodations (Disabilities)
Demand	for Education Use Educational Demand
Capital Outlay	(for Fixed Assets)
College Costs (Financing	for Individual Students) Use Paying for College
Writing	for Publication
English	for Science and Technology
English	for Special Purposes
Languages	for Special Purposes
Knowledge Base	for Teaching
Homes	for the Aged Use Personal Care Homes
Interpreting	for the Deaf Use Deaf Interpreting
	Force
Air	Force Bases Use Military Air Facilities
Labor	Force Development
	Force Field Analysis
Labor	Force
Labor	Force Nonparticipants
	Force (Physical) Use Force
Reduction in	Force
Labor	Force Surveys Use Occupational Surveys
Work	Force Use Labor Force
	Forced Choice Technique
Armed	Forces
	Forecast Use Prediction
Employment	Forecasts Use Employment Projections
	Foreign Countries
	Foreign Culture
	Foreign Diplomats
	Foreign Language Books
	Foreign Language Enrollment Use Language Enrollment
	Foreign Language Films
	Foreign Language Instruction Use Second Language Instruction
	Foreign Language Learning Use Second Language Learning
Language Learning	(Foreign) Use Second Language Learning
	Foreign Language Periodicals
	Foreign Language Programs Use Second Language Programs
State	Foreign Language Supervisors (1967 1980) Use Second Language Instruction and State Supervisors
	Foreign Language Teachers Use Language Teachers
	Foreign Language Teaching Use Second Language Instruction
	Foreign Languages Use Second Languages
	Foreign Languages in the Elementary School Use FLES
	Foreign Medical Graduates
	Foreign Nationals
Nonresident Students (1967 1980)	(Foreign) Use Foreign Students
	Foreign Policy
	Foreign Relations (1966 1976) Use International Relations
	Foreign Student Advisers
	Foreign Students
	Foreign Trained Physicians Use Foreign Medical Graduates
	Foreign Workers
	Foremen Use Supervisors
Farm	Foremen Use Crew Leaders
	Forensics Use Persuasive Discourse
Rain	Forest Preserves Use Rainforests
	Forester Aides Use Forestry Aides
	Forestry
	Forestry Aides
	Forestry Occupations
	Forgetting Use Memory
	Form Classes (Languages)
Agreements	(Formal) Use Contracts
	Formal Criticism (1969 1980)
	Formal Operations
	Formal Organizations Use Organizations (Groups)
Conversion	(Format) Use Data Conversion
Debate	Format
	Format (Publications) Use Layout (Publications)

Screen	Format Use Screen Design (Computers)
Test	Format
Concept	Formation
Habit	Formation
Policy	Formation
	Formative Evaluation
	Former Teachers (1967 1980)
Metal	Forming Occupations Use Metal Working
Negative	Forms (Language)
Pneumatic	Forms
Records	(Forms)
Mathematical	Formulas
Readability	Formulas
Scoring	Formulas
Parent	Forums Use Parent Conferences
	Fossil Fuels
	Fossils Use Paleontology
	Foster Care
Adult	Foster Care
	Foster Children
	Foster Family
	Foster Homes (1970 1982) (Adults) Use Adult Foster Care
	Foster Homes (1970 1982) (Children) Use Foster Care
	Foster Parents Use Foster Family
	Found Materials Use Found Objects
	Found Objects
	Found Spaces
	Foundation Courses (Introductory) Use Introductory Courses
	Foundation Courses (Required) Use Required Courses
	Foundation Programs
Educational	Foundations Use Philanthropic Foundations
	Foundations (Institutions) Use Philanthropic Foundations
	Foundations of Education
Philanthropic	Foundations
	Foundries
Iron	Foundries Use Foundries
Steel	Foundries Use Foundries
	Four Day Work Week Use Flexible Working Hours
	Four H Club Agents Use Extension Agents
	Fractions
Common	Fractions (1966 1980) Use Fractions
Decimal	Fractions
	Frail Elderly
	Franchising
	Franchising (Cable) Use Cable Franchising
Cable	Franchising
	Fraternities
	Fraud
	Free Choice Transfer Programs
	Free Education
	Free Enterprise System
Barrier	Free Environment (for Disabled) Use Accessibility (for Disabled)
Context	Free Grammar
	Free Market Use Free Enterprise System
	Free Play Use Play
	Free Schools
Distribution	Free Statistics Use Nonparametric Statistics
Culture	Free Tests (1967 1980) Use Culture Fair Tests
	Free Translation Use Translation
	Free Universities Use Experimental Colleges
	Free Writing
	Freedom
Academic	Freedom
Intellectual	Freedom
	Freedom of Information
	Freedom of Speech
	Freedom of the Press Use Freedom of Speech
	Freedom of Thought Use Intellectual Freedom
	Freedom Schools
Teaching	Freedom Use Academic Freedom
	Freedom to Read Use Intellectual Freedom
	Freehand Drawing
Drawing	(Freehand) Use Freehand Drawing
	Freewrites Use Free Writing
	French
	French Canadian Literature Use Canadian Literature
	French Canadians
	French Literature
	Frequency Distributions Use Statistical Distributions
Word	Frequency
	Freshman Composition
College	Freshmen
	Freshmen (1967 1980) (First Year College Students) Use College Freshmen
	Freshmen (1967 1980) (Grade 9) Use High School Freshmen
High School	Freshmen
User	Friendly Interface
	Friendship
Childhood	Friendship (1966 1980) Use Friendship
	Fringe Benefits
Employee	Fringe Benefits Use Fringe Benefits
Away	from the Job Training Use Off the Job Training
	Front End Systems (Computers) Use Gateway Systems
	Fruit and Vegetable Inspectors Use Food and Drug Inspectors

```
                        FTE   Use Full Time Equivalency
                        Fuel Consumption
                 Diesel Fuel   Use Diesel Engines and Fuels
                        Fuel Oil   Use Fossil Fuels and Oil
                        Fuels
                 Fossil Fuels
                        Ful   Use Fulani
                        Fula   Use Fulani
                        Fulani
                   Self Fulfilling Prophecies
                        Fulfulde   Use Fulani
                        Full Day Half Day Alternate Day   Use Alternate Day Schedules and Full Day Half Day Schedules
                        Full Day Half Day Schedules
                        Full Inclusion   Use Inclusive Schools
                        Full Service Schools (Human Services)   Use Integrated Services
                        Full State Funding
                        Full Text Databases
                        Full Time Equivalency
                        Full Time Faculty
                        Full Time Students
                        Full Time Teachers   Use Full Time Faculty
                 Agency Function   Use Agency Role
            Discriminant Function Analysis   Use Discriminant Analysis
           Institutional Function   Use Institutional Role
                        Function Words
                        Functional Illiteracy (1968 1980)   Use Functional Literacy
                        Functional Literacy
                        Functional Notional Syllabi   Use Notional Functional Syllabi
                        Functional Reading
                Notional Functional Syllabi
                        Functional Systems Theory   Use Systems Analysis
        Differential Item Functioning   Use Item Bias
        Brain Hemisphere Functions
               Counselor Functions (1967 1977)   Use Counselor Role
    Educational Production Functions   Use Productivity
             Government Functions   Use Government Role
                Guidance Functions (1968 1980)   Use Guidance Objectives
                        Functions (Mathematics)
              Production Functions   Use Productivity
                        Functions (Sociology)   Use Role
                        Functors   Use Function Words
                        Fund Raising
                        Fundamental Concepts
                        Fundamental Education (Adults)   Use Adult Basic Education
                        Fundamental Skills (Daily Living)   Use Daily Living Skills
                        Fundamental Skills (School)   Use Basic Skills
                        Funding   Use Financial Support
              Full State Funding
                Library Funding
               Endowment Funds
              Scholarship Funds
                 School Funds
                  Trust Funds   Use Trusts (Financial)
                        Fungi
                   Home Furnishings
                        Furniture
                        Furniture Arrangement
                        Furniture (Classroom)   Use Classroom Furniture
              Classroom Furniture
                        Furniture Design
                        Furniture Industry
                        Further Education   Use Adult Education
                        Fused Curriculum
                        Future Studies   Use Futures (of Society)
            Alternative Futures   Use Futures (of Society)
             Educational Futures   Use Educational Trends and Futures (of Society)
                        Futures (of Society)
                        Futures Planning   Use Long Range Planning
                        Futurism   Use Futures (of Society)
                        Futuristics   Use Futures (of Society)
                        Futurology   Use Futures (of Society)
                        G Scores   Use Grade Equivalent Scores
                        Ga
                        Gaelic (Irish)   Use Irish
                  Scots Gaelic
                        Gaelic (Scottish)   Use Scots Gaelic
                Reading Gain   Use Reading Improvement
            Achievement Gains
                    Art Galleries   Use Arts Centers
                 Squash (Game)
                        Game Theory
                        Gamekeeping   Use Wildlife Management
                        Games
               Academic Games   Use Educational Games
               Business Games   Use Management Games
              Childrens Games
              Classroom Games (1966 1980)   Use Class Activities and Educational Games
               Computer Games
             Educational Games
               Heuristic Games   Use Educational Games
             Management Games
                Olympic Games
                Reading Games
```

Summer Olympic	Games Use Olympic Games
Video	Games
Winter Olympic	Games Use Olympic Games and Winter Sports
	Ganda
Juvenile	Gangs
Generation	Gap
Parking	Garages Use Parking Facilities
	Garbage Use Solid Wastes
	Gardeners Use Gardening and Grounds Keepers
	Gardening
	Gardens
	Garment Industry Use Fashion Industry
Natural	Gas
Petroleum (Oil and	Gas) Use Fossil Fuels and Oil
	Gas Utilities Use Utilities
	Gas Welding Use Welding
	Gasoline
	Gateway Systems
	Gauges Use Measurement Equipment
Anti	Gay Bias Use Homophobia
	Gbaya
	Gbeya Use Gbaya
	GED Programs Use High School Equivalency Programs
	Gender Bias Use Sex Bias
	Gender Differences (Sex) Use Sex Differences
	Gender Discrimination Use Sex Discrimination
	Gender Identity (Sex) Use Sexual Identity
	Gender Issues
	Gender Role (Sex) Use Sex Role
	Gender (Sex) Use Sex
	Gender Stereotypes Use Sex Stereotypes
	Genealogy
	General and Special Education Relationship Use Regular and Special Education Relationship
	General Business Education Use Basic Business Education
	General Education
	General Educational Development Programs Use High School Equivalency Programs
	General High Schools (1966 1980) Use General Education
	General Mathematics
	General Mechanics Use Mechanics (Process)
	General Methods Courses Use Methods Courses
	General Practice (Medicine) Use Family Practice (Medicine)
	General Science
	General Semantics Use Semantics
	General Shop Use Shop Curriculum
	Generalizability Theory
	Generalization
Stimulus	Generalization
	Generation Gap
	Generative Grammar
Transformation	Generative Grammar (1968 1980) Use Transformational Generative Grammar
Transformational	Generative Grammar
	Generative Phonology
	Generative Transformational Grammar Use Transformational Generative Grammar
	Genetic Diversity Use Biodiversity
	Genetic Engineering
	Genetics
	Genocide
Literary	Genres
	Geochemistry
Areas	(Geographic) Use Geographic Regions
	Geographic Concepts
Depressed Areas	(Geographic) (1966 1980) Use Poverty Areas
	Geographic Dialects Use Regional Dialects
	Geographic Distribution
	Geographic Isolation
	Geographic Location
	Geographic Mobility (1980 1980) Use Migration
Physical Divisions	(Geographic)
Political Divisions	(Geographic)
	Geographic Regions
	Geography
Cultural	Geography Use Human Geography
Economic	Geography Use Human Geography
Historical	Geography Use Human Geography
Human	Geography
	Geography Instruction
Physical	Geography
Political	Geography Use Human Geography
Social	Geography Use Human Geography
Urban	Geography Use Human Geography
World	Geography
	Geology
	Geometric Concepts
	Geometric Constructions
	Geometrical Optics Use Optics
	Geometrodynamics Use Relativity
	Geometry
Analytic	Geometry
Coordinate	Geometry Use Analytic Geometry
Plane	Geometry
Solid	Geometry
Transformational	Geometry Use Transformations (Mathematics)
	Geophysics

Georgian   Use Caucasian Languages
Geoscience   Use Earth Science
Geothermal Energy
Geriatrics
German
German Literature
German Measles   Use Rubella
Gerontology
Educational   Gerontology
Gestalt Therapy
Gestation   Use Pregnancy
Gestures (Deaf Communication)   Use Sign Language
Gestures (Nonverbal Communication)   Use Body Language
Ghettos
Gifted
Academically   Gifted
Gifted Children   Use Gifted
Gifted Disabled
Gifted Disadvantaged
Gifted Handicapped   Use Gifted Disabled
Gifted Students   Use Academically Gifted
Gifted Teachers   Use Gifted
Gifted Youth   Use Gifted
Girls   Use Females
Girls Clubs (1966 1980)   Use Youth Clubs
Corporate   Giving   Use Corporate Support
Help   Giving   Use Helping Relationship
Glare
Glass
Glass Installers   Use Glaziers
Glass Walls
Safety   Glasses   Use Safety Equipment
Glaziers
Glee Clubs   Use Singing
Global Approach
Global Education
Global Perspectives   Use Global Approach
Global Studies Education   Use Global Education
Global Warming
Glossaries
Glottochronology
Glues   Use Adhesives
Goal Attainment   Use Success
Goal Orientation
Goals   Use Objectives
Counseling   Goals (1966 1980)   Use Counseling Objectives
Educational   Goals   Use Educational Objectives
Guidance   Goals   Use Guidance Objectives
Institutional   Goals   Use Organizational Objectives
Measurement   Goals (1966 1980)   Use Measurement Objectives
Educational   Goals of Students   Use Student Educational Objectives
Organizational   Goals   Use Organizational Objectives
Training   Goals   Use Training Objectives
Golf
Gonorrhea   Use Venereal Diseases
Good Citizenship   Use Citizenship
Goodness of Fit
Mother   Goose Rhymes   Use Nursery Rhymes
Governance
Governing Boards
College   Governing Councils
Government (Administrative Body)
Government Agencies   Use Public Agencies
City   Government
County   Government   Use Counties and Local Government
American   Government (Course) (1966 1980)   Use United States Government (Course)
United States   Government (Course)
Government Documents   Use Government Publications
Government Employees
Federal   Government
Government Functions   Use Government Role
Government Libraries
Local   Government
Municipal   Government   Use City Government
Government Policy   Use Public Policy
State   Government Programs   Use State Government and State Programs
Provincial   Government   Use State Government
Government Publications
School   Government Relationship   Use Government School Relationship
Government Role
Government School Relationship
Government Sector   Use Public Sector
Self   Government   Use Self Determination
Contracting Out (of   Government Services)   Use Privatization
State   Government
Government Structure   Use Governmental Structure
Student   Government
Tribal   Government
Trust Responsibility   (Government)
Governmental Structure
Grade 1
Grade 10
Grade 11

```
                                 Grade 12
          Seniors (1966 1980)    (Grade 12)   Use High School Seniors
                                 Grade 13 (1970 1980)   Use Postsecondary Education
                                 Grade 14 (1970 1980)   Use Postsecondary Education
                                 Grade 2
                                 Grade 3
                                 Grade 4
                                 Grade 5
                                 Grade 6
                                 Grade 7
                                 Grade 8
                                 Grade 9
         Freshmen (1967 1980)    (Grade 9)   Use High School Freshmen
                                 Grade a Year Integration (1966 1980)   Use School Desegregation
                                 Grade Average   Use Grade Point Average
                                 Grade Cards   Use Report Cards
                                 Grade Charts (1966 1980)
                                 Grade Equivalent Scales (1967 1980)   Use Grade Equivalent Scores
                                 Grade Equivalent Scores
                                 Grade Inflation
                                 Grade Levels   Use Instructional Program Divisions
                                 Grade Organization (1966 1980)   Use Instructional Program Divisions
                          Age    Grade Placement
                                 Grade Point Average
                                 Grade Prediction
                                 Grade Repetition
                 Retention (in   Grade)   Use Grade Repetition
                                 Grade Scores   Use Grade Equivalent Scores
                          Age    Grade Status   Use Age Grade Placement
                     Elementary  Grades (1966 1980)   Use Elementary Education
                       Inflated  Grades   Use Grade Inflation
                   Intermediate  Grades
                        Primary  Grades (1966 1980)   Use Primary Education
                                 Grades (Program Divisions)   Use Instructional Program Divisions
                                 Grades (Scholastic)
                      Secondary  Grades (1966 1980)   Use Secondary Education
                                 Grading
                       Contract  Grading   Use Grading and Performance Contracts
               Credit No Credit  Grading
                      Pass Fail  Grading
                 Pass No Credit  Grading   Use Credit No Credit Grading
                 Pass No Record  Grading   Use Credit No Credit Grading
                                 Graduate Ceremonies   Use Commencement Ceremonies
                                 Graduate Education   Use Graduate Study
                                 Graduate Medical Education
                                 Graduate Medical Students
                                 Graduate Professors (1966 1980)   Use Graduate School Faculty
                                 Graduate School Faculty
                                 Graduate Students
                                 Graduate Study
                                 Graduate Surveys
                                 Graduate Training   Use Graduate Study
                                 Graduates
                        College  Graduates
                  Foreign Medical Graduates
                    High School  Graduates
                                 Graduation
                                 Graduation Requirements
                                 Grain Elevator Occupations   Use Crop Processing Occupations
                                 Grain Marketing   Use Grains (Food)
                                 Grain Processing   Use Grains (Food)
                                 Grain Production   Use Grains (Food)
                                 Grains (Food)
                                 Grammar
                       Articles  (Grammar)   Use Determiners (Languages)
                          Case   (Grammar)
                   Context Free  Grammar
                     Generative  Grammar
     Generative Transformational Grammar   Use Transformational Generative Grammar
                       Prefixes  (Grammar)
                         Story   Grammar
                     Structural  Grammar
                        Tenses   (Grammar)
                    Traditional  Grammar
       Transformation Generative Grammar (1968 1980)   Use Transformational Generative Grammar
               Transformational  Grammar   Use Transformational Generative Grammar
     Transformational Generative Grammar
                                 Grammar Translation Method
                                 Grammatical Acceptability
                                 Grandchildren
                                 Granddaughters   Use Grandchildren
                                 Grandfathers   Use Grandparents
                                 Grandmothers   Use Grandparents
                                 Grandparents
                                 Grandsons   Use Grandchildren
                          Land   Grant Colleges   Use Land Grant Universities
                                 Grant Proposals   Use Grants and Program Proposals
                          Land   Grant Universities
                                 Grants
                         Block   Grants
                       Federal   Grants   Use Federal Aid
                      Incentive  Grants
                       Tuition   Grants
```

	Grantsmanship
Phoneme	Grapheme Correspondence
	Grapheme Phoneme Correspondence Use Phoneme Grapheme Correspondence
	Graphemes
	Graphic Arts
Computer	Graphics
Engineering	Graphics
	Graphing Calculators
	Graphs
Delay of	Gratification
Need	Gratification
	Gravitation Use Gravity (Physics)
	Gravity (Physics)
	Graying of Faculty Use Aging in Academia
	Grease Use Lubricants
	Greek
	Greek Americans
	Greek Civilization
Classical	Greek Use Greek
	Greek Literature
Modern	Greek Use Greek
	Greenhouse Effect
	Greenhouse Workers Use Nursery Workers (Horticulture)
	Greenhouses
	Greenlandic Use Inupiaq
	Gregariousness Use Interpersonal Competence
	Grief
	Grievance Procedures
Parent	Grievances
Parental	Grievances (1967 1980) Use Parent Grievances
	Grinding Machines Use Machine Tools
	Grocery Stores Use Food Stores
Personal	Grooming Use Hygiene
	Gross Scores Use Raw Scores
	Ground Water Supplies Use Groundwater
	Grounds Caretakers Use Grounds Keepers
	Grounds Keepers
	Groundwater
	Group Activities
	Group Adjustment Use Adjustment (to Environment)
	Group Behavior
Minority	Group Children
	Group Cohesiveness Use Group Unity
	Group Counseling
	Group Decision Support Systems Use Decision Support Systems and Group Dynamics
	Group Discussion
	Group Dynamics
	Group Experience
	Group Guidance
	Group Homes
Minority	Group Influences
	Group Instruction
Large	Group Instruction
Small	Group Instruction
	Group Intelligence Testing (1966 1980) Use Group Testing and Intelligence Tests
	Group Intelligence Tests (1966 1980) Use Group Testing and Intelligence Tests
	Group Interaction Use Group Dynamics
	Group Interests Use Interests
Focused	Group Interviews Use Focus Groups
	Group Living (1966 1977) Use Group Experience
	Group Membership
	Group Norms (1968 1980)
	Group Pacing Use Pacing
	Group Pressures Use Group Dynamics
	Group Processes Use Group Dynamics
	Group Reading (1966 1980)
	Group Relations (1966 1980) Use Group Dynamics
	Group Status
	Group Structure
Ethnic	Group Studies Use Ethnic Studies
Minority	Group Teachers
Nominal	Group Technique
	Group Testing
	Group Tests (1966 1980) Use Group Testing
	Group Therapy
	Group Unity
	Group Values Use Social Values
Ability	Grouping
Cluster	Grouping
Ethnic	Grouping (1966 1980)
Heterogeneous	Grouping
Homogeneous	Grouping
	Grouping (Instructional Purposes)
Mixed Age	Grouping
Multiage	Grouping Use Mixed Age Grouping
Nongraded Instructional	Grouping
	Grouping Procedures (1966 1980) Use Classification
Student	Grouping (1966 1980) Use Grouping (Instructional Purposes)
	Groups
Age	Groups
Associations	(Groups) Use Organizations (Groups)
Civic	Groups Use Community Organizations
Control	Groups

Developmental Differences (Age   Groups)   Use Age Differences and Individual Development
Disadvantaged   Groups (1966 1980)   Use Disadvantaged
Discussion   Groups
Ethnic   Groups
Ethnic Cultural   Groups   Use Ethnic Groups
Experimental   Groups
Focus   Groups
Support   Groups (Human Services)   Use Social Support Groups
Leaderless   Groups   Use Self Directed Groups
Listening   Groups
Low Income   Groups
Matched   Groups
Minority   Groups
Minority Language   Groups   Use Language Minorities
Classes   (Groups of Students)
Organization Size   (Groups)
Organizations   (Groups)
Parent Study   Groups   Use Parent Conferences
Peer   Groups
Racial Cultural   Groups   Use Ethnic Groups
Reference   Groups
Religious   Groups   Use Religious Cultural Groups
Religious Cultural   Groups
Segregationist   Groups   Use Segregationist Organizations
Self Directed   Groups
Self Evaluation   (Groups)
Self Guided   Groups   Use Self Directed Groups
Social Support   Groups
T   Groups (1967 1980)   Use Sensitivity Training
Grown Children   Use Adult Children
Rapid   Growth Communities   Use Boomtowns
Faculty   Growth   Use Faculty Development
Growth Motivation   Use Self Actualization
Growth Patterns (1966 1980)
Personal   Growth (1967 1980)   Use Individual Development
Plant   Growth
Population   Growth
Professional   Growth   Use Professional Development
Self   Growth   Use Individual Development
Guarani
Mbya   Guarani   Use Guarani
Tupi   Guarani   Use Guarani
Guaranteed Income
Coast   Guard Air Stations   Use Military Air Facilities
Guards (Border Patrol)   Use Immigration Inspectors
Guards (Security)   Use Security Personnel
Guerrilla Warfare   Use War
Look   Guess Method   Use Sight Method
Guessing (Tests)
Guidance
Career   Guidance
Guidance Centers
Continuous   Guidance (1966 1980)   Use Guidance
Guidance Counseling (1966 1980)   Use School Counseling
Guidance Counselors   Use School Counselors
Developmental   Guidance (1967 1980)   Use Guidance
Educational   Guidance (1966 1977)   Use Educational Counseling
Elementary School   Guidance (1967 1980)   Use School Guidance
Guidance Facilities (1967 1977)   Use Guidance Centers
Guidance Functions (1968 1980)   Use Guidance Objectives
Guidance Goals   Use Guidance Objectives
Group   Guidance
Guidance Objectives
Occupational   Guidance (1966 1980)   Use Career Guidance
Guidance Personnel
Post High School   Guidance
Guidance Programs
Classroom   Guidance Programs (1968 1980)
School   Guidance
Secondary School   Guidance   Use School Guidance
Guidance Services (1966 1980)   Use Guidance Programs
Guidance Specialists   Use Guidance Personnel and Specialists
Teacher   Guidance
Vocational   Guidance   Use Career Guidance
Guidebooks   Use Guides
Guided Design
Self   Guided Groups   Use Self Directed Groups
Guidelines
Facility   Guidelines
Guides
Administrator   Guides
Curriculum   Guides
Discussion   Guides   Use Discussion (Teaching Technique) and Teaching Guides
FLES   Guides (1967 1980)   Use Curriculum Guides and FLES
Health   Guides (1966 1980)   Use Guides and Health Materials
Language   Guides (1966 1980)
Leaders   Guides
Library   Guides
Literature   Guides (1966 1980)
Program   Guides
Resource   Guides (1966 1980)   Use Resource Materials
Rubrics (Scoring   Guides)   Use Scoring Rubrics
State Curriculum   Guides

```
            Study   Guides
          Teacher   Guides    Use Teaching Guides
         Teaching   Guides
                    Guilt
                    Gujarati
                    Gujerati    Use Gujarati
                    Gullah
                    Gun Control
                    Guns
                    Gymnasiums
                    Gymnastics
                    Gynecology
             Four   H Club Agents    Use Extension Agents
                    Habit Formation
                    Habitats
           Eating   Habits
        Listening   Habits
          Reading   Habits
           Speech   Habits
            Study   Habits
                    Habituation
                    Hagiographies (1971 1980)    Use Biographies
                    Haiku
                    Haitian Creole
                    Haitians
         Full Day   Half Day Alternate Day    Use Alternate Day Schedules and Full Day Half Day Schedules
                    Half Day Schedules    Use Full Day Half Day Schedules
          All Day   Half Day Schedules    Use Full Day Half Day Schedules
         Full Day   Half Day Schedules
                    Half Reversal Shift    Use Shift Studies
                    Halfway Houses    Use Group Homes and Rehabilitation Centers
        Residence   Halls    Use Dormitories
            Study   Halls    Use Study Centers
                    Hallways    Use Corridors
                    Hand Calculators    Use Calculators
              Eye   Hand Coordination
                    Hand Tools
                    Handball
             Team   Handball
                    Handbooks    Use Guides
          Faculty   Handbooks
 Health Activities   Handbooks (1966 1980)    Use Guides and Health Materials
          Library   Handbooks    Use Library Guides
             Left   Handed Writer
                    Handedness
                    Handicap Detection (1966 1980)    Use Disability Identification
                    Handicap Discrimination (1984 1994)    Use Disability Discrimination
                    Handicap Identification (1980 1994)    Use Disability Identification
                    Handicapped (1966 1980)    Use Disabilities
      Academically   Handicapped (1966 1980)
   Adventitiously   Handicapped (1975 1980)    Use Adventitious Impairments
          Aurally   Handicapped (1966 1980)    Use Hearing Impairments
                    Handicapped Children (1966 1980)
       Congenitally   Handicapped (1975 1980)    Use Congenital Impairments
Custodial Mentally   Handicapped (1968 1980)    Use Severe Mental Retardation
Educable Mentally   Handicapped (1966 1980)    Use Mild Mental Retardation
           Gifted   Handicapped    Use Gifted Disabled
         Language   Handicapped (1967 1980)    Use Language Impairments
          Mentally   Handicapped (1966 1980)    Use Mental Retardation
          Visually   Handicapped Mobility (1967 1994)    Use Visually Impaired Mobility
          Multiply   Handicapped (1967 1980)    Use Multiple Disabilities
    Neurologically   Handicapped (1966 1980)    Use Neurological Impairments
     Normalization   (Handicapped) (1974 1994)    Use Normalization (Disabilities)
          Visually   Handicapped Orientation (1967 1980)    Use Visually Impaired Mobility
    Orthopedically   Handicapped (1968 1980)    Use Physical Disabilities
      Perceptually   Handicapped (1966 1980)    Use Perceptual Impairments
        Physically   Handicapped (1966 1980)    Use Physical Disabilities
         Severely   Handicapped (1975 1980)    Use Severe Disabilities
           Speech   Handicapped (1967 1980)    Use Speech Impairments
                    Handicapped Students (1967 1980)
 Trainable Mentally   Handicapped (1967 1980)    Use Moderate Mental Retardation
          Visually   Handicapped (1966 1980)    Use Visual Impairments
                    Handicaps    Use Disabilities
         Language   Handicaps (1966 1994)    Use Language Impairments
        Perceptual   Handicaps (1980 1994)    Use Perceptual Impairments
         Physical   Handicaps (1966 1980)    Use Physical Disabilities
           Speech   Handicaps (1966 1994)    Use Speech Impairments
                    Handicrafts
 Manuscript Writing   (Handlettering)
             Food   Handling Facilities
                    Hands on Learning    Use Experiential Learning
                    Hands on Science
                    Handwriting
                    Handwriting Development (1966 1980)    Use Handwriting and Writing Skills
                    Handwriting Instruction (1966 1983)    Use Handwriting and Writing Instruction
                    Handwriting Materials (1966 1983)    Use Handwriting and Instructional Materials
                    Handwriting Readiness (1966 1983)    Use Handwriting and Writing Readiness
                    Handwriting Skills (1966 1983)    Use Handwriting and Writing Skills
                    Hangul    Use Korean
                    Hanja    Use Korean
                    Hankul    Use Korean
                    Happiness
                    Haptic Perception (1967 1980)    Use Tactual Perception
```

```
                      Sexual   Harassment
                               Hard of Hearing (1967 1980)   Use Partial Hearing
                               Harmony (Music)
                               Harvesting
                        Crop   Harvesting   Use Harvesting
                               Hashish   Use Marijuana
                               Hausa
                               Hawaiian
                               Hawaiians
                               Hazardous Materials
                               Hazardous Wastes   Use Hazardous Materials and Wastes
                               Hazing
                               Head Banging   Use Self Injurious Behavior
                               Head Injuries
                      Closed   Head Injuries   Use Head Injuries
                               Head Librarians   Use Library Directors
                     Subject   Headings   Use Subject Index Terms
                               Headlines
                  Department   Heads
                   Household   Heads   Use Heads of Households
                               Heads of Households
                               Health
                               Health Activities
                               Health Activities Handbooks (1966 1980)   Use Guides and Health Materials
                        Home   Health Aides
                               Health Behavior
                               Health Books (1966 1980)   Use Books and Health Materials
                       Child   Health Care   Use Child Health
                               Health Care Costs
                               Health Care Evaluation   Use Medical Care Evaluation
                     Primary   Health Care
                       Child   Health
                      Mental   Health Clinics
                   Community   Health (1966 1980)   Use Public Health
                               Health Conditions
                               Health Costs   Use Health Care Costs
                      Dental   Health
                               Health Education
                      Allied   Health Education   Use Allied Health Occupations Education
         Comprehensive School   Health Education
                   Emotional   Health   Use Mental Health
                               Health Facilities
                      Family   Health
                               Health Guides (1966 1980)   Use Guides and Health Materials
                               Health Insurance
                      Public   Health Laws (1966 1974)   Use Public Health Legislation
                      Public   Health Legislation
                               Health Maintenance Organizations
                               Health Materials
                      Mental   Health
                               Health Needs
                Occupational   Health   Use Occupational Safety and Health
        Occupational Safety and Health
                               Health Occupations
                      Allied   Health Occupations
                               Health Occupations Centers (1968 1980)
                               Health Occupations Education (1967 1980)   Use Allied Health Occupations Education
                      Allied   Health Occupations Education
                               Health Occupations Education (Vocational)   Use Allied Health Occupations Education and Vocational Education
                               Health Occupations Personnel   Use Health Personnel
                    Personal   Health   Use Hygiene
                               Health Personnel
                      Allied   Health Personnel
                    Physical   Health
                  Preventive   Health   Use Health Promotion
                     Special   Health Problems
                      Allied   Health Professions   Use Allied Health Occupations
            Clinical Teaching   (Health Professions)
                               Health Programs
         Comprehensive School   Health Programs   Use Comprehensive School Health Education
                      Mental   Health Programs
                               Health Promotion
                      Public   Health
                               Health Related Fitness
                               Health Related Professions   Use Allied Health Occupations
                      Mental   Health Resources   Use Mental Health Programs
                               Health Sciences Libraries   Use Medical Libraries
                               Health Service Personnel   Use Health Personnel
                               Health Service Workers   Use Health Personnel
                               Health Services
                   Community   Health Services
                     Migrant   Health Services
                      School   Health Services
        Occupational Safety and Health Standards   Use Labor Standards and Occupational Safety and Health
                               Health Workers   Use Health Personnel
                   Community   Health Workers   Use Community Health Services and Health Personnel
             Community Mental   Health Workers   Use Community Health Services and Mental Health Workers
                      Mental   Health Workers
                               Hearing Aids
                               Hearing Clinics (1968 1980)   Use Speech and Hearing Clinics
                  Speech and   Hearing Clinics
                               Hearing Conservation
                     Hard of   Hearing (1967 1980)   Use Partial Hearing
```

Profoundly	Hearing Impaired Use Deafness
	Hearing Impairments
	Hearing Loss (1967 1980) Use Hearing Impairments
Partial	Hearing
	Hearing (Physiology)
	Hearing Rehabilitation Use Hearing Therapy
	Hearing Tests Use Auditory Tests
	Hearing Therapists (1967 1980) Use Hearing Therapy and Therapists
	Hearing Therapy
	Hearings
Public	Hearings Use Hearings
	Heart Disorders
	Heart Rate
	Heat
	Heat Equations Use Thermodynamics
Insulation	(Heat) Use Thermal Insulation
	Heat Recovery
	Heating
	Heating Oils Use Fossil Fuels and Oil
Solar	Heating Use Heating and Solar Energy
	Hebrew
	Height
Body	Height
	Helicopter Pilots Use Aircraft Pilots
Self	Help Devices (Disabled) Use Assistive Devices (for Disabled)
	Help Giving Use Helping Relationship
Self	Help Programs
	Help Seeking
Temporary	Help Services Use Employment Services and Temporary Employment
	Helping Behavior Use Helping Relationship
Cross Age	Helping Use Cross Age Teaching
	Helping Relationship
	Helplessness
Learned	Helplessness Use Helplessness
Brain	Hemisphere Functions
	Hemispheric Specialization (Brain) Use Brain Hemisphere Functions
	Hemodynamics Use Blood Circulation
	Herbicides
	Heredity
Environment	Heredity Controversy Use Nature Nurture Controversy
	Heredity Environment Controversy Use Nature Nurture Controversy
Cultural	Heritage Use Cultural Background
	Heritage Education
Ethnic	Heritage Use Cultural Background
	Hermeneutics
	Heroin
	Heterogeneous Grouping
	Heterophoria (1968 1974) Use Strabismus
	Heterotropia (1968 1974) Use Strabismus
	Heuristic Games Use Educational Games
	Heuristics
	Hidden Curriculum
	Hierarchy Use Vertical Organization
	High Achievement
	High Achievers (1966 1980) Use High Achievement
	High Blood Pressure Use Hypertension
	High Interest Low Vocabulary Books
	High Risk Persons (1982 1990) Use At Risk Persons
	High Risk Students
	High School Academies (Career Development) Use Career Academies
	High School College Cooperation Use College School Cooperation
College	High School Cooperation (1967 1980) Use College School Cooperation
	High School Curriculum (1967 1980) Use Secondary School Curriculum
	High School Design (1966 1980) Use Educational Facilities Design
	High School Dropouts Use Dropouts
Post	High School Education Use Postsecondary Education
	High School Equivalency Programs
	High School Freshmen
	High School Graduates
Post	High School Guidance
	High School Libraries Use School Libraries
	High School Organization (1966 1980) Use School Organization
	High School Role (1966 1980) Use School Role
Junior	High School Role (1966 1980) Use School Role
	High School Seniors
	High School Students
Junior	High School Students
Senior	High School Students Use High School Students
	High School Supervisors (1966 1980) Use School Supervision
	High School Teachers Use Secondary School Teachers
Junior	High School Teachers Use Secondary School Teachers
	High Schools
Catholic	High Schools (1967 1980) Use Catholic Schools
Comprehensive	High Schools (1967 1980) Use High Schools
Continuation	High Schools (1968 1980) Use Continuation Students
General	High Schools (1966 1980) Use General Education
Junior	High Schools
Senior	High Schools (1966 1980) Use High Schools
Technical	High Schools Use Vocational High Schools
Vocational	High Schools
	High Stakes Tests
	High Technology Use Technological Advancement
	Higher Education

Admission Tests	(Higher Education) Use College Entrance Examinations
	Higher Education as a Field of Study Use Postsecondary Education as a Field of Study
	Higher Education Institutions Use Colleges
Private	Higher Education Use Higher Education and Private Education
Public	Higher Education Use Higher Education and Public Education
Performance Assessment	(Higher Order Learning) Use Performance Based Assessment
	Higher Order Skills Use Thinking Skills
	Highway Construction Use Road Construction
	Highway Engineering Use Civil Engineering
	Highway Engineering Aides
	Hindi
	Hiring (Personnel) Use Personnel Selection
	Hispanic American Culture
	Hispanic American Literature
	Hispanic American Students
	Hispanic Americans
	Historians
	Historic Sites
	Historical Criticism (1969 1980)
	Historical Geography Use Human Geography
	Historical Interpretation
	Historical Linguistics Use Diachronic Linguistics
	Historical Reviews (1966 1980) Use History
	Historical Sites Use Historic Sites
	Historically Black Colleges Use Black Colleges
Life	Histories Use Biographies
Medical Case	Histories
	Historiography
	History
African	History
American	History (1966 1980)
American Indian	History
Ancient	History
Applied	History Use Public History
Art	History
Asian	History
Black	History
Central American	History Use Latin American History
Community	History Use Local History
Constitutional	History
Contemporary	History Use Modern History
County	History Use Counties and Local History
	History Curriculum Use History Instruction
Diplomatic	History
	History Education Use History Instruction
Educational	History
European	History
Family	History
	History Instruction
Intellectual	History
Journalism	History
Language	History Use Diachronic Linguistics
Latin American	History
Literary	History
Local	History
Mathematics	History
Medieval	History
Mexican American	History
Middle Eastern	History
Modern	History
Near Eastern	History Use Middle Eastern History
Negro	History (1966 1977) Use Black History
North American	History
	History of Education Use Educational History
	History of Language Use Diachronic Linguistics
Oral	History
Public	History
Science	History
Science Education	History
Social	History
South American	History Use Latin American History
State	History
	History Textbooks
United States	History
Colonial	History (United States)
World	History
	Hmong
	Hmong People
	HMOs Use Health Maintenance Organizations
Managed Care	(HMOs) Use Health Maintenance Organizations
	Hobbies
Field	Hockey
Ice	Hockey
	Hokku Use Haiku
Job	Holding Patterns Use Employment Patterns
	Holding Power (of Schools) Use School Holding Power
School	Holding Power
Library	Holdings Use Library Collections
	Holidays
Religious	Holidays
	Holistic Approach
	Holistic Evaluation
	Holography

```
                              Holy Days    Use Religious Holidays
                              Home    Use Family Environment
                     Rest   Home Aides    Use Nurses Aides
                              Home and Family Life Education    Use Family Life Education
                              Home Appliance Repair    Use Appliance Repair
                              Home Attendants    Use Home Health Aides
                              Home Child Care    Use Child Rearing
                              Home Conditions    Use Family Environment
                              Home Day Care    Use Family Day Care
                              Home Demonstration Agents    Use Extension Agents
                              Home Economics
                              Home Economics Education
             Occupational   Home Economics
                              Home Economics Skills
                              Home Economics Teachers
                              Home Environment    Use Family Environment
                              Home Experience    Use Experiential Learning
                              Home Furnishings
                              Home Health Aides
                              Home Influence    Use Family Influence
                              Home Instruction
                              Home Life    Use Family Life
                              Home Management
          Work Stations   (Home or Office)    Use Workstations
                              Home Programs
                  School   Home Relationship    Use Family School Relationship
                              Home School Relationship    Use Family School Relationship
                              Home Schooling
                              Home Study
                              Home Visits
                              Homebound
                              Homebound Children (1966 1980)    Use Homebound
                              Homebound Teachers (1966 1980)    Use Itinerant Teachers
                              Homeless People
                              Homelessness    Use Homeless People
                              Homemakers
                              Homemakers Clubs (1966 1980)    Use Clubs and Homemaking Skills
               Displaced   Homemakers
                 Visiting   Homemakers
                              Homemaking Education (1967 1980)    Use Home Economics
                              Homemaking Skills
                              Homeowners
                  Foster   Homes (1970 1982) (Adults)    Use Adult Foster Care
               Boarding   Homes
                  Foster   Homes (1970 1982) (Children)    Use Foster Care
           Convalescent   Homes    Use Nursing Homes
                              Homes for the Aged    Use Personal Care Homes
                   Group   Homes
                 Nursing   Homes
          Personal Care   Homes
                     Rest   Homes    Use Personal Care Homes
                              Homework
                              Homicide
                              Homogeneous Grouping
                              Homonegativism    Use Homophobia
                              Homophobia
                              Homosexuality
                  Female   Homosexuality    Use Lesbianism
                              Honesty
                              Honor Codes    Use Codes of Ethics
                              Honor Societies
                              Honors Classes (1966 1980)    Use Honors Curriculum
                              Honors Courses    Use Honors Curriculum
                              Honors Curriculum
                              Hopi
                              Hopi (Tribe)
                              Horizontal Organization
                              Horologists    Use Watchmakers
                              Horology
                              Horseback Riding
                              Horses
                              Horticulture
                Nurseries   (Horticulture)
          Nursery Workers   (Horticulture)
                Ornamental   Horticulture Occupation (1967 1976)    Use Ornamental Horticulture Occupations
                Ornamental   Horticulture Occupations
                Ornamental   Horticulture
              Yard Workers   (Horticulture)    Use Grounds Keepers
                              Hospices (Terminal Care)
                              Hospital Attendants    Use Nurses Aides
                Veterinary   Hospital Attendants    Use Veterinary Assistants
                              Hospital Libraries
                              Hospital Personnel
                              Hospital Record Administrators    Use Medical Record Administrators
                              Hospital Record Technicians    Use Medical Record Technicians
                              Hospital Schools
                              Hospitality Occupations
                              Hospitalized Children
                              Hospitals
                Psychiatric   Hospitals
                  Teaching   Hospitals
        University Teaching   Hospitals    Use Teaching Hospitals
                              Hostility
```

Database	Hosts Use Online Vendors
	Hotels
	Hothouses Use Greenhouses
	Hotlines (Public)
Flexible Working	Hours
	Hours of Work Use Working Hours
Student Credit	Hours Use Credits
Study	Hours Use Study
Working	Hours
	House Plan
	Household Chores Use Housework
	Household Heads Use Heads of Households
	Household Occupations Use Household Workers and Service Occupations
	Household Science Use Consumer Science
	Household Workers
	Households Use Family (Sociological Unit)
Heads of	Households
Housekeeping	(Households) Use Housework
	Househusbands Use Homemakers
	Housekeepers
	Housekeeping Aides Use Housekeepers
	Housekeeping (Households) Use Housework
	Houseparents Use Resident Advisers
Field	Houses
Halfway	Houses Use Group Homes and Rehabilitation Centers
Publishing	Houses Use Publishing Industry
Settlement	Houses
	Housewives (1968 1980) Use Homemakers
	Housework
	Housing
Local	Housing Authorities (1966 1980) Use Housing
Black	Housing (1977 1980)
College	Housing
Student	Housing (College) Use College Housing
	Housing Deficiencies
	Housing Discrimination
	Housing Industry
Low Rent	Housing
	Housing Management Aides
Middle Income	Housing
Migrant	Housing
	Housing Needs
Negro	Housing (1966 1977)
	Housing Opportunities
	Housing Patterns (1966 1980) Use Residential Patterns
Public	Housing
Public	Housing Residents (1966 1980) Use Public Housing
Suburban	Housing
Teacher	Housing
	HTLV 3 Use Acquired Immune Deficiency Syndrome
	Hue Use Color
	Human Biology Use Biology
	Human Body
	Human Capital
	Human Development (1966 1980)
	Human Dignity
	Human Engineering (1967 1980) Use Human Factors Engineering
	Human Factors Engineering
	Human Geography
	Human Immunodeficiency Virus Use Acquired Immune Deficiency Syndrome
	Human Living (1966 1980)
	Human Performance Technology Use Performance Technology
	Human Posture
	Human Relations
	Human Relations Organizations (1966 1980) Use Human Relations Programs
	Human Relations Programs
	Human Relations Training Use Sensitivity Training
	Human Relations Units (1966 1980) Use Human Relations and Units of Study
	Human Resources
	Human Resources Development (Labor) Use Labor Force Development
	Human Rights Use Civil Liberties
	Human Services
Client Background	(Human Services) Use Client Characteristics (Human Services)
Client Characteristics	(Human Services)
Full Service Schools	(Human Services) Use Integrated Services
Support Groups	(Human Services) Use Social Support Groups
	Human Sexuality Use Sexuality
	Human T Cell Lymphotropic Virus Type 3 Use Acquired Immune Deficiency Syndrome
	Humaneness Use Altruism
	Humanism
	Humanistic Education
	Humanitarianism
	Humanities
	Humanities Instruction
	Humanization
	Humid Areas Use Humidity
	Humidity
Absolute	Humidity Use Humidity
Relative	Humidity Use Humidity
	Humor
	Hungarian
	Hunger
	Hurricanes

Animal	Husbandry
	Husbands Use Spouses
	Hvac Use Climate Control
	Hybrid Air Structures (1972 1980) Use Air Structures
	Hydraulics
	Hydrology
	Hygiene
Mental	Hygiene Use Mental Health
Dental	Hygienists
Oral	Hygienists Use Dental Hygienists
	Hymns
	Hyperactivity
	Hyperkinesis Use Hyperactivity
	Hypermedia
	Hyperopia
	Hypersensitivity Use Allergy
	Hypertension
	Hypertext Use Hypermedia
	Hypnosis
	Hypnotics Use Sedatives
	Hypothesis Testing
World War	I
	Ibo (1967 1993) Use Igbo
	ICAI Use Intelligent Tutoring Systems
	Ice Hockey
	Ice Skating
	Ichthyology
	Icibemba Use Bemba
Access to	Ideas Use Intellectual Freedom
Adoption	(Ideas)
Ownership of	Ideas Use Intellectual Property
	Identification
Ability	Identification
Delinquent	Identification (1966 1980) Use Delinquency and Identification
Disability	Identification
Dropout	Identification (1966 1980) Use Dropout Characteristics
Early	Identification
Ethnic	Identification Use Ethnicity
Handicap	Identification (1980 1994) Use Disability Identification
Plant	Identification
	Identification (Psychological) (1968 1980) Use Identification (Psychology)
	Identification (Psychology)
Racial	Identification
Racial Self	Identification Use Racial Identification
Talent	Identification
	Identification Tests (1966 1980) Use Tests
Racial	Identity Use Racial Identification
Gender	Identity (Sex) Use Sexual Identity
Sexual	Identity
	Ideography
	Ideology
	Idiomatic Expressions Use Idioms
	Idioms
	Igbo
World War	II
	III Child Care Use Sick Child Care
	Illegal Aliens Use Undocumented Immigrants
	Illegal Drug Use
	Illegal Immigrants (1976 1984) Use Undocumented Immigrants
Alien	Illegality Use Undocumented Immigrants
Immigrant	Illegality Use Undocumented Immigrants
	Illegitimacy Use Births to Single Women
	Illegitimate Births (1967 1995) Use Births to Single Women
	Illiteracy
Functional	Illiteracy (1968 1980) Use Functional Literacy
	Illiterate Adults (1966 1980) Use Adult Literacy and Illiteracy
Chronic	Illness
Mental	Illness (1966 1980) Use Mental Disorders
Terminal	Illness
	Illnesses Use Diseases
	Illocutionary Acts Use Speech Acts
	Illumination Levels (1968 1980) Use Lighting
Technical	Illustration
	Illustrations
Body	Image
Public	Image Use Public Opinion
Self	Image Use Self Concept
	Imagery
Eidetic	Imagery
Cultural	Images
Eidetic	Images (1967 1980) Use Eidetic Imagery
	Imagination
Racial	Imbalance Use Racial Balance
	Imitation
	Imitative Learning Use Observational Learning
	Immaturity (1966 1980) Use Maturity (Individuals)
Social	Immaturity (1966 1980) Use Maturity (Individuals)
	Immersion Programs
	Immigrant Illegality Use Undocumented Immigrants
	Immigrants
Illegal	Immigrants (1976 1984) Use Undocumented Immigrants
Internal	Immigrants Use Migrants
Undocumented	Immigrants

Immigration
Immigration Inspectors
Urban Immigration (1966 1976) Use Rural to Urban Migration
Acquired Immune Deficiency Syndrome
Immunization Programs
Human Immunodeficiency Virus Use Acquired Immune Deficiency Syndrome
Desegregation Impact Use Desegregation Effects
Economic Impact
Integration Impact Use Desegregation Effects
Visually Impaired Mobility
Profoundly Hearing Impaired Use Deafness
Impairment Severity Use Severity (of Disability)
Adventitious Impairments
Articulation Impairments
Congenital Impairments
Hearing Impairments
Language Impairments
Neurological Impairments
Perceptual Impairments
Speech Impairments
Visual Impairments
Equity (Impartiality) Use Justice
Impasse Resolution Use Negotiation Impasses
Negotiation Impasses
Imperative Mood Use Verbs
Imperialism
Cochlear Implants
Program Implementation
Imports
Impressionism
Impressionistic Criticism (1969 1980)
Improvement
Building Improvement (1966 1980) Use Facility Improvement
City Improvement (1966 1980) Use Urban Improvement
Curriculum Improvement Use Curriculum Development
Educational Improvement
Educational Facilities Improvement
Enunciation Improvement (1966 1980) Use Articulation (Speech) and Speech Improvement
Facility Improvement
Faculty Improvement Use Faculty Development
Instructional Improvement
Neighborhood Improvement
Program Improvement
Improvement Programs
Science Course Improvement Project (1967 1980) Use Science Course Improvement Projects
Science Course Improvement Projects
Reading Improvement
Sanitation Improvement (1966 1980) Use Sanitation
School Improvement (1966 1980) Use Educational Facilities Improvement
Speech Improvement
Staff Improvement (1966 1980) Use Staff Development
Student Improvement
Teacher Improvement
Urban Improvement
Writing Improvement
Improvisation
Impulse Control Use Self Control
Impulsivity Use Conceptual Tempo
Aging in Academia
Drug Testing (Presence in Body) Use Drug Use Testing
Rank in Class Use Class Rank
Master of Arts in College Teaching Use Masters Degrees
Reading in Content Areas Use Content Area Reading
Key Word in Context Use Permuted Indexes
Resident Students (1967 1980) (in District) Use Residence Requirements
Computer Uses in Education
Specialist in Education Degrees
Excellence in Education
Partnerships in Education
Partners in Education Projects Use Partnerships in Education
Reduction in Force
Retention (in Grade) Use Grade Repetition
Sexism in Language
In Loco Parentis
Patterns in Mathematics
Progressive Retardation (1966 1980) (in School) Use Educationally Disadvantaged
Registration in School Use School Registration
Retention (in School) Use School Holding Power
In School Suspension
Prayer in Schools Use School Prayer
Resident Students (1967 1980) (in State) Use In State Students
In State Students
Step in Step out Students Use Stopouts
Master of Arts in Teaching Use Masters Degrees
Master of Science in Teaching Use Masters Degrees
Foreign Languages in the Elementary School Use FLES
Physicians in Training Use Graduate Medical Students
Drug Exposure in Utero Use Prenatal Drug Exposure
Inadequate Employment Use Underemployment
Developmentally Inappropriate Education Use Developmentally Appropriate Practices
Incentive Grants
Incentive Systems (1967 1980) Use Incentives
Incentives

Achievement	Incentives Use Incentives
	Incest
	Incest Taboo Use Incest
	Incidence
Low	Incidence Disabilities
Disease	Incidence
	Incidental Learning
Critical	Incidents Method
	Inclusion (Education) Use Inclusive Schools
Full	Inclusion Use Inclusive Schools
	Inclusive Education Use Inclusive Schools
	Inclusive Schools
	Income
	Income Contingent Loans
Low	Income Counties
Family	Income
Low	Income Groups
Guaranteed	Income
Middle	Income Housing
Low	Income
	Income Patterns Use Income
Low	Income States
Negative	Income Tax Use Guaranteed Income
College Costs	(Incurred by Students) Use Student Costs
	Indemnity Bonds
Field	Independence Use Field Dependence Independence
Field Dependence	Independence
	Independent Colleges Use Private Colleges
	Independent Learning Use Independent Study
	Independent Living
	Independent Living Skills Use Daily Living Skills
	Independent Reading
	Independent Schools Use Private Schools
	Independent Students (Self Supporting) Use Self Supporting Students
	Independent Study
	Independent Variables Use Predictor Variables
	Index Numbers (Costs) Use Cost Indexes
	Index Terms Use Subject Index Terms
Subject	Index Terms
	Indexes
Citation	Indexes
Coordinate	Indexes
Cost	Indexes
KWIC	Indexes Use Permuted Indexes
KWOC	Indexes Use Permuted Indexes
	Indexes (Locaters) (1967 1980) Use Indexes
Permuted	Indexes
Post Coordinate	Indexes Use Coordinate Indexes
Price	Indexes Use Cost Indexes
Title Word	Indexes Use Permuted Indexes
Uniterm	Indexes Use Coordinate Indexes
	Indexing
Automatic	Indexing
Computer Assisted	Indexing Use Automatic Indexing
Machine Aided	Indexing Use Automatic Indexing
	Indian Controlled Schools Use American Indian Education and Tribally Controlled Education
American	Indian Culture
American	Indian Education
American	Indian History
American	Indian Languages
American	Indian Literature
Federal	Indian Relationship
Reservations	(Indian) (1971 1980) Use American Indian Reservations
American	Indian Reservations
American	Indian Studies
	Indians
American	Indians
Nonreservation American	Indians
Off Reservation American	Indians Use Nonreservation American Indians
Reservation American	Indians
Rural American	Indians
Urban American	Indians
	Indicative Mood Use Verbs
Social	Indicators
	Indifference Use Apathy
	Indigenous Personnel
	Indigenous Populations
	Individual Activities
	Individual Adjustment Use Adjustment (to Environment)
	Individual Autonomy Use Personal Autonomy
	Individual Characteristics
	Individual Counseling
	Individual Development
	Individual Differences
	Individual Dignity Use Human Dignity
Symptoms	(Individual Disorders)
	Individual Family Service Plans Use Individualized Family Service Plans
	Individual Instruction
	Individual Needs
	Individual Power
	Individual Psychology
	Individual Reading (1966 1980)
	Individual Rights Use Civil Liberties

College Costs (Financing for	Individual Students) Use Paying for College
	Individual Study (1966 1980) Use Independent Study
	Individual Testing
	Individual Tests (1966 1980) Use Individual Testing
	Individual Volition Use Individual Power
	Individualism
	Individualized Curriculum (1966 1980) Use Individualized Instruction
	Individualized Education Use Individualized Instruction
	Individualized Education Programs
	Individualized Family Service Plans
	Individualized Instruction
Clinical Teaching	(Individualized Instruction) Use Individualized Instruction
	Individualized Programs
	Individualized Reading
Aging	(Individuals)
Alternative Evaluation	(Individuals) Use Alternative Assessment
Assessment Instruments	(Individuals) Use Measures (Individuals)
Delayed Development	(Individuals) Use Developmental Delays
Developmental Patterns	(Individuals) Use Individual Development
Disposition	(Individuals) Use Personality
Maturity	(Individuals)
Measures	(Individuals)
Self Disclosure	(Individuals)
Self Evaluation	(Individuals)
Special Needs	(Individuals) Use Individual Needs
	Indo European Languages
	Indochinese
	Indochinese Americans Use Asian Americans and Indochinese
Bahasa	Indonesia Use Indonesian
	Indonesian
	Indonesian Languages
	Induction
Beginning Teacher	Induction
Entry Year Assistance (Teacher	Induction) Use Beginning Teacher Induction
Loop	Induction Systems
Teacher	Induction Use Teacher Orientation
	Inductive Methods (1967 1980) Use Induction
	Industrial and Organizational Psychology Use Industrial Psychology
	Industrial Arts
Painting	(Industrial Arts)
	Industrial Arts Shops Use School Shops
	Industrial Arts Teachers
	Industrial Communication Use Business Communication
	Industrial Crafts Use Industrial Arts
	Industrial Education
Trade and	Industrial Education
Vocational	Industrial Education Use Trade and Industrial Education
	Industrial Libraries Use Corporate Libraries
	Industrial Nations Use Developed Nations
Painting (1966 1980)	(Industrial) Use Painting (Industrial Arts)
	Industrial Personnel
	Industrial Psychology
	Industrial Relations (1969 1980) Use Labor Relations
	Industrial Robotics Use Robotics
	Industrial Structure
Trade and	Industrial Teachers
	Industrial Technology (1969 1980) Use Industry and Technology
	Industrial Technology Education Use Technology Education
	Industrial Training
	Industrial X Ray Operators Use Radiographers
	Industrialization
	Industry
Aerospace	Industry
Apparel	Industry Use Fashion Industry
Bakery	Industry
Banking	Industry Use Banking
Book	Industry Use Publishing Industry
Brick	Industry
Broadcast	Industry
Business Officials	(Industry) Use Administrators
Cement	Industry
Chemical	Industry
Clothing	Industry Use Fashion Industry
Company Size	(Industry) Use Organization Size (Groups)
Concrete	Industry Use Cement Industry
Construction	Industry
Electronics	Industry
Fashion	Industry
Feed	Industry
Film	Industry
Food Service	Industry (1967 1981) Use Food Service
Furniture	Industry
Garment	Industry Use Fashion Industry
Housing	Industry
Information	Industry
Insurance	Industry Use Insurance Companies
Lumber	Industry
Machinery	Industry
Machinery Manufacturing	Industry Use Machinery Industry
Manufacturing	Industry
Meat Packing	Industry
Metal	Industry
Petroleum	Industry

Publishing	Industry
School	Industry Relationship (1967 1980) Use School Business Relationship
	Industry School Relationship Use School Business Relationship
Service	Industry Use Service Occupations
Sightseeing	Industry Use Tourism
Steel	Industry (1967 1980) Use Metal Industry
Telephone Communications	Industry
Timber Based	Industry Use Lumber Industry
Tourist	Industry Use Tourism
	Ineligibility Use Disqualification
	Inequalities (1970 1980)
Educational	Inequality Use Equal Education
	Inequality (Mathematics)
	Infancy (1966 1980) Use Infants
	Infant Behavior
	Infant Care
	Infant Death Rate Use Infant Mortality and Mortality Rate
Sudden	Infant Death Syndrome
	Infant Mortality
British	Infant Schools
	Infant Schools (British Primary System) Use British Infant Schools
	Infants
Newborn	Infants Use Neonates
Premature	Infants
Ear	Infections (Middle Ear) Use Otitis Media
	Infectious Diseases (1966 1974) Use Communicable Diseases
Statistical	Inference
	Inferences
	Inferential Statistics Use Statistical Inference and Statistics
	Infirmaries Use Health Facilities
	Inflatable Structures Use Air Structures
	Inflated Grades Use Grade Inflation
Air	Inflated Structures (1972 1980) Use Air Structures
	Inflation (Economics)
Grade	Inflation
Community	Influence
Family	Influence
Home	Influence Use Family Influence
Parent	Influence
Peer	Influence
Teacher	Influence
	Influences
Biological	Influences
Black	Influences
Cultural	Influences
Economic	Influences Use Economic Factors
Enrollment	Influences
Environmental	Influences
Literary	Influences (1969 1980)
Minority Group	Influences
Perinatal	Influences
Political	Influences
Prenatal	Influences
Race	Influences (1966 1980) Use Racial Factors
Social	Influences
Socioeconomic	Influences
	Informal Assessment
	Informal Conversational Usage Use Standard Spoken Usage
	Informal Education
	Informal Leadership
	Informal Organization
	Informal Reading Inventories
	Informal Reading Inventory (1968 1980) Use Informal Reading Inventories
Native	Informants Use Native Speakers
	Informatics Use Information Science
Access to	Information
	Information and Referral Services Use Information Services and Referral
Authority Control	(Information)
	Information Brokers Use Information Scientists
	Information Centers
Community	Information Centers Use Community Information Services
Confidential	Information Use Confidentiality
Decoding	(Information) Use Coding
Career	Information Delivery Systems Use Career Information Systems
	Information Dissemination
Encoding	(Information) Use Coding
End Users	(Information) Use Users (Information)
Electronic	Information Exchange Use Information Networks and Telecommunications
Scholarly	Information Exchange Use Scholarly Communication
	Information Flow Use Information Transfer
Freedom of	Information
	Information Industry
	Information Literacy
	Information Management
Merchandise	Information
	Information Needs
	Information Networks
Occupational	Information
	Information Policy
Private	Information Use Confidentiality
	Information Processes (Psychological) Use Cognitive Processes
	Information Processing
Product	Information Use Merchandise Information

Information Professionals   Use Information Scientists
Information Resources Management   Use Information Management
Information Retrieval
Online   Information Retrieval   Use Online Searching
Relevance   (Information Retrieval)
Information Science
Science   Information   Use Scientific and Technical Information
Information Science Education
Scientific   Information   Use Scientific and Technical Information
Scientific and Technical   Information
Information Scientists
Information Seeking
Selective Dissemination of   Information
Information Services
Information Services (Community)   Use Community Information Services
Community   Information Services
Local   Information Services   Use Community Information Services
Information Skills
Information Sources
Information Specialists   Use Information Scientists
Information Storage
Information Storage (Psychology)   Use Encoding (Psychology)
Information Superhighway   Use Internet
Information Systems
Career   Information Systems
Dial Access   Information Systems
Management   Information Systems
Navigation   (Information Systems)
Occupational   Information Systems   Use Career Information Systems
Technical   Information   Use Scientific and Technical Information
Technological   Information   Use Scientific and Technical Information
Information Technology
Information Theory
Information Transfer
Information User Needs   Use User Needs (Information)
User Needs   (Information)
Information User Satisfaction   Use User Satisfaction (Information)
User Satisfaction   (Information)
Information Users   Use Users (Information)
Users   (Information)
Information Utilities (Online)   Use Online Vendors
Information Utilization
Rural   Inhabitants   Use Rural Population
Inhalation Therapists (1969 1985)   Use Respiratory Therapy and Therapists
Oxygen   Inhalation Therapy   Use Respiratory Therapy
Linguistic Difficulty   (Inherent)
Inhibition
Proactive   Inhibition   Use Inhibition
Reactive   Inhibition   Use Inhibition
Retroactive   Inhibition   Use Inhibition
Initial Expenses (1966 1980)   Use Expenditures
Minimum   Initial Expenses   Use Expenditures
Initial Teaching Alphabet
Minimally Brain   Injured (1966 1980)   Use Minimal Brain Dysfunction
Injuries
Closed Head   Injuries   Use Head Injuries
Head   Injuries
Self   Injurious Behavior
Traumatic Brain   Injury   Use Head Injuries and Neurological Impairments
Magnetic   Ink Character Recognition   Use Character Recognition
Inmates   Use Prisoners
Jail   Inmates   Use Prisoners
Inner City
Inner City Education   Use Urban Education
Inner Speech (Subvocal)
Innovation
Building   Innovation
Educational   Innovation
Instructional   Innovation
Teaching   Innovations   Use Instructional Innovation
Inns   Use Hotels
Inorganic Chemistry
Inplant Programs
Input Devices   Use Input Output Devices
Input Evaluation   Use Input Output Analysis
Language   Input   Use Linguistic Input
Linguistic   Input
Input Output
Input Output Analysis
Input Output Devices
Inquiry
Inquiry Training (1967 1980)   Use Inquiry
Insect Studies   Use Entomology
Insecticides
Insecurity (1966 1980)   Use Security (Psychology)
Economic   Insecurity   Use Poverty
Inservice Courses (1966 1980)   Use Inservice Education
Inservice Education
Inservice Education Programs   Use Inservice Education
Inservice Programs (1966 1980)   Use Inservice Education
Inservice Teacher Education
Inservice Teacher Training   Use Inservice Teacher Education
Inservice Teaching (1966 1980)   Use Inservice Education and Teaching (Occupation)

Inservice Teaching Experience   Use Teaching Experience
Inspection
Cosmetics   Inspectors   Use Food and Drug Inspectors
Dairy Product   Inspectors   Use Food and Drug Inspectors
Drug   Inspectors   Use Food and Drug Inspectors
Egg   Inspectors   Use Food and Drug Inspectors
Fish   Inspectors   Use Food and Drug Inspectors
Food   Inspectors   Use Food and Drug Inspectors
Food and Drug   Inspectors
Fruit and Vegetable   Inspectors   Use Food and Drug Inspectors
Immigration   Inspectors
Meat   Inspectors   Use Food and Drug Inspectors
Peanut   Inspectors   Use Food and Drug Inspectors
Processed Foods   Inspectors   Use Food and Drug Inspectors
Sanitary   Inspectors   Use Environmental Technicians
Marital   Instability
Floor   Installation   Use Flooring
Roof   Installation   Use Roofing
Glass   Installers   Use Glaziers
Institute Type Courses (1966 1980)   Use Institutes (Training Programs)
Science   Institutes (1967 1980)   Use Institutes (Training Programs) and Science Programs
Summer   Institutes (1967 1980)   Use Institutes (Training Programs) and Summer Programs
Technical   Institutes
Institutes (Training Programs)
Institution Libraries (1969 1980)   Use Institutional Libraries
Institutional Administration
Institutional Advancement
Institutional Assessment   Use Institutional Evaluation
Institutional Autonomy
Institutional Characteristics
Institutional Cooperation
Institutional Differences   Use Differences and Institutional Characteristics
Diversity   (Institutional)
Institutional Eligibility   Use Eligibility
Institutional Environment
Institutional Evaluation
Institutional Facilities (1967 1980)   Use Facilities
Institutional Function   Use Institutional Role
Institutional Goals   Use Organizational Objectives
Institutional Libraries
Institutional Mission
Institutional Objectives   Use Organizational Objectives
Institutional Personnel
Institutional Research
Institutional Role
Institutional Schools
Institutional Self Study   Use Self Evaluation (Groups)
Institutional Survival
Institutionalized (Persons) (1967 1976)   Use Institutionalized Persons
Institutionalized Persons
Institutions
Accreditation   (Institutions)
Black   Institutions
Comparable   Institutions   Use Peer Institutions
Correctional   Institutions
Corrective   Institutions (1966 1980)   Use Correctional Institutions
Developing   Institutions
Educational   Institutions   Use Schools
Foundations   (Institutions)   Use Philanthropic Foundations
Higher Education   Institutions   Use Colleges
Negro   Institutions (1966 1977)   Use Black Institutions
Social   Institutions (Organizations)   Use Institutions
Peer   Institutions
Residential   Institutions
Social   Institutions (Social Patterns)   Use Sociocultural Patterns
Instruction
Self   Instruction Aids   Use Autoinstructional Aids
Art Making   (Instruction)   Use Studio Art
Audiovisual   Instruction
Bibliographic   Instruction   Use Library Instruction
Biology   Instruction (1966 1980)   Use Biology and Science Instruction
Case Based   Instruction   Use Case Method (Teaching Technique)
Chemistry   Instruction (1967 1980)   Use Chemistry and Science Instruction
Clinical Teaching (Individualized   Instruction)   Use Individualized Instruction
Clothing   Instruction
College   Instruction
Computer Aided   Instruction   Use Computer Assisted Instruction
Computer Assisted   Instruction
Computer Based   Instruction   Use Computer Assisted Instruction
Computer Managed   Instruction
Conventional   Instruction
Cooking   Instruction
Course Integrated Library   Instruction
Course of   Instruction   Use Course Organization
Course Related Library   Instruction   Use Course Integrated Library Instruction
Curriculum Integrated Library   Instruction   Use Course Integrated Library Instruction
Deans of   Instruction   Use Academic Deans
Community Based   Instruction (Disabilities)
Economics   Instruction   Use Economics Education
English   Instruction
Ethical   Instruction
Excursions   (Instruction)   Use Field Trips
Field   Instruction

Foods	Instruction
Foreign Language	Instruction Use Second Language Instruction
Geography	Instruction
Group	Instruction
Handwriting	Instruction (1966 1983) Use Handwriting and Writing Instruction
History	Instruction
Home	Instruction
Humanities	Instruction
Individual	Instruction
Individualized	Instruction
Integrated Library	Instruction Use Course Integrated Library Instruction
Intelligent Computer Assisted	Instruction Use Intelligent Tutoring Systems
Language	Instruction (1966 1980)
Medium of	Instruction (Language) Use Language of Instruction
Language of	Instruction
Large Group	Instruction
Learner Controlled	Instruction
Library	Instruction
Mass	Instruction
Self	Instruction Materials Use Programmed Instructional Materials
Mathematics	Instruction
Moral	Instruction Use Ethical Instruction
Multilevel Classes (Second Language	Instruction)
Multimedia	Instruction
Native Language	Instruction
Nutrition	Instruction
Personalized	Instruction Use Individualized Instruction
Physics	Instruction (1966 1980) Use Physics and Science Instruction
Problem Oriented	Instruction Use Problem Based Learning
Programed	Instruction (1966 1994) Use Programmed Instruction
Programmed	Instruction
Programmed Self	Instruction Use Programmed Instruction
Pronunciation	Instruction
Reading	Instruction
Remedial	Instruction
Science	Instruction
Second Language	Instruction
Self	Instruction Use Independent Study
Self Paced	Instruction Use Individualized Instruction and Pacing
Sewing	Instruction
Small Group	Instruction
Speech	Instruction
Spelling	Instruction
Technical	Instruction Use Technical Education
Telephone	Instruction
Telephone Usage	Instruction
Televised	Instruction (1966 1974) Use Educational Television
Textiles	Instruction
Traditional	Instruction Use Conventional Instruction
Tutorial	Instruction Use Tutoring
Research and	Instruction Units
Writing	Instruction
	Instructional Aids (1966 1980) Use Educational Media
	Instructional Alternatives Use Nontraditional Education
	Instructional Design
	Instructional Development
	Instructional Effectiveness
	Instructional Films
Nongraded	Instructional Grouping
	Instructional Improvement
	Instructional Innovation
	Instructional Language Use Language of Instruction
	Instructional Leadership
Postsecondary	Instructional Level Use Postsecondary Education
Computer Aided	Instructional Management Use Computer Managed Instruction
Computer Based	Instructional Management Use Computer Managed Instruction
	Instructional Material Adaptation Use Media Adaptation
	Instructional Material Development Use Material Development
	Instructional Material Evaluation
	Instructional Material Selection Use Media Selection
	Instructional Materials
Bilingual	Instructional Materials
	Instructional Materials Centers (1966 1980) Use Learning Resources Centers
Programed	Instructional Materials (1980 1994) Use Programmed Instructional Materials
Programmed	Instructional Materials
	Instructional Media (1967 1980) Use Educational Media
	Instructional Methods Use Teaching Methods
	Instructional Outcomes Use Outcomes of Education
	Instructional Planning Use Instructional Development
	Instructional Program Divisions
	Instructional Programs (1966 1980)
Counseling	Instructional Programs (1967 1980)
Grouping	(Instructional Purposes)
	Instructional Radio Use Educational Radio
	Instructional Software Use Courseware
	Instructional Staff (1966 1980) Use Teachers
	Instructional Strategies Use Educational Strategies
	Instructional Student Costs
	Instructional Systems
Integrated	Instructional Systems (Computers) Use Integrated Learning Systems
	Instructional Teams Use Team Teaching
	Instructional Technology (1966 1978) Use Educational Technology
	Instructional Television (1966 1974) Use Educational Television

Instructional Trips (1966 1980)   Use Field Trips
Instructionally Effective Schools   Use School Effectiveness
Instructor Centered Television (1966 1980)   Use Educational Television
Instructor Coordinators
Instructor Manuals   Use Teaching Guides
Instructors   Use Teachers
Instrumental Conditioning   Use Operant Conditioning
Instrumentation
Instrumentation and Orchestration
Instrumentation Technicians
Brass Instruments
Combat Instruments   Use Weapons
Assessment Instruments (Individuals)   Use Measures (Individuals)
Measurement Instruments (1966 1980)
Musical Instruments
Potentiometers (Instruments)
String Instruments
Stringed Instruments   Use String Instruments
Wind Instruments
Woodwind Instruments
Acoustic Insulation
Insulation (Heat)   Use Thermal Insulation
Insulation (Sound)   Use Acoustic Insulation
Sound Insulation   Use Acoustic Insulation
Thermal Insulation
Insurance
Insurance Companies
Fire Insurance
Health Insurance
Insurance Industry   Use Insurance Companies
Insurance Occupations
Insurance Programs (1968 1980)   Use Insurance
Unemployment Insurance
Integers
Integrated Activities
Integrated Automated Library Systems   Use Integrated Library Systems
Integrated Classes   Use Classroom Desegregation
Integrated Colleges   Use College Desegregation
Integrated Curriculum
Integrated Education   Use Integrated Curriculum
Integrated Faculty   Use Faculty Integration
Integrated Instructional Systems (Computers)   Use Integrated Learning Systems
Integrated Learning   Use Integrated Activities and Learning Activities
Integrated Learning Systems
Computer Based Integrated Learning Systems   Use Integrated Learning Systems
Integrated Library Instruction   Use Course Integrated Library Instruction
Course Integrated Library Instruction
Curriculum Integrated Library Instruction   Use Course Integrated Library Instruction
Integrated Library Systems
Integrated Neighborhoods   Use Neighborhood Integration
Integrated Public Facilities (1966 1980)   Use Public Facilities and Racial Integration
Integrated Schools   Use School Desegregation
Integrated Services
Integrated Teaching Method   Use Integrated Activities and Teaching Methods
Classroom Integration (1967 1980)   Use Classroom Desegregation
College Integration (1966 1980)   Use College Desegregation
Integration (Disabled Students)   Use Mainstreaming
Integration Effects (1966 1980)   Use Desegregation Effects
Ethnic Integration   Use Social Integration
Faculty Integration
Grade a Year Integration (1966 1980)   Use School Desegregation
Integration Impact   Use Desegregation Effects
Intersensory Integration   Use Sensory Integration
Integration Litigation (1966 1980)   Use Desegregation Litigation
Integration Methods (1966 1980)   Use Desegregation Methods
Neighborhood Integration
Personnel Integration
Integration Plans (1966 1980)   Use Desegregation Plans
Integration (Racial)   Use Racial Integration
Racial Integration
Integration Readiness
School Integration (1966 1980)   Use School Desegregation
Sensory Integration
Integration (Social)   Use Social Integration
Social Integration
Social Class Integration   Use Social Integration
Integration Studies
Teacher Integration
Token Integration (1966 1980)   Use Tokenism
Voluntary Integration (1966 1980)   Use Voluntary Desegregation
Integrative Analysis   Use Meta Analysis
Integrity
Intellectronics   Use Bionics
Intellectual Development
Intellectual Disciplines
Intellectual Experience
Intellectual Freedom
Intellectual History
Intellectual Property
Anti Intellectualism
Intellectualization (1970 1980)   Use Abstract Reasoning
Intelligence
Intelligence Age   Use Mental Age

Artificial	Intelligence
	Intelligence Differences
	Intelligence Factors (1966 1980) Use Intelligence
	Intelligence Level (1966 1980) Use Intelligence
	Intelligence Measures Use Intelligence Tests
National	Intelligence Norm (1966 1980) Use Intelligence and National Norms
	Intelligence Quotient
Group	Intelligence Testing (1966 1980) Use Group Testing and Intelligence Tests
	Intelligence Tests
Group	Intelligence Tests (1966 1980) Use Group Testing and Intelligence Tests
Multiple	Intelligences
	Intelligent CAI Systems Use Intelligent Tutoring Systems
	Intelligent Computer Assisted Instruction Use Intelligent Tutoring Systems
	Intelligent Tutoring Systems
	Intelligent Video Use Interactive Video
Mutual	Intelligibility
	Intensive Language Courses
	Intention
	Intentional Learning
	Interaction
	Interaction Analysis Use Interaction
Aptitude Treatment	Interaction
Cultural	Interaction Use Cultural Exchange
Group	Interaction Use Group Dynamics
Parent Child	Interaction Use Parent Child Relationship
	Interaction Process Analysis
Racial	Interaction Use Racial Relations
School Community	Interaction Use School Community Relationship
Social	Interaction Use Interpersonal Relationship
Student Teacher	Interaction Use Teacher Student Relationship
Teacher Student	Interaction Use Teacher Student Relationship
Trait Treatment	Interaction Use Aptitude Treatment Interaction
Verbal	Interaction Use Verbal Communication
	Interactive Cable Television Use Interactive Television
	Interactive Satellite Television Use Interactive Television
	Interactive Searching (Online) Use Online Searching
	Interactive Systems (Online) Use Online Systems
	Interactive Television
	Interactive Video
	Interagency Cooperation (1967 1980) Use Agency Cooperation
	Interagency Coordination (1967 1980) Use Agency Cooperation and Coordination
	Interagency Planning (1966 1980) Use Agency Cooperation and Cooperative Planning
School Based	Interagency Services Use Integrated Services
	Intercollegiate Athletics Use College Athletics and Intercollegiate Cooperation
	Intercollegiate Cooperation
	Intercollegiate Programs (1967 1980) Use Intercollegiate Cooperation
	Intercommunication (1966 1980) Use Communication (Thought Transfer)
	Intercultural Communication
	Intercultural Education Use Multicultural Education
	Intercultural Programs
	Interdimensional Shift Use Shift Studies
	Interdisciplinary Approach
	Interdistrict Policies
	Interest (1967 1981) Use Interest (Finance)
	Interest Centers (Classroom) Use Learning Centers (Classroom)
Centers of	Interest (1966 1980) Use Learning Centers (Classroom)
Conflict of	Interest
Educational	Interest (1967 1980) Use Student Educational Objectives
	Interest (Finance)
	Interest Inventories
High	Interest Low Vocabulary Books
	Interest Research
	Interest Scales (1966 1980) Use Interest Inventories
	Interest Tests (1966 1980) Use Interest Inventories
	Interests
Childhood	Interests
Childrens	Interests Use Childhood Interests
Group	Interests Use Interests
Personal	Interests (1966 1980) Use Interests
Reading	Interests
Science	Interests
Student	Interests
Student Science	Interests (1967 1980) Use Science Interests
Vocational	Interests
	Interface Devices (Computers) Use Computer Interfaces
Man Machine	Interface Use Man Machine Systems
Special Regular Education	Interface Use Regular and Special Education Relationship
	Interface Systems (Cross Database) Use Gateway Systems
User Friendly	Interface
Computer	Interfaces
	Interfaith Relations
Dialect	Interference Use Dialects and Interference (Language)
	Interference (Language)
	Interference (Language Learning) (1968 1980) Use Interference (Language)
	Intergenerational Programs
	Intergovernmental Organizations Use International Organizations
	Intergroup Education
	Intergroup Relations
	Interinstitutional Cooperation (1968 1980) Use Institutional Cooperation
	Interior Decoration Use Interior Design
	Interior Design
	Interior Monologues Use Monologs
	Interior Space

	Interjudge Agreement Use Interrater Reliability
	Interlanguage
	Interlibrary Loans
	Intermarriage
Search	Intermediaries
	Intermediate Administrative Units
	Intermediate Grades
	Intermediate School Districts Use Intermediate Administrative Units
	Intermediate Service Districts Use Intermediate Administrative Units
	Intermode Differences
	Intern Teachers Use Teacher Interns
	Internal External Locus of Control Use Locus of Control
	Internal Immigrants Use Migrants
	Internal Medicine
	Internal Review (Organizations) Use Self Evaluation (Groups)
	Internal Scaling (1966 1980) Use Scaling
	Internation Behavior Use International Relations
	International Approach Use Global Approach
	International Communication
	International Cooperation
	International Crimes
	International Education
	International Educational Exchange
	International Law
	International Legal Analysis Use International Law
	International Organizations
	International Peace Use Peace
	International Policy Use Foreign Policy
	International Politics Use International Relations
	International Programs
	International Relations
	International Students Use Foreign Students
	International Studies
	International Technical Assistance Use International Programs and Technical Assistance
	International Torts Use International Law
	International Trade
	International Trade Vocabulary
	International War Use War
	Internet
	Internet Discussion Lists Use Listservs
	Interns (Medical) Use Graduate Medical Students
Teacher	Interns
Urban Teaching	Interns Use Teacher Interns and Urban Teaching
	Internship Programs
	Internships (Medical) Use Graduate Medical Education
	Interobserver Reliability Use Interrater Reliability
	Interpersonal Attraction
	Interpersonal Communication
	Interpersonal Competence
	Interpersonal Perception Use Social Cognition
	Interpersonal Problems (1966 1980) Use Interpersonal Relationship
	Interpersonal Relationship
	Interpersonal Skills Use Interpersonal Competence
Data	Interpretation
Environmental	Interpretation
Historical	Interpretation
Oral	Interpretation
Test	Interpretation
	Interpreters
Deaf	Interpreting
	Interpreting for the Deaf Use Deaf Interpreting
	Interpretive Reading (1966 1980)
	Interpretive Skills
	Interprofessional Relationship
	Interracial Adoption Use Transracial Adoption
	Interracial Offspring Use Multiracial Persons
	Interracial Relations Use Racial Relations
	Interrater Reliability
Cultural	Interrelationships
	Interscholastic Athletics Use Extramural Athletics
	Interschool Communication
	Interschool Visits Use School Visitation
	Interscorer Reliability Use Interrater Reliability
	Intersensory Integration Use Sensory Integration
	Intersession School Programs Use Vacation Programs
	Interstate Programs
	Interstate Workers (1966 1980) (Migrants) Use Migrant Workers
	Interval Pacing (1967 1980) Use Pacing
	Intervals
	Intervention
Crisis	Intervention
Early	Intervention
Prereferral	Intervention
	Interviewing Use Interviews
	Interviews
Employment	Interviews
Field	Interviews
Focused Group	Interviews Use Focus Groups
Job	Interviews Use Employment Interviews
Question Answer	Interviews (1966 1980) Use Interviews
	Intimacy
	Intonation
	Intonation Contours Use Intonation

Driving While	Intoxicated
Alcohol	Intoxication Use Alcohol Abuse
	Intramural Athletic Programs (1966 1980) Use Intramural Athletics
	Intramural Athletics
	Intramural Sports Use Intramural Athletics
	Intricacy Level Use Difficulty Level
	Intrinsic Motivation Use Self Motivation
	Introductory Courses
Foundation Courses	(Introductory) Use Introductory Courses
	Introjection Use Identification (Psychology)
	Introversion Use Extraversion Introversion
Extraversion	Introversion
	Intrusion Detectors Use Alarm Systems
	Intuition
	Inuit Use Inupiaq
	Inuit (People) Use Eskimos
	Inuktitut Use Inupiaq
	Inupiaq
	Inupiat Use Inupiaq
	Inupik Use Inupiaq
	Invalids Use Patients
	Invasion of Privacy Use Privacy
	Invented Spelling
Rhetorical	Invention
	Inventions
	Inventive Spelling Use Invented Spelling
Biographical	Inventories
Informal Reading	Inventories
Interest	Inventories
	Inventories (Measurement) Use Measures (Individuals)
Equipment	Inventory Use Facility Inventory
Facility	Inventory
Informal Reading	Inventory (1968 1980) Use Informal Reading Inventories
Materials	Inventory Use Facility Inventory
Property	Inventory Use Facility Inventory
	Investigations
	Investment
Citizen	Involvement Use Citizen Participation
Civic	Involvement Use Citizen Participation
Community	Involvement
Family	Involvement
Parent	Involvement Use Parent Participation
Participant	Involvement (1967 1980) Use Participation
School	Involvement
	IQ Use Intelligence Quotient
	Iris Reflex Use Pupillary Dilation
	Irish
Gaelic	(Irish) Use Irish
	IRM Use Information Management
	Iron Deficiency Anemia Use Anemia
	Iron Foundries Use Foundries
	Irony
	Iroquois (Tribe)
	IRT LTT Measurement Theory Use Item Response Theory
	Isiswati Use Siswati
	Islam
	Islamic Culture
Pacific	Islanders
Cultural	Isolation
Geographic	Isolation
	Isolation (Perceptual) Use Sensory Deprivation
Professional	Isolation
Social	Isolation
Publish or Perish	Issue
Bond	Issues
Controversial	Issues (Course Content)
Gender	Issues
Local	Issues
Moral	Issues
Political	Issues
Social	Issues Use Social Problems
	ITA Use Initial Teaching Alphabet
	Italian
	Italian Americans
	Italian Literature
	Item Analysis
	Item Banks
	Item Bias
	Item Characteristic Curve Theory Use Item Response Theory
	Item Difficulty Use Difficulty Level and Test Items
Differential	Item Functioning Use Item Bias
Differential	Item Performance Use Item Bias
	Item Pools Use Item Banks
	Item Response Theory
	Item Sampling
	Item Types Use Test Format
Test	Items
	ITFS Use Educational Television
	Itinerant Clinics (1966 1980) Use Mobile Clinics
	Itinerant Teachers
	ITV Use Educational Television
	Jail Inmates Use Prisoners
	JAN Technique Use Judgment Analysis Technique

```
                        Japanese
                        Japanese American Culture
                        Japanese Americans
                        Japanese Culture
                        Jargon
                        Javanese
                        Jazz
                        Jealousy
                        Jewish Stereotypes (1966 1980)   Use Ethnic Stereotypes and Jews
                        Jews
          American      Jews   Use Jews
                        Job Adjustment    Use Vocational Adjustment
                        Job Analysis
                        Job Applicants
                        Job Application
                        Job Banks
                        Job Behaviors   Use Job Skills
                        Job Change   Use Career Change
                        Job Clusters   Use Occupational Clusters
                        Job Conditions   Use Work Environment
                        Job Content   Use Occupational Information
                        Job Content Analysis   Use Job Analysis
                        Job Creation   Use Job Development
                        Job Descriptions   Use Occupational Information
                        Job Design   Use Job Development
                        Job Development
                        Job Discrimination    Use Equal Opportunities (Jobs)
                        Job Elimination   Use Job Layoff
                        Job Enrichment
                        Job Experience   Use Employment Experience
                        Job Families   Use Occupational Clusters
                        Job Family Relationship   Use Family Work Relationship
                        Job Holding Patterns   Use Employment Patterns
                        Job Interviews   Use Employment Interviews
                        Job Ladders   Use Career Ladders
                        Job Layoff
                        Job Literacy   Use Workplace Literacy
                        Job Loss Services   Use Outplacement Services (Employment)
                        Job Market (1966 1980)   Use Labor Market
                        Job Mobility   Use Occupational Mobility
                        Job Opportunities   Use Employment Opportunities
                        Job Performance
                        Job Placement
          Student       Job Placement   Use Job Placement and Student Employment
                        Job Redesign   Use Job Development
                        Job Related Literacy   Use Workplace Literacy
          Family        Job Relationship   Use Family Work Relationship
                        Job Restructuring   Use Job Development
                        Job Safety   Use Occupational Safety and Health
                        Job Sample Tests   Use Work Sample Tests
                        Job Samples   Use Work Sample Tests
                        Job Satisfaction
                        Job Search Methods
                        Job Security
                        Job Seekers   Use Job Applicants
                        Job Segregation   Use Occupational Segregation
                        Job Sharing
                        Job Simplification
                        Job Skills
                        Job Specifications   Use Occupational Information
                        Job Tenure (1967 1978)   Use Tenure
                        Job Training
                        Job Training Academies   Use Career Academies
     Away from the      Job Training   Use Off the Job Training
        Off the         Job Training
        On the          Job Training
                        Job Vacancies   Use Employment Opportunities
                        Job Vacancy Surveys   Use Occupational Surveys
          Multiple      Jobholding   Use Multiple Employment
                        Jobs (1966 1980)   Use Employment
  Equal Opportunities   (Jobs)
        Part Time       Jobs (1966 1980)   Use Part Time Employment
                        Jogging
                        Joint Occupancy   Use Shared Facilities
                        Journal Articles
                        Journal Writing
                        Journalism
          Broadcast     Journalism
                        Journalism Education
                        Journalism History
          New           Journalism
          Pictorial     Journalism   Use Photojournalism
          Radio         Journalism   Use Broadcast Journalism
                        Journalism Research
          Scholastic    Journalism
          Television    Journalism   Use Broadcast Journalism
                        Journals   Use Periodicals
          Articles      (Journals)   Use Journal Articles
          Dialog        Journals
          Dialogue      Journals   Use Dialog Journals
          Electronic    Journals
          Online        Journals   Use Electronic Journals
          Scholarly     Journals
```

```
           Student  Journals
                    Journey Workers   Use Skilled Workers
                    Joy   Use Happiness
                    Judaism
                    Judges
             Court  Judges
            Debate  Judges   Use Judges
         Aesthetic  Judgment   Use Aesthetic Values and Value Judgment
                    Judgment Analysis Technique
             Legal  Judgment   Use Court Litigation
          Clinical  Judgment (Medicine)   Use Medical Evaluation
             Moral  Judgment   Use Moral Values and Value Judgment
          Clinical  Judgment (Psychology)   Use Psychological Evaluation
             Value  Judgment
                    Judgmental Processes   Use Evaluative Thinking
                    Judicial Action   Use Court Litigation
                    Judicial Role   Use Court Role
                    Judicial System   Use Courts
                    Junior College Libraries (1966 1980)   Use College Libraries and Two Year Colleges
                    Junior College Students (1969 1980)   Use Two Year College Students
                    Junior Colleges (1966 1980)   Use Two Year Colleges
           Private  Junior Colleges   Use Private Colleges and Two Year Colleges
                    Junior High School Role (1966 1980)   Use School Role
                    Junior High School Students
                    Junior High School Teachers   Use Secondary School Teachers
                    Junior High Schools
           College  Juniors
                De  Jure Segregation
                    Juries
          Trial by  Jury   Use Juries
                    Justice
 Corrections (Criminal  Justice)   Use Correctional Rehabilitation
          Juvenile  Justice
          Juvenile  Justice System   Use Juvenile Justice
                    Juvenile Courts
                    Juvenile Delinquency   Use Delinquency
                    Juvenile Gangs
                    Juvenile Justice
                    Juvenile Justice System   Use Juvenile Justice
   Training Schools  (Juvenile Offenders)   Use Correctional Institutions
                    Juvenile Runaways   Use Runaways
                    Kabyle
                    Kannada
                    Kashmiri
                    Kechua   Use Quechua
            Animal  Keepers   Use Animal Caretakers
           Grounds  Keepers
                    Kernel Sentences
                    Key Word Access Points   Use Keywords
                    Key Word in Context   Use Permuted Indexes
                    Keyboarding (Data Entry)
          Computer  Keyboards   Use Keyboarding (Data Entry)
                    Keypunching   Use Keyboarding (Data Entry)
            Answer  Keys
           Scoring  Keys   Use Answer Keys
                    Keywords
                    Khalkha   Use Mongolian
                    Khmer (Language)   Use Cambodian
                    Khmer (People)   Use Cambodians
                    Kikongo Ya Leta   Use Kituba
             Mercy  Killing   Use Euthanasia
                    Kindergarten
                    Kindergarten Children
                    Kindergarten Teachers   Use Preschool Teachers
                    Kindness   Use Altruism
                    Kinescope Recordings
                    Kinescopes   Use Kinescope Recordings
                    Kinesics   Use Body Language
                    Kinesthesia   Use Kinesthetic Perception
                    Kinesthesis   Use Kinesthetic Perception
                    Kinesthetic Memory   Use Kinesthetic Perception
                    Kinesthetic Methods
                    Kinesthetic Perception
                    Kinetic Molecular Theory
                    Kinetics
                    Kinship
                    Kinship Role   Use Kinship
                    Kinship Terminology
                    Kirghiz (1968 1998)   Use Kyrgyz
                    Kirgiz   Use Kyrgyz
                    Kirundi
                    Kiswahili   Use Swahili
          Learning  Kits   Use Learning Modules
                    Kituba
          Right to  Know   Use Freedom of Information
                    Knowledge Base for Teaching
           Teacher  Knowledge Base   Use Knowledge Base for Teaching
 Teacher Education  Knowledge Base   Use Knowledge Base for Teaching
          Teaching  Knowledge Base   Use Knowledge Base for Teaching
                    Knowledge Based Systems   Use Expert Systems
                    Knowledge Level
              Meta  Knowledge   Use Metacognition
                    Knowledge of Results   Use Feedback
```

Pedagogical Content Knowledge
Prior Knowledge   Use Prior Learning
Knowledge Representation
Self Knowledge   Use Self Concept
Knowledge Structures   Use Cognitive Structures
Kodaly Method
Korean
Korean Americans
Korean Culture
Korean War
Krio   Use Sierra Leone Creole
Sierra Leone Krio   Use Sierra Leone Creole
Kurdish
KWIC Indexes   Use Permuted Indexes
KWOC Indexes   Use Permuted Indexes
Kyrghyz   Use Kyrgyz
Kyrgyz
Labeling (of Persons)
Product Labels   Use Merchandise Information
Labor
Labor Camps (1966 1980) (Migrants)   Use Migrant Housing
Child Labor
Labor (Childbirth)   Use Birth
Labor Conditions
Labor Demands
Agricultural Labor Disputes (1966 1980)   Use Labor Demands
Labor Economics
Labor Education
Farm Labor
Labor Force
Labor Force Development
Labor Force Nonparticipants
Labor Force Surveys   Use Occupational Surveys
Human Resources Development (Labor)   Use Labor Force Development
Labor Laws (1966 1974)   Use Labor Legislation
Child Labor Laws (1966 1974)   Use Child Labor and Labor Legislation
Labor Legislation
Child Labor Legislation (1966 1980)   Use Child Labor and Labor Legislation
Farm Labor Legislation (1966 1980)   Use Farm Labor and Labor Legislation
Labor Market
Mediation (Labor)   Use Arbitration
Labor Mobility   Use Occupational Mobility
Labor Needs
Labor Problems
Farm Labor Problems (1966 1980)   Use Farm Labor and Labor Problems
Labor Relations
Seasonal Labor (1966 1980)   Use Seasonal Employment
Skilled Labor (1966 1980)   Use Skilled Workers
Labor Standards
Labor Supply
Farm Labor Supply (1966 1980)   Use Farm Labor and Labor Supply
Supply of Labor   Use Labor Supply
Labor Turnover
Labor Unions (1966 1980)   Use Unions
Unskilled Labor (1966 1980)   Use Unskilled Workers
Labor Utilization
Laboratories
Audio Active Laboratories (1967 1980)   Use Language Laboratories
Audio Active Compare Laboratories (1967 1980)   Use Language Laboratories
Audio Passive Laboratories (1968 1980)   Use Language Laboratories
Audio Video Laboratories (1967 1980)   Use Audiovisual Centers
Autoinstructional Laboratories (1967 1980)   Use Learning Laboratories
Computer Based Laboratories (1967 1980)   Use Computer Assisted Instruction and Laboratories
Curriculum Laboratories   Use Curriculum Study Centers
Language Laboratories
Learning Laboratories
Mobile Laboratories
Reading Laboratories   Use Reading Centers
Regional Laboratories
Satellite Laboratories (1966 1980)   Use Satellites (Aerospace)
Science Laboratories
Training Laboratories (1967 1980)
Writing Laboratories
Laboratory Animals
Medical Laboratory Assistants
Laboratory Equipment
Language Laboratory Equipment (1966 1980)   Use Laboratory Equipment and Language Laboratories
Field Laboratory Experience   Use Field Experience Programs
Laboratory Experiments
Laboratory Manuals
Laboratory Preschools   Use Laboratory Schools and Preschool Education
Laboratory Procedures
Laboratory Safety
Laboratory Schools
Dental Laboratory Technicians   Use Dental Technicians
Laboratory Techniques (1967 1980)
Medical Laboratory Technologists   Use Medical Technologists
Laboratory Technology
Laboratory Training
Language Laboratory Use (1966 1980)   Use Language Laboratories
Laborers
Agricultural Laborers
Auxiliary Laborers

Experienced	Laborers (1966 1980) Use Laborers
Seasonal	Laborers
	Lacrosse
Career	Ladders
Job	Ladders Use Career Ladders
Cultural	Lag Use Culture Lag
Culture	Lag
	Laissez Faire Economy Use Free Enterprise System
	Lakhota Use Lakota
	Lakota
	Lakota (Tribe)
	Land Acquisition
	Land Colonization Use Land Settlement
	Land Grant Colleges Use Land Grant Universities
	Land Grant Universities
	Land Settlement
	Land Use
	Landladies Use Landlords
	Landlords
	Landscaping
	Language
	Language Ability (1966 1980)
	Language Acquisition
	Language Aids (1966 1980)
American Sign	Language
Contrastive	Language Analysis Use Contrastive Linguistics
	Language and Area Centers (1968 1980)
Whole	Language Approach
	Language Aptitude
	Language Arts
	Language Attitudes
	Language Attrition (Skills) Use Language Skill Attrition
	Language Awareness Use Metalinguistics
Body	Language
Foreign	Language Books
Second	Language Books Use Foreign Language Books
Child	Language
Chippewa	(Language) Use Ojibwa
	Language Classification
Code Switching	(Language)
Conversational	Language Courses
Intensive	Language Courses
Modern	Language Curriculum
	Language Development (1966 1980) Use Language Acquisition
Dialogs	(Language)
	Language Disabilities Use Language Impairments
Distinctive Features	(Language)
	Language Dominance
English (Second	Language)
	Language Enrichment
	Language Enrollment
Foreign	Language Enrollment Use Language Enrollment
Second	Language Enrollment Use Language Enrollment
Error Analysis	(Language)
	Language Evolution Use Diachronic Linguistics
	Language Experience Use Language Enrichment
	Language Experience Approach
Expressive	Language
Farsi	(Language) Use Persian
Figurative	Language
Foreign	Language Films
Second	Language Films Use Foreign Language Films
	Language Fluency
Minority	Language Groups Use Language Minorities
	Language Guides (1966 1980)
	Language Handicapped (1967 1980) Use Language Impairments
	Language Handicaps (1966 1994) Use Language Impairments
	Language History Use Diachronic Linguistics
History of	Language Use Diachronic Linguistics
	Language Impairments
	Language Input Use Linguistic Input
	Language Instruction (1966 1980)
Foreign	Language Instruction Use Second Language Instruction
Multilevel Classes (Second	Language Instruction)
Native	Language Instruction
Second	Language Instruction
Instructional	Language Use Language of Instruction
Interference	(Language)
Khmer	(Language) Use Cambodian
	Language Laboratories
	Language Laboratory Equipment (1966 1980) Use Laboratory Equipment and Language Laboratories
	Language Laboratory Use (1966 1980) Use Language Laboratories
Approximative Systems	(Language Learning) Use Interlanguage
Aural	Language Learning Use Aural Learning and Language Acquisition
	Language Learning (Foreign) Use Second Language Learning
Foreign	Language Learning Use Second Language Learning
Interference	(Language Learning) (1968 1980) Use Interference (Language)
	Language Learning Levels (1967 1980)
Second	Language Learning
Visual	Language Learning Use Language Acquisition and Visual Learning
	Language Loss (Skills) Use Language Skill Attrition
	Language Maintenance
Medium of Instruction	(Language) Use Language of Instruction

	Language Minorities
Negative Forms	(Language)
Nonsexist	Language Use Sexism in Language
	Language of Instruction
Oral	Language
Speech	Language Pathology
Speech and	Language Pathology Use Speech Language Pathology
Pattern Drills	(Language)
	Language Patterns
Basic	Language Patterns Use Language Patterns
Foreign	Language Periodicals
Second	Language Periodicals Use Foreign Language Periodicals
	Language Planning
	Language Processing
Natural	Language Processing
	Language Proficiency
Proficiency Tests	(Language) Use Language Proficiency and Language Tests
	Language Programs (1966 1980)
College	Language Programs (1967 1980)
College Second	Language Programs
Foreign	Language Programs Use Second Language Programs
Second	Language Programs
Receptive	Language
	Language Records (Phonograph) (1966 1980) Use Audiodisks
	Language Research
	Language Rhythm
Rhythm	(Language) Use Language Rhythm
	Language Role
Sexism in	Language
Sexist	Language Use Sexism in Language
Sign	Language
	Language Skill Attrition
	Language Skills
	Language Standardization
	Language Styles
State Foreign	Language Supervisors (1967 1980) Use Second Language Instruction and State Supervisors
Switching	(Language) Use Code Switching (Language)
Symbolic	Language
	Language Tapes Use Audiotape Recordings
	Language Teachers
Foreign	Language Teachers Use Language Teachers
Second	Language Teachers Use Language Teachers
Teaching	Language Use Language of Instruction
Foreign	Language Teaching Use Second Language Instruction
	Language Tests
Transformation Theory	(Language) (1967 1980) Use Linguistic Theory and Transformational Generative Grammar
Transformations	(Language) (1967 1980) Use Transformational Generative Grammar
	Language Typology
Natural	Language Understanding Systems Use Natural Language Processing
	Language Universals
Unwritten	Language (1968 1980)
Urban	Language
	Language Usage
Valence	(Language) Use Syntax
	Language Variation
Vocational English (Second	Language)
Written	Language
	Languages
African	Languages
Afro Asiatic	Languages
Altaic	Languages Use Uralic Altaic Languages
American Indian	Languages
Artificial	Languages
Athabascan	Languages Use Athapascan Languages
Athapascan	Languages
Australian Aboriginal	Languages
Austro Asiatic	Languages
Austronesian	Languages Use Malayo Polynesian Languages
Authoring	Languages Use Authoring Aids (Programming) and Programming Languages
Baltic	Languages
Bantu	Languages
Berber	Languages
Caucasian	Languages
Chad	Languages
Classical	Languages
Communicative Competence	(Languages)
Computer	Languages Use Programming Languages
Constructed	Languages Use Artificial Languages
Determiners	(Languages)
Dravidian	Languages
Eskimo Aleut	Languages
Fenno Ugric	Languages Use Finno Ugric Languages
Finno Ugric	Languages
	Languages for Special Purposes
Foreign	Languages Use Second Languages
Form Classes	(Languages)
Foreign	Languages in the Elementary School Use FLES
Indo European	Languages
Indonesian	Languages
Less Commonly Taught	Languages Use Uncommonly Taught Languages
Malayo Polynesian	Languages
Mayan	Languages
Melanesian	Languages

```
                Modern  Languages
             Mongolian  Languages
            Morphology  (Languages)
              National  Languages    Use Official Languages
             Neglected  Languages    Use Uncommonly Taught Languages
               Official Languages
            Programing  Languages (1969 1994)    Use Programming Languages
           Programming  Languages
               Romance  Languages
              Samoyed   Languages
                Second  Languages
                Semitic Languages
          Sino Tibetan  Languages
                 Slavic Languages
       Threshold Level  (Languages)
                  Tone  Languages
                 Turkic Languages
   Uncommonly Taught    Languages
             Unwritten  Languages
          Uralic Altaic Languages
            Uto Aztecan Languages
                        Lao
                        Laotian    Use Lao
                        Laotian Americans    Use Asian Americans and Laotians
                        Laotians
                        Lap Belts    Use Restraints (Vehicle Safety)
                        Laps    Use Learning Modules
                        Large Cities    Use Urban Areas
                        Large Group Instruction
                        Large Scale Production    Use Mass Production
                        Large Type Books    Use Large Type Materials
                        Large Type Materials
                        Laser Disks    Use Optical Disks
                        Laser Oscillators    Use Lasers
                        Lasers
       Light Amplifiers (Lasers)    Use Lasers
    Seniors (1966 1980)  (Last Year Undergraduates)    Use College Seniors
                        Latchkey Children
                        Late Adolescence    Use Late Adolescents
                        Late Adolescents
                        Late Registration
              Response  Latency    Use Reaction Time
                        Latent Trait Theory (1980 1990)    Use Item Response Theory
                        Lateral Dominance
                        Lathes    Use Machine Tools
                        Latin
                   Non  Latin Alphabets    Use Non Roman Scripts
American Literature (1966 1980)  (Latin America)    Use Latin American Literature
                        Latin American Culture
                        Latin American History
                        Latin American Literature
                        Latin Americans
                        Latin Literature
                        Latvian
                        Laundry Drycleaning Occupations
            Drycleaning Laundry Occupations    Use Laundry Drycleaning Occupations
             Advocates  (Law)    Use Lawyers
                 Civil  Law
        Constitutional  Law
              Criminal  Law
                        Law Enforcement
                        Law Enforcement Officers    Use Police
    Executions (Criminal Law)    Use Capital Punishment
         International  Law
                        Law Libraries
                        Law of Nations    Use International Law
                        Law of Primacy    Use Primacy Effect
                        Law Related Education
                School  Law
                        Law School Applicants    Use College Applicants and Law Schools
                        Law School Education    Use Legal Education (Professions)
                        Law Schools
             Solicitors (Law)    Use Lawyers
                        Law Students
                        Lawmakers    Use Legislators
                        Lawn Maintenance    Use Turf Management
                        Laws
            Child Labor Laws (1966 1974)    Use Child Labor and Labor Legislation
               Federal  Laws (1966 1974)    Use Federal Legislation
                 Labor  Laws (1966 1974)    Use Labor Legislation
        Minimum Wage   Laws (1966 1974)    Use Minimum Wage Legislation
         Public Health  Laws (1966 1974)    Use Public Health Legislation
     School Attendance  Laws (1966 1974)    Use School Attendance Legislation
                 State  Laws (1966 1974)    Use State Legislation
                        Lawyers
                        Lay People
                        Lay Teachers
                Carpet  Layers    Use Floor Layers
                 Floor  Layers
                        Laymen (1966 1980)    Use Lay People
                   Job  Layoff
               Display  Layout (Computers)    Use Screen Design (Computers)
                        Layout (Publications)
```

Street	Layouts Use Traffic Circulation
	Lc Classification Use Library of Congress Classification
	Lea Use School Districts
	Lead Lecture Plan (1966 1980) Use Lecture Method
	Lead Poisoning
	Leader Participation (1966 1980) Use Leadership
Team	Leader (Teaching) (1966 1980) Use Leaders and Team Teaching
	Leaderless Groups Use Self Directed Groups
	Leaders
Adult	Leaders (1967 1980) Use Leaders
Community	Leaders
Crew	Leaders
	Leaders Guides
Youth	Leaders
	Leadership
Black	Leadership
Informal	Leadership
Instructional	Leadership
Negro	Leadership (1966 1977) Use Black Leadership
Outdoor	Leadership
	Leadership Qualities
	Leadership Responsibility
Student	Leadership
	Leadership Styles
	Leadership Training
	Leaflets Use Pamphlets
	Lean Fat Ratio Use Body Composition
Learning to	Learn Use Learning Strategies
	Learned Helplessness Use Helplessness
	Learner Autonomy Use Personal Autonomy
	Learner Control Use Learner Controlled Instruction
	Learner Controlled Instruction
	Learner Outcomes Use Outcomes of Education
Slow	Learners
	Learning
Action	Learning Use Experiential Learning
Active	Learning
	Learning Activities
Activity	Learning (1968 1978) Use Experiential Learning
	Learning Activity Packages Use Learning Modules
	Learning Activity Packets Use Learning Modules
Adult	Learning
Adventure	Learning Use Adventure Education
Approximative Systems (Language	Learning) Use Interlanguage
Associative	Learning
Aural	Learning
Aural Language	Learning Use Aural Learning and Language Acquisition
	Learning Centers (Classroom)
Living	Learning Centers
	Learning Characteristics (1968 1980) Use Learning
Community Service	Learning Use Service Learning
Computer Assisted	Learning Use Computer Assisted Instruction
Constructivism	(Learning)
Continuous	Learning (1967 1980) Use Lifelong Learning
	Learning Contracts Use Performance Contracts
Student	Learning Contracts Use Performance Contracts
Maturation	Learning Controversy Use Nature Nurture Controversy
Cooperative	Learning
	Learning Cycles Use Learning Processes
	Learning Difficulties (1966 1980) Use Learning Problems
	Learning Disabilities
Specific	Learning Disabilities Use Learning Disabilities
Discovery	Learning
Discrimination	Learning
Engaged Time	(Learning) Use Time on Task
	Learning Experience
Clinical	Learning Experience Use Clinical Experience
Experiential	Learning
Exploratory	Learning Use Discovery Learning
Foreign Language	Learning Use Second Language Learning
Language	Learning (Foreign) Use Second Language Learning
Hands on	Learning Use Experiential Learning
Imitative	Learning Use Observational Learning
Incidental	Learning
Independent	Learning Use Independent Study
Integrated	Learning Use Integrated Activities and Learning Activities
Intentional	Learning
Interference (Language	Learning) (1968 1980) Use Interference (Language)
	Learning Kits Use Learning Modules
	Learning Laboratories
Language	Learning Levels (1967 1980)
Lifelong	Learning
Mastery	Learning
	Learning Maturation Controversy Use Nature Nurture Controversy
	Learning Modalities
Modular	Learning Use Learning Modules
	Learning Modules
	Learning Motivation
Multisensory	Learning
Nonverbal	Learning
	Learning Objectives Use Behavioral Objectives
Observational	Learning
	Learning Packages Use Learning Modules

Paired Associate Learning
Perceptual Motor Learning
Performance Assessment (Higher Order Learning)   Use Performance Based Assessment
Learning Plateaus
Preschool Learning (1966 1980)
Previous Learning   Use Prior Learning
Prior Learning
Prior Experiential Learning   Use Experiential Learning and Prior Learning
Problem Based Learning
Learning Problems
Learning Processes
Programmed Learning   Use Programmed Instruction
Learning Readiness
Learning Reinforcement   Use Reinforcement
Learning Resources   Use Educational Resources
Learning Resources Centers
Rote Learning
Second Language Learning
Self Directed Learning   Use Independent Study
Sensory Motor Learning   Use Perceptual Motor Learning
Sequential Learning
Serial Learning
Service Learning
Social Learning   Use Socialization
Learning Specialists (1966 1980)   Use Specialists
Learning Stations (Classroom)   Use Learning Centers (Classroom)
Learning Strategies
Student Controlled Learning   Use Learner Controlled Instruction
Learning Style   Use Cognitive Style
Symbolic Learning
Computer Based Integrated Learning Systems   Use Integrated Learning Systems
Integrated Learning Systems
Learning Theories
Academic Learning Time   Use Time on Task
Time Factors (Learning)
Learning to Learn   Use Learning Strategies
Toilet Learning   Use Toilet Training
Transfer of Learning   Use Transfer of Training
Transformation Theory (Adult Learning)   Use Learning Theories and Transformative Learning
Transformations (Adult Learning)   Use Transformative Learning
Transformative Learning
Verbal Learning
Visual Learning
Visual Language Learning   Use Language Acquisition and Visual Learning
Least Restrictive Environment (Disabled)   Use Mainstreaming
Least Squares Statistics
Leather
Leather Crafts   Use Leather
Leave of Absence (1968 1980)   Use Leaves of Absence
Early School Leavers   Use Dropouts
Leaves of Absence
Sabbatical Leaves
Lecture (1966 1980)   Use Lecture Method
Lecture Method
Lead Lecture Plan (1966 1980)   Use Lecture Method
Television Lecturers   Use Television Teachers
Left Handed Writer
Left Right Preference   Use Lateral Dominance
Legal Aid
Legal Aid Projects (1966 1980)   Use Legal Aid
International Legal Analysis   Use International Law
Legal Assistants
Citations (Legal)   Use Law Enforcement
Compliance (Legal)
Legal Costs
Legal Decisions   Use Court Litigation
Legal Education (1977 1986)
Legal Education (Professions)
Evidence (Legal)
Legal Judgment   Use Court Litigation
Legal Problems
Legal Responsibility
Legal Secretaries   Use Secretaries
Legal Segregation (1966 1980)   Use De Jure Segregation
Legal Services   Use Legal Aid
Legends
Legislation
Anti Discrimination Legislation   Use Civil Rights Legislation
Child Labor Legislation (1966 1980)   Use Child Labor and Labor Legislation
Civil Rights Legislation
Community Legislation   Use Local Legislation
Community Recreation Legislation (1966 1978)   Use Local Legislation and Recreation Legislation
Discriminatory Legislation
Drug Legislation
Educational Legislation
Farm Labor Legislation (1966 1980)   Use Farm Labor and Labor Legislation
Federal Legislation
Federal Recreation Legislation (1966 1978)   Use Federal Legislation and Recreation Legislation
Labor Legislation
Local Legislation
Local Recreation Legislation (1966 1978)   Use Local Legislation and Recreation Legislation
Minimum Wage Legislation
Public Health Legislation

Recreation	Legislation
School Attendance	Legislation
State	Legislation
State Recreation	Legislation (1966 1978) Use Recreation Legislation and State Legislation
	Legislative Discrimination Use Discriminatory Legislation
	Legislative Reference Libraries (1968 1980) Use Law Libraries
	Legislators
	Leisure Use Leisure Time
	Leisure Counseling Use Leisure Education
	Leisure Education
	Leisure Time
	Leisure Time Reading Use Recreational Reading
	Leitmotifs Use Motifs
	Leitmotivs Use Motifs
Book	Lending Use Library Circulation
Program	Length
Test	Length
Sierra	Leone Creole
Sierra	Leone Krio Use Sierra Leone Creole
	Lesbianism
	Less Commonly Taught Languages Use Uncommonly Taught Languages
	Lesson Notes Use Lesson Plans
	Lesson Observation Criteria
	Lesson Plans
	Lesson Units Use Units of Study
Kikongo Ya	Leta Use Kituba
	Letter Sound Correspondence Use Phoneme Grapheme Correspondence
	Letters (Alphabet)
Business	Letters Use Business Correspondence
	Letters (Correspondence)
Correspondence	(Letters) Use Letters (Correspondence)
Achievement	Level Use Achievement
Age	Level Use Age
Aspiration	Level Use Aspiration
Low	Level Aspiration (1966 1980) Use Aspiration
Complexity	Level (1968 1979) Use Difficulty Level
Difficulty	Level
Educational	Level Use Academic Achievement
Employment	Level
Intelligence	Level (1966 1980) Use Intelligence
Intricacy	Level Use Difficulty Level
Knowledge	Level
Threshold	Level (Languages)
Middle	Level Management Use Middle Management
Activity	Level (Motor Behavior) Use Physical Activity Level
Occupational	Level Use Employment Level
Occupational Aspiration	Level Use Occupational Aspiration
Physical Activity	Level
Postsecondary Instructional	Level Use Postsecondary Education
Precollege	Level Use High Schools
Reading	Level (1966 1980)
Socioeconomic	Level Use Socioeconomic Status
Adaptation	Level Theory
Abstraction	Levels (1968 1980) Use Abstract Reasoning
Grade	Levels Use Instructional Program Divisions
Illumination	Levels (1968 1980) Use Lighting
Language Learning	Levels (1967 1980)
Noise	Levels Use Noise (Sound)
	Lexicography
	Lexicology
	Lexicons Use Dictionaries
	Liability (Responsibility) Use Legal Responsibility
Police School	Liaison Use Police School Relationship
	Libel and Slander
	Liberal Arts
	Liberal Arts Majors (1967 1980) Use Liberal Arts and Majors (Students)
	Liberal Education Use General Education
	Liberalism
Womens	Liberation Use Feminism
Civil	Liberties
	Liberty Use Freedom
Personal	Liberty Use Civil Liberties
	Librarian Attitudes
Teacher	Librarian Cooperation Use Librarian Teacher Cooperation
	Librarian Teacher Cooperation
	Librarians
Head	Librarians Use Library Directors
Medical Record	Librarians (1969 1980) Use Medical Record Administrators
Reference	Librarians Use Librarians and Reference Services
	Librarianship Use Library Science
	Libraries
Academic	Libraries
Branch	Libraries
Childrens	Libraries
Classroom	Libraries (1966 1980) Use Instructional Materials
Collection Development	(Libraries) Use Library Collection Development
College	Libraries
Company	Libraries Use Corporate Libraries
Corporate	Libraries
County	Libraries
Depository	Libraries
Digital	Libraries Use Electronic Libraries
District	Libraries Use Regional Libraries

```
                Electronic  Libraries
        Elementary School  Libraries (1966 1980)   Use School Libraries
                  Federal  Libraries   Use Federal Government and Government Libraries
                     Film  Libraries
               Government  Libraries
          Health Sciences  Libraries   Use Medical Libraries
              High School  Libraries   Use School Libraries
                 Hospital  Libraries
               Industrial  Libraries   Use Corporate Libraries
              Institution  Libraries (1969 1980)   Use Institutional Libraries
            Institutional  Libraries
            Junior College  Libraries (1966 1980)   Use College Libraries and Two Year Colleges
                      Law  Libraries
     Legislative Reference  Libraries (1968 1980)   Use Law Libraries
                  Medical  Libraries
                   Mobile  Libraries   Use Bookmobiles
                 National  Libraries
                   Prison  Libraries
                Provincial  Libraries   Use State Libraries
                   Public  Libraries
                 Regional  Libraries
                 Research  Libraries
                 Satellite  Libraries   Use Branch Libraries
                   School  Libraries
                  Science  Libraries
    Science and Technology  Libraries   Use Science Libraries
          Secondary School  Libraries   Use School Libraries
                  Special  Libraries
                    State  Libraries
                Technical  Libraries   Use Science Libraries
        Technical Processes (Libraries)   Use Library Technical Processes
         Technical Services (Libraries)   Use Library Technical Processes
            Turnkey Systems (Libraries)   Use Integrated Library Systems
               University  Libraries (1968 1980)   Use College Libraries
                 Videotape  Libraries   Use Film Libraries
                   Virtual  Libraries   Use Electronic Libraries
                            Library Acquisition
                            Library Administration
                            Library Administrators
                            Library Aides   Use Library Technicians
                            Library Aids   Use Library Equipment
                            Library Associations
                            Library Automation
                            Library Cataloging   Use Cataloging
                            Library Catalogs
  Retrospective Conversion  (Library Catalogs)
                            Library Circulation
                            Library Clerks   Use Library Technicians
                            Library Clients   Use Users (Information)
                            Library Collection Development
                            Library Collections
                            Library Cooperation
                            Library Development
                            Library Directors
                            Library Education
                            Library Employees   Use Library Personnel
                            Library Equipment
                            Library Expenditures
                            Library Extension
                            Library Facilities
                            Library Finance   Use Library Funding
                            Library Fines   Use Fines (Penalties)
                            Library Funding
                            Library Guides
                            Library Handbooks   Use Library Guides
                            Library Holdings   Use Library Collections
                            Library Instruction
        Course Integrated  Library Instruction
           Course Related  Library Instruction   Use Course Integrated Library Instruction
      Curriculum Integrated  Library Instruction   Use Course Integrated Library Instruction
               Integrated  Library Instruction   Use Course Integrated Library Instruction
                            Library Loans   Use Library Circulation
                            Library Management   Use Library Administration
                            Library Material Selection
                            Library Materials
                            Library Mechanization   Use Library Automation
                            Library Networks
                            Library of Congress Classification
                            Library Organizations   Use Library Associations
                            Library Orientation   Use Library Instruction
                            Library Patrons   Use Users (Information)
                            Library Personnel
                            Library Planning
                            Library Policy
                            Library Programs (1966 1980)   Use Library Services
                            Library Reference Materials   Use Library Materials and Reference Materials
                            Library Reference Services (1968 1980)   Use Library Services and Reference Services
                            Library Research
                   Shared  Library Resources
                            Library Role
                            Library Schools
                            Library Science
                            Library Services
```

	Library Skills
	Library Specialists Use Librarians
	Library Standards
	Library Statistics
	Library Surveys
	Library Systems Use Library Networks
Decentralized	Library Systems (1968 1980) Use Decentralization and Library Networks
Integrated	Library Systems
Integrated Automated	Library Systems Use Integrated Library Systems
	Library Technical Assistants Use Library Technicians
	Library Technical Processes
	Library Technicians
	Library User Needs Use User Needs (Information)
	Library User Satisfaction Use User Satisfaction (Information)
	Library Users Use Users (Information)
Weeding	(Library)
	Licensed Nurses Use Nurses
	Licensing Use Certification
State	Licensing Boards
Counselor	Licensing Use Counselor Certification
	Licensing Examinations (Professions)
State Boards of	Licensing Use State Licensing Boards
	Lie Detectors Use Polygraphs
Animal	Life Use Animals
	Life Costs (Facilities and Equipment) Use Life Cycle Costing
	Life Cycle Costing
Family	Life Education
Home and Family	Life Education Use Family Life Education
	Life Events
Work	Life Expectancy
Family	Life
	Life Histories Use Biographies
Home	Life Use Family Life
Outlooks on	Life Use World Views
Philosophy of	Life Use World Views
Plant	Life Use Plants (Botany)
	Life Quality Use Quality of Life
Quality of	Life
Quality of Working	Life
	Life Satisfaction
	Life Sciences Use Biological Sciences
	Life Skills Use Daily Living Skills
Social	Life
	Life Span Education Use Lifelong Learning
	Life Style
Alternative	Life Styles Use Life Style
Urban	Life Use Urban Culture
	Life Views Use World Views
	Lifelong Education Use Lifelong Learning
	Lifelong Learning
	Lifetime Sports
	Lifting
	Light
	Light Amplifiers (Lasers) Use Lasers
	Light Radiation Use Light
	Lighted Playgrounds (1966 1980) Use Playgrounds
	Lighting
	Lighting Design
Flexible	Lighting Design
Outdoor	Lighting (1971 1980) Use Lighting
Television	Lighting
	Lights (1966 1980) Use Lighting
Television	Lights (1966 1980) Use Television Lighting
	Lignite Use Coal
Maximum	Likelihood Factor Analysis Use Factor Analysis and Maximum Likelihood Statistics
Maximum	Likelihood Statistics
	Likert Scales
Research	Limitations Use Research Problems
	Limited English Proficient Use Limited English Speaking
	Limited English Speaking
	Limits (Mathematics)
Raised	Line Drawings
On	Line Systems (1971 1980) Use Online Systems
Ancestral	Lineage Use Genealogy
	Linear Programing (1966 1994) Use Linear Programming
	Linear Programming
	Linear Regression Use Regression (Statistics)
	Linear Structural Equation Models Use Structural Equation Models
	Lingala
	Linguistic Anthropology Use Anthropological Linguistics
	Linguistic Awareness Use Metalinguistics
	Linguistic Borrowing
	Linguistic Competence
	Linguistic Difficulty (Contrastive) Use Interference (Language)
	Linguistic Difficulty (Inherent)
	Linguistic Input
	Linguistic Minorities Use Language Minorities
	Linguistic Patterns (1966 1980) Use Language Patterns
	Linguistic Performance
	Linguistic Research Use Language Research
	Linguistic Styles Use Language Styles
	Linguistic Theory
	Linguistic Universals Use Language Universals

Linguistics
Anthropological Linguistics
Applied Linguistics
Comparative Linguistics   Use Contrastive Linguistics
Computational Linguistics
Contrastive Linguistics
Descriptive Linguistics
Diachronic Linguistics
Historical Linguistics   Use Diachronic Linguistics
Mathematical Linguistics
Statistical Linguistics   Use Mathematical Linguistics
Structural Linguistics
Structural Analysis (Linguistics)
Synchronic Linguistics (1967 1980)   Use Descriptive Linguistics
Comprehensive Services (School Linked)   Use Integrated Services
School Linked Services   Use Integrated Services
Linking Agents
Cleft Lip (1967 1980)   Use Cleft Palate
Lipreading
Lisrel Type Models   Use Structural Equation Models
Mailing List Servers   Use Listservs
Listening
Listening Comprehension
Listening Comprehension Tests
Listening Groups
Listening Habits
Listening Skills
Listening Tests (1970 1980)   Use Listening Comprehension Tests
Basic Word Lists   Use Word Lists
Check Lists
Electronic Discussion Lists   Use Listservs
Film Lists   Use Filmographies
Internet Discussion Lists   Use Listservs
Phonograph Record Lists   Use Discographies
Word Lists
Listservs
Literacy
Adult Literacy
Child Parent Literacy   Use Family Literacy
Literacy Classes (1966 1980)   Use Literacy Education
Computer Literacy
Cultural Literacy
Early Literacy   Use Emergent Literacy
Literacy Education
Emergent Literacy
Family Literacy
Family English Literacy
Functional Literacy
Information Literacy
Job Literacy   Use Workplace Literacy
Job Related Literacy   Use Workplace Literacy
Mathematical Literacy   Use Numeracy
Occupational Literacy   Use Workplace Literacy
Parent Child Literacy   Use Family Literacy
Quantitative Literacy   Use Numeracy
Scientific Literacy
Literacy Skills   Use Literacy
Survival Literacy   Use Functional Literacy
Technological Literacy
Visual Literacy
Workplace Literacy
Literary Analysis (1968 1980)   Use Literary Criticism
Literary Classics   Use Classics (Literature)
Composition (Literary) (1966 1980)   Use Writing (Composition)
Composition Processes (Literary)   Use Writing Processes
Composition Skills (Literary) (1966 1980)   Use Writing Skills
Literary Conventions (1968 1980)   Use Literary Devices
Literary Criticism
Literary Devices
Dialogs (Literary)
Literary Discrimination (1966 1980)
Exposition (Literary)   Use Expository Writing
Literary Genres
Literary History
Literary Influences (1969 1980)
Literary Mood (1970 1980)
Parallelism (Literary)
English Neoclassic Literary Period (1968 1980)
Literary Perspective (1969 1980)
Prosody (Literary)   Use Poetry
Literary Styles
Symbols (Literary)
Literature
Adolescent Literature
African Literature
American Indian Literature
Literature Appreciation
Australian Literature
Baroque Literature
Biblical Literature
Black Literature
Bucolic Literature   Use Pastoral Literature
Canadian Literature

Central American	Literature Use Latin American Literature
Characterization	(Literature) (1969 1977) Use Characterization
Childrens	Literature
Classical	Literature
Classics	(Literature)
Czech	Literature
Eighteenth Century	Literature
English	Literature
Fifteenth Century	Literature
French	Literature
French Canadian	Literature Use Canadian Literature
German	Literature
Greek	Literature
	Literature Guides (1966 1980)
Hispanic American	Literature
Italian	Literature
Latin	Literature
American	Literature (1966 1980) (Latin America) Use Latin American Literature
Latin American	Literature
Medieval	Literature
Mexican American	Literature
Midtwentieth Century	Literature Use Twentieth Century Literature
Negro	Literature (1968 1977) Use Black Literature
Nineteenth Century	Literature
North American	Literature
Old English	Literature
Pastoral	Literature
Polish	Literature
	Literature Programs (1966 1980)
Renaissance	Literature
	Literature Reviews
Reviews of the	Literature Use Literature Reviews
Roman	Literature Use Latin Literature
Russian	Literature
	Literature Searches Use Bibliographies
Seventeenth Century	Literature
Sixteenth Century	Literature
South American	Literature Use Latin American Literature
Spanish	Literature
Spanish American	Literature (1969 1980) Use Hispanic American Literature
	Literature Surveys Use Literature Reviews
Twentieth Century	Literature
United States	Literature
American	Literature (1966 1980) (United States) Use United States Literature
Victorian	Literature
World	Literature
	Lithuanian
	Litigation Use Court Litigation
Court	Litigation
Desegregation	Litigation
Federal Court	Litigation (1966 1980) Use Court Litigation and Federal Courts
Integration	Litigation (1966 1980) Use Desegregation Litigation
State Court	Litigation Use Court Litigation and State Courts
Supreme Court	Litigation (1966 1980)
	Litter Use Solid Wastes
	Livestock
	Livestock Feed Stores Use Feed Stores
	Livestock Production Use Agricultural Production
	Livestock Technology Use Animal Husbandry
Communal	Living Use Collective Settlements and Group Experience
Dormitory	Living Use Dormitories and Group Experience
Family	Living Use Family Life
Fundamental Skills (Daily	Living) Use Daily Living Skills
Group	Living (1966 1977) Use Group Experience
Human	Living (1966 1980)
Independent	Living
	Living Learning Centers
Productive	Living (1967 1980) Use Quality of Life
	Living Quarters Use Housing
Daily	Living Skills
Independent	Living Skills Use Daily Living Skills
	Living Standards
Survival Skills (Daily	Living) Use Daily Living Skills
Faculty	Load Use Faculty Workload
Teacher	Load Use Teaching Load
Teaching	Load
Student	Loading Areas (1968 1980) Use Student Transportation
	Loan Applicants Use Financial Aid Applicants
	Loan Default
Student	Loan Programs
	Loan Repayment
	Loan Words Use Linguistic Borrowing
Defaulted	Loans Use Loan Default
Income Contingent	Loans
Interlibrary	Loans
Library	Loans Use Library Circulation
Scholarship	Loans (1966 1980) Use Scholarships and Student Loan Programs
	Lobbying
	Local Area Networks
	Local Autonomy (of Schools) Use School District Autonomy
	Local Color Writing
	Local Community Programs Use Community Programs
	Local Control (of Schools) Use School District Autonomy

Local Education Agencies   Use School Districts
Local Education Authorities   Use School Districts
Local Government
Local History
Local Housing Authorities (1966 1980)   Use Housing
Local Information Services   Use Community Information Services
Local Issues
Local Legislation
Local Norms
Local Recreation Legislation (1966 1978)   Use Local Legislation and Recreation Legislation
Local Unions (1966 1980)   Use Unions
Indexes   (Locaters) (1967 1980)   Use Indexes
Geographic   Location
Residential   Location   Use Place of Residence
School   Location
Locational Skills (Social Studies)
Locker Rooms
Loco Parentis   Use In Loco Parentis
In   Loco Parentis
Locomotive Engineers
Locus of Control
Internal External   Locus of Control   Use Locus of Control
Logarithms
Logic
Codes   (Logic)   Use Coding
Mathematical   Logic
Symbolic   Logic   Use Mathematical Logic
Logical Thinking
Student   Logs   Use Student Journals
Loneliness
Long Range Planning
Long Term Care
Long Term Memory
Long Term Planning   Use Long Range Planning
Longitudinal Studies
Look Guess Method   Use Sight Method
Look Say Method   Use Sight Method
Loop Induction Systems
Film   Loops   Use Filmstrips
Hearing   Loss (1967 1980)   Use Hearing Impairments
Job   Loss Services   Use Outplacement Services (Employment)
Language   Loss (Skills)   Use Language Skill Attrition
Achievement   Losses   Use Achievement Gains
Parking   Lots   Use Parking Facilities
Love
Low Ability Students (1967 1980)
Low Achievement
Low Achievement Factors (1966 1980)   Use Low Achievement
Low Achievers (1966 1980)   Use Low Achievement
Low Incidence Disabilities
Low Income
Low Income Counties
Low Income Groups
Low Income States
Low Level Aspiration (1966 1980)   Use Aspiration
Low Motivation (1966 1980)   Use Motivation
Low Rent Housing
Low Vision Aids
High Interest   Low Vocabulary Books
Lower Class
Lower Class Males (1966 1980)   Use Lower Class and Males
Lower Class Parents
Lower Class Students
Lower Middle Class
Loyalty Oaths
Lozanov Method   Use Suggestopedia
LRC   Use Learning Resources Centers
LSD   Use Lysergic Acid Diethylamide
IRT   LTT Measurement Theory   Use Item Response Theory
Lubricants
Luganda   Use Ganda
Lumber Industry
Lumbering   Use Lumber Industry
Luminescence
Lunar Exploration   Use Lunar Research
Lunar Research
Lunch Programs
Luo
Luso Brazilian Culture
Lying
Human T Cell   Lymphotropic Virus Type 3   Use Acquired Immune Deficiency Syndrome
Lyric Poetry
Lyric Poets   Use Poets
Lysergic Acid Diethylamide
Machine Aided Indexing   Use Automatic Indexing
Man   Machine Dialogs   Use Man Machine Systems
Machine Dictation   Use Dictation
Man   Machine Interface   Use Man Machine Systems
Production   Machine Operators   Use Machine Tool Operators
Sewing   Machine Operators
Sheet Metal   Machine Operators   Use Machine Tool Operators and Sheet Metal Work
Machine Readable Cataloging
Machine Readable Data Files   Use Databases

	Machine Readable Text Use Electronic Text
	Machine Repairers
	Machine Repairmen (1968 1980) Use Machine Repairers
Man	Machine Systems
	Machine Tool Operators
	Machine Tools
	Machine Translation
Agricultural	Machinery
	Machinery Industry
	Machinery Maintenance Workers Use Machine Repairers
	Machinery Manufacturing Industry Use Machinery Industry
Agricultural	Machinery Occupations
Business	Machines Use Office Machines
Grinding	Machines Use Machine Tools
Milling	Machines Use Machine Tools
Office	Machines
Self Pacing	Machines (1966 1980) Use Teaching Machines
Teaching	Machines
Test Scoring	Machines
Vending	Machines
	Machinists
Maintenance	Machinists Use Machine Repairers
	Macroeconomics
Teacher	Made Tests
	Magazine Articles Use Journal Articles
	Magazines Use Periodicals
Electronic	Magazines Use Electronic Journals
	Magistrates Use Court Judges
	Magnet Centers Use Magnet Schools
	Magnet Schools
	Magnetic Amplifiers Use Electronic Control
	Magnetic Disks
	Magnetic Ink Character Recognition Use Character Recognition
	Magnetic Tape Cartridges Use Magnetic Tape Cassettes
	Magnetic Tape Cassette Recorders (1970 1980) Use Magnetic Tape Cassettes and Tape Recorders
	Magnetic Tape Cassettes
	Magnetic Tapes
	Magnets
Permanent	Magnets Use Magnets
	Magnification Methods
	Magnitude of Effect Use Effect Size
	Maids (1968 1980) Use Household Workers
Electronic	Mail
	Mail Surveys
	Mailing List Servers Use Listservs
	Mainstreaming
	Maintenance
Computer Software	Maintenance Use Computer Software Development
Cultural	Maintenance
Equipment	Maintenance
Language	Maintenance
Lawn	Maintenance Use Turf Management
	Maintenance Machinists Use Machine Repairers
Health	Maintenance Organizations
School	Maintenance
	Maintenance Vehicles Use Service Vehicles
Machinery	Maintenance Workers Use Machine Repairers
	Majority Attitudes
	Majority Culture Use Middle Class Culture
College	Majors (1968 1980) Use Majors (Students)
Departmental	Majors Use Majors (Students)
Education	Majors
Liberal Arts	Majors (1967 1980) Use Liberal Arts and Majors (Students)
	Majors (Students)
	Make Believe Play Use Pretend Play
Tool and Die	Makers
Print	Making Arts Use Printmaking
Collaborative Decision	Making Use Participative Decision Making
Collective Decision	Making Use Participative Decision Making
Decision	Making
Art	Making (Instruction) Use Studio Art
Participative Decision	Making
Decision	Making Skills
Socially	Maladjusted (1966 1980) Use Social Adjustment
	Maladjusted Students Use Student Adjustment
	Maladjustment (1966 1980) Use Adjustment (to Environment)
Emotional	Maladjustment (1966 1980) Use Emotional Adjustment
Student	Maladjustment Use Student Adjustment
	Malagasy
	Malay
	Malayalam
	Malayo Polynesian Languages
	Male Role Use Males and Sex Role
	Males
Lower Class	Males (1966 1980) Use Lower Class and Males
	Malignant Neoplasms Use Cancer
Tumors	(Malignant) Use Cancer
	Malnutrition Use Nutrition
	Malpractice
Academic	Malpractice Use Educational Malpractice
Educational	Malpractice
	Man Days (1968 1980) Use Worker Days
	Man Machine Dialogs Use Man Machine Systems

Man Machine Interface   Use Man Machine Systems
Man Machine Systems
Managed Care (HMOs)   Use Health Maintenance Organizations
Computer   Managed Instruction
Management (1966 1980)   Use Administration
Housing   Management Aides
Behavioral Self   Management   Use Self Management
Management by Objectives
Class   Management (1966 1980)   Use Classroom Techniques
Classroom   Management   Use Classroom Techniques
Computer Aided Instructional   Management   Use Computer Managed Instruction
Computer Based Instructional   Management   Use Computer Managed Instruction
Construction   Management
Contingency   Management
Crisis   Management
Democratic   Management   Use Participative Decision Making
Management Development
Management Education (1967 1980)   Use Administrator Education
Educational   Management   Use Educational Administration
Energy   Management
Enrollment   Management
Family   Management (1966 1980)   Use Home Management
Farm   Management
Financial   Management   Use Money Management
Management Games
Home   Management
Information   Management
Information Resources   Management   Use Information Management
Management Information Systems
Library   Management   Use Library Administration
Middle   Management
Middle Level   Management   Use Middle Management
Money   Management
Office   Management
Participative   Management   Use Participative Decision Making
Management Personnel   Use Administrators
Personnel   Management
Records   Management
Research   Management   Use Research Administration
Risk   Management
School Based   Management
School Site   Management   Use School Based Management
Site Based   Management (Schools)   Use School Based Management
Self   Management
Small Business   Management   Use Business Administration and Small Businesses
Strategic   Management   Use Strategic Planning
Stress   Management
Management Systems
Database   Management Systems
File   Management Systems   Use Database Management Systems
Team   Management   Use Management Teams
Management Teams
Time   Management
Total Quality   Management
Management Training   Use Management Development
Turf   Management
Waste   Management   Use Waste Disposal
Wildlife   Management
Managerial Occupations
Managers   Use Administrators
Personnel   Managers   Use Personnel Directors
Women   Managers   Use Women Administrators
Manchu
Mandarin Chinese
Mandatory Continuing Education
Mandatory Courses   Use Required Courses
Mandatory Education   Use Compulsory Education
Mandatory Retirement
Mandingo
Mangala   Use Lingala
Object   Manipulation
Manipulative Materials
Comedy of   Manners   Use Comedy
Manpower   Use Labor Force
Manpower Development (1966 1980)   Use Labor Force Development
Manpower Needs (1968 1980)   Use Labor Needs
Scientific   Manpower (1967 1980)   Use Scientific Personnel
Manpower Utilization (1966 1980)   Use Labor Utilization
Manual Communication
Manuals (1966 1980)   Use Guides
Instructor   Manuals   Use Teaching Guides
Laboratory   Manuals
Test   Manuals
Equipment   Manufacturers
Manufacturing
Assembly   (Manufacturing)
Computer Aided Design and   Manufacturing   Use Computer Assisted Design and Computer Assisted Manufacturing
Computer Assisted   Manufacturing
Manufacturing Industry
Machinery   Manufacturing Industry   Use Machinery Industry
Manufacturing Methods   Use Manufacturing
Manufacturing Techniques   Use Manufacturing
Manuscript Writing (Handlettering)

	Manuscripts
	Maori
	Maori (People)
	Map Reading Skills Use Map Skills
	Map Skills
	Mapping (Cartography) Use Cartography
Cognitive	Mapping
Concept	Mapping
	Mappings (Mathematics) Use Functions (Mathematics)
	Maps
	Maranao
	Marathi
	Marching Bands Use Bands (Music)
	Marihuana (1969 1986) Use Marijuana
	Marijuana
	Marine Biology
	Marine Corps Air Stations Use Military Air Facilities
	Marine Education
	Marine Science Education Use Marine Education
	Marine Technicians
	Mariners Use Seafarers
	Marital Counseling Use Marriage Counseling
	Marital Instability
	Marital Satisfaction
	Marital Status
	Maritime Education
	Market Economy Use Free Enterprise System
Employment	Market Use Labor Market
Free	Market Use Free Enterprise System
Job	Market (1966 1980) Use Labor Market
Labor	Market
	Marketable Skills Use Employment Potential and Job Skills
	Marketing
Grain	Marketing Use Grains (Food)
Food	Markets Use Food Stores
Diacritical	Marking
	Marking (Scholastic) Use Grading
	Markov Chains Use Markov Processes
	Markov Processes
	Marks (Scholastic) Use Grades (Scholastic)
	Marksmanship
	Marriage
	Marriage Counseling
Exogamous	Marriage Use Intermarriage
	Married Persons Use Spouses
	Married Students
	Marshes Use Wetlands
Salt	Marshes Use Wetlands
	Marxian Analysis
	Marxism
	Marxist Criticism Use Marxian Analysis
	Masculinity
Optical	Masers Use Lasers
	Masonry
Brick	Masonry Use Bricklaying
	Masons (Trade) Use Masonry
Body	Mass Use Body Composition
	Mass Communications Use Mass Media
	Mass Culture Use Popular Culture
	Mass Instruction
	Mass Media
	Mass Media Effects
Media Role	(Mass Media) Use Mass Media Role
Media Use	(Mass Media) Use Mass Media Use
	Mass Media Role
	Mass Media Technology Use Communications and Mass Media
	Mass Media Use
	Mass Production
Weight	(Mass)
	Massed Negative Reinforcement Use Negative Reinforcement
	Master of Arts Degrees Use Masters Degrees
	Master of Arts in College Teaching Use Masters Degrees
	Master of Arts in Teaching Use Masters Degrees
	Master of Science Degrees Use Masters Degrees
	Master of Science in Teaching Use Masters Degrees
	Master Plans
	Master Tapes (Audio) (1968 1980) Use Audiotape Recordings
	Master Teachers
	Masters Degrees
	Masters Programs
	Masters Theses
	Mastery Learning
	Mastery Tests
	Matched Groups
	Matching Tests Use Objective Tests
	Mate Selection
	Material Adaptation Use Media Adaptation
Instructional	Material Adaptation Use Media Adaptation
	Material Culture
	Material Development
Instructional	Material Development Use Material Development
Instructional	Material Evaluation
Paper	(Material)

Material Research   Use Material Development
Material Selection   Use Media Selection
Instructional Material Selection   Use Media Selection
Library Material Selection
Reading Material Selection
Material Sources   Use Resource Materials
Dialectical Materialism   Use Marxism
Anechoic Materials   Use Acoustic Insulation
Art Materials
Audiovisual Materials   Use Audiovisual Aids
Bilingual Materials   Use Multilingual Materials
Bilingual Instructional Materials
Building Materials (1968 1980)   Use Construction Materials
Instructional Materials Centers (1966 1980)   Use Learning Resources Centers
Classroom Materials (1966 1980)   Use Instructional Materials
Construction Materials
Curriculum Materials   Use Instructional Materials
Dangerous Materials   Use Hazardous Materials
Educational Materials   Use Instructional Materials
FLES Materials (1967 1980)   Use FLES and Instructional Materials
Found Materials   Use Found Objects
Handwriting Materials (1966 1983)   Use Handwriting and Instructional Materials
Hazardous Materials
Health Materials
Instructional Materials
Materials Inventory   Use Facility Inventory
Large Type Materials
Library Materials
Library Reference Materials   Use Library Materials and Reference Materials
Manipulative Materials
Mathematics Materials
Multilingual Materials
Multimedia Materials
Nonbook Materials   Use Nonprint Media
Orientation Materials
Parent Materials
Parenting Materials   Use Parent Materials
Portfolios (Background Materials)
Print Media (Materials)   Use Printed Materials
Printed Materials
Programed Materials (1966 1980)   Use Programmed Instructional Materials
Programed Instructional Materials (1980 1994)   Use Programmed Instructional Materials
Programmed Instructional Materials
Protocol Materials
Readers (Materials)   Use Reading Materials
Reading Materials
Reference Materials
Resource Materials
Science Materials
Self Instruction Materials   Use Programmed Instructional Materials
Student Developed Materials
Supplementary Reading Materials
Tactile Materials   Use Manipulative Materials
Teacher Developed Materials
Teaching Materials   Use Instructional Materials
Telegraphic Materials
Visual Materials   Use Visual Aids
Mathematical Applications
Mathematical Aptitude
Mathematical Concepts
Mathematical Enrichment
Mathematical Experience (1966 1980)
Mathematical Expressions   Use Mathematical Formulas
Mathematical Formulas
Mathematical Linguistics
Mathematical Literacy   Use Numeracy
Mathematical Logic
Mathematical Models
Mathematical Patterns   Use Patterns in Mathematics
Mathematical Sentences   Use Mathematical Formulas
Mathematical Statistics   Use Statistics
Mathematical Vocabulary
Mathematicians
Mathematics
Mathematics Achievement
Mathematics Activities
Mathematics Anxiety
Approximation (Mathematics)   Use Estimation (Mathematics)
Mathematics Aptitude   Use Mathematical Aptitude
Mathematics Avoidance   Use Mathematics Anxiety
College Mathematics
Congruence (Mathematics)
Mathematics Curriculum
Mathematics Education
Elementary School Mathematics
Equations (Mathematics)
Estimation (Mathematics)
Field Properties (Mathematics)   Use Properties (Mathematics)
Functions (Mathematics)
General Mathematics
Mathematics History
Inequality (Mathematics)
Mathematics Instruction

Limits	(Mathematics)
Mappings	(Mathematics) Use Functions (Mathematics)
	Mathematics Materials
Mental	Mathematics Use Mental Computation
Modern	Mathematics
New	Mathematics Use Modern Mathematics
Patterns in	Mathematics
Practical	Mathematics (1966 1980) Use Mathematical Applications
Proof	(Mathematics)
Properties	(Mathematics)
Proportion	(Mathematics) Use Ratios (Mathematics)
Quantitative Tests (1980 1985)	(Mathematics) Use Mathematics Tests
Ratios	(Mathematics)
Reciprocals	(Mathematics)
Remedial	Mathematics
Secondary School	Mathematics
	Mathematics Skills
Story Problems	(Mathematics) Use Word Problems (Mathematics)
Symbols	(Mathematics)
	Mathematics Teachers
Technical	Mathematics
	Mathematics Tests
Transformations	(Mathematics)
Vectors	(Mathematics)
Volume	(Mathematics)
Word Problems	(Mathematics)
	Mathophobia Use Mathematics Anxiety
	Matrices
	Matriculation Use Admission (School)
	Matrix Sampling Use Item Sampling
Multiple	Matrix Sampling Use Item Sampling
	Matter
Density	(Matter)
	Maturation (1967 1980)
Learning	Maturation Controversy Use Nature Nurture Controversy
	Maturation Learning Controversy Use Nature Nurture Controversy
Career	Maturity Use Vocational Maturity
	Maturity (Individuals)
Social	Maturity (1966 1980) Use Maturity (Individuals)
	Maturity Tests
Vocational	Maturity
	Mauritian Creole
	Maximum Likelihood Factor Analysis Use Factor Analysis and Maximum Likelihood Statistics
	Maximum Likelihood Statistics
	Maya (People)
	Mayan Languages
	Mayans Use Maya (People)
	Mbya Guarani Use Guarani
Word	Meaning Use Semantics
German	Measles Use Rubella
Cubic	Measure Use Volume (Mathematics)
True	Measure Use True Scores
	Measurement
Cognitive	Measurement
Outcomes	Measurement (College) Use College Outcomes Assessment
Composition	Measurement Use Chemical Analysis
Curriculum Based	Measurement Use Curriculum Based Assessment
	Measurement Equipment
	Measurement Error Use Error of Measurement
Error of	Measurement
	Measurement Goals (1966 1980) Use Measurement Objectives
	Measurement Instruments (1966 1980)
Inventories	(Measurement) Use Measures (Individuals)
	Measurement Objectives
Predictive	Measurement
Standard Error of	Measurement (1970 1980) Use Error of Measurement
	Measurement Techniques
IRT LTT	Measurement Theory Use Item Response Theory
Affective	Measures
Association	Measures
Attitude	Measures
Creativity	Measures Use Creativity Tests
	Measures (Individuals)
Intelligence	Measures Use Intelligence Tests
Nondiscursive	Measures Use Visual Measures
Norm Referenced	Measures Use Norm Referenced Tests
Personality	Measures
Preventive	Measures Use Prevention
Projective	Measures
Self Concept	Measures
Significance	Measures Use Statistical Significance
Visual	Measures
	Meat
	Meat Inspectors Use Food and Drug Inspectors
	Meat Packing Industry
	Mechanical Design Technicians
	Mechanical Devices Use Mechanical Equipment
	Mechanical Drawing Use Engineering Drawing
	Mechanical Engineering Assistants Use Mechanical Design Technicians
	Mechanical Equipment
	Mechanical Skills
	Mechanical Teaching Aids (1966 1980) Use Educational Media
	Mechanical Translation Use Machine Translation

Air Conditioning Mechanics   Use Refrigeration Mechanics
Aircraft   Mechanics   Use Aviation Mechanics
Auto   Mechanics
Automobile   Mechanics   Use Auto Mechanics
Aviation   Mechanics
Classical   Mechanics   Use Mechanics (Physics)
Diesel   Mechanics   Use Auto Mechanics
Fluid   Mechanics
General   Mechanics   Use Mechanics (Process)
Auto   Mechanics (Occupation) (1968 1980)   Use Auto Mechanics
Farm   Mechanics (Occupation) (1967 1980)   Use Agricultural Machinery Occupations
Mechanics (Physics)
Power   Mechanics (1969 1980)   Use Power Technology
Mechanics (Process)
Quantum   Mechanics
Refrigeration   Mechanics
Shop   Mechanics   Use Machine Repairers
Small Engine   Mechanics
Agricultural   Mechanics (Subject)   Use Agricultural Engineering
Farm   Mechanics (Subject)   Use Agricultural Engineering
Truck   Mechanics   Use Auto Mechanics
Defense   Mechanisms
Mechanization   Use Automation
Library   Mechanization   Use Library Automation
Media Adaptation
Educational   Media Adaptation   Use Media Adaptation
Audiovisual   Media   Use Audiovisual Aids
Captioned   Media   Use Captions
School   Media Centers   Use Learning Resources Centers
Communications   Media   Use Mass Media
Educational   Media
Mass   Media Effects
Instructional   Media (1967 1980)   Use Educational Media
Mass   Media
Print   Media (Materials)   Use Printed Materials
Media Role (Mass   Media)   Use Mass Media Role
Media Use (Mass   Media)   Use Mass Media Use
News   Media
Nonprint   Media
Otitis   Media
Media Research
Mass   Media Role
Media Role (Mass Media)   Use Mass Media Role
Media Selection
Educational   Media Selection   Use Media Selection
Media Specialists
Media Technology (1968 1980)   Use Communications
Mass   Media Technology   Use Communications and Mass Media
Mass   Media Use
Media Use (Mass Media)   Use Mass Media Use
Visual   Media   Use Visual Aids
Computer   Mediated Communication
Mediation (Labor)   Use Arbitration
Peer   Mediation
Student   Mediation   Use Peer Mediation
Mediation Theory
Medical Assistance   Use Medical Services
Medical Assistants
Medical Associations
Medical Audit   Use Medical Care Evaluation
Medical Care   Use Medical Services
Medical Care Evaluation
Medical Case Histories
Medical Consultants
Medical Costs   Use Health Care Costs and Medical Services
Medical Doctors   Use Physicians
Medical Education
Graduate   Medical Education
Veterinary   Medical Education
Medical Evaluation
Fellows   (Medical)   Use Graduate Medical Students
Foreign   Medical Graduates
Interns   (Medical)   Use Graduate Medical Students
Internships   (Medical)   Use Graduate Medical Education
Medical Laboratory Assistants
Medical Laboratory Technologists   Use Medical Technologists
Medical Libraries
Allied   Medical Occupations   Use Allied Health Occupations
Medical Record Administrators
Medical Record Clerks   Use Medical Record Technicians
Medical Record Librarians (1969 1980)   Use Medical Record Administrators
Medical Record Technicians
Medical Research
Residency Programs   (Medical)   Use Graduate Medical Education
Residents   (Medical)   Use Graduate Medical Students
Medical School Applicants   Use College Applicants and Medical Schools
Medical School Faculty
Medical Schools
Medical Sciences   Use Medicine
Medical Secretaries   Use Secretaries
Medical Services
Medical Students
Graduate   Medical Students

	Medical Technicians Use Medical Laboratory Assistants
Emergency	Medical Technicians
	Medical Technologists
	Medical Treatment (1967 1980) Use Medical Services
	Medical Vocabulary
	Medicine
Clerkships	(Medicine) Use Clinical Experience
Clinical Judgment	(Medicine) Use Medical Evaluation
Clinical Professors (1967 1980)	(Medicine) Use Medical School Faculty
CPR	(Medicine) Use Cardiopulmonary Resuscitation
Externships	(Medicine) Use Clinical Experience
Family Practice	(Medicine)
General Practice	(Medicine) Use Family Practice (Medicine)
Internal	Medicine
Nuclear	Medicine Use Radiology
Preceptors	(Medicine) Use Physicians and Practicum Supervision
Preceptorships	(Medicine) Use Clinical Experience
Preventive	Medicine
Schools of	Medicine Use Medical Schools
Sport	Medicine Use Sports Medicine
Sports	Medicine
Nuclear	Medicine Technologists Use Radiologic Technologists
Veterinary	Medicine
X Rays	(Medicine) Use Radiology
	Medieval History
	Medieval Literature
	Medieval Romance (1969 1980) Use Medieval Literature
	Meditation
Transcendental	Meditation
	Medium of Instruction (Language) Use Language of Instruction
	Meetings
Colloquiums	(Meetings) Use Meetings
Planning	Meetings (1966 1980) Use Meetings
Staff	Meetings
	Melancholia Use Depression (Psychology)
	Melancholy Use Sadness
	Melanesian Languages
	Melody
Board of Education	Members Use Boards of Education
School Board	Members Use Boards of Education
Union	Members
Average Daily	Membership
Group	Membership
	Memorization
	Memorizing (1967 1980) Use Memorization
	Memory
	Memory Devices (Computers) Use Computer Storage Devices
Kinesthetic	Memory Use Kinesthetic Perception
Long Term	Memory
Photographic	Memory Use Eidetic Imagery
Short Term	Memory
	Men Use Males
Auto Parts	Men (1968 1980) Use Auto Parts Clerks
Deans of	Men Use Deans of Students
Enlisted	Men (1967 1976) Use Enlisted Personnel
	Mende
	Meningomyelocele Use Spina Bifida
	Menses Use Menstruation
	Menstruation
	Mental Ability Use Cognitive Ability
	Mental Age
	Mental Arithmetic Use Arithmetic and Mental Computation
	Mental Computation
	Mental Development (1966 1980) Use Cognitive Development
	Mental Disorders
	Mental Health
	Mental Health Clinics
	Mental Health Programs
	Mental Health Resources Use Mental Health Programs
	Mental Health Workers
Community	Mental Health Workers Use Community Health Services and Mental Health Workers
	Mental Hygiene Use Mental Health
	Mental Illness (1966 1980) Use Mental Disorders
	Mental Mathematics Use Mental Computation
Readiness	(Mental) (1966 1980) Use Readiness
	Mental Retardation
Borderline	Mental Retardation Use Slow Learners
Mild	Mental Retardation
Moderate	Mental Retardation
Severe	Mental Retardation
	Mental Rigidity
	Mental Tests (1966 1980) Use Psychological Testing
	Mentally Advanced Children Use Gifted
	Mentally Handicapped (1966 1980) Use Mental Retardation
Custodial	Mentally Handicapped (1968 1980) Use Severe Mental Retardation
Educable	Mentally Handicapped (1966 1980) Use Mild Mental Retardation
Trainable	Mentally Handicapped (1967 1980) Use Moderate Mental Retardation
Profoundly	Mentally Retarded Use Severe Mental Retardation
	Mentors
	Menu Driven Software
	Meo Use Hmong
	Meos Use Hmong People
	Merchandise Information

Merchandising
Merchants
Mercy Killing   Use Euthanasia
Mergers
Merit Pay
Merit Rating
Merit Rating Programs (1967 1980)   Use Merit Rating
Merit Scholarships

Computer Based	Message Systems Use Electronic Mail	

Meta Analysis
Meta Knowledge   Use Metacognition
Metabolism
Metacognition
Metal Finishing   Use Finishing
Metal Forming Occupations   Use Metal Working
Metal Industry

Sheet   Metal Machine Operators   Use Machine Tool Operators and Sheet Metal Work
Metal Trades   Use Metal Working
Sheet   Metal Work
Sheet   Metal Workers (1967 1981)   Use Sheet Metal Work
Metal Working
Metal Working Occupations (1968 1980)   Use Metal Working
Metalinguistics
Metallurgical Technicians
Metallurgy
Metals
Metamemory   Use Metacognition
Metaphors
Meteorology
Wind   (Meteorology)
Meters   Use Measurement Equipment
Parking   Meters (1968 1980)   Use Parking Controls
Critical Incidents   Method
Critical Path   Method
Design Construct   Method   Use Design Build Approach
Grammar Translation   Method
Integrated Teaching   Method   Use Integrated Activities and Teaching Methods
Kodaly   Method
Lecture   Method
Look Guess   Method   Use Sight Method
Look Say   Method   Use Sight Method
Lozanov   Method   Use Suggestopedia
Montessori   Method
Centroid   Method of Factor Analysis   Use Factor Analysis
Oral Communication   Method
Orff   Method
Phonic   Method   Use Phonics
Word   Method (Reading)   Use Sight Method
Serial   Method   Use Serial Learning
Sight   Method
Suzuki   Method
Case   Method (Teaching Technique)
Methodology (1966 1974)   Use Methods
MTMM   Methodology   Use Multitrait Multimethod Techniques
Q   Methodology
Research   Methodology
Scientific   Methodology
Social Science   Methodology   Use Research Methodology and Social Science Research
Methods
Audiolingual   Methods
Autoinstructional   Methods (1966 1980)   Use Programmed Instruction
Classroom   Methods   Use Classroom Techniques
Counseling   Methods   Use Counseling Techniques
Methods Courses
General   Methods Courses   Use Methods Courses
Special   Methods Courses   Use Methods Courses
Deductive   Methods (1967 1980)   Use Deduction
Desegregation   Methods
Educational   Methods
Enlargement   Methods   Use Magnification Methods
Evaluation   Methods
Inductive   Methods (1967 1980)   Use Induction
Instructional   Methods   Use Teaching Methods
Integration   Methods (1966 1980)   Use Desegregation Methods
Job Search   Methods
Kinesthetic   Methods
Magnification   Methods
Manufacturing   Methods   Use Manufacturing
Monte Carlo   Methods
Presentation   Methods   Use Teaching Methods
Project   Methods   Use Student Projects and Teaching Methods
Project Training   Methods (1968 1980)   Use Student Projects and Teaching Methods
Psychoeducational   Methods
Methods Research
Scientific   Methods   Use Scientific Methodology
Statistical   Methods   Use Statistical Analysis
Statistical Association   Methods   Use Correlation
Supervisory   Methods
Methods Teachers
Teaching   Methods
Testing   Methods   Use Testing
Training   Methods
Metis (People)

	Metric System
	Metrication Use Metric System
	Metropolitan Areas
	Mexican American Culture Use Hispanic American Culture and Mexican Americans
	Mexican American Education
	Mexican American History
	Mexican American Literature
	Mexican Americans
	Mexicans
	Miao Use Hmong
	Miaos Use Hmong People
	Microbiology
	Microcalorimeters Use Calorimeters
	Microcomputers
	Microcounseling
	Microeconomics
	Microelectronics
	Microfiche
	Microfilm
Computer Output	Microfilm
	Microfilming Use Microreproduction
	Microform Reader Printers (1971 1980) Use Microform Readers
	Microform Readers
	Microforms
	Micrographics Use Microreproduction
	Microimages Use Microforms
	Microminiature Electronics Use Microelectronics
	Microphones
	Microphotography Use Microreproduction
	Microprocessors Use Microcomputers
	Microreproduction
	Microscopes
	Microteaching
	Microtexts Use Microforms
	Microwave Relay Systems (1971 1980) Use Telecommunications
	Microworlds
Computer	Microworlds Use Microworlds
Computer Based	Microworlds Use Microworlds
	Midcareer Change Use Career Change and Midlife Transitions
	Middle Aged (1966 1980) Use Middle Aged Adults
	Middle Aged Adults
	Middle Class
	Middle Class College Students (1966 1980) Use College Students and Middle Class Students
	Middle Class Culture
	Middle Class Fathers (1966 1980) Use Fathers and Middle Class Parents
Lower	Middle Class
	Middle Class Mothers (1966 1980) Use Middle Class Parents and Mothers
	Middle Class Norm (1966 1980) Use Middle Class Standards
	Middle Class Parents
	Middle Class Standards
	Middle Class Students
	Middle Class Values (1966 1980) Use Middle Class Standards
	Middle Ear Disease Use Otitis Media
Ear Infections	(Middle Ear) Use Otitis Media
	Middle Eastern History
	Middle Eastern Studies
	Middle English
	Middle Income Housing
	Middle Level Management Use Middle Management
	Middle Management
	Middle School Students
	Middle School Teachers
	Middle Schools
	Midlife Use Middle Aged Adults
	Midlife Transitions
	Midmanagement Use Middle Management
	Midtwentieth Century Literature Use Twentieth Century Literature
	Midwifery Use Obstetrics
	Migrant Adult Education
	Migrant Adults Use Migrants
	Migrant Child Care Centers (1966 1980) Use Day Care Centers and Migrant Children
	Migrant Child Education (1967 1980) Use Migrant Education
	Migrant Children
	Migrant Education
	Migrant Employment
	Migrant Health Services
	Migrant Housing
	Migrant Population Use Migrants
	Migrant Problems
	Migrant Programs
	Migrant Projects Use Migrant Programs
Church	Migrant Projects (1966 1980) Use Church Programs and Migrant Programs
Community	Migrant Projects (1966 1980) Use Community Programs and Migrant Programs
	Migrant Schools (1966 1980) Use Migrant Education
	Migrant Transportation (1966 1980) Use Migrants and Transportation
	Migrant Welfare Services
	Migrant Worker Projects (1966 1980) Use Migrant Programs and Migrant Workers
	Migrant Workers
Agricultural	Migrant Workers Use Migrant Workers
	Migrant Youth
	Migrants
Agricultural	Migrants Use Migrants
Interstate Workers (1966 1980)	(Migrants) Use Migrant Workers

Labor Camps (1966 1980)	(Migrants) Use Migrant Housing
Native	Migrants Use Migrants
	Migration
	Migration Patterns
Rural to Urban	Migration
	Migration Trends Use Migration Patterns
Urban to Rural	Migration
Urban to Suburban	Migration
	Migratory Agricultural Workers Use Migrant Workers
	Migratory Children Use Migrant Children
	Mild Disabilities
	Mild Mental Retardation
	Milieu Therapy
	Militancy Use Activism
Teacher	Militancy
	Military Air Facilities
	Military Organizations
	Military Personnel
	Military Schools
	Military Science
	Military Service
	Military Training
Eight	Millimeter Projectors (1970 1980) Use Projection Equipment
Sixteen	Millimeter Projectors (1966 1980) Use Projection Equipment
	Milling Machines Use Machine Tools
	Millwork Use Cabinetmaking
	Mime Use Pantomime
	Mineral Oil Use Oil
	Mineralogy
	Minerals
Clay	Minerals Use Clay
	Miniaturized Electronics Use Microelectronics
	Minicomputers
	Minicourses
	Minimal Brain Dysfunction
	Minimal Competencies Use Minimum Competencies
	Minimal Competency Testing Use Minimum Competency Testing
	Minimally Brain Injured (1966 1980) Use Minimal Brain Dysfunction
	Minimum Competencies
	Minimum Competency Testing
	Minimum Initial Expenses Use Expenditures
	Minimum Operating Expenses Use Operating Expenses
	Minimum Wage
	Minimum Wage Laws (1966 1974) Use Minimum Wage Legislation
	Minimum Wage Legislation
	Mining
Coal	Mining Use Coal and Mining
	Ministers Use Clergy
	Minnesingers Use Poets
Language	Minorities
Linguistic	Minorities Use Language Minorities
Population	Minorities Use Minority Groups
	Minority Culture Use Minority Groups
	Minority Group Children
	Minority Group Influences
	Minority Group Teachers
	Minority Groups
	Minority Language Groups Use Language Minorities
	Minority Rights Use Civil Rights
	Minority Role (1966 1980) Use Minority Group Influences
	Miosis Use Myopia
	MIS Use Management Information Systems
	Misassignment of Teachers
	Misbehavior (1966 1980) Use Behavior Problems
	Misconceptions
	Miscue Analysis
	Miscue Taxonomy Use Miscue Analysis
	Misplaced Teachers Use Misassignment of Teachers
	Missing Children
Institutional	Mission
	Mission Statements
	Mississippi Band of Choctaw (Tribe)
	Mistaken Conceptions Use Misconceptions
	Mixed Age Grouping
Racially	Mixed Persons Use Multiracial Persons
	Mixed Race Persons Use Multiracial Persons
	Mnemonics
	Mobile Classrooms
	Mobile Clinics
	Mobile Educational Services
	Mobile Laboratories
	Mobile Libraries Use Bookmobiles
	Mobility
	Mobility Aids
Educational	Mobility
Faculty	Mobility
Family	Mobility
Geographic	Mobility (1980 1980) Use Migration
Job	Mobility Use Occupational Mobility
Labor	Mobility Use Occupational Mobility
Occupational	Mobility
Physical	Mobility
Social	Mobility

Student	Mobility
Teacher	Mobility Use Faculty Mobility
Visually Handicapped	Mobility (1967 1994) Use Visually Impaired Mobility
Visually Impaired	Mobility
Youth	Mobilization Use Youth Employment
Learning	Modalities
Response	Mode (1967 1980) Use Responses
	Model Programs Use Demonstration Programs
	Modeling (Psychological) (1977 1980) Use Modeling (Psychology)
	Modeling (Psychology)
	Models
Causal	Models
Collegial	Models Use Collegiality
Linear Structural Equation	Models Use Structural Equation Models
Lisrel Type	Models Use Structural Equation Models
Mathematical	Models
Role	Models
Structural Equation	Models
Student Writing	Models
Teaching	Models
Theoretical	Models Use Models
	Modems
	Moderate Mental Retardation
	Modern Greek Use Greek
	Modern History
	Modern Language Curriculum
	Modern Languages
	Modern Mathematics
	Modern Science (1966 1980) Use Sciences
	Modernism
Post	Modernism Use Postmodernism
	Modernization
Discourse	Modes
Behavior	Modification
Cognitive	Modification Use Cognitive Restructuring
Cognitive Behavior	Modification Use Behavior Modification and Cognitive Restructuring
	Modular Arithmetic
	Modular Building Design
	Modular Drafting Use Modular Building Design
	Modular Learning Use Learning Modules
	Modular Scheduling Use Flexible Scheduling
	Modulator Demodulators Use Modems
Learning	Modules
Schedule	Modules (1968 1980) Use Flexible Scheduling
	Mole Use Mossi
	Molecular Biology
Cellular	Molecular Biology Use Cytology and Molecular Biology
	Molecular Structure
Kinetic	Molecular Theory
	Monera
	Monetary Systems
Disbursements	(Money) Use Expenditures
	Money Management
	Money Systems (1966 1980) Use Monetary Systems
	Mong Use Hmong
	Mongol Use Mongolian
	Mongolian
	Mongolian Languages
	Mongolism (1968 1978) Use Downs Syndrome
	Monolingualism
	Monologs
	Monologues (1970 1980) Use Monologs
Interior	Monologues Use Monologs
	Monte Carlo Methods
	Montessori Method
Imperative	Mood Use Verbs
Indicative	Mood Use Verbs
Literary	Mood (1970 1980)
Subjunctive	Mood Use Verbs
	Moods
	Moonlighting Use Multiple Employment
	Moqui (Tribe) Use Hopi (Tribe)
	Moral Criticism (1969 1980)
	Moral Development
	Moral Instruction Use Ethical Instruction
	Moral Issues
	Moral Judgment Use Moral Values and Value Judgment
	Moral Values
	Morale
Teacher	Morale
	Morals Use Ethics
	More Use Mossi
	Morphemes
Suprasegmental	Morphemes Use Intonation
	Morphemics Use Morphology (Languages)
	Morphology (Languages)
	Morphophonemics
Infant	Mortality
	Mortality (Physiology) Use Death
	Mortality Rate
	Mortality (Research Studies) Use Attrition (Research Studies)
	Moslems Use Muslims
	Mossi

Motels   Use Hotels
Mother Absence   Use Motherless Family
Mother Attitudes
Single   Mother Births   Use Births to Single Women
Unmarried   Mother Births   Use Births to Single Women
Mother Goose Rhymes   Use Nursery Rhymes
Mother Role   Use Mothers and Parent Role
Motherese and Fatherese   Use Caregiver Speech and Parent Child Relationship
Motherhood   Use Mothers
Motherless Family
Mothers
Black   Mothers
Employed   Mothers   Use Employed Parents and Mothers
Middle Class   Mothers (1966 1980)   Use Middle Class Parents and Mothers
Negro   Mothers (1966 1977)   Use Black Mothers
Unwed   Mothers
Motifs
Motion
Motion Pictures   Use Films
Motivation
Achievement   Motivation   Use Achievement Need
Extrinsic   Motivation   Use Incentives
Growth   Motivation   Use Self Actualization
Intrinsic   Motivation   Use Self Motivation
Learning   Motivation
Low   Motivation (1966 1980)   Use Motivation
Reading   Motivation
Self   Motivation
Student   Motivation
Teacher   Motivation
Motivation Techniques
Motor Ability   Use Psychomotor Skills
(Motor Behavior)   Use Physical Activity Level
Activity Level   (Motor Behavior)   Use Physical Activity Level
Perceptual   Motor Coordination
Motor Development
Perceptual   Motor Learning
Sensory   Motor Learning   Use Perceptual Motor Learning
Motor Oil   Use Lubricants and Oil
Motor Reactions
Motor Skills   Use Psychomotor Skills
Motor Vehicles
Motorboat Operators   Use Boat Operators
Electric   Motors
Mourning   Use Grief
Movable Partitions
Movement   Use Motion
Movement Education
English Only   Movement
Northward   Movement   Use Migration
Official English   Movement   Use English Only Movement
Educational Excellence   Movement (United States)   Use Excellence in Education
Eye   Movements
Performance Assessment (Skilled Bodily   Movements)   Use Performance Tests
Population   Movements   Use Migration
MTMM Methodology   Use Multitrait Multimethod Techniques
Mulattoes   Use Multiracial Persons
Multiage Grouping   Use Mixed Age Grouping
Multicampus Colleges
Multicampus Districts
Multichannel Programing (1966 1980)   Use Programming (Broadcast)
Multicultural Education
Multicultural Textbooks
Multicultural Training   Use Cross Cultural Training
Multiculturalism   Use Cultural Pluralism
Multidimensional Scaling
Multidisciplinary Approach   Use Interdisciplinary Approach
Multiethnic Education   Use Multicultural Education
Multiethnic Training   Use Cross Cultural Training
Multigraded Classes
Multilateral Disarmament   Use Disarmament
Multilevel Classes (Second Language Instruction)
Multilingual Materials
Multilingualism
Multilithing   Use Reprography
Multimedia Instruction
Multimedia Materials
Multitrait   Multimethod Techniques
Multiple Choice Tests
Multiple Correlation   Use Correlation
Multiple Disabilities
Multiple Discriminant Analysis   Use Discriminant Analysis
Multiple Employment
Multiple Intelligences
Multiple Jobholding   Use Multiple Employment
Multiple Matrix Sampling   Use Item Sampling
Multiple Regression Analysis
Multiplication
Multiply Handicapped (1967 1980)   Use Multiple Disabilities
Multipurpose Classrooms
Multiracial Persons
Multisensory Learning
Multitrait Multimethod Techniques
Multiunit Schools

```
                         Multivariate Analysis
                         Multivariate Analysis of Variance   Use Multivariate Analysis
                         Multivariate Statistics   Use Multivariate Analysis
                         Municipal Government   Use City Government
                         Municipalities
                         Munukutaba   Use Kituba
                         Murder   Use Homicide
                         Muscle Sense   Use Kinesthetic Perception
                         Muscles   Use Muscular System
                         Muscular Activities   Use Motor Reactions
                         Muscular Exercise   Use Exercise and Muscular System
                         Muscular Extensions   Use Motor Reactions
                         Muscular Flexions   Use Motor Reactions
                         Muscular Strength
                         Muscular System
                         Musculoskeletal System
                         Museums
                         Music
                         Music Activities
              Applied    Music
                         Music Appreciation
                Asian    Music   Use Oriental Music
                Bands    (Music)
               Choral    Music
          Composition    (Music)   Use Musical Composition
                         Music Education
                         Music Facilities
              Harmony    (Music)
         Orchestration   (Music)   Use Instrumentation and Orchestration
              Oriental   Music
                  Pop    Music   Use Popular Music
              Popular    Music
             Practical   Music   Use Applied Music
              Ragtime    Music   Use Jazz
                         Music Reading
               Rhythm    (Music)
                 Rock    Music
                Swing    Music   Use Jazz
                         Music Teachers
                         Music Techniques
                Tempo    (Music)
                         Music Theory
                         Music Therapy
                Vocal    Music
                         Musical Composition
                         Musical Instruments
                         Musicians
                         Muslims
                 Self    Mutilation (1977 1993)   Use Self Injurious Behavior
                         Mutual Intelligibility
                         Mycology
                         Myelocele   Use Spina Bifida
                         Myelomeningocele   Use Spina Bifida
                         Myopia
                         Myosis   Use Myopia
                         Mysticism
                         Mythic Criticism (1969 1980)
                         Mythology
                         Myths   Use Mythology
                         N C Systems   Use Numerical Control
                         Narcotics
                         Narcotics Addiction   Use Drug Addiction
                         Narration
             Personal    Narratives
     Personal Accounts   (Narratives)   Use Personal Narratives
                         Natality   Use Birth Rate
               Navajo    (Nation)
                         National Achievement Tests   Use National Competency Tests
                         National Certification (Teaching)   Use National Teacher Certification
                         National Competency Tests
                         National Curriculum
              British    National Curriculum
                         National Defense
                         National Demography (1966 1980)   Use Demography
                         National Intelligence Norm (1966 1980)   Use Intelligence and National Norms
                         National Languages   Use Official Languages
                         National Libraries
                         National Norms
                         National Organizations
                         National Parks
                         National Programs
                         National Security
                         National Skill Standards   Use National Standards
                         National Socialism   Use Nazism
                         National Standards
                         National Surveys
                         National Teacher Certification
                         National Tests (of Achievement)   Use National Competency Tests
                         Nationalism
                Black    Nationalism   Use Black Power
              Foreign    Nationals
             Advanced    Nations   Use Developed Nations
            Developed    Nations
```

Developing	Nations
Economically Advanced	Nations Use Developed Nations
Emerging	Nations Use Developing Nations
Industrial	Nations Use Developed Nations
Law of	Nations Use International Law
Underdeveloped	Nations Use Developing Nations
	Native Informants Use Native Speakers
	Native Language Instruction
	Native Migrants Use Migrants
	Native Speakers
	Natives Use Indigenous Populations
Alaska	Natives
Canada	Natives
	Natural Disasters
	Natural Gas
	Natural Language Processing
	Natural Language Understanding Systems Use Natural Language Processing
	Natural Parents Use Biological Parents
	Natural Resources
	Natural Sciences
	Naturalism
	Naturalistic Observation
	Nature Centers
	Nature Nurture Controversy
	Nature of Science Use Scientific Principles
	Nature Trails Use Trails
	Navaho (1967 1978) Use Navajo
	Navajo
	Navajo (Nation)
	Naval Air Stations Use Military Air Facilities
	Navigation
	Navigation (Information Systems)
	Nazism
Neo	Nazism Use Nazism
	Near Eastern History Use Middle Eastern History
	Nearsightedness Use Myopia
Achievement	Need
Affiliation	Need
	Need Analysis (Student Financial Aid)
	Need Gratification
	Need Reduction Use Need Gratification
No	Need Scholarships
Status	Need
	Needle Trades
	Needs
	Needs Assessment
Childhood	Needs
Childrens	Needs Use Childhood Needs
Community	Needs
Construction	Needs
Data	Needs Use Information Needs
Design	Needs (1968 1980) Use Design Requirements
Educational	Needs
Emotional	Needs Use Psychological Needs
Evaluation	Needs
Facility	Needs Use Facility Requirements
Family	Needs
Financial	Needs
Health	Needs
Housing	Needs
Individual	Needs
Special	Needs (Individuals) Use Individual Needs
Information	Needs
Information User	Needs Use User Needs (Information)
User	Needs (Information)
Labor	Needs
Library User	Needs Use User Needs (Information)
Manpower	Needs (1968 1980) Use Labor Needs
Personnel	Needs
Physical Design	Needs (1968 1980) Use Design Requirements
Psychological	Needs
Psychological Design	Needs (1968 1980) Use Design Requirements
Research	Needs
Student	Needs
Special	Needs Students
	Negative Attitudes
	Negative Forms (Language)
	Negative Income Tax Use Guaranteed Income
	Negative Practice
	Negative Reinforcement
Massed	Negative Reinforcement Use Negative Reinforcement
Spaced	Negative Reinforcement Use Negative Reinforcement
	Negentropy Use Entropy
Child	Neglect
	Neglected Children (1977 1980) Use Child Neglect
	Neglected Languages Use Uncommonly Taught Languages
	Negligence
	Negotiation Agreements
Collective	Negotiation (1967 1977) Use Collective Bargaining
	Negotiation Impasses
Professional	Negotiation Use Collective Bargaining
	Negro Achievement (1966 1977) Use Black Achievement
	Negro Attitudes (1966 1977) Use Black Attitudes

Negro Businesses (1967 1977) Use Black Businesses
Negro Colleges (1968 1977) Use Black Colleges
Negro Community Use Black Community
Negro Culture (1966 1977) Use Black Culture
Negro Dialects (1966 1977) Use Black Dialects
Negro Education (1966 1977) Use Black Education
Negro Employment (1966 1977) Use Black Employment
Negro History (1966 1977) Use Black History
Negro Housing (1966 1977)
Negro Institutions (1966 1977) Use Black Institutions
Negro Leadership (1966 1977) Use Black Leadership
Negro Literature (1968 1977) Use Black Literature
Negro Mothers (1966 1977) Use Black Mothers
Negro Organizations (1966 1977) Use Black Organizations
Negro Population Trends (1966 1977) Use Black Population Trends
Negro Role (1966 1977) Use Black Influences
Negro Stereotypes (1966 1977) Use Black Stereotypes
Negro Students (1966 1977) Use Black Students
Negro Studies Use Black Studies
Negro Teachers (1966 1977) Use Black Teachers
Negro Youth (1966 1977) Use Black Youth
Negroes (1966 1977) Use Blacks
American Negroes Use Blacks
Neighborhood (1966 1980) Use Neighborhoods
Neighborhood Centers (1966 1980) Use Community Centers
Neighborhood Improvement
Neighborhood Integration
Neighborhood School Policy (1966 1980) Use Neighborhood Schools and School Policy
Neighborhood Schools
Neighborhood Settlements Use Settlement Houses
Neighborhoods
Integrated Neighborhoods Use Neighborhood Integration
Nembe
Neo Nazism Use Nazism
English Neoclassic Literary Period (1968 1980)
Neoclassicism
Neonates
Malignant Neoplasms Use Cancer
Neopsychoanalysis Use Psychiatry
Nepali
Anorexia Nervosa
Netsilik Use Inupiaq
Network Analysis
Networks
Communications Networks Use Communications
Computer Networks
Information Networks
Library Networks
Local Area Networks
Support Networks (Personal Assistance) Use Social Support Groups
Social Networks
Neurolinguistics
Neurological Defects (1966 1980) Use Neurological Impairments
Neurological Impairments
Neurological Organization
Neurologically Handicapped (1966 1980) Use Neurological Impairments
Neurology
Neuropsychology
Neurosis
Posttraumatic Neurosis Use Posttraumatic Stress Disorder
Neurotic Children (1966 1980) Use Neurosis
Fiscal Neutrality
Wealth Neutrality Use Fiscal Neutrality
New Federalism
New Journalism
New Mathematics Use Modern Mathematics
Newborn Infants Use Neonates
News Broadcasting Use Broadcast Journalism and News Reporting
News Media
News Reporting
Sports News Use Athletics and News Media
News Use Use Mass Media Use and News Media
News Writing
Newsletters
Newspapers
Class Newspapers (1967 1980) Use Class Activities and Student Publications
School Newspapers
College Night Use College Day
Night Schools (1966 1980) Use Evening Programs
Nightmares
Nineteenth Century Literature
Credit No Credit Grading
Pass No Credit Grading Use Credit No Credit Grading
No Need Scholarships
Pass No Record Grading Use Credit No Credit Grading
No Shows
Noise Control Use Noise (Sound)
Noise Levels Use Noise (Sound)
Noise Pollution Use Noise (Sound)
Noise (Sound)
Noise Testing Use Noise (Sound)
Nomads
Chemical Nomenclature

```
                        Nominal Group Technique
                        Nominals (1967 1980)   Use Nouns
            Political    Nominees   Use Political Candidates
                        Non English Speaking
                        Non Latin Alphabets   Use Non Roman Scripts
                        Non Roman Scripts
                        Non Western Civilization
                        Nonauthoritarian Classes
                        Nonbook Materials   Use Nonprint Media
                        Noncampus Colleges
                        Noncategorical Education
                        Noncollege Bound Students
                        Noncollege Preparatory Students (1967 1980)   Use Noncollege Bound Students
                        Noncompliance (Psychology)   Use Compliance (Psychology)
                        Noncredit Courses
                        Nondirective Counseling
                        Nondiscriminatory Education
                        Nondiscursive Measures   Use Visual Measures
                        Nonfarm Agricultural Occupations   Use Off Farm Agricultural Occupations
            Rural        Nonfarm Residents
                        Nonfiction
                        Nonformal Education
                        Nongovernmental Organizations
                        Nongraded Classes (1966 1980)   Use Nongraded Instructional Grouping
                        Nongraded Instructional Grouping
                        Nongraded Primary System (1966 1980)   Use Nongraded Instructional Grouping
                        Nongraded Student Evaluation
                        Nongraded System (1966 1980)   Use Nongraded Instructional Grouping
                        Noninstructional Responsibility
                        Noninstructional Student Costs
                        Nonmajors
                        Nonmarital Childbirth   Use Births to Single Women
                        Nonmetropolitan Areas
                        Nonorganic Failure to Thrive   Use Failure to Thrive
                        Nonparametric Statistics
        Labor Force     Nonparticipants
                        Nonprint Media
                        Nonprofessional Personnel
                        Nonprofit Organizations
                        Nonpublic Agencies   Use Private Agencies
                        Nonpublic Education   Use Private Education
                        Nonpublic School Aid (1972 1980)   Use Private School Aid
                        Nonpublic Schools   Use Private Schools
                        Nonpublic Sector   Use Private Sector
                        Nonreservation American Indians
                        Nonresident Farmers   Use Part Time Farmers
                        Nonresident Students (1967 1980) (Foreign)   Use Foreign Students
                        Nonresident Students (1967 1980) (Out of District)   Use Residence Requirements
                        Nonresident Students (1967 1980) (Out of State)   Use Out of State Students
                        Nonresidential Schools (1967 1980)   Use Commuter Colleges
                        Nonreversal Shift   Use Shift Studies
                        Nonroman Alphabets   Use Non Roman Scripts
                        Nonschool Educational Programs
                        Nonsexist Language   Use Sexism in Language
                        Nonspecialists   Use Lay People
                        Nonstandard Dialects
                        Nonteaching Duties   Use Noninstructional Responsibility
                        Nontenured Faculty
                        Nontenured Teachers   Use Nontenured Faculty
                        Nontraditional Careers   Use Nontraditional Occupations
                        Nontraditional Education
                        Nontraditional Occupations
                        Nontraditional Students
                        Nonverbal Ability
                        Nonverbal Communication
            Gestures     (Nonverbal Communication)   Use Body Language
                        Nonverbal Learning
                        Nonverbal Tests
        Middle Class    Norm (1966 1980)   Use Middle Class Standards
National Intelligence    Norm (1966 1980)   Use Intelligence and National Norms
                        Norm Referenced Measures   Use Norm Referenced Tests
                        Norm Referenced Tests
                        Normalization (Disabilities)
                        Normalization (Handicapped) (1974 1994)   Use Normalization (Disabilities)
                        Normative Behavior   Use Behavior Standards
                        Norms
            County       Norms   Use Local Norms
          District       Norms   Use Local Norms
            Group        Norms (1968 1980)
            Local        Norms
          National       Norms
    School District       Norms   Use Local Norms
            Social       Norms   Use Behavior Standards and Social Behavior
            State        Norms
            Test         Norms
                        North American Culture
                        North American English
                        North American History
                        North American Literature
                        North Americans
                        Northern Attitudes (1968 1980)   Use Regional Attitudes
                        Northern Schools (1966 1980)
                        Northward Movement   Use Migration
```

	Norwegian
	Notation Use Coding
Student	Notebooks (Diaries) Use Student Journals
Lesson	Notes Use Lesson Plans
	Notetaking
	Notional Functional Syllabi
Functional	Notional Syllabi Use Notional Functional Syllabi
	Nouns
	Novella Use Novels
	Novels
Sociological	Novels (1969 1980) Use Novels
	Novelty (Stimulus Dimension)
	Nuclear Arms Use Nuclear Weapons
	Nuclear Control Use Disarmament
	Nuclear Energy
	Nuclear Energy Occupations Use Energy Occupations and Nuclear Energy
	Nuclear Family
	Nuclear Medicine Use Radiology
	Nuclear Medicine Technologists Use Radiologic Technologists
	Nuclear Physics
	Nuclear Power Plant Technicians
	Nuclear Power Plants
	Nuclear Technology
	Nuclear Warfare
	Nuclear Weapons
	Nucleic Acids
	Numamiut Use Inupiaq
	Number Concepts
	Number Operations Use Arithmetic
	Number Skills Tests Use Mathematics Tests
	Number Systems
	Number Use Use Numbers
	Numbers
Index	Numbers (Costs) Use Cost Indexes
Prime	Numbers
Rational	Numbers
Whole	Numbers
	Numeracy
	Numeric Databases
	Numeric Filing Use Filing
	Numerical Control
	Nun Teachers (1966 1980) Use Nuns
	Nuns
	Nurse Practitioners
School	Nurse Practitioners Use Nurse Practitioners and School Nurses
	Nurseries (Horticulture)
	Nursery Rhymes
	Nursery Schools
	Nursery Workers (Horticulture)
	Nurses
	Nurses Aides
Certified	Nurses Use Nurses
Licensed	Nurses Use Nurses
Practical	Nurses (1967 1981) Use Nurses and Practical Nursing
Professional	Nurses Use Nurses
Registered	Nurses Use Nurses
School	Nurses
Teacher	Nurses (1966 1980) Use Nurses
	Nursing
	Nursing Aides Use Nurses Aides
	Nursing Assistants Use Nurses Aides
	Nursing Education
	Nursing Homes
Practical	Nursing
	Nursing Research
Vocational	Nursing Use Practical Nursing
Nature	Nurture Controversy
	Nutrient Deficiencies Use Nutrition
	Nutrition
	Nutrition Instruction
	Nutritional Deficiencies Use Nutrition
	Nyanja Use Chinyanja
Tohono	O Odham People
Loyalty	Oaths
	OBE Use Outcome Based Education
	Obedience
	Obesity
	Object Concept Use Object Permanence
	Object Manipulation
	Object Permanence
	Objective Referenced Tests Use Criterion Referenced Tests
	Objective Tests
	Objectively Scored Tests Use Objective Tests
	Objectives
Affective	Objectives
Behavioral	Objectives
Career	Objectives Use Career Choice
Cognitive	Objectives
Counseling	Objectives
Course	Objectives
Educational	Objectives
Guidance	Objectives
Institutional	Objectives Use Organizational Objectives

Learning Objectives   Use Behavioral Objectives
Management by Objectives
Measurement Objectives
Educational Objectives of Students   Use Student Educational Objectives
Organizational Objectives
Performance Objectives   Use Behavioral Objectives
Psychomotor Objectives
Student Educational Objectives
Training Objectives
Objectivity
Found Objects
Parental Obligations   Use Parent Responsibility
Oblique Rotation
Obscenity
Observation
Lesson Observation Criteria
Naturalistic Observation
Diversity (Cultural) as an Observation or a Fact   Use Cultural Differences
Participant Observation
Classroom Observation Techniques
Observational Learning
Obsolescence
Building Obsolescence
Skill Obsolescence
Obstetrics
Obtained Scores   Use Raw Scores
Occidental Civilization   Use Western Civilization
Joint Occupancy   Use Shared Facilities
Auto Mechanics (Occupation) (1968 1980)   Use Auto Mechanics
Companions (Occupation) (1968 1980)   Use Attendants
Farm Mechanics (Occupation) (1967 1980)   Use Agricultural Machinery Occupations
Ornamental Horticulture Occupation (1967 1976)   Use Ornamental Horticulture Occupations
Teaching (Occupation)
Occupational Adjustment   Use Vocational Adjustment
Admission Tests (Occupational)   Use Occupational Tests
Occupational Analysis   Use Job Analysis
Occupational Aspiration
Occupational Aspiration Level   Use Occupational Aspiration
Occupational Awareness   Use Career Awareness
Occupational Choice (1966 1980)   Use Career Choice
Occupational Clusters
Occupational Counseling   Use Career Counseling
Occupational Diseases
Supervised Occupational Experience (Agriculture)
Occupational Exploration   Use Career Exploration
Occupational Families   Use Occupational Clusters
Occupational Followup   Use Vocational Followup
Occupational Guidance (1966 1980)   Use Career Guidance
Occupational Health   Use Occupational Safety and Health
Occupational Home Economics
Occupational Information
Occupational Information Systems   Use Career Information Systems
Occupational Level   Use Employment Level
Occupational Literacy   Use Workplace Literacy
Occupational Mobility
Promotion (Occupational)
Occupational Psychology   Use Industrial Psychology
Occupational Safety and Health
Occupational Safety and Health Standards   Use Labor Standards and Occupational Safety and Health
Occupational Satisfaction   Use Job Satisfaction
Occupational Segregation
Occupational Succession   Use Occupational Mobility
Occupational Surveys
Occupational Tests
Occupational Therapists
Occupational Therapy
Occupational Therapy Assistants
Occupational Training   Use Job Training
Occupations
Administrative Occupations   Use Managerial Occupations
Agricultural Occupations
Agricultural Chemical Occupations
Agricultural Machinery Occupations
Agricultural Supply Occupations
Allied Health Occupations
Allied Medical Occupations   Use Allied Health Occupations
Blue Collar Occupations
Health Occupations Centers (1968 1980)
Child Care Occupations
Clerical Occupations
Construction Occupations   Use Building Trades
Crop Processing Occupations
Data Processing Occupations
Demand Occupations
Drycleaning Laundry Occupations   Use Laundry Drycleaning Occupations
Allied Health Occupations Education
Health Occupations Education (1967 1980)   Use Allied Health Occupations Education
Office Occupations Education
Health Occupations Education (Vocational)   Use Allied Health Occupations Education and Vocational Education
Electrical Occupations
Electromechanical Occupations   Use Electrical Occupations and Electromechanical Technology
Emerging Occupations
Energy Occupations

Farm	Occupations	
Farm Related	Occupations	Use Off Farm Agricultural Occupations
Finance	Occupations	
Food Processing	Occupations	
Food Service	Occupations (1968 1981)	Use Food Service
Forestry	Occupations	
Grain Elevator	Occupations	Use Crop Processing Occupations
Health	Occupations	
Hospitality	Occupations	
Household	Occupations	Use Household Workers and Service Occupations
Insurance	Occupations	
Laundry Drycleaning	Occupations	
Managerial	Occupations	
Metal Forming	Occupations	Use Metal Working
Metal Working	Occupations (1968 1980)	Use Metal Working
Nonfarm Agricultural	Occupations	Use Off Farm Agricultural Occupations
Nontraditional	Occupations	
Nuclear Energy	Occupations	Use Energy Occupations and Nuclear Energy
Off Farm Agricultural	Occupations	
Office	Occupations	
Ornamental Horticulture	Occupations	
Paramedical	Occupations (1967 1980)	Use Allied Health Occupations
Health	Occupations Personnel	Use Health Personnel
Professional	Occupations	
Public Service	Occupations	
Real Estate	Occupations	
Sales	Occupations	
Semiskilled	Occupations	
Service	Occupations	
Skilled	Occupations	
Structural Work	Occupations	Use Building Trades
Technical	Occupations	
Unskilled	Occupations	
White Collar	Occupations	
	Ocean Engineering	
	Oceanography	
	Oceanology (1966 1980)	Use Oceanography
	OCR	Use Character Recognition and Optical Scanners
	Ocular Refractive Errors	Use Ametropia
	Odes	
Tohono O	Odham People	
Leave	of Absence (1968 1980)	Use Leaves of Absence
Leaves	of Absence	
National Tests	(of Achievement)	Use National Competency Tests
Points	of Articulation	Use Articulation (Speech)
Bachelor	of Arts Degrees	Use Bachelors Degrees
Doctor	of Arts Degrees	
Master	of Arts Degrees	Use Masters Degrees
Master	of Arts in College Teaching	Use Masters Degrees
Master	of Arts in Teaching	Use Masters Degrees
Scope	of Bargaining	
Defamation	of Character	Use Libel and Slander
Mississippi Band	of Choctaw (Tribe)	
Library	of Congress Classification	
Internal External Locus	of Control	Use Locus of Control
Locus	of Control	
Analysis	of Covariance	
Victims	of Crime	
Schools	of Dentistry	Use Dental Schools
Stages	of Development	Use Developmental Stages
Severity	(of Disability)	
Adaptive Behavior	(of Disabled)	
Deinstitutionalization	(of Disabled)	
Nonresident Students (1967 1980) (Out	of District)	Use Residence Requirements
Boards	of Education	
Colleges	of Education	Use Schools of Education
Continuity	of Education	Use Developmental Continuity
Economics	of Education	Use Educational Economics
Equality	of Education	Use Equal Education
Foundations	of Education	
History	of Education	Use Educational History
Board	of Education Members	Use Boards of Education
Outcomes	of Education	
Board	of Education Policy	
Politics	of Education	
Results	of Education	Use Outcomes of Education
Role	of Education	
Board	of Education Role	
Schools	of Education	
Sociology	of Education	Use Educational Sociology
State Boards	of Education	
State Departments	of Education	
Supply	of Education	Use Educational Supply
Magnitude	of Effect	Use Effect Size
Retention	(of Employees)	Use Labor Turnover
Standard Error	of Estimate	Use Error of Measurement
Codes	of Ethics	
Centroid Method	of Factor Analysis	Use Factor Analysis
Deans	of Faculty	Use Academic Deans
Graying	of Faculty	Use Aging in Academia
Goodness	of Fit	
Contracting Out	(of Government Services)	Use Privatization
Delay	of Gratification	

Hard of Hearing (1967 1980)   Use Partial Hearing
Heads of Households
Ownership of Ideas   Use Intellectual Property
Freedom of Information
Selective Dissemination of Information
Course of Instruction   Use Course Organization
Deans of Instruction   Use Academic Deans
Language of Instruction
Medium of Instruction (Language)   Use Language of Instruction
Centers of Interest (1966 1980)   Use Learning Centers (Classroom)
Conflict of Interest
Supply of Labor   Use Labor Supply
History of Language   Use Diachronic Linguistics
Transfer of Learning   Use Transfer of Training
State Boards of Licensing   Use State Licensing Boards
Philosophy of Life   Use World Views
Quality of Life
Comedy of Manners   Use Comedy
Error of Measurement
Standard Error of Measurement (1970 1980)   Use Error of Measurement
Schools of Medicine   Use Medical Schools
Deans of Men   Use Deans of Students
Law of Nations   Use International Law
Labeling (of Persons)
Feminization of Poverty
Law of Primacy   Use Primacy Effect
Invasion of Privacy   Use Privacy
Termination of Programs   Use Program Termination
Error of Refraction   Use Ametropia
Board of Regents   Use Governing Boards
Directors of Research   Use Research Directors
Place of Residence
Allocation of Resources   Use Resource Allocation
Knowledge of Results   Use Feedback
Out of School Youth
Holding Power (of Schools)   Use School Holding Power
Local Autonomy (of Schools)   Use School District Autonomy
Local Control (of Schools)   Use School District Autonomy
Restructuring of Schools (United States)   Use School Restructuring
Bachelor of Science Degrees   Use Bachelors Degrees
Master of Science Degrees   Use Masters Degrees
Master of Science in Teaching   Use Masters Degrees
Nature of Science   Use Scientific Principles
Tests of Significance (1966 1980)   Use Statistical Significance
Futures (of Society)
Figures of Speech   Use Figurative Language
Freedom of Speech
Parts of Speech   Use Form Classes (Languages)
Nonresident Students (1967 1980) (Out of State)   Use Out of State Students
Out of State Students
Classes (Groups of Students)
Deans of Students
Educational Goals of Students   Use Student Educational Objectives
Educational Objectives of Students   Use Student Educational Objectives
Teacher Expectations of Students
Higher Education as a Field of Study   Use Postsecondary Education as a Field of Study
Postsecondary Education as a Field of Study
Units of Study (Subject Fields) (1966 1977)   Use Units of Study
Units of Study
Fear of Success
Student Evaluation of Teacher Performance
Clinical Supervision (of Teachers)
Misassignment of Teachers
State of the Art Reviews
Reviews of the Literature   Use Literature Reviews
Freedom of the Press   Use Freedom of Speech
Presidents of the United States
Freedom of Thought   Use Intellectual Freedom
Transfer of Training
Outcomes of Treatment
Termination of Treatment
Board of Trustees   Use Governing Boards
Analysis of Variance
Multivariate Analysis of Variance   Use Multivariate Analysis
Out of Wedlock Births   Use Births to Single Women
Deans of Women   Use Deans of Students
Hours of Work   Use Working Hours
Quality of Working Life
Off Campus Education   Use Extension Education
Off Campus Facilities
Off Campus Student Teaching   Use Student Teaching
Off Farm Agricultural Occupations
Off Reservation American Indians   Use Nonreservation American Indians
Off Site Training   Use Off the Job Training
Off the Job Training
Training Schools (Juvenile Offenders)   Use Correctional Institutions
Central Office Administrators
Office Automation
Office Communication   Use Organizational Communication
Office Education   Use Office Occupations Education
Office Machines
Office Management
Office Occupations

	Office Occupations Education
	Office Practice
	Office Supplies Use Supplies
Work Stations (Home or	Office) Use Workstations
	Officer Personnel
Admissions	Officers
Attendance	Officers
Border Patrol	Officers Use Immigration Inspectors
Chief Academic	Officers Use Academic Deans
Law Enforcement	Officers Use Police
Parole	Officers
Probation	Officers
Student Financial Aid	Officers
Truant	Officers Use Attendance Officers and Truancy
	Offices (Facilities)
Faculty	Offices Use Offices (Facilities)
Staff	Offices Use Offices (Facilities)
	Official English Movement Use English Only Movement
	Official Languages
City	Officials
County	Officials
Elected City	Officials Use City Officials
Business	Officials (Industry) Use Administrators
Public	Officials
School	Officials Use School Personnel
Business	Officials (School) Use School Business Officials
School Business	Officials
State	Officials
Adult	Offspring Use Adult Children
Interracial	Offspring Use Multiracial Persons
	Oglala Sioux (Tribe)
	Oil
Petroleum	(Oil and Gas) Use Fossil Fuels and Oil
Crude	Oil Use Oil
Fuel	Oil Use Fossil Fuels and Oil
Mineral	Oil Use Oil
Motor	Oil Use Lubricants and Oil
Petroleum	(Oil) Use Oil
Heating	Oils Use Fossil Fuels and Oil
	Ojibwa
	Ojibwa (Tribe) Use Chippewa (Tribe)
	Ojibway (Tribe) Use Chippewa (Tribe)
	Ojibwe (Tribe) Use Chippewa (Tribe)
	Okinawan
Old	Old Adults
Young	Old Adults
	Old Age Use Older Adults
	Old English
	Old English Literature
	Old Old Adults
	Older Adolescents Use Late Adolescents
	Older Adults
	Older Workers
	Olympic Games
Summer	Olympic Games Use Olympic Games
Winter	Olympic Games Use Olympic Games and Winter Sports
Special	Olympics
	Ombudsmen
	On Campus Students
State Committees	on Education Use State Boards of Education
Hands	on Learning Use Experiential Learning
Outlooks	on Life Use World Views
	On Line Systems (1971 1980) Use Online Systems
Hands	on Science
	On Site Tests Use Field Tests
Time	on Task
	On the Job Training
	Oncology
	One Parent Family
	One Room Schools Use One Teacher Schools
	One Teacher Schools
	Online Catalogs
Commercial Search Services	(Online) Use Online Vendors
	Online Information Retrieval Use Online Searching
Information Utilities	(Online) Use Online Vendors
Interactive Searching	(Online) Use Online Searching
Interactive Systems	(Online) Use Online Systems
	Online Journals Use Electronic Journals
	Online Public Access Catalogs Use Online Catalogs
	Online Reference Services Use Online Systems and Reference Services
	Online Searching
	Online Systems
	Online Vendors
English	Only Movement
	Onomastics
	Onomatology Use Onomastics
Co	Op Programs Use Cooperative Programs
	Opaque Projectors
	Open Admission Use Open Enrollment
	Open Area Schools Use Open Plan Schools
	Open Book Tests
	Open Circuit Television (1966 1980) Use Broadcast Television
	Open Education

	Open Enrollment
	Open Plan Schools
	Open Schools Use Open Education
	Open Universities
	Opera
	Operant Conditioning
Verbal	Operant Conditioning
Soap	Operas
	Operating Engineering
	Operating Expenses
Minimum	Operating Expenses Use Operating Expenses
	Operating Room Technicians Use Surgical Technicians
Building	Operation
	Operations Analysis Use Operations Research
Formal	Operations
Number	Operations Use Arithmetic
	Operations Research
	Operations (Surgery) Use Surgery
Beauty	Operators Use Cosmetology
Boat	Operators
Drill Press	Operators Use Machine Tool Operators
Farm	Operators Use Farmers
Industrial X Ray	Operators Use Radiographers
Machine Tool	Operators
Motorboat	Operators Use Boat Operators
Production Machine	Operators Use Machine Tool Operators
Punch Press	Operators Use Machine Tool Operators
Sewing Machine	Operators
Sheet Metal Machine	Operators Use Machine Tool Operators and Sheet Metal Work
	Ophthalmology
Counselor	Opinion Use Counselor Attitudes
	Opinion Papers
Press	Opinion
Public	Opinion
	Opinion Scales Use Attitude Measures
Student	Opinion (1966 1980) Use Student Attitudes
	Opinions
Administrator	Opinions Use Administrator Attitudes
Employee	Opinions Use Employee Attitudes
Employer	Opinions Use Employer Attitudes
Parent	Opinions Use Parent Attitudes
Teacher	Opinions Use Teacher Attitudes
	Opportunities
Career	Opportunities (1966 1980)
Cultural	Opportunities
Economic	Opportunities
Educational	Opportunities
Educational Equity	(Opportunities) Use Equal Education
Employment	Opportunities
Equal Educational	Opportunities Use Equal Education
Equity (Educational	Opportunities) Use Equal Education
Housing	Opportunities
Job	Opportunities Use Employment Opportunities
Equal	Opportunities (Jobs)
Research	Opportunities
Social	Opportunities (1966 1980) Use Social Mobility
Training	Opportunities Use Educational Opportunities
Youth	Opportunities
	Opportunity Classes (1966 1980) Use Special Classes
Compensatory	Opportunity Use Compensatory Education
Co	Ops Use Cooperatives
	Optical Character Recognition Use Character Recognition and Optical Scanners
	Optical Data Disks
Digital	Optical Data Disks Use Optical Data Disks
	Optical Disks
	Optical Masers Use Lasers
	Optical Scanners
	Optical Spectrum Use Light
	Optical Videodisks Use Optical Disks and Videodisks
	Optics
Geometrical	Optics Use Optics
Physical	Optics Use Optics
	Optional Branching (1966 1980) Use Branching
	Optional Courses Use Elective Courses
	Optometrists
	Optometry
Diversity (Cultural) as an Observation	or a Fact Use Cultural Differences
Work Stations (Home	or Office) Use Workstations
Publish	or Perish Issue
	Oral Communication (1966 1977) Use Speech Communication
	Oral Communication Method
	Oral English
	Oral Expression (1966 1977) Use Speech Communication
	Oral Facility Use Speech Skills
	Oral History
	Oral Hygienists Use Dental Hygienists
	Oral Interpretation
	Oral Language
	Oral Reading
	Oral Rehydration Therapy
	Oral Skills Use Speech Skills
Aural	Oral Skills Use Audiolingual Skills
	Oral Tradition

Orbiting Satellites   Use Satellites (Aerospace)
Orchestras
Repertory Orchestras   Use Orchestras
Symphony Orchestras   Use Orchestras
Instrumentation and Orchestration
Orchestration (Music)   Use Instrumentation and Orchestration
Birth Order
Performance Assessment (Higher Order Learning)   Use Performance Based Assessment
Higher Order Skills   Use Thinking Skills
Word Order
Serial Ordering
Orff Method
Orff Schulwerk Approach   Use Orff Method
Organ Donors   Use Tissue Donors
Organic Chemistry
Organic Curriculum   Use Student Centered Curriculum
Organization
Administrative Organization
Class Organization
Course Organization
Grade Organization (1966 1980)   Use Instructional Program Divisions
High School Organization (1966 1980)   Use School Organization
Horizontal Organization
Informal Organization
Neurological Organization
Pyramid Organization
School Organization
Six Three Three Organization   Use Instructional Program Divisions
Organization Size (Groups)
Vertical Organization
Organizational Change
Organizational Climate
Organizational Communication
Organizational Development
Organizational Effectiveness
Organizational Goals   Use Organizational Objectives
Organizational Objectives
Organizational Plans   Use Planning
Industrial and Organizational Psychology   Use Industrial Psychology
Organizational Psychology (Work Environment)   Use Industrial Psychology
Organizational Self Study   Use Self Evaluation (Groups)
Organizational Theories
Black Organizations
Civic Organizations   Use Community Organizations
Community Organizations
Faculty Organizations
Formal Organizations   Use Organizations (Groups)
Organizations (Groups)
Health Maintenance Organizations
Human Relations Organizations (1966 1980)   Use Human Relations Programs
Intergovernmental Organizations   Use International Organizations
Internal Review (Organizations)   Use Self Evaluation (Groups)
International Organizations
Library Organizations   Use Library Associations
Military Organizations
National Organizations
Negro Organizations (1966 1977)   Use Black Organizations
Nongovernmental Organizations
Nonprofit Organizations
Religious Organizations
Segregationist Organizations
Social Organizations
Social Institutions (Organizations)   Use Institutions
Student Organizations
Teacher Organizations   Use Teacher Associations
Voluntary Organizations   Use Voluntary Agencies
Advance Organizers
Oriental Americans   Use Asian Americans
Oriental Civilization   Use Non Western Civilization
Oriental Music
American Orientals   Use Asian Americans
Orientation
Career Orientation   Use Career Planning
Goal Orientation
Library Orientation   Use Library Instruction
Orientation Materials
School Orientation
Sexual Orientation
Space Orientation (1968 1980)
Staff Orientation
Teacher Orientation
Visually Handicapped Orientation (1967 1980)   Use Visually Impaired Mobility
Output Oriented Education   Use Competency Based Education
Problem Oriented Instruction   Use Problem Based Learning
Computer Oriented Programs
Output Oriented Teacher Education   Use Competency Based Teacher Education
Orienteering
Original Scores   Use Raw Scores
Original Sources   Use Primary Sources
Originality (1966 1980)   Use Creativity
Ethnic Origins
Ornamental Horticulture
Ornamental Horticulture Occupation (1967 1976)   Use Ornamental Horticulture Occupations

Ornamental Horticulture Occupations
Ornithology
Orthodontic Technicians   Use Dental Technicians
Orthodontics   Use Dentistry
Orthodontists   Use Dentists
Orthogonal Projection (1967 1980)   Use Orthographic Projection
Orthogonal Rotation
Orthographic Projection
Orthographic Symbols
Orthopedically Handicapped (1968 1980)   Use Physical Disabilities
Laser   Oscillators   Use Lasers
Ossetic
Osteopathy
Ostyak
Reading Aloud to   Others
Significant   Others
Otitis Media
Otological Tests   Use Auditory Tests
Nonresident Students (1967 1980)   (Out of District)   Use Residence Requirements
Contracting   Out (of Government Services)   Use Privatization
Out of School Youth
Nonresident Students (1967 1980)   (Out of State)   Use Out of State Students
Out of State Students
Out of Wedlock Births   Use Births to Single Women
Step in Step   out Students   Use Stopouts
Outcome Based Education
College   Outcomes Assessment
Outcomes Based Education   Use Outcome Based Education
Educational   Outcomes   Use Outcomes of Education
Instructional   Outcomes   Use Outcomes of Education
Learner   Outcomes   Use Outcomes of Education
Outcomes Measurement (College)   Use College Outcomes Assessment
Outcomes of Education
Outcomes of Treatment
Student   Outcomes   Use Outcomes of Education
Outdoor Activities
Outdoor Drama (1968 1980)   Use Drama and Outdoor Activities
Outdoor Education
Outdoor Leadership
Outdoor Lighting (1971 1980)   Use Lighting
Outdoor Theaters (1968 1980)   Use Outdoor Activities and Theaters
Outer Space Research   Use Space Exploration
Capital   Outlay (for Fixed Assets)
Course   Outlines   Use Course Descriptions
Outlining (Discourse)
Outlooks on Life   Use World Views
Outplacement Services (Employment)
Input   Output Analysis
Output Devices   Use Input Output Devices
Input   Output Devices
Input   Output
Computer   Output Microfilm
Output Oriented Education   Use Competency Based Education
Output Oriented Teacher Education   Use Competency Based Teacher Education
Community   Outreach   Use Outreach Programs
Outreach Counseling   Use Outreach Programs
Outreach Programs
Overachievement
Overachievers (1966 1980)   Use Overachievement
Overhead Projectors
Overhead Television (1966 1980)   Use Television
Overhead Transparencies   Use Transparencies
Overhead Transparency Projectors   Use Overhead Projectors
Overpopulation
Overseas Employment
Working   Overseas   Use Overseas Employment
Overt Response
Overtime
Overweight (Excessive Body Fat)   Use Obesity
Ownership
Ownership of Ideas   Use Intellectual Property
Oxidation
Oxygen Inhalation Therapy   Use Respiratory Therapy
Self   Paced Instruction   Use Individualized Instruction and Pacing
Pacific Americans
Pacific Islanders
Pacing
Group   Pacing   Use Pacing
Interval   Pacing (1967 1980)   Use Pacing
Self   Pacing Machines (1966 1980)   Use Teaching Machines
Self   Pacing   Use Pacing
Learning   Packages   Use Learning Modules
Learning Activity   Packages   Use Learning Modules
Learning Activity   Packets   Use Learning Modules
Meat   Packing Industry
Page Readers   Use Optical Scanners
Pain
Chronic   Pain   Use Chronic Illness and Pain
Sign   Painters
Painting (1966 1980) (Artistic)   Use Painting (Visual Arts)
Painting (1966 1980) (Industrial)   Use Painting (Industrial Arts)
Painting (Industrial Arts)
Painting (Visual Arts)

```
                        Paired Associate Learning
                        Palaeontology    Use Paleontology
              Cleft     Palate
                        Paleontology
           Cerebral     Palsy
                        Pamphlets
            Display     Panels (1968 1980)    Use Display Aids
                        Panjabi (1967 1994)    Use Punjabi
                        Pantomime
                        Papago
                        Papago (Tribe)    Use Tohono O Odham People
                        Paper (Material)
                        Paperback Books
         Conference     Papers
            Opinion     Papers
           Position     Papers
          Practicum     Papers
           Research     Papers (Students)
               Term     Papers    Use Research Papers (Students)
                        Paradigms    Use Models
                        Paradox
                        Paragraph Composition
                        Paragraphs
                        Paralanguage    Use Paralinguistics
                        Paralegal Education    Use Legal Assistants and Legal Education (Professions)
                        Paralegals    Use Legal Assistants
                        Paralinguistics
                        Parallelism (Literary)
                        Paramedical Occupations (1967 1980)    Use Allied Health Occupations
                        Paramedical Sciences    Use Medicine
                        Paramedics    Use Allied Health Personnel
                        Paranoid Behavior
                        Paraplegia    Use Neurological Impairments
                        Paraprofessional Personnel
                        Paraprofessional School Personnel
                        Parent Absence    Use One Parent Family
                        Parent as a Teacher    Use Parents as Teachers
                        Parent Aspiration
                        Parent Associations
                        Parent Attitudes
                        Parent Background
                        Parent Behavior    Use Parent Child Relationship
                        Parent Child Interaction    Use Parent Child Relationship
                        Parent Child Literacy    Use Family Literacy
                        Parent Child Relationship
                        Parent Conferences
            Teacher     Parent Conferences    Use Parent Teacher Conferences
            Teacher     Parent Cooperation    Use Parent Teacher Cooperation
                        Parent Counseling
                        Parent Education
                        Parent Empowerment
                One     Parent Family
             Single     Parent Family    Use One Parent Family
                Two     Parent Family    Use Nuclear Family
                        Parent Financial Contribution
                        Parent Forums    Use Parent Conferences
                        Parent Grievances
                        Parent Influence
                        Parent Involvement    Use Parent Participation
              Child     Parent Literacy    Use Family Literacy
                        Parent Materials
                        Parent Opinions    Use Parent Attitudes
                        Parent Participation
                        Parent Reaction (1966 1980)    Use Parent Attitudes
              Child     Parent Relationship    Use Parent Child Relationship
             School     Parent Relationship    Use Parent School Relationship
            Student     Parent Relationship    Use Parent Student Relationship
                        Parent Responsibility
                        Parent Rights
                        Parent Role
                        Parent School Relationship
                        Parent Skills    Use Parenting Skills
                        Parent Student Conferences (1967 1980)    Use Parent Teacher Conferences
                        Parent Student Relationship
                        Parent Study Groups    Use Parent Conferences
                        Parent Talk    Use Caregiver Speech and Parent Child Relationship
                        Parent Teacher Conferences
                        Parent Teacher Cooperation
                        Parent Workshops
                        Parental Aspiration (1966 1980)    Use Parent Aspiration
                        Parental Background (1966 1980)    Use Parent Background
                        Parental Financial Contribution (1978 1980)    Use Parent Financial Contribution
                        Parental Grievances (1967 1980)    Use Parent Grievances
                        Parental Obligations    Use Parent Responsibility
              Early     Parenthood
                        Parenthood Education
                        Parenting    Use Child Rearing
                        Parenting Materials    Use Parent Materials
                        Parenting Skills
           In Loco     Parentis
              Loco     Parentis    Use In Loco Parentis
                        Parents
         Adolescent     Parents    Use Early Parenthood
```

Adoptive	Parents
	Parents as Teachers
Biological	Parents
Birth	Parents Use Biological Parents
Catholic	Parents (1966 1980) Use Catholics and Parents
Cottage	Parents Use Resident Advisers
Disabled	Parents Use Parents with Disabilities
Dual Earner	Parents Use Employed Parents
Employed	Parents
Foster	Parents Use Foster Family
Lower Class	Parents
Middle Class	Parents
Natural	Parents Use Biological Parents
	Parents with Disabilities
Working	Parents (1966 1980) Use Employed Parents
	Parish Workers Use Church Workers
	Park Design
	Parking Areas (1966 1980) Use Parking Facilities
Street	Parking Areas Use Parking Facilities
	Parking Controls
	Parking Facilities
	Parking Garages Use Parking Facilities
	Parking Lots Use Parking Facilities
	Parking Meters (1968 1980) Use Parking Controls
	Parking Permits Use Parking Controls
	Parking Ramps Use Parking Facilities
	Parking Regulations Use Parking Controls
	Parks
Educational	Parks
National	Parks
	Parliamentary Procedures
	Parochial School Aid (1972 1980) Use Parochial Schools and Private School Aid
	Parochial Schools
	Parody
	Parole Officers
	Parsons Use Clergy
	Part Correlation Use Correlation
	Part Time Employment
	Part Time Faculty
	Part Time Farmers
	Part Time Jobs (1966 1980) Use Part Time Employment
	Part Time Students
	Part Time Teachers (1967 1980) Use Part Time Faculty
	Part Time Teaching (1967 1980) Use Part Time Faculty
	Part Time Work Use Part Time Employment
	Partial Correlation Use Correlation
	Partial Hearing
	Partial Vision
	Partially Sighted (1967 1980) Use Partial Vision
	Participant Characteristics
	Participant Involvement (1967 1980) Use Participation
	Participant Observation
	Participant Satisfaction
	Participation
Audience	Participation
Citizen	Participation
Classroom	Participation (1966 1980) Use Class Activities and Student Participation
Community	Participation Use Community Involvement
Family	Participation Use Family Involvement
Leader	Participation (1966 1980) Use Leadership
Parent	Participation
Public	Participation Use Citizen Participation
School	Participation Use School Involvement
Student	Participation
Teacher	Participation
	Participative Decision Making
	Participative Management Use Participative Decision Making
	Participative Problem Solving Use Participative Decision Making and Problem Solving
	Participatory Action Research Use Action Research and Participatory Research
	Participatory Research
Political	Parties
Folding	Partitions Use Movable Partitions
Movable	Partitions
	Partners in Education Projects Use Partnerships in Education
	Partnership Academies (School and Business) Use Career Academies
	Partnership Teachers
Educational	Partnerships Use Partnerships in Education
	Partnerships in Education
Auto	Parts Clerks
Auto	Parts Men (1968 1980) Use Auto Parts Clerks
	Parts of Speech Use Form Classes (Languages)
	Parturition Use Birth
	Pashto
	Pashtu Use Pashto
	Pass Fail Grading
	Pass No Credit Grading Use Credit No Credit Grading
	Pass No Record Grading Use Credit No Credit Grading
Audio	Passive Laboratories (1968 1980) Use Language Laboratories
	Pastes (Adhesives) Use Adhesives
	Pastoral Literature
	Pastoral Peoples Use Nomads
	Patents
	Path Analysis

Critical	Path Method
	Pathogenesis Use Pathology
	Pathology
Plant	Pathology
Speech	Pathology (1967 1994) Use Speech Language Pathology
Speech and Language	Pathology Use Speech Language Pathology
Speech Language	Pathology
	Pathways Use Trails
	Patient Care Evaluation Use Medical Care Evaluation
	Patient Education
	Patient Physician Relationship Use Physician Patient Relationship
Doctor	Patient Relationship Use Physician Patient Relationship
Physician	Patient Relationship
	Patients
	Patients (Persons) (1968 1980) Use Patients
	Patriotism
Guards (Border	Patrol) Use Immigration Inspectors
Border	Patrol Officers Use Immigration Inspectors
Library	Patrons Use Users (Information)
Coronary Prone Behavior	Pattern Use Type A Behavior
	Pattern Drills (Language)
	Pattern Recognition
	Patterned Behavior Use Behavior Patterns
	Patterned Responses
	Patternmaking
Arousal	Patterns
Attendance	Patterns
Basic Language	Patterns Use Language Patterns
Behavior	Patterns
Emotional	Patterns Use Psychological Patterns
Employment	Patterns
Error	Patterns
Feeder	Patterns
Growth	Patterns (1966 1980)
Housing	Patterns (1966 1980) Use Residential Patterns
	Patterns in Mathematics
Income	Patterns Use Income
Developmental	Patterns (Individuals) Use Individual Development
Job Holding	Patterns Use Employment Patterns
Language	Patterns
Linguistic	Patterns (1966 1980) Use Language Patterns
Mathematical	Patterns Use Patterns in Mathematics
Migration	Patterns
Posture	Patterns Use Human Posture
Psychological	Patterns
Residential	Patterns
Settlement	Patterns Use Land Settlement
Social Institutions (Social	Patterns) Use Sociocultural Patterns
Sociocultural	Patterns
Traffic	Patterns (1968 1980) Use Traffic Circulation
Equal	Pay Use Salary Wage Differentials
	Pay Equity Use Comparable Worth
Merit	Pay
Premium	Pay
	Paying for College
	Payroll Records
	Peace
International	Peace Use Peace
World	Peace Use Peace
	Peanut Inspectors Use Food and Drug Inspectors
	Pedagogical Content Knowledge
	Pedagogy Use Instruction
	Pedestrian Circulation Use Pedestrian Traffic
	Pedestrian Traffic
	Pediatrics
	Pediatrics Training (1966 1980) Use Pediatrics
	Peer Acceptance
	Peer Counseling
	Peer Evaluation
	Peer Groups
	Peer Influence
	Peer Institutions
	Peer Mediation
	Peer Pressure Use Peer Influence
	Peer Relationship
	Peer Review Use Peer Evaluation
	Peer Teaching
	Peer Tutoring Use Peer Teaching and Tutoring
Fines	(Penalties)
Death	Penalty Use Capital Punishment
	Pensions Use Retirement Benefits
Aboriginal	People Use Indigenous Populations
	People Days Use Worker Days
Hmong	People
Homeless	People
Inuit	(People) Use Eskimos
Khmer	(People) Use Cambodians
Lay	People
Maori	(People)
Maya	(People)
Metis	(People)
Pueblo	(People)
Street	People Use Homeless People

Tohono O Odham People
Vietnamese People
Peoples Education   Use Popular Education
Pastoral Peoples   Use Nomads
Expenditure per Student
Percent   Use Percentage
Percent Body Fat   Use Body Composition
Percentage
Perception
Auditory Perception
Perception (between Persons)   Use Social Cognition
Depth Perception
Haptic Perception (1967 1980)   Use Tactual Perception
Interpersonal Perception   Use Social Cognition
Kinesthetic Perception
Person Perception   Use Social Cognition
Role Perception
Social Perception   Use Social Cognition
Spatial Perception (1980 1981)   Use Spatial Ability
Tactual Perception
Perception Tests
Visual Perception
Perceptiveness (between Persons)   Use Interpersonal Competence and Social Cognition
Perceptual Deprivation   Use Sensory Deprivation
Perceptual Development
Perceptual Handicaps (1980 1994)   Use Perceptual Impairments
Perceptual Impairments
Isolation (Perceptual)   Use Sensory Deprivation
Perceptual Motor Coordination
Perceptual Motor Learning
Perceptual Style   Use Cognitive Style
Perceptually Handicapped (1966 1980)   Use Perceptual Impairments
Performance
Academic Performance (1966 1974)   Use Academic Achievement
Performance Appraisal (Personnel)   Use Personnel Evaluation
Performance Assessment (Higher Order Learning)   Use Performance Based Assessment
Performance Assessment (Skilled Bodily Movements)   Use Performance Tests
Performance Based Assessment
Performance Based Education (1974 1980)   Use Competency Based Education
Performance Based Evaluation   Use Performance Based Assessment
Performance Based Teacher Education (1972 1980)   Use Competency Based Teacher Education
Performance Contracts
Counselor Performance
Performance Criteria (1968 1980)
Differential Item Performance   Use Item Bias
Employee Performance   Use Job Performance
Work Performance Evaluation   Use Vocational Evaluation
Performance Factors
Job Performance
Linguistic Performance
Performance Objectives   Use Behavioral Objectives
Physical Performance   Use Physical Fitness
Performance Specifications (1969 1980)
Student Evaluation of Teacher Performance
Task Performance (1966 1980)
Performance Technology
Human Performance Technology   Use Performance Technology
Performance Tests
Work Evaluation (Performance)   Use Vocational Evaluation
Performing Arts   Use Theater Arts
Performing Arts Centers   Use Theaters
Perinatal Influences
English Neoclassic Literary Period (1968 1980)
Probationary Period
Periodical Articles   Use Journal Articles
Periodicals
Foreign Language Periodicals
Second Language Periodicals   Use Foreign Language Periodicals
Computer Peripherals
Publish or Perish Issue
Object Permanence
Permanent Education   Use Lifelong Learning
Permanent Magnets   Use Magnets
Education Permanente   Use Lifelong Learning
Permissive Environment
Parking Permits   Use Parking Controls
Permuted Indexes
Perquisites (Employment)   Use Fringe Benefits
Perseverance   Use Persistence
Persian
Tadjik Persian   Use Tajik
Persistence
Academic Persistence
Teacher Persistence
Teaching Persistence   Use Teacher Persistence
Whole Person Approach   Use Holistic Approach
Cardiac (Person) (1968 1980)   Use Heart Disorders
Person Days   Use Worker Days
Person Perception   Use Social Cognition
Personal Accounts (Narratives)   Use Personal Narratives
Personal Adjustment (1966 1980)   Use Adjustment (to Environment)
Support Networks (Personal Assistance)   Use Social Support Groups
Personal Autonomy

Personal Care Homes
Personal Computers   Use Microcomputers
Personal Development   Use Individual Development
Personal Empowerment   Use Empowerment
Personal Grooming   Use Hygiene
Personal Growth (1967 1980)   Use Individual Development
Personal Health   Use Hygiene
Personal Interests (1966 1980)   Use Interests
Personal Liberty   Use Civil Liberties
Personal Narratives
Personal Publishing   Use Desktop Publishing
Personal Relationship (1966 1974)   Use Interpersonal Relationship
Resumes   (Personal)
Personal Space
Personal Values (1966 1980)   Use Values
Personality
Adaptability   (Personality)   Use Adjustment (to Environment) and Personality Traits
Personality Assessment
Personality Change
Dependency   (Personality)
Personality Development
Personality Measures
Personality Problems
Personality Rating   Use Personality Assessment
Resilience   (Personality)
Personality Studies
Personality Tests (1968 1980)   Use Personality Measures
Personality Theories
Personality Traits
Personalized Instruction   Use Individualized Instruction
Personnel
Administrative   Personnel (1966 1980)   Use Administrators
Personnel Administrators   Use Personnel Directors
Agricultural   Personnel
Allied Health   Personnel
Assessment Centers   (Personnel)
Personnel Data
Personnel Development   Use Staff Development
Personnel Directors
School   Personnel Directors   Use Personnel Directors and School Personnel
Personnel Discharge   Use Dismissal (Personnel)
Personnel Dismissal   Use Dismissal (Personnel)
Dismissal   (Personnel)
Emergency Squad   Personnel
Enlisted   Personnel
Personnel Evaluation
Guidance   Personnel
Health   Personnel
Health Occupations   Personnel   Use Health Personnel
Health Service   Personnel   Use Health Personnel
Hiring   (Personnel)   Use Personnel Selection
Hospital   Personnel
Indigenous   Personnel
Industrial   Personnel
Institutional   Personnel
Personnel Integration
Library   Personnel
Personnel Management
Management   Personnel   Use Administrators
Personnel Managers   Use Personnel Directors
Military   Personnel
Personnel Needs
Nonprofessional   Personnel
Officer   Personnel
Paraprofessional   Personnel
Paraprofessional School   Personnel
Performance Appraisal   (Personnel)   Use Personnel Evaluation
Personnel Policy
Professional   Personnel
Student   Personnel Programs (1967 1980)   Use Student Personnel Services
Personnel Recruitment   Use Recruitment
Rescue Squad   Personnel   Use Emergency Squad Personnel
Personnel Role   Use Staff Role
School   Personnel
Clinic   Personnel (School) (1966 1980)   Use Allied Health Personnel and School Health Services
Scientific   Personnel
Search Committees   (Personnel)
Security   Personnel
Personnel Selection
Selection Committees   (Personnel)   Use Search Committees (Personnel)
Pupil   Personnel Services
Student   Personnel Services
Special   Personnel   Use Specialists
Personnel Tests   Use Occupational Tests
Student   Personnel Work (1967 1980)   Use Student Personnel Services
Pupil   Personnel Workers
Student   Personnel Workers
At Risk   Persons
Attractiveness (between   Persons)   Use Interpersonal Attraction
Biracial   Persons   Use Multiracial Persons
Divorced   Persons   Use Divorce
Exceptional   Persons (1978 1994)
High Risk   Persons (1982 1990)   Use At Risk Persons

Institutionalized	(Persons) (1967 1976) Use Institutionalized Persons
Institutionalized	Persons
Labeling (of	Persons)
Married	Persons Use Spouses
Mixed Race	Persons Use Multiracial Persons
Multiracial	Persons
Patients	(Persons) (1968 1980) Use Patients
Perception (between	Persons) Use Social Cognition
Perceptiveness (between	Persons) Use Interpersonal Competence and Social Cognition
Racially Mixed	Persons Use Multiracial Persons
African Centered	Perspective Use Afrocentrism
Literary	Perspective (1969 1980)
	Perspective Taking
Temporal	Perspective Use Time Perspective
Time	Perspective
	Perspective Transformation Use Transformative Learning
Global	Perspectives Use Global Approach
	Persuasive Discourse
	Pest Control Use Pests
	Pesticides
	Pests
	Petrography Use Petrology
	Petroleum Industry
	Petroleum (Oil) Use Oil
	Petroleum (Oil and Gas) Use Fossil Fuels and Oil
	Petrology
	Pets
	Peul Use Fulani
	Pharmaceutical Education
	Pharmacists
	Pharmacology
	Pharmacy
Program	Phaseout Use Program Termination
	Phenomenology
	Pheul Use Fulani
	Philanthropic Foundations
	Philanthropy Use Private Financial Support
	Philology Use Linguistics
	Philosophy
Educational	Philosophy
	Philosophy of Life Use World Views
School	Philosophy Use Educational Philosophy
School	Phobia
	Phonathons
Grapheme	Phoneme Correspondence Use Phoneme Grapheme Correspondence
	Phoneme Grapheme Correspondence
	Phonemes
Suprasegmental	Phonemes Use Suprasegmentals
	Phonemic Alphabets
	Phonemics
	Phonetic Analysis
	Phonetic Transcription
	Phonetics
Acoustic	Phonetics
	Phonic Method Use Phonics
	Phonics
Language Records	(Phonograph) (1966 1980) Use Audiodisks
	Phonograph Record Lists Use Discographies
	Phonograph Records (1966 1980) Use Audiodisks
	Phonological Borrowing Use Linguistic Borrowing
	Phonological Units (1966 1980) Use Phonemes
	Phonology
Generative	Phonology
Stress	(Phonology)
	Phonotape Recordings (1966 1978) Use Audiotape Recordings
	Photochemical Reactions
	Photochemistry Use Photochemical Reactions
	Photocomposition
	Photocopying Use Reprography
	Photographic Equipment
	Photographic Memory Use Eidetic Imagery
	Photographs
	Photography
	Photojournalism
	Photometric Brightness Use Luminescence
	Photoreproduction Use Reprography
	Photosynthesis
	Phrase Structure
	Physical Activities
	Physical Activity Level
	Physical Attractiveness
	Physical Characteristics
	Physical Chemistry
	Physical Conditioning Use Physical Fitness
	Physical Design Needs (1968 1980) Use Design Requirements
	Physical Development
	Physical Disabilities
	Physical Divisions (Geographic)
	Physical Education
Adapted	Physical Education
	Physical Education Facilities
	Physical Education Teachers
	Physical Educators Use Physical Education Teachers

Physical Environment
Physical Examinations
Physical Exercise   Use Exercise
Physical Facilities (1966 1980)   Use Facilities
Physical Fitness
Physical Fitness Tests
Force   (Physical)   Use Force
Physical Geography
Physical Handicaps (1966 1980)   Use Physical Disabilities
Physical Health
Physical Mobility
Physical Optics   Use Optics
Physical Performance   Use Physical Fitness
Physical Pressure   Use Pressure (Physics)
Physical Recreation Programs
Physical Sciences
Physical Self Concept   Use Body Image
Physical Strength   Use Muscular Strength
Test Characteristics   (Physical)   Use Test Format
Physical Tests   Use Physical Examinations
Physical Therapists
Physical Therapy
Physical Therapy Aides
Physical Therapy Attendants   Use Physical Therapy Aides
Physically Handicapped (1966 1980)   Use Physical Disabilities
Physician Patient Relationship
Patient   Physician Relationship   Use Physician Patient Relationship
Physicians
Physicians Assistants
Foreign Trained   Physicians   Use Foreign Medical Graduates
Physicians in Training   Use Graduate Medical Students
Physics
Acceleration (1966 1982)   (Physics)   Use Acceleration (Physics)
Acceleration   (Physics)
Atomic   Physics   Use Nuclear Physics
Physics Curriculum (1966 1980)   Use Physics and Science Curriculum
Diffusion (1967 1982)   (Physics)   Use Diffusion (Physics)
Diffusion   (Physics)
Physics Experiments (1966 1980)   Use Physics and Science Experiments
Gravity   (Physics)
Physics Instruction (1966 1980)   Use Physics and Science Instruction
Mechanics   (Physics)
Nuclear   Physics
Pressure   (Physics)
Physics Teachers (1967 1980)   Use Physics and Science Teachers
Physiological Chemistry   Use Biochemistry
Physiological Psychology   Use Psychophysiology
Physiology
Audition   (Physiology) (1967 1980)   Use Hearing (Physiology)
Exercise   (Physiology) (1969 1980)
Exercise   Physiology
Hearing   (Physiology)
Mortality   (Physiology)   Use Death
Piagetian Stages   Use Developmental Stages and Piagetian Theory
Piagetian Tasks   Use Developmental Tasks and Piagetian Theory
Piagetian Theory
Pictorial Journalism   Use Photojournalism
Pictorial Stimuli
Pictorial Tests   Use Visual Measures
Picture Books
Motion   Pictures   Use Films
Pidgins
Pilipino   Use Tagalog
Pilot Programs   Use Pilot Projects
Pilot Projects
Pilot Training   Use Flight Training
Aircraft   Pilots
Airline   Pilots   Use Aircraft Pilots
Airplane   Pilots   Use Aircraft Pilots
Commercial   Pilots   Use Aircraft Pilots
Helicopter   Pilots   Use Aircraft Pilots
Ping Pong   Use Table Tennis
Pipe Fitting   Use Plumbing
Place of Residence
Place Value
Placement
Advanced   Placement
Age Grade   Placement
College   Placement (1966 1980)   Use Student Placement
Job   Placement
Advanced   Placement Programs
Regular Class   Placement (1968 1978)   Use Mainstreaming
Student   Placement
Student Job   Placement   Use Job Placement and Student Employment
Teacher   Placement
Vocational   Placement   Use Job Placement
Plagiarism
Continuous Progress   Plan
House   Plan
Lead Lecture   Plan (1966 1980)   Use Lecture Method
Open   Plan Schools
Schools within a School   Plan   Use House Plan
Unit   Plan (1966 1980)

Planar Area   Use Area
Plane Geometry
Planetariums
Planetary Exploration   Use Space Exploration
Planned Communities
Planned Community (1966 1980)   Use Planned Communities
Planning
Academic   Planning   Use Educational Planning
Administrative   Planning   Use Planning
Campus   Planning
Career   Planning
City   Planning (1966 1980)   Use Urban Planning
College   Planning
Color   Planning
Planning Commissions
Community   Planning
Cooperative   Planning
Curriculum   Planning (1966 1980)   Use Curriculum Development
Educational   Planning
Educational Facilities   Planning
Estate   Planning
Facility   Planning
Family   Planning
Futures   Planning   Use Long Range Planning
Instructional   Planning   Use Instructional Development
Interagency   Planning (1966 1980)   Use Agency Cooperation and Cooperative Planning
Language   Planning
Library   Planning
Long Range   Planning
Long Term   Planning   Use Long Range Planning
Planning Meetings (1966 1980)   Use Meetings
Program   Planning (1966 1980)   Use Program Development
Regional   Planning
Research   Planning   Use Research Design
School   Planning (1966 1980)
Social   Planning
State   Planning   Use Statewide Planning
Statewide   Planning
Strategic   Planning
Urban   Planning
Building   Plans
Departmental Teaching   Plans (1968 1980)   Use Departments
Desegregation   Plans
Educational   Plans   Use Educational Planning
Individual Family Service   Plans   Use Individualized Family Service Plans
Individualized Family Service   Plans
Integration   Plans (1966 1980)   Use Desegregation Plans
Lesson   Plans
Master   Plans
Organizational   Plans   Use Planning
Rotation   Plans
Studio Floor   Plans (1966 1980)
Tutorial   Plans   Use Tutorial Programs
Voucher   Plans   Use Educational Vouchers
Plant Biology   Use Botany
Plant Diseases   Use Plant Pathology
Plant Growth
Plant Identification
Plant Life   Use Plants (Botany)
Plant Pathology
Plant Propagation
Plant Science (1967 1980)
Nuclear Power   Plant Technicians
Plantae   Use Plants (Botany)
Planting (1966 1980)   Use Horticulture
Crop   Planting   Use Agronomy and Horticulture
Plants (Botany)
Nuclear Power   Plants
School   Plants   Use Educational Facilities
Plastics
Plate Tectonics
Learning   Plateaus
Platform Diving   Use Diving
Platonic Criticism (1970 1980)
Platonism
Play
Childrens   Play   Use Play
Dramatic   Play
Fantasy   Play   Use Pretend Play
Free   Play   Use Play
Make Believe   Play   Use Pretend Play
Pretend   Play
Sociodramatic   Play   Use Dramatic Play
Symbolic   Play   Use Pretend Play
Therapeutic   Play   Use Play Therapy
Play Therapy
Playground Activities
Playgrounds
Lighted   Playgrounds (1966 1980)   Use Playgrounds
Role   Playing
Sight   Playing   Use Music Reading
Shadow   Plays   Use Theater Arts
Plays (Theatrical)   Use Drama

	Playwriting
Economic	Plight Use Poverty
	Plumbing
Cultural	Pluralism
	Pluralization Use Plurals
	Plurals
	Plurilingualism Use Multilingualism
Two	Plus Two Tech Prep Associate Degrees Use Associate Degrees and Tech Prep
Two	Plus Two Tech Prep Use Tech Prep
	Plyometrics
	Pneumatic Forms
	Pocket Calculators Use Calculators
	Pocket Computers Use Microcomputers
	Podiatry
	Poetry
Lyric	Poetry
	Poets
Lyric	Poets Use Poets
Grade	Point Average
Quality	Point Ratio Use Grade Point Average
Key Word Access	Points Use Keywords
	Points of Articulation Use Articulation (Speech)
	Poisoning
Lead	Poisoning
	Poisons
	Police
	Police Action
	Police Community Relationship
	Police Costs (1966 1980) Use Costs and Police
	Police Education
Community	Police Relationship Use Police Community Relationship
School	Police Relationship Use Police School Relationship
	Police School Liaison Use Police School Relationship
	Police School Relationship
	Police Seminars (1966 1980) Use Police Education
State	Police (1966 1980) Use Police
Interdistrict	Policies
	Policy
Administrative	Policy
	Policy Analysis
Board of Education	Policy
Diplomatic	Policy Use Foreign Policy
Discipline	Policy
Educational	Policy
Family Services	Policy Use Family Programs and Public Policy
Financial	Policy
Fiscal	Policy Use Financial Policy
Foreign	Policy
	Policy Formation
Government	Policy Use Public Policy
Information	Policy
International	Policy Use Foreign Policy
Library	Policy
Neighborhood School	Policy (1966 1980) Use Neighborhood Schools and School Policy
Personnel	Policy
Public	Policy
School	Policy
School Board	Policy Use Board of Education Policy
School District	Policy Use Board of Education Policy
	Policy Statements Use Position Papers
Transfer	Policy
	Polish
	Polish Americans
	Polish Literature
	Political Advocacy Use Lobbying
	Political Affiliation
	Political Attitudes
	Political Campaigns
	Political Candidates
	Political Correctness
	Political Divisions (Geographic)
	Political Geography Use Human Geography
	Political Influences
	Political Issues
	Political Nominees Use Political Candidates
	Political Parties
	Political Power
	Political Protest Use Activism
	Political Reform Use Social Action
	Political Refugees Use Refugees
	Political Science
	Political Socialization
	Politicalization Use Political Socialization
	Politically Correct Communication Use Political Correctness
	Politics
Educational	Politics Use Politics of Education
International	Politics Use International Relations
	Politics of Education
	Pollution
Air	Pollution
Atmospheric	Pollution Use Air Pollution
Air	Pollution Control (1967 1980) Use Air Pollution
Water	Pollution Control (1969 1980) Use Water Pollution

Noise	Pollution	Use Noise (Sound)
River	Pollution	Use Water Pollution
Stream	Pollution	Use Water Pollution
Water	Pollution	
Water	Polo	
	Polygons	
	Polygraphs	
	Polymers	
Malayo	Polynesian Languages	
	Polynomials	
	Pomo	
Ping	Pong	Use Table Tennis
Item	Pools	Use Item Banks
Swimming	Pools	
	Poor	Use Economically Disadvantaged
	Pop Culture	Use Popular Culture
	Pop Music	Use Popular Music
	Popular Culture	
	Popular Education	
	Popular Music	
	Popularity	
	Population Changes	Use Population Trends
	Population Distribution	
	Population Education	
	Population Growth	
Migrant	Population	Use Migrants
	Population Minorities	Use Minority Groups
	Population Movements	Use Migration
	Population Research	Use Demography
Rural	Population	
	Population Shifts	Use Migration
	Population Trends	
Black	Population Trends	
Negro	Population Trends (1966 1977)	Use Black Population Trends
Urban	Population	
Diffusion (1967 1982)	(Populations)	Use Population Distribution
Indigenous	Populations	
Risk	Populations	Use At Risk Persons
	Pornography	
	Portable Computers	Use Microcomputers
	Portable Facilities	Use Relocatable Facilities
	Portfolio Assessment	
	Portfolios (Background Materials)	
Character	Portrayal	Use Characterization
	Portuguese	
	Portuguese Americans	
	Position Papers	
	Positive Reinforcement	
	Post Coordinate Indexes	Use Coordinate Indexes
	Post Doctoral Education (1967 1980)	Use Postdoctoral Education
	Post High School Education	Use Postsecondary Education
	Post High School Guidance	
	Post Modernism	Use Postmodernism
	Post Secondary Education (1967 1978)	Use Postsecondary Education
	Post Testing (1966 1980)	Use Pretests Posttests
	Post Traumatic Stress Syndrome	Use Posttraumatic Stress Disorder
	Postdoctoral Education	
	Postmodernism	
Tuition	Postponement	Use Income Contingent Loans
	Postsecondary Education	
	Postsecondary Education as a Field of Study	
	Postsecondary Instructional Level	Use Postsecondary Education
Pretests	Posttests	
	Posttraumatic Neurosis	Use Posttraumatic Stress Disorder
	Posttraumatic Stress Disorder	
	Posture Development	Use Human Posture
Human	Posture	
	Posture Patterns	Use Human Posture
	Potable Water	Use Drinking Water
	Potential Dropouts	
Employment	Potential	
Scholastic	Potential	Use Academic Aptitude
	Potentiometers (Instruments)	
	Pottery	Use Ceramics
	Potty Training	Use Toilet Training
	Poverty	
	Poverty Areas	
	Poverty Factors	Use Economic Factors and Poverty
Feminization of	Poverty	
	Poverty Programs	
Anti	Poverty Programs	Use Poverty Programs
	Poverty Research (1970 1980)	Use Poverty
	Poverty Stricken	Use Economically Disadvantaged
Black	Power	
Fluid	Power Education (1967 1980)	Use Fluid Mechanics
Individual	Power	
	Power Mechanics (1969 1980)	Use Power Technology
Holding	Power (of Schools)	Use School Holding Power
Nuclear	Power Plant Technicians	
Nuclear	Power Plants	
Political	Power	
School Holding	Power	
	Power Structure	

	Power Technology
	Power Transfer Systems Use Kinetics
States	Powers
	Practical Arts
	Practical Mathematics (1966 1980) Use Mathematical Applications
	Practical Music Use Applied Music
	Practical Nurses (1967 1981) Use Nurses and Practical Nursing
	Practical Nursing
Drills	(Practice)
Educational	Practice (1967 1980) Use Educational Practices
Family	Practice (Medicine)
General	Practice (Medicine) Use Family Practice (Medicine)
Negative	Practice
Office	Practice
Research	Practice Relationship Use Research and Development and Theory Practice Relationship
Theory	Practice Relationship
Professional	Practice Schools Use Professional Development Schools
Supervised Farm	Practice (1966 1990) Use Supervised Occupational Experience (Agriculture)
Teacher Directed	Practice Use Teacher Guidance
	Practice Teaching Use Student Teaching
Developmentally Appropriate	Practices
Educational	Practices
Employment	Practices
Teaching	Practices Use Teaching Methods
	Practicum Papers
	Practicum Supervision
	Practicums
Nurse	Practitioners
School Nurse	Practitioners Use Nurse Practitioners and School Nurses
Dementia	Praecox Use Schizophrenia
	Pragmatics
	Praise
	Prayer in Schools Use School Prayer
School	Prayer
	Preachers Use Clergy
	Preadolescence Use Preadolescents
	Preadolescents
	Preceptors (Medicine) Use Physicians and Practicum Supervision
	Preceptorships (Medicine) Use Clinical Experience
Drawing	(Precision Draft) Use Drafting
	Precision Ratio Use Relevance (Information Retrieval)
	Precision Teaching
	Precollege Level Use High Schools
	Prediction
Achievement	Prediction Use Achievement and Prediction
Grade	Prediction
	Predictive Ability (Testing) (1966 1980) Use Predictive Measurement
Criterion Validity	(Predictive) Use Predictive Validity
	Predictive Measurement
	Predictive Validity
	Predictive Variables Use Predictor Variables
	Predictor Variables
	Predictors Use Predictor Variables
	Prefabrication
Dimensional	Preference
Left Right	Preference Use Lateral Dominance
Sexual	Preference Use Sexual Orientation
Design	Preferences
	Preferential Admission Use Selective Admission
	Prefixes (Grammar)
	Pregnancy
	Pregnant Students
	Prejudice Use Bias
Racial	Prejudice Use Racial Bias
Sex	Prejudice Use Sex Bias
	Prekindergarten Use Preschool Education
	Prekindergarten Classes Use Preschool Education
	Prekindergarten Teachers Use Preschool Teachers
	Premature Birth Use Premature Infants
	Premature Infants
	Premedical Students
	Premium Pay
	Prenatal Care
	Prenatal Drug Exposure
Cocaine	Prenatal Exposure Use Cocaine and Prenatal Drug Exposure
	Prenatal Exposure to Drugs Use Prenatal Drug Exposure
	Prenatal Influences
Two Plus Two Tech	Prep Associate Degrees Use Associate Degrees and Tech Prep
Tech	Prep
Two Plus Two Tech	Prep Use Tech Prep
Administrator	Preparation Use Administrator Education
College	Preparation
Counselor	Preparation Use Counselor Training
Employment	Preparation Use Job Training
Five Year Teacher	Preparation Programs Use Extended Teacher Education Programs
Teacher	Preparation Use Teacher Education
Textbook	Preparation
Noncollege	Preparatory Students (1967 1980) Use Noncollege Bound Students
	Prepositions
	Prereading Experience
	Prereferral Assessment Use Prereferral Intervention
	Prereferral Intervention
	Prerequisite Courses Use Prerequisites and Required Courses

Prerequisites
Preretirement Education
Preretirement Programs   Use Preretirement Education
Preschool Children
Preschool Clinics (1966 1980)   Use Clinics and Preschool Education
Preschool Curriculum
Preschool Education
Preschool Evaluation
Preschool Experience   Use Early Experience
Preschool Learning (1966 1980)
Preschool Programs (1966 1980)   Use Preschool Education
Preschool Teachers
Preschool Tests
Preschool Workshops (1966 1980)   Use Preschool Education and Workshops
Preschoolers   Use Preschool Children
Laboratory   Preschools   Use Laboratory Schools and Preschool Education
Reggio Emilia   Preschools   Use Preschool Education and Reggio Emilia Approach
Prescriptive Teaching   Use Diagnostic Teaching
Drug Testing   (Presence in Body)   Use Drug Use Testing
Color   Presentation (1969 1980)   Use Color
Presentation Methods   Use Teaching Methods
Preservation
Cultural   Preservation   Use Cultural Maintenance
Talent   Preservation   Use Talent Development
Rain Forest   Preserves   Use Rainforests
Preservice Education (1966 1980)   Use Preservice Teacher Education
Preservice Teacher Education
Preservice Teachers
Preservice Teaching Experience   Use Teaching Experience
Presidential Campaigns (United States)
Presidential Candidates (United States)   Use Political Candidates and Presidential Campaigns (United States)
Presidential Debates (United States)   Use Debate and Presidential Campaigns (United States)
Presidential Elections (United States)   Use Elections and Presidential Campaigns (United States)
Presidents
College   Presidents
Presidents of the United States
Women   Presidents   Use Presidents and Women Administrators
Press   Use News Media
Freedom of the   Press   Use Freedom of Speech
Drill   Press Operators   Use Machine Tool Operators
Punch   Press Operators   Use Machine Tool Operators
Press Opinion
Press Role   Use Mass Media Role and News Media
Drill   Presses   Use Machine Tools
Punch   Presses   Use Machine Tools
University   Presses
Pressure (1970 1980)
Absolute   Pressure   Use Pressure (Physics)
Ambient   Pressure   Use Pressure (Physics)
Fluid   Pressure   Use Pressure (Physics)
High Blood   Pressure   Use Hypertension
Peer   Pressure   Use Peer Influence
Physical   Pressure   Use Pressure (Physics)
Pressure (Physics)
Social   Pressure   Use Social Influences
Group   Pressures   Use Group Dynamics
Prestige
Prestressed Concrete
Pretechnology Programs
Pretend Play
Pretensioned Concrete   Use Prestressed Concrete
Pretesting
Pretests (1966 1980)   Use Pretests Posttests
Pretests Posttests
Prevalence   Use Incidence
Prevention
Accident   Prevention
Crime   Prevention
Delinquency   Prevention
Dropout   Prevention
Fire   Prevention   Use Fire Protection
Preventive Health   Use Health Promotion
Preventive Measures   Use Prevention
Preventive Medicine
Previous Learning   Use Prior Learning
Prevocational Education
Prevocational Training   Use Prevocational Education
Prewriting
Price Indexes   Use Cost Indexes
Priests
Primacy Effect
Law of   Primacy   Use Primacy Effect
Primary Education
Primary Grades (1966 1980)   Use Primary Education
Primary Health Care
Ungraded   Primary Programs (1966 1980)   Use Nongraded Instructional Grouping
Primary Sources
Infant Schools (British   Primary System)   Use British Infant Schools
Nongraded   Primary System (1966 1980)   Use Nongraded Instructional Grouping
Primatology
Prime Numbers
Principal Components Analysis   Use Factor Analysis
Principals

Assistant	Principals	
Beginning	Principals	
First Year	Principals	Use Beginning Principals
School	Principals	Use Principals
Vice	Principals	Use Assistant Principals
Administrative	Principles	
Educational	Principles	
Scientific	Principles	
	Print Making Arts Use Printmaking	
	Print Media (Materials) Use Printed Materials	
	Printed Materials	
	Printed Text Use Printed Materials	
Computer	Printers	
Microform Reader	Printers (1971 1980) Use Microform Readers	
	Printing	
	Printmaking	
	Printscript Use Manuscript Writing (Handlettering)	
	Prior Experiential Learning Use Experiential Learning and Prior Learning	
	Prior Knowledge Use Prior Learning	
	Prior Learning	
	Priority Determination Use Needs Assessment	
	Prison Education Use Correctional Education	
	Prison Libraries	
	Prison Sentences Use Sentencing	
	Prisoners	
	Prisons Use Correctional Institutions	
	Privacy	
Invasion of	Privacy Use Privacy	
	Private Agencies	
	Private Colleges	
	Private Education	
	Private Financial Support	
	Private Higher Education Use Higher Education and Private Education	
	Private Information Use Confidentiality	
	Private Junior Colleges Use Private Colleges and Two Year Colleges	
	Private School Aid	
	Private Schools	
	Private Sector	
	Private Universities Use Private Colleges	
	Privatization	
	Privileged Communication Use Confidentiality	
	Proactive Inhibition Use Inhibition	
	Probability	
	Probability Theory (1967 1980) Use Probability	
Academic	Probation	
	Probation Officers	
Scholastic	Probation Use Academic Probation	
	Probationary Period	
	Probationary Teachers Use Probationary Period	
	Problem Based Learning	
	Problem Centered Curriculum Use Problem Based Learning	
	Problem Children	
	Problem Drinking Use Alcohol Abuse	
	Problem Oriented Instruction Use Problem Based Learning	
	Problem Sets	
	Problem Solving	
Participative	Problem Solving Use Participative Decision Making and Problem Solving	
	Problems	
Adjustment	Problems (1966 1980) Use Adjustment (to Environment)	
Administrative	Problems	
Behavior	Problems	
City	Problems (1966 1980) Use Urban Problems	
Communication	Problems	
Community	Problems	
Curriculum	Problems	
Discipline	Problems	
Dropout	Problems (1966 1980) Use Dropouts	
Educational	Problems (1966 1980)	
Emotional	Problems	
Employment	Problems	
Evaluation	Problems	
Family	Problems	
Farm Labor	Problems (1966 1980) Use Farm Labor and Labor Problems	
Financial	Problems	
Interpersonal	Problems (1966 1980) Use Interpersonal Relationship	
Labor	Problems	
Learning	Problems	
Legal	Problems	
Story	Problems (Mathematics) Use Word Problems (Mathematics)	
Word	Problems (Mathematics)	
Migrant	Problems	
Personality	Problems	
Programing	Problems (1966 1980)	
Reading	Problems Use Reading Difficulties	
Research	Problems	
Social	Problems	
Special Health	Problems	
Student	Problems	
Suburban	Problems	
Testing	Problems	
Urban	Problems	
Welfare	Problems (1966 1980) Use Welfare Services	
World	Problems	

Youth Problems

Procedural Due Process Use Due Process

Cloze Procedure

Procedures Use Methods

Evaluation Procedures Use Evaluation Methods

Experimental Procedures Use Research Methodology

Grievance Procedures

Grouping Procedures (1966 1980) Use Classification

Laboratory Procedures

Parliamentary Procedures

Sorting Procedures (1966 1980) Use Classification

Teaching Procedures (1966 1980) Use Teaching Methods

Conference Proceedings

Interaction Process Analysis

Process Approach (Writing)

Writing Process Approach Use Process Approach (Writing)

Construction (Process)

Counseling Process Use Counseling

Due Process

Process Education

Process Evaluation Use Formative Evaluation

Mechanics (Process)

Procedural Due Process Use Due Process

Science Process Skills

Teaching (Process) Use Instruction

Process Writing Use Process Approach (Writing)

Writing as Process Use Process Approach (Writing)

Processed Foods Inspectors Use Food and Drug Inspectors

Cognitive Processes

Discovery Processes

Educational Processes Use Learning Processes

Group Processes Use Group Dynamics

Judgmental Processes Use Evaluative Thinking

Learning Processes

Technical Processes (Libraries) Use Library Technical Processes

Library Technical Processes

Composition Processes (Literary) Use Writing Processes

Markov Processes

Psychoeducational Processes (1966 1980) Use Psychoeducational Methods

Information Processes (Psychological) Use Cognitive Processes

Reading Processes

Statistical Processes Use Statistical Analysis

Thinking Processes Use Cognitive Processes

Thought Processes (1966 1980) Use Cognitive Processes

Writing Processes

Automatic Data Processing Use Data Processing

Data Processing Centers Use Computer Centers and Data Processing

Data Processing

Electronic Data Processing (1967 1980) Use Data Processing

Grain Processing Use Grains (Food)

Information Processing

Language Processing

Natural Language Processing

Crop Processing Occupations

Data Processing Occupations

Food Processing Occupations

Text Processing Use Word Processing

Word Processing

Procreation Use Reproduction (Biology)

Proctoring

Producer Services

Database Producers

Product Evaluation Use Summative Evaluation

Product Information Use Merchandise Information

Dairy Product Inspectors Use Food and Drug Inspectors

Product Labels Use Merchandise Information

Agricultural Production

Video Production Centers Use Television Studios

Crop Production Use Agricultural Production

Art Production Curriculum Use Studio Art

Film Production

Production Functions Use Productivity

Educational Production Functions Use Productivity

Grain Production Use Grains (Food)

Large Scale Production Use Mass Production

Livestock Production Use Agricultural Production

Production Machine Operators Use Machine Tool Operators

Mass Production

Film Production Specialists

Production Technicians

Production Techniques

Textbook Production Use Textbook Publication

Productive Living (1967 1980) Use Quality of Life

Productive Thinking

Productivity

Art Products

Teaching Profession Use Teaching (Occupation)

Academic Rank (Professional)

Professional Associations

Professional Autonomy

Professional Continuing Education

First Professional Degrees Use Degrees (Academic) and Professional Education

Professional Development

Professional Development Schools
Professional Education
Professional Growth   Use Professional Development
Professional Isolation
Professional Negotiation   Use Collective Bargaining
Professional Nurses   Use Nurses
Professional Occupations
Professional Personnel
Professional Practice Schools   Use Professional Development Schools
Professional Recognition
Professional Services
Professional Staff   Use Professional Personnel
Professional Standards   Use Standards
Professional Status   Use Professional Recognition
Professional Training
Information Professionals   Use Information Scientists
Allied Health Professions   Use Allied Health Occupations
Clinical Teaching (Health Professions)
Health Related Professions   Use Allied Health Occupations
Legal Education (Professions)
Licensing Examinations (Professions)
Professorial Rank   Use Academic Rank (Professional)
Aging Professoriate   Use Aging in Academia
Professors
Adjunct Professors   Use Adjunct Faculty
Clinical Professors (1967 1980) (Education)   Use Student Teacher Supervisors
Graduate Professors (1966 1980)   Use Graduate School Faculty
Clinical Professors (1967 1980) (Medicine)   Use Medical School Faculty
Women Professors (1966 1980)   Use Women Faculty
Proficiency Based Education   Use Competency Based Education
Proficiency Based Teacher Education   Use Competency Based Teacher Education
Language Proficiency
Proficiency Tests (Academic)   Use Achievement Tests
Proficiency Tests (Language)   Use Language Proficiency and Language Tests
Limited English Proficient   Use Limited English Speaking
Profile Evaluation (1966 1980)   Use Profiles
Profiles
Biographical Profiles   Use Biographical Inventories
Profound Disabilities   Use Severe Disabilities
Profoundly Hearing Impaired   Use Deafness
Profoundly Mentally Retarded   Use Severe Mental Retardation
Prognoses   Use Prognostic Tests
Prognostic Tests
Program Administration
Program Approval (Validation)   Use Program Validation
(Program) (1967 1980)   Use Articulation (Education)
Articulation
Program Attitudes
Program Budgeting
Program Content
Program Coordination (1966 1980)   Use Cooperative Programs and Coordination
Program Costs
Program Descriptions
Program Design
Program Development
Program Discontinuance   Use Program Termination
Grades (Program Divisions)   Use Instructional Program Divisions
Instructional Program Divisions
Computer Program Documentation   Use Computer Software
Program Effectiveness
Program Elimination   Use Program Termination
Program Evaluation
Program Guides
Program Implementation
Program Improvement
Program Length
Program Phaseout   Use Program Termination
Program Planning (1966 1980)   Use Program Development
Program Proposals
Program Termination
Program Validation
Programed Instruction (1966 1994)   Use Programmed Instruction
Programed Instructional Materials (1980 1994)   Use Programmed Instructional Materials
Programed Materials (1966 1980)   Use Programmed Instructional Materials
Programed Texts (1966 1980)   Use Programmed Instructional Materials and Textbooks
Programed Tutoring (1967 1994)   Use Programmed Tutoring
Programed Units (1966 1980)   Use Programmed Instruction and Units of Study
Programers (1967 1994)   Use Programmers
Programing (1966 1994)   Use Programming
Architectural Programing (1968 1994)   Use Architectural Programming
Authoring Aids (Programing) (1983 1994)   Use Authoring Aids (Programming)
Programing (Broadcast) (1971 1994)   Use Programming (Broadcast)
Programing Languages (1969 1994)   Use Programming Languages
Linear Programing (1966 1994)   Use Linear Programming
Multichannel Programing (1966 1980)   Use Programming (Broadcast)
Programing Problems (1966 1980)
Programmed Instruction
Programmed Instructional Materials
Programmed Learning   Use Programmed Instruction
Programmed Self Instruction   Use Programmed Instruction
Programmed Tutoring
Programmers
Programming
Architectural Programming

Authoring Aids	(Programming)
	Programming (Broadcast)
Computer	Programming Use Programming
	Programming Languages
Linear	Programming
Radio	Programming Use Programming (Broadcast)
Television	Programming Use Programming (Broadcast)
	Programs
Accelerated	Programs (1966 1980) Use Acceleration (Education)
Adult	Programs
Adult Education	Programs (1966 1980) Use Adult Education and Adult Programs
Adult Reading	Programs
Advanced	Programs (1966 1980)
Advanced Placement	Programs
After School	Programs
Anti Poverty	Programs Use Poverty Programs
Anti Segregation	Programs (1967 1980) Use Racial Integration
Assembly	Programs
Athletic	Programs (1966 1980) Use Athletics
Audiovisual	Programs (1966 1980) Use Audiovisual Instruction
Autoinstructional	Programs (1966 1980) Use Programmed Instruction
Bilingual Education	Programs
Bracero	Programs (1966 1980) Use Braceros
Breakfast	Programs
Building	Programs Use Construction Programs
Church	Programs
City Wide	Programs (1967 1980) Use Urban Programs
Civic	Programs Use Community Programs
Classroom Guidance	Programs (1968 1980)
Co Op	Programs Use Cooperative Programs
College	Programs
College Language	Programs (1967 1980)
College Second Language	Programs
College Work Study	Programs Use Work Study Programs
Community	Programs
Action	Programs (Community) (1966 1980) Use Community Action
Community Consultant	Programs (1966 1980) Use Consultation Programs
Community Recreation	Programs
Community School	Programs Use School Community Programs
Community Service	Programs (1966 1980) Use Community Services
Compensatory Education	Programs (1966 1980) Use Compensatory Education
Comprehensive	Programs
Comprehensive School Health	Programs Use Comprehensive School Health Education
Computer	Programs (1966 1984) Use Computer Software
Computer Oriented	Programs
Construction	Programs
Consultation	Programs
Cooperative	Programs
Cooperative Work Experience	Programs Use Cooperative Education
Counseling	Programs (1966 1980) Use Counseling Services
Counseling Instructional	Programs (1967 1980)
County	Programs
Day	Programs
Day Camp	Programs
Day Care	Programs (1966 1980) Use Day Care
Daytime	Programs (1967 1980) Use Day Programs
Demonstration	Programs
Developmental	Programs
Developmental Studies	Programs
Developmentally Appropriate	Programs Use Developmentally Appropriate Practices
Discussion	Programs (1966 1980) Use Discussion
Doctoral	Programs
Dropout	Programs
Educational	Programs (1966 1980)
Emergency	Programs
Employee Assistance	Programs
Employment	Programs
English	Programs (1966 1980) Use English Curriculum
Enrichment	Programs (1966 1980) Use Enrichment Activities
Evening	Programs
Evening Counseling	Programs (1966 1980) Use Counseling Services and Evening Programs
Exchange	Programs
Exemplary	Programs Use Demonstration Programs
Experimental	Programs
Extended Teacher Education	Programs
External Degree	Programs
Extramural Athletic	Programs (1966 1980) Use Extramural Athletics
Family	Programs
Federal	Programs
Feeder	Programs (1966 1980) Use Feeder Patterns
Field Experience	Programs
Five Year Teacher Preparation	Programs Use Extended Teacher Education Programs
FLES	Programs (1967 1980) Use FLES and Second Language Programs
Followup	Programs Use Followup Studies
Foreign Language	Programs Use Second Language Programs
Foundation	Programs
Free Choice Transfer	Programs
GED	Programs Use High School Equivalency Programs
General Educational Development	Programs Use High School Equivalency Programs
Guidance	Programs
Health	Programs
High School Equivalency	Programs
Home	Programs

Human Relations	Programs	
Immersion	Programs	
Immunization	Programs	
Improvement	Programs	
Individualized	Programs	
Individualized Education	Programs	
Inplant	Programs	
Inservice	Programs (1966 1980)	Use Inservice Education
Inservice Education	Programs	Use Inservice Education
Institutes (Training	Programs)	
Instructional	Programs (1966 1980)	
Insurance	Programs (1968 1980)	Use Insurance
Intercollegiate	Programs (1967 1980)	Use Intercollegiate Cooperation
Intercultural	Programs	
Intergenerational	Programs	
International	Programs	
Internship	Programs	
Intersession School	Programs	Use Vacation Programs
Interstate	Programs	
Intramural Athletic	Programs (1966 1980)	Use Intramural Athletics
Language	Programs (1966 1980)	
Library	Programs (1966 1980)	Use Library Services
Literature	Programs (1966 1980)	
Local Community	Programs	Use Community Programs
Lunch	Programs	
Masters	Programs	
Residency	Programs (Medical)	Use Graduate Medical Education
Mental Health	Programs	
Merit Rating	Programs (1967 1980)	Use Merit Rating
Migrant	Programs	
Model	Programs	Use Demonstration Programs
National	Programs	
Nonschool Educational	Programs	
Outreach	Programs	
Physical Recreation	Programs	
Pilot	Programs	Use Pilot Projects
Poverty	Programs	
Preretirement	Programs	Use Preretirement Education
Preschool	Programs (1966 1980)	Use Preschool Education
Pretechnology	Programs	
Reading	Programs	
Recreational	Programs	
Regional	Programs	
Rehabilitation	Programs	
Remedial	Programs	
Remedial Education	Programs	Use Remedial Programs
Remedial Reading	Programs (1966 1980)	Use Remedial Programs and Remedial Reading
Research	Programs	Use Research Projects
Resident Camp	Programs	
Residential	Programs	
Resource Room	Programs	
Restrictive Transfer	Programs (1966 1980)	Use Transfer Programs
School	Programs	Use School Activities
School Community	Programs	
School Recreational	Programs	
Science	Programs	
Second Language	Programs	
Self Help	Programs	
Sequential	Programs (1966 1980)	Use Sequential Approach
Sequential Reading	Programs (1966 1980)	Use Sequential Approach
Social Recreation	Programs (1966 1980)	Use Recreational Programs
Special	Programs	
Special Degree	Programs	
State	Programs	
State Government	Programs	Use State Government and State Programs
Statewide	Programs	Use State Programs
Student Exchange	Programs	
Student Loan	Programs	
Student Personnel	Programs (1967 1980)	Use Student Personnel Services
Study Release	Programs	Use Released Time
Summer	Programs	
Summer Science	Programs	
Supported Work	Programs	Use Supported Employment
Teacher	Programs (1966 1980)	Use Teacher Education Programs
Teacher Education	Programs	
Extended Degree	Programs (Teacher Education)	Use Extended Teacher Education Programs
Teacher Exchange	Programs	
Teaching	Programs (1966 1980)	
Technological	Programs	Use Science Programs
Telephone Solicitation	Programs	Use Phonathons
Termination of	Programs	Use Program Termination
Testing	Programs	
Time Shortened Degree	Programs	Use Acceleration (Education)
Transfer	Programs	
Transitional	Programs	
Tutorial	Programs	
Ungraded	Programs (1966 1980)	Use Nongraded Instructional Grouping
Ungraded Elementary	Programs (1966 1980)	Use Nongraded Instructional Grouping
Ungraded Primary	Programs (1966 1980)	Use Nongraded Instructional Grouping
Unified Studies	Programs (1966 1980)	Use Unified Studies Curriculum
Urban	Programs	
Vacation	Programs	
Validated	Programs	

Approved Programs (Validated)   Use Validated Programs
Weekend Programs
Wellness Programs   Use Wellness
Work Education Programs   Use Work Study Programs
Work Experience Programs
Work Study Programs
Youth Programs
Academic Progress   Use Academic Achievement
Economic Progress
Continuous Progress Plan
Flexible Progression
Progressive Education
Progressive Relaxation (1967 1980)   Use Relaxation Training
Progressive Retardation (1966 1980) (in School)   Use Educationally Disadvantaged
Project Applications (1967 1980)
Project Methods   Use Student Projects and Teaching Methods
Project Proposals   Use Program Proposals
Project Schools   Use Experimental Schools
Science Course Improvement Project (1967 1980)   Use Science Course Improvement Projects
Project Training Methods (1968 1980)   Use Student Projects and Teaching Methods
Projection Equipment
Orthogonal Projection (1967 1980)   Use Orthographic Projection
Orthographic Projection
Employment Projections
Enrollment Projections
Projective Measures
Projective Tests (1968 1980)   Use Projective Measures
Projectors   Use Projection Equipment
Eight Millimeter Projectors (1970 1980)   Use Projection Equipment
Film Projectors   Use Projection Equipment
Filmstrip Projectors
Opaque Projectors
Overhead Projectors
Overhead Transparency Projectors   Use Overhead Projectors
Sixteen Millimeter Projectors (1966 1980)   Use Projection Equipment
Slide Projectors   Use Projection Equipment
Transparency Projectors   Use Overhead Projectors
Projects (1966 1980)
Agricultural Research Projects (1966 1981)   Use Research Projects
Church Projects   Use Church Programs
Church Migrant Projects (1966 1980)   Use Church Programs and Migrant Programs
Class Projects   Use Class Activities
Community Projects   Use Community Programs
Community Migrant Projects (1966 1980)   Use Community Programs and Migrant Programs
Demonstration Projects (1966 1980)   Use Demonstration Programs
Family Projects (1966 1980)   Use Family Programs
Legal Aid Projects (1966 1980)   Use Legal Aid
Migrant Projects   Use Migrant Programs
Migrant Worker Projects (1966 1980)   Use Migrant Programs and Migrant Workers
Partners in Education Projects   Use Partnerships in Education
Pilot Projects
Research Projects
Science Projects
Science Course Improvement Projects
Student Projects
Proletariat   Use Working Class
Academic Promotion   Use Student Promotion
Faculty Promotion
Health Promotion
Promotion (Occupational)
Sales Promotion   Use Merchandising
Social Promotion
Student Promotion
Teacher Promotion
Prompting
Prompts   Use Cues
Coronary Prone Behavior Pattern   Use Type A Behavior
Pronominals   Use Pronouns
Pronouns
Pronunciation
Pronunciation Instruction
Proof (Mathematics)
Proofreading
Propaganda
Plant Propagation
Properties (Mathematics)
Field Properties (Mathematics)   Use Properties (Mathematics)
Property Accounting
Property Appraisal
Property Control   Use Property Accounting
Property Control Systems   Use Property Accounting
Intellectual Property
Property Inventory   Use Facility Inventory
Property Taxes
Self Fulfilling Prophecies
Prophylacticians   Use Dental Hygienists
Proportion (Mathematics)   Use Ratios (Mathematics)
Proposal Writing
Grant Proposals   Use Grants and Program Proposals
Program Proposals
Project Proposals   Use Program Proposals
Research Proposals
Proprietary Schools

Propulsion Development Technicians   Use Mechanical Design Technicians
Prose
Prosocial Behavior
Prosodic Features (Speech)   Use Suprasegmentals
Prosody (Literary)   Use Poetry
Prospective Teachers   Use Preservice Teachers
Prostheses
Cosmetic Prostheses (1967 1980)   Use Prostheses
Consumer Protection
Equal Protection
Fire Protection
Political Protest   Use Activism
Student Protest   Use Activism
Protestant Ethic   Use Work Ethic
Protestants
Protista   Use Protists
Protists
Protocol Analysis
Protocol Materials
Thinking Aloud Protocols   Use Protocol Analysis
Protoctista   Use Protists
Protozoa
Proverbs
Provincial Aid   Use State Aid
Provincial Government   Use State Government
Provincial Libraries   Use State Libraries
Provincial Regulation   Use State Regulation
Provincial Surveys   Use State Surveys
Safety Provisions   Use Safety
Proxemics   Use Personal Space
Proximity
Psychiatric Aides
Psychiatric Hospitals
Psychiatric Services
Psychiatric Technicians   Use Psychiatric Aides
Psychiatrists
Psychiatry
Psychoacoustics
Psychoanalysis   Use Psychiatry
Psychocatharsis   Use Catharsis
Psychoeducational Clinics
Psychoeducational Methods
Psychoeducational Processes (1966 1980)   Use Psychoeducational Methods
Psycholinguistics
Psychological Abuse   Use Emotional Abuse
Association (Psychological) (1968 1980)   Use Association (Psychology)
Psychological Characteristics
Psychological Conditioning   Use Conditioning
Psychological Design Needs (1968 1980)   Use Design Requirements
Psychological Education   Use Humanistic Education
Psychological Evaluation
Identification (Psychological) (1968 1980)   Use Identification (Psychology)
Information Processes (Psychological)   Use Cognitive Processes
Modeling (Psychological) (1977 1980)   Use Modeling (Psychology)
Psychological Needs
Psychological Patterns
Recall (Psychological) (1967 1980)   Use Recall (Psychology)
Psychological Research   Use Psychological Studies
Psychological Services
Psychological Studies
Psychological Testing
Psychological Tests (1966 1980)   Use Psychological Testing
Psychologists
School Psychologists
Psychology
Abnormal Psychology   Use Psychopathology
Association (Psychology)
Behaviorist Psychology   Use Behaviorism
Child Psychology
Clinical Psychology
Clinical Judgment (Psychology)   Use Psychological Evaluation
Cognitive Psychology
Community Psychology
Compliance (Psychology)
Congruence (Psychology)
Counseling Psychology
Denial (Psychology)
Depression (Psychology)
Developmental Psychology
Differential Psychology   Use Individual Psychology
Educational Psychology
Encoding (Psychology)
Experimental Psychology
Extinction (Psychology)
Identification (Psychology)
Individual Psychology
Industrial Psychology
Industrial and Organizational Psychology   Use Industrial Psychology
Information Storage (Psychology)   Use Encoding (Psychology)
Modeling (Psychology)
Noncompliance (Psychology)   Use Compliance (Psychology)
Occupational Psychology   Use Industrial Psychology
Physiological Psychology   Use Psychophysiology

Recall	(Psychology)
Recoding	(Psychology) Use Encoding (Psychology)
Recognition	(Psychology)
Rejection	(Psychology)
Resistance	(Psychology)
Retention	(Psychology)
School	Psychology
Security	(Psychology)
Social	Psychology
Sport	Psychology
Sports	Psychology Use Sport Psychology
Trust	(Psychology)
Withdrawal	(Psychology)
Withdrawal Tendencies	(Psychology) (1966 1980) Use Withdrawal (Psychology)
Organizational	Psychology (Work Environment) Use Industrial Psychology
	Psychometrics
	Psychometrists (1967 1980) Use Psychometrics
Coordination	(Psychomotor) Use Psychomotor Skills
	Psychomotor Objectives
	Psychomotor Skills
	Psychopathology
	Psychophysiology
	Psychosis
	Psychosomatic Diseases (1968 1980) Use Psychosomatic Disorders
	Psychosomatic Disorders
	Psychotherapy
	Psychotic Children (1966 1980) Use Psychosis
	PTSD Use Posttraumatic Stress Disorder
	Puberty
Online	Public Access Catalogs Use Online Catalogs
	Public Accommodations Use Public Facilities
Certified	Public Accountants
	Public Administration
	Public Administration Education
	Public Affairs Education
	Public Agencies
	Public Colleges
Community Agencies	(Public) (1966 1980) Use Public Agencies
	Public Demonstrations Use Demonstrations (Civil)
	Public Disclosure Use Disclosure
	Public Documents Use Government Publications
	Public Education
	Public Employees Use Government Employees
	Public Facilities
Integrated	Public Facilities (1966 1980) Use Public Facilities and Racial Integration
Segregated	Public Facilities (1966 1980) Use Public Facilities and Racial Segregation
	Public Health
	Public Health Laws (1966 1974) Use Public Health Legislation
	Public Health Legislation
	Public Hearings Use Hearings
	Public Higher Education Use Higher Education and Public Education
	Public History
Hotlines	(Public)
	Public Housing
	Public Housing Residents (1966 1980) Use Public Housing
	Public Image Use Public Opinion
	Public Libraries
	Public Officials
	Public Opinion
	Public Participation Use Citizen Participation
	Public Policy
	Public Relations
	Public School Adult Education
	Public School Systems (1966 1980) Use Public Schools and School Districts
	Public School Teachers
	Public Schools
	Public Sector
	Public Service
	Public Service Occupations
	Public Speaking
	Public Support
	Public Television
	Public Utilities Use Utilities
	Public Welfare Assistance Use Welfare Services
Textbook	Publication
Writing for	Publication
	Publications
Comics	(Publications)
Format	(Publications) Use Layout (Publications)
Government	Publications
Layout	(Publications)
Research Reviews	(Publications) (1966 1980)
School	Publications
Student	Publications
Textbook	Publications (1966 1980)
	Publicity
	Publicize (1968 1980)
	Publish or Perish Issue
Desktop	Publishing
Electronic	Publishing
Faculty	Publishing
	Publishing Houses Use Publishing Industry
	Publishing Industry

Personal	Publishing Use Desktop Publishing
Textbook	Publishing Use Textbook Publication
	Pueblo (People)
	Puerto Rican Culture
	Puerto Ricans
	Pulse Rate Use Heart Rate
	Punch Press Operators Use Machine Tool Operators
	Punch Presses Use Machine Tools
	Punctuation
	Punishment
Capital	Punishment
Corporal	Punishment
	Punjabi
	Puns
	Pupil Personnel Services
	Pupil Personnel Workers
	Pupillary Dilation
	Pupillary Reflex Use Pupillary Dilation
	Pupillary Response Use Pupillary Dilation
	Pupils Use Students
	Puppet Shows Use Puppetry
	Puppetry
	Puppets Use Puppetry
	Purchasing
Equipment	Purchasing Use Purchasing
Water	Purification Use Water Treatment
	Puritan Ethic Use Work Ethic
	Puritans
Educational	Purposes Use Educational Objectives
English for Academic	Purposes
English for Special	Purposes
Grouping (Instructional	Purposes)
Languages for Special	Purposes
	Pushto Use Pashto
	Pushtu Use Pashto
	Putonghua Use Mandarin Chinese
	Puzzles
	Pygmalion Effect Use Self Fulfilling Prophecies
	Pyramid Organization
	Q Analysis Use Q Methodology
	Q Methodology
	Q Sort (1967 1980) Use Q Methodology
	Q Technique Use Q Methodology
	Quadriplegia (1969 1980) Use Neurological Impairments
	Qualifications
Administrator	Qualifications
Counselor	Qualifications
Employment	Qualifications
Supervisor	Qualifications
Teacher	Qualifications
	Qualitative Research
Leadership	Qualities
Educational	Quality Assessment Use Educational Assessment and Educational Quality
	Quality Circles
	Quality Control
	Quality Education Use Educational Quality
Educational	Quality
Life	Quality Use Quality of Life
Total	Quality Management
	Quality of Life
	Quality of Working Life
	Quality Point Ratio Use Grade Point Average
Teacher	Quality Use Teacher Effectiveness
Teaching	Quality (1966 1980) Use Teacher Effectiveness
Water	Quality
	Quantitative Aptitude Use Mathematical Aptitude
	Quantitative Literacy Use Numeracy
	Quantitative Research (Statistics) Use Statistical Analysis
	Quantitative Tests (1980 1985) (Mathematics) Use Mathematics Tests
	Quantum Mechanics
	Quarter System
Living	Quarters Use Housing
	Quasiexperimental Design
	Quechua
	Question Answer Interviews (1966 1980) Use Interviews
	Questioning Techniques
	Questionnaires
Response Rates	(Questionnaires)
Return Rates	(Questionnaires) Use Response Rates (Questionnaires)
	Quiche
	Quizzes Use Tests
	Quotas
Intelligence	Quotient
	R and D Use Research and Development
	R D and E Use Research and Development
	Race
Caucasian	Race (1967 1980) Use Whites
	Race Influences (1966 1980) Use Racial Factors
Mixed	Race Persons Use Multiracial Persons
	Race Relations (1966 1980) Use Racial Relations
	Racial Attitudes
	Racial Balance
	Racial Bias

	Racial Characteristics (1966 1980)
	Racial Composition
	Racial Cultural Groups Use Ethnic Groups
	Racial Differences
	Racial Discrimination
	Racial Distribution
	Racial Factors
	Racial Identification
	Racial Identity Use Racial Identification
	Racial Imbalance Use Racial Balance
	Racial Integration
Integration	(Racial) Use Racial Integration
	Racial Interaction Use Racial Relations
	Racial Prejudice Use Racial Bias
	Racial Recognition (1966 1980) Use Racial Identification
	Racial Relations
	Racial Segregation
Segregation	(Racial) Use Racial Segregation
	Racial Self Identification Use Racial Identification
	Racially Balanced Schools
	Racially Mixed Persons Use Multiracial Persons
	Racism (1966 1980)
	Racket Sports Use Racquet Sports
	Racquet Sports
	Racquetball
	Radar
	Radiation
	Radiation Biology
	Radiation Damage Use Radiation Effects
	Radiation Effects
Solar	Radiation Energy Use Solar Energy
Light	Radiation Use Light
Solar	Radiation (1968 1983) Use Solar Energy
	Radiation Therapy Use Radiology
	Radiation Therapy Technologists Use Radiologic Technologists
Visible	Radiation Use Light
	Radio
Educational	Radio
Instructional	Radio Use Educational Radio
	Radio Journalism Use Broadcast Journalism
	Radio Programming Use Programming (Broadcast)
Television	Radio Repairers
	Radio Technology (1967 1980) Use Radio
	Radio Television Repairers Use Television Radio Repairers
	Radiobiology Use Radiation Biology
	Radiographers
	Radioisotopes
	Radiologic Technologists
	Radiology
	Ragtime Music Use Jazz
Air	Raid Shelters Use Fallout Shelters
	Rail Transportation
	Railroads Use Rail Transportation
	Railways Use Rail Transportation
Acid	Rain
	Rain Forest Preserves Use Rainforests
	Rainforests
Temperate	Rainforests Use Rainforests
Tropical	Rainforests Use Rainforests
	Raised Line Drawings
Salary	Raises Use Promotion (Occupational)
Consciousness	Raising
Fund	Raising
Parking	Ramps Use Parking Facilities
	Range (Distance) Use Distance
Long	Range Planning
Class	Rank
Faculty	Rank Use Academic Rank (Professional)
	Rank in Class Use Class Rank
Academic	Rank (Professional)
Professorial	Rank Use Academic Rank (Professional)
	Rape
Statutory	Rape Use Rape
	Rapid Growth Communities Use Boomtowns
	Rapid Reading (1966 1980) Use Speed Reading
	Rapport
Birth	Rate
Death	Rate Use Mortality Rate
Disease	Rate (1967 1980) Use Disease Incidence
Dropout	Rate
Enrollment	Rate
Fertility	Rate Use Birth Rate
Heart	Rate
Infant Death	Rate Use Infant Mortality and Mortality Rate
Mortality	Rate
Pulse	Rate Use Heart Rate
Reading	Rate
	Rate Tests Use Timed Tests
Transfer	Rates (College)
College Transfer	Rates Use Transfer Rates (College)
Response	Rates (Questionnaires)
Return	Rates (Questionnaires) Use Response Rates (Questionnaires)
Tax	Rates

Achievement	Rating
Merit	Rating
Personality	Rating Use Personality Assessment
Merit	Rating Programs (1967 1980) Use Merit Rating
	Rating Scales
Behavior	Rating Scales
Summated	Rating Scales Use Likert Scales
Teacher	Rating (1966 1977) Use Teacher Evaluation
Client Counselor	Ratio Use Counselor Client Ratio
Counselor Client	Ratio
Fat	Ratio Use Body Composition
Lean Fat	Ratio Use Body Composition
Precision	Ratio Use Relevance (Information Retrieval)
Quality Point	Ratio Use Grade Point Average
Recall	Ratio Use Relevance (Information Retrieval)
Student Teacher	Ratio (1966 1984) Use Teacher Student Ratio
Teacher Student	Ratio
	Rational Emotive Therapy
	Rational Numbers
	Rational Therapy (1968 1980) Use Rational Emotive Therapy
Contrast	Ratios Use Contrast
	Ratios (Mathematics)
	Rats
	Raw Scores
Industrial X	Ray Operators Use Radiographers
X	Ray Technologists Use Radiologic Technologists
Cathode	Ray Tube Terminals Use Video Display Terminals
X	Rays (Medicine) Use Radiology
Counselor	Reaction Use Counselor Attitudes
Parent	Reaction (1966 1980) Use Parent Attitudes
Student	Reaction
Teacher	Reaction Use Teacher Response
Situation	Reaction Tests Use Situational Tests
	Reaction Time
Chemical	Reactions
Motor	Reactions
Photochemical	Reactions
Stranger	Reactions
	Reactive Behavior (1966 1980) Use Responses
	Reactive Inhibition Use Inhibition
Freedom to	Read Use Intellectual Freedom
	Readability
	Readability Formulas
Machine	Readable Cataloging
Machine	Readable Data Files Use Databases
Machine	Readable Text Use Electronic Text
Microform	Reader Printers (1971 1980) Use Microform Readers
	Reader Response
	Reader Text Relationship
Document	Readers Use Optical Scanners
	Readers (Materials) Use Reading Materials
Microform	Readers
Page	Readers Use Optical Scanners
Retarded	Readers (1966 1980) Use Reading Difficulties
	Readers Theater
	Readiness
Desegregation	Readiness Use Integration Readiness
Disaster	Readiness Use Emergency Programs
Handwriting	Readiness (1966 1983) Use Handwriting and Writing Readiness
Integration	Readiness
Learning	Readiness
	Readiness (Mental) (1966 1980) Use Readiness
Reading	Readiness
School	Readiness
Reading	Readiness Tests
School	Readiness Tests
Writing	Readiness
	Reading
	Reading Ability
	Reading Achievement
Directed	Reading Activity
	Reading Aloud to Others
Applied	Reading (1966 1980) Use Reading
Whole Word	Reading Approach Use Sight Method
	Reading Assignments
	Reading Attitudes
Basal	Reading
Basic	Reading (1967 1980)
Beginning	Reading
	Reading Centers
	Reading Clinics (1966 1980) Use Reading Centers
Remedial	Reading Clinics (1966 1980) Use Reading Centers and Remedial Reading
	Reading Comprehension
	Reading Consultants
Content	Reading (1967 1980) Use Content Area Reading
Content Area	Reading
Corrective	Reading
Creative	Reading (1966 1980)
Critical	Reading
Decoding	(Reading)
	Reading Development (1966 1980)
Developmental	Reading (1966 1980)
	Reading Diagnosis

Reading Difficulties
Reading Difficulty (1966 1980)
Reading Disabilities   Use Reading Difficulties
Early   Reading
Elective   Reading (1966 1980)
Reading Enjoyment   Use Literature Appreciation
Factual   Reading (1966 1980)
Reading Failure
Functional   Reading
Reading Gain   Use Reading Improvement
Reading Games
Group   Reading (1966 1980)
Reading Habits
Reading Improvement
Reading in Content Areas   Use Content Area Reading
Independent   Reading
Individual   Reading (1966 1980)
Individualized   Reading
Reading Instruction
Reading Interests
Interpretive   Reading (1966 1980)
Informal   Reading Inventories
Informal   Reading Inventory (1968 1980)   Use Informal Reading Inventories
Reading Laboratories   Use Reading Centers
Leisure Time   Reading   Use Recreational Reading
Reading Level (1966 1980)
Reading Material Selection
Reading Materials
Supplementary   Reading Materials
Reading Motivation
Music   Reading
Oral   Reading
Reading Problems   Use Reading Difficulties
Reading Processes
Reading Programs
Adult   Reading Programs
Remedial   Reading Programs (1966 1980)   Use Remedial Programs and Remedial Reading
Sequential   Reading Programs (1966 1980)   Use Sequential Approach
Rapid   Reading (1966 1980)   Use Speed Reading
Reading Rate
Reading Readiness
Reading Readiness Tests
Recreational   Reading
Remedial   Reading
Reading Research
Score   Reading   Use Music Reading
Silent   Reading
Reading Skills
Map   Reading Skills   Use Map Skills
Survival   Reading Skills   Use Functional Reading
Skimming   (Reading)   Use Speed Reading
Reading Specialists   Use Reading Consultants
Speech   Reading   Use Lipreading
Reading Speed (1966 1977)   Use Reading Rate
Speed   Reading
Story   Reading
Reading Strategies
Sustained Silent   Reading
Reading Teachers
Reading Tests
Reading Therapy   Use Bibliotherapy
Word Associations   (Reading)   Use Associative Learning
Word Method   (Reading)   Use Sight Method
Reading Writing Relationship
Collected   Readings   Use Anthologies
Readings (Collections)   Use Anthologies
Real Estate
Real Estate Appraisal   Use Property Appraisal
Real Estate Occupations
Realia
Realism
Reality Therapy
Virtual   Reality
Self   Realization   Use Self Actualization
Child   Rearing
Abstract   Reasoning
Reasoning Skills   Use Thinking Skills
Recall (Psychological) (1967 1980)   Use Recall (Psychology)
Recall (Psychology)
Recall Ratio   Use Relevance (Information Retrieval)
Broadcast   Reception Equipment
Receptionists
Receptive Communication   Use Receptive Language
Receptive Language
Recess Breaks
Recidivism
Recipes (Food)
Welfare   Recipients
Reciprocal Teaching
Reciprocals (Mathematics)
Recoding (Psychology)   Use Encoding (Psychology)
Recognition (1967 1980)
Recognition (Achievement)

```
                  Character  Recognition
     Magnetic Ink Character  Recognition    Use Character Recognition
         Optical Character  Recognition    Use Character Recognition and Optical Scanners
                   Pattern  Recognition
              Professional  Recognition
                            Recognition (Psychology)
                    Racial  Recognition (1966 1980)    Use Racial Identification
                     Word  Recognition
                            Recombinant DNA    Use DNA and Genetic Engineering
                            Reconstruction Era
                    Social  Reconstruction    Use Social Change
                  Hospital  Record Administrators    Use Medical Record Administrators
                   Medical  Record Administrators
                            Record Clerks    Use File Clerks
                   Medical  Record Clerks    Use Medical Record Technicians
                  Pass No  Record Grading    Use Credit No Credit Grading
                   Medical  Record Librarians (1969 1980)    Use Medical Record Administrators
               Phonograph  Record Lists    Use Discographies
                  Hospital  Record Technicians    Use Medical Record Technicians
                   Medical  Record Technicians
                 Audiotape  Recorders
         Audiotape Cassette  Recorders    Use Audiotape Cassettes and Audiotape Recorders
      Magnetic Tape Cassette  Recorders (1970 1980)    Use Magnetic Tape Cassettes and Tape Recorders
                      Tape  Recorders
                 Videotape  Recorders
         Videotape Cassette  Recorders    Use Videotape Cassettes and Videotape Recorders
                 Audiodisc  Recordings (1980 1986)    Use Audiodisks
                 Audiotape  Recordings
                       CD  Recordings    Use Optical Disks
                 Kinescope  Recordings
                Phonotape  Recordings (1966 1978)    Use Audiotape Recordings
               Sound Tape  Recordings    Use Audiotape Recordings
                      Tape  Recordings
                Video Tape  Recordings (1966 1978)    Use Videotape Recordings
                 Videodisc  Recordings (1979 1986)    Use Videodisks
                 Videotape  Recordings
                            Recordkeeping
                  Academic  Records
                 Attendance  Records
               Bibliographic  Records
                     Case  Records
               Confidential  Records
                            Records (Forms)
                            Records Management
                   Payroll  Records
               Phonograph  Records (1966 1980)    Use Audiodisks
                 Language  Records (Phonograph) (1966 1980)    Use Audiodisks
                   Student  Records
                     Heat  Recovery
                            Recreation
                            Recreation Finances
                            Recreation Legislation
                Community  Recreation Legislation (1966 1978)    Use Local Legislation and Recreation Legislation
                   Federal  Recreation Legislation (1966 1978)    Use Federal Legislation and Recreation Legislation
                     Local  Recreation Legislation (1966 1978)    Use Local Legislation and Recreation Legislation
                     State  Recreation Legislation (1966 1978)    Use Recreation Legislation and State Legislation
                Community  Recreation Programs
                  Physical  Recreation Programs
                    Social  Recreation Programs (1966 1980)    Use Recreational Programs
               Therapeutic  Recreation
                            Recreation Therapy    Use Therapeutic Recreation
                            Recreational Activities
                            Recreational Facilities
                            Recreational Programs
                    School  Recreational Programs
                            Recreational Reading
                            Recreationists
                            Recruitment
                   Faculty  Recruitment
                 Personnel  Recruitment    Use Recruitment
                   Student  Recruitment
                   Teacher  Recruitment
                            Recurrent Education    Use Lifelong Learning
                            Recycling
                       Job  Redesign    Use Job Development
                            Redevelopment Areas    Use Urban Renewal
                    School  Redistricting (1966 1980)    Use School District Reorganization
                            Reduction in Force
                     Need  Reduction    Use Need Gratification
                            Redundancy
                            Reentry Students
                            Reentry Workers
                Curriculum  Reevaluation    Use Curriculum Evaluation
                    Review  (Reexamination)
                            Reference Books (1966 1980)    Use Reference Materials
                            Reference Groups
                            Reference Librarians    Use Librarians and Reference Services
                Legislative  Reference Libraries (1968 1980)    Use Law Libraries
                            Reference Materials
                    Library  Reference Materials    Use Library Materials and Reference Materials
                            Reference Services
            Computer Based  Reference Services    Use Online Systems and Reference Services
                    Library  Reference Services (1968 1980)    Use Library Services and Reference Services
```

Online Reference Services   Use Online Systems and Reference Services
Curriculum Referenced Assessment   Use Curriculum Based Assessment
Criterion Referenced Education   Use Competency Based Education
Norm Referenced Measures   Use Norm Referenced Tests
Criterion Referenced Teacher Education   Use Competency Based Teacher Education
Criterion Referenced Tests
Norm Referenced Tests
Objective Referenced Tests   Use Criterion Referenced Tests
Bibliographic References   Use Citations (References)
Citations (References)
Referral
Referral Services (Community)   Use Community Information Services and Referral
Employment Referral Services   Use Employment Services
Information and Referral Services   Use Information Services and Referral
Reflective Teaching
Reflectivity   Use Conceptual Tempo
Iris Reflex   Use Pupillary Dilation
Pupillary Reflex   Use Pupillary Dilation
Chain Reflexes (Behavior)   Use Behavior Chaining
Curriculum Reform   Use Curriculum Development
Educational Reform   Use Educational Change
Finance Reform
Political Reform   Use Social Action
Social Reform   Use Social Action
Tax Reform   Use Finance Reform
Error of Refraction   Use Ametropia
Refractive Errors   Use Ametropia
Ocular Refractive Errors   Use Ametropia
Refresher Courses
Refresher Training   Use Retraining
Refrigeration
Refrigeration Mechanics
Refugees
Political Refugees   Use Refugees
Refuse   Use Wastes
Regents   Use Trustees
Board of Regents   Use Governing Boards
Reggio Emilia Approach
Reggio Emilia Preschools   Use Preschool Education and Reggio Emilia Approach
Regional Attitudes
Regional Characteristics
Regional Cooperation
Regional Dialects
Regional Differences   Use Differences and Regional Characteristics
Regional Laboratories
Regional Libraries
Regional Planning
Regional Programs
Regional Schools
Geographic Regions
Registered Nurses   Use Nurses
College Registrars   Use Registrars (School)
Registrars (School)
College Registration   Use School Registration
Registration in School   Use School Registration
Late Registration
School Registration
Voter Registration
Multiple Regression Analysis
Regression Effects   Use Regression (Statistics)
Linear Regression   Use Regression (Statistics)
Regression (Statistics)
Eye Regressions (1966 1980)   Use Eye Movements
Regressors   Use Predictor Variables
Regular and Special Education Relationship
Regular Class Placement (1968 1978)   Use Mainstreaming
Special Education Regular Education Cooperation   Use Regular and Special Education Relationship
Special Regular Education Interface   Use Regular and Special Education Relationship
Special and Regular Education Relationship   Use Regular and Special Education Relationship
Federal Regulation
Provincial Regulation   Use State Regulation
State Regulation
Parking Regulations   Use Parking Controls
Traffic Regulations (1968 1980)   Use Traffic Control
Rehabilitation
Rehabilitation Centers
Correctional Rehabilitation
Rehabilitation Counseling
Delinquent Rehabilitation
Dropout Rehabilitation (1966 1980)   Use Dropout Programs
Drug Rehabilitation
Hearing Rehabilitation   Use Hearing Therapy
Rehabilitation Programs
Student Rehabilitation (1966 1980)   Use Rehabilitation
Vocational Rehabilitation
Rehearsals (Theater Arts)
Oral Rehydration Therapy
Reinforcement
Learning Reinforcement   Use Reinforcement
Massed Negative Reinforcement   Use Negative Reinforcement
Negative Reinforcement
Positive Reinforcement
Social Reinforcement

Spaced Negative	Reinforcement Use Negative Reinforcement
	Reinforcement Theory Use Reinforcement
	Reinforcers (1966 1980) Use Reinforcement
	Rejection (1966 1980) Use Rejection (Psychology)
	Rejection (Psychology)
School	Related Activities Use Extracurricular Activities
Church	Related Colleges
Law	Related Education
Health	Related Fitness
Course	Related Library Instruction Use Course Integrated Library Instruction
Job	Related Literacy Use Workplace Literacy
Farm	Related Occupations Use Off Farm Agricultural Occupations
Health	Related Professions Use Allied Health Occupations
Black White	Relations Use Racial Relations
Civic	Relations Use Community Relations
Community	Relations
Employee	Relations Use Labor Relations
Ethnic	Relations
Foreign	Relations (1966 1976) Use International Relations
Group	Relations (1966 1980) Use Group Dynamics
Human	Relations
Industrial	Relations (1969 1980) Use Labor Relations
Interfaith	Relations
Intergroup	Relations
International	Relations
Interracial	Relations Use Racial Relations
Labor	Relations
Human	Relations Organizations (1966 1980) Use Human Relations Programs
Human	Relations Programs
Public	Relations
Race	Relations (1966 1980) Use Racial Relations
Racial	Relations
Social	Relations (1966 1980)
Human	Relations Training Use Sensitivity Training
Human	Relations Units (1966 1980) Use Human Relations and Units of Study
White Black	Relations Use Racial Relations
	Relationship
Administrator Teacher	Relationship Use Teacher Administrator Relationship
Board Administrator	Relationship
Business School	Relationship Use School Business Relationship
Caregiver Child	Relationship
Child Parent	Relationship Use Parent Child Relationship
Client Counselor	Relationship Use Counselor Client Relationship
College Community	Relationship Use School Community Relationship
College Student	Relationship Use Student College Relationship
Community Police	Relationship Use Police Community Relationship
Community School	Relationship Use School Community Relationship
Counselor Client	Relationship
Doctor Patient	Relationship Use Physician Patient Relationship
Education Work	Relationship
Employee Employer	Relationship Use Employer Employee Relationship
Employer Employee	Relationship
Spatial	Relationship (Facilities)
Faculty College	Relationship
Family	Relationship
Family Job	Relationship Use Family Work Relationship
Family School	Relationship
Family Work	Relationship
Federal Indian	Relationship
Federal State	Relationship
General and Special Education	Relationship Use Regular and Special Education Relationship
Government School	Relationship
Helping	Relationship
Home School	Relationship Use Family School Relationship
Industry School	Relationship Use School Business Relationship
Interpersonal	Relationship
Interprofessional	Relationship
Job Family	Relationship Use Family Work Relationship
Parent Child	Relationship
Parent School	Relationship
Parent Student	Relationship
Patient Physician	Relationship Use Physician Patient Relationship
Peer	Relationship
Personal	Relationship (1966 1974) Use Interpersonal Relationship
Physician Patient	Relationship
Police Community	Relationship
Police School	Relationship
Reader Text	Relationship
Reading Writing	Relationship
Regular and Special Education	Relationship
Research Practice	Relationship Use Research and Development and Theory Practice Relationship
School Business	Relationship
School Community	Relationship
School Family	Relationship Use Family School Relationship
School Government	Relationship Use Government School Relationship
School Home	Relationship Use Family School Relationship
School Industry	Relationship (1967 1980) Use School Business Relationship
School Parent	Relationship Use Parent School Relationship
School Police	Relationship Use Police School Relationship
School Student	Relationship Use Student School Relationship
Sibling	Relationship
Spatial	Relationship (1966 1980)
Special and Regular Education	Relationship Use Regular and Special Education Relationship

```
          State Federal  Relationship   Use Federal State Relationship
   State School District  Relationship
        Student College  Relationship
         Student Parent  Relationship   Use Parent Student Relationship
         Student School  Relationship
        Student Teacher  Relationship (1966 1984)   Use Teacher Student Relationship
 Teacher Administrator  Relationship
        Teacher College  Relationship   Use Faculty College Relationship
        Teacher Student  Relationship
        Theory Practice  Relationship
       Work Education  Relationship   Use Education Work Relationship
           Work Family  Relationship   Use Family Work Relationship
                         Relative Humidity   Use Humidity
                         Relativity
         Progressive  Relaxation (1967 1980)   Use Relaxation Training
                         Relaxation Training
          Microwave  Relay Systems (1971 1980)   Use Telecommunications
                 Day  Release   Use Released Time
              Study  Release Programs   Use Released Time
               Work  Release   Use Released Time
                         Released Time
                         Relevance (Cultural)   Use Cultural Relevance
            Cultural  Relevance
          Curriculum  Relevance   Use Relevance (Education)
                         Relevance (Education)
         Educational  Relevance   Use Relevance (Education)
                         Relevance (Information Retrieval)
          Culturally  Relevant Education
                         Reliability
        Interobserver  Reliability   Use Interrater Reliability
           Interrater  Reliability
          Interscorer  Reliability   Use Interrater Reliability
                Test  Reliability
                         Relief (Art)
                         Relief Teachers   Use Substitute Teachers
                         Religion
         Comparative  Religion   Use Religion Studies
                         Religion Studies
                         Religious Agencies (1966 1980)   Use Religious Organizations
                         Religious Conflict
                         Religious Cultural Groups
                         Religious Differences
                         Religious Discrimination
                         Religious Education
                         Religious Factors
                         Religious Groups   Use Religious Cultural Groups
                         Religious Holidays
                         Religious Organizations
                         Religious Studies   Use Religion Studies
                         Relocatable Facilities
                         Relocation
                         Remarriage
                         Remedial Arithmetic (1966 1980)   Use Arithmetic and Remedial Mathematics
                         Remedial Courses (1966 1980)   Use Remedial Instruction
                         Remedial Education   Use Remedial Instruction
                         Remedial Education Programs   Use Remedial Programs
                         Remedial Instruction
                         Remedial Mathematics
                         Remedial Programs
                         Remedial Reading
                         Remedial Reading Clinics (1966 1980)   Use Reading Centers and Remedial Reading
                         Remedial Reading Programs (1966 1980)   Use Remedial Programs and Remedial Reading
                         Remedial Teachers
                         Remediation   Use Remedial Instruction
                         Remembering   Use Memory
                         Reminiscence
                         Remuneration   Use Compensation (Remuneration)
       Compensation  (Remuneration)
                         Renaissance Literature
               Urban  Renewal Agencies
               Urban  Renewal
                         Renovation   Use Improvement
            Building  Renovation   Use Facility Improvement
             School  Renovation   Use Educational Facilities Improvement
                Low  Rent Housing
         Curriculum  Reorganization   Use Curriculum Development
             School  Reorganization   Use School Organization
     School District  Reorganization
                         Repair
          Appliance  Repair
          Equipment  Repair   Use Equipment Maintenance
      Home Appliance  Repair   Use Appliance Repair
          Appliance  Repairers (1980 1981)   Use Appliance Repair
          Auto Body  Repairers
     Body and Fender  Repairers   Use Auto Body Repairers
            Machine  Repairers
    Radio Television  Repairers   Use Television Radio Repairers
    Television Radio  Repairers
              Watch  Repairers   Use Watchmakers
          Appliance  Repairing (1968 1981)   Use Appliance Repair
          Auto Body  Repairmen (1966 1980)   Use Auto Body Repairers
            Machine  Repairmen (1968 1980)   Use Machine Repairers
         Television  Repairmen (1968 1980)   Use Television Radio Repairers
```

Loan	Repayment
	Repertory Catalogs Use Union Catalogs
	Repertory Orchestras Use Orchestras
Grade	Repetition
	Repetitive Film Showings
	Report Cards
	Report Writing Use Technical Writing
Court	Reporters
News	Reporting
Sports	Reporting Use Athletics and News Reporting
	Reports
Annual	Reports
Conference	Reports (1967 1980)
Research	Reports
Scientific	Reports Use Research Reports
Technical	Reports (1968 1980) Use Research Reports
Knowledge	Representation
	Representatives Use Legislators
	Reproduction (Biology)
	Reproduction (Copying) Use Reprography
Copying	(Reproduction) Use Reprography
	Reprography
	Reputation
	Required Courses
Foundation Courses	(Required) Use Required Courses
Degree	Requirements
Design	Requirements
Diploma	Requirements Use Graduation Requirements
Facility	Requirements
Graduation	Requirements
Residence	Requirements
	Rescue
	Rescue Squad Personnel Use Emergency Squad Personnel
	Research
Action	Research
	Research Administration
	Research and Development
	Research and Development Centers
	Research and Instruction Units
Applied	Research Use Research
	Research Apprenticeships (1967 1981) Use Research Assistants
	Research Approaches Use Research Methodology
Architectural	Research
	Research Assistants
Basic	Research Use Research
Behavioral Science	Research
Biomedical	Research Use Biomedicine
Brain	Research Use Brain
Classroom	Research
	Research Committees
Communication	Research
	Research Coordinating Units
Creativity	Research
	Research Criteria (1967 1980)
Curriculum	Research
Deaf	Research (1968 1980) Use Deafness
	Research Design
	Research Directors
Directors of	Research Use Research Directors
Dropout	Research
Economic	Research
Educational	Research
Effective Schools	Research
Environmental	Research
Evaluation	Research
Evaluative	Research Use Evaluation Research
Exceptional Child	Research
Facility Utilization	Research
Institutional	Research
Interest	Research
Journalism	Research
Language	Research
	Research Libraries
Library	Research
	Research Limitations Use Research Problems
Linguistic	Research Use Language Research
Lunar	Research
	Research Management Use Research Administration
Material	Research Use Material Development
Media	Research
Medical	Research
	Research Methodology
Methods	Research
	Research Needs
Nursing	Research
Operations	Research
	Research Opportunities
Outer Space	Research Use Space Exploration
	Research Papers (Students)
Participatory	Research
Participatory Action	Research Use Action Research and Participatory Research
	Research Planning Use Research Design
Population	Research Use Demography

Poverty	Research (1970 1980) Use Poverty
	Research Practice Relationship Use Research and Development and Theory Practice Relationship
	Research Problems
	Research Programs Use Research Projects
	Research Projects
Agricultural	Research Projects (1966 1981) Use Research Projects
	Research Proposals
Psychological	Research Use Psychological Studies
Qualitative	Research
Reading	Research
	Research Reports
	Research Reviews (Publications) (1966 1980)
Scientific	Research
	Research Skills
Social Science	Research
	Research Specialists (Education) Use Educational Researchers
Speech Communication	Research Use Communication Research and Speech Communication
Quantitative	Research (Statistics) Use Statistical Analysis
Student	Research
	Research Studies Use Research Reports
Attrition	(Research Studies)
Mortality	(Research Studies) Use Attrition (Research Studies)
Television	Research
Textbook	Research
	Research Tools
	Research Universities
	Research Utilization
Writing	Research
	Researcher Characteristics Use Experimenter Characteristics and Researchers
	Researchers
Educational	Researchers
Teacher	Researchers
Teachers as	Researchers Use Teacher Researchers
	Resegregated Schools Use School Resegregation
School	Resegregation
	Resentment
	Reservation American Indians
Off	Reservation American Indians Use Nonreservation American Indians
American Indian	Reservations
	Reservations (Indian) (1971 1980) Use American Indian Reservations
	Resettlement Use Land Settlement
Rural	Resettlement
	Residence Factors Use Residence Requirements
	Residence Halls Use Dormitories
Place of	Residence
	Residence Requirements
	Residency Programs (Medical) Use Graduate Medical Education
	Resident Advisers
	Resident Assistants
	Resident Camp Programs
	Resident Students (1967 1980) (in District) Use Residence Requirements
	Resident Students (1967 1980) (in State) Use In State Students
	Resident Supervisors Use Resident Advisers
	Residential Care
	Residential Centers (1967 1980) Use Residential Institutions
	Residential Colleges
	Residential Desegregation Use Neighborhood Integration
	Residential Institutions
	Residential Location Use Place of Residence
	Residential Patterns
	Residential Programs
	Residential Schools
	Residents (Medical) Use Graduate Medical Students
Public Housing	Residents (1966 1980) Use Public Housing
Rural Farm	Residents
Rural Nonfarm	Residents
	Resilience (Personality)
	Resilient Floor Covering Use Flooring
	Resistance (Psychology)
	Resistance to Change
	Resistance to Temptation
Conflict	Resolution
Impasse	Resolution Use Negotiation Impasses
	Resource Allocation
	Resource Allocations (1966 1980) Use Resource Allocation
	Resource Centers
	Resource Guides (1966 1980) Use Resource Materials
	Resource Materials
	Resource Room Programs
	Resource Sharing Use Shared Resources and Services
	Resource Staff
	Resource Staff Role (1966 1980) Use Resource Staff
	Resource Teachers
	Resource Units
	Resources
Allocation of	Resources Use Resource Allocation
Shared	Resources and Services
Learning	Resources Centers
Coal	Resources Use Coal
Community	Resources
Curriculum	Resources Use Educational Resources
Depleted	Resources
Human	Resources Development (Labor) Use Labor Force Development

Educational	Resources
Family	Resources (1966 1980) Use Family Financial Resources
Family Financial	Resources
Human	Resources
Learning	Resources Use Educational Resources
Information	Resources Management Use Information Management
Mental Health	Resources Use Mental Health Programs
Natural	Resources
Shared Library	Resources
Teaching	Resources Use Educational Resources
Water	Resources
	Respiratory Therapy
	Respite Care
Audience	Response
	Response Bias (Tests) Use Response Style (Tests)
Conditioned	Response (1967 1980) Use Responses
Constructed	Response
	Response Contingent Testing Use Adaptive Testing
Covert	Response
Emotional	Response
	Response Latency Use Reaction Time
	Response Mode (1967 1980) Use Responses
Overt	Response
Pupillary	Response Use Pupillary Dilation
	Response Rates (Questionnaires)
Reader	Response
	Response Set (Tests) Use Response Style (Tests)
	Response Style (Tests)
Teacher	Response
Situation	Response Tests Use Situational Tests
Item	Response Theory
	Response Time Use Reaction Time
	Responses
Patterned	Responses
Student	Responses Use Student Reaction
	Responsibility
Administrator	Responsibility
Business	Responsibility
Child	Responsibility
Church	Responsibility
Citizen	Responsibility Use Citizenship Responsibility
Citizenship	Responsibility
Civic	Responsibility Use Citizenship Responsibility
Community	Responsibility
Educational	Responsibility
Employee	Responsibility
Trust	Responsibility (Government)
Leadership	Responsibility
Legal	Responsibility
Liability	(Responsibility) Use Legal Responsibility
Noninstructional	Responsibility
Parent	Responsibility
School	Responsibility
Social	Responsibility
Student	Responsibility
Teacher	Responsibility
Culturally	Responsive Education Use Culturally Relevant Education
	Rest Home Aides Use Nurses Aides
	Rest Homes Use Personal Care Homes
	Restaurants Use Dining Facilities
Self	Restraint Use Self Control
	Restraints (Vehicle Safety)
Child	Restraints (Vehicle Safety) Use Child Safety and Restraints (Vehicle Safety)
Social	Restrictions Use Social Mobility
	Restrictive Admission Use Selective Admission
Least	Restrictive Environment (Disabled) Use Mainstreaming
	Restrictive Transfer Programs (1966 1980) Use Transfer Programs
	Restrooms Use Toilet Facilities
Cognitive	Restructuring
Job	Restructuring Use Job Development
	Restructuring of Schools (United States) Use School Restructuring
School	Restructuring
	Results Based Education Use Outcome Based Education
Knowledge of	Results Use Feedback
	Results of Education Use Outcomes of Education
Test	Results
	Resumes (Personal)
Cardiopulmonary	Resuscitation
	Retail Training Use Distributive Education
	Retailing
	Retardation (1966 1980) Use Mental Retardation
Borderline Mental	Retardation Use Slow Learners
Educational	Retardation (1966 1980)
Progressive	Retardation (1966 1980) (in School) Use Educationally Disadvantaged
Mental	Retardation
Mild Mental	Retardation
Moderate Mental	Retardation
Severe Mental	Retardation
	Retarded Children (1966 1980) Use Mental Retardation
Profoundly Mentally	Retarded Use Severe Mental Retardation
	Retarded Readers (1966 1980) Use Reading Difficulties
	Retarded Speech Development (1968 1980) Use Delayed Speech
	Retention (1966 1980) Use Retention (Psychology)

Retention (in Grade)   Use Grade Repetition
Retention (in School)   Use School Holding Power
Retention (of Employees)   Use Labor Turnover
Retention (Psychology)
Retention Studies (1966 1980)   Use Retention (Psychology)
Retired Teachers   Use Teacher Retirement
Retirement
Retirement Benefits
Compulsory   Retirement   Use Mandatory Retirement
Early   Retirement
Mandatory   Retirement
Teacher   Retirement
Retraining
Vocational   Retraining (1966 1980)   Use Retraining
Retrenchment
Information   Retrieval
Online Information   Retrieval   Use Online Searching
Relevance (Information   Retrieval)
Retroactive Inhibition   Use Inhibition
Retrospective Conversion (Library Catalogs)
Return Rates (Questionnaires)   Use Response Rates (Questionnaires)
Reunions
Revenue   Use Income
Revenue Sharing
Reversal Shift   Use Shift Studies
Half   Reversal Shift   Use Shift Studies
Reverse Discrimination
Internal   Review (Organizations)   Use Self Evaluation (Groups)
Peer   Review   Use Peer Evaluation
Review (Reexamination)
Book   Reviews
Computer Software   Reviews
Software   Reviews (Computers)   Use Computer Software Reviews
Courseware   Reviews   Use Computer Software Reviews and Courseware
Historical   Reviews (1966 1980)   Use History
Literature   Reviews
Reviews of the Literature   Use Literature Reviews
Research   Reviews (Publications) (1966 1980)
State of the Art   Reviews
Test   Reviews
Revision (Written Composition)
Curriculum   Revisions   Use Curriculum Development
Cultural   Revitalization   Use Cultural Maintenance
Revolution
American   Revolutionary War   Use Revolutionary War (United States)
Revolutionary War (United States)
Self   Reward
Rewards
Rewriting   Use Revision (Written Composition)
Rezoning
Rezoning Districts   Use Rezoning
Rh Factors
Rhetoric
Rhetorical Community   Use Discourse Communities
Rhetorical Criticism
Rhetorical Invention
Rhetorical Theory
Rhyme
Mother Goose   Rhymes   Use Nursery Rhymes
Nursery   Rhymes
Rhythm (Language)   Use Language Rhythm
Language   Rhythm
Rhythm (Music)
Blue   Ribbon Commissions
Ribonucleic Acid   Use RNA
Puerto   Rican Culture
Puerto   Ricans
Horseback   Riding
Riff
Left   Right Preference   Use Lateral Dominance
Right to Know   Use Freedom of Information
Childrens   Rights
Civil   Rights
Human   Rights   Use Civil Liberties
Individual   Rights   Use Civil Liberties
Civil   Rights Legislation
Minority   Rights   Use Civil Rights
Parent   Rights
States   Rights   Use States Powers
Student   Rights
Teacher   Rights
Voting   Rights
Womens   Rights   Use Feminism
Mental   Rigidity
Rime (Sound)   Use Rhyme
Risk
Risk Management
At   Risk Persons
High   Risk Persons (1982 1990)   Use At Risk Persons
Risk Populations   Use At Risk Persons
High   Risk Students
River Pollution   Use Water Pollution
Rivers

	RNA
	Road Construction
	Road Signs Use Signs
	Robotics
Industrial	Robotics Use Robotics
	Robots Use Robotics
	Robustness (Statistics)
	Rock Music
	Rock Studies Use Petrology
	Rodenticides (1968 1980) Use Pesticides
	Role
Administrator	Role
Agency	Role
Assistant Superintendent	Role (1966 1980)
Black	Role (1977 1980) Use Black Influences
Board of Education	Role
Caregiver	Role
Child	Role
Church	Role
Citizen	Role
College	Role
Community	Role
	Role Conflict
Congress	Role Use Government Role
Counselor	Role
Court	Role
Delinquent	Role (1966 1980) Use Delinquency
Dropout	Role (1966 1980) Use Dropouts
Education	Role Use Role of Education
Elementary School	Role (1966 1980) Use School Role
Family	Role
Father	Role Use Fathers and Parent Role
Female	Role Use Females and Sex Role
Government	Role
High School	Role (1966 1980) Use School Role
Institutional	Role
Judicial	Role Use Court Role
Junior High School	Role (1966 1980) Use School Role
Kinship	Role Use Kinship
Language	Role
Library	Role
Male	Role Use Males and Sex Role
Mass Media	Role
Media	Role (Mass Media) Use Mass Media Role
Minority	Role (1966 1980) Use Minority Group Influences
	Role Models
Mother	Role Use Mothers and Parent Role
Negro	Role (1966 1977) Use Black Influences
	Role of Education
Parent	Role
	Role Perception
Personnel	Role Use Staff Role
	Role Playing
Press	Role Use Mass Media Role and News Media
Resource Staff	Role (1966 1980) Use Resource Staff
School	Role
School Board	Role Use Board of Education Role
Senior Teacher	Role (1966 1980) Use Master Teachers and Teacher Role
Sex	Role
Gender	Role (Sex) Use Sex Role
Social	Role Use Role
Staff	Role
Student	Role
Superintendent	Role (1966 1980) Use Superintendents
	Role Taking Use Perspective Taking
Teacher	Role
Television	Role Use Mass Media Role and Television
	Role Theory
	Roller Skating
CD	ROM Use Optical Data Disks
	Roman Literature Use Latin Literature
Non	Roman Scripts
	Romance Languages
Medieval	Romance (1969 1980) Use Medieval Literature
	Romanian
	Romanization
	Romanticism
	Roof Installation Use Roofing
	Roofers (1968 1981) Use Roofing and Skilled Workers
	Roofing
	Roofs Use Roofing
	Room Dividers Use Space Dividers
Resource	Room Programs
One	Room Schools Use One Teacher Schools
Operating	Room Technicians Use Surgical Technicians
Community	Rooms (1967 1980) Use Community Centers
Crafts	Rooms (1966 1980) Use Educational Facilities and Handicrafts
Locker	Rooms
Shop	Rooms Use School Shops
Windowless	Rooms
Epidemic	Roseola Use Rubella
Oblique	Rotation
Orthogonal	Rotation

Rotation Plans
Rote Learning
Roumanian   Use Romanian
Year   Round Schools
Rubella
Assessment   Rubrics   Use Scoring Rubrics
Scoring   Rubrics
Rubrics (Scoring Guides)   Use Scoring Rubrics
Rumanian (1980 1994)   Use Romanian
Runaways
Adult   Runaways   Use Runaways
Juvenile   Runaways   Use Runaways
Rundi   Use Kirundi
Running
Rural American Indians
Rural Areas
Rural Clinics (1966 1980)   Use Clinics and Rural Areas
Rural Development
Urban   Rural Differences   Use Rural Urban Differences
Rural Dropouts (1966 1981)   Use Dropouts
Rural Economics
Rural Education
Rural Environment
Rural Extension
Rural Family
Rural Farm Residents
Rural Inhabitants   Use Rural Population
Urban to   Rural Migration
Rural Nonfarm Residents
Rural Population
Rural Resettlement
Rural School Systems (1966 1980)   Use Rural Schools and School Districts
Rural Schools
Rural Sociology
Rural to Urban Migration
Rural Urban Differences
Rural Women
Rural Youth
Russian
Russian Literature
Sabbatical Leaves
Sadness
Safety
Agricultural   Safety
Occupational   Safety and Health
Occupational   Safety and Health Standards   Use Labor Standards and Occupational Safety and Health
Child   Safety
Child Restraints (Vehicle   Safety)   Use Child Safety and Restraints (Vehicle Safety)
Safety Education
Safety Equipment
Safety Glasses   Use Safety Equipment
Job   Safety   Use Occupational Safety and Health
Laboratory   Safety
Safety Provisions   Use Safety
Restraints (Vehicle   Safety)
School   Safety
Traffic   Safety
Sailing
Salaries
Contract   Salaries
Teacher   Salaries
Salary Differentials (1968 1980)   Use Salary Wage Differentials
Wage   Salary Differentials   Use Salary Wage Differentials
Salary Raises   Use Promotion (Occupational)
Salary Wage Differentials
Sales Clerks   Use Sales Workers
Sales Occupations
Sales Promotion   Use Merchandising
Sales Workers
Salesmanship
Salish
Salt Marshes   Use Wetlands
Samoan
Samoan Americans
American   Samoans   Use Samoan Americans
Samoyed Languages
Sample Size
Job   Sample Tests   Use Work Sample Tests
Work   Sample Tests
Job   Samples   Use Work Sample Tests
Work   Samples   Use Work Sample Tests
Sampling
Item   Sampling
Matrix   Sampling   Use Item Sampling
Multiple Matrix   Sampling   Use Item Sampling
Sanatoriums   Use Hospitals
Sanctions
Sango
Sanitary Facilities
Sanitary Inspectors   Use Environmental Technicians
Sanitary Technicians   Use Environmental Technicians
Sanitation
Sanitation Improvement (1966 1980)   Use Sanitation

	Sanskrit
	Sara
	Sarcasm Use Irony
	Sarcoma Use Cancer
	Satellite Facilities
	Satellite Laboratories (1966 1980) Use Satellites (Aerospace)
	Satellite Libraries Use Branch Libraries
Interactive	Satellite Television Use Interactive Television
	Satellites (Aerospace)
Artificial	Satellites Use Satellites (Aerospace)
Communication	Satellites (1967 1980) Use Communications Satellites
Communications	Satellites
Orbiting	Satellites Use Satellites (Aerospace)
	Satire
	Satisfaction
Community	Satisfaction
Employment	Satisfaction Use Job Satisfaction
Information User	Satisfaction Use User Satisfaction (Information)
User	Satisfaction (Information)
Job	Satisfaction
Library User	Satisfaction Use User Satisfaction (Information)
Life	Satisfaction
Marital	Satisfaction
Occupational	Satisfaction Use Job Satisfaction
Participant	Satisfaction
Vocational	Satisfaction Use Job Satisfaction
Work	Satisfaction Use Job Satisfaction
Anglo	Saxon Use Old English
Look	Say Method Use Sight Method
Large	Scale Production Use Mass Production
	Scales Use Measures (Individuals)
Behavior Rating	Scales
Grade Equivalent	Scales (1967 1980) Use Grade Equivalent Scores
Interest	Scales (1966 1980) Use Interest Inventories
Likert	Scales
Opinion	Scales Use Attitude Measures
Rating	Scales
Summated Rating	Scales Use Likert Scales
	Scaling
Internal	Scaling (1966 1980) Use Scaling
Multidimensional	Scaling
Optical	Scanners
Visual	Scanners Use Optical Scanners
Environmental	Scanning
	Schedule Modules (1968 1980) Use Flexible Scheduling
All Day Half Day	Schedules Use Full Day Half Day Schedules
Alternate Day	Schedules
Flexible	Schedules (1967 1980)
Full Day Half Day	Schedules
Half Day	Schedules Use Full Day Half Day Schedules
School	Schedules
Trimester	Schedules (1966 1980) Use Trimester System
	Scheduling
Alternate Day Block	Scheduling Use Alternate Day Schedules and Block Scheduling
Block	Scheduling
Broadcast	Scheduling Use Programming (Broadcast)
Fast Track	Scheduling
Flexible	Scheduling
Modular	Scheduling Use Flexible Scheduling
Body	Schema Use Body Image
	Schemata (Cognition)
	Schematic Studies
Conceptual	Schemes (1967 1980)
	Schizophrenia
	Scholarly Communication
	Scholarly Information Exchange Use Scholarly Communication
	Scholarly Journals
	Scholarly Writing
	Scholarship
	Scholarship Funds
	Scholarship Loans (1966 1980) Use Scholarships and Student Loan Programs
	Scholarships
Endowed	Scholarships Use Scholarships
Merit	Scholarships
No Need	Scholarships
	Scholastic Ability Use Academic Ability
	Scholastic Achievement Use Academic Achievement
	Scholastic Failure Use Academic Failure
Grades	(Scholastic)
	Scholastic Journalism
Marking	(Scholastic) Use Grading
Marks	(Scholastic) Use Grades (Scholastic)
	Scholastic Potential Use Academic Aptitude
	Scholastic Probation Use Academic Probation
High	School Academies (Career Development) Use Career Academies
	School Accidents
	School Accounting
	School Activities
After	School Activities (1967 1980) Use After School Programs
	School Adjustment Use Student Adjustment
	School Administration
	School Administrators Use Administrators
	School Admission Use Admission (School)

Admission	(School)
Public	School Adult Education
	School Age Day Care
	School Aid Use Educational Finance
Nonpublic	School Aid (1972 1980) Use Private School Aid
Parochial	School Aid (1972 1980) Use Parochial Schools and Private School Aid
Private	School Aid
	School Aides
Partnership Academies	(School and Business) Use Career Academies
Law	School Applicants Use College Applicants and Law Schools
Medical	School Applicants Use College Applicants and Medical Schools
	School Architecture (1966 1980) Use Educational Facilities Design
	School Attendance Use Attendance
	School Attendance Laws (1966 1974) Use School Attendance Legislation
	School Attendance Legislation
	School Attitudes
	School Based Interagency Services Use Integrated Services
	School Based Management
	School Board Members Use Boards of Education
	School Board Policy Use Board of Education Policy
	School Board Role Use Board of Education Role
	School Boards Use Boards of Education
State	School Boards Use State Boards of Education
	School Boundaries Use School Districts
	School Boycotts
	School Budget Elections
	School Buildings
	School Bus Drivers Use Bus Drivers and School Buses
	School Buses
	School Business Officials
Business Officials	(School) Use School Business Officials
	School Business Relationship
	School Cadres
	School Calendars (1967 1980) Use School Schedules
	School Catalogs
After	School Centers
	School Characteristics Use Institutional Characteristics
Elementary	School Children Use Elementary School Students
	School Choice
	School Climate Use Educational Environment
Clinic Personnel	(School) (1966 1980) Use Allied Health Personnel and School Health Services
	School Closing
	School College Cooperation Use College School Cooperation
High	School College Cooperation Use College School Cooperation
	School Community Communication Use School Community Relationship
	School Community Cooperation (1966 1980) Use School Community Relationship
	School Community Coordination Use School Community Relationship
	School Community Interaction Use School Community Relationship
	School Community Programs
	School Community Relationship
	School Conditions (1966 1980) Use Educational Environment
	School Consolidation Use Consolidated Schools
	School Construction
College	School Cooperation
College High	School Cooperation (1967 1980) Use College School Cooperation
	School Counseling
Elementary	School Counseling (1967 1980) Use School Counseling
Secondary	School Counseling Use School Counseling
	School Counselors
Elementary	School Counselors (1967 1980) Use School Counselors
Secondary	School Counselors (1967 1980) Use School Counselors
	School Culture
Elementary	School Curriculum
High	School Curriculum (1967 1980) Use Secondary School Curriculum
Secondary	School Curriculum
After	School Day Care (1978 1983) Use After School Programs and School Age Day Care
Extended	School Day
	School Demography
Department Directors	(School) (1966 1980) Use Department Heads
	School Desegregation
	School Design (1966 1980) Use Educational Facilities Design
Decentralized	School Design (1966 1980) Use Decentralization and Educational Facilities Design
High	School Design (1966 1980) Use Educational Facilities Design
Community	School Directors (1967 1980) Use Administrators and Community Schools
	School District Autonomy
	School District Norms Use Local Norms
	School District Policy Use Board of Education Policy
State	School District Relationship
	School District Reorganization
	School District Size
	School District Spending
	School District Wealth
	School Districts
County	School Districts
Intermediate	School Districts Use Intermediate Administrative Units
	School Dropouts Use Dropouts
High	School Dropouts Use Dropouts
After	School Education
Education Departments	(School) Use Schools of Education
Law	School Education Use Legal Education (Professions)
Post High	School Education Use Postsecondary Education
	School Effectiveness
	School Employees Use School Personnel

```
                                      School Enrollment   Use Enrollment
                                      School Entrance Age
                                      School Environment (1966 1980)   Use Educational Environment
                              High    School Equivalency Programs
                                      School Expansion
                                      School Experience   Use Educational Experience
                                      School Facilities   Use Educational Facilities
                            Dental    School Faculty   Use Dental Schools and Medical School Faculty
                          Graduate    School Faculty
                           Medical    School Faculty
                                      School Family Relationship   Use Family School Relationship
                                      School Finance   Use Educational Finance
                                      School Finance Equity   Use Educational Equity (Finance)
   Foreign Languages in the Elementary School   Use FLES
                              High    School Freshmen
                  Fundamental Skills  (School)   Use Basic Skills
                                      School Funds
                                      School Government Relationship   Use Government School Relationship
                              High    School Graduates
                                      School Guidance
                        Elementary    School Guidance (1967 1980)   Use School Guidance
                         Post High    School Guidance
                         Secondary    School Guidance   Use School Guidance
                     Comprehensive    School Health Education
                     Comprehensive    School Health Programs   Use Comprehensive School Health Education
                                      School Health Services
                                      School Holding Power
                                      School Home Relationship   Use Family School Relationship
                                      School Improvement (1966 1980)   Use Educational Facilities Improvement
                                      School Industry Relationship (1967 1980)   Use School Business Relationship
                                      School Integration (1966 1980)   Use School Desegregation
                                      School Involvement
                                      School Law
                             Early    School Leavers   Use Dropouts
                            Police    School Liaison   Use Police School Relationship
                                      School Libraries
                        Elementary    School Libraries (1966 1980)   Use School Libraries
                              High    School Libraries   Use School Libraries
                         Secondary    School Libraries   Use School Libraries
              Comprehensive Services  (School Linked)   Use Integrated Services
                                      School Linked Services   Use Integrated Services
                                      School Location
                                      School Maintenance
                        Elementary    School Mathematics
                         Secondary    School Mathematics
                                      School Media Centers   Use Learning Resources Centers
                                      School Newspapers
                                      School Nurse Practitioners   Use Nurse Practitioners and School Nurses
                                      School Nurses
                                      School Officials   Use School Personnel
                                      School Organization
                              High    School Organization (1966 1980)   Use School Organization
                                      School Orientation
                                      School Parent Relationship   Use Parent School Relationship
                                      School Participation   Use School Involvement
                                      School Personnel
                                      School Personnel Directors   Use Personnel Directors and School Personnel
                  Paraprofessional    School Personnel
                                      School Philosophy   Use Educational Philosophy
                                      School Phobia
                  Schools within a    School Plan   Use House Plan
                                      School Planning (1966 1980)
                                      School Plants   Use Educational Facilities
                                      School Police Relationship   Use Police School Relationship
                                      School Policy
                     Neighborhood     School Policy (1966 1980)   Use Neighborhood Schools and School Policy
                                      School Prayer
                                      School Principals   Use Principals
                                      School Programs   Use School Activities
                             After    School Programs
                         Community    School Programs   Use School Community Programs
                      Intersession    School Programs   Use Vacation Programs
   Progressive Retardation (1966 1980) (in School)   Use Educationally Disadvantaged
                                      School Psychologists
                                      School Psychology
                                      School Publications
                                      School Readiness
                                      School Readiness Tests
                                      School Recreational Programs
                                      School Redistricting (1966 1980)   Use School District Reorganization
                         Registrars   (School)
                                      School Registration
                      Registration in School   Use School Registration
                                      School Related Activities   Use Extracurricular Activities
                          Business    School Relationship   Use School Business Relationship
                         Community    School Relationship   Use School Community Relationship
                            Family    School Relationship
                        Government    School Relationship
                             Home     School Relationship   Use Family School Relationship
                          Industry    School Relationship   Use School Business Relationship
                            Parent    School Relationship
                            Police    School Relationship
                           Student    School Relationship
```

School Renovation   Use Educational Facilities Improvement
School Reorganization   Use School Organization
School Resegregation
School Responsibility
School Restructuring
Retention (in   School)   Use School Holding Power
School Role
Elementary   School Role (1966 1980)   Use School Role
High   School Role (1966 1980)   Use School Role
Junior High   School Role (1966 1980)   Use School Role
School Safety
School Schedules
Elementary   School Science
Secondary   School Science
School Secretaries
School Security
School Segregation
High   School Seniors
School Services (1966 1980)   Use Ancillary School Services
Ancillary   School Services
Auxiliary   School Services   Use Ancillary School Services
School Shops
School Site Management   Use School Based Management
School Sites   Use School Location
School Size
School Social Workers
School Space
School Statistics
School Student Relationship   Use Student School Relationship
Elementary   School Students
High   School Students
Junior High   School Students
Middle   School Students
Secondary   School Students
Senior High   School Students   Use High School Students
School Study Centers (1966 1980)   Use Study Centers
School Superintendents (1966 1980)   Use Superintendents
School Supervision
Elementary   School Supervisors (1966 1980)   Use School Supervision
High   School Supervisors (1966 1980)   Use School Supervision
School Supplies   Use Supplies
School Support
School Surveys
In   School Suspension
School Systems (1966 1980)   Use School Districts
County   School Systems (1967 1980)   Use County School Districts
Public   School Systems (1966 1980)   Use Public Schools and School Districts
Rural   School Systems (1966 1980)   Use Rural Schools and School Districts
School Taxes
Elementary   School Teachers
High   School Teachers   Use Secondary School Teachers
Junior High   School Teachers   Use Secondary School Teachers
Middle   School Teachers
Public   School Teachers
Secondary   School Teachers
Timetables   (School)   Use School Schedules
School to Work Transition   Use Education Work Relationship
School Transportation   Use Student Transportation
School Truancy   Use Truancy
After   School Tutoring (1966 1980)   Use After School Education and Tutoring
School Uniforms
School Vandalism
School Visitation
School Visits   Use School Visitation
Extended   School Year
Out of   School Youth
School Zoning
Effective   Schooling   Use School Effectiveness
Home   Schooling
Schools
Affiliated   Schools
Alternative   Schools (1972 1980)   Use Nontraditional Education
Area Vocational   Schools (1966 1980)   Use Regional Schools and Vocational Schools
Bilingual   Schools
Biracial   Schools (1966 1980)   Use School Desegregation
Biracial Elementary   Schools (1966 1980)   Use School Desegregation
Biracial Secondary   Schools (1966 1980)   Use School Desegregation
Boarding   Schools
British Infant   Schools
Infant   Schools (British Primary System)   Use British Infant Schools
Campus   Schools   Use Laboratory Schools
Catholic   Schools
Catholic Elementary   Schools (1967 1980)   Use Catholic Schools
Catholic High   Schools (1967 1980)   Use Catholic Schools
Centralized   Schools   Use Consolidated Schools
Charter   Schools
City   Schools   Use Urban Schools
Closed   Schools   Use School Closing
Commercial Correspondence   Schools   Use Correspondence Schools
Community   Schools
Comprehensive High   Schools (1967 1980)   Use High Schools
Consolidated   Schools
Continuation High   Schools (1968 1980)   Use Continuation Students

Contract Tribal	Schools	Use Tribally Controlled Education
Cooperating	Schools	Use Affiliated Schools
Correspondence	Schools	
Day	Schools	
Dental	Schools	
Desegregated	Schools	Use School Desegregation
Disadvantaged	Schools	
Elementary	Schools	
Experimental	Schools	
Folk	Schools	
Free	Schools	
Freedom	Schools	
General High	Schools (1966 1980)	Use General Education
High	Schools	
Holding Power (of	Schools)	Use School Holding Power
Hospital	Schools	
Full Service	Schools (Human Services)	Use Integrated Services
Inclusive	Schools	
Independent	Schools	Use Private Schools
Indian Controlled	Schools	Use American Indian Education and Tribally Controlled Education
Institutional	Schools	
Instructionally Effective	Schools	Use School Effectiveness
Integrated	Schools	Use School Desegregation
Junior High	Schools	
Training	Schools (Juvenile Offenders)	Use Correctional Institutions
Laboratory	Schools	
Law	Schools	
Library	Schools	
Local Autonomy (of	Schools)	Use School District Autonomy
Local Control (of	Schools)	Use School District Autonomy
Magnet	Schools	
Medical	Schools	
Middle	Schools	
Migrant	Schools (1966 1980)	Use Migrant Education
Military	Schools	
Multiunit	Schools	
Neighborhood	Schools	
Night	Schools (1966 1980)	Use Evening Programs
Nonpublic	Schools	Use Private Schools
Nonresidential	Schools (1967 1980)	Use Commuter Colleges
Northern	Schools (1966 1980)	
Nursery	Schools	
	Schools of Dentistry	Use Dental Schools
	Schools of Education	
	Schools of Medicine	Use Medical Schools
One Room	Schools	Use One Teacher Schools
One Teacher	Schools	
Open	Schools	Use Open Education
Open Area	Schools	Use Open Plan Schools
Open Plan	Schools	
Parochial	Schools	
Prayer in	Schools	Use School Prayer
Private	Schools	
Professional Development	Schools	
Professional Practice	Schools	Use Professional Development Schools
Project	Schools	Use Experimental Schools
Proprietary	Schools	
Public	Schools	
Racially Balanced	Schools	
Regional	Schools	
Effective	Schools Research	
Resegregated	Schools	Use School Resegregation
Residential	Schools	
Rural	Schools	
Secondary	Schools	
Senior High	Schools (1966 1980)	Use High Schools
Single Sex	Schools	
Site Based Management	(Schools)	Use School Based Management
Slum	Schools	
Small	Schools	
Southern	Schools (1966 1980)	
Special	Schools	
Special Service	Schools	Use Special Schools
Specialty	Schools	Use Proprietary Schools
State	Schools	
Suburban	Schools	
Summer	Schools	
Clinical	Schools (Teacher Education)	Use Professional Development Schools
Technical	Schools	Use Vocational Schools
Technical High	Schools	Use Vocational High Schools
Traditional	Schools	
Transitional	Schools	
Tribal	Schools	Use Tribally Controlled Education
Ungraded	Schools (1966 1980)	Use Nongraded Instructional Grouping
Restructuring of	Schools (United States)	Use School Restructuring
University	Schools	Use Laboratory Schools
Urban	Schools	
Vocational	Schools	
Vocational High	Schools	
	Schools within a School Plan	Use House Plan
Year Round	Schools	
	Schoolsickness	Use School Phobia
Orff	Schulwerk Approach	Use Orff Method

```
                      Science    Use Sciences
                      Science Achievement
                      Science Activities
                      Science and Society
         English for  Science and Technology
                      Science and Technology Libraries    Use Science Libraries
              Animal  Science (1967 1980)    Use Animal Husbandry
                      Science Careers
                      Science Clubs
             College  Science
            Computer  Science
                      Science Consultants
            Consumer  Science
                      Science Course Improvement Project (1967 1980)    Use Science Course Improvement Projects
                      Science Course Improvement Projects
                      Science Courses (1966 1980)    Use Science Curriculum
                      Science Curriculum
          Bachelor of  Science Degrees    Use Bachelors Degrees
           Master of  Science Degrees    Use Masters Degrees
      Demonstrations  (Science)
                      Science Departments
               Earth  Science
                      Science Education
           Aerospace  Science Education    Use Aerospace Education
            Computer  Science Education
                Fire  Science Education
                      Science Education History
         Information  Science Education
              Marine  Science Education    Use Marine Education
          Elementary  Science (1966 1980)    Use Elementary School Science
   Elementary School  Science
                      Science Equipment
                      Science Experiments
                      Science Facilities
                      Science Fairs
                      Science Fiction
             General  Science
            Hands on  Science
                      Science History
           Household  Science    Use Consumer Science
           Master of  Science in Teaching    Use Masters Degrees
                      Science Information    Use Scientific and Technical Information
         Information  Science
                      Science Institutes (1967 1980)    Use Institutes (Training Programs) and Science Programs
                      Science Instruction
                      Science Interests
             Student  Science Interests (1967 1980)    Use Science Interests
                      Science Laboratories
                      Science Libraries
             Library  Science
                      Science Materials
              Social  Science Methodology    Use Research Methodology and Social Science Research
            Military  Science
              Modern  Science (1966 1980)    Use Sciences
          Nature of  Science    Use Scientific Principles
               Plant  Science (1967 1980)
           Political  Science
                      Science Process Skills
                      Science Programs
             Summer  Science Programs
                      Science Projects
          Behavioral  Science Research
              Social  Science Research
    Secondary School  Science
                Soil  Science
  Structural Analysis  (Science)
                      Science Supervision
                      Science Teachers
                      Science Teaching Centers
                      Science Technology and Society    Use Science and Society
                 Sts  (Science Technology Society)    Use Science and Society
                      Science Tests
                      Science Units (1966 1980)    Use Science Curriculum and Units of Study
                      Sciences
           Aerospace  Sciences    Use Aerospace Technology
             Applied  Sciences    Use Technology
          Behavioral  Sciences
          Biological  Sciences
              Dental  Sciences    Use Dentistry
              Health  Sciences Libraries    Use Medical Libraries
                Life  Sciences    Use Biological Sciences
             Medical  Sciences    Use Medicine
             Natural  Sciences
         Paramedical  Sciences    Use Medicine
            Physical  Sciences
              Social  Sciences
               Space  Sciences
                      Scientific and Technical Information
                      Scientific Attitudes
                      Scientific Concepts
                      Scientific Creationism    Use Creationism
                      Scientific Enterprise
                      Scientific Information    Use Scientific and Technical Information
```

```
                        Scientific Literacy
                        Scientific Manpower (1967 1980)   Use Scientific Personnel
                        Scientific Methodology
                        Scientific Methods   Use Scientific Methodology
                        Scientific Personnel
                        Scientific Principles
                        Scientific Reports   Use Research Reports
                        Scientific Research
                        Scientists
          Information   Scientists
               Social   Scientists
                        Scope of Bargaining
                 Test   Score Decline
                        Score Reading   Use Music Reading
                        Score Theory   Use Test Theory
          Objectively   Scored Tests   Use Objective Tests
                        Scores
             Critical   Scores   Use Cutting Scores
                Crude   Scores   Use Raw Scores
              Cutting   Scores
            Declining   Scores   Use Test Score Decline
              Equated   Scores
                    G   Scores   Use Grade Equivalent Scores
                Grade   Scores   Use Grade Equivalent Scores
     Grade Equivalent   Scores
                Gross   Scores   Use Raw Scores
             Obtained   Scores   Use Raw Scores
             Original   Scores   Use Raw Scores
                  Raw   Scores
                 Test   Scores   Use Scores
                 True   Scores
             Weighted   Scores
                        Scoring
                        Scoring Formulas
              Rubrics   (Scoring Guides)   Use Scoring Rubrics
                        Scoring Keys   Use Answer Keys
                 Test   Scoring Machines
                        Scoring Rubrics
                        Scots Gaelic
               Gaelic   (Scottish)   Use Scots Gaelic
                        Screen Design (Computers)
                        Screen Education   Use Film Study
                        Screen Format   Use Screen Design (Computers)
                        Screening Tests
                        Screens (Displays)
               Uncial   Script   Use Manuscript Writing (Handlettering)
                        Scripts
           Non Roman   Scripts
                        Scuba Diving   Use Underwater Diving
                        Sculpture
                        SDI   Use Selective Dissemination of Information
                 Deep   Sea Diving   Use Underwater Diving
                        Seafarers
                        Seafood (1968 1980)   Use Food
                        Sealants   Use Adhesives
                        Seamen (1969 1980)   Use Seafarers
                        Seamstresses (1968 1980)   Use Needle Trades
                        Search and Seizure
                        Search Committees (Personnel)
                        Search Intermediaries
                  Job   Search Methods
           Commercial   Search Services (Online)   Use Online Vendors
                        Search Strategies
           Literature   Searches   Use Bibliographies
               Online   Searching
          Interactive   Searching (Online)   Use Online Searching
                        Seasonal Employment
                        Seasonal Labor (1966 1980)   Use Seasonal Employment
                        Seasonal Laborers
                        Seat Belts   Use Restraints (Vehicle Safety)
                        Second Language Books   Use Foreign Language Books
              English   (Second Language)
                        Second Language Enrollment   Use Language Enrollment
                        Second Language Films   Use Foreign Language Films
                        Second Language Instruction
     Multilevel Classes   (Second Language Instruction)
                        Second Language Learning
                        Second Language Periodicals   Use Foreign Language Periodicals
                        Second Language Programs
              College   Second Language Programs
                        Second Language Teachers   Use Language Teachers
    Vocational English   (Second Language)
                        Second Languages
                        Secondary Education
           Elementary   Secondary Education
                 Post   Secondary Education (1967 1978)   Use Postsecondary Education
                        Secondary Employment   Use Multiple Employment
                        Secondary Grades (1966 1980)   Use Secondary Education
                        Secondary School Counseling   Use School Counseling
                        Secondary School Counselors (1967 1980)   Use School Counselors
                        Secondary School Curriculum
                        Secondary School Guidance   Use School Guidance
                        Secondary School Libraries   Use School Libraries
```

	Secondary School Mathematics
	Secondary School Science
	Secondary School Students
	Secondary School Teachers
	Secondary Schools
Biracial	Secondary Schools (1966 1980) Use School Desegregation
	Secretaries
Administrative	Secretaries Use Secretaries
Executive	Secretaries Use Secretaries
Legal	Secretaries Use Secretaries
Medical	Secretaries Use Secretaries
School	Secretaries
	Sectarian Colleges Use Church Related Colleges
Cross	Sectional Studies
Government	Sector Use Public Sector
Nonpublic	Sector Use Private Sector
Private	Sector
Public	Sector
	Security (1967 1978)
Campus	Security Use School Security
Computer	Security
Emotional	Security Use Security (Psychology)
Employment	Security Use Job Security
Guards	(Security) Use Security Personnel
Job	Security
National	Security
	Security Personnel
	Security (Psychology)
School	Security
	Security Systems (Alarms) Use Alarm Systems
	Sedatives
Job	Seekers Use Job Applicants
Help	Seeking
Information	Seeking
	Segregated Public Facilities (1966 1980) Use Public Facilities and Racial Segregation
College	Segregation
De Facto	Segregation
De Jure	Segregation
Defacto	Segregation (1966 1980) Use De Facto Segregation
Dejure	Segregation (1966 1980) Use De Jure Segregation
Job	Segregation Use Occupational Segregation
Legal	Segregation (1966 1980) Use De Jure Segregation
Occupational	Segregation
Anti	Segregation Programs (1967 1980) Use Racial Integration
	Segregation (Racial) Use Racial Segregation
Racial	Segregation
School	Segregation
	Segregationist Groups Use Segregationist Organizations
	Segregationist Organizations
	Seismology
Search and	Seizure
	Seizures
	Selection
Administrator	Selection
Book	Selection Aids Use Selection Tools
	Selection Committees (Personnel) Use Search Committees (Personnel)
Competitive	Selection
Computer	Selection
Computer Software	Selection
Software	Selection (Computers) Use Computer Software Selection
Counselor	Selection
Courseware	Selection Use Computer Software Selection and Courseware
Educational Media	Selection Use Media Selection
Instructional Material	Selection Use Media Selection
Library Material	Selection
Mate	Selection
Material	Selection Use Media Selection
Media	Selection
Personnel	Selection
Reading Material	Selection
Site	Selection
Student	Selection Use Admission Criteria
Course	Selection (Students)
Teacher	Selection
Test	Selection
Textbook	Selection
	Selection Tools
	Selective Admission
	Selective Colleges
	Selective Dissemination of Information
	Self Abuse Use Self Destructive Behavior
	Self Actualization
	Self Advocacy
	Self Appraisal Use Self Evaluation (Individuals)
	Self Assessment Use Self Evaluation (Individuals)
	Self Attitude Tests Use Self Concept Measures
	Self Bias Use Egocentrism
	Self Care Skills
	Self Centeredness Use Egocentrism
	Self Concept
	Self Concept Measures
Physical	Self Concept Use Body Image
	Self Concept Tests (1971 1980) Use Self Concept Measures

Self Confidence   Use Self Esteem
Self Congruence
Self Contained Classrooms
Self Control
Self Destructive Behavior
Self Determination
Self Development   Use Self Actualization
Self Directed Classrooms (1966 1980)
Self Directed Groups
Self Directed Learning   Use Independent Study
Self Discipline   Use Self Control
Self Disclosure (Individuals)
Self Efficacy
Self Employment
Self Empowerment   Use Empowerment
Self Esteem
Self Evaluation (1966 1980)
Self Evaluation (Groups)
Self Evaluation (Individuals)
Self Expression
Self Fulfilling Prophecies
Self Government   Use Self Determination
Self Growth   Use Individual Development
Self Guided Groups   Use Self Directed Groups
Self Help Devices (Disabled)   Use Assistive Devices (for Disabled)
Self Help Programs
Racial   Self Identification   Use Racial Identification
Self Image   Use Self Concept
Self Injurious Behavior
Self Instruction   Use Independent Study
Self Instruction Aids   Use Autoinstructional Aids
Self Instruction Materials   Use Programmed Instructional Materials
Programmed   Self Instruction   Use Programmed Instruction
Self Knowledge   Use Self Concept
Self Management
Behavioral   Self Management   Use Self Management
Self Motivation
Self Mutilation (1977 1993)   Use Self Injurious Behavior
Self Paced Instruction   Use Individualized Instruction and Pacing
Self Pacing   Use Pacing
Self Pacing Machines (1966 1980)   Use Teaching Machines
Self Realization   Use Self Actualization
Self Restraint   Use Self Control
Self Reward
Institutional   Self Study   Use Self Evaluation (Groups)
Organizational   Self Study   Use Self Evaluation (Groups)
Independent Students   (Self Supporting)   Use Self Supporting Students
Self Supporting Students
Self Teaching   Use Independent Study
Self Understanding   Use Self Concept
Self Utilization   Use Self Actualization
Semantic Differential
Semantics
General   Semantics   Use Semantics
Semester Division (1966 1980)   Use Semester System
Semester System
Semiconductor Devices
Seminaries   Use Church Related Colleges and Theological Education
Seminars
Police   Seminars (1966 1980)   Use Police Education
Student   Seminars (1966 1980)   Use Seminars
Teacher   Seminars (1966 1980)   Use Teacher Workshops
Semiology   Use Semiotics
Semiotics
Semiskilled Occupations
Semiskilled Workers
Semitic Languages
Anti   Semitism
Academic   Senates (Colleges)   Use College Governing Councils
Faculty   Senates (Colleges)   Use College Governing Councils
University   Senates   Use College Governing Councils
Senators   Use Legislators
Senile Dementia Alzheimers Type   Use Alzheimers Disease
Senior Citizens (1967 1980)   Use Older Adults
Senior High School Students   Use High School Students
Senior High Schools (1966 1980)   Use High Schools
Senior Teacher Role (1966 1980)   Use Master Teachers and Teacher Role
Seniority
College   Seniors
Seniors (1966 1980) (Grade 12)   Use High School Seniors
High School   Seniors
Seniors (1966 1980) (Last Year Undergraduates)   Use College Seniors
Cutaneous   Sense (1968 1980)   Use Tactual Perception
Dermal   Sense   Use Tactual Perception
Muscle   Sense   Use Kinesthetic Perception
Sensitivity Training
Sensory Aids
Sensory Deprivation
Sensory Experience
Sensory Integration
Sensory Motor Learning   Use Perceptual Motor Learning
Sensory Training
Sentence Combining

Transformational	Sentence Combining Use Sentence Combining
	Sentence Diagraming
	Sentence Structure
	Sentences
Kernel	Sentences
Mathematical	Sentences Use Mathematical Formulas
Prison	Sentences Use Sentencing
	Sentencing
	Separation Anxiety
Church State	Separation Use State Church Separation
State Church	Separation
Fixed	Sequence
	Sequential Approach
	Sequential Learning
	Sequential Programs (1966 1980) Use Sequential Approach
	Sequential Reading Programs (1966 1980) Use Sequential Approach
	Serbocroatian
	Serial Association Use Serial Learning
	Serial Learning
	Serial Method Use Serial Learning
	Serial Ordering
	Serials
Mailing List	Servers Use Listservs
Education	Service Centers
Educational	Service Centers Use Education Service Centers
Intermediate	Service Districts Use Intermediate Administrative Units
	Service Education (1966 1980) Use Vocational Education
Civil	Service Employees Use Government Employees
Food	Service
	Service Industry Use Service Occupations
Food	Service Industry (1967 1981) Use Food Service
	Service Learning
Community	Service Learning Use Service Learning
Military	Service
	Service Occupations
Food	Service Occupations (1968 1981) Use Food Service
Public	Service Occupations
Health	Service Personnel Use Health Personnel
Individual Family	Service Plans Use Individualized Family Service Plans
Individualized Family	Service Plans
Community	Service Programs (1966 1980) Use Community Services
Public	Service
Full	Service Schools (Human Services) Use Integrated Services
Special	Service Schools Use Special Schools
Appliance	Service Technicians (1967 1980) Use Appliance Repair
Fixed	Service Television (1969 1980) Use Educational Television
	Service Vehicles
	Service Workers
Food	Service Workers (1968 1981) Use Food Service
Health	Service Workers Use Health Personnel
Worldwide Web	Service Use World Wide Web
Electrical Appliance	Servicemen (1968 1980) Use Appliance Repair
	Services
Ancillary	Services (1967 1980)
Ancillary School	Services
Attendance	Services (1968 1980) Use Attendance and Pupil Personnel Services
Auxiliary School	Services Use Ancillary School Services
Client Background (Human	Services) Use Client Characteristics (Human Services)
Client Characteristics (Human	Services)
Clinical	Services Use Clinics
Communications	Services Use Communications
Community	Services
Community Health	Services
Community Information	Services
Information	Services (Community) Use Community Information Services
Referral	Services (Community) Use Community Information Services and Referral
Computer Based Reference	Services Use Online Systems and Reference Services
Contracting Out (of Government	Services) Use Privatization
Counseling	Services
Current Awareness	Services Use Selective Dissemination of Information
Day Care	Services (1967 1980) Use Day Care
Employment	Services
Outplacement	Services (Employment)
Employment Referral	Services Use Employment Services
Exceptional Child	Services (1968 1980)
Extension	Services Use Extension Education
Financial	Services
Full Service Schools (Human	Services) Use Integrated Services
Guidance	Services (1966 1980) Use Guidance Programs
Health	Services
Human	Services
Information	Services
Information and Referral	Services Use Information Services and Referral
Integrated	Services
Job Loss	Services Use Outplacement Services (Employment)
Legal	Services Use Legal Aid
Technical	Services (Libraries) Use Library Technical Processes
Library	Services
Library Reference	Services (1968 1980) Use Library Services and Reference Services
Local Information	Services Use Community Information Services
Medical	Services
Migrant Health	Services
Migrant Welfare	Services

Mobile Educational Services
Commercial Search Services (Online)   Use Online Vendors
Online Reference Services   Use Online Systems and Reference Services
Family Services Policy   Use Family Programs and Public Policy
Producer Services
Professional Services
Psychiatric Services
Psychological Services
Pupil Personnel Services
Reference Services
School Services (1966 1980)   Use Ancillary School Services
School Based Interagency Services   Use Integrated Services
School Health Services
School Linked Services   Use Integrated Services
Comprehensive Services (School Linked)   Use Integrated Services
Shared Services (1974 1986)   Use Shared Resources and Services
Shared Resources and Services
Signal Services   Use Telecommunications
Social Services
Sociopsychological Services (1967 1980)   Use Psychological Services and Social Services
Special Services (1966 1980)   Use Services
Student Affairs Services   Use Student Personnel Services
Student Personnel Services
Support Groups (Human Services)   Use Social Support Groups
Support Systems (Services)   Use Services
Telephone Crisis Services   Use Hotlines (Public)
Temporary Help Services   Use Employment Services and Temporary Employment
Tutorial Services   Use Tutorial Programs
Welfare Services
Summer Session   Use Summer Schools
Double Sessions
Split Sessions   Use Double Sessions
Staggered Sessions   Use Extended School Day
Response Set (Tests)   Use Response Style (Tests)
Set Theory
Problem Sets
Agenda Setting
Accommodations for Disabled (Educational Settings)   Use Academic Accommodations (Disabilities)
Settlement Houses
Land Settlement
Settlement Patterns   Use Land Settlement
Collective Settlements
Communistic Settlements   Use Collective Settlements
Neighborhood Settlements   Use Settlement Houses
University Settlements   Use Settlement Houses
Seventeenth Century Literature
Severe Disabilities
Severe Mental Retardation
Severely Handicapped (1975 1980)   Use Severe Disabilities
Impairment Severity   Use Severity (of Disability)
Severity (of Disability)
Sewage   Use Waste Water
Sewing Instruction
Sewing Machine Operators
Sex
Sex Bias
Sex (Characteristics) (1966 1980)
Single Sex Colleges
Sex Differences
Sex Discrimination
Sex Education
Sex Fairness
Gender (Sex)   Use Sex
Gender Differences (Sex)   Use Sex Differences
Gender Identity (Sex)   Use Sexual Identity
Gender Role (Sex)   Use Sex Role
Sex Prejudice   Use Sex Bias
Sex Role
Single Sex Schools
Sex Stereotypes
Sexism   Use Sex Bias
Sexism in Language
Sexist Language   Use Sexism in Language
Sexual Abuse
Child Sexual Abuse   Use Child Abuse and Sexual Abuse
Sexual Assault   Use Sexual Abuse
Sexual Behavior   Use Sexuality
Sexual Harassment
Sexual Identity
Sexual Orientation
Sexual Preference   Use Sexual Orientation
Sexuality
Human Sexuality   Use Sexuality
Shade Trees   Use Trees
Shadow Plays   Use Theater Arts
Shapers   Use Machine Tools
Sharecroppers
Shared Facilities
Shared Library Resources
Shared Resources and Services
Shared Services (1974 1986)   Use Shared Resources and Services
Shared Time (Computers)   Use Time Sharing
Shared Time (Education)   Use Dual Enrollment

```
                          Sharing Behavior
                   Job    Sharing
              Resource    Sharing     Use Shared Resources and Services
               Revenue    Sharing
                  Time    Sharing
                  Work    Sharing     Use Job Sharing
                          Sheet Metal Machine Operators   Use Machine Tool Operators and Sheet Metal Work
                          Sheet Metal Work
                          Sheet Metal Workers (1967 1981)   Use Sheet Metal Work
                Answer    Sheets
                  Data    Sheets (1966 1980)   Use Worksheets
                          Sheltered Workshops
              Air Raid    Shelters    Use Fallout Shelters
                  Bomb    Shelters    Use Fallout Shelters
               Fallout    Shelters
       Extradimensional   Shift    Use Shift Studies
          Half Reversal   Shift    Use Shift Studies
       Interdimensional   Shift    Use Shift Studies
           Nonreversal    Shift    Use Shift Studies
              Reversal    Shift    Use Shift Studies
                          Shift Studies
            Population    Shifts    Use Migration
               Culture    Shock    Use Culture Conflict
                          Shona
                          Shop Curriculum
               General    Shop    Use Shop Curriculum
                          Shop Mechanics    Use Machine Repairers
                          Shop Rooms    Use School Shops
         Industrial Arts  Shops    Use School Shops
                School    Shops
                          Short Courses (1970 1980)    Use Minicourses
                          Short Stories
                          Short Term Memory
               Teacher    Shortage
                  Time    Shortened Degree Programs    Use Acceleration (Education)
                          Shorthand
         Repetitive Film  Showings
                    No    Shows
                Puppet    Shows    Use Puppetry
                          Shyness
                          SI Units    Use Metric System
                          Sibling Relationship
                          Siblings
                Eldest    Siblings    Use First Born
                          Sick Child Care
                          Sickle Cell Anemia
                          Sickle Cell Trait    Use Sickle Cell Anemia
                          Sicknesses    Use Diseases
                          SIDS    Use Sudden Infant Death Syndrome
                          Sierra Leone Creole
                          Sierra Leone Krio    Use Sierra Leone Creole
                          Sight    Use Vision
                          Sight Method
                          Sight Playing    Use Music Reading
                          Sight Singing    Use Music Reading
                          Sight Vocabulary
             Partially    Sighted (1967 1980)    Use Partial Vision
                          Sightseeing Industry    Use Tourism
                          Sign Language
              American    Sign Language
                          Sign Painters
                          Sign Writers    Use Sign Painters
                          Signal Services    Use Telecommunications
                          Signboards    Use Signs
                          Signed English    Use Manual Communication
                          Significance Measures    Use Statistical Significance
            Statistical   Significance
              Tests of    Significance (1966 1980)    Use Statistical Significance
                          Significant Others
                          Signs
                  Road    Signs    Use Signs
                Traffic    Signs (1968 1980)    Use Signs and Traffic Control
                          Silent Films    Use Films
                          Silent Reading
             Sustained    Silent Reading
                          Silent Speech    Use Inner Speech (Subvocal)
                          Similarity Transformations    Use Transformations (Mathematics)
                   Job    Simplification
                  Work    Simplification (1968 1980)    Use Job Simplification
                          Simulated Environment
                          Simulated Speech    Use Artificial Speech
                          Simulated Studies    Use Simulation
                          Simulation
              Computer    Simulation
                          Simulators (1967 1980)    Use Simulation
                          Singhalese
                          Singing
                 Sight    Singing    Use Music Reading
                          Single Concept Films
                          Single Mother Births    Use Births to Single Women
                          Single Parent Family    Use One Parent Family
                          Single Sex Colleges
                          Single Sex Schools
```

	Single Students	
Births to	Single Women	
	Sinhalese	Use Singhalese
	Sino Tibetan Languages	
	Sioux (Tribe)	
Oglala	Sioux (Tribe)	
Teton	Sioux (Tribe)	Use Lakota (Tribe)
	Sisters	Use Siblings
	Siswati	
	Site Analysis	
	Site Based Management (Schools)	Use School Based Management
	Site Development	
School	Site Management	Use School Based Management
	Site Selection	
On	Site Tests	Use Field Tests
Off	Site Training	Use Off the Job Training
Historic	Sites	
Historical	Sites	Use Historic Sites
School	Sites	Use School Location
Classroom	Situation	Use Classroom Environment
Behavioral	Situation Films	Use Protocol Materials
	Situation Reaction Tests	Use Situational Tests
	Situation Response Tests	Use Situational Tests
	Situational Determinants	Use Context Effect
	Situational Tests	
	Situational Therapy	Use Milieu Therapy
	Six Three Three Organization	Use Instructional Program Divisions
	Sixteen Millimeter Projectors (1966 1980)	Use Projection Equipment
	Sixteenth Century Literature	
Class	Size	
Community	Size	
Effect	Size	
Family	Size	
Organization	Size (Groups)	
Company	Size (Industry)	Use Organization Size (Groups)
Sample	Size	
School	Size	
School District	Size	
Ice	Skating	
Roller	Skating	
	Skeletal System	
	Skeletomuscular System	Use Musculoskeletal System
	Skiing	
	Skill Analysis	
Language	Skill Attrition	
	Skill Centers	
	Skill Development	
	Skill Obsolescence	
National	Skill Standards	Use National Standards
Performance Assessment	(Skilled Bodily Movements)	Use Performance Tests
	Skilled Labor (1966 1980)	Use Skilled Workers
	Skilled Occupations	
	Skilled Workers	
	Skills	
Agricultural	Skills	
Alphabetizing	Skills	
Audiolingual	Skills	
Aural Oral	Skills	Use Audiolingual Skills
Basic	Skills	
Business	Skills	
Cognitive	Skills	Use Thinking Skills
Communication	Skills	
Conference	Skills (Communication)	Use Communication Skills
Daily Living	Skills	
Fundamental	Skills (Daily Living)	Use Daily Living Skills
Survival	Skills (Daily Living)	Use Daily Living Skills
Decision Making	Skills	
Employable	Skills	Use Employment Potential and Job Skills
Handwriting	Skills (1966 1983)	Use Handwriting and Writing Skills
Higher Order	Skills	Use Thinking Skills
Home Economics	Skills	
Homemaking	Skills	
Independent Living	Skills	Use Daily Living Skills
Information	Skills	
Interpersonal	Skills	Use Interpersonal Competence
Interpretive	Skills	
Job	Skills	
Language	Skills	
Language Attrition	(Skills)	Use Language Skill Attrition
Language Loss	(Skills)	Use Language Skill Attrition
Library	Skills	
Life	Skills	Use Daily Living Skills
Listening	Skills	
Literacy	Skills	Use Literacy
Composition	Skills (Literary) (1966 1980)	Use Writing Skills
Map	Skills	
Map Reading	Skills	Use Map Skills
Marketable	Skills	Use Employment Potential and Job Skills
Mathematics	Skills	
Mechanical	Skills	
Motor	Skills	Use Psychomotor Skills
Oral	Skills	Use Speech Skills
Parent	Skills	Use Parenting Skills

```
        Parenting   Skills
     Psychomotor    Skills
         Reading    Skills
       Reasoning    Skills    Use Thinking Skills
        Research    Skills
     Fundamental    Skills (School)    Use Basic Skills
 Science Process    Skills
       Self Care    Skills
          Social    Skills    Use Interpersonal Competence
      Locational    Skills (Social Studies)
        Speaking    Skills    Use Speech Skills
          Speech    Skills
           Study    Skills
 Survival Reading   Skills    Use Functional Reading
         Teacher    Skills    Use Teaching Skills
        Teaching    Skills
     Test Taking    Skills    Use Test Wiseness
          Number    Skills Tests    Use Mathematics Tests
        Thinking    Skills
      Vocabulary    Skills
      Vocational    Skills    Use Job Skills
      Word Study    Skills
         Writing    Skills
                    Skimming (Reading)    Use Speed Reading
                    Skin Diving    Use Underwater Diving
                    Skits
                    Slander    Use Libel and Slander
        Libel and   Slander
                    Slavery
                    Slavic Languages
                    Sleep
                    Slide Projectors    Use Projection Equipment
                    Slides
                    Slovene    Use Slovenian
                    Slovenian
                    Slow Learners
                    Sludge
       Activated    Sludge    Use Sludge
                    Slum Children    Use Disadvantaged Youth
                    Slum Conditions (1966 1980)    Use Slum Environment
                    Slum Environment
                    Slum Schools
                    Slums
           Urban    Slums (1966 1980)    Use Slums
                    Small Arms    Use Guns
                    Small Business Management    Use Business Administration and Small Businesses
                    Small Businesses
                    Small Classes
                    Small Colleges
                    Small Engine Mechanics
                    Small Group Instruction
                    Small Schools
                    Small Towns
                    Smog    Use Air Pollution
                    Smoke Alarms    Use Alarm Systems
                    Smokestacks    Use Chimneys
                    Smoking
       Cigarette    Smoking    Use Smoking
                    Snack Bars    Use Dining Facilities
                    Snowskiing    Use Skiing
                    Soap Operas
                    Soccer
                    Sociability    Use Interpersonal Competence
                    Social Action
                    Social Adjustment
                    Social Agencies
      Atmosphere    (Social)    Use Social Environment
                    Social Attitudes
                    Social Awareness    Use Interpersonal Competence
                    Social Background
                    Social Behavior
            Anti    Social Behavior (1966 1980)    Use Antisocial Behavior
      Assistance    (Social Behavior)    Use Helping Relationship
                    Social Bias
                    Social Biology
                    Social Change
                    Social Characteristics
                    Social Class
                    Social Class Differences    Use Social Differences
                    Social Class Integration    Use Social Integration
                    Social Climate    Use Social Environment
                    Social Cognition
                    Social Competence    Use Interpersonal Competence
                    Social Context    Use Social Environment
                    Social Control
          Dating    (Social)
                    Social Desirability
                    Social Development
                    Social Dialects
                    Social Differences
                    Social Disadvantagement (1966 1980)    Use Disadvantaged
                    Social Discrimination
  Discrimination    (Social)    Use Social Discrimination
```

Discriminatory Attitudes	(Social) (1966 1980) Use Social Bias
	Social Distribution
	Social Drinking Use Drinking
	Social Environment
	Social Exchange Theory
	Social Experience
	Social Factors (1968 1980) Use Social Influences
	Social Geography Use Human Geography
	Social History
	Social Immaturity (1966 1980) Use Maturity (Individuals)
	Social Indicators
	Social Influences
	Social Institutions (Organizations) Use Institutions
	Social Institutions (Social Patterns) Use Sociocultural Patterns
	Social Integration
Integration	(Social) Use Social Integration
	Social Interaction Use Interpersonal Relationship
	Social Isolation
	Social Issues Use Social Problems
	Social Learning Use Socialization
	Social Life
	Social Maturity (1966 1980) Use Maturity (Individuals)
	Social Mobility
	Social Networks
	Social Norms Use Behavior Standards and Social Behavior
	Social Opportunities (1966 1980) Use Social Mobility
	Social Organizations
Social Institutions	(Social Patterns) Use Sociocultural Patterns
	Social Perception Use Social Cognition
	Social Planning
	Social Pressure Use Social Influences
	Social Problems
	Social Promotion
	Social Psychology
	Social Reconstruction Use Social Change
	Social Recreation Programs (1966 1980) Use Recreational Programs
	Social Reform Use Social Action
	Social Reinforcement
	Social Relations (1966 1980)
	Social Responsibility
	Social Restrictions Use Social Mobility
	Social Role Use Role
	Social Science Methodology Use Research Methodology and Social Science Research
	Social Science Research
	Social Sciences
	Social Scientists
	Social Services
	Social Skills Use Interpersonal Competence
	Social Status
	Social Stratification
	Social Structure
	Social Studies
Locational Skills	(Social Studies)
	Social Studies Units (1966 1980) Use Social Studies and Units of Study
	Social Support Groups
	Social Systems
	Social Theories
	Social Trends Use Sociocultural Patterns
	Social Values
	Social Welfare (1966 1980)
	Social Work
	Social Workers
School	Social Workers
	Socialism
National	Socialism Use Nazism
	Socialization
Political	Socialization
	Socially Advantaged Use Advantaged
	Socially Deviant Behavior (1966 1980) Use Antisocial Behavior
	Socially Disadvantaged (1966 1980) Use Disadvantaged
	Socially Maladjusted (1966 1980) Use Social Adjustment
	Societal Change Use Social Change
Honor	Societies
Tribal	Societies Use Tribes
Futures (of	Society)
Science and	Society
Science Technology and	Society Use Science and Society
Sts (Science Technology	Society) Use Science and Society
	Sociobiology
	Sociocultural Patterns
	Sociodrama (1966 1980) Use Role Playing
	Sociodramatic Play Use Dramatic Play
	Socioeconomic Background
	Socioeconomic Influences
	Socioeconomic Level Use Socioeconomic Status
	Socioeconomic Status
	Sociograms Use Sociometric Techniques
	Sociolinguistics
	Sociological Novels (1969 1980) Use Novels
	Sociological Studies Use Social Science Research and Sociology
Family	(Sociological Unit)
	Sociologists
	Sociology

Educational   Sociology
Functions   (Sociology)   Use Role
Sociology of Education   Use Educational Sociology
Rural   Sociology
Sociometric Techniques
Sociopsychological Services (1967 1980)   Use Psychological Services and Social Services
Soft Cover Books   Use Paperback Books
Softball
Water   Softening   Use Water Treatment
Computer   Software
Software (Computers)   Use Computer Software
Computer   Software Design   Use Computer Software Development
Computer   Software Development
Software Development (Computers)   Use Computer Software Development
Computer   Software Engineering   Use Computer Software Development
Computer   Software Evaluation
Software Evaluation (Computers)   Use Computer Software Evaluation
Instructional   Software   Use Courseware
Computer   Software Maintenance   Use Computer Software Development
Menu Driven   Software
Computer   Software Reviews
Software Reviews (Computers)   Use Computer Software Reviews
Computer   Software Selection
Software Selection (Computers)   Use Computer Software Selection
Soil Conservation
Soil Science
Solar Energy
Solar Heating   Use Heating and Solar Energy
Solar Radiation (1968 1983)   Use Solar Energy
Solar Radiation Energy   Use Solar Energy
Solar System
Telephone   Solicitation Programs   Use Phonathons
Solicitors (Law)   Use Lawyers
Solid Geometry
Solid Wastes
Soliloquies   Use Monologs
Participative Problem   Solving   Use Participative Decision Making and Problem Solving
Problem   Solving
Somali
Art   Song
Songs
Sonic Environment   Use Acoustical Environment
Sonnets
Sons
College   Sophomores
Sororities
Q   Sort (1967 1980)   Use Q Methodology
Sorting Procedures (1966 1980)   Use Classification
Sound   Use Acoustics
Sound Barriers   Use Acoustic Insulation
Letter   Sound Correspondence   Use Phoneme Grapheme Correspondence
Sound Effects
Sound Equipment   Use Audio Equipment
Sound Films (1966 1980)   Use Films
Sound Insulation   Use Acoustic Insulation
Insulation   (Sound)   Use Acoustic Insulation
Noise   (Sound)
Rime   (Sound)   Use Rhyme
Sound Spectrographs
Spectrographs   (Sound)   Use Sound Spectrographs
Sound Systems   Use Audio Equipment
Central   Sound Systems (1966 1980)   Use Audio Equipment
Sound Tape Recordings   Use Audiotape Recordings
Sound Tracks (1966 1980)
Sound Transmission   Use Acoustics
Volume   (Sound)   Use Noise (Sound)
Sound Waves   Use Acoustics
Soundproofing   Use Acoustic Insulation
Source Credibility   Use Credibility
Alternative Energy   Sources
Information   Sources
Material   Sources   Use Resource Materials
Original   Sources   Use Primary Sources
Primary   Sources
South American History   Use Latin American History
South American Literature   Use Latin American Literature
South Americans   Use Latin Americans
South Asian Civilization   Use Non Western Civilization
Southern Attitudes (1966 1980)   Use Regional Attitudes
Southern Citizens (1966 1980)
Southern Community (1966 1980)
Southern Schools (1966 1980)
Tribal   Sovereignty
Space
Space Classification
Space Dividers
Space Exploration
Interior   Space
Space Orientation (1968 1980)
Personal   Space
Outer   Space Research   Use Space Exploration
School   Space
Space Sciences

	Space Time Continuum Use Relativity
	Space Utilization
	Spaced Negative Reinforcement Use Negative Reinforcement
Found	Spaces
Attention	Span
Life	Span Education Use Lifelong Learning
Eye Voice	Span
	Spanish
	Spanish American Literature (1969 1980) Use Hispanic American Literature
	Spanish Americans
	Spanish Culture
	Spanish Literature
	Spanish Speaking
	Spatial Ability
	Spatial Perception (1980 1981) Use Spatial Ability
	Spatial Relationship (1966 1980)
	Spatial Relationship (Facilities)
Native	Speakers
	Speaking (1966 1980) Use Speech Communication
	Speaking Activities (1966 1980) Use Speech Communication
Choral	Speaking
Limited English	Speaking
Non English	Speaking
Public	Speaking
	Speaking Skills Use Speech Skills
Spanish	Speaking
	Special Admission Use Selective Admission
	Special and Regular Education Relationship Use Regular and Special Education Relationship
	Special Classes
	Special Counselors (1966 1980) Use Counselors and Specialists
	Special Creation Theory Use Creationism
	Special Degree Programs
	Special Education
	Special Education Regular Education Cooperation Use Regular and Special Education Relationship
General and	Special Education Relationship Use Regular and Special Education Relationship
Regular and	Special Education Relationship
	Special Education Teachers
	Special Effects
	Special Health Problems
	Special Libraries
	Special Methods Courses Use Methods Courses
	Special Needs (Individuals) Use Individual Needs
	Special Needs Students
	Special Olympics
	Special Personnel Use Specialists
	Special Programs
English for	Special Purposes
Languages for	Special Purposes
	Special Regular Education Interface Use Regular and Special Education Relationship
	Special Schools
	Special Service Schools Use Special Schools
	Special Services (1966 1980) Use Services
	Special Teachers Use Specialists
	Special Zoning
	Specialist in Education Degrees
	Specialists
Child Development	Specialists
Research	Specialists (Education) Use Educational Researchers
Evaluation	Specialists Use Evaluators
Film Production	Specialists
Guidance	Specialists Use Guidance Personnel and Specialists
Information	Specialists Use Information Scientists
Learning	Specialists (1966 1980) Use Specialists
Library	Specialists Use Librarians
Media	Specialists
Reading	Specialists Use Reading Consultants
	Specialization
Hemispheric	Specialization (Brain) Use Brain Hemisphere Functions
	Specialty Schools Use Proprietary Schools
Endangered	Species
	Specific Learning Disabilities Use Learning Disabilities
	Specifications
Educational	Specifications (1967 1980)
Facility	Specifications Use Facility Guidelines
Job	Specifications Use Occupational Information
Performance	Specifications (1969 1980)
	Spectator Traffic Control Use Traffic Control
	Spectators Use Audiences
	Spectrograms (1967 1980) Use Sound Spectrographs
	Spectrographs (Sound) Use Sound Spectrographs
Sound	Spectrographs
	Spectroscopy
Optical	Spectrum Use Light
Visible	Spectrum Use Light
	Speech
	Speech Acts
	Speech and Hearing Clinics
	Speech and Language Pathology Use Speech Language Pathology
Articulation	(Speech)
Artificial	Speech
Caregiver	Speech
	Speech Clinics (1968 1980) Use Speech and Hearing Clinics
	Speech Communication

```
                          Speech Communication Curriculum    Use Speech Communication and Speech Curriculum
                          Speech Communication Research    Use Communication Research and Speech Communication
                          Speech Compression
                   Cued   Speech
                          Speech Curriculum
                Delayed   Speech
               Retarded   Speech Development (1968 1980)    Use Delayed Speech
                          Speech Education (1966 1980)
                          Speech Evaluation
             Figures of   Speech    Use Figurative Language
             Freedom of   Speech
                          Speech Habits
                          Speech Handicapped (1967 1980)    Use Speech Impairments
                          Speech Handicaps (1966 1994)    Use Speech Impairments
                          Speech Impairments
                          Speech Improvement
                          Speech Instruction
                          Speech Language Pathology
               Parts of   Speech    Use Form Classes (Languages)
                          Speech Pathology (1967 1994)    Use Speech Language Pathology
      Prosodic Features   (Speech)    Use Suprasegmentals
                          Speech Reading    Use Lipreading
                 Silent   Speech    Use Inner Speech (Subvocal)
              Simulated   Speech    Use Artificial Speech
                          Speech Skills
                  Inner   Speech (Subvocal)
                          Speech Synthesizers
               Text to    Speech Synthesizers    Use Speech Synthesizers
              Synthetic   Speech    Use Artificial Speech
                          Speech Tests
                          Speech Therapists (1966 1980)    Use Speech Therapy and Therapists
                          Speech Therapy
                 Visible   Speech
                          Speeches
                          Speed Reading
               Reading    Speed (1966 1977)    Use Reading Rate
                          Speed Tests    Use Timed Tests
                          Spelling
               Creative   Spelling    Use Invented Spelling
                 Finger   Spelling
                          Spelling Instruction
               Invented   Spelling
               Inventive   Spelling    Use Invented Spelling
        School District   Spending
                          Sperm Donors    Use Tissue Donors
                          Spina Bifida
                          Spiral Curriculum
                          Spirituality
                          Split Sessions    Use Double Sessions
                          Split Time    Use Dual Enrollment
               Standard   Spoken Usage
               Employer   Sponsored Day Care    Use Employer Supported Day Care
                          Spontaneous Behavior
                Fencing   (Sport)
                          Sport Medicine    Use Sports Medicine
                          Sport Psychology
                          Sports    Use Athletics
                Aquatic   Sports
             Extramural   Sports    Use Extramural Athletics
              Intramural   Sports    Use Intramural Athletics
               Lifetime   Sports
                          Sports Medicine
                          Sports News    Use Athletics and News Media
                          Sports Psychology    Use Sport Psychology
                 Racket   Sports    Use Racquet Sports
                Racquet   Sports
                          Sports Reporting    Use Athletics and News Reporting
                  Team   Sports
                  Water   Sports    Use Aquatic Sports
                 Winter   Sports
                          Sportsmanship
                          Spouses
                          Spreadsheets
              Electronic   Spreadsheets    Use Spreadsheets
                          Springboard Diving    Use Diving
             Emergency   Squad Personnel
                Rescue   Squad Personnel    Use Emergency Squad Personnel
                   Chi    Square
                  Least   Squares Statistics
                          Squash (Game)
                Exhaust   Stacks    Use Chimneys
                          Staff Days    Use Worker Days
                          Staff Development
                          Staff Evaluation    Use Personnel Evaluation
                          Staff Improvement (1966 1980)    Use Staff Development
            Instructional   Staff (1966 1980)    Use Teachers
                          Staff Meetings
                          Staff Offices    Use Offices (Facilities)
                          Staff Orientation
            Professional   Staff    Use Professional Personnel
                Resource   Staff
                          Staff Role
                Resource   Staff Role (1966 1980)    Use Resource Staff
```

	Staff Utilization
Differentiated	Staffs
	Stage Theory Use Developmental Stages
	Stages (1969 1980) Use Stages (Facilities)
Developmental	Stages
	Stages (Facilities)
	Stages of Development Use Developmental Stages
Piagetian	Stages Use Developmental Stages and Piagetian Theory
	Staggered Sessions Use Extended School Day
High	Stakes Tests
	Stammering Use Stuttering
	Standard Error of Estimate Use Error of Measurement
	Standard Error of Measurement (1970 1980) Use Error of Measurement
	Standard Spoken Usage
Colloquial	Standard Usage Use Standard Spoken Usage
Language	Standardization
Alternatives to	Standardized Testing Use Alternative Assessment
	Standardized Tests
	Standards
Academic	Standards
Behavior	Standards
Environmental	Standards
Equipment	Standards
Facility	Standards Use Facility Guidelines
Food	Standards
Labor	Standards
Library	Standards
Living	Standards
Middle Class	Standards
National	Standards
National Skill	Standards Use National Standards
Occupational Safety and Health	Standards Use Labor Standards and Occupational Safety and Health
Professional	Standards Use Standards
State	Standards
Textbook	Standards
Advanced	Standing Examinations Use Equivalency Tests
	Stars
	State Action
	State Agencies
	State Aid
Federal	State Aid Use State Federal Aid
	State Assistance Use State Aid
	State Boards of Education
	State Boards of Licensing Use State Licensing Boards
	State Church Separation
	State Colleges
	State Committees on Education Use State Boards of Education
	State Court Litigation Use Court Litigation and State Courts
	State Courts
	State Curriculum Bulletins Use State Curriculum Guides
	State Curriculum Guides
	State Departments of Education
	State Education Agencies Use State Departments of Education
	State Federal Aid
	State Federal Relationship Use Federal State Relationship
	State Federal Support (1966 1977) Use State Federal Aid
	State Financial Aid Use State Aid
	State Foreign Language Supervisors (1967 1980) Use Second Language Instruction and State Supervisors
Full	State Funding
	State Government
	State Government Programs Use State Government and State Programs
	State History
	State Laws (1966 1974) Use State Legislation
	State Legislation
	State Libraries
	State Licensing Boards
Nonresident Students (1967 1980) (Out of	State) Use Out of State Students
	State Norms
	State of the Art Reviews
	State Officials
	State Planning Use Statewide Planning
	State Police (1966 1980) Use Police
	State Programs
	State Recreation Legislation (1966 1978) Use Recreation Legislation and State Legislation
	State Regulation
Federal	State Relationship
Resident Students (1967 1980) (in	State) Use In State Students
	State School Boards Use State Boards of Education
	State School District Relationship
	State Schools
Church	State Separation Use State Church Separation
	State Standards
In	State Students
Out of	State Students
	State Supervisors
	State Support Use State Aid
	State Supreme Courts Use State Courts
	State Surveys
	State Syllabi Use State Curriculum Guides
	State Universities
Mission	Statements
Policy	Statements Use Position Papers
Wage	Statements (1966 1980) Use Payroll Records

American Literature (1966 1980) (United States)   Use United States Literature
Civil War (United States)
Colonial History (United States)
Educational Excellence Movement (United States)   Use Excellence in Education
United States Government (Course)
United States History
United States Literature
Low Income States
States Powers
Presidential Campaigns (United States) .
Presidential Candidates (United States)   Use Political Candidates and Presidential Campaigns (United States)
Presidential Debates (United States)   Use Debate and Presidential Campaigns (United States)
Presidential Elections (United States)   Use Elections and Presidential Campaigns (United States)
Presidents of the United States
Restructuring of Schools (United States)   Use School Restructuring
Revolutionary War (United States)
States Rights   Use States Powers
Statewide Coordination   Use Statewide Planning
Statewide Planning
Statewide Programs   Use State Programs
Static Controls   Use Electronic Control
Learning Stations (Classroom)   Use Learning Centers (Classroom)
Coast Guard Air Stations   Use Military Air Facilities
Experiment Stations
Field Experiment Stations   Use Experiment Stations
Work Stations (Home or Office)   Use Workstations
Marine Corps Air Stations   Use Military Air Facilities
Naval Air Stations   Use Military Air Facilities
Statistical Analysis
Statistical Association Methods   Use Correlation
Statistical Bias
Statistical Bibliography   Use Bibliometrics
Statistical Data
Statistical Distributions
Statistical Inference
Statistical Linguistics   Use Mathematical Linguistics
Statistical Methods   Use Statistical Analysis
Statistical Processes   Use Statistical Analysis
Statistical Significance
Statistical Studies
Statistical Surveys
Statistical Theory   Use Statistics
Statistics
Bayesian Statistics
Comparative Statistics (1966 1980)   Use Comparative Analysis and Statistical Analysis
Distribution Free Statistics   Use Nonparametric Statistics
Distributions (Statistics)   Use Statistical Distributions
Employment Statistics
Inferential Statistics   Use Statistical Inference and Statistics
Least Squares Statistics
Library Statistics
Mathematical Statistics   Use Statistics
Maximum Likelihood Statistics
Multivariate Statistics   Use Multivariate Analysis
Nonparametric Statistics
Quantitative Research (Statistics)   Use Statistical Analysis
Regression (Statistics)
Robustness (Statistics)
School Statistics
Status
Age Grade Status   Use Age Grade Placement
Class Status   Use Social Status
Educational Status Comparison
Economic Status
Employment Status   Use Employment Level
Ethnic Status
Family Status
Group Status
Marital Status
Status Need
Professional Status   Use Professional Recognition
Social Status
Socioeconomic Status
Statutory Rape   Use Rape
Stealing
Steel Foundries   Use Foundries
Steel Industry (1967 1980)   Use Metal Industry
Stenographers (1966 1981)   Use Shorthand
Clerk Stenographers   Use Shorthand
Stenography (1967 1980)   Use Shorthand
Step in Step out Students   Use Stopouts
Step in Step out Students   Use Stopouts
Stepfamily
Stereochemistry
Stereopsis (1968 1980)   Use Depth Perception
Stereotypes
Black Stereotypes
Ethnic Stereotypes
Gender Stereotypes   Use Sex Stereotypes
Jewish Stereotypes (1966 1980)   Use Ethnic Stereotypes and Jews
Negro Stereotypes (1966 1977)   Use Black Stereotypes
Sex Stereotypes
Teacher Stereotypes

```
                        Stickers    Use Adhesives
                        Stimulants
                        Stimulation
                        Stimuli
             Auditory    Stimuli
               Aural    Stimuli (1966 1980)    Use Auditory Stimuli
           Electrical    Stimuli
            Pictorial    Stimuli
              Tactile    Stimuli
             Tactual    Stimuli    Use Tactile Stimuli
              Verbal    Stimuli
              Visual    Stimuli
                        Stimulus Behavior (1966 1980)    Use Responses
                        Stimulus Characteristics    Use Stimuli
         Conditioned    Stimulus (1966 1980)    Use Stimuli
                        Stimulus Devices (1966 1980)
             Novelty    (Stimulus Dimension)
                        Stimulus Generalization
                        Stimulus Synthesis    Use Patterned Responses
                        Stockpiles    Use Supplies
                        Stopouts
                        Storage
                        Storage Batteries    Use Electric Batteries
           Computer    Storage Devices
          Equipment    Storage
         Information    Storage
         Information    Storage (Psychology)    Use Encoding (Psychology)
             College    Stores
                Feed    Stores
               Food    Stores
             Grocery    Stores    Use Food Stores
       Livestock Feed    Stores    Use Feed Stores
             Feature    Stories
               Short    Stories
                        Story Grammar
                        Story Problems (Mathematics)    Use Word Problems (Mathematics)
                        Story Reading
                        Story Structure    Use Story Grammar
                        Story Telling
                        Strabismus
                        Stradaptive Testing    Use Adaptive Testing
               Fiscal    Strain    Use Financial Problems
                        Stranger Reactions
                        Strategic Management    Use Strategic Planning
                        Strategic Planning
             Change    Strategies
         Educational    Strategies
        Instructional    Strategies    Use Educational Strategies
            Learning    Strategies
            Reading    Strategies
             Search    Strategies
         Test Taking    Strategies    Use Test Wiseness
             Writing    Strategies
              Social    Stratification
                        Stream Pollution    Use Water Pollution
                        Streams    Use Rivers
                        Street Layouts    Use Traffic Circulation
                        Street Parking Areas    Use Parking Facilities
                        Street People    Use Homeless People
                        Strength (Biology)    Use Muscular Strength
            Muscular    Strength
            Physical    Strength    Use Muscular Strength
       Accents (Vocal    Stress)    Use Stress (Phonology)
        Posttraumatic    Stress Disorder
                        Stress Management
                        Stress (Phonology)
       Post Traumatic    Stress Syndrome    Use Posttraumatic Stress Disorder
                        Stress Variables
             Poverty    Stricken    Use Economically Disadvantaged
                        Strikes
             Teacher    Strikes
                        String Instruments
                        Stringed Instruments    Use String Instruments
                        Structural Analysis (1966 1980)
                        Structural Analysis (Linguistics)
                        Structural Analysis (Science)
                        Structural Arrangement    Use Organization
                        Structural Building Systems
                        Structural Elements (Construction)
                        Structural Equation Models
              Linear    Structural Equation Models    Use Structural Equation Models
                        Structural Grammar
                        Structural Linguistics
                        Structural Unemployment
                        Structural Work Occupations    Use Building Trades
              Atomic    Structure
            Authority    Structure    Use Power Structure
         Constituent    Structure    Use Phrase Structure
                Deep    Structure
              Factor    Structure
              Family    Structure
         Government    Structure    Use Governmental Structure
        Governmental    Structure
```

Group	Structure
Industrial	Structure
Molecular	Structure
Phrase	Structure
Power	Structure
Sentence	Structure
Social	Structure
Story	Structure Use Story Grammar
Surface	Structure
Text	Structure
Air	Structures
Air Inflated	Structures (1972 1980) Use Air Structures
Air Supported	Structures (1972 1980) Use Air Structures
Cognitive	Structures
Hybrid Air	Structures (1972 1980) Use Air Structures
Inflatable	Structures Use Air Structures
Knowledge	Structures Use Cognitive Structures
	Sts (Science Technology Society) Use Science and Society
	Student Ability (1966 1980) Use Academic Ability
	Student Achievement Use Academic Achievement
	Student Activities (Extraclass) Use Extracurricular Activities
	Student Adjustment
Foreign	Student Advisers
	Student Affairs Services Use Student Personnel Services
	Student Affairs Workers Use Student Personnel Workers
	Student Aid Use Student Financial Aid
	Student Alienation
	Student Application (1966 1980) Use College Applicants
	Student Appraisal Use Student Evaluation
	Student Aptitude Use Academic Aptitude
	Student Assignments Use Assignments
	Student Attitudes
	Student Attrition
	Student Behavior
	Student Centered Curriculum
	Student Centers Use Student Unions
	Student Certification
	Student Characteristics
	Student College Relationship
Parent	Student Conferences (1967 1980) Use Parent Teacher Conferences
	Student Controlled Learning Use Learner Controlled Instruction
	Student Costs
Instructional	Student Costs
Noninstructional	Student Costs
	Student Councils Use Student Government
	Student Credit Hours Use Credits
	Student Developed Materials
	Student Development
	Student Distribution (1966 1980)
Diversity	(Student)
	Student Educational Objectives
	Student Eligibility Use Eligibility
	Student Employment
	Student Empowerment
	Student Engaged Time Use Time on Task
	Student Enrollment (1966 1977) Use Enrollment
	Student Evaluation
Nongraded	Student Evaluation
	Student Evaluation of Teacher Performance
	Student Exchange Programs
Expenditure per	Student
	Student Experience
	Student Financial Aid
Need Analysis	(Student Financial Aid)
	Student Financial Aid Officers
	Student Government
	Student Grouping (1966 1980) Use Grouping (Instructional Purposes)
	Student Housing (College) Use College Housing
	Student Improvement
Teacher	Student Interaction Use Teacher Student Relationship
	Student Interests
	Student Job Placement Use Job Placement and Student Employment
	Student Journals
	Student Leadership
	Student Learning Contracts Use Performance Contracts
	Student Loading Areas (1968 1980) Use Student Transportation
	Student Loan Programs
	Student Logs Use Student Journals
	Student Maladjustment Use Student Adjustment
	Student Mediation Use Peer Mediation
	Student Mobility
	Student Motivation
	Student Needs
	Student Notebooks (Diaries) Use Student Journals
	Student Opinion (1966 1980) Use Student Attitudes
	Student Organizations
	Student Outcomes Use Outcomes of Education
	Student Parent Relationship Use Parent Student Relationship
	Student Participation
	Student Personnel Programs (1967 1980) Use Student Personnel Services
	Student Personnel Services
	Student Personnel Work (1967 1980) Use Student Personnel Services
	Student Personnel Workers

```
                                            Student Placement
                                            Student Problems
                                            Student Projects
                                            Student Promotion
                                            Student Protest   Use Activism
                                            Student Publications
                                 Teacher    Student Ratio
                                            Student Reaction
                                            Student Records
                                            Student Recruitment
                                            Student Rehabilitation (1966 1980)   Use Rehabilitation
                                 College    Student Relationship   Use Student College Relationship
                                  Parent    Student Relationship
                                  School    Student Relationship   Use Student School Relationship
                                 Teacher    Student Relationship
                                            Student Research
                                            Student Responses   Use Student Reaction
                                            Student Responsibility
                                            Student Rights
                                            Student Role
                                            Student School Relationship
                                            Student Science Interests (1967 1980)   Use Science Interests
                                            Student Selection   Use Admission Criteria
                                            Student Seminars (1966 1980)   Use Seminars
                                            Student Subcultures
                                            Student Surveys
                                            Student Teacher Attitudes
                                            Student Teacher Evaluation
                                            Student Teacher Interaction   Use Teacher Student Relationship
                                            Student Teacher Ratio (1966 1984)   Use Teacher Student Ratio
                                            Student Teacher Relationship (1966 1984)   Use Teacher Student Relationship
                                            Student Teacher Supervisors
                                            Student Teachers
                                            Student Teaching
                              Off Campus    Student Teaching   Use Student Teaching
                                            Student Testing (1966 1980)   Use Educational Testing
                                            Student Transfers   Use Transfer Students
                                            Student Transportation
                                            Student Travel   Use Travel
                                            Student Unions
                                            Student Violence   Use Violence
                                            Student Volunteers
                                            Student Welfare
                                            Student Writing Models
                                            Students
                                    Able    Students (1966 1978)   Use Academically Gifted
                                 Absence    (Students)   Use Attendance
                                   Adult    Students
                                Advanced    Students
                          Asian American    Students
                                Attrition    (Students)   Use Student Attrition
                                 Average    Students (1967 1980)   Use Students
                                Bilingual    Students
                                   Black    Students
                               Caucasian    Students (1967 1980)   Use White Students
                        Classes (Groups of  Students)
                                 College    Students
                            College Bound   Students
       College Costs (Financing for Individual  Students)   Use Paying for College
             College Costs (Incurred by    Students)   Use Student Costs
                         College Transfer   Students
                               Commuting    Students
                             Continuation   Students
                          Course Selection  (Students)
                                     Day    Students
                                Deans of    Students
                                  Dental    Students
                    Desegregation (Disabled  Students)   Use Mainstreaming
                       Educational Goals of  Students   Use Student Educational Objectives
                  Educational Objectives of  Students   Use Student Educational Objectives
                     Elementary School    Students
                            Emancipated    Students (1975 1980)   Use Self Supporting Students
                                 Evening    Students
                             Exceptional    Students (1966 1978)   Use Exceptional Persons (1978 1994)
                                 Foreign    Students
                            Nonresident    Students (1967 1980) (Foreign)   Use Foreign Students
   Freshmen (1967 1980) (First Year College  Students)   Use College Freshmen
                               Full Time    Students
                                  Gifted    Students   Use Academically Gifted
                                Graduate    Students
                         Graduate Medical   Students
                            Handicapped    Students (1967 1980)
                               High Risk    Students
                             High School    Students
                        Hispanic American   Students
                                Resident    Students (1967 1980) (in District)   Use Residence Requirements
                                In State    Students
                                Resident    Students (1967 1980) (in State)   Use In State Students
                    Integration (Disabled   Students)   Use Mainstreaming
                           International    Students   Use Foreign Students
                           Junior College   Students (1969 1980)   Use Two Year College Students
                     Junior High School    Students
                                    Law    Students
```

Low Ability	Students (1967 1980)	
Lower Class	Students	
Majors	(Students)	
Maladjusted	Students	Use Student Adjustment
Married	Students	
Medical	Students	
Middle Class	Students	
Middle Class College	Students (1966 1980)	Use College Students and Middle Class Students
Middle School	Students	
Negro	Students (1966 1977)	Use Black Students
Noncollege Bound	Students	
Noncollege Preparatory	Students (1967 1980)	Use Noncollege Bound Students
Nontraditional	Students	
On Campus	Students	
Nonresident	Students (1967 1980) (Out of District)	Use Residence Requirements
Out of State	Students	
Nonresident	Students (1967 1980) (Out of State)	Use Out of State Students
Part Time	Students	
Pregnant	Students	
Premedical	Students	
Reentry	Students	
Research Papers	(Students)	
Secondary School	Students	
Self Supporting	Students	
Independent	Students (Self Supporting)	Use Self Supporting Students
Senior High School	Students	Use High School Students
Single	Students	
Special Needs	Students	
Step in Step out	Students	Use Stopouts
Superior	Students (1966 1978)	Use Academically Gifted
Talented	Students (1966 1980)	Use Talent
Teacher Expectations of	Students	
Terminal	Students	
Transfer	Students	
Two Year College	Students	
Undergraduate	Students	
University	Students	Use College Students
Unmarried	Students	Use Single Students
White	Students	
African	Studies	
African American	Studies (1969 1977)	Use Black Studies
American	Studies	
American Indian	Studies	
Area	Studies	
Asian	Studies	
Attrition (Research	Studies)	
Bird	Studies	Use Ornithology
Black	Studies	
Canadian	Studies	
Case	Studies	
Correlation	Studies	Use Correlation
Cross Cultural	Studies	
Cross Sectional	Studies	
Unified	Studies Curriculum	
Dialect	Studies	
Case	Studies (Education) (1966 1980)	Use Case Studies
Global	Studies Education	Use Global Education
World	Studies Education	Use Global Education
Ethnic	Studies	
Ethnic Group	Studies	Use Ethnic Studies
Facility Case	Studies	
Feasibility	Studies	
Field	Studies	
Fish	Studies	Use Ichthyology
Followup	Studies	
Future	Studies	Use Futures (of Society)
Insect	Studies	Use Entomology
Integration	Studies	
International	Studies	
Locational Skills (Social	Studies)	
Longitudinal	Studies	
Middle Eastern	Studies	
Mortality (Research	Studies)	Use Attrition (Research Studies)
Negro	Studies	Use Black Studies
Personality	Studies	
Developmental	Studies Programs	
Unified	Studies Programs (1966 1980)	Use Unified Studies Curriculum
Psychological	Studies	
Religion	Studies	
Religious	Studies	Use Religion Studies
Research	Studies	Use Research Reports
Retention	Studies (1966 1980)	Use Retention (Psychology)
Rock	Studies	Use Petrology
Schematic	Studies	
Shift	Studies	
Simulated	Studies	Use Simulation
Social	Studies	
Sociological	Studies	Use Social Science Research and Sociology
Statistical	Studies	
Social	Studies Units (1966 1980)	Use Social Studies and Units of Study
Urban	Studies	
Use	Studies	
User	Studies	Use Use Studies

```
                          Womens  Studies
                                  Studio Art
                             Art  Studio Courses    Use Studio Art
                                  Studio Floor Plans (1966 1980)
                      Television  Studios
                                  Study
                                  Study Abroad
                            Case  Study Approach (Teaching)    Use Case Method (Teaching Technique)
                                  Study Carrels    Use Carrels
                                  Study Centers
                      Curriculum  Study Centers
                          School  Study Centers (1966 1980)    Use Study Centers
                          Cinema  Study    Use Film Study
                       Community  Study
                     Comparative  Study    Use Comparative Analysis
                  Correspondence  Study
                                  Study Facilities
                            Film  Study
                        Graduate  Study
                          Parent  Study Groups    Use Parent Conferences
                                  Study Guides
                                  Study Habits
                                  Study Halls    Use Study Centers
   Higher Education as a Field of  Study    Use Postsecondary Education as a Field of Study
                            Home  Study
                                  Study Hours    Use Study
                     Independent  Study
                      Individual  Study (1966 1980)    Use Independent Study
               Institutional Self  Study    Use Self Evaluation (Groups)
             Organizational Self  Study    Use Self Evaluation (Groups)
  Postsecondary Education as a Field of  Study
                    College Work  Study Programs    Use Work Study Programs
                            Work  Study Programs
                                  Study Release Programs    Use Released Time
                                  Study Skills
                            Word  Study Skills
                        Units of  Study (Subject Fields) (1966 1977)    Use Units of Study
                                  Study Trips    Use Field Trips
                   Undergraduate  Study
                        Units of  Study
                            Work  Study    Use Work Study Programs
                                  Stunts and Tumbling    Use Tumbling
                                  Stuttering
                   Architectural  Style    Use Architectural Character
                       Cognitive  Style
                        Learning  Style    Use Cognitive Style
                            Life  Style
                      Perceptual  Style    Use Cognitive Style
                        Response  Style (Tests)
                 Alternative Life  Styles    Use Life Style
                        Language  Styles
                      Leadership  Styles
                       Linguistic  Styles    Use Language Styles
                        Literary  Styles
                        Teaching  Styles
                                  Subculture (1967 1980)    Use Subcultures
                           Black  Subculture    Use Black Culture
                                  Subcultures
                         Student  Subcultures
                                  Subemployment (1968 1980)    Use Underemployment
                                  Subject Access    Use Indexing
             Agricultural Mechanics  (Subject)    Use Agricultural Engineering
                                  Subject Disciplines    Use Intellectual Disciplines
                  Farm Mechanics  (Subject)    Use Agricultural Engineering
                  Units of Study  (Subject Fields) (1966 1977)    Use Units of Study
                                  Subject Headings    Use Subject Index Terms
                                  Subject Index Terms
                        Academic  Subjects    Use Academic Education
                        Business  Subjects (1967 1980)    Use Business Education
                         Elective  Subjects (1966 1977)    Use Elective Courses
                                  Subjunctive Mood    Use Verbs
                                  Subprofessionals (1967 1977)    Use Paraprofessional Personnel
                                  Subsidies    Use Grants
                                  Substance Abuse
                           Toxic  Substances    Use Poisons
                                  Substitute Teachers
                                  Substitution Drills
                                  Subtraction
                                  Suburban Environment
                                  Suburban Housing
                        Urban to  Suburban Migration
                                  Suburban Problems
                                  Suburban Schools
                                  Suburban Youth
                                  Suburbs
                     Inner Speech  (Subvocal)
                                  Success
                        Academic  Success    Use Academic Achievement
                                  Success Avoidance    Use Fear of Success
                                  Success Factors (1968 1980)    Use Success
                         Fear of  Success
                     Occupational  Succession    Use Occupational Mobility
                                  Sudden Infant Death Syndrome
```

Suffixes
Suggestopedia
Suicide
Summated Rating Scales   Use Likert Scales
Summative Evaluation
Summer Institutes (1967 1980)   Use Institutes (Training Programs) and Summer Programs
Summer Olympic Games   Use Olympic Games
Summer Programs
Summer Schools
Summer Science Programs
Summer Session   Use Summer Schools
Summer Workshops (1966 1980)   Use Summer Programs and Workshops
Superconductors
Electronic   Superhighway   Use Internet
Information   Superhighway   Use Internet
Superintendent Role (1966 1980)   Use Superintendents
Assistant   Superintendent Role (1966 1980)
Superintendents
Assistant   Superintendents   Use Superintendents
School   Superintendents (1966 1980)   Use Superintendents
Superior Students (1966 1978)   Use Academically Gifted
Supermarkets   Use Food Stores
Supervised Farm Practice (1966 1990)   Use Supervised Occupational Experience (Agriculture)
Supervised Occupational Experience (Agriculture)
Supervising Teachers   Use Cooperating Teachers
Supervision
Clinical   Supervision (of Teachers)
Practicum   Supervision
School   Supervision
Science   Supervision
Teacher   Supervision
Supervisor Qualifications
Supervisor Training   Use Supervisory Training
Supervisors
College   Supervisors (1967 1980)   Use Student Teacher Supervisors
Elementary School   Supervisors (1966 1980)   Use School Supervision
High School   Supervisors (1966 1980)   Use School Supervision
Resident   Supervisors   Use Resident Advisers
State   Supervisors
State Foreign Language   Supervisors (1967 1980)   Use Second Language Instruction and State Supervisors
Student Teacher   Supervisors
Supervisory Activities (1968 1980)   Use Supervision
Supervisory Methods
Supervisory Training
Supplementary Education
Supplementary Educational Centers (1966 1980)   Use Education Service Centers and Supplementary Education
Supplementary Reading Materials
Supplementary Textbooks (1967 1980)   Use Supplementary Reading Materials and Textbooks
Supplies
Agricultural   Supplies
Farm   Supplies   Use Agricultural Supplies
Ground Water   Supplies   Use Groundwater
Office   Supplies   Use Supplies
School   Supplies   Use Supplies
Supply and Demand
Teacher   Supply and Demand
Educational   Supply
Farm Labor   Supply (1966 1980)   Use Farm Labor and Labor Supply
Labor   Supply
Agricultural   Supply Occupations
Supply of Education   Use Educational Supply
Supply of Labor   Use Labor Supply
Water   Supply   Use Water Resources
Child   Support
Community   Support
Corporate   Support
Economic   Support   Use Financial Support
Educational   Support   Use Educational Finance
Financial   Support
Support Groups (Human Services)   Use Social Support Groups
Social   Support Groups
Support Networks (Personal Assistance)   Use Social Support Groups
Private Financial   Support
Public   Support
School   Support
State   Support   Use State Aid
State Federal   Support (1966 1977)   Use State Federal Aid
Decision   Support Systems
Group Decision   Support Systems   Use Decision Support Systems and Group Dynamics
Support Systems (Services)   Use Services
Tax   Support (1966 1980)   Use Tax Allocation
Supported Competitive Employment   Use Supported Employment
Employer   Supported Day Care
Supported Employment
Air   Supported Structures (1972 1980)   Use Air Structures
Supported Work Programs   Use Supported Employment
Independent Students (Self   Supporting)   Use Self Supporting Students
Self   Supporting Students
Suppressor Variables
Suprasegmental Morphemes   Use Intonation
Suprasegmental Phonemes   Use Suprasegmentals
Suprasegmentals
Supreme Court Litigation (1966 1980)

	Supreme Courts (1966 1980)
State	Supreme Courts Use State Courts
	Surface Area Use Area
	Surface Finishing Use Finishing
	Surface Structure
	Surfing
Dental	Surgeons Use Dentists
	Surgery
Operations	(Surgery) Use Surgery
	Surgical Technicians
	Surrealism
	Survey Courses Use Introductory Courses
	Surveys
Community	Surveys
Educational	Surveys Use School Surveys
Employment	Surveys Use Occupational Surveys
Graduate	Surveys
Job Vacancy	Surveys Use Occupational Surveys
Labor Force	Surveys Use Occupational Surveys
Library	Surveys
Literature	Surveys Use Literature Reviews
Mail	Surveys
National	Surveys
Occupational	Surveys
Provincial	Surveys Use State Surveys
School	Surveys
State	Surveys
Statistical	Surveys
Student	Surveys
Teacher	Surveys
Telephone	Surveys
Television	Surveys
Institutional	Survival
	Survival Literacy Use Functional Literacy
	Survival Reading Skills Use Functional Reading
	Survival Skills (Daily Living) Use Daily Living Skills
	Suspension
In School	Suspension
	Sustainable Development
	Sustained Silent Reading
	Susu
	Suzuki Method
	Swahili
	Swamps Use Wetlands
	Swazi Use Siswati
	Swedish
	Swimming
	Swimming Pools
	Swing Music Use Jazz
	Switching (Language) Use Code Switching (Language)
Code	Switching (Language)
	Syllabi Use Course Descriptions
Functional Notional	Syllabi Use Notional Functional Syllabi
Notional Functional	Syllabi
State	Syllabi Use State Curriculum Guides
	Syllables
	Symbolic Coding Use Coding
	Symbolic Language
	Symbolic Learning
	Symbolic Logic Use Mathematical Logic
	Symbolic Play Use Pretend Play
	Symbolism
	Symbols (Literary)
	Symbols (Mathematics)
Orthographic	Symbols
	Symmetry
	Symphony Orchestras Use Orchestras
	Symposia (1967 1980) Use Conferences
	Symptoms (Individual Disorders)
	Synchronic Linguistics (1967 1980) Use Descriptive Linguistics
Acquired Immune Deficiency	Syndrome
Downs	Syndrome
Fetal Alcohol	Syndrome
Post Traumatic Stress	Syndrome Use Posttraumatic Stress Disorder
Sudden Infant Death	Syndrome
	Syntactic Borrowing Use Linguistic Borrowing
	Syntax
	Synthesis
Chemical	Synthesis Use Chemical Reactions
Stimulus	Synthesis Use Patterned Responses
Speech	Synthesizers
Text to Speech	Synthesizers Use Speech Synthesizers
Voice	Synthesizers Use Speech Synthesizers
	Synthetic Speech Use Artificial Speech
	Syphilis Use Venereal Diseases
Cardiovascular	System
Circulatory	System Use Cardiovascular System
Computer	System Design
Computer	System Development Use Computer System Design
Track	System (Education)
Free Enterprise	System
Infant Schools (British Primary	System) Use British Infant Schools
Judicial	System Use Courts

Juvenile Justice	System	Use Juvenile Justice
Metric	System	
Muscular	System	
Musculoskeletal	System	
Nongraded	System (1966 1980)	Use Nongraded Instructional Grouping
Nongraded Primary	System (1966 1980)	Use Nongraded Instructional Grouping
Quarter	System	
Semester	System	
Skeletal	System	
Skeletomuscular	System	Use Musculoskeletal System
Solar	System	
Trimester	System	
Vascular	System	Use Cardiovascular System
	Systematic Desensitization	Use Desensitization
Alarm	Systems	
Security	Systems (Alarms)	Use Alarm Systems
	Systems Analysis	
	Systems Analysts	
	Systems Approach	
Arithmetic	Systems	Use Number Systems
Augmentative Communication	Systems	Use Augmentative and Alternative Communication
Authoring	Systems	Use Authoring Aids (Programming)
	Systems Building	
Building	Systems	
Career Information	Systems	
Career Information Delivery	Systems	Use Career Information Systems
Central Sound	Systems (1966 1980)	Use Audio Equipment
Communications	Systems	Use Communications
Component	Systems	Use Building Systems
Component Building	Systems (1968 1976)	Use Building Systems
Computer Based Integrated Learning	Systems	Use Integrated Learning Systems
Computer Based Message	Systems	Use Electronic Mail
Front End	Systems (Computers)	Use Gateway Systems
Integrated Instructional	Systems (Computers)	Use Integrated Learning Systems
	Systems Concepts (1966 1980)	
County School	Systems (1967 1980)	Use County School Districts
Interface	Systems (Cross Database)	Use Gateway Systems
Database Management	Systems	
Decentralized Library	Systems (1968 1980)	Use Decentralization and Library Networks
Decision Support	Systems	
Delivery	Systems	
	Systems Development	
Dial Access Information	Systems	
Alternative Communication	Systems (Disabled)	Use Augmentative and Alternative Communication
Display	Systems	
Electric	Systems	Use Electrical Systems
Electrical	Systems	
Electronic Communications	Systems	Use Telecommunications
Expert	Systems	
Facsimile Communication	Systems (1968 1980)	Use Facsimile Transmission
File Management	Systems	Use Database Management Systems
Filing	Systems	Use Information Storage
Gateway	Systems	
Group Decision Support	Systems	Use Decision Support Systems and Group Dynamics
Incentive	Systems (1967 1980)	Use Incentives
Information	Systems	
Instructional	Systems	
Integrated Automated Library	Systems	Use Integrated Library Systems
Integrated Learning	Systems	
Integrated Library	Systems	
Intelligent CAI	Systems	Use Intelligent Tutoring Systems
Intelligent Tutoring	Systems	
Knowledge Based	Systems	Use Expert Systems
Approximative	Systems (Language Learning)	Use Interlanguage
Turnkey	Systems (Libraries)	Use Integrated Library Systems
Library	Systems	Use Library Networks
Loop Induction	Systems	
Man Machine	Systems	
Management	Systems	
Management Information	Systems	
Microwave Relay	Systems (1971 1980)	Use Telecommunications
Monetary	Systems	
Money	Systems (1966 1980)	Use Monetary Systems
N C	Systems	Use Numerical Control
Natural Language Understanding	Systems	Use Natural Language Processing
Navigation (Information	Systems)	
Number	Systems	
Occupational Information	Systems	Use Career Information Systems
On Line	Systems (1971 1980)	Use Online Systems
Online	Systems	
Interactive	Systems (Online)	Use Online Systems
Power Transfer	Systems	Use Kinetics
Property Control	Systems	Use Property Accounting
Public School	Systems (1966 1980)	Use Public Schools and School Districts
Rural School	Systems (1966 1980)	Use Rural Schools and School Districts
School	Systems (1966 1980)	Use School Districts
Support	Systems (Services)	Use Services
Social	Systems	
Sound	Systems	Use Audio Equipment
Structural Building	Systems	
Teaching	Systems	Use Teaching Methods
Telephone Communication	Systems (1967 1980)	Use Telephone Communications Systems
Telephone Communications	Systems	

	Systems Theory Use Systems Approach
Functional	Systems Theory Use Systems Analysis
Video	Systems Use Video Equipment
Video Cassette	Systems (1971 1980) Use Videotape Cassettes
Writing	Systems Use Written Language
Human	T Cell Lymphotropic Virus Type 3 Use Acquired Immune Deficiency Syndrome
	T Groups (1967 1980) Use Sensitivity Training
	Table Tennis
	Tables (Data)
Expectancy	Tables
Incest	Taboo Use Incest
Data	Tabulation Use Data Processing
	Tachistoscopes
	Tackboards Use Bulletin Boards
	Tactile Adaptation
	Tactile Materials Use Manipulative Materials
	Tactile Stimuli
	Tactual Perception
	Tactual Stimuli Use Tactile Stimuli
	Tactual Visual Tests
	Tadjik Persian Use Tajik
	Tagalog
	Tagmemic Analysis
	Tailored Testing Use Adaptive Testing
Computerized	Tailored Testing Use Adaptive Testing and Computer Assisted Testing
	Tailors Use Needle Trades
	Tajik
Perspective	Taking
Role	Taking Use Perspective Taking
Test	Taking Skills Use Test Wiseness
Test	Taking Strategies Use Test Wiseness
	Talent
Artistic	Talent Use Talent
	Talent Development
	Talent Identification
	Talent Preservation Use Talent Development
	Talent Tests Use Aptitude Tests
	Talent Utilization (1966 1980)
	Talented Students (1966 1980) Use Talent
Vocational	Talents Use Vocational Aptitude
	Tales
Fairy	Tales
Parent	Talk Use Caregiver Speech and Parent Child Relationship
	Talking Books
	Talks Use Speeches
	Tamil
	Taoism
Magnetic	Tape Cartridges Use Magnetic Tape Cassettes
Magnetic	Tape Cassette Recorders (1970 1980) Use Magnetic Tape Cassettes and Tape Recorders
Cassettes	(Tape) Use Magnetic Tape Cassettes
Magnetic	Tape Cassettes
	Tape Recorders
	Tape Recordings
Sound	Tape Recordings Use Audiotape Recordings
Video	Tape Recordings (1966 1978) Use Videotape Recordings
Master	Tapes (Audio) (1968 1980) Use Audiotape Recordings
Computer	Tapes Use Computer Storage Devices and Magnetic Tapes
Language	Tapes Use Audiotape Recordings
Magnetic	Tapes
	Taremiut Use Inupiaq
	Task Analysis
	Task Difficulty Use Difficulty Level
	Task Performance (1966 1980)
Time on	Task
Developmental	Tasks
Piagetian	Tasks Use Developmental Tasks and Piagetian Theory
	Taste (Aesthetics) Use Aesthetic Values
	Tatar
Less Commonly	Taught Languages Use Uncommonly Taught Languages
Uncommonly	Taught Languages
Ad Valorem	Tax Use Property Taxes
	Tax Allocation
	Tax Credits
Tuition	Tax Credits Use Tax Credits and Tuition
	Tax Deductions
	Tax Effort
	Tax Equity (Education) Use Educational Equity (Finance)
Negative Income	Tax Use Guaranteed Income
	Tax Rates
	Tax Reform Use Finance Reform
	Tax Support (1966 1980) Use Tax Allocation
	Taxes
Property	Taxes
School	Taxes
	Taxonomy (1967 1980) Use Classification
Miscue	Taxonomy Use Miscue Analysis
	Teacher Administrator Relationship
	Teacher Advancement Use Teacher Promotion
	Teacher Aides
Bilingual	Teacher Aides
	Teacher Alienation
	Teacher Associations
	Teacher Attendance

```
                            Teacher Attitudes
                 Student    Teacher Attitudes
                            Teacher Attrition    Use Faculty Mobility
                            Teacher Autonomy    Use Professional Autonomy
                            Teacher Background
                            Teacher Behavior
                            Teacher Burnout
                            Teacher Centers
                            Teacher Certificates (1967 1980)    Use Teacher Certification
                            Teacher Certification
             Alternative    Teacher Certification
                National    Teacher Certification
                            Teacher Characteristics
                            Teacher Collaboration
                            Teacher College Relationship    Use Faculty College Relationship
                            Teacher Competencies
                            Teacher Competency Testing
                  Parent    Teacher Conferences
                            Teacher Cooperation    Use Teacher Collaboration
               Counselor    Teacher Cooperation
                Librarian   Teacher Cooperation
                  Parent    Teacher Cooperation
                            Teacher Coordinators    Use Instructor Coordinators
                            Teacher Counselor Cooperation    Use Counselor Teacher Cooperation
                            Teacher Desegregation    Use Teacher Integration
                            Teacher Developed Materials
                            Teacher Directed Practice    Use Teacher Guidance
                            Teacher Discipline
                            Teacher Dismissal
                            Teacher Distribution
                            Teacher Education
                            Teacher Education Centers    Use Teacher Centers
          Clinical Schools  (Teacher Education)    Use Professional Development Schools
        Competency Based    Teacher Education
       Consequence Based    Teacher Education    Use Competency Based Teacher Education
      Criterion Referenced  Teacher Education    Use Competency Based Teacher Education
                            Teacher Education Curriculum
                 English    Teacher Education
 Extended Degree Programs   (Teacher Education)    Use Extended Teacher Education Programs
                Inservice   Teacher Education
                            Teacher Education Knowledge Base    Use Knowledge Base for Teaching
          Output Oriented   Teacher Education    Use Competency Based Teacher Education
       Performance Based    Teacher Education (1972 1980)    Use Competency Based Teacher Education
               Preservice   Teacher Education
      Proficiency Based     Teacher Education    Use Competency Based Teacher Education
                            Teacher Education Programs
                Extended    Teacher Education Programs
                            Teacher Educator Education
                            Teacher Educators
                            Teacher Effectiveness
                            Teacher Employment
                            Teacher Employment Benefits
                            Teacher Empowerment
                            Teacher Evaluation
                 Student    Teacher Evaluation
                            Teacher Exchange Programs
                            Teacher Expectations of Students
                            Teacher Experience (1966 1974)    Use Teaching Experience
                            Teacher Guidance
                            Teacher Guides    Use Teaching Guides
                            Teacher Housing
                            Teacher Improvement
                            Teacher Induction    Use Teacher Orientation
                Beginning   Teacher Induction
     Entry Year Assistance  (Teacher Induction)    Use Beginning Teacher Induction
                            Teacher Influence
                            Teacher Integration
                 Student    Teacher Interaction    Use Teacher Student Relationship
                            Teacher Interns
                            Teacher Knowledge Base    Use Knowledge Base for Teaching
                            Teacher Librarian Cooperation    Use Librarian Teacher Cooperation
                            Teacher Load    Use Teaching Load
                            Teacher Made Tests
                            Teacher Militancy
                            Teacher Mobility    Use Faculty Mobility
                            Teacher Morale
                            Teacher Motivation
                            Teacher Nurses (1966 1980)    Use Nurses
                            Teacher Opinions    Use Teacher Attitudes
                            Teacher Organizations    Use Teacher Associations
                            Teacher Orientation
               Parent as a  Teacher    Use Parents as Teachers
                            Teacher Parent Conferences    Use Parent Teacher Conferences
                            Teacher Parent Cooperation    Use Parent Teacher Cooperation
                            Teacher Participation
      Student Evaluation of  Teacher Performance
                            Teacher Persistence
                            Teacher Placement
                            Teacher Preparation    Use Teacher Education
                Five Year    Teacher Preparation Programs    Use Extended Teacher Education Programs
                            Teacher Programs (1966 1980)    Use Teacher Education Programs
                            Teacher Promotion
                            Teacher Qualifications
```

	Teacher Quality Use Teacher Effectiveness
	Teacher Rating (1966 1977) Use Teacher Evaluation
Student	Teacher Ratio (1966 1984) Use Teacher Student Ratio
	Teacher Reaction Use Teacher Response
	Teacher Recruitment
Administrator	Teacher Relationship Use Teacher Administrator Relationship
Student	Teacher Relationship (1966 1984) Use Teacher Student Relationship
	Teacher Researchers
	Teacher Response
	Teacher Responsibility
	Teacher Retirement
	Teacher Rights
	Teacher Role
Senior	Teacher Role (1966 1980) Use Master Teachers and Teacher Role
	Teacher Salaries
One	Teacher Schools
	Teacher Selection
	Teacher Seminars (1966 1980) Use Teacher Workshops
	Teacher Shortage
	Teacher Skills Use Teaching Skills
	Teacher Stereotypes
	Teacher Strikes
	Teacher Student Interaction Use Teacher Student Relationship
	Teacher Student Ratio
	Teacher Student Relationship
	Teacher Supervision
Student	Teacher Supervisors
	Teacher Supply and Demand
	Teacher Surveys
	Teacher Testing (for Competency) Use Teacher Competency Testing
	Teacher Trainers Use Teacher Educators
	Teacher Training Use Teacher Education
	Teacher Training Films Use Protocol Materials
Inservice	Teacher Training Use Inservice Teacher Education
	Teacher Transfer
	Teacher Travel Use Travel
	Teacher Turnover Use Faculty Mobility
	Teacher Unions Use Unions
	Teacher Wait Time Use Wait Time
	Teacher Welfare
	Teacher Workshops
	Teachers
Absence	(Teachers) Use Employee Absenteeism and Teacher Attendance
Art	Teachers
	Teachers as Researchers Use Teacher Researchers
Beginning	Teachers
Bilingual	Teachers
Black	Teachers
Business	Teachers Use Business Education Teachers
Business Education	Teachers
Chemistry	Teachers (1967 1980) Use Chemistry and Science Teachers
Circuit	Teachers Use Itinerant Teachers
Clinical Supervision (of	Teachers)
Coaching	Teachers (1966 1974) Use Tutors
Collaborative	Teachers Use Teacher Collaboration
College	Teachers (1967 1980) Use College Faculty
	Teachers Colleges (1966 1980) Use Schools of Education
Cooperating	Teachers
Disabled	Teachers Use Teachers with Disabilities
Distributive Education	Teachers
Elementary School	Teachers
English	Teachers
First Year	Teachers Use Beginning Teachers
FLES	Teachers (1967 1980) Use FLES and Language Teachers
Foreign Language	Teachers Use Language Teachers
Former	Teachers (1967 1980)
Full Time	Teachers Use Full Time Faculty
Gifted	Teachers Use Gifted
High School	Teachers Use Secondary School Teachers
Home Economics	Teachers
Homebound	Teachers (1966 1980) Use Itinerant Teachers
Industrial Arts	Teachers
Intern	Teachers Use Teacher Interns
Itinerant	Teachers
Junior High School	Teachers Use Secondary School Teachers
Kindergarten	Teachers Use Preschool Teachers
Language	Teachers
Lay	Teachers
Master	Teachers
Mathematics	Teachers
Methods	Teachers
Middle School	Teachers
Minority Group	Teachers
Misassignment of	Teachers
Misplaced	Teachers Use Misassignment of Teachers
Music	Teachers
Negro	Teachers (1966 1977) Use Black Teachers
Nontenured	Teachers Use Nontenured Faculty
Nun	Teachers (1966 1980) Use Nuns
Parents as	Teachers
Part Time	Teachers (1967 1980) Use Part Time Faculty
Partnership	Teachers
Physical Education	Teachers

Physics Teachers (1967 1980)   Use Physics and Science Teachers
Prekindergarten Teachers   Use Preschool Teachers
Preschool Teachers
Preservice Teachers
Probationary Teachers   Use Probationary Period
Prospective Teachers   Use Preservice Teachers
Public School Teachers
Reading Teachers
Relief Teachers   Use Substitute Teachers
Remedial Teachers
Resource Teachers
Retired Teachers   Use Teacher Retirement
Science Teachers
Second Language Teachers   Use Language Teachers
Secondary School Teachers
Special Teachers   Use Specialists
Special Education Teachers
Student Teachers
Substitute Teachers
Supervising Teachers   Use Cooperating Teachers
Television Teachers
Tenured Teachers   Use Tenured Faculty
Trade and Industrial Teachers
Traveling Teachers   Use Itinerant Teachers
Visiting Teachers   Use Itinerant Teachers
Vocational Agriculture Teachers (1967 1980)   Use Agricultural Education and Vocational Education Teachers
Vocational Education Teachers
Teachers with Disabilities
Women Teachers (1967 1980)   Use Women Faculty
Writing Teachers
Teaching (1966 1980)
Mechanical Teaching Aids (1966 1980)   Use Educational Media
Initial Teaching Alphabet
Alternative Certification (Teaching)   Use Alternative Teacher Certification
Teaching Alternatives   Use Nontraditional Education
Teaching Areas   Use Curriculum
Teaching Assignment (1966 1980)
Teaching Assistants
Teaching Benefits (1966 1980)   Use Teacher Employment Benefits
Block Time Teaching   Use Block Scheduling
Case Study Approach (Teaching)   Use Case Method (Teaching Technique)
Science Teaching Centers
Teaching Certificates   Use Teacher Certification
Collaborative Teaching   Use Team Teaching
College Teaching   Use College Instruction
Concept Teaching
Teaching Conditions
Cooperative Teaching (1966 1980)   Use Team Teaching
Teaching Core   Use Core Curriculum
Creative Teaching
Cross Age Teaching
Diagnostic Teaching
Dropout Teaching (1966 1980)   Use Dropout Programs
Effective Teaching (1966 1980)   Use Teacher Effectiveness
Episode Teaching (1967 1980)
Teaching Experience
Inservice Teaching Experience   Use Teaching Experience
Preservice Teaching Experience   Use Teaching Experience
Experimental Teaching
Teaching Facilities   Use Educational Facilities
Field Teaching   Use Field Instruction
Foreign Language Teaching   Use Second Language Instruction
Teaching Freedom   Use Academic Freedom
Teaching Guides
Clinical Teaching (Health Professions)
Teaching Hospitals
University Teaching Hospitals   Use Teaching Hospitals
Clinical Teaching (Individualized Instruction)   Use Individualized Instruction
Teaching Innovations   Use Instructional Innovation
Inservice Teaching (1966 1980)   Use Inservice Education and Teaching (Occupation)
Urban Teaching Interns   Use Teacher Interns and Urban Teaching
Teaching Knowledge Base   Use Knowledge Base for Teaching
Knowledge Base for Teaching
Teaching Language   Use Language of Instruction
Teaching Load
Teaching Machines
Master of Arts in Teaching   Use Masters Degrees
Master of Arts in College Teaching   Use Masters Degrees
Master of Science in Teaching   Use Masters Degrees
Teaching Materials   Use Instructional Materials
Integrated Teaching Method   Use Integrated Activities and Teaching Methods
Teaching Methods
Teaching Models
National Certification (Teaching)   Use National Teacher Certification
Teaching (Occupation)
Off Campus Student Teaching   Use Student Teaching
Part Time Teaching (1967 1980)   Use Part Time Faculty
Peer Teaching
Teaching Persistence   Use Teacher Persistence
Departmental Teaching Plans (1968 1980)   Use Departments
Practice Teaching   Use Student Teaching
Teaching Practices   Use Teaching Methods
Precision Teaching

```
           Prescriptive  Teaching   Use Diagnostic Teaching
                         Teaching Procedures (1966 1980)   Use Teaching Methods
                         Teaching (Process)   Use Instruction
                         Teaching Profession   Use Teaching (Occupation)
                         Teaching Programs (1966 1980)
                         Teaching Quality (1966 1980)   Use Teacher Effectiveness
            Reciprocal   Teaching
            Reflective   Teaching
                         Teaching Resources   Use Educational Resources
                  Self   Teaching   Use Independent Study
                         Teaching Skills
               Student   Teaching
                         Teaching Styles
                         Teaching Systems   Use Teaching Methods
                  Team   Teaching
            Team Leader  (Teaching) (1966 1980)   Use Leaders and Team Teaching
           Case Method   (Teaching Technique)
            Discussion   (Teaching Technique)
                         Teaching Techniques (1966 1980)   Use Teaching Methods
                 Urban   Teaching
                         Team Administration (1967 1980)   Use Management Teams
                         Team Counseling   Use Cocounseling
                         Team Handball
                         Team Leader (Teaching) (1966 1980)   Use Leaders and Team Teaching
                         Team Management   Use Management Teams
                         Team Sports
                         Team Teaching
                         Team Training
        Administrative   Teams   Use Management Teams
          Instructional  Teams   Use Team Teaching
            Management   Teams
                         Teamwork
                         Tech Prep
         Two Plus Two    Tech Prep Associate Degrees   Use Associate Degrees and Tech Prep
         Two Plus Two    Tech Prep   Use Tech Prep
                         Technical Assistance
          International   Technical Assistance   Use International Programs and Technical Assistance
               Library   Technical Assistants   Use Library Technicians
                         Technical Education
                         Technical Education Directors   Use Vocational Directors
                         Technical High Schools   Use Vocational High Schools
                         Technical Illustration
                         Technical Information   Use Scientific and Technical Information
        Scientific and   Technical Information
                         Technical Institutes
                         Technical Instruction   Use Technical Education
                         Technical Libraries   Use Science Libraries
                         Technical Mathematics
                         Technical Occupations
                         Technical Processes (Libraries)   Use Library Technical Processes
               Library   Technical Processes
                         Technical Reports (1968 1980)   Use Research Reports
                         Technical Schools   Use Vocational Schools
                         Technical Services (Libraries)   Use Library Technical Processes
                         Technical Writing
                         Technicians   Use Paraprofessional Personnel
          Agricultural   Technicians
      Appliance Service  Technicians (1967 1980)   Use Appliance Repair
   Biomedical Equipment  Technicians   Use Medical Laboratory Assistants
              Chemical   Technicians
                Dental   Technicians
      Dental Laboratory  Technicians   Use Dental Technicians
               Dietary   Technicians   Use Dietitians
             Electrical  Technicians   Use Electronic Technicians
            Electronic   Technicians
      Emergency Medical  Technicians
    Engine Development   Technicians   Use Mechanical Design Technicians
           Engineering   Technicians
         Environmental   Technicians
        Hospital Record  Technicians   Use Medical Record Technicians
        Instrumentation  Technicians
               Library   Technicians
                Marine   Technicians
      Mechanical Design  Technicians
               Medical   Technicians   Use Medical Laboratory Assistants
        Medical Record   Technicians
           Metallurgical Technicians
   Nuclear Power Plant   Technicians
        Operating Room   Technicians   Use Surgical Technicians
            Orthodontic  Technicians   Use Dental Technicians
            Production   Technicians
  Propulsion Development Technicians   Use Mechanical Design Technicians
            Psychiatric  Technicians   Use Psychiatric Aides
              Sanitary   Technicians   Use Environmental Technicians
               Surgical  Technicians
 Case Method (Teaching   Technique)
                Delphi   Technique
  Discussion (Teaching   Technique)
         Forced Choice   Technique
                  JAN    Technique   Use Judgment Analysis Technique
     Judgment Analysis   Technique
         Nominal Group   Technique
                    Q    Technique   Use Q Methodology
```

```
                          Techniques (1966 1974)    Use Methods
             Classroom    Techniques
 Classroom Observation    Techniques
                 Cloze    Techniques    Use Cloze Procedure
            Counseling    Techniques
             Culturing    Techniques
            Evaluation    Techniques (1966 1974)    Use Evaluation Methods
            Laboratory    Techniques (1967 1980)
         Manufacturing    Techniques    Use Manufacturing
           Measurement    Techniques
            Motivation    Techniques
 Multitrait Multimethod    Techniques
                 Music    Techniques
            Production    Techniques
           Questioning    Techniques
            Sociometric    Techniques
              Teaching    Techniques (1966 1980)    Use Teaching Methods
               Testing    Techniques    Use Testing
              Training    Techniques (1967 1980)    Use Training Methods
                          Technological Advancement
                          Technological Education    Use Technology Education
                          Technological Information    Use Scientific and Technical Information
                          Technological Literacy
                          Technological Programs    Use Science Programs
                          Technological Unemployment    Use Structural Unemployment
               Medical    Technologists
     Medical Laboratory    Technologists    Use Medical Technologists
       Nuclear Medicine    Technologists    Use Radiologic Technologists
      Radiation Therapy    Technologists    Use Radiologic Technologists
             Radiologic    Technologists
                 X Ray    Technologists    Use Radiologic Technologists
                          Technology
             Aerospace    Technology
               Science    Technology and Society    Use Science and Society
           Appropriate    Technology
              Aviation    Technology
            Behavioral    Technology    Use Behavioral Sciences
              Computer    Technology    Use Computers
                          Technology Education
             Industrial    Technology Education    Use Technology Education
           Educational    Technology
       Electromechanical    Technology
                Energy    Technology    Use Power Technology
           Engineering    Technology
  English for Science and    Technology
                  High    Technology    Use Technological Advancement
      Human Performance    Technology    Use Performance Technology
             Industrial    Technology (1969 1980)    Use Industry and Technology
           Information    Technology
          Instructional    Technology (1966 1978)    Use Educational Technology
            Laboratory    Technology
            Science and    Technology Libraries    Use Science Libraries
              Livestock    Technology    Use Animal Husbandry
            Mass Media    Technology    Use Communications and Mass Media
                 Media    Technology (1968 1980)    Use Communications
               Nuclear    Technology
           Performance    Technology
                 Power    Technology
                 Radio    Technology (1967 1980)    Use Radio
          Sts (Science    Technology Society)    Use Science and Society
            Television    Technology    Use Television
                          Technology Transfer
                  Plate    Tectonics
                          Teenagers (1966 1980)    Use Adolescents
                          TEFL    Use English (Second Language)
                          Telecommunication (1970 1980)    Use Telecommunications
                          Telecommunications
                          Teleconferencing
                          Telecourses
                          Telefacsimile    Use Facsimile Transmission
                          Telefax    Use Facsimile Transmission
                          Telegraphic Materials
                          Telegu    Use Telugu
                          Telephone Communication Systems (1967 1980)    Use Telephone Communications Systems
                          Telephone Communications Industry
                          Telephone Communications Systems
                          Telephone Crisis Services    Use Hotlines (Public)
                          Telephone Instruction
                          Telephone Solicitation Programs    Use Phonathons
                          Telephone Surveys
                          Telephone Usage Instruction
                          Telephones    Use Telephone Communications Systems
                          Teletext    Use Videotex
                          Televised Instruction (1966 1974)    Use Educational Television
                          Television
              Airborne    Television (1966 1980)    Use Television
             Broadcast    Television
                 Cable    Television
             Childrens    Television
          Closed Circuit    Television
                 Color    Television (1969 1980)    Use Color and Television
            Commercial    Television
                          Television Commercials
```

	Television Curriculum
Educational	Television
	Television Equipment Use Video Equipment
Fixed Service	Television (1969 1980) Use Educational Television
Instructional	Television (1966 1974) Use Educational Television
Instructor Centered	Television (1966 1980) Use Educational Television
Interactive	Television
Interactive Cable	Television Use Interactive Television
Interactive Satellite	Television Use Interactive Television
	Television Journalism Use Broadcast Journalism
	Television Lecturers Use Television Teachers
	Television Lighting
	Television Lights (1966 1980) Use Television Lighting
Open Circuit	Television (1966 1980) Use Broadcast Television
Overhead	Television (1966 1980) Use Television
	Television Programming Use Programming (Broadcast)
Public	Television
	Television Radio Repairers
Radio	Television Repairers Use Television Radio Repairers
	Television Repairmen (1968 1980) Use Television Radio Repairers
	Television Research
	Television Role Use Mass Media Role and Television
	Television Studios
	Television Surveys
	Television Teachers
	Television Technology Use Television
Two Way	Television Use Interactive Television
	Television Use Use Mass Media Use and Television Viewing
	Television Viewing
Story	Telling
	Telugu
	Temperament Use Personality
	Temperate Rainforests Use Rainforests
	Temperature
	Tempo (Cognition) Use Conceptual Tempo
Cognitive	Tempo Use Conceptual Tempo
Conceptual	Tempo
	Tempo (Music)
	Temporal Perspective Use Time Perspective
	Temporary Employment
	Temporary Facilities Use Relocatable Facilities
	Temporary Help Services Use Employment Services and Temporary Employment
Resistance to	Temptation
Withdrawal	Tendencies (Psychology) (1966 1980) Use Withdrawal (Psychology)
	TENES Use English (Second Language)
	TENL (1968 1980)
	Tennis
Table	Tennis
	Tenpins Use Bowling
	Tenses (Grammar)
Community	Tensions Use Community Problems
	Tenure
Job	Tenure (1967 1978) Use Tenure
	Tenured Faculty
	Tenured Teachers Use Tenured Faculty
Long	Term Care
Long	Term Memory
Short	Term Memory
	Term Papers Use Research Papers (Students)
Long	Term Planning Use Long Range Planning
Hospices	(Terminal Care)
	Terminal Education
	Terminal Illness
	Terminal Students
Cathode Ray Tube	Terminals Use Video Display Terminals
Computer	Terminals
Video Display	Terminals
	Termination of Programs Use Program Termination
	Termination of Treatment
Program	Termination
	Terminology Use Vocabulary
Kinship	Terminology
Index	Terms Use Subject Index Terms
Subject Index	Terms
	Terrorism
	Tertiary Education Use Postsecondary Education
	TESL Use English (Second Language)
	TESOL Use English (Second Language)
	Test Abuse Use Test Use
	Test Administration Use Testing
	Test Administrators Use Examiners
	Test Analysis Use Test Theory
	Test Anxiety
	Test Bias
	Test Books Use Tests
	Test Characteristics (Physical) Use Test Format
	Test Coaching
	Test Construction
	Test Content
	Test Design Use Test Construction
	Test Format
	Test Interpretation
	Test Items

	Test Length
	Test Manuals
	Test Norms
	Test Reliability
	Test Results
	Test Reviews
	Test Score Decline
	Test Scores Use Scores
	Test Scoring Machines
	Test Selection
	Test Taking Skills Use Test Wiseness
	Test Taking Strategies Use Test Wiseness
	Test Theory
	Test Type Use Test Format
	Test Use
	Test Validity
	Test Wiseness
	Testing
Adaptive	Testing
Alternatives to Standardized	Testing Use Alternative Assessment
Comparative	Testing
Computer Assisted	Testing
Computerized Adaptive	Testing Use Adaptive Testing and Computer Assisted Testing
Computerized Tailored	Testing Use Adaptive Testing and Computer Assisted Testing
Confidence	Testing
Drug Use	Testing
Educational	Testing
Flexilevel	Testing Use Adaptive Testing
Teacher	Testing (for Competency) Use Teacher Competency Testing
Group	Testing
Group Intelligence	Testing (1966 1980) Use Group Testing and Intelligence Tests
Hypothesis	Testing
Individual	Testing
	Testing Methods Use Testing
Minimal Competency	Testing Use Minimum Competency Testing
Minimum Competency	Testing
Noise	Testing Use Noise (Sound)
Post	Testing (1966 1980) Use Pretests Posttests
Predictive Ability	(Testing) (1966 1980) Use Predictive Measurement
Drug	Testing (Presence in Body) Use Drug Use Testing
	Testing Problems
	Testing Programs
Psychological	Testing
Response Contingent	Testing Use Adaptive Testing
Stradaptive	Testing Use Adaptive Testing
Student	Testing (1966 1980) Use Educational Testing
Tailored	Testing Use Adaptive Testing
Teacher Competency	Testing
	Testing Techniques Use Testing
	Tests
Abstraction	Tests (1967 1980) Use Cognitive Tests
Proficiency	Tests (Academic) Use Achievement Tests
Achievement	Tests
Affective	Tests (1971 1980) Use Affective Measures
Aptitude	Tests
Arithmetic	Tests Use Arithmetic and Mathematics Tests
Articulation	Tests Use Speech Tests
Association	Tests (1968 1980) Use Association Measures
Attitude	Tests (1966 1980) Use Attitude Measures
Audiometric	Tests
Auditory	Tests
Auditory Visual	Tests (1966 1980) Use Auditory Tests and Vision Tests
Biochemical	Tests Use Biochemistry
Cognitive	Tests
Creative Thinking	Tests Use Creativity Tests
Creativity	Tests
Criterion Referenced	Tests
Cross Cultural	Tests Use Culture Fair Tests
Culture Fair	Tests
Culture Free	Tests (1967 1980) Use Culture Fair Tests
Diagnostic	Tests
Distractors	(Tests)
Employment	Tests Use Occupational Tests
Equivalency	Tests
Essay	Tests
Field	Tests
Group	Tests (1966 1980) Use Group Testing
Group Intelligence	Tests (1966 1980) Use Group Testing and Intelligence Tests
Guessing	(Tests)
Hearing	Tests Use Auditory Tests
High Stakes	Tests
Admission	Tests (Higher Education) Use College Entrance Examinations
Identification	Tests (1966 1980) Use Tests
Individual	Tests (1966 1980) Use Individual Testing
Intelligence	Tests
Interest	Tests (1966 1980) Use Interest Inventories
Job Sample	Tests Use Work Sample Tests
Language	Tests
Proficiency	Tests (Language) Use Language Proficiency and Language Tests
Listening	Tests (1970 1980) Use Listening Comprehension Tests
Listening Comprehension	Tests
Mastery	Tests
Matching	Tests Use Objective Tests

Mathematics	Tests
Quantitative	Tests (1980 1985) (Mathematics) Use Mathematics Tests
Maturity	Tests
Mental	Tests (1966 1980) Use Psychological Testing
Multiple Choice	Tests
National Achievement	Tests Use National Competency Tests
National Competency	Tests
Nonverbal	Tests
Norm Referenced	Tests
Number Skills	Tests Use Mathematics Tests
Objective	Tests
Objective Referenced	Tests Use Criterion Referenced Tests
Objectively Scored	Tests Use Objective Tests
Occupational	Tests
Admission	Tests (Occupational) Use Occupational Tests
National	Tests (of Achievement) Use National Competency Tests
	Tests of Significance (1966 1980) Use Statistical Significance
On Site	Tests Use Field Tests
Open Book	Tests
Otological	Tests Use Auditory Tests
Perception	Tests
Performance	Tests
Personality	Tests (1968 1980) Use Personality Measures
Personnel	Tests Use Occupational Tests
Physical	Tests Use Physical Examinations
Physical Fitness	Tests
Pictorial	Tests Use Visual Measures
Preschool	Tests
Prognostic	Tests
Projective	Tests (1968 1980) Use Projective Measures
Psychological	Tests (1966 1980) Use Psychological Testing
Rate	Tests Use Timed Tests
Reading	Tests
Reading Readiness	Tests
Response Bias	(Tests) Use Response Style (Tests)
Response Set	(Tests) Use Response Style (Tests)
Response Style	(Tests)
School Readiness	Tests
Science	Tests
Screening	Tests
Self Attitude	Tests Use Self Concept Measures
Self Concept	Tests (1971 1980) Use Self Concept Measures
Situation Reaction	Tests Use Situational Tests
Situation Response	Tests Use Situational Tests
Situational	Tests
Speech	Tests
Speed	Tests Use Timed Tests
Standardized	Tests
Tactual Visual	Tests
Talent	Tests Use Aptitude Tests
Teacher Made	Tests
Timed	Tests
True False	Tests Use Objective Tests
Verbal	Tests
Vision	Tests
Vocational	Tests Use Occupational Tests
Work Sample	Tests
Writing	Tests
	Teton Dakota Use Lakota
	Teton Sioux (Tribe) Use Lakota (Tribe)
	Tetraplegia Use Neurological Impairments
Full	Text Databases
	Text Editing Use Word Processing
	Text Editors Use Computer Software and Word Processing
Electronic	Text
Machine Readable	Text Use Electronic Text
Printed	Text Use Printed Materials
	Text Processing Use Word Processing
Reader	Text Relationship
	Text Structure
	Text to Speech Synthesizers Use Speech Synthesizers
	Textbook Assignments (1966 1980) Use Assignments
	Textbook Bias
	Textbook Content
	Textbook Development Use Textbook Preparation
	Textbook Evaluation
	Textbook Preparation
	Textbook Production Use Textbook Publication
	Textbook Publication
	Textbook Publications (1966 1980)
	Textbook Publishing Use Textbook Publication
	Textbook Research
	Textbook Selection
	Textbook Standards
	Textbook Writing Use Textbook Preparation
	Textbooks
History	Textbooks
Multicultural	Textbooks
Supplementary	Textbooks (1967 1980) Use Supplementary Reading Materials and Textbooks
	Textile Finishing Use Finishing
	Textiles Instruction
Programed	Texts (1966 1980) Use Programmed Instructional Materials and Textbooks
	Textual Criticism (1969 1980)

	Thai
	Thanatology Use Death
Homes for	the Aged Use Personal Care Homes
State of	the Art Reviews
Writing Across	the Curriculum
Interpreting for	the Deaf Use Deaf Interpreting
Foreign Languages in	the Elementary School Use FLES
Away from	the Job Training Use Off the Job Training
Off	the Job Training
On	the Job Training
Reviews of	the Literature Use Literature Reviews
Freedom of	the Press Use Freedom of Speech
Presidents of	the United States
Web	(The) Use World Wide Web
	Theater Use Theater Arts
	Theater Arts
Rehearsals	(Theater Arts)
Readers	Theater
	Theaters
Outdoor	Theaters (1968 1980) Use Outdoor Activities and Theaters
Plays	(Theatrical) Use Drama
	Thefts Use Stealing
Book	Thefts (1969 1980) Use Books and Stealing
	Thematic Approach
	Theme Writing Use Writing (Composition)
	Theological Education
	Theoretical Criticism (1969 1980)
	Theoretical Models Use Models
	Theories
Behavior	Theories
Counseling	Theories
Educational	Theories
Learning	Theories
Organizational	Theories
Personality	Theories
Social	Theories
Adaptation Level	Theory
Transformation	Theory (Adult Learning) Use Learning Theories and Transformative Learning
Atomic	Theory
Attribution	Theory
Cell	Theory (1966 1980) Use Cytology
Chaos	Theory
Cognitive	Theory Use Epistemology
Communication	Theory Use Communication (Thought Transfer)
Communications	Theory Use Information Theory
Critical	Theory
Functional Systems	Theory Use Systems Analysis
Game	Theory
Generalizability	Theory
Information	Theory
IRT LTT Measurement	Theory Use Item Response Theory
Item Characteristic Curve	Theory Use Item Response Theory
Item Response	Theory
Kinetic Molecular	Theory
Transformation	Theory (Language) (1967 1980) Use Linguistic Theory and Transformational Generative Grammar
Latent Trait	Theory (1980 1990) Use Item Response Theory
Linguistic	Theory
Mediation	Theory
Music	Theory
Piagetian	Theory
	Theory Practice Relationship
Probability	Theory (1967 1980) Use Probability
Reinforcement	Theory Use Reinforcement
Rhetorical	Theory
Role	Theory
Score	Theory Use Test Theory
Set	Theory
Social Exchange	Theory
Special Creation	Theory Use Creationism
Stage	Theory Use Developmental Stages
Statistical	Theory Use Statistics
Systems	Theory Use Systems Approach
Test	Theory
	Therapeutic Communities Use Milieu Therapy
	Therapeutic Environment
	Therapeutic Play Use Play Therapy
	Therapeutic Recreation
	Therapeutics Use Therapy
	Therapists
Hearing	Therapists (1967 1980) Use Hearing Therapy and Therapists
Inhalation	Therapists (1969 1985) Use Respiratory Therapy and Therapists
Occupational	Therapists
Physical	Therapists
Speech	Therapists (1966 1980) Use Speech Therapy and Therapists
	Therapy
Physical	Therapy Aides
Art	Therapy
Occupational	Therapy Assistants
Physical	Therapy Attendants Use Physical Therapy Aides
Behavior	Therapy Use Behavior Modification
Cognitive	Therapy Use Cognitive Restructuring
Crisis	Therapy (1969 1980) Use Crisis Intervention
Dance	Therapy

```
              Drug  Therapy
       Educational  Therapy
     Environmental  Therapy     Use Milieu Therapy
           Gestalt  Therapy
             Group  Therapy
           Hearing  Therapy
            Milieu  Therapy
             Music  Therapy
        Occupational  Therapy
   Oral Rehydration  Therapy
 Oxygen Inhalation  Therapy     Use Respiratory Therapy
          Physical  Therapy
              Play  Therapy
         Radiation  Therapy     Use Radiology
          Rational  Therapy (1968 1980)   Use Rational Emotive Therapy
  Rational Emotive  Therapy
           Reading  Therapy     Use Bibliotherapy
           Reality  Therapy
        Recreation  Therapy     Use Therapeutic Recreation
       Respiratory  Therapy
        Situational  Therapy     Use Milieu Therapy
            Speech  Therapy
         Radiation  Therapy Technologists   Use Radiologic Technologists
                    Thermal Environment
                    Thermal Insulation
                    Thermodynamics
                    Thermomechanics   Use Thermodynamics
                    Thermophysics   Use Thermodynamics
                    Thermoscience   Use Thermodynamics
                    Thesauri
                    Theses
          Doctoral  Theses (1967 1980)   Use Doctoral Dissertations
           Masters  Theses
                    Thinking Aloud Protocols   Use Protocol Analysis
        Convergent  Thinking
          Creative  Thinking
          Critical  Thinking
         Divergent  Thinking
        Evaluative  Thinking
           Logical  Thinking
                    Thinking Processes   Use Cognitive Processes
        Productive  Thinking
                    Thinking Skills
          Creative  Thinking Tests   Use Creativity Tests
                    Third World Countries   Use Developing Nations
       Freedom of  Thought   Use Intellectual Freedom
                    Thought Processes (1966 1980)   Use Cognitive Processes
     Communication  (Thought Transfer)
                    Three Dimensional Aids
        Six Three  Three Organization   Use Instructional Program Divisions
               Six  Three Three Organization   Use Instructional Program Divisions
                    Three Year Bachelors Degrees   Use Acceleration (Education) and Bachelors Degrees
                    Threshold Level (Languages)
        Failure to  Thrive
 Nonorganic Failure to  Thrive   Use Failure to Thrive
                    Tibetan
              Sino  Tibetan Languages
                    Timber Based Industry   Use Lumber Industry
                    Time
 Academic Learning  Time   Use Time on Task
                    Time Allocation   Use Time Management
                    Time Blocks
            Shared  Time (Computers)   Use Time Sharing
             Space  Time Continuum   Use Relativity
  Degree Completion  Time   Use Time to Degree
            Shared  Time (Education)   Use Dual Enrollment
              Part  Time Employment
              Full  Time Equivalency
                    Time Estimation   Use Time Management
                    Time Factors (Learning)
              Full  Time Faculty
              Part  Time Faculty
              Part  Time Farmers
              Part  Time Jobs (1966 1980)   Use Part Time Employment
           Engaged  Time (Learning)   Use Time on Task
           Leisure  Time
                    Time Management
                    Time on Task
                    Time Perspective
          Reaction  Time
           Leisure  Time Reading   Use Recreational Reading
          Released  Time
          Response  Time   Use Reaction Time
                    Time Sharing
                    Time Shortened Degree Programs   Use Acceleration (Education)
             Split  Time   Use Dual Enrollment
   Student Engaged  Time   Use Time on Task
              Full  Time Students
              Part  Time Students
       Teacher Wait  Time   Use Wait Time
              Full  Time Teachers   Use Full Time Faculty
              Part  Time Teachers (1967 1980)   Use Part Time Faculty
             Block  Time Teaching   Use Block Scheduling
```

Part   Time Teaching (1967 1980)   Use Part Time Faculty
        Time to Degree
        Time Use Data   Use Time Management
        Time Utilization   Use Time Management
Viewing   Time (1968 1980)   Use Programming (Broadcast)
Wait   Time
Part   Time Work   Use Part Time Employment
        Timed Tests
        Timeout
        Timetables   Use Scheduling
        Timetables (School)   Use School Schedules
        Timidity   Use Shyness
        Tissue Donors
        Title Word Indexes   Use Permuted Indexes
Degrees   (Titles) (1966 1980)   Use Degrees (Academic)
Adults (30   to 45)
Back   to Basics
Resistance   to Change
Time   to Degree
Prenatal Exposure   to Drugs   Use Prenatal Drug Exposure
Access   to Education
Adjustment   (to Environment)
Access   to Ideas   Use Intellectual Freedom
Access   to Information
Right   to Know   Use Freedom of Information
Learning   to Learn   Use Learning Strategies
Reading Aloud   to Others
Freedom   to Read   Use Intellectual Freedom
Urban   to Rural Migration
Births   to Single Women
Text   to Speech Synthesizers   Use Speech Synthesizers
Alternatives   to Standardized Testing   Use Alternative Assessment
Urban   to Suburban Migration
Resistance   to Temptation
Failure   to Thrive
Nonorganic Failure   to Thrive   Use Failure to Thrive
Rural   to Urban Migration
School   to Work Transition   Use Education Work Relationship
        Tobacco
        Toddlers
        Tohono O Odham People
        Toilet Facilities
        Toilet Learning   Use Toilet Training
        Toilet Training
        Token Economy
        Token Integration (1966 1980)   Use Tokenism
        Tokenism
        Tone Languages
        Tool and Die Makers
Machine   Tool Operators
Hand   Tools
Machine   Tools
Research   Tools
Selection   Tools
        Topography
        Topology
        Tornadoes
        Torts
International   Torts   Use International Law
        Total Communication
        Total Quality Management
        Totalitarianism
        Tourism
        Tourist Courts   Use Hotels
        Tourist Industry   Use Tourism
Attitudes   toward Disabilities
        Tower Diving   Use Diving
Boom   Town Areas   Use Boomtowns
        Towns   Use Municipalities
Small   Towns
        Toxic Substances   Use Poisons
        Toxicology
        Toxins   Use Poisons
        Toys
        TQM   Use Total Quality Management
        Track and Field
Fast   Track Scheduling
        Track System (Education)
        Tracking (1968 1980)
Sound   Tracks (1966 1980)
        Tractors
        Trade and Industrial Education
        Trade and Industrial Teachers
International   Trade
Masons   (Trade)   Use Masonry
        Trade Unions   Use Unions
International   Trade Vocabulary
Building   Trades
Metal   Trades   Use Metal Working
Needle   Trades
Architectural   Tradition   Use Architectural Character
Oral   Tradition
        Traditional Classrooms   Use Self Contained Classrooms

Traditional Family Unit   Use Nuclear Family
Traditional Grammar
Traditional Instruction   Use Conventional Instruction
Traditional Schools
Traditionalism
Traditions (Culture)   Use Folk Culture
Traffic Accidents
Traffic Circulation
Traffic Control
Air   Traffic Control
Spectator   Traffic Control   Use Traffic Control
Traffic Flow   Use Traffic Circulation
Traffic Patterns (1968 1980)   Use Traffic Circulation
Pedestrian   Traffic
Traffic Regulations (1968 1980)   Use Traffic Control
Traffic Safety
Traffic Signs (1968 1980)   Use Signs and Traffic Control
Vehicular   Traffic
Tragedy
Trails
Nature   Trails   Use Trails
Trainable Mentally Handicapped (1967 1980)   Use Moderate Mental Retardation
Foreign   Trained Physicians   Use Foreign Medical Graduates
Trainees
Trainers
Coordinator   Trainers   Use Instructor Coordinators
Teacher   Trainers   Use Teacher Educators
Training
Job   Training Academies   Use Career Academies
Administrator   Training   Use Management Development
Training Allowances
Training Alternatives   Use Nontraditional Education
Assertive   Training   Use Assertiveness
Assertiveness   Training   Use Assertiveness
Attendant   Training (1968 1980)   Use Attendants and Job Training
Auditory   Training
Away from the Job   Training   Use Off the Job Training
Bicultural   Training   Use Cross Cultural Training
University   Training Centers   Use Teacher Centers
Vocational   Training Centers
Cooperative   Training   Use Cooperative Education
Corporate   Training   Use Industrial Training
Counselor   Training
Cross Cultural   Training
Custodian   Training
Driver   Training   Use Driver Education
Teacher   Training Films   Use Protocol Materials
Flight   Training
Training Goals   Use Training Objectives
Graduate   Training   Use Graduate Study
Human Relations   Training   Use Sensitivity Training
Industrial   Training
Inquiry   Training (1967 1980)   Use Inquiry
Inservice Teacher   Training   Use Inservice Teacher Education
Job   Training
Training Laboratories (1967 1980)
Laboratory   Training
Leadership   Training
Management   Training   Use Management Development
Training Methods
Project   Training Methods (1968 1980)   Use Student Projects and Teaching Methods
Military   Training
Multicultural   Training   Use Cross Cultural Training
Multiethnic   Training   Use Cross Cultural Training
Training Objectives
Occupational   Training   Use Job Training
Off Site   Training   Use Off the Job Training
Off the Job   Training
On the Job   Training
Training Opportunities   Use Educational Opportunities
Pediatrics   Training (1966 1980)   Use Pediatrics
Physicians in   Training   Use Graduate Medical Students
Pilot   Training   Use Flight Training
Potty   Training   Use Toilet Training
Prevocational   Training   Use Prevocational Education
Professional   Training
Institutes   (Training Programs)
Refresher   Training   Use Retraining
Relaxation   Training
Retail   Training   Use Distributive Education
Training Schools (Juvenile Offenders)   Use Correctional Institutions
Sensitivity   Training
Sensory   Training
Supervisor   Training   Use Supervisory Training
Supervisory   Training
Teacher   Training   Use Teacher Education
Team   Training
Training Techniques (1967 1980)   Use Training Methods
Toilet   Training
Transfer of   Training
Travel   Training
Undergraduate   Training   Use Undergraduate Study
Vocational   Training   Use Vocational Education

Volunteer Training
Weight Training   Use Weightlifting
Sickle Cell Trait   Use Sickle Cell Anemia
Latent Trait Theory (1980 1990)   Use Item Response Theory
Trait Treatment Interaction   Use Aptitude Treatment Interaction
Community Traits   Use Community Characteristics
Cultural Traits
Personality Traits
Tranquilizing Drugs   Use Sedatives
Transactional Analysis
Transcendental Meditation
Phonetic Transcription
Transcripts (Academic)   Use Academic Records
Communication (Thought Transfer)
Discrimination Transfer   Use Shift Studies
Information Transfer
Transfer of Learning   Use Transfer of Training
Transfer of Training
Transfer Policy
Transfer Programs
Free Choice Transfer Programs
Restrictive Transfer Programs (1966 1980)   Use Transfer Programs
Transfer Rates (College)
College Transfer Rates   Use Transfer Rates (College)
Transfer Students
College Transfer Students
Power Transfer Systems   Use Kinetics
Teacher Transfer
Technology Transfer
Transfers (1966 1980)
Student Transfers   Use Transfer Students
Transformation Generative Grammar (1968 1980)   Use Transformational Generative Grammar
Perspective Transformation   Use Transformative Learning
Transformation Theory (Adult Learning)   Use Learning Theories and Transformative Learning
Transformation Theory (Language) (1967 1980)   Use Linguistic Theory and Transformational Generative Grammar
Transformational Generative Grammar
Transformational Geometry   Use Transformations (Mathematics)
Transformational Grammar   Use Transformational Generative Grammar
Generative Transformational Grammar   Use Transformational Generative Grammar
Transformational Sentence Combining   Use Sentence Combining
Transformations (Adult Learning)   Use Transformative Learning
Transformations (Language) (1967 1980)   Use Transformational Generative Grammar
Transformations (Mathematics)
Similarity Transformations   Use Transformations (Mathematics)
Transformative Learning
Transhumance   Use Nomads
Transient Children
Transistors
School to Work Transition   Use Education Work Relationship
Transitional Classes (1966 1981)   Use Transitional Programs
Transitional Programs
Transitional Schools
Midlife Transitions
Translation
Free Translation   Use Translation
Machine Translation
Mechanical Translation   Use Machine Translation
Grammar Translation Method
Translators   Use Interpreters
Facsimile Transmission
Sound Transmission   Use Acoustics
Transparencies
Overhead Transparencies   Use Transparencies
Transparency Projectors   Use Overhead Projectors
Overhead Transparency Projectors   Use Overhead Projectors
Transplanting (1968 1980)   Use Horticulture
Transportation
Air Transportation
Bus Transportation
Migrant Transportation (1966 1980)   Use Migrants and Transportation
Rail Transportation
School Transportation   Use Student Transportation
Student Transportation
Transracial Adoption
Trash   Use Solid Wastes
Traumatic Brain Injury   Use Head Injuries and Neurological Impairments
Post Traumatic Stress Syndrome   Use Posttraumatic Stress Disorder
Travel
Student Travel   Use Travel
Teacher Travel   Use Travel
Travel Training
Traveling Teachers   Use Itinerant Teachers
Treaties
Treatment Centers   Use Clinics
Aptitude Treatment Interaction
Trait Treatment Interaction   Use Aptitude Treatment Interaction
Medical Treatment (1967 1980)   Use Medical Services
Outcomes of Treatment
Termination of Treatment
Waste Water Treatment   Use Waste Water and Water Treatment
Water Treatment
Trees
Family Trees   Use Genealogy

Shade	Trees Use Trees
	Trend Analysis
Agricultural	Trends
Black Population	Trends
Educational	Trends
Employment	Trends (1966 1980) Use Employment Patterns
Enrollment	Trends
Migration	Trends Use Migration Patterns
Negro Population	Trends (1966 1977) Use Black Population Trends
Population	Trends
Social	Trends Use Sociocultural Patterns
	Trial by Jury Use Juries
	Triangulation
	Tribal Colleges Use Tribally Controlled Education
	Tribal Government
	Tribal Schools Use Tribally Controlled Education
Contract	Tribal Schools Use Tribally Controlled Education
	Tribal Societies Use Tribes
	Tribal Sovereignty
	Tribally Controlled Education
Anishinabe	(Tribe) Use Chippewa (Tribe)
Cherokee	(Tribe)
Chippewa	(Tribe)
Choctaw	(Tribe)
Cree	(Tribe)
Hopi	(Tribe)
Iroquois	(Tribe)
Lakota	(Tribe)
Mississippi Band of Choctaw	(Tribe)
Moqui	(Tribe) Use Hopi (Tribe)
Oglala Sioux	(Tribe)
Ojibwa	(Tribe) Use Chippewa (Tribe)
Ojibway	(Tribe) Use Chippewa (Tribe)
Ojibwe	(Tribe) Use Chippewa (Tribe)
Papago	(Tribe) Use Tohono O Odham People
Sioux	(Tribe)
Teton Sioux	(Tribe) Use Lakota (Tribe)
Zuni	(Tribe)
	Tribes
	Trigonometry
	Trimester Schedules (1966 1980) Use Trimester System
	Trimester System
Airborne Field	Trips (1968 1980) Use Field Trips
Field	Trips
Instructional	Trips (1966 1980) Use Field Trips
Study	Trips Use Field Trips
Federal	Troops (1966 1980) Use Armed Forces
	Tropical Cyclones Use Hurricanes
	Tropical Rainforests Use Rainforests
	Troubadours Use Poets
	Troubleshooting
	Truancy
School	Truancy Use Truancy
	Truant Officers Use Attendance Officers and Truancy
	Truck Mechanics Use Auto Mechanics
	True False Tests Use Objective Tests
	True Measure Use True Scores
	True Scores
	Trust Funds Use Trusts (Financial)
	Trust (Psychology)
	Trust Responsibility (Government)
	Trustees
Board of	Trustees Use Governing Boards
Charitable	Trusts Use Trusts (Financial)
	Trusts (Financial)
	Trustworthiness Use Credibility
	Truthfulness Use Honesty
Cathode Ray	Tube Terminals Use Video Display Terminals
	Tuition
Deferred	Tuition Use Income Contingent Loans
	Tuition Grants
	Tuition Postponement Use Income Contingent Loans
	Tuition Tax Credits Use Tax Credits and Tuition
	Tumbling
Stunts and	Tumbling Use Tumbling
	Tumors (Malignant) Use Cancer
	Tupi Guarani Use Guarani
	Turf Management
	Turkic Languages
	Turkish
	Turnkey Building Use Design Build Approach
	Turnkey Systems (Libraries) Use Integrated Library Systems
Labor	Turnover
Teacher	Turnover Use Faculty Mobility
	Tutorial Instruction Use Tutoring
	Tutorial Plans Use Tutorial Programs
	Tutorial Programs
	Tutorial Services Use Tutorial Programs
	Tutoring
After School	Tutoring (1966 1980) Use After School Education and Tutoring
Peer	Tutoring Use Peer Teaching and Tutoring
Programed	Tutoring (1967 1994) Use Programmed Tutoring
Programmed	Tutoring

Intelligent	Tutoring Systems
	Tutors
	TV Use Television
	Twentieth Century Literature
	Twi Use Akan
	Twins
	Two Parent Family Use Nuclear Family
	Two Plus Two Tech Prep Use Tech Prep
	Two Plus Two Tech Prep Associate Degrees Use Associate Degrees and Tech Prep
Two Plus	Two Tech Prep Associate Degrees Use Associate Degrees and Tech Prep
Two Plus	Two Tech Prep Use Tech Prep
	Two Way Television Use Interactive Television
	Two Year College Degrees Use Associate Degrees
	Two Year College Students
	Two Year Colleges
Human T Cell Lymphotropic Virus	Type 3 Use Acquired Immune Deficiency Syndrome
	Type A Behavior
	Type B Behavior
Large	Type Books Use Large Type Materials
Institute	Type Courses (1966 1980) Use Institutes (Training Programs)
Large	Type Materials
Lisrel	Type Models Use Structural Equation Models
Senile Dementia Alzheimers	Type Use Alzheimers Disease
Test	Type Use Test Format
Item	Types Use Test Format
	Typewriting
	Typhoons Use Hurricanes
	Typing Use Typewriting
	Typists (1967 1981) Use Typewriting
Clerk	Typists Use Typewriting
	Typology (1967 1980) Use Classification
Language	Typology
	Tzeltal
	Tzendal Use Tzeltal
	Tzotzil
	UDC (Classification) Use Universal Decimal Classification
Fenno	Ugric Languages Use Finno Ugric Languages
Finno	Ugric Languages
	Ukrainian
	Ultramicrofiche Use Microfiche
	Uncial Script Use Manuscript Writing (Handlettering)
	Uncommonly Taught Languages
	Unconventional Warfare Use War
	Underachievement
	Underachievers (1966 1979) Use Underachievement
	Underdeveloped Nations Use Developing Nations
	Underemployed (1969 1980) Use Underemployment
	Underemployment
	Undergraduate Education Use Undergraduate Study
	Undergraduate Students
	Undergraduate Study
	Undergraduate Training Use Undergraduate Study
Seniors (1966 1980) (Last Year	Undergraduates) Use College Seniors
	Underground Facilities
	Underground Water Use Groundwater
	Underprivileged Use Disadvantaged
Cultural	Understanding Use Cultural Awareness
Self	Understanding Use Self Concept
Natural Language	Understanding Systems Use Natural Language Processing
	Underwater Diving
	Undocumented Immigrants
	Undocumented Workers Use Foreign Workers and Undocumented Immigrants
	Unemployed (1967 1980) Use Unemployment
	Unemployment
	Unemployment Insurance
Structural	Unemployment
Technological	Unemployment Use Structural Unemployment
	Ungraded Classes (1966 1980) Use Nongraded Instructional Grouping
	Ungraded Curriculum (1966 1980) Use Nongraded Instructional Grouping
	Ungraded Elementary Programs (1966 1980) Use Nongraded Instructional Grouping
	Ungraded Primary Programs (1966 1980) Use Nongraded Instructional Grouping
	Ungraded Programs (1966 1980) Use Nongraded Instructional Grouping
	Ungraded Schools (1966 1980) Use Nongraded Instructional Grouping
	Unification Use Group Unity
	Unified Studies Curriculum
	Unified Studies Programs (1966 1980) Use Unified Studies Curriculum
School	Uniforms
	Unilateral Disarmament Use Disarmament
	Union Catalogs
	Union Members
	Unions
College	Unions Use Student Unions
Labor	Unions (1966 1980) Use Unions
Local	Unions (1966 1980) Use Unions
Student	Unions
Teacher	Unions Use Unions
Trade	Unions Use Unions
	Unit Costs
Family (Sociological	Unit)
	Unit Plan (1966 1980)
Traditional Family	Unit Use Nuclear Family
American Literature (1966 1980)	(United States) Use United States Literature
Civil War	(United States)

Colonial History	(United States)
Educational Excellence Movement	(United States) Use Excellence in Education
	United States Government (Course)
	United States History
	United States Literature
Presidential Campaigns	(United States)
Presidential Candidates	(United States) Use Political Candidates and Presidential Campaigns (United States)
Presidential Debates	(United States) Use Debate and Presidential Campaigns (United States)
Presidential Elections	(United States) Use Elections and Presidential Campaigns (United States)
Presidents of the	United States
Restructuring of Schools	(United States) Use School Restructuring
Revolutionary War	(United States)
	Uniterm Indexes Use Coordinate Indexes
	Uniterms Use Subject Index Terms
Dramatic	Unities (1970 1980) Use Drama
Activity	Units
Continuing Education	Units
Experience	Units Use Activity Units
Human Relations	Units (1966 1980) Use Human Relations and Units of Study
Intermediate Administrative	Units
Lesson	Units Use Units of Study
	Units of Study
	Units of Study (Subject Fields) (1966 1977) Use Units of Study
Phonological	Units (1966 1980) Use Phonemes
Programed	Units (1966 1980) Use Programmed Instruction and Units of Study
Research and Instruction	Units
Research Coordinating	Units
Resource	Units
Science	Units (1966 1980) Use Science Curriculum and Units of Study
SI	Units Use Metric System
Social Studies	Units (1966 1980) Use Social Studies and Units of Study
Visual Display	Units Use Video Display Terminals
Ethnic	Unity Use Group Unity
Family	Unity Use Group Unity
Group	Unity
	Universal Decimal Classification
Decimal Classification	(Universal) Use Universal Decimal Classification
	Universal Education (1968 1976) Use Equal Education
Language	Universals
Linguistic	Universals Use Language Universals
	Universities
Extended	Universities Use Open Universities
Free	Universities Use Experimental Colleges
Land Grant	Universities
Open	Universities
Private	Universities Use Private Colleges
Research	Universities
State	Universities
Urban	Universities
	Universities without Walls Use Open Universities
	University Administration (1967 1980) Use College Administration
	University Characteristics Use Institutional Characteristics
	University Extension (1967 1980) Use Extension Education
	University Libraries (1968 1980) Use College Libraries
	University Presses
	University Schools Use Laboratory Schools
	University Senates Use College Governing Councils
	University Settlements Use Settlement Houses
	University Students Use College Students
	University Teaching Hospitals Use Teaching Hospitals
	University Training Centers Use Teacher Centers
	Unmarried Mother Births Use Births to Single Women
	Unmarried Students Use Single Students
	Unskilled Labor (1966 1980) Use Unskilled Workers
	Unskilled Occupations
	Unskilled Workers
	Untenured Faculty Use Nontenured Faculty
	Unwed Mothers
	Unwritten Language (1968 1980)
	Unwritten Languages
	Upgrading Use Improvement
Equipment	Upkeep Use Equipment Maintenance
	Upper Class
	Upper Division Colleges
	Uralic Altaic Languages
	Urban American Indians
	Urban Areas
	Urban Culture
	Urban Demography
	Urban Desegregation Use Racial Integration
Rural	Urban Differences
	Urban Dropouts (1966 1981) Use Dropouts
	Urban Education
	Urban Environment
	Urban Extension
	Urban Geography Use Human Geography
	Urban Immigration (1966 1976) Use Rural to Urban Migration
	Urban Improvement
	Urban Language
	Urban Life Use Urban Culture
Rural to	Urban Migration
	Urban Planning
	Urban Population

	Urban Problems
	Urban Programs
	Urban Renewal
	Urban Renewal Agencies
	Urban Rural Differences Use Rural Urban Differences
	Urban Schools
	Urban Slums (1966 1980) Use Slums
	Urban Studies
	Urban Teaching
	Urban Teaching Interns Use Teacher Interns and Urban Teaching
	Urban to Rural Migration
	Urban to Suburban Migration
	Urban Universities
	Urban Youth
	Urbanization
	Urdu
Colloquial Standard	Usage Use Standard Spoken Usage
Informal Conversational	Usage Use Standard Spoken Usage
Telephone	Usage Instruction
Language	Usage
Standard Spoken	Usage
Alcohol	Use Use Drinking
Fair	Use (Copyrights)
Time	Use Data Use Time Management
Drug	Use
Electronic Classroom	Use (1966 1980) Use Electronic Classrooms
Illegal Drug	Use
Land	Use
Language Laboratory	Use (1966 1980) Use Language Laboratories
Mass Media	Use
Media	Use (Mass Media) Use Mass Media Use
News	Use Use Mass Media Use and News Media
Number	Use Use Numbers
	Use Studies
Television	Use Use Mass Media Use and Television Viewing
Test	Use
Drug	Use Testing
	User Friendly Interface
	User Needs (Information)
Information	User Needs Use User Needs (Information)
Library	User Needs Use User Needs (Information)
	User Satisfaction (Information)
Information	User Satisfaction Use User Satisfaction (Information)
Library	User Satisfaction Use User Satisfaction (Information)
	User Studies Use Use Studies
	Users (Information)
Information	Users Use Users (Information)
End	Users (Information) Use Users (Information)
Library	Users Use Users (Information)
Computer	Uses in Education
Drug Exposure in	Utero Use Prenatal Drug Exposure
	Utilities
Bibliographic	Utilities
Electric	Utilities Use Utilities
Gas	Utilities Use Utilities
Information	Utilities (Online) Use Online Vendors
Public	Utilities Use Utilities
Water	Utilities Use Utilities
Cost	Utility Analysis Use Cost Effectiveness
Equipment	Utilization
Evaluation	Utilization
Information	Utilization
Labor	Utilization
Manpower	Utilization (1966 1980) Use Labor Utilization
Research	Utilization
Facility	Utilization Research
Self	Utilization Use Self Actualization
Space	Utilization
Staff	Utilization
Talent	Utilization (1966 1980)
Time	Utilization Use Time Management
	Uto Aztecan Languages
	Uzbek
Job	Vacancies Use Employment Opportunities
Job	Vacancy Surveys Use Occupational Surveys
	Vacation Programs
	Vacations
	Valence (Language) Use Syntax
Approved Programs	(Validated) Use Validated Programs
	Validated Programs
Program	Validation
Program Approval	(Validation) Use Program Validation
	Validity
Concurrent	Validity
Criterion	Validity (Concurrent) Use Concurrent Validity
Construct	Validity
Content	Validity
Predictive	Validity
Criterion	Validity (Predictive) Use Predictive Validity
Test	Validity
Ad	Valorem Tax Use Property Taxes
Assessed	Valuation
Diversity (Cultural) as a	Value Use Cultural Pluralism

```
                            Value Judgment
                  Place     Value
                            Values
              Aesthetic     Values
                            Values Clarification
             Democratic     Values
                            Values Education
                Ethical     Values (1966 1980)   Use Moral Values
                  Group     Values    Use Social Values
            Middle Class    Values (1966 1980)   Use Middle Class Standards
                  Moral     Values
               Personal     Values (1966 1980)   Use Values
                 Social     Values
                            Vandalism
                 School     Vandalism
            Independent     Variables   Use Predictor Variables
              Predictive    Variables   Use Predictor Variables
               Predictor    Variables
                 Stress     Variables
             Suppressor     Variables
            Analysis of     Variance
                  Error     Variance    Use Error of Measurement
   Multivariate Analysis of Variance    Use Multivariate Analysis
               Language     Variation
                            Vascular System    Use Cardiovascular System
                            Vectors (Mathematics)
              Fruit and     Vegetable Inspectors   Use Food and Drug Inspectors
         Child Restraints   (Vehicle Safety)    Use Child Safety and Restraints (Vehicle Safety)
              Restraints    (Vehicle Safety)
              Contractor    Vehicles    Use Service Vehicles
             Maintenance    Vehicles    Use Service Vehicles
                  Motor     Vehicles
                Service     Vehicles
                            Vehicular Circulation   Use Vehicular Traffic
                            Vehicular Traffic
                            Velocity
                            Vending Machines
                            Vendors
               Database     Vendors    Use Online Vendors
                 Online     Vendors
                            Venereal Diseases
                            Ventilation
                            Verbal Ability
                            Verbal Abuse
                            Verbal Communication
                            Verbal Development
                            Verbal Interaction    Use Verbal Communication
                            Verbal Learning
                            Verbal Operant Conditioning
                            Verbal Stimuli
                            Verbal Tests
                            Verbs
                  Audits    (Verification)
                            Versification (1969 1980)   Use Poetry
                            Vertical Organization
                            Veterans
                            Veterans Education
                Vietnam     Veterans
                            Veterinarians
                            Veterinary Assistants
                            Veterinary Hospital Attendants    Use Veterinary Assistants
                            Veterinary Medical Education
                            Veterinary Medicine
                            Vice Principals    Use Assistant Principals
                            Victims of Crime
                            Victorian Literature
                            Video Cassette Systems (1971 1980)   Use Videotape Cassettes
                            Video Display Terminals
                            Video Equipment
                            Video Games
              Intelligent   Video   Use Interactive Video
              Interactive   Video
                  Audio     Video Laboratories (1967 1980)   Use Audiovisual Centers
                            Video Production Centers   Use Television Studios
                            Video Systems   Use Video Equipment
                            Video Tape Recordings (1966 1978)   Use Videotape Recordings
                            Videodisc Recordings (1979 1986)   Use Videodisks
                            Videodisks
                Optical     Videodisks   Use Optical Disks and Videodisks
                            Videogames (Electronic)   Use Video Games
                            Videotape Cartridges   Use Videotape Cassettes
                            Videotape Cassette Recorders   Use Videotape Cassettes and Videotape Recorders
                            Videotape Cassettes
                            Videotape Libraries   Use Film Libraries
                            Videotape Recorders
                            Videotape Recordings
                            Videotex
                            Videotext   Use Videotex
                            Vietnam Veterans
                            Vietnam War
                            Vietnamese
                            Vietnamese Americans   Use Asian Americans and Vietnamese People
                            Vietnamese People
```

	Viewdata Use Videotex
Critical	Viewing
Television	Viewing
	Viewing Time (1968 1980) Use Programming (Broadcast)
Life	Views Use World Views
World	Views
	Village Extension Agents Use Extension Agents
	Violence
Family	Violence
Domestic	Violence (Family) Use Family Violence
Student	Violence Use Violence
	Viracnon Use Bikol
	Virtual Libraries Use Electronic Libraries
	Virtual Reality
Human Immunodeficiency	Virus Use Acquired Immune Deficiency Syndrome
Human T Cell Lymphotropic	Virus Type 3 Use Acquired Immune Deficiency Syndrome
	Viruses
	Visayan
	Visible Radiation Use Light
	Visible Spectrum Use Light
	Visible Speech
	Vision
Low	Vision Aids
Partial	Vision
	Vision Tests
School	Visitation
	Visiting Homemakers
	Visiting Teachers Use Itinerant Teachers
Farm	Visits
Home	Visits
Interschool	Visits Use School Visitation
School	Visits Use School Visitation
	Visual Acuity
	Visual Aids
	Visual Arts
Painting	(Visual Arts)
	Visual Discrimination
	Visual Display Units Use Video Display Terminals
	Visual Environment
	Visual Equipment Use Visual Aids
	Visual Impairments
	Visual Language Learning Use Language Acquisition and Visual Learning
	Visual Learning
	Visual Literacy
	Visual Materials Use Visual Aids
	Visual Measures
	Visual Media Use Visual Aids
	Visual Perception
	Visual Scanners Use Optical Scanners
	Visual Stimuli
Auditory	Visual Tests (1966 1980) Use Auditory Tests and Vision Tests
Tactual	Visual Tests
	Visualization
	Visually Handicapped (1966 1980) Use Visual Impairments
	Visually Handicapped Mobility (1967 1994) Use Visually Impaired Mobility
	Visually Handicapped Orientation (1967 1980) Use Visually Impaired Mobility
	Visually Impaired Mobility
	Visuospatial Ability Use Spatial Ability
	Vitae Use Resumes (Personal)
Curriculum	Vitae Use Resumes (Personal)
	Vocabulary
Aviation	Vocabulary
Banking	Vocabulary
Basic	Vocabulary
High Interest Low	Vocabulary Books
	Vocabulary Building Use Vocabulary Development
	Vocabulary Development
International Trade	Vocabulary
Mathematical	Vocabulary
Medical	Vocabulary
Sight	Vocabulary
	Vocabulary Skills
	Vocal Ensembles Use Singing
	Vocal Music
Accents	(Vocal Stress) Use Stress (Phonology)
	Vocational Academies Use Career Academies
	Vocational Adjustment
Agricultural Education	(Vocational) Use Agricultural Education and Vocational Education
	Vocational Agriculture (1967 1980) Use Agricultural Education and Vocational Education
	Vocational Agriculture Teachers (1967 1980) Use Agricultural Education and Vocational Education Teachers
	Vocational Aptitude
	Vocational Aspiration Use Occupational Aspiration
	Vocational Assessment Use Vocational Evaluation
	Vocational Awareness Use Career Awareness
	Vocational Business Education Use Business Education
	Vocational Change Use Career Change
	Vocational Choice Use Career Choice
	Vocational Counseling (1966 1980) Use Career Counseling
	Vocational Development (1967 1978) Use Career Development
	Vocational Directors
	Vocational Education
Adult	Vocational Education
	Vocational Education Directors Use Vocational Directors

```
                                    Vocational Education Teachers
                                    Vocational English (Second Language)
                                    Vocational Evaluation
                                    Vocational Followup
                                    Vocational Guidance   Use Career Guidance
        Health Occupations Education (Vocational)   Use Allied Health Occupations Education and Vocational Education
                                    Vocational High Schools
                                    Vocational Industrial Education   Use Trade and Industrial Education
                                    Vocational Interests
                                    Vocational Maturity
                                    Vocational Nursing   Use Practical Nursing
                                    Vocational Placement   Use Job Placement
                                    Vocational Rehabilitation
                                    Vocational Retraining (1966 1980)   Use Retraining
                                    Vocational Satisfaction   Use Job Satisfaction
                                    Vocational Schools
                               Area Vocational Schools (1966 1980)   Use Regional Schools and Vocational Schools
                                    Vocational Skills   Use Job Skills
                                    Vocational Talents   Use Vocational Aptitude
                                    Vocational Tests   Use Occupational Tests
                                    Vocational Training   Use Vocational Education
                                    Vocational Training Centers
                                    Vocational Work Experience   Use Cooperative Education
                                    Vocations   Use Occupations
                                    Vocoids   Use Vowels
                                    Vogul
                                    Voice Disorders
                                Eye Voice Span
                                    Voice Synthesizers   Use Speech Synthesizers
                                    Volcanoes
                                    Volcanology   Use Volcanoes
                                    Volition   Use Individual Power
                         Individual Volition   Use Individual Power
                                    Volleyball
                                    Volume (Mathematics)
                                    Volume (Sound)   Use Noise (Sound)
                                    Voluntary Agencies
                                    Voluntary Associations   Use Voluntary Agencies
                                    Voluntary Desegregation
                                    Voluntary Integration (1966 1980)   Use Voluntary Desegregation
                                    Voluntary Organizations   Use Voluntary Agencies
                                    Volunteer Training
                                    Volunteers
                            Student Volunteers
                                    Voter Registration
                                    Voting
                                    Voting Rights
                                    Voucher Plans   Use Educational Vouchers
                          Education Vouchers (1971 1980)   Use Educational Vouchers
                        Educational Vouchers
                                    Vowels
                             Salary Wage Differentials
                            Minimum Wage Laws (1966 1974)   Use Minimum Wage Legislation
                            Minimum Wage Legislation
                            Minimum Wage
                                    Wage Salary Differentials   Use Salary Wage Differentials
                                    Wage Statements (1966 1980)   Use Payroll Records
                                    Wages
                                    Wait Time
                            Teacher Wait Time   Use Wait Time
                                    Waiters and Waitresses
                        Waiters and Waitresses
                                    Walking
                                    Walleyes   Use Strabismus
                              Glass Walls
            Universities without Walls   Use Open Universities
                             Window Walls   Use Glass Walls
                                    War
            American Revolutionary War   Use Revolutionary War (United States)
                               Civil War   Use War
                                    War Crimes   Use International Crimes
                              World War I
                              World War II
                      International War   Use War
                             Korean War
                               Civil War (United States)
                      Revolutionary War (United States)
                            Vietnam War
                                    Warehouses
                             Atomic Warfare   Use Nuclear Warfare
                       Conventional Warfare   Use War
                          Guerrilla Warfare   Use War
                            Nuclear Warfare
                     Unconventional Warfare   Use War
                             Global Warming
                                    Washrooms   Use Toilet Facilities
                                    Waste Disposal
                                    Waste Management   Use Waste Disposal
                                    Waste Water
                                    Waste Water Treatment   Use Waste Water and Water Treatment
                                    Wastes
                          Hazardous Wastes   Use Hazardous Materials and Wastes
                              Solid Wastes
```

Watch Repairers Use Watchmakers
Watchmakers
Water
Chlorination (Water) Use Water Treatment
Clean Water Use Water Quality
Drinking Water
Water Pollution
Water Pollution Control (1969 1980) Use Water Pollution
Water Polo
Potable Water Use Drinking Water
Water Purification Use Water Treatment
Water Quality
Water Resources
Water Softening Use Water Treatment
Water Sports Use Aquatic Sports
Ground Water Supplies Use Groundwater
Water Supply Use Water Resources
Water Treatment
Waste Water Treatment Use Waste Water and Water Treatment
Underground Water Use Groundwater
Water Utilities Use Utilities
Waste Water
Water Works Use Utilities and Water Treatment
Waterskiing
Sound Waves Use Acoustics
Two Way Television Use Interactive Television
Wealth Neutrality Use Fiscal Neutrality
School District Wealth
Weapons
Arms (Weapons) Use Weapons
Nuclear Weapons
Weariness Use Fatigue (Biology)
Weather
Worldwide Web Service Use World Wide Web
Web (The) Use World Wide Web
World Wide Web
Webzines Use Electronic Journals
Out of Wedlock Births Use Births to Single Women
Weeding (Library)
Weeds
Compressed Work Week Use Flexible Working Hours
Four Day Work Week Use Flexible Working Hours
Weekend Programs
Weight (1968 1980)
Birth Weight
Body Weight
Weight (Mass)
Weight Training Use Weightlifting
Weighted Scores
Weightlifting
Welders (1968 1981) Use Welding
Welding
Acetylene Welding Use Welding
Arc Welding Use Welding
Gas Welding Use Welding
Welfare (1966 1980)
Welfare Agencies
Public Welfare Assistance Use Welfare Services
Child Welfare
Welfare Problems (1966 1980) Use Welfare Services
Welfare Recipients
Welfare Services
Migrant Welfare Services
Social Welfare (1966 1980)
Student Welfare
Teacher Welfare
Well Being
Wellness
Wellness Programs Use Wellness
Welsh
Weltanschauungen Use World Views
Western Civilization
Non Western Civilization
Wetlands
Wheel Chairs (1970 1981) Use Wheelchairs
Wheelchairs
Driving While Intoxicated
White Black Relations Use Racial Relations
White Collar Occupations
White Ethnics Use Whites
Black and White Films Use Films
White Flight Use Migration and Whites
Black White Relations Use Racial Relations
White Students
Whites
Whole Language Approach
Whole Numbers
Whole Person Approach Use Holistic Approach
Whole Word Reading Approach Use Sight Method
Wholesaling
Wholistic Approach Use Holistic Approach
City Wide Commissions (1966 1980) Use Planning Commissions and Urban Planning
City Wide Programs (1967 1980) Use Urban Programs

World	Wide Web
	Widowed
	Wilderness
	Wildlife
	Wildlife Management
	Wills
	Wind Energy
	Wind Instruments
	Wind (Meteorology)
	Window Walls Use Glass Walls
	Windowless Rooms
	Windows
	Winter Olympic Games Use Olympic Games and Winter Sports
	Winter Sports
	Wire Communications Use Telecommunications
	Wireless Communications Use Telecommunications
Test	Wiseness
Parents	with Disabilities
Teachers	with Disabilities
	Withdrawal (1966 1980) Use Withdrawal (Education)
Course	Withdrawal Use Withdrawal (Education)
Drug	Withdrawal Use Drug Rehabilitation
	Withdrawal (Drugs) Use Drug Rehabilitation
	Withdrawal (Education)
	Withdrawal (Psychology)
	Withdrawal Tendencies (Psychology) (1966 1980) Use Withdrawal (Psychology)
Schools	within a School Plan Use House Plan
Universities	without Walls Use Open Universities
	Wives Use Spouses
	Wolof
	Women Use Females
Abused	Women Use Battered Women
	Women Administrators
Battered	Women
Births to Single	Women
Deans of	Women Use Deans of Students
	Women Directors Use Women Administrators
Employed	Women
Enlisted	Women Use Enlisted Personnel
	Women Faculty
Farm	Women Use Rural Women
	Women Managers Use Women Administrators
	Women Presidents Use Presidents and Women Administrators
	Women Professors (1966 1980) Use Women Faculty
Rural	Women
	Women Teachers (1967 1980) Use Women Faculty
	Women Workers Use Employed Women
Working	Women (1968 1980) Use Employed Women
	Womens Athletics
	Womens Education
	Womens Liberation Use Feminism
	Womens Rights Use Feminism
	Womens Studies
	Wood Finishing Use Finishing
	Woodwind Instruments
	Woodworking
Key	Word Access Points Use Keywords
	Word Associations (Reading) Use Associative Learning
	Word Borrowing Use Linguistic Borrowing
	Word Frequency
Key	Word in Context Use Permuted Indexes
Title	Word Indexes Use Permuted Indexes
	Word Lists
Basic	Word Lists Use Word Lists
	Word Meaning Use Semantics
	Word Method (Reading) Use Sight Method
	Word Order
	Word Problems (Mathematics)
	Word Processing
Whole	Word Reading Approach Use Sight Method
	Word Recognition
	Word Study Skills
Function	Words
Loan	Words Use Linguistic Borrowing
	Work Use Employment
	Work Adjustment Use Vocational Adjustment
	Work and Education Use Education Work Relationship
	Work Attitudes
Employee	Work Attitudes Use Employee Attitudes and Work Attitudes
	Work Change Use Career Change
Education and	Work Use Education Work Relationship
	Work Education Programs Use Work Study Programs
	Work Education Relationship Use Education Work Relationship
	Work Enrichment Use Job Enrichment
	Work Environment
Organizational Psychology	(Work Environment) Use Industrial Psychology
	Work Ethic
	Work Evaluation (Performance) Use Vocational Evaluation
	Work Experience
	Work Experience Programs
Cooperative	Work Experience Programs Use Cooperative Education
Vocational	Work Experience Use Cooperative Education
	Work Family Relationship Use Family Work Relationship

	Work Force Use Labor Force
Hours of	Work Use Working Hours
	Work Life Expectancy
Structural	Work Occupations Use Building Trades
Part Time	Work Use Part Time Employment
	Work Performance Evaluation Use Vocational Evaluation
Supported	Work Programs Use Supported Employment
Education	Work Relationship
Family	Work Relationship
	Work Release Use Released Time
	Work Sample Tests
	Work Samples Use Work Sample Tests
	Work Satisfaction Use Job Satisfaction
	Work Sharing Use Job Sharing
Sheet Metal	Work
	Work Simplification (1968 1980) Use Job Simplification
Social	Work
	Work Stations (Home or Office) Use Workstations
Student Personnel	Work (1967 1980) Use Student Personnel Services
	Work Study Use Work Study Programs
	Work Study Programs
College	Work Study Programs Use Work Study Programs
School to	Work Transition Use Education Work Relationship
Compressed	Work Week Use Flexible Working Hours
Four Day	Work Week Use Flexible Working Hours
	Workbooks
	Workday Use Working Hours
	Worker Days
	Worker Evaluation Use Personnel Evaluation
Migrant	Worker Projects (1966 1980) Use Migrant Programs and Migrant Workers
Agricultural	Workers Use Agricultural Laborers
Agricultural Migrant	Workers Use Migrant Workers
Auxiliary	Workers Use Auxiliary Laborers
Beginning	Workers Use Entry Workers
Child Care	Workers (1967 1980) Use Child Caregivers
Church	Workers
Clerical	Workers
Community	Workers Use Community Organizations
Community Health	Workers Use Community Health Services and Health Personnel
Community Mental Health	Workers Use Community Health Services and Mental Health Workers
	Workers Compensation
Craft	Workers
Dislocated	Workers
Displaced	Workers Use Dislocated Workers
	Workers Education Use Labor Education
Entry	Workers
Food Service	Workers (1968 1981) Use Food Service
Foreign	Workers
Greenhouse	Workers Use Nursery Workers (Horticulture)
Health	Workers Use Health Personnel
Health Service	Workers Use Health Personnel
Nursery	Workers (Horticulture)
Yard	Workers (Horticulture) Use Grounds Keepers
Household	Workers
Journey	Workers Use Skilled Workers
Machinery Maintenance	Workers Use Machine Repairers
Mental Health	Workers
Migrant	Workers
Interstate	Workers (1966 1980) (Migrants) Use Migrant Workers
Migratory Agricultural	Workers Use Migrant Workers
Older	Workers
Parish	Workers Use Church Workers
Pupil Personnel	Workers
Reentry	Workers
Sales	Workers
School Social	Workers
Semiskilled	Workers
Service	Workers
Sheet Metal	Workers (1967 1981) Use Sheet Metal Work
Skilled	Workers
Social	Workers
Student Affairs	Workers Use Student Personnel Workers
Student Personnel	Workers
Undocumented	Workers Use Foreign Workers and Undocumented Immigrants
Unskilled	Workers
Women	Workers Use Employed Women
	Working Abroad Use Overseas Employment
	Working Class
	Working Conditions Use Work Environment
	Working Hours
Flexible	Working Hours
Quality of	Working Life
Metal	Working
Metal	Working Occupations (1968 1980) Use Metal Working
	Working Overseas Use Overseas Employment
	Working Parents (1966 1980) Use Employed Parents
	Working Women (1968 1980) Use Employed Women
Faculty	Workload
	Workmans Compensation (1966 1980) Use Workers Compensation
	Workplace Literacy
Water	Works Use Utilities and Water Treatment
	Worksheets
	Workshops

Drama	Workshops
Parent	Workshops
Preschool	Workshops (1966 1980) Use Preschool Education and Workshops
Sheltered	Workshops
Summer	Workshops (1966 1980) Use Summer Programs and Workshops
Teacher	Workshops
Writing	Workshops
	Workstations
Computer	Workstations Use Workstations
	Workweek Use Working Hours
	World Affairs
Third	World Countries Use Developing Nations
	World Geography
	World History
	World Literature
	World Peace Use Peace
	World Problems
	World Studies Education Use Global Education
	World Views
	World War I
	World War II
	World Wide Web
	Worldmindedness Use Global Approach
	Worldviews Use World Views
	Worldwide Approach Use Global Approach
	Worldwide Web Service Use World Wide Web
Comparable	Worth
	Wrestling
Left Handed	Writer
	Writers Use Authors
Sign	Writers Use Sign Painters
	Writing (1966 1980) Use Writing (Composition)
	Writing Ability
Academic	Writing Use Academic Discourse
	Writing Achievement
	Writing Across the Curriculum
	Writing Apprehension
	Writing as Process Use Process Approach (Writing)
	Writing Assignments
	Writing Attitudes
Basic	Writing
Beginning	Writing
	Writing Centers Use Writing Laboratories
Childrens	Writing
	Writing (Composition)
Content Area	Writing
Creative	Writing
Cursive	Writing
Descriptive	Writing
	Writing Development Use Writing (Composition)
Developmental	Writing Use Basic Writing
	Writing Difficulties
Direction	Writing (1966 1980)
	Writing Evaluation
	Writing Exercises
Expository	Writing
	Writing for Publication
Free	Writing
Manuscript	Writing (Handlettering)
	Writing Improvement
	Writing Instruction
Journal	Writing
	Writing Laboratories
Local Color	Writing
Student	Writing Models
News	Writing
Process	Writing Use Process Approach (Writing)
	Writing Process Approach Use Process Approach (Writing)
Process Approach	(Writing)
	Writing Processes
Proposal	Writing
	Writing Readiness
Reading	Writing Relationship
Report	Writing Use Technical Writing
	Writing Research
Scholarly	Writing
	Writing Skills
	Writing Strategies
	Writing Systems Use Written Language
	Writing Teachers
Technical	Writing
	Writing Tests
Textbook	Writing Use Textbook Preparation
Theme	Writing Use Writing (Composition)
	Writing Workshops
Cohesion	(Written Composition)
Revision	(Written Composition)
	Written Language
	WWW Use World Wide Web
Industrial	X Ray Operators Use Radiographers
	X Ray Technologists Use Radiologic Technologists
	X Rays (Medicine) Use Radiology
	Xenophobia Use Stranger Reactions

Xerography   Use Reprography
Kikongo   Ya Leta   Use Kituba
Yakut
Yard Workers (Horticulture)   Use Grounds Keepers
Entry   Year Assistance (Teacher Induction)   Use Beginning Teacher Induction
Three   Year Bachelors Degrees   Use Acceleration (Education) and Bachelors Degrees
Two   Year College Degrees   Use Associate Degrees
Freshmen (1967 1980) (First   Year College Students)   Use College Freshmen
Two   Year College Students
Two   Year Colleges
Extended School   Year
Grade a   Year Integration (1966 1980)   Use School Desegregation
First   Year Principals   Use Beginning Principals
Year Round Schools
Five   Year Teacher Preparation Programs   Use Extended Teacher Education Programs
First   Year Teachers   Use Beginning Teachers
Seniors (1966 1980) (Last   Year Undergraduates)   Use College Seniors
Yearbooks
Yiddish
Yoruba
Young Adolescents   Use Early Adolescents
Young Adults
Young Children
Young Farmer Education
Young Old Adults
Youth
Affluent   Youth
Youth Agencies
Black   Youth
Youth Clubs
Disadvantaged   Youth
Youth Employment
Farm   Youth   Use Rural Youth
Gifted   Youth   Use Gifted
Youth Leaders
Migrant   Youth
Youth Mobilization   Use Youth Employment
Negro   Youth (1966 1977)   Use Black Youth
Youth Opportunities
Out of School   Youth
Youth Problems
Youth Programs
Rural   Youth
Suburban   Youth
Urban   Youth
Yucatec
Yupik
Yurak
E   Zines   Use Electronic Journals
Zoning
Community   Zoning
School   Zoning
Special   Zoning
Zoology
Zoos
Zuni (Tribe)

Two-Way Hierarchical Term Display

The Hierarchical Display depicts families of Descriptors (generic trees) related by the taxonomic concept of ''class membership.'' Two-way visibility is provided for the broader-narrower relationships of every *Thesaurus* Descriptor. Generic trees are carried to their farthest extreme in both directions. Broader terms (i.e., BTs) are identified by preceding colons and appear above each file point (main entry). File point terms are bold. Narrower terms (i.e., NTs) are identified by preceding periods and are listed below each file point. Multiple colons or periods indicate successively broader or narrower levels of terms. Descriptors having neither BTs nor NTs in the display are ''hierarchical isolates.'' The display is filed word by word, ignoring spaces between words.

Abbreviations

Ability
. Academic Ability
. Cognitive Ability
.. Thinking Skills
. Competence
.. Interpersonal Competence
.. Minimum Competencies
.. Teacher Competencies
. Language Proficiency
. Language Fluency
. Threshold Level (Languages)
. Leadership
.. Black Leadership
.. Informal Leadership
.. Instructional Leadership
.. Outdoor Leadership
.. Student Leadership
. Nonverbal Ability
. Skills
.. Agricultural Skills
.. Basic Skills
... Alphabetizing Skills
.. Business Skills
... Bookkeeping
... Keyboarding (Data Entry)
... Recordkeeping
... Typewriting
.. Communication Skills
... Communicative Competence
(Languages)
.... Threshold Level (Languages)
.. Daily Living Skills
.. Self Care Skills
.. Decision Making Skills
.. Home Economics Skills
.. Homemaking Skills
.. Information Skills
... Library Skills
.. Interpretive Skills
.. Job Skills
.. Language Skills
... Audiolingual Skills
.... Listening Skills
.... Speech Skills
... Communicative Competence
(Languages)
.... Threshold Level (Languages)
... Reading Skills
.... Reading Comprehension
.... Reading Rate
... Vocabulary Skills
... Writing Skills
.. Locational Skills (Social Studies)
.. Map Skills
.. Mathematics Skills
.. Mechanical Skills
.. Minimum Competencies
.. Parenting Skills
.. Psychomotor Skills
... Marksmanship
... Object Manipulation
... Perceptual Motor Coordination
.... Eye Hand Coordination
.... Eye Voice Span
.. Research Skills
. Salesmanship
. Science Process Skills
.. Study Skills
... Word Study Skills
.. Teaching Skills
.. Thinking Skills
.. Visual Literacy
. Spatial Ability
. Verbal Ability
.. Reading Ability
... Reading Skills
.... Reading Comprehension
.... Reading Rate
.. Writing Ability
... Writing Skills

::::: Organization
:::: Classification
:: Grouping (Instructional Purposes)
: Homogeneous Grouping
Ability Grouping

: Identification
Ability Identification

Abortions

: Cognitive Processes
Abstract Reasoning
. Generalization
.. Stimulus Generalization

:: Literacy
: Language Arts
: Writing (Composition)
:::: Services
::: Information Services
:: Information Processing
: Documentation
Abstracting

:: Publications
: Reference Materials
Abstracts

: Ability
Academic Ability

: Accessibility (for Disabled)
**Academic Accommodations
(Disabilities)**

: Achievement
Academic Achievement
. Educational Attainment
. Student Promotion
.. Social Promotion

::: Guidance
:: Counseling
: Educational Counseling
Academic Advising

: Aptitude
Academic Aptitude

: Aspiration
Academic Aspiration

::::: Groups
:::: Personnel
::: School Personnel
::::: Groups
:::: Personnel
::: Professional Personnel
:: Faculty
:::: Groups
::: Personnel
:: Administrators
: Deans
Academic Deans

:::: Linguistics
::: Sociolinguistics
:: Language Variation
: Language Usage
: Language Styles
Academic Discourse

: Education
Academic Education

::: Behavior
:: Performance
: Failure
Academic Failure
. Reading Failure

: Freedom
Academic Freedom

:: Institutions
:: Information Sources
: Libraries
Academic Libraries
. College Libraries

:: Behavior
: Persistence
Academic Persistence

: Probationary Period
Academic Probation

:: Status
: Employment Level
Academic Rank (Professional)

:: Records (Forms)
: Student Records
Academic Records

: Standards
Academic Standards
. Graduation Requirements
.. Degree Requirements

:: Groups
: Gifted
Academically Gifted

**Academically Handicapped (1966
1980)**

: Flexible Progression
Acceleration (Education)

:: Scientific Concepts
: Motion
Acceleration (Physics)

:: Opportunities
: Educational Opportunities
Access to Education

Access to Information
. Freedom of Information

Accessibility (for Disabled)
. Academic Accommodations
(Disabilities)

: Prevention
Accident Prevention

Accidents
. School Accidents
. Traffic Accidents

: Responsibility
Accountability

::: Groups
:: Personnel
: Professional Personnel
Accountants
. Certified Public Accountants

: Technology
Accounting
. Property Accounting
. School Accounting

: Certification
Accreditation (Institutions)

::: Groups
:: Organizations (Groups)
: Agencies
Accrediting Agencies

Acculturation

Achievement
. Academic Achievement
.. Educational Attainment
.. Student Promotion
... Social Promotion
. Black Achievement
. Graduation
. High Achievement
. Knowledge Level
. Low Achievement
. Mathematics Achievement
. Overachievement
. Reading Achievement
. Scholarship
.. Scholarly Communication
.. Scholarly Writing
. Science Achievement
. Underachievement
. Writing Achievement

: Improvement
Achievement Gains

::: Needs
:: Individual Needs
: Psychological Needs
: Motivation
Achievement Need

: Measurement
Achievement Rating
. Grading
.. Credit No Credit Grading
.. Pass Fail Grading

:: Measures (Individuals)
: Tests
Achievement Tests
. Equivalency Tests
. Mastery Tests
. National Competency Tests

:: Pollution
: Water Pollution
:: Pollution
: Air Pollution
Acid Rain

: Matter
Acids

: Structural Elements (Construction)
Acoustic Insulation

::: Linguistics
:: Phonology
: Phonetics
Acoustic Phonetics

:: Environment
: Physical Environment
Acoustical Environment
. Noise (Sound)

:: Liberal Arts
: Sciences
Acoustics
. Psychoacoustics

: Viruses
::: Disabilities
:: Diseases
: Communicable Diseases
**Acquired Immune Deficiency
Syndrome**

:::: Liberal Arts
::: Humanities
:: Fine Arts
: Theater Arts
Acting

: Research
Action Research

: Learning
Active Learning

:: Behavior
: Social Behavior
Activism

Activities
. Art Activities
. Creative Activities
.. Brainstorming
.. Creative Art
... Creative Dramatics
.. Creative Expression
.. Creative Writing
.. Improvisation
. Cultural Activities
. Enrichment Activities
. Games
.. Childrens Games
.. Computer Games
.. Educational Games
... Reading Games
.. Management Games
.. Olympic Games
.. Puzzles
.. Video Games
. Group Activities
. Health Activities
.. Health Promotion
. Individual Activities
. Integrated Activities
.. Integrated Curriculum
. Learning Activities
.. Study
... Home Study
.... Homework

. . . Independent Study
. Lobbying
. Mathematics Activities
. Music Activities
. . Concerts
. . Instrumentation and Orchestration
. . Singing
. Outdoor Activities
. Physical Activities
. . Athletics
. . . Aquatic Sports
. . . . Diving
. . . . Sailing
. . . . Surfing
. . . . Swimming
. . . . Water Polo
. . . . Waterskiing
. . . Archery
. . . Bowling
. . . College Athletics
. . . Extramural Athletics
. . . Fencing (Sport)
. . . Golf
. . . Gymnastics
. . . . Tumbling
. . . Handball
. . . Intramural Athletics
. . . Lifetime Sports
. . . Olympic Games
. . . Orienteering
. . . Racquet Sports
. . . . Badminton
. . . . Racquetball
. . . . Squash (Game)
. . . . Tennis
. . . Roller Skating
. . . Special Olympics
. . . Table Tennis
. . . Team Sports
. . . . Baseball
. . . . Basketball
. . . . Field Hockey
. . . . Football
. . . . Ice Hockey
. . . . Lacrosse
. . . . Soccer
. . . . Softball
. . . . Team Handball
. . . . Volleyball
. . . . Water Polo
. . . Track and Field
. . . Weightlifting
. . . Winter Sports
. . . . Ice Hockey
. . . . Ice Skating
. . . . Skiing
. . . Womens Athletics
. . . Wrestling
. . Bicycling
. . Dance
. . Exercise
. . . Aerobics
. . . Calisthenics
. . . Plyometrics
. . Horseback Riding
. . Lifting
. . . Weightlifting
. . Running
. . . Jogging
. . Underwater Diving
. . Walking
. Play
. . Pretend Play
. Recreational Activities
. . Camping
. . Hobbies
. . Playground Activities
. . Recreational Reading
. Review (Reexamination)
. School Activities
. . Class Activities
. . Extracurricular Activities
. . Student Projects
. Science Activities
. . Science Fairs
. . Science Projects
. Television Viewing
. Travel

: : : Curriculum
: : Courses
: Units of Study
Activity Units

: : Theories
: Behavior Theories
Adaptation Level Theory

: : Education
: Special Education
: : Education
: Physical Education
Adapted Physical Education

: : Behavior
: Adjustment (to Environment)
Adaptive Behavior (of Disabled)

: : : Methods
: : Measurement Techniques
: Testing
Adaptive Testing

: : : Liberal Arts
: : Mathematics
: Arithmetic
Addition

: : Resources
: Supplies
Adhesives

: : : : : Linguistics
: : : : Descriptive Linguistics
: : : Grammar
: : Syntax
: Form Classes (Languages)
Adjectives

: : : : Groups
: : : Personnel
: : School Personnel
: : : : Groups
: : : Personnel
: : Professional Personnel
: Faculty
Adjunct Faculty

: Behavior
Adjustment (to Environment)
. Adaptive Behavior (of Disabled)
. Coping
. Emotional Adjustment
. Social Adjustment
. Student Adjustment
. Vocational Adjustment

: : : : Groups
: : : Personnel
: : Guidance Personnel
: Counselors
Adjustment Counselors

: Governance
Administration
. Building Operation
. Business Administration
. Construction Management
. Crisis Management
. Educational Administration
. . School Administration
. . . College Administration
. . . School Based Management
. Energy Management
. Enrollment Management
. Farm Management
. Home Management
. Information Management
. Records Management
. Institutional Administration
. . Library Administration
. . School Administration
. . . College Administration
. . . School Based Management
. Management by Objectives
. Middle Management
. Money Management
. Office Management
. Personnel Management
. Program Administration
. Public Administration
. Research Administration
. Risk Management
. Supervision
. . Practicum Supervision
. . Proctoring
. . School Supervision

. . Science Supervision
. . Teacher Supervision
. . . Clinical Supervision (of Teachers)
. Time Management
. Total Quality Management

Administrative Agencies (1966 1980)

: Change
Administrative Change

: Organization
Administrative Organization
. Centralization
. Decentralization
. Departments
. . English Departments
. . Science Departments
. . State Departments of Education
. Management Teams
. Participative Decision Making

: Policy
Administrative Policy
. Board of Education Policy

: Standards
Administrative Principles

: Problems
Administrative Problems

: Attitudes
Administrator Attitudes

: Behavior
Administrator Behavior
. Administrator Effectiveness

Administrator Characteristics

: : Education
: Professional Education
Administrator Education

: : Behavior
: Administrator Behavior
Administrator Effectiveness

: : Evaluation
: Personnel Evaluation
Administrator Evaluation

: : : Publications
: : Reference Materials
: Guides
Administrator Guides

: : Standards
: Qualifications
Administrator Qualifications

: Responsibility
Administrator Responsibility

: Role
Administrator Role

: : Selection
: Personnel Selection
Administrator Selection

: : Groups
: Personnel
Administrators
. Admissions Officers
. Assistant Principals
. Beginning Principals
. Central Office Administrators
. Coordinators
. . Audiovisual Coordinators
. . Instructor Coordinators
. Deans
. . Academic Deans
. . Deans of Students
. Department Heads
. Library Administrators
. . Library Directors
. Medical Record Administrators
. Personnel Directors
. Presidents
. . College Presidents
. . Presidents of the United States

. Principals
. Registrars (School)
. Research Directors
. School Business Officials
. Student Financial Aid Officers
. Superintendents
. Supervisors
. . Crew Leaders
. . State Supervisors
. . Student Teacher Supervisors
. Trustees
. Vocational Directors
. Women Administrators

Admission (School)
. College Admission
. Early Admission
. Open Enrollment
. Selective Admission

: : Standards
: Criteria
Admission Criteria

: : : Guidance
: : Counseling
: Educational Counseling
Admissions Counseling

: : : Groups
: : Personnel
: School Personnel
: : Groups
: : Personnel
: Administrators
Admissions Officers

: Attitudes
Adolescent Attitudes

: Behavior
Adolescent Behavior

: : Development
: Individual Development
Adolescent Development

: : : Liberal Arts
: : Humanities
: Literature
Adolescent Literature

: : Groups
: Age Groups
Adolescents

: : : Groups
: : Age Groups
: Children
Adopted Children

Adoption
. Transracial Adoption

Adoption (Ideas)

: : Groups
: Parents
Adoptive Parents

: : : Education
: : Elementary Secondary Education
: Elementary Education
: : Education
: Adult Education
Adult Basic Education

: : : Groups
: : Age Groups
: Adults
Adult Children

: : Guidance
: Counseling
Adult Counseling

: : : Services
: : Human Services
: Social Services
Adult Day Care

: : Development
: Individual Development
Adult Development

: : Groups
: Dropouts
: : : Groups
: : Age Groups
: Adults
Adult Dropouts

: Education
Adult Education
. Adult Basic Education
. Adult Vocational Education
. . Adult Farmer Education
. . Young Farmer Education
. Continuing Education
. . Mandatory Continuing Education
. . Professional Continuing Education
. Labor Education
. Migrant Adult Education
. Parent Education
. Preretirement Education
. Public School Adult Education
. Veterans Education

: : : : Groups
: : : Personnel
: : Professional Personnel
: Teachers
Adult Educators

: : Education
: Agricultural Education
: : : Education
: : Vocational Education
: : : Education
: : Adult Education
: Adult Vocational Education
Adult Farmer Education

: : : Services
: : Human Services
: Social Services
Adult Foster Care

: Learning
Adult Learning

: Literacy
Adult Literacy

: Programs
Adult Programs
. Adult Reading Programs
. High School Equivalency Programs

: : Programs
: Reading Programs
: : Programs
: Adult Programs
Adult Reading Programs

: : Groups
: Students
: : : Groups
: : Age Groups
: Adults
Adult Students

: : Education
: Vocational Education
: : Education
: Adult Education
Adult Vocational Education
. Adult Farmer Education
. Young Farmer Education

: : Groups
: Age Groups
Adults
. Adult Children
. Adult Dropouts
. Adult Students
. Adults (30 to 45)
. Middle Aged Adults
. Older Adults
. . Frail Elderly
. . Old Old Adults
. . Young Old Adults
. Young Adults

: : : Groups
: : Age Groups
: Adults
Adults (30 to 45)

: : Educational Media
: Instructional Materials
Advance Organizers

: : Curriculum
: Courses
Advanced Courses

: Placement
Advanced Placement

: Programs
Advanced Placement Programs

Advanced Programs (1966 1980)

: : Groups
: Students
Advanced Students

: Groups
Advantaged

: Disabilities
Adventitious Impairments

: : Education
: Outdoor Education
Adventure Education

: : : : Linguistics
: : : Descriptive Linguistics
: : : Grammar
: : Syntax
: Form Classes (Languages)
Adverbs

: : : : Services
: : : Information Services
: : Information Dissemination
: : Communication (Thought Transfer)
: Publicity
Advertising
. Television Commercials

: Committees
Advisory Committees

Advocacy
. Child Advocacy
. Self Advocacy

: : : Activities
: : Physical Activities
: Exercise
Aerobics

: Education
Aerospace Education
. Aviation Education

: : : Business
: : Industry
: Manufacturing Industry
Aerospace Industry

: Technology
Aerospace Technology
. Aviation Technology
. . Aviation Mechanics

: Education
Aesthetic Education
. Art Appreciation
. Film Study
. Music Appreciation

: Values
Aesthetic Values

: : : Liberal Arts
: : Humanities
: Philosophy
Aesthetics

: : : Needs
: : : Individual Needs

: Psychological Needs
Affection

: Behavior
Affective Behavior

: Measures (Individuals)
Affective Measures

: : Objectives
: Behavioral Objectives
Affective Objectives

: : Institutions
: Schools
Affiliated Schools

: : : Needs
: : Individual Needs
: Psychological Needs
Affiliation Need
. Peer Acceptance

Affirmative Action

: : : : : Linguistics
: : : : Descriptive Linguistics
: : : Grammar
: : Morphology (Languages)
: Morphemes
Affixes
. Prefixes (Grammar)
. Suffixes

: : Groups
: Youth
Affluent Youth

: Culture
African Culture

: : : : Liberal Arts
: : : Sciences
: : Social Sciences
: : : Liberal Arts
: : Humanities
: History
African History

: Languages
African Languages
. Akan
. Bantu Languages
. . Chinyanja
. . Ganda
. . Kirundi
. . Kituba
. . Lingala
. . Shona
. . Siswati
. . Swahili
. Basaa
. Bini
. Dyula
. Ewe
. Fulani
. Ga
. Gbaya
. Igbo
. Luo
. Mandingo
. Mende
. Mossi
. Nembe
. Sango
. Sara
. Susu
. Wolof
. Yoruba

: : : Liberal Arts
: : Humanities
: Literature
African Literature

: : Curriculum
: Area Studies
African Studies

: : Languages
: Indo European Languages
Afrikaans

: Languages
Afro Asiatic Languages
. Berber Languages
. . Kabyle
. . Riff
. Chad Languages
. . Hausa
. Semitic Languages
. . Amharic
. . Arabic
. . Hebrew
. Somali

Afrocentrism

: : Facilities
: Educational Facilities
After School Centers

: Education
After School Education

: Programs
After School Programs

: Individual Characteristics
Age
. Chronological Age
. Mental Age
. School Entrance Age

: : Differences
: Individual Differences
Age Differences

: Social Discrimination
Age Discrimination

: Placement
Age Grade Placement

: Groups
Age Groups
. Adolescents
. Adults
. . Adult Children
. . Adult Dropouts
. . Adult Students
. . Adults (30 to 45)
. . Middle Aged Adults
. . Older Adults
. . . Frail Elderly
. . . Old Old Adults
. . . Young Old Adults
. . Young Adults
. Children
. . Adopted Children
. . Foster Children
. . Grandchildren
. . Hospitalized Children
. . Latchkey Children
. . Migrant Children
. . Minority Group Children
. . Missing Children
. . Preadolescents
. . Problem Children
. . Transient Children
. . Young Children
. . . Infants
. . . . Neonates
. . . . . Premature Infants
. . . Kindergarten Children
. . . Preschool Children
. . . . Toddlers
. Early Adolescents
. Late Adolescents
. Mixed Age Grouping

: : Groups
: Organizations (Groups)
Agencies
. Accrediting Agencies
. Private Agencies
. Public Agencies
. . Planning Commissions
. . State Agencies
. . . State Departments of Education
. . . State Licensing Boards
. . Social Agencies
. . Welfare Agencies
. Urban Renewal Agencies
. Voluntary Agencies
. Youth Agencies

: : Behavior
: Cooperation
Agency Cooperation

: : Role
: Institutional Role
Agency Role

Agenda Setting

: : : Behavior
: : Social Behavior
: Antisocial Behavior
Aggression

: : Development
: Individual Development
Aging (Individuals)
. Aging in Academia

: Education
Aging Education

: : : Development
: : Individual Development
: Aging (Individuals)
Aging in Academia

: Business
Agribusiness

: : : Occupations
: : Agricultural Occupations
: Off Farm Agricultural Occupations
Agricultural Chemical Occupations

: : : Institutions
: : Schools
: Colleges
Agricultural Colleges

: Education
Agricultural Education
. Adult Farmer Education
. Supervised Occupational Experience
   (Agriculture)
. Young Farmer Education

: : Technology
: Engineering
Agricultural Engineering

: : : : : Groups
: : : : Personnel
: : : Nonprofessional Personnel
: : Unskilled Workers
: Laborers
: : : Groups
: : Personnel
: Agricultural Personnel
Agricultural Laborers
. Migrant Workers
. Seasonal Laborers

: Equipment
Agricultural Machinery

: : : Occupations
: : Agricultural Occupations
: Off Farm Agricultural Occupations
Agricultural Machinery Occupations

: Occupations
Agricultural Occupations
. Farm Occupations
. Off Farm Agricultural Occupations
. . Agricultural Chemical Occupations
. . Agricultural Machinery Occupations
. . Agricultural Supply Occupations
. . Crop Processing Occupations
. . Food Processing Occupations
. . Ornamental Horticulture
      Occupations

: : Groups
: Personnel
Agricultural Personnel
. Agricultural Laborers
. . Migrant Workers
. . Seasonal Laborers
. Agricultural Technicians
. Farmers
. . Dairy Farmers

. . Part Time Farmers
. . Sharecroppers

Agricultural Production

: Safety
Agricultural Safety

: : Ability
: Skills
Agricultural Skills

: : Resources
: Supplies
Agricultural Supplies

: : : Occupations
: : Agricultural Occupations
: Off Farm Agricultural Occupations
Agricultural Supply Occupations

: : : Groups
: : Personnel
: Paraprofessional Personnel
: : : Groups
: : Personnel
: Agricultural Personnel
Agricultural Technicians

Agricultural Trends

: Technology
Agriculture
. Agronomy
. Animal Husbandry
. Gardening
. Harvesting
. Horticulture
. . Ornamental Horticulture
. . . Floriculture
. . . Landscaping
. . . Turf Management

: : Technology
: Agriculture
Agronomy

: Climate Control
Air Conditioning

: Equipment
Air Conditioning Equipment

Air Flow

: Pollution
Air Pollution
. Acid Rain

: Facilities
Air Structures
. Pneumatic Forms

: Traffic Control
Air Traffic Control

: Transportation
Air Transportation

: : Groups
: Personnel
Aircraft Pilots

: Facilities
Airports

: : Languages
: African Languages
Akan

Alarm Systems

: : Groups
: North Americans
: : Groups
: Ethnic Groups
Alaska Natives

: : Languages
: Indo European Languages
Albanian

: : Behavior
: Substance Abuse
: : Behavior
: Drinking
Alcohol Abuse
. Alcoholism

: Education
Alcohol Education

Alcoholic Beverages

: : Disabilities
: Diseases
: : : Behavior
: : Substance Abuse
: : : Behavior
: : Drinking
: Alcohol Abuse
Alcoholism

: : Liberal Arts
: Mathematics
Algebra
. Matrices
. Polynomials
. Vectors (Mathematics)

: Methods
: : : : : Liberal Arts
: : : : Humanities
: : : Philosophy
: : Logic
: Mathematical Logic
: Mathematical Applications
Algorithms

: Psychological Patterns
Alienation
. Student Alienation
. Teacher Alienation

: : Literary Devices
: : Language
: Figurative Language
Allegory

: : Disabilities
: Diseases
Allergy

: : Occupations
: Health Occupations
Allied Health Occupations

: Education
Allied Health Occupations Education

: : : Groups
: : Personnel
: Health Personnel
Allied Health Personnel
. Dental Assistants
. Dental Hygienists
. Dental Technicians
. Dietitians
. Emergency Medical Technicians
. Environmental Technicians
. Home Health Aides
. Medical Assistants
. . Medical Laboratory Assistants
. Medical Record Administrators
. Medical Record Technicians
. Medical Technologists
. Nurses Aides
. Occupational Therapy Assistants
. Optometrists
. Physical Therapy Aides
. Physicians Assistants
. Psychiatric Aides
. Radiologic Technologists
. Surgical Technicians
. Therapists
. . Occupational Therapists
. . Physical Therapists
. Veterinary Assistants

: : : Ability
: : Skills
: Basic Skills
Alphabetizing Skills

Alphabets
. Cyrillic Alphabet
. Initial Teaching Alphabet
. Non Roman Scripts
. Phonemic Alphabets

: : Planning
: Scheduling
Alternate Day Schedules

: Evaluation
Alternative Assessment
. Performance Based Assessment

Alternative Energy Sources

: : Certification
: Teacher Certification
Alternative Teacher Certification

Altruism

: Groups
Alumni
. Graduates
. . College Graduates
. . Foreign Medical Graduates
. . High School Graduates

: : Groups
: Organizations (Groups)
Alumni Associations

: Education
Alumni Education

: : Disabilities
: Diseases
Alzheimers Disease

: : Literary Devices
: : Language
: Figurative Language
Ambiguity

American Culture (1966 1980)

: : Values
: Democratic Values
American Dream

American History (1966 1980)

: Culture
American Indian Culture

: Education
American Indian Education

: : : : Liberal Arts
: : : Sciences
: : Social Sciences
: : : Liberal Arts
: : Humanities
: History
American Indian History

: Languages
American Indian Languages
. Athapascan Languages
. Apache
. Navajo
. Aymara
. Cherokee
. Choctaw
. Cree
. Dakota
. Lakota
. Guarani
. Mayan Languages
. . Cakchiquel
. . Quiche
. . Tzeltal
. . Tzotzil
. . Yucatec
. Ojibwa
. Pomo
. Quechua
. Salish
. Uto Aztecan Languages
. . Hopi
. . Papago

: : : Liberal Arts
: : Humanities
: Literature
American Indian Literature

: : Geographic Regions
: Political Divisions (Geographic)
American Indian Reservations

: : Curriculum
: Ethnic Studies
American Indian Studies

: : Groups
: Ethnic Groups
American Indians
. Cherokee (Tribe)
. Chippewa (Tribe)
. Choctaw (Tribe)
. . Mississippi Band of Choctaw
      (Tribe)
. Cree (Tribe)
. Iroquois (Tribe)
. Maya (People)
. Navajo (Nation)
. Nonreservation American Indians
. . Rural American Indians
. . Urban American Indians
. Pueblo (People)
. . Hopi (Tribe)
. . Zuni (Tribe)
. Reservation American Indians
. Sioux (Tribe)
. . Lakota (Tribe)
. . . Oglala Sioux (Tribe)
. Tohono O Odham People

: : : : Communication (Thought
          Transfer)
: : : Augmentative and Alternative
        Communication
: : Manual Communication
: Language
: Sign Language
: Languages
American Sign Language

: : Curriculum
: Area Studies
American Studies

: : Disabilities
: Visual Impairments
Ametropia
. Hyperopia
. Myopia

: : : Languages
: : Afro Asiatic Languages
: Semitic Languages
Amharic

: : : Groups
: : Religious Cultural Groups
: Protestants
Amish

: : Disabilities
: Physical Disabilities
Amputations

: : : Equipment
: : Electronic Equipment
: Computers
Analog Computers

: : : : Methods
: : : Evaluation Methods
: : Data Analysis
: Statistical Analysis
Analysis of Covariance

: : : : Methods
: : : Evaluation Methods
: : Data Analysis
: Statistical Analysis
Analysis of Variance

: : : Liberal Arts
: : Mathematics
: Geometry
Analytic Geometry

Analytical Criticism (1969 1980)

: : : : Liberal Arts
: : : Sciences
: : Natural Sciences
: Biological Sciences
Anatomy

: : : : Liberal Arts
: : : Sciences
: : Social Sciences
: : : Liberal Arts
: : Humanities
: History
Ancient History

: : : Services
: : Human Services
: Social Services
Ancillary School Services
. Mobile Educational Services
. Pupil Personnel Services
. School Health Services
. Student Personnel Services

Ancillary Services (1967 1980)

Andragogy

Androgyny

: : Disabilities
: Diseases
Anemia
. Sickle Cell Anemia

: : Technology
: Medicine
Anesthesiology

: Psychological Patterns
Anger
. Hostility

: : Groups
: North Americans
: : Groups
: Ethnic Groups
Anglo Americans

: Behavior
Animal Behavior

: : : : Groups
: : : Personnel
: : Nonprofessional Personnel
: Semiskilled Workers
Animal Caretakers

: Facilities
Animal Facilities
. Zoos

: : Technology
: Agriculture
Animal Husbandry

Animals
. Birds
. Dinosaurs
. Horses
. Laboratory Animals
. Livestock
. Pets
. Rats

: : : Methods
: : Production Techniques
: Special Effects
Animation

: : : Publications
: : Reference Materials
: Bibliographies
Annotated Bibliographies

: : Publications
: Serials
: : Publications
: Reports
Annual Reports

: : : Disabilities
: : Diseases
: Eating Disorders
Anorexia Nervosa

Answer Keys

Answer Sheets

: : Publications
: Reference Materials
Anthologies

: Linguistics
: : : : Liberal Arts
: : : Sciences
: : Social Sciences
: Anthropology
Anthropological Linguistics

: : : Liberal Arts
: : Sciences
: Social Sciences
Anthropology
. Anthropological Linguistics
. Archaeology
. Educational Anthropology
. Ethnography
. Ethnology
. . Ethnomathematics

: Attitudes
Anti Intellectualism

Anti Semitism

: : Behavior
: Social Behavior
Antisocial Behavior
. Aggression
. Bullying
. Cheating
. Child Abuse
. Child Neglect
. Crime
. . Delinquency
. . International Crimes
. . . Genocide
. Driving While Intoxicated
. Elder Abuse
. Emotional Abuse
. Fraud
. Hazing
. Homicide
. Incest
. Sexual Abuse
. . Rape
. Sexual Harassment
. Stealing
. . Plagiarism
. Terrorism
. Vandalism
. . School Vandalism
. Verbal Abuse
. Violence
. . Family Violence

: : Literary Devices
: : Language
: Figurative Language
Antithesis

: Psychological Patterns
Anxiety
. Communication Apprehension
. Computer Anxiety
. Mathematics Anxiety
. Separation Anxiety
. Test Anxiety
. Writing Apprehension

: : : Languages
: : American Indian Languages
: Athapascan Languages
Apache

Apartheid

: Psychological Patterns
Apathy

: : : Disabilities
: : Physical Disabilities

: Neurological Impairments
: : Disabilities
: Language Impairments
Aphasia

: : Maintenance
: Repair
Appliance Repair

: Linguistics
Applied Linguistics

: : : : Liberal Arts
: : : Humanities
: : Fine Arts
: Music
Applied Music

: : : Training
: : Job Training
: On the Job Training
Apprenticeships

: Technology
Appropriate Technology

Aptitude
. Academic Aptitude
. Language Aptitude
. Mathematical Aptitude
. Vocational Aptitude

: : Measures (Individuals)
: Tests
Aptitude Tests
. Reading Readiness Tests
. School Readiness Tests

: : Relationship
: Interaction
Aptitude Treatment Interaction

: Facilities
Aquariums

: : : Activities
: : Physical Activities
: Athletics
Aquatic Sports
. Diving
. Sailing
. Surfing
. Swimming
. Water Polo
. Waterskiing

: : : Languages
: : Afro Asiatic Languages
: Semitic Languages
Arabic

: Groups
Arabs

Arbitration

: : : : Liberal Arts
: : : Sciences
: : Social Sciences
: Anthropology
Archaeology

: : : Activities
: : Physical Activities
: Athletics
Archery

: : : Groups
: : Personnel
: Professional Personnel
Architects

Architectural Barriers (1970 1980)

Architectural Character

: : : : : Liberal Arts
: : : : Humanities
: : : Fine Arts
: : Visual Arts
: Drafting
Architectural Drafting

: : Education
: Professional Education
Architectural Education

Architectural Programming

: Research
Architectural Research

: : : : Liberal Arts
: : : Humanities
: : Fine Arts
: Visual Arts
Architecture

: Information Sources
Archives

: : Scientific Concepts
: Space
: : Mathematical Concepts
: Geometric Concepts
Area

: Curriculum
Area Studies
. African Studies
. American Studies
. Asian Studies
. Canadian Studies
. Middle Eastern Studies

Aristotelian Criticism (1969 1980)

: : Liberal Arts
: Mathematics
Arithmetic
. Addition
. Division
. Modular Arithmetic
. Multiplication
. Subtraction

: : : Groups
: : Organizations (Groups)
: Military Organizations
Armed Forces

: : Languages
: Indo European Languages
Armenian

: Behavior Patterns
Arousal Patterns

Art
. Art Products
. Commercial Art
. Creative Art
. . Creative Dramatics

: Activities
Art Activities

: : Education
: Aesthetic Education
Art Appreciation

: Criticism
Art Criticism

: Education
Art Education
. Discipline Based Art Education
. Studio Art

Art Expression

: : : : : Liberal Arts
: : : : Sciences
: : : Social Sciences
: : : : Liberal Arts
: : : Humanities
: : History
: Intellectual History
Art History

Art Materials

: Art
Art Products

: : : : : : Liberal Arts
: : : : : Humanities
: : : : Fine Arts
: : : Music
: : Vocal Music
: Songs
Art Song

: : : : Groups
: : : Personnel
: : Professional Personnel
: Teachers
Art Teachers

: Therapy
Art Therapy

Articulation (Education)

: : Language Arts
: Speech
Articulation (Speech)

: : Disabilities
: Speech Impairments
Articulation Impairments

Artificial Intelligence
. Expert Systems
. . Intelligent Tutoring Systems

: Language
Artificial Languages
. Esperanto

: : Language Arts
: Speech
Artificial Speech

: Groups
Artists
. Musicians

: : Facilities
: Resource Centers
Arts Centers

: : Matter
: Minerals
Asbestos

: : Groups
: Students
: : : Groups
: : North Americans
: Asian Americans
Asian American Students

: : Groups
: North Americans
Asian Americans
. Asian American Students
. Chinese Americans
. Filipino Americans
. Japanese Americans
. Korean Americans

: : : : Liberal Arts
: : : Sciences
: : Social Sciences
: : : Liberal Arts
: : Humanities
: History
Asian History
. Korean War
. Vietnam War

: : Curriculum
: Area Studies
Asian Studies

: Construction Materials
Asphalts

Aspiration
. Academic Aspiration
. Occupational Aspiration
. Parent Aspiration

: : Technology
: Manufacturing
Assembly (Manufacturing)

: Programs
Assembly Programs

: Behavior
Assertiveness

: : Evaluation
: Property Appraisal
Assessed Valuation

: Facilities
Assessment Centers (Personnel)

: Instruction
Assignments
. Homework
. Reading Assignments
. Research Papers (Students)
. Writing Assignments

: : : Groups
: : Personnel
: School Personnel
: : : Groups
: : Personnel
: Administrators
Assistant Principals

**Assistant Superintendent Role
(1966 1980)**

: : Financial Support
: Student Financial Aid
Assistantships

: Equipment
Assistive Devices (for Disabled)
. Mobility Aids
. . Wheelchairs
. Prostheses
. . Cochlear Implants

: Degrees (Academic)
Associate Degrees

: Cognitive Processes
Association (Psychology)

: : Measures (Individuals)
: Projective Measures
Association Measures

: Learning
Associative Learning
. Paired Associate Learning

: : Disabilities
: Diseases
Asthma

: : : : Liberal Arts
: : : Sciences
: : Natural Sciences
: Physical Sciences
Astronomy

: Groups
At Risk Persons
. High Risk Students

: : Languages
: American Indian Languages
Athapascan Languages
. Apache
. Navajo

: Groups
Athletes

: : : Groups
: : Personnel
: Professional Personnel
Athletic Coaches

: Equipment
Athletic Equipment

: Facilities
Athletic Fields

: : Activities
: Physical Activities
Athletics

. Aquatic Sports
. . Diving
. . Sailing
. . Surfing
. . Swimming
. . Water Polo
. . Waterskiing
. Archery
. Bowling
. College Athletics
. Extramural Athletics
. Fencing (Sport)
. Golf
. Gymnastics
. . Tumbling
. Handball
. Intramural Athletics
. Lifetime Sports
. Olympic Games
. Orienteering
. Racquet Sports
. . Badminton
. . Racquetball
. . Squash (Game)
. . Tennis
. Roller Skating
. Special Olympics
. Table Tennis
. Team Sports
. . Baseball
. . Basketball
. . Field Hockey
. . Football
. . Ice Hockey
. . Lacrosse
. . Soccer
. . Softball
. . Team Handball
. . Volleyball
. . Water Polo
. Track and Field
. Weightlifting
. Winter Sports
. . Ice Hockey
. . Ice Skating
. . Skiing
. Womens Athletics
. Wrestling

: : Publications
: Reference Materials
Atlases

Atomic Structure

: Theories
Atomic Theory

: Behavior
Attachment Behavior

Attendance
. Average Daily Attendance
. College Attendance
. Teacher Attendance

: : : : Groups
: : : Personnel
: : School Personnel
: Pupil Personnel Workers
Attendance Officers

Attendance Patterns

: Records (Forms)
Attendance Records

: : : : Groups
: : : Personnel
: : Nonprofessional Personnel
: Service Workers
: : Groups
: Caregivers
Attendants

Attention

Attention Control

: Disabilities
Attention Deficit Disorders

: : Individual Characteristics
: Psychological Characteristics
Attention Span

: Change
Attitude Change

: Measures (Individuals)
Attitude Measures
. Likert Scales
. Semantic Differential

Attitudes
. Administrator Attitudes
. Adolescent Attitudes
. Anti Intellectualism
. Attitudes toward Disabilities
. Beliefs
. Black Attitudes
. Childhood Attitudes
. Community Attitudes
. . Community Satisfaction
. Computer Attitudes
. Counselor Attitudes
. Design Preferences
. Dropout Attitudes
. Educational Attitudes
. Employee Attitudes
. Employer Attitudes
. Family Attitudes
. Language Attitudes
. . Grammatical Acceptability
. Librarian Attitudes
. Majority Attitudes
. Negative Attitudes
. Opinions
. . Press Opinion
. . Public Opinion
. Parent Attitudes
. . Father Attitudes
. . Mother Attitudes
. Political Attitudes
. Program Attitudes
. Racial Attitudes
. Reading Attitudes
. Regional Attitudes
. Satisfaction
. . Community Satisfaction
. . Job Satisfaction
. . Life Satisfaction
. . Marital Satisfaction
. . Participant Satisfaction
. . User Satisfaction (Information)
. School Attitudes
. Scientific Attitudes
. Social Attitudes
. . Social Bias
. . . Ethnic Bias
. . . Homophobia
. . . Racial Bias
. . . Sex Bias
. . . . Sexism in Language
. . Social Desirability
. Sportsmanship
. Stereotypes
. . Ethnic Stereotypes
. . . Black Stereotypes
. . Sex Stereotypes
. . Teacher Stereotypes
. Student Attitudes
. Student Teacher Attitudes
. Teacher Attitudes
. Trust (Psychology)
. Work Attitudes
. . Job Satisfaction
. World Views
. Writing Attitudes

: Attitudes
Attitudes toward Disabilities

: : Theories
: Behavior Theories
Attribution Theory

Attrition (Research Studies)

: : Methods
: Evaluation Methods
Audience Analysis

Audience Awareness

: : Behavior
: Participation
Audience Participation

: : Behavior
: Responses
Audience Response
. Reader Response

: Groups
Audiences

: Equipment
Audio Equipment
. Audiodisks
. Audiotape Cassettes
. Audiotape Recorders
. Hearing Aids
. Microphones
. Sound Spectrographs
. Speech Synthesizers

: Nonprint Media
: Equipment
: Audio Equipment
Audiodisks

: : Methods
: : Educational Methods
: Teaching Methods
Audiolingual Methods

: : : Ability
: : Skills
: Language Skills
Audiolingual Skills
. Listening Skills
. Speech Skills

: : Technology
: Medicine
Audiology

: : : Measures (Individuals)
: : Tests
: Auditory Tests
Audiometric Tests

: : : : Resources
: : : Supplies
: : : Equipment
: : Electronic Equipment
: : Magnetic Tapes
: Magnetic Tape Cassettes
: : Equipment
: Audio Equipment
Audiotape Cassettes

: : : Equipment
: : Electronic Equipment
: Tape Recorders
: : Equipment
: Audio Equipment
Audiotape Recorders

: : Nonprint Media
: Tape Recordings
Audiotape Recordings

: Educational Media
Audiovisual Aids
. Instructional Films
. Protocol Materials

: : Facilities
: Resource Centers
: : Facilities
: Educational Facilities
Audiovisual Centers

: : Technology
: Communications
Audiovisual Communications
. Dial Access Information Systems
. Educational Radio
. Educational Television
. Loop Induction Systems

: : : Groups
: : Personnel
: School Personnel

: : : : Groups
: : : Personnel
: : Specialists
: Media Specialists
: : : Groups
: : Personnel
: : Administrators
: Coordinators
Audiovisual Coordinators

: : : : Methods
: : : Educational Methods
: : Teaching Methods
: Multimedia Instruction
Audiovisual Instruction

Auditing (Coursework)

: Facilities
Auditoriums

: : : Cognitive Processes
: : Perception
: Auditory Perception
Auditory Discrimination

: : Evaluation
: Medical Evaluation
Auditory Evaluation

: : Cognitive Processes
: Perception
Auditory Perception
. Auditory Discrimination

: Stimuli
Auditory Stimuli

: : Measures (Individuals)
: Tests
Auditory Tests
. Audiometric Tests

: : Training
: Sensory Training
Auditory Training

Audits (Verification)
. Communication Audits
. Energy Audits
. Financial Audits

: Communication (Thought Transfer)
Augmentative and Alternative Communication
. Manual Communication
. . Cued Speech
. . Finger Spelling
. . Sign Language
. . . American Sign Language
. Total Communication

: Learning
Aural Learning

: Languages
Australian Aboriginal Languages

: : : Liberal Arts
: : Humanities
: Literature
Australian Literature

: Languages
Austro Asiatic Languages
. Cambodian

Auteurism

Authoring Aids (Programming)

Authoritarianism

: : : : Services
: : : Information Services
: : Information Processing
: Documentation
Authority Control (Information)

: Groups
Authors
. Poets

: Disabilities
Autism

: : : : Groups
: : : Personnel
: : Nonprofessional Personnel
: Skilled Workers
Auto Body Repairers

: : Technology
: Mechanics (Process)
Auto Mechanics

: : : : Groups
: : : Personnel
: : Nonprofessional Personnel
: Sales Workers
Auto Parts Clerks

: : : : : Liberal Arts
: : : : Humanities
: : : Literature
: : : Prose
: : Nonfiction
: Literary Genres
: Biographies
Autobiographies

: Educational Media
Autoinstructional Aids
. Teaching Machines

: : : : : Services
: : : : Information Services
: : : Information Processing
: : Documentation
: Indexing
Automatic Indexing

: Technology
Automation
. Library Automation
. . Retrospective Conversion (Library Catalogs)
. Office Automation
. Robotics

: : : : : Groups
: : : : Personnel
: : : Nonprofessional Personnel
: : Unskilled Workers
: Laborers
Auxiliary Laborers

: Incidence
: Attendance
Average Daily Attendance

: : Incidence
: Enrollment Rate
Average Daily Membership

: : Education
: Aerospace Education
Aviation Education

: : Technology
: Mechanics (Process)
: : Technology
: : Aerospace Technology
: Aviation Technology
Aviation Mechanics

: : Technology
: Aerospace Technology
Aviation Technology
. Aviation Mechanics

: Vocabulary
Aviation Vocabulary

: : Evaluation
: Recognition (Achievement)
Awards

: : Languages
: American Indian Languages
Aymara

: : : Languages
: : Uralic Altaic Languages
: Turkic Languages
Azerbaijani

: Groups
Baby Boomers

: Degrees (Academic)
Bachelors Degrees

: Education
Back to Basics

Background
. Cultural Background
. Educational Background
. . Educational Experience
. Experience
. . Early Experience
. . Educational Experience
. . Emotional Experience
. . . Catharsis
. . Group Experience
. . Intellectual Experience
. . Learning Experience
. . . Clinical Experience
. . Life Events
. . Prereading Experience
. . Sensory Experience
. . . Figural Aftereffects
. . . Sensory Deprivation
. . Social Experience
. . Student Experience
. . Teaching Experience
. . Work Experience
. . . Employment Experience
. Parent Background
. Socioeconomic Background
. . Social Background
. . . Social Experience
. Teacher Background

Bacteria

: : : : Activities
: : : Physical Activities
: : Athletics
: Racquet Sports
Badminton

: : Business
: Industry
Bakery Industry

: : : : : : Liberal Arts
: : : : : Humanities
: : : : Fine Arts
: : : Music
: : Vocal Music
: Songs
: : : : : Liberal Arts
: : : : Humanities
: : : Literature
: : Poetry
: Lyric Poetry
: Literary Genres
Ballads

: : Languages
: Indo European Languages
Baltic Languages
. Latvian
. Lithuanian

: : Languages
: Indo European Languages
Baluchi

Bands (Music)

: : Business
: Industry
Banking

: Vocabulary
Banking Vocabulary

: : Languages
: African Languages
Bantu Languages
. Bemba
. Chinyanja
. Ganda
. Kirundi
. Kituba
. Lingala
. Shona

. Siswati
. Swahili

: : : : Groups
: : : Personnel
: : Nonprofessional Personnel
: Service Workers
Barbers

: : : Liberal Arts
: : Humanities
: Literature
Baroque Literature

: : Languages
: African Languages
Basaa

: : Instruction
: Reading Instruction
: : Literacy
: : Language Arts
: Reading
Basal Reading

: : : : Activities
: : : Physical Activities
: : Athletics
: Team Sports
Baseball

: : : Languages
: : Uralic Altaic Languages
: Turkic Languages
Bashkir

: Education
Basic Business Education

Basic Reading (1967 1980)

: : Ability
: Skills
Basic Skills
. Alphabetizing Skills

: Vocabulary
Basic Vocabulary

: : Instruction
: Writing Instruction
: : Literacy
: : Language Arts
: Writing (Composition)
Basic Writing

: : : : Activities
: : : Physical Activities
: : Athletics
: Team Sports
Basketball

: Languages
Basque

: : Groups
: Females
Battered Women

: : : Liberal Arts
: : Mathematics
: Statistics
: : : : Methods
: : : Evaluation Methods
: : Data Analysis
: Statistical Analysis
Bayesian Statistics

: : : Groups
: : Personnel
: School Personnel
: : : Groups
: : Personnel
: Administrators
Beginning Principals

: : Literacy
: : Language Arts
: Reading
Beginning Reading

: : Orientation
: Teacher Orientation
Beginning Teacher Induction

: : : : Groups
: : : Personnel
: : Professional Personnel
: Teachers
Beginning Teachers

: : Literacy
: : Language Arts
: Writing (Composition)
Beginning Writing

Behavior
. Adjustment (to Environment)
. . Adaptive Behavior (of Disabled)
. . Coping
. . Emotional Adjustment
. . Social Adjustment
. . Student Adjustment
. . Vocational Adjustment
. Administrator Behavior
. . Administrator Effectiveness
. Adolescent Behavior
. Affective Behavior
. Animal Behavior
. Assertiveness
. Attachment Behavior
. Child Behavior
. . Infant Behavior
. Competition
. . Competitive Selection
. Cooperation
. . Agency Cooperation
. . Community Cooperation
. . Compliance (Psychology)
. . . Compliance (Legal)
. . . Obedience
. . Educational Cooperation
. . . College School Cooperation
. . . Counselor Teacher Cooperation
. . . Intercollegiate Cooperation
. . . Librarian Teacher Cooperation
. . . Parent Teacher Cooperation
. . . Partnerships in Education
. . . Teacher Collaboration
. . Institutional Cooperation
. . . College School Cooperation
. . . Intercollegiate Cooperation
. . Library Cooperation
. . International Cooperation
. . Regional Cooperation
. Crying
. Drinking
. . Alcohol Abuse
. . . Alcoholism
. Drug Use
. . Drug Abuse
. . . Drug Addiction
. . Illegal Drug Use
. . Prenatal Drug Exposure
. Exploratory Behavior
. Group Behavior
. . Teamwork
. Health Behavior
. Hyperactivity
. Imitation
. Leadership Styles
. Life Style
. Modeling (Psychology)
. Paranoid Behavior
. Participation
. . Audience Participation
. . Citizen Participation
. . Community Involvement
. . Family Involvement
. . Parent Participation
. . School Involvement
. . Student Participation
. . Teacher Participation
. Performance
. . Counselor Performance
. . Failure
. . . Academic Failure
. . . . Reading Failure
. . Job Performance
. . Success
. Persistence
. . Academic Persistence
. . Teacher Persistence
. Physical Activity Level

. Resistance (Psychology)
. . Resistance to Change
. . Resistance to Temptation
. Response Style (Tests)
. . Guessing (Tests)
. Responses
. . Audience Response
. . . Reader Response
. . Burnout
. . . Teacher Burnout
. . Constructed Response
. . Covert Response
. . Dimensional Preference
. . Emotional Response
. . Motor Reactions
. . . Eye Movements
. . . . Eye Fixations
. . . . Pupillary Dilation
. . Overt Response
. . Patterned Responses
. . Stranger Reactions
. . Student Reaction
. . Teacher Response
. Self Control
. . Delay of Gratification
. . Self Management
. Self Destructive Behavior
. . Self Injurious Behavior
. . Suicide
. Smoking
. Social Behavior
. . Activism
. . Antisocial Behavior
. . . Aggression
. . . Bullying
. . . Cheating
. . . Child Abuse
. . . Child Neglect
. . . Crime
. . . . Delinquency
. . . . International Crimes
. . . . . Genocide
. . . . Driving While Intoxicated
. . . Elder Abuse
. . . Emotional Abuse
. . . Fraud
. . . Hazing
. . . Homicide
. . . Incest
. . . Sexual Abuse
. . . . Rape
. . . Sexual Harassment
. . . Stealing
. . . . Plagiarism
. . . Terrorism
. . . Vandalism
. . . . School Vandalism
. . . Verbal Abuse
. . . Violence
. . . . Family Violence
. . Conformity
. . Dissent
. . Help Seeking
. . Lying
. . Obedience
. . Prosocial Behavior
. . . Sharing Behavior
. . Social Adjustment
. Spontaneous Behavior
. Student Behavior
. . Student Adjustment
. . Student Participation
. . Student Reaction
. Substance Abuse
. . Alcohol Abuse
. . . Alcoholism
. . Drug Abuse
. . . Drug Addiction
. Teacher Behavior
. . Teacher Collaboration
. . Teacher Effectiveness
. . Teacher Militancy
. . Teacher Participation
. . Teacher Persistence
. . Teacher Response
. Type A Behavior
. Type B Behavior

: : Cognitive Processes
: Learning Processes
Behavior Chaining

: Change
Behavior Change

: : Development
: Individual Development
Behavior Development
. Habit Formation

: Disabilities
Behavior Disorders

: Conditioning
Behavior Modification
. Contingency Management
. Desensitization

Behavior Patterns
. Arousal Patterns
. Reading Habits
. Recidivism
. Speech Habits
. Study Habits
. Type A Behavior
. Type B Behavior

: Problems
Behavior Problems

: : Measures (Individuals)
: Rating Scales
Behavior Rating Scales

: Standards
Behavior Standards
. Codes of Ethics

: Theories
Behavior Theories
. Adaptation Level Theory
. Attribution Theory
. Mediation Theory

: Objectives
Behavioral Objectives
. Affective Objectives
. Cognitive Objectives
. Psychomotor Objectives

: Research
Behavioral Science Research
. Integration Studies
. Psychological Studies
. . Force Field Analysis
. . Interest Research
. . Personality Studies

: : Liberal Arts
: Sciences
Behavioral Sciences
. Ethology
. Psychology
. . Behaviorism
. . Child Psychology
. . Clinical Psychology
. . Cognitive Psychology
. . Community Psychology
. . Counseling Psychology
. . Developmental Psychology
. . Educational Psychology
. . Experimental Psychology
. . Individual Psychology
. . Industrial Psychology
. . Neuropsychology
. . Psychoacoustics
. . Psychometrics
. . Psychopathology
. . Psychophysiology
. . School Psychology
. . Social Psychology
. . Sport Psychology
. Sociobiology
. Sociology
. . Criminology
. . Educational Sociology
. . Rural Sociology
. . Social Psychology

: : : : Liberal Arts
: : : Sciences
: : Behavioral Sciences
: Psychology
Behaviorism

: Attitudes
Beliefs

: : : Languages
: : African Languages
: Bantu Languages
Bemba

: : Methods
: Evaluation Methods
Benchmarking

: : Languages
: Indo European Languages
Bengali

: : Languages
: Afro Asiatic Languages
Berber Languages
. Kabyle
. Riff

Bereavement

Bias
. Social Bias
. . Ethnic Bias
. . Homophobia
. . Racial Bias
. . Sex Bias
. . . Sexism in Language
. . Statistical Bias
. . Test Bias
. . Item Bias
. . Textbook Bias

: : : Liberal Arts
: : Humanities
: Literature
Biblical Literature

: : : : : Services
: : : : Information Services
: : : : Information Processing
: : : Documentation
: : Bibliometrics
: Citation Analysis
Bibliographic Coupling

: : Information Sources
: : Data
: Databases
Bibliographic Databases

: Records (Forms)
Bibliographic Records

: : Groups
: Organizations (Groups)
: : Networks
: : Information Networks
: Library Networks
Bibliographic Utilities

: : Publications
: Reference Materials
Bibliographies
. Annotated Bibliographies

: : : : Services
: : : Information Services
: : Information Processing
: Documentation
Bibliometrics
. Citation Analysis
. . Bibliographic Coupling

: Therapy
Bibliotherapy

: Cultural Pluralism
Biculturalism

: : Activities
: Physical Activities
Bicycling

Bidialectalism

Bids

: : : Languages
: : Indo European Languages

: Slavic Languages
Bielorussian

: : : Languages
: : Malayo Polynesian Languages
: Indonesian Languages
Bikol

: Education
Bilingual Education

: Programs
Bilingual Education Programs

: Multilingual Materials
: : Educational Media
: Instructional Materials
Bilingual Instructional Materials

: : Institutions
: Schools
Bilingual Schools

: : Groups
: Students
Bilingual Students

: : : : : Groups
: : : : Personnel
: : : School Personnel
: : : : Groups
: : : : Personnel
: : : Paraprofessional Personnel
: : Paraprofessional School Personnel
: Teacher Aides
Bilingual Teacher Aides

: : : : Groups
: : : Personnel
: : Professional Personnel
: Teachers
Bilingual Teachers

Bilingualism

: : Languages
: African Languages
Bini

: : : : Liberal Arts
: : : Sciences
: : Natural Sciences
: : Physical Sciences
: Chemistry
: : : Liberal Arts
: : Sciences
: Natural Sciences
: Biological Sciences
Biochemistry

Biodiversity

: : : : Liberal Arts
: : : Humanities
: : Philosophy
: Ethics
Bioethics

: : : Relationship
: : Interaction
: Feedback
: : : Liberal Arts
: : Sciences
: Natural Sciences
: Biological Sciences
Biofeedback

: Measures (Individuals)
Biographical Inventories

: : : : Liberal Arts
: : : Humanities
: : Literature
: Prose
: Nonfiction
: Literary Genres
Biographies
. Autobiographies

: Influences
Biological Influences
. Rh Factors

: : Groups
: Parents
Biological Parents

: : : Liberal Arts
: : Sciences
: Natural Sciences
Biological Sciences
. Anatomy
. Biochemistry
. Biofeedback
. Biology
. . Marine Biology
. . Microbiology
. . Molecular Biology
. . Radiation Biology
. . Social Biology
. Biomedicine
. Biophysics
. . Biomechanics
. . Bionics
. . . Robotics
. Biotechnology
. Botany
. Cytology
. Ecology
. Embryology
. Ethology
. Genetics
. . Genetic Engineering
. Mycology
. Physiology
. . Exercise Physiology
. . Psychophysiology
. Sociobiology
. Zoology
. . Entomology
. . Ichthyology
. . Ornithology
. . Primatology

: : : : Liberal Arts
: : : Sciences
: : Natural Sciences
: Biological Sciences
Biology
. Marine Biology
. Microbiology
. Molecular Biology
. Radiation Biology
. Social Biology

: : : : : : Liberal Arts
: : : : : Sciences
: : : : Natural Sciences
: : : Physical Sciences
: : Physics
: : : : Liberal Arts
: : : Sciences
: : Natural Sciences
: : Biological Sciences
: Biophysics
Biomechanics

: Equipment
Biomedical Equipment

: : Technology
: Medicine
: : : : Liberal Arts
: : : Sciences
: : Natural Sciences
: Biological Sciences
Biomedicine

: : : : : Liberal Arts
: : : : Sciences
: : : Natural Sciences
: : Physical Sciences
: : Physics
: : : : Liberal Arts
: : : Sciences
: : Natural Sciences
: : Biological Sciences
: Biophysics
Bionics
. Robotics

: : : : : Liberal Arts
: : : : Sciences
: : : Natural Sciences
: : Physical Sciences
: Physics

: : : : Liberal Arts
: : : Sciences
: : Natural Sciences
: Biological Sciences
Biophysics
. Biomechanics
. Bionics
. . Robotics

: Technology
: : : : Liberal Arts
: : : Sciences
: : Natural Sciences
: Biological Sciences
Biotechnology

: Committees
Biracial Committees

: Animals
Birds

Birth

: : : Organization
: : Group Structure
: Family Structure
Birth Order
. First Born

: Incidence
: : : : Liberal Arts
: : : Sciences
: : Social Sciences
: Demography
Birth Rate

: : : Individual Characteristics
: : Physical Characteristics
: Body Weight
Birth Weight

Births to Single Women

: Sexuality
Bisexuality

: Achievement
Black Achievement

: Attitudes
Black Attitudes

: Business
Black Businesses

: : : Institutions
: : Schools
: Colleges
: : Institutions
: Black Institutions
Black Colleges

: Community
Black Community

: Culture
Black Culture

: : Languages
: : : : Linguistics
: : : Sociolinguistics
: : Language Variation
: Dialects
Black Dialects

: Education
Black Education

: Employment
Black Employment

: : Groups
: Family (Sociological Unit)
Black Family

: : : : Liberal Arts
: : : Sciences
: : Social Sciences
: : : Liberal Arts
: : Humanities
: History
Black History

Black Housing (1977 1980)

: Influences
Black Influences

: Institutions
Black Institutions
. Black Colleges

: : Ability
: Leadership
Black Leadership

: : : Liberal Arts
: : Humanities
: Literature
Black Literature

: : : Groups
: : Parents
: : : Groups
: : Females
: Mothers
: : Groups
: Blacks
Black Mothers

: : Groups
: Organizations (Groups)
Black Organizations

: : : : : Liberal Arts
: : : : Sciences
: : : Social Sciences
: : Demography
: Population Trends
Black Population Trends

Black Power

: : : Attitudes
: : Stereotypes
: Ethnic Stereotypes
Black Stereotypes

: : Groups
: Students
: : Groups
: Blacks
Black Students

: : Curriculum
: Ethnic Studies
Black Studies

: : : : Groups
: : : Personnel
: : Professional Personnel
: Teachers
: : Groups
: Blacks
Black Teachers

: : Groups
: Youth
: : Groups
: Blacks
Black Youth

: Groups
Blacks
. Black Mothers
. Black Students
. Black Teachers
. Black Youth

: : Disabilities
: Visual Impairments
Blindness

: : Financial Support
: Grants
Block Grants

: : : Planning
: : Scheduling
: School Schedules
Block Scheduling

: Metabolism
Blood Circulation

: Occupations
Blue Collar Occupations

: : Groups
: Organizations (Groups)
Blue Ribbon Commissions

: Building Plans
Blueprints

: : Relationship
: Interpersonal Relationship
Board Administrator Relationship

: Groups
Board Candidates

: : Policy
: Administrative Policy
Board of Education Policy

: Role
Board of Education Role

: : Facilities
: Housing
Boarding Homes

: : Institutions
: Schools
: : Institutions
: Residential Institutions
Boarding Schools
. Residential Schools

: : : Groups
: : Organizations (Groups)
: Governing Boards
Boards of Education
. State Boards of Education

: : : : Groups
: : : Personnel
: : Nonprofessional Personnel
: Semiskilled Workers
Boat Operators

: : Individual Characteristics
: Physical Characteristics
Body Composition
. Obesity

: : Individual Characteristics
: Physical Characteristics
Body Height

: Self Concept
Body Image

: : Communication (Thought Transfer)
: Nonverbal Communication
Body Language

: : Individual Characteristics
: Physical Characteristics
Body Weight
. Birth Weight
. Obesity

Bond Issues

: : : Publications
: : Reference Materials
: : : Publications
: : Catalogs
: Library Catalogs
Book Catalogs

: Publications
Book Reviews

: : : Ability
: : Skills
: Business Skills
Bookkeeping

: : : Equipment
: : Motor Vehicles
: Service Vehicles
: : Equipment
: Library Equipment
Bookmobiles

: Publications
: Printed Materials
Books
. Foreign Language Books
. High Interest Low Vocabulary Books
. Paperback Books
. Picture Books
. Textbooks
. . History Textbooks
. . Multicultural Textbooks
. Yearbooks

: Facilities
Bookstores

: : : Geographic Regions
: : Urban Areas
: : Community
: : Municipalities
Boomtowns

: : : : Liberal Arts
: : : Sciences
: : Natural Sciences
: Biological Sciences
Botany

: : : Activities
: : Physical Activities
: Athletics
Bowling

: : : Groups
: : Latin Americans
: Mexicans
: : : Groups
: : Personnel
: Foreign Workers
Braceros

: : Language
: Written Language
Braille

Brain

: : Mobility
: Migration
Brain Drain

: : : Individual Characteristics
: : Physical Characteristics
: Neurological Organization
Brain Hemisphere Functions

: : Activities
: Creative Activities
Brainstorming

: : Institutions
: : Information Sources
: Libraries
Branch Libraries

: Methods
Branching

: : : Equipment
: : Musical Instruments
: Wind Instruments
Brass Instruments

: : Programs
: Health Programs
Breakfast Programs

: Nutrition
Breastfeeding

: : Business
: Industry
Brick Industry

: : Technology
: : Construction (Process)
: Masonry
Bricklaying

: : Institutions
: Schools
British Infant Schools

: : Curriculum
: National Curriculum
British National Curriculum

: : Business
: Industry
Broadcast Industry

: : Technology
: Journalism
Broadcast Journalism

: : Equipment
: Electronic Equipment
Broadcast Reception Equipment

: : : : Technology
: : : Communications
: : Telecommunications
: : Mass Media
: Television
Broadcast Television

: Religion
Buddhism

: Planning
Budgeting
. Program Budgeting

Budgets

: Change
Building Conversion

: Design
Building Design
. Modular Building Design

: Innovation
Building Innovation

: Obsolescence
Building Obsolescence

: : Governance
: Administration
Building Operation

Building Plans
. Blueprints

: Structural Elements (Construction)
Building Systems
. Structural Building Systems

: Occupations
Building Trades

: Facilities
Buildings
. School Buildings
. . College Buildings

: : Environment
: Physical Environment
Built Environment

: : : Languages
: : Indo European Languages
: Slavic Languages
Bulgarian

: : : Disabilities
: : Diseases
: Eating Disorders
Bulimia

: Visual Aids
Bulletin Boards

: : Publications
: Serials
Bulletins

: : : Behavior
: : Social Behavior
: Antisocial Behavior
Bullying

: Organization
Bureaucracy

: : : Languages
: : Uralic Altaic Languages
: Mongolian Languages
Buriat

: : Languages
: Sino Tibetan Languages
Burmese

: Culture
Burmese Culture

: : Behavior
: Responses
Burnout
. Teacher Burnout

: Languages
Burushaski

: : Groups
: Personnel
Bus Drivers

: Transportation
Bus Transportation

Business
. Agribusiness
. Black Businesses
. Industry
. . Bakery Industry
. . Banking
. . Brick Industry
. . Broadcast Industry
. . Construction Industry
. . . Housing Industry
. . Fashion Industry
. . Feed Industry
. . Film Industry
. . Information Industry
. . Insurance Companies
. . Lumber Industry
. . Manufacturing Industry
. . . Aerospace Industry
. . . Cement Industry
. . . Chemical Industry
. . . Electronics Industry
. . . Furniture Industry
. . . Machinery Industry
. . . Metal Industry
. . Meat Packing Industry
. . Petroleum Industry
. . Publishing Industry
. . . University Presses
. . Telephone Communications
       Industry
. . Tourism
. Small Businesses

: : Governance
: Administration
Business Administration

: : Education
: Professional Education
Business Administration Education

: : Communication (Thought Transfer)
: Organizational Communication
Business Communication
. Business Correspondence

: : Communication (Thought Transfer)
: Verbal Communication
: : : Communication (Thought
       Transfer)
: : Organizational Communication
: Business Communication
Business Correspondence

Business Cycles

: : Education
: Vocational Education
Business Education
. Office Occupations Education

: : Facilities
: Educational Facilities
Business Education Facilities

: : : : : Groups
: : : : Personnel
: : : Professional Personnel
: : Teachers
: Vocational Education Teachers
Business Education Teachers

: : : Languages
: : Indo European Languages
: English
Business English

: Responsibility
Business Responsibility

: : Ability
: Skills
Business Skills
. Bookkeeping
. Keyboarding (Data Entry)
. Recordkeeping
. Typewriting

: : Methods
: Desegregation Methods
Busing

: : Technology
: Woodworking
: Construction (Process)
Cabinetmaking

Cable Franchising

: : : : Technology
: : : Communications
: : Telecommunications
: : Mass Media
: Television
Cable Television

: : : Languages
: : American Indian Languages
: Mayan Languages
Cakchiquel

: Equipment
Calculators
. Graphing Calculators

: : Liberal Arts
: Mathematics
Calculus

: : : Activities
: : Physical Activities
: Exercise
Calisthenics

: : Equipment
: Measurement Equipment
Calorimeters

: : Languages
: Austro Asiatic Languages
Cambodian

: : Groups
: Indochinese
Cambodians

: : Activities
: Recreational Activities
Camping

: : : Planning
: : Facility Planning
: : Planning
: : Educational Planning
: Educational Facilities Planning
Campus Planning

: : : Facilities
: : Educational Facilities
: Educational Complexes
Campuses

: : Groups
: North Americans
: : Groups
: Ethnic Groups
Canada Natives
. Metis (People)

: : : : Liberal Arts
: : : Humanities
: : Literature
: North American Literature
Canadian Literature

: : Curriculum
: Area Studies
Canadian Studies

: : Disabilities
: Diseases
Cancer

: : : Languages
: : Sino Tibetan Languages
: Chinese
Cantonese

: Financial Support
Capital

: Expenditures
Capital Outlay (for Fixed Assets)

: : Reinforcement
: Punishment
Capital Punishment

: Social Systems
Capitalism
. Free Enterprise System

Capitalization (Alphabetic)

Captions

: : : Publications
: : Reference Materials
: : : Publications
: : Catalogs
: Library Catalogs
Card Catalogs

: : : : : Services
: : : : Human Services
: : : Health Services
: : Medical Services
: First Aid
Cardiopulmonary Resuscitation

Cardiovascular System

: : : Institutions
: : Schools
: Vocational Schools
: : : Organization
: : School Organization
: House Plan
Career Academies

: : : Development
: : Individual Development
: Career Development
Career Awareness

: Change
Career Change

: Selection
Career Choice

: : Guidance
: Counseling
: Guidance
: Career Guidance
Career Counseling

: : Development
: Individual Development
Career Development
. Career Awareness
. Career Exploration

: Education
Career Education

: : : Development
: : Individual Development
: Career Development
Career Exploration

: Guidance
Career Guidance
. Career Counseling

: Information Systems
Career Information Systems

: : Mobility
: Occupational Mobility
Career Ladders

Career Opportunities (1966 1980)

: Planning
Career Planning

Careers
. Science Careers

: : Relationship
: Interpersonal Relationship
Caregiver Child Relationship

: Role
Caregiver Role

: : Language Arts
: Speech
Caregiver Speech

: Groups
Caregivers
. Attendants
. Child Caregivers
. Family Caregivers

Caricatures (1966 1980)

: : Technology
: Woodworking
: Construction (Process)
Carpentry

: : Structural Elements (Construction)
: Flooring
Carpeting

: : : Facilities
: : Educational Facilities
: Study Facilities
Carrels

: : : : : Liberal Arts
: : : : Humanities
: : : Fine Arts
: : Visual Arts
: Graphic Arts
Cartography

: Visual Aids
Cartoons

: : Theories
: Linguistic Theory
Case (Grammar)

: : : Methods
: : Educational Methods
: Teaching Methods
Case Method (Teaching Technique)

: Records (Forms)
Case Records
. Medical Case Histories

: Research
: : Methods
: Evaluation Methods
Case Studies
. Cross Sectional Studies
. Facility Case Studies
. Longitudinal Studies
. . Followup Studies
. . . Graduate Surveys
. . . Vocational Followup

: Methods
Caseworker Approach

: : Groups
: Personnel
Caseworkers
. Parole Officers

. Probation Officers
. Social Workers
. . School Social Workers

: : Groups
: Social Class
Caste

: : : : Services
: : : Information Services
: : Information Processing
: Documentation
Cataloging
. Machine Readable Cataloging

: Publications
Catalogs
. Library Catalogs
. Book Catalogs
. . Card Catalogs
. . Union Catalogs
. Online Catalogs
. School Catalogs

: Financial Support
Categorical Aid

: : : Background
: : Experience
: Emotional Experience
Catharsis

: : : : Groups
: : : Personnel
: : Professional Personnel
: Teachers
Catholic Educators

: : : : Institutions
: : : Schools
: : Private Schools
: Parochial Schools
Catholic Schools

: : Groups
: Religious Cultural Groups
Catholics

: Languages
Caucasian Languages

: : : Methods
: : Simulation
: Models
Causal Models
. Structural Equation Models

: : : : Languages
: : : Malayo Polynesian Languages
: : Indonesian Languages
: Visayan
Cebuano

: Structural Elements (Construction)
Ceilings

: : : Business
: : Industry
: Manufacturing Industry
Cement Industry

Censorship

: : Data
: Statistical Data
Census Figures

: : : Groups
: : Personnel
: Administrators
Central Office Administrators

: : Organization
: Administrative Organization
Centralization

: : : : : Liberal Arts
: : : : Humanities
: : : Fine Arts
: : Visual Arts
: Handicrafts
Ceramics

: : : Disabilities
: : : Physical Disabilities
: : Neurological Impairments
: : Disabilities
: Congenital Impairments
Cerebral Palsy

Certification
. Accreditation (Institutions)
. Counselor Certification
. Student Certification
. Teacher Certification
. . Alternative Teacher Certification
. . National Teacher Certification

: : : : Groups
: : : Personnel
: : Professional Personnel
: Accountants
Certified Public Accountants

: : Languages
: Afro Asiatic Languages
Chad Languages
. Hausa

: Visual Aids
Chalkboards

: : Languages
: Malayo Polynesian Languages
Chamorro

Change
. Administrative Change
. Attitude Change
. Behavior Change
. Building Conversion
. Career Change
. Climate Change
. . Global Warming
. . . Greenhouse Effect
. Community Change
. Data Conversion
. . Retrospective Conversion (Library Catalogs)
. Economic Change
. Educational Change
. Life Events
. Media Adaptation
. . Tactile Adaptation
. Midlife Transitions
. Organizational Change
. . Mergers
. Personality Change
. Social Change
. . Modernization

: Groups
Change Agents
. Extension Agents
. Linking Agents

: Methods
Change Strategies

: Theories
Chaos Theory

: : : : Cognitive Processes
: : : Memory
: : Recognition (Psychology)
: Pattern Recognition
Character Recognition

: Literary Devices
Characterization

: : : Institutions
: : Schools
: Public Schools
Charter Schools

: Visual Aids
Charts
. Experience Charts
. Flow Charts

: : : Behavior
: : Social Behavior
: Antisocial Behavior
Cheating

: Records (Forms)
Check Lists

: : Methods
: Evaluation Methods
Chemical Analysis

: Chemical Reactions
Chemical Bonding

: : Technology
: Engineering
Chemical Engineering

Chemical Equilibrium

: : : Business
: : Industry
: Manufacturing Industry
Chemical Industry

: Vocabulary
Chemical Nomenclature

Chemical Reactions
. Chemical Bonding
. Oxidation
. Photochemical Reactions
. . Photosynthesis

: : : Groups
: : Personnel
: Paraprofessional Personnel
Chemical Technicians

: : : : Liberal Arts
: : : Sciences
: : Natural Sciences
: Physical Sciences
Chemistry
. Biochemistry
. Geochemistry
. Inorganic Chemistry
. Organic Chemistry
. Physical Chemistry
. . Electrochemistry
. Stereochemistry

: : : Languages
: : Uralic Altaic Languages
: Finno Ugric Languages
Cheremis

: : Languages
: American Indian Languages
Cherokee

: : Groups
: Tribes
: : : Groups
: : Ethnic Groups
: American Indians
Cherokee (Tribe)

: : : : Methods
: : : Evaluation Methods
: : Data Analysis
: Statistical Analysis
Chi Square

: : : Behavior
: : Social Behavior
: Antisocial Behavior
Child Abuse

: Advocacy
Child Advocacy

: Behavior
Child Behavior
. Infant Behavior

: : Occupations
: Service Occupations
Child Care Occupations

Child Care (1966 1980)

: : Groups
: Caregivers
Child Caregivers

Child Custody

: : Development
: Individual Development
Child Development

: : Facilities
: Educational Facilities
Child Development Centers

: : : Groups
: : Personnel
: Specialists
Child Development Specialists

: Health
Child Health

: Labor
Child Labor

: Language
Child Language

: Negligence
: : : Behavior
: : Social Behavior
: Antisocial Behavior
Child Neglect

: : : : Liberal Arts
: : : Sciences
: : Behavioral Sciences
: Psychology
Child Psychology

Child Rearing

: Responsibility
Child Responsibility

: Role
Child Role

: Safety
Child Safety

: Financial Support
Child Support

: : Quality of Life
: Well Being
Child Welfare

: Attitudes
Childhood Attitudes

: Interests
Childhood Interests

: : Needs
: Individual Needs
Childhood Needs

Childlessness

: : Groups
: Age Groups
Children
. Adopted Children
. Foster Children
. Grandchildren
. Hospitalized Children
. Latchkey Children
. Migrant Children
. Minority Group Children
. Missing Children
. Preadolescents
. Problem Children
. Transient Children
. Young Children
. . Infants
. . . Neonates
. . . Premature Infants
. . Kindergarten Children
. . Preschool Children
. . Toddlers

: : : : Liberal Arts
: : : Humanities
: : Fine Arts
: Visual Arts
Childrens Art

: : Activities
: Games
Childrens Games

: : Institutions
: : Information Sources
: Libraries
Childrens Libraries

: : : Liberal Arts
: : Humanities
: Literature
Childrens Literature

: Civil Liberties
Childrens Rights

: : : : Technology
: : : Communications
: : Telecommunications
: : Mass Media
: Television
Childrens Television

: : Literacy
: : Language Arts
: Writing (Composition)
Childrens Writing

: Structural Elements (Construction)
Chimneys

: : Languages
: Sino Tibetan Languages
Chinese
. Cantonese
. Foochow
. Mandarin Chinese

: : Groups
: Ethnic Groups
: : : Groups
: : North Americans
: Asian Americans
Chinese Americans

: Culture
Chinese Culture

: : : Languages
: : African Languages
: Bantu Languages
Chinyanja

: : Groups
: Tribes
: : : Groups
: : Ethnic Groups
: American Indians
Chippewa (Tribe)

: : Languages
: American Indian Languages
Choctaw

: : Groups
: Tribes
: : : Groups
: : Ethnic Groups
: American Indians
Choctaw (Tribe)
. Mississippi Band of Choctaw (Tribe)

: : : : : Liberal Arts
: : : : Humanities
: : : Fine Arts
: : Music
: Vocal Music
Choral Music

: : : : Liberal Arts
: : : Humanities
: : Fine Arts
: Theater Arts
Choral Speaking

: Religion
Christianity

: : Methods
: Laboratory Procedures
Chromatography

: : Disabilities
: Diseases
Chronic Illness

: : : : : Liberal Arts
: : : : Humanities
: : : Literature
: : Prose
: Nonfiction
: Literary Genres
Chronicles

: : Individual Characteristics
: Age
Chronological Age

: Programs
Church Programs

: : : Institutions
: : Schools
: Colleges
Church Related Colleges

: Responsibility
Church Responsibility

: : Role
: Institutional Role
Church Role

: : Groups
: Personnel
Church Workers

: Institutions
Churches

: : : Languages
: : Uralic Altaic Languages
: Turkic Languages
Chuvash

: : : : : Services
: : : : Information Services
: : : Information Processing
: : Documentation
: Bibliometrics
Citation Analysis
. Bibliographic Coupling

: : : Publications
: : Reference Materials
: Indexes
Citation Indexes

: : Publications
: Reference Materials
Citations (References)

: : Behavior
: Participation
Citizen Participation

: Role
Citizen Role

: : : Groups
: : Organizations (Groups)
: Community Organizations
Citizens Councils

: Status
Citizenship

: Education
Citizenship Education

: : Responsibility
: Social Responsibility
Citizenship Responsibility

: : : : Groups
: : : Organizations (Groups)
: : Government (Administrative Body)
: Local Government
City Government

: : : Groups
: : : Personnel
: : Government Employees
: Public Officials
City Officials

: : : Liberal Arts
: : Sciences
: Social Sciences
Civics

Civil Defense

Civil Disobedience

: : Technology
: Engineering
Civil Engineering

: : Standards
: Laws
Civil Law

Civil Liberties
. Childrens Rights
. Civil Rights
. . Equal Education
. . Equal Opportunities (Jobs)
. . . Occupational Segregation
. . Equal Protection
. . Voting Rights
. Due Process
. Freedom of Speech
. Parent Rights
. Student Rights
. Teacher Rights

: Civil Liberties
Civil Rights
. Equal Education
. Equal Opportunities (Jobs)
. . Occupational Segregation
. Equal Protection
. Voting Rights

: Legislation
Civil Rights Legislation

: : Conflict
: War
: : : : : Liberal Arts
: : : : Sciences
: : : Social Sciences
: : : : : Liberal Arts
: : : : Humanities
: : : History
: : North American History
: United States History
Civil War (United States)

: : Activities
: School Activities
Class Activities

Class Attitudes (1966 1980)

Class Average (1966 1980)

: Organization
Class Organization

Class Rank

Class Size

: Groups
Classes (Groups of Students)
. Multigraded Classes
. Multilevel Classes (Second Language
    Instruction)
. Nonauthoritarian Classes
. Small Classes
. Special Classes

: Conditioning
Classical Conditioning

: Languages
Classical Languages
. Latin
. Sanskrit

: : : Liberal Arts
: : Humanities
: Literature
Classical Literature
. Latin Literature

::: Liberal Arts
:: Humanities
: Literature
Classics (Literature)

: Organization
Classification
. Cluster Grouping
. Codification
. Coding
. Dewey Decimal Classification
. Discourse Modes
. Grouping (Instructional Purposes)
.. Heterogeneous Grouping
.. Homogeneous Grouping
... Ability Grouping
.. Nongraded Instructional Grouping
. Labeling (of Persons)
. Language Classification
.. Language Typology
. Library of Congress Classification
. Space Classification
. Universal Decimal Classification

: Communication (Thought Transfer)
Classroom Communication

: Social Integration
Classroom Desegregation

: Design
Classroom Design

:: Environment
: Educational Environment
Classroom Environment

:: Equipment
: Furniture
:: Equipment
: Educational Equipment
Classroom Furniture

Classroom Guidance Programs (1968 1980)

:: Methods
: Measurement Techniques
Classroom Observation Techniques

:: Research
: Educational Research
Classroom Research

:: Methods
: Educational Methods
Classroom Techniques

:: Facilities
: Educational Facilities
Classrooms
. Electronic Classrooms
. Mobile Classrooms
. Multipurpose Classrooms
. Self Contained Classrooms

Clay

: Sanitation
Cleaning
. Dishwashing

::: Facilities
:: Resource Centers
:: Information Sources
: Information Centers
Clearinghouses

:: Disabilities
: Speech Impairments
:: Disabilities
: Physical Disabilities
:: Disabilities
: Congenital Impairments
Cleft Palate

:: Groups
: Personnel
Clergy
. Priests

: Occupations
Clerical Occupations

::: Groups
:: Personnel
: Nonprofessional Personnel
Clerical Workers
. Court Reporters
. Examiners
. File Clerks
. Receptionists
. Secretaries
.. School Secretaries

Cliches

:: Environment
: Physical Environment
Client Characteristics (Human Services)

: Change
Climate

Climate Change
. Global Warming
.. Greenhouse Effect

Climate Control
. Air Conditioning
. Heat Recovery
. Heating
. Refrigeration
. Ventilation

: Identification
Clinical Diagnosis

::: Background
:: Experience
: Learning Experience
Clinical Experience

:::: Liberal Arts
::: Sciences
:: Behavioral Sciences
: Psychology
Clinical Psychology

:::: Governance
::: Administration
:: Supervision
: Teacher Supervision
Clinical Supervision (of Teachers)

::: Methods
:: Educational Methods
: Teaching Methods
Clinical Teaching (Health Professions)

Clinics
. Dental Clinics
. Mental Health Clinics
. Mobile Clinics
. Psychoeducational Clinics
. Speech and Hearing Clinics

:::: Technology
::: Communications
:: Telecommunications
:: Mass Media
: Television
Closed Circuit Television

Clothing
. School Uniforms

: Design
Clothing Design

: Instruction
Clothing Instruction

: Methods
Cloze Procedure

: Groups
Clubs
. Science Clubs
. Youth Clubs

::::: Methods
:::: Evaluation Methods
::: Data Analysis
:: Statistical Analysis

: Multivariate Analysis
Cluster Analysis

::: Institutions
:: Schools
: Colleges
Cluster Colleges

:: Organization
: Classification
Cluster Grouping

:: Resources
: Natural Resources
::: Resources
:: Natural Resources
:: Fuels
: Fossil Fuels
Coal

: Narcotics
Cocaine
. Crack

: Sensory Aids
::: Equipment
:: Assistive Devices (for Disabled)
: Prostheses
Cochlear Implants

:: Guidance
: Counseling
Cocounseling

Code Switching (Language)

:: Standards
: Behavior Standards
Codes of Ethics

:: Organization
: Classification
Codification

:: Organization
: Classification
Coding

: Education
Coeducation

: Ability
Cognitive Ability
. Thinking Skills

:: Development
: Individual Development
Cognitive Development
. Intellectual Development
. Perceptual Development
. Verbal Development
.. Language Acquisition

: Psychological Patterns
Cognitive Dissonance

:: Cognitive Processes
: Learning Processes
Cognitive Mapping

: Measurement
Cognitive Measurement

:: Objectives
: Behavioral Objectives
Cognitive Objectives

Cognitive Processes
. Abstract Reasoning
.. Generalization
... Stimulus Generalization
. Association (Psychology)
. Conflict Resolution
.. Peer Mediation
. Consciousness Raising
. Convergent Thinking
. Creative Thinking
.. Divergent Thinking
.. Productive Thinking
. Critical Thinking
.. Evaluative Thinking
... Value Judgment
. Decision Making

.. Participative Decision Making
. Encoding (Psychology)
. Intuition
. Language Processing
.. Expressive Language
.. Interference (Language)
.. Reading Processes
... Decoding (Reading)
.. Receptive Language
. Learning Processes
.. Behavior Chaining
.. Cognitive Mapping
.. Concept Formation
.. Discovery Processes
.. Extinction (Psychology)
.. Generalization
... Stimulus Generalization
.. Habituation
.. Memorization
.. Primacy Effect
. Logical Thinking
.. Deduction
.. Induction
. Memory
.. Eidetic Imagery
.. Long Term Memory
.. Recall (Psychology)
... Reminiscence
.. Recognition (Psychology)
... Pattern Recognition
.... Character Recognition
... Word Recognition
.. Retention (Psychology)
. Short Term Memory
.. Mental Computation
. Metacognition
.. Meditation
... Transcendental Meditation
. Perception
.. Auditory Perception
... Auditory Discrimination
.. Kinesthetic Perception
.. Tactual Perception
.. Visual Perception
... Depth Perception
... Visual Acuity
... Visual Discrimination
. Problem Solving
. Role Perception
. Serial Ordering
. Social Cognition
. Visualization

:::: Liberal Arts
::: Sciences
:: Behavioral Sciences
: Psychology
Cognitive Psychology

Cognitive Restructuring

Cognitive Structures

:: Individual Characteristics
: Psychological Characteristics
Cognitive Style
. Conceptual Tempo
. Field Dependence Independence

:: Measures (Individuals)
: Tests
Cognitive Tests
. Intelligence Tests
. Perception Tests
.. Tactual Visual Tests

:: Relationship
: Interpersonal Relationship
Cohabitation

:: Language Arts
: Rhetoric
Coherence

: Connected Discourse
Cohesion (Written Composition)

: Research
Cohort Analysis

Collage

Collective Bargaining
. Scope of Bargaining

: Community
Collective Settlements

: : : : Governance
: : : Administration
: : Institutional Administration
: : : : Governance
: : : Administration
: : Educational Administration
: School Administration
College Administration

: Admission (School)
College Admission

: Groups
College Applicants

: : : Activities
: : Physical Activities
: Athletics
College Athletics

: Attendance
College Attendance

: : : : Groups
: : : Students
: : Secondary School Students
: High School Students
College Bound Students

: : : Facilities
: : Educational Facilities
: : Facilities
: : Buildings
: School Buildings
College Buildings

: : Selection
: School Choice
College Choice

: Credits
College Credits

: Curriculum
College Curriculum
. College English
. College Mathematics
. College Science
. College Second Language Programs
. Education Courses
. Freshman Composition
. Postsecondary Education as a
    Field of Study
. Teacher Education Curriculum
. . Methods Courses

: Programs
College Day

: : Social Integration
: School Desegregation
College Desegregation

: : Curriculum
: English Curriculum
: : Curriculum
: College Curriculum
College English

: : Measures (Individuals)
: Tests
College Entrance Examinations

: : Environment
: Institutional Environment
: : Environment
: Educational Environment
College Environment

: : : : Groups
: : : Personnel
: : School Personnel
: : : : Groups
: : : Personnel
: : Professional Personnel

: Faculty
College Faculty
. College Presidents
. Counselor Educators
. Graduate School Faculty
. . Medical School Faculty
. Professors
. Student Teacher Supervisors
. Teacher Educators
. . Methods Teachers
. Teaching Assistants

: : : Groups
: : Students
: College Students
College Freshmen

: : Groups
: Organizations (Groups)
College Governing Councils

: : : Groups
: : Alumni
: Graduates
College Graduates

: : Facilities
: Housing
College Housing

: Instruction
College Instruction

: : : Groups
: : Students
: College Students
College Juniors

College Language Programs
      (1967 1980)

: : : Institutions
: : : Information Sources
: : Libraries
: Academic Libraries
College Libraries

: : Curriculum
: Mathematics Curriculum
: : Curriculum
: College Curriculum
College Mathematics

: Outcomes of Education
: : Evaluation
: Educational Assessment
College Outcomes Assessment

: : Planning
: Educational Planning
College Planning

: : : Education
: : Elementary Secondary Education
: Secondary Education
College Preparation

: : : : Groups
: : : Personnel
: : Administrators
: Presidents
: : : : : Groups
: : : : Personnel
: : : School Personnel
: : : : : Groups
: : : : Personnel
: : : Professional Personnel
: : Faculty
: College Faculty
College Presidents

: Programs
College Programs
. Doctoral Programs
. External Degree Programs
. Masters Programs

: : : Role
: : Institutional Role
: School Role
College Role

: : : Behavior
: : Cooperation
: Institutional Cooperation
: : : Behavior
: : Cooperation
: Educational Cooperation
College School Cooperation

: : Curriculum
: Science Curriculum
: : Curriculum
: College Curriculum
College Science

: : Programs
: Second Language Programs
: : Curriculum
: College Curriculum
College Second Language Programs

: : : Social Discrimination
: : Educational Discrimination
: School Segregation
College Segregation

: : : Groups
: : Students
: College Students
College Seniors

: : : Groups
: : Students
: College Students
College Sophomores

: Facilities
College Stores

: : Groups
: Students
College Students
. College Freshmen
. College Juniors
. College Seniors
. College Sophomores
. College Transfer Students
. Graduate Students
. . Dental Students
. . Law Students
. . Medical Students
. . . Graduate Medical Students
. In State Students
. On Campus Students
. Out of State Students
. Preservice Teachers
. . Student Teachers
. Resident Assistants
. Two Year College Students
. Undergraduate Students
. . Premedical Students

: : : Groups
: : Students
: Transfer Students
: : : Groups
: : Students
: College Students
College Transfer Students

: : Institutions
: Schools
Colleges
. Agricultural Colleges
. Black Colleges
. Church Related Colleges
. Cluster Colleges
. Commuter Colleges
. Dental Schools
. Developing Institutions
. Experimental Colleges
. Law Schools
. Library Schools
. Medical Schools
. Multicampus Colleges
. Noncampus Colleges
. Private Colleges
. Public Colleges
. . Community Colleges
. . State Colleges
. . . State Universities
. Residential Colleges
. Selective Colleges
. Single Sex Colleges

. Small Colleges
. Two Year Colleges
. . Community Colleges
. . Technical Institutes
. Universities
. . Land Grant Universities
. . Open Universities
. . Research Universities
. . State Universities
. . Urban Universities
. Upper Division Colleges

: : Relationship
: Interpersonal Relationship
Collegiality

: : : : : : Liberal Arts
: : : : : Sciences
: : : : Social Sciences
: : : : : Liberal Arts
: : : : Humanities
: : : History
: : North American History
: United States History
Colonial History (United States)

: : : Policy
: : Foreign Policy
: Imperialism
Colonialism

Color

: Planning
Color Planning

: : : : : Liberal Arts
: : : : Humanities
: : : Fine Arts
: : Theater Arts
: : : : Liberal Arts
: : : Humanities
: : Literature
: Drama
Comedy
. Skits

: Publications
Comics (Publications)

: : Evaluation
: Recognition (Achievement)
Commencement Ceremonies

: Art
Commercial Art

: : : : Technology
: : : Communications
: : Telecommunications
: : Mass Media
: Television
Commercial Television

Committees
. Advisory Committees
. Biracial Committees
. Research Committees
. Search Committees (Personnel)

: : Disabilities
: Diseases
Communicable Diseases
. Acquired Immune Deficiency
      Syndrome
. Rubella
. Venereal Diseases

Communication (Thought Transfer)
. Augmentative and Alternative
      Communication
. . Manual Communication
. . . Cued Speech
. . . Finger Spelling
. . . Sign Language
. . . . American Sign Language
. . Total Communication
. Classroom Communication
. Computer Mediated Communication
. . Electronic Mail
. . . Listservs
. . Electronic Publishing
. Development Communication

. Diffusion (Communication)
. Discussion
. . Group Discussion
. Intercultural Communication
. International Communication
. Interpersonal Communication
. Nonverbal Communication
. . Body Language
. . Eye Contact
. . Facial Expressions
. Organizational Communication
. . Business Communication
. . . Business Correspondence
. . Interschool Communication
. Propaganda
. Publicity
. . Advertising
. . . Television Commercials
. . Institutional Advancement
. Scholarly Communication
. Speech Communication
. . Oral Interpretation
. . Public Speaking
. Verbal Communication
. . Business Correspondence
. . Dictation
. . Letters (Correspondence)
. . Verbal Abuse

Communication Aids (for Disabled)

: : Psychological Patterns
: Anxiety
Communication Apprehension

: Audits (Verification)
Communication Audits

: Disabilities
Communication Disorders

: Problems
Communication Problems

: Research
Communication Research

: : Ability
: Skills
Communication Skills
. Communicative Competence
　　(Languages)
. . Threshold Level (Languages)

: Technology
Communications
. Audiovisual Communications
. . Dial Access Information Systems
. . Educational Radio
. . Educational Television
. . Loop Induction Systems
. Telecommunications
. . Communications Satellites
. . Computer Mediated Communication
. . . Electronic Mail
. . . . Listservs
. . . Electronic Publishing
. . Facsimile Transmission
. . Radio
. . . Educational Radio
. . Teleconferencing
. . Telephone Communications
　　　Systems
. . Television
. . . Broadcast Television
. . . Cable Television
. . . Childrens Television
. . . Closed Circuit Television
. . . Commercial Television
. . . Educational Television
. . . Interactive Television
. . . Public Television
. . Videotex

: : : Technology
: : Communications
: Telecommunications
: Satellites (Aerospace)
Communications Satellites

: : : Ability
: : Skills
: Language Skills

: : Ability
: : Skills
: Communication Skills
**Communicative Competence
　　(Languages)**
. Threshold Level (Languages)

: Social Systems
Communism

Community
. Black Community
. Collective Settlements
. Discourse Communities
. Municipalities
. . Boomtowns
. . Small Towns
. Neighborhoods
. Planned Communities

: Social Action
Community Action

: Attitudes
Community Attitudes
. Community Satisfaction

: : : Methods
: : Educational Methods
: Teaching Methods
**Community Based Instruction
　　(Disabilities)**

Community Benefits

: Facilities
Community Centers

: Change
Community Change

Community Characteristics
. Community Size

: : : : Institutions
: : : Schools
: : Colleges
: Two Year Colleges
: : : : Institutions
: : : Schools
: : Colleges
: Public Colleges
Community Colleges

: Governance
Community Control

: : Behavior
: Cooperation
Community Cooperation

: Coordination
Community Coordination

: Development
Community Development

: Education
Community Education

: : : Services
: : Human Services
: Health Services
: : Services
: Community Services
Community Health Services

: Influences
Community Influence

: : Services
: Information Services
: : Services
: Community Services
Community Information Services
. Hotlines (Public)

: : Behavior
: Participation
Community Involvement

: : Groups
: Leaders

: Groups
Community Leaders

: Needs
Community Needs

: : Groups
: Organizations (Groups)
Community Organizations
. Citizens Councils

: Planning
Community Planning

: Problems
Community Problems

: Programs
Community Programs
. Community Recreation Programs
. School Community Programs

: : : : Liberal Arts
: : : Sciences
: : Behavioral Sciences
: Psychology
Community Psychology

: : Programs
: Recreational Programs
: : Programs
: Community Programs
Community Recreation Programs

: Relationship
Community Relations

: Resources
Community Resources

: Responsibility
Community Responsibility

: Role
Community Role

: : Attitudes
: Satisfaction
: : Attitudes
: Community Attitudes
Community Satisfaction

: : Institutions
: Schools
Community Schools

: Services
Community Services
. Community Health Services
. Community Information Services
. . Hotlines (Public)

: Community Characteristics
Community Size

: Research
Community Study

Community Support

: : : Methods
: : Evaluation Methods
: Surveys
Community Surveys

: Zoning
Community Zoning

: : : Institutions
: : Schools
: Colleges
Commuter Colleges

: : Groups
: Students
Commuting Students

Comparable Worth

: : Methods
: Evaluation Methods
Comparative Analysis
. Educational Status Comparison

. Error Analysis (Language)

: Education
Comparative Education

: : : Methods
: : Measurement Techniques
: Testing
Comparative Testing

: Fundamental Concepts
Compensation (Concept)

: Expenditures
Compensation (Remuneration)

: Education
Compensatory Education

: Ability
Competence
. Interpersonal Competence
. Minimum Competencies
. Teacher Competencies

: Education
Competency Based Education
. Competency Based Teacher
　　Education

: : : Education
: : Professional Education
: Teacher Education
: Education
: Competency Based Education
Competency Based Teacher Education

: Behavior
Competition
. Competitive Selection

: Selection
: : Behavior
: Competition
Competitive Selection

: : : Behavior
: : Cooperation
: Compliance (Psychology)
Compliance (Legal)

: : Behavior
: Cooperation
Compliance (Psychology)
. Compliance (Legal)
. Obedience

: : Methods
: Evaluation Methods
Componential Analysis

: : : Individual Characteristics
: : Psychological Characteristics
: Intelligence
Comprehension
. Listening Comprehension
. Reading Comprehension

: Programs
Comprehensive Programs

: : Education
: Health Education
**Comprehensive School Health
　　Education**

: Education
Compulsory Education
. Home Schooling

: Mathematical Applications
Computation
. Estimation (Mathematics)
. Mental Computation

: Linguistics
Computational Linguistics
. Machine Translation

: : Psychological Patterns
: Anxiety
Computer Anxiety

: Design
Computer Assisted Design

: : : : Methods
: : : Educational Methods
: : Teaching Methods
: Programmed Instruction
: Computer Uses in Education
Computer Assisted Instruction
. Intelligent Tutoring Systems

: : Technology
: Manufacturing
Computer Assisted Manufacturing

: : : Methods
: : Measurement Techniques
: Testing
: Computer Uses in Education
Computer Assisted Testing

: Attitudes
Computer Attitudes

: : Facilities
: Resource Centers
Computer Centers

: : Activities
: Games
Computer Games

: : : : : Liberal Arts
: : : : Humanities
: : : Fine Arts
: : Visual Arts
: Graphic Arts
Computer Graphics

Computer Interfaces
. User Friendly Interface

: Technological Literacy
Computer Literacy

: Information Systems
: Computer Uses in Education
Computer Managed Instruction

: : : Technology
: : Communications
: Telecommunications
: Communication (Thought Transfer)
Computer Mediated Communication
. Electronic Mail
. Listservs
. Electronic Publishing

: Networks
Computer Networks
. Integrated Learning Systems
. Internet
. . World Wide Web
. Local Area Networks

: Programs
Computer Oriented Programs

: : : Visual Aids
: : Microforms
: Microfilm
Computer Output Microfilm

: : Equipment
: Electronic Equipment
Computer Peripherals
. Computer Storage Devices
. . Magnetic Disks
. . . Floppy Disks
. Input Output Devices
. . Computer Printers
. . Computer Terminals
. . . Video Display Terminals
. . Disk Drives
. . Optical Scanners
. Modems

: : : : Equipment
: : : Electronic Equipment
: : Computer Peripherals
: Input Output Devices
Computer Printers

: : : Liberal Arts
: : Sciences
: Information Science
Computer Science
. Programming

: : : Education
: : Professional Education
: Information Science Education
Computer Science Education

Computer Security

: Selection
Computer Selection

: : Methods
: Simulation
Computer Simulation
. Virtual Reality

: : Standards
: Specifications
Computer Software
. Courseware
. Microworlds
. Database Management Systems
. Menu Driven Software

: : Development
: Material Development
Computer Software Development
. Programming

: Evaluation
Computer Software Evaluation

: Publications
Computer Software Reviews

: : Selection
: Media Selection
Computer Software Selection

: : : Equipment
: : Electronic Equipment
: Computer Peripherals
Computer Storage Devices
. Magnetic Disks
. . Floppy Disks

: Design
Computer System Design
. Screen Design (Computers)

: : : : Equipment
: : : Electronic Equipment
: : Computer Peripherals
: Input Output Devices
Computer Terminals
. Video Display Terminals

Computer Uses in Education
. Computer Assisted Instruction
. . Intelligent Tutoring Systems
. Computer Assisted Testing
. Computer Managed Instruction
. Integrated Learning Systems
. Microworlds

: : Equipment
: Electronic Equipment
Computers
. Analog Computers
. Digital Computers
. Microcomputers
. Minicomputers

: : Cognitive Processes
: Learning Processes
Concept Formation

: Methods
Concept Mapping

: Instruction
Concept Teaching

Conceptual Schemes (1967 1980)

: : : Individual Characteristics
: : Psychological Characteristics

: Cognitive Style
Conceptual Tempo

: : Activities
: Music Activities
Concerts

: : : : Standards
: : : Criteria
: : Evaluation Criteria
: Validity
Concurrent Validity

Conditioning
. Behavior Modification
. . Contingency Management
. . Desensitization
. Classical Conditioning
. Operant Conditioning
. . Verbal Operant Conditioning

: : Publications
: Reports
Conference Papers

: : Publications
: Serials
Conference Proceedings

Conference Reports (1967 1980)

Conferences
. Parent Conferences
. Parent Teacher Conferences

: : : Methods
: : Measurement Techniques
: Testing
Confidence Testing

: Records (Forms)
Confidential Records

: : Relationship
: Privacy
Confidentiality

Conflict
. Conflict of Interest
. Culture Conflict
. Religious Conflict
. Revolution
. Role Conflict
. War
. . Civil War (United States)
. . Korean War
. . Nuclear Warfare
. . Revolutionary War (United States)
. . Vietnam War
. . World War I
. . World War II

: Conflict
Conflict of Interest

: Cognitive Processes
Conflict Resolution
. Peer Mediation

: : Behavior
: Social Behavior
Conformity

: Religion
Confucianism

: Disabilities
Congenital Impairments
. Cerebral Palsy
. Cleft Palate
. Downs Syndrome
. Fetal Alcohol Syndrome
. Spina Bifida

: : Mathematical Concepts
: Geometric Concepts
Congruence (Mathematics)

: Psychological Patterns
Congruence (Psychology)
. Self Congruence

Congruence (1970 1980)

: : : : : Linguistics
: : : : Descriptive Linguistics
: : : Grammar
: : Syntax
: Form Classes (Languages)
Conjunctions

Connected Discourse
. Cohesion (Written Composition)

: Cognitive Processes
Consciousness Raising

: Fundamental Concepts
Conservation (Concept)

Conservation (Environment)
. Energy Conservation
. . Heat Recovery
. Soil Conservation

: : Education
: Environmental Education
Conservation Education

Conservatism

: : Institutions
: Schools
Consolidated Schools

: : : : Linguistics
: : : Phonology
: : Phonemics
: Phonemes
Consonants

: : Groups
: Organizations (Groups)
Consortia

: : : : Liberal Arts
: : : Sciences
: : Social Sciences
: : Liberal Arts
: : Humanities
: History
Constitutional History

: : Standards
: Laws
Constitutional Law

: : : : : Standards
: : : : Criteria
: : : Evaluation Criteria
: : Validity
: Test Validity
Construct Validity

: : Behavior
: Responses
Constructed Response

Construction (Process)
. Cabinetmaking
. Carpentry
. Masonry
. . Bricklaying
. Prefabrication
. Road Construction
. School Construction

: Costs
Construction Costs

: : Business
: Industry
Construction Industry
. Housing Industry

: : Governance
: Administration
Construction Management

Construction Materials
. Asphalts
. Prestressed Concrete

: Needs
Construction Needs

: Programs
Construction Programs

: : Theories
: Learning Theories
Constructivism (Learning)

: : Groups
: Personnel
Consultants
. Medical Consultants
. Reading Consultants
. Science Consultants

: Programs
Consultation Programs

: : : : Liberal Arts
: : : Sciences
: : Social Sciences
: Economics
Consumer Economics

: Education
Consumer Education
. Consumer Science

Consumer Protection

: Technology
: : Education
: Consumer Education
Consumer Science

: : Methods
: Evaluation Methods
Content Analysis

: : Instruction
: Reading Instruction
: : Literacy
: : Language Arts
: Reading
Content Area Reading

: : Instruction
: Writing Instruction
: : Literacy
: : Language Arts
: Writing (Composition)
Content Area Writing
. Writing Across the Curriculum

: : : : : Standards
: : : : Criteria
: : : Evaluation Criteria
: : Validity
: Test Validity
Content Validity

: : Stimuli
: Cues
Context Clues

Context Effect

: : : : Theories
: : : Linguistic Theory
: : Generative Grammar
: Transformational Generative
　　Grammar
Context Free Grammar

: : Conditioning
: Behavior Modification
Contingency Management

Continuation Education (1968 1980)

: : Groups
: Students
Continuation Students

: : Education
: Adult Education
Continuing Education
. Mandatory Continuing Education
. Professional Continuing Education

: : Facilities
: Educational Facilities
Continuing Education Centers

: Credits
Continuing Education Units

: Curriculum
Continuous Progress Plan

Contraception

: : Income
: : Expenditures
: Salaries
Contract Salaries

Contracts
. Performance Contracts

Contrast

: Linguistics
Contrastive Linguistics

: Groups
Control Groups

Controlled Environment (1966 1980)

Controversial Issues (Course Content)

: : : Methods
: : Educational Methods
: Teaching Methods
Conventional Instruction

: Cognitive Processes
Convergent Thinking

: : Curriculum
: Modern Language Curriculum
: Curriculum
: Courses
Conversational Language Courses

: Instruction
Cooking Instruction

: : : : Groups
: : : Personnel
: : Nonprofessional Personnel
: Service Workers
Cooks

: : : : Groups
: : : Personnel
: : Professional Personnel
: Teachers
Cooperating Teachers

: Behavior
Cooperation
. Agency Cooperation
. Community Cooperation
. Compliance (Psychology)
. . Compliance (Legal)
. . Obedience
. Educational Cooperation
. . College School Cooperation
. . Counselor Teacher Cooperation
. . Intercollegiate Cooperation
. . Librarian Teacher Cooperation
. . Parent Teacher Cooperation
. . Partnerships in Education
. . Teacher Collaboration
. Institutional Cooperation
. . College School Cooperation
. . Intercollegiate Cooperation
. Library Cooperation
. International Cooperation
. Regional Cooperation

: : Education
: Vocational Education
Cooperative Education

: Learning
Cooperative Learning

: Planning
Cooperative Planning

: Programs
Cooperative Programs

: : Groups
: Organizations (Groups)
Cooperatives

: : : Publications
: : Reference Materials
: Indexes
Coordinate Indexes

Coordination
. Community Coordination

Coordination Compounds

: : : Groups
: : Personnel
: Administrators
Coordinators
. Audiovisual Coordinators
. Instructor Coordinators

: : Behavior
: Adjustment (to Environment)
Coping

: : Ownership
: Intellectual Property
Copyrights

: Curriculum
Core Curriculum

: : Reinforcement
: Punishment
Corporal Punishment

: Education
Corporate Education

: : : Institutions
: : : Information Sources
: : Libraries
: Special Libraries
Corporate Libraries

Corporate Support

: : Groups
: Organizations (Groups)
Corporations

: Education
Correctional Education

: : Institutions
: Residential Institutions
Correctional Institutions

: Rehabilitation
Correctional Rehabilitation
. Delinquent Rehabilitation

: : Instruction
: Reading Instruction
: : Literacy
: : Language Arts
: Reading
Corrective Reading

: : : : Methods
: : : Evaluation Methods
: : Data Analysis
: Statistical Analysis
Correlation

: : Institutions
: Schools
Correspondence Schools

: : Education
: Distance Education
Correspondence Study

: Facilities
Corridors

: Technology
Cosmetology

: : Methods
: Evaluation Methods
Cost Effectiveness

: Costs
Cost Estimates

Cost Indexes

Costs
. Construction Costs
. Cost Estimates
. Fees
. . Fines (Penalties)
. . Tuition
. Health Care Costs
. Interest (Finance)
. Legal Costs
. Program Costs
. Student Costs
. . Instructional Student Costs
. . . Tuition
. . Noninstructional Student Costs
. Unit Costs

: Guidance
Counseling
. Adult Counseling
. Career Counseling
. Cocounseling
. Educational Counseling
. . Academic Advising
. . Admissions Counseling
. Family Counseling
. Group Counseling
. Individual Counseling
. Marriage Counseling
. Nondirective Counseling
. Parent Counseling
. Peer Counseling
. Rehabilitation Counseling
. School Counseling

Counseling Effectiveness

**Counseling Instructional Programs
　　(1967 1980)**

: : Objectives
: Guidance Objectives
Counseling Objectives

: : : : Liberal Arts
: : : Sciences
: : Behavioral Sciences
: Psychology
Counseling Psychology

: : Services
: Human Services
Counseling Services

: Methods
Counseling Techniques

: Theories
Counseling Theories

: Attitudes
Counselor Attitudes

: Certification
Counselor Certification

Counselor Characteristics

: Ratios (Mathematics)
Counselor Client Ratio

: : Relationship
: Interpersonal Relationship
Counselor Client Relationship

: : : : : Groups
: : : : Personnel
: : : School Personnel
: : : : : Groups
: : : : Personnel
: : : Professional Personnel
: : Faculty
: College Faculty
Counselor Educators

: : Evaluation
: Personnel Evaluation
Counselor Evaluation

: : Behavior
: Performance
Counselor Performance

: : Standards
: Qualifications
Counselor Qualifications

: Role
Counselor Role

: : Selection
: Personnel Selection
Counselor Selection

: : : Behavior
: : Cooperation
: Educational Cooperation
Counselor Teacher Cooperation

: Training
Counselor Training

: : : Groups
: : Personnel
: Guidance Personnel
Counselors
. Adjustment Counselors
. Employment Counselors
. School Counselors

: Geographic Regions
Counties
. Low Income Counties

: : : Facilities
: : Public Facilities
: : : Institutions
: : : Information Sources
: : : Libraries
: : Public Libraries
County Libraries

: : : : Groups
: : : Personnel
: : Government Employees
: Public Officials
County Officials

: Programs
County Programs

: : : Groups
: : Organizations (Groups)
: School Districts
County School Districts

: : Organization
: Course Organization
Course Content

Course Descriptions

: Evaluation
Course Evaluation

: : Instruction
: Library Instruction
Course Integrated Library Instruction

: Objectives
Course Objectives

: Organization
Course Organization
. Course Content

: Selection
Course Selection (Students)

: Curriculum
Courses
. Advanced Courses
. Conversational Language Courses
. Credit Courses
. Education Courses
. Elective Courses
. Intensive Language Courses
. Introductory Courses
. Methods Courses
. Minicourses
. Noncredit Courses
. Practicums

. . Office Practice
. Refresher Courses
. Required Courses
. Telecourses
. United States Government (Course)
. Units of Study
. . Activity Units

: : Educational Media
: Instructional Materials
: : : Standards
: : Specifications
: Computer Software
Courseware
. Microworlds

: Standards
Court Doctrine

: : : : Groups
: : : Personnel
: : Government Employees
: Public Officials
: : Groups
: Judges
Court Judges

Court Litigation
. Desegregation Litigation

: : : : Groups
: : : Personnel
: : Nonprofessional Personnel
: Clerical Workers
Court Reporters

: : Role
: Institutional Role
Court Role

: Institutions
Courts
. Federal Courts
. Juvenile Courts
. State Courts

: : Behavior
: Responses
Covert Response

: : Narcotics
: Cocaine
Crack

: : : : Groups
: : : Personnel
: : Nonprofessional Personnel
: Skilled Workers
Craft Workers

Creationism

: Activities
Creative Activities
. Brainstorming
. Creative Art
. . Creative Dramatics
. Creative Expression
. Creative Writing
. Improvisation

: : Activities
: Creative Activities
: Art
Creative Art
. Creative Dramatics

: : Development
: Individual Development
Creative Development

: : : : : Liberal Arts
: : : : Humanities
: : : Fine Arts
: : Theater Arts
: Dramatics
: : Activities
: : Creative Activities
: : Art
: Creative Art
Creative Dramatics

: : Activities
: Creative Activities
Creative Expression

Creative Reading (1966 1980)

: : : Methods
: : Educational Methods
: Teaching Methods
Creative Teaching

: Cognitive Processes
Creative Thinking
. Divergent Thinking
. Productive Thinking

: : Literacy
: : Language Arts
: Writing (Composition)
: : Activities
: Creative Activities
Creative Writing

: : Individual Characteristics
: Psychological Characteristics
Creativity
. Imagination

: Research
Creativity Research

: : Measures (Individuals)
: Tests
Creativity Tests

: Records (Forms)
Credentials
. Educational Certificates
. Portfolios (Background Materials)
. Resumes (Personal)

: Relationship
Credibility

Credit (Finance)

: : Curriculum
: Courses
Credit Courses

: : : Measurement
: : Achievement Rating
: Grading
Credit No Credit Grading

Credits
. College Credits
. Continuing Education Units

: : Languages
: American Indian Languages
Cree

: : Groups
: Tribes
: : : Groups
: : Ethnic Groups
: American Indians
Cree (Tribe)

: Languages
: : : Linguistics
: : Sociolinguistics
: Language Variation
Creoles
. Gullah
. Haitian Creole
. Mauritian Creole
. Sierra Leone Creole

: : : : Groups
: : : Personnel
: : Administrators
: Supervisors
Crew Leaders

: : : Behavior
: : Social Behavior
: Antisocial Behavior
Crime
. Delinquency
. International Crimes
. . Genocide

: Prevention
Crime Prevention
. Delinquency Prevention

: : Standards
: Laws
Criminal Law

: Groups
Criminals

: : : : Liberal Arts
: : : Sciences
: : Social Sciences
: : : : Liberal Arts
: : : Sciences
: : Behavioral Sciences
: Sociology
Criminology

: Intervention
Crisis Intervention

: : Governance
: Administration
Crisis Management

: : Standards
Criteria
. Admission Criteria
. Evaluation Criteria
. . Reliability
. . . Interrater Reliability
. . . Test Reliability
. . Validity
. . . Concurrent Validity
. . . Predictive Validity
. . . Proof (Mathematics)
. . Test Validity
. . . . Construct Validity
. . . . Content Validity
. Lesson Observation Criteria

: : Measures (Individuals)
: Tests
Criterion Referenced Tests
. Mastery Tests

: Methods
Critical Incidents Method

: Methods
Critical Path Method

: : Literacy
: : Language Arts
: Reading
Critical Reading

: Theories
: : Research
: Social Science Research
Critical Theory

: Cognitive Processes
Critical Thinking
. Evaluative Thinking
. . Value Judgment

Critical Viewing

Criticism
. Art Criticism
. Feminist Criticism
. Film Criticism
. Literary Criticism
. . Rhetorical Criticism

: : : Occupations
: : Agricultural Occupations
: Off Farm Agricultural Occupations
Crop Processing Occupations

: : : Methods
: : Educational Methods
: Teaching Methods
Cross Age Teaching

: Research
Cross Cultural Studies

: Training
Cross Cultural Training

: : Research
: : : Methods
: : Evaluation Methods
: Case Studies
Cross Sectional Studies

Crowding

: Behavior
Crying

: : : : Liberal Arts
: : : Sciences
: : Natural Sciences
: Physical Sciences
Crystallography

: : Groups
: Latin Americans
Cubans

: : : Communication (Thought Transfer)
: : Augmentative and Alternative Communication
: Manual Communication
Cued Speech

: Stimuli
Cues
. Context Clues

: Activities
Cultural Activities

Cultural Awareness

: Background
Cultural Background

: : Facilities
: Resource Centers
Cultural Centers

: Environment
Cultural Context

: Differences
Cultural Differences

: Education
Cultural Education
. Heritage Education

: Enrichment
Cultural Enrichment

Cultural Exchange

Cultural Images

: Influences
Cultural Influences

: Relationship
Cultural Interrelationships

Cultural Isolation

Cultural Literacy

Cultural Maintenance

: Opportunities
Cultural Opportunities

Cultural Pluralism
. Biculturalism

Cultural Relevance
. Culturally Relevant Education

Cultural Traits

: Relevance (Education)
: Education
: Cultural Relevance
Culturally Relevant Education

Culture
. African Culture
. American Indian Culture
. Black Culture

. Burmese Culture
. Chinese Culture
. Dutch Culture
. Folk Culture
. Foreign Culture
. Islamic Culture
. Japanese Culture
. . Japanese American Culture
. Korean Culture
. Latin American Culture
. . Luso Brazilian Culture
. . Puerto Rican Culture
. Material Culture
. Middle Class Culture
. Non Western Civilization
. North American Culture
. . Hispanic American Culture
. . Japanese American Culture
. Oral Tradition
. Popular Culture
. School Culture
. Spanish Culture
. Subcultures
. . Student Subcultures
. Urban Culture
. Western Civilization

: Conflict
Culture Conflict

Culture Contact

: : Measures (Individuals)
: Tests
Culture Fair Tests

Culture Lag

: : Methods
: Laboratory Procedures
Culturing Techniques

: : : Individual Characteristics
: : Psychological Characteristics
: Personality Traits
Curiosity

Current Events

Curriculum
. Area Studies
. . African Studies
. . American Studies
. . Asian Studies
. . Canadian Studies
. . Middle Eastern Studies
. College Curriculum
. . College English
. . College Mathematics
. . College Science
. . College Second Language Programs
. . Education Courses
. . Freshman Composition
. . Postsecondary Education as a Field of Study
. . Teacher Education Curriculum
. . . Methods Courses
. Continuous Progress Plan
. Core Curriculum
. Courses
. . Advanced Courses
. . Conversational Language Courses
. . Credit Courses
. . Education Courses
. . Elective Courses
. . Intensive Language Courses
. . Introductory Courses
. . Methods Courses
. . Minicourses
. . Noncredit Courses
. . Practicums
. . . Office Practice
. . Refresher Courses
. . Required Courses
. . Telecourses
. . United States Government (Course)
. . Units of Study
. . . Activity Units
. Elementary School Curriculum
. . Elementary School Mathematics
. . Elementary School Science
. . FLES
. English Curriculum

. . College English
. . World Literature
. Ethnic Studies
. . American Indian Studies
. . Black Studies
. Experimental Curriculum
. Fused Curriculum
. Home Economics
. Honors Curriculum
. Integrated Curriculum
. Mathematics Curriculum
. . College Mathematics
. . Elementary School Mathematics
. . General Mathematics
. . Modern Mathematics
. . Secondary School Mathematics
. Military Science
. Modern Language Curriculum
. . Conversational Language Courses
. . FLES
. . Intensive Language Courses
. . Notional Functional Syllabi
. National Curriculum
. . British National Curriculum
. Preschool Curriculum
. Religion Studies
. Science Curriculum
. . College Science
. . Elementary School Science
. . General Science
. . Secondary School Science
. Secondary School Curriculum
. . Secondary School Mathematics
. . Secondary School Science
. Shop Curriculum
. Social Studies
. Speech Curriculum
. Spiral Curriculum
. Student Centered Curriculum
. Television Curriculum
. Unified Studies Curriculum
. Urban Studies
. Womens Studies

: : Evaluation
: Student Evaluation
Curriculum Based Assessment

: Design
Curriculum Design

: : Development
: Educational Development
Curriculum Development

: Enrichment
Curriculum Enrichment

: Evaluation
Curriculum Evaluation

: : : Publications
: : Reference Materials
: Guides
Curriculum Guides
. State Curriculum Guides

: Problems
Curriculum Problems

: : Research
: Educational Research
Curriculum Research

: : Facilities
: Resource Centers
: : Facilities
: Educational Facilities
Curriculum Study Centers

: : Language Arts
: Handwriting
Cursive Writing

: : Training
: Job Training
Custodian Training

: : Data
: Scores
Cutting Scores

: Technology
Cybernetics

: Alphabets
Cyrillic Alphabet

: : Disabilities
: Diseases
Cystic Fibrosis

: : : : Liberal Arts
: : : Sciences
: : Natural Sciences
: Biological Sciences
Cytology

: : : Languages
: : Indo European Languages
: Slavic Languages
Czech

: : : Liberal Arts
: : Humanities
: Literature
Czech Literature

: : Languages
: : Uralic Altaic Languages
: Mongolian Languages
Dagur

: : Ability
: Skills
Daily Living Skills
. Self Care Skills

: : : : Groups
: : : Personnel
: : Agricultural Personnel
: Farmers
Dairy Farmers

: : Languages
: American Indian Languages
Dakota
. Lakota

: : Activities
: Physical Activities
: : : Liberal Arts
: : Humanities
: Fine Arts
Dance

: Education
Dance Education

: Therapy
Dance Therapy

: : Languages
: Indo European Languages
Danish

Data
. Databases
. . Bibliographic Databases
. . Full Text Databases
. . Numeric Databases
. . Online Catalogs
. Personnel Data
. Profiles
. Scores
. . Cutting Scores
. . Equated Scores
. . Grade Equivalent Scores
. . Raw Scores
. . True Scores
. . Weighted Scores
. Statistical Data
. . Census Figures
. . Employment Statistics
. . . Worker Days
. . Library Statistics
. . Norms
. . . Local Norms
. . . National Norms
. . . State Norms
. . . Test Norms
. . School Statistics
. . Social Indicators

: : Methods
: Evaluation Methods
Data Analysis
. Data Collection
. . Sampling
. . . Item Sampling
. Data Interpretation
. Statistical Inference
. . Test Interpretation
. Statistical Analysis
. . Analysis of Covariance
. . Analysis of Variance
. . Bayesian Statistics
. . Chi Square
. . Correlation
. . Effect Size
. . Error of Measurement
. . Goodness of Fit
. . Item Analysis
. . Judgment Analysis Technique
. . Least Squares Statistics
. . Maximum Likelihood Statistics
. . Meta Analysis
. . Multivariate Analysis
. . . Cluster Analysis
. . . Discriminant Analysis
. . . Factor Analysis
. . . . Oblique Rotation
. . . . Orthogonal Rotation
. . . Multidimensional Scaling
. . . Path Analysis
. . Regression (Statistics)
. . . Multiple Regression Analysis
. . Robustness (Statistics)
. . Statistical Distributions
. Statistical Inference
. Statistical Significance
. Trend Analysis

: : : Services
: : Information Services
: Information Processing
: : Methods
: : Evaluation Methods
: Data Analysis
Data Collection
. Sampling
. . Item Sampling

: Change
Data Conversion
. Retrospective Conversion (Library
    Catalogs)

: : : Methods
: : Evaluation Methods
: Data Analysis
Data Interpretation
. Statistical Inference
. Test Interpretation

: : : Services
: : Information Services
: Information Processing
Data Processing
. Input Output
. . Keyboarding (Data Entry)
. Natural Language Processing
. Time Sharing

: Occupations
Data Processing Occupations

: Design
Database Design

: Management Systems
: : : Standards
: : Specifications
: Computer Software
Database Management Systems

: : Groups
: Organizations (Groups)
Database Producers

: Information Sources
: Data
Databases
. Bibliographic Databases
. Full Text Databases
. Numeric Databases
. Online Catalogs

: : Relationship
: Interpersonal Relationship
Dating (Social)

: : Groups
: Females
Daughters

: : Programs
: Recreational Programs
Day Camp Programs

: : : Services
: : Human Services
: Social Services
Day Care
. Employer Supported Day Care
. Family Day Care
. School Age Day Care
. Sick Child Care

: Facilities
Day Care Centers

Day Care Effects

: Programs
Day Programs

: : Institutions
: Schools
Day Schools

: : Groups
: Students
Day Students

: : : Social Discrimination
: : Racial Discrimination
: Racial Segregation
De Facto Segregation

: : : Social Discrimination
: : Racial Discrimination
: Racial Segregation
De Jure Segregation

: : Disabilities
: Multiple Disabilities
Deaf Blind

: Translation
Deaf Interpreting

: : Disabilities
: Hearing Impairments
Deafness

: : : : Groups
: : : Personnel
: : School Personnel
: : : : Groups
: : : Personnel
: : Professional Personnel
: Faculty
: : : Groups
: : Personnel
: Administrators
Deans
. Academic Deans
. Deans of Students

: : : : : Groups
: : : : Personnel
: : : School Personnel
: : : : : Groups
: : : : Personnel
: : : Professional Personnel
: : Faculty
: : : : Groups
: : : Personnel
: : Administrators
: Deans
Deans of Students

Death
. Homicide
. Infant Mortality
. . Sudden Infant Death Syndrome
. Suicide

: Language Arts
Debate

Debate Format

Debt (Financial)

: : Methods
: Troubleshooting
Debugging (Computers)

: : Organization
: Administrative Organization
Decentralization

Deception
. Fraud
. Lying

: : : : Symbols (Mathematics)
: : : Numbers
: : Rational Numbers
: Fractions
Decimal Fractions

: Cognitive Processes
Decision Making
. Participative Decision Making

: : Ability
: Skills
Decision Making Skills

: : Management Systems
: : Information Systems
: Management Information Systems
Decision Support Systems

: : Incidence
: Enrollment Rate
Declining Enrollment

: : : Cognitive Processes
: : Language Processing
: Reading Processes
Decoding (Reading)

: : Cognitive Processes
: Logical Thinking
Deduction

: : : : Theories
: : : Linguistic Theory
: : Generative Grammar
: Transformational Generative
    Grammar
Deep Structure

: Psychological Patterns
Defense Mechanisms
. Denial (Psychology)

Definitions

: : : Standards
: : Academic Standards
: Graduation Requirements
Degree Requirements

Degrees (Academic)
. Associate Degrees
. Bachelors Degrees
. Doctoral Degrees
. . Doctor of Arts Degrees
. Masters Degrees
. Specialist in Education Degrees

: Normalization (Disabilities)
Deinstitutionalization (of Disabled)

: : Behavior
: Self Control
Delay of Gratification

: : Disabilities
: Speech Impairments
Delayed Speech

: : : : Behavior
: : : Social Behavior
: : Antisocial Behavior
: Crime
Delinquency

Delinquency Causes

: : Prevention
: Crime Prevention
Delinquency Prevention

: : Rehabilitation
: Correctional Rehabilitation
Delinquent Rehabilitation

: Services
Delivery Systems
. Document Delivery

: Methods
Delphi Technique

: Occupations
Demand Occupations
. Emerging Occupations

: Values
Democratic Values
. American Dream

: : : Liberal Arts
: : Sciences
: Social Sciences
Demography
. Birth Rate
. Employment Patterns
. Geographic Distribution
. Mortality Rate
. Population Distribution
. . Ethnic Distribution
. . Racial Distribution
. Population Growth
. Population Trends
. . Black Population Trends
. Racial Composition
. Racial Balance
. Residential Patterns
. School Demography
. Teacher Distribution
. Social Distribution
. Urban Demography

: : Facilities
: Educational Facilities
Demonstration Centers

: Programs
Demonstration Programs

Demonstrations (Civil)

: : : Methods
: : Educational Methods
: Teaching Methods
Demonstrations (Educational)
. Demonstrations (Science)

: : : : Methods
: : : Educational Methods
: : Teaching Methods
: Demonstrations (Educational)
Demonstrations (Science)

: : Psychological Patterns
: Defense Mechanisms
Denial (Psychology)

: Scientific Concepts
Density (Matter)

: : : : Groups
: : : Personnel
: : Health Personnel
: Allied Health Personnel
Dental Assistants

: Clinics
Dental Clinics

: : Evaluation
: Medical Evaluation
Dental Evaluation

: : Health
: Physical Health
Dental Health

: : Communication (Thought Transfer)
: Verbal Communication
Dictation

Diction

: : Publications
: Reference Materials
Dictionaries
. Glossaries

Didacticism

: : Equipment
: Engines
Diesel Engines

: : Technology
: Medicine
Dietetics

: : : : Groups
: : : Personnel
: : Health Personnel
: Allied Health Personnel
Dietitians

Differences
. Cultural Differences
. Individual Differences
. . Age Differences
. . Intelligence Differences
. . Sex Differences
. Intermode Differences
. Racial Differences
. Religious Differences
. Rural Urban Differences
. Salary Wage Differentials
. Social Differences

: : : : : : Liberal Arts
: : : : : Humanities
: : : : Philosophy
: : : Logic
: : : Mathematical Logic
: : : Mathematical Applications
: : Mathematical Formulas
: Equations (Mathematics)
Differential Equations

: : Groups
: Personnel
Differentiated Staffs

Difficulty Level

: Communication (Thought Transfer)
Diffusion (Communication)

: : : : : : Liberal Arts
: : : : : Sciences
: : : : Natural Sciences
: : : : Physical Sciences
: : : Physics
: : Mechanics (Physics)
: Kinetics
Diffusion (Physics)

: : : Equipment
: : Electronic Equipment
: Computers
Digital Computers

Diglossia

: : Behavior
: Responses
Dimensional Preference

: Facilities
Dining Facilities

: Animals
Dinosaurs

: : : : Liberal Arts
: : : Sciences
: : : Social Sciences
: : : Liberal Arts
: : Humanities
: History
Diplomatic History

: : Instruction
: Reading Instruction
: : Literacy
: : Language Arts
: Reading
Directed Reading Activity

Direction Writing (1966 1980)

: : Publications
: Reference Materials
Directories

Disabilities
. Adventitious Impairments
. Attention Deficit Disorders
. Autism
. Behavior Disorders
. Communication Disorders
. Congenital Impairments
. . Cerebral Palsy
. . Cleft Palate
. . Downs Syndrome
. . Fetal Alcohol Syndrome
. . Spina Bifida
. Developmental Disabilities
. Diseases
. . Alcoholism
. . Allergy
. . Alzheimers Disease
. . Anemia
. . . Sickle Cell Anemia
. . Asthma
. . Cancer
. . Chronic Illness
. . Communicable Diseases
. . . Acquired Immune Deficiency
         Syndrome
. . . Rubella
. . . Venereal Diseases
. . Cystic Fibrosis
. . Diabetes
. . Drug Addiction
. . Eating Disorders
. . . Anorexia Nervosa
. . . Bulimia
. . Failure to Thrive
. . Fetal Alcohol Syndrome
. . Hypertension
. . Obesity
. . Occupational Diseases
. . Otitis Media
. . Poisoning
. . . Lead Poisoning
. . Seizures
. . Terminal Illness
. Hearing Impairments
. . Deafness
. . Partial Hearing
. Injuries
. . Head Injuries
. Language Impairments
. . Aphasia
. . Dyslexia
. Learning Disabilities
. Low Incidence Disabilities
. Mental Disorders
. . Emotional Disturbances
. . . Psychosomatic Disorders
. . Neurosis
. . Posttraumatic Stress Disorder
. . Psychosis
. . . Echolalia
. . . Schizophrenia
. Mental Retardation
. . Downs Syndrome
. . Mild Mental Retardation
. . Moderate Mental Retardation
. . Severe Mental Retardation
. Mild Disabilities
. . Mild Mental Retardation
. . Minimal Brain Dysfunction
. Multiple Disabilities
. . Deaf Blind
. Perceptual Impairments
. Physical Disabilities
. . Amputations
. . Cleft Palate
. . Heart Disorders
. . Neurological Impairments
. . . Aphasia
. . . Cerebral Palsy
. . . Epilepsy

. . . Minimal Brain Dysfunction
. Severe Disabilities
. . Psychosis
. . Echolalia
. . Schizophrenia
. Severe Mental Retardation
. Special Health Problems
. Speech Impairments
. . Articulation Impairments
. . Cleft Palate
. . Delayed Speech
. . Stuttering
. . Voice Disorders
. Visual Impairments
. . Ametropia
. . . Hyperopia
. . . Myopia
. . Blindness
. . Partial Vision
. . Strabismus

: Social Discrimination
Disability Discrimination

: Identification
Disability Identification

: Groups
Disadvantaged
. Disadvantaged Youth
. Economically Disadvantaged
. Educationally Disadvantaged
. Gifted Disadvantaged

: Environment
Disadvantaged Environment

: : Institutions
: Schools
Disadvantaged Schools

: : Groups
: Youth
: : Groups
: Disadvantaged
Disadvantaged Youth

Disarmament

Discipline
. Dismissal (Personnel)
. . Teacher Dismissal
. Expulsion
. Suspension
. . In School Suspension
. Teacher Discipline
. . Teacher Dismissal

: : Education
: Art Education
Discipline Based Art Education

: Policy
Discipline Policy

: Problems
Discipline Problems

Disclosure
. Self Disclosure (Individuals)

: : Publications
: Reference Materials
Discographies

: : : Methods
: : Evaluation Methods
: Structural Analysis (Linguistics)
Discourse Analysis

: Community
Discourse Communities

: : Organization
: Classification
Discourse Modes

: Learning
Discovery Learning

: : Cognitive Processes
: Learning Processes
Discovery Processes

: : : : : Methods
: : : : Evaluation Methods
: : : Data Analysis
: : Statistical Analysis
: Multivariate Analysis
Discriminant Analysis

: Learning
Discrimination Learning

: Legislation
Discriminatory Legislation

: Communication (Thought Transfer)
Discussion
. Group Discussion

: : : Methods
: : Educational Methods
: Teaching Methods
Discussion (Teaching Technique)

: Groups
Discussion Groups
. Focus Groups
. Listening Groups

Disease Control
. Fluoridation

: Incidence
Disease Incidence

: Disabilities
Diseases
. Alcoholism
. Allergy
. Alzheimers Disease
. Anemia
. . Sickle Cell Anemia
. Asthma
. Cancer
. Chronic Illness
. Communicable Diseases
. . Acquired Immune Deficiency
       Syndrome
. . Rubella
. . Venereal Diseases
. Cystic Fibrosis
. Diabetes
. Drug Addiction
. Eating Disorders
. . Anorexia Nervosa
. . Bulimia
. Failure to Thrive
. Fetal Alcohol Syndrome
. Hypertension
. Obesity
. Occupational Diseases
. Otitis Media
. Poisoning
. . Lead Poisoning
. Seizures
. Terminal Illness

: : Sanitation
: Cleaning
Dishwashing

: : : : Equipment
: : : Electronic Equipment
: : Computer Peripherals
: Input Output Devices
Disk Drives

: : Groups
: Personnel
Dislocated Workers

: Discipline
Dismissal (Personnel)
. Teacher Dismissal

: : Groups
: Females
Displaced Homemakers

: Visual Aids
Display Aids

Display Systems

Disqualification

: : Methods
: Laboratory Procedures
Dissection

: : Behavior
: Social Behavior
Dissent

Distance

: Education
Distance Education
. Correspondence Study

: Linguistics
Distinctive Features (Language)

Distractors (Tests)

: : Education
: Vocational Education
Distributive Education

: : : : : Groups
: : : : Personnel
: : : Professional Personnel
: : Teachers
: Vocational Education Teachers
Distributive Education Teachers

: : Cognitive Processes
: Creative Thinking
Divergent Thinking

Diversity (Faculty)

: Institutional Characteristics
Diversity (Institutional)

: Student Characteristics
Diversity (Student)

: : : : Activities
: : : Physical Activities
: : Athletics
: Aquatic Sports
Diving

: : : Liberal Arts
: : Mathematics
: Arithmetic
Division

Divorce

: Nucleic Acids
DNA

: : Degrees (Academic)
: Doctoral Degrees
Doctor of Arts Degrees

: Degrees (Academic)
Doctoral Degrees
. Doctor of Arts Degrees

: : : Publications
: : Reports
: Theses
Doctoral Dissertations

: : Programs
: College Programs
Doctoral Programs

: : : Services
: : Information Services
: Information Dissemination
: Services
: Delivery Systems
Document Delivery

: Nonprint Media
Documentaries

: : : Services
: : Information Services
: Information Processing
Documentation

. Abstracting
. Authority Control (Information)
. Bibliometrics
. . Citation Analysis
. . . Bibliographic Coupling
. Cataloging
. . Machine Readable Cataloging
. Filing
. Indexing
. . Automatic Indexing

Dogmatism

: : Groups
: Latin Americans
Dominicans

: Groups
Donors

: Structural Elements (Construction)
Doors

: : Facilities
: Housing
Dormitories

: : : Planning
: : Scheduling
: School Schedules
Double Sessions

: : : : Services
: : : Information Services
: : Information Processing
: Information Retrieval
Downloading

: : Disabilities
: Mental Retardation
: : Disabilities
: Congenital Impairments
Downs Syndrome

: : : : Liberal Arts
: : : Humanities
: : Fine Arts
: Visual Arts
Drafting
. Architectural Drafting
. Engineering Drawing
. Technical Illustration

: : : : Liberal Arts
: : : Humanities
: : Fine Arts
: Theater Arts
: : : Liberal Arts
: : Humanities
: Literature
Drama
. Comedy
. . Skits
. Scripts
. Soap Operas
. Tragedy

: Workshops
Drama Workshops

: : : Methods
: : Simulation
: Role Playing
Dramatic Play

: : : : Liberal Arts
: : : Humanities
: : Fine Arts
: Theater Arts
Dramatics
. Creative Dramatics

: Languages
Dravidian Languages
. Kannada
. Malayalam
. Tamil
. Telugu

Dreams
. Nightmares

: Standards
Dress Codes

: : : Methods
: : Educational Methods
: Teaching Methods
Drills (Practice)
. Pattern Drills (Language)
. . Substitution Drills

: Behavior
Drinking
. Alcohol Abuse
. . Alcoholism

: : Matter
: Water
Drinking Water

: Education
Driver Education

: Facilities
Driveways

: : : Behavior
: : Social Behavior
: Antisocial Behavior
Driving While Intoxicated

: Attitudes
Dropout Attitudes

Dropout Characteristics

: Prevention
Dropout Prevention

: : Programs
: Rehabilitation Programs
Dropout Programs

: Incidence
Dropout Rate

: Research
Dropout Research

: Groups
Dropouts
. Adult Dropouts

: Weather
: Natural Disasters
Drought

: : Behavior
: Substance Abuse
: : Behavior
: Drug Use
Drug Abuse
. Drug Addiction

: : : Behavior
: : Substance Abuse
: : : Behavior
: : Drug Use
: Drug Abuse
: : Disabilities
: Diseases
Drug Addiction

: Education
Drug Education

: : Legislation
: Public Health Legislation
Drug Legislation

: Rehabilitation
Drug Rehabilitation

: Therapy
Drug Therapy

: Behavior
Drug Use
. Drug Abuse
. . Drug Addiction
. Illegal Drug Use
. Prenatal Drug Exposure

: : Methods
: Evaluation Methods
Drug Use Testing

: : Groups
: Family (Sociological Unit)
Dual Career Family

: Enrollment
Dual Enrollment

: Civil Liberties
Due Process

: : : Languages
: : Malayo Polynesian Languages
: Indonesian Languages
Dusun

: : Languages
: Indo European Languages
Dutch

: Culture
Dutch Culture

: : Disabilities
: Language Impairments
Dyslexia

: : Languages
: African Languages
Dyula

: Admission (School)
Early Admission

: : Groups
: Age Groups
Early Adolescents

: Education
Early Childhood Education
. Preschool Education
. Primary Education

: : Background
: Experience
Early Experience

: Identification
Early Identification

: Intervention
Early Intervention
. Individualized Family Service Plans

Early Parenthood

: : Literacy
: : Language Arts
: Reading
Early Reading

: : Status
: Retirement
Early Retirement

Ears

: : : : Liberal Arts
: : : Sciences
: : Natural Sciences
: Physical Sciences
Earth Science
. Geochemistry
. Geology
. . Mineralogy
. . Paleontology
. . Petrology
. Geophysics
. . Plate Tectonics
. Hydrology
. Meteorology
. Oceanography
. Physical Geography
. Seismology
. . Plate Tectonics
. Soil Science

Earthquakes

: : Disabilities
: Diseases
Eating Disorders
. Anorexia Nervosa
. Bulimia

Eating Habits

: : : Disabilities
: : : Severe Disabilities
: : : Disabilities
: : Mental Disorders
: Psychosis
Echolalia

Echolocation

: Influences
Ecological Factors

: : : : Liberal Arts
: : : Sciences
: : Natural Sciences
: Biological Sciences
Ecology

: : : : Liberal Arts
: : : Sciences
: : Social Sciences
: Economics
Econometrics

: Change
Economic Change

: Environment
Economic Climate
. Inflation (Economics)

: Development
Economic Development
. Economic Progress

: Influences
Economic Factors

Economic Impact

: Opportunities
Economic Opportunities

: : Development
: Economic Development
Economic Progress

: : Research
: Social Science Research
Economic Research

: Status
Economic Status
. Poverty

: : Groups
: Disadvantaged
Economically Disadvantaged

: : : Liberal Arts
: : Sciences
: Social Sciences
Economics
. Consumer Economics
. Econometrics
. Educational Economics
. . Educational Finance
. Labor Economics
. Macroeconomics
. Microeconomics
. Rural Economics

: Education
Economics Education

Editing

: : Mass Media
: News Media
Editorials

: : Groups
: Personnel
Editors

Education
. Academic Education
. Adult Education
. . Adult Basic Education
. . Adult Vocational Education
. . . Adult Farmer Education
. . . Young Farmer Education
. . Continuing Education
. . . Mandatory Continuing Education
. . . Professional Continuing Education
. . Labor Education
. . Migrant Adult Education
. . Parent Education
. . Preretirement Education
. . Public School Adult Education
. . Veterans Education
. Aerospace Education
. . Aviation Education
. Aesthetic Education
. . Art Appreciation
. . Film Study
. . Music Appreciation
. After School Education
. Aging Education
. Agricultural Education
. . Adult Farmer Education
. . Supervised Occupational Experience
       (Agriculture)
. . Young Farmer Education
. Alcohol Education
. Allied Health Occupations Education
. Alumni Education
. American Indian Education
. Art Education
. . Discipline Based Art Education
. . Studio Art
. Back to Basics
. Basic Business Education
. Bilingual Education
. Black Education
. Career Education
. Citizenship Education
. Coeducation
. Community Education
. Comparative Education
. Compensatory Education
. Competency Based Education
. . Competency Based Teacher
       Education
. Compulsory Education
. . Home Schooling
. Consumer Education
. . Consumer Science
. Corporate Education
. Correctional Education
. Cultural Education
. . Heritage Education
. . Culturally Relevant Education
. Dance Education
. Distance Education
. . Correspondence Study
. Driver Education
. Drug Education
. Early Childhood Education
. . Preschool Education
. . Primary Education
. Economics Education
. Elementary Secondary Education
. . Elementary Education
. . . Adult Basic Education
. . . Primary Education
. . Secondary Education
. . . College Preparation
. Energy Education
. Environmental Education
. . Conservation Education
. . Environmental Interpretation
. Equal Education
. Extension Education
. . External Degree Programs
. . Library Extension
. . Rural Extension
. . Urban Extension
. Family Life Education
. . Parenthood Education
. . Sex Education
. Free Education
. General Education
. Global Education

. . International Education
. Health Education
. . Comprehensive School Health
       Education
. Humanistic Education
. Industrial Education
. Informal Education
. Inservice Education
. . Inservice Teacher Education
. Intergroup Education
. . Multicultural Education
. Journalism Education
. Law Related Education
. Leisure Education
. Literacy Education
. Marine Education
. . Maritime Education
. Mathematics Education
. Mexican American Education
. Migrant Education
. Music Education
. . Kodaly Method
. . Orff Method
. . Suzuki Method
. Noncategorical Education
. Nondiscriminatory Education
. Nonformal Education
. Nontraditional Education
. Open Education
. Outcome Based Education
. Outdoor Education
. . Adventure Education
. Patient Education
. Physical Education
. . Adapted Physical Education
. . Movement Education
. Police Education
. Popular Education
. Population Education
. Postsecondary Education
. . Higher Education
. . . Graduate Study
. . . . Graduate Medical Education
. . . . Postsecondary Education as a
          Field of Study
. . . Postdoctoral Education
. . . Undergraduate Study
. Private Education
. Process Education
. Professional Education
. . Administrator Education
. . Architectural Education
. . Business Administration Education
. . Engineering Education
. . Home Economics Education
. . Information Science Education
. . . Computer Science Education
. . . Library Education
. . Legal Education (Professions)
. . Medical Education
. . . Graduate Medical Education
. . . Nursing Education
. . . Pharmaceutical Education
. . . Veterinary Medical Education
. . Professional Continuing Education
. . Public Administration Education
. . Teacher Education
. . . Competency Based Teacher
          Education
. . . English Teacher Education
. . . Inservice Teacher Education
. . . Preservice Teacher Education
. . . . Student Teaching
. . . Teacher Educator Education
. . Theological Education
. Progressive Education
. Public Affairs Education
. Public Education
. . Public School Adult Education
. Religious Education
. Rural Education
. Safety Education
. Science Education
. Special Education
. . Adapted Physical Education
. Study Abroad
. Supplementary Education
. Technology Education
. Terminal Education
. Tribally Controlled Education
. Urban Education
. Values Education
. Vocational Education

. . Adult Vocational Education
. . . Adult Farmer Education
. . . Young Farmer Education
. . Business Education
. . . Office Occupations Education
. . Cooperative Education
. . Distributive Education
. . Occupational Home Economics
. . Prevocational Education
. . Technical Education
. . . Fire Science Education
. . . Tech Prep
. . Trade and Industrial Education
. Womens Education

: : Curriculum
: Courses
: : Curriculum
: College Curriculum
Education Courses

: : : Groups
: : Students
: Majors (Students)
Education Majors

: : Facilities
: Resource Centers
: : Facilities
: Educational Facilities
Education Service Centers

: Relationship
Education Work Relationship

: : Governance
: Administration
Educational Administration
. School Administration
. . College Administration
. . School Based Management

: Foundations of Education
: : : : Liberal Arts
: : : Sciences
: : Social Sciences
: Anthropology
Educational Anthropology

: Evaluation
Educational Assessment
. College Outcomes Assessment

: : Achievement
: Academic Achievement
Educational Attainment

: Attitudes
Educational Attitudes

: Background
Educational Background
. Educational Experience

: Outcomes of Education
Educational Benefits

: : Records (Forms)
: Credentials
Educational Certificates

: Change
Educational Change

: : Facilities
: Educational Facilities
Educational Complexes
. Campuses
. Educational Parks

: : Behavior
: Cooperation
Educational Cooperation
. College School Cooperation
. Counselor Teacher Cooperation
. Intercollegiate Cooperation
. Librarian Teacher Cooperation
. Parent Teacher Cooperation
. Partnerships in Education
. Teacher Collaboration

: : Guidance
: Counseling
Educational Counseling
. Academic Advising
. Admissions Counseling

Educational Demand

: Development
Educational Development
. Curriculum Development
. Instructional Development

: Identification
Educational Diagnosis
. Reading Diagnosis
. . Miscue Analysis

: Social Discrimination
Educational Discrimination
. School Segregation
. . College Segregation
. . School Resegregation

: Foundations of Education
: : : : Liberal Arts
: : : Sciences
: : Social Sciences
: Economics
Educational Economics
. Educational Finance

: Environment
Educational Environment
. Classroom Environment
. College Environment
. Teaching Conditions

: Equipment
Educational Equipment
. Classroom Furniture

Educational Equity (Finance)

: : Background
: Experience
: : Background
: Educational Background
Educational Experience

: Experiments
Educational Experiments

: Facilities
Educational Facilities
. After School Centers
. Audiovisual Centers
. Business Education Facilities
. Child Development Centers
. Classrooms
. . Electronic Classrooms
. . Mobile Classrooms
. . Multipurpose Classrooms
. . Self Contained Classrooms
. Continuing Education Centers
. Curriculum Study Centers
. Demonstration Centers
. Education Service Centers
. Educational Complexes
. . Campuses
. . Educational Parks
. Found Spaces
. Guidance Centers
. Learning Centers (Classroom)
. Learning Laboratories
. . Language Laboratories
. Learning Resources Centers
. Living Learning Centers
. Off Campus Facilities
. Physical Education Facilities
. Reading Centers
. School Buildings
. . College Buildings
. School Shops
. School Space
. Science Teaching Centers
. Skill Centers
. Student Unions
. Study Facilities
. . Carrels
. . Study Centers
. Vocational Training Centers
. Writing Laboratories

: Design
Educational Facilities Design

: : Improvement
: Facility Improvement
Educational Facilities Improvement

: : Planning
: Facility Planning
: : Planning
: Educational Planning
Educational Facilities Planning
. Campus Planning

: : Foundations of Education
: : : : : Liberal Arts
: : : : Sciences
: : : Social Sciences
: : Economics
: Educational Economics
Educational Finance

: : Activities
: Games
Educational Games
. Reading Games

: : : : Liberal Arts
: : : Sciences
: : Social Sciences
: Gerontology
Educational Gerontology

: : : : Liberal Arts
: : : Sciences
: : Social Sciences
: : : Liberal Arts
: : Humanities
: History
: Foundations of Education
Educational History
. Science Education History

: Improvement
Educational Improvement
. Instructional Improvement

: Innovation
Educational Innovation
. Instructional Innovation

: Legislation
Educational Legislation
. School Attendance Legislation

: Malpractice
Educational Malpractice

Educational Media
. Audiovisual Aids
. . Instructional Films
. . Protocol Materials
. Autoinstructional Aids
. . Teaching Machines
. Instructional Materials
. . Advance Organizers
. . Bilingual Instructional Materials
. . Courseware
. . . Microworlds
. . Experience Charts
. . Instructional Films
. . Laboratory Manuals
. . Learning Modules
. . Manipulative Materials
. . Problem Sets
. . Programmed Instructional Materials
. . Protocol Materials
. . Student Developed Materials
. . . Student Writing Models
. . Study Guides
. . Teacher Developed Materials
. . . Teacher Made Tests
. . Textbooks
. . . History Textbooks
. . . Multicultural Textbooks
. . Workbooks

: Methods
Educational Methods
. Classroom Techniques
. Educational Strategies
. Psychoeducational Methods
. Teaching Methods

. . Audiolingual Methods
. . Case Method (Teaching Technique)
. . Clinical Teaching (Health Professions)
. . Community Based Instruction (Disabilities)
. . Conventional Instruction
. . Creative Teaching
. . Cross Age Teaching
. . Demonstrations (Educational)
. . . Demonstrations (Science)
. . Diagnostic Teaching
. . Discussion (Teaching Technique)
. . Drills (Practice)
. . Pattern Drills (Language)
. . . Substitution Drills
. . Experimental Teaching
. . Grammar Translation Method
. . Guided Design
. . Individualized Instruction
. . Kinesthetic Methods
. . Kodaly Method
. . Language Experience Approach
. . Learner Controlled Instruction
. . Lecture Method
. . Montessori Method
. . Multimedia Instruction
. . . Audiovisual Instruction
. . Negative Practice
. . Oral Communication Method
. . . Lipreading
. . Orff Method
. . Peer Teaching
. . Precision Teaching
. . Programmed Instruction
. . . Computer Assisted Instruction
. . . . Intelligent Tutoring Systems
. . . Programmed Tutoring
. . Reciprocal Teaching
. . Reggio Emilia Approach
. . Sight Method
. . Suggestopedia
. . Suzuki Method
. . Telephone Instruction
. . Thematic Approach
. . Training Methods
. . . Management Games
. . . Microcounseling
. . . Microteaching
. . Whole Language Approach

: Mobility
Educational Mobility

: Needs
Educational Needs

: Objectives
Educational Objectives

: Opportunities
Educational Opportunities
. Access to Education

: : : Facilities
: : Educational Facilities
: Educational Complexes
Educational Parks

: : : Liberal Arts
: : Humanities
: Philosophy
: Foundations of Education
Educational Philosophy

: Planning
Educational Planning
. College Planning
. Educational Facilities Planning
. . Campus Planning

: Policy
Educational Policy

Educational Practices
. Developmentally Appropriate Practices

: Standards
: Foundations of Education
Educational Principles

Educational Problems (1966 1980)

Educational Programs (1966 1980)

: : : : Liberal Arts
: : : Sciences
: : Behavioral Sciences
: Psychology
: Foundations of Education
Educational Psychology

Educational Quality

: : : : Technology
: : : Communications
: : Telecommunications
: : Mass Media
: Radio
: Technology
: : : Communications
: Audiovisual Communications
Educational Radio

: Research
Educational Research
. Classroom Research
. Curriculum Research
. Effective Schools Research
. Reading Research
. Writing Research

: : : : Groups
: : : Personnel
: Professional Personnel
: Researchers
Educational Researchers
. Teacher Researchers

: Resources
Educational Resources
. Educational Supply

: Responsibility
Educational Responsibility

Educational Retardation (1966 1980)

: : : : Liberal Arts
: : : Sciences
: : Social Sciences
: : : : Liberal Arts
: : : Sciences
: : Behavioral Sciences
: Sociology
: Foundations of Education
Educational Sociology

Educational Specifications (1967 1980)

: : : Methods
: : Evaluation Methods
: Comparative Analysis
Educational Status Comparison

: : Methods
: Educational Methods
Educational Strategies

: : Resources
: Educational Resources
Educational Supply

: Technology
Educational Technology
. Instructional Systems
. Performance Technology

: : : : Technology
: : : Communications
: : Telecommunications
: : Mass Media
: Television
: Technology
: : Communications
: Audiovisual Communications
Educational Television

: : : Methods
: : Measurement Techniques
: Testing
Educational Testing

: Theories
: Foundations of Education
Educational Theories

: Therapy
Educational Therapy

Educational Trends

: : Financial Support
: Grants
Educational Vouchers

: : Groups
: Disadvantaged
Educationally Disadvantaged

: : : : Methods
: : : Evaluation Methods
: : Data Analysis
: Statistical Analysis
Effect Size

: : Research
: Educational Research
Effective Schools Research

Efficiency

: Psychological Patterns
Egocentrism

: : Cognitive Processes
: Memory
Eidetic Imagery

: : : Liberal Arts
: : Humanities
: Literature
Eighteenth Century Literature

: : : Behavior
: : Social Behavior
: Antisocial Behavior
Elder Abuse

: Selection
Elections
. School Budget Elections

: : Curriculum
: Courses
Elective Courses

Elective Reading (1966 1980)

: : Resources
: Supplies
: Equipment
Electric Batteries

: Equipment
Electric Circuits

: : Equipment
: Engines
Electric Motors

: Equipment
Electrical Appliances

: Occupations
Electrical Occupations

: Stimuli
Electrical Stimuli

Electrical Systems

: : : : Groups
: : : Personnel
: : Nonprofessional Personnel
: Skilled Workers
Electricians

Electricity

: : : : : : Liberal Arts
: : : : : Sciences
: : : : Natural Sciences
: : : Physical Sciences
: : Chemistry

: Physical Chemistry
Electrochemistry

: : Technology
: Medicine
Electroencephalography

: Equipment
Electromechanical Aids

: Technology
Electromechanical Technology

: : : Facilities
: : Educational Facilities
: Classrooms
Electronic Classrooms

Electronic Control

: Equipment
Electronic Equipment
. Broadcast Reception Equipment
. Computer Peripherals
. . Computer Storage Devices
. . . Magnetic Disks
. . . . Floppy Disks
. . Input Output Devices
. . . Computer Printers
. . . Computer Terminals
. . . . Video Display Terminals
. . Disk Drives
. . Optical Scanners
. . Modems
. Computers
. . Analog Computers
. . Digital Computers
. . Microcomputers
. . Minicomputers
. Magnetic Tapes
. . Magnetic Tape Cassettes
. . . Audiotape Cassettes
. . . Videotape Cassettes
. Microphones
. Optical Disks
. . Optical Data Disks
. Polygraphs
. Radar
. Semiconductor Devices
. . Transistors
. Sound Spectrographs
. Speech Synthesizers
. Tape Recorders
. . Audiotape Recorders
. . Videotape Recorders
. Video Equipment
. . Videodisks
. . Videotape Cassettes
. . Videotape Recorders

: : : Publications
: : Serials
: Periodicals
Electronic Journals

: : Institutions
: : Information Sources
: Libraries
Electronic Libraries

: : : : Technology
: : : Communications
: : Telecommunications
: : Communication (Thought Transfer)
: Computer Mediated Communication
Electronic Mail
. Listservs

: : Methods
: Production Techniques
: : : : Technology
: : : Communications
: : Telecommunications
: : Communication (Thought Transfer)
: Computer Mediated Communication
Electronic Publishing

: : : Groups
: : Personnel
: Paraprofessional Personnel
Electronic Technicians

: : Language
: Written Language
Electronic Text

: : : : : Liberal Arts
: : : : Sciences
: : : Natural Sciences
: : Physical Sciences
: Physics
Electronics
. Microelectronics

: : : Business
: : Industry
: Manufacturing Industry
Electronics Industry

: : Education
: Elementary Secondary Education
Elementary Education
. Adult Basic Education
. Primary Education

: Curriculum
Elementary School Curriculum
. Elementary School Mathematics
. Elementary School Science
. FLES

: : Curriculum
: Mathematics Curriculum
: : Curriculum
: Elementary School Curriculum
Elementary School Mathematics

: : Curriculum
: Science Curriculum
: : Curriculum
: Elementary School Curriculum
Elementary School Science

: : Groups
: Students
Elementary School Students

: : : : Groups
: : : Personnel
: : Professional Personnel
: Teachers
Elementary School Teachers

: : Institutions
: Schools
Elementary Schools

: Education
Elementary Secondary Education
. Elementary Education
. . Adult Basic Education
. . Primary Education
. Secondary Education
. . College Preparation

Eligibility

Elitism

: : : : Liberal Arts
: : : Sciences
: : Natural Sciences
: Biological Sciences
Embryology

: : : : : Groups
: : : : Personnel
: : : Nonprofessional Personnel
: : Service Workers
: Emergency Squad Personnel
: : : : Groups
: : : Personnel
: : Health Personnel
: Allied Health Personnel
Emergency Medical Technicians

: Programs
Emergency Programs

: : : : Groups
: : : Personnel
: : Nonprofessional Personnel
: Service Workers
Emergency Squad Personnel
. Emergency Medical Technicians

: Literacy
Emergent Literacy

: : Occupations
: Demand Occupations
Emerging Occupations

: : : Behavior
: : Social Behavior
: Antisocial Behavior
Emotional Abuse

: : Behavior
: Adjustment (to Environment)
Emotional Adjustment

: : Development
: Individual Development
Emotional Development

: : Disabilities
: Mental Disorders
Emotional Disturbances
. Psychosomatic Disorders

: : Background
: Experience
Emotional Experience
. Catharsis

: Problems
Emotional Problems

: : Behavior
: Responses
Emotional Response

: Psychological Patterns
Empathy

: : Groups
: Parents
Employed Parents

: : Groups
: Females
Employed Women
. Women Administrators
. Women Faculty

Employee Absenteeism

: Programs
Employee Assistance Programs

: Attitudes
Employee Attitudes

: Responsibility
Employee Responsibility

: : Groups
: Personnel
Employees
. Entry Workers

: Attitudes
Employer Attitudes

: : Relationship
: Interpersonal Relationship
Employer Employee Relationship

: : : : Services
: : : Human Services
: : Social Services
: Day Care
Employer Supported Day Care

: Groups
Employers

Employment
. Black Employment
. Migrant Employment
. Multiple Employment
. Overseas Employment
. Part Time Employment
. . Job Sharing
. Seasonal Employment
. Self Employment
. Student Employment
. Supported Employment

. Teacher Employment
. Temporary Employment
. Underemployment
. Youth Employment

: : : : Groups
: : : Personnel
: : Guidance Personnel
: Counselors
Employment Counselors

: : : Background
: : Experience
: Work Experience
Employment Experience

: : : : Methods
: : : Evaluation Methods
: : Interviews
Employment Interviews

: Status
Employment Level
. Academic Rank (Professional)
. Tenure

: Opportunities
Employment Opportunities
. Equal Opportunities (Jobs)
. . Occupational Segregation

: : : : Liberal Arts
: : : Sciences
: : Social Sciences
: Demography
Employment Patterns

Employment Potential

Employment Practices

: Problems
Employment Problems

: Programs
Employment Programs

: Prediction
Employment Projections

: : Standards
: Qualifications
Employment Qualifications

: : Services
: Human Services
Employment Services
. Outplacement Services (Employment)

: : Data
: Statistical Data
Employment Statistics
. Worker Days

Empowerment
. Parent Empowerment
. Student Empowerment
. Teacher Empowerment

: Facilities
Encapsulated Facilities

: Cognitive Processes
Encoding (Psychology)

: : Publications
: Reference Materials
Encyclopedias

: Wildlife
Endangered Species

: Financial Support
Endowment Funds

: Scientific Concepts
Energy
. Geothermal Energy
. Heat
. Radiation
. . Light
. . Nuclear Energy
. . Solar Energy

. Wind Energy

: Audits (Verification)
Energy Audits

: Conservation (Environment)
Energy Conservation
. Heat Recovery

: Education
Energy Education

: : Governance
: Administration
Energy Management

: Occupations
Energy Occupations

: Technology
Engineering
. Agricultural Engineering
. Chemical Engineering
. Civil Engineering
. Ocean Engineering
. Operating Engineering

: : : : : : Liberal Arts
: : : : : Humanities
: : : : Fine Arts
: : : Visual Arts
: : Graphic Arts
: Engineering Graphics
: : : : : Liberal Arts
: : : : Humanities
: : : Fine Arts
: : Visual Arts
: Drafting
Engineering Drawing

: : Education
: Professional Education
Engineering Education

: : : : : Liberal Arts
: : : : Humanities
: : : Fine Arts
: : Visual Arts
: Graphic Arts
Engineering Graphics
. Engineering Drawing

: : : Groups
: : Personnel
: Paraprofessional Personnel
Engineering Technicians
. Highway Engineering Aides

: Technology
Engineering Technology

: : : Groups
: : Personnel
: Professional Personnel
Engineers

: Equipment
Engines
. Diesel Engines
. Electric Motors

: : Languages
: Indo European Languages
English
. Business English
. English (Second Language)
. . English for Special Purposes
. . . English for Academic Purposes
. . . English for Science and
Technology
. . . Vocational English (Second
Language)
. Middle English
. North American English
. Old English
. Oral English

: : Language
: Second Languages
: : : Languages
: : Indo European Languages
: English
English (Second Language)

. English for Special Purposes
. . English for Academic Purposes
. . English for Science and Technology
. . Vocational English (Second
Language)

: Curriculum
English Curriculum
. College English
. World Literature

: : : Organization
: : Administrative Organization
: Departments
English Departments

English Education (1967 1980)

: : : Language
: : Languages for Special Purposes
: : : : Language
: : : Second Languages
: : : : Languages
: : : Indo European Languages
: : English
: English (Second Language)
: English for Special Purposes
English for Academic Purposes

: : : Language
: : Languages for Special Purposes
: : : : Language
: : : Second Languages
: : : : Languages
: : : Indo European Languages
: : English
: English (Second Language)
: English for Special Purposes
English for Science and Technology

: : Language
: Languages for Special Purposes
: : : Language
: : Second Languages
: : : Languages
: : Indo European Languages
: : English
: English (Second Language)
English for Special Purposes
. English for Academic Purposes
. English for Science and Technology
. Vocational English (Second
Language)

: : : Instruction
: : Humanities Instruction
: Native Language Instruction
English Instruction

: : : Liberal Arts
: : Humanities
: Literature
English Literature
. Old English Literature

**English Neoclassic Literary Period
(1968 1980)**

English Only Movement

: : : Education
: : Professional Education
: Teacher Education
English Teacher Education

: : : : : Groups
: : : : Personnel
: : : Professional Personnel
: : Teachers
: Language Teachers
English Teachers

: : : : Groups
: : : Personnel
: : Government Employees
: Military Personnel
Enlisted Personnel

Enrichment
. Cultural Enrichment
. Curriculum Enrichment
. Job Enrichment
. Language Enrichment

. Mathematical Enrichment

: Activities
Enrichment Activities

Enrollment
. Dual Enrollment
. Language Enrollment
. Student Attrition

: Influences
Enrollment Influences

: Management Systems
: : Governance
: Administration
Enrollment Management

: Prediction
Enrollment Projections

: Incidence
Enrollment Rate
. Average Daily Membership
. Declining Enrollment

Enrollment Trends

: : : : : Liberal Arts
: : : : Sciences
: : : Natural Sciences
: : Biological Sciences
: Zoology
Entomology

Entrepreneurship

: Scientific Concepts
Entropy

: : : Groups
: : Personnel
: Employees
Entry Workers

Environment
. Cultural Context
. Disadvantaged Environment
. Economic Climate
. . Inflation (Economics)
. Educational Environment
. . Classroom Environment
. . College Environment
. . Teaching Conditions
. Family Environment
. Institutional Environment
. . College Environment
. Organizational Climate
. Permissive Environment
. Physical Environment
. . Acoustical Environment
. . . Noise (Sound)
. . Built Environment
. . Climate
. . Thermal Environment
. . Visual Environment
. . Wilderness
. Rural Environment
. Simulated Environment
. Slum Environment
. Social Environment
. . Social Isolation
. Suburban Environment
. Therapeutic Environment
. Urban Environment
. Work Environment
. . Teaching Conditions

: Education
Environmental Education
. Conservation Education
. Environmental Interpretation

: Influences
Environmental Influences

: : Education
: Environmental Education
Environmental Interpretation

: Research
Environmental Research

: : Methods
: Evaluation Methods
Environmental Scanning

: Standards
Environmental Standards

: : : Groups
: : Personnel
: Paraprofessional Personnel
: : : : Groups
: : : Personnel
: : Health Personnel
: Allied Health Personnel
Environmental Technicians

Enzymes

: : : : Liberal Arts
: : : Humanities
: : Literature
: Poetry
: Literary Genres
Epics

: : Technology
: Medicine
Epidemiology

: : : Disabilities
: : Physical Disabilities
: Neurological Impairments
Epilepsy

Episode Teaching (1967 1980)

: : : Liberal Arts
: : Humanities
: Philosophy
Epistemology

: Education
: : Civil Liberties
: Civil Rights
Equal Education

: Facilities
Equal Facilities

: : Opportunities
: Employment Opportunities
: : Civil Liberties
: Civil Rights
Equal Opportunities (Jobs)
. Occupational Segregation

: : Civil Liberties
: Civil Rights
Equal Protection

: Financial Support
Equalization Aid

: : Data
: Scores
Equated Scores

: : : : : Liberal Arts
: : : : Humanities
: : : Philosophy
: : : Logic
: : Mathematical Logic
: : Mathematical Applications
: Mathematical Formulas
Equations (Mathematics)
. Differential Equations

Equipment
. Agricultural Machinery
. Air Conditioning Equipment
. Assistive Devices (for Disabled)
. . Mobility Aids
. . Wheelchairs
. . Prostheses
. . . Cochlear Implants
. Athletic Equipment
. Audio Equipment
. . Audiodisks
. . Audiotape Cassettes
. . Audiotape Recorders
. . Hearing Aids
. . Microphones
. . Sound Spectrographs

. . Speech Synthesizers
. Biomedical Equipment
. Calculators
. . Graphing Calculators
. Educational Equipment
. . Classroom Furniture
. Electric Batteries
. Electric Circuits
. Electrical Appliances
. Electromechanical Aids
. Electronic Equipment
. Broadcast Reception Equipment
. Computer Peripherals
. . . Computer Storage Devices
. . . . Magnetic Disks
. . . . . Floppy Disks
. . . Input Output Devices
. . . . Computer Printers
. . . . Computer Terminals
. . . . . Video Display Terminals
. . . . Disk Drives
. . . . Optical Scanners
. . . Modems
. . Computers
. . . Analog Computers
. . . Digital Computers
. . . Microcomputers
. . . Minicomputers
. . Magnetic Tapes
. . Magnetic Tape Cassettes
. . . . Audiotape Cassettes
. . . . Videotape Cassettes
. . Microphones
. . Optical Disks
. . . Optical Data Disks
. . Polygraphs
. . Radar
. . Semiconductor Devices
. . . Transistors
. . Sound Spectrographs
. . Speech Synthesizers
. Tape Recorders
. . . Audiotape Recorders
. . . Videotape Recorders
. . Video Equipment
. . . Videodisks
. . . Videotape Cassettes
. . . Videotape Recorders
. Engines
. . Diesel Engines
. . Electric Motors
. Furniture
. . Classroom Furniture
. Guns
. Hand Tools
. Home Furnishings
. Laboratory Equipment
. . Microscopes
. Library Equipment
. . Bookmobiles
. Machine Tools
. Measurement Equipment
. . Calorimeters
. . Polygraphs
. . Potentiometers (Instruments)
. . Sound Spectrographs
. Mechanical Equipment
. Motor Vehicles
. . Service Vehicles
. . . Bookmobiles
. . . School Buses
. . Tractors
. Musical Instruments
. . String Instruments
. . Wind Instruments
. . . Brass Instruments
. . . Woodwind Instruments
. Office Machines
. Photographic Equipment
. Projection Equipment
. . Filmstrip Projectors
. . Microform Readers
. . Opaque Projectors
. . Overhead Projectors
. . Tachistoscopes
. Safety Equipment
. . Restraints (Vehicle Safety)
. Science Equipment
. Space Dividers
. . Movable Partitions
. Test Scoring Machines
. Vending Machines

: Evaluation
Equipment Evaluation

: Maintenance
Equipment Maintenance

: : Groups
: Personnel
Equipment Manufacturers

: Standards
Equipment Standards

: Storage
Equipment Storage

Equipment Utilization

: : : Measures (Individuals)
: : Tests
: Achievement Tests
Equivalency Tests

: : : Methods
: : Evaluation Methods
: Comparative Analysis
Error Analysis (Language)

Error Correction

: : : : Methods
: : : Evaluation Methods
: : Data Analysis
: Statistical Analysis
Error of Measurement

Error Patterns

: Languages
Eskimo Aleut Languages
. Inupiaq
. Yupik

: Groups
Eskimos

: : Language
: Artificial Languages
Esperanto

: : : Measures (Individuals)
: : Tests
: Verbal Tests
Essay Tests

: : : : : Liberal Arts
: : : : Humanities
: : : Literature
: : Prose
: Nonfiction
: Literary Genres
Essays

: Planning
Estate Planning

: : Mathematical Applications
: Computation
Estimation (Mathematics)

: : : Languages
: : Uralic Altaic Languages
: Finno Ugric Languages
Estonian

Estuaries

: Instruction
Ethical Instruction

: : : Liberal Arts
: : Humanities
: Philosophy
Ethics
. Bioethics
. Work Ethic

: : : Attitudes
: : Social Attitudes
: : Bias
: Social Bias
Ethnic Bias

: Social Discrimination
Ethnic Discrimination

: : : : Liberal Arts
: : : Sciences
: : : Social Sciences
: : Demography
: Population Distribution
Ethnic Distribution

Ethnic Grouping (1966 1980)

: Groups
Ethnic Groups
. Alaska Natives
. American Indians
. . Cherokee (Tribe)
. . Chippewa (Tribe)
. . Choctaw (Tribe)
. . . Mississippi Band of Choctaw
    (Tribe)
. . Cree (Tribe)
. . Iroquois (Tribe)
. . Maya (People)
. . Navajo (Nation)
. . Nonreservation American Indians
. . . Rural American Indians
. . . Urban American Indians
. . Pueblo (People)
. . Hopi (Tribe)
. . Zuni (Tribe)
. . Reservation American Indians
. . Sioux (Tribe)
. . Lakota (Tribe)
. . . Oglala Sioux (Tribe)
. . Tohono O Odham People
. Anglo Americans
. Canada Natives
. . Metis (People)
. Chinese Americans
. Filipino Americans
. French Canadians
. Greek Americans
. Hawaiians
. Hmong People
. Italian Americans
. Japanese Americans
. Korean Americans
. Maori (People)
. Mexican Americans
. Polish Americans
. Portuguese Americans
. Samoan Americans
. Spanish Americans

Ethnic Origins

: : : Relationship
: : Human Relations
: Intergroup Relations
Ethnic Relations

: Status
Ethnic Status

: : Attitudes
: Stereotypes
Ethnic Stereotypes
. Black Stereotypes

: Curriculum
Ethnic Studies
. American Indian Studies
. Black Studies

: Sociocultural Patterns
Ethnicity

Ethnocentrism

: : : : Liberal Arts
: : : Sciences
: : Social Sciences
: Anthropology
Ethnography

: : : : Liberal Arts
: : : Sciences
: : Social Sciences
: Anthropology
Ethnology
. Ethnomathematics

: : Liberal Arts
: Mathematics
: : : : : Liberal Arts
: : : : Sciences
: : : Social Sciences
: : Anthropology
: Ethnology
Ethnomathematics

: : : : Liberal Arts
: : : Sciences
: : Natural Sciences
: Biological Sciences
: : : Liberal Arts
: : Sciences
: Behavioral Sciences
Ethology

: Technology
Etiology

: : Linguistics
: Diachronic Linguistics
Etymology
. Onomastics

: : : : Liberal Arts
: : : Sciences
: : Social Sciences
: : : Liberal Arts
: : Humanities
: History
European History

Euthanasia

Evaluation
. Alternative Assessment
. . Performance Based Assessment
. Computer Software Evaluation
. Course Evaluation
. Curriculum Evaluation
. Educational Assessment
. . College Outcomes Assessment
. Equipment Evaluation
. Formative Evaluation
. Holistic Evaluation
. Informal Assessment
. Institutional Evaluation
. Instructional Material Evaluation
. . Textbook Evaluation
. Medical Care Evaluation
. Medical Evaluation
. . Auditory Evaluation
. . Dental Evaluation
. . Physical Examinations
. . Speech Evaluation
. Needs Assessment
. Peer Evaluation
. Personnel Evaluation
. . Administrator Evaluation
. . Counselor Evaluation
. . Faculty Evaluation
. . Teacher Evaluation
. . . Student Evaluation of Teacher
    Performance
. Portfolio Assessment
. Preschool Evaluation
. Program Evaluation
. Property Appraisal
. . Assessed Valuation
. Psychological Evaluation
. . Personality Assessment
. Recognition (Achievement)
. . Awards
. . Commencement Ceremonies
. . Professional Recognition
. Self Evaluation (Groups)
. Self Evaluation (Individuals)
. Student Evaluation
. . Curriculum Based Assessment
. . Nongraded Student Evaluation
. Student Teacher Evaluation
. Summative Evaluation
. Vocational Evaluation
. Writing Evaluation

: : Standards
: Criteria
Evaluation Criteria
. Reliability
. . Interrater Reliability
. . Test Reliability

. Validity
. . Concurrent Validity
. . Predictive Validity
. . Proof (Mathematics)
. . Test Validity
. . . Construct Validity
. . . Content Validity

: Methods
Evaluation Methods
. Audience Analysis
. Benchmarking
. Case Studies
. . Cross Sectional Studies
. . Facility Case Studies
. . Longitudinal Studies
. . . Followup Studies
. . . . Graduate Surveys
. . . . Vocational Followup
. Chemical Analysis
. Comparative Analysis
. . Educational Status Comparison
. Error Analysis (Language)
. Componential Analysis
. Content Analysis
. Cost Effectiveness
. Data Analysis
. . Data Collection
. . . Sampling
. . . . Item Sampling
. . Data Interpretation
. . . Statistical Inference
. . . Test Interpretation
. . Statistical Analysis
. . . Analysis of Covariance
. . . Analysis of Variance
. . . Bayesian Statistics
. . . Chi Square
. . . Correlation
. . . Effect Size
. . . Error of Measurement
. . . Goodness of Fit
. . . Item Analysis
. . . Judgment Analysis Technique
. . . Least Squares Statistics
. . . Maximum Likelihood Statistics
. . . Meta Analysis
. . . Multivariate Analysis
. . . . Cluster Analysis
. . . . Discriminant Analysis
. . . . Factor Analysis
. . . . . Oblique Rotation
. . . . . Orthogonal Rotation
. . . . Multidimensional Scaling
. . . Path Analysis
. . . Regression (Statistics)
. . . . Multiple Regression Analysis
. . . Robustness (Statistics)
. . . Statistical Distributions
. . . Statistical Inference
. . . Statistical Significance
. . Trend Analysis
. Drug Use Testing
. Environmental Scanning
. Hypothesis Testing
. Input Output Analysis
. Inspection
. Interviews
. . Employment Interviews
. . Field Interviews
. Job Analysis
. Life Cycle Costing
. Need Analysis (Student Financial Aid)
. Phonetic Analysis
. Policy Analysis
. Pretesting
. Quality Control
. Readability Formulas
. Scoring Rubrics
. Site Analysis
. Skill Analysis
. Structural Analysis (Linguistics)
. . Discourse Analysis
. . Tagmemic Analysis
. Structural Analysis (Science)
. Surveys
. . Community Surveys
. . Graduate Surveys
. . Library Surveys
. . Mail Surveys
. . National Surveys
. . Occupational Surveys
. . School Surveys

. . State Surveys
. . Statistical Surveys
. . Student Surveys
. . Teacher Surveys
. . Telephone Surveys
. . Television Surveys
. Synthesis
. Task Analysis

: Needs
Evaluation Needs

: Problems
Evaluation Problems

: : Research
: Methods Research
Evaluation Research

: Information Utilization
Evaluation Utilization

: : Cognitive Processes
: Critical Thinking
Evaluative Thinking
. Value Judgment

: : Groups
: Personnel
Evaluators

: Programs
Evening Programs

: : Groups
: Students
Evening Students

Evidence (Legal)

: Development
Evolution
. Heredity

: : Languages
: African Languages
Ewe

: : : : Groups
: : : Personnel
: : Nonprofessional Personnel
: Clerical Workers
Examiners

Excellence in Education
. School Restructuring

**Exceptional Child Education
(1968 1980)**

: Research
Exceptional Child Research

**Exceptional Child Services (1968
1980)**

Exceptional Persons (1978 1994)

: Programs
Exchange Programs
. Student Exchange Programs
. Teacher Exchange Programs

: : Activities
: Physical Activities
Exercise
. Aerobics
. Calisthenics
. Plyometrics

Exercise (Physiology) (1969 1980)

: : : : : Liberal Arts
: : : : Sciences
: : : Natural Sciences
: : Biological Sciences
: Physiology
Exercise Physiology

: Nonprint Media
Exhibits
. Science Fairs

: : : Liberal Arts
: : Humanities
: Philosophy
Existentialism

: : Visual Aids
: Tables (Data)
Expectancy Tables

Expectation
. Self Fulfilling Prophecies
. Teacher Expectations of Students
. Work Life Expectancy

: Expenditures
Expenditure per Student

Expenditures
. Capital Outlay (for Fixed Assets)
. Compensation (Remuneration)
. Expenditure per Student
. Library Expenditures
. Merit Pay
. Operating Expenses
. Premium Pay
. Salaries
. . Contract Salaries
. . Teacher Salaries
. School District Spending
. Wages
. . Minimum Wage

: Background
Experience
. Early Experience
. Educational Experience
. Emotional Experience
. . Catharsis
. Group Experience
. Intellectual Experience
. Learning Experience
. . Clinical Experience
. Life Events
. Prereading Experience
. Sensory Experience
. . Figural Aftereffects
. . Sensory Deprivation
. Social Experience
. Student Experience
. Teaching Experience
. Work Experience
. . Employment Experience

: : Educational Media
: Instructional Materials
: : Visual Aids
: Charts
Experience Charts

: Learning
Experiential Learning
. Field Experience Programs
. . Supervised Occupational Experience
    (Agriculture)
. Internship Programs
. Service Learning

: Facilities
Experiment Stations

: : : Institutions
: : Schools
: Experimental Schools
: : : Institutions
: : Schools
: Colleges
Experimental Colleges

: Curriculum
Experimental Curriculum

: Groups
Experimental Groups

: Programs
Experimental Programs

: : : : Liberal Arts
: : : Sciences
: : Behavioral Sciences
: Psychology
Experimental Psychology

: : Institutions
: Schools
Experimental Schools
. Experimental Colleges

: : : Methods
: : Educational Methods
: Teaching Methods
Experimental Teaching

Experimenter Characteristics

Experiments
. Educational Experiments
. Laboratory Experiments
. Science Experiments

: Artificial Intelligence
Expert Systems
. Intelligent Tutoring Systems

: Behavior
Exploratory Behavior

: International Trade
Exports

: : Literacy
: : Language Arts
: Writing (Composition)
Expository Writing

Expressionism

: : Cognitive Processes
: Language Processing
Expressive Language

: Discipline
Expulsion

: : Groups
: Family (Sociological Unit)
Extended Family

: : : Planning
: : Scheduling
: School Schedules
Extended School Day

: : : Planning
: : Scheduling
: School Schedules
Extended School Year

: : Programs
: Teacher Education Programs
Extended Teacher Education Programs

: : : Groups
: : Personnel
: Government Employees
: : Groups
: Change Agents
Extension Agents

: Education
Extension Education
. External Degree Programs
. Library Extension
. Rural Extension
. Urban Extension

: : Education
: Extension Education
: Programs
: College Programs
External Degree Programs

: : Cognitive Processes
: Learning Processes
Extinction (Psychology)

: : Activities
: School Activities
Extracurricular Activities

: : : Activities
: : Physical Activities
: Athletics
Extramural Athletics

: : : Individual Characteristics
: : Psychological Characteristics
: Personality Traits
Extraversion Introversion

: : Communication (Thought Transfer)
: Nonverbal Communication
Eye Contact

: : : : Behavior
: : : Responses
: : Motor Reactions
: Eye Movements
Eye Fixations

: : : : Ability
: : : Skills
: : Psychomotor Skills
: Perceptual Motor Coordination
Eye Hand Coordination

: : : Behavior
: : Responses
: Motor Reactions
Eye Movements
. Eye Fixations

: : : : Ability
: : : Skills
: : Psychomotor Skills
: Perceptual Motor Coordination
Eye Voice Span

Eyes

: : Literary Genres
: Tales
Fables

: : Communication (Thought Transfer)
: Nonverbal Communication
Facial Expressions

Facilities
. Air Structures
. . Pneumatic Forms
. Airports
. Animal Facilities
. . Zoos
. Aquariums
. Assessment Centers (Personnel)
. Athletic Fields
. Auditoriums
. Bookstores
. Buildings
. . School Buildings
. . . College Buildings
. College Stores
. Community Centers
. Corridors
. Day Care Centers
. Dining Facilities
. Driveways
. Educational Facilities
. . After School Centers
. . Audiovisual Centers
. . Business Education Facilities
. . Child Development Centers
. . Classrooms
. . . Electronic Classrooms
. . . Mobile Classrooms
. . . Multipurpose Classrooms
. . . Self Contained Classrooms
. . Continuing Education Centers
. . Curriculum Study Centers
. . Demonstration Centers
. . Education Service Centers
. . Educational Complexes
. . Campuses
. . . Educational Parks
. . Found Spaces
. . Guidance Centers
. . Learning Centers (Classroom)
. . Learning Laboratories
. . . Language Laboratories
. . Learning Resources Centers
. . Living Learning Centers
. . Off Campus Facilities
. . Physical Education Facilities
. . Reading Centers
. . School Buildings
. . . College Buildings
. . School Shops

. School Space
. . Science Teaching Centers
. . Skill Centers
. . Student Unions
. . Study Facilities
. . . Carrels
. . . Study Centers
. . Vocational Training Centers
. . Writing Laboratories
. Encapsulated Facilities
. Equal Facilities
. Experiment Stations
. Fallout Shelters
. Feed Stores
. Field Houses
. Fisheries
. Flexible Facilities
. Food Handling Facilities
. Food Stores
. Foundries
. Gardens
. Greenhouses
. Gymnasiums
. Health Facilities
. . Nursing Homes
. Housing
. . Boarding Homes
. . College Housing
. . Dormitories
. . Group Homes
. . Hotels
. . Low Rent Housing
. . . Public Housing
. . Middle Income Housing
. . Migrant Housing
. . Suburban Housing
. . Teacher Housing
. Interior Space
. Laboratories
. . Learning Laboratories
. . Language Laboratories
. . Mobile Laboratories
. . Regional Laboratories
. . Science Laboratories
. . Writing Laboratories
. Library Facilities
. Locker Rooms
. Military Air Facilities
. Museums
. Music Facilities
. Nuclear Power Plants
. Nurseries (Horticulture)
. Offices (Facilities)
. Parking Facilities
. Parks
. . National Parks
. Planetariums
. Public Facilities
. . Public Libraries
. . . County Libraries
. . . Regional Libraries
. Recreational Facilities
. . Playgrounds
. Rehabilitation Centers
. Relocatable Facilities
. Research and Development Centers
. Resource Centers
. . Arts Centers
. . Audiovisual Centers
. . Computer Centers
. . Cultural Centers
. . Curriculum Study Centers
. . Education Service Centers
. . Information Centers
. . . Clearinghouses
. . Learning Centers (Classroom)
. . Learning Resources Centers
. . Nature Centers
. . Reading Centers
. . Teacher Centers
. Sanitary Facilities
. . Toilet Facilities
. Satellite Facilities
. Science Facilities
. . Science Laboratories
. . Science Teaching Centers
. Settlement Houses
. Shared Facilities
. Swimming Pools
. Television Studios
. Theaters
. Trails
. Underground Facilities

. Warehouses
. Windowless Rooms
. Workstations

: : Research
: : : Methods
: : Evaluation Methods
: Case Studies
Facility Case Studies

: Development
Facility Expansion
. School Expansion

: Guidelines
Facility Guidelines

: Improvement
Facility Improvement
. Educational Facilities Improvement

Facility Inventory

: Planning
Facility Planning
. Educational Facilities Planning
. . Campus Planning

: : Standards
: Specifications
Facility Requirements

: : Research
: Use Studies
Facility Utilization Research

: : : Technology
: : Communications
: Telecommunications
Facsimile Transmission

: : : : : Methods
: : : : Evaluation Methods
: : : Data Analysis
: : Statistical Analysis
: Multivariate Analysis
Factor Analysis
. Oblique Rotation
. Orthogonal Rotation

Factor Structure

Factual Reading (1966 1980)

: : : Groups
: : Personnel
: School Personnel
: : : Groups
: : Personnel
: Professional Personnel
Faculty
. Adjunct Faculty
. College Faculty
. College Presidents
. Counselor Educators
. Graduate School Faculty
. . Medical School Faculty
. Professors
. Student Teacher Supervisors
. Teacher Educators
. . Methods Teachers
. Teaching Assistants
. Deans
. Academic Deans
. Deans of Students
. Department Heads
. Faculty Advisers
. Full Time Faculty
. Nontenured Faculty
. Part Time Faculty
. Partnership Teachers
. Tenured Faculty
. Women Faculty

: : : : Groups
: : : Personnel
: : School Personnel
: : : Groups
: : Personnel
: Professional Personnel
: Faculty
Faculty Advisers

: Prose
Fiction
. Novels
. Science Fiction
. Short Stories

: Plants (Botany)
Field Crops
. Grains (Food)
. Tobacco

: : : Individual Characteristics
: : Psychological Characteristics
: Cognitive Style
Field Dependence Independence

: Programs
: : Learning
: Experiential Learning
Field Experience Programs
. Supervised Occupational Experience
   (Agriculture)

: : : : Activities
: : : Physical Activities
: : Athletics
: Team Sports
Field Hockey

: Facilities
Field Houses

: Instruction
Field Instruction

: : : Methods
: : Evaluation Methods
: Interviews
Field Interviews

: Research
Field Studies

: : Measures (Individuals)
: Tests
Field Tests

Field Trips
. Farm Visits

: : : Liberal Arts
: : Humanities
: Literature
Fifteenth Century Literature

: : : Background
: : Experience
: Sensory Experience
Figural Aftereffects

: Literary Devices
: Language
Figurative Language
. Allegory
. Ambiguity
. Antithesis
. Imagery
. Irony
. Metaphors
. Puns
. Symbols (Literary)

: : : : Groups
: : : Personnel
: : Nonprofessional Personnel
: Clerical Workers
File Clerks

: : : : Services
: : : Information Services
: : Information Processing
: Documentation
Filing

: : Groups
: Ethnic Groups
: : : Groups
: : North Americans
: Asian Americans
Filipino Americans

: Criticism
Film Criticism

: : Business
: Industry
Film Industry

: : : Institutions
: : : Information Sources
: : Libraries
: Special Libraries
Film Libraries

: : : : Liberal Arts
: : : Humanities
: : Fine Arts
: Visual Arts
: : Methods
: Production Techniques
Film Production

: : : Groups
: : Personnel
: Specialists
Film Production Specialists

: : Education
: Aesthetic Education
Film Study

: : Publications
: Reference Materials
Filmographies

: Visual Aids
: Nonprint Media
: Mass Media
Films
. Foreign Language Films
. Instructional Films
. Kinescope Recordings
. Single Concept Films

: : Visual Aids
: : Equipment
: Projection Equipment
Filmstrip Projectors

: Visual Aids
: Nonprint Media
Filmstrips

: Occupations
Finance Occupations

: Improvement
Finance Reform

: Groups
Financial Aid Applicants

: Audits (Verification)
Financial Audits

Financial Exigency

: Needs
Financial Needs

: Policy
Financial Policy

: Problems
Financial Problems

: Services
Financial Services

Financial Support
. Capital
. Categorical Aid
. Child Support
. Endowment Funds
. Equalization Aid
. Full State Funding
. Grants
. . Block Grants
. . Educational Vouchers
. . Incentive Grants
. . Tuition Grants
. Library Funding
. Private Financial Support
. Private School Aid
. Recreation Finances
. Revenue Sharing
. Scholarship Funds

. School Funds
. Student Financial Aid
. . Assistantships
. . Fellowships
. . Faculty Fellowships
. . Income Contingent Loans
. . Parent Financial Contribution
. . Scholarships
. . . Merit Scholarships
. . . . No Need Scholarships
. . . Tuition Grants
. Tax Allocation
. Training Allowances
. Unemployment Insurance
. Workers Compensation

: : Liberal Arts
: : Humanities
Fine Arts
. Dance
. Music
. . Applied Music
. . Harmony (Music)
. . Jazz
. . Melody
. . Oriental Music
. . Popular Music
. . Rock Music
. . Vocal Music
. . . Choral Music
. . . Songs
. . . . Art Song
. . . . Ballads
. . . . Hymns
. Theater Arts
. . Acting
. . Choral Speaking
. . Drama
. . . Comedy
. . . . Skits
. . . Scripts
. . . Soap Operas
. . . Tragedy
. . Dramatics
. . . Creative Dramatics
. . Opera
. . Pantomime
. . Puppetry
. . Readers Theater
. . Rehearsals (Theater Arts)
. Visual Arts
. . Architecture
. . Childrens Art
. . Design Crafts
. . Drafting
. . . Architectural Drafting
. . . Engineering Drawing
. . . Technical Illustration
. . Film Production
. . Freehand Drawing
. . Graphic Arts
. . Cartography
. . . Computer Graphics
. . . Engineering Graphics
. . . . Engineering Drawing
. . . Layout (Publications)
. . . Printing
. . Handicrafts
. . Ceramics
. . Painting (Visual Arts)
. . Photography
. . . Holography
. . Printmaking
. . Sculpture

: : Costs
: Fees
Fines (Penalties)

: : Language Arts
: Spelling
: : : Communication (Thought
      Transfer)
: : Augmentative and Alternative
      Communication
: Manual Communication
Finger Spelling

Finishing

: : : Languages
: : Uralic Altaic Languages

: Finno Ugric Languages
Finnish

: : Languages
: Uralic Altaic Languages
Finno Ugric Languages
. Cheremis
. Estonian
. Finnish
. Hungarian
. Ostyak
. Vogul

: : : : Groups
: : : Personnel
: : Nonprofessional Personnel
: Service Workers
Fire Fighters

: : Methods
: Insurance
Fire Insurance

: Safety
Fire Protection

: : : Education
: : Vocational Education
: Technical Education
Fire Science Education

: : : : Services
: : : Human Services
: : Health Services
: Medical Services
First Aid
. Cardiopulmonary Resuscitation

: : Groups
: Siblings
: : : : Organization
: : : Group Structure
: : Family Structure
: Birth Order
First Born

Fiscal Capacity
. School District Wealth

Fiscal Neutrality

: Facilities
Fisheries

: Methods
Fixed Sequence

: : Curriculum
: Modern Language Curriculum
: : Curriculum
: Elementary School Curriculum
FLES

: Facilities
Flexible Facilities

: : Design
: Lighting Design
Flexible Lighting Design

Flexible Progression
. Acceleration (Education)

Flexible Schedules (1967 1980)

: : : Planning
: : Scheduling
: School Schedules
Flexible Scheduling

: : : Planning
: : Scheduling
: Working Hours
Flexible Working Hours

: Training
Flight Training

Floods

: : : : Groups
: : : Personnel
: : Nonprofessional Personnel

: Skilled Workers
Floor Layers

: Structural Elements (Construction)
Flooring
. Carpeting

::::: Equipment
:::: Electronic Equipment
::: Computer Peripherals
:: Computer Storage Devices
: Magnetic Disks
Floppy Disks

:::: Technology
::: Agriculture
:: Horticulture
: Ornamental Horticulture
Floriculture

:: Visual Aids
: Charts
Flow Charts

:::::: Liberal Arts
::::: Sciences
:::: Natural Sciences
::: Physical Sciences
:: Physics
: Mechanics (Physics)
Fluid Mechanics

: Disease Control
Fluoridation

:: Groups
: Discussion Groups
Focus Groups

: Culture
Folk Culture

:: Institutions
: Schools
Folk Schools

::: Research
:::: Methods
::: Evaluation Methods
:: Case Studies
: Longitudinal Studies
Followup Studies
. Graduate Surveys
. Vocational Followup

:::: Languages
:: Sino Tibetan Languages
: Chinese
Foochow

Food
. Grains (Food)
. Meat

::: Groups
:: Personnel
: Government Employees
Food and Drug Inspectors

: Facilities
Food Handling Facilities

::: Occupations
:: Agricultural Occupations
: Off Farm Agricultural Occupations
Food Processing Occupations

:: Services
: Human Services
Food Service

: Standards
Food Standards

: Facilities
Food Stores

: Instruction
Foods Instruction

:::: Activities
::: Physical Activities
:: Athletics

: Team Sports
Football

: Scientific Concepts
Force

::: Research
:: Behavioral Science Research
: Psychological Studies
Force Field Analysis

:: Methods
: Measurement Techniques
Forced Choice Technique

: Geographic Regions
Foreign Countries

: Culture
Foreign Culture

::: Groups
:: Personnel
: Government Employees
Foreign Diplomats

:: Publications
:: Printed Materials
: Books
Foreign Language Books

:: Visual Aids
:: Nonprint Media
:: Mass Media
: Films
Foreign Language Films

::: Publications
:: Serials
: Periodicals
Foreign Language Periodicals

:::: Groups
::: Personnel
:: Professional Personnel
:::: Groups
::: Personnel
:: Health Personnel
: Physicians
::: Groups
:: Alumni
: Graduates
Foreign Medical Graduates

Foreign Nationals

: Policy
Foreign Policy
. Imperialism
.. Colonialism

::: Groups
:: Personnel
: School Personnel
Foreign Student Advisers

:: Groups
: Students
Foreign Students

:: Groups
: Personnel
Foreign Workers
. Braceros

: Technology
Forestry

::: Groups
:: Personnel
: Paraprofessional Personnel
Forestry Aides

: Occupations
Forestry Occupations

:::: Linguistics
::: Descriptive Linguistics
:: Grammar
: Syntax
Form Classes (Languages)
. Adjectives
. Adverbs

. Conjunctions
. Determiners (Languages)
. Function Words
. Nouns
. Prepositions
. Pronouns
. Verbs

Formal Criticism (1969 1980)

::: Individual Characteristics
:: Psychological Characteristics
: Intelligence
Formal Operations

: Evaluation
Formative Evaluation

Former Teachers (1967 1980)

:: Resources
: Natural Resources
: Fuels
Fossil Fuels
. Coal
. Gasoline
. Natural Gas

::: Services
:: Human Services
: Social Services
Foster Care

::: Groups
:: Age Groups
: Children
Foster Children

:: Groups
: Family (Sociological Unit)
Foster Family

Found Objects

:: Facilities
: Educational Facilities
Found Spaces

: State Aid
: Programs
Foundation Programs

Foundations of Education
. Educational Anthropology
. Educational Economics
.. Educational Finance
. Educational History
.. Science Education History
. Educational Philosophy
. Educational Principles
. Educational Psychology
. Educational Sociology
. Educational Theories

: Facilities
Foundries

::: Symbols (Mathematics)
:: Numbers
: Rational Numbers
Fractions
. Decimal Fractions

:::: Groups
::: Age Groups
:: Adults
: Older Adults
Frail Elderly

Franchising

:: Groups
: Organizations (Groups)
Fraternities

: Deception
::: Behavior
:: Social Behavior
: Antisocial Behavior
Fraud

:: Programs
: Transfer Programs
Free Choice Transfer Programs

: Education
Free Education

:: Social Systems
: Capitalism
Free Enterprise System

:: Institutions
: Schools
Free Schools

:: Literacy
: Language Arts
: Writing (Composition)
Free Writing

Freedom
. Academic Freedom
. Freedom of Information
. Freedom of Speech
. Intellectual Freedom

: Freedom
: Access to Information
Freedom of Information

: Freedom
: Civil Liberties
Freedom of Speech

:: Institutions
: Schools
Freedom Schools

:::: Liberal Arts
::: Humanities
:: Fine Arts
: Visual Arts
Freehand Drawing

::: Languages
:: Indo European Languages
: Romance Languages
French

:: Groups
: North Americans
: Groups
: Ethnic Groups
French Canadians

::: Liberal Arts
:: Humanities
: Literature
French Literature

:: Instruction
: Writing Instruction
:: Literacy
: Language Arts
: Writing (Composition)
:: Curriculum
: College Curriculum
Freshman Composition

:: Relationship
: Interpersonal Relationship
Friendship

Fringe Benefits

Fuel Consumption

Fuels
. Fossil Fuels
.. Coal
.. Gasoline
.. Natural Gas

:: Languages
: African Languages
Fulani

:: Planning
: Scheduling
Full Day Half Day Schedules

: State Aid
: Financial Support
Full State Funding

: : Information Sources
: : Data
: Databases
Full Text Databases

: Status
Full Time Equivalency

: : : : Groups
: : : Personnel
: : School Personnel
: : : : Groups
: : : Personnel
: : Professional Personnel
: Faculty
Full Time Faculty

: : Groups
: Students
Full Time Students

: : : : : Linguistics
: : : : Descriptive Linguistics
: : : Grammar
: : Syntax
: Form Classes (Languages)
Function Words

: Literacy
Functional Literacy
. Functional Reading

: : Literacy
: : Language Arts
: Reading
: Literacy
: Functional Literacy
Functional Reading

: : : : : Liberal Arts
: : : : : Humanities
: : : : Philosophy
: : : Logic
: : Mathematical Logic
: : Mathematical Applications
: Mathematical Formulas
Functions (Mathematics)

Fund Raising
. Grantsmanship

Fundamental Concepts
. Compensation (Concept)
. Conservation (Concept)
. Object Permanence

Fungi

: Equipment
Furniture
. Classroom Furniture

: Organization
Furniture Arrangement

: Design
Furniture Design

: : : Business
: : Industry
: Manufacturing Industry
Furniture Industry

: Curriculum
Fused Curriculum

Futures (of Society)

: : Languages
: African Languages
Ga

: Theories
: : Research
: Operations Research
Game Theory

: Activities
Games

. Childrens Games
. Computer Games
. Educational Games
. . Reading Games
. Management Games
. Olympic Games
. Puzzles
. Video Games

: : : Languages
: : African Languages
: Bantu Languages
Ganda

: : Technology
: Agriculture
Gardening

: Facilities
Gardens

: : : Resources
: : Natural Resources
: Fuels
: Fossil Fuels
Gasoline

Gateway Systems

: : Languages
: African Languages
Gbaya

Gender Issues

: : : : : Liberal Arts
: : : : Sciences
: : : Social Sciences
: : : Liberal Arts
: : : Humanities
: : History
: Family History
Genealogy

: Education
General Education

: : Curriculum
: Mathematics Curriculum
General Mathematics

: : Curriculum
: Science Curriculum
General Science

: Theories
Generalizability Theory

: : Cognitive Processes
: Learning Processes
: : Cognitive Processes
: Abstract Reasoning
Generalization
. Stimulus Generalization

Generation Gap

: : Theories
: Linguistic Theory
Generative Grammar
. Transformational Generative
        Grammar
. Context Free Grammar
. . Deep Structure
. . Kernel Sentences
. . Sentence Combining
. . Surface Structure

: : Linguistics
: Phonology
: : Theories
: Linguistic Theory
Generative Phonology

: Technology
: : : : : Liberal Arts
: : : : Sciences
: : : Natural Sciences
: : Biological Sciences
: Genetics
Genetic Engineering

: : : : Liberal Arts
: : : Sciences
: : Natural Sciences
: Biological Sciences
Genetics
. Genetic Engineering

: : : : : Behavior
: : : : Social Behavior
: : : Antisocial Behavior
: : Crime
: International Crimes
Genocide

: : : : : Liberal Arts
: : : : Sciences
: : : Natural Sciences
: : Physical Sciences
: Earth Science
: : : : Liberal Arts
: : : Sciences
: : Natural Sciences
: Physical Sciences
: Chemistry
Geochemistry

Geographic Concepts

: : : : Liberal Arts
: : : Sciences
: : Social Sciences
: Demography
Geographic Distribution

Geographic Isolation

Geographic Location

Geographic Regions
. Counties
. . Low Income Counties
. Developed Nations
. Developing Nations
. Foreign Countries
. Low Income States
. Metropolitan Areas
. . Suburbs
. Nonmetropolitan Areas
. Physical Divisions (Geographic)
. Political Divisions (Geographic)
. . American Indian Reservations
. Poverty Areas
. Slums
. Rural Areas
. Urban Areas
. Inner City
. . Municipalities
. . . Boomtowns
. . . Small Towns

: : : Liberal Arts
: : Sciences
: Social Sciences
Geography
. Human Geography
. Physical Geography
. World Geography

: Instruction
Geography Instruction

: : : : : Liberal Arts
: : : : Sciences
: : : Natural Sciences
: : Physical Sciences
: Earth Science
Geology
. Mineralogy
. Paleontology
. Petrology

: Mathematical Concepts
Geometric Concepts
. Area
. Congruence (Mathematics)
. Orthographic Projection
. Polygons
. Vectors (Mathematics)
. Volume (Mathematics)

: Visual Aids
Geometric Constructions

: : Liberal Arts
: : Mathematics
Geometry
. Analytic Geometry
. Plane Geometry
. . Polygons
. Solid Geometry
. Topology

: : : : : Liberal Arts
: : : : Sciences
: : : Natural Sciences
: : Physical Sciences
: Earth Science
Geophysics
. Plate Tectonics

: : Scientific Concepts
: Energy
Geothermal Energy

: : Technology
: Medicine
Geriatrics

: : Languages
: Indo European Languages
German
. Yiddish

: : : Liberal Arts
: : Humanities
: Literature
German Literature

: : : Liberal Arts
: : Sciences
: Social Sciences
Gerontology
. Educational Gerontology

: : Therapy
: Psychotherapy
: : Methods
: Holistic Approach
Gestalt Therapy

Ghettos

: Groups
Gifted
. Academically Gifted
. Gifted Disabled
. Gifted Disadvantaged

: : Groups
: Gifted
Gifted Disabled

: : Groups
: Gifted
: : Groups
: Disadvantaged
Gifted Disadvantaged

Glare

Glass

: Structural Elements (Construction)
Glass Walls

: : : : Groups
: : : Personnel
: : Nonprofessional Personnel
: Skilled Workers
Glaziers

: : Methods
: Holistic Approach
Global Approach
. Global Education
. . International Education

: : : Methods
: : Holistic Approach
: Global Approach
: Education
Global Education
. International Education

: : Change
: Climate Change
Global Warming
. Greenhouse Effect

: : : Publications
: : Reference Materials
: Dictionaries
Glossaries

: : Linguistics
: Diachronic Linguistics
Glottochronology

: Orientation
Goal Orientation

: : : Activities
: : Physical Activities
: Athletics
Golf

: : : : Methods
: : : Evaluation Methods
: : Data Analysis
: Statistical Analysis
Goodness of Fit

Governance
. Administration
. . Building Operation
. . Business Administration
. . Construction Management
. . Crisis Management
. . Educational Administration
. . . School Administration
. . . . College Administration
. . . . School Based Management
. . Energy Management
. . Enrollment Management
. . Farm Management
. . Home Management
. . Information Management
. . . Records Management
. . Institutional Administration
. . . Library Administration
. . . School Administration
. . . . College Administration
. . . . School Based Management
. . Management by Objectives
. . Middle Management
. . Money Management
. . Office Management
. . Personnel Management
. . Program Administration
. . Public Administration
. . Research Administration
. . Risk Management
. . Supervision
. . . Practicum Supervision
. . . Proctoring
. . . School Supervision
. . . Science Supervision
. . . Teacher Supervision
. . . . Clinical Supervision (of Teachers)
. . Time Management
. . Total Quality Management
. Community Control
. Federal Regulation
. State Regulation

: : Groups
: Organizations (Groups)
Governing Boards
. Boards of Education
. . State Boards of Education

: : Groups
: Organizations (Groups)
Government (Administrative Body)
. Federal Government
. Local Government
. . City Government
. State Government
. Student Government
. Tribal Government

: : Groups
: Personnel
Government Employees
. Extension Agents
. Food and Drug Inspectors
. Foreign Diplomats

. Immigration Inspectors
. Military Personnel
. . Enlisted Personnel
. . Officer Personnel
. Police
. Public Officials
. . City Officials
. . County Officials
. . Court Judges
. . Legislators
. . State Officials
. . . State Supervisors
. Public School Teachers

: : : Institutions
: : Information Sources
: : Libraries
: Special Libraries
Government Libraries
. National Libraries
. State Libraries

: Publications
Government Publications

: Role
Government Role

: Relationship
Government School Relationship
. State School District Relationship

: : Organization
: Group Structure
Governmental Structure

: Instructional Program Divisions
Grade 1

: Instructional Program Divisions
Grade 10

: Instructional Program Divisions
Grade 11

: Instructional Program Divisions
Grade 12

: Instructional Program Divisions
Grade 2

: Instructional Program Divisions
Grade 3

: Instructional Program Divisions
Grade 4

: Instructional Program Divisions
Grade 5

: Instructional Program Divisions
Grade 6

: Instructional Program Divisions
Grade 7

: Instructional Program Divisions
Grade 8

: Instructional Program Divisions
Grade 9

Grade Charts (1966 1980)

: : Data
: Scores
Grade Equivalent Scores

: Grades (Scholastic)
Grade Inflation

: Grades (Scholastic)
Grade Point Average

: Prediction
Grade Prediction

Grade Repetition

Grades (Scholastic)
. Grade Inflation
. Grade Point Average

: : Measurement
: Achievement Rating
Grading
. Credit No Credit Grading
. Pass Fail Grading

: : : Education
: : Professional Education
: Medical Education
: : : : Education
: : : Postsecondary Education
: : Higher Education
: Graduate Study
Graduate Medical Education

: : : : : Groups
: : : : Students
: : : College Students
: : Graduate Students
: Medical Students
Graduate Medical Students

: : : : : Groups
: : : : Personnel
: : : School Personnel
: : : : : Groups
: : : : Personnel
: : : Professional Personnel
: : Faculty
: College Faculty
Graduate School Faculty
. Medical School Faculty

: : : Groups
: : Students
: College Students
Graduate Students
. Dental Students
. Law Students
. Medical Students
. . Graduate Medical Students

: : : Education
: : Postsecondary Education
: Higher Education
Graduate Study
. Graduate Medical Education
. Postsecondary Education as a
    Field of Study

: : : Methods
: : Evaluation Methods
: Surveys
: : : : Research
: : : : : Methods
: : : : Evaluation Methods
: : : Case Studies
: : Longitudinal Studies
: Followup Studies
Graduate Surveys

: : Groups
: Alumni
Graduates
. College Graduates
. Foreign Medical Graduates
. High School Graduates

: Achievement
Graduation

: : Standards
: Academic Standards
Graduation Requirements
. Degree Requirements

: Food
: : Plants (Botany)
: Field Crops
Grains (Food)

: : Linguistics
: Descriptive Linguistics
Grammar
. Morphology (Languages)
. . Morphemes
. . . Affixes
. . . . Prefixes (Grammar)
. . . . Suffixes
. . . Negative Forms (Language)
. . . Plurals
. . . Tenses (Grammar)
. . Morphophonemics

. Syntax
. . Form Classes (Languages)
. . . Adjectives
. . . Adverbs
. . . Conjunctions
. . . Determiners (Languages)
. . . Function Words
. . . Nouns
. . . Prepositions
. . . Pronouns
. . . Verbs
. . Phrase Structure
. . Sentence Structure

: : : Methods
: : Educational Methods
: Teaching Methods
Grammar Translation Method

: : Attitudes
: Language Attitudes
Grammatical Acceptability

: : : Groups
: : Age Groups
: Children
Grandchildren

: : Groups
: Parents
Grandparents

: Financial Support
Grants
. Block Grants
. Educational Vouchers
. Incentive Grants
. Tuition Grants

: Fund Raising
Grantsmanship

: : Language
: Written Language
Graphemes

: : : : Liberal Arts
: : : Humanities
: : Fine Arts
: Visual Arts
Graphic Arts
. Cartography
. Computer Graphics
. Engineering Graphics
. . Engineering Drawing
. Layout (Publications)
. Printing

: : Equipment
: Calculators
Graphing Calculators

: Visual Aids
Graphs

: Scientific Concepts
Gravity (Physics)

: : Languages
: Indo European Languages
Greek

: : Groups
: North Americans
: : Groups
: Ethnic Groups
Greek Americans

Greek Civilization

: : : Liberal Arts
: : : Humanities
: Literature
Greek Literature

: : : Change
: : Climate Change
: Global Warming
Greenhouse Effect

: Facilities
Greenhouses

: : Psychological Patterns
: Sadness
Grief

: Methods
Grievance Procedures

: : : : Groups
: : : Personnel
: : Nonprofessional Personnel
: Semiskilled Workers
Grounds Keepers

: : : Resources
: : Natural Resources
: Water Resources
: : Matter
: Water
Groundwater

: Activities
Group Activities

: Behavior
Group Behavior
. Teamwork

: : Guidance
: Group Guidance
: Guidance
: Counseling
Group Counseling

: : Communication (Thought Transfer)
: Discussion
Group Discussion

: : Relationship
: Interaction
Group Dynamics

: : Background
: Experience
Group Experience

: Guidance
Group Guidance
. Group Counseling

: : Facilities
: Housing
Group Homes

: Instruction
Group Instruction
. Large Group Instruction
. Small Group Instruction

Group Membership
. Political Affiliation

Group Norms (1968 1980)

Group Reading (1966 1980)

: Status
Group Status
. Family Status

: Organization
Group Structure
. Family Structure
. . Birth Order
. . . First Born
. Governmental Structure

: : : Methods
: : Measurement Techniques
: Testing
Group Testing

: Therapy
Group Therapy

: : Relationship
: Interpersonal Relationship
Group Unity

: : Organization
: Classification
Grouping (Instructional Purposes)
. Heterogeneous Grouping
. Homogeneous Grouping

. . Ability Grouping
. Nongraded Instructional Grouping

Groups
. Advantaged
. Age Groups
. . Adolescents
. . Adults
. . . Adult Children
. . . Adult Dropouts
. . . Adult Students
. . . Adults (30 to 45)
. . . Middle Aged Adults
. . . Older Adults
. . . . Frail Elderly
. . . . Old Old Adults
. . . . Young Old Adults
. . . Young Adults
. . Children
. . . Adopted Children
. . . Foster Children
. . . Grandchildren
. . . Hospitalized Children
. . . Latchkey Children
. . . Migrant Children
. . . Minority Group Children
. . . Missing Children
. . . Preadolescents
. . . Problem Children
. . . Transient Children
. . . Young Children
. . . . Infants
. . . . . Neonates
. . . . . . Premature Infants
. . . . Kindergarten Children
. . . . Preschool Children
. . . . Toddlers
. . Early Adolescents
. . Late Adolescents
. . Mixed Age Grouping
. Alumni
. . Graduates
. . . College Graduates
. . . Foreign Medical Graduates
. . . High School Graduates
. Arabs
. Artists
. . Musicians
. At Risk Persons
. . High Risk Students
. Athletes
. Audiences
. Authors
. . Poets
. Baby Boomers
. Blacks
. . Black Mothers
. . Black Students
. . Black Teachers
. . Black Youth
. Board Candidates
. Caregivers
. . Attendants
. . Child Caregivers
. . Family Caregivers
. Change Agents
. . Extension Agents
. . Linking Agents
. Classes (Groups of Students)
. . Multigraded Classes
. . Multilevel Classes (Second
        Language Instruction)
. . Nonauthoritarian Classes
. . Small Classes
. . Special Classes
. Clubs
. . Science Clubs
. . Youth Clubs
. College Applicants
. Community Leaders
. Control Groups
. Criminals
. Dependents
. Disadvantaged
. . Disadvantaged Youth
. . Economically Disadvantaged
. . Educationally Disadvantaged
. . Gifted Disadvantaged
. Discussion Groups
. . Focus Groups
. . Listening Groups
. Donors
. Dropouts

. . Adult Dropouts
. Employers
. Eskimos
. Ethnic Groups
. . Alaska Natives
. . American Indians
. . . Cherokee (Tribe)
. . . Chippewa (Tribe)
. . . Choctaw (Tribe)
. . . . Mississippi Band of
           Choctaw (Tribe)
. . . Cree (Tribe)
. . . Iroquois (Tribe)
. . . Maya (People)
. . . Navajo (Nation)
. . . Nonreservation American Indians
. . . . Rural American Indians
. . . . Urban American Indians
. . . Pueblo (People)
. . . . Hopi (Tribe)
. . . . Zuni (Tribe)
. . . Reservation American Indians
. . . Sioux (Tribe)
. . . . Lakota (Tribe)
. . . . . Oglala Sioux (Tribe)
. . . Tohono O Odham People
. . Anglo Americans
. . Canada Natives
. . . Metis (People)
. . Chinese Americans
. . Filipino Americans
. . French Canadians
. . Greek Americans
. . Hawaiians
. . Hmong People
. . Italian Americans
. . Japanese Americans
. . Korean Americans
. . Maori (People)
. . Mexican Americans
. . Polish Americans
. . Portuguese Americans
. . Samoan Americans
. . Spanish Americans
. Experimental Groups
. Family (Sociological Unit)
. . Black Family
. . Dual Career Family
. . Extended Family
. . Foster Family
. . Nuclear Family
. . One Parent Family
. . . Fatherless Family
. . . Motherless Family
. . Rural Family
. . Stepfamily
. Females
. . Battered Women
. . Daughters
. . Displaced Homemakers
. . Employed Women
. . . Women Administrators
. . . Women Faculty
. . Mothers
. . . Black Mothers
. . . Unwed Mothers
. . Nuns
. . Pregnant Students
. . Rural Women
. Financial Aid Applicants
. Gifted
. . Academically Gifted
. . Gifted Disabled
. . Gifted Disadvantaged
. Heads of Households
. Homeless People
. Homemakers
. Homeowners
. Indians
. Indigenous Populations
. Indochinese
. . Cambodians
. . Laotians
. . Vietnamese People
. Institutionalized Persons
. . Prisoners
. Job Applicants
. Judges
. . Court Judges
. Juries
. Juvenile Gangs
. Labor Force Nonparticipants
. Landlords

. Language Minorities
. Latin Americans
. . Cubans
. . Dominicans
. . Haitians
. . Maya (People)
. . Mexicans
. . . Braceros
. . Puerto Ricans
. Lay People
. . Lay Teachers
. Leaders
. . Community Leaders
. . Youth Leaders
. Left Handed Writer
. Limited English Speaking
. Low Income Groups
. Males
. . Fathers
. . Sons
. Matched Groups
. Migrants
. . Immigrants
. . . Undocumented Immigrants
. . Migrant Children
. . Migrant Workers
. . Migrant Youth
. Nomads
. Refugees
. . Transient Children
. Minority Groups
. Multiracial Persons
. Native Speakers
. Spanish Speaking
. No Shows
. Non English Speaking
. North Americans
. . Alaska Natives
. . Anglo Americans
. . Asian Americans
. . . Asian American Students
. . . Chinese Americans
. . . Filipino Americans
. . . Japanese Americans
. . . Korean Americans
. . Canada Natives
. . . Metis (People)
. . French Canadians
. . Greek Americans
. . Hispanic Americans
. . . Hispanic American Students
. . . Mexican Americans
. . . Portuguese Americans
. . . Spanish Americans
. . Italian Americans
. . Pacific Americans
. . . Hawaiians
. . . Samoan Americans
. . Polish Americans
. Organizations (Groups)
. . Agencies
. . . Accrediting Agencies
. . . Private Agencies
. . . Public Agencies
. . . . Planning Commissions
. . . . State Agencies
. . . . . State Departments of Education
. . . . . State Licensing Boards
. . . Social Agencies
. . . . Welfare Agencies
. . . Urban Renewal Agencies
. . . Voluntary Agencies
. . . Youth Agencies
. . Alumni Associations
. . Bibliographic Utilities
. . Black Organizations
. . Blue Ribbon Commissions
. . College Governing Councils
. . Community Organizations
. . . Citizens Councils
. . Consortia
. . Cooperatives
. . Corporations
. . Database Producers
. . Faculty Organizations
. . Fraternities
. . Governing Boards
. . . Boards of Education
. . . . State Boards of Education
. . Government (Administrative Body)
. . . Federal Government
. . . Local Government
. . . . City Government

. . . State Government
. . . Student Government
. . . Tribal Government
. . Health Maintenance Organizations
. . Honor Societies
. . International Organizations
. . Military Organizations
. . . Armed Forces
. . National Organizations
. . Nongovernmental Organizations
. . Nonprofit Organizations
. . Online Vendors
. . Parent Associations
. . Political Parties
. . Professional Associations
. . . Library Associations
. . . Medical Associations
. . . Teacher Associations
. . Religious Organizations
. . Research Coordinating Units
. School Districts
. . County School Districts
. . Multicampus Districts
. Segregationist Organizations
. Social Organizations
. Sororities
. Student Organizations
. . Student Government
. . Student Unions
. Unions
. Pacific Islanders
. . Maori (People)
. . Pacific Americans
. . . Hawaiians
. . . Samoan Americans
. Parents
. . Adoptive Parents
. . Biological Parents
. . Employed Parents
. . Fathers
. . Grandparents
. . Lower Class Parents
. . Middle Class Parents
. . Mothers
. . . Black Mothers
. . . Unwed Mothers
. . Parents as Teachers
. . Parents with Disabilities
. Patients
. . Hospitalized Children
. Peer Groups
. Personnel
. . Administrators
. . . Admissions Officers
. . . Assistant Principals
. . . Beginning Principals
. . . Central Office Administrators
. . . Coordinators
. . . . Audiovisual Coordinators
. . . . Instructor Coordinators
. . . Deans
. . . . Academic Deans
. . . . Deans of Students
. . . Department Heads
. . . Library Administrators
. . . . Library Directors
. . . Medical Record Administrators
. . . Personnel Directors
. . . Presidents
. . . . College Presidents
. . . . Presidents of the United States
. . . Principals
. . . Registrars (School)
. . . Research Directors
. . . School Business Officials
. . . Student Financial Aid Officers
. . . Superintendents
. . . Supervisors
. . . . Crew Leaders
. . . . State Supervisors
. . . . Student Teacher Supervisors
. . . Trustees
. . . Vocational Directors
. . . Women Administrators
. . Agricultural Personnel
. . . Agricultural Laborers
. . . . Migrant Workers
. . . . Seasonal Laborers
. . . Agricultural Technicians
. . . Farmers
. . . . Dairy Farmers
. . . . Part Time Farmers
. . . . Sharecroppers

. . Aircraft Pilots
. . Bus Drivers
. . Caseworkers
. . . Parole Officers
. . . Probation Officers
. . . Social Workers
. . . . School Social Workers
. . Church Workers
. . . Clergy
. . . Priests
. . Consultants
. . . Medical Consultants
. . . Reading Consultants
. . . Science Consultants
. . Designers
. . Differentiated Staffs
. . Dislocated Workers
. . Editors
. . Employees
. . . Entry Workers
. . Equipment Manufacturers
. . Evaluators
. . Foreign Workers
. . . Braceros
. . Government Employees
. . . Extension Agents
. . . Food and Drug Inspectors
. . . Foreign Diplomats
. . . . Immigration Inspectors
. . . Military Personnel
. . . . Enlisted Personnel
. . . . Officer Personnel
. . . Police
. . . Public Officials
. . . . City Officials
. . . . County Officials
. . . . Court Judges
. . . . Legislators
. . . . State Officials
. . . . . State Supervisors
. . . Public School Teachers
. . Guidance Personnel
. . . Counselors
. . . . Adjustment Counselors
. . . . Employment Counselors
. . . . School Counselors
. . Health Personnel
. . . Allied Health Personnel
. . . . Dental Assistants
. . . . Dental Hygienists
. . . . Dental Technicians
. . . . Dietitians
. . . . Emergency Medical Technicians
. . . . Environmental Technicians
. . . . Home Health Aides
. . . . Medical Assistants
. . . . . Medical Laboratory Assistants
. . . . Medical Record Administrators
. . . . Medical Record Technicians
. . . . Medical Technologists
. . . . Nurses Aides
. . . . Occupational Therapy Assistants
. . . . Optometrists
. . . . Physical Therapy Aides
. . . . Physicians Assistants
. . . . Psychiatric Aides
. . . . Radiologic Technologists
. . . . Surgical Technicians
. . . . Therapists
. . . . . Occupational Therapists
. . . . . Physical Therapists
. . . . Veterinary Assistants
. . . Dentists
. . . Hospital Personnel
. . . . Medical Consultants
. . . . Mental Health Workers
. . . . Psychiatric Aides
. . . . Psychiatrists
. . . . School Psychologists
. . . Nurses
. . . . Nurse Practitioners
. . . . School Nurses
. . . Pharmacists
. . . Physicians
. . . . Foreign Medical Graduates
. . . . Psychiatrists
. . . Psychologists
. . . . School Psychologists
. . . Veterinarians
. . Indigenous Personnel
. . Industrial Personnel
. . Institutional Personnel
. . Interpreters

. . Library Personnel
. . . Librarians
. . . Library Administrators
. . . . Library Directors
. . . Library Technicians
. . . Medical Record Technicians
. . Merchants
. . Nonprofessional Personnel
. . . Clerical Workers
. . . . Court Reporters
. . . . Examiners
. . . . File Clerks
. . . . Receptionists
. . . . Secretaries
. . . . . School Secretaries
. . . . Sales Workers
. . . . . Auto Parts Clerks
. . . Semiskilled Workers
. . . . Animal Caretakers
. . . . Boat Operators
. . . . Grounds Keepers
. . . . Nursery Workers (Horticulture)
. . . . Sewing Machine Operators
. . . Service Workers
. . . . Attendants
. . . . Barbers
. . . . Cooks
. . . . Emergency Squad Personnel
. . . . . Emergency Medical Technicians
. . . . Fire Fighters
. . . . Household Workers
. . . . . Home Health Aides
. . . . Housekeepers
. . . . Housing Management Aides
. . . . Waiters and Waitresses
. . . Skilled Workers
. . . . Auto Body Repairers
. . . . Craft Workers
. . . . Electricians
. . . . Floor Layers
. . . . Glaziers
. . . . Locomotive Engineers
. . . . Machinists
. . . . Machine Repairers
. . . . Machine Tool Operators
. . . . . Tool and Die Makers
. . . . Sign Painters
. . . . Television Radio Repairers
. . . . Watchmakers
. . . Unskilled Workers
. . . . Laborers
. . . . . Agricultural Laborers
. . . . . . Migrant Workers
. . . . . Seasonal Laborers
. . . . Auxiliary Laborers
. . . Older Workers
. . Ombudsmen
. . Paraprofessional Personnel
. . . Agricultural Technicians
. . . Chemical Technicians
. . . Electronic Technicians
. . . Engineering Technicians
. . . . Highway Engineering Aides
. . . Environmental Technicians
. . . Forestry Aides
. . . Housing Management Aides
. . . Instrumentation Technicians
. . . Legal Assistants
. . . Marine Technicians
. . . Mechanical Design Technicians
. . . Metallurgical Technicians
. . . Nuclear Power Plant Technicians
. . . Paraprofessional School Personnel
. . . . School Aides
. . . . . Teacher Aides
. . . . . . Bilingual Teacher Aides
. . . Production Technicians
. . . Radiographers
. . . Veterinary Assistants
. . . Visiting Homemakers
. . Professional Personnel
. . . Accountants
. . . . Certified Public Accountants
. . . Architects
. . . Athletic Coaches
. . . Dentists
. . . Engineers
. . . Faculty
. . . . Adjunct Faculty
. . . . College Faculty
. . . . . College Presidents
. . . . . Counselor Educators
. . . . . Graduate School Faculty

. . . . . . Medical School Faculty
. . . . . Professors
. . . . . Student Teacher Supervisors
. . . . . Teacher Educators
. . . . . . Methods Teachers
. . . . . Teaching Assistants
. . . . Deans
. . . . . Academic Deans
. . . . . Deans of Students
. . . . Department Heads
. . . . Faculty Advisers
. . . . Full Time Faculty
. . . . Nontenured Faculty
. . . . Part Time Faculty
. . . . Partnership Teachers
. . . . Tenured Faculty
. . . . Women Faculty
. . . Information Scientists
. . . . Librarians
. . . . Search Intermediaries
. . . Lawyers
. . . Mathematicians
. . . Nurses
. . . . Nurse Practitioners
. . . . School Nurses
. . . Optometrists
. . . Pharmacists
. . . Physicians
. . . . Foreign Medical Graduates
. . . . Psychiatrists
. . . Psychologists
. . . . School Psychologists
. . . Research Directors
. . . Researchers
. . . . Educational Researchers
. . . . . Teacher Researchers
. . . Scientists
. . . Social Scientists
. . . . Historians
. . . . Sociologists
. . . Social Workers
. . . . School Social Workers
. . . Teachers
. . . . Adult Educators
. . . . Art Teachers
. . . . Beginning Teachers
. . . . Bilingual Teachers
. . . . Black Teachers
. . . . Catholic Educators
. . . . Cooperating Teachers
. . . . Elementary School Teachers
. . . . Home Economics Teachers
. . . . Industrial Arts Teachers
. . . . Instructor Coordinators
. . . . Itinerant Teachers
. . . . Language Teachers
. . . . . English Teachers
. . . . Lay Teachers
. . . . Master Teachers
. . . . Mathematics Teachers
. . . . Middle School Teachers
. . . . Minority Group Teachers
. . . . Music Teachers
. . . . Physical Education Teachers
. . . . Preschool Teachers
. . . . Public School Teachers
. . . . Reading Teachers
. . . . Remedial Teachers
. . . . Resource Teachers
. . . . Science Teachers
. . . . Secondary School Teachers
. . . . Special Education Teachers
. . . . Student Teachers
. . . . Substitute Teachers
. . . . Teacher Interns
. . . . Teacher Researchers
. . . . Teachers with Disabilities
. . . . Television Teachers
. . . . Tutors
. . . . Vocational Education Teachers
. . . . . Business Education Teachers
. . . . . Distributive Education Teachers
. . . . . Trade and Industrial Teachers
. . . . Writing Teachers
. . . Therapists
. . . . Occupational Therapists
. . . . Physical Therapists
. . . Veterinarians
. . Programmers
. Reentry Workers
. Research Assistants
. Resident Advisers
. Resident Assistants

.. Resource Staff
. School Personnel
.. Admissions Officers
... Assistant Principals
... Audiovisual Coordinators
... Beginning Principals
... Faculty
.... Adjunct Faculty
.... College Faculty
..... College Presidents
..... Counselor Educators
..... Graduate School Faculty
..... Medical School Faculty
..... Professors
..... Student Teacher Supervisors
..... Teacher Educators
..... Methods Teachers
..... Teaching Assistants
.... Deans
..... Academic Deans
..... Deans of Students
.... Department Heads
.... Faculty Advisers
.... Full Time Faculty
.... Nontenured Faculty
.... Part Time Faculty
.... Partnership Teachers
.... Tenured Faculty
.... Women Faculty
... Foreign Student Advisers
... Paraprofessional School Personnel
.... School Aides
.... Teacher Aides
..... Bilingual Teacher Aides
.... Principals
... Pupil Personnel Workers
.... Attendance Officers
... Registrars (School)
... School Business Officials
... School Cadres
... School Counselors
... School Nurses
... School Psychologists
... School Secretaries
... School Social Workers
... Student Financial Aid Officers
... Student Personnel Workers
.. Scientific Personnel
... Mathematicians
... Science Consultants
... Scientists
.. Security Personnel
.. Specialists
... Child Development Specialists
... Film Production Specialists
... Media Specialists
.... Audiovisual Coordinators
.. Systems Analysts
. Trainers
. Political Candidates
. Potential Dropouts
. Quality Circles
. Recreationists
. Reference Groups
. Religious Cultural Groups
.. Catholics
.. Jews
.. Muslims
.. Protestants
... Amish
... Puritans
. Research and Instruction Units
. Role Models
.. Mentors
. Runaways
. Rural Population
.. Rural American Indians
.. Rural Family
.. Rural Farm Residents
.. Rural Nonfarm Residents
.. Rural Women
.. Rural Youth
. Seafarers
. Self Directed Groups
. Siblings
.. First Born
.. Twins
. Slow Learners
. Social Class
.. Caste
.. Lower Class
.. Lower Middle Class
.. Middle Class

.. Upper Class
.. Working Class
. Social Support Groups
. Spouses
. Stopouts
. Students
.. Adult Students
.. Advanced Students
.. Asian American Students
.. Bilingual Students
.. Black Students
.. College Students
.. College Freshmen
.. College Juniors
.. College Seniors
.. College Sophomores
.. College Transfer Students
.. Graduate Students
... Dental Students
... Law Students
.... Medical Students
..... Graduate Medical Students
.. In State Students
.. On Campus Students
.. Out of State Students
.. Preservice Teachers
.. Student Teachers
.. Resident Assistants
.. Two Year College Students
.. Undergraduate Students
.. Premedical Students
. Commuting Students
. Continuation Students
. Day Students
. Elementary School Students
. Evening Students
. Foreign Students
. Full Time Students
. High Risk Students
. Hispanic American Students
. Lower Class Students
. Majors (Students)
.. Education Majors
. Married Students
. Middle Class Students
. Middle School Students
. Nonmajors
. Nontraditional Students
. Part Time Students
. Pregnant Students
. Reentry Students
. Secondary School Students
.. High School Students
... College Bound Students
... High School Freshmen
.... High School Seniors
.... Noncollege Bound Students
.. Junior High School Students
. Self Supporting Students
. Single Students
. Special Needs Students
. Student Volunteers
. Terminal Students
. Transfer Students
.. College Transfer Students
.. White Students
. Tissue Donors
. Trainees
. Tribes
.. Cherokee (Tribe)
.. Chippewa (Tribe)
.. Choctaw (Tribe)
... Mississippi Band of Choctaw
    (Tribe)
.. Cree (Tribe)
.. Hopi (Tribe)
.. Iroquois (Tribe)
.. Navajo (Nation)
.. Sioux (Tribe)
... Lakota (Tribe)
.... Oglala Sioux (Tribe)
.. Tohono O Odham People
.. Zuni (Tribe)
. Union Members
. Urban Population
.. Urban American Indians
.. Urban Youth
. Users (Information)
. Vendors
.. Merchants
.. Online Vendors
. Veterans
.. Vietnam Veterans

. Victims of Crime
. Volunteers
.. Student Volunteers
. Welfare Recipients
. Whites
.. White Students
. Widowed
. Youth
.. Affluent Youth
.. Black Youth
.. Disadvantaged Youth
.. Migrant Youth
.. Out of School Youth
.. Rural Youth
.. Suburban Youth
.. Urban Youth
. Youth Leaders

Growth Patterns (1966 1980)

: : Languages
: American Indian Languages
Guarani

: Income
Guaranteed Income

: : Behavior
: Response Style (Tests)
Guessing (Tests)

Guidance
. Career Guidance
.. Career Counseling
. Counseling
.. Adult Counseling
.. Career Counseling
.. Cocounseling
.. Educational Counseling
... Academic Advising
... Admissions Counseling
.. Family Counseling
.. Group Counseling
.. Individual Counseling
.. Marriage Counseling
.. Nondirective Counseling
.. Parent Counseling
.. Peer Counseling
.. Rehabilitation Counseling
.. School Counseling
. Group Guidance
.. Group Counseling
. Post High School Guidance
. School Guidance
.. School Counseling
. Teacher Guidance

: : Facilities
: Educational Facilities
Guidance Centers

: Objectives
Guidance Objectives
. Counseling Objectives

: : Groups
: Personnel
Guidance Personnel
. Counselors
.. Adjustment Counselors
.. Employment Counselors
.. School Counselors

: Programs
Guidance Programs

: : : Methods
: : Educational Methods
: Teaching Methods
Guided Design

Guidelines
. Facility Guidelines

: : Publications
: Reference Materials
Guides
. Administrator Guides
. Curriculum Guides
.. State Curriculum Guides
. Faculty Handbooks
. Laboratory Manuals
. Leaders Guides

. Library Guides
. Program Guides
. Study Guides
. Teaching Guides
. Test Manuals

Guilt

: : Languages
: Indo European Languages
Gujarati

: : Languages
: : : : Linguistics
: : : Sociolinguistics
: : Language Variation
: Creoles
Gullah

Gun Control

: Weapons
: Equipment
Guns

: Facilities
Gymnasiums

: : : Activities
: : Physical Activities
: Athletics
Gymnastics
. Tumbling

: : Technology
: Medicine
Gynecology

: : : Development
: : Individual Development
: Behavior Development
Habit Formation

Habitats

: : Cognitive Processes
: Learning Processes
Habituation

: : : : Liberal Arts
: : : Humanities
: : Literature
: Poetry
: Literary Genres
Haiku

: : Languages
: : : Linguistics
: : : Sociolinguistics
: : Language Variation
: Creoles
Haitian Creole

: : Groups
: Latin Americans
Haitians

: Equipment
Hand Tools

: : : Activities
: : Physical Activities
: Athletics
Handball

: : : Individual Characteristics
: : Physical Characteristics
: Lateral Dominance
Handedness
. Left Handed Writer

Handicapped Children (1966 1980)

Handicapped Students (1967 1980)

: : : : Liberal Arts
: : : Humanities
: : Fine Arts
: Visual Arts
Handicrafts
. Ceramics

Hands on Science

: Language Arts
Handwriting
. Cursive Writing
. Manuscript Writing (Handlettering)

: Psychological Patterns
Happiness

: : : : Liberal Arts
: : : Humanities
: : Fine Arts
: Music
Harmony (Music)

: : Technology
: Agriculture
Harvesting

: : : Languages
: : Afro Asiatic Languages
: Chad Languages
Hausa

: : Languages
: Malayo Polynesian Languages
Hawaiian

: : : Groups
: : Pacific Islanders
: : : Groups
: : North Americans
: Pacific Americans
: Groups
: Ethnic Groups
Hawaiians

Hazardous Materials
. Poisons
. . Pesticides
. . . Herbicides
. . . Insecticides

: : : Behavior
: : Social Behavior
: Antisocial Behavior
Hazing

: : Disabilities
: Injuries
Head Injuries

Headlines

: Groups
Heads of Households

Health
. Child Health
. Family Health
. Mental Health
. Occupational Safety and Health
. Physical Health
. . Dental Health
. . Physical Fitness
. . . Health Related Fitness
. Public Health
. Wellness

: Activities
Health Activities
. Health Promotion

: Behavior
Health Behavior

: Costs
Health Care Costs

Health Conditions

: Education
Health Education
. Comprehensive School Health
    Education

: Facilities
Health Facilities
. Nursing Homes

: : Methods
: Insurance
Health Insurance

: : Groups
: Organizations (Groups)
Health Maintenance Organizations

Health Materials

: Needs
Health Needs

: Occupations
Health Occupations
. Allied Health Occupations

**Health Occupations Centers
    (1968 1980)**

: : Groups
: Personnel
Health Personnel
. Allied Health Personnel
. . Dental Assistants
. . Dental Hygienists
. . Dental Technicians
. . Dietitians
. . Emergency Medical Technicians
. . Environmental Technicians
. . Home Health Aides
. . Medical Assistants
. . . Medical Laboratory Assistants
. . Medical Record Administrators
. . Medical Record Technicians
. . Medical Technologists
. . Nurses Aides
. . Occupational Therapy Assistants
. . Optometrists
. . Physical Therapy Aides
. . Physicians Assistants
. . Psychiatric Aides
. . Radiologic Technologists
. . Surgical Technicians
. . Therapists
. . . Occupational Therapists
. . Physical Therapists
. . Veterinary Assistants
. Dentists
. Hospital Personnel
. Medical Consultants
. Mental Health Workers
. . Psychiatric Aides
. . Psychiatrists
. . School Psychologists
. Nurses
. Nurse Practitioners
. . School Nurses
. Pharmacists
. Physicians
. . Foreign Medical Graduates
. . Psychiatrists
. Psychologists
. . School Psychologists
. Veterinarians

: Programs
Health Programs
. Breakfast Programs
. Immunization Programs
. Lunch Programs
. Mental Health Programs

: : Activities
: Health Activities
Health Promotion

: : : Health
: : Physical Health
: Physical Fitness
Health Related Fitness

: : Services
: Human Services
Health Services
. Community Health Services
. Hospices (Terminal Care)
. Long Term Care
. Medical Services
. First Aid
. . . Cardiopulmonary Resuscitation
. . Psychiatric Services
. Migrant Health Services

. Prenatal Care
. School Health Services

Hearing (Physiology)

: Sensory Aids
: : Equipment
: Audio Equipment
Hearing Aids

: Prevention
Hearing Conservation

: Disabilities
Hearing Impairments
. Deafness
. Partial Hearing

: Therapy
Hearing Therapy

Hearings

: : Disabilities
: Physical Disabilities
Heart Disorders

: Metabolism
Heart Rate

: : Scientific Concepts
: Energy
Heat

: : Conservation (Environment)
: Energy Conservation
: Climate Control
Heat Recovery

: Climate Control
Heating

: : : Languages
: : Afro Asiatic Languages
: Semitic Languages
Hebrew

: Scientific Concepts
Height

: : Behavior
: Social Behavior
Help Seeking

: : Relationship
: Interpersonal Relationship
Helping Relationship

Helplessness

: : : Hazardous Materials
: : Poisons
: Pesticides
Herbicides

: : Development
: Evolution
Heredity

: : Education
: Cultural Education
Heritage Education

: : : Liberal Arts
: : Humanities
: Philosophy
: Methods
Hermeneutics

: Narcotics
Heroin

: : : Organization
: : Classification
: Grouping (Instructional Purposes)
Heterogeneous Grouping

: Methods
Heuristics

Hidden Curriculum

: Achievement
High Achievement

: : Publications
: Printed Materials
: Books
High Interest Low Vocabulary Books

: : Groups
: Students
: Groups
: At Risk Persons
High Risk Students

: : Programs
: Adult Programs
High School Equivalency Programs

: : : : Groups
: : : Students
: : Secondary School Students
: High School Students
High School Freshmen

: : : Groups
: : Alumni
: Graduates
High School Graduates

: : : : Groups
: : : Students
: : Secondary School Students
: High School Students
High School Seniors

: : : Groups
: : Students
: Secondary School Students
High School Students
. College Bound Students
. High School Freshmen
. High School Seniors
. Noncollege Bound Students

: : : Institutions
: : Schools
: Secondary Schools
High Schools
. Vocational High Schools

: : Measures (Individuals)
: Tests
High Stakes Tests

: : Education
: Postsecondary Education
Higher Education
. Graduate Study
. . Graduate Medical Education
. . Postsecondary Education as a
    Field of Study
. Postdoctoral Education
. Undergraduate Study

: : : : Groups
: : : Personnel
: : Paraprofessional Personnel
: Engineering Technicians
Highway Engineering Aides

: : Languages
: Indo European Languages
Hindi

: : Culture
: North American Culture
Hispanic American Culture

: : : : : Liberal Arts
: : : : Humanities
: : : Literature
: : North American Literature
: United States Literature
Hispanic American Literature
. Mexican American Literature

: : Groups
: Students
: : : Groups
: : North Americans

: Hispanic Americans
Hispanic American Students

: : Groups
: North Americans
Hispanic Americans
. Hispanic American Students
. Mexican Americans
. Portuguese Americans
. Spanish Americans

: : : : Groups
: : : Personnel
: : Professional Personnel
: Social Scientists
Historians

Historic Sites

Historical Criticism (1969 1980)

Historical Interpretation

: : : : Liberal Arts
: : : Sciences
: : Social Sciences
: : Liberal Arts
: : Humanities
: History
Historiography

: : : Liberal Arts
: : Sciences
: Social Sciences
: : Liberal Arts
: Humanities
History
. African History
. American Indian History
. Ancient History
. Asian History
. . Korean War
. . Vietnam War
. Black History
. Constitutional History
. Diplomatic History
. Educational History
. Science Education History
. European History
. Family History
. Genealogy
. Historiography
. Intellectual History
. . Art History
. . Literary History
. Journalism History
. Latin American History
. Local History
. Mathematics History
. Medieval History
. Middle Eastern History
. Modern History
. North American History
. . United States History
. . . Civil War (United States)
. . . Colonial History (United States)
. . . Mexican American History
. . . Reconstruction Era
. . . Revolutionary War (United States)
. . . State History
. Oral History
. Public History
. Science History
. Social History
. World History
. . World War I
. . World War II

: : Instruction
: Humanities Instruction
History Instruction

: : : Educational Media
: : Instructional Materials
: : : Publications
: : Printed Materials
: : Books
: Textbooks
History Textbooks

: : Languages
: Sino Tibetan Languages
Hmong

: : Groups
: Ethnic Groups
Hmong People

: : Activities
: Recreational Activities
Hobbies

Holidays
. Religious Holidays

. Methods
Holistic Approach
. Gestalt Therapy
. Global Approach
. . Global Education
. . . International Education
. Systems Approach
. . Systems Building
. . . Design Build Approach
. Whole Language Approach

: Evaluation
Holistic Evaluation

: : : : : Liberal Arts
: : : : Humanities
: : : Fine Arts
: : Visual Arts
: Photography
Holography

: Curriculum
Home Economics

: : Education
: Professional Education
Home Economics Education

: : Ability
: Skills
Home Economics Skills

: : : : Groups
: : : Personnel
: : Professional Personnel
: Teachers
Home Economics Teachers

: Equipment
Home Furnishings

: : : : : Groups
: : : : Personnel
: : : Nonprofessional Personnel
: : Service Workers
: Household Workers
: : : : Groups
: : : Personnel
: : Health Personnel
: Allied Health Personnel
Home Health Aides

: Instruction
Home Instruction

: : Governance
: Administration
Home Management

: Programs
Home Programs

: : Education
: Compulsory Education
Home Schooling

: : : Activities
: : Learning Activities
: Study
Home Study
. Homework

: Methods
Home Visits

Homebound

: Groups
Homeless People

: Groups
Homemakers

: : Ability
: Skills
Homemaking Skills

: Groups
Homeowners

: : : : Activities
: : : Learning Activities
: : Study
: Home Study
: : Instruction
: Assignments
Homework

. Death
: : : Behavior
: : Social Behavior
: Antisocial Behavior
Homicide

: : : Organization
: : Classification
: Grouping (Instructional Purposes)
Homogeneous Grouping
. Ability Grouping

: : : Attitudes
: : Social Attitudes
: : Bias
: Social Bias
Homophobia

: Sexuality
Homosexuality
. Lesbianism

Honesty

: : Groups
: Organizations (Groups)
Honor Societies

: Curriculum
Honors Curriculum

: : : Languages
: : American Indian Languages
: Uto Aztecan Languages
Hopi

: : Groups
: Tribes
: : : Groups
: : : Ethnic Groups
: : American Indians
: Pueblo (People)
Hopi (Tribe)

: Organization
Horizontal Organization

: Technology
Horology

: : Activities
: Physical Activities
Horseback Riding

. Animals
Horses

: : Technology
: Agriculture
Horticulture
. Ornamental Horticulture
. . Floriculture
. . Landscaping
. . Turf Management

: : : Services
: : Human Services
: Health Services
Hospices (Terminal Care)

: : : : Institutions
: : : : Information Sources
: : : Libraries
: : Special Libraries
: Institutional Libraries
Hospital Libraries

: : : Groups
: : Personnel
: Health Personnel
Hospital Personnel

: : : : Institutions
: : : Schools
: : Special Schools
: Institutional Schools
Hospital Schools

: Occupations
: Service Occupations
Hospitality Occupations

: : Groups
: Patients
: : : Groups
: : Age Groups
: Children
Hospitalized Children

: Institutions
Hospitals
. Psychiatric Hospitals
. Teaching Hospitals

: : Psychological Patterns
: Anger
Hostility

: : Facilities
: Housing
Hotels

: : : Services
: : Information Services
: : Services
: : Community Services
: Community Information Services
Hotlines (Public)

: : Organization
: School Organization
House Plan
. Career Academies

: : : : Groups
: : : Personnel
: : Nonprofessional Personnel
: Service Workers
Household Workers
. Home Health Aides

: : : : Groups
: : : Personnel
: : Nonprofessional Personnel
: Service Workers
Housekeepers

Housework

: Facilities
Housing
. Boarding Homes
. College Housing
. Dormitories
. Group Homes
. Hotels
. Low Rent Housing
. . Public Housing
. Middle Income Housing
. Migrant Housing
. Suburban Housing
. Teacher Housing

Housing Deficiencies

: Social Discrimination
Housing Discrimination

: : : Business
: : Industry
: Construction Industry
Housing Industry

: : : : Groups
: : : Personnel
: : Nonprofessional Personnel
: Service Workers
: : : Groups
: : Personnel

: Paraprofessional Personnel
Housing Management Aides

: Needs
Housing Needs

: Opportunities
Housing Opportunities

Human Body

: Investment
Human Capital

Human Development (1966 1980)

Human Dignity

Human Factors Engineering

: : : : Liberal Arts
: : : Sciences
: : Social Sciences
: Geography
Human Geography

Human Living (1966 1980)

Human Posture

: Relationship
Human Relations
. Intergroup Relations
. . Ethnic Relations
. . Interfaith Relations
. . Racial Relations
. Peace
. Slavery

: Programs
Human Relations Programs

: Resources
Human Resources
. Labor Force
. Labor Supply

: Services
Human Services
. Counseling Services
. Employment Services
. . Outplacement Services (Employment)
. Food Service
. Health Services
. . Community Health Services
. . Hospices (Terminal Care)
. . Long Term Care
. . Medical Services
. . . First Aid
. . . . Cardiopulmonary Resuscitation
. . . Psychiatric Services
. . Migrant Health Services
. . Prenatal Care
. . School Health Services
. Integrated Services
. Psychological Services
. Social Services
. . Adult Day Care
. . Adult Foster Care
. . Ancillary School Services
. . . Mobile Educational Services
. . . Pupil Personnel Services
. . . School Health Services
. . . Student Personnel Services
. . Day Care
. . . Employer Supported Day Care
. . . Family Day Care
. . . School Age Day Care
. . . Sick Child Care
. . Foster Care
. . Social Work
. . Welfare Services
. . . Migrant Welfare Services

: : : Liberal Arts
: : Humanities
: Philosophy
Humanism

: Education
Humanistic Education

: Sociocultural Patterns
Humanitarianism

: Liberal Arts
Humanities
. Fine Arts
. . Dance
. . Music
. . . Applied Music
. . . Harmony (Music)
. . . Jazz
. . . Melody
. . . Oriental Music
. . . Popular Music
. . . Rock Music
. . . Vocal Music
. . . Choral Music
. . . . Songs
. . . . Art Song
. . . . Ballads
. . . . Hymns
. . Theater Arts
. . . Acting
. . . Choral Speaking
. . . Drama
. . . . Comedy
. . . . . Skits
. . . . Scripts
. . . . Soap Operas
. . . . Tragedy
. . . Dramatics
. . . . Creative Dramatics
. . . Opera
. . . Pantomime
. . . Puppetry
. . . Readers Theater
. . . Rehearsals (Theater Arts)
. . Visual Arts
. . . Architecture
. . . Childrens Art
. . . Design Crafts
. . . Drafting
. . . . Architectural Drafting
. . . . Engineering Drawing
. . . . Technical Illustration
. . . Film Production
. . . Freehand Drawing
. . . Graphic Arts
. . . . Cartography
. . . . Computer Graphics
. . . . Engineering Graphics
. . . . . Engineering Drawing
. . . . Layout (Publications)
. . . . Printing
. . . Handicrafts
. . . . Ceramics
. . . Painting (Visual Arts)
. . . Photography
. . . . Holography
. . . Printmaking
. . . Sculpture
. History
. . African History
. . American Indian History
. . Ancient History
. . Asian History
. . . Korean War
. . . Vietnam War
. . Black History
. . Constitutional History
. . Diplomatic History
. . Educational History
. . . Science Education History
. . European History
. . Family History
. . Genealogy
. . Historiography
. . Intellectual History
. . . Art History
. . . Literary History
. . Journalism History
. . Latin American History
. . Local History
. . Mathematics History
. . Medieval History
. . Middle Eastern History
. . Modern History
. . North American History
. . . United States History
. . . . Civil War (United States)
. . . . Colonial History (United States)
. . . . Mexican American History
. . . . Reconstruction Era

. . . . Revolutionary War (United States)
. . . State History
. . Oral History
. . Public History
. . Science History
. . Social History
. . World History
. . . World War I
. . . World War II
. Literature
. . Adolescent Literature
. . African Literature
. . American Indian Literature
. . Australian Literature
. . Baroque Literature
. . Biblical Literature
. . Black Literature
. . Childrens Literature
. . Classical Literature
. . . Latin Literature
. . Classics (Literature)
. . Czech Literature
. . Drama
. . . Comedy
. . . . Skits
. . . Scripts
. . . Soap Operas
. . . Tragedy
. . Eighteenth Century Literature
. . English Literature
. . . Old English Literature
. . Fifteenth Century Literature
. . French Literature
. . German Literature
. . Greek Literature
. . Italian Literature
. . Latin American Literature
. . Legends
. . Medieval Literature
. . Nineteenth Century Literature
. . North American Literature
. . . Canadian Literature
. . . United States Literature
. . . . Hispanic American Literature
. . . . . Mexican American Literature
. . Pastoral Literature
. . Poetry
. . . Epics
. . . Haiku
. . . Lyric Poetry
. . . . Ballads
. . . . Hymns
. . . . Odes
. . . . Sonnets
. . . Nursery Rhymes
. . Polish Literature
. . Prose
. . . Fiction
. . . . Novels
. . . . Science Fiction
. . . . Short Stories
. . . Nonfiction
. . . . Biographies
. . . . . Autobiographies
. . . . Chronicles
. . . . Diaries
. . . . . Dialog Journals
. . . . . Student Journals
. . . Essays
. . Renaissance Literature
. . Russian Literature
. . Seventeenth Century Literature
. . Sixteenth Century Literature
. . Spanish Literature
. . Twentieth Century Literature
. . Victorian Literature
. Philosophy
. Aesthetics
. . Educational Philosophy
. . Epistemology
. . Ethics
. . . Bioethics
. . . Work Ethic
. . Existentialism
. . Hermeneutics
. . Humanism
. . Logic
. . . Mathematical Logic
. . . . Algorithms
. . . . Mathematical Formulas
. . . . . Equations (Mathematics)
. . . . . . Differential Equations

. . . . Functions (Mathematics)
. . . . Polynomials
. . . Proof (Mathematics)
. . . Set Theory
. . Marxism
. . Phenomenology
. . Platonism
. . Semiotics
. . . Pragmatics
. . . Semantics
. . . . Lexicology
. . World Views

: Instruction
Humanities Instruction
. History Instruction
. Native Language Instruction
. English Instruction
. Second Language Instruction

Humanization

Humidity

Humor

: : : Languages
: : Uralic Altaic Languages
: Finno Ugric Languages
Hungarian

Hunger

: Weather
Hurricanes

: Technology
Hydraulics

: : : : : Liberal Arts
: : : : Sciences
: : : Natural Sciences
: : Physical Sciences
: Earth Science
Hydrology

Hygiene

: : : : : : Liberal Arts
: : : : : Humanities
: : : : Fine Arts
: : : Music
: : Vocal Music
: Songs
: : : : : Liberal Arts
: : : : Humanities
: : : Literature
: : Poetry
: Lyric Poetry
: Literary Genres
Hymns

: Behavior
Hyperactivity

Hypermedia

: : : Disabilities
: : Visual Impairments
: Ametropia
Hyperopia

: : Disabilities
: Diseases
Hypertension

Hypnosis

: : Methods
: Evaluation Methods
Hypothesis Testing

: : : : Activities
: : : Physical Activities
: : Athletics
: Winter Sports
: : : : Activities
: : : Physical Activities
: : Athletics
: Team Sports
Ice Hockey

: : : : Activities
: : : Physical Activities
: : Athletics
: Winter Sports
Ice Skating

: : : : : Liberal Arts
: : : : Sciences
: : : Natural Sciences
: : Biological Sciences
: Zoology
Ichthyology

Identification
. Ability Identification
. Clinical Diagnosis
. Disability Identification
. Early Identification
. Educational Diagnosis
. . Reading Diagnosis
. . . Miscue Analysis
. Plant Identification
. Racial Identification
. Talent Identification

: Psychological Patterns
Identification (Psychology)

: : Language
: Written Language
Ideography

Ideology

: Language Patterns
Idioms

: : Languages
: African Languages
Igbo

: : Behavior
: Drug Use
Illegal Drug Use

Illiteracy

: Visual Aids
Illustrations

: : Literary Devices
: : Language
: Figurative Language
Imagery

: : : Individual Characteristics
: : Psychological Characteristics
: Creativity
Imagination

: Behavior
Imitation

: : Programs
: Second Language Programs
Immersion Programs

: : Groups
: Migrants
Immigrants
. Undocumented Immigrants

: : Mobility
: Migration
Immigration

: : : Groups
: : Personnel
: Government Employees
Immigration Inspectors

: : Programs
: Health Programs
Immunization Programs

: : Policy
: Foreign Policy
Imperialism
. Colonialism

: International Trade
Imports

Impressionism

Impressionistic Criticism (1969 1980)

Improvement
. Achievement Gains
. Educational Improvement
. . Instructional Improvement
. Facility Improvement
. . Educational Facilities Improvement
. Finance Reform
. Neighborhood Improvement
. Program Improvement
. Reading Improvement
. Speech Improvement
. Student Improvement
. Teacher Improvement
. Urban Improvement
. . Urban Renewal
. Writing Improvement

: Programs
Improvement Programs
. Self Help Programs

: : Activities
: Creative Activities
Improvisation

In Loco Parentis

: : Discipline
: Suspension
In School Suspension

: : : Groups
: : Students
: College Students
In State Students

: : Financial Support
: Grants
Incentive Grants

Incentives

: : : Behavior
: : Social Behavior
: Antisocial Behavior
Incest

Incidence
. Average Daily Attendance
. Birth Rate
. Disease Incidence
. Dropout Rate
. Enrollment Rate
. . Average Daily Membership
. . Declining Enrollment
. Low Incidence Disabilities
. Mortality Rate
. Transfer Rates (College)

: Learning
Incidental Learning

: : Institutions
: Schools
Inclusive Schools

Income
. Family Income
. Guaranteed Income
. Interest (Finance)
. Low Income
. Merit Pay
. Premium Pay
. Salaries
. . Contract Salaries
. . Teacher Salaries
. Wages
. . Minimum Wage

: : Financial Support
: Student Financial Aid
Income Contingent Loans

Indemnity Bonds

Independent Living

: : Literacy
: : Language Arts

: Reading
Independent Reading

: : : Activities
: : Learning Activities
: Study
Independent Study

: : Publications
: Reference Materials
Indexes
. Citation Indexes
. Coordinate Indexes
. Permuted Indexes

: : : : Services
: : : Information Services
: : Information Processing
: Documentation
Indexing
. Automatic Indexing

: Groups
Indians

: : Groups
: Personnel
Indigenous Personnel

: Groups
Indigenous Populations

: Activities
Individual Activities

Individual Characteristics
. Age
. . Chronological Age
. . Mental Age
. . School Entrance Age
. Maturity (Individuals)
. . Vocational Maturity
. Physical Characteristics
. . Body Composition
. . . Obesity
. . Body Height
. . Body Weight
. . . Birth Weight
. . . Obesity
. . Lateral Dominance
. . Handedness
. . . Left Handed Writer
. . Muscular Strength
. . Neurological Organization
. . . Brain Hemisphere Functions
. . Race
. . Sex
. Psychological Characteristics
. . Attention Span
. . Cognitive Style
. . . Conceptual Tempo
. . . Field Dependence Independence
. . Creativity
. . . Imagination
. . Intelligence
. . . Comprehension
. . . . Listening Comprehension
. . . . Reading Comprehension
. . . Formal Operations
. . . Mental Age
. . . Multiple Intelligences
. . Personality Traits
. . . Curiosity
. . . Dependency (Personality)
. . . Extraversion Introversion
. . . Locus of Control
. . . Mental Rigidity
. . . Resilience (Personality)
. . Shyness
. . Schemata (Cognition)

: : Guidance
: Counseling
Individual Counseling

: Development
Individual Development
. Adolescent Development
. Adult Development
. Aging (Individuals)
. . Aging in Academia
. Behavior Development
. . Habit Formation

. Career Development
. . Career Awareness
. . Career Exploration
. Child Development
. Cognitive Development
. . Intellectual Development
. . Perceptual Development
. . Verbal Development
. . . Language Acquisition
. Creative Development
. Emotional Development
. Moral Development
. Personality Development
. Physical Development
. . Motor Development
. Skill Development
. Social Development
. Talent Development

: Differences
Individual Differences
. Age Differences
. Intelligence Differences
. Sex Differences

: Instruction
Individual Instruction
. Tutoring
. . Programmed Tutoring

: Needs
Individual Needs
. Childhood Needs
. Psychological Needs
. . Achievement Need
. . Affection
. . Affiliation Need
. . . Peer Acceptance
. . Personal Space
. . Security (Psychology)
. . Self Actualization
. . Status Need

Individual Power

: : : : Liberal Arts
: : : Sciences
: : Behavioral Sciences
: Psychology
Individual Psychology

Individual Reading (1966 1980)

: : : Methods
: : Measurement Techniques
: Testing
Individual Testing

Individualism

: : Programs
: Special Programs
Individualized Education Programs

: : Programs
: Special Programs
: : Intervention
: Early Intervention
Individualized Family Service Plans

: : : Methods
: : Educational Methods
: Teaching Methods
Individualized Instruction

: Programs
Individualized Programs

: : Instruction
: Reading Instruction
: : Literacy
: Language Arts
: Reading
Individualized Reading

: Languages
Indo European Languages
. Afrikaans
. Albanian
. Armenian
. Baltic Languages
. . Latvian
. . Lithuanian

. Baluchi
. Bengali
. Danish
. Dutch
. English
. . Business English
. . English (Second Language)
. . . English for Special Purposes
. . . . English for Academic Purposes
. . . . English for Science and
　　　Technology
. . . . Vocational English (Second
　　　Language)
. . Middle English
. . North American English
. . Old English
. . Oral English
. German
. . Yiddish
. Greek
. Gujarati
. Hindi
. Irish
. Kashmiri
. Kurdish
. Marathi
. Nepali
. Norwegian
. Ossetic
. Pashto
. Persian
. Punjabi
. Romance Languages
. . French
. . Italian
. . Latin
. . Portuguese
. . Romanian
. . Spanish
. Scots Gaelic
. Singhalese
. Slavic Languages
. . Bielorussian
. . Bulgarian
. . Czech
. . Polish
. . Russian
. . Serbocroatian
. . Slovenian
. . Ukrainian
. Swedish
. Tajik
. Urdu
. Welsh

: Groups
Indochinese
. Cambodians
. Laotians
. Vietnamese People

: : : Languages
: : Malayo Polynesian Languages
: Indonesian Languages
Indonesian

: : Languages
: Malayo Polynesian Languages
Indonesian Languages
. Bikol
. Dusun
. Indonesian
. Javanese
. Malagasy
. Malay
. Maranao
. Tagalog
. Visayan
. . Cebuano

: : Cognitive Processes
: Logical Thinking
Induction

Industrial Arts
. Painting (Industrial Arts)

: : : : Groups
: : : Personnel
: : Professional Personnel
: Teachers
Industrial Arts Teachers

: Education
Industrial Education

: : Groups
: Personnel
Industrial Personnel

: : : : Liberal Arts
: : : Sciences
: : Behavioral Sciences
: Psychology
Industrial Psychology

: Organization
Industrial Structure

: Training
Industrial Training

: Development
Industrialization

: Business
Industry
. Bakery Industry
. Banking
. Brick Industry
. Broadcast Industry
. Construction Industry
. . Housing Industry
. Fashion Industry
. Feed Industry
. Film Industry
. Information Industry
. Insurance Companies
. Lumber Industry
. Manufacturing Industry
. . Aerospace Industry
. . Cement Industry
. . Chemical Industry
. . Electronics Industry
. . Furniture Industry
. . Machinery Industry
. . Metal Industry
. Meat Packing Industry
. Petroleum Industry
. Publishing Industry
. . University Presses
. Telephone Communications Industry
. Tourism

Inequalities (1970 1980)

: Mathematical Concepts
Inequality (Mathematics)

: : Behavior
: Child Behavior
Infant Behavior

Infant Care

: Death
Infant Mortality
. Sudden Infant Death Syndrome

: : : : Groups
: : : Age Groups
: : Children
: Young Children
Infants
. Neonates
. Premature Infants

Inferences
. Statistical Inference

: : Environment
: Economic Climate
Inflation (Economics)

Influences
. Biological Influences
. . Rh Factors
. Black Influences
. Community Influence
. Cultural Influences
. Ecological Factors
. Economic Factors
. Enrollment Influences
. Environmental Influences
. Family Influence
. Minority Group Influences

. Parent Influence
. Peer Influence
. Performance Factors
. Perinatal Influences
. Political Influences
. Prenatal Influences
. . Prenatal Drug Exposure
. Racial Factors
. Religious Factors
. Social Influences
. Socioeconomic Influences
. Teacher Influence
. Time Factors (Learning)

: Evaluation
Informal Assessment

: Education
Informal Education

: : Ability
: Leadership
Informal Leadership

: Organization
Informal Organization

: : : : Measures (Individuals)
: : : Tests
: : Verbal Tests
: Reading Tests
Informal Reading Inventories

: : Facilities
: Resource Centers
: Information Sources
Information Centers
. Clearinghouses

: : Services
: Information Services
Information Dissemination
. Document Delivery
. Propaganda
. Publicity
. . Advertising
. . . Television Commercials
. . Institutional Advancement
. Selective Dissemination of
　Information

: : Business
: Industry
Information Industry

: Literacy
Information Literacy

: : Governance
: Administration
Information Management
. Records Management

: Needs
Information Needs

: Networks
Information Networks
. Internet
. . World Wide Web
. Library Networks
. . Bibliographic Utilities

: Policy
Information Policy
. Library Policy

: : Services
: Information Services
Information Processing
. Data Collection
. . Sampling
. . . Item Sampling
. Data Processing
. . Input Output
. . . Keyboarding (Data Entry)
. . . Natural Language Processing
. . Time Sharing
. Documentation
. . Abstracting
. . Authority Control (Information)
. . Bibliometrics
. . . Citation Analysis

. . . Bibliographic Coupling
. . Cataloging
. . . Machine Readable Cataloging
. . Filing
. . Indexing
. . . Automatic Indexing
. Information Retrieval
. . Downloading
. . Online Searching
. Information Storage
. Word Processing

: : : Services
: : Information Services
: Information Processing
Information Retrieval
. Downloading
. Online Searching

: : Liberal Arts
: Sciences
Information Science
. Computer Science
. . Programming
. Library Science

: : Education
: Professional Education
Information Science Education
. Computer Science Education
. Library Education

: : : Groups
: : Personnel
: Professional Personnel
Information Scientists
. Librarians
. Search Intermediaries

Information Seeking
. Search Strategies

: Services
Information Services
. Community Information Services
. . Hotlines (Public)
. Information Dissemination
. . Document Delivery
. . Propaganda
. . Publicity
. . . Advertising
. . . . Television Commercials
. . . Institutional Advancement
. . Selective Dissemination of
　　Information
. Information Processing
. . Data Collection
. . . Sampling
. . . . Item Sampling
. . Data Processing
. . . Input Output
. . . . Keyboarding (Data Entry)
. . . . Natural Language Processing
. . . Time Sharing
. . Documentation
. . . Abstracting
. . . Authority Control (Information)
. . . Bibliometrics
. . . . Citation Analysis
. . . . . Bibliographic Coupling
. . . . Cataloging
. . . . . Machine Readable Cataloging
. . . . Filing
. . . Indexing
. . . . Automatic Indexing
. . Information Retrieval
. . . Downloading
. . . Online Searching
. . Information Storage
. . Word Processing
. Library Services
. . Library Circulation
. . . Interlibrary Loans
. . Library Extension
. . Library Technical Processes
. . . Library Acquisition
. . . . Library Material Selection
. Reference Services
. Videotex

: : Ability
: Skills
Information Skills

. Library Skills

Information Sources
. Archives
. Databases
. . Bibliographic Databases
. . . Full Text Databases
. . Numeric Databases
. . Online Catalogs
. Information Centers
. . Clearinghouses
. Libraries
. . Academic Libraries
. . . College Libraries
. . Branch Libraries
. . Childrens Libraries
. . Depository Libraries
. . Electronic Libraries
. . Public Libraries
. . . County Libraries
. . . Regional Libraries
. . Research Libraries
. . School Libraries
. . Special Libraries
. . . Corporate Libraries
. . . Film Libraries
. . . Government Libraries
. . . . National Libraries
. . . . State Libraries
. . . Institutional Libraries
. . . . Hospital Libraries
. . . . Prison Libraries
. . . Law Libraries
. . Medical Libraries
. . . Science Libraries
. Primary Sources

: Storage
: : Services
: : Information Services
: Information Processing
Information Storage

Information Systems
. Career Information Systems
. Computer Managed Instruction
. Dial Access Information Systems
. Integrated Learning Systems
. Integrated Library Systems
. Management Information Systems
. . Decision Support Systems

: Technology
Information Technology

: Theories
Information Theory

Information Transfer

Information Utilization
. Evaluation Utilization
. Research Utilization

Inhibition

: Alphabets
Initial Teaching Alphabet

: Disabilities
Injuries
. Head Injuries

: : Geographic Regions
: Urban Areas
Inner City

: : Language Arts
: Speech
Inner Speech (Subvocal)

Innovation
. Building Innovation
. Educational Innovation
. . Instructional Innovation

: : : : : Liberal Arts
: : : : Sciences
: : : Natural Sciences
: : Physical Sciences
: Chemistry
Inorganic Chemistry

: Programs
Inplant Programs

: : : : Services
: : : Information Services
: : Information Processing
: Data Processing
Input Output
. Keyboarding (Data Entry)

: : Methods
: Evaluation Methods
Input Output Analysis

: : : Equipment
: : Electronic Equipment
: Computer Peripherals
Input Output Devices
. Computer Printers
. Computer Terminals
. . Video Display Terminals
. Disk Drives
. Optical Scanners

: Methods
Inquiry

: : : Hazardous Materials
: : Poisons
: Pesticides
Insecticides

: Education
Inservice Education
. Inservice Teacher Education

: : : Education
: : Professional Education
: Teacher Education
: Education
: Inservice Education
Inservice Teacher Education

: : Methods
: Evaluation Methods
Inspection

: Programs
Institutes (Training Programs)

: : Governance
: Administration
Institutional Administration
. Library Administration
. School Administration
. . College Administration
. . School Based Management

: : : : Services
: : : Information Services
: : Information Dissemination
: : Communication (Thought Transfer)
: Publicity
Institutional Advancement

Institutional Autonomy
. School Based Management

Institutional Characteristics
. Diversity (Institutional)
. School Size

: : Behavior
: Cooperation
Institutional Cooperation
. College School Cooperation
. Intercollegiate Cooperation
. Library Cooperation

: Environment
Institutional Environment
. College Environment

: Evaluation
Institutional Evaluation

: : : Institutions
: : : Information Sources
: : Libraries
: Special Libraries
Institutional Libraries
. Hospital Libraries
. Prison Libraries

: : Objectives
: Organizational Objectives
Institutional Mission

: : Groups
: Personnel
Institutional Personnel

: Research
Institutional Research

: Role
Institutional Role
. Agency Role
. Church Role
. Court Role
. Library Role
. School Role
. . College Role

: : : Institutions
: : Schools
: Special Schools
Institutional Schools
. Hospital Schools

Institutional Survival

: Groups
Institutionalized Persons
. Prisoners

Institutions
. Black Institutions
. . Black Colleges
. Churches
. Courts
. . Federal Courts
. . Juvenile Courts
. . State Courts
. Hospitals
. . Psychiatric Hospitals
. . Teaching Hospitals
. Libraries
. . Academic Libraries
. . . College Libraries
. . Branch Libraries
. . Childrens Libraries
. . Depository Libraries
. . Electronic Libraries
. . Public Libraries
. . . County Libraries
. . . Regional Libraries
. . Research Libraries
. . School Libraries
. . Special Libraries
. . . Corporate Libraries
. . . Film Libraries
. . . Government Libraries
. . . . National Libraries
. . . . State Libraries
. . . Institutional Libraries
. . . . Hospital Libraries
. . . . Prison Libraries
. . . Law Libraries
. . Medical Libraries
. . . Science Libraries
. Peer Institutions
. Philanthropic Foundations
. Residential Institutions
. . Boarding Schools
. . . Residential Schools
. . Correctional Institutions
. . Nursing Homes
. . Personal Care Homes
. . Residential Colleges
. Schools
. . Affiliated Schools
. . Bilingual Schools
. . Boarding Schools
. . . Residential Schools
. . British Infant Schools
. . Colleges
. . . Agricultural Colleges
. . . Black Colleges
. . . Church Related Colleges
. . . Cluster Colleges
. . . Commuter Colleges
. . . Dental Schools
. . . Developing Institutions
. . . Experimental Colleges
. . . Law Schools
. . . Library Schools

. . . Medical Schools
. . . Multicampus Colleges
. . . Noncampus Colleges
. . . Private Colleges
. . . Public Colleges
. . . . Community Colleges
. . . . State Colleges
. . . . . State Universities
. . . Residential Colleges
. . . Selective Colleges
. . . Single Sex Colleges
. . . Small Colleges
. . . Two Year Colleges
. . . . Community Colleges
. . . . Technical Institutes
. . . Universities
. . . . Land Grant Universities
. . . . Open Universities
. . . . Research Universities
. . . . State Universities
. . . . Urban Universities
. . . Upper Division Colleges
. . Community Schools
. . Consolidated Schools
. . Correspondence Schools
. . Day Schools
. . Disadvantaged Schools
. . Elementary Schools
. . Experimental Schools
. . Experimental Colleges
. . Folk Schools
. . Free Schools
. . Freedom Schools
. . Inclusive Schools
. . Laboratory Schools
. . Magnet Schools
. . Middle Schools
. . Military Schools
. . Multiunit Schools
. . Neighborhood Schools
. . Nursery Schools
. . Open Plan Schools
. . Private Schools
. . Parochial Schools
. . . Catholic Schools
. . Private Colleges
. . Proprietary Schools
. . Professional Development Schools
. . Public Schools
. . Charter Schools
. . Racially Balanced Schools
. . Regional Schools
. . Rural Schools
. . Schools of Education
. . Secondary Schools
. . . High Schools
. . . . Vocational High Schools
. . . Junior High Schools
. . Single Sex Schools
. . Single Sex Colleges
. . Slum Schools
. . Small Schools
. . . One Teacher Schools
. . . Small Colleges
. . Special Schools
. . . Institutional Schools
. . . . Hospital Schools
. . . Residential Schools
. . State Schools
. . . State Colleges
. . . . State Universities
. . Suburban Schools
. . Summer Schools
. . Traditional Schools
. . Transitional Schools
. . Urban Schools
. . . Urban Universities
. . Vocational Schools
. . . Career Academies
. . . Vocational High Schools
. . Year Round Schools

Instruction
. Assignments
. . Homework
. . Reading Assignments
. . Research Papers (Students)
. . Writing Assignments
. Clothing Instruction
. College Instruction
. Concept Teaching
. Cooking Instruction
. Ethical Instruction

. Field Instruction
. Foods Instruction
. Geography Instruction
. Group Instruction
. . Large Group Instruction
. . Small Group Instruction
. Home Instruction
. Humanities Instruction
. . History Instruction
. . Native Language Instruction
. . . English Instruction
. Second Language Instruction
. Individual Instruction
. . Tutoring
. . . Programmed Tutoring
. Library Instruction
. . Course Integrated Library Instruction
. Mass Instruction
. Mathematics Instruction
. . Remedial Mathematics
. Nutrition Instruction
. Reading Instruction
. . Basal Reading
. . Content Area Reading
. . Corrective Reading
. . Directed Reading Activity
. . Individualized Reading
. . Remedial Reading
. . Sustained Silent Reading
. Remedial Instruction
. . Remedial Mathematics
. . Remedial Reading
. Science Instruction
. Sewing Instruction
. Speech Instruction
. . Pronunciation Instruction
. Spelling Instruction
. Telephone Usage Instruction
. Test Coaching
. Textiles Instruction
. Writing Instruction
. . Basic Writing
. . Content Area Writing
. . . Writing Across the Curriculum
. . Freshman Composition
. . Process Approach (Writing)

: Design
Instructional Design

: : Development
: Educational Development
Instructional Development

Instructional Effectiveness

: : Educational Media
: Instructional Materials
: : Visual Aids
: Nonprint Media
: : Mass Media
: Films
: Educational Media
: : Audiovisual Aids
Instructional Films

: : Improvement
: Educational Improvement
Instructional Improvement

: : Innovation
: Educational Innovation
Instructional Innovation

: : Ability
: Leadership
Instructional Leadership

: Evaluation
Instructional Material Evaluation
. Textbook Evaluation

: Educational Media
Instructional Materials
. Advance Organizers
. Bilingual Instructional Materials
. Courseware
. Microworlds
. Experience Charts
. Instructional Films
. Laboratory Manuals
. Learning Modules

. Manipulative Materials
. Problem Sets
. Programmed Instructional Materials
. Protocol Materials
. Student Developed Materials
. . Student Writing Models
. Study Guides
. Teacher Developed Materials
. . Teacher Made Tests
. Textbooks
. . History Textbooks
. . Multicultural Textbooks
. Workbooks

Instructional Program Divisions
. Grade 1
. Grade 10
. Grade 11
. Grade 12
. Grade 2
. Grade 3
. Grade 4
. Grade 5
. Grade 6
. Grade 7
. Grade 8
. Grade 9
. Intermediate Grades
. Kindergarten

Instructional Programs (1966 1980)

: : Costs
: Student Costs
Instructional Student Costs
. Tuition

: : Technology
: Educational Technology
Instructional Systems

: : : : Groups
: : : Personnel
: : Professional Personnel
: Teachers
: : : : Groups
: : : Personnel
: : Administrators
: Coordinators
Instructor Coordinators

Instrumentation
. Visible Speech

: : Activities
: Music Activities
Instrumentation and Orchestration

: : : Groups
: : Personnel
: Paraprofessional Personnel
Instrumentation Technicians

: Methods
Insurance
. Fire Insurance
. Health Insurance
. Unemployment Insurance
. Workers Compensation

: : Business
: Industry
Insurance Companies

: Occupations
Insurance Occupations

: : : Symbols (Mathematics)
: : Numbers
: Rational Numbers
Integers
. Prime Numbers
. Whole Numbers

: Activities
Integrated Activities
. Integrated Curriculum

: : Activities
: Integrated Activities
: Curriculum
Integrated Curriculum

: Information Systems
: Computer Uses in Education
: : Networks
: Computer Networks
Integrated Learning Systems

: Online Systems
: Information Systems
Integrated Library Systems

: : Services
: Human Services
Integrated Services

: Readiness
Integration Readiness

: : Research
: Behavioral Science Research
Integration Studies

Integrity

: : : Development
: : Individual Development
: Cognitive Development
Intellectual Development

Intellectual Disciplines

: : Background
: Experience
Intellectual Experience

: Freedom
Intellectual Freedom

: : : : Liberal Arts
: : : Sciences
: : Social Sciences
: : : Liberal Arts
: : Humanities
: History
Intellectual History
. Art History
. Literary History

: Ownership
Intellectual Property
. Copyrights
. Patents

: : Individual Characteristics
: Psychological Characteristics
Intelligence
. Comprehension
. . Listening Comprehension
. . Reading Comprehension
. Formal Operations
. Mental Age
. Multiple Intelligences

: : Differences
: Individual Differences
Intelligence Differences

: Ratios (Mathematics)
Intelligence Quotient

: : : Measures (Individuals)
: : Tests
: Cognitive Tests
Intelligence Tests

: : Artificial Intelligence
: Expert Systems
: : : : : Methods
: : : : Educational Methods
: : : Teaching Methods
: : Programmed Instruction
: : Computer Uses in Education
: Computer Assisted Instruction
Intelligent Tutoring Systems

: : Curriculum
: Modern Language Curriculum
: : Curriculum
: Courses
Intensive Language Courses

Intention

: Learning
Intentional Learning

: Relationship
Interaction
. Aptitude Treatment Interaction
. Feedback
. . Biofeedback
. Group Dynamics

: : Methods
: Research Methodology
Interaction Process Analysis

: : : : Technology
: : : Communications
: : Telecommunications
: : Mass Media
: Television
Interactive Television

: Online Systems
Interactive Video

: : : Behavior
: : Cooperation
: Institutional Cooperation
: : : Behavior
: : Cooperation
: Educational Cooperation
Intercollegiate Cooperation

: Communication (Thought Transfer)
Intercultural Communication

: Programs
Intercultural Programs

: Methods
Interdisciplinary Approach

: Policy
Interdistrict Policies

: Income
: Costs
Interest (Finance)

: Measures (Individuals)
Interest Inventories

: : : Research
: : Behavioral Science Research
: Psychological Studies
Interest Research

Interests
. Childhood Interests
. Reading Interests
. Science Interests
. Student Interests
. Vocational Interests

: : : Relationship
: : Human Relations
: Intergroup Relations
Interfaith Relations

: : Cognitive Processes
: Language Processing
Interference (Language)

: Programs
Intergenerational Programs

: Education
Intergroup Education
. Multicultural Education

: : Relationship
: Human Relations
Intergroup Relations
. Ethnic Relations
. Interfaith Relations
. Racial Relations

: Design
Interior Design

: Facilities
Interior Space

: Language
Interlanguage

: : : : Services
: : : Information Services
: : Library Services
: Library Circulation
Interlibrary Loans

: : : Relationship
: : Interpersonal Relationship
: Marriage
Intermarriage

Intermediate Administrative Units

: Instructional Program Divisions
Intermediate Grades

: Differences
Intermode Differences

: : Technology
: Medicine
Internal Medicine

: Communication (Thought Transfer)
International Communication

: : Behavior
: Cooperation
International Cooperation

: : : : Behavior
: : : Social Behavior
: : Antisocial Behavior
: Crime
International Crimes
. Genocide

: : : : Methods
: : : Holistic Approach
: : Global Approach
: : Education
: Global Education
International Education

International Educational Exchange

: : Standards
: Laws
International Law

: : Groups
: Organizations (Groups)
International Organizations

: Programs
International Programs

: Relationship
International Relations

: : : Liberal Arts
: : Sciences
: Social Sciences
International Studies

International Trade
. Exports
. Imports

: Vocabulary
International Trade Vocabulary

: : Networks
: Information Networks
: : Networks
: Computer Networks
Internet
. World Wide Web

: Programs
: Learning
: Experiential Learning
Internship Programs

: : Relationship
: Interpersonal Relationship
Interpersonal Attraction
. Physical Attractiveness

: Communication (Thought Transfer)
Interpersonal Communication

: : Ability
: Competence
Interpersonal Competence

: Relationship
Interpersonal Relationship
. Board Administrator Relationship
. Caregiver Child Relationship
. Cohabitation
. Collegiality
. Counselor Client Relationship
. Dating (Social)
. Employer Employee Relationship
. Family Relationship
. . Parent Child Relationship
. . . Parent Student Relationship
. . Sibling Relationship
. Friendship
. Group Unity
. Helping Relationship
. Interpersonal Attraction
. . Physical Attractiveness
. Interprofessional Relationship
. Kinship
. Marriage
. . Intermarriage
. . Remarriage
. Peer Relationship
. Physician Patient Relationship
. Rapport
. Significant Others
. Teacher Administrator Relationship
. Teacher Student Relationship

: : Groups
: Personnel
Interpreters

Interpretive Reading (1966 1980)

: : Ability
: Skills
Interpretive Skills

: : Relationship
: Interpersonal Relationship
Interprofessional Relationship

: : : : Standards
: : : Criteria
: : Evaluation Criteria
: Reliability
Interrater Reliability

: : Communication (Thought Transfer)
: Organizational Communication
Interschool Communication

: Programs
Interstate Programs

Intervals

Intervention
. Crisis Intervention
. Early Intervention
. . Individualized Family Service Plans
. Prereferral Intervention

: : Methods
: Evaluation Methods
Interviews
. Employment Interviews
. Field Interviews

: Relationship
Intimacy

: : : Linguistics
: : Phonology
: Suprasegmentals
Intonation

: : : Activities
: : Physical Activities
: Athletics
Intramural Athletics

: : Curriculum
: Courses
Introductory Courses

: Cognitive Processes
Intuition

: : Languages
: Eskimo Aleut Languages
Inupiaq

: : Language Arts
: Spelling
Invented Spelling

Inventions

: Research
Investigations

Investment
. Human Capital

: : Languages
: Indo European Languages
Irish

: : : Literary Devices
: : Language
: Figurative Language
Irony

: : : Groups
: : Tribes
: : : Groups
: : Ethnic Groups
: American Indians
Iroquois (Tribe)

: Religion
Islam

: Culture
Islamic Culture

: : : Languages
: : Indo European Languages
: Romance Languages
Italian

: : Groups
: North Americans
: : Groups
: Ethnic Groups
Italian Americans

: : : Liberal Arts
: : Humanities
: Literature
Italian Literature

: : : : Methods
: : : Evaluation Methods
: : Data Analysis
: Statistical Analysis
Item Analysis

Item Banks

: : Bias
: Test Bias
Item Bias

: : Theories
: Test Theory
Item Response Theory

: : : : Liberal Arts
: : : Mathematics
: : Statistics
: : : : Services
: : : : Information Services
: : : Information Processing
: : : : : Methods
: : : : Evaluation Methods
: : : Data Analysis
: : Data Collection
: Sampling
Item Sampling

: : : : Groups
: : : Personnel
: : Professional Personnel

: Teachers
Itinerant Teachers

: Languages
Japanese
. Okinawan

: : Culture
: North American Culture
: : Culture
: Japanese Culture
Japanese American Culture

: : Groups
: Ethnic Groups
: : : Groups
: : North Americans
: Asian Americans
Japanese Americans

: Culture
Japanese Culture
. Japanese American Culture

: Vocabulary
Jargon

: : : Languages
: : Malayo Polynesian Languages
: Indonesian Languages
Javanese

: : : : Liberal Arts
: : : Humanities
: : Fine Arts
: Music
Jazz

: Psychological Patterns
Jealousy

: : Groups
: Religious Cultural Groups
Jews

: : Methods
: Evaluation Methods
Job Analysis

: Groups
Job Applicants

Job Application

Job Banks

: Development
Job Development
. Job Enrichment
. Job Simplification

: : Development
: Job Development
: Enrichment
Job Enrichment

: Reduction in Force
Job Layoff

: : Behavior
: Performance
Job Performance

: Placement
Job Placement
. Teacher Placement

: : Attitudes
: Work Attitudes
: : Attitudes
: Satisfaction
Job Satisfaction

: Methods
Job Search Methods

Job Security

: : Employment
: Part Time Employment
Job Sharing

: : : Development
: : Job Development
Job Simplification

: : : Ability
: Skills
Job Skills

: : Training
Job Training
. Custodian Training
. Off the Job Training
. On the Job Training
. . Apprenticeships

: : : Activities
: : Physical Activities
: Running
Jogging

: Publications
Journal Articles

: : Literacy
: : Language Arts
: Writing (Composition)
Journal Writing

: Technology
Journalism
. Broadcast Journalism
. New Journalism
. News Reporting
. News Writing
. Photojournalism
. Scholastic Journalism

: Education
Journalism Education

: : : : Liberal Arts
: : : Sciences
: : Social Sciences
: : : Liberal Arts
: : Humanities
: History
Journalism History

: : Research
: Media Research
Journalism Research

: Religion
Judaism

: Groups
Judges
. Court Judges

: : : : Methods
: : : Evaluation Methods
: : Data Analysis
: Statistical Analysis
Judgment Analysis Technique

: : : Groups
: : Students
: Secondary School Students
Junior High School Students

: : : Institutions
: : Schools
: Secondary Schools
Junior High Schools

: Groups
Juries

Justice
. Juvenile Justice

: : Institutions
: Courts
Juvenile Courts

: Groups
Juvenile Gangs

: Justice
Juvenile Justice

: : : Languages
: : Afro Asiatic Languages

: Berber Languages
Kabyle

: : Languages
: Dravidian Languages
Kannada

: : Languages
: Indo European Languages
Kashmiri

: : : : Theories
: : : Linguistic Theory
: : Generative Grammar
: Transformational Generative
Grammar
: : : Language Patterns
: : Paragraphs
: Sentences
Kernel Sentences

: : : : : Services
: : : : Information Services
: : : Information Processing
: : Data Processing
: Input Output
: : : Ability
: : Skills
: Business Skills
Keyboarding (Data Entry)

: Vocabulary
Keywords

: Instructional Program Divisions
Kindergarten

: : : : Groups
: : : Age Groups
: : Children
: Young Children
Kindergarten Children

: : Visual Aids
: : Nonprint Media
: : Mass Media
: Films
Kinescope Recordings

: : : Methods
: : Educational Methods
: Teaching Methods
Kinesthetic Methods

: : Cognitive Processes
: Perception
Kinesthetic Perception

: Theories
Kinetic Molecular Theory

: : : : : : Liberal Arts
: : : : : Sciences
: : : : Natural Sciences
: : : Physical Sciences
: : Physics
: Mechanics (Physics)
Kinetics
. Diffusion (Physics)

: : Relationship
: Interpersonal Relationship
Kinship

: Vocabulary
Kinship Terminology

: : : Languages
: : African Languages
: Bantu Languages
Kirundi

: : : Languages
: : African Languages
: Bantu Languages
Kituba

Knowledge Base for Teaching

: Achievement
Knowledge Level

Knowledge Representation

: : : Methods
: : Educational Methods
: Teaching Methods
: Education
: Music Education
Kodaly Method

: Languages
Korean

: : Groups
: Ethnic Groups
: : : Groups
: : North Americans
: Asian Americans
Korean Americans

: Culture
Korean Culture

: : Conflict
: War
: : : : Liberal Arts
: : : : Sciences
: : : Social Sciences
: : : : Liberal Arts
: : : Humanities
: : History
: Asian History
Korean War

: : Languages
: Indo European Languages
Kurdish

: : : Languages
: : Uralic Altaic Languages
: Turkic Languages
Kyrgyz

: : Organization
: Classification
Labeling (of Persons)

Labor
. Child Labor
. Farm Labor

Labor Conditions

Labor Demands

: : : : Liberal Arts
: : : Sciences
: : Social Sciences
: Economics
Labor Economics

: : Education
: Adult Education
Labor Education

: : Resources
: Human Resources
Labor Force

: Development
Labor Force Development
. Management Development
. Professional Development
. . Faculty Development
. Staff Development
. . Faculty Development

: Groups
Labor Force Nonparticipants

: Legislation
Labor Legislation

Labor Market
. Teacher Supply and Demand
. . Teacher Shortage

: Needs
Labor Needs
. Personnel Needs

: Problems
Labor Problems

: Relationship
Labor Relations

: Standards
Labor Standards

: : Resources
: Human Resources
Labor Supply

Labor Turnover

Labor Utilization
. Staff Utilization

: Facilities
Laboratories
. Learning Laboratories
. . Language Laboratories
. Mobile Laboratories
. Regional Laboratories
. Science Laboratories
. Writing Laboratories

: Animals
Laboratory Animals

: Equipment
Laboratory Equipment
. Microscopes

: Experiments
Laboratory Experiments

: : Educational Media
: Instructional Materials
: : : Publications
: : Reference Materials
: Guides
Laboratory Manuals

: Methods
Laboratory Procedures
. Chromatography
. Culturing Techniques
. Dissection

: Safety
Laboratory Safety

: : Institutions
: Schools
Laboratory Schools

Laboratory Techniques (1967 1980)

: Technology
Laboratory Technology

: Training
Laboratory Training

: : : : Groups
: : : Personnel
: : Nonprofessional Personnel
: Unskilled Workers
Laborers
. Agricultural Laborers
. . Migrant Workers
. Seasonal Laborers
. Auxiliary Laborers

: : : : Activities
: : : Physical Activities
: : Athletics
: Team Sports
Lacrosse

: : : Languages
: : American Indian Languages
: Dakota
Lakota

: : : Groups
: : Tribes
: : : : Groups
: : : Ethnic Groups
: : American Indians
: Sioux (Tribe)
Lakota (Tribe)
. Oglala Sioux (Tribe)

Land Acquisition

: : : : Institutions
: : : Schools
: : Colleges
: Universities
Land Grant Universities

: Land Use
Land Settlement
. Rural Resettlement

Land Use
. Land Settlement
. . Rural Resettlement
. Soil Conservation

: Groups
Landlords

: : : : Technology
: : : Agriculture
: : Horticulture
: Ornamental Horticulture
Landscaping

Language
. Artificial Languages
. . Esperanto
. Child Language
. Figurative Language
. . Allegory
. . Ambiguity
. . Antithesis
. . Imagery
. . Irony
. . Metaphors
. . Puns
. . Symbols (Literary)
. Interlanguage
. Language of Instruction
. Language Universals
. Languages for Special Purposes
. . English for Special Purposes
. . . English for Academic Purposes
. . . English for Science and
        Technology
. . . Vocational English (Second
        Language)
. Official Languages
. Oral Language
. Programming Languages
. Second Languages
. . English (Second Language)
. . . English for Special Purposes
. . . . English for Academic Purposes
. . . . English for Science and
          Technology
. . . . Vocational English (Second
          Language)
. Sign Language
. . American Sign Language
. Symbolic Language
. Tone Languages
. Uncommonly Taught Languages
. Unwritten Languages
. Urban Language
. Written Language
. . Braille
. . Electronic Text
. . Graphemes
. . Ideography
. . Orthographic Symbols
. . . Diacritical Marking
. . . Letters (Alphabet)
. . . Phonetic Transcription
. . Punctuation
. . Shorthand

Language Ability (1966 1980)

: : : : Development
: : : Individual Development
: : Cognitive Development
: Verbal Development
Language Acquisition

Language Aids (1966 1980)

**Language and Area Centers
(1968 1980)**

: Aptitude
Language Aptitude

Language Arts
. Debate
. Handwriting
. . Cursive Writing
. . Manuscript Writing (Handlettering)
. Listening
. Outlining (Discourse)
. Reading
. . Basal Reading
. . Beginning Reading
. . Content Area Reading
. . Corrective Reading
. . Critical Reading
. . Directed Reading Activity
. . Early Reading
. . Functional Reading
. . Independent Reading
. . Individualized Reading
. . Music Reading
. . Oral Reading
. . Reading Aloud to Others
. . Recreational Reading
. . Remedial Reading
. . Silent Reading
. . Speed Reading
. . Story Reading
. . Sustained Silent Reading
. Rhetoric
. . Coherence
. . Persuasive Discourse
. . Rhetorical Invention
. Speech
. . Articulation (Speech)
. . Artificial Speech
. . Caregiver Speech
. . Inner Speech (Subvocal)
. . Pronunciation
. . Speech Acts
. . Speech Compression
. Spelling
. . Finger Spelling
. . Invented Spelling
. Story Telling
. Writing (Composition)
. . Abstracting
. . Basic Writing
. . Beginning Writing
. . Childrens Writing
. . Content Area Writing
. . . Writing Across the Curriculum
. . Creative Writing
. . Descriptive Writing
. . Expository Writing
. . Free Writing
. . Freshman Composition
. . Journal Writing
. . Local Color Writing
. . News Writing
. . Notetaking
. . Paragraph Composition
. . Parallelism (Literary)
. . Playwriting
. . Proposal Writing
. . Scholarly Writing
. . Technical Writing
. . Writing for Publication

: Attitudes
Language Attitudes
. Grammatical Acceptability

: : Organization
: Classification
Language Classification
. Language Typology

Language Dominance

: Enrichment
Language Enrichment

: Enrollment
Language Enrollment

: : : Methods
: : Educational Methods
: Teaching Methods
Language Experience Approach

: : Ability
: Language Proficiency
Language Fluency

Language Guides (1966 1980)

: Disabilities
Language Impairments
. Aphasia
. Dyslexia

Language Instruction (1966 1980)

: : : Facilities
: : Laboratories
: : : Facilities
: : Educational Facilities
: Learning Laboratories
Language Laboratories

**Language Learning Levels (1967
1980)**

Language Maintenance

: Groups
Language Minorities

: Language
Language of Instruction

Language Patterns
. Idioms
. Language Rhythm
. Paragraphs
. . Sentences
. . . Kernel Sentences
. Phoneme Grapheme Correspondence

: : Linguistics
: Sociolinguistics
: Planning
Language Planning
. Language Standardization

: Cognitive Processes
Language Processing
. Expressive Language
. Interference (Language)
. Reading Processes
. . Decoding (Reading)
. Receptive Language

: Ability
Language Proficiency
. Language Fluency
. Threshold Level (Languages)

Language Programs (1966 1980)

: Research
Language Research
. Dialect Studies

: Language Patterns
Language Rhythm

: Role
Language Role

Language Skill Attrition

: : Ability
: Skills
Language Skills
. Audiolingual Skills
. . Listening Skills
. . Speech Skills
. Communicative Competence
    (Languages)
. . Threshold Level (Languages)
. Reading Skills
. . Reading Comprehension
. . Reading Rate
. Vocabulary Skills
. Writing Skills

: : Linguistics
: : Sociolinguistics
: : Planning
: Language Planning
Language Standardization

: : : Linguistics
: : Sociolinguistics
: Language Variation
: Language Usage
Language Styles
. Academic Discourse

: : : : Groups
: : : Personnel
: : Professional Personnel
: Teachers
Language Teachers
. English Teachers

: : : Measures (Individuals)
: : Tests
: Verbal Tests
Language Tests

: : : Organization
: : Classification
: Language Classification
Language Typology

: Language
Language Universals

Language Usage
. Language Styles
. . Academic Discourse
. Sexism in Language
. Standard Spoken Usage

: : Linguistics
: Sociolinguistics
Language Variation
. Creoles
. . Gullah
. . Haitian Creole
. . Mauritian Creole
. . Sierra Leone Creole
. Dialects
. . Black Dialects
. . Nonstandard Dialects
. . Regional Dialects
. . Social Dialects
. Language Styles
. . Academic Discourse
. Linguistic Borrowing
. Pidgins

Languages
. African Languages
. . Akan
. . Bantu Languages
. . . Bemba
. . . Chinyanja
. . . Ganda
. . . Kirundi
. . . Kituba
. . . Lingala
. . . Shona
. . . Siswati
. . . Swahili
. . Basaa
. . Bini
. . Dyula
. . Ewe
. . Fulani
. . Ga
. . Gbaya
. . Igbo
. . Luo
. . Mandingo
. . Mende
. . Mossi
. . Nembe
. . Sango
. . Sara
. . Susu
. . Wolof
. . Yoruba
. Afro Asiatic Languages
. . Berber Languages
. . . Kabyle
. . . Riff
. . Chad Languages

... Hausa
.. Semitic Languages
... Amharic
... Arabic
... Hebrew
.. Somali
. American Indian Languages
.. Athapascan Languages
... Apache
... Navajo
.. Aymara
.. Cherokee
.. Choctaw
.. Cree
.. Dakota
... Lakota
.. Guarani
.. Mayan Languages
... Cakchiquel
... Quiche
... Tzeltal
... Tzotzil
... Yucatec
.. Ojibwa
.. Pomo
.. Quechua
.. Salish
.. Uto Aztecan Languages
... Hopi
... Papago
. American Sign Language
. Australian Aboriginal Languages
. Austro Asiatic Languages
.. Cambodian
. Basque
. Burushaski
. Caucasian Languages
. Classical Languages
.. Latin
.. Sanskrit
. Creoles
.. Gullah
.. Haitian Creole
.. Mauritian Creole
. Sierra Leone Creole
. Dialects
.. Black Dialects
.. Nonstandard Dialects
. Regional Dialects
. Social Dialects
. Dravidian Languages
.. Kannada
.. Malayalam
.. Tamil
.. Telugu
. Eskimo Aleut Languages
.. Inupiaq
.. Yupik
. Indo European Languages
.. Afrikaans
.. Albanian
.. Armenian
.. Baltic Languages
... Latvian
... Lithuanian
.. Baluchi
.. Bengali
.. Danish
.. Dutch
.. English
... Business English
... English (Second Language)
.... English for Special Purposes
..... English for Academic Purposes
..... English for Science and
       Technology
..... Vocational English (Second
       Language)
... Middle English
... North American English
... Old English
... Oral English
.. German
... Yiddish
.. Greek
.. Gujarati
.. Hindi
.. Irish
.. Kashmiri
.. Kurdish
.. Marathi
.. Nepali
.. Norwegian

.. Ossetic
.. Pashto
.. Persian
.. Punjabi
.. Romance Languages
... French
... Italian
... Latin
... Portuguese
... Romanian
... Spanish
.. Scots Gaelic
.. Singhalese
.. Slavic Languages
.. Bielorussian
.. Bulgarian
.. Czech
.. Polish
.. Russian
.. Serbocroatian
.. Slovenian
.. Ukrainian
.. Swedish
.. Tajik
.. Urdu
.. Welsh
. Japanese
. Okinawan
. Korean
. Malayo Polynesian Languages
.. Chamorro
.. Hawaiian
.. Indonesian Languages
... Bikol
... Dusun
... Indonesian
... Javanese
... Malagasy
... Malay
... Maranao
... Tagalog
... Visayan
.... Cebuano
... Maori
.. Melanesian Languages
.. Samoan
. Modern Languages
. Pidgins
. Sino Tibetan Languages
.. Burmese
.. Chinese
... Cantonese
... Foochow
... Mandarin Chinese
.. Hmong
.. Lao
.. Thai
.. Tibetan
. Uralic Altaic Languages
.. Finno Ugric Languages
... Cheremis
... Estonian
... Finnish
... Hungarian
... Ostyak
... Vogul
.. Manchu
.. Mongolian Languages
... Buriat
... Dagur
... Mongolian
.. Samoyed Languages
... Yurak
.. Turkic Languages
... Azerbaijani
... Bashkir
... Chuvash
... Kyrgyz
... Tatar
... Turkish
... Uzbek
... Yakut
. Vietnamese

: Language
Languages for Special Purposes
. English for Special Purposes
.. English for Academic Purposes
.. English for Science and Technology
.. Vocational English (Second
   Language)

:: Languages
: Sino Tibetan Languages
Lao

:: Groups
: Indochinese
Laotians

:: Instruction
: Group Instruction
Large Group Instruction

: Reading Materials
Large Type Materials

Lasers

::: Groups
:: Age Groups
: Children
Latchkey Children

:: Groups
: Age Groups
Late Adolescents

: School Registration
Late Registration

:: Individual Characteristics
: Physical Characteristics
Lateral Dominance
. Handedness
.. Left Handed Writer

::: Languages
:: Indo European Languages
: Romance Languages
:: Languages
: Classical Languages
Latin

: Culture
Latin American Culture
. Luso Brazilian Culture
. Puerto Rican Culture

:::: Liberal Arts
::: Sciences
:: Social Sciences
::: Liberal Arts
:: Humanities
: History
Latin American History

::: Liberal Arts
:: Humanities
: Literature
Latin American Literature

: Groups
Latin Americans
. Cubans
. Dominicans
. Haitians
. Maya (People)
. Mexicans
.. Braceros
. Puerto Ricans

:::: Liberal Arts
::: Humanities
:: Literature
: Classical Literature
Latin Literature

::: Languages
:: Indo European Languages
: Baltic Languages
Latvian

:: Occupations
: Service Occupations
Laundry Drycleaning Occupations

Law Enforcement
. Police Action
.. Search and Seizure
. Sentencing

::: Institutions
::: Information Sources
:: Libraries

: Special Libraries
Law Libraries

: Education
Law Related Education

::: Institutions
:: Schools
: Colleges
Law Schools

:::: Groups
::: Students
:: College Students
: Graduate Students
Law Students

: Standards
Laws
. Civil Law
. Constitutional Law
. Criminal Law
. International Law
. School Law

::: Groups
:: Personnel
: Professional Personnel
Lawyers

: Groups
Lay People
. Lay Teachers

:::: Groups
::: Personnel
:: Professional Personnel
: Teachers
:: Groups
: Lay People
Lay Teachers

::::: Liberal Arts
:::: Humanities
::: Fine Arts
:: Visual Arts
: Graphic Arts
Layout (Publications)

::: Disabilities
:: Diseases
: Poisoning
Lead Poisoning

: Groups
Leaders
. Community Leaders
. Youth Leaders

::: Publications
:: Reference Materials
: Guides
Leaders Guides

: Ability
Leadership
. Black Leadership
. Informal Leadership
. Instructional Leadership
. Outdoor Leadership
. Student Leadership

Leadership Qualities

: Responsibility
Leadership Responsibility

: Behavior
Leadership Styles

: Training
Leadership Training

::: Methods
:: Educational Methods
: Teaching Methods
Learner Controlled Instruction

Learning
. Active Learning
. Adult Learning
. Associative Learning
.. Paired Associate Learning

. Aural Learning
. Cooperative Learning
. Discovery Learning
. Discrimination Learning
. Experiential Learning
.. Field Experience Programs
... Supervised Occupational
        Experience (Agriculture)
.. Internship Programs
.. Service Learning
. Incidental Learning
. Intentional Learning
. Lifelong Learning
. Mastery Learning
. Multisensory Learning
. Nonverbal Learning
.. Perceptual Motor Learning
. Observational Learning
. Prior Learning
. Problem Based Learning
. Rote Learning
. Second Language Learning
. Sequential Learning
. Serial Learning
. Symbolic Learning
. Transfer of Training
. Transformative Learning
. Verbal Learning
. Visual Learning

: Activities
Learning Activities
. Study
.. Home Study
... Homework
.. Independent Study

:: Facilities
: Resource Centers
: Facilities
: Educational Facilities
Learning Centers (Classroom)

: Disabilities
Learning Disabilities

:: Background
: Experience
Learning Experience
. Clinical Experience

:: Facilities
: Laboratories
: Facilities
: Educational Facilities
Learning Laboratories
. Language Laboratories

Learning Modalities

:: Educational Media
: Instructional Materials
Learning Modules

: Motivation
Learning Motivation

Learning Plateaus

: Problems
Learning Problems

: Cognitive Processes
Learning Processes
. Behavior Chaining
. Cognitive Mapping
. Concept Formation
. Discovery Processes
. Extinction (Psychology)
. Generalization
.. Stimulus Generalization
. Habituation
. Memorization
. Primacy Effect

: Readiness
Learning Readiness

:: Facilities
: Resource Centers
: Facilities
: Educational Facilities
Learning Resources Centers

. Methods
Learning Strategies
. Reading Strategies

: Theories
Learning Theories
. Constructivism (Learning)

::: Liberal Arts
:: Mathematics
: Statistics
::: Methods
::: Evaluation Methods
:: Data Analysis
: Statistical Analysis
Least Squares Statistics

Leather

Leaves of Absence
. Sabbatical Leaves

::: Methods
:: Educational Methods
: Teaching Methods
Lecture Method

:::: Individual Characteristics
::: Physical Characteristics
:: Lateral Dominance
: Handedness
: Groups
Left Handed Writer

Legal Aid

::: Groups
:: Personnel
: Paraprofessional Personnel
Legal Assistants

: Costs
Legal Costs

:: Education
: Professional Education
Legal Education (Professions)

Legal Education (1977 1986)

: Problems
Legal Problems

: Responsibility
Legal Responsibility
. Trust Responsibility (Government)

::: Liberal Arts
:: Humanities
: Literature
: Literary Genres
Legends

Legislation
. Civil Rights Legislation
. Discriminatory Legislation
. Educational Legislation
.. School Attendance Legislation
. Federal Legislation
. Labor Legislation
. Local Legislation
. Minimum Wage Legislation
. Public Health Legislation
. Drug Legislation
. Recreation Legislation
. State Legislation
.. School Attendance Legislation

:::: Groups
::: Personnel
:: Government Employees
: Public Officials
Legislators

: Education
Leisure Education

Leisure Time

:: Sexuality
: Homosexuality
Lesbianism

:: Standards
: Criteria
Lesson Observation Criteria

Lesson Plans

::: Language
:: Written Language
: Orthographic Symbols
Letters (Alphabet)

:: Communication (Thought Transfer)
: Verbal Communication
Letters (Correspondence)

: Technology
Lexicography

::::: Liberal Arts
:::: Humanities
::: Philosophy
::: Theories
::: Linguistic Theory
:: Semiotics
:: Linguistics
: Descriptive Linguistics
: Semantics
Lexicology

Libel and Slander

Liberal Arts
. Humanities
.. Fine Arts
... Dance
... Music
.... Applied Music
.... Harmony (Music)
.... Jazz
.... Melody
.... Oriental Music
.... Popular Music
.... Rock Music
.... Vocal Music
..... Choral Music
..... Songs
...... Art Song
...... Ballads
...... Hymns
... Theater Arts
.... Acting
.... Choral Speaking
.... Drama
..... Comedy
...... Skits
..... Scripts
..... Soap Operas
..... Tragedy
.... Dramatics
..... Creative Dramatics
.... Opera
.... Pantomime
.... Puppetry
.... Readers Theater
.... Rehearsals (Theater Arts)
.. Visual Arts
... Architecture
... Childrens Art
... Design Crafts
... Drafting
.... Architectural Drafting
.... Engineering Drawing
.... Technical Illustration
... Film Production
... Freehand Drawing
... Graphic Arts
.... Cartography
.... Computer Graphics
.... Engineering Graphics
..... Engineering Drawing
.... Layout (Publications)
... Printing
... Handicrafts
.... Ceramics
.... Painting (Visual Arts)
... Photography
.... Holography
.... Printmaking
... Sculpture
.. History
... African History
... American Indian History
... Ancient History

... Asian History
.... Korean War
.... Vietnam War
.. Black History
.. Constitutional History
.. Diplomatic History
.. Educational History
... Science Education History
.. European History
.. Family History
.. Genealogy
.. Historiography
.. Intellectual History
... Art History
... Literary History
... Journalism History
.. Latin American History
.. Local History
.. Mathematics History
.. Medieval History
.. Middle Eastern History
.. Modern History
.. North American History
... United States History
.... Civil War (United States)
.... Colonial History (United States)
..... Mexican American History
.... Reconstruction Era
.... Revolutionary War (United
        States)
.... State History
.. Oral History
.. Public History
.. Science History
.. Social History
.. World History
... World War I
... World War II
. Literature
.. Adolescent Literature
.. African Literature
.. American Indian Literature
.. Australian Literature
.. Baroque Literature
.. Biblical Literature
.. Black Literature
.. Childrens Literature
.. Classical Literature
... Latin Literature
.. Classics (Literature)
.. Czech Literature
.. Drama
... Comedy
.... Skits
... Scripts
... Soap Operas
... Tragedy
.. Eighteenth Century Literature
.. English Literature
... Old English Literature
.. Fifteenth Century Literature
.. French Literature
.. German Literature
.. Greek Literature
.. Italian Literature
.. Latin American Literature
.. Legends
.. Medieval Literature
.. Nineteenth Century Literature
.. North American Literature
... Canadian Literature
... United States Literature
.... Hispanic American Literature
..... Mexican American Literature
.. Pastoral Literature
.. Poetry
... Epics
... Haiku
... Lyric Poetry
.... Ballads
.... Hymns
.... Odes
.... Sonnets
... Nursery Rhymes
.. Polish Literature
.. Prose
... Fiction
.... Novels
.... Science Fiction
.... Short Stories
... Nonfiction
.... Biographies
..... Autobiographies

. . . . . Chronicles
. . . . Diaries
. . . . . . Dialog Journals
. . . . . . Student Journals
. . . . Essays
. . . Renaissance Literature
. . Russian Literature
. . Seventeenth Century Literature
. . Sixteenth Century Literature
. . Spanish Literature
. . Twentieth Century Literature
. . Victorian Literature
. . Philosophy
. . Aesthetics
. . . Educational Philosophy
. . . Epistemology
. . . Ethics
. . . . Bioethics
. . . Work Ethic
. . . Existentialism
. . . Hermeneutics
. . . Humanism
. . . Logic
. . . . Mathematical Logic
. . . . . Algorithms
. . . . . Mathematical Formulas
. . . . . . Equations (Mathematics)
. . . . Differential Equations
. . . . . Functions (Mathematics)
. . . . . . Polynomials
. . . . . Proof (Mathematics)
. . . . Set Theory
. . . Marxism
. . . Phenomenology
. . . Platonism
. . . Semiotics
. . . . Pragmatics
. . . . Semantics
. . . Lexicology
. . . World Views
. Mathematics
. Algebra
. . Matrices
. . Polynomials
. . Vectors (Mathematics)
. Arithmetic
. . Addition
. . Division
. . Modular Arithmetic
. . Multiplication
. . Subtraction
. Calculus
. Ethnomathematics
. Geometry
. . Analytic Geometry
. . Plane Geometry
. . Polygons
. . Solid Geometry
. . Topology
. Probability
. Statistics
. . Bayesian Statistics
. . Least Squares Statistics
. . Maximum Likelihood Statistics
. . Nonparametric Statistics
. . Sampling
. . . Item Sampling
. . . Statistical Distributions
. . Technical Mathematics
. Trigonometry
. Sciences
. Acoustics
. . Psychoacoustics
. Behavioral Sciences
. . Ethology
. . Psychology
. . . Behaviorism
. . . Child Psychology
. . . Clinical Psychology
. . . Cognitive Psychology
. . . Community Psychology
. . . Counseling Psychology
. . . Developmental Psychology
. . . Educational Psychology
. . . Experimental Psychology
. . . Individual Psychology
. . . Industrial Psychology
. . . Neuropsychology
. . . Psychoacoustics
. . . Psychometrics
. . . Psychopathology
. . . Psychophysiology
. . . School Psychology

. . . Social Psychology
. . . Sport Psychology
. . Sociobiology
. . Sociology
. . . Criminology
. . . Educational Sociology
. . . Rural Sociology
. . . Social Psychology
. Information Science
. . Computer Science
. . . Programming
. . . Library Science
. Natural Sciences
. . Biological Sciences
. . . Anatomy
. . . Biochemistry
. . . Biofeedback
. . . Biology
. . . . Marine Biology
. . . . Microbiology
. . . . Molecular Biology
. . . . Radiation Biology
. . . . Social Biology
. . . Biomedicine
. . . Biophysics
. . . . Biomechanics
. . . . Bionics
. . . . Robotics
. . . Biotechnology
. . . Botany
. . . Cytology
. . . Ecology
. . . Embryology
. . . Ethology
. . . Genetics
. . . . Genetic Engineering
. . . Mycology
. . . Physiology
. . . . Exercise Physiology
. . . . Psychophysiology
. . . . Sociobiology
. . . Zoology
. . . . Entomology
. . . . Ichthyology
. . . . Ornithology
. . . . Primatology
. . Physical Sciences
. . . Astronomy
. . . Chemistry
. . . . Biochemistry
. . . . Geochemistry
. . . . Inorganic Chemistry
. . . . Organic Chemistry
. . . . Physical Chemistry
. . . . . Electrochemistry
. . . . . Stereochemistry
. . . . Crystallography
. . . Earth Science
. . . . Geochemistry
. . . . Geology
. . . . . Mineralogy
. . . . . Paleontology
. . . . . Petrology
. . . . Geophysics
. . . . . Plate Tectonics
. . . . Hydrology
. . . . Meteorology
. . . . Oceanography
. . . . Physical Geography
. . . . Seismology
. . . . Plate Tectonics
. . . Soil Science
. . . Physics
. . . . Biophysics
. . . . Biomechanics
. . . . Bionics
. . . . . Robotics
. . . . Electronics
. . . . . Microelectronics
. . . . Mechanics (Physics)
. . . . . Fluid Mechanics
. . . . . Kinetics
. . . . . . Diffusion (Physics)
. . . . . Quantum Mechanics
. . . . Nuclear Physics
. . . . Optics
. . . . Thermodynamics
. . . . Spectroscopy
. Social Sciences
. . Anthropology
. . . Anthropological Linguistics

. . . Archaeology
. . . Educational Anthropology
. . . Ethnography
. . . Ethnology
. . . . Ethnomathematics
. . Civics
. . Demography
. . . Birth Rate
. . . Employment Patterns
. . . Geographic Distribution
. . . Mortality Rate
. . . Population Distribution
. . . . Ethnic Distribution
. . . . Racial Distribution
. . . Population Growth
. . . Population Trends
. . . . Black Population Trends
. . . Racial Composition
. . . . Racial Balance
. . . Residential Patterns
. . . School Demography
. . . Teacher Distribution
. . . Social Distribution
. . . Urban Demography
. . Economics
. . . Consumer Economics
. . . Econometrics
. . . Educational Economics
. . . . Educational Finance
. . . Labor Economics
. . . Macroeconomics
. . . Microeconomics
. . . Rural Economics
. . Geography
. . . Human Geography
. . . Physical Geography
. . . World Geography
. . Gerontology
. . . Educational Gerontology
. . History
. . . African History
. . . American Indian History
. . . Ancient History
. . . Asian History
. . . . Korean War
. . . . Vietnam War
. . . Black History
. . . Constitutional History
. . . Diplomatic History
. . . Educational History
. . . . Science Education History
. . . European History
. . . Family History
. . . . Genealogy
. . . Historiography
. . . Intellectual History
. . . . Art History
. . . . Literary History
. . . Journalism History
. . . Latin American History
. . . Local History
. . . Mathematics History
. . . Medieval History
. . . Middle Eastern History
. . . Modern History
. . . North American History
. . . United States History
. . . . Civil War (United States)
. . . . Colonial History (United States)
. . . . Mexican American History
. . . . Reconstruction Era
. . . . Revolutionary War (United States)
. . . . State History
. . . Oral History
. . . Public History
. . . Science History
. . . Social History
. . . World History
. . . . World War I
. . . . World War II
. . International Studies
. . Political Science
. . Social Studies
. . Sociology
. . . Criminology
. . . Educational Sociology
. . . Rural Sociology
. . . Social Psychology
. . Topography
. . Space Sciences

Liberalism

: Attitudes
Librarian Attitudes

: : : Behavior
: : Cooperation
: Educational Cooperation
Librarian Teacher Cooperation

: : : Groups
: : Personnel
: Library Personnel
: : : : Groups
: : : Personnel
: Professional Personnel
: Information Scientists
Librarians

: Institutions
: Information Sources
Libraries
. Academic Libraries
. . College Libraries
. Branch Libraries
. Childrens Libraries
. Depository Libraries
. Electronic Libraries
. Public Libraries
. . County Libraries
. . Regional Libraries
. Research Libraries
. School Libraries
. Special Libraries
. . Corporate Libraries
. . Film Libraries
. . Government Libraries
. . . National Libraries
. . . State Libraries
. . Institutional Libraries
. . . Hospital Libraries
. . . Prison Libraries
. . Law Libraries
. . Medical Libraries
. . Science Libraries

: : : : Services
: : : Information Services
: : Library Services
: Library Technical Processes
Library Acquisition
. Library Material Selection

: : : Governance
: : Administration
: Institutional Administration
Library Administration

: : : Groups
: : Personnel
: Library Personnel
: : : Groups
: : Personnel
: Administrators
Library Administrators
. Library Directors

: : : Groups
: : Organizations (Groups)
: Professional Associations
Library Associations

: : Technology
: Automation
Library Automation
. Retrospective Conversion (Library Catalogs)

: : Publications
: Reference Materials
: Publications
: Catalogs
Library Catalogs
. Book Catalogs
. Card Catalogs
. Union Catalogs

: : : Services
: : Information Services
: Library Services
Library Circulation
. Interlibrary Loans

: Development
Library Collection Development
. Weeding (Library)

: Library Materials
Library Collections

: : : Behavior
: : Cooperation
: Institutional Cooperation
Library Cooperation

: Development
Library Development

: : : : Groups
: : : Personnel
: : Library Personnel
: : : : Groups
: : : Personnel
: : Administrators
: Library Administrators
Library Directors

: : : Education
: : Professional Education
: Information Science Education
Library Education

: Equipment
Library Equipment
. Bookmobiles

: Expenditures
Library Expenditures

: : : Services
: : Information Services
: Library Services
: Education
: Extension Education
Library Extension

: Facilities
Library Facilities

: Financial Support
Library Funding

: : : Publications
: : Reference Materials
: Guides
Library Guides

: Instruction
Library Instruction
. Course Integrated Library Instruction

: : Selection
: Media Selection
: : : : : Services
: : : : Information Services
: : : Library Services
: : Library Technical Processes
: Library Acquisition
Library Material Selection

Library Materials
. Library Collections

: : Networks
: Information Networks
Library Networks
. Bibliographic Utilities

: : Organization
: Classification
Library of Congress Classification

: : Groups
: Personnel
Library Personnel
. Librarians
. Library Administrators
. . Library Directors
. Library Technicians
. . Medical Record Technicians

: Planning
Library Planning

: : Policy
: Information Policy
Library Policy

: Research
Library Research

: : Role
: Institutional Role
Library Role

: : : Institutions
: : Schools
: Colleges
Library Schools

: : : Liberal Arts
: : Sciences
: Information Science
Library Science

: : Services
: Information Services
Library Services
. Library Circulation
. Interlibrary Loans
. Library Extension
. Library Technical Processes
. Library Acquisition
. . . Library Material Selection

: : : Ability
: : Skills
: Information Skills
Library Skills

: Standards
Library Standards

: : Data
: Statistical Data
Library Statistics

: : : Methods
: : Evaluation Methods
: Surveys
Library Surveys

: : : Services
: : Information Services
: Library Services
Library Technical Processes
. Library Acquisition
. . Library Material Selection

: : : Groups
: : Personnel
: Library Personnel
Library Technicians
. Medical Record Technicians

: : Measures (Individuals)
: Tests
Licensing Examinations (Professions)

: : Methods
: Evaluation Methods
Life Cycle Costing

: : Background
: Experience
: Change
Life Events

: : Attitudes
: Satisfaction
Life Satisfaction

: Behavior
Life Style

: Learning
Lifelong Learning

: : : Activities
: : Physical Activities
: Athletics
Lifetime Sports

: : Activities
: Physical Activities
Lifting
. Weightlifting

: : : Scientific Concepts
: : Energy
: Radiation
Light

Lighting
. Television Lighting

: Design
Lighting Design
. Flexible Lighting Design

: : Measures (Individuals)
: Rating Scales
: : Measures (Individuals)
: Attitude Measures
Likert Scales

: Groups
Limited English Speaking

: Mathematical Concepts
Limits (Mathematics)

: Mathematical Applications
Linear Programming

: : : Languages
: : African Languages
: Bantu Languages
Lingala

: : : Linguistics
: : Sociolinguistics
: Language Variation
Linguistic Borrowing

: : Theories
: Linguistic Theory
Linguistic Competence

Linguistic Difficulty (Inherent)

Linguistic Input

: : Theories
: Linguistic Theory
Linguistic Performance

: Theories
Linguistic Theory
. Case (Grammar)
. Generative Grammar
. . Transformational Generative
      Grammar
. . . Context Free Grammar
. . . Deep Structure
. . . Kernel Sentences
. . . Sentence Combining
. . . Surface Structure
. Generative Phonology
. Linguistic Competence
. Linguistic Performance
. Semiotics
. . Pragmatics
. . Semantics
. . . Lexicology
. Structural Grammar
. Traditional Grammar

Linguistics
. Anthropological Linguistics
. Applied Linguistics
. Computational Linguistics
. . Machine Translation
. Contrastive Linguistics
. Descriptive Linguistics
. . Grammar
. . . Morphology (Languages)
. . . . Morphemes
. . . . . Affixes
. . . . . . Prefixes (Grammar)
. . . . . . Suffixes
. . . . Negative Forms (Language)
. . . . Plurals
. . . . Tenses (Grammar)
. . . . Morphophonemics
. . . Syntax
. . . . Form Classes (Languages)
. . . . . Adjectives
. . . . . Adverbs
. . . . . Conjunctions
. . . . . Determiners (Languages)

. . . . . Function Words
. . . . . Nouns
. . . . . Prepositions
. . . . . Pronouns
. . . . . Verbs
. . . . Phrase Structure
. . . . Sentence Structure
. . . Semantics
. . . . Lexicology
. Diachronic Linguistics
. . Etymology
. . . Onomastics
. . Glottochronology
. Distinctive Features (Language)
. Mathematical Linguistics
. Metalinguistics
. Neurolinguistics
. Paralinguistics
. Phonology
. . Generative Phonology
. . Phonemics
. . . Phonemes
. . . . Consonants
. . . . Vowels
. . Phonetics
. . . Acoustic Phonetics
. . . Phonics
. . Suprasegmentals
. . . Intonation
. . . Stress (Phonology)
. . Syllables
. Psycholinguistics
. Sociolinguistics
. . Dialect Studies
. . Language Planning
. . . Language Standardization
. . . Language Variation
. . . Creoles
. . . . Gullah
. . . . Haitian Creole
. . . . Mauritian Creole
. . . . Sierra Leone Creole
. . . Dialects
. . . . Black Dialects
. . . . Nonstandard Dialects
. . . . Regional Dialects
. . . . Social Dialects
. . . Language Styles
. . . . Academic Discourse
. . . . Linguistic Borrowing
. . . Pidgins
. Structural Linguistics

: : Groups
: Change Agents
Linking Agents

: : : : Methods
: : : Educational Methods
: : Teaching Methods
: Oral Communication Method
Lipreading

: Language Arts
Listening

: : : : Individual Characteristics
: : : Psychological Characteristics
: : Intelligence
: Comprehension
Listening Comprehension

: : : Measures (Individuals)
: : Tests
: Verbal Tests
Listening Comprehension Tests

: : Groups
: Discussion Groups
Listening Groups

Listening Habits

: : : : Ability
: : : Skills
: : Language Skills
: Audiolingual Skills
Listening Skills

: : : : : Technology
: : : : Communications
: : : Telecommunications
: : : Communication (Thought

Transfer)
: : Computer Mediated Communication
: Electronic Mail
Listservs

Literacy
. Adult Literacy
. Emergent Literacy
. Family Literacy
. . Family English Literacy
. Functional Literacy
. . Functional Reading
. Information Literacy
. Reading
. . Basal Reading
. . Beginning Reading
. . Content Area Reading
. . Corrective Reading
. . Critical Reading
. . Directed Reading Activity
. . Early Reading
. . Functional Reading
. . Independent Reading
. . Individualized Reading
. . Music Reading
. . Oral Reading
. . Reading Aloud to Others
. . Recreational Reading
. . Remedial Reading
. . Silent Reading
. . Speed Reading
. . Story Reading
. . Sustained Silent Reading
. Scientific Literacy
. Workplace Literacy
. Writing (Composition)
. . Abstracting
. . Basic Writing
. . Beginning Writing
. . Childrens Writing
. . Content Area Writing
. . . Writing Across the Curriculum
. . Creative Writing
. . Descriptive Writing
. . Expository Writing
. . Free Writing
. . Freshman Composition
. . Journal Writing
. . Local Color Writing
. . News Writing
. . Notetaking
. . Paragraph Composition
. . Parallelism (Literary)
. . Playwriting
. . Proposal Writing
. . Scholarly Writing
. . Technical Writing
. . Writing for Publication

: Education
Literacy Education

: Criticism
Literary Criticism
. Rhetorical Criticism

Literary Devices
. Characterization
. Dialogs (Literary)
. Figurative Language
. . Allegory
. . Ambiguity
. . Antithesis
. . Imagery
. . Irony
. . Metaphors
. . Puns
. Symbols (Literary)
. Monologs
. Motifs
. Narration

Literary Discrimination (1966 1980)

Literary Genres
. Ballads
. Biographies
. . Autobiographies
. Chronicles
. Diaries
. . Dialog Journals
. . Student Journals
. Epics

. Essays
. Haiku
. Hymns
. Legends
. Novels
. Odes
. Parody
. Satire
. Scripts
. Short Stories
. Skits
. Sonnets
. Tales
. . Fables
. . Fairy Tales

: : : : : Liberal Arts
: : : : Sciences
: : : Social Sciences
: : : : Liberal Arts
: : : Humanities
: : History
: Intellectual History
Literary History

Literary Influences (1969 1980)

Literary Mood (1970 1980)

Literary Perspective (1969 1980)

Literary Styles

: : Liberal Arts
: Humanities
Literature
. Adolescent Literature
. African Literature
. American Indian Literature
. Australian Literature
. Baroque Literature
. Biblical Literature
. Black Literature
. Childrens Literature
. Classical Literature
. . Latin Literature
. Classics (Literature)
. Czech Literature
. Drama
. . Comedy
. . . Skits
. . Scripts
. . Soap Operas
. . Tragedy
. Eighteenth Century Literature
. English Literature
. . Old English Literature
. Fifteenth Century Literature
. French Literature
. German Literature
. Greek Literature
. Italian Literature
. Latin American Literature
. Legends
. Medieval Literature
. Nineteenth Century Literature
. North American Literature
. . Canadian Literature
. . United States Literature
. . . Hispanic American Literature
. . . . Mexican American Literature
. Pastoral Literature
. Poetry
. . Epics
. . Haiku
. . Lyric Poetry
. . . Ballads
. . . Hymns
. . . Odes
. . . Sonnets
. . Nursery Rhymes
. Polish Literature
. Prose
. . Fiction
. . . Novels
. . . Science Fiction
. . . Short Stories
. . Nonfiction
. . Biographies
. . . Autobiographies
. . . Chronicles
. . . Diaries
. . . . Dialog Journals

. . . Student Journals
. . . Essays
. Renaissance Literature
. Russian Literature
. Seventeenth Century Literature
. Sixteenth Century Literature
. Spanish Literature
. Twentieth Century Literature
. Victorian Literature

Literature Appreciation

Literature Guides (1966 1980)

Literature Programs (1966 1980)

: Publications
Literature Reviews

: : : Languages
: : Indo European Languages
: Baltic Languages
Lithuanian

: Animals
Livestock

: : Facilities
: Educational Facilities
Living Learning Centers

: Standards
Living Standards

: Loan Repayment
Loan Default

Loan Repayment
. Loan Default

: Activities
Lobbying

: : Networks
: Computer Networks
Local Area Networks

: : Literacy
: : Language Arts
: Writing (Composition)
Local Color Writing

: : : Groups
: : Organizations (Groups)
: Government (Administrative Body)
Local Government
. City Government

: : : : Liberal Arts
: : : Sciences
: : : Social Sciences
: : : Liberal Arts
: : Humanities
: History
Local History

Local Issues

: Legislation
Local Legislation

: : : Data
: : Statistical Data
: Norms
Local Norms

: : Ability
: Skills
Locational Skills (Social Studies)

: Facilities
Locker Rooms

: : : : Groups
: : : Personnel
: : Nonprofessional Personnel
: Skilled Workers
Locomotive Engineers

: : : Individual Characteristics
: : Psychological Characteristics
: Personality Traits
Locus of Control

: : Symbols (Mathematics)
: Numbers
Logarithms

: : : Liberal Arts
: : Humanities
: Philosophy
Logic
. Mathematical Logic
. . Algorithms
. . Mathematical Formulas
. . . Equations (Mathematics)
. . . . Differential Equations
. . . Functions (Mathematics)
. . . Polynomials
. . Proof (Mathematics)
. . Set Theory

: Cognitive Processes
Logical Thinking
. Deduction
. Induction

: : Psychological Patterns
: Sadness
Loneliness

: Planning
Long Range Planning

: : : Services
: : Human Services
: Health Services
Long Term Care

: : Cognitive Processes
: Memory
Long Term Memory

: : Research
: : Methods
: : Evaluation Methods
: Case Studies
Longitudinal Studies
. Followup Studies
. . Graduate Surveys
. . Vocational Followup

: : : Technology
: : Communications
: Audiovisual Communications
Loop Induction Systems

Love

Low Ability Students (1967 1980)

: Achievement
Low Achievement

: Incidence
: Disabilities
Low Incidence Disabilities

: Income
Low Income

: : Geographic Regions
: Counties
Low Income Counties

: Groups
Low Income Groups

: Geographic Regions
Low Income States

: : Facilities
: Housing
Low Rent Housing
. Public Housing

: Sensory Aids
Low Vision Aids

: : Groups
: Social Class
Lower Class

: : Groups
: Parents
Lower Class Parents

: : Groups
: Students
Lower Class Students

: : Groups
: Social Class
Lower Middle Class

Loyalty Oaths

Lubricants

: : Business
: Industry
Lumber Industry

Luminescence

: : : Research
: : Scientific Research
: Space Exploration
Lunar Research

: : Programs
: Health Programs
Lunch Programs

: : Languages
: African Languages
Luo

: : Culture
: Latin American Culture
Luso Brazilian Culture

: : Behavior
: Social Behavior
: Deception
Lying

: : : : Liberal Arts
: : : Humanities
: : Literature
: Poetry
Lyric Poetry
. Ballads
. Hymns
. Odes
. Sonnets

Lysergic Acid Diethylamide

: : : : : Services
: : : : Information Services
: : : Information Processing
: : Documentation
: Cataloging
Machine Readable Cataloging

: : : : : Groups
: : : : Personnel
: : : Nonprofessional Personnel
: : Skilled Workers
: Machinists
Machine Repairers

: : : : : Groups
: : : : Personnel
: : : Nonprofessional Personnel
: : Skilled Workers
: Machinists
Machine Tool Operators

: Equipment
Machine Tools

: Translation
: : Linguistics
: Computational Linguistics
Machine Translation

: : : Business
: : Industry
: Manufacturing Industry
Machinery Industry

: : : : Groups
: : : Personnel
: : Nonprofessional Personnel
: Skilled Workers
Machinists
. Machine Repairers
. Machine Tool Operators

. Tool and Die Makers

: : : : Liberal Arts
: : : Sciences
: : Social Sciences
: Economics
Macroeconomics

: : Institutions
: Schools
Magnet Schools

: : : : Equipment
: : : Electronic Equipment
: : Computer Peripherals
: Computer Storage Devices
Magnetic Disks
. Floppy Disks

: : : Resources
: : Supplies
: : : Equipment
: Electronic Equipment
: Magnetic Tapes
Magnetic Tape Cassettes
. Audiotape Cassettes
. Videotape Cassettes

: : Resources
: Supplies
: : Equipment
: Electronic Equipment
Magnetic Tapes
. Magnetic Tape Cassettes
. . Audiotape Cassettes
. . Videotape Cassettes

Magnets

: Methods
Magnification Methods

: : : Methods
: : Evaluation Methods
: Surveys
Mail Surveys

: Placement
Mainstreaming

Maintenance
. Equipment Maintenance
. Preservation
. Repair
. . Appliance Repair
. School Maintenance

: Attitudes
Majority Attitudes

: : Groups
: Students
Majors (Students)
. Education Majors

: : : Languages
: : Malayo Polynesian Languages
: Indonesian Languages
Malagasy

: : : Languages
: : Malayo Polynesian Languages
: Indonesian Languages
Malay

: : Languages
: Dravidian Languages
Malayalam

: Languages
Malayo Polynesian Languages
. Chamorro
. Hawaiian
. Indonesian Languages
. . Bikol
. . Dusun
. . Indonesian
. . Javanese
. . Malagasy
. . Malay
. . Maranao
. . Tagalog
. . Visayan

. . . Cebuano
. Maori
. Melanesian Languages
. Samoan

: Groups
Males
. Fathers
. Sons

Malpractice
. Educational Malpractice

Man Machine Systems
. User Friendly Interface

: Management Systems
: : Governance
: Administration
Management by Objectives

: : Development
: Labor Force Development
Management Development

: : : : Methods
: : : Educational Methods
: : Teaching Methods
: Training Methods
: : Activities
: Games
Management Games

: Management Systems
: Information Systems
Management Information Systems
. Decision Support Systems

Management Systems
. Database Management Systems
. Enrollment Management
. Management by Objectives
. Management Information Systems
. . Decision Support Systems
. Total Quality Management

: : Organization
: Administrative Organization
Management Teams

: Occupations
Managerial Occupations

: : Languages
: Uralic Altaic Languages
Manchu

: : : Languages
: : Sino Tibetan Languages
: Chinese
Mandarin Chinese

: : : Education
: : Adult Education
: Continuing Education
Mandatory Continuing Education

: : Status
: Retirement
Mandatory Retirement

: : Languages
: African Languages
Mandingo

: : Educational Media
: Instructional Materials
Manipulative Materials

: : Communication (Thought Transfer)
: Augmentative and Alternative
    Communication
Manual Communication
. Cued Speech
. Finger Spelling
. Sign Language
. . American Sign Language

: Technology
Manufacturing
. Assembly (Manufacturing)
. Computer Assisted Manufacturing
. Mass Production

: Business
: Industry
Manufacturing Industry
. Aerospace Industry
. Cement Industry
. Chemical Industry
. Electronics Industry
. Furniture Industry
. Machinery Industry
. Metal Industry

: : Language Arts
: Handwriting
Manuscript Writing (Handlettering)

: Printed Materials
Manuscripts

: : Languages
: Malayo Polynesian Languages
Maori

: : Groups
: Pacific Islanders
: : Groups
: Ethnic Groups
Maori (People)

: : Ability
: Skills
Map Skills

: Visual Aids
Maps

: : : Languages
: : Malayo Polynesian Languages
: Indonesian Languages
Maranao

: : Languages
: Indo European Languages
Marathi

: Narcotics
Marijuana

: : : : : Liberal Arts
: : : : Sciences
: : : Natural Sciences
: : Biological Sciences
: Biology
Marine Biology

: Education
Marine Education
. Maritime Education

: : : Groups
: : Personnel
: Paraprofessional Personnel
Marine Technicians

Marital Instability

: : Attitudes
: Satisfaction
Marital Satisfaction

: Status
Marital Status

: : Education
: Marine Education
Maritime Education

: Technology
Marketing
. Merchandising
. Retailing
. Salesmanship
. Wholesaling

: : Methods
: Simulation
Markov Processes

: : : Ability
: : Skills
: Psychomotor Skills
Marksmanship

: : Relationship
: Interpersonal Relationship
Marriage
. Intermarriage
. Remarriage

: : Guidance
: Counseling
Marriage Counseling

: : Groups
: Students
Married Students

: Methods
Marxian Analysis

: : : Liberal Arts
: : Humanities
: Philosophy
Marxism

Masculinity

: Technology
: Construction (Process)
Masonry
. Bricklaying

: Instruction
Mass Instruction

Mass Media
. Films
. . Foreign Language Films
. . Instructional Films
. . Kinescope Recordings
. . Single Concept Films
. News Media
. . Editorials
. . Newspapers
. . . Newsletters
. . . School Newspapers
. Radio
. . Educational Radio
. Television
. . Broadcast Television
. . Cable Television
. . Childrens Television
. . Closed Circuit Television
. . Commercial Television
. . Educational Television
. . Interactive Television
. . Public Television

Mass Media Effects

: Role
Mass Media Role

Mass Media Use

: : Technology
: Manufacturing
Mass Production

Master Plans

: : : : Groups
: : : Personnel
: : Professional Personnel
: Teachers
Master Teachers

: Degrees (Academic)
Masters Degrees

: : Programs
: College Programs
Masters Programs

: : : Publications
: : Reports
: Theses
Masters Theses

: Learning
Mastery Learning

: : : Measures (Individuals)
: : Tests
: Criterion Referenced Tests
: : : Measures (Individuals)

: : Tests
: Achievement Tests
Mastery Tests

: Groups
Matched Groups

: Selection
Mate Selection

: Culture
Material Culture

: Development
Material Development
. Computer Software Development
. . Programming
. Test Construction

Mathematical Applications
. Algorithms
. Computation
. . Estimation (Mathematics)
. . Mental Computation
. Linear Programming
. Mathematical Formulas
. . Equations (Mathematics)
. . . Differential Equations
. . Functions (Mathematics)
. . Polynomials
. Word Problems (Mathematics)

: Aptitude
Mathematical Aptitude

Mathematical Concepts
. Geometric Concepts
. . Area
. . Congruence (Mathematics)
. . Orthographic Projection
. . Polygons
. . Vectors (Mathematics)
. . Volume (Mathematics)
. Inequality (Mathematics)
. Limits (Mathematics)
. Number Concepts
. . Modular Arithmetic
. . Place Value
. Patterns in Mathematics
. Properties (Mathematics)

: Enrichment
Mathematical Enrichment

Mathematical Experience (1966 1980)

: : : : : Liberal Arts
: : : : Humanities
: : : Philosophy
: : Logic
: Mathematical Logic
: Mathematical Applications
Mathematical Formulas
. Equations (Mathematics)
. . Differential Equations
. Functions (Mathematics)
. Polynomials

: Linguistics
Mathematical Linguistics

: : : : Liberal Arts
: : : Humanities
: : Philosophy
: Logic
Mathematical Logic
. Algorithms
. Mathematical Formulas
. . Equations (Mathematics)
. . . Differential Equations
. . Functions (Mathematics)
. . Polynomials
. Proof (Mathematics)
. Set Theory

: : : Methods
: : Simulation
: Models
Mathematical Models

: Vocabulary
Mathematical Vocabulary

: : : Groups
: : Personnel
: Scientific Personnel
: : : Groups
: : Personnel
: Professional Personnel
Mathematicians

: Liberal Arts
Mathematics
. Algebra
. . Matrices
. . Polynomials
. . Vectors (Mathematics)
. Arithmetic
. . Addition
. . Division
. . Modular Arithmetic
. . Multiplication
. . Subtraction
. Calculus
. Ethnomathematics
. Geometry
. . Analytic Geometry
. . Plane Geometry
. . . Polygons
. . Solid Geometry
. . Topology
. Probability
. Statistics
. . Bayesian Statistics
. . Least Squares Statistics
. . Maximum Likelihood Statistics
. . Nonparametric Statistics
. . Sampling
. . . Item Sampling
. . Statistical Distributions
. Technical Mathematics
. Trigonometry

: Achievement
Mathematics Achievement

: Activities
Mathematics Activities

: : Psychological Patterns
: Anxiety
Mathematics Anxiety

: Curriculum
Mathematics Curriculum
. College Mathematics
. Elementary School Mathematics
. General Mathematics
. Modern Mathematics
. Secondary School Mathematics

: Education
Mathematics Education

: : : : Liberal Arts
: : : Sciences
: : Social Sciences
: : : Liberal Arts
: : Humanities
: History
Mathematics History

: Instruction
Mathematics Instruction
. Remedial Mathematics

Mathematics Materials

: : Ability
: Skills
Mathematics Skills

: : : : Groups
: : : Personnel
: : Professional Personnel
: Teachers
Mathematics Teachers

: : Measures (Individuals)
: Tests
Mathematics Tests

: : : Liberal Arts
: : Mathematics
: Algebra
Matrices

Matter
. Acids
. Minerals
. . Asbestos
. Polymers
. Sludge
. Wastes
. . Solid Wastes
. . Waste Water
. Water
. . Drinking Water
. . Groundwater
. . Waste Water

Maturation (1967 1980)

: Individual Characteristics
Maturity (Individuals)
. Vocational Maturity

: : Measures (Individuals)
: Tests
Maturity Tests

: : Languages
: : : Linguistics
: : : Sociolinguistics
: : Language Variation
: Creoles
Mauritian Creole

: : : Liberal Arts
: : Mathematics
: Statistics
: : : : Methods
: : : Evaluation Methods
: : Data Analysis
: Statistical Analysis
Maximum Likelihood Statistics

: : Groups
: Latin Americans
: : : Groups
: : Ethnic Groups
: American Indians
Maya (People)

: : Languages
: American Indian Languages
Mayan Languages
. Cakchiquel
. Quiche
. Tzeltal
. Tzotzil
. Yucatec

Measurement
. Achievement Rating
. . Grading
. . . Credit No Credit Grading
. . . Pass Fail Grading
. Cognitive Measurement
. Merit Rating
. Predictive Measurement
. Scoring

: Equipment
Measurement Equipment
. Calorimeters
. Polygraphs
. Potentiometers (Instruments)
. Sound Spectrographs

Measurement Instruments (1966 1980)

: Objectives
Measurement Objectives

: Methods
Measurement Techniques
. Classroom Observation Techniques
. Forced Choice Technique
. Q Methodology
. Scaling
. . Multidimensional Scaling
. Scoring Formulas
. Sociometric Techniques
. Testing
. Adaptive Testing
. . Comparative Testing
. . Computer Assisted Testing
. . Confidence Testing

.. Educational Testing
.. Group Testing
.. Individual Testing
.. Minimum Competency Testing
.. Psychological Testing
.. Teacher Competency Testing

Measures (Individuals)
. Affective Measures
. Attitude Measures
.. Likert Scales
.. Semantic Differential
. Biographical Inventories
. Interest Inventories
. Personality Measures
.. Self Concept Measures
. Projective Measures
.. Association Measures
. Questionnaires
. Rating Scales
.. Behavior Rating Scales
.. Likert Scales
.. Semantic Differential
. Tests
.. Achievement Tests
... Equivalency Tests
... Mastery Tests
... National Competency Tests
.. Aptitude Tests
.. Reading Readiness Tests
... School Readiness Tests
.. Auditory Tests
... Audiometric Tests
.. Cognitive Tests
... Intelligence Tests
... Perception Tests
.... Tactual Visual Tests
.. College Entrance Examinations
.. Creativity Tests
.. Criterion Referenced Tests
.. Mastery Tests
.. Culture Fair Tests
.. Diagnostic Tests
.. Field Tests
.. High Stakes Tests
.. Licensing Examinations
   (Professions)
.. Mathematics Tests
.. Maturity Tests
.. Nonverbal Tests
.. Visual Measures
.. Norm Referenced Tests
.. Objective Tests
... Multiple Choice Tests
.. Occupational Tests
... Work Sample Tests
.. Open Book Tests
.. Performance Tests
.. Physical Fitness Tests
.. Preschool Tests
.. Pretests Posttests
.. Prognostic Tests
.. Science Tests
.. Screening Tests
.. Situational Tests
.. Standardized Tests
.. Teacher Made Tests
.. Timed Tests
.. Verbal Tests
... Essay Tests
... Language Tests
... Listening Comprehension Tests
... Reading Tests
.... Informal Reading Inventories
... Speech Tests
... Writing Tests
.. Vision Tests

: Food
Meat

:: Business
: Industry
Meat Packing Industry

::: Groups
:: Personnel
: Paraprofessional Personnel
Mechanical Design Technicians

: Equipment
Mechanical Equipment

:: Ability
: Skills
Mechanical Skills

::::: Liberal Arts
:::: Sciences
::: Natural Sciences
:: Physical Sciences
: Physics
Mechanics (Physics)
. Fluid Mechanics
. Kinetics
.. Diffusion (Physics)
. Quantum Mechanics

: Technology
Mechanics (Process)
. Auto Mechanics
. Aviation Mechanics
. Refrigeration Mechanics
. Small Engine Mechanics

: Change
Media Adaptation
. Tactile Adaptation

: Research
Media Research
. Journalism Research
. Television Research
. Textbook Research

: Selection
Media Selection
. Computer Software Selection
. Library Material Selection
. Reading Material Selection
. Textbook Selection

::: Groups
:: Personnel
: Specialists
Media Specialists
. Audiovisual Coordinators

:: Theories
: Behavior Theories
Mediation Theory

:::: Groups
::: Personnel
:: Health Personnel
: Allied Health Personnel
Medical Assistants
. Medical Laboratory Assistants

::: Groups
:: Organizations (Groups)
: Professional Associations
Medical Associations

: Evaluation
Medical Care Evaluation

:: Records (Forms)
: Case Records
Medical Case Histories

::: Groups
:: Personnel
: Health Personnel
::: Groups
:: Personnel
: Consultants
Medical Consultants

:: Education
: Professional Education
Medical Education
. Graduate Medical Education
. Nursing Education
. Pharmaceutical Education
. Veterinary Medical Education

: Evaluation
Medical Evaluation
. Auditory Evaluation
. Dental Evaluation
. Physical Examinations
. Speech Evaluation

::::: Groups
:::: Personnel

::: Health Personnel
:: Allied Health Personnel
: Medical Assistants
Medical Laboratory Assistants

::: Institutions
::: Information Sources
:: Libraries
: Special Libraries
Medical Libraries

:::: Groups
::: Personnel
:: Health Personnel
: Allied Health Personnel
::: Groups
:: Personnel
: Administrators
Medical Record Administrators

:::: Groups
::: Personnel
:: Library Personnel
: Library Technicians
::: Groups
:: Personnel
: Health Personnel
: Allied Health Personnel
Medical Record Technicians

: Research
Medical Research

:::::: Groups
::::: Personnel
:::: School Personnel
::::: Groups
:::: Personnel
::: Professional Personnel
:: Faculty
: College Faculty
: Graduate School Faculty
Medical School Faculty

::: Institutions
:: Schools
: Colleges
Medical Schools

::: Services
:: Human Services
: Health Services
Medical Services
. First Aid
.. Cardiopulmonary Resuscitation
. Psychiatric Services

:::: Groups
::: Students
:: College Students
: Graduate Students
Medical Students
. Graduate Medical Students

:::: Groups
::: Personnel
:: Health Personnel
: Allied Health Personnel
Medical Technologists

: Vocabulary
Medical Vocabulary

: Technology
Medicine
. Anesthesiology
. Audiology
. Biomedicine
. Dentistry
. Dietetics
. Electroencephalography
. Epidemiology
. Family Practice (Medicine)
. Geriatrics
. Gynecology
. Internal Medicine
. Neurology
. Nursing
.. Practical Nursing
. Obstetrics
. Oncology
. Ophthalmology
. Osteopathy

. Pathology
.. Plant Pathology
.. Psychopathology
. Speech Language Pathology
. Pediatrics
. Pharmacology
. Pharmacy
. Podiatry
. Preventive Medicine
. Primary Health Care
. Psychiatry
. Sports Medicine
. Surgery
. Toxicology
. Veterinary Medicine

:::: Liberal Arts
::: Sciences
:: Social Sciences
::: Liberal Arts
:: Humanities
: History
Medieval History

::: Liberal Arts
:: Humanities
: Literature
Medieval Literature

:: Cognitive Processes
: Metacognition
Meditation
. Transcendental Meditation

Meetings
. Reunions
. Seminars
. Staff Meetings

:: Languages
: Malayo Polynesian Languages
Melanesian Languages

:::: Liberal Arts
::: Humanities
:: Fine Arts
: Music
Melody

:: Cognitive Processes
: Learning Processes
Memorization

: Cognitive Processes
Memory
. Eidetic Imagery
. Long Term Memory
. Recall (Psychology)
. Reminiscence
. Recognition (Psychology)
.. Pattern Recognition
... Character Recognition
.. Word Recognition
. Retention (Psychology)
. Short Term Memory

:: Languages
: African Languages
Mende

Menstruation

::: Individual Characteristics
:: Psychological Characteristics
: Intelligence
:: Individual Characteristics
: Age
Mental Age

:: Mathematical Applications
: Computation
: Cognitive Processes
Mental Computation

: Disabilities
Mental Disorders
. Emotional Disturbances
.. Psychosomatic Disorders
. Neurosis
.. Posttraumatic Stress Disorder
. Psychosis
.. Echolalia
.. Schizophrenia

: Health
Mental Health

: Clinics
Mental Health Clinics

: : Programs
: Health Programs
Mental Health Programs

: : : Groups
: : Personnel
: Health Personnel
Mental Health Workers
. Psychiatric Aides
. Psychiatrists
. School Psychologists

: Disabilities
Mental Retardation
. Downs Syndrome
. Mild Mental Retardation
. Moderate Mental Retardation
. Severe Mental Retardation

: : : Individual Characteristics
: : Psychological Characteristics
: Personality Traits
Mental Rigidity

: : : : Methods
: : : Simulation
: : Models
: : Groups
: Role Models
Mentors

: : : Standards
: : Specifications
: Computer Software
Menu Driven Software

Merchandise Information

: : Technology
: Marketing
Merchandising

: : Groups
: Vendors
: : Groups
: Personnel
Merchants

: : Change
: Organizational Change
Mergers

: Income
: Expenditures
Merit Pay

: Measurement
Merit Rating

: : : Financial Support
: : Student Financial Aid
: Scholarships
Merit Scholarships
. No Need Scholarships

: : : : Methods
: : : Evaluation Methods
: : Data Analysis
: Statistical Analysis
Meta Analysis

Metabolism
. Blood Circulation
. Heart Rate

: Cognitive Processes
Metacognition
. Meditation
. . Transcendental Meditation

: : : Business
: : Industry
: Manufacturing Industry
Metal Industry

: Technology
Metal Working

. Sheet Metal Work

: Linguistics
Metalinguistics

: : : Groups
: : Personnel
: Paraprofessional Personnel
Metallurgical Technicians

: Technology
Metallurgy

Metals

: : Literary Devices
: : Language
: Figurative Language
Metaphors

: : : : : Liberal Arts
: : : : Sciences
: : : Natural Sciences
: : Physical Sciences
: Earth Science
Meteorology

Methods
. Algorithms
. Branching
. Caseworker Approach
. Change Strategies
. Cloze Procedure
. Concept Mapping
. Counseling Techniques
. Critical Incidents Method
. Critical Path Method
. Delphi Technique
. Desegregation Methods
. . Busing
. Educational Methods
. . Classroom Techniques
. . Educational Strategies
. . Psychoeducational Methods
. . Teaching Methods
. . . Audiolingual Methods
. . . Case Method (Teaching
      Technique)
. . . Clinical Teaching (Health
      Professions)
. . . Community Based Instruction
      (Disabilities)
. . . Conventional Instruction
. . . Creative Teaching
. . . Cross Age Teaching
. . . Demonstrations (Educational)
. . . . Demonstrations (Science)
. . . Diagnostic Teaching
. . . Discussion (Teaching Technique)
. . . Drills (Practice)
. . . . Pattern Drills (Language)
. . . . . Substitution Drills
. . . Experimental Teaching
. . . Grammar Translation Method
. . . Guided Design
. . . Individualized Instruction
. . . Kinesthetic Methods
. . . Kodaly Method
. . . Language Experience Approach
. . . Learner Controlled Instruction
. . . Lecture Method
. . . Montessori Method
. . . Multimedia Instruction
. . . . Audiovisual Instruction
. . . Negative Practice
. . . Oral Communication Method
. . . . Lipreading
. . . Orff Method
. . . Peer Teaching
. . . Precision Teaching
. . . Programmed Instruction
. . . . Computer Assisted Instruction
. . . . . Intelligent Tutoring Systems
. . . . Programmed Tutoring
. . . Reciprocal Teaching
. . . Reggio Emilia Approach
. . . Sight Method
. . . Suggestopedia
. . . Suzuki Method
. . . Telephone Instruction
. . . Thematic Approach
. . . Training Methods
. . . . Management Games

. . . . Microcounseling
. . . . Microteaching
. . . Whole Language Approach
. Evaluation Methods
. . Audience Analysis
. . Benchmarking
. . Case Studies
. . . Cross Sectional Studies
. . . Facility Case Studies
. . . Longitudinal Studies
. . . . Followup Studies
. . . . . Graduate Surveys
. . . . . Vocational Followup
. . Chemical Analysis
. . Comparative Analysis
. . . Educational Status Comparison
. . . Error Analysis (Language)
. . Componential Analysis
. . Content Analysis
. . Cost Effectiveness
. . Data Analysis
. . Data Collection
. . . Sampling
. . . . Item Sampling
. . Data Interpretation
. . . Statistical Inference
. . . . Test Interpretation
. . Statistical Analysis
. . . Analysis of Covariance
. . . Analysis of Variance
. . . Bayesian Statistics
. . . Chi Square
. . . Correlation
. . . . Effect Size
. . . Error of Measurement
. . . Goodness of Fit
. . . Item Analysis
. . . Judgment Analysis Technique
. . . Least Squares Statistics
. . . Maximum Likelihood Statistics
. . . Meta Analysis
. . . Multivariate Analysis
. . . . Cluster Analysis
. . . . Discriminant Analysis
. . . . Factor Analysis
. . . . . Oblique Rotation
. . . . . Orthogonal Rotation
. . . . Multidimensional Scaling
. . . . Path Analysis
. . . Regression (Statistics)
. . . . Multiple Regression Analysis
. . . Robustness (Statistics)
. . . Statistical Distributions
. . . Statistical Inference
. . . Statistical Significance
. . Trend Analysis
. Drug Use Testing
. Environmental Scanning
. Hypothesis Testing
. Input Output Analysis
. Inspection
. Interviews
. . Employment Interviews
. . Field Interviews
. Job Analysis
. Life Cycle Costing
. Need Analysis (Student
    Financial Aid)
. Phonetic Analysis
. Policy Analysis
. Pretesting
. Quality Control
. Readability Formulas
. Scoring Rubrics
. Site Analysis
. Skill Analysis
. Structural Analysis (Linguistics)
. . Discourse Analysis
. . Tagmemic Analysis
. . Structural Analysis (Science)
. Surveys
. . Community Surveys
. . Graduate Surveys
. . Library Surveys
. . Mail Surveys
. . National Surveys
. . Occupational Surveys
. . School Surveys
. . State Surveys
. . Statistical Surveys
. . Student Surveys
. . Teacher Surveys
. . Telephone Surveys

. . . Television Surveys
. . Synthesis
. . Task Analysis
. Fixed Sequence
. Grievance Procedures
. Hermeneutics
. Heuristics
. Holistic Approach
. Gestalt Therapy
. Global Approach
. . Global Education
. . . International Education
. Systems Approach
. . Systems Building
. . . Design Build Approach
. . Whole Language Approach
. Home Visits
. Inquiry
. Insurance
. . Fire Insurance
. . Health Insurance
. . Unemployment Insurance
. . Workers Compensation
. Interdisciplinary Approach
. Job Search Methods
. Laboratory Procedures
. . Chromatography
. . Culturing Techniques
. . Dissection
. Learning Strategies
. . Reading Strategies
. Magnification Methods
. Marxian Analysis
. Measurement Techniques
. . Classroom Observation Techniques
. . Forced Choice Technique
. . Q Methodology
. . Scaling
. . . Multidimensional Scaling
. . Scoring Formulas
. . Sociometric Techniques
. . Testing
. . . Adaptive Testing
. . . Comparative Testing
. . . Computer Assisted Testing
. . . Confidence Testing
. . . Educational Testing
. . . Group Testing
. . . Individual Testing
. . . Minimum Competency Testing
. . . Psychological Testing
. . . Teacher Competency Testing
. Motivation Techniques
. Music Techniques
. Network Analysis
. Nominal Group Technique
. Pacing
. Production Techniques
. Desktop Publishing
. Electronic Publishing
. Film Production
. Photocomposition
. Special Effects
. . Animation
. . Sound Effects
. Television Lighting
. Textbook Publication
. Prompting
. Questioning Techniques
. Research Methodology
. . Interaction Process Analysis
. . Multitrait Multimethod Techniques
. . Protocol Analysis
. . Scientific Methodology
. . Triangulation
. Sequential Approach
. Simulation
. . Computer Simulation
. . . Virtual Reality
. . Markov Processes
. Models
. . Causal Models
. . . Structural Equation Models
. . . Mathematical Models
. . Role Models
. . . Mentors
. . . Student Writing Models
. . . Teaching Models
. . Monte Carlo Methods
. Role Playing
. . Dramatic Play
. Supervisory Methods
. Systems Analysis

. Troubleshooting
. . Debugging (Computers)
. Writing Strategies

: : : Curriculum
: : College Curriculum
: Teacher Education Curriculum
: Curriculum
: Courses
Methods Courses

: Research
Methods Research
. Evaluation Research

: : : : : Groups
: : : : Personnel
: : : School Personnel
: : : : : Groups
: : : : Personnel
: : : Professional Personnel
: : Faculty
: : College Faculty
: Teacher Educators
Methods Teachers

: : : Groups
: : North Americans
: : Groups
: : Ethnic Groups
: Canada Natives
Metis (People)

: Standards
Metric System

: Geographic Regions
Metropolitan Areas
. Suburbs

: Education
Mexican American Education

: : : : : : Liberal Arts
: : : : : Sciences
: : : : Social Sciences
: : : : : Liberal Arts
: : : : Humanities
: : : History
: : North American History
: United States History
Mexican American History

: : : : : : Liberal Arts
: : : : : Humanities
: : : : Literature
: : : North American Literature
: : United States Literature
: Hispanic American Literature
Mexican American Literature

: : : Groups
: : North Americans
: : Hispanic Americans
: : Groups
: Ethnic Groups
Mexican Americans

: : Groups
: Latin Americans
Mexicans
. Braceros

: : : : : Liberal Arts
: : : : Sciences
: : : Natural Sciences
: : Biological Sciences
: Biology
Microbiology

: : : Equipment
: : Electronic Equipment
: Computers
Microcomputers

: : : : Methods
: : : Educational Methods
: : Teaching Methods
: Training Methods
Microcounseling

: : : : Liberal Arts
: : : Sciences

: : Social Sciences
: Economics
Microeconomics

: : : : : : Liberal Arts
: : : : : Sciences
: : : : Natural Sciences
: : : Physical Sciences
: : Physics
: Electronics
Microelectronics

: : Visual Aids
: Microforms
Microfiche

: : Visual Aids
: Microforms
Microfilm
. Computer Output Microfilm

: : Visual Aids
: : Equipment
: Projection Equipment
Microform Readers

: Visual Aids
Microforms
. Microfiche
. Microfilm
. . Computer Output Microfilm

: : Equipment
: Electronic Equipment
: : Equipment
: Audio Equipment
Microphones

: : Technology
: Reprography
Microreproduction

: : Equipment
: Laboratory Equipment
Microscopes

: : : : Methods
: : : Educational Methods
: : Teaching Methods
: Training Methods
Microteaching

: : : Educational Media
: : Instructional Materials
: : : Standards
: : : Specifications
: : Computer Software
: Courseware
: Computer Uses in Education
Microworlds

: : : Groups
: : Age Groups
: Adults
Middle Aged Adults

: : Groups
: Social Class
Middle Class

: Culture
Middle Class Culture

: : Groups
: Parents
Middle Class Parents

: Standards
Middle Class Standards

: : Groups
: Students
Middle Class Students

: : : : Liberal Arts
: : : Sciences
: : Social Sciences
: : : Liberal Arts
: : Humanities
: History
Middle Eastern History

: Curriculum
: Area Studies
Middle Eastern Studies

: : : Languages
: : Indo European Languages
: English
Middle English

: : Facilities
: Housing
Middle Income Housing

: : Governance
: Administration
Middle Management

: : Groups
: Students
Middle School Students

: : : : Groups
: : : Personnel
: : Professional Personnel
: Teachers
Middle School Teachers

: : Institutions
: Schools
Middle Schools

: Change
Midlife Transitions

: : Education
: Adult Education
Migrant Adult Education

: : Groups
: Migrants
: : : Groups
: : Age Groups
: Children
Migrant Children

: Education
Migrant Education

: Employment
Migrant Employment

: : : Services
: : Human Services
: Health Services
Migrant Health Services

: : Facilities
: Housing
Migrant Housing

: Problems
Migrant Problems

: Programs
Migrant Programs

: : : : Services
: : : Human Services
: : Social Services
: Welfare Services
Migrant Welfare Services

: : Groups
: Migrants
: : : : : Groups
: : : : Personnel
: : : Nonprofessional Personnel
: : Unskilled Workers
: : Laborers
: : : Groups
: : : Personnel
: : Agricultural Personnel
: Agricultural Laborers
Migrant Workers

: : Groups
: Youth
: : Groups
: Migrants
Migrant Youth

: Groups
Migrants

. Immigrants
. . Undocumented Immigrants
. Migrant Children
. Migrant Workers
. Migrant Youth
. Nomads
. Refugees
. Transient Children

: Mobility
Migration
. Brain Drain
. Family Mobility
. Immigration
. Migration Patterns
. Relocation
. . Rural Resettlement
. Rural to Urban Migration
. Student Mobility
. Urban to Rural Migration
. Urban to Suburban Migration

: : Mobility
: Migration
Migration Patterns

: Disabilities
Mild Disabilities
. Mild Mental Retardation
. Minimal Brain Dysfunction

: : Disabilities
: Mild Disabilities
: : Disabilities
: Mental Retardation
Mild Mental Retardation

: : Therapy
: Psychotherapy
Milieu Therapy

: Facilities
Military Air Facilities

: : Groups
: Organizations (Groups)
Military Organizations
. Armed Forces

: : : Groups
: : Personnel
: Government Employees
Military Personnel
. Enlisted Personnel
. Officer Personnel

: : Institutions
: Schools
Military Schools

: Curriculum
Military Science

Military Service

: Training
Military Training

: : : : : : Liberal Arts
: : : : : Sciences
: : : : Natural Sciences
: : : Physical Sciences
: : Earth Science
: Geology
Mineralogy

: Matter
Minerals
. Asbestos

: : : Equipment
: : Electronic Equipment
: Computers
Minicomputers

: : Curriculum
: Courses
Minicourses

: : : Disabilities
: : Physical Disabilities
: Neurological Impairments
: : Disabilities

: Mild Disabilities
Minimal Brain Dysfunction

: : Ability
: Skills
: : Ability
: Competence
Minimum Competencies

: : : Methods
: : Measurement Techniques
: Testing
Minimum Competency Testing

: : Income
: : Expenditures
: Wages
Minimum Wage

: Legislation
Minimum Wage Legislation

: Technology
Mining

: : : Groups
: : Age Groups
: Children
Minority Group Children

: Influences
Minority Group Influences

: : : : Groups
: : : Personnel
: : Professional Personnel
: Teachers
Minority Group Teachers

: Groups
Minority Groups

Misassignment of Teachers

Misconceptions

: : : Identification
: : Educational Diagnosis
: Reading Diagnosis
Miscue Analysis

: : : Groups
: : Age Groups
: Children
Missing Children

: : : Publications
: : Reports
: Position Papers
Mission Statements

: : : Groups
: : Tribes
: : : : Groups
: : : Ethnic Groups
: : American Indians
: Choctaw (Tribe)
Mississippi Band of Choctaw (Tribe)

: : Groups
: Age Groups
Mixed Age Grouping

Mnemonics

: : : Facilities
: : Educational Facilities
: Classrooms
Mobile Classrooms

: Clinics
Mobile Clinics

: : : : Services
: : : Human Services
: : Social Services
: Ancillary School Services
Mobile Educational Services

: : Facilities
: Laboratories
Mobile Laboratories

: Mobility
. Educational Mobility
. Migration
. . Brain Drain
. . Family Mobility
. . Immigration
. . Migration Patterns
. . Relocation
. . . Rural Resettlement
. . Rural to Urban Migration
. . Student Mobility
. . Urban to Rural Migration
. . Urban to Suburban Migration
. Occupational Mobility
. . Career Ladders
. . Faculty Mobility
. . Teacher Transfer
. Physical Mobility
. . Visually Impaired Mobility
. Social Mobility

: : Equipment
: Assistive Devices (for Disabled)
Mobility Aids
. Wheelchairs

: Behavior
Modeling (Psychology)

: : Methods
: Simulation
Models
. Causal Models
. . Structural Equation Models
. Mathematical Models
. Role Models
. . Mentors
. Student Writing Models
. Teaching Models

: : : Equipment
: : Electronic Equipment
: Computer Peripherals
Modems

: : Disabilities
: Mental Retardation
Moderate Mental Retardation

: : : : Liberal Arts
: : : Sciences
: : Social Sciences
: : Liberal Arts
: : Humanities
: History
Modern History

: Curriculum
Modern Language Curriculum
. Conversational Language Courses
. FLES
. Intensive Language Courses
. Notional Functional Syllabi

: Languages
Modern Languages

: : Curriculum
: Mathematics Curriculum
Modern Mathematics

Modernism

: : Change
: Social Change
: Development
Modernization

: : Mathematical Concepts
: Number Concepts
: : : Liberal Arts
: : Mathematics
: Arithmetic
Modular Arithmetic

: : Design
: Building Design
Modular Building Design

: : : : : Liberal Arts
: : : : Sciences
: : : Natural Sciences
: : Biological Sciences

: Biology
Molecular Biology

Molecular Structure

Monera

Monetary Systems

: : Governance
: Administration
Money Management

: : : Languages
: : Uralic Altaic Languages
: Mongolian Languages
Mongolian

: : Languages
: Uralic Altaic Languages
Mongolian Languages
. Buriat
. Dagur
. Mongolian

Monolingualism

: Literary Devices
Monologs

: : Methods
: Simulation
Monte Carlo Methods

: : : Methods
: : Educational Methods
: Teaching Methods
Montessori Method

: Psychological Patterns
Moods

Moral Criticism (1969 1980)

: : Development
: Individual Development
Moral Development

Moral Issues

: Values
Moral Values

: Psychological Patterns
Morale
. Teacher Morale

: : : : Linguistics
: : : Descriptive Linguistics
: : Grammar
: Morphology (Languages)
Morphemes
. Affixes
. . Prefixes (Grammar)
. . Suffixes
. Negative Forms (Language)
. Plurals
. Tenses (Grammar)

: : : Linguistics
: : Descriptive Linguistics
: Grammar
Morphology (Languages)
. Morphemes
. . Affixes
. . . Prefixes (Grammar)
. . Suffixes
. . Negative Forms (Language)
. . Plurals
. . Tenses (Grammar)
. Morphophonemics

: : : : Linguistics
: : : Descriptive Linguistics
: : Grammar
: Morphology (Languages)
Morphophonemics

: Incidence
Mortality Rate

: : Languages
: African Languages
Mossi

: : Attitudes
: Parent Attitudes
Mother Attitudes

: : : Groups
: : Family (Sociological Unit)
: One Parent Family
Motherless Family

: : Groups
: Parents
: Groups
: Females
Mothers
. Black Mothers
. Unwed Mothers

: Literary Devices
Motifs

: Scientific Concepts
Motion
. Acceleration (Physics)
. Velocity

Motivation
. Achievement Need
. Learning Motivation
. Reading Motivation
. Self Motivation
. Student Motivation
. Teacher Motivation

: Methods
Motivation Techniques

: : : Development
: : Individual Development
: Physical Development
Motor Development

: : Behavior
: Responses
Motor Reactions
. Eye Movements
. . Eye Fixations
. Pupillary Dilation

: Equipment
Motor Vehicles
. Service Vehicles
. . Bookmobiles
. . School Buses
. Tractors

: : Structural Elements (Construction)
: : Equipment
: Space Dividers
Movable Partitions

: : Education
: Physical Education
Movement Education

: : : Institutions
: : Schools
: Colleges
Multicampus Colleges

: : : Groups
: : Organizations (Groups)
: School Districts
Multicampus Districts

: : Education
: Intergroup Education
Multicultural Education

: : : Educational Media
: : Instructional Materials
: : : Publications
: : : Printed Materials
: : Books
: Textbooks
Multicultural Textbooks

:: : Methods
: : Measurement Techniques
: Scaling
: : : : : Methods
: : : : Evaluation Methods
: : : Data Analysis
: : Statistical Analysis
: Multivariate Analysis
Multidimensional Scaling

: : Groups
: Classes (Groups of Students)
Multigraded Classes

: : Groups
: Classes (Groups of Students)
Multilevel Classes (Second Language Instruction)

Multilingual Materials
. Bilingual Instructional Materials

Multilingualism

: : : Methods
: : Educational Methods
: Teaching Methods
Multimedia Instruction
. Audiovisual Instruction

Multimedia Materials

: : : Measures (Individuals)
: : Tests
: Objective Tests
Multiple Choice Tests

: Disabilities
Multiple Disabilities
. Deaf Blind

: Employment
Multiple Employment

: : : Individual Characteristics
: : Psychological Characteristics
: Intelligence
Multiple Intelligences

: : : : : Methods
: : : : Evaluation Methods
: : : Data Analysis
: : Statistical Analysis
: Regression (Statistics)
Multiple Regression Analysis

: : : Liberal Arts
: : Mathematics
: Arithmetic
Multiplication

: : : Facilities
: : Educational Facilities
: Classrooms
Multipurpose Classrooms

: Groups
Multiracial Persons

: Learning
Multisensory Learning

: : Methods
: Research Methodology
Multitrait Multimethod Techniques

: : Institutions
: Schools
Multiunit Schools

: : : : Methods
: : : Evaluation Methods
: : Data Analysis
: Statistical Analysis
Multivariate Analysis
. Cluster Analysis
. Discriminant Analysis
. Factor Analysis
. . Oblique Rotation
. . Orthogonal Rotation
. Multidimensional Scaling
. Path Analysis

: : Geographic Regions
: Urban Areas
: Community
Municipalities
. Boomtowns
. Small Towns

: : Individual Characteristics
: Physical Characteristics
Muscular Strength

: Musculoskeletal System
Muscular System

Musculoskeletal System
. Muscular System
. Skeletal System

: Facilities
Museums

: : : Liberal Arts
: : Humanities
: Fine Arts
Music
. Applied Music
. Harmony (Music)
. Jazz
. Melody
. Oriental Music
. Popular Music
. Rock Music
. Vocal Music
. . Choral Music
. . Songs
. . . Art Song
. . . Ballads
. . . Hymns

: Activities
Music Activities
. Concerts
. Instrumentation and Orchestration
. Singing

: : Education
: Aesthetic Education
Music Appreciation

: Education
Music Education
. Kodaly Method
. Orff Method
. Suzuki Method

: Facilities
Music Facilities

: : Literacy
: : Language Arts
: Reading
Music Reading

: : : : Groups
: : : Personnel
: : Professional Personnel
: Teachers
Music Teachers

: Methods
Music Techniques

: Theories
Music Theory

: Therapy
Music Therapy

Musical Composition

: Equipment
Musical Instruments
. String Instruments
. Wind Instruments
. . Brass Instruments
. . Woodwind Instruments

: : Groups
: Artists
Musicians

: : Groups
: Religious Cultural Groups
Muslims

Mutual Intelligibility

: : : : Liberal Arts
: : : Sciences
: : Natural Sciences
: Biological Sciences
Mycology

: : : Disabilities
: : Visual Impairments
: Ametropia
Myopia

Mysticism

Mythic Criticism (1969 1980)

Mythology

Narcotics
. Cocaine
. . Crack
. Heroin
. Marijuana
. Sedatives

: Literary Devices
Narration

: : : Measures (Individuals)
: : Tests
: Achievement Tests
National Competency Tests

: Curriculum
National Curriculum
. British National Curriculum

: National Security
National Defense

: : : : Institutions
: : : Information Sources
: : : Libraries
: : Special Libraries
: Government Libraries
National Libraries

: : : Data
: : Statistical Data
: Norms
National Norms

: : Groups
: Organizations (Groups)
National Organizations

: : Facilities
: Parks
National Parks

: Programs
National Programs

National Security
. National Defense

: Standards
National Standards

: : : Methods
: : Evaluation Methods
: Surveys
National Surveys

: : Certification
: Teacher Certification
National Teacher Certification

Nationalism
. Patriotism

: : Instruction
: Humanities Instruction
Native Language Instruction
. English Instruction

: Groups
Native Speakers

. Spanish Speaking

Natural Disasters
. Drought

: : : Resources
: : Natural Resources
: Fuels
: Fossil Fuels
Natural Gas

: : : : Services
: : : Information Services
: : Information Processing
: Data Processing
Natural Language Processing

: Resources
Natural Resources
. Coal
. Fossil Fuels
. Coal
. Gasoline
. Natural Gas
. Oil
. Water Resources
. . Groundwater
. . Rivers

: : Liberal Arts
: Sciences
Natural Sciences
. Biological Sciences
. . Anatomy
. . Biochemistry
. . Biofeedback
. . Biology
. . . Marine Biology
. . . Microbiology
. . . Molecular Biology
. . . Radiation Biology
. . . Social Biology
. . Biomedicine
. . Biophysics
. . . Biomechanics
. . . Bionics
. . . . Robotics
. . Biotechnology
. . Botany
. . Cytology
. . Ecology
. . Embryology
. . Ethology
. . Genetics
. . . Genetic Engineering
. . Mycology
. . Physiology
. . . Exercise Physiology
. . . Psychophysiology
. . Sociobiology
. . Zoology
. . . Entomology
. . . Ichthyology
. . . Ornithology
. . . Primatology
. Physical Sciences
. . Astronomy
. . Chemistry
. . . Biochemistry
. . . Geochemistry
. . . Inorganic Chemistry
. . . Organic Chemistry
. . . Physical Chemistry
. . . . Electrochemistry
. . . Stereochemistry
. . Crystallography
. . Earth Science
. . . Geochemistry
. . . Geology
. . . . Mineralogy
. . . . Paleontology
. . . Petrology
. . . Geophysics
. . . . Plate Tectonics
. . . Hydrology
. . . Meteorology
. . . Oceanography
. . . Physical Geography
. . . Seismology
. . . . Plate Tectonics
. . . Soil Science
. . Physics
. . . Biophysics

. . . . Biomechanics
. . . . Bionics
. . . . . Robotics
. . . . Electronics
. . . . . Microelectronics
. . . Mechanics (Physics)
. . . . Fluid Mechanics
. . . . Kinetics
. . . . . Diffusion (Physics)
. . . . Quantum Mechanics
. . . Nuclear Physics
. . . Optics
. . . Thermodynamics
. . Spectroscopy

Naturalism

: Observation
Naturalistic Observation

: : Facilities
: Resource Centers
Nature Centers

Nature Nurture Controversy

: : : : Languages
: : American Indian Languages
: Athapascan Languages
Navajo

: : Groups
: Tribes
: : : Groups
: : Ethnic Groups
: American Indians
Navajo (Nation)

Navigation
. Navigation (Information Systems)
. Orienteering

: Navigation
Navigation (Information Systems)

: Totalitarianism
: : Social Systems
: Fascism
Nazism

: : Methods
: Evaluation Methods
Need Analysis (Student Financial Aid)

Need Gratification

: Occupations
Needle Trades

Needs
. Community Needs
. Construction Needs
. Educational Needs
. Evaluation Needs
. Family Needs
. Financial Needs
. Health Needs
. Housing Needs
. Individual Needs
. . Childhood Needs
. . Psychological Needs
. . . Achievement Need
. . . Affection
. . . Affiliation Need
. . . . Peer Acceptance
. . . Personal Space
. . . Security (Psychology)
. . . Self Actualization
. . . Status Need
. Information Needs
. Labor Needs
. . Personnel Needs
. Research Needs
. Student Needs
. User Needs (Information)

: Evaluation
Needs Assessment

: Attitudes
Negative Attitudes

: : : : : Linguistics
: : : : Descriptive Linguistics
: : : Grammar
: : Morphology (Languages)
: Morphemes
Negative Forms (Language)

: : : Methods
: : Educational Methods
: Teaching Methods
Negative Practice

: Reinforcement
Negative Reinforcement

Negligence
. Child Neglect

Negotiation Agreements

Negotiation Impasses

Negro Housing (1966 1977)

: Improvement
Neighborhood Improvement

: Social Integration
Neighborhood Integration

: : Institutions
: Schools
Neighborhood Schools

: Community
Neighborhoods

: : Languages
: African Languages
Nembe

Neoclassicism

: : : : : Groups
: : : : Age Groups
: : : Children
: : Young Children
: Infants
Neonates

: : Languages
: Indo European Languages
Nepali

: Methods
Network Analysis

Networks
. Computer Networks
. . Integrated Learning Systems
. . Internet
. . . World Wide Web
. . Local Area Networks
. Information Networks
. . Internet
. . . World Wide Web
. . Library Networks
. . . Bibliographic Utilities
. Social Networks

: Linguistics
Neurolinguistics

: : Disabilities
: Physical Disabilities
Neurological Impairments
. Aphasia
. Cerebral Palsy
. Epilepsy
. Minimal Brain Dysfunction

: : Individual Characteristics
: Physical Characteristics
Neurological Organization
. Brain Hemisphere Functions

: : Technology
: Medicine
Neurology

: : : : Liberal Arts
: : : Sciences
: : Behavioral Sciences

: Psychology
Neuropsychology

: : Disabilities
: Mental Disorders
Neurosis
. Posttraumatic Stress Disorder

: Federalism
New Federalism

: : Technology
: Journalism
New Journalism

: Mass Media
News Media
. Editorials
. Newspapers
. . Newsletters
. . School Newspapers

: : Technology
: Journalism
News Reporting

: : Literacy
: : Language Arts
: Writing (Composition)
: Technology
: Journalism
News Writing

: : : Publications
: : Serials
: : : Mass Media
: : News Media
: Newspapers
Newsletters

: : Publications
: Serials
: : Mass Media
: News Media
Newspapers
. Newsletters
. School Newspapers

: Dreams
Nightmares

: : : Liberal Arts
: : Humanities
: Literature
Nineteenth Century Literature

: : : : Financial Support
: : : Student Financial Aid
: : Scholarships
: Merit Scholarships
No Need Scholarships

: Groups
No Shows

: : : Environment
: : Physical Environment
: Acoustical Environment
Noise (Sound)

: : Groups
: Migrants
Nomads

: Methods
Nominal Group Technique

: Groups
Non English Speaking

: Alphabets
Non Roman Scripts

: Culture
Non Western Civilization

: : Groups
: Classes (Groups of Students)
Nonauthoritarian Classes

: : : Institutions
: : Schools

: Colleges
Noncampus Colleges

: Education
Noncategorical Education

: : : : Groups
: : : Students
: : Secondary School Students
: High School Students
Noncollege Bound Students

: : Curriculum
: Courses
Noncredit Courses

: : Guidance
: Counseling
Nondirective Counseling

: Education
Nondiscriminatory Education

: : : : Liberal Arts
: : : Humanities
: : Literature
: Prose
Nonfiction
. Biographies
. . Autobiographies
. Chronicles
. Diaries
. . Dialog Journals
. . Student Journals
. Essays

: Education
Nonformal Education

: : Groups
: Organizations (Groups)
Nongovernmental Organizations

: : : Organization
: : Classification
: Grouping (Instructional Purposes)
Nongraded Instructional Grouping

: : Evaluation
: Student Evaluation
Nongraded Student Evaluation

: : Responsibility
: Teacher Responsibility
Noninstructional Responsibility

: : Costs
: Student Costs
Noninstructional Student Costs

: : Groups
: Students
Nonmajors

: Geographic Regions
Nonmetropolitan Areas

: : : Liberal Arts
: : Mathematics
: Statistics
Nonparametric Statistics

Nonprint Media
. Audiodisks
. Documentaries
. Exhibits
. . Science Fairs
. Films
. . Foreign Language Films
. . Instructional Films
. . Kinescope Recordings
. . Single Concept Films
. Filmstrips
. Optical Disks
. . Optical Data Disks
. Realia
. Tape Recordings
. . Audiotape Recordings
. . Videotape Recordings
. Transparencies
. Slides
. Videodisks

: : Groups
: Personnel
Nonprofessional Personnel
. Clerical Workers
. . Court Reporters
. . Examiners
. . File Clerks
. . Receptionists
. . Secretaries
. . . School Secretaries
. Sales Workers
. . Auto Parts Clerks
. Semiskilled Workers
. . Animal Caretakers
. . Boat Operators
. . Grounds Keepers
. . Nursery Workers (Horticulture)
. . Sewing Machine Operators
. Service Workers
. . Attendants
. . Barbers
. . Cooks
. . Emergency Squad Personnel
. . . Emergency Medical Technicians
. . Fire Fighters
. . Household Workers
. . . Home Health Aides
. . Housekeepers
. . Housing Management Aides
. . Waiters and Waitresses
. Skilled Workers
. . Auto Body Repairers
. . Craft Workers
. . Electricians
. . Floor Layers
. . Glaziers
. . Locomotive Engineers
. . Machinists
. . Machine Repairers
. . . Machine Tool Operators
. . . Tool and Die Makers
. . Sign Painters
. . Television Radio Repairers
. . Watchmakers
. Unskilled Workers
. Laborers
. . Agricultural Laborers
. . . Migrant Workers
. . . . Seasonal Laborers
. . . Auxiliary Laborers

: : Groups
: Organizations (Groups)
Nonprofit Organizations

: : : Groups
: : Ethnic Groups
: American Indians
Nonreservation American Indians
. Rural American Indians
. Urban American Indians

: Programs
Nonschool Educational Programs

: : Languages
: : : : Linguistics
: : : Sociolinguistics
: : Language Variation
: Dialects
Nonstandard Dialects

: : : : Groups
: : : Personnel
: : School Personnel
: : : : Groups
: : : Personnel
: : Professional Personnel
: Faculty
Nontenured Faculty

: Education
Nontraditional Education

: Occupations
Nontraditional Occupations

: : Groups
: Students
Nontraditional Students

: Ability
Nonverbal Ability

: Communication (Thought Transfer)
Nonverbal Communication
. Body Language
. Eye Contact
. Facial Expressions

: Learning
Nonverbal Learning
. Perceptual Motor Learning

: : Measures (Individuals)
: Tests
Nonverbal Tests
. Visual Measures

: : Measures (Individuals)
: Tests
Norm Referenced Tests

Normalization (Disabilities)
. Deinstitutionalization (of Disabled)

: : Data
: Statistical Data
Norms
. Local Norms
. National Norms
. State Norms
. Test Norms

: Culture
North American Culture
. Hispanic American Culture
. Japanese American Culture

: : : Languages
: : Indo European Languages
: English
North American English

: : : : Liberal Arts
: : : Sciences
: : Social Sciences
: : : Liberal Arts
: : Humanities
: History
North American History
. United States History
. . Civil War (United States)
. . Colonial History (United States)
. . Mexican American History
. . Reconstruction Era
. . Revolutionary War (United States)
. . State History

: : : Liberal Arts
: : Humanities
: Literature
North American Literature
. Canadian Literature
. United States Literature
. Hispanic American Literature
. . Mexican American Literature

: Groups
North Americans
. Alaska Natives
. Anglo Americans
. Asian Americans
. . Asian American Students
. . Chinese Americans
. . Filipino Americans
. . Japanese Americans
. . Korean Americans
. Canada Natives
. . Metis (People)
. French Canadians
. Greek Americans
. Hispanic Americans
. . Hispanic American Students
. . Mexican Americans
. . Portuguese Americans
. . Spanish Americans
. Italian Americans
. Pacific Americans
. . Hawaiians
. . Samoan Americans
. Polish Americans

Northern Schools (1966 1980)

: : Languages
: Indo European Languages
Norwegian

: : Literacy
: Language Arts
: Writing (Composition)
Notetaking

: : Curriculum
: Modern Language Curriculum
Notional Functional Syllabi

: : : : : Linguistics
: : : : Descriptive Linguistics
: : : Grammar
: : Syntax
: Form Classes (Languages)
Nouns

: Literary Genres
: : : : : Liberal Arts
: : : : Humanities
: : : Literature
: : Prose
: Fiction
Novels

Novelty (Stimulus Dimension)

: : : Scientific Concepts
: : Energy
: Radiation
Nuclear Energy

: : Groups
: Family (Sociological Unit)
Nuclear Family

: : : : : Liberal Arts
: : : : Sciences
: : : Natural Sciences
: : Physical Sciences
: Physics
Nuclear Physics

: : : Groups
: : Personnel
: Paraprofessional Personnel
Nuclear Power Plant Technicians

: Facilities
Nuclear Power Plants

: : Technology
: Power Technology
Nuclear Technology

: : Conflict
: War
Nuclear Warfare

: Weapons
Nuclear Weapons

Nucleic Acids
. DNA
. RNA

: Mathematical Concepts
Number Concepts
. Modular Arithmetic
. Place Value

: : Symbols (Mathematics)
: Numbers
Number Systems

: Symbols (Mathematics)
Numbers
. Logarithms
. Number Systems
. Rational Numbers
. . Fractions
. . . Decimal Fractions
. . Integers
. . . Prime Numbers
. . . Whole Numbers
. Reciprocals (Mathematics)

Numeracy

: : Information Sources
: Data
: Databases
Numeric Databases

Numerical Control

: : Groups
: Females
Nuns

: : : : Groups
: : : Personnel
: : Professional Personnel
: : : : Groups
: : : Personnel
: : Health Personnel
: Nurses
Nurse Practitioners

: Facilities
Nurseries (Horticulture)

: : : : Liberal Arts
: : : Humanities
: : Literature
: Poetry
Nursery Rhymes

: : Institutions
: Schools
Nursery Schools

: : : : Groups
: : : Personnel
: : Nonprofessional Personnel
: Semiskilled Workers
Nursery Workers (Horticulture)

: : : Groups
: : Personnel
: Professional Personnel
: : : Groups
: : Personnel
: Health Personnel
Nurses
. Nurse Practitioners
. School Nurses

: : : : Groups
: : : Personnel
: : Health Personnel
: Allied Health Personnel
Nurses Aides

: : Technology
: Medicine
Nursing
. Practical Nursing

: : : Education
: : Professional Education
: Medical Education
Nursing Education

: : Institutions
: Residential Institutions
: : Facilities
: Health Facilities
Nursing Homes

: Research
Nursing Research

Nutrition
. Breastfeeding

: Instruction
Nutrition Instruction

: : Behavior
: Social Behavior
: : Behavior
: : Cooperation
: Compliance (Psychology)
Obedience

: : Disabilities
: Diseases
: : : Individual Characteristics
: : Physical Characteristics

: Body Weight
: : : Individual Characteristics
: : Physical Characteristics
: Body Composition
Obesity

: : : Ability
: : : Skills
: Psychomotor Skills
Object Manipulation

: Fundamental Concepts
Object Permanence

: : Measures (Individuals)
: Tests
Objective Tests
. Multiple Choice Tests

Objectives
. Behavioral Objectives
. . Affective Objectives
. . Cognitive Objectives
. . Psychomotor Objectives
. Course Objectives
. Educational Objectives
. Guidance Objectives
. . Counseling Objectives
. Measurement Objectives
. Organizational Objectives
. . Institutional Mission
. Student Educational Objectives
. Training Objectives

Objectivity

: : : : : Methods
: : : : : Evaluation Methods
: : : : Data Analysis
: : : Statistical Analysis
: : Multivariate Analysis
: Factor Analysis
Oblique Rotation

Obscenity

Observation
. Naturalistic Observation
. Participant Observation
. School Visitation

: Learning
Observational Learning

Obsolescence
. Building Obsolescence
. Skill Obsolescence

: : Technology
: Medicine
Obstetrics

: Aspiration
Occupational Aspiration

Occupational Clusters

: : Disabilities
: Diseases
Occupational Diseases

: : Education
: Vocational Education
Occupational Home Economics

Occupational Information

: Mobility
Occupational Mobility
. Career Ladders
. Faculty Mobility
. Teacher Transfer

: Safety
: Health
Occupational Safety and Health

: : : Opportunities
: : : Employment Opportunities
: : : Civil Liberties
: : Civil Rights
: Equal Opportunities (Jobs)
Occupational Segregation

: : Methods
: : Evaluation Methods
: Surveys
Occupational Surveys

: : Measures (Individuals)
: Tests
Occupational Tests
. Work Sample Tests

: : : : Groups
: : : Personnel
: : Professional Personnel
: : : : : Groups
: : : : Personnel
: : : Health Personnel
: : Allied Health Personnel
: Therapists
Occupational Therapists

: Therapy
Occupational Therapy

: : : : Groups
: : : Personnel
: : Health Personnel
: Allied Health Personnel
Occupational Therapy Assistants

Occupations
. Agricultural Occupations
. . Farm Occupations
. . Off Farm Agricultural Occupations
. . . Agricultural Chemical Occupations
. . . Agricultural Machinery
        Occupations
. . . Agricultural Supply Occupations
. . . Crop Processing Occupations
. . . Food Processing Occupations
. . . Ornamental Horticulture
        Occupations
. Blue Collar Occupations
. Building Trades
. Clerical Occupations
. Data Processing Occupations
. Demand Occupations
. . Emerging Occupations
. Electrical Occupations
. Energy Occupations
. Finance Occupations
. Forestry Occupations
. Health Occupations
. . Allied Health Occupations
. Insurance Occupations
. Managerial Occupations
. Needle Trades
. Nontraditional Occupations
. Office Occupations
. Professional Occupations
. . Teaching (Occupation)
. . . Team Teaching
. . . Urban Teaching
. Public Service Occupations
. Real Estate Occupations
. Sales Occupations
. Semiskilled Occupations
. Service Occupations
. . Child Care Occupations
. . Hospitality Occupations
. . Laundry Drycleaning Occupations
. Skilled Occupations
. Technical Occupations
. Unskilled Occupations
. White Collar Occupations

: : Technology
: Engineering
Ocean Engineering

: : : : : Liberal Arts
: : : : Sciences
: : : Natural Sciences
: : Physical Sciences
: Earth Science
Oceanography

: : : : : Liberal Arts
: : : : Humanities
: : : Literature
: : Poetry
: Lyric Poetry
: Literary Genres
Odes

: : Facilities
: Educational Facilities
Off Campus Facilities

: : Occupations
: Agricultural Occupations
Off Farm Agricultural Occupations
. Agricultural Chemical Occupations
. Agricultural Machinery Occupations
. Agricultural Supply Occupations
. Crop Processing Occupations
. Food Processing Occupations
. Ornamental Horticulture Occupations

: : Training
: Job Training
Off the Job Training

: : Technology
: Automation
Office Automation

: Equipment
Office Machines

: : Governance
: Administration
Office Management

: Occupations
Office Occupations

: : : Education
: : Vocational Education
: Business Education
Office Occupations Education

: : : Curriculum
: : Courses
: Practicums
Office Practice

: : : : Groups
: : : Personnel
: : Government Employees
: Military Personnel
Officer Personnel

: Facilities
Offices (Facilities)

: Language
Official Languages

: : : : Groups
: : : Tribes
: : : : Groups
: : : : Ethnic Groups
: : : American Indians
: : Sioux (Tribe)
: Lakota (Tribe)
Oglala Sioux (Tribe)

: Resources
: Natural Resources
Oil

: : Languages
: American Indian Languages
Ojibwa

: : Languages
: Japanese
Okinawan

: : : Languages
: : Indo European Languages
: English
Old English

: : : : Liberal Arts
: : : Humanities
: : Literature
: English Literature
Old English Literature

: : : : Groups
: : : Age Groups
: : Adults
: Older Adults
Old Old Adults

: : : Groups
: : Age Groups
: Adults
Older Adults
. Frail Elderly
. Old Old Adults
. Young Old Adults

: : Groups
: Personnel
Older Workers

: : Activities
: Games
: : : Activities
: : Physical Activities
: Athletics
Olympic Games

: : Groups
: Personnel
Ombudsmen

: : : Groups
: : Students
: College Students
On Campus Students

: : Training
: Job Training
On the Job Training
. Apprenticeships

: : Technology
: Medicine
Oncology

: : Groups
: Family (Sociological Unit)
One Parent Family
. Fatherless Family
. Motherless Family

: : : Institutions
: : Schools
: Small Schools
One Teacher Schools

: Online Systems
: : Information Sources
: : Data
: Databases
: : Publications
: Catalogs
Online Catalogs

: : : : Services
: : : Information Services
: : Information Processing
: Information Retrieval
Online Searching

Online Systems
. Integrated Library Systems
. Interactive Video
. Online Catalogs

: : Groups
: Vendors
: : Groups
: Organizations (Groups)
Online Vendors

: : : Linguistics
: : Diachronic Linguistics
: Etymology
Onomastics

: : Visual Aids
: : Equipment
: Projection Equipment
Opaque Projectors

: : Measures (Individuals)
: Tests
Open Book Tests

: Education
Open Education

: Admission (School)
Open Enrollment

:: Institutions
: Schools
Open Plan Schools

:::: Institutions
::: Schools
:: Colleges
: Universities
Open Universities

:::: Liberal Arts
::: Humanities
:: Fine Arts
: Theater Arts
Opera

: Conditioning
Operant Conditioning
. Verbal Operant Conditioning

:: Technology
: Engineering
Operating Engineering

: Expenditures
Operating Expenses

: Research
Operations Research
. Game Theory

:: Technology
: Medicine
Ophthalmology

:: Publications
: Reports
Opinion Papers

: Attitudes
Opinions
. Press Opinion
. Public Opinion

Opportunities
. Cultural Opportunities
. Economic Opportunities
. Educational Opportunities
.. Access to Education
. Employment Opportunities
.. Equal Opportunities (Jobs)
... Occupational Segregation
. Housing Opportunities
. Research Opportunities
. Youth Opportunities

:: Nonprint Media
::: Equipment
:: Electronic Equipment
: Optical Disks
Optical Data Disks

: Nonprint Media
:: Equipment
: Electronic Equipment
Optical Disks
. Optical Data Disks

:::: Equipment
::: Electronic Equipment
:: Computer Peripherals
: Input Output Devices
Optical Scanners

::::: Liberal Arts
:::: Sciences
::: Natural Sciences
:: Physical Sciences
: Physics
Optics

::: Groups
:: Personnel
: Professional Personnel
:::: Groups
::: Personnel
:: Health Personnel
: Allied Health Personnel
Optometrists

: Technology
Optometry

::: Methods
:: Educational Methods
: Teaching Methods
Oral Communication Method
. Lipreading

::: Languages
:: Indo European Languages
: English
Oral English

:::: Liberal Arts
::: Sciences
:: Social Sciences
:: Liberal Arts
:: Humanities
: History
Oral History

:: Communication (Thought Transfer)
: Speech Communication
Oral Interpretation

: Language
Oral Language

:: Literacy
:: Language Arts
: Reading
Oral Reading

: Therapy
Oral Rehydration Therapy

: Culture
Oral Tradition

Orchestras

::: Methods
:: Educational Methods
: Teaching Methods
: Education
: Music Education
Orff Method

::::: Liberal Arts
:::: Sciences
::: Natural Sciences
:: Physical Sciences
: Chemistry
Organic Chemistry

Organization
. Administrative Organization
.. Centralization
.. Decentralization
.. Departments
... English Departments
... Science Departments
... State Departments of Education
.. Management Teams
.. Participative Decision Making
. Bureaucracy
. Class Organization
. Classification
.. Cluster Grouping
.. Codification
.. Coding
.. Dewey Decimal Classification
.. Discourse Modes
.. Grouping (Instructional Purposes)
... Heterogeneous Grouping
... Homogeneous Grouping
.... Ability Grouping
... Nongraded Instructional Grouping
.. Labeling (of Persons)
.. Language Classification
... Language Typology
.. Library of Congress Classification
.. Space Classification
.. Universal Decimal Classification
. Course Organization
.. Course Content
. Furniture Arrangement
. Group Structure
.. Family Structure
... Birth Order
.... First Born
. Governmental Structure
. Horizontal Organization
. Industrial Structure
. Informal Organization

. Power Structure
. Pyramid Organization
. School District Reorganization
. School Organization
.. House Plan
... Career Academies
. School Restructuring
. Social Structure
.. Social Stratification
. Vertical Organization

Organization Size (Groups)
. School District Size

: Change
Organizational Change
. Mergers

: Environment
Organizational Climate

: Communication (Thought Transfer)
Organizational Communication
. Business Communication
.. Business Correspondence
. Interschool Communication

: Development
Organizational Development

Organizational Effectiveness
. School Effectiveness

: Objectives
Organizational Objectives
. Institutional Mission

:: Theories
: Social Theories
Organizational Theories

: Groups
Organizations (Groups)
. Agencies
.. Accrediting Agencies
.. Private Agencies
.. Public Agencies
... Planning Commissions
... State Agencies
.... State Departments of Education
.... State Licensing Boards
.. Social Agencies
... Welfare Agencies
.. Urban Renewal Agencies
.. Voluntary Agencies
.. Youth Agencies
. Alumni Associations
. Bibliographic Utilities
. Black Organizations
. Blue Ribbon Commissions
. College Governing Councils
. Community Organizations
.. Citizens Councils
. Consortia
. Cooperatives
. Corporations
. Database Producers
. Faculty Organizations
. Fraternities
. Governing Boards
.. Boards of Education
... State Boards of Education
. Government (Administrative Body)
.. Federal Government
.. Local Government
... City Government
.. State Government
.. Student Government
.. Tribal Government
. Health Maintenance Organizations
. Honor Societies
. International Organizations
. Military Organizations
.. Armed Forces
. National Organizations
. Nongovernmental Organizations
. Nonprofit Organizations
. Online Vendors
. Parent Associations
. Political Parties
. Professional Associations
.. Library Associations
.. Medical Associations

.. Teacher Associations
. Religious Organizations
. Research Coordinating Units
. School Districts
.. County School Districts
.. Multicampus Districts
. Segregationist Organizations
. Social Organizations
.. Sororities
. Student Organizations
.. Student Government
.. Student Unions
. Unions

:::: Liberal Arts
::: Humanities
:: Fine Arts
: Music
Oriental Music

Orientation
. Goal Orientation
. School Orientation
. Sexual Orientation
. Staff Orientation
. Teacher Orientation
.. Beginning Teacher Induction

Orientation Materials

: Navigation
::: Activities
:: Physical Activities
: Athletics
Orienteering

::: Technology
:: Agriculture
: Horticulture
Ornamental Horticulture
. Floriculture
. Landscaping
. Turf Management

::: Occupations
:: Agricultural Occupations
: Off Farm Agricultural Occupations
Ornamental Horticulture Occupations

::::: Liberal Arts
:::: Sciences
::: Natural Sciences
:: Biological Sciences
: Zoology
Ornithology

:::::: Methods
::::: Evaluation Methods
:::: Data Analysis
::: Statistical Analysis
:: Multivariate Analysis
: Factor Analysis
Orthogonal Rotation

:: Mathematical Concepts
: Geometric Concepts
Orthographic Projection

:: Language
: Written Language
Orthographic Symbols
. Diacritical Marking
. Letters (Alphabet)
. Phonetic Transcription

:: Languages
: Indo European Languages
Ossetic

:: Technology
: Medicine
Osteopathy

::: Languages
:: Uralic Altaic Languages
: Finno Ugric Languages
Ostyak

:: Disabilities
: Diseases
Otitis Media

: : Groups
: Youth
Out of School Youth

: : : Groups
: : Students
: College Students
Out of State Students

: Education
Outcome Based Education

Outcomes of Education
. College Outcomes Assessment
. Educational Benefits

Outcomes of Treatment

: Activities
Outdoor Activities

: Education
Outdoor Education
. Adventure Education

: : Ability
: Leadership
Outdoor Leadership

: Language Arts
Outlining (Discourse)

: : : Services
: : Human Services
: Employment Services
Outplacement Services (Employment)

: Programs
Outreach Programs

: Achievement
Overachievement

: : Visual Aids
: : Equipment
: Projection Equipment
Overhead Projectors

Overpopulation

: Employment
Overseas Employment

: : Behavior
: Responses
Overt Response

Overtime

Ownership
. Intellectual Property
. . Copyrights
. . Patents
. Real Estate

: Chemical Reactions
Oxidation

: : Groups
: Pacific Islanders
: Groups
: North Americans
Pacific Americans
. Hawaiians
. Samoan Americans

: Groups
Pacific Islanders
. Maori (People)
. Pacific Americans
. . Hawaiians
. . Samoan Americans

: Methods
Pacing

Pain

: Industrial Arts
Painting (Industrial Arts)

: : : : Liberal Arts
: : : Humanities

: : Fine Arts
: Visual Arts
Painting (Visual Arts)

: : Learning
: Associative Learning
Paired Associate Learning

: : : : : Liberal Arts
: : : : Sciences
: : : Natural Sciences
: : : Physical Sciences
: : Earth Science
: Geology
Paleontology

: Publications
: Printed Materials
Pamphlets

: : : : Liberal Arts
: : : Humanities
: : Fine Arts
: Theater Arts
Pantomime

: : : Languages
: : American Indian Languages
: Uto Aztecan Languages
Papago

Paper (Material)

: : Publications
: : Printed Materials
: Books
Paperback Books

Paradox

: : Literacy
: : Language Arts
: Writing (Composition)
Paragraph Composition

: Language Patterns
Paragraphs
. Sentences
. . Kernel Sentences

: Linguistics
Paralinguistics

: : Literacy
: : Language Arts
: Writing (Composition)
Parallelism (Literary)

: Behavior
Paranoid Behavior

: : Groups
: Personnel
Paraprofessional Personnel
. Agricultural Technicians
. Chemical Technicians
. Electronic Technicians
. Engineering Technicians
. . Highway Engineering Aides
. Environmental Technicians
. Forestry Aides
. Housing Management Aides
. Instrumentation Technicians
. Legal Assistants
. Marine Technicians
. Mechanical Design Technicians
. Metallurgical Technicians
. Nuclear Power Plant Technicians
. Paraprofessional School Personnel
. . School Aides
. . Teacher Aides
. . . Bilingual Teacher Aides
. Production Technicians
. Radiographers
. Veterinary Assistants
. Visiting Homemakers

: : : Groups
: : Personnel
: School Personnel
: : : Groups
: : Personnel

: Paraprofessional Personnel
Paraprofessional School Personnel
. School Aides
. Teacher Aides
. . Bilingual Teacher Aides

: Aspiration
Parent Aspiration

: : Groups
: Organizations (Groups)
Parent Associations

: Attitudes
Parent Attitudes
. Father Attitudes
. Mother Attitudes

: Background
Parent Background

: : : Relationship
: : Interpersonal Relationship
: Family Relationship
Parent Child Relationship
. Parent Student Relationship

: Conferences
Parent Conferences

: : Guidance
: Counseling
Parent Counseling

: : Education
: Adult Education
Parent Education

: Empowerment
Parent Empowerment

: : Financial Support
: Student Financial Aid
Parent Financial Contribution

Parent Grievances

: Influences
Parent Influence

Parent Materials

: : Behavior
: Participation
Parent Participation

: Responsibility
Parent Responsibility

: Civil Liberties
Parent Rights

: Role
Parent Role
. Parents as Teachers

: : Relationship
: Family School Relationship
Parent School Relationship

: : : : Relationship
: : : Interpersonal Relationship
: : Family Relationship
: Parent Child Relationship
Parent Student Relationship

: Conferences
Parent Teacher Conferences

: : : Behavior
: : Cooperation
: Educational Cooperation
Parent Teacher Cooperation

: Workshops
Parent Workshops

: : Education
: Family Life Education
Parenthood Education

: : Ability
: Skills
Parenting Skills

: Groups
Parents
. Adoptive Parents
. Biological Parents
. Employed Parents
. Fathers
. Grandparents
. Lower Class Parents
. Middle Class Parents
. Mothers
. . Black Mothers
. . Unwed Mothers
. Parents as Teachers
. Parents with Disabilities

: : Groups
: Parents
: : Role
: Parent Role
Parents as Teachers

: : Groups
: Parents
Parents with Disabilities

: Design
Park Design

Parking Controls

: Facilities
Parking Facilities

: Facilities
Parks
. National Parks

: Standards
Parliamentary Procedures

: : : Institutions
: : Schools
: Private Schools
Parochial Schools
. Catholic Schools

: Literary Genres
Parody

: : : Groups
: : Personnel
: Caseworkers
Parole Officers

: Employment
Part Time Employment
. Job Sharing

: : : : Groups
: : : Personnel
: : School Personnel
: : : : Groups
: : : Personnel
: Professional Personnel
: Faculty
Part Time Faculty
. Partnership Teachers

: : : : Groups
: : : Personnel
: : Agricultural Personnel
: Farmers
Part Time Farmers

: : Groups
: Students
Part Time Students

: : Disabilities
: Hearing Impairments
Partial Hearing

: : Disabilities
: Visual Impairments
Partial Vision

Participant Characteristics

: Observation
Participant Observation

: : Attitudes
: Satisfaction
Participant Satisfaction

: Behavior
Participation
. Audience Participation
. Citizen Participation
. Community Involvement
. Family Involvement
. Parent Participation
. School Involvement
. Student Participation
. Teacher Participation

: : Cognitive Processes
: Decision Making
: Organization
: Administrative Organization
Participative Decision Making

: Research
Participatory Research

: : : : : Groups
: : : : Personnel
: : : School Personnel
: : : : Groups
: : : : Personnel
: : : Professional Personnel
: : Faculty
: Part Time Faculty
Partnership Teachers

: : : Behavior
: : Cooperation
: Educational Cooperation
Partnerships in Education

: : Languages
: Indo European Languages
Pashto

: : : Measurement
: : Achievement Rating
: Grading
Pass Fail Grading

: : : Liberal Arts
: : Humanities
: Literature
Pastoral Literature

: : Ownership
: Intellectual Property
Patents

: : : : : Methods
: : : : Evaluation Methods
: : : Data Analysis
: : Statistical Analysis
: Multivariate Analysis
Path Analysis

: : Technology
: Medicine
Pathology
. Plant Pathology
. Psychopathology
. Speech Language Pathology

: Education
Patient Education

: Groups
Patients
. Hospitalized Children

: Nationalism
Patriotism

: : : : Methods
: : : Educational Methods
: : Teaching Methods
: Drills (Practice)
Pattern Drills (Language)
. Substitution Drills

: : : Cognitive Processes
: : Memory
: Recognition (Psychology)
Pattern Recognition
. Character Recognition

: : Behavior
: Responses
Patterned Responses

Patternmaking

: Mathematical Concepts
Patterns in Mathematics

Paying for College

: Records (Forms)
Payroll Records

: : Relationship
: Human Relations
Peace

Pedagogical Content Knowledge

Pedestrian Traffic

: : Technology
: Medicine
Pediatrics

: : : : Needs
: : : Individual Needs
: : Psychological Needs
: Affiliation Need
Peer Acceptance

: : Guidance
: Counseling
Peer Counseling

: Evaluation
Peer Evaluation

: Groups
Peer Groups

: Influences
Peer Influence

: Institutions
Peer Institutions

: : Cognitive Processes
: Conflict Resolution
Peer Mediation

: : Relationship
: Interpersonal Relationship
Peer Relationship

: : : Methods
: : Educational Methods
: Teaching Methods
Peer Teaching

: Ratios (Mathematics)
Percentage

: Cognitive Processes
Perception
. Auditory Perception
. . Auditory Discrimination
. Kinesthetic Perception
. Tactual Perception
. Visual Perception
. . Depth Perception
. . Visual Acuity
. . Visual Discrimination

: : : Measures (Individuals)
: : Tests
: Cognitive Tests
Perception Tests
. Tactual Visual Tests

: : : Development
: : Individual Development
: Cognitive Development
Perceptual Development

: Disabilities
Perceptual Impairments

: : : Ability
: : Skills
: Psychomotor Skills
Perceptual Motor Coordination
. Eye Hand Coordination
. Eye Voice Span

: : Learning
: Nonverbal Learning
Perceptual Motor Learning

: Behavior
Performance
. Counselor Performance
. Failure
. . Academic Failure
. . . Reading Failure
. Job Performance
. Success

: : Evaluation
: Alternative Assessment
Performance Based Assessment

: Contracts
Performance Contracts

Performance Criteria (1968 1980)

: Influences
Performance Factors

Performance Specifications (1969 1980)

: : Technology
: Educational Technology
Performance Technology

: : Measures (Individuals)
: Tests
Performance Tests

: Influences
Perinatal Influences

: : Publications
: Serials
Periodicals
. Electronic Journals
. Foreign Language Periodicals
. Scholarly Journals

: Environment
Permissive Environment

: : : Publications
: : Reference Materials
: Indexes
Permuted Indexes

: : Languages
: Indo European Languages
Persian

: Behavior
Persistence
. Academic Persistence
. Teacher Persistence

Personal Autonomy

: : Institutions
: Residential Institutions
Personal Care Homes

: : Publications
: Reports
Personal Narratives

: : : Needs
: : Individual Needs
: Psychological Needs
Personal Space

Personality

: : Evaluation
: Psychological Evaluation
Personality Assessment

: Change
Personality Change

: : Development
: Individual Development
Personality Development

: Measures (Individuals)
Personality Measures
. Self Concept Measures

: Problems
Personality Problems

: : : Research
: : Behavioral Science Research
: Psychological Studies
Personality Studies

: Theories
Personality Theories

: : Individual Characteristics
: Psychological Characteristics
Personality Traits
. Curiosity
. Dependency (Personality)
. Extraversion Introversion
. Locus of Control
. Mental Rigidity
. Resilience (Personality)
. Shyness

: Groups
Personnel
. Administrators
. . Admissions Officers
. . Assistant Principals
. . Beginning Principals
. . Central Office Administrators
. . Coordinators
. . . Audiovisual Coordinators
. . . Instructor Coordinators
. . Deans
. . . Academic Deans
. . . Deans of Students
. . Department Heads
. . Library Administrators
. . . Library Directors
. . Medical Record Administrators
. . Personnel Directors
. . Presidents
. . . College Presidents
. . . Presidents of the United States
. . Principals
. . Registrars (School)
. . Research Directors
. . School Business Officials
. . Student Financial Aid Officers
. . Superintendents
. . Supervisors
. . . Crew Leaders
. . . State Supervisors
. . . Student Teacher Supervisors
. . Trustees
. . Vocational Directors
. . Women Administrators
. Agricultural Personnel
. . Agricultural Laborers
. . . Migrant Workers
. . . Seasonal Laborers
. . Agricultural Technicians
. . Farmers
. . . Dairy Farmers
. . . Part Time Farmers
. . . Sharecroppers
. Aircraft Pilots
. Bus Drivers
. Caseworkers
. . Parole Officers
. . Probation Officers
. . Social Workers
. . . School Social Workers
. Church Workers
. Clergy
. . Priests
. Consultants
. . Medical Consultants
. . Reading Consultants
. . Science Consultants
. Designers
. Differentiated Staffs
. Dislocated Workers

Pests

: : Business
: Industry
Petroleum Industry

: : : : : Liberal Arts
: : : : Sciences
: : : Natural Sciences
: : Physical Sciences
: Earth Science
: Geology
Petrology

: Animals
Pets

: : : Education
: : Professional Education
: Medical Education
Pharmaceutical Education

: : : Groups
: : Personnel
: Professional Personnel
: : : Groups
: : Personnel
: Health Personnel
Pharmacists

: : Technology
: Medicine
Pharmacology

: : Technology
: Medicine
Pharmacy

: : : Liberal Arts
: : Humanities
: Philosophy
Phenomenology

: Institutions
Philanthropic Foundations

: : Liberal Arts
: Humanities
Philosophy
. Aesthetics
. Educational Philosophy
. Epistemology
. Ethics
. . Bioethics
. . Work Ethic
. Existentialism
. Hermeneutics
. Humanism
. Logic
. . Mathematical Logic
. . . Algorithms
. . . Mathematical Formulas
. . . . Equations (Mathematics)
. . . . . Differential Equations
. . . . Functions (Mathematics)
. . . . Polynomials
. . . Proof (Mathematics)
. . Set Theory
. Marxism
. Phenomenology
. Platonism
. Semiotics
. . Pragmatics
. . Semantics
. . . Lexicology
. World Views

Phonathons

: Language Patterns
Phoneme Grapheme Correspondence

: : : Linguistics
: : Phonology
: Phonemics
Phonemes
. Consonants
. Vowels

: Alphabets
Phonemic Alphabets

: : Linguistics
: Phonology
Phonemics
. Phonemes
. Consonants
. . Vowels

: : Methods
: Evaluation Methods
Phonetic Analysis

: : : Language
: : Written Language
: Orthographic Symbols
Phonetic Transcription

: : Linguistics
: Phonology
Phonetics
. Acoustic Phonetics
. Phonics

: : : Linguistics
: : Phonology
: Phonetics
Phonics

: Linguistics
Phonology
. Generative Phonology
. Phonemics
. . Phonemes
. . . Consonants
. . . Vowels
. Phonetics
. . Acoustic Phonetics
. . Phonics
. Suprasegmentals
. . Intonation
. . Stress (Phonology)
. Syllables

: Chemical Reactions
Photochemical Reactions
. Photosynthesis

: : Methods
: Production Techniques
Photocomposition

: Visual Aids
: Equipment
Photographic Equipment

: Visual Aids
Photographs

: : : : Liberal Arts
: : : Humanities
: : Fine Arts
: Visual Arts
Photography
. Holography

: : Technology
: Journalism
Photojournalism

: : Chemical Reactions
: Photochemical Reactions
Photosynthesis

: : : : Linguistics
: : : Descriptive Linguistics
: : Grammar
: Syntax
Phrase Structure

: Activities
Physical Activities
. Athletics
. . Aquatic Sports
. . . Diving
. . . Sailing
. . . Surfing
. . . Swimming
. . . Water Polo
. . . Waterskiing
. . Archery
. . Bowling
. . College Athletics
. . Extramural Athletics
. . Fencing (Sport)

. . Golf
. . Gymnastics
. . . Tumbling
. . Handball
. . Intramural Athletics
. . Lifetime Sports
. . Olympic Games
. . Orienteering
. . Racquet Sports
. . . Badminton
. . . Racquetball
. . . Squash (Game)
. . . Tennis
. . Roller Skating
. . Special Olympics
. . Table Tennis
. . Team Sports
. . . Baseball
. . . Basketball
. . . Field Hockey
. . . Football
. . . Ice Hockey
. . . Lacrosse
. . . Soccer
. . . Softball
. . . Team Handball
. . . Volleyball
. . . Water Polo
. . Track and Field
. . Weightlifting
. . Winter Sports
. . . Ice Hockey
. . . Ice Skating
. . . Skiing
. . Womens Athletics
. . Wrestling
. Bicycling
. Dance
. Exercise
. . Aerobics
. . Calisthenics
. . Plyometrics
. Horseback Riding
. Lifting
. . Weightlifting
. Running
. . Jogging
. Underwater Diving
. Walking

: Behavior
Physical Activity Level

: : : Relationship
: : Interpersonal Relationship
: Interpersonal Attraction
Physical Attractiveness

: Individual Characteristics
Physical Characteristics
. Body Composition
. . Obesity
. Body Height
. Body Weight
. . Birth Weight
. . Obesity
. Lateral Dominance
. . Handedness
. . . Left Handed Writer
. Muscular Strength
. Neurological Organization
. . Brain Hemisphere Functions
. Race
. Sex

: : : : : Liberal Arts
: : : : Sciences
: : : Natural Sciences
: : Physical Sciences
: Chemistry
Physical Chemistry
. Electrochemistry

: : Development
: Individual Development
Physical Development
. Motor Development

: Disabilities
Physical Disabilities
. Amputations
. Cleft Palate
. Heart Disorders

. Neurological Impairments
. . Aphasia
. . Cerebral Palsy
. . Epilepsy
. . Minimal Brain Dysfunction

: Geographic Regions
Physical Divisions (Geographic)

: Education
Physical Education
. Adapted Physical Education
. Movement Education

: : Facilities
: Educational Facilities
Physical Education Facilities

: : : : Groups
: : : Personnel
: : Professional Personnel
: Teachers
Physical Education Teachers

: Environment
Physical Environment
. Acoustical Environment
. . Noise (Sound)
. Built Environment
. Climate
. Thermal Environment
. Visual Environment
. Wilderness

: : Evaluation
: Medical Evaluation
Physical Examinations

: : Health
: Physical Health
Physical Fitness
. Health Related Fitness

: : Measures (Individuals)
: Tests
Physical Fitness Tests

: : : : Liberal Arts
: : : Sciences
: : Social Sciences
: Geography
: : : : : Liberal Arts
: : : : Sciences
: : : Natural Sciences
: : Physical Sciences
: Earth Science
Physical Geography

: Health
Physical Health
. Dental Health
. Physical Fitness
. . Health Related Fitness

: Mobility
Physical Mobility
. Visually Impaired Mobility

: : Programs
: Recreational Programs
Physical Recreation Programs

: : : Liberal Arts
: : Sciences
: Natural Sciences
Physical Sciences
. Astronomy
. Chemistry
. . Biochemistry
. . Geochemistry
. . Inorganic Chemistry
. . Organic Chemistry
. . Physical Chemistry
. . . Electrochemistry
. . Stereochemistry
. Crystallography
. Earth Science
. . Geochemistry
. . Geology
. . . Mineralogy
. . . Paleontology
. . . Petrology
. . Geophysics

. . . Plate Tectonics
. Hydrology
. . Meteorology
. . Oceanography
. . Physical Geography
. . Seismology
. . . Plate Tectonics
. . Soil Science
. Physics
. . Biophysics
. . . Biomechanics
. . . Bionics
. . . . Robotics
. . Electronics
. . . Microelectronics
. . Mechanics (Physics)
. . . Fluid Mechanics
. . . Kinetics
. . . . Diffusion (Physics)
. . . Quantum Mechanics
. . Nuclear Physics
. . Optics
. . Thermodynamics
. Spectroscopy

: : : : Groups
: : : Personnel
: : Professional Personnel
: : : : : Groups
: : : : Personnel
: : : Health Personnel
: : Allied Health Personnel
: Therapists
Physical Therapists

: Therapy
Physical Therapy

: : : : Groups
: : : Personnel
: : Health Personnel
: Allied Health Personnel
Physical Therapy Aides

: : Relationship
: Interpersonal Relationship
Physician Patient Relationship

: : : Groups
: : Personnel
: Professional Personnel
: : : Groups
: : Personnel
: Health Personnel
Physicians
. Foreign Medical Graduates
. Psychiatrists

: : : : Groups
: : : Personnel
: : Health Personnel
: Allied Health Personnel
Physicians Assistants

: : : : Liberal Arts
: : : Sciences
: : Natural Sciences
: Physical Sciences
Physics
. Biophysics
. . Biomechanics
. . Bionics
. . . Robotics
. Electronics
. . Microelectronics
. Mechanics (Physics)
. . Fluid Mechanics
. . Kinetics
. . . Diffusion (Physics)
. . Quantum Mechanics
. Nuclear Physics
. Optics
. Thermodynamics

: : : : Liberal Arts
: : : Sciences
: : Natural Sciences
: Biological Sciences
Physiology
. Exercise Physiology
. Psychophysiology

: Theories
Piagetian Theory

: : Stimuli
: Visual Stimuli
Pictorial Stimuli

: : Publications
: : Printed Materials
: Books
Picture Books

: Languages
: : : Linguistics
: : Sociolinguistics
: Language Variation
Pidgins

: Programs
Pilot Projects

Place of Residence

: : Mathematical Concepts
: Number Concepts
Place Value

Placement
. Advanced Placement
. Age Grade Placement
. Job Placement
. . Teacher Placement
. Mainstreaming
. Student Placement

: : : : Behavior
: : : Social Behavior
: : Antisocial Behavior
: Stealing
Plagiarism

: : : Liberal Arts
: : Mathematics
: Geometry
Plane Geometry
. Polygons

: Facilities
Planetariums

: Community
Planned Communities

Planning
. Budgeting
. . Program Budgeting
. Career Planning
. Color Planning
. Community Planning
. Cooperative Planning
. Desegregation Plans
. Educational Planning
. . College Planning
. . Educational Facilities Planning
. . . Campus Planning
. Estate Planning
. Facility Planning
. . Educational Facilities Planning
. . . Campus Planning
. Family Planning
. Language Planning
. . Language Standardization
. Library Planning
. Long Range Planning
. Policy Formation
. Regional Planning
. Scheduling
. . Alternate Day Schedules
. . Fast Track Scheduling
. . Full Day Half Day Schedules
. . School Schedules
. . . Block Scheduling
. . . Double Sessions
. . . Extended School Day
. . . Extended School Year
. . . Flexible Scheduling
. . . Quarter System
. . . Semester System
. . . Trimester System
. . Working Hours
. . . Flexible Working Hours
. Social Planning
. Statewide Planning

. Strategic Planning
. Urban Planning

: : : : Groups
: : : Organizations (Groups)
: : Agencies
: Public Agencies
Planning Commissions

: Development
Plant Growth

: Identification
Plant Identification

: : : Technology
: : Medicine
: Pathology
Plant Pathology

Plant Propagation

Plant Science (1967 1980)

Plants (Botany)
. Field Crops
. . Grains (Food)
. . Tobacco
. Trees
. Weeds

Plastics

: : : : : : Liberal Arts
: : : : : Sciences
: : : : Natural Sciences
: : : Physical Sciences
: : Earth Science
: Seismology
: : : : : Liberal Arts
: : : : Sciences
: : : Natural Sciences
: : Physical Sciences
: Earth Science
: Geophysics
Plate Tectonics

Platonic Criticism (1970 1980)

: : : Liberal Arts
: : Humanities
: Philosophy
Platonism

: Activities
Play
. Pretend Play

: : Therapy
: : Recreation
: Therapeutic Recreation
Play Therapy

: : Activities
: Recreational Activities
Playground Activities

: : Facilities
: Recreational Facilities
Playgrounds

: : Literacy
: : Language Arts
: Writing (Composition)
Playwriting

: Technology
Plumbing

: : : : : Linguistics
: : : : Descriptive Linguistics
: : : Grammar
: : Morphology (Languages)
: Morphemes
Plurals

: : : Activities
: : Physical Activities
: Exercise
Plyometrics

: : Facilities
: Air Structures
Pneumatic Forms

: : Technology
: Medicine
Podiatry

: : : Liberal Arts
: : Humanities
: Literature
Poetry
. Epics
. Haiku
. Lyric Poetry
. . Ballads
. . Hymns
. . Odes
. . Sonnets
. Nursery Rhymes

: : Groups
: Authors
Poets

: : Disabilities
: Diseases
Poisoning
. Lead Poisoning

: Hazardous Materials
Poisons
. Pesticides
. . Herbicides
. . Insecticides

: : : Groups
: : Personnel
: Government Employees
Police

. Law Enforcement
Police Action
. Search and Seizure

: Relationship
Police Community Relationship

: Education
Police Education

: Relationship
Police School Relationship

Policy
. Administrative Policy
. . Board of Education Policy
. Discipline Policy
. Educational Policy
. Financial Policy
. Foreign Policy
. . Imperialism
. . . Colonialism
. Information Policy
. . Library Policy
. Interdistrict Policies
. Personnel Policy
. Public Policy
. School Policy
. Transfer Policy

: : Methods
: Evaluation Methods
Policy Analysis

: Planning
Policy Formation

: : : Languages
: : Indo European Languages
: Slavic Languages
Polish

: : Groups
: North Americans
: : Groups
: Ethnic Groups
Polish Americans

: : : Liberal Arts
: : Humanities
: Literature
Polish Literature

: Group Membership
Political Affiliation

: Attitudes
Political Attitudes

: Politics
Political Campaigns
. Presidential Campaigns (United States)

: Groups
Political Candidates

Political Correctness

: Geographic Regions
Political Divisions (Geographic)
. American Indian Reservations

: Influences
Political Influences

Political Issues

: : Groups
: Organizations (Groups)
Political Parties

Political Power

: : : Liberal Arts
: : Sciences
: Social Sciences
Political Science

: Socialization
Political Socialization

Politics
. Political Campaigns
. . Presidential Campaigns (United States)
. Politics of Education

: Politics
Politics of Education

Pollution
. Air Pollution
. . Acid Rain
. Water Pollution
. . Acid Rain

: : : : Liberal Arts
: : : Mathematics
: : Geometry
: Plane Geometry
: : Mathematical Concepts
: Geometric Concepts
Polygons

: : Equipment
: Measurement Equipment
: : Equipment
: Electronic Equipment
Polygraphs

: Matter
Polymers

: : : : : Liberal Arts
: : : : Humanities
: : : Philosophy
: : : Logic
: : Mathematical Logic
: : Mathematical Applications
: : Mathematical Formulas
: : : Liberal Arts
: : Mathematics
: Algebra
Polynomials

: : Languages
: American Indian Languages
Pomo

: Culture
Popular Culture

: Education
Popular Education

: : : : Liberal Arts
: : : Humanities
: : Fine Arts
: Music
Popular Music

Popularity

: : : : Liberal Arts
: : : Sciences
: : Social Sciences
: Demography
Population Distribution
. Ethnic Distribution
. Racial Distribution

: Education
Population Education

: Development
: : : : Liberal Arts
: : : Sciences
: : Social Sciences
: Demography
Population Growth

: : : : Liberal Arts
: : : Sciences
: : Social Sciences
: Demography
Population Trends
. Black Population Trends

Pornography

: Evaluation
Portfolio Assessment

: : Records (Forms)
: Credentials
Portfolios (Background Materials)

: : : Languages
: : Indo European Languages
: Romance Languages
Portuguese

: : : Groups
: : North Americans
: Hispanic Americans
: : Groups
: Ethnic Groups
Portuguese Americans

: : Publications
: Reports
Position Papers
. Mission Statements

: Reinforcement
Positive Reinforcement

: Guidance
Post High School Guidance

: : : Education
: : Postsecondary Education
: Higher Education
Postdoctoral Education

Postmodernism

: Education
Postsecondary Education
. Higher Education
. . Graduate Study
. . . Graduate Medical Education
. . . Postsecondary Education as a Field of Study
. . Postdoctoral Education
. . Undergraduate Study

: : : : Education
: : : Postsecondary Education
: : Higher Education
: Graduate Study
: : Curriculum
: College Curriculum
Postsecondary Education as a Field of Study

: : : Disabilities
: : Mental Disorders

: Neurosis
Posttraumatic Stress Disorder

: Groups
Potential Dropouts

: : Equipment
: Measurement Equipment
Potentiometers (Instruments)

: : Status
: Economic Status
Poverty

: Geographic Regions
Poverty Areas
. Slums

: Programs
Poverty Programs

: Organization
Power Structure

: Technology
Power Technology
. Nuclear Technology

Practical Arts

: : : Technology
: : Medicine
: Nursing
Practical Nursing

: : Publications
: Reports
Practicum Papers

: : : Governance
: : Administration
: Supervision
Practicum Supervision

: : Curriculum
: Courses
Practicums
. Office Practice

: : : : Liberal Arts
: : : Humanities
: : Philosophy
: : : Theories
: : Linguistic Theory
: Semiotics
Pragmatics

Praise

: : : Groups
: : Age Groups
: Children
Preadolescents

: : : Methods
: : Educational Methods
: Teaching Methods
Precision Teaching

Prediction
. Employment Projections
. Enrollment Projections
. Grade Prediction

: Measurement
Predictive Measurement

: : : : Standards
: : : Criteria
: : Evaluation Criteria
: Validity
Predictive Validity

Predictor Variables
. Suppressor Variables

: Construction (Process)
Prefabrication

: : : : : : Linguistics
: : : : : Descriptive Linguistics
: : : : Grammar
: : : Morphology (Languages)

: : Morphemes
: Affixes
Prefixes (Grammar)

Pregnancy

: : Groups
: Students
: Groups
: Females
Pregnant Students

: : : : : Groups
: : : : Age Groups
: : : Children
: : Young Children
: Infants
Premature Infants

: : : : Groups
: : : Students
: : College Students
: Undergraduate Students
Premedical Students

: Income
: Expenditures
Premium Pay

: : : Services
: : Human Services
: Health Services
Prenatal Care

: : Influences
: Prenatal Influences
: : Behavior
: Drug Use
Prenatal Drug Exposure

: Influences
Prenatal Influences
. Prenatal Drug Exposure

: : : : : Linguistics
: : : : Descriptive Linguistics
: : : Grammar
: : Syntax
: Form Classes (Languages)
Prepositions

: : Background
: Experience
Prereading Experience

: Intervention
Prereferral Intervention

Prerequisites

: : Education
: Adult Education
Preretirement Education

: : : : Groups
: : : Age Groups
: : Children
: Young Children
Preschool Children

: Curriculum
Preschool Curriculum

: : Education
: Early Childhood Education
Preschool Education

: Evaluation
Preschool Evaluation

Preschool Learning (1966 1980)

: : : : Groups
: : : Personnel
: : Professional Personnel
: Teachers
Preschool Teachers

: : Measures (Individuals)
: Tests
Preschool Tests

: Maintenance
Preservation

: : : Education
: : Professional Education
: Teacher Education
Preservice Teacher Education
. Student Teaching

: : : Groups
: : Students
: College Students
Preservice Teachers
. Student Teachers

: : Politics
: Political Campaigns
Presidential Campaigns (United States)

: : : Groups
: : Personnel
: Administrators
Presidents
. College Presidents
. Presidents of the United States

: : : : Groups
: : : Personnel
: : Administrators
: Presidents
Presidents of the United States

: : Attitudes
: Opinions
Press Opinion

: Scientific Concepts
Pressure (Physics)

Pressure (1970 1980)

: Reputation
Prestige

: Construction Materials
Prestressed Concrete

: Programs
Pretechnology Programs

: : Activities
: Play
Pretend Play

: : Methods
: Evaluation Methods
Pretesting

: : Measures (Individuals)
: Tests
Pretests Posttests

Prevention
. Accident Prevention
. Crime Prevention
. . Delinquency Prevention
. Dropout Prevention
. Hearing Conservation

: : Technology
: Medicine
Preventive Medicine

: : Education
: Vocational Education
Prevocational Education

: Writing Processes
Prewriting

: : : Groups
: : Personnel
: Clergy
Priests

: : Cognitive Processes
: Learning Processes
Primacy Effect

: : : Education
: : Elementary Secondary Education
: Elementary Education

: : Education
: Early Childhood Education
Primary Education

: : Technology
: Medicine
Primary Health Care

: Information Sources
Primary Sources

: : : : : Liberal Arts
: : : : Sciences
: : : Natural Sciences
: : Biological Sciences
: Zoology
Primatology

: : : : Symbols (Mathematics)
: : : Numbers
: : Rational Numbers
: Integers
Prime Numbers

: : : Groups
: : Personnel
: School Personnel
: : Groups
: : Personnel
: Administrators
Principals

Printed Materials
. Books
. . Foreign Language Books
. . High Interest Low Vocabulary Books
. Paperback Books
. Picture Books
. Textbooks
. . History Textbooks
. . Multicultural Textbooks
. Yearbooks
. Manuscripts
. Pamphlets

: : : : : Liberal Arts
: : : : Humanities
: : : Fine Arts
: : Visual Arts
: Graphic Arts
Printing

: : : : Liberal Arts
: : : Humanities
: : Fine Arts
: Visual Arts
Printmaking

: Learning
Prior Learning

: : : : Institutions
: : : : Information Sources
: : : Libraries
: : Special Libraries
: Institutional Libraries
Prison Libraries

: : Groups
: Institutionalized Persons
Prisoners

: Relationship
Privacy
. Confidentiality

: : : Groups
: : Organizations (Groups)
: Agencies
Private Agencies

: : : Institutions
: : Schools
: Private Schools
: : : Institutions
: : Schools
: Colleges
Private Colleges

: Education
Private Education

: Financial Support
Private Financial Support

: School Support
: Financial Support
Private School Aid

: : Institutions
: Schools
Private Schools
. Parochial Schools
. . Catholic Schools
. Private Colleges
. Proprietary Schools

Private Sector

Privatization

: : Liberal Arts
: Mathematics
Probability

: : : Groups
: : Personnel
: Caseworkers
Probation Officers

Probationary Period
. Academic Probation

: Learning
Problem Based Learning

: : : Groups
: : Age Groups
: Children
Problem Children

: : Educational Media
: Instructional Materials
Problem Sets

: Cognitive Processes
Problem Solving

Problems
. Administrative Problems
. Behavior Problems
. Communication Problems
. Community Problems
. Curriculum Problems
. Discipline Problems
. Emotional Problems
. Employment Problems
. Evaluation Problems
. Family Problems
. Financial Problems
. Labor Problems
. Learning Problems
. Legal Problems
. Migrant Problems
. Personality Problems
. Reading Difficulties
. Research Problems
. Social Problems
. Student Problems
. Suburban Problems
. Testing Problems
. Urban Problems
. World Problems
. Writing Difficulties
. Youth Problems

: : Instruction
: Writing Instruction
Process Approach (Writing)

: Education
Process Education

: : : Governance
: : Administration
: Supervision
Proctoring

: Services
Producer Services

: : : Groups
: : Personnel
: Paraprofessional Personnel
Production Technicians

: Methods
Production Techniques
. Desktop Publishing
. Electronic Publishing
. Film Production
. Photocomposition
. Special Effects
. . Animation
. Sound Effects
. Television Lighting
. Textbook Publication

: : Cognitive Processes
: Creative Thinking
Productive Thinking

Productivity

: : Groups
: Organizations (Groups)
Professional Associations
. Library Associations
. Medical Associations
. Teacher Associations

Professional Autonomy

: : Education
: Professional Education
: : : Education
: : Adult Education
: Continuing Education
Professional Continuing Education

: : Development
: Labor Force Development
Professional Development
. Faculty Development

: : Institutions
: Schools
Professional Development Schools

: Education
Professional Education
. Administrator Education
. Architectural Education
. Business Administration Education
. Engineering Education
. Home Economics Education
. Information Science Education
. . Computer Science Education
. . Library Education
. Legal Education (Professions)
. Medical Education
. . Graduate Medical Education
. . Nursing Education
. . Pharmaceutical Education
. . Veterinary Medical Education
. Professional Continuing Education
. Public Administration Education
. Teacher Education
. . Competency Based Teacher Education
. . English Teacher Education
. . Inservice Teacher Education
. . Preservice Teacher Education
. . . Student Teaching
. . Teacher Educator Education
. Theological Education

Professional Isolation

: Occupations
Professional Occupations
. Teaching (Occupation)
. . Team Teaching
. . Urban Teaching

: : Groups
: Personnel
Professional Personnel
. Accountants
. . Certified Public Accountants
. Architects
. Athletic Coaches
. Dentists
. Engineers
. Faculty
. . Adjunct Faculty
. . College Faculty
. . . College Presidents
. . . Counselor Educators

. . . Graduate School Faculty
. . . Medical School Faculty
. . . Professors
. . . Student Teacher Supervisors
. . . Teacher Educators
. . . . Methods Teachers
. . . Teaching Assistants
. . Deans
. . . Academic Deans
. . . Deans of Students
. . Department Heads
. . Faculty Advisers
. . Full Time Faculty
. . Nontenured Faculty
. . Part Time Faculty
. . . Partnership Teachers
. . Tenured Faculty
. . Women Faculty
. Information Scientists
. . Librarians
. . Search Intermediaries
. Lawyers
. Mathematicians
. Nurses
. . Nurse Practitioners
. . School Nurses
. Optometrists
. Pharmacists
. Physicians
. . Foreign Medical Graduates
. . Psychiatrists
. Psychologists
. . School Psychologists
. Research Directors
. Researchers
. . Educational Researchers
. . . Teacher Researchers
. Scientists
. Social Scientists
. . Historians
. . Sociologists
. Social Workers
. . School Social Workers
. Teachers
. . Adult Educators
. . Art Teachers
. . Beginning Teachers
. . Bilingual Teachers
. . Black Teachers
. . Catholic Educators
. . Cooperating Teachers
. . Elementary School Teachers
. . Home Economics Teachers
. . Industrial Arts Teachers
. . Instructor Coordinators
. . Itinerant Teachers
. . Language Teachers
. . . English Teachers
. . Lay Teachers
. . Master Teachers
. . Mathematics Teachers
. . Middle School Teachers
. . Minority Group Teachers
. . Music Teachers
. . Physical Education Teachers
. . Preschool Teachers
. . Public School Teachers
. . Reading Teachers
. . Remedial Teachers
. . Resource Teachers
. . Science Teachers
. . Secondary School Teachers
. . Special Education Teachers
. . Student Teachers
. . Substitute Teachers
. . Teacher Interns
. . Teacher Researchers
. . Teachers with Disabilities
. . Television Teachers
. . Tutors
. . Vocational Education Teachers
. . . Business Education Teachers
. . . Distributive Education Teachers
. . . Trade and Industrial Teachers
. . Writing Teachers
. Therapists
. . Occupational Therapists
. . Physical Therapists
. Veterinarians

: : Evaluation
: Recognition (Achievement)
Professional Recognition

: Services
Professional Services

: Training
Professional Training

: : : : : Groups
: : : : Personnel
: : : School Personnel
: : : : : Groups
: : : : Personnel
: : : Professional Personnel
: : Faculty
: College Faculty
Professors

: Data
Profiles

: : Measures (Individuals)
: Tests
Prognostic Tests

: : Governance
: Administration
Program Administration

: Attitudes
Program Attitudes

: : Planning
: Budgeting
Program Budgeting

Program Content

: Costs
Program Costs

Program Descriptions

: Design
Program Design

: Development
Program Development

Program Effectiveness

: Evaluation
Program Evaluation

: : : Publications
: : Reference Materials
: Guides
Program Guides

Program Implementation

: Improvement
Program Improvement

Program Length

Program Proposals
. Research Proposals

Program Termination

Program Validation

Programing Problems (1966 1980)

: : : Methods
: : Educational Methods
: Teaching Methods
Programmed Instruction
. Computer Assisted Instruction
. . Intelligent Tutoring Systems
. Programmed Tutoring

: : Educational Media
: Instructional Materials
Programmed Instructional Materials

: : : Instruction
: : Individual Instruction
: Tutoring
: : : : Methods
: : : Educational Methods
: : Teaching Methods
: Programmed Instruction
Programmed Tutoring

: : Groups
: Personnel
Programmers

: : : Development
: : Material Development
: Computer Software Development
: : : : Liberal Arts
: : : Sciences
: : Information Science
: Computer Science
Programming

Programming (Broadcast)

: Language
Programming Languages

Programs
. Adult Programs
. . Adult Reading Programs
. . High School Equivalency Programs
. Advanced Placement Programs
. After School Programs
. Assembly Programs
. Bilingual Education Programs
. Church Programs
. College Day
. College Programs
. . Doctoral Programs
. . External Degree Programs
. . Masters Programs
. Community Programs
. . Community Recreation Programs
. . School Community Programs
. Comprehensive Programs
. Computer Oriented Programs
. Construction Programs
. Consultation Programs
. Cooperative Programs
. County Programs
. Day Programs
. Demonstration Programs
. Developmental Programs
. . Developmental Studies Programs
. Emergency Programs
. Employee Assistance Programs
. Employment Programs
. Evening Programs
. Exchange Programs
. . Student Exchange Programs
. . Teacher Exchange Programs
. Experimental Programs
. Family Programs
. Federal Programs
. Field Experience Programs
. . Supervised Occupational Experience
       (Agriculture)
. Foundation Programs
. Guidance Programs
. Health Programs
. . Breakfast Programs
. . Immunization Programs
. . Lunch Programs
. . Mental Health Programs
. Home Programs
. Human Relations Programs
. Improvement Programs
. . Self Help Programs
. Individualized Programs
. Inplant Programs
. Institutes (Training Programs)
. Intercultural Programs
. Intergenerational Programs
. International Programs
. Internship Programs
. Interstate Programs
. Migrant Programs
. National Programs
. Nonschool Educational Programs
. Outreach Programs
. Pilot Projects
. Poverty Programs
. Pretechnology Programs
. Reading Programs
. . Adult Reading Programs
. Recreational Programs
. . Community Recreation Programs
. . Day Camp Programs
. . Physical Recreation Programs
. . Resident Camp Programs
. . School Recreational Programs
. Regional Programs

. Rehabilitation Programs
. . Dropout Programs
. . Remedial Programs
. Research Projects
. Residential Programs
. . Resident Camp Programs
. Science Course Improvement
       Projects
. Science Programs
. . Summer Science Programs
. Second Language Programs
. . College Second Language Programs
. . Immersion Programs
. Special Programs
. Individualized Education Programs
. Individualized Family Service Plans
. . Resource Room Programs
. . Special Degree Programs
. State Programs
. Student Loan Programs
. Summer Programs
. . Summer Science Programs
. Teacher Education Programs
. . Extended Teacher Education
       Programs
. Testing Programs
. Transfer Programs
. . Free Choice Transfer Programs
. Transitional Programs
. Tutorial Programs
. Urban Programs
. Vacation Programs
. Validated Programs
. Weekend Programs
. Work Experience Programs
. Work Study Programs
. Youth Programs

: Education
Progressive Education

Project Applications (1967 1980)

: Visual Aids
: Equipment
Projection Equipment
. Filmstrip Projectors
. Microform Readers
. Opaque Projectors
. Overhead Projectors
. Tachistoscopes

: Measures (Individuals)
Projective Measures
. Association Measures

Projects (1966 1980)

Promotion (Occupational)
. Faculty Promotion
. Teacher Promotion

: Methods
Prompting

: : : : : Linguistics
: : : : Descriptive Linguistics
: : : Grammar
: : Syntax
: Form Classes (Languages)
Pronouns

: : Language Arts
: Speech
Pronunciation

: : Instruction
: Speech Instruction
Pronunciation Instruction

: : : : Standards
: : : Criteria
: : Evaluation Criteria
: Validity
: : : : : Liberal Arts
: : : : Humanities
: : : Philosophy
: : Logic
: Mathematical Logic
Proof (Mathematics)

Proofreading

: : : Services
: : Information Services
: Information Dissemination
: Communication (Thought Transfer)
Propaganda

: Mathematical Concepts
Properties (Mathematics)

: : Technology
: Accounting
Property Accounting

: Evaluation
Property Appraisal
. Assessed Valuation

: Taxes
Property Taxes

: : Literacy
: : Language Arts
: Writing (Composition)
Proposal Writing

: : : Institutions
: : Schools
: Private Schools
Proprietary Schools

: : : Liberal Arts
: : Humanities
: Literature
Prose
. Fiction
. . Novels
. . Science Fiction
. . Short Stories
. Nonfiction
. . Biographies
. . . Autobiographies
. . Chronicles
. . Diaries
. . . Dialog Journals
. . . Student Journals
. . Essays

: : Behavior
: Social Behavior
Prosocial Behavior
. Sharing Behavior

: : Equipment
: Assistive Devices (for Disabled)
Prostheses
. Cochlear Implants

: : Groups
: Religious Cultural Groups
Protestants
. Amish
. Puritans

Protists

: : Methods
: Research Methodology
Protocol Analysis

: : Educational Media
: Instructional Materials
: : Educational Media
: Audiovisual Aids
Protocol Materials

Protozoa

Proverbs

Proximity

: : : : Groups
: : : Personnel
: : Health Personnel
: Mental Health Workers
: : : : Groups
: : : Personnel
: : Health Personnel
: Allied Health Personnel
Psychiatric Aides

: : Institutions
: Hospitals
Psychiatric Hospitals

: : : : Services
: : : Human Services
: : Health Services
: Medical Services
Psychiatric Services

: : : : Groups
: : : Personnel
: : Professional Personnel
: : : : Groups
: : : Personnel
: : Health Personnel
: Physicians
: : : Groups
: : : Personnel
: : Health Personnel
: Mental Health Workers
Psychiatrists

: : Technology
: Medicine
Psychiatry

: : : : Liberal Arts
: : : Sciences
: : Behavioral Sciences
: Psychology
: : Liberal Arts
: : Sciences
: Acoustics
Psychoacoustics

: Clinics
Psychoeducational Clinics

: : Methods
: Educational Methods
Psychoeducational Methods

: Linguistics
Psycholinguistics

: Individual Characteristics
Psychological Characteristics
. Attention Span
. Cognitive Style
. . Conceptual Tempo
. . Field Dependence Independence
. Creativity
. . Imagination
. Intelligence
. . Comprehension
. . . Listening Comprehension
. . . Reading Comprehension
. . Formal Operations
. . Mental Age
. . Multiple Intelligences
. Personality Traits
. . Curiosity
. . Dependency (Personality)
. . Extraversion Introversion
. . Locus of Control
. . Mental Rigidity
. . Resilience (Personality)
. . Shyness
. Schemata (Cognition)

: Evaluation
Psychological Evaluation
. Personality Assessment

: : Needs
: Individual Needs
Psychological Needs
. Achievement Need
. Affection
. Affiliation Need
. . Peer Acceptance
. Personal Space
. Security (Psychology)
. Self Actualization
. Status Need

Psychological Patterns
. Alienation
. . Student Alienation
. . Teacher Alienation
. Anger
. . Hostility

. Anxiety
. . Communication Apprehension
. . Computer Anxiety
. . Mathematics Anxiety
. . Separation Anxiety
. . Test Anxiety
. . Writing Apprehension
. Apathy
. Cognitive Dissonance
. Congruence (Psychology)
. . Self Congruence
. Defense Mechanisms
. . Denial (Psychology)
. Depression (Psychology)
. Egocentrism
. Empathy
. Fear
. . Fear of Success
. . School Phobia
. Happiness
. Identification (Psychology)
. Jealousy
. Moods
. Morale
. . Teacher Morale
. Rejection (Psychology)
. Resentment
. Resistance (Psychology)
. . Resistance to Change
. . Resistance to Temptation
. Sadness
. . Grief
. . Loneliness
. Withdrawal (Psychology)

: : Services
: Human Services
Psychological Services

: : Research
: Behavioral Science Research
Psychological Studies
. Force Field Analysis
. Interest Research
. Personality Studies

: : : Methods
: : Measurement Techniques
: Testing
Psychological Testing

: : : Groups
: : Personnel
: Professional Personnel
: : : Groups
: : Personnel
: Health Personnel
Psychologists
. School Psychologists

: : : Liberal Arts
: : Sciences
: Behavioral Sciences
Psychology
. Behaviorism
. Child Psychology
. Clinical Psychology
. Cognitive Psychology
. Community Psychology
. Counseling Psychology
. Developmental Psychology
. Educational Psychology
. Experimental Psychology
. Individual Psychology
. Industrial Psychology
. Neuropsychology
. Psychoacoustics
. Psychometrics
. Psychopathology
. Psychophysiology
. School Psychology
. Social Psychology
. Sport Psychology

: : : : Liberal Arts
: : : Sciences
: : Behavioral Sciences
: Psychology
Psychometrics

: : Objectives
: Behavioral Objectives
Psychomotor Objectives

: : Ability
: Skills
Psychomotor Skills
. Marksmanship
. Object Manipulation
. Perceptual Motor Coordination
. . Eye Hand Coordination
. . Eye Voice Span

: : : : Liberal Arts
: : : Sciences
: : Behavioral Sciences
: Psychology
: : : Technology
: : Medicine
: Pathology
Psychopathology

: : : : Liberal Arts
: : : Sciences
: : Behavioral Sciences
: Psychology
: : : : Liberal Arts
: : : Sciences
: : Natural Sciences
: : Biological Sciences
: Physiology
Psychophysiology

: : Disabilities
: Severe Disabilities
: : Disabilities
: Mental Disorders
Psychosis
. Echolalia
. Schizophrenia

: : : Disabilities
: : Mental Disorders
: Emotional Disturbances
Psychosomatic Disorders

: Therapy
Psychotherapy
. Gestalt Therapy
. Milieu Therapy
. Rational Emotive Therapy
. Reality Therapy
. Relaxation Training
. Transactional Analysis

Puberty

: : Governance
: Administration
Public Administration

: : Education
: Professional Education
Public Administration Education

: Education
Public Affairs Education

: : : Groups
: : Organizations (Groups)
: Agencies
Public Agencies
. Planning Commissions
. State Agencies
. . State Departments of Education
. . State Licensing Boards

: : : Institutions
: : Schools
: Colleges
Public Colleges
. Community Colleges
. State Colleges
. . State Universities

: Education
Public Education
. Public School Adult Education

: Facilities
Public Facilities
. Public Libraries
. . County Libraries
. . Regional Libraries

: Health
Public Health

: Legislation
Public Health Legislation
. Drug Legislation

: : : : Liberal Arts
: : : Sciences
: : Social Sciences
: : : Liberal Arts
: : Humanities
: History
Public History

: : : Facilities
: : Housing
: Low Rent Housing
Public Housing

: : Facilities
: Public Facilities
: : Institutions
: : Information Sources
: Libraries
Public Libraries
. County Libraries
. Regional Libraries

: : : Groups
: : Personnel
: Government Employees
Public Officials
. City Officials
. County Officials
. Court Judges
. Legislators
. State Officials
. . State Supervisors

: : Attitudes
: Opinions
Public Opinion

: Policy
Public Policy

: Relationship
Public Relations

: : Education
: Public Education
: : Education
: Adult Education
Public School Adult Education

: : : : Groups
: : : Personnel
: : Professional Personnel
: Teachers
: : : Groups
: : Personnel
: Government Employees
Public School Teachers

: : Institutions
: Schools
Public Schools
. Charter Schools

Public Sector

Public Service

: Occupations
Public Service Occupations

: : Communication (Thought Transfer)
: Speech Communication
Public Speaking

Public Support

: : : : Technology
: : : Communications
: : Telecommunications
: : Mass Media
: Television
Public Television

Publications
. Book Reviews
. Books
. . Foreign Language Books
. . High Interest Low Vocabulary
    Books

. . Paperback Books
. . Picture Books
. . Textbooks
. . . History Textbooks
. . . Multicultural Textbooks
. . Yearbooks
. Catalogs
. . Library Catalogs
. . . Book Catalogs
. . . Card Catalogs
. . . Union Catalogs
. . . Online Catalogs
. . School Catalogs
. Comics (Publications)
. Computer Software Reviews
. Government Publications
. Journal Articles
. Literature Reviews
. Pamphlets
. Reference Materials
. . Abstracts
. . Anthologies
. . Atlases
. . Bibliographies
. . . Annotated Bibliographies
. . Citations (References)
. . Dictionaries
. . . Glossaries
. . Directories
. . Discographies
. . Encyclopedias
. . Filmographies
. . Guides
. . . Administrator Guides
. . . Curriculum Guides
. . . . State Curriculum Guides
. . . Faculty Handbooks
. . . Laboratory Manuals
. . . Leaders Guides
. . . Library Guides
. . . Program Guides
. . . Study Guides
. . . Teaching Guides
. . . Test Manuals
. . Indexes
. . . Citation Indexes
. . . Coordinate Indexes
. . . Permuted Indexes
. . Library Catalogs
. . . Book Catalogs
. . . Card Catalogs
. . . Union Catalogs
. . Thesauri
. . Yearbooks
. Reports
. . Annual Reports
. . Conference Papers
. . Opinion Papers
. . Personal Narratives
. . Position Papers
. . . Mission Statements
. . Practicum Papers
. . Research Reports
. . Theses
. . . Doctoral Dissertations
. . . Masters Theses
. School Publications
. . Faculty Handbooks
. . School Catalogs
. . School Newspapers
. . Student Publications
. Serials
. . Annual Reports
. . Bulletins
. . Conference Proceedings
. . Newspapers
. . . Newsletters
. . . School Newspapers
. . Periodicals
. . . Electronic Journals
. . . Foreign Language Periodicals
. . . Scholarly Journals
. . Yearbooks
. State of the Art Reviews
. Test Reviews

: : : Services
: : Information Services
: Information Dissemination
: Communication (Thought Transfer)
Publicity
. Advertising
. . Television Commercials

. Institutional Advancement

Publicize (1968 1980)

Publish or Perish Issue

: : Business
: Industry
Publishing Industry
. University Presses

: : : Groups
: : Ethnic Groups
: American Indians
Pueblo (People)
. Hopi (Tribe)
. Zuni (Tribe)

: : Culture
: Latin American Culture
Puerto Rican Culture

: : Groups
: Latin Americans
Puerto Ricans

: : Language
: Written Language
Punctuation

: Reinforcement
Punishment
. Capital Punishment
. Corporal Punishment

: : Languages
: Indo European Languages
Punjabi

: : Literary Devices
: : Language
: Figurative Language
Puns

: : : : Services
: : : Human Services
: : Social Services
: Ancillary School Services
Pupil Personnel Services

: : : Groups
: : Personnel
: School Personnel
Pupil Personnel Workers
. Attendance Officers

: : : Behavior
: : Responses
: Motor Reactions
Pupillary Dilation

: : : : Liberal Arts
: : : Humanities
: : Fine Arts
: Theater Arts
Puppetry

Purchasing

: : : Groups
: : Religious Cultural Groups
: Protestants
Puritans

: : Activities
: Games
Puzzles

: Organization
Pyramid Organization

: : Methods
: Measurement Techniques
Q Methodology

: Standards
Qualifications
. Administrator Qualifications
. Counselor Qualifications
. Employment Qualifications
. Supervisor Qualifications
. Teacher Qualifications

: Research
Qualitative Research

: Groups
Quality Circles

: : Methods
: Evaluation Methods
Quality Control

: Quality of Life
. Quality of Working Life
. Well Being
. . Child Welfare
. . Student Welfare
. . Teacher Welfare
. . Wellness

: Quality of Life
Quality of Working Life

: : : : : Liberal Arts
: : : : Sciences
: : : : Natural Sciences
: : : Physical Sciences
: : Physics
: Mechanics (Physics)
Quantum Mechanics

: : : Planning
: : Scheduling
: School Schedules
Quarter System

: : Design
: Research Design
Quasiexperimental Design

: : Languages
: American Indian Languages
Quechua

: Methods
Questioning Techniques

: Measures (Individuals)
Questionnaires

: : : Languages
: : American Indian Languages
: Mayan Languages
Quiche

Quotas

: : Individual Characteristics
: Physical Characteristics
Race

: Attitudes
Racial Attitudes

: : : : : Liberal Arts
: : : : Sciences
: : : Social Sciences
: : Demography
: Racial Composition
Racial Balance

: : : Attitudes
: : Social Attitudes
: : Bias
: Social Bias
Racial Bias

Racial Characteristics (1966 1980)

: : : : Liberal Arts
: : : Sciences
: : Social Sciences
: Demography
Racial Composition
. Racial Balance

: Differences
Racial Differences

: Social Discrimination
Racial Discrimination
. Racial Segregation
. . De Facto Segregation
. . De Jure Segregation

: : : : : Liberal Arts
: : : : Sciences
: : : Social Sciences
: : Demography
: Population Distribution
Racial Distribution

: Influences
Racial Factors

: Identification
Racial Identification

: Social Integration
Racial Integration

: : : Relationship
: : Human Relations
: Intergroup Relations
Racial Relations

: : Social Discrimination
: Racial Discrimination
Racial Segregation
. De Facto Segregation
. De Jure Segregation

: : Institutions
: Schools
Racially Balanced Schools

Racism (1966 1980)

: : : Activities
: : Physical Activities
: Athletics
Racquet Sports
. Badminton
. Racquetball
. Squash (Game)
. Tennis

: : : : Activities
: : : Physical Activities
: : Athletics
: Racquet Sports
Racquetball

: : Equipment
: Electronic Equipment
Radar

: : Scientific Concepts
: Energy
Radiation
. Light
. Nuclear Energy
. Solar Energy

: : : : : Liberal Arts
: : : : Sciences
: : : Natural Sciences
: : Biological Sciences
: Biology
Radiation Biology

Radiation Effects

: : : Technology
: : Communications
: Telecommunications
: Mass Media
Radio
. Educational Radio

: : : Groups
: : Personnel
: Paraprofessional Personnel
Radiographers

Radioisotopes

: : : : Groups
: : : Personnel
: : Health Personnel
: Allied Health Personnel
Radiologic Technologists

: Technology
Radiology

: Transportation
Rail Transportation

Rainforests

: Visual Aids
: Sensory Aids
Raised Line Drawings

: : : : Behavior
: : : Social Behavior
: : Antisocial Behavior
: Sexual Abuse
Rape

: : Relationship
: Interpersonal Relationship
Rapport

: Measures (Individuals)
Rating Scales
. Behavior Rating Scales
. Likert Scales
. Semantic Differential

: : Therapy
: Psychotherapy
Rational Emotive Therapy

: : Symbols (Mathematics)
: Numbers
Rational Numbers
. Fractions
. . Decimal Fractions
. Integers
. . Prime Numbers
. . Whole Numbers

Ratios (Mathematics)
. Counselor Client Ratio
. Intelligence Quotient
. Percentage
. Relevance (Information Retrieval)
. Response Rates (Questionnaires)
. Tax Rates
. Teacher Student Ratio

: Animals
Rats

: : Data
: Scores
Raw Scores

Reaction Time

Readability

: : Methods
: Evaluation Methods
Readability Formulas

: : : Behavior
: : Responses
: Audience Response
Reader Response

: Relationship
Reader Text Relationship

: : : : Liberal Arts
: : : Humanities
: : Fine Arts
: Theater Arts
Readers Theater

Readiness
. Integration Readiness
. Learning Readiness
. Reading Readiness
. School Readiness
. Writing Readiness

: Literacy
: Language Arts
Reading
. Basal Reading
. Beginning Reading
. Content Area Reading
. Corrective Reading
. Critical Reading
. Directed Reading Activity
. Early Reading
. Functional Reading
. Independent Reading
. Individualized Reading

. Music Reading
. Oral Reading
. Reading Aloud to Others
. Recreational Reading
. Remedial Reading
. Silent Reading
. Speed Reading
. Story Reading
. Sustained Silent Reading

: : Ability
: Verbal Ability
Reading Ability
. Reading Skills
. . Reading Comprehension
. . Reading Rate

: Achievement
Reading Achievement

: : Literacy
: : Language Arts
: Reading
Reading Aloud to Others

: : Instruction
: Assignments
Reading Assignments

: Attitudes
Reading Attitudes

: : Facilities
: Resource Centers
: Facilities
: Educational Facilities
Reading Centers

: : : : Ability
: : : Verbal Ability
: : : Reading Ability
: : : : Ability
: : : Skills
: : Language Skills
: Reading Skills
: : : : Individual Characteristics
: : : Psychological Characteristics
: : Intelligence
: Comprehension
Reading Comprehension

: : : Groups
: : Personnel
: Consultants
Reading Consultants

Reading Development (1966 1980)

: : Identification
: Educational Diagnosis
Reading Diagnosis
. Miscue Analysis

: Problems
Reading Difficulties

Reading Difficulty (1966 1980)

: : : : Behavior
: : : Performance
: : Failure
: Academic Failure
Reading Failure

: : : Activities
: : Games
: Educational Games
Reading Games

: Behavior Patterns
Reading Habits

: Improvement
Reading Improvement

: Instruction
Reading Instruction
. Basal Reading
. Content Area Reading
. Corrective Reading
. Directed Reading Activity
. Individualized Reading
. Remedial Reading

. Sustained Silent Reading

: Interests
Reading Interests

Reading Level (1966 1980)

: : Selection
: Media Selection
Reading Material Selection

Reading Materials
. Large Type Materials
. Supplementary Reading Materials
. Telegraphic Materials

: Motivation
Reading Motivation

: : Cognitive Processes
: Language Processing
Reading Processes
. Decoding (Reading)

: Programs
Reading Programs
. Adult Reading Programs

: : : : Ability
: : : Verbal Ability
: : Reading Ability
: : : : Ability
: : : Skills
: : Language Skills
: Reading Skills
Reading Rate

: Readiness
Reading Readiness

: : : Measures (Individuals)
: : Tests
: Aptitude Tests
Reading Readiness Tests

: : Research
: Educational Research
Reading Research

: : : Ability
: : Verbal Ability
: Reading Ability
: : Ability
: : Skills
: Language Skills
Reading Skills
. Reading Comprehension
. Reading Rate

: : Methods
: Learning Strategies
Reading Strategies

: : : : Groups
: : : Personnel
: : Professional Personnel
: Teachers
Reading Teachers

: : : Measures (Individuals)
: : Tests
: Verbal Tests
Reading Tests
. Informal Reading Inventories

: Relationship
Reading Writing Relationship

: Ownership
Real Estate

: Occupations
Real Estate Occupations

: Nonprint Media
Realia

Realism

: : Therapy
: Psychotherapy
Reality Therapy

: : Cognitive Processes
: Memory
Recall (Psychology)
. Reminiscence

: : : : Groups
: : : Personnel
: : Nonprofessional Personnel
: Clerical Workers
Receptionists

: : Cognitive Processes
: Language Processing
Receptive Language

Recess Breaks

: Behavior Patterns
Recidivism

Recipes (Food)

: : : Methods
: : Educational Methods
: Teaching Methods
Reciprocal Teaching

: : Symbols (Mathematics)
: Numbers
Reciprocals (Mathematics)

: Evaluation
Recognition (Achievement)
. Awards
. Commencement Ceremonies
. Professional Recognition

: : Cognitive Processes
: Memory
Recognition (Psychology)
. Pattern Recognition
. . Character Recognition
. Word Recognition

Recognition (1967 1980)

: : : : : Liberal Arts
: : : : Sciences
: : : : Social Sciences
: : : : Liberal Arts
: : : : Humanities
: : : History
: : North American History
: United States History
Reconstruction Era

: : : Ability
: : Skills
: Business Skills
Recordkeeping

Records (Forms)
. Attendance Records
. Bibliographic Records
. Case Records
. . Medical Case Histories
. Check Lists
. Confidential Records
. Credentials
. . Educational Certificates
. . Portfolios (Background Materials)
. . Resumes (Personal)
. Farm Accounts
. Payroll Records
. Student Records
. . Academic Records
. . Report Cards
. Wills
. . Worksheets
. . Spreadsheets

: : : Governance
: : Administration
: Information Management
Records Management

Recreation
. Therapeutic Recreation
. . Play Therapy

: Financial Support
Recreation Finances

: Legislation
Recreation Legislation

: Activities
Recreational Activities
. Camping
. Hobbies
. Playground Activities
. Recreational Reading

: Facilities
Recreational Facilities
. Playgrounds

: Programs
Recreational Programs
. Community Recreation Programs
. Day Camp Programs
. Physical Recreation Programs
. Resident Camp Programs
. School Recreational Programs

: : Activities
: Recreational Activities
: : Literacy
: : Language Arts
: Reading
Recreational Reading

: Groups
Recreationists

Recruitment
. Faculty Recruitment
. Student Recruitment
. Teacher Recruitment

: : Sanitation
: Waste Disposal
Recycling

Reduction in Force
. Job Layoff

Redundancy

: : Groups
: Students
Reentry Students

: : Groups
: Personnel
Reentry Workers

: Groups
Reference Groups

: Publications
Reference Materials
. Abstracts
. Anthologies
. Atlases
. Bibliographies
. . Annotated Bibliographies
. Citations (References)
. Dictionaries
. . Glossaries
. Directories
. Discographies
. Encyclopedias
. Filmographies
. Guides
. . Administrator Guides
. . Curriculum Guides
. . . State Curriculum Guides
. . Faculty Handbooks
. . Laboratory Manuals
. . Leaders Guides
. . Library Guides
. . Program Guides
. . Study Guides
. . Teaching Guides
. . Test Manuals
. Indexes
. . Citation Indexes
. . Coordinate Indexes
. . Permuted Indexes
. Library Catalogs
. . Book Catalogs
. . Card Catalogs
. . Union Catalogs
. Thesauri
. Yearbooks

: : Services
: Information Services
Reference Services

Referral

Reflective Teaching

: : Curriculum
: Courses
Refresher Courses

: Climate Control
Refrigeration

: : Technology
: Mechanics (Process)
Refrigeration Mechanics

: : Groups
: Migrants
Refugees

: : : Methods
: : Educational Methods
: Teaching Methods
Reggio Emilia Approach

: Attitudes
Regional Attitudes

Regional Characteristics
. Regional Dialects

: : Behavior
: Cooperation
Regional Cooperation

: Regional Characteristics
: : Languages
: : : Linguistics
: : : Sociolinguistics
: : Language Variation
: Dialects
Regional Dialects

: : Facilities
: Laboratories
Regional Laboratories

: : : Facilities
: : Public Facilities
: : Institutions
: : : Information Sources
: : Libraries
: Public Libraries
Regional Libraries

: Planning
Regional Planning

: Programs
Regional Programs

: : Institutions
: Schools
Regional Schools

: : : Groups
: : Personnel
: School Personnel
: : : Groups
: : Personnel
: Administrators
Registrars (School)

: : : : Methods
: : : Evaluation Methods
: : Data Analysis
: Statistical Analysis
Regression (Statistics)
. Multiple Regression Analysis

: Relationship
**Regular and Special Education
    Relationship**

Rehabilitation
. Correctional Rehabilitation
. . Delinquent Rehabilitation
. Drug Rehabilitation
. Vocational Rehabilitation

: Facilities
Rehabilitation Centers

: : Guidance
: Counseling
Rehabilitation Counseling

: Programs
Rehabilitation Programs
. Dropout Programs

: : : : Liberal Arts
: : : Humanities
: : Fine Arts
: Theater Arts
Rehearsals (Theater Arts)

Reinforcement
. Negative Reinforcement
. Positive Reinforcement
. Punishment
. . Capital Punishment
. . Corporal Punishment
. Rewards
. . Self Reward
. Social Reinforcement
. Timeout
. Token Economy

: Psychological Patterns
Rejection (Psychology)

Relationship
. Community Relations
. Credibility
. Cultural Interrelationships
. Developmental Continuity
. Education Work Relationship
. Faculty College Relationship
. Family School Relationship
. . Parent School Relationship
. Family Work Relationship
. Federal Indian Relationship
. Federal State Relationship
. Government School Relationship
. . State School District Relationship
. Human Relations
. . Intergroup Relations
. . . Ethnic Relations
. . . Interfaith Relations
. . . Racial Relations
. Peace
. Slavery
. Interaction
. Aptitude Treatment Interaction
. . Feedback
. . . Biofeedback
. Group Dynamics
. International Relations
. Interpersonal Relationship
. . Board Administrator Relationship
. . Caregiver Child Relationship
. . Cohabitation
. . Collegiality
. . Counselor Client Relationship
. . Dating (Social)
. . Employer Employee Relationship
. . Family Relationship
. . . Parent Child Relationship
. . . . Parent Student Relationship
. . . Sibling Relationship
. . Friendship
. . Group Unity
. . Helping Relationship
. . Interpersonal Attraction
. . . Physical Attractiveness
. . Interprofessional Relationship
. . Kinship
. . Marriage
. . . Intermarriage
. . . Remarriage
. . Peer Relationship
. . Physician Patient Relationship
. . Rapport
. . Significant Others
. . Teacher Administrator Relationship
. . Teacher Student Relationship
. . Intimacy
. Labor Relations
. Police Community Relationship
. Police School Relationship
. Privacy
. . Confidentiality

. Public Relations
. Reader Text Relationship
. Reading Writing Relationship
. Regular and Special Education
   Relationship
. School Business Relationship
. School Community Relationship
. Science and Society
. Spatial Relationship (Facilities)
. State Church Separation
. Student School Relationship
. . Student College Relationship
. Supply and Demand
. . Teacher Supply and Demand
. . . Teacher Shortage
. Theory Practice Relationship

: Theories
: Scientific Concepts
Relativity

: : Therapy
: Psychotherapy
Relaxation Training

Released Time

Relevance (Education)
. Culturally Relevant Education

: Ratios (Mathematics)
Relevance (Information Retrieval)

: : : Standards
: : Criteria
: Evaluation Criteria
Reliability
. Interrater Reliability
. Test Reliability

Relief (Art)

Religion
. Buddhism
. Christianity
. Confucianism
. Islam
. Judaism
. Taoism

: Curriculum
Religion Studies

: Conflict
Religious Conflict

: Groups
Religious Cultural Groups
. Catholics
. Jews
. Muslims
. Protestants
. . Amish
. . Puritans

: Differences
Religious Differences

: Social Discrimination
Religious Discrimination

: Education
Religious Education

: Influences
Religious Factors

: Holidays
Religious Holidays

: : Groups
: Organizations (Groups)
Religious Organizations

: Facilities
Relocatable Facilities

: : Mobility
: Migration
Relocation
. Rural Resettlement

: : : Relationship
: : Interpersonal Relationship
: Marriage
Remarriage

: Instruction
Remedial Instruction
. Remedial Mathematics
. Remedial Reading

: : Instruction
: Remedial Instruction
: Instruction
: Mathematics Instruction
Remedial Mathematics

: Programs
Remedial Programs

: : Instruction
: Remedial Instruction
: : Instruction
: Reading Instruction
: : Literacy
: : Language Arts
: Reading
Remedial Reading

: : : : Groups
: : : Personnel
: : Professional Personnel
: Teachers
Remedial Teachers

: : : Cognitive Processes
: : Memory
: Recall (Psychology)
Reminiscence

: : : Liberal Arts
: : Humanities
: Literature
Renaissance Literature

: Maintenance
Repair
. Appliance Repair

Repetitive Film Showings

: : Records (Forms)
: Student Records
Report Cards

: Publications
Reports
. Annual Reports
. Conference Papers
. Opinion Papers
. Personal Narratives
. Position Papers
. . Mission Statements
. Practicum Papers
. Research Reports
. Theses
. . Doctoral Dissertations
. . Masters Theses

Reproduction (Biology)

: Technology
Reprography
. Microreproduction

Reputation
. Prestige

: : Curriculum
: Courses
Required Courses

Rescue

Research
. Action Research
. Architectural Research
. Behavioral Science Research
. . Integration Studies
. . Psychological Studies
. . . Force Field Analysis
. . . Interest Research
. . . Personality Studies
. Case Studies

. . Cross Sectional Studies
. . Facility Case Studies
. . Longitudinal Studies
. . . Followup Studies
. . . . Graduate Surveys
. . . . Vocational Followup
. Cohort Analysis
. Communication Research
. Community Study
. Creativity Research
. Cross Cultural Studies
. Dropout Research
. Educational Research
. . Classroom Research
. . Curriculum Research
. . Effective Schools Research
. . Reading Research
. . Writing Research
. Environmental Research
. Exceptional Child Research
. Feasibility Studies
. Field Studies
. Institutional Research
. Investigations
. Language Research
. . Dialect Studies
. Library Research
. Media Research
. . Journalism Research
. . Television Research
. . Textbook Research
. Medical Research
. Methods Research
. . Evaluation Research
. Nursing Research
. Operations Research
. . Game Theory
. Participatory Research
. Qualitative Research
. Schematic Studies
. Scientific Research
. Space Exploration
. . . Lunar Research
. Social Science Research
. . Critical Theory
. . Economic Research
. Statistical Studies
. Student Research
. Use Studies
. . Facility Utilization Research

: : Governance
: Administration
Research Administration

Research and Development

: Facilities
Research and Development Centers

: Groups
Research and Instruction Units

: : Groups
: Personnel
Research Assistants

: Committees
Research Committees

: : Groups
: Organizations (Groups)
Research Coordinating Units

Research Criteria (1967 1980)

: Design
Research Design
. Quasiexperimental Design

: : : Groups
: : Personnel
: Professional Personnel
: : : Groups
: : Personnel
: Administrators
Research Directors

: : Institutions
: : Information Sources
: Libraries
Research Libraries

: Methods
Research Methodology
. Interaction Process Analysis
. Multitrait Multimethod Techniques
. Protocol Analysis
. Scientific Methodology
. Triangulation

: Needs
Research Needs

: Opportunities
Research Opportunities

: : Instruction
: Assignments
Research Papers (Students)

: Problems
Research Problems

: Programs
Research Projects

: Program Proposals
Research Proposals

: : Publications
: Reports
Research Reports

**Research Reviews (Publications)
(1966 1980)**

: : Ability
: Skills
Research Skills

Research Tools

: : : : Institutions
: : : Schools
: : Colleges
: Universities
Research Universities

: Information Utilization
Research Utilization

: : : Groups
: : Personnel
: Professional Personnel
Researchers
. Educational Researchers
. . Teacher Researchers

: Psychological Patterns
Resentment

: : : Groups
: : Ethnic Groups
: American Indians
Reservation American Indians

: Standards
Residence Requirements

: : Groups
: Personnel
Resident Advisers
. Resident Assistants

: : : Groups
: : Personnel
: Resident Advisers
: : : Groups
: : Students
: College Students
Resident Assistants

: : Programs
: Residential Programs
: : Programs
: Recreational Programs
Resident Camp Programs

Residential Care

: : Institutions
: Residential Institutions
: : : Institutions
: : Schools

: Colleges
Residential Colleges

: Institutions
Residential Institutions
. Boarding Schools
.. Residential Schools
. Correctional Institutions
. Nursing Homes
. Personal Care Homes
. Residential Colleges

: : : : Liberal Arts
: : : Sciences
: : Social Sciences
: Demography
Residential Patterns

: Programs
Residential Programs
. Resident Camp Programs

: : : Institutions
: : Schools
: Special Schools
: : : Institutions
: : Schools
: Institutions
: : Residential Institutions
: Boarding Schools
Residential Schools

: : : Individual Characteristics
: : Psychological Characteristics
: Personality Traits
Resilience (Personality)

: Psychological Patterns
: Behavior
Resistance (Psychology)
. Resistance to Change
. Resistance to Temptation

: : Psychological Patterns
: : Behavior
: Resistance (Psychology)
Resistance to Change

: : Psychological Patterns
: : Behavior
: Resistance (Psychology)
Resistance to Temptation

Resource Allocation

: Facilities
Resource Centers
. Arts Centers
. Audiovisual Centers
. Computer Centers
. Cultural Centers
. Curriculum Study Centers
. Education Service Centers
. Information Centers
.. Clearinghouses
. Learning Centers (Classroom)
. Learning Resources Centers
. Nature Centers
. Reading Centers
. Teacher Centers

Resource Materials
. Resource Units

: : Programs
: Special Programs
Resource Room Programs

: : Groups
: Personnel
Resource Staff

: : : : Groups
: : : Personnel
: : Professional Personnel
: Teachers
Resource Teachers

: Resource Materials
Resource Units

Resources
. Community Resources

. Depleted Resources
. Educational Resources
.. Educational Supply
. Family Financial Resources
. Human Resources
.. Labor Force
.. Labor Supply
. Natural Resources
.. Coal
.. Fossil Fuels
... Coal
... Gasoline
... Natural Gas
.. Oil
.. Water Resources
... Groundwater
... Rivers
. Shared Resources and Services
.. Shared Facilities
.. Shared Library Resources
. Supplies
.. Adhesives
.. Agricultural Supplies
.. Electric Batteries
.. Magnetic Tapes
... Magnetic Tape Cassettes
.... Audiotape Cassettes
.... Videotape Cassettes

: Therapy
Respiratory Therapy

Respite Care

: Ratios (Mathematics)
Response Rates (Questionnaires)

: Behavior
Response Style (Tests)
. Guessing (Tests)

: Behavior
Responses
. Audience Response
. Reader Response
. Burnout
.. Teacher Burnout
. Constructed Response
. Covert Response
. Dimensional Preference
. Emotional Response
. Motor Reactions
.. Eye Movements
... Eye Fixations
.. Pupillary Dilation
. Overt Response
. Patterned Responses
. Stranger Reactions
. Student Reaction
. Teacher Response

Responsibility
. Accountability
. Administrator Responsibility
. Business Responsibility
. Child Responsibility
. Church Responsibility
. Community Responsibility
. Educational Responsibility
. Employee Responsibility
. Leadership Responsibility
. Legal Responsibility
.. Trust Responsibility (Government)
. Parent Responsibility
. School Responsibility
. Social Responsibility
.. Citizenship Responsibility
. Student Responsibility
. Teacher Responsibility
.. Noninstructional Responsibility

: : Equipment
: Safety Equipment
Restraints (Vehicle Safety)

: : Records (Forms)
: Credentials
Resumes (Personal)

: : Technology
: Marketing
Retailing

: : Cognitive Processes
: Memory
Retention (Psychology)

: Status
Retirement
. Early Retirement
. Mandatory Retirement
. Teacher Retirement

Retirement Benefits

: Training
Retraining

Retrenchment

: : : Technology
: : Automation
: Library Automation
: : Change
: Data Conversion
Retrospective Conversion (Library Catalogs)

: Meetings
Reunions

: Financial Support
: Federal Aid
Revenue Sharing

: Social Discrimination
Reverse Discrimination

: Activities
Review (Reexamination)

: Writing Processes
Revision (Written Composition)

: Conflict
Revolution

: : Conflict
: War
: : : : : Liberal Arts
: : : : Sciences
: : : Social Sciences
: : : : Liberal Arts
: : : Humanities
: : History
: : North American History
: United States History
Revolutionary War (United States)

: Reinforcement
Rewards
. Self Reward

: Zoning
Rezoning

: : Influences
: Biological Influences
Rh Factors

: Language Arts
Rhetoric
. Coherence
. Persuasive Discourse
. Rhetorical Invention

: : Criticism
: Literary Criticism
Rhetorical Criticism

: : Language Arts
: Rhetoric
Rhetorical Invention

: Theories
Rhetorical Theory

Rhyme

Rhythm (Music)
. Tempo (Music)

: : : Languages
: : Afro Asiatic Languages
: Berber Languages
Riff

Risk

: : Governance
: Administration
Risk Management

: : : Resources
: : Natural Resources
: Water Resources
Rivers

: Nucleic Acids
RNA

: Construction (Process)
Road Construction

: : : : : : : Liberal Arts
: : : : : : Sciences
: : : : : Natural Sciences
: : : : Physical Sciences
: : : Physics
: : : : : Liberal Arts
: : : : Sciences
: : : Natural Sciences
: : Biological Sciences
: Biophysics
: Bionics
: : Technology
: Automation
Robotics

: : : : Methods
: : : Evaluation Methods
: : Data Analysis
: Statistical Analysis
Robustness (Statistics)

: : : : Liberal Arts
: : : Humanities
: : Fine Arts
: Music
Rock Music

Role
. Administrator Role
. Board of Education Role
. Caregiver Role
. Child Role
. Citizen Role
. Community Role
. Counselor Role
. Family Role
. Government Role
. Institutional Role
.. Agency Role
.. Church Role
.. Court Role
.. Library Role
.. School Role
... College Role
. Language Role
. Mass Media Role
. Parent Role
.. Parents as Teachers
. Role of Education
. Sex Role
. Staff Role
. Student Role
. Teacher Role

: Conflict
Role Conflict

: : : Methods
: : Simulation
: Models
: Groups
Role Models
. Mentors

: Role
Role of Education

: Cognitive Processes
Role Perception

: : Methods
: Simulation
Role Playing
. Dramatic Play

: Theories
Role Theory

: : : Activities
: : Physical Activities
: Athletics
Roller Skating

: : Languages
: Indo European Languages
Romance Languages
. French
. Italian
. Latin
. Portuguese
. Romanian
. Spanish

: : : Languages
: : Indo European Languages
: Romance Languages
Romanian

Romanization

Romanticism

: Structural Elements (Construction)
Roofing

Rotation Plans

: Learning
Rote Learning

: Viruses
: : : Disabilities
: : Diseases
: Communicable Diseases
Rubella

: Groups
Runaways

: : Activities
: Physical Activities
Running
. Jogging

: : Groups
: Rural Population
: : : : Groups
: : : Ethnic Groups
: : American Indians
: Nonreservation American Indians
Rural American Indians

: Geographic Regions
Rural Areas

: Development
Rural Development

: : : : Liberal Arts
: : : Sciences
: : Social Sciences
: Economics
Rural Economics

: Education
Rural Education

: Environment
Rural Environment

: : Education
: Extension Education
Rural Extension

: : Groups
: Rural Population
: : Groups
: Family (Sociological Unit)
Rural Family

: : Groups
: Rural Population
Rural Farm Residents

: : Groups
: Rural Population
Rural Nonfarm Residents

: Groups
Rural Population
. Rural American Indians
. Rural Family
. Rural Farm Residents
. Rural Nonfarm Residents
. Rural Women
. Rural Youth

: : : Mobility
: : Migration
: : Relocation
: : Land Use
: Land Settlement
Rural Resettlement

: : Institutions
: Schools
Rural Schools

: : : : Liberal Arts
: : : Sciences
: : Social Sciences
: : : : Liberal Arts
: : : Sciences
: : Behavioral Sciences
: Sociology
Rural Sociology

: : Mobility
: Migration
Rural to Urban Migration

: Differences
Rural Urban Differences

: : Groups
: Rural Population
: : Groups
: Females
Rural Women

: : Groups
: Youth
: : Groups
: Rural Population
Rural Youth

: : : Languages
: : Indo European Languages
: Slavic Languages
Russian

: : : Liberal Arts
: : Humanities
: Literature
Russian Literature

: Leaves of Absence
Sabbatical Leaves

: Psychological Patterns
Sadness
. Grief
. Loneliness

Safety
. Agricultural Safety
. Child Safety
. Fire Protection
. Laboratory Safety
. Occupational Safety and Health
. School Safety
. . School Security
. Traffic Safety

: Education
Safety Education

: Equipment
Safety Equipment
. Restraints (Vehicle Safety)

: : : : Activities
: : : Physical Activities
: : Athletics
: Aquatic Sports
Sailing

: Income
: Expenditures
Salaries
. Contract Salaries

. Teacher Salaries

: Differences
Salary Wage Differentials

: Occupations
Sales Occupations

: : : Groups
: : Personnel
: Nonprofessional Personnel
Sales Workers
. Auto Parts Clerks

: : Ability
: Skills
: : Technology
: Marketing
Salesmanship

: : Languages
: American Indian Languages
Salish

: : Languages
: Malayo Polynesian Languages
Samoan

: : : Groups
: : Pacific Islanders
: : : Groups
: : North Americans
: Pacific Americans
: : Groups
: Ethnic Groups
Samoan Americans

: : Languages
: Uralic Altaic Languages
Samoyed Languages
. Yurak

Sample Size

: : : Liberal Arts
: : Mathematics
: Statistics
: : : : Services
: : : Information Services
: : Information Processing
: : : : Methods
: : : Evaluation Methods
: : Data Analysis
: Data Collection
Sampling
. Item Sampling

Sanctions

: : Languages
: African Languages
Sango

: Facilities
Sanitary Facilities
. Toilet Facilities

Sanitation
. Cleaning
. . Dishwashing
. Waste Disposal
. . Recycling

: : Languages
: Classical Languages
Sanskrit

: : Languages
: African Languages
Sara

: Facilities
Satellite Facilities

Satellites (Aerospace)
. Communications Satellites

: Literary Genres
Satire

: Attitudes
Satisfaction
. Community Satisfaction

. Job Satisfaction
. Life Satisfaction
. Marital Satisfaction
. Participant Satisfaction
. User Satisfaction (Information)

: : Methods
: Measurement Techniques
Scaling
. Multidimensional Scaling

: Planning
Scheduling
. Alternate Day Schedules
. Fast Track Scheduling
. Full Day Half Day Schedules
. School Schedules
. . Block Scheduling
. . Double Sessions
. . Extended School Day
. . Extended School Year
. . Flexible Scheduling
. . Quarter System
. . Semester System
. . Trimester System
. Working Hours
. . Flexible Working Hours

: : Individual Characteristics
: Psychological Characteristics
Schemata (Cognition)

: Research
Schematic Studies

: : : Disabilities
: : Severe Disabilities
: : : Disabilities
: : Mental Disorders
: Psychosis
Schizophrenia

: : Achievement
: Scholarship
: Communication (Thought Transfer)
Scholarly Communication

: : : Publications
: : Serials
: Periodicals
Scholarly Journals

: : Literacy
: Language Arts
: Writing (Composition)
: : Achievement
: Scholarship
Scholarly Writing

: Achievement
Scholarship
. Scholarly Communication
. Scholarly Writing

: Financial Support
Scholarship Funds

: : Financial Support
: Student Financial Aid
Scholarships
. Merit Scholarships
. No Need Scholarships
. Tuition Grants

: : Technology
: Journalism
Scholastic Journalism

: Accidents
School Accidents

: : Technology
: Accounting
School Accounting

: Activities
School Activities
. Class Activities
. Extracurricular Activities
. Student Projects

: : : Governance
: : Administration

: Institutional Administration
: : : Governance
: : : Administration
: Educational Administration
School Administration
. College Administration
. School Based Management

: : : : Services
: : : Human Services
: : Social Services
: Day Care
School Age Day Care

: : : : Groups
: : : Personnel
: : School Personnel
: : : Groups
: : : Personnel
: : Paraprofessional Personnel
: Paraprofessional School Personnel
School Aides

: : Legislation
: State Legislation
: : Legislation
: Educational Legislation
School Attendance Legislation

: Attitudes
School Attitudes

: : : : Governance
: : : Administration
: : Institutional Administration
: : : : Governance
: : : Administration
: : Educational Administration
: School Administration
: Institutional Autonomy
School Based Management

School Boycotts

: : Selection
: Elections
School Budget Elections

: : Facilities
: Educational Facilities
: .Facilities
: Buildings
School Buildings
. College Buildings

: : : Equipment
: : Motor Vehicles
: Service Vehicles
School Buses

: : : Groups
: : Personnel
: School Personnel
: : : Groups
: : Personnel
: Administrators
School Business Officials

: Relationship
School Business Relationship

: : : Groups
: : Personnel
: School Personnel
School Cadres

: : Publications
: School Publications
: : Publications
: Catalogs
School Catalogs

: Selection
School Choice
. College Choice

School Closing

: : Programs
: Community Programs
School Community Programs

: Relationship
School Community Relationship

: Construction (Process)
School Construction

: : Guidance
: School Guidance
: : Guidance
: Counseling
School Counseling

: : : Groups
: : Personnel
: School Personnel
: : : Groups
: : Personnel
: : Guidance Personnel
: Counselors
School Counselors

: Culture
School Culture

: : : : Liberal Arts
: : : Sciences
: : Social Sciences
: Demography
School Demography
. Teacher Distribution

: Social Integration
School Desegregation
. College Desegregation

School District Autonomy

: Organization
School District Reorganization

: Organization Size (Groups)
School District Size

: Expenditures
School District Spending

: Fiscal Capacity
School District Wealth

: : Groups
: Organizations (Groups)
School Districts
. County School Districts
. Multicampus Districts

: Organizational Effectiveness
School Effectiveness

: : Individual Characteristics
: Age
School Entrance Age

: : Development
: Facility Expansion
School Expansion

: Financial Support
School Funds

: Guidance
School Guidance
. School Counseling

: : : Services
: : Human Services
: Health Services
: : : : Services
: : : Human Services
: : Social Services
: Ancillary School Services
School Health Services

School Holding Power

: : Behavior
: Participation
School Involvement

: : Standards
: Laws
School Law

: : Institutions
: : Information Sources
: Libraries
School Libraries

School Location

: Maintenance
School Maintenance

: : Publications
: School Publications
: : : Publications
: : Serials
: : : Mass Media
: : News Media
: Newspapers
School Newspapers

: : : Groups
: : Personnel
: School Personnel
: : : : Groups
: : : Personnel
: : Professional Personnel
: : : Groups
: : : Personnel
: : Health Personnel
: Nurses
School Nurses

: Organization
School Organization
. House Plan
. . Career Academies
. School Restructuring

: Orientation
School Orientation

: : Groups
: Personnel
School Personnel
. Admissions Officers
. Assistant Principals
. Audiovisual Coordinators
. Beginning Principals
. Faculty
. . Adjunct Faculty
. . College Faculty
. . . College Presidents
. . . Counselor Educators
. . . Graduate School Faculty
. . . . Medical School Faculty
. . . Professors
. . . Student Teacher Supervisors
. . . Teacher Educators
. . . . Methods Teachers
. . . Teaching Assistants
. . Deans
. . . Academic Deans
. . . Deans of Students
. . Department Heads
. . Faculty Advisers
. . Full Time Faculty
. . Nontenured Faculty
. . Part Time Faculty
. . . Partnership Teachers
. . Tenured Faculty
. . Women Faculty
. Foreign Student Advisers
. Paraprofessional School Personnel
. . School Aides
. . Teacher Aides
. . . Bilingual Teacher Aides
. Principals
. Pupil Personnel Workers
. . Attendance Officers
. Registrars (School)
. School Business Officials
. School Cadres
. School Counselors
. School Nurses
. School Psychologists
. School Secretaries
. School Social Workers
. Student Financial Aid Officers
. Student Personnel Workers

: : Psychological Patterns
: Fear
School Phobia

School Planning (1966 1980)

: Policy
School Policy

School Prayer

: : : Groups
: : Personnel
: School Personnel
: : : : Groups
: : : Personnel
: : Professional Personnel
: : : : Groups
: : : Personnel
: : Health Personnel
: Psychologists
: : : : Groups
: : : Personnel
: : Health Personnel
: Mental Health Workers
School Psychologists

: : : : Liberal Arts
: : : Sciences
: : Behavioral Sciences
: Psychology
School Psychology

: Publications
School Publications
. Faculty Handbooks
. School Catalogs
. School Newspapers
. Student Publications

: Readiness
School Readiness

: : : Measures (Individuals)
: : Tests
: Aptitude Tests
School Readiness Tests

: : Programs
: Recreational Programs
School Recreational Programs

School Registration
. Late Registration

: : : Social Discrimination
: : Educational Discrimination
: School Segregation
School Resegregation

: Responsibility
School Responsibility

: : Organization
: School Organization
: Excellence in Education
School Restructuring

: : Role
: Institutional Role
School Role
. College Role

: Safety
School Safety
. School Security

: : Planning
: Scheduling
School Schedules
. Block Scheduling
. Double Sessions
. Extended School Day
. Extended School Year
. Flexible Scheduling
. Quarter System
. Semester System
. Trimester System

: : : : : Groups
: : : : Personnel
: : : Nonprofessional Personnel
: : Clerical Workers
: Secretaries
: : : Groups
: : Personnel

: School Personnel
School Secretaries

: : Safety
: School Safety
School Security

: : Social Discrimination
: Educational Discrimination
School Segregation
. College Segregation
. School Resegregation

: : Facilities
: Educational Facilities
School Shops

: Institutional Characteristics
School Size

: : : : Groups
: : : Personnel
: : Professional Personnel
: : : : Groups
: : : Personnel
: : Caseworkers
: Social Workers
: : : Groups
: : Personnel
: School Personnel
School Social Workers

: : Facilities
: Educational Facilities
School Space

: : Data
: Statistical Data
School Statistics

: : : Governance
: : Administration
: Supervision
School Supervision

School Support
. Private School Aid

: : : Methods
: : Evaluation Methods
: Surveys
School Surveys

: Taxes
School Taxes

: Clothing
School Uniforms

: : : : Behavior
: : : Social Behavior
: : Antisocial Behavior
: Vandalism
School Vandalism

: Observation
School Visitation

: Zoning
School Zoning

: Institutions
Schools
. Affiliated Schools
. Bilingual Schools
. Boarding Schools
. . Residential Schools
. British Infant Schools
. Colleges
. . Agricultural Colleges
. . Black Colleges
. . Church Related Colleges
. . Cluster Colleges
. . Commuter Colleges
. . Dental Schools
. . Developing Institutions
. . Experimental Colleges
. . Law Schools
. . Library Schools
. . Medical Schools
. . Multicampus Colleges
. . Noncampus Colleges
. . Private Colleges

. . Public Colleges
. . . Community Colleges
. . . State Colleges
. . . . State Universities
. . Residential Colleges
. . Selective Colleges
. . Single Sex Colleges
. . Small Colleges
. . Two Year Colleges
. . . Community Colleges
. . . Technical Institutes
. . Universities
. . . Land Grant Universities
. . . Open Universities
. . . Research Universities
. . . State Universities
. . . Urban Universities
. . Upper Division Colleges
. Community Schools
. Consolidated Schools
. Correspondence Schools
. Day Schools
. Disadvantaged Schools
. Elementary Schools
. . Experimental Colleges
. Folk Schools
. Free Schools
. Freedom Schools
. Inclusive Schools
. Laboratory Schools
. Magnet Schools
. Middle Schools
. Military Schools
. Multiunit Schools
. Neighborhood Schools
. Nursery Schools
. Open Plan Schools
. Private Schools
. . Parochial Schools
. . . Catholic Schools
. . Private Colleges
. . Proprietary Schools
. Professional Development Schools
. Public Schools
. Charter Schools
. Racially Balanced Schools
. Regional Schools
. Rural Schools
. Schools of Education
. Secondary Schools
. High Schools
. . Vocational High Schools
. . Junior High Schools
. Single Sex Schools
. . Single Sex Colleges
. Slum Schools
. Small Schools
. . One Teacher Schools
. . Small Colleges
. Special Schools
. . Institutional Schools
. . Hospital Schools
. . Residential Schools
. State Schools
. . State Colleges
. . . State Universities
. Suburban Schools
. Summer Schools
. Traditional Schools
. Transitional Schools
. Urban Schools
. . Urban Universities
. Vocational Schools
. . Career Academies
. . Vocational High Schools
. Year Round Schools

: : Institutions
: Schools
Schools of Education

: Achievement
Science Achievement

: Activities
Science Activities
. Science Fairs
. Science Projects

: Relationship
Science and Society

: Careers
Science Careers

: : Groups
: Clubs
Science Clubs

: : : Groups
: : Personnel
: Scientific Personnel
: : : Groups
: : Personnel
: Consultants
Science Consultants

: Programs
Science Course Improvement Projects

: Curriculum
Science Curriculum
. College Science
. Elementary School Science
. General Science
. Secondary School Science

: : : Organization
: : Administrative Organization
: Departments
Science Departments

: Education
Science Education

: : : : : Liberal Arts
: : : : Sciences
: : : Social Sciences
: : : Liberal Arts
: : : Humanities
: : History
: : Foundations of Education
: Educational History
Science Education History

: Equipment
Science Equipment

: Experiments
Science Experiments

: Facilities
Science Facilities
. Science Laboratories
. Science Teaching Centers

: : Activities
: Science Activities
: Nonprint Media
: Exhibits
Science Fairs

: : : : : Liberal Arts
: : : : Humanities
: : : Literature
: : Prose
: Fiction
Science Fiction

: : : : Liberal Arts
: : : Sciences
: : Social Sciences
: : Liberal Arts
: : Humanities
: History
Science History

: Instruction
Science Instruction

: Interests
Science Interests

: : Facilities
: Science Facilities
: : Facilities
: Laboratories
Science Laboratories

: : : Institutions
: : : Information Sources
: : Libraries
: Special Libraries
Science Libraries

Science Materials

: : Ability
: Skills
Science Process Skills

: Programs
Science Programs
. Summer Science Programs

: : Activities
: Science Activities
Science Projects

: : : Governance
: : Administration
: Supervision
Science Supervision

: : : : Groups
: : : Personnel
: : Professional Personnel
: Teachers
Science Teachers

: : Facilities
: Science Facilities
: : Facilities
: Educational Facilities
Science Teaching Centers

: : Measures (Individuals)
: Tests
Science Tests

: Liberal Arts
Sciences
. Acoustics
. . Psychoacoustics
. Behavioral Sciences
. . Ethology
. . Psychology
. . . Behaviorism
. . . Child Psychology
. . . Clinical Psychology
. . . Cognitive Psychology
. . . Community Psychology
. . . Counseling Psychology
. . . Developmental Psychology
. . . Educational Psychology
. . . Experimental Psychology
. . . Individual Psychology
. . . Industrial Psychology
. . . Neuropsychology
. . . Psychoacoustics
. . . Psychometrics
. . . Psychopathology
. . . Psychophysiology
. . . School Psychology
. . . Social Psychology
. . . Sport Psychology
. . Sociobiology
. . Sociology
. . . Criminology
. . . Educational Sociology
. . . Rural Sociology
. . . Social Psychology
. Information Science
. . Computer Science
. . . Programming
. . Library Science
. Natural Sciences
. . Biological Sciences
. . . Anatomy
. . . Biochemistry
. . . Biofeedback
. . . Biology
. . . . Marine Biology
. . . . Microbiology
. . . . Molecular Biology
. . . . Radiation Biology
. . . . Social Biology
. . . Biomedicine
. . . Biophysics
. . . . Biomechanics
. . . . Bionics
. . . . . Robotics
. . . . Biotechnology
. . . Botany
. . . Cytology
. . . Ecology
. . . Embryology
. . . Ethology

... Genetics
.... Genetic Engineering
... Mycology
... Physiology
.... Exercise Physiology
.... Psychophysiology
... Sociobiology
... Zoology
... Entomology
... Ichthyology
... Ornithology
... Primatology
.. Physical Sciences
... Astronomy
... Chemistry
.... Biochemistry
.... Geochemistry
.... Inorganic Chemistry
.... Organic Chemistry
.... Physical Chemistry
..... Electrochemistry
..... Stereochemistry
.... Crystallography
... Earth Science
.... Geochemistry
.... Geology
..... Mineralogy
..... Paleontology
..... Petrology
.... Geophysics
..... Plate Tectonics
.... Hydrology
.... Meteorology
.... Oceanography
.... Physical Geography
.... Seismology
.... Plate Tectonics
.... Soil Science
... Physics
.... Biophysics
..... Biomechanics
..... Bionics
...... Robotics
.... Electronics
..... Microelectronics
.... Mechanics (Physics)
..... Fluid Mechanics
..... Kinetics
...... Diffusion (Physics)
..... Quantum Mechanics
.... Nuclear Physics
.... Optics
... Thermodynamics
... Spectroscopy
. Social Sciences
.. Anthropology
... Anthropological Linguistics
... Archaeology
... Educational Anthropology
... Ethnography
... Ethnology
.... Ethnomathematics
.. Civics
.. Demography
... Birth Rate
... Employment Patterns
... Geographic Distribution
... Mortality Rate
... Population Distribution
.... Ethnic Distribution
.... Racial Distribution
... Population Growth
... Population Trends
.... Black Population Trends
... Racial Composition
.... Racial Balance
... Residential Patterns
... School Demography
.... Teacher Distribution
... Social Distribution
... Urban Demography
.. Economics
... Consumer Economics
... Econometrics
... Educational Economics
.... Educational Finance
... Labor Economics
... Macroeconomics
... Microeconomics
... Rural Economics
.. Geography
... Human Geography
... Physical Geography

... World Geography
.. Gerontology
... Educational Gerontology
.. History
... African History
... American Indian History
... Ancient History
... Asian History
.... Korean War
.... Vietnam War
... Black History
... Constitutional History
... Diplomatic History
... Educational History
.... Science Education History
... European History
... Family History
... Genealogy
... Historiography
... Intellectual History
... Art History
... Literary History
... Journalism History
... Latin American History
... Local History
... Mathematics History
... Medieval History
... Middle Eastern History
... Modern History
... North American History
.... United States History
..... Civil War (United States)
..... Colonial History (United States)
..... Mexican American History
..... Reconstruction Era
..... Revolutionary War (United
       States)
..... State History
... Oral History
... Public History
... Science History
... Social History
... World History
... World War I
... World War II
.. International Studies
.. Political Science
.. Social Studies
.. Sociology
... Criminology
... Educational Sociology
... Rural Sociology
... Social Psychology
. Topography
. Space Sciences

Scientific and Technical Information

: Attitudes
Scientific Attitudes

Scientific Concepts
. Density (Matter)
. Energy
.. Geothermal Energy
.. Heat
.. Radiation
... Light
... Nuclear Energy
.. Solar Energy
.. Wind Energy
. Entropy
. Force
. Gravity (Physics)
. Height
. Motion
.. Acceleration (Physics)
.. Velocity
. Pressure (Physics)
. Relativity
. Space
.. Area
.. Volume (Mathematics)
. Time
.. Time Blocks
. Weight (Mass)

Scientific Enterprise

: Literacy
Scientific Literacy

: : Methods
: Research Methodology
Scientific Methodology

: : Groups
: Personnel
Scientific Personnel
. Mathematicians
. Science Consultants
. Scientists

: Standards
Scientific Principles

: Research
Scientific Research
. Space Exploration
.. Lunar Research

: : : Groups
: : Personnel
: Scientific Personnel
: : Groups
: Personnel
: Professional Personnel
Scientists

: Collective Bargaining
Scope of Bargaining

: Data
Scores
. Cutting Scores
. Equated Scores
. Grade Equivalent Scores
. Raw Scores
. True Scores
. Weighted Scores

: Measurement
Scoring

: : Methods
: Measurement Techniques
Scoring Formulas

: : Methods
: Evaluation Methods
Scoring Rubrics

: : Languages
: Indo European Languages
Scots Gaelic

: : Design
: Computer System Design
Screen Design (Computers)

: : Measures (Individuals)
: Tests
Screening Tests

: Visual Aids
Screens (Displays)

: Literary Genres
: : : : : Liberal Arts
: : : : Humanities
: : : : Fine Arts
: : Theater Arts
: : : : Liberal Arts
: : : Humanities
: Literature
: Drama
Scripts

: : : : Liberal Arts
: : : Humanities
: : Fine Arts
: Visual Arts
Sculpture

: Groups
Seafarers

: : Law Enforcement
: Police Action
Search and Seizure

: Committees
Search Committees (Personnel)

: : : : Groups
: : : Personnel
: : Professional Personnel
: Information Scientists
Search Intermediaries

: Information Seeking
Search Strategies

: Employment
Seasonal Employment

: : : : : : Groups
: : : : : Personnel
: : : : Nonprofessional Personnel
: : : Unskilled Workers
: : Laborers
: : : Groups
: : Personnel
: : Agricultural Personnel
: Agricultural Laborers
Seasonal Laborers

: : Instruction
: Humanities Instruction
Second Language Instruction

: Learning
Second Language Learning

: Programs
Second Language Programs
. College Second Language Programs
. Immersion Programs

: Language
Second Languages
. English (Second Language)
.. English for Special Purposes
... English for Academic Purposes
... English for Science and
     Technology
... Vocational English (Second
     Language)

: : Education
: Elementary Secondary Education
Secondary Education
. College Preparation

: Curriculum
Secondary School Curriculum
. Secondary School Mathematics
. Secondary School Science

: : Curriculum
: Secondary School Curriculum
: Curriculum
: Mathematics Curriculum
Secondary School Mathematics

: : Curriculum
: Secondary School Curriculum
: : Curriculum
: Science Curriculum
Secondary School Science

: : Groups
: Students
Secondary School Students
. High School Students
.. College Bound Students
.. High School Freshmen
.. High School Seniors
.. Noncollege Bound Students
. Junior High School Students

: : : : Groups
: : : Personnel
: : Professional Personnel
: Teachers
Secondary School Teachers

: : Institutions
: Schools
Secondary Schools
. High Schools
.. Vocational High Schools
. Junior High Schools

: : : : Groups
: : : Personnel
: : Nonprofessional Personnel

: Clerical Workers
Secretaries
. School Secretaries

: : : Needs
: : Individual Needs
: Psychological Needs
Security (Psychology)

: : Groups
: Personnel
Security Personnel

Security (1967 1978)

: Narcotics
Sedatives

: : Groups
: Organizations (Groups)
Segregationist Organizations

: : : : : Liberal Arts
: : : : Sciences
: : : Natural Sciences
: : Physical Sciences
: Earth Science
Seismology
. Plate Tectonics

: : Disabilities
: Diseases
Seizures

Selection
. Career Choice
. Competitive Selection
. Computer Selection
. Course Selection (Students)
. Elections
. . School Budget Elections
. Mate Selection
. Media Selection
. . Computer Software Selection
. . Library Material Selection
. . Reading Material Selection
. . Textbook Selection
. Personnel Selection
. . Administrator Selection
. . Counselor Selection
. Teacher Selection
. School Choice
. . College Choice
. Site Selection
. Test Selection

Selection Tools

: Admission (School)
Selective Admission

: : : Institutions
: : Schools
: Colleges
Selective Colleges

: : : Services
: : Information Services
: Information Dissemination
Selective Dissemination of Information

: : : Needs
: : Individual Needs
: Psychological Needs
Self Actualization

: Advocacy
Self Advocacy

: : : Ability
: : Skills
: Daily Living Skills
Self Care Skills

Self Concept
. Body Image
. Self Congruence
. Self Esteem
. . Self Efficacy

: : Measures (Individuals)
: Personality Measures
Self Concept Measures

: Self Concept
: : Psychological Patterns
: Congruence (Psychology)
Self Congruence

: : : Facilities
: : Educational Facilities
: Classrooms
Self Contained Classrooms

: Behavior
Self Control
. Delay of Gratification
. Self Management

: Behavior
Self Destructive Behavior
. Self Injurious Behavior
. Suicide

Self Determination
. Tribal Sovereignty

Self Directed Classrooms (1966 1980)

: Groups
Self Directed Groups

: Disclosure
Self Disclosure (Individuals)

: : Self Concept
: Self Esteem
Self Efficacy

: Employment
Self Employment

: Self Concept
Self Esteem
. Self Efficacy

: Evaluation
Self Evaluation (Groups)

: Evaluation
Self Evaluation (Individuals)

Self Evaluation (1966 1980)

Self Expression

: Expectation
Self Fulfilling Prophecies

: : Programs
: Improvement Programs
Self Help Programs

: : Behavior
: Self Destructive Behavior
Self Injurious Behavior

: : Behavior
: Self Control
Self Management

: Motivation
Self Motivation

: : Reinforcement
: Rewards
Self Reward

: : Groups
: Students
Self Supporting Students

: : Measures (Individuals)
: Rating Scales
: : Measures (Individuals)
: Attitude Measures
Semantic Differential

: : : : Liberal Arts
: : : Humanities
: : Philosophy
: : Theories
: : Linguistic Theory

: Semiotics
: : Linguistics
: Descriptive Linguistics
Semantics
. Lexicology

: : : Planning
: : Scheduling
: School Schedules
Semester System

: : Equipment
: Electronic Equipment
Semiconductor Devices
. Transistors

: Meetings
Seminars

: : : Liberal Arts
: : Humanities
: Philosophy
: Theories
: Linguistic Theory
Semiotics
. Pragmatics
. Semantics
. . Lexicology

: Occupations
Semiskilled Occupations

: : : Groups
: : Personnel
: Nonprofessional Personnel
Semiskilled Workers
. Animal Caretakers
. Boat Operators
. Grounds Keepers
. Nursery Workers (Horticulture)
. Sewing Machine Operators

: : Languages
: Afro Asiatic Languages
Semitic Languages
. Amharic
. Arabic
. Hebrew

: Status
Seniority

: Training
Sensitivity Training

Sensory Aids
. Cochlear Implants
. Hearing Aids
. Low Vision Aids
. Raised Line Drawings
. Talking Books

: : : Background
: : Experience
: Sensory Experience
Sensory Deprivation

: : Background
: Experience
Sensory Experience
. Figural Aftereffects
. Sensory Deprivation

Sensory Integration

: Training
Sensory Training
. Auditory Training

: : : : Theories
: : : Linguistic Theory
: : Generative Grammar
: Transformational Generative Grammar
Sentence Combining

Sentence Diagraming

: : : : Linguistics
: : : Descriptive Linguistics
: : Grammar
: Syntax
Sentence Structure

: : Language Patterns
: Paragraphs
Sentences
. Kernel Sentences

: Law Enforcement
Sentencing

: : Psychological Patterns
: Anxiety
Separation Anxiety

: Methods
Sequential Approach

: Learning
Sequential Learning

: : : Languages
: : Indo European Languages
: Slavic Languages
Serbocroatian

: Learning
Serial Learning

: Cognitive Processes
Serial Ordering

: Publications
Serials
. Annual Reports
. Bulletins
. Conference Proceedings
. Newspapers
. . Newsletters
. . School Newspapers
. Periodicals
. . Electronic Journals
. . Foreign Language Periodicals
. . Scholarly Journals
. Yearbooks

: : Learning
: Experiential Learning
Service Learning

: Occupations
Service Occupations
. Child Care Occupations
. Hospitality Occupations
. Laundry Drycleaning Occupations

: : Equipment
: Motor Vehicles
Service Vehicles
. Bookmobiles
. School Buses

: : : Groups
: : Personnel
: Nonprofessional Personnel
Service Workers
. Attendants
. Barbers
. Cooks
. Emergency Squad Personnel
. . Emergency Medical Technicians
. Fire Fighters
. Household Workers
. . Home Health Aides
. Housekeepers
. . Housing Management Aides
. Waiters and Waitresses

Services
. Community Services
. . Community Health Services
. . Community Information Services
. . Hotlines (Public)
. Delivery Systems
. . Document Delivery
. Financial Services
. Human Services
. . Counseling Services
. . Employment Services
. . . Outplacement Services (Employment)
. . Food Service
. . Health Services
. . . Community Health Services
. . . Hospices (Terminal Care)
. . . Long Term Care

. . . Medical Services
. . . . First Aid
. . . . . Cardiopulmonary Resuscitation
. . . . Psychiatric Services
. . . Migrant Health Services
. . . Prenatal Care
. . School Health Services
. . Integrated Services
. Psychological Services
. Social Services
. . Adult Day Care
. . Adult Foster Care
. . Ancillary School Services
. . . Mobile Educational Services
. . . Pupil Personnel Services
. . . School Health Services
. . . Student Personnel Services
. . Day Care
. . . Employer Supported Day Care
. . . Family Day Care
. . . School Age Day Care
. . . Sick Child Care
. . Foster Care
. . Social Work
. . Welfare Services
. . . Migrant Welfare Services
. Information Services
. . Community Information Services
. . . Hotlines (Public)
. . Information Dissemination
. . Document Delivery
. . . Propaganda
. . . Publicity
. . . . Advertising
. . . . . Television Commercials
. . . . Institutional Advancement
. . . Selective Dissemination of
          Information
. . Information Processing
. . . Data Collection
. . . . Sampling
. . . . . Item Sampling
. . . Data Processing
. . . Input Output
. . . . . Keyboarding (Data Entry)
. . . . Natural Language Processing
. . . . Time Sharing
. . . Documentation
. . . . Abstracting
. . . . Authority Control (Information)
. . . . Bibliometrics
. . . . . Citation Analysis
. . . . . . Bibliographic Coupling
. . . . Cataloging
. . . . . Machine Readable Cataloging
. . . . Filing
. . . . Indexing
. . . . . Automatic Indexing
. . . Information Retrieval
. . . . Downloading
. . . . Online Searching
. . . Information Storage
. . Word Processing
. . Library Services
. . . Library Circulation
. . . . Interlibrary Loans
. . . Library Extension
. . . Library Technical Processes
. . . . Library Acquisition
. . . . . Library Material Selection
. . Reference Services
. . Videotex
. Producer Services
. Professional Services
. Shared Resources and Services
. . Shared Facilities
. . Shared Library Resources

: Theories
: : : : : Liberal Arts
: : : : Humanities
: : : Philosophy
: : Logic
: Mathematical Logic
Set Theory

: Facilities
Settlement Houses

: : : Liberal Arts
: : Humanities
: Literature
Seventeenth Century Literature

: Disabilities
Severe Disabilities
. Psychosis
. . Echolalia
. . Schizophrenia
. Severe Mental Retardation

: : Disabilities
: Severe Disabilities
: : Disabilities
: Mental Retardation
Severe Mental Retardation

Severity (of Disability)

: Instruction
Sewing Instruction

: : : : Groups
: : : Personnel
: : Nonprofessional Personnel
: Semiskilled Workers
Sewing Machine Operators

: : Individual Characteristics
: Physical Characteristics
Sex

Sex (Characteristics) (1966 1980)

: : : Attitudes
: : Social Attitudes
: : Bias
: Social Bias
Sex Bias
. Sexism in Language

: : Differences
: Individual Differences
Sex Differences

: Social Discrimination
Sex Discrimination
. Sexual Harassment

: : Education
: Family Life Education
Sex Education

Sex Fairness

: Role
Sex Role

: : Attitudes
: Stereotypes
Sex Stereotypes

: : : : Attitudes
: : : Social Attitudes
: : : Bias
: : Social Bias
: Sex Bias
: Language Usage
Sexism in Language

: : : Behavior
: : Social Behavior
: Antisocial Behavior
Sexual Abuse
. Rape

: : Social Discrimination
: Sex Discrimination
: : : Behavior
: : Social Behavior
: Antisocial Behavior
Sexual Harassment

Sexual Identity

: Orientation
Sexual Orientation

Sexuality
. Bisexuality
. Homosexuality
. . Lesbianism

: : : : Groups
: : : Personnel
: : Agricultural Personnel

: Farmers
Sharecroppers

: : Services
: : Resources
: : Shared Resources and Services
: Facilities
Shared Facilities

: : Services
: : Resources
: Shared Resources and Services
Shared Library Resources

: Services
: Resources
Shared Resources and Services
. Shared Facilities
. Shared Library Resources

: : : Behavior
: : Social Behavior
: Prosocial Behavior
Sharing Behavior

: : Technology
: Metal Working
Sheet Metal Work

: Workshops
Sheltered Workshops

Shift Studies

: : : Languages
: : African Languages
: Bantu Languages
Shona

: Curriculum
Shop Curriculum

: Literary Genres
: : : : : Liberal Arts
: : : : Humanities
: : : Literature
: : Prose
: Fiction
Short Stories

: : Cognitive Processes
: Memory
Short Term Memory

: : Language
: Written Language
Shorthand

: : : Individual Characteristics
: : Psychological Characteristics
: Personality Traits
Shyness

: : : Relationship
: : Interpersonal Relationship
: Family Relationship
Sibling Relationship

: Groups
Siblings
. First Born
. Twins

: : : : Services
: : : Human Services
: : Social Services
: Day Care
Sick Child Care

: : : Disabilities
: : Diseases
: Anemia
Sickle Cell Anemia

: : Languages
: : : : Linguistics
: : : Sociolinguistics
: : Language Variation
: Creoles
Sierra Leone Creole

: : : Methods
: : Educational Methods

: Teaching Methods
Sight Method

: Vocabulary
Sight Vocabulary

: : : Communication (Thought
          Transfer)
: : Augmentative and Alternative
          Communication
: Manual Communication
: Language
Sign Language
. American Sign Language

: : : : Groups
: : : Personnel
: : Nonprofessional Personnel
: Skilled Workers
Sign Painters

: : Relationship
: Interpersonal Relationship
Significant Others

: Visual Aids
Signs

: : Literacy
: Language Arts
: Reading
Silent Reading

: Environment
Simulated Environment

: Methods
Simulation
. Computer Simulation
. . Virtual Reality
. Markov Processes
. Models
. . Causal Models
. . . Structural Equation Models
. . Mathematical Models
. . Role Models
. . Mentors
. Student Writing Models
. Teaching Models
. Monte Carlo Methods
. Role Playing
. . Dramatic Play

: : Languages
: Indo European Languages
Singhalese

: : Activities
: Music Activities
Singing

: : Visual Aids
: : Nonprint Media
: : Mass Media
: Films
Single Concept Films

: : : Institutions
: : Schools
: Single Sex Schools
: : : Institutions
: : Schools
: Colleges
Single Sex Colleges

: : Institutions
: Schools
Single Sex Schools
. Single Sex Colleges

: : Groups
: Students
Single Students

: Languages
Sino Tibetan Languages
. Burmese
. Chinese
. . Cantonese
. Foochow
. . Mandarin Chinese
. Hmong
. Lao

. Thai
. Tibetan

: : Groups
: Tribes
: : : Groups
: : Ethnic Groups
: American Indians
Sioux (Tribe)
. Lakota (Tribe)
. . Oglala Sioux (Tribe)

: : : Languages
: : African Languages
: Bantu Languages
Siswati

: : Methods
: Evaluation Methods
Site Analysis

: Development
Site Development

: Selection
Site Selection

: : Measures (Individuals)
: Tests
Situational Tests

: : : Liberal Arts
: : Humanities
: Literature
Sixteenth Century Literature

: Musculoskeletal System
Skeletal System

: : : : Activities
: : : Physical Activities
: : Athletics
: Winter Sports
Skiing

: : Methods
: Evaluation Methods
Skill Analysis

: : Facilities
: Educational Facilities
Skill Centers

: : Development
: Individual Development
Skill Development

: Obsolescence
Skill Obsolescence

: Occupations
Skilled Occupations

: : : Groups
: : Personnel
: Nonprofessional Personnel
Skilled Workers
. Auto Body Repairers
. Craft Workers
. Electricians
. Floor Layers
. Glaziers
. Locomotive Engineers
. Machinists
. . Machine Repairers
. . Machine Tool Operators
. . Tool and Die Makers
. Sign Painters
. Television Radio Repairers
. Watchmakers

: Ability
Skills
. Agricultural Skills
. Basic Skills
. . Alphabetizing Skills
. Business Skills
. . Bookkeeping
. . Keyboarding (Data Entry)
. . Recordkeeping
. . Typewriting
. Communication Skills
. . Communicative Competence

(Languages)
. . . Threshold Level (Languages)
. Daily Living Skills
. . Self Care Skills
. Decision Making Skills
. Home Economics Skills
. Homemaking Skills
. Information Skills
. Library Skills
. Interpretive Skills
. Job Skills
. Language Skills
. . Audiolingual Skills
. . Listening Skills
. . Speech Skills
. . Communicative Competence
(Languages)
. . . Threshold Level (Languages)
. Reading Skills
. . Reading Comprehension
. . Reading Rate
. . Vocabulary Skills
. . Writing Skills
. Locational Skills (Social Studies)
. Map Skills
. Mathematics Skills
. Mechanical Skills
. Minimum Competencies
. Parenting Skills
. Psychomotor Skills
. . Marksmanship
. . Object Manipulation
. . Perceptual Motor Coordination
. . . Eye Hand Coordination
. . Eye Voice Span
. Research Skills
. Salesmanship
. Science Process Skills
. Study Skills
. . Word Study Skills
. Teaching Skills
. Thinking Skills
. Visual Literacy

: Literary Genres
: : : : : Liberal Arts
: : : : Humanities
: : : Fine Arts
: : : Theater Arts
: : : : Liberal Arts
: : : : Humanities
: : Literature
: : Drama
: Comedy
Skits

: : Relationship
: Human Relations
Slavery

: : Languages
: Indo European Languages
Slavic Languages
. Bielorussian
. Bulgarian
. Czech
. Polish
. Russian
. Serbocroatian
. Slovenian
. Ukrainian

Sleep

: : Visual Aids
: : Nonprint Media
: Transparencies
Slides

: : : Languages
: : Indo European Languages
: Slavic Languages
Slovenian

: Groups
Slow Learners

: Matter
Sludge

: Environment
Slum Environment

: : Institutions
: : Schools
Slum Schools

: : Geographic Regions
: Poverty Areas
Slums

: Business
Small Businesses

: : Groups
: Classes (Groups of Students)
Small Classes

: : : Institutions
: : Schools
: Small Schools
: : : Institutions
: : Schools
: Colleges
Small Colleges

: : Technology
: Mechanics (Process)
Small Engine Mechanics

: : Instruction
: Group Instruction
Small Group Instruction

: : Institutions
: Schools
Small Schools
. One Teacher Schools
. Small Colleges

: : : Geographic Regions
: : Urban Areas
: : Community
: Municipalities
Small Towns

: Behavior
Smoking

: : : : : Liberal Arts
: : : : Humanities
: : : Fine Arts
: : Theater Arts
: : : : Liberal Arts
: : : Humanities
: : Literature
: Drama
Soap Operas

: : : : Activities
: : : Physical Activities
: : Athletics
: Team Sports
Soccer

Social Action
. Community Action

: : Behavior
: Social Behavior
: : Behavior
: Adjustment (to Environment)
Social Adjustment

: : : Groups
: : Organizations (Groups)
: Agencies
Social Agencies
. Welfare Agencies

: Attitudes
Social Attitudes
. Social Bias
. . Ethnic Bias
. . Homophobia
. . Racial Bias
. . Sex Bias
. . . Sexism in Language
. Social Desirability

: : Background
: Socioeconomic Background
Social Background
. Social Experience

: Behavior
Social Behavior
. Activism
. Antisocial Behavior
. . Aggression
. . Bullying
. . Cheating
. . Child Abuse
. . Child Neglect
. . Crime
. . . Delinquency
. . . International Crimes
. . . Genocide
. . Driving While Intoxicated
. . Elder Abuse
. . Emotional Abuse
. . Fraud
. . Hazing
. . Homicide
. . Incest
. . Sexual Abuse
. . . Rape
. . Sexual Harassment
. . Stealing
. . . Plagiarism
. . Terrorism
. . Vandalism
. . . School Vandalism
. . Verbal Abuse
. . Violence
. . . Family Violence
. Conformity
. Dissent
. Help Seeking
. Lying
. Obedience
. Prosocial Behavior
. . Sharing Behavior
. Social Adjustment

: : Attitudes
: Social Attitudes
: Bias
Social Bias
. Ethnic Bias
. Homophobia
. Racial Bias
. Sex Bias
. . Sexism in Language

: : : : : Liberal Arts
: : : : Sciences
: : : Natural Sciences
: : Biological Sciences
: Biology
Social Biology

: Change
Social Change
. Modernization

Social Characteristics

: Groups
Social Class
. Caste
. Lower Class
. Lower Middle Class
. Middle Class
. Upper Class
. Working Class

: Cognitive Processes
Social Cognition

Social Control

: : Attitudes
: Social Attitudes
Social Desirability

: : Development
: Individual Development
Social Development

: : Languages
: : : : Linguistics
: : : Sociolinguistics
: : Language Variation
: Dialects
Social Dialects

: Differences
Social Differences

Social Discrimination
. Age Discrimination
. Disability Discrimination
. Educational Discrimination
. . School Segregation
. . . College Segregation
. . . School Resegregation
. Ethnic Discrimination
. Housing Discrimination
. Racial Discrimination
. . Racial Segregation
. . . De Facto Segregation
. . . De Jure Segregation
. Religious Discrimination
. Reverse Discrimination
. Sex Discrimination
. . Sexual Harassment

: : : : Liberal Arts
: : : Sciences
: : Social Sciences
: Demography
Social Distribution

: Environment
Social Environment
. Social Isolation

: : Theories
: Social Theories
Social Exchange Theory

: : : Background
: : Socioeconomic Background
: Social Background
: : Background
: Experience
Social Experience

: : : : Liberal Arts
: : : Sciences
: : Social Sciences
: : : Liberal Arts
: : Humanities
: History
Social History

: : Data
: Statistical Data
Social Indicators

: Influences
Social Influences

Social Integration
. Classroom Desegregation
. Neighborhood Integration
. Personnel Integration
. . Faculty Integration
. . Teacher Integration
. Racial Integration
. School Desegregation
. College Desegregation
. Voluntary Desegregation

: : Environment
: Social Environment
Social Isolation

Social Life

: Mobility
Social Mobility

: Networks
Social Networks

: : Groups
: Organizations (Groups)
Social Organizations

: Planning
Social Planning

: Problems
Social Problems

: : : Achievement
: : Academic Achievement

: Student Promotion
Social Promotion

: : : : Liberal Arts
: : : Sciences
: : Social Sciences
: : : : Liberal Arts
: : : Sciences
: : Behavioral Sciences
: Sociology
: : : Liberal Arts
: : : Sciences
: : Behavioral Sciences
: Psychology
Social Psychology

: Reinforcement
Social Reinforcement

Social Relations (1966 1980)

: Responsibility
Social Responsibility
. Citizenship Responsibility

: Research
Social Science Research
. Critical Theory
. Economic Research

: : Liberal Arts
: Sciences
Social Sciences
. Anthropology
. . Anthropological Linguistics
. . Archaeology
. . Educational Anthropology
. . Ethnography
. . Ethnology
. . . Ethnomathematics
. Civics
. Demography
. . Birth Rate
. . Employment Patterns
. . Geographic Distribution
. . Mortality Rate
. . Population Distribution
. . . Ethnic Distribution
. . . Racial Distribution
. . Population Growth
. . Population Trends
. . . Black Population Trends
. . Racial Composition
. . . Racial Balance
. . Residential Patterns
. . School Demography
. . . Teacher Distribution
. . Social Distribution
. . Urban Demography
. Economics
. . Consumer Economics
. . Econometrics
. . Educational Economics
. . . Educational Finance
. . Labor Economics
. . Macroeconomics
. . Microeconomics
. . Rural Economics
. Geography
. . Human Geography
. . Physical Geography
. . World Geography
. Gerontology
. . Educational Gerontology
. History
. . African History
. . American Indian History
. . Ancient History
. . Asian History
. . . Korean War
. . . Vietnam War
. . Black History
. . Constitutional History
. . Diplomatic History
. . Educational History
. . . Science Education History
. . European History
. . Family History
. . . Genealogy
. . Historiography
. . Intellectual History
. . . Art History
. . . Literary History

. . Journalism History
. . Latin American History
. . Local History
. . Mathematics History
. . Medieval History
. . Middle Eastern History
. . Modern History
. . North American History
. . . United States History
. . . . Civil War (United States)
. . . . Colonial History (United States)
. . . . Mexican American History
. . . . Reconstruction Era
. . . . Revolutionary War (United
States)
. . . . State History
. . Oral History
. . Public History
. . Science History
. . Social History
. . World History
. . . World War I
. . . World War II
. International Studies
. Political Science
. Social Studies
. Sociology
. . Criminology
. . Educational Sociology
. . Rural Sociology
. . Social Psychology
. Topography

: : : Groups
: : Personnel
: Professional Personnel
Social Scientists
. Historians
. Sociologists

: : Services
: Human Services
Social Services
. Adult Day Care
. Adult Foster Care
. Ancillary School Services
. . Mobile Educational Services
. . Pupil Personnel Services
. . School Health Services
. . Student Personnel Services
. Day Care
. . Employer Supported Day Care
. . Family Day Care
. . School Age Day Care
. . Sick Child Care
. Foster Care
. Social Work
. Welfare Services
. . Migrant Welfare Services

: Status
Social Status

: : Organization
: Social Structure
Social Stratification

: Organization
Social Structure
. Social Stratification

: : : Liberal Arts
: : Sciences
: Social Sciences
: Curriculum
Social Studies

: Groups
Social Support Groups

Social Systems
. Capitalism
. . Free Enterprise System
. Communism
. Fascism
. . Nazism
. Socialism

: Theories
Social Theories
. Organizational Theories
. Social Exchange Theory

: Values
Social Values

Social Welfare (1966 1980)

: : : Services
: : Human Services
: Social Services
Social Work

: : : Groups
: : Personnel
: Professional Personnel
: : : Groups
: : Personnel
: Caseworkers
Social Workers
. School Social Workers

: Social Systems
Socialism

Socialization
. Political Socialization

: : : : Liberal Arts
: : : Sciences
: : Natural Sciences
: Biological Sciences
: : : Liberal Arts
: : Sciences
: Behavioral Sciences
Sociobiology

Sociocultural Patterns
. Ethnicity
. Humanitarianism

: Background
Socioeconomic Background
. Social Background
. . Social Experience

: Influences
Socioeconomic Influences

: Status
Socioeconomic Status

: Linguistics
Sociolinguistics
. Dialect Studies
. Language Planning
. . Language Standardization
. Language Variation
. Creoles
. . Gullah
. . . Haitian Creole
. . . Mauritian Creole
. . . Sierra Leone Creole
. Dialects
. . Black Dialects
. . Nonstandard Dialects
. . Regional Dialects
. . Social Dialects
. Language Styles
. . Academic Discourse
. . Linguistic Borrowing
. Pidgins

: : : : Groups
: : : Personnel
: : Professional Personnel
: Social Scientists
Sociologists

: : : Liberal Arts
: : Sciences
: Social Sciences
: : : Liberal Arts
: : Sciences
: Behavioral Sciences
Sociology
. Criminology
. Educational Sociology
. Rural Sociology
. Social Psychology

: : Methods
: Measurement Techniques
Sociometric Techniques

: : : : Activities
: : : Physical Activities
: : Athletics
: Team Sports
Softball

: Land Use
: Conservation (Environment)
Soil Conservation

: : : : : Liberal Arts
: : : : Sciences
: : : Natural Sciences
: : Physical Sciences
: Earth Science
Soil Science

: : : Scientific Concepts
: : Energy
: Radiation
Solar Energy

Solar System

: : : Liberal Arts
: : Mathematics
: Geometry
Solid Geometry

: : Matter
: Wastes
Solid Wastes

: : Languages
: Afro Asiatic Languages
Somali

: : : : : Liberal Arts
: : : : Humanities
: : : Fine Arts
: : Music
: Vocal Music
Songs
. Art Song
. Ballads
. Hymns

: : : : : Liberal Arts
: : : : Humanities
: : : Literature
: : Poetry
: Lyric Poetry
: Literary Genres
Sonnets

: : Groups
: Males
Sons

: : Groups
: Organizations (Groups)
Sororities

: : : Methods
: : Production Techniques
: Special Effects
Sound Effects

: : Equipment
: Measurement Equipment
: : Equipment
: Electronic Equipment
: : Equipment
: Audio Equipment
Sound Spectrographs

Sound Tracks (1966 1980)

Southern Citizens (1966 1980)

Southern Community (1966 1980)

Southern Schools (1966 1980)

: Scientific Concepts
Space
. Area
. Volume (Mathematics)

: : Organization
: Classification
Space Classification

: Structural Elements (Construction)
: Equipment
Space Dividers
. Movable Partitions

: : Research
: Scientific Research
Space Exploration
. Lunar Research

Space Orientation (1968 1980)

: : Liberal Arts
: Sciences
Space Sciences

Space Utilization

: : : Languages
: : Indo European Languages
: Romance Languages
Spanish

: : : Groups
: : North Americans
: Hispanic Americans
: : Groups
: Ethnic Groups
Spanish Americans

: Culture
Spanish Culture

: : : Liberal Arts
: : Humanities
: Literature
Spanish Literature

: : Groups
: Native Speakers
Spanish Speaking

: Ability
Spatial Ability

: Relationship
Spatial Relationship (Facilities)

Spatial Relationship (1966 1980)

: : Groups
: Classes (Groups of Students)
Special Classes

: : Programs
: Special Programs
Special Degree Programs

: Education
Special Education
. Adapted Physical Education

: : : : Groups
: : : Personnel
: : Professional Personnel
: Teachers
Special Education Teachers

: : Methods
: Production Techniques
Special Effects
. Animation
. Sound Effects

: Disabilities
Special Health Problems

: : Institutions
: : Information Sources
: Libraries
Special Libraries
. Corporate Libraries
. Film Libraries
. Government Libraries
.. National Libraries
.. State Libraries
. Institutional Libraries
.. Hospital Libraries
.. Prison Libraries
. Law Libraries
. Medical Libraries
. Science Libraries

: Groups
: Students
Special Needs Students

: : : Activities
: : Physical Activities
: Athletics
Special Olympics

: Programs
Special Programs
. Individualized Education Programs
. Individualized Family Service Plans
. Resource Room Programs
. Special Degree Programs

: : Institutions
: Schools
Special Schools
. Institutional Schools
.. Hospital Schools
. Residential Schools

: Zoning
Special Zoning

: Degrees (Academic)
Specialist in Education Degrees

: : Groups
: Personnel
Specialists
. Child Development Specialists
. Film Production Specialists
. Media Specialists
.. Audiovisual Coordinators

Specialization

: Standards
Specifications
. Computer Software
.. Courseware
... Microworlds
.. Database Management Systems
.. Menu Driven Software
. Design Requirements
. Facility Requirements

: : : : Liberal Arts
: : : Sciences
: : Natural Sciences
: Physical Sciences
Spectroscopy

: Language Arts
Speech
. Articulation (Speech)
. Artificial Speech
. Caregiver Speech
. Inner Speech (Subvocal)
. Pronunciation
. Speech Acts
. Speech Compression

: : Language Arts
: Speech
Speech Acts

: Clinics
Speech and Hearing Clinics

: Communication (Thought Transfer)
Speech Communication
. Oral Interpretation
. Public Speaking

: : Language Arts
: Speech
Speech Compression

: Curriculum
Speech Curriculum

Speech Education (1966 1980)

: : Evaluation
: Medical Evaluation
Speech Evaluation

: Behavior Patterns
Speech Habits

: Disabilities
Speech Impairments
. Articulation Impairments
. Cleft Palate
. Delayed Speech
. Stuttering
. Voice Disorders

: Improvement
Speech Improvement

: Instruction
Speech Instruction
. Pronunciation Instruction

: : : Technology
: : Medicine
: Pathology
Speech Language Pathology

: : : : Ability
: : : Skills
: : Language Skills
: Audiolingual Skills
Speech Skills

: : Equipment
: Electronic Equipment
: : Equipment
: Audio Equipment
Speech Synthesizers

: : : Measures (Individuals)
: : Tests
: Verbal Tests
Speech Tests

: Therapy
Speech Therapy

Speeches

: : Literacy
: : Language Arts
: Reading
Speed Reading

: Language Arts
Spelling
. Finger Spelling
. Invented Spelling

: Instruction
Spelling Instruction

: : Disabilities
: Congenital Impairments
Spina Bifida

: Curriculum
Spiral Curriculum

Spirituality

: Behavior
Spontaneous Behavior

: : : : Liberal Arts
: : : Sciences
: : Behavioral Sciences
: Psychology
Sport Psychology

: : Technology
: Medicine
Sports Medicine

: Attitudes
Sportsmanship

: Groups
Spouses

: : Records (Forms)
: Worksheets
Spreadsheets

: : : : Activities
: : : Physical Activities
: : Athletics
: Racquet Sports
Squash (Game)

: : Development
: Labor Force Development
Staff Development
. Faculty Development

: Meetings
Staff Meetings

: Orientation
Staff Orientation

: Role
Staff Role

: Labor Utilization
Staff Utilization

: Structural Elements (Construction)
Stages (Facilities)

: Language Usage
Standard Spoken Usage

: : Measures (Individuals)
: Tests
Standardized Tests

Standards
. Academic Standards
. . Graduation Requirements
. . . Degree Requirements
. Administrative Principles
. Behavior Standards
. . Codes of Ethics
. Court Doctrine
. Criteria
. . Admission Criteria
. . Evaluation Criteria
. . . Reliability
. . . . Interrater Reliability
. . . . Test Reliability
. . . Validity
. . . . Concurrent Validity
. . . . Predictive Validity
. . . . Proof (Mathematics)
. . . . Test Validity
. . . . . Construct Validity
. . . . . Content Validity
. . Lesson Observation Criteria
. Dress Codes
. Educational Principles
. Environmental Standards
. Equipment Standards
. Food Standards
. Labor Standards
. Laws
. . Civil Law
. . Constitutional Law
. . Criminal Law
. . International Law
. . School Law
. Library Standards
. Living Standards
. Metric System
. Middle Class Standards
. National Standards
. Parliamentary Procedures
. Qualifications
. . Administrator Qualifications
. . Counselor Qualifications
. . Employment Qualifications
. . Supervisor Qualifications
. . Teacher Qualifications
. Residence Requirements
. Scientific Principles
. Specifications
. . Computer Software
. . . Courseware
. . . . Microworlds
. . . Database Management Systems
. . . Menu Driven Software
. Design Requirements
. Facility Requirements
. State Standards
. Textbook Standards

Stars

State Action

: : : : Groups
: : : Organizations (Groups)
: : Agencies

: Public Agencies
State Agencies
. State Departments of Education
. State Licensing Boards

State Aid
. Foundation Programs
. Full State Funding
. State Federal Aid

: : : : Groups
: : : Organizations (Groups)
: : Governing Boards
: Boards of Education
State Boards of Education

: Relationship
State Church Separation

: : : Institutions
: : Schools
: State Schools
: : : : Institutions
: : : Schools
: : Colleges
: Public Colleges
State Colleges
. State Universities

: : Institutions
: Courts
State Courts

: : : : Publications
: : : Reference Materials
: : Guides
: Curriculum Guides
State Curriculum Guides

: : : : : Groups
: : : : Organizations (Groups)
: : : Agencies
: : Public Agencies
: State Agencies
: : : Organization
: : Administrative Organization
: Departments
State Departments of Education

: State Aid
: Federal Aid
State Federal Aid

: : : Groups
: : Organizations (Groups)
: Government (Administrative Body)
State Government

: : : : : : Liberal Arts
: : : : : Sciences
: : : : Social Sciences
: : : : : Liberal Arts
: : : : Humanities
: : : History
: : North American History
: United States History
State History

: Legislation
State Legislation
. School Attendance Legislation

: : : : Institutions
: : : : Information Sources
: : : Libraries
: : Special Libraries
: Government Libraries
State Libraries

: : : : : Groups
: : : : Organizations (Groups)
: : : Agencies
: : Public Agencies
: State Agencies
State Licensing Boards

: : : Data
: : Statistical Data
: Norms
State Norms

: Publications
State of the Art Reviews

: : : : Groups
: : : Personnel
: : Government Employees
: Public Officials
State Officials
. State Supervisors

: Programs
State Programs

: Governance
State Regulation

: : Relationship
: Government School Relationship
State School District Relationship

: : Institutions
: Schools
State Schools
. State Colleges
. . State Universities

: Standards
State Standards

: : : : Groups
: : : Personnel
: : Administrators
: Supervisors
: : : : Groups
: : : Personnel
: : Government Employees
: : Public Officials
: State Officials
State Supervisors

: : : Methods
: : Evaluation Methods
: Surveys
State Surveys

: : : : Institutions
: : : Schools
: : Colleges
: Universities
: : : : Institutions
: : : Schools
: : State Schools
: : : : : Institutions
: : : : Schools
: : : Colleges
: : Public Colleges
: State Colleges
State Universities

States Powers

: Planning
Statewide Planning

: : : Methods
: : Evaluation Methods
: Data Analysis
Statistical Analysis
. Analysis of Covariance
. Analysis of Variance
. Bayesian Statistics
. Chi Square
. Correlation
. Effect Size
. Error of Measurement
. Goodness of Fit
. Item Analysis
. Judgment Analysis Technique
. Least Squares Statistics
. Maximum Likelihood Statistics
. Meta Analysis
. Multivariate Analysis
. . Cluster Analysis
. . Discriminant Analysis
. . Factor Analysis
. . . Oblique Rotation
. . . Orthogonal Rotation
. . Multidimensional Scaling
. . Path Analysis
. Regression (Statistics)
. . Multiple Regression Analysis
. Robustness (Statistics)
. Statistical Distributions
. Statistical Inference
. Statistical Significance

: Bias
Statistical Bias

: Data
Statistical Data
. Census Figures
. Employment Statistics
. . Worker Days
. Library Statistics
. Norms
. . Local Norms
. . National Norms
. . State Norms
. . Test Norms
. School Statistics
. Social Indicators

: : : Liberal Arts
: : Mathematics
: Statistics
: : : : Methods
: : : Evaluation Methods
: : Data Analysis
: Statistical Analysis
Statistical Distributions

: : : : Methods
: : : Evaluation Methods
: : Data Analysis
: Statistical Analysis
: Inferences
: : : : Methods
: : : Evaluation Methods
: : Data Analysis
: Data Interpretation
Statistical Inference

: : : : Methods
: : : Evaluation Methods
: : Data Analysis
: Statistical Analysis
Statistical Significance

: Research
Statistical Studies

: : : Methods
: : Evaluation Methods
: Surveys
Statistical Surveys

: : Liberal Arts
: Mathematics
Statistics
. Bayesian Statistics
. Least Squares Statistics
. Maximum Likelihood Statistics
. Nonparametric Statistics
. Sampling
. . Item Sampling
. Statistical Distributions

Status
. Citizenship
. Economic Status
. . Poverty
. Employment Level
. . Academic Rank (Professional)
. . Tenure
. Ethnic Status
. Full Time Equivalency
. Group Status
. . Family Status
. Marital Status
. Retirement
. . Early Retirement
. . Mandatory Retirement
. . Teacher Retirement
. Seniority
. Social Status
. Socioeconomic Status

: : : Needs
: : Individual Needs
: Psychological Needs
Status Need

: : : Behavior
: : Social Behavior
: Antisocial Behavior
Stealing
. Plagiarism

: : Groups
: Family (Sociological Unit)
Stepfamily

: : : : : Liberal Arts
: : : : Sciences
: : : Natural Sciences
: : Physical Sciences
: Chemistry
Stereochemistry

: Attitudes
Stereotypes
. Ethnic Stereotypes
. . Black Stereotypes
. Sex Stereotypes
. Teacher Stereotypes

: Stimuli
Stimulants

Stimulation

Stimuli
. Auditory Stimuli
. Cues
. . Context Clues
. Electrical Stimuli
. Stimulants
. Tactile Stimuli
. Verbal Stimuli
. Visual Stimuli
. . Pictorial Stimuli

Stimulus Devices (1966 1980)

: : : Cognitive Processes
: : Learning Processes
: : : Cognitive Processes
: : Abstract Reasoning
: Generalization
Stimulus Generalization

: Groups
Stopouts

Storage
. Equipment Storage
. Information Storage

Story Grammar

: : Literacy
: : Language Arts
: Reading
Story Reading

: Language Arts
Story Telling

: : Disabilities
: Visual Impairments
Strabismus

: : Behavior
: Responses
Stranger Reactions

: Planning
Strategic Planning

: : : Linguistics
: : Phonology
: Suprasegmentals
Stress (Phonology)

Stress Management

Stress Variables

Strikes
. Teacher Strikes

: : Equipment
: Musical Instruments
String Instruments

: : Methods
: Evaluation Methods
Structural Analysis (Linguistics)
. Discourse Analysis
. Tagmemic Analysis

: : Methods
: Evaluation Methods
Structural Analysis (Science)

Structural Analysis (1966 1980)

: : Structural Elements (Construction)
: Building Systems
Structural Building Systems

Structural Elements (Construction)
. Acoustic Insulation
. Building Systems
. . Structural Building Systems
. Ceilings
. Chimneys
. Doors
. Flooring
. . Carpeting
. Glass Walls
. Roofing
. Space Dividers
. . Movable Partitions
. Stages (Facilities)
. Thermal Insulation
. Windows

: : : : Methods
: : : Simulation
: : Models
: : Causal Models
Structural Equation Models

: : Theories
: Linguistic Theory
Structural Grammar

: Linguistics
Structural Linguistics

: Unemployment
Structural Unemployment

: : Behavior
: Student Behavior
: : Behavior
: Adjustment (to Environment)
Student Adjustment

: : Psychological Patterns
: Alienation
Student Alienation

: Attitudes
Student Attitudes

: Enrollment
Student Attrition

: Behavior
Student Behavior
. Student Adjustment
. Student Participation
. Student Reaction

: Curriculum
Student Centered Curriculum

: Certification
Student Certification

Student Characteristics
. Diversity (Student)

: : Relationship
: Student School Relationship
Student College Relationship

: Costs
Student Costs
. Instructional Student Costs
. . Tuition
. Noninstructional Student Costs

: : Educational Media
: Instructional Materials
Student Developed Materials
. Student Writing Models

: Development
Student Development

Student Distribution (1966 1980)

: Objectives
Student Educational Objectives

: Employment
Student Employment

: Empowerment
Student Empowerment

: Evaluation
Student Evaluation
. Curriculum Based Assessment
. Nongraded Student Evaluation

: : : Evaluation
: : Personnel Evaluation
: Teacher Evaluation
Student Evaluation of Teacher Performance

: : Programs
: Exchange Programs
Student Exchange Programs

: : Background
: Experience
Student Experience

: Financial Support
Student Financial Aid
. Assistantships
. Fellowships
. . Faculty Fellowships
. Income Contingent Loans
. Parent Financial Contribution
. Scholarships
. . Merit Scholarships
. . No Need Scholarships
. . Tuition Grants

: : : Groups
: : Personnel
: School Personnel
: : : Groups
: : Personnel
: Administrators
Student Financial Aid Officers

: : : Groups
: : Organizations (Groups)
: Student Organizations
: : Groups
: : Organizations (Groups)
: Government (Administrative Body)
Student Government

: Improvement
Student Improvement

: Interests
Student Interests

: : : : : : Liberal Arts
: : : : : Humanities
: : : : Literature
: : : Prose
: : Nonfiction
: : Literary Genres
: Diaries
Student Journals

: : Ability
: Leadership
Student Leadership

: Programs
Student Loan Programs

: : Mobility
: Migration
Student Mobility

: Motivation
Student Motivation

: Needs
Student Needs

: : Groups
: Organizations (Groups)
Student Organizations

. Student Government
. Student Unions

: : Behavior
: Student Behavior
: Behavior
: Participation
Student Participation

: : : : Services
: : : Human Services
: : Social Services
: Ancillary School Services
Student Personnel Services

: : : Groups
: : Personnel
: School Personnel
Student Personnel Workers

: Placement
Student Placement

: Problems
Student Problems

: : Activities
: School Activities
Student Projects

: : Achievement
: Academic Achievement
Student Promotion
. Social Promotion

: : Publications
: School Publications
Student Publications

: : Behavior
: Student Behavior
: : Behavior
: Responses
Student Reaction

: Records (Forms)
Student Records
. Academic Records
. Report Cards

: Recruitment
Student Recruitment

: Research
Student Research

: Responsibility
Student Responsibility

: Civil Liberties
Student Rights

: Role
Student Role

: Relationship
Student School Relationship
. Student College Relationship

: : Culture
: Subcultures
Student Subcultures

: : : Methods
: : Evaluation Methods
: Surveys
Student Surveys

: Attitudes
Student Teacher Attitudes

: Evaluation
Student Teacher Evaluation

: : : : Groups
: : : Personnel
: : Administrators
: Supervisors
: : : : Groups
: : : Personnel
: : School Personnel
: : : : Groups
: : : : Personnel

::: Professional Personnel
: Faculty
: College Faculty
Student Teacher Supervisors

:::: Groups
::: Personnel
:: Professional Personnel
: Teachers
:::: Groups
::: Students
:: College Students
: Preservice Teachers
Student Teachers

:::: Education
::: Professional Education
:: Teacher Education
: Preservice Teacher Education
Student Teaching

: Transportation
Student Transportation

::: Groups
:: Organizations (Groups)
: Student Organizations
:: Facilities
: Educational Facilities
Student Unions

:: Groups
: Volunteers
: Groups
: Students
Student Volunteers

:: Quality of Life
: Well Being
Student Welfare

::: Educational Media
:: Instructional Materials
: Student Developed Materials
:: Methods
:: Simulation
: Models
Student Writing Models

: Groups
Students
. Adult Students
. Advanced Students
. Asian American Students
. Bilingual Students
. Black Students
. College Students
.. College Freshmen
.. College Juniors
.. College Seniors
.. College Sophomores
.. College Transfer Students
. Graduate Students
... Dental Students
... Law Students
... Medical Students
.... Graduate Medical Students
.. In State Students
.. On Campus Students
.. Out of State Students
.. Preservice Teachers
... Student Teachers
.. Resident Assistants
.. Two Year College Students
.. Undergraduate Students
... Premedical Students
. Commuting Students
. Continuation Students
. Day Students
. Elementary School Students
. Evening Students
. Foreign Students
. Full Time Students
. High Risk Students
. Hispanic American Students
. Lower Class Students
. Majors (Students)
.. Education Majors
. Married Students
. Middle Class Students
. Middle School Students
. Nonmajors
. Nontraditional Students

. Part Time Students
. Pregnant Students
. Reentry Students
. Secondary School Students
.. High School Students
... College Bound Students
... High School Freshmen
... High School Seniors
... Noncollege Bound Students
.. Junior High School Students
. Self Supporting Students
. Single Students
. Special Needs Students
. Student Volunteers
. Terminal Students
. Transfer Students
.. College Transfer Students
. White Students

:: Education
: Art Education
Studio Art

Studio Floor Plans (1966 1980)

:: Activities
: Learning Activities
Study
. Home Study
.. Homework
. Independent Study

: Education
Study Abroad

::: Facilities
:: Educational Facilities
: Study Facilities
Study Centers

:: Facilities
: Educational Facilities
Study Facilities
. Carrels
. Study Centers

:: Educational Media
: Instructional Materials
::: Publications
:: Reference Materials
: Guides
Study Guides

: Behavior Patterns
Study Habits

:: Ability
: Skills
Study Skills
. Word Study Skills

:: Disabilities
: Speech Impairments
Stuttering

: Culture
Subcultures
. Student Subcultures

: Vocabulary
Subject Index Terms

: Behavior
Substance Abuse
. Alcohol Abuse
.. Alcoholism
. Drug Abuse
.. Drug Addiction

:::: Groups
::: Personnel
:: Professional Personnel
: Teachers
Substitute Teachers

::::: Methods
:::: Educational Methods
::: Teaching Methods
:: Drills (Practice)
: Pattern Drills (Language)
Substitution Drills

::: Liberal Arts
:: Mathematics
: Arithmetic
Subtraction

: Environment
Suburban Environment

:: Facilities
: Housing
Suburban Housing

: Problems
Suburban Problems

:: Institutions
: Schools
Suburban Schools

:: Groups
: Youth
Suburban Youth

:: Geographic Regions
: Metropolitan Areas
Suburbs

:: Behavior
: Performance
Success

:: Death
: Infant Mortality
Sudden Infant Death Syndrome

:::::: Linguistics
::::: Descriptive Linguistics
:::: Grammar
::: Morphology (Languages)
:: Morphemes
: Affixes
Suffixes

::: Methods
:: Educational Methods
: Teaching Methods
Suggestopedia

:: Behavior
: Self Destructive Behavior
: Death
Suicide

: Evaluation
Summative Evaluation

: Programs
Summer Programs
. Summer Science Programs

:: Institutions
: Schools
Summer Schools

:: Programs
: Summer Programs
:: Programs
: Science Programs
Summer Science Programs

Superconductors

::: Groups
:: Personnel
: Administrators
Superintendents

:: Programs
:: Learning
: Experiential Learning
: Field Experience Programs
:: Education
: Agricultural Education
Supervised Occupational Experience (Agriculture)

:: Governance
: Administration
Supervision
. Practicum Supervision
. Proctoring
. School Supervision
. Science Supervision

. Teacher Supervision
.. Clinical Supervision (of Teachers)

:: Standards
: Qualifications
Supervisor Qualifications

::: Groups
:: Personnel
: Administrators
Supervisors
. Crew Leaders
. State Supervisors
. Student Teacher Supervisors

: Methods
Supervisory Methods

: Training
Supervisory Training

: Education
Supplementary Education

: Reading Materials
Supplementary Reading Materials

: Resources
Supplies
. Adhesives
. Agricultural Supplies
. Electric Batteries
. Magnetic Tapes
.. Magnetic Tape Cassettes
... Audiotape Cassettes
... Videotape Cassettes

: Relationship
Supply and Demand
. Teacher Supply and Demand
.. Teacher Shortage

: Employment
Supported Employment

: Predictor Variables
Suppressor Variables

:: Linguistics
: Phonology
Suprasegmentals
. Intonation
. Stress (Phonology)

Supreme Court Litigation (1966 1980)

Supreme Courts (1966 1980)

::::: Theories
:::: Linguistic Theory
::: Generative Grammar
:: Transformational Generative
    Grammar
Surface Structure

:::: Activities
::: Physical Activities
:: Athletics
: Aquatic Sports
Surfing

:: Technology
: Medicine
Surgery

:::: Groups
::: Personnel
:: Health Personnel
: Allied Health Personnel
Surgical Technicians

Surrealism

:: Methods
: Evaluation Methods
Surveys
. Community Surveys
. Graduate Surveys
. Library Surveys
. Mail Surveys
. National Surveys
. Occupational Surveys
. School Surveys

. State Surveys
. Statistical Surveys
. Student Surveys
. Teacher Surveys
. Telephone Surveys
. Television Surveys

: Discipline
Suspension
. In School Suspension

: Development
Sustainable Development

: : Instruction
: Reading Instruction
: : Literacy
: : Language Arts
: Reading
Sustained Silent Reading

: : Languages
: African Languages
Susu

: : : Methods
: : Educational Methods
: Teaching Methods
: : Education
: Music Education
Suzuki Method

: : : Languages
: : African Languages
: Bantu Languages
Swahili

: : Languages
: Indo European Languages
Swedish

: : : : Activities
: : : Physical Activities
: : Athletics
: Aquatic Sports
Swimming

: Facilities
Swimming Pools

: : Linguistics
: Phonology
Syllables

: Language
Symbolic Language

: Learning
Symbolic Learning

Symbolism

: : Literary Devices
: : Language
: Figurative Language
Symbols (Literary)

Symbols (Mathematics)
. Numbers
. . Logarithms
. . Number Systems
. . Rational Numbers
. . . Fractions
. . . . Decimal Fractions
. . . Integers
. . . . Prime Numbers
. . . . Whole Numbers
. . Reciprocals (Mathematics)

Symmetry

Symptoms (Individual Disorders)

: : : Linguistics
: : Descriptive Linguistics
: Grammar
Syntax
. Form Classes (Languages)
. . Adjectives
. . Adverbs
. . Conjunctions
. . Determiners (Languages)
. . Function Words

. . Nouns
. . Prepositions
. . Pronouns
. . Verbs
. Phrase Structure
. Sentence Structure

: : Methods
: Evaluation Methods
Synthesis

: Methods
Systems Analysis

: : Groups
: Personnel
Systems Analysts

: : Methods
: Holistic Approach
Systems Approach
. Systems Building
. . Design Build Approach

: : : Methods
: : Holistic Approach
: Systems Approach
Systems Building
. Design Build Approach

Systems Concepts (1966 1980)

: Development
Systems Development

: : : Activities
: : Physical Activities
: Athletics
Table Tennis

: Visual Aids
Tables (Data)
. Expectancy Tables

: : Visual Aids
: : Equipment
: Projection Equipment
Tachistoscopes

: : Change
: Media Adaptation
Tactile Adaptation

: Stimuli
Tactile Stimuli

: : Cognitive Processes
: Perception
Tactual Perception

: : : : Measures (Individuals)
: : : Tests
: : Cognitive Tests
: Perception Tests
Tactual Visual Tests

: : : Languages
: : Malayo Polynesian Languages
: Indonesian Languages
Tagalog

: : : Methods
: : Evaluation Methods
: Structural Analysis (Linguistics)
Tagmemic Analysis

: : Languages
: Indo European Languages
Tajik

Talent

: : Development
: Individual Development
Talent Development

: Identification
Talent Identification

Talent Utilization (1966 1980)

: Literary Genres
Tales

. Fables
. Fairy Tales

: Sensory Aids
Talking Books

: : Languages
: Dravidian Languages
Tamil

: Religion
Taoism

: : Equipment
: Electronic Equipment
Tape Recorders
. Audiotape Recorders
. Videotape Recorders

: Nonprint Media
Tape Recordings
. Audiotape Recordings
. Videotape Recordings

: : Methods
: Evaluation Methods
Task Analysis

Task Performance (1966 1980)

: : : Languages
: : Uralic Altaic Languages
: Turkic Languages
Tatar

: Financial Support
Tax Allocation

Tax Credits

Tax Deductions

Tax Effort

: Ratios (Mathematics)
Tax Rates

Taxes
. Property Taxes
. School Taxes

: : Relationship
: Interpersonal Relationship
Teacher Administrator Relationship

: : : : Groups
: : : Personnel
: : School Personnel
: : : : Groups
: : : Personnel
: : Paraprofessional Personnel
: Paraprofessional School Personnel
Teacher Aides
. Bilingual Teacher Aides

: : Psychological Patterns
: Alienation
Teacher Alienation

: : : Groups
: : Organizations (Groups)
: Professional Associations
Teacher Associations

: Attendance
Teacher Attendance

: Attitudes
Teacher Attitudes

: Background
Teacher Background

: Behavior
Teacher Behavior
. Teacher Collaboration
. Teacher Effectiveness
. Teacher Militancy
. Teacher Participation
. Teacher Persistence
. Teacher Response

: : : Behavior
: : Responses
: Burnout
Teacher Burnout

: : Facilities
: Resource Centers
Teacher Centers

: Certification
Teacher Certification
. Alternative Teacher Certification
. National Teacher Certification

Teacher Characteristics
. Teaching Styles

: : Behavior
: Teacher Behavior
: : : Behavior
: Cooperation
: Educational Cooperation
Teacher Collaboration

: : Ability
: Competence
Teacher Competencies

: : : Methods
: : Measurement Techniques
: Testing
Teacher Competency Testing

: : Educational Media
: Instructional Materials
Teacher Developed Materials
. Teacher Made Tests

: Discipline
Teacher Discipline
. Teacher Dismissal

: : Discipline
: Teacher Discipline
: : Discipline
: Dismissal (Personnel)
Teacher Dismissal

: : : : : Liberal Arts
: : : : Sciences
: : : Social Sciences
: : Demography
: School Demography
Teacher Distribution

: : Education
: Professional Education
Teacher Education
. Competency Based Teacher
     Education
. English Teacher Education
. Inservice Teacher Education
. Preservice Teacher Education
. . Student Teaching
. Teacher Educator Education

: : Curriculum
: College Curriculum
Teacher Education Curriculum
. Methods Courses

: Programs
Teacher Education Programs
. Extended Teacher Education
     Programs

: : : Education
: : Professional Education
: Teacher Education
Teacher Educator Education

: : : : : Groups
: : : : Personnel
: : : School Personnel
: : : : Groups
: : : Personnel
: : Professional Personnel
: Faculty
: College Faculty
Teacher Educators
. Methods Teachers

: : Behavior
: Teacher Behavior
Teacher Effectiveness

: Employment
Teacher Employment

Teacher Employment Benefits

: Empowerment
Teacher Empowerment

: : Evaluation
: Personnel Evaluation
Teacher Evaluation
. Student Evaluation of Teacher
  Performance

: : Programs
: Exchange Programs
Teacher Exchange Programs

: Expectation
Teacher Expectations of Students

: Guidance
Teacher Guidance

: : Facilities
: Housing
Teacher Housing

: Improvement
Teacher Improvement

: Influences
Teacher Influence

: : Social Integration
: Personnel Integration
Teacher Integration

: : : : Groups
: : : Personnel
: : Professional Personnel
: Teachers
Teacher Interns

: : Measures (Individuals)
: Tests
: : : Educational Media
: : Instructional Materials
: Teacher Developed Materials
Teacher Made Tests

: : Behavior
: Teacher Behavior
Teacher Militancy

: : Psychological Patterns
: Morale
Teacher Morale

: Motivation
Teacher Motivation

: Orientation
Teacher Orientation
. Beginning Teacher Induction

: : Behavior
: Teacher Behavior
: : Behavior
: Participation
Teacher Participation

: : Behavior
: Teacher Behavior
: : Behavior
: Persistence
Teacher Persistence

: : Placement
: Job Placement
Teacher Placement

: Promotion (Occupational)
Teacher Promotion

: : Standards
: Qualifications
Teacher Qualifications

: Recruitment
Teacher Recruitment

: : : : Groups
: : : Personnel
: : Professional Personnel
: Teachers
: : : : : Groups
: : : : Personnel
: : : Professional Personnel
: : Researchers
: Educational Researchers
Teacher Researchers

: : Behavior
: Teacher Behavior
: : Behavior
: Responses
Teacher Response

: Responsibility
Teacher Responsibility
. Noninstructional Responsibility

: : Status
: Retirement
Teacher Retirement

: Civil Liberties
Teacher Rights

: Role
Teacher Role

: : Income
: Expenditures
: Salaries
Teacher Salaries

: : Selection
: Personnel Selection
Teacher Selection

: : : Relationship
: : Supply and Demand
: : Labor Market
: Teacher Supply and Demand
Teacher Shortage

: : Attitudes
: Stereotypes
Teacher Stereotypes

: Strikes
Teacher Strikes

: Ratios (Mathematics)
Teacher Student Ratio

: : Relationship
: Interpersonal Relationship
Teacher Student Relationship

: : : Governance
: : Administration
: Supervision
Teacher Supervision
. Clinical Supervision (of Teachers)

: : Relationship
: Supply and Demand
: Labor Market
Teacher Supply and Demand
. Teacher Shortage

: : : Methods
: : Evaluation Methods
: Surveys
Teacher Surveys

: : Mobility
: Occupational Mobility
Teacher Transfer

: : Quality of Life
: Well Being
Teacher Welfare

: Workshops
Teacher Workshops

: : : Groups
: : Personnel

: Professional Personnel
Teachers
. Adult Educators
. Art Teachers
. Beginning Teachers
. Bilingual Teachers
. Black Teachers
. Catholic Educators
. Cooperating Teachers
. Elementary School Teachers
. Home Economics Teachers
. Industrial Arts Teachers
. Instructor Coordinators
. Itinerant Teachers
. Language Teachers
. . English Teachers
. Lay Teachers
. Master Teachers
. Mathematics Teachers
. Middle School Teachers
. Minority Group Teachers
. Music Teachers
. Physical Education Teachers
. Preschool Teachers
. Public School Teachers
. Reading Teachers
. Remedial Teachers
. Resource Teachers
. Science Teachers
. Secondary School Teachers
. Special Education Teachers
. Student Teachers
. Substitute Teachers
. Teacher Interns
. Teacher Researchers
. Teachers with Disabilities
. Television Teachers
. Tutors
. Vocational Education Teachers
. . Business Education Teachers
. . Distributive Education Teachers
. . Trade and Industrial Teachers
. Writing Teachers

: : : : Groups
: : : Personnel
: : Professional Personnel
: Teachers
Teachers with Disabilities

: : Occupations
: Professional Occupations
Teaching (Occupation)
. Team Teaching
. Urban Teaching

Teaching Assignment (1966 1980)

: : : : : Groups
: : : : Personnel
: : : School Personnel
: : : : : Groups
: : : : Personnel
: : : Professional Personnel
: : Faculty
: College Faculty
Teaching Assistants

: : Environment
: Work Environment
: : Environment
: Educational Environment
Teaching Conditions

: : Background
: Experience
Teaching Experience

: : : Publications
: : Reference Materials
: Guides
Teaching Guides

: : Institutions
: Hospitals
Teaching Hospitals

: Faculty Workload
Teaching Load

: : Educational Media
: Autoinstructional Aids
Teaching Machines

: : Methods
: Educational Methods
Teaching Methods
. Audiolingual Methods
. Case Method (Teaching Technique)
. Clinical Teaching (Health
  Professions)
. Community Based Instruction
  (Disabilities)
. Conventional Instruction
. Creative Teaching
. Cross Age Teaching
. Demonstrations (Educational)
. . Demonstrations (Science)
. Diagnostic Teaching
. Discussion (Teaching Technique)
. Drills (Practice)
. . Pattern Drills (Language)
. . . Substitution Drills
. Experimental Teaching
. Grammar Translation Method
. Guided Design
. Individualized Instruction
. Kinesthetic Methods
. Kodaly Method
. Language Experience Approach
. Learner Controlled Instruction
. Lecture Method
. Montessori Method
. Multimedia Instruction
. . Audiovisual Instruction
. Negative Practice
. Oral Communication Method
. . Lipreading
. Orff Method
. Peer Teaching
. Precision Teaching
. Programmed Instruction
. . Computer Assisted Instruction
. . . Intelligent Tutoring Systems
. . Programmed Tutoring
. Reciprocal Teaching
. Reggio Emilia Approach
. Sight Method
. Suggestopedia
. Suzuki Method
. Telephone Instruction
. Thematic Approach
. Training Methods
. . Management Games
. . Microcounseling
. . Microteaching
. Whole Language Approach

: : : Methods
: : Simulation
: Models
Teaching Models

Teaching Programs (1966 1980)

: : Ability
: Skills
Teaching Skills

: Teacher Characteristics
Teaching Styles

Teaching (1966 1980)

: : : : Activities
: : : Physical Activities
: : Athletics
: Team Sports
Team Handball

: : : Activities
: : Physical Activities
: Athletics
Team Sports
. Baseball
. Basketball
. Field Hockey
. Football
. Ice Hockey
. Lacrosse
. Soccer
. Softball
. Team Handball
. Volleyball
. Water Polo

: : : Occupations
: : Professional Occupations
: Teaching (Occupation)
Team Teaching

: Training
Team Training

: : Behavior
: Group Behavior
Teamwork

: : : Education
: : Vocational Education
: Technical Education
Tech Prep

Technical Assistance

: : Education
: Vocational Education
Technical Education
. Fire Science Education
. Tech Prep

: : : : : Liberal Arts
: : : : Humanities
: : : Fine Arts
: : Visual Arts
: Drafting
Technical Illustration

: : : : Institutions
: : : Schools
: : Colleges
: Two Year Colleges
Technical Institutes

: : Liberal Arts
: Mathematics
Technical Mathematics

: Occupations
Technical Occupations

: : Literacy
: Language Arts
: Writing (Composition)
Technical Writing

: Development
Technological Advancement

Technological Literacy
. Computer Literacy

Technology
. Accounting
. . Property Accounting
. . School Accounting
. Aerospace Technology
. . Aviation Technology
. . . Aviation Mechanics
. Agriculture
. . Agronomy
. . Animal Husbandry
. . Gardening
. . Harvesting
. . Horticulture
. . . Ornamental Horticulture
. . . . Floriculture
. . . . Landscaping
. . . . Turf Management
. Appropriate Technology
. Automation
. . Library Automation
. . . Retrospective Conversion (Library Catalogs)
. . Office Automation
. . Robotics
. Biotechnology
. Communications
. . Audiovisual Communications
. . . Dial Access Information Systems
. . . Educational Radio
. . . Educational Television
. . . Loop Induction Systems
. . Telecommunications
. . . Communications Satellites
. . . Computer Mediated Communication
. . . . Electronic Mail
. . . . . Listservs

. . . Electronic Publishing
. . . Facsimile Transmission
. . . Radio
. . . . Educational Radio
. . . Teleconferencing
. . . Telephone Communications Systems
. . . Television
. . . . Broadcast Television
. . . . Cable Television
. . . . Childrens Television
. . . . Closed Circuit Television
. . . . Commercial Television
. . . . Educational Television
. . . . Interactive Television
. . . . Public Television
. . . Videotex
. Consumer Science
. Cosmetology
. Cybernetics
. Educational Technology
. Instructional Systems
. Performance Technology
. Electromechanical Technology
. Engineering
. . Agricultural Engineering
. . Chemical Engineering
. . Civil Engineering
. . Ocean Engineering
. . Operating Engineering
. . Engineering Technology
. Etiology
. Forestry
. Genetic Engineering
. Horology
. Hydraulics
. Information Technology
. Journalism
. . Broadcast Journalism
. . New Journalism
. . News Reporting
. . News Writing
. . Photojournalism
. . Scholastic Journalism
. Laboratory Technology
. Lexicography
. Manufacturing
. . Assembly (Manufacturing)
. . Computer Assisted Manufacturing
. . Mass Production
. Marketing
. . Merchandising
. . Retailing
. . Salesmanship
. . Wholesaling
. Masonry
. . Bricklaying
. Mechanics (Process)
. . Auto Mechanics
. . Aviation Mechanics
. . Refrigeration Mechanics
. . Small Engine Mechanics
. Medicine
. . Anesthesiology
. . Audiology
. . Biomedicine
. . Dentistry
. . Dietetics
. . Electroencephalography
. . Epidemiology
. . Family Practice (Medicine)
. . Geriatrics
. . Gynecology
. . Internal Medicine
. . Neurology
. . Nursing
. . . Practical Nursing
. . Obstetrics
. . Oncology
. . Ophthalmology
. . Osteopathy
. . Pathology
. . . Plant Pathology
. . . Psychopathology
. . . Speech Language Pathology
. . Pediatrics
. . Pharmacology
. . Pharmacy
. . Podiatry
. . Preventive Medicine
. . Primary Health Care
. . Psychiatry
. . Sports Medicine

. Surgery
. Toxicology
. . Veterinary Medicine
. Metal Working
. . Sheet Metal Work
. Metallurgy
. Mining
. Optometry
. Plumbing
. Power Technology
. . Nuclear Technology
. Radiology
. Reprography
. . Microreproduction
. Water Treatment
. Welding
. Wildlife Management
. Woodworking
. . Cabinetmaking
. . Carpentry

: Education
Technology Education

Technology Transfer

: : Technology
: Communications
Telecommunications
. Communications Satellites
. Computer Mediated Communication
. . Electronic Mail
. . . Listservs
. . Electronic Publishing
. Facsimile Transmission
. Radio
. . Educational Radio
. Teleconferencing
. Telephone Communications Systems
. Television
. . Broadcast Television
. . Cable Television
. . Childrens Television
. . Closed Circuit Television
. . Commercial Television
. . Educational Television
. . Interactive Television
. . Public Television
. Videotex

: : : Technology
: : Communications
: Telecommunications
Teleconferencing

: : Curriculum
: Courses
Telecourses

: Reading Materials
Telegraphic Materials

: : Business
: Industry
Telephone Communications Industry

: : : Technology
: : Communications
: Telecommunications
Telephone Communications Systems

: : : Methods
: : Educational Methods
: Teaching Methods
Telephone Instruction

: : : Methods
: : Evaluation Methods
: Surveys
Telephone Surveys

: Instruction
Telephone Usage Instruction

: : : Technology
: : Communications
: Telecommunications
: Mass Media
Television
. Broadcast Television
. Cable Television
. Childrens Television
. Closed Circuit Television

. Commercial Television
. Educational Television
. Interactive Television
. Public Television

: : : : Services
: : : Information Services
: : : Information Dissemination
: : : Communication (Thought Transfer)
: : Publicity
: Advertising
Television Commercials

: Curriculum
Television Curriculum

: : Methods
: Production Techniques
: Lighting
Television Lighting

: : : : Groups
: : : Personnel
: : Nonprofessional Personnel
: Skilled Workers
Television Radio Repairers

: : Research
: Media Research
Television Research

: Facilities
Television Studios

: : : Methods
: : Evaluation Methods
: Surveys
Television Surveys

: : : : Groups
: : : Personnel
: : Professional Personnel
: Teachers
Television Teachers

: Activities
Television Viewing

: : Languages
: Dravidian Languages
Telugu

Temperature

: Rhythm (Music)
Tempo (Music)

: Employment
Temporary Employment

TENL (1968 1980)

: : : : Activities
: : : Physical Activities
: : Athletics
: Racquet Sports
Tennis

: : : : : Linguistics
: : : : Descriptive Linguistics
: : : Grammar
: : Morphology (Languages)
: Morphemes
Tenses (Grammar)

: : Status
: Employment Level
Tenure

: : : : Groups
: : : Personnel
: : School Personnel
: : : Groups
: : : Personnel
: : Professional Personnel
: Faculty
Tenured Faculty

: Education
Terminal Education

:: Disabilities
: Diseases
Terminal Illness

:: Groups
: Students
Terminal Students

Termination of Treatment

::: Behavior
:: Social Behavior
: Antisocial Behavior
Terrorism

:: Psychological Patterns
: Anxiety
Test Anxiety

: Bias
Test Bias
. Item Bias

: Instruction
Test Coaching

:: Development
: Material Development
Test Construction

Test Content

Test Format

:::: Methods
::: Evaluation Methods
:: Data Analysis
: Data Interpretation
Test Interpretation

Test Items

Test Length

::: Publications
:: Reference Materials
: Guides
Test Manuals

::: Data
:: Statistical Data
: Norms
Test Norms

:::: Standards
::: Criteria
:: Evaluation Criteria
: Reliability
Test Reliability

Test Results

: Publications
Test Reviews

Test Score Decline

: Equipment
Test Scoring Machines

: Selection
Test Selection

: Theories
Test Theory
. Item Response Theory

Test Use

:::: Standards
::: Criteria
:: Evaluation Criteria
: Validity
Test Validity
. Construct Validity
. Content Validity

Test Wiseness

:: Methods
: Measurement Techniques
Testing
. Adaptive Testing

. Comparative Testing
. Computer Assisted Testing
. Confidence Testing
. Educational Testing
. Group Testing
. Individual Testing
. Minimum Competency Testing
. Psychological Testing
. Teacher Competency Testing

: Problems
Testing Problems

: Programs
Testing Programs

: Measures (Individuals)
Tests
. Achievement Tests
.. Equivalency Tests
.. Mastery Tests
.. National Competency Tests
. Aptitude Tests
.. Reading Readiness Tests
.. School Readiness Tests
. Auditory Tests
.. Audiometric Tests
. Cognitive Tests
.. Intelligence Tests
.. Perception Tests
... Tactual Visual Tests
. College Entrance Examinations
. Creativity Tests
. Criterion Referenced Tests
.. Mastery Tests
. Culture Fair Tests
. Diagnostic Tests
. Field Tests
. High Stakes Tests
. Licensing Examinations (Professions)
. Mathematics Tests
. Maturity Tests
. Nonverbal Tests
.. Visual Measures
. Norm Referenced Tests
. Objective Tests
.. Multiple Choice Tests
. Occupational Tests
.. Work Sample Tests
. Open Book Tests
. Performance Tests
. Physical Fitness Tests
. Preschool Tests
. Pretests Posttests
. Prognostic Tests
. Science Tests
. Screening Tests
. Situational Tests
. Standardized Tests
. Teacher Made Tests
. Timed Tests
. Verbal Tests
.. Essay Tests
.. Language Tests
.. Listening Comprehension Tests
.. Reading Tests
... Informal Reading Inventories
.. Speech Tests
.. Writing Tests
. Vision Tests

Text Structure

: Bias
Textbook Bias

Textbook Content

:: Evaluation
: Instructional Material Evaluation
Textbook Evaluation

Textbook Preparation

:: Methods
: Production Techniques
Textbook Publication

Textbook Publications (1966 1980)

:: Research
: Media Research
Textbook Research

: Selection
: Media Selection
Textbook Selection

: Standards
Textbook Standards

:: Educational Media
: Instructional Materials
:: Publications
: Printed Materials
: Books
Textbooks
. History Textbooks
. Multicultural Textbooks

: Instruction
Textiles Instruction

Textual Criticism (1969 1980)

:: Languages
: Sino Tibetan Languages
Thai

::: Liberal Arts
:: Humanities
: Fine Arts
Theater Arts
. Acting
. Choral Speaking
. Drama
.. Comedy
... Skits
.. Scripts
.. Soap Operas
.. Tragedy
. Dramatics
.. Creative Dramatics
. Opera
. Pantomime
. Puppetry
. Readers Theater
. Rehearsals (Theater Arts)

: Facilities
Theaters

::: Methods
:: Educational Methods
: Teaching Methods
Thematic Approach

:: Education
: Professional Education
Theological Education

Theoretical Criticism (1969 1980)

Theories
. Atomic Theory
. Behavior Theories
.. Adaptation Level Theory
.. Attribution Theory
.. Mediation Theory
. Chaos Theory
. Counseling Theories
. Critical Theory
. Educational Theories
. Game Theory
. Generalizability Theory
. Information Theory
. Kinetic Molecular Theory
. Learning Theories
.. Constructivism (Learning)
. Linguistic Theory
.. Case (Grammar)
.. Generative Grammar
... Transformational Generative
      Grammar
.... Context Free Grammar
.... Deep Structure
.... Kernel Sentences
.... Sentence Combining
.... Surface Structure
.. Generative Phonology
.. Linguistic Competence
.. Linguistic Performance
. Semiotics
.. Pragmatics
... Semantics
.... Lexicology
.. Structural Grammar

.. Traditional Grammar
. Music Theory
. Personality Theories
. Piagetian Theory
. Relativity
. Rhetorical Theory
. Role Theory
. Set Theory
. Social Theories
.. Organizational Theories
.. Social Exchange Theory
. Test Theory
.. Item Response Theory

: Relationship
Theory Practice Relationship

: Environment
Therapeutic Environment

: Therapy
: Recreation
Therapeutic Recreation
. Play Therapy

::: Groups
:: Personnel
: Professional Personnel
:::: Groups
::: Personnel
:: Health Personnel
: Allied Health Personnel
Therapists
. Occupational Therapists
. Physical Therapists

Therapy
. Art Therapy
. Bibliotherapy
. Dance Therapy
. Drug Therapy
. Educational Therapy
. Group Therapy
. Hearing Therapy
. Music Therapy
. Occupational Therapy
. Oral Rehydration Therapy
. Physical Therapy
. Psychotherapy
.. Gestalt Therapy
.. Milieu Therapy
.. Rational Emotive Therapy
.. Reality Therapy
.. Relaxation Training
.. Transactional Analysis
. Respiratory Therapy
. Speech Therapy
. Therapeutic Recreation
.. Play Therapy

:: Environment
: Physical Environment
Thermal Environment

: Structural Elements (Construction)
Thermal Insulation

::::: Liberal Arts
:::: Sciences
::: Natural Sciences
:: Physical Sciences
: Physics
Thermodynamics

:: Publications
: Reference Materials
Thesauri

:: Publications
: Reports
Theses
. Doctoral Dissertations
. Masters Theses

:: Ability
: Skills
:: Ability
: Cognitive Ability
Thinking Skills

: Visual Aids
Three Dimensional Aids

: : Ability
: Language Proficiency
: : : : Ability
: : : Skills
: : Language Skills
: : : : Ability
: : : Skills
: : Communication Skills
: Communicative Competence
　　(Languages)
Threshold Level (Languages)

: : Languages
: Sino Tibetan Languages
Tibetan

: Scientific Concepts
Time
. Time Blocks

: : Scientific Concepts
: Time
Time Blocks

: Influences
Time Factors (Learning)

: : Governance
: Administration
Time Management

Time on Task

Time Perspective

: : : : Services
: : : Information Services
: : Information Processing
: Data Processing
Time Sharing

Time to Degree

: : Measures (Individuals)
: Tests
Timed Tests

: Reinforcement
Timeout

: Groups
Tissue Donors

: : Plants (Botany)
: Field Crops
Tobacco

: : : : Groups
: : : Age Groups
: : Children
: Young Children
Toddlers

: : Groups
: Tribes
: : : Groups
: : Ethnic Groups
: American Indians
Tohono O Odham People

: : Facilities
: Sanitary Facilities
Toilet Facilities

: Training
Toilet Training

: Reinforcement
Token Economy

Tokenism

: Language
Tone Languages

: : : : : Groups
: : : : Personnel
: : : Nonprofessional Personnel
: : Skilled Workers
: Machinists
Tool and Die Makers

: : : Liberal Arts
: : Sciences
: Social Sciences
Topography

: : : Liberal Arts
: : Mathematics
: Geometry
Topology

: Weather
Tornadoes

Torts

: : Communication (Thought Transfer)
: Augmentative and Alternative
　　Communication
Total Communication

: Management Systems
: : Governance
: Administration
Total Quality Management

Totalitarianism
. Nazism

: : Business
: Industry
Tourism

: : Technology
: Medicine
Toxicology

Toys

: : : Activities
: : Physical Activities
: Athletics
Track and Field

Track System (Education)

Tracking (1968 1980)

: : Equipment
: Motor Vehicles
Tractors

: : Education
: Vocational Education
Trade and Industrial Education

: : : : : Groups
: : : : Personnel
: : : Professional Personnel
: : Teachers
: Vocational Education Teachers
Trade and Industrial Teachers

: : Theories
: Linguistic Theory
Traditional Grammar

: : Institutions
: Schools
Traditional Schools

Traditionalism

: Accidents
Traffic Accidents

Traffic Circulation

Traffic Control
. Air Traffic Control

: Safety
Traffic Safety

: : : : : Liberal Arts
: : : : Humanities
: : : Fine Arts
: : Theater Arts
: : : Liberal Arts
: : : Humanities
: : Literature
: Drama
Tragedy

: Facilities
Trails

: Groups
Trainees

: : Groups
: Personnel
Trainers

Training
. Counselor Training
. Cross Cultural Training
. Flight Training
. Industrial Training
. Job Training
. . Custodian Training
. . Off the Job Training
. . On the Job Training
. . . Apprenticeships
. Laboratory Training
. Leadership Training
. Military Training
. Professional Training
. Retraining
. Sensitivity Training
. Sensory Training
. . Auditory Training
. Supervisory Training
. Team Training
. Toilet Training
. Travel Training
. Volunteer Training

: Financial Support
Training Allowances

Training Laboratories (1967 1980)

: : : Methods
: : Educational Methods
: Teaching Methods
Training Methods
. Management Games
. Microcounseling
. Microteaching

: Objectives
Training Objectives

: : Therapy
: Psychotherapy
Transactional Analysis

: : : Cognitive Processes
: : Metacognition
: Meditation
Transcendental Meditation

: Learning
Transfer of Training

: Policy
Transfer Policy

: Programs
Transfer Programs
. Free Choice Transfer Programs

: Incidence
Transfer Rates (College)

: : Groups
: Students
Transfer Students
. College Transfer Students

Transfers (1966 1980)

: : : Theories
: : Linguistic Theory
: Generative Grammar
Transformational Generative Grammar
. Context Free Grammar
. Deep Structure
. Kernel Sentences
. Sentence Combining
. Surface Structure

Transformations (Mathematics)

: Learning
Transformative Learning

: : Groups
: Migrants
: : : Groups
: : Age Groups
: Children
Transient Children

: : : Equipment
: : Electronic Equipment
: Semiconductor Devices
Transistors

: Programs
Transitional Programs

: : Institutions
: Schools
Transitional Schools

Translation
. Deaf Interpreting
. Machine Translation

: Visual Aids
: Nonprint Media
Transparencies
. Slides

Transportation
. Air Transportation
. Bus Transportation
. Rail Transportation
. Student Transportation

: Adoption
Transracial Adoption

: Activities
Travel

: Training
Travel Training

Treaties

: Plants (Botany)
Trees

: : : Methods
: : Evaluation Methods
: Data Analysis
Trend Analysis

: : Methods
: Research Methodology
Triangulation

: : : Groups
: : Organizations (Groups)
: Government (Administrative Body)
Tribal Government

: Self Determination
Tribal Sovereignty

: Education
Tribally Controlled Education

: Groups
Tribes
. Cherokee (Tribe)
. Chippewa (Tribe)
. Choctaw (Tribe)
. . Mississippi Band of Choctaw
　　(Tribe)
. Cree (Tribe)
. Hopi (Tribe)
. Iroquois (Tribe)
. Navajo (Nation)
. Sioux (Tribe)
. . Lakota (Tribe)
. . . Oglala Sioux (Tribe)
. Tohono O Odham People
. Zuni (Tribe)

: : Liberal Arts
: Mathematics
Trigonometry

: : : Planning
: : Scheduling
: School Schedules
Trimester System

: Methods
Troubleshooting
. Debugging (Computers)

Truancy

: : Data
: Scores
True Scores

: Attitudes
Trust (Psychology)

: : Responsibility
: Legal Responsibility
Trust Responsibility (Government)

: : : Groups
: : Personnel
: Administrators
Trustees

Trusts (Financial)

: : : Costs
: : Student Costs
: Instructional Student Costs
: : Costs
: Fees
Tuition

: : : Financial Support
: : Student Financial Aid
: Scholarships
: : Financial Support
: Grants
Tuition Grants

: : : : Activities
: : : Physical Activities
: : Athletics
: Gymnastics
Tumbling

: : : : Technology
: : : Agriculture
: : Horticulture
: Ornamental Horticulture
Turf Management

: : Languages
: Uralic Altaic Languages
Turkic Languages
. Azerbaijani
. Bashkir
. Chuvash
. Kyrgyz
. Tatar
. Turkish
. Uzbek
. Yakut

: : : Languages
: : Uralic Altaic Languages
: Turkic Languages
Turkish

: Programs
Tutorial Programs

: : Instruction
: Individual Instruction
Tutoring
. Programmed Tutoring

: : : : Groups
: : : Personnel
: : Professional Personnel
: Teachers
Tutors

: : : Liberal Arts
: : Humanities
: Literature
Twentieth Century Literature

: : Groups
: Siblings
Twins

: : : Groups
: : Students

: College Students
Two Year College Students

: : : Institutions
: : Schools
: Colleges
Two Year Colleges
. Community Colleges
. Technical Institutes

: Behavior Patterns
: Behavior
Type A Behavior

: Behavior Patterns
: Behavior
Type B Behavior

: : : Ability
: : Skills
: Business Skills
Typewriting

: : : Languages
: : American Indian Languages
: Mayan Languages
Tzeltal

: : : Languages
: : American Indian Languages
: Mayan Languages
Tzotzil

: : : Languages
: : Indo European Languages
: Slavic Languages
Ukrainian

: Language
Uncommonly Taught Languages

: Achievement
Underachievement

: Employment
Underemployment

: : : Groups
: : Students
: College Students
Undergraduate Students
. Premedical Students

: : : Education
: : Postsecondary Education
: Higher Education
Undergraduate Study

: Facilities
Underground Facilities

: : Activities
: Physical Activities
Underwater Diving

: : : Groups
: : Migrants
: Immigrants
Undocumented Immigrants

Unemployment
. Structural Unemployment

: : Methods
: Insurance
: Financial Support
Unemployment Insurance

: Curriculum
Unified Studies Curriculum

: : : Publications
: : Reference Materials
: : : Publications
: : Catalogs
: Library Catalogs
Union Catalogs

: Groups
Union Members

: : Groups
: Organizations (Groups)
Unions

: Costs
Unit Costs

Unit Plan (1966 1980)

: : Curriculum
: Courses
United States Government (Course)

: : : : : Liberal Arts
: : : : Sciences
: : : Social Sciences
: : : Liberal Arts
: : Humanities
: : History
: North American History
United States History
. Civil War (United States)
. Colonial History (United States)
. Mexican American History
. Reconstruction Era
. Revolutionary War (United States)
. State History

: : : : Liberal Arts
: : : Humanities
: : Literature
: North American Literature
United States Literature
. Hispanic American Literature
. . Mexican American Literature

: : Curriculum
: Courses
Units of Study
. Activity Units

: : Organization
: Classification
Universal Decimal Classification

: : : Institutions
: : Schools
: Colleges
Universities
. Land Grant Universities
. Open Universities
. Research Universities
. State Universities
. Urban Universities

: : : Business
: : Industry
: Publishing Industry
University Presses

: Occupations
Unskilled Occupations

: : : Groups
: : Personnel
: Nonprofessional Personnel
Unskilled Workers
. Laborers
. . Agricultural Laborers
. . . Migrant Workers
. . . Seasonal Laborers
. . Auxiliary Laborers

: : : Groups
: : Parents
: : : Groups
: : Females
: Mothers
Unwed Mothers

Unwritten Language (1968 1980)

: Language
Unwritten Languages

: : Groups
: Social Class
Upper Class

: : : Institutions
: : Schools
: Colleges
Upper Division Colleges

: Languages
Uralic Altaic Languages
. Finno Ugric Languages
. . Cheremis
. . Estonian
. . Finnish
. . Hungarian
. . Ostyak
. . Vogul
. Manchu
. Mongolian Languages
. . Buriat
. . Dagur
. . Mongolian
. Samoyed Languages
. . Yurak
. Turkic Languages
. . Azerbaijani
. . Bashkir
. . Chuvash
. . Kyrgyz
. . Tatar
. . Turkish
. . Uzbek
. . Yakut

: : Groups
: Urban Population
: : : Groups
: : : Ethnic Groups
: : American Indians
: Nonreservation American Indians
Urban American Indians

: Geographic Regions
Urban Areas
. Inner City
. Municipalities
. . Boomtowns
. . Small Towns

: Culture
Urban Culture

: : : : Liberal Arts
: : : Sciences
: : Social Sciences
: Demography
Urban Demography

: Education
Urban Education

: Environment
Urban Environment

: : Education
: Extension Education
Urban Extension

: Improvement
Urban Improvement
. Urban Renewal

: Language
Urban Language

: Planning
Urban Planning

: Groups
Urban Population
. Urban American Indians
. Urban Youth

: Problems
Urban Problems

: Programs
Urban Programs

: : Improvement
: Urban Improvement
Urban Renewal

: : : Groups
: : Organizations (Groups)
: Agencies
Urban Renewal Agencies

: : Institutions
: Schools
Urban Schools

. Urban Universities

: Curriculum
Urban Studies

: : : Occupations
: : Professional Occupations
: Teaching (Occupation)
Urban Teaching

: : Mobility
: Migration
Urban to Rural Migration

: : Mobility
: Migration
Urban to Suburban Migration

: : : Institutions
: : Schools
: Urban Schools
: : : : Institutions
: : : Schools
: : Colleges
: Universities
Urban Universities

: : Groups
: Youth
: : Groups
: Urban Population
Urban Youth

: Development
Urbanization

: : Languages
: Indo European Languages
Urdu

: Research
Use Studies
. Facility Utilization Research

: Man Machine Systems
: Computer Interfaces
User Friendly Interface

: Needs
User Needs (Information)

: : Attitudes
: Satisfaction
User Satisfaction (Information)

: Groups
Users (Information)

Utilities

: : Languages
: American Indian Languages
Uto Aztecan Languages
. Hopi
. Papago

: : : Languages
: : Uralic Altaic Languages
: Turkic Languages
Uzbek

: Programs
Vacation Programs

Vacations

: Programs
Validated Programs

: : : Standards
: : Criteria
: Evaluation Criteria
Validity
. Concurrent Validity
. Predictive Validity
. Proof (Mathematics)
. Test Validity
. . Construct Validity
. . Content Validity

: : : Cognitive Processes
: : Critical Thinking

: Evaluative Thinking
Value Judgment

Values
. Aesthetic Values
. Democratic Values
. . American Dream
. Moral Values
. Social Values

: Education
Values Clarification

: Education
Values Education

: : : Behavior
: : Social Behavior
: Antisocial Behavior
Vandalism
. School Vandalism

: : Mathematical Concepts
: Geometric Concepts
: : : Liberal Arts
: : Mathematics
: Algebra
Vectors (Mathematics)

Vehicular Traffic

: : Scientific Concepts
: Motion
Velocity

: Equipment
Vending Machines

: Groups
Vendors
. Merchants
. Online Vendors

: : : Disabilities
: : Diseases
: Communicable Diseases
Venereal Diseases

: Climate Control
Ventilation

: Ability
Verbal Ability
. Reading Ability
. . Reading Skills
. . . Reading Comprehension
. . . Reading Rate
. Writing Ability
. . Writing Skills

: : Communication (Thought Transfer)
: Verbal Communication
: : : Behavior
: : Social Behavior
: Antisocial Behavior
Verbal Abuse

: Communication (Thought Transfer)
Verbal Communication
. Business Correspondence
. Dictation
. Letters (Correspondence)
. Verbal Abuse

: : : Development
: : Individual Development
: Cognitive Development
Verbal Development
. Language Acquisition

: Learning
Verbal Learning

: : Conditioning
: Operant Conditioning
Verbal Operant Conditioning

: Stimuli
Verbal Stimuli

: : Measures (Individuals)
: Tests
Verbal Tests
. Essay Tests

. Language Tests
. Listening Comprehension Tests
. Reading Tests
. . Informal Reading Inventories
. Speech Tests
. Writing Tests

: : : : Linguistics
: : : Descriptive Linguistics
: : Grammar
: : Syntax
: Form Classes (Languages)
Verbs

: Organization
Vertical Organization

: Groups
Veterans
. Vietnam Veterans

: : Education
: Adult Education
Veterans Education

: : : Groups
: : Personnel
: Professional Personnel
: : : Groups
: : Personnel
: Health Personnel
Veterinarians

: : : Groups
: : Personnel
: Paraprofessional Personnel
: : : : Groups
: : : Personnel
: : Health Personnel
: Allied Health Personnel
Veterinary Assistants

: : : Education
: : Professional Education
: Medical Education
Veterinary Medical Education

: : Technology
: Medicine
Veterinary Medicine

: Groups
Victims of Crime

: : : Liberal Arts
: : Humanities
: Literature
Victorian Literature

: : : : Equipment
: : : Electronic Equipment
: : : Computer Peripherals
: : Input Output Devices
: Computer Terminals
Video Display Terminals

: Visual Aids
: Equipment
: Electronic Equipment
Video Equipment
. Videodisks
. Videotape Cassettes
. Videotape Recorders

: : Activities
: Games
Video Games

: : Visual Aids
: : : Equipment
: : Electronic Equipment
: Video Equipment
: Nonprint Media
Videodisks

: : Visual Aids
: : : Equipment
: : Electronic Equipment
: Video Equipment
: : : : Resources
: : : Supplies
: : : Equipment
: : : Electronic Equipment

: : Magnetic Tapes
: Magnetic Tape Cassettes
Videotape Cassettes

: : Visual Aids
: : : Equipment
: : : Electronic Equipment
: Video Equipment
: : Equipment
: Electronic Equipment
: Tape Recorders
Videotape Recorders

: Visual Aids
: Nonprint Media
: Tape Recordings
Videotape Recordings

: : : Technology
: : Communications
: Telecommunications
: Services
: Information Services
Videotex

: : Groups
: Veterans
Vietnam Veterans

: : Conflict
: War
: : : : : Liberal Arts
: : : : Sciences
: : : Social Sciences
: : : : Liberal Arts
: : : Humanities
: : History
: Asian History
Vietnam War

: Languages
Vietnamese

: : Groups
: Indochinese
Vietnamese People

: : : Behavior
: : Social Behavior
: Antisocial Behavior
Violence
. Family Violence

: : : Methods
: : Simulation
: Computer Simulation
Virtual Reality

Viruses
. Acquired Immune Deficiency
         Syndrome
. Rubella

: : : Languages
: : Malayo Polynesian Languages
: Indonesian Languages
Visayan
. Cebuano

: Instrumentation
Visible Speech

Vision

: : Measures (Individuals)
: Tests
Vision Tests

: : : Groups
: : Personnel
: Paraprofessional Personnel
Visiting Homemakers

: : : Cognitive Processes
: : Perception
: Visual Perception
Visual Acuity

Visual Aids
. Bulletin Boards
. Cartoons
. Chalkboards
. Charts

. . Experience Charts
. . Flow Charts
. Diagrams
. Display Aids
. Films
. . Foreign Language Films
. . Instructional Films
. . Kinescope Recordings
. . Single Concept Films
. Filmstrips
. Geometric Constructions
. Graphs
. Illustrations
. Maps
. Microforms
. . Microfiche
. . Microfilm
. . . Computer Output Microfilm
. Photographic Equipment
. Photographs
. Projection Equipment
. . Filmstrip Projectors
. . Microform Readers
. . Opaque Projectors
. . Overhead Projectors
. . Tachistoscopes
. Raised Line Drawings
. Screens (Displays)
. Signs
. Tables (Data)
. . Expectancy Tables
. Three Dimensional Aids
. Transparencies
. . Slides
. Video Equipment
. . Videodisks
. . Videotape Cassettes
. . Videotape Recorders
. Videotape Recordings

: : : Liberal Arts
: : Humanities
: Fine Arts
Visual Arts
. Architecture
. Childrens Art
. Design Crafts
. Drafting
. . Architectural Drafting
. . Engineering Drawing
. . Technical Illustration
. Film Production
. Freehand Drawing
. Graphic Arts
. . Cartography
. . Computer Graphics
. . Engineering Graphics
. . . Engineering Drawing
. . Layout (Publications)
. . Printing
. Handicrafts
. Ceramics
. Painting (Visual Arts)
. Photography
. . Holography
. Printmaking
. Sculpture

: : : Cognitive Processes
: : Perception
: Visual Perception
Visual Discrimination

: : Environment
: Physical Environment
Visual Environment

: Disabilities
Visual Impairments
. Ametropia
. . Hyperopia
. . Myopia
. Blindness
. Partial Vision
. Strabismus

: Learning
Visual Learning

: : Ability
: Skills
Visual Literacy

: : : Measures (Individuals)
: : Tests
: Nonverbal Tests
Visual Measures

: : Cognitive Processes
: Perception
Visual Perception
. Depth Perception
. Visual Acuity
. Visual Discrimination

: Stimuli
Visual Stimuli
. Pictorial Stimuli

: Cognitive Processes
Visualization

: : Mobility
: Physical Mobility
Visually Impaired Mobility

Vocabulary
. Aviation Vocabulary
. Banking Vocabulary
. Basic Vocabulary
. Chemical Nomenclature
. International Trade Vocabulary
. Jargon
. Keywords
. Kinship Terminology
. Mathematical Vocabulary
. Medical Vocabulary
. Sight Vocabulary
. Subject Index Terms
. Word Lists

: Development
Vocabulary Development

: : : Ability
: : Skills
: Language Skills
Vocabulary Skills

: : : : Liberal Arts
: : : Humanities
: : Fine Arts
: Music
Vocal Music
. Choral Music
. Songs
. . Art Song
. . Ballads
. . Hymns

: : Behavior
: Adjustment (to Environment)
Vocational Adjustment

: Aptitude
Vocational Aptitude

: : : Groups
: : Personnel
: Administrators
Vocational Directors

: Education
Vocational Education
. Adult Vocational Education
. . Adult Farmer Education
. . Young Farmer Education
. Business Education
. . Office Occupations Education
. Cooperative Education
. Distributive Education
. Occupational Home Economics
. Prevocational Education
. Technical Education
. . Fire Science Education
. . Tech Prep
. Trade and Industrial Education

: : : : Groups
: : : Personnel
: : Professional Personnel
: Teachers
Vocational Education Teachers
. Business Education Teachers
. Distributive Education Teachers
. Trade and Industrial Teachers

: : : Language
: : Languages for Special Purposes
: : : : Language
: : Second Languages
: : : : : Languages
: : : : Indo European Languages
: : : English
: : English (Second Language)
: English for Special Purposes
Vocational English (Second Language)

: Evaluation
Vocational Evaluation

: : : : Research
: : : : : Methods
: : : : Evaluation Methods
: : Case Studies
: : Longitudinal Studies
: Followup Studies
Vocational Followup

: : : Institutions
: : Schools
: Vocational Schools
: : : : Institutions
: : : Schools
: : Secondary Schools
: High Schools
Vocational High Schools

: Interests
Vocational Interests

: : Individual Characteristics
: Maturity (Individuals)
Vocational Maturity

: Rehabilitation
Vocational Rehabilitation

: : Institutions
: Schools
Vocational Schools
. Career Academies
. Vocational High Schools

: : Facilities
: Educational Facilities
Vocational Training Centers

: : : Languages
: : Uralic Altaic Languages
: Finno Ugric Languages
Vogul

: : Disabilities
: Speech Impairments
Voice Disorders

Volcanoes

: : : : Activities
: : : Physical Activities
: : Athletics
: Team Sports
Volleyball

: : Scientific Concepts
: Space
: : Mathematical Concepts
: Geometric Concepts
Volume (Mathematics)

: : : Groups
: : Organizations (Groups)
: Agencies
Voluntary Agencies

: Social Integration
Voluntary Desegregation

: Training
Volunteer Training

: Groups
Volunteers
. Student Volunteers

Voter Registration

Voting

: : Civil Liberties
: Civil Rights
Voting Rights

: : : : Linguistics
: : : Phonology
: : Phonemics
: Phonemes
Vowels

: Income
: Expenditures
Wages
. Minimum Wage

Wait Time

: : : : Groups
: : : Personnel
: : Nonprofessional Personnel
: Service Workers
Waiters and Waitresses

: : Activities
: Physical Activities
Walking

: Conflict
War
. Civil War (United States)
. Korean War
. Nuclear Warfare
. Revolutionary War (United States)
. Vietnam War
. World War I
. World War II

: Facilities
Warehouses

: Sanitation
Waste Disposal
. Recycling

: : Matter
: Water
: Matter
: Wastes
Waste Water

: Matter
Wastes
. Solid Wastes
. Waste Water

: : : : Groups
: : : Personnel
: : Nonprofessional Personnel
: Skilled Workers
Watchmakers

: Matter
Water
. Drinking Water
. Groundwater
. Waste Water

: Pollution
Water Pollution
. Acid Rain

: : : : Activities
: : : Physical Activities
: : Athletics
: Team Sports
: : : : Activities
: : : Physical Activities
: : Athletics
: Aquatic Sports
Water Polo

Water Quality

: : Resources
: Natural Resources
Water Resources
. Groundwater
. Rivers

: Technology
Water Treatment

: : : : Activities
: : : Physical Activities
: : Athletics
: Aquatic Sports
Waterskiing

Weapons
. Guns
. Nuclear Weapons

Weather
. Drought
. Hurricanes
. Tornadoes

: : Development
: Library Collection Development
Weeding (Library)

: Plants (Botany)
Weeds

: Programs
Weekend Programs

: Scientific Concepts
Weight (Mass)

Weight (1968 1980)

: : Data
: Scores
Weighted Scores

: : : Activities
: : Physical Activities
: Lifting
: : : Activities
: : Physical Activities
: Athletics
Weightlifting

: Technology
Welding

: : : : Groups
: : : Organizations (Groups)
: : Agencies
: Social Agencies
Welfare Agencies

: Groups
Welfare Recipients

: : : Services
: : Human Services
: Social Services
Welfare Services
. Migrant Welfare Services

Welfare (1966 1980)

: Quality of Life
Well Being
. Child Welfare
. Student Welfare
. Teacher Welfare
. Wellness

: : Quality of Life
: Well Being
: Health
Wellness

: : Languages
: Indo European Languages
Welsh

: Culture
Western Civilization

Wetlands

: : : Equipment
: : Assistive Devices (for Disabled)
: Mobility Aids
Wheelchairs

: Occupations
White Collar Occupations

: : Groups
: Whites
: : Groups
: Students
White Students

: Groups
Whites
. White Students

: : : Methods
: : Educational Methods
: Teaching Methods
: : Methods
: Holistic Approach
Whole Language Approach

: : : : Symbols (Mathematics)
: : : Numbers
: : Rational Numbers
: Integers
Whole Numbers

: : Technology
: Marketing
Wholesaling

: Groups
Widowed

: : Environment
: Physical Environment
Wilderness

Wildlife
. Endangered Species

: Technology
Wildlife Management

: Records (Forms)
Wills

Wind (Meteorology)

: : Scientific Concepts
: Energy
Wind Energy

: : Equipment
: Musical Instruments
Wind Instruments
. Brass Instruments
. Woodwind Instruments

: Facilities
Windowless Rooms

: Structural Elements (Construction)
Windows

: : : Activities
: : Physical Activities
: Athletics
Winter Sports
. Ice Hockey
. Ice Skating
. Skiing

Withdrawal (Education)

: Psychological Patterns
Withdrawal (Psychology)

: : Languages
: African Languages
Wolof

: : : Groups
: : Females
: Employed Women
: : Groups
: : Personnel
: Administrators
Women Administrators

: : : : Groups
: : : Personnel
: : School Personnel
: : : : Groups
: : : Personnel
: : Professional Personnel
: Faculty

: : : Groups
: : Females
: Employed Women
Women Faculty

: : : Activities
: : Physical Activities
: Athletics
Womens Athletics

: Education
Womens Education

: Curriculum
Womens Studies

: : : Equipment
: : Musical Instruments
: Wind Instruments
Woodwind Instruments

: Technology
Woodworking
. Cabinetmaking
. Carpentry

Word Frequency

: Vocabulary
Word Lists

Word Order

. Mathematical Applications
Word Problems (Mathematics)

: : : Services
: : Information Services
: Information Processing
Word Processing

: : : Cognitive Processes
: : Memory
: Recognition (Psychology)
Word Recognition

: : : Ability
: : Skills
: Study Skills
Word Study Skills

: Attitudes
Work Attitudes
. Job Satisfaction

: Environment
Work Environment
. Teaching Conditions

: : : : Liberal Arts
: : : Humanities
: : Philosophy
: Ethics
Work Ethic

: : Background
: Experience
Work Experience
. Employment Experience

: Programs
Work Experience Programs

: Expectation
Work Life Expectancy

: : : Measures (Individuals)
: : Tests
: Occupational Tests
Work Sample Tests

: Programs
Work Study Programs

: : Educational Media
: Instructional Materials
Workbooks

: : : Data
: : Statistical Data
: Employment Statistics
Worker Days

: : Methods
: Insurance
: Financial Support
Workers Compensation

: : Groups
: Social Class
Working Class

: : Planning
: Scheduling
Working Hours
. Flexible Working Hours

: Literacy
Workplace Literacy

: Records (Forms)
Worksheets
. Spreadsheets

Workshops
. Drama Workshops
. Parent Workshops
. Sheltered Workshops
. Teacher Workshops
. Writing Workshops

: Facilities
Workstations

World Affairs

: : : : Liberal Arts
: : : Sciences
: : Social Sciences
: Geography
World Geography

: : : : Liberal Arts
: : : Sciences
: : Social Sciences
: Liberal Arts
: Humanities
: History
World History
. World War I
. World War II

: : Curriculum
: English Curriculum
World Literature

: Problems
World Problems

: : : Liberal Arts
: : Humanities
: Philosophy
: Attitudes
World Views

: : : : : Liberal Arts
: : : : Sciences
: : : Social Sciences
: : : : Liberal Arts
: : : Humanities
: : History
: World History
: : Conflict
: War
World War I

: : : : : Liberal Arts
: : : : Sciences
: : : Social Sciences
: : : : Liberal Arts
: : : Humanities
: : History
: World History
: : Conflict
: War
World War II

: : : Networks
: : Information Networks
: : : Networks
: : Computer Networks
: Internet
World Wide Web

: : : Activities
: : Physical Activities

: Athletics
Wrestling

: Literacy
: Language Arts
Writing (Composition)
. Abstracting
. Basic Writing
. Beginning Writing
. Childrens Writing
. Content Area Writing
. . Writing Across the Curriculum
. Creative Writing
. Descriptive Writing
. Expository Writing
. Free Writing
. Freshman Composition
. Journal Writing
. Local Color Writing
. News Writing
. Notetaking
. Paragraph Composition
. Parallelism (Literary)
. Playwriting
. Proposal Writing
. Scholarly Writing
. Technical Writing
. Writing for Publication

: : Ability
: Verbal Ability
Writing Ability
. Writing Skills

: Achievement
Writing Achievement

: : : Instruction
: : Writing Instruction
: : : Literacy
: : : Language Arts
: : Writing (Composition)
: Content Area Writing
Writing Across the Curriculum

: : Psychological Patterns
: Anxiety
Writing Apprehension

: Writing Exercises
: : Instruction
: Assignments
Writing Assignments

: Attitudes
Writing Attitudes

: Problems
Writing Difficulties

: Evaluation
Writing Evaluation

Writing Exercises
. Writing Assignments

: : Literacy
: : Language Arts

: Writing (Composition)
Writing for Publication

: Improvement
Writing Improvement

: Instruction
Writing Instruction
. Basic Writing
. Content Area Writing
. . Writing Across the Curriculum
. Freshman Composition
. Process Approach (Writing)

: : Facilities
: Laboratories
: : Facilities
: Educational Facilities
Writing Laboratories

Writing Processes
. Prewriting
. Revision (Written Composition)

: Readiness
Writing Readiness

: : Research
: Educational Research
Writing Research

: : : Ability
: : Verbal Ability
: Writing Ability
: : : Ability
: : Skills
: Language Skills
Writing Skills

: Methods
Writing Strategies

: : : : Groups
: : : Personnel
: : Professional Personnel
: Teachers
Writing Teachers

: : : Measures (Individuals)
: : Tests
: Verbal Tests
Writing Tests

: Workshops
Writing Workshops

: Language
Written Language
. Braille
. Electronic Text
. Graphemes
. Ideography
. Orthographic Symbols
. . Diacritical Marking
. . Letters (Alphabet)
. . Phonetic Transcription
. Punctuation
. Shorthand

: : : Languages
: : Uralic Altaic Languages
: Turkic Languages
Yakut

: : Institutions
: Schools
Year Round Schools

: : Publications
: Serials
: : Publications
: Reference Materials
: : Publications
: Printed Materials
: Books
Yearbooks

: : : Languages
: : Indo European Languages
: German
Yiddish

: : Languages
: African Languages
Yoruba

: : : Groups
: : Age Groups
: Adults
Young Adults

: : : Groups
: : Age Groups
: Children
Young Children
. Infants
. . Neonates
. . Premature Infants
. Kindergarten Children
. Preschool Children
. Toddlers

: : Education
: Agricultural Education
: : : Education
: : Vocational Education
: : : Education
: : Adult Education
: Adult Vocational Education
Young Farmer Education

: : : : Groups
: : : Age Groups
: : Adults
: Older Adults
Young Old Adults

: Groups
Youth
. Affluent Youth
. Black Youth
. Disadvantaged Youth
. Migrant Youth
. Out of School Youth
. Rural Youth
. Suburban Youth
. Urban Youth

: : : Groups
: : Organizations (Groups)
: Agencies
Youth Agencies

: : Groups
: Clubs
Youth Clubs

: Employment
Youth Employment

: : Groups
: Leaders
: Groups
Youth Leaders

: Opportunities
Youth Opportunities

: Problems
Youth Problems

: Programs
Youth Programs

: : : Languages
: : American Indian Languages
: Mayan Languages
Yucatec

: : Languages
: Eskimo Aleut Languages
Yupik

: : : Languages
: : Uralic Altaic Languages
: Samoyed Languages
Yurak

Zoning
. Community Zoning
. Rezoning
. School Zoning
. Special Zoning

: : : : Liberal Arts
: : : Sciences
: : Natural Sciences
: Biological Sciences
Zoology
. Entomology
. Ichthyology
. Ornithology
. Primatology

: : : Facilities
: : Animal Facilities
Zoos

: : Groups
: Tribes
: : : : Groups
: : : Ethnic Groups
: : American Indians
: Pueblo (People)
Zuni (Tribe)

Descriptor Groups and Descriptor Group Display

Descriptor Groups

The Descriptor groups offer a "table of contents" to the *Thesaurus*. The 41 Descriptor Groups are presented below in nine categories. A Scope Note for each Descriptor Group is provided.

Groups Related to LEARNING AND DEVELOPMENT

LEARNING AND PERCEPTION   110

Learning, conditioning, and reinforcement; cognition and thought processes; and perception. *See also* MEASUREMENT, THE EDUCATIONAL PROCESS: CLASSROOM PERSPECTIVES, and DISABILITIES.

INDIVIDUAL DEVELOPMENT AND CHARACTERISTICS   120

Attributes of the individual, i.e., psychological characteristics, aptitudes, abilities, behavior, needs, and attitudes; growth and development; age groups; and individual differences. *See also* MENTAL HEALTH and THE INDIVIDUAL IN SOCIAL CONTEXT.

Groups Related to PHYSICAL AND MENTAL CONDITIONS

HEALTH AND SAFETY   210

Medicine and health, health conditions and services, and diseases; health occupations; health facilities; professional and paraprofessional health education; parts of the body; and accidents and safety. *See also* DISABILITIES.

DISABILITIES   220

Physical and mental disabilities; special education; communication disorders, processes, and therapies; and equipment and personnel serving the disabled. *See also* LEARNING AND PERCEPTION and INDIVIDUAL DEVELOPMENT AND CHARACTERISTICS. For emotional and psychiatric conditions, *see* MENTAL HEALTH.

MENTAL HEALTH   230

Mental illness and mentally ill persons; therapies promoting mental welfare; mental health facilities and personnel; and psychology. *See also* COUNSELING.

COUNSELING   240

Guidance and counseling; guidance personnel; counseling techniques; and rehabilitation. *See also* MENTAL HEALTH.

Groups Related to EDUCATIONAL PROCESSES AND STRUCTURES

THE EDUCATIONAL PROCESS: CLASSROOM PERSPECTIVES   310

Procedures and processes characteristic of the classroom, i.e., instructional systems, teaching methods, classroom environment, and classroom management; and student/teacher behavior and interaction. *See also* CURRICULUM ORGANIZATION and groups related to curriculum areas. For instructional materials, *see* COMMUNICATIONS MEDIA and PUBLICATION/DOCUMENT TYPES. For specified types of students and teachers, *see* STUDENTS, TEACHERS, SCHOOL PERSONNEL.

THE EDUCATIONAL PROCESS: SCHOOL PERSPECTIVES   320

Procedures and processes beyond the classroom, but internal to the school, i.e., internal policy and administration, personnel practices, staff evaluation, curriculum and program development, student/school and teacher/administrator relationships. *See also* STUDENTS, TEACHERS, SCHOOL PERSONNEL. For types of schools and colleges, *see* EDUCATIONAL LEVELS, DEGREES, AND ORGANIZATIONS. For school facilities, *see* FACILITIES.

THE EDUCATIONAL PROCESS: SOCIETAL PERSPECTIVES   330

Procedures and processes related to the school in its social and educational environment, i.e., relations with parents, community, and society at large; relations and processes between schools and higher authorities, between schools and other agencies, and among schools; movement of staff and students; the role of schools in society; and the impacts of schools on society and of society on schools. Other educational factors beyond the single school. *See also* BIAS AND

EQUITY. For educational finance, *see* ECONOMICS AND FINANCE.

EDUCATIONAL LEVELS, DEGREES, AND ORGANIZATIONS   340

Grade levels; types of schools and colleges; school districts; educational credits and credentials. *See also* CURRICULUM ORGANIZATION. For school administration, *see* THE EDUCATIONAL PROCESS: SCHOOL PERSPECTIVES.

CURRICULUM ORGANIZATION   350

Units and sequences around which curriculum and instruction are organized; and attributes of curriculum structures as defined by time, sequence, special location, and other organizational concepts. For instructional processes, *see* THE EDUCATIONAL PROCESS: CLASSROOM PERSPECTIVES. For grade levels, *see* EDUCATIONAL LEVELS, DEGREES, AND ORGANIZATIONS.

STUDENTS, TEACHERS, SCHOOL PERSONNEL   360

Terms for students, teachers, administrators, and support personnel other than counselors (*see* COUNSELING) and library/media personnel (*see* INFORMATION / COMMUNICATIONS SYSTEMS). *See also* DISABILITIES for specialists serving the handicapped.

Groups Related to CURRICULUM AREAS

SUBJECTS OF INSTRUCTION   400

Terms representing subject matter (e.g., Civics) or curriculum areas (e.g., General Education) and terms precoordinating a subject area concept with a concept related to education, skills training, instruction, or curricula. Excludes those terms assigned to a group dealing with a specific curriculum area: *see* AGRICULTURE AND NATURAL RESOURCES, LANGUAGE AND SPEECH, MATHEMATICS, READING, and SCIENCE AND TECHNOLOGY for precoordinated terms in those areas. For professional and paraprofessional health education, *see* HEALTH AND SAFETY. *See also* ARTS, HUMANITIES, LANGUAGES, and PHYSICAL EDUCATION AND RECREATION for other terms frequently used to represent a subject of instruction.

AGRICULTURE AND NATURAL RESOURCES   410

Agriculture; forestry; agricultural education; agricultural occupations; agricultural products, materials, and facilities; natural resources; and pollution, conservation, and other environmental concerns.

ARTS   420

Fine arts, i.e., art, music, dance, and theater and dramatics; and commercial arts, i.e., graphic arts and design. *See also* COMMUNICATIONS MEDIA and HUMANITIES.

HUMANITIES   430

Literature and literary genres; criticism; history; philosophy; and religion. *See also* ARTS and PEOPLES AND CULTURES.

LANGUAGES   440

Human languages and language groups.

LANGUAGE AND SPEECH   450

Language and linguistics; grammar and parts of speech; language instruction; speech and speech education; and vocabulary. For terms related to writing and composition skills, *see* SUBJECTS OF INSTRUCTION. For speech disorders, *see* DISABILITIES. *See also* LANGUAGES and INDIVIDUAL DEVELOPMENT AND CHARACTERISTICS.

READING   460

Reading instruction and development; literacy; and reading facilities.

PHYSICAL EDUCATION AND RECREATION   470

Physical education, recreation, and sports.

MATHEMATICS   480

Mathematics and mathematics education; excludes statistical techniques (*see* MEASUREMENT).

SCIENCE AND TECHNOLOGY   490

Physical and biological sciences; scientific concepts; science education; engineering; and technology. For technical occupations, *see* OCCUPATIONS. For health sciences and medicine, *see* HEALTH AND SAFETY. *See also* AGRICULTURE AND NATURAL RESOURCES and EQUIPMENT.

Groups Related to HUMAN SOCIETY

THE INDIVIDUAL IN SOCIAL CONTEXT   510

Familial and other social influences on individual development; social attributes of individuals; individuals defined by social attributes and social roles; and personal relationships. *See also* INDIVIDUAL DEVELOPMENT AND CHARACTERISTICS, PEOPLES AND CULTURES, SOCIAL PROB-

LEMS, and BIAS AND EQUITY. For attributes of social groups, *see* SOCIAL PROCESSES AND STRUCTURES.

SOCIAL PROCESSES AND STRUCTURES   520

Attributes of society and of social groups; social programs and services; social institutions, values, and structures (e.g., family, community, and social classes); collective action and behavior; social originations; social life; and group relations. *See also* SOCIAL PROBLEMS, THE INDIVIDUAL IN SOCIAL CONTEXT, and BIAS AND EQUITY.

SOCIAL PROBLEMS   530

Behavioral and other social problems; individuals and groups defined by such problems. *See also* BIAS AND EQUITY.

BIAS AND EQUITY   540

Prejudice, stereotypes, discriminatory attitudes; segregation and integration; and equality and opportunity. *See also* THE EDUCATIONAL PROCESS: SOCIETAL PERSPECTIVES, and PEOPLES AND CULTURES.

HUMAN GEOGRAPHY   550

Demography; geographic distribution and migration of people; and urban and rural environments and conditions.

PEOPLES AND CULTURES   560

Culture and cultures; ethnic/racial groups; and religious groups.

Groups Related to SOCIAL/ ECONOMIC ENTERPRISE

GOVERNMENT AND POLITICS   610

Local, state, and federal government; government employees; law; political divisions and political systems; military organizations and war; political activism; and international relations. *See also* SOCIAL PROCESSES AND STRUCTURES, ECONOMICS AND FINANCE, and THE EDUCATIONAL PROCESS: SOCIETAL PERSPECTIVES. For military personnel, *see* OCCUPATIONS.

ECONOMICS AND FINANCE   620

Economics; individual and institutional finances; educational finance; budgeting and accounting; and taxes. *See also* LABOR AND EMPLOYMENT. For other aspects of educational administration, *see* THE EDUCATIONAL PROCESS: SCHOOL PERSPECTIVES.

LABOR AND EMPLOYMENT   630

Jobs, employment, and unemployment; employment practices; the labor force; skill levels of workers and personnel; job training; personnel management; working conditions and attitudes; employee-employer relations; and supervi-

sion. For specific job training areas, *see* SUBJECTS OF INSTRUCTION.

OCCUPATIONS   640

Occupations and occupational groups, excluding those assigned to a specialized category (*see* AGRICULTURE AND NATURAL RESOURCES, COUNSELING, HEALTH AND SAFETY, MENTAL HEALTH, etc., for occupations related to those areas).

BUSINESS, COMMERCE, AND INDUSTRY   650

Business, industries, transportation, and sales. *See also* AGRICULTURE AND NATURAL RESOURCES.

Groups Related to INFORMATION AND COMMUNICATIONS

INFORMATION/COMMUNICATIONS SYSTEMS   710

Information and communication processes, services, and systems; libraries and information centers; and library and information personnel. *See also* EQUIPMENT and COMMUNICATIONS MEDIA.

COMMUNICATIONS MEDIA   720

Print and nonprint media used in communication; and media production and personnel. *See also* EQUIPMENT and PUBLICATION/DOCUMENT TYPES.

PUBLICATION/DOCUMENT TYPES   730

Terms used frequently, though not exclusively, to describe the form of a document. For other terms used in this manner *see* TESTS AND SCALES, RESEARCH AND THEORY, and MEASUREMENT. A list of the terms that duplicate the Publication Type Codes, and therefore should only be used to refer to the subject of a document, appears in the front matter of the Thesaurus. *See also* COMMUNICATIONS MEDIA.

Groups Related to RESEARCH AND MEASUREMENT

RESEARCH AND THEORY   810

The research process; fields and types of research; and theories. Terms may be used to represent subject concepts or to classify research documents by their subject fields or methodological types; they may also be used to categorize theoretical research, research hypotheses, or other types of causal explanations emerging from research. For statistical and other methodologies of research, *see* MEASUREMENT. For tests and scales used in research, *see* TESTS AND SCALES.

MEASUREMENT   820

Testing and measurement; statistical and analytical techniques used in indexing to represent subjects of documents and also to indicate methodologies employed in a research document. Terms related to evaluation and criteria similarly may be used to indicate aspects of documents other than their subject. For types of research, *see* RESEARCH AND THEORY. For specific types of tests and scales, *see* TESTS AND SCALES.

TESTS AND SCALES   830

Testing and data-gathering instruments; may be used in indexing to represent subjects of documents and the presence of tests or scales in the documents. For the processes of testing and measurement, *see* MEASUREMENT.

Groups Related to FACILITIES AND EQUIPMENT

EQUIPMENT   910

Types of equipment and supplies; and equipment maintenance. *See* DISABILITIES for special equipment serving the handicapped. *See also* INFORMATION/COMMUNICATIONS SYSTEMS, COMMUNICATIONS MEDIA, and SCIENCE AND TECHNOLOGY.

FACILITIES   920

Design and construction of facilities; building materials and components; interior space; and types of facilities, excluding libraries, reading facilities, and facilities related to mental or physical health (for facilities in these areas, see specific Descriptor Groups). For occupations in the building trades, *see* OCCUPATIONS.

Descriptor Group Display

The Descriptor Groups offer a ''table of contents'' to the *Thesaurus*. A Descriptor Group Code appears within the main entry of each term in the Alphabetical Display of the *Thesaurus*. See the preceding Descriptor Groups section for Scope Notes about the various Descriptor Groups. Below is an alphabetical listing of all the Descriptors assigned to each Descriptor Group.

110 LEARNING AND PERCEPTION

Ability Identification
Abstract Reasoning
Active Learning
Adult Learning
Arousal Patterns
Associative Learning
Attention
Attention Control
Audience Response
Auditory Discrimination
Auditory Perception
Auditory Stimuli
Aural Learning
Behavior Chaining
Behavior Modification
Classical Conditioning
Cognitive Mapping
Cognitive Processes
Cognitive Psychology
Cognitive Restructuring
Cognitive Structures
Cognitive Style
Compensation (Concept)
Comprehension
Concept Formation
Concept Mapping
Conceptual Schemes (1967 1980)
Conceptual Tempo
Conditioning
Conservation (Concept)
Constructed Response
Constructivism (Learning)
Contingency Management
Convergent Thinking
Covert Response
Creative Thinking
Critical Thinking
Cues
Decision Making
Decision Making Skills
Deduction
Depth Perception
Dimensional Preference
Discovery Learning
Discovery Processes
Discrimination Learning
Divergent Thinking
Eidetic Imagery
Electrical Stimuli
Encoding (Psychology)
Epistemology
Evaluative Thinking
Extinction (Psychology)
Eye Fixations
Eye Movements
Familiarity
Field Dependence Independence
Figural Aftereffects
Formal Operations
Fundamental Concepts
Generalization

Habit Formation
Habituation
Hearing (Physiology)
Imitation
Incidental Learning
Induction
Inferences
Information Seeking
Intellectual Experience
Intentional Learning
Intuition
Kinesthetic Methods
Kinesthetic Perception
Learning
Learning Experience
Learning Modalities
Learning Motivation
Learning Plateaus
Learning Problems
Learning Processes
Learning Strategies
Listening Comprehension
Logical Thinking
Long Term Memory
Meditation
Memorization
Memory
Metacognition
Misconceptions
Mnemonics
Multisensory Learning
Negative Reinforcement
Nonverbal Learning
Novelty (Stimulus Dimension)
Obedience
Object Permanence
Objectivity
Observational Learning
Operant Conditioning
Overt Response
Paired Associate Learning
Patterned Responses
Perception
Perceptual Motor Learning
Pictorial Stimuli
Planning
Positive Reinforcement
Praise
Preschool Learning (1966 1980)
Primacy Effect
Prior Learning
Problem Solving
Productive Thinking
Pupillary Dilation
Reader Response
Recall (Psychology)
Recognition (Psychology)
Reference Groups
Reinforcement
Reminiscence
Retention (Psychology)
Review (Reexamination)

Role Models
Rote Learning
Schemata (Cognition)
Selection
Sensory Deprivation
Sensory Experience
Sensory Integration
Sequential Learning
Serial Learning
Serial Ordering
Short Term Memory
Social Cognition
Social Reinforcement
Stimulation
Stimuli
Stimulus Generalization
Suggestopedia
Symbolic Learning
Tactile Stimuli
Tactual Perception
Thinking Skills
Time Factors (Learning)
Time Perspective
Timeout
Token Economy
Transcendental Meditation
Transfer of Training
Transformative Learning
Value Judgment
Verbal Learning
Verbal Operant Conditioning
Verbal Stimuli
Vision
Visual Acuity
Visual Discrimination
Visual Learning
Visual Literacy
Visual Perception
Visual Stimuli
Visualization
World Views

120 INDIVIDUAL DEVELOPMENT

Ability
Academic Ability
Academic Aptitude
Academic Aspiration
Achievement
Achievement Need
Activities
Adolescent Attitudes
Adolescent Behavior
Adolescent Development
Adolescents
Adult Development
Adults
Adults (30 to 45)
Affection
Affective Behavior
Affiliation Need
Age

Age Differences
Age Groups
Aging (Individuals)
Altruism
Androgyny
Animal Behavior
Apathy
Aptitude
Aspiration
Assertiveness
Association (Psychology)
At Risk Persons
Attachment Behavior
Attention Span
Attitude Change
Attitudes
Authoritarianism
Background
Behavior
Behavior Change
Behavior Development
Behavior Patterns
Behavior Problems
Behaviorism
Beliefs
Biological Influences
Birth
Birth Order
Birth Weight
Bisexuality
Body Height
Body Image
Body Language
Body Weight
Brain Hemisphere Functions
Career Change
Career Choice
Career Development
Child Behavior
Child Development
Childhood Attitudes
Childhood Interests
Childhood Needs
Children
Chronological Age
Client Characteristics (Human Services)
Cognitive Ability
Cognitive Development
Cognitive Dissonance
Communication Apprehension
Communication Problems
Competence
Compliance (Psychology)
Creative Development
Creativity
Crying
Curiosity
Death
Delay of Gratification
Delayed Speech
Dependency (Personality)
Developmental Delays
Developmental Stages
Developmental Tasks
Dogmatism
Early Adolescents
Early Experience
Egocentrism
Emotional Development
Emotional Experience
Emotional Problems
Emotional Response
Empathy
Environmental Influences
Ethnicity
Exceptional Persons (1978 1994)
Expectation
Experience
Exploratory Behavior
Extraversion Introversion
Eye Contact
Eye Hand Coordination
Facial Expressions
Failure to Thrive
Fantasy
Females
Femininity

First Born
Gifted
Goal Orientation
Handedness
Happiness
Health Behavior
High Achievement
Homosexuality
Honesty
Identification (Psychology)
Imagination
Independent Living
Individual Characteristics
Individual Development
Individual Differences
Individual Needs
Individual Power
Infant Behavior
Infants
Inhibition
Integrity
Intellectual Development
Intelligence
Intelligence Differences
Intention
Interests
Interpersonal Competence
Intimacy
Kindergarten Children
Knowledge Level
Language Acquisition
Late Adolescents
Lateral Dominance
Learning Readiness
Left Handed Writer
Lesbianism
Life Events
Listening Habits
Listening Skills
Locus of Control
Love
Low Achievement
Males
Masculinity
Maturation (1967 1980)
Maturity (Individuals)
Mental Age
Mental Rigidity
Middle Aged Adults
Midlife Transitions
Modeling (Psychology)
Moral Development
Motivation
Motor Development
Motor Reactions
Multiple Intelligences
Muscular Strength
Nature Nurture Controversy
Need Gratification
Neonates
Nonverbal Ability
Nonverbal Communication
Occupational Aspiration
Old Old Adults
Older Adults
Opinions
Orientation
Overachievement
Parenting Skills
Participation
Perceptual Development
Perceptual Motor Coordination
Performance
Perinatal Influences
Persistence
Personal Space
Personality
Personality Change
Personality Development
Personality Traits
Perspective Taking
Physical Activity Level
Physical Attractiveness
Physical Characteristics
Physical Development
Preadolescents
Pregnancy

Premature Infants
Prenatal Influences
Preschool Children
Pretend Play
Prosocial Behavior
Psychological Characteristics
Psychological Needs
Psychological Patterns
Psychomotor Skills
Puberty
Race
Reaction Time
Readiness
Resentment
Resilience (Personality)
Resistance (Psychology)
Resistance to Change
Resistance to Temptation
Responses
Role Conflict
Sadness
Satisfaction
School Readiness
Self Actualization
Self Advocacy
Self Control
Self Disclosure (Individuals)
Self Efficacy
Self Esteem
Self Evaluation (Individuals)
Self Expression
Self Fulfilling Prophecies
Self Management
Self Motivation
Self Reward
Sex
Sex (Characteristics) (1966 1980)
Sex Differences
Sexual Identity
Sexual Orientation
Sexuality
Sharing Behavior
Shyness
Skill Development
Skills
Social Behavior
Social Development
Socialization
Space Orientation (1968 1980)
Spatial Ability
Specialization
Spontaneous Behavior
Status Need
Stranger Reactions
Talent
Talent Development
Toddlers
Trust (Psychology)
Twins
Type A Behavior
Type B Behavior
Underachievement
Vocational Aptitude
Vocational Interests
Vocational Maturity
Well Being
Wellness
Writing Achievement
Writing Apprehension
Writing Attitudes
Writing Difficulties
Writing Readiness
Young Adults
Young Children
Young Old Adults
Youth

210 HEALTH AND SAFETY

Abortions
Accident Prevention
Accidents
Acquired Immune Deficiency Syndrome
Alcoholic Beverages
Alcoholism
Allergy

Allied Health Occupations
Allied Health Occupations Education
Allied Health Personnel
Anemia
Anesthesiology
Anorexia Nervosa
Asthma
Audiology
Biomedicine
Blood Circulation
Body Composition
Brain
Breakfast Programs
Breastfeeding
Bulimia
Cancer
Cardiopulmonary Resuscitation
Cardiovascular System
Child Health
Child Safety
Chronic Illness
Cleaning
Clinical Diagnosis
Clinical Experience
Clinical Teaching (Health Professions)
Clothing
Cocaine
Communicable Diseases
Community Health Services
Contraception
Crack
Cystic Fibrosis
Dental Assistants
Dental Clinics
Dental Evaluation
Dental Health
Dental Hygienists
Dental Technicians
Dentistry
Dentists
Diabetes
Dietetics
Dietitians
Disease Control
Disease Incidence
Diseases
Dishwashing
Drinking
Drug Rehabilitation
Drug Therapy
Drug Use
Drug Use Testing
Ears
Eating Disorders
Eating Habits
Electroencephalography
Emergency Medical Technicians
Epidemiology
Etiology
Euthanasia
Exercise Physiology
Eyes
Family Health
Family Planning
Family Practice (Medicine)
Fatigue (Biology)
Fire Protection
First Aid
Fluoridation
Food
Food Service
Food Standards
Frail Elderly
Geriatrics
Graduate Medical Education
Gun Control
Gynecology
Hazardous Materials
Health
Health Activities
Health Conditions
Health Facilities
Health Maintenance Organizations
Health Needs
Health Occupations
Health Occupations Centers (1968 1980)
Health Personnel

Health Programs
Health Promotion
Health Related Fitness
Health Services
Hearing Conservation
Heart Disorders
Heart Rate
Heroin
Home Health Aides
Hospices (Terminal Care)
Hospital Personnel
Hospitalized Children
Hospitals
Human Body
Human Posture
Hunger
Hygiene
Hypertension
Immunization Programs
Infant Mortality
Injuries
Internal Medicine
Laboratory Safety
Lead Poisoning
Long Term Care
Lunch Programs
Lysergic Acid Diethylamide
Marijuana
Medical Assistants
Medical Care Evaluation
Medical Case Histories
Medical Consultants
Medical Education
Medical Evaluation
Medical Laboratory Assistants
Medical Record Administrators
Medical Record Technicians
Medical Services
Medical Technologists
Medical Vocabulary
Medicine
Menstruation
Metabolism
Migrant Health Services
Muscular System
Musculoskeletal System
Narcotics
Natural Disasters
Neurological Organization
Neurology
Nurse Practitioners
Nurses
Nurses Aides
Nursing
Nursing Education
Nutrition
Obesity
Obstetrics
Occupational Diseases
Occupational Safety and Health
Oncology
Ophthalmology
Optometrists
Optometry
Oral Rehydration Therapy
Osteopathy
Otitis Media
Outcomes of Treatment
Pain
Pathology
Patient Education
Patients
Pediatrics
Pharmaceutical Education
Pharmacists
Pharmacology
Pharmacy
Physical Examinations
Physical Fitness
Physical Health
Physical Therapists
Physical Therapy
Physical Therapy Aides
Physician Patient Relationship
Physicians
Physicians Assistants
Podiatry

Poisoning
Poisons
Practical Nursing
Prenatal Care
Prenatal Drug Exposure
Preventive Medicine
Primary Health Care
Public Health
Radiologic Technologists
Radiology
Rescue
Respiratory Therapy
Rh Factors
Risk
Rubella
Safety
Sanitation
School Accidents
School Health Services
Security (1967 1978)
Sedatives
Sick Child Care
Sickle Cell Anemia
Skeletal System
Sleep
Smoking
Special Health Problems
Sports Medicine
Stimulants
Sudden Infant Death Syndrome
Surgery
Surgical Technicians
Symptoms (Individual Disorders)
Terminal Illness
Termination of Treatment
Therapy
Tissue Donors
Tobacco
Toilet Training
Toxicology
Traffic Accidents
Traffic Safety
Venereal Diseases
Weapons

220 DISABILITIES

Academic Accommodations (Disabilities)
Academically Handicapped (1966 1980)
Accessibility (for Disabled)
Adapted Physical Education
Adaptive Behavior (of Disabled)
Adult Day Care
Adult Foster Care
Adventitious Impairments
Alzheimers Disease
American Sign Language
Ametropia
Amputations
Aphasia
Architectural Barriers (1970 1980)
Articulation Impairments
Assistive Devices (for Disabled)
Attention Deficit Disorders
Attitudes toward Disabilities
Augmentative and Alternative Communication
Autism
Blindness
Braille
Cerebral Palsy
Cleft Palate
Cochlear Implants
Communication Aids (for Disabled)
Communication Disorders
Community Based Instruction (Disabilities)
Congenital Impairments
Cued Speech
Daily Living Skills
Deaf Blind
Deaf Interpreting
Deafness
Deinstitutionalization (of Disabled)
Developmental Disabilities
Disabilities
Disability Identification
Downs Syndrome

Dyslexia
Echolocation
Educational Retardation (1966 1980)
Epilepsy
Exceptional Child Education (1968 1980)
Exceptional Child Services (1968 1980)
Fetal Alcohol Syndrome
Finger Spelling
Gifted Disabled
Group Homes
Handicapped Children (1966 1980)
Handicapped Students (1967 1980)
Head Injuries
Hearing Aids
Hearing Impairments
Hearing Therapy
Homebound
Hyperactivity
Hyperopia
Individualized Family Service Plans
Institutionalized Persons
Language Impairments
Large Type Materials
Learning Disabilities
Lipreading
Loop Induction Systems
Low Incidence Disabilities
Low Vision Aids
Mainstreaming
Manual Communication
Mental Retardation
Mild Disabilities
Mild Mental Retardation
Minimal Brain Dysfunction
Mobility Aids
Moderate Mental Retardation
Multiple Disabilities
Myopia
Neurological Impairments
Normalization (Disabilities)
Oral Communication Method
Parents with Disabilities
Partial Hearing
Partial Vision
Perceptual Impairments
Physical Disabilities
Physical Mobility
Prostheses
Raised Line Drawings
Residential Care
Respite Care
Seizures
Self Care Skills
Sensory Aids
Severe Disabilities
Severe Mental Retardation
Severity (of Disability)
Sheltered Workshops
Sign Language
Slow Learners
Special Education
Special Education Teachers
Special Olympics
Speech Impairments
Speech Language Pathology
Speech Therapy
Spina Bifida
Strabismus
Stuttering
Tactile Adaptation
Teachers with Disabilities
Total Communication
Travel Training
Visible Speech
Visual Impairments
Visually Impaired Mobility
Voice Disorders
Wheelchairs

230 MENTAL HEALTH

Adjustment (to Environment)
Aggression
Alienation
Anger
Anxiety

Art Therapy
Behavior Disorders
Bibliotherapy
Burnout
Catharsis
Child Psychology
Clinical Psychology
Community Psychology
Congruence (Psychology)
Coping
Crisis Intervention
Dance Therapy
Defense Mechanisms
Denial (Psychology)
Depression (Psychology)
Desensitization
Developmental Psychology
Dreams
Echolalia
Emotional Adjustment
Emotional Disturbances
Experimental Psychology
Fear
Fear of Success
Gestalt Therapy
Grief
Group Therapy
Guilt
Helplessness
Hostility
Hypnosis
Individual Psychology
Industrial Psychology
Jealousy
Life Satisfaction
Loneliness
Mental Disorders
Mental Health
Mental Health Clinics
Mental Health Programs
Mental Health Workers
Milieu Therapy
Moods
Morale
Music Therapy
Neuropsychology
Neurosis
Nightmares
Occupational Therapists
Occupational Therapy
Occupational Therapy Assistants
Paranoid Behavior
Personality Problems
Play Therapy
Posttraumatic Stress Disorder
Problem Children
Psychiatric Aides
Psychiatric Hospitals
Psychiatric Services
Psychiatrists
Psychiatry
Psychoeducational Clinics
Psychological Evaluation
Psychological Services
Psychologists
Psychology
Psychometrics
Psychopathology
Psychophysiology
Psychosis
Psychosomatic Disorders
Psychotherapy
Rational Emotive Therapy
Reality Therapy
Rejection (Psychology)
Relaxation Training
Schizophrenia
School Phobia
School Psychology
Security (Psychology)
Self Concept
Self Congruence
Self Destructive Behavior
Self Injurious Behavior
Separation Anxiety
Social Adjustment
Social Psychology

Sport Psychology
Stress Management
Stress Variables
Suicide
Therapeutic Environment
Therapeutic Recreation
Withdrawal (Psychology)

240 COUNSELING

Academic Advising
Adjustment Counselors
Admissions Counseling
Adult Counseling
Career Counseling
Career Guidance
Career Planning
Caseworker Approach
Caseworkers
Classroom Guidance Programs (1968 1980)
Cocounseling
Consultants
Consultation Programs
Counseling
Counseling Effectiveness
Counseling Instructional Programs (1967 1980)
Counseling Objectives
Counseling Psychology
Counseling Services
Counseling Techniques
Counseling Theories
Counselor Attitudes
Counselor Certification
Counselor Characteristics
Counselor Client Ratio
Counselor Client Relationship
Counselor Evaluation
Counselor Performance
Counselor Qualifications
Counselor Role
Counselor Selection
Counselor Teacher Cooperation
Counselor Training
Counselors
Delinquent Rehabilitation
Educational Counseling
Faculty Advisers
Family Counseling
Group Counseling
Group Guidance
Guidance
Guidance Centers
Guidance Objectives
Guidance Personnel
Guidance Programs
Helping Relationship
Hotlines (Public)
Individual Counseling
Laboratory Training
Marriage Counseling
Microcounseling
Nondirective Counseling
Parent Counseling
Peer Counseling
Post High School Guidance
Pupil Personnel Services
Pupil Personnel Workers
Referral
Rehabilitation
Rehabilitation Counseling
Rehabilitation Programs
Role Playing
School Counseling
School Counselors
School Guidance
Sensitivity Training
Social Support Groups
Student Personnel Services
Student Personnel Workers
Student Welfare
Teacher Guidance
Transactional Analysis

310 CLASSROOM PERSPECTIVES

Ability Grouping

Academic Achievement
Academic Failure
Academic Persistence
Acceleration (Education)
Achievement Gains
Advance Organizers
Affective Objectives
Andragogy
Aptitude Treatment Interaction
Assignments
Audiovisual Instruction
Behavioral Objectives
Case Method (Teaching Technique)
Class Activities
Class Average (1966 1980)
Class Organization
Class Rank
Class Size
Classes (Groups of Students)
Classroom Communication
Classroom Environment
Classroom Techniques
Cognitive Objectives
Computer Assisted Instruction
Computer Managed Instruction
Computer Simulation
Conventional Instruction
Cooperative Learning
Course Content
Course Evaluation
Course Objectives
Course Organization
Creative Activities
Creative Teaching
Cross Age Teaching
Cultural Enrichment
Curriculum Based Assessment
Curriculum Enrichment
Demonstrations (Educational)
Developmental Studies Programs
Developmentally Appropriate Practices
Diagnostic Teaching
Dialog Journals
Discussion (Teaching Technique)
Discussion Groups
Drills (Practice)
Educational Diagnosis
Educational Methods
Educational Strategies
Educational Therapy
Enrichment
Enrichment Activities
Episode Teaching (1967 1980)
Error Correction
Experience Charts
Experiential Learning
Experimental Teaching
Formative Evaluation
Global Approach
Grade Charts (1966 1980)
Grades (Scholastic)
Grading
Group Activities
Group Discussion
Group Instruction
Grouping (Instructional Purposes)
Guided Design
Heterogeneous Grouping
Home Study
Homework
Homogeneous Grouping
Honors Curriculum
Independent Study
Individual Activities
Individual Instruction
Individualized Instruction
Individualized Programs
Instruction
Instructional Design
Instructional Development
Instructional Effectiveness
Instructional Improvement
Instructional Innovation
Instructional Material Evaluation
Instructional Programs (1966 1980)
Instructional Systems
Integrated Activities

Intelligent Tutoring Systems
Interdisciplinary Approach
Intermode Differences
Knowledge Base for Teaching
Large Group Instruction
Learner Controlled Instruction
Learning Activities
Learning Centers (Classroom)
Lecture Method
Listening
Listening Groups
Management Games
Mastery Learning
Material Development
Microteaching
Mixed Age Grouping
Montessori Method
Motivation Techniques
Multigraded Classes
Multimedia Instruction
Negative Practice
Nonauthoritarian Classes
Notetaking
Object Manipulation
Outlining (Discourse)
Pacing
Participant Satisfaction
Pedagogical Content Knowledge
Peer Teaching
Performance Contracts
Performance Factors
Portfolio Assessment
Practicum Supervision
Precision Teaching
Prereferral Intervention
Problem Based Learning
Process Education
Proctoring
Programmed Instruction
Programmed Tutoring
Progressive Education
Prompting
Psychoeducational Methods
Psychomotor Objectives
Questioning Techniques
Reciprocal Teaching
Redundancy
Reflective Teaching
Reggio Emilia Approach
Remedial Instruction
Remedial Programs
Repetitive Film Showings
Research Papers (Students)
Resource Room Programs
Resource Units
Self Contained Classrooms
Self Directed Classrooms (1966 1980)
Sequential Approach
Simulated Environment
Simulation
Small Classes
Small Group Instruction
Special Classes
Student Behavior
Student Centered Curriculum
Student Development
Student Experience
Student Improvement
Student Interests
Student Journals
Student Motivation
Student Participation
Student Projects
Student Reaction
Study
Study Habits
Study Skills
Substitution Drills
Summative Evaluation
Task Performance (1966 1980)
Teacher Behavior
Teacher Competencies
Teacher Effectiveness
Teacher Expectations of Students
Teacher Improvement
Teacher Influence
Teacher Motivation

Teacher Response
Teacher Student Relationship
Teaching Conditions
Teaching Experience
Teaching Methods
Teaching Models
Teaching Skills
Teaching Styles
Teaching (1966 1980)
Team Teaching
Team Training
Test Anxiety
Test Coaching
Test Wiseness
Textbook Content
Thematic Approach
Time Management
Time on Task
Training Methods
Training Objectives
Tutorial Programs
Tutoring
Wait Time
Writing Assignments
Writing Exercises

320 SCHOOL PERSPECTIVES

Academic Probation
Academic Rank (Professional)
Academic Records
Academic Standards
Administration
Administrative Change
Administrative Organization
Administrative Policy
Administrative Principles
Administrative Problems
Administrator Attitudes
Administrator Behavior
Administrator Characteristics
Administrator Effectiveness
Administrator Evaluation
Administrator Qualifications
Administrator Responsibility
Administrator Role
Administrator Selection
Admission (School)
Admission Criteria
Advanced Placement
Advanced Placement Programs
Advanced Programs (1966 1980)
Advisory Committees
Age Grade Placement
Alternate Day Schedules
Alumni Education
Ancillary School Services
Attendance
Attendance Patterns
Attendance Records
Auditing (Coursework)
Average Daily Attendance
Average Daily Membership
Beginning Teacher Induction
Bus Transportation
Case Records
Clinical Supervision (of Teachers)
College Administration
College Admission
College Environment
College Governing Councils
College Instruction
College Planning
College Programs
Commencement Ceremonies
Comprehensive Programs
Computer Oriented Programs
Confidential Records
Course Selection (Students)
Credit No Credit Grading
Crisis Management
Critical Path Method
Curriculum Design
Curriculum Development
Curriculum Evaluation
Curriculum Problems

Degree Requirements
Dress Codes
Dropout Prevention
Dropout Programs
Early Admission
Educational Administration
Educational Environment
Educational Programs (1966 1980)
Educational Specifications (1967 1980)
Emergency Programs
Enrollment
Enrollment Influences
Enrollment Management
Experimental Programs
Faculty College Relationship
Faculty Development
Faculty Evaluation
Faculty Organizations
Faculty Promotion
Faculty Recruitment
Faculty Workload
Flexible Schedules (1967 1980)
Flexible Scheduling
Full Day Half Day Schedules
Full Time Equivalency
Grade Inflation
Grade Repetition
Graduation
Graduation Requirements
Improvement Programs
In School Suspension
Inservice Teacher Education
Institutional Administration
Institutional Characteristics
Institutional Environment
Institutional Evaluation
Institutional Mission
Instructional Leadership
Language Enrollment
Late Registration
Majors (Students)
Management by Objectives
Management Development
Management Systems
Management Teams
Merit Rating
Misassignment of Teachers
Nongraded Student Evaluation
Noninstructional Responsibility
Organization Size (Groups)
Organizational Change
Organizational Climate
Organizational Communication
Organizational Development
Organizational Effectiveness
Organizational Objectives
Participative Decision Making
Pass Fail Grading
Peer Evaluation
Peer Institutions
Preschool Evaluation
Program Administration
Program Attitudes
Program Content
Program Design
Program Development
Program Effectiveness
Program Evaluation
Program Implementation
Program Improvement
Program Termination
Publish or Perish Issue
Quality Circles
Recordkeeping
Risk Management
Rotation Plans
Scheduling
School Activities
School Administration
School Based Management
School Catalogs
School Construction
School Effectiveness
School Expansion
School Holding Power
School Maintenance
School Organization

School Orientation
School Policy
School Registration
School Safety
School Security
School Shops
School Size
School Space
School Supervision
School Uniforms
Science Clubs
Science Supervision
Search Committees (Personnel)
Selective Admission
Social Promotion
Special Programs
Staff Development
Staff Meetings
Staff Orientation
Staff Role
Staff Utilization
Student Adjustment
Student Alienation
Student Attitudes
Student Attrition
Student Characteristics
Student College Relationship
Student Evaluation
Student Evaluation of Teacher Performance
Student Government
Student Needs
Student Organizations
Student Placement
Student Promotion
Student Records
Student Recruitment
Student Role
Student School Relationship
Student Teacher Attitudes
Student Teacher Evaluation
Student Teaching
Student Transportation
Systems Approach
Systems Concepts (1966 1980)
Systems Development
Teacher Administrator Relationship
Teacher Alienation
Teacher Attendance
Teacher Attitudes
Teacher Background
Teacher Burnout
Teacher Characteristics
Teacher Collaboration
Teacher Discipline
Teacher Dismissal
Teacher Evaluation
Teacher Morale
Teacher Orientation
Teacher Participation
Teacher Promotion
Teacher Qualifications
Teacher Recruitment
Teacher Responsibility
Teacher Role
Teacher Selection
Teacher Student Ratio
Teacher Supervision
Teaching Assignment (1966 1980)
Teaching Load
Teaching Programs (1966 1980)
Textbook Evaluation
Textbook Selection
Total Quality Management
Transfers (1966 1980)
Validated Programs

330 SOCIETAL PERSPECTIVES

Academic Freedom
Access to Education
Accountability
Accreditation (Institutions)
Accrediting Agencies
Aging in Academia
Alternative Teacher Certification
American Indian Education

Articulation (Education)
Back to Basics
Bilingual Education
Black Achievement
Black Education
Board Administrator Relationship
Board of Education Policy
Board of Education Role
Boards of Education
Certification
Change Agents
Change Strategies
Coeducation
College Attendance
College Choice
College Day
College Outcomes Assessment
College Preparation
College Role
College School Cooperation
Community Benefits
Community Control
Community Involvement
Community Support
Compensatory Education
Competency Based Education
Competitive Selection
Compulsory Education
Computer Anxiety
Computer Attitudes
Computer Literacy
Computer Uses in Education
Consortia
Continuation Education (1968 1980)
Controversial Issues (Course Content)
Cooperative Programs
Corporal Punishment
Corporate Education
Correctional Education
Culturally Relevant Education
Declining Enrollment
Demonstration Programs
Discipline
Discipline Policy
Distance Education
Diversity (Faculty)
Diversity (Institutional)
Diversity (Student)
Dropout Attitudes
Dropout Characteristics
Dropout Rate
Dual Enrollment
Education
Education Work Relationship
Educational Attitudes
Educational Benefits
Educational Change
Educational Cooperation
Educational Demand
Educational Development
Educational History
Educational Improvement
Educational Innovation
Educational Legislation
Educational Malpractice
Educational Mobility
Educational Needs
Educational Objectives
Educational Opportunities
Educational Philosophy
Educational Planning
Educational Policy
Educational Practices
Educational Principles
Educational Problems (1966 1980)
Educational Quality
Educational Resources
Educational Responsibility
Educational Supply
Educational Technology
Educational Trends
Enrollment Rate
Enrollment Trends
Environmental Scanning
Excellence in Education
Exchange Programs
Expulsion

Faculty Mobility
Family School Relationship
Feeder Patterns
Free Choice Transfer Programs
Free Education
Governance
Governing Boards
Government School Relationship
Hidden Curriculum
Home Programs
Home Schooling
Home Visits
Honor Societies
In Loco Parentis
Individualized Education Programs
Informal Education
Information Literacy
Institutional Autonomy
Institutional Cooperation
Institutional Role
Institutional Survival
Integrated Services
Intellectual Freedom
Intercollegiate Cooperation
Intercultural Communication
Interdistrict Policies
Intergroup Education
International Communication
International Educational Exchange
Interschool Communication
Linking Agents
Long Range Planning
Mexican American Education
Migrant Adult Education
Migrant Education
Minimum Competencies
Mobile Educational Services
Noncategorical Education
Nonformal Education
Nonschool Educational Programs
Nontraditional Education
Open Enrollment
Outcome Based Education
Outcomes of Education
Outreach Programs
Parent Associations
Parent Conferences
Parent Education
Parent Grievances
Parent Participation
Parent School Relationship
Parent Student Relationship
Parent Teacher Conferences
Parent Teacher Cooperation
Parent Workshops
Parents as Teachers
Participant Characteristics
Partnerships in Education
Performance Technology
Police School Relationship
Policy
Policy Formation
Politics of Education
Popular Education
Portfolios (Background Materials)
Professional Autonomy
Professional Training
Program Validation
Proposal Writing
Public Relations
Public Service
Regional Cooperation
Regional Planning
Regular and Special Education Relationship
Relevance (Education)
Report Cards
Residence Requirements
Role of Education
Rural Education
Scholarship
School Attendance Legislation
School Attitudes
School Business Relationship
School Choice
School Closing
School Community Programs
School Community Relationship

School Demography
School District Autonomy
School District Reorganization
School District Size
School Entrance Age
School Involvement
School Law
School Location
School Planning (1966 1980)
School Prayer
School Responsibility
School Restructuring
School Role
School Visitation
School Zoning
Service Learning
Shared Resources and Services
State Boards of Education
State Departments of Education
State School District Relationship
Statewide Planning
Strategic Planning
Student Certification
Student Distribution (1966 1980)
Student Educational Objectives
Student Empowerment
Student Exchange Programs
Student Leadership
Student Mobility
Student Problems
Student Responsibility
Student Rights
Student Subcultures
Suspension
Teacher Associations
Teacher Certification
Teacher Distribution
Teacher Empowerment
Teacher Exchange Programs
Teacher Militancy
Teacher Persistence
Teacher Placement
Teacher Rights
Teacher Transfer
Teacher Welfare
Test Score Decline
Textbook Standards
Track System (Education)
Tracking (1968 1980)
Training
Transfer Policy
Transfer Programs
Transfer Rates (College)
Truancy
Urban Education
Urban Teaching
Veterans Education
Withdrawal (Education)
Womens Education

340 ED. LEVELS, DEGREES, ORGANIZATIONS

Adult Basic Education
Adult Education
Adult Programs
Affiliated Schools
Agricultural Colleges
Associate Degrees
Bachelors Degrees
Bilingual Schools
Black Colleges
Boarding Schools
British Infant Schools
Catholic Schools
Charter Schools
Church Related Colleges
Cluster Colleges
College Credits
Colleges
Community Colleges
Community Education
Community Schools
Commuter Colleges
Consolidated Schools
Continuing Education
Continuing Education Units

Correspondence Schools
County School Districts
Credentials
Credits
Day Schools
Degrees (Academic)
Dental Schools
Developing Institutions
Disadvantaged Schools
Doctor of Arts Degrees
Doctoral Degrees
Doctoral Programs
Early Childhood Education
Educational Certificates
Elementary Education
Elementary Schools
Elementary Secondary Education
Experimental Colleges
Experimental Schools
Extended Teacher Education Programs
Folk Schools
Free Schools
Freedom Schools
Grade 1
Grade 10
Grade 11
Grade 12
Grade 2
Grade 3
Grade 4
Grade 5
Grade 6
Grade 7
Grade 8
Grade 9
Graduate Study
High School Equivalency Programs
High Schools
Higher Education
Hospital Schools
Inclusive Schools
Institutional Schools
Instructional Program Divisions
Intermediate Administrative Units
Intermediate Grades
Junior High Schools
Kindergarten
Laboratory Schools
Land Grant Universities
Law Schools
Library Schools
Lifelong Learning
Magnet Schools
Mandatory Continuing Education
Masters Degrees
Masters Programs
Medical Schools
Middle Schools
Military Schools
Multicampus Colleges
Multicampus Districts
Multiunit Schools
Neighborhood Schools
Noncampus Colleges
Northern Schools (1966 1980)
Nursery Schools
One Teacher Schools
Open Universities
Parochial Schools
Postdoctoral Education
Postsecondary Education
Preschool Education
Primary Education
Private Colleges
Private Education
Private Schools
Professional Continuing Education
Professional Development Schools
Professional Education
Proprietary Schools
Public Colleges
Public Education
Public School Adult Education
Public Schools
Regional Schools
Research and Instruction Units
Research Coordinating Units

Research Universities
Residential Colleges
Residential Schools
Rural Schools
School Districts
Schools
Schools of Education
Secondary Education
Secondary Schools
Selective Colleges
Single Sex Colleges
Single Sex Schools
Slum Schools
Small Colleges
Small Schools
Southern Schools (1966 1980)
Special Degree Programs
Special Schools
Specialist in Education Degrees
State Colleges
State Schools
State Universities
Suburban Schools
Teaching Hospitals
Technical Institutes
Terminal Education
Traditional Schools
Transitional Programs
Transitional Schools
Tribally Controlled Education
Two Year Colleges
Undergraduate Study
Universities
Upper Division Colleges
Urban Schools
Urban Universities
Vocational High Schools
Vocational Schools

350 CURRICULUM ORGANIZATION

Activity Units
Advanced Courses
After School Education
After School Programs
Assembly Programs
Block Scheduling
British National Curriculum
Career Academies
College Curriculum
Continuous Progress Plan
Core Curriculum
Correspondence Study
Courses
Credit Courses
Curriculum
Day Programs
Departments
Double Sessions
Elective Courses
Elementary School Curriculum
English Departments
Evening Programs
Experimental Curriculum
Extended School Day
Extended School Year
Extension Education
External Degree Programs
Field Experience Programs
Field Instruction
Field Trips
Fixed Sequence
Flexible Progression
Fused Curriculum
Home Instruction
House Plan
Institutes (Training Programs)
Integrated Curriculum
Intellectual Disciplines
Internship Programs
Introductory Courses
Mass Instruction
Minicourses
National Curriculum
Noncredit Courses
Nongraded Instructional Grouping

Open Education
Practicums
Preschool Curriculum
Program Length
Quarter System
Refresher Courses
Required Courses
Residential Programs
Rural Extension
School Schedules
Science Departments
Secondary School Curriculum
Semester System
Seminars
Spiral Curriculum
Study Abroad
Summer Programs
Summer Schools
Supplementary Education
Teacher Workshops
Telecourses
Telephone Instruction
Time Blocks
Time to Degree
Trimester System
Unified Studies Curriculum
Unit Plan (1966 1980)
Units of Study
Urban Extension
Vacation Programs
Weekend Programs
Work Experience Programs
Workshops
Writing Workshops
Year Round Schools

360 STUDENTS, TEACHERS, SCHOOL PERSONNEL

Academic Deans
Academically Gifted
Adjunct Faculty
Administrators
Admissions Officers
Adult Educators
Adult Students
Advanced Students
Alumni
Art Teachers
Asian American Students
Assistant Principals
Assistant Superintendent Role (1966 1980)
Attendance Officers
Audiovisual Coordinators
Beginning Principals
Beginning Teachers
Bilingual Students
Bilingual Teacher Aides
Bilingual Teachers
Black Students
Black Teachers
Business Education Teachers
Catholic Educators
Central Office Administrators
Child Development Specialists
College Applicants
College Bound Students
College Faculty
College Freshmen
College Graduates
College Juniors
College Presidents
College Seniors
College Sophomores
College Students
College Transfer Students
Commuting Students
Continuation Students
Cooperating Teachers
Coordinators
Counselor Educators
Day Students
Deans
Deans of Students
Dental Students
Department Heads

Differentiated Staffs
Distributive Education Teachers
Education Majors
Educational Researchers
Elementary School Students
Elementary School Teachers
English Teachers
Evaluators
Evening Students
Faculty
Financial Aid Applicants
Foreign Medical Graduates
Foreign Student Advisers
Foreign Students
Former Teachers (1967 1980)
Full Time Faculty
Full Time Students
Graduate Medical Students
Graduate School Faculty
Graduate Students
Graduates
High Risk Students
High School Freshmen
High School Graduates
High School Seniors
High School Students
Hispanic American Students
Home Economics Teachers
In State Students
Industrial Arts Teachers
Instructor Coordinators
Itinerant Teachers
Junior High School Students
Language Teachers
Law Students
Lay Teachers
Low Ability Students (1967 1980)
Lower Class Students
Married Students
Master Teachers
Mathematics Teachers
Medical School Faculty
Medical Students
Methods Teachers
Middle Class Students
Middle School Students
Middle School Teachers
Minority Group Teachers
Music Teachers
Noncollege Bound Students
Nonmajors
Nontenured Faculty
Nontraditional Students
Ombudsmen
On Campus Students
Out of State Students
Paraprofessional School Personnel
Part Time Faculty
Part Time Students
Partnership Teachers
Physical Education Teachers
Potential Dropouts
Pregnant Students
Premedical Students
Preschool Teachers
Preservice Teachers
Principals
Professors
Public School Teachers
Reading Consultants
Reading Teachers
Reentry Students
Registrars (School)
Remedial Teachers
Resident Advisers
Resident Assistants
Resource Staff
Resource Teachers
School Aides
School Business Officials
School Cadres
School Nurses
School Personnel
School Psychologists
School Secretaries
School Social Workers
Science Teachers

Secondary School Students
Secondary School Teachers
Self Supporting Students
Single Students
Special Needs Students
Specialists
State Supervisors
Student Financial Aid Officers
Student Teacher Supervisors
Student Teachers
Student Volunteers
Students
Substitute Teachers
Superintendents
Teacher Aides
Teacher Educators
Teacher Interns
Teacher Researchers
Teachers
Teaching Assistants
Television Teachers
Tenured Faculty
Terminal Students
Trade and Industrial Teachers
Transfer Students
Trustees
Tutors
Two Year College Students
Undergraduate Students
Vocational Directors
Vocational Education Teachers
White Students
Women Administrators
Women Faculty
Writing Teachers

400 SUBJECTS OF INSTRUCTION

Academic Discourse
Academic Education
Administrator Education
Adult Vocational Education
Adventure Education
African Studies
Aging Education
Alcohol Education
Alphabetizing Skills
American Indian Studies
American Studies
Anthropology
Archaeology
Architectural Education
Area Studies
Asian Studies
Auditory Training
Basic Business Education
Basic Skills
Basic Writing
Beginning Writing
Behavioral Sciences
Black Studies
Business Administration Education
Business Education
Business English
Business Skills
Canadian Studies
Career Awareness
Career Education
Career Exploration
Cartography
Childrens Writing
Citizenship Education
Civics
Clothing Instruction
College English
Communication Skills
Comparative Education
Competency Based Teacher Education
Comprehensive School Health Education
Computer Science Education
Concept Teaching
Consumer Education
Consumer Science
Content Area Writing
Cooking Instruction
Cooperative Education

Course Integrated Library Instruction
Creative Writing
Criminology
Critical Viewing
Cross Cultural Studies
Cross Cultural Training
Cultural Education
Current Events
Cursive Writing
Custodian Training
Debate
Descriptive Writing
Direction Writing (1966 1980)
Distributive Education
Driver Education
Drug Education
Economics Education
Education Courses
Educational Anthropology
Educational Gerontology
Educational Psychology
Educational Sociology
Energy Education
English Curriculum
English Education (1967 1980)
English Instruction
English Teacher Education
Ethical Instruction
Ethnic Studies
Ethnography
Ethnology
Expository Writing
Family Life Education
Film Study
Fire Science Education
Flight Training
Foods Instruction
Foundations of Education
Free Writing
Freshman Composition
General Education
Geographic Concepts
Geography
Geography Instruction
Gerontology
Global Education
Handwriting
Health Education
Heritage Education
Home Economics
Home Economics Education
Home Economics Skills
Home Management
Homemaking Skills
Humanistic Education
Industrial Arts
Industrial Education
Industrial Training
Information Science Education
International Education
International Studies
Invented Spelling
Journal Writing
Journalism Education
Law Related Education
Leadership Training
Legal Education (Professions)
Legal Education (1977 1986)
Leisure Education
Liberal Arts
Library Education
Library Instruction
Literature Appreciation
Literature Programs (1966 1980)
Locational Skills (Social Studies)
Logic
Map Skills
Marine Education
Marksmanship
Mechanical Skills
Methods Courses
Middle Eastern Studies
Military Science
Military Training
Nutrition Instruction
Occupational Home Economics
Office Occupations Education

Office Practice
Outdoor Education
Paragraph Composition
Parenthood Education
Police Education
Political Science
Population Education
Postsecondary Education as a Field of Study
Practical Arts
Preretirement Education
Preservice Teacher Education
Pretechnology Programs
Prevocational Education
Prewriting
Process Approach (Writing)
Public Administration Education
Public Affairs Education
Public Speaking
Religious Education
Revision (Written Composition)
Safety Education
Sensory Training
Sewing Instruction
Sex Education
Shop Curriculum
Shorthand
Social Sciences
Social Studies
Sociology
Spelling
Spelling Instruction
Supervisory Training
Teacher Education
Teacher Education Curriculum
Teacher Education Programs
Teacher Educator Education
Tech Prep
Technical Education
Telephone Usage Instruction
Television Curriculum
Textiles Instruction
Theological Education
Trade and Industrial Education
Typewriting
United States Government (Course)
Urban Studies
Values Clarification
Values Education
Veterinary Medical Education
Vocational Education
Volunteer Training
Womens Studies
World Geography
Writing (Composition)
Writing Ability
Writing Across the Curriculum
Writing Improvement
Writing Instruction
Writing Processes
Writing Skills
Writing Strategies

410 AGRICULTURE AND NATURAL RESOURCES

Acid Rain
Adult Farmer Education
Agribusiness
Agricultural Chemical Occupations
Agricultural Education
Agricultural Engineering
Agricultural Laborers
Agricultural Machinery
Agricultural Machinery Occupations
Agricultural Occupations
Agricultural Personnel
Agricultural Production
Agricultural Safety
Agricultural Skills
Agricultural Supplies
Agricultural Supply Occupations
Agricultural Technicians
Agricultural Trends
Agriculture
Agronomy
Air Pollution
Animal Husbandry

Asbestos
Birds
Braceros
Coal
Conservation (Environment)
Conservation Education
Crew Leaders
Crop Processing Occupations
Dairy Farmers
Depleted Resources
Drinking Water
Drought
Ecological Factors
Endangered Species
Energy Audits
Energy Conservation
Energy Management
Environment
Environmental Education
Environmental Interpretation
Estuaries
Experiment Stations
Extension Agents
Farm Accounts
Farm Labor
Farm Management
Farm Occupations
Farm Visits
Farmers
Feed Industry
Feed Stores
Fertilizers
Field Crops
Fisheries
Floriculture
Forestry
Forestry Aides
Forestry Occupations
Fossil Fuels
Fuel Consumption
Fuels
Gardening
Gardens
Gasoline
Grains (Food)
Greenhouse Effect
Greenhouses
Grounds Keepers
Groundwater
Habitats
Harvesting
Herbicides
Horses
Horticulture
Insecticides
Landscaping
Livestock
Lumber Industry
Meat
Minerals
Mining
Natural Gas
Natural Resources
Nurseries (Horticulture)
Nursery Workers (Horticulture)
Off Farm Agricultural Occupations
Oil
Ornamental Horticulture
Ornamental Horticulture Occupations
Part Time Farmers
Pesticides
Pests
Plant Growth
Plant Identification
Plant Pathology
Plant Propagation
Plant Science (1967 1980)
Pollution
Rainforests
Recycling
Rivers
Rural Farm Residents
Sharecroppers
Sludge
Soil Conservation
Soil Science
Solid Wastes

Supervised Occupational Experience (Agriculture)
Sustainable Development
Tractors
Trees
Turf Management
Veterinary Medicine
Waste Disposal
Waste Water
Wastes
Water Pollution
Water Quality
Water Resources
Weeds
Wetlands
Wilderness
Wildlife
Wildlife Management
Young Farmer Education

420 ARTS

Acting
Aesthetic Education
Applied Music
Architects
Architecture
Art
Art Activities
Art Appreciation
Art Criticism
Art Education
Art Expression
Art History
Art Materials
Art Products
Art Song
Artists
Bands (Music)
Brass Instruments
Caricatures (1966 1980)
Ceramics
Childrens Art
Choral Music
Choral Speaking
Clothing Design
Collage
Color Planning
Commercial Art
Computer Assisted Design
Concerts
Contrast
Creative Art
Creative Dramatics
Creative Expression
Dance
Dance Education
Design
Design Crafts
Design Preferences
Discipline Based Art Education
Drama Workshops
Dramatic Play
Dramatics
Fine Arts
Found Objects
Freehand Drawing
Furniture Design
Graphic Arts
Handicrafts
Harmony (Music)
Hymns
Improvisation
Instrumentation and Orchestration
Interior Design
Jazz
Kodaly Method
Manuscript Writing (Handlettering)
Melody
Music
Music Activities
Music Appreciation
Music Education
Music Reading
Music Techniques
Music Theory
Musical Composition

Musical Instruments
Musicians
Opera
Oral Interpretation
Orchestras
Orff Method
Oriental Music
Painting (Visual Arts)
Pantomime
Photography
Popular Music
Printmaking
Puppetry
Readers Theater
Rehearsals (Theater Arts)
Relief (Art)
Rhythm (Music)
Rock Music
Sculpture
Singing
Skits
Songs
String Instruments
Studio Art
Suzuki Method
Tempo (Music)
Theater Arts
Visual Arts
Vocal Music
Wind Instruments
Woodwind Instruments

430 HUMANITIES

Adolescent Literature
Aesthetics
African History
African Literature
Allegory
Ambiguity
American History (1966 1980)
American Indian History
American Indian Literature
Analytical Criticism (1969 1980)
Ancient History
Antithesis
Aristotelian Criticism (1969 1980)
Asian History
Audience Awareness
Australian Literature
Auteurism
Authors
Ballads
Baroque Literature
Biblical Literature
Bioethics
Black History
Black Literature
Buddhism
Canadian Literature
Characterization
Childrens Literature
Christianity
Chronicles
Civil War (United States)
Classical Literature
Classics (Literature)
Cliches
Colonial History (United States)
Comedy
Confucianism
Constitutional History
Creationism
Czech Literature
Dialogs (Literary)
Diaries
Didacticism
Drama
Eighteenth Century Literature
English Literature
English Neoclassic Literary Period (1968 1980)
Epics
Essays
Ethics
European History
Existentialism

Expressionism
Fables
Fairy Tales
Family History
Fiction
Fifteenth Century Literature
Figurative Language
Film Criticism
Formal Criticism (1969 1980)
French Literature
Genealogy
German Literature
Greek Civilization
Greek Literature
Haiku
Hispanic American Literature
Historical Criticism (1969 1980)
Historical Interpretation
Historiography
History
History Instruction
Humanism
Humanities
Humanities Instruction
Humor
Imagery
Impressionism
Impressionistic Criticism (1969 1980)
Individualism
Intellectual History
Irony
Islam
Italian Literature
Journalism History
Judaism
Korean War
Latin American History
Latin American Literature
Latin Literature
Legends
Literary Criticism
Literary Devices
Literary Discrimination (1966 1980)
Literary Genres
Literary History
Literary Influences (1969 1980)
Literary Mood (1970 1980)
Literary Perspective (1969 1980)
Literary Styles
Literature
Local Color Writing
Local History
Lyric Poetry
Medieval History
Medieval Literature
Metaphors
Mexican American History
Mexican American Literature
Middle Eastern History
Modern History
Modernism
Monologs
Moral Criticism (1969 1980)
Motifs
Mysticism
Mythic Criticism (1969 1980)
Mythology
Narration
Naturalism
Neoclassicism
New Journalism
Nineteenth Century Literature
Nonfiction
North American History
North American Literature
Novels
Nursery Rhymes
Odes
Old English Literature
Oral History
Paradox
Parallelism (Literary)
Parody
Pastoral Literature
Phenomenology
Philosophy
Platonic Criticism (1970 1980)

Platonism
Playwriting
Poetry
Poets
Polish Literature
Postmodernism
Prose
Proverbs
Public History
Puns
Realism
Reconstruction Era
Religion
Religion Studies
Renaissance Literature
Revolutionary War (United States)
Rhetoric
Rhetorical Criticism
Rhetorical Invention
Rhetorical Theory
Rhyme
Romanticism
Russian Literature
Satire
Science Fiction
Seventeenth Century Literature
Short Stories
Sixteenth Century Literature
Social History
Sonnets
Spanish Literature
Spirituality
State History
Surrealism
Symbolism
Symbols (Literary)
Tales
Taoism
Textual Criticism (1969 1980)
Theoretical Criticism (1969 1980)
Tragedy
Twentieth Century Literature
United States History
United States Literature
Victorian Literature
Vietnam War
World History
World Literature
World War I
World War II

440 LANGUAGES

African Languages
Afrikaans
Afro Asiatic Languages
Akan
Albanian
American Indian Languages
Amharic
Apache
Arabic
Armenian
Artificial Languages
Athapascan Languages
Australian Aboriginal Languages
Austro Asiatic Languages
Aymara
Azerbaijani
Baltic Languages
Baluchi
Bantu Languages
Basaa
Bashkir
Basque
Bemba
Bengali
Berber Languages
Bielorussian
Bikol
Bini
Bulgarian
Buriat
Burmese
Burushaski
Cakchiquel

Cambodian
Cantonese
Caucasian Languages
Cebuano
Chad Languages
Chamorro
Cheremis
Cherokee
Chinese
Chinyanja
Choctaw
Chuvash
Classical Languages
Cree
Creoles
Czech
Dagur
Dakota
Danish
Dravidian Languages
Dusun
Dutch
Dyula
English
English (Second Language)
English for Academic Purposes
English for Science and Technology
English for Special Purposes
English Only Movement
Eskimo Aleut Languages
Esperanto
Estonian
Ewe
Finnish
Finno Ugric Languages
Foochow
French
Fulani
Ga
Ganda
Gbaya
German
Greek
Guarani
Gujarati
Gullah
Haitian Creole
Hausa
Hawaiian
Hebrew
Hindi
Hmong
Hopi
Hungarian
Igbo
Indo European Languages
Indonesian
Indonesian Languages
Inupiaq
Irish
Italian
Japanese
Javanese
Kabyle
Kannada
Kashmiri
Kirundi
Kituba
Korean
Kurdish
Kyrgyz
Lakota
Languages
Languages for Special Purposes
Lao
Latin
Latvian
Lingala
Lithuanian
Luo
Malagasy
Malay
Malayalam
Malayo Polynesian Languages
Manchu
Mandarin Chinese
Mandingo

Maori
Maranao
Marathi
Mauritian Creole
Mayan Languages
Melanesian Languages
Mende
Middle English
Modern Languages
Mongolian
Mongolian Languages
Mossi
Navajo
Nembe
Nepali
Norwegian
Ojibwa
Okinawan
Old English
Ossetic
Ostyak
Papago
Pashto
Persian
Pidgins
Polish
Pomo
Portuguese
Punjabi
Quechua
Quiche
Riff
Romance Languages
Romanian
Russian
Salish
Samoan
Samoyed Languages
Sango
Sanskrit
Sara
Scots Gaelic
Semitic Languages
Serbocroatian
Shona
Sierra Leone Creole
Singhalese
Sino Tibetan Languages
Siswati
Slavic Languages
Slovenian
Somali
Spanish
Susu
Swahili
Swedish
Tagalog
Tajik
Tamil
Tatar
Telugu
Thai
Tibetan
Turkic Languages
Turkish
Tzeltal
Tzotzil
Ukrainian
Uralic Altaic Languages
Urdu
Uto Aztecan Languages
Uzbek
Vietnamese
Visayan
Vocational English (Second Language)
Vogul
Welsh
Wolof
Yakut
Yiddish
Yoruba
Yucatec
Yupik
Yurak

450 LANGUAGE AND SPEECH

Acoustic Phonetics
Adjectives
Adverbs
Affixes
Alphabets
Anthropological Linguistics
Applied Linguistics
Articulation (Speech)
Artificial Speech
Audiolingual Methods
Audiolingual Skills
Aviation Vocabulary
Banking Vocabulary
Basic Vocabulary
Bidialectalism
Bilingual Education Programs
Bilingualism
Black Dialects
Capitalization (Alphabetic)
Caregiver Speech
Case (Grammar)
Child Language
Code Switching (Language)
Coherence
Cohesion (Written Composition)
College Language Programs (1967 1980)
College Second Language Programs
Communicative Competence (Languages)
Componential Analysis
Computational Linguistics
Conjunctions
Connected Discourse
Consonants
Context Free Grammar
Contrastive Linguistics
Conversational Language Courses
Cyrillic Alphabet
Debate Format
Deep Structure
Descriptive Linguistics
Determiners (Languages)
Diachronic Linguistics
Diacritical Marking
Dialects
Dialogs (Language)
Diction
Diglossia
Discourse Analysis
Discourse Modes
Distinctive Features (Language)
Error Analysis (Language)
Etymology
Expressive Language
FLES
Form Classes (Languages)
Function Words
Generative Grammar
Generative Phonology
Glottochronology
Grammar
Grammar Translation Method
Grammatical Acceptability
Graphemes
Ideography
Idioms
Immersion Programs
Inner Speech (Subvocal)
Intensive Language Courses
Interference (Language)
Interlanguage
International Trade Vocabulary
Interpretive Skills
Intonation
Jargon
Kernel Sentences
Keywords
Kinship Terminology
Language
Language Ability (1966 1980)
Language Aids (1966 1980)
Language Aptitude
Language Arts
Language Attitudes
Language Classification
Language Dominance

Language Enrichment
Language Experience Approach
Language Fluency
Language Instruction (1966 1980)
Language Learning Levels (1967 1980)
Language Maintenance
Language Minorities
Language of Instruction
Language Patterns
Language Planning
Language Processing
Language Proficiency
Language Programs (1966 1980)
Language Rhythm
Language Role
Language Skill Attrition
Language Skills
Language Standardization
Language Styles
Language Typology
Language Universals
Language Usage
Language Variation
Letters (Alphabet)
Limited English Speaking
Linguistic Borrowing
Linguistic Competence
Linguistic Difficulty (Inherent)
Linguistic Input
Linguistic Performance
Linguistic Theory
Linguistics
Mathematical Linguistics
Metalinguistics
Modern Language Curriculum
Monolingualism
Morphemes
Morphology (Languages)
Morphophonemics
Multilevel Classes (Second Language Instruction)
Multilingualism
Mutual Intelligibility
Native Language Instruction
Native Speakers
Negative Forms (Language)
Neurolinguistics
Non English Speaking
Non Roman Scripts
Nonstandard Dialects
North American English
Notional Functional Syllabi
Nouns
Official Languages
Onomastics
Oral English
Oral Language
Orthographic Symbols
Paragraphs
Paralinguistics
Pattern Drills (Language)
Persuasive Discourse
Phoneme Grapheme Correspondence
Phonemes
Phonemic Alphabets
Phonemics
Phonetic Analysis
Phonetic Transcription
Phonetics
Phonology
Phrase Structure
Plurals
Pragmatics
Prefixes (Grammar)
Prepositions
Pronouns
Pronunciation
Pronunciation Instruction
Psycholinguistics
Punctuation
Receptive Language
Regional Dialects
Romanization
Second Language Instruction
Second Language Learning
Second Language Programs
Second Languages
Semantics

Semiotics
Sentence Combining
Sentence Diagraming
Sentence Structure
Sentences
Sexism in Language
Social Dialects
Sociolinguistics
Spanish Speaking
Speech
Speech Acts
Speech Communication
Speech Compression
Speech Curriculum
Speech Education (1966 1980)
Speech Evaluation
Speech Habits
Speech Improvement
Speech Instruction
Speech Skills
Standard Spoken Usage
Stress (Phonology)
Structural Analysis (Linguistics)
Structural Analysis (1966 1980)
Structural Grammar
Structural Linguistics
Suffixes
Suprasegmentals
Surface Structure
Syllables
Symbolic Language
Syntax
Tagmemic Analysis
TENL (1968 1980)
Tenses (Grammar)
Threshold Level (Languages)
Tone Languages
Traditional Grammar
Transformational Generative Grammar
Translation
Uncommonly Taught Languages
Unwritten Language (1968 1980)
Unwritten Languages
Urban Language
Verbal Ability
Verbal Communication
Verbal Development
Verbs
Vocabulary
Vocabulary Development
Vocabulary Skills
Vowels
Whole Language Approach
Word Frequency
Word Order
Written Language

460 READING

Adult Literacy
Adult Reading Programs
Basal Reading
Basic Reading (1967 1980)
Beginning Reading
Cloze Procedure
Content Area Reading
Context Clues
Corrective Reading
Creative Reading (1966 1980)
Critical Reading
Decoding (Reading)
Developmental Reading (1966 1980)
Directed Reading Activity
Early Reading
Elective Reading (1966 1980)
Emergent Literacy
Eye Voice Span
Factual Reading (1966 1980)
Family English Literacy
Family Literacy
Functional Literacy
Functional Reading
Group Reading (1966 1980)
Illiteracy
Independent Reading
Individual Reading (1966 1980)

Individualized Reading
Initial Teaching Alphabet
Interpretive Reading (1966 1980)
Literacy
Literacy Education
Miscue Analysis
Oral Reading
Phonics
Prereading Experience
Readability
Readability Formulas
Reader Text Relationship
Reading
Reading Ability
Reading Achievement
Reading Aloud to Others
Reading Assignments
Reading Attitudes
Reading Centers
Reading Comprehension
Reading Development (1966 1980)
Reading Diagnosis
Reading Difficulties
Reading Difficulty (1966 1980)
Reading Failure
Reading Games
Reading Habits
Reading Improvement
Reading Instruction
Reading Interests
Reading Level (1966 1980)
Reading Material Selection
Reading Motivation
Reading Processes
Reading Programs
Reading Rate
Reading Readiness
Reading Skills
Reading Strategies
Reading Writing Relationship
Recreational Reading
Remedial Reading
Sight Method
Sight Vocabulary
Silent Reading
Speed Reading
Story Grammar
Story Reading
Supplementary Reading Materials
Sustained Silent Reading
Text Structure
Word Recognition
Word Study Skills
Workplace Literacy

470 PHYSICAL EDUCATION AND RECREATION

Aerobics
Aquatic Sports
Archery
Athletes
Athletic Coaches
Athletic Fields
Athletics
Badminton
Baseball
Basketball
Bicycling
Bowling
Calisthenics
Camping
Childrens Games
College Athletics
Community Recreation Programs
Day Camp Programs
Diving
Exercise
Exercise (Physiology) (1969 1980)
Extracurricular Activities
Extramural Athletics
Fencing (Sport)
Field Hockey
Football
Games
Golf
Gymnastics

Handball
Hobbies
Horseback Riding
Ice Hockey
Ice Skating
Intramural Athletics
Jogging
Lacrosse
Leisure Time
Lifetime Sports
Movement Education
Olympic Games
Orienteering
Outdoor Activities
Outdoor Leadership
Physical Activities
Physical Education
Physical Recreation Programs
Play
Playground Activities
Plyometrics
Racquet Sports
Racquetball
Recess Breaks
Recreation
Recreational Activities
Recreational Programs
Recreationists
Resident Camp Programs
Roller Skating
Running
Sailing
School Recreational Programs
Skiing
Soccer
Softball
Sportsmanship
Squash (Game)
Surfing
Swimming
Table Tennis
Team Handball
Team Sports
Tennis
Toys
Track and Field
Tumbling
Underwater Diving
Volleyball
Walking
Water Polo
Waterskiing
Weightlifting
Winter Sports
Womens Athletics
Wrestling

480 MATHEMATICS

Addition
Algebra
Algorithms
Analytic Geometry
Area
Arithmetic
Bayesian Statistics
Calculus
College Mathematics
Computation
Congruence (Mathematics)
Decimal Fractions
Differential Equations
Distance
Division
Elementary School Mathematics
Equations (Mathematics)
Estimation (Mathematics)
Ethnomathematics
Expectancy Tables
Fractions
Functions (Mathematics)
General Mathematics
Geometric Concepts
Geometric Constructions
Geometry
Incidence

Inequality (Mathematics)
Integers
Limits (Mathematics)
Linear Programming
Logarithms
Markov Processes
Mathematical Applications
Mathematical Aptitude
Mathematical Concepts
Mathematical Enrichment
Mathematical Experience (1966 1980)
Mathematical Formulas
Mathematical Logic
Mathematical Vocabulary
Mathematics
Mathematics Achievement
Mathematics Activities
Mathematics Anxiety
Mathematics Curriculum
Mathematics Education
Mathematics History
Mathematics Instruction
Mathematics Skills
Matrices
Mental Computation
Metric System
Modern Mathematics
Modular Arithmetic
Multiplication
Nonparametric Statistics
Number Concepts
Number Systems
Numbers
Numeracy
Orthographic Projection
Patterns in Mathematics
Percentage
Place Value
Plane Geometry
Polygons
Polynomials
Prime Numbers
Probability
Proof (Mathematics)
Properties (Mathematics)
Rational Numbers
Ratios (Mathematics)
Reciprocals (Mathematics)
Regression (Statistics)
Remedial Mathematics
Secondary School Mathematics
Set Theory
Solid Geometry
Statistical Distributions
Statistical Inference
Statistics
Subtraction
Symbols (Mathematics)
Symmetry
Technical Mathematics
Topography
Topology
Transformations (Mathematics)
Trigonometry
Vectors (Mathematics)
Volume (Mathematics)
Whole Numbers
Word Problems (Mathematics)

490 SCIENCE AND TECHNOLOGY

Acceleration (Physics)
Acids
Acoustics
Aerospace Education
Aerospace Technology
Air Flow
Air Traffic Control
Alternative Energy Sources
Anatomy
Animals
Astronomy
Atomic Structure
Atomic Theory
Automation
Aviation Education

Aviation Technology
Bacteria
Biochemistry
Biodiversity
Biofeedback
Biological Sciences
Biology
Biomechanics
Bionics
Biophysics
Biotechnology
Botany
Chemical Analysis
Chemical Bonding
Chemical Engineering
Chemical Equilibrium
Chemical Nomenclature
Chemical Reactions
Chemistry
Chromatography
Civil Engineering
Clay
Climate
Climate Change
Climate Control
College Science
Color
Coordination Compounds
Crystallography
Culturing Techniques
Cytology
Demonstrations (Science)
Density (Matter)
Diffusion (Physics)
Dinosaurs
Dissection
DNA
Earth Science
Earthquakes
Ecology
Electricity
Electrochemistry
Electromechanical Technology
Electronic Control
Electronics
Elementary School Science
Embryology
Energy
Engineering
Engineering Drawing
Engineering Education
Engineering Graphics
Engineering Technology
Entomology
Entropy
Enzymes
Ethology
Evolution
Floods
Fluid Mechanics
Force
Fungi
General Science
Genetic Engineering
Genetics
Geochemistry
Geology
Geophysics
Geothermal Energy
Global Warming
Gravity (Physics)
Hands on Science
Heat
Height
Heredity
Horology
Human Factors Engineering
Humidity
Hurricanes
Hydraulics
Hydrology
Ichthyology
Inorganic Chemistry
Intervals
Inventions
Kinetic Molecular Theory
Kinetics

Laboratory Animals
Laboratory Experiments
Laboratory Procedures
Laboratory Techniques (1967 1980)
Laboratory Technology
Lasers
Light
Luminescence
Magnets
Marine Biology
Maritime Education
Matter
Mechanics (Physics)
Metallurgy
Metals
Meteorology
Microbiology
Microelectronics
Mineralogy
Molecular Biology
Molecular Structure
Monera
Motion
Mycology
Natural Sciences
Navigation
Noise (Sound)
Nuclear Energy
Nuclear Physics
Nuclear Technology
Nuclear Weapons
Nucleic Acids
Obsolescence
Ocean Engineering
Oceanography
Optics
Organic Chemistry
Ornithology
Oxidation
Paleontology
Petrology
Pets
Photochemical Reactions
Photosynthesis
Physical Chemistry
Physical Geography
Physical Sciences
Physics
Physiology
Plants (Botany)
Plate Tectonics
Polymers
Power Technology
Preservation
Pressure (Physics)
Pressure (1970 1980)
Primatology
Protists
Protozoa
Proximity
Psychoacoustics
Quantum Mechanics
Radiation
Radiation Biology
Radiation Effects
Radioisotopes
Rats
Relativity
Reproduction (Biology)
RNA
Robotics
Satellites (Aerospace)
Science Achievement
Science Activities
Science and Society
Science Careers
Science Course Improvement Projects
Science Curriculum
Science Education
Science Education History
Science Experiments
Science Fairs
Science History
Science Instruction
Science Interests
Science Process Skills
Science Programs

Science Projects
Sciences
Scientific and Technical Information
Scientific Attitudes
Scientific Concepts
Scientific Enterprise
Scientific Literacy
Scientific Methodology
Scientific Personnel
Scientific Principles
Secondary School Science
Seismology
Social Biology
Sociobiology
Solar Energy
Solar System
Space
Space Exploration
Space Sciences
Spectroscopy
Stars
Stereochemistry
Structural Analysis (Science)
Summer Science Programs
Technological Advancement
Technological Literacy
Technology
Technology Education
Technology Transfer
Temperature
Thermodynamics
Time
Tornadoes
Velocity
Viruses
Volcanoes
Water
Water Treatment
Weather
Weight (Mass)
Wind (Meteorology)
Wind Energy
Zoology

510 THE INDIVIDUAL IN SOCIAL CONTEXT

Adopted Children
Adoptive Parents
Adult Children
Adult Dropouts
Advantaged
Affluent Youth
Bereavement
Biological Parents
Black Mothers
Black Youth
Caregiver Child Relationship
Caregiver Role
Caregivers
Child Responsibility
Child Role
Consciousness Raising
Dating (Social)
Daughters
Dependents
Displaced Homemakers
Dropouts
Dual Career Family
Economic Status
Educational Attainment
Educational Background
Educational Experience
Educational Status Comparison
Employed Parents
Ethnic Status
Family Attitudes
Family Caregivers
Family Characteristics
Family Environment
Family Influence
Family Involvement
Family Life
Family Relationship
Family Role

Family Status
Father Attitudes
Fatherless Family
Fathers
Foster Children
Foster Family
Friendship
Grandchildren
Grandparents
Group Membership
Heads of Households
Homeowners
Immigrants
Interaction
Interpersonal Attraction
Interpersonal Communication
Interpersonal Relationship
Latchkey Children
Leaders
Lower Class Parents
Marital Satisfaction
Marital Status
Mate Selection
Middle Class Parents
Migrant Children
Migrant Youth
Migrants
Minority Group Children
Mother Attitudes
Motherless Family
Mothers
One Parent Family
Out of School Youth
Parent Aspiration
Parent Attitudes
Parent Background
Parent Child Relationship
Parent Influence
Parent Responsibility
Parent Role
Parents
Peer Acceptance
Peer Influence
Peer Relationship
Permissive Environment
Personal Autonomy
Racial Differences
Rapport
Recognition (1967 1980)
Refugees
Religious Differences
Role Perception
Rural Family
Rural Nonfarm Residents
Rural Women
Rural Youth
Sex Role
Sibling Relationship
Siblings
Significant Others
Social Attitudes
Social Background
Social Characteristics
Social Control
Social Differences
Social Environment
Social Experience
Social Influences
Social Responsibility
Social Status
Socioeconomic Background
Socioeconomic Influences
Socioeconomic Status
Sons
Spouses
Stopouts
Suburban Youth
Transient Children
Undocumented Immigrants
Unwed Mothers
Urban Youth
Veterans
Victims of Crime
Vietnam Veterans
Welfare Recipients
Widowed
Youth Leaders

520 SOCIAL PROCESSES AND STRUCTURES

Adoption
Adoption (Ideas)
Advocacy
Aesthetic Values
Agenda Setting
Alumni Associations
American Dream
Ancillary Services (1967 1980)
Awards
Behavior Standards
Births to Single Women
Black Attitudes
Black Community
Black Family
Black Influences
Black Institutions
Black Organizations
Brainstorming
Bureaucracy
Capital Punishment
Censorship
Centralization
Change
Child Advocacy
Child Care (1966 1980)
Child Custody
Child Rearing
Child Welfare
Childlessness
Childrens Rights
Church Programs
Church Responsibility
Church Role
Church Workers
Class Attitudes (1966 1980)
Clubs
Codes of Ethics
Cohabitation
Collegiality
Committees
Communication (Thought Transfer)
Communication Audits
Community
Community Action
Community Attitudes
Community Characteristics
Community Cooperation
Community Coordination
Community Influence
Community Leaders
Community Needs
Community Organizations
Community Programs
Community Relations
Community Resources
Community Responsibility
Community Role
Community Satisfaction
Community Services
Competition
Confidentiality
Conflict of Interest
Conflict Resolution
Conformity
Conservatism
Consumer Protection
Context Effect
Cooperation
Cooperative Planning
Coordination
Correctional Rehabilitation
Credibility
Crime Prevention
Criteria
Crowding
Cultural Influences
Cultural Pluralism
Culture Conflict
Day Care
Day Care Effects
Decentralization
Deception
Delinquency Prevention
Delivery Systems
Development

Development Communication
Developmental Continuity
Developmental Programs
Differences
Discourse Communities
Disqualification
Divorce
Early Intervention
Early Parenthood
Eligibility
Elitism
Empowerment
Extended Family
Family (Sociological Unit)
Family Day Care
Family Needs
Family Programs
Family Size
Family Structure
Family Work Relationship
Foreign Nationals
Foster Care
Fraternities
Futures (of Society)
Gender Issues
Group Behavior
Group Dynamics
Group Experience
Group Norms (1968 1980)
Group Status
Group Structure
Group Unity
Groups
Growth Patterns (1966 1980)
Help Seeking
Holidays
Horizontal Organization
Human Development (1966 1980)
Human Living (1966 1980)
Human Relations
Human Resources
Human Services
Humanitarianism
Humanization
Ideology
Improvement
Incentives
Infant Care
Influences
Informal Leadership
Informal Organization
Innovation
Institutional Personnel
Institutions
Interfaith Relations
Intergenerational Programs
Intergroup Relations
Intermarriage
International Cooperation
Interprofessional Relationship
Intervention
Kinship
Lay People
Leadership
Leadership Qualities
Leadership Responsibility
Leadership Styles
Legal Aid
Liberalism
Library Associations
Life Style
Living Standards
Low Income Groups
Lower Class
Lower Middle Class
Majority Attitudes
Marriage
Mass Media Effects
Mass Media Role
Medical Associations
Meetings
Mentors
Mergers
Middle Class
Middle Class Standards
Migrant Programs
Migrant Welfare Services

Minority Group Influences
Minority Groups
Modernization
Moral Issues
Moral Values
National Organizations
Needs
No Shows
Nongovernmental Organizations
Nonprofit Organizations
Nuclear Family
Objectives
Organization
Organizations (Groups)
Parent Empowerment
Parent Rights
Peer Groups
Peer Mediation
Placement
Police Community Relationship
Political Socialization
Popularity
Power Structure
Prerequisites
Prestige
Prevention
Privacy
Private Agencies
Professional Associations
Professional Isolation
Professional Recognition
Professional Services
Programs
Punishment
Pyramid Organization
Quality of Life
Recognition (Achievement)
Regional Programs
Relationship
Religious Factors
Religious Holidays
Religious Organizations
Remarriage
Reputation
Resources
Responsibility
Reunions
Rewards
Role
Rural Sociology
Sanctions
School Age Day Care
Self Directed Groups
Self Help Programs
Sentencing
Services
Slavery
Social Action
Social Agencies
Social Change
Social Class
Social Desirability
Social Indicators
Social Life
Social Mobility
Social Organizations
Social Relations (1966 1980)
Social Services
Social Stratification
Social Structure
Social Systems
Social Values
Social Welfare (1966 1980)
Sociocultural Patterns
Sororities
Southern Community (1966 1980)
Standards
Status
Stepfamily
Talent Utilization (1966 1980)
Teamwork
Traditionalism
Transracial Adoption
Upper Class
Urban Programs
Values
Vertical Organization

Voluntary Agencies
Welfare Agencies
Welfare Services
Welfare (1966 1980)
Work Ethic
Working Class
Youth Agencies
Youth Clubs
Youth Programs

530 SOCIAL PROBLEMS

Alcohol Abuse
Antisocial Behavior
Battered Women
Bullying
Cheating
Child Abuse
Child Neglect
Community Problems
Conflict
Crime
Criminals
Delinquency
Delinquency Causes
Discipline Problems
Driving While Intoxicated
Drug Abuse
Drug Addiction
Elder Abuse
Emotional Abuse
Family Problems
Family Violence
Feminization of Poverty
Fraud
Generation Gap
Hazing
Homeless People
Homicide
Housing Deficiencies
Illegal Drug Use
Incest
International Crimes
Juvenile Gangs
Libel and Slander
Lying
Malpractice
Marital Instability
Migrant Problems
Missing Children
Negligence
Obscenity
Plagiarism
Poverty
Prisoners
Problems
Rape
Recidivism
Runaways
School Vandalism
Sexual Abuse
Sexual Harassment
Social Isolation
Social Problems
Stealing
Substance Abuse
Urban Problems
Vandalism
Verbal Abuse
Violence
World Problems
Youth Problems

540 BIAS AND EQUITY

Affirmative Action
Afrocentrism
Age Discrimination
Anti Intellectualism
Anti Semitism
Apartheid
Bias
Biracial Committees
Black Leadership
Black Power
Black Stereotypes

Busing
Caste
Civil Rights
Classroom Desegregation
College Desegregation
College Segregation
Comparable Worth
Cultural Images
Cultural Opportunities
Culture Fair Tests
De Facto Segregation
De Jure Segregation
Desegregation Effects
Desegregation Litigation
Desegregation Methods
Desegregation Plans
Disability Discrimination
Disadvantaged
Disadvantaged Youth
Discriminatory Legislation
Economic Opportunities
Economically Disadvantaged
Educational Discrimination
Educational Parks
Educationally Disadvantaged
Equal Education
Equal Facilities
Equal Opportunities (Jobs)
Equal Protection
Ethnic Bias
Ethnic Discrimination
Ethnic Relations
Ethnic Stereotypes
Ethnocentrism
Faculty Integration
Feminism
Feminist Criticism
Gifted Disadvantaged
Homophobia
Housing Discrimination
Housing Opportunities
Human Dignity
Human Relations Programs
Inequalities (1970 1980)
Integration Readiness
Item Bias
Labeling (of Persons)
Multicultural Education
Multicultural Textbooks
Negative Attitudes
Neighborhood Integration
Nondiscriminatory Education
Nontraditional Occupations
Occupational Segregation
Opportunities
Personnel Integration
Political Correctness
Quotas
Racial Attitudes
Racial Balance
Racial Bias
Racial Characteristics (1966 1980)
Racial Discrimination
Racial Factors
Racial Identification
Racial Integration
Racial Relations
Racial Segregation
Racially Balanced Schools
Racism (1966 1980)
Religious Conflict
Religious Discrimination
Reverse Discrimination
School Boycotts
School Desegregation
School Resegregation
School Segregation
Segregationist Organizations
Sex Bias
Sex Discrimination
Sex Fairness
Sex Stereotypes
Social Bias
Social Discrimination
Social Integration
Stereotypes
Teacher Integration

Teacher Stereotypes
Test Bias
Textbook Bias
Tokenism
Voluntary Desegregation
Youth Opportunities

550 HUMAN GEOGRAPHY

Appropriate Technology
Baby Boomers
Birth Rate
Black Housing (1977 1980)
Black Population Trends
Boomtowns
Brain Drain
Collective Settlements
Community Change
Community Development
Community Planning
Community Size
Community Zoning
Counties
Demography
Disadvantaged Environment
Ethnic Distribution
Ethnic Grouping (1966 1980)
Family Mobility
Geographic Distribution
Geographic Isolation
Geographic Location
Geographic Regions
Ghettos
Human Geography
Immigration
Indigenous Populations
Inner City
Land Settlement
Land Use
Low Income Counties
Low Income States
Low Rent Housing
Metropolitan Areas
Middle Income Housing
Migration
Migration Patterns
Mobility
Mortality Rate
Municipalities
Negro Housing (1966 1977)
Neighborhood Improvement
Neighborhoods
Nonmetropolitan Areas
Overpopulation
Physical Divisions (Geographic)
Place of Residence
Planned Communities
Population Distribution
Population Growth
Population Trends
Poverty Areas
Public Housing
Racial Composition
Racial Distribution
Regional Attitudes
Regional Characteristics
Relocation
Residential Patterns
Rural Areas
Rural Development
Rural Environment
Rural Population
Rural Resettlement
Rural to Urban Migration
Rural Urban Differences
Slum Environment
Slums
Small Towns
Social Distribution
Suburban Environment
Suburban Housing
Suburban Problems
Suburbs
Travel
Urban Areas
Urban Demography

Urban Environment
Urban Improvement
Urban Planning
Urban Population
Urban Renewal
Urban to Rural Migration
Urban to Suburban Migration
Urbanization

560 PEOPLES AND CULTURES

Acculturation
African Culture
Alaska Natives
American Culture (1966 1980)
American Indian Culture
American Indians
Amish
Anglo Americans
Arabs
Asian Americans
Biculturalism
Black Culture
Blacks
Burmese Culture
Cambodians
Canada Natives
Catholics
Cherokee (Tribe)
Chinese Americans
Chinese Culture
Chippewa (Tribe)
Choctaw (Tribe)
Cree (Tribe)
Cubans
Cultural Activities
Cultural Awareness
Cultural Background
Cultural Context
Cultural Differences
Cultural Exchange
Cultural Interrelationships
Cultural Isolation
Cultural Literacy
Cultural Maintenance
Cultural Relevance
Cultural Traits
Culture
Culture Contact
Culture Lag
Dominicans
Dutch Culture
Eskimos
Ethnic Groups
Ethnic Origins
Filipino Americans
Folk Culture
Foreign Culture
French Canadians
Greek Americans
Haitians
Hawaiians
Hispanic American Culture
Hispanic Americans
Hmong People
Hopi (Tribe)
Indians
Indochinese
Intercultural Programs
Iroquois (Tribe)
Islamic Culture
Italian Americans
Japanese American Culture
Japanese Americans
Japanese Culture
Jews
Korean Americans
Korean Culture
Lakota (Tribe)
Laotians
Latin American Culture
Latin Americans
Luso Brazilian Culture
Maori (People)
Material Culture
Maya (People)

Metis (People)
Mexican Americans
Mexicans
Middle Class Culture
Mississippi Band of Choctaw (Tribe)
Multiracial Persons
Muslims
Navajo (Nation)
Nomads
Non Western Civilization
Nonreservation American Indians
North American Culture
North Americans
Oglala Sioux (Tribe)
Oral Tradition
Pacific Americans
Pacific Islanders
Polish Americans
Portuguese Americans
Protestants
Pueblo (People)
Puerto Rican Culture
Puerto Ricans
Puritans
Religious Cultural Groups
Reservation American Indians
Rural American Indians
Samoan Americans
School Culture
Sioux (Tribe)
Spanish Americans
Spanish Culture
Subcultures
Tohono O Odham People
Tribes
Urban American Indians
Urban Culture
Vietnamese People
Western Civilization
Whites
Zuni (Tribe)

610 GOVERNMENT AND POLITICS

Activism
Administrative Agencies (1966 1980)
Agencies
Agency Cooperation
Agency Role
American Indian Reservations
Armed Forces
Blue Ribbon Commissions
Board Candidates
Cable Franchising
Capitalism
Citizen Participation
Citizen Role
Citizens Councils
Citizenship
Citizenship Responsibility
City Government
City Officials
Civil Defense
Civil Disobedience
Civil Law
Civil Liberties
Civil Rights Legislation
Colonialism
Communism
Compliance (Legal)
Constitutional Law
County Officials
County Programs
Court Doctrine
Court Judges
Court Litigation
Court Role
Courts
Criminal Law
Democracy
Democratic Values
Demonstrations (Civil)
Developed Nations
Developing Nations
Diplomatic History
Disarmament

Dissent
Drug Legislation
Due Process
Elections
Environmental Standards
Evidence (Legal)
Fascism
Federal Courts
Federal Government
Federal Indian Relationship
Federal Legislation
Federal Programs
Federal Regulation
Federal State Relationship
Federalism
Foreign Countries
Foreign Diplomats
Foreign Policy
Free Enterprise System
Freedom
Freedom of Information
Freedom of Speech
Genocide
Government (Administrative Body)
Government Employees
Government Role
Governmental Structure
Hearings
Imperialism
International Law
International Organizations
International Programs
International Relations
Interstate Programs
Juries
Justice
Juvenile Courts
Juvenile Justice
Labor Legislation
Law Enforcement
Laws
Legal Problems
Legal Responsibility
Legislation
Legislators
Lobbying
Local Government
Local Issues
Local Legislation
Marxism
Military Organizations
Minimum Wage Legislation
National Defense
National Programs
National Security
National Standards
Nationalism
Nazism
New Federalism
Nuclear Warfare
Parliamentary Procedures
Patents
Patriotism
Peace
Planning Commissions
Police Action
Political Affiliation
Political Attitudes
Political Campaigns
Political Candidates
Political Divisions (Geographic)
Political Influences
Political Issues
Political Parties
Political Power
Politics
Presidential Campaigns (United States)
Presidents of the United States
Press Opinion
Public Administration
Public Agencies
Public Health Legislation
Public Officials
Public Opinion
Public Policy
Public Support
Recreation Legislation

Revolution
Rezoning
Search and Seizure
Self Determination
Social Planning
Socialism
Southern Citizens (1966 1980)
Special Zoning
State Action
State Agencies
State Church Separation
State Courts
State Government
State Legislation
State Licensing Boards
State Officials
State Programs
State Regulation
State Standards
States Powers
Supreme Court Litigation (1966 1980)
Supreme Courts (1966 1980)
Technical Assistance
Terrorism
Torts
Totalitarianism
Treaties
Tribal Government
Tribal Sovereignty
Trust Responsibility (Government)
Urban Renewal Agencies
Voter Registration
Voting
Voting Rights
War
World Affairs
Zoning

620 ECONOMICS AND FINANCE

Accounting
Assessed Valuation
Assistantships
Banking
Bids
Block Grants
Bond Issues
Bookkeeping
Budgeting
Budgets
Business Cycles
Capital
Capital Outlay (for Fixed Assets)
Categorical Aid
Child Support
Construction Costs
Consumer Economics
Contract Salaries
Contracts
Corporate Support
Cost Effectiveness
Cost Estimates
Cost Indexes
Costs
Credit (Finance)
Debt (Financial)
Donors
Econometrics
Economic Change
Economic Climate
Economic Development
Economic Factors
Economic Impact
Economic Progress
Economics
Educational Economics
Educational Equity (Finance)
Educational Finance
Educational Vouchers
Efficiency
Endowment Funds
Equalization Aid
Estate Planning
Expenditure per Student
Expenditures
Faculty Fellowships

Family Financial Resources
Family Income
Federal Aid
Fees
Fellowships
Finance Reform
Financial Audits
Financial Exigency
Financial Needs
Financial Policy
Financial Problems
Financial Services
Financial Support
Fines (Penalties)
Fire Insurance
Fiscal Capacity
Fiscal Neutrality
Foundation Programs
Full State Funding
Fund Raising
Grants
Grantsmanship
Guaranteed Income
Health Care Costs
Health Insurance
Human Capital
Incentive Grants
Income
Income Contingent Loans
Indemnity Bonds
Inflation (Economics)
Input Output Analysis
Instructional Student Costs
Insurance
Interest (Finance)
Investment
Labor Economics
Legal Costs
Library Expenditures
Library Funding
Life Cycle Costing
Loan Default
Loan Repayment
Low Income
Macroeconomics
Merit Scholarships
Microeconomics
Monetary Systems
Money Management
Need Analysis (Student Financial Aid)
No Need Scholarships
Noninstructional Student Costs
Operating Expenses
Ownership
Parent Financial Contribution
Paying for College
Philanthropic Foundations
Phonathons
Poverty Programs
Private Financial Support
Private School Aid
Private Sector
Privatization
Productivity
Program Budgeting
Program Costs
Property Accounting
Property Appraisal
Property Taxes
Public Sector
Purchasing
Recreation Finances
Resource Allocation
Retrenchment
Revenue Sharing
Rural Economics
Salary Wage Differentials
Scholarship Funds
Scholarships
School Accounting
School Budget Elections
School District Spending
School District Wealth
School Funds
School Support
School Taxes
State Aid

State Federal Aid
Student Costs
Student Financial Aid
Student Loan Programs
Supply and Demand
Tax Allocation
Tax Credits
Tax Deductions
Tax Effort
Tax Rates
Taxes
Teacher Salaries
Training Allowances
Trusts (Financial)
Tuition
Tuition Grants
Unit Costs
Wills
Work Study Programs

630 LABOR AND EMPLOYMENT

Apprenticeships
Arbitration
Auxiliary Laborers
Black Employment
Career Ladders
Career Opportunities (1966 1980)
Careers
Child Labor
Collective Bargaining
Compensation (Remuneration)
Dislocated Workers
Dismissal (Personnel)
Early Retirement
Employed Women
Employee Absenteeism
Employee Assistance Programs
Employee Attitudes
Employee Responsibility
Employees
Employer Attitudes
Employer Employee Relationship
Employer Supported Day Care
Employers
Employment
Employment Counselors
Employment Experience
Employment Interviews
Employment Level
Employment Opportunities
Employment Patterns
Employment Potential
Employment Practices
Employment Problems
Employment Programs
Employment Qualifications
Employment Services
Entry Workers
Flexible Working Hours
Foreign Workers
Fringe Benefits
Grievance Procedures
Indigenous Personnel
Inplant Programs
Inservice Education
Job Analysis
Job Applicants
Job Application
Job Development
Job Enrichment
Job Layoff
Job Performance
Job Placement
Job Satisfaction
Job Search Methods
Job Security
Job Sharing
Job Simplification
Job Skills
Job Training
Labor
Labor Conditions
Labor Demands
Labor Education
Labor Force

Labor Force Development
Labor Force Nonparticipants
Labor Market
Labor Needs
Labor Problems
Labor Relations
Labor Standards
Labor Supply
Labor Turnover
Labor Utilization
Laborers
Leaves of Absence
Lifting
Loyalty Oaths
Mandatory Retirement
Merit Pay
Middle Management
Migrant Employment
Migrant Workers
Minimum Wage
Multiple Employment
Negotiation Agreements
Negotiation Impasses
Nonprofessional Personnel
Occupational Information
Occupational Mobility
Off the Job Training
Older Workers
On the Job Training
Outplacement Services (Employment)
Overseas Employment
Overtime
Paraprofessional Personnel
Part Time Employment
Payroll Records
Personnel
Personnel Data
Personnel Evaluation
Personnel Management
Personnel Needs
Personnel Policy
Personnel Selection
Premium Pay
Probationary Period
Professional Development
Professional Personnel
Promotion (Occupational)
Qualifications
Quality of Working Life
Recruitment
Reduction in Force
Reentry Workers
Released Time
Resumes (Personal)
Retirement
Retirement Benefits
Retraining
Sabbatical Leaves
Salaries
Scope of Bargaining
Seasonal Employment
Seasonal Laborers
Self Employment
Semiskilled Workers
Seniority
Skill Obsolescence
Skilled Workers
Strikes
Structural Unemployment
Student Employment
Supervision
Supervisor Qualifications
Supervisory Methods
Supported Employment
Teacher Employment
Teacher Employment Benefits
Teacher Retirement
Teacher Shortage
Teacher Strikes
Teacher Supply and Demand
Temporary Employment
Tenure
Trainees
Trainers
Underemployment
Unemployment
Unemployment Insurance

Union Members
Unions
Unskilled Workers
Vacations
Vocational Adjustment
Vocational Rehabilitation
Volunteers
Wages
Work Attitudes
Work Environment
Work Experience
Work Life Expectancy
Worker Days
Workers Compensation
Working Hours
Youth Employment

640 OCCUPATIONS

Accountants
Aircraft Pilots
Animal Caretakers
Appliance Repair
Architectural Drafting
Attendants
Auto Body Repairers
Auto Mechanics
Auto Parts Clerks
Aviation Mechanics
Barbers
Blue Collar Occupations
Boat Operators
Bricklaying
Building Trades
Bus Drivers
Cabinetmaking
Carpentry
Certified Public Accountants
Chemical Technicians
Child Care Occupations
Child Caregivers
Clergy
Clerical Occupations
Clerical Workers
Cooks
Cosmetology
Court Reporters
Craft Workers
Data Processing Occupations
Demand Occupations
Designers
Drafting
Electrical Occupations
Electricians
Electronic Technicians
Emergency Squad Personnel
Emerging Occupations
Energy Occupations
Engineering Technicians
Engineers
Enlisted Personnel
Environmental Technicians
Examiners
File Clerks
Finance Occupations
Finishing
Fire Fighters
Floor Layers
Food and Drug Inspectors
Food Processing Occupations
Glaziers
Highway Engineering Aides
Historians
Homemakers
Hospitality Occupations
Household Workers
Housekeepers
Housework
Housing Management Aides
Immigration Inspectors
Industrial Personnel
Instrumentation Technicians

Insurance Occupations
Interpreters
Judges
Landlords
Laundry Drycleaning Occupations
Lawyers
Legal Assistants
Locomotive Engineers
Machine Repairers
Machine Tool Operators
Machinists
Managerial Occupations
Marine Technicians
Mathematicians
Mechanical Design Technicians
Mechanics (Process)
Merchants
Metal Working
Metallurgical Technicians
Military Personnel
Military Service
Needle Trades
Nuclear Power Plant Technicians
Nuns
Occupational Clusters
Occupations
Office Occupations
Officer Personnel
Operating Engineering
Painting (Industrial Arts)
Parole Officers
Patternmaking
Personnel Directors
Plumbing
Police
Presidents
Priests
Printing
Probation Officers
Production Technicians
Professional Occupations
Public Service Occupations
Radiographers
Real Estate Occupations
Receptionists
Refrigeration Mechanics
Repair
Research Assistants
Research Directors
Researchers
Sales Occupations
Sales Workers
Science Consultants
Scientists
Seafarers
Secretaries
Security Personnel
Semiskilled Occupations
Service Occupations
Service Workers
Sewing Machine Operators
Sheet Metal Work
Sign Painters
Skilled Occupations
Small Engine Mechanics
Social Scientists
Social Work
Social Workers
Sociologists
Supervisors
Systems Analysts
Teaching (Occupation)
Technical Occupations
Television Radio Repairers
Therapists
Tool and Die Makers
Troubleshooting
Unskilled Occupations
Vendors
Veterinarians
Veterinary Assistants
Visiting Homemakers
Waiters and Waitresses
Watchmakers
Welding
White Collar Occupations
Woodworking

650 BUSINESS, COMMERCE, AND INDUSTRY

Aerospace Industry
Air Transportation
Assembly (Manufacturing)
Bakery Industry
Black Businesses
Brick Industry
Broadcast Industry
Business
Business Administration
Business Communication
Business Correspondence
Business Responsibility
Cement Industry
Chemical Industry
Computer Assisted Manufacturing
Construction Industry
Cooperatives
Corporations
Electronics Industry
Entrepreneurship
Equipment Manufacturers
Exports
Fashion Industry
Film Industry
Franchising
Furniture Industry
Housing Industry
Imports
Industrial Structure
Industrialization
Industry
Information Industry
Inspection
Insurance Companies
International Trade
Machinery Industry
Manufacturing
Manufacturing Industry
Marketing
Mass Production
Meat Packing Industry
Merchandise Information
Merchandising
Metal Industry
Office Automation
Office Management
Petroleum Industry
Producer Services
Publishing Industry
Quality Control
Rail Transportation
Real Estate
Retailing
Salesmanship
Small Businesses
Telephone Communications Industry
Tourism
Transportation
University Presses
Wholesaling

710 INFORMATION/COMMUNICATIONS SYSTEMS

Abbreviations
Abstracting
Academic Libraries
Access to Information
Archives
Artificial Intelligence
Authority Control (Information)
Automatic Indexing
Bibliographic Coupling
Bibliographic Databases
Bibliographic Utilities
Book Catalogs
Branch Libraries
Branching
Card Catalogs
Career Information Systems
Cataloging
Catalogs
Character Recognition
Childrens Libraries
Citation Indexes

Classification
Clearinghouses
Codification
Coding
College Libraries
Communications
Communications Satellites
Community Information Services
Computer Graphics
Computer Interfaces
Computer Mediated Communication
Computer Networks
Computer Science
Computer Security
Computer Selection
Computer Software Development
Computer Software Evaluation
Computer Software Selection
Computer System Design
Conferences
Copyrights
Corporate Libraries
County Libraries
Cybernetics
Data
Data Conversion
Data Processing
Database Design
Database Management Systems
Database Producers
Databases
Debugging (Computers)
Decision Support Systems
Definitions
Depository Libraries
Desktop Publishing
Dewey Decimal Classification
Dial Access Information Systems
Diffusion (Communication)
Disclosure
Display Systems
Document Delivery
Documentation
Downloading
Editors
Electronic Libraries
Electronic Mail
Electronic Publishing
Electronic Text
Expert Systems
Facsimile Transmission
Fair Use (Copyrights)
Feedback
Filing
Film Libraries
Full Text Databases
Gateway Systems
Government Libraries
Hospital Libraries
Indexing
Information Centers
Information Dissemination
Information Management
Information Needs
Information Networks
Information Policy
Information Processing
Information Retrieval
Information Science
Information Scientists
Information Services
Information Skills
Information Sources
Information Storage
Information Systems
Information Technology
Information Transfer
Information Utilization
Input Output
Institutional Libraries
Integrated Learning Systems
Integrated Library Systems
Intellectual Property
Interactive Video
Interlibrary Loans
Internet
Job Banks

Keyboarding (Data Entry)
Law Libraries
Learning Resources Centers
Lexicography
Lexicology
Librarian Attitudes
Librarian Teacher Cooperation
Librarians
Libraries
Library Acquisition
Library Administration
Library Administrators
Library Automation
Library Catalogs
Library Circulation
Library Collection Development
Library Collections
Library Cooperation
Library Development
Library Directors
Library Extension
Library Material Selection
Library Materials
Library Networks
Library of Congress Classification
Library Personnel
Library Planning
Library Policy
Library Role
Library Science
Library Services
Library Skills
Library Standards
Library Technical Processes
Library Technicians
Listservs
Local Area Networks
Machine Readable Cataloging
Machine Translation
Man Machine Systems
Management Information Systems
Medical Libraries
National Libraries
Natural Language Processing
Navigation (Information Systems)
Networks
Numeric Databases
Numerical Control
Online Catalogs
Online Searching
Online Systems
Online Vendors
Pattern Recognition
Photocomposition
Prison Libraries
Programing Problems (1966 1980)
Programmers
Programming
Programming Languages
Public Libraries
Records Management
Reference Services
Regional Libraries
Relevance (Information Retrieval)
Reprography
Research Libraries
Retrospective Conversion (Library Catalogs)
School Libraries
Science Libraries
Screen Design (Computers)
Search Intermediaries
Search Strategies
Selection Tools
Selective Dissemination of Information
Shared Library Resources
Social Networks
Special Libraries
Spreadsheets
State Libraries
Subject Index Terms
Telecommunications
Teleconferencing
Telephone Communications Systems
Time Sharing
Union Catalogs
Universal Decimal Classification
User Friendly Interface

User Needs (Information)
User Satisfaction (Information)
Users (Information)
Videotex
Weeding (Library)
Word Processing
World Wide Web

720 COMMUNICATIONS MEDIA

Advertising
Animation
Audience Participation
Audiences
Audiodisks
Audiotape Cassettes
Audiotape Recordings
Audiovisual Aids
Audiovisual Communications
Bibliographic Records
Bibliographies
Books
Broadcast Journalism
Broadcast Television
Cable Television
Captions
Cartoons
Charts
Childrens Television
Closed Circuit Television
Comics (Publications)
Commercial Television
Computer Games
Computer Output Microfilm
Computer Software
Conference Papers
Conference Proceedings
Courseware
Diagrams
Dictation
Dictionaries
Directories
Discussion
Display Aids
Doctoral Dissertations
Documentaries
Editing
Editorials
Educational Games
Educational Media
Educational Radio
Educational Television
Electronic Journals
Exhibits
Faculty Publishing
Feature Stories
Film Production
Film Production Specialists
Films
Filmstrips
Floppy Disks
Flow Charts
Foreign Language Films
Graphs
Guides
Headlines
High Interest Low Vocabulary Books
Holography
Hypermedia
Illustrations
Institutional Advancement
Instructional Films
Interactive Television
Journal Articles
Journalism
Kinescope Recordings
Layout (Publications)
Letters (Correspondence)
Magnetic Disks
Magnetic Tape Cassettes
Magnetic Tapes
Magnification Methods
Manipulative Materials
Maps
Mass Media
Mass Media Use

Masters Theses
Media Adaptation
Media Selection
Media Specialists
Menu Driven Software
Microfiche
Microfilm
Microforms
Microreproduction
Microworlds
Multilingual Materials
Multimedia Materials
News Media
News Reporting
News Writing
Newspapers
Nonprint Media
Optical Data Disks
Optical Disks
Paperback Books
Photographs
Photojournalism
Picture Books
Popular Culture
Pornography
Practicum Papers
Primary Sources
Printed Materials
Production Techniques
Programming (Broadcast)
Proofreading
Propaganda
Protocol Materials
Public Television
Publications
Publicity
Publicize (1968 1980)
Radio
Realia
Recipes (Food)
Reference Materials
Reports
Research Reports
Scholarly Communication
Scholarly Journals
Scholarly Writing
Scholastic Journalism
School Newspapers
School Publications
Serials
Signs
Single Concept Films
Slides
Soap Operas
Sound Effects
Sound Tracks (1966 1980)
Special Effects
Specifications
Speeches
Story Telling
Student Developed Materials
Student Publications
Student Writing Models
Talking Books
Tape Recordings
Technical Illustration
Technical Writing
Telegraphic Materials
Television
Television Commercials
Television Viewing
Textbook Preparation
Textbook Publication
Theses
Three Dimensional Aids
Transparencies
Video Games
Videodisks
Videotape Cassettes
Videotape Recordings
Virtual Reality
Visual Aids
Writing for Publication

730 PUBLICATION/DOCUMENT TYPES

Abstracts
Administrator Guides
Annotated Bibliographies
Annual Reports
Answer Keys
Answer Sheets
Anthologies
Atlases
Authoring Aids (Programming)
Autobiographies
Autoinstructional Aids
Bilingual Instructional Materials
Biographies
Book Reviews
Bulletins
Census Figures
Check Lists
Citations (References)
Computer Software Reviews
Conference Reports (1967 1980)
Coordinate Indexes
Course Descriptions
Curriculum Guides
Discographies
Employment Projections
Employment Statistics
Encyclopedias
Enrollment Projections
Faculty Handbooks
Filmographies
Foreign Language Books
Foreign Language Periodicals
Glossaries
Government Publications
Guidelines
Health Materials
History Textbooks
Indexes
Instructional Materials
Laboratory Manuals
Language Guides (1966 1980)
Leaders Guides
Learning Modules
Lesson Plans
Library Guides
Library Statistics
Literature Guides (1966 1980)
Literature Reviews
Manuscripts
Master Plans
Mathematical Models
Mathematics Materials
Mission Statements
Models
Newsletters
Opinion Papers
Orientation Materials
Pamphlets
Parent Materials
Periodicals
Permuted Indexes
Personal Narratives
Position Papers
Profiles
Program Descriptions
Program Guides
Program Proposals
Programmed Instructional Materials
Project Applications (1967 1980)
Puzzles
Reading Materials
Records (Forms)
Research Reviews (Publications) (1966 1980)
Resource Materials
School Statistics
Science Materials
Scripts
State Curriculum Guides
State of the Art Reviews
Study Guides
Tables (Data)
Teacher Developed Materials
Teaching Guides
Test Manuals
Test Reviews

Textbook Publications (1966 1980)
Textbooks
Thesauri
Word Lists
Workbooks
Worksheets
Yearbooks

810 RESEARCH AND THEORY

Action Research
Adaptation Level Theory
Architectural Research
Attribution Theory
Attrition (Research Studies)
Audience Analysis
Behavior Theories
Behavioral Science Research
Case Studies
Chaos Theory
Citation Analysis
Classroom Research
Communication Research
Community Study
Community Surveys
Content Analysis
Creativity Research
Critical Theory
Cross Sectional Studies
Curriculum Research
Data Collection
Dialect Studies
Difficulty Level
Dropout Research
Economic Research
Educational Assessment
Educational Experiments
Educational Research
Educational Theories
Effective Schools Research
Environmental Research
Evaluation Research
Exceptional Child Research
Experimenter Characteristics
Experiments
Facility Case Studies
Facility Utilization Research
Feasibility Studies
Field Interviews
Field Studies
Followup Studies
Game Theory
Generalizability Theory
Graduate Surveys
Hermeneutics
Heuristics
Holistic Approach
Information Theory
Inquiry
Institutional Research
Integration Studies
Interest Research
Interviews
Investigations
Item Response Theory
Journalism Research
Knowledge Representation
Language Research
Learning Theories
Library Research
Library Surveys
Longitudinal Studies
Lunar Research
Mail Surveys
Marxian Analysis
Media Research
Mediation Theory
Medical Research
Methods
Methods Research
National Surveys
Needs Assessment
Nursing Research
Occupational Surveys
Operations Research
Organizational Theories

Participatory Research
Personality Studies
Personality Theories
Piagetian Theory
Pilot Projects
Projects (1966 1980)
Protocol Analysis
Psychological Studies
Qualitative Research
Quasiexperimental Design
Reading Research
Research
Research Administration
Research and Development
Research Committees
Research Criteria (1967 1980)
Research Design
Research Methodology
Research Needs
Research Opportunities
Research Problems
Research Projects
Research Proposals
Research Skills
Research Tools
Research Utilization
Response Rates (Questionnaires)
Role Theory
Schematic Studies
School Surveys
Scientific Research
Self Evaluation (Groups)
Shift Studies
Social Exchange Theory
Social Science Research
Social Theories
State Surveys
Statistical Studies
Statistical Surveys
Student Research
Student Surveys
Surveys
Teacher Surveys
Telephone Surveys
Television Research
Television Surveys
Test Theory
Textbook Research
Theories
Theory Practice Relationship
Use Studies
Vocational Followup
Writing Research

820 MEASUREMENT

Achievement Rating
Adaptive Testing
Alternative Assessment
Analysis of Covariance
Analysis of Variance
Assessment Centers (Personnel)
Auditory Evaluation
Audits (Verification)
Benchmarking
Bibliometrics
Causal Models
Chi Square
Classroom Observation Techniques
Cluster Analysis
Cluster Grouping
Cognitive Measurement
Cohort Analysis
Comparative Analysis
Comparative Testing
Computer Assisted Testing
Concurrent Validity
Confidence Testing
Congruence (1970 1980)
Construct Validity
Content Validity
Control Groups
Correlation
Critical Incidents Method
Criticism
Cutting Scores

Data Analysis
Data Interpretation
Delphi Technique
Discriminant Analysis
Distractors (Tests)
Early Identification
Educational Testing
Effect Size
Equated Scores
Error of Measurement
Error Patterns
Evaluation
Evaluation Criteria
Evaluation Methods
Evaluation Needs
Evaluation Problems
Evaluation Utilization
Experimental Groups
Factor Analysis
Factor Structure
Failure
Focus Groups
Force Field Analysis
Forced Choice Technique
Goodness of Fit
Grade Equivalent Scores
Grade Point Average
Grade Prediction
Group Testing
Guessing (Tests)
Holistic Evaluation
Hypothesis Testing
Identification
Individual Testing
Informal Assessment
Intelligence Quotient
Interaction Process Analysis
Interrater Reliability
Item Analysis
Item Sampling
Judgment Analysis Technique
Least Squares Statistics
Lesson Observation Criteria
Local Norms
Matched Groups
Maximum Likelihood Statistics
Measurement
Measurement Objectives
Measurement Techniques
Meta Analysis
Minimum Competency Testing
Monte Carlo Methods
Multidimensional Scaling
Multiple Regression Analysis
Multitrait Multimethod Techniques
Multivariate Analysis
National Norms
National Teacher Certification
Naturalistic Observation
Network Analysis
Nominal Group Technique
Norms
Oblique Rotation
Observation
Orthogonal Rotation
Participant Observation
Path Analysis
Performance Based Assessment
Performance Criteria (1968 1980)
Performance Specifications (1969 1980)
Personality Assessment
Policy Analysis
Prediction
Predictive Measurement
Predictive Validity
Predictor Variables
Pretesting
Psychological Testing
Q Methodology
Raw Scores
Reliability
Response Style (Tests)
Robustness (Statistics)
Sample Size
Sampling
Scaling
Scores

Scoring
Scoring Formulas
Scoring Rubrics
Self Evaluation (1966 1980)
Skill Analysis
Sociometric Techniques
State Norms
Statistical Analysis
Statistical Bias
Statistical Data
Statistical Significance
Structural Equation Models
Success
Suppressor Variables
Synthesis
Systems Analysis
Talent Identification
Task Analysis
Teacher Competency Testing
Test Construction
Test Content
Test Format
Test Interpretation
Test Items
Test Length
Test Norms
Test Reliability
Test Results
Test Selection
Test Use
Test Validity
Testing
Testing Problems
Testing Programs
Trend Analysis
Triangulation
True Scores
Validity
Vocational Evaluation
Weight (1968 1980)
Weighted Scores
Writing Evaluation

830 TESTS AND SCALES

Achievement Tests
Affective Measures
Aptitude Tests
Association Measures
Attitude Measures
Audiometric Tests
Auditory Tests
Behavior Rating Scales
Biographical Inventories
Cognitive Tests
College Entrance Examinations
Creativity Tests
Criterion Referenced Tests
Diagnostic Tests
Equivalency Tests
Essay Tests
Field Tests
High Stakes Tests
Informal Reading Inventories
Intelligence Tests
Interest Inventories
Item Banks
Language Tests
Licensing Examinations (Professions)
Likert Scales
Listening Comprehension Tests
Mastery Tests
Mathematics Tests
Maturity Tests
Measures (Individuals)
Multiple Choice Tests
National Competency Tests
Nonverbal Tests
Norm Referenced Tests
Objective Tests
Occupational Tests
Open Book Tests
Perception Tests
Performance Tests
Personality Measures
Physical Fitness Tests

Preschool Tests
Pretests Posttests
Problem Sets
Prognostic Tests
Projective Measures
Questionnaires
Rating Scales
Reading Readiness Tests
Reading Tests
School Readiness Tests
Science Tests
Screening Tests
Self Concept Measures
Semantic Differential
Situational Tests
Speech Tests
Standardized Tests
Tactual Visual Tests
Teacher Made Tests
Tests
Timed Tests
Verbal Tests
Vision Tests
Visual Measures
Work Sample Tests
Writing Tests

910 EQUIPMENT

Adhesives
Air Conditioning Equipment
Alarm Systems
Analog Computers
Athletic Equipment
Audio Equipment
Audiotape Recorders
Biomedical Equipment
Bookmobiles
Broadcast Reception Equipment
Bulletin Boards
Calculators
Calorimeters
Carrels
Chalkboards
Classroom Furniture
Computer Peripherals
Computer Printers
Computer Storage Devices
Computer Terminals
Computers
Diesel Engines
Digital Computers
Disk Drives
Educational Equipment
Electric Batteries
Electric Circuits
Electric Motors
Electrical Appliances
Electromechanical Aids
Electronic Equipment
Engines
Equipment
Equipment Evaluation
Equipment Maintenance
Equipment Standards
Equipment Storage
Equipment Utilization
Filmstrip Projectors
Furniture
Glass
Graphing Calculators
Guns
Hand Tools
Heat Recovery
Home Furnishings
Input Output Devices
Instrumentation
Laboratory Equipment
Leather
Library Equipment
Lubricants
Machine Tools
Measurement Equipment
Measurement Instruments (1966 1980)
Mechanical Equipment
Microcomputers

Microform Readers
Microphones
Microscopes
Minicomputers
Modems
Motor Vehicles
Office Machines
Opaque Projectors
Optical Scanners
Overhead Projectors
Paper (Material)
Photographic Equipment
Plastics
Polygraphs
Potentiometers (Instruments)
Projection Equipment
Radar
Restraints (Vehicle Safety)
Safety Equipment
School Buses
Science Equipment
Screens (Displays)
Semiconductor Devices
Service Vehicles
Sound Spectrographs
Speech Synthesizers
Stimulus Devices (1966 1980)
Superconductors
Supplies
Tachistoscopes
Tape Recorders
Teaching Machines
Television Lighting
Test Scoring Machines
Transistors
Vending Machines
Video Display Terminals
Video Equipment
Videotape Recorders

920 FACILITIES

Acoustic Insulation
Acoustical Environment
After School Centers
Air Conditioning
Air Structures
Airports
Animal Facilities
Aquariums
Architectural Character
Architectural Programming
Arts Centers
Asphalts
Audiovisual Centers
Auditoriums
Blueprints
Boarding Homes
Bookstores
Building Conversion
Building Design
Building Innovation
Building Obsolescence
Building Operation
Building Plans
Building Systems
Buildings
Built Environment
Business Education Facilities
Campus Planning
Campuses
Carpeting
Ceilings
Child Development Centers
Chimneys
Churches
Classroom Design
Classrooms
Clinics
College Buildings
College Housing
College Stores
Community Centers
Computer Centers
Construction (Process)
Construction Management

Construction Materials
Construction Needs
Construction Programs
Continuing Education Centers
Controlled Environment (1966 1980)
Correctional Institutions
Corridors
Cultural Centers
Curriculum Study Centers
Day Care Centers
Demonstration Centers
Design Build Approach
Design Requirements
Dining Facilities
Doors
Dormitories
Driveways
Education Service Centers
Educational Complexes
Educational Facilities
Educational Facilities Design
Educational Facilities Improvement
Educational Facilities Planning
Electrical Systems
Electronic Classrooms
Encapsulated Facilities
Facilities
Facility Expansion
Facility Guidelines
Facility Improvement
Facility Inventory
Facility Planning
Facility Requirements
Fallout Shelters
Fast Track Scheduling
Field Houses
Flexible Facilities
Flexible Lighting Design
Flooring
Food Handling Facilities
Food Stores
Found Spaces
Foundries
Furniture Arrangement
Glare
Glass Walls
Gymnasiums
Heating
Historic Sites
Hotels
Housing
Housing Needs
Interior Space
Laboratories
Land Acquisition
Language and Area Centers (1968 1980)
Language Laboratories
Learning Laboratories
Library Facilities
Lighting
Lighting Design
Living Learning Centers
Locker Rooms
Maintenance
Masonry
Migrant Housing
Military Air Facilities
Mobile Classrooms
Mobile Clinics
Mobile Laboratories
Modular Building Design
Movable Partitions
Multipurpose Classrooms
Museums
Music Facilities
National Parks
Nature Centers
Nuclear Power Plants
Nursing Homes
Off Campus Facilities
Offices (Facilities)
Open Plan Schools
Park Design
Parking Controls
Parking Facilities
Parks
Pedestrian Traffic

Personal Care Homes
Physical Education Facilities
Physical Environment
Planetariums
Playgrounds
Pneumatic Forms
Prefabrication
Prestressed Concrete
Public Facilities
Recreational Facilities
Refrigeration
Regional Laboratories
Rehabilitation Centers
Relocatable Facilities
Research and Development Centers
Residential Institutions
Resource Centers
Road Construction
Roofing
Sanitary Facilities
Satellite Facilities
School Buildings
Science Facilities
Science Laboratories

Science Teaching Centers
Settlement Houses
Shared Facilities
Site Analysis
Site Development
Site Selection
Skill Centers
Space Classification
Space Dividers
Space Utilization
Spatial Relationship (Facilities)
Spatial Relationship (1966 1980)
Speech and Hearing Clinics
Stages (Facilities)
Storage
Structural Building Systems
Structural Elements (Construction)
Student Unions
Studio Floor Plans (1966 1980)
Study Centers
Study Facilities
Swimming Pools
Systems Building
Teacher Centers

Teacher Housing
Television Studios
Theaters
Thermal Environment
Thermal Insulation
Toilet Facilities
Traffic Circulation
Traffic Control
Trails
Training Laboratories (1967 1980)
Underground Facilities
Utilities
Vehicular Traffic
Ventilation
Visual Environment
Vocational Training Centers
Warehouses
Windowless Rooms
Windows
Workstations
Writing Laboratories
Zoos

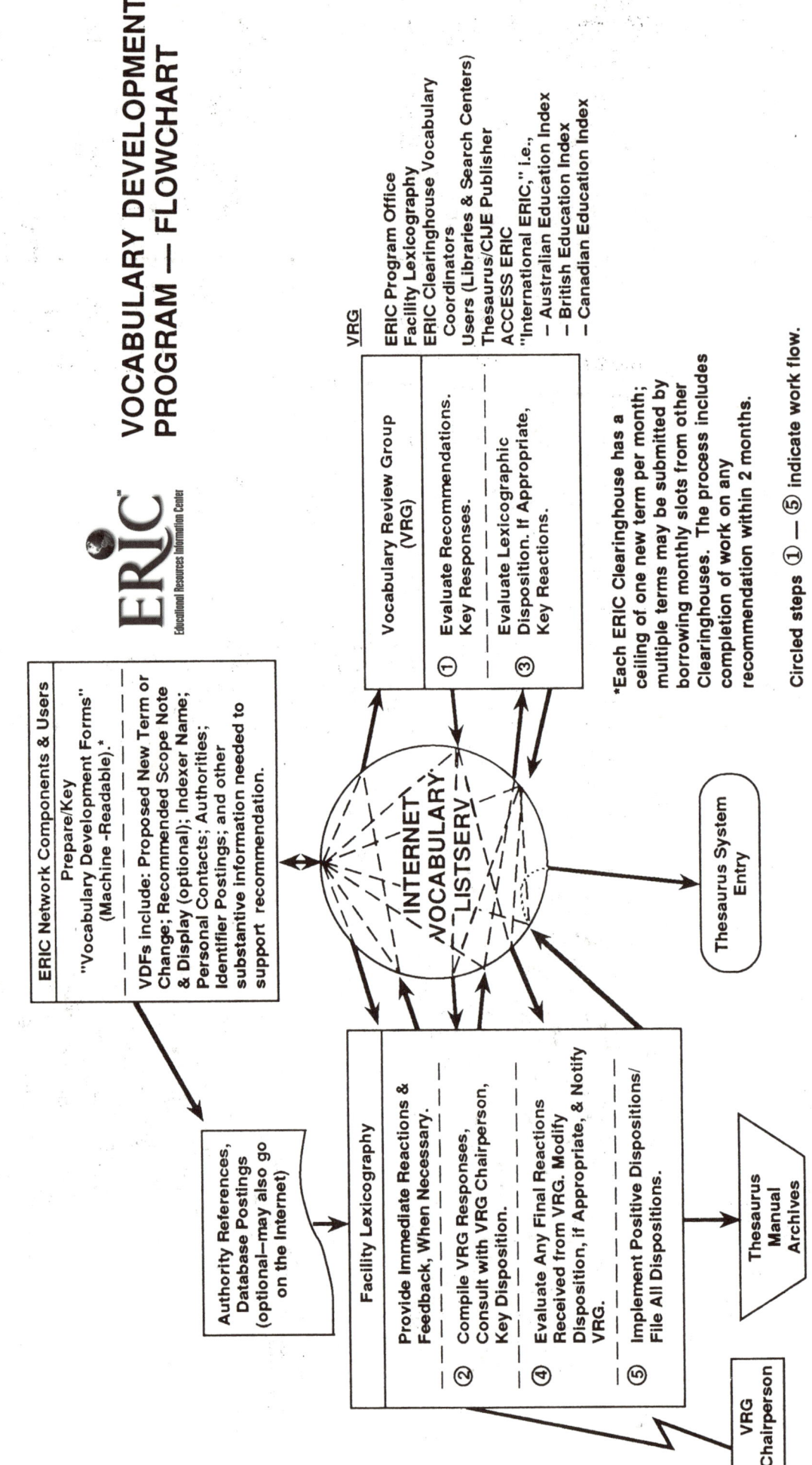

VOCABULARY DEVELOPMENT PROGRAM — FLOWCHART

ERIC
Educational Resources Information Center

ERIC Network Components & Users

Prepare/Key
"Vocabulary Development Forms"
(Machine -Readable).*

VDFs include: Proposed New Term or Change; Recommended Scope Note & Display (optional); Indexer Name; Personal Contacts; Authorities; Identifier Postings; and other substantive information needed to support recommendation.

Authority References, Database Postings (optional—may also go on the Internet)

INTERNET VOCABULARY LISTSERV

VRG

ERIC Program Office
Facility Lexicography
ERIC Clearinghouse Vocabulary Coordinators
Users (Libraries & Search Centers)
Thesaurus/CIJE Publisher
ACCESS ERIC
"International ERIC," i.e.,
 – Australian Education Index
 – British Education Index
 – Canadian Education Index

Vocabulary Review Group (VRG)

① Evaluate Recommendations. Key Responses.

③ Evaluate Lexicographic Disposition. If Appropriate, Key Reactions.

*Each ERIC Clearinghouse has a ceiling of one new term per month; multiple terms may be submitted by borrowing monthly slots from other Clearinghouses. The process includes completion of work on any recommendation within 2 months.

Circled steps ① — ⑤ indicate work flow.

Facility Lexicography

Provide Immediate Reactions & Feedback, When Necessary.

② Compile VRG Responses. Consult with VRG Chairperson, Key Disposition.

④ Evaluate Any Final Reactions Received from VRG. Modify Disposition, if Appropriate, & Notify VRG.

⑤ Implement Positive Dispositions/ File All Dispositions.

Thesaurus System Entry

Thesaurus Manual Archives

VRG Chairperson